Merry Christmas
Chuch —
Christmas 2002.
Love
Margie.

RECORDS OF NORTH AMERICAN BIG GAME

11TH EDITION

Records of North American Big Game, 11th Edition

Edited by C. Randall Byers and George A. Bettas

Library of Congress Catalog Card Number: 99-63185
ISBN: 0-940864-35-5
Published August 1999

Published in the United States of America
by the
Boone and Crockett Club
250 Station Drive
Missoula, Montana 59801
Phone (406) 542-1888
Fax (406) 542-0784
Toll-Free (888) 840-4868
www.boone-crockett.org

Painting by Bob Kuhn

RECORDS OF NORTH AMERICAN BIG GAME

11TH EDITION

A Book of the Boone and Crockett Club Containing Tabulations of Outstanding North American Big-Game Trophies, Compiled from Data in the Club's Big-Game Records Archives.

Edited by

C. Randall Byers

George A. Bettas

1999

BOONE AND CROCKETT CLUB

Missoula, Montana

DEDICATION

Phil Wright, 1914-1997

GEORGE A. BETTAS
VICE PRESIDENT OF
COMMUNICATIONS
Boone and Crockett Club

This 11th Edition of the Boone and Crockett Club's All-Time records book is dedicated to Philip L. Wright. Phil passed away at his home in Missoula, Montana, on July 16, 1997. He was a man who was a distinguished teacher, a dedicated father and husband and a man who stood for what is highest and most worthy in hunting ethics and sportsmanship. Phil's membership in the Club and his dedication to the work of the Club will stand as a standard of excellence for all Club members, current and future. While it is fitting that the Club dedicate the eleventh edition of the Boone and Crockett Club's **Records of North American Big Game** to Phil, no such work can adequately express the degree of regret and sense of personal loss felt by Phil's family, students, colleagues, and members of the Boone and Crockett Club. Phil Wright was a pleasant companion and a loyal friend who will be remembered with love and admiration.

Phil had been a Boone and Crockett official measurer for 20 years when he was proposed for membership in the Boone and Crockett Club by Dr. Charles Nadler in 1971. Seconding letters were written by Dan Poole, J.P. Linduska and Lloyd W. Swift. In his letter proposing Phil Wright for regular membership, Dr. Nadler cited Phil's exemplary career as a professor and chairman of the University of Montana Department of Zoology.

Phil's first university teaching position was at the University of Montana in 1939. He taught courses including elementary zoology, histology, comparative anatomy, human physiology, parasitology and wildlife techniques. Phil was best known for the mammalogy courses that he taught at the university for 46 years and the ornithology courses he taught for 38 years. Phil's teaching spanned the time from the infancy of the zoology department in 1939 to his retirement in 1985. Phil's courses were legendary for their overwhelming content and his high expectations for mastery of the material. Phil was a demanding, but highly respected and loved teacher. He was known for his storytelling during his classes much like his storytelling in his work with the Boone and Crockett Club. Phil's stories were

PHIL BEGAN TO DEVELOP AND MAINTAIN A COLLECTION OF BIRDS AND ANIMALS AT THE UNIVERSITY OF MONTANA IN 1939 AND DEVOTED MORE THAN 56 YEARS TO COLLECTING SPECIMENS AND ESTABLISHING ONE OF THE LARGEST ZOOLOGICAL COLLECTIONS IN THE NORTHERN ROCKY MOUNTAIN REGION.

detailed and always contained a "lesson." They were a rich collection of his experiences and recollections of important happenings, issues, and cases.

Phil was chairman of the University of Montana Department of Zoology for 14 years during the late 1950s and 60s when the department started a Ph.D. program in 1960. That program has to date produced over 50 doctoral recipients. Among university faculty it is somewhat unique to find a faculty member who is both a great teacher and an equally good researcher. Phil Wright was both. In addition to the many different research projects for which Phil was responsible, the students voted him one of the 20 outstanding professors at the University of Montana in 1969.

Nadler described Phil's activities as a Boone and Crockett measurer. He noted, "Phil Wright has been an official measurer since 1951, has measured over 100 heads that are listed in the 1952, 1958, and 1964 records books... This list of scientific and common names utilized in the 1964 records book was prepared by Wright at the request of Milford Baker and Bob Waters. Finally, he served on the 1971 Panel of Judges for the 14th N.A.B.G. Competition; there he displayed an empathy for the 'art' of measuring passed down by the older members and indicated a willingness to record as much 'art' as possible in an objectively written set of instructions directed toward the clarification of measuring controversies... he offers unique promises as a potential member of the N.A.B.G. Committee who respects the problems, traditions, and 'art' of our present measuring system but also is willing to improve and refine its applications with scientific objectivity." Nadler concluded by stating, "Despite his many accomplishments, Phil Wright will be greatly honored by membership and will work hard to further the objectives of the Boone and Crockett Club." Those of us who know Phil well also know how deeply honored he was to be a regular member of the Boone and Crockett Club. Everyone knows how hard he worked to further the objectives of the Club and the leadership he provided for the records program.

Phil Wright began to develop and maintain a collection of birds and animals at the University of Montana in 1939 and devoted more than 56 years to collecting specimens and establishing one of the largest zoological collections in the Northern Rocky Mountain region. There are over 17,000 specimens housed in the museum including many valuable and irreplaceable specimens of both birds and mammals. On May 5, 1997, the faculty of the University of Montana's biological science division named the collection in Phil's honor. It is officially known as the Philip L. Wright Zoological Museum. During the dedication ceremony, Phil's colleagues praised his excellence in teaching and research. Professor Emeritus H. Richard Fevold wrote: "...There are few people who have contributed more to their students, their profession and to the University of Montana than Phil Wright..." "No other faculty member in the state (or nation for that matter) has influenced as many nationally prominent wildlife biologists," noted Phil's colleagues.

In addition to being a wonderful teacher and scholar, Phil

PHIL AND HEDWIG AT A SKI RACE IN WEST YELLOWSTONE (1993); PHIL WITH A BIGHORN SHEEP HE HARVESTED; PHIL AND MARGARET AT COURAGEOUS LAKE (1985); CLUB MEMBERS (CLOCKWISE FROM TOP RIGHT) GUIDO RAHR, CRAIG BODDINGTON, ARTHUR POPHAM, GEORGE BETTAS AND GUEST BOB MUNSON JOINED PHIL AT A CLUB DINNER IN DALLAS, TX; AND PHIL MEASURING A TROPHY AT THE 21ST AWARDS JUDGES' PANEL.

Wright was an eager hunter. His interest in the outdoors and wildlife began when he was ten years old at which time he attempted to photograph English sparrows through a window with an old box camera. His interest in birds from that age on became a focal point of his life and involved many hours afield collecting bird specimens and banding birds. Phil recalled this interest while being interviewed by Dan Hall for the Boone and Crockett Club's Oral History Project. "I was interested in birds initially and I seemed to have a natural interest in hunting as a boy. I remember standing for long periods at displays in sporting goods stores in the hunting season where they displayed guns and mounted pheasants. Also as a boy, I remember trips to the Boston Society of Natural History where mounted birds were on display and I spent a lot of time there. It was remarkable because neither of my parents had much interest in the outdoors."

Phil first began big game hunting in western Montana in September 1941 when he backpacked into the South Fork of the Flathead Country (now called Bob Marshall Wilderness). Since that time Phil noted in 1971, "I have taken at least one of every Montana big game species except cougar, which have not interested me, and grizzly bear of which only a handful are taken each year." Phil described his interest in hunting whitetail deer in his 1971 Club personal data record. "During the past three years in Montana, I have been hunting whitetails almost exclusively as this species offers the greatest challenge. I agree with Grancel Fitz that obtaining a big whitetail buck by still hunting is the most difficult of all feats in big game hunting. We have some excellent whitetails in Montana although I have never gotten one that was close to record size" In regard to elk, Phil noted, " The finest wapiti head I have gotten was in the Bob Marshall in 1942, but my partners and I were doing our own packing and we couldn't fit the head on the pack horse! We were forced to leave the head in the woods." In addition to hunting extensively in Montana, Phil hunted big game in British Columbia, Alaska, Northwest Territories and Africa.

Aldo Leopold asked Phil to measure all the trophies in Wisconsin in 1937 for the Boone and Crockett Club. Because of the press of other duties at The University of Wisconsin, Phil had to decline the assignment, but some fellow graduate students took the measurements for the Wisconsin heads for the 1939 record book. In about 1947, the Boone and Crockett Club sent out information to various colleges and universities and museums announcing a Competition for big game trophies. Phil had a number of cougar skulls in his collection at the University of Montana that had been donated by local hunters. The University entered a couple of those skulls and received awards from the first Boone and Crockett Club Competition. As the one in charge of the museum, the classification of the specimens and their life histories became part of Phil's course in mammalogy so it was natural that he continued to obtain specimens that could be entered in this Competition.

In 1950, when Samuel B. Webb was trying to recruit official measurers from all over the country he invited Phil to serve as one of the initial official measurers. There were about 30 original measurers and at the time of his death, Phil Wright was the only one who was still active as an official measurer. When Grancel Fitz was active Phil wrote him on several occasions about problems that arose in measuring heads. Just before his death, Grancel asked Phil on behalf of the Club's editorial committee to prepare a list of up-to-date scientific names for the various big game species. The 1964 record book used that list without substantial change.

From the time Phil became a regular member of the Boone and Crockett Club in 1971, he was an integral part of the big game records program and contributed a great deal of his time to working with and refining the records program. Phil was a judge for three Awards Programs and Consultant for five others. He was Chairman of Judges for the 16th Awards Program. Phil became chairman of the Records Committee in 1978 and served as chairman for nine years.

Phil Wright was elected as an Honorary Life Member of the Boone and Crockett Club in 1984 and was awarded the Club's highest honor, the Sagamore Hill Award in May 1996 "For lifelong commitment to conservation; For dedication to the principles of fair chase and scientific integrity with the records program."

Phil Wright loved to tell stories and he relived his hunting adventures through his story telling. One of Phil's best friends and favorite hunting companions was Dr. Robert F. Wallace of Pullman, Washington. It was Bob Wallace who sparked my interest in the Boone and Crockett Club. He knew a great deal about the history of the Club and the individuals who were members of the Club. Although I was only familiar with the Club's records program, I learned about the history, traditions, and membership of the Boone and Crockett Club from Bob. Bob introduced me to Phil and I immediately felt the warmth and sincerity of Phil's friendship.

Bob became acquainted with Phil Wright when Bob moved from his faculty position in the economics department at Washington State University to Missoula to become the Chair of the Economics Department at the University of Montana in 1961. At the time Phil Wright was the Chair of the Zoology Department. Over the following nine years Bob and Phil became very close friends and hunting partners. Phil and Bob hit it off right away. Phil welcomed Bob and took him to his favorite hunting places. Phil knew the area and Bob was a discoverer so they found a lot of great places to hunt. At the time Bob owned a wonderful English pointer named Joe. Phil had Tana, a very good golden retriever. Often they would go to the Flathead Valley. That was their favorite place. It had lots and lots of pheasants. Phil liked to tell Bob the story about a man who was a very good fisherman. "He's like us when it comes to hunting we always get our limit," Phil exclaimed!

Bob summarized his years of friendship and hunting adventures with Phil Wright by simply saying, "We had some dandy adventures...."

I too, had some dandy adventures with Phil, some of them afield but most of them vicariously over a cup of coffee. Although I knew Phil for only ten short years I feel privileged to have had the opportunity to share this time with him. As I sit through Club meetings and the endless meetings of the Big Game Records Committee my thoughts sometimes drift and I ask myself, what would Phil say or think about the subject at hand. I have so much that I want to tell him and I find that I did not learn nearly enough from him. We will all miss Phil's serious attention to detail, his wry sense of humor, his stories, and his dedication to the Club. But most of all we will miss him as one of the most wonderful friends any of us could have ever known. ∎

22ND BIG GAME AWARDS
1992-1994 ▲ DALLAS, TX

AWARDS JUDGES' PANELS

23RD BIG GAME AWARDS
1995-1997 ▲ RENO, NV

Hunting North American Big Game

C. RANDALL BYERS

CHAIRMAN
Records of North
American Big Game
Committee

This edition of *Records of North American Big Game* is dedicated to Dr. Philip Wright. George Bettas, editor of *Fair Chase* magazine and current Vice President of Communications for the Club prepared the dedication. Those of us who knew and worked closely with Phil have mourned his passing yet his legacy lives on. Phil worried enough for all of us about the measuring system and insuring comparability and accuracy in its application. He personally trained many of the Boone and Crockett measurers who daily volunteer their time and effort on behalf of the Club. By worrying for all of us, Phil insured the records are what they are today and left many of us in a far better position to follow in his footsteps.

This is a book about hunting North American big game animals. This, too, is a book about the Boone and Crockett Club. In part, they belong together, especially when one views the selective hunting and trophy recognition aspects of fair chase pursuit that the lists in the later part of this book display. Since the mid-thirties the Boone and Crockett Club has published lists of outstanding examples of North American big game specimens primarily taken by sport hunters under fair chase conditions. For more than 50 years, when hunters gathered and talked about getting one that will make the book, they were speaking of having an animal large enough to exceed the Boone and Crockett Club's minimum levels for entry into this All-Time records book.

And as you can see by looking through this book, many have succeeded. More than 17,100 record-class entries are acknowledged in these pages. Countless hours of efforts, days in the woods, and evenings around campfires have passed to provide this tribute to sport hunting and modern game management. And while the recording of trophies has been taking place by the Club since the 1930s, the practices and principles it has espoused since its founding in 1887 laid the groundwork for much of the success and hunting ethic we have today.

As a hunting book, it provides a historical reference to

22ND AWARDS JUDGES' PANEL. (L-R) ROBERT E. ESTES, PHILIP L. WRIGHT, PAUL D. WEBSTER, HOMER SAYE, JIMMIE E. ENGELMANN, FRANK COOK, JACK GRAHAM, RONALD L. BOUCHER, HORACE G. GORE (KNEELING), FREDERICK J. KING, GERARD BEAULIEU, WILLIAM L. COOPER, C. RANDALL BYERS, AND JACK RENEAU.

23RD AWARDS JUDGES' PANEL. (STANDING L-R) GERARD BEAULIEU, HOMER SAYE, LARRY R. CAREY, FRANK COOK, FREDERICK J. KING, BUCK BUCKNER, L. VICTOR CLARK, WILLIAM C. MACCARTY III, ROGER W. ATWOOD, GLENN E. HISEY, PAUL D. WEBSTER. (KNEELING L-R) WAYNE N. CAPURRO, GEORGE K. TSUKAMOTO, C. RANDALL BYERS, JACK GRAHAM, RON BOUCHER AND JACK RENEAU.

how things were and how they are. More than 4,300 new entries appear in these lists from the time the 10th Edition of **Records of North American Big Game** appeared. Since the publication of the 10th Edition the minimum score for muskox has risen as has the minimum for Columbia blacktail deer while the minimums for typical and non-typical mule deer have decreased. Among these pages you will find the "hunt" stories for the 35 World's Record trophies listed in the various categories of North American big game. True, not all the animals shown here were taken by hunters as these lists also contain picked up trophies and some of unknown origin. But those animals too reflect the management and habitat conditions that allowed them to develop as exceptional representatives of their species.

Eight new World's Records (pictured at left) appear in this edition as compared to the 10th Edition. These include Milo Hanson's record whitetail deer and John Crouse's exceptional Alaska-Yukon moose scoring 261-5/8 points. New World's Records in both the typical and non-typical American elk categories exist: Alonzo Winter's 442-5/8 typical bull and the 465-2/8 non-typical bull that was picked up in Upper Arrow Lake in British Columbia. The 133 Sitka blacktail deer taken by Peter Bond is a new World's Record and another from the Canadian provinces. The top of the muskox records has been nearly rewritten in these past two recording periods. Bob Black has the distinction of being the World's Record holder for both the Boone and Crockett Club and the Pope and Young Club muskox with his 127 bull. Don Hotter's 433-4/8 Central Canada barren ground caribou, an Award winner in the 22nd Awards Program tops this relatively new category. When this category was established a few short years ago, many believed the largest representatives of this group of caribou from the central regions of northern Canada would never top 400! The remaining new World's Record is another picked up trophy, a Pacific walrus from Alaska scoring 147-4/8.

A number of updates have been made to trophies contained in this 11th Edition. Editing of records and updating owner information is an on going part of the activities of the Boone and Crockett Club's office operations. Director of Big Game Records, Jack Reneau, has spent numerous hours on updating and proofing the records to insure their completeness and accuracy. In addition, the Club has made an effort to update many of the asterisked trophies which have appeared in past editions. Those that were not resolved were dropped. The remaining asterisked trophies which appear in this edition are from only the 22nd and 23rd Awards Periods.

CLOCKWISE FROM TOP LEFT CORNER: NON-TYPICAL AMERICAN ELK (465-2/8); CENTRAL CANADA BARREN GROUND CARIBOU (433-4/8); TYPICAL AMERICAN ELK (442-5/8); PACIFIC WALRUS (147-4/8); ALASKA-YUKON MOOSE (261-5/8); MUSKOX (127); SITKA BLACKTAIL (133) AND IN THE CENTER TYPICAL WHITETAIL (213-5/8)

Still this is a book that is more than a simple listing of animals and hunters and owners names; it is a book about hunting and hunting perspectives. President Dan Pedrotti opens with a discussion of Hunting in the Twenty-first Century, certainly an issue that concerns all readers of this publication. His beginning is prefaced with a quote from Club founder, Theodore Roosevelt. The message that begins the TR quote "In a civilized and cultivated country wild animals only continue to exist at all

Photographs by Ron Anfinson and Mike Biggs

when preserved by sportsmen" embodies the spirit of the Boone and Crockett Club. It is the underlying theme for much of the material that appears within these pages. President Pedrotti lays forth many of the key issues we, as hunters, face today. He also provides an answer – a possible solution – to these issues. Just as TR and his colleagues faced significant challenges at the beginning of the twentieth century, so do we today. And, just as the Boone and Crockett Club played a key role in the preservation of our sport hunting tradition then, so shall it again today as concerned sportsmen and sportswomen face challenges, albeit different ones, to our huntable wildlife populations.

A book of records is a snapshot of the past. Still this edition also shows what will be – a glimpse into the future. In addition to President Pedrotti's look to the future, Jon Fischer and William E. Clark have written a chapter (which first appeared in the Spring 1999 issue of *Fair Chase*) on the success of the tule elk program in California. This program has restored a once remnant group of these animals to a large, huntable population. While this edition does not contain a listing of record class tule elk, the next will as the Boone and Crockett Club has adopted the tule elk as its newest category for recognition in future record books and is currently accepting entries for these "smaller" elk from the California marsh lands. The success with the tule elk demonstrates what sport hunters, working with game managers and landholders can accomplish. Cooperative habitat programs, hunters working with game divisions and land managers, and economic support from sportsman dollars will be key to our hunting future.

Historical side notes interspersed throughout this book document the past efforts of the members of the Boone and Crockett Club. These mini-biographies, prepared by Club member Hudson DeCray who personally has a fine antelope and mountain caribou in the record listings, document but a brief portion of the many contributions of the Boone and Crockett Club and its members to the hunting conservation movement. Many of the past Club members are well known to the conservation community. Names such as Gifford Pinchot, Aldo Leopold, and Theodore Roosevelt are oft repeated as the leaders of hunting, conservation and ethical sportsmanship. You will find others in these pages, while less well known, who have played vastly important roles in shaping the highly successful hunting opportunities we have today. Current members of the Club continue in this tradition as we move to the new millennia.

Included in this book you will also encounter some breathtaking wildlife art. The names are ones recognized worldwide for their talent as wildlife artists – Bierstadt, Coheleach, Kuhn, Lambson and Rungius. What is less well-known perhaps is that all of these artists are current or past members of the Boone and Crockett Club. Director of Publications for the Boone and Crockett Club, Julie Tripp, has once again used her artistic talents to present a stylish layout for this material. She has worked closely with the artists and owners of the paintings chosen for this edition to bring their many great works together for you to enjoy.

No hunting book is complete without hunting stories and campfire reflections. Long time hunter, Club member and conservationist, Art Popham, shares his thoughts on hunting ethics. Art's hunting adventures cover many years as he reflects on one of his partner's, Jack O'Connor's, advice. Three outstanding contemporary outdoor writers have contributed to this latest edition. Craig Boddington adds his thoughts in "Inches Aren't Everything." Tom McIntyre provides an interesting perspective on high tech aspects, which now impact members of the hunting community. Jim Zumbo discusses a hunt with the Inuits of the frozen north. Jim's reflections on his guide Salamonie Jaw's understanding of his hunting environment and in his confidence in his ability to deal with these conditions and elements as they arose certainly provide the fodder for another good campfire tale. Craig, Jim and Tom are all Professional members of the Club and strong supporters of the hunting ethic that has become synonymous with Boone and Crockett. Despite very different topics in these three chapters, you will find the common theme. Craig notes we "hunt because we are hunters." Tom indicates our goal "is to hunt." In similar fashion, Jim comments we "were in no hurry to hunt. The next morning would come soon enough." As I read these words, these stories, I am reminded we each set our own very personal terms under which we pursue and harvest game animals. The precepts of fair chase guide our actions as do our own hunting mores. Yet, as President Pedrotti notes "we must put aside our differences" in order to insure this heritage through the 21st century."

And there is more; stories for each of the 35 World's Records that top each of the trophy listings appear. In no other publication can one find an encapsulated account for each outstanding trophy. These accounts are far ranging from the chase for the Chadwick ram to the discovery of the highest scoring North American elk found floating near a ferry terminal in British Columbia.

If you enjoy the sport and heritage of hunting, and if you share the concern for sustainable future populations of big game animals, I am sure you will find material within these pages of interest. I know I have! ∎

Hunting in the 21st Century

DANIEL A. PEDROTTI
PRESIDENT
Boone and Crockett Club

"In a civilized and cultivated country wild animals only continue to exist at all when preserved by sportsmen. The excellent people who protest against all hunting and consider sportsmen as enemies of wildlife (do not understand) the fact that in reality the genuine Sports man is, by all odds, the most important factor in keeping the larger and more valuable wild creatures from total extermination."
— PRESIDENT THEODORE ROOSEVELT

The turn of the 19th century was marked by futurists' portrayal of life as they envisioned it "a hundred years hence," or what they thought this planet would look like at the close of the century they were entering. Among the predictions in the December 1900 issue of *Ladies' Home Journal* is the profound yet widely accepted statement "there will be no wild animals except in menageries." (*Corpus Christi Caller-Times* article by Madeline Baro, Associated Press, March 13, 1999)

Today, as we approach the turn of the 20th century, we are blessed with thriving populations of most all species of wildlife. For this, we owe a huge debt of gratitude to the optimists who refused to believe the doomsayers and used their energy, resources and political clout to provide us with the wildlife, hunting and conservation heritage that we have enjoyed and enhanced.

As we enter the new century, it is fitting that we contemplate what will happen in the next 100 years. We are faced with many of the same, and a few new, obstacles that led to the gloom and doom of the nay-sayers of December 1900. Rising human population, urbanization, habitat loss, the animal rights movement, anti-hunting coalitions, reduced freedom due to more government regulation, and fewer hunters as a percentage of our population will all test our convictions. Yet, why don't we hear dire predictions on the future of our hunting heritage? Are we naive? Is it apathy? Are we too full of confidence due to our past success? Are we better armed

THE BOONE AND CROCKETT CLUB WAS FOUNDED BY THEODORE ROOSEVELT AND SEVERAL LIKE-MINDED SPORTSMAN FRIENDS IN 1887. THE MISSION OF THE CLUB WAS TO PROMOTE TWO MAJOR GOALS: THE CONSERVATION OF CRITICAL WILDLIFE HABITAT AND THE PRINCIPLE OF HUNTING IN FAIR CHASE.

due to our awareness of the problems? Do we have more resources available? With the answer to all these questions being "yes," one has to consider how our efforts and results will be graded by the generation enjoying the turn of the 21st century.

Dr. Jack Ward Thomas, Boone and Crockett Club Professor at the University of Montana, has compared the decade from 1995 to 2005 to the decade at the close of the last century in that wildlife conservation was at a crisis level. The actions taken then were obviously responsible for the present improved condition of our lands and wildlife. We can assume that the next five to ten years will see little change in our current situation due to the momentum created in the recent past, but what of the next 25 or 50 years? For a clear perspective, the factors that will shape hunting in the first century of the next millennium can be divided between negative and positive influences.

NEGATIVE INFLUENCES

The two major negatives are habitat loss and anti-hunting forces. These two factors carry a long list of causes and effects. Habitat loss is linked to human population growth, urbanization and the increase in ranchettes owned by individuals near wildlife winter ranges. The increased demand for both non-renewable resources and more outdoor experiences by non-consumptive users also will play a major role. With the anti-hunting movement, we are seeing a myriad of organizations and coalitions capitalizing on many issues that strengthen their claims. With calculated abandon, these organizations have been planting the seeds of anti-hunter bias at all education levels. Their effectiveness at generating anti-hunter sentiment has resulted in continued attacks on our 2nd Amendment rights, unnecessary infringements on hunter's rights, and hunter harassment. Anti-hunting sentiment even seems to be reflected in some government agency policies, which restrict access to public lands, hunting methods and sportfishing opportunity. Especially troubling is the appearance of an anti-hunting sentiment among some federal wildlife agency employees responsible for meeting some of the greatest wildlife management challenges upon which our hunting heritage depends. Poor hunter image and hunter apathy continue to feed the anti-hunting fire storm.

An additional negative influence relates to the enforcement of game laws. Looking back over a century of conservation in the United States, it is clear that law enforcement officers – State and Federal – have played a critical role. As human populations continue to increase and wildlife habitats shrink, it is essential that law enforcement personnel and legitimate hunters consider themselves allies. Unfortunately, in some cases, we are seeing the opposite. There are signs of deterioration in this critical relationship that must be addressed if the welfare of hunters is to be assured, and conservation laws effectively enforced.

Some activities by enforcement personnel are considered by hunters to be unjustified and inappropriate, including arrogance, intimidation, and discourtesy when dealing with hunters. Urgent steps should be taken immediately to change this destructive perception. Agency heads – and the leaders in law enforcement – must be ever vigilant that officers are well-trained, highly motivated and devoted to a work and service ethic that is based on courtesy, respect and sensitivity to all people, and to hunters in particular.

Hunters, on the other hand, are dependent on law enforcement for the perpetuation of hunting and are likewise obligated to treat law enforcement officers with courtesy and respect. The role of law enforcement officers, be they state or federal, is to insure compliance with the laws, rules and regulations and their job is tough. These rules and regulations exist to ensure the welfare of wildlife and the future of hunting. Only through mutual respect can our hunting future be protected and many opportunities for unfavorable media attention be avoided.

POSITIVE INFLUENCES

Habitat conservation, increases in wildlife populations and pro-hunting forces are at the top of the list of positives that will shape hunting in the next ten years. Under habitat conservation, the proven benefits of hunting and wildlife viewing on private lands has come to the forefront to encourage reform. The creation of conservation easements and land acquisitions by conservation organizations has expanded the boundaries of protected and managed lands. Cooperation between permitees on grazing allotments on public lands, and members of conservation organizations and wildlife agencies has also helped to reverse the trend of increasing habitat deterioration and loss.

These conservation efforts, and a better understanding of disease control, have contributed to an increase in our wildlife populations. Also contributing to this increase is the expertise demonstrated by state and federal wildlife agencies. With funding through license fees, excise taxes and contributions from hunter-conservation organizations, agencies have been able to effectively implement the most modern management tools. There is cause for concern however as costs increase and income remains constant or declines.

Pro-hunting forces have caused the growth of species specific hunter-conservation organizations. These groups not only contribute necessary financial support, they also provide dedicated manpower. Pro-hunting groups create an awareness of the many problems facing wildlife and the real threat of anti-hunting efforts. These groups are also responsible for an increase of pro-hunting education at all levels and the improved image of hunters through more knowledge of ethical hunting.

The Silver Anniversary Edition of *Petersen's HUNTING* magazine, November 1998, featured a series of essays on "The Future of Hunting" by a number of today's most influential people in the shooting, hunting and conservation arenas. As one reads through these excellent articles, five themes appear to dominate the thinking of these leaders. In order of their frequency of occurrence in the articles they are as follows:

1. Hunters must extol their contributions to wildlife that have led to our present abundance, and communicate these facts to those who disagree with us, and be willing to listen as well as preach.
2. We must expose more young people to the best of shooting sports, encourage our children and grandchildren to participate in outdoor oriented sports, make

ourselves mentors for their friends, and inject some reality regarding the contributions and value of hunter-conservationists, into the educational systems of this country, especially kindergarten through the 12th grade.

3. We must recognize that hunters are a minority, that fewer hunters make wildlife management more expensive and that as hunting becomes more expensive, hunting numbers further decline.

4. We must put aside our differences and unite our various species specific hunter-conservation groups into a coalition that understands the issues that are winnable, be ready, and capable of combating the sophisticated public relations techniques used by the anti's and the media, and we must be willing to reach out to others who reject our sport due to the lack of understanding our motives.

5. We must become politically involved and put wildlife management back into the hands of the professionals and remove it from those who use the ballot box to frustrate the work of our great wildlife system which is managed by highly trained wildlife professionals.

These themes indeed present some excellent opportunities for the future enjoyment of wildlife and hunting, but how do we develop and implement a strategy to accomplish these objectives? The foreword of *Boone and Crockett Club's 23rd Big Game Awards* lists an alphabet of conservation organizations representing millions of dedicated sportsmen and women. Each of these groups has its own agenda and many overlap; however we currently do not possess a mechanism for uniting these many efforts.

We may have the answer. The Boone and Crockett Club is in the process of structuring a "Wildlife Conservation Partners Summit" that will provide a forum for all concerned with the future of our wildlife heritage to come together and develop policies that will be needed for wildlife and hunting in the next century. Such an effort will not be without risk and conflict, as different factions attempt to influence outcomes, but we must be willing to take risk. It is my belief that in the end consensus on most key issues is possible if participants remember that the welfare of wildlife is always the major goal.

A long term plan, starting with an inventory of all our wildlife resources, broken into shorter segments, with a moving strategy that can be evaluated every five years and revised accordingly, could evolve from this meeting. In 1974, a meeting of all parties concerned with wild sheep was held in Missoula, Montana, and out of that symposium came an understanding that helped wild sheep numbers in North America increase by more than 40 percent in the past 25 years. Our summit could create similar results for the other key species. It could also develop plans to deal with the negative influences described above.

The 11th edition of *Records of North American Big Game* is the final version to be published in this century. It is also the largest to date, containing over 17,100 trophies that meet the stringent qualifications imposed by the Boone and Crockett Club. This represents an increase of 33 percent over the 10th edition published in 1993.

Based on our tradition of releasing this record book every six years, the final book of the 21st century (28th Edition) will be published in 2095. Ever wonder what the 28th edition of *Records of North American Big Game* will look like? Sportsmen and conservationists of today will be judged by its contents. Will we be admired and emulated for our successes as we have honored the generations of the late 1900s who helped shape today's wildlife hunting heritage, or will this epoch in human history be forgotten along with the great hunting and conservation traditions we have enjoyed?

The quantity of hunting opportunities in the 21st century, as well as the quality of the experiences, are in our hands, but we **must act effectively now** as I know we will. As a result, I believe that we will share a place in history along side those who gave us our present abundance, and future generations will be as proud as we are today. ■

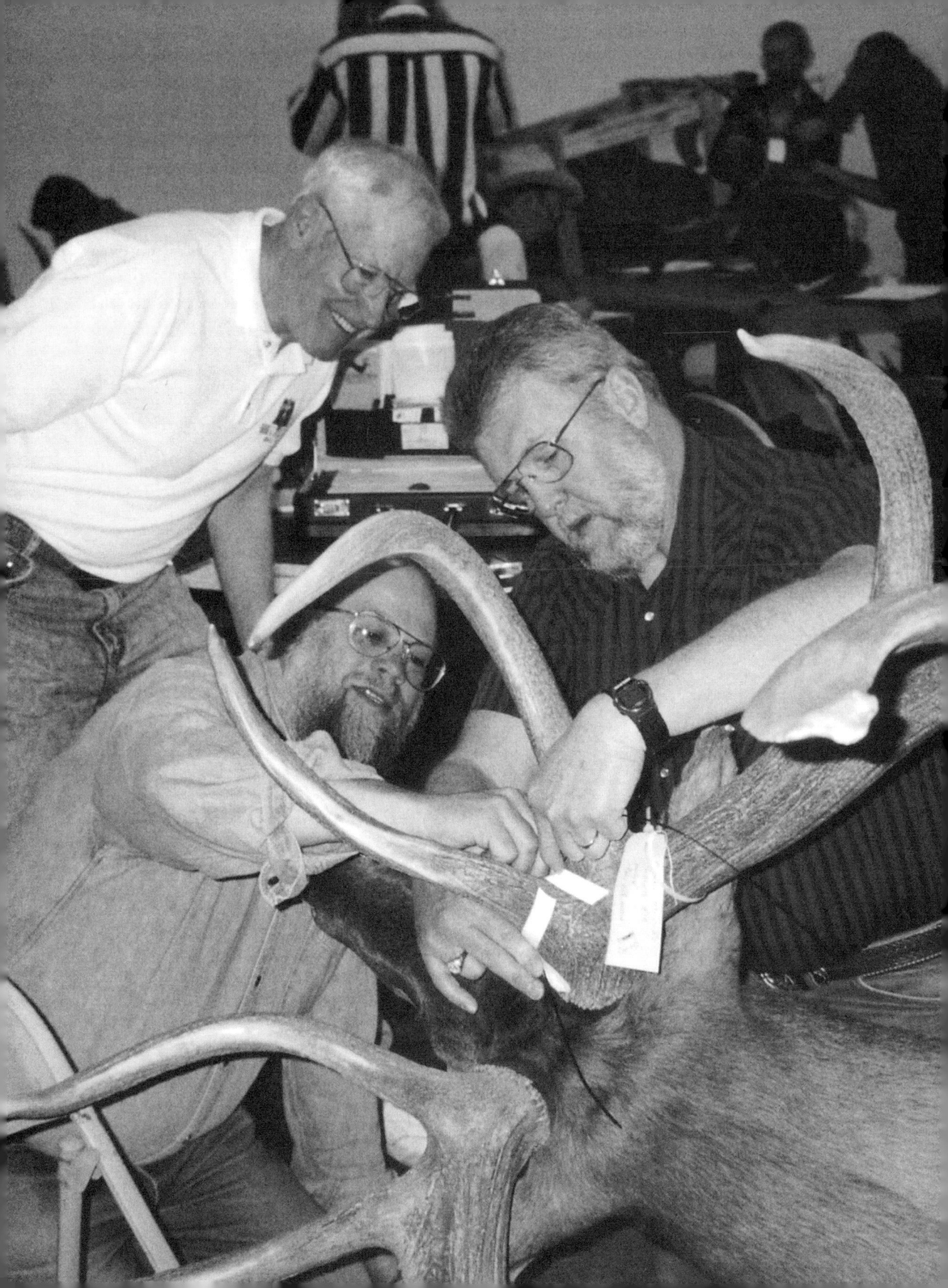

Records of N.A. Big Game

MEASURING CONSULTANT, JACK GRAHAM WATCHES FELLOW MEMBERS OF THE JUDGES' PANEL, RONALD L. BOUCHER (LEFT) AND ROGER W. ATWOOD, MARK THE BASE LINE OF THE BROW TINE ON THE NEW WORLD'S RECORD TYPICAL AMERICAN ELK TAKEN BY ALONZO WINTERS IN 1968. THIS ELK IS JUST ONE OF THE EIGHT NEW WORLD'S RECORDS IN THIS BOOK.

TABLE OF CONTENTS

Continued

RECORDS OF NORTH AMERICAN BIG GAME

11TH EDITION

CHAPTER ONE

Inches Aren't Everything

COL. CRAIG
BODDINGTON USMCR
PROFESSIONAL MEMBER
Boone and Crockett Club

The listings in this volume are a celebration of the biggest and best North American trophies known to exist. Perhaps the proper phrase is "the best North American trophies in history," for this book is history. It is the oldest system keeping records on North American big game, and it has the most rigorous acceptance requirements and the highest standards. All of the trophies listed herein that were taken by hunters have been certified as being legally taken, and taken in fair chase. These are the biggest and the best . . . but no one should consider that phrase to be all-inclusive or all-pervasive.

Rather, these are the largest trophies, in accordance with Boone and Crockett's system of trophy measurement, that have been submitted for official measurement since the first edition of this book generations ago. We know that there are great trophies out there that have not been submitted for measurement. Some will surface someday, and many will not. While we do know this to be true, realistically we might also suppose that there are other great trophies lost forever to the sands of time. The trophies listed herein go back more than century, in itself a noteworthy achievement. But it would be impudent and arrogant not to suppose that some Indian or early European settler might not have, over the many centuries, taken a whitetail larger than any listed herein. Or that another Indian, or perhaps an early fur trapper, might not have taken a wapiti or mule deer larger than any listed herein. These things we are unlikely to ever know, but we do know that each and every trophy listed in this "all-time records book" is a superlative representative of his kind.

Every hunter listed with a trophy has beaten the odds to gain his or her measure of immortality in these timeless listings. Those whose trophies are near the top have beaten truly spectacular odds, in some cases their trophies representing one superlative animal out of tens of thousands harvested. All of us as hunters must admire the fine animals listed in this volume . . . and, as humans, it would be most unnatural not to feel at least a small tinge of jealousy toward their fortunate owners. Should we

THIS COLORADO BULL IS FAR, FAR SHORT OF MEETING THE MINIMUMS FOR THIS BOOK. THIS DOESN'T BOTHER ME IN THE LEAST. HE IS A NICE BULL, TAKEN FAIR AND SQUARE ON PUBLIC LAND, AND I WILL ALWAYS BE PROUD OF HIM.

also feel a measure of universal respect toward the many hundreds of hunters listed herein? My answer to that is yes . . . and no.

No two hunts are alike, and none of the trophies listed in this volume were harvested under identical circumstances. Some of these great trophies came as a result of extreme and lengthy effort. Some were taken easily in a chance encounter. Some were taken by experienced, veteran hunters. Others were taken by newcomers to the sport. In some cases the hunter knew the quality of the animal in his or her sights; in other cases the potential for a "book listing" was unknown until much later.

The taking of a North American trophy qualifying for this or any other edition of *Records of North American Big Game* is a major event in any hunter's life, and I would never wish to suggest it should be less. Whether the event came about as a result of a well-planned campaign, or largely by accident, the holder of a great North American trophy is almost instantly cast into the role of an authority on the subject. So much so that some have launched lucrative careers on the basis of one fortunate encounter with a truly great animal! I find this more amusing than bothersome. The animal grew to whatever proportions he grew, and by everything we have learned about his tribe in the last century, if that animal is listed herein, then he was a magnificent specimen of his kind. The animal has my admiration and respect, but I tend to want to know a little more about the circumstances under which that animal was harvested before I accord the same honor to the hunter.

Except for this. Even with the very best planning and in the very best area, there is never any guarantee that a given hunter will be fortunate enough to encounter the kind of animal that will earn him and it a place in this book. I do not necessarily believe that hunting is a matter of blind luck; I believe that luck is greatly assisted by preparation, effort, persistence, and smart hunting techniques. Even so, there is an element of chance that places a great animal before one hunter and not another. Sometimes the hunter who works the hardest gets the greatest trophy . . . but not always. However, for every great trophy that is taken, there are almost certainly others that could have been taken, but were not.

Every hunter has his or her stories about the one that got away. Heaven knows I have mine. This is also part of the game. Sometimes great animals are seen just for a moment, with no shots possible. Other times they are missed . . . and many times the mere sight of their majestic horns or antlers causes the onset of a bout of buck fever so severe that no shots are fired, even when there could well have been.

Some of the trophies in this book were taken by hunters who studied maps and other references, then backpacked alone into remote wilderness and came back with their prizes. Other trophies were particular animals that were known and patterned and hunted hard, sometimes for several seasons, before they were brought to bag. Still others were taken in chance encounters. So I cannot accord an equal level of respect for the hunting accomplishments displayed in this volume. Except. Regardless of the circumstances, fortune smiled in giving these hunters an opportunity to

NORTH TO SOUTH, EAST TO WEST, OUR NORTH AMERICAN CONTINENT OFFERS A WONDERFUL DIVERSITY OF GAME AND HUNTING OPPORTUNITIES. THE RECORD-BOOK ANIMALS ARE OUT THERE – BUT THEY ARE NOT COMMON, AND THE OPPORTUNITIES ARE NOT EVENLY DISTRIBUTED.

4

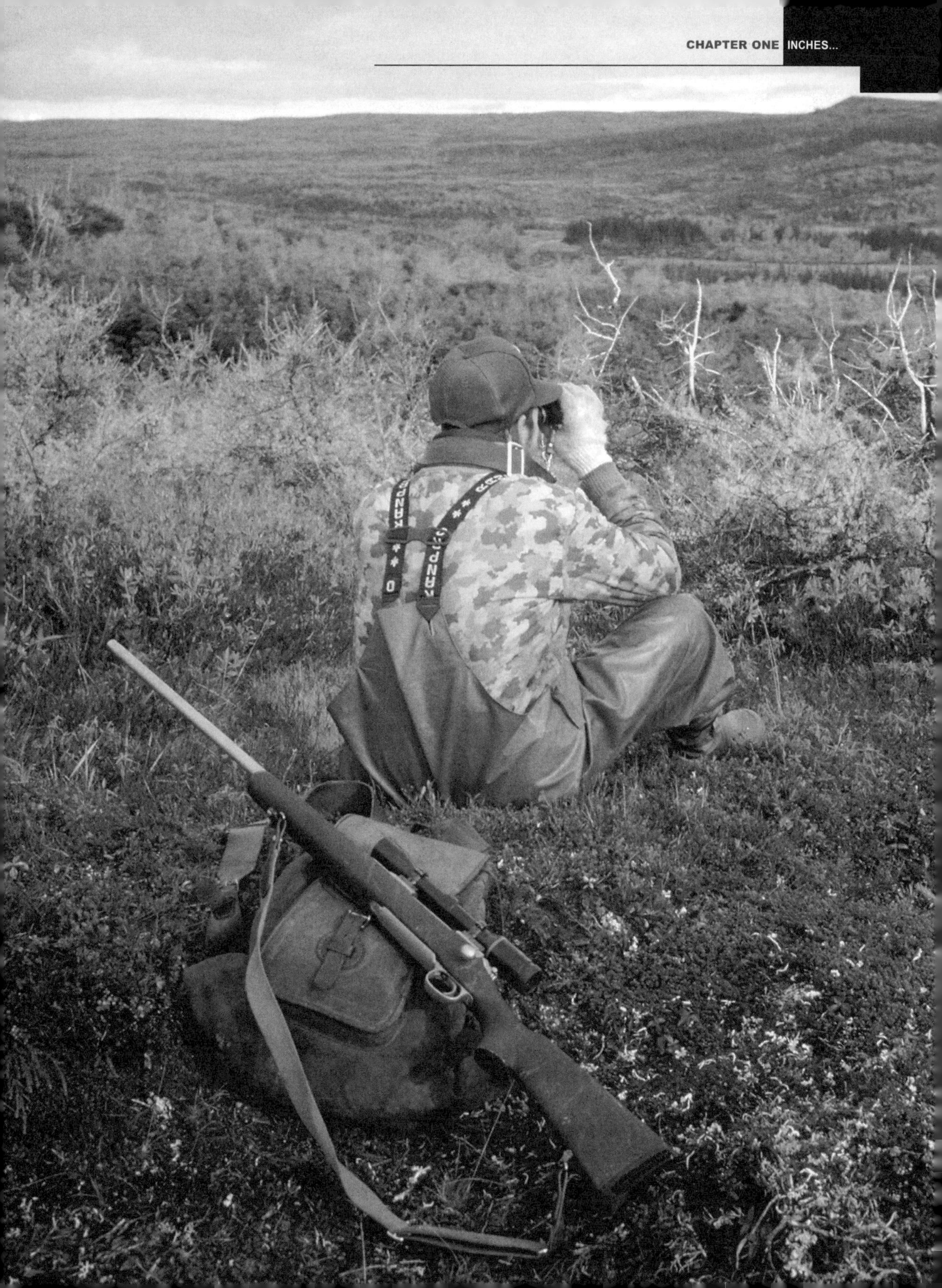

take their wonderful prizes. And that is where fortune stopped playing a part.

Every single hunter represented in this volume did a great many things right when that opportunity was presented. Every single one was able to fight off buck fever and make the right decisions and the right moves that resulted in a bullet or arrow being launched in the right direction. In some cases this was skill born of long experience; in other cases it was instinctual. Perhaps in most cases it was a bit of both. But this I have unqualified respect for! Hunters who take a great trophy early in their career will hear a great deal about "beginner's luck." Bunk! Any hunter who is listed in this volume did a whole lot of things right that have nothing to do with luck, and each deserves much credit for coolness and efficiency in that moment of truth.

Unfortunately, the reality is that very few of us, among the millions of American hunters, will ever learn how well or how poorly we would handle an encounter with a trophy large enough to gain us fame and immortality in these pages. Part of the prestige of this book is that its standards are so damnably high; in many of the categories an animal that qualifies for inclusion is literally one in tens of thousands. Not all of us will see such a creature, even in a lifetime of hard hunting.

This is not due entirely to the high standards that have been set over time. We in North America have the greatest hunting opportunities found on this planet – but our opportunities are not altogether equal. With almost any variety of game, there are some areas that produce large trophies on a regular basis, some that only rarely produce large specimens, and other areas that almost never do. This disparity may be caused by management practices, genetics, food, minerals, climate . . . or, more likely, a combination of factors. This is neither fair nor unfair; it just is.

Ours is a free country. Those who have the desire, flexibility, and financial ability can travel to the better trophy areas – but not everyone can. This does not mean that hunters who live and hunt in poor trophy country aren't as good hunters as those who live and hunt where the big ones grow. They may well be better hunters, but if animals large enough to make these hallowed listings simply don't exist where they hunt, then their names will never be seen herein.

This business of some areas being better than others is not the only limiting factor. For an increasing number of species, especially in the West, some of our very best trophy opportunities are found in areas that require beating the odds in exceptionally difficult draws. The research is there to be done, and it can be done quite easily. It doesn't take a rocket scientist to figure out that, if you could draw a tag in Montana's Rock Creek area, you would have a very good chance at a bighorn ram that would make these listings. Or, if you could draw a mule deer tag in Utah's Paunsaugant, you might take the mule deer of a lifetime. Knowing these things doesn't help all that much if you must beat odds of 50 or 100 to one to get a tag. Here luck isn't just a small factor; it's everything. Without luck in the draw, all the research and all the hunting skill in the world won't get you in the door.

THE ONLY THING WRONG WITH THIS ALBERTA WHITETAIL IS THAT HE ISN'T MINE; HE WAS TAKEN BY MY GOOD FRIEND, CRAIG LEERBERG. THIS IS THE KIND OF BUCK WE ALL DREAM ABOUT, AND THAT HOPE KEEPS US COMING BACK YEAR AFTER YEAR.

There are other very good areas that are privately owned.

I HAVE NEVER BEEN PAR-
TICULARLY GOOD AT
SITTING STILL. REGARD-
LESS OF THE GAME, MY
FAVORITE KIND OF HUNT-
ING IS WITH BINOCULARS
AND LEGS... PREFERABLY
IN THAT ORDER.

Photograph courtesy of Craig Boddington

While the wildlife present is in public stewardship, our system respects private property, and it gives the landowner the right to decide how his land is utilized, and by whom. This is part of the American dream, so I have no problem with it. I certainly want to have a say over who comes in my house, and a rancher should have the same say-so on his property. That's fine, but it means that some private land is accessible, some is accessible only to friends and relatives of the landowner, and some is accessible only for a fee. We are also built around a market economy, so if some private landowners or Indian Reservations that have done exceptionally good game management are able to command high fees for the opportunity they offer, no one who believes in our system should have a problem with that. But it all means that opportunity to take record-class animals is not altogether equal.

Secretly (if not openly!), I think most of us would be pleased to see our name plastered all over this book. We all hunt for different reasons. A very, very few of us are unabashedly obsessed with seeing our name in these pages. A few more are simply competitive by nature, driven to excel in whatever they pursue. Neither bothers me, so long as all the rules of sportsmanship are adhered to. More of us, I suspect, hunt because we are hunters. It is recreation in the great outdoors, and offers tasty venison and the occasional trophy as by-products. Few of us today are truly "meat hunters" in the sense that venison is survival . . . but more of us consider ourselves meat hunters than trophy hunters. That said, there are very, very few self-proclaimed meat hunters who, in open season and with a tag in hand, would allow an animal of Boone and Crockett proportions to walk by! But not all of us will live long enough to have such an opportunity.

There was a time when the listings in this book – more specifically, my ability to get my name in this book – seemed exceptionally important. Today I'm not so sure. I am genuinely happy for each and every hunter listed herein, and I'm also grateful to them. Collectively, their entries provide all of us a yardstick of excellence, a means for knowing how large the antlers, horns, and skulls of our North American big game animals can be, and thus establishing sound criteria for selective hunting. I'm also grateful to them for giving us all hope, witnessed by the incredible number of new entries in this last Twentieth Century edition. After all, regardless of where we hunt and what the real odds might be, who among us doesn't harbor just a wee hope, on every day afield, that this will be the day that a monster crosses our path?

As the years go by, I am more and more convinced that this hope and anticipation are more important than the actual inches of antler, horn, or bone. I have never taken a whitetail deer large enough to qualify for this records book. I am hardly alone; there are as many as 10 million whitetail hunters on this continent, and just a couple thousand entries! In fact, even my vocation, avocation, and passion lead me to pursue whitetails in some very good places, it is quite likely that I will never take a whitetail that is big enough and perfect enough to qualify.

That doesn't bother me. Every day I step into the whitetail woods there is hope. This will be the day that the monster of all monsters will step out of the morning mists and pause broadside. I

A FEW YEARS EARLIER, IN GENTLY ROLLING COUNTRY THAT WAS FULL OF RAMS, I TOOK A MUCH LARGER BIGHORN THAN THIS. I CAN'T SAY THAT I VALUE THIS WYOMING RAM MORE, BUT HE CAME AT THE END OF A LONG AND DIFFICULT HUNT, A REAL SHEEP HUNT, AND I VALUE HIM JUST AS MUCH.

can see the gleam of his immense rack, and the rifle is steady. We all harbor that secret hope, and what would the deer woods be without it?

What we do with that hope varies. Some people, perhaps better men than I, continue to search until the last hour of the last day, and go home happy knowing they have tried. I don't consciously drop my standards as the days pass, but with stories to write and a great fondness for whitetail backstrap, I try not to let my hopes and dreams interfere with reality. My reality is that a buck I would take on the last day is probably a buck I should take on the first day. That reality does not diminish my vision of the great buck that will appear someday, somewhere. Nor does it diminish the tremendous thrill I have received from every single buck I have been fortunate enough to take, whether large, small, or just plain average.

Effort counts, too. In fact, effort counts a great deal. For many years I have considered the Rocky Mountain bighorn sheep to be the ultimate North American big game animal. You may choose the elk, the grizzly bear, even the whitetail, and these three are also favorites of mine. But the bighorn sheep and all he symbolizes is my choice. I put in for the draw tags for many years, and I backpacked into Montana's "unlimited permit" country as well. If effort counts, in that country you will receive your full measure – even if you don't get a ram, and I did not.

Then I drew a permit in the Butte Highlands, one of Montana's really good areas. It was a wonderful hunt, and I was rewarded with a great ram. After applying for 20-some years and busting my tail in the unlimited permit country, I probably deserved it (although no more than anyone else). Except it wasn't really a sheep hunt. This was relatively low, rolling country, and there were rams everywhere. I'm sure I saw 150 rams, and the hunt was much more similar to a good pronghorn hunt. I prize that ram, you bet . . . but I vaguely regretted not having the high country experience I had dreamed of for so long.

Just four years later I drew a Wyoming bighorn permit. Be careful what you wish for in life, because you just might get it. This was a real sheep hunt, and a long sheep hunt, and a tough sheep hunt. More than once I kicked myself for mentally regretting how easy that Montana hunt had been. I knew I had brought the pain on myself! On the tenth day, all of them spent fighting a terrible cold and the last three with broken ribs from a fall off a horse, after spending a long night huddled around a fire with no gear, I shot a very nice, very pretty, fully mature bighorn ram. He is not even in the same class as my Montana ram, but I prize him just as much because hunting him was the bighorn hunting experience I had always dreamed of (and then some!). Effort counts.

IT WASN'T FAR FROM THIS SPOT THAT I MISSED THE LARGEST ELK, AND ONE OF THE HIGHEST-QUALITY ANIMALS OF <u>ANY</u> SPECIES – THAT I HAVE EVER HAD A CHANCE AT. IT WAS STILL A BEAUTIFUL DAY ON THE MOUNTAIN.

Undoubtedly that is one of the reasons why I enjoy elk hunting as much as I do. I am not a good stand hunter. I admire those who can sit in a treestand day after day, enjoying the woods and waiting for a whitetail. I can do it when I must, but I'm terrified of heights and I hate to sit still. I much prefer hunting with binoculars and legs rather than sheer determined patience. Elk hunting is some of the most physical hunting that I know, under most circumstances even more physical than sheep hunting.

Our elk is a fairly democratic animal, especially with today's burgeoning herds. There are special places, and a quick look at the elk listings in this book will reveal them – but a monster could turn up (and occasionally does) almost anywhere. Even though it is possible, usually I don't hold out for, or even seek, a monster. I have no place to put such a trophy, and any nice bull is a difficult enough prize to be considered a really fine trophy. Once, just once, I consciously went after the biggest bull in the woods.

Well I should have. I drew an Arizona elk tag in a very good area, an area that definitely held the bull of a lifetime. Just this once, it made sense to go look for him. We found him, too, far up on a steep slope, bedded in bare-limbed late-season aspen. I waited him out, and when he stood and came out into the open I had my moment of truth with the trophy of a lifetime.

Thanks to my choice of profession, I have been fortunate to have hunted a great deal. I have taken some very fine trophies over the years. Some have come easily and some not. I have certainly never gone out of my way to make things harder than they needed to be – that will take care of itself – but I have always stayed in good shape, and I can usually get where I need to in order to make a shot. I have always practiced my shooting, and usually I can handle that department as well. On this morning in Arizona, I got to where I needed to get to. I took my time and set my pack over a boulder, and I waited for the right presentation. Then I missed the biggest elk I have ever had a chance to take.

The shot was a long one, but I knew how to do it and I had the right equipment. I just didn't do what I know how to do, and all the excuses in the world won't change that. The funny thing is that it doesn't bother me much. Maybe not at all. We tried, and we had a chance. You can't ask for much more than that.

The next evening was my last, and at last light I took a very nice young bull – with a much more difficult shot than the one I missed the day before. If I were a fatalist, I'd say it just wasn't meant to be. But I'm much more of a realist, and the reality is that I simply blew it. It happens, and it will undoubtedly happen again . . . hopefully not on such a great animal. But, then, I am most unlikely to ever have another chance on an elk like that! And yet the fact that I blew it doesn't detract from the memories of a great hunt. We worked hard and we tried. That bull will never grace my wall, nor the pages of this book – at least not with my name next to it – but I'll never forget those long minutes, watching him bedded, nor the majesty with which he swaggered into that snowy clearing.

I have been extremely fortunate; that great bull standing in a clearing high in Arizona's mountains is not the only truly magnificent trophy I have ever had a chance at. But you can bet he is the one I remember best. If I work at it long enough, I will convince myself that I prefer remembering him that way! ■

Col. Craig Boddington of Paso Robles, California, is a professional member of the Boone and Crockett Club and senior field editor of Petersen's HUNTING *and* GUNS & AMMO *magazines. He is also a regular contributor to* Fair Chase *magazine. Craig is also the author of numerous hunting and gun books. He has over 25 years of service in the U.S. Marine Corps.*

THE NEXT DAY WAS MY LAST. JUST AT DARK I TOOK THIS YOUNG BULL – THOUGH NOT QUITE AS FAR, TECHNICALLY A FAR MORE DIFFICULT SHOT THAN I MISSED ON THE BIG BOY. LARGE TROPHIES HAVE A WAY OF MESSING WITH HUNTERS' MINDS, AND NO ONE HAS ENOUGH EXPERIENCE TO BE IMMUNE!

CHAPTER TWO

High Tech and Hunting

THOMAS McINTYRE
PROFESSIONAL MEMBER
Boone and Crockett Club

Trying to differentiate between hunters and tech-nologists is like trying to say that falcons are separate from birds. Among all the predators, humans, from the earliest stages of their evolution, were uniquely dependent upon technology in order to become hunters. It is, in fact, technology —the modification and manipulation of natural objects to accomplish various tasks, or in other words the manufacture and use of tools — along with language makes us human.

We are not naturally suited to chase and capture game, particular large ungulates. We walk, it has been noted, no faster than the chicken, and at a dead run are not likely to overtake anything much more fleet than a porcupine. We are, as a species, gifted with enormous stamina (few wild animals could sustain the distance and competitive pace of a marathon race, for example); but while we might conceivably wear an animal out over a long-distance pursuit, we are then faced with the matter of how to dispatch it. Noticeably lacking in fang and claw, we at first undoubtedly resorted (à la the primates in *2001*) to blunt objects, whether a femur or wooden club or stone, as our killing tools. What allowed us to do so was the fact that while we might have been physically unprepossessing, at least on the outside, we had on the inside of our skulls quite oversized brains that allowed us to see how we might pick up such inanimate objects and wield them to our benefit.

Other animals, of course, from chimpanzees to otters also use simple hand tools, whether a twig to probe for termites in a log or a rock to crack the shells of mollusks. Humans, though, not only go farther by fabricating tools (whether sharpening the end of a stick to make it a stabbing tool, or fracturing a rock to turn it into an edged, cutting one), but also by seeing beyond their use in the hand alone. The development of hunting tools is one of a progression toward force-at-a-distance weapons with ever increasing ranges and velocities. The wooden spear went from a thrusting weapon

TODAY ADVANCED TECH-NOLOGY THREATENS TO BLIND EVEN THESE "PURIST" PURSUITS WITH SCIENCE, AND AT BEST BLUR THE CLOSER CONNECTION BETWEEN PREDATOR AND QUARRY THAT WAS BEING SOUGHT THROUGH THEM. DOES THIS LOOK LIKE A "PRIMITIVE" WEAPON?

to a throwing one topped with a knapped stone point to one made even more lethal by the addition of a spear thrower, such as the atlatl. After the spear thrower came the bow and arrow (one of human technology's most ingenious and beneficial leaps), which was continually refined to become ever more efficient.

Nonetheless, to become an effective archer required no small amount of talent and a good deal of practice. The crossbow was devised as a means of shortcutting the lengthy process of acquiring archery skills. Anyone who had the strength to draw a crossbow had only then to aim it and press a trigger to launch a bolt. The firearms that followed in the wake of the crossbow (and adopted many of its designs, such as the shoulder stock) demanded even less training.

Still, the bow was considered the far more lethal hunting tool until well into the 18th century. And it was not until the advent of the percussion firearm, and the acceptance of riflings, not to mention sights, that the gun, or rifle, became the weapon of choice for the hunter. From there, technological advances in the rifle came on steadily, with first the breechloading cartridge rifle replacing the muzzleloader, the lever superseding the single-shot action, then the bolt. With the addition of the telescopic sight, it would have seemed that hunting technology would have reached its apex, and for many decades this was not far off the mark.

I can recall a veteran brown bear guide in Alaska telling me in the late '70s that the technology of hunting had advanced very little from the Griffin & Howe rifle of the '30s, or from the rubber boot and the down jacket of roughly the same period. It was his opinion, to paraphrase the words of the show tune, that things had gone about fer as they could go, and were unlikely to go much ferther. He died shortly after that, and did not witness the brave new world that came rapidly on.

In the last twenty years we have seen, among many, many other wonders, waterproof boots that not only keep our feet warm in the cold, but free of sweat in the warm, letting us enjoy the historically unprecedented phenomenon of actually hunting dry shod. Down has been replaced with lighter, better insulating materials that maintain their warmth even when wet, and seldom get wet due to the breathable yet rain-resistant fabrics now used in a garment's outer shell. And these are nothing compared to the changes in the hunting rifle.

A generation ago, the state-of-the-art hunting rifle weighed in at nine or ten pounds, had a wooden stock, a fixed-power scope that might or might not fog up in a light mist, and two or three types of bullets to choose from. Today, six- to seven-pound rifles are not uncommon; stocks are synthetic for reduced weight and elimination of any change due to the vagaries of weather; scopes are fully waterproof variables with multi-coated lenses and extra-large objectives to give unsurpassed light transmission; sometimes dozens of different bullets, from plastic tipped to coated to solid copper, are available for any particular caliber. Add to that the use of stainless steel and even more exotic alloys, along with new metal treatments, to create virtually rust-free rifles; cryogenic and barrel-polishing processes for increased accuracy; built-in bipods; and various styles of porting for

reduced recoil, and it is obviously not your father's deer rifle anymore.

Today, a rifle capable of making 400-, even 500-yard shots at last light in a driving sleet storm is nearly pro forma. It also conforms to the age-old trend of hunters being able to increase both the physical and psychological distance between themselves and their prey. Since the first hunter let a spear leave his hand by hurling it, we have been able to move farther and farther away from the game. This is a natural progression, to be sure, and with it has come a greater, perhaps even counterbalancing ability to kill more swiftly and humanely. Still, there is something in this that threatens ultimately to sever the intimate connection between the hunter and hunted, that connection being one of the elements that draws humans to the hunt to begin with. Certainly, the rise of bowhunting and muzzleloader-hunting, now decades ago, owes much to a desire to maintain and intensify this connection by demanding that a hunter place himself in greater proximity to the game because of the limited range of his weapon.

RANGEFINDERS CAN MAKE FOR MORE ACCURATE AND, THEREFORE, CLEANER KILLS. IF ONLY IT ENDED THERE...

Today, though, the advanced technology of overdraw compound bows with 80% letoffs (allowing a hunter to hold a 75-

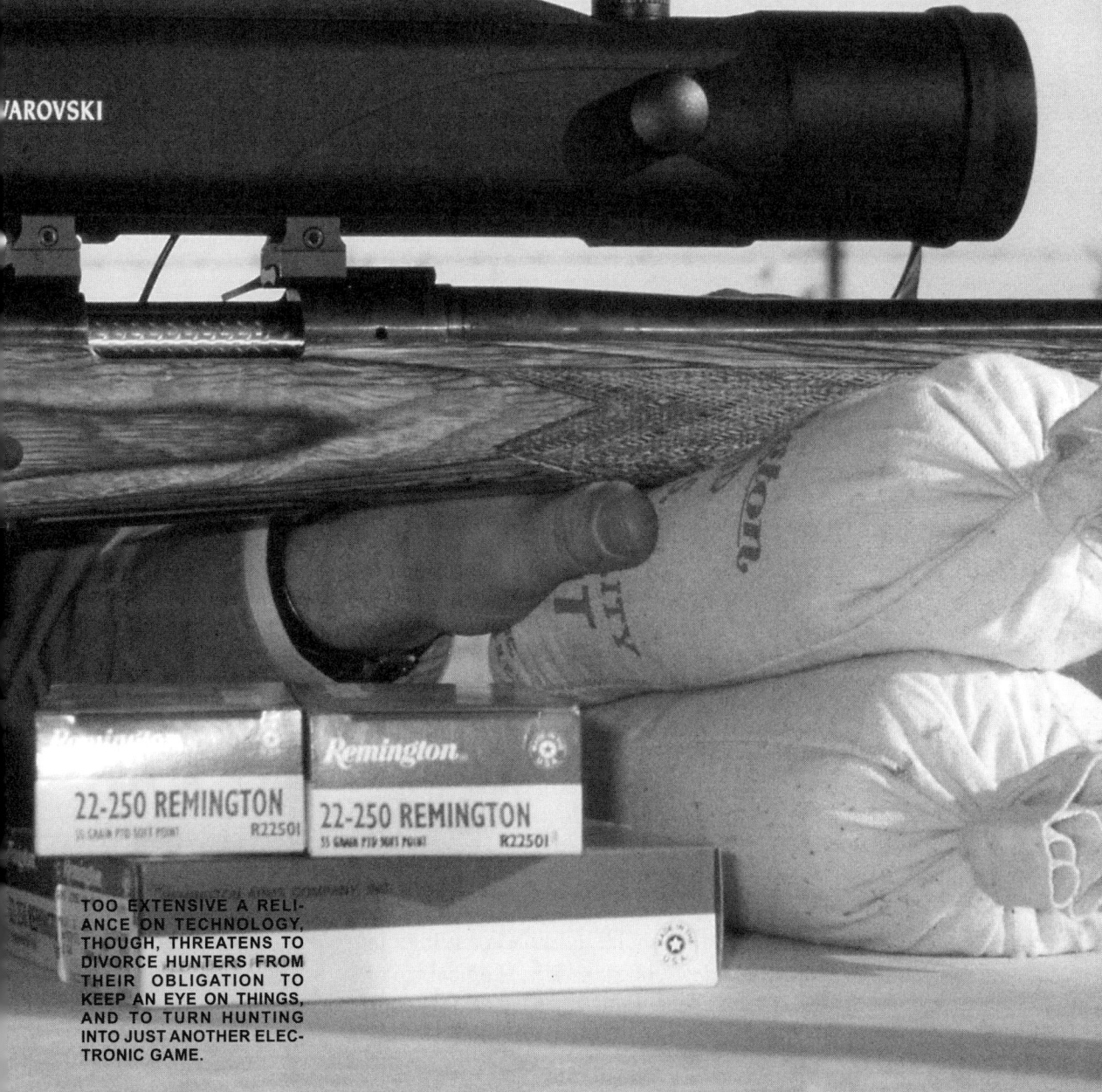

VAROVSKI

22-250 REMINGTON
55 GRAIN PTD SOFT POINT   R22501

Remington

22-250 REMINGTON
55 GRAIN PTD SOFT POINT   R22501

TOO EXTENSIVE A RELI-
ANCE ON TECHNOLOGY,
THOUGH, THREATENS TO
DIVORCE HUNTERS FROM
THEIR OBLIGATION TO
KEEP AN EYE ON THINGS,
AND TO TURN HUNTING
INTO JUST ANOTHER ELEC-
TRONIC GAME.

Photograph courtesy of Tom McIntyre

21

pound bow at full-draw almost indefinitely with only 15-pounds of energy), peep sights, release aids, and mechanical broadheads whose blades fly open on contact; and in-line muzzleloaders using shotgun primers and powder pellets, scoped sights, and saboted 250-grain jacketed bullets capable of velocities substantially above 2000-feet-per-second, threatens to blind even these "purist" pursuits with science, and at best blur the closer connection between predator and quarry that was being sought through them. Worse than this, though, are the so-called high-tech "hunting aids" that threaten not merely to blur, but to obliterate almost completely that ancient and essential connection.

We are told, far too often by outdoor publications and on television hunting programs and by self-proclaimed experts, that no modern hunter is complete without his laser rangefinder, night-vision binocular, global-positioning system (GPS), pocket citizen-band (CB) radio, electronic hearing-enhancement device, ATV, and cellular phone; not, in short, until he is outfitted like some Imperial Stormtrooper out of *Star Wars*. Logical, and legal, arguments can be made for the use of all of the above: Rangefinders can make for more accurate and, therefore, cleaner

LOGICAL, AND LEGAL, ARGUMENTS CAN BE MADE FOR MANY OF THESE NEW TECHNOLOGIES. GPS UNITS CAN KEEP HUNTERS FROM GETTING LOST IN THE WOODS, BUT THE GREATER OUR RELIANCE ON TECHNOLOGY, THE MORE LIKELY WE ARE TO MISTAKE THE PROCESS FOR THE FINAL GOAL — TO HUNT.

Photograph courtesy of Tom McIntyre

kills; GPSes can keep hunters from getting lost in the woods; CBs and cellular phones can summon help in the event of an emergency, etc. If only it ended there...

The applications of technology to hunting, though, also extend to infrared trail counters to keep a tally of the animals passing by, and camera "surveillance systems" that will photograph that big buck that is coming to a scrape or beneath our stand when we are away from it. In Quebec, it is possible to obtain a weekly printout pinpointing the location of radio-collared caribou in various herds, as monitored by satellite. Timed electronic feeders can summon game as surely as a picnic basket beckons ants. Special nutrients and minerals may be supplied to enhance antler growth. Perhaps worst of all is the application of eugenics to certain high-demand big-game, such as whitetail, where they are being intensely managed on private (and sometimes enclosed) land, all in the hopes of producing extraordinary "trophy" heads. Here is a case of using technology not simply to manipulate the sticks and stones around us, but the very environment and the basic nature of the prey species itself.

The most serious risk in all this is not just a faulty connection with the wildlife we hunt, and the wildlands in which we hunt it, but an outright sense of detachment from the totality of both. The greater our reliance on technology, the more likely we are to mistake the process for the final goal. That goal, by the way, is not to kill an animal. The goal is to hunt, to rejoin as profoundly as possible with our primitive self and to experience the environment, and our relationship to the animals in it, as we once did when we dwelled in our first, natural state; to relive as truly as we can a time definitely devoid of microchips. The kill, while vital, is not even the last act of such a hunt, the hunt is not complete until we have packed in the carcass, skinned it out, butchered it, and not least, eaten the meat, the same kind of meat that sustained us for hundreds of thousands of years before we even dreamed of culture and science. Yet the surfeit of modern technology threatens to short-circuit that more complex purpose by focusing all the attention of the hunt on the kill, none of it designed to deepen or broaden our experience of the hunting grounds, but actually to filter most of it out and narrow and compress our field of vision onto the quarry alone, the quarry reduced to no more than a score to be posted on a display.

The real danger is that the more detached we become, the more likely we are to feel no concern for the overall fate of the game we pursue or the country through which we pursue it. If all we see in our rangefinders, or hear of over our CBs, is a single, trophy animal, then we are less likely to worry about all the other, non-trophy animals that live with it, or the condition of the environment in which they live. Hunters have always been in the forefront of conservation because they have always been the ones most "out there," most alert to the changes taking place, and the ones most ready to speak out against them when necessary. Too extensive a reliance on technology, though, threatens to divorce hunters from their obligation to keep an eye on things, and to turn hunting into just another electronic game, something only different from the video hunting games already on the market by virtue of its being played in the open, rather than in front of a television or computer screen.

Let's be honest: Hunters are technologists and always have been. Much of technology has improved the quality of hunting as a whole (few of us, I think, would prefer to subject an animal to the sort of death it might suffer by a spear, rather than the humane death made possible by the modern bow and arrow or rifle). I will be honest enough to say that I like the comfort of high-tech hunting clothes and boots, and the lightness and accuracy of my rifle with its synthetic stock and large-objective scope, not to mention the superior performance of its bullets. I'm sure that others could say the same about many of the other high-tech devices listed above, and that they feel they can utilize any and all of them not just legally, but morally and ethically. The difference, at least for me, is that I have chosen the technology I have because it distracts me less from my experience of the hunt; with no sopping clothes to make me uncomfortable and no boat-anchor of a rifle to weigh me down, I am free to concentrate more fully on the hunt itself. Carrying more technology would not create more clarity; in all likelihood it would only produce more electronic "snow" and white noise. When I hunt, I want to see and hear as acutely as I can; but I also want, as

TODAY'S MUZZLELOADERS USE SABOTED 250-GRAIN JACKETED BULLETS CAPABLE OF VELOCITIES SUBSTANTIALLY ABOVE 2000 FEET-PER-SECOND ARE FAR CRY FROM THE "PRIMITIVE" WEAPON.

much as I can, to see and hear with my own eyes and ears. The more I minimize my use of technology, the closer I draw to the game, which has only its own eyes and ears to defend itself. And what is hunting if it is not about getting as close to the game as it is humanly, rather than technologically, possible to do so? ■

Tom McIntyre, a member, both Regular and Professional, of the Boone and Crockett Club for over 10 years, was for nearly 20 years the Hunting Editor at Sports Afield *magazine. He is now a contributing editor at* Field & Stream, *as well as writing for* Gray's Sporting Journal, Rifle, Bugle, Hunting, Men's Journal, *and* The Field *in England. Tom is the author of four books, his latest on the shooting sports from Lyons Press. Tom lives in north-central Wyoming with his wife Elaine, son Bryan Ruark, one cat Tiger Lily, and a lumpen Lab Beckett.*

CHAPTER THREE

Hunting With Inuits

JIM ZUMBO
PROFESSIONAL MEMBER
Boone and Crockett Club

The far north has always held a special appeal. It is a land of unforgiveness, where a simple mistake may cost you your life. Nowhere else in North America does one face the extreme perils of nature than in the north. Human comfort becomes the highest of priorities. Survival may require hard work, taking up most hours of the day. Luxuries are brief and basic, dependent on a person's astuteness and the weather.

Always the weather. Most human activities in the far north are scheduled according to nature's whims. To be sure, the weather is a part of life everywhere in the world, from thunderstorms to tornadoes, hurricanes, droughts, and floods. But in the north it can be counted on to be extreme — for the best part of every year. Bitterly cold sub-zero temperatures and gale force winds are a fact of life. Add to this bleak description the very short, insect-ridden summers, and the very long, 20-hour dark winter days, and you have a region where humanity battles valiantly with the elements.

There are no palm trees here, no white sandy beaches, no trees bearing exotic fruits. Unlike the natives in the tropics, whose stereotype is dancing in grass skirts, the Arctic Inuits cope with this planet's most challenging climate. They are a people of improvisation, of incredible outdoor skills, of amazing tenacity.

Here is a place where the need to stay warm cannot be satisfied by simply building a fire, for there is no firewood. The tundra is a seemingly barren landscape that supports lichens and dwarfed shrubbery that seldom grows higher than a child's knee. Yesterday, natives used whale oil and then coal oil for heat; today more modern fuels are burned.

MY FIRST TRIP TO THE TREE-LESS NORTH WAS A HUNT FOR CARIBOU ON BAFFIN ISLAND. HUNTING WITH OUTFITTER JEROME KNAP, THE PLAN WAS TO NAVI-GATE ACROSS 80 MILES OF THE ARCTIC OCEAN IN FREIGHTER CANOES.

My first trip to the treeless north was a hunt for caribou on Baffin Island. Hunting with outfitter Jerome Knap, the plan was to navigate across 80 miles of the Arctic Ocean in freighter canoes. We were told that our party was the first group of non-native hunters to ever hunt the region, and it was with a bit of trepidation and exhilaration that we climbed

aboard the canoes at Cape Dorset.

My guide, Salamonie Jaw, spoke poor English, but he was nevertheless able to communicate fairly well. Our canoe, powered by a 35 hp outboard, was 24 feet long and easily held the guide, me, two other hunters, and all our gear.

An elderly Inuit who was designated as chief took the lead. His canoe was trailed by six others, each carrying hunters and gear. We totaled seven Inuits and 18 hunters in all.

As we left the rocky coast, I assumed we'd all be traveling in a group so each canoe was within sight of each other. After all, that only made good sense, because several of the Inuit guides had never been to the area we were going to, including Salamonie. Good sense, however, isn't exactly a quality that's seen much in the far North. This isn't a negative critique of the native people, but a look at reality. As we soon learned, they are so incredibly rugged and self-reliant that they don't use logic in the manner we do.

We'd gone about 10 miles, each canoe a small spot on the ocean; some in front of us and some behind. As we traveled, the canoes became farther and farther apart. Salamonie made no attempt to close the gap; he was perfectly content to do his own thing.

Presently Salamonie pointed the canoe toward a rocky bay and left the parade of other canoes. I thought perhaps he wanted to gas up or take a nature break, but when he beached the canoe and calmly set up a pot on a small propane burner on the canoe floor, I was perplexed.

"What are we doing, Salamonie," I asked pleasantly.

"We drink tea," he responded. "Time for tea."

Noting that all the canoes were now well ahead of us, I asked the obvious question.

"Do you know where we're going"? I queried.

"No," he responded simply, and that was that.

Now I was carefully weighing my words, because it was necessary that the Inuit comprehend the next point.

"If you don't know where we're going," I said, "shouldn't we be following the other canoes?"

Salamonie digested that bit of information, and then it appeared that a light went on in his head.

"You right," he said. "No time for tea."

At that our guide put away the tea makings, fired up the outboard, and we were once again cruising along the ocean, but this time the other canoes were barely visible. They were just tiny dots in the huge expanse of sea that was now beginning to come alive. A stiff breeze came up, creating whitecaps and significant rollers. Suddenly the big 24-foot craft didn't seem so big anymore as we pitched and lurched in the growing waves.

Salamonie's actions were exemplary of Inuit thinking. The fact that he'd never been to that spot wasn't a worry. He was so independent, and so used to reckoning on his own, that he'd

AS WE LEFT THE ROCKY COAST, I ASSUMED WE'D ALL BE TRAVELING IN A GROUP SO EACH CANOE WAS WITHIN SIGHT OF EACH OTHER. AFTER ALL, THAT ONLY MADE GOOD SENSE, BECAUSE SEVERAL OF THE INUIT GUIDES HAD NEVER BEEN TO THE AREA WE WERE GOING TO, INCLUDING SALAMONIE.

somehow find his way. Time was unimportant. I was awed and impressed.

Shortly afterward, we passed an island that was nothing but a pile of rocks. To our amazement, a bunch of dogs appeared and ran along the waterline, barking incessantly. This was a sight worth pondering: what were a dozen dogs doing on a small, barren island?

Salamonie answered the question before we asked it.

"Dogs free on island," he said. "Not free in town. Always tied up."

"What do they eat?", one of our party asked.

Salamonie shrugged. "Anything," he said. "Every few days somebody brings fish or bones or garbage. Dogs eat good."

Now the rollers grew stronger. The wind picked up considerably, and I began to wonder how much punishment the canoe would take as it rose and fell with the demands of the sea.

Soon Salamonie turned the craft away from the open ocean and headed toward a rocky island. The rest of our party had already pulled up to shore and were breaking out gear as we arrived.

"Sea too strong," Salamonie said. "We stay here until it get quiet."

That was perfectly fine with us.

It didn't take long to set up the tent. As added insurance, we tied large rocks all the way around in preparation for the storm that we were expecting. The Inuits are big on radio communications; there was a constant chatter between our camp and other groups scattered in the northland. A serious blow was in the forecast.

The wind increased during the night to the point where I wondered if our tent would stay erect. Our party was quite comfortable, tucked in warm sleeping bags with a kerosene heater to warm the shelter.

Sometime during the night I felt a serious breeze on my face. A gap in the tent wall had opened, allowing the cold air in. The wind was now almost gale force, tearing at the ropes and fabric with mighty gusts. I worked to repair the tent wall, and I can recall the eerie feeling as I toiled outside. Illuminated in the starlight were the rest of the tents, each of them protecting humans inside. The ocean raged a few yards away, and the wind seethed through our remote outpost. It amazed me that we were where we were, toughing out a storm that would have killed us if we didn't have proper shelters. Indeed, the Inuits were survivors.

That point was driven home even more clearly the next day when our entire group of guides left camp in two boats, leaving the rest of us to wonder what was going on. The wind had subsided some, but not enough to risk taking on the rest of the journey, especially a 25 mile crossing that would move us through an enormous open-water area with no islands to run to in case of danger. The crossing would have to be made in reasonably calm water.

THEY SELDOM KILLED OLDER BULLS, AND SINCE WE WERE THE FIRST HUNTERS THEY'D EVER GUIDED, THEY WEREN'T INTO EVALUATING ANTLERS.

30

THERE ARE NO PALM
TREES HERE, NO WHITE
SANDY BEACHES, NO
TREES BEARING EXOTIC
FRUITS.

Photograph courtesy of Jim Zumbo

We heard distant shots a couple hours after the guides had left, but we had no clue what they were up to. They finally showed up several hours later, the bows of their canoes splatting the heaving ocean swells as they made their way back to our island.

Salamonie nonchalantly told us what they'd done.

"We shoot geese and ducks," he said, "and cook them in pot. Good stuff."

After further inquiry, the Inuit told us that he and his pals had killed some waterfowl, tossed them in a pot of boiling water, feathers and innards and all, and ate them after they had cooked a bit.

The fact that the Inuits left all their puzzled hunters in camp without any explanation of their plans made no difference. For all we knew, we were abandoned forever on the island. Interesting people, these Inuits. I marveled at them more and more as time passed.

Salamonie pulled a stunt the next day that was unbelievable. Underway to our hunting camp once again, he'd spotted some ducks crossing in front of the canoe. He grabbed a very rusted .22 that leaned against the gunwale, and drew a bead on one of the ducks.

Mind you, we are in a craft that's crashing down from one wave to the other. The Inuit is using a rifle that looks like it sunk with the Titanic. You can imagine our astonishment when the little .22 bullet hit the duck smartly and sent it plummeting into the ocean. Never in my life had I seen such an incredible shot.

Soon it was time to cross the big bay. Luck was on our side, since the ocean calmed somewhat and the crossing was easily accomplished. Icebergs drifted about, and seals romped about around our boat. A couple hunters had seal tags, but none were able to connect. I was disappointed, because I wanted to see how the seals were processed by the natives.

Finally we neared camp. As we pulled up to the shore, a small bunch of bull caribou ran off over a little rise. Some of the hunters could stand it no longer, and despite a bit of advice to hold off until bigger bulls were spotted, they had none of it. Fifteen minutes later several shots rang out; the hunt was over for a half dozen hunters who'd scored on mediocre bulls.

Since it was late in the day when we arrived, we set up camp and were in no hurry to hunt. The next morning would come soon enough.

As we cruised away from camp soon after sunup, a lone bull appeared in the tundra close to shore. Salamonie gave the thumbs-up sign, but we weren't too sure. We'd been told that the Inuits had no experience in trophy hunting — to them a small bull or cow or calf was prime meat. They seldom killed older bulls, and since we were the first hunters they'd ever guided, they weren't into evaluating antlers.

I MADE THE TRIP IN LATE AUGUST RATHER THAN THE TRADITIONAL SPRING HUNT BECAUSE I'D LIVE WITH SEVERAL INUIT FAMILIES AS THEY FISHED FOR THEIR WINTER SUPPLY OF CHAR AND TROUT.

Nonetheless, the bull looked fine to us, and one of our party made a stalk. His bull was down soon afterward, and we loaded it into the canoe after dressing it.

Before nightfall, the other hunter and I had taken our bulls, all of them in the velvet and in prime condition.

When it was time to pack up and leave, we made another interesting discovery. Behind the tent the Inuits lived in was a large pile of raw, meatless caribou ribs. Salamonie explained they'd eaten the rib meat as a delicacy. I was convinced these people could survive anywhere.

Salamonie made a most distressing announcement as we loaded the canoe.

"Maybe not have enough gas to get home," he said with amazing calmness.

"What should we do?" I said, noting that several other canoes, some of which held extra gas, were taking off for the 80 mile journey.

"My brother maybe have more gas," Salamonie said.

I had no idea Salamonie's brother was among our party.

"Where's your brother?" I asked.

Salamonie looked at the remaining Inuits who hadn't left yet, and then gazed out into the ocean.

"Out there," Salamonie responded, pointing to a boat half a mile distant racing away. We'd never catch up, since we had another half hour's work to do before we could leave.

It occurred to me that Salamonie hadn't done any advance thinking about the issue of inadequate gas, but he had a solution that might work.

"If we make it through cut with tide high, we maybe get home," he said. "If tide low and we have to go around, we don't get home. Run out of gas."

"Then what?"

Salamonie had no answer. He simply shrugged, but he smiled. Any non-Inuit might have panicked at this point, but Salamonie wasn't concerned. I had the feeling he'd been there and done that many times before.

The cut was actually a 15-yard gap in a 20 mile-long peninsula. Making it through the cut should have been a top priority, but Salamonie wasn't in much of a hurry as he readied the canoe and lashed down the gear.

Rain pelted us hard as we finally got under way, and I kept looking at the high tide mark on the distant shoreline. This adventure was not quite over.

The cut finally appeared and Salamonie finally expressed some emotion.

"Aieeeee," he said. "Maybe not make it. Tide too low."

THE HUNT WAS EVERY-THING I'D HOPED FOR — AND THEN SOME. I'D TAKEN A FINE MUSKOX

The three of us hunters looked at each other . It was almost humorous, but we weren't laughing.

"We try anyway," Salamonie said with a big grin. "Maybe get across."

We tried, and we made it, though the prop cleared the rocks by a mere inch or two. Five minutes later and we wouldn't have cleared the cut.

About 10 miles from camp, Salamonie pointed to a small rocky island that couldn't have been more than a quarter mile long. There was nothing on the island except for some old structures that had been blown down long ago. He smiled, with a sort of distant look that we didn't understand.

"I born there," he said with pride.

Perhaps the most indelible sight, one which I failed to record with my camera, was a family of Inuits returning from a seal hunt. As they slowly approached the shore with a dead seal draped over the bow, other villagers ran down amidst barking dogs and shouting youngsters. The look of pride on the faces of the victorious hunters was a beautiful sight, each of them beaming and gesturing toward the seal.

Another hunt with Inuits is vivid in my memory. This was an arctic adventure for muskox out of Cambridge Bay. I made the trip in late August rather than the traditional spring hunt because I'd live with several Inuit families as they fished for their winter supply of char and trout.

The hunt was everything I'd hoped for — and then some. I'd taken a fine muskox with my guide, and later accompanied several families as they speared and netted fish at a falls.

One day, we took a break from fishing to have lunch. The Inuits merrily ate their fish raw, including the roe and livers. Though I'm a sushi fan, this fish was rather bland and tasteless, but I made a valiant effort to eat a few bites.

One of the Inuit children ran up with an armload of tiny willow branches, the biggest as thick as a cigar, and prepared a small fire. Producing an eight-inch frying pan, salt, pepper, and butter from his parent's boat, he fried some fresh arctic char for me. I've never had better fish in my life.

Another day we explored and searched for cranberries that grew on tiny ankle-high bushes. I accompanied a family consisting of the two parents and four children. Though I managed to fill my bucket, I was most interested in watching this family as they merrily laughed and played in the tundra, No soccer fields here, no traffic, and no malls to hang around in. These people were living life at its fullest, taking every day as it came.

But, as they say, life is change. Traditions are modified by technology. Even the remote arctic cannot resist progress.

I discussed dogsleds and their waning popularity with my guide.

"In the old days, we all used dogsleds to get around in the winter," he told me, "now we use snowmobiles."

"How did you navigate?" I asked.

"By the moon, stars, wind direction, all sorts of natural features," he answered.

Then his expression changed. The grin faded to a look of displeasure.

"The ways of the new world have taken over," he said wistfully. "We now use a GPS to find our way around."

That statement left me searching for a comment, but I could find none. Perhaps my romantic notions of humans fighting for survival in this harsh land are selfish. I live in a land of luxury, of high tech gadgetry that makes my life comfortable. Should we expect less of these people in the north?

When it came time to leave, we were told the first big snowstorm was coming. I was heading for another two or three months of decent weather in Wyoming, but the Inuits at Cambridge Bay were gearing up for snow.

It would be a long, cold, dark winter, but my new Inuit friends seemed not to care. Technology or not, nature was still a powerful force to be reckoned with. ■

Jim Zumbo of Cody, Wyoming, is the Hunting Editor for Outdoor Life *magazine and is the author of numerous outdoor books on topics from humorous tales to cooking venison. Jim has two college degrees in forestry and wildlife management and worked as forester and wildlife biologist for 15 years before joining the* Outdoor Life *staff in 1978. Jim has been a professional member of the Boone and Crockett Club since 1997.*

CHAPTER FOUR

Artwork by B&C Members

The following 32 pages include reproductions of artwork created by Boone and Crockett Club members past and present.

Albert Bierstadt

Albert Bierstadt, an early member of the Boone and Crockett Club, was born near Dusseldorf, Germany, in 1830, and moved to New Bedford, Massachusetts, with his family in 1832. He was educated in New Bedford, but studied art in Germany and Italy for four years while still in his early twenties.

Upon his return to the United States in 1857, Albert went west the following year for the first time with General F.W. Lander's expedition to find a new wagon route to the Pacific. On this trip, and subsequent trips to the Rocky Mountains, Albert made sketches and collected materials for future paintings. While he is best known for his heroic-size Western landscapes, he also painted Native Americans and wildlife. His works are in the Corcoran Gallery and the U.S. Capitol in Washington, D.C., the Hermitage in Russia, the Buffalo Bill Historical Center, Cody, Wyoming, and the Montreal Museum, to mention only a few.

Albert was elected a National Academician in England in 1860. He was a member of the Union League Club, the Century Association, the National Academy of Design, as well as many European art institutions. He received numerous awards for his work from foreign countries, including France, Russia, Turkey, Bavaria, Belgium, Austria, and Germany.

Near the end of his life Albert's popularity as an artist waned, and he died in obscurity. His artwork was "rediscovered" by a new generation after his death, and now enjoys a considerable following. ■

OPPOSITE
YELLOWSTONE FALLS (1881) ■ ALBERT BIERSTADT
COURTESY OF BUFFALO BILL HISTORICAL CENTER, CODY, WY
GIFT OF MR. AND MRS. LLOYD TAGGART

ISLAND LAKE, WIND RIVER RANGE, WYOMING (1861) ■
ALBERT BIERSTADT

COURTESY OF BUFFALO BILL HISTORICAL CENTER, CODY, WY

PREVIOUS PAGE
LAST OF THE BUFFALO (1888) ■ ALBERT BIERSTADT

COURTESY OF BUFFALO BILL HISTORICAL CENTER, CODY, WY
GERTRUDE VANDERBILT WHITNEY TRUST FUND PURCHASE

DEER IN MOUNTAIN HOME ■ ALBERT BIERSTADT

COURTESY OF BUFFALO BILL HISTORICAL CENTER, CODY, WY
GIFT OF JOSEPH M. ROEBLING

44

46

Guy Coheleach

In the last nine years Guy Coheleach has had one man exhibitions at major museums in 18 cities across America from New York to Los Angeles. Guy's paintings have received the Award of Excellence of the Society of Animal Artists an unprecedented seven times. This most prestigious honor is awarded by curators and professors of fine art from museums and universities across America.

The subject of two films, *Guy Coheleach and the Bald Eagle* and *Quest: An Artist and His Prey*, Guy has also been the focus of articles in *Reader's Digest, Saturday Evening Post*, and numerous regional art and wildlife magazines. *The Big Cats: The Paintings of Guy Coheleach* by Abrams was a Book of the Month Club Selection in 1982. Both it and his *Coheleach: Master of the Wild* are out of print. *Guy Coheleach's Animal Art* by DDR Publishing is still in print.

In 1972 Guy was run down by an elephant in Zambia. "This is exactly what has made him one of the best wild animal painters in the world admired by both scientists and art critics," says Pat Robertson in *Sporting Classics*.

Guy's endowment to the University of Tennessee provides about six full scholarships to the School of Wildlife Management each year. ∎

MUTTON CHASE ■ GUY COHELEACH

OPPOSITE
LAST WATERHOLE ■ GUY COHELEACH

LEOPARAL VIC FALLS ■ GUY COHELEACH

SERIOUS BUSINESS ■ GUY COHELEACH

Bob Kuhn

Bob was born in Buffalo, New York, in 1920. His artistic skills were honed at Pratt Institute and at the Art Student's League in New York City where his instructors gave him little encouragement to use wildlife as subject matter.

While on active duty in the Merchant Marines during World War II, Bob began his career by illustrating books. His art has appeared in books such as *Big Red, How's Inky?, Elmer Keith's Big Game Hunting*, and *Shots at Whitetail*, to mention only a few. After the war he was an illustrator for a number of outdoor magazines, including *Field and Stream* and *Outdoor Life*.

Bob's first one-man show was at the New York Abercrombie and Fitch Gallery in 1965. He quit illustrating in 1970 to pursue a full-time career in the fine arts.

Bob is a member of the National Academy of Western Art. He has won the Prix de West from the National Cowboy Hall of Fame. He has received five Awards of Merit from the Society of Animal Artists, and was honored with the Rungius Medal from the National Museum of Wildlife Art, Jackson Hole, Wyoming. Most recently, Bob received the Artist of the Year Award given by the Friends of Western Art, honoring a Tucson area artist who paints in the Western genre. ∎

NOMAD ∎ BOB KUHN

HIGH RIDGE RAMS ■ BOB KUHN

55

DAVY CROCKETT AND BEAR ■ BOB KUHN
NATIONAL MUSEUM OF WILDLIFE ART

BOONE AND MOUNTAIN LION ■ **BOB KUHN**
NATIONAL MUSEUM OF WILDLIFE ART

RESPITE ■ BOB KUHN

Hayden Lambson

Hayden graduated from B.Y.U. in 1970 and pursued a career with the Boy Scouts of America for six years immediately following graduation. He turned his full attention to art in 1976.

Hayden began his print business in 1982. His honors include: Artist of the Year for Whitetails Unlimited in 1988; Artist of the Year for the Foundation for North American Wild Sheep in 1990; Artist of the Quarter for the Rocky Mountain Elk Foundation, winter 1991; and Artist of the Year for the Minnesota Deer Hunter's Association in 1992.

Many of Hayden's paintings have been published as greeting cards and prints by Leanin' Tree, the National Rifle Association, Whitetails Unlimited, the National Wild Turkey Federation, and others. His work has graced the covers and contents of many Boone and Crockett Club publications.

Hayden's art work has been featured in magazines such as *Art West*, *Hunter's Quest*, *Wildlife Art News*, *Idaho Wildlife*, and many others. His art work has also been instrumental in raising thousands of dollars each year for conservation groups.

Other works of Hayden include: Nova Scotia habitat stamp print, Manitoba Wildlife Federation Habitat Stamp, New Brunswick Conservation Fund stamp and print, a six piece Alaskan series for the Bradford Exchange, and a limited edition print for Cabela's. ■

BIGHORN SHEEP ■ HAYDEN LAMBSON

MULE DEER ■ HAYDEN LAMBSON

GRIZZLIES ■ HAYDEN LAMBSON

63

TEXAS WHITETAIL ■ HAYDEN LAMBSON

ELK CROSSING ■ HAYDEN LAMBSON

65

OLD BALDFACE ■ **CARL RUNGIUS**
NATIONAL MUSEUM OF WILDLIFE ART

Carl Rungius

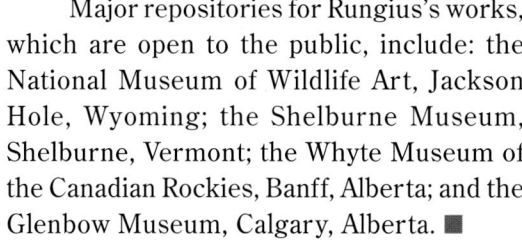

Carl Rungius is recognized as one of North America's greatest wildlife painters. He was born near Berlin in 1869 and moved to New York City in 1894. He attended the Berlin Art School, the School of Applied Arts and the Academy of Fine Arts.

In addition to being a member of the Boone and Crockett Club, Carl belonged to many professional organizations such as the National Academy of Design, National Arts Club, The Society of Animal Painters and Sculptors and the League of American Artists. His works included wildlife, western subjects and landscapes. He received many accolades for his art including the prestigious Altman Prize, the Vezin Prize, Ellen P. Speyer Memorial Prize and the Carnegie Prize, to mention only a few.

After moving to the United States, Carl lived in New York and traveled to Wyoming, New Brunswick, Yukon Territory and Alberta where he did countless sketches and painted. From 1921 until his death in 1959, Carl maintained two studio-homes — one in Banff, Alberta, and the other in New York City.

Major repositories for Rungius's works, which are open to the public, include: the National Museum of Wildlife Art, Jackson Hole, Wyoming; the Shelburne Museum, Shelburne, Vermont; the Whyte Museum of the Canadian Rockies, Banff, Alberta; and the Glenbow Museum, Calgary, Alberta. ■

FOLLOWING PAGE
UNDER PYRAMID PEAK ■ CARL RUNGIUS
NATIONAL MUSEUM OF WILDLIFE ART

IN THE CLOUDS ■ CARL RUNGIUS
NATIONAL MUSEUM OF WILDLIFE ART

67

69

The Ethics of Hunting

ARTHUR C. POPHAM
EMERITUS MEMBER
Boone and Crockett Club

I believe that what may be called the ethics of how we hunt overlays and supplements the basic "Rules Of Fair Chase", as prescribed by the Boone and Crockett Club for entry of trophy animals in its *Records of North American Big Game*. Those rules are fully set out elsewhere in this volume, in their current form, and are accepted as a general basic guide for sportsmanship in the methods of pursuit of big game animals.

I recall their formulation many years ago by the Records Committee, and often, after Committee meetings, spent many very late hours with Grancel Fitz, a noted hunter and writer, and his wife Betty at their New York apartment, surrounded by Grancel's marvelous trophies. She, for many years was the Committee's devoted secretary, and we sought to clearly and unmistakably express the ideas for those rules previously discussed by the Committee.

These have been updated regularly over the years to deal with the changing mechanical, electronic, biological and other developments that may be applied to the pursuit of game.

But these Rules of Fair Chase deal basically with the manner of <u>pursuit</u> of game. I have conferred with a number of Boone and Crockett members of wide hunting experience, who feel as I do that there is another standard that comes into play in that final moment of trigger pressure that determines how the animal being taken may expire. Preparation of this is what may be called the ethical side of hunting.

Webster's Dictionary defines "ethics" as "The study of standards of conduct and moral judgment."

My thoughts and experiences as set out here will be concerned with the "standards of conduct" in <u>how</u> we hunt the game animals in an ethical manner to that final moment, rather than with any "moral judgment" of <u>whether</u> it is ethical or acceptable to do so.

I am assuming that most of those reading this have now well-satisfied their own ethical sense of the propriety of the well-conducted hunting sport, and they may be devoted participants.

JACK O'CONNOR COMPOSED THIS PICTURE OF ART POPHAM ON THEIR FIRST OF MANY HUNTS TOGETHER -- KAIBAB FOREST, NORTHERN ARIZONA, 1934

No doubt there is some connection or crossover effect between the two defining concepts of whether or how we hunt, for when hunting is conducted in an ethical manner it may, indeed, mollify or diffuse some of the arguments made against the practice generally.

Just to illustrate how some individuals may have their own distorted concepts of what generally constitutes accepted ethical conduct, and those who may suffer from its breaches, I can't resist recounting the old story of the fellow who inquired of a friend, "Just what is all this talk about something called 'ethics'? What does it mean?"

The friend replied, "Well, it's the way you do things. Suppose I ran a clothing store with my partner and he is out to lunch and I am minding the store, when a customer comes in and buys a $50 coat. He pays me with a $50 bill and just before he is going out the door, I see that there is another $50 bill stuck to it. That is where the 'ethics' comes in: Should I tell the customer? Should I tell my partner?"

So, who gets hurt when there is a misconception or breach of what constitutes a reasonably ethical standard of conduct?

In the hunting world, it's first of all, and directly, the poorly and painfully taken animals that suffer the most. Then the concept and perpetuation of the sport itself is damaged. But maybe, although not with the animals' physical pain, but even more lastingly, it is the hunter himself who is affected by a loss of self esteem for his lapse and its abiding memory.

Hunting to an ethical conclusion leading to a satisfying outcome in that final moment calls for sound and thoughtful planning and preparation for the whole process of a long trip. This may cover the many aspects of such an operation, from careful selection and study of the terrain considered, and the weather expected, the suitable clothing for performing in it, selection of competent outfitters and guides, the reliability of the transport and camping equipment, and realistic visualization as far as possible of all the imaginable situations and problems ahead and their solutions.

Certainly, there are countless unforeseeable obstacles in a trip to the top of the highest mountain at the edge of nowhere, for an elusive quarry. It is mostly when weather, equipment, or unanticipated situations have gone sour that the temptation of accepting "situation ethics" may rule on a hunt. Compromised decisions made then may be long rued.

Yet such failure or loss may be a necessary learning process, and proper preparation next time may avoid many such misfortunes. Perhaps it may minimize or overcome the huge element of the sheer bad luck possible on a long and difficult search for the trophy of your dreams.

One thing is sure: The ultimate point and the whole climax of a laborious trip is to make a well placed shot with the effective power to give an immediate kill of the game pursued.

This process requires the initial selection of the proper firearm and cartridges and sighting equipment, and a gun stock and steadying gun sling that fit. It then calls for acquiring practiced familiarity and skill with that combination.

Nothing pays off better when the final moment of the trip arrives than getting a quick and accurate sight picture of the vulnerable target area. The best training for this is hours of dry-firing at pictures or cutouts of the animals sought.

Learn to drop quickly to a comfortable, steady, sitting position with sling in place for sighting above grass, as a prone view is often blocked.

High grass can be a real heartbreaker. I will never forget, near the end of a Tanganyika safari in 1957 when I still needed a greater kudu. Finally, I had a fine one standing broadside in good range, the only bull seen on the trip.

But the grass between us was so high I had, literally, to stand on the highest tiptoe to get my sight on the animal, which was about to take off. I could not hold steadily on it as I rocked back and forth, with the scope's cross hairs moving up and down. However, trying to time the movement, I squeezed of a shot, and still have etched in my memory the picture of the cross hairs some 2 inches below the bull's chest as the gun fired, and he ran off.

The ethics were compromised, but sometimes there is little choice, and nothing but my psyche was hurt.

On your dryfiring practice, after each "shot" instantly grasp the bolt handle and operate it rapidly as to reload and get back to the trigger, until this becomes automatic for a follow up shot, if needed.

Some fifty years ago I witnessed a sad example of what can happen when failing to be properly armed. I and two hunter friends were booked for a thirty-day horse pack trip with the Yukon Territory's most famous outfitter and perennial local hero. We were well equipped, superbly armed and well practiced, and were about ready for anything. But at the last minute before we set out, the outfitter had brought along a young hunter for just a few days to see if he could quickly bag a Dall's sheep and leave.

The young man was likable and pleasant, and his brief inclusion did not seriously affect our plans. But it had been a spur-of-the-moment arrangement and he was ill prepared.

He had brought a slide-action Remington rifle with open iron sights and no shooting sling. I can't recall if it was a .32 Remington Rimless or a .35 Remington caliber of similar ballistics of about 2,200 feet per second velocity and a similar number of muzzle energy foot pounds.

My plain-spoken old hunting companion of many years, Jack O'Connor, in his standard *Big-Game Rifle Book* (page 125, in the chapter devoted to suitable guns for forest deer hunting) says, "I have heard hunters argue that the .32 Special killed better than the .30-.30. As the figures show, such argument is simply ridiculous."

Compared with the sling-equipped, scope-sighted, custom-expanded chamber version of the .300 Magnum caliber rifle, similar to Weatherby's, that I was shooting on the trip, with muzzle velocity of some 3,289 F.P.S. and energy of 4,300 F.P., it was clear our friend was seriously under-gunned and handicapped for such long-range mountain shooting.

But when a moderate-sized white ram appeared near camp one evening, the young hunter excitedly said he wanted to take it, as he had to leave the next morning. So he sat down with his open sights and no steadying sling and at some 175 yards did hit the sheep

but far back in the left hip area, where blood appeared. The ram did not go down, but limped over the rim of a nearby deep canyon. With darkness approaching, the guides did not search for the ram that night and could not find it the next day, when the hunter left.

It was a sad experience for him, and certainly for the ram, which could have been killed cleanly and properly by a reasonably well-trained shooter with adequate equipment.

The whole occurrence put something of a pallor on the beginning of our long hunt. However, with our own good preparation and equipment it turned out exceedingly well on Dall's sheep, grizzlies and moose.

The satisfaction derived from a well-planned, well pre-pared and well-executed hunting trip is boundless, whether a brief local foray or a lengthy and difficult journey. Not all cir-cumstances may permit it, but when the game is taken by an instant kill, certainly the memories of it remain brighter and happier. I like to think of a bighorn ram in the Rockies of Brit-ish Columbia that I needed for a planned museum habitat group. The guide and I watched across the wide canyon as the ram lay down in a rock cleft. We planned and carefully executed a

THE URIAL OF EASTERN IRAN IS A LOVELY SHEEP WITH ITS FLOWING RUFF. ART TOOK THIS RAM NEARLY 30 YEARS AGO WHILE ON A SCIENTIFIC HUNT.

Photograph reprinted from *Stalking Big Game From Desert to Tundra*

long, roundabout stalk to where I could be in a good position to shoot. Through the scope, I could see his lambent amber eyes slowly close in sleep. At the shot, the ram's head just dropped forward. He never moved. He felt nothing.

In the good days of Iran, I was enlisted to secure sterile tissue samples from each of the three types of sheep in the country to establish that the central mountains red sheep is a true intergrade between the western Armenian sheep, with supracervical horns, and the eastern area urial with a handsome chest ruff.

The urial was taken like the bighorn, above, after a long, circuitous stalk while sleeping, in a nearly identical manner, and the memory stays green.

(The tissue samples, taken under difficult conditions, were kept sterile, and chromosome counts did, indeed, demonstrate, that the red sheep is a true intergrade between the Armenian sheep and the urial, so the trip was a scientific and ethical success.)

There is a strange, basic dichotomy in the ethical hunter, who loves and respects the fine game animals that he instinctively seeks to stalk and kill. He admires the telescopic eyesight and equally incredible scenting ability of the mountain sheep, and its instant flight from any danger perceived; or the awesome strength of the grizzly bear, digging out huge boulders to reach a burrowed ground squirrel, then hopping about, quick as a cat, to capture it; or the mountain goat's casual leaps from rock-to-rock across chasms dizzying to us; or the whitetail deer's cleverly circling to watch its back track for danger; or the antelope's dazzling speed, that lead us to seek and challenge them on their own ground.

But when we do so, we owe it to them to do our very best to avoid making them suffer.

I may seem, sometimes, to take all of our developed skills, efforts, fortitude, self-denials and physical and mental strengths to do so, but that is truly ethical hunting and is, indeed, what I believe makes it worthwhile. ■

Arthur C. Popham has been a Regular member of the Boone and Crockett Club since 1960 and became an Emeritus member in 1993. Art is involved with creating large animal habitat groups at the Kansas City Museum of History and Science. He has written articles for outdoor publications for over 50 years and is the author of Stalking Big Game from Desert to Tundra *– a collection of his hunting experiences over the years and throughout the world.*

CHAPTER SIX

California's Tule Elk

JON K. FISCHER
PROGRAM COORDINATOR
California Department of
Fish and Game

WILLIAM E. CLARK
RETIRED - INVESTIGATIONS
LABORATORY
California Department of
Fish and Game

It was dark by the time the ten of us sloshed through the marsh to the bull, which had been taken moments before sundown the first day of California's 1995 Grizzly Island tule elk season. Its massive 9X8 rack, although only about 35 inches wide, had impressive crown points and would score well.

The bulk of our work lay ahead of us though, because the bull had spent its last moments on a small patch of dry ground surrounded by 200 yards of brackish marsh that we had to cross before he could be loaded onto a trailer for transport back to camp. It was tempting to clean and quarter him where he lay, but then we would be unable to get weight and body measurements, important information from tule elk on quality habitat. The evening's mosquito bloom quickly encouraged us to slide the elk onto a makeshift canvas litter and begin carrying it toward the trailer approximately 1/4 mile away. Carrying the bull provided time for reflection, not just on the hunt, but on the recovery of tule elk from the teetering edge of extinction. This was a conservation success story made possible by the intervention of private individuals, management actions of wildlife agencies, and financial contributions of sportsmen groups.

Historical records indicate that there were about 500,000 tule elk in California during pristine times. They inhabited the Central Valley and were probably named for the marsh tule patches they preferred. They also were found in grassland and woodland areas of the Coast Range.

Even in the 1840s explorers still observed huge concentrations of elk in California. But by 1863 they had been nearly wiped out. Exotic grasses, livestock, agriculture, and market shooting all contributed to their demise. European settlers brought livestock and European grasses. The non-native grasses replaced many native plants eaten by the elk, and livestock competed for the food that was left. Swamp lands that had sustained elk were drained and used to grow crops. And when gold was discovered in 1848, elk, bighorn sheep, prong-

A TULE ELK BULL IN THE TUPMAN AREA -- LIKE ROOSEVELT'S ELK, ANTLERS OF MATURE TULE ELK BULLS TEND TO BE STOCKY AND HAVE CROWN POINTS.

horn, and other species were shot for food to the point of decimation.

At the time these same trends were occurring elsewhere in the United States. While the discovery of gold was unique to California, the presence of exotic grasses, livestock, and the explosion of agriculture affected elk subspecies from other states. The eastern elk subspecies was wiped out from its range east of the Mississippi River, and by the early 1900s, the Merriams subspecies probably was extirpated from its range in the southwestern United States.

In California, the decline was dramatic and severe. The state's abundant tule elk populations were relegated to just a few animals in the San Joaquin Valley. Local lore contends that in 1874, the last pair of tule elk were found in a remote marsh near Buena Vista Lake. Henry Miller, a cattle baron who owned the property, ordered that the elk were to be protected, perhaps the first elk conservation effort in the state.

Had it not been for Miller, we probably would not have been at Grizzly Island, some 65 miles southwest of Sacramento, laboring under the effort of carrying this bull. Part of the San Francisco Bay Delta, most of the 11,500 acre island is owned by the State of California. Approximately 3,000 acres is privately owned waterfowl and pheasant clubs. The Department of Fish and Game manages state property at Grizzly Island. Tule elk freely roam the state and private land at Grizzly Island, and a few adjacent islands.

The peat soil characteristic of Grizzly Island made carrying the bull like walking on a three foot thick sponge. We fell like dominos each time one of us stumbled. It was slow going. The size of this bull was truly impressive, and the irony was not lost on us that some people refer to tule elk as "dwarf" elk. We rested as we saw headlights approaching the spot where our vehicles were parked approximately 300 yards away.

Most of our group of elk packers had heard of Henry Miller and knew he was credited with saving tule elk from extinction. Thanks to his protection, by 1905 there were 145 elk on his land. But they were trampling habitat and fences, causing $5,000 to $10,000 each year in depredation damages. Miller decided to relocate some of the elk by using cowboys to rope and hogtie them causing plenty of injuries to man and beast alike.

In 1914, the California Academy of Sciences agreed to capture and relocate the troublesome elk. They baited elk into traps, loaded them into cattle trucks, and actually managed to relocate 146 animals to 19 different sites throughout the state. Despite this early success, the capture and relocation process was stressful and eventually most of the relocated animals died. But by 1940, tule elk were established at three locations in California.

TULE ELK BULLS IN A CAPTURE PEN IN OWENS VALLEY -- HUNDREDS OF ELK HAVE BEEN CAPTURED USING CORRAL TRAPS, WITH MUCH LESS STRESS THAN OTHER METHODS.

There were no relocation efforts involving tule elk from 1940 to 1970. But there were plenty of conflicts involving elk and fences, livestock, agricultural crops, and even golf courses. As a result of these conflicts and a growing environmental concern, in 1971 the California Legislature passed a bill requiring the Department of Fish and Game to relocate tule elk to suitable locations within the state. The bill also prohibited tule elk

NET-GUNNING A BULL AT
THE GRIZZLY ISLAND WILD-
LIFE AREA -- THE DE-
PARTMENT NOW RELIES
HEAVILY ON THIS METHOD
TO CAPTURE ELK.

Photograph by Jeanne Clark©

hunting, although tule elk were never state or federally listed as threatened or endangered. Similar legislation was passed at the federal level.

So in the early 1970s, the Department had to develop capture, handling and transport techniques that would safeguard this fragile population. There was little information or practical experience regarding the capture, handling, or transport of elk, except for the stories of cowboys roping elk and the 1914 California Academy of Sciences captures. The Department also had to find suitable sites to sustain the relocated animals. Concerted efforts were made to find public lands with suitable forage and cover, away from agricultural operations, and where new herds would have room to grow.

When it came to capture the elk, earlier "rodeo" method was considered too stressful and risky, so Fish and Gamers began by using a helicopter to select individual animals and chemically immobilize them with a drug-filled dart. Many drug "cocktails" were tried before an efficient and safe combination of drugs was identified.

The Department also developed physical techniques for handling the immobilized animals, such as removing the bulls' antlers, lifting and moving them, and developing safe trailering techniques for these 300 to 900 pound animals. Trailers were specially constructed of heavy gauge steel, with several partitioned areas and special ventilation and cooling systems. Males, females, and calves were separated to prevent fighting and trampling injuries.

The Department relied on chemical immobilization for several years. But the process was expensive, very slow (only one animal could be caught at a time) and the chemicals that caught the animals also caused them stress. During this period of time, Fish and Gamers noticed that the elk could be herded somewhat. Keying off the California Academy of Science's success, in 1979 the Department began to catch elk in large numbers by using a helicopter to herd them into large enclosures. Once captured, the elk could be worked into smaller, partitioned areas and processed for transport. Hundreds of elk were captured using corral traps, with much less stress.

While this was a great improvement over darting, it was very labor intensive. Specially-built panels were constantly shipped across the state and it took lots of people to construct the traps and catch pens. During the mid 1980s Department personnel began to use a net gun (.308 rifle that deploys a 15 x 15 foot large mesh net) shot from a helicopter to catch bighorn sheep, antelope, and deer. They hadn't used the net gun on elk, fearing injury to both the animals and people attempting to restrain them. But this method had been used extensively in New Zealand on elk and red deer.

In 1993, the Department asked capture experts from New Zealand to demonstrate their method for netgunning elk. It only took a few animals to see the merits of this approach. Overnight, this method was seized as perhaps the most selective, safe, and efficient method for capturing these large cervids. The Department now relies heavily on netgunning to capture elk, but also still uses bait traps and darting in selective cases.

AIRLIFTING A DARTED BULL TO A PEN AT THE GRIZZLY ISLAND WILDLIFE AREA -- THIS PROCESS WAS EXPENSIVE, VERY SLOW AND THE CHEMICALS CAUSED THE ANIMALS STRESS. EVENTUALLY, THE DEPARTMENT GOT AWAY FROM CHEMICAL IMMOBILIZATION AND BEGAN USING A HERDING TECHNIQUE.

Photograph by Jeanne Clark©

At Grizzly Island, the headlights brought into view a truck with a 12 foot aluminum skiff in back. Our makeshift canvas litter was not effective. With five people on each side, we were constantly stumbling over each other as we tried to walk on the spongy peat. However, the load was too heavy to carry with four on a side. Finally someone suggested putting the elk inside the skiff and skidding it across the saltgrass and pickelweed and through the marsh. Although a bit hard on the skiff, this method worked well. In moments we skidded the elk to a shallow canal, and with the use of a winch, pulled it across the canal and into the trailer for transport back to camp.

Back at camp, the bull was processed by volunteers from conservation organizations such as Safari Club International, Rocky Mountain Elk Foundation, and the Boone and Crockett Club. Although numerous Grizzly Island tule elk bulls have tipped the scale at more than 800 pounds, we were amazed to see this one balanced out at 910 pounds. So much for its reputation of being a dwarf elk.

Some have called tule elk dwarf elk because they were smaller than Rocky Mountain and Roosevelt's elk. But historical reports of tule elk weight involved locations where their habitat was less than optimal. Scientists observing tule elk under these conditions probably saw animals that were much smaller than they might have been with good forage. Since the relocation program has been in effect, tule elk relocated to places with good forage such as Grizzly Island and San Luis National Wildlife Refuge have sometimes been larger than Roosevelt's elk in California.

Other physical traits distinguishing tule elk from Rocky Mountain and Roosevelt elk are much more subtle. Like Roosevelt's elk, antlers of mature tule elk bulls tend to be stocky and have crown points. Palmation in the crown region, and extra projections from the first and second tines also may be observed in tule elk. While pelage in tule elk may be lighter than that of either Roosevelt's or Rocky Mountain elk, there is enough variation to make this characteristic unreliable. Because of such subtle differences, geographic location continues to be one of the best factors to distinguish between elk subspecies in California.

Since 1970, the Department of Fish and Game has worked with other wildlife agencies and conservation organizations to capture and relocate more than 1,000 individuals of this subspecies to reestablish tule elk in suitable parts of California. Statewide, the tule elk population has grown from approximately 600 animals in 1970 to more than 3,400 animals in 23 different herds today. But the conflicts and private property damage initially experienced by Henry Miller still exist today in some areas, exacerbated by California's growing human population of more than 32 million. Recognizing the role that regulated hunting can have in reducing such conflicts, in 1987 the California Legislature passed a bill that allowed tule elk hunting to resume. The Fish and Game Commission authorized public tule elk hunting at two locations in 1989. Annually since then, the Commission has authorized tule elk hunting and acted to expand hunting opportunities .

THE RECOVERY OF TULE ELK FROM THE TEETERING EDGE OF EXTINCTION IS A CONSERVATION SUCCESS STORY MADE POSSIBLE BY THE INTERVENTION OF PRIVATE INDIVIDUALS, MANAGEMENT ACTIONS OF WILDLIFE AGENCIES AND FINANCIAL CONTRIBUTIONS OF SPORTSMEN'S GROUPS.

In 1998, tule elk hunting occurred at eight public hunt locations and an additional 13 ranches qualified under the state's Private Lands Program. That same year, the Boone and Crockett Club marked another milestone in the recovery of tule elk by establishing a separate category in their Records of North American Big Game. Minimum qualifying score for this category is 270 for the Awards book and 285 for the All-Time book. After examining unofficial records of tule elk taken during the last 10 years, it is possible that a large bull taken from any of the established hunt zones has the potential to meet the minimum score. Besides Grizzly Island in Solano County, it is likely that tule elk bulls from Inyo, Mendocino, Monterey and San Luis Obispo counties may score in excess of 300 points.

The green score of the 1995 Grizzly Island bull was approximately 360 points. A life-size mount of the bull was prepared and is now on display at the World Wildlife Museum in Stockton, California. Although this one is still the largest tule elk (by weight), two or three other bulls have been taken since 1995 that should exceed this score. As we helped to measure and record this 360 point bull, we couldn't help but reflect with satisfaction upon the long journey tule elk have made from the brink of extinction to thriving herds that are capable of producing world class bulls. ■

IN 1998, THE BOONE AND CROCKETT CLUB ESTABLISHED A NEW CATEGORY FOR TULE ELK. THE MAP ABOVE SHOWS THE BOUNDARIES FOR ENTRY INTO THE CLUB'S AWARDS PROGRAM. MINIMUM SCORES ARE 270 AND 285 FOR THE AWARD AND ALL-TIME BOOKS RESPECTIVELY.

Jon K. Fischer works for the California Department of Fish and Game as the statewide elk program coordinator. William E. Clark recently retired from the California Department of Fish and Game's Wildlife Investigations Laboratory where he oversaw many of the capture and reintroduction efforts involving elk, bighorn sheep and pronghorn.

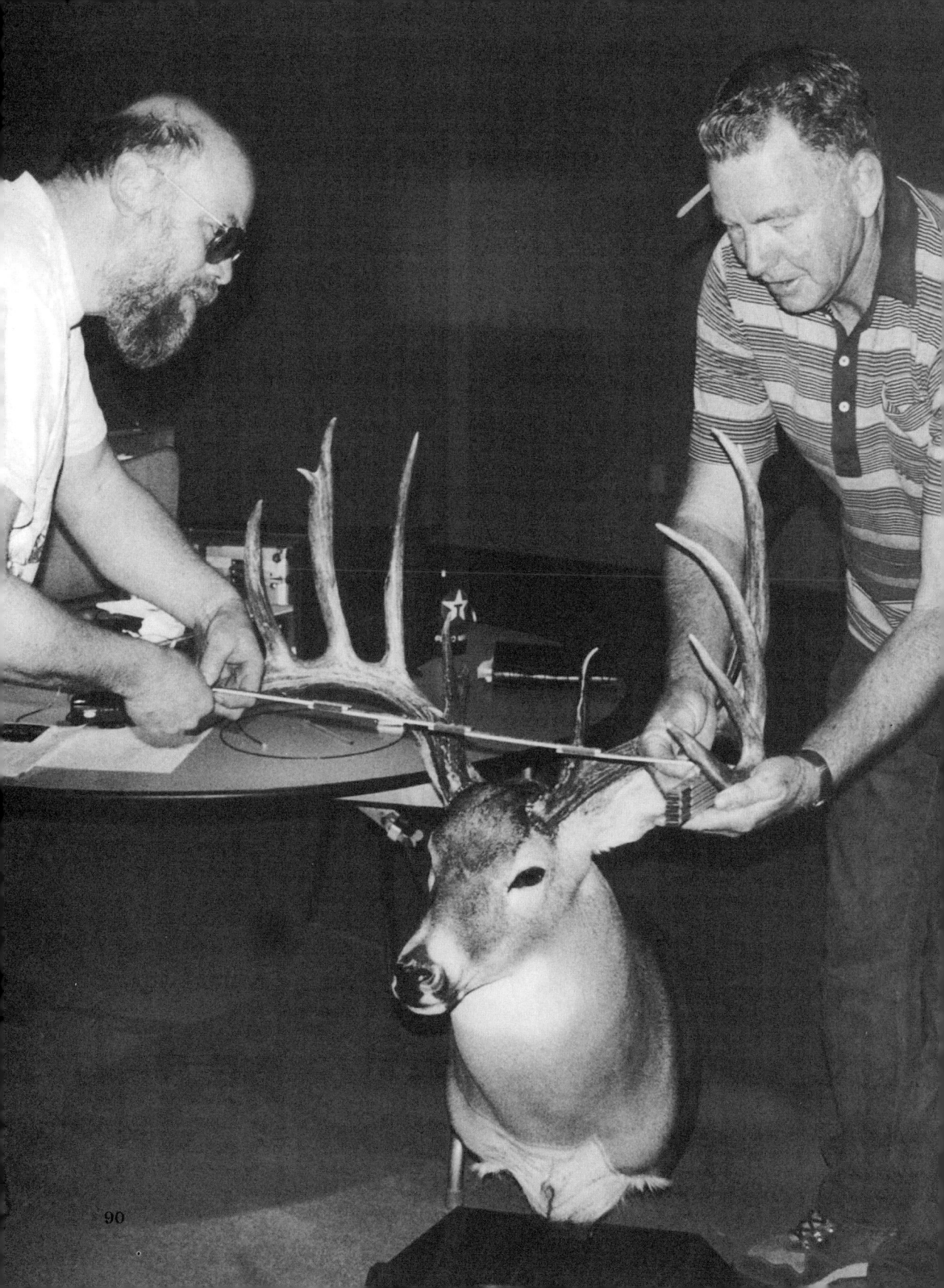

Recorded Trophies

JACK RENEAU
DIRECTOR OF
BIG GAME RECORDS
Boone and Crockett Club

The trophy data shown herein have been taken from score charts in the Records Archives of the Boone and Crockett Club. Trophies listed are those that continue to meet minimum scores and other stated requirements of trophy entry for the program. This edition includes entries from the 10th edition of the all time records book, *Records of North American Big Game*, as well as entries from the 22nd (1992-1994) and 23rd (1995-1997) Awards Entry Periods that meet or exceed the all-time minimum entry scores for each category.

The final scores and rank shown are official, except for those trophies shown with an asterisk. The asterisk is assigned to trophies whose entry scores are subject to certification by an Awards Judges' Panel. The asterisk can be removed (except in the case of potential World's Records), by submitting two additional, independent scorings by official measurers of the Boone and Crockett Club. The Records Committee of the Club will review the three scorings available (original plus two additional), and determine which, if any, will be accepted in lieu of the Awards Judges' Panel measurement. When the score has been accepted as final by the Records Committee, the asterisk will be removed in future editions of the all-time records book, *Records of North American Big Game*, and other publications. In the case of a potential World's Record trophy, the trophy must come before an Awards Judges' Panel at the end of an Awards Entry Period. Only an Awards Judges' Panel can certify a World's Record and finalize its score.

Asterisked trophies are shown at the end of the listings for their category. They are not ranked as their final score is subject to revision by an Awards Judges' Panel or by the submission of additional, official scorings, as described above.

There are fewer asterisked trophies in this edition of the records book than in past editions because the Club's Records Committee made a concerted effort to verify final scores of trophies asterisked in past editions. Trophies with scores that were verified as outlined above have taken their

RONALD L. BOUCHER, LEFT, AND JIMMIE E. ENGELMANN, MEMBERS OF THE 22ND AWARDS JUDGES' PANEL MEASURE THE INSIDE SPREAD OF THE NEW WORLD'S RECORD TYPICAL WHITE-TAIL DEER TAKEN BY MILO N. HANSON NEAR BIGGAR, SASKATCHEWAN, IN 1993.

POSTAL CODES ABBREVIATIONS

UNITED STATES
AL Alabama
AK Alaska
AZ Arizona
AR Arkansas
CA California
CO Colorado
CT Connecticut
DE Delaware
FL Florida
GA Georgia
ID Idaho
IL Illinois
IN Indiana
IA Iowa
KS Kansas
KY Kentucky
LA Louisiana
MA Massachusetts
ME Maine
MD Maryland
MI Michigan
MN Minnesota
MS Mississippi
MO Missouri
MT Montana
NE Nebraska
NV Nevada
NH New Hampshire
NJ New Jersey
NM New Mexico
NY New York
NC North Carolina
ND North Dakota
OH Ohio
OK Oklahoma
OR Oregon
PA Pennsylvania
RI Rhode Island
SC South Carolina
SD South Dakota
TN Tennessee
TX Texas
UT Utah
VT Vermont
VA Virginia
WA Washington
WV West Virginia
WI Wisconsin
WY Wyoming

CANADA
AB Alberta
BC British Columbia
LB Labrador*
MB Manitoba
NB New Brunswick
NF Newfoundland
NT Northwest Territories
NS Nova Scotia
ON Ontario
QC Quebec
SK Saskatchewan
YT Yukon Territory

*LB is used to designate location of kill for Quebec-Labrador caribou taken in the Labrador region of Newfoundland.

MEXICO
MX used for all trophies taken in Mexico.

rightful place in the listings, while those that were not verified were dropped from this book. Dropped trophies can be added to future editions if their scores are verified as outlined above. In actuality, the only asterisked trophies in this edition are trophies from the 22nd and 23rd Awards Programs with scores that were not verified by their respective Awards Judges' Panels.

There are a few other changes worth noting that have taken place since the last edition of the all-time records book. The most significant are those involving changes in minimum scores. The all-time minimum score for typical mule deer was lowered from 195 points to 190 points, and the minimum score for non-typical mule deer was lowered from 240 points to 230 points. Also, the minimum score for Columbia blacktail deer was raised from 130 points to 135 points.

The only other significant change in the trophy listings concerns the abbreviations of state and provincial names under locations of kill for each category. This is the first edition to use standard postal code abbreviations for states and provinces. Not only are these codes shorter, allowing more room for each trophy's data, but they are more recognizable than the codes used in previous editions. A complete listing of postal codes used in this edition is shown in the table to the left.

The scientific and vernacular names, and the sequence of presentation, follow that suggested in the *Revised Checklist of North American Mammals North of Mexico, 1979* (J. Knox, et al., Texas Tech University, Dec. 14, 1979.) Note that "PR" preceding date of kill indicates "prior to" the date shown for kill.

GEOGRAPHIC BOUNDARIES

Geographic boundaries are of considerable importance in the records keeping. The records keeping is set up only for native North American big-game animals. For such purposes, the southern boundary is defined as the south boundary of Mexico. The northern limit for trophies that may inhabit the offshore waters, such as polar bear and walrus, is the limit of the continent and associated waters held by the United States, Canada or Greenland. Continental limited and associated waters define the east and west boundaries for all categories.

In addition to the broad geographic boundaries described above, carefully described geographic boundaries are necessary in certain categories that closely resemble each other, due to the fact they are set up to recognize subspecies. Examples include Wyoming and Canada moose, Columbia and Sitka blacktail deer, and others. For these cases, specific boundary descriptions are spelled out for the smaller category to prevent specimens of the larger being erroneously entered and thus receiving undue recognition.

Categories for which such boundaries are spelled out include: grizzly and brown bear; American and Roosevelt's elk; mule, Columbia and Sitka blacktail deer; whitetail and Coues' deer; Canada, Alaska-Yukon and Wyoming moose; barren ground, Central Canada barren ground, mountain, woodland and Quebec-Labrador caribou; bighorn, desert, Dall's and Stone's sheep; and Atlantic and Pacific walrus.

In addition, special considerations are also spelled out for certain other animals. For example, bison exist today as wild, free-ranging herds in their original setting only in Alaska and Canada. Bison from the lower 48 states are, in many cases, semi-domesticated and regulated as domestic livestock. Thus, hunter-taken trophies from the lower 48 states are acceptable for listing in the records book(s) only if they were taken in a state that recognizes bison as wild and free-ranging, and which requires a hunting license and/or big-game tag for such hunting. If bison from the lower 48 states are invited and sent into an Awards Judges' Panel, the trophy can only receive a certificate of merit. Bison from most herds in Canada and Alaska are eligible to receive awards medals.

Detailed descriptions of the applicable geographic boundaries are given in the trophy data section for the affected categories. Hunters are encouraged to read and understand such boundaries while planning hunting trips in order to avoid possible disappointment.

SAGAMORE HILL AWARD

The Sagamore Hill Medal is given by the Roosevelt family in memory of Theodore Roosevelt (Founder and first President of the Boone and Crockett Club), Theodore Roosevelt, Jr., and Kermit Roosevelt. It was created in 1948. It may be awarded by the Big Game Final Awards Judges' Panel, if in their opinion there is an outstanding trophy worthy of great distinction. Only one may be given in any Big Game Awards program. A special award may also be presented by the Executive Committee of the Boone and Crockett Club for distinguished devotion to the objectives of the Club. The Sagamore Hill Medal is the highest award given by the Boone and Crockett Club. This edition of the All-Time records book highlights those trophies that have received this distinguished award by listing the trophy in bold type and including an image of the Sagamore Hill Medal next to the trophy photo where available. ■

SAGAMORE HILL AWARDS

1948 - Robert C. Reeve - Alaska brown bear
1949 - E.C. Haase - Rocky Mountain goat
1950 - Dr. R.C. Bentzen - typical wapiti
1951 - George H. Lesser - woodland caribou
1953 - Edison A. Pillmore - typical mule deer
1957 - Frank Cook - Dall's sheep
1959 - Fred C. Mercer - typical wapiti
1961 - Harry L. Swank, Jr. - Dall's sheep
1963 - Norman Blank - Stone's sheep
1965 - Melvin J. Johnson - typical whitetail
1973 - Doug Burris, Jr., - typical mule deer
1976 - Garry Beaubien - mountain caribou
1986 - Michael J. O'Haco - pronghorn
1989 - Gene C. Alford - cougar
1992 - Charles E. Erickson, Jr., - non-typical Coues' whitetail

SPECIAL SAGAMORE HILL AWARD RECIPIENTS

1952 - DeForest Grant
1968 - Richard King Mellon
1977 - Robert Munro Ferguson
1987 - C.R. "Pink" Gutermuth
1992 - William I. Spencer
1996 - Philip L. Wright
1997 - George C. Hixon

BLACK BEAR
WORLD'S RECORD

RANK
World's Record

SCORE
23 $^{10}/_{16}$

LOCATION
San Pete Co., UT

HUNTER
Picked Up

OWNERS
A.R. Lund and
M. Daniels

DATE KILLED
1975

On July 1, 1975, the World's Record skull for a black bear (*Ursus americanus*) was found along the edge of the Manti-La Sal National Forest, about seven miles east of Ephraim, Utah. Out west, black bears are occasionally seen in sub-alpine meadows, but they generally prefer the shelter of trees, where they quietly move in and out along the edges of the forest. Such was the setting where Merrill Daniels and Alma Lund contemplated their discovery. Daniels and Lund were unable to determine the cause of death but did recognize the immensity of the old carcass that was slowly decaying in the summer heat. In the past, when many trophy-sized black bears were scored by measuring hides, this could have been a tough call. Using Boone and Crockett's system for measuring the bear's immense skull, the duo received an entry score of 23-10/16. However, because the score exceeded the previous record by more than an inch, their incredible find was greeted with skepticism. With the concurrence of the trophy owners, the skull was shipped to Washington D.C., where it was examined by experts at the Smithsonian Institution.

After undergoing careful comparisons with type specimens, as well as other identification criteria, the final assessment was that this was indeed a bona fide black bear skull. In 1980, the trophy was awarded a Certificate of Merit in recognition of its outstanding trophy character at the 17th North American Big Game Awards. Pick-ups are included, in order to enhance the scientific value of the records and to complete the standard by which sportsmen can judge their best trophies. San Pete County, Utah, was also the location of the previous state record trophy taken by Rex W. Peterson accompanied by Richard Hardy in 1970, which scored 22-6/16. Bears taken in Arizona and Colorado during the 1960s have also received impressive scores. ■

BLACK BEAR
WORLD'S RECORD SCORECHART

Measurements are taken with calipers or by using parallel perpendiculars, to the nearest one-sixteenth of an inch, without reduction of fractions. Official measurements cannot be taken until the skull has air dried for at least 60 days after the animal was killed. All adhering flesh, membrane and cartilage must be completely removed before official measurements are taken.

A. **Greatest Length** is measured between perpendiculars parallel to the long axis of the skull, without the lower jaw and excluding malformations.

B. **Greatest Width** is measured between perpendiculars at right angles to the long axis.

Records of
North American
Big Game

250 Station Drive
Missoula, MT 59801
(406) 542-1888

BOONE AND CROCKETT CLUB®

OFFICIAL SCORING SYSTEM FOR NORTH AMERICAN BIG GAME TROPHIES

BEAR

MINIMUM SCORES

	AWARDS	ALL-TIME
black bear	20	21
grizzly bear	23	24
Alaska brown bear	26	28
polar bear	27	27

KIND OF BEAR (check one)
- ■ black bear
- ☐ grizzly
- ☐ Alaska brown bear
- ☐ polar

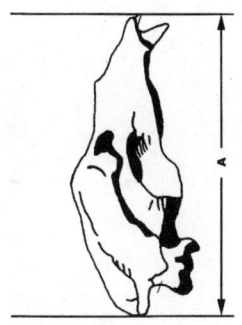

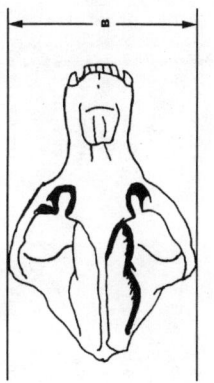

SEE OTHER SIDE FOR INSTRUCTIONS	MEASUREMENTS
A. Greatest Length Without Lower Jaw	14 12/16
B. Greatest Width	8 14/16
FINAL SCORE	23 10/16

Exact Locality Where Killed: San Pete Co., UT

Date Killed: July 1, 1976   Hunter: Picked Up

Owner: Alma R. Lund and Merrill Daniels

Owner's Address: Telephone #:

Guide's Name and Address:

Remarks: (Mention Any Abnormalities or Unique Qualities)

I, __Glenn C. Sanderson__ , certify that I have measured this trophy on __03/11/1980__
PRINT NAME   MM/DD/YYYY

at __Missouri Department of Conservation__   __Jefferson City__   __MO__
STREET ADDRESS   CITY   STATE/PROVINCE

and that these measurements and data are, to the best of my knowledge and belief, made in accordance with the instructions given.

Witness: __F. Cook__   Signature: __Glenn C. Sanderson__   I.D. Number:
                                      B&C OFFICIAL MEASURER

BLACK BEAR

Ursus americanus and related subspecies

MINIMUM SCORE 21

Score	Greatest Length of Skull Without Lower Jaw	Greatest Width of Skull	Locality	Hunter	Owner	Date Killed	Rank
23 10/16	14 12/16	8 14/16	Sanpete Co., UT	Picked Up	A.R. Lund & M. Daniels	1975	1
23 7/16	14 8/16	8 15/16	Lycoming Co., PA		PA Game Comm.	1987	2
23 3/16	13 15/16	9 4/16	Mendocino Co., CA	Robert J. Shuttleworth, Jr.	Robert J. Shuttleworth, Jr.	1993	3
22 15/16	13 14/16	9 1/16	Kuiu Island, AK	Craig D. Martin	Craig D. Martin	1996	4
22 13/16	14 1/16	8 12/16	Ventura Co., CA	Loren C. Nodolf	Loaned to B&C Natl. Coll.	1990	5
22 11/16	14 5/16	8 6/16	Bradford Co., PA	Chad M. Reed	Chad M. Reed	1991	6
22 11/16	13 13/16	8 14/16	Bronson Lake, SK	Stanley Benson	Stanley Benson	1997	6
22 9/16	14 6/16	8 3/16	Greenlee Co., AZ	William H. Slater	William H. Slater	1987	8
22 9/16	13 12/16	8 13/16	Carbon Co., PA	Joseph M. Legotti	Joseph M. Legotti	1991	8
22 9/16	14 7/16	8 2/16	Jefferson Co., PA	Frank A. Rottman	B&C National Collection	1991	8
22 9/16	13 14/16	8 11/16	Prince of Wales Island, AK	Mark T. Young	Mark T. Young	1993	8
22 8/16	14 6/16	8 2/16	Porcupine Plain, SK	Calvin Parsons	Calvin Parsons	1977	12
22 8/16	14 1/16	8 7/16	Gila Co., AZ	Fred Peters	Fred Peters	1985	12
22 8/16	13 13/16	8 11/16	Rockingham Co., VA	Roger O. Wyant	Roger O. Wyant	1994	12
22 8/16	14	8 8/16	Monroe Co., PA	Thomas Q. Vasey	Thomas Q. Vasey	1995	12
22 7/16	13 11/16	8 12/16	Sevier Co., UT	Picked Up	UT Div. of Wildl. Resc.	1982	16
22 6/16	13 11/16	8 11/16	Sanpete Co., UT	R.W. Peterson & R.S. Hardy	Rex W. Peterson	1970	17
22 6/16	14 3/16	8 3/16	Gila Co., AZ	Roy A. Stewart	Roy A. Stewart	1978	17
22 6/16	13 11/16	8 11/16	Lycoming Co., PA	John C. Whyne	John C. Whyne	1983	17
22 6/16	13 12/16	8 10/16	Gronlid, SK	Floyd Forster	Floyd Forster	1992	17
22 6/16	13 12/16	8 10/16	Bedford Co., PA	James E. Deneen	James E. Deneen	1995	17
22 4/16	13 9/16	8 11/16	Apache Co., AZ	R.R. Barney & H.E. Booher	Richard R. Barney	1968	22
22 4/16	14 1/16	8 3/16	Ft. Apache Res., AZ	Jimmie C. James	Jimmie C. James	1971	22
22 4/16	13 15/16	8 5/16	Nestor Falls, ON	Vicki M. Blender	Vicki M. Blender	1995	22
22 4/16	13 11/16	8 9/16	Greenlee Co., AZ	Brian Reece	Brian Reece	1996	22
22 3/16	13 13/16	8 6/16	Frog Lake, AB	Darren Daniel	Darren Daniel	1983	26
22 3/16	14 1/16	8 2/16	Aitkin Co., MN	Picked Up	Greg & Gary Kullhem	1992	26
22 3/16	13 7/16	8 12/16	Barron Co., WI	Mike T. Losey	Mike T. Losey	1995	26
22 3/16	13 12/16	8 7/16	Kanabec Co., MN	Corey A. Gilbertson	Corey A. Gilbertson	1996	26
22 2/16	13 13/16	8 5/16	Graham Co., AZ	Peter C. Knagge	Peter C. Knagge	1982	30
22 2/16	13 11/16	8 7/16	Sanpete Co., UT	Larry W. Cox	Larry W. Cox	1987	30
22 2/16	13 14/16	8 4/16	Queen Charlotte Islands, BC	Craig N. Beachy	Craig N. Beachy	1988	30
22 2/16	13 12/16	8 6/16	Kern Co., CA	Danny R. Thomas	Danny R. Thomas	1988	30
22 2/16	13 6/16	8 12/16	Mendocino Co., CA	Jay Bromley	Jay Bromley	1991	30
22 2/16	13 8/16	8 10/16	Clark Co., WI	Daniel L. Kizewski	Daniel L. Kizewski	1993	30
22 2/16	13 13/16	8 5/16	Mendocino Co., CA	Chris Brennan	Chris Brennan	1995	30
22 1/16	13 11/16	8 6/16	Uintah Co., UT	Hal Mecham	Hal Mecham	1975	37
22 1/16	13 13/16	8 4/16	Arran, SK	Harry Kushniryk	Harry Kushniryk	1981	37

			Locality	Hunter	Owner	Date	Rank
22 1/16	13 15/16	8 2/16	Fox Creek, AB	Richard Raiwet	Richard Raiwet	1992	37
22	13 6/16	8 10/16	Hahns Peak, CO	W.L. Cave	W.L. Cave	1964	40
22	13 8/16	8 9/16	Graham Co., AZ	Thomas E. Klepfer	Thomas E. Klepfer	1972	40
22	13 12/16	8 4/16	Garfield Co., CO	Joseph R. Maynard	Joseph R. Maynard	1977	40
22	13 10/16	8 6/16	Hamilton Co., NY	Samuel A. Johnson	Samuel A. Johnson	1986	40
22	13 13/16	8 3/16	Maknak, MB	Cory A. Pardon	Cory A. Pardon	1986	40
22	13 7/16	8 9/16	Roscommon Co., MI	Matthew A. Gettler	Matthew A. Gettler	1987	40
22	13 11/16	8 5/16	Carbon Co., UT	Michael J. Hreinson	Michael J. Hreinson	1987	40
22	13 7/16	8 4/16	Prince of Wales Island, AK	John W. Simons	John W. Simons	1987	40
22	13 12/16	8 4/16	Prince of Wales Island, AK	George P. Mann	George P. Mann	1991	40
22	13 14/16	8 2/16	Prince of Wales Island, AK	Stanley L. Parkerson	Stanley L. Parkerson	1991	40
22	13 10/16	8 6/16	Gila Co., AZ	Steven J. Stayner	Steven J. Stayner	1991	40
22	13 10/16	8 6/16	Los Angeles Co., CA	Joe L. Clay	Joe L. Clay	1992	40
22	13 8/16	8 8/16	Lycoming Co., PA	Clarence G. Eppley	Clarence G. Eppley	1992	40
22	13 9/16	8 7/16	Menominee Co., MI	Michael L. Hesyck	Michael L. Hesyck	1992	40
22	14 2/16	7 14/16	Tioga Co., PA	Ronald E. Andrus	Ronald E. Andrus	1994	40
22	13 6/16	8 10/16	Aitkin Co., MN	Joel J. Stang	Joel J. Stang	1995	40
22	13 11/16	8 5/16	Pine Co., MN	Darrin G. Stream	Darrin G. Stream	1995	40
22	14	8	Essex Co., NY	Anthony J. Ploufe	Anthony J. Ploufe	1996	40
21 15/16	13 3/16	8 12/16	Land O' Lakes, WI	Ed Strobel	Ed Strobel	1953	58
21 15/16	13 13/16	8 2/16	Swan River, MB	Jim E. Russell	Jim E. Russell	1973	58
21 15/16	13 13/16	8 10/16	Lincoln Co., WY	C. William Redshaw	C. William Redshaw	1976	58
21 15/16	13 12/16	8 3/16	Clearfield Co., PA	Dwayne B. DeLattre	Dwayne B. DeLattre	1987	58
21 15/16	13 9/16	8 6/16	Russell, MB	Gerry Mushumanski	Gerry Mushumanski	1987	58
21 15/16	13 12/16	8 3/16	Gila Co., AZ	Thomas Alvin	Thomas Alvin	1990	58
21 15/16	14 6/16	7 9/16	Birdtail Creek, MB	Barry Minshull	Barry Minshull	1990	58
21 15/16	13 12/16	8 3/16	Cambria Co., PA	Frank J. Mehalko, Sr.	Frank J. Mehalko, Sr.	1992	58
21 15/16	13 9/16	8 6/16	Riverton, MB	Samuel J. Amodeo	Samuel J. Amodeo	1995	58
21 15/16	13 13/16	8 2/16	Queen Charlotte Islands, BC	Philip Giesbrecht	Philip Giesbrecht	1995	58
21 15/16	13 10/16	8 5/16	Graham Co., AZ	Mark D. Morris	Mark D. Morris	1995	58
21 15/16	13 14/16	8 1/16	Shawano Co., WI	Rick A. Much	Rick A. Much	1997	58
21 14/16	13 11/16	8 3/16	Smithers, BC	Native American	Jack Adams	1975	70
21 14/16	13 10/16	8 4/16	Lincoln Co., WI	Robert P. Faufau	Robert P. Faufau	1981	70
21 14/16	13 7/16	8 7/16	Grant Co., NM	Mark J. Miller	Mark J. Miller	1983	70
21 14/16	13 12/16	8 2/16	Hirsch Creek, BC	Cecil W. Brown	Cecil W. Brown	1984	70
21 14/16	13 9/16	8 5/16	Luzerne Co., PA	Adrian C. Robbins	Adrian C. Robbins	1989	70
21 14/16	13 12/16	8 2/16	Tyrrell Co., NC	Albert J. Blase	Albert J. Blase	1996	70
21 14/16	13 9/16	8 5/16	Chimdemash Creek, BC	Randy Kucharysen	Randy Kucharysen	1997	70
21 13/16	13 9/16	8 4/16	Ft. Apache Res., AZ	G. Boyd, P. Ellsworth & G. Brewer	Greg Boyd	1964	77
21 13/16	13 7/16	8 6/16	Tatlanika River, AK	Barry W. Campbell	Barry W. Campbell	1966	77
21 13/16	13 8/16	8 5/16	Ft. Apache Res., AZ	Gary W. Sholl	Gary W. Sholl	1969	77
21 13/16	13 9/16	8 4/16	Graham Co., AZ	Bruce Liddy	Bruce Liddy	1976	77
21 13/16	13 6/16	8 7/16	Carbon Co., PA	Robert F. Kulp	Robert F. Kulp	1983	77
21 13/16	13 6/16	8 6/16	Big River, SK	William Dear	William Dear	1985	77
21 13/16	14 6/16	7 7/16	St. Johns Co., FL	Picked Up	FL Game & Fresh Water Fish Comm.	1985	77
21 13/16	13 12/16	8 1/16	Aitkin Co., MN	Picked Up	MN Dept. of Natl. Resc.	1988	77
21 13/16	13 4/16	8 9/16	Menominee Co., MI	Andrew M. Bray	Ray Bray	1989	77

BLACK BEAR

Ursus americanus and related subspecies

Score	Greatest Length of Skull Without Lower Jaw	Greatest Width of Skull	Locality	Hunter	Owner	Date Killed	Rank
21 13/16	13 3/16	8 10/16	Price Co., WI	John W. Marshall	John W. Marshall	1993	77
21 13/16	14	7 13/16	Douglas Co., WI	Annette C. Lehman	Annette C. Lehman	1995	77
21 13/16	13 12/16	8 1/16	White Co., GA	John M. Wood	John M. Wood	1995	77
21 13/16	13 5/16	8 8/16	Prince of Wales Island, AK	Dyrk T. Eddie	Dyrk T. Eddie	1996	77
21 12/16	13 3/16	8 9/16	Delta Co., CO	Quincy Hines	Quincy Hines	1967	90
21 12/16	13 10/16	8 2/16	Bayfield Co., WI	Byron Bird, Jr.	Byron Bird, Jr.	1976	90
21 12/16	13 14/16	7 14/16	California Creek, AK	Boyd J. Blair	Boyd J. Blair	1976	90
21 12/16	13 5/16	8 4/16	Gila Co., AZ	Mike Lisk	Mike Lisk	1984	90
21 12/16	13 10/16	8 2/16	Garfield Co., UT	Clint Mecham	Clint Mecham	1985	90
21 12/16	13 11/16	8 1/16	Greenwater Lake, SK	John Woulfe	John Woulfe	1987	90
21 12/16	13 4/16	8 8/16	Huerfano Co., CO	Harvey R. Newcomb	Harvey R. Newcomb	1988	90
21 12/16	13 5/16	8 7/16	Lily Lake, BC	James W. Zevely	James W. Zevely	1990	90
21 12/16	14	7 12/16	Chowan Co., NC	George D. Copeland, Sr.	George D. Copeland, Sr.	1991	90
21 12/16	13 8/16	8 4/16	Makinak, MB	Wendell Hanson	Wendell Hanson	1991	90
21 12/16	13 10/16	8 2/16	Alonsa, MB	Cory Mozdzen	Cory Mozdzen	1991	90
21 12/16	13 8/16	8 4/16	Prince of Wales Island, AK	Kleigh C. Hirschi	Kleigh C. Hirschi	1992	90
21 12/16	13 2/16	8 10/16	Ventura Co., CA	Joey La Salle	Joey La Salle	1992	90
21 12/16	13 9/16	8 3/16	Gila Co., AZ	John W. Oberg	John W. Oberg	1992	90
21 12/16	13 12/16	8	Pine Co., MN	Fred Olander	Fred Olander	1992	90
21 12/16	13 2/16	8 10/16	Trinity Co., CA	Blue Millsap	Blue Millsap	1994	90
21 12/16	13	8 12/16	Graham Co., AZ	Lee A. Malaby	Lee A. Malaby	1995	90
21 12/16	13 11/16	8 1/16	Maricopa Co., AZ	Trent P. Thornton	Trent P. Thornton	1995	90
21 11/16	13 5/16	8 6/16	Mendocino Co., CA	E.J. Vamm	Univ. Calif. Museum	1928	108
21 11/16	13 6/16	8 5/16	Gila Co., AZ	Clay Warden	Milo Warden	1975	108
21 11/16	13 5/16	8 6/16	Menominee Co., MI	Ray Bray	Andy Bray	1984	108
21 11/16	13 5/16	8 6/16	Kern Co., CA	George H. Hershberger	George H. Hershberger	1985	108
21 11/16	13 7/16	8 4/16	Karta Bay, AK	Donald J. McNeil	Douglas A. McNeil	1985	108
21 11/16	13 15/16	7 12/16	Hyde Co., NC	Gurnwood L. Radcliff, Jr.	Gurnwood L. Radcliff, Jr.	1986	108
21 11/16	13 6/16	8 5/16	Cass Co., MN	Anne M. Zahalka	Anne M. Zahalka	1986	108
21 11/16	13 11/16	8	Prairie River, SK	Gregory Stabrylla	Gregory Stabrylla	1987	108
21 11/16	13 7/16	8 4/16	Queen Charlotte Islands, BC	Kurt M. Saffarek	Kurt M. Saffarek	1988	108
21 11/16	13 6/16	8 5/16	Prince of Wales Island, AK	Richard J. Asplund	Richard J. Asplund	1990*	108
21 11/16	13 15/16	7 12/16	Porcupine Hills, SK	Richard K. McLean	Richard K. McLean	1990	108
21 11/16	13 5/16	8 6/16	Ventura Co., CA	Marsha Vaughan	Marsha Vaughan	1990	108
21 11/16	13 9/16	8 2/16	Tyrrell Co., NC	Hank D. Rose, Jr.	NC Wildl. Resc. Comm.	1993	108
21 11/16	13 13/16	7 14/16	Rusk Co., WI	Gregory J. Baneck	Gregory J. Baneck	1995	108
21 11/16	13 6/16	8 5/16	Washburn Co., WI	Keith W. Dahlstrom	Keith W. Dahlstrom	1996	108
21 11/16	13 4/16	8 7/16	Olha, MB	Gary G. Lex	Gary G. Lex	1996	108

Score			Locality	By whom killed	Owner	Date	Rank
21 11/16	13 8/16	8 3/16	Prince of Wales Island, AK	Kurt G. Kruger	Kurt G. Kruger	1997	108
21 10/16	13	8 10/16	Mendocino Co., CA	Andy Bowman	Univ. Calif. Museum	1930	125
21 10/16	13	8 10/16	Custer Co., ID	Robert L. Caskey	Robert L. Caskey	1967	125
21 10/16	13 5/16	8 5/16	Lake Co., OR	Martin V. Pernoll	Martin V. Pernoll	1967	125
21 10/16	13 12/16	7 14/16	Piscataquis Co., ME	J.D. Flowers	J.D. Flowers	1980	125
21 10/16	13 4/16	8 6/16	Grande Cache, AB	Laurier Adam	Laurier Adam	1984	125
21 10/16	13 8/16	8 2/16	Gila Co., AZ	Harold W. Mosser	Harold W. Mosser	1985	125
21 10/16	13 9/16	8 1/16	Prairie River, SK	Tim P. Matzinger	Tim P. Matzinger	1989	125
21 10/16	13 2/16	8 8/16	Gila Co., AZ	Fred Peters	Fred Peters	1989	125
21 10/16	13 10/16	8	Alcona Co., MI	Randy L. Schultz	Randy L. Schultz	1989	125
21 10/16	13 7/16	8 3/16	Graham Co., AZ	S. Kim Bonnett	S. Kim Bonnett	1990	125
21 10/16	13 10/16	8 4/16	Bucareli Bay, AK	Dwight B. Leister, Jr.	Dwight B. Leister, Jr.	1990	125
21 10/16	13 3/16	8 7/16	Sullivan Co., NY	Daniel O'Keefe	Daniel O'Keefe	1991	125
21 10/16	13 2/16	8 8/16	Ventura Co., CA	Chris Ames	Chris Ames	1992	125
21 10/16	13 7/16	8 3/16	Sawyer Co., WI	Brad A. Beise	Brad A. Beise	1992	125
21 10/16	13 8/16	8 2/16	Grant Co., WV	Carnie Carr, Jr.	Carnie Carr, Jr.	1993	125
21 10/16	13 10/16	8 6/16	Peace River, AB	Richard A. Walker	Richard A. Walker	1993	125
21 10/16	13 6/16	8 4/16	Glenn Co., CA	John H. Knight	John H. Knight	1994	125
21 10/16	13 6/16	7 13/16	Graham Co., AZ	Jeffrey D. Warren	Jeffrey D. Warren	1994	125
21 10/16	13 13/16	8	Prince of Wales Island, AK	Gerald Baty	Gerald Baty	1996	125
21 10/16	13 10/16	8 1/16	Marathon Co., WI	David S. Williamson	David S. Williamson	1996	125
21 10/16	13 9/16	8 5/16	Qu'Appelle River, SK	Lyle Gorecki	Lyle Gorecki	1997	125
21 9/16	13 4/16	8 6/16	Garfield Co., CO	Robert C. Maurer	Robert C. Maurer	1955	146
21 9/16	13 3/16	8 3/16	Collbran, CO	O.K. Clifton	O.K. Clifton	1957	146
21 9/16	13 6/16	8 3/16	Williams Fork River, CO	C. Stehle & J. Grove	Clyde Stehle	1958	146
21 9/16	13 4/16	8 5/16	Vilas Co., WI	WI Dept. of Natl. Resc.	Neal Long Taxidermy	1959	146
21 9/16	13 6/16	8 4/16	Mesa Co., CO	Hartle V. Morris	Hartle V. Morris	1962	146
21 9/16	13 5/16	8 2/16	Clinton Co., PA	Donald Sorgen	Donald Sorgen	1968	146
21 9/16	13 7/16	8 5/16	Vilas Co., WI	John J. Volkmann	John J. Volkmann	1973	146
21 9/16	13 2/16	8 7/16	Ouray Co., CO	Thomas C. Middleton	Thomas C. Middleton	1978	146
21 9/16	13 4/16	8 5/16	Zeballos, BC	Gary M. Biggar	Gary M. Biggar	1983	146
21 9/16	13 6/16	8 3/16	Catron Co., NM	Sam Ray	Sam Ray	1983	146
21 9/16	13 11/16	7 14/16	Tyrrell Co., NC	Larry D. Bailey	Larry D. Bailey	1987	146
21 9/16	13 9/16	8	Tioga Co., PA	Thomas B. Gamble	Thomas B. Gamble	1987	146
21 9/16	13 13/16	8 6/16	Pelican Lake, MB	Rick D. Oliphant	Rick D. Oliphant	1987	146
21 9/16	13 2/16	7 12/16	Collier Co., FL	Picked Up	FL Game & Fresh Water Fish Comm.	1988	146
21 9/16	13 7/16	8 7/16	Thorne River, AK	Ernest W. McLean	Ernest W. McLean	1989	146
21 9/16	13 3/16	8 2/16	Deena Creek, BC	William H. Hintze	William H. Hintze	1992	146
21 9/16	13 7/16	8 6/16	Burnt Bay, NF	Ewen K. Whiteway	Ewen K. Whiteway	1992	146
21 9/16	13 2/16	8 2/16	Ouray Co., CO	Lee Gabardi	Lee Gabardi	1993	146
21 9/16	13 5/16	8 5/16	Sawyer Co., WI	Kevin R. Samuel	Kevin R. Samuel	1993	146
21 9/16	13 4/16	8	Dunn Co., WI	Richard E. Anderson	Richard E. Anderson	1995	146
21 9/16	13 8/16	8 1/16	Rusk Co., WI	Dennis F. Grimme	Dennis F. Grimme	1995	146
21 8/16	13 1/16	8 7/16	Gallatin River, WY	J.P.V. Evans	U.S. Natl. Museum	1914	167
21 8/16	13 9/16	7 15/16	Bayfield Co., WI	Earl B. Johnson	Earl B. Johnson	1953	167
21 8/16	13 8/16	8 8/16	Lincoln Co., WY	Picked Up	Matt Failoni	1965	167
21 8/16	13 5/16	8 3/16	Forest Co., WI	Richard Ruthven	WI Buck & Bear Club	1968	167

BLACK BEAR

Ursus americanus americanus and related subspecies

Score	Greatest Length of Skull Without Lower Jaw	Greatest Width of Skull	Locality	Hunter	Owner	Date Killed	Rank
21 8/16	13 5/16	8 3/16	Chiricahua Butte, AZ	W.O. Morrison	W.O. Morrison	1969	167
21 8/16	13 6/16	8 2/16	Lincoln Co., WY	Charles R. Nixon	Charles R. Nixon	1973	167
21 8/16	13 7/16	8 1/16	Augusta Co., VA	Joseph R. Lam	Joseph R. Lam	1977	167
21 8/16	13 4/16	8 4/16	Ventura Co., CA	James B. Wade	James B. Wade	1977	167
21 8/16	13 1/16	8 7/16	Apache Co., AZ	Joseph H. Lyman	Fred Peters	1978	167
21 8/16	13 7/16	8 1/16	Rossburn, MB	Unknown	Randall J. Bean	1980	167
21 8/16	13 3/16	8 5/16	Garfield Co., CO	Robert W. Jackson	Robert W. Jackson	1980	167
21 8/16	12 14/16	8 10/16	Harrison Hot Springs, BC	Domenico Abbinante	Domenico Abbinante	1982	167
21 8/16	13 5/16	8 3/16	Bonneville Co., ID	George R. Adams	George R. Adams	1982	167
21 8/16	13 6/16	8 2/16	Gila Co., AZ	Rick Corven	R. Corven & R. Gifford	1983	167
21 8/16	13	8 6/16	Pike Co., PA	Paul D. Longenbach	Paul D. Longenbach	1983	167
21 8/16	13 11/16	7 13/16	Douglas Co., WI	Picked Up	WI Dept. of Natl. Resc.	1984	167
21 8/16	13 6/16	8 2/16	Marshall Co., MN	James E. Kelley	J. & B. Zimpel	1984	167
21 8/16	12 15/16	8 9/16	Mesa Co., CO	Rem B. Bennett, Jr.	Rem B. Bennett, Jr.	1986	167
21 8/16	13 6/16	8 2/16	Navajo Co., AZ	Fred Peters	Fred Peters	1987	167
21 8/16	13 6/16	8 2/16	Sarkar Creek, AK	Robert F. Ellebruch	Robert F. Ellebruch	1988	167
21 8/16	13 10/16	7 14/16	Lake Co., FL	Picked Up	FL Game & Fresh Water Fish Comm.	1989	167
21 8/16	13 5/16	8 3/16	Gila Co., AZ	Don Hoey	Don Hoey	1989	167
21 8/16	13 4/16	8 4/16	Stove Lake, SK	David Prince	David Prince	1990	167
21 8/16	13 3/16	8 5/16	Clinton Co., NY	Todd F. Rabideau	Todd F. Rabideau	1990	167
21 8/16	13 2/16	8 6/16	Prince of Wales Island, AK	James W. Cook	James W. Cook	1992	167
21 8/16	13 5/16	8 3/16	Westmoreland Co., PA	Wayne E. Toth	Wayne E. Toth	1993	167
21 8/16	13 6/16	8 2/16	Bradford Co., PA	Robert C. Beebe	Robert C. Beebe	1994	167
21 8/16	13 11/16	7 13/16	Bladen Co., NC	Michael Burgess	Michael Burgess	1994	167
21 8/16	13 5/16	8 3/16	Piney, MB	Paul E. Asmundson	Paul E. Asmundson	1995	167
21 8/16	13 7/16	8 1/16	Florence Co., WI	Richard T. Slattery	Richard T. Slattery	1995	167
21 8/16	13 6/16	8 2/16	Sullivan Co., PA	John C. Koller	John C. Koller	1996	167
21 8/16	13 1/16	8 7/16	Grant Co., NM	Mark J. Miller	Mark J. Miller	1996	167
21 8/16	13	8 6/16	Sandoval Co., NM	Thomas D. Stromei	Thomas D. Stromei	1996	167
21 8/16	13 11/16	7 13/16	Rennell Sound, BC	Philip Giesbrecht	Philip Giesbrecht	1997	167
21 8/16	13 3/16	8 5/16	Prince of Wales Island, AK	Eric H. Wietfeld	Eric H. Wietfeld	1997	167
21 7/16	13 2/16	8 5/16	Mariposa Co., CA	Bert Palmberg	Bert Palmberg	1957	202
21 7/16	13 2/16	8 5/16	Wales Is., AK	Picked Up	L.R. Hall	1962	202
21 7/16	13 3/16	8 4/16	Megal Mt., NF	Ben Hillicoss	Ben Hillicoss	1963	202
21 7/16	13 7/16	8	Albemarle Co., VA	Grover F. Sites	Grover F. Sites	1964	202
21 7/16	13 3/16	8 4/16	Pierce Co., WA	T. Johnson & B. Paque	Tracy Johnson	1968	202
21 7/16	13 6/16	8 1/16	McKean Co., PA	Picked Up	PA Game Comm.	1969	202
21 7/16	13 4/16	8 3/16	Douglas Co., WI	Kenneth J. Burton	Kenneth J. Burton	1972	202

			Locality	Hunter	Owner	Date	Rank
21 7/16	13	8 7/16	Nordegg, AB	Leo F. Hermary	Leo F. Hermary	1977	202
21 7/16	13 4/16	8 3/16	Pierceland, SK	Bryce Burgess	Bryce Burgess	1980	202
21 7/16	13 12/16	7 11/16	Sevier Co., UT	Milton L. Robb	Milton L. Robb	1980	202
21 7/16	13 4/16	8 3/16	Iron Co., WI	Gary G. Johnson	Gary G. Johnson	1982	202
21 7/16	13 10/16	7 13/16	Flat Lake, AB	Dale T. Loosemore	Dale T. Loosemore	1983	202
21 7/16	13 8/16	7 15/16	Simonette River, AB	Richard Mellon	Richard Mellon	1983	202
21 7/16	13 4/16	8 3/16	Gila Co., AZ	D. Highly Falkner	D. Highly Falkner	1984	202
21 7/16	13 3/16	8 4/16	Cholmondeley Sound, AK	Philip A. Indovina	Philip A. Indovina	1984	202
21 7/16	13 11/16	7 12/16	Peesane, SK	Peter Janzen	Peter Janzen	1984	202
21 7/16	13 3/16	8 4/16	Greenlee Co., AZ	Robin W. Bechtel	Robin W. Bechtel	1985	202
21 7/16	13 3/16	8 4/16	Fox Creek, AB	William Hellebrand	William Hellebrand	1985	202
21 7/16	13 3/16	8 3/16	Tokeen, AK	Terry D. Denmon	Terry D. Denmon	1986	202
21 7/16	13 2/16	8 5/16	Somerset Co., PA	Ralph T. Meyers	Ralph T. Meyers	1987	202
21 7/16	13 6/16	8 1/16	Loon Lake, SK	Wyatt Barnes	Wyatt Barnes	1988	202
21 7/16	13 9/16	7 14/16	Smoky River, AB	Gary G. Dumdei	Gary G. Dumdei	1989	202
21 7/16	13 7/16	8	Kupreanof Island, AK	David K. Mueller	David K. Mueller	1989	202
21 7/16	13 6/16	8 1/16	Carrot River, SK	Hanz F. Meyer	Hanz F. Meyer	1991	202
21 7/16	13 2/16	8 5/16	Douglas Co., WI	Richard J. Rohlfs	Richard J. Rohlfs	1991	202
21 7/16	13 11/16	7 12/16	Gordondale, AB	Zigmund J. Kertenis, Jr.	Zigmund J. Kertenis, Jr.	1993	202
21 7/16	13 6/16	8 1/16	Clearfield Co., PA	James A. Mihalko	James A. Mihalko	1993	202
21 7/16	13 4/16	8 3/16	Roseau Co., MN	Kevin D. Johnson	Kevin D. Johnson	1994	202
21 7/16	13 6/16	8 1/16	McAuley, MB	Jamie B. Poole	Jamie B. Poole	1994	202
21 7/16	13 6/16	8 1/16	Price Co., WI	Peter E. Dickmann	Donald L. Cramer	1996	202
21 7/16	13 1/16	8 6/16	Ventura Co., CA	Mark Karluk	Mark Karluk	1996	202
21 7/16	13	8 7/16	Menominee Co., MI	Jacqueline M. Piatt	Jacqueline M. Piatt	1997	202
21 6/16	13 1/16	8 5/16	Prince of Wales Island, AK	Picked Up	Robert Kase	PR 1954	234
21 6/16	13 13/16	7 9/16	Sandpoint, ID	Ronald L. Book	Ronald L. Book	1969	234
21 6/16	12 12/16	8 10/16	Franklin Co., NY	James Donner	James Donner	1970	234
21 6/16	13 5/16	8 1/16	Reserve, NM	C.J. McElroy	C.J. McElroy	1970	234
21 6/16	13 11/16	7 11/16	Pike Co., PA	Robert Loux	Robert Loux	1971	234
21 6/16	13 2/16	8 4/16	Prince of Wales Island, AK	John Stubbs	John Stubbs	1973	234
21 6/16	13 6/16	8	Bayfield Co., WI	Larry L. Frye	Larry L. Frye	1975	234
21 6/16	13 10/16	7 12/16	Carbon Co., UT	R. Peterson & R.S. Hardy	Rex Peterson	1975	234
21 6/16	13	7 12/16	Humboldt Co., CA	Dean Earley	Dean Earley	1977	234
21 6/16	12 13/16	8 9/16	Pitkin Co., CO	Chris Green	Chris Green	1980	234
21 6/16	13 2/16	8 4/16	Thorne Bay, AK	Tod L. Reichert	Tod L. Reichert	1985	234
21 6/16	13 3/16	8 3/16	Klawock, AK	Tom R. Engel	Tom R. Engel	1987	234
21 6/16	13 6/16	8	Grant Co., WV	Carnie Carr, Sr.	Carnie Carr, Sr.	1988	234
21 6/16	13 10/16	7 12/16	Graham Co., AZ	Timm J. Haas	Timm J. Haas	1988	234
21 6/16	13 7/16	7 14/16	Cattaraugus Co., NY	John M. Abrams, Sr.	John M. Abrams, Sr.	1989	234
21 6/16	13 5/16	8 1/16	Potter Co., PA	Earl E. Carolus	Earl E. Carolus	1989	234
21 6/16	12 13/16	8 9/16	Craven Co., NC	Todd A. Brewer	Todd A. Brewer	1991	234
21 6/16	13 2/16	8 4/16	York Co., NB	Kenneth J. Fluck	Kenneth J. Fluck	1991	234
21 6/16	13 4/16	8 2/16	Mendocino Co., CA	R. Larry Hyder	R. Larry Hyder	1991	234
21 6/16	13 1/16	8 5/16	Plumas Co., CA	Monty D. McCormick	Monty D. McCormick	1992	234
21 6/16	13 4/16	8 2/16	Taylor Co., WI	Kenneth R. Cisewski	Kenneth R. Cisewski	1993	234
21 6/16	13 5/16	8 1/16	Gila Co., AZ	Becky Jo Smith	Becky Jo Smith	1993	234

Ursus americanus americanus and related subspecies

Score	Greatest Length of Skull Without Lower Jaw	Greatest Width of Skull	Locality	Hunter	Owner	Date Killed	Rank
21 6/16	12 14/16	8 8/16	Mendocino Co., CA	Lawrence E. Taylor	Lawrence E. Taylor	1993	234
21 6/16	13 5/16	8 1/16	Menominee Co., MI	Linda K. Nowack	Linda K. Nowack	1995	234
21 6/16	13 4/16	8 2/16	Price Co., WI	Patrick H. Sheldon	Patrick H. Sheldon	1995	234
21 6/16	13 10/16	7 12/16	Mahnomen Co., MN	Michael J. Ahles	Michael J. Ahles	1996	234
21 6/16	13 7/16	7 15/16	Oakburn, MB	Marv Biadasz	Marv Biadasz	1996	234
21 6/16	13 4/16	8 2/16	Clark Co., WI	Larry L. Osegard	Larry L. Osegard	1996	234
21 5/16	13 1/16	8 4/16	Colorado	E.T. Seton	U.S. Natl. Museum	1897	262
21 5/16	13 6/16	7 15/16	Yarmouth Co., NS	John L. Bastey	John L. Bastey	1945	262
21 5/16	12 15/16	8 6/16	Centre Co., PA	Picked Up	Wayne B. Harpster	1946	262
21 5/16	13 3/16	8 2/16	Rockbridge Co., VA	Richard L. Merchant	Richard L. Merchant	1953	262
21 5/16	13	8 5/16	Buffalo Park, CO	John L. Howard	John L. Howard	1958	262
21 5/16	13 5/16	8	Coburn Lake, CA	Lauren A. Johnson	Lauren A. Johnson	1960	262
21 5/16	13 2/16	8 3/16	Olympic Pen., WA	Bert Klineburger	Bert Klineburger	1963	262
21 5/16	12 15/16	8 6/16	Cynthia, AB	R. LeVoir	R. LeVoir	1968	262
21 5/16	13 3/16	8 2/16	Mendocino Co., CA	Gene H. Whitney	Gene H. Whitney	1971	262
21 5/16	13 5/16	8	Vilas Co., WI	Michael G. Duwe	Michael G. Duwe	1972	262
21 5/16	13 4/16	8 1/16	Lincoln Co., WY	Gregg G. Fisher	Gregg G. Fisher	1975	262
21 5/16	13 7/16	7 14/16	Gila Co., AZ	Larry S. Behrends	Larry S. Behrends	1976	262
21 5/16	13 11/16	7 10/16	Langlade Co., WI	Michael Steliga	Michael Steliga	1981	262
21 5/16	13 5/16	8	Santa Barbara Co., CA	Picked Up	John L. Mussell	1982	262
21 5/16	13 8/16	7 13/16	Rockingham Co., VA	Roger O. Wyant	Roger O. Wyant	1984	262
21 5/16	13	8 5/16	Mendocino Co., CA	John Jacobs	John Jacobs	1985	262
21 5/16	13 2/16	8 3/16	Navajo Co., AZ	D. Howard Mullins	D. Howard Mullins	1986	262
21 5/16	13 4/16	8 1/16	Gila Co., AZ	Neil L. Sullivan	Neil L. Sullivan	1986	262
21 5/16	13 8/16	7 13/16	Pine Co., MN	Harland Johnson	Harland Johnson	PR 1987	262
21 5/16	13 2/16	8 3/16	Prince of Wales Island, AK	Mark S. Rodin	Mark S. Rodin	1987	262
21 5/16	12 13/16	8 8/16	Rio Blanco Co., CO	Jason Steiner	Jason Steiner	1987	262
21 5/16	13 5/16	8	Potter Co., PA	Gary R. Sellers	Gary R. Sellers	1989	262
21 5/16	13 8/16	7 13/16	Hudson Bay, SK	Jim Strini	Jim Strini	1989	262
21 5/16	13 3/16	8 2/16	Swan River, MB	Linda A. Nuss	Linda A. Nuss	1990	262
21 5/16	12 14/16	8 7/16	Sawyer Co., WI	Mark R. Heath	Mark R. Heath	1991	262
21 5/16	13 2/16	8 3/16	Swan River, MB	Richard C. Weber	Richard C. Weber	1991	262
21 5/16	13 8/16	7 13/16	Sawyer Co., WI	Stephan E. Bouton	Stephan E. Bouton	1992	262
21 5/16	13 3/16	8 2/16	Forest Co., PA	Raymond A. Egan III	Raymond A. Egan III	1992	262
21 5/16	13 4/16	8 1/16	Meadow Lake, SK	Jack B. Kambeitz	Jack B. Kambeitz	1992	262
21 5/16	13 2/16	8 3/16	Kuiu Island, AK	David K. Mueller	David K. Mueller	1992	262
21 5/16	12 12/16	8 9/16	Williams Creek, BC	Wayne P. Topolewski	Wayne P. Topolewski	1992	262
21 5/16	13 4/16	8 1/16	Round Lake, SK	Floyd Forster	Floyd Forster	1994	262

Score	Greatest Length of Skull	Greatest Width of Skull	Locality	Hunter	Owner	Date Killed	Rank
21 5/16	13 7/16	7 14/16	Rossburn, MB	Curtis L. Hahn	Curtis L. Hahn	1994	262
21 5/16	12 15/16	8 6/16	Garfield Co., CO	Ted R. Bina	Ted R. Bina	1995	262
21 5/16	13 9/16	7 12/16	Deep Lake, MB	Kenneth B. Cherepak	Kenneth B. Cherepak	1995	262
21 5/16	13 6/16	7 15/16	Horseshoe Lake, AB	Darren Daniel	Darren Daniel	1995	262
21 5/16	13 5/16	8	Shawano Co., WI	Scott A. Johnson	Scott A. Johnson	1995	262
21 5/16	13 5/16	8 5/16	San Bernardino Co., CA	Rahul T. Mathur	Rahul T. Mathur	1995	262
21 5/16	13 5/16	8	Lincoln Co., WI	Richard H. Rollmann	Richard H. Rollmann	1996	262
21 5/16	13 11/16	8 10/16	Hyde Co., NC	David M. Blalock	David M. Blalock	1996	262
21 5/16	13 2/16	8 3/16	Falher, AB	Stephen L. Collins	Stephen L. Collins	1996	262
21 5/16	13	8 5/16	Delaware Co., NY	William S. Hoover	William S. Hoover	1996	262
21 5/16	13 3/16	8	Prince of Wales Island, AK	David K. Mueller	David K. Mueller	1997	262
21 4/16	13 1/16	8 2/16	Carswell Lake, SK	David A. Whitcomb	David A. Whitcomb	1928	307
21 4/16	13 15/16	8 4/16	Stenen, SK	J. Stephen Williams	J. Stephen Williams	1952	307
21 4/16	13 3/16	7 6/16	Cochise Co., AZ	Unknown	Univ. of Calif. Mus.	1956	307
21 4/16	13 6/16	8 1/16	Los Angeles Co., CA	Picked Up	Anselmo Lewis	1957	307
21 4/16	13 6/16	7 14/16	Shoshone River, WY	Loren L. Lutz	Loren L. Lutz	1965	307
21 4/16	13 8/16	7 14/16	Michigan	Albert Erickson	Albert Erickson	1967	307
21 4/16	13 2/16	7 12/16	Arizona	Paul B. Reynolds	Paul B. Reynolds	1968	307
21 4/16	13 9/16	8 2/16	Olympic Pen., WA	Bert Klineburger	Bert Klineburger	1968	307
21 4/16	12 12/16	7 11/16	Curry Co., OR	Joe W. Latimer	Joe W. Latimer	1969	307
21 4/16	12 11/16	8 8/16	Sawyer Co., WI	Ted Roberts	Ted Roberts	1970	307
21 4/16	13 1/16	8 9/16	Hudson Bay, SK	Neil Southam	Neil Southam	1974	307
21 4/16	13 6/16	8 3/16	Williams, AZ	James E. Coy	James E. Coy	1975	307
21 4/16	13	8 3/16	Snowmass, CO	Ronald D. Vincent	Ronald D. Vincent	1980	307
21 4/16	13 7/16	7 14/16	Marquette Co., MI	David L. Pietro	David L. Pietro	1980	307
21 4/16	13 7/16	8 4/16	Tehama Co., CA	Jim Cox	Jim Cox	1982	307
21 4/16	13 2/16	7 13/16	Pinal Co., AZ	Bruce R. Gifford	Bruce R. Gifford	1982	307
21 4/16	13 2/16	7 13/16	Khyex River, BC	Edward Dickens	Edward Dickens	1985	307
21 4/16	13 4/16	8 2/16	Sawyer Co., WI	Harvey W. Klein	Harvey W. Klein	1987	307
21 4/16	13 4/16	8 2/16	Vanderhoof, BC	William Stanley	William Stanley	1988	307
21 4/16	13	8	Mille Lacs Co., MN	Timothy J. Dusbabek	Timothy J. Dusbabek	1988	307
21 4/16	13 7/16	8	Greenlee Co., AZ	Bart Bledsoe	Bart Bledsoe	1988	307
21 4/16	13 1/16	8 4/16	Navajo Co., AZ	Fred Peters	Fred Peters	1989	307
21 4/16	13 5/16	7 13/16	Catron Co., NM	Gary L. Raney	Gary L. Raney	1989	307
21 4/16	13 2/16	8 3/16	Peace River, BC	Ivan Brausse	Ivan Brausse	1990	307
21 4/16	13 2/16	7 15/16	Pasquia Hills, SK	Patrick G. Povah	Patrick G. Povah	1990	307
21 4/16	13	8 2/16	Aroostook Co., ME	John S. Drost	John S. Drost	1991	307
21 4/16	13 9/16	8 2/16	Shasta Co., CA	Richard L. Moore	Richard L. Moore	1992	307
21 4/16	13 3/16	8 4/16	Crow Wing Co., MN	Robert H. Hartigan	Robert H. Hartigan	1993	307
21 4/16	12 15/16	7 11/16	Alpena Co., MI	Fred C. Webber	Fred C. Webber	1993	307
21 4/16	13	8 1/16	Cass Co., MN	Bradley T. Anderson	Bradley T. Anderson	1993	307
21 4/16	13 4/16	8 5/16	Greenlee Co., AZ	Brody J. Bonnett	Brody J. Bonnett	1993	307
21 4/16	13 4/16	8 4/16	Prince of Wales Island, AK	George P. Mann	George P. Mann	1993	307
21 4/16	13 2/16	8	Menominee Co., MI	Todd D. Powers	Todd D. Powers	1993	307
21 4/16	13 5/16	8 2/16	Mendocino Co., CA	Steven W. Shelton	Steven W. Shelton	1993	307
21 4/16	13 2/16	7 15/16	Greenlee Co., AZ	Picked Up	Steven J. Stayner	1993	307
21 4/16	13 2/16	8 2/16	Gila Co., AZ	Fred Peters	Fred Peters	1994	307

BLACK BEAR

Ursus americanus americanus and related subspecies

Score	Greatest Length of Skull Without Lower Jaw	Greatest Width of Skull	Locality	Hunter	Owner	Date Killed	Rank
21 4/16	13 6/16	7 14/16	Prince of Wales Island, AK	Carl F. Sellers	Carl F. Sellers	1994	307
21 4/16	13 6/16	7 14/16	Mantagao Lake, MB	Joseph D. Belas	Joseph D. Belas	1995	307
21 4/16	13 4/16	8	Wadena Co., MN	Bonita G. Newhouse	Bonita G. Newhouse	1995	307
21 4/16	13 7/16	7 13/16	Porcupine Plain, SK	Royce P. Reavley	Royce P. Reavley	1995	307
21 4/16	13 8/16	7 12/16	Chippewa Co., WI	Lavern M. Vetterkind	Lavern M. Vetterkind	1995	307
21 4/16	13 4/16	8	Greenlee Co., AZ	Bill Hudzietz	Bill Hudzietz	1996	307
21 4/16	13 8/16	7 12/16	Beltrami Co., MN	Picked Up	Larry D. Johnson	1996	307
21 4/16	13 1/16	8 3/16	Gila Co., AZ	Leonardo E. Murdock	Leonardo E. Murdock	1996	307
21 3/16	13 6/16	7 13/16	Queen Charlotte Islands, BC	C. de Blois Green	Univ. Calif. Museum	1911	349
21 3/16	13 2/16	8 1/16	Bayfield Co., WI	G. Michaels	Gerald M. Weber	1966	349
21 3/16	13 8/16	7 11/16	Alberta	James C. Wynne	James C. Wynne	1966	349
21 3/16	12 15/16	8 4/16	Alberta	F.A. Stromstedt	Univ. of Calgary	1967	349
21 3/16	13	8 3/16	Thurston Co., WA	Hugh M. Oliver	Hugh M. Oliver	1969	349
21 3/16	13 1/16	8 2/16	Graham Co., AZ	O. Dale Porter	O. Dale Porter	1970	349
21 3/16	12 15/16	8 4/16	Eagle Co., CO	Charles T. Coffman	Charles T. Coffman	1971	349
21 3/16	13 4/16	7 15/16	Ashland Co., WI	Herman Straubel	Herman Straubel	1972	349
21 3/16	12 13/16	8 6/16	Madison Co., MT	Gerald D. Morgan	Gerald D. Morgan	1974	349
21 3/16	13 1/16	8 2/16	Stonecliffe, ON	Robert M. Weir	Robert M. Weir	1974	349
21 3/16	13 1/16	8 2/16	Oneida Co., WI	Fred C. Hageny	Fred C. Hageny	1975	349
21 3/16	13 4/16	7 15/16	Gila Co., AZ	Kae L. Brockermeyer	Kae L. Brockermeyer	1977	349
21 3/16	12 15/16	8 4/16	Carbon Co., WY	Hugh D. Beavers, Jr.	Hugh D. Beavers, Jr.	1981	349
21 3/16	12 14/16	8 5/16	Routt Co., CO	Picked Up	Steven R. Beckwith	1981	349
21 3/16	13 3/16	8	Clinton Co., PA	Orwin W. Srock	Orwin W. Srock	1981	349
21 3/16	12 15/16	8 4/16	Slave Lake, AB	Dwight E. Diehl	Dwight E. Diehl	1982	349
21 3/16	12 11/16	8 8/16	Yolo Co., CA	Walter D. Foster	Walter D. Foster	1983	349
21 3/16	13 1/16	8 2/16	Neck Lake, AK	F.A. Lonsway, Jr.	F.A. Lonsway, Jr.	1983	349
21 3/16	13 5/16	7 14/16	McBride Lake, SK	Maurice Maurer	Maurice Maurer	1984	349
21 3/16	12 10/16	8 9/16	Chuwhels Mt., BC	Ronald J. Couture	Ronald J. Couture	1986	349
21 3/16	13 1/16	8 2/16	Valleyview, AB	Alfred Heschl	Alfred Heschl	1986	349
21 3/16	13 7/16	7 12/16	Minitonas, MB	Scott Ward	Scott Ward	1986	349
21 3/16	13 6/16	7 13/16	Washington Co., ME	John S. Barmby	John S. Barmby	1987	349
21 3/16	13 2/16	8 1/16	Lincoln Co., WI	Daniel L. Lemke	Daniel L. Lemke	1987	349
21 3/16	13 2/16	8 1/16	Whiteshell Lake, MB	Paul D. Pauls	Paul D. Pauls	1987	349
21 3/16	13 3/16	8	Mesa Co., CO	Marilyn J. Scott	Marilyn J. Scott	1987	349
21 3/16	13	8 3/16	Eaglehead Lake, ON	Ty Sweeney	Ty Sweeney	1987	349
21 3/16	12 14/16	8 5/16	Coconino Co., AZ	Russell M. Watkins	Russell M. Watkins	1987	349
21 3/16	13 4/16	7 15/16	Aitkin Co., MN	Picked Up	S. & P. Gelhar	1988	349
21 3/16	13 8/16	7 11/16	Jim Lake, SK	James A. Lynn	James A. Lynn	1988	349

104

Score	L	W	Locality	Owner	Hunter	Date Killed	Rank
21 3/16	13	8 3/16	Red Deer River, SK	Gordon Paproski	Gordon Paproski	1988	349
21 3/16	13 2/16	8 1/16	Kuiu Island, AK	Michael D. Speigle	Michael D. Speigle	1989	349
21 3/16	13 8/16	7 11/16	Westmoreland Co., PA	Clyde A. Tantlinger	Clyde A. Tantlinger	1989	349
21 3/16	13 3/16	8 2/16	Prince of Wales Island, AK	George P. Mann	George P. Mann	1990	349
21 3/16	13 1/16	7 13/16	Catron Co., NM	John M. Burton, Jr.	John M. Burton, Jr.	1991	349
21 3/16	13 6/16	7 12/16	Fort McMurray, AB	Karl F. Falch	Karl F. Falch	1991	349
21 3/16	13 7/16	8	Canora, SK	Rodney S. Petrychyn	Rodney S. Petrychyn	1991	349
21 3/16	13 3/16	7 13/16	Prince of Wales Island, AK	L. Scott Robinson	L. Scott Robinson	1991	349
21 3/16	13 6/16	7 13/16	Fort a la Corne, SK	Larry Zens	Larry Zens	1992	349
21 3/16	13 3/16	7 15/16	Oldman Lake, SK	Robert L. Fitzsimonds	Robert L. Fitzsimonds	1994	349
21 3/16	13 4/16	7 13/16	Socorro Co., NM	William F. Gorman	William F. Gorman	1994	349
21 3/16	13 6/16	8	Gila Co., AZ	Gary D. Gorsuch	Gary D. Gorsuch	1994	349
21 3/16	13 3/16	7 12/16	Greenwater Lake, ON	Kevin J. Wagner	Kevin J. Wagner	1994	349
21 3/16	13 7/16	8 1/16	Apache Co., AZ	Benny White	Benny White	1994	349
21 3/16	13 2/16	7 13/16	Lincoln Co., WI	Jesse J. Hoffman	Jesse J. Hoffman	1996	349
21 3/16	13 3/16	7 14/16	Beaver River, SK	Jason Toews	Jason Toews	1997	349
21 3/16	13 5/16	8 2/16	Kupreanof Island, AK	Richard L. Tshudy	Richard L. Tshudy	1997	349
21 2/16	13	7 12/16	Kuiu Island, AK	L.W. Potter	L.W. Potter	1951	396
21 2/16	13 6/16	8 6/16	Lincoln Co., WY	Ralph Langford	R. Langford & W.R. Ryan	1955	396
21 2/16	12 12/16	7 15/16	Essex Co., NY	NY Dept. of Env. Cons.	William R. Waddell	1955	396
21 2/16	13 3/16	8	Los Angeles Co., CA	Leo J. Reihsen	Leo J. Reihsen	1961	396
21 2/16	13	7 6/16	Mammoth Mt., CA	Clarke Merrill	Clarke Merrill	1963	396
21 2/16	13 12/16	8 3/16	Chinitna Bay, AK	Basil C. Bradbury	Basil C. Bradbury	1964	396
21 2/16	12 15/16	8 6/16	Chelan Co., WA	Virgil R. Bedient	Virgil R. Bedient	1965	396
21 2/16	12 12/16	7 13/16	Collbran, CO	Raymond R. Lyons	R.R. Lyons & H.V. Morris	1965	396
21 2/16	13 5/16	8 2/16	Shasta Co., CA	Ivan L. Marx	Ivan L. Marx	1965	396
21 2/16	13	8 4/16	Mesa Co., CO	Waldemar R. Kuenzel, Jr.	Waldemar R. Kuenzel, Jr.	1966	396
21 2/16	13	8	Trinity Co., CA	Picked Up	Robert E. Frost	1967	396
21 2/16	12 14/16	8 8/16	Raven Lake, BC	Robert G. Wardian	Robert G. Wardian	1967	396
21 2/16	12 10/16	7 11/16	Montrose Co., CO	Earl L. Markley	Earl L. Markley	1970	396
21 2/16	13 7/16	7 1/16	Clam Lake, WI	Picked Up	M. Reynolds & J. Olson	PR 1971	396
21 2/16	14 1/16	8	Sublette Co., WY	A. Jack Welch	A. Jack Welch	1971	396
21 2/16	13 2/16	7 12/16	Lake Co., CA	David C. Sharp	David C. Sharp	1972	396
21 2/16	13 6/16	7 14/16	Gila Co., AZ	Daniel J. Urban	Daniel J. Urban	1972	396
21 2/16	13 4/16	8 1/16	Gunnison Co., CO	Dick Cooper	Dick Cooper	1977	396
21 2/16	13 1/16	8 2/16	Gila Co., AZ	Robert E. Barnes	Robert E. Barnes	1978	396
21 2/16	13	8 1/16	Ethelbert, MB	Paul A. Bormes	Paul A. Bormes	1979	396
21 2/16	13 1/16	8 10/16	Lodgepole, AB	Jim H. Van Manen	Jim H. Van Manen	1979	396
21 2/16	13 8/16	8	Graham Island, BC	Roger Britton	Roger Britton	1982	396
21 2/16	13 2/16	8 2/16	Fox Creek, AB	Brent E. Eeles	Brent E. Eeles	1982	396
21 2/16	13 2/16	8 2/16	Preeceville, SK	David S. Hodgin	David S. Hodgin	1982	396
21 2/16	13	8 6/16	Goose River, AB	Thomas Barker	T. Barker & R. Mompere	1983	396
21 2/16	12 12/16	7 15/16	Marquette Co., MI	Gerald J. Isetts, Sr.	Gerald J. Isetts, Sr.	1984	396
21 2/16	13 3/16	8 2/16	Hudson Bay, SK	Neil Southam	Neil Southam	1984	396
21 2/16	13	8 6/16	Terra Nova River, NF	James A. Young	James A. Young	1986	396
21 2/16	13 2/16	8	Montmorency Co., MI	Kenneth R. Reed	Kenneth R. Reed	1986	396
21 2/16	12 15/16	8 3/16	Gallatin Co., MT	Steven M. Steele	Steven M. Steele	1986	396

Ursus americanus americanus and related subspecies

Score	Greatest Length of Skull Without Lower Jaw	Greatest Width of Skull	Locality	Hunter	Owner	Date Killed	Rank
21 2/16	13	8 2/16	Caribou Co., ID	Ronald J. Thompson	Ronald J. Thompson	1986	396
21 2/16	13 3/16	7 15/16	Beltrami Co., MN	Douglas P. Budensiek	Douglas P. Budensiek	1987	396
21 2/16	13 9/16	7 9/16	Gila Co., AZ	Jesse L. Enterkin, Jr.	Jesse L. Enterkin, Jr.	1987	396
21 2/16	13 8/16	7 10/16	Marco, MB	Erwin Weidenfeld	Erwin Weidenfeld	1987	396
21 2/16	12 13/16	8 5/16	Pencil Lake, ON	Michael F. Gerber	Michael F. Gerber	1988	396
21 2/16	13 2/16	8	Kuiu Island, AK	Robert M. Teskey	Robert M. Teskey	1988	396
21 2/16	13 4/16	7 14/16	Turtle Lake, SK	Tony L. Johnson	Tony L. Johnson	1989	396
21 2/16	13 2/16	8	Cold Lake, AB	Dean Herron	Dean Herron	1990	396
21 2/16	13 3/16	7 15/16	Bjorkdale, SK	Clayton R. Shiels	Clayton R. Shiels	1990	396
21 2/16	12 14/16	8 4/16	Humboldt Co., CA	Conrad H. Will	Conrad H. Will	1990	396
21 2/16	13 4/16	7 14/16	Chinaman Lake, BC	Fred Becker	Fred Becker	1991	396
21 2/16	13 4/16	8 1/16	Craven Co., NC	Eddie C. Bridges	Eddie C. Bridges	1991	396
21 2/16	13 1/16	8 1/16	Moresby Island, BC	Roger W. Robinson	Roger W. Robinson	1991	396
21 2/16	12 12/16	8 6/16	Mitkof Island, AK	Robert W. Anderson	Robert W. Anderson	1993	396
21 2/16	13	8 2/16	Rogersville, NB	Larry Dominguez	Larry Dominguez	1993	396
21 2/16	13 1/16	8 1/16	King Co., WA	Timothy C. Fish	Timothy C. Fish	1993	396
21 2/16	13 7/16	7 11/16	Price Co., WI	Picked Up	William D. Janak	1993	396
21 2/16	13 11/16	7 7/16	Clinton Co., PA	Richard T. Kordes	Richard T. Kordes	1993	396
21 2/16	13 5/16	7 13/16	San Bernardino Co., CA	Rodney K. McGee	Rodney K. McGee	1993	396
21 2/16	13 2/16	8	Clearfield Co., PA	Donald C. Miller III	Donald C. Miller III	1993	396
21 2/16	13 2/16	8	Tyrrell Co., NC	Ed Wilkerson	NC State Mus. Natl. Sci.	1993	396
21 2/16	13 7/16	7 11/16	Kuiu Island, AK	Thomas E. Phillippe, Sr.	Thomas E. Phillippe, Sr.	1993	396
21 2/16	13 8/16	7 10/16	Craven Co., NC	Eddie C. Bridges	Eddie C. Bridges	1994	396
21 2/16	13 3/16	7 15/16	Fort a la Corne, SK	Gerald Gilmore	Gerald Gilmore	1994	396
21 2/16	12 13/16	8 5/16	Pine Co., MN	Picked Up	MN Dept. of Natl. Resc.	1994	396
21 2/16	13	8 2/16	Catron Co., NM	Joe W. Murdock	Joe W. Murdock	1994	396
21 2/16	13 6/16	7 12/16	Hyde Co., NC	Stephen R. Bathon	Stephen R. Bathon	1995	396
21 2/16	13 5/16	7 13/16	Rockingham Co., VA	Charles G. Carter	Charles G. Carter	1995	396
21 2/16	13 4/16	7 14/16	Oconto Co., WI	Patrick J. Gauthier	Patrick J. Gauthier	1995	396
21 2/16	13 9/16	7 9/16	Clarion Co., PA	Todd W. Miller	Todd W. Miller	1995	396
21 2/16	13 8/16	7 10/16	Onslow Co., NC	John R. Sewell	John R. Sewell	1995	396
21 2/16	13	8 2/16	Hodgson, MB	Linda Cherepak	Linda Cherepak	1996	396
21 2/16	13 6/16	7 12/16	Mesa Co., CO	Stephen J. Gray	Stephen J. Gray	1996	396
21 2/16	13 3/16	7 15/16	Preeceville, SK	David O. Guthrel	David O. Guthrel	1996	396
21 2/16	13 10/16	7 8/16	Coos Co., NH	Gary J. Russell	Gary J. Russell	1996	396
21 1/16	13 3/16	7 14/16	Indian Lake, LA	B.V. Lilly	U.S. Natl. Museum	1904	461
21 1/16	13 3/16	7 14/16	Coahuila, MX	B.V. Lilly	U.S. Natl. Museum	1906	461
21 1/16	13 7/16	7 10/16	Santa Barbara Co., CA	Charles Tant	Univ. Calif. Museum	1940	461

21 1/16	13 2/16	7 15/16	Columbia Co., WA	Fred Van Arsdol	Glenn Ford	1954	461
21 1/16	13 2/16	7 15/16	Mt. Gentry, AZ	Cliff Edwards	Cliff Edwards	1960	461
21 1/16	12 12/16	8 5/16	Paonia, CO	William O. Good	William O. Good	1960	461
21 1/16	12 8/16	8 9/16	Steamboat Springs, CO	Norman Garwood	Norman Garwood	1964	461
21 1/16	13 3/16	7 14/16	Peace River, AB	Don W. Caldwell	Don W. Caldwell	1965	461
21 1/16	13	8 1/16	Piscataquis Co., ME	J.D. Flowers	J.D. Flowers	1966	461
21 1/16	13 2/16	7 15/16	Gila Co., AZ	George L. Massingill	George L. Massingill	1971	461
21 1/16	13	8 1/16	Price Co., WI	Joseph Valiga	J. Hanson & J. Valiga	1971	461
21 1/16	13 3/16	7 14/16	Iron Co., WI	Gerald Brauer	Gerald Brauer	1972	461
21 1/16	12 13/16	8 4/16	San Carlos Indian Res., AZ	Michael D. Gunnett	Michael D. Gunnett	1973	461
21 1/16	13 6/16	7 11/16	Hubbard Co., MN	Dean J. Como	Dean J. Como	1974	461
21 1/16	13 3/16	7 14/16	Graham Island, BC	Roger Britton	Roger Britton	1978	461
21 1/16	12 15/16	8 2/16	Logan Lake, BC	Norman W. Dougan	Norman W. Dougan	1978	461
21 1/16	12 15/16	8 2/16	Greenlee Co., AZ	Michael W. Goodyear	Michael W. Goodyear	1979	461
21 1/16	13 10/16	7 7/16	Graham Island, BC	Roger Britton	Roger Britton	1980	461
21 1/16	13 1/16	8	Spirit River, AB	John Dobish	John Dobish	1982	461
21 1/16	12 15/16	8 2/16	Teller Co., CO	Samuel T. Harrelson, Jr.	Samuel T. Harrelson, Jr.	1982	461
21 1/16	12 13/16	8 4/16	Apache Co., AZ	William J. Morris	William J. Morris	1985	461
21 1/16	12 14/16	8 3/16	Cook Co., MN	Kevin R. Johnson	K. Johnson, G. Bjerkness, & S. Borud	1986	461
21 1/16	12 15/16	8 2/16	Menominee Co., MI	Manfred L. Pfitzer	Manfred L. Pfitzer	1986	461
21 1/16	13 5/16	7 12/16	Valley River, MB	Craig Kozak	Craig Kozak	1987	461
21 1/16	13 4/16	7 13/16	Gila Co., AZ	Daniel G. Robinett	Daniel G. Robinett	1987	461
21 1/16	13 1/16	8	Charlevoix Co., MI	Gerald L. Fuller	Gerald L. Fuller	1988	461
21 1/16	12 13/16	8 4/16	Klakas Inlet, AK	Stephen P. Harvey	Stephen P. Harvey	1988	461
21 1/16	12 15/16	8 2/16	Eagle Lake, SK	Randall N. Olejnik	Randall N. Olejnik	1988	461
21 1/16	12 14/16	8 3/16	St. Louis Co., MN	Jonathan E. Polecheck	Jonathan E. Polecheck	1989	461
21 1/16	12 12/16	8 5/16	Orange Co., NY	George E. Decker	George E. Decker	1992	461
21 1/16	13	8 1/16	Prince of Wales Island, AK	Hanson E. Fitte	Hanson E. Fitte	1993	461
21 1/16	13 3/16	7 14/16	Pierce Co., WI	Steven J. Hlavacek	Steven J. Hlavacek	1993	461
21 1/16	13 2/16	7 15/16	Trinity Co., CA	Dorrel K. Byrd	Dorrel K. Byrd	1994	461
21 1/16	12 13/16	8 4/16	Trinity Co., CA	Curt M. Connor	Curt M. Connor	1995	461
21 1/16	13 6/16	7 11/16	Otter Lake, MB	William A. Guelzow, Jr.	William A. Guelzow, Jr.	1995	461
21 1/16	12 10/16	8 7/16	Smoky Lake, AB	Lawrence L. Piquette	Lawrence L. Piquette	1995	461
21 1/16	13 2/16	7 15/16	Bayfield Co., WI	Thomas C. Albrecht	Thomas C. Albrecht	1996	461
21 1/16	13 1/16	8	Prince of Wales Island, AK	Shawn P. Price	Shawn P. Price	1996	461
21 1/16	13 3/16	7 14/16	Round Lake, SK	Floyd Forster	Floyd Forster	1997	461
21	12 15/16	8 1/16	Queen Charlotte Islands, BC	Douglas McIntyre	Unknown	PR 1959	500
21	12 10/16	8 6/16	Vancouver, BC	Elmer E. Kurrus, Jr.	Elmer E. Kurrus, Jr.	1964	500
21	13	8	Hamilton Co., NY	NY Dept. of Env. Cons.	James McIntyre	1965	500
21	12 12/16	8 4/16	Collbran, CO	Cecil E. Alumbaugh, Jr.	Cecil E. Alumbaugh, Jr.	1967	500
21	12 11/16	8 5/16	Oconto Co., WI	Calvin E. Schindel	Calvin E. Schindel	1968	500
21	13 2/16	7 14/16	Overflowing River, MB	Victor Kostiniuk	Victor Kostiniuk	1971	500
21	12 15/16	8 1/16	Garfield Co., CO	J.D. Liles	J.D. Liles	1974	500
21	13 2/16	7 14/16	St. Louis Co., MN	Robert J. Manteuffel	Robert J. Manteuffel	1977	500
21	13	8	Routt Co., CO	Jerome W. Keyes, Jr.	Jerome W. Keyes, Jr.	1980	500
21	13 4/16	7 12/16	Wasatch Co., UT	UT Div. of Wildl. Resc.	Picked Up	1980	500
21	13 4/16	7 12/16	Hamilton Co., NY	Marshall E. Conklin	Marshall E. Conklin	1981	500

BLACK BEAR

Ursus americanus americanus and related subspecies

Score	Greatest Length of Skull Without Lower Jaw	Greatest Width of Skull	Locality	Hunter	Owner	Date Killed	Rank
21	12 7/16	8 9/16	Fremont Co., WY	Timothy B. Hill	Timothy B. Hill	1981	500
21	12 12/16	8 4/16	Bradford Co., PA	Ray B. Moyer	Ray B. Moyer	1981	500
21	13 2/16	7 14/16	Coconino Co., AZ	Michael P. Whelan	Michael P. Whelan	1981	500
21	13	8	Fort Assiniboine, AB	George Plashka	George Plashka	1982	500
21	13 3/16	7 13/16	Langlade Co., WI	Michael Steliga	Michael Steliga	1982	500
21	12 14/16	8 2/16	Macon Co., NC	C. Rick Jones	C. Rick Jones	1983	500
21	13 2/16	7 14/16	Ostenfeld, MB	Erik Thienpondt	Erik Thienpondt	1983	500
21	13 2/16	7 14/16	Santa Barbara Co., CA	Picked Up	Marshall Munger	1984	500
21	13	8	Cholmondeley Sound, AK	Gerry D. Downey	Gerry D. Downey	1985	500
21	13 1/16	7 15/16	Garfield Co., CO	Gordon L. Haxton	Gordon L. Haxton	1985	500
21	12 10/16	8 6/16	Echouani Lake, QC	Collins F. Kellogg	Collins F. Kellogg	1985	500
21	13 3/16	7 13/16	Wild Goose, ON	William G. Tellijohn	William G. Tellijohn	1985	500
21	13 3/16	7 13/16	Graham Co., AZ	Mark J. Bensley	Mark J. Bensley	1986	500
21	13 6/16	7 10/16	Ogemaw Co., MI	William D. Massey	William D. Massey	1987	500
21	13 1/16	7 15/16	Carrot River, SK	Demetry Procyk	Demetry Procyk	1987	500
21	13 6/16	7 10/16	Muriel Lake, AB	Edward R. Rempel	Edward R. Rempel	1988	500
21	13 2/16	7 14/16	Gates Co., NC	John W. Whitehurst, Jr.	John W. Whitehurst, Jr.	1988	500
21	13	8	Carbon Co., UT	Lonnie K. Bell	Lonnie K. Bell	1989	500
21	12 13/16	8 3/16	Iron Co., WI	Todd J. Brauer	Todd J. Brauer	1989	500
21	13 2/16	7 14/16	Peace River, AB	Danny de Melo	Danny de Melo	1989	500
21	12 15/16	8 1/16	Brokenhead River, MB	Michael E. Vandenbosch	Michael E. Vandenbosch	1989	500
21	13	8	LeDomaine, QC	Anthony Becciro	Anthony Becciro	1990	500
21	12 10/16	8 6/16	Greenlee Co., AZ	Robin W. Bechtel	Robin W. Bechtel	1990	500
21	13	8	Beaufort Co., NC	Marlow V. Jones	Marlow V. Jones	1990	500
21	12 12/16	8 4/16	Peace River, AB	Kent S. Anderson	Kent S. Anderson	1991	500
21	13 4/16	7 12/16	Onanole, MB	Robert J. Grosfield	Robert J. Grosfield	1992	500
21	12 13/16	8 3/16	Prince of Wales Island, AK	Matthew Heller	Matthew Heller	1992	500
21	13 2/16	7 14/16	Peace River, AB	G. Byron Horn	G. Byron Horn	1992	500
21	12 14/16	8 2/16	Price Co., WI	Paul A. Quinn	Paul A. Quinn	1992	500
21	13 8/16	7 8/16	Indiana Co., PA	William G. Shank	William G. Shank	1992	500
21	13 4/16	7 12/16	Clark Co., WI	Don A. Ziemann	Don A. Ziemann	1992	500
21	13 4/16	7 12/16	Otero Co., NM	Woodie B. Howell	Woodie B. Howell	1993	500
21	13 6/16	7 10/16	Hyde Co., NC	Chuck Blalock	Chuck Blalock	1994	500
21	12 15/16	8 1/16	Painted Rock Island, ON	Harry D. Brickley	Harry D. Brickley	1994	500
21	13 4/16	7 12/16	Aroostook Co., ME	George W. Cameron	George W. Cameron	1994	500
21	12 14/16	8 2/16	Bay Tree, AB	Sedgwick B. Loyd II	Sedgwick B. Loyd II	1994	500
21	13	8	Hyde Co., NC	Benjamin Simmons III	Benjamin Simmons III	1994	500
21	13 6/16	7 10/16	Hyde Co., NC	Charlie E. Vandiford	Charlie E. Vandiford	1994	500

21	13 ^{7}/$_{16}$	7 ^{9}/$_{16}$	Tyrrell Co., NC	Edward R. Wilkerson	Edward R. Wilkerson	1994	500
21	12 ^{14}/$_{16}$	8 ^{2}/$_{16}$	Tuolumne Co., CA	Stacy J. Willoughby	Stacy J. Willoughby	1994	500
21	12 ^{10}/$_{16}$	8 ^{6}/$_{16}$	Ulster Co., NY	Thomas Nolan	Thomas Nolan	1995	500
21	12 ^{14}/$_{16}$	8 ^{2}/$_{16}$	Washburn Co., WI	Sonjonae L. Setser	Sonjonae L. Setser	1995	500
21	13 ^{3}/$_{16}$	7 ^{13}/$_{16}$	Barron Co., WI	Jeffrey P. Tomesh	Jeffrey P. Tomesh	1995	500
21	13	8	Whale Passage, AK	Eric L. Whary	Eric L. Whary	1995	500
21	13 ^{1}/$_{16}$	7 ^{15}/$_{16}$	Bradford Co., PA	J. Martin Alles	J. Martin Alles	1996	500
21	13	8	Stevens Co., WA	Tom Balis	Tom Balis	1996	500
21	13 ^{3}/$_{16}$	7 ^{13}/$_{16}$	Humboldt Co., CA	Jerry R. Cardoza	Jerry R. Cardoza	1996	500
21	13 ^{7}/$_{16}$	7 ^{9}/$_{16}$	Sawyer Co., WI	Chris L. Duerst	Chris L. Duerst	1996	500
21	12 ^{11}/$_{16}$	8 ^{5}/$_{16}$	Delaware Co., NY	James D. Muench	James D. Muench	1996	500
21	12 ^{14}/$_{16}$	8 ^{2}/$_{16}$	Marathon Co., WI	Orville J. Sazama	Orville J. Sazama	1996	500
21	12 ^{14}/$_{16}$	8 ^{2}/$_{16}$	Smeaton, SK	Paul C. Sills	Paul C. Sills	1997	500
22 ^{6}/$_{16}$*	14 ^{2}/$_{16}$	8 ^{4}/$_{16}$	Punnichy, SK	Peter Hunter	Peter Hunter	1995	500

* Final score is subject to revision by additional verifying measurements.

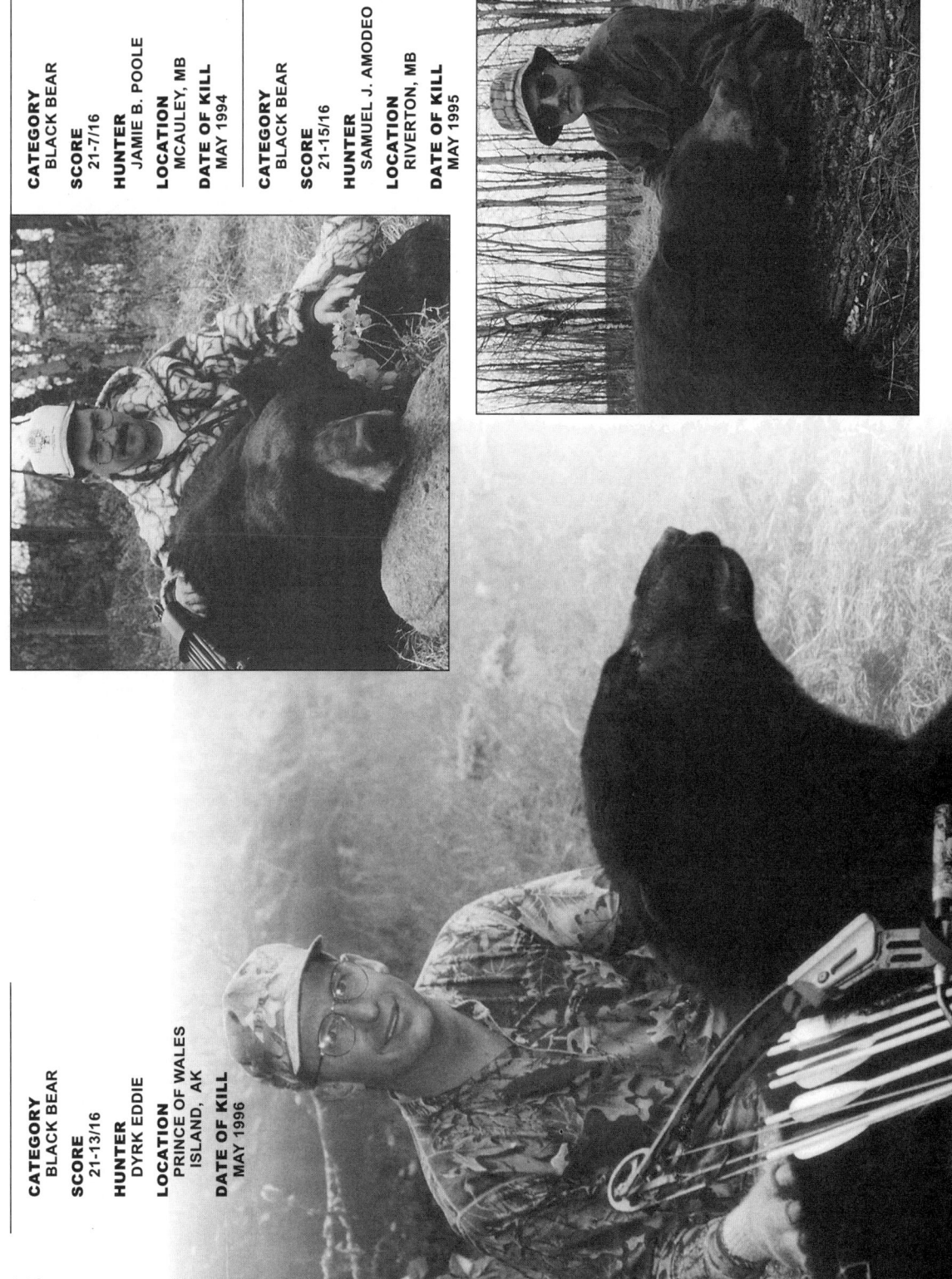

CATEGORY
BLACK BEAR

SCORE
21-7/16

HUNTER
JAMIE B. POOLE

LOCATION
MCAULEY, MB

DATE OF KILL
MAY 1994

CATEGORY
BLACK BEAR

SCORE
21-15/16

HUNTER
SAMUEL J. AMODEO

LOCATION
RIVERTON, MB

DATE OF KILL
MAY 1995

CATEGORY
BLACK BEAR

SCORE
21-13/16

HUNTER
DYRK EDDIE

LOCATION
PRINCE OF WALES
ISLAND, AK

DATE OF KILL
MAY 1996

ALASKA BROWN BEAR AND GRIZZLY BEAR BOUNDARIES

The big brown bears are found on Kodiak and Afognak Islands, the Alaska Peninsula, and eastward and southeastward along the coast of Alaska. The smaller interior grizzly is found in the remaining parts of the continent. The boundary between the two was first defined as an imaginary line extending 75 miles inland from the coast of Alaska. Later this boundary was more precisely defined with the current definition as follows (Alaska brown bear is shaded area of map):

A line of separation between the larger coastal brown bear and the smaller interior grizzly has been developed such that west and south of this line (to and including Unimak Island) bear trophies are recorded as Alaska brown bear. North and east of this line, bear trophies are recorded as grizzly bear. The boundary line description is as follows: Starting at Pearse Canal and following the Canadian-Alaskan boundary northwesterly to Mt. St. Elias on the 141 degree meridian; thence north along the Canadian-Alaskan boundary to Mt. Natazhat; thence west northwest along the divide of the Wrangell Range to Mt. Jarvis at the western end of the Wrangell Range; thence north along the divide of the Mentasta Range to Mentasta Pass; thence in a general westerly direction along the divide of the Alaska Range to Houston Pass; thence westerly following the 62nd parallel of latitude to the Bering Sea. ■

YUKOKN TERRITORY

ALASKA

62°

GRIZZLY BEAR
WORLD'S RECORD

There is a three-way tie for the World's Record grizzly bear (*Ursus arctos horribilis*) beginning in 1970 with a find in Bella Coola Valley, British Columbia, by James G. Shelton. The Final Judging on Shelton's pick-up would confirm a score of 27-2/16, which was recorded in the 1981 edition. This trophy would be tied a year later by an equally huge grizzly taken in the same province along the Dean River by Roger J. Pentecost. Pentecost shared his story that colorfully describes the momentous hunting event that he shared with his son.

"Suddenly, off to our left about 70 feet away and partly obscured by a cedar, something started to move slowly up out of the ground. It was a massive head in profile, followed by an enormous shoulder hump. We froze. Here was what we had come all this way for – a good bear. But really, I never wanted it quite so close. As I readied my Husqvarna, I heard Jason close his gun.

"For what seemed to be a long time, I had an excellent side shot. I squeezed the shot off. But, the bear, instead of falling over dead, rose up out of the hollow in the ground and turned toward us. Here it was, coming right at us. I aimed at his shoulder, still hardly believing he wasn't down. This next shot hit his side. This turned him, and he plunged off sideways into a thick area of alders, windfalls and devils club. As he was going in, I placed a third shot.

"All hell seemed to break loose in that small wooded area. It was too thick to see what was happening, but boy, could we hear the bear snorting, growling, grunting and gasp-ing draughts of breath. It was a simply enormous and rather frightening sound. I looked back at Jason and Wayne. They looked as apprehensive as I felt. I knew a grizzly could explode out of that cover like an 'express train', with none of the bush slowing him down at all, and leap 15 feet in a bound."

Entered in the 19th Awards, Pentecost's trophy would stand alone for nearly a decade as the largest hunter-taken trophy for a grizzly. However, it was matched again in 1991 by Theodore Kurdziel, Jr., during a hunt on the frozen landscape along the Inglutalik River near Koyuk, Alaska. Kurdziel gave an equally fine account describing the pinnacle of his hunting story.

"Suddenly the bear appeared about 40 yards ahead, running for me at full speed. Steve could not see him from his position. The bear, his hackles raised, looked as mad as a guard dog protecting his turf. I shouldered my rifle and found the grizzly in my scope. The only shot I had was at the bear's head, so I held off until the bear was about 20 yards away. At that point, he stumbled momentarily and exposed his chest, and I fired instinctively. The bear spun around like a top and ran uphill, more or less angling toward Steve. I shot again, hitting the bear in the neck.

When we walked up to that mountain of a bear, we were awestruck by his size. I did not care at that point whether he was a Boone and Crockett bear or not. All I knew was that I had experienced a close-range encounter with one of the most imposing gorgeous creatures on earth, and I had survived." ■

GRIZZLY BEAR
WORLD'S RECORD SCORECHART

Measurements are taken with calipers or by using parallel perpendiculars, to the nearest one-sixteenth of an inch, without reduction of fractions. Official measurements cannot be taken until the skull has air dried for at least 60 days after the animal was killed. All adhering flesh, membrane and cartilage must be completely removed before official measurements are taken.

A. **Greatest Length** is measured between perpendiculars parallel to the long axis of the skull, without the lower jaw and excluding malformations.

B. **Greatest Width** is measured between perpendiculars at right angles to the long axis.

TROPHY INFO

RANK
World's Record
(3-way tie)

SCORE
27 2/16

LOCATION
a) Bella Coola Valley, B.C.
b) Dean River, B.C.
c) Inglutalik River, AK

HUNTERS
a) Picked Up
b) Roger Pentecost
c) Theodore Kurdziel, Jr.

OWNER
a) James G. Shelton
b) Roger J. Pentecost
c) Theodore Kurdziel, Jr.

DATE KILLED
a) 1970
b) 1982
c) 1991

Records of
North American
Big Game

250 Station Drive
Missoula, MT 59801
(406) 542-1888

BOONE AND CROCKETT CLUB®
OFFICIAL SCORING SYSTEM FOR NORTH AMERICAN BIG GAME TROPHIES

BEAR

	MINIMUM SCORES	
	AWARDS	ALL-TIME
black bear	20	21
grizzly bear	23	24
Alaska brown bear	26	28
polar bear	27	27

KIND OF BEAR (check one)
☐ black bear
■ grizzly
☐ Alaska brown bear
☐ polar

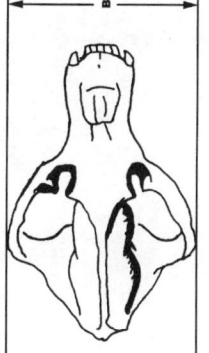

SEE OTHER SIDE FOR INSTRUCTIONS

	MEASUREMENTS
A. Greatest Length Without Lower Jaw	17 8/16
B. Greatest Width	9 12/16
FINAL SCORE	27 2/16

Exact Locality Where Killed: **Bella Coola Valley, BC**

Date Killed: **1970**   Hunter: **Picked Up**

Owner: **James G. Shelton**   Telephone #:

Owner's Address:

Guide's Name and Address:

Remarks: (Mention Any Abnormalities or Unique Qualities)

I, _____**Bernard A. Fashingbauer**_____ , certify that I have measured this trophy on ___**03/01/1971**___
          PRINT NAME   MM/DD/YYYY

at **Carnegie Museum** _____ **Pittsburgh** _____ **PA** ____
          STREET ADDRESS   CITY   STATE/PROVINCE

and that these measurements and data are, to the best of my knowledge and belief, made in accordance with the instructions given.

Witness: ___**Charles E. Wilson, Jr.**___   Signature: ___**B.A. Fashingbauer**___   I.D. Number [   ]
                                                                              B&C OFFICIAL MEASURER

COPYRIGHT © 1999 BY BOONE AND CROCKETT CLUB®

113

GRIZZLY BEAR
Ursus arctos horribilis

Score	Greatest Length of Skull Without Lower Jaw	Greatest Width of Skull	Locality	Hunter	Owner	Date Killed	Rank
27 2/16	17 6/16	9 12/16	Bella Coola Valley, BC	Picked Up	James G. Shelton	1970	1
27 2/16	16 14/16	10 4/16	Dean River, BC	Roger J. Pentecost	Lynn Allen	1982	1
27 2/16	17 3/16	9 15/16	Inglutalik River, AK	Theodore Kurdziel, Jr.	Theodore Kurdziel, Jr.	1991	1
26 14/16	16 14/16	10	Teklanika River, AK	D. Alan McCaleb	D. Alan McCaleb	1989	4
26 14/16	16 6/16	10 8/16	Anahim Lake, BC	Denis E. Schiller	D.E. Schiller & K. Karran	1990	4
26 13/16	16 11/16	10 2/16	Wakeman River, BC	Harry Leggett, Jr.	Harry Leggett, Jr.	1980	6
26 13/16	16 9/16	10 4/16	Devil Mt., AK	Russell J. Lewis	Russell J. Lewis	1993	6
26 11/16	16 11/16	10	Shaktoolik River, AK	Hans Hartwig	B&C National Collection	1993	8
26 10/16	16 10/16	10	Rivers Inlet, BC	F. Nygaard	Univ. of B.C.	1954	9
26 10/16	17	9 10/16	Lonesome Lake, BC	J. Turner	Douglas Kenefick	1965	9
26 9/16	16 4/16	10 5/16	Ungalik River, AK	Stanley F. Smith	S. Smith & G. Fait	1983	11
26 8/16	16 10/16	9 14/16	Yanert Glacier, AK	Xavier T. Riedmiller	Xavier T. Riedmiller	1970	12
26 7/16	16 11/16	9 12/16	Casadepaga River, AK	Carl O. Merchant	Carl O. Merchant	1996	13
26 6/16	16 6/16	10	Bella Coola, BC	Walter C. Shutts	Walter C. Shutts	1957	14
26 6/16	16 12/16	9 10/16	Farewell Lake, AK	John C. Schwietert	John C. Schwietert	1968	14
26 6/16	16 8/16	9 14/16	Seaskinnish Creek, BC	Paddy H.S. Wong	Fred Y.C. Wong	1982	14
26 6/16	16 5/16	10 1/16	Cluculz Creek, BC	Thomas C. Roberson	Thomas C. Roberson	1983	14
26 6/16	16 10/16	9 12/16	Tonzona River, AK	Fred M. Corriea	Fred M. Corriea	1997	14
26 6/16	16 4/16	10 2/16	Little Tahltan River, BC	Duane A. Enders	Duane A. Enders	1997	14
26 5/16	16 10/16	9 11/16	Slave Lake, AB	B. Twin & D. Auger	R.W.H. Eben-Ebenau	1953	20
26 5/16	16 5/16	10	Knights Inlet, BC	Thomas N. Bernard	Thomas N. Bernard	1967	20
26 5/16	16 15/16	9 6/16	Swan Hills, AB	Wilfred Hartfelder	Wilfred Hartfelder	1974	20
26 5/16	16 1/16	10 4/16	Devereux Creek, BC	Raymond Ferrieri	Raymond Ferrieri	1994	20
26 5/16	16 2/16	10 3/16	Koyuk River, AK	Remo Pizzagalli	Remo Pizzagalli	1996	20
26 4/16	16 10/16	9 10/16	Elliott Hwy., AK	Unknown	AK Dept. of Fish & Game	1967	25
26 4/16	16 12/16	9 8/16	Tatshenshini River, BC	William G. Underhill	William G. Underhill	1970	25
26 4/16	16 5/16	9 15/16	Ferry, AK	Jamie C. Smyth	Jamie C. Smyth	1973	25
26 4/16	16 1/16	10 3/16	Nulato Hills, AK	Randy A. Tarnowski	Randy A. Tarnowski	1978	25
26 4/16	16 1/16	9 4/16	Kakwa River, AB	Klaus Wernsdorf	Klaus Wernsdorf	1979	25
26 4/16	16 4/16	10	Nenana River, AK	Stan W. Hughes	Stan W. Hughes	1995	25
26 3/16	17	9 3/16	Tatla Lake, BC	Robert L. Tuma	Robert L. Tuma	1971	31
26 3/16	16 1/16	10 7/16	Buckland River, AK	Bill McDavid	Bill McDavid	1977	31
26 3/16	16 12/16	9 8/16	Bear Lake, BC	DeVern Gardner	DeVern Gardner	1984	31
26 2/16	16 10/16	9 8/16	Nechako River, BC	R.J. Nielsen	R.J. Nielsen	1971	34
26 2/16	16	10 3/16	Kantishna River, AK	Theodore B. Kelly, Jr.	Theodore B. Kelly, Jr.	1972	34
26 2/16	16 5/16	9 13/16	Kwatna Bay, AK	J.G. Bartlett	J.G. Bartlett	1976	34
26 2/16	15 13/16	10 5/16	Chiroskey River, AK	Harold L. Ahlberg	Harold L. Ahlberg	1992	34
26 2/16	16 5/16	9 13/16	Post River, AK	Jack J. Tuso	Jack J. Tuso	1997	34

26 1/16	16 1/16	10	Smiths Inlet, BC	Donald M. Swarthout	Donald M. Swarthout	1963	39
26 1/16	16 4/16	9 13/16	Camelback Mt., AK	Thomas E. Smith	Thomas E. Smith	1985	39
26 1/16	16	10 1/16	Bendelben Mts., AK	Ronald E. Taig	Ronald E. Taig	1992	39
26 1/16	16 3/16	9 14/16	Klinaklini River, BC	Morris Trace	Morris Trace	1995	39
26 1/16	16 5/16	9 12/16	Inglutalik River, AK	John J. McPartlin	John J. McPartlin	1996	39
26	16	10	Lake Minchumina, AK	Val J. Blackburn	Val J. Blackburn	1956	44
26	17	9	Bella Coola, BC	J. Harstad	John Lesowski	1959	44
26	16 1/16	9 15/16	Tweedsmuir Park, BC	Michael R. Caspersen	Michael R. Caspersen	1969	44
26	16 8/16	9 8/16	Kobuk River, AK	Charlie Horner	Charlie Horner	1971	44
26	16 2/16	9 14/16	Meziadin Lake, BC	Peter Martinson	Peter Martinson	1987	44
25 15/16	15 12/16	10 3/16	Rapids Roadhouse, AK	H. Herring	H. Herring	1964	49
25 15/16	16 3/16	9 12/16	Bella Coola, BC	Bernard J. Meinerz	Bernard J. Meinerz	1968	49
25 15/16	16 3/16	9 12/16	Klinaklini River, BC	Jerry Stubblefield	Jerry Stubblefield	1970	49
25 15/16	16	9 15/16	Iskut River, BC	Fritz A. Nachant	Fritz A. Nachant	1980	49
25 15/16	15 10/16	10 5/16	Tubukutulik River, AK	William A. Brooks, Sr.	William A. Brooks, Sr.	1986	49
25 15/16	15 15/16	10	Tatlawiksuk River, AK	William H. Green	Mrs. William H. Green	1988	49
25 15/16	15 13/16	10 2/16	Morice River, BC	Josef Martinek	Josef Martinek	1991	49
25 15/16	16 7/16	9 8/16	Poplar Lake, BC	Dick Van Barneveld	Dick Van Barneveld	1996	49
25 14/16	16	9 14/16	Telkwa River, BC	Matt Helstrom	Lowell A. Davison	1957	57
25 14/16	16 9/16	9 5/16	Owikeno Lake, BC	Alexander M. Peterson	Alexander M. Peterson	1959	57
25 14/16	16	9 14/16	Christmas Mt., AK	Mark E. Gilson	Mark E. Gilson	1980	57
25 14/16	16 2/16	9 12/16	Muskeg River, AB	Dale B. Kolberg	Dale B. Kolberg	1981	57
25 14/16	16 5/16	9 9/16	Gardner Canal, BC	Steven B. Garland	Steven B. Garland	1984	57
25 13/16	15 15/16	9 14/16	Wood River, AK	Horace Black	Horace Black	1963	62
25 13/16	16 9/16	9 4/16	Bella Coola, BC	Roger L. Adams	Roger L. Adams	1965	62
25 13/16	16 7/16	9 6/16	Spatsizi River, BC	Howard W. Gambrell	Howard W. Gambrell	1985	62
25 12/16	15 13/16	9 15/16	Alaska Range, AK	Elmer R. Schlachter	Elmer R. Schlachter	1971	65
25 12/16	16 2/16	9 10/16	Kwatna River, BC	Robert C. Riggs	Robert C. Riggs	1981	65
25 12/16	16	9 12/16	Hanna Ridge, BC	Dale T. Dean	Dale T. Dean	1984	65
25 12/16	16	9 12/16	Bond Sound, BC	William Kemp, Jr.	William Kemp, Jr.	1985	65
25 12/16	16 2/16	9 10/16	Klinaklini River, BC	Leonard E. Ellis	Leonard E. Ellis	1991	65
25 11/16	16 3/16	9 8/16	Owikeno Lake, BC	W.W. Meeker	W.W. Meeker	1959	70
25 11/16	15 11/16	10	Tatshenshini River, BC	Robert E. Miller	Robert E. Miller	1974	70
25 11/16	15 11/16	9 4/16	Kimsquit River, BC	Norman E. Kinsey	Norman E. Kinsey	1977	70
25 11/16	16	10	Meziadin Lake, BC	J.D. Jensen & R.S. Curtis	Jae D. Jensen	1979	70
25 11/16	16 4/16	9 7/16	Knight Inlet, BC	Charles E. Gromatzky	Charles E. Gromatzky	1988	70
25 11/16	16 2/16	9 9/16	Babine River, BC	Robert V. Ellis	Robert V. Ellis	1991	70
25 11/16	15 12/16	9 15/16	Paragon River, AK	Gregory D. Yon	Gregory D. Yon	1992	70
25 10/16	16 1/16	9 9/16	Bralorne, BC	Bert Klineburger	Bert Klineburger	1956	77
25 10/16	16 3/16	9 7/16	Dease River, BC	Herb Klein	Herb Klein	1960	77
25 10/16	16 2/16	9 8/16	Eagle Creek, WY	Picked Up	L.L. Lutz & H. Sanford	1961	77
25 10/16	16	9 10/16	Brooks Range, AK	John H. Epp	John H. Epp	1965	77
25 10/16	15 6/16	10 4/16	Nabesna River, AK	Jack A. Shane, Sr.	Jack A. Shane, Sr.	1966	77
25 10/16	16 2/16	9 8/16	Kuskokwim River, AK	George Panagos	George Panagos	1968	77
25 10/16	15 15/16	9 11/16	Tok River, AK	Robert S. Thompson	Robert S. Thompson	1974	77
25 10/16	16	9 10/16	Machmell River, BC	Herbert J. Wenk	Herbert J. Wenk	1975	77
25 10/16	15 14/16	9 12/16	Sheslay River, BC	John Welsh	John Welsh	1983	77

GRIZZLY BEAR

Ursus arctos horribilis

Score	Greatest Length of Skull Without Lower Jaw	Greatest Width of Skull	Locality	Hunter	Owner	Date Killed	Rank
25 10/16	15 14/16	9 12/16	Kuskokwim River, AK	Thomas J. Stolsky	Thomas J. Stolsky	1992	77
25 9/16	16	9 9/16	Missouri Breaks, MT	E.S. Cameron	U.S. Natl. Museum	1890	87
25 9/16	16 4/16	9 5/16	Klinaklini River, BC	Grancel Fitz	Mrs. Grancel Fitz	1953	87
25 9/16	16	9 9/16	Kitseguecla Mts., BC	Jack Adams	Jack Adams	1975	87
25 9/16	16 3/16	9 6/16	Carpenter Lake, BC	Jim Sprangers	Jim Sprangers	1982	87
25 9/16	16 1/16	9 8/16	Klinaklini River, BC	Homer Harvey	Homer Harvey	1987	87
25 9/16	15 11/16	9 14/16	Tok River, AK	Phillip A. Wolfe	Phillip A. Wolfe	1993	87
25 8/16	16 2/16	9 6/16	Owikeno Lake, BC	J.C. Russell	J.C. Russell	1957	93
25 8/16	16	9 8/16	Maxan Lake, BC	Alfred E. Matthew	Alfred E. Matthew	1967	93
25 8/16	15 15/16	9 9/16	Wakeman Sound, BC	Dennis King	Dennis King	1969	93
25 8/16	16	9 8/16	Cassiar Mts., BC	Arlow Lothe	Arlow Lothe	1969	93
25 8/16	15 12/16	9 12/16	McKinley River, AK	John R. Cardis	John R. Cardis	1970	93
25 8/16	16	9 8/16	Big River, AK	George Engel	George Engel	1976	93
25 8/16	16 3/16	9 5/16	Prince Rupert, BC	Murray B. Wilson	Murray B. Wilson	1979	93
25 8/16	16 8/16	9	King Salmon Creek, BC	John K. Fritze	John K. Fritze	1980	93
25 8/16	15 12/16	9 12/16	Kuskokwim River, AK	Bernard V. Davis	Bernard V. Davis	1983	93
25 8/16	16 2/16	9 6/16	Iskut River, BC	Robin Buchanan	Robin Buchanan	1987	93
25 8/16	15 15/16	9 9/16	Ospika River, BC	Frank H. Gunther	Frank H. Gunther	1987	93
25 8/16	15 12/16	9 12/16	Sand Creek, AK	Picked Up	B. & T. Jorgensen	1994	93
25 7/16	15 12/16	9 12/16	Upper Boulder River, MT	Ted Johnston	E.C. Cates	1934	105
25 7/16	16	9 11/16	Tweedsmuir Park, BC	Lloyd B. Walker	Lloyd B. Walker	1950	105
25 7/16	15 13/16	9 10/16	Clearwater River, AB	Jack Allen	Jack Allen	1957	105
25 7/16	15 4/16	10 3/16	Zohini Creek, BC	Paul R. Beebe	Paul R. Beebe	1967	105
25 7/16	16 10/16	8 13/16	Nordegg, AB	Charles W. Matter	Charles W. Matter	1974	105
25 7/16	15 14/16	9 9/16	Kitlope River, BC	Darryl W. Hodson	Darryl W. Hodson	1975	105
25 7/16	15 4/16	10 3/16	Lakelse River, BC	William J. Harvey, Jr.	William J. Harvey, Jr.	1979	105
25 7/16	16 2/16	9 5/16	Andreafsky River, AK	John C. Bruno	John C. Bruno	1981	105
25 7/16	15 9/16	9 9/16	Toad River, BC	Paul E. Robey	Paul E. Robey	1981	105
25 7/16	15 14/16	9 10/16	Wedeene River, BC	Stuart Haslett	Stuart Haslett	1983	105
25 7/16	15 13/16	9 14/16	Skeena Mts., BC	Thomas J. Grogan	Thomas J. Grogan	1989	105
25 6/16	15 9/16	9	Slave Lake, AB	R.W.H. Eben-Ebenau	R.W.H. Eben-Ebenau	1944	116
25 6/16	16 6/16	9 5/16	Kleena Kleene, BC	A.W. Travis	A.W. Travis	1961	116
25 6/16	16 1/16	9 13/16	Northway, AK	James A. Johnson	James A. Johnson	1964	116
25 6/16	15 9/16	9 12/16	Edson, AB	Jack Armstrong	Jack Armstrong	1967	116
25 6/16	15 10/16	9 6/16	Mussel Inlet, BC	Victor W. Budd	Victor W. Budd	1967	116
25 6/16	16	10 3/16	Brooks Range, AK	Rusty Pickus	Rusty Pickus	1979	116
25 6/16	15 3/16	10 2/16	Kuskokwim River, AK	Michael T. Carlucci	Michael T. Carlucci	1981	116
25 6/16	15 12/16	9 10/16	Bond Sound, BC	James H. Garner	James H. Garner	1982	116

			Locality	Hunter	Owner	Date	Rank
25 6/16	15 13/16	9 9/16	Liard River, BC	Norman F. Schenk	Norman F. Schenk	1986	116
25 6/16	16 2/16	9 4/16	Bella Coola, BC	G. Thierbach & F. Rad	George Thierbach	1987	116
25 6/16	16 6/16	9	Jennings River, BC	Jeffrey S. Shoaf	Jeffrey S. Shoaf	1993	116
25 6/16	15 12/16	9 10/16	Suskwa River, BC	Debra Nelson	Debra Nelson	1994	116
25 6/16	16 4/16	9 2/16	Casadepaga River, AK	Fred D. Chadwick	Fred D. Chadwick	1995	129
25 5/16	15 13/16	9 8/16	Anahim Lake, BC	Ace Demers	Ace Demers	1951	129
25 5/16	15 14/16	9 7/16	Kwatna River, BC	Walter W. Butcher	Walter W. Butcher	1954	129
25 5/16	15 1/16	10 4/16	Granite Lake, YT	Jim Papst	Jim Papst	1969	129
25 5/16	15 12/16	9 9/16	Kobuk River, AK	Hugh H. Chatham, Jr.	Hugh H. Chatham, Jr.	1971	129
25 5/16	15 8/16	9 13/16	Eutsuk Lake, BC	W.R. Macfarlane	W.R. Macfarlane	1974	129
25 5/16	15 12/16	9 9/16	Brooks Range, AK	Warren K. Parker	Warren K. Parker	1979	129
25 5/16	16 1/16	9 4/16	Scoop Lake, BC	Darrell A. Farr	Dwight E. Farr	1981	129
25 5/16	16 4/16	9 1/16	Skowquiltz River, BC	Robert C. McEntee	Robert C. McEntee	1981	129
25 5/16	15 7/16	9 14/16	Tonzona River, AK	George G. Houser	George G. Houser	1985	129
25 5/16	16 4/16	9 1/16	Pilgrim Springs, AK	Troy L. Nance	Troy L. Nance	1993	129
25 5/16	15 15/16	9 15/16	Kwiniuk River, AK	Bruce M. Stoner	Bruce M. Stoner	1994	129
25 5/16	15 10/16	9 11/16	Deadlock Mt., AK	Richard R. Lindsay	Richard R. Lindsay	1995	129
25 5/16	15 12/16	9 9/16	Solo Lake, AK	Robert P. Robb	Robert P. Robb	1995	129
25 4/16	16	9 4/16	Anahim Lake, BC	C.D. Carrington	Univ. Calif. Museum	1957	142
25 4/16	16 3/16	9 1/16	Cascade Inlet, BC	Walter A. Frame	Walter A. Frame	1964	142
25 4/16	15 9/16	9 11/16	Salmon River, BC	Al Rand	Al Rand	1964	142
25 4/16	15 8/16	9 12/16	Yanert River, AK	Herbert A. Biss	Herbert A. Biss	1965	142
25 4/16	15 6/16	9 5/16	Anahim Lake, BC	Bernard Nofziger	Bernard Nofziger	1970	142
25 4/16	15 13/16	9 7/16	Kynoch Inlet, BC	P.J. Kennedy	W.G. Hawes	1971	142
25 4/16	15 15/16	9 5/16	Berland River, AB	Donald Brockman	Donald Brockman	1978	142
25 4/16	15 12/16	9 8/16	Alaska Range, AK	David L. Kulzer	David L. Kulzer	1979	142
25 4/16	15 10/16	9 10/16	Gisasa River, AK	Billy R. Deligans, Jr.	Billy R. Deligans, Jr.	1985	142
25 4/16	15 2/16	9 2/16	Dazell Creek, AK	Armand J. Giannini	Armand J. Giannini	1988	142
25 4/16	16 4/16	9	Trapper Lake, BC	John Kloosterman	John Kloosterman	1991	142
25 3/16	15 7/16	9 12/16	Bella Coola, BC	Umberto Benedet	Umberto Benedet	1957	153
25 3/16	16 4/16	8 15/16	Wrangell Mts., AK	Peter W. Bading	Peter W. Bading	1963	153
25 3/16	15 9/16	9 10/16	Teller, AK	Harry Armitage	Harry Armitage	1965	153
25 3/16	15 1/16	10 2/16	Motase Lake, BC	Joel Franzoia	Joel Franzoia	1970	153
25 3/16	15 9/16	9 10/16	Anahim Lake, BC	Lloyd E. Nygaard	Lloyd E. Nygaard	1973	153
25 3/16	16 2/16	9 1/16	McClinchy River, BC	Picked Up	Bernie Gano	PR 1974	153
25 3/16	15 8/16	9 2/16	Bella Coola, BC	Richard K. Miller	Richard K. Miller	1975	153
25 3/16	15 6/16	9 11/16	Thutade Lake, BC	James H. Glover	James H. Glover	1977	153
25 3/16	15 5/16	9 8/16	American River, AK	John M. Griffith, Jr.	John M. Griffith, Jr.	1977	153
25 3/16	15 9/16	9 13/16	Andreafsky River, AK	James P. Barkman	James P. Barkman	1980	153
25 3/16	15 3/16	9 14/16	Ogilvie Mts., YT	Stanton E. Wilson	Stanton E. Wilson	1981	153
25 3/16	16	9 10/16	Kingcome River, BC	Graydon A. Peat	Graydon A. Peat	1983	153
25 3/16	15 14/16	9 10/16	Nunakogok River, AK	Randy Jackson	Randy Jackson	1984	153
25 3/16	15 8/16	9 3/16	Boston Creek, AK	Sigurd E. Murphy	Sigurd E. Murphy	1987	153
25 3/16	15 11/16	9 5/16	Salcha River, AK	Danny E. Walker	Danny E. Walker	1987	153
25 3/16	16 1/16	9 11/16	Bella Coola River, BC	Craig A. Crichton	Craig A. Crichton	1996	153
25 2/16	15 10/16	9 2/16	Fremont Co., WY	Unknown	Warren V. Spriggs, Sr.	1947	169
25 2/16	15 14/16	9 4/16	Yellowstone River, WY	Bill Nymeyer	Jack H. White	1960	169

GRIZZLY BEAR

Ursus arctos horribilis

Score	Greatest Length of Skull Without Lower Jaw	Greatest Width of Skull	Locality	Hunter	Owner	Date Killed	Rank
25 ²/₁₆	16 ²/₁₆	9	Lignite, AK	Leonard Spencer	Leonard Spencer	1963	169
25 ²/₁₆	16 ²/₁₆	9	Mentasta Mts., AK	Basil C. Bradbury	Basil C. Bradbury	1965	169
25 ²/₁₆	15 ¹³/₁₆	9 ⁵/₁₆	Kotzebue, AK	F.W. Hatterscheidt	F.W. Hatterscheidt	1968	169
25 ²/₁₆	16	9 ²/₁₆	Bella Coola, BC	Howard Morrisey	Howard Morrisey	1971	169
25 ²/₁₆	15 ⁶/₁₆	9 ¹²/₁₆	McGrath, AK	Curtis C. Classen	Curtis C. Classen	1974	169
25 ²/₁₆	15 ⁸/₁₆	9 ¹⁰/₁₆	Butedale, BC	Walter R. Peters	Walter R. Peters	1974	169
25 ²/₁₆	15 ¹²/₁₆	9 ⁶/₁₆	Parsnip River, BC	Graham Markland	Graham Markland	1977	169
25 ²/₁₆	16	9 ²/₁₆	Cluculz Creek, BC	Ed Roberson	Ed Roberson	1978	169
25 ²/₁₆	15 ⁶/₁₆	9 ¹²/₁₆	Beaver Creek, AK	Abram Walter	Abram Walter	1979	169
25 ²/₁₆	15 ¹⁰/₁₆	9 ⁸/₁₆	Blue Ridge, AB	Thomas E. Deacon	Thomas E. Deacon	1983	169
25 ²/₁₆	15 ²/₁₆	10	Kemano River, BC	Victor L. Sensenig	Victor L. Sensenig	1983	169
25 ²/₁₆	15 ¹²/₁₆	9 ⁶/₁₆	Toklat River, AK	Marvin Carkhuff	Marvin Carkhuff	1987	169
25 ²/₁₆	15 ⁶/₁₆	9 ¹²/₁₆	Dease Lake, BC	John Flynn	John Flynn	1988	169
25 ²/₁₆	16 ²/₁₆	9	Noomst Creek, BC	Marc A. Laynes	Marc A. Laynes	1988	169
25 ¹/₁₆	15 ¹¹/₁₆	9 ⁶/₁₆	Teton Co., WY	C.C. Craven	Jackson Hole Museum	1938	185
25 ¹/₁₆	15 ¹³/₁₆	9 ⁴/₁₆	Knight Inlet, BC	Frederic N. Dodge	Frederic N. Dodge	1954	185
25 ¹/₁₆	15 ¹⁴/₁₆	9 ³/₁₆	Bella Coola, BC	L. Rowe Davidson	L. Rowe Davidson	1958	185
25 ¹/₁₆	15 ¹⁰/₁₆	9 ⁷/₁₆	Caribou Flats, BC	Edward Escott	Edward Escott	1962	185
25 ¹/₁₆	15 ¹¹/₁₆	9 ⁶/₁₆	Yanert River, AK	E.G. Brust, Jr.	E.G. Brust, Jr.	1964	185
25 ¹/₁₆	16 ³/₁₆	8 ¹⁴/₁₆	Selby River, AK	Kenneth T. Alt	Kenneth T. Alt	1965	185
25 ¹/₁₆	15 ⁸/₁₆	9 ⁹/₁₆	Bob Quinn Lake, BC	Dave Miscavish	Dave Miscavish	1971	185
25 ¹/₁₆	15 ²/₁₆	9 ¹⁵/₁₆	Pikmiktalik River, AK	Donald B. Huffines	Donald B. Huffines	1984	185
25 ¹/₁₆	15 ¹²/₁₆	9 ⁵/₁₆	Euchiniko Lakes, BC	Native American	Mark J. Simonson	1986	185
25 ¹/₁₆	15 ¹⁰/₁₆	9 ⁷/₁₆	Morice River, BC	Doug W. Six	Doug W. Six	1991	185
25 ¹/₁₆	15 ¹²/₁₆	9 ⁵/₁₆	Alsek River, BC	Roy S. Bowers	Roy S. Bowers	1994	185
25	16 ³/₁₆	8 ¹³/₁₆	Lewistown, MT	Mildred Connor	U.S. Natl. Museum	1888	196
25	16	9	Atnarko River, BC	David Maytag	H.J. Borden	1959	196
25	15 ⁹/₁₆	9 ⁷/₁₆	Nabesna River, AK	Marven Henriksen	Marven Henriksen	1964	196
25	15 ¹¹/₁₆	9 ⁵/₁₆	Yellowstone Natl. Park, WY	Picked Up	John C. Kirk	PR 1965	196
25	15	10	Kotzebue, AK	Glen E. Park	Glen E. Park	1965	196
25	15 ⁴/₁₆	9 ¹²/₁₆	Hart Peaks, BC	T.T. Stroup	T.T. Stroup	1966	196
25	15 ³/₁₆	9 ¹³/₁₆	Mt. Hayes, AK	Benjamin H. Robson	Benjamin H. Robson	1968	196
25	15 ⁴/₁₆	9 ¹²/₁₆	Noomst Creek, BC	James G. Shelton	James G. Shelton	1970	196
25	15 ⁸/₁₆	9 ⁸/₁₆	Stikine River, BC	Donald R. McClure, Sr.	Donald R. McClure, Sr.	1971	196
25	15 ¹⁰/₁₆	9 ⁶/₁₆	Tacu River, BC	W.N. Olson	W.N. Olson	1971	196
25	15 ¹³/₁₆	9 ³/₁₆	Hinton, AB	Oliver Hannula	Oliver Hannula	1972	196
25	15 ¹⁵/₁₆	9 ¹/₁₆	Whitecourt, AB	Sid Wheeler	Sid Wheeler	1974	196
25	15 ⁸/₁₆	9 ⁸/₁₆	Richland Co., MT	Picked Up	Jack Stewart	1976	196

			Locality			Date	Rank
25	14 14/16	10 2/16	Fortymile River, AK	James B. DeMoss	James B. DeMoss	1980	196
25	16 1/16	8 15/16	Owikeno Lake, BC	Robert K. Fisher	Robert K. Fisher	1981	196
25	15 13/16	9 3/16	Bella Coola River, BC	James G. Shelton	James G. Shelton	1983	196
25	15 6/16	9 10/16	Koyuk River, AK	John Macaluso	John Macaluso	1985	196
25	16 9/16	8 7/16	Chincaga River, AB	Bernd Licht	Bernd Licht	1989	196
25	15 9/16	9 7/16	Dunedin River, BC	E.M. Takahashi	E.M. Takahashi	1992	196
25	15 14/16	9 2/16	Noatak River, AK	Kenneth C. Thomas	Kenneth C. Thomas	1992	196
25	15 10/16	9 6/16	Ungalik River, AK	Donald R. Card	Donald R. Card	1996	196
24 15/16	15 6/16	9 9/16	Taseko Lakes, BC	A. Cecil Henry	A. Cecil Henry	1956	217
24 15/16	15 4/16	9 11/16	Ootsa Lake, BC	John Block	J. Block & D. Vantine	1965	217
24 15/16	15 7/16	9 8/16	Dudidontu River, BC	Bob Loewenstein	Bob Loewenstein	1965	217
24 15/16	15 14/16	9 1/16	Teller, AK	Jack D. Putnam	Jack D. Putnam	1965	217
24 15/16	15 10/16	9 5/16	Lakelse River, BC	Victor Lepp	Victor Lepp	1968	217
24 15/16	15 12/16	9 3/16	Wrangell Mts., AK	James E. Saxton	James E. Saxton	1977	217
24 15/16	15 13/16	9 2/16	Nusatsum River, BC	Randy Svisdahl	Picked Up	1980	217
24 15/16	15 6/16	9 9/16	Tonzona River, AK	Wayne J. Pensenstadler	Wayne J. Pensenstadler	1982	217
24 15/16	15 5/16	9 10/16	Tetsa River, BC	John J. Belous	John J. Belous	1985	217
24 15/16	15 7/16	9 8/16	Maroon Creek, BC	Roger M. Britton	Roger M. Britton	1988	217
24 14/16	16 2/16	8 12/16	Atnarko, BC	Chicago Nat. Hist. Mus.	F.N. Bard	1938	227
24 14/16	15 12/16	9 2/16	Chilcotin, BC	R.J. Pop	R.J. Pop & J. Beban	1954	227
24 14/16	15 7/16	9 7/16	Chisana, AK	Larry Folger	Larry Folger	1957	227
24 14/16	15 6/16	9 5/16	Atnarko River, BC	Carl Molander	Carl Molander	1957	227
24 14/16	15 11/16	9 3/16	Meziadin Lake, BC	Larry T. Spangler	Larry T. Spangler	1962	227
24 14/16	15 4/16	9 10/16	Brooks Range, AK	E. Wayne Gilley	E. Wayne Gilley	1963	227
24 14/16	15 13/16	9 1/16	Alaska Range, AK	Jack Williamson	Jack Williamson	1963	227
24 14/16	15 2/16	9 12/16	Shishmaref, AK	James Harrower	James Harrower	1964	227
24 14/16	16 3/16	8 11/16	Taku River, BC	Robert J. Lacy	Robert J. Lacy	1964	227
24 14/16	15 7/16	8 11/16	Knights Inlet, BC	Levon Bender	Levon Bender	1965	227
24 14/16	15 7/16	9 7/16	Brooks Range, AK	W.F. Krebill	W.F. Krebill	1966	227
24 14/16	15 6/16	9 8/16	Cassiar Mts., BC	H. Kenneth Seiferd	H. Kenneth Seiferd	1966	227
24 14/16	15 7/16	9 7/16	McGregor Mts., BC	Edward Johnson	Edward Johnson	1967	227
24 14/16	15 9/16	9 5/16	McGregor River, BC	C.C. Carpenter	C.C. Carpenter	1968	227
24 14/16	15 12/16	9 2/16	Telkwa River, BC	Richard Pohlschneider	Richard Pohlschneider	1969	227
24 14/16	15 6/16	9 11/16	Seaskinnish Creek, BC	Thomas D.J. Fulko	Thomas D.J. Fulko	1977	227
24 14/16	15 3/16	9 6/16	Klutina River, AK	Robert M. Decker	Robert M. Decker	1979	227
24 14/16	15 8/16	9 4/16	Tatla Lake, BC	Donald L. Gardner	Donald L. Gardner	1980	227
24 14/16	15 10/16	9 4/16	Andreafsky River, AK	James W. Latreille	James W. Latreille	1980	227
24 14/16	15 15/16	8 15/16	Barney Creek, BC	Roy Pattison	Roy Pattison	1984	227
24 14/16	15 4/16	9 10/16	Squirrel River, AK	William M. Eubank	William M. Eubank	1988	227
24 14/16	15 8/16	9 2/16	Grayling Fork, YT	Michael L. Rogers	Michael L. Rogers	1991	227
24 14/16	15 12/16	9 2/16	Meziadin Lake, BC	C. Don Wall	C. Don Wall	1991	227
24 14/16	15 5/16	9 9/16	Nazcha Creek, BC	Ken Moffett	Ken Moffett	1992	227
24 14/16	15 3/16	9 11/16	Knight Inlet, BC	Robert E. Sheets	Robert E. Sheets	1992	227
24 14/16	15 10/16	9 4/16	Nation River, YT	Daniel J. Jones	Daniel J. Jones	1993	227
24 13/16	15 8/16	9 6/16	Peace River, BC	Lee Johnson	Lee Johnson	1995	227
24 13/16	15 7/16	9 6/16	Chisana River, AK	Larry Folger	Larry Folger	1957	254
24 13/16	15 9/16	9 4/16	Livengood, AK	Ada Holst	Ada Holst	1961	254

GRIZZLY BEAR
Ursus arctos horribilis

Score	Greatest Length of Skull Without Lower Jaw	Greatest Width of Skull	Locality	Hunter	Owner	Date Killed	Rank
24 13/16	15 3/16	9 10/16	Tatla Lake, BC	R.D. Brooks	R.D. Brooks	1962	254
24 13/16	15 12/16	9 1/16	Warden Creek, AB	Harvey R. Cook	Harvey R. Cook	1964	254
24 13/16	15 12/16	9 1/16	Chetwynd, BC	William E. Dugger	William E. Dugger	1964	254
24 13/16	15 5/16	9 8/16	Tonzona River, AK	Francis Kernan	Francis Kernan	1964	254
24 13/16	15 4/16	9 9/16	Clarence Lake, AK	E.A. Munroe	E.A. Munroe	1964	254
24 13/16	15 6/16	9 7/16	Slim Lake, BC	Freda Stalder	Freda Stalder	1968	254
24 13/16	15 4/16	9 9/16	Noatak River, AK	John E. Batson	John E. Batson	1970	254
24 13/16	15 11/16	9 2/16	Telkwa Range, BC	Jack Adams	Jack Adams	1978	254
24 13/16	15 15/16	8 14/16	Kiibella River, BC	Larry Sawchuk	Larry Sawchuk	1984	254
24 13/16	15 14/16	8 15/16	Burnt Trail Creek, BC	Tom Housh	Tom Housh	1985	254
24 13/16	15 8/16	9 5/16	Noatak River, AK	Dave R. Cerenzia	Dave R. Cerenzia	1987	254
24 13/16	15 5/16	9 8/16	Bear River, AK	Richard M. Cowles	Richard M. Cowles	1987	254
24 13/16	15 10/16	9 3/16	Trident Glacier, AK	Glenn J. Rasmussen	Glenn J. Rasmussen	1992	254
24 13/16	15 13/16	9	Bella Coola River, BC	Byron K. McGaffey	Byron K. McGaffey	1993	254
24 13/16	15	9 13/16	Pitmegea River, AK	Scott R. Ravenscroft	Scott R. Ravenscroft	1993	254
24 12/16	15 8/16	9 4/16	Spanish Lake, BC	Bill Niemi	Bill Niemi	1953	271
24 12/16	15 6/16	9 6/16	Sheep Creek, AB	Robert V. Broadbent	Robert V. Broadbent	1963	271
24 12/16	15	9 12/16	Brooks Range, AK	Lewis A. Meyers	Lewis A. Meyers	1964	271
24 12/16	15 10/16	9 2/16	Terminus Mt., BC	Herb Klein	Herb Klein	1965	271
24 12/16	15 8/16	9 4/16	Kitimat, BC	Hans Lackner	Hans Lackner	1969	271
24 12/16	15 3/16	9 9/16	Burrage Creek, BC	Jack Worthy	Jack Worthy	1970	271
24 12/16	15 15/16	8 13/16	Toklat River, AK	George P. Mann	George P. Mann	1971	271
24 12/16	15 9/16	9 3/16	Bella Coola, BC	Joe M. Colvin	Joe M. Colvin	1973	271
24 12/16	15 4/16	9 8/16	Alaska Range, AK	Earl K. Edstrom	Earl K. Edstrom	1976	271
24 12/16	15 8/16	9 4/16	Wigwam River, BC	Ray S. Koontz	Ray S. Koontz	1977	271
24 12/16	15	9 12/16	Turnagain River, BC	Arthur E. Crawford	Arthur E. Crawford	1980	271
24 12/16	15 6/16	9 6/16	Norton Sound, AK	Lewis E. Henyon	Lewis E. Henyon	1984	271
24 12/16	16 2/16	8 10/16	Tsayta Lake, BC	Vincent A. Pisani	Vincent A. Pisani	1986	271
24 12/16	15 15/16	8 13/16	Teklanika River, AK	Kenneth E. Abel	Kenneth E. Abel	1990	271
24 12/16	15 7/16	9 5/16	Valemount, BC	Mark G. Holt	Mark G. Holt	1992	271
24 12/16	15 4/16	9 8/16	Pilgrim River, AK	Brent E. Chadwick	Brent E. Chadwick	1995	271
24 12/16	15 10/16	9 2/16	Minaker River, BC	Fred A. Parent	Fred A. Parent	1995	271
24 12/16	15 8/16	9 4/16	Telegraph Creek, BC	Keith C. Caldwell	Keith C. Caldwell	1996	271
24 12/16	15 7/16	9 5/16	White River, YT	Roger D. Evans	Roger D. Evans	1996	271
24 12/16	15 8/16	9 4/16	Fraser River, BC	Randy W. Kolida	Randy W. Kolida	1996	271
24 11/16	15 2/16	9 9/16	Stevens Lake, BC	R.L. Hambrick	R.L. Hambrick	1965	291
24 11/16	15 4/16	9 7/16	Tok River, AK	Lewis B. Wyman	Lewis B. Wyman	1965	291
24 11/16	15 4/16	9 7/16	Alaska Range, AK	Tony Caputo	Tony Caputo	1967	291

Score	Length	Width	Locality	Owner	Hunter	Date	Rank
24 11/16	15 14/16	8 13/16	Lesser Slave Lake, AB	James Erickson	Picked Up	1967	291
24 11/16	15	9 11/16	MacMillan Plateau, YT	Paul Yeager	Paul Yeager	1967	291
24 11/16	15 8/16	9 3/16	Butte Inlet, BC	Thomas M. Utigard	Thomas M. Utigard	1970	291
24 11/16	15 6/16	9 5/16	Kuzitrin River, AK	H. Doak Neal	H. Doak Neal	1976	291
24 11/16	15	9 11/16	Toklat River, AK	Timothy A. Sanderson	Timothy A. Sanderson	1976	291
24 11/16	15 3/16	9 8/16	Toad River, BC	Bruce H. Morrill	Bruce H. Morrill	1980	291
24 11/16	15 9/16	9 2/16	Kwatna Bay, BC	Norman C. Roettger	Norman C. Roettger	1982	291
24 11/16	15 9/16	9 2/16	American Creek, AK	Marvin H. Hanebuth	Marvin H. Hanebuth	1986	291
24 11/16	15 6/16	9 5/16	Cadomin, AB	Pemble Davis	Pemble Davis	1987	291
24 11/16	15 13/16	8 14/16	Moses Inlet, BC	Robert E. Johnson	Robert E. Johnson	1989	291
24 11/16	15 9/16	9 2/16	Muskwa River, BC	Benjamin F. Kirkham	Benjamin F. Kirkham	1990	291
24 11/16	15 9/16	9 2/16	Kirbyville Creek, BC	Gary L. Drager	Gary L. Drager	1992	291
24 11/16	15 5/16	9 6/16	Sheep Mt., AK	Norman W. Schmidt	Norman W. Schmidt	1994	291
24 11/16	15 3/16	9 8/16	Koyuk River, AK	Peter J. Pizzagalli	Peter J. Pizzagalli	1996	291
24 10/16	15 8/16	9 2/16	Camp Island Lake, BC	Harold L. Jones	Harold L. Jones	1965	308
24 10/16	15 5/16	9 6/16	Point Hope, AK	Richard K. Siller	Richard K. Siller	1965	308
24 10/16	15 11/16	9 5/16	Brooks Range, AK	T.W. Bohannan	T.W. Bohannan	1968	308
24 10/16	15 4/16	8 15/16	Seymour Inlet, BC	Tim Fischer	Tim Fischer	1969	308
24 10/16	15 2/16	9 6/16	Wiseman, AK	David L. Howard	David L. Howard	1970	308
24 10/16	15 2/16	9 8/16	Toklat River, AK	Gary Miller	Gary Miller	1972	308
24 10/16	15 4/16	9 8/16	Mosley Creek, BC	Charles Harvey	Charles Harvey	1976	308
24 10/16	15 6/16	9 4/16	Alaska Range, AK	Victor Geibel	Victor Geibel	1978	308
24 10/16	15 3/16	9 7/16	Toklat River, AK	Howard W. Neice	Howard W. Neice	1981	308
24 10/16	14 12/16	9 14/16	Pilgrim River, AK	Karen J. Chadwick	Karen J. Chadwick	1982	308
24 10/16	15 14/16	8 14/16	John River, AK	Rick J. Schikora	Rick J. Schikora	1982	308
24 10/16	15 12/16	8 12/16	Swan Hills, AB	Henry H. Foisy	Henry H. Foisy	1988	308
24 10/16	14 15/16	9 11/16	Mt. Miller, YT	Doug White	Doug White	1990	308
24 10/16	15 8/16	9 4/16	Gold Bridge, BC	J. Gregory Boyd	J. Gregory Boyd	1993	308
24 10/16	15 5/16	9 2/16	Horse Range Creek, BC	Guyle G. Cox	Guyle G. Cox	1993	308
24 10/16	15 5/16	9 4/16	Morice River, BC	Tom Wiggins	Tom Wiggins	1993	308
24 9/16	15 13/16	9 1/16	Whiteswan Lake, BC	A.C. Gilbert	A.C. Gilbert	1937	324
24 9/16	15 4/16	8 12/16	Tatla Lake, BC	D. McDermott	D. McDermott	1954	324
24 9/16	16 1/16	9 5/16	Bella Coola, BC	William P. Mastrangel	William P. Mastrangel	1956	324
24 9/16	15 6/16	9 6/16	Atnarko River, BC	Martin Anderson	Martin Anderson	1957	324
24 9/16	15 5/16	9 2/16	Owikeno Lake, BC	Norman W. Garwood	Norman W. Garwood	1960	324
24 9/16	15 1/16	9 5/16	Hulahula River, AK	Richard Sjoden	Richard Sjoden	1963	324
24 9/16	15 9/16	8 8/16	Ray Mts., AK	Mario Grassi	Mario Grassi	1965	324
24 9/16		9 3/16	Anahim Lake, BC	M.V. Nearing	M.V. Nearing	1966	324
24 9/16		9 4/16	Meziadin Lake, BC	Teuvo Pahti	Teuvo Pahti	1968	324
24 9/16			Tok River, AK	John W. Waller	John W. Waller	1968	324
24 9/16			Cape Lisburne, AK	Gerrit N. Vandenberg	Gerrit N. Vandenberg	1969	324
24 9/16			Kispiox River, BC	W.J. Love	W.J. Love	1971	324
24 9/16	16	9	Graham River, BC	Edward F. Lundberg	Edward F. Lundberg	1976	324
24 9/16	14 15/16	8 9/16	Yanert River, AK	Robert J. Barham	Robert J. Barham	1977	324
24 9/16	15	9 10/16	Quesnel Lake, BC	Thomas E. Phillippe, Sr.	Thomas E. Phillippe, Sr.	1978	324
24 9/16	15 13/16	8 12/16	Chuckwalla River, BC	George B. Morris	George B. Morris	1979	324
24 9/16	15 7/16	9 2/16	Motase Peak, BC	Roger L. Pock	Roger L. Pock	1984	324

GRIZZLY BEAR

Ursus arctos horribilis

Score	Greatest Length of Skull Without Lower Jaw	Greatest Width of Skull	Locality	Hunter	Owner	Date Killed	Rank
24 9/16	15 1/16	9 8/16	Brooks Range, AK	Tim D. Hiner	Tim D. Hiner	1992	324
24 9/16	14 13/16	9 12/16	Kukpowruk River, AK	Alan J. Amundson	Alan J. Amundson	1993	324
24 8/16	15 2/16	9 6/16	Cassiar Mts., BC	Elgin T. Gates	Elgin T. Gates	1953	343
24 8/16	14 11/16	9 13/16	Mt. McKinley, AK	Howard W. Pollock	Howard W. Pollock	1953	343
24 8/16	15	9 8/16	Bella Coola, BC	James A. Perry	H.J. Borden	1959	343
24 8/16	15 4/16	9 4/16	Big Delta, AK	Harold E. Hogan	Harold E. Hogan	1961	343
24 8/16	14 15/16	9 9/16	Tatla Lake, BC	Harold A. Cowman	Harold A. Cowman	1964	343
24 8/16	15 13/16	8 11/16	Kleena Kleene River, BC	Martin J. Durkan	Martin J. Durkan	1966	343
24 8/16	15 1/16	9 7/16	Brooks Range, AK	Jerry N. Martin	Jerry N. Martin	1968	343
24 8/16	15 2/16	9 6/16	Kotzebue, AK	C.J. McElroy	C.J. McElroy	1968	343
24 8/16	15 1/16	9 7/16	Brooks Range, AK	Rick Reakoff	Rick Reakoff	1969	343
24 8/16	15 2/16	9 6/16	Tweedsmuir Park, BC	Tom & Clara Ritter	Tom & Clara Ritter	1969	343
24 8/16	14 11/16	9 13/16	Lakelse River, BC	Kolbjorn Eide	Kolbjorn Eide	1970	343
24 8/16	14 14/16	9 10/16	Miner Lake, BC	Dwight E. Farr, Jr.	Dwight E. Farr, Jr.	1971	343
24 8/16	15 6/16	9 2/16	Coast Range, BC	L.D. Hirzel & J. Petersen	Laverne D. Hirzel	1971	343
24 8/16	14 12/16	9 12/16	Stikine River, BC	Fred P. Grob	Fred P. Grob	1973	343
24 8/16	15 5/16	9 3/16	Colville River, AK	Richard A. McClellan	Richard A. McClellan	1974	343
24 8/16	15 5/16	9 3/16	Tonzona River, BC	Jill L. Nunley	Jill L. Nunley	1974	343
24 8/16	14 13/16	9 11/16	Ogilvie Mts., YT	Vearl Fowler	Vearl Fowler	1976	343
24 8/16	15 2/16	9 6/16	Brooks Range, AK	Calvin Danzig	Calvin Danzig	1977	343
24 8/16	15 4/16	9 4/16	Fraser River, BC	Paul F. Bays, Sr.	Paul F. Bays, Sr.	1978	343
24 8/16	15 7/16	9 1/16	Kugururok River, AK	Bruce A. Moe	Bruce A. Moe	1978	343
24 8/16	15 9/16	8 15/16	Table River, BC	George W. Morris	George W. Morris	1978	343
24 8/16	15	9 8/16	Terminus Mt., BC	William E. Greehey	William E. Greehey	1982	343
24 8/16	15 1/16	9 7/16	Koyuk, AK	K. James Malady III	K. James Malady III	1985	343
24 8/16	15 9/16	8 15/16	Brazeau Mts., AB	Richard F. Edmonds, Jr.	Richard F. Edmonds, Jr.	1986	343
24 8/16	15 9/16	8 15/16	Kuskokwim River, AK	Jerome D. Melbinger	Jerome D. Melbinger	1986	343
24 8/16	14 14/16	9 10/16	Greyling Creek, YT	Lee A. Hickey, Sr.	Lee A. Hickey, Sr.	1987	343
24 8/16	15	9 8/16	Buckland River, AK	Curtis R. Cebulski	Doug Christiansen	1988	343
24 8/16	15 6/16	9 2/16	Norton Sound, AK	Jerry W. Peterman	Jerry W. Peterman	1988	343
24 8/16	15 2/16	9 6/16	Bowser Lake, BC	Raymond J. Kotera	Raymond J. Kotera	1990	343
24 8/16	14 8/16	10	Eli River, AK	Gary A. Habe	Gary A. Habe	1992	343
24 8/16	15 7/16	9 1/16	Tatla Lake, BC	Morris Monita	Morris Monita	1993	343
24 8/16	15 5/16	9 3/16	Cariboo River, BC	Peter P.K. Grundmann	Peter P.K. Grundmann	1996	343
24 8/16	15 4/16	9 4/16	Ducette Peak, BC	Rainer Maas	Rainer Maas	1997	343
24 7/16	15	9 7/16	Cold Fish Lake, BC	William E. Goudey	William E. Goudey	1956	376
24 7/16	15 8/16	8 15/16	Dease River, BC	John Caputo	John Caputo	1958	376
24 7/16	15 6/16	9 1/16	Brooks Range, AK	Bobbie J. Cavnar	Bobbie J. Cavnar	1966	376

24 7/16	15 5/16	McClaren Glacier, AK	9 2/16	Gordon S. Pleiss	Gordon S. Pleiss	1967	376
24 7/16	15 7/16	Brooks Range, AK	9	Don Elder	Don Elder	1968	376
24 7/16	15 4/16	Ocena Falls, BC	9 3/16	Richard D. Dimick	Richard D. Dimick	1969	376
24 7/16	15 2/16	Colville River, AK	9 5/16	Alfonso I. Casso	Alfonso I. Casso	1970	376
24 7/16	15 6/16	Grande Cache, AB	9 1/16	Laurier Adam	Laurier Adam	1976	376
24 7/16	15 8/16	Kelly Creek, AK	8 15/16	Rick H. Jackson	Rick H. Jackson	1980	376
24 7/16	15 5/16	Wood River, AK	9 2/16	Kerry Q. Gronewold	Kerry Q. Gronewold	1984	376
24 7/16	14 15/16	Wulik River, AK	9 8/16	Bill Dress	Peter W. Dress	1986	376
24 7/16	15 6/16	Dore River, BC	9 1/16	Brian C. Jeck	Brian C. Jeck	1987	376
24 7/16	14 15/16	Nation River, AK	9 8/16	Robert W. Stenehjem	Robert W. Stenehjem	1987	376
24 7/16	14 15/16	Big River, AK	9 8/16	William J. Schilling	William J. Schilling	1992	376
24 7/16	15 8/16	Raley Creek, BC	8 15/16	Randy Kucharyshen	Randy Kucharyshen	1994	376
24 7/16	15 1/16	Black Lake, YT	9 6/16	Thomas P. Bruner	Thomas P. Bruner	1995	376
24 6/16	15	Alaska Hwy. Mile 175, BC	9 6/16	Selmer Torrison	Selmer Torrison	1958	392
24 6/16	15 6/16	Willow River, BC	9	Eric Hanet	Eric Hanet	1962	392
24 6/16	15 4/16	Alaska Range, AK	9 6/16	Hank Kramer	Hank Kramer	1964	392
24 6/16	14 10/16	Yanert River, AK	9 4/16	P.W. LaHaye	P.W. LaHaye	1965	392
24 6/16	15 5/16	Alaska Range, AK	9 12/16	Alberto Pipia	Alberto Pipia	1966	392
24 6/16	15 6/16	Atlin, BC	9 1/16	Jack E. Carpenter	Jack E. Carpenter	1967	392
24 6/16	14 15/16	Brooks Range, AK	9	Paul H. Magee	Paul H. Magee	1967	392
24 6/16	14 12/16	Prince George, BC	9 7/16	Wayne H. Laursen	Wayne H. Laursen	1969	392
24 6/16	15	Colville River, AK	9 10/16	E.H. Borchers, Jr.	E.H. Borchers, Jr.	1970	392
24 6/16	15 8/16	Wrangell Mts., AK	9	Victor W. Bullard	Victor W. Bullard	1971	392
24 6/16	14 14/16	Ogilvie Mts., YT	8 14/16	Philip R. Murphy	Philip R. Murphy	1972	392
24 6/16	15 4/16	Cassiar Mts., BC	9 8/16	Monte Hofstrand	Monte Hofstrand	1975	392
24 6/16	14 11/16	Kelly River, AK	9 2/16	James B. Goodman	J.B. Goodman & E. Remsing	1976	392
24 6/16	15	Alaska Range, AK	9 11/16	Larry W. Casey	Steve Casey	1977	392
24 6/16	15 2/16	Murray River, BC	9 6/16	Carl Kortmeyer	Carl Kortmeyer	1980	392
24 6/16	15 4/16	Nalbeelah Creek, BC	9 4/16	Wayne Moon	Wayne Moon	1983	392
24 6/16	15 10/16	Clyak River, BC	8 12/16	Marvin Opp	Marvin Opp	1983	392
24 6/16	15 2/16	Tagagawik River, AK	9 4/16	Roland L. Quimby	Roland L. Quimby	1983	392
24 6/16	15 5/16	Knight Inlet, BC	9 1/16	Norman W. Dougan	Norman W. Dougan	1984	392
24 6/16	15 10/16	Macoun Creek, BC	8 12/16	Martin McIlroy	Martin McIlroy	1984	392
24 6/16	15 7/16	Poutang Creek, BC	8 15/16	Irvin H. Brown	Irvin H. Brown	1990	392
24 6/16	15 10/16	Phillips Creek, BC	9 4/16	Paul L. VanMeter	Paul L. VanMeter	1991	392
24 6/16	15 1/16	Wakeman River, BC	8 12/16	Peter Morrison	Peter Morrison	1992	392
24 6/16	15	Swift River, BC	9 1/16	Scott Fontaine	Scott Fontaine	1993	392
24 6/16	14 10/16	Tetlin River, AK	9 6/16	Zach Pallister	Zach Pallister	1994	392
24 6/16	15 6/16	Shaktoolik River, AK	9 12/16	Charles M. Walraven	Charles M. Walraven	1995	392
24 5/16	15 9/16	Nenana River, AK	9	James E. Boyd	James E. Boyd	1997	392
24 5/16	15 6/16	Kitimat, BC	8 12/16	Ewald Kirschner	Ewald Kirschner	1958	419
24 5/16	15 8/16	Bear Berry, AB	8 15/16	Phil Temple	Phil Temple	1958	419
24 5/16	14 6/16	Blackstone River, AB	9 15/16	Wilhelm Eichenauer	Wilhelm Eichenauer	1963	419
24 5/16	15 2/16	Teller, AK	9 3/16	Bill Glunt	Bill Glunt	1965	419
24 5/16	15 7/16	Cassiar Mts., BC	8 14/16	Henry E. High	Henry E. High	1965	419
24 5/16	15 4/16	Nabesna River, AK	9 1/16	C.W. Houle	C.W. Houle	1965	419
24 5/16	15 4/16	Tetachuck Lake, BC	9 1/16	Torben Dahl	Torben Dahl	1966	419

GRIZZLY BEAR
Ursus arctos horribilis

Score	Greatest Length of Skull Without Lower Jaw	Greatest Width of Skull	Locality	Hunter	Owner	Date Killed	Rank
24 5/16	14 10/16	9 11/16	Brooks Range, AK	Robert L. Cohen	Robert L. Cohen	1967	419
24 5/16	16	8 5/16	Edson, AB	Otto Braaz	Otto Braaz	1969	419
24 5/16	14 14/16	9 7/16	Toba Inlet, BC	Jack C. Glover	Jack C. Glover	1970	419
24 5/16	15 7/16	8 14/16	Chatsquot Creek, BC	Roger J. Ahern	Roger J. Ahern	1978	419
24 5/16	15 7/16	8 14/16	Graham River, BC	William J. Fogarty, Jr.	William J. Fogarty, Jr.	1978	419
24 5/16	14 15/16	9 6/16	Selwyn Creek, YT	Rod G. Hardie	Rod G. Hardie	1979	419
24 5/16	15 6/16	8 15/16	Cranberry River, BC	Fred Y.C. Wong	Albert Wong	1982	419
24 5/16	14 15/16	9 6/16	Baird Mts., AK	Howard L. Olson	Howard L. Olson	1985	419
24 5/16	15 4/16	9 1/16	Stikine River, BC	Frederick L. Wood III	Frederick L. Wood III	1986	419
24 5/16	15	9 5/16	Mt. Fairplay, AK	David G. Kelleyhouse	David G. Kelleyhouse	1987	419
24 5/16	15 3/16	9 2/16	Poktonik Mts., AK	John W. Bania	John W. Bania	1989	419
24 5/16	15 6/16	8 15/16	Squirrel River, AK	Walter J. Miller	Walter J. Miller	1990	419
24 5/16	15 1/16	9 4/16	Horton River, NT	Victor E. Moss	Victor E. Moss	1990	419
24 5/16	14 11/16	9 10/16	Ungalik River, AK	Barry Kutun	Barry Kutun	1993	419
24 5/16	14 15/16	9 6/16	Yanert Fork, AK	Randy F. Stout	Randy F. Stout	1994	419
24 5/16	15 1/16	9 4/16	Chalco Creek, BC	Clifton Keel, Jr.	Clifton Keel, Jr.	1997	419
24 5/16	14 9/16	9 12/16	Green Creek, YT	Richard P. Musselman	Richard P. Musselman	1997	419
24 4/16	15 8/16	8 12/16	Dease Lake, BC	G.C.F. Dalziel	G.C.F. Dalziel	1956	443
24 4/16	15 13/16	9 7/16	Selkirk Mt., BC	Eli Paulson	Eli Paulson	1957	443
24 4/16	15 10/16	8 10/16	South Hay River, AB	Bert Shearer	Bert Shearer	1957	443
24 4/16	14 6/16	9 14/16	Kotzebue, AK	Don D. Giles	Don D. Giles	1965	443
24 4/16	15 4/16	9	Kuskokwim River, AK	Edward W. Williams	Edward W. Williams	1967	443
24 4/16	14 14/16	9 6/16	Brooks Range, AK	Stanley Blazovich	Stanley Blazovich	1970	443
24 4/16	15 10/16	8 10/16	Bella Coola, BC	Howard Creason	Howard Creason	1971	443
24 4/16	15 7/16	8 13/16	Sheep Creek, AB	Rolly Balzer	Rolly Balzer	1972	443
24 4/16	14 10/16	9 10/16	Nilkitkwa River, BC	Roger Britton	Roger Britton	1976	443
24 4/16	15 4/16	9	Trout Lake, BC	Paul L. Reese	Paul L. Reese	1982	443
24 4/16	14 12/16	9 8/16	Luwa Mt., BC	Joel B. Benner	Joel B. Benner	1985	443
24 4/16	15 1/16	9 3/16	Knight Inlet, BC	Steven C. Gromatzky	Steven C. Gromatzky	1988	443
24 4/16	15	9 4/16	Gathto Creek, BC	James I. Scott	James I. Scott	1988	443
24 4/16	15 8/16	8 12/16	Thutade Lake, BC	George R. Kennedy, Jr.	George R. Kennedy, Jr.	1992	443
24 4/16	15	9 4/16	Chisana River, AK	Shelby R. Smithey	Shelby R. Smithey	1994	443
24 4/16	15 8/16	8 12/16	Scoop Lake, BC	Mark S. Coles	Mark S. Coles	1996	443
24 4/16	14 10/16	9 10/16	Unalakleet, AK	Stanley R. Godfrey	Stanley R. Godfrey	1997	443
24 3/16	15 2/16	9 1/16	Nabesna, AK	Ernest B. Schur	Ernest B. Schur	1958	460
24 3/16	14 14/16	9 5/16	Moose Creek, BC	R. Angell	R. Angell	1964	460
24 3/16	15 8/16	8 11/16	Gardiner, MT	Marguerite McDonald	Marguerite McDonald	1964	460
24 3/16	15 2/16	9 1/16	Toba Inlet, BC	Kenneth L. Wagner, Jr.	Kenneth L. Wagner, Jr.	1968	460

24 3/16	14 14/16	9 5/16	Likely, BC	Louis Tremblay	Louis Tremblay	1970	460
24 3/16	15 1/16	9 2/16	Alaska Range, AK	Gilbert L. Shelton	Gilbert L. Shelton	1975	460
24 3/16	15 2/16	9 1/16	Parsnip River, BC	Richard O.A. Gunther	Richard O.A. Gunther	1976	460
24 3/16	14 5/16	9 14/16	Tetlin Indian Res., AK	Robert B. Rhyne	Robert B. Rhyne	1976	460
24 3/16	14 13/16	9 6/16	Kuskokwim River, AK	Roger J. Ahern	Roger J. Ahern	1977	460
24 3/16	15 6/16	8 13/16	Big River, AK	Dale G. Moffat	Dale G. Moffat	1977	460
24 3/16	15 8/16	8 11/16	Nusatsum River, BC	Randy Svisdahl	Randy Svisdahl	1983	460
24 3/16	15	9 3/16	White Creek, AK	J.H. Harvey & V. Landt	John H. Harvey, Jr.	1985	460
24 3/16	14 15/16	9 4/16	Squirrel River, AK	Bob L. Eubank	Bob L. Eubank	1986	460
24 3/16	14 15/16	9 4/16	Monashee Mts., BC	Georg Frisch	Georg Frisch	1986	460
24 3/16	14 14/16	9 5/16	Sinclair Mills, BC	Steven L. Gingras	Steven L. Gingras	1986	460
24 3/16	15 6/16	8 13/16	Christmas Creek, AK	Charles L. Fuller	Charles L. Fuller	1988	460
24 3/16	14 14/16	9 5/16	Henry Creek, AK	Ray S. Smith	Ray S. Smith	1990	460
24 3/16	15 2/16	9 1/16	Nuka River, AK	Gene Hynes	Gene Hynes	1991	460
24 3/16	15 5/16	8 14/16	Ghost Lake, BC	Thomas J. Pagel	Thomas J. Pagel	1991	460
24 3/16	15 9/16	8 10/16	Lake Owikeno, BC	Robert Smink	Robert Smink	1993	460
24 3/16	15 2/16	9 1/16	Colville River, AK	Thomas D. Suedmeier	Thomas D. Suedmeier	1993	460
24 3/16	15 4/16	8 15/16	Sulphur Creek, BC	Bud Dow	Bud Dow	1996	460
24 2/16	15 2/16	9 1/16	John Hansen Lake, AK	Beverly A. Wiesner	Beverly A. Wiesner	1997	483
24 2/16	15 3/16	8 15/16	Chisana River, AK	Larry Folger	Larry Folger	1961	483
24 2/16	14 15/16	9 3/16	McDonnell Lake, BC	W.C. Gardiner	W.C. Gardiner	1966	483
24 2/16	15 2/16	9	Dawson City, YT	Donald R. Hull	Donald R. Hull	1971	483
24 2/16	15 9/16	8 9/16	Bella Coola, BC	Hugh M. Klein	Hugh M. Klein	1972	483
24 2/16	15	9 2/16	Sikanni Chief River, BC	Dale E. Mirr	Dale E. Mirr	1973	483
24 2/16	15 4/16	8 14/16	Quintette Mt., BC	Dennis J. Brady	Dennis J. Brady	1977	483
24 2/16	15 1/16	9 1/16	Chatanika River, AK	Robert L. Nelson	Robert L. Nelson	1981	483
24 2/16	15 9/16	8 9/16	Koeye River, BC	William H. Dunstan IV	William H. Dunstan IV	1983	483
24 2/16	15 10/16	8 8/16	Kuskokwim River, AK	Anthony J. Bianchi	Anthony J. Bianchi	1984	483
24 2/16	15 10/16	8 8/16	Deep Valley Creek, AB	Gerald Desjardins	Gerald Desjardins	1984	483
24 2/16	15	9 2/16	Casadepaga River, AK	Richard L. Hoffman	Richard L. Hoffman	1987	483
24 2/16	14 12/16	9 6/16	Mason River, NT	Gary G. Dumdei	Gary G. Dumdei	1992	483
24 2/16	14 14/16	9 4/16	Noatak River, AK	David M. Smith	David M. Smith	1994	483
24 2/16	14 14/16	9 4/16	Anvik River, AK	Chilton E. Miles, Jr.	Chilton E. Miles, Jr.	1996	483
24 1/16	15 10/16	8 7/16	Owikeno Lake, BC	R.C. Bentzen	R.C. Bentzen	1960	497
24 1/16	15 3/16	8 14/16	Flathead Co., MT	T.H. Soldowski	T.H. Soldowski	1963	497
24 1/16	14 12/16	9 5/16	Brooks Range, AK	Ted Schlaepfer	Ted Schlaepfer	1964	497
24 1/16	14 14/16	9 3/16	Nabesna River, AK	F.C. Hibben	F.C. Hibben	1967	497
24 1/16	14 15/16	9 2/16	Quesnel, BC	Larry Chaves	Larry Chaves	1968	497
24 1/16	14 9/16	9 8/16	Toklat River, AK	Ronald Lauretti	Ronald Lauretti	1971	497
24 1/16	15 7/16	8 10/16	California Creek, AK	Boyd J. Blair	Boyd J. Blair	1975	497
24 1/16	14 15/16	9 2/16	Gataga River, BC	James E. Carson	James E. Carson	1977	497
24 1/16	15 2/16	8 15/16	Tatlatui Lake, BC	Paul S. Burke, Jr.	Paul S. Burke, Jr.	1978	497
24 1/16	14 14/16	9 3/16	Sukunka River, BC	Albert R. Heikel, Jr.	Albert R. Heikel, Jr.	1979	497
24 1/16	15	9 1/16	King Salmon River, BC	Phil Forte	Phil Forte	1981	497
24 1/16	15 1/16	9	Noatak River, AK	Stephen P. Connell	Stephen P. Connell	1984	497
24 1/16	15 11/16	9 6/16	Pine River, BC	Brian R. Goates	Brian R. Goates	1985	497
24 1/16	15 5/16	8 12/16	Little Red Rock Creek, AB	Patrick Casey	P. Casey & B. Winters	1987	497

GRIZZLY BEAR

Ursus arctos horribilis

Score	Greatest Length of Skull Without Lower Jaw	Greatest Width of Skull	Locality	Hunter	Owner	Date Killed	Rank
24 1/16	15 1/16	9	Hunter Creek, AK	Leonard L. Taig	Leonard L. Taig	1992	497
24 1/16	15 3/16	8 14/16	Blackman Creek, BC	James A. Springer	James A. Springer	1994	497
24	15 5/16	8 11/16	Bella Coola, BC	Wynn Beebe	Wynn Beebe	1960	513
24	15 4/16	8 12/16	Wood River, AK	Gordon Studer	Gordon Studer	1963	513
24	15 2/16	8 14/16	Cantwell, AK	Donald R. Johnson	Donald R. Johnson	1964	513
24	14 11/16	9 5/16	Little Tok River, AK	Herbert F. Fassler	Herbert F. Fassler	1966	513
24	15	9	Fernie, BC	James Sloan	James Sloan	1967	513
24	14 14/16	9 2/16	Fairbanks, AK	Rudolf von Strasser	Rudolf von Strasser	1968	513
24	15 12/16	8 4/16	Bella Coola, BC	Alton A. Myhrvold	Alton A. Myhrvold	1969	513
24	14 9/16	9 7/16	Alaska Range, AK	R.A. Schriewer	R.A. Schriewer	1969	513
24	14 14/16	9 2/16	Canyon Lake, BC	Luther E. Lilly	Luther E. Lilly	1970	513
24	14 9/16	9 7/16	Ayiyak River, AK	Tom Toscano	Tom Toscano	1971	513
24	14 12/16	9 4/16	Kuskokwim Mts., AK	James V. Travis	James V. Travis	1974	513
24	15 4/16	8 12/16	Ram River, AB	Howard Bugg	Howard Bugg	1976	513
24	14 12/16	9 4/16	Andreafsky River, AK	Bruce K. Kent	Bruce K. Kent	1980	513
24	15 5/16	8 11/16	Kitsumkalum River, BC	Bill Gourlie	Bill Gourlie	1984	513
24	14 11/16	9 5/16	Kelly River, AK	Thomas W. Becker	Thomas W. Becker	1986	513
24	14 12/16	9 4/16	Stikine River, BC	Lynn F. Greenlee	Lynn F. Greenlee	1987	513
24	15 1/16	8 15/16	Draney Inlet, BC	Tim Dernbach	Tim Dernbach	1988	513
24	14 14/16	9 2/16	Nome River, AK	Samuel J. Nicolosi, Jr.	Samuel J. Nicolosi, Jr.	1990	513
24	14 8/16	9 8/16	Koyuk River, AK	Thomas A. Vaughn	Thomas A. Vaughn	1990	513
24	15 1/16	8 15/16	Bastille Creek, BC	Robert Learie	Robert Learie	1991	513
24	14 13/16	9 3/16	Talik Ridge, AK	William J. Papineau	William J. Papineau	1991	513
24	15	9	Caribou Creek, AK	Lee M. Wahlund	Lee M. Wahlund	1991	513
24	14 12/16	9 4/16	Toklat River, AK	James W. Rodgers	James W. Rodgers	1993	513

CATEGORY
GRIZZLY BEAR

SCORE
26-5/16

HUNTER
REMO PIZZAGALLI

LOCATION
KOYUK RIVER, AK

DATE OF KILL
APRIL 1996

CATEGORY
GRIZZLY BEAR

SCORE
25-5/16

HUNTER
RICHARD R. LINDSAY

LOCATION
DEADLOCK MT., AK

DATE OF KILL
APRIL 1995

CATEGORY
GRIZZLY BEAR

SCORE
25-1/16

HUNTER
DOUG W. SIX

LOCATION
MORICE RIVER, BC

DATE OF KILL
MAY 1991

ALASKA BROWN BEAR

WORLD'S RECORD

RANK
World's Record

SCORE
30 12/16

LOCATION
Kodiak Island, AK

HUNTER
Roy Lindsley

OWNER
Los Angeles County
Museum

DATE KILLED
1952

Alaska's Kodiak Island, just below Cook Inlet, supports the largest land-based carnivores in the world. The World's Record for the Alaska brown bear (*Ursus arctos middendorffi*) continues to hold with a score at 30-12/16 after being taken in late May, 1952, near Karluk Lake, Kodiak Island. This immense bear was collected by a scientific expedition headed by Melville N. Lincoln and was sponsored by a habitat group affiliated with the Los Angeles County Museum. The actual shot was made by Roy R. Lindsley, an employee of the U.S. Fish and Wildlife Service in Kodiak, who was working in co-operation with the scientists. Lindsley, who had never before shot an Alaska brown bear, had many years of experience working among these intelligent giants Technically, the Alaska brown bear and grizzly bear are classified as the same species, *Ursus arctos*. The Alaska brown bears that have been genetically and physically isolated on Kodiak Island have slightly varied skull proportions, claw shape and dentition that have set them apart from browns found elsewhere in Alaska, and are therefore classified as a separate subspecies. A mature boar can weigh as much as 1,500 pounds after feeding on Coho salmon during the autumn season, and when he rises upright from the river bank to test the coastal winds, may stand well over nine feet tall. As a seasoned observer, Lindsley knew that he would need a heavy bullet that could deliver sufficient force in order to make a clean kill and prevent the possibility of the bear charging or running away. He took down the record-sized male brown bear using the 180-grain bullet in a .30-06 rifle. Nearly ten years later, another large Alaska brown bear was harvested from Kodiak Island after being shot by Erling Hansen. Scored at 30-11/16, Hansen's trophy placed second in the 1961 Competition. ∎

ALASKA BROWN BEAR
WORLD'S RECORD SCORECHART

Measurements are taken with calipers or by using parallel perpendiculars, to the nearest one-sixteenth of an inch, without reduction of fractions. Official measurements cannot be taken until the skull has air dried for at least 60 days after the animal was killed. All adhering flesh, membrane and cartilage must be completely removed before official measurements are taken.

A. **Greatest Length** is measured between perpendiculars parallel to the long axis of the skull, without the lower jaw and excluding malformations.
B. **Greatest Width** is measured between perpendiculars at right angles to the long axis.

Records of
North American
Big Game

250 Station Drive
Missoula, MT 59801
(406) 542-1888

BOONE AND CROCKETT CLUB®
OFFICIAL SCORING SYSTEM FOR NORTH AMERICAN BIG GAME TROPHIES

BEAR

	MINIMUM SCORES	
	AWARDS	ALL-TIME
black bear	20	21
grizzly bear	23	24
Alaska brown bear	26	28
polar bear	27	27

KIND OF BEAR (check one)
☐ black bear
☐ grizzly
■ Alaska brown bear
☐ polar

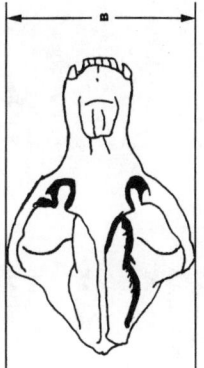

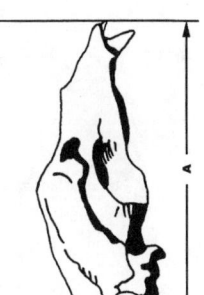

SEE OTHER SIDE FOR INSTRUCTIONS	MEASUREMENTS
A. Greatest Length Without Lower Jaw	17 15/16
B. Greatest Width	12 13/16
FINAL SCORE	30 12/16

Exact Locality Where Killed: **Karluk Lake, AK**

Date Killed: **May 28, 1952** Hunter: **Roy Lindsley**

Owner: **Los Angeles County Museum** Telephone #:

Owner's Address:

Guide's Name and Address:

Remarks: (Mention Any Abnormalities or Unique Qualities)

I, _____**Grancel Fitz**_____ , certify that I have measured this trophy on _____**03/11/1953**_____
PRINT NAME   MM/DD/YYYY

at **5 Tudor City Place**   **New York**   **N Y**
STREET ADDRESS   CITY   STATE/PROVINCE

and that these measurements and data are, to the best of my knowledge and belief, made in accordance with the instructions given.

Witness: _____**Samuel B. Webb**_____ Signature: _____**Grancel Fitz**_____ I.D. Number ☐☐☐
                                                                                        B&C OFFICIAL MEASURER

ALASKA BROWN BEAR

Ursus arctos middendorffi and certain related subspecies

MINIMUM SCORE 28

Score	Greatest Length of Skull Without Lower Jaw	Greatest Width of Skull	Locality	Hunter	Owner	Date Killed	Rank
30 12/16	17 15/16	12 13/16	Kodiak Island, AK	Roy Lindsley	Los Angeles Co. Museum	1952	1
30 11/16	18 10/16	12 1/16	Kodiak Island, AK	Erling Hansen	Erling Hansen	1961	2
30 9/16	18 7/16	12 2/16	Kodiak Island, AK	Fred A. Henton	Los Angeles Co. Museum	1938	3
30 8/16	18 12/16	11 12/16	Bear River, AK	Cap Wagner	Univ. Calif. Museum	PR 1908	4
30 8/16	18	12 8/16	Kodiak Island, AK	W.S. Brophy, Jr. & W.E. McClure	W.S. Brophy III	1966	4
30 7/16	19 13/16	10 10/16	Port Heiden, AK	Herschel A. Lamb	Herschel A. Lamb	1961	6
30 5/16	18	12 5/16	Deadman Bay, AK	Grancel Fitz	Mrs. Grancel Fitz	1955	7
30 4/16	18 12/16	11 8/16	Kodiak Island, AK	Donald S. Hopkins	Unknown	1940	8
30 4/16	18 12/16	11 8/16	Kodiak Island, AK	Jack Roach	Jack Roach	1947	8
30 4/16	18	12 4/16	Kodiak Island, AK	T.H. McGregor	T.H. McGregor	1960	8
30 4/16	18 5/16	11 15/16	Kodiak Island, AK	Will Gay	Will Gay	1997	8
30 3/16	18 2/16	12 1/16	Kodiak Island, AK	W.J. Fisher	U.S. Natl. Museum	PR 1904	12
30 3/16	18	12 3/16	Kodiak Island, AK	Oliver L. Durbin	Ben Hurtado	1952	12
30 3/16	18 12/16	11 7/16	Kodiak Island, AK	A.L. Hooker	A.L. Hooker	1958	12
30 2/16	18	12 2/16	Uyak Bay, AK	Walter H. White	B&C National Collection	1954	15
30 2/16	18 7/16	11 11/16	Kodiak Island, AK	Dave Connor	Dave Connor	1957	15
30 1/16	18 1/16	12	Kodiak Island, AK	Seymour P. Smith	U.S. Natl. Museum	1927	17
30 1/16	18 3/16	11 14/16	Kodiak Island, AK	John M. Tait	John M. Tait	1957	17
30 1/16	18 4/16	11 15/16	Alinchak Bay, AK	Clarence R. Scott	Clarence R. Scott	1961	17
30 1/16	18 12/16	11 5/16	Cold Bay, AK	Randy J. Cain	Randy J. Cain	1992	17
29 15/16	18 6/16	11 9/16	Kodiak Island, AK	Donald S. Hopkins	Unknown	1939	21
29 15/16	18 6/16	11 9/16	Kodiak Island, AK	Samuel Atkinson	Samuel & Florence Atkinson	1953	21
29 14/16	18 2/16	11 12/16	Unimak Island, AK	Fred W. Shield	Fred W. Shield	1950	23
29 14/16	18	11 14/16	Kodiak Island, AK	Unknown	Kim Clark	1958	23
29 14/16	17 15/16	11 15/16	Kodiak Island, AK	H.F. Primosch	H.F. Primosch	1959	23
29 14/16	18	11 14/16	Aliulik Pen., AK	Cindy L. Rhodes	Cindy L. Rhodes	1997	23
29 13/16	17 9/16	12 4/16	Nelson Lagoon, AK	Unknown	Harry H. Webb	1946	27
29 13/16	**18 5/16**	**11 8/16**	**Cold Bay, AK**	**Robert C. Reeve**	**Am. Mus. Nat. Hist.**	**1948**	**27**
29 13/16	18 6/16	11 7/16	Alaska Pen., AK	Lud W. Rettig	Denver Mus. Nat. Hist.	1955	27
29 13/16	18 5/16	11 8/16	Alaska Pen., AK	Don Johnson	Don Johnson	1962	27
29 13/16	17 14/16	11 15/16	Sturgeon River, AK	W. Ted Burger	W. Ted Burger	1985	27
29 13/16	17 13/16	11 15/16	Kodiak Island, AK	William D. Holmes	William D. Holmes	1957	32
29 12/16	18 11/16	11 1/16	Alaska Pen., AK	Russell J. Uhl	Russell J. Uhl	1963	32
29 11/16	17 13/16	11 14/16	Kodiak Island, AK	Herman Gibson	Herman Gibson	1951	34
29 11/16	17 9/16	12 2/16	Kodiak Island, AK	James H. Nash	James H. Nash	1954	34
29 11/16	17 12/16	11 15/16	Kodiak Island, AK	A.J. Taylor & E.A. Chappell	Allen J. Taylor	1976	34
29 10/16	17 13/16	11 13/16	Kodiak Island, AK	Eddie W. Stinnett	Eddie W. Stinnett	1974	37
29 9/16	19 1/16	10 8/16	Unimak Island, AK	A.C. Gilbert	A.C. Gilbert	1950	38

Score	Length	Width	Locality	Hunter	Owner	Date	Rank
29 9/16	17 7/16	12 2/16	Kodiak, AK	Peter W. Bading	Peter W. Bading	1964	38
29 8/16	17 14/16	11 10/16	Kodiak Island, AK	E.M. & H. Rusten	Elmer M. Rusten	1941	40
29 8/16	18 14/16	10 10/16	Mother Goose Lake, AK	Tom Moore	Chicago Nat. Hist. Mus.	1947	40
29 8/16	17 13/16	11 11/16	Kodiak Island, AK	F.W. Crail	F.W. Crail	1950	40
29 8/16	17 10/16	11 14/16	Kodiak Island, AK	W.H. Cothrum	W.H. Cothrum	1953	40
29 8/16	18 6/16	11 2/16	Cold Bay, AK	W.P. Waltz	W.P. Waltz	1953	40
29 8/16	17 12/16	11 12/16	Kodiak Island, AK	Carlos Alden	Carlos Alden	1956	40
29 8/16	18 4/16	11 4/16	Alaska Pen., AK	Charles Gates	Charles Gates	1960	40
29 8/16	18	11 8/16	Alaska Pen., AK	Sam Pancotto	Sam Pancotto	1963	40
29 8/16	18 2/16	11 6/16	Port Heiden, AK	Robert J. Miller	Robert J. Miller	1971	40
29 8/16	17 12/16	11 12/16	Sturgeon River, AK	Anthony Gioffre	Anthony Gioffre	1984	40
29 8/16	18 1/16	11 7/16	Kaiuguak Bay, AK	Martin H. Shaft	Martin H. Shaft	1990	40
29 7/16	17 10/16	11 13/16	Kodiak Island, AK	Robert R. Snodgrass	Robert R. Snodgrass	1949	51
29 7/16	17 8/16	11 15/16	Deadman Bay, AK	Ira M. Piper	Ira M. Piper	1954	51
29 7/16	17 11/16	11 12/16	Kodiak Island, AK	Keith Chisholm	Keith Chisholm	1956	51
29 7/16	17 13/16	11 10/16	Kodiak Island, AK	Richard Van Dyke	Richard Van Dyke	1957	51
29 7/16	17 13/16	11 10/16	Kodiak Island, AK	H.I.H. Prince Abdorreza Pahlavi	H.I.H. Prince Abdorreza Pahlavi	1967	51
29 7/16	17 15/16	11 8/16	Cold Bay, AK	Jiro Miyamoto	Jiro Miyamoto	1992	51
29 6/16	18 2/16	11 4/16	Pavlof Bay, AK	Willie Pavlof	U.S. Natl. Museum	1897	57
29 6/16	17 13/16	11 9/16	Belkofski Bay, AK	Laurenti Kuzakin	U.S. Natl. Museum	1897	57
29 6/16	17 15/16	11 7/16	Pavlof Bay, AK	H. Cutting	U.S. Natl. Museum	1917	57
29 6/16	18	11 8/16	Cold Bay, AK	Ira A. Minnick	U.S. Natl. Museum	1923	57
29 6/16	18 5/16	11 11/16	Alaska Pen., AK	E.I. Garrett	Am. Mus. Nat. Hist.	1926	57
29 6/16	17 9/16	11 13/16	Kodiak Island, AK	John S. Day	John S. Day	1953	57
29 6/16	17 6/16	12	Amook Island, AK	Albert C. Bledsoe	Albert C. Bledsoe	1959	57
29 6/16	18 3/16	11 3/16	Kodiak Island, AK	Herb Klein	Herb Klein	1965	57
29 6/16	18 6/16	11 6/16	Stepovak Bay, AK	Roy Fencl	Roy Fencl	1966	57
29 5/16	18 7/16	10 14/16	Cold Bay, AK	Edwin Mallinkrodt, Jr.	U.S. Natl. Museum	1920	66
29 5/16	17 12/16	11 9/16	Sand Lake, AK	William A. Fisher	William A. Fisher	1953	66
29 5/16	18 1/16	11 8/16	Kodiak Island, AK	Picked Up	Am. Mus. Nat. Hist.	PR 1957	66
29 5/16	17 13/16	11 4/16	Braided Creek, AK	Robert L. Coleman	Robert L. Coleman	1991	66
29 5/16	17 12/16	11 9/16	Kodiak Island, AK	Jerry D. Johnson	Jerry D. Johnson	1996	66
29 4/16	17 14/16	11 14/16	Kodiak Island, AK	A.C. Skinner, Jr.	A.C. Skinner, Jr.	1951	71
29 4/16	17 6/16	11 6/16	Kodiak Island, AK	H.R. Eavey & H. Wright	Harry R. Eavey	1960	71
29 4/16	17 5/16	11 2/16	Alaska Pen., AK	Johnnie White	Horns of Hunter Tr. Post	1962	71
29 4/16	18 2/16	11	Alaska Pen., AK	H.S. Kamil	H.S. Kamil	1963	71
29 4/16	18 4/16	11 9/16	Port Heiden, AK	Ashley C. Sanders	Ashley C. Sanders	1965	71
29 4/16	17 11/16	11 11/16	Deadman Bay, AK	George W. Aldredge	George W. Aldredge	1996	71
29 4/16	17 9/16	10 9/16	Spiridon Lake, AK	Dennis S. Boyer	Dennis S. Boyer	1997	71
29 3/16	18 10/16	11 4/16	Alaska Pen., AK	J.A. Atkinson	Am. Mus. Nat. Hist.	1948	78
29 3/16	17 15/16	11 9/16	Port Moller Bay, AK	A.M. Harper	A.M. Harper	1949	78
29 3/16	17 10/16	11 6/16	Kodiak Island, AK	Fred B. Hawk	Fred B. Hawk	1959	78
29 3/16	17 13/16	11 4/16	Kodiak Island, AK	William H. Sleith	Lutz Junior Museum	1966	78
29 3/16	17 15/16	11 15/16	Port Heiden, AK	Ralph E. Smith	Ralph E. Smith	1966	78
29 3/16	18 9/16	10 10/16	Mother Goose Lake, AK	Robert Denis	Robert Denis	1967	78
29 3/16	18	11 3/16	Alaska Pen., AK	Peter Ma	Peter Ma	1990	78
29 3/16	18 5/16	10 14/16	Alaska Pen., AK	T. Michael McMahon	T. Michael McMahon	1994	78

ALASKA BROWN BEAR

Ursus arctos middendorffi and certain related subspecies

Score	Greatest Length of Skull Without Lower Jaw	Greatest Width of Skull	Locality	Hunter	Owner	Date Killed	Rank
29 2/16	17 10/16	11 8/16	Kodiak Island, AK	Mrs. J. Watson Webb	Mrs. J. Watson Webb	1948	86
29 2/16	17 14/16	11 4/16	Alaska Pen., AK	Mrs. John J. Louis, Jr.	Mrs. John J. Louis, Jr.	1955	86
29 2/16	17 15/16	11 3/16	Kodiak Island, AK	Alan O. Hickok	Alan O. Hickok	1957	86
29 2/16	17 11/16	11 7/16	Port Moller, AK	Milton Knapp	Milton Knapp	1960	86
29 2/16	17 10/16	11 8/16	Kodiak Island, AK	Edward F. Pedersen, Jr.	Edward F. Pedersen, Jr.	1961	86
29 2/16	18 3/16	10 15/16	Alaska Pen., AK	Kenneth Richmond	Kenneth Richmond	1962	86
29 2/16	17 10/16	11 8/16	Alaska Pen., AK	Wesley Pollock	Wesley Pollock	1964	86
29 2/16	18 3/16	10 15/16	Ugashik, AK	Joseph K. Link	Buffalo Mus. of Sci.	1966	86
29 2/16	18 2/16	11	Alaska Pen., AK	Richard Hodous	Richard Hodous	1966	86
29 3/16	17 7/16	11 11/16	Kodiak Island, AK	John F. Ries	John F. Ries	1967	86
29 2/16	18 10/16	10 8/16	Balboa Bay, AK	William C. LeMasters	William C. LeMasters	1994	86
29 1/16	17 8/16	11 9/16	Kodiak Island, AK	John C. Ayres	Signa J. Byers	1934	97
29 1/16	17 10/16	11 7/16	Kodiak Island, AK	H.H. Kissinger	H.H. Kissinger	1961	97
29 1/16	17 11/16	11 6/16	Port Heiden, AK	Marshall Carr	Marshall Carr	1963	97
29 1/16	17 11/16	11 6/16	Ugashik Lakes, AK	George Purdie	George Purdie	1963	97
29 1/16	18 2/16	10 15/16	Port Moller, AK	Russell H. Underdahl	Russell H. Underdahl	1967	97
29 1/16	17 15/16	11 2/16	Cold Bay, AK	George Caswell	George Caswell	1984	97
29 1/16	17 12/16	11 5/16	Fraser Lake, AK	Randy D. Klingenmeyer	Randy D. Klingenmeyer	1991	97
29	17 10/16	11 6/16	Kodiak Island, AK	John Fox	John Fox	1959	104
29	17 14/16	11 2/16	Kodiak Island, AK	Raymond C. Boystel	Raymond C. Boystel	1963	104
29	18 2/16	10 14/16	Cold Bay, AK	J.S. Parker	J.S. Parker	1964	104
29	17 12/16	11 4/16	Cold Bay, AK	Fritz A. Nachant	Fritz A. Nachant	1965	104
29	18 6/16	10 10/16	Yakutat, AK	Jack DeWald	Jack DeWald	1973	104
29	17 15/16	11 1/16	Kodiak Island, AK	Creig M. Sharp	Creig M. Sharp	1977	104
29	18 3/16	10 13/16	Alaska Pen., AK	Johnnie R. Lowe	Johnnie R. Lowe	1979	104
29	17 12/16	11 4/16	Shearwater Bay, AK	Chester E. Chellman	Chester E. Chellman	1987	104
29	17 12/16	11 4/16	Kiavak Bay, AK	John L. Largura	John L. Largura	1987	104
29	17 14/16	11 2/16	Amber Bay, AK	Richard M. Welch	Richard M. Welch	1988	104
29	17 8/16	11 8/16	Middle Bay, AK	Royal V. Large, Jr.	Royal V. Large, Jr.	1990	104
29	17 5/16	11 11/16	Kodiak Island, AK	James D. Nyce	James D. Nyce	1990	104
29	18 3/16	10 13/16	Karluk Lake, AK	Robert W. Stevens	Robert W. Stevens	1990	104
28 15/16	17 11/16	11 2/16	Port Moller Bay, AK	C.A. Stenger	C.A. Stenger	1951	117
28 15/16	17 13/16	11 2/16	Alaska Pen., AK	G.W. Folta	G.W. Folta	1954	117
28 15/16	17 6/16	11 9/16	Kodiak Island, AK	Robert T. Leever	Robert T. Leever	1959	117
28 15/16	17 12/16	11 3/16	Kodiak Island, AK	H.T. Hilderbrandt	H.T. Hilderbrandt	1961	117
28 15/16	17 15/16	11	Sand Lake, AK	J.J. Stallone	J.J. Stallone	1962	117
28 15/16	17 14/16	11 1/16	Port Moller, AK	Andrew S. Allen	Andrew S. Allen	1963	117
28 15/16	17 8/16	11 7/16	Kodiak Island, AK	Stephen A. Mihal	Stephen A. Mihal	1969	117

Score	Length	Width	Locality	Hunter	Owner	Date	Rank
28 15/16	17 11/16	11 4/16	Alaska Pen., AK	James A. Johnson	James A. Johnson	1970	117
28 15/16	17 4/16	11 11/16	Kodiak Island, AK	Robert E. Pippen	Robert E. Pippen	1975	117
28 15/16	18 1/16	10 14/16	Mother Goose Lake, AK	John H. Buckman	John H. Buckman	1976	117
28 15/16	17 7/16	11 8/16	Kiliuda Bay, AK	Dean J. Walden	Dean J. Walden	1980	117
28 15/16	18 4/16	10 11/16	Stepovak Bay, AK	Kurt A. Haskin	Kurt A. Haskin	1986	117
28 15/16	18 7/16	10 8/16	Alaska Pen., AK	Ron D. King	Ron D. King	1988	117
28 15/16	17 8/16	11 7/16	Olga Bay, AK	Alan O'Neil	Alan O'Neil	1988	117
28 15/16	17 5/16	11 10/16	Kodiak Island, AK	Geoffrey H.S. House	Geoffrey H.S. House	1989	117
28 15/16	17 6/16	11 9/16	Dog Salmon River, AK	John H. Sholtiss	John H. Sholtiss	1989	117
28 15/16	17 14/16	11 1/16	Kodiak Island, AK	George Pappas	George Pappas	1992	117
28 14/16	17 13/16	11 1/16	Yakataga Beach, AK	Stanley P. Young	Stanley P. Young	1933	134
28 14/16	16 12/16	12 4/16	Kodiak Island, AK	A.J. Casper	A.J. Casper	1936	134
28 14/16	17 7/16	11 7/16	Kodiak Island, AK	Jack Honhart	Jack Honhart	1952	134
28 14/16	18 5/16	10 9/16	Alaska Pen., AK	Herb Elliott	Herb Elliott	1960	134
28 14/16	17 6/16	11 6/16	Kodiak Island, AK	Maurice S. Ireland	Maurice S. Ireland	1961	134
28 14/16	18 5/16	10 9/16	Alaska Pen., AK	Ethel Prine	Ethel Prine	1964	134
28 14/16	18	10 14/16	Alaska Pen., AK	Richard Kilbane	Richard Kilbane	1965	134
28 14/16	17 5/16	11 9/16	Kodiak Island, AK	William B. Valen	William B. Valen	1965	134
28 14/16	17 14/16	11	Skwentna River, AK	Gerald N. Felando	Gerald N. Felando	1971	134
28 14/16	17 12/16	11 2/16	Alaska Pen., AK	Richard N. Von	Richard N. Von	1975	134
28 14/16	17 12/16	11 6/16	Kodiak Island, AK	Robert A. Wainscott	Robert A. Wainscott	1978	134
28 14/16	17 3/16	11 11/16	Olga Bay, AK	William G. James	William G. James	1989	134
28 14/16	18 5/16	10 9/16	Muddy River, AK	Chung C. Huang	Chung C. Huang	1990	134
28 14/16	17 12/16	11 2/16	Meshik River, AK	R. Jackson Willingham	R. Jackson Willingham	1990	134
28 14/16	18 11/16	10 3/16	Cold Bay, AK	Dick A. Jacobs	Dick A. Jacobs	1991	134
28 14/16	17 5/16	11 9/16	Zachar Bay, AK	Richard E. Metzger	Richard E. Metzger	1992	134
28 14/16	17 8/16	11 6/16	Olga Bay, AK	Harvey R. Carson	Harvey R. Carson	1993	134
28 14/16	17 9/16	11 5/16	Aliulik Pen., AK	Annemarie Rome	Annemarie Rome	1993	134
28 13/16	18 2/16	10 11/16	Hoodoo Lake, AK	A.C. Gilbert	A.C. Gilbert	1950	152
28 13/16	17 4/16	11 9/16	Port Heiden, AK	John Du Puy	John Du Puy	1951	152
28 13/16	17 12/16	11 1/16	Fraser Lake, AK	Rupert Chisholm	Rupert Chisholm	1956	152
28 13/16	17 15/16	10 14/16	Alaska Pen., AK	Elgin T. Gates	Elgin T. Gates	1960	152
28 13/16	17 13/16	11 13/16	Kodiak Island, AK	Charles Daniels	Charles Daniels	1962	152
28 13/16	17 6/16	11 7/16	Kodiak, AK	Hal Waugh	Hal Waugh	1964	152
28 13/16	17 12/16	11 1/16	Alaska Pen., AK	Ernest Rush, Jr.	Ernest Rush, Jr.	1966	152
28 13/16	17 10/16	11 3/16	Deadman Bay, AK	Michael R. Anderson	Michael R. Anderson	1971	152
28 13/16	17 8/16	11 5/16	Herring Bay, AK	Michael F. Short	Michael F. Short	1983	152
28 13/16	17 14/16	10 15/16	Beaver Bay, AK	Jesse T. Kirk	Jesse T. Kirk	1988	152
28 13/16	17 13/16	11	Kejulik River, AK	Yuko Sato	Yuko Sato	1993	152
28 12/16	18	10 12/16	Sand Lake, AK	A.C. Gilbert	A.C. Gilbert	1939	163
28 12/16	18 2/16	10 10/16	Sand Lake, AK	Jules V. Lane	Jules V. Lane	1939	163
28 12/16	18 4/16	10 8/16	Pavlof Bay, AK	Robert R. Stewart	Robert R. Stewart	1949	163
28 12/16	18 2/16	10 10/16	Alaska Pen., AK	Harry H. Webb	Harry H. Webb	1952	163
28 12/16	17 5/16	11 7/16	Kodiak Island, AK	Robert D. Boone	Robert D. Boone	1960	163
28 12/16	17 11/16	11 11/16	Alaska Pen., AK	Bert Klineburger	Bert Klineburger	1961	163
28 12/16	17 12/16	11	Alaska Pen., AK	Hans O. Meissner	Hans O. Meissner	1961	163
28 12/16	17 11/16	11 1/16	Karluk Lake, AK	Alberto F. Ruiloha	Alberto F. Ruiloha	1962	163

ALASKA BROWN BEAR

Ursus arctos middendorffi and certain related subspecies

Score	Greatest Length of Skull Without Lower Jaw	Greatest Width of Skull	Locality	Hunter	Owner	Date Killed	Rank
28 12/16	16 14/16	11 14/16	Kodiak Island, AK	Vernon C. Jensen	Vernon C. Jensen	1963	163
28 12/16	17 2/16	11 10/16	Alaska Pen., AK	Bert Klineburger	Bert Klineburger	1964	163
28 12/16	17 9/16	11 3/16	Kodiak Island, AK	Joe M. Floyd, Jr.	Joe M. Floyd, Jr.	1966	163
28 12/16	17 15/16	10 13/16	Kodiak Island, AK	Clyde Ormond	Clyde Ormond	1968	163
28 12/16	18 2/16	10 10/16	Cold Bay, AK	Ted J. Forsi	Ted J. Forsi	1975	163
28 12/16	17 4/16	11 8/16	Kodiak Island, AK	Roy H. Tyler	Roy H. Tyler	1977	163
28 12/16	17 4/16	11 8/16	Kaiugnak Bay, AK	Dale E. Machacek	Dale E. Machacek	1984	163
28 12/16	17 5/16	11 7/16	Red Lake, AK	Joe B. Brewster	Joe B. Brewster	1985	163
28 12/16	17 14/16	10 14/16	Lilly Lake, AK	Darryl W. Indvik	Darryl W. Indvik	1987	163
28 12/16	17 3/16	11 9/16	Deadman Bay, AK	Marvin Shick	Marvin Shick	1989	163
28 12/16	17 8/16	11 4/16	Uganik Bay, AK	George M. Schmidt	George M. Schmidt	1992	163
28 12/16	17 12/16	11	Dog Salmon Creek, AK	Gene J. Brzek	Gene J. Brzek	1995	163
28 11/16	18 4/16	10 7/16	Cinder River, AK	George W. Vaughan	George W. Vaughan	1951	183
28 11/16	17 6/16	11 5/16	Kodiak Island, AK	John Treillet	John Treillet	1953	183
28 11/16	18 7/16	11 5/16	Kodiak Island, AK	Harold J. Ahrendt	Harold J. Ahrendt	1957	183
28 11/16	17 3/16	10 4/16	Alaska Pen., AK	Edward R. Crooks	Edward R. Crooks	1958	183
28 11/16	18 2/16	11 8/16	Kodiak Island, AK	Anthony A. Caldrone	Anthony A. Caldrone	1962	183
28 11/16	17 15/16	10 9/16	Alaska Pen., AK	Basil C. Bradbury	Basil C. Bradbury	1963	183
28 11/16	17 7/16	10 12/16	Afognak Island, AK	Clyde Gett	Clyde Gett	1969	183
28 11/16	17 5/16	11 4/16	Afognak Island, AK	Charles Hettman	Charles Hettman	1969	183
28 11/16	17 3/16	10 5/16	Afognak Island, AK	William A. Bardot	William A. Bardot	1972	183
28 11/16	18 6/16	11 8/16	Bear Lake, AK	Leon A. Naccarato	Leon A. Naccarato	1980	183
28 11/16	17 3/16	11 3/16	Deadman Bay, AK	James S. Fogel	James S. Fogel	1982	183
28 11/16	17 8/16	10 14/16	Kodiak Island, AK	Terry M. Webb	Terry M. Webb	1986	183
28 11/16	17 13/16	10 15/16	Cold Bay, AK	Simon Aragi	Simon Aragi	1988	183
28 11/16	17 12/16	10 15/16	Cold Bay, AK	John F. Bermen	John F. Bermen	1988	183
28 10/16	18 3/16	10 8/16	Littlejohn Lagoon, AK	Anthony C. Henry	Anthony C. Henry	1990	200
28 10/16	17 6/16	11 5/16	Kodiak Island, AK	John T. Dembowiak	John T. Dembowiak	1992	200
28 10/16	17 5/16	11 6/16	Deadman Bay, AK	Raymond L. Holmes	Raymond L. Holmes	1993	200
28 10/16	18 6/16	10 4/16	Pavlof Bay, AK	R.H. Rockwell	U.S. Natl. Museum	1921	200
28 10/16	17 2/16	10 8/16	Alaska Pen., AK	Harry H. Webb	Harry H. Webb	1952	200
28 10/16	17 11/16	10 15/16	Alaska Pen., AK	Arthur C. Popham, Jr.	Arthur C. Popham, Jr.	1953	200
28 10/16	17 3/16	11 7/16	Kodiak Island, AK	Kenneth D. Landes	Kenneth D. Landes	1954	200
28 10/16	17 9/16	11 1/16	Kodiak Island, AK	Pat Soderburg	Pat Soderburg	1959	200
28 10/16	17 4/16	11 6/16	Alaska Pen., AK	Selmer Torrison	Selmer Torrison	1959	200
28 10/16	18 1/16	10 9/16	Alaska Pen., AK	Win Condict	Win Condict	1960	200
28 10/16	17 4/16	11 6/16	Cordova, AK	Wallace Fields	Wallace Fields	1962	200
28 10/16	17 12/16	10 14/16	Kodiak Island, AK	Alfonso Pasquel	Alfonso Pasquel	1962	200

Score	Length	Width	Locality	Hunter	Owner	Date	Rank
$28\ ^{10}/_{16}$	$17\ ^{8}/_{16}$	$11\ ^{2}/_{16}$	Alaska Pen., AK	Frederick O. Kielmam	Frederick O. Kielmam	1963	200
$28\ ^{10}/_{16}$	$17\ ^{3}/_{16}$	$11\ ^{7}/_{16}$	Kodiak, AK	Michael Friedland	Michael Friedland	1964	200
$28\ ^{10}/_{16}$	$17\ ^{9}/_{16}$	$11\ ^{1}/_{16}$	Alaska Pen., AK	Ed Shapiro	Ed Shapiro	1964	200
$28\ ^{10}/_{16}$	$17\ ^{5}/_{16}$	$11\ ^{5}/_{16}$	Kodiak Island, AK	John E. Crook	John E. Crook	1965	200
$28\ ^{10}/_{16}$	$17\ ^{8}/_{16}$	$11\ ^{2}/_{16}$	Pavlof Bay, AK	William M. Kessner	William M. Kessner	1965	200
$28\ ^{10}/_{16}$	$17\ ^{10}/_{16}$	11	Kodiak Island, AK	Alex W. McCoy III	Alex W. McCoy III	1965	200
$28\ ^{10}/_{16}$	$17\ ^{8}/_{16}$	$11\ ^{2}/_{16}$	Alaska Pen., AK	C.J. McElroy	C.J. McElroy	1965	200
$28\ ^{10}/_{16}$	$17\ ^{12}/_{16}$	$10\ ^{14}/_{16}$	Port Gravina, AK	Norton T. Montague	Norton T. Montague	1967	200
$28\ ^{10}/_{16}$	$17\ ^{1}/_{16}$	$11\ ^{9}/_{16}$	Kodiak Island, AK	Louis R. Kaminsky	Louis R. Kaminsky	1972	200
$28\ ^{10}/_{16}$	$17\ ^{4}/_{16}$	$11\ ^{6}/_{16}$	Olga Bay, AK	Doug Latimer	Doug Latimer	1980	200
$28\ ^{10}/_{16}$	$17\ ^{14}/_{16}$	$10\ ^{12}/_{16}$	Long Bay, AK	Delbert E. Starr	Delbert E. Starr	1984	200
$28\ ^{10}/_{16}$	$17\ ^{5}/_{16}$	$11\ ^{5}/_{16}$	Kodiak, AK	Larry L. Stephens	Larry L. Stephens	1984	200
$28\ ^{10}/_{16}$	17	$11\ ^{10}/_{16}$	Kaguyak Bay, AK	Robert W. Bundtzen	Robert W. Bundtzen	1989	200
$28\ ^{10}/_{16}$	$17\ ^{2}/_{16}$	$11\ ^{8}/_{16}$	Kodiak Island, AK	John D. Powers	John D. Powers	1989	200
$28\ ^{10}/_{16}$	$17\ ^{14}/_{16}$	$10\ ^{12}/_{16}$	Alaska Pen., AK	James L. Kedrowski	James L. Kedrowski	1990	200
$28\ ^{10}/_{16}$	18	$10\ ^{10}/_{16}$	Aniakchak River, AK	Jeffrey D. Lapp	Jeffrey D. Lapp	1992	200
$28\ ^{10}/_{16}$	$17\ ^{14}/_{16}$	$10\ ^{12}/_{16}$	Hoodoo Lake, AK	Jerry B. Cotner	Jerry B. Cotner	1994	200
$28\ ^{10}/_{16}$	$17\ ^{12}/_{16}$	$10\ ^{14}/_{16}$	Sunday Creek, AK	Neil D. McKenzie	Neil D. McKenzie	1996	200
$28\ ^{9}/_{16}$	$17\ ^{8}/_{16}$	$11\ ^{1}/_{16}$	Alaska Pen., AK	Charles S. King	Camp Fire Club	1922	227
$28\ ^{9}/_{16}$	$17\ ^{11}/_{16}$	$10\ ^{14}/_{16}$	Kodiak Island, AK	Peggy M. Noles	Peggy M. Noles	1962	227
$28\ ^{9}/_{16}$	$17\ ^{7}/_{16}$	$11\ ^{2}/_{16}$	Kodiak Island, AK	Charles Askins	Charles Askins	1963	227
$28\ ^{9}/_{16}$	$17\ ^{5}/_{16}$	$11\ ^{4}/_{16}$	Becharof Lake, AK	Robert J. Brocker	Robert J. Brocker	1964	227
$28\ ^{9}/_{16}$	$17\ ^{6}/_{16}$	$11\ ^{3}/_{16}$	Cordova, AK	Marvin Kocurek	Marvin Kocurek	1966	227
$28\ ^{9}/_{16}$	$17\ ^{12}/_{16}$	$10\ ^{13}/_{16}$	Alaska Pen., AK	Robert L. Helms	Robert L. Helms	1966	227
$28\ ^{9}/_{16}$	$17\ ^{4}/_{16}$	$11\ ^{5}/_{16}$	Alaska Pen., AK	George H. Landreth	George H. Landreth	1973	227
$28\ ^{9}/_{16}$	18	$10\ ^{9}/_{16}$	Chichagof Island, AK	Stewart N. Shaft	Stewart N. Shaft	1975	227
$28\ ^{9}/_{16}$	$17\ ^{9}/_{16}$	11	Alaska Pen., AK	James B. Lindahl	James B. Lindahl	1987	227
$28\ ^{9}/_{16}$	$17\ ^{6}/_{16}$	$11\ ^{3}/_{16}$	Talkeetna Mts., AK	Max C. Schwab	Max C. Schwab	1989	227
$28\ ^{9}/_{16}$	$17\ ^{2}/_{16}$	$11\ ^{7}/_{16}$	Sitkalidak Island, AK	Travis L. Barber	Travis L. Barber	1991	227
$28\ ^{9}/_{16}$	$17\ ^{6}/_{16}$	$11\ ^{3}/_{16}$	Kodiak Island, AK	Robert K. Deligans	Robert K. Deligans	1992	227
$28\ ^{9}/_{16}$	$17\ ^{4}/_{16}$	$11\ ^{5}/_{16}$	Spiridon Bay, AK	Michael H. Bolo	Michael H. Bolo	1992	227
$28\ ^{9}/_{16}$	$16\ ^{12}/_{16}$	$11\ ^{13}/_{16}$	Uganik Bay, AK	Jay M. Haverstick	Jay M. Haverstick	1993	227
$28\ ^{9}/_{16}$	$17\ ^{3}/_{16}$	$11\ ^{6}/_{16}$	Olga Bay, AK	John B. Martin	John B. Martin	1994	227
$28\ ^{8}/_{16}$	$17\ ^{6}/_{16}$	$11\ ^{3}/_{16}$	Dog Salmon Creek, AK	Gary R. Ploeckelmann	Gary R. Ploeckelmann	1994	227
$28\ ^{8}/_{16}$	18	$10\ ^{9}/_{16}$	Kodiak Island, AK	Mrs. Donald S. Hopkins	Unknown	1939	227
$28\ ^{8}/_{16}$	$17\ ^{2}/_{16}$	$11\ ^{6}/_{16}$	Herendeen Bay, AK	Arthur Johnson	Univ. of Alaska	1950	243
$28\ ^{8}/_{16}$	$16\ ^{10}/_{16}$	$11\ ^{14}/_{16}$	Caribou Lake, AK	W.A. Heldt	W.A. Heldt	1956	243
$28\ ^{8}/_{16}$	$17\ ^{4}/_{16}$	$11\ ^{4}/_{16}$	Kodiak Island, AK	Gloria T. Zerega	Gloria T. Zerega	1956	243
$28\ ^{8}/_{16}$	17	$11\ ^{8}/_{16}$	Kodiak Island, AK	W.M. Hollinger	W.M. Hollinger	1958	243
$28\ ^{8}/_{16}$	$17\ ^{12}/_{16}$	$10\ ^{12}/_{16}$	Kodiak Island, AK	Ross Beach	Ross Beach	1963	243
$28\ ^{8}/_{16}$	$17\ ^{14}/_{16}$	$10\ ^{10}/_{16}$	Port Heiden, AK	Chic Kawahara	Chic Kawahara	1963	243
$28\ ^{8}/_{16}$	$17\ ^{4}/_{16}$	$11\ ^{4}/_{16}$	Alaska Pen., AK	W.H. Picher	W.H. Picher	1964	243
$28\ ^{8}/_{16}$	$17\ ^{6}/_{16}$	$11\ ^{2}/_{16}$	Unimak Island, AK	Richard A. Guthrie	Richard A. Guthrie	1974	243
$28\ ^{8}/_{16}$	$17\ ^{10}/_{16}$	$10\ ^{14}/_{16}$	Deadman Bay, AK	Frank Alabiso	Frank Alabiso	1976	243
$28\ ^{8}/_{16}$	$17\ ^{10}/_{16}$	$10\ ^{14}/_{16}$	Pavlof Bay, AK	Melvin Gillis	Melvin Gillis	1976	243
$28\ ^{8}/_{16}$	$17\ ^{10}/_{16}$	$10\ ^{14}/_{16}$	Karluk Lake, AK	Paul W. Hansen	Paul W. Hansen	1983	243
$28\ ^{8}/_{16}$	$17\ ^{4}/_{16}$	$11\ ^{4}/_{16}$	Kiavak Bay, AK	Robert J. Welsh, Jr.	Robert J. Welsh, Jr.	1987	243

ALASKA BROWN BEAR

Ursus arctos middendorffi and certain related subspecies

Score	Greatest Length of Skull Without Lower Jaw	Greatest Width of Skull	Locality	Hunter	Owner	Date Killed	Rank
28 8/16	17 12/16	10 12/16	Ash Creek, AK	Phil N. Alward	Phil N. Alward	1988	243
28 8/16	17 4/16	11 4/16	Viekoda Bay, AK	Houston Smith	Houston Smith	1989	243
28 8/16	17 8/16	11	Kodiak Island, AK	Andrew J. Fierro	Andrew J. Fierro	1991	243
28 8/16	16 15/16	11 9/16	Deadman Bay, AK	John L. Spencer	John L. Spencer	1991	243
28 8/16	17 14/16	10 10/16	Cold Bay, AK	Charles W. Drechsel III	Charles W. Drechsel III	1992	243
28 8/16	17 4/16	11 4/16	Malina Bay, AK	Ron T. Schmitz	Ron T. Schmitz	1994	243
28 8/16	17 6/16	10 6/16	Cinder River, AK	A.J. Foyt III	A.J. Foyt III	1995	243
28 7/16	18 2/16	11 1/16	Alaska Pen., AK	William Ronning	Lloyd Ronning	1958	263
28 7/16	16 12/16	11 11/16	Kodiak Island, AK	Bill Polland	Bill Polland	1959	263
28 7/16	17 15/16	10 8/16	Cold Bay, AK	Virgil Brill	Virgil Brill	1960	263
28 7/16	17 10/16	10 13/16	Alaska Pen., AK	Milton L. Knapp	Milton L. Knapp	1961	263
28 7/16	17 2/16	11 5/16	Kodiak Island, AK	Edward F. Pedersen	Edward F. Pedersen	1961	263
28 7/16	17 5/16	11 2/16	Kodiak Island, AK	Frank Rogers	Frank Rogers	1961	263
28 7/16	17 9/16	10 14/16	Alaska Pen., AK	Kenneth Golden	Kenneth Golden	1962	263
28 7/16	17 7/16	11	Afognak Island, AK	Robert Munger	Robert Munger	1962	263
28 7/16	17 13/16	10 10/16	Alaska Pen., AK	Sam Pancotto	Sam Pancotto	1962	263
28 7/16	17 13/16	10 10/16	Alaska Pen., AK	Dennis Burke	Dennis Burke	1964	263
28 7/16	17 10/16	10 13/16	Ugashik Lakes, AK	James E. Egger	James E. Egger	1966	263
28 7/16	17 11/16	10 12/16	Kodiak Island, AK	William A. Ross, Jr.	William A. Ross, Jr.	1968	263
28 7/16	17 2/16	11 5/16	Kodiak Island, AK	M.H. Brock	M.H. Brock	1971	263
28 7/16	17 11/16	10 12/16	Alaska Pen., AK	James E. Otto	James E. Otto	1973	263
28 7/16	17 4/16	11 3/16	Kodiak Island, AK	Virgil J. Sheppard	Virgil J. Sheppard	1978	263
28 7/16	17 8/16	10 15/16	Uganik River, AK	Donald W. Baxter	Donald W. Baxter	1985	263
28 7/16	17 8/16	10 15/16	Uganik Bay, AK	Mark T. Jacobson	Mark T. Jacobson	1989	263
28 7/16	18	10 7/16	Cold Bay, AK	George A. Bettas	George A. Bettas	1990	263
28 7/16	17 14/16	10 9/16	Karluk Lake, AK	Stanley N. Kaneshiro	Stanley N. Kaneshiro	1990	263
28 7/16	17 4/16	11 3/16	Uganik Island, AK	David S. Collett-Paule	James J. Brooks	1991	263
28 7/16	17 8/16	10 15/16	Unimak Island, AK	Danny V. Grangaard	Danny V. Grangaard	1991	263
28 7/16	17 9/16	10 14/16	Sandy River, AK	Lawrence W. Frisoli	Lawrence W. Frisoli	1992	263
28 7/16	17	11 7/16	Kodiak Island, AK	Kelly McClain	Kelly McClain	1993	263
28 7/16	17 1/16	11 6/16	Seven Rivers, AK	Karen H. Parks	Karen H. Parks	1993	263
28 7/16	16 10/16	11 13/16	Kodiak Island, AK	Gary F. Bogner	Gary F. Bogner	1994	263
28 7/16	17 13/16	10 10/16	Alaska Pen., AK	Stephen C. Walker	Stephen C. Walker	1994	263
28 7/16	17 11/16	10 12/16	Uyak Bay, AK	William E. Wilson	William E. Wilson	1996	263
28 6/16	17 15/16	10 7/16	Moroski Bay, AK	Ivan Katchinof	U.S. Natl. Museum	1897	290
28 6/16	17 14/16	10 8/16	Sand Lake, AK	Mrs. J. Watson Webb	Mrs. J. Watson Webb	1939	290
28 6/16	17 9/16	10 13/16	Kodiak Island, AK	Martin J. Coyne	Martin J. Coyne	1960	290
28 6/16	17 11/16	10 11/16	Alaska Pen., AK	Alberto Pipia	Alberto Pipia	1965	290

Score	Length	Width	Locality	Hunter	Owner	Date	Rank
28 6/16	17 8/16	10 14/16	Alaska Pen., AK	John F. Ault	John F. Ault	1967	290
28 6/16	17 4/16	11 2/16	Prince William Sound, AK	Ron Kacsmaryk	Ron Kacsmaryk	1970	290
28 6/16	17 14/16	11 8/16	Port Heiden, AK	Jack Holland, Jr.	Jack Holland, Jr.	1976	290
28 6/16	16 12/16	11 10/16	Kodiak Island, AK	Darrel Williams	Earl Hahn	1976	290
28 6/16	17 4/16	11 2/16	Port Heiden, AK	Russ McLennan	Russ McLennan	1980	290
28 6/16	17 2/16	11 4/16	Larsen Bay, AK	Sherron G. Perry	Sherron G. Perry	1983	290
28 6/16	17	11 6/16	Olga Bay, AK	David B. Colclough	David B. Colclough	1989	290
28 6/16	17 15/16	10 7/16	Pavlof Bay, AK	John R. Sullivan	John R. Sullivan	1989	290
28 6/16	17 2/16	11 4/16	Karluk River, AK	Terry J. Leffler	Terry J. Leffler	1990	290
28 6/16	17 2/16	11 4/16	Alaska Pen., AK	Robert W. Orzechowski	Robert W. Orzechowski	1991	290
28 6/16	17 3/16	11 3/16	Kodiak Island, AK	Thomas W. Triplett	Thomas W. Triplett	1997	290
28 5/16	17 14/16	10 7/16	Pavlof Bay, AK	Peter Ruppi	U.S. Natl. Museum	1897	305
28 5/16	17 4/16	11 1/16	Captain Harbor, AK	Tarleton F. Smith	MI State Univ. Mus.	1949	305
28 5/16	17 4/16	11 1/16	Cold Bay, AK	L.S. Kuter	L.S. Kuter	1952	305
28 5/16	16 14/16	11 7/16	Kodiak Island, AK	C.D. Fuller & F.C. Miller	C.D. Fuller & F.C. Miller	1959	305
28 5/16	17 4/16	11 7/16	Kodiak Island, AK	J.D. Roebuck	J.D. Roebuck	1960	305
28 5/16	17 14/16	10 7/16	Port Heiden, AK	John S. Cochran, Jr.	John S. Cochran, Jr.	1964	305
28 5/16	17 9/16	10 12/16	Alaska Pen., AK	J.B. Kerley	J.B. Kerley	1964	305
28 5/16	17 8/16	10 13/16	Mother Goose Lake, AK	H.T. Sliger	H.T. Sliger	1965	305
28 5/16	17 3/16	11 2/16	Kodiak Island, AK	Jerry Coon	Jerry Coon	1965	305
28 5/16	18	10 5/16	Port Heiden, AK	Leonard W. Bruns	Leonard W. Bruns	1967	305
28 5/16	18	10 8/16	Kodiak Island, AK	Chris Klineburger	Chris Klineburger	1967	305
28 5/16	16 15/16	11 6/16	Kodiak Island, AK	King Mahendra of Nepal	King Mahendra of Nepal	1968	305
28 5/16	17 6/16	10 15/16	Kodiak Island, AK	Theodore J. Schorsch, Sr.	Theodore J. Schorsch, Sr.	1976	305
28 5/16	18	10 5/16	Alaska Pen., AK	Keith W. Bates	Keith W. Bates	1981	305
28 5/16	17 3/16	11 2/16	Dog Salmon Creek, AK	John D. Valle	John D. Valle	1982	305
28 5/16	18	10 5/16	Foot Bay, AK	Larry A. McComb	Larry A. McComb	1984	305
28 5/16	17 9/16	10 12/16	Cold Bay, AK	Kenneth C. Hayden	Kenneth C. Hayden	1984	305
28 5/16	17 13/16	10 8/16	Cold Bay, AK	Timothy Orton	Timothy Orton	1985	305
28 5/16	17 7/16	10 14/16	Stuyahok River, AK	William S. Greene, Jr.	William S. Greene, Jr.	1988	305
28 5/16	16 12/16	11 9/16	Kodiak Island, AK	Roy F. Bain	Roy F. Bain	1989	305
28 5/16	17	11 5/16	Kaguyak Bay, AK	Arnold F. Thibault	Arnold F. Thibault	1990	305
28 5/16	17 4/16	11 1/16	Kodiak Island, AK	J. Dorsey Smith	J. Dorsey Smith	1993	305
28 5/16	17 12/16	11 4/16	Kiliuda Bay, AK	Teresa I. Ramos	Teresa I. Ramos	1994	305
28 5/16	18 1/16	10 9/16	Cinder River, AK	Scott M. Ackelson	Scott M. Ackelson	1996	305
28 5/16	17 12/16	9 13/16	Mt. Veniaminof, AK	Steve D. Adams	Steve D. Adams	1996	305
28 4/16	17	10 8/16	Port Moller, AK	Harry H. Webb	Harry H. Webb	1953	330
28 4/16	17 4/16	11 4/16	Afognak Island, AK	T.E. Shillingburg	T.E. Shillingburg	1954	330
28 4/16	17 8/16	11	Kodiak Island, AK	Edward M. Simko	Edward M. Simko	1957	330
28 4/16	17 9/16	11 8/16	Alaska Pen., AK	Willie D. Payton	Willie D. Payton	1959	330
28 4/16	17 4/16	10 11/16	Kodiak Island, AK	Jeffrey G. Burmeister	Jeffrey G. Burmeister	1960	330
28 4/16	18 4/16	10	Alaska Pen., AK	Jean Branson	Jean Branson	1962	330
28 4/16	17	11 4/16	Uganik Bay, AK	J. Coker & J. Meagher	Jerry Coker	1963	330
28 4/16	17 3/16	11 1/16	Kodiak Island, AK	Roy M. Champayne	Roy M. Champayne	1965	330
28 4/16	16 12/16	11 8/16	Kodiak Island, AK	Keith Honhart	Keith Honhart	1965	330
28 4/16	16 15/16	11 5/16	Kodiak Island, AK	James E. Nelson	James E. Nelson	1979	330
28 4/16	17 4/16	11	Olga Bay, AK	Allan E. Bergland	Allan E. Bergland	1981	330

ALASKA BROWN BEAR

Ursus arctos middendorffi and certain related subspecies

Score	Greatest Length of Skull Without Lower Jaw	Greatest Width of Skull	Locality	Hunter	Owner	Date Killed	Rank
28 4/16	17 12/16	10 8/16	Cinder River, AK	Javier Zubia	Javier Zubia	1981	330
28 4/16	17 9/16	10 11/16	Unimak Island, AK	John D. Frost	John D. Frost	1985	330
28 4/16	17 5/16	10 15/16	Alaska Pen., AK	H. Blake Allen	H. Blake Allen	1986	330
28 4/16	17 1/16	11 3/16	Kiavak Bay, AK	Garry V. Woodman	Garry V. Woodman	1992	330
28 4/16	17 6/16	10 14/16	Funny River, AK	Brian L. Larion	Brian L. Larion	1993	330
28 4/16	17	11 4/16	Kodiak Island, AK	Sam A. Francis	Sam A. Francis	1997	330
28 3/16	17 4/16	10 15/16	Aniakchak Bay, AK	Francis J. Fabick	Francis J. Fabick	1949	347
28 3/16	17 1/16	11 2/16	Kodiak Island, AK	Raymond A. Du Four	Raymond A. Du Four	1959	347
28 3/16	17 14/16	10 5/16	Alaska Pen., AK	Kenneth Holland	Kenneth Holland	1959	347
28 3/16	17 2/16	11 1/16	Kodiak Island, AK	William Offenheim	William Offenheim	1960	347
28 3/16	17 7/16	10 12/16	Alaska Pen., AK	Elmer Graham	Elmer Graham	1961	347
28 3/16	16 15/16	11 4/16	Kodiak Island, AK	Frank Hollendonner	Frank Hollendonner	1961	347
28 3/16	18	10 3/16	Port Moller, AK	John D. Phillips	John D. Phillips	1961	347
28 3/16	17 4/16	10 15/16	Port Heiden, AK	Michael Ferrell	Michael Ferrell	1964	347
28 3/16	18 4/16	9 15/16	Port Moller, AK	Ray Eyler	Ray Eyler	1966	347
28 3/16	17 6/16	10 13/16	Talkeetna Mts., AK	Robert W. Holladay	Robert W. Holladay	1966	347
28 3/16	16 15/16	11 4/16	Kodiak Island, AK	T. Kimball Hill	T. Kimball Hill	1967	347
28 3/16	17 5/16	10 14/16	Cathedral Valley, AK	J.M. Norton	J.M. Norton	1982	347
28 3/16	17 13/16	10 6/16	Volcano Bay, AK	L. Clark Kiser	L. Clark Kiser	1984	347
28 3/16	17 1/16	11 2/16	Red Lake, AK	Richard H. Neville	Richard H. Neville	1984	347
28 3/16	16 13/16	11 6/16	Kaguyak Bay, AK	Jack D. Revelle	Jack D. Revelle	1984	347
28 3/16	17 15/16	10 4/16	Cold Bay, AK	Carlos F.S. Schutz	Carlos F.S. Schutz	1990	347
28 3/16	17 3/16	11	Chekok Creek, AK	Dana L. Timaeus	Dana L. Timaeus	1995	347
28 2/16	16 11/16	11 7/16	Kodiak Island, AK	J. Watson Webb	J. Watson Webb	1948	364
28 2/16	17 12/16	10 6/16	Alaska Pen., AK	J.D. Jones	J.D. Jones	1954	364
28 2/16	18 1/16	10 1/16	Cold Bay, AK	Lewis E. Yearout	Lewis E. Yearout	1956	364
28 2/16	17	11 2/16	Kodiak Island, AK	Merril R. Reller	Merril R. Reller	1958	364
28 2/16	17 8/16	10 10/16	Cinder River, AK	Russell Cutter	Russell Cutter	1960	364
28 2/16	17 1/16	11 1/16	Kodiak Island, AK	Jim Alexander	Jim Alexander	PR 1961	364
28 2/16	17 10/16	10 8/16	Port Heiden, AK	Herman Kuchanek	Herman Kuchanek	1961	364
28 2/16	17 12/16	10 6/16	Alaska Pen., AK	Mrs. Sam Pancotto	Mrs. Sam Pancotto	1962	364
28 2/16	17 8/16	10 10/16	Alaska Pen., AK	Charles L. Ball, Jr.	Charles L. Ball, Jr.	1964	364
28 2/16	16 9/16	11 9/16	Kodiak Island, AK	Gordon G. Maclean	Gordon G. Maclean	1964	364
28 2/16	17 8/16	10 10/16	Unimak Island, AK	Don Burk	Don Burk	1966	364
28 2/16	17 12/16	10 6/16	Cold Bay, AK	Robert Hansen	Robert Hansen	1966	364
28 2/16	16 8/16	11 10/16	Eagle Harbor, AK	James T. Harrell	James T. Harrell	1966	364
28 2/16	17 10/16	10 8/16	Cold Bay, AK	John D. Jones	John D. Jones	1966	364
28 2/16	17 10/16	10 8/16	Alaska Pen., AK	Francis S. Levien	Francis S. Levien	1968	364

Score	Length of Skull	Width of Skull	Locality	By whom killed	Owner	Date	Rank
28 2/16	17 5/16	10 13/16	Afognak Island, AK	Laszlo Lemhenyi-Hanko	Laszlo Lemhenyi-Hanko	1970	364
28 2/16	17 5/16	10 13/16	Kodiak Island, AK	Dwight Hildebrandt	Dwight Hildebrandt	1971	364
28 2/16	16 9/16	11 9/16	Kodiak Island, AK	Bart D'Averso	Bart D'Averso	1974	364
28 2/16	17 3/16	10 15/16	Great Salmon Lake, AK	Siegfried Kube	Siegfried Kube	1974	364
28 2/16	17 2/16	11	Afognak Island, AK	Picked Up	David L. Lazer	PR 1976	364
28 2/16	17 4/16	10 14/16	Kodiak Island, AK	Charles A. Goldenberg	Charles A. Goldenberg	1978	364
28 2/16	17	11	Spiridon Lake, AK	Chris T. Hinchey	Bear Arms	1983	364
28 2/16	17 7/16	10 11/16	Cold Bay, AK	Lonnie W. McCurry, Sr.	Lonnie W. McCurry, Sr.	1984	364
28 2/16	17 1/16	11 1/16	Afognak Island, AK	Donald E. Peterson	Donald E. Peterson	1984	364
28 2/16	17 10/16	10 8/16	Cold Bay, AK	George A. Bettas	George A. Bettas	1986	364
28 2/16	17 12/16	10 13/16	Kiavak Bay, AK	Wayne E. Clark	Wayne E. Clark	1987	364
28 2/16	17 12/16	10 6/16	Pumice Creek, AK	Tony E. Jorgenson	Tony E. Jorgenson	1988	364
28 2/16	16 6/16	11 12/16	Meshik Lake, AK	Richard L. DeFelice	Richard L. DeFelice	1989	364
28 2/16	16 15/16	11 3/16	Uyak Bay, AK	Picked Up	Randy C. Arsenault	PR 1990	364
28 2/16	17 5/16	10 13/16	Karluk Lake, AK	Robert W. Stevens III	Robert W. Stevens III	1990	364
28 2/16	17 4/16	10 14/16	Port Heiden, AK	Florentino G. Escobedo	Florentino G. Escobedo	1991	364
28 2/16	17 2/16	11	Akwe River, AK	Roger R. Reck	Roger R. Reck	1991	364
28 2/16	17 6/16	10 12/16	Kodiak Island, AK	Michael P. Horstman	Michael P. Horstman	1992	364
28 2/16	16 13/16	11 5/16	Wildman Lake, AK	William M. Sumner	William M. Sumner	1993	364
28 2/16	17 10/16	10 8/16	Traders Mt., AK	Phillip D. Wagner	Phillip D. Wagner	1993	364
28 2/16	16 12/16	11 2/16	Glacier Bay, AK	Robert M. Daggett	Robert M. Daggett	1995	364
28 2/16	16 15/16	10 15/16	Uganik Bay, AK	William N. Adkins	William N. Adkins	1996	364
28 1/16	18	10 1/16	Port Moller, AK	Enos A. Axtell	Enos A. Axtell	1950	401
28 1/16	16 12/16	11 5/16	Alaska Pen., AK	R.H. Blum	R.H. Blum	1954	401
28 1/16	17	11 1/16	Kodiak Island, AK	Richard O. Daniels	Richard O. Daniels	1958	401
28 1/16	17 4/16	10 13/16	Kodiak Island, AK	Joe Maxwell	Joe Maxwell	1959	401
28 1/16	17 4/16	10 7/16	Kodiak Island, AK	L.W. Zeug	L.W. Zeug	1959	401
28 1/16	17 11/16	10 6/16	Alaska Pen., AK	Roscoe S. Mosiman	Roscoe S. Mosiman	1960	401
28 1/16	17	11 1/16	Cold Bay, AK	Keith C. Brown	Keith C. Brown	1962	401
28 1/16	16 15/16	11 2/16	Alaska Pen., AK	Bill Boone	Bill Boone	1964	401
28 1/16	17 8/16	10 8/16	Kodiak Island, AK	Dan G. Brown	Dan G. Brown	1967	401
28 1/16	17 9/16	10 1/16	Kodiak Island, AK	Cary E. Weldon	Cary E. Weldon	1968	401
28 1/16	18	10 1/16	Kodiak Island, AK	Bill Ulich	Bill Ulich	1976	401
28 1/16	18	10 12/16	Olga Bay, AK	Robert N. Wainscott	Robert N. Wainscott	1982	401
28 1/16	17 5/16	10 8/16	Port Heiden, AK	William H.F. Wiltshire	William H.F. Wiltshire	1984	401
28 1/16	17 9/16	10 11/16	Alaska Pen., AK	Kurt R. Clark	Kurt R. Clark	1986	401
28 1/16	17 7/16	10 5/16	Sturgeon River, AK	Michael R. Dullen	Michael R. Dullen	1987	401
28 1/16	17 12/16	10 6/16	Canoe Bay, AK	John E. Hoye	John E. Hoye	1987	401
28 1/16	17 11/16	11 9/16	Kodiak Island, AK	Bruce T. Berger	Bruce T. Berger	1988	401
28 1/16	16 8/16	10 14/16	Cinder River, AK	Keith Pilz	Keith Pilz	1989	401
28 1/16	17 3/16	10 14/16	Stepovak Bay, AK	Martin G. Glover	Martin G. Glover	1990	401
28 1/16	17 2/16	10 6/16	Afognak Island, AK	Gary M. Allen	Gary M. Allen	1993	401
28 1/16	17 10/16	11	Uganik Bay, AK	Edwin E. Orr	Edwin E. Orr	1993	401
28	17 2/16	10 14/16	Alaska Pen., AK	Harold Dugdale	Harold Dugdale	1954	422
28	17 15/16	10 1/16	Alaska Pen., AK	Robert D. Jones, Jr.	Robert D. Jones, Jr.	1955	422
28	17	11	Kodiak Island, AK	Harry F. Weyher	Harry F. Weyher	1958	422
28	17 15/16	10 1/16	Alaska Pen., AK	Fred Bear	Fred Bear	1960	422

ALASKA BROWN BEAR

Ursus arctos middendorffi and certain related subspecies

Score	Greatest Length of Skull Without Lower Jaw	Greatest Width of Skull	Locality	Hunter	Owner	Date Killed	Rank
28	17 12/16	10 4/16	Alaska Pen., AK	Wendell S. Fletcher	Wendell S. Fletcher	1960	422
28	17 7/16	10 9/16	Alaska Pen., AK	W.T. Yoshimoto	W.T. Yoshimoto	1961	422
28	17 3/16	10 13/16	Alaska Pen., AK	Gilbert Elton	Mrs. Gilbert Elton	1962	422
28	17 12/16	10 4/16	Port Moller, AK	Harry J. Armitage	Harry J. Armitage	1963	422
28	17 3/16	10 13/16	Kodiak Island, AK	Dean Herring	Dean Herring	1963	422
28	17 9/16	10 7/16	Alaska Pen., AK	James D. Smith	James D. Smith	1967	422
28	18	10	Alaska Pen., AK	Peter Santin	Peter Santin	1968	422
28	17 14/16	10 2/16	Alaska Pen., AK	Rudy Tuten	Rudy Tuten	1968	422
28	17	11	Alaska Pen., AK	James J. Fraioli	James J. Fraioli	1969	422
28	17 12/16	10 4/16	Alaska Pen., AK	Larry Lassley	Larry Lassley	1970	422
28	18	10	Chilkoot River, AK	Philip Nare	Philip Nare	1975	422
28	16 10/16	11 6/16	Ugak Bay, AK	Arnie Gutenkauf	Arnie Gutenkauf	1981	422
28	17 12/16	10 4/16	Windy Bay, AK	Archie H. Stevens, Sr.	Archie H. Stevens, Sr.	1982	422
28	16 15/16	11 1/16	Skilak Glacier, AK	Richard W. Carlock	Richard W. Carlock	1983	422
28	17 4/16	10 12/16	Afognak Lake, AK	Picked Up	Leon A. Metz	1984	422
28	17 5/16	10 11/16	Copper River, AK	Roger R. Card	Roger R. Card	1985	422
28	17 9/16	10 7/16	Cold Bay, AK	John D. Teeter	John D. Teeter	1988	422
28	17	11	Sulna Bay, AK	Theodore A. Mallett	Theodore A. Mallett	1989	422
28	17	11	Uganik Bay, AK	Donald M. Sitton	Donald M. Sitton	1990	422
28	17 1/16	10 15/16	Pedro Bay, AK	Fred W. Amyotte	Fred W. Amyotte	1991	422
28	16 12/16	11 4/16	Uganik Bay, AK	Gene J. Brzek	Gene J. Brzek	1991	422
28	17 4/16	10 12/16	Kiliuda Bay, AK	Theodore A. Mallett	Theodore A. Mallett	1994	422
28	17 7/16	10 9/16	Upper Ugashik Lake, AK	Michael A. Telles	Michael A. Telles	1994	422

CATEGORY
ALASKA BROWN BEAR

SCORE
30-4/16

HUNTER
WILL GAY

LOCATION
KODIAK ISLAND, AK

DATE OF KILL
APRIL 1997

CATEGORY
ALASKA BROWN BEAR

SCORE
30-1/16

HUNTER
RANDY J. CAIN

LOCATION
COLD BAY, AK

DATE OF KILL
MAY 1992

CATEGORY
ALASKA BROWN BEAR

SCORE
28-7/16

HUNTER
GEORGE A. BETTAS

LOCATION
COLD BAY, AK

DATE OF KILL
MAY 1990

141

CATEGORY
ALASKA BROWN BEAR

SCORE
29-7/16

HUNTER
JIRO MIYAMOTO

LOCATION
COLD BAY, AK

DATE OF KILL
MAY 1992

CATEGORY
ALASKA BROWN BEAR

SCORE
28-15/16

HUNTER
GEORGE PAPPAS

LOCATION
KODIAK ISLAND, AK

DATE OF KILL
MAY 1992

CATEGORY
ALASKA BROWN BEAR

SCORE
29-14/16

HUNTER
CINDY L. RHODES

LOCATION
ALIULIK PEN., AK

DATE OF KILL
APRIL 1997

FRED BEAR
1902-1988

Considered by many as the "father" of modern archery, Fred Bear was a brilliantly innovative designer of archery products, a successful manufacturer, adventurer and author. Born in 1902 in Pennsylvania, he began building archery equipment in 1927. He started hunting with a bow in 1929 and harvested a variety of game animals in North America and Africa, including high-ranking Stone's sheep and Alaska brown bear. He was awarded several key patents in the evolution of archery equipment. He was a member of the Boone and Crockett Club, the Adventurer's Club, the Explorer's Club and a charter member of the Pope and Young Club. Bear was also inducted into the Hunting Hall of Fame. ■

POLAR BEAR
WORLD'S RECORD

TROPHY INFO

RANK
World's Record

SCORE
29 $^{15}/_{16}$

LOCATION
Kotzebue, AK

HUNTER
Shelby Longoria

OWNER
Shelby Longoria

DATE KILLED
1963

The polar bear (Ursus maritimus) taken by Shelby Longoria of Matamoros, Mexico, continues to hold the World's Record. In the spring of 1963, Longoria headed from his home south of the border toward the far north, embarking on what would become a harrowing yet rewarding adventure. Choosing from outfitters who operated out of Cape Lisburne, Point Hope, and as far north as Point Barrow, Longoria made a decision to hunt out of Kotzebue, Alaska. Spring in the North American Arctic can be an ideal window for hunting as warm flickers of light provide a pleasing contrast to the dark tones of winter. However, unlike the polar bear that is partially insulated by their long, shaggy coats, it is possible for a man to die from exposure within a matter of minutes if he should plunge into the cold polar seas. This was only one of many dangers that lingered as Longoria and his guides searched the windswept and wave-sculpted ice fields near the Bering Strait and Chukchi Sea for the grandest bear they could find.

Nearly a hundred miles offshore, the hunting expedition located a promising ivory-white bear wandering against a treacherous background pocketed with bulging mounds of splintered ice. Utilizing powerful hindquarters and long legs with partially webbed feet, "bears of the sea" have been spotted swimming up to 300 miles from shore and are capable of bounding completely out of the water onto an ice floe. After undertaking a contrastingly dangerous landing on the sea ice, Longoria continued to stalk his prey through the frozen maze before eventually bagging the impressive polar bear. Scoring 29-15/16, Longoria's trophy topped the former record held by Tom Bolack. It should be noted that polar bears are extremely capable hunters due to their nearly exclusive carnivorous diet. As a result of this adaptation to their environment, these bears typically have longer, narrower skulls than the Alaska brown bear. ∎

144

POLAR BEAR
WORLD'S RECORD SCORECHART

Measurements are taken with calipers or by using parallel perpendiculars, to the nearest one-sixteenth of an inch, without reduction of fractions. Official measurements cannot be taken until the skull has air dried for at least 60 days after the animal was killed. All adhering flesh, membrane and cartilage must be completely removed before official measurements are taken.

A. **Greatest Length** is measured between perpendiculars parallel to the long axis of the skull, without the lower jaw and excluding malformations.

B. **Greatest Width** is measured between perpendiculars at right angles to the long axis.

Records of
North American
Big Game

BOONE AND CROCKETT CLUB®

250 Station Drive
Missoula, MT 59801
(406) 542-1888

OFFICIAL SCORING SYSTEM FOR NORTH AMERICAN BIG GAME TROPHIES

BEAR

MINIMUM SCORES

	AWARDS	ALL-TIME
black bear	20	21
grizzly bear	23	24
Alaska brown bear	26	28
polar bear	27	27

KIND OF BEAR (check one)

- ☐ black bear
- ☐ grizzly
- ☐ Alaska brown bear
- ■ polar

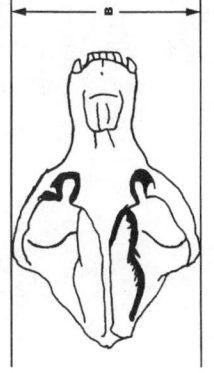

SEE OTHER SIDE FOR INSTRUCTIONS

	MEASUREMENTS
A. Greatest Length Without Lower Jaw	18 8/16
B. Greatest Width	11 7/16
FINAL SCORE	29 15/16

Exact Locality Where Killed: **Kotzebue, AK**

Date Killed: **April 11, 1983** Hunter: **Shelby Longoria**

Owner: **Shelby Longoria** Telephone #:

Owner's Address:

Guide's Name and Address:

Remarks: (Mention Any Abnormalities or Unique Qualities)

I, ___**Elgin T. Gates**___ , certify that I have measured this trophy on ___**03/06/1984**___

PRINT NAME   MM/DD/YYYY

at __**Carnegie Museum**__   __**Pittsburgh**__   __**PA**__

STREET ADDRESS   CITY   STATE/PROVINCE

and that these measurements and data are, to the best of my knowledge and belief, made in accordance with the instructions given.

Witness: ___**John H. Batten**___ Signature: ___**Elgin T. Gates**___ I.D. Number: _____

                               B&C OFFICIAL MEASURER

POLAR BEAR
Ursus maritimus

Score	Greatest Length of Skull Without Lower Jaw	Greatest Width of Skull	Locality	Hunter	Owner	Date Killed	Rank
29 15/16	18 8/16	11 7/16	Kotzebue, AK	Shelby Longoria	Shelby Longoria	1963	1
29 1/16	18 2/16	10 15/16	Kotzebue, AK	Louis Mussatoo	Louis Mussatoo	1965	2
28 12/16	17 13/16	10 15/16	Point Hope, AK	Tom F. Bolack	Tom F. Bolack	1958	3
28 12/16	17 11/16	11 1/16	Kotzebue, AK	Bill Nottley	Bill Nottley	1967	3
28 10/16	18	10 10/16	Little Diomede Island, AK	Richard G. Van Vorst	Richard G. Van Vorst	1963	5
28 10/16	17 8/16	11 2/16	Chukchi Sea, AK	Jack D. Putnam	Jack D. Putnam	1965	5
28 9/16	17 6/16	11 3/16	Kotzebue, AK	E.A. McCracken	E.A. McCracken	1966	7
28 8/16	17 6/16	11 2/16	Kotzebue, AK	Curtis S. Williams, Jr.	Curtis S. Williams, Jr.	1967	8
28 8/16	17 10/16	10 14/16	Kotzebue, AK	Winfred L. English	Winfred L. English	1968	8
28 7/16	17 5/16	11 2/16	Point Hope, AK	Rodney Lincoln	J.A. Columbus	1954	10
28 6/16	17 6/16	11	St. Lawrence Island, AK	H.B. Collins, Jr.	U.S. Natl. Museum	1929	11
28 6/16	17 8/16	10 14/16	Point Hope, AK	Clifford Thom	Clifford Thom	1964	11
28 6/16	17 3/16	11 3/16	Diomede Islands, AK	Stephen Pyle III	Stephen Pyle III	1965	11
28 5/16	17 10/16	10 11/16	Teller, AK	Walter Simas	Walter Simas	1966	14
28 4/16	18 2/16	10 2/16	Kotzebue, AK	Peter W. Bading	Peter W. Bading	1960	15
28 4/16	17 9/16	10 11/16	Big Diomede Island, AK	Vance A. Halverson	Vance A. Halverson	1963	15
28 4/16	17 7/16	10 13/16	Teller, AK	Jack C. Phillips	Jack C. Phillips	1964	15
28 3/16	17 9/16	10 10/16	Diomede Islands, AK	Louis F. Kincaid	Louis F. Kincaid	1955	18
28 3/16	17 15/16	10 4/16	Kotzebue, AK	Finis G. Cooper	Los Angeles Co. Museum	1959	18
28 3/16	17 12/16	10 7/16	Kotzebue, AK	S.D. Slaughter	S.D. Slaughter	1962	18
28 3/16	17 6/16	10 13/16	Kotzebue, AK	Harold Trulin	Harold Trulin	1962	18
28 3/16	17 6/16	10 13/16	Kotzebue, AK	C.J. McElroy	C.J. McElroy	1965	18
28 2/16	17 3/16	10 15/16	Big Diomede Island, AK	Francis Bogon	Francis Bogon	1957	23
28 2/16	17 6/16	10 12/16	Point Hope, AK	Pete Kesselring	Pete Kesselring	1957	23
28 2/16	17 1/16	11 1/16	Chukchi Sea, AK	Horace Steele	Horace Steele	1963	23
28 1/16	18 1/16	10	St. Paul Island, AK	C.H. Townsend	U.S. Natl. Museum	1875	26
28 1/16	17 6/16	10 11/16	Kotzebue, AK	Don Jahns	Don Jahns	1961	26
28	17 8/16	10 8/16	Point Hope, AK	Tommy Thompson	Pablo B. Romero	1958	28
28	17 7/16	10 9/16	Kotzebue, AK	Rupert Chisholm	Rupert Chisholm	1959	28
28	17 6/16	10 10/16	Point Hope, AK	William Stevenson	William Stevenson	1959	28
28	17 10/16	10 6/16	Kotzebue, AK	W.H. Hagenmeyer	W.H. Hagenmeyer	1961	28
28	17 5/16	10 11/16	Kotzebue, AK	Alberto Pipia	Alberto Pipia	1964	28
28	17 8/16	10 8/16	Kotzebue, AK	Leonard W. Bruns	Leonard W. Bruns	1966	28
27 15/16	17 6/16	10 9/16	Diomede Islands, AK	Russell C. Cutter	Russell C. Cutter	1960	34
27 15/16	17 8/16	10 7/16	Kotzebue, AK	Blair Truitt	Blair Truitt	1960	34
27 15/16	17 9/16	10 6/16	Kotzebue, AK	Jess L. Ferguson	Jess L. Ferguson	1961	34
27 15/16	17 4/16	10 11/16	Kotzebue, AK	William H. Smith, Jr.	William H. Smith, Jr.	1961	34
27 15/16	17 9/16	10 6/16	Kotzebue, AK	James S. Martin	James S. Martin	1962	34

Score	Length	Width	Locality	Hunter	Owner	Rank	Date
27 15/16	17 11/16	10 4/16	Teller, AK	R. Lynn Ross	R. Lynn Ross	34	1966
27 14/16	17 4/16	10 10/16	Point Barrow, AK	James W. Brooks	Univ. of Alaska	40	1952
27 14/16	17 10/16	10 4/16	Kotzebue, AK	Roy E. Weatherby	Roy E. Weatherby	40	1959
27 14/16	17 5/16	10 12/16	Kotzebue, AK	Don R. Downey	Don R. Downey	40	1960
27 14/16	17 2/16	10 9/16	Chukchi Sea, AK	C.D. Dofflemyer	C.D. Dofflemyer	40	1961
27 14/16	17 13/16	10 12/16	Kotzebue, AK	Nikolaus Koenig	Nikolaus Koenig	40	1966
27 13/16	17 7/16	10	Point Hope, AK	Hugh O'Dower	Hugh O'Dower	45	1959
27 13/16	17 8/16	10 6/16	Point Hope, AK	William P. Boone	William P. Boone	45	1960
27 13/16	17 3/16	10 5/16	Kotzebue, AK	Helen Burnett	Helen Burnett	45	1962
27 13/16	16 15/16	10 10/16	Cape Lisburne, AK	Charles Renaud	Charles Renaud	45	1963
27 13/16	17 4/16	10 14/16	Alaska Coast	Dale H. Wolff	Dale H. Wolff	45	1963
27 13/16	17 7/16	10 9/16	Chukchi Sea, AK	Lowell M. Cooke	Lowell M. Cooke	45	1965
27 13/16	17 5/16	10 6/16	Cape Lisburne, AK	Robert M. Mallett	Robert M. Mallett	45	1967
27 12/16	17 5/16	10 7/16	Kotzebue, AK	Edward M. Simko	Edward M. Simko	52	1956
27 12/16	17 6/16	10 6/16	Little Diomede Island, AK	J.E. Ottoviano	J.E. Ottoviano	52	1958
27 12/16	17 8/16	10 6/16	Kotzebue, AK	D.V. Merrick	D.V. Merrick	52	1959
27 12/16	17	10 4/16	Point Hope, AK	Owen K. Murphy	Owen K. Murphy	52	1959
27 12/16	17 2/16	10 12/16	Kotzebue, AK	A.H. Woodward, Jr.	A.H. Woodward, Jr.	52	1959
27 12/16	17 5/16	10 10/16	Kotzebue, AK	Arthur W. Clark	Arthur W. Clark	52	1963
27 12/16	17 4/16	10 8/16	Teller, AK	Louis Menegas	Louis Menegas	52	1963
27 11/16	17 4/16	10 8/16	Teller, AK	Earl W. Nystrom	Earl W. Nystrom	61	1965
27 11/16	16 4/16	11 7/16	Kotzebue, AK	William M. Kessner	William M. Kessner	61	1966
27 11/16	17 6/16	10 5/16	Kotzebue, AK	Arthur W. Smith	Arthur W. Smith	61	1963
27 11/16	17 7/16	10 4/16	Kotzebue, AK	Andrew S. Allen	Andrew S. Allen	61	1965
27 10/16	16 11/16	10 15/16	Kotzebue, AK	Patricia T. Bergstrom	Patricia T. Bergstrom	64	1965
27 10/16	17 6/16	10 6/16	Kotzebue, AK	Joe Foss	Joe Foss	64	1960
27 10/16	16 15/16	10 11/16	Little Diomede Island, AK	C.T. Kraftmeyer	C.T. Kraftmeyer	64	1962
27 10/16	17 4/16	10 6/16	Kotzebue, AK	Willard R. Skousen	Willard R. Skousen	64	1962
27 10/16	17 4/16	10 10/16	Kotzebue, AK	George P. Whittington	George P. Whittington	64	1962
27 10/16	17	10 4/16	Kotzebue, AK	Kenneth W. Vaughn	Kenneth W. Vaughn	64	1963
27 10/16	17 6/16	10 6/16	Point Hope, AK	Norma Wahrer	Norma Wahrer	64	1963
27 9/16	17 6/16	10 2/16	Kotzebue, AK	Robert L. Cohen	Robert L. Cohen	71	1966
27 9/16	17 7/16	10 3/16	Point Hope, AK	T.E. Shillingburg	T.E. Shillingburg	71	1957
27 9/16	17 6/16	10 12/16	Cape Thompson, AK	Daniel H. Cuddy	Daniel H. Cuddy	71	1959
27 9/16	16 13/16	10 5/16	Chukchi Sea, AK	Angelo Alessio	Angelo Alessio	71	1963
27 9/16	17 4/16	10 5/16	Point Hope, AK	Pat Auld	Pat Auld	71	1964
27 9/16	17 3/16	10 6/16	Diomede Islands, AK	Tony Oney	Tony Oney	71	1964
27 8/16	17 2/16	10 3/16	Kotzebue, AK	Harry D. Tousley	Harry D. Tousley	76	1961
27 8/16	17 5/16	10 3/16	Cape Lisburne, AK	Willard E. Flynn	Willard E. Flynn	76	1963
27 8/16	17 5/16	10 8/16	Point Hope, AK	Edward Frecker	Edward Frecker	76	1963
27 8/16	17	10	Kotzebue, AK	Ted Lick	Ted Lick	76	1965
27 8/16	17 1/16	10 7/16	Kotzebue, AK	Russell J. Uhl	Russell J. Uhl	76	1965
27 8/16	16 9/16	10 14/16	Pond Inlet, NT	Thomas H. Viuf	Thomas H. Viuf	76	1996
27 7/16	16 7/16	10 1/16	Kotzebue, AK	Mahlon T. Everhart	Mahlon T. Everhart	82	1959
27 7/16	17 5/16	10 2/16	Little Diomede Island, AK	Herb Klein	Herb Klein	82	1960
27 7/16	16 15/16	10 8/16	Kotzebue, AK	Gregory E. Koshell	Gregory E. Koshell	82	1961
27 7/16	16 15/16		Polar Circle, AK	Aurelio Caccomo	Aurelio Caccomo	82	1965

Score	Greatest Length of Skull Without Lower Jaw	Greatest Width of Skull	Locality	Hunter	Owner	Date Killed	Rank
27 7/16	16 7/16	10	Kotzebue, AK	Andrew De Matteo	Andrew De Matteo	1965	82
27 6/16	16 11/16	10 11/16	Wales, AK	Eskimo	Univ. of Alaska	1956	87
27 6/16	16 15/16	10 7/16	Cape Lisburne, AK	J.S. Lichtenfels	J.S. Lichtenfels	1957	87
27 6/16	17	10 6/16	Kotzebue, AK	W.H. Cato, Jr.	W.H. Cato, Jr.	1960	87
27 6/16	17 5/16	10 1/16	Kotzebue, AK	Gene Klineburger	Gene Klineburger	1963	87
27 6/16	17 3/16	10 3/16	Teller, AK	James O. Campbell	James O. Campbell	1964	87
27 6/16	17	10 6/16	Little Diomede Island, AK	Bob Payne	Bob Payne	1964	87
27 6/16	16 10/16	10 12/16	Kotzebue, AK	Glen E. Park	Glen E. Park	1965	87
27 6/16	16 13/16	10 9/16	Chukchi Sea, AK	Terry Kennedy	Terry Kennedy	1967	87
27 6/16	17	10 6/16	Kotzebue, AK	Harry Daum	Harry Daum	1971	87
27 5/16	16 13/16	10 8/16	Kotzebue, AK	W.L. Coleman	W.L. Coleman	1961	96
27 5/16	16 15/16	10 6/16	Point Barrow, AK	Bert Klineburger	Bert Klineburger	1963	96
27 5/16	17 1/16	10 4/16	Point Hope, AK	Charles A. McKinsey	Charles A. McKinsey	1963	96
27 5/16	17 1/16	10 4/16	Point Hope, AK	Sherman R. Whitmore	Sherman R. Whitmore	1963	96
27 5/16	16 9/16	10 12/16	Big Diomede Island, AK	Basil C. Bradbury	Basil C. Bradbury	1964	96
27 5/16	17 1/16	10 4/16	Bering Strait, AK	William D. Backman, Jr	William D. Backman, Jr.	1965	96
27 5/16	16 12/16	10 9/16	Kotzebue, AK	Lewis Figone	Lewis Figone	1965	96
27 5/16	16 12/16	10 9/16	Point Barrow, AK	James Senn	James Senn	1965	96
27 5/16	16 2/16	10 3/16	Point Hope, AK	R.K. Siller	R.K. Siller	1965	96
27 5/16	16 15/16	10 6/16	Kotzebue, AK	Gene Barrow	Gene Barrow	1966	96
27 5/16	17 4/16	10 1/16	Point Hope, AK	E.F. Simon	E.F. Simon	1968	96
27 4/16	16 13/16	10 7/16	Wales, AK	Eldon Brant	Univ. of Alaska	1957	107
27 4/16	17	10 4/16	Point Hope, AK	Charles Brauch	Charles Brauch	1960	107
27 4/16	16 12/16	10 8/16	Cape Lisburne, AK	Richard Hanks	Richard Hanks	1962	107
27 4/16	17 1/16	10 3/16	Point Hope, AK	C. Sam Sparks	C. Sam Sparks	1962	107
27 4/16	16 14/16	10 6/16	Kotzebue, AK	Ralph Lenheim	Ralph Lenheim	1964	107
27 4/16	16 15/16	10 5/16	Kotzebue, AK	Bill Taylor	Bill Taylor	1964	107
27 4/16	16 14/16	10 6/16	Teller, AK	Joseph O. Porter, Sr.	Joseph O. Porter, Sr.	1965	107
27 4/16	17	10 4/16	Kotzebue, AK	Russell Underdahl	Russell Underdahl	1965	107
27 3/16	17 5/16	9 14/16	Nome, AK	J.H. Rogers	J.H. Rogers	1956	115
27 3/16	17 5/16	9 14/16	Bering Strait, AK	Henry S. Budney	Henry S. Budney	1959	115
27 3/16	16 11/16	10 8/16	Kotzebue, AK	Bud Lotstedt	Bud Lotstedt	1959	115
27 3/16	16 13/16	10 6/16	Point Hope, AK	Kenneth Holland	Kenneth Holland	1960	115
27 3/16	17 4/16	9 15/16	Point Hope, AK	Bert Klineburger	Bert Klineburger	1961	115
27 3/16	16 12/16	10 7/16	Point Hope, AK	Richard Hanks	Richard Hanks	1962	115
27 3/16	16 13/16	10 6/16	Chukchi Sea, AK	Chas. P. Adkins	Chas. P. Adkins	1964	115
27 3/16	17 3/16	10	Kotzebue, AK	Barbara Sjoden	Barbara Sjoden	1966	115
27 3/16	17 1/16	10 2/16	Kotzebue, AK	Bernard Domries	Bernard Domries	1970	115

Score	Length	Width	Locality	Owner	Hunter	Date Killed	Rank
27 3/16	16 13/16	10 6/16	Banks Island, NT	Robert B. Nancarrow	Robert B. Nancarrow	1997	115
27 2/16	16 11/16	10 7/16	Point Hope, AK	Finis Gilbert	Finis Gilbert	1959	125
27 2/16	17 4/16	9 14/16	Point Hope, AK	C.C. Irving	C.C. Irving	1960	125
27 2/16	16 13/16	10 5/16	Kotzebue, AK	John F. Meyer	John F. Meyer	1960	125
27 2/16	16 15/16	10 3/16	Kotzebue, AK	W.T. Yoshimoto	W.T. Yoshimoto	1962	125
27 2/16	16 12/16	10 6/16	Point Barrow, AK	Frank Bydalek	Frank Bydalek	1963	125
27 2/16	17	10 2/16	Kotzebue, AK	E.B. Schur	E.B. Schur	1964	125
27 2/16	16 14/16	10 4/16	Chuckchi Sea, AK	R.G. Howlett	R.G. Howlett	1965	125
27 2/16	16 12/16	10 6/16	Shishmaref, AK	R.V. Hoyt & W.H. Otis	R.V. Hoyt & W.H. Otis	1965	125
27 1/16	16 15/16	10 2/16	Cape Lisburne, AK	Howard W. Pollock	Howard W. Pollock	1957	133
27 1/16	16 13/16	10 4/16	Kotzebue, AK	Glenn B. Walker	Glenn B. Walker	1959	133
27 1/16	17 7/16	9 10/16	Kotzebue, AK	True Davis	True Davis	1961	133
27 1/16	16 13/16	10 4/16	Point Hope, AK	Bill Ellis	Bill Ellis	1962	133
27 1/16	16 12/16	10 5/16	Diomede Islands, AK	Flavy Davis	Flavy Davis	1963	133
27 1/16	16 11/16	10 6/16	Little Diomede Island, AK	Tony Oney	Tony Oney	1963	133
27 1/16	16 10/16	10 7/16	Kotzebue, AK	Fritz Worster	Fritz Worster	1965	133
27 1/16	16 11/16	10 6/16	Kotzebue, AK	Marshall Johnson	Marshall Johnson	1965	133
27	16 14/16	10 2/16	Point Barrow, AK	George W. Roberts	George W. Roberts		142
27	16 15/16	10 1/16	Kotzebue, AK	U.S. Natl. Museum	T.L. Richardson	1917	142
27	17 2/16	9 14/16	Point Hope, AK	Dick Drew	Unknown	1959	142
27	16 7/16	10 9/16	Point Barrow, AK	T.A. Warren	T.A. Warren	1959	142
27	16 14/16	10 2/16	Kotzebue, AK	Clifford H. Dietz	Clifford H. Dietz	1960	142
27	16 12/16	10 4/16	Kotzebue, AK	Henry Blackford	Henry Blackford	1961	142
27	16 12/16	10 4/16	Kotzebue, AK	Cinn. Mus. Nat. Hist.	James T. Byrnes	1963	142
27	16 12/16	10 4/16	Kotzebue, AK	William A. Bond	William A. Bond	1964	142
27	16 8/16	10 8/16	Kotzebue, AK	Norman W. Garwood	Norman W. Garwood	1964	142
27	16 14/16	10 2/16	Kotzebue, AK	Charles E. Shedd	Charles E. Shedd	1964	142
27	16 9/16	10 7/16	Shishmaref, AK	Howard R. Driskell	Howard R. Driskell	1972	142
27 3/16 *	16 8/16	10 11/16	Banks Island, NT	James R. Gall	James R. Gall	1997	142

* Final score is subject to revision by additional verifying measurements.

CATEGORY
POLAR BEAR

SCORE
27-3/16

HUNTER
JAMES R. GALL

LOCATION
BANKS ISLAND, NT

DATE OF KILL
MARCH 1997

JAGUAR
WORLD'S RECORD

In 1965, C.J. McElroy returned from the jungle of Sinaola, Mexico, with a World's Record jaguar (*Felis onca*) scoring 18-7/16.

Hunting under the cover of night, McElroy adapted himself to the methods of this formidable predator, enduring oppressive heat, foul smelling swamps, ticks, chiggers and snakes, which jaguars prey on as regular reptile killers. It was a hunting experience that would remain with McElroy. Two years after taking the trophy, McElroy gave a hair-raising account of his encounter in an article for *Outdoor Life*. It reveals that at one point during the chase, the hunter became the hunted.

"The tigre was bleeding heavily, and his trail led us out of the grass and into thick jungle. About 100 yards farther, Hugo made a discovery that shook us. The trail of blood circled, and we were crossing the cat's original trail. There was some conversation in Spanish that I didn't understand. Then Hugo looked at me grimly.

"'The tigre is behind us!' he said.

"Hugo's words hit me with full impact. I knew that a wounded animal considering attack often doubles back to ambush the trackers from the rear. I still was confident in my ability with a rifle, and I believed I could kill the cat quickly if I had any chance at all."

Even though McElroy was shooting a light 100 grain bullet, his ability with a Winchester .270 saved his hide from the potentially fatal impact of the jaguar's teeth. The hunter and his guides emerged from a long night in the bush with what they knew was a magnificent trophy. On May 4, 1966, at the Club's 12th Biennial Awards dinner at the Carnegie Museum, McElroy's jaguar was officially recognized as the best taken in North America. McElroy's estimated 270 pound jaguar beat Jack Funk's 1924 record that scored 18-5/16 points and was killed in Cibecue, Arizona. Sadly for hunters, the joint pressures of agriculture and development drove the last jaguars from the U.S. in the 1940s and continue to lead to the loss of habitat for the largest North American cat. ∎

JAGUAR
WORLD'S RECORD SCORECHART

Measurements are taken with calipers or by using parallel perpendiculars, to the nearest one-sixteenth of an inch, without reduction of fractions. Official measurements cannot be taken until the skull has air dried for at least 60 days after the animal was killed. All adhering flesh, membrane and cartilage must be completely removed before official measurements are taken.

A. **Greatest Length** is measured between perpendiculars parallel to the long axis of the skull, without the lower jaw and excluding malformations.

B. **Greatest Width** is measured between perpendiculars at right angles to the long axis.

Records of
North American
Big Game

250 Station Drive
Missoula, MT 59801
(406) 542-1888

BOONE AND CROCKETT CLUB®

OFFICIAL SCORING SYSTEM FOR NORTH AMERICAN BIG GAME TROPHIES

COUGAR AND JAGUAR

MINIMUM SCORES		
	AWARDS	ALL-TIME
cougar	14 - 8/16	15
jaguar	14 - 8/16	14 - 8/16

KIND OF CAT (check one)
☐ cougar
■ jaguar

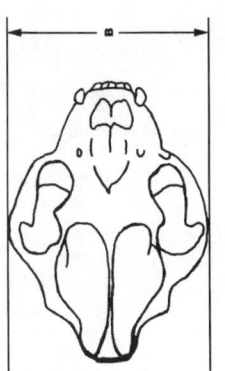

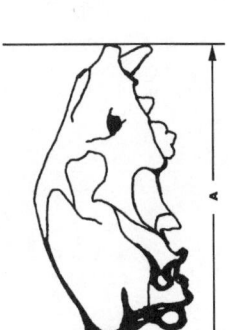

SEE OTHER SIDE FOR INSTRUCTIONS

	MEASUREMENTS
A. Greatest Length Without Lower Jaw	10 15/16
B. Greatest Width	7 8/16
FINAL SCORE	**18 7/16**

Exact Locality Where Killed: **Sinaola, MX**

Date Killed: **March 24, 1965** Hunter: **C.J. McElroy**

Owner: **C.J. McElroy**   Telephone #:

Owner's Address:

Guide's Name and Address:

Remarks: (Mention Any Abnormalities or Unique Qualities)

I, __**John E. Hammett**__ , certify that I have measured this trophy on __**02/28/1966**__
PRINT NAME   MM/D/D/YYYY

at __**Carnegie Museum**__   __**Pittsburgh**__   __**PA**__
STREET ADDRESS   CITY   STATE/PROVINCE

and that these measurements and data are, to the best of my knowledge and belief, made in accordance with the instructions given.

Signature: __**John E. Hammett**__   I.D. Number:
B&C OFFICIAL MEASURER

Witness: __**John H. Batten**__

JAGUAR

Felis onca hernandesii and related subspecies

MINIMUM SCORE 14 8/16

Score	Greatest Length of Skull Without Lower Jaw	Greatest Width of Skull	Locality	Hunter	Owner	Date Killed	Rank
18 7/16	10 15/16	7 8/16	Sinaola, MX	C.J. McElroy	C.J. McElroy	1965	1
18 5/16	10 14/16	7 7/16	Cibecue, AZ	Jack Funk	U.S. Natl. Mus.	1924	2
18 3/16	10 15/16	7 4/16	Nogales, AZ	Fred Ott	U.S. Natl. Mus.	1926	3
18 2/16	11	7 2/16	Vera Cruz, MX	E.W. Nelson & E.A. Goldman	U.S. Natl. Mus.	1894	4
17 15/16	10 9/16	7 6/16	Tehuantepec, MX	Francis Sumuchrast	U.S. Natl. Mus.	PR 1869	5
17 13/16	10 9/16	7 4/16	Guadalajara, MX	Elgin T. Gates	Elgin T. Gates	1954	6
17 11/16	10 11/16	7	Campeche, MX	Jacinta S. Dorantes	Squire Haskins	1960	7
17 10/16	10 9/16	7 1/16	Chiapas, MX	E.W. Nelson & E.A. Goldman	U.S. Natl. Mus.	1900	8
17 8/16	10 6/16	7	Tamaulipas, MX	Henderson Coquat	M. Nowotny	1940	9
17 8/16	10 8/16	7	Campeche, MX	Alex Hudson III	Alex Hudson III	1962	9
17 7/16	10 7/16	7	Tamaulipas, MX	Unknown	Bond Carroll	1959	11
17 6/16	10 7/16	6 15/16	Nayarit, MX	Aldegundo Garza de Leon	Aldegundo Garza de Leon	1969	12
17 2/16	10 6/16	6 12/16	Mills Co., TX	H.D. Attwater	U.S. Natl. Mus.	1903	13
17 2/16	10 5/16	6 13/16	Nayarit, MX	P. Mueller & D.O. Rudin	P. Mueller & D.O. Rudin	1959	13
17	10 4/16	6 12/16	Nayarit, MX	Graciano Guichard	Graciano Guichard	1969	15
16 15/16	10 4/16	6 11/16	Tamaulipas, MX	Squire Haskins	Dallas Mus. Nat. Hist.	1957	16
16 14/16	10 2/16	6 12/16	Helvetia, AZ	E.J. O'Doherty	U.S. Natl. Mus.	1917	17
16 14/16	10 5/16	6 9/16	Sonora, MX	Frank C. Hibben	Frank C. Hibben	1934	17
16 14/16	10 5/16	6 9/16	Sonora, MX	Frank C. Hibben	Frank C. Hibben	1934	17
16 14/16	10 4/16	6 10/16	Nayarit, MX	J.F. Brinkley	J.F. Brinkley	1959	17
16 13/16	9 12/16	7 2/16	Tampico, MX	Hector Elizondo	Hector Elizondo	1962	22
16 13/16	10 5/16	6 8/16	Nayarit, MX	G. Hooker & L. Stephens	George Hooker	1957	22
16 13/16	10 4/16	6 9/16	Tabasco, MX	W.T. Yoshimoto	W.T. Yoshimoto	1971	22
16 12/16	10 1/16	6 11/16	Nayarit, MX	Herb Klein	Herb Klein	1955	24
16 12/16	10 3/16	6 9/16	Nayarit, MX	Picked Up	Lawson E. Miller, Jr.	1959	24
16 11/16	9 15/16	6 12/16	Oaxaca, MX	Charles Oertel	U.S. Natl. Mus.	1899	26
16 11/16	9 14/16	6 13/16	Sonora, MX	Dick Wooddell	Dick Wooddell	1955	26
16 11/16	10 1/16	6 10/16	Ft. Apache Res., AZ	Russell Culbreath	Russell Culbreath	1964	26
16 10/16	9 11/16	6 15/16	Nayarit, MX	John Ryan	John Ryan	1962	29
16 10/16	9 14/16	6 12/16	Nayarit, MX	Morton J. Greene	Morton J. Greene	1965	29
16 9/16	9 14/16	6 11/16	Vera Cruz, MX	A. Wetmore & J. Canela	U.S. Natl. Mus.	1939	31
16 9/16	9 15/16	6 10/16	Tamaulipas, MX	Juan Lebeira	Juan Lebeira	1965	31
16 6/16	9 14/16	6 8/16	Tamaulipas, MX	Alex Hudson	Alex Hudson	1964	33
16 6/16	9 14/16	6 7/16	Nayarit, MX	William J. Campbell	William J. Campbell	1970	33
16 5/16	9 12/16	6 9/16	Nayarit, MX	George H. Hodges, Jr.	George H. Hodges, Jr.	1960	35
16 5/16	9 12/16	6 9/16	Nayarit, MX	O.J. Fletcher	O.J. Fletcher	1964	35
16 4/16	9 11/16	6 9/16	Nayarit, MX	Charles Binney II	443rd Hunting Club	1965	37
16 3/16	9 11/16	6 8/16	Nayarit, MX	Ventura G. Cosio	Ventura G. Cosio	1965	38

16 2/16	9 9/16	6 9/16	Arizona	Arvid F. Benson	Arvid F. Benson	1961	39
16 2/16	9 11/16	6 7/16	Tamaulipas, MX	Juan A. Saenz, Jr.	Juan A. Saenz, Jr.	1970	39
16 1/16	9 9/16	6 8/16	Tamaulipas, MX	A.D. Stenger	A.D. Stenger	1957	41
16	9 2/16	6 14/16	Tamaulipas, MX	Frank R. Denman	Frank R. Denman	1966	42
15 15/16	9 6/16	6 9/16	Tamaulipas, MX	Patrick W. Frederick	Patrick W. Frederick	1983	43
15 13/16	9 10/16	6 3/16	Tamaulipas, MX	Winfred L. English	Winfred L. English	1966	44
15 8/16	9 5/16	6 3/16	Nayarit, MX	Roy E. Cooper	Roy E. Cooper	1960	45
15 8/16	9 5/16	6 3/16	Nayarit, MX	Gene Biddle	Gene Biddle	1961	45
15 8/16	8 14/16	6 10/16	Tamaulipas, MX	O.A. Washburn	O.A. Washburn	1964	45
15 6/16	9 1/16	6 5/16	Patagonia Mts., AZ	Laurence L. McGee	Univ. of AZ	1965	48
15 5/16	9 1/16	6 4/16	Nayarit, MX	Jimmie Underwood	Steve M. Matthes	1963	49
15 2/16	9 2/16	6	Nayarit, MX	James G. Shirley, Jr.	James G. Shirley, Jr.	1959	50
15 1/16	9	6 1/16	Big Lake, AZ	Terry D. Penrod	Terry D. Penrod	1963	51
14 15/16	9	5 15/16	Nayarit, MX	E.W. Ennis, Jr.	E.W. Ennis, Jr.	1956	52
14 14/16	9 11/16	6 3/16	Nogales, AZ	John F. Nutt	John F. Nutt	1958	53
14 14/16	9	5 14/16	Nayarit, MX	Glenn W. Slade, Jr.	Glenn W. Slade, Jr.	1960	53
14 12/16	8 15/16	5 13/16	Nayarit, MX	Cecil M. Hopper	Cecil M. Hopper	1971	55
14 9/16	8 14/16	5 11/16	Santa Cruz Co., AZ	Ed Scarla	Ed Scarla	1959	56

COUGAR
WORLD'S RECORD

RANK
World's Record

SCORE
16 $^{4/16}$

LOCATION
Tatlayoko Lake, BC

HUNTER
Douglas E. Schuk

OWNER
Charles M. Travers

DATE KILLED
1979

The World's Record for a cougar (Felis concolor) has held for two decades with a score of 16-4/16. Currently owned by Charles M. Travers, this cougar was taken by Douglas E. Schuk on the wintry afternoon of February 12, 1979. Schuk's hounds trailed the big tom through 32 inches of snow that had blanketed Tatlayoko Lake, British Columbia. At 3:00 p.m., Schuk's dogs closed in as the sun descended toward the far coastal mountains. Usually hunters recognize when a cat has been brought to bay as the excited tone of their dogs is answered by the shrill whistle of the cornered prey. Though cougars are generally tremulous in such circumstances, cats that can weigh up to 227 pounds are quite capable of taking out a hound with the rake of their powerful paws. Having taken a considerable amount of time and dedication to train his fine pack of dogs, Schuk knew he had to make a clean kill or there might be a very real risk of injury to his four-legged hunting companions. Using his .308, Schuk assuredly took down the impressive, snow-speckled cat.

Charles Travers later acquired the skull of the tom. When he had it measured, it was hard to believe. The entry measurement was well above the long standing 1964 record of 16 taken by Garth Roberts in Garfield County, Utah. As a potential record, it had to come before the Final Awards Judges Panel. They too found it to score better than the record and confirmed it as the new World's Record for the category.

Since it was no longer owned by the hunter, it was eligible only for a Certificate of Merit.

Schuk's World's Record cougar was nearly matched by a cougar taken in Idaho's Selway-Bitterroot Wilderness by Gene R. Alford of Kamiah, Idaho. Alford's cougar, taken on a solo month-long wilderness hunt in 1988 missed the World's Record by 1/16 of an inch. Alford's cougar was awarded the Sagamore Hill Medal for the uniqueness of the hunt and the manner in which Alford's pursuit of this magnificent cat epitomized the essence of the Boone and Crockett Club's fair chase ethic.

The original World's Record was taken by President Theodore Roosevelt in 1901 near Meeker, Colorado, and scored at 15-12/16. Predominately gray in their northern range, Theodore Roosevelt shot both slate-gray and red pumas in Colorado, thus revealing that there is a considerable variation in the color of this American wild cat. ∎

COUGAR
WORLD'S RECORD SCORECHART

Measurements are taken with calipers or by using parallel perpendiculars, to the nearest one-sixteenth of an inch, without reduction of fractions. Official measurements cannot be taken until the skull has air dried for at least 60 days after the animal was killed. All adhering flesh, membrane and cartilage must be completely removed before official measurements are taken.

A. Greatest Length is measured between perpendiculars parallel to the long axis of the skull, without the lower jaw and excluding malformations.

B. Greatest Width is measured between perpendiculars at right angles to the long axis.

Records of
North American
Big Game

250 Station Drive
Missoula, MT 59801
(406) 542-1888

BOONE AND CROCKETT CLUB®
OFFICIAL SCORING SYSTEM FOR NORTH AMERICAN BIG GAME TROPHIES

COUGAR AND JAGUAR

KIND OF CAT (check one)

■ cougar
□ jaguar

MINIMUM SCORES

	AWARDS	ALL-TIME
cougar	14-8/16	15
jaguar	14-8/16	14-8/16

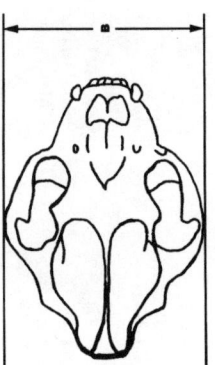

	MEASUREMENTS
SEE OTHER SIDE FOR INSTRUCTIONS	
A. Greatest Length Without Lower Jaw	9 9/16
B. Greatest Width	6 11/16
FINAL SCORE	16 4/16

Exact Locality Where Killed: **Tatlayoko Lake, BC**

Date Killed: **Feb. 12, 1979**   Hunter: **Douglas E. Schuk**

Owner: **Charles M. Travers**   Telephone #:

Owner's Address:

Guide's Name and Address:

Remarks: (Mention Any Abnormalities or Unique Qualities)

I, **Ed Williamson** , certify that I have measured this trophy on **06/20/1983**

    PRINT NAME   MM/DD/YYYY

at **Dallas Museum of Natural History**   **Dallas**   **TX**

  STREET ADDRESS   CITY   STATE/PROVINCE

and that these measurements and data are, to the best of my knowledge and belief, made in accordance with the instructions given.

Signature: **Ed Williamson**   I.D. Number:

                       B&C OFFICIAL MEASURER

Witness: **Frank Cook**

155

COUGAR

Felis concolor hippolestes and related subspecies

MINIMUM SCORE 15

Score	Greatest Length of Skull Without Lower Jaw	Greatest Width of Skull	Locality	Hunter	Owner	Date Killed	Rank
16 4/16	9 9/16	6 11/16	Tatlayoko Lake, BC	Douglas E. Schuk	Charles M. Travers	1979	1
16 3/16	9 8/16	6 11/16	Idaho Co., ID	Gene R. Alford	B&C National Collection	1988	2
16 1/16	9 7/16	6 10/16	Park Co., WY	Scott M. Moore	Scott M. Moore	1993	3
16	9 4/16	6 12/16	Garfield Co., UT	Garth Roberts	R. Scott Jarvie	1964	4
15 15/16	9 1/16	6 14/16	Clearwater River, AB	Walter R. Weller	Walter R. Weller	1973	5
15 14/16	9 2/16	6 12/16	Walla Walla Co., WA	Robert A. Klicker	Robert A. Klicker	1988	6
15 12/16	9 5/16	6 7/16	Meeker, CO	Theodore Roosevelt	U.S. Natl. Museum	1901	7
15 12/16	9 2/16	6 10/16	Dutch Creek, AB	Edward D. Burton	Edward D. Burton	1954	7
15 12/16	9 1/16	6 11/16	Okanagan Lake, BC	Ted Razook	Ted Razook	1973	7
15 12/16	9 5/16	6 7/16	Mesa Co., CO	Robert R. Meyer	Robert R. Meyer	1978	7
15 12/16	9 4/16	6 8/16	Lincoln Co., MT	Stan D. Stamey	Stan D. Stamey	1994	7
15 11/16	9 4/16	6 7/16	Darby, MT	Lowell Hayes	Sherman L. Hayes	1953	12
15 11/16	9	6 11/16	Selway River, ID	Gene R. Alford	Gene R. Alford	1961	12
15 11/16	9 3/16	6 8/16	Selway River, ID	Gene R. Alford	Gene R. Alford	1961	12
15 11/16	9 3/16	6 8/16	Valley Co., ID	Louis Rebillet	Louis Rebillet	1961	12
15 11/16	9 3/16	6 8/16	Fisher Creek, AB	John Cassidy	John Cassidy	1985	12
15 11/16	9 2/16	6 9/16	Okanagan Lake, BC	D. Cooper & M. Hubbard	Dusty R. Cooper	1985	12
15 11/16	9 4/16	6 7/16	Idaho Co., ID	Richard C. Farthing	Richard C. Farthing	1988	12
15 11/16	9 4/16	6 7/16	Eagle Co., CO	Layne K. Wing	Layne K. Wing	1990	12
15 10/16	9 3/16	6 7/16	Catherine Creek, OR	Ron Lay	Ron Lay	1966	20
15 10/16	9	6 10/16	Tatla Lake, BC	Harold J. Coult	Harold J. Coult	1986	20
15 10/16	9 3/16	6 7/16	Shoshone Co., ID	Henry L. Chandler	Henry L. Chandler	1992	20
15 10/16	9 1/16	6 9/16	Garfield Co., UT	Robin Siegfried	Robin Siegfried	1992	20
15 9/16	9 2/16	6 7/16	Carbon Co., UT	H. Alan Foster	H. Alan Foster	1959	24
15 9/16	9 3/16	6 6/16	Okanogan Co., WA	Mike Lynch	Mike Lynch	1964	24
15 9/16	9 2/16	6 7/16	Salmon River, ID	Doug Kittredge	Doug Kittredge	1971	24
15 9/16	9	6 9/16	Gallatin Co., MT	Tracy J. Peterson	Tracy J. Peterson	1984	24
15 9/16	9 2/16	6 7/16	Carbon Co., UT	Robert F. McLawhorn	Robert F. McLawhorn	1985	24
15 9/16	9 2/16	6 7/16	Elko Co., NV	Joel C. Brown	Joel C. Brown	1986	24
15 9/16	9 2/16	6 7/16	Flathead Co., MT	Rusby Seabaugh	Brad Seabaugh	1986	24
15 9/16	9 2/16	6 7/16	Idaho Co., ID	Randy L. Waddell	Randy L. Waddell	1990	24
15 9/16	9 3/16	6 6/16	Rio Arriba Co., NM	Robert J. Seeds	Robert J. Seeds	1995	24
15 9/16	9 2/16	6 6/16	Pondera Co., MT	Daneil L. Swanson	Daneil L. Swanson	1996	24
15 8/16	9 2/16	6 6/16	Cottonwood, NV	Berkley Hunt	Berkley Hunt	1962	34
15 8/16	9	6 8/16	Porcupine Hills, AB	Edward D. Burton	Edward D. Burton	1965	34
15 8/16	9 2/16	6 6/16	Huerfano Co., CO	J.D. Dodge	J.D. Dodge	1971	34
15 8/16	9 8/16	6	Priest Lake, ID	Ron Book	Ron Book	1972	34
15 8/16	9 1/16	6 7/16	Lincoln Co., MT	Robert Fleshman	Gary Grenfell	1975	34

			Locality	By whom killed	Owner	Date	Rank
15 8/16	9 1/16	6 7/16	Loblaw Creek, AB	John A. Jorgensen	John A. Jorgensen	1977	34
15 8/16	9	6 8/16	Idaho Co., ID	Jerry J. James	Jerry J. James	1982	34
15 8/16	9	6 8/16	Bannock Co., ID	Frank N. Hough	Frank N. Hough	1985	34
15 8/16	9 2/16	6 6/16	Rio Blanco Co., CO	Robert L. Raley	Robert L. Raley	1985	34
15 8/16	9 3/16	6 5/16	Rio Arriba Co., NM	Dick Ray	Dick Ray	1985	34
15 8/16	9	6 8/16	Wallowa Co., OR	Robin D. Dickenson	Robin D. Dickenson	1987	34
15 8/16	9 3/16	6 5/16	Robbins Range, BC	R.J. Petrie & G. Schweitzer	Robert J. Petrie	1987	34
15 8/16	9 4/16	6 4/16	Montrose Co., CO	Kendall Hamilton	Kendall Hamilton	1988	34
15 8/16	9 4/16	6 4/16	Boise Co., ID	Ron E. Romig	Ron E. Romig	1988	34
15 8/16	9 2/16	6 6/16	Clallam Co., WA	John M. Rawlings	John M. Rawlings	1990	34
15 8/16	8 15/16	6 9/16	Gila Co., AZ	Stephen D. Hornady	Stephen D. Hornady	1991	34
15 8/16	9 1/16	6 7/16	Bragg Creek, AB	Drew Ramsay	Drew Ramsay	1991	34
15 8/16	9	6 8/16	Sanders Co., MT	Wayne M. Foley	Wayne M. Foley	1993	34
15 8/16	9 3/16	6 5/16	Lemhi Co., ID	Michael A. Judas	Michael A. Judas	1995	34
15 7/16	8 15/16	6 8/16	Coleman, AB	H. Freeman & D. Girardi	H. Freeman & D. Girardi	1963	53
15 7/16	9	6 7/16	Kootenay, BC	Melvin E. Almas	Melvin E. Almas	1965	53
15 7/16	9 3/16	6 4/16	Coal Canyon, CO	Larry Bamford	Larry Bamford	1967	53
15 7/16	9 1/16	6 6/16	Lewis & Clark Co., MT	Ron Jenkins	R. Jenkins & J. Lee	1967	53
15 7/16	9 1/16	6 6/16	Rio Blanco Co., CO	Ronald D. Vincent	Ronald D. Vincent	1970	53
15 7/16	9 2/16	6 5/16	Columbia Co., WA	William R. Randall	William R. Randall	1972	53
15 7/16	8 13/16	6 10/16	Gold Creek, BC	Donovan W. Ellis	Donovan W. Ellis	1981	53
15 7/16	9 2/16	6 5/16	Lemhi Co., ID	David W. Thompson	David W. Thompson	1983	53
15 7/16	9	6 7/16	Columbia Co., WA	Curtis D. Neal	Curtis D. Neal	1986	53
15 7/16	9 1/16	6 6/16	Lewis & Clark Co., MT	Mike Barthelmess	M. Barthelmess & D. Wilson	1987	53
15 7/16	9 2/16	6 5/16	Idaho Co., ID	Harold A. Kottre	Harold A. Kottre	1988	53
15 7/16	9 1/16	6 6/16	Pend Oreille Co., WA	Wesley M. Kreiger	Wesley M. Kreiger	1988	53
15 7/16	8 15/16	6 8/16	Ferry Co., WA	John P. Peruchini	John P. Peruchini	1989	53
15 7/16	9 4/16	6 3/16	Colfax Co., NM	Robert M. Werley	Robert M. Werley	1989	53
15 7/16	9 2/16	6 5/16	Gila Co., AZ	Antonio E. Ornes	Antonio E. Ornes	1991	53
15 7/16	9	6 7/16	Ravalli Co., MT	Paul R. Begins	Paul R. Begins	1992	53
15 7/16	8 15/16	6 8/16	Clearwater Co., ID	Dennis L. Butler	Dennis L. Butler	1992	53
15 7/16	9 3/16	6 4/16	Wallowa Co., OR	Benjamin D. Grote	Benjamin D. Grote	1992	53
15 7/16	8 15/16	6 8/16	Colfax Co., NM	Donald P. Travis	Donald P. Travis	1994	53
15 7/16	9 4/16	6 3/16	Williams Lake, BC	Dennis R. Beebe	Dennis R. Beebe	1995	53
15 7/16	9 2/16	6 5/16	Yahk River, BC	Gerry Tames	Gerry Tames	1995	53
15 7/16	9	6 7/16	Union Co., OR	Michael C. Bennett	Michael C. Bennett	1996	53
15 6/16	9 5/16	6 2/16	Twin Lakes, BC	T. Philcox & G. Thomas	Tim Philcox	1996	53
15 6/16	9 1/16	6 6/16	Latah Co., ID	Don Scoles	Tyson Scoles	1996	53
15 6/16	9 1/16	6 6/16	Madison Co., MT	Cody Stemler	Cody Stemler	1996	53
15 6/16	9 1/16	6 5/16	Wind River Mts., WY	M. Abbott Frazier	U.S. Natl. Museum	1892	78
15 6/16	8 14/16	6 8/16	Okanogan Co., WA	Merle Hooshagen	Merle Hooshagen	1957	78
15 6/16	8 14/16	6 6/16	Young, AZ	Ed Scarla	Ed Scarla	1958	78
15 6/16	9 4/16	6 2/16	Sedalia, CO	Walt Paulk	Walt Paulk	1961	78
15 6/16	8 13/16	6 9/16	Fernie, BC	Oscar Jansen	Oscar Jansen	1964	78
15 6/16	9 2/16	6 4/16	West Salt Creek, CO	Hartle V. Morris	Hartle V. Morris	1964	78
15 6/16	8 14/16	6 8/16	Mineral Co., MT	Richard Ramberg	Richard Ramberg	1964	78
15 6/16	8 13/16	6 9/16	Natal, BC	Dick Ritco	Dick Ritco	1964	78

COUGAR

Felis concolor hippolestes and related subspecies

Score	Greatest Length of Skull Without Lower Jaw	Greatest Width of Skull	Locality	Hunter	Owner	Date Killed	Rank
15 6/16	9	6 6/16	Missoula Co., MT	Jim Zeiler	William W. Zeiler	1966	78
15 6/16	9	6 6/16	Sanders Co., MT	Lloyd F. Behling	Lloyd F. Behling	1969	78
15 6/16	9 1/16	6 5/16	Bull River, BC	Henry Fercho	Henry Fercho	1976	78
15 6/16	9 2/16	6 4/16	Colfax Co., NM	Marta S. Burnside	Marta S. Burnside	1977	78
15 6/16	9 1/16	6 5/16	Mesa Co., CO	Jack Harrison	Jack Harrison	1980	78
15 6/16	8 11/16	6 11/16	Taos Co., NM	George P. Mann	George P. Mann	1981	78
15 6/16	8 14/16	6 8/16	Lewis & Clark Co., MT	Wayne L. Beach	Wayne L. Beach	1983	78
15 6/16	9 5/16	6 1/16	Socorro Co., NM	Edwin E. Finkbeiner	Edwin E. Finkbeiner	1984	78
15 6/16	9 1/16	6 5/16	Benewah Co., ID	Kurt R. Morris	Kurt R. Morris	1984	78
15 6/16	9	6 6/16	Missoula Co., MT	Bruce E. Parker	Bruce E. Parker	1984	78
15 6/16	9 1/16	6 5/16	Clearwater Co., ID	Daniel J. Greve	Daniel J. Greve	1985	78
15 6/16	9	6 6/16	Idaho Co., ID	Ralph L. Hatter	Ralph L. Hatter	1987	78
15 6/16	8 15/16	6 7/16	Mineral Co., MT	James E. Miller III	James E. Miller III	1988	78
15 6/16	8 14/16	6 8/16	James River, AB	Susan M. Geduhn	S. Geduhn & F. Geduhn	1989	78
15 6/16	9	6 6/16	Rio Arriba Co., NM	James E. Kapuscinski	James E. Kapuscinski	1989	78
15 6/16	9	6 6/16	Highwood River, AB	G. Burton & J.D. Gordon	G. Burton & J.D. Gordon	1990	78
15 6/16	8 15/16	6 7/16	Nez Perce Co., ID	Rob Courville	Rob Courville	1990	78
15 6/16	8 14/16	6 8/16	Coldstream Creek, BC	Christopher P. Barker	Christopher P. Barker	1992	78
15 6/16	9 4/16	6 2/16	Mora Co., NM	Andrew J. Ortega	Andrew J. Ortega	1992	78
15 6/16	9	6 6/16	Elmore Co., ID	Kelly Dougherty	Kelly Dougherty	1993	78
15 6/16	9	6 6/16	Idaho Co., ID	Mark L. Dunham	Mark L. Dunham	1994	78
15 6/16	9	6 6/16	Flathead Co., MT	Sidney E. Taylor	Sidney E. Taylor	1995	78
15 6/16	9 1/16	6 5/16	N. Saskatchewan River, AB	Lyle G. Andersen	Lyle G. Andersen	1996	78
15 6/16	9 3/16	6 3/16	Columbia Co., WA	Brian W. Hergert	Brian W. Hergert	1996	78
15 6/16	9	6 6/16	Mineral Co., MT	Michael R. Borden	Michael R. Borden	1997	78
15 5/16	8 14/16	6 7/16	Hamilton, MT	Lloyd Thompson	U.S. Natl. Museum	1922	111
15 5/16	8 12/16	6 9/16	Clearwater River, AB	William A. Schutte	William A. Schutte	1935	111
15 5/16	8 13/16	6 8/16	Missoula Co., MT	Ronald Thompson	U.S. Natl. Museum	1936	111
15 5/16	8 15/16	6 6/16	East Kootenay, BC	Martin Marigeau	C. Garrett	1940	111
15 5/16	8 15/16	6 6/16	Clearwater Co., ID	Andy Eatmon	H.H. Schnetler	1953	111
15 5/16	8 13/16	6 8/16	Spanish Fork Canyon, UT	R. Jones & G. Pierce	Ronald Jones	1954	111
15 5/16	8 15/16	6 6/16	Granite Co., MT	Oscar E. Nelson	Oscar E. Nelson	1961	111
15 5/16	8 15/16	6 6/16	Idaho Co., ID	W. & D. England	Wayne England	1962	111
15 5/16	9 2/16	6 3/16	Eagle Nest, NM	Hal Vaught	Hal Vaught	1963	111
15 5/16	9 2/16	6 3/16	Lake Quinault, WA	C.A. Heppe	C.A. Heppe	1964	111
15 5/16	8 13/16	6 8/16	Okanogan Co., WA	Clyde A. Paul	Clyde A. Paul	1965	111
15 5/16	9 1/16	6 4/16	Lac La Hache, BC	Andy Hagberg	Andy Hagberg	1967	111
15 5/16	9 1/16	6 4/16	Elk City, ID	W. Goodwin & D. Baldwin	David Baldwin	1969	111

Score	Length	Width	Locality	Hunter	Owner	Date	Rank
15 5/16	8 15/16	6 6/16	Grand Junction, CO	John Lamicq, Jr.	John Lamicq, Jr.	1969	111
15 5/16	9 4/16	6 1/16	Elko Co., NV	Kenneth A. Johnson	Kenneth A. Johnson	1974	111
15 5/16	9	6 5/16	Okanogan Co., WA	Joel N. Hughes	Joel N. Hughes	1975	111
15 5/16	8 13/16	6 8/16	Osoyoos, BC	Alvin L. Reiff	Alvin L. Reiff	1975	111
15 5/16	8 15/16	6 6/16	Lemhi Co., ID	Larry L. Schweitzer	Larry L. Schweitzer	1975	111
15 5/16	9	6 5/16	Hardesty Creek, AB	John T. Shillingburg	John T. Shillingburg	1976	111
15 5/16	9	6 5/16	Custer Co., ID	Florence Buxton	Florence Buxton	1977	111
15 5/16	8 15/16	6 6/16	Jumpingpound Creek, AB	Max W. Good	Max W. Good	1978	111
15 5/16	8 15/16	6 6/16	Mineral Co., MT	Dennis E. Moos	Dennis E. Moos	1979	111
15 5/16	8 15/16	6 6/16	Wallowa Co., OR	Duane E. Neuschwander	Duane E. Neuschwander	1980	111
15 5/16	8 15/16	6 6/16	Pend Oreille Co., WA	Jack Schulte	Jack Schulte	1981	111
15 5/16	9	6 5/16	Rio Blanco Co., CO	Rocky O. Alburtiss	Rocky O. Alburtiss	1987	111
15 5/16	9 1/16	6 4/16	Beaverhead Co., MT	R.C. Carlson & O.D. Perala	R.C. Carlson & O.D. Perala	1987	111
15 5/16	8 15/16	6 6/16	Dutch Creek, AB	Darryl C. Naslund	Darryl C. Naslund	1988	111
15 5/16	9 2/16	6 3/16	Ravalli Co., MT	Edward J. Pines III	Edward J. Pines III	1988	111
15 5/16	8 15/16	6 6/16	Lewis & Clark Co., MT	Clyde S. Lankford	Clyde S. Lankford	1991	111
15 5/16	9 1/16	6 4/16	Boise Co., ID	Donald G. Thurston	Donald G. Thurston	1991	111
15 5/16	8 15/16	6 6/16	Ravalli Co., MT	Dean Irwin	Dean Irwin	1992	111
15 5/16	9 1/16	6 4/16	Flathead Co., MT	James L. Bates	James L. Bates	1994	111
15 5/16	8 15/16	6 6/16	Albany Co., WY	Dennis D. Church	Dennis D. Church	1994	111
15 5/16	9	6 5/16	Duchesne Co., UT	Ferdell K. Day	Ferdell K. Day	1994	111
15 5/16	9	6 5/16	Las Animas Co., CO	Picked Up	Phillip L. Ehrlich	PR 1994	111
15 5/16	9	6 5/16	Shoshone Co., ID	Peter J. Gardner	Peter J. Gardner	1994	111
15 5/16	8 14/16	6 7/16	Delta Co., CO	William E. Kallister	William E. Kallister	1995	111
15 5/16	9	6 5/16	Lemhi Co., ID	Mike B. Woltering	Mike B. Woltering	1995	111
15 5/16	9 1/16	6 4/16	Idaho Co., ID	Arthur W. Swanstrom	Arthur W. Swanstrom	1997	111
15 4/16	8 15/16	6 5/16	Okanogan Co., WA	Merle Hooshagen	Merle Hooshagen	1956	150
15 4/16	9	6 4/16	Wells Gray Park, BC	Colin Mann	Colin Mann	1960	150
15 4/16	8 13/16	6 7/16	Union Co., OR	Don Haefer	W.H. Miller	1961	150
15 4/16	8 13/16	6 7/16	Motoqua, UT	Basil C. Bradbury	Basil C. Bradbury	1963	150
15 4/16	8 15/16	6 5/16	Missoula Co., MT	Richard Ramberg	Maurice Hornocker	1964	150
15 4/16	9	6 4/16	Canim Lake, BC	H.C. Nickelsen	H.C. Nickelsen	1964	150
15 4/16	8 14/16	6 6/16	Salmon River, ID	Aaron U. Jones	Aaron U. Jones	1967	150
15 4/16	9	6 4/16	Missoula Co., MT	B. Stanley & C. Johnson	Bob Stanley	1967	150
15 4/16	9	6 4/16	Snake River, ID	Dee M. Cannon	Dee M. Cannon	1968	150
15 4/16	9	6 4/16	Okanogan Co., WA	Louis J. Ayers	Louis J. Ayers	1969	150
15 4/16	8 15/16	6 5/16	Sandpoint, ID	George C. Taft	George C. Taft	1969	150
15 4/16	8 13/16	6 7/16	Sanders Co., MT	Edna Hill	Edna Hill	1970	150
15 4/16	9 3/16	6 1/16	Beaver Creek, AB	Oscar Markle	Oscar Markle	1970	150
15 4/16	8 15/16	6 5/16	Vernal, UT	Harold Schneider	Harold Schneider	1970	150
15 4/16	9	6 4/16	Ravalli Co., MT	Larry A. Rose	Larry A. Rose	1973	150
15 4/16	9 2/16	6 2/16	Nakusp, BC	Glen Olson	Glen Olson	1974	150
15 4/16	8 15/16	6 5/16	Lincoln Co., MT	Wayne B. Hunt	Wayne B. Hunt	1975	150
15 4/16	9	6 4/16	Mineral Co., MT	Irving H. Ratnour	Irving H. Ratnour	1975	150
15 4/16	8 15/16	6 5/16	Meldrum Creek, BC	Walter A. Riemer	Walter A. Riemer	1977	150
15 4/16	9	6 4/16	Oliver, BC	Walter Snoke	Walter Snoke	1977	150
15 4/16	8 14/16	6 6/16	Rio Arriba Co., NM	Anderson Bakewell	Anderson Bakewell	1978	150

Felis concolor hippolestes and related subspecies

Score	Greatest Length of Skull Without Lower Jaw	Greatest Width of Skull	Locality	Hunter	Owner	Date Killed	Rank
15 4/16	9	6 4/16	Threepoint Creek, AB	Robert C. Dickson	R.C. Dickson & R.J. Dickson, Jr.	1978	150
15 4/16	8 15/16	6 5/16	Idaho Co., ID	Ralph E. Close	Ralph E. Close	1980	150
15 4/16	8 14/16	6 6/16	Baker Co., OR	Joe J. Lay	Joe J. Lay	1981	150
15 4/16	8 14/16	6 6/16	Broadwater Co., MT	Ray Toombs	Ray Toombs	1982	150
15 4/16	9 2/16	6 2/16	Colfax Co., NM	Ronald G. Troyer	Ronald G. Troyer	1982	150
15 4/16	8 13/16	6 7/16	Wallowa Co., OR	Donna Lancaster	Donna Lancaster	1983	150
15 4/16	8 15/16	6 5/16	Lewis & Clark Co., MT	Robert A. Soukkala	Robert A. Soukkala	1983	150
15 4/16	9 2/16	6 2/16	Mill Creek, AB	Warren R. Burton	Warren R. Burton	1984	150
15 4/16	8 14/16	6 6/16	Dolores Co., CO	Bruce Nay	Bruce Nay	1984	150
15 4/16	9 2/16	6 2/16	Colfax Co., NM	L. Profazi & R. Troyer	Louie Profazi	1984	150
15 4/16	9	6 4/16	Coconino Co., AZ	Gregg A. Thurston	Gregg A. Thurston	1984	150
15 4/16	9	6 4/16	Sevier Co., UT	John R. Blanton	John R. Blanton	1985	150
15 4/16	9	6 4/16	Rio Arriba Co., NM	Ray B. Bailey	Ray B. Bailey	1986	150
15 4/16	9	6 4/16	Madison Co., MT	Stephen P. Connell	Stephen P. Connell	1986	150
15 4/16	9	6 4/16	Uintah Co., UT	Albert L. Farace	Albert L. Farace	1986	150
15 4/16	9	6 4/16	Columbia Co., WA	Gregory P. Leid	Gregory P. Leid	1987	150
15 4/16	9 1/16	6 3/16	Porcupine Hills, AB	Lyle Czember	Lyle Czember	1988	150
15 4/16	8 15/16	6 5/16	Cassia Co., ID	Charles W. Eagleson	Charles W. Eagleson	1988	150
15 4/16	8 15/16	6 5/16	Wallowa Co., OR	Mark D. Armstrong	Mark D. Armstrong	1989	150
15 4/16	9 1/16	6 3/16	Rio Blanco Co., CO	William E. Pipes III	William E. Pipes III	1989	150
15 4/16	8 14/16	6 6/16	Shoshone Co., ID	Darrell G. Holmquist	Darrell G. Holmquist	1990	150
15 4/16	8 13/16	6 7/16	Shoshone Co., ID	Picked Up	Tracy L. Skay	1990	150
15 4/16	8 15/16	6 5/16	Whaleback Ridge, AB	Sally A. Kloosterman	Sally A. Kloosterman	1991	150
15 4/16	8 13/16	6 7/16	Jumping Pond, AB	Fred Schrader	Fred Schrader	1991	150
15 4/16	9 1/16	6 3/16	Clearwater Co., ID	Robert J. Barnett	Robert J. Barnett	1992	150
15 4/16	9 2/16	6 2/16	Columbia Co., WA	Mark Jenkins	Mark Jenkins	1992	150
15 4/16	9	6 4/16	Ravalli Co., MT	Walter R. Willey, Jr.	Walter R. Willey, Jr.	1992	150
15 4/16	8 15/16	6 5/16	Wallowa Co., OR	Benjamin D. Grote	Benjamin D. Grote	1993	150
15 4/16	8 15/16	6 5/16	Carbon Co., UT	Kenny E. Leo	Kenny E. Leo	1993	150
15 4/16	9	6 4/16	Utah Co., UT	Bob Kaid	Bob Kaid	1994	150
15 4/16	9 2/16	6 2/16	Flathead Co., MT	Shawn P. Price	Shawn P. Price	1994	150
15 4/16	9	6 4/16	Rio Arriba Co., NM	Robert J. Seeds	Robert J. Seeds	1992	150
15 4/16	8 15/16	6 4/16	Likely, BC	James Dunigan	James Dunigan	1996	150
15 4/16	8 15/16	6 5/16	Cartier Creek, AB	Douglas G. Jones	Douglas G. Jones	1997	150
15 3/16	8 15/16	6 4/16	East Kootenay, BC	Martin Marigeau	C. Garrett	1940	205
15 3/16	8 13/16	6 6/16	Ventura Co., CA	Warren C. Johnston	Warren C. Johnston	1953	205
15 3/16	8 14/16	6 2/16	Churn Creek, BC	J.R. Aitchison	J.R. Aitchison	1956	205
15 3/16	9 1/16	6 2/16	Nelson, BC	R.A. Rutherglen	Univ. of BC	1956	205

Score	Greatest Length	Greatest Width	Locality	Owner	By	Date	Rank
15 3/16	8 14/16	6 5/16	Saratoga, WY	Win Condict	Win Condict	1961	205
15 3/16	8 14/16	6 5/16	Pincher Creek, AB	Harry R. Freeman	Harry R. Freeman	1961	205
15 3/16	8 14/16	6 5/16	Trout Creek, AB	Kenny McRae	Kenny McRae	1961	205
15 3/16	8 14/16	6 5/16	McGregor Lake, AB	A.C. Wilson	Gus Daley	1962	205
15 3/16	8 14/16	6 5/16	Oliver, BC	Allan Nichol	Allan Nichol	1963	205
15 3/16	9	6 3/16	Okanogan Co., WA	Mike Lynch	Mike Lynch	1964	205
15 3/16	8 15/16	6 4/16	Tatlayoko Lake, BC	C.L. Anderson	C.L. Anderson	1967	205
15 3/16	8 11/16	6 8/16	Oroville, WA	Leon Fleming	L. Fleming & J. Lemaster	1967	205
15 3/16	8 15/16	6 4/16	Whitecourt, AB	K.J. Stanton	K.J. Stanton	1967	205
15 3/16	9 3/16	6	Meeker, CO	Jack Cadario	Jack Cadario	1968	205
15 3/16	8 14/16	6 5/16	Orofino, ID	Fairly Bonner	Fairly Bonner	1969	205
15 3/16	8 15/16	6 4/16	Falkland, BC	Earl Carlson	Wildl. Tax. Studios	1974	205
15 3/16	8 15/16	6 4/16	Prouton Lakes, BC	G.C. Ridley & R. Gillespie	G.C. Ridley & R. Gillespie	1976	205
15 3/16	9 3/16	6	Emery Co., UT	Dan Scartezina	Dan Scartezina	1976	205
15 3/16	9 2/16	6 1/16	Garfield Co., UT	William A. Coats	William A. Coats	1978	205
15 3/16	8 15/16	6 4/16	Mt. Evans, BC	Larry N. Dent	Larry N. Dent	1980	205
15 3/16	8 14/16	6 5/16	Stevens Co., WA	William K. Bean	William K. Bean	1981	205
15 3/16	8 10/16	6 9/16	Ferry Co., WA	Richard A. Bonander	Richard A. Bonander	1981	205
15 3/16	8 13/16	6 6/16	Silver Creek, AB	John E. Cassidy	John E. Cassidy	1981	205
15 3/16	8 14/16	6 5/16	Rio Blanco Co., CO	Robert L. Raley	Robert L. Raley	1983	205
15 3/16	8 14/16	6 5/16	Plumbob Mt., BC	Andreas Felber	Andreas Felber	1985	205
15 3/16	8 14/16	6 5/16	Hot Springs Co., WY	Dan B. Artery	Dan B. Artery	1986	205
15 3/16	8 13/16	6 6/16	Idaho Co., ID	Richard Farthing	Steve C. Ryan	1987	205
15 3/16	8 14/16	6 5/16	Clearwater Co., ID	Mike T. McCain	Mike T. McCain	1988	205
15 3/16	9 1/16	6 2/16	Lincoln Co., MT	Jon G. Clark	Jon G. Clark	1989	205
15 3/16	8 13/16	6 6/16	Mt. Thynne, BC	Cliff C. Cory	Cliff C. Cory	1989	205
15 3/16	8 14/16	6 5/16	Porcupine Hills, AB	Sidney Websdale	Sidney Websdale	1989	205
15 3/16	8 15/16	6 4/16	Idaho Co., ID	Stephan Galles	Stephan Galles	1990	205
15 3/16	8 11/16	6 8/16	Larimer Co., CO	Peter A. Larson	Peter A. Larson	1990	205
15 3/16	9 2/16	6 1/16	San Miguel Co., NM	Robert J. Seeds	Robert J. Seeds	1990	205
15 3/16	8 15/16	6 4/16	Archuleta Co., CO	Charles T. Ames	Charles T. Ames	1991	205
15 3/16	8 14/16	6 5/16	Clearwater Co., ID	Donald K. Cooper	Donald K. Cooper	1991	205
15 3/16	9 1/16	6 2/16	Moffat Co., CO	Robert W. Dager	Robert W. Dager	1991	205
15 3/16	8 14/16	6 5/16	Coleman, AB	Jerry Fisher	Jerry Fisher	1991	205
15 3/16	8 14/16	6 5/16	Boundary Co., ID	Ron R. Frederickson	Ron R. Frederickson	1991	205
15 3/16	9 1/16	6 2/16	Elk River, BC	Jim Musil	Jim Musil	1991	205
15 3/16	8 15/16	6 4/16	Eagle Co., CO	Jeffrey S. Shoaf	Jeffrey S. Shoaf	1991	205
15 3/16	8 13/16	6 6/16	Whiskey Creek, AB	Dennis Watson	Dennis Watson	1992	205
15 3/16	9 1/16	6 2/16	Bannock Co., ID	Brad Hough	Brad Hough	1992	205
15 3/16	8 15/16	6 4/16	Gila Co., AZ	Fred Peters	Fred Peters	1992	205
15 3/16	8 15/16	6 4/16	Ram Mt., AB	Stanley D. Simpson	Stanley D. Simpson	1992	205
15 3/16	8 15/16	6 4/16	San Miguel Co., NM	Paul W. Brown	Paul W. Brown	1993	205
15 3/16	8 13/16	6 6/16	Boundary Co., ID	Tom D. Neuburg	Tom D. Neuburg	1993	205
15 3/16	9 1/16	6 2/16	Barkshanty Creek, BC	Daryl Donald	Daryl Donald	1994	205
15 3/16	8 13/16	6 6/16	Rio Arriba Co., NM	Robert J. Seeds	Robert J. Seeds	1994	205
15 3/16	9 1/16	6 2/16	McGregor Lake, AB	Frederick S. Fish	Frederick S. Fish	1995	205
15 3/16	8 15/16	6 4/16	Ravalli Co., MT	Gregory Sketas	Gregory Sketas	1995	205

COUGAR

Felis concolor hippolestes and related subspecies

Score	Greatest Length of Skull Without Lower Jaw	Greatest Width of Skull	Locality	Hunter	Owner	Date Killed	Rank
15 3/16	8 14/16	6 5/16	Garfield Co., WA	DeWayne L. Straube	DeWayne L. Straube	1995	205
15 3/16	9 1/16	6 2/16	Tooele Co., UT	Ed R. Sheets	Ed R. Sheets	1996	205
15 3/16	8 14/16	6 5/16	Garfield Co., CO	Daryl G. Speck	Daryl G. Speck	1996	205
15 3/16	8 15/16	6 4/16	Benewah Co., ID	Kurt R. Morris	Kurt R. Morris	1997	205
15 2/16	8 12/16	6 6/16	East Kootenay, BC	Martin Marigeau	C. Garrett	1940	260
15 2/16	8 14/16	6 4/16	Benewak Co., ID	Karl Paulson	Karl Paulson	1945	260
15 2/16	9 1/16	6 1/16	Salmon River, ID	Bob Hagel	Bob Hagel	1950	260
15 2/16	8 15/16	6 3/16	Strawberry, AZ	Irene Morden	Irene Morden	1958	260
15 2/16	8 14/16	6 4/16	Pine, AZ	C.J. Prock	C.J. Prock	1958	260
15 2/16	9 1/16	6 1/16	New Harmony, UT	Art Coates	Art Coates	1962	260
15 2/16	9	6 2/16	Allison, CO	Georgianna Etheridge	Georgianna Etheridge	1962	260
15 2/16	8 12/16	6 6/16	Coleman, AB	T. & C. Michalsky	T. & C. Michalsky	1962	260
15 2/16	8 11/16	6 7/16	Lendrum Creek, AB	Gary G. Giese	Gary G. Giese	1964	260
15 2/16	8 14/16	6 4/16	Parowan, UT	William Mastrangel	William Mastrangel	1964	260
15 2/16	8 14/16	6 4/16	Reserve, NM	Wilmer C. Hansen	Wilmer C. Hansen	1966	260
15 2/16	8 15/16	6 3/16	Saratoga, WY	Win Condict	Win Condict	1967	260
15 2/16	8 12/16	6 6/16	Little Fort, BC	Earl E. Hill	Earl E. Hill	1968	260
15 2/16	8 15/16	6 3/16	Duchesne Co., UT	Clyde C. Edwards	Clyde C. Edwards	1969	260
15 2/16	8 12/16	6 6/16	Okanogan Valley, WA	Patrick M. Davis	Patrick M. Davis	1970	260
15 2/16	8 14/16	6 4/16	Manzano Mts., NM	C.J. McElroy	C.J. McElroy	1970	260
15 2/16	9	6 2/16	Graveyard Creek, BC	Rod G. Hardie	Rod G. Hardie	1972	260
15 2/16	8 14/16	6 4/16	Duchesne Co., UT	Richard B. Sydnor, Jr.	Richard B. Sydnor, Jr.	1972	260
15 2/16	8 14/16	6 4/16	Stevens Co., WA	Leroy W. Kindsvogel	WA State U. Alumni Assoc.	1972	260
15 2/16	8 12/16	6 6/16	Ferry Co., WA	Paul L. Watts	Paul L. Watts	1972	260
15 2/16	8 13/16	6 5/16	Lincoln Co., MT	Katherine Kimberlin	Katherine Kimberlin	1973	260
15 2/16	9	6 2/16	Carbon Co., UT	L.A. Grelling	L.A. Grelling	1974	260
15 2/16	9	6 2/16	Pend Oreille Co., WA	Robert J. Robertson	Robert J. Robertson	1974	260
15 2/16	8 11/16	6 7/16	Granby River, BC	Everett B. Pannkuk, Jr.	Everett B. Pannkuk, Jr.	1977	260
15 2/16	8 12/16	6 6/16	Idaho Co., ID	Lawrence L. Seiler	Lawrence L. Seiler	1977	260
15 2/16	8 15/16	6 3/16	Uintah Co., UT	Dale Larson	Dale Larson	1978	260
15 2/16	8 13/16	6 5/16	Cascade Range, BC	Dennis C. Roach	Dennis C. Roach	1978	260
15 2/16	8 14/16	6 4/16	Mt. Roderick, BC	Gail Holderman	Gail Holderman	1979	260
15 2/16	9 1/16	6 1/16	Colfax Co., NM	Philip H. Whitley	Philip H. Whitley	1980	260
15 2/16	8 14/16	6 4/16	Stevens Co., WA	Fritz G. Nagel	Fritz G. Nagel	1981	260
15 2/16	8 13/16	6 5/16	Archuleta Co., CO	Judd Cooney	Judd Cooney	1982	260
15 2/16	8 14/16	6 4/16	Adams Co., ID	Warren J. Masson	Warren J. Masson	1982	260
15 2/16	8 12/16	6 6/16	Garfield Co., CO	Leslie H. Brewster	Leslie H. Brewster	1983	260
15 2/16	8 14/16	6 4/16	Sanders Co., MT	Conrad P. Anderson	Conrad P. Anderson	1984	260

Score	Length	Width	Location	Owner	Hunter	Date	Rank
15 2/16	8 12/16	6 6/16	Wallowa Co., OR	Samuel E. Briscoe	Samuel E. Briscoe	1984	260
15 2/16	8 11/16	6 7/16	Gallatin Co., MT	David M. Tofte	David M. Tofte	1984	260
15 2/16	8 12/16	6 6/16	Little White Mt., BC	Thomas M. Lavelle	Thomas M. Lavelle	1986	260
15 2/16	8 13/16	6 5/16	Latah Co., ID	Terry L. Watkins	Terry L. Watkins	1986	260
15 2/16	8 15/16	6 3/16	Clearwater Co., ID	Michael J. Kennedy	Michael J. Kennedy	1987	260
15 2/16	8 13/16	6 5/16	Union Co., OR	Francis G. Culver	Francis G. Culver	1988	260
15 2/16	8 13/16	6 5/16	Castle River, AB	Duane B. Schultz	Duane B. Schultz	1988	260
15 2/16	8 13/16	6 5/16	Utah Co., UT	Brent M. Taylor	Brent M. Taylor	1988	260
15 2/16	8 12/16	6 6/16	Lake Co., MT	Kevin J. Warning	Kevin J. Warning	1989	260
15 2/16	9 1/16	6 1/16	Woods Lake, BC	Sean MacKenzie	S. MacKenzie & B. Jaeger	1990	260
15 2/16	9	6 2/16	Taos Co., NM	William L. Porteous	William L. Porteous	1990	260
15 2/16	8 15/16	6 3/16	Park Co., CO	Jack P. Van Vianen	Jack P. Van Vianen	1990	260
15 2/16	8 12/16	6 6/16	San Miguel Co., CO	Charles M. Karp	Charles M. Karp	1991	260
15 2/16	8 13/16	6 5/16	Missoula Co., MT	Kenneth P. Schoening	Kenneth P. Schoening	1991	260
15 2/16	8 15/16	6 3/16	Missoula Co., MT	Steve B. Tenold	Steve B. Tenold	1991	260
15 2/16	8 15/16	6 3/16	Duchesne Co., UT	Jet C. Abegglen	Jet C. Abegglen	1992	260
15 2/16	8 13/16	6 5/16	Chimney Peak, AB	Derek A. Burdeny	Derek A. Burdeny	1992	260
15 2/16	8 10/16	6 8/16	Lincoln Co., MT	James R. Eff	James R. Eff	1992	260
15 2/16	9	6 2/16	Idaho Co., ID	William D. Ketcham II	Ben F. Ketcham	1992	260
15 2/16	8 15/16	6 3/16	Mineral Co., MT	Luke Cowan	Luke Cowan	1993	260
15 2/16	8 15/16	6 3/16	Shoshone Co., ID	Randy L. Fort	Randy L. Fort	1993	260
15 2/16	8 11/16	6 7/16	Kootenay Lake, BC	Robert Kuny	Robert Kuny	1993	260
15 2/16	9	6 2/16	Stevens Co., WA	William D. MeWhinney	William D. MeWhinney	1993	260
15 2/16	8 12/16	6 6/16	Park Co., MT	Primo Scapin	Primo Scapin	1993	260
15 2/16	8 15/16	6 3/16	Kootenay River, BC	Brian Schuck	Brian Schuck	1993	260
15 2/16	9 1/16	6 1/16	Okanogan Co., WA	David J. Burdulis	David J. Burdulis	1994	260
15 2/16	9 1/16	6 1/16	Uintah Co., UT	Shawn A. Labrum	Shawn A. Labrum	1994	260
15 2/16	8 14/16	6 4/16	Gold Creek, BC	Dean W. Hogaboam	Dean W. Hogaboam	1995	260
15 2/16	8 15/16	6 3/16	Idaho Co., ID	Allen D. Jones	Allen D. Jones	1995	260
15 2/16	9	6 2/16	Okanagan, BC	Jose L. Perez	Jose L. Perez	1995	260
15 2/16	9	6 2/16	Gila Co., AZ	Felix E. Sanchez	Felix E. Sanchez	1995	260
15 2/16	8 15/16	6 3/16	Flathead Co., MT	Curtis B. Stene	Curtis B. Stene	1995	260
15 2/16	8 14/16	6 4/16	Clallam Co., WA	Richard L. Deane	Richard L. Deane	1996	260
15 2/16	8 15/16	6 3/16	Elko Co., NV	Kazushige Harada	Kazushige Harada	1996	260
15 2/16	9 1/16	6 1/16	Kobau Mt., BC	James E. Riley	James E. Riley	1996	260
15 2/16	8 12/16	6 6/16	Rio Arriba Co., NM	Robert J. Seeds	Robert J. Seeds	1996	260
15 2/16	9	6 2/16	Archuleta Co., CO	Dolores E. Adams	Dolores E. Adams	1997	260
15 2/16	8 9/16	6 9/16	Monroe Lake, BC	Terry Faiers	Terry Faiers	1997	260
15 1/16	9	6 2/16	Bonner Co., ID	Don P. Miller II	Don P. Miller II	1997	260
15 1/16	8 13/16	6 4/16	Princeton, BC	C.F. Gigot	Alan Gill	1948	333
15 1/16	8 13/16	6 4/16	Okanogan Co., WA	Francis Randall	Francis Randall	1948	333
15 1/16	8 15/16	6 2/16	Saratoga, WY	Win Condict	Win Condict	1954	333
15 1/16	8 9/16	6 8/16	Ferris Mts., WY	Win Condict	W. Condict & E. Levasseur	1959	333
15 1/16	8 14/16	6 3/16	Cat Creek, AB	Hyrum R. Baker	Hyrum R. Baker	1960	333
15 1/16	9	6 1/16	Wild Horse Basin, WY	Win Condict	Win Condict	1961	333
15 1/16	8 13/16	6 4/16	Custer Co., ID	Joe Blackburn	Joe Blackburn	1962	333
15 1/16	8 14/16	6 3/16	Oliver, BC	Allan Nichol	Allan Nichol	1963	333

COUGAR

Felis concolor hippolestes and related subspecies

Score	Greatest Length of Skull Without Lower Jaw	Greatest Width of Skull	Locality	Hunter	Owner	Date Killed	Rank
15 1/16	9	6 1/16	Clearwater River, ID	Ted Hall	Ted Hall	1964	333
15 1/16	8 12/16	6 5/16	Idaho Co., ID	Elliot V. Nelson	Elliot V. Nelson	1965	333
15 1/16	8 14/16	6 3/16	Mineral Co., MT	Richard Ramberg	R. & N. Ramberg	1966	333
15 1/16	8 12/16	6 5/16	Missoula Co., MT	William Zeiler	William Zeiler	1966	333
15 1/16	8 14/16	6 3/16	Clearwater Co., ID	Robert W. Haskin	Robert W. Haskin	1967	333
15 1/16	8 13/16	6 4/16	Lincoln Co., MT	H.M. Johnston	H.M. Johnston	1967	333
15 1/16	8 13/16	6 4/16	S. Castle River, AB	James F. Simpson	James F. Simpson	1967	333
15 1/16	9 1/16	6	Price, UT	Robert H. Elder	Robert H. Elder	1968	333
15 1/16	8 13/16	6 4/16	Little Fort, BC	Earl E. Hill	Earl E. Hill	1968	333
15 1/16	8 15/16	6 2/16	Oroville, WA	Dan Lynch	Dan Lynch	1968	333
15 1/16	8 14/16	6 3/16	Douglas Co., CO	C.R. Anderson & E.H. Brown	Charles R. Anderson	1969	333
15 1/16	9 1/16	6	Sunflower, AZ	John C. Shaw	John C. Shaw	1969	333
15 1/16	8 12/16	6 5/16	Mineral Co., MT	William E. Bullock	William E. Bullock	1971	333
15 1/16	9 1/16	6	Gunlock, UT	L. Dean Taylor	L. Dean Taylor	1971	333
15 1/16	8 14/16	6 3/16	Pima Co., AZ	George W. Parker	George W. Parker	1972	333
15 1/16	9	6 1/16	Superior, MT	James L. Schaeffer	James L. Schaeffer	1972	333
15 1/16	8 13/16	6 4/16	Uintah Co., UT	Brent L. Winchester	Brent L. Winchester	1972	333
15 1/16	8 13/16	6 4/16	Emery Co., UT	Sharon A. Burkett	Sharon A. Burkett	1973	333
15 1/16	8 15/16	6 2/16	Granite Co., MT	James A. Raikos	James A. Raikos	1973	333
15 1/16	8 14/16	6 3/16	Idaho Co., ID	Chester D. Haight	Chester D. Haight	1975	333
15 1/16	8 15/16	6 2/16	Lake Co., MT	J.E. McCreedy & R.E. Seabaugh	James McCreedy	1977	333
15 1/16	8 13/16	6 4/16	Pend Oreille Co., WA	William M. Day	William M. Day	1978	333
15 1/16	8 15/16	6 2/16	Pimainus Hills, BC	Norman W. Dougan	Norman W. Dougan	1978	333
15 1/16	8 15/16	6 2/16	Wallowa Co., OR	Rollie Mattson	Rollie Mattson	1978	333
15 1/16	8 12/16	6 5/16	Nez Perce Co., ID	Pete M. Baughman, Jr.	Pete M. Baughman, Jr.	1979	333
15 1/16	9 1/16	6	Piute Co., UT	Fred J. Markley	Fred J. Markley	1979	333
15 1/16	8 14/16	6 3/16	Mill Creek, AB	Richard C. Davidson	Richard C. Davidson	1980	333
15 1/16	8 15/16	6 2/16	Rio Arriba Co., NM	Joseph Strasser, Jr.	Joseph Strasser, Jr.	1980	333
15 1/16	9	6 1/16	Wallowa Co., OR	William E. Hosford	William E. Hosford	1982	333
15 1/16	8 13/16	6 4/16	Erickson Creek, BC	R. John Kovak	R. John Kovak	1982	333
15 1/16	8 14/16	6 3/16	Idaho Co., ID	Roy M. Schumacher	Roy M. Schumacher	1984	333
15 1/16	8 13/16	6 4/16	Garfield Co., CO	Jay H. Kneasel	Jay H. Kneasel	1985	333
15 1/16	8 13/16	6 4/16	Whitney Creek, AB	Bryne J. Lengyel	Bryne J. Lengyel	1985	333
15 1/16	9 1/16	6	Lincoln Co., MT	Gary C. Cargill	Gary C. Cargill	1986	333
15 1/16	8 13/16	6 4/16	Newington Creek, BC	James W. Anderson	James W. Anderson	1987	333
15 1/16	8 14/16	6 3/16	Garfield Co., CO	Joseph S. Arrain	Joseph S. Arrain	1987	333
15 1/16	8 15/16	6 4/16	Idaho Co., ID	Ronald R. Feist	Ronald R. Feist	1987	333
15 1/16	8 15/16	6 2/16	Clearwater Co., ID	Charles C. Smith	Charles C. Smith	1987	333

Score	Greatest Length of Skull	Greatest Width of Skull	Locality	By Whom Killed	Owner	Date	Rank
15 1/16	8 11/16	6 6/16	Shoshone Co., ID	David K. Mueller	David K. Mueller	1988	333
15 1/16	8 14/16	6 3/16	Apache Co., AZ	Fred Peters	Fred Peters	1988	333
15 1/16	9	6 1/16	Missoula Co., MT	Kenneth P. Schoening	Kenneth P. Schoening	1988	333
15 1/16	8 13/16	6 4/16	Clallam Co., WA	John R. Franz	John R. Franz	1989	333
15 1/16	8 12/16	6 5/16	Hinton, AB	Rodney M. Janz	Rodney M. Janz	1989	333
15 1/16	8 14/16	6 3/16	Daggett Co., UT	T.C. Benson & L.V. Massey	Todd C. Benson	1990	333
15 1/16	8 12/16	6 5/16	Flathead Co., MT	Robert D. Boutang	Robert D. Boutang	1990	333
15 1/16	8 11/16	6 6/16	Utah Co., UT	Mary L. Brooks	Mary L. Brooks	1990	333
15 1/16	8 14/16	6 3/16	Rio Blanco Co., CO	Gerald L. Dowling	Gerald L. Dowling	1990	333
15 1/16	9	6 1/16	Millard Co., UT	Edwin A. Lewis	Edwin A. Lewis	1990	333
15 1/16	8 14/16	6 3/16	Bragg Creek, AB	Drew Ramsay	Drew Ramsay	1990	333
15 1/16	8 13/16	6 4/16	Dolores Co., CO	Anthony S. Wagner	Anthony S. Wagner	1991	333
15 1/16	8 14/16	6 3/16	Bonner Co., ID	Paul R. Allen	Paul R. Allen	1991	333
15 1/16	8 12/16	6 5/16	Latah Co., ID	Stephan D. Galles	Stephan D. Galles	1991	333
15 1/16	8 15/16	6 2/16	Cross River, BC	Mike J. McBride	Mike J. McBride	1992	333
15 1/16	9	6 1/16	Missoula Co., MT	John F. Haviland	John F. Haviland	1992	333
15 1/16	8 14/16	6 3/16	Missoula Co., MT	Robert J. Matye	Robert J. Matye	1992	333
15 1/16	8 10/16	6 7/16	Sanders Co., MT	Phillip J. Taylor	Phillip J. Taylor	1992	333
15 1/16	8 14/16	6 3/16	Chelan Co., WA	Douglas W. Thies	Douglas W. Thies	1992	333
15 1/16	8 13/16	6 4/16	Lincoln Co., MT	William R. Vyvyan	William R. Vyvyan	1993	333
15 1/16	9	6 1/16	Carbon Co., UT	Ray T. Bridge	Ray T. Bridge	1993	333
15 1/16	8 14/16	6 3/16	Shoshone Co., ID	Shawn Frederickson	Shawn Frederickson	1993	333
15 1/16	8 11/16	6 6/16	Montrose Co., CO	Kevin W. Smith	Kevin W. Smith	1993	333
15 1/16	8 14/16	6 3/16	Douglas Co., OR	Greg A. Thomas	Greg A. Thomas	1994	333
15 1/16	8 14/16	6 3/16	Boundary Co., ID	Ronald R. Frederickson	Ronald R. Frederickson	1994	333
15 1/16	8 14/16	6 3/16	Sanders Co., MT	Dennis J. Gripp	Dennis J. Gripp	1994	333
15 1/16	8 15/16	6 2/16	Teton Co., MT	Ivan L. Irwin	Ivan L. Irwin	1994	333
15 1/16	8 14/16	6 3/16	San Miguel Co., NM	James O. Pittman, Jr.	James O. Pittman, Jr.	1994	333
15 1/16	8 13/16	6 4/16	Wallowa Co., OR	Picked Up	Timothy J. Schommer	PR 1994	333
15 1/16	9	6 1/16	Rio Arriba Co., NM	Robert J. Seeds	Robert J. Seeds	1991	333
15 1/16	8 14/16	6 3/16	Whiskey Creek, AB	Stephen Dyke	Stephen Dyke	1995	333
15 1/16	9	6 1/16	Missoula Co., MT	Brad R. Tacke	Brad R. Tacke	1995	333
15 1/16	8 14/16	6 3/16	Stillwater Co., MT	John D. Devitt	John D. Devitt	1996	333
15 1/16	9	6 1/16	Summit Co., UT	Thomas G. Dunlap	Thomas G. Dunlap	1996	333
15 1/16	8 12/16	6 5/16	Grand Co., CO	Ken A. Krien	Ken A. Krien	1996	333
15 1/16	8 13/16	6 4/16	Las Animas Co., CO	Norman R. Noe	Norman R. Noe	1996	333
15 1/16	8 15/16	6 2/16	St. Mary River, BC	Joe Roberts	Joe Roberts	1996	333
15 1/16	8 14/16	6 3/16	Park Co., MT	William D. Bradley	William D. Bradley	1997	333
15 1/16	9	6 1/16	Grand Co., CO	Richard F. Karbowski	Richard F. Karbowski	1997	333
15 1/16	9	6 1/16	Penticton, BC	Brian K. Mortz	Brian K. Mortz	1997	333
15	9	6	Columbia River, WA	J.K. Townsend	Acad. Nat. Sci., Phil.	1834	419
15	9	6	Dotsero, CO	J.T. Meirer	Univ. of Kansas Mus.	1887	419
15	8 12/16	6 4/16	Lincoln Co., MT	Frank Haacke	Univ. of Mont. Zool. Mus.	1950	419
15	8 15/16	6 1/16	Salmon River, ID	Bob Hagel	Bob Hagel	1953	419
15	8 13/16	6 3/16	Iron Co., UT	James A. Worthen	James A. Worthen	1958	419
15	8 11/16	6 5/16	Elko Co., NV	Earl Dudley	Earl Dudley	1959	419
15	8 15/16	6 1/16	Invermere, BC	R.A. Merkner	R.A. Merkner	1959	419

Felis concolor hippolestes and related subspecies

Score	Greatest Length of Skull Without Lower Jaw	Greatest Width of Skull	Locality	Hunter	Owner	Date Killed	Rank
15	8 14/16	6 2/16	Salmon River, ID	Roy Tumilsen	Roy Tumilsen	1959	419
15	8 13/16	6 3/16	Flat Creek, AB	Hyrum R. Baker	Hyrum R. Baker	1960	419
15	8 8/16	6 8/16	Magdalena Mts., NM	Frank C. Hibben	Frank C. Hibben	1960	419
15	8 13/16	6 3/16	Cranbrook, BC	Unknown	Aasland Taxidermy	1961	419
15	8 12/16	6 4/16	Onyx, CA	Ray Mallory	Larry Mansfield	1961	419
15	8 12/16	6 4/16	Powell Co., MT	Copenhaver Bros.	Norris Pratt	1961	419
15	8 14/16	6 2/16	Lumby, BC	Ronald Catt	Ronald Catt	1962	419
15	9	6	Jesmond, BC	Charlie Coldwell	Charlie Coldwell	1963	419
15	8 10/16	6 6/16	Socorro Co., NM	Hugh Olney	Hugh Olney	1964	419
15	8 12/16	6 4/16	Mesa Co., CO	John Adams	John Adams	1965	419
15	9	6	Grass Valley, OR	Danny Henderson	Danny Henderson	1965	419
15	8 13/16	6 3/16	Grand Forks, BC	Clarence C. Bahr	Clarence C. Bahr	1966	419
15	8 12/16	6 4/16	West Kootenay, BC	M.E. Goddard	M.E. Goddard	1966	419
15	8 11/16	6 5/16	Darfield, BC	Ted Scott	Ted Scott	1966	419
15	8 12/16	6 4/16	Idaho Co., ID	Jack D. Sheppard	Jack D. Sheppard	1966	419
15	8 13/16	6 3/16	Selway River, ID	Ken Wolfinbarger	Ken Wolfinbarger	1966	419
15	8 12/16	6 4/16	Fisher Creek, AB	Perry Jacobson	Perry Jacobson	1967	419
15	8 14/16	6 2/16	Hanksville, UT	Eddie D. Scheinost	Eddie D. Scheinost	1967	419
15	8 12/16	6 4/16	Ferndale, MT	Loren R. Wittrock	Loren R. Wittrock	1967	419
15	8 14/16	6 2/16	Wolf Creek, MT	Gus R. Wolfe	G.R. Wolfe & J. Lee	1967	419
15	8 11/16	6 5/16	Alpine Co., CA	Jeffrey A. Brent	Jeffrey A. Brent	1968	419
15	8 13/16	6 3/16	Spanish Fork Canyon, UT	Richard C. Smith	Richard C. Smith	1968	419
15	8 11/16	6 5/16	Mizzezula Mts., BC	Bengt G. Bjalme	Bengt G. Bjalme	1969	419
15	8 15/16	6 1/16	Canon City, CO	Dale R. Leonard	Dale R. Leonard	1969	419
15	8 10/16	6 6/16	Ferry Co., WA	John D. Mercer	John D. Mercer	1969	419
15	8 14/16	6 2/16	Lucile, ID	Carl P. Bentz	Mrs. W.H. Prescott, Jr.	1969	419
15	8 12/16	6 4/16	Stevens Co., WA	N. Willey & L. Hedrick	N. Willey & L. Hedrick	1969	419
15	8 12/16	6 4/16	Wells, NV	Marvin Johnson	Marvin Johnson	1970	419
15	8 13/16	6 3/16	Canon City, CO	Glen Rosengarten	Glen Rosengarten	1970	419
15	8 13/16	6 3/16	Kootenai Co., ID	George H. Daly	George H. Daly	1971	419
15	9	6	Antelope Pass, CO	Phil Nichols	Phil Nichols	1971	419
15	8 12/16	6 4/16	Stevens Co., WA	Roger Lofts	Roger Lofts	1971	419
15	8 14/16	6 2/16	Las Animas Co., CO	Marion M. Snyder	Mike Powell	1974	419
15	8 14/16	6 2/16	Millard Co., UT	Picked Up	UT Div. of Wildl. Resc.	1974	419
15	8 12/16	6 4/16	Ashcroft, BC	Ken Kilback	Ken Kilback	1975	419
15	8 13/16	6 3/16	Huerfano Co., CO	Sheila D. Bisgard	Sheila D. Bisgard	1977	419
15	8 14/16	6 2/16	Latah Co., ID	Earl Landrus	Earl Landrus	1977	419
15	8 13/16	6 3/16	Prouton Lakes, BC	G.C. Ridley	G.C. Ridley & R. Gillespie	1977	419

15	8 12/16	6 4/16	Union Co., OR	Brian Spencer	Brian Spencer	1977	419
15	8 11/16	6 5/16	Stevens Co., WA	Roger A. Rasching	Roger A. Rasching	1979	419
15	8 15/16	6 1/16	Skookumchuck Creek, BC	Jack Walkley, Jr.	Jack Walkley, Jr.	1979	419
15	8 11/16	6 5/16	Nine Mile Creek, BC	Ray Carry	Ray Carry	1980	419
15	8 14/16	6 2/16	Madison Co., MT	George A. Dieruf	George A. Dieruf	1980	419
15	9	6	Washington Co., UT	J. Phil Goodson	J. Phil Goodson	1980	419
15	8 11/16	6 5/16	San Miguel Co., CO	James N. McHolme	James N. McHolme	1981	419
15	8 15/16	6 1/16	Millard Co., UT	William J. Alldredge	William J. Alldredge	1982	419
15	8 12/16	6 4/16	Rio Arriba Co., NM	Michael Ray	Michael Ray	1982	419
15	8 10/16	6 6/16	Teton Co., MT	Richard Klick	John F. Sulik	1982	419
15	8 14/16	6 2/16	Gila Co., AZ	William T. Haney	William T. Haney	1983	419
15	8 10/16	6 6/16	Wallowa Co., OR	Edward Cranston	Edward Cranston	1984	419
15	8 11/16	6 5/16	Ashnola River, BC	Bill Bryant	Bill Bryant	1985	419
15	8 13/16	6 3/16	Mesa Co., CO	Lawrence C. Glass	Lawrence C. Glass	1985	419
15	8 13/16	6 3/16	San Miguel Co., CO	Jerry J. Jergins	Jerry J. Jergins	1985	419
15	8 15/16	6 1/16	Dolores Co., CO	Ray E. Ables	Ray E. Ables	1986	419
15	9	6	Rio Grande Co., CO	Richard J. Dugas	Richard J. Dugas	1986	419
15	8 14/16	6 2/16	Idaho Co., ID	John G. Klauss	John G. Klauss	1986	419
15	8 15/16	6 1/16	Lewis & Clark Co., MT	Jim Foster	Jim Foster	1987	419
15	8 12/16	6 4/16	Dolores Co., CO	Richard S. Inman	Richard S. Inman	1987	419
15	8 14/16	6 2/16	Deadeye Creek, BC	Claude W. Rohrbaugh	Claude W. Rohrbaugh	1987	419
15	8 11/16	6 5/16	Columbia Co., WA	David N. Bowen	David N. Bowen	1988	419
15	8 13/16	6 3/16	Ferry Co., WA	Arthur E. Crate	Arthur E. Crate	1988	419
15	8 12/16	6 4/16	Big Horn Co., WY	Brant Z. Hilman	Brant Z. Hilman	1988	419
15	8 13/16	6 3/16	Summers Creek, BC	Jack Sprayberry	Jack Sprayberry	1988	419
15	8 12/16	6 4/16	Clear Creek Co., CO	Garry E. Fry	Garry E. Fry	1989	419
15	8 13/16	6 3/16	Pillow Lake, BC	K.T. Michie & T. Wasylyszyn	Kent T. Michie	1989	419
15	8 12/16	6 4/16	Porcupine Hills, AB	Dennis M. Olson	Dennis M. Olson	1989	419
15	8 14/16	6 2/16	Rio Arriba Co., NM	Robert J. Seeds	Robert J. Seeds	1989	419
15	9	6	Elmore Co., ID	Ed J. Strayhorn	Ed J. Strayhorn	1989	419
15	8 11/16	6 5/16	Cotton Creek, BC	Ed Swanson, Jr.	Ed Swanson, Jr.	1989	419
15	8 11/16	6 5/16	Bob Creek, AB	Tom Ellis	Tom Ellis	1990	419
15	8 15/16	6 1/16	Grand Co., UT	Darin King	Darin King	1990	419
15	8 11/16	6 2/16	Carbon Co., UT	Roy R. Wheeler, Jr.	Roy R. Wheeler, Jr.	1990	419
15	8 14/16	6 4/16	Kane Co., UT	Robert A. Carlson	Robert A. Carlson	1991	419
15	8 12/16	6 6/16	Granite Co., MT	Hal W. Johnson	Hal W. Johnson	1991	419
15	8 10/16	6 3/16	Eagle Co., CO	James R. Johnston	James R. Johnston	1991	419
15	8 13/16	6 4/16	Spokane Co., WA	Colin F. MacRae	Colin F. MacRae	1991	419
15	8 12/16	6 1/16	Duchesne Co., UT	Lonnie L. Ritchey	Lonnie L. Ritchey	1991	419
15	8 15/16	6 5/16	Wallowa Co., OR	Sharron K. Tarter	Sharron K. Tarter	1991	419
15	8 11/16	6 5/16	Fergus Co., MT	Charles R. Taylor	Charles R. Taylor	1991	419
15	8 11/16	6 2/16	Columbia Co., WA	Paul R. Becker	Paul R. Becker	1992	419
15	8 14/16	6 5/16	Garfield Co., UT	Gregory A. Nixon	Gregory A. Nixon	1992	419
15	8 11/16	6 2/16	Eagle Co., CO	Dwain Spray	Dwain Spray	1992	419
15	9	6	Las Animas Co., CO	Rick E. Tenreiro	Rick E. Tenreiro	1992	419
15	9	6	Lander Co., NV	Travis S. Edgar	Travis S. Edgar	1993	419
15	8 14/16	6 2/16	Utah Co., UT	Jerome F. Heckman, Jr.	Jerome F. Heckman, Jr.	1993	419

COUGAR

Felis concolor hippolestes and related subspecies

Score	Greatest Length of Skull Without Lower Jaw	Greatest Width of Skull	Locality	Hunter	Owner	Date Killed	Rank
15	8 13/16	6 3/16	Wallowa Co., OR	Dwayne E. Heikes	Dwayne E. Heikes	1993	419
15	8 14/16	6 2/16	Okanogan Co., WA	Harlan R. Tverberg	Harlan R. Tverberg	1993	419
15	8 11/16	6 5/16	Park Co., WY	Jack E. Potter	Jack E. Potter	1994	419
15	8 13/16	6 3/16	Ram River, AB	John M. Straughan	John M. Straughan	1994	419
15	8 13/16	6 3/16	Hawkins Creek, BC	Ross S. Priest	Ross S. Priest	1995	419
15	8 3/16	6 13/16	Powell Co., MT	David F. Skaw	David F. Skaw	1995	419
15	8 12/16	6 4/16	Duchesne Co., UT	Gary A. Durfee	Gary A. Durfee	1996	419
15	8 10/16	6 6/16	Stillwater Co., MT	Darrell G. Holmquist	Darrell G. Holmquist	1996	419
15	8 13/16	6 3/16	Rio Blanco Co., CO	Lyle R. Sigg	Lyle R. Sigg	1996	419
15	8 14/16	6 2/16	Idaho Co., ID	Garold J. Skluzacek	Garold J. Skluzacek	1996	419
15	8 12/16	6 4/16	Routt Co., CO	Bob Barnes	Bob Barnes	1997	419
15	8 15/16	6 1/16	Catron Co., NM	Kenneth E. Justus	Kenneth E. Justus	1997	419
15 14/16*	9 1/16	5 15/16	Routt Co., CO	Tavis D. Rogers	Tavis D. Rogers	1997	419
15 11/16*	9 3/16	6 11/16	Canim Lake, BC	Alejandro Vidaurreta	Alejandro Vidaurreta	1992	419
15 9/16*	9 3/16	6 8/16	Clearwater Co., ID	Dwight Snyder	Dwight Snyder	1990	419
	9 1/16	6 8/16	Umatilla Co., OR	David L. Bradshaw	David L. Bradshaw	1994	

* Final score is subject to revision by additional verifying measurements.

GENE ALFORD RECEIVING THE SAGAMORE HILL AWARD FROM DR. RED DUKE AT THE BOONE AND CROCKETT CLUB'S 20TH AWARDS BANQUET IN 1989.

CATEGORY
COUGAR

SCORE
15-7/16

HUNTER
MICHAEL C. BENNETT

LOCATION
UNION CO., OR

DATE OF KILL
OCTOBER 1996

CATEGORY
COUGAR

SCORE
15

HUNTER
DWAIN SPRAY

LOCATION
EAGLE CO., CO

DATE OF KILL
DECEMBER 1992

CATEGORY
COUGAR

SCORE
15-5/16

HUNTER
DENNIS D. CHURCH

LOCATION
ALBANY CO., WY

DATE OF KILL
NOVEMBER 1994

ATLANTIC WALRUS
WORLD'S RECORD

The story surrounding this big game World's Record cannot be traced much further back than the 1950s. It was at this time that Roy Vail of Warwick, New York, came across a unique find, the tremendous tusks of an Atlantic walrus (*Odobenus rosmarus rosmarus*). Vail, an importer-exporter of fine hunting supplies, purchased the loose tusks from a G.I. who had brought them back from his tour in Greenland. Having a good eye and genuine interest, Vail had a feeling that the tusks may just measure up as a Boone and Crockett record. On January 14, 1955, the trophy became the new World's Record at 118-6/8 and was generously donated to the National Collection of Heads and Horns.

The immensity of these ivory tusks sparks the imagination. The size of this Atlantic walrus may very well have been 12 feet long and weighed over 3,000 pounds. Tusks such as these would have indicated a superior social rank, providing ample protection during aggressive encounters with rivals as well as natural predators such as polar bears and killer whales. While diving for food, the walrus may have used the tusks to stir up clams and other shellfish along the sea bottom, and after resurfacing, as hooks to climb out of the water or to break up an ice floe for breathing holes.

Following Vail's donation, the record tusks became an educational tool that exhibited an insight into this incredible animal's behavior as well as the way of life of an ancient people. For thousands of years, the walrus has been hunted

by the Inuit of Greenland for food and fuel, as well as for making tools, sleds, boats, shelter and clothing. However, there are others that value the ivory tusks of the walrus merely for their monetary worth. This could very well have been the malicious intent underlying their theft from National Collection in 1974. ■

TROPHY INFO

RANK
World's Record

SCORE
118 6/8

LOCATION
Greenland

HUNTER
Unknown

OWNER
Unknown

DATE KILLED
Prior to 1955

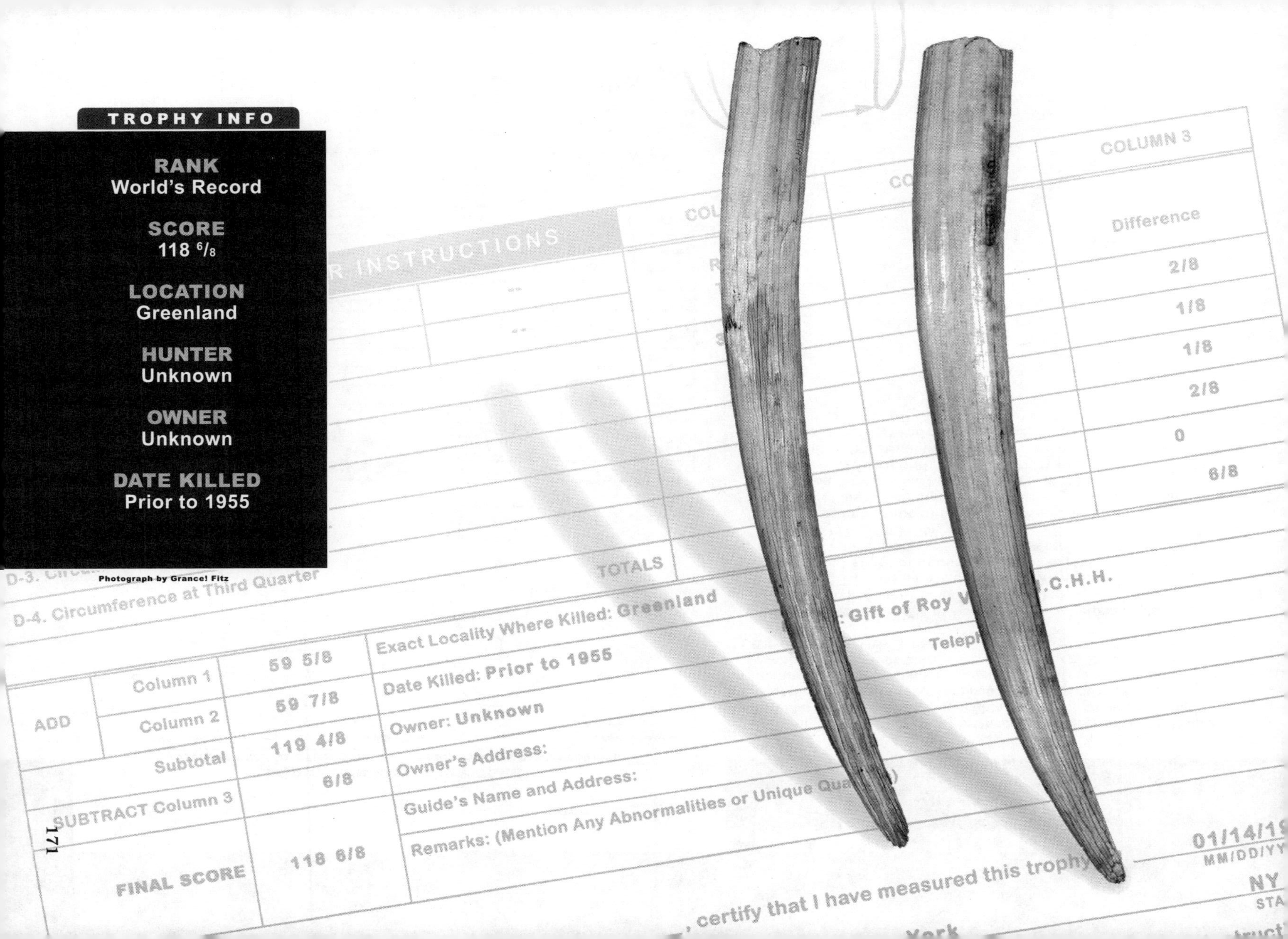

Photograph by Grancel Fitz

COLUMN 3
Difference
2/8
1/8
1/8
2/8
0
6/8

: Gift of Roy V... C.H.H.

Telephone

TOTALS

Exact Locality Where Killed: Greenland

Date Killed: Prior to 1955

Owner: Unknown

Owner's Address:

Guide's Name and Address:

Remarks: (Mention Any Abnormalities or Unique Qua...)

ADD	Column 1	59 5/8
	Column 2	59 7/8
	Subtotal	119 4/8
SUBTRACT Column 3		6/8
FINAL SCORE		118 6/8

D-3. CIR...

D-4. Circumference at Third Quarter

R INSTRUCTIONS

01/14/19
MM/DD/YY

NY
STA...

, certify that I have measured this trophy

York

All measurements must be made with a 1/4-inch wide flexible steel tape to the nearest one-eighth of an inch. Enter fractional figures in eighths, without reduction. Tusks should be removed from mounted specimens for measuring. Official measurements cannot be taken until tusks have air dried for at least 60 days after the animal was killed.

A. Greatest spread is measured between perpendiculars at a right angle to the center line of the skull.

B. Tip to Tip Spread is measured between tips of tusks.

C. Entire Length of Loose Tusk is measured over outer curve from a point in line with the greatest projecting edge of the base to a point in line with tip.

D-1. Circumference of Base is measured at a right angle to axis of tusk. Do not follow irregular edge of tusk; the line of measurement must be entirely on tusk material.

D-2-3-4. Divide length of longer tusk by four. Starting at base, mark both tusks at these quarters (even though the other tusk is shorter) and measure circumferences at these marks.

Records of
North American
Big Game

250 Station Drive
Missoula, MT 59801
(406) 542-1888

BOONE AND CROCKETT CLUB®
OFFICIAL SCORING SYSTEM FOR NORTH AMERICAN BIG GAME TROPHIES

WALRUS

MINIMUM SCORES	AWARDS	ALL-TIME
Atlantic	95	95
Pacific	100	100

KIND OF WALRUS (check one)
■ Atlantic
☐ Pacific

SEE OTHER SIDE FOR INSTRUCTIONS		COLUMN 1 Right Tusk	COLUMN 2 Left Tusk	COLUMN 3 Difference
A. Greatest Spread (If possible)	::			
B. Tip to Tip Spread (If possible)	::			
C. Entire Length of Loose Tusk		30 5/8	30 3/8	2/8
D-1. Circumference of Base		8 3/8	8 4/8	1/8
D-2. Circumference at First Quarter		8 2/8	8 3/8	1/8
D-3. Circumference at Second Quarter		7	7 2/8	2/8
D-4. Circumference at Third Quarter		5 3/8	5 3/8	0
	TOTALS	59 6/8	59 7/8	6/8

ADD	Column 1	59 6/8	Exact Locality Where Killed: Greenland
	Column 2	59 7/8	Date Killed: Prior to 1955 Hunter: Gift of Roy Vail to N.C.H.H.
	Subtotal	119 4/8	Owner: Unknown Telephone #:
SUBTRACT Column 3		6/8	Owner's Address:
			Guide's Name and Address:
FINAL SCORE		118 6/8	Remarks: (Mention Any Abnormalities or Unique Qualities)

I, **Samuel B. Webb**, certify that I have measured this trophy on **01/14/1955**
PRINT NAME   MM/DD/YYYY

at **5 Tudor City Place**   **New York**   **NY**
STREET ADDRESS   CITY   STATE/PROVINCE

and that these measurements and data are, to the best of my knowledge and belief, made in accordance with the instructions given.

Witness: **Betty Fitz**   Signature: **Samuel B. Webb**   I.D. Number
                                          B&C OFFICIAL MEASURER

ATLANTIC WALRUS

Odobenus rosmarus rosmarus

MINIMUM SCORE 95

Score	Entire Length of Loose Tusk		Circumference of Base		Circumference at Third Quarter		Locality	Hunter	Owner	Date Killed	Rank
	R	L	R	L	R	L					
118 6/8	30 5/8	30 3/8	8 3/8	8 4/8	5 3/8	5 3/8	Greenland	Gift of Roy Vail to NCHH	Unknown	PR 1955	1
117 6/8	27 1/8	26 3/8	9 2/8	9 2/8	5 6/8	5 7/8	Greenland	Unknown	Zool. Mus., Copenhagen	PR 1951	2
116 6/8	29 3/8	29 3/8	7 3/8	7 4/8	6	5 7/8	Greenland	Unknown	Zool. Mus., Copenhagen	PR 1951	3
114	28 6/8	28	7 4/8	7 1/8	6	5 7/8	Greenland	Unknown	Zool. Mus., Copenhagen	PR 1951	4
105	25	25	7	7	5 4/8	5 4/8	Greenland	Unknown	Demarest Memorial Mus.	1909	5
103 4/8	24 6/8	25	7 4/8	7 7/8	5 2/8	5	Crockerland, Greenland	D.B. MacMillan	Am. Mus. Nat. Hist.	PR 1916	6
100 6/8	23 7/8	23 5/8	7 4/8	7 2/8	5 2/8	5 3/8	Unknown	Unknown	Zool. Mus., Copenhagen	PR 1951	7
98 4/8	22 3/8	20 7/8	8 2/8	8 3/8	4 7/8	4 5/8	Arctic Ocean	Gift of Peary Arctic Club	Am. Mus. Nat. Hist.	PR 1899	8
98 4/8	24 4/8	24	6 7/8	6 7/8	5 2/8	5 1/8	Crockerland, Greenland	D.B. MacMillan	Am. Mus. Nat. Hist.	PR 1916	8

PACIFIC WALRUS
NEW WORLD'S RECORD

Searching the shores of Bristol Bay, Alaska, in 1997, Ralph Young picked up one of the latest big game World's Record, the colossal tusks of a Pacific walrus (*Odebenus rosmarus divergens*).

Young, who is Commodore of the Naknek Yacht Club, uses his pilot boat to guide barges en route to the salmon canneries along the interior of Bristol Bay. As a man of the sea, an avid hunter, and a pilot who uses his plane to beachcomb "Alaska style," Young has a zest for exploring the Alaskan frontier. He is well aware that the sea deposits many of its treasures in the area, having found Japanese glass ball floats and several walrus and whales. This was particularly evident following a large storm that swept the coast for several days leaving behind a wealth of debris washed upon the shores.

"On July 5, the engine of my Super Cub coughed and soon settled into its normal steady hum over the muddy salmon-filled waters of Bristol Bay. The wind was gusty and soon the far shore came into view. The tide had reached its lowest point as vast expanses of wet mud and sand became dominant. Alaska is said to be twice the size of Texas, but at low tide, Alaska seems three times the size of Texas. Up ahead on the beach, I spotted a gray oblong form washed up on the sand. As I flew over, two white, ivory tusks could be seen against the contrasting sand. There was a small strip of gravel near the high tide breaker line and the Cub gently alighted on the mark. An axe made the removal of the ivory and mask

from the mountain of walrus an easy task. Soon the little Cub was up and heading for the area of Cape Constantine. I spotted another giant monarch up ahead, close to some hard-pack sand. (Certain areas contain soft sand that, when exposed by the tide, can grip a plane's tires and flip it over.) The tusks seemed to be thicker than others, as I worked to remove them."

Aware that the Pacific walrus may not be hunted by non-native people and may only be possessed in compliance with the 1972 Marine Mammals Protection Act, Young took them to the Alaska Department of Fish and Game and had them sealed and registered. However, he did not remove the tusks from the skull until a friend, who was visiting Naknek for the autumn Caribou hunt, convinced him to do so.

"Upon my friend's arrival, he was excited at the size of the tusks, but said they had to be removed from the skull to determine their true size. We took them down to the boat yard and boiled them. After four hours of boiling water filling the air with a unique scent, they were ready to be removed. Heavy gloves gripped the hot tusks as they were slammed down on a 2x12, held in a vise to break them loose. The tape showed each tusk in excess of 36" and nearly 10" around each base."

Scored at 147-4/8, the tusks were judged to be worthy of the Certificate of Merit and became a highlight of Young's years of beachcombing. ∎

	COLUMN 1	COLUMN 2	COLUMN 3
	Right Tusk	Left Tusk	Difference
	37 7/8	36 7/8	0
	9 7/8	9 7/8	1/8
	10 5/8	10 6/8	2/8
	9 4/8	9 2/8	0
	7 1/8	7 1/8	1 3/8
	75	73 7/8	

	13 7/8	
	11 1/8	

Locality Where Killed: Bay, AK

Date Killed: 1997   Hunter: Picked Up

Owner: Ralph Young

Owner's Address:

Telephone

Guides Name and Address:

Remarks: (Mention Any Abnormalities or Unique Qualities)

Examiner

ADD	Column 1	75
	Column 2	73 7/8
	Subtotal	148 7/8
SUBTRACT Column 3		1 3/8
FINAL SCORE		147 4/8

George Tsukamoto

Sparks
CITY

, certify that I have measured

STA

in accordance with the instruct

175

All measurements must be made with a 1/4-inch wide flexible steel tape to the nearest one-eighth of an inch. Enter fractional figures in eighths, without reduction. Tusks should be removed from mounted specimens for measuring. Official measurements cannot be taken until tusks have air dried for at least 60 days after the animal was killed.

A. Greatest spread is measured between perpendiculars at a right angle to the center line of the skull.

B. Tip to Tip Spread is measured between tips of tusks.

C. Entire Length of Loose Tusk is measured over outer curve from a point in line with the greatest projecting edge of the base to a point in line with tip.

D-1. Circumference of Base is measured at a right angle to axis of tusk. Do not follow irregular edge of tusk; the line of measurement must be entirely on tusk material.

D-2-3-4. Divide length of longer tusk by four. Starting at base, mark both tusks at these quarters (even though the other tusk is shorter) and measure circumferences at these marks.

Records of
North American
Big Game

250 Station Drive
Missoula, MT 59801
(406) 542-1888

BOONE AND CROCKETT CLUB®

OFFICIAL SCORING SYSTEM FOR NORTH AMERICAN BIG GAME TROPHIES

WALRUS

KIND OF WALRUS (check one)
☐ Atlantic
☑ Pacific

MINIMUM SCORES
	AWARDS	ALL-TIME
Atlantic	95	95
Pacific	100	100

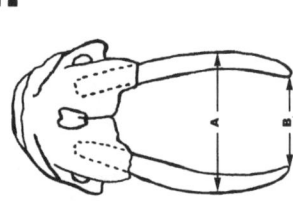

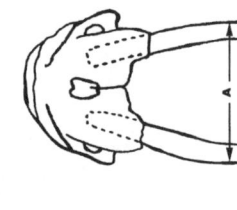

SEE OTHER SIDE FOR INSTRUCTIONS		COLUMN 1	COLUMN 2	COLUMN 3
		Right Tusk	Left Tusk	Difference
A. Greatest Spread (If possible)	13 7/8			
B. Tip to Tip Spread (If possible)	11 1/8			
C. Entire Length of Loose Tusk		37 7/8	36 7/8	1
D-1. Circumference of Base		9 7/8	9 7/8	0
D-2. Circumference at First Quarter		10 5/8	10 6/8	1/8
D-3. Circumference at Second Quarter		9 4/8	9 2/8	2/8
D-4. Circumference at Third Quarter		7 1/8	7 1/8	0
TOTALS		75	73 7/8	1 3/8

	Column 1	75
ADD	Column 2	73 7/8
	Subtotal	148 7/8
SUBTRACT Column 3		1 3/8
FINAL SCORE		147 4/8

Exact Locality Where Killed: **Bristol Bay, AK**

Date Killed: **1997**   Hunter: **Picked Up**

Owner: **Ralph Young**   Telephone #:

Owner's Address:

Guide's Name and Address:

Remarks: (Mention Any Abnormalities or Unique Qualities)

I, **George Tsukamoto** , certify that I have measured this trophy on **04/27/1998**
      PRINT NAME   MM/DD/YYYY

at **1080 Icehouse Ave.**   **Sparks**   **NV**
      STREET ADDRESS   CITY   STATE/PROVINCE

and that these measurements and data are, to the best of my knowledge and belief, made in accordance with the instructions given.

Witness: **Gerard Beaulieu**   Signature: **George Tsukamoto**   I.D. Number:
                                                      B&C OFFICIAL MEASURER

PACIFIC WALRUS
Odobenus rosmarus divergens

Score	Entire Length of Loose Tusk R	L	Circumference of Base R	L	Circumference at Third Quarter R	L	Locality	Hunter	Owner	Date Killed	Rank
147 4/8	37 7/8	36 7/8	9 7/8	9 7/8	7 1/8	7 1/8	Bristol Bay, AK	Picked Up	Ralph Young	1997	1
145 6/8	32 2/8	32 1/8	12 2/8	13	7 2/8	7 1/8	Point Hope, AK	Eskimos	Jonas Bros. of Seattle	1957	2
142 2/8	40 1/8	39 6/8	9 5/8	9 4/8	5 4/8	5 5/8	Bering Sea, AK	Bill Foster	Foster's Bighorn Rest.	1940	3
138 4/8	35 2/8	35 1/8	9 3/8	9 2/8	6 6/8	6 2/8	St. Lawrence Island, AK	Valentin De Madariaga	Valentin De Madariaga	1976	4
137 2/8	36 2/8	36 2/8	9 7/8	10 2/8	6	6 1/8	Alaska	Gift of N.A. Caesar to NCHH	Unknown	PR 1910	5
136 4/8	32 6/8	32 4/8	9 5/8	9 3/8	7 4/8	7 2/8	Port Moller, AK	Picked Up	Larry R. Rivers	1981	6
136 2/8	35 6/8	35	9 5/8	9 3/8	6 3/8	6	Bristol Bay, AK	Eskimo	James W. Brooks	1955	7
135	38	36 3/8	9	9 4/8	5 6/8	5 6/8	Alaska	Picked Up	Paul Umlauf	1970	8
134 6/8	34	34 2/8	9 3/8	9 4/8	6	6	Wainwright, AK	Helen Burnett	Helen Burnett	1964	9
133 6/8	32 2/8	32 6/8	9 4/8	9 4/8	6 6/8	6 7/8	Diomede Islands, AK	Eskimo	Univ. of Iowa Mus.	1893	10
133 6/8	34 4/8	36 3/8	8 7/8	8 5/8	6 7/8	6 4/8	Togiak Bay, AK	Picked Up	Bill Renfrew	1949	10
133 4/8	32 6/8	32	9 1/8	9 1/8	7 2/8	7 1/8	Port Heiden, AK	Picked Up	John T. Taylor	1980	10
133 4/8	37 3/8	37 2/8	7 4/8	7 5/8	6 1/8	6 3/8	Cape Seniavin, AK	Picked Up	Patrick C. Martin	1985	13
133	35	35 2/8	8 4/8	8 4/8	6	6	St. Lawrence Island, AK	Eskimo	Eugene Saxton	1956	14
132 6/8	36 2/8	37 3/8	8 1/8	8	6 2/8	6	Port Moller, AK	Picked Up	R. Hammack & J. Hammack	1984	15
132 4/8	38 1/8	37 6/8	8 5/8	8 6/8	5 4/8	5 5/8	Alaska	Unknown	Harvard Univ. Museum	1870	16
132 4/8	37 6/8	35 3/8	8 6/8	8 6/8	6 2/8	5 5/8	St. Lawrence Island, AK	Eskimo	Adventurers Club of N.Y.	1964	16
132 4/8	34 1/8	34	9 3/8	9 3/8	6 2/8	5 7/8	Hazen Bay, AK	Daniel B. Moore	Daniel B. Moore	1979	16
132 2/8	33 6/8	32 5/8	10 3/8	9	6 5/8	6 4/8	St. Lawrence Island, AK	Robert F. Hurford	Robert F. Hurford	1959	19
132	35 2/8	34	9 2/8	8 7/8	7 1/8	5 7/8	Savoonga, AK	Unknown	Victor Rovier	1967	20
132	29	28 6/8	10 4/8	10 5/8	7 3/8	6 7/8	Savoonga, AK	Gordon Iya	C. Vernon Humble	1977	20
131 4/8	36 3/8	35 2/8	8 4/8	8 4/8	5 5/8	5 5/8	Bering Sea, AK	Gift of W.H. White	Am. Mus. Nat. Hist.	1916	22
131 2/8	33 1/8	33 4/8	8 6/8	8 4/8	6 4/8	6 4/8	Wainwright, AK	Eskimo	Ken Armstrong	PR 1946	23
131 2/8	34 3/8	34 6/8	9 1/8	9	5 7/8	5 7/8	Togiak Bay, AK	Picked Up	Clifford H. Driskell	1968	23
131 2/8	31 5/8	31 6/8	8 5/8	9 4/8	6 6/8	6 4/8	Savoonga, AK	Robert M. Vinovich	Robert M. Vinovich	1976	23
131	33 5/8	34 2/8	8 5/8	8 5/8	6 2/8	6 2/8	Hagemeister Island, AK	Picked Up	Frank M. Thomason	1964	26
130 6/8	33 5/8	32 3/8	8 7/8	9 1/8	6 3/8	6 4/8	St. Lawrence Island, AK	Peter W. Bading	Peter W. Bading	1960	27
130 6/8	31 6/8	32 4/8	8 7/8	9 1/8	6 7/8	7	Port Moller, AK	Picked Up	John Sarvis	1980	27
130 4/8	34 7/8	34 4/8	8 2/8	8	6 1/8	6 1/8	St. Lawrence Island, AK	Unknown	Univ. of Alaska	PR 1939	29
130 4/8	36 4/8	35 7/8	8 4/8	8	6 3/8	5 6/8	St. Lawrence Island, AK	George H. Landreth	George H. Landreth	1967	29
130 2/8	34 6/8	35	9	8 6/8	5 6/8	5 4/8	Point Barrow, AK	Eskimos	William E. Moss	1952	31
130 2/8	31 2/8	32	8 7/8	8 7/8	7 2/8	7 1/8	St. Lawrence Island, AK	Grancel Fitz	Mrs. Grancel Fitz	1957	31
129 4/8	34 6/8	33 4/8	8 3/8	8 6/8	6 4/8	6 1/8	Bering Sea, AK	Joseph J. Cafmeyer	Joseph J. Cafmeyer	1976	33
129 4/8	32	32	9	8 5/8	6 7/8	6 4/8	Izembek Lagoon, AK	Picked Up	John Sarvis	1981	33
129 4/8	32 5/8	32 7/8	8 5/8	8 5/8	6 2/8	6 3/8	Port Heiden, AK	Picked Up	Donald R. Warren	1982	33
128 4/8	36	35 4/8	7 7/8	8	5 4/8	5 6/8	Goodnews Bay, AK	Picked Up	David S. Haeg	1994	36
128	30 6/8	30 4/8	9 2/8	9 2/8	7 1/8	7	Savoonga, AK	William M. Wheless III	William M. Wheless III	1977	37
127 6/8	32 7/8	33	9	8 7/8	6	5 5/8	Nome, AK	Charles F. Kleptz	Charles F. Kleptz	1978	38

PACIFIC WALRUS
Odobenus rosmarus divergens

MINIMUM SCORE 100

Score	Entire Length of Loose Tusk R	L	Circumference of Base R	L	Circumference at Third Quarter R	L	Locality	Hunter	Owner	Date Killed	Rank
127 4/8	35 6/8	34 4/8	8 5/8	8 2/8	5 4/8	5 2/8	St. Lawrence Island, AK	Chris Klineburger	Chris Klineburger	1961	39
127 4/8	32 2/8	30 3/8	9	8 6/8	6 6/8	6 6/8	Port Heiden, AK	Picked Up	Larry R. Rivers	1981	39
127 2/8	33 7/8	34 6/8	8 1/8	8 3/8	5 4/8	5 6/8	Wainwright, AK	J. Richard Reuter III	J. Richard Reuter III	1970	41
127	32 4/8	32 4/8	8 3/8	8 3/8	6 1/8	6	Point Barrow, AK	Karl W. Opryshek	Karl W. Opryshek	1965	42
127	33	32 7/8	8 5/8	9	5 6/8	6	St. Lawrence Island, AK	Norman W. Garwood	Norman W. Garwood	1976	42
127	32 4/8	32 5/8	8 4/8	9	6	6 2/8	St. Lawrence Island, AK	Dick Ullery	Dick Ullery	1976	42
127	34 2/8	34 2/8	7 6/8	7 5/8	6	6 1/8	Cape Pierce, AK	Picked Up	David S. Haeg	1992	42
126 4/8	31 6/8	31 6/8	8 6/8	8 7/8	6 1/8	6 1/8	Gambell, AK	Eskimo	Mike W. Millar	1982	46
126 2/8	32 3/8	32 7/8	8 5/8	8 4/8	5 6/8	5 6/8	St. Lawrence Island, AK	Martin J. Foerster	Martin J. Foerster	1958	47
126 2/8	31 6/8	31 1/8	9	8 6/8	6 2/8	6 2/8	Point Barrow, AK	Eskimos	Walter O. Sinn	1958	47
126 2/8	34 3/8	34 4/8	8	8 1/8	5 3/8	5 6/8	Savoonga, AK	Unknown	Wayne S. Weiler	1978	47
126	33 4/8	33	8	8	5 6/8	6 1/8	Alaska Pen., AK	Unknown	Sam Pancotto	1962	50
126	31 1/8	31 3/8	8 4/8	8 3/8	6 6/8	6 7/8	Bering Sea, AK	Wakon I. Redbird	Wakon I. Redbird	1977	50
125 6/8	34 2/8	34 5/8	7 6/8	7 6/8	5 6/8	5 7/8	St. Lawrence Island, AK	Eskimos	Sidney T. Shore	1950	52
125 6/8	30 4/8	31 1/8	9 5/8	9 3/8	6 1/8	6	St. Lawrence Island, AK	F.J. Bremer	F.J. Bremer	1971	52
125	35	34 4/8	8 6/8	8 5/8	4 7/8	4 7/8	Bering Sea, AK	Manfred O. Schroeder	Manfred O. Schroeder	1977	54
125	30 7/8	30 6/8	9 1/8	9 4/8	5 7/8	5 7/8	Gambell, AK	Charles McLaughlin	Charles McLaughlin	1978	55
124 6/8	33 6/8	33 5/8	8 2/8	8 3/8	5 2/8	5	Bering Sea, AK	Henry A. Snow	Snow Museum	1923	56
124 6/8	30 7/8	32	9 1/8	9 4/8	5 3/8	5 6/8	St. Lawrence Island, AK	Bert Klineburger	Bert Klineburger	1962	56
124 6/8	31 7/8	32 7/8	8 2/8	8 2/8	5 7/8	5 7/8	Cape Seniavin, AK	Picked Up	Tom Atkins	1990	56
124 4/8	32 4/8	31 5/8	8 7/8	8 2/8	5 7/8	5 7/8	St. Lawrence Island, AK	Tim Gollorgeren	George H. Landreth	1966	59
124 4/8	32 7/8	32 4/8	7 5/8	7 1/8	6 1/8	7 1/8	Pilot Point, AK	Picked Up	Dick Gunlogson	PR 1969	59
124 4/8	36 2/8	35 5/8	7	7 1/8	5 1/8	5 3/8	Nunivak Island, AK	Terry Yager	Terry Yager	1977	59
124 4/8	31 2/8	30 4/8	8 3/8	8 3/8	6 3/8	6 2/8	Hagemeister Island, AK	Picked Up	Lloyd D. Friend	1979	59
124 2/8	31 5/8	31 6/8	8	7 7/8	6 2/8	6 2/8	Port Moller, AK	Picked Up	Daniel W. Wray	1995	64
124	32 6/8	33 1/8	8	8 4/8	5 6/8	6	Bering Sea, AK	F.E. Klinesmith	Am. Mus. Nat. Hist.	PR 1951	65
123 6/8	35	33 6/8	7 3/8	7 5/8	5 6/8	6	St. Lawrence Island, AK	Bert Klineburger	Bert Klineburger	1969	66
123 6/8	34 7/8	33 4/8	7 6/8	7 3/8	5 1/8	5 6/8	Little Diomede Island, AK	Eskimo	James W. Brooks	1953	66
123 6/8	33 7/8	33 3/8	8 3/8	8	6 2/8	6 3/8	Bering Sea, AK	Dick Salemi	Dick Salemi	1978	66
123 4/8	29 3/8	29 1/8	9	8 6/8	6 2/8	6 3/8	St. Lawrence Island, AK	C.J. McElroy	C.J. McElroy	1968	68
123 4/8	31 5/8	32	9	8 1/8	5 5/8	5 7/8	Bering Sea, AK	Dan H. Brainard	Dan H. Brainard	1977	68
123 4/8	30	29 7/8	9 4/8	9 4/8	5 5/8	5 5/8	Bering Sea, AK	Arthur H. Bullerdick	Arthur H. Bullerdick	1978	68
123 2/8	34	31 7/8	8 4/8	8 4/8	6 3/8	5 3/8	Alaskan Arctic	Eskimo	Robert C. Reeve	PR 1955	71
123 2/8	32 3/8	32 2/8	7 4/8	7 4/8	6 3/8	6 1/8	Nakuck, AK	Unknown	Leonard Schwah	1964	71
123 2/8	28 5/8	28 2/8	9 7/8	9 7/8	6 2/8	6 4/8	Teller, AK	W.J. Glunt	W.J. Glunt	1965	71
123	32 5/8	32 1/8	7 4/8	7 7/8	6 3/8	6 7/8	Cape Constantine, AK	Picked Up	Ray Tremblay	1960	74
123	31	31	8 2/8	8	6 2/8	6	St. Lawrence Island, AK	F. Phillips Williamson	F. Phillips Williamson	1961	74
123	33	32 5/8	7 5/8	7 6/8	6	5 5/8	Nunivak Island, AK	Arvid F. Benson	Arvid F. Benson	1970	74
122 6/8	32 3/8	31 2/8	8	7 6/8	6	6 4/8	Alaska	George Wright	Acad. Nat. Sci., Phil.	1960	77

Score							Locality	Owner	By Whom Killed	Date Killed	Rank
122 6/8	32 5/8	31 6/8	8 1/8	8 1/8	5 6/8	5 6/8	Savoonga, AK	Lynn M. Castle	Lynn M. Castle	1971	77
122 4/8	32 1/8	31 4/8	8 3/8	8 4/8	5 7/8	5 6/8	St. Lawrence Island, AK	Herb Klein	Herb Klein	1959	79
122 4/8	32 2/8	31 4/8	8	8 2/8	5 4/8	5 5/8	Savoonga, AK	William W. Garrison	William W. Garrison	1971	79
122 2/8	30	32 2/8	8 2/8	8 2/8	6 3/8	6 2/8	Walrus Island, AK	Robert C. Reeve	Unknown	1962	81
122	27 2/8	28 6/8	10 2/8	10 2/8	6	6	Diomede Islands, AK	Tony Oney	Tony Oney	1964	82
122	31 4/8	31 1/8	9 1/8	9 2/8	5 7/8	5 3/8	St. Lawrence Island, AK	Ted Lick	Ted Lick	1970	82
121 6/8	31 7/8	32 6/8	8 1/8	8 6/8	5 3/8	5 4/8	Diomede Islands, AK	Tony Oney	Jim Harrower	1964	84
121 4/8	31 6/8	31	8 1/8	8 4/8	5 4/8	5 4/8	Savoonga, AK	Gerald G. Balciar	Gerald G. Balciar	1971	85
121 2/8	31 2/8	31 6/8	8 3/8	8 3/8	5 3/8	5 6/8	Savoonga, AK	Lowell C. Hansen II	Lowell C. Hansen II	1978	86
121 2/8	33 7/8	29 3/8	8 1/8	8 2/8	6 7/8	5 3/8	Alaska Pen., AK	Richard A. Pulley	Picked Up	1994	86
121	33 2/8	34 1/8	7 5/8	7 6/8	5 5/8	5 3/8	Bering Sea, AK	Elmer Keith	Eskimo	1956	88
121	28	28 5/8	11 2/8	9 6/8	5 6/8	5 7/8	Little Diomede Island, AK	William H. Picher	William H. Picher	1966	88
121	29 4/8	29 4/8	8 2/8	8 2/8	6 3/8	6	Nunivak Island, AK	C. Vernon Humble	C. Vernon Humble	1977	88
120 6/8	29 1/8	29 1/8	8 3/8	8 3/8	5 3/8	5 7/8	Little Diomede Island, AK	Robert Curtis	Robert Curtis	1963	91
120 6/8	33 6/8	34	7	6 7/8	5 3/8	5 4/8	Point Hope, AK	Don Johnson	Don Johnson	1963	91
120 6/8	29 7/8	30 4/8	8 7/8	8 7/8	6	6	Cape Thompson, AK	Nick Petropolis	Eskimo	PR 1965	91
120 6/8	29	30 1/8	9	9	5 7/8	5 6/8	Gambell, AK	L. Keith Mortensen	L. Keith Mortensen	1978	91
120 4/8	33 4/8	33 4/8	7	7 1/8	5 2/8	5 3/8	Alaska	Acad. Nat. Sci., Phil.	S.R. Caldwell	1902	95
120 2/8	28 7/8	29 1/8	9 1/8	9 1/8	5 4/8	5 4/8	Savoonga, AK	Werner-Rolf Muno	Werner-Rolf Muno	1971	96
120 2/8	30 2/8	29 4/8	8 3/8	8 3/8	5 7/8	5 7/8	Hazen Bay, AK	Richard D. Dimick	Richard D. Dimick	1979	96
120	27 5/8	30 3/8	9 1/8	6 1/8	6	6	Bristol Bay, AK	Foster H. Thompson	Eskimo	PR 1959	98
120	29	29	8 4/8	8	5 2/8	5 2/8	St. Lawrence Island, AK	Sarkis Atamian	Sarkis Atamian	1968	98
120	30 4/8	33	8 4/8	8 4/8	5 6/8	5 6/8	Bering Sea, AK	George L. Hall	George L. Hall	1977	98
119 6/8	29 2/8	30 6/8	8 7/8	8 7/8	6	6	Savoonga, AK	Ed Cox, Jr.	Ed Cox, Jr.	1977	101
119 6/8	28 1/8	31 6/8	9 3/8	8 7/8	6 6/8	6 5/8	Bristol Bay, AK	Eddie Clark	Picked Up	1990	101
119 2/8	33 1/8	28	7 1/8	7 1/8	6 1/8	6 1/8	Bering Sea, AK	Gary Babcock	Unknown	PR 1975	103
119 2/8	31 2/8	31 1/8	7 6/8	8	5 4/8	5 4/8	Savoonga, AK	Douglas E. Miller	Douglas E. Miller	1976	103
119	30 3/8	30	8	8	5 7/8	5 7/8	Port Moller, AK	Bob Stokes	Picked Up	1961	105
118 4/8	31 4/8	31 4/8	9 1/8	9 1/8	5 5/8	5 1/8	Diomede Islands, AK	Harry J. Armitage	Harry J. Armitage	1965	106
118 4/8	28 3/8	28 6/8	8 2/8	8 4/8	6 2/8	5 7/8	St. Lawrence Island, AK	Alice J. Landreth	Alice J. Landreth	1967	106
118 4/8	29 3/8	28 7/8	8 7/8	8 3/8	6 1/8	5 6/8	St. Lawrence Island, AK	Wilbur L. Leworthy	Wilbur L. Leworthy	1970	106
118 4/8	29 2/8	28 2/8	8 4/8	8 7/8	6 6/8	6 6/8	Savoonga, AK	Clifford Patz	Clifford Patz	1979	106
118 2/8	31 4/8	32	7 4/8	7 4/8	5 1/8	5 1/8	Little Diomede Island, AK	Jack Schwabland	Jack Schwabland	1978	110
117 2/8	30 4/8	29 4/8	7 7/8	7 7/8	5 5/8	5 5/8	St. Lawrence Island, AK	Robert Curtis	Robert Curtis	1963	111
117 2/8	29 4/8	29	8	8	6	6	Little Diomede Island, AK	C. Pitt Sanders	C. Pitt Sanders	1978	111
116 6/8	28	30 1/8	8 5/8	8 2/8	6 4/8	5 7/8	Savoonga, AK	Tony Oney	Eskimos	1962	113
116 4/8	26 7/8	28	8 6/8	8 5/8	6	6	Nunivak Island, AK	Arnold Carlson	Arnold Carlson	1971	114
116 4/8	27 2/8	28 6/8	8 7/8	8 6/8	6	6	Savoonga, AK	Darrell D. Wells	Darrell D. Wells	1978	114
116 2/8	29	28 4/8	8 4/8	8	6	6	Point Hope, AK	R. & C. Ballow	Unknown	PR 1994	116
116	29 3/8	29	8	8	5 7/8	5 5/8	Bering Sea, AK	William C. Penttila	Picked Up	1965	117
116	28	28	8 3/8	8 3/8	5 6/8	5 5/8	St. Lawrence Island, AK	Hugh L. Nichols, Jr.	Hugh L. Nichols, Jr.	1972	117
115 6/8	30 3/8	29 6/8	8 6/8	8 2/8	5 1/8	5 1/8	Savoonga, AK	U.S. Natl. Mus.	Hugh H. Logan	1962	119
115 6/8	27 3/8	31 4/8	8 1/8	8	6 3/8	6	Diomede Islands, AK	Peter A. Bossart	Peter A. Bossart	1972	119
115 4/8	28 7/8	29	7 6/8	8 1/8	5 7/8	6	Savoonga, AK	Gerald L. Warnock	Gerald L. Warnock	1977	119
115 4/8	29 6/8	29 6/8	7 7/8	8	5 3/8	5 3/8	St. Lawrence Island, AK	Univ. of Alaska	Unknown	1953	122
115 4/8	30 2/8	30 1/8	7 4/8	7 5/8	5 4/8	5 3/8	St. Lawrence Island, AK	W.T. Yoshimoto	W.T. Yoshimoto	1962	122
115 4/8	27 2/8	25 2/8	9 2/8	9 2/8	6 1/8	6 1/8	Little Diomede Island, AK	Basil C. Bradbury	Basil C. Bradbury	1964	122

Score	Entire Length of Loose Tusk R	L	Circumference of Base R	L	Circumference at Third Quarter R	L	Locality	Hunter	Owner	Date Killed	Rank
115 2/8	30 4/8	31	7 2/8	7 4/8	5 1/8	5 3/8	Little Diomede Island, AK	Jack D. Putnam	Jack D. Putnam	1965	125
115 2/8	27 6/8	31 6/8	8 6/8	8 7/8	5 5/8	5 2/8	Nunivak Island, AK	Lloyd Ward	Lloyd Ward	1971	125
115	31 1/8	30 7/8	6 7/8	7	5 4/8	5 6/8	Savoonga, AK	John Estes	John Estes	1978	127
114 6/8	29 6/8	29 4/8	7 6/8	7 6/8	5 3/8	5	Point Hope, AK	Eskimo	Jonas Bros. of Alaska	1958	128
114 6/8	29	29 5/8	7 3/8	7 5/8	5 6/8	5 6/8	Kigluaik Mts., AK	Russell H. Underdahl	Russell H. Underdahl	1978	128
114 4/8	29 3/8	29 4/8	8 2/8	8 2/8	5 1/8	5 1/8	Savoonga, AK	Richard G. Van Vorst	Richard G. Van Vorst	1976	130
114	26 4/8	26 6/8	9 5/8	9 6/8	5 2/8	5 1/8	Kotzebue, AK	E.B. Rhodes	E.B. Rhodes	1964	131
113 6/8	28 7/8	26 5/8	9	9 1/8	5 1/8	5 2/8	St. Lawrence Island, AK	Maitland Armstrong	Maitland Armstrong	1961	132
113 6/8	26	26 1/8	8 2/8	8 1/8	6 1/8	6	Point Hope, AK	Glenn W. Slade	Glenn W. Slade	1961	132
113 6/8	29	29 5/8	7 5/8	7 6/8	5 2/8	5 3/8	Point Hope, AK	Eskimos	John W. Elmore	1966	132
113 6/8	29 4/8	28 2/8	7 3/8	7 3/8	5 6/8	5 5/8	St. Lawrence Island, AK	Denver D. Coleman	Denver D. Coleman	1968	132
113 6/8	28 4/8	28 5/8	7 5/8	7 5/8	5 6/8	5 4/8	St. Lawrence Island, AK	Dick Davis	Dick Davis	1976	132
113 6/8	31 3/8	30 5/8	7 3/8	7 2/8	5 1/8	5 1/8	Savoonga, AK	Warren K. Parker	Warren K. Parker	1979	132
113 4/8	28 7/8	28 5/8	7 5/8	7 4/8	5 4/8	5 4/8	Savoonga, AK	Tom Andersen	Tom Andersen	1978	138
113 2/8	27 5/8	27 2/8	8 6/8	8 3/8	5 3/8	5 3/8	St. Lawrence Island, AK	W. Brandon Macomber	W. Brandon Macomber	1965	139
113 2/8	28 1/8	28 3/8	8 2/8	8 3/8	5	5 3/8	Nunivak Island, AK	C.R. Feazell	C.R. Feazell	1972	139
113 2/8	27 5/8	27 5/8	7 5/8	7 5/8	6 2/8	5 7/8	Bering Sea, AK	Jack Holland	Jack Holland	1978	139
113	29 5/8	29 4/8	8 1/8	8	5	5	St. Lawrence Island, AK	Jim Roe	Jim Roe	1969	142
113	30 4/8	29 1/8	7 2/8	7 3/8	5 4/8	5 4/8	St. Lawrence Island, AK	I.D. Shapiro	I.D. Shapiro	1970	142
113	28	27	8 3/8	8	5 5/8	5 3/8	St. Lawrence Island, AK	Gail W. Holderman	Gail W. Holderman	1976	142
113	27 1/8	26	8 1/8	8	4 7/8	6 1/8	Bering Sea, AK	Jon E. Holland	Jon E. Holland	1978	142
113	31 7/8	31	6 6/8	6 6/8	4 7/8	4 6/8	St. Lawrence Island, AK	G.A. Treschow	G.A. Treschow	1979	142
112 6/8	27 7/8	27 6/8	8 2/8	8 1/8	5 3/8	5 1/8	St. Lawrence Island, AK	Alfred F. Corwin	Alfred F. Corwin	1964	147
112 4/8	28 1/8	27 7/8	7 7/8	7 4/8	5 5/8	6 2/8	St. Lawrence Island, AK	Henry K. Leworthy	Henry K. Leworthy	1970	148
112 4/8	27 7/8	27 6/8	8 2/8	8 2/8	5 4/8	5 4/8	Togiak Bay, AK	Picked Up	Lloyd E. Zeman	PR 1970	148
112 4/8	28 6/8	27 5/8	7 5/8	7 4/8	5 6/8	5 5/8	Savoonga, AK	Harm De Boer	Harm De Boer	1972	148
112 4/8	25	23 6/8	8 6/8	8 5/8	6 4/8	6 6/8	Nunivak Island, AK	W.K. Leech	W.K. Leech	1972	148
112 2/8	29 4/8	28 7/8	7 4/8	7 6/8	5 1/8	5	St. Lawrence Island, AK	Eskimo	George H. Landreth	1966	152
111 6/8	27 4/8	32 1/8	8 6/8	8 4/8	4 4/8	6	Point Hope, AK	Gary D'Aigle	Gary D'Aigle	1968	153
111 6/8	30 4/8	26 4/8	8 1/8	7 6/8	5 7/8	5 5/8	St. Lawrence Island, AK	Don L. Corley	Don L. Corley	1977	153
111 6/8	30 4/8	29 5/8	6 7/8	6 7/8	5 3/8	5 2/8	Strogonof Point, AK	Picked Up	Brian G. Oldfield	1993	153
111	28 3/8	28 1/8	7	6 7/8	5 5/8	5 5/8	Savoonga, AK	Robert E. Speegle	Robert E. Speegle	1972	156
111	28 5/8	30	7 7/8	8	4 5/8	4 7/8	St. Lawrence Island, AK	Don B. Skidmore	Don B. Skidmore	1977	156
110 6/8	29 1/8	30 1/8	7 6/8	7 6/8	4 6/8	4 6/8	Savoonga, AK	John M. Blair	John M. Blair	1971	158
110 4/8	29 7/8	27 5/8	6 3/8	7 3/8	5 6/8	5 7/8	St. Lawrence Island, AK	Hugh H. Logan	Los Angeles Co. Mus.	1962	159
110 2/8	27 6/8	27 4/8	8	7 4/8	5 4/8	5 1/8	St. Lawrence Island, AK	Robert Rood	Robert Rood	1966	160
110 2/8	27	26 4/8	8 1/8	8	5 4/8	5 3/8	Kuskokwim Bay, AK	James Lewis	Steve Bayless	1969	160
110 2/8	30 4/8	30 3/8	6 5/8	6 5/8	4 7/8	4 6/8	Nunivak Island, AK	Arthur LaCapria	Arthur LaCapria	1971	160
110 2/8	27 6/8	28	7 6/8	7 7/8	5	5	Point Barrow, AK	Cecil M. Hopper	Cecil M. Hopper	1972	160

Score						Locality	Hunter	Owner	Date Killed	Rank
110 2/8	28 6/8	28 6/8	7 3/8	7 2/8	5 1/8 / 4 7/8	St. Lawrence Island, AK	Wayne S. Weiler	Wayne S. Weiler	1972	160
110 2/8	28 3/8	28 2/8	7 2/8	7 2/8	5 2/8 / 5 2/8	St. Lawrence Island, AK	James A. Bush, Jr.	James A. Bush, Jr.	1979	160
110 2/8	29 7/8	29 1/8	7 3/8	7 3/8	4 7/8 / 4 6/8	St. Lawrence Island, AK	Val Tibbetts	Val Tibbetts	1979	160
110	28 6/8	28 6/8	7 1/8	7 2/8	5 2/8 / 5 2/8	Nelson Island, AK	Picked Up	Brent R. Akers	1987	167
109 6/8	28 1/8	28 2/8	7 3/8	7 4/8	5 / 5	Point Franklin, AK	Michael R. Bogan	Michael R. Bogan	1978	168
109 4/8	26 4/8	26 2/8	8 2/8	8 2/8	5 / 5	Savoonga, AK	Richard A. Furniss	Richard A. Furniss	1972	169
109 4/8	27 6/8	27 5/8	8	8	4 7/8 / 5 3/8	St. Lawrence Island, AK	Mahlon T. White	Mahlon T. White	1977	169
108 6/8	28 6/8	27 1/8	7 7/8	7 2/8	5 6/8 / 5 3/8	St. Lawrence Island, AK	T.E. Shillingburg	T.E. Shillingburg	1961	171
108 4/8	30 6/8	30 7/8	7	6 7/8	4 4/8 / 5 4/8	Wainwright, AK	Delano J. Lietzau	Delano J. Lietzau	1978	172
108 2/8	27	30	7 3/8	7 1/8	5 1/8 / 5 1/8	Little Diomede Island, AK	Barrie White	Barrie White	1963	173
107 2/8	26 5/8	28 4/8	7 6/8	7 6/8	4 6/8 / 4 7/8	Bering Sea, AK	Gary Boychuk	Gary Boychuk	1977	174
107	27 2/8	27 5/8	7 2/8	7 2/8	5 1/8 / 5 1/8	St. Lawrence Island, AK	W.A. Bond	W.A. Bond	1964	175
106	26 5/8	26	7 3/8	7 2/8	5 4/8 / 5 1/8	Savoonga, AK	Jon G. Koshell	Jon G. Koshell	1972	176
104 4/8	23 3/8	23 3/8	7 3/8	7 1/8	6 2/8 / 6 2/8	St. Lawrence Island, AK	L.M. Cole	L.M. Cole	1964	177
104 4/8	26 6/8	26 7/8	7 5/8	7 4/8	4 6/8 / 4 5/8	Bering Sea, AK	Rudolf Sand	Rudolf Sand	1971	177
104 4/8	26 4/8	26 4/8	7 4/8	7 7/8	4 7/8 / 5	Savoonga, AK	Andrew A. Samuels, Jr.	Andrew A. Samuels, Jr.	1979	177
104	24 7/8	26	8	8	5 / 5 2/8	St. Lawrence Island, AK	Norman S. MacPhee	B&C National Collection	1978	180
104	27 7/8	26 3/8	6 4/8	6 4/8	5 1/8 / 5 4/8	Wainwright, AK	Donald R. Theophilus	Donald R. Theophilus	1978	180
103 2/8	26	26 1/8	6 6/8	6 6/8	4 7/8 / 5	Point Barrow, AK	Glenn W. Slade	Glenn W. Slade	1968	182
103 2/8	26 1/8	27 4/8	6 3/8	6 2/8	5 1/8 / 4 5/8	St. Lawrence Island, AK	Gunther Matschke	Gunther Matschke	1972	182
102 6/8	27 3/8	28 2/8	6 5/8	6 3/8	5 5/8 / 5 4/8	Port Moller, AK	Picked Up	Dan Lynch	1966	184
102	28 2/8	25 3/8	7 4/8	7 4/8	5 4/8 / 4 5/8	St. Lawrence Island, AK	Dalton Foster	Dalton Foster	1961	185
102	25 3/8	25	7 5/8	7 4/8	4 5/8 / 4 5/8	Savoonga, AK	Robert J. Bartlett	Robert J. Bartlett	1979	185
101 2/8	24 6/8	26 7/8	6 7/8	7	4 2/8 / 4 6/8	St. Lawrence Island, AK	Eskimo	Steve Fowler	1967	187
147 *	37 2/8	37	10	10 1/8	7 4/8 / 7 4/8	Egegik Bay, AK	Picked Up	George G. Tibbetts, Jr.	1970	

* Final score is subject to revision by additional verifying measurements.

AMERICAN ELK - TYPICAL ANTLERS
NEW WORLD'S RECORD

Growing up in the White Mountains of eastern Arizona has given Alan C. Ellsworth the opportunity to see some great elk. However, he never would have imagined what was going to take place on February 28, 1995.

"Being a local antler buyer, I was leaving my home to pick up some antlers. As I was waiting at the intersection to pull onto Main Street, a blue Dodge pickup loaded with a washer and dryer, along with a great elk rack, drove by. As I pulled onto Main, behind the truck, I was in awe of the faded elk rack. It was turned upside down, straddling the dryer. My first thought was, 'There's a 400 point bull!' I followed the truck for about a mile, guessing the 6x6 would score about 420 points. The truck turned into a local restaurant and I had to see the bull up close, so I turned in as well.

"To make the story short, I was able to purchase the elk. I took the rack back home, quickly put a tape to it, and came up with a score of 438. Telling my wife, Debby, that we may have a new state record, I hurried out the door to get back to my antler business. While I was gone I kept thinking, 'I must have made a mistake on my score.' I didn't think it was that big. When I returned home that night, I remeasured the huge rack. This time a lot slower! After double checking everything I came up with a score of 445-4/8. Now I was really excited, but also in disbelief! Could I possibly have a new World's Record?"

A week later an official Boone and Crockett measurer, Robin Bechtel, scored the elk at 447-7/8 points. Ellsworth's

trophy went on to break the Arizona state record that April with another score of 446-2/8. However, in order to take the World's Record at Boone and Crockett's 23rd Awards program, Ellsworth would need to provide some additional history on the great 6x6.

Backtracking, Ellsworth traced the story to the previous owner's brother, Alonzo (Lon) Winters of Globe, Arizona. Winters, since deceased, was a second generation cattle rancher who grew up enjoying the outdoors of Arizona. Riding through the White Mountains during the fall of 1968, Winters and close friend, Bill Vogt, spotted the magnificent animal near the Black River. Winters took the elk down using his Savage Model 99 .308, and avoiding incident, the hunters headed out of the canyon with their prize packed on their horses. Later though, Ellsworth noted one minor dilemma Winters had to overcome.

"Tagging his elk presented a problem. In 1968, the Arizona Game and Fish game tags were a metal band. Lon was unable to fit this tag on the large elk, so he notched the bull's antler between the G-4 and G-5 points, so he could properly tag his elk. His children can remember eating elk burger that winter, and the rack was stored for years in the garage. Friends and relatives remember how proud Lon was when he showed them his trophy."

Nearly 30 years later, Ellsworth must have felt similar pride as he concluded the fine elk hunting story with a triumphant ending, a new World's Record scoring 442-5/8 points. ∎

TROPHY INFO

RANK
New World's Record

SCORE
442 5/8

LOCATION
White Mountains, AZ

HUNTER
Alonzo Winters

OWNER
Alan C. Ellsworth

DATE KILLED
1968

183

All measurements must be made with a 1/4-inch wide flexible steel tape to the nearest one-eighth of an inch. (Note: A flexible steel cable can be used to measure points and main beams only.) Enter fractional figures in eighths, without reduction. Official measurements cannot be taken until the antlers have air dried for at least 60 days after the animal was killed.

A. Number of Points on Each Antler: To be counted a point, the projection must be at least one inch long, with length exceeding width at one inch or more of length. All points are measured from tip of point to nearest edge of beam as illustrated. Beam tip is counted as a point but not measured as a point.

B. Tip to Tip Spread is measured between tips of main beams.

C. Greatest Spread is measured between perpendiculars at a right angle to the center line of the skull at widest part, whether across main beams or points.

D. Inside Spread of Main Beams is measured at a right angle to the center line of the skull at widest point between main beams. Enter this measurement again as the Spread Credit if it is less than or equal to the length of the longer antler; if greater, enter longer antler length for Spread Credit.

E. Total of Lengths of all Abnormal Points: Abnormal Points are those non-typical in location (such as points originating from a point or from bottom or sides of main beam) or pattern (extra points, not generally paired). Measure in usual manner and record in appropriate blanks.

F. Length of Main Beam is measured from the center of the lowest outside edge of burr over the outer side to the most distant point of the main beam. The point of beginning is that point on the burr where the center line along the outer side of the beam intersects the burr, then following generally the line of the illustration.

G-1-2-3-4-5-6-7. Length of Normal Points: Normal points project from the top or front of the main beam in the general pattern illustrated. They are measured from nearest edge of main beam over outer curve to tip. Lay the tape along the outer curve of the beam so that the top edge of the tape coincides with the top edge of the beam on both sides of point to determine the baseline for point measurement. Record point length in appropriate blanks.

H-1-2-3-4. Circumferences are taken as detailed in illustration for each measurement.

Records of North American Big Game

BOONE AND CROCKETT CLUB®

250 Station Drive
Missoula, MT 59801
(406) 542-1888

OFFICIAL SCORING SYSTEM FOR NORTH AMERICAN BIG GAME TROPHIES

TYPICAL
AMERICAN ELK (WAPITI)

MINIMUM SCORES
AWARDS   ALL-TIME
360   375

Detail of Point Measurement

Abnormal Points

	Right Antler	Left Antler
		2 1/8
		2 1/8
SUBTOTALS		2 1/8
TOTAL TO E		2 1/8

SEE OTHER SIDE FOR INSTRUCTIONS

A. No. Points on Right Antler	6	No. Points on Left Antler	7
B. Tip to Tip Spread	47	C. Greatest Spread	52
D. Inside Spread of Main Beams	47 4/8	SPREAD CREDIT MAY EQUAL BUT NOT EXCEED LONGER ANTLER	

	COLUMN 1	COLUMN 2	COLUMN 3	COLUMN 4
	Spread Credit	Right Antler	Left Antler	Difference
	47 4/8			
E. Total of Lengths of Abnormal Points				2 1/8
F. Length of Main Beam		56 2/8	56 2/8	0
G-1. Length of First Point		22 2/8	25 6/8	3 4/8
G-2. Length of Second Point		29	25 6/8	3 2/8
G-3. Length of Third Point		22 3/8	23 5/8	1 2/8
G-4. Length of Fourth Point		24 5/8	22	2 5/8
G-5. Length of Fifth Point		19	17 2/8	1 6/8
G-6. Length of Sixth Point, If Present				
G-7. Length of Seventh Point, If Present				
H-1. Circumference at Smallest Place Between First and Second Points		11	10 2/8	6/8
H-2. Circumference at Smallest Place Between Second and Third Points		8	7 6/8	2/8
H-3. Circumference at Smallest Place Between Third and Fourth Points		8 1/8	8 4/8	3/8
H-4. Circumference at Smallest Place Between Fourth and Fifth Points		6 5/8	7 7/8	1 2/8
TOTALS	47 4/8	207 2/8	205	17 1/8

Exact Locality Where Killed: White Mountains, AZ	
Date Killed: 1968	Hunter: Alonzo Winters
Owner: Alan C. Ellsworth	Telephone #:
Owner's Address:	
Guide's Name and Address:	
Remarks: (Mention Any Abnormalities or Unique Qualities)	

ADD	Column 1	47 4/8
	Column 2	207 2/8
	Column 3	205
	Subtotal	459 6/8
SUBTRACT Column 4		17 1/8
FINAL SCORE		442 5/8

AMERICAN ELK - TYPICAL ANTLERS

Cervus elaphus nelsoni and related subspecies

MINIMUM SCORE 375

Score	Length of Main Beam R	L	Inside Spread	Circumference at Smallest Place Between First and Second Points R	L	Number of Points R	L	Locality	Hunter	Owner	Date Killed	Rank
442 5/8	56 2/8	56 2/8	47 4/8	11	10 2/8	6	7	White Mts., AZ	Alonzo Winters	Alan C. Ellsworth	1968	1
442 3/8	55 5/8	59 5/8	45 4/8	12 1/8	11 2/8	8	7	Dark Canyon, CO	John Plute	Ed Rozman	1899	2
441 6/8	61 6/8	61 2/8	47	10 2/8	9 7/8	8	7	Big Horn Mts., WY	Unknown	Jackson Hole Museum	1890	3
421 4/8	55 4/8	58 2/8	39	11 2/8	10 6/8	7	7	Gila Co., AZ	James C. Littleton	James C. Littleton	1985	4
420 4/8	56 4/8	56 2/8	45 6/8	9	9 2/8	7	7	Yakima Co., WA	Charles F. Gunnier	Charles F. Gunnier	1990	5
419 5/8	62 3/8	62 2/8	49 2/8	10 3/8	10 3/8	6	8	Panther River, AB	Clarence Brown	Clarence Brown	1977	6
419 4/8	59 7/8	60 1/8	53	9 2/8	9 3/8	7	7	Madison Co., MT	Fred C. Mercer	Fred C. Mercer	1958	7
418 7/8	58	55	43 1/8	10 5/8	11 3/8	6	7	Wyoming	J.G. Millais	G. Kenneth Whitehead	1886	8
418	63 2/8	64 2/8	38 2/8	10 1/8	9 6/8	7	7	Crook Co., OR	Hugh P. Evans	Joseph S. Jessel, Jr.	1942	9
418	54 1/8	50 4/8	44 2/8	8 4/8	8 4/8	6	6	Muddywater River, AB	Bruce W. Hale	Bruce W. Hale	1971	9
417 3/8	62	59 4/8	47 3/8	9 2/8	9 3/8	8	8	Park Co., WY	Merwin D. Martin	Loaned to B&C Natl. Coll.	1991	11
412 5/8	51 6/8	51 1/8	42 5/8	10	9 1/8	9	8	Wieser River, ID	Elmer Bacus	Elmer Bacus	1954	12
410	56	53 4/8	44 2/8	8 6/8	8 1/8	7	7	Unknown	Picked Up	Neil R. Hinton	1943	13
407	56 7/8	56 6/8	43 4/8	9 4/8	8 4/8	8	7	Summit Co., CO	Robert G. Young	Robert G. Young	1967	14
406 7/8	52 7/8	52 6/8	49 3/8	8 6/8	9 2/8	6	6	Duck Mt., MB	Herb Andres	Larry L. Huffman	1980	15
405 7/8	53 4/8	55 5/8	44 6/8	8 5/8	8 5/8	6	8	Ft. Apache Res., AZ	Roy R. Blythe	Roy R. Blythe	1970	16
404 6/8	58 6/8	57	47 2/8	9 5/8	9 1/8	8	7	Mineral Co., MT	Carl B. Snyder	Warren G. Stone	1959	17
402 5/8	59 1/8	59 6/8	44 1/8	9 1/8	8 5/8	7	7	Red Deer River, AB	Henry Folkman	Henry Folkman	1946	18
402 3/8	59 4/8	62 1/8	47 7/8	8 2/8	8 6/8	8	7	San Miguel Co., CO	Lewis Fredrickson	Jay Scott	1954	19
401 7/8	55 3/8	54 4/8	45 3/8	9 6/8	9 4/8	6	6	Kootenay Lake, BC	Picked Up	Rick D. Armstrong	1986	20
401 7/8	57 4/8	58 4/8	42 4/8	9 4/8	9 2/8	6	7	Apache Co., AZ	Bruce R. Keller	Bruce R. Keller	1987	20
401 6/8	58 3/8	57 5/8	47 2/8	7 7/8	8	6	6	Teton Co., WY	Douglas Spicer	Douglas Spicer	1972	22
401 4/8	53 1/8	55 1/8	44 4/8	7 7/8	8 1/8	7	7	Park Co., MT	Wayne A. Hertzler	Wayne A. Hertzler	1977	23
401 3/8	60 4/8	64 5/8	43 7/8	9 3/8	9	7	6	Grant Co., OR	James T. Sproul	James T. Sproul	1972	24
400 7/8	59 3/8	59 3/8	47 5/8	8 4/8	8 2/8	7	7	Rock Lake, AB	Ray Hindmarsh	Ray Hindmarsh	1963	25
400 7/8	59 2/8	64 3/8	50	8 4/8	8 2/8	7	8	Navajo Co., AZ	Marvin W. Wuertz	Marvin W. Wuertz	1993	25
400 4/8	59 4/8	61	48 4/8	8 2/8	8 5/8	8	7	Routt Co., CO	Lewis Frederickson	Lewis Frederickson	1953	27
400 4/8	59 1/8	60 1/8	42 6/8	9 3/8	10	7	7	Owyhee Co., ID	Cecil R. Coonts	Cecil R. Coonts	1965	27
400 2/8	56	55 2/8	46	8 2/8	8 4/8	7	7	Jackson Hole, WY	C. Atkins & O. Maynard	Thomas Myers	1947	29
400	56 2/8	57	49	9 1/8	9 1/8	7	7	Crook Co., OR	Picked Up	Randall L. Ryerse	1984	30
399 3/8	58 3/8	58	49 3/8	9 2/8	9 1/8	6	6	Coconino Co., AZ	Terry J. Rice	Terry J. Rice	1979	31
399 2/8	59 5/8	57 4/8	47 3/8	7 7/8	7 5/8	8	7	Ram River, AB	Ralph A. Fry	Ralph A. Fry	1952	32
398 7/8	56 4/8	56 4/8	39 5/8	9 6/8	10 3/8	6	6	Navajo Co., AZ	Terry C. Hickson	Terry C. Hickson	1997	33
398 5/8	57 2/8	53 4/8	40 5/8	9	9 2/8	8	8	Lewis & Clark Co., MT	Richard Mosher	J.A. Iverson	1953	34
398	50 5/8	50 7/8	39 4/8	10 5/8	11	7	7	Mora Co., NM	Bernabe Alcon	Don Schaufler	1963	35
398	50 3/8	53 5/8	46 6/8	8 4/8	8 4/8	6	6	Pincher Creek, AB	Monty F. Adams	Pat Adams	1977	35

Score	L. Main Beam R	L. Main Beam L	Inside Spread	Circ. R	Circ. L	Pts. R	Pts. L	Locality	By Whom Killed	Owner	Date	Rank
397 7/8	52	55 1/8	52 1/8	8 1/8	7 6/8	7	7	Sublette Co., WY	Ray Daugherty	Aldon L. Hale	1950	37
397 6/8	53	53	44 2/8	8 7/8	9	8	7	Cascade Co., MT	John W. Campbell	John W. Campbell	1955	38
397 2/8	50 2/8	50 6/8	45 2/8	9 6/8	9 5/8	8	7	Gunnison Co., CO	John R. Burritt	John R. Burritt	1970	39
397 1/8	51 7/8	51 7/8	33 7/8	10 1/8	10 5/8	8	6	Lincoln Co., NV	Michael A. Trousdale	Michael A. Trousdale	1994	40
396 6/8	56 1/8	56 3/8	43 4/8	9 7/8	10 6/8	6	6	Volunteer Canyon, AZ	Lamar Haines	Lamar Haines	1960	41
396 6/8	59 6/8	57 6/8	44	8 1/8	7 6/8	7	6	Coconino Co., AZ	Aaron M. Lowry	Aaron M. Lowry	1995	41
396 2/8	48	50 4/8	32 4/8	10	9 4/8	7	7	Duck Mt., MB	Paul Kirkowich	Paul Kirkowich	1960	43
396 1/8	51 5/8	50 2/8	49 7/8	7 4/8	7 4/8	8	6	Rock Lake, AB	Harold R. Vaughn	Harold R. Vaughn	1968	44
395 4/8	57 5/8	60 1/8	47	8 1/8	8 6/8	6	6	Fremont Co., WY	Roger Linnell	Roger Linnell	1955	45
395 1/8	56 2/8	51 2/8	43 6/8	10 2/8	9 5/8	6	6	Silver Bow Co., MT	Wayne Estep	Wayne Estep	1966	45
395 1/8	56 4/8	57 2/8	46 5/8	10 2/8	9 3/8	8	6	Wallowa Co., OR	Lawton McDaniel	Lawton McDaniel	1935	47
395 1/8	52	51 4/8	41 3/8	9 2/8	9 2/8	6	7	Coconino Co., AZ	Picked Up	John C. McClendon	1995	47
395	56 2/8	56 2/8	48 7/8	8 7/8	9	6	7	Salmon Natl. For., ID	Fred W. Thomson	Fred W. Thomson	1964	49
395	59 4/8	59	44 6/8	7 7/8	7 7/8	7	7	Apache Co., AZ	R. Steve Bass	R. Steve Bass	1993	49
394 6/8	54 2/8	60 7/8	47 2/8	8 2/8	8 4/8	7	6	Jefferson Co., MT	John Willard	John Willard	1953	51
394 4/8	55	57 5/8	52 4/8	10	9 4/8	6	6	Beaverhead Co., MT	Gwyn Brown	Gwyn Brown	1944	52
394 4/8	53 4/8	53 2/8	46 4/8	8 7/8	8 7/8	7	6	Idaho Co., ID	L.M. White	L.M. White	1977	52
394 4/8	55 2/8	54 6/8	37	9 2/8	10	6	6	Duck Mt., MB	Melvin J. Podaima	Melvin J. Podaima	1991	52
394 2/8	56 7/8	57 2/8	42 6/8	9 2/8	7 6/8	6	6	Panther River, AB	Picked Up	George Browne	1938	55
394 2/8	53 2/8	56 2/8	41 2/8	8 1/8	9 2/8	6	6	Hoback Rim, WY	Clyde Robbins	George Franz	1940	55
394 2/8	53 1/8	55 3/8	45 2/8	9 1/8	8 3/8	6	6	Elkwater, AB	Roy Crawford	Roy Crawford	1976	55
394 2/8	54 2/8	51 4/8	47 7/8	9 6/8	9 2/8	6	6	Baca Co., CO	David B. Martin	David B. Martin	1994	55
394 1/8	58	58 4/8	46 7/8	8	10 2/8	7	6	Lincoln Co., WY	Roland Smith	Leon C. Smith	1930	59
393 7/8	57 1/8	58	43 7/8	9 1/8	8	6	7	Apache Co., AZ	T.R. Tidwell	T.R. Tidwell	1983	60
393 5/8	56 2/8	52 4/8	42 5/8	7 6/8	9 4/8	7	7	Elmore Co., ID	Picked Up	Joe Adams	PR 1955	61
393 4/8	50	51 3/8	40 4/8	10 2/8	8 1/8	7	6	White Pine Co., NV	Paul Green	Paul Green	1993	62
393 2/8	53 5/8	51 6/8	46 2/8	8 3/8	10	6	6	Big Horn Co., WY	Edwin Shaffer	Edwin Shaffer	1946	63
393 2/8	55 2/8	54 4/8	51 4/8	9 4/8	8 2/8	6	6	Watertown Natl. Park, AB	Alan Foster	Alan Foster	1952	63
393 2/8	58 6/8	52 1/8	45 2/8	9 5/8	9 4/8	7	6	Winchester, ID	Doyle Shriver	Doyle Shriver	1954	63
393 2/8	63 1/8	64 4/8	44 2/8	8 6/8	9 6/8	6	7	Socorro Co., NM	Floyd R. Owens	Floyd R. Owens	1977	63
393 1/8	56 3/8	59 2/8	47 1/8	8 7/8	8 6/8	6	7	Kittitas Co., WA	Paul Anderson	Paul Anderson	1927	67
392 5/8	58 7/8	58 4/8	48 5/8	9	9	7	6	Panther River, AB	Bill Brooks	Bill Brooks	1955	68
392 4/8	51 3/8	51 1/8	42 3/8	7 7/8	7 7/8	7	7	Buford, CO	Picked Up	Robert T. Fulton	PR 1967	69
392 3/8	53 4/8	54 4/8	46 3/8	8 3/8	8 6/8	6	6	Umatilla Co., OR	Picked Up	Robert L. Brown	1982	70
392 3/8	54	54 6/8	41 7/8	9 4/8	10	6	6	Apache Co., AZ	McLean Bowman	McLean Bowman	1989	70
392	54 6/8	56 6/8	45 2/8	10	8 7/8	6	6	Jackson Co., CO	James A. Baller	North Park State Bank	1969	72
391 6/8	54 4/8	53	46	7 7/8	7 7/8	6	6	Thoroughfare Creek, WY	Thomas A. Yawkey	Thomas A. Yawkey	1936	73
391 6/8	52 6/8	53 6/8	35 6/8	7 7/8	9	6	6	Slater, CO	W.J. Bracken	W.J. Bracken	1963	73
391 4/8	54 5/8	56 3/8	43 2/8	9 1/8	9	6	7	Mt. Evans, CO	Unknown	Frank Brady	1874	75
391 4/8	52 2/8	52 7/8	51 2/8	8 5/8	8 2/8	6	6	Big Horn Mts., WY	Robert K. Hamilton	Robert K. Hamilton	1954	75
391 3/8	55 7/8	50 3/8	39 3/8	7 2/8	9 5/8	7	7	Grand Lake, CO	John Holzwarth	John Holzwarth	1949	77
390 6/8	53 5/8	54 3/8	49 6/8	9 3/8	9	7	6	Clearwater River, AB	Bob Dial	Bob Dial	1955	78
390 6/8	59 6/8	58	42	8 7/8	8 4/8	7	7	Caribou Co., ID	Ken Homer	Ken Homer	1963	78
390 6/8	57 3/8	57 2/8	51 2/8	8 6/8	9 1/8	6	6	Apache Co., AZ	Robert M. Brittingham	Robert M. Brittingham	1990	78
390 3/8	57 1/8	54 1/8	40 1/8	9 2/8	9 1/8	7	6	Hoback Canyon, WY	Picked Up	Spanky Greenville	1977	81
390 3/8	57	60 2/8	42 7/8	9 1/8	9 1/8	6	6	Valencia Co., NM	Sam Jaksick, Jr.	Sam Jaksick, Jr.	1997	81
390 2/8	55	55 4/8	49 2/8	8 6/8	8 6/8	7	7	Hood River Co., OR	Bill Tensen	Bill Tensen	1980	83

AMERICAN ELK - TYPICAL ANTLERS

Cervus elaphus nelsoni and related subspecies

Score	Length of Main Beam R	L	Inside Spread	Circumference at Smallest Place Between First and Second Points R	L	Number of Points R	L	Locality	Hunter	Owner	Date Killed	Rank
390 2/8	51 1/8	52 1/8	49	9 2/8	8 7/8	7	6	Las Animas Co., CO	Robert A. Schnee	Robert A. Schnee	1993	83
389 6/8	56 3/8	55 7/8	39 4/8	8 5/8	8 5/8	6	7	Navajo Co., AZ	Fred Fortier	Fred Fortier	1985	85
389 5/8	50 2/8	53	50 3/8	8	7 6/8	6	7	Park Co., MT	Thomas B. Adams	Jack Adams	1932	86
389 5/8	56 5/8	52 5/8	52 5/8	9 2/8	9 2/8	7	7	Fort a la Corne, SK	Jim Crozier	Jim Crozier	1955	86
389 5/8	55 1/8	54	45 7/8	7 7/8	8 1/8	7	7	Park Co., MT	Butch Kuflak	Butch Kuflak	1990	86
389 4/8	55 4/8	56 2/8	45	10 5/8	10	6	6	Helena, MT	Picked Up	Robert L. Smith	1964	89
389 4/8	57 3/8	55 2/8	42	8	8	6	6	Bitterroot Area, MT	Unknown	John Le Blanc	1965	89
389 4/8	53 7/8	54 7/8	46	8 7/8	8 7/8	6	6	Big Horn Co., WY	Floyd A. Clark	Floyd A. Clark	1976	89
389 3/8	56 5/8	60 5/8	43 7/8	8 3/8	8 2/8	6	6	Salmon River, ID	Unknown	John M. Anderson	1915	92
389 2/8	49 4/8	51 1/8	42 6/8	12 2/8	12 3/8	6	7	Nez Perce Co., ID	Picked Up	Michael Throckmorton	1949	93
389 2/8	49 7/8	48 1/8	40	10 7/8	10 3/8	6	6	Saskatchewan	Unknown	B.P.O.E. Lodge	PR 1956	93
389	51	48 3/8	41 6/8	8 2/8	8 2/8	6	6	Meacham, OR	H.M. Bailey	H.M. Bailey	1963	95
388 7/8	56	55 4/8	46 3/8	9 6/8	8 6/8	6	6	Jackson Hole, WY	Unknown	William Sonnenburg	PR 1912	96
388 6/8	50 6/8	47 2/8	45 6/8	10	9 4/8	7	6	Larimer Co., CO	John Zimmerman	Ft. Collins Mus.	PR 1890	97
388 6/8	56 1/8	55 1/8	41 3/8	10 3/8	10 4/8	8	7	Graham Co., AZ	Hans Veit Toerring	Hans Veit Toerring	1994	97
388 4/8	55 6/8	56 1/8	44 4/8	9 4/8	9 5/8	6	6	Platte Co., WY	Mike C. Boughton	Mike C. Boughton	1995	99
388 3/8	53 5/8	55	47 1/8	9	9 3/8	7	6	Coconino Co., AZ	Picked Up	Tim Cotten	PR 1982	100
388 2/8	62 4/8	63 5/8	49 2/8	9 3/8	9 1/8	7	9	Unknown	Unknown	Carnegie Mus.	PR 1966	101
388 2/8	52 5/8	51 3/8	39	10 1/8	10 1/8	6	6	Gila Co., AZ	Fred B. Dickey	Fred B. Dickey	1984	101
388 2/8	56 1/8	54 7/8	40	9 2/8	9 7/8	7	6	Sentinel Mt., BC	Martin Braun	Martin Braun	1986	101
388 2/8	59 1/8	59	54	7 5/8	7 6/8	6	6	Cutoff Creek, AB	Joe A. Riviera	Joe A. Riviera	1986	101
388 1/8	56 3/8	56 4/8	46 4/8	8 3/8	8 4/8	8	7	Slocan River, BC	Trevor W. Stetsko	Trevor W. Stetsko	1991	105
388	57 1/8	55 1/8	55	8 6/8	8 1/8	7	6	Medicine Lodge Creek, ID	D.W. Marshall & E.J. Stacy	D.W. Marshall & E.J. Stacy	1961	106
388	53 2/8	53 6/8	48 2/8	9	9 3/8	6	6	Madison Co., MT	Terry Carlson	Christine Mullikin	1961	106
388	55 4/8	54 4/8	50 2/8	8 4/8	9	8	9	Converse Co., WY	Jerry F. Cook	J.F. Cook & Mrs. P. Muchmore	1965	106
387 7/8	54 4/8	55 5/8	44 5/8	9 6/8	9 5/8	7	6	Kelly, WY	Roger Penney	Bernard Bronk	1963	109
387 7/8	55 3/8	57	37 2/8	10	9 5/8	7	6	Grant Co., OR	Arnold Troph	Arnold Troph	1966	109
387 7/8	52 1/8	53	44 5/8	7 7/8	8	6	6	Lincoln, WY	Dexter R. Gardner	Dexter R. Gardner	1967	109
387 6/8	57 6/8	56 4/8	51	8	7 7/8	6	6	Big Horn Mts., WY	Elgin T. Gates	Elgin T. Gates	1954	112
387 6/8	50 2/8	51 7/8	43 2/8	9 5/8	10 2/8	6	6	Fremont, ID	Charles A. Preston	Charles A. Preston	1963	112
387 5/8	60 2/8	60	42 7/8	9	8 7/8	7	7	Cherokee Co., IA	C.A. Stiles	Jim Haas	PR 1900	114
387 5/8	58 1/8	56	39 1/8	8 7/8	9 1/8	7	7	Yarrow Creek, AB	D. Belyea	D. Belyea	1970	114
387 5/8	50 7/8	51 6/8	41 5/8	8 3/8	8 5/8	6	6	Washington Co., ID	Rick H. Moser	Raymond R. Cross	1994	114
387 4/8	49 1/8	49 1/8	41 7/8	8 7/8	8 7/8	7	6	Grant Co., OR	Andy Chambers	Andy Chambers	1959	117
387 4/8	56 5/8	58 2/8	44 2/8	9	9	6	7	Sage Creek, MT	Joseph A. Vogel	Joseph A. Vogel	1970	117
387 3/8	52 2/8	52 3/8	47 3/8	8 1/8	8 1/8	6	6	Park Co., MT	Lawrence P. Deering	Lawrence P. Deering	1978	119

Score	Length of Main Beam R	Length of Main Beam L	Inside Spread	Circumference R	Circumference L	Points R	Points L	Locality	Hunter	Owner	Date	Rank
387 3/8	52 3/8	50 4/8	46 3/8	9 7/8	9 6/8	7	7	Johnson Co., WY	Wallace D. Ramsbottom	Wallace D. Ramsbottom	1996	119
387 2/8	54 7/8	54 7/8	39	8 4/8	8 1/8	8	7	Navajo Co., AZ	Leo W. Mack, Jr.	Leo W. Mack, Jr.	1995	121
387 1/8	58 1/8	54 6/8	46	9 5/8	9 5/8	8	7	Meagher Co., MT	Bud McLees	B. McLees & H. Zehntner	1971	122
387	55	55 4/8	54 4/8	8 7/8	8 2/8	7	8	Chama, NM	Herb Klein	Herb Klein	1952	123
386 7/8	48 6/8	47 2/8	54 4/8	9 4/8	8 5/8	8	8	Powell Co., MT	Mildred Eder	Mildred Eder	1969	124
386 7/8	58 4/8	61 6/8	41 7/8	8 7/8	8 7/8	6	7	Otero Co., NM	William M. Wheless III	Picked Up	1981	124
386 6/8	52 2/8	51 5/8	34 4/8	10 3/8	10 2/8	6	6	Powell Co., MT	Thomas W. Moen	Unknown	1960	126
386 6/8	61 6/8	61 7/8	47 4/8	8 7/8	9 1/8	6	7	Flathead Co., MT	Floyd L. Jackson	Floyd L. Jackson	1976	126
386 5/8	59 3/8	60	52 1/8	9 6/8	9 1/8	7	6	Panther River, AB	Leonard L. Hengen	Leonard L. Hengen	1977	128
386 4/8	59	57	45	9	9	7	7	Cache Co., UT	L. Dwight Israelsen	Greg Nielsen	1937	129
386 4/8	49 2/8	50 3/8	39 6/8	8 6/8	9 2/8	7	6	Nez Perce Co., ID	H.H. Schnettler	H.H. Schnettler	1957	129
386 4/8	55 6/8	55 5/8	42	10	8 6/8	6	6	Smoky River, AB	Stephen Trulik	Stephen Trulik	1963	129
386 4/8	56 2/8	54 6/8	44	8 5/8	8 6/8	6	6	Coconino Co., AZ	Lee Clemson	Lee Clemson	1974	129
386 2/8	56 3/8	57 4/8	46 6/8	9 3/8	9 1/8	6	6	Carbon Co., UT	Edward C. Jessen	Edward C. Jessen	1961	133
386 2/8	52 4/8	54 1/8	48	8 7/8	8 7/8	6	6	Delta Co., CO	Bert Johnson	Bert Johnson	1974	133
386 2/8	59 6/8	60 4/8	47 4/8	9 7/8	9 6/8	6	6	Benewah Co., ID	Lee C. Mowreader	Lee C. Mowreader	1992	133
386 1/8	57	57 1/8	57 1/8	7 7/8	8 5/8	6	6	Forest Gate Store, SK	Edwin L. Roberts	Edwin L. Roberts	1962	136
386 1/8	59 1/8	58	58	10 3/8	9 4/8	6	6	Mescalero Apache Res., NM	Larry W. Bailey, Sr.	Larry W. Bailey, Sr.	1974	136
386 1/8	55 1/8	54 2/8	36 5/8	7 3/8	7 1/8	6	6	Apache Co., AZ	Don K. Callahan	Don K. Callahan	1993	136
386	53 7/8	55 4/8	53 1/8	9 6/8	9 6/8	6	6	Valley Co., ID	Kenny Poe	Denny Young	1957	139
386	52 4/8	53	51	8 4/8	8 4/8	7	6	Big Horn Mts., WY	Fred Gray	Unknown	1966	139
385 7/8	49 1/8	51 7/8	48 2/8	7 7/8	7 7/8	6	6	Shoshone Co., ID	Jerry Nearing	Jerry Nearing	1976	141
385 6/8	56 7/8	56 1/8	44 3/8	7 7/8	8 4/8	6	7	Big Smoky River, AB	Fred T. Huntington, Jr.	Fred T. Huntington, Jr.	1961	142
385 6/8	52 4/8	56	40 4/8	9	9 3/8	8	7	Apache Co., AZ	Jay A. Kellett	Jay A. Kellett	1993	142
385 5/8	59 6/8	56 6/8	41 2/8	8 7/8	8 1/8	8	6	Ft. Apache Res., AZ	Glen Daly	Glen Daly	1957	144
385 5/8	53	53	40 3/8	8 4/8	9 1/8	6	6	Kootenai Co., ID	Arth Day	Arth Day	1971	144
385 5/8	52 7/8	54 7/8	46 7/8	9 3/8	8 2/8	6	6	Wheeler Co., OR	Ronny E. Rhoden	Ronny E. Rhoden	1986	144
385 4/8	56 2/8	57 3/8	37 4/8	8 2/8	10 5/8	6	6	Emery Co., UT	Russell N. Wimmer	Neville L. Wimmer	1939	147
385 3/8	55 4/8	55 2/8	47 3/8	10 1/8	9	6	6	Teton Co., WY	Timothy D. Riordan	Gene J. Riordan	1960	148
385 3/8	57 2/8	55 7/8	42 5/8	8	10 5/8	6	6	Sanders Co., MT	George R. Johnson	George R. Johnson	1977	148
385 3/8	51 1/8	54 2/8	41 1/8	10 7/8	9 7/8	6	6	Otero Co., NM	Gregory C. Saunders	Gregory C. Saunders	1985	148
385 2/8	53 3/8	52 2/8	34 7/8	10 1/8	8 6/8	7	6	Apache Co., AZ	Herman C. Meyer	Herman C. Meyer	1991	151
385 1/8	48 5/8	49 3/8	48 4/8	8 3/8	11 4/8	6	6	Trappers Lake, CO	Byron W. Kneff	Byron W. Kneff	1954	152
385 1/8	51	51	46 5/8	11	10	6	8	Grande Cache Lake, AB	Kenneth A. Evans	Kenneth A. Evans	1966	152
385 1/8	56 7/8	56 7/8	44 3/8	8 3/8	8 2/8	7	6	Bozeman, MT	Robert B. McKnight	Robert B. McKnight	1966	152
385 1/8	46	48 2/8	46 6/8	7 6/8	8 3/8	6	6	Lincoln Co., WY	Ken Clark	Ken Clark	1979	152
385	54 7/8	53 3/8	43 7/8	8	8 7/8	6	6	Madison Co., MT	Boyd J. VanFleet	Boyd J. VanFleet	1991	156
384 7/8	56 6/8	57 2/8	36 4/8	9 3/8	9	6	7	Sanders Co., MT	Brett M. Fisher	Brett M. Fisher	1994	157
384 6/8	55 3/8	54 3/8	50	9 2/8	9 6/8	6	6	Clearwater River, AB	William Lenz	William Lenz	1966	158
384 6/8	54	54	44	10 1/8	10	6	7	Hualapai Indian Res., AZ	Tod Reichert	Tod Reichert	1975	158
384 6/8	56 2/8	58 4/8	44 3/8	9 4/8	8 7/8	6	6	Ft. Apache Res., AZ	Jim P. Caires	Jim P. Caires	1978	158
384 6/8	60	60 2/8	47 1/8	9 5/8	8 7/8	7	7	Apache Co., AZ	Herman C. Meyer	H.C. Meyer & J.T. Caid	1982	158
384 5/8	55 3/8	54 6/8	40 5/8	8 4/8	8 2/8	6	7	Ram River, AB	Joe Kramer	Joe Kramer	1966	162
384 5/8	57 6/8	56 6/8	43 4/8	8 7/8	9 3/8	6	6	Graham Co., AZ	Laura R. Williams	Laura R. Williams	1986	162
384 4/8	57	57	43	9 5/8	8 1/8	7	7	Bonneville Co., ID	David W. Anderson	David W. Anderson	1967	164
384 4/8	53 4/8	53 2/8	49 1/8	8 5/8	9 5/8	7	7	Bonneville Co., ID	Keith W. Hadley	Keith W. Hadley	1972	164
384 3/8	59 3/8	59 2/8	49 1/8	7 6/8	7 5/8	6	7	Jackson Hole, WY	Francis X. Bouchard	Francis X. Bouchard	1956	166

AMERICAN ELK - TYPICAL ANTLERS

Cervus elaphus nelsoni and related subspecies

Score	Length of Main Beam R	L	Inside Spread	Circumference at Smallest Place Between First and Second Points R	L	Number of Points R	L	Locality	Hunter	Owner	Date Killed	Rank
384 3/8	59	58 4/8	46 3/8	10 5/8	9 3/8	6	6	Beaverhead Co., MT	Phil Matovich	Phil Matovich	1960	166
384 3/8	54 5/8	54 5/8	50 7/8	9 7/8	9 2/8	6	6	Clear Creek Co., CO	John Wallace	John Wallace	1973	166
384 2/8	61 7/8	64 6/8	40 6/8	11	10 4/8	6	8	Ft. Apache Res., AZ	Ralph C. Winkler, Jr.	Ralph C. Winkler, Jr.	1977	169
384 2/8	58 1/8	60 6/8	49 3/8	10	8 3/8	6	7	Apache Co., AZ	Roy W. Baker	Roy W. Baker	1980	169
384 2/8	58	58	43	8	7 7/8	6	6	Catron Co., NM	Robert J. Seeds	Robert J. Seeds	1996	169
384 1/8	57 2/8	56 7/8	32 4/8	9 5/8	9 7/8	6	7	Navajo Co., AZ	Dennis K. Frandsen	Dennis K. Frandsen	1994	172
384	58 7/8	56 4/8	44	9 6/8	9 1/8	6	7	Willow Creek, MT	Mike Miles	Mike Miles	1958	173
384	53 2/8	51 1/8	48 3/8	8 5/8	8 2/8	6	7	Meagher Co., MT	Frank W. Fuller	Frank W. Fuller	1963	173
384	56 4/8	54	47	7 6/8	8 1/8	7	7	Costilla Co., CO	William E. Carl	William E. Carl	1967	173
384	52 5/8	53 6/8	41 1/8	11 4/8	11 1/8	7	7	Otero Co., NM	Robert McCasland	Robert McCasland	1992	173
384	58 7/8	60	41 4/8	9 5/8	9 6/8	7	6	Otero Co., NM	George R. Sellers	George R. Sellers	1992	173
383 6/8	53 6/8	54	43 4/8	9 4/8	9 5/8	6	6	Unknown	Unknown	S. Side Cody Elk Club	1939	178
383 6/8	54	51 5/8	46	8 7/8	9	6	6	Las Animas Co., CO	Michael W. Marbach	Michael W. Marbach	1993	178
383 5/8	54 6/8	55 3/8	54 4/8	8 2/8	8	6	7	Apache Co., AZ	Randall S. Ulmer	Randall S. Ulmer	1987	180
383 4/8	51 3/8	51 3/8	48 4/8	9 5/8	9 5/8	6	6	Unknown	Unknown	N. Side Cody Elk Club	PR 1967	181
383 3/8	53 5/8	55	50 1/8	8 2/8	8	6	6	Maycroft, AB	Steve Kubasek	Steve Kubasek	1957	182
383 2/8	52 2/8	52	41 6/8	9 4/8	9 2/8	6	7	Nez Perce Co., ID	Thenton L. Todd	Thenton L. Todd	1956	183
383 2/8	55 5/8	53 1/8	45	10 3/8	10 5/8	7	7	Coconino Co., AZ	Jay E. Elmer	Jay E. Elmer	1979	183
383 1/8	58 1/8	54 4/8	53 1/8	9	9 6/8	6	6	Snowy Range, WY	Kermit Platt	Kermit Platt	1961	185
383	55	55	52 2/8	9 3/8	8 6/8	6	8	Coconino Co., AZ	Gene Bird	Gene Bird	1972	186
383	52 1/8	52 3/8	51 4/8	9 5/8	9	6	6	Panther River, AB	Thomas Coupland	Echoglen Taxidermy	1984	186
382 7/8	53 4/8	51 4/8	47 4/8	9 7/8	10 2/8	7	8	Blacktail Creek, MT	Floyd E. Winn	Floyd E. Winn	1959	188
382 7/8	54 3/8	52 7/8	43 5/8	8 6/8	8 5/8	6	8	Castle River, AB	Albert Truant	Albert Truant	1970	188
382 7/8	59 6/8	59 6/8	42 5/8	8 6/8	8 6/8	6	6	Graham Co., AZ	Mark R. Herfort	Mark R. Herfort	1994	188
382 6/8	56 1/8	54 5/8	41 5/8	9 7/8	10 2/8	7	6	Rattlesnake Mt., WY	Bob Edgar	Bob Edgar	1966	191
382 6/8	56 7/8	55 4/8	48	9 3/8	10 5/8	6	6	Apache Co., AZ	William E. Moss	William E. Moss	1985	191
382 5/8	52 3/8	52 3/8	36 5/8	9 2/8	9	7	7	Kootenai Co., ID	Terry Cozad	Terry Cozad	1968	193
382 5/8	55 4/8	57 4/8	38 4/8	9 5/8	8 7/8	6	7	San Juan Co., UT	Kirk E. Winward	Kirk E. Winward	1997	193
382 4/8	49 6/8	48	32 7/8	14 4/8	13	9	7	Elbow River, AB	Harold F. Mailman	Harold F. Mailman	1964	195
382 4/8	56 6/8	56 7/8	41 6/8	8 7/8	9 2/8	7	7	Summit Co., CO	Marshall Sherman	Marshall Sherman	1966	195
382 4/8	49	48 5/8	36 6/8	8 5/8	8 6/8	6	6	Teton Co., WY	Randy Johnston	Randy Johnston	1970	195
382 4/8	54	55 1/8	40 6/8	8 4/8	9 1/8	7	7	Cascade Co., MT	Robert J. Gliko	Robert J. Gliko	1983	195
382 3/8	53 3/8	54	50 5/8	8 4/8	8 4/8	7	7	Sublette Co., WY	Frank Dew	Frank Dew	1931	199
382 3/8	49 6/8	52 1/8	35 5/8	11	10 1/8	6	6	Mormon Lake, AZ	Wayne A. Barry	John E. Rhea	1965	199
382 2/8	55 4/8	55	47 4/8	7 4/8	7 2/8	6	6	Gallatin Co., MT	Henry Lambert	Charles F. Miller	1923	201
382 2/8	58 4/8	62 6/8	48	8	7 4/8	6	6	Williams, AZ	Oscar B. Skaggs	Oscar B. Skaggs	1954	201

Score	Main Beam R	Main Beam L	Inside Spread	Circ. R	Circ. L	Pts. R	Pts. L	Locality	Hunter	Owner	Date	Rank
382 2/8	54 2/8	56 6/8	44 2/8	9	8 4/8	7	7	Clark Co., ID	John Larick, Jr.	John Larick, Jr.	1963	201
382 2/8	55 7/8	53 3/8	39 2/8	9 2/8	9 1/8	7	7	Grant Co., OR	Drake J. Davis	Drake J. Davis	1981	201
382 2/8	48	49 5/8	39 2/8	8 6/8	8 2/8	7	7	Apache Co., AZ	R. Steve Bass	R. Steve Bass	1992	201
382 2/8	50 5/8	49 1/8	50	8	7 5/8	6	7	Colfax Co., NM	Claude W. Hudson III	Claude W. Hudson III	1994	201
382 1/8	57 3/8	55 7/8	44 3/8	8 1/8	8 2/8	6	6	Bob Marshall Wilder., MT	Gene E. Trenary	Gene E. Trenary	1958	207
382 1/8	54 3/8	54 6/8	45 7/8	9 2/8	8 2/8	7	8	Gallatin Co., MT	A. Francis Bailey	A. Francis Bailey	1966	207
382	52 2/8	51 1/8	47 2/8	8 7/8	8 6/8	6	8	Missoula Co., MT	Fritz Frey	Clifford Frey	1943	209
382	53 2/8	51 1/8	48	7 6/8	9 1/8	8	7	Little Cimmaron, CO	Newell Beauchamp	Bud Lovato	1957	209
381 7/8	59 5/8	58	52 1/8	10 2/8	7 5/8	7	6	Gallatin Co., MT	H.K. Shields	H.K. Shields	1958	211
381 6/8	52 2/8	52	49 7/8	9 6/8	9 3/8	7	6	Beaverhead Co., MT	C.L. Jensen	C.L. Jensen	1960	212
381 6/8	55 2/8	57 1/8	41	9 1/8	9 6/8	7	8	Red Deer River, AB	Allan E. Brown	Allan E. Brown	1980	212
381 6/8	50 3/8	49 7/8	42	9 2/8	8 7/8	8	7	Madison Co., MT	Allan L. Mintken	Allan L. Mintken	1986	212
381 6/8	56 1/8	55	44 4/8	9 3/8	8 5/8	7	7	Waterton River, AB	Keith A. Keeler	Keith A. Keeler	1989	212
381 6/8	54 3/8	52 5/8	38 4/8	10 4/8	10	7	7	Otero Co., NM	David U. Inge	David U. Inge	1990	212
381 5/8	54 7/8	56 3/8	40 1/8	9 5/8	8	6	7	Rich Co., UT	Walter R. Moore	Kirk W. Moore	1935	217
381 5/8	56 2/8	56 2/8	41 5/8	9 7/8	10 1/8	6	6	Granite Co., MT	Jeff Conn	Jeff Conn	1971	217
381 5/8	59 6/8	58	39 7/8	10 4/8	9 2/8	6	6	Coconino Co., AZ	George E. Long	George E. Long	1985	217
381 5/8	58 2/8	52 4/8	39 5/8	9 6/8	10 1/8	7	6	Apache Co., AZ	McLean Bowman	McLean Bowman	1990	217
381 5/8	52	52	41 7/8	9 5/8	10 2/8	6	6	Platte Co., WY	James L. Brown	James L. Brown	1995	217
381 4/8	56 4/8	57 2/8	42 4/8	10 3/8	9 2/8	6	6	Fremont Co., WY	John S. Maxson	John S. Maxson	1954	222
381 4/8	51 7/8	50 6/8	40 4/8	9	10 4/8	7	7	Fergus Co., MT	Joe R. Odom	Joe R. Odom	1994	222
381 3/8	57 2/8	57 7/8	41 1/8	9	9 4/8	6	6	Park Co., MT	Edward F. Skillman	Edward F. Skillman	1968	224
381 3/8	55 4/8	54 5/8	37 4/8	8 6/8	9 1/8	6	6	Larimer Co., CO	Earl L. Erbes	Earl L. Erbes	1972	224
381 3/8	56 4/8	56 6/8	43 7/8	8 2/8	8 5/8	6	6	White Pine Co., NV	Michael N. Kalafatic	Michael N. Kalafatic	1985	224
381 2/8	57	55 4/8	34 7/8	8 5/8	9 4/8	6	9	Catron Co., NM	Gary F. Jamieson	Gary F. Jamieson	1993	224
381 2/8	55 1/8	55 1/8	44 2/8	8	8 6/8	8	6	Kittitas Co., WA	Clinton W. Morrow	Clinton W. Morrow	1957	228
381 1/8	57 5/8	56 1/8	50	10	9 1/8	6	8	Mora Co., NM	Andrew J. Ortega	Andrew J. Ortega	1989	228
381 1/8	49 6/8	51 4/8	45 1/8	9 4/8	7 3/8	6	8	Laramie Peak, WY	Lawrence Prager	Lawrence Prager	1958	230
381	56 3/8	56 3/8	39 7/8	8 5/8	9	6	6	Flathead Co., MT	Earl Weaver, Jr.	Earl Weaver, Jr.	1962	230
381	51 2/8	50 5/8	48 4/8	7 7/8	8 2/8	7	7	Gallatin Co., MT	Jack Bauer	Jack Bauer	1961	232
381	48	54 4/8	43 6/8	10 2/8	7 5/8	8	7	Big Horn Co., MT	Jerry Barnes	Jerry Barnes	1962	232
381	54	53 4/8	40 4/8	8	8 7/8	7	8	Bonneville Co., ID	Mrs. E. LaRene Smith	Mrs. E. LaRene Smith	1966	232
380 6/8	51 7/8	51	48 6/8	9	7 6/8	7	7	Gallatin Co., MT	Gerald Schroeder	Gerald Schroeder	1977	232
380 5/8	50 6/8	54 6/8	43 6/8	8 6/8	9 7/8	6	6	Park Co., MT	John Caputo	John Caputo	1968	236
380 5/8	57 4/8	55	47 5/8	8 1/8	9 7/8	6	6	Hayden, CO	Mike Holliday	Mike Holliday	1966	237
380 5/8	54 2/8	53 4/8	43 7/8	9	7 4/8	6	6	Sevier Co., UT	Miles A. Anderson	Miles A. Anderson	1970	237
380 5/8	54 3/8	57	51 3/8	8 6/8	9 3/8	6	6	Chaffee Co., CO	Anton Purkat	Anton Purkat	1972	237
380 5/8	56 5/8	56 5/8	42 3/8	7 5/8	8 1/8	6	6	Apache Co., AZ	Don L. Corley	Don L. Corley	1984	237
380 5/8	52 4/8	52 6/8	44 3/8	8 1/8	8 6/8	6	6	Apache Co., AZ	Pat C. Beaird	Pat C. Beaird	1995	237
380 4/8	62 7/8	63 2/8	41	8 5/8	8 6/8	6	7	Payson, AZ	Harold Foard	Harold Foard	1947	242
380 3/8	56 3/8	58	47 1/8	8 3/8	7 5/8	6	6	Harney Co., OR	Pat L. Wheeler	Pat L. Wheeler	1967	243
380 3/8	58	53 2/8	44 1/8	8 6/8	8 3/8	7	7	Catron Co., NM	Donald Parks, Jr.	Donald Parks, Jr.	1988	243
380 3/8	53 4/8	53 4/8	51 7/8	8 1/8	8 6/8	6	6	Rich Co., UT	Fahy S. Robinson, Jr.	Fahy S. Robinson, Jr.	1988	243
380 3/8	53 2/8	57 4/8	47 7/8	8 5/8	8 3/8	7	6	Grant Co., NM	Ken D. Lewis	Ken D. Lewis	1995	243
380 2/8	57 7/8	57 2/8	49 4/8	8 5/8	8 7/8	6	7	Madison Co., MT	Phil Hensel	Phil Hensel	1959	247
380 2/8	56 1/8	57 3/8	46 4/8	8 3/8	8 3/8	7	7	Lewis Co., WA	Charles Rudolph	Charles Rudolph	1973	247
380 2/8	57 4/8	54 1/8	45	8 7/8	8 7/8	6	7	Coconino Co., AZ	Doug Kittredge	Doug Kittredge	1975	247

AMERICAN ELK - TYPICAL ANTLERS
Cervus elaphus nelsoni and related subspecies

Score	Length of Main Beam		Inside Spread	Circumference at Smallest Place Between First and Second Points		Number of Points		Locality	Hunter	Owner	Date Killed	Rank
	R	L		R	L	R	L					
380 2/8	58 7/8	58 3/8	42 2/8	9 4/8	8 6/8	7	6	Granite Co., MT	Richard Shoner	Richard Shoner	1977	247
380 2/8	53 2/8	55 6/8	55 6/8	9 6/8	9 7/8	7	7	Las Animas Co., CO	Picked Up	Crawford Ranch	1987	247
380 1/8	59 1/8	58 2/8	50 5/8	7 6/8	7 3/8	6	6	Beaverhead Co., MT	Edward Konda	Edward Konda	1947	252
380	54	53 5/8	48 2/8	8 7/8	8 4/8	7	7	Spring Creek, AB	A.C. Bair	A.C. Bair	1948	253
380	53 2/8	56 2/8	50 3/8	10 3/8	9 7/8	7	6	Ft. Apache Res., AZ	George E. Crosby	George E. Crosby	1957	253
380	51 5/8	51 6/8	41 6/8	7 6/8	8 3/8	6	6	Duck Mt., MB	G.N. Burton	G.N. Burton	1965	253
380	50 4/8	50 3/8	35	8	8 2/8	7	6	Navajo Co., AZ	Gerry J. Tod	Gerry J. Tod	1990	253
379 7/8	58 6/8	57 2/8	47 3/8	9 1/8	8 4/8	6	6	Routt Co., CO	Walter R. Ducey	Walter R. Ducey	1961	257
379 7/8	56 7/8	56 2/8	42	8 1/8	8 4/8	8	6	Graham Co., AZ	Gerald Williams	Gerald Williams	1985	257
379 7/8	51 5/8	47 2/8	36 7/8	8 3/8	8 3/8	6	6	Apache Co., AZ	Thomas G. Kempken	Thomas G. Kempken	1994	257
379 6/8	58 3/8	58 4/8	45 2/8	9 2/8	9 6/8	6	6	Ruby Mts., MT	Jack Ballard	Jack Ballard	1960	260
379 6/8	50 2/8	51 4/8	45 4/8	9 4/8	9 4/8	6	6	Rock Lake, AB	Jim Soneff	Jim Soneff	1961	260
379 6/8	57 2/8	57 2/8	40 4/8	7 6/8	7 6/8	6	6	Big Horn Co., MT	George F. Gamble	George F. Gamble	1968	260
379 6/8	54	54 6/8	45 6/8	7 7/8	7 1/8	6	6	Daisy Pass, MT	Larry R. Price	Larry R. Price	1971	260
379 6/8	52	51 6/8	36 2/8	10	10	9	8	Adams Co., ID	William V. Baker	William V. Baker	1976	260
379 6/8	58 2/8	58 4/8	46 6/8	8 6/8	8 6/8	7	7	Grant Co., NM	Tony R. Grijalva	Tony R. Grijalva	1983	260
379 6/8	51 2/8	53 6/8	45 6/8	9 2/8	9 5/8	7	7	Park Co., WY	Timothy D. Metzler	Timothy D. Metzler	1994	260
379 6/8	54 7/8	56 6/8	41 2/8	9	8 7/8	6	6	Cibola Co., NM	Picked Up	Robert J. Seeds	1997	260
379 5/8	57	53 1/8	48 1/8	9 2/8	9 2/8	6	6	Big Horn Mts., WY	Unknown	L.M. Brownell	1956	268
379 5/8	53 7/8	48 2/8	55	8 2/8	8 4/8	7	7	Valley Co., ID	Joe Gisler	Joe Gisler	1961	268
379 4/8	51 7/8	52 3/8	39	9 7/8	9 7/8	6	6	Madison Co., MT	LeRoy Schweitzer	LeRoy Schweitzer	1964	270
379 3/8	54	52 6/8	42 3/8	8	7 4/8	6	6	Unknown	Gift of Arch. Rogers to NCHH	Unknown	PR 1951	271
379 3/8	60 1/8	61 1/8	45 5/8	8 7/8	8 3/8	6	6	Coconino Co., AZ	Tammy J. Otero	Tammy J. Otero	1984	271
379 3/8	51 2/8	47	42 3/8	9 4/8	9 7/8	6	6	Otero Co., NM	Hubert R. Kennedy	Hubert R. Kennedy	1985	271
379 3/8	52 4/8	53 6/8	40 1/8	11 1/8	12	6	6	Sierra Co., NM	James D. Wagner	James D. Wagner	1986	271
379 3/8	50	55 1/8	36 5/8	9 6/8	9 5/8	7	7	Red Deer River, SK	Emile Casavant	Emile Casavant	1997	271
379 2/8	55 7/8	56 1/8	44 4/8	9	8 7/8	6	6	Bozeman, MT	K.L. Berry	K.L. Berry	1959	276
379 2/8	58 3/8	57 2/8	41 6/8	9	9 4/8	6	6	Sierra Blanca Lake, AZ	Joseph A. Rozum	Joseph A. Rozum	1965	276
379 2/8	54 7/8	56 4/8	40 4/8	8 2/8	8 1/8	6	6	Sanders Co., MT	Robert L. Coates	Robert L. Coates	1974	276
379 2/8	57 1/8	55 5/8	41 6/8	8 1/8	8	6	6	Fremont Co., WY	Larry C. Nicholas	Frank J. Vrablic	1976	276
379 2/8	53 4/8	52 2/8	44	8	8 4/8	6	6	Yakima Co., WA	Donald G. Stein	Donald G. Stein	1985	276
379 2/8	53 2/8	53 4/8	41 4/8	8 5/8	8 7/8	6	6	Whirlpool River, MB	Rudy R. Usick	Rudy R. Usick	1989	276
379 2/8	56 3/8	57 1/8	53 2/8	8 6/8	8 3/8	6	6	Coconino Co., AZ	Fred Williams	Fred Williams	1990	276
379 1/8	56	57 4/8	33 7/8	8 6/8	9 1/8	6	6	Duvernay Bridge, AB	Alec Mitchell	Alec Mitchell	1917	283
379 1/8	56 6/8	56 1/8	45 5/8	9 5/8	9 3/8	7	7	Coconino Co., AZ	Charles M. Krieger	Charles M. Krieger	1992	283
379	50 4/8	51 1/8	40 6/8	9	8 6/8	6	6	Big Creek, ID	Picked Up	George Dovel	1963	285

Score	Main Beam R	Main Beam L	Inside Spread	Circ. R	Circ. L	Points R	Points L	Locality	By Whom Killed	Owner	Date Killed	Rank
379	49	50 4/8	39	10 1/8	10 1/8	8	6	Teton Park, WY	S.M. Vilven	S.M. Vilven	1964	285
379	50 7/8	51	44 4/8	10 2/8	9 7/8	6	6	Petroleum Co., MT	Lana J. Sluggett	Lana J. Sluggett	1984	285
379	52 4/8	53 2/8	40 6/8	8 3/8	8 2/8	7	7	Albany Co., WY	Carl G. Gross	Carl G. Gross	1995	285
379	57 3/8	56 5/8	44 6/8	10 4/8	10 2/8	6	6	Moffat Co., CO	Rod B. Morrison	Rod B. Morrison	1996	285
378 7/8	57 5/8	58 6/8	47 1/8	8 2/8	8 4/8	6	6	Carbon Co., WY	Donal F. Mueller	Donal F. Mueller	1964	290
378 7/8	56 6/8	56 1/8	46 5/8	8	8 4/8	6	6	Wildhay River, AB	Richard Clouthier	Richard Clouthier	1973	290
378 6/8	55	54 4/8	45	7 4/8	8	6	6	Gallatin Co., MT	Ted Shook	Ted Shook	1966	292
378 6/8	54 6/8	52 7/8	44 2/8	9 6/8	9 7/8	6	5	Otter Lake, MB	Walter Giesbrecht	Walter Giesbrecht	1989	292
378 5/8	52	55 2/8	47 7/8	8 6/8	8 7/8	7	6	Dutch Creek, AB	Harold King	Harold King	1951	294
378 4/8	52 7/8	54 5/8	42 4/8	10	9 3/8	6	7	Park Co., WY	Kenneth Smith	Kenneth Smith	1954	295
378 4/8	54 3/8	55 3/8	45 2/8	8 6/8	8 6/8	6	6	Shoshone Co., ID	Edward L. Bradford	Edward L. Bradford	1963	295
378 4/8	58 3/8	56 3/8	43 6/8	8 3/8	8 4/8	6	6	Beaverhead Co., MT	Milton F. Steele	Milton F. Steele	1963	295
378 4/8	51 3/8	49 6/8	40 2/8	9 1/8	9 3/8	6	6	Park Co., MT	M.J. Young	M.J. Young	1967	295
378 4/8	50 1/8	50 3/8	36 2/8	11 1/8	11 5/8	8	7	Idaho Co., ID	Johnny Bliznak	Johnny Bliznak	1990	295
378 4/8	56 3/8	57 3/8	50 6/8	9 1/8	10 1/8	6	6	Apache Co., AZ	Robert E. Sterling	Robert E. Sterling	1991	295
378 3/8	49 5/8	49 7/8	42 7/8	8 5/8	8 4/8	7	7	San Juan Co., UT	Jeffery B. Booey	Jeffery B. Booey	1997	301
378 2/8	51 4/8	52 6/8	50	10	10	7	7	White River, CO	Art Wright	Art Wright	1953	302
378 2/8	43 4/8	47 3/8	47 3/8	9 6/8	9 6/8	7	8	Duck Mt., MB	John D. Harbarenko	John D. Harbarenko	1973	302
378 1/8	60 5/8	58 1/8	47 5/8	8 3/8	8 1/8	7	7	Walla Walla Co., WA	Kathy Lilya	Warren Robison	1955	304
378 1/8	53 4/8	54 7/8	52 5/8	7 5/8	7 5/8	7	6	Navajo Co., AZ	Stanford H. Atwood, Jr.	Stanford H. Atwood, Jr.	1987	304
378 1/8	52 4/8	53 2/8	39 7/8	6 7/8	7 1/8	7	8	Langill Lake, BC	Gary D. Fodor	Gary D. Fodor	1989	304
378	49 3/8	50 2/8	39 5/8	8 6/8	8 1/8	7	6	Richard's Peak, MT	Richard Eastman	Albert Sales	1931	307
378	56 1/8	54 1/8	44 2/8	7 6/8	7 6/8	7	8	Gunnison, CO	Ed Lattimore, Jr.	Ed Lattimore, Jr.	1966	307
378	55	54	46 7/8	9 2/8	8 4/8	7	7	Catron Co., NM	Jayson W. Lucero	Jayson W. Lucero	1997	307
377 7/8	52 7/8	53 6/8	47 1/8	9 4/8	8 4/8	7	7	Baker Co., OR	Donald B. Martin	Donald B. Martin	1961	310
377 6/8	51 3/8	52 3/8	45	8 3/8	8	7	7	Routt Co., CO	Tom Nidey	Tom Nidey	1959	311
377 6/8	56 6/8	55 6/8	41 6/8	8 2/8	8 2/8	10	7	Sanders Co., MT	Steve Barnes	Steve Barnes	1973	311
377 6/8	53 3/8	53 4/8	41 6/8	9 5/8	9	9	9	Mistatim, SK	Peter Hrbachek	Peter Hrbachek	1984	311
377 5/8	54 2/8	54 5/8	40 6/8	8 1/8	8 6/8	9	9	Apache Co., AZ	A.C. Goodell	A.C. Goodell	1963	314
377 5/8	53 7/8	53 3/8	51 7/8	8 6/8	9	6	6	Beaverhead Co., MT	Edmund J. Giebel	Edmund J. Giebel	1981	314
377 4/8	54 3/8	51 5/8	45 5/8	8 6/8	8 4/8	7	6	Granite Co., MT	Tom Villeneue	Tom Villeneue	1966	316
377 4/8	52 2/8	53 1/8	42 2/8	8 5/8	9 1/8	6	6	Ft. Apache Res., AZ	Gary Marsh	Picked Up	1971	316
377 4/8	47 5/8	47 2/8	45	8 4/8	8 4/8	6	6	Gunnison Co., CO	Leo Welch	Leo Welch	1972	316
377 4/8	52 2/8	54	41 4/8	8 6/8	8 6/8	6	6	Park Co., WY	Jon M. Mekeal	Jon M. Mekeal	1984	316
377 3/8	59	55	39 3/8	9 7/8	9 7/8	7	6	Teton Co., WY	Walter V. Solinski	Walter V. Solinski	1962	320
377 3/8	60	58	41 7/8	8 4/8	11	6	6	Sanders Co., MT	Allen White	Allen White	1968	320
377 3/8	53 1/8	52	46 1/8	9 1/8	8 4/8	6	6	Missoula Co., MT	Tom Schenarts	Tom Schenarts	1970	320
377 3/8	49 3/8	49 7/8	40 3/8	10 2/8	11 2/8	6	6	Petroleum Co., MT	Jack Atcheson, Jr.	Jack Atcheson, Jr.	1990	320
377 2/8	53 5/8	53 6/8	49 2/8	8 2/8	8 2/8	7	7	Gallatin Range, MT	Earl Dehart, Sr.	E. Dehart, Sr., P. Van Beek, & H. Prestine	1960	324
377 2/8	55 4/8	60 1/8	50 6/8	10 3/8	9 7/8	6	6	Show Low, AZ	Michael Pew	Michael Pew	1964	324
377 2/8	56	55 2/8	40 2/8	11	11	6	6	Park Co., WY	M.J. Rickman & E.R. Rickman, Jr.	Mary J. Rickman	1965	324
377 2/8	54 2/8	54 2/8	44 2/8	8 1/8	8 2/8	7	7	Apache Co., AZ	Donald E. Franklin	Donald E. Franklin	1981	324
377 1/8	53	51 6/8	45 4/8	8 5/8	9	6	8	Sublette Co., WY	Ted Dew	Ted Dew	1928	328
377	54 6/8	54 1/8	47 2/8	8 5/8	9 2/8	7	6	Brazeau River, AB	Ted Loblaw	Ted Loblaw	1960	329
377	45 6/8	46 4/8	42 2/8	7 2/8	7 4/8	7	7	Navajo Co., AZ	Melvin Nolte, Jr.	Melvin Nolte, Jr.	1983	329

AMERICAN ELK - TYPICAL ANTLERS

Cervus elaphus nelsoni and related subspecies

Score	Length of Main Beam R	L	Inside Spread	Circumference at Smallest Place Between First and Second Points R	L	Number of Points R	L	Locality	Hunter	Owner	Date Killed	Rank
377	49 4/8	48 1/8	39	7 1/8	7 4/8	7	7	Clearwater River, AB	Don H. Grimes	Don H. Grimes	1985	329
377	58 5/8	56 4/8	47 4/8	8 6/8	8 1/8	7	7	Benton Co., WA	Daniel J. Bishop	Daniel J. Bishop	1988	329
376 7/8	55	55 6/8	38 2/8	9 5/8	10 2/8	7	6	Jackson Hole, WY	H.M. Hanna	M.H. Haskell	PR 1890	333
376 7/8	56 4/8	57 2/8	52 7/8	7 3/8	7 7/8	6	6	Park Co., WY	Warren C. Cubbage	Warren C. Cubbage	1957	333
376 7/8	54 4/8	54 5/8	57 2/8	6 6/8	6 7/8	6	6	Routt Co., CO	J.L. Bailey	J.L. Bailey	1963	333
376 7/8	46 6/8	45 6/8	42 6/8	10	9 6/8	6	6	Flotten Lake, SK	Garry G. Ronald	Garry G. Ronald	1987	333
376 6/8	56 2/8	54 4/8	44 6/8	9 4/8	9 3/8	7	7	Big Horn Mts., WY	Unknown	A.W. Hendershot	1912	337
376 6/8	51 2/8	52 4/8	48 2/8	8 4/8	8 3/8	8	7	Lewis & Clark Co., MT	Cameron G. Mielke	Cameron G. Mielke	1964	337
376 6/8	61	58 7/8	51	8 3/8	7 3/8	8	7	Teton Co., WY	Ward Keevert	Ward Keevert	1968	337
376 6/8	59 3/8	59 7/8	45 4/8	10	9 2/8	8	7	Crook Co., OR	Picked Up	Larry E. Miller	1983	337
376 6/8	51 2/8	51 6/8	40	8 1/8	8 1/8	7	7	Fremont Co., ID	Phil S. Borresen	Phil S. Borresen	1996	337
376 5/8	58 6/8	56 3/8	48 1/8	7 6/8	7 6/8	6	6	Granby, CO	Melvin Van Lewen	CO Div. of Wildl.	1961	342
376 5/8	48	50 1/8	39 3/8	8 5/8	8 7/8	7	7	Teton Co., ID	Edwin E. Schiess	Tim Schiess	1966	342
376 4/8	56 5/8	57	39 4/8	9 3/8	9 5/8	7	7	Highwood River, AB	Leonard Edwards	Ralph Seitz	1956	344
376 4/8	55 1/8	53 4/8	49 6/8	8 2/8	8 5/8	8	7	Albany Co., WY	Jerry F. Cook	Jerry F. Cook	1965	344
376 3/8	48 4/8	49 2/8	40 3/8	8	8 1/8	7	7	White River, CO	Ron Vance	Ronald Crawford	1957	346
376 3/8	49 3/8	49 7/8	41 5/8	7 7/8	7 4/8	6	6	Radium, CO	Bill Mercer	Bill Mercer	1964	346
376 3/8	54 2/8	55 5/8	43 3/8	9	9 1/8	7	7	Rocky Mt. House, AB	George P. Ebl	George P. Ebl	1966	346
376 3/8	55 6/8	55	30 2/8	8 6/8	8 4/8	7	7	Valley Co., ID	Ron Gastelecutto	Ron Gastelecutto	1985	346
376 3/8	55 4/8	55 5/8	39 1/8	9	9	6	6	Gunnison Co., CO	Gerald J. Obertino	Gerald J. Obertino	1986	346
376 1/8	58 3/8	56 4/8	42 1/8	8 4/8	8 2/8	6	6	Lincoln Co., NM	Jim Carter	Jim Carter	1981	351
376 1/8	55 4/8	54 6/8	38 1/8	8 2/8	8 2/8	6	6	White Pine Co., NV	Robert A. Jackson	Robert A. Jackson	1994	351
376 1/8	55 6/8	54	47 3/8	8 2/8	8 1/8	6	7	Albany Co., WY	Dean D. Dick	Dean D. Dick	1996	351
376 1/8	55 4/8	57 3/8	49 1/8	9	9 7/8	6	6	Cibola Co., NM	Bruce T. Berger	Bruce T. Berger	1997	351
376	49 6/8	51	39 2/8	9	8 5/8	6	6	Clark Co., ID	Bud Gifford	Darrell D. Riste	1951	355
376	60 4/8	59	44 4/8	7 5/8	8	6	6	Almont, CO	John Schwartz	John Schwartz	1961	355
376	55	54 1/8	42	9 3/8	9 1/8	6	6	Dormer River, AB	D.C. Thomas	D.C. Thomas	1978	355
376	47 5/8	50 1/8	48 6/8	10 1/8	10 1/8	7	8	Apache Co., AZ	William C. Moore	William C. Moore	1983	355
375 7/8	54 6/8	54 4/8	43 5/8	8 4/8	8 5/8	8	8	Flathead Co., MT	Pat Roth	Pat Roth	1966	359
375 7/8	52	54 6/8	37 3/8	9	8 5/8	8	8	Apache Co., AZ	McLean Bowman	McLean Bowman	1986	359
375 7/8	55 1/8	52 5/8	52 5/8	8 1/8	8 1/8	6	6	Morgan Co., UT	Vernon A. Ridd	Vernon A. Ridd	1995	359
375 6/8	54 6/8	50 4/8	43	8 4/8	8 2/8	6	6	Big Horn Mts., WY	Robert F. Retzlaff	Robert F. Retzlaff	1957	362
375 6/8	57 2/8	57 7/8	43	7 2/8	7 3/8	6	6	Buck Creek, WY	Andrew W. Heard, Jr.	Andrew W. Heard, Jr.	1958	362
375 6/8	50 3/8	50 6/8	40 4/8	9 4/8	10 4/8	6	6	Crow Valley, CO	Dale R. Leonard	Dale R. Leonard	1961	362
375 6/8	55 1/8	54 4/8	39 4/8	8 7/8	8 2/8	6	6	North Fall Creek, WY	Picked Up	Bob F. Penny	1981	362
375 6/8	52 1/8	50 4/8	37 2/8	8 4/8	7 7/8	7	7	Shoshone Co., ID	Ralph H. Brandvold, Jr.	Ralph H. Brandvold, Jr.	1983	362

Score	Length of Main Beam R	Length of Main Beam L	Inside Spread	Circumference R	Circumference L	Points R	Points L	Locality	Hunter	Owner	Date Killed	Rank
375 6/8	49 3/8	49 6/8	38	9 6/8	9 4/8	6	6	Glenboro, MB	Peter Sawatzky	Peter Sawatzky	1992	362
375 6/8	56 5/8	53 4/8	47 2/8	7 5/8	8	6	6	Coconino Co., AZ	Randy S. Ulmer	Randy S. Ulmer	1997	362
375 5/8	58	59 6/8	40 3/8	10 2/8	10 1/8	7	7	Unknown	Unknown	Demarest Mem. Museum PR	1952	369
375 5/8	54 3/8	51 3/8	43 7/8	9	9 1/8	7	7	Madison River, MT	Dale A. Hancock	Dale A. Hancock	1967	369
375 5/8	48	54 1/8	46 7/8	8 2/8	8 3/8	6	7	Sanders Co., MT	Tony B. Cox	Tony B. Cox	1980	369
375 5/8	57 6/8	51 6/8	48 4/8	8 5/8	8 2/8	7	6	Rich Co., UT	Bill L. Shupe	Bill L. Shupe	1996	369
375 4/8	50	55 2/8	48 4/8	8 7/8	8 1/8	6	6	Jefferson Co., MT	Ralph J. Huckaba	Ralph J. Huckaba	1949	373
375 4/8	47 6/8	53 2/8	34 1/8	8 4/8	9 1/8	6	6	Fremont Co., WY	Edward J. Patik	Edward J. Patik	1962	373
375 4/8	55 1/8	52 6/8	42 4/8	7 6/8	8 1/8	8	8	Powell Co., MT	Allan F. Kruse	Allan F. Kruse	1977	373
375 4/8	52	54	43 6/8	9	9	7	7	Skamania Co., WA	Kevin Schmid	Kevin Schmid	1990	373
375 3/8	51 1/8	52	44 7/8	9 2/8	10 1/8	6	6	Jefferson Co., MT	Mrs. Lou Sweet	Mrs. Lou Sweet	1924	377
375 3/8	58 7/8	56 6/8	43 1/8	7 6/8	8 2/8	6	7	Teton Co., WY	Unknown	Nathan E. Hindman PR	1950	377
375 3/8	52 6/8	54 6/8	44 5/8	8 3/8	9 1/8	7	7	Snake River, WY	W.H. Robinson	W.H. Robinson	1957	377
375 3/8	49	50 6/8	39 7/8	9	8 3/8	6	6	Park Co., MT	Bruce Brown	Bruce Brown	1967	377
375 3/8	58 1/8	59 1/8	37 3/8	7 5/8	7 5/8	6	6	Beaverhead Co., MT	Harold F. Krieger, Jr.	Harold F. Krieger, Jr.	1970	377
375 3/8	59 2/8	60 4/8	45 2/8	8 4/8	8 6/8	6	6	Apache Co., AZ	Picked Up	H. Jack Corbin	1989	377
375 3/8	52 7/8	53 3/8	40 1/8	8 7/8	8 5/8	6	7	Apache Co., AZ	Michael S. Muhlbauer	Michael S. Muhlbauer	1989	377
375 3/8	54 4/8	55 3/8	49	8 7/8	9	6	6	Apache Co., AZ	Lee M. Bass	Lee M. Bass	1995	377
375 2/8	51 4/8	55 3/8	36 2/8	9 3/8	9 6/8	6	6	Jackson, WY	Bill Blanchard	Bill Blanchard	1954	385
375 2/8	55 2/8	53 1/8	47 2/8	7 7/8	7 4/8	7	7	Ten Sleep, WY	Kenneth Hadland	Kenneth Hadland	1959	385
375 2/8	53	52 3/8	41	8 7/8	8 7/8	8	8	Craig, CO	Kenneth W. Cramer	Kenneth W. Cramer	1960	385
375 2/8	55 3/8	52	41 2/8	10	10 4/8	8	8	Natrona Co., WY	Victor R. Jackson	Victor R. Jackson	1976	385
375 2/8		55 3/8		8 3/8	8 3/8	6	6	Colfax Co., NM	Slim Pickens	Margaret M. Lindley	1981	385
375 1/8	56	55	38	8 4/8	8 4/8	6	6	Albany Co., WY	Don Stewart	Don Stewart	1981	391
375 1/8	52	53 4/8	39 3/8	9	10	7	6	Prince Albert, SK	Unknown	Lucky Lake Sask. Elks	1926	391
375	58 4/8	58 5/8	37 3/8	10 2/8	9 7/8	7	7	Tonto Lake, AZ	Louise F. Campbell	Louise F. Campbell	1967	393
375	57 1/8	54	38	8	8	6	7	Denton Co., TX	O.Z. Finley	Joe B. Finley, Jr.	1934	393
375	52 6/8	52 5/8	47 4/8	8 6/8	9	7	7	Fremont Co., ID	Eva Calonge	Eva Calonge	1960	393
375	57 3/8	54 4/8	41 2/8	9 3/8	9 5/8	6	6	Park Co., MT	Robert M. Brogan	Robert M. Brogan	1972	393
375	59	58 6/8	42 2/8	9 7/8	9 2/8	6	6	Lewis & Clark Co., MT	James Bollinger	James Bollinger	1982	393
375	57 1/8	58 1/8	42 6/8	9 1/8	8 6/8	6	6	Wheeler Co., OR	William K. Bartlett	William K. Bartlett	1986	393
375	57 7/8	57 5/8	49 4/8	6 7/8	7 3/8	6	6	Coconino Co., AZ	Arthur D. Ortiz	Arthur D. Ortiz	1993	393
375	48 2/8	50 2/8	46 4/8	8 1/8	8 4/8	6	6	Wyoming	Unknown	Randy Clark	1994	393
403*	57 1/8	57 2/8	43	8 7/8	8 7/8	6	6	Billings Co., ND	Douglas J. Jahnke	Douglas J. Jahnke	1997	
392*	52 4/8	53 3/8	36 4/8	10 3/8	10 4/8	6	6	Campbell Co., WY	Paul Wollenman	Paul Wollenman	1996	

* Final score is subject to revision by additional verifying measurements.

CATEGORY
AMERICAN ELK
NON-TYPICAL ANTLERS

SCORE
422-3/8

HUNTER
JOHN J. LOMONACO

LOCATION
NAVAJO CO., AZ

DATE OF KILL
SEPTEMBER 1992

CATEGORY
AMERICAN ELK
TYPICAL ANTLERS

SCORE
397-1/8

HUNTER
MICHAEL A. TROUSDALE

LOCATION
LINCOLN CO., NV

DATE OF KILL
NOVEMBER 1994

CATEGORY
AMERICAN ELK
TYPICAL ANTLERS

SCORE
375-2/8

HUNTER
SLIM PICKENS

LOCATION
COLFAX CO., NM

DATE OF KILL
OCTOBER 1981

196

B&C HISTORY

JAY N. "DING" DARLING
1876-1962

He was a newspaper reporter, author, cartoonist and winner, in 1924, of the Pulitzer Prize for the "best cartoon" published in any American newspaper during the preceding year. He was a leading conservationist with a deep and abiding interest in wildlife. As such he was probably the first to draw attention to the plight of the Florida Key Deer in the late 1950s. Ding designed the first Federal Duck Stamp in 1934. The Boone and Crockett Club bestowed him with an Honorary Life Membership in 1959. ∎

THE LAST OF THE TOY DEER OF THE FLORIDA KEYS

THE SMALLEST SPECIES OF DEER IN NORTH AMERICA, ALONE, UNGUARDED AND ON THE WAY OUT!

AMERICAN ELK - NON-TYPICAL ANTLERS
NEW WORLD'S RECORD

On July 30, 1994, a huge elk was found floating in the Upper Arrow Lake of British Columbia. Conservation Officer, Jim Beck seized the salvaged antlers from a resident who had cut them from the rapidly decomposing body.

Though investigation into the cause of death would prove unsuccessful, Beck knew right off that this rack was deserving of a Boone and Crockett measurement. What he didn't know was the stir it was about to cause in an area of the Kootenays already known for its trophy bulls. With nine and eleven points on the right and left, respectively, the non-typical antlers tallied an entry score of 456-3/8 with a total of 47-3/8 inches of abnormal points. This was enough to potentially become the new World's Record.

Once the case was closed, the antlers were transferred to Rick Morley, Regional Fish and Wildlife Manager in Nelson, British Columbia. Officially measured at 465-2/8 points, the non-typical American elk was declared the new World's Record by the 23rd Awards Judges' Panel. Interestingly, it was noted that the antlers were partially in velvet at the time of the bull's death and some of the main points had not fully hardened, indicating that they could have grown larger!

Elk management over the last 20 years in the Arrow Lakes portion of the Kootenays has deliberately aimed to produce trophy elk. Elk have gradually spread through this region from transplants in the 1950s and 1970s. Bull elk hunting, using a lottery permit system called Limited Entry Hunting (LEH), has been used since the early 1980s to control the harvest of bulls.

The management objective was to allow a significant number of bulls to reach 10 years of age or more, so they would have the body mass and condition to produce maximum growth. New populations were also given time to establish before very conservative hunts were initiated. West Kootenay hunter support for this management plan has been high since hunters recognize that the area is not capable of supporting large numbers of elk. They support the concept of managing for quality over quantity. Many of British Columbia's record elk antlers have resulted from this management strategy.

The Government of British Columbia plans to keep the antlers as a testimonial to the importance of elk in the Kootenay Region of British Columbia. Since 1995, the antlers have been treated by taxidermists, cleaned, dyed and put on a plaque for easier display. Efforts are being made to use the antlers to generate funds for elk management. These include the funds raised at Rocky Mountain Elk Foundation banquets and commissions on art work. Other means of generating funds for elk management, short of selling the antlers, will continue as well. ■

TROPHY INFO

RANK
New World's Record

SCORE
465 5/8

LOCATION
Upper Arrow Lake, BC

HUNTER
Picked Up

OWNER
BC Environment

DATE KILLED
1994

Photograph by Ron Anfinson

	COLUMN 1 Spread Credit	COLUMN 2 Right Antler	COLUMN 3 Left Antler	Difference
	49 2/8	49 2/8	46 3/8	2 7/8
		26 1/8	25 5/8	4/8
		23	23 4/8	4/8
		22	22 1/8	1/8
		20 2/8	17 6/8	4/8
		14 2/8	10 6/8	4/8
		8 5/8		6/8
		9 3/8	7 2/8	1/8
			9 2/8	1/8
		13 6/8		0
		85 1/8		3 7/8
			14 1/8	

C. Greatest Spread 49 2/8

SPREAD CREDIT MAY EQUAL BUT
NOT EXCEED LONGER ANTLER

Length of Sixth Point, If Present

G-6. Length of Seventh Point, If Present

G-7. Length of Seventh Point, If Present

H-1. Circumference at Smallest Place Between First and Second Points

H-2. Circumference at Smallest Place Between Second and Third and Fourth

H-3. Circumference at Smallest Place Between Fourth and Fifth Points

H-4. Circumference at Smallest Place Between Fourth and Fifth Points

TOTALS

Hunter: Picked Up

Exact Locality Where Killed: Upper Arrow

Date Killed: 1994

Owner: British Columbia Environment

Telephone #:

Column 1	49 2/8
Column 2	190
	85 1/8

AMERICAN ELK
NON-TYPICAL ANTLERS
WORLD'S RECORD SCORECHART

Records of
North American
Big Game

250 Station Drive
Missoula, MT 59801
(406) 542-1888

BOONE AND CROCKETT CLUB®

OFFICIAL SCORING SYSTEM FOR NORTH AMERICAN BIG GAME TROPHIES

NON-TYPICAL
AMERICAN ELK (WAPITI)

MINIMUM SCORES
AWARDS   ALL-TIME
385   385

Detail of Point Measurement

	Abnormal Points	
	Right Antler	Left Antler
	15	11 1/8
	4 6/8	9 6/8
	4	3 6/8
		1 4/8
		5 1/8
SUBTOTALS	23 6/8	31 2/8
E. TOTAL	55	

	COLUMN 1	COLUMN 2	COLUMN 3	COLUMN 4
	Spread Credit	Right Antler	Left Antler	Difference
	49 2/8			
F. Length of Main Beam		49 2/8	46 3/8	2 7/8
G-1. Length of First Point		26 1/8	25 5/8	4/8
G-2. Length of Second Point		23	23 4/8	4/8
G-3. Length of Third Point		22	22 1/8	1/8
G-4. Length of Fourth Point		20 2/8	17 6/8	2 4/8
G-5. Length of Fifth Point		14 2/8	10 6/8	3 4/8
G-6. Length of Sixth Point, If Present				
G-7. Length of Seventh Point, If Present				
H-1. Circumference at Smallest Place Between First and Second Points		8 6/8	8 6/8	1/8
H-2. Circumference at Smallest Place Between Second and Third Points		7 2/8	7 2/8	0
H-3. Circumference at Smallest Place Between Third and Fourth Points		9 3/8	9 2/8	1/8
H-4. Circumference at Smallest Place Between Fourth and Fifth Points		9 7/8	13 6/8	3 7/8
TOTALS	49 2/8	190	185 1/8	14 1/8

SEE OTHER SIDE FOR INSTRUCTIONS		
A. No. Points on Right Antler	9	No. Points on Left Antler	11
B. Tip to Tip Spread	50 5/8	C. Greatest Spread	61
D. Inside Spread of Main Beams	51 1/8	SPREAD CREDIT MAY EQUAL BUT NOT EXCEED LONGER ANTLER	

	Column 1	49 2/8	Exact Locality Where Killed: Upper Arrow Lake, BC
ADD	Column 2	190	Date Killed: 1994	Hunter: Picked Up
	Column 3	185 1/8	Owner: British Columbia Environment	Telephone #:
	Subtotal	424 3/8	Owner's Address:
SUBTRACT Column 4	14 1/8		Guide's Name and Address:
	Subtotal	410 2/8	Remarks: (Mention Any Abnormalities or Unique Qualities)
Add Line E Total	55		
FINAL SCORE	465 2/8		

COPYRIGHT © 1999 BY BOONE AND CROCKETT CLUB®

All measurements must be made with a 1/4-inch wide flexible steel tape to the nearest one-eighth of an inch. (Note: A flexible steel cable can be used to measure points and main beams only.) Enter fractional figures in eighths, without reduction. Official measurements cannot be taken until the antlers have air dried for at least 60 days after the animal was killed.

A. Number of Points on Each Antler: To be counted a point, the projection must be at least one inch long, with length exceeding width at one inch or more of length. All points are measured from tip of point to nearest edge of beam as illustrated. Beam tip is counted as a point but not measured as a point.

B. Tip to Tip Spread is measured between tips of main beams.

C. Greatest Spread is measured between perpendiculars at a right angle to the center line of the skull at widest part, whether across main beams or points.

D. Inside Spread of Main Beams is measured at a right angle to the center line of the skull at widest point between main beams. Enter this measurement again as the Spread Credit if it is less than or equal to the length of the longer antler; if greater, enter longer antler length for Spread Credit.

E. Total of Lengths of all Abnormal Points: Abnormal Points are those non-typical in location (such as points originating from a point or from bottom or sides of main beam) or pattern (extra points, not generally paired). Measure in usual manner and record in appropriate blanks.

F. Length of Main Beam is measured from the center of the lowest outside edge of burr over the outer side to the most distant point of the main beam. The point of beginning is that point on the burr where the center line along the outer side of the beam intersects the burr, then following generally the line of the illustration.

G-1-2-3-4-5-6-7. Length of Normal Points: Normal points project from the top or front of the main beam in the general pattern illustrated. They are measured from nearest edge of main beam over outer curve to tip. Lay the tape along the outer curve of the beam so that the top edge of the tape coincides with the top edge of the beam on both sides of point to determine the baseline for point measurement. Record point length in appropriate blanks.

H-1-2-3-4. Circumferences are taken as detailed in illustration for each measurement.

Cervus elaphus nelsoni and related subspecies

MINIMUM SCORE 385

Score	Length of Main Beam		Inside Spread	Circumference at Smallest Place Between First and Second Points		Number of Points		Locality	Hunter	Owner	Date Killed	Rank
	R	L		R	L	R	L					
465 2/8	49 2/8	46 3/8	51 1/8	8 5/8	8 6/8	9	11	Upper Arrow Lake, BC	Picked Up	BC Environment	1994	1
449 7/8	55 1/8	53 7/8	44	8 7/8	9 4/8	8	7	Golden Valley Co., ND	Kevin D. Fugere	Kevin D. Fugere	1997	2
447 1/8	54 1/8	52 5/8	39 7/8	11	10 2/8	9	9	Gilbert Plains, MB	James R. Berry	D.J. Hollinger & B. Howard	1961	3
445 5/8	58	57 7/8	41 6/8	9 2/8	10	8	8	Apache Co., AZ	Jerry J. Davis	Jerry J. Davis	1984	4
432 5/8	56 7/8	57 3/8	35 3/8	9 6/8	9 7/8	8	9	Gila Co., AZ	Nathaniel Boni	Alan C. Ellsworth	1994	5
430 6/8	46 5/8	51 5/8	45 3/8	8 6/8	9 4/8	10	9	Fraser River, BC	Ben Young	John Young	1980	6
423 4/8	51 4/8	50 6/8	44 7/8	8 4/8	7 7/8	8	7	Granite Co., MT	Lee F. Tracy	Lee F. Tracy	1971	7
423	53 4/8	52 3/8	40	8 2/8	8 6/8	8	10	Coconino Co., AZ	James L. Ludvigson	James L. Ludvigson	1985	8
422 3/8	51 6/8	52 2/8	40 3/8	10	9 6/8	8	8	Navajo Co., AZ	John J. LoMonaco	John J. LoMonaco	1992	9
417 6/8	58 1/8	52 1/8	47 4/8	9 3/8	9 2/8	7	9	Catron Co., NM	Martin D. Huggins	Martin D. Huggins	1992	10
417	57 5/8	56 5/8	48 4/8	10 6/8	9 6/8	7	6	Coconino Co., AZ	Timothy A. Pender	Picked Up	1993	11
416 4/8	51 2/8	50 6/8	43 5/8	9 2/8	9 2/8	9	9	Navajo Co., AZ	John A. Gulius	John A. Gulius	1990	12
415 2/8	54	55	42 6/8	8 7/8	9 4/8	8	8	Johnson Co., WY	Rod M. Odenbach	Rod M. Odenbach	1993	13
414 6/8	49 4/8	54 2/8	45 3/8	9 5/8	10 3/8	9	8	Graham Co., AZ	Curley Bush, Jr.	Alan C. Ellsworth	1995	14
414 4/8	53 3/8	54 6/8	40 1/8	9 5/8	10 2/8	7	9	White Pine Co., NV	James A. Cook	James A. Cook	1996	15
414	48 2/8	48 2/8	46 7/8	7 3/8	6 5/8	9	10	Taos Co., NM	Lou A. DePaolis	Bass Pro Shops F. & W. Mus.	1974	16
412 6/8	54 3/8	54 7/8	38 5/8	11 2/8	10 5/8	8	6	Apache Co., AZ	James P. Brooks	James P. Brooks	1997	17
411 1/8	55 4/8	55 3/8	41 2/8	10 3/8	9 7/8	10	9	Navajo Co., AZ	Dennis G. Hall	Dennis G. Hall	1996	18
410 1/8	46 3/8	47 1/8	50	9 6/8	9 3/8	11	10	Taos Co., NM	Picked Up	P.R. Ridilla & B. Adams	1993	19
410 1/8	54 6/8	50 6/8	45 3/8	9 4/8	8 7/8	7	7	White Pine Co., NV	George J. Brown	George J. Brown	1997	19
408 5/8	57 1/8	58 1/8	41	9 5/8	11 1/8	8	8	Apache Co., AZ	Herman C. Meyer	Herman C. Meyer	1992	21
408 4/8	50 7/8	47 1/8	41 5/8	8 5/8	9 5/8	9	9	Lincoln Co., MT	Picked Up	Grant Garcia	1995	22
408	51 7/8	50 6/8	39 7/8	7 7/8	8 6/8	7	8	Sanders Co., MT	John Fitchett	John Fitchett	1980	23
408	53 5/8	53	40 6/8	9	9 1/8	7	8	Apache Co., AZ	J.G. Brittingham & W. Dale	Jack G. Brittingham	1987	23
407 6/8	54 6/8	54 2/8	40 4/8	9	8	8	8	Granite Co., MT	Scott Hicks	Scott Hicks	1971	25
407 3/8	54 6/8	52 6/8	40 3/8	8 5/8	7 6/8	8	7	Lincoln Co., MT	Terry V. Crooks	Terry V. Crooks	1996	26
406 7/8	48 1/8	47 2/8	34 7/8	8 2/8	7 4/8	7	8	Apache Co., AZ	Joe W. Carroll	Joe W. Carroll	1982	27
406 4/8	53 6/8	54 2/8	42 2/8	7 5/8	7 1/8	10	9	King Co., WA	John Greiner	Alan C. Ellsworth	1953	28
406 2/8	49 4/8	49 6/8	41 2/8	9	10 1/8	9	10	Fremont Co., WY	Unknown	Warren V. Spriggs, Sr.	PR 1952	29
406	57 2/8	54 2/8	40 4/8	10 2/8	10 1/8	9	9	Coconino Co., AZ	Clifford Happy	Clifford Happy	1994	30
405 4/8	54 3/8	51 7/8	44	8 6/8	9	9	8	Granite Co., MT	Arthur W. Lundgren	Grace Lundgren	1946	31
405 3/8	54 2/8	54 7/8	46 5/8	10 4/8	9 5/8	8	7	Wallowa Co., OR	George Rogers	BPOE LaGrande Lodge 433	1933	32
405 3/8	59 4/8	58 1/8	40 2/8	8 4/8	8 2/8	7	8	Vermilion River, MB	Ernie M. Bernat	Ernie M. Bernat	1986	32
404 4/8	55	61	46 4/8	7 7/8	8 1/8	7	6	Lewis & Clark Co., MT	Clinton L. Pierson	Clinton L. Pierson	PR 1935	34
404 1/8	51 6/8	52 5/8	37 2/8	9 7/8	10 1/8	7	9	Jefferson Co., CO	Chris White	Chris White	1993	35
403 7/8	46 5/8	52	32 4/8	10 3/8	10 6/8	8	9	Shoshone Co., ID	Fred S. Scott	D.J. Hollinger & B. Howard	1964	36

Score	Beam R	Beam L	Inside Spread	Circ. R	Circ. L	Pts. R	Pts. L	Locality	Hunter	Owner	Date	Rank
403 7/8	51 4/8	47 2/8	43 1/8	9 2/8	9	9	7	White Pine Co., NV	Geoffrey H.S. House	Geoffrey H.S. House	1994	36
403 3/8	49 5/8	58 3/8	38 2/8	9 1/8	9 6/8	8	8	Coconino Co., AZ	Robert B. Krogh, Jr.	Robert B. Krogh, Jr.	1983	38
403 3/8	57	59 3/8	47 3/8	9 2/8	9 4/8	7	7	Yellowstone Co., MT	Charles A. Solem	Charles A. Solem	1995	38
403 2/8	54 5/8	52 4/8	47 4/8	8 6/8	9 2/8	9	6	Park Co., MT	Gary Beley	Gary Beley	1964	40
403 1/8	51 7/8	51 7/8	38 7/8	8 7/8	9 2/8	7	9	Big Horn Co., WY	Unknown	Steve Crossley	PR 1985	41
403	52 5/8	52 3/8	57 1/8	8 7/8	8 4/8	10	8	Uinta Co., WY	Steven W. Condos	Norman Heater	1967	42
403	48 2/8	49	43 6/8	8	9	8	8	Lincoln Co., MT	Delbert Bowe	Delbert Bowe	1992	42
402 7/8	48 6/8	50	39	8 2/8	8 3/8	7	11	Powell Co., MT	Donald A. Roberson	Donald A. Roberson	1987	44
402 4/8	53 1/8	49 4/8	47 2/8	8 4/8	8 5/8	7	7	Idaho	Unknown	William J. Barry	PR 1960	45
402 2/8	55 6/8	55 7/8	50 1/8	9 7/8	10 1/8	7	7	Dogrib Creek, AB	Robert H. Jochim	Robert H. Jochim	1984	46
402 1/8	48 5/8	49 2/8	41	11 5/8	11 7/8	8	8	Morton Co., KS	Jeff A. Newton	Jeff A. Newton	1988	47
402	51 7/8	46 3/8	38 3/8	8 6/8	8 2/8	8	9	Lundar, MB	Picked Up	Fred Thorkelson	1980	48
401 7/8	51 6/8	50	49 2/8	9 4/8	9 4/8	9	7	Beaverhead Co., MT	Ben C. Holland	Ben C. Holland	1953	49
401 6/8	52 1/8	50 1/8	50 4/8	7 3/8	7 2/8	7	8	Rock Lake, AB	Harold R. Vaughn	Harold R. Vaughn	1968	50
401 5/8	53 5/8	55 5/8	43 3/8	7 7/8	7 4/8	7	7	Cowlitz Co., WA	Unknown	Steve Crossley	1959	51
401 4/8	48	45 1/8	39 1/8	11 5/8	11	8	11	Teton Co., WY	Douglas G. DeVivo	Douglas G. DeVivo	1992	52
401 1/8	51 3/8	51 3/8	47 6/8	9 1/8	9 4/8	8	6	Fremont Co., WY	Bud Cantleberry	Robert E. Cantleberry	1948	53
400 6/8	51 2/8	52	50 3/8	8 5/8	8 3/8	9	8	Madison Co., MT	Arthur A. Cooper	Arthur A. Cooper	1962	54
400 6/8	54 3/8	54	48 3/8	10 2/8	10 1/8	8	8	Mesa Co., CO	William C. Parrish	William C. Parrish	1994	54
400 5/8	53 2/8	52 7/8	46 7/8	8 4/8	8 6/8	7	8	Montana	Unknown	William C. Perkins	PR 1870	56
400 4/8	54 7/8	54 6/8	40 5/8	7 4/8	7 2/8	10	7	Whipsaw Creek, BC	Harold Margerison	Harold Margerison	1960	57
400	55 3/8	53 4/8	42 2/8	9 7/8	9 5/8	6	7	Routt Co., CO	William E. Goosman	William E. Goosman	1939	58
400	55 1/8	53	41 6/8	9	10	12	8	Wallowa Co., OR	William L. Hamilton	William L. Hamilton	1982	58
400	56 5/8	51 3/8	43 2/8	8 5/8	8 7/8	8	7	Apache Co., AZ	Ben Hollingsworth, Jr.	Ben Hollingsworth, Jr.	1995	58
398 5/8	52	52 3/8	43 5/8	9 1/8	9 5/8	7	7	Pierce Co., WA	Larry N. Mohler	Larry N. Mohler	1991	61
398 4/8	52 7/8	51 4/8	42 3/8	10 1/8	10 1/8	7	9	Morton Co., KS	Camron Paxton	Camron Paxton	1987	62
398 1/8	52 2/8	55	44 2/8	8 5/8	8 3/8	8	7	Park Co., MT	Picked Up	O. Cline Stelzig	1972	63
397 4/8	47 7/8	51 6/8	35 2/8	8 5/8	8 1/8	8	7	Apache Co., AZ	McLean Bowman	McLean Bowman	1994	64
397 2/8	53 2/8	51 6/8	45 4/8	9 2/8	8 6/8	8	8	Powell Co., MT	Rex Sorenson	Univ. of Mont. Zool. Mus.	1952	65
395 3/8	51 5/8	50 7/8	40 4/8	8 7/8	9	8	8	Apache Co., AZ	Mark W. White, Jr.	Mark W. White, Jr.	1983	66
395 2/8	55 6/8	58 1/8	57	8 6/8	8 4/8	7	8	Apache Co., AZ	Edward Boutonnet	Edward Boutonnet	1992	67
395 1/8	50 3/8	48 6/8	46 7/8	9 1/8	9 6/8	8	9	Hot Springs Co., WY	Unknown	Michael F. Conner	PR 1940	68
394 6/8	56	55	35 6/8	9	9 6/8	8	6	Otero Co., NM	Kelly R. Ginn	Kelly R. Ginn	1991	69
394 4/8	53	55 5/8	51 7/8	8 1/8	7 7/8	8	7	Sublette Co., WY	Charles R. Pennock	Charles R. Pennock	PR 1942	70
394 4/8	47 4/8	50	41 4/8	8	7 5/8	7	7	Lytton Creek, BC	Cliff L. Loring	Cliff L. Loring	1984	70
394 3/8	40 2/8	39 2/8	34 3/8	10 2/8	10	14	11	Carberry, MB	Brent Maxwell	Brent Maxwell	1991	72
394 1/8	58	56 6/8	44 6/8	8 7/8	8	6	8	Apache Co., AZ	Richard R. Childress	Richard R. Childress	1991	73
393 6/8	54 5/8	55 6/8	46 6/8	7 5/8	7 4/8	7	7	Navajo Co., AZ	Larry G. Van Hassle	Burke Hudnall	1990	74
393 3/8	50 2/8	48 4/8	41 2/8	9 5/8	10 1/8	8	8	Shoshone Co., ID	Hugh M. Kitzmiller	John M. Kitzmiller	1974	75
392 5/8	56 3/8	56 1/8	46 7/8	7 7/8	8	6	8	Coconino Co., AZ	John L. Hontalas	John L. Hontalas	1990	76
392 4/8	46	47 5/8	41 6/8	12	12 1/8	7	8	Otero Co., NM	David U. Inge	David U. Inge	1989	77
392	54 6/8	54	45 1/8	9 3/8	9 6/8	8	7	Mohave Co., AZ	Alfred L. McMicking	Alfred L. McMicking	1989	78
391 5/8	50 6/8	51 1/8	37 6/8	9 2/8	9 6/8	7	8	Petroleum Co., MT	Russ Allen	Russ Allen	1995	79
390 7/8	43 6/8	45 2/8	41	9 4/8	9 3/8	8	7	Apache Co., AZ	Theodore E. Dugey, Jr.	Theodore E. Dugey, Jr.	1978	80
390 7/8	52 6/8	46	46	9 7/8	9 2/8	8	8	Sublette Co., WY	Dale A. Shaklee	Dale A. Shaklee	1993	80
390 5/8	50 6/8	51 1/8	42 5/8	9 5/8	11	7	8	Apache Co., AZ	Hyland B. Erickson	Hyland B. Erickson	1995	82
390 2/8	46 4/8	49	38 2/8	8 3/8	8 1/8	10	11	Adams Co., ID	Robert F. Hughes	Robert F. Hughes	1995	83

AMERICAN ELK - NON-TYPICAL ANTLERS

Cervus elaphus nelsoni and related subspecies

Score	Length of Main Beam		Inside Spread	Circumference at Smallest Place Between First and Second Points		Number of Points		Locality	Hunter	Owner	Date Killed	Rank
	R	L		R	L	R	L					
388 3/8	50	51 2/8	41 4/8	9	8 7/8	7	8	Glacier Co., MT	John D. Fitzgerald	John D. Fitzgerald	1990	84
388 3/8	53	50 4/8	53 6/8	10 7/8	11	6	7	Platte Co., WY	Gary A. Pagel	Gary A. Pagel	1993	84
386 5/8	51 7/8	50 6/8	45 7/8	8 7/8	8 4/8	8	7	Beaverhead Co., MT	Unknown	William H. Flesch	PR 1962	86
386 5/8	44 6/8	46 1/8	38	9 6/8	9 6/8	5	6	Gallatin Co., MT	Tom Satre	Tom Satre	1966	86
386 4/8	54 3/8	53 6/8	44	8 7/8	9	8	6	Apache Co., AZ	Alan Hamberlin	Alan Hamberlin	1994	88
386 2/8	44 3/8	47 4/8	43 4/8	8 7/8	9	9	6	Socorro Co., NM	Richard P. Gould	Richard P. Gould	1990	89
386 2/8	50	50 1/8	41 4/8	8 6/8	8 4/8	7	7	Otero Co., NM	William M. Pitcher	William M. Pitcher	1992	89
385 6/8	51 6/8	51 7/8	38 6/8	8 7/8	9 2/8	8	8	Apache Co., AZ	R.G. Fraser, Sr. & M. Gatewood	Ronald G. Fraser, Sr.	1995	91
385 1/8	50 5/8	48 6/8	40 4/8	7 5/8	7 4/8	9	8	Latah Co., ID	James A. Carpenter	James A. Carpenter	1985	92
385 1/8	63 2/8	63 6/8	49 7/8	8	7 4/8	7	7	Greenwater Lake Park, SK	Joseph C. Chernysh	Joseph C. Chernysh	1995	92
385 1/8	48 7/8	50	36 1/8	8 6/8	8	7	7	Clearwater Co., ID	Tim Papineau	Tim Papineau	1996	92
385	57 2/8	57 3/8	36 7/8	10 4/8	10 5/8	7	6	Navajo Co., AZ	David W. Baxter	David W. Baxter	1991	95
385	55 5/8	55 4/8	42 1/8	9 1/8	9 1/8	8	7	Navajo Co., AZ	Dennis K. Frandsen	Dennis K. Frandsen	1993	95
415 6/8*	58 2/8	52 3/8	40 2/8	10 5/8	10 5/8	8	7	Madison Co., MT	Michael Gecho	Michael Gecho	1958	
410 4/8*	55 5/8	55 2/8	46 6/8	11 3/8	11 6/8	6	7	Unknown	Unknown	James R. Britton	PR 1994	

* Final score is subject to revision by additional verifying measurements.

CATEGORY
AMERICAN ELK
NON-TYPICAL ANTLERS

SCORE
414-4/8

HUNTER
JAMES A. COOK

LOCATION
WHITE PINE CO., NV

DATE OF KILL
SEPTEMBER 1996

CATEGORY
AMERICAN ELK
NON-TYPICAL ANTLERS

SCORE
385-1/8

HUNTER
TIM PAPINEAU

LOCATION
CLEARWATER CO., ID

DATE OF KILL
OCTOBER 1996

205

ROOSEVELT'S ELK
WORLD'S RECORD

As a result of sound management and hunting regulations, the Roosevelt's elk (*Cervus canadensis roosevelti*) continues to thrive within the deep coastal forest of the Northwest. In 1989, after being drawn for a limited permit, Wayne Coe and his hunting partner, Sid McKay, decided to search for Roosevelt's elk on Vancouver Island, British Columbia.

The men drove to the end of the main logging road along the Tsitika River and scouted for signs of elk several hours without success. On the way back, Coe spotted what appeared to be the hindquarters of an elk.

"I promptly grabbed my binoculars and my .300 Weatherby Magnum. Next, Sid and I scrambled 300 yards up the brush covered hillside in an effort to get a better look.

"Using my binoculars, I located the elk just inside some heavy timber, approximately 250 yards from our vantage point. Clearly, the animal in my view was a bull elk. I quickly concluded that I had better take advantage of this great opportunity as the season was soon to draw to a close. I told Sid that we ought to make an attempt at it.

"I located a good, steady rest for shooting and patiently waited for the elk to turn broadside. All I could see in my scope was an area from the bottom of his ear to half way up his antlers. I waited for what seemed like an eternity. Eventually, I became anxious, considering the possibility that the elk might flee before I decided to shoot.

"I told Sid I was going to attempt a shot at the elk's head. My first shot missed, but it did not cause the elk to re-

treat. Instead, he picked his head up a little more. I put the cross hairs of my scope on the elk's ear and squeezed the trigger. Sid exclaimed, 'It's a hit!'

"Together, we scrambled 250 yards or so up the hill to the place where the elk disappeared from sight. We found the bull dead, right where he had stood. Both Sid and I were shocked at his size. However, neither of us had any idea of the actual size of my trophy."

Friends encouraged Coe to have the bull officially scored by the Boone and Crockett Club. With a final score of 388-3/8 points, Coe's trophy exceeded the top scoring bull elk in the 9th edition by four points. It was certified as the World's Record at the 21st Big Game Awards Program in Milwaukee in 1992. ∎

ROOSEVELT'S ELK BOUNDARIES

The Roosevelt's elk category was established in 1980. All other elk varieties, primarily from the Rocky Mountains, are now referred to as American elk (typical and non-typical). Roosevelt's elk trophies have thicker, shorter antlers, and many of the largest trophies develop crown points, a very distinctive feature.

Roosevelt's elk are acceptable from Del Norte, Humboldt and Trinity Counties, California, as well as that portion of Siskiyou County west of I-5 in Northern California; from west of Highway I-5 in Oregon and Washington; from Vancouver Island, B.C.; and from Afognak and Raspberry Islands of Alaska. The Alaskan animals are a result of a successful transplant from the Peninsula of Washington.

Photograph by Wm. H. Nesbitt

207

ROOSEVELT'S ELK
WORLD'S RECORD SCORECHART

All measurements must be made with a 1/4-inch wide flexible steel tape to the nearest one-eighth of an inch. (Note: A flexible steel cable can be used to measure points and main beams only.) Enter fractional figures in eighths, without reduction. Official measurements cannot be taken until the antlers have air dried for at least 60 days after the animal was killed.

A. Number of Points on Each Antler: to be counted a point, the projection must be at least one inch long, with length exceeding width at one inch or more of length. All points are measured from tip of point to nearest edge of beam as illustrated. Beam tip is counted as a point but not measured as a point.

B. Tip to Tip Spread is measured between tips of main beams.

C. Greatest Spread is measured between perpendiculars at a right angle to the center line of the skull at widest part, whether across main beams or points.

D. Inside Spread of Main Beams is measured at a right angle to the center line of the skull at widest point between main beams. Enter this measurement again as the Spread Credit if it is less than or equal to the length of the longer antler; if greater, enter longer antler length for Spread Credit.

E. Total of Lengths of all Abnormal Points: Abnormal Points are those non-typical in location or pattern occurring below G-4. Measure in usual manner and record in appropriate blanks. **Note: do not confuse with Crown Points that may occur in the vicinity of G-4, G-5, G-6, etc.**

F. Length of Main Beam is measured from the center of the lowest outside edge of burr over the outer side to the most distant point of the main beam. The point of beginning is that point on the burr where the center line along the outer side of the beam intersects the burr, then following generally the line of the illustration.

G-1-2-3-4-5-6-7. Length of Normal Points: Normal points project from the top or front of the main beam in the general pattern illustrated. They are measured from nearest edge of main beam over outer curve to tip. Lay the tape along the outer curve of the beam so that the top edge of the tape coincides with the top edge of the beam on both sides of point to determine the baseline for point measurement. Record point length in appropriate blanks.

H-1-2-3-4. Circumferences are taken as detailed in illustration for each measurement.

I. Crown Points: From the well-defined Royal on out to end of beam, all points other than the normal points in their typical locations are Crown Points. This includes points occurring on the Royal, on other normal points, on Crown Points, and on the bottom and sides of main beam after the Royal. Measure and record in appropriate blanks provided and add to score below.

Records of
North American
Big Game

250 Station Drive
Missoula, MT 59801
(406) 542-1888

BOONE AND CROCKETT CLUB®
OFFICIAL SCORING SYSTEM FOR NORTH AMERICAN BIG GAME TROPHIES
ROOSEVELT'S AND TULE ELK

MINIMUM SCORES	AWARDS	ALL-TIME
Roosevelt's	275	290
	270	285
Tule	285	

KIND OF ELK (check one)
☑ Roosevelt's
☐ Tule

	Crown Points	
	Right Antler	Left Antler
	11 2/8	12 7/8
	2 5/8	
	2	
	7 2/8	
I. Crown Points Total		36

Abnormal Points

	Right Antler	Left Antler
	1 5/8	
TOTAL TO E		1 5/8

Detail of Point Measurement

		COLUMN 1	COLUMN 2	COLUMN 3	COLUMN 4
		Spread Credit	Right Antler	Left Antler	Difference
A. No. Points on Right Antler	11				
	No. Points on Left Antler	8			
B. Tip to Tip Spread	39				
	C. Greatest Spread	46 4/8			
D. Inside Spread of Main Beams	36 1/8	SPREAD CREDIT MAY EQUAL BUT NOT EXCEED LONGER ANTLER	36 1/8			
E. Total of Lengths of Abnormal Points					1 5/8
F. Length of Main Beam			44 2/8	46 7/8	2 5/8
G-1. Length of First Point			15 7/8	18 1/8	2 2/8
G-2. Length of Second Point			16 6/8	17 1/8	3/8
G-3. Length of Third Point			19 6/8	20 4/8	6/8
G-4. Length of Fourth Point			17	15 5/8	1 3/8
G-5. Length of Fifth Point			12 2/8	12 2/8	0
G-6. Length of Sixth Point, If Present			0	3 7/8	3 7/8
G-7. Length of Seventh Point, If Present					
H-1. Circumference at Smallest Place Between First and Second Points			11 2/8	11 2/8	0
H-2. Circumference at Smallest Place Between Second and Third Points			7 7/8	7 3/8	4/8
H-3. Circumference at Smallest Place Between Third and Fourth Points			7 3/8	7 5/8	2/8
H-4. Circumference at Smallest Place Between Fourth and Fifth Points			7	6 4/8	4/8
	TOTALS	36 1/8	159 3/8	167 1/8	10 2/8

ADD	Column 1	36 1/8	Exact Locality Where Killed: Taitika River, BC	
	Column 2	159 3/8	Date Killed: Nov. 4, 1989	Hunter: Wayne Coe
	Column 3	167 1/8	Owner: Wayne Coe	Telephone #:
	Total of I	36	Owner's Address:	
	Subtotal	398 5/8	Guide's Name and Address:	
SUBTRACT	Column 4	10 2/8	Remarks: (Mention Any Abnormalities or Unique Qualities)	
	FINAL SCORE	388 3/8		

COPYRIGHT © 1999 BY BOONE AND CROCKETT CLUB®

SEE OTHER SIDE FOR INSTRUCTIONS

209

ROOSEVELT'S ELK

Cervus elaphus roosevelti

MINIMUM SCORE 290

Score	Length of Main Beam R	L	Inside Spread	Circumference at Smallest Place Between First and Second Points R	L	Number of Points R	L	Locality	Hunter	Owner	Date Killed	Rank
388 3/8	44 2/8	46 7/8	36 1/8	11 2/8	11 2/8	11	8	Tsitika River, BC	Wayne Coe	Wayne Coe	1989	1
384 3/8	48 4/8	49	41 1/8	8 7/8	9 4/8	9	8	Clatsop Co., OR	Robert Sharp	Robert Sharp	1949	2
380 6/8	52 3/8	52 6/8	45 1/8	8 3/8	8 1/8	8	8	Jefferson Co., WA	Sam Argo	Sam Argo	1983	3
378 5/8	53 2/8	51 3/8	37	8 7/8	8 5/8	7	9	Clatsop Co., OR	Fred M. Williamson	Loaned to B&C Natl. Coll.	1947	4
376 3/8	53 2/8	52 3/8	41 5/8	10 1/8	10 3/8	8	7	Clallam Co., WA	Picked Up	Roy C. Ewen	1912	5
376 1/8	51	49 1/8	38	10 1/8	10 3/8	8	7	Wahkiakum Co., WA	Norman G. Williams	Norman G. Williams	1948	6
368	53 4/8	54	39 5/8	8 7/8	8 2/8	7	9	Vancouver Island, BC	Lawrence A. Ondzik	Alf Spineto	1981	7
367 6/8	47 4/8	47 6/8	42 7/8	9 5/8	10	8	7	Woss Lake, BC	Johnny Bliznak	Johnny Bliznak	1992	8
367 5/8	50 3/8	53	37 4/8	9	8 5/8	7	7	Clatsop Co., OR	Pravomil Raichl	Pravomil Raichl	1959	9
367	51 6/8	51 4/8	43 2/8	9 6/8	9 6/8	6	6	Mason Co., WA	Unknown	George B. Putnam	1900	10
366 5/8	43	45 5/8	35 4/8	9 6/8	9 5/8	7	8	Columbia Co., OR	Floyd M. Lindberg	Floyd M. Lindberg	1962	11
363 1/8	46 6/8	46 5/8	43 4/8	9	9	8	7	Clatsop Co., OR	Oliver W. Dunsmoor	John R. Wall	PR 1938	12
362 6/8	45 7/8	45 5/8	37 4/8	9 4/8	9 1/8	7	7	Lincoln Co., OR	James H. Flescher	James H. Flescher	1955	13
358 6/8	51 4/8	51 4/8	42 2/8	9 6/8	10 2/8	7	7	Clatsop Co., OR	Donald A. Schoenborn	Eric Schoenborn	1939	14
358 5/8	55 4/8	53 4/8	42	9 5/8	8 7/8	8	7	Tillamook Co., OR	Albert Hoffarber	Ray Hoffarber	1940	15
353 4/8	52	53 3/8	38 4/8	8 5/8	9 1/8	6	9	Washington Co., OR	Kenneth R. Adamson	Kenneth R. Adamson	1985	16
352 5/8	53 2/8	50 5/8	40 6/8	9 6/8	9 5/8	8	7	Coos Co., OR	Bill Mattoon	Douglas County Mus.	PR 1907	17
351 7/8	46 4/8	49 2/8	46 6/8	9 4/8	9 4/8	8	9	Clatsop Co., OR	Steven E. Fick	Steven E. Fick	1995	18
351 5/8	45	45 5/8	40 2/8	9 1/8	9 7/8	8	9	Menzies Bay, BC	Gordon J. Birgbauer, Jr.	Gordon J. Birgbauer, Jr.	1991	19
351 4/8	45 3/8	46 4/8	41 2/8	10	10 1/8	7	7	Sayward, BC	Ken Thulin	Ken Thulin	1996	20
350 3/8	47 6/8	47 4/8	35 7/8	11 1/8	11 7/8	7	7	Coos Co., OR	E.V. Schmidt	Steve Crossley	1948	21
347 6/8	41 3/8	42 3/8	46 2/8	8 2/8	8	7	7	Tillamook Co., OR	Bud Davis	Herb W. Davis	1957	22
347	47 2/8	46 4/8	44 2/8	9 1/8	9 1/8	8	7	Columbia Co., OR	Al Glenn	Al Glenn	1955	23
345 6/8	51 5/8	51 3/8	40 5/8	11 1/8	11 1/8	6	7	Columbia Co., OR	Unknown	Harold E. Stepp	1962	24
344 4/8	49 5/8	47 7/8	38 6/8	8 2/8	8 5/8	7	6	Campbell River, BC	James D. Verbrugge	James D. Verbrugge	1995	25
344 2/8	49 2/8	47 5/8	40	8 4/8	8 5/8	7	7	Jefferson Co., WA	Carroll E. Koenke	Carroll E. Koenke	1966	26
343 2/8	55	56 4/8	34 3/8	7 2/8	7 4/8	6	6	Humboldt Co., CA	Picked Up	Gary Backanen	1992	27
342 1/8	52	50 4/8	34 5/8	9 5/8	10 3/8	6	7	Jefferson Co., WA	Ralph Warren	Ralph Warren	1972	28
341 2/8	45 1/8	42 4/8	44 6/8	9 6/8	9 3/8	7	8	Josephine Co., OR	Robert Veatch	Cass E. Raymond	1992	29
341	45 1/8	45 2/8	33 5/8	10 3/8	10	8	8	Columbia Co., OR	Derl Roberts	Derl Roberts	1965	30
341	47	47	38 7/8	8 7/8	9 3/8	8	7	Lewis Co., WA	Keith A. Heldreth	Keith A. Heldreth	1988	30
340 4/8	46 1/8	45	36	9 3/8	9	6	8	Columbia Co., OR	Bud Holmes	Sam Woody	1962	32
340 2/8	49	46 4/8	43 5/8	9 5/8	9 5/8	7	8	Clatsop Co., OR	Fain J. Little	Fain J. Little	1945	33
339 6/8	45 5/8	45 4/8	42 6/8	8 3/8	8	8	7	Gold River, BC	William H. Taylor	William H. Taylor	1987	34
338	43 4/8	44 1/8	41 1/8	9 7/8	9 1/8	7	7	Tillamook Co., OR	Tony W. Hancock	Tony W. Hancock	1985	35
337 5/8	57 5/8	53 2/8	33 2/8	7 2/8	7 5/8	8	8	Humboldt Co., CA	Picked Up	Gary Backanen	1992	36

Score								Locality	Hunter	Owner	Date	Rank
337 4/8	52 3/8	50 3/8	34 3/8	9	9	9	9	Greenstone Creek, BC	Gerald L. Warnock	Gerald L. Warnock	1989	37
337 1/8	49 5/8	52	30 2/8	9 1/8	9	6	7	Wahkiakum Co., WA	E.L. McKie & T. Faubian	E.L. McKie	1962	38
337 1/8	46	44 4/8	37 6/8	8 7/8	8 7/8	7	7	Jefferson Co., WA	Dave D. Godfrey	Dave D. Godfrey	1966	38
336 6/8	50 4/8	47 6/8	39	8	8 6/8	7	6	Tillamook Co., OR	Gary L. Cox	Gary L. Cox	1965	40
336 4/8	46 6/8	46 6/8	40 3/8	8 7/8	9 1/8	6	7	Oregon Coast Range, OR	Unknown	Richard Leach	PR 1981	41
336 2/8	46	48 3/8	40	8 3/8	9 1/8	7	7	Clallam Co., WA	Howard M. Cameron	Lawrence C. Cameron	1936	42
335 7/8	48 6/8	48 2/8	33 6/8	9 4/8	9 6/8	8	6	Union Bay, BC	Louis C. Podgorenko	Louis C. Podgorenko	1996	43
335 4/8	45 1/8	44 3/8	42	10 2/8	10 3/8	7	7	Clallam Co., WA	George R. Ames	George R. Ames	1956	44
335 1/8	51 2/8	51 7/8	42 1/8	10 1/8	8 1/8	6	8	Clatsop Co., OR	Picked Up	Andy Mendenhall, Jr.	1978	45
334 7/8	45	45 4/8	39 4/8	8 2/8	9 6/8	7	7	White River, BC	Sid D. Rajala	Sid D. Rajala	1994	46
334 4/8	52	52 1/8	43 1/8	9 4/8	11	7	8	Clallam Co., WA	Albert Clevenger	Albert Clevenger	1931	47
334 3/8	49 1/8	47 6/8	35 6/8	11	10 2/8	6	7	Clatsop Co., OR	Charles L. Smith	Daniel L. Smith	1960	48
333 3/8	49	47 3/8	45	10 2/8	9 1/8	8	8	Jefferson Co., WA	Louis Ehlers	Donald G. Hyatt	PR 1954	49
332 3/8	51 6/8	51 4/8	41 2/8	8 6/8	8 5/8	8	8	Humboldt Co., CA	Picked Up	Leo Prshora	1955	50
332 2/8	49	48 4/8	45	8 1/8	9	8	8	Tillamook Co., OR	Robert B. Thornton	Dale R. Thornton	1964	51
332	49 6/8	44 6/8	40 6/8	8 4/8	7 7/8	7	7	Wahkiakum Co., WA	Kyle J. Parker	Kyle J. Parker	1996	52
331 5/8	53 2/8	55 1/8	38 2/8	7 1/8	9	6	6	Siskiyou Co., CA	William D. Johnson	William D. Johnson	1997	53
330 5/8	51	50 1/8	38 4/8	8 7/8	8 2/8	6	6	Nanaimo Lakes, BC	Picked Up	Eric D. Martin	1988	54
330	48 7/8	50 1/8	39 3/8	8 5/8	8 5/8	6	6	Tillamook Co., OR	Gary H. Purdy	Gary H. Purdy	1969	55
329 5/8	46 4/8	46 4/8	38 4/8	8 5/8	11	6	6	Vancouver Island, BC	Wayne H. Zaccarelli	Wayne H. Zaccarelli	1981	56
328 7/8	47 4/8	46	44 4/8	10 3/8	10 3/8	6	6	Clallam Co., WA	Daniel D. Hinchen	Daniel D. Hinchen	1976	57
327 4/8	48 5/8	50 5/8	42 3/8	8 3/8	8 1/8	7	8	Tillamook Co., OR	Picked Up	Dave Griffith	1958	58
327 3/8	50 5/8	50	40 5/8	8 7/8	9 1/8	6	7	Clatsop Co., OR	Billy L. Jasper	Billy L. Jasper	1946	59
327 2/8	49 4/8	50 5/8	38 4/8	9 4/8	9 7/8	6	6	Del Norte Co., CA	Patrick J. Papasergia	Patrick J. Papasergia	1996	60
327	54 1/8	54 2/8	40	7 5/8	7 7/8	7	7	Pacific Co., WA	Donald Beasley	Donald Beasley	1963	61
326 4/8	49 6/8	49 2/8	33 6/8	8 1/8	8 1/8	7	7	Wahkiakum Co., WA	Otis E. Wright	Otis E. Wright	1966	62
326 1/8	47 3/8	47 6/8	43 2/8	7 2/8	8	8	7	Wahkiakum Co., WA	Robert B. Seaberg	Robert B. Seaberg	1958	63
325 5/8	50	49	43 6/8	9	9 6/8	7	8	Columbia Co., WA	Edgar J. Rea	Edgar J. Rea	1973	64
325 3/8	52 4/8	51	39 1/8	9 1/8	8 2/8	8	6	Siskiyou Co., CA	Jeremy W. Johnson	Jeremy W. Johnson	1997	65
325 1/8	50 1/8	47 4/8	36 5/8	8 7/8	8 6/8	6	7	Ucona River, BC	Norman W. Dougan	Norman W. Dougan	1986	66
324 7/8	43	43	43	10	10 5/8	7	5	Jefferson Co., WA	Vern Gedelman	Michael O'Dell	PR 1967	67
324 4/8	40 6/8	44 2/8	43 6/8	7 7/8	7 6/8	7	6	Jefferson Co., WA	Newton P. Morris	Newton P. Morris	1975	68
324 2/8	51 4/8	47 4/8	39 6/8	9 4/8	9 2/8	6	6	Vernon Lake, BC	George R. Banning	George R. Banning	1997	68
324 2/8	44	43 4/8	44	8 1/8	7 3/8	6	7	Jefferson Co., WA	Larry W. Haddock	Larry W. Haddock	1988	70
323 4/8	52	51 3/8	40	10 1/8	9 4/8	8	8	Clatsop Co., OR	David Tweedle	Scott A. Seppa	1938	71
323 2/8	45 5/8	47	37 7/8	7 2/8	7 1/8	7	7	Clatsop Co., OR	Clarence V. Jurhs	Clarence V. Jurhs	1958	72
323	47 6/8	44 5/8	38 1/8	8 7/8	9 2/8	7	7	Columbia Co., OR	William E. Curtis	Duane M. Bernard	1952	73
322 3/8	44 6/8	45 2/8	41 3/8	8 5/8	9 1/8	8	8	Lincoln Co., OR	James R. Goodwin	James R. Goodwin	1960	74
322 2/8	43 2/8	41	42 2/8	10 3/8	10 3/8	7	7	Clatsop Co., OR	Reed Holding	Reed Holding	1939	75
322 2/8	45 3/8	45 3/8	42 2/8	11 4/8	11	6	6	Polk Co., OR	R.L. Stamps	R.L. Stamps	1985	75
322 1/8	47 1/8	51 1/8	32 5/8	8 6/8	8 6/8	7	7	Tillamook Co., OR	Stanley E. Kephart	Stanley E. Kephart	1964	77
320 4/8	49 6/8	48 2/8	42 4/8	8 4/8	8 1/8	6	6	Mason Co., WA	Tony J. Bogachus	Tony J. Bogachus	1955	78
320 2/8	43 1/8	43 5/8	47 1/8	8 5/8	8 4/8	6	6	Columbia Co., OR	Harry R. Olsen	Harry R. Olsen	1961	78
320 2/8	43 2/8	48 6/8	42 2/8	10 6/8	10 6/8	7	5	Clatsop Co., OR	Jack O. Bay	Jack O. Bay	1963	80
320 1/8	43 7/8	45 2/8	38 2/8	7 5/8	7 6/8	8	6	Columbia Co., OR	Larry G. Behrend	Howard C. Behrend	1973	80
319 5/8	49 4/8	47 6/8	39 7/8	6 7/8	6 6/8	7	6	Clatsop Co., OR	Picked Up	John T. Mee	1969	82
318 5/8	48	49 2/8	40	8 2/8	8	6	7	Del Norte Co., CA	Richard K. Armas	Richard K. Armas	1988	83

ROOSEVELT'S ELK

Cervus elaphus roosevelti

Score	Length of Main Beam R	L	Inside Spread	Circumference at Smallest Place Between First and Second Points R	L	Number of Points R	L	Locality	Hunter	Owner	Date Killed	Rank
318 3/8	41 3/8	41 1/8	36 2/8	9	8 6/8	8	7	Grilise Creek, BC	Jack Foord	Jack Foord	1984	84
317 3/8	43 4/8	44 3/8	42 2/8	7 6/8	8 4/8	7	7	Tillamook Co., OR	Thomas G. Tompkins	Thomas G. Tompkins	1952	85
317 2/8	41 3/8	41 5/8	37 6/8	9	8 7/8	6	7	Columbia Co., OR	Max Oblack	Max Oblack	1967	86
316 6/8	51 3/8	49	39	8 6/8	9 7/8	6	7	Columbia Co., OR	Harry R. Olsen	Harry R. Olsen	1969	87
316 5/8	45 4/8	45 4/8	41 5/8	8 6/8	8 6/8	6	6	Lincoln Co., OR	Verlin H. Rhoades	Verlin H. Rhoades	1944	88
316 3/8	41 6/8	41 5/8	38 3/8	9 1/8	8 6/8	6	6	Clallam Co., WA	Daniel M. Hilt	Daniel M. Hilt	1982	88
316 5/8	44 5/8	46	36 7/8	9 7/8	10 1/8	7	6	Bonanza Lake, BC	Cameron W. Blacklock	Cameron W. Blacklock	1994	88
316 2/8	43 2/8	42 3/8	39 2/8	9 4/8	9 2/8	5	7	Columbia Co., OR	Everett Girt	James Girt	1951	91
316	47 3/8	46 5/8	43 1/8	10 3/8	10 1/8	6	6	Jefferson Co., WA	Hans Norbisrath	Hans Norbisrath	1966	92
315 4/8	48 2/8	47 7/8	42	9 4/8	9	6	6	Columbia Co., OR	William E. Curtis	Duane M. Bernard	1965	93
314 6/8	46 6/8	46 6/8	42 2/8	8	8 5/8	7	8	Columbia Co., OR	Picked Up	Harold E. Stepp	1962	94
314 4/8	52 1/8	49 2/8	36 3/8	9 5/8	9 3/8	6	6	Coos Co., OR	Robert D. Dunson	Robert D. Dunson	1982	95
314 3/8	45 7/8	46 1/8	41 5/8	8 4/8	8	7	7	Clatsop Co., OR	Robert L. Brown	Robert L. Brown	1966	96
312 7/8	43 5/8	45 1/8	43 4/8	8	7 5/8	7	8	Clallam Co., WA	Donald W. Coman	Donald W. Coman	1981	97
312 4/8	45 7/8	44 2/8	39 4/8	8 2/8	8 3/8	6	6	Nimpkish River, BC	Noel J. Poux	Noel J. Poux	1993	98
312 1/8	48 5/8	46 5/8	34 3/8	8 5/8	8 2/8	6	7	Clallam Co., WA	Michael L. Fisher	Michael L. Fisher	1993	99
311 2/8	47 6/8	40 3/8	41 2/8	8 6/8	8 6/8	7	7	Jefferson Co., WA	Walter L. Campbell	Walter L. Campbell	1987	100
310 5/8	43 4/8	44 6/8	38 2/8	7 7/8	7 3/8	7	7	Clallam Co., WA	Daniel M. Hilt	Daniel M. Hilt	1958	101
310 4/8	44 3/8	44	33 6/8	9 5/8	9 6/8	7	7	Clatsop Co., OR	Elman Peterson, Jr.	Elman Peterson, Jr.	1968	102
310 2/8	44 1/8	44 6/8	43 2/8	8 3/8	9 3/8	8	5	Clatsop Co., OR	Donald R. Chisholm	D.R. Chisholm & A. Holdridge	1957	103
310 1/8	44 5/8	44 4/8	34	10 2/8	9 3/8	7	7	Jefferson Co., WA	Howard L. Hilt	Michael R. Raffaell	1969	104
309 6/8	43 1/8	48 1/8	31 6/8	9 2/8	9 4/8	7	7	Clatsop Co., OR	Terry E. Andrews	Terry E. Andrews	1984	105
309 1/8	47 3/8	43 7/8	37 7/8	9 2/8	8 7/8	6	6	Clatsop Co., OR	Valentine T. Mueller	John A. Mueller	1938	106
308 3/8	48	48	41 5/8	9 7/8	9 2/8	6	7	Coos Co., OR	Dean Dunson	Dean Dunson	1986	107
307 6/8	44 5/8	46 4/8	35 4/8	8 7/8	8 6/8	6	6	Clallam Co., WA	David R. Hansen	David R. Hansen	1996	108
307 4/8	46 1/8	45 6/8	40 6/8	7 7/8	7 7/8	7	7	Tillamook Co., OR	John A. Wehinger	John A. Wehinger	1964	109
307 4/8	43 5/8	41 7/8	46 6/8	9 1/8	10 6/8	7	7	Clallam Co., WA	Kermit Guenkel	Kermit Guenkel	1972	109
306 7/8	46 3/8	45 1/8	37 4/8	7 6/8	8 3/8	7	7	Memekay River, BC	Harold Ratushniak	Harold Ratushniak	1993	111
306 6/8	50 2/8	50 4/8	38 6/8	7 6/8	8	6	6	Polk Co., OR	James E. Wallen	James E. Wallen	1980	112
306 4/8	47	47 5/8	43 5/8	7 5/8	7 6/8	6	6	Humboldt Co., CA	Michael L. Johnson	Michael L. Johnson	1976	113
306	40 4/8	39 3/8	40 4/8	9 1/8	9 4/8	7	7	Washington Co., OR	Michael R. Jamieson	Michael R. Jamieson	1982	114
304 6/8	49	41 1/8	39 1/8	9 7/8	9 3/8	6	7	Clatsop Co., OR	William D. Mellinger	William D. Mellinger	1958	115
304 4/8	47 1/8	46	36 4/8	7 7/8	8 2/8	6	6	Jefferson Co., WA	Dennis Potter	Dennis Potter	1970	116
304 4/8	45	46 1/8	42 4/8	8 2/8	8 5/8	6	6	Muchalat Lake, BC	Michael H. Baturin	Michael H. Baturin	1994	116
304 3/8	46 2/8	46 3/8	47 1/8	10	9 5/8	6	6	Grays Harbor Co., WA	Richard B. Grinols	Richard B. Grinols	1992	118
304 1/8	39 6/8	38 1/8	31 1/8	8	7 6/8	8	8	Yamhill Co., OR	Kevin E. Mishler	Kevin E. Mishler	1989	119

Score	Length Main Beam R	Length Main Beam L	Inside Spread	Circ. R	Circ. L	Points	Locality	Points	Hunter	Owner	Date	Rank
303 6/8	42 2/8	45 7/8	36 4/8	9 3/8	9 4/8	7	Gold River, BC	7	Abe Dougan	Abe Dougan	1988	120
303	47 4/8	47 6/8	42 2/8	9	8 6/8	7	Jefferson Co., WA	5	C.F. & C.H. Bernhardt	C.F. & C.H. Bernhardt	1972	121
302 6/8	50	50	36 7/8	7 3/8	7 3/8	6	Jefferson Co., WA	6	Gary Talley	Gary Talley	1981	122
302 6/8	45 6/8	44 3/8	37 2/8	8 6/8	8 6/8	6	Grays Harbor Co., WA	6	Donald M. Vestal	Dean Vestal	1981	122
302 6/8	49	49 1/8	38 4/8	7 7/8	7 7/8	6	Columbia Co., OR	9	Picked Up	Rick A. Hood	1991	122
302 5/8	41	39 6/8	44	9 7/8	9 5/8	6	Lincoln Co., OR	6	Michael Kosydar	Michael Kosydar	1985	125
302 1/8	41 3/8	41 2/8	37 5/8	8 2/8	8 4/8	8	Wahkiakum Co., WA	8	Kyle J. Parker	Kyle J. Parker	1990	126
301 6/8	43	43 7/8	36 2/8	8 6/8	9 4/8	8	Clatsop Co., OR	6	Pravomil Raichl	Pravomil Raichl	1963	127
301 1/8	46 5/8	44	34 2/8	8 5/8	8 2/8	7	Jefferson Co., WA	6	C.F. & C.H. Bernhardt	C.F. & C.H. Bernhardt	1973	128
301	42 5/8	42 6/8	41	9	9 6/8	7	Coos Co., OR	7	Picked Up	William H. Flesch	1993	129
300 7/8	44	43 5/8	41	9 3/8	9 5/8	6	Vancouver Island, BC	7	William C. Holcombe	William C. Holcombe	1989	130
300 5/8	37 7/8	36 6/8	37 1/8	8 2/8	7 4/8	8	Mason Co., WA	6	David J. Beerbower	David J. Beerbower	1983	131
300 2/8	43	40 6/8	37 4/8	9	8 4/8	6	Columbia Co., OR	6	Harry R. Olsen	Harry R. Olsen	1963	132
299 6/8	48 7/8	49 1/8	37 2/8	8 2/8	7 7/8	6	Lincoln Co., OR	7	Jullian Smallwood	Gerald Smallwood	1945	133
299 5/8	41 1/8	42 1/8	33 6/8	9 1/8	9 5/8	6	Grays Harbor Co., WA	7	Robert Lentz	Robert Lentz	1948	134
299 4/8	42 2/8	40 7/8	39	8 2/8	7 7/8	7	Lincoln Co., OR	7	Gene Nyhus	Gene Nyhus	1950	135
299 3/8	43	44 2/8	36 4/8	7 5/8	7 2/8	7	Cowlitz Co., WA	6	Daniel L. Howe	Daniel L. Howe	1996	136
299 2/8	42 4/8	41 6/8	46 4/8	7 2/8	7 5/8	6	Columbia Co., OR	6	Charles H. Atkins	Charles H. Atkins	1964	137
298 6/8	41 2/8	40 7/8	38 6/8	8 1/8	7 7/8	8	Jefferson Co., WA	8	Douglas A. Smith	Douglas A. Smith	1989	138
298 5/8	43 4/8	50 6/8	39 6/8	8 4/8	8	6	Clatsop Co., OR	6	Harold O. Hundere	Harold O. Hundere	1943	139
298 3/8	43 5/8	44 1/8	38 3/8	8	8 1/8	8	White River, BC	8	Harvey J. King	Harvey J. King	1987	140
298 2/8	47	44 3/8	37 4/8	7 6/8	7 4/8	6	Columbia Co., OR	7	Nicholas A. Berg	Nicholas A. Berg	1963	141
298 2/8	42 5/8	43 1/8	40 6/8	8 4/8	8 7/8	7	Polk Co., OR	6	R.L. Stamps	R.L. Stamps	1981	141
298 2/8	47 6/8	47 2/8	40 5/8	8 2/8	9	6	Humboldt Co., CA	6	Eugene M. Boyd IV	Eugene M. Boyd IV	1988	141
297 6/8	46	45 7/8	42 7/8	7 7/8	7 3/8	6	Clallam Co., WA	6	Arnold J. LaGambina	Arnold J. LaGambina	1988	144
297 4/8	48 1/8	45 4/8	40 5/8	8 3/8	7 6/8	7	Siskiyou Co., CA	6	Michael R. Bell	Michael R. Bell	1996	145
297 1/8	47 2/8	45 6/8	36 7/8	8	9	6	Clallam Co., WA	6	Ronald W. Sanchez	Ronald W. Sanchez	1988	146
296 6/8	43 1/8	42 4/8	34 7/8	9 2/8	9 3/8	6	Clallam Co., WA	6	Randy F. Mesenbrink	Randy F. Mesenbrink	1977	147
296 6/8	44 1/8	42 2/8	47 6/8	8 5/8	8 4/8	6	Clallam Co., WA	5	Aubrey F. Taylor	Aubrey F. Taylor	1984	147
296 1/8	46 6/8	42 1/8	35 2/8	7 7/8	8 2/8	7	Jefferson Co., WA	7	Max E. Graves	Max E. Graves	1970	149
296	39	39 3/8	36 6/8	7 5/8	7 7/8	7	Yamhill Co., OR	7	Steven E. Anderson	Steven E. Anderson	1983	150
295 7/8	46	46 6/8	41 5/8	8 3/8	7 5/8	7	Jefferson Co., WA	6	Newton P. Morris	Newton P. Morris	1970	151
295 5/8	44 3/8	44 1/8	39 3/8	8	7 6/8	6	Lincoln Co., OR	6	Picked Up	Chad J. Kimsey	1985	152
295 4/8	50 3/8	50	41	8 2/8	8	6	Columbia Co., OR	6	Reed Holding	Reed Holding	1950	153
294 7/8	39 7/8	41 6/8	34 6/8	7 7/8	8 1/8	6	Clatsop Co., OR	6	Picked Up	Robert L. Brown	1965	154
294 5/8	45 4/8	45 4/8	43 1/8	9	8 3/8	6	Clatsop Co., OR	6	Nolen R. Schoenborn	Nolen R. Schoenborn	1944	155
294 1/8	46 5/8	46 1/8	45 2/8	8 2/8	7 1/8	7	Washington Co., OR	7	John A. Beavers, Jr.	John A. Beavers, Jr.	1976	156
293 7/8	46 1/8	43 3/8	36 7/8	7 6/8	7 6/8	6	Tillamook Co., OR	6	Steven F. Kellow	Steven F. Kellow	1979	157
293 4/8	43 5/8	43 6/8	39 7/8	8	8	8	Lincoln Co., OR	8	Timothy A. Landis	Timothy A. Landis	1993	158
293 1/8	44 1/8	42 2/8	41 3/8	8 4/8	8 2/8	6	Jefferson Co., WA	6	William H. Boatman	William H. Boatman	1951	159
291 4/8	42	42 1/8	33 7/8	8 7/8	8 2/8	7	Tillamook Co., OR	7	Picked Up	Tim J. Christensen	1975	160
291 3/8	38 2/8	38 7/8	35 1/8	8 1/8	7	6	Clatsop Co., OR	6	Picked Up	Robert L. Brown	1979	161
291 1/8	43 5/8	43 5/8	43 6/8	6 6/8	6 7/8	6	Jefferson Co., WA	8	George R. Bernethy	George R. Bernethy	1956	162
290 7/8	41 6/8	40 4/8	37 4/8	9 3/8	9	6	Coos Co., OR	6	Gerald W. Hurst	Gerald W. Hurst	1979	163
290 7/8	45 6/8	44 1/8	42 5/8	8 6/8	7 7/8	7	Jefferson Co., WA	6	William A. Harrison	William A. Harrison	1984	163
290 2/8	44 1/8	44 2/8	39 4/8	8 6/8	7 5/8	7	White River, BC	7	George A. Colegrave	George A. Colegrave	1994	165
290 1/8	42 4/8	42 1/8	37 6/8	7 5/8	8 3/8	7	Lincoln Co., OR	7	Terry W. Smith	Terry W. Smith	1997	166

ROOSEVELT'S ELK

Cervus elaphus roosevelti

Score	Length of Main Beam		Inside Spread	Circumference at Smallest Place Between First and Second Points		Number of Points		Locality	Hunter	Owner	Date Killed	Rank
	R	L		R	L	R	L					
365 2/8*	43	46 7/8	37	9 3/8	9 7/8	8	8	Memekay River, BC	Armande Graham	Armande Graham	1994	
353 1/8*	51 1/8	51 3/8	36	9 1/8	9 5/8	6	6	Bonanza Lake, BC	Wes Swain	Wes Swain	1996	
342 4/8*	43 5/8	47 4/8	44 7/8	8 7/8	9 7/8	7	7	Nimpkish River, BC	Larry X. Hodgson	Larry X. Hodgson	1992	

* Final score is subject to revision by additional verifying measurements.

CATEGORY
ROOSEVELT'S ELK

SCORE
327

HUNTER
PATRICK J. PAPASERGIA

LOCATION
DEL NORTE CO., CA

DATE OF KILL
SEPTEMBER 1996

CATEGORY
ROOSEVELT'S ELK

SCORE
351-4/8

HUNTER
KEN THULIN

LOCATION
SAYWARD, BC

DATE OF KILL
OCTOBER 1996

CATEGORY
ROOSEVELT'S ELK

SCORE
304-3/8

HUNTER
RICHARD B. GRINOLS

LOCATION
GRAYS HARBOR CO., WA

DATE OF KILL
OCTOBER 1992

215

MULE DEER - TYPICAL ANTLERS
WORLD'S RECORD

Doug Burris, Jr. began hunting the Dolores County area of Colorado in 1969. On his first three hunts, he took three nice bucks that any hunter would be proud to hang over their mantle. Little did Burris realize, however, that on his fourth trip he would shake the very foundation of the hunting community with a trophy that would surpass the World's Record.

On opening day of the 1972 season, Burris and his three companions, Jack Smith, Robbie Roe and Bruce Winters, piled into their Jeep before dawn and headed out. Working their way up one of the many mountain roads on the San Juan National Forest, Burris dropped the hunters off at regular intervals. Roe was the first, followed by Winters and then Smith. Burris continued on up the mountain. The day was rainy but all agreed to hunt until dark.

All the bucks the Texans saw that day were small and no one fired a shot. On the second day, Roe and Winters both took nice five-pointers, while Smith and Burris remained empty-handed. On the third day, Burris decided to go after a buck a friend had seen in Proven Canyon the day before. About mid-morning, Burris spotted two nice bucks feeding in a clearing about 500 yards away. While he watched these two bucks, a third one came into view.

Burris knew immediately that the latter buck had to be exceptional as he could see antlers even without the aid of binoculars. He decided to make the stalk. For the better part

of an hour, Burris slowly and quietly worked his way through the oak brush. About the time he felt he had cut the distance in half, he nearly stepped on a doe bedded down in the underbrush. She exploded out of the brush, and the three bucks Burris was stalking scattered in all different directions. Burris had time for one quick shot with his .264 Winchester magnum, and the largest buck crumpled in mid stride.

Upon closer examination, Burris realized he had an unbelievable trophy. In 1974, at the 15th North American Big Game Awards Program held in Atlanta, Georgia, Burris' World's Record was confirmed. With a final score of 225-6/8 points, Burris' buck took the first place award for the typical mule deer category in addition to the coveted Sagamore Hill Award for the finest trophy taken.

When the so-called "double-penalty" was dropped for excessive spread at a later date by the Club's Records Committee, the final score of Burris' buck increased by 6/8 of an inch to 226-4/8 points. ■

Reprinted with permission from Colorado's Biggest Bucks and Bulls

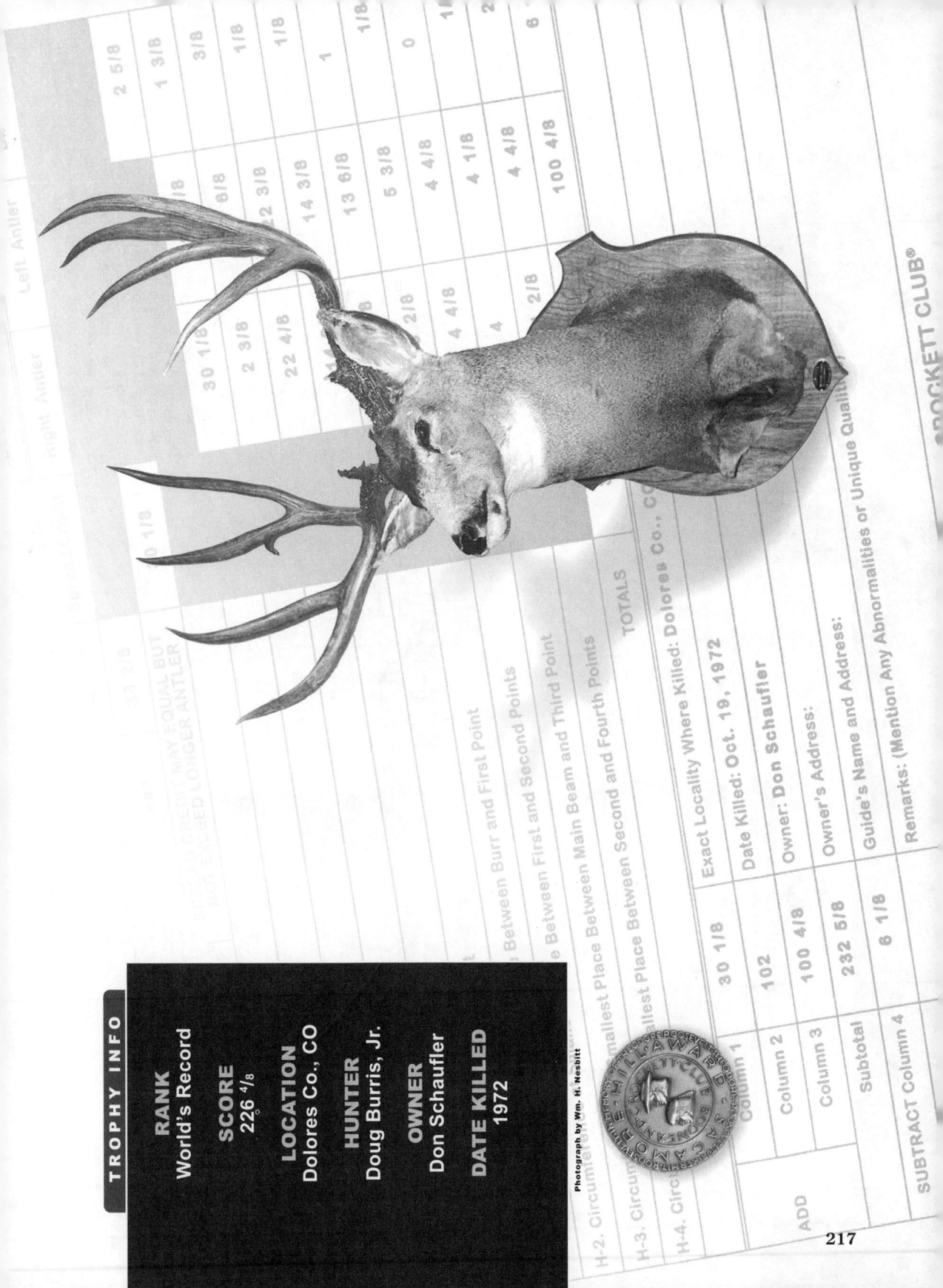

TROPHY INFO

RANK
World's Record

SCORE
226 4/8

LOCATION
Dolores Co., CO

HUNTER
Doug Burris, Jr.

OWNER
Don Schaufler

DATE KILLED
1972

Photograph by Wm. H. Nesbitt

BOONE & CROCKETT CLUB®

	Right Antler	Left Antler	
			2 5/8
			1 3/8
			3/8
		6/8	1/8
30 1/8			1/8
2 3/8		2 3/8	
22 4/8		14 3/8	1
		13 6/8	1/8
		5 3/8	1/8
		4 4/8	0
4 4/8		4 1/8	1
4		4 4/8	2
2/8		4 4/8	6
		100 4/8	

BE NO CREDIT MAY EQUAL BUT
MUST EXCEED LONGER ANTLER

33 2/8

0 1/8

H-2. Circumference at smallest Place Between Burr and First Point

H-3. Circumference at smallest Place Between First and Second Points

H-4. Circumference at smallest Place Between Main Beam and Third Point

Circumference at smallest Place Between Second and Fourth Points

TOTALS

Column 1	30 1/8	Exact Locality Where Killed: Dolores Co., CO
Column 2	102	Date Killed: Oct. 19, 1972
Column 3	100 4/8	Owner: Don Schaufler
Subtotal	232 5/8	Owner's Address:
ADD		Guide's Name and Address:
SUBTRACT Column 4	6 1/8	Remarks: (Mention Any Abnormalities or Unique Qualities)

MULE DEER
TYPICAL ANTLERS
WORLD'S RECORD SCORECHART

Records of
North American
Big Game

250 Station Drive
Missoula, MT 59901
(406) 542-1888

BOONE AND CROCKETT CLUB®
OFFICIAL SCORING SYSTEM FOR NORTH AMERICAN BIG GAME TROPHIES
TYPICAL
MULE DEER AND BLACKTAIL DEER

MINIMUM SCORES	AWARDS	ALL-TIME
mule deer	180	190
Columbia blacktail	125	135
Sitka blacktail	100	108

KIND OF DEER (check one)
- ■ mule deer
- □ Columbia blacktail
- □ Sitka blacktail

Detail of Point Measurement

Abnormal Points	Right Antler	Left Antler
	2 5/8	2 5/8
SUBTOTALS		2 5/8
TOTAL TO E		2 5/8

SEE OTHER SIDE FOR INSTRUCTIONS	COLUMN 1 Spread Credit	COLUMN 2 Right Antler	COLUMN 3 Left Antler	COLUMN 4 Difference
A. No. Points on Right Antler: 6 — No. Points on Left Antler: 5				
B. Tip to Tip Spread	28 5/8			
C. Greatest Spread	33 2/8			
D. Inside Spread of Main Beams 30 7/8	SPREAD CREDIT MAY EQUAL BUT NOT EXCEED LONGER ANTLER	30 1/8		
E. Total of Lengths of Abnormal Points				2 5/8
F. Length of Main Beam		30 1/8	28 6/8	1 3/8
G-1. Length of First Point, If Present		2 3/8	2 6/8	3/8
G-2. Length of Second Point		22 4/8	22 3/8	1/8
G-3. Length of Third Point, If Present		14 2/8	14 3/8	1/8
G-4. Length of Fourth Point, If Present		14 6/8	13 6/8	1
H-1. Circumference at Smallest Place Between Burr and First Point		5 2/8	5 3/8	1/8
H-2. Circumference at Smallest Place Between First and Second Points		4 4/8	4 4/8	0
H-3. Circumference at Smallest Place Between Main Beam and Third Point		4	4 1/8	1/8
H-4. Circumference at Smallest Place Between Second and Fourth Points		4 2/8	4 4/8	2/8
TOTALS	30 1/8	102	100 4/8	6 1/8

	Column 1	30 1/8	Exact Locality Where Killed: Dolores Co., CO
ADD	Column 2	102	Date Killed: Oct. 19, 1972 — Hunter: Doug Burris, Jr.
	Column 3	100 4/8	Owner: Don Schaufler — Telephone #:
	Subtotal	232 5/8	Owner's Address:
SUBTRACT	Column 4	6 1/8	Guide's Name and Address:
	FINAL SCORE	226 4/8	Remarks: (Mention Any Abnormalities or Unique Qualities)

COPYRIGHT © 1999 BY BOONE AND CROCKETT CLUB®

All measurements must be made with a 1/4-inch wide flexible steel tape to the nearest one-eighth of an inch. (Note: A flexible steel cable can be used to measure points and main beams only.) Enter fractional figures in eighths, without reduction. Official measurements cannot be taken until the antlers have air dried for at least 60 days after the animal was killed.

A. Number of Points on Each Antler: To be counted a point, the projection must be at least one inch long, with length exceeding width at one inch or more of length. All points are measured from tip of point to nearest edge of beam. Beam tip is counted as a point but not measured as a point.

B. Tip to Tip Spread is measured between tips of main beams.

C. Greatest Spread is measured between perpendiculars at a right angle to the center line of the skull at widest part, whether across main beams or points.

D. Inside Spread of Main Beams is measured at a right angle to the center line of the skull at widest point between main beams. Enter this measurement again as the Spread Credit if it is less than or equal to the length of the longer antler; if greater, enter longer antler length for Spread Credit.

E. Total of Lengths of all Abnormal Points: Abnormal Points are those non-typical in location such as points originating from a point (exception: G-3 originates from G-2 in perfectly normal fashion) or from bottom or sides of main beam, or any points beyond the normal pattern of five (including beam tip) per antler. Measure each abnormal point in usual manner and enter in appropriate blanks.

F. Length of Main Beam is measured from the center of the lowest outside edge of burr over the outer side to the most distant point of the Main Beam. The point of beginning is that point on the burr where the center line along the outer side of the beam intersects the burr, then following generally the line of the illustration.

G-1-2-3-4. Length of Normal Points: Normal points are the brow tines and the upper and lower forks as shown in the illustration. They are measured from nearest edge of main beam over outer curve to tip. Lay the tape along the outer curve of the beam so that the top edge of the tape coincides with the top edge of the beam on both sides of point to determine the baseline for point measurement. Record point lengths in appropriate blanks.

H-1-2-3-4. Circumferences are taken as detailed in illustration for each measurement. If brow point is missing, take H-1 and H-2 at smallest place between burr and G-2. If G-3 is missing, take H-3 halfway between the base and tip of G-2. If G-4 is missing, take H-4 halfway between G-2 and tip of main beam.

TROPHY INFO

RANK
3

SCORE
216 2/8

LOCATION
Coconino Co., AZ

HUNTER
Picked Up

OWNER
B&C National Collection

DATE KILLED
1994

Photograph by Ron Anfinson

TROPHY INFO

RANK
2

SCORE
217

LOCATION
Hoback Canyon, WY

HUNTER
Unknown

OWNER
Jackson Hole Museum

DATE KILLED
1925

Photograph by Alex Rota

MULE DEER - TYPICAL ANTLERS

Odocoileus hemionus hemionus and certain related subspecies

MINIMUM SCORE 190

Score	Length of Main Beam R	L	Inside Spread	Circumference at Smallest Place Between Burr and First Point R	L	Number of Points R	L	Locality	Hunter	Owner	Date Killed	Rank
226 4/8	30 1/8	28 6/8	30 7/8	5 2/8	5 3/8	6	5	Dolores Co., CO	Doug Burris, Jr.	Don Schaufler	1972	1
217	28 4/8	28 2/8	26 6/8	5 5/8	5 6/8	6	6	Hoback Canyon, WY	Unknown	Jackson Hole Museum	1925	2
216 2/8	28 2/8	28 3/8	26 2/8	4 7/8	4 7/8	5	5	Coconino Co., AZ	Picked Up	B&C National Collection	1994	3
215 5/8	26 7/8	28 1/8	29 4/8	5 3/8	5 3/8	5	7	Uinta Co., WY	Gary L. Albertson	Don Schaufler	1960	4
215 5/8	27 3/8	27 1/8	28 6/8	5 4/8	5 4/8	5	6	Franklin Co., ID	Ray Talbot	Loaned to B&C Natl. Coll.	1961	4
214 3/8	27 5/8	27 4/8	31 3/8	4 7/8	4 7/8	5	5	Gypsum Creek, CO	Paul A. Muehlbauer	Paul A. Muehlbauer	1967	6
213 1/8	25 7/8	24 7/8	26	5	4 7/8	5	5	Moffat Co., CO	Unknown	David W. Blaker	1982	7
212 6/8	26 6/8	26 7/8	25 4/8	5 2/8	5 2/8	6	5	Gem Co., ID	Kirk Payne	Kirk Payne	1967	8
212 6/8	28 1/8	28 2/8	26 4/8	4 6/8	5	6	5	Bonneville Co., ID	J. Larry Barr	J. Larry Barr	1996	8
212 1/8	26 3/8	26 6/8	26 4/8	6 1/8	6 1/8	8	6	San Juan Co., UT	V.R. Rayburn	V.R. Rayburn	1973	10
212 1/8	28 1/8	28 5/8	24 5/8	5 1/8	5	5	5	Idaho Co., ID	Urban H. Riener	Masters Trophy Coll.	1979	10
212	29	27	21 4/8	5 4/8	5 4/8	5	5	Grand Co., CO	Wesley B. Brock	Wesley B. Brock	1963	12
211 7/8	28 6/8	28	27 6/8	6 5/8	6 5/8	6	6	Chama, NM	Joseph A. Garcia	Masters Trophy Coll.	1965	13
211 7/8	30 3/8	30 1/8	25 3/8	5	5	5	5	Adams Co., ID	Boyd W. Dennis	Boyd W. Dennis	1970	13
211 7/8	25 6/8	26 7/8	26 7/8	5 2/8	5 2/8	5	5	Park Co., WY	Picked Up	Don Schaufler	1995	13
211 6/8	29 7/8	29 6/8	30 3/8	4 5/8	4 5/8	7	8	Teton Co., WY	Robert V. Parke	Robert V. Parke	1967	16
211 1/8	28 7/8	28 7/8	32 6/8	5 4/8	5 4/8	5	5	Cache Co., UT	Unknown	Don Schaufler	PR 1950	17
210 4/8	27 3/8	28	19 4/8	5 7/8	5 7/8	5	5	Morgan Co., UT	K.P. Rafton	Don Schaufler	1973	18
210 3/8	28	27 6/8	23 1/8	4 5/8	4 6/8	6	6	Madison Co., ID	Todd L. Landon	Todd L. Landon	1986	19
210 2/8	29 1/8	29 2/8	27	5 2/8	5 2/8	6	5	Southern Ute Res., CO	Jack D. Johnston	Jack D. Johnston	1963	20
210 2/8	27 7/8	27 4/8	31 4/8	5 1/8	5	5	5	Delta Co., CO	Tom Donaldson	Tom Donaldson	1972	20
210 1/8	28 3/8	28 7/8	30 4/8	4 7/8	4 6/8	6	6	Boulder Co., CO	Unknown	Don Schaufler	PR 1965	22
210	26 2/8	26 4/8	25 4/8	5 2/8	5 1/8	6	6	Manti-Lasal Mts., UT	William Norton	William Norton	1970	23
209 5/8	29 7/8	29 2/8	29 2/8	5 2/8	5 2/8	5	7	Montrose Co., CO	Mike Thomas	Mike Thomas	1974	24
209 5/8	27 4/8	27 7/8	28 7/8	5 5/8	5 5/8	5	5	Rio Arriba Co., NM	Kelly Baird	Kelly Baird	1984	24
209 5/8	27 5/8	26 5/8	30 6/8	4 7/8	5 2/8	6	8	Coconino Co., AZ	Unknown	John C. McClendon	PR 1985	24
209 4/8	28 7/8	29 6/8	28	5 7/8	5 7/8	6	8	Wallowa Co., OR	John C. Evans	Stan J. Neitling, Jr.	1920	27
209 3/8	26 4/8	25 6/8	23	5 1/8	5 2/8	8	5	Kansas	Brad Hughes	Don Schaufler	1984	28
209 3/8	26 1/8	25 5/8	23 7/8	5	4 6/8	5	5	Lincoln Co., WY	L. Victor Clark	L. Victor Clark	1992	28
209 2/8	27 6/8	27 1/8	27 4/8	5	5 6/8	5	5	Amherst Mt., CO	Herbert Graham	Mrs. W.J. Graham	1963	30
209 2/8	28	29 4/8	28 4/8	4 7/8	4 6/8	5	5	Rich Co., UT	Dee Hildt	Dee Hildt	1968	30
209	24 4/8	25 4/8	24 1/8	6 1/8	6 2/8	5	7	Saquache Co., CO	William B. Pennington	William B. Pennington	1967	32
209	26 7/8	27	24 2/8	5 6/8	5 6/8	5	5	Boise Co., ID	Charles Root	Soron Root	1970	32
208 6/8	27 6/8	26 7/8	26 2/8	5 1/8	5	6	5	North Kaibab, AZ	Horace T. Fowler	Horace T. Fowler	1938	34
208 6/8	24 4/8	24 6/8	17 4/8	5 3/8	5 3/8	6	6	Garfield Co., CO	George Shearer	Richard L. Baker	1952	34
208 6/8	26	27 3/8	26 4/8	5 2/8	5 2/8	6	5	Rio Arriba Co., NM	James R. Odiorne, Jr.	James R. Odiorne, Jr.	1978	34

Score	Main Beam R	Main Beam L	Inside Spread	Circ. R	Circ. L	Pts. R	Pts. L	Locality	Hunter	Owner	Date	Rank
208 5/8	26 7/8	27 1/8	27 2/8	5	5	5	5	Mesa Co., CO	Robert L. Zaina	Robert L. Zaina	1960	37
208	29	26 4/8	34 3/8	5 1/8	5	5	5	Utah Co., UT	Ned H. Losser	Ned H. Losser	1972	38
208	26 6/8	26 6/8	31 6/8	5 1/8	5 3/8	6	6	Franklin Co., ID	Herb Voyler, Jr.	Herb Voyler, Jr.	1972	38
207 6/8	25 5/8	26	23 2/8	5 1/8	4 7/8	5	5	Gem Co., ID	Thomas A. Sutton	Thomas A. Sutton	1991	40
207 4/8	27 4/8	26	24	4 7/8	4 7/8	5	5	Washington Co., UT	John K. Frei	Don Schaufler	1987	41
207 3/8	28 1/8	29 4/8	28 7/8	5 6/8	5 5/8	9	9	Mesa Co., CO	Wally Bruegman	Wally Bruegman	1972	42
207 2/8	28 5/8	27 1/8	28 1/8	6 5/8	6 4/8	6	6	Montrose Co., CO	Bill Crouch	Don Schaufler	1974	43
207 1/8	26 6/8	26 2/8	24 1/8	5 6/8	5 4/8	6	6	Golden, CO	Harold B. Moser	Harold B. Moser	1967	44
207	31 6/8	27 2/8	27 4/8	7	7	5	5	Split Rock, WY	Herb Klein	Herb Klein	1960	45
207	28	28 2/8	29	6	6	6	6	Montrose, CO	Warren S. Bachhofer	Warren S. Bachhofer	1966	45
207	26 7/8	28	26 5/8	5 3/8	5 3/8	5	5	Lincoln Co., WY	Al Firenze, Sr.	Al Firenze, Jr.	1969	45
207	25 2/8	26 2/8	21	6 2/8	6 2/8	4	4	Franklin Co., ID	Unknown	L. Dwight Israelsen	PR 1970	45
207	28 3/8	29 3/8	27	5 4/8	5 4/8	7	5	Kane Co., UT	Picked Up	John K. Springer	1986	45
206 7/8	29	29 2/8	29 7/8	5 5/8	5 3/8	5	6	Washington Co., ID	E. Jack Raby	E. Jack Raby	1968	50
206 7/8	26 1/8	25 7/8	21 3/8	5 3/8	4 7/8	6	5	Montrose Co., CO	W.L. Boynton	W.L. Boynton	1973	50
206 6/8	27	27 4/8	29 4/8	6 2/8	6 1/8	8	8	Pagosa Springs, CO	Richard V. Price	Richard V. Price	1962	52
206 6/8	26 3/8	25 6/8	28 2/8	5 1/8	4 7/8	5	6	Pagosa Springs, CO	Henry Trujillo, Jr.	Henry Trujillo, Jr.	1963	52
206 6/8	28 2/8	27 6/8	20 4/8	5	5 3/8	5	5	Rio Arriba Co., NM	Robert J. Seeds	Robert J. Seeds	1996	52
206 5/8	27 4/8	28 3/8	28 7/8	4 6/8	4 6/8	6	6	Coconino Co., AZ	Lamell Ellsworth	Lamell Ellsworth	1971	55
206 4/8	28 7/8	28 5/8	25 1/8	5 2/8	5 1/8	7	7	New Mexico	Unknown	C. & J. Neill	PR 1956	56
206 3/8	27 2/8	27 7/8	28 1/8	5 1/8	5 1/8	5	5	Eagle Co., CO	Harold Taylor	Fred Palmer	1960	57
206 3/8	27 4/8	26 3/8	26 7/8	5 2/8	5 3/8	5	5	Rio Arriba Co., NM	Jim Roddie	Jim Roddie	1971	57
206 3/8	26 5/8	26 5/8	24 3/8	5 1/8	5 1/8	6	6	Coconino Co., AZ	Robert C. Kaufman	Robert C. Kaufman	1978	57
206 3/8	26 6/8	26 3/8	28 3/8	4 7/8	4 7/8	6	6	Coconino Co., AZ	Katie A. Norman	Katie A. Norman	1990	57
206 2/8	26	27 4/8	26 4/8	5	5	5	5	Rio Arriba Co., NM	Harley Hinds	Oran M. Roberts	1963	61
206 2/8	28 6/8	28 6/8	22 4/8	6	6	9	9	Montrose Co., CO	Patrick E. Courtin, Jr.	Patrick E. Courtin, Jr.	1972	61
206 2/8	26 5/8	27 5/8	23 4/8	5 7/8	5 7/8	5	5	Mesa Co., CO	Picked Up	James S. Bennett	1974	61
206 1/8	26 3/8	26 3/8	26 7/8	6	6	5	5	Peterson, UT	Paul Crittenden	Paul Crittenden	PR 1965	64
206 1/8	25 1/8	25 1/8	25 2/8	5 1/8	5 1/8	5	5	Idaho Co., ID	William B. Joyner	William B. Joyner	1965	64
206	24	22 1/8	25	6 1/8	6 1/8	6	6	Eagle, CO	Harold L. Loesch	Harold L. Loesch	1967	66
206	27 6/8	28 4/8	31	5 1/8	5 1/8	5	5	Crooked Creek, AB	Chad J. Lyttle	Chad J. Lyttle	1996	66
205 6/8	26 6/8	27 6/8	25 2/8	5 2/8	5 2/8	7	7	Kanab, UT	Loyd A. Folkstad	Loyd A. Folkstad	1968	68
205 6/8	24 3/8	24 3/8	23 4/8	5 4/8	5 4/8	5	5	Eagle Co., CO	Mark A. McCormick	Mark A. McCormick	1981	68
205 5/8	28 7/8	27 3/8	28 7/8	5 3/8	5 3/8	5	5	Washington Co., UT	William C. Cloyd	William C. Cloyd	1994	70
205 4/8	25 3/8	25 3/8	22 7/8	5 4/8	5 4/8	6	6	Kremmling, CO	Larry Bell	Larry Bell	1962	71
205 4/8	29 1/8	28 4/8	27 5/8	5 2/8	5 1/8	4	5	Carbondale, CO	Richard Cobb	Richard Cobb	1962	71
205 4/8	26 2/8	25 5/8	28 4/8	5 6/8	5 6/8	5	5	Gunnison Co., CO	William T. Peacock	Ralph L. McKinley	1962	71
205 4/8	26 6/8	25 7/8	24 6/8	5 1/8	4 6/8	5	5	Lincoln Co., WY	John E. Myers	John E. Myers	1968	71
205 4/8	26 4/8	26 4/8	25 2/8	5 4/8	5 3/8	6	6	Lincoln Co., NV	Erich P. Burkhard	Erich P. Burkhard	1983	71
205 4/8	26 2/8	26 2/8	23 5/8	5 3/8	5 4/8	6	7	Rio Arriba Co., NM	Picked Up	Eudane Vicenti	1993	71
205 3/8	26 6/8	27	26 7/8	5 3/8	5 3/8	5	5	Starkey, OR	H.M. Bailey	H.M. Bailey	1963	77
205 2/8	27	28	30 1/8	4 7/8	4 4/8	5	5	Montrose Co., CO	Joe M. Gardner	Z. Gardner Holland	1954	78
205 2/8	27 1/8	27 6/8	28 1/8	5	5	5	5	Carbon Co., WY	Shelly R. Risner	Shelly R. Risner	1986	78
205 1/8	25 6/8	26 3/8	25 5/8	4 4/8	4 5/8	7	7	Morgan Co., UT	Gale Allen	Gale Allen	1946	80
205 1/8	30	28 4/8	23 5/8	5	5	5	5	San Juan Co., NM	David A. Brooks	David A. Brooks	1995	80
204 7/8	27	27 2/8	23 5/8	5 5/8	5 4/8	6	6	Delta Co., CO	Frank Peterson	Frank Peterson	1956	82
204 7/8	26 4/8	26 3/8	26 3/8	5 2/8	5 2/8	5	5	Southern Ute Res., CO	Nolan Martins	Nolan Martins	1967	82

MULE DEER - TYPICAL ANTLERS

Odocoileus hemionus hemionus and certain related subspecies

Score	Length of Main Beam R	L	Inside Spread	Circumference at Smallest Place Between Burr and First Point R	L	Number of Points R	L	Locality	Hunter	Owner	Date Killed	Rank
204 6/8	25 2/8	25	24 2/8	4 6/8	4 7/8	5	5	Colorado	Unknown	D.J. Hollinger & B. Howard	PR 1990	84
204 6/8	25	24 3/8	25 4/8	5 3/8	5 3/8	5	5	Colorado	Unknown	Don Schaufler	PR 1992	84
204 5/8	25 5/8	24 3/8	19 4/8	5 5/8	5 4/8	7	5	Eagle Co., CO	Robert V. Doerr	Robert V. Doerr	1982	86
204 3/8	26 1/8	26 4/8	20 5/8	5 6/8	5 5/8	5	5	Grand Junction, CO	Charles M. Bentley	Michael N. Bentley	1962	87
204 3/8	29 2/8	30 1/8	35	4 4/8	4 5/8	5	5	Sonora, MX	David V. Collis	David V. Collis	1986	87
204 2/8	26	26 2/8	22 2/8	5 4/8	5 4/8	5	5	Garfield Co., UT	James D. Perkins	James D. Perkins	1969	89
204 1/8	28 6/8	30 4/8	24 1/8	4 5/8	4 7/8	6	6	Jicarilla Apache Res., NM	Juan Monarco	Juan Monarco	1960	90
204 1/8	27 5/8	26 1/8	25 1/8	5	5	5	5	Hinsdale Co., NM	Norman E. Ebbley	Jim Temple	1961	90
204 1/8	24 6/8	26	27 6/8	4 7/8	4 7/8	6	5	Morgan Co., UT	Kenneth R. Dickamore	Kenneth R. Dickamore	1967	90
204 1/8	27 2/8	27	25 7/8	5 2/8	5 2/8	6	5	Rio Arriba Co., NM	Waymon Burkhalter	Waymon Burkhalter	1992	90
204	27	27 3/8	24	5 4/8	5 3/8	5	5	Pitkin Co., CO	Jens O. Solberg	Jens O. Solberg	1950	94
204	28 3/8	28 4/8	23 7/8	5 4/8	5 6/8	6	6	Arizona	Unknown	Don Schaufler	PR 1988	94
204	27 3/8	23 4/8	25	5 2/8	5 2/8	5	5	Kane Co., UT	Wade E. Ramsay	Wade E. Ramsay	1995	94
203 7/8	**24 5/8**	**26**	**24 4/8**	**5 7/8**	**5 6/8**	**6**	**6**	**North Park, CO**	**Edison A. Pillmore**	**Mrs. Edison A. Pillmore**	**1949**	**97**
203 7/8	26 3/8	27 5/8	26 3/8	5 2/8	5 3/8	6	6	Mesa Creek, CO	Ed Craig	Jerome Craig	1951	97
203 7/8	29 3/8	29 4/8	25 5/8	5 6/8	5 5/8	5	5	Jicarilla Apache Res., NM	Dick Wright	Dick Wright	1966	97
203 7/8	25 6/8	28 4/8	18 7/8	6 2/8	5 5/8	5	5	Apache Co., AZ	Picked Up	Mike A. Searles	1994	97
203 6/8	27	28 3/8	22 7/8	4 3/8	4 3/8	6	6	Montezuma Co., CO	Bob Meese	Don Schaufler	1970	101
203 5/8	28 3/8	27 3/8	24 4/8	5 7/8	5 6/8	6	6	La Plata Co., CO	B.E. Gressett	B.E. Gressett	1950	102
203 5/8	24 5/8	25 5/8	25 6/8	4 5/8	4 6/8	5	5	Mesa Co., CO	William P. Burger	William P. Burger	1957	102
203 5/8	28 6/8	30 2/8	30 1/8	5	5	5	5	Grand Co., UT	Glen Dumas	S. Kim Bonnett	PR 1960	102
203 5/8	28 5/8	28 7/8	27 7/8	5 2/8	5 3/8	7	5	Caribou Co., ID	William E. Van Antwerp	William E. Van Antwerp	1992	102
203 4/8	25 7/8	29 5/8	27 6/8	5 4/8	5 2/8	5	5	Kaibab Natl. For., AZ	Herb Graham	Herb Graham	1939	106
203 4/8	27 2/8	24	24 2/8	5 4/8	5 3/8	5	5	Elko Co., NV	C.H. Wahl	C.H. Wahl	1953	106
203 4/8	26 5/8	27 3/8	25 4/8	5 4/8	5 4/8	5	5	Mohave Co., AZ	Nick Papac	Nick Papac	1964	106
203 4/8	27	28 1/8	24 4/8	5 4/8	5 4/8	6	6	Rio Arriba Co., NM	Arnold Wendt	John W. Hughes	1965	106
203 4/8	28	26 5/8	30 5/8	5 4/8	5 2/8	6	5	Adams Co., ID	Roy Eastlick	Roy Eastlick	1975	106
203 4/8	27 5/8	28 3/8	25	4 5/8	4 6/8	5	7	Garfield Co., CO	John T. Sewell	John T. Sewell	1985	106
203 2/8	25 7/8	28	22 4/8	4 4/8	4 4/8	6	6	White River, CO	Ron Vance	Ronald Crawford	1943	112
203 2/8	25 3/8	25 7/8	24 6/8	4 6/8	4 5/8	6	7	Crook Co., WY	Ora McGurn	Bob R. Butler	1957	112
203 2/8	28	28 4/8	29 6/8	5 2/8	5 2/8	5	5	De Beque, CO	Francis A. Moore	Francis A. Moore	1962	112
203 2/8	25 6/8	26 6/8	23 3/8	4 6/8	4 7/8	6	6	Garfield Co., UT	James D. Perkins	Mrs. James D. Perkins	1965	112
203 2/8	27 1/8	26 6/8	22 2/8	4 7/8	4 6/8	5	5	Collbran, CO	Joe R. Colingo	Joe R. Colingo	1973	112
203 1/8	26 2/8	26 6/8	27 1/8	5 6/8	5 6/8	5	5	North Kaibab, AZ	Monico Marquez	Monico Marquez	1957	117
203 1/8	22 5/8	22 7/8	27 6/8	5 3/8	6 3/8	6	6	Hayden, CO	M.W. Giboney	M.W. Giboney	1959	117
203 1/8	25 7/8	26 6/8	24	5	5 1/8	5	6	Fremont Co., ID	Michael W.G. Neff	Michael W.G. Neff	1990	117

Score	L.R	L.L	Spread	C.R	C.L	R	L	Locality	By Whom Killed	Owner	Date	Rank
203	25 2/8	26 5/8	25 5/8	5 4/8	5 3/8	5	6	Bonneville Co., ID	Jay Hoover	Don Schaufler	1966	120
203	25	23 5/8	24	5 2/8	5 2/8	5	5	Mesa Co., CO	James K. Scott	James K. Scott	1966	120
203	26 3/8	25 5/8	27 1/8	5 4/8	5 6/8	9	8	Montrose Co., CO	Earl L. Markley	Aly M. Bruner	1968	120
203	24 2/8	24 5/8	23 5/8	4 6/8	4 6/8	5	7	Flathead Co., MT	Fran Cahoon	Don Schaufler	1989	120
202 7/8	26 3/8	26 3/8	26 3/8	5 2/8	5 7/8	5	5	Adams Co., ID	James S. Denney	James S. Denney	1939	124
202 7/8	26	23	23	5 2/8	5 2/8	5	5	Lincoln Co., WY	Monte J. Brough	Monte J. Brough	1968	124
202 7/8	25 3/8	24 7/8	23 7/8	4 7/8	4 7/8	6	7	Idaho Co., ID	Myron L. Gilbert	Myron L. Gilbert	1975	124
202 6/8	28 2/8	29 2/8	19 2/8	6 6/8	6 7/8	5	5	Ouray Co., CO	Jewel E. Schottel	Jewel E. Schottel	1966	127
202 6/8	26 3/8	25 5/8	25 4/8	5 3/8	5 2/8	5	5	Rio Arriba Co., NM	James F. Leveritt, Jr.	James F. Leveritt, Jr.	1980	127
202 6/8	27 1/8	26 1/8	21 5/8	5 1/8	5 1/8	5	5	Ouray Co., CO	Louis V. Schlosser	Louis V. Schlosser	1965	129
202 5/8	26 2/8	26 1/8	25 1/8	5	5 1/8	5	5	Adams Co., ID	David J. Couch	David J. Couch	1970	129
202 5/8	29 2/8	29	26 2/8	4 7/8	4 7/8	5	6	Bear Lake Co., ID	Alan R. Crane	Alan R. Crane	1962	131
202 4/8	30 4/8	30	29 4/8	5 2/8	5 1/8	6	7	Park Co., WY	Paul M. Rothermel, Jr.	Paul M. Rothermel, Jr.	1962	131
202 4/8	27 4/8	27 6/8	21 2/8	5 3/8	5 7/8	6	4	Mesa Co., CO	Jack Thompson	Jack Thompson	1968	131
202 4/8	26 7/8	24 7/8	27	5 1/8	5 2/8	6	6	Rio Arriba Co., NM	Gerald J. Weber	Gerald J. Weber	1970	131
202 4/8	29 5/8	29 5/8	21 6/8	5 1/8	5	4	6	Garfield Co., CO	James S. Harden	James S. Harden	1982	131
202 4/8	25 6/8	25 6/8	30 3/8	5 3/8	5 3/8	7	6	Jicarilla Apache Res., NM	Theodore Serafin	Theodore Serafin	1959	136
202 3/8	26 3/8	25 5/8	23 5/8	5 6/8	5 6/8	7	7	Boulder Co., CO	Bob Wallace	Bob Wallace	1963	136
202 3/8	26 1/8	26 1/8	24 5/8	5 3/8	5 4/8	8	5	Baker Co., OR	Brett N. Hayes	Brett N. Hayes	1982	136
202 3/8	27 1/8	27 1/8	28 3/8	5 3/8	6	5	5	Sublette Co., WY	Derek L. Kendrick	Derek L. Kendrick	1992	136
202 3/8	25 6/8	26	21 4/8	5 6/8	5 1/8	5	5	Coconino Co., AZ	Steve B. Parizek	Steve B. Parizek	1993	136
202 3/8	27 2/8	25 6/8	26	5 2/8	5 2/8	6	7	Pagosa Springs, CO	Allen R. Arnwine	Allen R. Arnwine	1960	141
202 2/8	30 2/8	31 3/8	31 3/8	5 2/8	5	10	7	Carbon Co., UT	Robert R. Henderson	Robert R. Henderson	1965	141
202 2/8	28	29 6/8	20 6/8	4 7/8	4 7/8	4	5	Archuleta Co., CO	Duane Yearwood	Duane Yearwood	1973	141
202 2/8	26 7/8	27	26	5	5 3/8	9	6	Bear Lake Co., ID	David L. Williams	Raymond L. Williams	1949	144
202	26 4/8	27 6/8	27 6/8	5 6/8	5 6/8	6	6	Lincoln Co., MT	William E. Hubbard	William E. Hubbard	1963	144
202	27 4/8	25 4/8	29 4/8	6 3/8	6 3/8	6	6	Gunnison Natl. For., CO	James M. Newsom	James M. Newsom	1963	144
202	26	27 1/8	24 2/8	5 1/8	5 1/8	5	6	Montrose Co., CO	Kenneth Klees	Kenneth Klees	1966	144
202	26 1/8	24 6/8	27 5/8	5 2/8	5 2/8	5	5	Chelan Co., WA	Unknown	James M. Brown	PR 1970	144
202	26 1/8	26 4/8	27 4/8	5 4/8	5 4/8	5	5	Sweetwater Co., WY	Arnold A. Bethke	Arnold A. Bethke	1976	144
202	29	26 1/8	21 4/8	5 1/8	5 1/8	5	5	Idaho Co., ID	John H. Davis	John H. Davis	1981	144
202	27 1/8	27 6/8	25 6/8	4 7/8	5	5	5	Unknown	Picked Up	Dale Selby	1982	144
202	26 1/8	27 3/8	29	5 2/8	5	5	5	Hidalgo Co., NM	Matt Evans	Matt Evans	1985	144
202	27 2/8	26 1/8	25 6/8	5 4/8	5 3/8	5	5	Elko Co., NV	Arlo M. Hummell	Arlo M. Hummell	1989	144
201 7/8	26 5/8	26 4/8	26 6/8	6 1/8	6 1/8	5	5	Coconino Co., AZ	Donald Vanderwall	Donald Vanderwall	1992	144
201 7/8	27	27 2/8	27 3/8	5 2/8	5 2/8	6	6	Daggett Co., UT	Earl Eldredge	Phil Brotherson	1940	155
201 7/8	26	26 5/8	26 3/8	4 7/8	5	5	6	Dolores Co., CO	Leonard J. Ashcraft	Leonard J. Ashcraft	1958	155
201 6/8	25 7/8	26 5/8	21 2/8	5 1/8	5 1/8	5	5	Union Co., OR	Brian M. Erwin	Brian M. Erwin	1991	155
201 6/8	26	26	26	5 3/8	5 3/8	5	5	Afton, WY	Bernard Domries	Bernard Domries	1967	158
201 6/8	26 6/8	26 3/8	26 4/8	5 2/8	5 2/8	6	5	Saddle Hills, AB	Dale Ophus	Dale Ophus	1989	158
201 6/8	26 2/8	26 1/8	27 1/8	4 7/8	4 7/8	5	6	Washoe Co., NV	Gordon Frazier	Ron W. Biggs	1991	158
201 6/8	26 4/8	26 4/8	25 2/8	5	5	5	6	Montrose Co., CO	Allan K. Slafter	Allan K. Slafter	1994	158
201 5/8	24 1/8	24 2/8	23 3/8	5 1/8	5 1/8	5	5	Gunnison Co., CO	Robert D. Rader	Robert D. Rader	1966	162
201 5/8	26 6/8	25 6/8	25 1/8	5 3/8	5 3/8	5	5	Cheyenne Co., KS	Jim Sutton	Don Schaufler	PR 1972	162
201 5/8	26 2/8	27 3/8	28 4/8	5 2/8	5 2/8	6	6	Eagle Co., CO	Richard C. Bergquist	Richard C. Bergquist	1981	162
201 5/8	27 3/8	26 2/8	24 3/8	5 4/8	5 4/8	6	5	Baker Co., OR	Terry Williams	Terry Williams	1988	162
201 4/8	26	26	26	5	5	5	5	Garfield Co., CO	Unknown	Ronald E. McKinney	1954	166

MULE DEER - TYPICAL ANTLERS

Odocoileus hemionus hemionus and certain related subspecies

Score	Length of Main Beam R	L	Inside Spread	Circumference at Smallest Place Between Burr and First Point R	L	Number of Points R	L	Locality	Hunter	Owner	Date Killed	Rank
201 4/8	23	24	20	5 4/8	5 2/8	6	6	Moffat Co., CO	Carl E. Jacobson	Carl E. Jacobson	1967	166
201 4/8	26 6/8	24 7/8	28 4/8	6 3/8	6	5	5	Chama, NM	James W. Smith II	James W. Smith II	1969	166
201 4/8	26 3/8	25 3/8	24 2/8	5 3/8	5 2/8	5	5	Malheur Co., OR	David L. Bauer	David L. Bauer	1971	166
201 4/8	28 1/8	28 3/8	22 7/8	5 6/8	5 4/8	5	7	Ravalli Co., MT	Sherman L. Williams	Sherman L. Williams	1973	166
201 4/8	27 1/8	26 2/8	22 6/8	5 1/8	5 2/8	5	5	Adams Co., ID	Gary D. Lewis	Gary D. Lewis	1990	166
201 4/8	28 7/8	27 6/8	23 3/8	5 3/8	5 2/8	7	6	Mesa Co., CO	Michael W. Laws	Michael W. Laws	1996	166
201 3/8	25 4/8	26 1/8	30 1/8	6 1/8	6	5	5	Archuleta Co., CO	Joe Moore	Joe Moore	1962	173
201 3/8	27 6/8	27 6/8	25 3/8	5 4/8	5 4/8	7	7	Blaine Co., ID	Brent Jones	Brent Jones	1965	173
201 3/8	25 5/8	26 4/8	25 3/8	5 4/8	5 4/8	5	5	Grand Junction, CO	William C. Byrd	William C. Byrd	1967	173
201 3/8	25 6/8	24 5/8	20 7/8	5 3/8	5 3/8	5	5	Unknown	Unknown	Matthew N. Davis	PR 1970	173
201 3/8	26 3/8	26 3/8	25 4/8	5 5/8	5 5/8	6	5	Rio Arriba Co., NM	Donald W. Johnson	Donald W. Johnson	1970	173
201 3/8	30 1/8	28 2/8	28 7/8	4 5/8	4 6/8	5	5	Wasatch Co., UT	Paul Probst	Paul Probst	1971	173
201 3/8	25 6/8	24 6/8	23 1/8	5 4/8	5 4/8	5	5	Montrose Co., CO	Grant Morlang	Grant Morlang	1972	173
201 3/8	28 3/8	29 7/8	34 2/8	5 3/8	5 6/8	4	5	Butte Co., ID	John A. Little	John A. Little	1981	173
201 3/8	26 5/8	25 7/8	23 3/8	5 2/8	5 2/8	6	7	Sublette Co., WY	Jerry C. Lopez	Jerry C. Lopez	1985	173
201 2/8	28	29	28	5	4 6/8	6	6	Bayfield, CO	D. Rockwell	D. Rockwell	1956	182
201 2/8	26 6/8	27 6/8	26 6/8	6	6	6	6	Jicarilla Apache Res., NM	Anthony Julian	Anthony Julian	1961	182
201 2/8	28 4/8	28 3/8	24	5 1/8	5 3/8	5	5	Chama, NM	Emitt W. Mundy	Emitt W. Mundy	1961	182
201 1/8	29 1/8	29 2/8	31	5 2/8	5 3/8	7	8	Sanpete Co., UT	Roger M. Allred	Roger M. Allred	1958	185
201 1/8	26 2/8	26 2/8	25 3/8	5	4 7/8	5	5	Cameo, CO	Thomas C. Krauss	Thomas C. Krauss	1962	185
201 1/8	26 4/8	27 2/8	26 6/8	6 3/8	6 5/8	5	7	Bayfield, CO	Les Patrick	Les Patrick	1966	185
201 1/8	25 6/8	26 1/8	26 4/8	5	5 4/8	5	6	Jicarilla Apache Res., NM	Arnold Cassador	Arnold Cassador	1967	185
201	28 2/8	28 6/8	28 6/8	5	5 2/8	6	4	Summit Co., UT	Clinton A. Larson	Clinton A. Larson	1949	189
201	29	26 2/8	22 6/8	6 1/8	6 1/8	6	8	Grand Junction, CO	Ernest Mancuso	Ernest Mancuso	1954	189
201	25	25 1/8	24 4/8	4 7/8	5	5	5	Dolores Co., CO	Mark Loverin	Mark Loverin	1978	189
201	26 2/8	26 2/8	23 6/8	5 1/8	5 1/8	5	5	La Plata Co., CO	Larry Pennington	Larry Pennington	1978	189
201	26 6/8	26 1/8	24 5/8	5 1/8	5 2/8	7	5	Idaho	Unknown	Rick Stover	PR 1990	189
201	23 2/8	24	23 1/8	5 2/8	5 3/8	7	8	Fremont Co., ID	Kenneth E. Stevens	Kenneth E. Stevens	1996	189
200 7/8	30 4/8	25 7/8	28 3/8	4 6/8	4 4/8	5	5	Elko Co., NV	Harry Irland	Mrs. Harry Irland	1919	195
200 7/8	28	28 4/8	25 4/8	5 2/8	5 2/8	6	6	Collbran, CO	Homer O. Hartley	Homer O. Hartley	1962	195
200 6/8	26 7/8	26 3/8	23	4 6/8	4 7/8	5	5	Provo Canyon, UT	Karl D. Zaugg	Karl D. Zaugg	1948	197
200 6/8	26 2/8	28	25 6/8	5 4/8	5 4/8	5	5	Malheur Co., OR	Raymond Duncan	Raymond Duncan	1949	197
200 6/8	27 1/8	25 2/8	22 4/8	5 7/8	5 6/8	5	5	Eagle Co., CO	John Robertson	John Robertson	1958	197
200 6/8	27	27 3/8	26	5	5 1/8	5	5	Southern Ute Res., CO	Jerry E. Morgan	Jerry E. Morgan	1965	197
200 6/8	26	26 6/8	23 4/8	5 6/8	5 4/8	6	7	Delta, CO	Emil Warber, Jr.	Emil Warber, Jr.	1966	197
200 6/8	25 2/8	25 2/8	26 7/8	5 3/8	5 2/8	5	7	Boise Co., ID	Delbert W. Crawford	Delbert W. Crawford	1969	197

Score	Beam R	Beam L	Spread	Circ. R	Circ. L	Pts R	Pts L	Locality	Hunter	Owner	Date	Rank
200 6/8	28 5/8	28 4/8	23	5 2/8	5 2/8	8	5	Gunnison Co., CO	James B. Holbrooks	James B. Holbrooks	1977	197
200 6/8	27 2/8	27 7/8	21 2/8	5 6/8	5 5/8	5	5	Merritt, BC	Cory Christensen	Cory Christensen	1989	197
200 5/8	27	27	26 4/8	5	4 6/8	7	9	Ogden, UT	Carl F. Worden	Carl F. Worden	1948	205
200 5/8	25 2/8	25 2/8	25 2/8	5 2/8	5	6	6	Lincoln Co., WY	John Myers	John Myers	1973	205
200 5/8	25	27	26 5/8	5 1/8	5	5	5	La Plata Co., CO	Unknown	Ronald F. Lax	1979	205
200 5/8	26 7/8	25 7/8	27 5/8	5	5 3/8	5	5	Yavapai Co., AZ	Joseph C. Pecha	Joseph C. Pecha	1983	205
200 4/8	27 5/8	26 7/8	27 6/8	5 1/8	5 1/8	5	6	Bear Lake Co., ID	Frank Bidart	Frank Bidart	1965	209
200 4/8	27 5/8	28 5/8	28 2/8	4 7/8	4 7/8	6	5	Utah Co., UT	Elroy A. Loveridge	Elroy A. Loveridge	1965	209
200 4/8	25 6/8	27	23 6/8	5 1/8	5 1/8	5	5	Bear Lake Co., ID	Lee Bridges	Lee Bridges	1966	209
200 4/8	26 6/8	26 4/8	23	5 3/8	5 3/8	5	6	Caribou Co., ID	Herb Voyler, Jr.	Herb Voyler, Jr.	1972	209
200 4/8	26	27 2/8	30 5/8	5 3/8	5 4/8	6	5	Adams Co., ID	Roy Eastlick	Roy Eastlick	1974	209
200 4/8	25 4/8	25	25	4 6/8	4 6/8	5	5	Eagle Co., CO	Jack Stevens	Jack Stevens	1975	209
200 4/8	27 4/8	27 3/8	31	5 4/8	5 5/8	5	5	Madison Co., MT	Glenn S. Shelton	Glenn S. Shelton	1976	209
200 4/8	24 6/8	24	23 3/8	5	4 6/8	5	6	Dolores Co., CO	James L. Horneck	James L. Horneck	1988	209
200 4/8	27	27	24	5 2/8	5	6	5	Rio Arriba Co., NM	Jay Walker	Jay Walker	1993	209
200 3/8	27 4/8	27 5/8	27 1/8	5 3/8	5 4/8	4	4	Okanogan Co., WA	E.R. Crooks	E.R. Crooks	1939	218
200 3/8	29 1/8	27 4/8	26 1/8	5 1/8	5 4/8	7	7	Uncompahgre Natl. For., CO	Richard M. Holbrook	Richard M. Holbrook	1972	218
200 3/8	25 7/8	26 7/8	24 4/8	5 6/8	5 1/8	7	7	Gypsum, CO	Gene D. Lintz	Gene D. Lintz	1974	218
200 3/8	25 1/8	29 1/8	20 1/8	5 6/8	5 2/8	6	6	Duchesne Co., UT	William E. Lewis	William E. Lewis	PR 1980	218
200 2/8	28 3/8	25 7/8	23 6/8	4 7/8	5 6/8	6	6	Battle Mt., WY	Ron Vance	Ronald Crawford	1963	222
200 2/8	26	25	25	5	5 6/8	5	5	Southern Ute Res., CO	Arthur Burch	Steven Burch	1966	222
200 2/8	26 4/8	29 7/8	22 4/8	4 6/8	5	6	6	Mesa Co., CO	Mitchell J. Sacco	Mitchell J. Sacco	1966	222
200 2/8	26	26 4/8	26 4/8	4 5/8	4 7/8	6	6	Ouray Co., CO	Joseph T. Hollingshead	Joseph T. Hollingshead	1967	222
200 2/8	27	26	27	4 7/8	4 6/8	4	4	Asotin Co., WA	Grant E. Holcomb	Grant E. Holcomb	1975	222
200 2/8	28 5/8	27	26 7/8	5	4 7/8	5	5	Montrose Co., CO	Nelson Harding	Nelson Harding	1985	222
200 2/8	24 1/8	27 5/8	26	4 6/8	5	6	6	Sevier Co., UT	Mayben J. Crane	Mayben J. Crane	1987	222
200 2/8	27 2/8	25 7/8	19 6/8	4 6/8	4 6/8	5	5	Bonneville Co., ID	Richard A. Kelley	Richard A. Kelley	1990	222
200 2/8	27 1/8	25 2/8	25 2/8	5 4/8	4 6/8	5	5	Boise Co., ID	Richard L. Jakomeit	Richard L. Jakomeit	1992	222
200 1/8	27 1/8	23 6/8	19 3/8	5 6/8	5 4/8	6	6	Cashmere, WA	John F. Schurle	William H. Schott	1913	231
200 1/8	27 3/8	26 3/8	19	4 6/8	5 5/8	6	6	Ruby Mt., NV	Earl Frantzen	Earl Frantzen	1941	231
200 1/8	23 6/8	27 3/8	27 3/8	5 3/8	4 6/8	5	5	Mesa Co., CO	John M. Domingos	John M. Domingos	1965	231
200 1/8	28 6/8	24 7/8	28 3/8	5 5/8	5 2/8	5	5	Mohave Co., AZ	Jay M. Ogden	Jay M. Ogden	1990	231
200	25 4/8	27 2/8	25 7/8	4 6/8	5 5/8	5	5	Summit Co., CO	Picked Up	Bill Knorr	1959	235
200	27	24 4/8	26	4 6/8	4 6/8	5	5	Piedra River, CO	Glenn A. Smith	Glenn A. Smith	1960	235
200	25 4/8	26 2/8	27	6 1/8	6 1/8	5	5	Silt, CO	George McCoy	George McCoy	1961	235
200	27 4/8	24 2/8	25 2/8	6 3/8	6 3/8	6	6	Garfield Co., CO	Picked Up	John F. Frost	1963	235
200	28 7/8	27	28 5/8	5 2/8	5 3/8	6	6	Mouqi, AZ	Tom Corey	Tom Corey	1964	235
200	29 7/8	27 4/8	29 3/8	6	5 7/8	6	6	Park Co., CO	Jim Fitzgerald	Rob Firth	1971	235
200	28	29 6/8	24 4/8	4 7/8	4 7/8	5	5	Eagle Co., CO	Dale R. Leonard	David P. Moore	1976	235
200	26	28	21 6/8	5 5/8	5 5/8	5	5	Hot Springs Co., WY	Basil C. Bradbury	Basil C. Bradbury	1977	235
200	24 4/8	27 1/8	26	5 2/8	5 2/8	5	5	Coconino Co., AZ	Adam R. Kowalski, Jr.	Adam R. Kowalski, Jr.	1995	235
199 7/8	21 7/8	25 7/8	24 4/8	5 1/8	5 1/8	7	7	Jackson Co., CO	G.B. Berger, Jr.	Denver Mus. Nat. Hist.	1934	244
199 7/8	25 1/8	24 7/8	21 7/8	5 6/8	5 6/8	5	5	Disappointment Creek, CO	Clifford Le Neve	Clifford Le Neve	1954	244
199 7/8	23 2/8	22 6/8	25 1/8	6	6	6	6	Jicarilla Apache Res., NM	Anthony Julian	Anthony Julian	1961	244
199 7/8	25 3/8	24 4/8	23 1/8	5 1/8	5 1/8	5	5	Uncompahgre Natl. For., CO	H.E. Gerhart	H.E. Gerhart	1963	244
199 7/8	27 4/8	27 5/8	26 1/8	4 5/8	4 6/8	7	6	Lincoln Co., WY	John D. Murphy	John D. Murphy	1963	244
199 7/8	24 1/8	24 1/8	25 1/8	5 4/8	5 4/8	5	5	Stillwater Co., MT	Basil C. Bradbury	Basil C. Bradbury	1965	244

MULE DEER - TYPICAL ANTLERS

Odocoileus hemionus hemionus and certain related subspecies

Score	Length of Main Beam R	L	Inside Spread	Circ. R	L	Points R	L	Locality	Hunter	Owner	Date Killed	Rank
199 7/8	26 4/8	26 4/8	24 4/8	4 7/8	4 7/8	6	6	Eagle Co., CO	George S. Burton	Betty Burton	1967	244
199 7/8	25 7/8	27 2/8	25 7/8	4 7/8	5	7	6	Coconino Co., AZ	John L. Johnson	John L. Johnson	1972	244
199 7/8	25 1/8	25 7/8	24 3/8	6 5/8	6 6/8	5	5	Wallowa Co., OR	Wilford E. Hingston	Wilford E. Hingston	1996	244
199 6/8	29 7/8	29	21 5/8	5 2/8	5 2/8	6	8	Montrose Co., CO	James O. McCleary	John E. McCleary	1951	253
199 6/8	25 1/8	25 3/8	25	5 1/8	5 1/8	5	5	Grant Co., OR	Steve M. Stevenson	Steve M. Stevenson	1982	253
199 6/8	26 6/8	25 4/8	24 5/8	5 3/8	5	6	5	Kane Co., UT	Gilbert T. Adams	Gilbert T. Adams	1993	253
199 6/8	24 5/8	25 6/8	22	5	5	6	6	Diefenbaker Lake, SK	Warren M. Heatherington	Warren M. Heatherington	1996	253
199 5/8	27 5/8	26	21 5/8	5 5/8	5 6/8	5	5	Princeton, BC	Buddy D. Baker	Buddy D. Baker	1979	257
199 5/8	27 5/8	25 4/8	26 4/8	5 2/8	5 3/8	7	6	Garfield Co., UT	Picked Up	Don Schaufler	PR 1980	257
199 5/8	25 4/8	24 2/8	21 7/8	6 1/8	6	5	5	Humboldt Co., NV	Robert L. Swinney	Robert L. Swinney	1982	257
199 5/8	26 6/8	26 5/8	26 7/8	5	4 6/8	5	6	Archuleta Co., CO	Charles W. Pearson	Charles W. Pearson	1995	257
199 4/8	28 2/8	27 3/8	28	6 1/8	6 2/8	8	8	Pagosa Springs, CO	Perry Dixon	Perry Dixon	1957	261
199 4/8	26 2/8	28 4/8	28 7/8	4 6/8	4 7/8	7	7	Salmon River, ID	C.A. Schwope	C.A. Schwope	1959	261
199 4/8	24 2/8	24 2/8	21 2/8	5 5/8	5 5/8	5	5	Bonneville Co., ID	Leonard J. Vella	Leonard J. Vella	1972	261
199 4/8	25 5/8	26 4/8	23 6/8	4 7/8	5	6	6	Sanpete Co., UT	Kevin P. Price	Kevin P. Price	1973	261
199 4/8	25	25 4/8	26	4 6/8	5	5	5	Dolores Co., CO	Kenneth L. Peters	Kenneth L. Peters	1976	261
199 4/8	26 7/8	27 3/8	25 6/8	5 6/8	5 6/8	4	4	Medicine Hat, AB	Duncan Baldie	D. Baldie & K.W. McKenzie	1981	261
199 3/8	26 5/8	26 4/8	25 5/8	5 2/8	5 2/8	6	6	Mesa Co., CO	Picked Up	Greg Duff	1949	267
199 3/8	27 3/8	28	25 1/8	5 4/8	6	4	4	Silt, CO	V.M. Spiller	V.M. Spiller	1961	267
199 3/8	25 5/8	26 3/8	26 4/8	4 5/8	4 3/8	5	4	San Miguel Co., NM	Frank Mata	Robert Cordova	1965	267
199 3/8	27	27 6/8	23 7/8	5 4/8	5 4/8	4	4	Rio Arriba Co., NM	John A. Farrell	John A. Farrell	1966	267
199 3/8	26 7/8	25 7/8	24 4/8	5 6/8	5 5/8	5	6	Rio Arriba Co., NM	Johnny L. Montgomery	Johnny L. Montgomery	1967	267
199 3/8	26 4/8	28 4/8	24 1/8	5 1/8	5 2/8	7	5	Harney Co., OR	John A. Echanis	John A. Echanis	1995	267
199 2/8	25 2/8	25 2/8	25	5 2/8	5 4/8	5	5	Washoe Co., NV	Joseph N. Ruscigno	Joseph N. Ruscigno	1955	273
199 2/8	27 1/8	24 6/8	26	5	5 2/8	7	7	Beechy, SK	Marvin Taylor	Marvin Taylor	1961	273
199 2/8	25 3/8	24 6/8	21 5/8	5 6/8	5 3/8	8	5	Archuleta Co., CO	Kenneth Hunter	LeRoy C. Haug	1962	273
199 2/8	27 5/8	28	25 4/8	5 2/8	5 2/8	5	5	Strawberry, UT	Steve Payne	Steve Payne	1962	273
199 2/8	27 4/8	26 1/8	26 4/8	5 1/8	5 1/8	5	5	Eagle Co., CO	Howard Stoker	Howard Stoker	1965	273
199 2/8	26 1/8	25 1/8	24 1/8	5 6/8	5 5/8	6	6	Hidden Canyon, AZ	Milton Wyman	Milton Wyman	1972	273
199 2/8	26 4/8	26 2/8	27 4/8	5 6/8	5 5/8	5	5	Grand Co., UT	Picked Up	Jon P. Leatham	1976	273
199 2/8	26 6/8	26 4/8	25 5/8	5 3/8	5 3/8	7	5	Eagle Co., CO	Anthony W. DeToy	Anthony W. DeToy	1978	273
199 2/8	25 2/8	25 1/8	25 1/8	5 2/8	5 2/8	7	6	Garfield Co., CO	Gary W. Hartley	Gary W. Hartley	1978	273
199 2/8	28 5/8	27 6/8	25	5 4/8	5 4/8	5	5	Gable Mt., BC	Jack V. Quiring	Jack V. Quiring	1988	273
199 2/8	26 6/8	26 3/8	25 3/8	5 3/8	4 7/8	6	6	Great Sand Hills, SK	Howard Jackle	Howard Jackle	1991	273
199 1/8	28 6/8	30 4/8	25 6/8	5 7/8	5 4/8	9	6	Coconino Co., AZ	John R. Fogle	John R. Fogle	1992	273
199 1/8	28 3/8	27 2/8	27 6/8	6	5 6/8	8	6	Jicarilla Apache Res., NM	David L. Chandler	David L. Chandler	1961	285

226

Score	Main Beam R	Main Beam L	Inside Spread	Circ. R	Circ. L	Pts R	Pts L	Locality	Hunter	Owner	Date Killed	Rank
199 1/8	25	24 3/8	24 3/8	5 6/8	5 5/8	6	5	San Juan Co., UT	Phyllis O. Crookston	Phyllis O. Crookston	1971	285
199 1/8	27	26 2/8	27 2/8	5 5/8	5 4/8	5	5	Laramie Co., WY	David L. Shannon	David L. Shannon	1981	285
199 1/8	25 4/8	25 3/8	23 3/8	5 6/8	6	5	5	Morgan Co., UT	H. Ritman Jons	H. Ritman Jons	1987	285
199 1/8	27	28 3/8	27 6/8	5 3/8	5 4/8	8	6	Bonneville Co., ID	Scott B. Huntsman	Scott B. Huntsman	1992	285
199 1/8	27	26	29 3/8	4 7/8	5 1/8	6	5	Maple Bush, SK	Dallas E. Wilm	Dallas E. Wilm	1996	285
199	26 6/8	27 1/8	26 2/8	5 4/8	5 1/8	5	5	Echo, UT	Wilford Zaugg	Wilford Zaugg	1958	291
199	25 1/8	26 3/8	23 4/8	5	5	5	5	Park Co., WY	Lois M. Pelzel	Lois M. Pelzel	1965	291
199	24 2/8	24 2/8	21	4 7/8	5 2/8	6	6	Mohave Co., AZ	William M. Berger, Jr.	William M. Berger, Jr.	1973	291
199	24 7/8	23 6/8	23 3/8	5 1/8	4 6/8	5	5	Power Co., ID	Jim A. Rose	Jim A. Rose	1977	291
198 7/8	28 4/8	27 7/8	24 1/8	5 7/8	5 7/8	4	5	San Juan Co., UT	Bradley J. Young	Bradley J. Young	1991	296
198 7/8	26 5/8	27 1/8	26 5/8	5 7/8	6	5	7	Jicarilla Apache Res., NM	Anthony Julian	Jicarilla Apache Res.	1961	296
198 7/8	26 4/8	24 2/8	24 2/8	5 1/8	5 7/8	7	5	Burns, CO	Charles D. Rush	Charles D. Rush	1967	296
198 7/8	26	25 7/8	21 3/8	5 1/8	5	5	5	Rio Arriba Co., NM	Ernest Petago	Ernest Petago	1994	296
198 6/8	23 4/8	22 2/8	21 6/8	6 3/8	6 3/8	5	7	Hines Creek, AB	Charles Lundgard	Charles Lundgard	1960	299
198 6/8	32 7/8	32 4/8	25 3/8	5	5 3/8	7	6	Dulce, NM	Picked Up	Everett M. Vigil	1967	299
198 6/8	26	27 6/8	27 4/8	5 1/8	5	7	6	Mohave Co., AZ	William C. Cloyd	William C. Cloyd	1994	299
198 6/8	26 3/8	26 7/8	26 1/8	4 5/8	5 1/8	6	5	Unknown	Ed Bastian	William H. Lilienthal	PR 1939	299
198 5/8	27 4/8	28 1/8	25 7/8	5	4 7/8	7	6	Colorado	Unknown	Don Schaufler	PR 1960	302
198 5/8	26 2/8	27 2/8	24 5/8	5 4/8	5	6	7	Carbondale, CO	Ralph Clock	Ralph Clock	1961	302
198 5/8	26	25 3/8	28	5 3/8	5 3/8	7	5	Rio Arriba Co., NM	Stanley Davis	Stanley Davis	1965	302
198 5/8	24 4/8	24 7/8	24 1/8	4 7/8	4 6/8	6	5	Swan Valley, ID	Harry G. Brinkley, Jr.	Harry G. Brinkley, Jr.	1966	302
198 5/8	25 1/8	25 2/8	23 5/8	4 7/8	4 7/8	5	5	Carbon Co., WY	M. Gary Muske	M. Gary Muske	1968	302
198 5/8	25	24 7/8	24 7/8	5 1/8	5 3/8	6	5	Elmore Co., ID	William Hartwig	William Hartwig	1984	302
198 5/8	26 2/8	26 2/8	29 4/8	5	4 6/8	6	5	Pueblo Co., CO	James L. Bradley	James L. Bradley	1986	302
198 5/8	25 2/8	26 5/8	21 7/8	5	5 1/8	5	6	Rio Arriba Co., NM	Picked Up	Larry Panzy	1994	302
198 4/8	28	26 1/8	28 2/8	5	5	5	6	Kaibab Natl. For., AZ	W.O. Hart	W.O. Hart	1946	311
198 4/8	29	27 2/8	27 2/8	5 5/8	5 4/8	6	9	Del Norte, CO	Esequiel Trujillo	Esequiel Trujillo	1947	311
198 4/8	25 5/8	25 6/8	20 4/8	5	5	5	5	Tabiona, UT	Picked Up	H.A. Zumbrock	1957	311
198 4/8	27	26 2/8	28 6/8	5	5	5	6	North Kaibab, AZ	Simon C. Krevitsky	Simon C. Krevitsky	1963	311
198 4/8	26 4/8	26 7/8	29 2/8	6 1/8	5 6/8	5	4	San Juan Co., NM	Dan R. Anderson	Dan R. Anderson	1964	311
198 4/8	26	25 4/8	21 4/8	5 3/8	5 2/8	4	5	Routt Co., CO	Lloyd D. Kindsfater	Lloyd D. Kindsfater	1966	311
198 4/8	29	28 7/8	22 4/8	5 1/8	5 1/8	5	6	Dark Canyon, CO	O.P. McGuire	O.P. McGuire	1966	311
198 4/8	28 5/8	28 4/8	24 5/8	4 6/8	5 3/8	6	6	Afton, WY	Ray M. Vincent	Ray M. Vincent	1967	311
198 3/8	29 5/8	30	28 4/8	5 2/8	4 5/8	6	6	La Plata Co., CO	Pauline J. Bostic	Pauline J. Bostic	1971	320
198 3/8	26 6/8	26 5/8	28	6	5 7/8	6	5	Moffat Co., CO	Lucille Gooch	George Gooch	1951	320
198 3/8	25	25 5/8	26	4 5/8	4 5/8	6	6	Mt. Trumbull, AZ	E.O. Brown	E.O. Brown	1960	320
198 3/8	25	25 4/8	19 5/8	5 2/8	5 2/8	5	7	Bonneville Co., ID	Tony Dawson	Tony Dawson	1973	320
198 3/8	26 4/8	26 7/8	23 2/8	4 6/8	4 6/8	6	5	Montrose Co., CO	Allan K. Slafter	Allan K. Slafter	1989	320
198 3/8	27 3/8	26 7/8	28 7/8	4 7/8	4 7/8	7	6	Washoe Co., NV	Jerry W. Lowery	Jerry W. Lowery	1995	320
198 2/8	26 4/8	27 4/8	26 4/8	5	5	5	5	Summit Co., CO	Picked Up	Louis Ceriani	PR 1965	325
198 2/8	25 6/8	25 5/8	24 3/8	5 2/8	5 4/8	6	6	Sonora, MX	Heinz G. Holdorf	Heinz G. Holdorf	1966	325
198 2/8	26 2/8	26	26 6/8	5 1/8	4 7/8	5	5	Gunnison Co., CO	Bobby J. Watson	Bobby J. Watson	1975	325
198 2/8	24 4/8	25	25 3/8	5 4/8	5 1/8	5	5	Coconino Co., AZ	Dale C. Morse	Dale C. Morse	1977	325
198 2/8	28 2/8	28 3/8	27	5 4/8	5 7/8	7	5	Bonneville Co., ID	Thomas N. Thiel	Thomas N. Thiel	1987	325
198 2/8	27 1/8	27 4/8	24 7/8	5 7/8	5 7/8	5	5	Rio Arriba Co., NM	Charles Tapia	Charles Tapia	1991	325
198 2/8	27 1/8	24 6/8	27	5	5	5	5	Rio Arriba Co., NM	Robert J. Seeds	Robert J. Seeds	1992	325
198 1/8	25 3/8	26	25 2/8	5 4/8	5 4/8	4	5	Irwin, ID	Chet Warwick	Chet Warwick	1959	332

227

MULE DEER - TYPICAL ANTLERS

Odocoileus hemionus hemionus and certain related subspecies

Score	Length of Main Beam		Inside Spread	Circumference at Smallest Place Between Burr and First Point		Number of Points		Locality	Hunter	Owner	Date Killed	Rank
	R	L		R	L	R	L					
198 1/8	25 3/8	26 1/8	23 7/8	5 6/8	5 7/8	5	6	Bayfield, CO	C. Ben Boyd	C. Ben Boyd	1967	332
198 1/8	25 1/8	26 1/8	25 7/8	5 4/8	5 4/8	5	6	Routt Co., CO	William E. Goswick	William E. Goswick	1968	332
198 1/8	27 4/8	27 2/8	23 2/8	5	5	7	6	Montrose Co., CO	Robert A. Klatt	Robert A. Klatt	1975	332
198 1/8	26 5/8	25 5/8	28	4 6/8	4 7/8	5	5	Wallowa Co., OR	Dan L. Gober	Dan L. Gober	1980	332
198 1/8	25 4/8	26 1/8	26 2/8	5 2/8	5 2/8	5	5	Natrona Co., WY	Kerry J. Clegg	Kerry J. Clegg	1983	332
198 1/8	26 6/8	27 5/8	24 5/8	5 1/8	5 1/8	6	8	Colorado	Unknown	Unknown	PR 1989	332
198 1/8	26 2/8	25 6/8	22 1/8	5 2/8	5 2/8	5	8	Unknown	Unknown	Lunds Wildlife Exhibit	1931	339
198	25 1/8	25 2/8	22 4/8	5 1/8	5	5	4	Davis Co., UT	Carl D. Craig	Jay D. Craig	1939	339
198	25 2/8	25 5/8	22 4/8	6 1/8	6	4	4	Garfield Co., CO	Leroy Failor	Leroy Failor	1944	339
198	25 4/8	24 6/8	25 1/8	5 4/8	5 3/8	6	5	Smithfield Canyon, UT	Stanley Richardson	Stanley Richardson	1961	339
198	23 7/8	25 4/8	27 1/8	4 7/8	4 7/8	7	7	Gunnison Co., CO	E.D. Palmer	E.D. Palmer	1962	339
198	25	25	22 4/8	5 6/8	5 6/8	5	5	Montpelier, ID	Charles R. Mann	Charles R. Mann	1973	339
198	24	24 7/8	22 4/8	6 1/8	6 6/8	7	5	Eagle Co., CO	Larry Schlasinger	Larry Schlasinger	1978	339
198	27	26 1/8	28 6/8	4 6/8	5 3/8	4	5	Hinsdale Co., CO	Alan L. VanDenBerg	Alan L. VanDenBerg	1978	339
197 7/8	27 7/8	27	26 2/8	5 2/8	5	5	8	Chaffee Co., CO	Marguerite Hill	Marguerite Hill	1956	347
197 7/8	25 2/8	25 1/8	24 5/8	4 6/8	4 7/8	5	6	Kaibab Natl. For., AZ	Eoans Pababla	Eoans Pababla	1957	347
197 7/8	27 6/8	27 7/8	28 5/8	5 1/8	5 3/8	5	5	San Miguel Co., CO	Everett Stutler	Everett Stutler	1965	347
197 7/8	26 1/8	27 4/8	24 1/8	4 7/8	5	5	5	Rio Blanco Co., CO	Gary L. Bicknell	D.J. Hollinger & B. Howard	1967	347
197 7/8	28 1/8	27 6/8	24 5/8	5 2/8	5 3/8	5	5	Rossland, BC	Robert Simm	Robert Simm	1968	347
197 7/8	28 6/8	28 6/8	25 6/8	5	5	6	5	Eagle Co., CO	Lee Frudden	Lee Frudden	1978	347
197 7/8	26 2/8	26 5/8	27 4/8	5 2/8	5 3/8	5	5	Elmore Co., ID	Bud Abele	Bud Abele	1981	347
197 7/8	28 3/8	28 2/8	25 7/8	5 6/8	5 5/8	7	6	Blaine Co., ID	James D. Scarrow	James D. Scarrow	1983	347
197 7/8	25 7/8	25	21 7/8	5 2/8	5 1/8	5	5	Malheur Co., OR	Gerald L. Warnock	Gerald L. Warnock	1996	347
197 6/8	27 2/8	28	25 2/8	4 6/8	4 6/8	5	5	Encampment, WY	Ralph E. Platt, Jr.	Ralph E. Platt, Jr.	1936	356
197 6/8	25 4/8	25 7/8	23 6/8	5 2/8	5 2/8	6	6	Elk Ridge, UT	Bill King	Joseph Fitting	1956	356
197 6/8	27 4/8	26 2/8	24 4/8	4 6/8	4 6/8	5	5	Jefferson Co., MT	James W. Rowe	James W. Rowe	1964	356
197 6/8	26 5/8	27 5/8	23 7/8	4 6/8	5	8	8	Teton Co., WY	John W. Farlow, Jr.	John W. Farlow, Jr.	1971	356
197 6/8	24 3/8	26 4/8	27 3/8	5	5 1/8	5	5	Bonneville Co., ID	Preston L. Winchell	Preston L. Winchell	1974	356
197 6/8	26 6/8	24 7/8	23 6/8	5 3/8	5 4/8	5	5	Botanie Lake, BC	Dennis R. Milton	Dennis R. Milton	1991	356
197 5/8	25 1/8	25	27 5/8	5 1/8	5 3/8	8	6	Summit Co., UT	Wendell M. Smith	Nathan H. Smith	1954	362
197 5/8	24 3/8	24 1/8	24 7/8	4 7/8	5	5	5	Ashton, ID	Earl Johnson	O.M. Corbett	1959	362
197 5/8	22 7/8	22	22 1/8	4 4/8	4 4/8	5	5	Major, SK	Art Heintz	Art Heintz	1961	362
197 5/8	27	26 6/8	22 7/8	5 7/8	5 5/8	6	6	San Miguel Co., CO	Virgil L. Burbridge	Jerry D. Burbridge	1964	362
197 5/8	23 5/8	29 5/8	21 3/8	5	5	5	5	Eagle Co., CO	Joseph Sokel, Jr.	Steve J. Sokel	1965	362
197 5/8	25 4/8	26 5/8	29 4/8	5 5/8	5 5/8	5	5	Elko Co., NV	Manfred E. Koska	Manfred E. Koska	1966	362
197 5/8	28 6/8	27 4/8	23 1/8	5 1/8	5 1/8	5	5	Kootenay River, BC	Raymond Carry	Raymond Carry	1982	362

Score	R. Beam	L. Beam	Spread	Circ.	Circ.	Pts	Pts	Locality	Owner	Hunter	Date	Rank
197 5/8	25 6/8	26 1/8	19 5/8	5 2/8	5 2/8	5	5	Beechy, SK	Brett E. Seidle	Brett E. Seidle	1983	362
197 5/8	26 7/8	27 3/8	26	5	4 7/8	5	6	Uintah Co., UT	Robert C. Chapoose, Jr.	Robert C. Chapoose, Jr.	1987	362
197 4/8	24	26	21 2/8	5 4/8	5 6/8	5	5	Moffat Co., CO	Russ H. Winslow	Russ H. Winslow	1967	371
197 4/8	26 3/8	25 7/8	24 7/8	4 6/8	4 7/8	6	5	Uinta Co., WY	Ken L. Vernon	Ken L. Vernon	1968	371
197 4/8	24 6/8	27	23 4/8	6	5 7/8	9	8	Routt Co., CO	William E. Goswick	William E. Goswick	1969	371
197 4/8	26	26 2/8	23 2/8	5 2/8	5 1/8	6	5	Rio Arriba Co., NM	Jerry Longenbaugh	Jerry Longenbaugh	1969	371
197 4/8	27	25 5/8	27	5 3/8	5 2/8	5	5	Rio Arriba Co., NM	Louis N. Burgess	Louis N. Burgess	1970	371
197 4/8	29 3/8	27 6/8	22 2/8	5 3/8	5 3/8	5	6	Grant Co., WA	D.J. Hollinger & B. Howard	Unknown	PR 1970	371
197 4/8	22 1/8	24	24	5 5/8	5 5/8	6	6	Gunnison Co., CO	Thomas Gray, Jr.	Thomas Gray, Jr.	1980	371
197 4/8	27 2/8	27 1/8	23 6/8	4 3/8	4 3/8	4	4	Bonneville Co., ID	LaDon Harriell	LaDon Harriell	1982	371
197 4/8	29	28 2/8	20 7/8	4 5/8	4 2/8	6	6	Idaho Co., ID	Marvin L. Lindquist	Marvin L. Lindquist	1988	371
197 4/8	28 1/8	27 3/8	26 1/8	5	5	5	9	Tompkins, SK	Edward J. Hardin	Edward J. Hardin	1994	371
197 4/8	27 4/8	26 1/8	23	4 7/8	5	6	5	Archuleta Co., CO	Lansing Kothmann	Lansing Kothmann	1957	371
197 3/8	26 7/8	26 5/8	24 5/8	5	5	5	5	Rio Blanco Co., CO	Jack Thompson	Picked Up	PR 1957	381
197 3/8	27 1/8	25	22 3/8	5 4/8	5 4/8	5	5	Currant Creek, UT	Morris Kidd	Morris Kidd	1960	381
197 3/8	26 5/8	27 4/8	24 2/8	5	5	5	5	Montrose, CO	H.R. Clark	H.R. Clark	1961	381
197 3/8	26 6/8	27 5/8	26 3/8	4 6/8	5 2/8	6	6	Fremont Co., ID	Stanley A. Gilgen	Stanley A. Gilgen	1964	381
197 3/8	25 5/8	26	25 4/8	5 2/8	5 4/8	5	5	Pagosa Springs, CO	John D. Guess	John D. Guess	1966	381
197 3/8	26	27 1/8	26 1/8	5 3/8	5 4/8	6	5	Apache Mesa, NM	Tom Martine	Tom Martine	1970	381
197 3/8	26 2/8	26 2/8	23 2/8	5 6/8	5 5/8	6	5	Gunnison Co., CO	Mark L. Hanna	Mark L. Hanna	1980	381
197 3/8	28 7/8	28 6/8	23 4/8	5 4/8	5 4/8	7	6	Garfield Co., UT	James R. McCourt	James R. McCourt	1985	381
197 3/8	24 7/8	24 5/8	27 2/8	4 4/8	4 5/8	5	5	Lincoln Co., WY	Kim L. King	Kim L. King	1990	381
197 2/8	26 4/8	26 4/8	21 6/8	6 6/8	7	7	7	Beechy, SK	Pete Perrin	Pete Perrin	1947	391
197 2/8	27 3/8	27 3/8	27 1/8	5 2/8	5 4/8	6	6	Afton, WY	Robert Williams	Robert Williams	1960	391
197 2/8	29 4/8	30 2/8	28 6/8	5 4/8	5 5/8	7	7	Harney Co., OR	Guy E. Osborne	Guy E. Osborne	1963	391
197 2/8	26 1/8	26 4/8	23 6/8	5 4/8	5 5/8	6	6	Custer Co., CO	Jerome L. DeGree	Jerome L. DeGree	1972	391
197 2/8	26 2/8	26 1/8	21 2/8	4 3/8	4 4/8	7	7	Weber Co., UT	Abe B. Murdock	Abe B. Murdock	1972	391
197 2/8	23	24	25	4 6/8	4 4/8	5	5	Elko Co., NV	John C. Burman	John C. Burman	1980	391
197 2/8	26 5/8	25 7/8	26 4/8	5 2/8	5 3/8	6	6	Blaine Co., ID	Bart Hofmann	Bart Hofmann	1980	391
197 2/8	24 4/8	24 4/8	23 2/8	4 6/8	4 6/8	5	5	Flathead Co., MT	James E. Betters	James E. Betters	1986	391
197 2/8	24 5/8	23 4/8	24 2/8	5 3/8	5 3/8	5	6	Elbert Co., CO	Francis Wilson	Francis Wilson	1993	391
197 1/8	25 1/8	24 3/8	25 5/8	4 3/8	4 2/8	5	6	Morgan Co., UT	Gayle Allen	Gayle Allen	1948	400
197 1/8	27 1/8	26 7/8	29 7/8	6 4/8	6 1/8	5	6	Gunnison Co., CO	Ted Wolcott, Jr.	Ted Wolcott, Jr.	1961	400
197 1/8	26 5/8	27 6/8	26 3/8	5 1/8	5 2/8	5	5	Ashwood, OR	Harvey Rhoads	Harvey Rhoads	1962	400
197 1/8	27	28	30	5 3/8	5 3/8	7	7	Delta Co., CO	B. Allan Jones	B. Allan Jones	1977	400
197 1/8	28 1/8	27 3/8	22 7/8	5	5	5	5	Mesa Co., CO	Willis A. Kinsey	Willis A. Kinsey	1978	400
197	25 4/8	25 6/8	25	5 1/8	5 2/8	6	6	Sonora, MX	J.G. Cigarroa, Sr.	J.G. Cigarroa, Sr.	1957	405
197	27 4/8	26 3/8	29 3/8	5 4/8	5 6/8	5	5	Jackson Co., CO	Jerry Haldeman	Alvin Bush	1961	405
197	24 2/8	25 4/8	25 2/8	5 2/8	5 4/8	5	5	Grand Co., CO	Woodrow W. Dixon	Woodrow W. Dixon	1962	405
197	26 4/8	26 4/8	27 5/8	5 3/8	5 3/8	6	6	Rio Arriba Co., NM	Ross Lopez	Ross Lopez	1964	405
197	26 6/8	26	28 4/8	5 3/8	5 3/8	5	5	Archuleta Co., CO	Hugh W. Gardner	Hugh W. Gardner	1971	405
197	24 7/8	22	22	4 7/8	4 6/8	5	5	Franklin Co., ID	Robert C. Porter	Robert C. Porter	1972	405
197	25 2/8	25	25	4 7/8	4 7/8	5	5	Camas Co., ID	Bret C. Silver	Bret C. Silver	1980	405
197	25 3/8	22 3/8	22 3/8	5	5	5	5	Utah Co., UT	L. Doug Carlton	L. Doug Carlton	1982	405
197	25 7/8	21 7/8	21 7/8	5 3/8	5 3/8	6	6	Suffern Lake, SK	Macklin Wildl. Fed.	Picked Up	PR 1992	405
197	25 7/8	26	22 3/8	5 5/8	5 5/8	7	7	Grant Co., OR	Bruce J. Brothers	Bruce J. Brothers	1993	405
196 7/8	24	24 5/8	26 4/8	5 1/8	5 2/8	6	5	North Kaibab, AZ	Alex J. Haas	Alex J. Haas	1961	415

MULE DEER - TYPICAL ANTLERS

Odocoileus hemionus hemionus and certain related subspecies

Score	Length of Main Beam R	L	Inside Spread	Circumference at Smallest Place Between Burr and First Point R	L	Number of Points R	L	Locality	Hunter	Owner	Date Killed	Rank
196 7/8	26 2/8	25 5/8	23 7/8	4 7/8	5	5	5	Mesa Co., CO	Carl England	James B. Sisco III	PR 1966	415
196 7/8	24 5/8	24 4/8	22 5/8	5 6/8	5 5/8	5	5	Boise Co., ID	Andrew T. Rogers	Andrew T. Rogers	1967	415
196 7/8	25 6/8	24	21 5/8	5 2/8	5 4/8	5	5	Lincoln Co., MT	Dennis J. Hauke	Dennis J. Hauke	1973	415
196 7/8	27 5/8	27	25 1/8	5 1/8	5 1/8	5	5	Scherf Creek, BC	Manuela Selby	Manuela Selby	1984	415
196 7/8	25 3/8	25 2/8	25 3/8	5	5	5	5	Lincoln Co., WY	William L. Lewis	William L. Lewis	1990	415
196 6/8	24 4/8	23 6/8	24 4/8	5 3/8	5 2/8	7	5	Bear Lake Co., ID	Nels H. Pehrson	Ralph V. Pehrson	1936	421
196 6/8	27 1/8	27 7/8	26	5 1/8	5 1/8	7	5	Eagle Co., CO	Picked Up	Don Schaufler	PR 1964	421
196 6/8	25 1/8	25 4/8	24 4/8	5 2/8	5 5/8	5	5	Delta, CO	Howard G. Reed	Howard G. Reed	1968	421
196 6/8	23 3/8	24 1/8	22 4/8	5 1/8	5 2/8	5	5	Bonneville Co., ID	William G. Pine	William G. Pine	1969	421
196 6/8	24 2/8	23 4/8	23 1/8	6 3/8	6 2/8	5	6	De Beque, CO	Walter C. Friauf	Walter C. Friauf	1970	421
196 6/8	26 1/8	26	22 2/8	5	5	5	5	San Juan Natl. For., CO	Wilford E. Seymour, Jr.	Wilford E. Seymour, Jr.	1974	421
196 6/8	25 4/8	24 4/8	26 1/8	5 1/8	4 6/8	5	5	Unknown	Picked Up	Curt M. Funk	1983	421
196 6/8	24	24 1/8	23 6/8	5 7/8	6 1/8	5	6	Coconino Co., AZ	James D. Wagner	James D. Wagner	1986	421
196 6/8	24 4/8	23 4/8	22 6/8	5 5/8	5 6/8	5	5	Kane Co., UT	Sam Jaksick, Jr.	Sam Jaksick, Jr.	1995	421
196 5/8	27 2/8	26 6/8	25 6/8	6	6	6	6	Chelan Co., WA	George Bolton	Welcome Sauer	1930	430
196 5/8	26	26 6/8	24 1/8	4 4/8	4 6/8	5	5	Slater, CO	W.J. Bracken	W.J. Bracken	1959	430
196 5/8	26 2/8	26 7/8	23 3/8	6 5/8	5 3/8	8	8	Moffat Co., CO	Tran Canton	Tran Canton	1960	430
196 5/8	26	25 7/8	22 6/8	4 4/8	4 6/8	6	5	Dubois, WY	P.C. Alfred Dorow	P.C. Alfred Dorow	1960	430
196 5/8	27 6/8	24 2/8	22 5/8	5 4/8	5 4/8	5	5	Grand Mesa, CO	Marvin L. Shepard	Marvin L. Shepard	1960	430
196 5/8	26 5/8	26 4/8	27 2/8	4 7/8	4 7/8	6	6	Mesa Co., CO	Bill Styers	Bill Styers	1964	430
196 5/8	25 6/8	25 5/8	24 2/8	5	4 7/8	7	7	Summit Co., UT	Jerry L. Henriod	Jerry L. Henriod	1967	430
196 5/8	22	22 6/8	21 5/8	5	5 1/8	7	6	Lemhi Co., ID	Hubert M. Livingston	Hubert M. Livingston	1967	430
196 5/8	24 7/8	25	23 5/8	4 4/8	4 5/8	5	5	Maybell, CO	James W. Johnson	James W. Johnson	1968	430
196 5/8	23 7/8	24	22 5/8	4 6/8	4 7/8	5	5	Lincoln Co., WY	Chester P. Michalski	Chester P. Michalski	1974	430
196 5/8	26 7/8	26 7/8	24 5/8	5 3/8	5 3/8	6	6	Eureka Co., NV	Michael G. Miller	Michael G. Miller	1995	430
196 5/8	26	25 6/8	21 3/8	4 7/8	4 7/8	5	5	Teton Co., ID	J. Scott Shipton	J. Scott Shipton	1995	430
196 5/8	27 3/8	27 6/8	24	5 4/8	5 1/8	7	7	Rio Arriba Co., NM	Picked Up	Elliot L. Vigil	1996	430
196 4/8	25	24 5/8	28 4/8	4 4/8	4 4/8	6	5	McKenzie Co., ND	Roy Mitten, Sr.	Roy Mitten, Jr.	1937	443
196 4/8	26 3/8	27 5/8	27 5/8	5	4 7/8	5	6	Missouri River, ND	Unknown	Robert L. Klisares	PR 1958	443
196 4/8	24 5/8	25 5/8	25 1/8	5 2/8	5 1/8	7	5	Flathead River, MT	Stanley Rauscher	Stanley Rauscher	1959	443
196 4/8	23 2/8	22 6/8	19 6/8	5 1/8	5	5	5	Garfield Co., CO	Elmer Nelson	Elmer Nelson	1962	443
196 4/8	24 2/8	25 1/8	21	6 1/8	6 1/8	5	5	Vernal, UT	Selby G. Tanner	Selby G. Tanner	1966	443
196 4/8	22 1/8	22 2/8	23 5/8	5 3/8	5 4/8	5	6	Summit Co., CO	Steve Orecchio	Steve Orecchio	1967	443
196 4/8	26 2/8	26 1/8	25 2/8	5 2/8	5 6/8	6	5	Morgan Co., UT	Elwood Williams	Elwood Williams	1968	443
196 4/8	25 3/8	24 5/8	23	5 5/8	5 7/8	5	5	Southern Ute Res., CO	William C. Forsyth	William C. Forsyth	1974	443
196 4/8	23 5/8	23 5/8	23	5 2/8	5 2/8	5	5	Powell Co., MT	Raymond A. Fitzgerald	Raymond A. Fitzgerald	1983	443

Score	Main Beam R	Main Beam L	Inside Spread	Circ.	Circ.	Circ.	Pts. R	Pts. L	Locality	Hunter	Owner	Date	Rank
196 4/8	27 5/8	26 2/8	24 7/8	5 4/8	5 4/8	5 4/8	7	4	Bonneville Co., ID	Michael Pinkham	Michael Pinkham	1985	443
196 4/8	25 1/8	26 6/8	25 7/8	5 2/8	5 2/8	5 2/8	5	7	Wasco Co., OR	Steven W. Forman	Steven W. Forman	1986	443
196 4/8	24	25 1/8	24 4/8	4 5/8	4 5/8	4 5/8	5	7	Teton Co., WY	John C. Branca III	John C. Branca III	1991	443
196 4/8	23 2/8	25 4/8	25	5	5	5	5	5	Oneida Co., ID	Russell P. Roe	Russell P. Roe	1996	443
196 3/8	24 4/8	25 1/8	24 6/8	5 3/8	5 3/8	5 3/8	5	6	Powell Co., MT	Stanley F. Malcolm	Stanley F. Malcolm	1958	456
196 3/8	24 4/8	26	26 4/8	5 2/8	5 2/8	5 2/8	4	5	Durango, CO	Ronald Chitwood	Ronald Chitwood	1964	456
196 3/8	28 1/8	28 1/8	26 1/8	5	5	5	5	5	Uncompahgre Plateau, CO	Earl L. Markley	Earl L. Markley	1969	456
196 3/8	26 3/8	27 1/8	25 1/8	5 4/8	5 6/8	5 4/8	6	6	Sublette Co., WY	S. Kim Bonnett	S. Kim Bonnett	1978	456
196 3/8	28 3/8	28 4/8	23 5/8	5 3/8	5 3/8	5 3/8	5	7	Beaver Co., UT	Dawson Barnes	Dawson Barnes	1992	461
196 2/8	27 4/8	27 1/8	25 1/8	5 1/8	5 1/8	5 1/8	5	7	Lincoln Co., MT	Tommy Boothman	Tommy Boothman	1960	461
196 2/8	27 1/8	27 3/8	25 1/8	5 4/8	5 4/8	5 4/8	6	5	Sweetwater Co., WY	Donald H. Pabst	Donald H. Pabst	1962	461
196 2/8	25 4/8	25 4/8	23 6/8	5 3/8	5 3/8	5 3/8	6	5	Ravalli Co., MT	Gary Godfrey	Calvin D. Kluth	1965	461
196 2/8	22 5/8	22 5/8	22 5/8	5 3/8	5 3/8	5 3/8	7	6	Millard Co., UT	Burnell Washburn	Burnell Washburn	1967	461
196 2/8	23 7/8	23 7/8	26 1/8	6	6	6	6	5	Chama, NM	Laura Wilson	Laura Wilson	1967	461
196 2/8	23 4/8	24	25	4 5/8	4 5/8	4 5/8	5	5	Big Horn Mts., WY	Ruth Davis	Ruth Davis	1968	461
196 2/8	20 6/8	26	26 4/8	5 4/8	5 4/8	5 4/8	5	5	Dawes Co., NE	Terry L. Sandstrom	Terry L. Sandstrom	1969	461
196 2/8	26	27 1/8	27 1/8	5 4/8	5 4/8	5 4/8	9	7	Rio Arriba Co., NM	B.D. Shipwash	B.D. Shipwash	1970	461
196 2/8	24 7/8	23 7/8	25 7/8	5 4/8	5 4/8	5 4/8	6	6	Idaho	Unknown	D.J. Hollinger & B. Howard PR	1971	461
196 2/8	25 4/8	27 2/8	27 3/8	5 2/8	5 6/8	5 6/8	8	5	Meeker, CO	Mike Murphy	Mike Murphy	1972	461
196 2/8	20 6/8	22 4/8	25 6/8	5 3/8	5 2/8	5 2/8	6	6	Bingham Co., ID	Thomas D. Robison	Thomas D. Robison	1972	461
196 2/8	22 4/8	25 4/8	25 4/8	5 1/8	5	5	5	5	Meeker, CO	Max R. Zoeller	Max R. Zoeller	1986	475
196 2/8	25 5/8	25 4/8	27 5/8	5	5	5	5	5	Baker Co., OR	Vivian M. Zikmund	Vivian M. Zikmund	1989	475
196 2/8	26	27 1/8	26	5 3/8	5 4/8	5 4/8	6	6	San Juan Co., UT	John Rowley	John Rowley	1960	475
196 1/8	28 4/8	26	27 3/8	6 1/8	6	6	7	7	Jicarilla Apache Res., NM	Tim Vicenti	Tim Vicenti	1960	475
196 1/8	22 3/8	27 7/8	27 7/8	5 1/8	5 1/8	5 1/8	6	6	Chama, NM	Jerry Washburn	Jerry Washburn	1966	475
196 1/8	27	26	27	5 7/8	5 7/8	5 7/8	9	7	Boise Co., ID	H.L. Rice	H.L. Rice	1968	480
196 1/8	24 4/8	25 2/8	24 4/8	5 4/8	5 3/8	5 4/8	7	5	Uncompahgre Natl. For., CO	Harry L. Whitlock	Harry L. Whitlock	1981	480
196 1/8	23 5/8	25 5/8	23 5/8	4 7/8	4 6/8	4 7/8	4	4	Eagle Co., CO	Jeffery D. Harrison	Jeffery D. Harrison		480
196	25 3/8	26 6/8	25 3/8	5 2/8	5 3/8	5 2/8	5	7	Kaibab Natl. For., AZ	Graves Peeler	John E. Conner Museum PR	1930	480
196	23 3/8	26	23 3/8	5 1/8	5	5 3/8	7	5	North Kaibab, AZ	John D. McNeley	John D. McNeley	1948	480
196	22 4/8	24 1/8	22 4/8	5 6/8	5	5 1/8	5	5	Kaibab Natl. For., AZ	Elgin T. Gates	Elgin T. Gates	1958	480
196	27 2/8	27 4/8	27 6/8	5 6/8	5 6/8	5 6/8	5	6	Huerfano Co., CO	Frank C. Hibben	Frank C. Hibben	1963	480
196	25 1/8	25 1/8	27 1/8	5 3/8	5 3/8	5 4/8	5	6	Delta, CO	Alvin T. Stivers	Alvin T. Stivers	1965	480
196	24	24 4/8	25	5	5	5	8	8	Corwin Springs, MT	Donald Strazzabosco	Donald Strazzabosco	1966	480
196	29 2/8	29 2/8	24 4/8	5	5	5	5	5	Jicarilla Apache Res., NM	Collins F. Kellogg	Collins F. Kellogg	1973	480
196	23	28	25 4/8	5 6/8	5 5/8	5 5/8	6	6	Franklin Co., ID	Larry W. Cross	Larry W. Cross	1974	480
196	25 6/8	25 1/8	25 1/8	6	5 7/8	5 7/8	5	5	Ferry Co., WA	Owen R. Burgess	Owen R. Burgess	1982	491
196	29 1/8	26 4/8	28 2/8	5 3/8	5 2/8	5 2/8	5	5	Elko Co., NV	Johnny W. Filippini	Johnny W. Filippini	1991	491
195 7/8	22	26 2/8	25 4/8	4 7/8	4 7/8	4 7/8	6	5	Fremont Co., WY	Peter R. Ardlen	Peter R. Ardlen	1992	491
195 7/8	26 4/8	27 6/8	25 7/8	4 6/8	4 6/8	4 6/8	7	6	Lassen Co., CA	Sulo E. Lakso	Tracy A. Jenkins	1943	491
195 7/8	27 6/8	26 4/8	26 6/8	5 3/8	5 3/8	5 3/8	5	6	Rio Blanco Co., CO	Randy Kruse	Randy Kruse	1951	491
195 7/8	26 2/8	25 7/8	26 5/8	5 6/8	5 6/8	5 6/8	7	7	Bannock Co., ID	William J. Barry	William J. Barry	1956	491
195 7/8	26 6/8	26 7/8	26 5/8	5 4/8	5 4/8	5 4/8	6	6	Southern Ute Res., CO	Richard Schmidt	Southern Ute Tribe	1960	491
195 7/8	28 5/8	28	26 5/8	5 5/8	5 5/8	5 5/8	8	6	Cache Co., UT	Richard E. Reeder	Richard E. Reeder	1968	491
195 7/8	27 4/8	26 5/8	24 7/8	5 5/8	5 5/8	5 5/8	5	5	San Miguel Co., CO	Jerry E. Albin	Jerry E. Albin	1972	491
195 7/8	27	28 4/8	27	5 3/8	5 3/8	5 3/8	7	7	Franklin Co., ID	Melvin S. Thomson	Melvin S. Thomson	1987	491
195 7/8	28	27 6/8	24 3/8	4 6/8	4 6/8	4 6/8	5	5	Teton Co., WY	Lewis E. Sharp	Lewis E. Sharp	1990	491

MULE DEER - TYPICAL ANTLERS

Odocoileus hemionus hemionus and certain related subspecies

Score	Length of Main Beam R	L	Inside Spread	Circumference at Smallest Place Between Burr and First Point R	L	Number of Points R	L	Locality	Hunter	Owner	Date Killed	Rank
195 7/8	28	28	26 1/8	5 4/8	5 5/8	5	4	Rio Arriba Co., NM	Arlene Perea	Arlene Perea	1991	491
195 7/8	25 2/8	23 5/8	19 1/8	5 5/8	5 3/8	5	5	Teton Co., WY	Douglas L. Wynn	Douglas L. Wynn	1994	491
195 7/8	24	24 7/8	24 7/8	4 5/8	4 4/8	6	5	Teton Co., WY	Frank E. Baldwin	Frank E. Baldwin	1995	491
195 6/8	27 3/8	28 2/8	26 3/8	5 4/8	5 5/8	7	6	Custer Co., ID	Sylvester Potaman	W. Douglas Lightfoot	1900	502
195 6/8	25 3/8	25 2/8	23 4/8	5 1/8	5	5	5	Jefferson Co., CO	Lloyd O. Rauchfuss	Lloyd O. Rauchfuss	1947	502
195 6/8	26 5/8	26 6/8	28 2/8	5 1/8	5 1/8	6	6	Eagle Co., CO	Orlo E. Park	Orlo E. Park	1954	502
195 6/8	27	23 7/8	24 2/8	5 2/8	5 1/8	5	6	Huerfano Co., CO	Mike Disert	Janet D. Wasson	1954	502
195 6/8	27 4/8	29	26 2/8	5 5/8	5 4/8	7	9	Keating, OR	Al Delepierre	Francis A. Delepierre	1966	502
195 6/8	25 4/8	26 4/8	24 6/8	4 6/8	4 6/8	5	5	Gunnison, CO	Randall R. Kieft	Randall R. Kieft	1967	502
195 6/8	28 7/8	28 4/8	28 4/8	5 1/8	5 3/8	5	5	Grant Co., OR	Larry Parlette	Larry Parlette	1967	502
195 6/8	24 6/8	25 2/8	22 6/8	5	5	5	7	Montrose Co., CO	Larry D. Bitta	Larry D. Bitta	1969	502
195 6/8	22 7/8	24 6/8	23 5/8	5 3/8	5 2/8	6	6	Gunnison Co., CO	George L. Hoffman, Jr.	George L. Hoffman, Jr.	1972	502
195 6/8	25 3/8	24 3/8	24 6/8	4 5/8	4 5/8	5	5	Teton Co., WY	Joel M. Leatham	Joel M. Leatham	1979	502
195 6/8	26	28	33	5 5/8	5 4/8	5	5	Grant Co., OR	Gordon E. Mitchell	Gordon E. Mitchell	1982	502
195 6/8	25 6/8	25 3/8	24 1/8	6 2/8	6 2/8	6	6	Eagle Co., CO	James B. Mesecke	James B. Mesecke	1985	502
195 6/8	24 5/8	26 1/8	24	5 1/8	5 1/8	5	5	Caribou Co., ID	John B. Kochever	John B. Kochever	1986	502
195 6/8	27	27	27 7/8	5 3/8	5 3/8	5	5	Kiskatinaw River, BC	Tim Roberts	Tim Roberts	1994	502
195 6/8	26 6/8	26 6/8	23	4 2/8	4 3/8	5	6	Potter Co., TX	Mickey G. VanHuss	Mickey G. VanHuss	1996	502
195 5/8	26 6/8	27 1/8	26 1/8	4 7/8	4 6/8	5	5	Ravalli Co., MT	William H. Cowan	William H. Cowan	1959	517
195 5/8	27 4/8	27 6/8	24 1/8	6	5 7/8	7	7	Slocan Valley, BC	John Braun	John Braun	1962	517
195 5/8	30 5/8	29	26 4/8	6 2/8	6 2/8	6	8	Jicarilla Apache Res., NM	Eldrid Vigil	Eldrid Vigil	1962	517
195 5/8	28 3/8	27	34 7/8	5	4 7/8	6	6	Idaho	Wayne Urdahl	Don Schaufler	PR 1964	517
195 5/8	25 1/8	25 4/8	21 3/8	4 6/8	4 4/8	5	4	Pitkin Co., CO	William F. Kirby	William F. Kirby	1966	517
195 5/8	27 5/8	25 3/8	20 5/8	4 7/8	4 6/8	5	5	Delta Co., CO	Royce J. Carville	Royce J. Carville	1974	517
195 5/8	25 3/8	25 4/8	21 3/8	5 2/8	5	5	5	Grand Co., CO	C. Jay Stout	C. Jay Stout	1981	517
195 5/8	26 1/8	26 1/8	24	5	5	6	6	Washington Co., UT	Scott M. Bulloch	Scott M. Bulloch	1985	517
195 5/8	26 5/8	27	24 3/8	5 2/8	5 2/8	9	5	Archuleta Co., CO	Matthew J. Arkins	Matthew J. Arkins	1986	517
195 5/8	24 7/8	24 4/8	22 3/8	5 4/8	5 4/8	5	5	Cibola Co., NM	Picked Up	Craig C. Sanchez	1988	517
195 5/8	25 3/8	25 3/8	26 3/8	5 3/8	5 5/8	5	5	Huerfano Co., CO	Hub R. Grounds	Hub R. Grounds	1989	517
195 5/8	25 6/8	25 7/8	26 2/8	5 4/8	5 2/8	5	5	Mesa Co., CO	John F. Stewart	John F. Stewart	1989	517
195 4/8	26 4/8	26 4/8	24 2/8	5 3/8	5 2/8	5	5	Princeton, BC	Glen Stadler	Glen Stadler	1958	529
195 4/8	25 1/8	25 4/8	22 6/8	5 1/8	5 2/8	5	5	Grover, UT	Vicki Davis	R.J. Davis	1959	529
195 4/8	26 3/8	25 1/8	26 2/8	5 3/8	5 2/8	5	5	Raton, NM	Unknown	John H. Steinle III	1963	529
195 4/8	24 2/8	24 7/8	24 2/8	5 2/8	5 2/8	7	6	Garfield Co., CO	Billy R. Babb	Billy R. Babb	1969	529
195 4/8	24 2/8	25	20 4/8	5 6/8	5 7/8	5	5	Montrose, CO	Tony L. Hill	Tony L. Hill	1969	529
195 4/8	25 2/8	27 1/8	22 7/8	5 6/8	5 4/8	6	6	Flathead Co., MT	Sharon M. Gaughan	B&C National Collection	1980	529

Score	Length of Main Beam R	Length of Main Beam L	Inside Spread	Greatest Spread	Circumference R	Circumference L	Points R	Points L	Locality	Hunter	Owner	Date Killed	Rank
195 4/8	26 3/8	26 5/8	25 2/8	26 5/8	5 6/8	5 5/8	5	5	Sanders Co., MT	William B. Hart	William B. Hart	1984	529
195 4/8	26	26 1/8	25 4/8	26	5	5	5	6	Bear Lake Co., ID	Joseph R. Given	Joseph R. Given	1985	529
195 3/8	25 4/8	24 2/8	24 5/8	25	5 2/8	5	5	4	Rio Arriba Co., NM	Robert W. Highfill	Robert W. Highfill	1964	537
195 3/8	28 4/8	28 4/8	25 5/8	28 4/8	5 2/8	5 2/8	5	7	Mohave Co., AZ	Bob B. Coker	Bob B. Coker	1972	537
195 3/8	27 5/8	27 5/8	30 7/8	27 5/8	4 4/8	4 3/8	5	5	Niobrara Co., WY	Unknown	Barry Dampman	1975	537
195 3/8	27 3/8	26 7/8	26 5/8	27 3/8	4 6/8	4 6/8	5	5	Natrona Co., WY	Richard Ullery	Richard Ullery	1977	537
195 3/8	26 4/8	25 7/8	26 3/8	26 4/8	5 2/8	5 1/8	6	5	Moffat Co., CO	Frank J. Kubin	Frank J. Kubin	1978	537
195 3/8	26 3/8	26	26 1/8	26 3/8	4 6/8	4 6/8	6	5	Frontier Co., NE	Brent S. Klein	Brent S. Klein	1984	537
195 3/8	25	25 2/8	25 1/8	25	4 4/8	4 4/8	5	5	Wallowa Co., OR	Michael R. Shirley	Michael R. Shirley	1986	537
195 3/8	25	25 5/8	25 5/8	25	5 2/8	5 3/8	5	5	Garfield Co., UT	John E. Braithwaite	John E. Braithwaite	1987	537
195 3/8	28 4/8	28 4/8	28 6/8	28 4/8	5 5/8	5 4/8	6	5	Apache Co., AZ	William D. Beck	William D. Beck	1991	537
195 3/8	29 1/8	27 7/8	25 7/8	27 3/8	5 3/8	4 6/8	6	5	Gunnison Co., CO	Herman F. Tomky	Russell J. Tomky	1937	537
195 2/8	24 4/8	24 3/8	24 6/8	24 5/8	4 6/8	4 5/8	6	5	Moffat Co., CO	Orville R. Meineke	Craig Sports	1964	546
195 2/8	26 4/8	26 4/8	27	27 1/8	5 7/8	5 7/8	5	5	Lewis & Clark Co., MT	Edward A. Ipser	Edward A. Ipser	1965	546
195 2/8	27 1/8	26 1/8	27	25 1/8	5 2/8	5 1/8	6	6	Marble, CO	Donald E. Alfson	Donald E. Alfson	1966	546
195 2/8	26 4/8	26 4/8	25 7/8	25 1/8	5 1/8	5 1/8	7	5	Davis Co., UT	David R. Allen	David R. Allen	1968	546
195 2/8	25	25	24 4/8	24 4/8	5 7/8	5 7/8	5	5	Davis Co., UT	Mitchell L. Cochran	Mitchell L. Cochran	1972	546
195 2/8	28 5/8	28 1/8	29	29 7/8	5 7/8	5 5/8	5	5	Niobrara Co., WY	David E. Pauna	David E. Pauna	1976	546
195 2/8	26 4/8	25 5/8	26 4/8	25 5/8	4 2/8	4 2/8	5	5	Antelope Lake, SK	Doug Westergaard	Doug Westergaard	1977	546
195 2/8	23 3/8	24 6/8	21 4/8	24 6/8	5 1/8	5 1/8	5	5	Sublette Co., WY	John R. Birchett	John R. Birchett	1981	546
195 2/8	24 4/8	24 4/8	23 4/8	25	5 2/8	5	5	5	Twin Falls Co., ID	Alvin Tollini	Alvin Tollini	1990	546
195 2/8	26 4/8	26 4/8	25 1/8	24 6/8	4 6/8	4 6/8	7	6	Nez Perce Co., ID	Patrick G. Sinclair	Patrick G. Sinclair	1991	546
195 2/8	28 1/8	27 7/8	24 2/8	24 3/8	4 2/8	4 2/8	4	4	Crook Co., OR	Leah D. Robertson	Leah D. Robertson	1995	546
195 2/8	27 6/8	25 2/8	22	22	4 6/8	4 4/8	5	5	Rio Arriba Co., NM	Robert J. Seeds	Robert J. Seeds	1995	546
195 1/8	25 2/8	25	22 1/8	25 2/8	5 1/8	5 1/8	5	5	Elko Co., NV	Donald G. Heidtman	Donald G. Heidtman	1954	559
195 1/8	25 2/8	24 3/8	22 2/8	24 4/8	5 2/8	5 6/8	5	6	Utah	Unknown	Jarvie Taxidermy	1959	559
195 1/8	24 3/8	24 2/8	24 1/8	24 2/8	5 5/8	5 5/8	6	6	Rio Arriba Co., NM	Eddie W. Brieno, Jr.	Eddie W. Brieno, Jr.	1965	559
195 1/8	26 1/8	26 3/8	24 1/8	24 1/8	5 7/8	5 7/8	6	5	Montrose Co., CO	Eldon L. Webb	Eldon L. Webb	1965	559
195 1/8	27	29 5/8	29 1/8	29 5/8	6	6	5	5	Fruitvale, BC	Allan Endersby	Allan Endersby	1968	559
195 1/8	25	25	22 4/8	22 4/8	4 7/8	5	5	5	Idaho Co., ID	Gary BeVan	Gary BeVan	1970	559
195 1/8	26 5/8	26 1/8	24 7/8	24 7/8	5 1/8	4 7/8	6	7	Coconino Co., AZ	Gary R. Clark	Gary R. Clark	1972	559
195 1/8	27 3/8	28 2/8	27 1/8	27 1/8	5 5/8	5 5/8	5	5	Kane Co., UT	Cecil Hunt	Cecil Hunt	1987	559
195	26 1/8	26 1/8	26 1/8	26 1/8	5	5	6	5	Rio Arriba Co., NM	David Shadrick	David Shadrick	1988	568
195	27 4/8	27 4/8	21 4/8	27 4/8	4 4/8	5 1/8	5	6	Powder River Co., MT	Roy Dahlby	Michael R. Dahlby	1963	568
195	27	25 6/8	28 1/8	25 7/8	5 7/8	5 7/8	6	6	Elko Co., NV	Steve Beneto, Sr.	Steve Beneto, Sr.	1966	568
195	27 1/8	26 1/8	22 4/8	22 4/8	5 6/8	5 6/8	5	5	Sun River, MT	Dick Lyman	Dick Lyman	1966	568
195	25 1/8	25 1/8	25	24 7/8	4 7/8	4 4/8	5	6	Rio Arriba Co., NM	Pat Wilson	John Lind, Jr.	1967	568
195	25 2/8	25 2/8	22 2/8	24 6/8	4 5/8	4 6/8	5	6	Beaver Co., UT	Unknown	Mark R. Dotson	1969	568
195	25 6/8	25 6/8	23 4/8	25 7/8	5 7/8	5 7/8	5	6	Mesa Co., CO	Paul Roddam, Jr.	Paul Roddam, Jr.	1969	568
195	26	25 5/8	22 3/8	25 5/8	5	5	7	6	Larimer Co., CO	Michael D. Blehm	Michael D. Blehm	1972	568
195	24 2/8	24 6/8	22 4/8	24 4/8	6 1/8	6 2/8	5	6	Sublette Co., WY	Norm Busselle	Norm Busselle	1977	568
195	24 6/8	24 7/8	22 4/8	24 6/8	5 1/8	5	5	6	Rio Blanco Co., CO	Gene Lawrence	Gene Lawrence	1977	568
195	27 1/8	26 5/8	27 1/8	27 1/8	5 2/8	5 3/8	5	6	Carbon Co., UT	Thomas E. Wilson	Thomas E. Wilson	1988	568
195	24	24 6/8	28	26 5/8	5 1/8	5 1/8	7	5	Rio Arriba Co., NM	Donald G. Sams	Donald G. Sams	1992	568
194 7/8	26 4/8	26 6/8	21 3/8	26 6/8	5 3/8	5 3/8	5	5	Blaine Co., ID	Elliot K. Vigil	Elliot K. Vigil	1997	579
194 6/8	25 4/8	24 6/8	23 1/8	24 6/8	4 3/8	4 3/8	6	6	Rio Arriba Co., NM	Unknown	Jarvie Taxidermy	1947	580
194 6/8	28	27 5/8	26 7/8	27 5/8	4 7/8	4 5/8	6	8	Grand Co., UT	Richard V. Beesley	Richard V. Beesley	1986	580

MULE DEER - TYPICAL ANTLERS

Odocoileus hemionus hemionus and certain related subspecies

Score	Length of Main Beam R	L	Inside Spread	Circumference at Smallest Place Between Burr and First Point R	L	Number of Points R	L	Locality	Hunter	Owner	Date Killed	Rank
194 5/8	28 3/8	28 3/8	26 6/8	5 5/8	5 5/8	6	7	Duchesne Co., UT	Kate Hamilton	Raymond R. Cross	1948	582
194 5/8	25 7/8	25 4/8	25 1/8	4 6/8	5 2/8	5	5	Weber River, UT	Desmond Shields	Desmond Shields	1960	582
194 5/8	24 7/8	25 2/8	21 3/8	4 5/8	4 5/8	6	6	Cabri Lake, SK	Dean R. Francis	Dean R. Francis	1991	582
194 5/8	26	28 2/8	25 7/8	5 4/8	5 4/8	7	5	Adams Co., CO	Daniel L. Kraft	Daniel L. Kraft	1995	582
194 5/8	27 5/8	28	24 4/8	4 6/8	4 5/8	6	7	Rio Arriba Co., NM	Patrick Notsinneh	Patrick Notsinneh	1995	582
194 4/8	25 6/8	25 2/8	23 2/8	5	5 1/8	5	5	Eagle Co., CO	William E. Pipes III	William E. Pipes III	1984	587
194 2/8	26	24 4/8	27 4/8	4 6/8	4 7/8	5	5	Grant Co., OR	Richard W. Erickson	Richard W. Erickson	1994	588
194 1/8	25 7/8	25	23 6/8	4 6/8	4 6/8	6	6	Hanksville, UT	Ernie Shirley	Ray Epps	1950	589
194 1/8	26	25 4/8	21	5	5	6	5	Delta Co., CO	Bill Rainer	Bill Rainer	1977	589
194 1/8	25 2/8	25	21 4/8	5	4 7/8	5	5	Petroleum Co., MT	Christopher G. Basham	Christopher G. Basham	1994	589
194	25 1/8	25 4/8	27 4/8	5 4/8	5 4/8	5	5	Rio Arriba Co., NM	C.J. McElroy	C.J. McElroy	1970	592
194	23 3/8	25 1/8	22 4/8	4 6/8	4 7/8	5	5	Sublette Co., WY	James J. McBride	James J. McBride	1979	592
193 6/8	27 6/8	27 2/8	29 4/8	5 5/8	5 3/8	4	5	Cimarron, CO	Reynolds L. Vanstrom	Reynolds L. Vanstrom	1960	594
193 6/8	25	26 2/8	22	4 4/8	4 5/8	6	5	Smoky River, AB	Jeffrey S. Reichert	Jeffrey S. Reichert	1989	594
193 6/8	26	26 6/8	27 1/8	4 2/8	4 1/8	6	5	Lander Co., NV	Picked Up	John W. Filippini	1992	594
193 5/8	27	25 3/8	26 1/8	5 4/8	5 5/8	5	5	Rio Arriba Co., NM	David W. DeMello	David W. DeMello	1994	597
193 5/8	23 3/8	23 2/8	23 6/8	5 4/8	5 4/8	6	5	Eagle Co., CO	William E. Pipes III	William E. Pipes III	1995	597
193 4/8	27 1/8	26 7/8	24 4/8	5 4/8	5 5/8	6	6	Garfield Co., CO	Marvin A. Meyers	Marvin A. Meyers	1982	599
193 4/8	23 7/8	25	25 1/8	5	4 7/8	5	5	Gem Co., ID	David W. Bowman	David W. Bowman	1995	599
193 4/8	25 3/8	25 6/8	23	5 4/8	5 7/8	5	6	Sonora, MX	Gregory F. Lucero	Gregory F. Lucero	1996	599
193 3/8	26 7/8	27 2/8	23 3/8	4 7/8	4 7/8	5	5	Washoe Co., NV	Barbara M. Conley	Barbara M. Conley	1987	602
193 3/8	25 3/8	24 2/8	22 6/8	5	5	6	5	Rio Arriba Co., NM	Edward C. Joseph	Edward C. Joseph	1995	602
193 3/8	28 2/8	28	24 7/8	5 1/8	5 1/8	6	5	Baker Co., OR	Anthony A. Myers	Anthony A. Myers	1996	602
193 2/8	26	26 7/8	25 2/8	6 1/8	6 1/8	5	6	Gunnison Co., CO	Bill Morrow	Nancy Morrow	1960	605
193 2/8	23 6/8	24	22 2/8	5 2/8	5 4/8	6	6	Franklin Co., ID	L. Munk & T. Braegger	Larry Munk	1990	605
193	26 7/8	24 1/8	23	5 4/8	5 4/8	5	5	Malheur Co., OR	LeRoy Zollo	Nick Spiropolos	1978	607
193	27 4/8	27 7/8	24 6/8	4 6/8	4 6/8	5	5	Owyhee Co., ID	Bob Lambert	Jerome E. Arledge	PR 1980	607
193	25 2/8	27 6/8	29	5 4/8	5 5/8	7	6	Kane Co., UT	Unknown	D.J. Hollinger & B. Howard	PR 1983	607
193	25 5/8	23 7/8	21 4/8	5 1/8	5	5	5	Gem Co., ID	Blaine L. Hyde	Blaine L. Hyde	1995	607
192 7/8	25 1/8	26	20 3/8	4 6/8	5	6	5	Colorado	Unknown	Unknown	1953	611
192 7/8	23 1/8	25 6/8	24 5/8	5	5	6	5	Swan Lake, BC	Jurgen Schulz	Jurgen Schulz	1995	611
192 6/8	26	25 6/8	21 2/8	5 4/8	5 5/8	6	5	Gunnison Co., CO	Stephen A. Mahurin	Stephen A. Mahurin	1968	613
192 6/8	27 1/8	27 1/8	28 3/8	5 4/8	5 4/8	5	6	Lincoln Co., WY	William D. Tate	William D. Tate	1981	613
192 6/8	26 2/8	26 6/8	24 2/8	5	5 1/8	5	5	Kane Co., UT	Steven A. Wilson	Steven A. Wilson	1991	613
192 5/8	25	24 1/8	20 6/8	5 1/8	5 1/8	5	6	Park Co., WY	LaVerne M. Nelson	LaVerne M. Nelson	1992	616
192 5/8	23 6/8	24 3/8	21 3/8	4 4/8	4 6/8	5	5	Unknown	Unknown	Jerome E. Arledge	PR 1993	616

Score	Main Beam R	Main Beam L	Inside Spread	Circ. R	Circ. L	Pts. R	Pts. L	Locality	By Whom Killed	Owner	Date	Rank
192 5/8	27 1/8	25 6/8	23	5 6/8	5 7/8	7	6	Montana	Unknown	James B. Sisco III	PR 1995	616
192 4/8	24 4/8	25	20 1/8	5	5	5	6	Bear Lake Co., ID	Lee Bridges	Lee Bridges	1967	619
192 4/8	28 2/8	26 3/8	27	6 1/8	6 2/8	5	5	Rio Arriba Co., NM	Charles Tapia	Charles Tapia	1993	619
192 4/8	29	27 7/8	28	6	6	4	5	Grant Co., OR	Don Messenger	Don Messenger	1994	619
192 3/8	24 7/8	24 7/8	24 1/8	5 2/8	5 4/8	5	5	Platte Co., WY	Robby McAllister	Robby McAllister	1992	622
192 3/8	26 3/8	26 6/8	25 5/8	5 1/8	5 3/8	5	5	Williams Lake, BC	Evan D. Howarth	Evan D. Howarth	1994	622
192 3/8	24 6/8	25 5/8	23 3/8	5 1/8	5 1/8	5	5	Powder River Co., MT	Eric A. DeVuyst	Eric A. DeVuyst	1995	622
192 2/8	26 4/8	27 3/8	22 6/8	6 3/8	5 1/8	7	6	Eagle Co., CO	Ronald L. McCall	Ronald L. McCall	1996	625
192 1/8	25 4/8	25 2/8	23 3/8	4 7/8	4 7/8	7	8	Bonneville Co., ID	Glen M. Brown	Glen M. Brown	1949	626
192 1/8	25 4/8	26 1/8	26 1/8	5 2/8	5 1/8	7	7	Duchesne Co., UT	Dennis F. Mower	Dennis F. Mower	1969	626
192 1/8	28 4/8	27 4/8	28 7/8	6	5 5/8	7	6	Malheur Co., OR	William T. Monson	William T. Monson	1995	626
192	26 4/8	25 7/8	27 7/8	5 3/8	5 3/8	5	5	Delta Co., CO	James W. Arellano	James W. Arellano	1977	629
192	23 3/8	24 6/8	22 4/8	5	5	5	5	Larimer Co., CO	Picked Up	John R. Steffes, Sr.	PR 1990	629
192	26 6/8	26 2/8	25 6/8	5	4 7/8	5	5	Teton Co., WY	Steven G. Coy	Steven G. Coy	1992	629
192	25 5/8	25 4/8	20 4/8	4 3/8	4 3/8	5	5	Park Co., WY	Richard L. Kempka	Richard L. Kempka	1994	629
192	23 2/8	23	21 4/8	5 4/8	5 6/8	7	5	Wayne Co., UT	Ivan B. Henderson	Ivan B. Henderson	1996	629
192	25 1/8	26 3/8	24 1/8	5	5 4/8	6	5	Arapahoe Co., CO	Daniel K. Madajski	Daniel K. Madajski	1996	629
191 7/8	25 2/8	24 7/8	23 5/8	4 7/8	5	5	5	Carbondale River, AB	Michael Pearce	Michael Pearce	1992	635
191 7/8	26	26	27 3/8	5	5	5	5	Kane Co., UT	Scott S. Snyder	Scott S. Snyder	1995	635
191 6/8	25 2/8	25 4/8	25 2/8	4 7/8	4 4/8	5	6	Gooding Co., ID	Mark Moncrief	Mark E. Moncrief	1994	637
191 6/8	28 5/8	28	28	5 6/8	5 4/8	5	5	Rio Arriba Co., NM	Leroy TeCube	Leroy TeCube	1995	637
191 6/8	24 2/8	24 2/8	21	4 6/8	4 6/8	6	6	Kane Co., UT	James D. Delaney	James D. Delaney	1997	639
191 5/8	26 3/8	26 1/8	25 4/8	5 2/8	5	7	7	Coconino Co., AZ	Steven G. Mallory	Steven G. Mallory	1988	640
191 4/8	25 5/8	25 2/8	24 7/8	4 7/8	4 7/8	6	5	Grant Co., NM	Robin W. Bechtel	Robin W. Bechtel	1988	641
191 3/8	27 2/8	26 6/8	25 5/8	5 5/8	5 5/8	5	5	Rio Arriba Co., NM	Michael B. O'Banion	Michael B. O'Banion	1993	641
191 3/8	26 1/8	26 1/8	24 4/8	5 5/8	5 4/8	6	6	Forest Lake, BC	Gordon Simpson	Gordon Simpson	1994	641
191 2/8	25 7/8	25 4/8	24 6/8	5	5	5	5	Gunnison Co., CO	Tim Hays	Tim Hays	1981	644
191 2/8	24 5/8	24 6/8	24 5/8	4 6/8	4 4/8	5	5	Morrow Co., OR	Russell D. Britt	Russell D. Britt	1990	644
191 2/8	27 6/8	27 6/8	26	4 3/8	4 3/8	5	4	Idaho	Unknown	Jerome E. Arledge	PR 1992	644
191 2/8	25 2/8	25 2/8	22 2/8	5 5/8	5 5/8	5	5	Rio Arriba Co., NM	D. Boone Kuersteiner	D. Boone Kuersteiner	1994	644
191 2/8	24	24	22 4/8	4 5/8	4 5/8	4	4	Gem Co., ID	Troy A. Gaskell	Troy A. Gaskell	1994	644
191 1/8	24 3/8	24 1/8	24 3/8	5	5	5	5	Moffat Co., CO	Len E. Mayfield	Len E. Mayfield	1995	649
191 1/8	26 1/8	26 1/8	23 1/8	4 5/8	4 6/8	6	6	Rich Co., UT	Carl Nelson	Brian C. Nelson	1959	649
191 1/8	27 1/8	27 4/8	22 1/8	4 3/8	4 4/8	5	5	Washoe Co., NV	Jay Walker	Jay Walker	PR 1960	649
191 1/8	26 4/8	26 3/8	26 1/8	4 4/8	4 7/8	5	5	Grand Co., CO	Zane Palmer	Zane Palmer	1967	649
191 1/8	23 3/8	25 1/8	23 3/8	5 5/8	5 5/8	5	5	Uintah Co., UT	Robert B. Keel	Robert B. Keel	1981	649
191 1/8	26 5/8	24 6/8	24 6/8	5 1/8	5	5	4	Unita Co., WY	Daniel T. Begley	Daniel T. Begley	1986	649
191 1/8	28 2/8	28 1/8	26 3/8	5 7/8	5 7/8	6	6	Teton Co., WY	Buck Taylor	Buck Taylor	1995	649
191	26 4/8	26 4/8	27 3/8	5 2/8	5 2/8	6	6	Kane Co., UT	Edward B. Franceschi, Jr.	Edward B. Franceschi, Jr.	1969	655
191	25 4/8	25 1/8	25 1/8	4 6/8	4 5/8	5	6	Elmore Co., ID	Michael H. Felton	Michael H. Felton	1990	655
190 7/8	27 4/8	27 7/8	27	4 6/8	4 7/8	6	6	Unknown	Unknown	Don Schaufler	1980	657
190 7/8	24 4/8	24 6/8	24	5 2/8	5 2/8	8	8	Las Animas Co., CO	Robert D. Davidson	Robert D. Davidson	PR 1986	657
190 7/8	28	28	25 6/8	5 1/8	5 2/8	5	5	Fall River Co., SD	Art Thomsen	Art Thomsen	1995	657
190 6/8	27	26 1/8	20 4/8	4 6/8	4 6/8	5	5	Jackson Co., CO	Guy Amburgey	Guy Amburgey	1953	660
190 6/8	26	25 1/8	25 2/8	5 1/8	5 3/8	5	5	Granite Co., MT	Larry Peterman	Larry Peterman	1969	660
190 5/8	26 2/8	27 7/8	28 4/8	5 7/8	5 7/8	7	7	Archuleta Co., CO	Lansing Kothmann	Lansing Kothmann	1976	660
190 5/8	24 1/8	24 6/8	25	6 2/8	5 6/8	6	5	Douglas Co., CO	Harold A. Weippert	Harold A. Weippert	1958	663

235

MULE DEER - TYPICAL ANTLERS

Odocoileus hemionus hemionus and certain related subspecies

Score	Length of Main Beam R	L	Inside Spread	Circumference at Smallest Place Between Burr and First Point R	L	Number of Points R	L	Locality	Hunter	Owner	Date Killed	Rank
190 5/8	23 4/8	23 6/8	24	5	4 6/8	6	8	Boise Co., ID	Donald I. Mace	Donald I. Mace	1994	663
190 5/8	25 6/8	26 1/8	22 5/8	5	4 6/8	5	5	Las Animas Co., CO	Mark W. Streissguth	Mark W. Streissguth	1994	663
190 4/8	26	25 4/8	21 6/8	5 1/8	5 1/8	6	5	Garfield Co., CO	Donald M. Alburtus	Dennis J. DaSilva	1963	667
190 4/8	26 6/8	27 3/8	27	5 1/8	5 1/8	5	5	Garfield Co., CO	William D. Tate	William D. Tate	1978	667
190 4/8	25 1/8	25 4/8	26 4/8	5	4 6/8	5	5	Archuleta Co., CO	James M. Russell III	James M. Russell III	1985	667
190 3/8	24 7/8	25 3/8	26	4 4/8	4 4/8	5	5	Mesa, CO	Robert W. Hill	Robert W. Hill	1963	670
190 3/8	26	27 5/8	20 1/8	4 5/8	4 5/8	5	5	Lemhi Co., ID	Mac A. Hughes	Brad Sweeney	1978	670
190 3/8	25 1/8	26 3/8	26 3/8	5 4/8	5 5/8	7	6	Franklin Co., ID	Samuel L. Smith	Samuel L. Smith	1981	670
190 3/8	25 4/8	25 1/8	21 5/8	4 4/8	4 6/8	5	8	Lincoln Co., WY	Jerry A. McAllister	Jerry A. McAllister	1990	670
190 3/8	25 4/8	26 5/8	24 5/8	5	5 1/8	6	5	Yale, BC	Lewis B. Butcher	Lewis B. Butcher	1994	670
190 3/8	25 5/8	25 2/8	26 1/8	4 6/8	4 5/8	5	5	Deschutes Co., OR	Ronald J. Robinson, Jr.	Ronald J. Robinson, Jr.	1995	670
190 3/8	27 6/8	27 1/8	27 7/8	5 2/8	5 2/8	8	6	Delta Co., CO	Joe Alexander	Joe Alexander	1996	670
190 2/8	21 3/8	23 3/8	21 7/8	4 3/8	4 6/8	6	5	Boise Co., ID	Rickey D. Addison	Rickey D. Addison	1984	677
190 2/8	25 2/8	25 1/8	23	5	4 7/8	5	5	Rich Co., UT	Troy Howard	Troy Howard	1992	677
190 2/8	24 4/8	23 6/8	21	4 6/8	4 5/8	5	7	Sounding Lake, AB	Brian J. Rehman	Brian J. Rehman	1992	677
190 2/8	22 6/8	23 2/8	24 3/8	4 6/8	4 6/8	5	5	Butte Co., ID	Keith G. Palmer	Keith G. Palmer	1995	677
190 2/8	22 4/8	23 5/8	20 4/8	4 5/8	4 5/8	5	5	Humboldt Co., NV	Daniel A. Hinz	Daniel A. Hinz	1997	677
190 1/8	26 4/8	26 7/8	25 2/8	5	5 1/8	5	6	Rio Arriba Co., NM	Vernon R. Chapman	Vernon R. Chapman	1985	682
190	27 2/8	26 3/8	21 6/8	4 7/8	4 7/8	7	7	Missoula Co., MT	James A. Schwartz	James A. Schwartz	1987	683
190	27 2/8	27 5/8	27 4/8	4 6/8	4 7/8	7	7	Carbon Co., WY	Stephen M. Murnan	Stephen M. Murnan	1990	683
190	24 1/8	24 2/8	19 5/8	5 2/8	5 1/8	5	6	Rich Co., UT	Ernie Davis	Ernie Davis	1992	683
190	24 6/8	27 2/8	25 2/8	5 1/8	5 1/8	6	5	Baker Co., OR	Mike Raney	Mike Raney	1996	683
190	26 6/8	26 6/8	25	4 5/8	4 6/8	6	6	Unknown	Unknown	Robert H. Arledge	PR 1997	683

B&C HISTORY

GEORGE EASTMAN
1854-1932

A "professional member" of the Boone and Crockett Club, George Eastman was the preeminent pioneer in the field of photography. His research led to milestone developments of film, film processing and cameras. He introduced the Kodak camera in 1888. Located in Rochester, New York, the Eastman Kodak Company became the driving force in putting affordable cameras and film in most American households. Having no immediate family, his philanthropies were legendary: donating large sums of money to such institutions as the University of Rochester and the Massachusetts Institute of Technology. He died in 1932. ∎

CATEGORY
MULE DEER
TYPICAL ANTLERS

SCORE
204-1/8

HUNTER
WAYMON BURKHALTER

LOCATION
RIO ARRIBA CO., NM

DATE OF KILL
DECEMBER 1992

CATEGORY
MULE DEER
TYPICAL ANTLERS

SCORE
199-6/8

HUNTER
GILBERT T. ADAMS

LOCATION
KANE CO., UT

DATE OF KILL
SEPTEMBER 1993

CATEGORY
MULE DEER
TYPICAL ANTLERS

SCORE
192

HUNTER
STEVEN G. COY

LOCATION
TETON CO., WY

DATE OF KILL
SEPTEMBER 1992

238

MULE DEER - NON-TYPICAL ANTLERS
WORLD'S RECORD

Perhaps one of the most outstanding trophies ever recorded is the World's Record non-typical mule deer. This deer was taken in 1926 near Chip Lake, Alberta, by Ed Broder who gave a colorful account of his hunt.

"On November 25, 1926, I and two friends, driving an old 1914 Model T Ford, left Edmonton for Chip Lake, Alberta, a distance of approximately 100 miles. The weather was 20°F with a foot of soft snow. At a sawmill camp, near Chip Lake, we made arrangements to hire a team of horses and a sleigh to haul our gear and equipment. Finding a good cabin near the lake, we used this instead of putting up our tent.

"It was about 1 p.m. when I left camp and set out through some heavy timber and soon came across a large deer track, following the deer tracks for a half mile, I found where he had bedded down. Knowing the deer could not be too far away, I tracked him off the timber ridge, through a jackpine swamp. There I found that two moose had crossed the deer tracks. I had to make a decision as to whether to go after the moose or the deer. Through past experiences I knew moose would travel farther and faster than deer, and with only a short time before dark, I decided to carry on with the deer. Following these tracks through the swamp I came up onto a higher land with a clearing not too far off. In this clearing I spotted the deer; he was approximately, 200 yards away, standing and feeding with his back to me. So immediately I had to make a guess as to when and how to shoot. The distance was right but his

position was wrong. I knew I had to select a rear shot. The shot would have to be placed high in the spine, so I pulled up my .32 Winchester Special to a firing position, waited for his head to rise so as to back up a high spine shot. I fired and the animal dropped; I had broken its spine. 'What a rack that one's got,' was the first thing I thought."

At 355-2/8, the final score replaced the former World's Record by over half as many points, but it was not officially scored until 1960. However, the rack was impressive enough that a drawing of it appeared in the 1939 edition of *North American Big Game*. Broder acknowledged his record with the determined words of a true sportsman.

"I started hunting in the year 1909 and have never missed a season since; I am now 72 and in fair health and who can tell, I may yet beat my old 1926 record!" ■

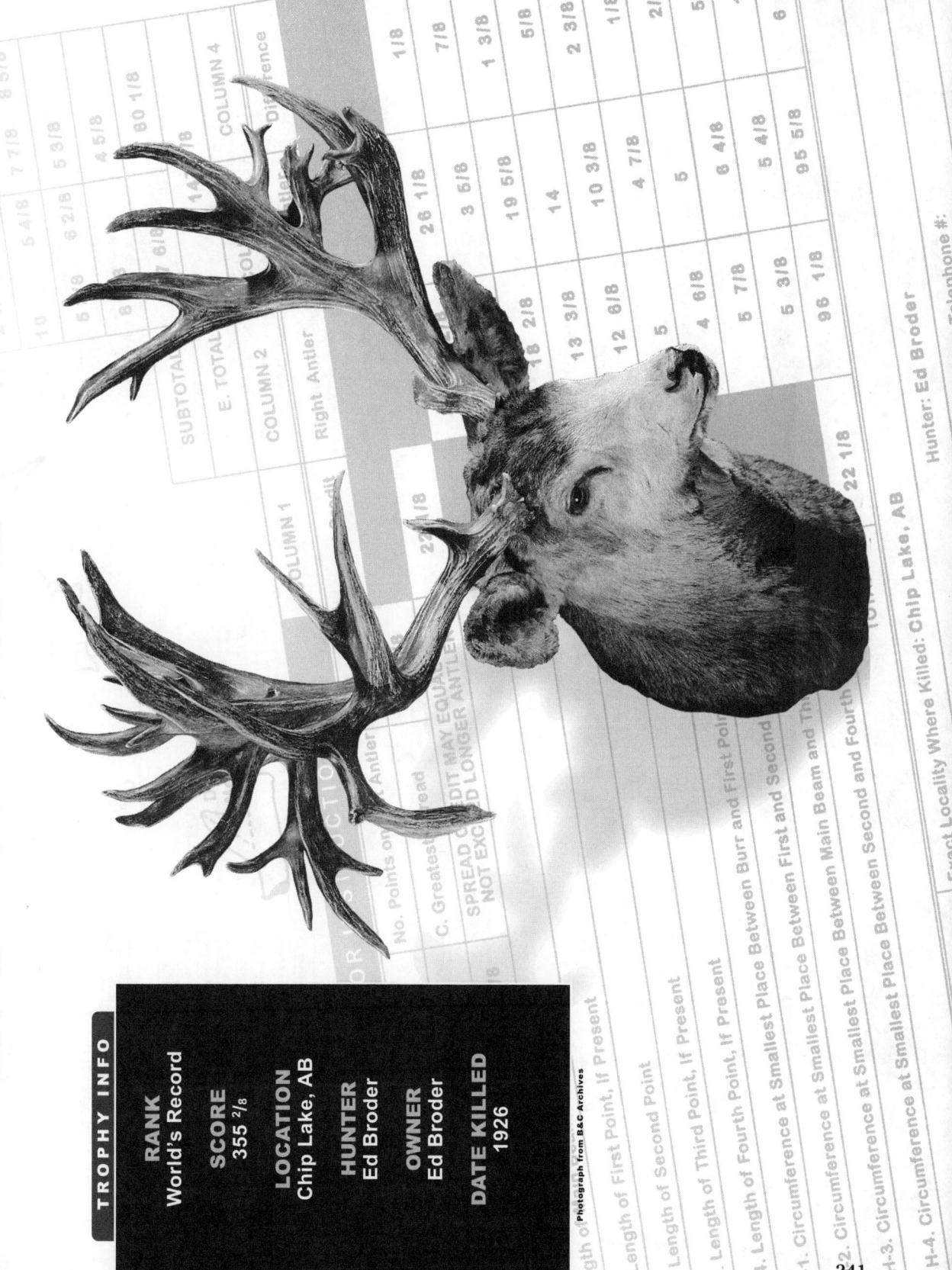

TROPHY INFO

RANK
World's Record

SCORE
355 2/8

LOCATION
Chip Lake, AB

HUNTER
Ed Broder

OWNER
Ed Broder

DATE KILLED
1926

Length of First Point, If Present

G-1. Length of First Point, If Present

G-2. Length of Second Point

G-3. Length of Third Point, If Present

G-4. Length of Fourth Point, If Present

H-1. Circumference at Smallest Place Between Burr and First Point

H-2. Circumference at Smallest Place Between First and Second

2. Circumference at Smallest Place Between Main Beam and Th

H-3. Circumference at Smallest Place Between Second and Fourth

H-4. Circumference at Smallest Place Between

Exact Locality Where Killed: Chip Lake, AB

Hunter: Ed Broder

Telephone #:

241

MULE DEER
NON-TYPICAL ANTLERS
WORLD'S RECORD SCORECHART

Records of
North American
Big Game

250 Station Drive
Missoula, MT 59801
(406) 542-1888

BOONE AND CROCKETT CLUB®

OFFICIAL SCORING SYSTEM FOR NORTH AMERICAN BIG GAME TROPHIES

NON-TYPICAL MULE DEER

MINIMUM SCORES
AWARDS   ALL-TIME
215   230

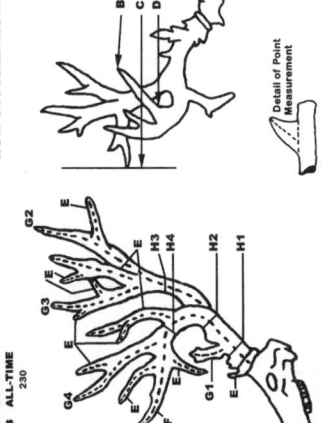

Detail of Point Measurement

	Abnormal Points	
	Right Antler	Left Antler
	5 1/8	2 2/8	1 2/8	1 4/8
	8 3/8	6 7/8	5 1/8	1 7/8
	2	1 7/8	3 6/8	2 7/8
	1 2/8	2 6/8	2 3/8	1 2/8
	3 2/8	8 1/8	2 7/8	1 2/8
	2 4/8	8 2/8	8	1 4/8
	10	5 4/8	7 7/8	8 5/8
	5 2/8	6 2/8	5 3/8	
	8 1/8		4 6/8	
SUBTOTALS	87 6/8		80 1/8	
E. TOTAL		147 7/8		

SEE OTHER SIDE FOR INSTRUCTIONS	COLUMN 1	COLUMN 2	COLUMN 3	COLUMN 4
		Spread Credit	Right Antler	Left Antler	Difference
A. No. Points on Right Antler	22				
No. Points on Left Antler	21				
B. Tip to Tip Spread	16				
C. Greatest Spread	38 5/8				
D. Inside Spread of Main Beams	22 1/8	SPREAD CREDIT MAY EQUAL BUT NOT EXCEED LONGER ANTLER	22 1/8		
E. Total of Lengths of all Abnormal Points					
F. Length of Main Beam			26 2/8	26 1/8	1/8
G-1. Length of First Point, If Present			4 4/8	3 5/8	7/8
G-2. Length of Second Point			18 2/8	19 5/8	1 3/8
G-3. Length of Third Point, If Present			13 3/8	14	5/8
G-4. Length of Fourth Point, If Present			12 6/8	10 3/8	2 3/8
H-1. Circumference at Smallest Place Between Burr and First Point			5	4 7/8	1/8
H-2. Circumference at Smallest Place Between First and Second Points			4 6/8	5	2/8
H-3. Circumference at Smallest Place Between Main Beam and Third Point			5 7/8	6 4/8	5/8
H-4. Circumference at Smallest Place Between Second and Fourth Points			5 3/8	5 4/8	1/8
TOTALS		22 1/8	96 1/8	95 5/8	6 4/8

ADD	Column 1	22 1/8	Exact Locality Where Killed: Chip Lake, AB	
	Column 2	96 1/8	Date Killed: Nov. 26, 1926	Hunter: Ed Broder
	Column 3	95 5/8	Owner: Ed Broder	Telephone #:
	Subtotal	213 7/8	Owner's Address:	
SUBTRACT Column 4		6 4/8	Guide's Name and Address:	
	Subtotal	207 3/8	Remarks: (Mention Any Abnormalities or Unique Qualities)	
	ADD Line E Total	147 7/8		
	FINAL SCORE	355 2/8		

All measurements must be made with a 1/4-inch wide flexible steel tape to the nearest one-eighth of an inch. (Note: A flexible steel cable can be used to measure points and main beams only.) Enter fractional figures in eighths, without reduction. Official measurements cannot be taken until the antlers have air dried for at least 60 days after the animal was killed.

A. **Number of Points** on Each Antler: To be counted a point, the projection must be at least one inch long, with length exceeding width at one inch or more of length. All points are measured from tip of point to nearest edge of beam as illustrated. Beam tip is counted as a point but not measured as a point.

B. **Tip to Tip Spread** is measured between tips of main beams.

C. **Greatest Spread** is measured between perpendiculars at a right angle to the center line of the skull at widest part, whether across main beams or points.

D. **Inside Spread of Main Beams** is measured at a right angle to the center line of the skull at widest point between main beams. Enter this measurement again as the Spread Credit if it is less than or equal to the length of the longer antler; if greater, enter longer antler length for Spread Credit.

E. **Total of Lengths of all Abnormal Points:** Abnormal Points are those non-typical in location such as points originating from a point (exception: G-3 originates from G-2 in perfectly normal fashion) or from bottom or sides of main beam, or any points beyond the normal pattern of five (including beam tip) per antler. Measure each abnormal point in usual manner and enter in appropriate blanks.

F. **Length of Main Beam** is measured from the center of the lowest outside edge of burr over the outer side to the most distant point of the main beam. The point of beginning is that point on the burr where the center line along the outer side of the beam intersects the burr, then following generally the line of the illustration.

G-1-2-3-4. **Length of Normal Points:** Normal points are the brow tines and the upper and lower forks as shown in the illustration. They are measured from nearest edge of main beam over outer curve to tip. Lay the tape along the outer curve of the beam so that the top edge of the tape coincides with the top edge of the beam on both sides of point to determine the baseline for point measurement. Record point lengths in appropriate blanks.

H-1-2-3-4. **Circumferences** are taken as detailed in illustration for each measurement. If brow point is missing, take H-1 and H-2 at smallest place between burr and tip of G-2. If G-3 is missing, take H-3 halfway between burr and tip of G-2. If G-4 is missing, take H-4 halfway between G-2 and tip of main beam.

MULE DEER - NON-TYPICAL ANTLERS

Odocoileus hemionus hemionus and certain related subspecies

MINIMUM SCORE 230

Score	Length of Main Beam R	L	Inside Spread	Circumference at Smallest Place Between Burr and First Point R	L	Number of Points R	L	Locality	Hunter	Owner	Date Killed	Rank
355 2/8	26 2/8	26 1/8	22 1/8	5	4 7/8	22	21	Chip Lake, AB	Ed Broder	Ed Broder	1926	1
339 2/8	20 6/8	20 4/8	14 7/8	6 4/8	6 2/8	24	23	Okanagan, BC	Unknown	D.J. Hollinger & B. Howard	PR 1890	2
330 1/8	23 2/8	22	9 4/8	8 2/8	8 3/8	21	28	Box Elder Co., UT	Alton Hunsaker	D.J. Hollinger & B. Howard	1943	3
325 6/8	24 5/8	23 5/8	21 6/8	4 6/8	4 7/8	21	21	Nye Co., NV	Clifton Fauria	Don Schaufler	1955	4
324 1/8	25 5/8	25 1/8	32 7/8	6 5/8	6 5/8	16	17	North Kaibab, AZ	William L. Murphy	Michael R. Karam	1943	5
321 1/8	28 1/8	25 4/8	26 5/8	6 7/8	6 7/8	17	25	Umatilla Co., OR	Albert C. Peterson	Don Schaufler	1925	6
320 4/8	23 5/8	24 7/8	25	6	6 2/8	17	20	Madison Co., ID	Grover Browning	D.J. Hollinger & B. Howard	1960	7
319 4/8	24 2/8	24	23 5/8	7 7/8	7 1/8	27	23	Mariposa Co., CA	Harold R. Laird	Don Schaufler	1972	8
311 6/8	26 7/8	24 7/8	24 1/8	6 1/8	6 5/8	22	21	Kaibab, AZ	Vernor Wilson	Don Schaufler	1941	9
306 7/8	30 3/8	30 5/8	24 3/8	5 2/8	5 4/8	16	18	Montezuma Co., CO	Lloyd Pyle	Don Schaufler	1972	10
306 2/8	28 6/8	27 4/8	22 6/8	5 6/8	5 4/8	14	23	Norwood, CO	Steve H. Herndon	V.D. & D.F. Holleman	1954	11
306 2/8	29	28 5/8	28 7/8	5 4/8	5 5/8	18	18	Chama, NM	Joseph A. Garcia	Don Schaufler	1963	11
305 6/8	23 7/8	24 1/8	21 3/8	6 1/8	6 4/8	17	17	Shasta Co., CA	Artie McGram	Artie McGram	1987	13
305 3/8	25 1/8	26 4/8	22 2/8	4 6/8	4 5/8	13	17	Boise Co., ID	Babe Hansen	Don Schaufler	1928	14
303 6/8	26 4/8	26 7/8	24 3/8	5 2/8	5	13	11	Eagle Co., CO	James Austill	Don Schaufler	1962	15
302 4/8	25 1/8	26 2/8	25 2/8	5 7/8	6 3/8	18	14	Paonia, CO	Louis H. Huntington, Jr.	Louis H. Huntington, Jr.	1965	16
302	26 7/8	26 2/8	21 5/8	6 3/8	6 5/8	21	15	Iron Co., UT	Darwin Hulett	Don Schaufler	1950	17
300 7/8	24	22 6/8	29 4/8	5 5/8	5 3/8	17	16	Bonneville Co., ID	Brett J. Sauer	Don Schaufler	1985	18
300	27	25 6/8	23 1/8	5 3/8	5 3/8	14	12	Mesa Co., CO	George Blackmon, Jr.	Don Schaufler	1961	19
299 5/8	26 6/8	28 1/8	29 1/8	6 2/8	5 2/8	19	17	Elk Creek, CO	Andrew Daum	Unknown	1886	20
299 1/8	27 7/8	28 3/8	24 4/8	5 6/8	5 4/8	13	16	Eureka Co., NV	Dan Avery, Jr.	Don Schaufler	1968	21
299	27 3/8	27 2/8	27 4/8	5 1/8	5 1/8	16	22	Lake Co., OR	Jack Aldredge	Don Schaufler	1948	22
298 5/8	26 1/8	26	24 6/8	5 5/8	6	14	13	California	Unknown	D.J. Hollinger & B. Howard	1940	23
297 7/8	29 1/8	27 5/8	35 4/8	5 4/8	5 3/8	20	18	Malheur Co., OR	Bradley Barclay	Bradley Barclay	1971	24
297 5/8	26 1/8	26 3/8	26 3/8	6 4/8	6 6/8	17	15	Larimer Co., CO	Jack Autrey	Linda Guy	1941	25
296 2/8	30 1/8	30 2/8	26 5/8	5 7/8	5 7/8	12	14	Mesa Co., CO	Unknown	Don Schaufler	PR 1981	26
294 4/8	25 2/8	24 2/8	21 6/8	6 1/8	5 5/8	15	11	Elmore Co., ID	Robert H. Arledge	Robert H. Arledge	1997	27
294 1/8	27 1/8	26 1/8	24 3/8	5 7/8	5 6/8	14	16	Coconino Co., AZ	Philip K. Coffeen	William A. Coffeen	1939	28
293 7/8	26 4/8	24 6/8	27 6/8	5 6/8	5 4/8	18	16	Wyoming	J.B. Marvin, Jr.	Unknown	PR 1924	29
293 6/8	26 7/8	26 3/8	27 3/8	5 3/8	5 5/8	12	12	Garfield Co., UT	Lloyd Barton	Lloyd Barton	1993	30
288 6/8	30 4/8	31 6/8	26 5/8	6 5/8	6 3/8	12	10	Chama, NM	Frank B. Maestas	Aly M. Bruner	1962	31
288 2/8	25	25 7/8	26	6	6	16	13	Hailey, ID	Robby Miller	Don Schaufler	1969	32
286 3/8	29 4/8	29 6/8	35 4/8	5 1/8	5 1/8	13	13	Eagle Co., CO	Albert L. Mulnix	Don Schaufler	1928	33
286 1/8	21 2/8	22 7/8	20 6/8	4 5/8	4 4/8	14	21	Unknown	Walt Mednick	Ike Foster	PR 1940	34
286 1/8	27	26 6/8	26 1/8	5 2/8	5 3/8	12	20	Utah Co., UT	Joe Allen	Todd L. Johnson	PR 1950	34
286 1/8	24 4/8	25	26 4/8	5	5	12	13	Elko Co., NV	Joseph W. Dooley	Raymond R. Cross	1954	34

Score	Length of Main Beam R	Length of Main Beam L	Inside Spread	Circumference R	Circumference L	Points R	Points L	Locality	By Whom Killed	Owner	Date Killed	Rank
285 7/8	27 1/8	27 6/8	26 7/8	6	6 1/8	19	16	Adams Co., ID	Picked Up	Raymond R. Cross	PR 1968	37
284 3/8	27 4/8	24 3/8	26	5 1/8	5 2/8	15	15	Duchesne Co., UT	Clyde Lambert	Lucy L. Back	1935	38
284	25 7/8	26 3/8	24 1/8	5 2/8	5 4/8	15	15	Provo River, UT	Melvin T. Ashton	Don Schaufler	1961	39
283 4/8	26 4/8	27 5/8	28 3/8	5	5 2/8	14	14	Lewis Co., WA	Quinten R. Grow	Desiree Gillingham	1943	40
283 1/8	28 5/8	28 3/8	22 2/8	5	4 7/8	14	14	Teton Co., ID	Unknown	D.J. Hollinger & B. Howard	PR 1980	41
283	28	29 2/8	24 3/8	8	7 7/8	14	13	Rose Creek, UT	Verl N. Creager	Verl N. Creager	1960	42
282 6/8	24 4/8	24 2/8	25 4/8	5 4/8	5 2/8	14	16	Cabri, SK	Robert Comba	Don Schaufler	1962	43
282 3/8	22 5/8	21 3/8	22 1/8	4 6/8	5 1/8	18	15	North Kaibab, AZ	Robert C. Rantz	Robert C. Rantz	1969	44
282 2/8	25 3/8	25 6/8	24	7	6 2/8	17	13	Saskatchewan	Herman Cox	Herman Cox	1947	45
281 6/8	28 6/8	27 6/8	25 6/8	5 6/8	5 3/8	13	11	Kaibab Natl. For., AZ	Unknown	Don Schaufler	PR 1950	46
281 3/8	28 2/8	28 2/8	21 2/8	6	5 6/8	19	22	Idaho	Unknown	Don Schaufler	PR 1950	47
280 4/8	27	26 6/8	23 4/8	6	6	15	14	Gem Co., ID	Ronald S. Holbrook	Ronald S. Holbrook	1982	48
280 2/8	25 7/8	24 4/8	24 2/8	6	6	10	15	Otthon, SK	Unknown	Don Schaufler	1940	49
280 2/8	29	31 2/8	29 4/8	5 1/8	5 4/8	11	16	Coconino Co., AZ	Unknown	Marlen D. Murphy	1941	49
280 2/8	24 6/8	21 6/8	21 6/8	4 4/8	4 4/8	16	11	Franklin Co., ID	M. Powell & D. Auld, Jr.	D.J. Hollinger & B. Howard	PR 1980	49
279 6/8	26 6/8	24 2/8	17 3/8	6 4/8	5 4/8	18	10	Kaibab Natl. For., AZ	Unknown	Miroy Powell	1950	52
279 5/8	21 7/8	22 5/8	30 4/8	6 2/8	6 3/8	8	17	Cuprum, ID	Ed Martin	Ed Martin	1966	53
278 7/8	24 4/8	26	18	5 1/8	4 7/8	12	11	Montrose Co., CO	Keith Thaute	Keith Thaute	1961	54
278 7/8	26 7/8	24 6/8	24 6/8	6 3/8	6 2/8	12	12	Eagle Co., CO	Dale L. Becker	Dale L. Becker	1978	54
278 3/8	27 2/8	26	26	5 3/8	5 3/8	11	13	Soda Springs, ID	Jack White	Don Schaufler	1957	56
277 6/8	28 1/8	28	28	6 1/8	6	11	12	Rio Arriba Co., NM	James Duran	Robert J. Seeds	1959	57
277 2/8	23 6/8	25 1/8	19 2/8	5 2/8	5 2/8	20	10	Morgan Co., UT	Jim Kilfoil	Gilbert Francis	1938	58
277 1/8	25 2/8	24 7/8	25 6/8	5 2/8	5 2/8	16	16	Colorado	Native American	Charles McAden	1930	59
277 1/8	26 1/8	24 6/8	20 5/8	5 6/8	5 7/8	14	13	Bly, OR	Alice C. O'Brien	Don Schaufler	1949	59
276 4/8	26 5/8	25 6/8	23 6/8	6	6	11	15	Glenwood Springs, CO	Larry Prehm	Spanky Greenville	1967	61
275 7/8	29 2/8	28 3/8	27 5/8	5 6/8	5	11	15	Highland Mts., MT	Peter Zemljak, Sr.	Peter Zemljak	1962	62
275 6/8	25 4/8	25 1/8	27 5/8	5 1/8	5 1/8	11	13	Dahlton, SK	Jim Hewitt	Jim Hewitt	1932	63
275 6/8	24 5/8	26	24 2/8	6 6/8	6 2/8	13	16	Red Deer River, SK	K. Michael Weisbrod	K. Michael Weisbrod	1992	63
275 2/8	28 2/8	23 2/8	23	5 6/8	5 6/8	14	13	Rio Arriba Co., NM	Unknown	Don Schaufler	PR 1955	65
274 7/8	23 6/8	23 6/8	24 5/8	5 4/8	5 4/8	10	4	Ruby Mts., MT	Peter Zemljak	Peter Zemljak	1960	66
274 7/8	27 7/8	24 2/8	25 4/8	5 7/8	5 6/8	11	11	Delta Co., CO	Robert G. Wilson	Robert G. Wilson	1989	67
274 6/8	23 2/8	26 1/8	24	6 1/8	6 1/8	8	12	Unknown	Picked Up	Carl D. Rey	1952	68
274 5/8	26	28 2/8	23 4/8	5 4/8	5 4/8	11	13	Pueblo Co., CO	Unknown	Butler Ranch	1988	69
274 2/8	28 3/8	24 5/8	23 2/8	5 4/8	5 2/8	14	13	Sublett, ID	Mrs. Jack Keen	Mr. & Mrs. Jack Keen	1957	70
274 1/8	21 7/8	24	24 5/8	5 6/8	5 5/8	11	11	Fremont Co., ID	David L. Maurer	David L. Maurer	1979	70
274 1/8	22 1/8	24	24 1/8	5 7/8	5 4/8	8	6	Beaver, UT	Murray Bohn	Parowan Rod & Gun Club	1920	72
273 7/8	24 1/8	24 2/8	23 6/8	5	4 7/8	11	11	North Fork, ID	James D. Edwards	ID Fish & Game Dept.	1967	72
273 6/8	29	29 2/8	26 6/8	6 1/8	6 1/8	8	12	Kane Co., UT	Waldon Ballard	Alice Ballard	1950	74
273 6/8	28	24 2/8	23 3/8	5 4/8	5 4/8	15	15	Hayden, CO	Roy I. Roney	CO Div. of Wildl.	1930	75
273 5/8	28 3/8	26 1/8	28 2/8	5	5	15	18	Klamath Co., OR	J.J. McDaniels	Roy I. Roney	1952	75
273	26	23 7/8	28 3/8	6 1/8	6 1/8	15	16	Morgan Co., UT	Harold B. Rollins	J.J. McDaniels	1944	77
273	21 7/8	20 5/8	24	7 4/8	6 6/8	23	18	Idaho	Unknown	Harold B. Rollins	PR 1943	78
272 7/8	22 1/8	24	24	5 7/8	5 6/8	10	13	Madison Co., MT	Ray Ypma	Ray Ypma	1946	78
272 5/8	24 1/8	26 2/8	24 1/8	5 4/8	5 4/8	16	16	Caribou Co., ID	Picked Up	Don Schaufler	1948	80
272 4/8	29	28	21 5/8	5 5/8	5 2/8	16	14	Glenwood Springs, CO	William L. Kurtz	William L. Kurtz	1967	81
272 3/8	28 3/8	27 2/8	21 2/8	6 3/8	6 2/8	19	17	Eagle Co., CO	Eddie Stephenson, Jr.	Eddie Stephenson, Jr.	1978	82
272 3/8	28 4/8	28 2/8	28 4/8	5 1/8	5 5/8	11	12	Albany Co., WY	S.A. Lawson	Acad. Nat. Sci., Phil.	1905	83

MULE DEER - NON-TYPICAL ANTLERS

Odocoileus hemionus hemionus and certain related subspecies

Score	Length of Main Beam R	L	Inside Spread	Circumference at Smallest Place Between Burr and First Point R	L	Number of Points R	L	Locality	Hunter	Owner	Date Killed	Rank
271 2/8	24 3/8	24 4/8	20	4 6/8	5 1/8	13	14	East Canyon, UT	Joseph H. Greenig	Mrs. Joseph H. Greenig	1947	84
270 7/8	25 6/8	26 7/8	23	5 2/8	5 2/8	12	11	Sanpete Co., UT	Preston Bown	Don Schaufler	1963	85
270 6/8	23 2/8	24 6/8	23 4/8	5 3/8	5 3/8	10	13	Carbon Co., WY	Edward Vigil	Michelle Ferguson	PR 1950	86
270 6/8	26 6/8	26 3/8	20 1/8	5 4/8	5 4/8	13	11	Colorado	Floyd Hill	Don Schaufler	1958	86
270 6/8	28 6/8	28 2/8	27 6/8	5 7/8	5 7/8	15	15	Crook Co., OR	C.F. Cheney	C.F. Cheney	1962	86
270 5/8	23 6/8	24 3/8	21 1/8	4 3/8	4 3/8	10	12	Big Horn Co., MT	R. Turnsback & J.V. Elsen	William Erdmann	1961	89
270 3/8	24	25	27 4/8	5 6/8	6	10	10	Kaibab Natl. For., AZ	Dean Naylor	D.B. Sanford	1948	90
270 3/8	23 7/8	25 4/8	27 5/8	5	4 6/8	11	13	Mesa Co., CO	Todd McKay	Todd McKay	1994	90
270 2/8	29 2/8	32 1/8	28	4 6/8	4 6/8	12	13	North Kaibab, AZ	Thomas M. Knoles, Jr.	Thomas M. Knoles, Jr.	1944	92
269 4/8	28 3/8	28 7/8	25 7/8	5 5/8	6	14	13	Owyhee Co., ID	Frank Cogdill	Raymond R. Cross	1939	93
268 6/8	28 3/8	28 4/8	24 6/8	5 5/8	5 5/8	12	13	Kaibab Natl. For., AZ	Milroy Powell	Milroy Powell	1952	94
268 5/8	24 2/8	22 7/8	27	6	6 3/8	14	15	Grant Co., OR	Lige Davis	Coy Johnston	1941	95
268 5/8	27	25 1/8	25 1/8	5	5 4/8	14	14	Leader, SK	Cocks Brothers	Richard Jensen	1954	95
268 4/8	21 3/8	23 6/8	17 4/8	6 5/8	6 5/8	17	16	Cascade Co., MT	Unknown	Kent Austin	PR 1980	97
268 3/8	25 4/8	27 5/8	23	6 1/8	6	17	11	Delta Co., CO	Shirley Smith	Shirley Smith	1962	98
268 1/8	24 6/8	23 7/8	25 7/8	5 1/8	4 7/8	12	11	Teton Co., ID	Picked Up	Don Schaufler	1984	99
268 1/8	29 6/8	27 7/8	26 2/8	5 3/8	5 2/8	10	10	Gallatin Co., MT	Michael O. Wold	Michael O. Wold	1992	99
267 5/8	26 4/8	25 7/8	26 3/8	4 7/8	4 6/8	13	18	Jicarilla Apache Res., NM	Byrd L. Minter, Jr.	Byrd L. Minter, Jr.	1961	101
267 5/8	23 2/8	23 3/8	23 5/8	4 7/8	4 6/8	18	16	Idaho Co., ID	Alan B. Hermann	Alan B. Hermann	1991	101
267 4/8	24	25 3/8	18 2/8	6 2/8	7 2/8	16	15	Mariposa Co., CA	Ray Douglas	John Douglas	1948	103
267 1/8	23 7/8	25 3/8	24 2/8	5 2/8	5 4/8	15	11	Eagle Co., CO	Josef Langegger	Josef Langegger	1969	104
266 7/8	26	25 1/8	22 4/8	6 4/8	6 1/8	13	15	Wyoming	J.L. Kemmerer	Am. Mus. Nat. Hist.	1905	105
266 7/8	22 5/8	22 7/8	18 6/8	5 1/8	5 1/8	8	8	Draper, UT	Glenn W. Furrow	Glenn W. Furrow	1962	105
266 5/8	25 5/8	25 2/8	20 6/8	5	5	13	11	Philip, SD	Clifford Ramsey	Clifford Ramsey	1959	107
266 2/8	24 4/8	24 7/8	21	5 3/8	5 4/8	12	18	Park Co., MT	Benton R. Venable	Benton R. Venable	1945	108
266 2/8	27	28 3/8	24 1/8	6 1/8	5 5/8	15	9	Mohave Co., AZ	Carl A. Luedeman	Carl A. Luedeman	1993	108
266 1/8	22 4/8	22 7/8	16 4/8	5 4/8	5 1/8	16	13	Stevens Co., WA	Joe C. Mally	Steve Mally	1933	110
266	25 3/8	24 2/8	27 7/8	5 6/8	5 5/8	16	20	Grant Co., OR	Harold T. Oathes	Harold T. Oathes	1965	111
266	29 3/8	27	22 7/8	5	5 2/8	11	10	Cassia Co., ID	Ken McDaniels	Don Schaufler	1972	111
265 7/8	25 5/8	26 4/8	27 6/8	5 4/8	5 6/8	8	12	Sidney, MT	Buster Dodson	F.P. Murray	1954	113
265 7/8	23 5/8	24 1/8	22 7/8	5 5/8	5 6/8	20	15	Powder River Co., MT	Michael A. Siewert	Michael A. Siewert	1987	113
265 6/8	25 6/8	25 6/8	24 1/8	5 1/8	5 4/8	11	13	Cache Co., UT	Jerry S. Wuthrich	Jerry S. Wuthrich	1966	115
265 5/8	24 7/8	26 7/8	27 2/8	6 7/8	6 5/8	16	14	Chama, NM	Stephanie D. Tartaglia	Stephanie D. Tartaglia	1966	116
265 3/8	26 6/8	27	23 4/8	5 3/8	5 2/8	21	16	Custer Co., ID	Merle Markle	D.J. Hollinger & B. Howard	1949	117
265 3/8	25 6/8	25 1/8	21 5/8	5 3/8	5 3/8	13	14	Tyaughton River, BC	Terry E. Crawford	Terry E. Crawford	1970	117
265 2/8	24 5/8	25 7/8	23 1/8	4 4/8	4 5/8	19	13	Beaver Co., UT	Blaine Blackett	Don Schaufler	1938	119

Score	Main Beam R	Main Beam L	Circ. R	Circ. L	Inside Spread	Points R	Points L	Locality	Hunter	Owner	Date	Rank
265 2/8	25 6/8	24 2/8	5 6/8	5 2/8	18	22	18	Blue Mts., WA	Frank Henriksen	Frank Henriksen	1961	119
265 1/8	25	24 2/8	5	5	23	9	11	Sweetwater Co., WY	Unknown	John Cheese	PR 1940	121
265 1/8	26	25 2/8	4 6/8	4 5/8	20 6/8	10	10	Hayes Co., NE	Charles J. Hogeland	Charles J. Hogeland	1994	121
265	24	24 2/8	4 7/8	4 7/8	19 4/8	13	15	Custer Co., NE	John L. Simmons	John L. Simmons	1986	123
264 5/8	26	26 5/8	5 4/8	5 6/8	22 4/8	18	13	Bannock Co., ID	Jarel Neeser	Jarel Neeser	1974	124
264 4/8	28 6/8	27 5/8	5 1/8	5 1/8	23 4/8	13	14	Idaho	Ken Potts	Don Schaufler	1962	125
264 3/8	26	27 5/8	5 4/8	5 3/8	21 4/8	13	10	Gunnison Co., CO	Gordon E. Blay	Gorden E. Blay	1975	126
264 2/8	24 4/8	26 2/8	5 3/8	5 3/8	21	7	13	Southern Utah	Unknown	Earl Mecham	1932	127
264 2/8	29 2/8	28 6/8	4 7/8	4 7/8	27 6/8	12	9	Utah	Garth Barrett	Don Schaufler	PR 1978	127
264 1/8	22 5/8	22	4 5/8	4 5/8	20 2/8	13	14	Coconino Co., AZ	Gilbert T. Adams	Gilbert T. Adams	1989	129
264	25 5/8	26 1/8	6 2/8	5 7/8	22 7/8	14	13	Elko Co., NV	Jim Stichter	Jim Stichter	1965	130
263 6/8	27 6/8	28 1/8	5 4/8	5 4/8	25 7/8	13	10	Harney Co., OR	Dave Morris	Don Schaufler	1960	131
263 6/8	26 5/8	26 5/8	5	5	22 2/8	16	14	Sanpete Co., UT	Wayne Dwyer	Raymond R. Cross	1974	131
263 4/8	26 5/8	26 4/8	5	5	23 6/8	12	12	Montrose, CO	Robert L. Price	Robert L. Price	1963	133
263 3/8	26	26	5 1/8	4 7/8	24 7/8	12	12	Lincoln Co., WY	Joe Welch	Don Schaufler	1940	134
263 1/8	27 4/8	27 7/8	6 2/8	6 1/8	26 4/8	20	13	Bigwood River, ID	Robert C. Young	Robert C. Young	1956	135
263	26 3/8	26 1/8	5	5	25 4/8	12	12	Kaibab Natl. For., AZ	Unknown	Bob Housholder	1940	136
262 7/8	28 2/8	27 5/8	6	6	19	12	14	Kane Co., UT	Bob Talbott	Don Schaufler	1958	137
262 7/8	27 4/8	27 1/8	5	5	25 1/8	12	15	Teton Co., WY	Thomas R. Ford	Thomas R. Ford	1984	137
262 5/8	26 2/8	24	4 6/8	4 7/8	23 7/8	14	12	Dawson Co., MT	Johnny Scheitlin	Bob Scheitlin	1949	139
262 4/8	28 2/8	28 2/8	5 4/8	5 4/8	24	14	15	Tierra Amarilla, NM	Jack Verner	Jack Verner	1947	140
262 3/8	29	29	6 2/8	6 4/8	28 2/8	10	11	Brush Creek, CO	Pat Lovato, Jr.	Pat Lovato, Jr.	1966	141
262 3/8	30 7/8	27 6/8	5 3/8	5 6/8	29 4/8	10	13	Franklin Co., ID	Pete Taullie	Pete Taullie	1967	141
262 1/8	25 6/8	29 3/8	5 6/8	5 3/8	23 3/8	15	12	Montana	Lester Lowe	D.J. Hollinger & B. Howard	1933	143
262 1/8	26 5/8	30 7/8	5 2/8	4 7/8	29 3/8	17	16	John Day River, OR	Unknown	Nick M. Messmer	PR 1943	143
262	24 2/8	25 6/8	4 6/8	4 6/8	24 6/8	14	15	Utah Co., UT	Glen E. Park	Glen E. Park	1962	145
262	25 7/8	26 5/8	4 7/8	5	24 6/8	14	14	Gallatin Co., MT	Michael D. Atwood	Michael D. Atwood	1967	145
261 6/8	24 4/8	24 2/8	5	5 4/8	21	16	16	Heber Mt., UT	Clifford R. Plum	Clifford R. Plum	1932	147
261 5/8	25	25 7/8	5 4/8	4 7/8	20 5/8	10	12	Blaine Co., ID	DuWayne C. Bailey	DuWayne C. Bailey	1963	148
261 3/8	25 4/8	24 4/8	4 7/8	5	23 6/8	10	10	Iron Creek, WA	Roger A. Crowder	Roger A. Crowder	1957	149
261 2/8	25 2/8	25	5 2/8	5 1/8	27 2/8	19	13	Rio Blanco Co., CO	Win Coultas	Win Coultas	1924	150
261 1/8	23	25 4/8	4 6/8	5 2/8	24 3/8	13	12	Kaibab Natl. For., AZ	L.C. Denny, Jr.	L.C. Denny, Jr.	1961	151
261	29 4/8	25 2/8	5 4/8	5 1/8	21 3/8	12	12	Rooks Co., KS	Unknown	Larry Arndt	1930	152
260 6/8	26 5/8	23	5	5 7/8	20	14	14	Ada Co., ID	Lee Odle	Lee Odle	1965	153
260 6/8	25 5/8	25 1/8	5 4/8	4 7/8	32 6/8	13	13	Kaibab Natl. For., AZ	Howard R. Cromwell	Raymond R. Cross	1975	153
260 4/8	23 1/8	26 3/8	4 7/8	5 7/8	24 6/8	14	14	Boise, ID	David Bevly	David Bevly	1949	155
260 2/8	26 7/8	25 5/8	5 7/8	6	22 2/8	17	17	Pinedale, WY	George M. Tweedy	George M. Tweedy	1946	156
260 2/8	26	23 1/8	5 7/8	4 5/8	26 6/8	13	13	Newcastle, UT	James H. Straley	Monte W. Straley	1965	156
260 1/8	22 7/8	26 7/8	4 6/8	5 1/8	25 4/8	20	20		Unknown	UT Div. of Wildl. Resc.	1961	158
260	27 2/8	26	5	5	21 2/8	11	11	Caribou Co., ID	Arthur H. Summers	Arthur H. Summers	1966	159
260	25 7/8	22 7/8	5 6/8	6 2/8	20	13	13	Mohave Co., AZ	John W. Sokatch	John W. Sokatch	1978	159
259 7/8	25 1/8	27 2/8	4 7/8	4 6/8	27 2/8	11	11	Kanab, UT	Arthur Glover	Arthur Glover	1947	161
259 7/8	28 4/8	25 1/8	5	5	24 6/8	8	10	Caribou Co., ID	Jerry Hunt	Jerry Hunt	1966	161
259 7/8	24 3/8	28 4/8	5 7/8	5 5/8	22 2/8	12	15	Catron Co., NM	Jeff K. Gunnell	Jeff K. Gunnell	1981	161
259 6/8	24 7/8	24 2/8	5 3/8	5 3/8	27 4/8	13	13	Routt Co., NM	R.V. Rhoads	Cecil R. Weston	1949	164
259 6/8	25 7/8	25 7/8	6 3/8	5 7/8	21 3/8	15	14	Gooding Co., ID	Charles Hollingsworth	Charles Hollingsworth	1970	164
259 5/8	27 2/8	26 6/8	5 2/8	5 2/8	24 1/8	12	13	Glendo, WY	Rudolph B. Johnson	Rudolph B. Johnson	1961	166

MULE DEER - NON-TYPICAL ANTLERS

Odocoileus hemionus hemionus and certain related subspecies

Score	Length of Main Beam R	L	Inside Spread	Circumference at Smallest Place Between Burr and First Point R	L	Number of Points R	L	Locality	Hunter	Owner	Date Killed	Rank
259 4/8	24 3/8	24	25 3/8	5	5 2/8	13	15	Boise Co., ID	LeRoy Massey	LeRoy Massey	1959	167
259 3/8	27 3/8	29 2/8	24 6/8	5 6/8	5 4/8	13	13	Iron Co., UT	Mont Hunter	Mont Hunter	1939	168
259 3/8	23 4/8	23 4/8	21 6/8	5	5	15	16	Idaho Co., ID	Unknown	Raymond R. Cross	PR 1940	168
259	28 1/8	26 6/8	28 4/8	7 1/8	6 6/8	12	12	Coconino Co., AZ	Lue O. Nulliner	Lue O. Nulliner	1968	170
258 7/8	28 5/8	27 7/8	28 2/8	4 6/8	4 7/8	13	13	North Kaibab, AZ	Marvin Fridenmaker	Marvin Fridenmaker	1968	171
258 6/8	27 5/8	27 6/8	24 5/8	5	5	15	10	Valley Co., ID	Larry Dwonch	Larry Dwonch	1972	172
258 6/8	21	22	16 2/8	10	5	18	18	Sweetwater Co., WY	John A. Fabian	John A. Fabian	1974	172
258 6/8	26	25 2/8	18 2/8	4 5/8	4 4/8	13	11	Washington Co., UT	Brian A. Bowler	Brian A. Bowler	1989	172
258 6/8	24 6/8	25	22 6/8	5 6/8	5 2/8	9	18	Decatur Co., KS	Lance W. Randolph	Lance W. Randolph	1996	172
258 5/8	25 3/8	25 4/8	21	5 2/8	5 3/8	12	10	Elko Co., NV	Edward J. Giauque	Edward J. Giauque	1960	176
258 4/8	25 4/8	26 6/8	24 4/8	5 6/8	5 4/8	11	9	Grand Co., UT	Vernon K. Heller	Vernon K. Heller	1971	177
258 3/8	27	28 4/8	25 1/8	5 1/8	5 1/8	11	11	Monte Vista, CO	Geis Nettlebeck	Phil Skinner	1956	178
258 2/8	29 5/8	30 5/8	29 3/8	6 6/8	6 7/8	15	14	Rock Creek, BC	George Whiting	B.C. Game Dept.	1909	179
258 1/8	27 1/8	25 6/8	23 2/8	5 7/8	5 7/8	11	13	Morgan Co., UT	Martin Harris	Rodney D. Layton	1935	180
258 1/8	27 3/8	26 4/8	23 6/8	5 1/8	5 1/8	13	14	Atlanta, ID	Kenneth E. Potts	Kenneth E. Potts	1968	180
258 1/8	25 4/8	24 7/8	27 3/8	5 7/8	6	8	9	Sheridan Co., KS	John Simpson	Don Schaufler	PR 1969	180
258	20 4/8	22 1/8	19 3/8	4 2/8	4 5/8	13	13	Cimarron, NM	Ralph L. Smith	Don Schaufler	1957	183
258	26 5/8	29	27 6/8	5 4/8	5 3/8	14	16	Coconino Co., AZ	William T. Parsons	William T. Parsons	1967	183
257 7/8	27 1/8	26	26 7/8	5 7/8	5 6/8	14	14	Jicarilla Apache Res., NM	Henry Callado	Henry Callado	1961	185
257 6/8	27 6/8	26 5/8	27 4/8	6 1/8	6 4/8	10	12	Apache Co., AZ	Lamell Ellsworth	Lamell Ellsworth	1992	185
257 6/8	28 3/8	27 1/8	24 2/8	5 4/8	5 4/8	9	13	Leclerc Creek, WA	Ernest Fait	Ernest Fait	1960	187
257 5/8	27 2/8	29	28 7/8	5 5/8	5 5/8	15	14	Kaibab Natl. For., AZ	Graves Peeler	John E. Connor Museum	1946	188
257 5/8	25 7/8	26 5/8	25 1/8	5 6/8	5 5/8	12	11	Kaibab Natl. For., AZ	Graves Peeler	John E. Connor Museum	1947	188
257 5/8	24 2/8	26 7/8	20 6/8	5 3/8	5 4/8	11	13	Hell's Hole, AZ	D.L. DeMente	D.L. DeMente	1965	188
257 5/8	25 3/8	25 2/8	24	4 7/8	5 1/8	12	12	Rio Blanco Co., CO	Rachael Palmer	Rachael Palmer	1970	188
257 4/8	24 5/8	23	19 2/8	5 4/8	5 4/8	11	11	Encampment, WY	Sam Whitney	Mrs. Sam Whitney	1946	192
257 4/8	28 7/8	28 6/8	27 7/8	4 6/8	4 7/8	18	10	Utah Co., UT	J. Clyde Burgess	Dave Burgess	1949	192
257 4/8	25 3/8	26	27 2/8	5 4/8	5 4/8	9	14	Blaine Co., ID	Philip T. Homer	Philip T. Homer	1983	192
257 4/8	23 6/8	24 1/8	20 2/8	5 6/8	5 4/8	12	10	Sanpete Co., UT	Dan J. Keller	Dan J. Keller	1986	192
257 4/8	24 2/8	25 5/8	23	6 5/8	5 2/8	15	12	Coconino Co., AZ	Dale McKinnon	Dale McKinnon	1995	192
257 3/8	24 6/8	26 3/8	23 1/8	4 6/8	4 7/8	12	8	New Castle, CO	Unknown	A.E. Hudson	1952	197
257 2/8	28 1/8	28 4/8	28 5/8	5 4/8	5 4/8	11	15	Sevier Co., UT	Reed Hintze	Don Schaufler	1939	198
257 1/8	25 2/8	24 7/8	19	5 6/8	5 3/8	10	8	Juab Co., UT	P.L. Jones	Nelson L. Jones	1949	199
257	26 7/8	26	24 2/8	5	4 7/8	12	12	Cache Co., UT	Harold S. Shandrew	Harold S. Shandrew	1958	200
257	29 1/8	27 7/8	26 2/8	4 6/8	4 6/8	10	10	Madison Co., ID	Grover Browning	D.J. Hollinger & B. Howard	1959	200
256 7/8	26 5/8	27 2/8	22 6/8	5 3/8	5 6/8	20	14	Chadron, NE	Art Thomsen	Art Thomsen	1960	202

Score	Main Beam R	Main Beam L	Inside Spread	Circ. R	Circ. L	Pts. R	Pts. L	Locality	Hunter	Owner	Date	Rank
256 7/8	23 7/8	22 4/8	21 4/8	4 1/8	4 6/8	12	13	Elmore Co., ID	Paul Vetter	Paul Vetter	1972	202
256 7/8	25 5/8	26 1/8	22 6/8	5 3/8	5 5/8	10	15	Moose Creek, AB	Henry Thomas	Henry Thomas	1993	202
256 6/8	24 6/8	26 4/8	20 4/8	5	5 1/8	12	15	Hoback Basin, WY	Buck Heide	Buck Heide	1968	205
256 6/8	28	28 6/8	26 1/8	5 4/8	5 6/8	13	13	Bannock Co., ID	Unknown	Don Schaufler	PR 1982	205
256 5/8	25 7/8	27 2/8	25 6/8	5 3/8	5 3/8	14	13	Jicarilla Apache Res., NM	Picked Up	S.L. Canterbury III	1967	207
256 4/8	26 2/8	26 1/8	22	5 5/8	5 3/8	12	11	Douglas Co., CO	Adolph A. Larsen	Don Schaufler	1926	208
256 4/8	26 5/8	25 1/8	21	4 7/8	4 7/8	10	19	Summit Co., UT	Glen Holtman	Glen Holtman	1946	208
256 4/8	24	24 5/8	25 2/8	6	6 1/8	12	11	Portreeve, SK	Mike Spies	Mike Spies	1947	208
256 4/8	28 3/8	28 4/8	22	5 1/8	5 1/8	10	9	Baker Co., OR	Thomas M. Rousseau	Thomas M. Rousseau	1988	208
256 2/8	27 4/8	27 4/8	26 4/8	4 7/8	5 1/8	10	8	Mt. Trumbull, AZ	Ervin M. Schmutz	Ervin M. Schmutz	1965	212
256 2/8	27 4/8	25 4/8	27 4/8	4 5/8	4 5/8	10	14	Caribou Co., ID	Unknown	D.J. Hollinger & B. Howard	PR 1970	212
256 2/8	28 4/8	28 6/8	29 3/8	6 2/8	6 3/8	11	12	Missoula Co., MT	Leland Crow	Don Schaufler	1952	212
256 1/8	23 7/8	24 7/8	32 5/8	4 7/8	5 1/8	12	13	East Zion, UT	Raymond Pocta	Raymond Pocta	1963	214
256 1/8	22 7/8	22 4/8	25	4 5/8	5	14	12	Irwin, ID	Hale K. Charlton	Hale K. Charlton	1966	214
256 1/8	26 2/8	26 2/8	20 1/8	4 6/8	4 5/8	15	13	Summit Lake, BC	Herald A. Friedenberger	Herald A. Friedenberger	1988	214
256 1/8	24 4/8	26 7/8	21 6/8	5	4 6/8	13	13	Garfield Co., UT	James D. Perkins	James D. Perkins	1959	214
256	26 5/8	26 5/8	25 1/8	5 4/8	5	16	9	Gem Co., ID	Jay P. Baker	Jay P. Baker	1981	218
256	23	24 1/8	22 6/8	9 4/8	6 5/8	18	12	Unknown	Unknown	Buckhorn Mus. & Saloon, Ltd.	1901	218
255 7/8	26 5/8	26 7/8	26 5/8	5 4/8	5	11	9	Cache Co., UT	Roland Leishman	Roland Leishman	1980	220
255 6/8	25 2/8	25 7/8	24 3/8	5 2/8	5 2/8	12	12	Idaho	Unknown	D.J. Hollinger & B. Howard	PR 1948	221
255 5/8	23 3/8	23 5/8	25 5/8	4 5/8	4 4/8	12	12	Coconino Co., AZ	Glenn A. Hunt	Glenn A. Hunt	1985	222
255 4/8	28	27 3/8	28 2/8	5 6/8	5 7/8	14	12	Garfield Co., CO	Louis Lindauer	Louis Lindauer	1932	223
255 2/8	25 2/8	24 7/8	22 1/8	5 7/8	5 5/8	10	9	Eagle Co., CO	Lloyd Murphy	Don Schaufler	1936	224
255 2/8	26	26 5/8	25 1/8	4 3/8	4 5/8	9	9	Rio Arriba Co., NM	Gene Garcia	Gene Garcia	1964	224
255 2/8	25 6/8	26 6/8	26	4 7/8	5 4/8	10	11	Hells Canyon, ID	Basil C. Bradbury	Basil C. Bradbury	1955	224
255 1/8	25	25	25	5 6/8	5	7	9	Eagle Co., CO	Dennis Martinson	Dennis Martinson	1980	227
255 1/8	27 6/8	27	24 3/8	4 7/8	4 6/8	10	13	Fremont Co., ID	Dale Sanderson	Don Schaufler	1953	227
255	21 5/8	22 4/8	19 7/8	5	5 5/8	9	9	Dunkley Flat, CO	Richard A. Gorden	Richard A. Gorden	1966	229
255	26 6/8	25 4/8	21 5/8	5 5/8	4 6/8	8	8	Adams Co., ID	Fred Bain	Raymond R. Cross	1974	229
255	25 1/8	24	23 4/8	5 4/8	5 2/8	13	15	Maloy, AB	Otto Schmalzbauer	Otto Schmalzbauer	1930	229
254 4/8	25 1/8	24 1/8	18 5/8	4 6/8	4 6/8	16	12	Utah	Unknown	D.J. Hollinger & B. Howard	PR 1960	232
254 4/8	30	28 6/8	21 1/8	6 2/8	6 4/8	7	8	Columbine, CO	M.A. Story	M.A. Story	1955	232
254 2/8	24 4/8	25 2/8	23 4/8	4 5/8	4 6/8	9	10	Jefferson Co., CO	Larry J. Jones	Larry J. Jones	1994	234
254 1/8	26 7/8	26 7/8	23 7/8	6 1/8	6 1/8	13	9	Wyoming	Unknown	D.J. Hollinger & B. Howard	PR 1960	235
254	25	25	21 5/8	6 1/8	4 6/8	9	12	Mohave Co., AZ	Manuel Machado	Manuel Machado	1973	236
253 6/8	25 6/8	25 6/8	25 6/8	4 6/8	5 1/8	11	11	East End, SK	Henry Leroy	Henry Leroy	1960	237
253 4/8	24 6/8	25 1/8	25	5 2/8	5 4/8	11	10	Silt, CO	George McCoy	George McCoy	1961	238
253 3/8	27 6/8	26 6/8	21	5 3/8	5 2/8	13	17	Meeker, CO	George R. Howey	Robert L. Howey	1917	240
253 3/8	24 4/8	24 3/8	20 4/8	5 2/8	5 3/8	11	13	Georgetown, CO	George Lappin	Doug Grubbe	1947	240
253 3/8	20 1/8	22 1/8	22 6/8	5 3/8	5 3/8	11	11	Rawlins, WY	A.H. Henkel	A.H. Henkel	1952	240
253 3/8	24 3/8	26 6/8	20 5/8	5 2/8	5 5/8	15	22	Utah Co., UT	Paul H. Mitchell	Paul H. Mitchell	1953	240
253 2/8	24 2/8	24 3/8	24 6/8	5 2/8	5 1/8	15	17	Salmon, ID	Ben H. Quick	Ben H. Quick	1960	244
253 1/8	26 1/8	25 2/8	23 2/8	5 4/8	5 4/8	16	12	Sweetwater Co., WY	John C. Erickson	M. Painovich & J. Etcheverry	1932	245
253	25 5/8	25 1/8	23 2/8	5 1/8	6	10	13	Elko Co., NV	Joseph Souza	Joseph Souza	1953	246
253	22 4/8	25 4/8	19 1/8	6	5 4/8	11	11	Paonia, CO	F.F. Parham	F.F. Parham	1961	246
252 7/8	18 6/8	18 6/8	19 1/8	5 4/8	5 4/8	11	22	Boise Co., ID	Dennis D. Snider	Dennis D. Snider	1983	248
252 6/8	25 2/8	24 3/8	22 4/8	5	5	12	17	Wyoming	Unknown	Don Schaufler	PR 1970	249

MULE DEER - NON-TYPICAL ANTLERS

Odocoileus hemionus hemionus and certain related subspecies

Score	Length of Main Beam R	L	Inside Spread	Circumference at Smallest Place Between Burr and First Point R	L	Number of Points R	L	Locality	Hunter	Owner	Date Killed	Rank
252 6/8	25 6/8	24 6/8	25 6/8	5 5/8	5 5/8	10	14	Fremont Co., ID	Trevor D. Larson	Trevor D. Larson	1990	249
252 5/8	26 7/8	28 7/8	29 1/8	5 3/8	5 5/8	15	13	Kaibab Natl. For., AZ	Graves Peeler	Graves Peeler	PR 1951	251
252 5/8	20 5/8	21 7/8	18 3/8	4 5/8	4 6/8	12	13	Valley Co., ID	Picked Up	Raymond R. Cross	PR 1989	251
252 4/8	23 1/8	26 4/8	21 1/8	5 4/8	5 4/8	12	12	Sonora, MX	Fredric W. Decker	Fredric W. Decker	1997	253
252 2/8	23 4/8	22	14 5/8	5 6/8	5 6/8	16	15	Glacier Co., MT	Bob Scriver	Philip Schlegel	1934	254
252 2/8	30	30	26 6/8	6	5 4/8	15	14	Garfield Co., CO	B.J. Slack	Aly M. Bruner	1973	254
252 1/8	25 1/8	24 1/8	21 5/8	4 6/8	4 7/8	11	10	Salina Canyon, UT	James C. Larsen	James C. Larsen	1969	256
252 1/8	28 6/8	28 6/8	28 3/8	5 4/8	5 3/8	11	10	Elmore Co., ID	Bud Abele	Bud Abele	1996	256
252	22 7/8	22 1/8	24 6/8	5 4/8	5 4/8	18	16	Grease Creek, AB	Jack McCallum	J.H. Fry	PR 1940	258
252	24 7/8	23	24 5/8	5	5	9	13	Eagle Co., CO	Richard G. Lundock	Richard G. Lundock	1945	258
252	26	25 2/8	20 3/8	6	6 4/8	14	14	Box Elder Co., UT	Mr. Selman	D.J. Hollinger & B. Howard	1951	258
251 7/8	22	24 1/8	17 1/8	4 6/8	4 5/8	10	10	Salem, UT	John Vincent	John Vincent	1956	261
251 6/8	24	25 4/8	20	5 1/8	5	13	14	Gem Co., ID	A.K. England	Roscoe E. Ferris	1969	262
251 6/8	25 2/8	25 7/8	23	6 3/8	6	7	14	Washington Co., UT	Richard S. Mansker	Richard S. Mansker	1990	262
251 5/8	27 4/8	25 2/8	23 6/8	5 2/8	5 2/8	9	14	Gunnison Co., CO	John M. Ringler	John M. Ringler	1956	264
251 5/8	24 1/8	26 1/8	21	5 1/8	5 4/8	10	14	Roan Creek, CO	Anthony Morabito	Anthony Morabito	1965	264
251 4/8	28 1/8	26 4/8	23 2/8	5 2/8	5 4/8	13	13	Grand Co., UT	Picked Up	Glen Holtman	1976	266
251 4/8	29 1/8	28 2/8	22 1/8	5 7/8	5 5/8	14	9	Martha Creek, BC	Charles J. McKinney	Charles J. McKinney	1992	266
251 3/8	26 7/8	26	31 1/8	5 5/8	5 3/8	18	12	Wayne Co., UT	Chuck Simmons	Chuck Simmons	1988	268
251 2/8	29	27 2/8	26 4/8	5 6/8	7 1/8	13	13	Wyoming	Unknown	D.J. Hollinger & B. Howard	PR 1970	269
251 2/8	25 1/8	25	25 6/8	5	5	12	11	Rosebud Co., MT	John P. Garner	Don Schaufler	1978	269
251 1/8	27 5/8	25 6/8	25 7/8	5 3/8	5 2/8	10	9	Meeker, CO	Henry Zietz, Jr.	Henry Zietz, Jr.	1955	271
251 1/8	28 1/8	27 7/8	26 3/8	6	6 1/8	10	9	Iron Co., UT	James C. Howard	James C. Howard	1987	271
251	28 6/8	28 1/8	24 4/8	5	4 7/8	10	9	Washington	Unknown	D.J. Hollinger & B. Howard	1936	273
251	25 1/8	26 1/8	26 1/8	5 1/8	5 1/8	13	14	Adams Co., ID	Clark Childers	Clark Childers	1955	273
250 7/8	26 4/8	27 2/8	24	5 4/8	6	19	13	Chelan Co., WA	Ben R. Williamson	Vera T. Williamson	1951	275
250 6/8	29	29 1/8	35 1/8	5 4/8	5 3/8	11	13	Pagosa Springs, CO	Thomas Jarrett	Thomas Jarrett	1962	276
250 6/8	26 4/8	27 4/8	28 3/8	5 1/8	5 2/8	11	11	Idaho	Unknown	D.J. Hollinger & B. Howard	PR 1970	276
250 6/8	30	29 1/8	28 7/8	6 2/8	6 2/8	11	12	Apache Co., AZ	Perry D. Null	Perry D. Null	1993	276
250 5/8	25 3/8	25 3/8	22 2/8	5 1/8	5 1/8	13	10	Millard Co., UT	Walter D. LeFevre	Walter D. LeFevre	1968	279
250 4/8	29 7/8	26 7/8	22 4/8	6 2/8	8	7	13	Kunard Valley, ID	Ralph D. Hogan	Ralph D. Hogan	1966	280
250 4/8	26 1/8	27 3/8	28 4/8	5	5	12	10	Washington	Picked Up	Pat Redding	PR 1973	280
250 4/8	26	27 2/8	27 3/8	5 4/8	6	11	9	Quesnel, BC	Picked Up	Paul W. Stafford	1984	280
250 4/8	29	26 7/8	30 2/8	5 4/8	5 6/8	10	13	Shoshone Co., ID	Ron L. Purnell	Ron L. Purnell	1987	280
250 3/8	29	28 4/8	27 4/8	5 1/8	4 6/8	10	12	Moffat Co., CO	Unknown	Aly M. Bruner	1960	284
250 3/8	26 2/8	24 7/8	25 4/8	5	5	10	10	Cedaredge, CO	E.K. Plante	E.K. Plante	1963	284

Score								Locality	Hunter	Owner	Date	Rank
250 3/8	26 2/8	26 5/8	28 1/8	4 6/8	5	10	12	Petroleum Co., MT	Lawrence T. Keenan	Lawrence T. Keenan	1979	284
250 1/8	22 7/8	23 4/8	17 7/8	4 5/8	4 6/8	14	14	Sheridan Co., WY	Richard Legerski	Richard Legerski	1976	287
250 1/8	26	26	24	5 4/8	5 6/8	15	11	Montezuma Co., CO	Jack E. Reed	Jack E. Reed	1981	287
250	25	25 1/8	25 1/8	6 5/8	6 2/8	10	10	Elko Co., NV	Joseph Brodnick	J. & B. Brodnick	1965	289
250	28 4/8	29 5/8	28 4/8	4 6/8	4 2/8	11	10	Summit Co., UT	David Montoya	D.J. Hollinger & B. Howard	1976	289
250	27 1/8	25	21 4/8	6 5/8	6 4/8	14	14	Mohave Co., AZ	Douglas C. Mallory	Douglas C. Mallory	1980	289
249 6/8	21 6/8	23 3/8	23 3/8	6 2/8	5 7/8	12	12	Mt. Dellenbaugh, AZ	Ted Riggs	Don Schaufler	1965	292
249 6/8	25 2/8	24 7/8	22	5	4 7/8	10	14	Red Willow Co., NE	Delman H. Tuller	Delman H. Tuller	1965	292
249 5/8	25 7/8	26 2/8	23	5	5 3/8	11	10	Colorado	Unknown	Don Schaufler	PR 1960	294
249 3/8	24 2/8	25	19 6/8	5 4/8	5 3/8	12	9	Routt Co., CO	Howard Stoker	Howard Stoker	1958	295
249 3/8	27 4/8	27	27 5/8	6 1/8	6 2/8	7	11	Adams Co., ID	Howard E. Paradis	Howard E. Paradis	1966	295
249 3/8	24 6/8	25	22 6/8	5 4/8	5 4/8	18	16	Owyhee Co., ID	Tom Tomlinson	Raymond R. Cross	1968	295
249 2/8	28 4/8	26 1/8	29 1/8	5 6/8	6 1/8	14	10	Klamath Co., OR	Fred Teeny	Rick Teeny	1947	298
249 2/8	23 4/8	23 5/8	20 7/8	5	4 5/8	12	10	Mesa Co., CO	Gene Cavanagh	Gene Cavanagh	1967	298
249 2/8	26 5/8	26 2/8	21 4/8	6 6/8	6 4/8	21	22	Adams Co., ID	Charles H. Daniels	Raymond R. Cross	1975	298
249 2/8	23 5/8	24 3/8	27	4 6/8	4 6/8	10	10	Lincoln Co., WY	Robert J. Stallone	Robert J. Stallone	1986	298
249 1/8	26	25 4/8	25 1/8	5 1/8	5 1/8	8	11	Kaibab, AZ	Robert G. McDonald	Robert G. McDonald	1969	302
249	23 4/8	25 1/8	23 1/8	5 3/8	5	14	10	Minturn, CO	John F. Baldauf	L.F. Nowotny	1941	303
249	29 7/8	27 7/8	25 6/8	5 1/8	5 1/8	11	8	Jemez Mts., NM	Max S. Jenson	Max S. Jenson	1962	303
249	26 7/8	26 7/8	26 7/8	5 6/8	5 1/8	8	10	New Castle, CO	William Wiedenfeld	William Wiedenfeld	1969	303
248 6/8	25 4/8	27	28	5 5/8	5 6/8	9	14	Okanogan Co., WA	Fred C. Heuer	Raymond R. Cross	1940	306
248 5/8	25 6/8	26 6/8	33 6/8	6 2/8	5 2/8	14	10	Franklin Co., ID	Joan Butterworth	Quinten Butterworth	1961	307
248 4/8	25 1/8	25 4/8	25 1/8	5 6/8	5 5/8	13	11	Kaibab Natl. For., AZ	H.W. Meisch	H.W. Meisch	1942	308
248 4/8	27 3/8	29 2/8	20 4/8	5 2/8	6	15	16	Baker Co., OR	Wally Hutton	R. Dwayne Wright	1964	308
248 4/8	26 4/8	27 2/8	29 2/8	6 2/8	5 2/8	13	13	Sevier Co., UT	Orson Lance	Orson Lance	1969	308
248 3/8	26 6/8	26 3/8	23 4/8	5 4/8	5 3/8	10	16	Kaibab Natl. For., AZ	O.M. Corbett	O.M. Corbett	1953	311
248 3/8	25 1/8	24 4/8	25 1/8	5 5/8	5 1/8	10	12	Mesa Co., CO	Edwin Baal	Edwin Baal	1988	311
248 3/8	27 6/8	29 2/8	27 2/8	6 1/8	6 2/8	10	9	Costilla Co., CO	Ronald E. Lewis	Ronald E. Lewis	1988	311
248 2/8	24	24	22 5/8	5 3/8	5 3/8	13	8	Elko Co., NV	Gary Murphy	Bart Druehl	PR 1947	314
248 2/8	25	25	26 7/8	7	7	12	12	Kaibab Natl. For., AZ	Graves Peeler	Graves Peeler	PR 1951	314
248 1/8	24 4/8	24 7/8	19 7/8	4 4/8	4 4/8	9	8	Colorado	Unknown	D.J. Hollinger & B. Howard	PR 1980	314
248 1/8	25 7/8	24 7/8	22 6/8	5 1/8	5	11	10	Rio Blanco Co., CO	Claude E. Shults	Claude E. Shults	1956	317
248	25 4/8	25	23	5	5	15	18	San Juan Natl. For., CO	Leland R. Tate	Leland R. Tate	1973	317
248	23 3/8	22 4/8	23 2/8	5 6/8	5 6/8	12	14	Val Marie, SK	J. Milton Brown	J. Milton Brown	1958	319
248	26	27 1/8	22	5	5	12	9	Pinedale, WY	Lyle Rosendahl	Lyle Rosendahl	1960	319
248	25 5/8	26 4/8	24 7/8	5 2/8	5 2/8	11	10	Columbine, CO	Bobby McLaughlin	Bobby McLaughlin	1962	319
248	26 2/8	26	27 7/8	4 4/8	4 4/8	13	9	Uintah Co., UT	Mabel Henry	Don Schaufler	1966	319
247 7/8	26 1/8	24	26	5 4/8	5 2/8	17	11	Idaho Co., ID	Howard Springston	Raymond R. Cross	1939	323
247 7/8	25 3/8	25 3/8	25	6	6	16	11	Norwood, CO	Walter L. Reisbeck	Walter L. Reisbeck	1951	323
247 7/8	21 6/8	21 2/8	24 6/8	5 7/8	5 4/8	9	10	Cabri, SK	Enos Mitchell, Jr.	Enos Mitchell, Jr.	1960	323
247 7/8	26	25 6/8	25 3/8	5 4/8	5 4/8	19	17	Weber Co., UT	John Lindsay	Robert R. Donaldson	1966	323
247 7/8	24	26	20 7/8	5	5	14	13	Asotin Co., WA	David G. Bennett	David G. Bennett	1971	323
247 6/8	22 5/8	23 6/8	19 2/8	4 3/8	5	10	13	Grand Co., UT	Bruce M. Turnbow	Bruce M. Turnbow	1967	328
247 6/8	23 5/8	22 6/8	22 2/8	5	5 1/8	11	16	Shoshone Co., ID	Gary J. Finney	Gary J. Finney	1983	328
247 5/8	26 7/8	24 7/8	24 4/8	6	5 7/8	10	13	Waterton Park, AB	Eric Westergreen	Eric Westergreen	1941	330
247 5/8	24 1/8	26	26 5/8	7 3/8	7 5/8	16	20	Hinsdale Co., CO	Fred Jardine	Fred Jardine	1966	330
247 5/8	25 4/8	25 2/8	22 2/8	6 1/8	6	12	16	Mohave Co., AZ	Brad L. Johnson	Brad L. Johnson	1986	330

MULE DEER - NON-TYPICAL ANTLERS

Odocoileus hemionus hemionus and certain related subspecies

Score	Length of Main Beam R	L	Inside Spread	Circumference at Smallest Place Between Burr and First Point R	L	Number of Points R	L	Locality	Hunter	Owner	Date Killed	Rank
247 4/8	22 6/8	27	31 6/8	6	6 6/8	14	13	Tooele Co., UT	Murray G. Loveless	Murray G. Loveless	1949	333
247 4/8	25 2/8	24 7/8	24 3/8	6 2/8	5 6/8	12	16	Bend, OR	L.M. Martinson	L.M. Martinson	1949	333
247 4/8	28 3/8	28 5/8	28 3/8	5 1/8	5	9	10	Archuleta Co., CO	Vince Plaskett	Vince Plaskett	1970	333
247 3/8	27 5/8	28 4/8	33 6/8	6 1/8	6 4/8	11	12	Missoula Co., MT	Harold Wample	Ralph Raymond	1949	336
247 3/8	28 6/8	28 1/8	25 2/8	5	5	10	9	Eagle Co., CO	Earl M. Johnson	Earl M. Johnson	1966	336
247 3/8	22 5/8	22 6/8	22 5/8	4 4/8	4 4/8	11	9	Fremont Co., ID	Donald R. Craig	Donald R. Craig	1982	336
247 2/8	24 3/8	24 1/8	24 7/8	5 3/8	5 5/8	13	10	Owyhee Co., ID	Elwin J. Saxton	Raymond R. Cross	1975	339
247 2/8	18 1/8	23 4/8	19 2/8	5	4 7/8	8	11	Elko Co., NV	Picked Up	Ron Druck	1980	339
247 1/8	30 4/8	30 3/8	28 3/8	6 1/8	6 2/8	11	11	Drummond, MT	Tom Brosovich	Tom Brosovich	1957	341
247 1/8	26 2/8	25	27 2/8	4 6/8	4 5/8	12	9	Whitebird, ID	Harold Gustin	Wayne Demaray	1965	341
247 1/8	28 3/8	27 7/8	25	6 1/8	6	10	15	San Miguel Co., CO	W.F. Grice	W.F. Grice	1978	341
247 1/8	25 7/8	28 6/8	23 7/8	5 6/8	5 4/8	7	10	Carbon Co., UT	Ralph A. Sanich	Ralph A. Sanich	1986	341
247	29 7/8	28 6/8	24 5/8	6	5 4/8	14	16	Elko Co., NV	Walter B. Hester	Walter B. Hester	1957	345
247	23 4/8	24 2/8	21 1/8	4 7/8	4 7/8	11	8	Montrose Co., CO	Thomas M. Bost	Thomas M. Bost	1967	345
246 7/8	23 5/8	23	26 4/8	5 1/8	5 1/8	11	10	Craig, CO	Fred E. Trouth	Fred E. Trouth	1960	347
246 7/8	25 5/8	26 2/8	26 5/8	5 5/8	5 5/8	10	7	Carbon Co., UT	Sherman R. Jensen, Jr.	Sherman R. Jensen, Jr.	1965	347
246 7/8	27 2/8	21 3/8	29 2/8	5 2/8	5 4/8	14	14	Needle Peak, ID	Michael G. Cameron	Michael G. Cameron	1966	347
246 7/8	24 6/8	24 4/8	21 3/8	5 7/8	5 7/8	10	10	Gallatin Co., MT	C. Martin Wood III	C. Martin Wood III	1994	347
246 6/8	23 4/8	21	26 3/8	6 2/8	6 4/8	13	14	Modoc Co., CA	Bill Foster	Foster's Bighorn Rest.	1930	351
246 6/8	24 6/8	24 7/8	22 1/8	4 5/8	4 6/8	10	14	Lawrence Co., SD	Unknown	Old Style Saloon	1945	351
246 6/8	26 6/8	26 4/8	20 7/8	4 7/8	4 7/8	10	15	Rio Blanco Co., CO	James A. Cook	James A. Cook	1963	351
246 6/8	24 2/8	23 3/8	25 1/8	5 2/8	5 2/8	13	11	Eagle Co., CO	William M. Nickels	William M. Nickels	1963	351
246 3/8	24 7/8	25	26	5 4/8	5 2/8	9	11	Glenwood Springs, CO	Grady P. Lester	Grady P. Lester	1959	355
246 3/8	24 7/8	24 6/8	25 1/8	5 2/8	5 2/8	11	14	Kaibab Natl. For., AZ	Elgin T. Gates	Elgin T. Gates	1960	355
246 2/8	28 1/8	26 6/8	28 2/8	5 1/8	4 6/8	8	9	Eagle Co., CO	Charles H. Thornberg	Charles H. Thornberg	1949	357
246 2/8	23 4/8	24 1/8	26 4/8	5 1/8	5 1/8	12	11	Ravalli Co., MT	Lloyd G. Hunter	Lloyd G. Hunter	1963	357
246 1/8	26 6/8	25 4/8	25 4/8	5 3/8	5 4/8	12	10	Mesa Co., CO	Joseph J. Pitcherella	Joseph J. Pitcherella	1972	359
246	26 7/8	25 3/8	26 4/8	5	4 6/8	9	13	Cherokee Co., IA	C.A. Stiles	Jim Haas	PR 1900	360
246	23 5/8	26 1/8	24 1/8	6 3/8	5 6/8	14	13	Mesa Co., CO	Harry A. Gay	Harry A. Gay	1962	360
246	27 1/8	26 5/8	31 6/8	5 5/8	5 5/8	8	8	Mohave Co., AZ	Bernard E. Anderson	Bernard E. Anderson	1969	360
245 7/8	23 1/8	24 5/8	17 6/8	4 7/8	5 2/8	14	16	Tyee Lake, BC	Harold Bartha	Harold Bartha	1961	363
245 7/8	24 1/8	23 4/8	22 3/8	4 2/8	4 3/8	11	9	Idaho Co., ID	Unknown	D.J. Hollinger & B. Howard	PR 1970	363
245 6/8	27 1/8	28 2/8	24 4/8	5 6/8	5 7/8	11	9	Rio Arriba Co., NM	Kenneth W. Lee	Kenneth W. Lee	1971	365
245 5/8	27 5/8	28	23 3/8	5 1/8	5 7/8	13	11	Rio Blanco Co., CO	Charlie Grove	Dorothy Shults	1934	366
245 5/8	25 5/8	24 4/8	24	5 3/8	5 2/8	13	12	Latah Co., ID	Leonard Gunnerson	Michael R. Damery	PR 1944	366
245 5/8	26 4/8	26 6/8	22 2/8	5	5 3/8	10	10	Montana	Unknown	D.J. Hollinger & B. Howard	PR 1968	366

Score	Length of Main Beam R	Length of Main Beam L	Inside Spread	Circumference R	Circumference L	Points R	Points L	Locality	Hunter	Owner	Date Killed	Rank
245 5/8	27 2/8	28 2/8	23 2/8	5 3/8	5 4/8	9	8	Eagle Co., CO	James Caraccioli	James Caraccioli	1978	366
245 3/8	24 1/8	24 6/8	21 7/8	5	5	11	10	Broadwater Co., MT	Harry Neafus	Dwayne Frandsen	PR 1870	370
245 3/8	28 2/8	24	31 6/8	5 1/8	5 1/8	10	7	Saquache Co., CO	Walter A. Larsen	Walter A. Larsen	1962	370
245 2/8	24 6/8	24 6/8	24 3/8	5 1/8	5	18	12	Lac La Biche, AB	Julius Hagen	Olaf Hagen	1945	372
245 2/8	26 5/8	27 4/8	21 2/8	5 6/8	5 6/8	8	10	Jicarilla Apache Res., NM	Arthur Wanoskea	Arthur Wanoskea	1960	372
245 2/8	28	27 5/8	33 4/8	4 7/8	4 6/8	8	8	Fergus Co., MT	Unknown	Don Schaufler	PR 1965	372
245 2/8	23 2/8	22 3/8	20 2/8	6 3/8	6 3/8	9	9	Rio Arriba Co., NM	Robert B. Loring	Robert B. Loring	1995	372
245 1/8	27 1/8	25 3/8	25 4/8	5 3/8	5 3/8	7	7	Coconino Co., AZ	Edward H. Abplanalp	Edward H. Abplanalp	1947	376
245 1/8	24	23 2/8	20 2/8	5 4/8	5 3/8	10	12	Power Co., ID	Mark B. Cooper	D.J. Hollinger & B. Howard	1984	376
245	26 6/8	22 5/8	18 5/8	7	6 5/8	9	12	Mt. Trumbull, AZ	Tony Stromei	Tony Stromei	1960	378
245	25 6/8	25 5/8	29 6/8	5 4/8	5 5/8	17	14	Bonner Co., ID	Dick Sherwood	Dick Sherwood	1963	378
245	26 7/8	26 1/8	24 1/8	5 2/8	5 3/8	12	15	Kane Co., UT	Koyle T. Cram	Koyle T. Cram	1966	378
245	30	26 3/8	27 5/8	5 2/8	5 2/8	6	12	Okanagan Valley, BC	Dan Osborne	Don Schaufler	1969	378
244 7/8	28 3/8	28 5/8	25	6 4/8	5 5/8	9	11	Eagle, CO	Robert Rambo	Robert Rambo	1963	382
244 7/8	25 6/8	26 4/8	22 1/8	4 7/8	4 7/8	11	9	Lincoln Co., WY	Brian H. Suter	Brian H. Suter	1981	382
244 5/8	25 6/8	26 3/8	22 3/8	4 7/8	4 7/8	8	12	Summit Co., UT	Dewey R. Saxton	Dewey R. Saxton	1965	384
244 5/8	25 1/8	25 3/8	22 1/8	5 2/8	5 1/8	10	8	Park Co., MT	Unknown	Don Schaufler	PR 1968	384
244 5/8	25 5/8	24 2/8	22 1/8	5 6/8	5 6/8	14	13	Teton Co., WY	Vern Shinkle	Vern Shinkle	1968	384
244 5/8	25 5/8	25 4/8	20 3/8	5 1/8	5 1/8	13	10	Delta Co., CO	Neil A. Briscoe, Jr.	Neil A. Briscoe, Jr.	1969	384
244 5/8	26	25	18 6/8	5 4/8	5 5/8	20	15	Rossland, BC	Victor Mattiazzi	Victor Mattiazzi	1970	384
244 4/8	24 6/8	26 6/8	26	4 6/8	5	11	11	Kaibab Natl. For., AZ	C.M. Randal, Jr.	C.M. Randal, Jr.	1953	389
244 4/8	24 3/8	19 7/8	26	4 7/8	5 1/8	14	11	Wyoming	Unknown	D.J. Hollinger & B. Howard	PR 1990	390
244 2/8	25 1/8	24 5/8	22 5/8	5	5	13	12	Wasatch Co., UT	Unknown	Ted Clegg	1938	391
244 2/8	24 4/8	26 2/8	28 4/8	5 6/8	5 6/8	8	9	Kaibab Natl. For., AZ	Ray Ramsey	Ray Ramsey	1952	391
244 2/8	28 4/8	28 7/8	30 1/8	5 4/8	5 2/8	9	8	Oak Creek, CO	Scott C. Hinkle	Scott C. Hinkle	1961	391
244 2/8	22 6/8	21 6/8	19 4/8	4 7/8	4 4/8	13	9	Fremont Co., WY	Warren V. Spriggs	Warren V. Spriggs	1962	391
244 2/8	25 6/8	26 3/8	22 7/8	5 2/8	5 2/8	13	13	San Juan Co., UT	Phil Acton	Phil Acton	1966	391
244 2/8	27 3/8	29 2/8	29 6/8	5 3/8	5 2/8	9	9	Montrose Co., CO	Jim Herndon	Mrs. Jim Herndon	1974	391
244 2/8	23 1/8	25	23 6/8	5 5/8	5 2/8	12	9	Mesa Co., CO	Thomas S. Hundley	Thomas S. Hundley	1986	391
244 1/8	25	26 4/8	29 2/8	5 6/8	5 3/8	11	12	Split Rock, WY	Herb Klein	Herb Klein	1957	398
244 1/8	24 2/8	25 1/8	27	5 1/8	5 1/8	14	11	Mesa Co., CO	Edward B. Walsh	Mrs. Edward B. Walsh	1960	398
244 1/8	25 1/8	22 6/8	23 2/8	5 3/8	5 2/8	12	14	Grand Co., CO	Kenneth H. Newbury	Kenneth H. Newbury	1966	398
244 1/8	24 2/8	24 2/8	28	4 4/8	4 4/8	9	12	Big Horn Co., WY	Picked Up	Henry D. Frey	1978	398
244	26 4/8	27 1/8	28	4 6/8	4 6/8	9	9	East Canyon, UT	Ronald E. Coburn	Ronald E. Coburn	1961	402
243 7/8	23 6/8	23 7/8	26	4 6/8	4 6/8	9	10	Utah Co., UT	Zenneth K. Chamberlain	Zenneth K. Chamberlain	1956	403
243 7/8	24 1/8	27	24 6/8	4 4/8	4 4/8	18	11	St. Cyr Hills, SK	Raymond Jeancart	Raymond Jeancart	1963	403
243 7/8	23 3/8	23 4/8	21 3/8	4 3/8	4 3/8	11	10	Malheur Co., OR	Larry L. Herron	Larry L. Herron	1983	403
243 6/8	27 2/8	27 3/8	27 3/8	5 5/8	5 4/8	16	18	Slave Lake, AB	R.W.H. Eben-Ebenau	R.W.H. Eben-Ebenau	1930	406
243 6/8	26	22 4/8	26 3/8	6 2/8	6 2/8	10	10	San Miguel Co., CO	Ben Crandell	Ben Crandell	1939	406
243 6/8	26 5/8	24 5/8	29 7/8	5 4/8	5 4/8	9	9	Apache Co., AZ	Jay M. Ogden	Jay M. Ogden	1991	406
243 6/8	22 6/8	25 7/8	26 3/8	4 7/8	4 7/8	13	12	Montrose, SK	Gordon G. Pattison	Gordon G. Pattison	1992	406
243 6/8	24 2/8	23 6/8	22 7/8	5 4/8	4 5/8	11	10	Veteran, AB	Frank Geduhn	Frank Geduhn	1994	406
243 5/8	23 6/8	23 2/8	26 6/8	4 7/8	4 6/8	9	7	Cache Co., UT	Albert C. Steffenhagen	A. Ladell Atkinson	1924	411
243 5/8	27 1/8	25 6/8	23 3/8	4 6/8	4 5/8	10	11	Gunnison Co., CO	Unknown	D.J. Hollinger & B. Howard	PR 1970	411
243 4/8	21 6/8	22 7/8	23	5	5 4/8	10	13	Clear Creek Co., ID	Louis I. Kingsley	Louis I. Kingsley	1981	413
243 4/8	24	21 6/8	21 5/8	5 5/8	5 4/8	14	14	Unknown	David Bicknell	D.J. Hollinger & B. Howard	PR 1986	413
243 4/8	22 2/8	18 1/8	23 5/8	4 5/8	5	14	11	Cibola Co., NM	Fred R. Valdez, Jr.	Don Schaufler	1986	413

MULE DEER - NON-TYPICAL ANTLERS

Odocoileus hemionus hemionus and certain related subspecies

Score	Length of Main Beam R	L	Inside Spread	Circumference at Smallest Place Between Burr and First Point R	L	Number of Points R	L	Locality	Hunter	Owner	Date Killed	Rank
243 2/8	28 4/8	28 1/8	25 5/8	4 6/8	4 7/8	10	10	Colorado	Unknown	D.J. Hollinger & B. Howard	1954	416
243 1/8	29 2/8	28 2/8	28 6/8	4 6/8	5 2/8	8	9	Harrison Gulch, CO	George R. Mattern	Aly M. Bruner	1958	417
243 1/8	24 4/8	24 3/8	21 1/8	5	5	12	7	Converse Co., WY	William E. Goswick	William E. Goswick	1968	417
243 1/8	25 4/8	23 4/8	25 1/8	5 4/8	5 7/8	8	11	Fremont Co., ID	Larry D. Hawker	Larry D. Hawker	1970	417
243	25 7/8	25 6/8	20	5 2/8	5	15	12	Crook Co., OR	Wes Mitts	Wes Mitts	1936	420
243	25	25 5/8	20 4/8	7 1/8	5 2/8	15	11	Winthrop, WA	Bruce Miller	Bruce Miller	1941	420
243	25 6/8	27 2/8	29	5 3/8	5 3/8	11	10	Elko Co., NV	Paul Giuliani	Paul Giuliani	1971	420
242 7/8	24 4/8	24 1/8	22 6/8	4 7/8	5	10	11	Sheridan, WY	J.M. Blakeman	J.M. Blakeman	1952	423
242 7/8	29 6/8	30	28 4/8	5 1/8	5	12	8	Unknown	Unknown	Alan C. Ellsworth	PR 1960	423
242 7/8	22 4/8	23 7/8	26 4/8	5 4/8	5 3/8	10	12	Gem Co., ID	Roland Bright	Roland Bright	1965	423
242 7/8	26 4/8	26 2/8	22 3/8	5 5/8	5 7/8	11	16	Gem Co., ID	Cary G. Cada	Raymond R. Cross	1975	423
242 5/8	25	26 3/8	18 3/8	6	5 6/8	11	10	Baison, ID	Daniel E. Osborne	Daniel E. Osborne	1959	427
242 5/8	27 3/8	26 7/8	25 5/8	5 7/8	5 6/8	12	9	Sanders Co., MT	Robert D. Frisk	Robert D. Frisk	1974	427
242 4/8	27 2/8	25 3/8	29 4/8	5	5	10	11	Blaine Co., ID	Roger A. Crowder	Roger A. Crowder	1957	429
242 4/8	27 4/8	27 5/8	25 4/8	6 1/8	5 6/8	9	8	Hinsdale Co., CO	Picked Up	Rick House	1991	429
242 3/8	23 1/8	22 3/8	17 3/8	4 7/8	5	12	12	Arborfield, SK	Joseph Fournier	Joseph Fournier	1930	431
242 2/8	24 2/8	21 5/8	25 4/8	5 6/8	5 6/8	15	10	Iron Co., UT	Unknown	Don Schaufler	PR 1958	432
242 2/8	23 2/8	23	20 2/8	5 3/8	5 6/8	12	17	Middle Park, CO	Picked Up	Karl H. Knorr	PR 1961	432
242 2/8	25 4/8	25 3/8	23 2/8	5	4 7/8	9	12	Rabbit Ears Pass, CO	Douglas Valentine	Douglas Valentine	1964	432
242 2/8	24	25 2/8	21	6	6	9	11	Rio Arriba Co., NM	Elvon DeVaney	Shannon DeVaney	1971	432
242 1/8	20 7/8	23 2/8	17 4/8	6	5 7/8	12	11	Bear Lake Co., ID	Gordon Millward	Gordon Millward	1960	436
242 1/8	28	27 6/8	22 1/8	6 1/8	6 1/8	9	11	Hinsdale Co., CO	Robert N. Gale	Robert N. Gale	1970	436
242 1/8	26	25 4/8	28	5 2/8	5 2/8	12	10	S. Saskatchewan River, AB	Bill Crose	Bill Crose	1973	436
242 1/8	25 6/8	25 5/8	23 2/8	5 4/8	5 4/8	10	14	Clinton, BC	Terry Lacey	Terry Lacey	1994	436
242 1/8	26 3/8	26 1/8	23 7/8	5 7/8	5 7/8	9	15	Klamath Co., OR	Jamie M. York	Jamie M. York	1995	436
242	26 2/8	26 6/8	28 1/8	5 4/8	5 4/8	10	8	Garfield Co., CO	Corinne Fields	Corinne Fields	1946	441
242	22 6/8	23 5/8	18 6/8	5 4/8	5 7/8	12	14	Porcupine Ridge, BC	Daniel J. Stanek	Daniel J. Stanek	1981	441
242	25 7/8	26 2/8	26 2/8	5 1/8	5 1/8	14	8	Jefferson Co., OR	Unknown	Rick Berreth	1985	441
241 7/8	24 5/8	24 2/8	25	5 2/8	5 2/8	11	19	Madison Co., ID	Spencer L. Darrar	Spencer L. Darrar	1953	444
241 7/8	22 5/8	20 2/8	20 2/8	5 1/8	5 1/8	9	10	Sanders Co., MT	Grover Browning	D.J. Hollinger & B. Howard	1962	444
241 7/8	21	18	14 7/8	4 3/8	5 3/8	12	15	Grand Co., CO	Buzz Faro	Buzz Faro	1963	444
241 7/8	24 2/8	25 6/8	24 5/8	5 3/8	5	10	11	La Plata Co., CO	Ricky Dixon	D.J. Hollinger & B. Howard	1978	444
241 7/8	26 4/8	26 2/8	30 6/8	4 5/8	4 6/8	10	9	Great Sand Hills, SK	Randall N. Bostick	Randall N. Bostick	1984	444
241 7/8	24	25 4/8	18 5/8	5 7/8	6	14	11	Bear Lake Co., ID	A. Bruce LaRose	A. Bruce LaRose	1989	444
241 6/8	27 2/8	27 2/8	26 6/8	4 6/8	5	8	10		Len E. Mayfield	Len E. Mayfield	1972	450
241 6/8	25 6/8	26 3/8	31 1/8	5	5	11	9	Idaho	Unknown	D.J. Hollinger & B. Howard	PR 1980	450

Score	Main Beam R	Main Beam L	Inside Spread	Circ. R	Circ. L	Pts R	Pts L	Locality	By Whom Killed	Owner	Date Killed	Rank
241 6/8	24 7/8	23 5/8	21 6/8	5 6/8	6	17	19	Hot Springs Co., WY	John A. Kotan, Jr.	Picked up	1983	450
241 6/8	26	26	26	4	4 5/8	9	9	Park Co., WY	Troy A. Jones	Troy A. Jones	1997	450
241 5/8	27 1/8	27	23 4/8	6	5 3/8	13	10	Adams Co., ID	Joseph N. Ruscigno	Joseph N. Ruscigno	1960	454
241 5/8	22 3/8	22 3/8	21 7/8	6 2/8	6 2/8	15	16	Red Deer River, AB	Carl J. Peterson	Carl J. Peterson	1993	454
241 4/8	27	27	27	5	5 3/8	8	7	Socorro Co., NM	James T. Everheart	James T. Everheart	1973	456
241 4/8	25 1/8	25 7/8	23 3/8	4 4/8	4 4/8	10	9	Summit Co., CO	Robert R. Ross	Robert R. Ross	1974	456
241 4/8	27 2/8	27	22 5/8	5 3/8	5 3/8	17	12	Douglas Co., CO	Donald E. Ditmars	Donald E. Ditmars	1994	456
241 3/8	22 3/8	23 7/8	20 4/8	5 1/8	5 2/8	10	12	Adams Co., ID	Peter Renberg	Peter Renberg	1963	459
241 3/8	26 6/8	24 7/8	24 3/8	5	5 1/8	12	13	Salmon River, ID	Richard Shilling	Richard Shilling	1965	459
241 3/8	19	24 6/8	20	6 2/8	6 4/8	12	15	Nakusp, BC	Frank Vicen	Frank Vicen	1967	459
241 3/8	27 1/8	26 1/8	26 1/8	5 5/8	5 4/8	13	11	Kane Co., UT	Aivars O. Berkis	Aivars O. Berkis	1987	459
241 2/8	26 6/8	25 1/8	18 6/8	5	5	10	13	Oak Creek, CO	Richard J. Peltier	Richard J. Peltier	1967	463
241 1/8	24 3/8	24 5/8	24 6/8	5 7/8	5 7/8	16	12	Bloom Creek, BC	Ron Yerbury	Ron Yerbury	1992	464
241 1/8	27 1/8	26 1/8	26 6/8	6 3/8	6 1/8	11	10	Lincoln Co., WY	Mark C. Lafferty	Mark C. Lafferty	1994	464
241	26 6/8	25 7/8	26 7/8	6	5 5/8	9	8	Fremont Co., ID	Don Schaufler	Don Freeman	1953	466
241	25 6/8	27	25 6/8	5	5 1/8	8	11	Colorado	Aly M. Bruner	Nolan Allen	PR 1969	466
241	26 2/8	27 3/8	26 3/8	4 6/8	4 6/8	11	6	Lewis & Clark Co., MT	Mike Filcher	Mike Filcher	1972	466
240 7/8	27	27 5/8	27 3/8	5 2/8	5 1/8	6	9	New Castle, CO	Harold F. Auld	Harold F. Auld	1960	469
240 7/8	27 7/8	27 5/8	25 2/8	5 3/8	5 1/8	7	12	Rio Arriba Co., NM	Douglas Bryant	Douglas Bryant	1988	469
240 7/8	27 4/8	28 2/8	22	5 7/8	6	7	11	Coconino Co., AZ	Robert B. Metzgus	Robert B. Metzgus	1993	469
240 6/8	26 3/8	25 6/8	23 6/8	5 6/8	5 5/8	9	9	Colorado	Darryl Powell	Unknown	PR 1970	472
240 6/8	27	25 6/8	27 1/8	5 1/8	5 7/8	10	10	Eagle Co., CO	Steve B. Humann	Steve B. Humann	1982	472
240 5/8	26 4/8	27 6/8	23 2/8	5 7/8	6	10	13	Kaibab Natl. For., AZ	Bert E. George	Bert E. George	1949	474
240 5/8	22	23 2/8	21	6	4 7/8	10	9	Elko Co., NV	George M. Boman	George M. Boman	1956	474
240 5/8	26	26 1/8	26 1/8	4 7/8	5 4/8	11	12	Lincoln Co., WY	D.J. Hollinger & B. Howard	Unknown	PR 1965	474
240 4/8	26 4/8	27	21 4/8	5 4/8	5 4/8	10	9	Modoc Co., CA	Niilo Niemi	Niilo Niemi	1968	477
240 4/8	27 1/8	25 4/8	27 1/8	6 2/8	5 6/8	9	8	La Plata Co., CO	Cullen Wagoner	Cullen Wagoner	1976	477
240 4/8	25 4/8	22	22 6/8	5 3/8	5 3/8	10	11	Eagle Co., CO	James P. Hale	James P. Hale	1979	477
240 4/8	23 6/8	23 5/8	23 2/8	5 1/8	5 1/8	11	14	Morgan Co., UT	Pietro De Santis	Pietro De Santis	1982	477
240 4/8	23	24 4/8	24 4/8	5 2/8	5 2/8	15	14	Garfield Co., CO	James E. Powell, Jr.	James E. Powell, Jr.	1983	477
240 4/8	25 5/8	24 4/8	21 6/8	5 4/8	5 4/8	10	9	Great Sand Hills, SK	Emile T. Paradis	Emile T. Paradis	1989	477
240 3/8	22	22 3/8	22 3/8	4 5/8	4 4/8	13	11	Coconino Co., AZ	Craig R. Dunlap	Craig R. Dunlap	1993	484
240 2/8	22 3/8	24 5/8	21 7/8	5 5/8	5 5/8	13	12	Missoula Co., MT	Richard A. Gendrow	Richard A. Gendrow	1973	485
240 2/8	27 3/8	27 1/8	23 1/8	5 1/8	5 2/8	9	11	Mt. Dellenbaugh, AZ	Edwin R. Riggs	Edwin R. Riggs	1964	485
240 2/8	28 4/8	24 4/8	26 4/8	6 3/8	6 4/8	9	8	Crook Co., OR	Charles H. Kies	Charles H. Kies	1995	485
240 2/8	27	26 4/8	27	5 2/8	5 2/8	13	7	Unknown	Darryl Powell	Unknown	PR 1995	485
240 1/8	22 7/8	22 6/8	22 2/8	5 2/8	5 2/8	9	11	Yuma Co., CO	Vernon E. Young	Vernon E. Young	1995	489
240 1/8	24 2/8	24	24 5/8	5 7/8	5 6/8	13	12	Harney Co., OR	R.G. Creager	R.G. Creager	1957	489
240	23 1/8	23 1/8	19 6/8	5 5/8	5 5/8	12	10	Elmore Co., ID	Phillip K. Messer	Phillip K. Messer	1971	491
240	28	28	23 2/8	5 4/8	5 4/8	7	10	Kamloops, BC	Ralph McLean	Ralph McLean	1960	491
240	25 1/8	24 4/8	25	4 6/8	4 6/8	12	8	Grand Valley, CO	Ed Peters, Jr.	Ed Peters, Jr.	1962	491
240	26 1/8	28 5/8	23 3/8	5 6/8	5 6/8	9	13	San Juan Wilder., CO	Tommie Cornelius	Tommie Cornelius	1967	491
239 7/8	27 6/8	27 7/8	27 1/8	5	5	8	13	Frenchman River, SK	Edward J. Hardin	Edward J. Hardin	1992	495
239 4/8	24 6/8	23 7/8	25	5 3/8	5 3/8	12	15	Diefenbaker Lake, SK	Anthony J. Pyette	Anthony J. Pyette	1996	496
239 4/8	25 1/8	25 1/8	19 2/8	5 5/8	5 5/8	14	13	Pondera Co., MT	Dan Mougeot	Dan Mougeot	1961	496
239 2/8	27 4/8	29 2/8	24 5/8	5 4/8	5 5/8	12	14	Washington Co., UT	Doug McKnight	Doug McKnight	1967	497
239 1/8	26 1/8	27 1/8	25	4 7/8	4 6/8	11	11	Summit Co., CO	Fred H. Palmer	Fred H. Palmer	1959	498

MULE DEER - NON-TYPICAL ANTLERS

Odocoileus hemionus hemionus and certain related subspecies

Score	Length of Main Beam		Inside Spread	Circumference at Smallest Place Between Burr and First Point		Number of Points		Locality	Hunter	Owner	Date Killed	Rank
	R	L		R	L	R	L					
239 1/8	29	26 4/8	31 2/8	4 7/8	5 3/8	8	11	Lucky Lake, SK	Dan Mosley	Dan Mosley	1996	498
239	24 1/8	25 3/8	24 5/8	4 7/8	5	13	8	Wallace Co., KS	Rudolph A. Busen	Rudolph A. Busen	1993	500
238 6/8	26 2/8	26 3/8	28	4 7/8	4 6/8	11	9	Lincoln Co., WY	Waylon G. Beckstrom	Waylon G. Beckstrom	1997	501
238 4/8	27	27 1/8	28 7/8	6 1/8	5 4/8	17	13	Pima Co., AZ	Richard M. Cordora	Richard M. Cordora	1989	502
238 4/8	26 2/8	25 6/8	23 7/8	5 1/8	5 2/8	11	13	Coconino Co., AZ	Gilbert T. Adams	Gilbert T. Adams	1992	502
238 2/8	23 6/8	24 1/8	26 5/8	5 1/8	5	16	11	Walsh, AB	Rick M. MacDonald	Rick M. MacDonald	1987	504
237 6/8	25 3/8	25 2/8	25	4 5/8	4 5/8	9	11	Coconino Co., AZ	Ronald J. Wolosyn	Ronald J. Wolosyn	1992	505
237 6/8	23 7/8	23 1/8	20 1/8	5 5/8	5 4/8	13	10	Caribou Co., ID	Robert L. Rigby	Robert L. Rigby	1996	505
237 5/8	25 4/8	26	21 7/8	4 7/8	4 6/8	8	9	Lynx Creek, BC	J. Gregory Simmons	J. Gregory Simmons	1989	507
237 3/8	27 2/8	23 7/8	20 2/8	4 6/8	5 4/8	8	13	Hawley Creek, ID	Clifford Nealis	Clifford Nealis	1960	508
237 3/8	23 6/8	23 2/8	23 3/8	5 5/8	5 7/8	11	12	Bonneville Co., ID	Bert L. Freed	Bert L. Freed	1987	508
236 7/8	26 2/8	27 2/8	30 4/8	4 4/8	4 5/8	9	9	Lincoln Co., WY	Terry Barton	D.J. Hollinger & B. Howard	1989	510
236 7/8	24 6/8	24	17 7/8	4 7/8	4 6/8	9	9	Ft. St. John, BC	Jos Van Hage	Jos Van Hage	1994	510
236 2/8	25 1/8	23 6/8	17 7/8	5 3/8	5 6/8	10	10	Kane Co., UT	Ken Church	Ken Church	1987	512
236 1/8	26 3/8	26	20 3/8	5 7/8	6 1/8	16	12	Rio Arriba Co., NM	Shane Vigil	Shane Vigil	1997	513
236	26 5/8	27	28 1/8	5	5	10	10	Ravalli Co., MT	Daniel I. Cainan	B&C National Collection	1957	514
236	28 6/8	28 2/8	29 4/8	4 7/8	4 6/8	9	9	Antelope Lake, SK	Roland Joubert	Roland Joubert	1993	514
235 5/8	24 6/8	24 4/8	23	5	5	13	10	Cypress Hills, SK	Margie R. Stabler	Margie R. Stabler	1994	516
235 3/8	25 1/8	24 6/8	20 3/8	5 2/8	5	10	12	Ferry Co., WA	Jack Ledgerwood	Kelly Ledgerwood	1938	517
235 3/8	25 2/8	24 7/8	27 6/8	5 2/8	5 6/8	7	11	Cassia Co., ID	Picked Up	Keith G. Palmer	1996	517
234 3/8	25 7/8	26	26	5 1/8	5 3/8	7	9	Fremont Co., WY	Gail E. Folston	Gail E. Folston	1968	519
234 2/8	29	28 4/8	28 2/8	6 3/8	6 4/8	9	13	Boise Co., ID	Lowell B. Nosker	Lowell B. Nosker	1946	520
234 1/8	26 2/8	26	25 7/8	5 1/8	5 2/8	9	8	Gunnison Co., CO	Jack E. Moermond	Jack E. Moermond	1970	521
233 7/8	23 5/8	24 1/8	19 3/8	4 6/8	4 7/8	13	9	Colorado	Unknown	Darryl Powell	PR 1992	522
233 6/8	26 3/8	24 6/8	22 2/8	4 2/8	5 4/8	12	10	Rio Blanco Co., CO	Robert E. Buckles	Robert E. Buckles	1960	523
232 7/8	28 2/8	26 2/8	21 6/8	4 5/8	4 6/8	7	10	Arizona	Brian Quintero	D.J. Hollinger & B. Howard	1986	524
232 7/8	28 3/8	27 4/8	23 3/8	5 3/8	5 2/8	9	11	Caribou Co., ID	Michael H. Ferrera	Michael H. Ferrera	1992	524
232 5/8	24 4/8	25 7/8	17 5/8	4 3/8	4 3/8	13	10	Teton Co., WY	Bruce K. McRae	Bruce K. McRae	1986	526
232 3/8	27 2/8	26 5/8	22 2/8	5 3/8	5 5/8	14	9	Colorado	Unknown	Melvin A. Mitchell, Jr.	PR 1900	527
232	23 1/8	24	18 3/8	5 3/8	5 3/8	10	17	Grand Co., CO	William L. Henry	William L. Henry	1986	528
231 7/8	24 6/8	24 6/8	23 5/8	5 6/8	5 4/8	9	10	Bear Lake Co., ID	George L. Clifford	George L. Clifford	1966	529
231 7/8	25 5/8	30 2/8	25 2/8	5	4 7/8	11	9	Rio Arriba Co., NM	Dan F. Holleman	Vernon D. Holleman	1966	529
231 2/8	21 1/8	21 3/8	20	5 4/8	5 2/8	7	8	Lincoln Co., NV	Leo W. Mack, Jr.	Leo W. Mack, Jr.	1995	531
231 1/8	23 1/8	24 5/8	22 1/8	4 6/8	4 6/8	11	7	Eagle Co., CO	Mike Crites	Mike Crites	1996	532
231	23 7/8	26	19 3/8	5 7/8	5 4/8	11	13	Teton Co., ID	Unknown	D.J. Hollinger & B. Howard	1979	533
230 5/8	24 1/8	25 2/8	27 4/8	5	5 4/8	7	10	San Juan Co., UT	Gregory S. Amaral	Gregory S. Amaral	1988	534

Score								Locality	Hunter	Owner	Date	Rank
230 $^5/_8$	28 $^1/_8$	27 $^6/_8$	31 $^1/_8$	5 $^4/_8$	5 $^2/_8$	10	10	Mohave Co., AZ	Ross A. Ray	Ross A. Ray	1996	534
230 $^3/_8$	23 $^7/_8$	24 $^1/_8$	22 $^2/_8$	5 $^1/_8$	5 $^3/_8$	9	8	Eagle Co., CO	Ted R. Ramirez	Ted R. Ramirez	1996	536
230 $^1/_8$	27	25 $^2/_8$	22	5	5	10	12	Baker Co., OR	Unknown	D.J. Hollinger & B. Howard	PR 1970	537
230	24 $^4/_8$	23	25 $^4/_8$	5	5	12	12	Washoe Co., NV	Jason Langslet	Jason Langslet	1995	538
259 $^1/_8$*	26 $^5/_8$	26 $^5/_8$	23 $^7/_8$	5 $^7/_8$	5 $^6/_8$	12	13	Otero Co., CO	John N. Lucero	John N. Lucero	1995	

* Final score is subject to revision by additional verifying measurements.

Photograph courtesy of Kevin Harris

CATEGORY
MULE DEER
NON-TYPICAL ANTLERS

SCORE
264-1/8

HUNTER
GILBERT T. ADAMS

LOCATION
COCONINO CO., AZ

DATE OF KILL
DECEMBER 1989

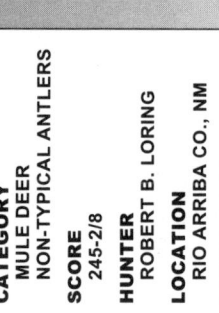

CATEGORY
MULE DEER
NON-TYPICAL ANTLERS

SCORE
245-2/8

HUNTER
ROBERT B. LORING

LOCATION
RIO ARRIBA CO., NM

DATE OF KILL
DECEMBER 1995

CATEGORY
MULE DEER
NON-TYPICAL ANTLERS

SCORE
294-4/8

HUNTER
ROBERT H. ARLEDGE

LOCATION
ELMORE CO., ID

DATE OF KILL
OCTOBER 1997

MULE DEER, COLUMBIA AND SITKA BLACKTAIL DEER BOUNDARIES

The problem of properly defining the boundary between the large antlered mule deer, which ranges widely over most of the western third of the United States and western Canada, and its smaller relatives, the Columbia and Sitka blacktails of the West Coast, has been difficult from the beginning of the records keeping. The three varieties belong to the same species and thus are able to interbreed readily where their ranges meet. The intent of the Club in drawing suitable boundary lines is to exclude intergrades from each of the three categories. These boundaries have been redrawn as necessary, as more details have become known about the precise ranges of these animals.

The current boundary for mule and Columbia blacktail deer is as follows:

BRITISH COLUMBIA — Starting at the Washington-British Columbia border, blacktail deer range runs west of the height of land between the Skagit and and the Chilliwack Ranges, intersecting the Fraser River opposite the mouth of Ruby Creek, then west to and up Harrison Lake to and up Tipella Creek to the height of land in Garibaldi Park and northwesterly along this divide past Alta Lake, Mt. Dalgleish and Mt. Waddington, thence north to Bella Coola. From Bella Coola, the boundary continues north to the head of Dean Channel, Gardner Canal and Douglas Channel to the town of Anyox, then due west to the Alaska-British Columbia border, which is then followed south to open water. This boundary excludes the area west of the Klesilkwa River and the west side of the Lillooet River.

WASHINGTON — Beginning at the Washington-British Columbia border, the boundary line runs south along the west boundary of North Cascades National Park to the range line between R10E and R11E, Willamette Meridian, which is then followed directly south to its intersection with the township line between T18N and T17N, which is then followed westward until it connects with the north border of Mt. Rainier National Park, then along the north, west and south park boundaries until it intersects with the range line between R9E and R10E, Willamette Meridian, which is then followed directly south to the Columbia River near Cook.

OREGON — Beginning at Multnomah Falls on the Columbia River, the boundary runs south along the western boundary of the National Forest to Tiller in Douglas County, then south along Highway 227 to Highway 62 at Trail, then south following Highway 62 to Medford, from which the boundary follows the range line between R1W and R2W, Willamette Meridian, to the California border.

CALIFORNIA — Beginning in Siskiyou County at the Oregon-California border, the boundary lies between townships R8W and R9W M.D.M., extending south to and along the Klamath River to Hamburg, then south along the road to Scott Bar, continuing south and then east on the unimproved road from Scott Bar to its intersection with the paved road to Mugginsville, then south through Mugginsville to State Highway 3, which is then followed to Douglas City in Trinity County, from which the line runs east on State Highway 299 to Interstate 5. The line follows Interstate 5 south to the area of Anderson, where the Sacramento River moves east of Interstate 5, following the Sacramento River until it joins with the San Joaquin River, which is followed to the south border of Stanislaus County. The line then runs west along this border to the east border of Santa Clara County. The east and south borders of Santa Clara County are then followed to the south border of Santa Cruz County, which is then followed to the edge of Monterey Bay.

On the Queen Charlotte Islands of British Columbia and along the coast of Alaska ranges another subspecies of mule deer, the Sitka blacktail. Accordingly, after a compilation of scores of the largest Sitka blacktail deer trophies from southern Alaska (including those from Kodiak Island where they have been transplanted), a separate trophy category was established for Sitka blacktail deer in 1984 with a minimum all-time records book entry score of 108.

Sitka blacktails have been transplanted to the Queen Charlotte Islands and are abundant there. Thus, the acceptable area for this category includes southeastern Alaska and the Queen Charlotte Islands of British Columbia. ∎

COLUMBIA BLACKTAIL DEER
WORLD'S RECORD

On a dank October morning in 1953, Lester H. Miller found himself face to face with an extraordinary Columbia blacktail deer (*Odocoileus hemionus columbianus*). He had been waiting for this moment a long time.

From the very first day Miller saw this buck in 1950, he knew he had to have him, no matter the cost in time or effort. For almost four years Miller stalked, drove thickets and took stands in the Upper Lincoln Creek Area of Lewis County, Washington, in pursuit of a near mythical buck that, except for an occasional sighting, eluded him and every hunter in the region.

"At Grange meetings, livestock auctions, and wherever people gathered in the nearby towns of Chehalis, Centralia, Fords Prairie, or Adna, it was not unusual to hear someone mention this majestic animal. Mostly, they would talk about his huge antlers, four points or bigger. Of course, the stories grew in the telling and soon he was almost a legend. Although I had twice jumped this deer out of his bed, and had seen him running down a runway on three or four different occasions, I still had never fired a shot at him, fearful that I might wound him and not make a clean kill."

Unhampered by the weight of his gun, Miller found himself spending the greater part of every day in the off-season cold-tracking, but occasionally hot on the trail of the Columbia blacktail. Gradually he began to familiarize himself with the deer's whereabouts hoping to catch an occasional glimpse in order to rid himself of the buck fever that was running so high.

He continued to keep tabs on the buck right up to that fateful October morning in 1953. Waiting in the final shadows of darkness, Miller's luck was about to change as the early autumn light signaled opening day of the season. After several false starts, Miller found himself on the right track following a muddy trail until he came across the ghostly figures of some deer disappearing into the alder trees. A huge four-pointer came into range, but Miller held back his instinct to shoot. It was not "The King." Miller continued on, making his way up the side of a ridge toward an opening in the timber.

"In the middle of the clearing, 80 yards away, stood my buck! He was quartering away from me, looking downhill right at me. I raised my gun and fired. The bullet struck him behind the shoulder and went into the heart. He went down in his tracks and never moved.

"I have killed many bull elk in my lifetime. But, no animal has ever had the impact on me that this huge buck had when I looked down on him as he lay there on the side of that ridge."

"The antlers were awesome to see with their spread and color and symmetry. In addition, they were hanging heavy with moss and lichen that he had accumulated while feeding or "horning" the alders and willows along the creek."

Scored at 182-2/8, the story behind the World's Record Columbia blacktail would be retold by Miller for years as an endless stream of visitors came to see and admire his renowned trophy. ∎

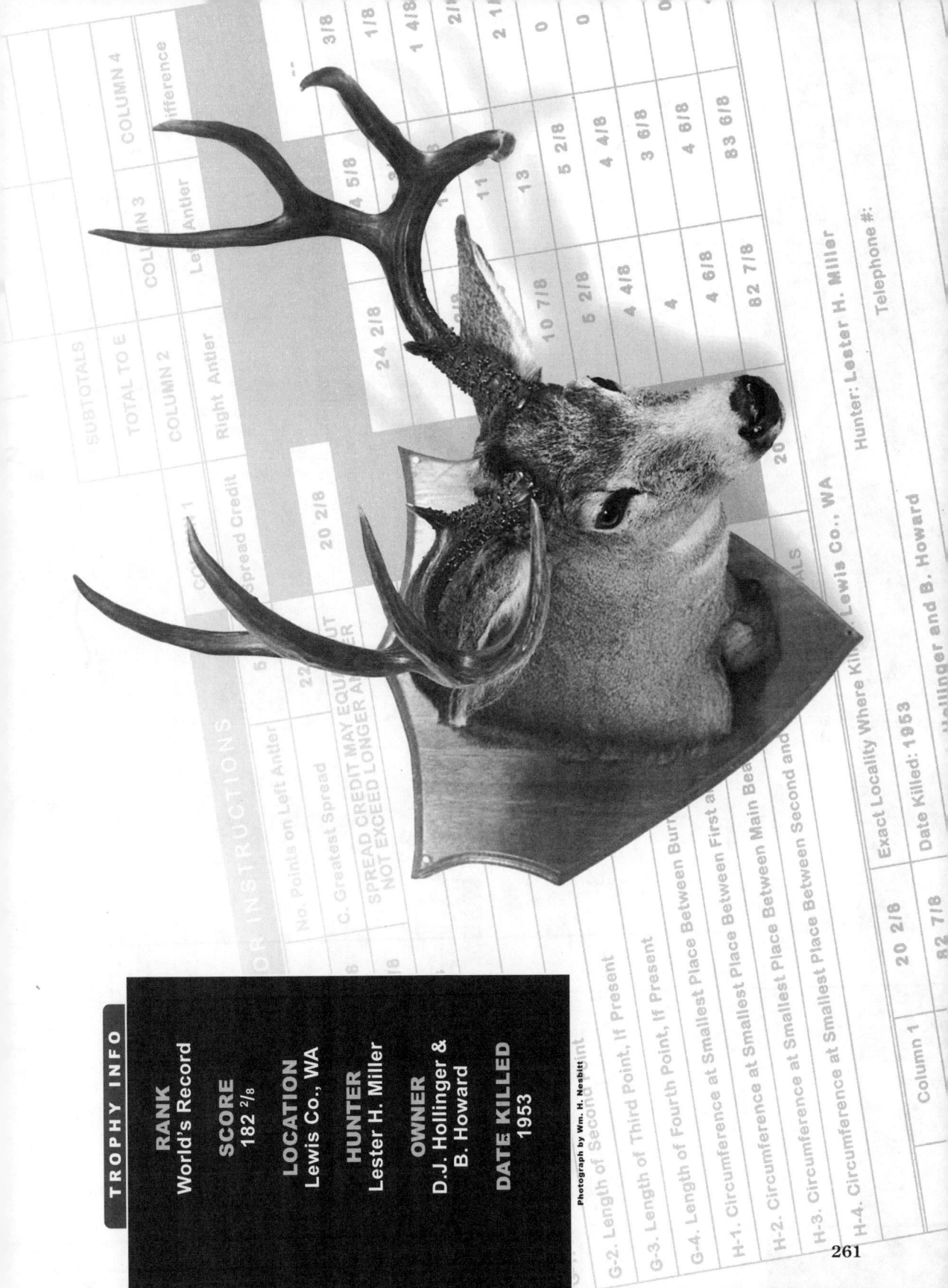

TROPHY INFO

RANK
World's Record

SCORE
182 2/8

LOCATION
Lewis Co., WA

HUNTER
Lester H. Miller

OWNER
D. J. Hollinger &
B. Howard

DATE KILLED
1953

Photograph by Wm. H. Nesbitt

COLUMBIA BLACKTAIL DEER
WORLD'S RECORD SCORECHART

All measurements must be made with a 1/4-inch wide flexible steel tape to the nearest one-eighth of an inch. (Note: A flexible steel cable can be used to measure points and main beams only.) Enter fractional figures in eighths, without reduction. Official measurements cannot be taken until the antlers have air dried for at least 60 days after the animal was killed.

A. Number of Points on Each Antler: To be counted a point, the projection must be at least one inch long, with length exceeding width at one inch or more of length. All points are measured from tip of point to nearest edge of beam. Beam tip is counted as a point but not measured as a point.

B. Tip to Tip Spread is measured between tips of main beams.

C. Greatest Spread is measured between perpendiculars at a right angle to the center line of the skull at widest part, whether across main beams or points.

D. Inside Spread of Main Beams is measured at a right angle to the center line of the skull at widest point between main beams. Enter this measurement again as the Spread Credit if it is less than or equal to the length of the longer antler; if greater, enter longer antler length for Spread Credit.

E. Total of Lengths of all Abnormal Points: Abnormal Points are those non-typical in location such as points originating from a point (exception: G-3 originates from G-2 in perfectly normal fashion) or from bottom or sides of main beam, or any points beyond the normal pattern of five (including beam tip) per antler. Measure each abnormal point in usual manner and enter in appropriate blanks.

F. Length of Main Beam is measured from the center of the lowest outside edge of burr over the outer side to the most distant point of the Main Beam. The point of beginning is that point on the burr where the center line along the outer side of the beam intersects the burr, then following generally the line of the illustration.

G-1-2-3-4. Length of Normal Points: Normal points are the brow tines and the upper and lower forks as shown in the illustration. They are measured from nearest edge of main beam over outer curve to tip. Lay the tape along the outer curve of the beam so that the top edge of the tape coincides with the top edge of the beam on both sides of point to determine the baseline for point measurement. Record point lengths in appropriate blanks.

H-1-2-3-4. Circumferences are taken as detailed in illustration for each measurement. If brow point is missing, take H-1 and H-2 at smallest place between burr and G-2. If G-3 is missing, take H-3 halfway between the base and tip of G-2. If G-4 is missing, take H-4 halfway between G-2 and tip of main beam.

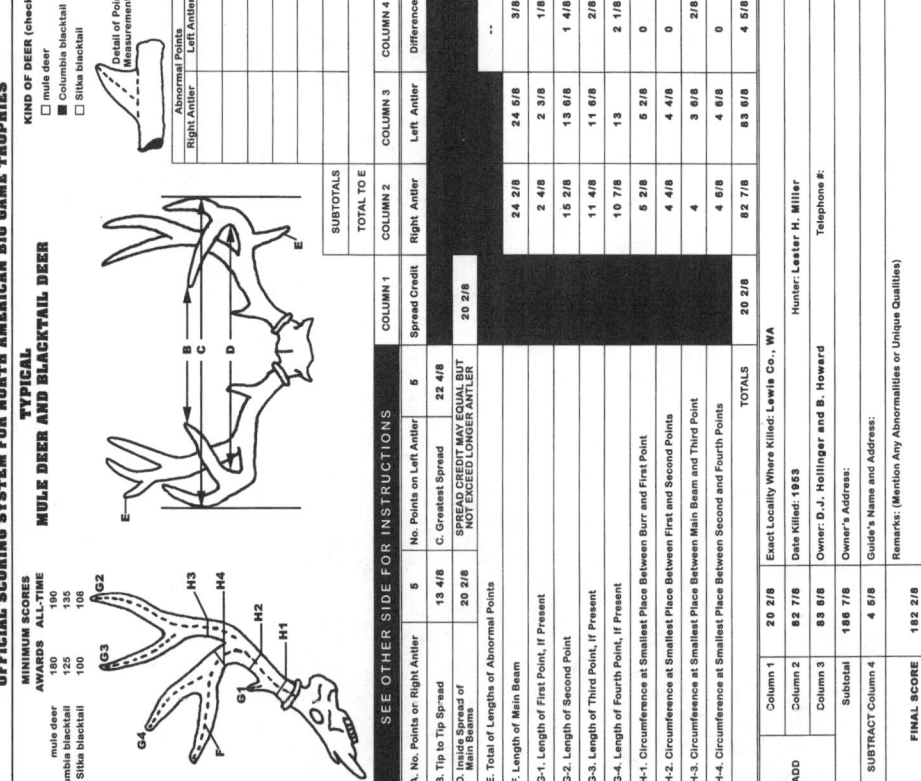

Records of
North American
Big Game

250 Station Drive
Missoula, MT 59801
(406) 542-1888

BOONE AND CROCKETT CLUB®

OFFICIAL SCORING SYSTEM FOR NORTH AMERICAN BIG GAME TROPHIES

	MINIMUM SCORES	
	AWARDS	ALL-TIME
mule deer	180	190
Columbia blacktail	125	135
Sitka blacktail	100	108

TYPICAL MULE DEER AND BLACKTAIL DEER

KIND OF DEER (check one)
☐ mule deer
☑ Columbia blacktail
☐ Sitka blacktail

	Abnormal Points	
	Right Antler	Left Antler
		3/8
		1/8
		1 4/8
		2/8
		2 1/8

SUBTOTALS
TOTAL TO E

SEE OTHER SIDE FOR INSTRUCTIONS	COLUMN 1	COLUMN 2	COLUMN 3	COLUMN 4
	Spread Credit	Right Antler	Left Antler	Difference
A. No. Points or Right Antler 5				
No. Points on Left Antler 5				
B. Tip to Tip Spread 13 4/8				
C. Greatest Spread 22 4/8				
D. Inside Spread of Main Beams 20 2/8	20 2/8			
SPREAD CREDIT MAY EQUAL BUT NOT EXCEED LONGER ANTLER				
E. Total of Lengths of Abnormal Points				--
F. Length of Main Beam		24 2/8	24 5/8	3/8
G-1. Length of First Point, If Present		2 4/8	2 3/8	1/8
G-2. Length of Second Point		15 2/8	13 6/8	1 4/8
G-3. Length of Third Point, If Present		11 4/8	11 6/8	2/8
G-4. Length of Fourth Point, If Present		10 7/8	13	2 1/8
H-1. Circumference at Smallest Place Between Burr and First Point		5 2/8	5 2/8	0
H-2. Circumference at Smallest Place Between First and Second Points		4 4/8	4 4/8	0
H-3. Circumference at Smallest Place Between Main Beam and Third Point		4	3 6/8	2/8
H-4. Circumference at Smallest Place Between Second and Fourth Points		4 6/8	4 6/8	0
TOTALS	20 2/8	82 7/8	83 6/8	4 5/8

	Column 1	20 2/8	Exact Locality Where Killed: Lewis Co., WA	
ADD	Column 2	82 7/8	Date Killed: 1953	Hunter: Lester H. Miller
	Column 3	83 6/8	Owner: D.J. Hollinger and B. Howard	Telephone #:
	Subtotal	186 7/8	Owner's Address:	
SUBTRACT	Column 4	4 5/8	Guide's Name and Address:	
FINAL SCORE		182 2/8	Remarks: (Mention Any Abnormalities or Unique Qualities)	

COPYRIGHT © 1999 BY BOONE AND CROCKETT CLUB®

Detail of Point Measurement

263

COLUMBIA BLACKTAIL DEER

Odocoileus hemionus columbianus

MINIMUM SCORE 135

Score	Length of Main Beam R	L	Inside Spread	Circumference at Smallest Place Between Burr and First Point R	L	Number of Points R	L	Locality	Hunter	Owner	Date Killed	Rank
182 2/8	24 2/8	24 5/8	20 2/8	5 2/8	5 2/8	5	5	Lewis Co., WA	Lester H. Miller	D.J. Hollinger & B. Howard	1953	1
175 2/8	22 5/8	22	17 1/8	4 6/8	4 6/8	6	5	Mendocino Co., CA	Clem Coughlin	D. & J. Phillips	1981	2
172 2/8	26 3/8	25 7/8	20 4/8	5 2/8	5 3/8	7	7	Marion Co., OR	B.G. Shurtleff	B.G. Shurtleff	1969	3
171 6/8	24 3/8	24 2/8	22 2/8	5 6/8	5 2/8	5	6	Skagit Co., WA	Harry M. Kay	Dan Heasley	1939	4
170 6/8	23 1/8	24	21 4/8	5 3/8	5 4/8	5	5	Elk City, OR	Clark D. Griffith	Clark D. Griffith	1962	5
170 2/8	25 6/8	25 5/8	20 2/8	4 5/8	4 6/8	5	5	Jackson Co., OR	Dennis R. King	King Tax. Studios	1970	6
170 1/8	23	22 6/8	19 5/8	5	4 6/8	5	5	Linn Co., OR	Woodrow W. Gibbs	Woodrow W. Gibbs	1963	7
170	23 2/8	24	20 2/8	4 3/8	4 3/8	5	5	Jackson Co., OR	Wayne Despain	Wayne Despain	1989	8
169 3/8	23 2/8	22 7/8	18 3/8	5 7/8	6 1/8	6	6	Lewis Co., WA	Larry V. Taylor	Thomas Gogan	1941	9
168 3/8	24 5/8	23 6/8	19 1/8	4 5/8	4 6/8	5	5	Jackson Co., OR	Fred H. Bean	Riley F. Bean	1970	10
168 2/8	22 4/8	21 4/8	21 4/8	5 2/8	5 1/8	5	5	Lake Co., CA	Bob DeShields	D. & J. Phillips	1953	11
168	24 2/8	24 6/8	19	4 6/8	4 7/8	5	5	Jackson Co., OR	Fred H. Bean	Riley F. Bean	1951	12
167 4/8	24 2/8	24 3/8	19 4/8	4 7/8	5	5	6	Marion Co., OR	Robert L. Brown	Robert L. Brown	1980	13
167 2/8	24 3/8	26	16 1/8	6	6	7	7	Lewis Co., WA	Maurice D. Heldreth	Loaned to B&C Natl. Coll.	1976	14
166 2/8	23 2/8	24 3/8	26 5/8	5 4/8	5 1/8	6	6	Glenn Co., CA	Peter Gerbo	Dennis P. Garcia	1949	15
165 6/8	22 6/8	23	20 6/8	4 6/8	4 6/8	5	5	Curry Co., OR	Si Pellow	Si Pellow	1988	16
165 4/8	23 6/8	24 5/8	21 6/8	5 1/8	5 1/8	4	4	Yamhill Co., OR	Jim McKinley	Jim McKinley	1971	17
165 1/8	21 4/8	21 7/8	18 5/8	4 4/8	4 4/8	5	5	Jackson Co., OR	Jay Walker	Jay Walker	1983	18
164 1/8	20 5/8	20 4/8	21 2/8	4 6/8	4 5/8	6	5	Cowlitz Co., WA	Harold Melland	Harold Melland	1962	19
164 1/8	21 7/8	20 2/8	17 5/8	4 4/8	4 4/8	5	5	Mendocino Co., CA	Mervin E. Lee	Mildred Lee	1995	19
163 7/8	21 7/8	21 7/8	19 5/8	4 4/8	4 4/8	5	5	Lincoln Co., OR	Picked Up	B. & S. Wales	1987	21
163 6/8	22 3/8	21 4/8	18	5	5	5	5	Jackson Co., OR	Donald G. Spence	Donald G. Spence	1982	22
163 1/8	23 3/8	21 5/8	20 4/8	5	4 7/8	7	6	Siskiyou Co., CA	Frank Barago	Frank Barago	1945	23
163 1/8	21 3/8	22 5/8	19 1/8	5 1/8	5	5	5	Eugene, OR	Russell Thomas	Russell Thomas	1964	23
162 6/8	25	25 2/8	23 2/8	4 5/8	4 6/8	7	7	Pierce Co., WA	Dick Allen	Craig Allen	1952	25
162 3/8	22	22 1/8	18 1/8	4 4/8	4 4/8	5	5	Trinity Co., CA	Sidney A. Nystrom	Sidney A. Nystrom	1961	26
162 2/8	24 5/8	25 1/8	19 2/8	4 2/8	4 2/8	5	5	Glenn Co., CA	Roger L. Spencer	Roger L. Spencer	1956	27
160 7/8	23 3/8	23 3/8	19 3/8	4 6/8	4 5/8	6	6	Jackson Co., OR	G. Scott Jennings	G. Scott Jennings	1972	28
160 5/8	20 5/8	21 4/8	16 5/8	4 5/8	4 5/8	4	4	Camas Valley, OR	Bernard L. Den	Bernard L. Den	1958	29
160 4/8	23 5/8	24 3/8	21	4 7/8	4 7/8	5	6	Siskiyou Co., CA	John L. Masters	John L. Masters	1967	30
160 3/8	23 1/8	23 5/8	26 5/8	4	4	6	6	Trinity Co., CA	A.H. Hilbert	Jack T. Brusatori	1929	31
160 3/8	22 7/8	23 1/8	17 7/8	4 2/8	4 1/8	5	5	Jackson Co., OR	Mickey C. Haynes	Travis J. Harvey	1989	31
160 1/8	25 1/8	24 7/8	24 7/8	5	5 5/8	5	4	Trinity Co., CA	Lorio Verzasconi	Lorio Verzasconi	1946	33
159 7/8	22 2/8	21 7/8	16 3/8	4	4	5	5	Siskiyou Co., CA	John C. Ley	E.R. Cummins	1937	34
159 7/8	22 5/8	22 3/8	21 7/8	4 5/8	4 4/8	5	5	Siskiyou Co., CA	Francis M. Sullivan	Francis M. Sullivan	1951	34
159 6/8	25 6/8	24 4/8	22 4/8	4 6/8	4 4/8	6	6	Jackson Co., OR	Frank Chapman	Frank Chapman	1965	36

Score	L. R	L. L	Spread	Circ. R	Circ. L	Pts. R	Pts. L	Locality	Hunter	Owner	Date	Rank
159 6/8	21	21 1/8	12 3/8	5 4/8	5 5/8	5	6	Humboldt Co., CA	Picked Up	D. & J. Phillips	1968	36
159 6/8	24 3/8	24 1/8	16 1/8	4 5/8	4 6/8	5	8	Jackson Co., OR	Douglas L. Milburn	Douglas L. Milburn	1985	36
159 4/8	24 4/8	23 6/8	14 7/8	4 5/8	4 4/8	6	6	Mendocino Co., CA	Russ McLennan	Russ McLennan	1984	39
159 2/8	24 7/8	24	24 4/8	4 4/8	5 2/8	4	5	Whatcom Co., WA	Paul A. Braddock	Paul A. Braddock	1963	40
159 2/8	24 7/8	22 4/8	19 4/8	4 4/8	4 4/8	5	5	Josephine Co., OR	Wayne Despain	Wayne Despain	1979	40
159 2/8	22 4/8	22 7/8	18 2/8	4 3/8	4 4/8	5	6	Jackson Co., OR	Jeffrey S. Sedey	Jeffrey S. Sedey	1988	40
159 1/8	21 7/8	20 7/8	19 1/8	4 6/8	4 6/8	5	5	Trinity Co., CA	A.H. Hilbert	A.H. Hilbert	1939	43
159	22 2/8	22 1/8	18 6/8	5 2/8	5 1/8	6	5	Lewis Co., WA	Larry F. Smith	Picked Up	1996	44
158 6/8	22	22 1/8	17 4/8	4 3/8	4 4/8	5	5	Marion Co., OR	Bradley M. Brenden	Bradley M. Brenden	1973	45
158 4/8	24	24 4/8	22 5/8	4 5/8	4 5/8	6	5	Trinity Co., CA	David Phillips	David Phillips	1974	46
158 2/8	24 4/8	23 7/8	19 6/8	4 6/8	4 6/8	6	6	Josephine Co., OR	James E. Brierley	James E. Brierley	1983	47
158 2/8	22 6/8	24 4/8	18 6/8	5 2/8	4 5/8	5	5	Lewis Co., WA	Keith A. Heldreth	Keith A. Heldreth	1984	47
158	22 7/8	23 2/8	18 4/8	4 6/8	4 6/8	5	5	Camas Valley, OR	Frank Kinnan	Frank Kinnan	1968	49
158	21 7/8	21 7/8	18 2/8	4 4/8	4 4/8	5	5	Trinity Co., CA	Charles A. Strickland	Charles A. Strickland	1984	49
158	23 4/8	23	18 3/8	4 4/8	4 3/8	5	5	Siskiyou Co., CA	Robert J. Ayers	Robert J. Ayers	1996	49
157 5/8	22 6/8	23 3/8	21 5/8	4 2/8	4 3/8	5	5	Shasta Co., CA	Richard L. Sobrato	Richard L. Sobrato	1969	52
157 4/8	21 2/8	19 4/8	20 7/8	4 7/8	5	5	5	Yamhill Co., OR	Henry Davenport	Henry Davenport	1932	53
157 1/8	22 1/8	23 1/8	23 1/8	4 5/8	4 5/8	7	7	Jackson Co., OR	Riley F. Bean	Fred H. Bean	1947	54
157 1/8	23	23 6/8	17 5/8	4 2/8	4 4/8	5	5	Jackson Co., OR	Marty Artoff	Marty Artoff	1980	54
157	24 7/8	26 1/8	24 1/8	5	5 1/8	5	7	Santa Clara Co., CA	Brud Eade	Brud Eade	1961	56
156 6/8	23	22 7/8	25 1/8	4 6/8	5	5	5	Benton Co., OR	Donald G. Breese	Donald G. Breese	1951	57
156 6/8	22 2/8	21 3/8	20 2/8	4 5/8	4 4/8	5	5	Pierce Co., WA	Horst A. Vierthaler	Horst A. Vierthaler	1963	57
156 6/8	23	23 7/8	16 6/8	4 6/8	4 6/8	7	7	Trinity Co., CA	Charles Hageman	Picked Up	1994	57
156 4/8	22 4/8	21 6/8	17	3 5/8	3 6/8	5	5	King Co., WA	Byron Gusa	Byron Gusa	1980	60
156 4/8	19 6/8	19 7/8	16 6/8	4 3/8	4 2/8	6	6	Lincoln Co., OR	Bruce G. Wales	Bruce G. Wales	1985	60
156 1/8	22 2/8	22	20 2/8	4 4/8	4 4/8	6	6	Lincoln Co., OR	Robert G. Biron	Robert G. Biron	1963	62
156	25	23 2/8	21	4 4/8	4 4/8	5	5	Polk Co., OR	Wayne Bond	Wayne Bond	1965	63
155 7/8	23 1/8	23 7/8	16 2/8	4 6/8	4 7/8	7	5	Pierce Co., WA	J. Bennett & F. Duell	J. Bennett & F. Duell	1983	64
155 7/8	23 1/8	23 1/8	17 3/8	4	4 2/8	5	5	Tehama Co., CA	George R. Chaffin	G.R. Chaffin & S. Bennett	1995	64
155 3/8	21 4/8	21	15 1/8	4 3/8	4 3/8	5	5	Tehama Co., CA	Carol F. Williams	Carol F. Williams	1948	66
155 3/8	26 2/8	25 7/8	25 7/8	4 4/8	4 4/8	7	7	Jackson Co., CA	Gary B. Christlieb	Gary B. Christlieb	1979	66
155 2/8	21 5/8	21 6/8	23 1/8	3 4/8	3 4/8	5	5	Trinity Co., CA	Fred Heider	Fred Heider	1927	68
155 2/8	21 7/8	20 2/8	17 6/8	4 2/8	4 2/8	5	5	King Co., WA	Horst A. Vierthaler	Horst A. Vierthaler	1960	68
155 2/8	22 3/8	23 1/8	20 6/8	5	5	4	5	Jackson Co., OR	L.M. Morgan & L. Miller	Lewis M. Morgan	1971	68
155 1/8	22 1/8	22 7/8	19 2/8	4 7/8	5 3/8	5	5	Mendocino Co., CA	Gary Land	Gary Land	1972	72
155 1/8	21	21 6/8	18 5/8	4 3/8	5 3/8	4	4	Shasta Co., CA	Vance Corrigan	Vance Corrigan	1956	72
155	24	23	21	4 1/8	4 4/8	6	5	Tehama Co., CA	Ben M. Youtsey	Ben M. Youtsey	1995	74
154 7/8	22 2/8	20 7/8	19 5/8	4	4	4	4	Linn Co., OR	Don L. Twito	Don L. Twito	1971	75
154 6/8	22 4/8	23 4/8	18	4 5/8	4 6/8	6	6	Cowlitz Co., WA	Bud Whittle	Bud Whittle	1957	75
154 6/8	20 4/8	20 3/8	20 4/8	4 5/8	4 5/8	4	4	Mendocino Co., CA	W.A. McAllister	W.A. McAllister	1968	75
154 6/8	21 1/8	21 3/8	18 1/8	4 2/8	4 2/8	6	6	Mendocino Co., CA	Andy Amerson	Andy Amerson	1993	78
154 5/8	24	22 7/8	23 3/8	4 3/8	4 4/8	5	5	Humboldt Co., CA	Phillip Brown	Phillip Brown	1962	78
154 2/8	24 7/8	24 3/8	21	4 7/8	4 6/8	6	7	Siskiyou Co., CA	Darrell R. Jones	Darrell R. Jones	1984	80
154 1/8	20 3/8	20 2/8	17 5/8	5	5 1/8	5	5	Jackson Co., OR	Mary L. Hannah	Mary L. Hannah	1988	81
154 1/8	20 4/8	20 4/8	18 1/8	4 4/8	4 4/8	6	5	Lane Co., OR	Eldon Lundy	Eldon Lundy	1943	81
154 1/8	21 6/8	22 2/8	18 6/8	4 6/8	4 7/8	6	7	Glenn Co., CA	Mitchell A. Thorson	Mitchell A. Thorson	1969	83
154	26 4/8	25 7/8	28 6/8	4 4/8	4 6/8	6	6	Trinity Co., CA	A.H. Hilbert	A.H. Hilbert	1930	83

COLUMBIA BLACKTAIL DEER

Odocoileus hemionus columbianus

Score	Length of Main Beam R	L	Inside Spread	Circumference at Smallest Place Between Burr and First Point R	L	Number of Points R	L	Locality	Hunter	Owner	Date Killed	Rank
154	24 4/8	24 3/8	19 5/8	4 7/8	4 4/8	5	5	Josephine Co., OR	Wayne H. Breeze	Wayne H. Breeze	1986	83
154	23 3/8	23 3/8	23 3/8	4 1/8	4 2/8	6	6	Josephine Co., OR	Ryan Kinghorn	Ryan Kinghorn	1989	83
153 7/8	22	22 1/8	17	4 5/8	4 5/8	6	5	Jefferson Co., WA	Picked Up	Wayne Brown	PR 1940	86
153 6/8	22 5/8	23 1/8	17 7/8	5 4/8	5 5/8	6	5	Thurston Co., WA	Denise A. George	Denise A. George	1987	87
153 4/8	21 3/8	20 7/8	17 6/8	4 6/8	4 7/8	5	5	Linn Co., OR	Greg L. Anderson	Greg L. Anderson	1983	88
153 3/8	21 5/8	20 5/8	19 1/8	5 2/8	5 2/8	6	7	Columbia Co., OR	J.H. Roberts	OR Fish & Wildl. Div.	1946	89
153 3/8	24 5/8	24 4/8	18 5/8	4 6/8	4 7/8	5	5	Clallam Co., WA	Picked Up	Lawrence J. Bourm	1949	89
153 3/8	21 2/8	21 5/8	17 4/8	5	5	6	5	Tehama Co., CA	James L. Carr	James L. Carr	1979	89
153 2/8	20 1/8	20 4/8	21 1/8	4 3/8	4 1/8	5	5	Pierce Co., WA	Brooks Carmichael	Brooks Carmichael	1971	92
153 1/8	22 4/8	22	19 7/8	5 1/8	5 2/8	6	6	Canton Creek, OR	Marell Abeene	Marell Abeene	1967	93
153 1/8	20 2/8	20	17 1/8	4 6/8	4 6/8	5	5	Humboldt Co., CA	Paul M. Mustain	Paul M. Mustain	1975	93
153	22 6/8	23 6/8	14 6/8	4 3/8	4 5/8	6	6	Siskiyou Co., CA	John Carmichael	John Carmichael	1969	95
152 6/8	21 6/8	21 7/8	21 1/8	4 6/8	4 3/8	8	7	Tehama Co., CA	Randy E. Reno	Randy E. Reno	1995	96
152 5/8	23 6/8	22 7/8	18 5/8	5	5 2/8	5	4	Trinity Co., CA	Allen Brownfield	Jason Brownfield	1979	97
152 5/8	22 1/8	22	19 5/8	4	4 3/8	5	5	Mendocino Co., CA	Harold D. Schneider	H.D. & M.J. Schneider	1979	97
152 4/8	23	23	20	4	4	6	7	Tehama Co., CA	Don Strickler	Don Strickler	1979	99
152 4/8	22	21 2/8	18 4/8	5 1/8	5	6	6	Mendocino Co., CA	Richard C. Martin	Richard C. Martin	1990	99
152 2/8	20 7/8	21	20 2/8	4 1/8	4 1/8	4	4	Douglas Co., OR	Ronald L. Sherva	Ronald L. Sherva	1987	101
152 1/8	22 4/8	21 4/8	17 7/8	4 2/8	4 1/8	5	5	Trinity Co., CA	Robert V. Strickland	Robert V. Strickland	1966	102
152 1/8	20 4/8	21 1/8	17 4/8	5 5/8	5 7/8	7	6	Pemberton, BC	Jim Decker	Jim Decker	1968	102
152 1/8	22 2/8	21 1/8	22	4 3/8	4 3/8	5	5	Josephine Co., OR	Bob Ferreira	Bob Ferreira	1988	102
152	23 3/8	22 7/8	21 6/8	4 4/8	4 4/8	6	5	Yolo Co., CA	Herman Darneille	E.L. Gallup	1943	105
152	20 6/8	21 7/8	15 2/8	4 6/8	4 7/8	6	6	Clackamas Co., OR	Larry W. Peterson	Larry W. Peterson	1980	105
151 7/8	25	24 3/8	20 3/8	4 3/8	4 5/8	5	5	Jackson Co., OR	David Ellefson	David Ellefson	1972	107
151 7/8	21 6/8	22	20 1/8	5	5	6	5	Tehama Co., CA	Gerald R. Cardoza, Jr.	Gerald R. Cardoza, Jr.	1994	107
151 6/8	22 2/8	22 4/8	17 4/8	5 4/8	5 1/8	6	6	Glide, OR	William Cellers	William Cellers	1947	109
151 5/8	20 3/8	20 1/8	22 4/8	4 5/8	4 4/8	5	5	Mendocino Co., CA	Bill L. Conn	Bill L. Conn	1969	110
151 5/8	22 1/8	21 7/8	22 5/8	4 6/8	4 6/8	5	5	Siskiyou Co., CA	Jim A. Turnbow	Jim A. Turnbow	1973	110
151 5/8	21	21 3/8	15 5/8	4 1/8	4	5	5	Trinity Co., CA	Dean Giordanella	Dean Giordanella	1994	110
151 4/8	20 3/8	19 1/8	16 4/8	4 5/8	4 7/8	5	5	Marion Co., OR	John Davenport	John Davenport	1958	113
151 4/8	22 7/8	21 3/8	17 5/8	4 1/8	4 2/8	6	6	Douglas Co., OR	Robert Shrode	Robert Shrode	1959	113
151 4/8	21 6/8	21 6/8	16	5 1/8	5 3/8	5	5	Whatcom Co., WA	Steve V. McIvor	Steve V. McIvor	1994	113
151 3/8	23 1/8	22 6/8	19 4/8	5	5	6	6	Josephine Co., OR	E.L. McKie & S.E. McKie	Ernie L. McKie	1977	116
151 1/8	21 5/8	21 5/8	16 1/8	4	4	4	4	Josephine Co., OR	Jim Wineteer	Jim Wineteer	1980	117
151	20 4/8	21 6/8	17 2/8	4 6/8	4 6/8	6	6	Lewis Co., WA	Norman Henspeter	Norman Henspeter	1941	118
151	20 1/8	21	19 2/8	4 2/8	4 1/8	5	5	Humboldt Co., CA	Elgin T. Gates	Elgin T. Gates	1952	118

Score	Beam R	Beam L	Inside Spread	Circ. 1	Circ. 2	Circ. 3	Pts. R	Pts. L	Locality	Owner	Hunter	Date	Rank
151	23 2/8	24	17 4/8	5 3/8	5 3/8	5 3/8	7	6	Lewis Co., WA	Harold Gossard	George V. Bagley	1967	118
150 7/8	21 7/8	22	19 5/8	4 4/8	4 5/8	4 5/8	5	5	Jackson Co., OR	Darrell Leek	Darrell Leek	1974	121
150 6/8	22	21 4/8	17	4 2/8	4 2/8	4 2/8	5	5	Siskiyou Co., CA	Raymond Whittaker	Raymond Whittaker	1978	122
150 6/8	21 6/8	22 2/8	18 3/8	4 7/8	4 6/8	4 6/8	5	5	Santa Clara Co., CA	Robert L. Fellom	Robert L. Fellom	1997	122
150 5/8	21 4/8	20 7/8	16 5/8	5 4/8	5 6/8	5 4/8	5	5	Yamhill Co., OR	Russell W. Byers	Russell W. Byers	1961	124
150 4/8	24 1/8	24 2/8	19 5/8	5 1/8	5	5 1/8	6	6	Trinity Co., CA	E.L. Brightenstine	E.L. Brightenstine	1978	125
150 1/8	20 3/8	21	14 1/8	5 2/8	5 2/8	5 2/8	5	5	Lewis Co., WA	Carroll H. Fenn	Carroll H. Fenn	1959	126
150 1/8	22 4/8	22	16 1/8	4 1/8	4 1/8	4 1/8	5	5	Napa Co., CA	Robert G. Wiley	Robert G. Wiley	1965	126
150 1/8	21	21	20 1/8	3 7/8	3 7/8	3 7/8	5	6	Trinity Co., CA	Thomas L. Hough	Thomas L. Hough	1969	126
150 1/8	22 7/8	23 1/8	19 3/8	4 6/8	4 7/8	4 6/8	5	5	Clackamas Co., OR	E. Clint Kuntz	E. Clint Kuntz	1981	126
150 1/8	21	22 2/8	17 7/8	4 6/8	4 6/8	4 6/8	5	4	Lane Co., OR	Gene C. Rolston	Gene C. Rolston	1983	131
150	24	25 1/8	24	4 4/8	4 5/8	4 4/8	4	5	Napa Co., CA	W.C. Lambert	W.C. Lambert	1957	131
150	22 5/8	22 7/8	19 4/8	5 5/8	5 6/8	5 5/8	5	5	King Co., WA	Roscoe Rainey	Roscoe Rainey	1963	131
150	20 5/8	21 5/8	16 6/8	4 7/8	5	4 7/8	5	4	Douglas Co., OR	Norman Burnett	Norman Burnett	1967	131
150	20 7/8	20 2/8	20	5 3/8	5 3/8	5 3/8	4	5	Lake Co., CA	Bruce Strickler	Bruce Strickler	1970	131
150	20 4/8	21 7/8	16 6/8	4 2/8	4 2/8	4 2/8	5	5	Tehama Co., CA	Marion F. Foster	Barbara J. Foster	1971	131
150	21 5/8	21 4/8	21 2/8	4 2/8	4 2/8	4 2/8	5	5	Trinity Co., CA	Richard E. Keller	Richard E. Keller	1995	131
149 7/8	23 2/8	22 5/8	17 3/8	4 1/8	4 1/8	4 1/8	6	5	Siskiyou Co., CA	John R. Adams	John R. Adams	1985	137
149 7/8	21 2/8	20 4/8	16 1/8	4 2/8	4 1/8	4 1/8	5	5	Trinity Co., CA	Steven E. Delaney	Steven E. Delaney	1992	137
149 7/8	22 4/8	21 7/8	16 1/8	4 4/8	4 4/8	4 4/8	5	6	Lane Co., OR	Robert P. Mann	Robert P. Mann	1995	137
149 6/8	22 7/8	22	18 7/8	5	5	5	5	5	Siskiyou Co., CA	Emit C. Jones	Emit C. Jones	1961	140
149 5/8	20	22 7/8	17 7/8	4 4/8	4 4/8	4 4/8	5	5	Humboldt Co., CA	Robert C. Stephens	Robert C. Stephens	1961	141
149 5/8	22 7/8	22 4/8	17 1/8	4 3/8	4 5/8	4 5/8	5	5	Clackamas Co., OR	Ray W. Bunnell	Ray W. Bunnell	1970	141
149 4/8	22 5/8	21	20 6/8	5 1/8	5 2/8	5 1/8	5	5	Glenn Co., CA	George Stewart, Jr.	George Stewart, Jr.	1957	143
149 4/8	21 1/8	21 4/8	23	5 1/8	5	5	5	5	Mendocino Co., CA	C.W. Bill King	C.W. Bill King	1993	143
149 3/8	20 5/8	22 5/8	17 5/8	5	5	5	5	5	Cowlitz Co., WA	Milton C. Gudgell	Milton C. Gudgell	1957	145
149 3/8	22 3/8	21 2/8	20 3/8	5 2/8	5 4/8	5 4/8	5	5	Trinity Co., CA	Lyle L. Johnson	Lyle L. Johnson	1979	145
149 3/8	23 7/8	26 5/8	20 5/8	4 5/8	4 4/8	4 5/8	5	5	Tehama Co., CA	Bill F. Stevenson	Bill F. Stevenson	1989	145
149 3/8	22 2/8	23 6/8	19 7/8	4 4/8	4 4/8	4 4/8	5	8	Clackamas Co., OR	David P. Prom	David P. Prom	1995	145
149 2/8	24 3/8	24 3/8	17 6/8	5 4/8	5 4/8	5 4/8	8	5	Trinity Co., CA	Lauren A. Johnson	Lauren A. Johnson	1964	149
149 2/8	20 2/8	20 3/8	14 6/8	4	4	4	5	5	Clackamas Co., OR	Lance V. Bentz	Lance V. Bentz	1980	149
149 2/8	21 6/8	22 6/8	19 4/8	4 2/8	4 2/8	4 2/8	5	5	Lane Co., OR	Richard C. MacKenzie	Richard C. MacKenzie	1983	149
149 1/8	21 4/8	22 7/8	16 1/8	4 7/8	4 7/8	4 7/8	5	5	Clallam Co., WA	Otis Dahman	E.A. Dahman	1943	149
148 7/8	22 1/8	23 1/8	18	5	5	5	6	5	Humboldt Co., CA	F. Joe Parker	F. Joe Parker	1946	152
148 6/8	24 5/8	24 2/8	20 2/8	4 7/8	5 1/8	5 1/8	5	5	Tillamook Co., OR	Fred Dick	Fred Dick	1948	153
148 6/8	22 5/8	22 6/8	15 6/8	4 6/8	4 6/8	4 6/8	5	5	Trinity Co., CA	Donald A. Dunn	Donald A. Dunn	1993	154
148 5/8	21 3/8	21 5/8	18 5/8	4 1/8	4 1/8	4 1/8	5	6	Lane Co., OR	Bill Sparks	Bill Sparks	1970	154
148 5/8	20 6/8	20 2/8	17 3/8	4	4	4	6	5	Jackson Co., OR	Jay Walker	Jay Walker	1975	154
148 4/8	23 2/8	22 7/8	20 6/8	4 5/8	4 5/8	4 5/8	5	6	Mendocino Co., CA	N.D. Windbigler	N.D. Windbigler	1969	156
148 4/8	22 5/8	22 1/8	16 6/8	4 4/8	4 4/8	4 4/8	6	5	Skamania Co., WA	Alan D. Borroz	Alan D. Borroz	1978	156
148 4/8	21 6/8	22 6/8	15 6/8	5 3/8	5 6/8	5 6/8	5	5	Linn Co., OR	Marlin D. Brinkley	Marlin D. Brinkley	1982	158
148 3/8	21 2/8	21	19 5/8	4 3/8	4 2/8	4 2/8	5	10	Douglas Co., OR	Unknown	Bud Jackson	1929	158
148 3/8	21 7/8	21 1/8	18 6/8	4 2/8	4 1/8	4 1/8	5	5	Marion Co., OR	Mike Fenimore	Mike Fenimore	1961	158
148 3/8	23	22 5/8	19 5/8	4 6/8	4 5/8	4 5/8	6	6	Clallam Co., WA	Nick R.D. Henry	Nick R.D. Henry	1992	161
148 2/8	22 4/8	23	17 6/8	5 1/8	5 1/8	5 1/8	6	6	Josephine Co., OR	Riley F. Bean	Riley F. Bean	1954	161
148 2/8	24	24 4/8	23 4/8	6 2/8	5 6/8	6 2/8	6	6	Shasta Co., CA	Jerry W. Sander	Jerry W. Sander	1977	164
148 1/8	21 6/8	22 1/8	18 6/8	5	5 1/8	5	8	7	Trinity Co., CA	Dean Tackette	Dean Tackette	1981	166

COLUMBIA BLACKTAIL DEER
Odocoileus hemionus columbianus

Score	Length of Main Beam R	L	Inside Spread	Circumference at Smallest Place Between Burr and First Point R	L	Number of Points R	L	Locality	Hunter	Owner	Date Killed	Rank
148 1/8	23 4/8	22 4/8	15 5/8	5 1/8	5 1/8	6	5	Clackamas Co., OR	Steven C. Oaks	Steven C. Oaks	1986	166
147 7/8	22	22 3/8	18 5/8	4 1/8	4 2/8	5	5	Glenn Co., CA	Emmet T. Frye	Emmet T. Frye	1937	168
147 7/8	20 6/8	20 7/8	21 6/8	5	4 7/8	5	5	Trinity Co., CA	Chauncy Willburn	Chauncy Willburn	1955	168
147 7/8	22 1/8	22 2/8	18 5/8	4 2/8	4 3/8	6	6	Humboldt Co., CA	Melvin H. Kadle	Melvin H. Kadle	1979	168
147 7/8	23 1/8	24 1/8	17	4 2/8	4 3/8	6	5	Josephine Co., OR	Ken Wilson	Ken Wilson	1995	168
147 5/8	23	23 6/8	19 5/8	4 4/8	4 3/8	5	4	Santa Clara Co., CA	Maitland Armstrong	Maitland Armstrong	1944	172
147 5/8	22 3/8	22 7/8	22 3/8	4 5/8	4 5/8	4	4	Mendocino Co., CA	Richard Sterling	Richard Sterling	1986	172
147 4/8	21 4/8	22 1/8	16 4/8	4	4	5	5	Mendocino Co., CA	Picked Up	Eugene E. Rentsch	1995	174
147 4/8	22 6/8	23 4/8	19 6/8	4 2/8	4 3/8	4	5	Jackson Co., OR	Mike Taylor	Mike Taylor	1969	175
147 2/8	27	26 5/8	21 3/8	5 4/8	5 6/8	0	0	Marion Co., OR	James C. Tennimon	James C. Tennimon	1988	175
147 1/8	21 2/8	21	16 7/8	4 3/8	4 3/8	5	6	Trinity Co., CA	Craig L. Brown	Craig & Joy Brown	1980	177
147 1/8	22 4/8	23 3/8	21 7/8	4 2/8	4 5/8	6	5	Trinity Co., CA	Barry D. Keyes	Barry D. Keyes	1992	177
147 1/8	22	21 2/8	17 3/8	4 5/8	4 7/8	5	4	Jackson Co., OR	Robert J. Rhodes	Robert J. Rhodes	1995	177
147	20	20 4/8	21 4/8	5	5	5	5	King Co., WA	Robert B. Gracey	Robert B. Gracey	1963	180
147	18	18 2/8	17	4 3/8	4 2/8	5	5	Siskiyou Co., CA	Ray Whittaker	Ray Whittaker	1966	180
147	22 2/8	22 3/8	19 6/8	4 3/8	4 3/8	5	5	Mendocino Co., CA	David W. Wilson	David W. Wilson	1993	180
146 7/8	22 4/8	22 2/8	15 1/8	5 3/8	5 3/8	5	5	Clallam Co., WA	Charles W. Lockhart	Charles W. Lockhart	1946	183
146 6/8	20	20 4/8	18 4/8	4 3/8	4 3/8	5	5	Siskiyou Co., CA	Richard Silva	Richard Silva	1958	184
146 6/8	21 4/8	21 5/8	18 4/8	4 7/8	5	6	5	Camas Valley, OR	Adam J. Hipp	Adam J. Hipp	1961	184
146 5/8	21 6/8	21	16 3/8	4 3/8	4 3/8	5	5	Coos Co., OR	Pete Serafin	Pete Serafin	1968	186
146 4/8	20 1/8	20 2/8	18 1/8	4 2/8	4 2/8	5	5	Clackamas Co., OR	Stan K. Naylor	Stan K. Naylor	1990	186
146 4/8	22 6/8	22 7/8	22	5 2/8	5 4/8	5	5	King Co., WA	Leo Klinkhammer	Leo Klinkhammer	1961	188
146 4/8	21 2/8	21 2/8	17 2/8	4 6/8	4 7/8	5	5	Glenn Co., CA	Lawrence E. Germeshausen	Lawrence E. Germeshausen	1983	188
146 4/8	19 7/8	19 6/8	19 4/8	4 6/8	4 5/8	5	6	Norrish Creek, BC	Cliff L. Loring	Cliff L. Loring	1990	188
146 3/8	23 4/8	23 6/8	24 6/8	4 5/8	4 5/8	5	5	Trinity Co., CA	Carroll E. Dow	Carroll E. Dow	1962	191
146 3/8	21 5/8	22	17 5/8	3 6/8	3 6/8	5	5	Trinity Co., CA	David J. Deininger	David J. Deininger	1992	191
146 2/8	20 7/8	21 4/8	14 2/8	4 4/8	4 4/8	5	5	Douglas Co., OR	Bernard H. Schum	Bernard H. Schum	1966	193
146 2/8	21 6/8	22 3/8	13 6/8	5 6/8	5 6/8	5	5	Shasta Co., CA	William H. Taylor	William H. Taylor	1971	193
146 2/8	21 7/8	21 6/8	16 2/8	3 7/8	3 7/8	5	5	Humboldt Co., CA	Charles R. Jurin	Charles R. Jurin	1988	193
146 2/8	25 3/8	24 5/8	16 2/8	5 1/8	5	8	7	Mason Co., WA	David D. Johnston	David D. Johnston	1996	193
146 1/8	23 1/8	23 5/8	19 1/8	4	4 5/8	4	4	Trinity Co., CA	Kenneth M. Brown	Kenneth M. Brown	1972	197
146 1/8	22 1/8	22 4/8	14 5/8	4 5/8	4 3/8	0	0	Lewis Co., WA	Keith A. Heldreth	Keith A. Heldreth	1988	197
146 1/8	22 2/8	23 4/8	19 1/8	3 7/8	4 2/8	4	5	Mendocino Co., CA	Brad B. Pitt	Brad B. Pitt	1994	197
146	20 2/8	20 7/8	15 2/8	5	5	5	5	Little Fall Creek, OR	Gene B. Johnson	Gene B. Johnson	1963	200
146	22 6/8	22 2/8	19 2/8	4 4/8	4 5/8	5	5	Mendocino Co., CA	Brian E. Hornberger	Brian E. Hornberger	1991	200
146	20 5/8	21 5/8	21 4/8	4 3/8	4 2/8	5	5	Mendocino Co., CA	Renaldo J. Marin	Renaldo J. Marin	1993	200

Score	Main Beam R	Main Beam L	Inside Spread	Circ. R	Circ. L	Pts R	Pts L	Locality	By Whom Killed	Owner	Date	Rank
146	22	21	22	4 2/8	4 2/8	5	5	Mendocino Co., CA	Cliff E. Jacobson	Cliff E. Jacobson	1996	200
145 7/8	23 4/8	23 3/8	22	5 3/8	5 4/8	6	8	Lake Co., CA	Floyd Goodrich	Mrs. William Olson	1926	204
145 7/8	22	23 5/8	16 3/8	4 5/8	4 7/8	5	5	Napa Co., CA	C.H.N. Dailey	Tony Stoer	1948	204
145 7/8	24 5/8	22 4/8	19	5 5/8	5 6/8	6	5	Linn Co., OR	Harold Tonkin	C. Vernon Humble	1954	204
145 7/8	22 6/8	22 6/8	21 7/8	4 2/8	4 1/8	6	5	Shasta Co., CA	Gary J. Miller	Gary J. Miller	1968	204
145 7/8	21 7/8	21	14 5/8	4 2/8	4 2/8	5	5	Yamhill Co., OR	Dwight A. Homestead	Dwight A. Homestead	1992	204
145 6/8	22 2/8	20 5/8	17	5 3/8	6	5	6	King Co., WA	Terry Flowers	Terry Flowers	1959	209
145 6/8	19 4/8	20 2/8	14 6/8	4 1/8	4 1/8	6	5	Whatcom Co., WA	Dennis Miller	Dennis Miller	1970	209
145 5/8	22 4/8	23	18 7/8	4 1/8	3 7/8	6	6	Humboldt Co., CA	Joe Dickerson	Jay Grunert	1962	211
145 5/8	22 4/8	21 1/8	19 5/8	3 7/8	4 1/8	5	5	Siskiyou Co., CA	Wallace D. Barlow	Wallace D. Barlow	1985	211
145 4/8	20 1/8	20 4/8	14 2/8	4 2/8	4 7/8	5	5	Jackson Co., OR	Gary D. Kaiser	Gary D. Kaiser	1967	213
145 4/8	21 1/8	20	16 2/8	4 7/8	4 7/8	6	5	Douglas Co., OR	Daniel J. Fisher	Daniel J. Fisher	1973	213
145 4/8	21 3/8	21 1/8	21 3/8	4 5/8	4 6/8	5	6	Mendocino Co., CA	Kenneth A. Bovero	Kenneth A. Bovero	1993	213
145 3/8	22 3/8	21	23 4/8	4 5/8	4	5	5	Mendocino Co., CA	Paul M. Holleman II	Paul M. Holleman II	1976	216
145 3/8	23 3/8	21	21	4 1/8	4	6	5	Trinity Co., CA	Donald A. Dunn	Donald A. Dunn	1992	216
145 2/8	22 6/8	22	22 6/8	4	4 7/8	6	4	Harrison Lake, BC	Lloyd L. Ward, Jr.	Lloyd L. Ward, Jr.	1947	218
145 2/8	22 5/8	17 5/8	17 2/8	4 4/8	5 2/8	5	5	Jackson Co., OR	Bill Hays	Bill Hays	1968	218
145 2/8	20 2/8	21 2/8	16 2/8	5 4/8	5 1/8	5	5	Marion Co., OR	James J. Edgell	James J. Edgell	1979	218
145 2/8	21	21	21	5 1/8	4 4/8	7	9	Tehama Co., CA	Clint Heiber	Clint Heiber	1979	218
145 2/8	22 5/8	22 5/8	22 7/8	4 3/8	5 2/8	6	5	Josephine Co., OR	Jim Breeze	Jim Breeze	1986	218
145 1/8	23	23	23 3/8	5 1/8	5 3/8	5	5	Tehama Co., CA	Lamar G. Hanson	Lamar G. Hanson	1972	223
145 1/8	23 4/8	23 4/8	16 3/8	5	5	6	6	Pierce Co., WA	Robert L. Armstrong	Robert L. Armstrong	1978	223
145 1/8	22 6/8	22 6/8	16 7/8	4 6/8	4 3/8	5	5	Lane Co., OR	Boyd Iverson	Boyd Iverson	1982	223
145 1/8	21 7/8	21 7/8	19 4/8	4 3/8	5 1/8	5	5	Lane Co., OR	Kevin M. Albin	Kevin M. Albin	1990	223
145	21 2/8	21 2/8	17 1/8	4 3/8	4 4/8	6	6	Trinity Co., CA	Gene Shannon	Daniel M. Phillips	1990	223
145	21 4/8	20 7/8	19 6/8	4 7/8	4 2/8	6	5	Humboldt Co., CA	Marvin D. Stapp	Marvin D. Stapp	1965	228
145	19 6/8	21 7/8	19 2/8	4 5/8	4 4/8	5	6	Douglas Co., OR	Larry E. Waller	Larry E. Waller	1980	228
144 7/8	19 2/8	19 2/8	21 2/8	5 1/8	4 1/8	6	5	Mendocino Co., CA	Ralph I. Sibley	Ralph I. Sibley	1986	228
144 7/8	22 2/8	21 4/8	21 4/8	4 4/8	5	6	7	Whatcom Co., WA	Harry E. Williams	Harry E. Williams	1992	228
144 7/8	23 7/8	23 7/8	14 4/8	4 2/8	5 2/8	5	6	Clatsop Co., OR	Pravomil Raichl	Pravomil Raichl	1959	232
144 7/8	20 6/8	20 4/8	13 3/8	4 1/8	3 4/8	5	5	Lane Co., OR	Clair R. Thomas	Clair R. Thomas	1959	232
144 7/8	22 1/8	22 1/8	22 7/8	5 1/8	4 6/8	6	5	Jackson Co., OR	Riley F. Bean	Riley F. Bean	1971	232
144 7/8	25	25 4/8	21	5	6	5	6	Skamania Co., WA	Fred W. Campbell	Fred W. Campbell	1992	232
144 6/8	21 6/8	21 6/8	18 3/8	5 2/8	4 3/8	5	6	King Co., WA	R. Walter Williams	R. Walter Williams	1956	236
144 6/8	20 4/8	20	19 4/8	3 4/8	4 2/8	6	4	Mendocino Co., CA	Richard Vannelli	Richard Vannelli	1970	236
144 6/8	22 4/8	22 4/8	22 4/8	4 6/8	4 4/8	5	6	Lincoln Co., OR	William D. Harmon	OR Fish & Wildl. Div.	1976	236
144 6/8	21 3/8	22 3/8	19 5/8	6	6	6	6	Skamania Co., WA	Melvin D. Robertson	Melvin D. Robertson	1983	236
144 6/8	22 2/8	22 1/8	17 7/8	4 4/8	4 2/8	6	5	Santa Clara Co., CA	Dean P. Filice	Dean P. Filice	1996	236
144 5/8	21 4/8	20	18	4 3/8	4	5	5	Josephine Co., OR	Jerry C. Sparlin	Jerry C. Sparlin	1963	241
144 5/8	22 6/8	22 4/8	21 5/8	4 2/8	4 2/8	5	5	Jackson Co., OR	Dean P. Pasche	Dean P. Pasche	1988	241
144 5/8	20 1/8	20 1/8	16 1/8	4 4/8	4 4/8	5	5	Benton Co., OR	Gerald L. Hibbs	Gerald L. Hibbs	1990	241
144 5/8	21 2/8	21 2/8	19 1/8	4 4/8	4	5	5	Linn Co., OR	Donald J. Semolke	Donald J. Semolke	1990	241
144 5/8	23 1/8	23 1/8	19 4/8	4 3/8	4 2/8	5	5	Shasta Co., CA	Ernie Young	Chet Young	1953	245
144 4/8	21 3/8	21 4/8	16 2/8	4 2/8	4 3/8	5	5	Clackamas Co., OR	John R. Vollmer, Jr.	John R. Vollmer, Jr.	1960	245
144 4/8	21 6/8	21 6/8	17 2/8	4 3/8	4 2/8	5	5	Powers, OR	Ray A. Davis	Ray A. Davis	1968	245
144 4/8	21 2/8	21 2/8	17	3 7/8	3 6/8	4	4	Snohomish Co., WA	Roy Shogren	Roy Shogren	1979	245
144 4/8	21	20 7/8	15 4/8	4 1/8	4 3/8	5	5	Benton Co., OR	Lance M. Holm	Lance M. Holm	1988	245

COLUMBIA BLACKTAIL DEER
Odocoileus hemionus columbianus

Score	Length of Main Beam R	L	Inside Spread	Circumference at Smallest Place Between Burr and First Point R	L	Number of Points R	L	Locality	Hunter	Owner	Date Killed	Rank
144 4/8	20 5/8	21 2/8	16 4/8	4 6/8	4 7/8	5	5	Clark Co., WA	Raymond M. Gibson	Raymond M. Gibson	1992	245
144 4/8	22 6/8	20 6/8	14 2/8	4 4/8	4 5/8	5	6	Clackamas Co., OR	Gregory A. Latimer	Gregory A. Latimer	1992	245
144 3/8	22 1/8	23 3/8	21 3/8	5	5 2/8	5	4	Santa Clara Co., CA	Maitland Armstrong	Maitland Armstrong	1946	252
144 3/8	20 3/8	24 4/8	21 5/8	4 1/8	4	4	5	Siskiyou Co., CA	Floyd B. Hoisington	Floyd B. Hoisington	1976	252
144 3/8	21	20 7/8	16 5/8	4 7/8	4 5/8	4	5	Humboldt Co., CA	Gerald Wescott	Gerald Wescott	1980	252
144 3/8	20 4/8	20 7/8	14 7/8	4 4/8	4 5/8	5	5	Humboldt Co., CA	Richard G. Van Vorst	Richard G. Van Vorst	1990	252
144 3/8	20 1/8	22	19 1/8	4 4/8	4 4/8	5	5	Alameda Co., CA	Anthony S. Webb	Anthony S. Webb	1990	252
144 3/8	22 3/8	24 4/8	18 3/8	5	5	6	6	Jefferson Co., WA	John E. Shultz	John E. Shultz	1991	252
144 3/8	23 3/8	23 6/8	20 5/8	3 7/8	3 7/8	4	4	Mendocino Co., CA	Jack J. Tuso	Jack J. Tuso	1997	252
144 2/8	20 3/8	21 6/8	17 2/8	4 4/8	4 5/8	5	5	Jackson Co., OR	Warren Pestka	Warren Pestka	1974	259
144 2/8	20 2/8	19 6/8	20 3/8	3 6/8	3 6/8	6	5	Josephine Co., OR	Clinton Moore	Clinton Moore	1975	259
144 2/8	21 6/8	21 3/8	15 6/8	4 6/8	4 6/8	6	5	Marion Co., OR	Arthur L. Schmidt	Arthur L. Schmidt	1978	259
144 2/8	21	22 4/8	20 4/8	4 4/8	4 4/8	5	5	Mendocino Co., CA	Frank Kester	Frank Kester	1981	259
144 1/8	21 7/8	21 3/8	17 7/8	4 5/8	4 4/8	5	5	Siskiyou Natl. For., OR	Dennis E. Bourn	Dennis E. Bourn	1971	263
144	20 7/8	20 4/8	17 2/8	4 4/8	4 5/8	5	5	Skamania Co., WA	Wayne Crockford	Wayne Crockford	1960	264
144	21 2/8	21 5/8	17	4 7/8	5 1/8	5	5	Linn Co., OR	Ed A. Taylor	Ed A. Taylor	1981	264
144	21 3/8	21 2/8	18	4 3/8	4 3/8	6	6	Clackamas Co., OR	Picked Up	Bob K. Oka	1993	264
143 7/8	21 7/8	23	20 6/8	5	4 5/8	6	6	Linn Co., OR	Clarence Howe	Clarence Howe	1941	267
143 7/8	23 4/8	22 7/8	21 3/8	5	4 6/8	5	5	Clackamas Co., OR	Richard G. Mathis	Richard G. Mathis	1965	267
143 7/8	20 5/8	19 5/8	20 3/8	5	5 1/8	5	5	Humboldt Co., CA	Lois C. Miller	Lois C. Miller	1986	267
143 7/8	20 3/8	20 2/8	18 1/8	4 4/8	4 3/8	5	5	Siskiyou Co., CA	Frank L. Galea	Frank L. Galea	1996	267
143 7/8	22 2/8	22 5/8	16	3 7/8	3 7/8	5	5	Siskiyou Co., CA	Dave E. Scheve	Dave E. Scheve	1996	267
143 6/8	19 3/8	20 2/8	16	4 6/8	4 7/8	5	5	Squamish, BC	B. Miller	B. Miller	1962	272
143 6/8	20 1/8	20 2/8	16 4/8	5	5	5	5	Lewis Co., WA	Bill W. Latimer	Bill W. Latimer	1974	272
143 6/8	20 5/8	20 2/8	19 7/8	5 2/8	5 2/8	6	6	Tehama Co., CA	Clint Heiber	Clint Heiber	1978	272
143 6/8	19 5/8	19 4/8	15 2/8	4 7/8	4 6/8	6	6	Mendocino Co., CA	Mark Ciancio	Mark Ciancio	1986	272
143 6/8	20 6/8	20 3/8	15 4/8	5 2/8	4 7/8	5	5	Humboldt Co., CA	Hartwell A. Burnett	Hartwell A. Burnett	1988	272
143 5/8	21 2/8	21 2/8	17 7/8	5 6/8	5 7/8	5	5	Grays Harbor Co., WA	E. & R. Dierick	E. & R. Dierick	1958	277
143 5/8	20 4/8	20 4/8	18 5/8	4 4/8	4 4/8	4	4	Siskiyou Co., CA	Emit C. Jones	Emit C. Jones	1960	277
143 5/8	20 5/8	19 3/8	18 5/8	4 1/8	4 2/8	5	5	Trinity Co., CA	Kenneth L. Cogle, Jr.	Kenneth L. Cogle, Jr.	1985	277
143 5/8	21 3/8	21 5/8	17 7/8	4 4/8	4 5/8	5	5	Jefferson Co., WA	Earl L. Woodley	Earl L. Woodley	1994	277
143 4/8	21 4/8	22 5/8	16 2/8	4 1/8	4 3/8	5	5	Clark Co., WA	A.W. Gerber	Earl Gerber	1929	281
143 4/8	21 4/8	21 1/8	21 4/8	4 4/8	4 4/8	5	4	Snoqualmie, WA	Milton L. James	Milton L. James	1964	281
143 4/8	21 3/8	20 7/8	16 6/8	4 5/8	4 5/8	5	5	Jackson Co., OR	Jay Walker	Jay Walker	1978	281
143 4/8	21	20 4/8	17	4 6/8	4 6/8	5	5	Trinity Co., CA	Barry Griffin	Barry Griffin	1983	281
143 4/8	22	23	16 4/8	3 7/8	4	5	5	Josephine Co., OR	Virgil Welch	Virgil Welch	1983	281

Score	R Beam	L Beam	Inside Spread	R Circ.	L Circ.	R Pts	L Pts	Locality	Owner	Hunter	Date	Rank
143 4/8	22 6/8	22 4/8	20	4 2/8	4 3/8	5	5	Mendocino Co., CA	Arnold E. Dado	Arnold E. Dado	1993	281
143 3/8	20	20 1/8	15 3/8	4 7/8	4 7/8	5	5	Chehalis River, BC	Clair A. Howard	Clair A. Howard	1971	287
143 3/8	19 2/8	18 7/8	18 3/8	3 4/8	3 4/8	5	5	Mendocino Co., CA	Larry G. Miller	Larry G. Miller	1978	287
143 2/8	21 6/8	21 5/8	19	4 5/8	4 5/8	5	5	Linn Co., OR	B&C National Collection	Basil C. Bradbury	1960	289
143 2/8	22 3/8	22 6/8	21 4/8	4 2/8	4 2/8	5	5	Lake Co., CA	Mario Sereni, Jr.	Mario Sereni, Jr.	1965	289
143 2/8	19 5/8	19 4/8	17 2/8	4	4	5	6	Humboldt Co., CA	Jack Stedman	Jack Stedman	1965	289
143 2/8	20 6/8	19 6/8	19	4 7/8	4 7/8	7	7	Jones Lake, BC	James Haslam	James Haslam	1967	289
143 2/8	20 2/8	20 4/8	18 6/8	4 5/8	4 5/8	5	5	Jackson Co., OR	Riley F. Bean	Riley F. Bean	1972	289
143 2/8	26	26	25	4 6/8	4 6/8	5	5	Mendocino Co., CA	George W. Rogers	George W. Rogers	1977	289
143 2/8	20 3/8	20 4/8	15	4 6/8	4 7/8	8	7	Shasta Co., CA	Brad E. Wittner	Brad E. Wittner	1989	289
143 2/8	21 2/8	21 3/8	18 2/8	5 1/8	5 1/8	5	5	Josephine Co., OR	Jaime L. Torres	Jaime L. Torres	1990	289
143 2/8	20	20 7/8	15 6/8	4	4	5	5	Shasta Co., CA	Ben Brackett	Ben Brackett	1993	289
143 1/8	21 4/8	22	17 3/8	4 4/8	4 4/8	6	6	Benton Co., OR	A.C. Nelson	A.C. Nelson	1957	298
143 1/8	22	22 1/8	18 1/8	4 1/8	4	5	5	Humboldt Co., CA	Mitchell A. Thorson	Mitchell A. Thorson	1965	298
143 1/8	21 6/8	22 2/8	17 1/8	4 1/8	4 1/8	5	5	Humboldt Co., CA	Eddie L. Mendes	Eddie L. Mendes	1992	298
143	22 3/8	22 3/8	18	4 2/8	4 2/8	4	4	Josephine Co., OR	Riley F. Bean	Riley F. Bean	1956	301
142 7/8	22	22	16 3/8	4 4/8	4 4/8	4	4	Clackamas Co., OR	Larry R. Tracy	Larry R. Tracy	1965	302
142 7/8	23 5/8	22 1/8	21 1/8	5 1/8	5 6/8	5	5	Clackamas Co., OR	Ross A. Gordon	Ross A. Gordon	1989	302
142 7/8	23 1/8	22 2/8	17 3/8	4	4 2/8	5	5	Tehema Co., CA	Randy Croote	Randy Croote	1993	302
142 6/8	21 2/8	22 4/8	19 4/8	4 6/8	5	5	5	Linn Co., OR	R. Reid & D. Liles	R. Reid & D. Liles	1982	305
142 6/8	23 2/8	21 7/8	17 2/8	3 7/8	4	4	4	Linn Co., OR	Kenneth W. Wegner	Kenneth W. Wegner	1982	305
142 6/8	20 4/8	22	20 7/8	4 4/8	3 7/8	5	5	Josephine Co., OR	Reginald P. Breeze	Reginald P. Breeze	1986	305
142 6/8	20 1/8	20 1/8	20 5/8	5 4/8	5 6/8	5	5	Mendocino Co., CA	Steen C. Henriksen	Steen C. Henriksen	1996	305
142 5/8	22 3/8	20 2/8	17 1/8	4 2/8	4 1/8	5	5	Marion Co., OR	Robert E. Bochsler	Robert E. Bochsler	1950	309
142 5/8	19 4/8	22 3/8	17 7/8	4 6/8	4 6/8	5	5	Jackson Co., OR	Nancy Sequeira	Leonard B. Sequeira	1959	309
142 5/8	20 2/8	19 4/8	16 5/8	4	4	4	4	Santa Clara Co., CA	Ray & Neal Haera	Picked Up	PR 1966	309
142 5/8	22 6/8	20	19 7/8	4 1/8	4 2/8	5	5	Santa Clara Co., CA	Russel Rasmussen	Picked Up	PR 1966	309
142 5/8	22 5/8	22 6/8	19 7/8	4 2/8	4 3/8	5	5	Trinity Co., CA	Larry Brown	Larry Brown	1979	309
142 5/8	21 4/8	18 3/8	19 7/8	4 4/8	4 7/8	4	4	Tehama Co., CA	Kenneth R. Hall	Kenneth R. Hall	1979	309
142 5/8	23 1/8	21 6/8	20 1/8	4 6/8	4 7/8	7	7	Mendocino Co., CA	Warren F. Coffman	Warren F. Coffman	1989	309
142 5/8	22	22 7/8	17 7/8	4 2/8	4 3/8	5	5	Trinity Co., CA	Robert T. Edwards	Robert T. Edwards	1991	309
142 5/8	20	18 3/8	16 5/8	4 3/8	4 1/8	5	5	Chilliwack Lake, BC	Blair R. Houdayer	Blair R. Houdayer	1992	309
142 4/8	19 6/8	22 7/8	13 3/8	4 6/8	4 5/8	4	4	Trinity Co., CA	Jace Comfort	Jace Comfort	1965	318
142 4/8	22 2/8	22	15	4 5/8	4 6/8	5	5	Chilliwack, BC	Frank Rosenauer	Frank Rosenauer	1967	318
142 4/8	18 3/8	22 7/8	16 6/8	4 3/8	4 3/8	6	6	Clackamas Co., OR	Henry A. Charriere	Henry A. Charriere	1970	318
142 4/8	21 6/8	21 1/8	21	3 7/8	3 7/8	5	5	Jackson Co., OR	Donald G. Spence	Donald G. Spence	1980	318
142 4/8	22 4/8	20 7/8	15 4/8	4 6/8	4 6/8	5	5	Mendocino Co., CA	Jerry C. Russell	Jerry C. Russell	1993	318
142 3/8	21 1/8	20 7/8	17 3/8	4 3/8	4 3/8	5	5	Laytonville, CA	Byron J. Rowland, Jr.	Byron J. Rowland, Jr.	1964	323
142 3/8	20 6/8	19 3/8	19 3/8	4	4	4	4	Humboldt Co., CA	Darol L. Damm	Darol L. Damm	1976	323
142 3/8	20 6/8	20 5/8	19 1/8	4 6/8	4 5/8	5	5	Humboldt Co., CA	James L. Sloan	James L. Sloan	1992	323
142 2/8	23 4/8	23 2/8	17	4 2/8	4 1/8	5	6	Mendocino Co., CA	James A. Shelton	James A. Shelton	1944	326
142 2/8	20 7/8	20 7/8	16 2/8	4 3/8	4 3/8	6	6	Jackson Co., OR	Eileen F. Damone	Eileen F. Damone	1976	326
142 2/8	20 6/8	20 6/8	19 6/8	4	4	6	6	Trinity Co., CA	Donald A. Dunn	Donald A. Dunn	1981	326
142 1/8	21 3/8	22 3/8	19 7/8	5 1/8	5 1/8	5	5	Shasta Co., CA	Richard R. Lowell	Richard R. Lowell	1953	329
142 1/8	23 5/8	22 2/8	16 7/8	4 5/8	4 4/8	5	5	Linn Co., OR	Jack V. Logozzo	Bob L. Brazeale	1972	329
142 1/8	21 3/8	21 3/8	16 3/8	4 4/8	4 3/8	5	5	Lane Co., OR	William Jordan	William Jordan	1982	329
142 1/8	20 4/8	19 5/8	15 5/8	4 4/8	4 3/8	5	5	Lewis Co., WA	Michael H. Carle	Michael H. Carle	1989	329

Score	Length of Main Beam R	L	Inside Spread	Circumference at Smallest Place Between Burr and First Point R	L	Number of Points R	L	Locality	Hunter	Owner	Date Killed	Rank
142 1/8	22	22	20 3/8	4 3/8	4 1/8	4	4	Siskiyou Co., CA	John T. Scheffler	John T. Scheffler	1992	329
142 1/8	20 4/8	20 2/8	15 3/8	4 2/8	4	6	8	Tehama Co., CA	Michael R. Weber	Michael R. Weber	1996	329
142	20 1/8	20 6/8	17	4 3/8	4 2/8	5	5	Cowlitz Co., WA	Harold C. Johnson	Harold C. Johnson	1947	335
142	21 6/8	22 5/8	20 2/8	4 5/8	4 6/8	6	6	Mt. Sheazer, WA	Joseph B. Wilcox	Joseph B. Wilcox	1953	335
142	24	23 5/8	16 7/8	5 1/8	5 6/8	8	5	Marion Co., OR	Hugh W. Gardner	Hugh W. Gardner	1966	335
142	24 6/8	24 6/8	17	5	5	4	5	Skamania Co., WA	Ted Howell	Ted Howell	1968	335
142	25 3/8	24	18 3/8	7	6 4/8	7	4	Doty, WA	Leslie A. Lusk	Leslie A. Lusk	1973	335
142	23	20 7/8	21 4/8	4 4/8	4 4/8	5	5	Skamania Co., WA	Herbert P. Roberts	Herbert P. Roberts	1983	335
141 7/8	20 7/8	21 3/8	18 1/8	5 5/8	5 5/8	4	4	Whatcom Co., WA	Kjell A. Thompson	Kjell A. Thompson	1963	341
141 7/8	21 4/8	21 2/8	17 7/8	4 7/8	5	5	5	Trinity Co., CA	Pedro H. Henrich	Pedro H. Henrich	1977	341
141 7/8	21 4/8	21 4/8	16 5/8	4 2/8	4 1/8	5	5	Lincoln Co., OR	Roy A. Parks	Roy A. Parks	1984	341
141 7/8	21 6/8	21 4/8	17 6/8	3 7/8	4	6	5	Trinity Co., CA	Melvin M. Clair	Melvin M. Clair	1992	341
141 7/8	21 3/8	21 2/8	15	5	4 4/8	7	6	Lane Co., OR	Picked Up	Dana H. Clay	1995	341
141 6/8	22 7/8	22 2/8	17 5/8	4 5/8	4 6/8	6	7	Pierce Co., WA	Joseph Kominski	Joseph Kominski	1954	346
141 6/8	21 3/8	21 3/8	19 2/8	4 4/8	4 4/8	5	5	Lane Co., OR	Jerry Shepard	Jerry Shepard	1954	346
141 6/8	19 7/8	19 3/8	16 4/8	4 7/8	4 7/8	5	5	Hobart, WA	Donald R. Heinle	Donald R. Heinle	1958	346
141 6/8	20 2/8	20 7/8	18 2/8	4 5/8	4 4/8	5	5	Linn Co., OR	Eugene L. Wilson	Eugene L. Wilson	1982	346
141 5/8	19 7/8	19 6/8	20 3/8	4	4 2/8	5	5	Trinity Co., CA	A.H. Hilbert	A.H. Hilbert	PR 1955	350
141 5/8	23	22 5/8	15 7/8	5 2/8	4 7/8	5	5	Skamania Co., WA	E. Gerald Tikka	E. Gerald Tikka	1987	350
141 5/8	21 1/8	21 6/8	18 5/8	3 6/8	3 6/8	5	5	Mendocino Co., CA	Lanny G. King	Lanny G. King	1992	350
141 4/8	20 2/8	20 6/8	17 6/8	4 7/8	5	5	5	Morton, WA	Ralph W. Cournyer	Ralph W. Cournyer	1962	353
141 4/8	22	22 5/8	15 4/8	5 2/8	5 1/8	5	5	Pierce Co., WA	Ron Dick	Ron Dick	1965	353
141 4/8	21 2/8	21 1/8	16 2/8	4 2/8	4 2/8	5	5	Mendocino Co., CA	Greg Rocha	Greg Rocha	1985	353
141 4/8	20 7/8	20 4/8	20	4 4/8	4 4/8	5	5	Del Norte Co., CA	Les Johnson	Les Johnson	1986	353
141 3/8	22 5/8	23 2/8	20	5 3/8	5 4/8	6	6	Pierce Co., WA	Delmer H. Stotler	Delmer H. Stotler	1957	357
141 3/8	19 6/8	19 7/8	17 6/8	4 7/8	4 6/8	7	6	Harrison Lake, BC	D. Harrison	D. Harrison	1963	357
141 3/8	22 1/8	21 5/8	18 7/8	4 7/8	4 5/8	5	4	Trinity Co., CA	Larry Brown	Larry Brown	1980	357
141 3/8	21 2/8	21 7/8	16 7/8	4 3/8	4 1/8	6	5	Mendocino Co., CA	Gene V. Bradley	Gene V. Bradley	1988	357
141 2/8	25 6/8	25 3/8	21 5/8	5 4/8	5 6/8	6	6	Pierce Co., WA	John Streepy, Sr.	John Streepy, Sr.	1956	361
141 2/8	21 4/8	20 6/8	18 2/8	4 3/8	4 2/8	5	5	Marion Co., OR	Arthur L. Schmidt	Arthur L. Schmidt	1986	361
141 2/8	21 4/8	20 4/8	18	4 2/8	4 4/8	5	5	Trinity Co., CA	Barry D. Keyes	Barry D. Keyes	1989	361
141 2/8	21 5/8	21 4/8	16	3 6/8	4	5	5	Trinity Co., CA	Donald A. Dunn	Donald A. Dunn	1996	361
141 1/8	22 2/8	22 4/8	17 7/8	4 6/8	4 6/8	5	5	Pierce Co., WA	Jerry E. Burke	Jerry E. Burke	1980	365
141 1/8	23 3/8	23 2/8	17 5/8	4 2/8	4 4/8	6	6	Jackson Co., OR	Harold R. Embury	Harold R. Embury	1985	365
141 1/8	21	21	19 3/8	4 6/8	4 5/8	5	5	Clallam Co., WA	David P. Sanford	David P. Sanford	1989	365
141	21 3/8	21 1/8	17	3 7/8	4 1/8	5	5	Humboldt Co., CA	Allen Pierce, Jr.	Allen Pierce, Jr.	1959	368

Score	L. Main Beam R	L. Main Beam L	Inside Spread	Circ. R	Circ. L	Pts R	Pts L	Locality	Hunter	Owner	Date	Rank
141	20 2/8	19 6/8	14	4	4	5	4	Lane Co., OR	Richard Porter	Ruel Holt	1962	368
141	21	20 2/8	19 4/8	4 4/8	4 4/8	4	5	Mendocino Co., CA	Richard Vannelli	Richard Vannelli	1970	368
141	23	24 4/8	22	5 4/8	5 4/8	6	7	Mendocino Co., CA	Gerald W. Whitmire	Gerald W. Whitmire	1976	368
141	22 4/8	21 3/8	20	3 6/8	4 3/8	5	7	Mendocino Co., CA	Richard L. Valladao	Richard L. Valladao	1993	368
140 7/8	22 2/8	25 7/8	12 3/8	7 4/8	6 5/8	7	5	Clallam Co., WA	Frank Foldi	Steve Crossley	1958	373
140 7/8	21 1/8	20 1/8	21 1/8	4 4/8	4 3/8	5	5	Shasta Co., CA	Dave Swenson	Dave Swenson	1968	373
140 7/8	23 3/8	23 7/8	16 5/8	4	3 7/8	5	5	Mendocino Co., CA	Douglas W. Lim	Douglas W. Lim	1981	373
140 7/8	23 7/8	17 4/8	18 6/8	5	5	8	10	Polk Co., OR	Gale A. Draper	Gale A. Draper	1984	373
140 6/8	17 6/8	21	17 2/8	4	4 5/8	6	5	Lewis Co., WA	Nick Nilson	Nick Nilson	1944	377
140 6/8	21	23 4/8	20 6/8	4 4/8	4	5	5	Mendocino Co., CA	Bill L. Conn	Bill L. Conn	1968	377
140 6/8	23 4/8	23	18 6/8	5 1/8	4 6/8	4	5	Mendocino Co., CA	Robert Lynch	Robert Lynch	1971	377
140 6/8	23	24 1/8	20	5 4/8	5 4/8	5	5	Mendocino Co., CA	Jerry D. Smith	Jerry D. Smith	1978	377
140 6/8	21 3/8	22 1/8	16 1/8	5	4 4/8	7	6	Trinity Co., CA	H. James Tonkin, Jr.	H. James Tonkin, Jr.	1995	377
140 5/8	23	21 7/8	18 3/8	4 6/8	4 6/8	5	5	Shasta Co., CA	Luther Clements	R.H. Bernhardy	1944	382
140 5/8	21	21	18 6/8	4 6/8	4 7/8	5	6	Glacier, WA	John J.A. Weatherby	John J.A. Weatherby	1965	382
140 5/8	21	20 4/8	18 4/8	5	4 7/8	6	6	Clark Co., WA	Wayne G. Place	Wayne G. Place	1995	382
140 4/8	19 4/8	20	17 2/8	4 4/8	4 4/8	5	5	Trinity Co., CA	Loran G. August	Larry Brown	1980	385
140 4/8	20	20 7/8	18 2/8	4 6/8	4 7/8	6	6	Yamhill Co., OR	Richard Watts	Richard Watts	1981	385
140 4/8	20 7/8	21 3/8	14 2/8	4 1/8	4 1/8	5	5	Mendocino Co., CA	Jay M. Gates III	Jay M. Gates III	1986	385
140 4/8	21 1/8	21 4/8	15	4 2/8	4 1/8	5	5	Trinity Co., CA	Jerry R. Cardoza	Jerry R. Cardoza	1996	385
140 3/8	22	21 4/8	16 5/8	4 3/8	3 7/8	5	5	Humboldt Co., CA	George S. Johnson	Roy F. Johnson	1934	389
140 3/8	21	21 2/8	17 7/8	4	4	5	5	Siskiyou Co., CA	Rodney Irwin	Rodney Irwin	1966	389
140 3/8	24 3/8	24 2/8	17 3/8	4 2/8	4 2/8	4	4	Jackson Co., OR	John T. Mee	John T. Mee	1974	389
140 3/8	22 6/8	23 5/8	19 5/8	4 6/8	4 7/8	4	4	Clackamas Co., OR	Anthony W. Wood	Anthony W. Wood	1996	389
140 2/8	21	20 7/8	19 6/8	5	5	5	5	Mendocino Co., CA	Harry S. Richardson	Harry S. Richardson	1952	393
140 2/8	21 4/8	21 4/8	19 6/8	3 7/8	3 7/8	5	5	Lewis Co., WA	Earl E. Hamlow, Jr.	Earl E. Hamlow, Jr.	1977	393
140 2/8	20 4/8	21 3/8	16 2/8	4 5/8	4 5/8	5	4	Trinity Co., CA	Randy J. Brossard	Randy J. Brossard	1978	393
140 2/8	22	21	23 4/8	4 3/8	4 7/8	4	5	Mendocino Co., CA	Charles E. Davy	Charles E. Davy	1983	393
140 1/8	21 2/8	21 2/8	15 6/8	4 2/8	4 2/8	5	5	Mendocino Co., CA	Clarence W. Nelson	Clarence W. Nelson	1948	397
140 1/8	23 7/8	22 7/8	18 1/8	4 4/8	5	6	6	Lewis Co., WA	George Nichols	George Nichols	1964	397
140 1/8	20 4/8	20 4/8	16 3/8	4 2/8	4 3/8	4	4	Santa Clara Co., CA	Dick Sullivan	Dick Sullivan	1977	397
140 1/8	20 7/8	20 7/8	16 5/8	4 3/8	4 3/8	5	5	Lincoln Co., OR	Darrel R. Grishaber	Darrel R. Grishaber	1984	397
140 1/8	19	19	16 5/8	4 6/8	3 7/8	7	6	Snohomish Co., WA	Kenneth A. Peterson	Kenneth A. Peterson	1985	397
140 1/8	21 1/8	21 3/8	16 3/8	4	4	4	4	Siskiyou Co., CA	Rickford M. Fisher	Rickford M. Fisher	1986	397
140 1/8	21 6/8	22 1/8	17 1/8	4 4/8	4 4/8	5	5	Trinity Co., CA	Wayne Sorensen	C.W. Sorensen	1986	397
140 1/8	22	21 4/8	19 1/8	3 6/8	3 6/8	4	4	Jackson Co., OR	Ronald L. Sherva	Ronald L. Sherva	1989	397
140 1/8	18 4/8	20 2/8	17 3/8	4 3/8	4 3/8	5	5	Santa Clara Co., CA	Darin S. Filice	Darin S. Filice	1995	397
140	20 2/8	20 1/8	16	4 6/8	4 7/8	6	7	Mendocino Co., CA	Roy Bergstrom	Roy Bergstrom	1966	406
140	23 1/8	21 3/8	17 6/8	4	4	5	5	Jackson Co., OR	Riley F. Bean	Riley F. Bean	1967	406
140	22 4/8	22 1/8	18	5 2/8	5 5/8	5	5	Mendocino Co., CA	Nick Deffterios	Nick Deffterios	1970	406
140	21	21	17	4 6/8	5	8	6	Polk Co., OR	Harold E. Stepp	Harold E. Stepp	1970	406
140	22	21 5/8	17 6/8	4 1/8	4 1/8	5	5	Humboldt Co., CA	Carl A. Anderson	Carl A. Anderson	1980	406
140	21 5/8	21 5/8	19	4 2/8	3 7/8	5	5	Trinity Co., CA	William J. Olson	William J. Olson	1981	406
140	20 4/8	20 4/8	17 2/8	3 6/8	3 6/8	7	7	Siskiyou Co., CA	Doug Weinrich	Doug Weinrich	1993	406
139 7/8	20 7/8	20 7/8	18 7/8	5	5	5	5	Jackson Co., OR	Dale E. Hoskins	Dale E. Hoskins	1946	413
139 7/8	19	18 6/8	15 5/8	4	4	4	4	Siskiyou Co., CA	Roy Eastlick	Roy Eastlick	1954	413
139 7/8	22 1/8	20 7/8	21 3/8	5	5	5	5	Trinity Co., CA	Craig L. Brown	Craig & Joy Brown	1981	413

COLUMBIA BLACKTAIL DEER
Odocoileus hemionus columbianus

Score	Length of Main Beam R	L	Inside Spread	Circumference at Smallest Place Between Burr and First Point R	L	Number of Points R	L	Locality	Hunter	Owner	Date Killed	Rank
139 7/8	23 2/8	22 2/8	17 6/8	4 7/8	5	5	6	Pierce Co., WA	John E. Mowatt	John E. Mowatt	1994	413
139 7/8	21 4/8	22	18 1/8	4 1/8	4 1/8	5	5	Mendocino Co., CA	David A. Chandler	David A. Chandler	1997	413
139 7/8	20 5/8	20 2/8	17 5/8	6	5 5/8	6	8	Humboldt Co., CA	Jace Comfort	Jace Comfort	1997	413
139 6/8	21 1/8	21 3/8	18 6/8	5	4 6/8	5	5	Thurston Co., WA	Eric Anderson	Eric Anderson	1937	419
139 6/8	20 5/8	21 7/8	16 2/8	4 6/8	4 6/8	6	6	Linn Co., OR	Gregory E. France	Gregory E. France	1961	419
139 6/8	21 5/8	22 4/8	16	4 1/8	4	5	5	Shasta Co., CA	Warren Hunter	Warren Hunter	1964	419
139 6/8	20 6/8	19 6/8	18 1/8	4 4/8	4 2/8	5	6	Josephine Co., OR	Richard H. Caswell	Richard H. Caswell	1969	419
139 6/8	19 6/8	19 7/8	18 6/8	4	4	5	5	Lewis Co., WA	Keith A. Heldreth	Keith A. Heldreth	1989	419
139 6/8	22 2/8	22 5/8	21 4/8	3 3/8	3 5/8	5	5	Trinity Co., CA	Andrew C. Hiebert	Andrew C. Hiebert	1993	419
139 6/8	21 4/8	21 6/8	17	4	4	5	5	Douglas Co., OR	Robert L. Baumgardner	Robert L. Baumgardner	1994	419
139 5/8	21 2/8	21 2/8	14 4/8	4 2/8	4 2/8	6	5	Cowlitz Co., WA	David A. Martin	David A. Martin	1962	426
139 5/8	20 2/8	19 6/8	16 6/8	4 5/8	4 5/8	6	6	Yamhill Co., OR	Mark J. Plummer	Mark J. Plummer	1994	426
139 4/8	21 7/8	21 5/8	20 4/8	4 1/8	4 2/8	5	5	Lane Co., OR	Gene Tinker	Gene Tinker	1955	428
139 4/8	21 7/8	21 1/8	17 2/8	3 4/8	3 4/8	7	5	Jackson Co., OR	Arthur A. Ekerson	Arthur A. Ekerson	1966	428
139 4/8	22 2/8	21 5/8	16	4 6/8	4 6/8	4	5	Lewis Co., WA	Kevin Pointer	Kevin Pointer	1972	428
139 4/8	20 7/8	22 3/8	19 4/8	4 7/8	4 5/8	6	7	Jackson Co., OR	Everett B. Music, Jr.	Everett B. Music, Jr.	1985	428
139 4/8	22	22 3/8	20	4 1/8	4 2/8	5	5	Humboldt Co., CA	Robert B. Feamster	Robert B. Feamster	1996	428
139 4/8	20 2/8	22	15 6/8	4 3/8	4 2/8	5	5	Mendocino Co., CA	Jack J. Tuso	Jack J. Tuso	1996	428
139 3/8	19 4/8	19 5/8	20 6/8	4 2/8	4 2/8	6	5	Mendocino Co., CA	Walter R. Schubert	Walter R. Schubert	1952	434
139 3/8	20 1/8	22 5/8	15 5/8	4 1/8	4 1/8	5	5	Whatcom Co., WA	Kim S. Scott	Kim S. Scott	1959	434
139 3/8	24 5/8	23 3/8	21 5/8	4 7/8	4 7/8	5	5	Trinity Co., CA	Andy Burgess	Andy Burgess	1964	434
139 3/8	21 4/8	21 5/8	22 5/8	4 3/8	4 1/8	5	5	Siskiyou Co., CA	Loren L. Lutz	Loren L. Lutz	1964	434
139 3/8	21 4/8	21 1/8	17 7/8	4 3/8	4 4/8	5	5	Monmouth, OR	Roy W. Miller	Roy W. Miller	1967	434
139 3/8	19 2/8	19 5/8	19 5/8	3 6/8	3 6/8	5	5	Marion Co., OR	Robert W. Hickman	Randall W. Hickman	1974	434
139 3/8	20 7/8	20 6/8	19 5/8	4 6/8	4 5/8	5	5	Marion Co., OR	Richard A. Hart	Richard A. Hart	1982	434
139 3/8	21	21	19 1/8	3 6/8	4 7/8	4	5	Mendocino Co., CA	Donald A. Dunn	Donald A. Dunn	1992	434
139 2/8	18 7/8	19 4/8	14 6/8	4 1/8	4 1/8	5	4	Humboldt Co., CA	Jeff Bryant	Jeff Bryant	1964	442
139 2/8	21 3/8	21 1/8	20 1/8	3 3/8	3 5/8	4	6	Trinity Co., CA	Gary L. Mayberry	Gary L. Mayberry	1968	442
139 2/8	22 5/8	23 3/8	18 6/8	5 1/8	4 3/8	7	4	Josephine Co., OR	David L. Teasley	David L. Teasley	1986	442
139 2/8	21 7/8	21	17 1/8	3 7/8	3 7/8	5	6	Trinity Co., CA	Terry H. Walker	Terry H. Walker	1986	442
139 2/8	21	20 4/8	16 7/8	4	4	4	4	Humboldt Co., CA	Daniel D. Zent	Daniel D. Zent	1991	442
139 2/8	20 5/8	22 3/8	20	4 1/8	3 7/8	5	5	Douglas Co., OR	Ken Wilson	Ken Wilson	1992	442
139 2/8	23 7/8	22	16 4/8	4	4 3/8	6	6	Siskiyou Co., CA	Thomas K. Higgs	Thomas K. Higgs	1993	442
139 1/8	21 7/8	21 1/8	18 6/8	3 7/8	4 1/8	4	5	Florence, OR	Edwin C. Stevens	Warner Pinkney	1928	450
139 1/8	22	21 2/8	18 5/8	4 2/8	4 2/8	5	5	Humboldt Co., CA	George E. Watson	George E. Watson	1933	450

Score	L. R	L. L	Inside Spread	Circ. R	Circ. L	Pts R	Pts L	Locality	Hunter	Owner	Date	Rank
139 1/8	22 1/8	22	17 5/8	4	5 6/8	5	4	Mendocino Co., CA	John Winn, Jr.	John Winn, Jr.	1972	450
139	21 1/8	22 3/8	16 2/8	4 5/8	4 5/8	5	5	Jefferson Co., WA	Aubrey F. Taylor	Picked Up	1947	453
139	20	20 5/8	16 4/8	4 6/8	4 4/8	5	5	Lewis Co., WA	Mike Cournyer	Mike Cournyer	1964	453
139	21 7/8	21 1/8	15 7/8	4 3/8	4 6/8	6	6	Lane Co., OR	Ruel Holt	Picked Up	1964	453
139	19 3/8	19 3/8	18 2/8	4 1/8	4	5	5	Douglas Co., OR	Richard Wigle	Richard Wigle	1968	453
139	21 2/8	21 3/8	16 4/8	3 7/8	3 7/8	5	5	Marion Co., OR	Gene Collier	Gene Collier	1983	453
139	22	21 6/8	17 2/8	4	4 1/8	4	5	Trinity Co., CA	Roger J. Scala	Roger J. Scala	1990	453
138 7/8	21 2/8	20 7/8	17 2/8	5	5 1/8	5	5	Polk Co., OR	Jimmy L. Smithey	Jimmy L. Smithey	1990	460
138 7/8	19 7/8	19 7/8	15 7/8	4 4/8	4 4/8	5	4	Pacific Co., WA	Russell Case	Russell Case	1956	460
138 7/8	21	22 2/8	20 5/8	4 5/8	4 2/8	4	5	Siskiyou Co., CA	Darrell Nowdesha	Darrell Nowdesha	1961	460
138 7/8	23 7/8	24 2/8	18 4/8	4 4/8	4 4/8	5	5	Tiller, OR	Ronald Elliott	Ronald Elliott	1963	460
138 7/8	19 1/8	20 5/8	15 3/8	5	4 7/8	6	5	Trinity Co., CA	William O. Louderback	William O. Louderback	1963	460
138 7/8	20 4/8	20 5/8	16 5/8	4 2/8	4 2/8	5	5	Tillamook Co., OR	Henry Naegeli	Henry Naegeli	1970	460
138 7/8	23	22 6/8	19 4/8	4 3/8	4 3/8	7	5	Josephine Co., OR	Bobby G. Farmer, Jr.	Picked Up	1979	460
138 6/8	21 3/8	21 7/8	19 5/8	4 3/8	4 5/8	4	5	Mendocino Co., CA	Donald W. Biggs	Donald W. Biggs	1992	468
138 6/8	21	22 3/8	15 5/8	5	5	5	5	Whatcom Co., WA	Michael D. Scott	Michael D. Scott	1994	468
138 6/8	20 2/8	21 3/8	15 6/8	5 1/8	5 2/8	5	7	Snohomish Co., WA	Walter J. Kau	Walter J. Kau	1950	468
138 6/8	23 3/8	23	16	4 4/8	4 5/8	5	6	Pierce Co., WA	James Latimer	James Latimer	1962	468
138 6/8	21 3/8	20 4/8	15 4/8	4	4 1/8	5	5	Humboldt Co., CA	Larry Bowermaster	Larry Bowermaster	1964	468
138 6/8	20 2/8	21 3/8	16	4 5/8	4 5/8	5	5	Chipmunk Creek, BC	Larri H. Woodrow	Larri H. Woodrow	1987	468
138 6/8	22 2/8	21 1/8	15 4/8	4 1/8	3 7/8	5	5	Mendocino Co., CA	Gordon O. Hanson	Gordon O. Hanson	1988	468
138 5/8	18 4/8	18	22 2/8	3 6/8	3 6/8	5	5	Mendocino Co., CA	Richard L. Moore	Richard L. Moore	1988	475
138 5/8	22 3/8	25 2/8	16 2/8	3 6/8	5	5	4	Mendocino Co., CA	Thomas R. Erasmy	Thomas R. Erasmy	1993	475
138 4/8	21	21	18	5	4 7/8	5	5	Clatsop Co., OR	Russell L. Hemphill	Russell L. Hemphill	1972	477
138 4/8	19 3/8	19 5/8	20 6/8	5	4	5	6	Linn Co., OR	Jeff B. Garber	Jeff B. Garber	1987	477
138 4/8	22 4/8	22 7/8	21	5	4	5	4	Mendocino Co., CA	Jess Jones	Jess Jones	1950	477
138 4/8	21 1/8	20	15 5/8	4	4 3/8	5	5	Siskiyou Co., CA	Bob Courts	Bob Courts	1965	477
138 3/8	19 4/8	19 4/8	14 6/8	4 3/8	4	5	6	Siskiyou Co., CA	John Carmichael	John Carmichael	1969	481
138 3/8	20 7/8	20 7/8	18 6/8	4	4 5/8	5	5	Mendocino Co., CA	John D. Tuso	John D. Tuso	1997	481
138 3/8	22	22	18 2/8	4 6/8	4 5/8	5	5	Clackamas Co., OR	Wes Mitts	J.B. Mitts	1896	481
138 3/8	22 4/8	22 2/8	17 2/8	4 7/8	5 4/8	5	6	Pierce Co., WA	George W. Halcott	George W. Halcott	1966	481
138 2/8	20 4/8	20 1/8	18	5 3/8	4 1/8	5	5	Humboldt Co., CA	Garry Hughes	Garry Hughes	1968	485
138 2/8	21 4/8	21 4/8	20 5/8	4 4/8	4 3/8	4	5	Trinity Co., CA	Stanley A. Apuli	Stanley A. Apuli	1991	485
138 2/8	22	22	16 3/8	4 1/8	5 3/8	5	5	Trinity Co., CA	Daniel M. Phillips	E.G. Palmrose	1940	485
138 2/8	21 4/8	21 4/8	18	5 2/8	4 4/8	5	5	Snohomish Co., WA	James McCarthy	James McCarthy	1961	485
138 2/8	22	22	18 5/8	5 2/8	3 7/8	5	5	Tehama Co., CA	Robert L. Armanasco	Robert L. Armanasco	1968	485
138 2/8	18 6/8	18 6/8	18 2/8	4	3 6/8	5	4	Trinity Co., CA	Thomas A. Pettigrew, Jr.	Thomas A. Pettigrew, Jr.	1972	485
138 2/8	21 1/8	21 2/8	16 2/8	3 6/8	4 3/8	5	5	Marion Co., OR	Gene Collier	Gene Collier	1974	485
138 1/8	18	18	15 6/8	4 1/8	5 1/8	5	5	Linn Co., OR	Douglas J. Morehead	Douglas J. Morehead	1984	493
138	19 5/8	20 4/8	17 6/8	5	4 3/8	6	5	Mendocino Co., CA	Kenzia L. Drake	Kenzia L. Drake	1985	494
138	18 5/8	18 5/8	15 6/8	4 4/8	4 3/8	5	5	Trinity Co., CA	Monte D. Matheson	Monte D. Matheson	1990	494
138	19 6/8	19 6/8	17 4/8	4 3/8	4 5/8	5	6	Columbia Co., OR	Steve Crossley	Virginia L. Brown	1981	494
138	19 3/8	20 1/8	14 4/8	4 2/8	4 2/8	5	5	Douglas Co., OR	Will H. Brown	Will H. Brown	1948	497
137 7/8	22 3/8	21 7/8	16 2/8	4 6/8	5	5	5	Marion Co., OR	Frank C. Bersin	Frank C. Bersin	1977	497
137 7/8	20 4/8	20 3/8	17 1/8	4 1/8	4 5/8	5	5	Mendocino Co., CA	Brian K. Isaac	Brian K. Isaac	1985	497
137 7/8	20 4/8	20 3/8	16 7/8	4 7/8	4 2/8	5	6	Yamhill Co., OR	Wallace Hill	Wallace Hill	1963	497
137 7/8	19 4/8	19 4/8	15	4 4/8	4 2/8	6	5	Shasta Co., CA	Paul G. Carter	Paul G. Carter	1964	497

COLUMBIA BLACKTAIL DEER
Odocoileus hemionus columbianus

Score	Length of Main Beam R	L	Inside Spread	Circumference at Smallest Place Between Burr and First Point R	L	Number of Points R	L	Locality	Hunter	Owner	Date Killed	Rank
137 7/8	18 4/8	17 5/8	17 3/8	4	4	5	5	Trinity Co., CA	Picked Up	North Coast Tax.	1965	497
137 7/8	20 5/8	20 5/8	16 6/8	4 5/8	4 6/8	6	5	Vancouver Island, BC	Gordie Simpson	Gordie Simpson	1966	497
137 7/8	18	18 5/8	18 5/8	5	4 5/8	4	4	Santa Clara Co., CA	Farber L. Johnston, Jr.	Farber L. Johnston, Jr.	1967	497
137 7/8	21	21	16	5	4 7/8	5	6	Trinity Co., CA	Daniel M. Phillips	Daniel M. Phillips	1993	497
137 6/8	21 2/8	22 1/8	16 7/8	4 3/8	4 3/8	6	6	Douglas Co., OR	Charles A. Cantwell	Dave Cantwell	1962	503
137 6/8	19 1/8	19 6/8	19 6/8	4	4	4	4	Siskiyou Co., CA	Robert L. Miller	Robert L. Miller	1985	503
137 6/8	20 2/8	20 7/8	19 6/8	3 6/8	3 7/8	4	5	Trinity Co., CA	Kevin Clair	Kevin Clair	1986	503
137 6/8	20 5/8	20 2/8	18 6/8	3 5/8	3 5/8	5	5	Trinity Co., CA	Gary A. Bradford	Gary A. Bradford	1996	503
137 5/8	20 4/8	20 3/8	19 5/8	4 4/8	4 5/8	5	5	Mendocino Co., CA	P.R. Borton	John R. Borton	1965	507
137 5/8	19 7/8	19 5/8	17 5/8	4 4/8	4 6/8	7	5	Napa Co., CA	Bruce D. Ringsmith	Bruce D. Ringsmith	1967	507
137 5/8	20 1/8	19 7/8	15 6/8	4 6/8	4 6/8	6	5	Lewis Co., WA	Larry L. Larson	Larry L. Larson	1978	507
137 5/8	20 3/8	21 1/8	20 7/8	4 1/8	4	4	4	Trinity Co., CA	Kenzia L. Drake	Kenzia L. Drake	1994	507
137 4/8	19 3/8	21 1/8	17	4	4 1/8	5	5	Trinity Co., CA	Picked Up	Philip Grunert	1967	511
137 4/8	21 1/8	21 1/8	19	4 1/8	4 3/8	5	5	Trinity Co., CA	Philip Grunert	Craig & Joy Brown	1982	511
137 4/8	22	21 7/8	19 2/8	4 4/8	4 4/8	5	5	Linn Co., OR	Manny M. Kurtz	Manny M. Kurtz	1993	511
137 4/8	20 2/8	20 3/8	20 2/8	4 4/8	4 4/8	4	5	Santa Clara Co., CA	Ray Le Deit	Ray Le Deit	1997	511
137 3/8	20 4/8	21 2/8	19 1/8	4 6/8	4 6/8	5	5	Trinity Co., CA	Donald A. Dunn	Donald A. Dunn	1977	515
137 3/8	20 3/8	20	21 5/8	3 6/8	3 4/8	5	4	Jackson Co., OR	Jay Walker	Jay Walker	1981	515
137 3/8	20 4/8	21 7/8	18 7/8	4 6/8	4 5/8	5	5	Mendocino Co., CA	Carlton C. White	Carlton C. White	1983	515
137 3/8	20 6/8	21 2/8	17 6/8	4 1/8	4 1/8	6	5	Trinity Co., CA	Robert E. Fulmer	Robert E. Fulmer	1993	515
137 2/8	19 3/8	20 7/8	18	4 2/8	4 1/8	5	5	Douglas Co., OR	Bernard L. Den	Bernard L. Den	1934	519
137 2/8	19 6/8	20	15	4 3/8	4 1/8	5	5	Douglas Co., OR	Francis R. Young	Francis R. Young	1972	519
137 2/8	20 5/8	21 4/8	17 6/8	5 2/8	4 7/8	8	5	Jackson Co., OR	Michael E. Earnest	Michael E. Earnest	1992	519
137 2/8	21 7/8	21 6/8	16	3 7/8	3 5/8	5	4	Jackson Co., OR	Ernie MacKenzie	Ernie MacKenzie	1992	519
137 2/8	21 6/8	22 3/8	16 6/8	4 3/8	4 2/8	5	5	Lake Co., CA	Kevin R. Smith	Kevin R. Smith	1997	519
137 1/8	21 3/8	19 2/8	15 7/8	4 2/8	4 2/8	5	5	Douglas Co., OR	Peter Serafin	Peter Serafin	1932	524
137 1/8	20 4/8	20 1/8	15 5/8	4 5/8	4 6/8	5	5	Tillamook Co., OR	Iola M. Pfaff	Iola M. Pfaff	1940	524
137 1/8	20	20 5/8	23 2/8	4 3/8	4 3/8	5	6	Shasta Co., CA	Jack Floyd	Jack Floyd	1957	524
137 1/8	23	22 4/8	22 7/8	5	4 6/8	5	4	Tehama Co., CA	Clint Heiber	Clint Heiber	1977	524
137 1/8	20 4/8	21 1/8	19 2/8	4 4/8	4 4/8	5	7	Douglas Co., OR	Jerry A. Caster	Jerry A. Caster	1989	524
137 1/8	23 5/8	23 4/8	18 3/8	4 3/8	4 3/8	6	5	Jackson Co., OR	Peter Buist	Peter Buist	1995	524
137	20 4/8	21	21 6/8	3 7/8	3 6/8	5	5	Siskiyou Co., CA	Shirley Eastlick	Shirley Eastlick	1962	530
137	24	23 6/8	21 2/8	4 3/8	4 3/8	4	5	King Co., WA	Douglas F. Dammarell	Douglas F. Dammarell	1974	530
137	20	19 5/8	15 6/8	4 6/8	4 6/8	5	5	Polk Co., OR	Ralph Cooper	Ralph Cooper	1978	530
137	22	21 3/8	19 2/8	4 7/8	4 7/8	4	4	Mendocino Co., CA	Shelby Bagley	Shelby Bagley	1991	530
137	21 2/8	19 6/8	18	4 2/8	4 2/8	5	5	Clackamas Co., OR	Mark Perez	Mark Perez	1991	530

Score	Length of Main Beam R	Length of Main Beam L	Inside Spread	Circumference R	Circumference L	Points R	Points L	Locality	Hunter	Owner	Date	Rank
137	20 1/8	21 2/8	16 6/8	4 7/8	4 6/8	5	5	Pierce Co., WA	Glenn T. Litzau	Glenn T. Litzau	1992	530
136 7/8	21 3/8	20 7/8	17 5/8	4 2/8	4 4/8	5	4	Lewis Co., WA	Allen J. Roehrick	Allen J. Roehrick	1968	536
136 7/8	20 1/8	20 3/8	16 1/8	4 6/8	4 3/8	5	6	Humboldt Co., CA	Michael M. Golightly	Michael M. Golightly	1991	536
136 7/8	21 3/8	20 5/8	18 1/8	5 2/8	5 2/8	6	6	Linn Co., OR	Terry L. Moore	Terry L. Moore	1993	536
136 6/8	21 3/8	21	14	4 7/8	4 6/8	5	5	King Co., WA	Ed Lochus	George B. Johnson	1930	539
136 6/8	21 6/8	23	18 2/8	4 5/8	5	4	4	Shasta Co., CA	Vance Corrigan	Vance Corrigan	1957	539
136 6/8	19 3/8	20	14 3/8	4 1/8	4 1/8	6	6	Lewis Co., WA	Mark G. Frohmader	Mark G. Frohmader	1969	539
136 6/8	20 5/8	21 1/8	16	4 5/8	4 6/8	5	5	Pierce Co., WA	Patrick M. Blackwell	Patrick M. Blackwell	1971	539
136 5/8	21 4/8	22 1/8	19 5/8	5 6/8	5 2/8	5	5	Tillamook Co., OR	J.A. Aaron	J.A. Aaron	1943	543
136 5/8	21 6/8	22 3/8	19	4 1/8	4	4	5	Arlington, WA	Ernest J. Kaesther	Ernest J. Kaesther	1959	543
136 5/8	22 4/8	21 1/8	15 7/8	3 4/8	3 6/8	5	5	Marion Co., OR	Ronald A. Bersin	Ronald A. Bersin	1978	543
136 5/8	20 2/8	20	20 1/8	4 7/8	4 5/8	5	4	Jackson Co., OR	Alberto L. Garcia	Alberto L. Garcia	1988	543
136 4/8	20 3/8	20 1/8	18 4/8	4 4/8	4 4/8	5	5	Grays Harbor Co., WA	Joseph S. Prohaska	Stephen H. Prohaska	1952	547
136 4/8	23 4/8	22 1/8	18	4 6/8	4 6/8	5	5	Ukiah, CA	Charles Tollini	Charles Tollini	1960	547
136 4/8	22	22	18 2/8	5	4 1/8	5	5	Lewis Co., WA	Larry F. Smith	Larry F. Smith	1964	547
136 4/8	21 5/8	21 1/8	18 4/8	4 2/8	4 7/8	4	5	Mendocino Co., CA	Jeff P. Leyden	Jeff P. Leyden	1993	547
136 4/8	20 2/8	20 1/8	18 4/8	4	5	6	8	Clackamas Co., OR	Stan K. Naylor	Stan K. Naylor	1994	547
136 3/8	20 2/8	19 7/8	19 1/8	4 3/8	4 1/8	5	4	Douglas Co., OR	Gerry F. Edwards	Gerry F. Edwards	1971	552
136 3/8	21 4/8	21	15 7/8	5 1/8	4 2/8	5	5	Tillamook Co., OR	Guy L. Thompson	Guy L. Thompson	1983	552
136 3/8	20 3/8	20 4/8	15 3/8	3 3/8	4 7/8	5	5	Marion Co., OR	Albert F. Brundidge	Albert F. Brundidge	1990	552
136 2/8	20 6/8	20 4/8	16	4 7/8	3 5/8	5	4	Jackson Co., OR	Martin G. Durbin	Ellis A. Jones	1921	555
136 2/8	20 3/8	21 3/8	20 2/8	3 3/8	4 1/8	4	5	Covelo, CA	David G. Cox	David G. Cox	1967	555
136 2/8	21 6/8	22	17	4 7/8	5 2/8	5	5	Yamhill Co., OR	Monty Dickey	Monty Dickey	1967	555
136 2/8	19 1/8	19 2/8	21 4/8	5	4 7/8	5	5	Siskiyou Co., CA	Wayne G. Rose	Wayne G. Rose	1977	555
136 2/8	20 7/8	20 3/8	16	4 3/8	4 2/8	5	5	Coos Co., OR	Ken Wilson	Ken Wilson	1985	555
136 2/8	19 6/8	20 1/8	16 5/8	4 7/8	4 4/8	6	6	Clackamas Co., OR	Loren R. Schilperoort	Loren R. Schilperoort	1990	555
136 2/8	19	18 6/8	19 2/8	4 3/8	5	5	5	Mendocino Co., CA	Denyse C. Linde	Denyse C. Linde	1997	555
136 1/8	20 4/8	20	14 5/8	5	5 2/8	6	6	Whatcom Co., WA	Dick Vander Yacht	Dick Vander Yacht	1960	562
136 1/8	22 2/8	21 3/8	15 1/8	4 3/8	4 2/8	5	5	Jackson Co., OR	Nancy J. Eden	Nancy J. Eden	1971	562
136 1/8	21 6/8	23	14 6/8	5 2/8	5	8	8	Pierce Co., WA	Randy Fisk	Randy Fisk	1982	562
136	21 4/8	21	19	5 1/8	5 1/8	6	6	Santa Clara Co., CA	Mrs. Maitland Armstrong	Mrs. Maitland Armstrong	1956	565
136	21 4/8	21	17	4 4/8	4 3/8	5	5	Mendocino Natl. For., CA	Edward Q. Garayalde	Edward Q. Garayalde	1966	565
136	23 1/8	19 2/8	19 2/8	4 7/8	4 7/8	5	3	Tehama Co., CA	Robert L. Armanasco	Robert L. Armanasco	1968	565
136	20 4/8	19 6/8	21 6/8	4 7/8	4 6/8	6	4	San Mateo Co., CA	Dan Caughey, Sr.	Dan Caughey, Sr.	1973	565
136	20 4/8	19 6/8	19	4	4 1/8	6	4	Trinity Co., CA	Richard G. Shelton	Richard G. Shelton	1973	565
136	18 7/8	19 2/8	19 2/8	4 7/8	4	5	5	Trinity Co., CA	John P. Morton	John P. Morton	1987	565
136	22 1/8	19 7/8	19 2/8	4	4 2/8	5	5	Mendocino Co., CA	George A. Deffterios	George A. Deffterios	1996	565
136	18 5/8	19 1/8	18 6/8	4 1/8	4 4/8	5	5	Columbia Co., OR	Jasson Kyser	Jasson Kyser	1996	565
135 7/8	22 1/8	22 2/8	15 7/8	4 6/8	4 2/8	5	5	Langley, BC	Charles R. Yeomans	James G. Hill	1959	573
135 7/8	19 2/8	19 3/8	17 3/8	4 4/8	4 4/8	4	5	Jackson Co., OR	Mrs. Ila B. Bethany	Mrs. Ila B. Bethany	1972	573
135 7/8	20 3/8	21 1/8	16 1/8	4 4/8	4 2/8	4	4	Tehama Co., CA	John A. Crockett	John A. Crockett	1982	573
135 7/8	20 1/8	20 4/8	16 7/8	4 2/8	4 4/8	5	5	Snohomish Co., WA	Edmund L. Hurst	Edmund L. Hurst	1984	573
135 7/8	21 1/8	20 1/8	16 5/8	5	4 2/8	5	5	Lane Co., OR	Aaron D. Helfrich	Aaron D. Helfrich	1992	573
135 6/8	20 2/8	19 4/8	18 2/8	4 5/8	4 4/8	5	5	Powell River, BC	Paddy Price	Duncan Formby	1939	578
135 6/8	21 2/8	20 4/8	19 4/8	4 7/8	4 2/8	4	4	Trinity Co., CA	Roy J. Renner	Roy J. Renner	1965	578
135 6/8	20 5/8	19 7/8	18	3 3/8	4	4	4	Linn Co., OR	Gene Collier	Gene Collier	1966	578
135 6/8	20 5/8	19 7/8	15	5 4/8	5 4/8	6	5	Whatcom Co., WA	Jack R. Teeter	Jack R. Teeter	1969	578

COLUMBIA BLACKTAIL DEER

Odocoileus hemionus columbianus

Score	Length of Main Beam R	L	Inside Spread	Circumference at Smallest Place Between Burr and First Point R	L	Number of Points R	L	Locality	Hunter	Owner	Date Killed	Rank
135 6/8	18 4/8	19 1/8	16 4/8	5 2/8	5 3/8	5	6	Linn Co., OR	Joel B. Care	Joel B. Care	1977	578
135 6/8	20	20 2/8	17 2/8	4 6/8	4 6/8	5	5	Cowlitz Co., WA	William R. Gottfryd	William R. Gottfryd	1986	578
135 6/8	16 4/8	20 6/8	16 3/8	5 1/8	5 1/8	6	5	Marion Co., OR	Joseph V. Pileggi	Joseph V. Pileggi	1988	578
135 6/8	20 4/8	20 4/8	16	4 2/8	4 1/8	5	5	Mendocino Co., CA	Phyllis W. Stevenson	Phyllis W. Stevenson	1992	578
135 6/8	19 4/8	20 1/8	14 4/8	3 7/8	3 7/8	5	5	Washington Co., OR	Joseph G. Jaquith	Joseph G. Jaquith	1994	578
135 6/8	20 3/8	20 6/8	15 4/8	4 1/8	4	5	5	Lane Co., OR	Robert J. McClory	Robert J. McClory	1994	578
135 6/8	19 6/8	19 3/8	17 5/8	4 3/8	4 1/8	4	4	Clallam Co., WA	Gary L. Smith	Gary L. Smith	1956	588
135 5/8	22 4/8	23 2/8	20 1/8	4 4/8	4 3/8	4	4	Pierce Co., WA	Mark A. Dye	Mark A. Dye	1987	588
135 5/8	20 2/8	21 2/8	15 1/8	4 1/8	4 1/8	5	5	Humboldt Co., CA	Michael M. Golightly	Michael M. Golightly	1990	588
135 5/8	23 7/8	23 6/8	20 4/8	4 7/8	4 4/8	4	5	Mendocino Co., CA	Ray D. MacDonald, Jr.	Ray D. MacDonald, Jr.	1990	588
135 4/8	20 4/8	20 1/8	16 6/8	3 6/8	3 7/8	5	5	Lewis Co., WA	Oren Layton	Oren Layton	1977	592
135 4/8	20 1/8	20 6/8	17 4/8	4 3/8	4 3/8	5	5	Trinity Co., CA	Robert T. Hammaker	Robert T. Hammaker	1988	592
135 4/8	20	21 5/8	15 4/8	4 3/8	4 3/8	5	6	Benton Co., OR	Mark A. Morris	Mark A. Morris	1990	592
135 4/8	18 3/8	18 3/8	16	4 2/8	4 3/8	5	5	Mendocino Co., CA	Ricky Stoddard	Ricky Stoddard	1996	592
135 3/8	21 5/8	21 2/8	17 6/8	4 6/8	4 5/8	6	6	Clark Co., WA	Francis E. Gillette	Francis E. Gillette	1934	596
135 3/8	21 7/8	21 6/8	16 5/8	5 1/8	5	5	5	King Co., WA	Ernest Zwiefelhofer	Wayne Ferderer	1941	596
135 2/8	19 6/8	20	15	3 4/8	3 3/8	4	4	Trinity Co., CA	Andy Burgess	Andy Burgess	1959	598
135 2/8	19 1/8	19 4/8	13 2/8	3 4/8	3 4/8	5	5	Humboldt Co., CA	Christopher A. Umbertus	Christopher A. Umbertus	1981	598
135 2/8	23 1/8	22 5/8	14 6/8	4 5/8	4 3/8	5	5	Lincoln Co., OR	David K. Oleman, Jr.	David K. Oleman, Jr.	1990	598
135 2/8	21 6/8	21 4/8	14 3/8	4	4	6	5	Lane Co., OR	Lorrie A. Nyseth	Lorrie A. Nyseth	1992	598
135 2/8	21	21 1/8	18 6/8	4 2/8	4 2/8	5	5	Humboldt Co., CA	Richard J. Banko, Jr.	Richard J. Banko, Jr.	1996	598
135 2/8	19 3/8	19 4/8	16 2/8	4 2/8	4 3/8	5	5	Lane Co., OR	Bill A. Parsons	Bill A. Parsons	1996	598
135 1/8	20 2/8	20 1/8	15 3/8	3 6/8	3 6/8	5	5	Jackson Co., OR	Valton G. Albert	Valton G. Albert	1991	604
135 1/8	21	20 7/8	17 1/8	4 6/8	4 6/8	5	5	Trinity Co., CA	Michael L. Rudick	Michael L. Rudick	1997	604
135	19	19 5/8	15 4/8	4 1/8	4 2/8	5	5	Humboldt Co., CA	Edward F. Burgess	Edward F. Burgess	1965	606
135	19 1/8	19 4/8	15 4/8	4 3/8	4 3/8	5	5	Clackamas Co., OR	Ray W. Bunnell	Ray W. Bunnell	1978	606
135	20	19 7/8	16 2/8	4 1/8	4 1/8	5	5	Whatcom Co., WA	Dennis R. Beebe	Dennis R. Beebe	1981	606
135	18 6/8	18 6/8	15 6/8	4 3/8	4 2/8	5	5	Trinity Co., CA	Andrew M. Felt	Andrew M. Felt	1986	606
135	22 6/8	23 2/8	20	4 4/8	4 3/8	4	4	Mendocino Co., CA	Rodney E. Carley	Rodney E. Carley	1989	606
135	20 7/8	21	17 4/8	4	3 7/8	5	5	Lincoln Co., OR	Bill H. Henderson	Bill H. Henderson	1995	606
157 2/8*	21	22	21 4/8	4 4/8	4 4/8	5	5	Mendocino Co., CA	Fred A. Hollenback	Fred A. Hollenback	1956	606
154*	22	23 7/8	22 2/8	4 3/8	4 4/8	5	4	Mendocino Co., CA	William E. Soekland	William E. Soekland	1994	

* Final score is subject to revision by additional verifying measurements.

CATEGORY
COLUMBIA BLACKTAIL

SCORE
143-4/8

HUNTER
ARNOLD E. DADO

LOCATION
MENDOCINO CO., CA

DATE OF KILL
SEPTEMBER 1993

CATEGORY
COLUMBIA BLACKTAIL

SCORE
140-6/8

HUNTER
H. JAMES TONKIN, JR.

LOCATION
TRINITY CO., CA

DATE OF KILL
OCTOBER 1995

CATEGORY
COLUMBIA BLACKTAIL

SCORE
142-5/8

HUNTER
BLAIR R. HOUDAYER

LOCATION
CHILLIWACK LAKE, BC

DATE OF KILL
NOVEMBER 1992

SITKA BLACKTAIL DEER
NEW WORLD'S RECORD

Bob Graham was visiting a shop in British Columbia when he spotted the captivating trophy of a Sitka blacktail (*Odocoileus hemionus sitkensis*). Graham offered to buy the rack, but Peter Bond turned the offer down. Upon hearing this conversation, Bond's son began to wonder what the story was behind the mount. After all, his father had always been a meat hunter and not a trophy hunter. The time had arrived for Peter Bond to recount the memorable evening of September 10, 1970.

"Graham Island, in the Queen Charlotte Island's chain, is the land of plenty for lovers of seafood and wild game. In the 1960s, a boat came once a week in good weather with our Woodwords Food or Sears order, and the mail. The only beef to be purchased was frozen New Zealand beef at a great cost, so we lived off the land. The blacktail deer had no predators except the occasional black bear and man. We were permitted to take 10 deer each year since the deer were small — 40 to 50 pounds dressed.

"On one hunt, I was by myself, on my way into camp in the evening, when I spotted several deer around a backline; but they were 600 yards away on a spur road. I decided to walk closer to get a good shot. When I closed to within 350 yards a couple of does got nervous, so I decided I had to shoot from there. As I put my trusty Weatherby 3x7 scope on each deer, looking for a buck, I ran into the biggest rack I had seen on the island.

"At first I thought it was a deer looking at me through a bush. I studied the buck for a while and when his head moved, looking away from me, I realized what I was looking at was all antler. I was still confused because the buck's body appeared too small for that rack size. All I could see was his head and the top of its back. I thought for a moment the buck was standing behind an old windfall or a dip in the ground. As I am never much on the chase of a wounded animal, I leveled my .300 Weatherby, 120 grain load on the top of his neck, just behind his rack, and let go.

"The buck instantly disappeared from sight, but I was sure he was hit. I climbed up the hill to find my buck had dropped where he stood. To my surprise it was a very large buck, the largest I had seen on the Charlottes'. The buck dressed out at 110 pounds. Also, to my surprise, he had been lying down. That was why his body looked so small."

Having never been one to have his kills mounted, Bond made an exception with this buck. However, Bond never realized he had shot a World's Record. Luckily Graham's persistence and efforts to preserve the great buck prevailed. Now both the new owner and the old hunter can share a pride in the Certificate of Merit awarded by Boone and Crockett Club at the 23rd Awards Program in Reno, Nevada. ■

Photograph courtesy of Jack Graham

TROPHY INFO

RANK
New World's Record

SCORE
133

LOCATION
Juskatla, BC

HUNTER
Peter Bond

OWNER
Bob Graham

DATE KILLED
1970

	SUBTOTALS		COLUMN 1	COLUMN 2 Right Antler	COLUMN 3 Left Antler	COLUMN 4 Difference
		TOTAL TO E	Spread Credit			
Spread Credit			19 6/8			
C. Greatest Spread						

G-3. Le...

G-4. Length of Fourth Point, if Present

G-4. Length of Fourth Place Between Burr and First Point

H-1. Circumference at Smallest Place Between First and Second Points

H-2. Circumference at Smallest Place Between Main Beam and Third Point

H-3. Circumference at Smallest Place Between Second and Fourth Points

H-4. Circumference at Smallest Place Between Second...

Exact Locality Where Killed: Juska...

Date Killed: Sept. 10, 1970

Owner: Bob Graham

Owner's Address:

Telephone #:

	Column 1	19 6/8
	Column 2	58 5/8
	Column 3	58 3/8
ADD		

SITKA BLACKTAIL DEER
WORLD'S RECORD SCORECHART

250 Station Drive
Missoula, MT 59801
(406) 542-1888

BOONE AND CROCKETT CLUB®

TYPICAL
MULE DEER AND BLACKTAIL DEER

OFFICIAL SCORING SYSTEM FOR NORTH AMERICAN BIG GAME TROPHIES

	MINIMUM SCORES	
	AWARDS	ALL-TIME
mule deer	180	190
Columbia blacktail	125	135
Sitka blacktail	100	108

KIND OF DEER (check one)
- ☐ mule deer
- ☐ Columbia blacktail
- ■ Sitka blacktail

Detail of Point Measurement

	Abnormal Points	
	Right Antler	Left Antler
SUBTOTALS		
TOTAL TO E		

SEE OTHER SIDE FOR INSTRUCTIONS		COLUMN 1	COLUMN 2	COLUMN 3	COLUMN 4
		Spread Credit	Right Antler	Left Antler	Difference
A. No. Points on Right Antler	5				
No. Points on Left Antler	5				
B. Tip to Tip Spread	15 5/8				
C. Greatest Spread	23 2/8				
D. Inside Spread of Main Beams	19 6/8	SPREAD CREDIT MAY EQUAL BUT NOT EXCEED LONGER ANTLER	19 6/8			
E. Total of Lengths of Abnormal Points					··
F. Length of Main Beam			20 4/8	19 4/8	1
G-1. Length of First Point, If Present			2 4/8	1 7/8	5/8
G-2. Length of Second Point			9 4/8	9 3/8	1/8
G-3. Length of Third Point, If Present			5 2/8	5 4/8	2/8
G-4. Length of Fourth Point, If Present			6 7/8	8 2/8	1 3/8
H-1. Circumference at Smallest Place Between Burr and First Point			3 6/8	3 6/8	0
H-2. Circumference at Smallest Place Between First and Second Points			3 4/8	3 3/8	1/8
H-3. Circumference at Smallest Place Between Main Beam and Third Point			3	3 1/8	1/8
H-4. Circumference at Smallest Place Between Second and Fourth Points			3 6/8	3 6/8	0
TOTALS		19 6/8	58 5/8	58 3/8	3 6/8

	Column 1	19 6/8	Exact Locality Where Killed: Juskatla, BC	
ADD	Column 2	58 5/8	Date Killed: Sept. 10, 1970	Hunter: Peter Bond
	Column 3	58 3/8	Owner: Bob Graham	Telephone #:
	Subtotal	136 6/8	Owner's Address:	
SUBTRACT Column 4	3 6/8	Guide's Name and Address:	
FINAL SCORE	133	Remarks: (Mention Any Abnormalities or Unique Qualities)	

All measurements must be made with a 1/4-inch wide flexible steel tape to the nearest one-eighth of an inch. (Note: A flexible steel cable can be used to measure points and main beams only.) Enter fractional figures in eighths, without reduction. Official measurements cannot be taken until the antlers have air dried for at least 60 days after the animal was killed.

A. Number of Points on Each Antler: To be counted a point, the projection must be at least one inch long, with length exceeding width at one inch or more of length. All points are measured from tip of point to nearest edge of beam. Beam tip is counted as a point but not measured as a point.

B. Tip to Tip Spread is measured between tips of main beams.

C. Greatest Spread is measured between perpendiculars at a right angle to the center line of the skull at widest part, whether across main beams or points.

D. Inside Spread of Main Beams is measured at a right angle to the center line of the skull at widest point between main beams. Enter this measurement again as the Spread Credit if it is less than or equal to the length of the longer antler; if greater, enter longer antler length for Spread Credit.

E. Total of Lengths of all Abnormal Points: Abnormal Points are those non-typical in location such as points originating from a point (exception: G-3 originates from G-2 in perfectly normal fashion) or from bottom or sides of main beam, or any points beyond the normal pattern of five (including beam tip) per antler. Measure each abnormal point in usual manner and enter in appropriate blanks.

F. Length of Main Beam is measured from the center of the lowest outside edge of burr over the outer side to the most distant point of the Main Beam. The point of beginning is that point on the burr where the center line along the outer side of the beam intersects the burr, then following generally the line of the illustration.

G-1-2-3-4. Length of Normal Points: Normal points are the brow tines and the upper and lower forks as shown in the illustration. They are measured from nearest edge of main beam over outer curve to tip. Lay the tape along the outer curve of the beam so that the top edge of the tape coincides with the top edge of the beam on both sides of point to determine the baseline for point measurement. Record point lengths in appropriate blanks.

H-1-2-3-4. Circumferences are taken as detailed in illustration for each measurement. If brow point is missing, take H-1 and H-2 at smallest place between burr and G-2. If G-3 is missing, take H-3 halfway between the base and tip of G-2. If G-4 is missing, take H-4 halfway between G-2 and tip of main beam.

TROPHY INFO

RANK
3

SCORE
126 3/8

LOCATION
Sunny Hay Mt., AK

HUNTER
Harry R. Horner

OWNER
Harry R. Horner

DATE KILLED
1987

Photograph by Wm. H. Nesbitt

TROPHY INFO

RANK
2

SCORE
128

LOCATION
Kodiak Island, AK

HUNTER
Unknown

OWNER
Craig Allen

DATE KILLED
1985

Photograph by Wm. H. Nesbitt

283

SITKA BLACKTAIL DEER

Odocoileus hemionus sitkensis

MINIMUM SCORE 108

Score	Length of Main Beam R	L	Inside Spread	Circumference at Smallest Place Between Burr and First Point R	L	Number of Points R	L	Locality	Hunter	Owner	Date Killed	Rank
133	20 4/8	19 4/8	19 6/8	3 6/8	3 6/8	5	5	Juskatla, BC	Peter Bond	Bob Graham	1970	1
128	19 6/8	19	19 4/8	4 7/8	4 7/8	5	5	Kodiak Island, AK	Unknown	Craig Allen	1985	2
126 3/8	18 5/8	19 4/8	14 5/8	4	4 1/8	5	6	Sunny Hay Mt., AK	Harry R. Horner	Harry R. Horner	1987	3
126 2/8	19 6/8	20 3/8	16 3/8	4 5/8	4 4/8	5	6	Control Lake, AK	William B. Steele, Jr.	William B. Steele, Jr.	1987	4
125 7/8	17 7/8	18 6/8	13 5/8	4	4	4	4	Tenakee Inlet, AK	Donald E. Thompson	Donald E. Thompson	1964	5
124 2/8	19 1/8	18 2/8	14 4/8	4 3/8	4	5	5	Exchange Cove, AK	Daniel J. Leo	Daniel J. Leo	1986	6
123 4/8	21 4/8	20 3/8	17 6/8	3 6/8	3 6/8	4	4	Uganik Bay, AK	Donna D. Braendel	Donna D. Braendel	1983	7
123 3/8	18 4/8	18 3/8	14 4/8	4 3/8	4 1/8	5	5	Prince of Wales Island, AK	Kenneth W. Twitchell	Kenneth W. Twitchell	1987	8
120 4/8	18 4/8	16 1/8	14 6/8	3 7/8	4 1/8	5	5	Cleveland Pen., AK	Dennis E. Northrup	Dennis E. Northrup	1986	9
120 1/8	17 6/8	17 6/8	16 3/8	4 5/8	4 4/8	5	5	Halibut Bay, AK	James W. Bickman	James W. Bickman	1987	10
118 5/8	17	16 6/8	15 1/8	3 7/8	3 7/8	5	5	Uganik Lake, AK	Larry D. Leuenberger	Larry D. Leuenberger	1985	11
118 3/8	19	17 1/8	14 7/8	4	4 1/8	5	5	Prince of Wales Island, AK	Johnnie R. Laird	Johnnie R. Laird	1987	12
117 4/8	17	16 6/8	15 2/8	3 7/8	3 7/8	5	5	Shrubby Island, AK	Alfred Oglend	Alfred Oglend	1986	13
117 1/8	16 4/8	16 4/8	13 1/8	4 1/8	4 2/8	5	6	Baird Peak, AK	William C. Dunham	William C. Dunham	1984	14
117 1/8	16 6/8	17 4/8	16 7/8	4 3/8	4 4/8	5	4	Mitkof Island, AK	Andrew Wright	Andrew Wright	1991	14
116 4/8	17 5/8	17 6/8	14 2/8	3 7/8	3 6/8	5	5	Kupreanof Island, AK	John N. Williams	John N. Williams	1995	16
116	17 2/8	16 5/8	16	4 1/8	3 6/8	5	5	Kiliuda Bay, AK	Timothy Tittle	Timothy Tittle	1984	17
115 6/8	18 6/8	18 6/8	17 2/8	4 2/8	4	5	5	Kodiak Island, AK	Daniel J. Folkman	Daniel J. Folkman	1991	18
115 6/8	18 4/8	18 2/8	13 4/8	4	4 1/8	5	5	Olga Bay, AK	Terry L. Wingert	Terry L. Wingert	1994	18
114 7/8	15 7/8	16 1/8	14 3/8	3 7/8	4	5	6	Control Lake, AK	Timothy C. Winsenberg	Timothy C. Winsenberg	1985	20
114 7/8	17 7/8	19 1/8	17 5/8	4	4 2/8	5	5	Dall Island, AK	Picked Up	Lynn W. Merrill	1987	20
114 4/8	17 2/8	17 2/8	13 4/8	4 2/8	4 2/8	5	4	Sharatin Bay, AK	H. Arthur Peck	H. Arthur Peck	1984	22
114 3/8	17 4/8	18 3/8	15 3/8	4 4/8	4 2/8	5	5	Hobart Bay, AK	Terry LaFrance	Terry LaFrance	1988	23
114	15 7/8	16	13 6/8	4	3 7/8	5	5	Olga Bay, AK	Frank E. Entsminger	Frank E. Entsminger	1986	24
113 6/8	17 5/8	19 1/8	16 2/8	3 2/8	3 2/8	4	4	Long Island, AK	Picked Up	Allan C. Merrill	1987	25
113 5/8	17 4/8	17 7/8	14 7/8	4 1/8	4 2/8	5	5	Kodiak Island, AK	William C. Hayes	William C. Hayes	1991	26
113 4/8	18 4/8	18 1/8	15 4/8	3 5/8	3 4/8	4	4	Viekoda Bay, AK	Edward R. Hajdys	Edward R. Hajdys	1980	27
113 1/8	17	17 7/8	15	3 5/8	3 5/8	5	5	Tokeen Island, AK	Picked Up	Vaughn R. Ross	1986	27
113 1/8	17 5/8	18 7/8	16 1/8	3 6/8	3 7/8	5	5	Wadding Cove, AK	Kurt W. Kuehl	Kurt W. Kuehl	1984	29
113	16 1/8	16 4/8	13 6/8	4 3/8	4 2/8	5	5	Zarembo Island, AK	Scott D. Newman	Scott D. Newman	1993	30
112 7/8	17	18	15 1/8	3 6/8	3 6/8	5	5	Kodiak Island, AK	Gene Coughlin	Gene Coughlin	1984	31
112 4/8	17 6/8	17 3/8	16	3 7/8	4 1/8	5	5	Prince of Wales Island, AK	William H. Welton	William H. Welton	1988	32
112 3/8	16 6/8	16 7/8	13 5/8	3 5/8	4 2/8	5	5	Kodiak Island, AK	Keith M. Nowell	Keith M. Nowell	1986	33
112 3/8	18 2/8	17 7/8	17 5/8	4	4	7	6	Alder Creek, AK	Richard L. Reeves	Richard L. Reeves	1988	33
112 3/8	19 4/8	19 7/8	17 5/8	4 1/8	4 1/8	4	4	Prince of Wales Island, AK	David L. Hahnes	David L. Hahnes	1990	33
112 2/8	17 5/8	17 2/8	16 4/8	4 1/8	3 7/8	5	5	Uganik Lake, AK	George W. Gozelski	George W. Gozelski	1983	36

Score	Length R	Length L	Inside Spread	Circ. R	Circ. L	Points R	Points L	Locality	Hunter	Owner	Date	Rank
112 2/8	19 2/8	19	16 4/8	4 3/8	4 2/8	4	4	Olga Bay, AK	John D. Frost	John D. Frost	1987	36
112 2/8	17 3/8	17	15 6/8	3 6/8	3 6/8	6	6	Big Salt Lake, AK	Roy Weatherford	Roy Weatherford	1988	36
112 1/8	17	16 2/8	15 5/8	4 1/8	4	5	5	Alitak Bay, AK	Dale J. Bunnage	Dale J. Bunnage	1988	39
112	17 1/8	16 7/8	15 2/8	4 2/8	4 3/8	5	5	Kaiugnak Bay, AK	Damian M. Baptiste	Damian M. Baptiste	1994	40
111 7/8	18 5/8	18 5/8	15 5/8	3 7/8	4 1/8	5	5	Uganik Bay, AK	Jeff A. Buffum	Jeff A. Buffum	1987	41
111 7/8	15 3/8	15	14 3/8	4	4	4	5	Kodiak Island, AK	Brad Holloway	Brad Holloway	1996	41
111 3/8	18	17 5/8	15 5/8	4	4 1/8	5	5	Uyak Bay, AK	Charlie W. Hastings	Charlie W. Hastings	1986	43
111 3/8	18	17 6/8	16 3/8	4 1/8	3 7/8	4	5	Spiridon Lake, AK	David H. Raskey	David H. Raskey	1986	43
111 3/8	18 3/8	18 1/8	15 5/8	3 7/8	3 7/8	5	4	Kodiak Island, AK	Craig T. Boddington	Craig T. Boddington	1992	43
111	16 3/8	16 5/8	14 2/8	3 7/8	3 6/8	5	5	Karluk Lake, AK	Ted H. Spraker	Ted H. Spraker	1983	46
110 7/8	17 4/8	17 6/8	15 7/8	3 6/8	3 7/8	4	4	Kodiak Island, AK	Ronnie L. Aldridge	Ronnie L. Aldridge	1989	47
110 7/8	17 6/8	16 4/8	12 3/8	3 7/8	3 7/8	5	5	Queen Charlotte Islands, BC	Gordon O. Tolman	Gordon O. Tolman	1990	47
110 6/8	16 4/8	18 2/8	14 6/8	3 6/8	3 7/8	5	5	Zarembo Island, AK	Helen G. Keller	Helen G. Keller	1993	49
110 5/8	19 1/8	19 1/8	15 5/8	3 7/8	3 5/8	5	5	Afognak Island, AK	Dale W. Grove	Dale W. Grove	1987	50
110 5/8	16 4/8	16 4/8	14 7/8	3 5/8	3 4/8	5	6	Amook Island, AK	Bob Price	Bob Price	1990	50
110 5/8	17 4/8	17 4/8	15 5/8	3 4/8	3 6/8	4	5	Prince of Wales Island, AK	Edward E. Toribio	Edward E. Toribio	1992	50
110 4/8	20 4/8	19	15 7/8	4 2/8	3 7/8	5	5	Klawock Lake, AK	Chris J. Blanc	Chris J. Blanc	1983	53
110 4/8	17 4/8	17 4/8	16 7/8	3 7/8	3 7/8	5	5	Kodiak Island, AK	William N. Krenz	William N. Krenz	1988	53
110 4/8	16 7/8	16 3/8	16 2/8	3 3/8	3 4/8	5	6	Zachar Bay, AK	Leslie Branson	Leslie Branson	1994	53
110 3/8	16 5/8	18 1/8	13 7/8	4 1/8	4 1/8	5	5	Hidden Basin, AK	Don J. Edwards	Don J. Edwards	1987	56
110 2/8	18 6/8	18	14 2/8	3 7/8	3 7/8	5	6	Kodiak Island, AK	R. Fred Fortier	R. Fred Fortier	1988	57
110 2/8	16 5/8	16 5/8	15	3 7/8	3 7/8	5	5	Halibut Bay, AK	Mike D. O'Malley	Mike D. O'Malley	1993	57
110 1/8	18 1/8	17 7/8	15 4/8	4 2/8	4	6	5	Outlet Cape, AK	Henry T. Hamelin	Henry T. Hamelin	1981	59
110 1/8	18	17 3/8	14 1/8	4 1/8	4 1/8	5	5	Ratz Harbor, AK	Gerald Hedges	Gerald Hedges	1985	59
110 1/8	16 5/8	15 6/8	15 5/8	4 5/8	3 7/8	6	6	Deadman Bay, AK	Donald W. Simmons	Donald W. Simmons	1989	59
110 1/8	17 7/8	17 5/8	15 3/8	3 5/8	4 6/8	5	5	Mitkof Island, AK	Joseph G. Doerr	Joseph G. Doerr	1992	59
109 7/8	17	14 7/8	17 5/8	3 5/8	3 4/8	4	6	Kosciusko Island, AK	Michael C. Fezatte	Michael C. Fezatte	1983	63
109 6/8	18 2/8	17 3/8	17 3/8	3 5/8	4	5	5	Cleveland Pen., AK	Dennis E. Northrup	Dennis E. Northrup	1983	64
109 5/8	19	18 4/8	17	3 6/8	4 4/8	4	5	Terror Bay, AK	Christopher L. Linford	Christopher L. Linford	1987	65
109 5/8	17 7/8	17 7/8	18 2/8	3 5/8	3 5/8	4	5	Olga Bay, AK	Ronnie L. Aldridge	Ronnie L. Aldridge	1988	65
109 4/8	18 1/8	18 1/8	14 7/8	3 5/8	3 6/8	5	5	Uganik Bay, AK	Harvey D. Harms	Harvey D. Harms	1982	67
109 4/8	18 4/8	18 4/8	17 2/8	4	3 7/8	5	5	Elbow Mt., AK	Henry B. Lewandowski	Henry B. Lewandowski	1994	67
109 3/8	16	16	15 4/8	3 6/8	3 5/8	5	5	Kodiak Island, AK	Gary L. McKay	Gary L. McKay	1991	69
109 3/8	18 2/8	18 2/8	15 5/8	3 5/8	3 6/8	4	6	Uganik Bay, AK	Remo Pizzagalli	Remo Pizzagalli	1991	69
109 2/8	18 4/8	18 4/8	15 2/8	4	4	5	5	Uyak Bay, AK	Bradley A. Pope	Bradley A. Pope	1986	71
109 2/8	18 3/8	18 3/8	14 7/8	3 7/8	3 5/8	5	5	Olga Bay, AK	David G. Kelleyhouse	David G. Kelleyhouse	1987	71
109 1/8	17 4/8	17 4/8	16 7/8	4	3 7/8	4	4	Kupreanof Pen., AK	John B. Murray	John B. Murray	1982	73
109 1/8	17 7/8	17 7/8	16 4/8	4 1/8	3 6/8	5	5	Ugak Bay, AK	Donald H. Tetzlaff	Donald H. Tetzlaff	1984	73
109	15 5/8	15 5/8	15	3 6/8	4	5	5	Uganik Bay, AK	Karl G. Braendel	Karl G. Braendel	1982	75
109	16	16	15 6/8	3 7/8	4	5	5	Kodiak Island, AK	D. Roger Liebner	D. Roger Liebner	1983	75
109	17 5/8	17 5/8	15 7/8	3 6/8	4 1/8	5	5	Dall Island, AK	Sharla L. Merrill	Sharla L. Merrill	1985	75
109	17 3/8	17 3/8	14 7/8	3 4/8	3 6/8	5	5	Terror Bay, AK	John R. Odom III	John R. Odom III	1985	75
108 7/8	17 7/8	17 7/8	17 2/8	3 3/8	3 7/8	5	5	Karluk Lake, AK	Wayne J. Jalbert	Wayne J. Jalbert	1993	79
108 7/8	17 3/8	17 3/8	14 4/8	4	3 4/8	5	5	Granite Mt., AK	Johnnie R. Laird	Johnnie R. Laird	1994	79
108 6/8	17 4/8	17 4/8	14 4/8	3 6/8	3 3/8	5	5	Barling Bay, AK	Guy C. Powell	Guy C. Powell	1984	81
108 6/8	17 7/8	17 7/8	13 7/8	3 6/8	3 6/8	5	5	Larsen Bay, AK	David Fischer	David Fischer	1994	81
108 5/8	16 5/8	16 5/8	13 7/8	3 6/8	4	5	5	Uganik Bay, AK	Patrick M. Barwick	Patrick M. Barwick	1988	83

SITKA BLACKTAIL DEER

Odocoileus hemionus sitkensis

Score	Length of Main Beam R	L	Inside Spread	Circumference at Smallest Place Between Burr and First Point R	L	Number of Points R	L	Locality	Hunter	Owner	Date Killed	Rank
108 4/8	19 3/8	19 6/8	15	4	4	4	4	Cleveland Pen., AK	Dennis E. Northrup	Dennis E. Northrup	1985	84
108 4/8	16 4/8	15	15	4 5/8	4 6/8	5	6	Cape Uyak, AK	Richard H. Dykema	Richard H. Dykema	1986	84
108 4/8	15 5/8	16 2/8	11 6/8	3 6/8	3 5/8	5	5	Winter Harbor, AK	Rocky C. Littleton	Rocky C. Littleton	1988	84
108 4/8	17 3/8	17	15 2/8	4 1/8	4	5	5	Prince of Wales Island, AK	Brooke P. Drexler	Brooke P. Drexler	1994	84
108 2/8	18 7/8	19 2/8	15 7/8	4 4/8	4 7/8	7	5	Whale Passage, AK	Howard W. Honsey	Howard W. Honsey	1985	88
108 2/8	17 4/8	16 4/8	12 4/8	3 6/8	3 6/8	5	5	Uganik Bay, AK	John R. Primasing, Jr.	John R. Primasing, Jr.	1995	88
108 1/8	15 6/8	15 1/8	14 5/8	3 7/8	4	5	5	Kodiak Island, AK	Kenneth G. Gerg	Kenneth G. Gerg	1988	90
108	16 6/8	17 3/8	14 4/8	3 6/8	3 6/8	5	5	Kizhuyak Bay, AK	Gene D. Carter	Gene D. Carter	1987	91
117 5/8*	16 2/8	17 3/8	15 5/8	4 4/8	4 3/8	5	5	Red Bay, AK	Randy S. Otos	Randy S. Otos	1987	
114*	16 4/8	17 1/8	13 4/8	3 4/8	3 4/8	5	5	Prince of Wales Island, AK	Robert D. Steward	Robert D. Steward	1991	

* Final score is subject to revision by additional verifying measurements.

CATEGORY
SITKA BLACKTAIL

SCORE
115-6/8

HUNTER
TERRY L. WINGERT

LOCATION
OLGA BAY, AK

DATE OF KILL
OCTOBER 1994

B&C HISTORY

GEORGE BIRD GRINNELL
1849-1938

Together with Theodore Roosevelt, George Bird Grinnell was one of the founding members of the Boone and Crockett Club in December of 1887. He served as its president from 1918 to 1927. He founded the Audubon Society in 1886. The establishment of Glacier National Park in 1910 came about largely due to the efforts of Dr. Grinnell. He developed a great interest in the Plains Indians and was considered the leading authority on the Blackfoot, Cheyenne, and Pawnee Nations. He was editor-in-chief of *Forest and Stream* magazine, the leading outdoor magazine of its time. He is considered one of the preeminent conservationists in the early history of the movement. ■

287

WHITETAIL DEER - TYPICAL ANTLERS
NEW WORLD'S RECORD

Working long days as a grain and cattle farmer in Biggar, Saskatchewan, Milo N. Hanson is not a man who has the time or money to hunt all over the continent, but then again he hasn't had to go that far. Hunting on his property in 1992, Hanson ended up reaping more from his fields than the usual autumn harvest.

"On the night of November 22, we had fresh snow, and I called the guys to plan our hunt.

"The next morning, I met my neighbor John Yaroshko and we drove to meet Walter Meger and Rene Igini. When we pulled up I knew something was happening because they were excited. They said they spotted the monster buck entering a willow run and not coming out.

"Rene walked the track while the rest of us surrounded the willows. I took a position that would keep the buck from running south onto nearby posted land. The buck bolted, giving me my first look at it. Believe me, my heart was pumping! We shot but missed it.

"Rene stayed on its tracks, and eventually lost the buck in a maVze of other deer tracks because its tracks weren't large. Just when we were getting frustrated and ready to move on, the big buck ran out of an aspen bluff and headed into a willow run on my land. We posted ourselves around the willows, and Rene walked the buck's tracks. The buck ran flat out about 150 yards broadside from John and me. I think we both got buck fever this time! We fired several shots, but missed the racing buck.

"We moved up to the next willow run, and when the buck ran out it turned straight away from me. I fired and the buck went down to its knees. 'You got him!' John hollered.

"The buck got up and ran into a nearby aspen bluff. I ran up the hill to where it disappeared, and saw it below me, standing still. I aimed through my 4-power scope and fired another shot with my .308 Winchester Model 88 lever-action. Down it went. I saw its head over a clump of willows. To ensure it stayed down, I fired another shot and the hunt ended.

"Shooting this buck gave me a feeling I will probably never experience again, even though I had no idea it would be declared the new Boone and Crockett Club World's Record in Dallas, Texas, at the 22nd Big Game Awards Program. I had never seen a bigger buck. The buck left me shaking."

Life on the farm took a turn. Following pre-preliminary measurements that put the whitetail in the running for the new World's Record, Hanson found his home under siege from journalists, promoters, collectors and well-wishers. After the 60-day drying period, Norm Parchewsky, Robert Allemand, and Allan Holtvogt, all Boone and Crockett official measurers, scored the buck at 213-1/8 in a scoring ceremony attended by more than 400 people.

At the 22nd Big Game Awards Program, the Boone and Crockett Club Judges' Panel declared Hanson's buck the new World's Record typical whitetail with a final and official score of 213-5/8 points. ∎

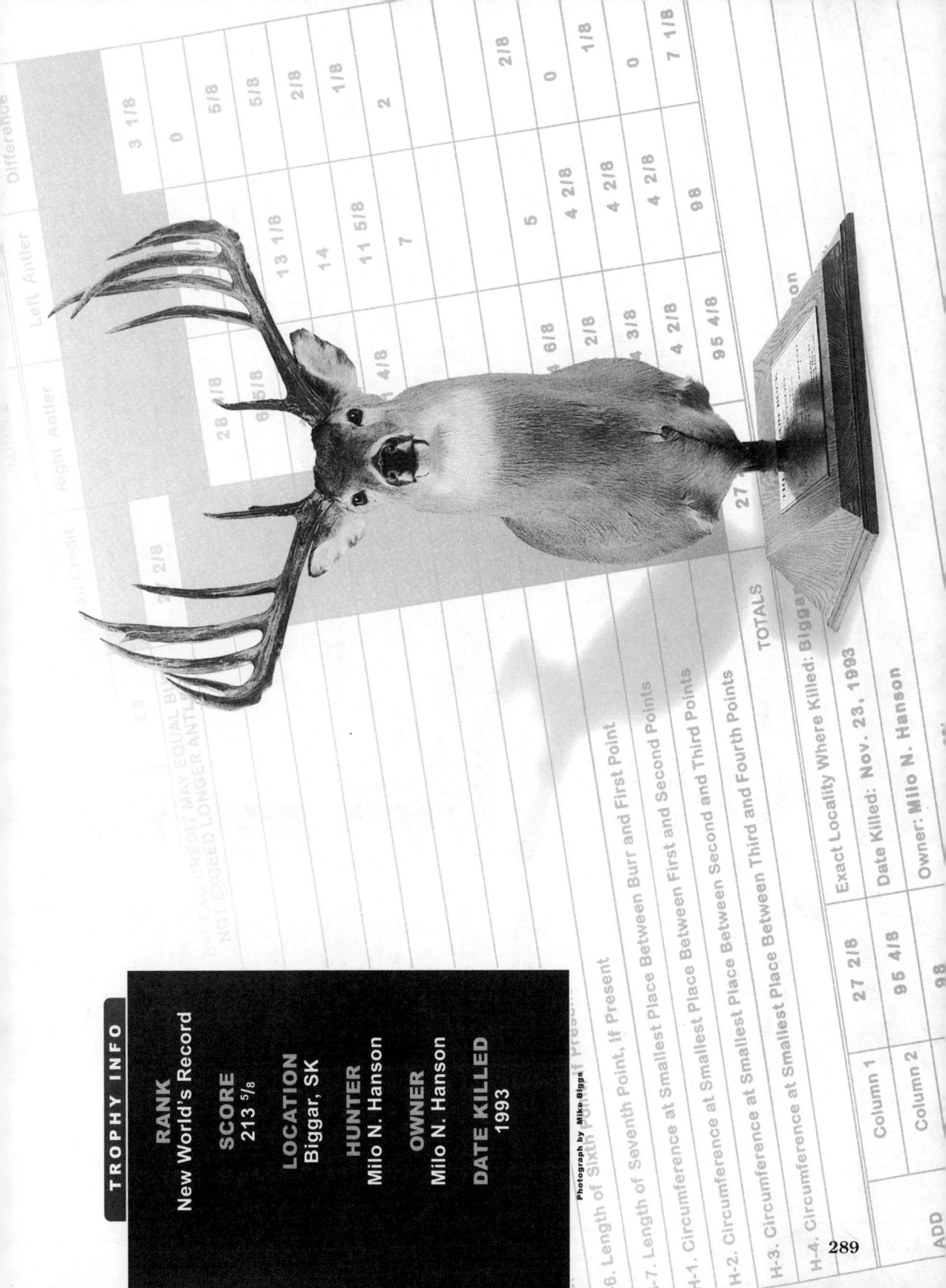

Photograph by Mike Biggs

TROPHY INFO

RANK
New World's Record

SCORE
213 5/8

LOCATION
Biggar, SK

HUNTER
Milo N. Hanson

OWNER
Milo N. Hanson

DATE KILLED
1993

	Right Antler	Left Antler	Difference
	2/8	3 1/8
	29	
	28 6/8		0
	6 5/8		
		13 1/8	5/8
		14	5/8
		11 5/8	2/8
	4 4/8	2	1/8
	4 6/8	7	2
	2/8	5	2/8
	4 3/8	4 2/8	0
	4 2/8	4 2/8	1/8
	95 4/8	98	0
	27		7 1/8

H-6. Length of Sixth Point, If Present

G-7. Length of Seventh Point, If Present

H-1. Circumference at Smallest Place Between Burr and First Point

H-2. Circumference at Smallest Place Between First and Second Points

H-3. Circumference at Smallest Place Between Second and Third Points

H-4. Circumference at Smallest Place Between Third and Fourth Points

TOTALS

Exact Locality Where Killed: Biggar

Date Killed: Nov. 23, 1993

Owner: Milo N. Hanson

	Column 1	Column 2
Column 1	27 2/8	
Column 2	95 4/8	
	98	

ADD

SPREAD CREDIT MAY EQUAL B
NOT EXCEED LONGER ANTL

289

Records of
North American
Big Game

250 Station Drive
Missoula, MT 59901
(406) 542-1888

BOONE AND CROCKETT CLUB®

OFFICIAL SCORING SYSTEM FOR NORTH AMERICAN BIG GAME TROPHIES

TYPICAL
WHITETAIL AND COUES' DEER

MINIMUM SCORES	AWARDS	ALL-TIME
whitetail	160	170
Coues'	100	110

KIND OF DEER (check one)
■ whitetail
☐ Coues'

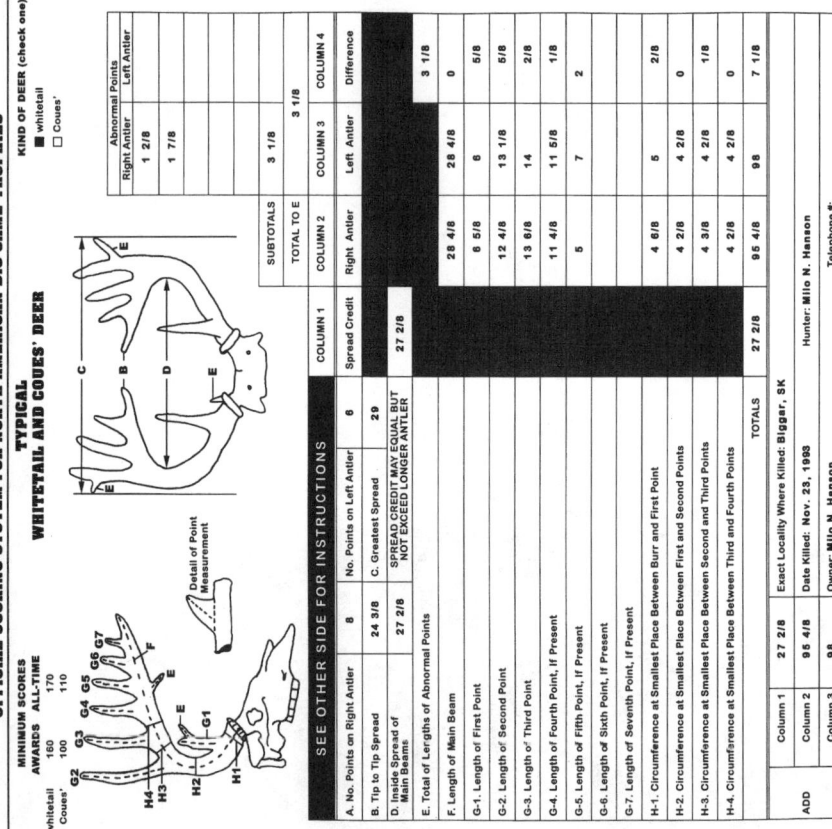

Detail of Point
Measurement

		Abnormal Points	
		Right Antler	Left Antler
		1 2/8	
		1 7/8	
SUBTOTALS		3 1/8	
TOTAL TO E			3 1/8

SEE OTHER SIDE FOR INSTRUCTIONS			COLUMN 1	COLUMN 2	COLUMN 3	COLUMN 4
A. No. Points on Right Antler	8	No. Points on Left Antler	6	Spread Credit	Right Antler	Left Antler	Difference
B. Tip to Tip Spread	24 3/8	C. Greatest Spread	29				
D. Inside Spread of Main Beams	27 2/8	SPREAD CREDIT MAY EQUAL BUT NOT EXCEED LONGER ANTLER		27 2/8			3 1/8
E. Total of Lengths of Abnormal Points							0
F. Total of Length of Main Beam				28 4/8	28 4/8	0
G-1. Length of First Point				6 5/8	6	5/8
G-2. Length of Second Point				12 4/8	13 1/8	5/8
G-3. Length o' Third Point				13 6/8	14	2/8
G-4. Length of Fourth Point, If Present				11 4/8	11 5/8	1/8
G-5. Length of Fifth Point, If Present				5	7	2
G-6. Length of Sixth Point, If Present						
G-7. Length of Seventh Point, If Present						
H-1. Circumference at Smallest Place Between Burr and First Point				4 6/8	5	2/8
H-2. Circumference at Smallest Place Between First and Second Points				4 2/8	4 2/8	0
H-3. Circumference at Smallest Place Between Second and Third Points				4 3/8	4 2/8	1/8
H-4. Circumference at Smallest Place Between Third and Fourth Points				4 2/8	4 2/8	0
TOTALS				27 2/8	95 4/8	98	7 1/8

		Exact Locality Where Killed: Bigar, SK	
ADD	Column 1	27 2/8	Date Killed: Nov. 23, 1993	Hunter: Milo N. Hanson
	Column 2	95 4/8	Owner: Milo N. Hanson	Telephone #:
	Column 3	98	Owner's Address:	
	Subtotal	220 6/8	Guide's Name and Address:	
SUBTRACT Column 4	7 1/8	Remarks: (Mention Any Abnormalities or Unique Qualities)	
FINAL SCORE	213 5/8		

COPYRIGHT © 1999 BY BOONE AND CROCKETT CLUB®

All measurements must be made with a 1/4-inch wide flexible steel tape to the nearest one-eighth of an inch. (Note: A flexible steel cable can be used to measure points and main beams only.) Enter fractional figures in eighths, without reduction. Official measurements cannot be taken until the antlers have air dried for at least 60 days after the animal was killed.

A. Number of Points on Each Antler: To be counted a point, the projection must be at least one inch long, with the length exceeding width at one inch or more of length. All points are measured from tip of point to nearest edge of beam as illustrated. Beam tip is counted as a point but not measured as a point.

B. Tip to Tip Spread is measured between tips of main beams.

C. Greatest Spread is measured between perpendiculars at a right angle to the center line of the skull at widest part, whether across main beams or points.

D. Inside Spread of Main Beams is measured at a right angle to the center line of the skull at widest point between main beams. Enter this measurement again as the Spread Credit if it is less than or equal to the length of the longer antler; if greater, enter longer antler length for Spread Credit.

E. Total of Lengths of all Abnormal Points: Abnormal Points are those non-typical in location (such as points originating from a point or from bottom or sides of main beam) or extra points beyond the normal pattern of points. Measure in usual manner and enter in appropriate blanks.

F. Length of Main Beam is measured from the center of the lowest outside edge of burr over the outer side to the most distant point of the main beam. The point of beginning is that point on the burr where the center line along the outer side of the beam intersects the burr, then following generally the line of the illustration.

G-1-2-3-4-5-6-7. Length of Normal Points: Normal points project from the top of the main beam. They are measured from nearest edge of main beam over outer curve to tip. Lay the tape along the outer curve of the beam so that the top edge of the tape coincides with the top edge of the beam on both sides of the point to determine the baseline for point measurements. Record point lengths in appropriate blanks.

H-1-2-3-4. Circumferences are taken as detailed in illustration for each measurement. If brow point is missing, take H-1 and H-2 at smallest place between burr and G-2. If G-4 is missing, take H-4 halfway between G-3 and tip of main beam.

Photograph by Wm. H. Nesbitt

Photograph courtesy of Charles T. Arnold

WHITETAIL DEER - TYPICAL ANTLERS

Odocoileus virginianus virginianus and certain related subspecies

MINIMUM SCORE 170

Score	Length of Main Beam R	L	Inside Spread	Circumference at Smallest Place Between Burr and First Point R	L	Number of Points R	L	Locality	Hunter	Owner	Date Killed	Rank
213 5/8	28 4/8	28 4/8	27 2/8	4 6/8	5	8	6	Biggar, SK	Milo N. Hanson	Milo N. Hanson	1993	1
206 1/8	30	30	20 1/8	6 2/8	6 1/8	5	5	Burnett Co., WI	James Jordan	Larry L. Huffman	1914	2
205	26 6/8	25 4/8	24 2/8	4 6/8	4 6/8	6	6	Randolph Co., MO	Larry W. Gibson	MO Show-Me Big Bucks Club	1971	3
204 4/8	**27 5/8**	**26 6/8**	**23 5/8**	**6 1/8**	**6 2/8**	**7**	**6**	**Peoria Co., IL**	**Mel Johnson**	**Larry L. Huffman**	**1965**	**4**
204 2/8	26 4/8	22 6/8	25 1/8	5 1/8	5 1/8	7	10	Beaverdam Creek, AB	Stephen Jansen	Stephen Jansen	1967	5
202 6/8	28	27 1/8	21 2/8	5 3/8	5 3/8	9	8	Barrier Valley, SK	Bruce Ewen	Bruce Ewen	1992	6
202	31 2/8	31	23 5/8	5 7/8	6	8	8	Beltrami Co., MN	John A. Breen	Larry L. Huffman	1918	7
201 4/8	27 5/8	29 1/8	23	5 5/8	5 2/8	6	6	Hamilton Co., IA	Wayne A. Bills	Larry L. Huffman	1974	8
201	26 2/8	26 2/8	15 5/8	4 5/8	4 7/8	8	6	Kittson Co., MN	Wayne G. Stewart	Wayne G. Stewart	1961	9
200 2/8	26 3/8	27 1/8	24	5	4 7/8	6	7	Whitkow, SK	Peter J. Swistun	Peter J. Swistun	1983	10
200 2/8	32	32 4/8	28 3/8	5 4/8	5 3/8	9	8	Macon Co., IL	Brian S. Damery	Bass Pro Shops F. & W. Mus.	1993	10
199 5/8	30 1/8	28	29 1/8	5 3/8	5 3/8	6	6	Edmonton, AB	Don McGarvey	Don McGarvey	1991	12
199 4/8	27 2/8	26 2/8	20	5 4/8	5 1/8	8	5	Clark Co., MO	Jeffrey A. Brunk	Jeffrey A. Brunk	1969	13
199 3/8	27 3/8	27 4/8	22 3/8	4 4/8	4 6/8	6	7	Missoula Co., MT	Thomas H. Dellwo	Bass Pro Shops F. & W. Mus.	1974	14
199 2/8	28 7/8	29	25 6/8	5	5 1/8	6	6	Lake of the Woods Co., MN	Vernon Jensen	Vernon Jensen	1954	15
199 2/8	27	27 1/8	21 4/8	5 2/8	5	5	5	Flathead Co., MT	Kent Petry	Larry L. Huffman	1966	15
198 3/8	29 5/8	29 4/8	18 1/8	4 6/8	4 6/8	6	8	Allegany Co., NY	Roosevelt Luckey	NY Dept. of Env. Cons.	1939	17
198 2/8	27 5/8	26 7/8	20 2/8	5	5	6	8	Nemaha Co., KS	Dennis P. Finger	Dennis P. Finger	1974	18
198 1/8	29 4/8	29 4/8	19 5/8	4 6/8	4 7/8	9	8	Decatur Co., IA	Kenneth Tilford	Jack G. Brittingham	1985	19
198	29 2/8	29 4/8	20 2/8	5 2/8	5 1/8	9	7	Jackson Co., MI	Troy A. Stephens	MI Whitetail Hall of Fame Mus.	1996	20
197 7/8	27 4/8	27 2/8	19 4/8	4 6/8	4 6/8	8	9	Assiniboine River, MB	Larry H. MacDonald	Larry H. MacDonald	1980	21
197 6/8	29 2/8	30	20 4/8	5 6/8	5 7/8	6	5	Wright Co., MN	Curtis F. Van Lith	Larry L. Huffman	1986	22
197 5/8	27 2/8	27 5/8	21 6/8	5 2/8	5 4/8	7	8	Wood Co., WI	Joe Haske	Goldie Haske	1945	23
197 3/8	29 1/8	29 7/8	21	5 1/8	5 2/8	9	7	Mann Lakes, AB	Lawrence J. Youngman	Lawrence J. Youngman	1992	24
197 2/8	25 4/8	27 2/8	32	5 2/8	5 3/8	6	7	Comanche Co., KS	Picked Up	H. James Reimer	1991	25
197 1/8	31	29 7/8	21 2/8	6 1/8	6 5/8	7	7	Macoupin Co., IL	Kevin L. Naugle	Bass Pro Shops F. & W. Mus.	1988	26
196 4/8	28 6/8	27 5/8	24 2/8	4 6/8	4 6/8	8	6	Maverick Co., TX	Tom McCulloch	McLean Bowman	1963	27
196 4/8	27	26 1/8	22 4/8	4 5/8	4 5/8	8	7	Des Moines Co., IA	Michael R. Edle	Michael R. Edle	1989	27
196 3/8	28 7/8	30 5/8	22 1/8	6 5/8	7	7	5	Plymouth Co., IA	Picked Up	H. James Reimer	1952	29
196 1/8	27 1/8	26 4/8	24 5/8	4 6/8	4 6/8	8	9	McMullen Co., TX	Milton P. George	John L. Stein	1906	30
195 7/8	26 4/8	27 1/8	21 1/8	4 1/8	4 1/8	6	6	Anoka Co., MN	Barry Peterson	Barry Peterson	1995	31
195 5/8	28 4/8	27 6/8	22 1/8	5 6/8	5 7/8	6	7	Marshall Co., MN	Robert Sands	Robert Sands	1960	32
195 4/8	25 3/8	25 7/8	19	4 7/8	4 7/8	9	7	Porcupine Plain, SK	Philip Philipowich	Philip Philipowich	1985	33
195 2/8	28 6/8	28 2/8	20 6/8	5 1/8	5	6	6	Pierce Co., ND	Kevin L. Bruner	Kevin L. Bruner	1994	34
195 1/8	28 6/8	28 4/8	20 3/8	4 7/8	5	5	5	Parke Co., IN	B. Dodd Porter	B. Dodd Porter	1985	35
195 1/8	25 6/8	28 1/8	19 6/8	5 2/8	5 2/8	8	5	Brightsand Lake, SK	Larry Pellerin	D.J. Hollinger & B. Howard	1993	35

Score	Length R	Length L	Inside Spread	Circ. R	Circ. L	Points R	Points L	Locality	Hunter	Owner	Date	Rank
194 7/8	26 7/8	27 2/8	23 1/8	6 1/8	5 6/8	7	7	Leavenworth Co., KS	William R. Mikijanis	William R. Mikijanis	1985	37
194 4/8	25 7/8	25 6/8	18 6/8	5 1/8	5 2/8	7	7	Monroe Co., IA	Lloyd Goad	Larry L. Huffman	1962	38
194 4/8	26 2/8	26	18 7/8	5 6/8	5 4/8	8	9	Nipawin, SK	Gerald Whitehead	Gerald Whitehead	1990	38
194 3/8	29 1/8	28 6/8	23 5/8	5 1/8	5 1/8	5	8	Warren Co., IA	Forest H. Richardson	Larry L. Huffman	1989	40
194 2/8	26 5/8	25	21	4 6/8	5	6	6	Jones Co., IA	Robert Miller	Larry L. Huffman	1977	41
194 2/8	30 6/8	30 3/8	24 7/8	5 3/8	5 2/8	9	9	Vigo Co., IN	D. Bates & S. Winkler	D. Bates & S. Winkler	1983	41
194 1/8	30	30 1/8	19 4/8	4 6/8	5	7	6	Dakota Co., NE	E. Keith Fahrenholz	E. Keith Fahrenholz	1966	43
193 6/8	24 5/8	24 4/8	18 1/8	5	5	7	7	Christopher Lake, SK	Jerry Thorson	Jerry Thorson	1959	44
193 6/8	29 5/8	30	23 1/8	5 4/8	5 4/8	6	6	Antigonish Co., NS	Kevin Boyle	Bass Pro Shops F. & W. Mus.	1987	44
193 4/8	29	29 5/8	23 7/8	4 4/8	5 3/8	6	6	Linn Co., IA	Picked Up	Gary W. Bowen	1994	46
193 3/8	28 6/8	28 6/8	21 2/8	4 4/8	4 4/8	5	5	Itasca Co., MN	Picked Up	Paul M. Shaw	1935	47
193 3/8	26	25 6/8	22 2/8	5 6/8	5 4/8	5	8	Aroostook Co., ME	Ronnie Cox	Bass Pro Shops F. & W. Mus.	1965	47
193 3/8	28 3/8	28 3/8	22 2/8	5 2/8	5 2/8	6	8	Jackson Co., MI	Craig Calderone	Bass Pro Shops F. & W. Mus.	1986	47
193 3/8	29 4/8	29 1/8	24 6/8	5 2/8	5 2/8	7	5	Chitek Lake, SK	David L. Wilson	David L. Wilson	1992	47
193	26	26	25	5 3/8	5 5/8	6	6	South Dakota	Unknown	Eugene J. Lodermeier	1964	51
192 7/8	27 4/8	27 2/8	19 3/8	4 3/8	4 5/8	8	9	York Co., ME	Alphonse Chase	Earl Taylor	1920	52
192 7/8	28 1/8	28 1/8	19 7/8	5 7/8	6	10	7	Williamson Co., IL	A. & J. Albers	A. & J. Albers	1991	52
192 7/8	26 6/8	25 6/8	18 4/8	5 1/8	5 1/8	7	6	Wabatansik Creek, AB	Norman Trudeau	Norman Trudeau	1992	52
192 7/8	25 6/8	25 7/8	18 5/8	5 4/8	5 3/8	6	9	Makwa Lake, SK	Ken Brown	Ken Brown	1993	52
192 6/8	30 1/8	28 3/8	21 2/8	5 2/8	5 2/8	5	6	Lucas Co., IA	Picked Up	H. James Reimer	1992	56
192 3/8	24 1/8	23 6/8	17 3/8	5	4 6/8	6	6	Monroe Co., IN	Donald L. Fritch	Donald L. Fritch	1992	57
192 3/8	28 4/8	28 2/8	19 4/8	5 7/8	5 4/8	9	9	Monroe Co., IA	Roy E. Allison	Roy E. Allison	1995	57
192 2/8	27 2/8	27 3/8	22 6/8	4 2/8	4 4/8	6	6	Frio Co., TX	Basil Dailey	John L. Stein	1903	59
192 2/8	28 2/8	28 7/8	23 5/8	5 3/8	5 4/8	5	6	Pope Co., MN	Roger Syrstad	Roger Syrstad	1989	59
192	27 1/8	27 2/8	19	4 5/8	4 5/8	6	6	Pine Co., MN	Frank Worlickey	Robert Worlickey	1952	61
192	27 4/8	28	19 2/8	4 6/8	4 6/8	6	6	Lyman Co., SD	Bob Weidner	E.N. Eichler	1957	61
192	24 3/8	23 5/8	17	4 7/8	4 6/8	8	8	Clay Co., MN	Mark L. Peterson	Mark L. Peterson	1984	61
191	30 5/8	30 7/8	19 2/8	5	5	6	7	Charles Mix Co., SD	John Simon	John Simon	PR 1970	64
191 7/8	29 5/8	30 1/8	20 4/8	5 7/8	5 7/8	9	9	Wayne Co., IL	Leo E. Elliott	Leo E. Elliott	1990	64
191 7/8	27	26	19 6/8	4 6/8	4 6/8	5	5	Hudson Bay, SK	George Chalus	Larry L. Huffman	1973	66
191 6/8	27 7/8	28	21	5	5	7	7	Union Co., IL	Everett F. Ellis	Everett F. Ellis	1994	66
191 6/8	26 5/8	26 2/8	19	5 1/8	5 1/8	6	6	Flathead Co., MT	Earl T. McMaster	Larry L. Huffman	1963	68
191 5/8	26	26 1/8	21 7/8	4 6/8	4 4/8	5	5	Goodhue Co., MN	David C. Klatt	Bass Pro Shops F. & W. Mus.	1985	68
191 5/8	25	25	22 7/8	5	5 1/8	6	6	Albany Co., WY	Robert D. Ross	Robert D. Ross	1986	68
191 4/8	25 5/8	27 4/8	20	4 3/8	4 4/8	5	6	Chautauqua Co., KS	Michael A. Young	Michael A. Young	1973	71
191 3/8	26 5/8	26 5/8	27 5/8	6 1/8	6 1/8	5	6	Vilas Co., WI	Robert Hunter	May Docken	1910	72
191 3/8	31 6/8	31 1/8	25 5/8	4 7/8	5 1/8	5	5	Meade Co., KY	Picked Up	William N. Burrell	1977	72
191	24 6/8	24 6/8	20 2/8	5 7/8	5 7/8	6	5	Scott Co., IA	Jeffery L. Whisker	Larry L. Huffman	1993	74
190 7/8	28 1/8	27 1/8	19 5/8	4 4/8	4 4/8	5	5	Lyon Co., KS	Jamie Fowler	Jamie Fowler	1992	75
190 5/8	26 3/8	26 3/8	20 7/8	4 5/8	4 5/8	7	5	Geary Co., KS	Gary L. Taylor	Gary L. Taylor	1994	77
190 5/8	25 2/8	25 4/8	19 5/8	4 4/8	4 5/8	7	5	Buffalo Lake, AB	Eugene L. Boll	Eugene L. Boll	1969	77
190 5/8	22 4/8	22 4/8	17 6/8	6	6	5	6	Polk Co., IA	Richard B. Swim	Richard B. Swim	1981	77
190 5/8	28	28	19 4/8	5 6/8	5 6/8	5	5	Parke Co., IN	Tony A. Trotter	Tony A. Trotter	1992	77
190 4/8	29	29	22 3/8	5 1/8	5 2/8	6	6	Monona Co., IA	Jeffery D. Scott	Jeffery D. Scott	1996	80
190 3/8	27 3/8	27 6/8	20 4/8	4 5/8	4 5/8	5	6	Pettis Co., MO	Jesse A. Perry	Jesse A. Perry	1986	81
190 3/8	27	27	22 6/8	5 6/8	5 7/8	10	6	Republic Co., KS	John M. Nylund	John M. Nylund	1995	81
190 2/8	26 1/8	23 1/8	25 7/8	4 2/8	4 3/8	6	7	Shackelford Co., TX	Steven W. O'Carroll	John L. Stein	1991	83

WHITETAIL DEER - TYPICAL ANTLERS

Odocoileus virginianus virginianus and certain related subspecies

Score	Length of Main Beam R	L	Inside Spread	Circumference at Smallest Place Between Burr and First Point R	L	Number of Points R	L	Locality	Hunter	Owner	Date Killed	Rank
190 2/8	25 6/8	26 2/8	21 3/8	5	4 5/8	13	13	Pike Co., IN	Vince Brock	Vince Brock	1993	83
190 1/8	26 4/8	27	18 4/8	6 1/8	5 7/8	9	7	Randolph Co., IL	Kevin Leemon	Kevin Leemon	1990	85
190	24 2/8	25 2/8	20 6/8	5	5	7	6	Dimmit Co., TX	C.P. Howard	C.P. Howard	1950	86
190	29 1/8	29	24 6/8	5 2/8	5 2/8	6	6	Fremont Co., IA	Randall D. Forney	Randall D. Forney	1971	86
190	29 2/8	31 1/8	23	5 1/8	5	6	6	Cherokee Co., IA	Dennis R. Vaudt	Dennis R. Vaudt	1974	86
190	27 5/8	26 6/8	19 4/8	5	4 7/8	5	5	Clinton Co., IA	Merwin E. Koch	Merwin E. Koch	1994	86
190	25	24 7/8	23 4/8	4 7/8	5	7	7	Callaway Co., MO	Ben Barks	Ben Barks	1995	86
190	31 2/8	31 2/8	24 6/8	5 4/8	5 2/8	5	5	Page Co., IA	Arlen D. Meyer	Arlen D. Meyer	1996	86
189 7/8	29 4/8	29 6/8	19 5/8	5	4 7/8	9	6	Trempealeau Co., WI	Emil Stelmach	Emil Stelmach	1959	92
189 7/8	26 6/8	26 1/8	22 1/8	4 7/8	5 1/8	5	6	Henry Co., IL	Reginald M. Anseeuw	Reginald M. Anseeuw	1992	92
189 7/8	25 5/8	26 4/8	23 2/8	5 7/8	6 1/8	6	6	Sangamon Co., IL	Leo J. Romanotto	Leo J. Romanotto	1994	92
189 5/8	29 2/8	29 2/8	21 4/8	4 7/8	4 6/8	5	6	Tabor, SD	Duane Graber	Sam Peterson	1954	95
189 5/8	26 3/8	27 3/8	25 1/8	6 2/8	6 7/8	9	7	Schuyler Co., IL	Picked Up	Bass Pro Shops F. & W. Mus.	1990	95
189 5/8	28	28 3/8	21 6/8	4 5/8	4 7/8	6	7	Ministikwan Lake, SK	James L. Cohick	James L. Cohick	1992	95
189 4/8	25 4/8	24 7/8	20	5	4 6/8	6	7	Monmouth Co., NJ	Scott W. Borden	Scott W. Borden	1995	98
189 3/8	28 2/8	27 2/8	20 1/8	4 1/8	4 1/8	5	5	McKenzie Co., ND	Gene Veeder	Legendary Whitetails	1972	99
189 3/8	25 7/8	24 1/8	23 1/8	6 2/8	6 2/8	6	7	Fillmore Co., MN	Tom Norby	Tom Norby	1975	99
189 3/8	24 6/8	24 6/8	23 6/8	5	4 7/8	7	6	Henry Co., IA	Lamonte A. Stark	Bass Pro Shops F. & W. Mus.	1984	99
189 3/8	29 1/8	29 1/8	19 2/8	5 1/8	5 2/8	8	6	Union Co., IA	Christopher C. Jimerson	Christopher C. Jimerson	1995	99
189 2/8	29 7/8	29	22 3/8	4 4/8	4 5/8	7	6	Hubbard Co., MN	Hans Lorentzen	Danny L. Cole	PR 1944	103
189 1/8	26	26 5/8	17 3/8	5 6/8	5 6/8	8	9	Douglas Co., WI	Bryan Lawler	Larry L. Huffman	1946	104
189 1/8	28	28 1/8	23 5/8	4 4/8	4 5/8	5	7	Blaine Co., MT	Kenneth Morehouse	Kenneth Morehouse	1959	104
189 1/8	27 5/8	26 6/8	25 7/8	5 1/8	5 2/8	6	6	Nuckolls Co., NE	Van Shotzman	Van Shotzman	1968	104
189 1/8	27 6/8	28 3/8	20 1/8	5	5 1/8	6	6	Allamakee Co., IA	Randy L. Petersburg	Randy L. Petersburg	1996	104
189	26 6/8	25 6/8	20 2/8	5 5/8	5 3/8	6	6	Shelby Co., KY	Frank W. Kendall	Frank W. Kendall	1971	108
189	25 1/8	25 4/8	17 2/8	4 5/8	4 4/8	6	6	Crawford Co., AR	Tom Sparks, Jr.	Tom Sparks, Jr.	1975	108
189	25 4/8	25 4/8	23 2/8	5 1/8	5 1/8	8	8	Red Deer Lake, MB	Will Bigelow	Will Bigelow	1986	108
188 7/8	28 2/8	27 3/8	19 2/8	5 1/8	5 1/8	6	7	Shelby Co., IL	James M. Holley	James M. Holley	1995	111
188 6/8	25 3/8	25 3/8	16 2/8	5 2/8	5 3/8	6	6	Shenandoah Co., VA	Gene Wilson	Gene Wilson	1985	112
188 6/8	26 6/8	28 5/8	18 4/8	5 3/8	5 3/8	5	5	Shelby Co., IL	Elmer Agney	Elmer Agney	1992	112
188 6/8	29	29 2/8	22 2/8	4 6/8	4 6/8	5	6	Crawford Co., WI	Eli D. Randall	Eli D. Randall	1995	112
188 5/8	25 5/8	27 3/8	19 7/8	4 3/8	4 4/8	5	5	Flathead Co., MT	Len E. Patterson	Len E. Patterson	1992	115
188 5/8	27 4/8	29 1/8	20 5/8	5 2/8	5	6	7	Lewis Co., KY	Ben C. Johnson	Ben C. Johnson	1993	115
188 4/8	25	26 3/8	22 5/8	4 7/8	4 6/8	5	6	Burstall, SK	W.P. Rolick	W.P. Rolick	1957	117
188 4/8	27 2/8	24 5/8	22 2/8	5 6/8	5 5/8	5	5	Metiskow, AB	Norman T. Salminen	Norman T. Salminen	1977	117
188 4/8	27 2/8	28 7/8	20 1/8	5	4 7/8	8	8	Riley Co., KS	Robert E. Luke	Robert E. Luke	1984	117

Score	Main Beam R	Main Beam L	Inside Spread	Circ. R	Circ. L	Pts. R	Pts. L	Locality	Hunter	Owner	Date	Rank
188 4/8	22 2/8	24 2/8	17	4 6/8	4 5/8	8	6	Crawford Co., WI	Roger W. Salmon	Roger W. Salmon	1986	117
188 4/8	27 1/8	27 2/8	20 6/8	6 6/8	6 4/8	5	5	Souris River, MB	Wes Todoruk	Wes Todoruk	1986	117
188 3/8	24 2/8	26 4/8	18 6/8	5 5/8	5 5/8	8	7	Sanford, MB	Picked Up	MB Wildl. Branch	1982	122
188 3/8	28 4/8	28 2/8	17 7/8	5 3/8	5 4/8	10	10	Red Deer, AB	Edwin Koberstein	Edwin Koberstein	1991	122
188 3/8	27 6/8	27 6/8	21 7/8	5	5 1/8	5	5	Peoria Co., IL	Jill M. Adcock	Jill M. Adcock	1993	122
188 2/8	28 1/8	28 6/8	25 7/8	4 4/8	4 5/8	5	5	Cowley Co., KS	Armand L. Hillier	Armand L. Hillier	1996	125
188	27 1/8	28 6/8	19	5 1/8	5 2/8	6	7	Marshall Co., MN	Paul J. Wolf	Paul J. Wolf	1991	126
188	27 6/8	28 4/8	21 2/8	5 6/8	6	7	7	Chisago Co., MN	John B. Nelson	John B. Nelson	1992	126
187 7/8	25 5/8	26 1/8	21 3/8	4 6/8	4 6/8	7	7	Zavala Co., TX	Donald Rutledge	Frank Rutledge	1946	128
187 7/8	27 4/8	28 7/8	19 5/8	5	5	6	5	Langlade Co., WI	Kory J. Schumacher	Kory J. Schumacher	1994	128
187 6/8	27 4/8	27 7/8	25 2/8	5 2/8	5 3/8	6	6	Union Co., KY	Charles Meuth	Larry S. Melton	1964	130
187 6/8	28	28 4/8	20 6/8	5 6/8	5 6/8	6	6	Houston Co., MN	Donald M. Grant	Donald M. Grant	1978	130
187 6/8	25 5/8	26 4/8	19	4 6/8	5 1/8	5	5	Johnson Co., IA	Gregg R. Redlin	Gregg R. Redlin	1983	130
187 6/8	25 5/8	23 2/8	17 2/8	6	5 6/8	6	8	Mantagao Lake, MB	Picked Up	Mel Podaima	1988	130
187 5/8	25 5/8	29 6/8	21	5	5 1/8	6	6	Clinton Co., MO	Scott E. Looney	Scott E. Looney	1994	135
187 5/8	29 7/8	27 6/8	19 6/8	5	5	5	5	Starr Co., TX	Picked Up	Jack F. Quist	1945	135
187 5/8	28 2/8	25	20 1/8	5 2/8	5 1/8	6	8	Emmons Co., ND	Joseph F. Bosch	Joseph F. Bosch	1959	135
187 5/8	25	25 2/8	19 2/8	5 2/8	5 3/8	6	6	Winona Co., MN	Ken W. Koenig	Ken W. Koenig	1976	135
187 5/8	25 2/8	27 1/8	17	5 3/8	5 2/8	7	6	Bourbon Co., KS	Picked Up	George J. McLiney, Jr.	1990	139
187 4/8	27	27 4/8	24 6/8	5 3/8	5 3/8	5	7	Winona Co., MN	Dan Groebner	Dan Groebner	1974	139
187 4/8	28 3/8	27 4/8	19 5/8	5 2/8	4 7/8	9	8	Brown Co., IL	Charles A. Howell	Charles A. Howell	1988	139
187 4/8	26 7/8	27 2/8	26 2/8	4 7/8	4 5/8	8	8	Zapata Co., TX	Phillip T. Stringer	Phillip T. Stringer	1992	139
187 4/8	28	28 1/8	21	4 7/8	5 3/8	5	5	Miami Co., OH	Dale L. Bevington	Dale L. Bevington	1996	139
187 3/8	26 7/8	27	21 3/8	5	5	7	6	Plunkett, SK	Myles Mann	Myles Mann	1996	144
187 2/8	30 6/8	30 3/8	30 3/8	4 6/8	5 3/8	8	8	Warren Co., IA	Dwight E. Green	Dwight E. Green	1964	144
187 2/8	29	28 5/8	26 4/8	5 2/8	5 2/8	5	5	Lyon Co., MN	Lynn Jackson	Dick Rossum	1967	144
187 2/8	26	26 2/8	19 4/8	5 1/8	5 1/8	8	8	Scotland Co., MO	Robin Berhorst	Robin Berhorst	1971	144
187 2/8	26 3/8	25	18 6/8	4 4/8	4 5/8	7	7	McLean Co., ND	Frank O. Bauman	Donald Bauman	1986	148
187 1/8	26 4/8	26 5/8	19 4/8	4 6/8	4 7/8	6	7	Cooper Co., MO	Joe Ditto	Joe Ditto	1974	148
187 1/8	26 6/8	26 4/8	18 7/8	4 7/8	5 7/8	6	6	Pulaski Co., KY	Scott Abbott	Scott Abbott	1982	148
187 1/8	27 7/8	27 3/8	18 7/8	5	5	5	6	Mercer Co., MO	Picked Up	Bob Summers	1986	148
187 1/8	27 2/8	27 6/8	17 7/8	5 2/8	4 5/8	8	7	Montgomery Co., IN	Larry E. Lawson	Larry E. Lawson	1988	148
187 1/8	26 1/8	26 1/8	24 1/8	4 7/8	5 1/8	5	6	Rossburn, MB	G. Wayne Preston	G. Wayne Preston	1994	148
187 1/8	28	28 3/8	22 3/8	5 1/8	4 3/8	7	6	Hocking Co., OH	Stephen C. Corley	Stephen C. Corley	1995	154
187	26 7/8	27	21 6/8	4 4/8	5	6	6	Des Moines Co., IA	Jim Brislawn	Connie Compton	PR 1993	154
187	26 7/8	26 2/8	18	4 4/8	5 2/8	7	7	Warren Co., IL	John K. Poole	John K. Poole	1994	156
186 7/8	29 5/8	29	20 1/8	4 7/8	5 3/8	5	5	Arkansas Co., AR	Walter Spears	Walter Spears	1952	156
186 7/8	25 5/8	25 3/8	19 1/8	5	5 5/8	8	8	Atchison Co., MO	Mike Moody	Mike Moody	1968	156
186 7/8	27 7/8	27 2/8	20 5/8	5 4/8	4 6/8	5	5	Andrew Co., MO	Kenneth Till	Kenneth Till	1989	156
186 7/8	26 3/8	26 7/8	17 4/8	5 2/8	4 7/8	6	5	Adair Co., IA	Dennis J. Gruss	Dennis J. Gruss	1995	161
186 7/8	27 1/8	27	20 4/8	5	5 2/8	7	6	Lewis Co., KY	W. David Mains	W. David Mains	1996	161
186 6/8	28 4/8	27 5/8	19	5 3/8	5 5/8	7	7	St. Louis Co., MN	Unknown	George W. Flaim	PR 1983	163
186 6/8	26 7/8	26 2/8	23	5 5/8	4 6/8	8	5	Logan Co., OH	Bernard R. Hines	Bernard R. Hines	1990	164
186 5/8	29 1/8	29 7/8	16 7/8	4 6/8	4 7/8	5	10	Langlade Co., WI	Fred J. Hofmann	Fred J. Hofmann	1994	164
186 4/8	29 7/8	24 7/8	19 6/8	4 7/8	5 2/8	7	7	Becker Co., MN	Ilo Dugger	Jeff Dugger	1930	164
186 4/8	24 4/8	26	22	5 1/8	4 4/8	6	7	Pine Co., MN	Unknown	Ralph Blessum	PR 1970	164
186 4/8	27 6/8	28 4/8	20 2/8	4 4/8	4 3/8	5	6	Monroe Co., IA	Picked Up	H. James Reimer	1992	164

WHITETAIL DEER - TYPICAL ANTLERS

Odocoileus virginianus virginianus and certain related subspecies

Score	Length of Main Beam R	L	Inside Spread	Circumference at Smallest Place Between Burr and First Point R	L	Number of Points R	L	Locality	Hunter	Owner	Date Killed	Rank
186 4/8	28 6/8	28	26 2/8	5 4/8	5 5/8	5	5	Coles Co., IL	Charles H. McElwee	Charles H. McElwee	1994	164
186 4/8	26 6/8	27 6/8	16 2/8	6 1/8	6 3/8	5	5	Monona Co., IA	David L. Zima	David L. Zima	1996	164
186 3/8	27 5/8	27 1/8	20 4/8	6 1/8	5 6/8	7	6	Morris Co., KS	Garold D. Miller	Garold D. Miller	1969	169
186 3/8	30 2/8	29	22 5/8	4 4/8	4 5/8	5	5	Flathead Co., MT	Unknown	Wayne D. Williamson	1973	169
186 3/8	26 1/8	26 3/8	18 6/8	4 7/8	4 7/8	7	5	Otter Tail Co., MN	Robert Ames	David R. Brigan	1977	169
186 3/8	26 2/8	27 2/8	20 4/8	5 2/8	5 2/8	8	7	Ontonagon Co., MI	Unknown	Mac's Taxidermy	1980	169
186 3/8	28 5/8	28 4/8	20 7/8	5 3/8	5 2/8	5	5	Pike Co., IL	Merle L. Shull	Merle L. Shull	1985	169
186 3/8	28	28	23 1/8	4 6/8	4 6/8	5	6	Lee Co., AL	Picked Up	George P. Mann	1986	169
186 3/8	26 4/8	26	20	5 7/8	5 6/8	5	6	Monona Co., IA	Mark Maynard	Mark Maynard	1992	169
186 3/8	27 7/8	29 2/8	19 1/8	4 7/8	5 6/8	6	7	Greene Co., IL	Picked Up	Cory L. Walker	1992	169
186 3/8	25	25 3/8	21 7/8	5 4/8	5 4/8	6	5	Rocky Mt. House, AB	Wyndell A. Wroten	Wyndell A. Wroten	1992	169
186 3/8	25 4/8	24 6/8	18 4/8	5 6/8	5 6/8	8	8	Adams Co., CO	David A. McCracken	David A. McCracken	1996	169
186 2/8	25 2/8	25 6/8	21	4 6/8	4 6/8	6	6	La Salle Co., TX	Herman C. Schliesing	Herman C. Schliesing	1967	179
186 2/8	27 4/8	27 4/8	18	4 6/8	4 6/8	8	10	Kenedy Co., TX	Jack Van Cleve III	McGill Estate	1972	179
186 2/8	25	25 4/8	22 4/8	5	5 2/8	6	7	Laclede Co., MO	Larry Ogle	Larry Ogle	1972	179
186 2/8	28 6/8	29 1/8	19	5 2/8	5 1/8	8	5	Hancock Co., ME	Gerald C. Murray	Gerald C. Murray	1984	179
186 2/8	29 1/8	29	22	4 7/8	4 6/8	5	6	Carter Co., KY	Herman G. Holbrooks	Herman G. Holbrooks	1989	179
186 2/8	25 7/8	27 4/8	20 3/8	4 6/8	5	7	7	Bayfield Co., WI	Ken T. Johnson	Ken T. Johnson	1994	179
186 1/8	25 1/8	26 2/8	20 1/8	4 6/8	4 7/8	6	6	Roane Co., TN	W.A. Foster	W.A. Foster	1959	185
186 1/8	28	26 2/8	21 4/8	6 1/8	6	8	5	Waupaca Co., WI	Fred Penny	Dale Trinrud	1963	185
186 1/8	29 4/8	29 2/8	21	4 6/8	4 5/8	8	9	Zavala Co., TX	Picked Up	Paul W. Sanders, Jr.	1965	185
186 1/8	28 4/8	27 6/8	18 5/8	5 6/8	6	5	5	St. Louis Co., MN	Unknown	George W. Flaim	1980	185
186 1/8	27 4/8	26 5/8	20 7/8	5	5 6/8	5	6	St. Louis Co., MN	Mark O. DuLong	Mark O. DuLong	1988	185
186 1/8	26 2/8	25 4/8	22	6	5 5/8	6	5	Pope Co., IL	Picked Up	Jim Frailey	1990	185
186 1/8	29 1/8	27 1/8	19 4/8	5 3/8	5 2/8	5	5	Camrose, AB	Dale A. Broker	Dale A. Broker	1992	185
186 1/8	27 6/8	27 3/8	20 1/8	5 1/8	5 1/8	5	5	Buchanan Co., IA	Gary W. Rasmussen	Gary W. Rasmussen	1994	185
186	30 5/8	31 3/8	26 3/8	5 1/8	5	5	9	Itasca Co., MN	Knud W. Jensen	Larry L. Huffman	1955	193
186	25 1/8	25 3/8	19	4 3/8	4 3/8	6	6	Flathead Co., MT	Douglas G. Mefford	Douglas G. Mefford	1966	193
186	30	29 4/8	22	6	5 4/8	6	5	Warren Co., KY	Arnold M. Bush	Arnold M. Bush	1986	193
186	25 5/8	25 6/8	23	5 3/8	5 2/8	6	7	Union Co., IA	Christine A. Weeks	Christine A. Weeks	1991	193
185 7/8	28 5/8	28 3/8	20 5/8	5 2/8	5 2/8	5	5	Beltrami Co., MN	Picked Up	Jerome D. Erdahl	1987	197
185 7/8	29 7/8	30 1/8	19 5/8	5	5 1/8	6	6	Prairie Co., AR	Lonnie W. Copeland	Jack G. Brittingham	1992	197
185 5/8	24 3/8	25	19 5/8	4 6/8	4 5/8	6	8	Nenzel, NE	Richard Kehr	Richard Kehr	1965	199
185 5/8	25 2/8	25 4/8	19 2/8	4 5/8	4 3/8	6	7	Dallas Co., MO	James E. Headings	James E. Headings	1986	199
185 4/8	26 6/8	27 1/8	22	4 5/8	4 5/8	6	6	Otter Tail Co., MN	Orris T. Neirby	Orris T. Neirby	1942	201
185 4/8	27 7/8	25 6/8	18 7/8	5 3/8	5 5/8	8	7	Zapata Co., TX	Jesus Lopez	John L. Stein	1969	201

Score	Length R	Length L	Inside Spread	Circ. R	Circ. L	Pts R	Pts L	Locality	By Whom Killed	Owner	Date	Rank
185 4/8	26 3/8	26 2/8	20 2/8	4 6/8	4 6/8	5	5	Sussex Co., DE	Herbert N. Milam	Herbert N. Milam	1978	201
185 4/8	29	28 1/8	24 6/8	5 3/8	5 2/8	5	6	Benton Co., MN	Clifford G. Knier	Clifford G. Knier	1992	201
185 3/8	26 4/8	27	19 4/8	5 2/8	5 1/8	7	10	Marshall Co., MN	Donald W. Wilkens	Donald W. Wilkens	1973	205
185 3/8	27 6/8	28 1/8	20 5/8	4 7/8	4 7/8	5	5	Canwood, SK	Clark Heimbechner	Clark Heimbechner	1984	205
185 3/8	29	28 1/8	23	4 7/8	5 1/8	9	5	Riley Co., KS	Robert L. Tully	Robert L. Tully	1988	205
185 3/8	27 7/8	27 7/8	21 5/8	5 1/8	5	5	5	Helene Lake, SK	Wayne A. Foster	Wayne A. Foster	1991	205
185 3/8	27 7/8	27 7/8	23 3/8	5 1/8	4 2/8	5	6	Woodlands, MB	Picked Up	Brant J. Mueller	1994	205
185 3/8	27	27	19 5/8	4 3/8	5 2/8	6	6	Harrison Co., MO	John W. Rhea II	John W. Rhea II	1995	205
185 2/8	29 2/8	30	30 2/8	5 2/8	5	8	8	Todd Co., KY	C.W. Shelton	Larry L. Huffman	1964	211
185 1/8	25 3/8	25 6/8	25 6/8	4 6/8	5	7	6	Webb Co., TX	Henderson Coquat	Henderson Coquat	1949	212
185 1/8	29 2/8	29 5/8	29 5/8	5 1/8	5 2/8	7	7	Warren Co., IA	Joyce McCormick	Joyce McCormick	1968	212
185 1/8	27 7/8	27 1/8	19 1/8	5	5	6	7	Harrison Co., IA	Marvin E. Tippery	Marvin E. Tippery	1971	212
185 1/8	27 4/8	26 2/8	23 1/8	5 1/8	4 5/8	6	8	Franklin Co., IN	Gayle Fritsch	Gayle Fritsch	1972	212
185 1/8	28	27 4/8	18 6/8	4 6/8	5	5	7	Porter Co., IN	Mathieu J. Price	Mathieu J. Price	1990	212
185 1/8	26 3/8	26 3/8	24 7/8	5 7/8	5 7/8	6	6	Bonnyville, AB	Richard A. Rhoden	Richard A. Rhoden	1996	212
185	25	25 2/8	19 2/8	4 6/8	4 6/8	6	6	Frio Co., TX	Loyd Nail	Steve L. Smith	1941	218
185	26 7/8	26 7/8	18 6/8	5 1/8	5 1/8	6	5	Carter Co., MO	Richard N. Goggin	Richard N. Goggin	1963	218
185	28 5/8	28 5/8	18 6/8	4 3/8	4 4/8	5	7	Vernon Co., WI	Harold Christianson	Harold Christianson	1968	218
185	25 7/8	25 7/8	19	4 7/8	4 7/8	7	8	Winona Co., MN	Ronald Bunke	B., S., & B. Bunke	1973	218
185	27 2/8	27 4/8	18 6/8	5 4/8	5 3/8	6	7	Putnam Co., IN	Earl G. McCammack	Earl G. McCammack	1985	218
185	27	27	17 5/8	6	5 7/8	10	7	Seward Co., KS	Michael D. Gatlin	Michael D. Gatlin	1987	218
184 7/8	26 6/8	26 5/8	27	5 6/8	5 7/8	7	7	Delaware Co., IA	R.E. Stewart	R.E. Stewart	1953	224
184 7/8	25 1/8	24 4/8	17 7/8	5 1/8	5 1/8	6	8	Yellowstone Co., MT	Picked Up	Dennis Helmey	1984	224
184 7/8	28	28	23 4/8	6	6	9	6	Vermilion, AB	C. Letawsky & B. Myshak	C. Letawsky & B. Myshak	1986	224
184 7/8	26 3/8	26 3/8	21	5 7/8	6	6	6	Baraga Co., MI	Louis J. Roy	Louis J. Roy	1987	224
184 7/8	24 4/8	23 5/8	17 3/8	5 5/8	5 6/8	6	7	Aitken Creek, BC	Guyle G. Cox	Guyle G. Cox	1990	224
184 7/8	25 2/8	25 2/8	18	5	4 7/8	5	7	Dallas Co., MO	Lynn Garner	Lynn Garner	1992	224
184 6/8	28 6/8	28 5/8	21 6/8	5 4/8	5 1/8	6	7	Madison Parish, LA	John Lee	Donald R. Broadway	1943	230
184 6/8	25 4/8	25 4/8	19 4/8	5 1/8	5 1/8	7	9	Morrison Co., MN	Mr. Holt	Michael J. Kampa	PR 1960	230
184 6/8	26 7/8	26 7/8	27 6/8	5 3/8	5 3/8	8	6	Desha Co., AR	Lee Perry	Walter Brock	1961	230
184 6/8	24 1/8	24 1/8	24 4/8	5 4/8	5 3/8	6	6	Dore Lake, SK	Garvis C. Coker	Garvis C. Coker	1971	230
184 6/8	26 3/8	26 2/8	21 2/8	4 6/8	4 6/8	7	6	Starr Co., TX	Harry Richardson, Jr.	Harry Richardson, Jr.	1973	230
184 6/8	26 7/8	26 7/8	24 2/8	4 5/8	4 5/8	5	5	Greene Co., PA	Ivan Parry	Ivan Parry	1974	230
184 6/8	26	26	20 6/8	6 1/8	6	6	5	Muskingum Co., OH	Dale Hartberger	Dale Hartberger	1981	230
184 6/8	27	27	27 4/8	5 4/8	5 4/8	5	8	Sauk Co., WI	Jeffrey J. Wilson	Jeffrey J. Wilson	1995	230
184 6/8	26 6/8	27 7/8	19 4/8	5	4 7/8	6	7	St. Brieux, SK	Ted Gaillard	Ted Gaillard	1996	230
184 5/8	28 2/8	28 2/8	27 6/8	4 4/8	4 5/8	6	5	Washington Co., ME	Unknown	Chuck P. Vose	1944	239
184 5/8	26	25 1/8	22	5 3/8	5 3/8	6	5	Polk Co., NE	Keith Houdersheldt	Keith Houdersheldt	1985	239
184 5/8	28 2/8	28 2/8	21 7/8	5 2/8	5 1/8	6	6	Nuevo Leon, MX	Charles H. Priess	Charles H. Priess	1985	239
184 5/8	29	24 4/8	23 2/8	5 4/8	5 3/8	5	5	Hudson Bay, SK	Picked Up	Wade Hersikorn	1986	239
184 5/8	24 7/8	27 2/8	19 3/8	5 3/8	5 4/8	5	6	Phelps Co., MO	Donald E. Davidson	Donald E. Davidson	1988	239
184 5/8	27	27 1/8	15 7/8	5 5/8	6 1/8	8	6	Paddle River, AB	Gregory D. Graff	Gregory D. Graff	1988	239
184 5/8	27 1/8	25 2/8	21	4 4/8	4 4/8	6	8	McDonough Co., IL	Louise Thompson	Louise Thompson	1991	239
184 4/8	26 1/8	28 4/8	22 5/8	5 1/8	5 3/8	5	5	Bandera Co., TX	Picked Up	Wyatt Birkner	1949	246
184 4/8	26 5/8	28 3/8	22 4/8	5 6/8	5 6/8	10	8	Bossier Parish, LA	Earnest O. McCoy	Lucille McCoy	1961	246
184 4/8	28	27 6/8	20 2/8	5 1/8	5 1/8	5	5	Ravalli Co., MT	Picked Up	Walter R. Willey	1978	246
184 4/8	23 4/8	23 4/8	17	4 6/8	4 6/8	6	6	Fayette Co., TN	Benny M. Johnson	Benny M. Johnson	1979	246

WHITETAIL DEER - TYPICAL ANTLERS

Odocoileus virginianus virginianus and certain related subspecies

Score	Length of Main Beam R	L	Inside Spread	Circumference at Smallest Place Between Burr and First Point R	L	Number of Points R	L	Locality	Hunter	Owner	Date Killed	Rank
184 4/8	30 3/8	30 4/8	20 4/8	5	5 1/8	7	7	Chase Co., KS	Thomas D. Mosher	Thomas D. Mosher	1984	246
184 4/8	26 7/8	26 3/8	19 7/8	4 4/8	4 4/8	7	7	Missoula Co., MT	Jack Greenwood	Jack Greenwood	1985	246
184 4/8	26 4/8	26	19	5 1/8	5 2/8	7	6	Smoky Lake, AB	Brendon Rezewski	Brendon Rezewski	1995	253
184 3/8	27	26	17 7/8	4 6/8	4 6/8	5	5	St. Louis Co., MN	Unknown	Dick Rossum	1935	253
184 3/8	28 4/8	29	25 5/8	5 6/8	5 7/8	5	7	Kingsbury Co., SD	Rudy F. Weigel	Rudy F. Weigel	1960	253
184 3/8	26	26 6/8	20 6/8	5 3/8	5 6/8	5	6	Paulding Co., GA	Floyd Benson	Floyd Benson	1962	253
184 3/8	26 5/8	26	19	5 1/8	5	6	6	Keokuk Co., IA	Randy D. Schmidt	Randy D. Schmidt	1995	253
184 2/8	28 2/8	27 6/8	24	5	5 1/8	5	6	Franklin Parish, LA	H.B. Womble	Carey D. McCoy	1914	257
184 2/8	29 1/8	28 2/8	18 6/8	4 7/8	5	6	7	Hardin Co., IA	Robert D. Imsland	Robert D. Imsland	1985	257
184 2/8	25 5/8	24 7/8	17 6/8	5 2/8	5 1/8	6	6	Dooly Co., GA	Joe Morgan	Joe Morgan	1985	257
184 2/8	25 1/8	28 4/8	23 1/8	5	5	5	6	Dilberry Lake, AB	Scott M. Rowein	Scott M. Rowein	1992	257
184 2/8	29 5/8	27 3/8	21	5 6/8	5 6/8	5	5	Jackson Co., IA	Unknown	Charles E. Matthiesen	PR 1994	257
184 2/8	24 7/8	24 6/8	18 4/8	5 6/8	5 7/8	7	7	Meeting Lake, SK	Dennis Woloshyn	Dennis Woloshyn	1996	257
184 1/8	26 7/8	27 6/8	21	5	5	8	7	Marshall Co., MN	Alvin C. Westerlund	Alvin C. Westerlund	1953	263
184 1/8	29	31	20 5/8	5 5/8	4 4/8	6	5	Vinton Co., OH	Dan F. Allison	Dan F. Allison	1965	263
184 1/8	31 3/8	29	24	6	6	8	8	Waldo Co., ME	Christopher Ramsey	Bass Pro Shops F. & W. Mus.	1983	263
184 1/8	25 3/8	25 4/8	18 1/8	4 4/8	4 5/8	6	6	Carroll Co., OH	Timothy F. Treadway	Timothy F. Treadway	1989	263
184 1/8	26 3/8	26 6/8	17 3/8	5	5 1/8	6	6	Muhlenberg Co., KY	Chad Mathis	Chad Mathis	1995	263
184	25 2/8	25 1/8	16 2/8	4 3/8	4 3/8	6	6	Arkansas Co., AR	Willard L. Harper	Delwyn E. Harper	1946	268
184	27 4/8	29 1/8	18 4/8	5	4 7/8	5	5	Newton Co., GA	Gene Almand	Duncan A. Dobie	1966	268
184	24 5/8	24 4/8	18 5/8	5 1/8	5 2/8	7	6	Menominee Co., WI	Keith Miller	Charles Loberg	1969	268
184	28 1/8	27 6/8	20 5/8	5 2/8	5 1/8	6	6	Saline Co., KS	James R. Bell	James R. Bell	1985	268
184	25	24 4/8	17 4/8	4 1/8	4	6	6	Hart Co., GA	Kenton L. Adams	Kenton L. Adams	1986	268
184	28 6/8	27 6/8	20 4/8	4 5/8	4 5/8	6	7	Grayson Co., KY	Floyd Stone	Floyd Stone	1987	268
184	28 4/8	29 1/8	24 7/8	5	5 1/8	7	9	Allamakee Co., IA	William P. Mitchell	W. Mitchell & J. Bakewell	1989	268
184	27 2/8	26	20 4/8	5 6/8	5 4/8	5	5	Wapello Co., IA	Raymond M. Todey	Raymond M. Todey	1993	268
183 7/8	27 7/8	28 3/8	20 1/8	6 2/8	6 5/8	6	7	Taylor Co., IA	Wayne Swartz	Spanky Greenville	1953	276
183 7/8	28	27 1/8	19 6/8	5	4 7/8	7	5	Forest Co., WI	James M. Thayer	James M. Thayer	1980	276
183 7/8	26 6/8	27 6/8	23 2/8	4 3/8	4 3/8	6	5	White Co., AR	W.A. Harden & C. Craven	Wilburn A. Harden	1993	276
183 6/8	26 7/8	25 1/8	18 6/8	5 4/8	5 4/8	7	7	Pepin Co., WI	LaVerne Anibas	LaVerne Anibas	1965	279
183 6/8	26 7/8	27 6/8	19 2/8	4 3/8	4 4/8	6	6	Clinton Co., IN	Stuart C. Snodgrass	Stuart C. Snodgrass	1977	279
183 6/8	30 7/8	29 7/8	24	5 5/8	5 4/8	5	8	Morris Co., KS	Craig C. Johnson	Craig C. Johnson	1991	279
183 6/8	28 7/8	29 1/8	19 4/8	4 4/8	4 4/8	5	5	Sumner Co., KS	Larry D. Bacon	Larry D. Bacon	1995	279
183 5/8	27 1/8	26	23 2/8	4 6/8	4 6/8	7	6	Buffalo Co., WI	Lee F. Spittler	Mrs. Lee F. Spittler	1953	283
183 4/8	26 6/8	26 6/8	18 2/8	5 3/8	5 4/8	5	6	Sumner, MO	Marvin F. Lentz	Marvin F. Lentz	1968	284
183 4/8	29 7/8	29 3/8	23 7/8	5 4/8	5 6/8	8	8	Holmes River, BC	Randy Lloyd	Randy Lloyd	1991	284

Score	Main Beam R	Main Beam L	Inside Spread	Circ. R	Circ. L	Pts. R	Pts. L	Locality	Hunter	Owner	Date	Rank
183 4/8	26 5/8	27 6/8	24 7/8	6 6/8	6 2/8	5	7	Madison Co., IA	Roy P. Mikesell	Roy P. Mikesell	1995	284
183 3/8	21 5/8	23 3/8	19 3/8	5 4/8	5 2/8	7	9	Flathead Co., MT	Unknown	Edwin M. Sager	1957	287
183 3/8	27 1/8	26 4/8	18 5/8	4 3/8	4 4/8	8	9	Dorchester Co., MD	John R. Seifert, Jr.	John R. Seifert, Jr.	1973	287
183 3/8	27 5/8	27 4/8	20 5/8	5 2/8	5 2/8	5	6	Drew Co., AR	Jimmy Monk	Jimmy Monk	1978	287
183 3/8	26 7/8	27 2/8	18 7/8	5 3/8	5 2/8	6	6	McLean Co., KY	Larry G. Porter	Larry G. Porter	1980	287
183 3/8	26 7/8	27 2/8	19 7/8	5 4/8	5 3/8	5	6	St. Louis Co., MN	Unknown	George W. Flaim	1982	287
183 3/8	28 5/8	29 5/8	18 5/8	5 2/8	5 3/8	5	5	Franklin Co., ME	Real Boulanger	Real Boulanger	1990	287
183 3/8	27 5/8	27 1/8	20 1/8	5 4/8	5 3/8	5	5	Talbot Co., MD	Petey L. Councell	Petey L. Councell	1994	287
183 3/8	27 2/8	25	21 5/8	5	5	5	5	La Salle Co., IL	Bernard Ernat	Bernard Ernat	1996	287
183 2/8	26 7/8	26 7/8	16	4 1/8	4 4/8	7	5	Ashland Co., WI	Unknown	Martin Bonack	1900	295
183 2/8	25 5/8	26	19	4 4/8	4 4/8	6	7	St. Louis Co., MN	Unknown	Kenneth Wilson	PR 1917	295
183 2/8	29 1/8	28 3/8	20 4/8	4 4/8	4 7/8	6	6	Shawnee Co., KS	Mark W. Young	Mark W. Young	1990	295
183 2/8	26 5/8	26 5/8	20 4/8	5	4 6/8	5	6	Custer Co., MT	Dennis Young	Dennis Young	1994	295
183 2/8	29 1/8	29 6/8	27	4 6/8	4 6/8	6	5	Whiteside Co., IL	Jacob A. Amesquita	Jacob A. Amesquita	1995	295
183 2/8	28 7/8	27 6/8	18 5/8	5 6/8	5 6/8	5	6	Knox Co., IL	Bradley A. Wunder	Bradley A. Wunder	1995	295
183 2/8	24 4/8	22 6/8	18 7/8	5 6/8	5	7	7	Invermay, SK	Trevor Jennings	Trevor Jennings	1996	295
183 2/8	29 5/8	30 5/8	22 1/8	5	5 4/8	7	7	Guthrie Co., IA	Don McCarty	Chad Redfern	1962	295
183 1/8	27 7/8	28 6/8	20 5/8	5	4 5/8	6	6	Duval Co., TX	Charles Drennan	Bill Carter	1973	302
183 1/8	25 3/8	26 1/8	21 5/8	4 6/8	5 2/8	7	6	Nuevo Leon, MX	Thomas D. Brittingham	Thomas D. Brittingham	1990	302
183 1/8	27 1/8	27 2/8	19 3/8	5	4 6/8	6	8	Crawford Co., WI	Ray Volkert	Brant J. Mueller	1990	302
183 1/8	26 1/8	26 1/8	21 1/8	4 6/8	5	6	6	Wabash Co., IL	Dale E. Strockbine	Dale E. Strockbine	1994	302
183 1/8	27 1/8	27 7/8	18 6/8	5	4 5/8	6	6	Desha Co., AR	R.J. Diekhoff	Franzen Bros.	1954	302
183	26 2/8	25	19 6/8	4 5/8	4 4/8	8	9	Piedmont Lake, OH	J. Rumbaugh & J. Ruyan	J. Rumbaugh & J. Ruyan	1958	307
183	25 6/8	26	21	4 6/8	5 5/8	5	5	Red Deer River, AB	Picked Up	Ovar Uggen	1966	307
183	26 3/8	25 3/8	23	5 5/8	5	5	5	Emmet Co., IA	Bill Walstead	Bill Walstead	1974	307
183	28 4/8	28 1/8	20 4/8	5 5/8	5 5/8	6	6	Union Co., IA	Randy G. Hall	Randy G. Hall	1986	307
182 7/8	26 1/8	26 1/8	19 3/8	5	4 7/8	8	8	Lorne, MB	Alain G. Comte	Alain G. Comte	1987	314
182 7/8	26 6/8	28 4/8	18 5/8	5 5/8	5 5/8	5	6	Van Buren Co., IA	Picked Up	Timothy J. Wilson	1990	314
182 7/8	27 7/8	28 2/8	21 1/8	4 7/8	5 3/8	5	7	Iosco Co., MI	Harvey H. Keast	Harvey H. Keast	1938	314
182 7/8	27 4/8	28 2/8	19 3/8	5 5/8	6	6	5	Hale Co., AL	James C. Bailey	James C. Bailey	1974	314
182 7/8	26 4/8	25 6/8	19 2/8	5 3/8	5 3/8	6	5	Lyon Co., MN	Jim Anderson	LuAnn Anderson	1975	314
182 7/8	28 5/8	28 5/8	19	5 6/8	5	6	7	Wayne Co., OH	Gary E. Landry	Gary E. Landry	1975	314
182 7/8	29 1/8	28 3/8	20 1/8	5 2/8	4 6/8	7	6	Oromocto River, NB	Bruce MacGougan	Bruce MacGougan	1984	314
182 6/8	27 2/8	27 3/8	19 2/8	5	4 1/8	8	7	Noxubee Co., MS	Glen D. Jourdon	Glen D. Jourdon	1986	321
182 6/8	22	23 1/8	19 5/8	4 6/8	5	6	5	Rock Island Co., IL	Clifton C. Webster	Clifton C. Webster	1986	321
182 6/8	28 2/8	28	22 6/8	4 3/8	6 2/8	6	6	Vilas Co., WI	George Sparks	Mac's Taxidermy	1942	321
182 6/8	28 4/8	25 4/8	19 3/8	4 7/8	4 4/8	8	6	Osage Co., MO	Picked Up	Ralph Reynolds	1972	321
182 6/8	26	28 6/8	18	6 3/8	4 3/8	6	8	Webb Co., TX	George Strait	George Strait	1988	321
182 6/8	28 2/8	28 6/8	19	4 4/8	5 1/8	9	8	Labette Co., KS	David W. Steeby	David W. Steeby	1989	321
182 6/8	27 5/8	25 1/8	19 4/8	4 3/8	4 7/8	6	7	Lee Co., IA	John L. Kite	John L. Kite	1990	321
182 5/8	25 3/8	24 3/8	22	5 2/8	5 5/8	6	6	Coahuila, MX	Manuel A. Flores Rojas	Manuel A. Flores Rojas	1990	329
182 5/8	24 5/8	28 6/8	20 6/8	5	5 5/8	8	7	Pembina River, AB	Curtis R. Siegfried	Curtis R. Siegfried	1991	329
182 5/8	28 6/8	28 6/8	22 6/8	5 6/8	5 7/8	5	5	La Salle Co., TX	Daniel A. Herson	Daniel A. Herson	1995	329
182 5/8	27 6/8	28 4/8	21 5/8	5 5/8	5 1/8	7	8	Virden, MB	Darryl Gray	Darryl Gray	1957	329
182 5/8	23 6/8	24 1/8	19 4/8	5 2/8	5 1/8	6	6	Yuma Co., CO	Ivan W. Rhodes	Ivan W. Rhodes	1978	329
182 5/8	28 3/8	28 4/8	24 1/8	5 1/8		6	6	Jefferson Co., IA	William J. Waugh	William J. Waugh	1985	329
182 5/8	24 6/8	26 3/8	18 1/8	5		5	5	Jones Co., SD	Richard A. Gordon	Richard A. Gordon	1989	329

WHITETAIL DEER - TYPICAL ANTLERS

Odocoileus virginianus virginianus and certain related subspecies

Score	Length of Main Beam R	L	Inside Spread	Circumference at Smallest Place Between Burr and First Point R	L	Number of Points R	L	Locality	Hunter	Owner	Date Killed	Rank
182 5/8	24	23 4/8	21 6/8	6 6/8	6 5/8	8	7	Crawford Creek, SK	Dale C. Conacher	Dale C. Conacher	1991	329
182 5/8	21 5/8	21 2/8	14 2/8	5 5/8	5 4/8	8	7	Noble Co., OH	William J. Estadt	William J. Estadt	1993	329
182 5/8	24	23 7/8	20 1/8	5 4/8	5 3/8	5	5	Boundary Co., ID	Aaron M. McNall	Aaron M. McNall	1993	329
182 5/8	24 4/8	23 5/8	20 5/8	4 6/8	4 6/8	6	7	Mantagao Lake, MB	Stephen Obelnicki	Stephen Obelnicki	1993	329
182 5/8	25 4/8	26 4/8	20 1/8	5 7/8	5 7/8	8	6	Jefferson Co., IL	Jerry R. Simmons	Jerry R. Simmons	1993	329
182 5/8	27 6/8	28 5/8	19 2/8	5 4/8	5 6/8	7	5	Republic Co., KS	Jody Hadachek	Jody Hadachek	1995	329
182 4/8	28 5/8	29	23 6/8	5 3/8	5 1/8	7	5	Carrot River, SK	Lori Lonson	J.D. Andrews	1960	339
182 4/8	27	26 6/8	18 4/8	5 3/8	5 3/8	7	5	Warren Co., MO	Donald L. Tanner	Donald L. Tanner	1968	339
182 4/8	28 3/8	27 1/8	23 4/8	5 5/8	5 5/8	7	7	Kanabec Co., MN	Steven R. Berg	Steven R. Berg	1973	339
182 3/8	28 1/8	27 3/8	20 5/8	5 4/8	5 4/8	5	5	Itasca Co., MN	Harry Haug	Harry Haug	1959	342
182 3/8	28 2/8	27 2/8	17 1/8	5 2/8	5 4/8	6	6	St. Louis Co., MN	Unknown	John R. Steffes, Sr.	PR 1960	342
182 3/8	27	26 5/8	23 1/8	5 7/8	5 7/8	6	5	Waubausee Co., KS	Norman Anderson	Norman Anderson	1966	342
182 3/8	25 5/8	25 1/8	18 1/8	4 6/8	4 6/8	6	6	Marshall Co., IA	Barbara Daniel	Terry Daniel	1967	342
182 3/8	25 4/8	25 6/8	21 3/8	6	5 6/8	5	6	Freeborn Co., MN	Robert H. Dowd	Robert H. Dowd	1969	342
182 3/8	28 1/8	27 1/8	21 5/8	4 4/8	4 5/8	6	6	Braxton Co., WV	William D. Given	William D. Given	1976	342
182 3/8	28 3/8	27 3/8	19 1/8	4 3/8	4 4/8	5	6	Buffalo Co., WI	Anthony F. Wolfe	Anthony F. Wolfe	1984	342
182 3/8	26 5/8	26 7/8	15 6/8	5 5/8	5 6/8	6	6	Unknown	Unknown	Rick Stover	PR 1993	342
182 3/8	26 4/8	25 5/8	22	5 6/8	6	6	7	Derwent, AB	Michael A. Miller	Michael A. Miller	1994	342
182 3/8	25 5/8	26	19 7/8	4 2/8	4 3/8	6	6	S. Saskatchewan River, SK	Jim Clary	Jim Clary	1996	342
182 2/8	27 7/8	26 6/8	23 4/8	5 5/8	5 7/8	5	5	Monroe Co., IA	Elisha G. Hugen	Elisha G. Hugen	1996	342
182 2/8	27 3/8	27	20 4/8	4 7/8	5	7	5	Sullivan Co., PA	Floyd Reibson	Maynard Reibson	1930	353
182 2/8	27 1/8	26 4/8	19 6/8	5 1/8	5 2/8	5	5	Claiborne Co., MS	R.L. Bobo	R.L. Bobo	1955	353
182 2/8	27 1/8	26 6/8	19 3/8	4 7/8	5 1/8	6	6	Nicollet Co., MN	T.J. Merkley	T.J. Merkley	1966	353
182 2/8	26	26 4/8	18 1/8	5 2/8	5 1/8	5	5	Park Co., MT	Jim Whitt	Jim Whitt	1983	353
182 2/8	28 1/8	27	20	5 3/8	5 5/8	5	6	Champaign Co., IL	Tom Babb	Tom Babb	1985	353
182 2/8	29 3/8	29	19 4/8	5 7/8	6	5	6	Forest Co., WI	Richard J. Moore	Richard J. Moore	1987	353
182 2/8	24 4/8	25 4/8	17 2/8	5 4/8	6	6	6	Stearns Co., MN	Michael G. Maki	Michael G. Maki	1988	353
182 2/8	27 1/8	25 6/8	23 4/8	5 3/8	5 4/8	5	5	Hancock Co., IL	Robert A. Reed	Robert A. Reed	1988	353
182 1/8	26 5/8	26 7/8	18 6/8	6 4/8	6	7	7	Keokuk Co., IA	Willaim Musgrove	William H. Lilienthal	1977	361
182 1/8	25 6/8	25 2/8	22 7/8	5 6/8	5 5/8	5	5	Round Lake, SK	Jesse Bates	Jesse Bates	1984	361
182 1/8	27 4/8	26 6/8	24	5 1/8	5	6	6	Frontier Co., NE	Robert G. Bortner	Robert G. Bortner	1985	361
182 1/8	27	26 7/8	22 1/8	5 1/8	5 2/8	5	5	Lincoln Co., MO	David L. Mudd	David L. Mudd	1988	361
182 1/8	28	27 4/8	25 4/8	6	6 2/8	7	6	MacCafferty Lake, AB	Alan S. Bell	Alan S. Bell	1990	361
182 1/8	28	28 1/8	22	5	5	6	6	Hardin Co., OH	Tim Campbell	Tim Campbell	1991	361
182 1/8	29 5/8	30 5/8	24	5	5	6	7	Clark Co., IN	William F. Mills II	William F. Mills II	1995	361
182 1/8	28 2/8	27 4/8	23 1/8	4 7/8	4 6/8	7	8	Adair Co., MO	Selby Lusher	Selby Lusher	1996	361

Score	Main Beam R	Main Beam L	Inside Spread	Circ. R	Circ. L	Points R	Points L	Locality	By Whom Killed	Owner	Date Killed	Rank
182	24 4/8	25	23	4	4 3/8	7	7	Zap, ND	Wally Duckwitz	Sioux Sporting Goods	1962	369
182	28 1/8	28 4/8	22 6/8	4 5/8	4 4/8	5	5	St. Louis Co., MN	Unknown	George W. Flaim	1975	369
182	24 7/8	24 5/8	18 4/8	5 4/8	5 6/8	5	5	Polk Co., MN	E. Norgaard, M. Sorenson, D. Sorenson & K. Oraskovich	E. Norgaard, M. Sorenson, & D. Sorenson	1986	369
182	27 7/8	28 4/8	21 4/8	5 1/8	5 1/8	6	6	Monona Co., IA	Jerry W. Conover	Jerry W. Conover	1990	369
182	23	25	19	5 3/8	5 3/8	6	6	Crawford Co., WI	Andrew D. Marg	Andrew D. Marg	1995	369
181 7/8	26 3/8	26 3/8	21 1/8	4 7/8	5	6	6	Jackson Co., IA	Ambrose Beck	Ambrose Beck	1963	374
181 7/8	26 7/8	26 7/8	23 3/8	5 3/8	5 4/8	8	7	Cottonwood Co., MN	Picked Up	MN Div. of Fish & Wildl.	1963	374
181 7/8	24 5/8	27 1/8	26 2/8	5 7/8	5 7/8	7	6	Todd Co., MN	Alvin Tvrdik	Alvin Tvrdik	1965	374
181 7/8	24 4/8	25 1/8	15 5/8	4 3/8	4 3/8	6	6	McMullen Co., TX	Oscar Hassette	Bill Carter	1971	374
181 7/8	26 4/8	24 4/8	21 3/8	4 6/8	4 6/8	5	5	Hotchkiss, AB	Andy G. Petkus	Andy G. Petkus	1984	374
181 7/8	26 5/8	26 2/8	21 5/8	4 4/8	4 4/8	5	5	Clearwater Co., ID	Richard E. Carver	Richard E. Carver	1985	374
181 7/8	27 4/8	26 5/8	20 5/8	4 4/8	4 4/8	5	6	Whitman Co., WA	George A. Cook III	George A. Cook III	1985	374
181 7/8	24 6/8	27 3/8	17 1/8	5 4/8	5 4/8	6	7	Lesser Slave Lake, AB	Picked Up	Jerry Napier	1985	374
181 7/8	28 5/8	27 5/8	22 1/8	5	5	5	5	Coahuila, MX	German Lopez Flores	German Lopez Flores	1986	374
181 7/8	25 4/8	25 2/8	23 5/8	5 2/8	5 2/8	5	5	Guilford Co., NC	Terry E. Daffron	Terry E. Daffron	1987	374
181 7/8	26 3/8	27 4/8	21 1/8	5	5	5	5	Alice Lake, AB	Dave S. Sietz	Dave S. Sietz	1989	374
181 7/8	27	25 4/8	22 1/8	5 2/8	5 1/8	6	6	Wright Co., MN	Craig S. Hansen	Craig S. Hansen	1992	374
181 7/8	25 1/8	26 3/8	23 6/8	5	5 3/8	8	9	Ghost River, AB	Dean Lee	Dean Lee	1995	374
181 6/8	23 6/8	24 7/8	20 6/8	5 3/8	6	5	5	Lyon Co., KS	Kenneth C. Haynes	Kenneth C. Haynes	1969	387
181 6/8	26 1/8	27 2/8	17 6/8	6 1/8	6	5	7	Wabasha Co., MN	Lee G. Partington	Lee G. Partington	1971	387
181 6/8	26 6/8	23 3/8	24	4 6/8	4 6/8	7	6	Nuevo Leon, MX	J.P. Davis	J.P. Davis	1985	387
181 6/8	25 5/8	26 4/8	23 6/8	4 7/8	5	7	7	Montgomery Co., MD	Gary F. Menso	Gary F. Menso	1985	387
181 6/8	27 5/8	25 5/8	21 4/8	4 3/8	4 4/8	5	5	Sussex Co., DE	Donald L. Betts	Donald L. Betts	1989	387
181 6/8	27 5/8	26 6/8	21 2/8	5 3/8	5	6	6	Bourbon Co., KS	Larry Daly	Larry Daly	1990	387
181 6/8	27 7/8	27 7/8	18 4/8	5 2/8	5 2/8	7	7	Davis Co., IA	Craig S. Heaverlo	Craig S. Heaverlo	1994	387
181 5/8	24 1/8	28 3/8	21 5/8	5 2/8	5 2/8	6	6	Ionia Co., MI	Lester Bowen	Richard Bowen	1947	394
181 5/8	28 2/8	27 7/8	21 3/8	4 1/8	4 6/8	6	6	La Salle Co., TX	Buck Turman	Lawson W. Walden	1947	394
181 5/8	25 6/8	24 1/8	19 7/8	5 4/8	4 8/8	6	6	Pierce Co., WI	Raymond G. Miller, Sr.	Raymond G. Miller, Sr.	1960	394
181 5/8	26 4/8	28 2/8	19 7/8	6 3/8	5 4/8	7	7	Wilkinson Co., MS	Ronnie P. Whitaker	Ronnie P. Whitaker	1981	394
181 5/8	28	25	21 5/8	4 6/8	6 1/8	6	6	Wabash Co., IL	Mike Drone	Mike Drone	1987	394
181 5/8	27 2/8	27 2/8	25 3/8	4 6/8	4 6/8	6	5	Blaine Co., MT	David A. Sprinkle	David A. Sprinkle	1989	394
181 5/8	27	25 7/8	22 1/8	6 7/8	6 7/8	5	6	Porcupine Hills, SK	Brian R. Anderson	Brian R. Anderson	1993	394
181 5/8	28 5/8	28	17 5/8	4 6/8	4 6/8	6	7	Pike Co., IL	George R. Metcalf	George R. Metcalf	1995	394
181 5/8	26 5/8	27 2/8	19 3/8	5 2/8	5 2/8	5	6	Des Moines Co., IA	Joseph J. Birkenstock	Joseph J. Birkenstock	1996	394
181 5/8	24 7/8	27	24 1/8	4 5/8	4 5/8	6	5	Nipawin, SK	Steve Clifford	Steve Clifford	1996	394
181 5/8	29	28	24 1/8	5 3/8	5 1/8	5	7	Racine Co., WI	Andrae D'Acquisto	Andrae D'Acquisto	1996	394
181 4/8	25 2/8	25 7/8	23 5/8	4 5/8	4 6/8	6	6	Oxford Co., ME	Dean W. Peaco	Dean W. Peaco	1953	405
181 4/8	28 4/8	24 7/8	22 7/8	5 7/8	5 7/8	7	7	Licking Co., OH	Arlee McCullough	Arlee McCullough	1962	405
181 4/8	26	29	22	5 3/8	5 3/8	5	5	Wadena Co., MN	Lester Zentner, Jr.	E.E. Patson	1962	405
181 4/8	25 4/8	25 2/8	18 6/8	5 2/8	5 1/8	9	9	Canton, IL	Arnold C. Hegele	Arnold C. Hegele	1968	405
181 4/8	26 1/8	28 4/8	22 6/8	5 6/8	5 2/8	6	6	Pine Lake, AB	Robert Crosby	Robert Crosby	1977	405
181 4/8	26 6/8	26	20 2/8	4 6/8	4 5/8	6	7	Trempealeau Co., WI	Randy A. Hoff	Randy A. Hoff	1987	405
181 4/8	26 7/8	27	18 2/8	5	5 3/8	7	6	Will Co., IL	James J.A. O'Keefe	James J.A. O'Keefe	1989	405
181 4/8	26 7/8	26 1/8	21	4 4/8	4 1/8	5	5	Wayne Co., IA	Picked Up	Ron King	1990	405
181 4/8	29 1/8	29	21	5 1/8	5	7	7	Grant Co., WI	Charles P. Fralick	Charles P. Fralick	1996	405

WHITETAIL DEER - TYPICAL ANTLERS

Odocoileus virginianus virginianus and certain related subspecies

Score	Length of Main Beam R	L	Inside Spread	Circumference at Smallest Place Between Burr and First Point R	L	Number of Points R	L	Locality	Hunter	Owner	Date Killed	Rank
181 3/8	27 4/8	27 5/8	20 6/8	4 4/8	4 4/8	7	6	Portage Co., OH	Robert M. Smith	Robert M. Smith	1953	414
181 3/8	25 2/8	24 3/8	21 2/8	5 6/8	5 6/8	7	6	Southey, SK	A.K. Flaman	Sam Peterson	1955	414
181 3/8	24 7/8	27 4/8	18 1/8	5	5	6	7	Orange Co., NY	Roy Vail	Roy Vail	1960	414
181 3/8	24 7/8	24 5/8	18 5/8	6 5/8	6 2/8	6	7	Pope Co., IL	Jack A. Higgs	Jack A. Higgs	1963	414
181 3/8	28	26 6/8	18 5/8	4 5/8	4 6/8	6	5	Polk Co., IA	Bob Boydston	Kevin Freymiller	1972	414
181 3/8	26 2/8	27 6/8	19 3/8	5	5	5	5	Houston Co., MN	Picked Up	Robert A. Morken	1980	414
181 3/8	26	25	17 5/8	4 5/8	4 5/8	6	6	Winona Co., MN	Kenneth W. Schreiber	Kenneth W. Schreiber	1980	414
181 3/8	24 1/8	24	20 4/8	5 1/8	5 3/8	6	8	Harding Co., SD	Cregg Else	Cregg Else	1985	414
181 3/8	27 4/8	26 7/8	18 4/8	5 1/8	5 1/8	5	7	Warren Co., IN	Todd J. Hemke	Todd J. Hemke	1987	414
181 3/8	24 6/8	26 3/8	19 7/8	5 1/8	4 7/8	6	6	Adair Co., IA	Gale D. Johnston	Gale D. Johnston	1995	414
181 3/8	28 2/8	29 3/8	21 2/8	5 5/8	5 3/8	8	7	Stafford Co., KS	Aaron W. King	Aaron W. King	1995	414
181 2/8	26 5/8	26	21 2/8	5 3/8	5 3/8	7	7	Sheridan Co., MT	Arthur M. Hagan, Sr.	Ken Hagan	1957	425
181 2/8	25 2/8	25 7/8	25 7/8	5 1/8	5 4/8	5	6	Hardin Co., KY	Thomas L. House	Thomas L. House	1963	425
181 2/8	25	25 2/8	21	4 3/8	4 3/8	6	6	Lafayette Co., WI	Michael Morrissey	Michael Morrissey	1982	425
181 2/8	27 7/8	28 2/8	20 6/8	5 2/8	5 3/8	5	6	Scotland Co., MO	Jerry Kennedy	Jerry Kennedy	1989	425
181 2/8	25 6/8	27	19 5/8	5	5	6	6	McBride Lake, SK	Bryan Rothenburger	Bryan Rothenburger	1993	425
181 2/8	28 2/8	27 7/8	23 6/8	4 7/8	4 7/8	6	5	Sangamon Co., IL	Jack D. Davis	Jack D. Davis	1995	425
181 2/8	26 2/8	25 2/8	22 2/8	4 7/8	4 5/8	5	6	Will Co., IL	Jozef H. Skubisz	Jozef H. Skubisz	1996	425
181 1/8	27 1/8	27 1/8	21 6/8	5 2/8	5 4/8	7	7	Elk River, MN	John E. Bush	Larry L. Huffman	1870	432
181 1/8	27 3/8	28	20 7/8	5 2/8	5 3/8	6	7	Polk Co., MN	Henry Cook	Steven D. Cook	1938	432
181 1/8	27 6/8	26 2/8	17 3/8	5 4/8	5 4/8	5	5	Waldo Co., ME	Clarendon Pomeroy	Larry C. Pomeroy	1946	432
181 1/8	26 1/8	25 3/8	18 5/8	5	5	6	5	Frio Co., TX	Warren Smith	Roy Hindes	PR 1950	432
181 1/8	27 3/8	27 6/8	20 7/8	6 2/8	5 6/8	10	7	Empress, SK	Don Leach	Don Leach	1960	432
181 1/8	24 5/8	25 1/8	20 5/8	5 3/8	5 2/8	7	7	Wood River, SK	Jeremy Egan	Jeremy Egan	1990	432
181 1/8	25 5/8	25 6/8	20	5 1/8	5	7	7	Crawford Co., WI	Randall E. Kreuscher	Randall E. Kreuscher	1992	432
181	25 7/8	24 6/8	22 3/8	4 7/8	5 3/8	6	8	Beltrami Co., MN	Robert C. Shaw	Robert C. Shaw	1910	439
181	26 3/8	26 2/8	20 2/8	4 7/8	5	6	5	Ransom Co., ND	Gerald V. Sweet	Gerald V. Sweet	1959	439
181	25 6/8	26 5/8	19	5 6/8	5	5	5	Langlade Co., WI	Elroy W. Timm	Elroy W. Timm	1959	439
181	27	26 5/8	20	5 7/8	5 7/8	6	6	Stettler, AB	Archie Smith	Archie Smith	1962	439
181	28 3/8	28 4/8	20	4 4/8	4 4/8	5	5	Wood Co., WI	James D. Wyman	James D. Wyman	1977	439
181	26 5/8	26 2/8	21 2/8	6 2/8	6 3/8	7	8	Lac qui Parle Co., MN	Mary A. Barvels	Mary A. Barvels	1978	439
181	27 7/8	27	20 3/8	5 1/8	5 1/8	8	7	Gallatin Co., KY	Kenneth D. Hoffman	Kenneth D. Hoffman	1979	439
181	27 1/8	27 2/8	20 7/8	5 2/8	5 2/8	7	8	Foam Lake, SK	Ray Howe	Ray Howe	1991	439
181	27 6/8	26 6/8	20 6/8	5 3/8	5 4/8	9	7	Adair Co., MO	Michael D. Hill	Michael D. Hill	1992	439
180 7/8	26 5/8	28	17 3/8	4 4/8	4 4/8	5	5	Marinette Co., WI	Albert Giese	Kenneth J. Giese	1938	448
180 7/8	29	29 6/8	20 4/8	5 2/8	5 2/8	7	6	Jones Co., GA	James H.C. Kitchens	James H.C. Kitchens	1957	448

Score	Main Beam R	Main Beam L	Inside Spread	Circ. R	Circ. L	Pts R	Pts L	Locality	Hunter	Owner	Date Killed	Rank
180 7/8	22 1/8	23 1/8	16 7/8	5 3/8	5 1/8	7	8	Chicot Co., AR	Lee R. Mathews	Henry Mathews	1963	448
180 7/8	29 6/8	29 2/8	24 1/8	5 2/8	5	6	5	Keya Paha Co., NE	Steve R. Pecsenye	Steve R. Pecsenye	1966	448
180 7/8	25 7/8	25 3/8	17 7/8	5 1/8	5 1/8	6	7	Castor, AB	Norman D. Stienwand	Norman D. Stienwand	1981	448
180 7/8	28 5/8	27 7/8	22 1/8	5 2/8	5 3/8	5	6	Polk Co., MN	Daniel Omdahl	Daniel Omdahl	1987	448
180 7/8	26 4/8	26 6/8	22	5 2/8	5	7	5	Wayne Co., IA	Richard L. Spencer	Richard L. Spencer	1990	448
180 7/8	26 7/8	26 5/8	22 1/8	5 3/8	5 3/8	5	5	Cedar Co., IA	Glenn U. Farrington	Glenn U. Farrington	1994	448
180 7/8	27	25 6/8	19 7/8	5 3/8	5 2/8	5	5	Adair Co., IA	Picked Up	Jerry Funke	1995	448
180 7/8	27 2/8	26 6/8	21 5/8	5 2/8	5 4/8	5	5	Rush Co., IN	Cain M. Grocox	Cain M. Grocox	1995	448
180 7/8	26 6/8	25 7/8	19	5 4/8	5 2/8	8	8	Dafoe, SK	Jamin Bolt	Jamin Bolt	1996	448
180 6/8	30	29 4/8	23 4/8	5 6/8	5 6/8	5	6	Hancock Co., ME	Cyrus H. Whitaker	Orrin W. Whitaker	1912	459
180 6/8	31 6/8	31 2/8	19 4/8	6	5 5/8	6	8	New Brunswick	Unknown	Acad. Nat. Sci., Phil.	1937	459
180 6/8	26 6/8	26	25	5 5/8	4 4/8	6	9	Dimmit Co., TX	Edward Gardner	Edward Gardner	1937	459
180 6/8	26 3/8	26 1/8	18 2/8	5 2/8	5 5/8	5	5	Jefferson Co., IA	James J. Hoskins	James J. Hoskins	1982	459
180 6/8	25 4/8	25 7/8	19	4 7/8	5 1/8	5	6	Marshall Co., MN	Scott T. Rabehl	Scott T. Rabehl	1987	459
180 6/8	27 2/8	28 3/8	22	5 1/8	5	6	5	Pike Lake, SK	Roger Ireland	Roger Ireland	1990	459
180 6/8	27 6/8	27 6/8	26	4 4/8	5 1/8	5	7	Sounding Lake, AB	Morris Thompson	Morris Thompson	1993	459
180 5/8	25	23 4/8	19 2/8	4 7/8	4 4/8	5	5	Maverick Co., TX	Jim Webb	Richard H. Bennett	1912	466
180 5/8	24 7/8	25 1/8	27 6/8	5 3/8	4 6/8	4	7	Treasure Co., MT	Jack Welch	Jack Welch	1958	466
180 5/8	25	23 6/8	18 3/8	4 7/8	5 3/8	7	7	Cheat Mt., WV	Joseph V. Volitis	Larry L. Huffman	1969	466
180 5/8	25	28 3/8	23 3/8	4 4/8	5	6	7	St. Landry Parish, LA	Shawn P. Ortego	Shawn P. Ortego	1975	466
180 5/8	29 6/8	29 3/8	18 7/8	4 5/8	4 4/8	8	5	Adams Co., IL	Kenneth E. Klauser	Kenneth E. Klauser	1990	466
180 5/8	25 6/8	24 7/8	22 5/8	6 2/8	4 3/8	5	5	Jim Hogg Co., TX	Michael L. Vickers	Michael L. Vickers	1991	466
180 5/8	26	26 3/8	19 3/8	5 4/8	6 4/8	6	6	Tuscarawas Co., OH	Thomas K. Winters	Thomas K. Winters	1991	466
180 5/8	27 6/8	27 2/8	21 3/8	5 1/8	5 4/8	6	6	Good Spirit Lake, SK	Grant Landstad	Grant Landstad	1993	466
180 5/8	26 3/8	26 2/8	23 3/8	4 7/8	5	5	8	Turner Co., SD	Nicklaus J. Schrag	Nicklaus J. Schrag	1996	466
180 4/8	29 2/8	28 4/8	18 3/8	4 6/8	4 6/8	6	5	Iron Co., MI	John Schmidt	Bob Schmidt	1927	475
180 4/8	28	26 2/8	20 6/8	4 6/8	5 2/8	6	7	Jim Hogg Co., TX	Roy L. Henry	Roy L. Henry	1958	475
180 4/8	27 6/8	26 2/8	26 6/8	5	4 6/8	7	7	Madison Parish, LA	Buford Perry	Buford Perry	1961	475
180 4/8	27 1/8	26 6/8	20	5 2/8	4 7/8	6	6	Adams Co., IA	Dale D. Blazek	Dale D. Blazek	1962	475
180 4/8	23 5/8	27	16 6/8	5 1/8	5	6	5	Andrew Co., MO	Virgil M. Ashley	Virgil M. Ashley	1967	475
180 4/8	28	23 5/8	17 2/8	4 7/8	5 1/8	6	6	Leflore Co., MS	W.F. Smith	W.F. Smith	1968	475
180 4/8	26 7/8	27	22 7/8	4 3/8	4 7/8	6	6	Clay Co., SD	James E. Olson	James E. Olson	1975	475
180 4/8	30	29 1/8	19	4 5/8	4 3/8	8	8	Okanogan Co., WA	Joe Peone	Joe Peone	1983	475
180 4/8	25 6/8	26 2/8	24 5/8	5 3/8	4 4/8	7	6	Carver Co., MN	Stephen M. Polston	Stephen M. Polston	1985	475
180 4/8	27 3/8	27 3/8	17 4/8	5 2/8	5 1/8	6	6	Portage Co., OH	Michael J. Simons	Michael J. Simons	1990	475
180 4/8	25 6/8	25 7/8	20	5 4/8	5 4/8	5	5	Livingston Co., MO	Jack Hampton	Jack Hampton	1991	475
180 4/8	24 7/8	24 7/8	22 2/8	5 1/8	5 2/8	5	5	Henry Co., IA	Jeff L. Weigert	Jeff L. Weigert	1994	475
180 4/8	27 7/8	27 7/8	21	4 3/8	5 6/8	5	10	Holt Co., NE	Fred L. Kubik	Fred L. Kubik	1995	475
180 4/8	27	27	22 2/8	5 2/8	5 4/8	9	7	Dubois Co., IN	Kenneth R. Hasenour	Kenneth R. Hasenour		475
180 3/8	30 2/8	30	21 1/8	5 1/8	5 3/8	6	6	Livingston Co., NY	Edward Beare	Edward Beare	1943	489
180 3/8	26 4/8	27	23 1/8	4 6/8	4 3/8	8	6	Sheboygan Co., WI	Unknown	James K. Lawton	1955	489
180 3/8	24 4/8	24 4/8	20 2/8	5 6/8	5 4/8	7	8	Ovando, MT	Clinton Berry	Clinton Berry	1957	489
180 3/8	25 6/8	26 3/8	19 1/8	5 1/8	5	8	7	Stoughton, SK	Joe Zbeetnoff	Joe Zbeetnoff	1961	489
180 3/8	26 6/8	25 5/8	21 5/8	6 2/8	6 3/8	6	7	Aitkin Co., MN	Donald J. Sorenson	Donald J. Sorenson	1963	489
180 3/8	27 5/8	26	20 1/8	4 5/8	4 5/8	5	6	Antler Lake, AB	German Wagenseil	German Wagenseil	1964	489
180 3/8	30 4/8	29 2/8	21 5/8	5 7/8	5 7/8	4	4	Hand Co., SD	Vernon Winter	J.D. Andrews	1965	489
180 3/8	30	30	22 3/8	4 5/8	4 5/8	6	8	Meeker Co., MN	Stanley M. Messner	Stanley M. Messner	1981	489

303

WHITETAIL DEER - TYPICAL ANTLERS

Odocoileus virginianus virginianus and certain related subspecies

Score	Length of Main Beam		Inside Spread	Circumference at Smallest Place Between Burr and First Point		Number of Points		Locality	Hunter	Owner	Date Killed	Rank
	R	L		R	L	R	L					
180 3/8	27	28 1/8	17 6/8	4 5/8	4 5/8	9	6	Huron Co., MI	Picked Up	Ray W. Hatfield	1985	489
180 3/8	25 1/8	24 7/8	17 2/8	4 7/8	4 5/8	7	6	Story Co., IA	Richard L. Borton	Richard L. Borton	1987	489
180 3/8	25 1/8	24 4/8	20 1/8	5	5	6	6	St. Louis Co., MN	Unknown	George W. Flaim	PR 1992	489
180 3/8	22 7/8	23 6/8	19 7/8	5	4 7/8	7	6	Nuevo Leon, MX	Melbourn Shillings	Melbourn Shillings	1992	489
180 3/8	28 1/8	28	19 6/8	5 5/8	5 3/8	6	4	Menard Co., IL	Ronald J. Wadsworth	Ronald J. Wadsworth	1993	489
180 3/8	26 5/8	27 3/8	21 1/8	5 1/8	5 2/8	5	5	Crane Lake, SK	Darron J. Corfield	Darron J. Corfield	1994	489
180 3/8	27 4/8	27 1/8	19 5/8	4 4/8	4 3/8	8	8	Dakota Co., MN	William E. Urbaniak	William E. Urbaniak	1996	489
180 2/8	28 2/8	27 7/8	20 2/8	4 7/8	4 7/8	6	6	Texas	Alfred Schroeder	John E. Hamilton	PR 1926	504
180 2/8	26 4/8	25	22 5/8	5 4/8	5 2/8	7	7	Lumsden, SK	Mike Lukas	E.M. Gazda	1959	504
180 2/8	28 1/8	28 4/8	18 4/8	4 6/8	4 6/8	5	5	Newton Co., GA	David Moon	David Moon	1972	504
180 2/8	26 6/8	26 3/8	20 2/8	4 7/8	4 5/8	6	6	Meeker Co., MN	Harold Nistler	William H. Lilienthal	PR 1975	504
180 2/8	24 1/8	26 6/8	19 1/8	5	4 6/8	6	6	Madison Co., IA	Carl W. Schroder	Carl W. Schroder	1977	504
180 2/8	26 3/8	26 3/8	18 2/8	4 5/8	4 5/8	6	6	Eau Claire Co., WI	Dennis B. Bryan	Dennis B. Bryan	1979	504
180 2/8	27 1/8	27 1/8	19 4/8	4 4/8	4 4/8	5	5	Iowa	Unknown	Tom Williams	PR 1984	504
180 2/8	25 1/8	25 3/8	20 4/8	4 4/8	4 3/8	5	5	Yuma Co., CO	Jeff L. Mekelburg	Jeff L. Mekelburg	1989	504
180 2/8	26 5/8	27 5/8	21 1/8	5 1/8	5 1/8	6	6	Drew Co., AR	Terry Tackette	Terry Tackette	1989	504
180 2/8	26 6/8	27 4/8	22 4/8	5	4 6/8	6	7	Polk Co., IA	Jeff P. Susic	Jeff P. Susic	1990	504
180 2/8	30	28 3/8	23 4/8	5	5	6	6	Pepin Co., WI	William J. Bates	William J. Bates	1991	504
180 2/8	25 2/8	25 7/8	20 4/8	4 7/8	4 6/8	5	5	Monroe Co., IA	Michael R. Maddy	Michael R. Maddy	1992	504
180 2/8	26 1/8	26 1/8	17 4/8	4 6/8	4 7/8	7	8	Cowley Co., KS	Thomas W. Jackson	Thomas W. Jackson	1994	504
180 2/8	28 4/8	27 6/8	21 1/8	5	5 2/8	6	8	Allamakee Co., IA	David L. Goedert	David L. Goedert	1995	504
180 2/8	25 3/8	25 6/8	20 1/8	4 7/8	4 6/8	8	7	Jefferson Co., WI	Randy Latsch	Randy Latsch	1995	504
180 2/8	26 7/8	28 5/8	19 4/8	5 2/8	5 1/8	5	6	Madison Co., MS	Stephen C. Greer	Stephen C. Greer	1996	504
180 1/8	23 3/8	23 5/8	17 5/8	5 2/8	5 2/8	5	5	Maryfield, SK	Donald Cook	Richard Christoforo	1956	520
180 1/8	25 4/8	26 6/8	17 3/8	4 7/8	4 6/8	7	6	Ashland Co., WI	Audrey Kundinger	Audrey Kundinger	1961	520
180 1/8	26 4/8	26 5/8	20 1/8	4 4/8	4 5/8	6	6	Phelps Co., MO	William A. Hagenhoff	William A. Hagenhoff	1973	520
180 1/8	24	24 4/8	19 1/8	4 7/8	5	7	6	Vermilion, AB	Ralph M. McDonald	Ralph M. McDonald	1975	520
180 1/8	25 1/8	24 4/8	26 7/8	5 6/8	5 4/8	6	7	Hardisty, AB	George R. Walker	George R. Walker	1977	520
180 1/8	27	26	15 7/8	4 7/8	4 6/8	5	5	Chariton Co., MO	Ricky Pearman	Ricky Pearman	1982	520
180 1/8	25 1/8	25 1/8	19 1/8	5 2/8	5 2/8	6	6	Cottonwood Co., MN	Charles C. Burnham	Charles C. Burnham	1983	520
180 1/8	24	24 4/8	19 4/8	5 1/8	5	7	5	Hubbard Co., MN	Larry D. Dierks	Larry D. Dierks	1984	520
180 1/8	29 7/8	28 6/8	25 1/8	5 1/8	5 3/8	5	5	Caroline Co., MD	Unknown	Charles D. Anderson	1987	520
180 1/8	26 1/8	25 6/8	20 1/8	5 2/8	5 2/8	5	5	Jackson Co., SD	Timothy J. Kelley	Timothy J. Kelley	1988	520
180 1/8	25 6/8	25 4/8	22 1/8	4 3/8	4 2/8	6	6	Parry, SK	Doug Hennie	Doug Hennie	1993	520
180 1/8	26 4/8	26 1/8	20	4 7/8	4 6/8	6	6	Montgomery Co., TN	Lonnie Hulse	Lonnie Hulse	1995	520
180 1/8	27 2/8	24 4/8	15 3/8	4 6/8	4 7/8	6	5	Macon Co., MO	M.F. Rickwa & S.M. Rickwa	M.F. Rickwa & S.M. Rickwa	1995	520

Score									Locality	Hunter	Owner	Date	Rank
180	27 5/8	27 6/8	20	4 7/8	5	4 7/8	5	6	Oneida Co., WI	Milo K. Fields	Milo K. Fields	1938	533
180	26 6/8	27 6/8	19 6/8	4 4/8	4 4/8	4 4/8	7	5	Desha Co., AR	Turner Neal	Turner Neal	1962	533
180	26	25 7/8	19	4 7/8	5	4 7/8	10	7	Zavala Co., TX	Mrs. Richard King III	Mrs. Richard King III	1966	533
180	25 7/8	25 5/8	19 4/8	6 1/8	5 7/8	6 1/8	6	8	Big Horn Co., MT	Clair W. Jensen	Clair W. Jensen	1967	533
180	26 7/8	25 5/8	20 4/8	5 7/8	5 5/8	5 7/8	5	7	Castor, AB	Kenneth Larson	Kenneth Larson	1969	533
180	26 4/8	27 1/8	18 2/8	5 5/8	4 7/8	5 3/8	6	5	Edwards Co., KS	David R. Cross	David R. Cross	1985	533
180	25 2/8	25 6/8	22 7/8	4 7/8	4 5/8	5 4/8	7	8	Pulaski Co., IL	Picked Up	Pat Kearny	1988	533
180	26 7/8	28	19 4/8	4 4/8	4 5/8	4 4/8	6	6	Florence Co., WI	Dale E. Samsa	Dale E. Samsa	1988	533
180	25 6/8	25 4/8	20	5 4/8	5 6/8	5 4/8	6	5	Dawson Creek, BC	H. Peter Bruhs	H. Peter Bruhs	1989	533
180	25 4/8	25 6/8	19 4/8	5 1/8	5 1/8	5 1/8	10	5	Pembina River, AB	Joe Jandl	Joe Jandl	1989	533
180	23 5/8	25 2/8	19 5/8	5 2/8	5	5 3/8	7	7	Torch River, SK	David Matchett	David Matchett	1991	533
180	24 5/8	24 5/8	22 6/8	5	5	5	5	5	Helene Lake, SK	Kevin R. Garner	Kevin R. Garner	1993	533
180	24 4/8	25 3/8	23 3/8	7	7	7	7	5	Boone Co., IA	Loren H. Phipps	Loren H. Phipps	1993	533
180	25 7/8	26	20 2/8	5 1/8	5 3/8	5 1/8	5	6	Brown Co., IL	Rocco Gibala	Rocco Gibala	1995	533
179 7/8	25 3/8	27 1/8	19	5 1/8	5	5	9	7	Hancock Co., ME	Butler B. Dunn	Butler B. Dunn	1930	547
179 7/8	27 6/8	26 6/8	19 7/8	5 4/8	5 4/8	5 4/8	5	6	Hamiota, MB	Alan J. Sheridan	Alan J. Sheridan	1984	547
179 7/8	26 1/8	28	19 4/8	5 3/8	5 3/8	5 3/8	6	6	Nicollet Co., MN	Joe Welter	Joe Welter	1987	547
179 7/8	26 2/8	26 3/8	19 5/8	5 1/8	5 1/8	5 1/8	6	5	Tensas Parish, LA	Anthony Guice	Anthony Guice	1995	547
179 7/8	28 5/8	28 3/8	20 4/8	4 6/8	4 6/8	4 6/8	5	6	Hancock Co., ME	Larry Snell	M. Don Betts	1884	551
179 6/8	27 1/8	29 3/8	21 2/8	4 7/8	5	5	7	7	Steele Co., MN	Elmer Janning	Elmer Janning	1972	551
179 6/8	28 1/8	26 4/8	22 2/8	4 6/8	4 6/8	4 6/8	6	6	Aitkin Co., MN	Harland A. Kern	Harland A. Kern	1973	551
179 6/8	29 1/8	28	21	5 6/8	5 8/8	5 6/8	7	6	Longview, AB	Eldred Umbach	Eldred Umbach	1977	551
179 6/8	26 7/8	26 5/8	21 4/8	4 5/8	4 4/8	4 4/8	7	7	Woodbury Co., IA	Harlan L. Allison	Harlan L. Allison	1979	551
179 6/8	26 3/8	26 2/8	19 6/8	4 6/8	4 5/8	4 5/8	6	6	Jim Hogg Co., TX	William B. Van Fleet	William B. Van Fleet	1979	551
179 6/8	25 6/8	26 6/8	21 5/8	5 2/8	5 3/8	5 3/8	6	5	Penobscot Co., ME	Dale Rustin	Dale Rustin	1984	551
179 6/8	27	26 6/8	15 6/8	4 5/8	4 4/8	4 4/8	7	8	Clark Co., IL	Robert E. Sweitzer	Robert E. Sweitzer	1994	551
179 6/8	25 1/8	24 7/8	20	4 6/8	4 6/8	4 6/8	6	5	Valhalla Centre, AB	Terry D. Hagman	Terry D. Hagman	1995	551
179 6/8	25 3/8	26	19 1/8	5 4/8	5 4/8	5 3/8	7	7	Decatur Co., IA	Wayne W. Owens	Wayne W. Owens	1995	551
179 5/8	25 4/8	25 7/8	19 5/8	6	6	6	7	6	Rumsey, AB	Arley Harder	Arley Harder	1969	561
179 5/8	28 6/8	27 6/8	21	4 6/8	5	5	6	5	Putnam Co., MO	Wes A. Seaton	Wes A. Seaton	1992	561
179 5/8	29 6/8	29	21 3/8	4 5/8	4 7/8	4 7/8	6	5	Haughton Co., MI	Matthew R. Usitalo	Matthew R. Usitalo	1992	561
179 4/8	23 4/8	23 5/8	19 2/8	4 6/8	4 5/8	4 5/8	6	6	Coronation, AB	Harold McKnight	Harold McKnight	1969	564
179 4/8	26 5/8	26 6/8	20	5 3/8	5 3/8	5 3/8	5	5	Sandridge, MB	Robert Anderson	Robert Anderson	1971	564
179 4/8	24 1/8	24 2/8	19 2/8	5 2/8	5 2/8	5 2/8	5	5	Spokane Co., WA	Bert E. Smith	Bert E. Smith	1972	564
179 4/8	27 5/8	27 3/8	19 7/8	5	5	5	6	6	Elk Co., KS	Lowell E. Howell	Lowell E. Howell	1973	564
179 4/8	27 3/8	28 4/8	20 1/8	5 3/8	5 3/8	5 3/8	6	5	Pawnee Co., NE	Kenneth C. Mort	Kenneth C. Mort	1975	564
179 4/8	24 1/8	25 3/8	19 5/8	4 7/8	4 7/8	4 7/8	7	8	Chouteau Co., MT	Richard L. Charlson	Richard L. Charlson	1977	564
179 4/8	26 3/8	26 5/8	22 3/8	4 2/8	4 3/8	4 3/8	5	6	Grant Co., WI	Rick L. Parker	Rick L. Parker	1982	564
179 4/8	26 2/8	26 2/8	19 5/8	5 6/8	5 3/8	5 3/8	6	5	Whitemud River, MB	L. Greg Fehr	L. Greg Fehr	1985	564
179 4/8	27 3/8	27 2/8	20 2/8	4 7/8	5 6/8	5 6/8	5	6	Cremona, AB	E. Roger Jackson	E. Roger Jackson	1985	564
179 4/8	28 3/8	28 5/8	21	4 4/8	4 4/8	4 4/8	6	5	Collingsworth Co., TX	Picked Up	F. Gus Reinarz	1987	564
179 4/8	28 1/8	28 1/8	19 6/8	6 1/8	6 1/8	6 1/8	6	5	Clarke Co., IA	Rodney D. Hommer	Rodney D. Hommer	1990	564
179 4/8	24 6/8	24 1/8	22	5 4/8	5 3/8	5 3/8	6	6	Yankee Lake, SK	Leo Stieb	Leo Stieb	1990	564
179 4/8	30 1/8	29 2/8	23	4 6/8	5	4 6/8	5	5	Litchfield Co., CT	Garry J. Lovrin	Garry J. Lovrin	1993	564
179 3/8	29	29 2/8	19 7/8	4 6/8	4 5/8	4 5/8	8	10	Essex Co., NY	Herbert Jaquish	Herbert Jaquish	1953	577
179 3/8	28 5/8	28	20 7/8	5 6/8	5 6/8	5 6/8	5	5	Parkman, SK	Harold Larsen	Sam Peterson	1958	577
179 3/8	26 1/8	26 2/8	17 7/8	4 7/8	4 7/8	4 7/8	6	6	Vernon Co., WI	Alois V. Schendel	Alois V. Schendel	1966	577

305

Odocoileus virginianus virginianus and certain related subspecies

Score	Length of Main Beam R	L	Inside Spread	Circumference at Smallest Place Between Burr and First Point R	L	Number of Points R	L	Locality	Hunter	Owner	Date Killed	Rank
179 3/8	26	26 2/8	17 3/8	6	5 5/8	6	6	Oberon, MB	Arnold W. Poole	Arnold W. Poole	1968	577
179 3/8	26 1/8	26	22 5/8	4 5/8	4 6/8	7	7	Pelican Mt., AB	Harold B. Biggs	Harold B. Biggs	1993	577
179 3/8	26 3/8	25 7/8	22 1/8	5	5	6	7	Allamakee Co., IA	Picked Up	David Gordon	1994	577
179 3/8	27 6/8	26 4/8	18 3/8	5 5/8	5 5/8	6	6	Sherman Co., NE	Richard McCauley, Jr.	Richard McCauley, Jr.	1994	577
179 3/8	25 3/8	27 7/8	21	5 3/8	5 4/8	6	7	Jennings Co., IN	Dennis L. Day	Dennis L. Day	1995	577
179 3/8	25	24 4/8	18 3/8	5 2/8	5 3/8	6	6	Lincoln Co., MO	Alfred W. Masterson	Alfred W. Masterson	1995	577
179 3/8	26 7/8	27 5/8	19 5/8	4 2/8	4 2/8	5	5	St. Lawrence Co., NY	Craig A. Morrill	Craig A. Morrill	1995	577
179 3/8	25	25 4/8	19 5/8	4 4/8	4 6/8	8	7	Priddis, AB	Jeffrey C. Dunn	Jeffrey C. Dunn	1996	577
179 3/8	26 1/8	26 6/8	22	4 6/8	4 6/8	8	6	Anoka Co., MN	Thomas M. Evertz	Thomas M. Evertz	1996	577
179 2/8	27 2/8	27 1/8	23 3/8	5	5 2/8	9	11	Prairie Co., AR	Charles Newsom	Charles Newsom	1962	589
179 2/8	28 5/8	28 5/8	20 6/8	5 2/8	5 3/8	6	5	Koochiching Co., MN	Ted Davis	Marc M. Jackson	1963	589
179 2/8	27 6/8	27	20	5 4/8	5 6/8	9	9	Cypress Hills, SK	Raymond McCrea	Raymond McCrea	1964	589
179 2/8	25 4/8	24 6/8	21 3/8	4 5/8	4 6/8	7	7	Lamar Co., GA	Gary Littlejohn	Gary Littlejohn	1968	589
179 2/8	26 5/8	25 5/8	17 7/8	5	4 6/8	7	7	Worth Co., IA	John Janssen	John Janssen	1976	589
179 2/8	26 7/8	28	16	4 4/8	4 3/8	6	5	Ashland Co., WI	Jack D. Hultman	Jack D. Hultman	1981	589
179 2/8	28 1/8	28 4/8	25 2/8	4 5/8	4 5/8	6	5	Webster Co., IA	Douglas W. Baedke	Douglas W. Baedke	1982	589
179 2/8	24 2/8	24 2/8	19 4/8	4 4/8	4 5/8	6	6	Dimmit Co., TX	William M. Knolle	William M. Knolle	1982	589
179 2/8	23 6/8	25 1/8	19 2/8	5 5/8	5 5/8	7	7	Buffalo Co., WI	Jerome Kulig	Jerome Kulig	1984	589
179 2/8	25 4/8	25 6/8	20 6/8	5	5	6	7	Hinds Co., MS	Marlon Stokes	Marlon Stokes	1988	589
179 2/8	28 7/8	27 1/8	19 2/8	5 3/8	5 3/8	5	5	Peoria Co., IL	Christopher M. McNulty	Christopher M. McNulty	1994	589
179 2/8	25 4/8	25 6/8	23 2/8	5 1/8	5 2/8	9	9	Unknown	Picked Up	David Gheen	1995	589
179 2/8	27 6/8	27 7/8	21	4 5/8	5 1/8	6	6	Henry Co., VA	Tony E. Meade	Tony E. Meade	1995	589
179 1/8	28 6/8	27 1/8	18 2/8	4 4/8	4 4/8	6	6	Twiggs Co., GA	Cy Smith	Duncan A. Dobie	1970	602
179 1/8	27 3/8	27 7/8	21 3/8	5 7/8	5 7/8	5	6	Renville Co., MN	Todd Swartz	Todd Swartz	1984	602
179 1/8	24 5/8	25 4/8	15 7/8	4 7/8	5	7	6	Dallas Co., IA	Steven W. Hick	Steven W. Hick	1992	602
179 1/8	28 4/8	28 1/8	21 3/8	4 7/8	5	6	7	Butler Co., KS	Donald B. Williamson	Donald B. Williamson	1994	602
179 1/8	25 6/8	25 6/8	16 3/8	4 4/8	5 4/8	6	5	Macoupin Co., IL	William T. Wiser, Sr.	William T. Wiser, Sr.	1994	602
179	25	23 7/8	18 2/8	5 2/8	5 3/8	5	6	Chippewa Co., WI	John F. Kukuska	John F. Kukuska	1931	607
179	27 1/8	25 5/8	19 4/8	5 5/8	5 4/8	6	7	Sherburne Co., MN	Victor Nagel	Victor Nagel	1956	607
179	26 6/8	26 2/8	21 4/8	4 4/8	4 6/8	5	6	Jasper Co., GA	Hubert R. Moody	Hubert R. Moody	1957	607
179	25 6/8	25 6/8	19 3/8	5	5 1/8	6	6	Waldersee, MB	W. Wutke	W. Wutke	1959	607
179	28 4/8	28 5/8	20 6/8	4 5/8	4 7/8	5	5	Dooly Co., GA	Shannon Akin	Shannon Akin	1981	607
179	27 4/8	29 4/8	20 2/8	4 6/8	4 6/8	6	7	Logan Co., OH	Gregory K. Snyder	Greta J. Snyder	1982	607
179	27 6/8	29 1/8	20 7/8	5 6/8	5 5/8	8	11	Perry Co., IL	Roy A. Smith	Roy A. Smith	1987	607
179	26 2/8	26 5/8	21	4 7/8	5	5	5	Monroe Co., MO	Tommy Garnett	Tommy Garnett	1988	607
179	27 2/8	26 4/8	19 1/8	5 1/8	5 4/8	5	6	Pictou Co., NS	Earl Perry	Earl Perry	1990	607

Score	Main Beam R	Main Beam L	Inside Spread	Circ. R	Circ. L	Pts R	Pts L	Locality	Hunter	Owner	Date	Rank
179	27 6/8	27 6/8	17 4/8	4 4/8	4 3/8	6	6	Benton Co., MN	Michael A. Gapinski	Michael A. Gapinski	1991	607
179	27 7/8	29 1/8	21 4/8	5 4/8	5 2/8	6	6	Union Co., IA	Richard Reed	Richard Reed	1996	607
178 7/8	24 3/8	28	21 7/8	5 3/8	5 3/8	6	6	Monroe Co., OH	Roger E. Schumacher	Roger E. Schumacher	1958	618
178 7/8	28 1/8	26 2/8	19 5/8	4 6/8	4 6/8	6	6	Van Buren Co., IA	Noel E. Harlan	Noel E. Harlan	1984	618
178 7/8	28 3/8	28 3/8	19 1/8	5	5	5	5	Pierce Lake, SK	Edwin Johnson	Edwin Johnson	1984	618
178 7/8	30	29 4/8	18 1/8	4 5/8	4 5/8	5	5	Whiteside Co., IL	Bernard J. Higley, Jr.	Bernard J. Higley, Jr.	1990	618
178 7/8	26 4/8	26 4/8	22 7/8	5 4/8	5	5	5	Coahuila, MX	Donald R. Summers	Donald R. Summers	1990	618
178 7/8	30	28 5/8	21 1/8	4 1/8	5	5	5	Scioto Co., OH	Craig D. Smith	Craig D. Smith	1991	618
178 6/8	27 3/8	27 5/8	20 7/8	5 2/8	5 1/8	8	9	Texas	Unknown	Buckhorn Mus. & Saloon, Ltd.	PR 1920	624
178 6/8	26	25	22 7/8	5 3/8	5 4/8	6	6	Elkhorn, MB	Jerry May	Jerry May	1959	624
178 6/8	27 6/8	27 6/8	25 4/8	5 2/8	5 2/8	5	6	Windthorst, SK	Clarence E. Genest	Clarence E. Genest	1965	624
178 6/8	26	26 5/8	21 2/8	5 2/8	5 2/8	8	6	McPherson Co., KS	Larry D. Daniel	Larry D. Daniel	1967	624
178 6/8	27	24 4/8	22 1/8	5 7/8	5 7/8	7	7	Breton, AB	George Clark	George Clark	1981	624
178 6/8	26 2/8	27 2/8	20 6/8	5	5	6	6	Aroostook Co., ME	John R. Hardy	John R. Hardy	1983	624
178 6/8	28 1/8	27 3/8	21 3/8	4 4/8	4 2/8	5	6	Corson Co., SD	Dean Little Dog	Dick Rossum	1984	624
178 6/8	27	27	19 2/8	4 5/8	4 6/8	5	6	Webb Co., TX	M.J. Satcher	M.J. Satcher	1987	624
178 6/8	25 7/8	26 4/8	22 2/8	4 6/8	4 6/8	6	6	Vilna, AB	M.M. Berrien, Jr.	M.M. Berrien, Jr.	1990	624
178 6/8	26	25 7/8	16	4 5/8	4 6/8	6	6	Shawano Co., WI	Gregory L. Teske	Gregory L. Teske	1991	624
178 6/8	29 2/8	27 6/8	21 5/8	5 5/8	5 3/8	7	7	Hancock Co., IL	Carl A. Lee	Carl A. Lee	1996	624
178 5/8	25 6/8	27 2/8	20 2/8	5 4/8	5 4/8	6	5	Bolivar Co., MS	Grady Robertson	Merigold Hunting Club	1951	635
178 5/8	28 7/8	27	24	5 1/8	5 1/8	5	7	Beechy, SK	Archie D. McRae	Archie D. McRae	1957	635
178 5/8	26 3/8	27 3/8	23 1/8	5 6/8	4 6/8	7	5	Hamilton Co., IA	Harrison McIntre	William H. Lilienthal	PR 1960	635
178 5/8	27	26 4/8	20 4/8	4 3/8	4 3/8	6	6	Harlan Co., NE	Don Tripe	Don Tripe	1962	635
178 5/8	28 4/8	28 1/8	16 7/8	5 4/8	5 4/8	6	7	St. Louis Co., MN	Picked Up	Jerome L. Schaller	1966	635
178 5/8	27 7/8	29 2/8	26 3/8	5 3/8	5 2/8	7	5	Debden, SK	Henry Rydde	Henry Rydde	1969	635
178 5/8	28 5/8	26 3/8	20	5 2/8	5 1/8	5	7	Thomas Co., GA	Clyde E. Anderson	Clyde E. Anderson	1973	635
178 5/8	24 1/8	24 7/8	20 4/8	4 7/8	4 7/8	7	7	Pincher Creek, AB	Unknown	H. Bruce Freeman	1977	635
178 5/8	27 2/8	26 4/8	21 5/8	5 3/8	5 3/8	5	5	St. Louis Co., MN	John Nordenstam	George W. Flaim	1978	635
178 5/8	27	26 4/8	21 1/8	5 1/8	4 4/8	5	5	Scott Co., TN	Charles H. Smith	Charles H. Smith	1980	635
178 5/8	25 4/8	25 5/8	22 7/8	5 3/8	5	5	5	Itasca Co., MN	Gino P. Maccario	Gino P. Maccario	1985	635
178 5/8	27 3/8	27 1/8	24 1/8	4 4/8	5 2/8	6	6	Crawford Co., WI	Dale Check, Jr.	Dale Check, Jr.	1985	635
178 5/8	24 7/8	25 1/8	18 1/8	5	4 7/8	5	7	Grant Co., WI	I. James Meng	I. James Meng	1986	635
178 5/8	25 4/8	26 1/8	20 1/8	5 6/8	5 3/8	6	7	Caldwell Co., MO	Jack L. Murray	Jack L. Murray	1987	635
178 5/8	25 7/8	23 7/8	18 7/8	4 6/8	5 1/8	7	8	Grundy Co., IL	Charles H. Frantini	Charles H. Frantini	1987	635
178 5/8	23 7/8	24 7/8	21 3/8	4 5/8	5	7	5	Flat Lake, AB	Paul Franchuk	Paul Franchuk	1988	635
178 5/8	24 7/8	26 2/8	19 5/8	4 4/8	5 4/8	5	5	Jones Co., IA	Dennis Boots	Dennis Boots	1988	635
178 5/8	26	26	20 3/8	4 2/8	4 6/8	6	6	Riley Co., KS	Colt Knutson	Colt Knutson	1989	635
178 5/8	27 1/8	27 5/8	20 1/8	5 4/8	4 5/8	8	8	Roseau Co., MN	Jeffrey Benson	Jeffrey Benson	1991	635
178 5/8	25 5/8	26 1/8	18 6/8	4 7/8	4 5/8	8	6	Saskatoon, SK	Patrick D. Shendruk	Patrick D. Shendruk	1992	635
178 5/8	28 3/8	28 1/8	17 7/8	4 3/8	4 2/8	6	6	Monroe Co., NY	David P. Ives	David P. Ives	1993	635
178 5/8	25 7/8	25 7/8	21 7/8	5 4/8	5 4/8	6	7	Crittenden Co., KY	Mendel Davidson	Mendel Davidson	1994	635
178 5/8	23 2/8	23 2/8	20 7/8	5 2/8	4 7/8	7	5	La Salle Co., IL	Larry G. Simmons	Larry G. Simmons	1995	635
178 4/8	26 4/8	26 1/8	28 2/8	4 3/8	4 3/8	5	7	Beltrami Co., MN	Arthur I. Hill	Arthur A. Hill	1954	658
178 4/8	26 6/8	24 6/8	21 3/8	5 4/8	5 4/8	7	7	Addy, WA	Irving Naff	Irving Naff	1957	658
178 4/8	24 6/8	25	23 2/8	5 2/8	5 2/8	6	6	McMullen Co., TX	D.H. Waldron	D.H. Waldron	1964	658
178 4/8	25	25 3/8	16 1/8	4 7/8	4 5/8	6	6	Yuma Co., CO	Terry M. Scheidecker	Terry M. Scheidecker	1979	658
178 4/8	25 1/8	27 3/8	18 6/8	4 7/8	4 5/8	6	6	Cumberland Co., ME	Patrick D. Wescott	Patrick D. Wescott	1980	658

WHITETAIL DEER - TYPICAL ANTLERS

Odocoileus virginianus virginianus and certain related subspecies

Score	Length of Main Beam R	L	Inside Spread	Circumference at Smallest Place Between Burr and First Point R	L	Number of Points R	L	Locality	Hunter	Owner	Date Killed	Rank
178 4/8	24 2/8	25 2/8	18 1/8	5 5/8	5 5/8	5	6	St. Clair Co., IL	Emil W. Kromat	Emil W. Kromat	1981	658
178 4/8	26 2/8	25 3/8	21	5 3/8	5 3/8	5	5	Scotland Co., MO	Picked Up	Roland E. Meyer	1984	658
178 4/8	26 1/8	27 3/8	22 6/8	4 3/8	4 4/8	6	5	Edmonson Co., KY	Picked Up	Joseph G. Saling	1984	658
178 4/8	25 1/8	25	18 4/8	4 7/8	4 6/8	5	5	Fulton Co., IL	Locie L. Murphy	Locie L. Murphy	1985	658
178 4/8	25 1/8	25 4/8	19 4/8	5 3/8	5 3/8	5	5	Firdale, MB	Randall J. Bean	Randall J. Bean	1988	658
178 4/8	30 4/8	30 3/8	18 2/8	6 2/8	5 6/8	10	8	Nance Co., NE	Robert J. Ziemba	Robert J. Ziemba	1988	658
178 4/8	27 4/8	27 2/8	19 6/8	4 7/8	5 3/8	6	8	Blue Earth Co., MN	Harry J. Baker	Harry J. Baker	1991	658
178 4/8	29 4/8	28 6/8	22 4/8	4 7/8	5 1/8	6	5	Iosco Co., MI	Frederic J. Latta	Frederic J. Latta	1991	658
178 3/8	25 1/8	26 1/8	21 1/8	4 5/8	4 7/8	6	6	Clinton Co., IL	Richard V. Spihlmann	Richard V. Spihlmann	1961	671
178 3/8	26 7/8	26 5/8	24 3/8	5 4/8	5 2/8	6	5	Aitkin Co., MN	George E. Jenks	George E. Jenks	1969	671
178 3/8	27	27 3/8	17 5/8	4 3/8	4 4/8	5	5	Queens Co., NB	Bert Bourque	Bert Bourque	1970	671
178 3/8	26 5/8	26 3/8	19 7/8	5 3/8	4 3/8	5	5	Fillmore Co., MN	Alanson W. Hamernik, Jr.	Alanson W. Hamernik, Jr.	1970	671
178 3/8	27 2/8	26	17 1/8	5 2/8	5	7	8	Carroll Co., AR	Roy F. Bartlett	Roy F. Bartlett	1975	671
178 3/8	25 3/8	28 1/8	20	5 5/8	5 4/8	7	6	Allamakee Co., IA	Stanley L. Jarosh	Stanley L. Jarosh	1976	671
178 3/8	28 4/8	28 7/8	23 7/8	5 1/8	5 2/8	7	8	Lincoln Co., MN	Larry Lustfield	Larry Lustfield	1976	671
178 3/8	28 4/8	27 7/8	17 1/8	4 7/8	4 6/8	6	6	Dubuque Co., IA	Clay W. Gronen	Clay W. Gronen	1978	671
178 3/8	23 1/8	24 2/8	25	5 6/8	6	6	7	Gregory Co., SD	Ronald L. Larson	Ronald L. Larson	1980	671
178 3/8	27 2/8	26 4/8	18 5/8	4 6/8	4 6/8	6	6	Goochland Co., VA	Edward W. Fielder	Edward W. Fielder	1981	671
178 3/8	26 4/8	25	19	4 7/8	4 6/8	6	6	Jo Daviess Co., IL	Gary J. Flynn	Gary J. Flynn	1986	671
178 3/8	27 3/8	27 3/8	22 4/8	5 3/8	5 3/8	7	7	Phillips Co., AR	Christopher Warren	Christopher Warren	1993	671
178 3/8	26 7/8	26 5/8	16 7/8	5 1/8	5 2/8	5	5	Keya Paha Co., NE	Joseph V. Bauer	Joseph V. Bauer	1994	671
178 3/8	25 5/8	26	22 1/8	6	6 2/8	7	6	Tippecanoe Co., IN	Robert Whitus	Robert Whitus	1994	671
178 3/8	29 4/8	30 2/8	18 4/8	5 5/8	5 2/8	7	6	Bourbon Co., KS	Ronald D. Pfeiffer	Ronald D. Pfeiffer	1995	671
178 3/8	24 4/8	26 1/8	18 5/8	4 2/8	4 2/8	5	5	Fayette Co., IA	Richard A. Wulfekuhle	Richard A. Wulfekuhle	1995	671
178 2/8	25 4/8	26 1/8	18 4/8	4 7/8	4 7/8	5	5	Shawano Co., WI	Picked Up	Ray T. Charles	1953	687
178 2/8	26 5/8	26 1/8	20 6/8	4 6/8	4 6/8	5	5	Pawnee Co., NE	Picked Up	Gale Sup	1960	687
178 2/8	25 7/8	25	23	5 5/8	5 5/8	7	5	Pope Co., MN	Greg Kobbermann	Greg Kobbermann	1976	687
178 2/8	27 6/8	28 3/8	19 4/8	4 4/8	4 4/8	6	5	Crawford Co., WI	Lance Bangen	Brant J. Mueller	PR 1980	687
178 2/8	27 6/8	27 3/8	24 6/8	4 3/8	4 3/8	6	6	Wallowa Co., OR	Sterling K. Shaver	Sterling K. Shaver	1982	687
178 2/8	27 4/8	27	19 6/8	4 3/8	4 4/8	5	5	Tuscarawas Co., OH	Raymond D. Gerber, Jr.	Raymond D. Gerber, Jr.	1983	687
178 2/8	26 6/8	28 1/8	19 6/8	5 4/8	5 4/8	7	7	Ohio Co., KY	Earl R. Trogden	Earl R. Trogden	1986	687
178 2/8	28	25 7/8	21 2/8	5 1/8	5 3/8	5	5	Lawrence Co., IL	Brian M. Dining	Brian M. Dining	1987	687
178 2/8	28 5/8	27 5/8	21	4 4/8	4 4/8	7	6	Richland Co., ND	Jeffrey D. Krabbenhoft	Jeffrey D. Krabbenhoft	1993	687
178 2/8	26 7/8	25 7/8	21 6/8	4 5/8	4 5/8	7	6	Clay Co., MN	Darrin D. Tonsfeldt	Darrin D. Tonsfeldt	1993	687
178 1/8	24 1/8	23 5/8	19 1/8	4 4/8	4 5/8	8	8	Dismal River, NE	Gift of G.B. Grinnell to NCHH	Unknown	PR 1909	697
178 1/8	28 2/8	26 7/8	18 7/8	4 7/8	5	5	7	Concrete, ND	Lawrence E. Vandal	Lawrence E. Vandal	1947	697

Score	Main Beam R	Main Beam L	Inside Spread	Circ. R	Circ. L	Pts R	Pts L	Locality	By Whom Killed	Owner	Date	Rank
178 1/8	24 6/8	25 5/8	25 6/8	4 3/8	4 3/8	6	6	Kent Co., MD	Herman Gravatt	Donald P. Travis	1955	697
178 1/8	27 5/8	27 4/8	17 4/8	4 7/8	4 7/8	8	7	Iron Co., WI	DuWayne A. Weichel	Robert G. Steidtmann	1957	697
178 1/8	28 1/8	28 1/8	18 1/8	4 6/8	4 6/8	5	5	Iron Co., MI	James Locke	Brant J. Mueller	1960	697
178 1/8	29 1/8	28 4/8	18 4/8	4 7/8	4 7/8	7	5	Harlan Co., NE	Duane E. Johnson	Duane E. Johnson	1967	697
178 1/8	26 5/8	26 5/8	20 4/8	4 2/8	4 3/8	5	6	Vonda, SK	Orest Hilkewich	Orest Hilkewich	1980	697
178 1/8	27 4/8	27 4/8	21 1/8	5 5/8	5 5/8	5	5	Price Co., WI	Terry Staroba	Terry Staroba	1983	697
178 1/8	28 5/8	29	21 7/8	5 5/8	5 5/8	7	5	Aroostook Co., ME	Gary G. Saucier	Gary G. Saucier	1987	697
178 1/8	24	23 3/8	16 3/8	4 4/8	4 4/8	5	6	Teton Co., MT	Ivan F. Holland	Ivan F. Holland	1991	697
178 1/8	29 1/8	28	19 5/8	4 3/8	4 3/8	7	7	Arkansas Co., AR	Roger Hansell	Roger Hansell	1992	697
178 1/8	26 6/8	26 4/8	19 1/8	5 4/8	5 3/8	5	5	Dallas Co., IA	Picked Up	William H. Lilienthal	1995	697
178	27	27 2/8	17 4/8	5	5	7	7	Price Co., IA	Emery Swan	Emery Swan	1949	709
178	26 7/8	27 2/8	21 6/8	4 3/8	4 3/8	6	6	Clark Co., MO	Allen L. Courtney	Allen L. Courtney	1966	709
178	24 1/8	25 3/8	16 6/8	4 7/8	4 7/8	6	6	Hillsdale Co., MI	Dudley N. Spade	Dudley N. Spade	1972	709
178	25	24 6/8	17 2/8	4 6/8	4 5/8	6	7	Washington Co., IA	Brad Gardner	Vaughn Wilkins	1978	709
178	27 5/8	27 2/8	20	5 1/8	5 2/8	7	7	Price Co., WI	John E. Martinson	John E. Martinson	1981	709
178	25 1/8	26 2/8	22 6/8	6	5 1/8	5	5	Union Co., KY	Gary L. Gibson	Gary L. Gibson	1983	709
178	29	30 2/8	25	6	6	9	9	Appanoose Co., IA	Steve G. Huff	Steve G. Huff	1988	709
178	25 4/8	25 1/8	18 5/8	4 1/8	4 1/8	7	7	Caswell Co., NC	Picked Up	Jimmy Koger	1988	709
178	29 5/8	28 2/8	21	5 2/8	5 3/8	6	5	Macon Co., MO	Charles L. Harrington	Charles L. Harrington	1992	709
178	28 2/8	27 5/8	19 3/8	5 1/8	5 2/8	7	6	Shell Lake, SK	Brent Brewer	Brent Brewer	1994	709
178	25 7/8	26 2/8	18 1/8	5 2/8	5 1/8	6	5	Decatur Co., IA	Picked Up	Jeffrey R. Danner	1995	709
177 7/8	29 2/8	28 4/8	18 2/8	5 3/8	5 5/8	5	7	Burnett Co., WI	John Backlund	Lester Thor	1916	720
177 7/8	27	27	20 3/8	5	5	6	6	Chicot Co., AR	George Matthews	W.T. Haynes	1923	720
177 7/8	28	27 4/8	20 3/8	5 6/8	5 6/8	5	5	Iron Co., MI	Felix Brzoznowski	Joseph Brzoznowski	1939	720
177 7/8	24 2/8	23 7/8	19 3/8	4 6/8	4 4/8	7	7	Ymir, BC	Frank Gowing	Frank Gowing	1961	720
177 7/8	25 7/8	25 1/8	24 3/8	5	5 1/8	6	6	Wibaux Co., MT	Dan Amunrud	David Welliever	1967	720
177 7/8	26 3/8	26 6/8	22 1/8	5 2/8	5 2/8	6	6	Christian Co., IL	Rodney J. Gorden	Rodney J. Gorden	1974	720
177 7/8	27 6/8	26 1/8	18 5/8	5 3/8	5 1/8	7	6	Haralson Co., GA	Picked Up	Alfred Wright	1982	720
177 7/8	26 4/8	23	23	5	5	7	9	Jefferson Co., MT	Tracy Forcella	Tracy Forcella	1983	720
177 7/8	26 6/8	26 6/8	18 2/8	4 3/8	4 3/8	6	6	Penobscot Co., ME	Andrew B. Alexander	Andrew B. Alexander	1985	720
177 7/8	22 4/8	23 2/8	17 4/8	5 2/8	5 2/8	8	7	Cass Co., ND	Joe D. Chesley	Joe D. Chesley	1987	720
177 7/8	25	25 4/8	17	5	5 1/8	7	6	Vilas Co., WI	Dean A. Casper	Dean A. Casper	1990	720
177 7/8	28 6/8	26 5/8	23 7/8	5 4/8	5 3/8	6	10	St. Marys Co., MD	Timothy B. Moore	Timothy B. Moore	1990	720
177 7/8	24 3/8	24	18 5/8	4 6/8	4 5/8	6	6	Harper Co., OK	Scott Davis	Scott Davis	1993	720
177 7/8	27	27 2/8	19 5/8	5 4/8	5 3/8	5	7	Rosieisle, MB	Richard A. Fay	Richard A. Fay	1995	720
177 7/8	27 4/8	27 2/8	18 7/8	5 4/8	5 4/8	7	6	Bates Co., MO	Daniel P. White	Daniel P. White	1995	720
177 7/8	25 5/8	22	19 5/8	4 2/8	4 4/8	8	7	Ontario Co., NY	Stephen E. McAllister	Stephen E. McAllister	1996	720
177 6/8	24 5/8	24 7/8	19	4 5/8	4 6/8	6	6	Paxton, NE	Ole Herstedt	Ole Herstedt	1956	736
177 6/8	24	24	22	4 4/8	4 4/8	6	6	Kleberg Co., TX	Elaine A. O'Brien	Patrick O'Brien	1972	736
177 6/8	26 6/8	22 6/8	22 6/8	5	5	5	6	Atoka Co., OK	Skip Rowell	Skip Rowell	1972	736
177 6/8	23 4/8	24	24	5	4 6/8	6	6	Duval Co., TX	Harry Heimer	Harry Heimer	1974	736
177 6/8	26 5/8	27 4/8	23 4/8	4 6/8	4 4/8	6	6	Stearns Co., MN	Robert G. Schwarz	Robert G. Schwarz	1975	736
177 6/8	26 4/8	26 4/8	18 2/8	4 5/8	5 1/8	5	5	Shaunavon, SK	Stan J. Crawford	Stan J. Crawford	1979	736
177 6/8	24 3/8	23 5/8	19	4 6/8	4 6/8	7	7	Clark Co., MO	Billie G. Noble	Billie G. Noble	1985	736
177 6/8	25 7/8	26 4/8	18	4 3/8	4 2/8	5	5	Kankakee Co., IL	Robert R. Tolmer, Jr.	Robert R. Tolmer, Jr.	1987	736
177 6/8	25 4/8	26 3/8	20 2/8	5 1/8	5 1/8	6	6	Pendleton Co., KY	Daniel Michalski	Daniel Michalski	1988	736
177 6/8	26 2/8	27 2/8	18 2/8	5 4/8	5 4/8	6	7	Antler River, SK	Larry Sterling	Larry Sterling	1989	736

Odocoileus virginianus virginianus and certain related subspecies

Score	Length of Main Beam R	L	Inside Spread	Circumference at Smallest Place Between Burr and First Point R	L	Number of Points R	L	Locality	Hunter	Owner	Date Killed	Rank
177 6/8	27 6/8	28 1/8	19 1/8	4 3/8	4 4/8	7	8	Anderson Co., KS	Randall R. West	Randall R. West	1990	736
177 6/8	26 4/8	26 5/8	20 7/8	4 6/8	4 6/8	5	6	Lincoln Co., MT	Bernard B. White	Bernard B. White	1990	736
177 6/8	31	29	23	5	5	5	7	Washington Co., ME	Edward S. Welsh, Jr.	Edward S. Welsh, Jr.	1992	736
177 6/8	29	27 7/8	20	5 2/8	5 2/8	6	7	St. Louis Co., MN	Ronald R. Anderson	Ronald R. Anderson	1994	736
177 6/8	26 5/8	27 4/8	19 6/8	4 6/8	4 6/8	5	5	Sumner Co., KS	Alan K. Boyle	Alan K. Boyle	1995	736
177 5/8	26 5/8	25 5/8	19 7/8	5 1/8	5	6	5	Crow Wing Co., MN	Gil Atwater	Donald McNevin	1926	751
177 5/8	24 6/8	23 3/8	24 7/8	5 1/8	5 2/8	7	6	Dimmit Co., TX	Carter Younts	Carter Younts	1963	751
177 5/8	25 5/8	26 3/8	19 1/8	5 4/8	5 3/8	5	5	Endeavor, WI	Terry L. Halgrimson	Terry L. Halgrimson	1971	751
177 5/8	26 2/8	26 6/8	22 6/8	4 7/8	4 7/8	7	7	Wabasha Co., MN	Bruce J. Hall	Bruce J. Hall	1972	751
177 5/8	25	24 3/8	17 6/8	4 1/8	4 1/8	6	6	Macon Co., GA	James W. Athon	Mike's Gun Shop	1976	751
177 5/8	25	25 4/8	17 5/8	5	5 2/8	6	6	Macon Co., GA	Dalton H. Cannon	Dalton H. Cannon	1977	751
177 5/8	24 4/8	25 3/8	18 3/8	5 1/8	5 1/8	6	7	Jim Hogg Co., TX	Howard Sturgess	Lawson W. Walden	PR 1982	751
177 5/8	29	28 2/8	22	4 4/8	4 4/8	7	8	Harrison Co., OH	Mark Dulkoski	Mark Dulkoski	1984	751
177 5/8	25 5/8	25 5/8	19 5/8	5 3/8	5 3/8	5	5	Washburn Co., WI	Patrick Henk	Patrick Henk	1984	751
177 5/8	26	25 6/8	21 3/8	4 5/8	4 5/8	5	5	Idaho Co., ID	Donna M. Knight	Donna M. Knight	1986	751
177 5/8	27 6/8	28 5/8	18	5 5/8	5 4/8	6	6	Colquitt Co., GA	Timothy Carter	Timothy Carter	1990	751
177 5/8	23 4/8	25 7/8	20 7/8	5 1/8	5 4/8	7	9	Morrison Co., MN	Jeanne Backowski-Jensen	Jeanne Backowski-Jensen	1991	751
177 5/8	27 7/8	27	19 2/8	6 3/8	6 5/8	9	9	Marshall Co., KS	Terre J. Carter	Terre J. Carter	1992	751
177 5/8	25 7/8	25 3/8	18 1/8	4 6/8	4 6/8	7	6	Kittson Co., MN	Picked Up	Derry Jones	1993	751
177 5/8	26 5/8	25	17 7/8	5 1/8	5 1/8	5	5	Nemaha Co., KS	Stephen C. Damron	Stephen C. Damron	1995	751
177 5/8	26 1/8	26 1/8	22 3/8	5 6/8	5 5/8	5	5	Winneshiek Co., IA	Glen J. Gienau	Glen J. Gienau	1995	751
177 5/8	28 5/8	28 2/8	20 1/8	4 4/8	4 4/8	6	6	Berkshire Co., MA	William E. Tatro	William E. Tatro	1995	751
177 5/8	28	28 2/8	21 3/8	5 1/8	5 1/8	5	5	Concordia Parish, LA	John W. King	John W. King	1996	751
177 4/8	26	26 4/8	21 5/8	4 5/8	4 4/8	8	8	Oneida Co., WI	Elmer Ahlborn	Gene Ahlborn	1926	769
177 4/8	27 6/8	27 4/8	23 4/8	5	5	6	7	Dimmit Co., TX	Tom Brady	McLean Bowman	1926	769
177 4/8	27 2/8	27 7/8	20	4 6/8	4 5/8	7	5	Marinette Co., WI	Henry L. Hoffman	Henry L. Hoffman	1942	769
177 4/8	25	24 4/8	21 1/8	5 2/8	5 4/8	5	6	Dundurn, SK	L.B. Galbraith	L.B. Galbraith	1956	769
177 4/8	26 1/8	26	21	4	4 1/8	5	5	Bedford Co., PA	Raymond Miller	Raymond Miller	1957	769
177 4/8	28 5/8	29 2/8	18 3/8	5 5/8	5 5/8	6	9	Cass Co., MN	Larry K. Sherman	Larry K. Sherman	1964	769
177 4/8	28 2/8	28 3/8	22 4/8	5 6/8	5 6/8	5	6	Beltrami Co., MN	Sheldon M. Stockdale	Sheldon M. Stockdale	1968	769
177 4/8	25 7/8	26 2/8	16 4/8	4 7/8	4 5/8	7	7	Wisconsin	Unknown	Brant J. Mueller	PR 1975	769
177 4/8	26	26 4/8	24	5	5	6	6	Montana	Unknown	John L. Stein	1983	769
177 4/8	28 3/8	28 4/8	23 5/8	4 3/8	4 3/8	8	5	Otter Tail Co., MN	Robert J. Perszyk	Robert J. Perszyk	1985	769
177 4/8	26	28	21 6/8	5 6/8	5 3/8	7	6	Krydor, SK	Julian Shewchuk	Julian Shewchuk	1985	769
177 4/8	29 7/8	28 6/8	21 6/8	4 6/8	4 7/8	5	5	Grayson Co., KY	David W. Mercer	David W. Mercer	1986	769
177 4/8	26 3/8	26 2/8	20 4/8	5	5	6	5	Swan River, MB	Myles T. Keller	Myles T. Keller	1994	769

Score	Main Beam R	Main Beam L	Inside Spread	Circ. R	Circ. L	Points R	Points L	Locality	Hunter	Owner	Date	Rank
177 4/8	26 3/8	25 6/8	17	4 6/8	4 6/8	6	6	Torquay, SK	Wayne Daae	Wayne Daae	1996	769
177 3/8	25 4/8	25 4/8	18	6	6 2/8	5	6	Hall Co., NE	Charles R. Babel	C.P. Medore	1969	783
177 3/8	27	26 2/8	23 1/8	5	5 1/8	5	5	Menominee Co., WI	William Matchapatow, Sr.	William Matchapatow, Sr.	1981	783
177 3/8	26	26	20 2/8	5 3/8	5 2/8	6	5	Greene Co., IA	David A. Reichel	David A. Reichel	1981	783
177 3/8	27 1/8	26 3/8	20 3/8	5 4/8	5 4/8	6	6	Rusk Co., WI	Roger V. Carlson	Roger V. Carlson	1983	783
177 3/8	27 3/8	28	16 5/8	5	5	6	5	Claiborne Parish, LA	Steven L. Morton	Steven L. Morton	1986	783
177 3/8	29 1/8	30 1/8	24 7/8	6 4/8	6 2/8	9	9	Menominee Co., WI	Jeff N. Dixon	Jeff N. Dixon	1987	783
177 3/8	29 2/8	29 1/8	24 2/8	5	5 1/8	6	6	Clinton Co., IA	Picked Up	William H. Lilienthal	1990	783
177 3/8	25 4/8	27 1/8	22 3/8	5 1/8	5 4/8	6	5	Chautauqua Co., KS	Wesley D. Coldren	Wesley D. Coldren	1991	783
177 3/8	27 3/8	27 1/8	18 6/8	5 4/8	5 5/8	9	9	Weasel Creek, AB	Ray M. Fels	Ray M. Fels	1991	783
177 3/8	26	25 7/8	20 3/8	4 5/8	4 6/8	6	6	Vermilion River, AB	Larry Flaata	Larry Flaata	1995	783
177 2/8	26 6/8	25 3/8	26 2/8	5 1/8	5 1/8	7	7	Webb Co., TX	Unknown	Eugene Roberts	1924	793
177 2/8	27 5/8	28 3/8	19 4/8	4 6/8	4 6/8	7	7	Pine Co., MN	C. Foster & E. Kepler	Lois Youngbauer	1930	793
177 2/8	24 1/8	24 5/8	22 2/8	4 1/8	4 2/8	5	5	La Salle Co., TX	T.H. Barker	Michael R. Barker	1939	793
177 2/8	29 1/8	29 2/8	21	4 5/8	4 6/8	5	5	Buffalo Co., WI	George W. Kees	George W. Kees	1957	793
177 2/8	28 1/8	28	20 6/8	4 6/8	4 6/8	5	5	Augusta Co., VA	Donald W. Houser	Donald W. Houser	1963	793
177 2/8	28 1/8	24 3/8	21 5/8	4 1/8	4 1/8	8	9	Golden Valley Co., ND	Allen Goltz	Allen Goltz	1964	793
177 2/8	26 5/8	27 3/8	22	4 6/8	4 4/8	7	7	Guthrie Co., IA	Picked Up	Dalton H. Hoover	1970	793
177 2/8	27 4/8	27 1/8	21 2/8	5 1/8	5	5	5	Rainy River, ON	Lynn Wilson	Lynn Wilson	1972	793
177 2/8	29 4/8	30 2/8	18 2/8	6 5/8	6 3/8	6	6	Geary Co., KS	Kelly D. Gulker	Kelly D. Gulker	1982	793
177 2/8	25 5/8	25 7/8	18 2/8	4 6/8	4 6/8	6	6	Richland Co., WI	Dewitt S. Pulham	Dewitt S. Pulham	1982	793
177 2/8	27 5/8	29	21 7/8	6	6	5	6	Litchfield Co., CT	Picked Up	Rickey A. Vincent	1984	793
177 2/8	27	26 3/8	17 3/8	4 6/8	4 4/8	8	7	Montgomery Co., KY	Bobby M. Dale	Bobby M. Dale	1986	793
177 2/8	27 4/8	26 7/8	20 6/8	5	5	5	5	Belmont Co., OH	Kevin A. Grimes	Kevin A. Grimes	1987	793
177 2/8	27 4/8	28 3/8	18 6/8	4 5/8	4 7/8	7	7	Clarke Co., IA	Richard Bassett	Richard Bassett	1989	793
177 2/8	24 2/8	23 4/8	20 2/8	5	5	6	6	Sawyer Co., WI	William H. Laney	William H. Laney	1991	793
177 2/8	27	25 6/8	19 4/8	5 4/8	5 4/8	6	6	Somerset Co., ME	Richard D. Hagerty	Richard D. Hagerty	1993	793
177 2/8	25 4/8	25	16 7/8	4 7/8	4 7/8	6	6	Pushmataha Co., OK	Herbert W. Savage	Herbert W. Savage	1994	793
177 1/8	25 5/8	26 1/8	19	5 1/8	5 2/8	7	10	Newcastle, WY	H.W. Julien	H.W. Julien	1954	810
177 1/8	27	27	18 1/8	4 6/8	4 7/8	6	5	Gregory Co., SD	Harold Deering	Harold Deering	1969	810
177 1/8	26 7/8	27 1/8	22 1/8	5	4 7/8	5	6	Harrison Co., KY	Picked Up	George Simpson	1978	810
177 1/8	26 3/8	25 5/8	21 6/8	5 2/8	5 3/8	6	8	Calhoun Co., IL	Paul V. Stumpf	Paul V. Stumpf	1979	810
177 1/8	27 2/8	27	21 7/8	4 4/8	4 4/8	6	5	Walworth Co., WI	Daniel J. Brede	Daniel J. Brede	1984	810
177 1/8	25 5/8	25 5/8	22 3/8	4 6/8	4 6/8	6	5	Thorsby, AB	Adam Tomaszewski	Adam Tomaszewski	1985	810
177 1/8	28	26 7/8	21 1/8	5 7/8	5 7/8	5	5	Kittson Co., MN	Unknown	George W. Flaim	1987	810
177 1/8	25 7/8	25 7/8	18 5/8	4 5/8	4 5/8	8	6	Forest Co., WI	Carl S. Ernst	Carl S. Ernst	1990	810
177 1/8	27 1/8	28 6/8	21 2/8	4 6/8	4 6/8	7	5	St. Croix Co., WI	Phillip R. Hovde	Phillip R. Hovde	1990	810
177 1/8	26 4/8	27	19 4/8	4 6/8	4 7/8	6	5	Cass Co., IA	Cleve H. Powell	Cleve H. Powell	1990	810
177 1/8	27 7/8	26 3/8	18 4/8	4 7/8	5 6/8	7	6	Wolf Lake, AB	Keith W. Hamilton	Keith W. Hamilton	1992	810
177 1/8	25 2/8	24 7/8	20 7/8	5	5	7	7	Ogle Co., IL	Daniel L. Bouton	Daniel L. Bouton	1993	810
177 1/8	27 1/8	27 1/8	20 7/8	5 2/8	5 1/8	5	5	Toole Co., MT	Anthony W. Enos	Anthony W. Enos	1994	810
177 1/8	25 7/8	25 7/8	18 1/8	4 6/8	4 7/8	5	5	Davis Co., IA	Michael G. White	Michael G. White	1995	810
177	28 1/8	28	17 2/8	4 6/8	4 6/8	6	7	Bayfield Co., WI	Elof E. Sjostrom	Mrs. Elof E. Sjostrom	1932	824
177	25 1/8	25 3/8	17 2/8	5 1/8	5	7	7	Rainy River, ON	Robert K. Hayes	Robert K. Hayes	1949	824
177	26 2/8	25 6/8	19 7/8	5 1/8	5 1/8	8	10	Kandiyohi Co., MN	Dale E. Nelson	Scott Nelson	1949	824
177	23 4/8	24 2/8	16 6/8	5	4 7/8	7	6	St. Louis Co., MN	Chuck Perkins	Chuck Perkins	1964	824
177	25	26	19 1/8	6	5 7/8	6	5	Gage Co., NE	Art Wallman	Art Wallman	1968	824

Odocoileus virginianus virginianus and certain related subspecies

Score	Length of Main Beam R	L	Inside Spread	Circumference at Smallest Place Between Burr and First Point R	L	Number of Points R	L	Locality	Hunter	Owner	Date Killed	Rank
177	26 2/8	27 6/8	18 4/8	4 4/8	4 6/8	5	5	Cass Co., IN	Herbert R. Frushour	Herbert R. Frushour	1974	824
177	28 7/8	28 6/8	22 3/8	4 1/8	4	6	5	Jasper Co., IN	Dan Haskins	Douglas R. Plourde	1975	824
177	28 1/8	26 1/8	20 7/8	5 4/8	5 6/8	7	6	Innisfree, AB	Donald M. Baranec	Donald M. Baranec	1984	824
177	24 7/8	25	16 2/8	5 1/8	5 1/8	8	9	Daly, MB	Bruce A. Crofton	Bruce A. Crofton	1984	824
177	23 7/8	25 1/8	14 3/8	5 2/8	5 1/8	11	7	Lundar, MB	Fred Thorkelson	Fred Thorkelson	1986	824
177	26 2/8	26 1/8	20 4/8	4 3/8	4 5/8	6	6	Muscatine Co., IA	Jack Van Nice	Jack Van Nice	1986	824
177	23 4/8	22 6/8	16 4/8	4 6/8	4 6/8	6	5	Harrison Co., IA	Craig D. Mitchell	Craig D. Mitchell	1988	824
177	28 2/8	28 1/8	18 3/8	5	5	8	6	Baltimore Co., MD	Richard B. Traband	Richard B. Traband	1990	824
177	26 1/8	25 1/8	19 6/8	4 3/8	4 3/8	6	6	Macon Co., MO	Wilbert R. Freeman	Wilbert R. Freeman	1991	824
177	26	27 3/8	21 6/8	5 3/8	5	10	6	Lewis Co., KY	David E. Henderson	David E. Henderson	1994	824
176 7/8	25 5/8	27 4/8	22 4/8	5	5 1/8	9	6	Prince George Co., VA	Fred W. Collins	Fred W. Collins	1949	839
176 7/8	28	26 7/8	16 2/8	3 7/8	3 6/8	5	7	Day Co., SD	William B. Davis	William B. Davis	1959	839
176 7/8	27 2/8	28 4/8	24 2/8	4 4/8	4 4/8	5	6	Lincoln Co., WI	Edmond H. Pay	Edmond H. Pay	1959	839
176 7/8	25 4/8	26	19 7/8	5 5/8	5 4/8	5	5	Pierson, MB	Bud Smith	Bud Smith	1960	839
176 7/8	29 2/8	28 3/8	23	5 7/8	5 4/8	5	6	Logan Co., OH	David Sutherly	David Sutherly	1975	839
176 7/8	25 2/8	25 5/8	22 1/8	4 6/8	5	5	5	Butler Co., KS	Craig D. Waltman	Craig D. Waltman	1982	839
176 7/8	27 3/8	27 2/8	20 3/8	4 5/8	4 5/8	5	5	Pierce Co., WI	John M. Oelke	John M. Oelke	1984	839
176 7/8	25 6/8	25 2/8	18 1/8	4 5/8	4 7/8	7	7	McDonough Co., IL	Richard F. Krohe	Richard F. Krohe	1986	839
176 7/8	27 4/8	28	25 3/8	5 6/8	5 6/8	5	5	Marion Co., OH	Thomas A. Bridenstine	Thomas A. Bridenstine	1987	839
176 7/8	27 1/8	27 6/8	18 5/8	4 4/8	4 5/8	5	5	Cass Co., IL	Mark A. Kluckman	Mark A. Kluckman	1988	839
176 7/8	30	28	29 5/8	5 4/8	5 4/8	4	4	Unknown	Unknown	R. Rogers and R. Scott	PR 1988	839
176 7/8	27 4/8	27 5/8	21 1/8	4 5/8	4 4/8	5	5	Warren Co., OH	Richard M. Barhorst	Richard M. Barhorst	1990	839
176 7/8	26 7/8	26 6/8	21 3/8	5 5/8	5 4/8	5	5	Saline Co., IL	Edward L. Brown	Edward L. Brown	1991	839
176 7/8	24 1/8	25 7/8	20 7/8	5 1/8	5	6	6	Jackson Co., MI	David M. Lindeman	David M. Lindeman	1991	839
176 7/8	28 1/8	28 6/8	19 1/8	4 7/8	4 7/8	6	5	Qu'Appelle River, SK	W. Leo Bumphrey	W. Leo Bumphrey	1992	839
176 7/8	27 1/8	27 1/8	21 6/8	5 5/8	5 4/8	6	5	Medina Co., OH	Bradley K. Shafer	Bradley K. Shafer	1994	839
176 7/8	25 7/8	25 3/8	17 4/8	4 6/8	5	6	5	Sullivan Co., IN	Larry A. Nash	Larry A. Nash	1995	839
176 6/8	27 1/8	26	20 7/8	5 2/8	5 2/8	5	6	Vilas Co., WI	Porter Dean	Safari North Tax.	1938	856
176 6/8	26 3/8	25	19	5 3/8	5 4/8	12	6	Langlade Co., WI	Jack Ryan	LaVern Emerich	1950	856
176 6/8	25 5/8	27 3/8	20 6/8	5 7/8	5 1/8	6	6	Clinton Co., MI	Ray Sadler	Ray Sadler	1963	856
176 6/8	26 3/8	26	19 2/8	4 4/8	4 4/8	6	6	Winona Co., MN	Harry M. Timm	Harry M. Timm	1964	856
176 6/8	26 3/8	26 2/8	18 4/8	5	5 3/8	5	5	Knox Co., NE	Alvin Zimmerman	Spanky Greenville	1966	856
176 6/8	25 2/8	25	23 4/8	4 4/8	4 6/8	6	6	Frankfort, KS	Ray A. Mosher	Ray A. Mosher	1966	856
176 6/8	26 5/8	26 4/8	21 4/8	5 2/8	5 3/8	5	5	Pine Co., MN	Kim Shira	Kim Shira	1977	856
176 6/8	26 4/8	25 6/8	20 2/8	4 6/8	4 7/8	6	6	Muscatine Co., IA	Donald L. McCullough	Donald L. McCullough	1980	856
176 6/8	27	27 7/8	22 2/8	5 5/8	5 7/8	5	5	Buffalo Co., WI	Dean Broberg	Dean Broberg	1985	856

Score	L. Main Beam R	L. Main Beam L	Inside Spread	Circ. R	Circ. L	Pts R	Pts L	Locality	Hunter	Owner	Date	Rank
176 6/8	24 5/8	24 4/8	19 4/8	5	5 3/8	6	6	Miami Co., KS	Richard T. Hale	Richard T. Hale	1985	856
176 6/8	23 6/8	22 3/8	16 2/8	4 1/8	4 1/8	7	7	Idaho Co., ID	Edward D. Moore	Edward D. Moore	1986	856
176 6/8	23 6/8	25 1/8	19 2/8	5 4/8	5 2/8	9	8	Saskatchewan	Unknown	D. Ross Sayrs	1986	856
176 6/8	25	26 1/8	20 5/8	6 2/8	5 7/8	6	6	Adams Co., WI	Mark R. Faber	Mark R. Faber	1987	856
176 6/8	25 6/8	26 5/8	17	5 2/8	5 1/8	7	6	Idaho Co., ID	Frank J. Loughran	Frank J. Loughran	1987	856
176 6/8	26 1/8	23 7/8	20 3/8	5 3/8	5 4/8	5	6	Linn Co., IA	Douglas D. Kriegel	Douglas D. Kriegel	1988	856
176 6/8	26	27 4/8	22 7/8	4 5/8	5 1/8	5	7	McHenry Co., IL	Eugene Melby	Eugene Melby	1988	856
176 6/8	26 2/8	27 4/8	23	5	4 7/8	6	6	Sturgeon River, AB	Michael G. Schmermund	Michael G. Schmermund	1990	856
176 6/8	25 1/8	25 7/8	21 4/8	4 5/8	4 6/8	6	6	Kane Co., IL	Mark O. DuLong	Mark O. DuLong	1991	856
176 6/8	23 7/8	24 6/8	17 6/8	4 5/8	4 4/8	9	7	Moose Mt., SK	Dwight C. Tonn	Dwight C. Tonn	1991	856
176 6/8	27	26 5/8	18 3/8	4 2/8	4 2/8	6	7	Rusk Co., WI	Kent E. Lund	Kent E. Lund	1992	856
176 6/8	27 6/8	28 3/8	18 4/8	5 1/8	5 2/8	5	8	Morris Co., KS	Nathan D. Muncy	Nathan D. Muncy	1992	856
176 6/8	25 1/8	25 2/8	17 6/8	5 6/8	5 3/8	6	6	Van Buren Co., IA	Bruce C. Spiller	Bruce C. Spiller	1995	856
176 6/8	25 6/8	25 4/8	21 1/8	4 6/8	4 6/8	6	7	Bureau Co., IL	John Binz	John Binz	1996	856
176 6/8	26 3/8	26 7/8	23 6/8	6 2/8	5 5/8	7	6	Jefferson Co., IL	Steve S. Shields	Steve S. Shields	1996	856
176 6/8	28 5/8	29 1/8	20	4 6/8	4 7/8	5	6	Jackson Co., MO	Charles H. Williams	Charles H. Williams	1996	856
176 5/8	26 2/8	24 6/8	27 2/8	5	5	6	5	Hayes Co., TX	Bill Kuykendall	Bill Kuykendall	1925	881
176 5/8	23 3/8	24 2/8	16 7/8	4 6/8	4 3/8	9	9	Welsh Co., TX	Antonio Gonzalez	Edmundo R. Gonzalez, Jr.	1929	881
176 5/8	28	23 3/8	21 5/8	4 6/8	4 4/8	7	7	Mifflin Co., PA	John Zerba	Kenneth Zerba	1936	881
176 5/8	25 4/8	28	21 7/8	4 5/8	4 7/8	5	5	Bolivar Co., MS	Sidney D. Sessions	Sidney D. Sessions	1952	881
176 5/8	24 2/8	25 4/8	17 6/8	5	5 1/8	8	8	Washington	Unknown	Jonas Bros. of Seattle	PR 1953	881
176 5/8	27 2/8	24 1/8	20 5/8	5 1/8	5 1/8	5	5	Winona Co., MN	Robert J. Haessig	Robert J. Haessig	1961	881
176 5/8	25	27 4/8	23 2/8	5	5	6	6	Roberts Co., SD	Fred Kuehl	J.D. Andrews	1964	881
176 5/8	26 1/8	25	21 1/8	5 1/8	5	7	7	Rusk Co., SD	Ercel Dustin	Ercel Dustin	1966	881
176 5/8	25 6/8	23 2/8	17 3/8	4 2/8	4 2/8	5	5	Meade Co., SD	Jerry Humble	Jerry Humble	1970	881
176 5/8	25 7/8	26 5/8	21 1/8	6 1/8	6 1/8	6	6	Buffalo, AB	Bob Fraleigh	Bob Fraleigh	1978	881
176 5/8	28 6/8	26 1/8	19 1/8	5 2/8	5 3/8	7	7	Dickinson Co., KS	Robert L. Aldrich	Robert L. Aldrich	1986	881
176 5/8	25	28	19 6/8	5 7/8	5 7/8	7	7	Pigeon Lake, AB	Milton Fawcett	Milton Fawcett	1991	881
176 5/8	25 5/8	24 6/8	18 5/8	4 4/8	4 6/8	6	6	Henderson Co., IL	Quinton R. Koch	Quinton R. Koch	1991	881
176 5/8	26 3/8	26 6/8	20 5/8	5 6/8	5 6/8	9	9	McHenry Co., IL	David J. Binz	David J. Binz	1992	881
175 5/8	25 2/8	28	22 3/8	5 3/8	5 3/8	5	7	Kleberg Co., TX	Donald M. Brock, Jr.	Donald M. Brock, Jr.	1993	881
175 5/8	26	26 3/8	18 3/8	5 6/8	5 5/8	5	5	Grant Co., MN	W.R. Freeburg & C. Adams	William R. Freeburg	1993	881
176 4/8	27	25 2/8	23 5/8	4 7/8	4 5/8	7	7	La Porte Co., IN	Alicia Boguslawski	Alicia Boguslawski	1995	881
176 4/8	27 5/8	26	22 6/8	5 1/8	5 3/8	6	7	Fairfield Co., OH	Harold R. McCafferty	Harold R. McCafferty	1996	881
176 4/8	24 5/8	27	19 4/8	4 5/8	4 5/8	7	7	Charlotte Co., NB	Albert E. Dewar	Albert E. Dewar	1960	899
176 4/8	23 4/8	27 5/8	22	5 3/8	5 5/8	5	6	Esterhazy, SK	Albert Kristoff	Albert Kristoff	1960	899
176 4/8	26 6/8	24 6/8	18 4/8	5 1/8	5 1/8	6	6	Itasca Co., MN	Jim Soukup	Jim Soukup	1960	899
176 4/8	23 5/8	23 4/8	17 4/8	5 4/8	5 3/8	6	6	St. Louis Co., MN	Michael J. Nielsen	Michael J. Nielsen	1962	899
176 4/8	24 2/8	22	19	3 7/8	4 1/8	6	6	Shackelford Co., TX	H.V. Stroud	H.V. Stroud	1964	899
176 4/8	23	26 6/8	16 4/8	4 4/8	4 3/8	6	9	Carrizo Springs, TX	Lin F. Nowotny	Lin F. Nowotny	1966	899
176 4/8	25	23 5/8	19 4/8	4 4/8	4 3/8	7	7	Crawford Co., WI	Louis Franks	Louis Franks	1969	899
176 4/8	26 6/8	25 2/8	26 6/8	4 2/8	4 4/8	6	6	Houston Co., MN	James L. Reinhart	James L. Reinhart	1971	899
176 4/8	27 3/8	23	21 2/8	4 3/8	4 4/8	6	5	Sanders Co., MT	Dallas J.C. Nelson	Dallas J.C. Nelson	1983	899
176 4/8	28	25	19 2/8	4 6/8	4 6/8	7	8	Jim Hogg Co., TX	Picked Up	Eddie Garza	1990	899
176 4/8	25 7/8	27	21 4/8	6	5 1/8	10	10	Davis Co., IA	Jeffrey A. Getz	Jeffrey A. Getz	1991	899
176 4/8	26 1/8	26 6/8	23 6/8	5 4/8	5 1/8	5	6	Todd Co., MN	Walter Zastrow	Walter Zastrow	1991	899
176 4/8	22 6/8	27 3/8	17 6/8	5 3/8	5 2/8	6	6	Turtle Mt., MB	David Murray	David Murray	1992	899

WHITETAIL DEER - TYPICAL ANTLERS

Odocoileus virginianus virginianus and certain related subspecies

Score	Length of Main Beam R	L	Inside Spread	Circumference at Smallest Place Between Burr and First Point R	L	Number of Points R	L	Locality	Hunter	Owner	Date Killed	Rank
176 4/8	27 2/8	26 6/8	20 3/8	5	5	6	5	Linn Co., IA	David E. Heck	David E. Heck	1994	899
176 4/8	27 5/8	28 6/8	21 3/8	5 5/8	5 4/8	8	7	Chisholm, AB	Paul Murray	Paul Murray	1994	899
176 4/8	26	26 4/8	18 4/8	5 3/8	5 3/8	5	6	Duck Mt., MB	Kevin E. Scott	Kevin E. Scott	1996	899
176 3/8	26	26 5/8	20 5/8	5 4/8	5 6/8	7	5	Baraga Co., MI	Paul Korhonen	Paul Korhonen	1945	915
176 3/8	26 1/8	25 5/8	22 4/8	5 7/8	5 6/8	5	6	Koochiching Co., MN	Picked Up	James R. Smith	1957	915
176 3/8	28 1/8	28	19 6/8	5 1/8	4 7/8	7	7	St. Louis Co., MN	Howard Maki	Howard Maki	1958	915
176 3/8	27 7/8	26 3/8	18 5/8	4 7/8	4 7/8	6	6	Cherokee Co., IA	Bob Roberts	Bob Roberts	1963	915
176 3/8	27 2/8	26 3/8	21 1/8	4 6/8	4 5/8	8	7	Otter Tail Co., MN	Steven C. Stinar	Steven C. Stinar	1968	915
176 3/8	25	25 1/8	17 5/8	4 5/8	5 1/8	6	5	Stockton, MB	Robert R. Blain	Robert R. Blain	1977	915
176 3/8	28	27	20 5/8	4 7/8	4 7/8	5	6	Montgomery Co., IA	Stanley D. Means	Stanley D. Means	1977	915
176 3/8	25 1/8	25 3/8	20 2/8	5 1/8	5 2/8	5	7	Wright Co., MO	Mike Napier	Mike Napier	1986	915
176 3/8	26 6/8	25 7/8	18 7/8	5 2/8	5 3/8	5	7	Fremont Co., IA	Scott J. Carnes	Scott J. Carnes	1987	915
176 3/8	25 6/8	25 4/8	20 1/8	4 4/8	4 4/8	6	6	Logan Co., OH	Larry D. Hyzer	Larry D. Hyzer	1987	915
176 3/8	22 3/8	24 5/8	21 7/8	5 2/8	5 1/8	6	6	Champaign Co., OH	David A. Owen	David A. Owen	1988	915
176 3/8	27 2/8	28	20 5/8	5 2/8	5 2/8	4	4	Boulder Co., CO	Picked Up	Michael J. Scrivner	1989	915
176 3/8	24 5/8	24 3/8	17 1/8	4 7/8	4 7/8	7	6	Round Lake, SK	Randy Tulloch	Randy Tulloch	1989	915
176 3/8	27 3/8	26 5/8	21 6/8	5 3/8	5 4/8	5	6	Hamilton Co., IL	Dennis W. Woolard, Jr.	Dennis W. Woolard, Jr.	1989	915
176 3/8	27 3/8	28 4/8	23 3/8	5 2/8	5 2/8	10	10	Cypress Hills, SK	Dwight W. Dobson	Dwight W. Dobson	1990	915
176 3/8	25 4/8	25 5/8	18 1/8	5	5	6	6	Fremont, SK	Earl M. Gilles	Earl M. Gilles	1992	915
176 3/8	28 3/8	24 2/8	18 1/8	5 3/8	5 2/8	8	6	Craven, SK	Steven G. Ries	Steven G. Ries	1993	915
176 3/8	28	28	21 4/8	6 2/8	5 7/8	6	9	Geary Co., KS	Donald J. Ereth	Donald J. Ereth	1994	915
176 3/8	27 4/8	29 3/8	21 3/8	5 2/8	5 1/8	5	6	Marion Co., OH	David B. Lafferty	David B. Lafferty	1994	915
176 3/8	28 4/8	28 3/8	22 3/8	4 7/8	4 6/8	5	5	Rock Island Co., IL	Douglas J. Grudzinski	Douglas J. Grudzinski	1995	915
176 3/8	27 7/8	28 1/8	20 5/8	5 4/8	5 3/8	5	5	Knox Co., IL	Jason McCulloch	Jason McCulloch	1996	915
176 2/8	24 7/8	26 1/8	21	4 1/8	4	6	6	Karnes Co., TX	Gideon Pace	Steve Mansfield	PR 1905	936
176 2/8	25 6/8	28 6/8	25 4/8	4 7/8	5	5	5	Erie Co., NY	Wesley H. Iulg	Wesley H. Iulg	1944	936
176 2/8	25 6/8	25 7/8	20 3/8	5 4/8	5 4/8	7	6	Rappahannock Co., VA	George W. Beahm	George W. Beahm	1959	936
176 2/8	23	25 5/8	18 6/8	5	4 7/8	5	5	Swanson, SK	L.S. Wood	L.S. Wood	1959	936
176 2/8	25 2/8	26 4/8	22 2/8	5	5	6	6	Des Moines Co., IA	Virgil Landrum	Virgil Landrum	1960	936
176 2/8	24 4/8	26 4/8	17 1/8	5 4/8	5 4/8	8	7	Warren Co., NY	Frank Dagles	Frank Dagles	1961	936
176 2/8	28 4/8	27 4/8	25	5 4/8	5 4/8	5	4	Washington Co., NE	Albert Ohrt	Spanky Greenville	1962	936
176 2/8	28 4/8	29 2/8	20 6/8	5 4/8	5 4/8	5	5	Richland Parish, LA	Willard Roberson	Willard Roberson	1968	936
176 2/8	26 1/8	28 5/8	23 2/8	4 3/8	4 3/8	5	5	Houston Co., MN	Harold Kruse	Brant J. Mueller	1975	936
176 2/8	30	28 2/8	23	6 1/8	6 1/8	7	6	Coshocton Co., OH	James R. Gardner	James R. Gardner	1976	936
176 2/8	26 7/8	27 4/8	21 6/8	4 4/8	4 5/8	5	5	St. Louis Co., MN	Picked Up	George W. Flaim	1978	936
176 2/8	24 6/8	24 5/8	19 2/8	4 7/8	4 5/8	5	6	Ravalli Co., MT	Jerry Saunders	William Garbo, Jr.	1981	936

Score	Length R	Length L	Inside Spread	Circ R	Circ L	Pts R	Pts L	Locality	Hunter	Owner	Date	Rank
176 2/8	28	26 4/8	21	5 4/8	5 4/8	8	7	Macon Co., GA	Charles M. Wilson	Charles M. Wilson	1981	936
176 2/8	28 2/8	27 5/8	21	4 6/8	4 7/8	7	5	Houston Co., MN	John W. Zahrte	John W. Zahrte	1981	936
176 2/8	24 7/8	25 4/8	20 6/8	4 7/8	4 5/8	6	6	Troup Co., GA	Claude A. McKibben, Jr.	James E. Lasater	1984	936
176 2/8	26 2/8	26 3/8	20 4/8	5 1/8	4 6/8	5	5	Litchfield Co., CT	Frederick H. Clymer	Frederick H. Clymer	1987	936
176 2/8	28 3/8	29 4/8	23 2/8	6 2/8	5 2/8	5	6	Aroostook Co., ME	Daniel T. Geary	Daniel T. Geary	1989	936
176 2/8	24 5/8	23 1/8	15 6/8	4 6/8	6	7	7	Converse Co., WY	Basil C. Bradbury	Basil C. Bradbury	1990	936
176 2/8	27	27	21 4/8	5 4/8	4 6/8	5	5	Dauphin, MB	Unknown	Wayne Selby	PR 1990	936
176 2/8	25 5/8	27 4/8	18	4 7/8	5 2/8	7	7	Bon Homme Co., SD	Lonnie L. Huber	Lonnie L. Huber	1991	936
176 2/8	26 2/8	25 5/8	18 4/8	5 4/8	4 7/8	6	8	Brown Co., IL	Picked Up	William S. Boyd	PR 1992	936
176 2/8	25 6/8	26 2/8	20 6/8	5 6/8	5 4/8	6	5	Lucas Co., IA	Corey E. Gwinn	Corey E. Gwinn	1992	936
176 2/8	28	26	24 2/8	5 5/8	5 6/8	6	5	Nuckolls Co., NE	Tim Brewster	Tim Brewster	1993	936
176 2/8	26 6/8	26 3/8	20 3/8	5 2/8	5 5/8	5	6	Moose Creek, SK	Joseph Romer	Joseph Romer	1993	936
176 2/8	23 6/8	23 3/8	19 4/8	4 5/8	5 3/8	8	7	Walworth Co., WI	Thomas G. Senft	Thomas G. Senft	1993	936
176 2/8	24 7/8	24 1/8	15 6/8	5	4 5/8	8	7	St. Louis Co., MN	Brian J. Keating	Brian J. Keating	1995	936
176 2/8	27 1/8	26 2/8	24	4 2/8	5	6	6	Washington Co., KS	Roger W. Novak	Roger W. Novak	1995	936
176 2/8	24 3/8	24 3/8	18 2/8	5 4/8	4 3/8	5	5	Monroe Co., IN	Chad A. DeGolyer	Chad A. DeGolyer	1996	936
176 1/8	28	28	21 2/8	6 7/8	5 4/8	6	9	Florence Co., WI	Theron A. Meyer, Sr.	Theron A. Meyer, Sr.	1943	964
176 1/8	25 3/8	25 3/8	19 7/8	5 7/8	6 6/8	7	7	Goodhue Co., MN	David Anderson	David Anderson	1960	964
176 1/8	25 6/8	26 1/8	20 5/8	5 5/8	5 6/8	5	5	Door Co., WI	Unknown	Steve Pluff	PR 1973	964
176 1/8	25 1/8	26 1/8	24 1/8	4 4/8	5 5/8	5	6	Assiniboine River, MB	G.G. Graham	G.G. Graham	1984	964
176 1/8	25 7/8	25 7/8	19 1/8	5 3/8	4 4/8	5	6	Grunthal, MB	Edwin Froese	Edwin Froese	1986	964
176 1/8	23 4/8	25 5/8	21 1/8	4 4/8	5 2/8	9	5	Pierce Lake, SK	Edwin Johnson	Edwin Johnson	1989	964
176 1/8	24 1/8	24 1/8	19 5/8	5 4/8	4 7/8	5	5	Jackson Co., IA	Roy O. Lindemier	Roy O. Lindemier	1990	964
176 1/8	27 1/8	27 4/8	23 5/8	4 7/8	5	6	5	Johnson Co., MO	James A. Stephens	James A. Stephens	1990	964
176 1/8	28 4/8	26	23 6/8	5	5	5	5	Randolph Co., GA	Jeff Hill	Jeff Hill	1991	964
176 1/8	25 7/8	25 7/8	18 5/8	5 1/8	5 2/8	6	6	Brown Co., KS	Dennis P. Finger	Dennis P. Finger	1992	964
176 1/8	26 6/8	26 6/8	19 5/8	5 2/8	5 5/8	6	6	Jackson Co., IL	Aaron E. Harsy	Aaron E. Harsy	1994	964
176 1/8	30 4/8	30 2/8	20 2/8	5 2/8	5 3/8	5	5	Lucas Co., IA	Justin J. Adams	Justin J. Adams	1995	964
176	28 5/8	29 6/8	17 5/8	5 3/8	3 7/8	8	8	Florence Co., WI	John G. Kozicki	Vernon J. Kozicki	1936	976
176	24 4/8	24 7/8	17 4/8	4	4 4/8	8	6	Bradford Co., PA	Clyde H. Rinehuls	Clyde H. Rinehuls	1944	976
176	28 3/8	28 5/8	17 6/8	4 4/8	5 2/8	5	5	Koochiching Co., MN	John A. Lind	John M. Lind	1956	976
176	27	29	20 4/8	5 6/8	5 6/8	5	5	Dawson Co., NE	Unknown	Spanky Greenville	1957	976
176	23 7/8	27	19 3/8	5 6/8	5 3/8	6	7	Lyon Co., IA	Duane K. Rohde	Duane K. Rohde	1964	976
176	26	23 7/8	20	5 4/8	4 7/8	5	5	Veblen, SD	Don W. Cimburek	Don W. Cimburek	1966	976
176	24 5/8	24 5/8	21 6/8	4 7/8	5	5	5	Russell Co., KS	Don Mai	Don Mai	1981	976
176	26	26 3/8	18 4/8	6 2/8	4 7/8	6	5	Racine Co., WI	Daniel P. Cramer	Daniel P. Cramer	1985	976
176	26 4/8	26 4/8	20	4 6/8	5 1/8	5	7	Nemaha Co., KS	Joseph L. Schmelzle	Joseph L. Schmelzle	1985	976
176	26 2/8	26 3/8	16	5 1/8	4 3/8	6	6	Goodhue Co., MN	Martin H. Bollum	Martin H. Bollum	1986	976
176	23 7/8	23 7/8	24 5/8	4 4/8	5 4/8	5	5	Ghost Lake, AB	Viktor Nill	Viktor Nill	1989	976
176	24 1/8	24 1/8	27 3/8	5 3/8	4 7/8	5	5	Duck Lake, SK	Larry Attig	Larry Attig	1993	976
176	27 3/8	27 3/8	20 7/8	4 7/8	5	7	7	Redwater, AB	Tim T. Bourne	Tim T. Bourne	1993	976
176	26 7/8	26 6/8	21 2/8	4 2/8	4 7/8	4	6	Butler Co., OH	Chris Allen	Chris Allen	1994	976
176	30	30	18 7/8	5 6/8	4 2/8	5	5	Pickens Co., SC	William C. Wyatt	William C. Wyatt	1994	976
176	27 2/8	26 6/8	19	5 3/8	5 6/8	6	6	Buffalo Co., WI	Guy A. Hansen	Guy A. Hansen	1995	976
176	26 6/8	27 2/8	19	4 6/8	5 3/8	5	7	Butler Co., OH	Rick Sizemore	Rick Sizemore	1995	976
176	27 2/8	28 5/8	27	5 3/8	4 6/8	7	8	Montgomery Co., MO	Dave Knoepflein	Dave Knoepflein	1996	976
175 7/8	24 3/8	27	20 5/8	4 3/8	4 3/8	5	6	Kinney Co., TX	Walter Griener	John L. Stein	1935	994

315

WHITETAIL DEER - TYPICAL ANTLERS

Odocoileus virginianus virginianus and certain related subspecies

Score	Length of Main Beam R	L	Inside Spread	Circumference at Smallest Place Between Burr and First Point R	L	Number of Points R	L	Locality	Hunter	Owner	Date Killed	Rank
175 7/8	26 1/8	26 4/8	20 3/8	4 3/8	4 3/8	7	7	Lewis Co., NY	Andrew Lustyik	Andrew F. Lustyik	1942	994
175 7/8	23	23 1/8	16 7/8	5 1/8	5 1/8	5	5	Hanley, SK	G. Koyl & W. King	Gavin Koyl	1964	994
175 7/8	24 6/8	25 6/8	17 1/8	4 5/8	4 4/8	5	5	Logan Co., CO	Picked Up	Marvin Gardner	1971	994
175 7/8	26 3/8	26 3/8	17 1/8	4 6/8	4 6/8	6	7	Brooks Co., GA	Joseph J. Freeman	Joseph J. Freeman	1978	994
175 7/8	26 5/8	27	21 7/8	4 3/8	4 3/8	5	6	Swift Co., MN	Kim Manska	Kim Manska	1982	994
175 7/8	27	26 6/8	22 5/8	4 4/8	4 4/8	5	5	Sundre, AB	Russell D. Holmes	Russell D. Holmes	1984	994
175 7/8	27 5/8	27 1/8	22 5/8	6 5/8	6 2/8	9	7	Pouce Coupe River, BC	Dale Callahan	Dale Callahan	1986	994
175 7/8	25 6/8	25 5/8	21 2/8	6	5 6/8	6	6	Haron Co., OH	Royal R. Chisholm	Royal R. Chisholm	1988	994
175 7/8	25 2/8	25 1/8	16 3/8	5	5 2/8	6	5	Barrhead, AB	Hugh L. Schmaus	Hugh L. Schmaus	1990	994
175 7/8	28 3/8	27 7/8	22 5/8	5	4 6/8	6	6	Washburn Co., WI	Terry A. Severson	Terry A. Severson	1991	994
175 7/8	26 1/8	26 4/8	19 5/8	5 2/8	5 3/8	5	5	Huron Co., OH	Donald W. Howard	Donald W. Howard	1992	994
175 7/8	23 4/8	25	17 1/8	5 2/8	5 2/8	6	6	Johnson Co., IL	Thomas F. Byrne	Thomas F. Byrne	1993	994
175 7/8	24 4/8	25 1/8	17 5/8	5 1/8	5 1/8	5	5	Putnam Co., IN	Picked Up	Terry Outcalt	1993	994
175 7/8	24 7/8	25 2/8	19 2/8	5 4/8	5 2/8	9	6	Bennett Lake, ON	Randy M. Love	Randy M. Love	1994	994
175 7/8	24 3/8	27	18	4 5/8	4 5/8	5	6	Buffalo Co., WI	Larry L. Bloom	Larry L. Bloom	1995	994
175 7/8	26 2/8	24 6/8	19 1/8	4 6/8	5 2/8	5	6	Boone Co., IA	Monte A. Carlson	Monte A. Carlson	1995	994
175 7/8	26 1/8	25 1/8	20 7/8	4 5/8	4 6/8	8	8	Pulaski Co., AR	Charles L. Marcum, Jr.	Charles L. Marcum, Jr.	1996	994
175 6/8	25 6/8	26	20 2/8	4	4	6	6	Webb Co., TX	William Bretthauer, Sr.	George H. Glass	1915	1012
175 6/8	21 6/8	23 2/8	18	4 4/8	4 5/8	6	6	St. Onge, SD	Don Ridley	Don Ridley	1957	1012
175 6/8	25 3/8	26 1/8	19 6/8	5 3/8	5 3/8	5	5	Southey, SK	J.A. Maier	J.A. Maier	1958	1012
175 6/8	26 4/8	25 3/8	16 7/8	5 4/8	5 4/8	8	6	Cuming Co., NE	Herman Blankenau	Herman Blankenau	1963	1012
175 6/8	22 6/8	24 5/8	20	5	5	6	6	Burleigh Co., ND	Earl Haakenson	Earl Haakenson	1963	1012
175 6/8	29 3/8	29 5/8	28 4/8	6	6	5	7	Randolph Co., IL	Picked Up	Larry L. Huffman	1965	1012
175 6/8	26 5/8	27 2/8	19 6/8	4 6/8	4 7/8	6	7	Cypress River, MB	Murray Jones	Murray Jones	1973	1012
175 6/8	26 4/8	27 6/8	20 2/8	5 2/8	5 2/8	5	5	Nine Mile Brook, NB	Leopold Leblanc	Jim Oickle	1973	1012
175 6/8	24 6/8	24 5/8	17 7/8	6 2/8	6 3/8	8	10	Marshall Co., MN	Ell-Kay B. Foss	Ell-Kay B. Foss	1974	1012
175 6/8	27 2/8	26 7/8	22 6/8	5 4/8	5	7	6	Webb Co., TX	Norman Frede	John L. Stein	1978	1012
175 6/8	25 4/8	26 4/8	20	5 3/8	5 2/8	6	6	Dimmit Co., TX	George E. Light III	George E. Light III	1979	1012
175 6/8	26 2/8	26 5/8	22 4/8	5 1/8	5	5	6	Pope Co., IL	Picked Up	James W. Seets	PR 1982	1012
175 6/8	26 3/8	25	21 4/8	5 4/8	5 5/8	6	6	Crawford Co., WI	David R. Kluesner	David R. Kluesner	1985	1012
175 6/8	26 3/8	24 5/8	19 6/8	5 5/8	5 7/8	5	6	Nemaha Co., KS	Kevin L. Kramer	Kevin L. Kramer	1988	1012
175 6/8	28 6/8	29 1/8	21 4/8	5 7/8	5 5/8	8	8	Williamson Co., IL	Timothy S. Holmes	Timothy S. Holmes	1991	1012
175 6/8	29 5/8	28 6/8	21	5 3/8	5 3/8	5	5	Kent Co., MI	Ronald L. Visser	Ronald L. Visser	1992	1012
175 6/8	30	27 5/8	18 5/8	5 7/8	6	6	6	Montgomery Co., IA	Randy L. Wienhold	Randy L. Wienhold	1992	1012
175 6/8	26	25 4/8	21	4 4/8	4 4/8	6	6	Faribault Co., MN	Lyle D. Ihle	Lyle D. Ihle	1995	1012
175 6/8	26 5/8	26 7/8	18 5/8	4 5/8	4 6/8	6	5	Rock Co., WI	Neil Laube	Neil Laube	1965	1030

Score	Main Beam R	Main Beam L	Inside Spread	Circ. R	Circ. L	Pts. R	Pts. L	Locality	By whom killed	Owner	Date Killed	Rank
175 5/8	26 5/8	25 6/8	17 5/8	5 1/8	5 1/8	5	5	Mellette Co., SD	Ben Krogman	Ben Krogman	1969	1030
175 5/8	27 6/8	27 3/8	19 5/8	4 6/8	4 6/8	6	5	Goodhue Co., MN	Ellsworth Ramseier	Chuck Ramseier	1972	1030
175 5/8	24 7/8	25 1/8	25 1/8	4 4/8	4 4/8	7	7	Lake Co., MT	Kenneth D. Johnson	Kenneth D. Johnson	1974	1030
175 5/8	26	27 4/8	18 1/8	4 4/8	4 6/8	6	5	Allegany Co., NY	William L. Damon	William L. Damon	1981	1030
175 5/8	25 5/8	25	17 7/8	4 5/8	4 5/8	7	6	Benewah Co., ID	Carl Groth	Carl Groth	1982	1030
175 5/8	24 2/8	26	17 1/8	5 1/8	5 1/8	5	6	Unknown	Unknown	Brad Lewis	PR 1985	1030
175 5/8	26	26	20 6/8	4 4/8	4 5/8	6	6	Warren Co., IA	Art L. Daniels	Art L. Daniels	1986	1030
175 5/8	24 1/8	23 4/8	17 3/8	4 6/8	4 6/8	7	7	Woodbury Co., IA	Paul Feddersen	Paul Feddersen	1988	1030
175 5/8	25 5/8	25 6/8	19 3/8	4 1/8	4	7	9	Lucas Co., IA	Dean E. Chandler	Dean E. Chandler	1991	1030
175 5/8	28	28 2/8	21 4/8	5 1/8	5 1/8	6	5	Morgan Co., OH	John E. Hite	John E. Hite	1991	1030
175 5/8	25 3/8	26 3/8	22	5	4 6/8	6	5	Sullivan Co., IN	Steven L. Hobbs	Steven L. Hobbs	1991	1030
175 5/8	26	26	20 5/8	4 6/8	4 6/8	7	7	Big Horn Co., MT	Darell R. Webber	Darell R. Webber	1992	1030
175 5/8	24 6/8	24 6/8	17 5/8	4 6/8	4 5/8	5	5	Pottawatomie Co., KS	Orten L. Dodds	Orten L. Dodds	1993	1030
175 5/8	26 5/8	26 3/8	24 5/8	5 6/8	5 6/8	7	7	Randolph Co., IL	Larry A. Ruebke	Larry A. Ruebke	1994	1030
175 5/8	28 4/8	25 7/8	20 5/8	5 4/8	5 5/8	8	8	Bayfield Co., WI	Lorry A. Hagstrom	Lorry A. Hagstrom	1995	1030
175 4/8	30 5/8	28 6/8	23 3/8	5 5/8	6 1/8	5	5	Bucks Co., PA	Albert J. Muntz	Albert J. Muntz	1830	1047
175 4/8	25 5/8	25	21 2/8	5 2/8	5	6	6	McKean Co., PA	Arthur Young	C.R. Studholme	1954	1047
175 4/8	27	25 4/8	21 2/8	5 1/8	5 1/8	5	5	Pepin Co., WI	Carl E. Frick	Carl E. Frick	1962	1047
175 4/8	25 6/8	25 4/8	25 4/8	6 1/8	5 5/8	5	5	Corning, MO	Orrie L. Schaeffer	Orrie L. Schaeffer	1963	1047
175 4/8	25 5/8	27	20 4/8	4 4/8	4 4/8	5	5	Dodge Co., NE	Leroy W. Ahrndt	Leroy W. Ahrndt	1963	1047
175 4/8	27	29	22 3/8	5 7/8	5 6/8	7	8	Jo Daviess Co., IL	J.O. Engebretson	J.O. Engebretson	1967	1047
175 4/8	30 2/8	27 1/8	21 3/8	5 3/8	5 2/8	6	5	Trigg Co., KY	Picked Up	L.J. Hendon	1973	1047
175 4/8	29	28	20 2/8	5 1/8	5	6	6	Mille Lacs Co., MN	John Krol	Ronald D. Evensen	1973	1047
175 4/8	26 5/8	27 7/8	21	5 1/8	5 1/8	5	5	Renville Co., MN	Larry D. Youngs	Larry D. Youngs	1975	1047
175 4/8	26 7/8	25 7/8	21 2/8	5 1/8	5 1/8	5	5	Winnebago Co., IA	Joel Kingland	Joel Kingland	1983	1047
175 4/8	26 3/8	25 5/8	20 1/8	4 7/8	4 7/8	8	5	Buffalo Co., WI	Picked Up	Charles G. Dienger	1985	1047
175 4/8	25 5/8	26 3/8	16 5/8	5 4/8	5 3/8	7	8	Canaan, NB	Marcel Poirier	Marcel Poirier	1987	1047
175 4/8	26 3/8	25 6/8	16 2/8	5 2/8	4 7/8	7	10	Macon Co., GA	Charles W. Haynie	Charles W. Haynie	1987	1047
175 4/8	26 2/8	26 3/8	19 6/8	5 2/8	5 2/8	6	6	Wabasha Co., MN	Ronald V. Hurlburt	Ronald V. Hurlburt	PR 1989	1047
175 4/8	24 5/8	26 4/8	22 6/8	4 6/8	5 1/8	5	5	Maine	Unknown	Richard Arsenault	1991	1047
175 3/8	25 7/8	27 3/8	22 3/8	5 2/8	5 2/8	6	5	Jo Daviess Co., IL	Richard J. McCartin, Sr.	Richard J. McCartin, Sr.	1991	1066
175 3/8	26 4/8	26 4/8	22 3/8	5	5	5	7	Logan Co., KY	Mark H. Hall	Mark H. Hall	1992	1066
175 3/8	26 5/8	26 7/8	21 2/8	4 5/8	4 5/8	5	5	Wayne Co., IN	Michael H. Baker	Michael H. Baker	1993	1066
175 3/8	25 1/8	25 2/8	23 4/8	5	4 6/8	5	5	Houston Co., MN	Wesley Lapham	Wesley Lapham	1993	1066
175 3/8	30 1/8	30 4/8	23 4/8	4 6/8	5	9	9	Wayne Co., IL	Donald L. Sutton	Donald L. Sutton	1994	1066
175 3/8	26 5/8	26 5/8	19 3/8	5 2/8	4 5/8	6	6	Endeavour, SK	Alfred Norman	Terry L. Amos	1954	1066
175 3/8	26 1/8	25 4/8	23 3/8	5 5/8	5 2/8	5	5	Bridgeford, SK	Elgin T. Gates	Elgin T. Gates	1958	1066
175 3/8	27 1/8	26 6/8	18 4/8	5 2/8	5 5/8	5	5	Worth Co., GA	Picked Up	L. Edwin Massey	1962	1066
175 3/8	25 2/8	25 4/8	20 1/8	5 2/8	5 2/8	6	6	Gallia Co., OH	Jack Auxier	Jack Auxier	1969	1066
175 3/8	24 5/8	25 2/8	20 4/8	5 5/8	5 2/8	5	5	Williamson Co., IL	Lewis F. Simon	Lewis F. Simon	1973	1066
175 3/8	24	22 2/8	21 4/8	4 7/8	4 7/8	6	6	Monroe Co., OH	David Mancano	David Mancano	1976	1066
175 3/8	29 1/8	28 7/8	18 1/8	5 2/8	5 2/8	8	6	Wright Co., IA	Picked Up	Ron Schaumburg	1976	1066
175 3/8	25	25	22 3/8	4 1/8	4 2/8	6	6	Dimmit Co., TX	Betsy Campbell	Betsy Campbell	1978	1066
175 3/8	29 6/8	28 5/8	17 6/8	4 6/8	4 6/8	6	5	Todd Co., KY	Gary W. Crafton	Gary W. Crafton	1981	1066
175 3/8	28 3/8	23 2/8	16 3/8	4 4/8	4 1/8	6	6	Carroll Co., IA	Edward L. Golay	Edward L. Golay	1984	1066
175 3/8	22 4/8	23 2/8	17 7/8	4 2/8	4 1/8	6	6	White Co., AR	Jerry Parish	Jerry Parish	1984	1066
175 3/8	26	25 4/8	17 7/8	5 3/8	5 3/8	6	5	Clark Co., IL	Gary L. Lovell	Gary L. Lovell	1986	1066

WHITETAIL DEER - TYPICAL ANTLERS

Odocoileus virginianus virginianus and certain related subspecies

Score	Length of Main Beam R	L	Inside Spread	Circumference at Smallest Place Between Burr and First Point R	L	Number of Points R	L	Locality	Hunter	Owner	Date Killed	Rank
175 3/8	26	25 5/8	18 7/8	5 6/8	5 7/8	5	5	Carberry, MB	H. & B. Calvert	H. & B. Calvert	1987	1066
175 3/8	25 6/8	26 1/8	22 3/8	4 7/8	5 1/8	6	7	Collingsworth Co., TX	Eugene Hanna	John L. Stein	1988	1066
175 3/8	27	26 6/8	16 6/8	4 7/8	4 7/8	6	6	Boone Co., IA	James D. Champion	James D. Champion	1991	1066
175 3/8	27 2/8	27 2/8	19 3/8	5	4 7/8	6	6	Worcester Co., MA	Thomas W. Bombard	Thomas W. Bombard	1992	1066
175 3/8	28 4/8	29 2/8	20 5/8	4 6/8	4 6/8	5	5	Mississippi Co., AR	Luther Gifford	Luther Gifford	1994	1066
175 3/8	25 4/8	25 5/8	20 1/8	5	5 1/8	5	5	Basin Lake, SK	Kurt R. Moorman	Kurt R. Moorman	1996	1066
175 2/8	25 5/8	25 5/8	19 4/8	4 4/8	4 6/8	5	5	Bayfield Co., WI	Bill Holiday	Douglas R. Plourde	PR 1920	1084
175 2/8	22 7/8	22 7/8	19	4 5/8	4 5/8	6	6	Encinal, TX	W.S. Benson, Sr.	W.S. Benson III	1928	1084
175 2/8	26 4/8	26 3/8	21 6/8	4 5/8	4 5/8	6	6	Lake Co., MN	John Brassill	Lorraine Brassill	1951	1084
175 2/8	27 2/8	27 3/8	15 4/8	5 2/8	6	6	8	Cherokee Co., IA	Unknown	H. James Reimer	1954	1084
175 2/8	24 2/8	24 6/8	20	4 2/8	4 2/8	6	6	Aitkin Co., MN	Terry Kullhem	Terry Kullhem	1958	1084
175 2/8	27 3/8	27 7/8	22 4/8	5 1/8	5	6	7	Kittson Co., MN	Fred Bloomquist	Gordon Johnson	1962	1084
175 2/8	24	23 6/8	19 6/8	5 4/8	5 5/8	6	5	Qu'Appelle, SK	Douglas Garden	Douglas Garden	1965	1084
175 2/8	30 3/8	22 6/8	21 2/8	5 2/8	5 1/8	7	5	Clinton Co., IN	William W. Cripe	William W. Cripe	1974	1084
175 2/8	26 2/8	26 2/8	21	4 4/8	4 3/8	6	6	Texas	Elmo Wilson	Joe B. Wilson	PR 1975	1084
175 2/8	28 1/8	28 6/8	17 6/8	5 2/8	5 2/8	6	5	Val Marie, SK	Leon Perrault	Leon Perrault	1977	1084
175 2/8	26 1/8	25 6/8	21 1/8	5 1/8	5 2/8	8	6	Wilkinson Co., MS	Johnnie J. Leake, Jr.	Johnnie J. Leake, Jr.	1978	1084
175 2/8	28 2/8	28 3/8	19 6/8	5 1/8	5 2/8	7	5	Fulton Co., IN	Larry A. Croxton	Larry A. Croxton	1984	1084
175 2/8	27 1/8	27	19	6	6 1/8	5	5	Union Co., IL	Randy Edmonds	Randy Edmonds	1984	1084
175 2/8	25	24 4/8	17	4 7/8	5	6	6	Russell, MB	Emile DeCorby	Emile DeCorby	1986	1084
175 2/8	25 3/8	26 3/8	23 4/8	5 5/8	5 7/8	6	6	Krydor, SK	Lorne M. Shewchuk	Lorne M. Shewchuk	1986	1084
175 2/8	23 2/8	24 1/8	19 6/8	4 7/8	4 5/8	5	5	Mayerthorpe, AB	Gregory Graff	Gregory Graff	1987	1084
175 2/8	25	25 1/8	18 6/8	5	5	5	5	Aitkin Co., MN	Picked Up	Steven M. Landrus	1988	1084
175 2/8	30	28 3/8	22	6 1/8	6 1/8	8	7	Schuyler Co., IL	Rodney C. Chute	Rodney C. Chute	1989	1084
175 2/8	26 6/8	27 4/8	23	5 1/8	5 3/8	6	6	Henry Co., IL	Bradley DeMay	Bradley DeMay	1989	1084
175 2/8	28 6/8	30 7/8	19 2/8	4 7/8	4 7/8	5	5	Van Buren Co., MI	Daryl D. Kovach	Daryl D. Kovach	1989	1084
175 2/8	25 6/8	26 2/8	19 5/8	4 3/8	4 4/8	5	7	Jo Daviess Co., IL	Michael J. Traum	Michael J. Traum	1989	1084
175 2/8	25 2/8	26 1/8	20 2/8	5 2/8	5 2/8	5	5	Ohio Co., KY	James B. Wettstain	James B. Wettstain	1989	1084
175 2/8	27 1/8	27 2/8	21 1/8	5 4/8	5 4/8	9	9	Greene Co., IL	Picked Up	Mark B. Thompson	1991	1084
175 2/8	25 6/8	26 7/8	15 2/8	4 4/8	4 4/8	6	6	Frio Co., TX	India N. Shackelford	India N. Shackelford	1992	1084
175 2/8	24 2/8	23 5/8	18 1/8	5 3/8	5 4/8	7	8	Pembina River, AB	Curtis R. Siegfried	Curtis R. Siegfried	1992	1084
175 2/8	26 3/8	25 4/8	19 5/8	5 1/8	5 3/8	8	7	Meadow Lake, SK	Joseph V. Caccamo, Jr.	Joseph V. Caccamo, Jr.	1995	1084
175 2/8	27 7/8	28 4/8	18 4/8	4 6/8	5 2/8	5	5	Meade Co., KY	David M. Jupin	David M. Jupin	1995	1084
175 2/8	26 5/8	28 3/8	21 4/8	5 2/8	5 2/8	5	5	Clayton Co., IA	Thomas J. Shea	Thomas J. Shea	1995	1084
175 1/8	28	27 6/8	25	4 7/8	4 6/8	8	7	Waldo Co., ME	Unknown	Kenneth T. Winters	1924	1112
175 1/8	26 2/8	27 2/8	19 5/8	4 4/8	4 7/8	5	5	Alger Co., MI	Warren Beebe	Donald J. Docking	1936	1112

Score								Locality			Date	Rank
175 1/8	26 7/8	25 7/8	17 4/8	5 1/8	5 1/8	5	6	Taylor Co., WI	Jack L. Dittrich	Jack L. Dittrich	1945	1112
175 1/8	23 5/8	22 7/8	22 3/8	5 5/8	5 6/8	5	5	Chedderville, AB	Larry Trimble	Larry Trimble	1963	1112
175 1/8	25 5/8	25 5/8	22 1/8	4 5/8	4 5/8	5	5	Gerald, SK	Ken Cherewka	Ken Cherewka	1964	1112
175 1/8	27 4/8	28 5/8	22 3/8	4 6/8	4 7/8	5	7	Roberts Co., SD	Rudy Duwenhoegger, Jr.	Rudy Duwenhoegger, Jr.	1966	1112
175 1/8	25 6/8	27	20 2/8	5	5	8	7	Menominee Co., WI	Gerald Ponfil	Gerald Ponfil	1968	1112
175 1/8	25 6/8	25 2/8	16 7/8	5 3/8	5 3/8	6	7	Howard Co., IA	Russell L. Stevenson, Jr.	Russell L. Stevenson, Jr.	1971	1112
173 1/8	25 7/8	26 5/8	22 4/8	5 1/8	5 1/8	6	6	Sac Co., IA	Randy J. Bentsen	Randy J. Bentsen	1973	1112
173 1/8	25 5/8	25 5/8	24 2/8	4 7/8	4 7/8	6	5	Lincoln Co., MN	Robert R. Bushman	Robert R. Bushman	1973	1112
175 1/8	27 1/8	25 5/8	18 3/8	5	5	5	6	Houston Co., MN	Craig F. Swenson	Craig F. Swenson	1973	1112
175 1/8	24 7/8	26 1/8	20 7/8	4 4/8	4 4/8	7	6	Lac qui Parle Co., MN	Harold Kittelson	Harold Kittelson	1976	1112
175 1/8	25 4/8	24 5/8	19 7/8	5 1/8	5 2/8	5	6	Shaunavon, SK	Richard Klink	Richard Klink	1981	1112
175 1/8	22 1/8	22 7/8	20 5/8	5 2/8	5	6	6	Marinette Co., WI	John Nielson	John Nielson	1983	1112
175 1/8	27 3/8	27 1/8	21 2/8	6	5 7/8	6	6	Wetzel Co., WV	Matthew Scheibelhood	Matthew Scheibelhood	1984	1112
175 1/8	23 7/8	24 4/8	17 3/8	4 4/8	4 5/8	5	6	Kings Co., NB	Wayne F. Anderson	Wayne F. Anderson	1987	1112
175 1/8	27 5/8	27 1/8	19 6/8	5 5/8	5 3/8	6	7	Marquette Co., MI	Andrew E. Cook II	Andrew E. Cook II	1987	1112
175 1/8	27 3/8	27 6/8	20 7/8	5 4/8	5 5/8	6	7	Des Moines Co., IA	Gordon F. Roebeck	Gordon F. Roebeck	1987	1112
175 1/8	24 5/8	25 4/8	17 5/8	5 4/8	5 4/8	7	5	Witchekan Lake, SK	Brent A. Smith	Brent A. Smith	1987	1112
175 1/8	27 5/8	26 4/8	17 2/8	4 4/8	4 6/8	5	8	Crawford Co., IA	Kermit Greenstreet	Kermit Greenstreet	1989	1112
175 1/8	25 1/8	24 5/8	23 7/8	6 2/8	6 2/8	8	6	Otero Co., CO	Kenny D. Mills	Kenny D. Mills	1992	1112
175 1/8	23	23 7/8	17 1/8	5	5 1/8	5	5	Loon Lake, SK	Thomas P. Shields	Thomas P. Shields	1992	1112
175 1/8	26 3/8	26 2/8	19 7/8	5 1/8	5 2/8	9	9	Butler Co., KS	Paul E. Kemp	Paul E. Kemp	1993	1112
175 1/8	27 1/8	28 2/8	24 3/8	4 2/8	4 3/8	7	6	Penobscot Co., ME	Peter A. Duncombe	Peter A. Duncombe	1994	1112
175 1/8	26 6/8	29	19 7/8	5	5	5	9	Cole Co., MO	Brian L. Bruemmer	Brian L. Bruemmer	1995	1112
175 1/8	27	26 7/8	20 1/8	5 6/8	5 7/8	7	6	Scott Co., IA	Jeffrey R. Coonts	Jeffrey R. Coonts	1996	1112
175 1/8	26 4/8	25 5/8	17 3/8	5	5	6	6	Jackfish Lake, SK	Dan Fitch	Dan Fitch	1996	1112
175	28 7/8	29 3/8	19 5/8	4 3/8	4 3/8	5	5	Wells Co., TX	Ryan C. Howard	Ryan C. Howard	1996	1112
175	26 2/8	26	18 4/8	4 4/8	4 5/8	5	6	Webb Co., TX	Leslie G. Fisher	Leslie G. Fisher, Jr.	1935	1140
175	28	27 1/8	18 6/8	4 6/8	5	6	7	Minnesota	Floyd Baade	Maverick Russell	1944	1140
175	28 6/8	29 3/8	22 2/8	5 1/8	5 2/8	7	6	Pope Co., MN	Picked Up	R. Benson & K. Wick	1957	1140
175	25 6/8	25 1/8	21	3 7/8	4 4/8	5	5	New Salem, ND	John T. Cartwright	John T. Cartwright	1957	1140
175	24 3/8	22 3/8	18 6/8	4 7/8	4 4/8	5	7	La Salle Co., TX	Leonard W. Bouldin	Leonard W. Bouldin	1972	1140
175	28 4/8	28 3/8	18 2/8	4 4/8	4 4/8	7	6	La Salle Co., TX	Phil Lyne	Phil Lyne	1972	1140
175	23 2/8	24	19 6/8	5 2/8	5 1/8	5	5	Harrison Co., MO	Carl J. Graham	Carl J. Graham	1973	1140
175	28 2/8	27 5/8	18 1/8	4 7/8	5	5	6	Louisa Co., IA	Glen D. Brandt	Glen D. Brandt	1974	1140
175	28 5/8	29 1/8	21 5/8	5	5 1/8	5	7	Henry Co., IA	Richard Doggett	Richard Doggett	1975	1140
175	25 3/8	25 4/8	19 2/8	5 4/8	5 4/8	5	6	Itasca Co., MN	David A. Frandsen	David A. Frandsen	1982	1140
175	31 3/8	31	23 2/8	5 1/8	5 1/8	6	7	Mower Co., MN	Scott R. Lau	Scott R. Lau	1983	1140
175	26	27 4/8	21	5 4/8	5 4/8	6	5	Jim Hogg Co., TX	Carl D. Ellis	Lee H. Lytton, Jr.	1984	1140
175	25 3/8	24 3/8	17 5/8	5 2/8	5 2/8	7	5	Hardin Co., OH	Roger E. Titus	Roger E. Titus	1988	1140
175	27	27	21	4 1/8	4 3/8	5	7	Riverdale, MB	David Hofer, Jr.	David Hofer, Jr.	1989	1140
175	27 6/8	28 6/8	19	4 6/8	5 3/8	6	6	Lee Co., IA	Stephen D. McKeehan, Jr.	Stephen D. McKeehan, Jr.	1989	1140
175	26 3/8	25 4/8	17	5 3/8	5 3/8	6	7	Bureau Co., IL	Paul S. Cobane III	Paul S. Cobane III	1990	1140
175	26 5/8	26 5/8	19 2/8	4 5/8	4 5/8	6	6	Rochester, AB	Terry Hill	Terry Hill	1991	1140
175	27	27 7/8	21	5	5 1/8	6	7	Dubuque Co., IA	Lawrence E. Blatz	Lawrence E. Blatz	1992	1140
175	27 4/8	27 7/8	21	5 1/8	5	7	9	Stearns Co., MN	Gregory M.J. Gunnerson	Gregory M.J. Gunnerson	1992	1140
175	26 2/8	28 2/8	22	5	5	5	5	Bjork Lake, SK	Don C. Wright	James E. Nelson	1992	1140
175	25 2/8	25 2/8	18 2/8	5 3/8	5 4/8	7	7	McKenzie Co., ND	Larry D. Schultz	Larry D. Schultz	1992	1140

WHITETAIL DEER - TYPICAL ANTLERS

Odocoileus virginianus virginianus and certain related subspecies

Score	Length of Main Beam R	L	Inside Spread	Circumference at Smallest Place Between Burr and First Point R	L	Number of Points R	L	Locality	Hunter	Owner	Date Killed	Rank
175	24 6/8	25 1/8	19 6/8	4 4/8	4 3/8	6	8	Maverick Co., TX	William M. Wheless III	William M. Wheless III	1992	1140
175	25 3/8	25 4/8	17 4/8	4	4 1/8	6	6	Maverick Co., TX	Gary L. Braun	Gary L. Braun	1993	1140
175	28 3/8	28 5/8	21	5 4/8	5 3/8	5	7	Schuyler Co., IL	Marc S. Anthony	Marc S. Anthony	1995	1140
175	27 6/8	26 6/8	21 2/8	4 6/8	4 6/8	6	6	Clayton Co., IA	Clifton L. Kauffman	Clifton L. Kauffman	1996	1140
174 7/8	24 3/8	24 2/8	23 6/8	4 7/8	4 7/8	7	7	Delta Co., MI	Will Wellman	Delor J. Wellman	1930	1165
174 7/8	26 5/8	25	22 6/8	5 3/8	5 4/8	6	9	Rivers, MB	N. Manchur	N. Manchur	1954	1165
174 7/8	28 1/8	28 1/8	21 3/8	5	5	4	4	Burnett Co., WI	Myles T. Keller	Myles T. Keller	1977	1165
174 7/8	25 2/8	25 5/8	16 5/8	4 4/8	5	6	6	Fillmore Co., MN	Daniel M. Hansen	Daniel M. Hansen	1979	1165
174 7/8	25 5/8	25 6/8	21 3/8	4 7/8	4 6/8	5	6	Jo Daviess Co., IL	W.V. Patrick	Jerry Patrick	1983	1165
174 7/8	25 1/8	25 1/8	20 6/8	4 1/8	4 3/8	8	7	Polk Co., TX	Charlie L. Albertson	Charlie L. Albertson	1984	1165
174 7/8	26 1/8	26 1/8	18 4/8	5 1/8	5 1/8	7	6	Stevens Co., WA	Clifton W. Hamilton	Clifton W. Hamilton	1990	1165
174 7/8	23 3/8	23 5/8	16 7/8	4 3/8	4 4/8	5	5	Dent Co., MO	Thomas P. Wylie	Thomas P. Wylie	1990	1165
174 7/8	27 5/8	27 5/8	20 1/8	4 3/8	4 3/8	6	6	Clinton Co., IL	Mark A. Porter	Mark A. Porter	1991	1165
174 7/8	28 3/8	28 6/8	18 7/8	4 3/8	4 3/8	7	5	Warren Co., IA	Picked Up	John I. Kunert	PR 1992	1165
174 7/8	25 7/8	26 4/8	19 2/8	5 1/8	4 7/8	5	6	Washtenaw Co., MI	Michael F. Burger	Michael F. Burger	1993	1165
174 7/8	25 3/8	25 1/8	17 5/8	5 3/8	5 2/8	5	6	Scott Co., IN	Henry E. Reynolds	Henry E. Reynolds	1994	1165
174 7/8	26 1/8	25 7/8	19 5/8	5 1/8	5 2/8	5	5	Woods Co., OK	Eddie Mustard	Eddie Mustard	1995	1165
174 7/8	22	22 3/8	18 5/8	5 3/8	5 4/8	6	6	Langbank, SK	Allan Brehaut	Allan Brehaut	1996	1165
174 6/8	26 2/8	27 4/8	21	5 6/8	5 6/8	8	6	Hayward, WI	Bill Metcalf	John Metcalf	1924	1179
174 6/8	27 2/8	29 1/8	21 2/8	5 1/8	5	5	5	Coahoma Co., MS	O.P. Gilbert	O.P. Gilbert	1960	1179
174 6/8	23 6/8	24 4/8	17 5/8	6	5 6/8	6	7	Lancaster Co., NE	Vaughn Wright	Phillip Wright	1960	1179
174 6/8	28 4/8	29	18 6/8	5 2/8	5 2/8	7	7	Essex Co., NY	Richard Olcott	Richard Olcott	1967	1179
174 6/8	24 6/8	24 2/8	18 2/8	4 4/8	4 4/8	6	6	Isanti Co., MN	Larry Roos	Larry Roos	1971	1179
174 6/8	28 3/8	27 6/8	21	4 6/8	4 5/8	5	5	Maine	Unknown	Warren H. Delaware	PR 1977	1179
174 6/8	24 4/8	24 3/8	19 4/8	5 2/8	5 1/8	9	9	Unknown	Unknown	Gerald Hillman	PR 1978	1179
174 6/8	27 2/8	27 2/8	21 2/8	5 1/8	5 1/8	8	7	Clayton Co., IA	James Trappe	James Trappe	1980	1179
174 6/8	26 5/8	26 1/8	20 1/8	4 4/8	4 6/8	6	5	Talbot Co., GA	Harold Cole, Sr.	Harold Cole, Sr.	1985	1179
174 6/8	27 4/8	28	19 4/8	5 2/8	5 3/8	6	5	Lake William, NS	Neil G. Oickle	Neil G. Oickle	1985	1179
174 6/8	25 5/8	24	18	4 7/8	5	6	6	Fisher Branch, MB	Paul Sanduliak	Paul Sanduliak	1985	1179
174 6/8	24 6/8	26 3/8	21 3/8	5 2/8	5 2/8	5	6	Shannon Co., MO	Picked Up	Scott D. Lindsey	1992	1179
174 6/8	23 3/8	24 4/8	23	5 3/8	5 2/8	5	5	Lincoln Co., MT	Daniel P. Murray	Daniel P. Murray	1993	1179
174 6/8	26 6/8	26	20 6/8	4 6/8	4 5/8	6	5	Jo Daviess Co., IL	Steven C. Rosenthal	Steven C. Rosenthal	1993	1179
174 6/8	23 3/8	23 7/8	16	4 7/8	4 7/8	6	6	Coahuila, MX	Gustavo Garza	Gustavo Garza	1994	1179
174 6/8	26 7/8	26 7/8	20	5	5	5	5	Fayette Co., IA	Gerald E. Gress	Gerald E. Gress	1995	1179
174 6/8	28 7/8	26 3/8	20 3/8	4 6/8	4 7/8	6	7	Medina Co., OH	Charles M. Hummel	Charles M. Hummel	1996	1179
174 6/8	27 2/8	26 7/8	17	4 3/8	4 4/8	6	7	Allamakee Co., IA	Dave Moritz, Jr.	Dave Moritz, Jr.	1996	1179

Score	Main Beam R	Main Beam L	Inside Spread	Circ. R	Circ. L	Pts R	Pts L	Locality	Hunter	Owner	Date	Rank
174 5/8	27 1/8	27 2/8	20 3/8	4 5/8	4 5/8	5	7	Isanti Co., MN	Unknown	Pete Thiry	PR 1940	1197
174 5/8	25	25 2/8	24 3/8	4 2/8	4 3/8	7	7	Kleberg Co., TX	C.T. Burris	Darrell Pitts	1959	1197
174 5/8	24 2/8	24 3/8	19 6/8	5 4/8	5 1/8	7	6	Manitoba	C.S. Browning	C.S. Browning	1960	1197
174 5/8	25 2/8	21 4/8	18 3/8	5 1/8	4 7/8	5	6	Butler Co., IA	Vernon Simon	Vernon Simon	1972	1197
174 5/8	22 4/8	22 5/8	17 1/8	5	5	7	6	Jefferson Co., KS	Keith D. Hendrix	Keith D. Hendrix	1973	1197
174 5/8	24	28 1/8	18 3/8	4 4/8	4 5/8	5	5	Meeker Co., MN	James L. Mattson	James L. Mattson	1973	1197
174 5/8	29 4/8	26 2/8	21 7/8	6	6	6	9	Otter Tail Co., MN	Oames C. Vonderbruggen	Oames C. Vonderbruggen	1976	1197
174 5/8	26	25 4/8	21 1/8	5 3/8	5 3/8	5	6	Baldonnel, BC	D. Ian Williams	D. Ian Williams	1978	1197
174 5/8	26 4/8	27 5/8	19 5/8	4 7/8	5 1/8	8	5	Des Moines Co., IA	Gene L. McAlister	Gene L. McAlister	1980	1197
174 5/8	27 5/8	25	18 1/8	5 2/8	5 2/8	6	5	Jasper Co., IL	Harold L. Ochs	Harold L. Ochs	1982	1197
174 5/8	25 1/8	28	18 3/8	5 1/8	5 3/8	5	7	Door Co., WI	Patrick D. Madden	Patrick D. Madden	1984	1197
174 5/8	28 2/8	25 3/8	16 5/8	5 3/8	6 5/8	5	5	Livingston Co., MI	Nicholas S. Converse	Nicholas S. Converse	1987	1197
174 5/8	26	28	22 5/8	6 7/8	5 4/8	8	6	Johnson Co., MO	Thomas E. White	Thomas E. White	1987	1197
174 5/8	28 6/8	24 3/8	22 3/8	5 5/8	5 4/8	6	8	Beaver Co., OK	Tanner Alexander	Tanner Alexander	1990	1197
174 5/8	24	28 1/8	20 4/8	5 3/8	5 4/8	5	9	Ray Co., MO	Dennis B. Bales	Dennis B. Bales	1990	1197
174 5/8	28 2/8	25 3/8	21 5/8	5 2/8	4 4/8	6	5	Jackson Co., MI	Louise S. Klarr	Louise S. Klarr	1990	1197
174 5/8	26 2/8	25 5/8	19 1/8	4 5/8	4 4/8	5	5	Delaware Co., OH	Robert J. Miller	Robert J. Miller	1990	1197
174 5/8	25 1/8	27 5/8	18 7/8	4 4/8	4 7/8	5	6	Buffalo Co., WI	Daniel L. Scharmer	Daniel L. Scharmer	1990	1197
174 5/8	27 5/8	26 6/8	30 4/8	5 1/8	5	5	6	Larimer Co., CO	George S. Sumter, Jr.	George S. Sumter, Jr.	1990	1197
174 5/8	29 2/8	27	20 1/8	4 4/8	4 6/8	6	5	Jefferson Co., OH	Walter R. Sutton	Walter R. Sutton	1991	1197
174 5/8	27	26 5/8	20 3/8	5 3/8	5 3/8	6	6	Jackson Co., IA	Ronald J. Casel	Ronald J. Casel	1992	1197
174 5/8	27 2/8	26 4/8	19 3/8	6 2/8	6 2/8	8	6	Jefferson Co., IL	Brian G. Pierce	Brian G. Pierce	1992	1197
174 5/8	27 1/8	25 6/8	20 3/8	4 5/8	4 6/8	5	7	Webb Co., TX	Edward O. Radke	Edward O. Radke	1992	1197
174 5/8	26 5/8	26 3/8	20 7/8	4 6/8	4 5/8	7	5	St. Louis Co., MN	Unknown	George W. Flaim	PR 1993	1197
174 5/8	26 3/8	25	17 5/8	4 6/8	4 5/8	5	8	Lodgepole, AB	Frank Spilak	Frank Spilak	1995	1197
174 5/8	25 6/8	25 2/8	16 7/8	6	6	6	7	St. Francis Co., AR	J.S. & J.R. Cook	J.S. & J.R. Cook	1996	1197
174 5/8	24 7/8	24 6/8	20 3/8	5 1/8	5 7/8	6	5	Saskatoon, SK	Kelly D. Day	Kelly D. Day	1996	1197
174 4/8	25 6/8	26	16 6/8	4 6/8	5 2/8	7	5	Marquette Co., MI	Henry L. Terres	Bass Pro Shops F. & W. Mus.	1944	1224
174 4/8	22 5/8	24 1/8	16 7/8	5 2/8	4 6/8	6	6	Koochiching Co., MN	Unknown	Michael Murphy	PR 1950	1224
174 4/8	26 4/8	25 2/8	16 6/8	5 3/8	5 1/8	5	7	Fort Steele, BC	John Lum	John Lum	1958	1224
174 4/8	27 3/8	27 7/8	19 4/8	4 6/8	5 2/8	6	5	Buffalo Co., WI	Unknown	Douglas R. Plourde	1961	1224
174 4/8	22 4/8	23 2/8	20 4/8	5 1/8	5 6/8	6	5	Butler Co., KY	Lonnie D. Hardin	Lonnie D. Hardin	1966	1224
174 4/8	22 6/8	24 6/8	19 5/8	5	5 2/8	6	6	Powell Co., MT	Dave Rittenhouse	Dave Rittenhouse	1973	1224
174 4/8	24 2/8	27 3/8	18	5 3/8	5 2/8	5	5	McKenzie Co., ND	Ben Dekker	Ben Dekker	1976	1224
174 4/8	26 3/8	24 6/8	20 2/8	5 2/8	4 6/8	6	7	Jensen Reservoir, AB	Gary Stanford	Gary Stanford	1976	1224
174 4/8	27 4/8	27 5/8	19 1/8	4 1/8	5 1/8	5	6	Charlotte Co., VA	Jerry C. Claybrook	Jerry C. Claybrook	1977	1224
174 4/8	28 2/8	28 2/8	21	5 2/8	5 4/8	6	7	Knox Co., ME	Robert E. Young	Robert E. Young	1979	1224
174 4/8	24 7/8	24 7/8	17	4 2/8	4	7	7	Boone Co., IA	Curtis A. Lind	Curtis A. Lind	1982	1224
174 4/8	27 2/8	27 2/8	20 6/8	5 2/8	5 2/8	5	5	La Salle Co., TX	H.C. Eppright	H.C. Sims	1982	1224
174 4/8	27 6/8	27 6/8	18 3/8	5 2/8	4 6/8	6	5	Lee Co., IL	Fred L. Schimel	Fred L. Schimel	1988	1224
174 4/8	29	28 1/8	18	5 1/8	5 1/8	8	5	Calhoun Co., IL	Michael L. Moore	Michael L. Moore	1989	1224
174 4/8	28 2/8	29 5/8	19 7/8	5	5 1/8	6	7	McDonough Co., IL	Gary Shelley	Gary Shelley	1991	1224
174 4/8	27 3/8	27 5/8	16	5 3/8	5 4/8	6	6	Washington Co., IN	Michael L. Bledsoe	Michael L. Bledsoe	1992	1224
174 4/8	25 6/8	27 5/8	24 7/8	5 2/8	4 8/8	5	7	Nicollet Co., MN	Ambrose R. McCabe	Ambrose R. McCabe	1992	1224
174 4/8	24 2/8	24 2/8	17 6/8	4 1/8	4 1/8	6	6	Wolfe Co., KY	Toy E. Hazenfield	Toy E. Hazenfield	1993	1224
174 4/8	24 2/8	24 2/8	23 4/8	5 1/8	5 1/8	5	5	Glaslyn, SK	Roger D. Matheny	Roger D. Matheny	1993	1224
174 4/8	26 2/8	25 3/8	17 5/8	5 4/8	5 4/8	8	9	Hamilton Co., IA	Todd L. Darling	Todd L. Darling	1994	1224

WHITETAIL DEER - TYPICAL ANTLERS

Odocoileus virginianus virginianus and certain related subspecies

Score	Length of Main Beam R	L	Inside Spread	Circumference at Smallest Place Between Burr and First Point R	L	Number of Points R	L	Locality	Hunter	Owner	Date Killed	Rank
174 4/8	25 5/8	26 2/8	19 7/8	5 2/8	5 4/8	6	5	Wright Co., MN	Michael J. Buennich	Michael J. Buennich	1995	1224
174 3/8	27 6/8	27 6/8	21 5/8	5 5/8	5 2/8	5	8	Guthrie Co., IA	Larry R. Belding	Larry R. Belding	1965	1245
174 3/8	24 7/8	23 6/8	17 7/8	5 5/8	5 1/8	5	5	Aitkin Co., MN	Christopher W. Steinke	Christopher W. Steinke	1969	1245
174 3/8	28 1/8	26 7/8	23 5/8	5 3/8	5 4/8	6	5	Knox Co., MO	Jon Simmons	Jon Simmons	1972	1245
174 3/8	25 4/8	26 3/8	18 3/8	4 6/8	5	9	8	Marshall Co., KS	Michael J. Krogman	Michael J. Krogman	1981	1245
174 3/8	26 2/8	25 2/8	20 5/8	4 4/8	4 2/8	5	5	McCreary Co., KY	Richmond Keeton	Ruby Keeton	1982	1245
174 3/8	27 2/8	25 2/8	23 6/8	5 1/8	5	5	7	Geary Co., KS	James Brethour	James Brethour	1984	1245
174 3/8	25 2/8	25 3/8	20 1/8	4 5/8	4 6/8	5	7	Goshen Co., WY	Casey L. Hunter	Casey L. Hunter	1984	1245
174 3/8	24	24	17 4/8	5 4/8	5 4/8	8	7	Sawyer Co., WI	Patrick E. Jasper	Patrick E. Jasper	1985	1245
174 3/8	28	28 4/8	21 2/8	4 6/8	4 7/8	5	6	La Crosse Co., WI	Kevin M. Kastenschmidt	Kevin M. Kastenschmidt	1986	1245
174 3/8	26 4/8	26 4/8	23 2/8	5 2/8	5 2/8	6	7	Trempealeau Co., WI	Laverne Killian, Jr.	Laverne Killian, Jr.	1986	1245
174 3/8	27 1/8	27 1/8	21 3/8	6 2/8	5 2/8	5	5	Itasca Co., MN	Mark O. DuLong	Mark O. DuLong	1987	1245
174 3/8	28 3/8	26 2/8	23 1/8	4 3/8	4 4/8	7	7	Dimmit Co., TX	Steven W. Vaughn	Steven W. Vaughn	1987	1245
174 3/8	26 2/8	25	17 3/8	5 2/8	5 7/8	6	5	N. Saskatchewan River, AB	James S. Romanchuk	James S. Romanchuk	1988	1245
174 3/8	25 4/8	25 4/8	19 5/8	4 2/8	4 3/8	5	5	Jackson Co., IN	Max E. Gambrel	Max E. Gambrel	1989	1245
174 3/8	26	26 6/8	21 7/8	5 4/8	5 4/8	5	5	Hardin Co., OH	Ron Hamilton	Ron Hamilton	1989	1245
174 3/8	27	27 6/8	22 7/8	5 2/8	5 2/8	8	7	Warren Co., IA	Craig O. Carpenter	Craig O. Carpenter	1990	1245
174 3/8	27 7/8	28	28	5 3/8	5 3/8	5	5	Washenaw Co., MI	Picked Up	Comm. Bucks of Mich.	1991	1245
174 3/8	24 4/8	24 2/8	17 1/8	4 7/8	5 1/8	7	7	Roddick Lake, SK	Peter J. Laroque	Peter J. Laroque	1993	1245
174 3/8	28 5/8	28 5/8	21 2/8	5 2/8	5 3/8	6	7	Barber Co., KS	James B. Talbott	James B. Talbott	1993	1245
174 3/8	26 1/8	25 6/8	15 6/8	5	4 7/8	6	5	Bayfield Co., WI	Steven W. Schilthelm	Steven W. Schilthelm	1994	1245
174 3/8	26 1/8	25 5/8	16 3/8	4 5/8	4 4/8	6	6	Newton Co., MO	Scott Wolfe	Scott Wolfe	1994	1245
174 3/8	23 4/8	23 4/8	19 3/8	5 2/8	5 3/8	6	6	Marion Co., KS	Matt E. Vaughn	Matt E. Vaughn	1995	1245
174 2/8	28 2/8	27 3/8	25 2/8	5 2/8	5 4/8	4	4	Cerralvo, MX	Unknown	Antonio G. Gonzalez	1900	1267
174 2/8	25 4/8	26	20	4 4/8	4 4/8	6	8	Zavala Co., TX	Ernest Holdsworth	E.M. Holdsworth	1908	1267
174 2/8	25 3/8	26 3/8	22	4 5/8	4 4/8	5	5	Livingston Co., NY	Kenneth Bowen	Kenneth Bowen	1941	1267
174 2/8	24 6/8	24 2/8	22	4 6/8	4 6/8	6	6	Dimmit Co., TX	Red Tollet	McLean Bowman	1958	1267
174 2/8	21 4/8	22	17	4 6/8	4 5/8	6	6	Cass Co., TX	R.J. Perkins	John D. Small	1963	1267
174 2/8	28 3/8	28 2/8	22 2/8	5 4/8	5 4/8	4	4	Cass Co., IA	Cecil Erickson	Cecil Erickson	1975	1267
174 2/8	23 3/8	23 6/8	15 6/8	4 4/8	4 5/8	10	9	La Salle Co., TX	Walter L. Taylor	Walter L. Taylor	1979	1267
174 2/8	26 1/8	26 5/8	22 6/8	5	4 7/8	7	6	Clearwater Co., ID	Douglas B. Crockett	Douglas B. Crockett	1983	1267
174 2/8	27 7/8	27	21 2/8	5 1/8	5 1/8	5	5	Ashland Co., WI	Kelly J. McClaire	Kelly J. McClaire	1986	1267
174 2/8	27 6/8	26 5/8	19 4/8	5 2/8	6 1/8	5	5	Butler Co., PA	Ralph Stoltenberg, Jr.	Ralph Stoltenberg, Jr.	1986	1267
174 2/8	27 5/8	25 7/8	19 5/8	4 7/8	4 6/8	7	7	Monona Co., IA	Larry R. Peterson	Larry R. Peterson	1990	1267
174 2/8	27 1/8	27 1/8	23 4/8	4 6/8	4 6/8	5	5	Dimmit Co., TX	Picked Up	John I. Kunert	PR 1991	1267
174 2/8	25 3/8	25	22 2/8	4 6/8	4 1/8	5	6	Leask, SK	Brian Brad	Brian Brad	1994	1267

Score	Main Beam R	Main Beam L	Inside Spread	Circ. R	Circ. L	Pts R	Pts L	Locality	Hunter	Owner	Date	Rank
174 2/8	24 2/8	25 3/8	17 2/8	6 1/8	5 4/8	8	8	St. Francis Co., AR	Brice Fletcher II	Brice Fletcher II	1995	1267
174 2/8	27 4/8	27 5/8	20 3/8	5 2/8	5 2/8	5	6	Highland Co., OH	Jeffrey A. Cooper	Jeffrey A. Cooper	1996	1267
174 1/8	27	27	21 1/8	5 2/8	5 5/8	7	6	Aroostook Co., ME	Unknown	Vern Black	1930	1282
174 1/8	27 3/8	26 3/8	16 7/8	4 3/8	4 2/8	6	7	Essex Co., NY	Denny Mitchell	Lewis P. Evans	1933	1282
174 1/8	28 1/8	27 1/8	24 7/8	5 1/8	5 1/8	6	6	Mahnomen Co., MN	Rolland Agnew	James Frazee	1941	1282
174 1/8	25 3/8	25 3/8	19 2/8	5 4/8	5 4/8	6	6	Pierson, MB	Art Minshull	Brad Minshull	PR 1950	1282
174 1/8	27	26 5/8	18 4/8	4 5/8	4 6/8	6	5	Buffalo Co., WI	Apolinary Sonsalla	Apolinary Sonsalla	1959	1282
174 1/8	25	25	16 6/8	4 7/8	4 6/8	8	7	Callaway Co., MO	Jac LaFon	Jac LaFon	1968	1282
174 1/8	23 5/8	24 5/8	19 5/8	5 4/8	5 4/8	5	5	Blackfoot, AB	Thomas J. Slager	Thomas J. Slager	1969	1282
174 1/8	26	25 6/8	18 5/8	4 6/8	4 7/8	6	6	Iowa Co., IA	Ronald L. Brecht	Ronald L. Brecht	1973	1282
174 1/8	26 4/8	26 3/8	20	4 7/8	5	6	6	Anarchist Mt., BC	George Urban	George Urban	1980	1282
174 1/8	24 5/8	23 2/8	20 6/8	5 1/8	5 2/8	5	6	Johnson Co., KS	Ralph E. Schlagel	Ralph E. Schlagel	1984	1282
174 1/8	27	26 1/8	20 7/8	6 4/8	6 7/8	7	7	Tuscarawas Co., OH	Dennis J. May, Jr.	Dennis J. May, Jr.	1985	1282
174 1/8	25 6/8	25 5/8	19 6/8	5	4 7/8	6	6	McDonough Co., IL	Jack C. Icenogle	Jack C. Icenogle	1986	1282
174 1/8	27 3/8	26 4/8	18 1/8	5 4/8	5 4/8	6	5	Clarke Co., IA	Lee R. Lundstrom	Lee R. Lundstrom	1987	1282
174 1/8	26 3/8	26 4/8	20 7/8	4 7/8	4 7/8	5	5	Amherstview, ON	Tony H. Stranak	Tony H. Stranak	1987	1282
174 1/8	23 7/8	23 5/8	18 1/8	5	5	5	5	Goodhue Co., MN	Tom Nesseth	Tom Nesseth	1988	1282
174 1/8	25	25 4/8	19 2/8	5 3/8	5 4/8	6	6	Mason Co., KY	Rocky L. Hamm	Rocky L. Hamm	1989	1282
174 1/8	24 3/8	25 4/8	19 2/8	4 2/8	4 2/8	6	7	Day Co., SD	Vernon L. Skoba	Vernon L. Skoba	1990	1282
174 1/8	25 5/8	25 6/8	20 7/8	5 1/8	5 6/8	6	6	Seneca Co., OH	Patrick J. Gillig	Patrick J. Gillig	1990	1282
174 1/8	28 4/8	28 3/8	22 3/8	5 1/8	5 1/8	6	5	Wright Co., MN	William J. Stuhr	William J. Stuhr	1991	1282
174 1/8	26	24 4/8	18 7/8	5 3/8	5 4/8	5	6	Stockholm, SK	Rienhold S. Kulcsar	Rienhold S. Kulcsar	1991	1282
174 1/8	27 2/8	25 4/8	20 6/8	5	5	6	5	Freeborn Co., MN	Charles D. Stadheim	Charles D. Stadheim	1991	1282
174 1/8	25 2/8	27	21 3/8	4 7/8	5	5	5	Chisago Co., MN	Richard A. Townsend	Richard A. Townsend	1993	1282
174 1/8	26 2/8	27	20	4 5/8	5 1/8	7	7	Adams Co., IL	Robert Daly	Robert Daly	1993	1282
174 1/8	25 3/8	25 2/8	18 4/8	4 5/8	4 6/8	6	6	Brown Co., NE	Marvin D. Hart	Marvin D. Hart	1994	1282
174 1/8	28	27 2/8	25	5 4/8	5 6/8	6	5	Montgomery Co., IL	Justin K. Arndt	Justin K. Arndt	1994	1282
174 1/8	27 2/8	24 7/8	17 1/8	4	3 7/8	6	7	Archer Co., TX	Wade G. Schreiber	Wade G. Schreiber	1995	1282
174	24 7/8	26	16 1/8	4 5/8	4 6/8	5	5	Livingston Co., MI	Dolores E. Kassuba	Dolores E. Kassuba	1949	1310
174	26	26 5/8	22 1/8	5 2/8	5 1/8	7	7	Coahoma Co., MS	William L. Walters	William L. Walden	1961	1310
174	26 5/8	27 5/8	24 7/8	5 1/8	5 1/8	6	6	La Salle Co., TX	Unknown	E.B. Shaw	1970	1310
174	28	28	24 7/8	5	5	7	7	Bulyea, SK	W.H. Dodsworth	W.H. Dodsworth	1987	1310
174	26 1/8	26 1/8	20 4/8	4 6/8	4 5/8	5	5	Jefferson Co., WI	Gary A. Coates	Gary A. Coates	1988	1310
174	26 4/8	26 3/8	17 5/8	4 4/8	4 4/8	5	5	Mills Co., IA	Rick W. Elliott	Rick W. Elliott	1988	1310
174	29 1/8	28 3/8	24	5 2/8	5 1/8	5	5	Jefferson Co., NY	James S. Hoar	James S. Hoar	1989	1310
174	27 6/8	28 4/8	19 6/8	4 3/8	4 4/8	6	5	Whitley Co., KY	Edward S. Pittman	Edward S. Pittman	1991	1310
174	26 3/8	26 2/8	17 6/8	4 2/8	4 2/8	6	6	Harrison Co., IA	Ricky G. Seydel	Ricky G. Seydel	1991	1310
174	26 5/8	26 5/8	18 3/8	5 4/8	5 4/8	7	6	Swan River, MB	Picked Up	Clint Martin	1993	1310
174	21 6/8	21 3/8	15 4/8	4 3/8	4 4/8	7	7	Dawson Co., MT	Clayton L. Verke	Clayton L. Verke	1994	1310
174	24 1/8	24 2/8	16 6/8	5 1/8	5	6	6	Chase Co., NE	Kent E. Wasieleski	Kent E. Wasieleski	1995	1310
174	25 7/8	25 7/8	21	4 7/8	4 6/8	6	6	Lake of the Prairies, SK	Brian Wonitowy	Brian Wonitowy	1995	1310
174	27	28 1/8	23	5 1/8	5 1/8	6	6	Brown Co., SD	John F. Culp	John F. Culp	1996	1310
174	25 7/8	26 3/8	23	6	6	8	8	Vermilion Co., IL	Alex L. Ramm	Alex L. Ramm	1996	1310
174	26 4/8	26 4/8	18	5	5	5	5	La Salle Co., IL	Michael Armstrong	Michael Armstrong		1310
174	29 3/8	29 7/8	19	4 5/8	4 7/8	4	4	Johnson Co., KS	Kevin M. Hancock	Kevin M. Hancock		1310
173 7/8	24 5/8	23 7/8	23 3/8	5 1/8	4 7/8	8	7	Dundurn, SK	Herb Wilson	Herb Wilson	1960	1325
173 7/8	26	25 4/8	19 3/8	5	5	6	6	Starr Co., TX	Leonard A. Schwarz	Leonard A. Schwarz	1965	1325

WHITETAIL DEER - TYPICAL ANTLERS

Odocoileus virginianus virginianus and certain related subspecies

Score	Length of Main Beam R	L	Inside Spread	Circumference at Smallest Place Between Burr and First Point R	L	Number of Points R	L	Locality	Hunter	Owner	Date Killed	Rank
173 7/8	25 7/8	25 7/8	20 7/8	5 1/8	4 7/8	5	5	Floyd Co., IA	James R. Lines	James R. Lines	1968	1325
173 7/8	27	26 1/8	19 3/8	5 6/8	5 4/8	6	5	Henry Co., IA	Marion L. Shappell	Marion L. Shappell	1970	1325
173 7/8	25 6/8	24 2/8	20 1/8	5 1/8	5 2/8	7	6	Ohio Co., KY	Rolly Tichenor	Rolly Tichenor	1982	1325
173 7/8	28 6/8	27 5/8	18 5/8	5 3/8	5 3/8	6	7	Penobscot Co., ME	Gregory A. York	Gregory A. York	1986	1325
173 7/8	26 1/8	26	19	4 6/8	5	6	8	Barrhead, AB	C.J. Fuller	C.J. Fuller	1992	1325
173 7/8	24 3/8	23 1/8	18 2/8	4 7/8	5	5	7	Esterhazy, SK	Garry Hawcutt	Garry Hawcutt	1992	1325
173 7/8	24	24 1/8	22 3/8	6 4/8	6 2/8	5	6	Ralls Co., MO	Nicholas D. Mudd	Nicholas D. Mudd	1992	1325
173 7/8	27	26 7/8	16 4/8	5	5	6	5	Rocky Mt. House, AB	Daniel F. Breton	Daniel F. Breton	1994	1325
173 7/8	26 3/8	27 7/8	21 4/8	6 1/8	5 7/8	6	6	Will Co., IL	Harry D. Hammock	Harry D. Hammock	1995	1325
173 7/8	25 3/8	26 2/8	20 2/8	4 7/8	4 7/8	7	6	Blue Earth Co., MN	Jeffery L. Zimmerman	Jeffery L. Zimmerman	1995	1325
173 7/8	28	28	17 3/8	4 2/8	4	5	6	Drew Co., AR	Ronald E. Pearce	Ronald E. Pearce	1996	1325
173 6/8	27 1/8	26 1/8	19 4/8	5 2/8	5 3/8	6	7	Florence Co., WI	Mark Shaw	Walter Knutson	1902	1338
173 6/8	26 6/8	27 1/8	19 7/8	5 5/8	5 3/8	7	5	Mercer Co., IL	Floyd A. Clark	Floyd A. Clark	1961	1338
173 6/8	26	26	18 6/8	5 7/8	6 1/8	6	5	Colfax Co., NE	Leonard Bowman	Leonard Bowman	1962	1338
173 6/8	24 3/8	23 6/8	18 2/8	4 6/8	4 4/8	6	7	Lucas Co., IA	James E. Wolfe	James E. Wolfe	1964	1338
173 6/8	27	26 6/8	21 4/8	5	5	7	9	Bullitt Co., KY	George W. Owens	George W. Owens	1965	1338
173 6/8	26 6/8	27 6/8	20 3/8	5 7/8	5 4/8	9	6	Bonner Co., ID	Robert L. Campbell	Robert L. Campbell	1967	1338
173 6/8	25	25 3/8	22 4/8	5 1/8	5	5	5	McAuley, MB	Alex D. Vallance	Alex D. Vallance	1967	1338
173 6/8	26	25 7/8	17 4/8	4 7/8	4 6/8	6	6	Johnson Co., IA	Godfrey Rhyme	William H. Lilienthal	PR 1968	1338
173 6/8	25 1/8	25 5/8	18 6/8	5 3/8	5 4/8	7	6	Knox Co., NE	Paul H. Klawitter	Paul H. Klawitter	1968	1338
173 6/8	23 2/8	24	19 6/8	4 6/8	4 6/8	6	6	Dimmit Co., TX	Booth W. Petry	Booth W. Petry	1970	1338
173 6/8	25 6/8	25 6/8	19 6/8	4 1/8	4 4/8	5	5	Pulaski Co., IL	Rose M. Blanchard	Rose M. Blanchard	1973	1338
173 6/8	28 1/8	28 1/8	20 6/8	5 1/8	5 2/8	6	6	Bayfield Co., WI	Henry Pajtash	Henry Pajtash	1978	1338
173 6/8	25 5/8	26 1/8	22 1/8	4 3/8	4 7/8	6	5	Des Moines Co., IA	Richard R. Hassell	Richard R. Hassell	1979	1338
173 6/8	26 6/8	25 6/8	18 4/8	4 3/8	4 3/8	6	6	Livingston Co., MI	Terry J. Kemp	Terry J. Kemp	1979	1338
173 6/8	26 6/8	26 6/8	19 1/8	4 7/8	4 7/8	5	7	Minburn, AB	Joseph R. McGillis	Joseph R. McGillis	1981	1338
173 6/8	24 1/8	24 1/8	17 6/8	4 6/8	4 6/8	6	6	Regina, SK	Don Wolk	Don Wolk	1982	1338
173 6/8	25 2/8	25 3/8	18 2/8	4 3/8	4 4/8	7	7	Carroll Co., GA	Ken Yearta	Ken Yearta	1983	1338
173 6/8	24	24 4/8	18	4 4/8	4 4/8	6	6	Marshall Co., MN	Neil Jacobson	Neil Jacobson	1984	1338
173 6/8	24 5/8	24 4/8	23 4/8	5 2/8	5 4/8	6	5	Hart Creek, BC	Greg Lamontange	Greg Lamontange	1984	1338
173 6/8	26 1/8	25	21 5/8	4 4/8	4 4/8	6	5	Winneshiek Co., IA	Herbert I. Amundson	Herbert I. Amundson	1985	1338
173 6/8	26 4/8	25 4/8	18 6/8	4 2/8	4 2/8	7	6	Stephens Co., TX	Robert L. Murphy	Robert L. Murphy	1986	1338
173 6/8	26 1/8	26 2/8	18 7/8	5 3/8	5 3/8	6	8	Schoolcraft Co., MI	Thomas J. Haas	Thomas J. Haas	1987	1338
173 6/8	25 5/8	25 1/8	18 4/8	5 6/8	5 6/8	5	5	Lincoln Co., NE	Raymond E. Blede	Raymond E. Blede	1988	1338
173 6/8	29 3/8	28 4/8	20 6/8	5 5/8	5 4/8	6	6	Mahaska Co., IA	Gareth P. Vande Klieft	Gareth P. Vande Klieft	1988	1338
173 6/8	25 3/8	26 6/8	19 3/8	4 5/8	4 5/8	6	5	Warren Co., IA	Wayne E. Bueltel	Wayne E. Bueltel	1989	1338

Score	L.R	L.L	Spread	Cir.R	Cir.L	Pts.R	Pts.L	Locality	By	Owner	Date	Rank
173 6/8	25 6/8	26 6/8	20	4 5/8	4 5/8	5	5	Dawson Co., NE	Michael L. Seaman	Michael L. Seaman	1989	1338
173 6/8	26 4/8	25 2/8	21 4/8	5 2/8	5 3/8	6	5	Mercer Co., IL	Clarence R. Howard	Clarence R. Howard	1990	1338
173 6/8	23 6/8	24 5/8	22	4 3/8	4 2/8	7	7	Grant Co., NE	Barry Leach	Barry Leach	1991	1338
173 6/8	26 4/8	26 4/8	20	5	5 2/8	7	5	Clinton Co., IA	Picked Up	Wayne Fowler	1992	1338
173 6/8	27 1/8	26	20 4/8	4 2/8	4 1/8	5	5	Vermillion Co., IN	Brian W. Meeker	Brian W. Meeker	1992	1338
173 6/8	26 6/8	27 3/8	23 3/8	4 5/8	4 5/8	6	7	Dolcy Lake, AB	Joseph P. Baker	Joseph P. Baker	1993	1338
173 6/8	27 1/8	26	23 6/8	4 6/8	4 7/8	6	6	St. Lina, AB	Don Felts	Don Felts	1993	1338
173 6/8	28 6/8	26	22 3/8	6	6	7	7	Sublette, KS	Neal Heaton	Neal Heaton	1993	1338
173 6/8	25	23 6/8	19	5	4 6/8	6	7	Meadow Lake, SK	Ike Rainey	Ike Rainey	1993	1338
173 6/8	26 5/8	26 5/8	19 6/8	5 2/8	5 3/8	6	7	Union Co., KY	Robert C. Caudill	Robert C. Caudill	1995	1338
173 6/8	30 6/8	31 2/8	19 4/8	5 3/8	5 2/8	7	6	Owen Co., IN	Troy C. Denney	Troy C. Denney	1995	1338
173 6/8	25 2/8	24 2/8	19 5/8	5 4/8	4 4/8	6	8	Webb Co., TX	Hunter McGrath	Hunter McGrath	1995	1338
173 6/8	24 2/8	25 3/8	20 6/8	5	5	8	5	Atchison Co., MO	Robert B. Tussing	Robert B. Tussing	1995	1338
173 6/8	28 2/8	27 7/8	24 4/8	5	5	4	5	Clinton Co., IA	Patrick J. Hall	Patrick J. Hall	1996	1338
173 5/8	25	24 5/8	17 5/8	4 4/8	5	5	5	Sawyer Co., WI	Maurice Peterson	Mac's Taxidermy	1940	1377
173 5/8	26 6/8	26 6/8	22 5/8	5 2/8	5 2/8	7	6	Alberta	Frank Lind	Frank Lind	1952	1377
173 5/8	26 2/8	26 4/8	19 7/8	4 2/8	4 2/8	6	7	Winona Co., MN	John W. Brand	John W. Brand	1969	1377
173 5/8	27	27	18 3/8	5	5	8	5	Gentry Co., MO	William F. Oberbeck	William F. Oberbeck	1969	1377
173 5/8	25 2/8	25 2/8	19 1/8	4 6/8	4 6/8	6	6	Webb, SK	Roger R. Zimmer	Roger R. Zimmer	PR 1976	1377
173 5/8	26 6/8	25 4/8	20 5/8	4 7/8	4 7/8	6	6	Valley Co., MT	Scott Fossum	Scott Fossum	1978	1377
173 5/8	22 6/8	22 5/8	22 5/8	4 2/8	4 2/8	6	6	Lowndes Co., MS	Geraline Holliman	Geraline Holliman	1982	1377
173 5/8	25	25	22 6/8	5 3/8	5 3/8	4	7	Woods Co., OK	Jack Clover	Jack Clover	1983	1377
173 5/8	27 5/8	28 1/8	20 7/8	5 4/8	5 4/8	5	6	Flathead Co., MT	Mike J. Beaty	Mike J. Beaty	1984	1377
173 5/8	28 3/8	28 5/8	19 1/8	5	5	5	5	Morris Co., KS	Wayne Kasten	Wayne Kasten	1985	1377
173 5/8	24	22 2/8	18 5/8	4 7/8	4 7/8	5	6	Plymouth Co., IA	Pat Kenaley	Pat Kenaley	1986	1377
173 5/8	25 3/8	26	20 3/8	4 4/8	4 4/8	6	5	Fillmore Co., MN	Kelly J. McQuay	Kelly J. McQuay	1986	1377
173 5/8	28	26 4/8	18 1/8	4 5/8	4 6/8	5	6	Roseau Co., MN	David A. Harmon	David A. Harmon	1987	1377
173 5/8	25 5/8	27 2/8	18 7/8	5 5/8	5 5/8	7	5	Pike Co., IL	Jimmy Howard	Jimmy Howard	1989	1377
173 5/8	27 3/8	27 7/8	19 7/8	6 4/8	6 4/8	8	6	Duck Creek, SK	Barry Marquette	Barry Marquette	1991	1377
173 5/8	25 2/8	25 1/8	18 6/8	4 6/8	4 6/8	8	5	Bottineau Co., ND	Alvin A. Hall	Alvin A. Hall	1993	1377
173 5/8	27 4/8	28 1/8	23 3/8	4 2/8	4 1/8	6	8	Unknown	Unknown	Rick Stover	PR 1993	1377
173 5/8	28 1/8	26 6/8	25 1/8	4 4/8	4 6/8	8	8	Will Co., IL	Jeremy L. Johnson	Jeremy L. Johnson	1994	1377
173 5/8	27 5/8	22 6/8	22 3/8	5 1/8	5 1/8	6	6	Renville Co., ND	Shawna R. Atwood	Shawna R. Atwood	1995	1377
173 5/8	23 1/8	23 5/8	17 6/8	5 3/8	5 3/8	9	8	Otter Tail Co., MN	Terry D. Krumwiede	Terry D. Krumwiede	1995	1377
173 5/8	24 2/8	30	25 3/8	5 2/8	5 2/8	6	6	Jackson Co., MO	Michael J. Sytkowski	Michael J. Sytkowski	1995	1377
173 5/8	30 1/8	25 1/8	19 4/8	4 1/8	4 1/8	6	5	Buffalo Co., WI	James R. Gabrick	James R. Gabrick	1996	1377
173 5/8	25 3/8	25 1/8	19 1/8	4 7/8	4 7/8	8	6	Atwater, SK	Gary Griffith	Gary Griffith	1996	1377
173 4/8	25 1/8	27 1/8	16	4 7/8	4 7/8	7	5	Zavala Co., TX	Roger Morris	Alvin Morris	1931	1400
173 4/8	26 6/8	27 6/8	18 2/8	5	5	5	5	Winona Co., MN	Raymond A. Manion	Raymond A. Manion	1950	1400
173 4/8	28	27	20 6/8	4 6/8	4 4/8	5	5	Augusta Co., VA	David H. Wolfe	David H. Wolfe	1957	1400
173 4/8	26 4/8	29 7/8	18	4 3/8	4 3/8	8	5	Livingston Co., MI	Paul M. Peckens	Paul M. Peckens	1959	1400
173 4/8	28 3/8	28 4/8	20 5/8	5	5	6	7	St. Louis Co., MN	Clarence Lindstrom	Donald A. Fondrick	1960	1400
173 4/8	23 7/8	23 6/8	18 6/8	4 6/8	4 6/8	6	6	Shelby Co., TN	John J. Heirigs	John J. Heirigs	1962	1400
173 4/8	23 6/8	24 7/8	17	5 7/8	5 6/8	7	6	Clover Leaf, MB	Walter Lucko	Walter Lucko	1962	1400
173 4/8	24 3/8	25	20 1/8	5 3/8	5 2/8	5	6	Tuffnell, SK	Ed Mattson	Ed Mattson	1964	1400
173 4/8	30 5/8	29 6/8	20 7/8	5 3/8	5 2/8	5	5	Todd Co., KY	Troy L. Harris	Troy L. Harris	1965	1400
173 4/8	28	27 4/8	21 6/8	5 1/8	4 7/8	5	5	Union Co., IA	Danny E. Abbott	Danny E. Abbott	1966	1400

WHITETAIL DEER - TYPICAL ANTLERS

Odocoileus virginianus virginianus and certain related subspecies

Score	Length of Main Beam R	L	Inside Spread	Circumference at Smallest Place Between Burr and First Point R	L	Number of Points R	L	Locality	Hunter	Owner	Date Killed	Rank
173 4/8	26	26	21	5 3/8	5 1/8	5	5	Vilas Co., WI	Unknown	Donald Krueger	1967	1400
173 4/8	28 4/8	27 1/8	22 1/8	5 6/8	5 2/8	5	5	Ellsworth Co., KS	Monte Hudson	Monte Hudson	1986	1400
173 4/8	24 2/8	24 2/8	20 2/8	4 7/8	4 7/8	7	7	Tamaulipas, MX	John F. Sontag, Jr.	John F. Sontag, Jr.	1987	1400
173 4/8	25 7/8	27	23	5	5 1/8	5	5	McHenry Co., IL	Gordon R. Sunderlage	Gordon R. Sunderlage	1987	1400
173 4/8	25 5/8	25 3/8	18	5	5	6	6	Barber Co., KS	James R. Schreiner	James R. Schreiner	1990	1400
173 4/8	24 7/8	25 6/8	22 4/8	4 7/8	4 7/8	5	5	Maverick Co., TX	Clifton F. Douglass III	Clifton F. Douglass III	1991	1400
173 4/8	24 5/8	25 5/8	21 4/8	4 6/8	4 6/8	7	9	Rodgers Co., OK	Marc Thompson	Marc Thompson	1991	1400
173 4/8	24 7/8	24 7/8	18	5 1/8	5 2/8	5	5	Allen Co., IN	Douglas R. Hill	Douglas R. Hill	1993	1400
173 4/8	25 3/8	25 2/8	20	4 1/8	4 5/8	5	5	Seneca Co., OH	Peter Lammers	Peter Lammers	1993	1400
173 4/8	25 6/8	25	16 3/8	4 4/8	4 3/8	6	6	Coahuila, MX	Fernando G. Fuentes	Fernando G. Fuentes	1994	1400
173 4/8	27 2/8	28	19 2/8	4 2/8	4 3/8	7	7	Flathead Co., MT	Ed M. Peter, Jr.	Ed M. Peter, Jr.	1994	1400
173 3/8	28 5/8	29 3/8	23 2/8	6 3/8	6 2/8	7	8	Ontario Co., NY	Martin Solway	NY Dept. of Env. Cons.	1946	1421
173 3/8	27 6/8	28 1/8	20 1/8	4 5/8	4 5/8	6	6	Clarion Co., PA	Mead R. Kiefer	Mead R. Kiefer	1947	1421
173 3/8	26 3/8	26 3/8	19 1/8	5 3/8	5 3/8	7	7	Arkansas Co., AR	Jimmy Hanson	Jimmy Hanson	1948	1421
173 3/8	25 6/8	26 2/8	17 5/8	4 4/8	4 4/8	5	5	Clarion Co., PA	Picked Up	Fred Gallagher	1954	1421
173 3/8	26 4/8	26 6/8	20 1/8	5	4 7/8	6	5	St. George, NB	Gilbert Leavitt	Gilbert Leavitt	1962	1421
173 3/8	27	27 2/8	21 4/8	5 2/8	5 4/8	5	5	Lewis Co., KY	Darrell Tully	Darrell Tully	1968	1421
173 3/8	23 3/8	23 3/8	23 3/8	5 1/8	5 1/8	5	5	Rosebud Co., MT	Ted Millhollin	Ted Millhollin	1975	1421
173 3/8	24 4/8	25 5/8	16 7/8	5 1/8	5 1/8	5	5	Valley Co., MT	Steve K. Sukut	Steve K. Sukut	1978	1421
173 3/8	26 1/8	25 5/8	18 6/8	5	5	5	5	Keya Paha Co., NE	Gene F. Pool	Gene F. Pool	1980	1421
173 3/8	27 4/8	27 4/8	17 1/8	4 5/8	4 6/8	7	5	Clay Co., KS	Charles A. Hammons	Charles A. Hammons	1984	1421
173 3/8	28 7/8	28 1/8	19 1/8	4 7/8	5 2/8	5	6	Monona Co., IA	Steve D. Maher	Steve D. Maher	1986	1421
173 3/8	27 3/8	26 5/8	19 3/8	4 6/8	4 6/8	6	5	Pend Oreille Co., WA	Tom R. Lentz	Tom R. Lentz	1987	1421
173 3/8	26 6/8	26 5/8	24 2/8	4 4/8	4 5/8	6	6	Bullitt Co., KY	Leon R. Allen	Leon R. Allen	1988	1421
173 3/8	26 5/8	26 1/8	18 7/8	4 6/8	4 5/8	7	9	Montgomery Co., IL	Douglas C. Furtwengler	Douglas C. Furtwengler	1988	1421
173 3/8	26 3/8	26 6/8	25 7/8	4 5/8	4 5/8	6	6	Riley Co., KS	Russell S. Santo	Russell S. Santo	1989	1421
173 3/8	23 3/8	26 7/8	18 6/8	5 3/8	5 4/8	7	7	Coles Co., IL	Thomas D. Simmering	Thomas D. Simmering	1989	1421
173 3/8	26	25 4/8	18 1/8	4 1/8	4 3/8	6	5	Chautauqua Co., KS	Wesley D. Coldren	Wesley D. Coldren	1992	1421
173 3/8	24 6/8	25 1/8	21 1/8	4 6/8	4 7/8	5	5	Pembina River, AB	Adrian Marr	Adrian Marr	1993	1421
173 3/8	25 2/8	25	17 5/8	5 1/8	5	7	5	Coahoma Co., MS	Richard D. Powell	Richard D. Powell	1994	1421
173 3/8	26 3/8	24 6/8	16 5/8	5 6/8	5 6/8	6	5	Bent Co., CO	Rick J. Tokarski	Rick J. Tokarski	1994	1421
173 3/8	27 2/8	27	28 7/8	5	5 1/8	5	6	Kane Co., IL	James Meyer	James Meyer	1995	1421
173 3/8	27 5/8	27 2/8	20 7/8	5 5/8	5 3/8	8	8	Fayette Co., WV	Richard L. Schoolcraft	Richard L. Schoolcraft	1995	1421
173 3/8	30 4/8	30 6/8	21 4/8	4 7/8	4 6/8	6	6	Miami Co., OH	Mike Newman	Mike Newman	1996	1421
173 2/8	25 5/8	25 7/8	19	4 2/8	4 1/8	6	6	Texas	Unknown	Marvin Schwarz	PR 1940	1444
173 2/8	30 3/8	29 6/8	21 1/8	5	5 7/8	6	8	Chicot Co., AR	Yan Sturdivant	Bruce Sturdivant	1951	1444

Score	R. Beam	L. Beam	Inside Spread	R. Circ.	L. Circ.	R. Pts.	L. Pts.	Locality	Hunter	Owner	Date	Rank
173 2/8	25 6/8	24 2/8	25 2/8	5 4/8	5 1/8	6	7	Price Co., WI	Clarence Parmelee	J.D. Andrews	1959	1444
173 2/8	24 3/8	25 3/8	20 6/8	4 5/8	4 6/8	5	5	Bemersyde, SK	R.L. McCullough	R.L. McCullough	1959	1444
173 2/8	26	26 6/8	20	4	4	7	5	Lincoln Co., AR	Billy McGriff	Billy McGriff	1962	1444
173 2/8	25 5/8	25 6/8	21	6	5 6/8	5	8	Whitewood, SK	L. Reichel	L. Reichel	1964	1444
173 2/8	26 7/8	24 3/8	20 6/8	5 2/8	5	5	5	Antler, SK	Elmer Lowry	Elmer Lowry	1966	1444
173 2/8	29	29 4/8	20	5 1/8	5 2/8	5	6	Furnas Co., NE	Marvin F. Wieland	Marvin F. Wieland	1969	1444
173 2/8	27 3/8	25 3/8	18 4/8	4	4 1/8	6	6	Decatur Co., TN	Glen D. Odle	Glen D. Odle	1972	1444
173 2/8	25 3/8	25 3/8	21 6/8	4 3/8	4 4/8	6	5	Lyman Co., SD	William G. Psychos	William G. Psychos	1972	1444
173 2/8	28	28 4/8	20 5/8	5 2/8	5 2/8	8	9	Allen Co., KY	Terry W. Sims	Terry W. Sims	1979	1444
173 2/8	26 7/8	28 5/8	23 5/8	4 2/8	4 4/8	6	6	Warren Co., MO	Jerome E. Ley	Jerome E. Ley	1980	1444
173 2/8	24 7/8	26	17 6/8	4 3/8	4 2/8	6	6	Kent Co., DE	William R. Conner	William R. Conner	1984	1444
173 2/8	25 5/8	25 3/8	19	4 6/8	4 6/8	5	5	Battle River, AB	Steven M. Cooper	Steven M. Cooper	1984	1444
173 2/8	24 4/8	22 5/8	19 4/8	5	5 5/8	8	8	Eagle Creek, SK	Perry Haanen	Perry Haanen	1984	1444
173 2/8	26 4/8	26 5/8	19	4 1/8	5	5	5	Chisago Co., MN	Roger A. Peterson	Roger A. Peterson	1984	1444
173 2/8	25 4/8	25 4/8	21 2/8	5 3/8	5 2/8	5	5	Webb Co., TX	Frank J. Sitterle	Frank J. Sitterle	1987	1444
173 2/8	27 5/8	27 5/8	20 6/8	5	5	6	6	Calhoun Co., IL	Picked Up	Dean Diaz	1990	1444
173 2/8	30 1/8	26 6/8	17 4/8	5 2/8	5 2/8	5	5	Woodbury Co., IA	Jim C. Jepson	Jim C. Jepson	1990	1444
173 2/8	26 3/8	24 6/8	19	4 2/8	4 2/8	5	5	Chicot Co., AR	James W. Brown	James W. Brown	1991	1444
173 2/8	26	24 6/8	22	4 6/8	4 5/8	5	8	La Salle Co., TX	Wayne W. Webb	Wayne W. Webb	1992	1444
173 2/8	27 2/8	25 5/8	20 3/8	5 2/8	5 4/8	9	5	Cass Co., MN	Picked Up	Robert Johnson	1993	1444
173 2/8	25 7/8	25 6/8	17 2/8	5	5	5	5	Loon Lake, SK	J. Ronnie Ray	J. Ronnie Ray	1993	1444
173 2/8	22 2/8	21 5/8	19 3/8	5 2/8	5 1/8	4	6	Sagamon Co., IL	Brian Daily	Brian Daily	1995	1444
173 2/8	27 1/8	28 1/8	18	4 5/8	4 6/8	5	6	Delaware Co., OH	John W. Hill, Jr.	John W. Hill, Jr.	1996	1444
173 2/8	25 7/8	25 5/8	18 2/8	4 7/8	5	6	5	Jackson Co., IA	Pat J. Schilling	Pat J. Schilling	1996	1444
173 1/8	26	26 6/8	21 7/8	5 5/8	5 3/8	5	6	St. Louis Co., MN	Unknown	George W. Flaim	1934	1470
173 1/8	27 4/8	26 3/8	20 3/8	5	5	7	7	Marie, SK	King Trew	King Trew	1957	1470
173 1/8	23 6/8	23 6/8	19 2/8	5	5	6	6	Estuary, SK	Melvin J. Anderson	Melvin J. Anderson	1962	1470
173 1/8	23 3/8	23 3/8	18 3/8	5	4	6	6	Slope Co., ND	Robert L. Stroup	Robert L. Stroup	1967	1470
173 1/8	28 5/8	28 6/8	22 2/8	4	5 7/8	6	6	Wabaunsee Co., KS	James D. Downey	James D. Downey	1970	1470
173 1/8	26 1/8	24 6/8	21 1/8	5 4/8	4 6/8	5	5	Lake Co., MT	Darrell Brist	Darrell Brist	1971	1470
173 1/8	29 3/8	28 7/8	25 1/8	4 7/8	3 7/8	6	4	Fillmore Co., MN	Gerry D. Arnold	Gerry D. Arnold	1973	1470
173 1/8	26	26 6/8	18 5/8	4 1/8	4 5/8	6	6	White Co., TN	Sam H. Langford	Sam H. Langford	1980	1470
173 1/8	26 5/8	27 6/8	19 5/8	4 4/8	4 3/8	7	6	Shelby Co., MO	William A. Light, Jr.	William A. Light, Jr.	1981	1470
173 1/8	24 4/8	25 3/8	16 3/8	4 3/8	4 3/8	5	5	Big Muddy Valley, SK	Lyndon T. Ross	Lyndon T. Ross	1984	1470
173 1/8	26 2/8	26 6/8	20 5/8	4 2/8	4 2/8	5	5	Adams Co., OH	Mark N. Barnes	Mark N. Barnes	1986	1470
173 1/8	28	28 2/8	21 5/8	4 6/8	4 6/8	7	5	Dunn Co., WI	Jack K. Dodge	Jack K. Dodge	1987	1470
173 1/8	27 1/8	27 3/8	20 2/8	4 6/8	4 6/8	5	7	Ralls Co., MO	Picked Up	Les James	1988	1470
173 1/8	27 7/8	27 3/8	20 3/8	4 2/8	4 4/8	5	5	Allegan Co., MI	Charles O. Hooper	Charles O. Hooper	1990	1470
173 1/8	26 4/8	26 2/8	20 1/8	4 4/8	4 6/8	5	5	Pottawatomie Co., KS	Donald L. Smith	Donald L. Smith	1990	1470
173 1/8	25 1/8	26	18 1/8	4 6/8	4 5/8	8	8	Latah Co., ID	John D. Kauffman	John D. Kauffman	1991	1470
173 1/8	25 5/8	26 2/8	19 1/8	4 6/8	4 6/8	6	6	Mohaska Co., IA	Ted Smith	Ted Smith	1991	1470
173 1/8	27 3/8	27 3/8	21 4/8	4 4/8	4 4/8	7	5	Buffalo Co., WI	Dale M. Komro	Dale M. Komro	1992	1470
173 1/8	26	25 6/8	17	4 6/8	4 5/8	6	7	Lincoln Co., MO	Daniel A. Narup	Daniel A. Narup	1992	1470
173 1/8	24 4/8	24 4/8	20 3/8	4 7/8	4 7/8	5	5	Crawford Co., OH	Roger C. Rothhaar	Roger C. Rothhaar	1993	1470
173 1/8	24 7/8	24 7/8	16 2/8	5 1/8	5 1/8	6	5	Dodge Co., GA	Paul W. Smith	Paul W. Smith	1993	1470
173 1/8	24 6/8	24 6/8	21 5/8	4 4/8	4 4/8	5	7	Jackson Co., IN	Sean C. Ashley	Sean C. Ashley	1994	1470
173 1/8	25	24 6/8	17 7/8	5	5	5	5	Greene Co., IN	J.D. Holtsclaw & K.J. Hobson	J.D. Holtsclaw & K.J. Hobson	1994	1470

327

WHITETAIL DEER - TYPICAL ANTLERS

Odocoileus virginianus virginianus and certain related subspecies

Score	Length of Main Beam R	L	Inside Spread	Circumference at Smallest Place Between Burr and First Point R	L	Number of Points R	L	Locality	Hunter	Owner	Date Killed	Rank
173 1/8	26 6/8	26 7/8	19 6/8	5 3/8	5 3/8	6	6	Gibbons, AB	Thomas Kampjes	Thomas Kampjes	1994	1470
173 1/8	25 5/8	25	21 1/8	4 2/8	4 2/8	7	6	Kansas	Unknown	James B. Sisco III	PR 1995	1470
173 1/8	24	24 4/8	21 1/8	5 2/8	5	5	5	Winneshiek Co., IA	Kenny J. White	Kenny J. White	1995	1470
173 1/8	26 2/8	25 6/8	18	4 3/8	4 4/8	6	7	White Co., AR	Ricky S. Cantrell	Ricky S. Cantrell	1996	1470
173 1/8	26 3/8	26 2/8	19 5/8	5 3/8	5 4/8	5	5	Macon Co., IL	Stuart A. Wolken	Stuart A. Wolken	1996	1470
173	29 1/8	28 7/8	21	4 7/8	4 6/8	8	8	Bayfield Co., WI	Unknown	Eagle Knob Lodge	PR 1930	1498
173	25 7/8	25 6/8	22	4 7/8	4 7/8	8	8	Pope Co., MN	Unknown	Tom Hammer	PR 1960	1498
173	28 7/8	28 4/8	17 2/8	4 6/8	4 5/8	6	7	Mellette Co., SD	Calvin R. Joy	Calvin R. Joy	1963	1498
173	25 5/8	27 4/8	25 3/8	5 7/8	5 6/8	6	5	Pawnee Co., NE	Gary G. Habegger	Gary G. Habegger	1967	1498
173	28 2/8	27	21 2/8	5 6/8	5 5/8	6	7	Oconto Co., WI	Donald P. Wimmer	Donald P. Wimmer	1969	1498
173	28 3/8	27 4/8	21	4 6/8	4 6/8	7	6	Koochiching Co., MN	Unknown	Marc M. Jackson	PR 1974	1498
173	28	28 7/8	20 4/8	4 6/8	4 5/8	5	5	Sandusky Co., OH	Harold M. Chalfin	Harold M. Chalfin	1975	1498
173	28	28 2/8	21 7/8	5 3/8	5 3/8	7	6	Howard Co., MO	Thomas R. Banning	Thomas R. Banning	1978	1498
173	26 5/8	25 3/8	19 4/8	4 7/8	5 1/8	6	8	Owen Co., KY	Roger Breeden	Roger Breeden	1978	1498
173	28 4/8	28 2/8	25	4 2/8	4 2/8	7	7	Dimmit Co., TX	George Light IV	George Light IV	1979	1498
173	25 2/8	24 2/8	21 7/8	4 5/8	4 6/8	9	6	Hidalgo Co., TX	William L. Turk	William L. Turk	1979	1498
173	27 1/8	27 2/8	21 6/8	4 5/8	4 5/8	5	6	Cook Co., MN	Wesley A. Nelson	Wesley A. Nelson	1980	1498
173	26	26	21	4 5/8	4 6/8	6	6	Somerset Co., ME	Charles A. Moulton	Charles A. Moulton	1981	1498
173	24 4/8	25 5/8	16 7/8	3 7/8	3 6/8	6	7	Trinity Co., TX	Don Knight	Don Knight	1983	1498
173	27	27 2/8	23 5/8	5 7/8	6 1/8	6	7	Doniphan Co., KS	Charles A. Staudenmier	Charles A. Staudenmier	1983	1498
173	23 2/8	25 5/8	19 5/8	4 6/8	4 6/8	7	8	Bunder Lake, AB	Steve Swinhoe	Steve Swinhoe	1983	1498
173	24 5/8	24 7/8	16 4/8	5 3/8	5 2/8	5	5	Bonnyville, AB	Lionel P. Tercier	Lionel P. Tercier	1983	1498
173	25 4/8	25 1/8	19 4/8	4 5/8	4 5/8	5	5	Sullivan Co., TN	C. Alan Altizer	C. Alan Altizer	1984	1498
173	26 4/8	25 7/8	18 4/8	4 6/8	4 6/8	5	6	Becker Co., MN	Albert E. Jahnke	Albert E. Jahnke	1985	1498
173	28 1/8	29 4/8	24 4/8	4 6/8	4 6/8	5	6	Jefferson Co., OH	Adam Firm	Adam Firm	1987	1498
173	25 1/8	24 7/8	18 6/8	5 1/8	4 7/8	6	5	Fairfield Co., OH	James Carmichael	James Carmichael	1988	1498
173	27 1/8	27 1/8	21 2/8	5 1/8	5 1/8	5	7	Shawnee Co., KS	Frank R. Murray	Frank R. Murray	1989	1498
173	27	26	20 1/8	4 1/8	4 2/8	6	7	Big Horn Co., WY	Daniel D. Wood	Daniel D. Wood	1989	1498
173	25 4/8	26 2/8	21 6/8	4 7/8	4 6/8	6	6	Pepin Co., WI	William A. Gray	William A. Gray	1990	1498
173	24	25 2/8	18 6/8	4 6/8	4 5/8	5	5	Sheridan Co., WY	Robert G. Green	Robert G. Green	1991	1498
173	27 1/8	27	21 1/8	5 2/8	5 2/8	7	6	Monroe Co., IA	Richard A. Bishop	Richard A. Bishop	1992	1498
173	23 6/8	24	19	4 6/8	4 7/8	6	5	Westlock, AB	Billy W. Kothmann	Billy W. Kothmann	1992	1498
173	26 5/8	26 6/8	17	5 1/8	5 1/8	6	6	Davis Co., IA	Picked Up	James E. Pierceall	1992	1498
173	27 5/8	28	19	4 3/8	4 1/8	7	6	Flathead Co., MT	Derek Schulz	Derek Schulz	1992	1498
173	28 6/8	29 3/8	21 6/8	5 4/8	5 6/8	4	4	Caroline Co., MD	Jay Downes, Jr.	Jay Downes, Jr.	1993	1498
173	26 2/8	26 6/8	17 6/8	5 2/8	5 1/8	6	6	Muhlenberg Co., KY	Larry Vincent	Larry Vincent	1993	1498

Score	Main Beam R	Main Beam L	Inside Spread	Circ. R	Circ. L	Pts R	Pts L	Locality	Hunter	Owner	Date	Rank
173	27 6/8	27	18 2/8	4 4/8	4 3/8	8	7	Johnson Co., NE	Kent Hippen	Kent Hippen	1994	1498
173	24 7/8	24 3/8	20	5 5/8	5 3/8	5	5	St. Croix Co., WI	James A. O'Keefe	James A. O'Keefe	1994	1498
173	23 7/8	23 5/8	19 2/8	5 6/8	5 7/8	7	7	Whitewood Lake, SK	Geordie D. McKay	Geordie D. McKay	1995	1498
173	27 1/8	25 4/8	19 4/8	5 2/8	5 1/8	9	8	Clay Co., MO	Neal B. Breshears	Neal B. Breshears	1996	1498
172 7/8	26	27	20 4/8	4 7/8	5	7	9	Harrison Co., IA	Dell C. Wohlers	Dell C. Wohlers	1996	1534
172 7/8	25 5/8	25 6/8	22 5/8	4 3/8	4 4/8	6	7	Windthorst, SK	Jack Glover	Jack Glover	1951	1534
172 7/8	25	25 3/8	20 2/8	5 4/8	5 3/8	7	6	McHenry Co., ND	David Medalen	David Medalen	1959	1534
172 7/8	24 3/8	24 6/8	20 1/8	4 3/8	4 2/8	5	7	Ashland Co., WI	Einar Sein	Rick Iacono	1965	1534
172 7/8	26 1/8	26 4/8	16 7/8	5 4/8	5 4/8	6	5	Olmsted Co., MN	Wesley W. Holtz	Wesley W. Holtz	1966	1534
172 7/8	27	26 1/8	18	4 1/8	4 2/8	6	6	Newton Co., GA	L.W. Shirley, Jr.	L.W. Shirley; Jr.	1967	1534
172 7/8	26 2/8	27	21 7/8	5 3/8	5 3/8	6	5	Seneca Co., NY	Martin J. Way	Martin J. Way	1968	1534
172 7/8	26 5/8	27 1/8	19 7/8	4 6/8	4 5/8	5	6	Williamson Co., IL	Picked Up	John L. Roseberry	1975	1534
172 7/8	25 1/8	24 3/8	24 3/8	5 4/8	5 4/8	6	8	Cascade Co., MT	Skip Halmes	Skip Halmes	1976	1534
172 7/8	28 2/8	28 7/8	28 7/8	5 1/8	5 2/8	5	6	Granville Co., NC	James M. Wilkerson	James M. Wilkerson	1981	1534
172 7/8	23	22 3/8	22 3/8	4 3/8	4 3/8	6	8	Dallas Co., IA	Gordon Cochran	Gordon Cochran	1982	1534
172 7/8	27 3/8	26	20	4 6/8	4 6/8	7	6	Heard Co., GA	Keith McCullough	Keith McCullough	1987	1534
172 7/8	26 5/8	25 7/8	22 5/8	4 6/8	4 6/8	6	10	Pike Co., IL	Robert L. Hubbell	Robert L. Hubbell	1987	1534
172 7/8	27 3/8	27 4/8	20 6/8	4	4	5	6	Jefferson Co., IN	Chet A. Nolan	Chet A. Nolan	1988	1534
172 7/8	27 1/8	26 6/8	19 6/8	5 3/8	5	7	6	Vermilion Co., IL	Edwin B. Gudgel	Edwin B. Gudgel	1989	1534
172 7/8	27	27	18 5/8	4 7/8	4 5/8	6	6	Jackson Co., IA	Picked Up	Roy Rathje	1991	1534
172 7/8	28 4/8	29 3/8	24 7/8	4 6/8	4 6/8	5	5	McMullen Co., TX	Steve Best	Steve Best	1992	1534
172 7/8	25 1/8	25 1/8	16 5/8	5 1/8	5 1/8	5	4	Sullivan Co., NH	Gordon E. Adams	Gordon E. Adams	1992	1534
172 7/8	29	29	20 5/8	4 1/8	4 2/8	7	6	Kootenai Co., ID	Kevin L. Lundblad	Kevin L. Lundblad	1994	1534
172 7/8	24 3/8	25 2/8	18	5 7/8	5 7/8	8	5	Schoolcraft Co., MI	Lanny D. Higley	Lanny D. Higley	1994	1534
172 7/8	28 2/8	27 4/8	18 3/8	4 7/8	4 7/8	7	7	Huron Co., OH	James A. McMorrow	James A. McMorrow	1996	1534
172 6/8	27	27	21 7/8	5	5	6	8	Fillmore Co., MN	Susan M. LeGare-Gulden	Susan M. LeGare-Gulden	1996	1555
172 6/8	26 7/8	26 7/8	19	4 5/8	4 5/8	5	7	Woodruff, WI	Unknown	Mac's Taxidermy	1918	1555
172 6/8	25 1/8	25 1/8	18 6/8	4 6/8	4 6/8	6	6	Somerset Co., PA	Edward B. Stutzman	Edward B. Stutzman, Jr.	1945	1555
172 6/8	26 1/8	23 6/8	19	4 6/8	4 6/8	5	7	Trempealeau Co., WI	Henry M. Hoff	Henry M. Hoff	1956	1555
172 6/8	25 6/8	23 4/8	21 4/8	5	5	5	6	Waldo Co., ME	Wallace Humphrey	Arthur Humphrey	1963	1555
172 6/8	23 2/8	23 3/8	24	4 6/8	5	5	6	Pope Co., IL	George Koderhandt, Sr.	David Koderhandt	1963	1555
172 6/8	27 5/8	27 5/8	20 2/8	4 4/8	4 4/8	5	5	Webb Co., TX	B.A. Vineyard	B.A. Vineyard	1964	1555
172 6/8	28 2/8	28 2/8	22 4/8	5 6/8	5 6/8	5	5	Vilas Co., WI	James Homan	Brant J. Mueller	1967	1555
172 6/8	28 6/8	28 6/8	15 4/8	4 4/8	4 4/8	6	7	Spokane Co., WA	Maurice Robinette	Maurice Robinette	1968	1555
172 6/8	27	27	22 4/8	4 5/8	4 5/8	5	6	Custer Co., MT	Picked Up	George A. Bettas	1974	1555
172 6/8	25 4/8	25 4/8	23 7/8	6 4/8	6 4/8	5	4	Louisa Co., IA	Merrill Flake	Monna B. Flake	1974	1555
172 6/8	27	27	20 4/8	5 3/8	5 3/8	6	5	Boone Co., IA	Lonne L. Tracy	Lonne L. Tracy	1975	1555
172 6/8	28 2/8	28 2/8	20 3/8	6	6	6	6	Allamakee Co., IA	Picked Up	Tom Kernat, Sr.	1976	1555
172 6/8	24 1/8	24 2/8	22 2/8	4 7/8	5 1/8	6	6	Dimmit Co., TX	David R. Park	David R. Park, Jr.	1978	1555
172 6/8	25 1/8	24 3/8	21 2/8	5	5	7	7	Edgerton, AB	Richard T. Abbott	Richard T. Abbott	1980	1555
172 6/8	26 1/8	26 5/8	16 5/8	3 7/8	3 7/8	6	6	Mitchell Co., IA	Dan A. Block	Dan A. Block	1981	1555
172 6/8	24 3/8	23 4/8	17 6/8	5 5/8	5 5/8	6	5	Surry Co., VA	Edward B. Jones	Edward B. Jones	1984	1555
172 6/8	27 2/8	26 3/8	22	6 2/8	6 2/8	5	6	Fayette Co., IA	Greg P. Bordignon	Greg P. Bordignon	1987	1555
172 6/8	24 5/8	25 1/8	20 2/8	5	5	5	5	Ashland Co., WI	Picked Up	David Sanborn	PR 1987	1555
172 6/8	27 6/8	27 4/8	18	4 6/8	4 6/8	5	7	Henderson Co., IL	Larry Spiker	William H. Lilienthal	1988	1555
172 6/8	27 6/8	27 6/8	24 4/8	5 4/8	5 4/8	6	5	Stafford Co., KS	Donald G. Fisher	Donald G. Fisher	1989	1555
172 6/8	25 5/8	26	18 7/8	4 7/8	4 7/8	5	6	Bee Co., TX	John W. Galloway	John W. Galloway	1990	1555

WHITETAIL DEER - TYPICAL ANTLERS

Odocoileus virginianus virginianus and certain related subspecies

Score	Length of Main Beam R	L	Inside Spread	Circumference at Smallest Place Between Burr and First Point R	L	Number of Points R	L	Locality	Hunter	Owner	Date Killed	Rank
172 6/8	26 2/8	27 7/8	18 4/8	4 3/8	4 2/8	4	5	Pike Co., OH	James W. Howard	James W. Howard	1990	1555
172 6/8	27 1/8	27 1/8	21 1/8	4 4/8	4 3/8	6	7	Renville Co., MN	Elroy E. Kuglin	Elroy E. Kuglin	1990	1555
172 6/8	26 4/8	27 3/8	20	4 6/8	4 6/8	6	5	Crawford Creek, SK	Scott Macnab	Scott Macnab	1990	1555
172 6/8	27 1/8	27 7/8	17 4/8	5	5 1/8	5	5	Mitchell Co., GA	Al Collins	Al Collins	1991	1555
172 6/8	29 4/8	26 2/8	22 6/8	6 1/8	6 2/8	7	6	Richland Co., IL	Donald L. Ginder	Donald L. Ginder	1991	1555
172 6/8	26 5/8	27	22 3/8	5 3/8	5 2/8	6	8	Cheshire Co., NH	Peter J. Krochunas	Peter J. Krochunas	1991	1555
172 6/8	28	28 7/8	19 2/8	5 1/8	5 1/8	6	5	Moultrie Co., IL	Joseph D. Nelson	Joseph D. Nelson	1991	1555
172 6/8	25 3/8	24 7/8	18 2/8	4 1/8	4 2/8	6	6	Johnson Co., NE	Dan Hollatz	Dan Hollatz	1992	1555
172 6/8	26 5/8	26 4/8	18 6/8	4 5/8	4 5/8	5	5	Manitowoc Co., WI	Stephen J. Kortens	Stephen J. Kortens	1992	1555
172 6/8	26 5/8	25 2/8	20 4/8	4 6/8	4 4/8	5	5	Horsehide Creek, SK	Gene Markowsky	Gene Markowsky	1992	1555
172 6/8	26	24 1/8	22 7/8	4 5/8	4 5/8	6	5	Seminole Co., OK	Lester H. Reich	Lester H. Reich	1994	1555
172 6/8	27	26 4/8	21 5/8	5 3/8	5 6/8	9	9	Menominee Co., WI	Marvin R. Ninham	Marvin R. Ninham	1995	1555
172 6/8	26 1/8	25 3/8	17 4/8	4 5/8	4 6/8	7	6	Cass Co., IA	Tom M. Roberts	Tom M. Roberts	1995	1555
172 6/8	25 4/8	25 4/8	17 4/8	4 6/8	4 5/8	6	7	Keokuk Co., IA	Michael A. Veres	Michael A. Veres	1995	1555
172 6/8	26	26 4/8	18	5 5/8	5 5/8	6	6	Washington Co., KS	Todd Jueneman	Todd Jueneman	1996	1555
172 6/8	27 2/8	27 7/8	20 3/8	4 5/8	5 1/8	6	9	Washington Co., PA	Ronald J. LaBrosse, Jr.	Ronald J. LaBrosse, Jr.	1996	1555
172 5/8	24 2/8	24 4/8	21 1/8	5 2/8	5	6	6	Frio Co., TX	Unknown	Roy Hindes	PR 1940	1592
172 5/8	25 4/8	26 3/8	20 5/8	4 5/8	4 4/8	5	5	Greene Co., AR	Unknown	Harry Willcockson	PR 1940	1592
172 5/8	25 4/8	26	22 6/8	4 3/8	4 4/8	6	5	Esterhazy, SK	J. Weise	J. Weise	1960	1592
172 5/8	24	24 3/8	23 5/8	4 3/8	4 3/8	7	7	San Patricio Co., TX	Mary L. Edwards	Mary L. Edwards	1967	1592
172 5/8	25 1/8	24 5/8	19 1/8	5 7/8	5 6/8	7	5	Shoal Lake, MB	Gary Phillips	Gary Phillips	1967	1592
172 5/8	26 7/8	25 5/8	18 4/8	5 4/8	5 3/8	5	5	Cass Co., MI	Ben R. Williams	Ben R. Williams	1971	1592
172 5/8	24 1/8	23	18 1/8	4 3/8	4 3/8	6	6	Tuscarawas Co., OH	Charles Kerns	Charles Kerns	1972	1592
172 5/8	26 6/8	25	17 2/8	4 5/8	4 7/8	9	6	Knox Co., ME	Willis A. Moody, Jr.	Willis A. Moody, Jr.	1974	1592
172 5/8	27 6/8	28 1/8	22 3/8	4 6/8	4 6/8	5	5	Koochiching Co., MN	Unknown	Marc M. Jackson	PR 1977	1592
172 5/8	26 3/8	26 4/8	21 3/8	4 7/8	4 7/8	5	7	Highland Co., OH	Wilbur D. Rhoads	Wilbur D. Rhoads	1979	1592
172 5/8	28 4/8	28	22	6 2/8	6 3/8	8	8	Adams Co., MS	Adrian L. Stallone	Adrian L. Stallone	1983	1592
172 5/8	24 7/8	25 7/8	25 1/8	4 7/8	4 7/8	5	5	Barren Co., KY	Billy N. Short	Billy N. Short	1984	1592
172 5/8	25 3/8	25 6/8	18 3/8	5	5 2/8	6	6	Sauk Co., WI	Terry A. Diske	Terry A. Diske	1987	1592
172 5/8	25 1/8	27	20 1/8	5 6/8	5 2/8	6	6	Surry Co., VA	Picked Up	Virginia L. Logan	1987	1592
172 5/8	22 5/8	23 3/8	19 7/8	4 5/8	4 4/8	6	6	Short Creek, SK	Neil Fornwald	Neil Fornwald	1989	1592
172 5/8	26 7/8	27 1/8	18 7/8	5 2/8	5 4/8	5	5	Rosebud Co., MT	Michael E. Gayheart	Michael E. Gayheart	1989	1592
172 5/8	26 2/8	25 6/8	18 6/8	5 3/8	5 5/8	5	7	Douglas Co., MO	Virgil Churchill	Virgil Churchill	1990	1592
172 5/8	26 7/8	27 1/8	19 2/8	4 4/8	4 4/8	5	6	Lyon Co., KS	Dale L. Hellman	Dale L. Hellman	1990	1592
172 5/8	26 6/8	27 1/8	22 3/8	5 1/8	5 2/8	4	4	Jackson Co., IA	Robert R. Morehead	Robert R. Morehead	1990	1592
172 5/8	26 4/8	26 1/8	17 1/8	4 2/8	4 1/8	5	5	Wayne Co., KY	Ronald G. Sexton	Ronald G. Sexton	1990	1592

Score	Main Beam R	Main Beam L	Inside Spread	Circ. R	Circ. L	Pts. R	Pts. L	Locality	Hunter	Owner	Date	Rank
172 5/8	27 1/8	26 4/8	21 2/8	4 7/8	5 2/8	5	6	Marshall Co., IL	Oscar C. Weber	Oscar C. Weber	1991	1592
172 5/8	25 1/8	25 2/8	16 5/8	4 4/8	4 4/8	5	6	Stewart Co., TN	Thomas M. Bowers	Thomas M. Bowers	1992	1592
172 5/8	23 4/8	23 1/8	20 1/8	5	5 2/8	6	7	Dawson Creek, BC	J. Grant Bowie	J. Grant Bowie	1992	1592
172 5/8	25 2/8	25 1/8	20 4/8	6 2/8	6	6	7	Crawford Co., IA	Picked Up	S.L. Reetz & J. Shumate	1992	1592
172 5/8	26 5/8	25 1/8	18 6/8	5 4/8	5 4/8	5	5	Buffalo Lake, SK	Garth Sander	Garth Sander	1992	1592
172 5/8	25 6/8	24 5/8	20 7/8	5	5	5	5	Holmes Co., OH	Sam Anderson	Sam Anderson	1994	1592
172 5/8	25 7/8	27	18 3/8	4 3/8	4 2/8	7	5	Ringgold Co., IA	Herbert J. Weigel	Herbert J. Weigel	1994	1592
172 5/8	26 1/8	26 4/8	19 6/8	4 6/8	4 6/8	7	7	Long Lake, AB	Gerald Bodner	Gerald Bodner	1995	1592
172 5/8	25 5/8	24 7/8	18 2/8	5 3/8	5 1/8	5	5	N. Saskatchewan River, SK	Blaine LaRose	Blaine LaRose	1995	1592
172 5/8	26 2/8	24 7/8	17 7/8	4 5/8	4 4/8	5	7	Eastland Co., TX	Kevin L. Reed	Kevin L. Reed	1995	1592
172 5/8	25 1/8	25 6/8	17	4 7/8	4 7/8	6	5	Menard Co., IL	Jeffrey M. Balding	Jeffrey M. Balding	1996	1592
172 5/8	26 2/8	25	24 1/8	5 1/8	5 2/8	5	5	Acton-Vale, QC	Guy Cusson	Guy Cusson	1996	1592
172 5/8	27 5/8	26 6/8	19 7/8	5 4/8	5 4/8	4	5	Coles Co., IL	Shane D. Duzan	Shane D. Duzan	1996	1592
172 5/8	25 4/8	26	20 1/8	5	4 7/8	5	6	Fayette Co., IL	Joseph M. Kirk	Joseph M. Kirk	1996	1592
172 5/8	26 1/8	26	20 7/8	4 6/8	4 5/8	5	5	Kootenai Co., ID	Shane Moyer	Shane Moyer	1996	1592
172 4/8	25 6/8	27	20 2/8	5 2/8	5	6	6	Cotulla, TX	George E. Light III	George E. Light III	1959	1627
172 4/8	24 4/8	24 4/8	18 4/8	4 4/8	4 4/8	6	6	Webb Co., TX	A.M. Russell	A.M. Russell	1961	1627
172 4/8	27 3/8	26 7/8	22 5/8	4 6/8	5 1/8	5	5	Laird, SK	A.E. Nikkel	A.E. Nikkel	1963	1627
172 4/8	27 3/8	26 6/8	21 2/8	4	4	5	4	Zavala Co., TX	Gaston F. Maurin	Clint Arnold	1964	1627
172 4/8	26 5/8	26 5/8	19	5 5/8	5 3/8	5	6	Fillmore Co., MN	Picked Up	William H. Lilienthal	1965	1627
172 4/8	26 4/8	27 2/8	24	4 3/8	5 3/8	5	5	Fort Knox, KY	E.G. Christian	E.G. Christian	1966	1627
172 4/8	27 5/8	27	23 3/8	5 3/8	5 1/8	7	7	Daugherty Co., GA	J.P. Flournoy	J.P. Flournoy	1969	1627
172 4/8	24 4/8	24 3/8	20	5	5	6	6	Chauvin, AB	Ron D. Jakimchuk	Ron D. Jakimchuk	1971	1627
172 4/8	26 7/8	25 2/8	19	4 6/8	4 5/8	6	5	Randolph Co., GA	Robert D. Bell	Robert D. Bell	1979	1627
172 4/8	24 3/8	25 2/8	23 4/8	5 6/8	5 4/8	8	7	Muhlenberg Co., KY	Dennis Nolen	Dennis Nolen	1982	1627
172 4/8	26 4/8	26 2/8	21 7/8	5 2/8	5 2/8	6	6	Muskingum Co., OH	Michael Wilson	Michael Wilson	1982	1627
172 4/8	23 5/8	25 2/8	20	6 1/8	5 7/8	6	5	Franklin Co., IL	Joseph S. Smothers	Joseph S. Smothers	1984	1627
172 4/8	29 4/8	28 6/8	20	5 3/8	5 2/8	6	5	Iron Co., WI	Dale D. Tuszke	Dale D. Tuszke	1987	1627
172 4/8	22	25 5/8	23 7/8	4 7/8	4 6/8	5	5	Smoky River, AB	Bevar C. Rose	Bevar C. Rose	1988	1627
172 4/8	26 2/8	26 4/8	20 4/8	5 1/8	5 3/8	6	5	Battle River, SK	Marcus E. Christensen	Marcus E. Christensen	1990	1627
172 4/8	24	23 6/8	20 4/8	5 3/8	5 4/8	6	7	Hillsdale Co., MI	Ronald Bexfield	Ronald Bexfield	1991	1627
172 4/8	25 4/8	25 2/8	18	5 5/8	6	6	6	Marion Co., IL	Turley Crisp	Turley G. Crisp	1991	1627
172 4/8	27 5/8	27 3/8	20 2/8	4 7/8	4 6/8	8	9	Ringgold Co., IA	Michele Hanks	Michele Hanks	1991	1627
172 4/8	26 2/8	25 4/8	17 6/8	4 5/8	4 5/8	8	6	Dawson Co., NE	Edward D. Miller	Edward D. Miller	1992	1627
172 4/8	22 2/8	23 3/8	18 1/8	4 4/8	4 3/8	7	7	Guilford Co., NC	Kim L. Farnstrom	Kim L. Farnstrom	1992	1627
172 4/8	29 1/8	27 5/8	19 2/8	5	5	5	5	Lucas Co., IA	Rodney D. Summers	Rodney D. Summers	1993	1627
172 4/8	26 2/8	26 5/8	21	4 6/8	4 6/8	5	5	Stafford Co., KS	Perry L. Klages, Jr.	Perry L. Klages, Jr.	1994	1627
172 4/8	27 7/8	28 4/8	16 2/8	5	5	5	6	Bond Co., IL	Alan Baldwin	Alan Baldwin	1995	1627
172 4/8	24 5/8	26 7/8	16 6/8	4 2/8	4 3/8	5	5	Colquitt Co., GA	William G. Brown	William G. Brown	1995	1627
172 4/8	26 5/8	27 4/8	17 2/8	4 4/8	4 5/8	5	5	Taylor Co., WI	Alan Whitaker	Alan Whitaker	1996	1627
172 3/8	26 6/8	26 7/8	19 2/8	4 6/8	5	5	7	Rainy Lake, ON	Karl Raatz	Kathleen Powell	1939	1652
172 3/8	27	28	23 6/8	4 6/8	4 6/8	7	8	Hamilton Co., NY	Floyd Kielczewski	Floyd Kielczewski	1953	1652
172 3/8	27	26	21	5 2/8	5 3/8	7	5	Brookings, SD	Unknown	Donald K. Hamilton	1956	1652
172 3/8	27 4/8	27 2/8	20 4/8	6	6 1/8	5	6	Monroe Co., MO	Paul W. Back	Paul W. Back	1967	1652
172 3/8	26	26 2/8	19 5/8	4 6/8	4 6/8	5	5	Snider Mt., NB	Clark E. Bray	Clark E. Bray	1967	1652
172 3/8	29 5/8	29 1/8	20 3/8	4 2/8	4 4/8	5	6		Jack W. Brown	Jack W. Brown	1975	1652
172 3/8	27 6/8	26 5/8	17 1/8	4 3/8	4 4/8	8	5	Kanabec Co., MN	Gregory L. Schultz	Gregory L. Schultz	1976	1652

WHITETAIL DEER - TYPICAL ANTLERS

Odocoileus virginianus virginianus and certain related subspecies

Score	Length of Main Beam R	L	Inside Spread	Circumference at Smallest Place Between Burr and First Point R	L	Number of Points R	L	Locality	Hunter	Owner	Date Killed	Rank
172 3/8	27 6/8	28 2/8	17 2/8	4 6/8	4 5/8	6	5	Decatur Co., TN	Danny Pope	Danny Pope	1982	1652
172 3/8	24 5/8	24 3/8	18	4 6/8	4 7/8	8	7	Rusk Co., WI	Randy A. Jochem	Randy A. Jochem	1984	1652
172 3/8	30 1/8	30 3/8	22 3/8	5 4/8	5 4/8	9	9	Porcupine Plain, SK	Kim Mikkonen	Kim Mikkonen	1985	1652
172 3/8	27 6/8	26 5/8	16	4 6/8	4 6/8	5	6	Dane Co., WI	Randy L. Letlebo	Randy L. Letlebo	1987	1652
172 3/8	26 4/8	26 7/8	16 2/8	5	4 6/8	5	7	Mercer Co., MO	Jarin J. Simpson	Jarin J. Simpson	1988	1652
172 3/8	27 6/8	26 7/8	18	5 6/8	5 2/8	7	7	Boone Co., IA	Kevin A. Anderson	Kevin A. Anderson	1989	1652
172 3/8	26 3/8	26 1/8	19 1/8	4 6/8	4 7/8	7	5	Monona Co., IA	Larry Hieber	Larry Hieber	1989	1652
172 3/8	24 6/8	24 6/8	17 5/8	4 3/8	4 3/8	5	5	Dearborn Co., IN	Walter C. Drake	Walter C. Drake	1990	1652
172 3/8	27	26 7/8	19 1/8	5	4 7/8	5	5	Johnson Co., KS	David T. Reed	David T. Reed	1990	1652
172 3/8	27	27 3/8	23 5/8	5 3/8	5 3/8	6	5	McHenry Co., IL	Kevin Rubow	Kevin Rubow	1990	1652
172 3/8	26 3/8	26 6/8	22 1/8	4 7/8	4 7/8	5	6	Harrison Co., KY	Charles B. Burgess	Charles B. Burgess	1993	1652
172 3/8	29 6/8	30 2/8	21 2/8	4 5/8	5	4	6	Prince Georges Co., MD	Lance D. Canter	Lance D. Canter	1993	1652
172 3/8	28 3/8	27 5/8	21 1/8	4 4/8	4 3/8	6	6	Bedford Co., VA	Robert A. McGann	Robert A. McGann	1993	1652
172 3/8	28	27 5/8	18 3/8	4 2/8	4 3/8	5	5	Jackson Co., WI	J. Esanbock & M. Finch	J. Esanbock & M. Finch	1994	1652
172 3/8	26 5/8	27 5/8	18 7/8	5	5	5	5	La Salle Co., IL	William J. Keith	William J. Keith	1994	1652
172 3/8	23 5/8	24	16 2/8	4 7/8	4 7/8	8	8	Sheridan Co., MT	Kent G. Unhjem	Kent G. Unhjem	1994	1652
172 3/8	24 5/8	26 1/8	16 6/8	5 3/8	5	6	5	Queen Annes Co., MD	Paul A. Pletzer	Paul A. Pletzer	1995	1652
172 3/8	24	24 1/8	17 3/8	4 5/8	4 6/8	6	6	Sounding Lake, AB	Neil Scammell	Neil Scammell	1995	1652
172 3/8	26 7/8	27 4/8	18 3/8	4 6/8	4 5/8	6	5	Greeley Co., NE	Alan D. Vanosdall	Alan D. Vanosdall	1995	1652
172 2/8	27 7/8	28	20	4 6/8	4 5/8	5	6	Lincoln Co., WI	Ronald F. Lax	Ronald F. Lax	1928	1678
172 2/8	24 6/8	24 3/8	18	4 4/8	4 5/8	6	6	Vilas Co., WI	Alfred Theilig	J. James Froelich	1936	1678
172 2/8	26 7/8	27	20 6/8	4 5/8	4 5/8	5	5	St. Louis Co., MN	Ray Hermanson	George W. Flaim	1942	1678
172 2/8	28 6/8	26 4/8	21 5/8	4 1/8	4 3/8	6	6	Bedford Co., PA	Everett Larson	John F. Sharpe	1942	1678
172 2/8	26 4/8	25 6/8	20	6	6	7	7	Weyburn, SK	John F. Sharpe	Wifred LaValley	1958	1678
172 2/8	25 6/8	26 3/8	20	5 1/8	5 1/8	5	5	Jones Co., SD	Wifred LaValley	J.D. Andrews	1960	1678
172 2/8	27 4/8	26 4/8	19 4/8	4 5/8	4 6/8	6	8	Manor, SK	Walter Prahl	Albert McConnell	1962	1678
172 2/8	25 4/8	25 2/8	23 5/8	5 1/8	5 1/8	5	7	Flathead Co., MT	Albert McConnell	Lonny Hanson	1963	1678
172 2/8	23	23	19	5	5 1/8	6	7	Adams Co., WI	Lonny Hanson	W.R. Ingraham	1965	1678
172 2/8	31 4/8	30 7/8	23 5/8	4 7/8	5 1/8	6	5	Perry Co., IL	W.R. Ingraham	Raymond E. Haertling	1968	1678
172 2/8	25 4/8	22 4/8	23 3/8	4 7/8	5	7	6	Perry Co., IL	Raymond E. Haertling	Ralph J. Przygoda, Jr.	1978	1678
172 2/8	25 6/8	24 2/8	20	4 5/8	4 5/8	6	8	Perkins Co., SD	Ralph J. Przygoda, Jr.	Randy G. Swenson	1979	1678
172 2/8	24 6/8	25 3/8	18 2/8	5 2/8	5 1/8	6	5	Trego Co., KS	Randy G. Swenson	Alan Baldwin	1982	1678
172 2/8	25 7/8	25 6/8	20 2/8	4 4/8	4 4/8	5	5	Cattaraugus Co., NY	Alan Baldwin	Thomas J. Hinchey	1982	1678
172 2/8	26 2/8	25 1/8	22	5	5	7	5	Pendleton Co., KY	Thomas J. Hinchey	Kevin L. Galloway	1983	1678
172 2/8	24 7/8	25	18 2/8	4 7/8	5	6	5	Putman Co., GA	Kevin L. Galloway	Spunky Thornton	1983	1678
172 2/8	26 2/8	25	18 7/8	5	5	6	6	Stewart Co., TN	Spunky Thornton	Joe K. Sanders	1984	1678

Score	Main Beam R	Main Beam L	Inside Spread	Circ.	Circ.	Pts R	Pts L	Locality	By Whom Killed	Owner	Date	Rank
172 2/8	27 6/8	30	20 4/8	5 4/8	5 4/8	7	8	Minnedosa River, MB	Eric W.C. Abel	Eric W.C. Abel	1986	1678
172 2/8	27 1/8	27	22	5	5 3/8	5	5	Jefferson Co., IA	Paul Hagist, Jr.	Paul Hagist, Jr.	1986	1678
172 2/8	26 7/8	27 6/8	26 2/8	4 3/8	4 2/8	5	6	Saunders Co., NE	John I. Kunert	John I. Kunert	1986	1678
172 2/8	24 2/8	25	18 1/8	4 3/8	4 2/8	5	8	Minnesota	Unknown	Jeff A. Puhl	PR 1987	1678
172 2/8	26 2/8	25 5/8	23 4/8	4 4/8	4 4/8	6	6	Scott Co., MN	Kenneth J. Scherer	Kenneth J. Scherer	1987	1678
172 2/8	22 7/8	27 1/8	16 3/8	5 4/8	5 3/8	6	8	Rainy Lake, MN	Andrew Brigham	Andrew Brigham	1989	1678
172 2/8	26 1/8	26 6/8	21	5 2/8	5 4/8	7	8	Norman Co., MN	Corey Hoseth	Corey Hoseth	1989	1678
172 2/8	26	26	22	5 4/8	5 2/8	8	8	Washtenaw Co., MI	Guy A. Miller	Guy A. Miller	1989	1678
172 2/8	25 1/8	25	18	5	5 2/8	5	5	Union Co., IL	Richard A. Sotiropoulos	Richard A. Sotiropoulos	1990	1678
172 2/8	26 3/8	25	21 2/8	5	5	6	6	Coahuila, MX	G. Rone Allen	G. Rone Allen	1992	1678
172 2/8	27 2/8	26	20	4 6/8	4 6/8	5	6	Miami Co., OH	Donald J. Boehmer, Jr.	Donald J. Boehmer, Jr.	1992	1678
172 2/8	27 4/8	27 3/8	20	5 3/8	5 3/8	6	6	Christian Co., KY	Randall G. Joiner	Randall G. Joiner	1992	1678
172 2/8	26 3/8	25 5/8	19 5/8	5	5	5	6	Sussex Co., DE	David T. Murray	David T. Murray	1992	1678
172 2/8	24 2/8	25 4/8	18	4	4	7	6	Mercer Co., MO	Brad Holt	Brad Holt	1993	1678
172 2/8	27 3/8	27 6/8	21 3/8	5 6/8	5 5/8	6	6	Norton Co., KS	Jim Keenan	Jim Keenan	1993	1678
172 2/8	26 2/8	26	22 4/8	4 6/8	4 6/8	8	8	Clayton Co., IA	Scott L. Doerring	Scott L. Doerring	1995	1678
172 2/8	26	25 7/8	19 7/8	5	5	6	6	Lee Co., IA	Chris L. Schiller	Chris L. Schiller	1995	1678
172 2/8	25 5/8	25 2/8	18	4 7/8	4 7/8	5	5	Brandon, MB	Robert W. Jonasson	Robert W. Jonasson	1996	1678
172 2/8	29 2/8	28 6/8	17 6/8	4 7/8	5	5	5	St. Louis Co., MN	Picked Up	Jerome L. Schaller	1996	1678
172 1/8	24 2/8	24 7/8	19 5/8	4 3/8	4 4/8	5	5	Wyandotte Co., KS	Earl A. Cooksey	Earl A. Cooksey	1922	1714
172 1/8	25 6/8	25 5/8	19 3/8	5 4/8	5 2/8	5	5	Juneau Co., WI	Unknown	Clark G. Gallup	1949	1714
172 1/8	26 1/8	26 2/8	19 3/8	4 4/8	4 4/8	6	5	St. Louis Co., MN	Luke Schoeppner	Ted Schoeppner	1955	1714
172 1/8	28 1/8	28 1/8	25 5/8	5	5	6	5	Morson, ON	Almer Godin	Almer Godin	1957	1714
172 1/8	30 1/8	30 1/8	20 7/8	4 7/8	5 1/8	5	6	Fillmore Co., MN	C.J. Semmen & G. Lea	Charles J. Semmen	1961	1714
172 1/8	26 3/8	26 4/8	21 5/8	5 1/8	4 6/8	5	5	Pickens Co., AL	Walter Jaynes	Walter Jaynes	1968	1714
172 1/8	27	27 3/8	23 2/8	4 6/8	4 6/8	8	8	Hughes Co., SD	Mark Lilevjen	Mark Lilevjen	1971	1714
172 1/8	28 5/8	28 3/8	19 2/8	5	4 5/8	7	7	Coshocton Co., OH	Virgil E. Carpenter	Virgil E. Carpenter	1972	1714
172 1/8	27 2/8	26 5/8	18 6/8	4 6/8	4 3/8	7	6	Queen Annes Co., MD	James R. Spies, Jr.	James R. Spies, Jr.	1976	1714
172 1/8	24	24 4/8	20 6/8	5 1/8	5 1/8	5	8	Fillmore Co., MN	Murrel Mathison	Murrel Mathison	1977	1714
172 1/8	25 3/8	24 2/8	21 5/8	4 3/8	4 3/8	7	6	Wabasha Co., MN	Timothy R. Pries	Timothy R. Pries	1977	1714
172 1/8	25 1/8	25 5/8	16 4/8	4 7/8	4 7/8	6	6	Winona Co., MN	Robert J. Cordie	Robert J. Cordie	1979	1714
172 1/8	26 1/8	25	18 5/8	5 5/8	5 5/8	6	8	Clinton Co., IA	R. Dean Grimes	R. Dean Grimes	1984	1714
172 1/8	24 7/8	24	18 6/8	4 6/8	4 6/8	7	6	Clinton Co., IL	James D. Rueter	James D. Rueter	1984	1714
172 1/8	27 6/8	27 1/8	19 4/8	4 5/8	4 5/8	6	7	Granville Co., NC	Dudley Barnes	Dudley Barnes	1985	1714
172 1/8	25 7/8	25 7/8	20 3/8	4 3/8	4 3/8	7	5	Buffalo Co., WI	Aaron Comero	Aaron Comero	1986	1714
172 1/8	24 1/8	24 5/8	19 6/8	5 3/8	5 3/8	5	6	Louisa Co., IA	John Bloomer	John Bloomer	1987	1714
172 1/8	25	25 5/8	18 3/8	5 4/8	5 4/8	7	7	Lac Emilien, AB	Dennis Ewanec	Dennis Ewanec	1987	1714
172 1/8	27 2/8	26 7/8	21 1/8	5 6/8	5 6/8	6	5	Chase Co., KS	Picked Up	Darwin Bailey	1989	1714
172 1/8	26 2/8	26 4/8	20 1/8	5 5/8	5 5/8	4	4	Jennings Co., IN	Gerald G. Powers	Gerald G. Powers	1989	1714
172 1/8	25 1/8	24 6/8	22 5/8	5 7/8	5 7/8	7	8	Lake Co., IL	Mark J. Kramer	Mark J. Kramer	1990	1714
172 1/8	24 6/8	27 4/8	17 5/8	4 1/8	4 3/8	8	8	Dooly Co., GA	Marty T. McNulty	Marty T. McNulty	1990	1714
172 1/8	27 4/8	22 6/8	22 6/8	5 4/8	4 1/8	6	6	Smoky River, AB	Lawrence Zawacki	Lawrence Zawacki	1990	1714
172 1/8	22 6/8	27 3/8	22 3/8	5 3/8	5 4/8	6	6	Goose Lake, SK	Joe W. Schmidt	Joe W. Schmidt	1991	1714
172 1/8	27 3/8	25 6/8	19 3/8	4 6/8	5 5/8	4	4	Genesee Co., MI	David C. Bastion	David C. Bastion	1992	1714
172 1/8	25 2/8	26 3/8	19 3/8	4 7/8	5 3/8	5	5	Miller Co., MO	Jim L. Bell	Jim L. Bell	1992	1714
172 1/8	23 7/8	23 3/8	18 1/8	4 4/8	4 6/8	6	6	Harrison Co., IA	Picked Up	Chad M. Kuhns	1994	1714
172 1/8	27 1/8	26 5/8	20 6/8	5 7/8	6	6	6	Butler Co., KY	Bradley D. Cardwell	Bradley D. Cardwell	1995	1714

Odocoileus virginianus virginianus and certain related subspecies

Score	Length of Main Beam R	L	Inside Spread	Circumference at Smallest Place Between Burr and First Point R	L	Number of Points R	L	Locality	Hunter	Owner	Date Killed	Rank
172 1/8	24 4/8	23 7/8	18 5/8	4 5/8	4 6/8	6	6	Kenedy Co., TX	Lee M. Bass	Lee M. Bass	1996	1714
172 1/8	29 3/8	30 2/8	21	5	4 4/8	7	8	Rock Co., WI	Steven W. Kravick	Steven W. Kravick	1996	1714
172	28 4/8	28	19 4/8	5 7/8	5 6/8	5	5	Carlton Co., MN	Picked Up	John R. Steffes, Sr.	1937	1744
172	26 4/8	25 2/8	19 1/8	5 2/8	5 3/8	5	6	Oconto Co., WI	Henry J. Bredael	Henry J. Bredael	1939	1744
172	25 4/8	26 3/8	19 6/8	4 7/8	4 6/8	5	5	Sauk Co., WI	Rudy Lehnherr	Philip J. Rouse	1946	1744
172	24 4/8	23 6/8	17	5 2/8	5 4/8	5	5	Neepawa, MB	Jim Sinclair	Jim Sinclair	1947	1744
172	25 6/8	26 7/8	24 2/8	5 2/8	5 1/8	6	6	Woodbury Co., IA	Harold Horsley	Harold Horsley	1956	1744
172	25 2/8	25 6/8	18 4/8	5 3/8	5 2/8	5	7	Henderson Co., IL	Harry M. Carner	Harry M. Carner	1959	1744
172	26 2/8	27 2/8	18 5/8	5 5/8	5 5/8	9	8	Wadena, SK	Edgar Smale	Edgar Smale	1959	1744
172	26 4/8	23	21 4/8	4 6/8	4 6/8	5	6	Buffalo Co., WI	Ralph Duellman	Ralph Duellman	1960	1744
172	24 3/8	24	17 7/8	5 2/8	5 2/8	5	6	N. Battleford, SK	Dick Napastuk	Dick Napastuk	1962	1744
172	26 1/8	25	24 2/8	4 5/8	4 4/8	5	5	Bearden, AR	Buddy Wise	Buddy Wise	1962	1744
172	24 1/8	24 1/8	20 2/8	6 5/8	6 4/8	8	7	Butts Co., GA	Jack Hammond	Jack Hammond	1963	1744
172	25	26 4/8	21 4/8	5 1/8	5 2/8	5	5	Parkman, SK	A.T. Mair	A.T. Mair	1963	1744
172	24 6/8	24 6/8	17 2/8	4 3/8	4 4/8	6	5	Joseph Plains, ID	Jim Felton	Jim Felton	1965	1744
172	23 7/8	23 4/8	18 6/8	4 4/8	4 4/8	5	5	Fergus Co., MT	Bill Scott	Martin J. Kilham, Jr.	1973	1744
172	25 5/8	24 5/8	25 6/8	5 1/8	5 4/8	5	6	Perry Co., OH	Bill Pargeon	Bill Pargeon	1976	1744
172	25	25 2/8	18 6/8	5 2/8	5 2/8	6	5	Adams Co., MS	Nan F. New	Nan F. New	1977	1744
172	25 1/8	26	19 3/8	5 2/8	4 7/8	7	5	Furnas Co., NE	Marvin A. Briegel	Marvin A. Briegel	1980	1744
172	26	25 6/8	22 3/8	4 4/8	4 3/8	6	7	Muskingum Co., OH	David R. Hatfield	David R. Hatfield	1980	1744
172	27 3/8	27 1/8	19 3/8	4 4/8	4 4/8	5	6	Marshall Co., MN	Keith D. Anderson	Keith D. Anderson	1982	1744
172	24 6/8	25 6/8	22 6/8	5 3/8	5 3/8	5	6	Miami Co., KS	Dan R. Moore	Dan R. Moore	1982	1744
172	24	25 7/8	18	4 2/8	4 2/8	6	5	Tift Co., GA	Mayo Tucker	Mayo Tucker	1982	1744
172	27 3/8	28 3/8	18 2/8	5	5 1/8	5	5	Westmoreland Co., NB	Edgar Cormier	Edgar Cormier	1983	1744
172	25 7/8	25 2/8	19	4 5/8	4 5/8	5	5	Waukesha Co., WI	Donald R. Friedlein	Donald R. Friedlein	1983	1744
172	29 5/8	29 4/8	22 2/8	5 4/8	5 4/8	4	4	Edwards Co., IL	Picked Up	George W. Flaim	1985	1744
172	26 1/8	26 3/8	17 4/8	5	4 6/8	5	6	Dodge Co., WI	Dennis E. Schulteis	Dennis E. Schulteis	1985	1744
172	27	27	17 1/8	4 6/8	5 2/8	6	5	Caroline Co., MD	Garey N. Brown	Garey N. Brown	1986	1744
172	25 4/8	25 4/8	17 4/8	4 4/8	4 4/8	6	6	Coahuila, MX	Picked Up	Carl Kallina	1986	1744
172	25 6/8	26 4/8	21 6/8	4 6/8	4 4/8	6	6	Henderson Co., KY	Gary Hancock	Gary Hancock	1990	1744
172	23 7/8	23 5/8	15 6/8	4 2/8	4	5	5	Callaway Co., MO	Picked Up	Larry W. Quick	1990	1744
172	24 4/8	25 3/8	18	4 6/8	4 6/8	6	7	Harrison Co., MO	Timothy E. Black	Timothy E. Black	1991	1744
172	24 2/8	24 7/8	19 3/8	4 7/8	4 7/8	10	5	De Kalb Co., MO	Dean Davis	Dean Davis	1991	1744
172	26 3/8	24 6/8	19 1/8	5 1/8	5 1/8	5	9	Battle River, SK	Robert J. Bullock	Robert J. Bullock	1992	1744
172	24 5/8	22 7/8	18 6/8	4 6/8	4 4/8	6	5	Daviess Co., MO	David K. DeWeese	David K. DeWeese	1992	1744
172	27 5/8	28	23 5/8	5 5/8	6	6	6	Greene Co., IL	B. David McCarthy	B. David McCarthy	1992	1744

Score	Length of Main Beam R	L	Inside Spread	Circumference R	L	Points R	L	Locality	Hunter	Owner	Date Killed	Rank
172	22 2/8	22	16 2/8	5	5	7	8	Ebel Creek, SK	Cory Zastrizny	Cory Zastrizny	1992	1744
172	26	26 3/8	19 5/8	5 7/8	5 4/8	5	6	Buffalo Co., WI	James L. Sturz	James L. Sturz	1994	1744
172	25 7/8	26 3/8	20 4/8	5 4/8	6 1/8	6	7	Hillsdale Co., MI	Art P. Toney	Art P. Toney	1994	1744
172	26 2/8	26	20	5 3/8	5 3/8	5	6	Arkansas Co., AR	Donald R. Sweetin	Donald R. Sweetin	1996	1744
171 7/8	27 6/8	27 2/8	20 1/8	5	5	8	5	Madison Parish, LA	M.L. Arnold	David D. Arnold	1941	1782
171 7/8	25 4/8	27	16 4/8	5 7/8	5 7/8	6	6	Scotch Bay, MB	W.J. Harker	W.J. Harker	1951	1782
171 7/8	27	27 1/8	21 4/8	6 3/8	6 5/8	5	6	Fillmore Co., MN	Maynard Howe	Maynard Howe	1957	1782
171 7/8	26 1/8	27	20 5/8	4 6/8	4 5/8	5	5	Houston Co., MN	Donald R. Sobolik	Donald R. Sobolik	1958	1782
171 7/8	26 1/8	25 6/8	20 1/8	5 1/8	5 2/8	7	6	Aroostook Co., ME	Julian B. Perry	Julian B. Perry	1962	1782
171 7/8	25 3/8	25 7/8	18 2/8	4 7/8	5 1/8	8	5	Prairie Co., AR	C.L. Vanhouten	C.L. Vanhouten	1964	1782
171 7/8	24 6/8	26	17 2/8	4 2/8	4 2/8	5	7	Duval Co., TX	Dan Harrison	Mike Pillow	1969	1782
171 7/8	25 4/8	25 7/8	18 4/8	5 3/8	5 3/8	6	7	Union Co., IA	Darrell M. Gutz	Darrell M. Gutz	1973	1782
171 7/8	25 2/8	26 1/8	21 1/8	5	4 4/8	5	6	Oxford Co., ME	Picked Up	Francis Ontengco	1980	1782
171 7/8	25	24 4/8	20	5	5	5	5	Washington Co., OH	Thomas E. Burnette	Thomas E. Burnette	1982	1782
171 7/8	26 2/8	26 4/8	24 1/8	4 4/8	4 4/8	5	6	Scotland Co., MO	David R. Smith	David R. Smith	1984	1782
171 7/8	25 2/8	25 7/8	18 5/8	4 7/8	4 7/8	6	6	Lafayette Co., AR	Billy D. Bland, Jr.	Billy D. Bland, Jr.	1986	1782
171 7/8	26 5/8	26 1/8	20 3/8	5 1/8	5 1/8	5	6	Clayton Co., IA	Michael A. Roussel	Michael A. Roussel	1986	1782
171 7/8	27	27	19	4 7/8	4 6/8	6	5	Grundy Co., TN	Wilson W. Weaver	Wilson W. Weaver	1987	1782
171 7/8	27 5/8	26 6/8	21 5/8	4 4/8	4 3/8	6	6	Lucas Co., IA	Tim M. Whitlatch	Tim M. Whitlatch	1989	1782
171 7/8	24 3/8	23 4/8	18 2/8	5 1/8	5 2/8	5	6	Dunn Co., ND	Doug L. Martin	Doug L. Martin	1991	1782
171 7/8	27 7/8	27 6/8	20 5/8	5	4 7/8	5	6	Whiteside Co., IL	Ann M. Ryan	Ann M. Ryan	1991	1782
171 7/8	27 6/8	27 7/8	22 2/8	5 1/8	5 1/8	4	6	Cross Co., AR	Mark C. Taylor	Mark C. Taylor	1992	1782
171 7/8	25 5/8	24 6/8	16 5/8	5	5 1/8	5	6	Winneshiek Co., IA	Richard A. Bollman	Richard A. Bollman	1993	1782
171 7/8	29 6/8	30 3/8	21 3/8	4 6/8	4 5/8	5	6	Jones Co., IA	Michael L. First	Michael L. First	1993	1782
171 7/8	27 4/8	26 7/8	20 7/8	4 7/8	4 6/8	6	5	Jo Daviess Co., IL	Donald W. Hansen, Jr.	Donald W. Hansen, Jr.	1994	1782
171 7/8	27 4/8	28 2/8	17 7/8	4 7/8	4 7/8	5	5	Pulaski Co., AR	Charles L. Marcum, Jr.	Charles L. Marcum, Jr.	1994	1782
171 7/8	25 7/8	26 1/8	19 4/8	4 5/8	4 5/8	6	5	Portage Co., WI	Lawrence P. Wierzba	Lawrence P. Wierzba	1994	1782
171 6/8	28 1/8	28	17 7/8	5 2/8	5 3/8	5	6	Almonte, ON	Scott K. Camp	Scott K. Camp	1995	1809
171 6/8	26 3/8	26 3/8	21 3/8	5	5	5	5	Henderson Co., KY	Aaron D. Parrish	Aaron D. Parrish	1995	1809
171 6/8	26 6/8	26 6/8	19 7/8	4 7/8	4 7/8	7	5	Muhlenberg Co., KY	Creighton Spurlock	Creighton Spurlock	1995	1809
171 6/8	24 2/8	24 2/8	22 7/8	5 3/8	5 3/8	8	8	Peoria Co., IL	Richard W. Winship	Richard W. Winship	1996	1809
171 6/8	26 5/8	26 4/8	18	4 6/8	4 6/8	5	5	Niagara, WI	Francis H. Van Ginkel	David Watson	1945	1809
171 6/8	26	27	18 4/8	6 2/8	6 2/8	5	5	St. Louis Co., MN	Paul S. Paulson	Paul S. Paulson	1946	1809
171 6/8	25	24 6/8	22	4 6/8	4 6/8	7	6	Maverick Co., TX	Harry Garner	Harry Garner	1962	1809
171 6/8	24 6/8	27 1/8	19	5 2/8	5 2/8	6	6	Turtle Mt., MB	Roy Hainsworth	Roy Hainsworth	1963	1809
171 6/8	27 1/8	26 5/8	21 5/8	4 4/8	4 4/8	6	9	Asquith, SK	M.S. Vanin	M.S. Vanin	1963	1809
171 6/8	25 6/8	25 6/8	18 2/8	4 1/8	4 1/8	5	5	Maple Creek, SK	G.J. Burch	G.J. Burch	1967	1809
171 6/8	24 4/8	24 3/8	17 1/8	5 6/8	5 5/8	8	8	Muscatine Co., IA	Larry Dipple	Larry Dipple	1967	1809
171 6/8	26 3/8	26 1/8	20 5/8	5 3/8	5 6/8	6	6	St. Louis Co., MN	Unknown	David G. Gagnon	PR 1970	1809
171 6/8	28 4/8	27 2/8	19 3/8	4 7/8	4 7/8	4	6	Buffalo Co., WI	Richard Schultz	Richard Schultz	1973	1809
171 6/8	25 1/8	26 2/8	18 4/8	4 5/8	4 5/8	6	5	Dawes Co., NE	Tim Morava	Tim Morava	1974	1809
171 6/8	27 3/8	27 3/8	21	5 6/8	5 6/8	5	5	Adams Co., IL	R.C. Stephens	R.C. Stephens	1975	1809
171 6/8	26 2/8	25 5/8	24 1/8	5 3/8	5 3/8	6	6	Clinton Co., NY	William J. Branch	William J. Branch	1982	1809
171 6/8	25 5/8	26 3/8	19 7/8	4 5/8	4 5/8	7	10	Perry Co., IL	Daniel P. Hollenkamp	Daniel P. Hollenkamp	1982	1809
171 6/8	26 6/8	23 2/8	19 4/8	4 6/8	4 6/8	10	8	Gray Creek, BC	Ross Oliver	Ross Oliver	1983	1809
171 6/8	24 4/8	26 3/8	20 4/8	4 6/8	4 6/8	4	5	Van Buren Co., MI	Ronald E. Eldred	Ronald E. Eldred	1985	1809
171 6/8	28 3/8	29 2/8	23 7/8	6	6	8	8	Taylor Co., GA	Picked Up	Charles L. Childree		1809

WHITETAIL DEER - TYPICAL ANTLERS

Odocoileus virginianus virginianus and certain related subspecies

Score	Length of Main Beam R	L	Inside Spread	Circumference at Smallest Place Between Burr and First Point R	L	Number of Points R	L	Locality	Hunter	Owner	Date Killed	Rank
171 6/8	25 5/8	25 6/8	16	5 3/8	5 3/8	5	5	Peace River, AB	Austin V. Cowan, Jr.	Austin V. Cowan, Jr.	1988	1809
171 6/8	26 2/8	26	21 6/8	4 7/8	4 7/8	5	5	Garden Co., NE	Doreen R. Lawrence	Doreen R. Lawrence	1989	1809
171 6/8	24 5/8	24 7/8	19 7/8	4 7/8	5 1/8	6	6	Tunica Co., MS	Delton D. Davis	Delton D. Davis	1990	1809
171 6/8	24 6/8	23 4/8	20 6/8	4 6/8	4 6/8	5	5	Dunn Co., WI	James W. Belmore	James W. Belmore	1991	1809
171 6/8	26 5/8	25 3/8	21 6/8	5 1/8	5 1/8	6	6	Webb Co., TX	David W. Bivins	David W. Bivins	1992	1809
171 6/8	27 5/8	25 3/8	18	5 1/8	5 2/8	9	8	Miami Co., KS	Garth S. Davis	Garth S. Davis	1992	1809
171 6/8	28 1/8	29	19	5	5 3/8	7	6	Campbell Creek, AB	K. Ryan & B. Winters	Ken Ryan	1992	1809
171 6/8	28	25 4/8	19 1/8	5	5 3/8	7	9	Endeavour, SK	Jeffery A. Duckworth	Jeffery A. Duckworth	1993	1809
171 6/8	27 7/8	29 3/8	22 6/8	5 5/8	5 5/8	7	6	Hancock Co., IL	Garold E. McConnull	Garold E. McConnull	1993	1809
171 6/8	26 6/8	27 3/8	20 2/8	4 3/8	4 4/8	5	6	Telfair Co., GA	Craig Walker	Craig Walker	1993	1809
171 6/8	27 3/8	27 5/8	18 5/8	4 3/8	4 3/8	7	7	Juneau Co., WI	Thomas J. Brien	Thomas J. Brien	1994	1809
171 6/8	26 3/8	26 1/8	19 6/8	4 6/8	4 6/8	5	5	Lone Rock, SK	Keith R. Fournier	Keith R. Fournier	1994	1809
171 6/8	26 3/8	25 7/8	14 6/8	4 3/8	4 3/8	5	6	Grayson Co., KY	Jurl Huffman	Jurl Huffman	1994	1809
171 6/8	28 5/8	27 1/8	19 2/8	4 5/8	4 6/8	5	7	Washtenaw Co., MI	Richard J. Degrand	Richard J. Degrand	1995	1809
171 6/8	26 4/8	26 5/8	19	5 2/8	5 5/8	5	5	Osage Co., OK	Don Gaddis	Don Gaddis	1995	1809
171 6/8	28 1/8	28 1/8	22 1/8	5 2/8	5 1/8	6	5	Jackson Co., IA	Rodger L. Johnson	Rodger L. Johnson	1995	1809
171 6/8	28 4/8	28 4/8	24 4/8	5	5 1/8	7	9	Allamakee Co., IA	Gregg N. Klein	Gregg N. Klein	1995	1809
171 6/8	23 4/8	22 6/8	16 2/8	5 2/8	5 6/8	6	6	Grande Prairie, AB	Theodore H. Stegman	Theodore H. Stegman	1995	1809
171 6/8	26 6/8	26 5/8	18 6/8	3 6/8	3 6/8	6	6	Anderson Co., KS	Gary Shields	Gary Shields	1996	1809
171 5/8	25	25 5/8	16 2/8	4 3/8	4 3/8	6	5	Koochiching Co., MN	Ray W. Bastin	Ray W. Bastin	1930	1844
171 5/8	24 4/8	24 6/8	19 4/8	5	5	9	10	Morton Co., ND	Dick Eastman	Sioux Sporting Goods	1955	1844
171 5/8	22 1/8	23	19	5 2/8	5 4/8	5	6	Tensas Parish, LA	Jim Keahey	Gerald P. Begnaud, Jr.	1960	1844
171 5/8	25 6/8	26 4/8	20 6/8	5 1/8	5 1/8	7	6	Hanley, SK	L.R. Libke	L.R. Libke	1961	1844
171 5/8	26	25 3/8	24 4/8	4 6/8	4 7/8	8	8	Langbank, SK	Thomas K. Grimm	Thomas K. Grimm	1968	1844
171 5/8	26 4/8	28 4/8	20 1/8	4 6/8	5	6	5	Meeker Co., MN	Ronald E. Lampi	Ronald E. Lampi	1973	1844
171 5/8	27 2/8	27	17 6/8	4 4/8	4 6/8	6	6	Willowbrook, SK	William Hrebenik	William Hrebenik	1976	1844
171 5/8	25 1/8	26 1/8	16 7/8	4	4	7	7	Baldwin Co., GA	Picked Up	E. Donald Graham	1977	1844
171 5/8	27	25 5/8	18 2/8	5 2/8	5 2/8	6	6	Otter Tail Co., MN	Carl D. Hill	Carl D. Hill	1977	1844
171 5/8	25 3/8	24 7/8	18 3/8	4 6/8	4 5/8	5	6	Grant Co., MN	Gary P. Kollman	Gary P. Kollman	1980	1844
171 5/8	27 3/8	27 4/8	18 3/8	5	4 6/8	6	5	Riley Co., KS	Mick McCallister	Mick McCallister	1980	1844
171 5/8	26	26	17 3/8	4 3/8	4 3/8	5	5	Crawford Co., MO	Chris Glaser	Fred Glaser	1982	1844
171 5/8	27 1/8	25 7/8	20	4 7/8	5	6	6	Pocahontas Co., IA	Larry G. Almond	Larry G. Almond	1983	1844
171 5/8	25 4/8	26 5/8	19 3/8	5 5/8	5 6/8	7	7	Bonnell Brook, NB	Steve R. McCutcheon	Steve R. McCutcheon	1984	1844
171 5/8	24 2/8	23 2/8	16 1/8	4 6/8	4 6/8	6	6	Carlton Co., MN	Charles Ditmarsen	Charles Ditmarsen	1985	1844
171 5/8	26 3/8	25 5/8	19 3/8	5 2/8	5 2/8	5	5	Logan Co., KY	Alan M. Scott	Alan M. Scott	1987	1844
171 5/8	25 6/8	24 6/8	21 6/8	4 6/8	4 6/8	7	5	Mercer Co., OH	Daniel J. Garman	Daniel J. Garman	1988	1844

Score	Main Beam R	Main Beam L	Inside Spread	Circ. R	Circ. L	Pts R	Pts L	Locality	Hunter	Owner	Date Killed	Rank
171 5/8	26 4/8	26 3/8	18 3/8	5 4/8	5 5/8	8	9	Anderson Co., KY	Blaine K. Price	Blaine K. Price	1990	1844
171 5/8	24 1/8	23 6/8	19 7/8	4 7/8	4 6/8	6	6	La Salle Co., TX	Harvey N. Bouldin, Jr.	Harvey N. Bouldin, Jr.	1992	1844
171 5/8	27 7/8	27 3/8	17 3/8	4 2/8	4 2/8	5	5	Trempealeau Co., WI	Scott D. Schank	Scott D. Schank	1993	1844
171 5/8	28	29 2/8	22 1/8	5 4/8	5 2/8	7	6	Warren Co., MO	Scott Parker	Scott Parker	1994	1844
171 5/8	27 7/8	26 5/8	18 1/8	4 2/8	5 2/8	6	6	Penobscot Co., ME	David Nadeau	David Nadeau	1995	1844
171 5/8	25 7/8	27 4/8	18 1/8	4 7/8	4 5/8	5	5	Lucas Co., IA	Picked Up	Harry Nicholson	1995	1844
171 5/8	26	21 7/8	18 3/8	5 2/8	5 2/8	5	5	Douglas Co., KS	Jerry S. Pippen	Jerry S. Pippen	1995	1844
171 5/8	27 1/8	25 2/8	22 5/8	5 5/8	5 4/8	5	5	Fremont Co., IA	Ryan T. Knapp	Ryan T. Knapp	1996	1844
171 5/8	24	26	21 6/8	4 4/8	4 7/8	6	6	Turtle Lake, SK	Andrew M. Milanowski	Andrew M. Milanowski	1996	1844
171 4/8	25 5/8	24	24	4 5/8	5 2/8	7	6	Wood Co., WI	Unknown	Joe Hutwagner	1918	1870
171 4/8	25 1/8	26 1/8	17 4/8	4 5/8	5 2/8	6	7	Delta Co., MI	Lawrence Charles	Bass Pro Shops F. & W. Mus.	PR 1941	1870
171 4/8	24 6/8	26 1/8	20 4/8	5 2/8	5 1/8	6	6	Hayter, AB	H.D.L. Loucks	H.D.L. Loucks	1953	1870
171 4/8	26 3/8	26	19 2/8	5	4 7/8	5	6	Woodlands Dist., MB	Bill Rutherford	Bill Rutherford	1961	1870
171 4/8	27 2/8	26 3/8	21 6/8	5 6/8	5 7/8	11	9	Clay Co., MN	Clint Foslien	Clint Foslien	1965	1870
171 4/8	26	27 2/8	23 6/8	4 7/8	4 3/8	7	7	Schroon Lake, NY	Richard E. Johndrow	Richard E. Johndrow	1968	1870
171 4/8	26	26	23 2/8	5 1/8	5	5	5	Hamilton Co., IA	Picked Up	Jerry Price	1972	1870
171 4/8	28 6/8	26 6/8	22 7/8	5 2/8	5 1/8	8	8	Lac qui Parle Co., MN	Wayne A. Hegland	Wayne A. Hegland	1977	1870
171 4/8	25 3/8	26 6/8	22	4 6/8	4 7/8	5	5	Southampton Co., VA	Sam J. Pope, Jr.	Davis-Ridley Hunt Club	1978	1870
171 4/8	26	25	22 6/8	4 6/8	4 7/8	6	6	Steele Co., MN	Craig Evans	Craig Evans	1978	1870
171 4/8	25	24 5/8	18 2/8	4 3/8	4 4/8	5	5	Clearwater Co., MN	Peter Tranby	Peter Tranby	1978	1870
171 4/8	24 5/8	25 4/8	19 6/8	4 5/8	4 6/8	5	5	Cherry Co., NE	Jim R. Monnier	Jim R. Monnier	1981	1870
171 4/8	25 4/8	30 1/8	19 2/8	5 3/8	5 2/8	4	5	Union Co., KY	Wayne Gibson	Wayne Gibson	1982	1870
171 4/8	30 1/8	25	27 2/8	4 3/8	3 6/8	4	4	Rusk Co., WI	Luke Dernovsek III	Luke Dernovsek III	1983	1870
171 4/8	25	27 1/8	20 4/8	4 5/8	4 5/8	6	6	Becker Co., MN	Kraig J. Ketter	Kraig J. Ketter	1983	1870
171 4/8	27 1/8	24 5/8	18 6/8	5	4 7/8	6	6	Crooked Lake, AB	Bruce J. Ferguson	Bruce J. Ferguson	1984	1870
171 4/8	24 5/8	24 7/8	21 3/8	4 7/8	5 2/8	8	8	Latah Co., ID	Darwin L. Baker	Darwin L. Baker	1986	1870
171 4/8	24 7/8	26 1/8	19 4/8	4 4/8	4 4/8	6	6	Rocky Mt. House, AB	Lloyd Cadrain	Lloyd Cadrain	1987	1870
171 4/8	26 1/8	26	20 1/8	4 7/8	5	8	8	Unknown	Unknown	Jerry L. Johnson	PR 1987	1870
171 4/8	26 6/8	26 7/8	17 2/8	4 6/8	4 6/8	5	5	Licking Co., OH	Michael E. Fleitz	Michael E. Fleitz	1988	1870
171 4/8	26 6/8	25 2/8	19 6/8	4 6/8	4 5/8	5	5	Washtenaw Co., MI	Michael C. Lamirand	Michael C. Lamirand	1988	1870
171 4/8	25 1/8	25 5/8	23 6/8	5 2/8	5 3/8	6	6	Kankakee Co., IL	Dennis Schneider	Dennis Schneider	1988	1870
171 4/8	26 7/8	27	17	4 7/8	4 7/8	8	8	Bollinger Co., MO	Darrell L. Bostic	Darrell L. Bostic	1989	1870
171 4/8	25 5/8	25 7/8	18	4 6/8	4 6/8	5	5	Ballard Co., KY	Howard P. Gardner	Howard P. Gardner	1989	1870
171 4/8	27 7/8	28 2/8	21	5 3/8	5 3/8	5	5	Lenawee Co., MI	Robert E. Knight	Robert E. Knight	1989	1870
171 4/8	28 2/8	26 3/8	17 6/8	4 4/8	4 4/8	5	5	Clay Co., KS	Eldyn W. Peck	Eldyn W. Peck	1989	1870
171 4/8	26 7/8	25 2/8	17 5/8	5 1/8	5 1/8	6	6	Scotland Co., MO	Harry Robeson	Harry Robeson	1989	1870
171 4/8	26 3/8	24 3/8	18 6/8	5 2/8	5 2/8	5	5	Rock Island Co., IL	David Parchert	David Parchert	1990	1870
171 4/8	26 4/8	25 3/8	21	4 5/8	4 5/8	5	5	Greene Co., IN	Jason B. Anderson	Jason B. Anderson	1991	1870
171 4/8	25 3/8	24 3/8	21 2/8	4 2/8	4 2/8	5	5	Iowa	Unknown	William H. Lilienthal	PR 1991	1870
171 4/8	24 3/8	26 5/8	16	4 2/8	5 1/8	6	6	Sangamon Co., IL	Michael R. Vincent	Michael R. Vincent	1991	1870
171 4/8	27	24 1/8	18 4/8	5	5	6	6	Whiteside Co., IL	William D. Kruse	William D. Kruse	1992	1870
171 4/8	27	26 2/8	21 4/8	4 6/8	4 6/8	5	5	Jasper Co., IL	Rick N. Strole	Rick N. Strole	1992	1870
171 4/8	24 1/8	26 6/8	22 6/8	5 1/8	5 1/8	6	6	Harrison Co., KY	Ronald Daugherty	Ronald Daugherty	1994	1870
171 4/8	26 7/8	21	21	4 7/8	4 7/8	5	5	Thunder Hill, SK	James R. Riddick	James R. Riddick	1994	1870
171 4/8	24	23 7/8	17	4 7/8	4 7/8	5	5	Treesbank, MB	Tom J. Gross	Tom J. Gross	1995	1870
171 4/8	26 5/8	21 7/8	21 1/8	4 1/8	4 2/8	9	9	Buffalo Pound Lake, SK	Troy E. Riche	Troy E. Riche	1995	1870
171 4/8	28 1/8	26	18 5/8	4 6/8	4 4/8	6	5	Jefferson Co., WI	Bradley J. Hering	Bradley J. Hering	1996	1870

WHITETAIL DEER - TYPICAL ANTLERS

Odocoileus virginianus virginianus and certain related subspecies

Score	Length of Main Beam		Inside Spread	Circumference at Smallest Place Between Burr and First Point		Number of Points		Locality	Hunter	Owner	Date Killed	Rank
	R	L		R	L	R	L					
171 4/8	28 2/8	27 4/8	20	4 5/8	4 6/8	6	6	Carlton Co., MN	Vincent A. Mullen, Sr.	Vincent A. Mullen, Sr.	1996	1870
171 3/8	26 5/8	26 6/8	21 5/8	4 4/8	4 4/8	9	7	Juneau Co., WI	Fay Hammersley	Fay Hammersley	1938	1909
171 3/8	26	26 3/8	17 6/8	4 4/8	4 3/8	6	7	Herkimer Co., OH	John Christie	John Christie	1957	1909
171 3/8	25 3/8	25 3/8	26 3/8	5 1/8	5 2/8	5	6	Whatshan Lake, BC	Ernest Roberts	Ernest Roberts	1957	1909
171 3/8	31 1/8	29	16	5	5	7	9	Frio Co., TX	Leonard Van Horn	Leonard Van Horn	1962	1909
171 3/8	24 3/8	24 3/8	18 5/8	4 3/8	4 3/8	6	6	Parker Co., TX	Velton L. Ford	Velton L. Ford	1963	1909
171 3/8	26	24 4/8	15 1/8	4 3/8	5 3/8	7	6	La Salle Co., TX	Charles D. Johnson	Charles D. Johnson	1964	1909
171 3/8	22 5/8	22 4/8	18	5 3/8	5 3/8	7	6	Grenfell, SK	George DeMontigny	George DeMontigny	1965	1909
171 3/8	25 2/8	25 2/8	19 3/8	4 2/8	4 3/8	6	7	Oceana Co., MI	Delos Highland	Delos Highland	1967	1909
171 3/8	25 3/8	26 6/8	18 5/8	5 3/8	5 2/8	5	5	Forest Co., WI	Chester Cox, Jr.	Chester Cox, Jr.	1969	1909
171 3/8	22 3/8	23 1/8	14 5/8	5	5	7	6	Metaline Falls Co., WA	Scott Hicks	Scott Hicks	1970	1909
171 3/8	23 4/8	24 2/8	23 1/8	4 7/8	4 7/8	5	5	Kandiyohi Co., MN	Werner B. Reining	Werner B. Reining	1974	1909
171 3/8	25 2/8	24 5/8	22 5/8	5	5	6	6	Pope Co., MN	Corbin G. Corson	Corbin G. Corson	1975	1909
171 3/8	25 2/8	25 3/8	25 2/8	4 3/8	4 4/8	7	6	Bennett Co., SD	Dave Risse	Dave Risse	1975	1909
171 3/8	24 4/8	23 6/8	21 5/8	4 4/8	4 4/8	5	5	Athabasca River, AB	Ron J. Holm	Ron J. Holm	1977	1909
171 3/8	25 3/8	26 2/8	16 2/8	4 6/8	4 6/8	6	7	Pike Co., IL	John C. Shover	John C. Shover	1979	1909
171 3/8	26 1/8	26 2/8	23 2/8	5 4/8	5 5/8	5	6	Buffalo Co., WI	Donald C. Neitzel	Donald C. Neitzel	1981	1909
171 3/8	27 2/8	27 2/8	21 2/8	5	4 7/8	7	6	Boyd Co., NE	Scott A. Sperling	Scott A. Sperling	1982	1909
171 3/8	28	27 1/8	18 4/8	4 4/8	4 7/8	6	6	Kalamazoo Co., MI	Harvey B. Braden	Harvey B. Braden	1984	1909
171 3/8	25 7/8	26 3/8	21 3/8	5 1/8	5 1/8	8	10	Douglas Co., MN	Gregory A. Dropik	Gregory A. Dropik	1984	1909
171 3/8	27 2/8	28 2/8	18 1/8	4 4/8	4 4/8	5	5	Sumner Co., KS	Jeff D. Ehlers	Jeff D. Ehlers	1984	1909
171 3/8	26 7/8	26 6/8	17 7/8	4 7/8	4 6/8	8	6	Turner Co., GA	Jerry S. Cook	Jerry S. Cook	1986	1909
171 3/8	20 4/8	22	19 1/8	4 7/8	5 1/8	6	6	Webb Co., TX	Robert Deligans	Kent Deligans	1986	1909
171 3/8	23 1/8	23	18	5	5	6	5	Washington Co., MO	Jerry D. Bouse	Jerry D. Bouse	1987	1909
171 3/8	23 3/8	23 6/8	18 3/8	4 5/8	4 5/8	5	5	Stonewall Co., TX	Jay W. Knorr	Jay W. Knorr	1987	1909
171 3/8	25 1/8	25 2/8	18 7/8	4 6/8	4 6/8	5	5	Washington Co., KY	Robert F. Medley	Robert F. Medley	1988	1909
171 3/8	26 5/8	25 5/8	19 6/8	5	5	6	6	Washington Co., WI	Joseph E. Kohler	Joseph E. Kohler	1989	1909
171 3/8	27	26 6/8	21 2/8	4 3/8	4 3/8	6	7	Custer Co., NE	Larry C. Beitel	Larry C. Beitel	1990	1909
171 3/8	23 7/8	24 5/8	18 7/8	5	5 2/8	5	6	Wabamun, AB	Greg Crain	Greg Crain	1992	1909
171 3/8	24 3/8	24 7/8	21 1/8	5	4 7/8	5	5	Jersey Co., IL	Louis E. Johnson	Louis E. Johnson	1992	1909
171 3/8	26 4/8	26 6/8	18 5/8	5 3/8	5 2/8	5	7	Howard Co., MO	Derrick Powell	Derrick Powell	1992	1909
171 3/8	26 1/8	27	20 7/8	6	6	6	7	Washburn Co., WI	Dale M. Swan	Dale M. Swan	1992	1909
171 3/8	27 4/8	27 4/8	19 2/8	4 5/8	4 6/8	7	8	Madison Co., IL	Keith T. Probst	Keith T. Probst	1993	1909
171 3/8	24 6/8	24 7/8	17 1/8	4 5/8	4 6/8	6	6	Dimmit Co., TX	Robert E. Zaiglin	Robert E. Zaiglin	1993	1909
171 3/8	29 2/8	27 4/8	21 2/8	4 6/8	4 7/8	6	5	Clark Co., OH	David A. Arrington	David A. Arrington	1994	1909
171 3/8	27 2/8	27 2/8	19 5/8	5 6/8	6	7	7	Crooked Lake, SK	John Duryba	John Duryba	1994	1909

Score						R	L	Locality	Hunter	Owner	Killed	Entered
171 3/8	27 3/8	26 5/8	19 5/8	4 7/8	4 7/8	7	8	Biggar, SK	Milo N. Hanson	Milo N. Hanson	1994	1909
171 3/8	27 2/8	27 4/8	20 7/8	4 4/8	4 6/8	7	5	Labette Co., KS	Dorothea L. Ludwig	Dorothea L. Ludwig	1994	1909
171 3/8	27	27 6/8	21 3/8	5	5	6	6	Washington Co., WI	Daniel J. Hanrahan	Daniel J. Hanrahan	1995	1909
171 3/8	21 5/8	22 6/8	17 2/8	5	4 7/8	10	6	N. Saskatchewan River, AB	Picked Up	Dale Loosemore	1995	1909
171 3/8	27 4/8	26 2/8	20 5/8	5	4 7/8	5	6	Bayne, SK	William Matsalla	William Matsalla	1995	1909
171 2/8	28 2/8	28 3/8	28	5 2/8	5 7/8	6	9	Somerset Co., PA	Paul E. Walker	Paul E. Walker	1941	1949
171 2/8	29 2/8	28 6/8	19 2/8	4 6/8	4 4/8	6	5	Arkansas Co., AR	Wilbur Stephens	Wilbur Stephens	1953	1949
171 2/8	25 6/8	25 7/8	21 3/8	5	5	6	5	Gregory Co., SD	Leonard L. Nespor	Leonard L. Nespor	1956	1949
171 2/8	25 6/8	25 7/8	19 4/8	5 3/8	5 2/8	6	6	Bayfield Co., WI	Lawrence Stumo	Lawrence Stumo	1956	1949
171 2/8	27	26 4/8	21 4/8	5 6/8	4 5/8	7	5	Waldo Co., ME	Paul K. Nickerson	Paul K. Nickerson	1957	1949
171 2/8	26 4/8	26 6/8	20 3/8	5 6/8	5 6/8	6	6	O'Brien Co., IA	George Sleeper	William H. Lilienthal	1959	1949
171 2/8	26 2/8	25	22 4/8	5	5	7	5	Macintosh, ON	Richard Kouhi	Richard Kouhi	1967	1949
171 2/8	25 4/8	25 3/8	19 4/8	4 6/8	5	6	5	Webb Co., TX	Ernie Pavlas	Ernie Pavlas	1970	1949
171 2/8	26 7/8	25 6/8	18 2/8	5 1/8	5 2/8	5	5	Beltrami Co., MN	Mickey Ewing	Mickey Ewing	1981	1949
171 2/8	26	26	18	5 5/8	5	7	6	Lucas Co., IA	James L. Barlow	James L. Barlow	1985	1949
171 2/8	21 1/8	21	16 7/8	5 1/8	5	8	6	Yuma Co., CO	John O. Cletcher	John O. Cletcher	1985	1949
171 2/8	24	23 7/8	19 4/8	5 4/8	5 4/8	5	5	Pembina Co., ND	Lee Einarson	Lee Einarson	1986	1949
171 2/8	23 1/8	24	16 6/8	4 2/8	4 2/8	5	5	Lake Co., MT	Del A. Niemeyer	Del A. Niemeyer	1986	1949
171 2/8	26 3/8	24 4/8	18 6/8	4 4/8	4 4/8	5	5	Oyen, AB	Daryl Peers	Daryl Peers	1986	1949
171 2/8	27 3/8	27	21	4 5/8	4 5/8	5	5	Randolph Co., IL	Steven R. Thompson	Steven R. Thompson	1986	1949
171 2/8	29 6/8	27 4/8	22 4/8	4 6/8	4 6/8	5	5	Ringgold Co., IA	John H. Good	John H. Good	1988	1949
171 2/8	26 2/8	26 1/8	20 6/8	5	5 2/8	5	5	Marshall Co., IA	Dale E. Smith	Dale E. Smith	1988	1949
171 2/8	23 2/8	23 2/8	20 6/8	6	5 7/8	6	6	Adams Co., IA	Gary D. Maatsch	Gary D. Maatsch	1990	1949
171 2/8	26 6/8	27 3/8	20 4/8	4 2/8	4 1/8	5	5	Missoula Co., MT	James R. Zullo	James R. Zullo	1990	1949
171 2/8	27 5/8	27 2/8	19 1/8	5 1/8	5 1/8	6	6	Henry Co., IL	Kevin P. Casteel	Kevin P. Casteel	1992	1949
171 2/8	26	25 7/8	18 1/8	5	5	7	7	Duck Lake, SK	Colin P. Laroque	Colin P. Laroque	1992	1949
171 2/8	25	25 4/8	19 6/8	4 6/8	4 6/8	6	5	Linn Co., MO	Bryan H. Mueller	Bryan H. Mueller	1992	1949
171 2/8	24	23 5/8	17 2/8	4 3/8	4 2/8	6	6	Lincoln Co., MO	F. Neil Norton	F. Neil Norton	1992	1949
171 2/8	24 6/8	23 5/8	20	5	5	6	6	Racine Co., WI	Charles Michna	Charles Michna	1993	1949
171 2/8	27 3/8	27 6/8	19 6/8	4 5/8	4 4/8	5	5	Todd Co., SD	Timothy E. Guerue	Timothy E. Guerue	1994	1949
171 2/8	25 5/8	26	17 2/8	4 5/8	4 5/8	5	5	Pepin Co., WI	Sharon M. Bauer	Sharon M. Bauer	1995	1949
171 2/8	25 7/8	26 7/8	18 4/8	5	5	5	5	Saline Co., MO	Jeffrey E. Edwards	Jeffrey E. Edwards	1995	1949
171 2/8	25	25 5/8	20 2/8	5 1/8	4 5/8	5	5	Bartholomew Co., IN	Gary B. Owsley	Gary B. Owsley	1995	1949
171 2/8	26 1/8	26	21	5	4 4/8	7	7	Warren Co., IL	R. Craig Akers	R. Craig Akers	1996	1949
171 2/8	25	26 3/8	20 6/8	4 4/8	4 4/8	6	6	Union Co., IA	Trevor Paulus	Trevor Paulus	1996	1949
171 1/8	27 1/8	27 3/8	20 2/8	5 4/8	5 2/8	5	5	Coshocton Co., OH	Michael H. Wills	Michael H. Wills	1996	1949
171 1/8	24 7/8	25 3/8	21 1/8	4 6/8	4 4/8	5	5	Sanders Co., MT	William Brox	Henry C. Bennett	1948	1980
171 1/8	27 4/8	27 4/8	21 1/8	4 2/8	4 2/8	6	6	Charlevoix Co., MI	Noel Thomson	Ivan Thomson	1957	1980
171 1/8	22 6/8	21	18 5/8	5 2/8	5 1/8	6	6	Medicine Hat, AB	Frank Chevalier	Marcel Houle	1958	1980
171 1/8	24 7/8	25	21	6	6	5	5	Penobscot Co., ME	Kenneth Scott	Kenneth W. Bennett	1960	1980
171 1/8	26	26 7/8	16 7/8	5 6/8	5 6/8	5	5	Douglas Co., MN	James M. Bircher	James M. Bircher	1962	1980
171 1/8	27 2/8	27 1/8	18	4 4/8	4 4/8	8	5	Alger Co., MI	Shirley L. Robare	Shirley L. Robare	1963	1980
171 1/8	23 2/8	23 1/8	20 6/8	5 2/8	5	6	6	Whitewood, SK	W. Cook	W. Cook	1966	1980
171 1/8	27	27	20 3/8	4 6/8	4 7/8	6	6	Polk Co., WI	Harold Dau	Harold Dau	1966	1980
171 1/8	23 6/8	24 7/8	15 7/8	4	4 3/8	7	7	Jackson Co., SD	Dale Jarman	Dale Jarman	1968	1980
171 1/8	25 5/8	26 7/8	16 1/8	4 3/8	4 3/8	7	7	Menominee Co., WI	Vyron N. Dixon, Sr.	Vyron N. Dixon, Sr.	1975	1980
171 1/8	26 7/8	27	18 7/8	5	5 1/8	5	5	Lafayette Co., AR	Picked Up	John Upton		1980

WHITETAIL DEER - TYPICAL ANTLERS

Odocoileus virginianus virginianus and certain related subspecies

Score	Length of Main Beam R	Length of Main Beam L	Inside Spread	Circumference at Smallest Place Between Burr and First Point R	Circumference at Smallest Place Between Burr and First Point L	Number of Points R	Number of Points L	Locality	Hunter	Owner	Date Killed	Rank
171 1/8	26	24 7/8	16 5/8	4 2/8	4 2/8	5	5	Koochiching Co., MN	Picked Up	Marc M. Jackson	1977	1980
171 1/8	23 4/8	23 4/8	18 3/8	7 2/8	6 3/8	5	5	Bayfield Co., WI	James A. Peters	James A. Peters	1979	1980
171 1/8	26 6/8	26 6/8	19 3/8	4 2/8	4 4/8	5	5	Unknown	Unknown	Keith Spencer	PR 1981	1980
171 1/8	23 7/8	23 5/8	17 1/8	5 2/8	5 1/8	8	8	Otter Tail Co., MN	Thomas E. Berger	Thomas E. Berger	1985	1980
171 1/8	27 2/8	27 3/8	21 5/8	5 6/8	5 4/8	5	4	Fulton Co., NY	Kenneth R. Mowrey, Jr.	Kenneth R. Mowrey, Jr.	1985	1980
171 1/8	25 5/8	25 2/8	19 5/8	5 4/8	5 5/8	5	6	Howard Brook, NB	Ralph L. Orser	Ralph L. Orser	1986	1980
171 1/8	28 5/8	26 6/8	20 1/8	5	5	6	6	Livingston Co., MO	Richard L. West	Richard L. West	1986	1980
171 1/8	28 5/8	25	17 6/8	4 7/8	5	6	8	Hubbard Co., MN	Merald D. Folkestad	Merald D. Folkestad	1987	1980
171 1/8	26 1/8	26 2/8	22 7/8	5 6/8	6 4/8	5	5	Van Buren Co., IA	Walter S. Church	Walter S. Church	1988	1980
171 1/8	25 3/8	25 2/8	20 1/8	5 2/8	5 3/8	5	5	Clark Co., OH	Lafayette Boggs III	Lafayette Boggs III	1991	1980
171 1/8	25 5/8	25 6/8	19 2/8	4 4/8	4 5/8	7	7	Pike Co., IL	Jarrod Kirk	Jarrod Kirk	1991	1980
171 1/8	25 3/8	26	21 4/8	6	5 6/8	7	6	Jersey Co., IL	Allen E. Conrad	Allen E. Conrad	1992	1980
171 1/8	26 4/8	26 3/8	20 7/8	5 7/8	5 6/8	6	9	Coffey Co., KS	Gerald L. Garrett	Gerald L. Garrett	1992	1980
171 1/8	28 1/8	27 1/8	24 6/8	6 5/8	6 2/8	5	7	Perth, ON	Robert J. Moir	Robert J. Moir	1992	1980
171 1/8	24 6/8	25 1/8	17 4/8	4 4/8	4 4/8	7	5	Flathead Co., MT	Gary Packer	Gary Packer	1992	1980
171 1/8	25 3/8	24 7/8	16 2/8	4 5/8	4 7/8	7	6	Dunn Co., WI	Jamie W. Mittlestadt	Jamie W. Mittlestadt	1993	1980
171 1/8	25 2/8	24 5/8	18 4/8	4 6/8	4 6/8	6	7	Huard Lake, SK	Garner H. Travelpiece	Garner H. Travelpiece	1994	1980
171 1/8	28 4/8	28	18 6/8	4 6/8	4 6/8	6	8	Franklin Co., ME	Michael J. Zubiate	Michael J. Zubiate	1994	1980
171 1/8	27 4/8	25 6/8	22 3/8	5 5/8	5 5/8	5	5	Buffalo Co., WI	George Clausen	George Clausen	1995	1980
171 1/8	26 5/8	27 1/8	17 3/8	5 6/8	5 4/8	5	5	Dane Co., WI	Miles Weaver	Miles Weaver	1996	1980
171	28 6/8	28 5/8	20	5	5	4	5	Windsor Co., VT	Picked Up	Alfred A. Durkee	1935	2011
171	26 4/8	26 4/8	19 1/8	4 7/8	5	7	6	Sherwood, ND	Roy Foss	Roy Foss	1947	2011
171	27 1/8	26 3/8	19 4/8	4 4/8	4 4/8	5	5	Hampshire Co., WV	Conda L. Shanholtz	Conda L. Shanholtz	1958	2011
171	28 2/8	25 6/8	24 2/8	5 4/8	5 4/8	5	4	Brown Co., SD	Anthony B. Goldade	Anthony B. Goldade	1960	2011
171	23 5/8	26	19 2/8	5 1/8	5 1/8	5	6	Windthorst, SK	Thomas Dovell	Thomas Dovell	1961	2011
171	28 5/8	27 7/8	20 4/8	5 7/8	5 6/8	7	7	Perkins Co., SD	Ethel Schrader	Ethel Schrader	1963	2011
171	22 6/8	20 4/8	19 5/8	4 1/8	4 1/8	7	8	Antelope Co., NE	Leo M. Beelart	Leo M. Beelart	1964	2011
171	26 2/8	25 6/8	20 5/8	5 2/8	6	6	6	Buffalo Co., WI	Clarence H. Castleberg, Jr.	Clarence H. Castleberg, Jr.	1964	2011
171	26	24 4/8	19 6/8	4 2/8	4 1/8	5	5	Wabasha Co., MN	John W. Mussell	John W. Mussell	1966	2011
171	24 4/8	25 2/8	17 2/8	5	5	6	5	Ray Co., MO	Darle R. Siegel	Darle R. Siegel	1966	2011
171	25 2/8	24 4/8	21	4 6/8	4 6/8	6	5	Seven Persons, AB	Haven Lane	Haven Lane	1968	2011
171	23 6/8	26 7/8	21	4 5/8	4 6/8	5	5	Speers, SK	Charles E. Strautman	Charles E. Strautman	1969	2011
171	28 1/8	26 7/8	18 3/8	5 3/8	5 2/8	8	8	Lyman Co., SD	Art Zimbelmann	Art Zimbelmann	1973	2011
171	26 2/8	24 4/8	26 2/8	5 3/8	5 2/8	7	8	Otter Tail Co., MN	Lawrence J. Anderson	Lawrence J. Anderson	1974	2011
171	27	26 5/8	17 2/8	5 2/8	5 3/8	6	5	Pierce Co., WI	Picked Up	Roger Hines	1975	2011
171	26	26	20	5	4 6/8	5	5	Aroostook Co., ME	Roland L. Demers	Roland L. Demers	1983	2011

Score	Main Beam R	Main Beam L	Inside Spread	Circ. R	Circ. L	Pts. R	Pts. L	Locality	Owner	Hunter	Date Killed	Rank
171	25 2/8	24	15 6/8	5 1/8	5 2/8	5	5	Christian Co., MO	Melba J. Herndon	Melba J. Herndon	1983	2011
171	25 2/8	25 4/8	19 2/8	4 7/8	4 7/8	6	5	Okanagan Range, BC	Dennis A. Dorholt	Picked Up	1984	2011
171	28 5/8	30 4/8	22 5/8	5 2/8	5 1/8	4	6	Penobscot Co., ME	Samuel C. Hands	Samuel C. Hands	1985	2011
171	27	26 5/8	20 2/8	4 3/8	4 3/8	6	6	Independence Co., AR	G. Covington & A. Schnitjer	Greg Covington	1986	2011
171	23 3/8	24 3/8	19	5	5 1/8	7	7	Comanche Co., KS	Frankie Felton	Frankie Felton	1986	2011
171	25 7/8	26 2/8	20 2/8	5	4 4/8	7	7	Pike Co., IN	Robert Jensen	Robert Jensen	1986	2011
171	24 3/8	23 7/8	20 6/8	4 1/8	4 1/8	6	6	Boone Co., IN	Phil Lemond	Phil Lemond	1988	2011
171	24 2/8	23 4/8	17 4/8	4 4/8	4 7/8	5	5	Williamson Co., IL	Kevin L. Albert	Kevin L. Albert	1988	2011
171	26 2/8	21 6/8	21 6/8	4 7/8	5 4/8	5	5	Okemasis Lake, SK	Ronnie G. Fletcher	Ronnie G. Fletcher	1989	2011
171	26 2/8	25 4/8	21 4/8	5 4/8	5	5	6	Wabasha Co., MN	Rick Galloway	Rick Galloway	1989	2011
171	25 7/8	26 2/8	19 3/8	5	5 1/8	6	5	Nuevo Leon, MX	Thomas J. Mullenbach	Thomas J. Mullenbach	1989	2011
171	26	26 2/8	21 2/8	5 3/8	5 1/8	5	5	Davis Co., IA	Farryl Holub	Farryl Holub	1991	2011
171	27 2/8	26 4/8	23 4/8	5 4/8	5 2/8	5	6	Peoria Co., IL	IA Dept. of Natl. Resc.	Picked Up	1991	2011
171	24 6/8	25	18 6/8	4 5/8	4 4/8	6	5	La Porte Co., IN	Leslie G. Shipp	Leslie G. Shipp	1991	2011
171	25 2/8	23 7/8	20	5 2/8	5 4/8	6	6	Lincoln Co., IN	Josh Skalka	Picked Up	1991	2011
171	24 4/8	24 7/8	17 2/8	5 4/8	4 4/8	6	5	Livingston Co., IL	Clell T. Gooch, Jr.	Clell T. Gooch, Jr.	1992	2011
171	26 4/8	27 2/8	20 4/8	4 4/8	4 7/8	5	5	Marshall Hill, NB	Lloyd D. Kemnetz, Jr.	Lloyd D. Kemnetz, Jr.	1992	2011
171	27 5/8	27	20 2/8	4 6/8	4 6/8	5	5	Nez Perce Co., ID	Michael J. Maxwell	Michael J. Maxwell	1992	2011
171	25	25 4/8	19 2/8	4 2/8	4 6/8	6	7	Marinette Co., WI	Paul A. Eke	Paul A. Eke	1993	2011
171	26 1/8	17 2/8	20 2/8	4 5/8	5	5	6	Vernon Co., WI	Roger W. Gusick	Roger W. Gusick	1993	2011
171	25	25 2/8	17 2/8	5 7/8	5 7/8	5	5	Fisher Branch, MB	Larry C. Hooverson	Larry C. Hooverson	1993	2011
171	24 7/8	24 7/8	18 4/8	4 7/8	4 4/8	7	5	Kleberg Co., TX	Garth J. Lagimodiere	Garth J. Lagimodiere	1993	2011
171	24	24 1/8	21 1/8	4 6/8	4 6/8	5	7	Lac La Biche, AB	Darwin D. Baucum	Darwin D. Baucum	1994	2011
171	27 5/8	27 5/8	23 2/8	4 2/8	4 6/8	5	5	Somerset Co., MD	Ken Harris	Ken Harris	1994	2011
171	29 4/8	27 7/8	20 4/8	5 1/8	5 1/8	6	6	Alexander Co., IL	Lloyd B. Bloodsworth	Lloyd B. Bloodsworth	1995	2011
171	29	29 1/8	26 4/8	6	6	4	6	Sedgwick Co., KS	Robert A. Kaufman	Robert A. Kaufman	1995	2011
171	26 4/8	27 1/8	23 5/8	4 7/8	4 7/8	6	6	St. Clair Co., MI	John E. McMurry	John E. McMurry	1995	2011
171	25 6/8	26	22 4/8	5 1/8	5 1/8	5	6	Blue Earth Co., MN	John Pierce	John Pierce	1995	2011
171	24 6/8	24 6/8	18	5 1/8	6 2/8	5	5	Crittenden Co., KY	Robert E. Richards	Robert E. Richards	1995	2011
171	25 3/8	24 3/8	18 2/8	6 3/8	4 4/8	6	5	Union Co., IA	Marshall Tennison	Marshall Tennison	1995	2011
171	26 5/8	26 5/8	18 5/8	4 4/8	4 4/8	6	6	Minnehaha Co., SD	Steven A. Wearmouth	Steven A. Wearmouth	1996	2011
171	27 7/8	27 1/8	18 4/8	3 7/8	3 7/8	6	6	Wadena Co., MN	Carl L. Murra	Carl L. Murra	1996	2011
170 7/8	29	29	18 5/8	6 2/8	6 1/8	8	8	Marinette Co., WI	Thomas W. Goddard	Charles Rader	1909	2060
170 7/8	28 1/8	29	20 1/8	4 6/8	4 6/8	8	8	Issaquena Co., MS	Alford M. Cooley	Warren A. Miller	1920	2060
170 7/8	26 3/8	27 1/8	19 2/8	5	5	4	5	Cass Co., MN	George W. Flaim	Orland Weekley	1929	2060
170 7/8	26 4/8	26	21 5/8	5 2/8	5 3/8	5	5	Frio Co., TX	Lex Stewart	Lex Stewart	1930	2060
170 7/8	24 5/8	24 5/8	17 6/8	5	5	6	5	Delta Co., MI	Mary J. Wellman	Jim Lawson	1939	2060
170 7/8	26 2/8	25 7/8	16 6/8	5 4/8	5 4/8	7	7	Bath Co., VA	Maurice Smith	Maurice Smith	1953	2060
170 7/8	27 1/8	26 3/8	19 1/8	4 7/8	4 6/8	5	5	Bayfield Co., WI	John Kavajecz	John Kavajecz	1964	2060
170 7/8	26 3/8	27 1/8	20 3/8	4	4 1/8	5	5	Beltrami Co., MN	Kenneth Slechta	Kenneth Slechta	1965	2060
170 7/8	30	30	20 4/8	5	5 1/8	6	6	Des Moines Co., IA	Craig A. Field	Craig A. Field	1967	2060
170 7/8	26 4/8	27 4/8	20 2/8	5	5	5	5	Kingman, AB	Robert D. Kozack	Robert D. Kozack	1971	2060
170 7/8	26 7/8	21 1/8	21 1/8	5 2/8	5 2/8	5	7	Holmes Co., OH	Ken Taylor	Ken Taylor	1975	2060
170 7/8	25 3/8	18 3/8	21 2/8	5 7/8	5 6/8	7	7	Tippecanoe Co., IN	Harold A. Anthrop	Harold A. Anthrop	1976	2060
170 7/8	27	24 5/8	18 3/8	5	5	6	6	Steuben Co., NY	Duane L. Horton	Duane L. Horton	1976	2060
170 7/8	25 2/8	26 5/8	23 1/8	4 7/8	5	8	8	McDonald Lake, NS	Frederick Zwarum	Frederick Zwarum	1976	2060

341

WHITETAIL DEER - TYPICAL ANTLERS

Odocoileus virginianus virginianus and certain related subspecies

Score	Length of Main Beam		Inside Spread	Circumference at Smallest Place Between Burr and First Point		Number of Points		Locality	Hunter	Owner	Date Killed	Rank
	R	L		R	L	R	L					
170 7/8	26 3/8	26 5/8	17 7/8	4 2/8	4 1/8	5	6	Sherburne Co., MN	Merlin F. Kittelson	Merlin F. Kittelson	1977	2060
170 7/8	25 7/8	25 5/8	17 5/8	5 4/8	5 4/8	5	5	Washington Co., ME	Merle G. Michaud	Merle G. Michaud	1979	2060
170 7/8	23 7/8	25 5/8	22	5 1/8	5 1/8	7	7	Henry Co., IA	Lewis E. Dallmeyer	Lewis E. Dallmeyer	1981	2060
170 7/8	27 2/8	26 5/8	22 2/8	5 2/8	5 2/8	8	6	Warren Co., IA	Gary L. Johnson	Gary L. Johnson	1981	2060
170 7/8	25 5/8	24 6/8	22 5/8	5	5 7/8	6	7	Burleigh Co., ND	Ronald C. Wagner	Ronald C. Wagner	1982	2060
170 7/8	29	29 3/8	21 5/8	6 3/8	5 3/8	4	4	Shelby Co., IL	Paul Marley	Paul Marley	1985	2060
170 7/8	30 4/8	30 2/8	24 7/8	4 2/8	4 2/8	5	5	Alexander Co., IL	Kenneth L. Karhliker	Kenneth L. Karhliker	1986	2060
170 7/8	26	26 7/8	16 3/8	4 5/8	4 5/8	5	5	Grundy Co., MO	Bill Zang	Bill Zang	1986	2060
170 7/8	27 4/8	28 4/8	21 4/8	4 7/8	5	7	8	Leavenworth Co., KS	Jacob W. Dragieff	Jacob W. Dragieff	1987	2060
170 7/8	23 4/8	23 5/8	18 7/8	4 6/8	4 6/8	6	7	Polk Co., WI	Timothy J. Droher	Timothy J. Droher	1988	2060
170 7/8	25 2/8	26 3/8	17 3/8	4 3/8	4 3/8	6	6	Crawford Co., WI	Dale M. Hanson	Dale M. Hanson	1988	2060
170 7/8	26	25 5/8	21 1/8	4 2/8	4 2/8	6	6	Eau Claire Co., WI	John F. Prissel	John F. Prissel	1988	2060
170 7/8	26 4/8	25 7/8	17 1/8	5 2/8	5 2/8	5	5	Houston Co., MN	Tony S. Rostad	Tony S. Rostad	1988	2060
170 7/8	28 5/8	28 6/8	26 2/8	5 3/8	5 2/8	5	5	Jackson Co., IA	Clarence E. Gartman	Clarence E. Gartman	1989	2060
170 7/8	26 2/8	25 7/8	18 6/8	5 2/8	5	5	5	Lamont, AB	Allen C. Johnston	Allen C. Johnston	1989	2060
170 7/8	26 4/8	25 6/8	19 2/8	5 1/8	5 2/8	7	7	Monona Co., IA	Byron S. Mesenbrink	Byron S. Mesenbrink	1989	2060
170 7/8	24	25 2/8	20 1/8	4 7/8	4 7/8	6	6	Knox Co., IL	Carl A. Swanson	Carl A. Swanson	1989	2060
170 7/8	25 7/8	26 1/8	16 6/8	4 4/8	4 3/8	6	5	Monroe Co., AR	William E. Bartlett	William E. Bartlett	1990	2060
170 7/8	27 4/8	26 5/8	21 5/8	5	5	6	8	Wapello Co., IA	Ray L. Schafer	Ray L. Schafer	1990	2060
170 7/8	28 1/8	27	21 5/8	4 6/8	4 7/8	5	5	Polk Co., WI	Dennis R. Measner	Dennis R. Measner	1991	2060
170 7/8	26 1/8	25 6/8	20 7/8	4 5/8	4 5/8	7	5	Sumner Co., KS	Hiram Tucker, Jr.	Hiram Tucker, Jr.	1992	2060
170 7/8	24	23 6/8	17 7/8	5 3/8	5 2/8	5	5	Jones Creek, SK	Andre Verville	Andre Verville	1992	2060
170 7/8	24 5/8	24 7/8	19 1/8	5	4 7/8	6	6	Christian Co., KY	Nicholas J. Gresham	Nicholas J. Gresham	1993	2060
170 7/8	26 4/8	27 7/8	19 1/8	4 3/8	4 4/8	6	6	St. Clair Co., IL	Donald F. Mehrtens	Donald F. Mehrtens	1993	2060
170 7/8	25 5/8	25 7/8	21 5/8	5 4/8	5 1/8	5	5	Wabasha Co., MN	Terry P. Ryan	Terry P. Ryan	1993	2060
170 7/8	26 1/8	23 5/8	21 1/8	5 4/8	5 1/8	5	5	Van Buren Co., MI	Donald J. Hamilton, Jr.	Donald J. Hamilton, Jr.	1994	2060
170 7/8	26	26	17 3/8	5 2/8	5	6	6	Vinton Co., OH	Mark Nusbaum	Mark Nusbaum	1994	2060
170 7/8	27 3/8	27 6/8	19 5/8	4 4/8	4 3/8	6	7	Montgomery Co., OH	Lee H. White	Lee H. White	1995	2060
170 6/8	28 4/8	28 1/8	24 6/8	4 2/8	4 1/8	6	8	Zapata Co., TX	G.O. Elliff	Michael Elliff	1926	2102
170 6/8	27	26 2/8	18	4 4/8	4 3/8	5	5	Eau Claire Co., WI	Kenneth W. Kling	Mrs. Kenneth W. Kling	1938	2102
170 6/8	24 6/8	23 4/8	19 2/8	5 6/8	6 5/8	6	5	Aitkin Co., MN	Unknown	George W. Flaim	PR 1947	2102
170 6/8	26 3/8	27 2/8	19 4/8	4 5/8	4 5/8	6	6	Kasshabog Lake, ON	Clarence Holdcroft	Jim Holdcroft	PR 1948	2102
170 6/8	25 6/8	26 7/8	19 1/8	4 6/8	4 5/8	6	5	Bayfield Co., WI	Sigurd A. Sandstrom	Sigurd A. Sandstrom	1955	2102
170 6/8	25 6/8	26	21	5 4/8	5 2/8	5	5	Dimmit Co., TX	J.H. Hixon	J.H. Hixon	1958	2102
170 6/8	25 2/8	24 4/8	24 2/8	4 5/8	4 6/8	6	5	Elbow, SK	W.H. Crossman	W.H. Crossman	1959	2102
170 6/8	25 3/8	25 1/8	19 4/8	5 3/8	5 3/8	7	6	Gerald, SK	Jerry Norek	Jerry Norek	1959	2102

Score	Main Beam R	Main Beam L	Inside Spread	Circ. R	Circ. L	Points R	Points L	Locality	Hunter	Owner	Date	Rank
170 6/8	27 4/8	26 6/8	18	5	5 2/8	6	7	Chicot Co., AR	Mrs. L.M. Hamilton	Mrs. L.M. Hamilton	1960	2102
170 6/8	24	24	21 2/8	5	5 1/8	6	6	Arnes, MB	T. Litwin	T. Litwin	1963	2102
170 6/8	25 7/8	25 3/8	16 2/8	4 6/8	4 4/8	5	5	Union Co., AR	Chester New	Chester New	1968	2102
170 6/8	24 6/8	25 6/8	19	4 7/8	4 6/8	5	5	Guysborough Co., NS	Roy B. Simpson	Roy B. Simpson	1968	2102
170 6/8	25 7/8	25 6/8	20	4 6/8	4 6/8	5	5	Carroll Co., MD	Wes McKenzie	Wes McKenzie	1971	2102
170 6/8	27 2/8	27 1/8	18 4/8	4 2/8	4 4/8	5	6	Kent Co., MD	Thomas C. Duff, Jr.	Thomas C. Duff, Jr.	1973	2102
170 6/8	28	28	21 3/8	5 3/8	5 3/8	6	5	Penobscot Co., ME	William Stratton	William Stratton	1974	2102
170 6/8	27 2/8	26 4/8	20	4 4/8	4 4/8	6	6	Howell Co., MO	Roy W. Woodson	Roy W. Woodson	1974	2102
170 6/8	26	26 1/8	19 2/8	4 7/8	5	6	5	Seneca Co., OH	Cheyenne Bloom	Cheyenne Bloom	1980	2102
170 6/8	23 7/8	23 4/8	19 2/8	4 6/8	4 6/8	5	5	Winn Parish, LA	William C. Erwin	William C. Erwin	1980	2102
170 6/8	24 4/8	24 1/8	16 4/8	4	4	7	7	Harris Co., GA	Gorman S. Riley	Gorman S. Riley	1983	2102
170 6/8	23 4/8	23 3/8	19 5/8	4 6/8	4 5/8	5	5	Great Sand Hills, SK	Ralph Cervo	Ralph Cervo	1984	2102
170 6/8	26 2/8	25 6/8	19	5 2/8	5 1/8	6	6	Coles Co., IL	Jeff D. Shrader	Jeff D. Shrader	1990	2102
170 6/8	23 3/8	23 3/8	18	4 1/8	4 1/8	6	7	Chisago Co., MN	Gary Thomas	Gary Thomas	1990	2102
170 6/8	24 5/8	23 5/8	14 6/8	4 3/8	4 3/8	7	5	Jackson Co., MI	Richard J. Galicki	Richard J. Galicki	1991	2102
170 6/8	25 1/8	25 1/8	20	4 7/8	4 7/8	5	5	Richland Co., OH	Curt McBride	Curt McBride	1991	2102
170 6/8	28 5/8	29 1/8	20 4/8	5 2/8	5 2/8	6	5	Laurens Co., GA	Darrell Evans	Darrell Evans	1992	2102
170 6/8	27 3/8	29 3/8	28 7/8	5	5 1/8	8	6	Calling Lake, AB	Fred J. Rein	Fred J. Rein	1993	2102
170 6/8	27 4/8	26 7/8	18 5/8	4 7/8	4 7/8	6	6	Putnam Co., IN	Mark L. Goodpaster	Mark L. Goodpaster	1995	2102
170 6/8	28 4/8	26 7/8	18 7/8	4 4/8	4 3/8	6	5	Tazewell Co., IL	Steve R. Larimore	Steve R. Larimore	PR 1995	2102
170 6/8	28 2/8	26 3/8	19 2/8	5 5/8	5 5/8	6	5	Saskatchewan	Unknown	James B. Sisco III	1996	2102
170 6/8	24 6/8	24 6/8	24 4/8	4 6/8	4 6/8	5	7	Kenedy Co., TX	John A. Cardwell	John A. Cardwell	1996	2102
170 6/8	25 4/8	24 7/8	18 6/8	5	5	7	6	Derwent, AB	Vincent D. Charchun	Vincent D. Charchun	1996	2102
170 5/8	23 6/8	23 6/8	17 5/8	4 4/8	4 4/8	6	6	Kinney Co., TX	Don T. Barksdale	Marshall E. Kuykendall	1925	2133
170 5/8	25 3/8	24 3/8	20 5/8	5 1/8	5 1/8	6	10	Pennington Co., SD	Glen Wilson	Dick Rossum	1946	2133
170 5/8	21 5/8	21 7/8	15 3/8	4 5/8	4 5/8	6	6	Allegan Co., MI	William Caywood	William Caywood	1948	2133
170 5/8	27 2/8	27 3/8	20 4/8	5 2/8	5 2/8	8	8	Sawyer Co., WI	Virgil A. Scanlon	Virgil A. Scanlon	1959	2133
170 5/8	25 6/8	25 5/8	18 3/8	4 6/8	4 6/8	6	6	Lake Co., MN	Unknown	George W. Flaim	1960	2133
170 5/8	26 1/8	26 1/8	19 3/8	4 5/8	4 7/8	6	6	Jasper Co., GA	Gordon W. Cown	Gordon W. Cown	1961	2133
170 5/8	27 1/8	23 2/8	17 7/8	5	4 7/8	5	5	St. Charles Co., MO	Oscar Mallinckrodt	Oscar Mallinckrodt	1962	2133
170 5/8	22 5/8	26 5/8	19 3/8	4 6/8	4 6/8	5	5	Douglas Co., WI	George Pettingill	George Pettingill	1963	2133
170 5/8	27 5/8	26 1/8	18 5/8	5 1/8	5	7	7	Wawota, SK	Benjamin F. Kregel	Benjamin F. Kregel	1965	2133
170 5/8	25 2/8	27 2/8	21 6/8	5 4/8	5 4/8	5	5	Sherburne Co., MN	Sylvester Zormeier	Sylvester Zormeier	1967	2133
170 5/8	27 2/8	27 2/8	18 3/8	4 3/8	4 3/8	6	6	Price Co., WI	Nyle H. Rodman	Nyle H. Rodman	1970	2133
170 5/8	26 2/8	26 2/8	18 1/8	4 3/8	4 3/8	6	6	Shannon Co., MO	Garry Bland	Garry Bland	1971	2133
170 5/8	26 1/8	25 4/8	19 3/8	4 2/8	4 2/8	5	5	Boyd Co., NE	Leonard Reiser	Leonard Reiser	1973	2133
170 5/8	28 1/8	27 1/8	24 5/8	5 2/8	5 1/8	6	6	Cedar Co., IA	Robert G. Grunder	Robert G. Grunder	1974	2133
170 5/8	29 3/8	29 4/8	21	4 6/8	4 6/8	7	6	Christian Co., KY	Henry J. Oliver	Henry J. Oliver	1978	2133
170 5/8	27	27	19 5/8	5 1/8	5	6	5	St. Louis Co., MN	Unknown	George W. Flaim	PR 1979	2133
170 5/8	26 2/8	26 6/8	20 5/8	5	5	5	5	Clayton Co., IA	Todd A. Moon	Todd A. Moon	1979	2133
170 5/8	24 3/8	26 4/8	17 3/8	5 1/8	5 1/8	5	5	St. Marys Co., MD	Brian M. Boteler	Brian M. Boteler	1980	2133
170 5/8	26 7/8	25 4/8	18 2/8	5 4/8	5 2/8	7	5	Atchison Co., MO	Roy E. Munsey	Roy E. Munsey	1980	2133
170 5/8	25 5/8	26	20 3/8	4 4/8	4 5/8	6	6	Berrien Co., MI	G. Steven Abdoe	G. Steven Abdoe	1982	2133
170 5/8	26 6/8	27 2/8	21	6	6	6	6	Lyon Co., KS	Bill D. Hollond	Bill D. Hollond	1984	2133
170 5/8	22 4/8	24 6/8	16 6/8	4 6/8	4 6/8	7	7	Webster Parish, LA	Henry G. Gregory	Henry G. Gregory	1985	2133
170 5/8	25 2/8	27 1/8	16	4 7/8	4 7/8	6	7	Big Stone Co., MN	Jeffrey A. Thielke	Jeffrey A. Thielke	1985	2133
170 5/8	24 1/8	24 6/8	16 7/8	4 6/8	4 6/8	5	5	Kings Co., NB	Allen MacDonald	Allen MacDonald	1986	2133

343

WHITETAIL DEER - TYPICAL ANTLERS

Odocoileus virginianus virginianus and certain related subspecies

Score	Length of Main Beam R	L	Inside Spread	Circumference at Smallest Place Between Burr and First Point R	L	Number of Points R	L	Locality	Hunter	Owner	Date Killed	Rank
170 5/8	25 2/8	26 6/8	20 2/8	6	5 7/8	7	6	Prowers Co., CO	Douglas W. Kuhns	Douglas W. Kuhns	1987	2133
170 5/8	24 6/8	25 1/8	20 6/8	4 5/8	4 4/8	7	8	Henry Co., IA	Michael S. Matthews	Michael S. Matthews	1988	2133
170 5/8	27 3/8	27 7/8	18 5/8	5 4/8	5 4/8	5	6	Grundy Co., MO	Michael C. Weathers	Michael C. Weathers	1988	2133
170 5/8	27 6/8	29 4/8	23 3/8	5 4/8	5 3/8	7	8	Sawyer Co., WI	Thorvald Skar	James M. Skar	PR 1990	2133
170 5/8	28 1/8	28 4/8	23 3/8	5 6/8	5 5/8	4	5	Polk Co., MN	D. Keith Thunem, Jr.	D. Keith Thunem, Jr.	1990	2133
170 5/8	26 2/8	26 5/8	18	4 6/8	4 7/8	5	6	Mervin, SK	Terry Brett	Terry Brett	1991	2133
170 5/8	24 2/8	24 3/8	17 4/8	5 4/8	5 4/8	6	6	Rocky Mt. House, AB	Robin L. McDonald	Robin L. McDonald	1991	2133
170 5/8	24 2/8	23 6/8	23 3/8	3 7/8	3 7/8	6	5	Crook Co., WY	Rick Shannon	Rick Shannon	1991	2133
170 5/8	26	25	20 2/8	4 7/8	4 7/8	6	6	Lee Co., GA	Stan R. Steiner	Stan R. Steiner	1991	2133
170 5/8	24 6/8	25 3/8	19 4/8	5 5/8	5 5/8	6	7	Aroostook Co., ME	Douglas P. Legasse	Douglas P. Legasse	1993	2133
170 5/8	26 4/8	27 2/8	17 3/8	5 4/8	5 2/8	7	6	Spokane Co., WA	Laura M. Kaiser	Laura M. Kaiser	1994	2133
170 5/8	25 5/8	25 1/8	17 6/8	5 6/8	5 5/8	7	7	St. Anne Lake, AB	Allen T. Carstairs	Allen T. Carstairs	1995	2133
170 5/8	26 7/8	25 7/8	18 5/8	5 1/8	5 1/8	6	6	Warren Co., IA	Martin L. Gehringer	Martin L. Gehringer	1995	2133
170 5/8	25 1/8	25 7/8	21 2/8	5 5/8	5 5/8	5	7	Melfort, SK	Dave Parfitt	Dave Parfitt	1995	2133
170 5/8	26 4/8	25 3/8	18 2/8	6	5 6/8	6	6	Spruce Lake, SK	Shawn Bleakney	Shawn Bleakney	1996	2133
170 4/8	26 1/8	25 4/8	20 4/8	4 6/8	4 5/8	6	6	Beltrami Co., MN	Hank Sandland	Hank Sandland	1931	2172
170 4/8	25 7/8	25 7/8	18 6/8	4 6/8	4 5/8	6	6	Pend Oreille Co., WA	Picked Up	Eugene M. Bailey	1944	2172
170 4/8	25 2/8	24 5/8	18	4 4/8	4 4/8	5	6	Douglas Co., MN	August P.J. Nelson	Roger M. Holmes	1946	2172
170 4/8	27	27 2/8	20 6/8	5 2/8	5 2/8	6	5	Desha Co., AR	Bob Norris	Bob Norris	1948	2172
170 4/8	23 5/8	26 1/8	22 4/8	5 6/8	5 7/8	5	5	Kittson Co., MN	Unknown	George W. Flaim	PR 1950	2172
170 4/8	25 3/8	25 4/8	18 3/8	5 2/8	5 2/8	6	6	Monroe Co., GA	T.E. Land	Jerry Moseley	1958	2172
170 4/8	25 4/8	24 5/8	19 1/8	4 7/8	4 5/8	8	7	Craven, SK	Ted Paterson	Ted Paterson	1960	2172
170 4/8	21	22 6/8	17 3/8	5 2/8	5 3/8	7	6	Great Sand Hills, SK	Picked Up	Frank Yeast	PR 1960	2172
170 4/8	24 2/8	24	20 6/8	5 6/8	5 6/8	5	5	Preeceville, SK	Vernon Hoffman	Vernon Hoffman	1965	2172
170 4/8	25 4/8	25 1/8	16 7/8	5 3/8	5 5/8	5	5	Marengo Co., AL	Frank W. Gardner	Frank W. Gardner	1967	2172
170 4/8	26	25 3/8	19	4 2/8	4 2/8	6	8	Henry Co., IA	Gerald Bailey	Gerald Bailey	1970	2172
170 4/8	27 2/8	28 5/8	21 2/8	5 1/8	5 2/8	5	5	Bedford Co., VA	W. Bane Bowyer	W. Bane Bowyer	1972	2172
170 4/8	27 4/8	27 2/8	20 2/8	5 4/8	5 3/8	5	5	St. Louis Co., MN	Unknown	David R. Brigan	1974	2172
170 4/8	24 2/8	25 2/8	19	4 2/8	4 4/8	6	6	La Salle Co., TX	Jerome Knebel	Jerome Knebel	1974	2172
170 4/8	26 4/8	25	17 7/8	5 1/8	5 1/8	6	6	Winona Co., MN	Sam Nottleman	Sam Nottleman	1977	2172
170 4/8	27	27 4/8	23 4/8	4 2/8	4 2/8	5	6	Webb Co., TX	R.W. Mann	R.W. Mann	1979	2172
170 4/8	29 6/8	29 2/8	21 2/8	4 6/8	4 4/8	7	8	Sherburne Co., MN	Curtis G. Nelson	Curtis G. Nelson	1981	2172
170 4/8	25 1/8	25 1/8	19	3 7/8	4 1/8	6	5	Sullivan Co., MO	Randy Tucker	Randy Tucker	1981	2172
170 4/8	25 2/8	24 2/8	16 4/8	5	5	7	7	Oneida Co., WI	Leonard E. Westberg	Leonard E. Westberg	1981	2172
170 4/8	26 1/8	25 4/8	18	4 4/8	4 4/8	5	5	Marshall Co., IN	Alan R. Collins	Alan R. Collins	1982	2172
170 4/8	24	24 2/8	19 2/8	4 5/8	4 6/8	5	5	Day Co., SD	Credan Ewalt	Credan Ewalt	1982	2172

Score	R. Main Beam	L. Main Beam	Inside Spread	R. Circ.	L. Circ.	R. Pts.	L. Pts.	Locality	Owner	Hunter	Date	Rank
170 4/8	28 5/8	28	20	5	5	8	8	Todd Co., MN	Freddie H. Peterson	Freddie H. Peterson	1982	2172
170 4/8	26 6/8	26 3/8	17 3/8	4	4	6	5	Houston Co., MN	Kenneth Carlson	Kenneth Carlson	1983	2172
170 4/8	25 6/8	25 2/8	17	4 6/8	4 5/8	7	6	Madison Co., IA	Merle Allen	Merle Allen	1984	2172
170 4/8	24 7/8	24 1/8	21	5	4 7/8	5	5	Chippewa Co., MI	Paul Slawski	Paul Slawski	1984	2172
170 4/8	26 2/8	25 4/8	18 4/8	5 3/8	5 3/8	5	9	Keya Paha Co., NE	Michael L. LeZotte	Michael L. LeZotte	1986	2172
170 4/8	26 3/8	26	22 4/8	5 3/8	5 3/8	5	5	Oak Mts., NB	Michael E. Mertz	Michael E. Mertz	1986	2172
170 4/8	23 4/8	24 1/8	18 4/8	4 5/8	4 4/8	6	5	Logan Co., ND	Jon M. Midthun	Jon M. Midthun	1986	2172
170 4/8	25 4/8	25 3/8	18 2/8	5 1/8	5	5	7	Lesser Slave Lake, AB	Adriaan Mik	Adriaan Mik	1987	2172
170 4/8	27 2/8	26 5/8	20 2/8	4 3/8	4 2/8	5	5	Buffalo Co., WI	Stephen F. Lang	Stephen F. Lang	1987	2172
170 4/8	26 1/8	26 5/8	20 5/8	4 5/8	4 6/8	5	7	Des Moines Co., IA	Lewis Mehaffy	Lewis Mehaffy	1987	2172
170 4/8	28 1/8	29	21 4/8	5	5	6	5	Rockingham Co., NC	Lindsey H. Watkins	Lindsey H. Watkins	1988	2172
170 4/8	27 1/8	26 7/8	21 6/8	4 5/8	4 5/8	5	6	Washington Co., MN	Peter J. Mogren	Peter J. Mogren	1988	2172
170 4/8	24 7/8	25 4/8	20 6/8	4 2/8	4 2/8	5	5	Clay Co., NE	James R. Vaughn	James R. Vaughn	1989	2172
170 4/8	23 6/8	23 3/8	18 4/8	4 3/8	4 2/8	6	6	Bradley Co., AR	Joe Hairston	Joe Hairston	1989	2172
170 4/8	26 4/8	28	18 5/8	4 3/8	4 3/8	6	6	Clinton Co., IA	Scott Jacobsen	Scott Jacobsen	1990	2172
170 4/8	25 3/8	24 7/8	20	5 3/8	5 2/8	6	6	Vilas Co., WI	Rick R. Lax	Rick R. Lax	1991	2172
170 4/8	26 3/8	25 3/8	19 6/8	4 2/8	4 2/8	5	5	Rock Island Co., IL	Joseph V. De Schepper	Joseph V. De Schepper	1991	2172
170 4/8	26 6/8	26 2/8	21 2/8	5 3/8	5 3/8	7	6	Jasper Co., IL	Joseph W. McIntyre	Joseph W. McIntyre	1991	2172
170 4/8	24 6/8	24 5/8	18	4 7/8	4 7/8	7	7	Pawnee Co., NE	Kenneth C. Mort	Kenneth C. Mort	1991	2172
170 4/8	25 4/8	24 7/8	22 2/8	5 1/8	5 1/8	5	5	Pike Co., IL	Donald E. Stefancic, Sr.	Donald E. Stefancic, Sr.	1992	2172
170 4/8	23 7/8	26	19 6/8	5 2/8	5 5/8	5	5	Chitek Lake, SK	Timothy E. Baxley	Timothy E. Baxley	1992	2172
170 4/8	26 3/8	23 1/8	20 6/8	4 6/8	4 6/8	6	6	Muskingum Co., OH	Kevin A. Berton	Kevin A. Berton	1994	2172
170 4/8	25 5/8	25 3/8	19 6/8	5 3/8	5 2/8	7	7	Appanoose Co., IA	John M. Aiello	John M. Aiello	1994	2172
170 4/8	25 4/8	26	19 2/8	4 1/8	4 2/8	6	6	Atascosa Co., TX	James C. Coffman	James C. Coffman	1994	2172
170 4/8	26 1/8	26 5/8	21 5/8	4 6/8	4 6/8	5	6	Livingston Co., IL	Alan E. Gray	Alan E. Gray	1994	2172
170 4/8	24 6/8	24 4/8	21	4 6/8	4 6/8	8	8	Carroll Co., KY	Tracey D. Kelley	Tracey D. Kelley	1994	2172
170 3/8	25 2/8	25 3/8	17	4 5/8	4 5/8	5	5	Madison Co., IN	Larry Shannon	George Groff	PR 1900	2219
170 3/8	25 5/8	25 1/8	16 4/8	4 7/8	4 7/8	6	6	Price Co., WI	Melvin Guenther	N.J. Groelle	1905	2219
170 3/8	25 5/8	25 1/8	22 2/8	3 7/8	3 7/8	9	9	Travis Co., TX	W.A. Brown	W.A. Brown	1922	2219
170 3/8	26	26	19 1/8	5 3/8	5 3/8	6	6	Woodruff Co., AR	R.L. Taylor	R.L. Taylor	1960	2219
170 3/8	27 3/8	26 2/8	25 6/8	5 4/8	5 4/8	5	5	Fort Qu'Appelle, SK	L.A. Magnuson	L.A. Magnuson	1962	2219
170 3/8	28 5/8	28 2/8	21 6/8	4 6/8	4 6/8	6	6	Hall Co., NE	Gust Bergman	Gust Bergman	1965	2219
170 3/8	25 2/8	25 4/8	23 3/8	5 2/8	5 2/8	5	5	Grant Co., SD	James Boerger	James Boerger	1965	2219
170 3/8	28 1/8	25 5/8	25 7/8	5	4 6/8	4	4	Saline Co., IL	Jack Crain	Jack Crain	1966	2219
170 3/8	25	25	21 4/8	4 7/8	5	5	4	Webb Co., TX	Clarence Zieschang	Clarence Zieschang	1966	2219
170 3/8	26 2/8	26	20 3/8	5 2/8	5 2/8	5	5	Portage La Prairie, MB	Robert Boyachek	Robert Boyachek	1967	2219
170 3/8	24 4/8	23 4/8	22	5 2/8	5 2/8	8	7	Duval Co., TX	R.L. Kruger	R.L. Kruger	1968	2219
170 3/8	28 5/8	28 4/8	23 4/8	5 1/8	5 1/8	8	8	Kingsbury Co., SD	Jerry Ellingson	Jerry Ellingson	1969	2219
170 3/8	26 1/8	26 1/8	21 1/8	4 7/8	4 7/8	7	7	Buffalo Co., WI	Lee E. Lang	Lee E. Lang	1969	2219
170 3/8	24 2/8	24 2/8	19 7/8	5	5	5	5	Buffalo Co., WI	Brant J. Mueller	Ralph Pella	1970	2219
170 3/8	25 5/8	25 2/8	22 6/8	5 2/8	5 4/8	5	5	Lac qui Parle Co., MN	Paul W. Hill	Paul W. Hill	1974	2219
170 3/8	29 4/8	28 7/8	17 7/8	4 2/8	4 2/8	8	8	Muskingum Co., OH	John H. O'Flaherty	John H. O'Flaherty	1976	2219
170 3/8	25 6/8	26 1/8	18 5/8	4 7/8	4 7/8	5	5	Newago Co., MI	Dennis Carlson	Dennis Carlson	1978	2219
170 3/8	26 6/8	26 3/8	17 3/8	4 3/8	4 3/8	6	6	Coweta Co., GA	Douglas R. Freeman	Douglas R. Freeman	1978	2219
170 3/8	29 5/8	29 3/8	26	5 1/8	5 3/8	7	5	Dimmit Co., TX	McLean Bowman	McLean Bowman	1981	2219
170 3/8	24 3/8	23 6/8	15 7/8	4 4/8	4 4/8	5	4	Wilcox Co., GA	Scott H. Urguhart	Scott H. Urguhart	1981	2219
170 3/8	27 4/8	25 4/8	21 1/8	6 7/8	6 4/8	6	4	Franklin Co., KS	Fran E. Wiederholt	Judy E. Wiederholt	1981	2219

WHITETAIL DEER - TYPICAL ANTLERS

Odocoileus virginianus virginianus and certain related subspecies

Score	Length of Main Beam R	L	Inside Spread	Circumference at Smallest Place Between Burr and First Point R	L	Number of Points R	L	Locality	Hunter	Owner	Date Killed	Rank
170 3/8	25 5/8	26 3/8	17 7/8	4 4/8	4 4/8	6	5	Decatur Co., IA	Julian J. Toney	Julian J. Toney	1982	2219
170 3/8	25 4/8	25 4/8	18 6/8	5 2/8	4 7/8	6	6	Wilkinson Co., GA	James W. Whitaker	James W. Whitaker	1982	2219
170 3/8	25 7/8	25 6/8	18 7/8	5 1/8	5 2/8	6	6	Beltrami Co., MN	Floyd Hlucny	Floyd Hlucny	1985	2219
170 3/8	26 1/8	26 4/8	19 5/8	4 4/8	4 2/8	6	7	Haskell Co., OK	Loyd Long	Loyd Long	1985	2219
170 3/8	23 1/8	23 2/8	19 5/8	4 6/8	4 5/8	6	6	Niobrara Co., WY	Joseph A. Perry III	Joseph A. Perry III	1985	2219
170 3/8	23 7/8	23 7/8	19 7/8	4 6/8	4 6/8	5	5	Emmet Co., MI	Jeffrey A. Phillips	Jeffrey A. Phillips	1985	2219
170 3/8	25 2/8	24	16 4/8	4 4/8	4 5/8	8	9	Cow Lake, AB	Edward J. Burns	Edward J. Burns	1986	2219
170 3/8	25 6/8	25 3/8	15 7/8	4 6/8	4 5/8	5	5	Baraga Co., MI	Howard D. Musick	Howard D. Musick	1987	2219
170 3/8	23 2/8	24 2/8	17	4 1/8	4 2/8	7	7	Marshall Co., MN	John R. O'Donnell	John R. O'Donnell	1988	2219
170 3/8	25	22 6/8	18 1/8	4 5/8	4 5/8	6	5	Pottawatomie Co., KS	Larry C. Schroeder	Larry C. Schroeder	1988	2219
170 3/8	27 4/8	27 5/8	23 1/8	5	5	5	5	Orange Co., IN	John W. Matthew	John W. Matthew	1989	2219
170 3/8	25	25 1/8	18 3/8	5 2/8	5	6	6	Griffin, SK	Leonard Mitchall	Leonard Mitchall	1989	2219
170 3/8	27 5/8	27 3/8	17 7/8	5	5	5	5	Montcalm Co., MI	Michael R. Nelson	Michael R. Nelson	1989	2219
170 3/8	27	26 4/8	19 7/8	4 2/8	4 3/8	5	5	Bruton, ON	Mark Vesters	Mark Vesters	1989	2219
170 3/8	27 1/8	27 5/8	20 1/8	5 1/8	4 7/8	5	5	Warren Co., IA	Lanny Caligiuri	Lanny Caligiuri	1990	2219
170 3/8	28 3/8	28 1/8	21 5/8	4 6/8	4 5/8	6	6	Dubuque Co., IA	Richard S. Hillard	Richard S. Hillard	1990	2219
170 3/8	25 2/8	25 2/8	18 7/8	5 4/8	5 4/8	7	7	Mercer Co., MO	Robert W. Vasey	Robert W. Vasey	1990	2219
170 3/8	26 6/8	26 2/8	17 7/8	4 6/8	4 6/8	5	5	McCook Co., SD	Unknown	Sam A. Wilson	PR 1990	2219
170 3/8	26	25 5/8	18 7/8	5 6/8	5 4/8	7	5	Coffey Co., KS	Glen R. Freeman	Glen R. Freeman	1991	2219
170 3/8	26 1/8	26 1/8	17 3/8	5	4 5/8	5	5	Harrison Co., MO	Glen D. Gentry	Glen D. Gentry	1991	2219
170 3/8	27 3/8	28 4/8	18 5/8	4 5/8	4 6/8	7	6	Howard Co., IA	Clarence Mincks	Clarence Mincks	1991	2219
170 3/8	26 6/8	26 5/8	18	5 1/8	5 1/8	6	5	Ziebach Co., SD	James S. Nelson IV	James S. Nelson IV	1992	2219
170 3/8	27 1/8	27 3/8	22 1/8	4 3/8	4 4/8	5	5	Grafton Co., NH	William M. Gordon	William M. Gordon	1993	2219
170 3/8	23 6/8	24	17 7/8	4	4 1/8	6	6	Maverick Co., TX	Jay C. Harmon	Jay C. Harmon	1994	2219
170 3/8	26 1/8	27 6/8	20 6/8	4 5/8	4 6/8	5	5	Warren Co., IA	Bruce L. Hupke	Bruce L. Hupke	1994	2219
170 3/8	27 1/8	27 1/8	19 2/8	5 1/8	5	6	6	Le Sueur Co., MN	Roy H. Krohn	Roy H. Krohn	1994	2219
170 3/8	27 5/8	27 5/8	21 5/8	4 6/8	4 7/8	5	5	Jasper Co., IL	Skip Moore	Skip Moore	1994	2219
170 3/8	27 4/8	27 6/8	22 2/8	5 2/8	5	6	7	Crawford Co., KS	David E. Onelio	David E. Onelio	1994	2219
170 3/8	25 3/8	27 6/8	23 5/8	5 4/8	5 4/8	5	5	Shelby Co., OH	Buck Siler	Buck Siler	1994	2219
170 3/8	23 6/8	24 3/8	18 5/8	4 4/8	4 5/8	5	5	Meagher Co., MT	Randy L. Kunkle	Randy L. Kunkle	1995	2219
170 3/8	28 4/8	27 1/8	23 2/8	5 6/8	5 6/8	8	5	Carroll Co., OH	Myron L. Miller	Myron L. Miller	1995	2219
170 3/8	26 5/8	26 4/8	19 6/8	5 1/8	5 1/8	7	6	Grundy Co., IL	Robert Alfonso, Jr.	Robert Alfonso, Jr.	1996	2219
170 3/8	24 6/8	24 4/8	16 7/8	5	4 7/8	6	6	Juneau Co., WI	Gaylord J. Downing	Gaylord J. Downing	1996	2219
170 3/8	23	23 2/8	17 3/8	5 6/8	5 7/8	6	6	McHenry Co., IL	Donald E. Hoey	Donald E. Hoey	1996	2219
170 3/8	25 4/8	25 3/8	19 3/8	4 2/8	4 2/8	6	5	St. Croix Co., WI	Earl L. Neumann	Earl L. Neumann	1996	2219
170 2/8	26 7/8	26 4/8	20 1/8	5 1/8	5 1/8	6	5	Shawano Co., WI	Jule Vandergate	Don E. Smith	1932	2275

Score	Main Beam R	Main Beam L	Spread	Circ. R	Circ. L	Pts R	Pts L	Locality	Hunter	Owner	Date	Rank
170 2/8	27 1/8	26 7/8	18 6/8	5 1/8	5 2/8	6	6	Florence Co., WI	Unknown	David G. Mueller	1940	2275
170 2/8	24 2/8	25 5/8	17 2/8	4 4/8	4 3/8	7	6	Marinette Co., WI	Phillip Marquis	Phillip Marquis	1944	2275
170 2/8	24 6/8	23 6/8	18	4 3/8	4 3/8	8	6	Polk Co., WI	Robert G. Overman	Robert G. Overman	1945	2275
170 2/8	27	27 1/8	19 2/8	4 3/8	4 4/8	7	5	Webb Co., TX	Roy C. Rice	Roy C. Rice	1948	2275
170 2/8	24 3/8	25 2/8	16 6/8	5 2/8	5 3/8	5	5	Carlton Co., MN	Unknown	George W. Flaim	1950	2275
170 2/8	27 2/8	26 6/8	20	5 2/8	5 2/8	5	5	Dafoe, SK	A. Linder	A. Linder	1959	2275
170 2/8	25 3/8	26 3/8	19 4/8	4 6/8	4 6/8	5	6	Calhoun Co., AR	George M. Gorman	George M. Gorman	1961	2275
170 2/8	24 4/8	24	19 4/8	5 1/8	5 2/8	6	7	McMullen Co., TX	Earl Welch	Earl Welch	1964	2275
170 2/8	26 2/8	25 7/8	22	4 3/8	4 3/8	6	6	Lestock, SK	Zoltan Blaskovich	Zoltan Blaskovich	1965	2275
170 2/8	24 3/8	24 7/8	21 6/8	4 5/8	4 4/8	5	9	Avonlea, SK	Doug English	Doug English	1965	2275
170 2/8	28 6/8	29 1/8	19 5/8	5 4/8	4 5/8	5	8	Blue Earth Co., MN	Roland Bode	Roland Bode	1967	2275
170 2/8	24 6/8	24 3/8	19 5/8	4 4/8	4 4/8	8	7	Jim Hogg Co., TX	Tom P. Hayes	Tom P. Hayes	1968	2275
170 2/8	23 2/8	24 2/8	15	4 4/8	4 4/8	8	5	Spokane Co., WA	Edward A. Floch, Jr.	Edward A. Floch, Jr.	1970	2275
170 2/8	23 6/8	26 4/8	18 2/8	5 2/8	5 4/8	5	6	Oglethorpe Co., GA	H.D. Cannon	H.D. Cannon	1971	2275
170 2/8	27 4/8	25 5/8	18	4 6/8	4 6/8	6	7	Houston Co., MN	Randy J. Benson	Randy J. Benson	1972	2275
170 2/8	27 4/8	27 5/8	19 7/8	4 6/8	4 4/8	7	6	Jefferson Co., OH	James S. Pratt	James S. Pratt	1976	2275
170 2/8	23 7/8	22 4/8	17 4/8	4 4/8	4 6/8	5	5	Hopkins Co., KY	Michael E. Dillingham	Michael E. Dillingham	1977	2275
170 2/8	25 2/8	24 6/8	19 4/8	5 1/8	5 2/8	4	4	Bradley Co., AR	Brad J. Davis	Brad J. Davis	1979	2275
170 2/8	27 1/8	27 2/8	21	5 3/8	5 3/8	6	5	Lee Co., AL	George P. Mann	George P. Mann	1980	2275
170 2/8	25 6/8	25	16 6/8	4 3/8	4 4/8	6	5	Olmsted Co., MN	James L. Miller	James L. Miller	1981	2275
170 2/8	26 6/8	26 7/8	22 2/8	5 6/8	5 6/8	5	5	Riley Co., KS	Paul K. Byarlay	Paul K. Byarlay	1983	2275
170 2/8	25 1/8	26	20 4/8	6 7/8	6 7/8	6	6	Ribstone Creek, AB	David H. Crum	David H. Crum	1984	2275
170 2/8	25 3/8	25 5/8	18 4/8	4 5/8	4 4/8	5	5	Adair Co., IA	Gale D. Johnston	Gale D. Johnston	1984	2275
170 2/8	24 6/8	26 1/8	18	5	5	6	5	Pembina River, MB	Bernie Thiessen	Bernie Thiessen	1987	2275
170 2/8	24 2/8	24 2/8	19 6/8	4 7/8	4 7/8	5	5	Winneshiek Co., IA	David Hageman	David Hageman	1988	2275
170 2/8	24 2/8	25 5/8	18	4 7/8	4 7/8	8	7	Pend Oreille Co., WA	George T. Law	George T. Law	1988	2275
170 2/8	26 3/8	26 1/8	19 6/8	4 3/8	4 3/8	5	7	Whitley Co., KY	Shevelery C. Sturgill	Shevelery C. Sturgill	1988	2275
170 2/8	26 1/8	28 3/8	25 2/8	4 2/8	4 3/8	7	6	Houston Co., MN	Omer M. Wangen	Omer M. Wangen	1988	2275
170 2/8	25 4/8	26 1/8	19 1/8	5 4/8	5 5/8	6	5	Clayton Co., IA	Myles T. Keller	Myles T. Keller	1989	2275
170 2/8	24 4/8	24 6/8	19 2/8	4 1/8	4 1/8	5	5	Jackson Co., OH	Roger K. Saltsman	Roger K. Saltsman	1989	2275
170 2/8	28 4/8	26	20 2/8	4 7/8	4 7/8	7	5	Adams Co., OH	R. Scott Boschert	R. Scott Boschert	1990	2275
170 2/8	26	25 6/8	26 6/8	4 4/8	4 6/8	5	4	Washington Co., ME	Phillip R. Dobbins	Phillip R. Dobbins	1990	2275
170 2/8	26 2/8	25 5/8	22 6/8	4 7/8	6	6	7	Lafayette Co., WI	Everette F. Mau	Everette F. Mau	1990	2275
170 2/8	27 6/8	26 2/8	19 3/8	5 6/8	5 6/8	5	6	Knox Co., OH	Ralph D. Wiley	Ralph D. Wiley	1990	2275
170 2/8	27	27 4/8	17	4 5/8	4 5/8	5	5	Macon Co., MO	Renee L. DeWeese	Renee L. DeWeese	1991	2275
170 2/8	25 4/8	25 6/8	18	4 1/8	5 2/8	6	8	Meade Co., KY	Paul E. Ice	Paul E. Ice	1991	2275
170 2/8	24 4/8	25 5/8	26	5 2/8	4 5/8	6	6	Washtenaw Co., MI	Tod G. Jaggi	Tod G. Jaggi	1991	2275
170 2/8	25 5/8	25 7/8	19 1/8	4 5/8	5 2/8	5	5	Fillmore Co., MN	Terry L. Rasmussen	Terry L. Rasmussen	1991	2275
170 2/8	26 3/8	27	20 4/8	5 1/8	5 3/8	5	5	Lincoln Co., CO	Joseph C. Fox	Joseph C. Fox	1992	2275
170 2/8	24 4/8	25 4/8	17	5 3/8	4 3/8	5	6	Ogle Co., IL	Dick V. Lalowski	Dick V. Lalowski	1992	2275
170 2/8	25 7/8	26	18 6/8	4 3/8	5 1/8	6	5	Dimmit Co., TX	Glenn H. Lau	Glenn H. Lau	1992	2275
170 2/8	27 2/8	26 2/8	18 6/8	5 1/8	5	5	6	Aroostook Co., ME	Peter C. Pedro	Peter C. Pedro	1992	2275
170 2/8	25	24 3/8	18 2/8	5	4 6/8	6	4	Platte Co., WY	Johnny Wehrmann	Johnny Wehrmann	1992	2275
170 2/8	25 3/8	25 3/8	20 6/8	4 6/8	4 6/8	5	5	Tippecanoe Co., IN	Jimmy M. Crites	Jimmy M. Crites	1993	2275
170 2/8	27 5/8	27 4/8	19 6/8	4 7/8	4 6/8	5	6	Page Co., IA	Arlen D. Meyer	Arlen D. Meyer	1993	2275
170 2/8	27 1/8	26 2/8	22 2/8	5 2/8	5	5	5	Chisago Co., MN	John B. Nelson	John B. Nelson	1993	2275
170 2/8	30 2/8	29 2/8	21 1/8	4 7/8	4 7/8	6	6	St. Louis Co., MN	Charles R. Wagaman	Charles R. Wagaman	1993	2275

WHITETAIL DEER - TYPICAL ANTLERS

Odocoileus virginianus virginianus and certain related subspecies

Score	Length of Main Beam R	L	Inside Spread	Circumference at Smallest Place Between Burr and First Point R	L	Number of Points R	L	Locality	Hunter	Owner	Date Killed	Rank
170 2/8	26 3/8	26 4/8	19 7/8	4 3/8	4 5/8	6	7	Van Buren Co., IA	Dennis R. Besick	Dennis R. Besick	1994	2275
170 2/8	27 5/8	26 6/8	23 6/8	5	5 3/8	6	7	Madison Co., MS	David G. McAdory	David G. McAdory	1994	2275
170 2/8	26 6/8	25 7/8	20	5 2/8	5 2/8	6	6	Hennepin Co., MN	Picked Up	Charles G. Nordstrom	1994	2275
170 2/8	26 2/8	25 7/8	19 2/8	4 3/8	4 4/8	5	5	Boone Co., IL	Matthew L. Schaller	Matthew L. Schaller	1994	2275
170 2/8	25 2/8	25 1/8	17 1/8	4 7/8	4 6/8	8	11	Logan Co., KY	Jim F. Sweeney	Jim F. Sweeney	1994	2275
170 2/8	27	26 3/8	21 4/8	5	5 1/8	8	8	St. Charles Co., MO	Leroy H. Vehige	Leroy H. Vehige	1994	2275
170 2/8	26 2/8	25 5/8	19 4/8	5	5	5	6	Jackson Co., SD	Jean Amiotte	Jean Amiotte	1995	2275
170 2/8	26 6/8	28	21 3/8	5 5/8	5 6/8	6	6	Hardisty, AB	David W. Higman	David W. Higman	1995	2275
170 2/8	28 1/8	27 4/8	22 6/8	5 3/8	4 6/8	7	6	Edgar Co., IL	Sharon McDaniel	Sharon McDaniel	1995	2275
170 2/8	25 2/8	24 2/8	20 5/8	5 2/8	5 3/8	6	6	Clay Co., IL	Jeremy D. Current	Jeremy D. Current	1996	2275
170 1/8	25 7/8	27 6/8	19	5 2/8	5 2/8	5	6	Minnesota	Unknown	William H. Lilienthal	PR 1950	2333
170 1/8	26 5/8	27	19 3/8	5 7/8	5 7/8	8	9	Massanutton Mt., VA	Lloyd Lam	Lloyd Lam	1955	2333
170 1/8	28 5/8	29	23 3/8	4 2/8	4 3/8	4	5	Faribault Co., MN	Harlan Francis	Harlan Francis	1956	2333
170 1/8	25 3/8	24 6/8	16 5/8	4 7/8	5	6	7	St. Louis Co., MN	Allan Ramstad	Allan Ramstad	1959	2333
170 1/8	30	27 5/8	23 1/8	4 2/8	4 2/8	6	7	Bayfield Co., WI	Roy Jacobson	David R. Jacobson	1960	2333
170 1/8	23 7/8	22 7/8	16 1/8	5 5/8	5 5/8	7	6	Swift Current, SK	Brian Baumann	Brian Baumann	1966	2333
170 1/8	27 6/8	24 7/8	20 7/8	4 7/8	4 7/8	6	6	Jackson Co., OH	Theodore R. Yates	Theodore R. Yates	1967	2333
170 1/8	23 6/8	25 6/8	20 5/8	4 2/8	4 3/8	6	6	Marinette Co., WI	Leonard Schartner	Leonard Schartner	1968	2333
170 1/8	26 1/8	26	21 1/8	4 6/8	4 6/8	6	6	Lake Co., MN	Ed Gregorich	George W. Flaim	1969	2333
170 1/8	24 3/8	24 2/8	18 1/8	4 4/8	4 2/8	5	5	Pincher Creek, AB	Dave Simpson	Dave Simpson	1971	2333
170 1/8	24 2/8	25 4/8	15 3/8	6	5 7/8	5	5	Iowa Co., IA	Edward E. Best	Edward E. Best	1972	2333
170 1/8	24 5/8	25 4/8	19	5 5/8	4 4/8	7	5	Warren Co., IA	Arnold J. Hoch	Arnold J. Hoch	1975	2333
170 1/8	23 7/8	24 7/8	18 3/8	4 7/8	4 6/8	5	5	Oglethorpe Co., GA	Robert C. Thaxton	Robert C. Thaxton	1978	2333
170 1/8	22 4/8	25 5/8	20 5/8	4 6/8	4 5/8	6	6	Logan Co., IL	Gary L. Humbert	Gary L. Humbert	1979	2333
170 1/8	22 3/8	24 3/8	16 1/8	4 7/8	4 7/8	7	6	Morehouse Parish, LA	Johnnie Kovac, Jr.	Johnnie Kovac, Jr.	1979	2333
170 1/8	20 6/8	21 4/8	16 7/8	4 5/8	4 5/8	6	5	Smoky River, AB	Bernie Reiswig	Bernie Reiswig	1980	2333
170 1/8	25 4/8	25 7/8	22 2/8	4 5/8	4 3/8	6	7	Winona Co., MN	Roger J. Traxler	Roger J. Traxler	1980	2333
170 1/8	26 7/8	27	19 5/8	5 1/8	5 4/8	7	7	Breckinridge Co., KY	Thomas F. Dean	Thomas F. Dean	1982	2333
170 1/8	27	27 1/8	19	4 6/8	4 6/8	7	6	Cook Co., MN	William Bohnen	William Bohnen	1984	2333
170 1/8	24 3/8	22 6/8	18 3/8	5	5 1/8	8	6	Sanders Co., MT	Richard Lukes	Richard Lukes	1984	2333
170 1/8	25 6/8	25 2/8	21 3/8	4 4/8	4 5/8	6	5	Mower Co., MN	Robert D. Plumb	Robert D. Plumb	1984	2333
170 1/8	25 7/8	25 7/8	21 5/8	4 4/8	4 5/8	6	6	Pulaski Co., MO	Chuck Adkins	Chuck Adkins	1986	2333
170 1/8	27 1/8	27 2/8	20 3/8	5 6/8	5 6/8	5	5	Essex Co., VT	Kevin A. Brockney	Kevin A. Brockney	1986	2333
170 1/8	22 3/8	22 3/8	15 5/8	5 3/8	5 2/8	5	5	Greene Co., IA	Charles Gunn	Charles Gunn	1986	2333
170 1/8	26 4/8	27	20 3/8	4 6/8	4 7/8	7	7	Vermilion River, AB	Vince V. Philipps	Vince V. Philipps	1986	2333
170 1/8	28 6/8	28 1/8	23	5	5	6	7	Winona Co., MN	Picked Up	Gary L. Bornfleth	1987	2333

Score	Main Beam R	Main Beam L	Inside Spread	Circ. R	Circ. L	Pts R	Pts L	Locality	Hunter	Owner	Date	Rank
170 1/8	26 7/8	26	20 7/8	4 6/8	4 6/8	5	6	Harford Co., MD	Edward C. Garrison	Edward C. Garrison	1987	2333
170 1/8	25 6/8	25 1/8	17 5/8	5 5/8	5 5/8	5	5	Comal Co., TX	Lyman Skolaut	Lyman Skolaut	1987	2333
170 1/8	25 4/8	25 3/8	23 1/8	5	5	5	6	Lycoming Co., PA	Richard C. Tebbs, Jr.	Richard C. Tebbs, Jr.	1987	2333
170 1/8	27 3/8	26	22 1/8	4 7/8	4 7/8	5	5	Coahuila, MX	Rodolfo F. Barrera	Rodolfo F. Barrera	1988	2333
170 1/8	27 7/8	26 4/8	18 7/8	5 1/8	5 4/8	5	6	Montgomery Co., MO	Kenneth B. Maskey	Kenneth B. Maskey	1988	2333
170 1/8	28 1/8	29 4/8	23 7/8	5 1/8	5 1/8	7	5	Douglas Co., KS	Picked Up	Frank Virchow	1988	2333
170 1/8	23 3/8	27 4/8	20 5/8	4 6/8	4 7/8	5	5	Racine Co., WI	Michael H. Poeschel	Michael H. Poeschel	1989	2333
170 1/8	25 2/8	26 5/8	17 6/8	5 6/8	5 6/8	6	6	Saginaw Co., MI	Scott M. Hutchins	Scott M. Hutchins	1990	2333
170 1/8	23 6/8	23 1/8	15 3/8	4 5/8	4 6/8	6	6	Webb Co., TX	Gerald W. Rentz, Jr.	Gerald W. Rentz, Jr.	1990	2333
170 1/8	26	25 5/8	20 1/8	5 3/8	5 3/8	7	6	Perry Co., IL	Stephen E. Brand	Stephen E. Brand	1991	2333
170 1/8	26 6/8	26 4/8	24 2/8	5	5 1/8	6	6	La Crosse Co., WI	Scott R. Wavra	Scott R. Wavra	1991	2333
170 1/8	28 2/8	27 4/8	23	4 6/8	4 6/8	6	6	Lake Co., IL	John W. Schnider, Jr.	John W. Schnider, Jr.	1992	2333
170 1/8	25 2/8	25 6/8	17 1/8	5 6/8	5 6/8	6	5	Butler Co., KY	David W. Alford	David W. Alford	1993	2333
170 1/8	26 3/8	26 1/8	20 3/8	5	5	6	6	Webb Co., TX	Picked Up	William O. Carter	1993	2333
170 1/8	26 7/8	25	23 1/8	4 7/8	4 7/8	5	5	Iroquois Co., IL	Picked Up	Michael L. Krumweide	1993	2333
170 1/8	30	29	21 5/8	6 1/8	6 1/8	5	5	Elk Co., KS	Michael L. Krumweide	Michael L. Krumweide	1993	2333
170 1/8	25 3/8	24 3/8	21 5/8	5 5/8	5 5/8	4	4	Jim Hogg Co., TX	Terry L. Tindle	Terry L. Tindle	1994	2333
170 1/8	25 5/8	25 5/8	21 5/8	5 2/8	5 1/8	5	5	Pine Creek, AB	Frances Weil	Frances Weil	1994	2333
170 1/8	26 6/8	30 1/8	21 6/8	5 2/8	5 2/8	8	8	Muhlenberg Co., KY	Daniel W. LaPierre	Daniel W. LaPierre	1994	2333
170 1/8	28 4/8	25 3/8	18	4 3/8	4 3/8	4	4	Adams Co., IL	Jamie G. Noble	Jamie G. Noble	1994	2333
170 1/8	26 7/8	25 4/8	21 2/8	5 4/8	5	5	5	Sullivan Co., IN	Jeffrey J. Rakers	Jeffrey J. Rakers	1995	2333
170 1/8	25 4/8	24 4/8	17 7/8	5 1/8	5	9	8	Athabasca River, AB	Troy J. Rambis	Troy J. Rambis	1995	2333
170 1/8	24 4/8	26 7/8	22 7/8	5	5	8	5	Douglas Co., WI	Patrick S. Casey	Patrick S. Casey	1995	2333
170 1/8	26 7/8	23 7/8	18 5/8	4 2/8	4 3/8	5	6	Dunn Co., WI	Duane Christiansen	Duane Christiansen	1995	2333
170 1/8	25 4/8	27 2/8	17	5 2/8	5 2/8	6	6	Otter Tail Co., MN	Jan J. Finley	Jan J. Finley	1995	2333
170 1/8	25 3/8	24 2/8	21 3/8	4 6/8	4 6/8	5	7	Hubbard, SK	Clarence P. Janota	Clarence P. Janota	1995	2333
170 1/8	24 2/8	25 7/8	18 4/8	4 5/8	4 5/8	6	5	Branch Co., MI	Randle R. Litke	Randle R. Litke	1995	2333
170 1/8	25 3/8	28 7/8	26 1/8	5 5/8	5 5/8	5	5	Allamakee Co., IA	Lionel Rokosh	Lionel Rokosh	1995	2333
170 1/8	28 7/8	24 7/8	18 6/8	4 7/8	4 6/8	5	7	Clayton Co., IA	Jeffrey M. Stauffer	Jeffrey M. Stauffer	1996	2333
170 1/8	24 7/8	26 4/8	22 7/8	4 7/8	4 5/8	6	5	Alberta Beach, AB	Eric W. Thorstenson	Eric W. Thorstenson	1996	2333
170 1/8	26 4/8	27	25 5/8	5	5	5	5	Clark Co., IN	Thomas G. Baumgartner	Thomas G. Baumgartner	1996	2333
170 1/8	24 2/8	25 5/8	19 3/8	4 2/8	4 4/8	6	6	Ashland Co., OH	Rodney M. Janz	Rodney M. Janz	1996	2333
170 1/8	25 4/8	24 3/8	19 5/8	4 1/8	4 1/8	6	6	Roseau Co., MN	Daniel H. Lenfert	Daniel H. Lenfert	1996	2333
170 1/8	25 6/8	25 6/8	20 1/8	6	6	8	6	Nuevo Laredo, MX	Steven J. Orchard	Steven J. Orchard	1996	2333
170 1/8	26 5/8	27 6/8	21 1/8	4 7/8	4 7/8	5	5	Schoolcraft Co., MI	R.E. Putney & F. Walker	Rodney E. Putney	1996	2333
170	26	26 6/8	17 5/8	4 1/8	4 1/8	7	7	Oiltown, TX	John F. Taylor	John F. Taylor	PR 1918	2394
170	24 2/8	24 2/8	18 4/8	4 4/8	4 6/8	6	6	Blair Co., PA	Harold P. Dixner	J. Kenneth Dixner	1941	2394
170	25 5/8	24 1/8	21 6/8	6 4/8	6 4/8	10	10	Virden, MB	L.D. Roberts	L.D. Roberts	1943	2394
170	26 4/8	27	23	4 4/8	4 4/8	5	5	Webb Co., TX	Claude Feathers	Claude Feathers	1951	2394
170	27	28	22 4/8	5 1/8	5 1/8	5	5	Chippewa Co., WI	Jessie Byer	Jessie Byer	1957	2394
170	28 7/8	27 5/8	20	6 7/8	6 7/8	5	5	Fullerton, NE	Herbert Zieschang	Herbert Zieschang	1959	2394
170	27 4/8	27 6/8	23 1/8	5 4/8	5 4/8	5	5	W. Feliciana Parish, LA	John J. Scheidler	Jim Falls Lions Club	1959	2394
170	26 2/8	25 2/8	21	5 2/8	5 1/8	7	5	Henderson Co., IL	Truman Lauterback	Truman Lauterback	1960	2394
170	23 2/8	26	19 6/8	4	4 1/8	6	6	Atascosa Co., TX	Jerry Loper	Jerry Loper	1960	2394
170	27 5/8	24 1/8	24 1/8	4 1/8	4 1/8	8	8	Flathead Co., MT	Donald R. Vaughn	Donald R. Vaughn	1961	2394
170	26 5/8	24 5/8	17 7/8	4 4/8	4 4/8	6	6	Stevens Co., WA	Ben H. Moore, Jr.	Ben H. Moore, Jr.	1966	2394
170	26 1/8	22 7/8	18 4/8	4 6/8	4 7/8	6	5		Dave Delap	Dave Delap	1966	2394
170									Clair Kelso	Clair Kelso	1966	2394

WHITETAIL DEER - TYPICAL ANTLERS

Odocoileus virginianus virginianus and certain related subspecies

Score	Length of Main Beam R	L	Inside Spread	Circumference at Smallest Place Between Burr and First Point R	L	Number of Points R	L	Locality	Hunter	Owner	Date Killed	Rank
170	26 4/8	26 5/8	17 4/8	4 6/8	4 7/8	7	5	Bates Co., MO	Gary Rosier	Gary Rosier	1969	2394
170	28 3/8	25 6/8	21 1/8	5 2/8	5 3/8	6	7	Hancock Co., IL	Henry F. Collins	Henry F. Collins	1973	2394
170	26 3/8	24 5/8	19 6/8	5 2/8	5 1/8	5	5	Shelby Co., MO	Rusty D. Gander	Rusty D. Gander	1973	2394
170	26 4/8	25 5/8	19 5/8	4 5/8	4 4/8	6	6	York Co., ME	Aubin Huertas	Aubin Huertas	1973	2394
170	28 4/8	27 3/8	21 4/8	4 7/8	5	8	7	Latah Co., ID	Lewis L. Turcott	Lewis L. Turcott	1974	2394
170	24 3/8	23 2/8	20 6/8	4 7/8	4 6/8	5	5	Scotland Co., MO	Chester J. Young	Chester J. Young	1974	2394
170	26	26	21	4 4/8	4 3/8	7	6	Dunn Co., WI	James W. Seehaver	James W. Seehaver	1976	2394
170	25 3/8	25 2/8	18	4 5/8	4 5/8	7	6	Ballard Co., KY	Rudolf Koranchan, Jr.	Rudolf Koranchan, Jr.	1977	2394
170	25 3/8	27 4/8	21	4 6/8	5	7	4	Androscoggin Co., ME	Ricky D. Cavers	Ricky D. Cavers	1981	2394
170	28 3/8	26 7/8	19 3/8	4 4/8	4 5/8	7	6	Des Moines Co., IA	Dean A. Dravis	Dean A. Dravis	1983	2394
170	26 2/8	26 6/8	20 2/8	4 7/8	4 5/8	5	7	Wapello Co., IA	George C. Ellis	George C. Ellis	1984	2394
170	25 6/8	25 6/8	16 5/8	4 7/8	5	5	8	Harrison Co., IA	Rodney P. Stahlnecker	Rodney P. Stahlnecker	1984	2394
170	29 1/8	27 7/8	23 4/8	5 4/8	5 4/8	6	6	Penobscot Co., ME	Picked Up	Tad D. Proudlove	1985	2394
170	27 7/8	27 6/8	18 6/8	4 6/8	4 6/8	7	7	Putnam Co., MO	Unknown	Terry L. Gates	PR 1986	2394
170	27 5/8	27 5/8	21 6/8	5 5/8	5 2/8	5	5	Jefferson Co., WI	Robert L. Becker	Robert L. Becker	1987	2394
170	26 7/8	27 2/8	20 4/8	5 4/8	5 6/8	5	5	Jones Co., IA	James L. Coyle	James L. Coyle	1988	2394
170	28	28 1/8	18 5/8	4 4/8	4 4/8	8	7	Dane Co., WI	Patrick D. Anderson	Patrick D. Anderson	1989	2394
170	28 4/8	26 7/8	20	4 4/8	4 4/8	5	5	Madison Co., IA	Terry L. Snyder	Terry L. Snyder	1989	2394
170	26	26 1/8	19 2/8	4 2/8	4 2/8	7	5	Webster Co., IA	Picked Up	Clare E. Bailey	1990	2394
170	26	27	19 4/8	4 6/8	4 7/8	6	5	Jackson Co., MI	Michael D. Fitzgerald	Michael D. Fitzgerald	1990	2394
170	29 3/8	27 5/8	21	4 5/8	4 6/8	5	7	Sounding Lake, AB	Bill Kostenuk	Bill Kostenuk	1990	2394
170	24 2/8	24 2/8	18 2/8	3 7/8	3 7/8	8	8	Hyde Co., SD	Matthew Kusser	Matthew Kusser	1990	2394
170	25 6/8	25 4/8	16 1/8	5 4/8	5 3/8	6	7	Tift Co., GA	Alan Parrish	Alan Parrish	1990	2394
170	28 3/8	27 4/8	17 4/8	4 1/8	4	6	6	Worth Co., GA	Travis Strenth	Travis Strenth	1990	2394
170	25 7/8	26 1/8	16 3/8	4 4/8	4 4/8	7	5	Boone Co., MO	Norman M. Barrows	Norman M. Barrows	1991	2394
170	28 1/8	27 3/8	21 3/8	5 5/8	5 6/8	9	9	Bond Co., IL	Mark A. Carr	Mark A. Carr	1991	2394
170	25 2/8	26 2/8	20 3/8	5 1/8	5 2/8	9	7	Montgomery Co., IA	Jerry A. Foote	Jerry A. Foote	1991	2394
170	23 7/8	23 7/8	18 2/8	5 2/8	6	6	7	Marion Co., IA	Helen Hall	Helen Hall	1991	2394
170	28 1/8	28 2/8	18 2/8	5	5 1/8	7	6	Ripley Co., IN	Robert N. Hughes	Robert N. Hughes	1991	2394
170	28 7/8	27 3/8	23 1/8	4 2/8	4 2/8	5	6	McHenry Co., IL	Daniel L. Doherty	Daniel L. Doherty	1992	2394
170	24 5/8	24 5/8	20 6/8	5 7/8	6	5	5	Buffalo Co., WI	Gary G. Ruff	Gary G. Ruff	1992	2394
170	26 1/8	25 2/8	17 4/8	4 6/8	5 1/8	6	6	Crow Wing Co., MN	Unknown	Calvin L. Seguin	PR 1992	2394
170	27 1/8	27 2/8	18 2/8	4 6/8	4 7/8	7	6	Bottineau Co., ND	Ryan M. Bernstein	Ryan M. Bernstein	1993	2394
170	24 7/8	24 4/8	18 2/8	5	4 7/8	5	5	Porcupine Forest, SK	Jeff B. Brigham	Jeff B. Brigham	1993	2394
170	25 4/8	25 1/8	20 2/8	5 6/8	5 5/8	5	5	McHenry Co., IL	Mike R. Fischer	Mike R. Fischer	1993	2394
170	25	24 6/8	23 4/8	5 1/8	5 1/8	6	6	De Witt Co., IL	Charles A. Leimbach	Charles A. Leimbach	1994	2394

170	25 6/8	27 5/8	22 2/8	5	5 2/8	4	4	Brown Co., IL	Paul I. Reid	Paul I. Reid	1994	2394
170	23 7/8	24 3/8	16 6/8	4 7/8	5	7	6	Harrison Co., IN	Phillip L. Whiteman	Phillip L. Whiteman	1994	2394
170	27 5/8	26 3/8	19 6/8	4 6/8	4 6/8	5	5	Wayne Co., KY	Danny Phillips	Danny Phillips	1995	2394
170	24 4/8	25	17 6/8	4 3/8	4 2/8	6	5	Porcupine Plain, SK	Picked Up	Terry L. Amos	1996	2394
170	28 4/8	27 2/8	21 6/8	4 1/8	4 1/8	5	5	Cross Co., AR	Clay C. Bassham	Clay C. Bassham	1996	2394
170	24 1/8	25 4/8	18	4 3/8	4 3/8	6	5	Washington Co., OH	Robert L. Clark, Jr.	Robert L. Clark, Jr.	1996	2394
194*	27 4/8	27 1/8	19	4 4/8	4 4/8	5	5	Johnson Co., IA	Steven E. Tyer	Steven E. Tyer	1994	2394

* Final score is subject to revision by additional verifying measurements.

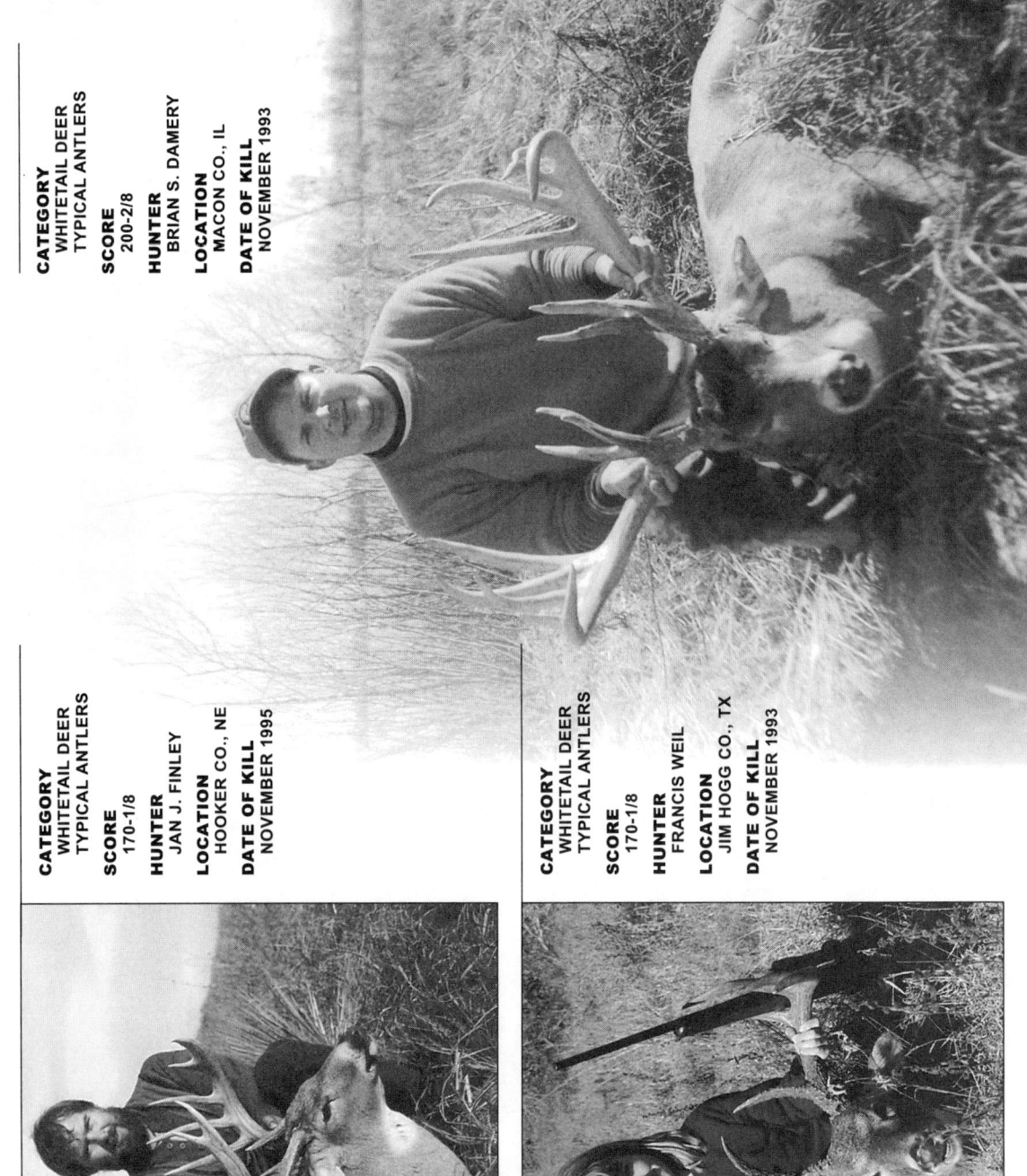

CATEGORY
WHITETAIL DEER
TYPICAL ANTLERS

SCORE
200-2/8

HUNTER
BRIAN S. DAMERY

LOCATION
MACON CO., IL

DATE OF KILL
NOVEMBER 1993

CATEGORY
WHITETAIL DEER
TYPICAL ANTLERS

SCORE
170-1/8

HUNTER
JAN J. FINLEY

LOCATION
HOOKER CO., NE

DATE OF KILL
NOVEMBER 1995

CATEGORY
WHITETAIL DEER
TYPICAL ANTLERS

SCORE
170-1/8

HUNTER
FRANCIS WEIL

LOCATION
JIM HOGG CO., TX

DATE OF KILL
NOVEMBER 1993

CATEGORY
WHITETAIL DEER
TYPICAL ANTLERS

SCORE
170-1/8

HUNTER
JOHN W. SCHNIDER, JR.

LOCATION
LAKE CO., IL

DATE OF KILL
OCTOBER 1992

CATEGORY
WHITETAIL DEER
TYPICAL ANTLERS

SCORE
181-5/8

HUNTER
ANDRAE D'ACQUISTO

LOCATION
RACINE CO., WI

DATE OF KILL
SEPTEMBER 1996

CATEGORY
WHITETAIL DEER
TYPICAL ANTLERS

SCORE
188-6/8

HUNTER
ELI D. RANDALL

LOCATION
CRAWFORD CO., WI

DATE OF KILL
NOVEMBER 1995

353

CATEGORY
WHITETAIL DEER
TYPICAL ANTLERS

SCORE
175

HUNTER
WILLIAM M. WHELESS III

LOCATION
MAVERICK CO., TX

DATE OF KILL
DECEMBER 1992

CATEGORY
WHITETAIL DEER
TYPICAL ANTLERS

SCORE
170-1/8

HUNTER
CLARENCE P. JANOTA

LOCATION
DUNN CO., WI

DATE OF KILL
OCTOBER 1995

CATEGORY
WHITETAIL DEER
TYPICAL ANTLERS

SCORE
172-5/8

HUNTER
J. GRANT BOWIE

LOCATION
DAWSON CREEK, BC

DATE OF KILL
NOVEMBER 1992

C.R. "PINK" GUTERMUTH
1900-1988

One of the "giants" in the conservation movement, Pink Gutermuth was directly involved in every major national conservation issue and legislation for more than a half century. Born in Fort Wayne, Indiana, he attended Notre Dame University and graduated from the American Institute of Banking in 1927. He served as vice president of the Wildlife Management Institute from 1945 until retirement in 1971. Founder and past president of the World Wildlife Fund USA, he was also the founder of the Wildlife Foundation. He was President of the National Rifle Association from 1973-1975. Pink received numerous awards from many conservation organizations, including the prestigious Sagamore Hill Award from Boone and Crockett Club. ∎

Although several all-time typical whitetail trophies have been from Missouri, it was not until the fall of 1981 that this state acquired the bragging rights to the World's Record non-typical whitetail deer (*Odocoileus virginianus*).

On November 15, 1981, David Beckman met Conservation Agent Michael Helland along a road in northern St. Louis County, Missouri. Beckman had killed a deer and he asked Helland to officially check and seal it, to save the drive to an official check station.

They talked for a few minutes after sealing the deer, and then Beckman drove away. Not long after leaving Helland, Beckman saw a dead buck with a very large rack lying inside a fence along the road. Knowing that the deer was on private property and that he would not be able to retrieve it, Beckman decided to find Helland and tell him of his discovery.

Agent Helland obtained permission of the landowner to recover the carcass. With the help of friends, he skinned the deer and removed the rack that weighed over 11 pounds. It was estimated that the deer weighed over 250 pounds. Examination of the teeth revealed that the monstrously large deer was only 5-1/2 years old. Cause of death could not be determined, but it did not appear to have been shot.

Winter is a busy time of year for conservation agents. The rack was forgotten until after the first of the year when Helland took the cape and rack to a taxidermist friend. The taxidermist to whom he took it recognized its outstanding trophy character. Helland arranged to have the trophy scored by Dean Murphy, a Boone and Crockett Club official measurer. With the help of Wayne Porath, deer biologist for the Missouri Department of Conservation, Murphy scored the trophy for entry into the 18th Awards Entry Period at 325-7/8. Later it was officially scored at 333-7/8, and became the new World's Record non-typical whitetail.

All persons involved agreed that a trophy of this stature should be held in public ownership and on public display for everyone to enjoy. Accordingly, the Missouri Department of Conservation was assumed possession of the marvelous antlers. ∎

WHITETAIL DEER
NON-TYPICAL ANTLERS
WORLD'S RECORD SCORECHART

All measurements must be made with a 1/4-inch wide flexible steel tape to the nearest one-eighth of an inch. (Note: A flexible steel cable can be used to measure points and main beams only.) Enter fractional figures in eighths, without reduction. Official measurements cannot be taken until the antlers have air dried for at least 60 days after the animal was killed.

A. Number of Points on Each Antler: To be counted a point, the projection must be at least one inch long, with the length exceeding width at one inch or more of length. All points are measured from tip of point to nearest edge of beam as illustrated. Beam tip is counted as a point but not measured as a point.

B. Tip to Tip Spread is measured between tips of main beams.

C. Greatest Spread is measured between perpendiculars at a right angle to the center line of the skull at widest part, whether across main beams or points.

D. Inside Spread of Main Beams is measured at a right angle to the center line of the skull at widest point between main beams. Enter this measurement again as the Spread Credit if it is less than or equal to the length of the longer antler; if greater, enter longer antler length for Spread Credit.

E. Total of Lengths of all Abnormal Points: Abnormal Points are those non-typical in location (such as points originating from a point or from bottom or sides of main beam) or extra points beyond the normal pattern of points. Measure in usual manner and enter in appropriate blanks.

F. Length of Main Beam is measured from the center of the lowest outside edge of burr over the outer side to the most distant point of the main beam. The point of beginning is that point on the burr where the center line along the outer side of the beam intersects the burr, then following generally the line of the illustration.

G-1-2-3-4-5-6-7. Length of Normal Points: Normal points project from the top of the main beam. They are measured from nearest edge of main beam over outer curve to tip. Lay the tape along the outer curve of the beam so that the top edge of the tape coincides with the top edge of the beam on both sides of the point to determine the baseline for point measurement. Record point lengths in appropriate blanks.

H-1-2-3-4. Circumferences are taken as detailed in illustration for each measurement. If brow point is missing, take H-1 and H-2 at smallest place between burr and G-2. If G-1 is missing, take H-4 halfway between G-3 and tip of main beam.

Records of
North American
Big Game

BOONE AND CROCKETT CLUB®

250 Station Drive
Missoula, MT 59801
(406) 542-1888

OFFICIAL SCORING SYSTEM FOR NORTH AMERICAN BIG GAME TROPHIES

NON-TYPICAL
WHITETAIL AND COUES' DEER

MINIMUM SCORES		
	AWARDS	ALL-TIME
whitetail	185	195
Coues'	105	120

KIND OF DEER (check one)
☑ whitetail
☐ Coues'

Detail of Point Measurement

Abnormal Points

Right Antler		Left Antler	
3 1/8	5 3/8	1 3/8	1 4/8
5 5/8	6	1	2 1/8
4 3/8	8	1 1/8	4 7/8
2 4/8	7	2 1/8	1 1/8
5 4/8	7	9 4/8	2 7/8
12 5/8		2 6/8	7 2/8
11 3/8		7 3/8	9 4/8
4 6/8		1 6/8	4
3 2/8		10	3
7 6/8		5 4/8	4 6/8
SUBTOTALS	94 2/8	6 2/8	89 6/8
E. TOTAL			184

SEE OTHER SIDE FOR INSTRUCTIONS	COLUMN 1	COLUMN 2	COLUMN 3	COLUMN 4
	Spread Credit	Right Antler	Left Antler	Difference
A. No. Points on Right Antler	19			
B. Tip to Tip Spread	27	No. Points on Left Antler	26	
		C. Greatest Spread	33 3/8	
D. Inside Spread of Main Beams	23 3/8	SPREAD CREDIT MAY EQUAL BUT NOT EXCEED LONGER ANTLER	23 3/8	
F. Length of Main Beam		24 1/8	23 3/8	6/8
G-1. Length of First Point		8 1/8	7	1 1/8
G-2. Length of Second Point		7 1/8	8 1/8	1
G-3. Length of Third Point		8 3/8	7 6/8	1 3/8
G-4. Length of Fourth Point, If Present				
G-5. Length of Fifth Point, If Present				
G-6. Length of Sixth Point, If Present				
G-7. Length of Seventh Point, If Present				
H-1. Circumference at Smallest Place Between Burr and First Point		5 1/8	5 1/8	0
H-2. Circumference at Smallest Place Between First and Second Points		4 4/8	4 4/8	0
H-3. Circumference at Smallest Place Between Second and Third Points		7 6/8	6 5/8	1 1/8
H-4. Circumference at Smallest Place Between Third and Fourth Points		3 1/8	3 7/8	6/8
TOTALS	23 3/8	66 2/8	66 3/8	6 1/8

ADD	Column 1	23 3/8	Exact Locality Where Killed: St. Louis Co., MO
	Column 2	66 2/8	Date Killed: Nov. 15, 1981 Hunter: Picked Up
	Column 3	66 3/8	Owner: Missouri Dept. of Conservation Telephone #:
	Subtotal	156	Owner's Address:
SUBTRACT	Column 4	6 1/8	Guide's Name and Address:
	Subtotal	149 7/8	Remarks: (Mention Any Abnormalities or Unique Qualities)
	ADD Line E Total	184	
	FINAL SCORE	333 7/8	

COPYRIGHT © 1999 BY BOONE AND CROCKETT CLUB®

MINIMUM SCORE 195 · *Odocoileus virginianus virginianus* and certain related subspecies

Score	Length of Main Beam		Inside Spread	Circumference at Smallest Place Between Burr and First Point		Number of Points		Locality	Hunter	Owner	Date Killed	Rank
	R	L		R	L	R	L					
333 7/8	24 1/8	23 3/8	23 3/8	5 1/8	5 1/8	19	25	St. Louis Co., MO	Picked Up	MO Dept. of Cons.	1981	1
328 2/8	25 5/8	24 4/8	24 3/8	6 2/8	5 6/8	23	22	Portage Co., OH	Picked Up	Larry L. Huffman	1940	2
295 6/8	21 2/8	18 2/8	22 3/8	5 5/8	5 3/8	21	24	Winston Co., MS	Tony Fulton	Tony Fulton	1995	3
284 3/8	21 4/8	19 6/8	16 2/8	4 4/8	4 4/8	21	26	McCulloch Co., TX	Unknown	Buckhorn Mus. & Saloon, Ltd.	1892	4
282	26 1/8	27	24 3/8	6 5/8	6 2/8	15	14	Clay Co., IA	Larry Raveling	Larry L. Huffman	1973	5
281 6/8	22 1/8	20 6/8	17 6/8	5 2/8	5	14	16	Tensas Parish, LA	James H. McMurray	James H. McMurray	1994	6
280 4/8	25 3/8	25 2/8	19 6/8	6 1/8	6 4/8	16	13	Shawnee Co., KS	Joseph H. Waters	Brad Gsell	1987	7
279 6/8	27 6/8	26	21 6/8	6	6	13	14	Whitemud Creek, AB	Neil J. Morin	Neil J. Morin	1991	8
277 5/8	27 5/8	28 4/8	24 6/8	6	6 1/8	17	16	Hardisty, AB	Doug Klinger	Doug Klinger	1976	9
277 3/8	28 1/8	28 3/8	21 1/8	6 5/8	6 7/8	19	18	Hall Co., NE	Del Austin	Larry L. Huffman	1962	10
273 6/8	27 3/8	27 5/8	20 6/8	6	6	19	16	West Afton River, NS	Alexander C. MacDonald	Bass Pro Shops F. & W. Mus.	1960	11
272	23 7/8	25	17 5/8	6 2/8	5 6/8	23	16	Junction, TX	Picked Up	Fred Mudge	1925	12
268 5/8	20 6/8	24 6/8	14 2/8	6 4/8	5 3/8	20	21	Norman Co., MN	Mitchell A. Vakoch	Bass Pro Shops F. & W. Mus.	1974	13
268	25 4/8	25	18	4 3/8	4 7/8	15	16	Idaho	Unknown	D.J. Hollinger & B. Howard	PR 1982	14
267 7/8	25	24 4/8	22 6/8	6 1/8	6 2/8	20	18	Shoal Lake, AB	Jerry Froma	Jerry Froma	1984	15
267 4/8	26 6/8	27 6/8	29 1/8	5 1/8	5 6/8	16	23	Idaho	Unknown	Jack Brittingham	PR 1923	16
267 3/8	25 4/8	28 2/8	20	6 5/8	6 3/8	18	7	Peoria Co., IL	Richard A. Pauli	Richard A. Pauli	1983	17
265 3/8	25 7/8	26	18 3/8	6 6/8	6 5/8	16	17	White Fox, SK	Elburn Kohler	Larry L. Huffman	1957	18
262 1/8	24 1/8	25 2/8	20	6 2/8	6 4/8	14	17	Ross Co., OH	Jay Pfankuch	Brad Gsell	1995	19
259 7/8	27	28 4/8	22 1/8	5	5 6/8	27	9	Perry Co., AL	Jon G. Moss	Jon G. Moss	1989	20
259 5/8	26 7/8	26 7/8	20 3/8	6	5 4/8	14	13	Chariton Co., MO	Duane R. Linscott	Jon G. Moss	1985	21
259	25 4/8	26 7/8	19 5/8	6 1/8	5 7/8	15	16	Washington Co., ME	Hill Gould	Bass Pro Shops F. & W. Mus.	1910	22
258 6/8	22 4/8	26 2/8	23 6/8	6 4/8	6	17	15	Republic Co., KS	John O. Band	Bass Pro Shops F. & W. Mus.	1965	23
258 6/8	24 3/8	25 4/8	22 7/8	5 4/8	5 5/8	15	15	Edgar Co., IL	Ernest R. Hires	Bass Pro Shops F. & W. Mus.	1994	23
258 4/8	27 3/8	29	19 5/8	5 7/8	6	16	17	Steep Rock, MB	John DeLorme	Bass Pro Shops F. & W. Mus.	1973	25
258 2/8	27	26 6/8	19 5/8	4 7/8	4 6/8	17	17	Becker Co., MN	J.J. Matter	J.J. Matter	1973	26
258 2/8	28 5/8	28 1/8	24 1/8	7	6 7/8	10	14	Louisa Co., IA	Lyle E. Spitznogle	Bass Pro Shops F. & W. Mus.	1982	26
258 2/8	23	23	16 2/8	6 4/8	6 1/8	14	15	Cheyenne Co., CO	Michael J. Okray	Bass Pro Shops F. & W. Mus.	1992	26
258 1/8	23 1/8	24 4/8	18 3/8	5 3/8	5 4/8	17	12	Cedar Co., IA	Picked Up	Bass Pro Shops F. & W. Mus.	1988	29
257 6/8	24 3/8	22 1/8	22 1/8	6 3/8	6 3/8	9	17	Nez Perce Co., ID	John D. Powers, Jr.	Bass Pro Shops F. & W. Mus.	1983	30
257 4/8	29 1/8	28 2/8	21	5 5/8	5 3/8	15	15	Warren Co., VA	James W. Smith	James W. Smith	1992	31
257 1/8	25 5/8	23 5/8	16 2/8	4 6/8	4 4/8	21	17	Elkhorn, MB	Harvey Olsen	Harvey Olsen	1973	32
256 7/8	28 3/8	27 6/8	21	5 1/8	5 4/8	18	17	Jackson Co., IA	David B. Manderscheid	Larry L. Huffman	1977	33
256 5/8	29 1/8	27 7/8	24 6/8	6 5/8	6 1/8	14	17	Holmes Co., OH	Picked Up	OH Dept. of Natl. Resc.	1975	34
256 2/8	28 7/8	28 1/8	20 4/8	6 5/8	6 4/8	11	16	Monona Co., IA	Carroll E. Johnson	Carroll E. Johnson	1968	35
256 1/8	28 7/8	26 5/8	23 3/8	7 5/8	7 2/8	18	13	Marshall Co., SD	Francis Fink	J.D. Andrews	1948	36

Score								Locality	By whom killed	Owner	Date Killed	Rank
256 1/8	30 1/8	29	21 7/8	5 3/8	5 5/8	11	16	McDonough Co., IL	Brian E. Bice	Larry L. Huffman	1992	36
255 4/8	23 2/8	22 7/8	18 1/8	5 6/8	5 5/8	18	15	Pigeon Lake, AB	Leo Eklund	Leo Eklund	1973	38
254 6/8	28 3/8	27	20 2/8	5 2/8	5	14	17	Stanley, ND	Roger Ritchie	Roger Ritchie	1968	39
253	28	28	21 4/8	5 5/8	5 6/8	14	26	Goldenville, NS	Neil MacDonald	Bass Pro Shops F. & W. Mus.	1945	40
253	29 7/8	27 2/8	24	5 3/8	5 4/8	12	14	Miami Co., KS	Kenneth R. Cartwright	Bass Pro Shops F. & W. Mus.	1994	40
252 2/8	23 4/8	25	21 3/8	4 7/8	5 1/8	17	12	Concordia Parish, LA	J.D. Shields	J. Logan Sewell	1948	42
252 1/8	25 6/8	28 3/8	19 5/8	5 3/8	5 6/8	9	9	Hill Co., MT	Frank A. Pleskac	Dick Idol	1968	43
252	24 3/8	25 2/8	19 1/8	5 7/8	5 4/8	11	16	Lee Co., IA	Carl Wenke	G. Bowen & B. Wohlers	1972	44
251 4/8	26 3/8	27 5/8	22 7/8	5 4/8	5 3/8	17	14	Beltrami Co., MN	Rodney Rhineberger	Bass Pro Shops F. & W. Mus.	1976	45
251 4/8	26 5/8	26 6/8	22 6/8	6	5 6/8	13	10	Meeting Lake, SK	Greg Brataschuk	Brad Gsell	1987	45
251 1/8	28 2/8	28	19	5 6/8	5 6/8	12	13	Mitchell Co., KS	Theron E. Wilson	Theron E. Wilson	1974	47
250 6/8	25 3/8	28	15 1/8	5	5	19	13	South Dakota	Howard Eaton	Jack Brittingham	1870	48
250 6/8	27 2/8	25 4/8	23 4/8	5 4/8	5 3/8	12	12	Richland Co., OH	David D. Dull	David D. Dull	1987	48
250 2/8	24 5/8	25 2/8	16 1/8	7 1/8	7	16	12	Washington Co., KS	Picked Up	Gale Sup	1988	50
250 1/8	27 3/8	28	19	5 7/8	6 1/8	16	17	Rainy Lake, ON	Grant Gustafson	Grant Gustafson	1995	51
250	29 5/8	30 1/8	23 4/8	6 2/8	6 1/8	15	13	Clearwater Co., MN	Ernest Sauer	Duane O. Bagley Wildl. Mus.	1931	52
249 7/8	26 5/8	25 6/8	23 2/8	4 1/8	4 2/8	12	22	Kings Co., NB	Ronald Martin	Bass Pro Shops F. & W. Mus.	1946	53
249 3/8	26 3/8	26 3/8	21 3/8	5 1/8	5	14	14	Rockingham Co., VA	Jeffery W. Hensley	Jeffery W. Hensley	1990	54
249 2/8	29 6/8	28 7/8	21 3/8	5 2/8	5 2/8	10	14	Fillmore Co., MN	Dallas R. Henn	Bass Pro Shops F. & W. Mus.	1961	55
249 1/8	26 2/8	26 7/8	19 2/8	6 4/8	6 2/8	12	20	Lily, SD	Jerry Roitsch	J.D. Andrews	1965	56
248 7/8	27 6/8	27 2/8	20 1/8	5 7/8	5 7/8	8	10	Greenwood Co., KS	Clifford G. Pickell	Bass Pro Shops F. & W. Mus.	1968	57
248 6/8	27 4/8	28 1/8	20 5/8	6	5 7/8	18	19	Warren Co., IA	Larry J. Caldwell	Larry J. Caldwell	1990	58
248 5/8	25	24	20 5/8	5 1/8	5 2/8	16	16	Snowy Mts., MT	Unknown	McLean Bowman	PR 1980	59
248 4/8	22 6/8	24 3/8	22	5 7/8	5 7/8	13	11	Moose Mt. Park, SK	Walter Bartko	George Hooey	1964	60
248 4/8	28	27 4/8	23 5/8	7 7/8	7 4/8	15	13	Fulton Co., IN	Robert S. Sears	Bass Pro Shops F. & W. Mus.	1990	60
248 1/8	26 5/8	26 1/8	18 1/8	6 1/8	5 7/8	16	19	Millet, AB	Donald Mayer	D.J. Hollinger & B. Howard	1995	60
248 1/8	31 1/8	32 1/8	22 6/8	5 2/8	5 4/8	15	15	Penobscot Co., ME	Unknown	James L. Mason, Sr.	1945	63
247 7/8	26 1/8	26	19 5/8	5 5/8	5 4/8	13	17	Frio Co., TX	Raul Rodriquez II	Raul Rodriquez II	1966	64
247 2/8	25 4/8	25 3/8	24 6/8	5 1/8	6 1/8	16	16	Johnston Co., OK	Bill M. Foster	Bill M. Foster	1970	65
246 3/8	27 1/8	26 1/8	29 3/8	6 6/8	6 6/8	9	14	Anderson Co., KS	Richard T. Stahl	Bass Pro Shops F. & W. Mus.	1992	66
245 7/8	31 2/8	27 6/8	25 3/8	5 6/8	5 6/8	11	14	Elk River, BC	James I. Brewster	James I. Brewster	1905	67
245 5/8	25 5/8	25 8/8	24 2/8	5 2/8	5 2/8	12	12	Itasca Co., MN	Peter Rutkowski	Bass Pro Shops F. & W. Mus.	1942	68
245 4/8	24 6/8	25 2/8	16 5/8	5 3/8	5	18	12	Carrot River, SK	Picked Up	Ken Halloway	1962	69
245 4/8	21 5/8	21 5/8	18 6/8	6 1/8	6 2/8	16	15	Kittson Co., MN	Lyndon K. Westerberg	Lyndon K. Westerberg	1990	69
245 3/8	27 7/8	27 5/8	17 4/8	5 7/8	6 1/8	14	14	Itasca Co., MN	Mike Hammer	Bass Pro Shops F. & W. Mus.	1956	71
245	24	24 4/8	20 6/8	5 3/8	5 4/8	15	15	Buffalo Co., WI	Elmer F. Gotz	Elmer F. Gotz	1973	72
244 6/8	27 4/8	27	17 4/8	5 2/8	5 2/8	18	13	Monroe Co., IA	Robert N. Wonderlich	Bass Pro Shops F. & W. Mus.	1970	73
244 2/8	25 4/8	28	16 5/8	5 5/8	5 3/8	13	13	Allegany Co., NY	Homer Boylan	Harry J. Boylan	1939	74
244 2/8	27	20 7/8	16 1/8	4 7/8	4 2/8	18	14	Zavala Co., TX	John R. Campbell	John L. Stein	1947	74
244 1/8	20 7/8	20	20 6/8	4 6/8	4 7/8	11	10	Sangamon Co., IL	William E. Hood	William E. Hood	1991	76
244	27 4/8	28	20 2/8	5 5/8	5	8	10	Becker Co., MN	James Saurdoff	Bass Pro Shops F. & W. Mus.	1985	77
243 7/8	25 4/8	30 3/8	16 2/8	8 2/8	8 2/8	18	15	Wirral, NB	H. Glenn Johnston	Arnold Alward	1962	78
243 7/8	26 7/8	26 3/8	20 4/8	6 5/8	7 1/8	14	13	Cook Co., IL	Picked Up	Jeffrey A. DeVroy	1995	78
243 5/8	26 3/8	26 5/8	22 2/8	5 1/8	5	11	15	Govan, SK	A.W. Davis	Bass Pro Shops F. & W. Mus.	1951	80
243 3/8	24 1/8	24 1/8	24 1/8	4 5/8	4 6/8	21	9	Mahoning Co., OH	David L. Klemm	Larry L. Huffman	1980	81
242 7/8	27 7/8	29 7/8	17 7/8	4 7/8	5 2/8	21	21	Pope Co., IL	William E. Henderson	William E. Henderson	1991	82
242 6/8	24	24 4/8	18 6/8	6 2/8	6	22	18	Bedford Co., VA	Walter Hatcher	Walter Hatcher	1993	83

WHITETAIL DEER - NON-TYPICAL ANTLERS

Odocoileus virginianus virginianus and certain related subspecies

Score	Length of Main Beam R	L	Inside Spread	Circumference at Smallest Place Between Burr and First Point R	L	Number of Points R	L	Locality	Hunter	Owner	Date Killed	Rank
242 5/8	27 2/8	26 1/8	17 2/8	6	5 4/8	13	16	Nance Co., NE	Robert E. Snyder	Bass Pro Shops F. & W. Mus.	1961	84
242 4/8	26 4/8	27	20 6/8	5 1/8	5 1/8	10	12	S. Saskatchewan River, SK	Earl W. Green	Bass Pro Shops F. & W. Mus.	1993	85
242 2/8	24 3/8	21 5/8	20 5/8	6 1/8	6 5/8	18	14	Auburnville, NB	John L. MacKenzie	Arnold Alward	1958	86
241 7/8	26 1/8	25 2/8	20 1/8	4 5/8	5	14	19	Flathead Co., MT	George Woldstad	George Woldstad	1960	87
241 7/8	22 2/8	28 3/8	19	5 3/8	5	15	11	Lyon Co., KS	Picked Up	D.J. Hollinger & B. Howard	1996	87
241 5/8	25	24 4/8	21 3/8	6 2/8	6 2/8	19	11	Manitoba	Unknown	Jack Brittingham	1984	89
241 3/8	29 2/8	25 7/8	19 3/8	5 2/8	5	9	11	Wisconsin	Unknown	Robert Kietzman	1940	90
241 1/8	26 4/8	26 1/8	18 1/8	6 1/8	6	19	18	Bighill Creek, AB	Donald D. Dwernychuk	Donald D. Dwernychuk	1984	91
240 7/8	28	28 6/8	20 2/8	6 3/8	6 2/8	13	10	Lewis Co., KY	Anthony D. Mefford	Anthony D. Mefford	1996	92
240 6/8	25 5/8	26 2/8	17 2/8	5 2/8	5 1/8	17	20	St. Louis Co., MN	John Cesarek	John Cesarek	1964	93
240 6/8	26 2/8	25 7/8	20 7/8	7 4/8	7 2/8	13	13	Clay Co., KS	Picked Up	H. James Reimer	1989	93
240 6/8	28 3/8	28 6/8	19 1/8	5 2/8	5 2/8	18	15	Wapello Co., IA	Picked Up	IA Dept. of Natl. Resc.	1991	93
240 4/8	24 5/8	24 5/8	18 7/8	6 3/8	6 3/8	12	18	Tisdale, SK	John Law	John Law	1988	96
240 3/8	24 2/8	24 6/8	18 5/8	7 2/8	7 2/8	18	20	Monroe Co., GA	John L. Hatton, Jr.	John L. Hatton, Jr.	1973	97
240	26 4/8	26	21 5/8	5 4/8	5 4/8	15	11	Kerr Co., TX	Walter R. Schreiner	Charles Schreiner III	1905	98
240	28 5/8	27 5/8	17	5 1/8	5 2/8	10	11	Allen Co., KS	Doug Whitcomb	John L. Stein	1987	98
239 4/8	25 7/8	25 6/8	17 2/8	4 4/8	4 4/8	10	12	Meeker Co., MN	Michael D. Dick	Michael D. Dick	1994	100
239 1/8	31 1/8	29 2/8	22 1/8	5 7/8	5 4/8	9	11	Illinois	William Seidel	Wayne Williamson	1987	101
239	28	29 2/8	22 3/8	5 7/8	5 5/8	13	13	Lyon Co., KS	Don E. Roberts	Bass Pro Shops F. & W. Mus.	1987	102
239	26 2/8	27 1/8	16 3/8	5 3/8	5 3/8	11	8	Montgomery Co., KS	Picked Up	H. James Reimer	1992	102
238 7/8	22 4/8	21 6/8	18 1/8	5	5 2/8	17	15	Crook Co., WY	Picked Up	J.D. Andrews	1962	104
238 6/8	22 6/8	22 2/8	18 3/8	5	5	18	15	Mahoning Co., OH	Ronald K. Osborne	Bass Pro Shops F. & W. Mus.	1986	105
238 6/8	26 2/8	25 3/8	20 5/8	6 7/8	7 2/8	11	12	Fulton Co., IL	Neil M. Booth	Neil M. Booth	1988	105
238 4/8	28 3/8	28 6/8	15 6/8	5 3/8	5 2/8	9	9	Piscataquis Co., ME	Christian B. Oberholser, Jr.	Christian B. Oberholser, Jr.	1996	107
238 3/8	28	26 6/8	22 7/8	6	5 4/8	12	10	Assiniboine River, MB	Doug Hawkins	Doug Hawkins	1981	108
238 2/8	24 3/8	25 2/8	22 6/8	6 2/8	7 4/8	12	11	Potter Co., SD	Larry Nylander	Donna Nylander	1963	109
238 2/8	27 1/8	26 2/8	21 4/8	5 5/8	5 7/8	17	17	Bay Co., MI	Paul M. Mickey	Paul M. Mickey	1976	109
238 2/8	27 6/8	28 1/8	19 6/8	6 3/8	6 2/8	15	17	Barren Co., KY	Picked Up	Ed Rigdon	1995	109
238 1/8	24 2/8	21 7/8	22	5 2/8	5 2/8	13	15	Whitewood, SK	Jack Davidge	Jack Davidge	1967	112
238 1/8	26 4/8	27 5/8	27	5 3/8	5 6/8	12	17	Madison Co., IL	Joe Bardill	Patrick Bardill	1985	112
238	26 4/8	27 6/8	23 6/8	5 6/8	5 7/8	12	8	Keya Paha Co., NE	Donald B. Phipps	Donald B. Phipps	1969	114
237 6/8	23 4/8	22 3/8	15	6	6	15	12	Henderson Co., IL	Robert E. Todd	Robert E. Todd	1978	115
237 6/8	27 2/8	27 6/8	19 5/8	5 4/8	5 4/8	14	17	Meadow Lake, SK	Picked Up	Darrell Roney	1996	115
237 5/8	25	22 7/8	17 3/8	5 2/8	5 2/8	18	18	Cross Co., AR	Picked Up	Kevin Ward	1994	117
237 3/8	24 2/8	23 7/8	20 2/8	5 4/8	5 4/8	12	16	Whiteshell, MB	Angus McVicar	Angus McVicar	1925	118
237	26 6/8	25 6/8	21 1/8	6 7/8	6 7/8	10	16	Barber Co., KS	Ronald D. Wilt	Cleon Almond	1986	119

Score								Locality	By Whom Killed	Owner	Date	Rank
237	27 5/8	26 3/8	22 4/8	5 5/8	5 7/8	14	12	Madison Co., IA	Picked Up	IA Dept. of Natl. Resc.	PR 1989	119
237	24 4/8	25 4/8	23	6 3/8	5 7/8	16	9	Douglas Co., KS	Terry D. Mayle	Terry D. Mayle	1994	119
236 7/8	28	27	25 3/8	5 3/8	5 4/8	11	10	Dallas Co., IA	Russ A. Clarken	Russ A. Clarken	1994	122
236 7/8	24 2/8	26 4/8	18 6/8	5 7/8	5 7/8	13	12	Preble Co., OH	Bruce A. Turner	Bruce A. Turner	1994	122
236 7/8	24 7/8	24 7/8	18 2/8	5 1/8	4 6/8	18	7	Beltrami Co., MN	Edwin C. Moe	Edwin C. Moe	1995	122
236 5/8	27 7/8	26	21 3/8	5 6/8	5 2/8	14	17	Pend Oreille Co., WA	George Gretener	John E. Gretener	PR 1931	125
236 5/8	27 2/8	26 1/8	20 1/8	7 1/8	6 6/8	11	9	Pike Co., IL	Floyd Pursley	Floyd Pursley	1987	125
236 4/8	24 6/8	25	20 5/8	5 4/8	5	17	12	Reserve, SK	Harry Nightingale	Legendary Whitetails	1959	127
236 3/8	25 7/8	23 6/8	20 3/8	5 4/8	5 4/8	14	16	Union Co., KY	Wilbur E. Buchanan	Wilbur E. Buchanan	1970	128
236 1/8	27	27 2/8	20 4/8	4 3/8	4 2/8	15	15	St. Joseph Co., MI	Kenneth L. Moore, Jr.	Kenneth L. Moore, Jr.	1995	129
236	22 3/8	27 2/8	19 5/8	5 4/8	5 1/8	11	12	Winona Co., MN	Francis A. Pries	Bass Pro Shops F. & W. Mus.	1964	130
235 4/8	29 2/8	27 1/8	22 7/8	5 7/8	5 6/8	13	13	Ashtabula Co., OH	James L. Clark	Bass Pro Shops F. & W. Mus.	1957	131
235 4/8	25 4/8	24 5/8	19 6/8	5 4/8	5 7/8	9	10	Pipestone Valley, SK	E.J. Marshall	E.J. Marshall	1958	131
235 3/8	21 7/8	22 6/8	21 6/8	6 2/8	6	13	20	Harding Co., SD	J.H. Krueger & R. Keeton	Larry L. Huffman	1965	133
235 1/8	24	23 7/8	21 2/8	5	4 7/8	14	10	Frio Co., TX	C.J. Stolle	John F. Stolle	1919	134
234 5/8	23 5/8	24	19 4/8	5 7/8	6 1/8	15	15	Nebraska	Picked Up	L.B. Philips	PR 1972	135
234 5/8	28 6/8	23 3/8	17 1/8	6 4/8	6 4/8	9	12	Round Lake, ON	Picked Up	Harry Jones	1990	135
234 5/8	27	28	25	6 2/8	6 2/8	8	7	Gallatin Co., IL	Scott G. Bosaw	Scott G. Bosaw	1994	135
234 4/8	29	28 2/8	20 7/8	5 6/8	5 3/8	14	16	Stevens Co., WA	Larry G. Gardner	Legendary Whitetails	1953	138
234 2/8	27 3/8	26 5/8	20 1/8	7 1/8	7	10	12	Alfalfa Co., OK	Loren Tarrant	Loren Tarrant	1984	139
234 1/8	25 7/8	27 4/8	17 2/8	4 2/8	4 5/8	6	10	Glacier Co., MT	Unknown	Larry W. Lander	PR 1968	140
234 1/8	26 7/8	26 3/8	20 2/8	6 2/8	5 5/8	16	14	Minnesota	Unknown	Gale Sup	PR 1985	140
234 1/8	26 1/8	26	21 1/8	6 2/8	6	14	14	Hamilton Co., IL	Mark A. Potts	Mark A. Potts	1995	140
234	26 7/8	26 4/8	18 5/8	6 6/8	6 6/8	14	12	Lac qui Parle Co., MN	Clifford A. Estlie	Clifford A. Estlie	1991	143
233 7/8	27	26 7/8	21 4/8	5 5/8	5 3/8	16	15	Loraine, WI	Homer Pearson	Larry L. Huffman	1937	144
233 7/8	23 6/8	22 4/8	16 5/8	5 7/8	6	9	14	Tompkins, SK	Don Stueck	McLean Bowman	1961	144
233 6/8	26	27	18	5 2/8	6	14	16	Carroll Co., IN	James R. Houston, Jr.	James R. Houston, Jr.	1995	144
233 6/8	26 2/8	22 4/8	21 1/8	4 6/8	5 4/8	13	13	Thompson Creek, WA	George Sly, Jr.	George Sly, Jr.	1964	147
233 6/8	28 2/8	27	22	4 7/8	5 4/8	13	13	Custer Co., NE	Lonnie E. Poland	Lonnie E. Poland	1986	147
233 3/8	30 5/8	26	21 2/8	5	5	11	13	Morrow Co., OH	Religh D. Martin	Religh D. Martin	1995	147
233 3/8	25 3/8	29 7/8	19 4/8	5 3/8	5 3/8	12	8	Carlton Co., MN	Peter Antonson	Roy Ober	PR 1938	150
233 3/8	27	26 4/8	18 3/8	5 6/8	5 6/8	13	12	Pueblo Co., CO	Raymond A. Vertovec	Raymond A. Vertovec	1994	150
233 2/8	27 2/8	25 5/8	18 6/8	5 3/8	4 7/8	9	11	Switzerland Co., IN	Henry Mitchell	Larry L. Huffman	1972	152
233 2/8	26 7/8	26 2/8	24 6/8	4 7/8	4 5/8	9	9	Acadia Valley, AB	James J. Niwa	James J. Niwa	1973	152
233 1/8	29 2/8	29	20 4/8	4 3/8	5 6/8	14	9	Condon Lakes, NS	Don McDonnell	Don McDonnell	1987	154
233	20 2/8	23 4/8	19 6/8	5 6/8	6 4/8	12	7	Punnichy, SK	Steve Kapay	Gale Sup	1968	155
232 7/8	25 7/8	26	18 7/8	5 1/8	5	13	11	Montana	Unknown	Raymond R. Cross	PR 1950	156
232 7/8	29 1/8	28 1/8	26 7/8	5 4/8	5 4/8	10	12	Montgomery Co., IA	Picked Up	Dirk M. Paul	1988	156
232 5/8	28 3/8	29	23 6/8	5 3/8	5 2/8	9	9	Wabasha Co., MN	Robert R. Friese	Robert R. Friese	1948	158
232 5/8	23 2/8	23 7/8	18 2/8	6 5/8	7	15	11	Winfield, AB	Harry O. Hueppelshevser	Harry O. Hueppelshevser	1986	158
232 4/8	29 2/8	23 3/8	18 7/8	5	5	14	18	Buckingham Co., VA	James R. Shumaker	James R. Shumaker	1986	160
232 4/8	26 3/8	19 6/8	23 2/8	6 7/8	4 4/8	11	12	Breathitt Co., KY	Delmar R. Hounshell	Delmar R. Hounshell	1990	161
232 3/8	25 2/8	24 2/8	19 6/8	5 4/8	5 3/8	12	9	Glendon, AB	John Diedrich	John Diedrich	1995	161
232 2/8	23 3/8	22 7/8	17 2/8	5 4/8	5 6/8	12	18	Thorsby, AB	Robert G. MacRae	Robert G. MacRae	1987	163
232 1/8	24 5/8	24 5/8	16 4/8	4 6/8	4 7/8	11	11	McLean Co., ND	Olaf P. Anderson	Larry L. Huffman	1886	164
232	25 6/8	25	17	6	6	18	11	Waukesha Co., WI	John Herr, Sr.	Mac's Taxidermy	1955	165
232	30 1/8	30 7/8	18 7/8	5 4/8	5 3/8	11	8	Barron Co., WI	Wayne F. Lindemans	Wayne F. Lindemans	1988	165

WHITETAIL DEER - NON-TYPICAL ANTLERS

Odocoileus virginianus virginianus and certain related subspecies

Score	Length of Main Beam R	L	Inside Spread	Circumference at Smallest Place Between Burr and First Point R	L	Number of Points R	L	Locality	Hunter	Owner	Date Killed	Rank
231 7/8	24	22 2/8	18	5 5/8	5 4/8	10	20	Harris, SK	Herman Cox	R.M. Burnett	1954	167
231 6/8	26 1/8	25 3/8	23 2/8	6	6 1/8	11	13	Peace River, AB	Terry Doll	Terry Doll	1978	168
231 5/8	28 1/8	26 5/8	19 2/8	5 1/8	5 1/8	11	11	Dane Co., WI	Dennis D. Shanks	Dennis D. Shanks	1979	169
231 4/8	29 4/8	29 4/8	18 6/8	6 2/8	6 1/8	14	13	Perry Co., IL	Unknown	Bass Pro Shops F. & W. Mus.	1968	170
231 4/8	25 7/8	26 4/8	27 3/8	6 1/8	6 2/8	11	14	Logan Co., IL	Donald D. Stiner	Donald D. Stiner	1993	170
231 3/8	29 3/8	27 4/8	23 1/8	4 3/8	4 3/8	9	10	Licking Co., OH	Norman L. Myers	Norman L. Myers	1964	172
231 3/8	28	28 4/8	26 1/8	6 6/8	6 3/8	9	9	Holland, MB	W. Ireland	John L. Stein	1968	172
231 2/8	25 6/8	26 3/8	18 4/8	5	4 7/8	17	13	Forest Co., WI	Robert Jacobson	Robert Jacobson	1958	174
231 2/8	26 1/8	30 1/8	20 6/8	5 2/8	5 1/8	10	9	Renville Co., MN	James L. Rath	Larry L. Huffman	1977	174
231 1/8	19 5/8	22 3/8	20 4/8	6	5 7/8	12	12	Lac qui Parle Co., MN	Willard Evans	Paul Evans	1951	176
231 1/8	28 3/8	28 4/8	24 2/8	5 1/8	5 3/8	12	9	Winona Co., MN	Robert E. Bains	Robert E. Bains	1973	176
231 1/8	25 3/8	25 7/8	21 4/8	5 6/8	5 6/8	14	12	Henry Co., IA	Wendell R. Prottsman	Wendell R. Prottsman	1988	176
231	26	25 7/8	18	5	5	14	12	Stevens Co., WA	Joe Bussano	Joe Bussano	1946	179
231	27 5/8	28	21 2/8	5 2/8	5 1/8	8	7	Cass Co., MN	L.S. Hanson	Joel H. Karvonen	1970	179
230 7/8	26 2/8	28 4/8	19 7/8	5 2/8	5	12	13	West Kootenay, BC	Karl H. Kast	Karl H. Kast	1940	181
230 7/8	25 4/8	25 2/8	21 5/8	5 1/8	5 1/8	12	14	Provost, AB	Richard C. Nelson	Richard C. Nelson	1990	181
230 6/8	27 5/8	27 2/8	19 3/8	5 7/8	6	14	16	Red Deer, AB	Delmer E. Johnson	Larry L. Huffman	1973	183
230 5/8	25 1/8	26 4/8	28 4/8	6 1/8	6 3/8	13	11	Iron Co., MI	Carl Runyan	Larry L. Huffman	1942	184
230 2/8	26 1/8	26	19 1/8	5	5 1/8	11	11	Todd Co., MN	John Berscheit	John Berscheit	1976	185
230 2/8	30	30	23 7/8	5 5/8	5 6/8	9	13	Walworth Co., WI	F. Dan Dinelli	F. Dan Dinelli	1992	185
230 1/8	27 2/8	27 1/8	18	5 3/8	5 3/8	15	11	Pope Co., MN	Harvey J. Erickson	Harvey J. Erickson	1974	187
230 1/8	25 6/8	24 7/8	18 5/8	4 6/8	4 7/8	12	11	Guthrie Co., IA	Todd A. Hawley	Todd A. Hawley	1982	187
230	26 6/8	26	22 2/8	6 3/8	6 1/8	13	12	Schoolcraft Co., MI	Bill Ogle	MI Whitetail Hall of Fame Mus.	1943	189
230	25 1/8	25 2/8	23 7/8	5 5/8	5 4/8	14	16	Bayfield Co., WI	Picked Up	Brant J. Mueller	1958	189
230	27 1/8	28 1/8	19 7/8	5	5	11	8	Houston Co., MN	Winnie Papenfuss	Winnie Papenfuss	1973	189
230	24 5/8	24 2/8	21 7/8	4 7/8	4 6/8	14	13	Clayton Co., IA	Fredrick A. Becker	Fredrick A. Becker	1993	189
229 7/8	27 4/8	26 7/8	19 7/8	6 4/8	6 2/8	13	11	Jackson Co., IN	Larry E. Deaton	Larry E. Deaton	1990	193
229 6/8	26 1/8	26	21 5/8	5 1/8	5 1/8	12	13	Decatur Co., IA	Edgar Shields	Edgar Shields	1986	194
229 4/8	28 5/8	28 4/8	20 4/8	5 3/8	5 3/8	9	8	Dewey Co., OK	Ricky C. Watt	Ricky C. Watt	1987	195
229 4/8	24 2/8	24 5/8	19 3/8	5	4 7/8	10	10	Marshall Co., IL	Daniel R. Ferguson	Daniel R. Ferguson	1994	195
229 4/8	27 5/8	26 2/8	21 3/8	6 7/8	6 6/8	13	9	Polk Co., IA	Terry M. Long	Terry M. Long	1995	195
229 3/8	27 7/8	26 6/8	23 6/8	5 3/8	5 4/8	8	8	Wapello Co., IA	Robert D. Harding	Robert D. Harding	1985	198
229 3/8	26 2/8	26 3/8	19 3/8	5 6/8	5 5/8	13	9	Montgomery Co., IL	Lee A. Heldebrandt	Lee A. Heldebrandt	1996	198
229 2/8	27	28 5/8	21 1/8	7	6 2/8	8	15	Linn Co., KS	Merle C. Beckman	Merle C. Beckman	1984	200
229 2/8	21 4/8	21 4/8	16 3/8	5 5/8	5 4/8	15	13	Flathead Co., MT	Carl E. Goetsch	Carl E. Goetsch	1992	200
229 2/8	26 4/8	26 3/8	22 2/8	4 2/8	4 3/8	11	12	Lincoln Co., MT	Picked Up	Steve Crossley	1994	200

Score	Main Beam R	Main Beam L	Inside Spread	Pts R	Pts L	Circ. R	Circ. L	Locality	Hunter	Owner	Date	Rank
229	27 4/8	27 1/8	16 2/8	8	9	6 7/8	6 2/8	Lake Co., IL	Rodney J. Rasmussen	Rodney J. Rasmussen	1995	203
228 7/8	27 2/8	28 2/8	18 5/8	11	10	5 7/8	6	Cherryfield, ME	Flora Campbell	Dick Idol	1953	204
228 6/8	24 5/8	24 3/8	18 1/8	18	14	6	5 6/8	Fulton Co., OH	Bernard Williamson III	Bernard Williamson III	1989	205
228 4/8	26	24	20 6/8	10	13	5 2/8	5 2/8	Montgomery Co., MD	John W. Poole	John W. Poole	1987	206
228 4/8	28 3/8	28 6/8	19 5/8	14	11	6 2/8	5 2/8	Lake Co., MN	Lisa A. Baxter	Lisa A. Baxter	1991	206
228 3/8	26 4/8	26 4/8	23	13	10	5 3/8	5 4/8	Kiowa Co., KS	Lance P. Ringler	Lance A. Baxter	1993	209
228 2/8	29 2/8	26 6/8	21	13	14	5 2/8	5 2/8	Cable, WI	Charles Berg	Eva M. Fisher	1910	210
228 1/8	29	28 7/8	20 1/8	13	13	5 6/8	6	Maine	Henry A. Caesar	Unknown	PR 1911	210
228 1/8	27	28 4/8	21 6/8	11	10	5 1/8	5 5/8	Bureau Co., IL	Keith F. VanderMeersch	Keith F. VanderMeersch	1992	210
227 6/8	25	21 6/8	17	13	17	6 4/8	6	Des Moines Co., IA	Edgar J. Steward	Edgar J. Steward	1990	212
227 4/8	25 2/8	25 3/8	18 4/8	16	9	6 4/8	6 4/8	Bayfield Co., WI	Earl Holt	Mrs. Earl Holt	1934	213
227 1/8	26 2/8	27 1/8	20 2/8	12	8	5 2/8	5 2/8	Pullman, WA	Glenn C. Paulson	Glenn C. Paulson	1965	213
227 2/8	26 5/8	26 4/8	29	11	10	6	6 1/8	Pembina River, AB	Joe Oleksiw	Joe Oleksiw	1992	215
227 1/8	27 3/8	26	16 3/8	8	9	4 6/8	4 6/8	Clark Co., WI	Edward W. Schoen	Edward W. Schoen	1955	216
227 1/8	23 6/8	24	21 4/8	8	14	4 4/8	4 4/8	Dimmit Co., TX	Stuart W. Stedman	Stuart W. Stedman	1990	216
227 1/8	26 6/8	24 7/8	18 6/8	11	14	5 1/8	4 7/8	Sang Lake, AB	V. Lynn Steeves	V. Lynn Steeves	1992	216
227	26 2/8	25 7/8	21 4/8	19	10	6 1/8	6 2/8	Concordia Parish, LA	Picked Up	Sandra Leger	1969	219
227	26 6/8	26 5/8	24 1/8	12	11	7 2/8	7 4/8	Miami Co., KS	Gary A. Smith	Larry L. Huffman	1970	219
227	25 3/8	26 1/8	17 2/8	13	12	5 1/8	5	Jackson Co., NE	Picked Up	H. James Reimer	1989	219
227	30 4/8	26 1/8	18	9	11	5 6/8	6	Lucas Co., IA	Picked Up	H. James Reimer	1992	219
227	28 1/8	29 4/8	23 1/8	10	10	6 2/8	6 6/8	Decatur Co., IA	Jack J. Schuler, Jr.	Jack J. Schuler, Jr.	1995	219
226 7/8	27 4/8	30 2/8	20 2/8	13	13	5	5	Dimmit Co., TX	Lake Webb	Warren N. Webb	1937	224
226 6/8	28 2/8	25 5/8	15 5/8	22	25	4 7/8	5 2/8	Rusk Co., WI	Joe Michalets	John R. Michalets	1911	225
226 6/8	26	28 2/8	22 1/8	10	12	5 4/8	5 5/8	Manor, SK	Stan Balkwill	Legendary Whitetails	1960	225
226 5/8	26 4/8	26 6/8	18 7/8	7	9	6	5 6/8	Pulaski Co., KY	H.C. Sumpter	H.C. Sumpter	1984	227
226 4/8	22 2/8	26	24 7/8	11	12	4 7/8	4 5/8	La Salle Co., TX	A.L. Lipscomb, Sr.	John L. Stein	1909	228
226 4/8	24 3/8	21 3/8	19 2/8	13	11	4 6/8	4 5/8	Muskingum Co., OH	Rex A. Thompson	Rex A. Thompson	1981	228
226 4/8	27 4/8	26 1/8	22	12	10	6 7/8	6 5/8	Linn Co., KS	Jerry O. Hampton	Larry L. Huffman	1988	228
226 4/8	27 3/8	27 4/8	20 3/8	11	12	4 7/8	4 7/8	Plymouth Co., IA	Ronald H. Junck	Ronald H. Junck	1995	228
226 3/8	26 2/8	25 7/8	18 2/8	10	8	5 5/8	5 3/8	Nez Perce Co., ID	Mrs. Ralph Bond	Mrs. Ralph Bond	1964	232
226 3/8	25 3/8	27 3/8	22 7/8	8	10	5 4/8	5 4/8	Clark Co., IN	Robert L. Bromm, Sr.	Robert L. Bromm, Sr.	1985	232
226 2/8	28 3/8	26 6/8	24 5/8	10	11	6 2/8	6	Warren Co., OH	Daniel H. Detrick	Daniel H. Detrick	1989	234
226 2/8	24 7/8	27 2/8	22 7/8	11	10	5 4/8	5 4/8	Amherst Co., VA	Picked Up	Brent W. Campbell	1994	234
226 1/8	26 3/8	25 3/8	22 3/8	12	14	5 1/8	5	Kimble Co., TX	Coke R. Stevenson	Marguerite K. Stevenson	1934	236
226 1/8	25 2/8	25 5/8	20 3/8	10	10	5 2/8	4 7/8	Trumbull Co., OH	Paul E. Lehman	Paul E. Lehman	1948	236
226	26 7/8	23 4/8	26 2/8	11	11	5	5	Winona Co., MN	Terry D. Masso	Terry D. Masso	1991	238
225 6/8	24 5/8	27 3/8	26 3/8	7	9	4 4/8	4 2/8	La Porte Co., IN	David Grundy	Don Schaufler	1987	239
225 6/8	25 4/8	26 7/8	21 5/8	9	8	5 2/8	5 2/8	Yellow Medicine Co., MN	Glen Bullick	Glen Bullick	1989	239
225 5/8	29 2/8	25 3/8	16 4/8	11	14	5 6/8	5 6/8	Laclede Co., MO	Picked Up	Scott Luthy	PR 1993	241
225 5/8	23 5/8	29 1/8	23 4/8	9	8	6 1/8	6 1/8	St. Louis Co., MN	Elmer H. Sellin	Larry L. Huffman	1938	242
225 3/8	16 7/8	23 4/8	16 7/8	13	10	6 3/8	6 1/8	Fayette Co., IA	Duane J. Cahoy	Duane J. Cahoy	1975	242
225 3/8	26 2/8	23 5/8	24 3/8	12	13	5 2/8	5	St. Lawrence Co., NY	Kenneth M. Locy	Kenneth M. Locy	1992	242
225 3/8	21 6/8	24 7/8	24	9	13	5 2/8	5 3/8	Scott Co., IA	Rick Porske	Rick Porske	1996	242
225 1/8	22 4/8	24 5/8	17 1/8	10	13	4 7/8	5	Burnet Co., TX	Mr. Stevens	Mclean Bowman	1938	246
225 1/8	31	22 4/8	23 4/8	9	11	5 6/8	5 5/8	Nodaway Co., MO	Ken Barcus	Larry L. Huffman	1982	246
225 1/8	27 4/8	30 6/8	22 6/8	8	9	5 2/8	5	Comanche Co., OK	Michael C. Apoka	Michael C. Apoka	1993	246
225	26 6/8	27 7/8	20 2/8	10	13	5 7/8	5 7/8	Barber Co., KS	Picked Up	Larry L. Huffman	1979	249

Odocoileus virginianus virginianus and certain related subspecies

Score	Length of Main Beam R	L	Inside Spread	Circumference at Smallest Place Between Burr and First Point R	L	Number of Points R	L	Locality	Hunter	Owner	Date Killed	Rank
225	24 1/8	24 7/8	24 7/8	4 7/8	5	11	9	Londes Co., MS	Richard Herring	Richard Herring	1988	249
225	25 6/8	24 5/8	23	5	4 7/8	12	14	Alameda Dam, SK	Duane Gervais	Duane Gervais	1992	249
224 7/8	20 2/8	24 2/8	17	8	5 5/8	19	11	Kinney Co., TX	Unknown	Joe L. Collins	1900	252
224 6/8	27	26 7/8	27 1/8	5 2/8	5 2/8	11	10	Mills Co., IA	James C. Reed	James C. Reed	1988	253
224 6/8	22 5/8	24 2/8	15 1/8	5 4/8	5 2/8	16	15	La Salle Co., TX	Minnie D.B. Haynes	Minnie D.B. Haynes	1992	253
224 6/8	28 2/8	28 2/8	20 4/8	5 5/8	5 7/8	9	9	Ross Co., OH	Richard F. Barnett	Richard F. Barnett	1995	253
224 5/8	24 6/8	27 1/8	25 1/8	5 7/8	5 4/8	15	7	Perry Co., AL	Robert E. Royster	Robert E. Royster	1976	256
224 4/8	25 3/8	27 6/8	20 2/8	5 5/8	5 4/8	9	8	Cass Co., MN	Roy K. Blowers, Sr.	Roy K. Blowers, Sr.	1947	257
224 4/8	26	26 3/8	25 6/8	5 6/8	5 6/8	11	14	Rock Co., WI	Joseph T. Fisher	Joseph T. Fisher	1988	257
224 4/8	25 7/8	26 5/8	21 3/8	6	6	20	13	Unknown	Unknown	Rick Stover	PR 1993	257
224 3/8	26 7/8	27	21 2/8	5 1/8	5 2/8	8	7	Lac qui Parle Co., MN	Mike Unzen	Mike Unzen	1969	260
224 2/8	26 4/8	27 6/8	20 5/8	5	5 1/8	11	11	Salmon River, NB	Ford Fulton	Legendary Whitetails	1966	261
224 2/8	23 2/8	23 2/8	22	5 3/8	5 2/8	18	15	Pine Co., MN	Greg S. Blom	Greg S. Blom	1980	261
224 1/8	25	24 7/8	19 6/8	4 5/8	4 3/8	12	13	Crook Co., WY	John S. Mahoney	John S. Mahoney	1947	263
224 1/8	25 6/8	26 7/8	28 3/8	6 5/8	6 2/8	9	8	Monona Co., IA	David Freihage	Bass Pro Shops F. & W. Mus.	1991	263
224	29 4/8	29 2/8	20	6 2/8	5 4/8	15	13	Minnesota	Unknown	Harvard Univ. Mus.	1890	265
224	23 1/8	24	17 6/8	4 6/8	5	16	12	Lincoln Co., MT	Ray Baenen	Ed Boyes	1935	265
224	31	31 2/8	19 2/8	5 3/8	5 2/8	11	11	Hancock Co., IL	Ronald A. Paul	Larry L. Huffman	1968	265
224	29 2/8	29 2/8	27	5 2/8	5 3/8	7	14	Hancock Co., ME	Picked Up	Wesley B. Starn	PR 1975	265
224	24 4/8	24 2/8	16 6/8	6	6 1/8	13	10	Torch River, SK	Gus Fomradas	Helmut Fomradas	1993	265
223 6/8	28	28	25 5/8	7 1/8	6 4/8	10	11	Greene Co., IL	Terry L. Walters	Terry L. Walters	1982	270
223 6/8	25 1/8	24 2/8	16 3/8	4 3/8	4 3/8	10	13	Nuevo Leon, MX	Ron Kolpin	Ron Kolpin	1983	270
223 5/8	28	28 3/8	18 7/8	4 7/8	4 7/8	10	12	Woods Co., OK	Monty E. Pfleider	Monty E. Pfleider	1987	272
223 5/8	25 5/8	24 4/8	19 5/8	5 6/8	5 6/8	13	16	Manitoba	Unknown	Wayne Selby	PR 1987	272
223 5/8	24 6/8	24 6/8	24 2/8	6	6 2/8	8	14	Wabash Co., IL	Tim W. Stout	Bass Pro Shops F. & W. Mus.	1988	272
223 5/8	23 5/8	24 5/8	17	5 5/8	5 4/8	10	12	Stevens Co., WA	Mike W. Naff	Mike W. Naff	1992	272
223 4/8	23 7/8	21 1/8	17	5 1/8	5 3/8	18	13	Richland Co., MT	Verner King	Verner King	1960	276
223 4/8	21 3/8	23	23 4/8	4 1/8	4 2/8	19	11	Hawkins Co., TN	Luther E. Fuller	Luther E. Fuller	1984	276
223 4/8	26 3/8	27 4/8	23 2/8	6 4/8	6 4/8	8	13	Turtle Lake, SK	Blaine LaRose	Blaine LaRose	1996	276
223 3/8	28 2/8	27 5/8	24 1/8	5 4/8	5 2/8	10	11	Maine	Frank Maxwell	David G. Cordray	1900	279
223 3/8	20 7/8	24 5/8	19	5 5/8	5 3/8	19	12	Cochin, SK	Vic Pearsall	Vic Pearsall	1960	279
223 3/8	22 5/8	20 5/8	12 5/8	8 1/8	8 7/8	12	12	Madison Co., IA	Duane Fick	Duane Fick	1972	279
223 3/8	24 7/8	26 1/8	20 2/8	5 5/8	5 5/8	11	15	Jefferson Co., KS	David P. Haeusler	David P. Haeusler	1990	279
223 3/8	30 1/8	29 2/8	24	5 5/8	5 5/8	12	12	Iron Co., WI	Parker E. Milewski	Parker E. Milewski	1994	279
223 2/8	24 3/8	27 3/8	25	4 4/8	4 5/8	12	12	Madison Co., TX	B.C. Bienek	B.C. Bienek	1967	284
223 1/8	23 7/8	24 5/8	15	6	5 6/8	21	12	Sumter Co., AL	James L. Spidle, Sr.	Elizabeth McCormick	PR 1942	285

Score	Main Beam R.	Main Beam L.	Inside Spread	Circ. R.	Circ. L.	Pts. R.	Pts. L.	Locality	By Whom Killed	Owner	Date Killed	Rank
223 1/8	23 6/8	24 1/8	18 3/8	5 3/8	5 4/8	21	14	McCreary Co., KY	James H. Sanders	James H. Sanders	1957	285
223 1/8	29 7/8	29 5/8	21 1/8	4 3/8	4 3/8	12	8	Wyandotte Co., KS	Randy W. Tillery	Randy W. Tillery	1988	285
223 1/8	26 4/8	25 5/8	25 1/8	5 2/8	5 4/8	10	9	Republic Co., KS	Roy C. Wilson	Roy C. Wilson	1995	285
223 1/8	19 7/8	19 2/8	18 2/8	7 6/8	8 2/8	6	10	Van Buren Co., IA	Picked Up	Wade Roberts	1979	285
223	26 6/8	27 6/8	19 7/8	5 7/8	5 7/8	12	12	Murray Co., MN	Clyde Robbins	David C. Robbins	1964	289
222 7/8	27 5/8	28 1/8	18 6/8	5	5	7	7	Coles Co., IL	Kim L. Boes	Larry L. Huffman	1989	290
222 7/8	24 4/8	23 4/8	17 7/8	5 4/8	5 6/8	8	8	Rusk Co., WI	Raymond Charlevois	Philip Schlegel	1936	290
222 6/8	21 4/8	22 7/8	16 1/8	5 7/8	5 3/8	11	10	Itasca Co., MN	Picked Up	James R. Smith	1936	292
222 6/8	27	25 5/8	19 2/8	5 3/8	5 7/8	9	12	Mair, SK	R.A. McGill	R.A. McGill	1952	292
222 5/8	24 6/8	23 7/8	18 5/8	5 1/8	5 5/8	9	9	Edgerton, AB	Nick Leskow	Mr. & Mrs. M. Melom	1964	294
222 5/8	25 4/8	26 6/8	22 1/8	6	5 5/8	11	9	Henderson Co., KY	Ronnie D. Stacy	Russell Thornberry	1992	294
222 5/8	24 2/8	25 4/8	20 6/8	5 6/8	5 3/8	16	10	Ostrea Lake, NS	Verden M. Baker	Ronnie D. Stacy	1949	294
222 4/8	25 4/8				5 2/8	14	11		John L. Stein	John L. Stein		297
222 4/8	25 1/8	23 6/8	21 1/8	5 3/8	6 2/8	10	13	Richland Co., WI	Janice K. Beranek	Janice K. Beranek	1983	297
222 4/8	25 2/8	24 1/8	18 2/8	6 1/8	5 5/8	14	12	Davis Co., IA	James L. Fine	James L. Fine	1987	297
222 3/8	24 2/8	25 6/8	19 1/8	5 6/8	4 3/8	15	14	Itasca Co., MN	Lumie Jackson	Rick Ferguson	1942	300
222 3/8	23 3/8	23 3/8	18	4 2/8	6 7/8	9	7	Ashley Co., AR	Picked Up	Al Billgisher	1959	300
222 3/8	27 3/8	27 5/8	22 3/8	6 5/8	6	9	14	Stearns Co., MN	Richard E. Sand	Richard E. Sand	1988	300
222 3/8	27 2/8	27 2/8	18 1/8	6 5/8	5	11	10	Macoupin Co., IL	Paul Luttmann	Lewis F. Smith	1993	300
222 3/8	25	25	17 4/8	5	4 4/8	14	12	Dallas Co., IA	Chris S. Wilson	Chris S. Wilson	1996	300
222 1/8	26 2/8	25 7/8	17 3/8	5 6/8	4 7/8	12	10	Hancock Co., IA	Jerry M. Monson	William H. Lilienthal	1977	305
222 1/8	27 1/8	27 1/8	22 3/8	4 6/8	5 1/8	11	11	Cass Co., MN	Marvel R. Utke	Marvel R. Utke	1977	305
222 1/8	26 5/8	28 1/8	22 2/8	4 7/8	5 1/8	11	11	Latah Co., ID	Randy L. Clemenhagen	Randy L. Clemenhagen	1995	305
221 7/8	26 6/8	26	21 3/8	5 4/8	4 3/8	12	14	Tama Co., IA	Charles Upah	Richard Upah	1959	308
221 7/8	25 4/8	26 4/8	16 4/8	4 3/8	5 6/8	9	13	Trigg Co., KY	Bill McWhirter	Bill McWhirter	1982	308
221 7/8	28 2/8	28	25 7/8	5 5/8	5	13	10	Texas	Unknown	Lawson W. Walden	PR 1988	308
221 6/8	23 2/8	25 7/8	21 5/8	5	5 4/8	10	11	Snipe Lake, AB	Robert Dickson, Sr.	Robert Dickson, Sr.	1984	311
221 5/8	25 2/8	24 6/8	23 7/8	5	5	12	12	Clearwater Co., MN	Kevin Crane	Kevin Crane	1994	312
221 4/8	27 4/8	27 5/8	15 5/8	5 4/8	5 4/8	12	12	Michigan	Unknown	MI Whitetail Hall of Fame Mus.	PR 1964	313
221 4/8	30	29 2/8	23 3/8	6 2/8	6 2/8	12	21	Humboldt Co., IA	Donald Crossley	Donald Crossley	1971	313
221 4/8	25	20 7/8	21 2/8	6 1/8	5 4/8	10	12	Hancock Co., IL	Neal C. Meyer	Neal C. Meyer	1987	313
221 4/8	27 4/8	27 5/8	20 3/8	4 6/8	5 4/8	11	10	Pike Co., MO	Billy J. Schanks	Billy J. Schanks	1991	313
221 3/8	29 3/8	29 5/8	19	5 5/8	10	12	13	Dewey Co., SD	Leo Fischer	Leo Fischer	1958	317
221 3/8	21 6/8	19 4/8	17 1/8	6 3/8	7 7/8	11	13	Anne Arundel Co., MD	Unknown	Fred Horn	1979	317
221 3/8	26 3/8	25	19 2/8	4 5/8	4 4/8	16	11	Louisa Co., VA	Picked Up	James T. Rapalee	1981	317
221 2/8	22 5/8	23 6/8	17 1/8	4 7/8	4 7/8	13	19	Itasca Co., MN	Richard I. Goble	Richard I. Goble	1955	320
221 2/8	20 5/8	20 5/8	19 2/8	5 4/8	5	10	11	Holmes Co., MS	Milton Parrish	Milton Parrish	1970	320
221 2/8	28 5/8	28 7/8	22 3/8	4 5/8	5 4/8	15	11	Franklin Co., KS	Marvin R. Smith	Brad Sowter	1988	320
221 2/8	25 7/8	26 2/8	18 1/8	5 5/8	4 5/8	15	14	Lapeer Co., MI	Picked Up	William Schmidt, Jr.	1993	320
221 1/8	27 2/8	29 4/8	22 6/8	4 4/8	4 5/8	9	9	Jefferson Co., IA	Daniel R. Thurman	Daniel R. Thurman	1979	324
221	29 1/8	29	23 4/8	6 7/8	4 4/8	17	12	Pike Co., IL	Frank C. Skelton	Frank C. Skelton	1987	325
220 7/8	23 1/8	23 7/8	14 4/8	6 6/8	6 6/8	9	11	Pembina Co., ND	Gary F. Bourbanis	Gary F. Bourbanis	1985	326
220 7/8	27 6/8	27 7/8	22 6/8	5 7/8	5 7/8	9	8	Sauk Co., WI	Bryan J. McGann	Bryan J. McGann	1986	326
220 7/8	26 1/8	27 1/8	19 4/8	5 2/8	5 3/8	11	15	Ross Co., OH	Tommy E. Dailey	Tommy E. Dailey	1993	326
220 6/8	26 2/8	25 6/8	19 6/8	6 1/8	6 3/8	12	9	Anoka Co., MN	Donald Torgerson	Bass Pro Shops F. & W. Mus.	1946	329
220 6/8	26 4/8	27 2/8	20 6/8	5 2/8	5 1/8	10	13	Dallas Co., IA	Picked Up	Gale Sup	1992	329
220 5/8	29 1/8	28 2/8	27 1/8	5 4/8	5 6/8	13	12	Kittson Co., MN	Todd J. Porter	Dick Rossum	1986	331
220 5/8	28	28	21 3/8	6 2/8	6 2/8	12	8	Jefferson Co., IA	Mike Laux	Bass Pro Shops F. & W. Mus.	1990	331

WHITETAIL DEER - NON-TYPICAL ANTLERS

Odocoileus virginianus virginianus and certain related subspecies

Score	Length of Main Beam R	L	Inside Spread	Circumference at Smallest Place Between Burr and First Point R	L	Number of Points R	L	Locality	Hunter	Owner	Date Killed	Rank
220 4/8	28 6/8	28 7/8	20 2/8	5 5/8	5 6/8	9	8	Dixon Co., NE	Otto D. Kneifl	Otto D. Kneifl	1964	333
220 4/8	30	30 6/8	20 5/8	4 7/8	4 6/8	12	9	Mercer Co., IL	Roger D. Hultgren	Roger D. Hultgren	1970	333
220 3/8	25 1/8	25 6/8	18 6/8	5	5	14	13	Olmsted Co., MN	E.E. Comartin III	E.E. Comartin, Jr.	1963	335
220 3/8	27 1/8	27	19 7/8	5 6/8	5 5/8	10	12	Todd Co., MN	Gary V. Martin	Gary V. Martin	1992	335
220 2/8	28 2/8	28 4/8	21	5	5	9	8	Zavala Co., TX	J.D. Jarratt	J.D. Jarratt	1930	337
220 2/8	25	26 4/8	19 1/8	5 4/8	5 4/8	11	12	Union Co., IA	George Foster	George Foster	1968	337
220 2/8	27 4/8	27 1/8	19	5 1/8	4 7/8	13	13	Caldwell Co., KY	Loyd Holt	Loyd Holt	1984	337
220 2/8	29 4/8	31 2/8	22 4/8	5 7/8	5 6/8	14	8	Prince Georges Co., MD	Robert Y. Clagett, Jr.	Robert Y. Clagett, Jr.	1995	337
220 1/8	27 4/8	27 5/8	24 3/8	4 7/8	4 6/8	12	9	Redvers, SK	Ira E. Sampson	Ira E. Sampson	1969	341
220	28 1/8	26 5/8	18 5/8	4 7/8	4 5/8	15	9	Wayne Co., IA	Dallas Patterson	Dallas Patterson	1975	342
219 7/8	27 2/8	27 6/8	19 7/8	6	6	10	10	Genesee Co., NY	Robert Wood	Robert Wood	1944	343
219 7/8	25 4/8	25 7/8	20 4/8	5 3/8	5 3/8	11	10	Clearwater Co., ID	Kipling D. Manfull	Kipling D. Manfull	1989	343
219 7/8	23 4/8	26 1/8	23 2/8	5 2/8	5 5/8	11	8	Saskatchewan River, SK	Don Thorimbert	Don Thorimbert	1996	343
219 6/8	19 1/8	23 1/8	18 4/8	4 4/8	4 6/8	15	15	Caddo Parish, LA	William D. Ethredge, Jr.	William D. Ethredge, Jr.	1988	346
219 6/8	25	27 7/8	21 1/8	5 4/8	5 5/8	10	15	N. Saskatchewan River, SK	Terry D. Redpath	Terry D. Redpath	1993	346
219 6/8	25 4/8	26 2/8	23 7/8	5 1/8	5 1/8	9	10	Christian Co., IL	Eric D. Garrett	Eric D. Garrett	1994	346
219 5/8	24 5/8	25 1/8	21 1/8	5 7/8	6 3/8	13	12	Warren Co., MO	James E. Williams	James E. Williams	1959	349
219 5/8	22 7/8	24 2/8	16 5/8	4 5/8	4 4/8	13	10	Black Hawk, ON	Picked Up	Marc M. Jackson	1990	349
219 4/8	27	27 2/8	24 2/8	5 6/8	6 1/8	11	11	Lake of the Woods Co., MN	Thomas Barden	Robert V. Ellenson	PR 1951	351
219 4/8	26 5/8	26 1/8	21 2/8	5	5	11	8	Sumner Co., KS	Picked Up	Greg L. Hill	1987	351
219 3/8	27 4/8	27 4/8	20	5 2/8	5 2/8	11	10	Webb Co., TX	Richard O. Rivera	John L. Stein	1972	353
219 3/8	28 1/8	27 5/8	20 5/8	4 5/8	4 4/8	12	17	Webster Co., IA	David Propst	David Propst	1987	353
219 3/8	25 2/8	24	17 4/8	5 4/8	5 5/8	12	15	Maine	Unknown	Gale Sup	PR 1988	353
219 2/8	26	30 5/8	19 2/8	6 2/8	6 2/8	13	11	Buffalo Co., WI	Glenn Lehman	Glenn Lehman	1958	356
219 2/8	23 6/8	23 5/8	23 2/8	4 4/8	4 5/8	12	12	Mud Creek, AB	Hank Stainbrook	Caroline Supplies Ltd.	1971	356
219 2/8	24 6/8	24 6/8	21 6/8	5 4/8	5 4/8	9	11	Aroostook Co., ME	Harold C. Kitchin	Harold C. Kitchin	1973	356
219 2/8	26 2/8	26 6/8	22 3/8	4 7/8	5	11	12	Midway, BC	Gordon Kamigochi	Gordon Kamigochi	1980	356
219 1/8	27	27	18 2/8	5 4/8	5 6/8	9	15	Flathead Co., MT	R.C. Garrett	R.C. Garrett	1962	360
219 1/8	22 5/8	22 5/8	18 4/8	5 1/8	5	17	13	Pontotoc Co., OK	Timothy F. Harris	Timothy F. Harris	1996	360
219	27 3/8	27	17 6/8	5 6/8	5 7/8	8	11	Morrison Co., MN	Michael R. Langin	Michael R. Langin	1992	362
218 7/8	28 1/8	27 7/8	20	5 2/8	4 7/8	12	11	Florence Co., WI	W.C. Gotstein	Larry L. Huffman	1914	363
218 7/8	29 2/8	28 6/8	21	5 4/8	5 4/8	6	11	Waldo Co., ME	Roy C. Guse	J. Bruce Probert	1957	363
218 7/8	22 6/8	23 3/8	15 4/8	7 3/8	7 1/8	16	11	Bay of Fundy, NS	Basil S. Lewis	Basil S. Lewis	1983	363
218 7/8	25 3/8	22 4/8	18 7/8	4 5/8	4 7/8	12	12	Marshall Co., IA	Picked Up	Charles E. Lewis	1989	363
218 7/8	26 6/8	25 5/8	20 3/8	6	6	8	12	St. Joseph Co., MI	Picked Up	Rex A. Mayer	PR 1989	363
218 6/8	23 5/8	24 7/8	19 2/8	6 2/8	5 4/8	14	7	Morrison Co., MN	Wilfred LeBlanc	George W. Flaim	1938	368

Score	Main Beam R	Main Beam L	Inside Spread	Circ. R	Circ. L	Points R	Points L	Locality	Hunter	Owner	Date	Rank
218 6/8	29 4/8	29 3/8	23 3/8	6	6	11	9	Williamson Co., IL	Carl W. Norris	Carl W. Norris	1994	368
218 5/8	25	25 2/8	14 4/8	5 1/8	5 1/8	13	15	Itasca Co., MN	John W. Pierson, Sr.	John W. Pierson, Sr.	1945	370
218 5/8	26 2/8	25 6/8	18 4/8	4 4/8	4 4/8	9	11	Chariton Co., MO	Stanley McSparren	Stanley McSparren	1979	370
218 5/8	28 6/8	27 4/8	20	6	6 1/8	14	11	St. Louis Co., MN	Unknown	George W. Flaim	PR 1983	370
218 5/8	25 3/8	27	18	6 3/8	6 7/8	17	13	Otter Tail Co., MN	Gerald P. Lucas	Gerald P. Lucas	1985	370
218 5/8	24 5/8	24 6/8	18 5/8	5 7/8	4 7/8	9	10	Page Co., IA	John L. Novy	John L. Novy	1989	370
218 5/8	23 5/8	23 5/8	17 1/8	4 7/8	5 2/8	7	12	Dawson Creek, BC	John D. Todd	John D. Todd	1992	370
218 4/8	27	26 3/8	18 7/8	5 3/8	5 5/8	12	8	Sawyer Co., WI	Walter Kittleson	Walter Kittleson	1920	376
218 4/8	26 2/8	26 3/8	17 2/8	5 5/8	7 5/8	8	12	St. Martin Parish, LA	Drew Ware	Gary S. Crnko	1941	376
218 4/8	23 1/8	22 7/8	20 5/8	7 1/8	5 7/8	9	9	Logan Co., KY	Robert L. Schrader, Jr.	Robert L. Schrader, Jr.	1987	376
218 3/8	27	24 3/8	17	5 5/8	5 5/8	9	12	La Crosse Co., WI	Daniel P. Cavadini	J.D. Andrews	1951	379
218 3/8	20 7/8	24 3/8	19 3/8	4 6/8	5 2/8	13	15	South Goodeve, SK	Fred Bohay	Fred Bohay	1958	379
218 3/8	24 7/8	25 5/8	23 2/8	5 2/8	5 4/8	10	11	Keweenaw Co., MI	Bernard J. Murn	Bernard J. Murn	1980	379
218 3/8	23	26	16 7/8	5 4/8	5 1/8	15	11	Itasca Co., MN	Unknown	George W. Flaim	1983	379
218 3/8	29 2/8	29 5/8	19 5/8	5 1/8	5 3/8	12	10	Fillmore Co., MN	Darrel R. Highum	Darrel R. Highum	1989	379
218 2/8	29 3/8	29 7/8	23 4/8	5 3/8	5 4/8	7	7	Allamakee Co., IA	Bernard Rank	Larry L. Huffman	1963	384
218 2/8	27	26 7/8	18 6/8	5 6/8	5 3/8	7	7	Waukesha Co., WI	Picked Up	WI Dept. of Natl. Resc.	1986	384
218	25 4/8	25 4/8	19	5 3/8	4 5/8	11	8	Otter Tail Co., MN	Dennis A. Pearson	Dennis A. Pearson	1977	386
217 7/8	23 4/8	23 4/8	19 4/8	4 5/8	5 4/8	11	15	Dimmit Co., TX	Unknown	McLean Bowman	1920	387
217 7/8	27 7/8	28 2/8	21 3/8	5 4/8	6 1/8	10	10	Maries Co., MO	Gerald R. Dake	Gerald R. Dake	1974	387
217 7/8	24 4/8	26 5/8	20	6 1/8	5 3/8	18	16	Cherokee Co., KS	Craig E. Ruddick	Craig E. Ruddick	1983	387
217 7/8	24	22 4/8	21 1/8	5 3/8	5 1/8	8	14	Washakie Co., WY	Kenneth A. Fossum	Kenneth A. Fossum	1991	387
217 6/8	26 2/8	24	18 6/8	5 1/8	6 1/8	12	20	Macoupin Co., IL	Albert Grichnik	Albert Grichnik	1966	391
217 6/8	27 6/8	24	20 3/8	4 7/8	4 6/8	11	12	Otoe Co., NE	Douglas E. Gregg	Douglas E. Gregg	1994	391
217 5/8	28 4/8	28 7/8	20 5/8	6 1/8	6	14	11	Clark Co., IL	David P. Mosley	David P. Mosley	1995	394
217 5/8	27 3/8	24 6/8	23	5 3/8	5 5/8	13	9	Carroll Co., MS	Mark T. Hathcock	Mark T. Hathcock	1978	394
217 5/8	28 6/8	27 2/8	14 6/8	6	5 1/8	9	14	Hardin Co., KY	Michael F. Meredith	Michael F. Meredith	1980	394
217 5/8	26	23 2/8	18 5/8	5 1/8	4 4/8	12	15	Flagstaff, AB	Craig A. Miller	Craig A. Miller	1990	394
217 4/8	24 4/8	24 3/8	17 3/8	4 4/8	6 2/8	11	16	Tobin Lake, SK	Picked Up	SK Parks & Renew. Resc.	1991	398
217 4/8	25 5/8	25	19 4/8	6 2/8	4 6/8	13	16	Aitkin Co., MN	Fred C. Melichar	Fred C. Melichar	1973	398
217 4/8	24 6/8	24 6/8	19 1/8	4 6/8	4 6/8	11	12	Hardin Co., IA	Picked Up	W.H. Lilienthal & J. Bruce	1987	398
217 3/8	24 2/8	26 1/8	20 3/8	5	5 2/8	10	13	Allamakee Co., IA	George A. Smith	George A. Smith	1991	401
217 3/8	22 7/8	23 6/8	13	4 6/8	5 2/8	8	7	Weston Co., WY	Harry Phillips	Harry Phillips	1957	401
217 3/8	27	28 5/8	18 3/8	5 2/8	5 4/8	10	11	Meeker Co., MN	Steven R. Turek	Steven R. Turek	1982	401
217 3/8	30 4/8	29	28 4/8	5 4/8	4 3/8	12	15	Cross Co., AR	Randal Harris	Randal Harris	1986	401
217 2/8	27 5/8	29 2/8	18 7/8	4 3/8	5 7/8	11	8	Dewer River, NS	Alan Fahey	Alan Fahey	1989	405
217 2/8	29 2/8	29 4/8	20	5 6/8	4 6/8	13	9	St. Louis Co., MN	Unknown	George W. Flaim	1957	405
217 2/8	23 3/8	23 1/8	19	5 2/8	5 7/8	7	11	Sprucehome, SK	Tom Pillar	Tom Pillar	1957	405
217 2/8	22	20	20	4 5/8	5	8	11	Talbot Co., MD	Vincent L. Jordan, Sr.	Vincent L. Jordan, Sr.	1974	405
217 2/8	29 6/8	29 5/8	25 3/8	5 2/8	4 6/8	13	12	Mills Co., IA	Rick W. Elliott	Rick W. Elliott	1976	405
217 2/8	28 6/8	28 6/8	21 6/8	4 7/8	5 4/8	6	7	Clark Co., MO	Lawrence L. Paul	Lawrence L. Paul	1977	405
217 2/8	23 6/8	23 6/8	19	5 4/8	4 2/8	5	8	Hudson Bay, SK	Ron Kenyon	Ron Kenyon	1987	405
217 1/8	30	29 2/8	21 2/8	4 6/8	5	12	10	Kandiyohi Co., MN	Picked Up	Dean Salzl	1988	413
217	24 5/8	24 2/8	17 4/8	5	6 3/8	13	12	Dallas Co., AL	Robert Tate	Robert Tate	1988	414
217	25 2/8	27 6/8	20 6/8	6 3/8	5 7/8	11	14	Sturgeon River, SK	Francis Rask	Francis Rask	1995	414
217	23 6/8	23 6/8	17 1/8	5 7/8	4 6/8	12	8	Unknown	Charles H. Reames	Ronald L. Christensen	PR 1872	414
217	23	25 4/8	25 7/8	4 6/8	5 6/8	11	11	Isle of Wight Co., VA	Peter F. Crocker, Jr.	Peter F. Crocker, Jr.	1963	414

WHITETAIL DEER - NON-TYPICAL ANTLERS

Odocoileus virginianus virginianus and certain related subspecies

Score	Length of Main Beam R	L	Inside Spread	Circumference at Smallest Place Between Burr and First Point R	L	Number of Points R	L	Locality	Hunter	Owner	Date Killed	Rank
217	29	27 4/8	19 4/8	5 4/8	5 4/8	10	9	Fulton Co., IL	Picked Up	Larry L. Huffman	1990	414
217	30 7/8	28 6/8	18 4/8	5 2/8	5	9	10	Dearborn Co., IN	Jerry L. Irvine	Jerry L. Irvine	1990	414
217	23 2/8	22 1/8	20 2/8	4 7/8	4 6/8	15	10	Love Co., OK	Greg French	Greg French	1996	414
216 7/8	26 7/8	24 7/8	17 2/8	6	5 7/8	12	17	Concordia Parish, LA	Richard Dale	J. Logan Sewell	1956	419
216 7/8	19 1/8	21 1/8	13 7/8	7	6 5/8	12	15	Brown Co., SD	Francis Shattuck	J.D. Andrews	1960	419
216 7/8	27 3/8	28 7/8	21 6/8	5 2/8	5 1/8	12	12	Wilson Co., KS	Gilbert J. McGee	Gilbert J. McGee	1988	419
216 7/8	25 3/8	28 1/8	19 7/8	6	5 5/8	13	10	Howard Co., IN	Jason E. Young	Jason E. Young	1995	419
216 6/8	26	24 4/8	22 3/8	5 2/8	5 1/8	11	13	Kathryn, ND	Gerald R. Elsner	Gerald R. Elsner	1963	423
216 6/8	25 1/8	24 4/8	18 2/8	6 3/8	6 4/8	10	13	Barber Co., KS	Robert L. Rose	Robert L. Rose	1972	423
216 6/8	24 4/8	24 1/8	17	7	7 1/8	11	11	Lake of the Woods Co., MN	Andy Streiff	Andy Streiff	1974	423
216 6/8	26 3/8	26 1/8	25 1/8	5	5 4/8	7	11	Brown Co., IL	David R. Herschelman	David R. Herschelman	1991	423
216 6/8	29	27 3/8	22 7/8	6 2/8	6 4/8	13	13	Charles Co., MD	Brian G. Klaas	Brian G. Klaas	1993	423
216 6/8	25	25	18	5 6/8	5 7/8	12	14	Menard Co., IL	Randy Boyle	Randy Boyle	1995	423
216 5/8	24 4/8	23 5/8	17 2/8	5 2/8	5 3/8	12	13	Dickinson Co., MI	Earl Wilt	Richard H. Wilt	1943	429
216 4/8	25 2/8	27 3/8	23	5	5	12	10	Surry Co., VA	Stanley M. Hall	Stanley M. Hall	1986	430
216 4/8	18	18	17	5 4/8	5 6/8	14	13	Macon Co., AL	George B. Bulls	George B. Bulls	1995	430
216 4/8	27 6/8	26 1/8	19 2/8	5	5 4/8	9	10	Jefferson Co., MO	Picked Up	Jeff L. Vaughan	1995	430
216 3/8	26	24 4/8	18 6/8	5 3/8	5 6/8	14	17	Comanche Co., OK	Dwight O. Allen	Dwight O. Allen	1962	433
216 3/8	26	25 5/8	17 4/8	5 4/8	5 4/8	10	9	Clay Co., IA	Blaine Salzkorn	Blaine Salzkorn	1970	433
216 3/8	26 6/8	26 3/8	20 3/8	4 7/8	5	9	10	Powhatan Co., VA	William E. Schaefer	William E. Schaefer	1970	433
216 2/8	30	28 2/8	23	5 7/8	5 5/8	7	9	Blue Earth Co., MN	Marion Abbas	Harold Abbas	1961	436
216 2/8	23 5/8	24	18 4/8	4 4/8	4 4/8	10	8	Buchanan, SK	Mike Spezrivka	Linda Christoforo	1961	436
216 2/8	26 5/8	27 5/8	20 3/8	5 6/8	5 7/8	10	14	Richland Co., MT	Joseph P. Culbertson	Joseph P. Culbertson	1972	436
216 2/8	25	24 3/8	19	6 7/8	7	10	11	Porter Co., IN	Lester W. Fornshell	Lester W. Fornshell	1994	436
216 2/8	28 7/8	26 7/8	23 3/8	4 7/8	5 1/8	10	9	Floyd Co., VA	Ronnie T. Perdue	Ronnie T. Perdue	1996	436
216 1/8	25 2/8	23 4/8	19 6/8	4 4/8	4 3/8	13	12	Gillespie Co., TX	J.C. Park	John L. Stein	1932	441
216 1/8	23 1/8	19 4/8	15 2/8	5 3/8	6 1/8	15	16	Itasca Co., MN	Thomas Thurstin	Thomas Thurstin	1977	441
216	29 4/8	29 4/8	19 1/8	5 2/8	5 2/8	11	10	Prairie Co., AR	Cecil M. Miller	Cecil M. Miller	1973	443
216	24 1/8	24 1/8	19 3/8	5 1/8	4 6/8	14	9	Manitoba	Unknown	Robert J. Winnekens	1990	443
216	25 3/8	25 6/8	19 2/8	5 3/8	5 2/8	11	9	Jackson Co., IA	Picked Up	Douglas J. Horst	1992	443
215 7/8	25	24 4/8	24 3/8	6 6/8	6	11	12	Long Pine, NE	Picked Up	Duane Lotspeich	1964	446
215 7/8	29 6/8	27 7/8	16 7/8	6 1/8	6 4/8	13	13	Putnam Co., GA	Thomas H. Cooper	Thomas H. Cooper	1974	446
215 7/8	27 1/8	26 5/8	27 7/8	6	5 2/8	6	6	Schuyler Co., IL	Donald E. Ziegenbein	Donald E. Ziegenbein	1981	446
215 7/8	27 1/8	27 5/8	22 2/8	5 5/8	5 6/8	9	13	Wabasha Co., MN	Leroy Goranson	Leroy Goranson	1990	446
215 6/8	24 4/8	24 4/8	23 3/8	6 2/8	7 4/8	10	12	Chippewa Co., MN	Micheal Allickson	Micheal Allickson	1974	450
215 6/8	26	25 1/8	24 2/8	4 3/8	5 2/8	6	11	Macoupin Co., IL	Allen E. McKee	Allen E. McKee	1992	450

Score	Main Beam R	Main Beam L	Inside Spread	Circ. R	Circ. L	Points R	Points L	Locality	Hunter	Owner	Date	Rank
215 5/8	26	25 6/8	20	5 5/8	5 6/8	16	12	Iron Co., MI	C. & R. Lester	C. & R. Lester	1970	452
215 5/8	28	28	20 2/8	5 2/8	5 1/8	10	9	Worth Co., MO	B.M. & R. Nonneman	B.M. & R. Nonneman	1974	452
215 5/8	28 2/8	29 2/8	18 6/8	4 6/8	4 5/8	9	11	Wise Co., VA	Edison Holcomb	Edison Holcomb	1987	452
215 5/8	24 4/8	21 3/8	17 6/8	5 3/8	6	11	13	Huron Co., MI	Patrick L. Flanagan, Jr.	Patrick L. Flanagan, Jr.	1990	452
215 4/8	26 7/8	26 6/8	19 3/8	5 3/8	5 3/8	10	9	Morrison Co., MN	James P. Poser	James P. Poser	1978	456
215 4/8	29 1/8	29 4/8	23 2/8	6 1/8	6 2/8	11	13	Wayne Co., IN	Clyde L. Day	Clyde L. Day	1986	456
215 4/8	24 3/8	24 3/8	21 7/8	6 3/8	5 1/8	11	8	Schuyler Co., IL	Raymond Shouse	Raymond Shouse	1993	456
215 4/8	28 2/8	28 2/8	24 5/8	6 4/8	6 3/8	9	11	Fulton Co., IL	Roger H. Mann	Roger H. Mann	1994	460
215 3/8	21	23 4/8	15	7 2/8	6 6/8	12	15	Trinity Co., TX	Earl Smith	Lawson W. Walden	1965	460
215 3/8	29 4/8	21	23 7/8	5 6/8	5 6/8	8	8	Lafayette Co., WI	Roger Vickers	Roger Vickers	1969	462
215 2/8	24 3/8	29 4/8	18 2/8	5 3/8	5 3/8	9	9	Fillmore Co., MN	George E. Holets	George E. Holets	1960	462
215 2/8	21	24 3/8	21	4	4	9	16	Parker Co., TX	Pleasant Mitchell	Pleasant Mitchell	1982	462
215 1/8	25 6/8	19	24	6	6	11	9	Cass Co., IL	David G. Bolletto	David G. Bolletto	1988	464
215 1/8	25 2/8	25 6/8	22 1/8	6 7/8	6 4/8	11	10	Winnebago Co., IL	Dennis F. Shipler	Dennis F. Shipler	1990	464
215 1/8	25 5/8	24	23 4/8	5 2/8	5 2/8	11	11	Jefferson Co., NE	Gary A. Hellbusch	Gary A. Hellbusch	1994	464
215	23 2/8	25 3/8	15 5/8	5 6/8	5 4/8	17	13	Fergus Co., MT	Robert D. Fleherty	Robert D. Fleherty	1958	467
215	26 3/8	25 4/8	15 6/8	5 2/8	5 2/8	13	13	Fillmore Co., MN	Picked Up	Jeffrey S. Mackey	1968	467
215	25 4/8	25 6/8	22 7/8	5	5	11	12	Stevens Co., WA	Unknown	Dick Rossum	PR 1989	467
215	30 3/8	25 4/8	18 1/8	5 7/8	5 7/8	10	8	Allen Co., KS	James W. Baker	James W. Baker	1992	467
215	25 1/8	30	24 3/8	4 4/8	4 5/8	11	15	Wood River, SK	Scott Cowie	Scott Cowie	1997	467
214 7/8	25 2/8	24 5/8	17	4 6/8	4 6/8	9	12	Aweme, MB	Criddle Bros.	Criddle Bros.	1954	472
214 7/8	24 6/8	24 4/8	12 4/8	5 2/8	5 1/8	15	10	St. John Co., NB	T. Emery	New Brunswick Mus.	1968	472
214 7/8	21 3/8	26 6/8	21 3/8	5 6/8	4 6/8	12	9	Big Horn Co., WY	Michael K. Smith	Michael K. Smith	1987	472
214 6/8	24 7/8	23 1/8	26 7/8	4 3/8	4 3/8	13	7	Quinlan Creek, NS	Fred Doucette	Fred Doucette	1962	475
214 6/8	27 6/8	24 7/8	22 2/8	7 2/8	6	13	8	Hitchcock Co., NE	David W. Oates	David W. Oates	1985	475
214 6/8	26 6/8	27 6/8	21 6/8	5	4 7/8	9	8	Decatur Co., IA	Dean D. Grimm	Dean D. Grimm	1988	475
214 6/8	27	28	17 2/8	5 5/8	5 6/8	10	14	Roseau River, MB	Darcy J. Stewart	Darcy J. Stewart	1990	475
214 5/8	26 3/8	26 3/8	16 5/8	5	4 7/8	15	12	Koochiching Co., MN	Unknown	Wilbur Tilander	1956	479
214 5/8	25 7/8	25 7/8	18	6 1/8	5 7/8	13	8	Turtle Lake, SK	Scott Macnab	Scott Macnab	1993	479
214 5/8	24 5/8	24 5/8	23	5	5 1/8	9	9	Pike Co., IL	David B. Crown	David B. Crown	1995	479
214 4/8	28	28	20 1/8	5 2/8	5	11	12	Swift Co., IL	Leonard N. Kanuit	Leonard N. Kanuit	1972	482
214 4/8	26 4/8	26 4/8	28 6/8	5 7/8	5 7/8	15	10	De Witt Co., IL	Kelly E. Riggs	Kelly E. Riggs	1996	482
214 3/8	23 4/8	23 4/8	15 3/8	5 2/8	5 2/8	11	10	Price Co., WI	Henry J. Copt	James A. Copt	1926	484
214 3/8	25	25	14 2/8	5 1/8	5	14	11	Missoula Co., MT	Lyle Pettit	Lyle Pettit	1962	484
214 3/8	23 2/8	23 2/8	17 5/8	5	5	11	13	Bayfield Co., WI	Clarence Lauer	Mrs. Clarence Lauer	1963	484
214 3/8	27 3/8	27 3/8	18 3/8	5 1/8	5 2/8	14	8	Roseau Co., MN	Warren Tveit	Warren Tveit	PR 1976	484
214 2/8	24 1/8	24 1/8	20 4/8	6 4/8	6 2/8	8	8	Crook Co., WY	Clinton Berry	Clinton Berry	1953	484
214 2/8	24 6/8	24 6/8	16 5/8	4 5/8	4 6/8	9	12	Unknown	Unknown	Kent Austin	PR 1991	488
214 2/8	22 5/8	22 5/8	17 1/8	6 2/8	5 6/8	13	15	Monona Co., IA	Brian R. Hebb	Brian R. Hebb	1996	488
214 2/8	23 4/8	23 4/8	17 3/8	5 4/8	5 6/8	13	14	Atchison Co., MO	Warren E. Davis	Warren E. Davis	1983	488
214	23 6/8	23 6/8	23 1/8	4 4/8	4 4/8	10	9	Clay Co., MN	Dean Klemetson	Dean Klemetson	1984	491
214	28 6/8	28 6/8	21	5 2/8	5 2/8	14	9	Hamilton Co., IA	Picked Up	Larry L. Huffman	1987	491
214	26 3/8	26 3/8	18	5 7/8	5 7/8	17	12	Sawyer Co., WI	Charles Ross	Charles Ross	1949	491
213 7/8	25	25	16 5/8	5 3/8	5 3/8	12	8	Bresaylor, SK	Barry Braun	Barry Braun	1966	494
213 7/8	27 3/8	27 3/8	19 3/8	5 1/8	4 7/8	9	10	Pottawatomie Co., KS	Picked Up	Tim Wanklyn	1974	494
213 7/8	28 5/8	28 5/8	18 2/8	5 2/8	5 2/8	10	10	Botetourt Co., VA	Craig A. Brogan	Craig A. Brogan	1989	494
213 7/8	23 3/8	23 3/8	20 7/8	6 3/8	6 6/8	15	11	Athabasca River, AB	Todd Armstrong	Todd Armstrong	1990	494

Odocoileus virginianus virginianus and certain related subspecies

Score	Length of Main Beam		Inside Spread	Circumference at Smallest Place Between Burr and First Point		Number of Points		Locality	Hunter	Owner	Date Killed	Rank
	R	L		R	L	R	L					
213 7/8	25 6/8	27 5/8	20 7/8	6 1/8	6 6/8	7	9	Pope Co., IL	Jason B. Potts	Jason B. Potts	1995	494
213 6/8	26 5/8	26 3/8	26 5/8	5 3/8	5 4/8	10	10	Lycoming Co., PA	Al Prouty	Al Prouty	1949	500
213 6/8	23 7/8	24 4/8	18 6/8	4 6/8	5	10	11	Webb Co., TX	Unknown	John B. Collier	1961	500
213 6/8	30 2/8	30 6/8	26 5/8	4 6/8	4 7/8	10	9	Fayette Co., IL	Sammy D. Diveley	Sammy D. Diveley	1990	500
213 6/8	26 1/8	26 7/8	19 6/8	5 4/8	5 6/8	14	13	Adams Co., IL	Michelle L. Hunter	Michelle L. Hunter	1991	500
213 6/8	28 4/8	27 2/8	20	5 6/8	5 4/8	12	14	Cass Co., IL	Vince C. Brewer	Vince C. Brewer	1993	500
213 5/8	24 2/8	24 2/8	17 1/8	5 6/8	5 5/8	12	6	Beltrami Co., MN	Unknown	Jim Smith	1924	505
213 5/8	22 7/8	22 6/8	13 5/8	3 6/8	3 7/8	9	18	Webb Co., TX	Unknown	Miguil Harper	PR 1950	505
213 5/8	29 3/8	29 6/8	21 4/8	5 7/8	5 7/8	7	9	Guthrie Co., IA	Merle Shirbrown	Sherrill Shirbrown	1963	505
213 5/8	23	23 7/8	16 2/8	6	6 1/8	10	12	Buffalo Co., WI	Norman C. Ratz	Ed Klink	1968	505
213 5/8	27 1/8	24 6/8	23 6/8	5 4/8	7	9	9	Bonner Co., ID	Rodney Thurlow	Rodney Thurlow	1968	505
213 5/8	18 5/8	18 1/8	17 5/8	4 1/8	4	14	15	Washington Co., TX	Thomas N. Holle	Thomas N. Holle	1987	505
213 5/8	24 7/8	25 6/8	19 7/8	6 2/8	6 2/8	12	13	Ogle Co., IL	Jerome F. Bruns	Jerome F. Bruns	1994	505
213 5/8	27 4/8	26 2/8	20 1/8	5 4/8	5 6/8	11	11	Ogle Co., IL	Jeffrey R. Breen	Jeffrey R. Breen	1995	505
213 4/8	22 1/8	23 1/8	19 2/8	5	5	15	15	Texas	Unknown	Buckhorn Mus. & Saloon, Ltd.	PR 1950	513
213 4/8	26 3/8	23 2/8	18 6/8	6 1/8	6 4/8	12	11	Rochester, AB	Lamar A. Windberg	Lamar A. Windberg	1973	513
213 4/8	25 4/8	26	22	6 2/8	6 1/8	11	13	Pike Co., IL	Donald L. Roseberry	Michael R. Roseberry	1984	513
213 3/8	25 4/8	24 5/8	18 5/8	4 7/8	4 7/8	9	9	Midale, SK	Picked Up	Dick Rossum	1969	516
213 3/8	31 1/8	27 6/8	18 6/8	5 5/8	6 6/8	11	13	Cumberland Co., VA	Jimmy E. Dedmond	Jimmy E. Dedmond	1995	516
213 2/8	27 2/8	27 1/8	18 5/8	5	5 1/8	7	8	Fillmore Co., MN	Steven A. Johnson	Steven A. Johnson	1988	518
213 2/8	26 4/8	26 2/8	20 2/8	5 2/8	5 3/8	10	13	Cold Lake, AB	John F. Koreman	John F. Koreman	1991	518
213 1/8	28 7/8	28 6/8	19	4 7/8	4 7/8	10	10	Michigan	Unknown	Keith H. Lundberg	PR 1941	520
213 1/8	22	22	17	5 1/8	5 1/8	12	10	Havre, MT	Unknown	Frank English	1950	520
213 1/8	24 4/8	25	20 6/8	5 6/8	6 2/8	9	11	Milwaukee Co., WI	Picked Up	WI Dept. of Natl. Resc.	1988	520
213	27	27 7/8	15 5/8	4 6/8	4 6/8	14	12	St. Louis Co., MN	Walfred Olson	Erling H. Olson	1935	523
213	24 4/8	24	17 5/8	4 7/8	4 5/8	10	10	Kinney Co., TX	Rankin F. O'Neill	John L. Stein	1960	523
213	25 7/8	24 1/8	20 6/8	5 4/8	5 6/8	5	15	Rush Lake, SK	Jim Runzer	Murray Bromley	1966	523
212 7/8	24 4/8	22 5/8	17 6/8	4 6/8	4 6/8	12	9	Boone Co., IA	Orlin Sorber	Ron Sorber	1973	526
212 7/8	30	23 3/8	21 1/8	5 2/8	5	7	12	Waukesha Co., WI	Max Mollgaard	Max Mollgaard	1976	526
212 7/8	25 5/8	29 1/8	20 6/8	5 3/8	5 2/8	10	13	Otter Tail Co., MN	Harold L. Collins	Harold L. Collins	1985	526
212 6/8	27 1/8	26 7/8	18 1/8	5 2/8	5 2/8	14	16	Lewis & Clark Co., MT	Mr. LeFleur	L.S. Kuter	1952	529
212 6/8	24 2/8	23 2/8	19 5/8	4 2/8	4 4/8	14	9	McCurtain Co., OK	Robert H. Crenshaw	Robert H. Crenshaw	1988	529
212 6/8	24 3/8	28 3/8	28 3/8	5 2/8	5 1/8	11	6	Illinois	Picked Up	John Brewer	1989	529
212 6/8	24 5/8	26 2/8	24 6/8	4 7/8	5 1/8	8	14	Fremont Co., IA	Picked Up	Jeff Haning	1989	529
212 6/8	25 3/8	26 3/8	24 1/8	5 4/8	5 3/8	7	8	Long Lake, AB	Philip H. Preisel	Philip H. Preisel	1995	529
212 6/8	25 4/8	25 4/8	22 7/8	4 7/8	5 1/8	10	9	Shell Lake, SK	Robert Barlow	Robert Barlow	1996	529

Score						R	L	Locality	Hunter	Owner	Date	Rank
212 5/8	25 3/8	25 4/8	23 6/8	4 2/8	4 4/8	11	11	Lincoln Co., MT	Charles F. Woods, Jr.	Charles F. Woods, Jr.	1973	535
212 5/8	29 6/8	28 2/8	23 7/8	5 7/8	5 7/8	10	9	Lake Co., MT	Dennis Courville	Dennis Courville	1975	535
212 5/8	21 3/8	20 1/8	16 5/8	4	4	14	16	Brooks Co., TX	Ken Smith	Lawson W. Walden	1975	535
212 5/8	23 7/8	23 5/8	18 3/8	6 1/8	6 3/8	12	12	Alberta	Picked Up	D.J. Hollinger & B. Howard	1980	535
212 5/8	24 6/8	25 2/8	17 6/8	5	5	11	13	Glentworth, SK	Garnet Fortnum	Garnet Fortnum	1984	535
212 5/8	23 2/8	24 5/8	29 1/8	5 4/8	5 4/8	11	9	Appanoose Co., IA	Picked Up	IA Dept. of Natl. Resc.	1991	535
212 5/8	25 2/8	26 4/8	21 3/8	5 4/8	5 4/8	11	9	Pelican River, AB	John Kozyra	John Kozyra	1993	535
212 5/8	29 1/8	28 5/8	19 7/8	5 5/8	5 5/8	11	13	Madison Co., IN	Michael A. Wallace	Michael A. Wallace	1993	535
212 5/8	25 1/8	24 2/8	21 6/8	6 1/8	6 1/8	6	10	Page Co., IA	Kevin L. Reints	Kevin L. Reints	1995	535
212 3/8	24 6/8	23 6/8	18 2/8	5	5	10	12	Alger Co., MI	Karl Beck	Rick Johnson	1934	544
212 3/8	29	28 4/8	24 3/8	5 6/8	5 6/8	11	10	Hershey, NE	Ray Liles	Spanky Greenville	1959	544
212 3/8	23 2/8	23 4/8	18 4/8	4 7/8	4 7/8	10	10	Rosebud Co., MT	Picked Up	Art F. Hayes III	1979	544
212 2/8	25	25 4/8	19 4/8	5 2/8	5 2/8	11	13	Webb Co., TX	Claude W. King	Claude W. King	1949	547
212 2/8	26 6/8	26 1/8	23 6/8	5 4/8	5 3/8	9	7	Houston Co., MN	Alfred C. Pieper	Alfred C. Pieper	1977	547
212 2/8	23 1/8	25 1/8	20 3/8	5 1/8	5	11	10	Gregory Co., SD	Picked Up	J.D. Andrews	1983	547
212 2/8	28 2/8	28 6/8	24 4/8	5 3/8	5	9	8	Madison Co., IA	Larry D. Bain	Larry D. Bain	1984	547
212 2/8	27 4/8	27 2/8	20 2/8	7 4/8	6	9	9	Van Buren Co., IA	Chris E. Clingan	Chris E. Clingan	1993	547
212 2/8	25 3/8	25 3/8	22 5/8	5 5/8	5 5/8	9	9	Langenburg, SK	Hartley Biley	Hartley Biley	1996	547
212 1/8	24	24 3/8	20 1/8	5	5	16	13	Minnesota	Unknown	John R. Steffes, Sr.	PR 1960	553
212 1/8	26 5/8	25 6/8	20	4 7/8	5	9	8	Stevens Co., MN	Ronald J. Mohr	Ronald J. Mohr	1963	553
212 1/8	28 1/8	28 1/8	21 6/8	5 3/8	6	8	10	Woodbury Co., IA	Harold M. Leonard	Harold M. Leonard	1965	553
212 1/8	23 3/8	23	20 3/8	5	5 2/8	8	7	Minnedosa, MB	Albert Pfau	Albert Pfau	1966	553
212 1/8	27	27 2/8	19 6/8	5 2/8	5 3/8	14	16	St. Louis Co., MN	Robert J. LaPine	Robert J. LaPine	1968	553
212	28 1/8	28	18 1/8	5 4/8	5 4/8	8	8	Winona Co., MN	Donald J. Mehren	Donald J. Mehren	1985	553
212	26 7/8	25	16 7/8	4 7/8	5 1/8	14	13	Becker Co., MN	Unknown	John R. Steffes, Sr.	1922	559
212	29	27 4/8	23 6/8	6 7/8	6 5/8	8	9	Iron Co., MI	Ben Komblevicz	Duaine K. Wenzel	1942	559
212	20 5/8	20 7/8	16 5/8	6 2/8	6 3/8	11	12	Wibaux Co., MT	Roy Berg	Daniel Burnosky	PR 1963	559
212	28 3/8	28 3/8	20 4/8	5 6/8	6	6	9	Greene Co., IA	Don Buswell	Don Buswell	1973	559
212	29 4/8	29 4/8	19 1/8	5 1/8	5 1/8	11	11	Vermilion, AB	Derry Heathcote	Derry Heathcote	1995	559
211 7/8	25 6/8	26 3/8	24 1/8	5 7/8	5 7/8	14	11	Raymore, SK	Adolf Wulff	Adolf Wulff	1951	564
211 7/8	25	25 4/8	20 2/8	4 6/8	4 6/8	10	12	Rockingham Co., VA	Dorsey O. Breeden	Dorsey O. Breeden	1966	564
211 7/8	22	23 2/8	21 4/8	4 4/8	4 4/8	15	15	Crook Co., WY	Curtis U. Nelson	Curtis U. Nelson	1971	564
211 7/8	24 1/8	24 4/8	19 5/8	4 7/8	4 7/8	11	8	Van Buren Co., IA	Loras R. Ernzen	Loras R. Ernzen	1988	564
211 7/8	27 6/8	27	18 6/8	5 6/8	5 6/8	12	8	Waukesha Co., WI	Patrick F. Cherone III	Patrick F. Cherone III	1989	564
211 6/8	26 3/8	26	24 7/8	5 2/8	5 2/8	11	6	Marion Co., IA	Paul J. Pearson	Paul J. Pearson	1964	569
211 6/8	22 3/8	25 5/8	21	5	5	11	11	Cottonwood Co., MN	James A. Sykora	James A. Sykora	1981	569
211 6/8	26 5/8	27 7/8	18 4/8	5 1/8	4 6/8	12	12	Roseau Co., MN	Edward L. Quiring	Edward L. Quiring	1988	569
211 5/8	23 1/8	22 5/8	13 4/8	7	5 4/8	18	11	Alda, NE	Donald Knuth	Donald Knuth	1964	572
211 5/8	28 2/8	28 4/8	23	5 7/8	6	11	11	Glaslyn, SK	Carl R. Frohaug	Carl R. Frohaug	1981	572
211 5/8	26 3/8	23 3/8	20 2/8	5 1/8	6 1/8	9	12	Adams Co., OH	William J. DeCamp	William J. DeCamp	1987	572
211 5/8	23 2/8	23 2/8	16	4 5/8	4 5/8	13	14	Rains Co., TX	Tommy Couch	Lawson W. Walden	PR 1988	572
211 4/8	26 4/8	27	20 3/8	6 1/8	6 2/8	11	11	Hillsborough Co., NH	Curtiss Whipple	Herman Whipple	1947	576
211 4/8	27 2/8	25 6/8	20 2/8	5 3/8	5 3/8	10	9	Minnesota	Picked Up	David Cater	1960	576
211 4/8	25 3/8	25	18 3/8	5 1/8	4 7/8	14	17	St. Louis Co., MN	John E. Peterson, Jr.	John E. Peterson, Jr.	1963	576
211 4/8	23 2/8	23 2/8	13 6/8	6 2/8	5 6/8	12	10	Dodge Co., WI	Michael A. Koehler	Michael A. Koehler	1984	576
211 4/8	23 3/8	23	18 6/8	4 7/8	5	13	14	Worth Co., GA	Wade Patterson	Wade Patterson	1988	576
211 3/8	27 3/8	24 4/8	20 3/8	4 7/8	4 5/8	12	12	Dimmit Co., TX	L.C. Wright	H.R. Wright	1927	581

Odocoileus virginianus virginianus and certain related subspecies

Score	Length of Main Beam		Inside Spread	Circumference at Smallest Place Between Burr and First Point		Number of Points		Locality	Hunter	Owner	Date Killed	Rank
	R	L		R	L	R	L					
211 3/8	24 7/8	25 2/8	16 6/8	5 6/8	5 6/8	11	10	Borden, SK	Leonard Verishine	Leonard Verishine	1972	581
211 3/8	26 2/8	26 6/8	23 4/8	5 2/8	5 3/8	12	9	Polk Co., IA	Picked Up	IA Dept. of Natl. Resc.	1993	581
211 2/8	24 5/8	26 6/8	14 7/8	6	6 2/8	9	8	Kittson Co., MN	Picked Up	Floyd R. Nelson	1942	584
211 2/8	27 7/8	27	19 2/8	6 2/8	6 1/8	8	9	Marshall Co., MN	Picked Up	Robert Sands	1959	584
211 2/8	23 2/8	24 4/8	16 6/8	5 7/8	5 7/8	10	9	Hughenden, AB	Morris Sather	Morris Sather	1966	584
211 2/8	26 1/8	25 5/8	19 4/8	4 2/8	4 2/8	9	7	Stearns Co., MN	Ronald Steil	Ronald Steil	1983	584
211 2/8	24 2/8	23 4/8	19 5/8	5 6/8	5 6/8	9	8	Spokane Co., WA	Cary C. Janson	Cary C. Janson	1992	584
211 2/8	29 2/8	29	24	5 1/8	5 3/8	7	7	Athabasca, AB	Tim M. Shmigelsky	Tim M. Shmigelsky	1995	584
211 1/8	27 5/8	28	18 6/8	5 6/8	5 6/8	9	10	Itasca Co., MN	Glen V. Jones	Mark W. Jones	PR 1948	590
211 1/8	26 5/8	26	22 4/8	5 1/8	5	9	9	Clarke Co., IA	Randy J. Showers	Randy J. Showers	1991	590
211 1/8	26 5/8	26 1/8	21 3/8	5 4/8	5 4/8	9	11	Rich Lake, AB	Sammy J. Schrimsher	Sammy J. Schrimsher	1994	590
211	23 6/8	23 4/8	16 3/8	6	6	12	13	Dimmit Co., TX	D.V. Day	McLean Bowman	1948	593
211	29 1/8	30	19 1/8	5 2/8	5 4/8	13	6	Allen Co., KY	Danny R. Towe	Ben & Seth Towe	1987	593
211	27 3/8	28 4/8	22 2/8	6 4/8	6 3/8	10	11	Rock Co., WI	Kevin C. Viken	Kevin C. Viken	1990	593
211	27 1/8	26	20 1/8	6 6/8	6 6/8	9	13	Monroe Co., IA	Picked Up	IA Dept. of Natl. Resc.	1991	593
211	29	29 6/8	22	5 6/8	5 6/8	7	8	Gallia Co., OH	Robert D. Wallis	Robert D. Wallis	1992	593
211	21 4/8	21 6/8	15 3/8	4	4	8	11	Mercer Co., MO	Treve A. Gray	Treve A. Gray	1995	593
211	27	26 4/8	19 3/8	4 4/8	4 4/8	9	10	Lenawee Co., MI	Paul T. Kintner	Paul T. Kintner	1996	593
210 7/8	24 2/8	24 1/8	18 1/8	5 2/8	5 2/8	11	11	Stevens Co., WA	Charles Tucker	Charles Tucker	1966	600
210 7/8	23 1/8	22 6/8	21 1/8	4 6/8	4 6/8	11	13	Patience Lake, SK	Rick Schindel	Rick Schindel	1990	600
210 7/8	25 3/8	27	20 1/8	6 2/8	6 6/8	11	9	Peoria Co., IL	Picked Up	Randy L. Isbell	1995	600
210 6/8	23 6/8	25 4/8	22	5	5	11	8	Coahuila, MX	Picked Up	John L. Stein	1981	603
210 6/8	26 2/8	26 7/8	21 1/8	5 5/8	5 4/8	12	9	Todd Co., MN	Paul E. Berscheit	Paul E. Berscheit	1990	603
210 6/8	27 6/8	25	20 4/8	5 3/8	5 5/8	10	13	Grafton Co., NH	David C. Braley	David C. Braley	1991	603
210 6/8	26 2/8	28 3/8	23 6/8	5	5	8	9	Lincoln Co., MT	Glen Savage	Patrick W. Savage	1934	606
210 5/8	28 5/8	26	24 6/8	6	6 4/8	8	8	Walworth Co., SD	H.F. McClellan, Sr.	H.F. McClellan, Sr.	1952	606
210 5/8	24 7/8	25 7/8	18 6/8	5 6/8	5 5/8	14	10	Renville Co., ND	Glen Southam	Glen Southam	1978	606
210 5/8	25 7/8	27 1/8	20 3/8	6	5 4/8	7	7	Waukesha Co., WI	Gerald J. Roethle, Jr.	Gerald J. Roethle, Jr.	1991	606
210 5/8	26 6/8	27 2/8	22 1/8	6	6	9	8	Ogle Co., IL	Daniel M. Pierce	Daniel M. Pierce	1994	606
210 4/8	26 7/8	25 6/8	20	5 1/8	5 1/8	12	11	Dane Co., WI	LaVerne W. Marten	LaVerne W. Marten	1970	611
210 4/8	26 1/8	26	21 7/8	5 1/8	5 2/8	14	11	Stearns Co., MN	Kim C. Kirckof	Kim C. Kirckof	1992	611
210 4/8	27 2/8	27 5/8	23 5/8	4 3/8	4 3/8	10	8	Pope Co., MN	Scott G. Finn	Scott G. Finn	1993	611
210 4/8	25 6/8	26 3/8	19 6/8	6 1/8	6 1/8	10	12	Wabaunsee Co., KS	Ron E. Pletcher	Ron E. Pletcher	1994	611
210 3/8	28 4/8	27 4/8	21 4/8	5	5 1/8	9	10	Marinette Co., WI	George E. Bierstaker	Mrs. G.E. Bierstaker	1947	615
210 3/8	24 3/8	25	19 2/8	5	5	13	12	Lyon Co., KY	Roy D. Lee	Roy D. Lee	1975	615
210 2/8	28 4/8	27 6/8	20 4/8	5 4/8	5 6/8	11	9	Louisa Co., IA	Picked Up	William H. Lilienthal	1959	617

Score								Locality	Hunter	Owner	Date	Rank
210 2/8	26 4/8	25 2/8	21 4/8	5 3/8	5 3/8	8	9	Columbiana Co., OH	Harold L. Hawkins	Harold L. Hawkins	1981	617
210 2/8	28 3/8	28 3/8	23 6/8	5 6/8	5 5/8	12	7	Washburn Co., WI	Dennis Loreth	William H. Lilienthal	1982	617
210 2/8	25 3/8	26	26 6/8	8 2/8	5 4/8	13	7	Fremont Co., IA	Mike Moody	Mike Moody	1990	617
210 2/8	29	27	19 1/8	5 1/8	5	10	11	Grayson Co., KY	Adam Pence	Adam Pence	1994	617
210 1/8	26 7/8	26 5/8	20	5 1/8	4 6/8	10	7	Crawford Co., GA	Walter Keel	Grace Stinson	1971	622
210 1/8	25 1/8	25 1/8	20 6/8	5 2/8	5	10	9	White Co., AR	Chester Weathers, Sr.	Chester Weathers, Jr.	1973	622
210 1/8	23 4/8	24	18 5/8	5 1/8	5	9	7	Harris, SK	Kenneth M. Lepp	Kenneth M. Lepp	1985	622
210 1/8	24 1/8	24 7/8	21 5/8	4 6/8	5	14	12	Chain Lakes, AB	Jim Chapman	Jim Chapman	1989	622
210 1/8	23 6/8	24 1/8	20 2/8	5 4/8	5 1/8	9	10	Macomb Co., MI	Bob H. Dismuke	Bob H. Dismuke	1992	622
210 1/8	26 4/8	23 3/8	20 6/8	5 3/8	5 4/8	15	16	Madison Co., IA	Andy A. Ross	Andy A. Ross	1994	622
210	26 5/8	27 2/8	17 5/8	5 6/8	5 6/8	13	9	Vilas Co., WI	Elmer T. Reise	John A. Kellett	1940	628
210	26	26 1/8	18	5 5/8	5 4/8	9	9	Glenewen, SK	H. Frew	H. Frew	1955	628
210	27 5/8	25	24 2/8	5 2/8	5 2/8	9	7	Lee Co., IA	Picked Up	Mike Conger	1978	628
210	23 4/8	23 6/8	20 3/8	5 7/8	6 2/8	9	8	Gregory Co., SD	Richard C. Berte	Richard C. Berte	1982	628
210	28 3/8	26	26 5/8	4 7/8	4 7/8	7	13	Calvert Co., MD	Robert E. Barnett	Robert E. Barnett	1984	628
210	26 2/8	25 1/8	19 6/8	4 5/8	4 4/8	8	7	Dallas Co., IA	Picked Up	William H. Lilienthal	1989	628
209 7/8	25 2/8	24 1/8	22 4/8	4 4/8	4 5/8	9	9	Maryfield, SK	W.W. Nichol	W.W. Nichol	1967	634
209 7/8	25 4/8	24 1/8	18 1/8	4 5/8	4 4/8	10	15	Pine Co., MN	Scott A. Miller	Scott A. Miller	1980	634
209 7/8	20 6/8	19 7/8	19 6/8	4 7/8	4 6/8	13	11	Hawkins Co., TN	Johnny W. Byington	Johnny W. Byington	1982	634
209 7/8	29	28 2/8	18 4/8	5 4/8	5 3/8	10	8	Todd Co., KY	Kenny V. Wilson	Kenny V. Wilson	1990	634
209 6/8	27	27 2/8	17 1/8	5 2/8	5 1/8	11	10	Koochiching Co., MN	Harry Van Keuren	Louis E. Muench	1929	638
209 6/8	24 6/8	24 2/8	20 7/8	5 6/8	5 3/8	10	10	Franklin Co., MS	Ronnie Strickland	Ronnie Strickland	1981	638
209 6/8	23 2/8	24 1/8	20 7/8	4 4/8	4 6/8	8	11	Edwards Co., KS	Tim C. Schaller	Tim C. Schaller	1984	638
209 6/8	25 2/8	25 2/8	16	5 1/8	5 6/8	10	9	Oak Lake, MB	Michael W. Leochko	Michael W. Leochko	1985	638
209 6/8	25 6/8	25	19 5/8	4 5/8	5 6/8	14	18	Pulaski Co., KY	Alan Sidwell	Alan Sidwell	1988	638
209 6/8	26 4/8	26 7/8	18 1/8	6	6	12	10	Union Co., IN	Billy G. Finch	Billy G. Finch	1989	638
209 6/8	26 5/8	27 5/8	20 7/8	5 3/8	5 5/8	9	8	Sangamon Co., IL	Mark A. Rademaker	Mark A. Rademaker	1994	638
209 5/8	25 1/8	25 3/8	16 5/8	5 3/8	5 2/8	13	12	Jefferson Co., AR	Kenneth Colson	Kenneth Colson	1968	645
209 5/8	24 4/8	25 3/8	22 4/8	4 6/8	5	10	11	Butler Co., KY	Dean A. Hannold	Dean A. Hannold	1979	645
209 5/8	26 4/8	26 4/8	16 7/8	5 1/8	5 1/8	13	12	McCreary Co., KY	Picked Up	Johnny Farmer	1983	645
209 5/8	25 4/8	25 3/8	21 5/8	5 3/8	5 2/8	10	8	Franklin Co., VA	Timothy J. Wright	Timothy J. Wright	1989	645
209 5/8	25 2/8	27 4/8	21 1/8	5 2/8	4 7/8	11	11	Harrison Co., IA	James A. Spelman	James A. Spelman	1991	645
209 4/8	23 3/8	23 1/8	22 5/8	4 7/8	5	10	14	Webb Co., TX	A. Holden	McLean Bowman	1940	650
209 4/8	25	24 2/8	19 2/8	4 5/8	4 1/8	8	9	Sterling Co., TX	Sam E. Kapavik	Sam E. Kapavik	1973	650
209 4/8	28 3/8	27 5/8	22 5/8	5	5	11	9	White Co., IL	David J. South	David J. South	1991	650
209 3/8	26 1/8	26 1/8	21	5 1/8	5 1/8	13	9	La Salle Co., TX	Unknown	E.T. Reilly	1931	650
209 3/8	24 2/8	24 2/8	17 1/8	4 4/8	4 4/8	13	10	Crook Co., WY	Roy H. Lubbert	Murphy's Tavern	1967	653
209 3/8	23 5/8	21 6/8	16 6/8	4 3/8	4 4/8	11	10	Grant Co., WI	Tim Yanna	Tim Yanna	1982	653
209 3/8	28 3/8	30 3/8	24 4/8	5 3/8	5 4/8	9	7	Jefferson Co., IN	Tim L. Brawner	Tim L. Brawner	1989	653
209 3/8	27 6/8	26 7/8	29 2/8	5 6/8	5 1/8	9	9	Keokuk Co., IA	Michael D. Hoover	Michael D. Hoover	1991	653
209 3/8	26 4/8	26 7/8	22 7/8	6 4/8	5 6/8	11	11	Pittsburg Co., OK	William R. Starry	William R. Starry	PR 1994	653
209 2/8	26 6/8	26 6/8	20 1/8	5 1/8	5	9	10	Racine Co., WI	Unknown	Lon M. Swatek	1994	653
209 2/8	23 7/8	22	16 4/8	4 7/8	6 2/8	10	8	Clarke Co., IA	James C. Reed	James C. Reed	1988	660
209 2/8	25 1/8	26	19 1/8	5	5	8	13	Person Co., NC	Stuart E. Gentry	Stuart E. Gentry	1996	660
209 1/8	26 3/8	26 3/8	19 1/8	5 4/8	5 4/8	15	13	Keweenaw Co., MI	Nathan E. Ruonavaara	Nathan E. Ruonavaara	1946	662
209 1/8	26	26 2/8	19 3/8	4 7/8	5	10	8	Clinton Co., IA	Gregory Stewart	Gregory Stewart	1963	662
209 1/8	23 4/8	24 4/8	16 6/8	4 3/8	4 2/8	12	14	Kenedy Co., TX	Dick Roberts	Dick Roberts	1988	662

WHITETAIL DEER - NON-TYPICAL ANTLERS

Odocoileus virginianus virginianus and certain related subspecies

Score	Length of Main Beam R	L	Inside Spread	Circumference at Smallest Place Between Burr and First Point R	L	Number of Points R	L	Locality	Hunter	Owner	Date Killed	Rank
209 1/8	26	25 7/8	22 4/8	5	5	9	8	Monroe Co., IA	Kelly J. Willis	Kelly J. Willis	1988	662
209 1/8	27 6/8	30 5/8	19 6/8	6 3/8	6 3/8	8	10	Monona Co., IA	Vincent P. Jauron	Vincent P. Jauron	1990	662
209 1/8	23 4/8	22 7/8	17 3/8	5 6/8	5 4/8	10	12	Riley Co., KS	Jerry P. McIntyre	Jerry P. McIntyre	1994	662
209	26 7/8	28 2/8	23 6/8	5 4/8	5 4/8	8	9	Lee Co., IA	Glenn L. Carter II	Glenn L. Carter II	1984	668
209	26 4/8	25 6/8	20 5/8	4 7/8	5	11	10	Hughes Co., OK	Lane Grimes	Lane Grimes	1987	668
208 7/8	25 1/8	26	21 6/8	5	4 7/8	8	10	Atchison Co., MO	Kenneth W. Lee	Kenneth W. Lee	1964	670
208 7/8	24 5/8	23 3/8	18 4/8	4 2/8	4 2/8	11	16	Bradley Co., AR	Carthel Forte	Carthel Forte	1971	670
208 7/8	29 4/8	27 5/8	18 4/8	4 6/8	4 6/8	14	10	Washington Co., ME	Robert E. Cooke	Robert E. Cooke	1972	670
208 7/8	26 7/8	26 7/8	26 6/8	5 3/8	5 3/8	10	8	Charles Co., MD	Robert A. Boarman	Robert A. Boarman	1984	670
208 7/8	27 1/8	27	23 5/8	6 3/8	6	11	13	Rideau River, ON	Harry Rathwell	Harry Rathwell	1988	670
208 6/8	27 1/8	26 6/8	20 4/8	5 3/8	5 1/8	7	10	Crook Co., WY	Joe Engelhaupt	Joe Engelhaupt	1956	675
208 6/8	24	24 2/8	19 2/8	5	5 1/8	13	12	Daniel Boone Natl. For., KY	Richard G. Lohre	Richard G. Lohre	1968	675
208 6/8	26 3/8	27 4/8	21 7/8	5 3/8	5 4/8	9	8	Unknown	Unknown	David A. Boys	PR 1982	675
208 5/8	27 4/8	28	22	6	5 7/8	10	8	Taylor Co., WI	Unknown	Mac's Taxidermy	PR 1945	678
208 5/8	19 6/8	23 4/8	18 4/8	5	5	11	10	Beaufort Co., SC	John M. Wood	John M. Wood	1971	678
208 5/8	26 2/8	24 3/8	20 4/8	6 3/8	7 1/8	10	12	Woodbury Co., IA	Ronald J. Eickhold	Ronald J. Eickhold	1977	678
208 5/8	27	26 1/8	20 4/8	5 1/8	5 1/8	8	8	Dunn Co., WI	Milburn Fleege	Brant J. Mueller	1986	678
208 5/8	27	26 5/8	22 4/8	4 6/8	5	9	12	St. Francis Co., AR	George W. Hobson	George W. Hobson	1987	678
208 4/8	26 6/8	27 3/8	21 6/8	6	6 1/8	9	8	Itasca Co., MN	Unknown	William L. Achman	1945	683
208 4/8	30 5/8	29 2/8	17 3/8	5 1/8	5 1/8	7	9	Day Co., SD	Unknown	J.D. Andrews	PR 1950	683
208 4/8	28	27 1/8	23 5/8	6 2/8	6 1/8	11	10	Dixon Co., NE	Dan Greeny	Dan Greeny	1969	683
208 4/8	22	21 4/8	17 4/8	5	5	12	13	Webb Co., TX	Travis D. Kelly	Travis D. Kelly	1978	683
208 4/8	30 5/8	30 2/8	20 6/8	5 5/8	5 4/8	7	8	Ford Co., KS	Picked Up	Larry L. Huffman	1985	683
208 4/8	25 1/8	25 3/8	17 5/8	5 4/8	5 5/8	10	13	Fulton Co., IL	Jeffrey C. Warmath	Jeffrey C. Warmath	1995	683
208 3/8	25 2/8	28 2/8	18 7/8	5 1/8	4 7/8	13	13	St. Louis Co., MN	Unknown	George W. Flaim	PR 1940	689
208 3/8	27 5/8	28 1/8	21 7/8	5	4 7/8	11	7	Decatur Co., GA	James L. Darley	James L. Darley	1964	689
208 3/8	21 6/8	23 7/8	24 1/8	5	4 7/8	8	8	Prairie Co., MT	Charles Danielson	Charles Danielson	1969	689
208 3/8	24 4/8	24 4/8	17 7/8	4 3/8	4 5/8	13	10	Isanti Co., MN	Richard C. Hansen	Richard C. Hansen	1995	689
208 2/8	27	26 2/8	18 2/8	5 4/8	5 6/8	10	7	Frio Co., TX	Unknown	Roy Hindes	PR 1950	693
208 2/8	27	26 1/8	20 4/8	4 7/8	4 6/8	11	11	St. Louis Co., MN	Walter H. Enzenauer	Walter H. Enzenauer	1961	693
208 2/8	27	26	22 2/8	5 4/8	5 3/8	10	7	St. Louis Co., MN	Ed Mikulich	Terry Mikulich	1964	693
208 2/8	26 5/8	24	19 3/8	5 3/8	7 3/8	10	10	Chauvin, AB	Picked Up	Shane Hansen	1981	693
208 2/8	24 3/8	19	19	5	5	7	11	Monona Co., IA	Rob L. Cadwallader	Rob L. Cadwallader	1984	693
208 2/8	28 6/8	24 6/8	21 4/8	5	5 4/8	9	13	Price Co., WI	Robin J. Manning	Robin J. Manning	1993	693
208 2/8	25	25 5/8	17	4 5/8	4 4/8	11	12	Van Buren Co., TN	A. Duane Hodges	A. Duane Hodges	1994	693
208 2/8	25 7/8	22 2/8	17 3/8	6 1/8	6	10	13	Washington Co., OH	Robert R. Zimmerman	Robert R. Zimmerman	1995	693

Score						Points R	Points L	Locality	Hunter	Owner	Date	Rank
208 1/8	30	23 6/8	31 2/8	5 3/8	5 4/8	8	8	Hancock Co., ME	Hollis Staples	Doug Scott	1922	701
208 1/8	25 7/8	19 6/8	24 5/8	4 6/8	4 4/8	8	8	Griswold, MB	J.V. Parker	J.V. Parker	1946	701
208 1/8	25 6/8	18 2/8	24 2/8	4 7/8	5	12	12	Mexico	Unknown	William M. Day	1959	701
208 1/8	24 1/8	20 2/8	25 2/8	6 2/8	4 7/8	13	12	Antelope Co., NE	Leon McCoy	Leon McCoy	1965	701
208 1/8	28 1/8	26 1/8	30 1/8	4 7/8	5	10	8	Atkinson Hwy., NE	Russell Angus	Russell Angus	1966	701
208 1/8	25 2/8	25 2/8	26 1/8	4 7/8	4 7/8	9	9	Beaverhill Lake, AB	Dean Hrehirchuk	Dean Hrehirchuk	1989	701
208 1/8	26 6/8	19 1/8	26 5/8	5 3/8	5 4/8	11	11	Brown Co., IL	Mark V. Piazza	Mark V. Piazza	1989	701
208 1/8	25 1/8	19 3/8	25 5/8	4 6/8	4 6/8	11	8	Peterson, SK	Albert Huber	Albert Huber	1993	701
208	27	21 5/8	26	4 5/8	4 7/8	9	10	Rainy River, ON	Leroy Berglund	Marc M. Jackson	PR 1930	709
208	25 4/8	19 6/8	25	4 5/8	4 5/8	9	10	Chesaw, WA	Charles Eder	Charles Eder	1967	709
208	26 3/8	15	26	4 1/8	4 1/8	14	8	Buena Vista Co., IA	Robert L. Vierow	Robert L. Vierow	1982	709
208	28 1/8	22	30	5 2/8	5 4/8	8	11	Lucas Co., IA	Mitch W. Hosler	Mitch W. Hosler	1991	709
208	22	25 2/8	22 2/8	6 1/8	6 3/8	11	6	Olmsted Co., MN	Glen E. Leighton	Glen E. Leighton	1991	709
208	21 2/8	17 4/8	24 5/8	9 2/8	5	15	10	Bath Co., KY	William Shields	William Shields	1993	709
208	24 4/8	19 1/8	26 2/8	4 7/8	4 6/8	8	8	Wayne Co., IA	George M. Tonelli	George M. Tonelli	1993	709
207 7/8	24 6/8	15 5/8	25 5/8	4 5/8	4 2/8	7	9	McMullen Co., TX	Robert L. Hodges	William D. Connally	1924	716
207 7/8	23 7/8	21 3/8	23 5/8	5 5/8	5 5/8	13	19	Suffolk Co., NY	George Hackal	Gary C. Boyer	1950	716
207 7/8	29 5/8	24 4/8	31 1/8	5 1/8	5 3/8	11	7	Port Royal, PA	C. Ralph Landis	Ruth V. Landis	1951	716
207 7/8	24 4/8	20 3/8	23 6/8	5 7/8	5 6/8	10	12	Fond du Lac Co., WI	Henry Theisen	Henry Theisen	1956	716
207 7/8	23 7/8	19	25 2/8	5 1/8	5	11	14	Perkins Co., SD	W.E. Brown	Dick Rossum	1957	716
207 7/8	26 5/8	22 2/8	24 5/8	5 3/8	5 2/8	10	10	Monona Co., IA	Robert V. Dean	Vernon R. Dean	1968	716
207 7/8	23 4/8	24 2/8	26	5 6/8	5 4/8	7	9	Monitor, AB	Raymond Worobo	Raymond Worobo	1979	716
207 7/8	30 3/8	23 7/8	31 2/8	6 2/8	6 1/8	11	10	Assiniboine River, MB	Terry L. Simcox	Terry L. Simcox	1987	716
207 7/8	23 6/8	15 6/8	24 4/8	5	5	9	9	Ribstone Creek, AB	Trevor C. Thorpe	Trevor C. Thorpe	1992	716
207 7/8	25 3/8	25 7/8	25 7/8	7	6 7/8	9	9	Breckinridge Co., KY	Joseph T. Smith	Joseph T. Smith	1993	716
207 7/8	22 2/8	15 4/8	22 2/8	5	5	8	7	Lee Co., IA	Timothy A. Miller	Timothy A. Miller	1994	716
207 6/8	27	25 4/8	27 5/8	6 6/8	6 4/8	14	16	Kleberg Co., TX	Unknown	King Ranch	1940	727
207 6/8	29	28 2/8	28 4/8	6 1/8	6	9	9	Aroostook Co., ME	Alfred Wardwell	Alfred Wardwell	1945	727
207 6/8	22 4/8	24 4/8	24 6/8	5	5 2/8	8	7	Henry Co., IL	Richard Vyneman	Richard Vyneman	1992	727
207 6/8	24 4/8	24 2/8	25 1/8	6 6/8	6 6/8	9	9	MacNutt, SK	Delwin Andres	Delwin Andres	1993	727
207 6/8	18	22 6/8	18 1/8	5	5	10	9	Edgeley, SK	Ian G. Gilchrist	Ian G. Gilchrist	1995	727
207 6/8	25 4/8	16 4/8	25 4/8	4 7/8	5	14	13	Cross Co., AR	Picked Up	Aaron Mauldin	PR 1996	727
207 5/8	27 1/8	15 4/8	26 5/8	6 6/8	6 6/8	11	7	Argenteuil Co., QC	R. Desjardins & A. Dobie	R. Desjardins & R. Morrison	1959	733
207 5/8	24 2/8	22 2/8	23 6/8	5 6/8	6	11	9	Lincoln Co., MN	Joe Ness	Joe Ness	1961	733
207 5/8	20 5/8	17 5/8	20 5/8	6	6	7	8	Moosomin, SK	Leslie Hanson	Sam Peterson	1961	733
207 5/8	25 4/8	19 6/8	25 4/8	6	5 2/8	10	17	Seward Co., NE	Ladislav Dolezal	Ladislav Dolezal	1964	733
207 5/8	30 1/8	21 2/8	29 3/8	5 1/8	6 2/8	11	7	Keephills, AB	Unknown	William J. Greenhough	PR 1970	733
207 5/8	24	20 1/8	23 6/8	6 3/8	4 6/8	10	9	Webster Co., IA	Larry E. Iles	Larry E. Iles	1979	733
207 5/8	25	23 6/8	25	6 2/8	5 6/8	8	8	Buffalo Co., WI	Dennis M. Eberhart	Dennis M. Eberhart	1984	733
207 5/8	27 2/8	20 3/8	28 3/8	4 6/8	4 4/8	8	14	Gentry Co., MO	Eric D. Sybert	Eric D. Sybert	1990	733
207 5/8	28 7/8	23 2/8	27 6/8	6 1/8	4 7/8	12	11	Penobscot Co., ME	Picked Up	Randall Madden	1995	733
207 4/8	25 2/8	19 5/8	24 6/8	4 7/8	5 2/8	10	9	Barron Co., WI	Charles Slayton	Gordon Lee	PR 1920	742
207 4/8	23 4/8	16 2/8	22 1/8	5 2/8	5 2/8	12	11	Burnett Co., WI	Harold Miller	Mac's Taxidermy	1938	742
207 4/8	22 1/8	18 5/8	29 1/8	5 3/8	5 3/8	9	10	Lawrence Co., SD	Ernest C. Larive	J.D. Andrews	1957	742
207 4/8	26 4/8	29 1/8	26 4/8	5 2/8	5 2/8	7	10	Portageville, NY	Howard W. Smith	Howard W. Smith	1959	742
207 4/8	26 5/8	18 7/8	25 5/8	5 2/8	5 2/8	8	8	Comanche Co., KS	Picked Up	Larry L. Huffman	1984	742
207 4/8	27	17 7/8	26 3/8	5 1/8	5 1/8	8	9	Macoupin Co., IL	John D. Carey	John D. Carey	1991	742

WHITETAIL DEER - NON-TYPICAL ANTLERS

Odocoileus virginianus virginianus and certain related subspecies

Score	Length of Main Beam R	L	Inside Spread	Circumference at Smallest Place Between Burr and First Point R	L	Number of Points R	L	Locality	Hunter	Owner	Date Killed	Rank
207 3/8	25 4/8	25 6/8	20 4/8	4 1/8	4 3/8	8	12	Langlade Co., WI	Henry L. Schewe	John R. Konkel	1907	748
207 3/8	25 3/8	26	26 3/8	5 2/8	5 3/8	8	11	Aitkin Co., MN	Viola Scott	Viola S. Weimer	1954	748
207 3/8	28 7/8	29 1/8	18 5/8	6 5/8	6 2/8	10	10	Lincoln Co., MO	Melvin Zumwalt	Melvin Zumwalt	1955	748
207 3/8	24 3/8	25 3/8	21 3/8	5	5 2/8	9	15	Throckmorton Co., TX	Jack Carlile	Watt R. Matthews	1960	748
207 3/8	28 3/8	27 6/8	21 2/8	5 6/8	5 7/8	10	11	Roberts Co., SD	Delbert Lackey	Delbert Lackey	1975	748
207 3/8	25 7/8	25 4/8	20 2/8	4 4/8	4 4/8	10	8	Zapata Co., TX	Romeo H. Garcia	Romeo H. Garcia	1977	748
207 3/8	25 7/8	26 3/8	17 4/8	6 2/8	6 1/8	12	9	Dane Co., WI	Todd J. DeForest	Todd J. DeForest	1989	748
207 2/8	24 4/8	19 5/8	11 7/8	5 6/8	5 5/8	11	17	Oroville, WA	Victor E. Moss	Victor E. Moss	1967	755
207 2/8	27 1/8	26 5/8	18 3/8	5 2/8	5 1/8	7	10	Drayton Valley, AB	Hassib Halabi	Hassib Halabi	1977	755
207 2/8	23 4/8	24 4/8	19	5	5 1/8	12	8	Unknown	Unknown	John L. Stein	PR 1979	755
207 2/8	30 1/8	29 5/8	21	5 5/8	5 4/8	8	7	Andrew Co., MO	Frank Kelso	Delores C. Kelso	1981	755
207 2/8	26 2/8	22 7/8	18 2/8	6	6 5/8	9	11	Brown Co., NE	Terry J. Graff	Terry J. Graff	1987	755
207 2/8	26 2/8	25 5/8	18 7/8	5 3/8	5 3/8	7	7	Adair Co., MO	Kevin Elsea	Kevin Elsea	1988	755
207 2/8	23 4/8	23 7/8	20 2/8	6 1/8	6 3/8	15	10	Swan Plain, SK	Gary A. Markofer	Gary A. Markofer	1991	755
207 2/8	26 3/8	24 6/8	19 5/8	5 2/8	5 4/8	7	13	Crawford Co., WI	Brent Swiggum	Brent Swiggum	1991	755
207 1/8	28 5/8	28 4/8	18 4/8	6	5 5/8	10	10	St. Louis Co., MO	Unknown	Kent Austin	1958	763
207 1/8	25 7/8	24 3/8	20 6/8	5 1/8	5 2/8	9	10	Provost, AB	Michael D. Kerley	Michael D. Kerley	1977	763
207 1/8	22	23 7/8	19 2/8	8	8 5/8	14	13	Buffalo Co., NE	Unknown	John L. Stein	1978	763
207 1/8	23 4/8	23 4/8	15 6/8	4 7/8	4 6/8	11	8	Traverse Co., MN	Joel E. Kuschel	Joel E. Kuschel	1996	763
207 1/8	29 3/8	28 4/8	25 4/8	5 5/8	5 4/8	8	7	Page Co., IA	Jeremy Williams	Jeremy Williams	1997	763
207	23 4/8	23 1/8	18 4/8	5 6/8	6 4/8	16	13	Bayfield Co., WI	Francis F. Zifko	Francis F. Zifko	1954	768
207	26 6/8	26	19 1/8	5 6/8	5 7/8	9	13	Cowley Co., KS	Joyce A. Williams	Joyce A. Williams	1983	768
207	26 4/8	27 1/8	25	5 4/8	5 2/8	10	8	Stark Co., OH	Tad E. Crawford	Tad E. Crawford	1987	768
207	23 7/8	23 6/8	20	5 6/8	5 6/8	7	11	Eagle Creek, SK	Perry Haanen	Perry Haanen	1993	768
207	22 7/8	23 4/8	18 6/8	6 4/8	6 2/8	9	11	Davis Co., IA	David L. Johnson	David L. Johnson	1994	768
206 7/8	24 3/8	25	16 5/8	5 5/8	5 3/8	14	9	Oneida Co., WI	Clarence Staudenmayer	Clarence Staudenmayer	1942	773
206 7/8	25	24 1/8	18	5 2/8	5 3/8	10	12	Loup Co., NE	T.A. Brandenburg	Dick Rossum	1963	773
206 7/8	23 4/8	25 5/8	18 4/8	5 1/8	4 7/8	14	12	Horicon Marsh, WI	Picked Up	Ronald A. Lillge	1966	773
206 7/8	28 6/8	30 3/8	23 4/8	6 1/8	5 6/8	11	10	Claiborne Parish, LA	J.H. Thurmon	J.H. Thurmon	1970	773
206 7/8	25 4/8	25 6/8	21 6/8	5 6/8	5 6/8	10	9	Pine Lake, AB	Richard D. Doan	Leila R. Doan	1979	773
206 7/8	26 2/8	29 5/8	27 7/8	5 2/8	5 4/8	11	10	Wright Co., MN	Richard A. Erickson	Richard A. Erickson	1983	773
206 7/8	25 5/8	27 1/8	22 4/8	4 5/8	4 6/8	11	9	Maple Creek, SK	Theodore Reierson	Theodore Reierson	1984	773
206 7/8	20 4/8	21 3/8	14 5/8	5 1/8	5	11	9	Whitemouth River, MB	Tom Clark, Jr.	Tom Clark, Jr.	1987	773
206 7/8	28 3/8	27 7/8	20 1/8	5 2/8	5 1/8	9	6	Stearns Co., MN	Steven J. Sperl	Steven J. Sperl	1987	773
206 7/8	24 7/8	24 6/8	20	5 3/8	5 2/8	13	12	Baxter Lake, AB	Terry F. Ermel	Terry F. Ermel	1988	773
206 7/8	28 1/8	27 1/8	21 4/8	5 4/8	5	12	14	Dodge Co., WI	Steven J. Schultz	Steven J. Schultz	1989	773

Score	Length of Main Beam R	Length of Main Beam L	Inside Spread	Circumference R	Circumference L	Points R	Points L	Locality	Hunter	Owner	Date Killed	Rank
206 7/8	25	22 5/8	18 6/8	5 6/8	4 7/8	9	11	Deserters Creek, AB	Duane Paisley	Duane Paisley	1992	773
206 7/8	30 5/8	29 3/8	21 6/8	5 1/8	5 1/8	8	9	McPherson Co., KS	Dennis G. Bordner	Dennis G. Bordner	1994	773
206 7/8	26 3/8	25	17 2/8	5 6/8	5 7/8	11	8	Hamilton Co., OH	Mickey E. Lotz	Mickey E. Lotz	1995	773
206 7/8	23 7/8	25	19 6/8	5 4/8	5 3/8	10	9	Douglas Co., WI	Neil R. Hagen	Neil R. Hagen	1996	773
206 6/8	25 4/8	25 4/8	24	5 4/8	5 4/8	7	11	Beechy, SK	Harold Penner	Spanky Greenville	1959	788
206 6/8	25 4/8	25 4/8	17 2/8	5 4/8	5 4/8	8	7	Grant Parish, LA	Richard D. Ellison, Jr.	Richard D. Ellison, Jr.	1969	788
206 6/8	25 6/8	23 3/8	23 7/8	5 4/8	5 5/8	12	8	Somerset Co., ME	Mark T. Lary	Mark T. Lary	1979	788
206 6/8	26 7/8	27	20 1/8	5	5	7	10	Buffalo Co., WI	Monte R. Nichols	Monte R. Nichols	1996	788
206 5/8	26 5/8	25 2/8	19 7/8	5 1/8	5	11	9	Outlook, SK	Unknown	Dick Rossum	1971	792
206 5/8	26	24 2/8	19 6/8	5 3/8	5 2/8	7	12	Chase Co., KS	Jay A. Talkington	Jay A. Talkington	1983	792
206 5/8	26	25 3/8	20 1/8	5 5/8	5 4/8	9	7	Iowa Co., IA	Picked Up	Ralph McBride	1990	792
206 5/8	24 5/8	24 3/8	19 6/8	6	6 1/8	8	11	Kevisville, AB	Brian R. McKain	Brian R. McKain	1990	792
206 5/8	24	23 3/8	23	4 5/8	4 4/8	9	12	Marshall Co., KY	Perry Beyer, Jr.	Perry Beyer, Jr.	1996	792
206 4/8	21 1/8	21 1/8	16 6/8	5 7/8	5 7/8	10	12	Chippewa Co., MI	John Nevins	Bass Pro Shops F. & W. Mus.	1904 PR	797
206 4/8	22 1/8	22 2/8	19 4/8	5	5	10	13	Brooks Co., TX	John E. Wilson	James M. Hancock, Jr.	1947	797
206 4/8	23 1/8	23 1/8	16 4/8	5 4/8	5	14	8	Norman Co., MN	Unknown	Tom Williams	1950	797
206 4/8	23 2/8	24 7/8	17 7/8	6 4/8	6 4/8	12	9	Yankton Co., SD	William Sees	William Sees	1973	797
206 4/8	26 1/8	26 1/8	19 2/8	6 3/8	6 1/8	11	6	Lac qui Parle Co., MN	Steven J. Karels	Steven J. Karels	1974	797
206 4/8	26 7/8	27 4/8	20 5/8	5 1/8	5 3/8	10	9	Lawrence Co., IL	Shirley Lewis	Shirley Lewis	1976	797
206 4/8	28 4/8	24 7/8	26 7/8	5	5	15	13	Madison Co., GA	Picked Up	GA Dept. of Natl. Resc.	1993	797
206 3/8	16 5/8	18 7/8	15 7/8	4 5/8	4 5/8	11	11	Webb Co., TX	Willard V. Brenizer	Gerry Elliff	1942	804
206 3/8	22 7/8	23 2/8	19	4 7/8	5	12	12	Menard Co., IL	Frank C. Pickett	Frank C. Pickett	1985	804
206 3/8	24 6/8	20 6/8	18 3/8	5	5	12	10	Clay Co., IN	Jason S. Shaw	Jason S. Shaw	1989	804
206 3/8	26 7/8	26 7/8	19	5 2/8	5 5/8	9	9	Adams Co., OH	James M. Wilson	James M. Wilson	1989	804
206 3/8	29 6/8	28 5/8	22 2/8	5 4/8	4 6/8	9	9	Colquitt Co., GA	Picked Up	GA Dept. of Natl. Resc.	1990	804
206 3/8	24 6/8	24 7/8	14	4 5/8	4 6/8	7	8	Cass Co., IA	Rodney A. Watson	Rodney A. Watson	1993	804
206 3/8	27 7/8	27 7/8	20	4 6/8	4 7/8	9	11	Kuroki, SK	Picked Up	K. Ian Cooper	1995	804
206 2/8	25	25	18 6/8	5 7/8	5 7/8	9	11	Cortland Co., NY	Hank Hayes	Interlaken Sportsmans Club	1947	811
206 2/8	28 4/8	28 5/8	25	5 6/8	5 6/8	7	9	Cotulla, TX	George E. Light III	George E. Light III	1950	811
206 2/8	25 4/8	25	16 6/8	5	5	10	13	Piscataquis Co., ME	Ralph E. Dow	Ralph E. Dow	1964	811
206 2/8	31	31	22 7/8	6	6	8	9	Lincoln Co., MT	Larry H. Beller	Larry H. Beller	1985	811
206 2/8	24 1/8	24 1/8	19	5 3/8	5 3/8	9	8	Benton Co., MN	Kenneth R. Nodo	Kenneth R. Nodo	1987	811
206 2/8	31 5/8	29 3/8	23 4/8	4 4/8	4 5/8	10	10	McLennan, AB	Gordon E. Ristow	Gordon E. Ristow	1993	811
206 1/8	26 5/8	26 4/8	19 7/8	5 1/8	5 1/8	15	10	Loon Lake, WA	Bill Quirt	Bill Quirt	1955	817
206 1/8	22	22	20 7/8	4 6/8	4 6/8	15	9	Kisbey, SK	J. Harrison	J. Harrison	1956	817
206 1/8	22 2/8	22 5/8	18 4/8	5 1/8	5 1/8	10	8	Lincoln Co., WI	Picked Up	Louis Pond	1974 PR	817
206 1/8	23 2/8	22 5/8	18 1/8	5 4/8	5 4/8	8	9	Dunn Co., ND	Kenneth E. DeLap	Kenneth E. DeLap	1982	817
206 1/8	25 4/8	25 3/8	17 4/8	5 2/8	6	12	12	Osage Co., OK	Wesley D. Coldren	Wesley D. Coldren	1986	817
206 1/8	26 3/8	26 2/8	19 7/8	5 4/8	5 5/8	10	12	Lake of the Woods Co., MN	Keith D. Yahnke	Keith D. Yahnke	1987	817
206 1/8	25 1/8	25 1/8	21	5 2/8	5 1/8	7	7	Union Co., OH	Henry W. Leistritz	Henry W. Leistritz	1989	817
206	23 5/8	23	18 6/8	4 6/8	4 6/8	11	11	Cameron Co., PA	William P. Rhines	David Rhines	1910	824
206	26 5/8	25 4/8	16 6/8	5 3/8	5 3/8	8	8	McMullen Co., TX	Robert L. Hodges	Robert L. Connally	1925	824
206	25 6/8	24 3/8	15 6/8	4 7/8	4 7/8	10	14	St. Louis Co., MN	Earl Skarp	George W. Flaim	1938	824
206	25	24 3/8	24 3/8	5 1/8	5	8	7	Queen Annes Co., MD	Kenneth J. Houtz	Kenneth J. Houtz	1992	824
206	24 1/8	25 1/8	17 5/8	5 3/8	5 3/8	8	11	Shoshone Co., ID	Marion G. Macaluso	Marion G. Macaluso	1993	824
205 7/8	28 6/8	27 4/8	17 1/8	5 4/8	5 4/8	8	17	Steuben Co., NY	Fred J. Kelley	Fred J. Kelley	1938	829
205 7/8	23 4/8	23 4/8	19 3/8	6 1/8	5 7/8	7	8	Swift Co., MN	A.P. Vander Weyst	A.P. Vander Weyst	1954	829

WHITETAIL DEER - NON-TYPICAL ANTLERS

Odocoileus virginianus virginianus and certain related subspecies

Score	Length of Main Beam R	L	Inside Spread	Circumference at Smallest Place Between Burr and First Point R	L	Number of Points R	L	Locality	Hunter	Owner	Date Killed	Rank
205 7/8	25 6/8	25 4/8	20 6/8	4 4/8	4 3/8	10	10	Houston Co., TX	Gary Rogers	Gary Rogers	1969	829
205 7/8	25	23 2/8	20 2/8	6	6	13	12	Missoula Co., MT	Unknown	John L. Stein	1973	829
205 7/8	27 4/8	28 6/8	19 4/8	5	5 1/8	10	8	Switzerland Co., IN	Paul Graf	Paul Graf	1981	829
205 7/8	23 2/8	23 3/8	17 5/8	5 4/8	5 4/8	9	13	Clark Co., MO	Allen L. Courtney	Allen L. Courtney	1983	829
205 7/8	24 7/8	23 5/8	20	6	5 4/8	14	11	Battle River, AB	Bryan Champagne	Bryan Champagne	1987	829
205 7/8	28 1/8	28	25 4/8	7	6 6/8	11	11	Atchison Co., MO	Larry Poppa	Larry Poppa	1990	829
205 7/8	28 2/8	27 4/8	23 2/8	5 2/8	5 6/8	5	11	Breckinridge Co., KY	Bruce Parris	Bruce Parris	1991	829
205 6/8	25 3/8	26 4/8	18 1/8	4 5/8	4 4/8	11	9	Minnesota	Unknown	Greg Jensen	1965	838
205 6/8	23 1/8	21 4/8	21	4 7/8	4 4/8	12	12	Lowndes Co., MS	Joe W. Shurden	Joe W. Shurden	1976	838
205 6/8	24 3/8	24	21	5	5 2/8	9	9	Ritchie Co., WV	Charles E. Bailey, Jr.	Charles E. Bailey, Jr.	PR 1979	838
205 6/8	26 2/8	25 2/8	15 6/8	5 7/8	6	14	10	Koochiching Co., MN	Unknown	Marc M. Jackson	1979	838
205 6/8	23 5/8	23	20 3/8	5 4/8	5 3/8	8	8	Cloud Co., KS	Gary G. Pingel	Gary G. Pingel	1982	838
205 6/8	26 2/8	25 5/8	19 2/8	5 6/8	6	8	8	Lucas Co., IA	William F. Bingaman	William F. Bingaman	1991	838
205 5/8	23 3/8	24 2/8	20 6/8	5 6/8	5 6/8	15	10	Orange Co., NY	Unknown	Victor T. Zarnock	PR 1944	844
205 5/8	26	25 2/8	21 2/8	5 4/8	5 7/8	14	9	Cottonwood Co., MN	Larry G. Gravley	Larry G. Gravley	1975	844
205 5/8	28	27 4/8	18 6/8	6 4/8	6 3/8	10	13	Spencer Co., KY	Phillip W. Lawson	Phillip W. Lawson	1989	844
205 5/8	24 6/8	25	21 4/8	5 1/8	5	14	12	Fellers Heights, BC	Billy L. Franks	Billy L. Franks	1995	844
205 4/8	27 2/8	25 4/8	22 4/8	5 5/8	5 6/8	9	9	Roseau Co., MN	Erwin Klaassen	Erwin Klaassen	1955	848
205 4/8	25 4/8	25 4/8	17 7/8	4 7/8	5 1/8	9	12	Charlotte Co., NB	Clayton Tatton	J.D. Andrews	1959	848
205 4/8	25	25 6/8	19 4/8	6 1/8	5 6/8	11	7	Adams Co., IL	Eldon K. Dagley	Eldon K. Dagley	1981	848
205 4/8	23 5/8	23	19 6/8	5 5/8	5 6/8	12	16	St. Louis Co., MN	Picked Up	George W. Flaim	1985	848
205 4/8	26	25 7/8	20 2/8	5 4/8	5 6/8	8	8	Washington Co., MN	Lonnie J. Diethert	Lonnie J. Diethert	1987	848
205 4/8	25 4/8	26 1/8	23 3/8	4 6/8	4 6/8	10	6	Ram River, AB	William Howard	William Howard	1988	848
205 4/8	21	21 3/8	17 3/8	5 1/8	5 1/8	18	16	Edgefield Co., SC	Bradley E. Means	Bradley E. Means	1994	848
205 4/8	23 5/8	22 7/8	19	4 1/8	4 1/8	9	11	Armit River, SK	Marvin B. Borsa	Marvin B. Borsa	1995	848
205 3/8	23 3/8	21 7/8	18 7/8	4 7/8	5	6	6	Kelvington, SK	D. Minor	D. Minor	1954	856
205 3/8	25 3/8	27 1/8	22 2/8	4 1/8	4 1/8	10	9	Trempealeau Co., WI	Dennis L. Ulberg	Dennis L. Ulberg	1968	856
205 3/8	22 4/8	23 2/8	17	6	6	10	12	Todd Co., MN	Mark A. Miksche	Mark A. Miksche	1979	856
205 3/8	27 1/8	25 7/8	21	6 2/8	6	8	12	Louisa Co., IA	Daniel Kaufman	Daniel Kaufman	1984	856
205 3/8	24 7/8	24 1/8	17 4/8	4 5/8	4 6/8	8	9	Wadena Co., MN	Donald R. Brockob	Donald R. Brockob	1990	856
205 3/8	25 1/8	24	15	6	7 3/8	8	12	Beltrami Co., MN	Matt E. Stone	Matt E. Stone	1990	856
205 3/8	26 3/8	24 6/8	16 4/8	4 5/8	4 5/8	10	11	Duval Co., TX	Daniel A. Pedrotti	Daniel A. Pedrotti	1995	856
205 3/8	20 4/8	23 1/8	20 6/8	5 4/8	5 3/8	9	9	St. Anne Lake, AB	Allen H. Wilkie	Allen H. Wilkie	1995	856
205 3/8	25 5/8	23 6/8	18 4/8	5 6/8	5 4/8	10	8	Dallas Co., IA	Picked Up	Jeff Kempf	PR 1996	856
205 2/8	24	23 5/8	27	5 4/8	5 4/8	11	8	Hungry Hollow, SK	K.W. Henderson	K.W. Henderson	1954	865
205 2/8	28 6/8	29 2/8	18 7/8	5 4/8	4 4/8	10	11	Effingham Co., IL	Allen K. Bandelow	Allen K. Bandelow	1991	865

Score	Main Beam R	Main Beam L	Inside Spread	Circ. R	Circ. L	Pts R	Pts L	Locality	Hunter	Owner	Date	Rank
205 2/8	27 5/8	27 1/8	19 4/8	5	5	7	11	Cross Co., AR	Gordon R. Banton	Gordon R. Banton	1992	865
205 2/8	25	25	16 3/8	5 1/8	5 3/8	14	11	Willow Brook, SK	Alvie Warcomika	Alvie Warcomika	1993	865
205 1/8	26 4/8	24 4/8	20 3/8	4 7/8	5	10	9	Leross, SK	R. Weger	R. Weger	1961	869
205 1/8	26 6/8	25 4/8	20 3/8	5 4/8	5 4/8	11	9	Rat River, MB	Ken L. Maxymowich	Ken L. Maxymowich	1987	869
205 1/8	24 5/8	24 4/8	20 2/8	4 7/8	5	13	11	Antler, SK	Regina K.V. Ross	Regina K.V. Ross	1987	869
205 1/8	22 2/8	29	14 6/8	5	4 6/8	12	13	Bonner Co., ID	Clinton M. Hackney	Clinton M. Hackney	1990	869
205 1/8	28 7/8	25 1/8	24 1/8	4 1/8	4 4/8	9	8	Erie Co., NY	Mark C. Surdi	Mark C. Surdi	1996	869
205	21	21	18	6 1/8	5 7/8	14	5	Boundary Co., ID	Lee Mahler	Lee Mahler	1961	874
205	26 3/8	26 4/8	16 7/8	6	5 5/8	12	9	St. Louis Co., MN	Ed Nelson	George W. Flaim	1964	874
205	25 5/8	24 5/8	22 1/8	5 4/8	5 4/8	7	11	Jo Daviess Co., IL	David L. Virtue	David L. Virtue	1990	874
205	25 3/8	25	24 1/8	4	3 7/8	9	10	Peoria Co., IL	Picked Up	Dick Rossum	1991	874
205	25 4/8	24 4/8	18 7/8	5 5/8	5 5/8	12	10	Marathon Co., WI	Joshua J. Erdman	Joshua J. Erdman	1994	874
205	24 2/8	22 4/8	18	4 7/8	4 5/8	9	11	Carroll Co., IL	Robert D. Guenzler	Robert D. Guenzler	1994	874
205	27 1/8	27 1/8	19 3/8	5 3/8	5 1/8	9	11	Guthrie Co., IA	James C. Long	James C. Long	1994	874
204 7/8	27 3/8	25 6/8	17 6/8	4 5/8	4 6/8	12	13	Union Co., IA	Jeff J. Tussey	Jeff J. Tussey	1995	882
204 7/8	26 3/8	26 4/8	21 4/8	5 1/8	4 6/8	6	8	Trempealeau Co., WI	Ralph Klimek	Ralph Klimek	1960	882
204 7/8	25 2/8	25 2/8	21 7/8	5	5 3/8	13	12	Roseau Co., MN	Andy Streiff	Andy Streiff	1967	882
204 7/8	25 4/8	26 3/8	21 2/8	4 5/8	5 4/8	13	9	Bentley, AB	Stanley A. Anderson	Stanley A. Anderson	1968	882
204 7/8	26	24 5/8	18 5/8	5 1/8	4 6/8	9	8	Winona Co., MN	Picked Up	Gary Bornfleth	1979	882
204 7/8	27 2/8	25 6/8	18 4/8	4 5/8	5 1/8	7	12	Battle River, SK	Corey M. Young	Corey M. Young	1992	882
204 6/8	21 2/8	22 2/8	23 6/8	5	4 5/8	11	8	Anson Co., NC	Keith M. Reese	Keith M. Reese	1994	888
204 6/8	22 7/8	24 1/8	21 2/8	5 2/8	4 7/8	7	8	Koochiching Co., MN	H.T. Hanson	Kevin Blomer	1920	888
204 6/8	23 4/8	23 4/8	15 2/8	5 7/8	6 6/8	9	14	Moose Jaw, SK	Earl Sears	Earl Sears	1958	888
204 6/8	25 4/8	22 6/8	22 6/8	5 6/8	5 4/8	8	10	Lowndes Co., MS	Picked Up	Thomas B. Yeatman	1959	888
204 6/8	28 4/8	26 5/8	21 7/8	4 4/8	5 7/8	10	9	Gilmer Co., WV	Brooks Reed	Brooks Reed	1960	888
204 6/8	23 1/8	24 2/8	19 7/8	5 1/8	5 6/8	10	10	Saskatchewan River, MB	Dieter Boehner	Dieter Boehner	1973	888
204 6/8	28 4/8	27 6/8	26 1/8	5 4/8	4 5/8	8	12	Stearns Co., MN	Curt Fettig	Curt Fettig	1975	888
204 6/8	26 7/8	25 7/8	21 1/8	5 2/8	5	8	7	Innisfree, AB	Donald Baranec	Donald Baranec	1977	888
204 6/8	26 3/8	26 4/8	19 2/8	6	5 3/8	6	8	Washington Co., IN	David Souder	David Souder	PR 1994	888
204 5/8	24 4/8	23 7/8	17 6/8	4 4/8	5 4/8	11	8	Davis Co., IA	Unknown	William H. Lilienthal	1996	899
204 5/8	27 2/8	24 4/8	20 4/8	5 2/8	6 1/8	10	16	Clay Co., KS	Rob W. Boling	Rob W. Boling	1996	899
204 5/8	26 5/8	26 6/8	19 7/8	5	4 4/8	11	10	St. Anne Lake, AB	Todd K. Kirk	Todd K. Kirk	1906	899
204 5/8	23 4/8	26 1/8	16 1/8	4 7/8	5 2/8	10	12	Bandera Co., TX	August Dienger	Larry L. Stahl	PR 1930	899
204 5/8	23 4/8	23 4/8	21 1/8	6 4/8	5	12	8	Unknown	Unknown	John A. Jarosz	1992	899
204 5/8	25 4/8	25 5/8	16 3/8	4 7/8	4 7/8	11	12	Okanogan Co., WA	Matthew B. King	Matthew B. King	1994	899
204 5/8	27 3/8	27 2/8	20 4/8	5 1/8	6 4/8	9	10	Bull River, BC	Gary Nonis	Gary Nonis	1994	899
204 4/8	26 6/8	26 5/8	21 2/8	4 6/8	4 7/8	8	10	Cloud Co., KS	Darrell L. Zimmerman	Darrell L. Zimmerman	1994	904
204 4/8	23 4/8	24	18 3/8	5 2/8	5 2/8	11	12	Jackson Co., OH	Bernard Tennant	Bernard Tennant	1960	904
204 4/8	30	21 6/8	20 4/8	4 7/8	4 6/8	10	11	Love Co., OK	William B. Heller	William B. Heller	1970	904
204 4/8	22 2/8	28 6/8	14 7/8	5 5/8	5 2/8	10	10	Monroe Co., MO	Rogelio L. Bautista	Rogelio L. Bautista	1996	904
204 3/8	28 6/8	29	19 3/8	4 7/8	4 7/8	10	7	Valley City, ND	William F. Cruff	George W. Flaim	1955	907
204 3/8	26 7/8	26 4/8	18 7/8	5 5/8	5 5/8	7	12	Newport, WA	David R. Buchite	David R. Buchite	1960	907
204 3/8	24 4/8	24 4/8	20 3/8	5 1/8	5 6/8	11	12	Harrison Co., IA	Raymond McDaniel	Raymond McDaniel	1970	907
204 3/8	27 3/8	27 3/8	20 4/8	5 6/8	5 2/8	13	8	Waukesha Co., WI	Unknown	Mac's Taxidermy	PR 1975	907
204 3/8	23 4/8	24	14 7/8	5 2/8	5 3/8	10	12	Clearwater Co., MN	Gilbert Oien	Vance R. Norgaard	1976	907
204 3/8	25	25 6/8	19 3/8	5 3/8	5 4/8	10	10	Nanton, AB	Barry Flipping	Barry Flipping	1986	907
204 3/8	24 5/8	26 6/8	18 7/8	5 4/8	—	13	11	Rock Island Co., IL	Jeff B. Davis	Jeff B. Davis	1990	907

Odocoileus virginianus virginianus and certain related subspecies

Score	Length of Main Beam R	L	Inside Spread	Circumference at Smallest Place Between Burr and First Point R	L	Number of Points R	L	Locality	Hunter	Owner	Date Killed	Rank
204 3/8	25 4/8	25 2/8	16 7/8	5 4/8	5 7/8	9	9	Jefferson Co., KS	Michael D. Wright	Michael D. Wright	1995	907
204 2/8	23	23	17 2/8	4 6/8	4 4/8	11	15	Crook Co., WY	David Sipe	David Sipe	1956	915
204 2/8	23 2/8	23 7/8	17 2/8	5 6/8	5 3/8	12	12	Rainy Lake, ON	Rod Hebert	Rod Hebert	1969	915
204 2/8	25 2/8	25 5/8	23 2/8	6 5/8	6 4/8	9	10	Meeker Co., MN	Walter J. Tintes	Walter J. Tintes	1975	915
204 2/8	25 5/8	23 1/8	17 1/8	5 1/8	5 4/8	7	15	Silver Lake, AB	Edwin Nelson	Gary Padleski	1980	915
204 2/8	26 2/8	26 4/8	22 2/8	4 6/8	4 6/8	5	8	Boone Co., MO	Calvin E. Brown	Calvin E. Brown	1985	915
204 2/8	27 3/8	27 7/8	21 4/8	6 2/8	6	9	8	Yuma Co., CO	Jeff L. Mekelburg	Jeff L. Mekelburg	1986	915
204 2/8	30	27 6/8	21 2/8	6 3/8	6 4/8	6	11	Cass Co., IL	J. David Bartels	J. David Bartels	1989	915
204 2/8	29 1/8	27 7/8	23 3/8	6 2/8	6	4	4	Ashland Co., OH	Keith A. Beringo	Keith A. Beringo	1991	915
204 2/8	25 6/8	25 3/8	18 2/8	5 1/8	5 3/8	10	12	Livingston Co., IL	Michael T. Schopp	Michael T. Schopp	1996	915
204 1/8	28 1/8	27 2/8	22 3/8	6	5 4/8	10	12	Lyon Co., MN	Ray Evans	David C. Johnson	1940	924
204 1/8	28	27 3/8	24 5/8	5 2/8	5 2/8	8	11	Pope Co., MN	LeRoy D. Hausmann	LeRoy D. Hausmann	1967	924
204 1/8	25 6/8	25 7/8	18 6/8	3 4/8	3 5/8	9	8	Dodge Co., WI	Wesley G. Braunschweig	Wesley G. Braunschweig	1976	924
204 1/8	28 5/8	25 7/8	22 2/8	5 7/8	6 1/8	12	9	Charlotte Co., NB	Gary L. Lister	Gary L. Lister	1984	924
204 1/8	26 5/8	26 2/8	22	5	4 7/8	7	9	Dubuque Co., IA	Joe J. Rettenmeier	Joe J. Rettenmeier	1987	924
204 1/8	25 2/8	26 1/8	18 3/8	5 5/8	5 5/8	14	11	Douglas Co., MN	Samuel Knapp	Samuel Knapp	1993	924
204 1/8	27 1/8	26 6/8	21	6 2/8	5 6/8	7	9	Crawford Co., WI	Francis J. Manning	Francis J. Manning	1994	924
204 1/8	25 4/8	26 3/8	19 5/8	5 2/8	5 2/8	11	10	Pike Co., MO	Robert J. Jeffries	Robert J. Jeffries	1995	924
204 1/8	25 4/8	25 1/8	19 7/8	5 5/8	5 6/8	12	11	Van Buren Co., IA	Geoffrey N. Phillips	Geoffrey N. Phillips	1995	924
204	27 6/8	27 3/8	21 1/8	4 7/8	5 1/8	9	14	Sutton Co., TX	L.H. McMillan	L.H. McMillan	1961	933
204	26 1/8	27 3/8	16 2/8	5 1/8	5 3/8	10	11	Carlton Co., MN	Erick Zack	Glen Van Guilder	1964	933
204	27 2/8	25 2/8	21 7/8	5 2/8	5 3/8	7	12	Sheep River, AB	Walter L. Brown	Walter L. Brown	1966	933
204	26 1/8	25 5/8	18 6/8	5 3/8	5 2/8	13	10	Grant Co., MN	Douglas S. Olson	Douglas S. Olson	1977	933
204	23 5/8	23 6/8	18 3/8	5 7/8	5 6/8	13	14	Holbein, SK	Jesse Bates	Jesse Bates	1981	933
204	26 6/8	27 1/8	21 7/8	5 1/8	5 4/8	9	11	Webster Co., KY	Jeff Robinson	Jeff Robinson	1982	933
204	26 3/8	26 7/8	17 4/8	5 1/8	5	8	9	Beltrami Co., MN	Terence C. Derosier	Terence C. Derosier	1991	933
204	28 2/8	28 5/8	23 3/8	5 1/8	5 1/8	8	8	Rockbridge Co., VA	Michael J. Shifflett	Michael J. Shifflett	1993	933
204	27 1/8	25 2/8	16 6/8	5 4/8	5 6/8	14	12	Webster Co., MS	William D. Eshee III	William D. Eshee III	1996	933
203 7/8	27 4/8	27 4/8	17 4/8	4 6/8	4 6/8	11	8	Eastland Co., TX	Picked Up	William B. Wright, Jr.	1920	942
203 7/8	25	25 4/8	18	4 7/8	4 6/8	8	11	McMullen Co., TX	Bruce Phillips	Jeffery C. Phillips	1941	942
203 7/8	22	22 5/8	19	5 1/8	5 1/8	10	10	Pope Co., MN	Irwin E. Strangeland	Irwin E. Strangeland	1980	942
203 7/8	23	18 7/8	16 2/8	4 3/8	4 4/8	11	14	Eaton Co., MI	Mark R. Janousek	Mark R. Janousek	1991	942
203 7/8	24 4/8	25 5/8	22 6/8	4 7/8	5 1/8	6	9	Portage Co., OH	Lee C. Morris	Lee C. Morris	1994	942
203 6/8	28	27 3/8	20	5 1/8	5 3/8	7	10	George Lake, NB	Henry Kirk	Ron Kirk	1903	947
203 6/8	23 5/8	24 6/8	14 5/8	5 3/8	4 7/8	11	8	Dickinson Co., MI	Harold Eskil	Bass Pro Shops F. & W. Mus.	1929	947
203 6/8	24 2/8	25 3/8	16 5/8	4	3 7/8	8	8	Maverick Co., TX	Picked Up	Richard H. Bennett	1941	947

Score	Main Beam R	Main Beam L	Inside Spread	Circ. R	Circ. L	Points R	Points L	Locality	By Whom Killed	Owner	Date	Rank
203 6/8	28	27 1/8	19 7/8	4 7/8	4 7/8	10	9	Phillips Co., AR	N.V. Hyde, Jr.	Dolph Horton	1948	947
203 6/8	26 2/8	25	17 6/8	4 4/8	4 4/8	9	8	McCurtain Co., OK	Gary L. Birge	Gary L. Birge	1981	947
203 6/8	22 4/8	23	16 1/8	5 7/8	5 7/8	11	12	Pike Co., IL	Randall B. Long	Randall B. Long	1987	947
203 6/8	27 3/8	25 6/8	19 6/8	5 5/8	5 4/8	16	7	Hart Co., KY	Terry Melvin	Picked Up	1992	947
203 5/8	24 6/8	23 6/8	19 6/8	5 4/8	5 4/8	10	8	Washtenaw Co., MI	Ronald R. Chabot	Ronald R. Chabot	1996	955
203 5/8	28	26 6/8	15 5/8	6 6/8	6 6/8	18	13	Chariton Co., MO	Vernon Sower	Vernon Sower	1953	955
203 5/8	30 6/8	23	15	6	5 6/8	8	14	Meigs Co., OH	Wesley Gilkey	Wesley Gilkey	1970	955
203 5/8	25 2/8	23 2/8	17 3/8	5 6/8	6 2/8	10	9	Grand Forks Co., ND	Thomas G. Bernotas	Thomas G. Bernotas	1975	955
203 5/8	27 3/8	28	17 5/8	5 7/8	5 7/8	14	9	Page Co., IA	Rodney S. Brooks	Picked Up	1981	955
203 5/8	23 3/8	24	15 7/8	4 7/8	4 5/8	13	9	Sabine Co., TX	Joe R. Dickerson	Marvin E. Dickerson	1981	955
203 5/8	26 3/8	24 3/8	21 7/8	5 7/8	5 5/8	12	11	St. Louis Co., MN	Phillip A. Roalstad	Picked Up	1981	955
203 5/8	25 1/8	25 1/8	17 5/8	5	5 2/8	9	11	Warren Co., IA	Ted Miller	Ted Miller	1986	964
203 5/8	30 4/8	30 4/8	21 3/8	5 3/8	5 1/8	10	11	Monona Co., IA	Robert S. Jensen	Robert S. Jensen	1991	964
203 5/8	23 6/8	23 6/8	15 2/8	6	6	10	10	Chariton Co., MO	Ann Walton	Kevin N. Stroup	1995	964
203 4/8	25 1/8	25	22	4 5/8	4 6/8	13	12	Live Oak Co., TX	Henderson Coquat	Alec Coker	1916	964
203 4/8	25 2/8	24 4/8	16 4/8	5 5/8	5 6/8	9	13	Kootenai Co., ID	Kevin L. Lundblad	A.P. Hegge	1929	964
203 4/8	27 5/8	28	23 3/8	4 7/8	5 2/8	9	8	Jones Co., GA	Mrs. Curtis F. Long	Curtis F. Long	1965	964
203 4/8	22 1/8	24	18 6/8	5 2/8	5 1/8	8	9	Lincoln Co., MT	Sean M. Blackley	Sean M. Blackley	1990	964
203 4/8	27 2/8	27	19 6/8	4 6/8	4 6/8	9	11	Upper Cutbank, BC	William E. Eckert	William E. Eckert	1990	964
203 4/8	25 3/8	24 6/8	19 1/8	5 2/8	5 2/8	9	10	Appanoose Co., IA	Clem A. Herman	Clem A. Herman	1990	964
203 4/8	24	22 5/8	16 5/8	6	6 4/8	14	12	Putnam Co., MO	Casey R. Hartlip	Casey R. Hartlip	1993	964
203 4/8	28 3/8	28	23 5/8	6	6 4/8	9	7	Prince Georges Co., MD	Charles C. Blankenship, Jr.	Charles C. Blankenship, Jr.	1995	964
203 4/8	24 2/8	24 6/8	16	6	6	7	11	Lincoln Co., NE	Truman A. Burch III	Truman A. Burch III	1996	964
203 3/8	26 4/8	27 4/8	16	5 6/8	5 6/8	8	9	St. Louis Co., MN	Eino W. Nurmi	Eino W. Nurmi	1934	973
203 3/8	25 2/8	25 2/8	21 5/8	5	5	10	10	Okanogan Co., WA	Michael A. Anderson	Michael A. Anderson	1961	973
203 3/8	24 1/8	24 1/8	21	5 3/8	5 4/8	8	10	Olmsted Co., MN	Logan Behrens	Logan Behrens	1961	973
203 3/8	23 2/8	23 2/8	19 2/8	6	6 1/8	8	8	Piapot, SK	Frank Kelly	John R. Steffes, Sr.	1966	973
203 3/8	26 1/8	26 2/8	17 6/8	5 4/8	5 4/8	8	10	Olmsted Co., MN	Daniel J. Bernard	Daniel J. Bernard	1967	973
203 3/8	24 2/8	25	19	4 7/8	5 1/8	10	13	Marquette Co., WI	Joseph E. Bell	Jeffrey L. Morgan	1969	973
203 3/8	24 1/8	23	20 2/8	6 2/8	6 4/8	7	13	Dunn Co., WI	Terry J. Evenson	Terry J. Evenson	1987	973
203 3/8	27 2/8	27 2/8	21 4/8	5 2/8	5	10	10	Fayette Co., IA	Steve M. Loban	Steve M. Loban	1995	973
203 3/8	28 2/8	28 2/8	22 2/8	5 6/8	5 6/8	8	7	Fulton Co., IL	Russell G. White	Russell G. White	1996	982
203 2/8	23 7/8	23 7/8	17 2/8	5 3/8	5 1/8	13	13	Esterhazy, SK	Walter Tucker	Walter Tucker	1966	982
203 2/8	26 6/8	27 1/8	16 6/8	5 6/8	5 6/8	10	10	Marinette Co., WI	Marvin E. Holmgren	Marvin E. Holmgren	1986	982
203 2/8	25 1/8	24 6/8	18 7/8	5 1/8	5 3/8	12	11	McHenry Co., ND	Garry L. Heizelman	Garry L. Heizelman	1987	982
203 2/8	25 2/8	25 2/8	16 1/8	5 1/8	5 1/8	13	9	Scott Co., IA	Marv A. Schmidt, Jr.	Marv A. Schmidt, Jr.	1987	982
203 2/8	23 6/8	24	19 6/8	7 6/8	6 1/8	9	14	Ross Co., OH	Scott Zurmehly	Scott Zurmehly	1987	982
203 2/8	23 6/8	23 4/8	15 5/8	5 3/8	5 3/8	11	12	Churchbridge, SK	Kevin W. Prince	Kevin W. Prince	1991	982
203 2/8	25 2/8	24 4/8	21 7/8	4 5/8	4 5/8	10	12	Sanders Co., MT	Donald W. Heerdt	Donald W. Heerdt	1992	982
203 2/8	26 2/8	25 6/8	18 4/8	5 7/8	5 7/8	9	11	McLeod Co., MN	William Sandman	William Sandman	1994	982
203 2/8	28 4/8	28 4/8	23	5 6/8	5 1/8	10	13	W. Feliciana Parish, LA	Estus S. Sykes	Estus S. Sykes	1994	982
203 2/8	27 2/8	26	21 5/8	5 3/8	5 7/8	12	7	Decatur Co., IA	Kenneth R. Jones	Kenneth R. Jones	1995	982
203 2/8	26 7/8	26 7/8	22 2/8	5	5	13	9	Andrew Co., MO	James C. Schweizer	James C. Schweizer	1995	982
203 2/8	24 1/8	23 7/8	20 4/8	5 7/8	4 7/8	9	9	Jefferson Co., NE	Greg D. Hansmire	Greg D. Hansmire	1996	982
203 1/8	25 5/8	23 5/8	16	4 6/8	4 4/8	11	10	Koochiching Co., MN	George W. Flaim	Unknown	1934	994
203 1/8	24 3/8	23 7/8	17 6/8	4 4/8	4 6/8	13	9	Kootenai Co., ID	William M. Ziegler	William M. Ziegler	1965	994
203 1/8	27 5/8	28 1/8	21	4 6/8	4 7/8	9	7	Pawnee Co., NE	Virgil J. Fisher	Virgil J. Fisher	1970	994

WHITETAIL DEER - NON-TYPICAL ANTLERS

Odocoileus virginianus virginianus and certain related subspecies

Score	Length of Main Beam R	L	Inside Spread	Circumference at Smallest Place Between Burr and First Point R	L	Number of Points R	L	Locality	Hunter	Owner	Date Killed	Rank
203 1/8	23 7/8	24 4/8	19 6/8	5 4/8	5 7/8	10	12	Wetzel Co., WV	Tom Kirkhart	Tom Kirkhart	1981	994
203 1/8	23 5/8	23 2/8	16 6/8	5 2/8	5 2/8	10	12	Roosevelt Co., MT	Jerry L. Altland	Jerry L. Altland	1991	994
203 1/8	22 4/8	19 1/8	14 3/8	4 4/8	4 4/8	10	13	Campbell Co., WY	Picked Up	John P. Riley	1992	994
203 1/8	29 2/8	28 2/8	19 3/8	5 3/8	5 3/8	11	8	Swan River, SK	Edwin E. Orr	Edwin E. Orr	1993	994
203 1/8	24 6/8	24 3/8	21 4/8	6 5/8	6 6/8	8	12	Greenwood Co., KS	Paul E. Bunyard	Paul E. Bunyard	1994	994
203 1/8	26 2/8	26	19 4/8	5	5 1/8	8	10	Lafayette Co., WI	Vernus Larson	Vernus Larson Estate	1995	994
203	26 2/8	26 1/8	15	5 2/8	5 1/8	9	11	Hancock Co., IL	S.E. Brockschmidt	S.E. Brockschmidt	1958	1003
203	26 3/8	25 4/8	18 4/8	4 5/8	5	10	8	Madison Co., IA	Joe Bruns	Tim Bruns	1967	1003
203	28 4/8	27 3/8	21 7/8	5 5/8	5 5/8	9	8	Guthrie Co., IA	Ronald R. Hoyt	Ronald R. Hoyt	1974	1003
203	27	23 6/8	18 1/8	5 2/8	5 4/8	8	9	Lee Co., IA	Wayne L. McClain	Wayne L. McClain	1980	1003
203	26 1/8	27 6/8	17 4/8	4 6/8	4 5/8	9	8	Jefferson Co., KS	Dale Heston	Dale Heston	1982	1003
203	24	23 6/8	15	4 6/8	4 7/8	9	12	Wayne Co., KY	Jack L. Keith	Jack L. Keith	1990	1003
203	28 6/8	26 4/8	25 2/8	6 1/8	6 1/8	7	7	Coles Co., IL	Richard A. Miller	Richard A. Miller	1991	1003
203	25 6/8	26 2/8	21 2/8	4 5/8	4 6/8	7	10	Du Page Co., IL	Kevin J. Moran	Kevin J. Moran	1995	1003
202 7/8	25 1/8	24 2/8	23 7/8	5	5	7	10	Marinette Co., WI	Theodore Maes	Theodore Maes	1932	1011
202 7/8	27 7/8	26 2/8	18	5 2/8	5 3/8	12	7	Du Page Co., IL	Picked Up	E. Dolf Pfefferkorn	1962	1011
202 7/8	24 4/8	24 2/8	19	6	5 7/8	10	10	Kingman Co., KS	Picked Up	Michael L. Piaskowski	1966	1011
202 7/8	30 1/8	29 6/8	21	6 3/8	5 3/8	8	7	Houston Co., MN	John B. Broers	John B. Broers	1991	1011
202 7/8	25 3/8	26 7/8	20 1/8	5 5/8	5 5/8	11	12	Decatur Co., IA	Kevin J. Anderson	Kevin J. Anderson	1992	1011
202 7/8	27 2/8	28 3/8	22 6/8	5 4/8	5 5/8	10	8	Brown Co., IL	Sylvan Purcell, Jr.	Sylvan Purcell, Jr.	1992	1011
202 7/8	26	26	19 1/8	5 2/8	5 2/8	10	10	Clearwater Co., MN	Donald E. Holm	Donald E. Holm	1993	1011
202 7/8	25 2/8	24 4/8	18 2/8	6 3/8	6 2/8	10	11	Saline Co., IL	Lindy R. Potts	Lindy R. Potts	1995	1011
202 6/8	22 3/8	22	18	5 6/8	5 1/8	7	8	Garrison, ND	Clarence Hummel	Clarence Hummel	1961	1019
202 6/8	25 1/8	24 5/8	20 7/8	5 7/8	5 7/8	9	14	Warren Co., IA	Leland Cortum	Leland Cortum	1969	1019
202 6/8	25	25 1/8	17 2/8	5 4/8	5 3/8	9	9	Chautauqua Co., KS	John L. Brown	John L. Brown	1990	1019
202 6/8	24 7/8	22 6/8	15 5/8	4 4/8	4 4/8	12	10	Kenedy Co., TX	Alex Hixon	Alex Hixon	1993	1019
202 6/8	24 6/8	22	20	5 4/8	5 1/8	10	8	Hamilton Co., OH	Vernon Smith	Vernon Smith	1993	1019
202 5/8	26 7/8	26 7/8	23 1/8	4 5/8	4 5/8	9	10	Kleberg Co., TX	Richard J. Mills	Richard J. Mills	1926	1024
202 5/8	26 3/8	23 4/8	18 6/8	4 7/8	5	9	11	Grafton Co., NH	Picked Up	Robert Hoffman	PR 1945	1024
202 5/8	22 5/8	23 3/8	18 4/8	4 6/8	4 6/8	16	9	Carroll Co., MS	George Galey	Terry Galey	1960	1024
202 5/8	29	29 3/8	20 6/8	4 7/8	4 7/8	9	9	Dane Co., WI	Ray S. Outhouse	Ray S. Outhouse	1964	1024
202 5/8	23	24	14 7/8	5 6/8	5 4/8	9	9	Unknown	Unknown	Ralph W. Jones	PR 1984	1024
202 5/8	26 2/8	26 2/8	19	4 6/8	4 6/8	8	11	Columbia Co., WI	William M. Bletsch	William M. Bletsch	1992	1024
202 5/8	25 1/8	25 6/8	18 7/8	5 3/8	4 7/8	9	9	Pike Co., IL	Brian M. Hill	Brian M. Hill	1994	1024
202 5/8	21	23	17 4/8	5 1/8	4 7/8	13	11	St. Louis Co., MN	Timothy Rosendahl	Timothy Rosendahl	1995	1024
202 4/8	24 7/8	24 6/8	23 3/8	4 7/8	5	10	11	Texas	Unknown	Buckhorn Mus. & Saloon, Ltd.	PR 1920	1032

Score	Main Beam R	Main Beam L	Inside Spread	Circ. R	Circ. L	Pts. R	Pts. L	Locality	Hunter	Owner	Date Killed	Rank
202 4/8	24 4/8	24 6/8	16 4/8	5	4 7/8	13	12	Missoula Co., MT	Robert A. Bracken	Unknown	1962	1032
202 4/8	26 2/8	25 3/8	22 1/8	5 1/8	5 2/8	9	8	Spokane Co., WA	Dick Rossum	Unknown	PR 1989	1032
202 4/8	22 4/8	25 4/8	19 4/8	6 3/8	5 2/8	11	9	Boundary Co., ID	Steve Crossley	Picked Up	1990	1032
202 4/8	27 5/8	29 7/8	22 4/8	5 7/8	6 1/8	7	6	St. Louis Co., MN	Jeff P. Marczak	Jeff P. Marczak	1991	1032
202 3/8	26	26	21 2/8	5 4/8	5 4/8	11	12	Koochiching Co., MN	George A. Balaski	George A. Balaski	1955	1037
202 3/8	26 4/8	24 5/8	17 5/8	4 7/8	5 2/8	8	9	Lac qui Parle Co., MN	Donald M. Nygaard	Donald M. Nygaard	1958	1037
202 3/8	26 1/8	27	20 7/8	5	5 1/8	10	10	Aitkin Co., MN	Joe Clarke	Joe Clarke	1960	1037
202 3/8	23 5/8	25 3/8	16 5/8	4 5/8	4 5/8	11	6	Crook Co., WY	Marshall Miller	Marshall Miller	1968	1037
202 3/8	26 2/8	25 4/8	18 1/8	4 7/8	4 6/8	10	7	Cass Co., MN	Hollace Brockoff	Hollace Brockoff	1976	1037
202 3/8	25 7/8	24 6/8	22 7/8	5 6/8	6	9	13	Delaware Co., OH	Duane E. Robinson	Duane E. Robinson	1980	1037
202 3/8	26 1/8	26 6/8	26 1/8	5 7/8	5 7/8	11	13	Washington Co., IL	Richard C. Keller	Richard C. Keller	1986	1037
202 3/8	23 1/8	26 3/8	20 1/8	6	6 2/8	10	6	Lake Co., MN	Lawrence J. Simonich	Lawrence J. Simonich	1987	1037
202 3/8	26 7/8	28 2/8	22 7/8	6 1/8	4 5/8	9	9	Douglas Co., MN	Timothy C. Sukke	Timothy C. Sukke	1988	1037
202 3/8	26 4/8	26 1/8	19	4 5/8	5 1/8	8	8	Thomas Co., GA	Rolf Kauka	Rolf Kauka	1991	1037
202 2/8	27 5/8	27 2/8	24 1/8	5	4 7/8	9	7	Bond Co., IL	Douglas E. Hays	Douglas E. Hays	1992	1049
202 2/8	26 7/8	26 3/8	25 2/8	4 3/8	5 1/8	9	9	Chisago Co., MN	John W. Holmblad	John W. Holmblad	1992	1049
202 2/8	21 6/8	22 4/8	22	5	4 7/8	12	7	Fergus Co., MT	Harold K. Stewart	Harold K. Stewart	1948	1049
202 2/8	25 1/8	24 7/8	19 2/8	4 6/8	5 2/8	9	9	East Kooteney, BC	Andrew W. Rosicky	Andrew W. Rosicky	1956	1049
202 2/8	26 1/8	23 1/8	26 6/8	5 2/8	5 7/8	8	10	Waldo Co., ME	James A. Tripp, Sr.	James A. Tripp, Sr.	1959	1049
202 2/8	28 4/8	28 3/8	20 1/8	6 2/8	5 7/8	8	7	Oglethorpe Co., GA	J. Richard Mocko	J. Richard Mocko	1983	1049
202 1/8	27 6/8	26 2/8	19 3/8	5 6/8	5 1/8	12	9	Louisa Co., IA	Robert L. McFadden	Robert L. McFadden	1986	1055
202 1/8	25 4/8	24 3/8	17 5/8	5	4 7/8	9	9	Lenawee Co., MI	Fredrick M. Hood, Jr.	Fredrick M. Hood, Jr.	1988	1055
202 1/8	25 1/8	25 2/8	22 6/8	4 7/8	6 2/8	9	9	Zehner, SK	Lee Danison	Lee Danison	1958	1055
202 1/8	26 1/8	26 4/8	19 3/8	6 1/8	4 6/8	8	7	Gary, SD	Dennis Cole	Dennis Cole	1960	1055
202	25 4/8	25 4/8	19 1/8	4 5/8	5 4/8	10	11	Pennington Co., MN	R. Scott Sorvig	R. Scott Sorvig	1980	1060
202	28 7/8	28 1/8	16 7/8	5 6/8	6 2/8	15	11	Oktibbeha Co., MS	Oliver H. Lindig	Oliver H. Lindig	1983	1060
202	27 5/8	27 2/8	15	6 1/8	6 1/8	7	9	Peoria Co., IL	Leonard A. Asbell	Leonard A. Asbell	1993	1060
202	27	27	22 5/8	6 1/8	6	6	11	Bayfield Co., WI	Larry L. Huffman	Native American	1960	1060
202	28 6/8	28 6/8	15 5/8	5 2/8	5 2/8	12	10	Nodaway Co., MO	Richard L. Stewart	Richard L. Stewart	1972	1060
202	26 7/8	26 7/8	23 4/8	5 7/8	5	13	7	Powell Co., KY	Hershel Ingram	Hershel Ingram	1980	1060
202	26 6/8	26 6/8	26 6/8	6 1/8	6 3/8	8	10	Knox Co., ME	Skip Black	Skip Black	1981	1060
202	25 3/8	19 6/8	18 3/8	5 5/8	5 5/8	10	10	Monona Co., IA	Gary W. Anfinson	Gary W. Anfinson	1988	1060
202	24	24 3/8	19 2/8	5 4/8	5 4/8	12	9	Roberts Co., SD	Ronnie A. Bucklin	Ronnie A. Bucklin	1988	1060
202	25	25	14 7/8	7 2/8	6 6/8	8	12	Platte Co., MO	Steven Richardson	Steven Richardson	1991	1060
201 7/8	23 6/8	24 1/8	23 5/8	4 7/8	5 1/8	9	8	Manito Lake, SK	Barry Manchester	Barry Manchester	1992	1070
201 7/8	24 1/8	23 5/8	18	4 7/8	5 7/8	16	10	Pushmataha Co., OK	Lucas Young	Lucas Young	1993	1070
201 7/8	23 5/8	26 1/8	18 5/8	4 4/8	4 4/8	8	7	Callaway Co., MO	Marc E. Meng	Marc E. Meng	1995	1070
201 7/8	26 4/8	24 1/8	14 5/8	5 7/8	5 6/8	8	8	Itasca Co., MN	Lewis R. Rocco, Jr.	Lewis Rocco, Sr.	1944	1070
201 7/8	25	25	19 7/8	5 6/8	5 6/8	10	9	Winnebago Co., IA	Peter G. Weiss	Unknown	PR 1957	1070
201 7/8	25 4/8	24	23 4/8	5 4/8	5 4/8	9	7	Burmis, AB	Joe Tapay	Joe Tapay	1964	1070
201 7/8	24 2/8	25	22	6	6	9	8	Todd Co., KY	Russell E. Carver	Russell E. Carver	1966	1070
201 7/8	29 4/8	28 4/8	17 2/8	5 1/8	5 1/8	11	11	Itasca Co., MN	J. Gorden & G. Dopp	Picked Up	1981	1070
201 7/8	27	27	17 4/8	5 3/8	5 5/8	8	7	Louisa Co., IA	Jason Gapinski	Jason Gapinski	1987	1070
201 7/8	28 2/8	25 2/8	20 1/8	5	4 6/8	8	7	Anderson Co., KS	Arthur O. Bell	Arthur O. Bell	1990	1070
201 7/8	26 1/8	27 2/8	20 2/8	4 6/8	6 1/8	7	11	Kiowa Co., KS	Jimmie L. Spencer	Jimmie L. Spencer	1991	1070
201 7/8	25 7/8	25 3/8	16	6 1/8	4 1/8	9	9	Pembina River, AB	Gordon Modanese	Gordon Modanese	1995	1070
201 6/8	24 1/8	24 6/8	19 3/8	4 2/8	4 1/8	12	12	Texas	Buckhorn Mus. & Saloon, Ltd.	Unknown	PR 1920	1079

WHITETAIL DEER - NON-TYPICAL ANTLERS

Odocoileus virginianus virginianus and certain related subspecies

Score	Length of Main Beam R	L	Inside Spread	Circ. at Smallest Place Between Burr and First Point R	L	Number of Points R	L	Locality	Hunter	Owner	Date Killed	Rank
201 6/8	23 3/8	23 4/8	19 7/8	4 6/8	4 4/8	10	10	Custer Co., SD	Unknown	Kenny Spring	PR 1940	1079
201 6/8	24	24	17 6/8	6	6	17	15	Wilkinson Co., MS	Jimmy Ashley	Jimmy Ashley	1985	1079
201 6/8	25 2/8	24 6/8	18 7/8	5 7/8	5 6/8	8	7	Van Buren Co., IA	Randy Kramer	Randy Kramer	1989	1079
201 6/8	29	25 6/8	25	5 5/8	5 7/8	8	11	Plamondon, AB	Steve K. Swinhoe	Steve K. Swinhoe	1996	1079
201 5/8	25 5/8	24 3/8	17 2/8	4 3/8	4 4/8	9	9	Cass Co., MN	Guy Chisholm	Charles F. Green	1945	1084
201 5/8	24 2/8	24 7/8	21	5	5	8	8	Brown Co., SD	Wallace Labisky	J.D. Andrews	1962	1084
201 5/8	27 6/8	22 2/8	20 5/8	5 6/8	5 5/8	15	12	Sisseton, SD	Truman M. Nelson	Truman M. Nelson	1967	1084
201 5/8	27	26 6/8	18	5 6/8	5 6/8	16	16	Charlevoix Co., MI	Robert V. Doerr	Robert V. Doerr	1973	1084
201 5/8	25	24 7/8	17 1/8	5 2/8	5 1/8	10	8	Ohaton, AB	Curtis R. Siegfried	Curtis R. Siegfried	1976	1084
201 5/8	25 1/8	24 7/8	19 7/8	6 3/8	6 1/8	7	7	Baraga Co., MI	Dennis D. Bess	Dennis D. Bess	1981	1084
201 5/8	27	26	18 3/8	5 5/8	5 6/8	7	8	Johnson Co., IA	Duane E. Papke	Duane E. Papke	1981	1084
201 5/8	25 2/8	26 6/8	21 6/8	4 7/8	5	10	10	Howard Co., MO	Gregory A. O'Brian	Gregory A. O'Brian	1983	1084
201 5/8	26 4/8	26 2/8	24 7/8	5 1/8	5	8	8	Clinton Co., MO	David E. Eads	David E. Eads	1989	1084
201 5/8	24 2/8	24 6/8	16 6/8	5 6/8	5 5/8	15	15	Kane Co., IL	Keith R. Kampert	Keith R. Kampert	1991	1084
201 5/8	23 5/8	22 7/8	20 2/8	4 6/8	4 6/8	11	11	Candle Lake, SK	Brian F. Prior	Brian F. Prior	1993	1084
201 5/8	29 6/8	28 2/8	22	5 6/8	5 4/8	10	9	Madison Co., IA	Raymond Dawson	Raymond Dawson	1994	1084
201 5/8	26 1/8	25 3/8	21 1/8	5 2/8	5 1/8	6	6	Roanoke Co., VA	James D. Scott	James D. Scott	1994	1084
201 5/8	25 6/8	26 2/8	19 7/8	5 1/8	5 1/8	13	10	Sheboygan Co., WI	Darren T. Winter	Darren T. Winter	1995	1084
201 5/8	28 6/8	28 4/8	19 1/8	4 7/8	4 7/8	10	10	Sumner Co., KS	Jeremy A. Schroeder	Jeremy A. Schroeder	1996	1084
201 4/8	22 3/8	23 3/8	16 5/8	4 1/8	4 2/8	9	9	Campbell Co., SD	Edward J. Torigian	J.D. Andrews	1957	1099
201 4/8	22 5/8	23	15 4/8	4 3/8	4 4/8	8	8	Monroe Co., AR	Hugh Erwin	Randy Erwin	1962	1099
201 4/8	25 2/8	23 1/8	16 5/8	4 5/8	5 2/8	14	13	Stevens Co., WA	Robert W. Newell	Robert W. Newell	1963	1099
201 4/8	28 5/8	28 1/8	22 1/8	5 3/8	5 1/8	8	9	Brown Co., NE	R.L. Tinkham	R.L. Tinkham	1965	1099
201 4/8	29 7/8	28 5/8	19 7/8	5 2/8	5 4/8	10	10	Hubbard Co., MN	Duane G. Lorsung	Duane G. Lorsung	1973	1099
201 4/8	22	29 2/8	23 6/8	6	6	10	8	Barber Co., KS	Joe Ash	Joe Ash	1975	1099
201 4/8	28 5/8	25 6/8	18 3/8	6 7/8	6 7/8	7	7	Flathead Co., MT	Barry L. Wensel	Barry L. Wensel	1976	1099
201 4/8	28 3/8	27 6/8	17 7/8	4 6/8	4 7/8	7	8	Clayton Co., IA	Paul C. Crawford	Paul C. Crawford	1987	1099
201 4/8	24 7/8	26 1/8	20 2/8	6 6/8	6 3/8	8	8	Allamakee Co., IA	Daniel J. Gallagher	Daniel J. Gallagher	1989	1099
201 4/8	22 4/8	21 2/8	14	5 2/8	5 6/8	13	13	Wayne Co., MO	David L. Hays	David L. Hays	1992	1099
201 4/8	25 6/8	25	21 4/8	5 5/8	5 6/8	10	9	Douglas Co., MN	Gerald F. Hoppe	Gerald F. Hoppe	1992	1099
201 4/8	25 4/8	25 5/8	19 3/8	4 7/8	5	9	10	Ebel Creek, SK	Barry D. Koshman	Barry D. Koshman	1992	1099
201 4/8	25 5/8	24 4/8	19 6/8	5 7/8	5	11	13	Fulton Co., IL	John R. Rosas	John R. Rosas	1994	1099
201 4/8	25 1/8	25 7/8	18 7/8	6 4/8	5 7/8	7	9	Sumner Co., KS	Bradley A. Smith	Bradley A. Smith	1994	1099
201 4/8	28 4/8	29	21 1/8	6	5 7/8	8	9	Dane Co., WI	Picked Up	Susan Clack	1995	1099
201 4/8	22 6/8	23 3/8	21 1/8	5 2/8	5 2/8	14	9	Athabasca, AB	Aldo B. Zanon	Aldo B. Zanon	1995	1099
201 3/8	24 1/8	23 5/8	17 3/8	5 3/8	5 4/8	11	14	Wakulla Co., FL	Clark Durrance	Clark Durrance	1941	1115

Score	L	L	Spread	Circ	Circ	R	L	Locality	Hunter	Owner	Date	Rank
201 3/8	26 3/8	25 7/8	18 4/8	5 2/8	5 1/8	10	8	St. Louis Co., MN	Andrew G. Groen	Andrew G. Groen	1958	1115
201 3/8	21 1/8	21 6/8	21 3/8	5 2/8	4 6/8	16	11	Bonner Co., ID	Leroy Coleman	Leroy Coleman	1960	1115
201 3/8	26 4/8	27	18 5/8	4 6/8	4 7/8	9	10	Concordia Parish, LA	G.O. McGuffee	G.O. McGuffee	1963	1115
201 3/8	26 6/8	26 6/8	19 3/8	5 5/8	5 3/8	13	9	Swift Co., MN	Joel T. Schmidt	Joel T. Schmidt	1973	1115
201 3/8	24 5/8	25 2/8	15 7/8	5 6/8	5 1/8	15	17	Pushmataha Co., OK	Maurice Jackson	Maurice Jackson	1975	1115
201 3/8	24 7/8	25 1/8	19	5 2/8	5 3/8	12	12	Queen Annes Co., MD	Franklin E. Jewell	Franklin E. Jewell	1978	1115
201 3/8	28 2/8	29	15	4 6/8	4 7/8	6	11	Monona Co., IA	Thomas R. Flynn	Thomas R. Flynn	1989	1115
201 3/8	26 6/8	26 3/8	20	5 5/8	5 4/8	9	11	Kiowa Co., CO	Dale A. Dilulo	Dale A. Dilulo	1991	1115
201 3/8	25 5/8	27 7/8	20 4/8	4 5/8	4 6/8	9	9	Donovan, SK	Glen E. Kristoff	Glen E. Kristoff	1992	1115
201 3/8	24 4/8	25 3/8	20 2/8	5	4 6/8	14	10	Grayson Co., TX	Donnie M. Brewer	Donnie M. Brewer	1995	1115
201 3/8	24 6/8	23	16 7/8	5 4/8	5 2/8	9	12	Morton Co., ND	Paul R. Shannon	Paul R. Shannon	1995	1115
201 3/8	30 4/8	29 2/8	21 6/8	5 3/8	5 7/8	10	8	Greene Co., OH	Richard D. Steen	Richard D. Steen	1996	1115
201 2/8	26 7/8	26 4/8	16	5 3/8	5 5/8	17	7	Pennington Co., MN	Glenn Tasa	Glenn Tasa	1940	1128
201 2/8	24 6/8	26 5/8	18 1/8	4 5/8	4 6/8	12	14	Dickinson Co., MI	Gene R. Barlament	Unknown	1948	1128
201 2/8	23 4/8	25 2/8	22 4/8	4 2/8	4 2/8	13	10	San Saba Co., TX	Ted J. Bode	Ted J. Bode	1965	1128
201 2/8	30 6/8	28	17 5/8	4 7/8	4 6/8	8	9	Cumberland Co., KY	Ewing Groce	Ewing Groce	1968	1128
201 2/8	27 3/8	27 3/8	16 5/8	4 6/8	5 4/8	11	7	Itasca Co., MN	Cecil L. Johnson	Cecil L. Johnson	1976	1128
201 2/8	28 3/8	28 5/8	23 1/8	4 7/8	4 6/8	12	10	Coshocton Co., OH	Lou L. Rogers	Lou L. Rogers	1979	1128
201 2/8	21 1/8	20 7/8	16 2/8	5 3/8	5 5/8	10	9	McLeod River, AB	Roy Schueler	Roy Schueler	1992	1128
201 2/8	24 7/8	26 4/8	19 5/8	5 4/8	5 4/8	8	9	High Prairie, AB	Leo Morawski	Leo Morawski	1997	1128
201 1/8	28 2/8	27 3/8	16 5/8	5 1/8	5 1/8	9	9	Arkansas Co., AR	Daniel B. Bullock	Daniel B. Bullock	1953	1136
201 1/8	29 2/8	28 5/8	21 2/8	4 6/8	4 6/8	9	11	Unknown	Larry D. Bollier	Unknown	PR 1957	1136
201 1/8	26 3/8	22 3/8	16 3/8	5 2/8	5 2/8	13	8	Slope Co., ND	J.D. Andrews	Arthur Hegge	1961	1136
201 1/8	23	22 5/8	14 5/8	4 6/8	5 1/8	10	9	Westmoreland Co., PA	Richard K. Mellon	Richard K. Mellon	1966	1136
201 1/8	25	25 1/8	20 4/8	6 1/8	6 4/8	8	7	Freeborn Co., MN	Jim Palmer	Jim Palmer	1972	1136
201 1/8	25 4/8	25 4/8	18 2/8	5	4 7/8	10	9	Butler Co., NE	James L. Sklenar	James L. Sklenar	1973	1136
201 1/8	20 3/8	19 3/8	20 3/8	4	4 2/8	9	9	Lincoln Co., AR	H.R. Morgan, Jr.	H.R. Morgan, Jr.	1977	1136
201 1/8	25 2/8	26 1/8	20 1/8	5 4/8	5 1/8	8	10	Jackson Co., MI	Steven G. Crocker	Steven G. Crocker	1989	1136
201 1/8	27 2/8	27 2/8	20 6/8	5 6/8	5 7/8	11	9	Carroll Co., IL	Mel Landwehr	Mel Landwehr	1991	1136
201 1/8	28	26 2/8	16 5/8	4 2/8	4 2/8	11	11	King Edward Lake, BC	Reiny Lippert	Reiny Lippert	1994	1136
201 1/8	26 7/8	23 2/8	15 5/8	6 1/8	6 3/8	14	12	Jackson Co., IL	Allen S. Casten	Allen S. Casten	1996	1136
201	23 6/8	22 7/8	15 2/8	5 3/8	5 3/8	9	13	Delta Co., MI	Ernest B. Fosterling	Ernest B. Fosterling	1953	1147
201	22 4/8	26 4/8	20 3/8	4 4/8	4 5/8	11	8	Cessford, AB	Russell C. Chapman	Russell C. Chapman	1966	1147
201	25 7/8	27 6/8	21 4/8	5 4/8	5 5/8	10	8	Mercer Co., IL	Gerald L. Olson	Gerald L. Olson	1972	1147
201	27 1/8	27	21 3/8	5	5	10	7	Empress, AB	David Booker	David Booker	1979	1147
201	26 1/8	25	22 5/8	4 6/8	4 6/8	9	9	Crawford Co., WI	Lloyd C. Rickleff	Lloyd C. Rickleff	1989	1147
201	25 4/8	26 1/8	22 2/8	5 7/8	5 7/8	6	13	Wilkinson Co., GA	E. Dwaine Davis	E. Dwaine Davis	1990	1147
201	22 1/8	25 6/8	15 4/8	5 1/8	7 2/8	9	8	Jasper Co., MO	Richard Morris	Picked Up	1991	1147
200 7/8	23 4/8	24 5/8	20 1/8	5 3/8	5 2/8	11	9	Mandan, ND	Peter Voigt	Virgil Chadwick	1957	1154
200 7/8	23	23 7/8	19	4 7/8	4 7/8	10	11	Rusk Co., WI	Gerald Cleven	Gerald Cleven	1963	1154
200 7/8	26 1/8	26 4/8	18	5 2/8	5 1/8	11	10	Desha Co., AR	Harold Farmer	Edgar Farmer	1963	1154
200 7/8	23 4/8	24 3/8	21	4 4/8	4 5/8	8	7	Kleberg Co., TX	John A. Larkin	Picked Up	1982	1154
200 7/8	24	22 5/8	22 1/8	5 1/8	6 3/8	10	12	Davis Co., IA	Roger G. Pettit	R.G. Pettit & W. Van Mersberger	1988	1154
200 7/8	25 3/8	25 1/8	20	5 2/8	5 1/8	8	13	Morgan Co., KY	Greg Powers	Greg Powers	1989	1154
200 7/8	26 1/8	22 7/8	18 3/8	5 1/8	4 7/8	13	14	Davison Co., SD	Louis W. Cooper	Louis W. Cooper	1990	1154
200 7/8	23 6/8	19 4/8	20	4 5/8	4 5/8			Pulaski Co., AR	Lyle K. Sinkey	Lyle K. Sinkey	1994	1154

WHITETAIL DEER - NON-TYPICAL ANTLERS

Odocoileus virginianus virginianus and certain related subspecies

Score	Length of Main Beam R	L	Inside Spread	Circumference at Smallest Place Between Burr and First Point R	L	Number of Points R	L	Locality	Hunter	Owner	Date Killed	Rank
200 6/8	24 1/8	24 3/8	17 6/8	5	5	11	9	Juneau Co., WI	Anchor Nelson	Larry L. Huffman	1946	1162
200 6/8	24 4/8	24	18 2/8	5 1/8	5	10	8	Morrison Co., MN	Elmer J. Hollenkamp	Elmer J. Hollenkamp	1977	1162
200 6/8	24 7/8	25 7/8	25 1/8	6 4/8	6 6/8	9	11	Wapello Co., IA	Rod A. McKelvey	Rod A. McKelvey	1983	1162
200 6/8	25 1/8	26	13 7/8	6 5/8	6 5/8	8	10	Saskatchewan	Picked Up	Ron Lavoie	1989	1162
200 6/8	27 1/8	26 2/8	17 7/8	4 4/8	4 3/8	11	9	Coahuila, MX	Biff MacCollum	Biff MacCollum	1992	1162
200 6/8	25 6/8	24 4/8	18	4 7/8	4 6/8	16	12	Okanogan Co., WA	Fred R. Miller	Fred R. Miller	1993	1162
200 6/8	26 5/8	25	16 7/8	4 7/8	4 6/8	8	8	Wapello Co., IA	Michael W. Garber	Michael W. Garber	1996	1162
200 5/8	28	27 6/8	22 1/8	5 3/8	5 2/8	8	7	Jackson Co., OH	Glenn McCall	Glenn McCall	1970	1169
200 5/8	26 7/8	26 7/8	18 6/8	5 7/8	5 6/8	10	7	Washington Co., IA	Bruce Guy	Bruce Guy	1973	1169
200 5/8	25	26 1/8	18 7/8	4 5/8	4 5/8	7	7	Clayton Co., IA	Dorrance Arnold	Dorrance Arnold	1977	1169
200 5/8	26 2/8	26 2/8	14	4 5/8	4 7/8	6	9	Texas Co., OK	Jeffrey T. Wright	Jeffrey T. Wright	1987	1169
200 5/8	24 6/8	24 6/8	22 2/8	5 4/8	5 5/8	10	9	Harper Co., KS	Robert A. Thomas	Robert A. Thomas	1990	1169
200 5/8	26 5/8	25 3/8	20 3/8	5 5/8	5 5/8	11	9	Mitchell Co., IA	Dean A. Beyer	Dean A. Beyer	1991	1169
200 5/8	24 5/8	23 5/8	19 5/8	5 4/8	5 3/8	8	9	Pembina Valley, MB	Claude R.J. Chappellaz	Claude R.J. Chappellaz	1992	1169
200 5/8	26 2/8	25 2/8	18 3/8	5 2/8	5 2/8	8	9	Madison Co., IA	Steve A. Marsh	Steve A. Marsh	1994	1169
200 5/8	23 4/8	24 1/8	18 4/8	4 5/8	4 6/8	8	11	Grayson Co., TX	Forrest L. Robertson	Forrest L. Robertson	1995	1169
200 4/8	23 5/8	21 4/8	21 1/8	4 5/8	4 4/8	8	9	Uvalde Co., TX	W.S. Gordon	1st State Bank of Uvalde	1923	1178
200 4/8	25 2/8	25 2/8	23	6 1/8	6 1/8	9	6	Brentford, SD	S.C. Mitchell	S.C. Mitchell	1948	1178
200 4/8	25 1/8	22 4/8	19 6/8	6	6	10	10	Wainwright, AB	Paul Pryor	Paul Pryor	1968	1178
200 4/8	24 5/8	24 7/8	19 7/8	5 4/8	5 4/8	12	10	Geauga Co., OH	Rudy C. Grecar	Rudy C. Grecar	1969	1178
200 4/8	26 2/8	27 1/8	19 6/8	4 1/8	4 2/8	8	8	Kleberg Co., TX	Charles Hoge	Charles Hoge	1976	1178
200 4/8	27	26 2/8	22	5 5/8	5 7/8	8	8	Clearwater Co., MN	Ronald O. Halvorson	Ronald O. Halvorson	1987	1178
200 4/8	25 5/8	27 5/8	16 6/8	4 5/8	4 5/8	10	7	Howard Co., IA	Victor J. Buresh	Victor J. Buresh	1990	1178
200 4/8	23 1/8	23 2/8	19 2/8	5 3/8	4 7/8	11	9	Clinton Co., MO	R. Rea Norton	R. Rea Norton	1991	1178
200 4/8	24 6/8	22 4/8	18	4 3/8	4 4/8	8	10	Crook Co., WY	Paul L. Wolz	Paul L. Wolz	1967	1186
200 3/8	23 5/8	24	18 6/8	4 6/8	4 6/8	8	8	Lake of the Woods Co., MN	Mark H. Hagen	Mark H. Hagen	1974	1186
200 3/8	25 4/8	27	19 1/8	6 4/8	5 4/8	10	10	Tuscarawas Co., OH	Michael D. Korns, Sr.	Michael D. Korns, Sr.	1978	1186
200 3/8	27	23 1/8	24 5/8	5 2/8	5	8	7	Knox Co., OH	Albert Hall	Albert Hall	1983	1186
200 3/8	25	26 2/8	17 4/8	4 6/8	4 7/8	11	10	Nez Perce Co., ID	Tim C. Baldwin	Tim C. Baldwin	1987	1186
200 3/8	25 2/8	22 1/8	21 4/8	5 1/8	5 2/8	9	11	Fremont Co., WY	Wallace M. Oldman	Wallace M. Oldman	1989	1186
200 3/8	25 3/8	27 2/8	20 4/8	5 3/8	5 5/8	6	6	Logan Co., CO	Picked Up	Dennis D. Reid	1994	1186
200 3/8	25 6/8	25 7/8	20 3/8	4 4/8	4 5/8	8	8	Branch Co., MO	Mitchell S. Brock	Mitchell S. Brock	1995	1186
200 3/8	29 1/8	29 6/8	21 3/8	5 4/8	5 6/8	7	8	Marion Co., IA	Louis L. Floden	Louis L. Floden	1996	1186
200 3/8	20 1/8	21 4/8	13 4/8	4 6/8	4 4/8	13	11	Powder River Co., MT	Levi Mitchell	Levi Mitchell	1996	1186
200 2/8	24 7/8	25	21 5/8	5 3/8	4 7/8	11	10	Swift Co., MN	George Piotter	George Piotter	1983	1196
200 2/8	26 2/8	26	19	5	5 2/8	13	14	Delaware Co., OH	Franklin D. Ronk	Franklin D. Ronk	1990	1196

Score	Length R	Length L	Spread	Circ.	Circ.	Pts R	Pts L	Locality	Owner	Hunter	Date	Rank
200 2/8	26 7/8	27 4/8	20 2/8	5 5/8	5 5/8	8	8	Wyandot Co., OH	Anthony Gentile	Anthony Gentile	1991	1196
200 2/8	26 4/8	26 2/8	25	4 5/8	4 4/8	9	9	Live Oak Co., TX	E.W. Douglass	E.W. Douglass	1993	1196
200 2/8	24 4/8	24 5/8	19 5/8	4 5/8	4 4/8	12	11	Koochiching Co., MN	Jack Karsnia	Jack Karsnia	1994	1196
200 1/8	27	26 4/8	21 7/8	5 6/8	5 5/8	9	9	Itasca Co., MN	Clyde Sucher	James Davidson	1926	1201
200 1/8	26	24 2/8	23	6	6	9	12	Parrsboro, NS	Allison Smith	Edward B. Shaw	1960	1201
200 1/8	27 3/8	26 6/8	21 2/8	4 7/8	5 1/8	11	12	Kandiyohi Co., MN	Robert J. Custer	Robert J. Custer	1966	1201
200 1/8	24 3/8	24 5/8	20 4/8	5	5	9	8	Blaine Co., NE	Pauline C. Sander	Pauline C. Sander	1983	1201
200 1/8	24 3/8	25 4/8	18 2/8	5 1/8	5 2/8	12	7	Dallas Co., AL	H. Lloyd Morris	H. Lloyd Morris	1989	1201
200 1/8	27 1/8	27 4/8	23	6 2/8	6 4/8	7	11	Smoky Lake, AB	Brent Weber	Brent Weber	1991	1201
200 1/8	23 5/8	24 1/8	17	5 6/8	5 5/8	10	8	Parke Co., IN	Chris Ebersole	Chris Ebersole	1992	1201
200 1/8	25 4/8	26 3/8	20 3/8	5 3/8	5 2/8	8	8	Indian Lake, SK	Glen Lantz	Glen Lantz	1992	1201
200 1/8	25	28 3/8	23 5/8	5 4/8	5 3/8	9	9	Macoupin Co., IL	John M. Ragusa	John M. Ragusa	1992	1201
200 1/8	26 3/8	26 7/8	20 7/8	5 1/8	5 2/8	11	9	St. Louis Co., MN	Picked Up	John R. Steffes, Sr.	1992	1201
200 1/8	28 5/8	27	19 3/8	5 3/8	5 1/8	12	7	Ogle Co., IL	Theodore H. Hysell	Theodore H. Hysell	1993	1201
200 1/8	31	30	22 2/8	4 5/8	4 6/8	8	9	Coshocton Co., OH	Edward J. Page	Edward J. Page	1993	1201
200 1/8	26 2/8	24 4/8	19 3/8	4 6/8	4 6/8	10	13	Holt Co., MO	Bruce Copsey	Bruce Copsey	1994	1201
200	29 5/8	29	18 5/8	5 4/8	5 3/8	11	7	Dallas Co., IA	Andy J. Lounsbury	Andy J. Lounsbury	1996	1215
200	25 1/8	25 4/8	18 4/8	4 7/8	4 5/8	12	10	Outlook, SK	Earl B. Schmitt	Earl B. Schmitt	1966	1215
200	26 2/8	25 2/8	21 7/8	5 7/8	5 4/8	6	12	Todd Co., MN	James J. Carr	James J. Carr	1978	1215
200	19 5/8	18 1/8	17 1/8	5 1/8	4 7/8	11	11	Crook Co., WY	Ralph R. Van Beck	Ralph R. Van Beck	1989	1215
200	27	25 6/8	22 3/8	5 2/8	5 4/8	12	10	Boone Co., IN	John E. Wright	John E. Wright	1989	1215
200	24 6/8	25	20 5/8	5 4/8	5 4/8	10	9	Monona Co., IA	Picked Up	Timothy C. Ashley	PR 1990	1215
200	25 5/8	25 5/8	18 2/8	4 6/8	4 6/8	7	8	Stearns Co., MN	David L. LaVoi	David L. LaVoi	1990	1215
200	22 5/8	18 7/8	20 1/8	5 5/8	5 5/8	8	12	Stevens Co., WA	Ronald F. Barber	Ronald F. Barber	1991	1215
199 7/8	24 1/8	23 2/8	19	4 6/8	4 6/8	6	6	Queens Lake, NB	George Lacey	Wendell Lacey	1915	1222
199 7/8	20 1/8	20 7/8	14	5	5 1/8	7	10	Hickory Co., MO	Darwin L. Stogsdill	Darwin L. Stogsdill	1971	1222
199 7/8	28 1/8	28 5/8	19 1/8	6	6	14	8	Peesane, SK	Pete Prosofsky	Pete Prosofsky	1982	1222
199 7/8	29 4/8	28 4/8	18 2/8	5 1/8	5 3/8	8	10	Cheyenne Co., KS	Picked Up	William H. Lilienthal	1986	1222
199 7/8	27	26 5/8	19 7/8	5	5 1/8	10	11	Knox Co., IL	Rodney G. Eklund	Rodney G. Eklund	1990	1222
199 6/8	28 6/8	26 5/8	19 2/8	6	6 4/8	9	8	Meigs Co., OH	Cody R. Boothe	Cody R. Boothe	1970	1227
199 6/8	26 5/8	27 2/8	18 5/8	4 2/8	5 2/8	7	7	Harris Co., GA	Kenneth H. Brown	Kenneth H. Brown	1974	1227
199 6/8	23 2/8	24	17 4/8	5 3/8	5 1/8	9	9	Rochester, AB	James Weismantel	James Weismantel	1979	1227
199 6/8	23 3/8	22 4/8	15 5/8	6	6 3/8	8	13	Duck Mt., MB	Picked Up	Jim Whitt	PR 1986	1227
199 6/8	25 2/8	24 7/8	27	5 2/8	5 3/8	13	11	Musquodoboit River, NS	David W. Brown	David W. Brown	1993	1227
199 6/8	24 6/8	27 5/8	22 5/8	9 6/8	9 6/8	9	10	Edgar Co., IL	Brad Davis	Brad Davis	1996	1227
199 6/8	24 2/8	26 2/8	20 2/8	4 5/8	4 6/8	10	9	Crawford Co., IL	John M. Kane	John M. Kane	1996	1227
199 5/8	24 7/8	23 5/8	21 2/8	5 7/8	5 7/8	9	7	Baraga Co., MI	William Simula	William Simula	1925	1234
199 5/8	29	27 7/8	19 4/8	6 3/8	6 1/8	8	6	Jefferson Co., WI	Jerome Stockheimer	Jerome Stockheimer	1968	1234
199 5/8	27 4/8	27 5/8	20 7/8	4 6/8	4 5/8	9	11	Hopkins Co., KY	Dwight L. Mason	Dwight L. Mason	1979	1234
199 5/8	25 2/8	22	18 4/8	6 2/8	6 4/8	8	12	Clinton Co., IA	Arlo Ketelsen	Arlo Ketelsen	1985	1234
199 5/8	27 7/8	27 3/8	23 2/8	5 4/8	5 4/8	8	8	Labette Co., KS	John L. Bryant	John L. Bryant	1987	1234
199 5/8	30 1/8	29 6/8	20 4/8	4 7/8	5 2/8	10	10	Hopkins Co., KY	Picked Up	James D. Spurlock	1988	1234
199 5/8	25 6/8	25 1/8	24 6/8	5 1/8	5	8	7	Pend Oreille Co., WA	John C. Kroker	John C. Kroker	1989	1234
199 5/8	24 6/8	27 6/8	19 4/8	4 3/8	4 5/8	10	12	Dimmit Co., TX	John T. Brannan III	John T. Brannan III	1992	1234
199 4/8	29 1/8	29 3/8	19 3/8	5 6/8	5 3/8	7	9	Jackson Co., OH	Jerry W. Butcher	Jerry W. Butcher	1992	1234
199 4/8	25 7/8	26 1/8	19 7/8	7 2/8	6 4/8	10	20	Gregory Co., SD	Fred Gnirk	Adeline Gnirk	1958	1243
199 4/8	25 2/8	25 2/8	20 6/8	5 4/8	5 1/8	8	8	Aitkin Co., MN	Sanford Patrick	Sanford Patrick	1963	1243

WHITETAIL DEER - NON-TYPICAL ANTLERS

Odocoileus virginianus virginianus and certain related subspecies

Score	Length of Main Beam R	L	Inside Spread	Circumference at Smallest Place Between Burr and First Point R	L	Number of Points R	L	Locality	Hunter	Owner	Date Killed	Rank
199 4/8	23 6/8	23 5/8	17 6/8	5 4/8	5 4/8	10	10	Flathead Co., MT	Unknown	Tom Williams	PR 1980	1243
199 4/8	26 2/8	25 4/8	17 5/8	5	5 1/8	13	11	St. Francois Co., MO	Henry A. Hull	Henry A. Hull	1984	1243
199 4/8	27 5/8	28	22 2/8	5 4/8	5 3/8	8	8	Linn Co., IA	Don J. Jilovec	Don J. Jilovec	1988	1243
199 4/8	28 4/8	28 3/8	21 6/8	5 1/8	5 1/8	10	6	Sangamon Co., IL	Kenneth J. Barlow	Kenneth J. Barlow	1991	1243
199 4/8	26 2/8	27 2/8	22 4/8	5 1/8	5	9	15	Cross Co., AR	Picked Up	William Loyd, Jr.	1992	1243
199 3/8	27 2/8	28	20 4/8	6 1/8	5 4/8	8	9	Chisago Co., MN	Helmer Benson	Jeff Benson	1965	1250
199 3/8	28	26 4/8	21 6/8	5 6/8	5 6/8	10	8	Clark Co., MO	Bob Arnold	Bob Arnold	1973	1250
199 3/8	22 7/8	22 3/8	20 1/8	6	6	11	9	Morgan Co., IL	David W. Roehrs	David W. Roehrs	1979	1250
199 3/8	20	17 1/8	18 5/8	4 7/8	4 5/8	17	12	Van Buren Co., MI	Michael A. DeRosa	Michael A. DeRosa	1989	1250
199 3/8	27 1/8	24 7/8	21 2/8	4 5/8	4 7/8	10	7	Iowa	Unknown	Charles E. Matthiesen	PR 1995	1250
199 2/8	24 6/8	25 4/8	14	5 2/8	5 1/8	13	9	Richland Co., MT	Aron Schmierer	Raymond Schmierer	1952	1255
199 2/8	21 4/8	21 5/8	20 6/8	5 6/8	5 6/8	8	8	Jasmin, SK	Richard Gill	Richard Gill	1958	1255
199 2/8	29 1/8	28 1/8	21 3/8	5	5	7	8	Todd Co., MN	Wayne V. Jensen	Wayne V. Jensen	1965	1255
199 2/8	28 7/8	27 3/8	23 5/8	5 2/8	5 2/8	7	9	Winston Co., AL	James W. Huckbay	James W. Huckbay	1973	1255
199 2/8	27 7/8	26 7/8	24 7/8	5 4/8	5 5/8	9	9	Delta Co., MI	Derwood Moore	Michael Waldvogel	1977	1255
199 2/8	28 3/8	28	18 5/8	6 3/8	6 3/8	8	8	Fountain Co., IN	Ken S. Harmeson	Ken S. Harmeson	1989	1255
199 2/8	26 3/8	25 5/8	19 7/8	5	4 7/8	8	10	Trigg Co., KY	Picked Up	Michael Shelton	1990	1255
199 1/8	26 3/8	26	24 1/8	5 4/8	5 2/8	11	11	Meade Co., SD	Donald Trohkimoinen	Donald Trohkimoinen	1966	1262
199 1/8	21 7/8	24 6/8	20	4 6/8	4 7/8	12	10	Clinton Co., NY	Unknown	William F. Mathieson	PR 1971	1262
199 1/8	25 2/8	25 7/8	17 4/8	5 1/8	5 2/8	10	13	St. Louis Co., MN	Orville Schultz	Orville Schultz	1978	1262
199 1/8	28 3/8	26 6/8	21 3/8	6	5 7/8	10	8	Macoupin Co., IL	Jerry A. Dittmer	Jerry A. Dittmer	1994	1262
199	22 7/8	21	17 7/8	5 3/8	5	13	7	Clark Co., WI	George Mashin	Douglas Wampole	1946	1266
199	23 2/8	22 4/8	15 2/8	5	5	10	9	Harrison Co., IA	Chester R. Hilton	Chester R. Hilton	1958	1266
199	25 1/8	26	19 2/8	5 6/8	5 5/8	9	6	Grattan Creek, AB	Torleif A. Larson	Torleif A. Larson	1968	1266
199	24 2/8	24 7/8	19 4/8	5	5 1/8	13	8	Penobscot Co., ME	Picked Up	Todd Africano	1971	1266
199	25	24 6/8	16 3/8	5 3/8	5 6/8	9	8	Cottonwood Co., MN	Lane L. Horn	Lane L. Horn	1972	1266
199	27 6/8	27 1/8	22 3/8	5 2/8	5 3/8	8	8	Adams Co., IL	Jerry Schaller	Jerry Schaller	1974	1266
199	26 3/8	25	19 1/8	5 1/8	5	10	8	Yellow Medicine Co., MN	William A. Botten	William A. Botten	1976	1266
199	26 1/8	26 3/8	19 6/8	5 4/8	5 4/8	10	8	Jackson Co., IA	John T. Kremer	John T. Kremer	1983	1266
199	24 7/8	27 2/8	19 7/8	5	5	8	7	Westaskiwin, AB	John Miller	John Miller	1984	1266
199	23 7/8	23 7/8	18	4 4/8	4 3/8	8	9	Crawford Co., WI	Jeff Sheckler	Jeff Sheckler	1989	1266
199	29 6/8	28 4/8	20	6 6/8	7	8	10	Lake Co., IL	Steven Hysell	Steven Hysell	1994	1266
199	26 1/8	25 7/8	19 7/8	4 4/8	4 5/8	6	8	Vernon Co., WI	Manuel M. Bahr	Manuel M. Bahr	1995	1266
199	27 7/8	27 2/8	18 4/8	4 6/8	5	7	7	Macoupin Co., IL	Jon D. DeNeef	Jon D. DeNeef	1995	1266
199	24 4/8	26	20	5	5 1/8	9	9	Harrison Co., IN	Timothy P. Uhl	Timothy P. Uhl	1995	1266
199	28 4/8	26 2/8	26 3/8	4 7/8	4 7/8	6	9	La Salle Co., IL	Hank J. Walsh III	Hank J. Walsh III	1995	1266

Score	Main Beam R	Main Beam L	Inside Spread	Circ. R	Circ. L	Points R	Points L	Locality	Hunter	Owner	Date Killed	Rank
198 7/8	24 4/8	28 3/8	24 7/8	6 4/8	7 3/8	7	9	Unknown	Unknown	Max E. Chittick	1900	1281
198 7/8	25	23 2/8	16 5/8	5 1/8	5 1/8	11	11		G. Huls & B.L. Arfmann	Chester S. Jones	1973	1281
198 7/8	26 7/8	25 6/8	21 4/8	5 4/8	5 2/8	10	7	Weston Co., WY	Ray N. Strand	Ray N. Strand	1976	1281
198 7/8	29 2/8	28 3/8	24 6/8	5 4/8	4 7/8	8	7	Chippewa Co., MN	William L. Wagner	William L. Wagner	1982	1281
198 7/8	24	25 2/8	22 3/8	5 4/8	5 6/8	11	13	Ripley Co., IN	Leo M. Schmaus	Leo M. Schmaus	1985	1281
198 7/8	27	26 7/8	17 7/8	4 6/8	4 6/8	7	7	Morse River, AB	Oscar Howard	Oscar Howard	1989	1281
198 7/8	24 2/8	24 3/8	18 2/8	6 2/8	6 2/8	5	5	Logan Co., KY	Thomas Free	Thomas Free	1992	1281
198 7/8	28 5/8	28 4/8	21 1/8	6 2/8	6 2/8	13	5	Pembina River, AB	Picked Up	Michael W. Welker	1992	1281
198 7/8	25 4/8	28 1/8	18 4/8	4 7/8	5 2/8	10	10	Bollinger Co., MO	James M. Bowker	James M. Bowker	1995	1281
198 7/8	25 6/8	25 1/8	20 3/8	5 6/8	5 6/8	9	11	Greene Co., IL	Kenneth L. Harmon	Kenneth L. Harmon	1995	1281
198 6/8	25 4/8	25 4/8	18 4/8	5 4/8	5 2/8	9	11	Richardson Co., NE	John Baker	Don Anderson	1910	1291
198 6/8	28 4/8	28 4/8	21 4/8	5 4/8	4 3/8	7	9	Aitkin Co., MN	Unknown	George W. Flaim	1965	1291
198 6/8	29 7/8	27 1/8	15 7/8	5 3/8	5 3/8	11	5	Crow Wing Co., MN	Phillip S. Hansen	Phillip S. Hansen	1973	1291
198 6/8	24 6/8	25 3/8	24	5 7/8	6 2/8	5	9	Fillmore Co., MN	Gerald K. Sorenson	Gerald K. Sorenson	1977	1291
198 6/8	28 6/8	28 4/8	23 2/8	5 7/8	5 6/8	9	8	Lake of the Woods Co., MN	Thomas K. Ernst	Thomas K. Ernst	1978	1291
198 6/8	25 1/8	27 4/8	15 4/8	5	5 4/8	13	8	Gallatin Co., KY	Rod Buck	Rod Buck	1984	1291
198 6/8	26 4/8	25 2/8	17 3/8	6 1/8	5 3/8	10	8	Buffalo Co., WI	Hans Van Vlaanderen	Hans Van Vlaanderen	1986	1291
198 6/8	25 4/8	24 7/8	19 2/8	6 2/8	6	11	8	James River, AB	Picked Up	Chris K. Foster	1989	1291
198 6/8	25 5/8	24 7/8	19 3/8	4 7/8	4 7/8	10	11	Rappahannock Co., VA	Roger Woodcock	Wayne Perry	1989	1291
198 6/8	22 5/8	24 5/8	15	6 5/8	5 5/8	7	7	Jefferson Co., WI	John A. Brown	Roger Woodcock	1989	1291
198 6/8	23 7/8	23 7/8	19 6/8	4 4/8	4 2/8	9	7	Peoria Co., IL	Brady Weiss	John A. Brown	1992	1291
198 6/8	26 5/8	26 3/8	20	5 6/8	5 4/8	11	15	Randolph Co., IL	Robert D. Adamson	Brady Weiss	1993	1291
198 6/8	28 3/8	27 4/8	23 4/8	6 1/8	6 2/8	6	13	Buffalo Co., WI	Unknown	Robert D. Adamson	1995	1291
198 5/8	24 3/8	24 2/8	17 7/8	5 4/8	6 4/8	8	11	Rock Co., WI	Eino Macki	Harold Burrows	PR 1920	1304
198 5/8	26 7/8	26 1/8	18 3/8	5 4/8	5 5/8	9	7	Hayward, WI	Raymond Cowan	Bass Pro Shops F. & W. Mus.	1930	1304
198 5/8	26 4/8	27 5/8	22 2/8	6 7/8	5 5/8	10	6	Iron Co., MI	Larry Bickham	Raymond Cowan	1961	1304
198 5/8	26 1/8	26 1/8	22 4/8	5	4 7/8	8	7	Concordia Parish, LA	Stanley Elam	Larry Bickham	1962	1304
198 5/8	26 2/8	26 6/8	17 4/8	5 2/8	5 4/8	9	6	Webb Co., TX	Paul M. Krueger	Stanley Elam	1962	1304
198 5/8	25 3/8	25 2/8	23 2/8	5	5	8	12	Jackson Co., OH	William H. Rutledge	Paul M. Krueger	1977	1304
198 5/8	23 6/8	22 2/8	22 4/8	4 6/8	5	9	9	Will Co., IL	Thomas D. Flannigan	William H. Rutledge	1977	1304
198 5/8	25 5/8	25 6/8	21 3/8	5 5/8	5 7/8	7	8	Hamilton Co., IL	Freddie Cooper	Thomas D. Flannigan	1989	1304
198 5/8	28 5/8	27 2/8	22 1/8	5 5/8	6 2/8	12	9	Franklin Co., IL	Philip D. Springer	Freddie Cooper	1990	1304
198 5/8	22	22	20 2/8	4 6/8	4 5/8	7	14	Dawsons Creek, BC	Picked Up	Philip D. Springer	1990	1304
198 5/8	25 4/8	23 5/8	18 2/8	6 3/8	6 2/8	12	9	Pleasantdale, SK	Roger A. LeBrun	Don Kjelshus	PR 1992	1304
198 5/8	24 3/8	22 5/8	21 3/8	5 7/8	5 7/8	6	9	Otter Tail Co., MN	George W. Flaim	Roger A. LeBrun	1992	1304
198 4/8	27 3/8	27	22 2/8	5 3/8	5 1/8	11	8	Kanabec Co., MN	Unknown	George W. Flaim	1927	1316
198 4/8	25 2/8	25 6/8	19 2/8	4 6/8	4 6/8	10	9	Cheboygan Co., MI	Maurice G. Fullerton	Robert G. Fullerton	1943	1316
198 4/8	26 4/8	22 5/8	18 7/8	5 6/8	5 5/8	9	12	Clay Co., MN	F.W. Kolle	Kolle Farms, Inc.	1946	1316
198 4/8	26	26	21	4 4/8	4 4/8	12	9	Forest Co., WI	John Lehner	Eric Lehner	1946	1316
198 4/8	24 2/8	23 1/8	18	5 2/8	5 4/8	9	8	Cow Creek, WY	Thelma Martens	Thelma Martens	1951	1316
198 4/8	24	23 5/8	19	5 5/8	5 6/8	8	8	Itasca Co., MN	Wayne W. Blesi, Jr.	Wayne W. Blesi, Jr.	1968	1316
198 4/8	23 7/8	23 7/8	17 1/8	4 6/8	4 7/8	9	10	Iroquois Co., IL	Charles E. Crow	Charles E. Crow	1974	1316
198 4/8	26 2/8	24 2/8	21 5/8	4 7/8	4 6/8	8	9	Lincoln Co., MN	Dennis G. Geiken	Dennis G. Geiken	1980	1316
198 4/8	28 1/8	28 1/8	19 7/8	4 6/8	4 6/8	10	12	Madison Co., IA	Elvin H. Dickinson	Elvin H. Dickinson	1982	1316
198 4/8	22 6/8	27 3/8	21 1/8	5 2/8	4 5/8	9	7	Wheeler Co., GA	David Frost	David Frost	1982	1316
198 4/8	25	26 2/8	23 5/8	4 6/8	4 6/8	12	8	Webb Co., TX	Alvin C. Santleben, Jr.	Alvin C. Santleben, Jr.	1983	1316
198 4/8	26 1/8	26 2/8	22 5/8	6	5 4/8	8	8	Perry Co., OH	Donald J. Griggs	Donald J. Griggs	1988	1316

WHITETAIL DEER - NON-TYPICAL ANTLERS

Odocoileus virginianus virginianus and certain related subspecies

Score	Length of Main Beam R	L	Inside Spread	Circumference at Smallest Place Between Burr and First Point R	L	Number of Points R	L	Locality	Hunter	Owner	Date Killed	Rank
198 4/8	26 3/8	26 6/8	19 7/8	4 6/8	4 4/8	10	9	Arborfield, SK	Terry G. Haugo	Terry G. Haugo	1989	1316
198 4/8	24	23 7/8	21 2/8	4 5/8	4 3/8		7	Lake Co., MT	Mike Gouge	Jim G. Ferguson III	1990	1316
198 4/8	22 3/8	17 4/8	13 6/8	5 2/8	5 1/8	15	14	Hamilton Co., TX	Randy L. Wright	Randy L. Wright	1992	1316
198 4/8	21 6/8	25 2/8	15	7 2/8	7	13	8	Adams Co., IL	Rick L. Dormire	Rick L. Dormire	1993	1316
198 4/8	26 5/8	26 4/8	20 5/8	5 5/8	5 4/8	7	10	Meacham, SK	Darren B. Maroniuk	Darren B. Maroniuk	1993	1316
198 4/8	26 7/8	28 1/8	19 2/8	5 2/8	5 1/8	8	10	Wallace Co., KS	Kent E. Rains	Kent E. Rains	1993	1316
198 3/8	25 7/8	27	20 3/8	5	5 1/8	9	9	Uvalde Co., TX	George Judson, Jr.	George Judson, Jr.	1958	1334
198 3/8	25 7/8	26 6/8	19 5/8	4 6/8	5	9	9	Rappahannock Co., VA	Collis W. Dodson, Jr.	Collis W. Dodson, Jr.	1966	1334
198 3/8	26 2/8	26 1/8	17 5/8	4 2/8	4 2/8	8	10	Montgomery Co., TN	Clarence McElhaney	Clarence McElhaney	1978	1334
198 3/8	25	24 5/8	22 4/8	5 2/8	5 1/8	8	9	Adams Co., IL	Eldie J. Miller	Eldie J. Miller	1980	1334
198 3/8	27	25 6/8	21 6/8	5	4 7/8	10	9	Clark's Brook, NB	Bernard V. Sharp	Bernard V. Sharp	1985	1334
198 3/8	23 6/8	23 3/8	19 7/8	5 2/8	5 2/8	9	7	Pottawattamie Co., IA	Rodney P. Stahlnecker	Rodney P. Stahlnecker	1991	1334
198 3/8	25 3/8	24 4/8	18 1/8	5 2/8	5	7	10	Pike Lake, SK	Robert J. MacDonald	Robert J. MacDonald	1992	1334
198 2/8	23 3/8	22 5/8	21 6/8	5	5	9	12	Crow Wing Co., MN	Harold B. Stotts	Harold B. Stotts	1941	1341
198 2/8	23 5/8	23 1/8	19 4/8	5 7/8	5 7/8	8	8	Rock Co., NE	Gerald M. Lewis	Gerald M. Lewis	1966	1341
198 2/8	27 3/8	27 4/8	22 2/8	6 1/8	6 3/8	5	8	Unknown	Unknown	John L. Stein	PR 1968	1341
198 2/8	27	26 2/8	21	4 7/8	4 5/8	8	9	Cass Co., MN	Timothy L. Anderson	Timothy L. Anderson	1987	1341
198 2/8	26 4/8	26 6/8	17 6/8	4 6/8	5 1/8	7		Madison Co., IA	Dan L. Bush	Dan L. Bush	1987	1341
198 2/8	24 6/8	24 6/8	16 3/8	5 4/8	5 7/8	10	15	Rock Co., NE	Picked Up	Dan L. Sandall	1987	1341
198 2/8	26 7/8	26 5/8	19 7/8	5	5 2/8	9	8	Decatur Co., IA	Julian J. Toney	Julian J. Toney	1991	1341
198 2/8	25 2/8	25	16 5/8	5 1/8	5 2/8	12	9	Osage Co., KS	Jerry L. Sand	Jerry L. Sand	1992	1341
198 2/8	25 4/8	26 1/8	21 6/8	6	6 2/8	12	11	Wayne Co., IA	Dan L. Bishop	Dan L. Bishop	1993	1341
198 2/8	25 4/8	24 7/8	20 6/8	4 6/8	5	9	8	Rochester, AB	Vern E. Alton	Vern E. Alton	1995	1341
198 1/8	21 7/8	21 2/8	17	4 7/8	5	13	12	Nelway, BC	Edward John	Edward John	1935	1351
198 1/8	27 6/8	28 2/8	22 4/8	4 6/8	4 6/8	7		Harrison Co., OH	Roy Hines	Roy Hines	1959	1351
198 1/8	25 3/8	25	23	5 1/8	5 2/8	10	10	Koochiching Co., MN	Maris Stolcers	Maris Stolcers	1963	1351
198 1/8	27	26 3/8	20 2/8	5	5 1/8	10	7	Hocking Co., OH	Hugh Cox	Hugh Cox	1964	1351
198 1/8	24 6/8	24 3/8	19 6/8	5 5/8	5 4/8	10	9	Kootenai Co., ID	Frank J. Cheney	ID Dept. Fish & Game	1967	1351
198 1/8	26 3/8	26 6/8	22 6/8	5 3/8	5 4/8	12	10	Iron Co., WI	Ben Benzine	Timothy C. Ashley	1968	1351
198 1/8	25 6/8	26 2/8	20 2/8	4 6/8	4 6/8	10	6	Carrot River, SK	Wayne W. Karlin	Wayne W. Karlin	1989	1351
198 1/8	25	24 1/8	24 4/8	5 3/8	5 5/8	6	6	Unknown	Unknown	Rick Stover	PR 1990	1351
198 1/8	26 3/8	28 6/8	22 5/8	5 4/8	5 6/8	8	10	Lawrence Co., OH	Eugene Baisden	Eugene Baisden	1991	1351
198 1/8	30 1/8	29 5/8	22 4/8	4 6/8	4 3/8	8	8	Jefferson Co., OH	William H. Ferguson III	William H. Ferguson III	1992	1351
198 1/8	22 3/8	21 6/8	18	5	4 6/8	9	12	Calhoun Co., MI	William D. Vickers	William D. Vickers	1994	1351
198 1/8	29	28 5/8	18 5/8	5	5 2/8	12	13	Itasca Co., MN	Dennis C. Campbell	Dennis C. Campbell	1995	1351
198 1/8	28 3/8	26 5/8	20 5/8	5 4/8	5 5/8	10	14	Chippewa Co., MI	Timothy Spence	Timothy Spence	1995	1351

Score	R. Main Beam	L. Main Beam	Inside Spread	Circ.	Circ.	Points R	Points L	Locality	Hunter	Owner	Date Killed	Rank
198	26 1/8	24 4/8	23	7 4/8	6 2/8	9	7	Valley, NE	Ivan Masher	Ivan Masher	1961	1364
198	25 5/8	25 2/8	17 5/8	6 2/8	6 4/8	9	10	Osage Co., KS	Joe A. Rose, Jr.	Joe A. Rose, Jr.	1977	1364
198	25 7/8	23 4/8	17 5/8	5	5	8	8	Assiniboine River, MB	James A. Roberts	James A. Roberts	1980	1364
198	27 6/8	27 3/8	21 4/8	5 2/8	5 3/8	6	9	Louisa Co., IA	William H. Lilienthal	Larry Soteros	1981	1364
198	28 6/8	27 3/8	21 7/8	5 6/8	5 3/8	8	10	Christian Co., IL	Jack B. Hartwig	Jack B. Hartwig	1987	1364
198	28 3/8	26 2/8	18 3/8	5	4 6/8	9	10	Edgar Co., IL	Aaron C. Bishop	Aaron C. Bishop	1990	1364
198	26	26 2/8	20	5 6/8	5 7/8	7	11	McLeod Co., MN	Owen L. Knacke	Owen L. Knacke	1990	1364
198	27	27 4/8	20 4/8	5	5 1/8	10	9	Jo Daviess Co., IL	Victor W. Rogers	Victor W. Rogers	1990	1364
198	25 4/8	22 3/8	20 5/8	5 4/8	6 2/8	9	12	Kipling, SK	Robert Lyons	Robert Lyons	1993	1364
198	24 3/8	24 1/8	13 5/8	4 2/8	5 2/8	11	9	Brown Co., SD	Paul J. Hill	Paul J. Hill	1994	1364
197 7/8	25 4/8	25	18 1/8	4 7/8	5 4/8	10	12	Clearwater Co., MN	Danny L. Cole	Unknown	PR 1975	1374
197 7/8	27 4/8	27 1/8	25	5 3/8	5	9	9	Cheyenne Co., NE	Reid Block	Reid Block	1984	1374
197 7/8	24 4/8	24 4/8	17 2/8	5 1/8	5	9	10	Keokuk Co., IA	Bradley J. Messenger	Bradley J. Messenger	1988	1374
197 7/8	25	25	25 1/8	5 2/8	5 4/8	12	11	St. John River, NB	James A. Perruso	James A. Perruso	1988	1374
197 7/8	24 7/8	25 5/8	19 6/8	5 6/8	5	10	9	Riley Co., KS	Gary L. Schroller	Gary L. Schroller	1990	1374
197 7/8	26 5/8	24 6/8	23 2/8	6	6	7	9	Eagle Creek, SK	Preston Haanen	Preston Haanen	1992	1374
197 7/8	22 2/8	25 5/8	22 2/8	5 1/8	5 1/8	8	12	Latah Co., ID	Dean C. Weyen	Dean C. Weyen	1992	1374
197 7/8	22 5/8	23	19 2/8	4 7/8	4 7/8	10	10	Cross Co., AR	Jimmy W. Rhodes	Picked Up	1993	1374
197 7/8	23 7/8	25 7/8	25 7/8	4 2/8	4 3/8	8	13	Hunt Co., TX	Wade Grimes	Wade Grimes	1994	1374
197 7/8	24 6/8	22 5/8	18	5 2/8	5	11	11	Great Sand Hills, SK	Craig Schwengler	Craig Schwengler	1996	1374
197 6/8	23 5/8	25 1/8	16 2/8	4 5/8	5	10	8	Hunters, WA	Rachel Mally	Rachel Mally	1961	1384
197 6/8	25 6/8	26 2/8	20 2/8	4 7/8	5 4/8	9	11	Riceville, MT	James R. Eastman	James R. Eastman	1965	1384
197 6/8	24	26 4/8	17	5 3/8	4 4/8	10	7	Langham, SK	Leonard Waldner	Leonard Waldner	1967	1384
197 6/8	24 5/8	24 4/8	18 4/8	4 4/8	4 2/8	11	9	Prowers Co., CO	Samuel S. Pattillo	Samuel S. Pattillo	1988	1384
197 6/8	26	24 6/8	13 4/8	4 2/8	4 7/8	7	5	Box Elder Creek, SK	David A. Thomson	David A. Thomson	1991	1384
197 6/8	24 3/8	26 1/8	19 3/8	4 7/8	4 6/8	12	10	York Co., PA	Kevin R. Brumgard	Kevin R. Brumgard	1992	1384
197 6/8	26 7/8	26 5/8	16	4 6/8	4 4/8	8	12	Edmonson Co., KY	Rex Hurt	Picked Up	1992	1384
197 6/8	26 2/8	27 7/8	16 6/8	4 4/8	4 4/8	8	9	Dimmit Co., TX	Michael H. Oldfather	Michael H. Oldfather	1992	1384
197 6/8	23 6/8	25 2/8	19 4/8	5 5/8	5 3/8	8	8	Spy Hill, SK	William Gilchuk	William Gilchuk	1996	1384
197 5/8	20	23 5/8	20 6/8	4 7/8	5 3/8	9	10	Luce Co., MI	Jim Deavereaux	Sid Jones	1917	1393
197 5/8	22 7/8	24	18	4 6/8	4 6/8	11	8	Sawyer Co., WI	Brant J. Mueller	Unknown	1940	1393
197 5/8	24 4/8	28 2/8	17 7/8	5 1/8	5 1/8	7	11	Sawyer Co., WI	James Borman	James Borman	1945	1393
197 5/8	23 3/8	24 6/8	20 3/8	5 7/8	5 6/8	10	9	Marathon Co., WI	Todd Rheinschmidt	Boots Greiner	1951	1393
197 5/8	31 5/8	24	15 6/8	5 1/8	5 1/8	5	6	Geauga Co., OH	Edward Dooner	Edward Dooner	1956	1393
197 5/8	24	28	25 2/8	5 2/8	4 6/8	11	9	Pennington Co., SD	Dick Rossum	Lynn Williams	1958	1393
197 5/8	28	27 3/8	21	4 6/8	5	8	8	Jo Daviess Co., IL	David H. Carpenter	David H. Carpenter	1962	1393
197 5/8	25 1/8	25 2/8	22 4/8	5 7/8	5	9	9	Blue Earth Co., MN	Daniel R. Nelson	Daniel R. Nelson	1981	1393
197 5/8	26 5/8	25 5/8	20 5/8	5 4/8	5	8	11	Monona Co., IA	Larry Koch	Picked Up	1987	1393
197 5/8	28	28	21 5/8	5 5/8	5	9	8	Adams Co., IL	Daniel J. Schlosser	Daniel J. Schlosser	1987	1393
197 5/8	28 4/8	29 3/8	22 5/8	5 1/8	5	10	7	Stephenson Co., IL	Richard M. Keller	Richard M. Keller	1988	1393
197 5/8	28 2/8	28 2/8	19	5 3/8	5	7	9	Thurston Co., NE	Rudy Reichelt	Picked Up	1989	1393
197 5/8	24 7/8	25 1/8	16 7/8	4 5/8	4 7/8	7	7	McDonough Co., IL	Jeffrey W. Foxall	Jeffrey W. Foxall	1990	1393
197 5/8	26	26 5/8	21 5/8	5 6/8	5 4/8	10	9	Morris Co., KS	John H. Payne	John H. Payne	1992	1393
197 5/8	26 5/8	27	20 5/8	5 2/8	5 2/8	10	8	Pierce Co., WI	Marilyn Wilkinson	Charles L. Wilkinson	1993	1393
197 5/8	24	24 6/8	16 4/8	4 7/8	5 1/8	9	8	Monroe Co., IA	Raymond F. Hinkel	Raymond F. Hinkel	1995	1393
197 4/8	25 6/8	25 6/8	25	5 4/8	5	10	9	Pope Co., IL	Joe C. Schwegman	Joe C. Schwegman	1961	1409
197 4/8	26 4/8	26 4/8	25 5/8	5	5	11	7	Wainwright, AB	George Bauman	George Bauman	1967	1409

Odocoileus virginianus virginianus and certain related subspecies

Score	Length of Main Beam R	L	Inside Spread	Circumference at Smallest Place Between Burr and First Point R	L	Number of Points R	L	Locality	Hunter	Owner	Date Killed	Rank
197 4/8	25	23 7/8	22 2/8	5 3/8	5 4/8	7	7	Johnson Co., IA	Dennis R. Ballard	Dennis R. Ballard	1971	1409
197 4/8	24 4/8	24 6/8	21 6/8	7	6 7/8	8	10	Chippewa Co., MN	Dean D. Anspach	Dean D. Anspach	1973	1409
197 4/8	25 7/8	25 6/8	20 1/8	6 1/8	6 1/8	11	10	Garfield Co., OK	Derald D. Crissup	Derald D. Crissup	1980	1409
197 4/8	25 3/8	26 3/8	16 7/8	5 1/8	5 3/8	6	8	Lyon Co., KS	John R. Clifton	John R. Clifton	1984	1409
197 4/8	26 3/8	27 3/8	18	4 6/8	4 5/8	10	12	Dooly Co., GA	Wayne Griffin	Wayne Griffin	1984	1409
197 4/8	27 6/8	26 3/8	19 6/8	5 1/8	5 3/8	7	7	Clay Co., SD	Curtis Gregg	Curtis Gregg	1988	1409
197 4/8	27	24 2/8	17 4/8	5 7/8	5 7/8	8	7	Comanche Co., KS	Allan Prasser	Brant J. Mueller	1989	1409
197 4/8	27 1/8	27	20 1/8	5 2/8	5 3/8	9	9	Boone Co., IA	Grant E. Saunders	Grant E. Saunders	1990	1409
197 4/8	26 6/8	26 4/8	19 1/8	5 1/8	5 1/8	7	7	Independence Co., AR	Terry L. Pease	Terry L. Pease	1993	1409
197 4/8	23 3/8	23	19 1/8	4 6/8	4 7/8	8	8	Lee Co., IA	Carl A. Bell	Carl A. Bell	1995	1409
197 4/8	26 5/8	25	19 6/8	5 5/8	6 3/8	8	9	Buffalo Co., WI	Dennis L. Mackeben	Dennis L. Mackeben	1995	1409
197 4/8	25 3/8	26 3/8	22 6/8	5 2/8	5 2/8	11	8	Tuscarawas Co., OH	Michael W. McKenzie	Michael W. McKenzie	1995	1409
197 4/8	29	29 5/8	27 2/8	5 4/8	5 4/8	9	9	Pike Co., IL	Donald Reynolds	Donald Reynolds	1996	1409
197 3/8	25	26	17 4/8	5 5/8	5 5/8	9	10	Stevens Co., WA	Coulston W. Drummond	Coulston W. Drummond	1948	1424
197 3/8	24 4/8	22 4/8	18 6/8	6 2/8	5 7/8	9	12	Buffalo Co., WI	Walter Mengelt	Timothy W. Trones	1957	1424
197 3/8	24	26 5/8	16 4/8	5 6/8	5 6/8	9	10	Newton Co., GA	R.H. Bumbalough	R.H. Bumbalough	1969	1424
197 3/8	27 3/8	26 3/8	20 4/8	5 2/8	5 2/8	8	9	Faribault Co., MN	Randy L. Sandt	Randy L. Sandt	1982	1424
197 3/8	22 2/8	23 7/8	21 6/8	5 6/8	5 1/8	14	10	Marshall Co., KS	Lloyd Wenzl	Lloyd Wenzl	1983	1424
197 3/8	26 5/8	27 2/8	16 5/8	5 1/8	5 1/8	8	14	Kittson Co., MN	Unknown	George W. Flaim	PR 1988	1424
197 3/8	26 3/8	26 7/8	17 3/8	5 1/8	5 2/8	10	12	Douglas Co., MN	Unknown	Wayne G. Nevar	PR 1988	1424
197 3/8	29 1/8	27 2/8	18	4 7/8	5 3/8	8	11	Anoka Co., MN	Dale M. Zimmerman	Dale M. Zimmerman	1990	1424
197 3/8	23 7/8	21 7/8	24	5 2/8	6	7	10	Gallia Co., OH	Jimmy W. Brumfield	Jimmy W. Brumfield	1992	1424
197 3/8	24 6/8	24 3/8	16 2/8	4 3/8	4 4/8	9	9	Cold Lake, SK	Anthony Clemenza, Jr.	Anthony Clemenza, Jr.	1994	1424
197 3/8	24 3/8	24 4/8	20 1/8	5 2/8	5 3/8	8	7	Clark Co., SD	Steven R. Frank	Steven R. Frank	1995	1424
197 3/8	24 6/8	24 6/8	16	6 6/8	7	8	17	Perry Co., IL	Dwayne Rogers	Dwayne Rogers	1996	1424
197 2/8	26 2/8	26 6/8	20	5 2/8	5 1/8	10	7	Iron Co., WI	Unknown	Henry C. Gilbertson	PR 1940	1436
197 2/8	27 4/8	26 5/8	21	5	5	8	9	Hancock Co., ME	Hollis Patterson	Reginald R. Clark	PR 1950	1436
197 2/8	23 2/8	26 1/8	17 1/8	5 4/8	6 1/8	10	9	Stanton, NE	Peter Bartman III	Peter Bartman III	1963	1436
197 2/8	29 7/8	30	21 1/8	5 5/8	5 4/8	6	8	Douglas Co., MN	David S. Paulson	David S. Paulson	1966	1436
197 2/8	23	24	20	6 2/8	5 6/8	10	8	Chouteau Co., MT	J. Burton Long	J. Burton Long	1975	1436
197 2/8	27 4/8	26 3/8	20	5	5	12	11	Tiudish River, NS	Clayton Ward	Clayton Ward	1982	1436
197 2/8	24 5/8	24 3/8	18 5/8	4 4/8	4 3/8	9	14	Redvers, SK	Eugene M. Gazda	Eugene M. Gazda	1984	1436
197 2/8	23 4/8	24 4/8	23 4/8	4 5/8	4 7/8	10	11	Scott Co., IN	Wilson D. Barger	Wilson D. Barger	1991	1436
197 2/8	27	27 2/8	17 1/8	4 1/8	4 3/8	11	8	McCreary Co., KY	Curtis Morrow	Curtis Morrow	1996	1436
197 2/8	27 6/8	25 1/8	21	5 4/8	5 3/8	9	8	Sangamon Co., IL	Robert W. Penwell	Robert W. Penwell	1996	1436
197 1/8	27 5/8	27 2/8	21 4/8	4 5/8	4 7/8	9	9	Becker Co., MN	Unknown	George W. Flaim	1924	1446

Score	Main Beam R	Main Beam L	Inside Spread	Circ. R	Circ. L	Pts. R	Pts. L	Locality	Hunter	Owner	Date Killed	Rank
197 1/8	24 3/8	24 1/8	18 3/8	5 6/8	5 3/8	17	14	Edmonson Co., KY	Leroy Wilson	Leroy Wilson	1963	1446
197 1/8	20 6/8	20 5/8	18 4/8	4 5/8	4 6/8	13	17	Kenedy Co., TX	Manuel Amaya	Arturo R. Amaya	1969	1446
197 1/8	23	22 7/8	17 7/8	5 1/8	4 6/8	10	9	Noble Co., OK	Kenneth R. Bright	Kenneth R. Bright	1982	1446
197 1/8	28 2/8	26 6/8	18 7/8	5 1/8	5 1/8	9	11	Worth Co., MO	Gary G. Kinder	Gary G. Kinder	1982	1446
197 1/8	25 3/8	25 2/8	21	5 2/8	5 7/8	10	7	Jefferson Co., IL	Unknown	Jeff Sartaine	1983	1446
197 1/8	26 1/8	26 3/8	17 3/8	4 6/8	4 6/8	8	9	Jackson Co., MO	Jim Martin	Jim Martin	1984	1446
197 1/8	27 4/8	27 3/8	18 3/8	4 5/8	4 5/8	9	9	Clay Co., TX	Dale L. Coleman	Dale L. Coleman	1988	1446
197 1/8	22 6/8	24 4/8	17 3/8	6 3/8	4 5/8	8	6	Caldwell Co., MO	James B. Nickels	James B. Nickels	1990	1446
197 1/8	26 6/8	26 3/8	19 3/8	5	5	11	11	Franklin Co., KS	Ron R. Rumford	Ron R. Rumford	1992	1446
197 1/8	26 2/8	25	18 3/8	5	5 3/8	6	7	Preeceville, SK	Dale Prestie	Dale Prestie	1996	1446
197	23 4/8	26 3/8	19 4/8	4 4/8	5	11	9	Oak River, MB	Sam Henry	J.J. Henry	1946	1457
197	27 5/8	27 6/8	20 4/8	5 1/8	4 5/8	7	13	Cook Co., MN	Edwin F. Niemeyer	Helen Niemeyer	1947	1457
197	28 2/8	26 5/8	22 7/8	5 5/8	5 3/8	8	8	Houghton Co., MI	Edward Heinonen	Bass Pro Shops F. & W. Mus.	1970	1457
197	26 5/8	26 4/8	22 1/8	6	6	6	9	Fayette Co., IA	Stanley E. Harrison	Stanley E. Harrison	1973	1457
197	24 2/8	26 4/8	25 3/8	5	5 1/8	8	9	Kootenai Co., ID	D.L. Whatcott & R.C. Carlson	D.L. Whatcott & R.C. Carlson	1980	1457
197	29 3/8	25 3/8	21 6/8	5 2/8	4 4/8	14	14	Bedford Co., VA	John P. Kirby, Sr.	John P. Kirby, Sr.	1981	1457
197	22 1/8	21 1/8	15 4/8	5 4/8	5	11	11	Rosebud Co., MT	Mark D. Holmes	Mark D. Holmes	1983	1457
197	24 3/8	24 1/8	18	5	5	7	8	Souris River, MB	Picked Up	T. Allan Good	1986	1457
197	23 6/8	23 4/8	20 4/8	6	6	9	14	Barber Co., KS	Lewis M. Mull	Lewis M. Mull	1986	1457
197	22	22 5/8	14 5/8	5 1/8	5 1/8	13	11	Montgomery Co., IA	Picked Up	M. & S. Philby	1988	1457
196 7/8	26 2/8	26	20 6/8	5 1/8	5 1/8	11	12	St. Louis Co., MN	James A. Guist	James A. Guist	1963	1467
196 7/8	27 1/8	27 2/8	23 2/8	5 2/8	5 2/8	10	5	Macon Co., GA	Major Beard	Major Brannon	1972	1467
196 7/8	27 2/8	23 4/8	18 5/8	5	5	12	13	Caddo Parish, LA	Robert W. Anderson	Robert W. Anderson	1983	1467
196 7/8	23 4/8	24 6/8	19	5 3/8	5 3/8	10	8	Edmunds Co., SD	Melvin Borkirchert	Melvin Borkirchert	1983	1467
196 7/8	24 6/8	26 5/8	19 2/8	4 4/8	4 4/8	7	8	Pepin Co., WI	Jerry R. Breitung	Jerry R. Breitung	1985	1467
196 7/8	26 5/8	24 2/8	22 6/8	4 4/8	4 4/8	7	7	Wayne Co., IA	Marshall V. Ruble	Marshall V. Ruble	1985	1467
196 7/8	24 2/8	22 1/8	17 1/8	6	6	11	9	Trigg Co., KY	Homer Stevens, Jr.	Homer Stevens, Jr.	1986	1467
196 7/8	22 6/8	23	23 1/8	4 4/8	4 4/8	8	9	Yazoo Co., MS	Eddie J. Alias, Jr.	Eddie J. Alias, Jr.	1989	1467
196 7/8	23	25 1/8	18 5/8	4 2/8	4 6/8	11	11	Jackson Co., MI	Herb C. Miller, Jr.	Herb C. Miller, Jr.	1993	1467
196 7/8	25 1/8	26	18	5 2/8	5	8	9	McLean Co., KY	John D. Greenfield	John D. Greenfield	1996	1467
196 7/8	26	26	17 6/8	5	5 1/8	8	10	Linn Co., IA	James L. Newman	James L. Newman	1996	1467
196 6/8	21 6/8	22 2/8	17 5/8	5 6/8	5 3/8	8	8	Vilas Co., WI	Joe Wilfer	Rick Iacono	1934	1478
196 6/8	22 2/8	23 1/8	18 2/8	4 6/8	5 3/8	9	8	Perry Co., PA	Kenneth Reisinger	Kenneth Reisinger	1949	1478
196 6/8	26 2/8	26	19 1/8	5 2/8	5 6/8	9	10	Unicoi Co., TN	Elmer Payne	Elmer Payne	1972	1478
196 6/8	25	25 1/8	21 4/8	5 2/8	5	13	10	Lake Co., MN	Unknown	George W. Flaim	PR 1984	1478
196 6/8	26 7/8	26 7/8	21	5 4/8	5 3/8	7	8	McHenry Co., IL	Timothy A. Schulze	Timothy A. Schulze	1989	1478
196 6/8	28 2/8	28	20 3/8	6	5 3/8	7	9	Athabasca, AB	Robert Camarillo	Robert Camarillo	1994	1478
196 6/8	24 5/8	24 5/8	20	4 4/8	5 6/8	9	6	Licking Co., OH	Michael E. Evans, Sr.	Michael E. Evans, Sr.	1994	1478
196 6/8	25 4/8	27 5/8	18 6/8	5 3/8	4 4/8	9	9	Clinton Co., IA	Robert W. Franks	Robert W. Franks	1994	1478
196 6/8	27	28 2/8	20	4 2/8	5 3/8	10	12	Birch Lake, SK	Brent V. Trumbo	Brent V. Trumbo	1994	1478
196 6/8	24 1/8	24 2/8	19	4 2/8	4 2/8	16	14	Stephens Co., TX	Thomas N. Clark	Lawson W. Walden	1995	1478
196 6/8	24 2/8	24 2/8	21 5/8	6 1/8	6 1/8	8	6	Jackson Co., IA	James L. Beetem	James L. Beetem	1996	1478
196 5/8	26 2/8	26 4/8	26 4/8	5 7/8	5 7/8	10	10	Buffalo Co., WI	Bill Black, Sr.	Tom Black	1956	1489
196 5/8	26 5/8	25 7/8	23 6/8	5 6/8	5 6/8	11	11	Delta Co., MI	Frans Kuula	Bass Pro Shops F. & W. Mus.	1967	1489
196 5/8	28 7/8	25 4/8	15 5/8	5 4/8	4 6/8	10	12	Westchester Co., NY	Picked Up	John J. Vitale	1968	1489
196 5/8	21 2/8	20 5/8	19 4/8	4 7/8	4 7/8	10	12	Wilkinson Co., MS	Robert D. Sullivan	Robert D. Sullivan	1982	1489

Odocoileus virginianus virginianus and certain related subspecies

Score	Length of Main Beam		Inside Spread	Circumference at Smallest Place Between Burr and First Point		Number of Points		Locality	Hunter	Owner	Date Killed	Rank
	R	L		R	L	R	L					
196 6/8	25 6/8	25 1/8	20 6/8	5 7/8	5 5/8	9	8	Van Buren Co., IA	Kenneth R. Barker	Kenneth R. Barker	1984	1489
196 5/8	30 2/8	30 3/8	20 5/8	5 6/8	5 6/8	9	7	Langlade Co., WI	Thomas G. Jahnke	Thomas G. Jahnke	1990	1489
196 5/8	26 7/8	26 3/8	21 7/8	4 4/8	4 5/8	7	7	Clarke Co., IL	Picked Up	William H. Lilienthal	PR 1990	1489
196 5/8	26 4/8	27 6/8	20 6/8	4 7/8	4 6/8	8	6	Scott Co., IL	Michael G. Schildman	Michael G. Schildman	1992	1489
196 4/8	26 6/8	28 5/8	19	5	4 7/8	8	8	Desha Co., AR	Turner Neal	Turner Neal	1955	1497
196 4/8	24 1/8	23 3/8	18 2/8	5 1/8	5 2/8	9	8	Trigg Co., KY	Jeffery Taylor	Jeffery Taylor	1983	1497
196 4/8	27	27 7/8	23 6/8	5 1/8	5	10	10	Garland Co., AR	Eldon G. Sisney	Eldon G. Sisney	1986	1497
196 4/8	26 4/8	25 6/8	18 5/8	4 7/8	5	8	11	Lucas Co., AR	Steve Shanks	Steve Shanks	1987	1497
196 4/8	25 6/8	26 4/8	25 3/8	4 6/8	4 6/8	9	8	Jackson Co., OH	Francis L. Ray	Francis L. Ray	1988	1497
196 4/8	27	26 4/8	19 2/8	4 4/8	4 6/8	11	8	Franklin Co., IN	Cory A. Rogers	Cory A. Rogers	1996	1497
196 3/8	22 4/8	23	23 6/8	6 3/8	6	10	11	Dunn Co., WI	Unknown	Brant J. Mueller	PR 1940	1503
196 3/8	23 6/8	24 4/8	20 2/8	4 4/8	4 7/8	8	7	Texas	Unknown	Roy Hindes	PR 1950	1503
196 3/8	25 1/8	25 2/8	17 6/8	4 5/8	4 6/8	9	6	Webb Co., TX	R. Blair James	R. Blair James	1954	1503
196 3/8	25 6/8	24 4/8	22 7/8	5	5 2/8	7	9	Prairie River, SK	Herb Kopperud	Herb Kopperud	1959	1503
196 3/8	24 3/8	18 6/8	24	5 4/8	5 3/8	9	10	Clark Co., IL	Mary K. LeCrone	Mary K. LeCrone	1982	1503
196 3/8	24 7/8	25 2/8	15 3/8	4 6/8	4 7/8	10	12	Lee Co., IA	Douglas W. Hopp	Douglas W. Hopp	1984	1503
196 3/8	26 2/8	25 7/8	18 3/8	4 4/8	4 5/8	11	8	Price Co., WI	John R. Lemke	John R. Lemke	1986	1503
196 3/8	25 4/8	26 5/8	20 1/8	6	6 1/8	12	11	Magaguadowic Lake, NB	Albert Fawcett	Albert Fawcett	1988	1503
196 3/8	27	26 1/8	17 7/8	5 7/8	5 6/8	8	11	Houghton Co., MI	Robert L. Marr	Robert L. Marr	1990	1503
196 3/8	22 5/8	26 2/8	17 3/8	5 1/8	4 4/8	10	6	Coahuila, MX	Jeanie D. Willard	Jeanie D. Willard	1993	1503
196 3/8	23 2/8	23 5/8	23 5/8	5 1/8	5 1/8	8	7	Pierceland, SK	Robert B. Rhyne	Robert B. Rhyne	1994	1503
196 3/8	28 4/8	27	21 3/8	4 6/8	5	9	7	Ringgold Co., IA	Frank J. Scovel	Frank J. Scovel	1994	1503
196 3/8	25 6/8	24 2/8	19 1/8	5 6/8	5 4/8	10	9	Ellis Co., KS	Douglas W. Carmichael	Douglas W. Carmichael	1996	1503
196 2/8	25 4/8	25 7/8	19 6/8	5 3/8	5 5/8	11	9	Winneshiek Co., IA	Picked Up	William H. Lilienthal	1940	1516
196 2/8	22 4/8	22 4/8	20 4/8	4 6/8	4 6/8	14	12	Delta Co., MI	William H. Johnson	Bass Pro Shops F. & W. Mus.	PR 1951	1516
196 2/8	23 2/8	23 1/8	17 5/8	5 2/8	4 7/8	11	7	Lake of the Woods Co., MN	Ralph Rehder	Ralph Rehder	1951	1516
196 2/8	24	24 5/8	22	4 7/8	5 5/8	11	10	Crook Co., WY	Donald W. Clements	Colleen B. Clements	1958	1516
196 2/8	28 4/8	27 5/8	22 4/8	5	4 7/8	6	6	Henry Co., KY	Picked Up	Michael L. Roberts	1965	1516
196 2/8	29 3/8	29 2/8	22 4/8	5	5 1/8	10	10	Crow Wing Co., MN	LeRoy E. Pelarski	LeRoy E. Pelarski	1975	1516
196 2/8	27	25 1/8	27	6 3/8	6 1/8	7	14	Dorchester Co., MD	Kevin R. Coulbourne	Kevin R. Coulbourne	1979	1516
196 2/8	23 7/8	25 6/8	17 3/8	5 5/8	6	10	9	Otter Tail Co., MN	William J. Klyve	William J. Klyve	1987	1516
196 2/8	25 6/8	23 2/8	22 3/8	5 3/8	5 4/8	11	8	Webster Co., KY	Timothy J. Shelton	Timothy J. Shelton	1993	1516
196 2/8	26 6/8	26 7/8	22 4/8	4 2/8	5 4/8	6	8	Butler Co., KY	Bradley S. Pharris	Bradley S. Pharris	1996	1516
196 2/8	27 6/8	24 3/8	18 1/8	3 7/8	4 2/8	11	11	Edwards Co., IL	David Broster	David Broster	1996	1516
196 2/8	24 7/8	24 6/8	18 4/8	5 2/8	5 4/8	8	7	Louisa Co., IA	Tony Thomas	Tony Thomas	1996	1516
196 1/8	24 3/8	24 1/8	19 3/8	5 4/8	5 6/8	8	11	Nemaha Co., NE	Picked Up	Gale Sup	1975	1528

Score	Main Beam R	Main Beam L	Inside Spread	Circ. R	Circ. L	Pts R	Pts L	Locality	Hunter	Owner	Date	Rank
196 1/8	24 4/8	26	17 2/8	5 7/8	5 6/8	11	10	McCreary Co., KY	Jack W. Bailey	Jack W. Bailey	1976	1528
196 1/8	25 5/8	24 4/8	16 7/8	5	4 7/8	11	10	Wyoming Co., NY	Eric D. Baney	Eric D. Baney	1985	1528
196 1/8	26 4/8	21 7/8	19 3/8	5 5/8	5 5/8	9	7	Henderson Co., IL	Bruce Keever	Bruce Keever	1992	1528
196 1/8	25 2/8	25 1/8	20 2/8	5 1/8	5 2/8	7	7	Ketchen, SK	Vernon C. Hoffman	Vernon C. Hoffman	1993	1528
196 1/8	28	27 1/8	18 7/8	4 1/8	4 4/8	9	7	Guthrie Co., IA	Terry D. Danielson	Terry D. Danielson	1995	1528
196 1/8	23 4/8	23 4/8	18 1/8	5 4/8	5 4/8	9	9	Jefferson Co., IN	Bill A. Knoblock	Bill A. Knoblock	1996	1528
196 1/8	22 6/8	24 5/8	19 4/8	5 3/8	5 4/8	14	8	Rumsey, AB	Greg Smith	Greg Smith	1996	1528
196	25	24 2/8	20	4 6/8	4 6/8	8	8	Forest Co., WI	Aaron E. Huettl	Aaron E. Huettl	1939	1536
196	27 7/8	26 2/8	15 4/8	5 2/8	5 2/8	12	8	Marinette Co., WI	Brant J. Mueller	Joseph Braun	1940	1536
196	25 5/8	25 1/8	16 1/8	5 1/8	5 1/8	7	15	Westmoreland Co., PA	Edward G. Ligus	Edward G. Ligus	1956	1536
196	26 4/8	25 6/8	18 7/8	5 2/8	5 2/8	6	12	Buffalo Co., WI	William A. Gatzlaff	William A. Gatzlaff	1970	1536
196	28 7/8	30 4/8	25 1/8	5 4/8	5 4/8	12	7	Missoula Co., MT	David Cabral	David Cabral	1984	1536
196	25 2/8	25 4/8	19 6/8	4 6/8	4 6/8	13	9	Annapolis Valley, NS	James D. Pladson	James D. Pladson	1987	1536
196	26 5/8	24 7/8	17 2/8	5 3/8	5 4/8	10	7	Dubuque Co., IA	Terry D. Freese	Terry D. Freese	1990	1536
196	24	24 4/8	18 5/8	4 5/8	4 6/8	10	12	Richland Co., WI	Jeff DuCharme	Picked Up	1992	1536
196	20 6/8	24 6/8	16 2/8	4	4	8	9	McNairy Co., TN	Bradley S. Koeppel	Bradley S. Koeppel	1993	1536
196	21 5/8	22	13 2/8	5 6/8	6 2/8	8	9	Muscatine Co., IA	James D. Evans	James D. Evans	1995	1536
196	24 1/8	28 3/8	22	3 6/8	3 6/8	5	6	Harlan Co., KY	Lester S. Whitehead	Lester S. Whitehead	1996	1536
195 7/8	25	25	23 6/8	6	6	8	7	Webb Co., TX	Vernon L. Watson	Charles J. Schelper, Sr.	1930	1547
195 7/8	26 3/8	25 4/8	19 2/8	5 5/8	4 7/8	10	8	Beltrami Co., MN	James Gorden	Ollie Jamtaas	1938	1547
195 7/8	25 4/8	25 1/8	18 6/8	4 5/8	4 4/8	7	10	Allamakee Co., IA	John L. Cahalan	John L. Cahalan	1953	1547
195 7/8	21 4/8	21 6/8	20 6/8	5 2/8	5 2/8	9	8	La Salle Co., TX	Steve A. Meyer	Steve A. Meyer	1968	1547
195 7/8	27 1/8	25 2/8	20 2/8	5	4 7/8	11	9	Grant Co., WI	Roger Derrickson	Roger Derrickson	1973	1547
195 7/8	29 1/8	21 7/8	21 6/8	5 4/8	5 5/8	8	8	Perry Co., OH	Pearl R. Wiseman	Pearl R. Wiseman	1976	1547
195 7/8	30	30 1/8	21 7/8	5 5/8	6	7	10	Jackson Co., MI	Ronald D. Murphy	Picked Up	1984	1547
195 7/8	28	27	21 2/8	4 7/8	4 7/8	6	6	Meade Co., KY	J. Mark Stull	J. Mark Stull	1984	1547
195 7/8	24 5/8	23 7/8	18 2/8	4 5/8	5 1/8	7	9	Monroe Co., MS	Kenneth A. Dye	Kenneth A. Dye	1986	1547
195 7/8	23 1/8	23 4/8	19	4 2/8	4 3/8	9	7	Latah Co., ID	Cecil H. Cameron	Cecil H. Cameron	1989	1547
195 7/8	26 6/8	26 4/8	23 6/8	4 3/8	4 2/8	8	8	Webb Co., TX	Marko Barrett	Marko Barrett	1993	1547
195 7/8	24 3/8	24 4/8	26 6/8	5	5	9	6	Kenedy Co., TX	Michael D. Fain	Michael D. Fain	1993	1547
195 7/8	28	28 5/8	20 1/8	5 7/8	5 3/8	8	7	Wayne Co., IA	Michael S. Perkins	Michael S. Perkins	1995	1547
195 6/8	28 6/8	30 2/8	22	5 3/8	5 3/8	7	8	Illinois	Ed Feist	Unknown	1945	1560
195 6/8	26 4/8	27 4/8	19 6/8	5 2/8	5 4/8	11	10	Moosomin, SK	Tom Ryan	Tom Ryan	1961	1560
195 6/8	25	25	20 2/8	5 6/8	5	10	7	St. Louis Co., MN	Mike Desanto	Mike Desanto	1963	1560
195 6/8	28 2/8	29 5/8	16 4/8	5	5	7	8	Douglas Co., WI	Buckhorn of Gordon, Inc.	Unknown	PR 1970	1560
195 6/8	24 2/8	24 6/8	18 3/8	6 5/8	7	7	8	Wetaskiwin, AB	Lewis D. Callies	Lewis D. Callies	1972	1560
195 6/8	24 6/8	26 5/8	19 5/8	6 3/8	4 3/8	11	12	Roseau Co., MN	George H. Tepley	George H. Tepley	1984	1560
195 6/8	25 7/8	25 7/8	27 6/8	5 2/8	4 4/8	14	8	Greenwater Creek, SK	Edward R. Mielke	Picked Up	1988	1560
195 6/8	26 2/8	24 4/8	17 6/8	4 4/8	4 2/8	9	8	Coal Co., OK	Todd Tobey	Todd Tobey	1988	1560
195 6/8	21 6/8	24 6/8	20 7/8	4 7/8	4 5/8	15	10	Ashland Co., OH	Michael R. Dull	Michael R. Dull	1992	1560
195 6/8	25 7/8	25 6/8	20 5/8	4 1/8	4	10	12	Howard Co., MO	Daniel A. Larkin	Daniel A. Larkin	1993	1560
195 6/8	23	23	17	4 5/8	4 5/8	9	8	Bonner Co., ID	Brian T. Farley	Picked Up	PR 1994	1560
195 6/8	24	24	20	5 1/8	5 1/8	9	8	Missoula Co., MT	Eugene L. Tripp, Sr.	Eugene L. Tripp, Sr.	1994	1560
195 6/8	25	25 4/8	17 4/8	5 4/8	5 6/8	6	9	Washington Co., ME	James H. Guertin	James H. Guertin	1995	1560
195 6/8	24 4/8	24 4/8	19 4/8	4 4/8	4 4/8	8	10	Lee Co., IA	Jesse W. Logan	Jesse W. Logan	1996	1560
195 5/8	23 2/8	22 2/8	19 2/8	4 4/8	4 4/8	12	12	Florence Co., WI	Joseph R. Szczepanski, Jr.	Joseph R. Szczepanski, Jr.	PR 1945	1574
195 5/8	25 4/8	25 6/8	19	6 1/8	6	10	10	Parkman, SK	H.E. Kennett	H.E. Kennett	1949	1574

WHITETAIL DEER - NON-TYPICAL ANTLERS

Odocoileus virginianus virginianus and certain related subspecies

Score	Length of Main Beam R	L	Inside Spread	Circumference at Smallest Place Between Burr and First Point R	L	Number of Points R	L	Locality	Hunter	Owner	Date Killed	Rank
195 5/8	25 5/8	24 2/8	19 1/8	5 4/8	5 5/8	8	16	Carlton Co., MN	Nick Rukovina	George W. Flaim	1960	1574
195 5/8	24 6/8	25 3/8	21 3/8	5 5/8	5 4/8	11	9	Jackson Co., MN	Allan Amundson	Allan Amundson	1973	1574
195 5/8	25 4/8	25 6/8	19 1/8	5	5 2/8	8	8	Duffield, AB	Robert A. Schaefer	Robert A. Schaefer	1980	1574
195 5/8	23 7/8	24 2/8	13	5	5 2/8	14	10	Adams Co., MS	Kathleen McGehee	Kathleen McGehee	1981	1574
195 5/8	26 2/8	26 1/8	21 3/8	5 3/8	5 2/8	8	7	Story Co., IA	Jordan L. Larson	Jordan L. Larson	1983	1574
195 5/8	21 4/8	22 4/8	16 7/8	4 4/8	4 4/8	11	14	Menard Co., TX	Don N. Jones, Jr.	Lawson W. Walden	1987	1574
195 5/8	24 6/8	24 7/8	19 2/8	5 2/8	5	10	9	Nez Perce Co., ID	Paul S. Snider	Paul S. Snider	1989	1574
195 5/8	25 6/8	26 6/8	19 5/8	5 3/8	5 2/8	6	10	Unknown	Unknown	C.J. Fuller	PR 1993	1574
195 5/8	24 2/8	24 3/8	13 7/8	5 3/8	5 6/8	8	9	Appanoose Co., IA	Brent Carlson	Brent Carlson	1994	1574
195 5/8	28 1/8	27 5/8	21 4/8	5 3/8	5 4/8	8	7	Brown Co., IL	Brian Matsko	Brian Matsko	1994	1574
195 5/8	27 3/8	27 3/8	19 7/8	5 2/8	5 2/8	9	10	Allamakee Co., IA	Gary L. Mezera	Gary L. Mezera	1994	1574
195 5/8	20 6/8	21 4/8	17 3/8	5 7/8	5 3/8	12	9	Stafford Co., KS	Kenneth R. Van Winkle	Kenneth R. Van Winkle	1994	1574
195 5/8	24 1/8	23 5/8	21 7/8	4 4/8	4 2/8	12	11	Livingston Co., MI	Patrick M. Harris	Patrick M. Harris	1995	1574
195 4/8	24	23 5/8	21 2/8	4 7/8	5 1/8	14	9	Wisconsin	Unknown	Brant J. Mueller	PR 1942	1589
195 4/8	28	27 7/8	24 3/8	4 4/8	4 4/8	9	11	La Salle Co., TX	Unknown	John C. Korbell	1952	1589
195 4/8	24 7/8	25 1/8	20	5 1/8	4 7/8	10	10	Eau Claire Co., WI	Sylvester Champa	Sylvester Champa	1959	1589
195 4/8	24 5/8	24 1/8	17 6/8	4 4/8	4 2/8	9	9	Maverick Co., TX	Ronald K. Hudson	Ronald K. Hudson	1971	1589
195 4/8	28 5/8	27 3/8	21 2/8	4	4	8	7	Fillmore Co., MN	Jim Sletten	Mrs. Jim Sletten	1974	1589
195 4/8	26	25 3/8	16 6/8	4 7/8	4 6/8	10	7	Winona Co., MN	Patrick Bartholomew	Patrick Bartholomew	1976	1589
195 4/8	25 6/8	16 2/8	20 6/8	6	6	7	7	Bureau Co., IL	Picked Up	John Cotter	1976	1589
195 4/8	26 3/8	27 2/8	20 2/8	5 1/8	4 7/8	11	9	Kanabec Co., MN	Kenneth L. Smith	Kenneth L. Smith	1976	1589
195 4/8	27	26	20 3/8	5 6/8	5 6/8	7	9	Dorchester Co., MD	Charles D. Anderson	Charles D. Anderson	1978	1589
195 4/8	21 3/8	22 4/8	17 2/8	5	5	10	8	Carlisle Co., KY	William H. Deane IV	William H. Deane IV	1979	1589
195 4/8	25 3/8	24 3/8	21 6/8	4 3/8	4 4/8	7	10	Worth Co., GA	Shane Calhoun	Shane Calhoun	1985	1589
195 4/8	28 6/8	27 5/8	18 2/8	4 7/8	5 3/8	10	15	Hamilton Co., IL	Douglas P. Collins	Douglas P. Collins	1985	1589
195 4/8	21 6/8	23 7/8	22 1/8	4 7/8	5 2/8	9	13	St. Louis Co., MN	LeRoy N. Nelson	LeRoy N. Nelson	1987	1589
195 4/8	26 2/8	27 6/8	17 4/8	5	5	10	8	Peoria Co., IL	Jerry T. Wyatt	Jerry T. Wyatt	1989	1589
195 4/8	21 4/8	23 4/8	15 2/8	6 1/8	4 2/8	11	8	Jessamine Co., KY	Tony W. Drury	Tony W. Drury	1991	1589
195 4/8	25 6/8	24	15 3/8	4 3/8	4 3/8	11	9	Allegan Co., MI	Jason A. Newman	Jason A. Newman	1994	1589
195 4/8	23 5/8	24 5/8	20 7/8	4 5/8	4 7/8	9	11	Uvalde Co., TX	Gary G. Patterson	Gary G. Patterson	1996	1589
195 3/8	23 7/8	24 2/8	18 3/8	4 3/8	4 3/8	11	11	Pope Co., MN	Kenneth M. Besonen	Kenneth M. Besonen	1975	1606
195 3/8	27 3/8	29 7/8	20 5/8	6	5 4/8	6	7	Colquitt Co., GA	Olen P. Ross	Olen P. Ross	1976	1606
195 3/8	20 1/8	22 4/8	16 2/8	7 3/8	7 5/8	10	12	Beltrami Co., MN	John G. Binsfeld	John G. Binsfeld	1980	1606
195 3/8	25 2/8	26 3/8	20 1/8	5 3/8	5 2/8	11	8	Grassland, AB	Frederick Neumann	Frederick Neumann	1980	1606
195 3/8	25 4/8	25 4/8	22 4/8	5	4 6/8	9	12	Webb Co., TX	Sidney A. Lindsay, Jr.	Sidney A. Lindsay, Jr.	1983	1606
195 3/8	26 3/8	26	20 2/8	6	5 7/8	9	8	Scott Co., IA	Jeffrey Rasche	Jeffrey Rasche	1989	1606

Score	Main Beam R	Main Beam L	Inside Spread	Circ. R	Circ. L	Pts R	Pts L	Locality	By Whom Killed	Owner	Date	Rank
195 3/8	24 2/8	23	18 2/8	5 1/8	5 2/8	9	11	N. Saskatchewan River, AB	Thomas J. Procinsky	Thomas J. Procinsky	1990	1606
195 3/8	26 5/8	26 3/8	22 7/8	4 4/8	4 5/8	8	10	Jackson Co., IL	Robert L. Koehn	Robert L. Koehn	1991	1606
195 3/8	25 6/8	26 1/8	14 6/8	6 4/8	6 3/8	11	10	Hart Co., KY	Robbie Toms	Robbie Toms	1991	1606
195 3/8	27 1/8	26 4/8	19 3/8	4 6/8	5	10	7	Henry Co., IN	Donn W. Duncan	Donn W. Duncan	1994	1606
195 3/8	27 4/8	28 4/8	19 5/8	4 5/8	4 6/8	9	7	Pottawatomie Co., KS	Thomas G. Holthaus	Thomas G. Holthaus	1994	1606
195 3/8	27 4/8	26 7/8	20 5/8	5 1/8	5	7	6	Dane Co., WI	Gaylord N. Denner	Gaylord N. Denner	1995	1606
195 3/8	25 2/8	25 2/8	19 7/8	4 1/8	4 2/8	7	7	Rock Co., WI	Dennis A. Losey	Dennis A. Losey	1995	1606
195 3/8	25 3/8	25 6/8	19 2/8	4 2/8	4 2/8	7	8	Lewis Co., KY	Chris McCane	Chris McCane	1996	1606
195 2/8	26	24 6/8	20 5/8	6 2/8	6 3/8	9	9	Rusk Co., WI	Alexander King	Roger King	1890	1620
195 2/8	28 4/8	27 2/8	18 4/8	4 7/8	4 6/8	11	8	Du Charme Coulee, WI	Eugene E. Morovitz	Eugene E. Morovitz	1959	1620
195 2/8	25	23 4/8	17 3/8	5 4/8	5 3/8	11	8	Pottawattmie Co., IA	Ted Houser	Ted Houser	1968	1620
195 2/8	24 4/8	22	22 2/8	4 3/8	4 2/8	12	11	Kenedy Co., TX	Don E. Harrison	Don E. Harrison	1975	1620
195 2/8	25 3/8	25 5/8	21	5 3/8	5 3/8	12	13	Stevens Co., WA	Floyd E. Newell	Floyd E. Newell	1981	1620
195 2/8	28 3/8	28 3/8	20	6	6	9	8	Somerset Co., ME	David A. McAllister	David A. McAllister	1985	1620
195 2/8	24	24 4/8	16 7/8	5 1/8	5	8	8	Chitek Lake, SK	Charles E. Gambino	Charles E. Gambino	1990	1620
195 2/8	11 2/8	12 4/8	17 5/8	4 1/8	4	21	16	Grimes Co., TX	Walter Schroeder, Jr.	Walter Schroeder, Jr.	1990	1620
195 1/8	23 2/8	24 6/8	15 7/8	4 5/8	4 5/8	8	8	Witchekan Lake, SK	Kim Tiringer	Kim Tiringer	1990	1634
195 1/8	20	19 3/8	22 7/8	5 6/8	5 3/8	8	8	Adams Co., IL	Thomas D. Stice	Thomas D. Stice	1991	1634
195 1/8	19 3/8	23 2/8	19 4/8	5	5	8	10	Lily Lake, AB	Richard J. Leclercq	Richard J. Leclercq	1993	1634
195 1/8	26	26	15 7/8	5 2/8	5 3/8	8	8	Dakota Co., MN	Mark A. LeMay	Mark A. LeMay	1993	1634
195 1/8	25 1/8	25 1/8	17 3/8	5 1/8	5 1/8	7	9	Grady Co., OK	Robert J. Rempe	Robert J. Rempe	1994	1634
195 1/8	24 3/8	24 3/8	15 3/8	4 6/8	4 6/8	11	11	Copiah Co., MS	Bill Kimble	Bill Kimble	1995	1634
195 1/8	22 2/8	23 1/8	18	4 3/8	4 3/8	6	17	Carlton Co., MN	Unknown	George W. Flaim	1910	1634
195 1/8	20 3/8	20	20 7/8	4 3/8	4 4/8	7	13	Bonner Co., ID	George B. Hatley	George B. Hatley	1939	1634
195 1/8	25 5/8	25 5/8	15	5 5/8	5 2/8	7	7	Buffalo Co., WI	Maynard Trones	Maynard Trones	1958	1634
195 1/8	27 2/8	27 2/8	21	5	5	15	14	Washington Co., ME	M. Chandler Stith	M. Chandler Stith	1963	1634
195 1/8	23 2/8	23 2/8	18 6/8	4 4/8	4 6/8	9	9	Zapata Co., TX	Corando Mirelez	Corando Mirelez	1966	1634
195 1/8	26	26	23 2/8	5 2/8	5 2/8	6	8	Dorchester Co., MD	Carroll R. Seegard	Charles D. Anderson	1974	1634
195 1/8	27	24 2/8	15 3/8	5 2/8	5 2/8	10	9	Whitman Co., WA	R. & R. Boyer	R. & R. Boyer	1975	1634
195 1/8	24 2/8	23 4/8	19 4/8	5	4 7/8	8	10	Macon Co., GA	Wesley Jones	Wesley Jones	1986	1634
195 1/8	23 1/8	23 5/8	20 5/8	5 2/8	5 1/8	8	9	Holmes Co., OH	Randy J. Strohminger	Randy J. Strohminger	1987	1634
195 1/8	26 7/8	27 4/8	19 2/8	6	6 1/8	8	8	Massac Co., IL	Kent Sommer	Kent Sommer	1989	1634
195 1/8	26 7/8	25 5/8	21 5/8	4 6/8	4 6/8	9	7	Otter Tail Co., MN	Thomas E. Joseph, Jr.	Thomas E. Joseph, Jr.	1992	1634
195 1/8	25 3/8	27	17 6/8	4 4/8	4 4/8	8	9	Polk Co., WI	Michael J. Wilson	Michael J. Wilson	1992	1634
195 1/8	26	26	12 4/8	5 4/8	5 4/8	7	9	Lucas Co., IA	Picked Up	Don Jessop	1993	1634
195 1/8	25 4/8	25 4/8	17 3/8	5 2/8	5 2/8	7	7	Newton Co., MO	W.P. & J.R. Pritchard	W.P. & J.R. Pritchard	1993	1634
195 1/8	22 7/8	22 7/8	17 1/8	5 4/8	5 4/8	7	10	Ashland Co., WI	Jerry M. Anderson	Jerry M. Anderson	1995	1634
195 1/8	27	27	15 5/8	4 6/8	4 6/8	9	8	Otter Tail Co., MN	Allen Antonsen	Allen Antonsen	1995	1634
195 1/8	26 4/8	26 4/8	19 1/8	4 2/8	4 2/8	9	7	Cecil Co., MD	Charles M. Crouse	Charles M. Crouse	1995	1634
195 1/8	25 1/8	25 7/8	20 2/8	4 3/8	4 3/8	10	8	Lonoke Co., AR	John W. Henderson	John W. Henderson	1995	1634
195 1/8	27	27	20 3/8	5	5	7	9	Bath Co., VA	Joe W. Bond	Joe W. Bond	1996	1634
195	26 3/8	25 3/8	20 3/8	5 3/8	5 4/8	7	9	Dickinson Co., MI	Ed Hogberg	Michael Waldvogel	PR 1921	1653
195	27 2/8	24 6/8	21 5/8	5 4/8	5 3/8	9	7	Windham Co., CT	Harold Tanner	Warren W. Rogers	1970	1653
195	25 6/8	25 3/8	20 3/8	5 4/8	5 2/8	11	13	Guthrie Co., IA	Tom C. Klever	Tom C. Klever	1982	1653
195	22 4/8	25 6/8	20 3/8	4 5/8	4 5/8	8	9	Calhoun Co., IL	Roger F. Becker	Roger F. Becker	1983	1653
195	25 4/8	25	18 6/8	5	5	10	9	Clarke Co., IA	Picked Up	Jeff Jorgenson	1985	1653
195	27 5/8	27 1/8	20	5	5	9	8	Montgomery Co., IA	Mark L. King	Mark L. King	1985	1653

WHITETAIL DEER - NON-TYPICAL ANTLERS

Odocoileus virginianus virginianus and certain related subspecies

Score	Length of Main Beam R	L	Inside Spread	Circumference at Smallest Place Between Burr and First Point R	L	Number of Points R	L	Locality	Hunter	Owner	Date Killed	Rank
195	23 1/8	21 4/8	17 1/8	4 4/8	4 4/8	9	10	Kenedy Co., TX	Phil Lyne	Phil Lyne	1986	1653
195	25 3/8	22 6/8	20 6/8	5 6/8	5 3/8	9	8	Henderson Co., IL	George S. Worley	William H. Lilienthal	1989	1653
195	25 6/8	26 1/8	17	4 3/8	4 3/8	11	7	Goodhue Co., MN	Darrin L. Goplen	Darrin L. Goplen	1990	1653
195	27 7/8	28 1/8	22 5/8	5 6/8	5 6/8	7	9	Lac du Bonnet, MB	Brad Ehinger	Brad Ehinger	1993	1653
195	24	24	20 2/8	4 7/8	4 6/8	9	8	Rusk Co., WI	Jon R. Lane	Jon R. Lane	1993	1653
195	24 1/8	23 5/8	15 7/8	5	5 2/8	7	9	Bayfield Co., WI	Bradley A. Kuhnert	Bradley A. Kuhnert	1994	1653
195	24 7/8	24 4/8	19 5/8	5 5/8	5 1/8	9	8	Marquette Co., WI	Donald E. Voskuil	Donald E. Voskuil	1994	1653
195	27 4/8	27 7/8	20 2/8	4 6/8	5 2/8	9	10	Jersey Co., IL	Glenn A. Wilson	Glenn A. Wilson	1994	1653
195	25 6/8	27 2/8	20 1/8	5 1/8	5	11	9	Westmoreland Co., PA	Eugene W. Livingston	Eugene W. Livingston	1995	1653
195	25 4/8	26 1/8	22	5 6/8	5 6/8	7	11	Darke Co., OH	Bob Spitler	Bob Spitler	1995	1653
195	25 4/8	26 1/8	22	5 4/8	5 3/8	8	9	McLean Co., IL	Frank G. Bartels	Frank G. Bartels	1996	1653
195	27 3/8	27	18 5/8	5 1/8	4 7/8	7	10	Guthrie Co., IA	Chad Laabs	Chad Laabs	1996	1653
195	25 7/8	25 3/8	20 6/8	4 6/8	4 7/8	7	10	Jasper Co., IA	Ronald D. Steenhoek	Ronald D. Steenhoek	1996	1653
263 6/8*	23 7/8	25	26 6/8	5 4/8	5 3/8	14	15	Ashern, MB	Graeme E. McGinnis	Graeme E. McGinnis	1994	
256 7/8*	26 6/8	26 3/8	20	5	5	16	14	Adams Co., IL	Todd R. Hurley	Todd R. Hurley	1995	
244 3/8*	23 4/8	24 1/8	20	5 5/8	5 7/8	12	14	Knox Co., IL	Karl R. Jones	Karl R. Jones	1992	

* Final score is subject to revision by additional verifying measurements.

HORACE M. ALBRIGHT
1890-1987

Albright was a central figure in the American conservation movement in the first half of the twentieth century. Born in Bishop, California, in 1890, he attended a one-room school house where he graduated from high school with three other students. He completed his undergraduate work at Cal Berkeley and received his law degree at Georgetown. He helped found the National Park Service and was its director from 1929 to 1933. He was also superintendent of Yellowstone National Park and helped found Mt. McKinley National Park in Alaska. He joined the Boone and Crockett Club in 1922 and was an active member until his death. ∎

CATEGORY
WHITETAIL DEER
NON-TYPICAL ANTLERS

SCORE
212-6/8

HUNTER
PHILIP H. PREISEL

LOCATION
LONG LAKE, AB

DATE OF KILL
NOVEMBER 1995

CATEGORY
WHITETAIL DEER
NON-TYPICAL ANTLERS

SCORE
203

HUNTER
KEVIN J. MORAN

LOCATION
DU PAGE CO., IL

DATE OF KILL
NOVEMBER 1995

CATEGORY
WHITETAIL DEER
NON-TYPICAL ANTLERS

SCORE
198-4/8

HUNTER
KENT E. RAINS

LOCATION
WALLACE CO., KS

DATE OF KILL
DECEMBER 1993

CATEGORY
WHITETAIL DEER
NON-TYPICAL ANTLERS

SCORE
203-1/8

HUNTER
EDWIN E. ORR

LOCATION
SWAN RIVER, SK

DATE OF KILL
NOVEMBER 1993

CATEGORY
WHITETAIL DEER
NON-TYPICAL ANTLERS

SCORE
206-7/8

HUNTER
DENNIS G. BORDNER

LOCATION
MCPHERSON CO., KS

DATE OF KILL
NOVEMBER 1994

CATEGORY
WHITETAIL DEER
NON-TYPICAL ANTLERS

SCORE
281-6/8

HUNTER
JAMES H. MCMURRAY

LOCATION
TENSAS PARISH, LA

DATE OF KILL
JANUARY 1994

COUES' WHITETAIL DEER - TYPICAL ANTLERS

As trophy measurements were reviewed for the 1955 Competition, judges were startled by a Coues' whitetail deer entry from Ed Stockwell of Pima County, Arizona. Stockwell had also added an equally amazing account of his hunt.

In 1958, after hunting all morning in the Santa Rita Mountains of southern Arizona, my partner and I were heading back to camp. There was a low but very rugged mountain to one side, and we decided to hunt around it. I began a slanting climb along the slope. My buddy took a lower route. There were lots of big rocks and impassable bluffs. Angling around them, I kept working upward until suddenly I was on top, and then, while going through the rocky terrain toward the smoother eastern slope, I jumped a big buck that had a small spike with him.

"As only the big antlers showed up behind a rocky ridge, I ran to get a better view. The big buck disappeared. Just as I was giving him up, he moved from behind a large oak tree and started down the slope, giving me a clear shot. I dropped him at about 60 yards. Evidently I had come up the side of the mountain that he used as his sneak exit, and it was probably due to this that I got such a good chance at him. My rifle was a .300 Savage, without a scope."

Scored at no less than 143, Ed Stockwell's trophy initially raised a few doubts in regard to its classification. The situation called for a careful examination of this head to make sure that it hadn't come from one of the larger whitetail races,

even though the Coues' whitetail deer range is not known to touch that of the bigger whitetails. By getting most of its water from cactus, this species has adapted to the dry country where most whitetails are incapable of surviving. After only a brief study of this rack it was verified that it had every characteristic of Coues' deer conformation. Although the antler beams were a trifle shorter than those of the 1952 leader, what set the official new World's Record apart at 144-1/8 was a massiveness that Coues' deer antlers very rarely show. ∎

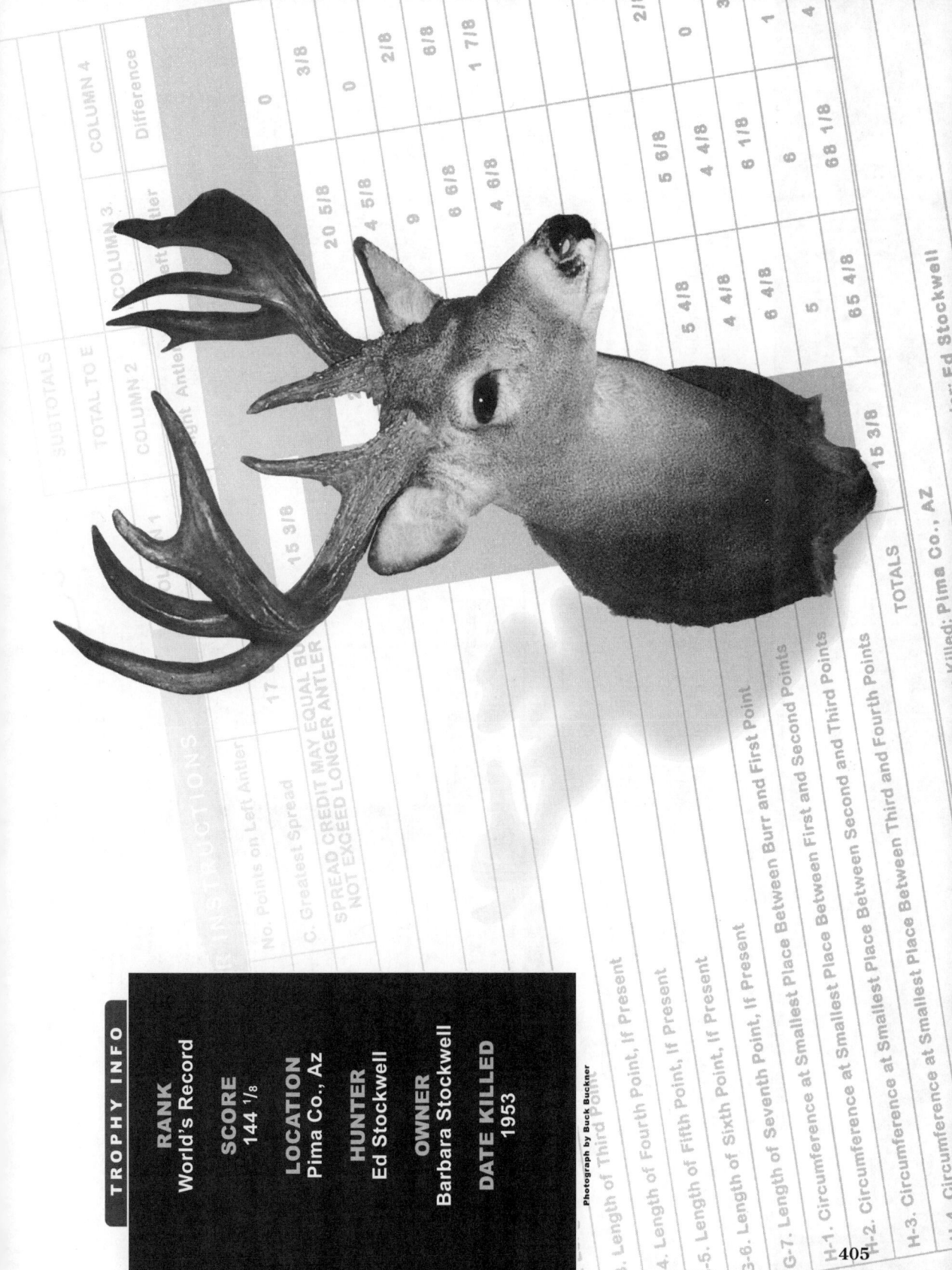

TROPHY INFO

RANK
World's Record

SCORE
144 1/8

LOCATION
Pima Co., Az

HUNTER
Ed Stockwell

OWNER
Barbara Stockwell

DATE KILLED
1953

Photograph by Buck Buckner

COUES' WHITETAIL DEER
TYPICAL ANTLERS
WORLD'S RECORD SCORECHART

All measurements must be made with a 1/4-inch wide flexible steel tape to the nearest one-eighth of an inch. (Note: A flexible steel cable can be used to measure points and main beams only.) Enter fractional figures in eighths, without reduction. Official measurements cannot be taken until the antlers have air dried for at least 60 days after the animal was killed.

A. Number of Points on Each Antler: To be counted a point, the projection must be at least one inch long, with the length exceeding width at one inch or more of length. All points are measured from tip of point to nearest edge of beam as illustrated. Beam tip is counted as a point but not measured as a point.

B. Tip to Tip Spread is measured between tips of main beams.

C. Greatest Spread is measured between perpendiculars at a right angle to the center line of the skull at widest part, whether across main beams or points.

D. Inside Spread of Main Beams is measured at a right angle to the center line of the skull at widest point between main beams. Enter this measurement again as the Spread Credit if it is less than or equal to the length of the longer antler; if greater, enter longer antler length for Spread Credit.

E. Total of Lengths of all Abnormal Points: Abnormal Points are those non-typical in location (such as points originating from a point or from bottom or sides of main beam) or extra points beyond the normal pattern of points. Measure in usual manner and enter in appropriate blanks.

F. Length of Main Beam is measured from the center of the lowest outside edge of burr over the outer side to the most distant point of the main beam. The point of beginning is that point on the burr where the center line along the outer side of the beam intersects the burr, then following generally the line of the illustration.

G-1-2-3-4-5-6-7. Length of Normal Points: Normal points project from the top of the main beam. They are measured from nearest edge of main beam over outer curve to tip. Lay the tape along the outer curve of the beam so that the top edge of the tape coincides with the top edge of the beam on both sides of the point to determine the baseline for point measurements. Record point lengths in appropriate blanks.

H-1-2-3-4. Circumferences are taken as detailed in illustration for each measurement. If brow point is missing, take H-1 and H-2 at smallest place between burr and G-2. If G-4 is missing, take H-4 halfway between G-3 and tip of main beam.

Records of
North American
Big Game

250 Station Drive
Missoula, MT 59801
(406) 542-1888

BOONE AND CROCKETT CLUB®

OFFICIAL SCORING SYSTEM FOR NORTH AMERICAN BIG GAME TROPHIES

TYPICAL
WHITETAIL AND COUES' DEER

MINIMUM SCORES	AWARDS	ALL-TIME
whitetail	160	170
Coues'	100	110

KIND OF DEER (check one)
☐ whitetail
☒ Coues'

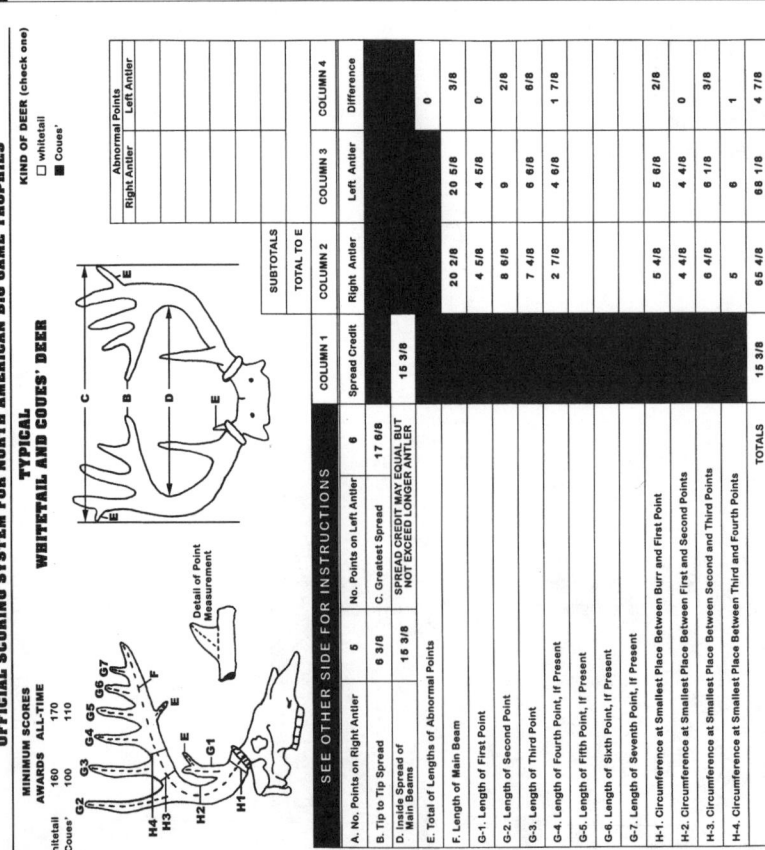

Detail of Point Measurement

Abnormal Points	
Right Antler	Left Antler
SUBTOTALS	
TOTAL TO E	

SEE OTHER SIDE FOR INSTRUCTIONS	COLUMN 1 Spread Credit	COLUMN 2 Right Antler	COLUMN 3 Left Antler	COLUMN 4 Difference
A. No. Points on Right Antler 5	No. Points on Left Antler 6			
B. Tip to Tip Spread 6 3/8	C. Greatest Spread 17 6/8			
D. Inside Spread of Main Beams 15 3/8	SPREAD CREDIT MAY EQUAL BUT NOT EXCEED LONGER ANTLER	15 3/8		
E. Total of Lengths of Abnormal Points				0
F. Length of Main Beam		20 2/8	20 5/8	3/8
G-1. Length of First Point		4 5/8	4 5/8	0
G-2. Length of Second Point		8 6/8	9	2/8
G-3. Length of Third Point		7 4/8	6 6/8	6/8
G-4. Length of Fourth Point, If Present		2 7/8	4 6/8	1 7/8
G-5. Length of Fifth Point, If Present				
G-6. Length of Sixth Point, If Present				
G-7. Length of Seventh Point, If Present				
H-1. Circumference at Smallest Place Between Burr and First Point		5 4/8	5 6/8	2/8
H-2. Circumference at Smallest Place Between First and Second Points		4 4/8	4 4/8	0
H-3. Circumference at Smallest Place Between Second and Third Points		6 4/8	6 1/8	3/8
H-4. Circumference at Smallest Place Between Third and Fourth Points		5	6	1
TOTALS	15 3/8	65 4/8	68 1/8	4 7/8

ADD	Column 1	15 3/8	Exact Locality Where Killed: Pima Co., AZ	
	Column 2	65 4/8	Date Killed: 1953	Hunter: Ed Stockwell
	Column 3	68 1/8	Owner: Barbara Stockwell	Telephone #:
	Subtotal	149	Owner's Address:	
SUBTRACT Column 4		4 7/8	Guide's Name and Address:	
FINAL SCORE		144 1/8	Remarks: (Mention Any Abnormalities or Unique Qualities)	

COPYRIGHT © 1999 BY BOONE AND CROCKETT CLUB®

Photograph by Wm. H. Nesbitt

Photograph by Ron Anfinson

MINIMUM SCORE 110

Odocoileus virginianus couesi

Score	Length of Main Beam R	L	Inside Spread	Circumference at Smallest Place Between Burr and First Point R	L	Number of Points R	L	Locality	Hunter	Owner	Date Killed	Rank
144 1/8	20 2/8	20 5/8	15 3/8	5 4/8	5 6/8	5	5	Pima Co., AZ	Ed Stockwell	Barbara Stockwell	1953	1
143	19 7/8	20 3/8	13 2/8	4 6/8	4 6/8	5	5	Navajo Co., AZ	Larry Johnson	Alan C. Ellsworth	1995	2
134 4/8	20 5/8	21 1/8	16	4 5/8	4 3/8	5	5	Grant Co., NM	Victor P. Giacoletti, Jr.	Victor P. Giacoletti, Jr.	1981	3
133	20 6/8	19 7/8	18	3 7/8	3 7/8	6	6	Pima Co., AZ	Michael E. Duperret	Loaned to B&C Natl. Coll.	1990	4
131 7/8	19 6/8	19 2/8	16 1/8	4 2/8	4 2/8	5	5	Cochise Co., AZ	George W. Kouts	George W. Kouts	1935	5
130 5/8	20 5/8	19 3/8	14 5/8	3 2/8	3 2/8	5	5	Chihuahua, MX	Wayne Kleinman	Wayne Kleinman	1958	6
130 4/8	20 6/8	20 6/8	15 6/8	4 6/8	4 5/8	8	6	Pima Co., AZ	Kim J. Poulin	Kim J. Poulin	1981	7
128	21 1/8	20	19 2/8	4 6/8	4 4/8	4	4	Grant Co., NM	Ramon C. Borrego	Ramon C. Borrego	1988	8
126 6/8	21 6/8	19 6/8	14	4	4 2/8	6	5	Cochise Co., AZ	Mike Kasun	Mike Kasun, Jr.	1959	9
126 5/8	19 4/8	18 6/8	11 1/8	4 5/8	4 3/8	5	6	Pima Co., AZ	DeWayne M. Hanna	DeWayne M. Hanna	1977	9
126 1/8	19 5/8	19 7/8	16 2/8	3 7/8	3 7/8	6	6	Pima Co., AZ	Robert G. McDonald	Robert G. McDonald	1986	11
125 4/8	18 6/8	19	16 2/8	3 6/8	3 6/8	5	5	Arivaca, AZ	Gerald Harris	Gerald Harris	1953	12
125	19 6/8	19 7/8	15 4/8	4 1/8	4 1/8	5	5	Ft. Apache Res., AZ	Picked Up	Jerry S. Pippen	PR 1969	13
125	21	20 6/8	16 2/8	4 3/8	4 4/8	4	5	Sonora, MX	Enrique Barrett	Enrique Barrett	1995	13
124 7/8	18 4/8	18 5/8	12 6/8	4 4/8	4 5/8	6	4	Hidalgo Co., NM	Martha M. Montes	Martha M. Montes	1994	15
124 5/8	19 6/8	19	14 1/8	4	4 1/8	6	6	Rincon Mts., AZ	James Pfersdorf	Mrs. J.E. Pfersdorf, Sr.	1936	16
124 5/8	18 2/8	18 7/8	13 5/8	3 6/8	3 6/8	5	5	Sonora, MX	Enrique Lares	Enrique Lares	1959	16
124	19 1/8	19 1/8	16 6/8	3 7/8	3 7/8	5	5	Greenlee Co., AZ	Ronald H. Gerdes	Ronald H. Gerdes	1993	18
123 7/8	17 2/8	17 3/8	13 7/8	4 3/8	4 3/8	6	6	Gila Co., AZ	Stephen P. Hayes	Stephen P. Hayes	1965	19
123 7/8	21 3/8	19 5/8	15 3/8	4 2/8	4 1/8	5	4	Pima Co., AZ	Kenneth R. Murray	Kenneth R. Murray	1996	19
123 6/8	18 2/8	17 7/8	14 2/8	4 4/8	4 4/8	6	6	Cochise Co., AZ	Larry Vance, Jr.	Larry Vance, Jr.	1985	21
122 7/8	18 7/8	18 2/8	14 1/8	4 1/8	4	5	5	Chiricahua Mts., AZ	Roger Becksted	Roger Becksted	1960	22
122 4/8	22	20 4/8	15 2/8	3 1/8	3 2/8	5	5	Sonora, MX	Lloyd L. Ward, Jr.	Lloyd L. Ward, Jr.	1945	23
121 5/8	20 1/8	19 3/8	15 5/8	4 2/8	4	4	4	Pima Co., AZ	Joe Fanning	Joe Fanning	1964	24
121 3/8	19	17 6/8	14 1/8	4	3 6/8	6	6	Santa Rita Mts., AZ	Max E. Wilson	Max E. Wilson	1965	25
121 1/8	16 1/8	17	10 7/8	3 4/8	3 4/8	6	6	Santa Rita Mts., AZ	George Shaar	George Shaar	1964	26
121 1/8	19 5/8	19 2/8	15 7/8	3 7/8	3 7/8	5	5	Pima Co., AZ	T. Reed Scott	T. Reed Scott	1975	27
121	20 3/8	19 5/8	13	3 7/8	3 7/8	5	5	Sierra Madre Mts., MX	Herb Klein	Herb Klein	1965	28
120 7/8	20 7/8	19 4/8	16 3/8	4 3/8	4 1/8	5	6	Santa Rita Mts., AZ	Harold Lyons	Harold Lyons	1956	29
120 6/8	19 4/8	18 2/8	14 4/8	4	4	5	5	Sonora, MX	Manuel A. Caravantez	Manuel A. Caravantez	1960	30
120 5/8	19	19 2/8	12 1/8	4 2/8	4 4/8	5	5	Sonora, MX	George W. Parker	George W. Parker	1969	31
120 5/8	20 1/8	19 2/8	16 3/8	3 5/8	3 6/8	4	4	Cochise Co., AZ	Becki D. Goffrier	Becki D. Goffrier	1984	31
120 4/8	17 6/8	18 3/8	13	4 2/8	4	4	4	Sonora, MX	Diego G. Sada	Diego G. Sada	1969	33
120 3/8	19 6/8	20 6/8	16 7/8	4 2/8	4 2/8	5	5	Sonora, MX	J. Marvin Smith III	J. Marvin Smith III	1990	34
120 1/8	18	18 5/8	13 5/8	4	4	5	6	Baboquivari Mts., AZ	Homer R. Edds	Homer R. Edds	1961	35
119 7/8	20 7/8	21 2/8	17 5/8	4 1/8	3 7/8	4	4	Gila Co., AZ	Tom Connolly	Tom Connolly	1960	36

Score								Locality	By	Owner	Date	Rank
119 7/8	20 2/8	20 4/8	15 1/8	4 4/8	4 6/8	4	5	Sonora, MX	Picked Up	George W. Parker	1960	36
119 6/8	20 1/8	19	12 2/8	4	4 1/8	5	4	Canelo Hills, AZ	George W. Parker	George W. Parker	1960	38
119 6/8	19 3/8	19 4/8	13 2/8	3 7/8	3 6/8	5	5	Hidalgo Co., NM	Frank L. Riley	Frank L. Riley	1990	38
119 3/8	19 6/8	20 1/8	12	3 7/8	3 7/8	6	6	Canelo Hills, AZ	A.R. Anglen	A.R. Anglen	1967	40
119 2/8	16 7/8	18 6/8	15	3 7/8	3 7/8	7	6	Sonora, MX	Bert M. Pringle	Mrs. Bert M. Pringle	1952	41
119 2/8	18	19 2/8	15 4/8	4 1/8	3 7/8	4	4	Sonora, MX	Michael Lonuzzi	Michael Lonuzzi	1996	41
119 1/8	18	19 2/8	10 5/8	5	5 3/8	6	6	Santa Rita Mts., AZ	Monte L. Colvin	Monte L. Colvin	1965	43
119 1/8	19 6/8	19	14 3/8	3 5/8	3 3/8	4	4	Cochise Co., AZ	James A. Leiendecker	James A. Leiendecker	1986	43
119 1/8	18 2/8	18	15 3/8	3 7/8	3 7/8	4	4	Pima Co., AZ	Scott Davis	Scott Davis	1995	43
119	17 5/8	17 4/8	13 6/8	3 4/8	3 5/8	7	6	Hidalgo Co., NM	Jesse E. Williams	Jesse E. Williams	1971	46
118 5/8	19 5/8	19 7/8	14 5/8	4 4/8	4 3/8	4	4	Chiricahua Mts., AZ	Ward Becksted	Ward Becksted	1958	47
118 3/8	18 6/8	18 7/8	13 7/8	3 4/8	3 6/8	4	4	Hidalgo Co., NM	Michael E. Duperret	M.E. Duperret & J.K. Volk	1993	48
118 1/8	17 1/8	17 3/8	15 1/8	3 7/8	3 7/8	5	5	Santa Cruz Co., AZ	David W. Ahnell	David W. Ahnell	1977	49
118	16 6/8	16 5/8	14 1/8	4 1/8	4 2/8	8	7	Washington Mts., AZ	Ralph Vaga	Ralph Vaga	1962	50
118	18 2/8	19 2/8	12 6/8	3 5/8	3 7/8	4	4	Santa Cruz Co., AZ	Michael L. Valenzuela	Michael L. Valenzuela	1982	50
118	17 7/8	18 1/8	13	4 1/8	4	7	7	Pima Co., AZ	Larry C. Dixon	Larry C. Dixon	1995	50
117 7/8	18 1/8	18 1/8	16 5/8	4	4	4	5	Rincon Mts., AZ	Picked Up	H.L. Russell	1963	53
117 7/8	19 5/8	19 4/8	12 3/8	4 1/8	3 7/8	6	6	Santa Rita Mts., AZ	George Shaar	George Shaar	1965	53
117 6/8	18 6/8	17 7/8	14	3 5/8	3 5/8	4	5	Canelo Hills, AZ	Raymond J. Kassler	Raymond J. Kassler	1958	55
117 5/8	20 3/8	20	18 5/8	4 2/8	4	4	4	Libertad, MX	Abe R. Hughes	Abe R. Hughes	1967	56
117 4/8	17 7/8	17 1/8	14 4/8	4 6/8	4 5/8	4	4	Graham Co., AZ	Steven J. Stayner	Steven J. Stayner	1993	57
117 3/8	17 4/8	17 1/8	14 3/8	4 3/8	4 3/8	4	4	Atasco Mts., AZ	F.O. Haskell	F.O. Haskell	1939	58
117 3/8	17 2/8	17 2/8	12 5/8	3 6/8	3 6/8	5	6	Sicritta Mts., AZ	George S. Tsaguris	George S. Tsaguris	1958	58
117 3/8	19 2/8	19 3/8	16 3/8	3 6/8	3 6/8	4	4	Sonora, MX	Charles B. Leonard	Charles B. Leonard	1974	58
117 2/8	19	19 3/8	11 6/8	4 7/8	4 4/8	8	8	Santa Rita Mts., AZ	George L. Garlits	George L. Garlits	1957	61
117 2/8	17 6/8	18 2/8	17 5/8	4 4/8	4 2/8	4	4	Chiricahua Mts., AZ	Picked Up	Warren A. Cartier	1963	61
117 2/8	18	18	12	3 5/8	3 4/8	5	5	Tumacacori Mts., AZ	Charles H. Pennington	Charles H. Pennington	1968	61
117	18 3/8	18 2/8	14 2/8	4 1/8	4 2/8	4	4	Cochise Co., AZ	W.R. Tanner	Fred Tanner	1941	64
117	18 7/8	19 1/8	16	3 6/8	3 6/8	7	6	Pima Co., AZ	Arthur L. Butler	Arthur L. Butler	1974	64
116 7/8	18 1/8	17 3/8	13 1/8	3 6/8	3 6/8	5	6	Santa Cruz Co., AZ	Seymour H. Levy	Seymour H. Levy	1967	66
116 7/8	19	19 6/8	16 3/8	4	3 6/8	5	6	Pima Co., AZ	Arcenio G. Valdez	Arcenio G. Valdez	1971	66
116 6/8	17 7/8	18 3/8	14	4 7/8	5	4	4	Coconino Co., AZ	Clay McDonald	Clay McDonald	1985	68
116 6/8	18 2/8	18 1/8	15 4/8	4 5/8	4 3/8	5	5	Yavapai Co., AZ	Kevin S. Stimple	Kevin S. Stimple	1992	68
116 5/8	17 5/8	19	14 3/8	4	4	4	4	Santa Rita Mts., AZ	Mike Holloran	Mike Holloran	1962	70
116 4/8	17 2/8	17 3/8	14 7/8	4 6/8	4 5/8	5	5	Gila Co., AZ	Richard A. Thom	Richard A. Thom	1978	70
116 4/8	19 5/8	20 2/8	14 5/8	3 7/8	3 6/8	6	6	Gila Co., AZ	Nathan Ellison	Nathan Ellison	1950	72
116 3/8	19 2/8	19	14 7/8	4 1/8	4 2/8	5	5	Blue River, AZ	Earl H. Harris	Earl H. Harris	1965	73
116 2/8	15 2/8	16 4/8	13 4/8	4 3/8	4 3/8	6	6	Chiricahua Mts., AZ	Freeman Neal	R.M. Woods	1947	74
116 2/8	16 2/8	16 5/8	14	4	4	5	5	Graham Co., AZ	Dale J. Holladay	Dale J. Holladay	1984	74
116 1/8	19 4/8	19 5/8	12 7/8	3 6/8	3 6/8	4	4	Greenlee Co., AZ	Richard A. Benson	Richard A. Benson	1991	76
116	17 4/8	17 3/8	13 2/8	4 6/8	4 7/8	4	4	Santa Cruz Co., AZ	Ben Richardson	Ben Richardson	1978	77
116	19	18 7/8	14	3 5/8	3 5/8	4	4	Santa Cruz Co., AZ	Jeffrey C. Lichtenwalter	Jeffrey C. Lichtenwalter	1982	77
115 7/8	18 6/8	16 7/8	14 3/8	4 6/8	4 6/8	5	5	Sonora, MX	Berry B. Brooks	Berry B. Brooks	1954	79
115 7/8	19 2/8	18 6/8	14 1/8	4 1/8	4	7	7	Yavapai Co., AZ	Robert W. Gaylor	Robert W. Gaylor	1987	79
115 5/8	18 5/8	18 4/8	14 3/8	3 6/8	3 7/8	5	5	Breadpan Mt., AZ	Mitchell R. Holder	Mitchell R. Holder	1966	81
115 4/8	15 6/8	16 6/8	13	4	4 2/8	4	4	Santa Rita Mts., AZ	Picked Up	James Bramhall	PR 1963	82
115 4/8	18 2/8	18 2/8	15	4	4	5	4	Cochise Co., AZ	Bill Byrd	Bill Byrd	1983	82

COUES' WHITETAIL DEER - TYPICAL ANTLERS

Odocoileus virginianus couesi

Score	Length of Main Beam R	L	Inside Spread	Circumference at Smallest Place Between Burr and First Point R	L	Number of Points R	L	Locality	Hunter	Owner	Date Killed	Rank
115 4/8	18	17 1/8	15 4/8	4 2/8	4 2/8	5	4	Gila Co., AZ	Doug J. Althoff	Doug J. Althoff	1985	82
115 3/8	19 1/8	19 5/8	19 5/8	3 7/8	3 6/8	4	4	Pima Co., AZ	William H. Taylor	William H. Taylor	1986	85
115 2/8	17 2/8	17	13 4/8	5	4 7/8	5	4	Santa Rita Mts., AZ	Denis Wolstenholme	Denis Wolstenholme	1958	86
115 2/8	18	20 1/8	15	4	4	5	4	Cerro Colo. Mts., AZ	Manuel V. Guillen	Manuel V. Guillen	1962	86
115 2/8	20 4/8	19 4/8	12 6/8	4 2/8	4 3/8	5	5	Santa Rita Mts., AZ	Bill J. Ford	Bill J. Ford	1965	86
115 2/8	20 1/8	19	16 4/8	4 2/8	4 3/8	5	5	Catalina Mts., AZ	Jim Stough	Jim Stough	1972	86
115	19 6/8	19 5/8	17 6/8	4 2/8	4 1/8	4	4	Baboquivari Mts., AZ	Karl G. Ronstadt	Karl G. Ronstadt	1967	90
115	19 6/8	20 1/8	18 2/8	4	4	4	4	Coconino Co., AZ	Picked Up	Jerry C. Walters	PR 1970	90
115	18 4/8	18 1/8	16 6/8	4	4	5	5	Pima Co., AZ	Glen A. Elmer	Glen A. Elmer	1980	90
115	18 6/8	18	17 2/8	4	4	5	5	Pinal Co., AZ	George Martin	George Martin	1983	90
114 7/8	18 2/8	18 6/8	12 3/8	4 7/8	4 7/8	4	4	Ruby, AZ	Richard McDaniel	Richard McDaniel	1963	94
114 7/8	20	19 4/8	16 1/8	3 6/8	3 6/8	5	4	Santa Rita Mts., AZ	John H. Lake	John H. Lake	1965	94
114 6/8	18	19	13 1/8	4 3/8	4 2/8	5	5	Sonora, MX	Carlos G. Hermosillo	Carlos G. Hermosillo	1995	94
114 6/8	16 6/8	16 6/8	13 6/8	4 1/8	4 1/8	5	5	Chihuahua, MX	Tom Jones	George B. Johnson	1932	97
114 6/8	19 5/8	19 3/8	14 5/8	4 4/8	4 5/8	6	8	Chiricahua Mts., AZ	John Miller	John Miller	1949	97
114 6/8	17 4/8	16	15 2/8	4 5/8	4 4/8	4	5	Santa Rita Mts., AZ	Art Pollard	Art Pollard	1951	97
114 6/8	17 2/8	17 4/8	16 2/8	4 2/8	4	4	4	Cochise Co., AZ	Rudy Alvarez	Rudy Alvarez	1960	97
114 6/8	18 3/8	18	15 1/8	4	3 7/8	6	5	Canelo Hills, AZ	Guy Perry	Guy Perry	1960	97
114 6/8	16 6/8	16 4/8	11	4 2/8	4 3/8	5	7	Santa Rita Mts., AZ	John Bessett	John Bessett	1965	97
114 5/8	17 5/8	17 5/8	14 4/8	4	4 1/8	5	5	Nogales, AZ	Arthur N. Lindsey	Arthur N. Lindsey	1967	97
114 5/8	15 2/8	14 7/8	14 3/8	3 4/8	3 5/8	5	5	Gila Co., AZ	J. Bradley Johns	J. Bradley Johns	1992	104
114 5/8	18 6/8	19 2/8	15 5/8	4	3 7/8	5	5	Sonora, MX	David A. Miller	David A. Miller	1992	104
114 4/8	19 3/8	20 4/8	15	4 2/8	4 4/8	4	4	Graham Mts., AZ	Robert Stonoff	Robert Stonoff	1962	106
114 4/8	15 6/8	16 1/8	12 4/8	3 7/8	4 1/8	6	4	Patagonia Mts., AZ	Verna Conlisk ·	Verna Conlisk ·	1964	106
114 4/8	17 5/8	17 1/8	13 7/8	3 5/8	3 5/8	6	5	Cherry Creek, AZ	Alan G. Adams	Alan G. Adams	1968	106
114 4/8	15 6/8	15 4/8	14 2/8	3 5/8	3 5/8	5	5	Chiricahua Mts., MX	Elgin T. Gates	Elgin T. Gates	1968	106
114 4/8	19 6/8	18 3/8	14 4/8	3 6/8	3 6/8	4	4	Pima Co., AZ	James M. Machac	James M. Machac	1985	106
114 4/8	18	17 5/8	15	4 2/8	4 1/8	4	4	Gila Co., AZ	Dallas J. Duhamell, Jr.	Dallas J. Duhamell, Jr.	1990	106
114 3/8	18	18 3/8	12 5/8	4	3 7/8	4	4	Atasco Mts., AZ	Antonio Lopez	Antonio Lopez	1961	112
114 2/8	18 4/8	15 7/8	15 2/8	4 3/8	4 2/8	5	6	Catalina Mts., AZ	Wayne L. Heckler	Wayne L. Heckler	1958	113
114 2/8	16 2/8	17 1/8	11 5/8	4	4 2/8	5	6	Canelo, AZ	Earl Stillson	Earl Stillson	1967	113
114 2/8	20 7/8	17 4/8	17	4 2/8	4 2/8	5	5	Grant Co., NM	Picked Up	Victor P. Giacoletti, Jr.	1985	113
114 1/8	18 7/8	16 3/8	14 1/8	4 4/8	4 2/8	4	4	Sonora, MX	Unknown	Bill Quimby	PR 1965	116
114 1/8	17 2/8	17 2/8	16 7/8	3 4/8	3 4/8	5	5	Yavapai Co., AZ	Jim D. Snodgrass	Jim D. Snodgrass	1983	116
114	18 4/8	18 1/8	10 4/8	3 6/8	3 6/8	4	4	Animas Mts., NM	Frank C. Hibben	Frank C. Hibben	1955	118
113 7/8	18 4/8	17 6/8	14 2/8	3 5/8	3 4/8	4	5	Galiuro Mts., AZ	Clifford Kouts	Clifford Kouts	1964	119

Score								Locality	Hunter	Owner	Year
113 7/8	20 1/8	19 7/8	12	4 5/8	4 5/8	5	5	Santa Rita Mts., AZ	Joe Moore	Joe Moore	1968
113 7/8	17	16 1/8	14 5/8	3 4/8	3 3/8	5	5	Sonora, MX	James W. Hutcheson	James W. Hutcheson	1996
113 6/8	18 2/8	18 4/8	13 4/8	3 6/8	3 6/8	8	8	Chihuahua, MX	Herb Klein	Herb Klein	1957
113 6/8	15 4/8	16	13 6/8	4	4	5	5	Mt. Graham, AZ	Bill Sizer	Bill Sizer	1963
113 6/8	17 3/8	16	13 5/8	4 2/8	4 5/8	6	7	Galiuro Mts., AZ	Doran V. Porter	Doran V. Porter	1966
113 6/8	18	17 7/8	14 6/8	4	4	5	4	Pima Co., AZ	Richard Huber	Richard N. Huber	1979
113 6/8	18 4/8	18	13 2/8	3 6/8	4	5	4	Pima Co., AZ	Andy A. Ramirez	Andy A. Ramirez	1979
113 5/8	19	17 6/8	16 5/8	4 1/8	3 7/8	5	5	Graham Mts., AZ	J.H. Hunt	J.H. Hunt	1962
113 5/8	19	18 6/8	17 1/8	4 1/8	3 7/8	4	4	Pinal Co., AZ	Randall E. Martin	Randall E. Martin	1992
113 4/8	19 2/8	19 2/8	15	3 6/8	3 7/8	4	4	Sonora, MX	George W. Parker	George W. Parker	1947
113 4/8	16 7/8	16 2/8	12 4/8	3 7/8	4	4	4	Santa Rita Mts., AZ	Jack Englet	Jack Englet	1962
113 4/8	19 6/8	19	14 2/8	4 1/8	3 6/8	6	6	Santa Rita Mts., AZ	George W. Parker	George W. Parker	1962
113 4/8	17 4/8	17 1/8	12 2/8	4 5/8	3 7/8	6	6	Santa Cruz Co., AZ	Robert A. Smith	Robert A. Smith	1985
113 3/8	16	16 3/8	12 5/8	4	4	4	4	Santa Teresa Mts., AZ	D.B. Sanford	D.B. Sanford	1950
113 3/8	17 3/8	16 7/8	13 3/8	4	4 4/8	5	5	Tumacacori Mts., AZ	Tom W. Caid	Tom W. Caid	1958
113 3/8	18	17	14 3/8	4 4/8	4 2/8	4	4	Four Peaks Mt., AZ	Carl J. Slagel	Carl J. Slagel	1963
113 3/8	16 5/8	16 4/8	12 4/8	3 6/8	4	4	4	Pima Co., AZ	Sam E. Harrison, Jr.	Sam E. Harrison, Jr.	1969
113 2/8	16 7/8	16 7/8	14 4/8	4	4 4/8	4	4	Santa Rita Mts., AZ	Donna Greene	Donna Greene	1958
113 2/8	18 7/8	17 5/8	14 4/8	4 1/8	3 6/8	5	5	Tumacacori Mts., AZ	Carlos G. Touche	Carlos G. Touche	1961
113 2/8	18	17	14 2/8	4 1/8	4	5	5	Santa Cruz Co., AZ	Hector Guglielmo	Hector Guglielmo	1984
113 2/8	19 3/8	18 5/8	16	4 4/8	4 1/8	5	4	Gila Co., AZ	David W. Miller, Jr.	David W. Miller, Jr.	1984
113 1/8	20 1/8	19 6/8	19	4 2/8	4 4/8	4	4	Chiricahua Mts., AZ	Ralph Hopkins	Fred Tanner	1928
113 1/8	15 6/8	16 2/8	15 4/8	3 6/8	4 1/8	6	6	Grant Co., NM	Andrew A. Musacchio	Andrew A. Musacchio	1985
113	18 1/8	18 1/8	18	3 6/8	4 4/8	5	5	Canelo Hills, AZ	Carlos Ochoa	Carlos Ochoa	1955
113	19	18 7/8	12 2/8	4 2/8	4 2/8	4	4	Tumacacori Mts., AZ	Basil C. Bradbury	Basil C. Bradbury	1968
112 7/8	17	17	14 5/8	3 4/8	3 6/8	5	5	Ruby, AZ	Roger Scott	Roger Scott	1962
112 7/8	18 3/8	17 6/8	14 5/8	3 6/8	4 2/8	4	4	Catron Co., NM	Picked Up	Mark Barboa	1994
112 7/8	17 5/8	18 2/8	13 1/8	5 1/8	3 4/8	4	4	Gila Co., AZ	James J. Zanzot	James J. Zanzot	1995
112 6/8	17 5/8	18 4/8	14 4/8	4 4/8	4 1/8	6	6	Baboquivari Mts., AZ	Charles R. Whitfield	Charles R. Whitfield	1969
112 6/8	17 4/8	18 6/8	15 7/8	4 7/8	4 6/8	6	5	Cochise Co., AZ	Mike York	Mike York	1973
112 5/8	18 1/8	17 2/8	14 1/8	4	4 6/8	6	6	Sonora, MX	Henry Lares	Henry Lares	1959
112 5/8	18 6/8	18 6/8	13 1/8	3 4/8	3 7/8	4	4	Sonora, MX	William W. Sharp	William W. Sharp	1968
112 5/8	17 6/8	17 6/8	15 3/8	5	3 5/8	6	5	Greenlee Co., AZ	John W. Barber	John W. Barber	1985
112 4/8	17 3/8	17 4/8	15	4 2/8	4 7/8	4	4	Gila Co., AZ	R.T. Beach & L.A. Mossinger	Ronald T. Beach	1974
112 4/8	14 6/8	14 6/8	13	3 5/8	4 3/8	4	5	Pima Co., AZ	Gary D. Ramirez	Gary D. Ramirez	1993
112 3/8	17 3/8	17	15 5/8	4 1/8	3 4/8	6	6	White Mts., AZ	Dennis E. Nolen	Dennis E. Nolen	1961
112 3/8	19	19 5/8	13 3/8	4 2/8	4 2/8	5	5	Santa Cruz Co., AZ	W.C. Grant	W.C. Grant	1973
112 2/8	19 6/8	19 1/8	11 6/8	4 4/8	4 4/8	4	4	Sonora, MX	George W. Parker	George W. Parker	1960
112 2/8	18	17 6/8	17	3 4/8	3 5/8	5	5	Maricopa Co., AZ	Gary D. Nichols	Gary D. Nichols	1980
112 2/8	16 2/8	16	13 2/8	4	3 7/8	5	5	Pima Co., AZ	William W. Sharp	William W. Sharp	1981
112 2/8	17 3/8	17 5/8	15	4 6/8	4 6/8	5	5	Pima Co., AZ	Angel J. Yslas	Angel J. Yslas	1994
112 1/8	18 2/8	18 6/8	15 5/8	4 4/8	4 2/8	4	4	Cochise Co., AZ	Edwin L. Hawkins	Edwin L. Hawkins	1977
112 1/8	17 2/8	17 1/8	14 4/8	3 7/8	3 7/8	6	7	Pima Co., AZ	David J. Vancas	David J. Vancas	1985
112 1/8	18 3/8	18 2/8	10 7/8	3 7/8	3 7/8	5	4	Pima Co., AZ	Travis D. Robbins	Travis D. Robbins	1992
112	18 7/8	18 3/8	17 1/8	4 4/8	4 3/8	4	4	Bartlett Mts., AZ	Keith Robbins	Keith Robbins	1957
112	17 2/8	18	14 2/8	3 6/8	3 6/8	5	5	Baboquivari Mts., AZ	Jesse Genin	Jesse Genin	1961
112	15 4/8	15 6/8	12 4/8	3 6/8	3 7/8	5	5	Greenlee Co., AZ	Jerald S. Wager	Jerald S. Wager	1982

Odocoileus virginianus couesi

Score	Length of Main Beam R	L	Inside Spread	Circumference at Smallest Place Between Burr and First Point R	L	Number of Points R	L	Locality	Hunter	Owner	Date Killed	Rank
111 7/8	18 6/8	17 6/8	13 7/8	4	4	4	4	Canelo Hills, AZ	Walter G. Sheets	Walter G. Sheets	1959	167
111 7/8	20 5/8	20 5/8	15 3/8	4	4	4	6	Greenlee Co., AZ	Ronald H. Gerdes	Ronald H. Gerdes	1992	167
111 6/8	17 1/8	16 4/8	13 2/8	3 2/8	3 2/8	5	5	Gila Co., AZ	Karl J. Payne	Karl J. Payne	1955	169
111 6/8	17	17 1/8	11 6/8	3 5/8	3 5/8	5	5	Catron Co., NM	Charles Tapia	Charles Tapia	1959	169
111 6/8	18 6/8	19 5/8	14 1/8	4 5/8	3 7/8	6	5	Patagonia Mts., AZ	Norval L. Wesson	Norval L. Wesson	1967	169
111 6/8	18 2/8	18 5/8	14 4/8	3 5/8	3 4/8	5	5	Baboquivari Mts., AZ	Stanley W. Gaines	Stanley W. Gaines	1971	169
111 6/8	17 1/8	16 5/8	14	3 7/8	3 7/8	4	5	Pima Co., AZ	George V. Borquez	George V. Borquez	1979	169
111 6/8	16 5/8	16 6/8	12 3/8	4 4/8	4 4/8	5	8	Cochise Co., AZ	Gregory F. Lucero	Gregory F. Lucero	1991	169
111 5/8	18 7/8	19	14 6/8	4 3/8	4 3/8	5	6	Santa Rita Mts., AZ	Rick Detwiler	Rick Detwiler	1968	175
111 4/8	20 1/8	19 5/8	14 2/8	4	3 7/8	5	5	Sonora, MX	George W. Parker	George W. Parker	1926	176
111 4/8	17 4/8	18	15	3 6/8	4	4	4	Santa Rita Mts., AZ	Tom L. Swanson	Tom L. Swanson	1965	176
111 4/8	17 6/8	17 7/8	15 4/8	4 6/8	4 4/8	5	4	Coconino Co., AZ	Dennis L. Campbell	Picked Up	1987	176
111 4/8	18 2/8	17 7/8	17 6/8	4 2/8	4 1/8	5	4	Graham Co., AZ	Robert L. Osborn	Robert L. Osborn	1993	176
111 3/8	20 6/8	21 2/8	12 3/8	3 6/8	3 4/8	4	4	Sierra Madre Mts., MX	Herb Klein	Herb Klein	1965	180
111 3/8	18 6/8	18 2/8	12 5/8	3 6/8	3 6/8	5	5	Pima Co., AZ	Unknown	Ruel Holt	PR 1974	180
111 3/8	17 6/8	18 5/8	16 5/8	4 1/8	4 1/8	4	4	Santa Cruz Co., AZ	Frank Yubeta III	Frank Yubeta III	1983	180
111 2/8	17 6/8	17	15 2/8	4	4	4	4	Graham Co., AZ	C.R. Hale	C.R. Hale	1958	183
111 2/8	18 7/8	19 5/8	11 6/8	3 4/8	3 4/8	4	4	Sonora, MX	George W. Parker	George W. Parker	1960	183
111 2/8	19 2/8	19 4/8	16 6/8	4	4	5	5	Graham Mts., AZ	Bill Barney	Bill Barney	1962	183
111 2/8	19 1/8	19	15 6/8	4 2/8	4 3/8	4	4	Atascosa Mt., AZ	Henry B. Carrillo	Henry B. Carrillo	1964	183
111 2/8	17 5/8	17 3/8	11 2/8	4	3 6/8	6	6	Santa Rita Mts., AZ	Lon E. Bothwell	Lon E. Bothwell	1969	183
111 2/8	16 4/8	16 4/8	15 2/8	3 4/8	3 4/8	5	5	Santa Cruz Co., AZ	Robert L. Rabb	Robert L. Rabb	1977	183
111 2/8	16 2/8	15 6/8	12 3/8	4	3 6/8	6	6	Hidalgo Co., NM	Jess Jones	Jess Jones	1993	183
111 1/8	17 5/8	17 6/8	16	4 1/8	3 7/8	5	5	Sonora, MX	Joe Daneker, Jr.	Joe Daneker, Jr.	1973	190
111 1/8	17 5/8	17 4/8	14 5/8	4 1/8	4 1/8	5	5	Cochise Co., AZ	Harvey G. Ward, Jr.	Harvey G. Ward, Jr.	1988	190
111 1/8	18	17	14 5/8	4	3 7/8	5	5	Pinal Co., AZ	John P. Garcia	John P. Garcia	1991	190
111	17 6/8	17 6/8	17 6/8	3 7/8	3 7/8	4	4	Pima Co., AZ	William G. Roberts	William G. Roberts	1992	193
111	18 6/8	17 2/8	15	4	4	4	4	Pima Co., AZ	Michael W. Lynch	Michael W. Lynch	1996	193
110 7/8	19 2/8	19 4/8	13 1/8	3 6/8	3 6/8	4	4	Chiricahua Mts., AZ	Wayne A. Dirst	Wayne A. Dirst	1954	195
110 7/8	17 2/8	18 6/8	11 2/8	4	4 1/8	5	5	Canelo Hills, AZ	Bill Fidelo	Bill Fidelo	1958	195
110 7/8	19 3/8	19	15 7/8	3 6/8	3 5/8	5	7	Rincon Mts., AZ	Ollie O. Barney, Jr.	Ollie O. Barney, Jr.	1961	195
110 7/8	16 6/8	16 5/8	13 1/8	4	4	6	4	Pima Co., AZ	William W. Sharp	William W. Sharp	1974	195
110 7/8	18 6/8	19 2/8	15 6/8	4 2/8	4 3/8	5	5	Gila Co., AZ	Kristin M. Currie	Kristin M. Currie	1994	195
110 6/8	18	18 2/8	13 4/8	3 6/8	3 6/8	4	5	Catalina Mts., AZ	H.C. Ruff	H.C. Ruff	1959	200
110 6/8	18 5/8	18 2/8	15 6/8	4	4	4	4	Santa Rita Mts., AZ	John S. McFarling	John S. McFarling	1965	200
110 5/8	18 5/8	18 4/8	15	3 2/8	3 5/8	5	4	Pima Co., AZ	David E. Furnas	David E. Furnas	1990	202

Score						Points R	Points L	Locality	Owner	Hunter	Date	Rank
110 5/8	17 5/8	17 2/8	18	3 5/8	3 5/8	4	4	Pima Co., AZ	James E. Hatcher	James E. Hatcher	1993	202
110 5/8	17 2/8	17	11 3/8	3 4/8	3 4/8	5	5	Chihuahua, MX	David A. Miller	David A. Miller	1997	202
110 4/8	16 7/8	17 6/8	14 2/8	4 4/8	4 4/8	4	4	Canelo Mts., AZ	Otto L. Fritz	Otto L. Fritz	1947	205
110 4/8	16 7/8	16 6/8	14 2/8	4 1/8	4	5	5	Tumacacori Mts., AZ	John Doyle	John Doyle	1966	205
110 4/8	18	18 4/8	14 2/8	3 3/8	4 2/8	4	4	Sonora, MX	Ricardo Andrade	Ricardo Andrade	1988	205
110 4/8	18 6/8	18 3/8	14 6/8	4 2/8	4	4	5	Pima Co., AZ	William T. Crutchley	William T. Crutchley	1992	205
110 3/8	17 7/8	17 7/8	13 7/8	4 1/8	3 4/8	4	4	Santa Rita Mts., AZ	Edward L. Blixt	Edward L. Blixt	1946	209
110 3/8	18 7/8	18 4/8	12 6/8	3 7/8	3 4/8	4	4	Santa Rita Mts., AZ	Lyle K. Sowls	Lyle K. Sowls	1956	209
110 3/8	17 6/8	18 6/8	15 7/8	3 6/8	4 6/8	4	5	Hidalgo Co., NM	Ronald M. Gerdes	Ronald M. Gerdes	1979	209
110 2/8	17	16 3/8	14	4 6/8	4	5	5	Gila Co., AZ	William P. Hampton, Jr.	William P. Hampton, Jr.	1976	212
110 2/8	16	15 4/8	15 4/8	4 1/8	4	4	4	Hidalgo Co., NM	Jay M. Gates III	Jay M. Gates III	1981	212
110 2/8	18 6/8	17 5/8	16	3 7/8	3 6/8	5	5	Yavapai Co., AZ	David G. Mattausch	David G. Mattausch	1984	212
110 2/8	19 1/8	16 3/8	15 7/8	4 4/8	4 6/8	4	4	Payson, AZ	Fred J. Nobbe, Jr.	Fred J. Nobbe, Jr.	1994	212
110 1/8	16 7/8	19 2/8	16 3/8	3 5/8	3 5/8	5	4	Santa Cruz Co., AZ	Richard Noonan	Picked Up	PR 1963	216
110 1/8	19 2/8	16 3/8	11 5/8	4 4/8	4 3/8	4	5	Hidalgo Co., NM	David A. Miller	David A. Miller	1977	216
110 1/8	16 1/8	17	12 3/8	4 7/8	4 4/8	4	4	Pima Co., AZ	Neuman Sanford	Neuman Sanford	1981	216
110 1/8	16 4/8	17 6/8	16 4/8	4 5/8	4 6/8	4	4	Cochise Co., AZ	Andy C. Strebe	Andy C. Strebe	1981	216
110 1/8	18 2/8	18 6/8	14 2/8	4 2/8	4 3/8	5	5	Cochise Co., AZ	Richard T. Ziehmer	Richard T. Ziehmer	1995	216
110	19 4/8	17 6/8	14 5/8	4 6/8	5	4	5	Sonora, MX	Enrique C. Cicero	Enrique C. Cicero	1966	221
110	18 1/8	18 2/8	18 1/8	3 6/8	4	4	6	Cochise Co., AZ	Bill Saathoff	Bill Saathoff	1987	221
110	18 1/8	19 7/8	15 4/8	4 3/8	4	5	4	Pima Co., AZ	David E. Furnas	David E. Furnas	1991	221
119 4/8*	19 7/8	19 7/8	15 4/8	4 2/8	4	5	4	Cochise Co., AZ	James A. Hall	James A. Hall	1991	
119 4/8*	18 4/8	18 2/8	16 4/8	4 2/8	4 1/8	4	4	Gila Co., AZ	Allen J. Anspach	Allen J. Anspach	1992	

* Final score is subject to revision by additional verifying measurements.

CATEGORY
COUES' WHITETAIL DEER
TYPICAL ANTLERS

SCORE
119-2/8

HUNTER
MICHAEL LONUZZI

LOCATION
SONORA, MX

DATE OF KILL
JANUARY 1996

CATEGORY
COUES' WHITETAIL DEER
TYPICAL ANTLERS

SCORE
110-7/8

HUNTER
KRISTIN M. CURRIE

LOCATION
GILA CO., AZ

DATE OF KILL
DECEMBER 1994

CATEGORY
COUES' WHITETAIL DEER
TYPICAL ANTLERS

SCORE
125

HUNTER
ENRIQUE BARRETT

LOCATION
SONORA, MX

DATE OF KILL
DECEMBER 1995

B&C HISTORY

WILLIAM T. HORNADAY
1854-1937

Born in 1854, this Indiana farm boy, was to become one of the Nation's most eloquent leaders in the protection of wildlife. His early interest was in scientific taxidermy. He founded the National Society of American Taxidermists in New York in 1880. He was appointed chief taxidermist of the U.S. National Museum in Washington, D.C. Later, as director of the New York Zoological Society, he supervised the building and administration of the Bronx Zoo. He wrote hundreds of newspaper and magazine articles and over 20 books in the field of conservation. He was a leading influence in the passage of the Federal Migratory Bird Law and the 1911 Fur Seal Treaty. But his greatest victory was probably his successful fight to preserve the American bison from extermination. ■

415

In January 1988, while hunting quail in the Patagonia Mountains of Arizona, Walter H. Pollock spotted the seemingly light and graceful rack of a Coues' whitetail deer.

"We had hunted most of the morning, with some success, and we were returning to the vehicles when, as I was walking through a little glen, something lying on the ground caught my eye.

"I walked over and saw small deer antlers lying on the ground, just waiting to be picked up. All that remained, besides the skull and antlers, was a small amount of hair that formed an outline of the deer's body. I thought these were small antlers because I am used to looking at mule deer antlers back in Colorado. I remembered that Steve Hopkins, a local taxidermist, had told me that if I ever found any Coues' deer antlers, he could always use them in his practice.

"After we arrived back in Patagonia, I was unloading the wood when my host, Dennis Parker, drove up and asked how we did. I told him that we had found five coveys and a deer rack. He took a look at the antlers and his eyes got big. He said he had been looking for a rack like this for ages. He said it probably would place in the Boone and Crockett records book."

The rack was taken to a shop in Tucson, Arizona, where John Doyle officially measured the magnificent specimen at around 159 points.

"When Steve called me in a couple of days with the news,

I knew I had literally stumbled into the records book."

Officially scored at 158-4/8, this new World's Record non-typical Coues' deer is now on continuing display in the Boone and Crockett Club's National Collection of Heads and Horns in the Buffalo Bill: Historical Center, Cody, Wyoming. Walter Pollock came to an agreement with the Boone and Crockett Club during the 20th Awards activities to make a continuing loan of this trophy to the Club's collection so that the vast numbers of hunters and others who visit the Buffalo Bill Historical Center each year can enjoy seeing the finest known specimen of this category. A few years later, Mr. Pollock made his loan permanent when he donated it to Boone and Crockett Club's National Collection of Heads and Horns. ■

TROPHY INFO

RANK World's Record
SCORE 158 4/8
LOCATION Santa Cruz Co., AZ
HUNTER Picked Up
OWNER B&C Natl. Collection
DATE KILLED 1988

Photograph by Tim E. Kelly

417

COUES' WHITETAIL DEER
NON-TYPICAL ANTLERS
WORLD'S RECORD SCORECHART

Records of
North American
Big Game

BOONE AND CROCKETT CLUB®
OFFICIAL SCORING SYSTEM FOR NORTH AMERICAN BIG GAME TROPHIES
NON-TYPICAL WHITETAIL AND COUES' DEER

250 Station Drive
Missoula, MT 59801
(406) 542-1888

MINIMUM SCORES	AWARDS	ALL-TIME
whitetail	185	195
Coues'	105	120

Detail of Point Measurement

KIND OF DEER (check one)
□ whitetail
■ Coues'

	Abnormal Points	
	Right Antler	Left Antler
	1 7/8	3 1/8
	1 7/8	6 2/8
	6 1/8	3 5/8
	2 6/8	2 2/8
	1 6/8	2 4/8
	2	2 1/8
	4 5/8	1 3/8
SUBTOTALS	21	21 2/8
E. TOTAL	42 2/8	

SEE OTHER SIDE FOR INSTRUCTIONS

A. No. Points on Right Antler	11	No. Points on Left Antler	11
B. Tip to Tip Spread	6 3/8	C. Greatest Spread	18 1/8
D. Inside Spread of Main Beams	12 6/8	SPREAD CREDIT MAY EQUAL BUT NOT EXCEED LONGER ANTLER	

	COLUMN 1 Spread Credit	COLUMN 2 Right Antler	COLUMN 3 Left Antler	COLUMN 4 Difference
	12 6/8			
F. Length of Main Beam		17 1/8	16 7/8	2/8
G-1. Length of First Point		7 1/8	7 1/8	0
G-2. Length of Second Point		9	8 2/8	6/8
G-3. Length of Third Point		5 3/8	6 3/8	1
G-4. Length of Fourth Point, If Present				
G-5. Length of Fifth Point, If Present				
G-6. Length of Sixth Point, If Present				
G-7. Length of Seventh Point, If Present				
H-1. Circumference at Smallest Place Between Burr and First Point		3 7/8	4 1/8	2/8
H-2. Circumference at Smallest Place Between First and Second Points		4 3/8	4 1/8	2/8
H-3. Circumference at Smallest Place Between Second and Third Points		3 5/8	3 7/8	2/8
H-4. Circumference at Smallest Place Between Third and Fourth Points		2 4/8	2 5/8	1/8
TOTALS	12 6/8	53	53 3/8	2 7/8

ADD	Column 1	12 6/8
	Column 2	53
	Column 3	53 3/8
	Subtotal	119 1/8
SUBTRACT	Column 4	2 7/8
	Subtotal	116 2/8
	ADD Line E Total	42 2/8
	FINAL SCORE	158 4/8

Exact Locality Where Killed: Santa Cruz Co., AZ
Date Killed: Prior to 1988   Hunter: Picked Up
Owner: Natl. Coll. of Heads and Horns   Telephone #:
Owner's Address:
Guide's Name and Address:
Remarks: (Mention Any Abnormalities or Unique Qualities)
Donated by Walter H. Pollock

All measurements must be made with a 1/4-inch wide flexible steel tape to the nearest one-eighth of an inch. (Note: A flexible steel cable can be used to measure points and main beams only.) Enter fractional figures in eighths, without reduction. Official measurements cannot be taken until the antlers have air dried for at least 60 days after the animal was killed.

A. **Number of Points on Each Antler:** To be counted a point, the projection must be at least one inch long, with the length exceeding width at one inch or more of length. All points are measured from tip of point to nearest edge of beam as illustrated. Beam tip is counted as a point but not measured as a point.

B. **Tip to Tip Spread** is measured between tips of main beams.

C. **Greatest Spread** is measured between perpendiculars at a right angle to the center line of the skull at widest part, whether across main beams or points.

D. **Inside Spread of Main Beams** is measured at a right angle to the center line of the skull at widest point between main beams. Enter this measurement again as the Spread Credit if it is less than or equal to the length of the longer antler; if greater, enter longer antler length for Spread Credit.

E. **Total of Lengths of all Abnormal Points:** Abnormal Points are those non-typical in location (such as points originating from a point or from bottom or sides of main beam) or extra points beyond the normal pattern of points. Measure in usual manner and enter in appropriate blanks.

F. **Length of Main Beam** is measured from the center of the lowest outside edge of burr over the outer side to the most distant point of the main beam. The point of beginning is that point on the burr where the center line along the outer side of the beam intersects the burr, then following generally the line of the illustration.

G-1-2-3-4-5-6-7. **Length of Normal Points:** Normal points project from the top of the main beam. They are measured from nearest edge of main beam over outer curve to tip. Lay the tape along the outer curve of the beam so that the top edge of the tape coincides with the top edge of the beam on both sides of the point to determine the baseline for point measurement. Record point lengths in appropriate blanks.

H-1-2-3-4. **Circumferences** are taken as detailed in illustration for each measurement. If brow point is missing, take H-1 and H-2 at smallest place between burr and G-2. If G-4 is missing, take H-4 halfway between G-3 and tip of main beam.

COUES' WHITETAIL DEER - NON-TYPICAL ANTLERS

Odocoileus virginianus couesi

MINIMUM SCORE 120

Score	Length of Main Beam R	L	Inside Spread	Circumference at Smallest Place Between Burr and First Point R	L	Number of Points R	L	Locality	Hunter	Owner	Date Killed	Rank
158 4/8	17 1/8	16 7/8	12 6/8	3 7/8	4 1/8	11	11	Santa Cruz Co., AZ	Picked Up	B&C National Collection	1988	1
155	19	20	16 6/8	4 7/8	4 5/8	9	8	Gila Co., AZ	Charles E. Erickson, Jr.	Charles E. Erickson, Jr.	1988	2
151 4/8	18 4/8	18 5/8	15 6/8	5 4/8	5 4/8	9	8	Cochise Co., AZ	Charles C. Mabry	Don Schaufler	1929	3
150 5/8	18 4/8	19	12 5/8	4 3/8	4 4/8	8	8	Sasabe, AZ	Robert Rabb	Robert Rabb	1954	4
150 3/8	18 3/8	18	15 2/8	4 3/8	4 3/8	7	7	Pima Co., AZ	Jeffrey K. Volk	J.K. Volk & M.E. Duperret	1992	5
149 7/8	17 2/8	18 5/8	13 3/8	4 6/8	4 2/8	10	8	Chiricahua Mts., AZ	Marvin R. Hardin	Marvin R. Hardin	1950	6
148 6/8	16 3/8	15 7/8	18 4/8	4 6/8	4 4/8	12	8	Gila Co., AZ	Clay E. Goldman	Clay E. Goldman	1993	7
143 6/8	17 3/8	16 5/8	14 5/8	4 2/8	5	6	9	Pima Co., AZ	Oscar C. Truex	Oscar C. Truex	1983	8
142 7/8	20 4/8	18 7/8	13 3/8	4 4/8	4 5/8	9	7	Apache Indian Res., AZ	Native American	AZ Game & Fish Dept.	1950	9
142 6/8	17 6/8	17 1/8	14 2/8	4 6/8	4 5/8	8	8	Pinal Mts., AZ	Phil Rothengatter	Phil Rothengatter	1967	10
139 7/8	18 3/8	18 3/8	15	4 7/8	4 7/8	8	6	Patagonia Mts., AZ	Howard W. Drake	Howard W. Drake	1968	11
137 6/8	19 4/8	19 2/8	14 5/8	4 4/8	4 4/8	6	7	Patagonia Mts., AZ	Ivan J. Buttram	Ivan J. Buttram	1969	12
137 3/8	16 6/8	16 7/8	13 6/8	4 5/8	4 5/8	8	8	Gila Co., AZ	Cal W. Bryant	Cal W. Bryant	1991	13
134 6/8	18 7/8	18 6/8	13 5/8	3 7/8	3 6/8	6	8	Sonora, MX	David A. Miller	David A. Miller	1990	14
134 3/8	21 3/8	21	16 6/8	4 5/8	4 4/8	8	5	Cochise Co., AZ	Brian Childers	Brian Childers	1990	15
134 2/8	20 6/8	20 4/8	13 5/8	4 2/8	4 3/8	7	8	Yavapai Co., AZ	William B. Bullock	William B. Bullock	1986	16
134 2/8	17 7/8	16 5/8	13 1/8	4 5/8	4 5/8	6	7	Sonora, MX	Unknown	Ronald D. Hyatt	PR 1986	16
132 3/8	17 4/8	17 1/8	13 7/8	5	5	6	6	Gila Co., AZ	Dale J. Little	Dale J. Little	1989	18
132	20	19 7/8	14 5/8	3 6/8	3 6/8	5	5	Sonora, MX	Picked Up	Harry P. Samarin	PR 1988	19
131 5/8	18 2/8	18 2/8	13	4 6/8	4 6/8	8	5	Cochise Co., AZ	Phil M. Krentz	Phil M. Krentz	1991	20
131 3/8	19 1/8	18 1/8	14 7/8	3 7/8	4 1/8	6	6	Cochise Co., AZ	Erik M. Thorsrud	Erik M. Thorsrud	1986	21
131 2/8	16 1/8	18	13 5/8	6 6/8	5	9	8	Gila Co., AZ	Nathan E. Ellison	Nathan E. Ellison	1958	22
130 3/8	17 2/8	17 5/8	13 2/8	4 1/8	4 2/8	7	9	Santa Cruz Co., AZ	Jack Everhart	Fred Baker	1946	23
130 2/8	14 5/8	15 7/8	10 1/8	5	3 7/8	10	7	Rincon Mts., AZ	Velton Clark	Velton Clark	1962	24
130 1/8	17	18 3/8	14 5/8	4 3/8	4 2/8	8	8	Yavapai Co., AZ	David K. Moore	David K. Moore	1988	25
130	17 3/8	16 2/8	13 7/8	4 3/8	5 2/8	6	11	Whetstone Range, AZ	Unknown	Roger Clyne	PR 1967	26
129 5/8	19 6/8	19 7/8	16 6/8	3 4/8	3 5/8	7	8	Cochise Co., AZ	James C. Cornelius	James C. Cornelius	1994	27
128 3/8	17 4/8	17 6/8	15 1/8	4 2/8	4 1/8	5	7	Pima Co., AZ	Gary D. Gorsuch	Gary D. Gorsuch	1992	28
128	18 6/8	19 1/8	16 2/8	5 2/8	4 3/8	5	8	Santa Cruz Co., AZ	Carlos G. Touche	Carlos G. Touche	1968	29
127 6/8	17 2/8	17 3/8	13 4/8	4 1/8	4 2/8	6	6	Hidalgo Co., NM	Michael C. Finley	Michael C. Finley	1983	30
127 5/8	20	18 2/8	18	4 7/8	4 7/8	6	5	Pima Co., AZ	Robert E. Pierce	R.E. Pierce & D. May	1993	31
127 1/8	19 4/8	19 5/8	13 3/8	4 2/8	4 2/8	7	8	Sonora, MX	Picked Up	D.J. Hollinger & B. Howard	1993	32
127	17 6/8	18 2/8	13 2/8	4 5/8	4 5/8	7	7	Santa Cruz Co., AZ	David A. Miller	David A. Miller	1979	33
126 5/8	17 6/8	17 5/8	13 3/8	4	4	9	6	Gila Co., AZ	Paul A. Stewart	Paul A. Stewart	1992	34
126 1/8	14 7/8	15 2/8	11 2/8	4 5/8	4 6/8	8	6	Pima Co., AZ	William F. Crull	William F. Crull	1979	35
125 7/8	16 7/8	16 2/8	13 4/8	4 4/8	4 2/8	6	8	Pima Co., AZ	Fred W. Havens	Fred W. Havens	1966	36

Score								Locality	Hunter	Owner	Date Killed	Rank
125 7/8	18 7/8	17 7/8	12 1/8	4	4	6	8	Arizona	Picked Up	Michael J. Tamboli	PR 1976	36
125 3/8	15 3/8	16 4/8	13 6/8	4 2/8	4 3/8	9	6	Sonora, MX	Enrique C. Cicero	Enrique C. Cicero	1967	38
125 1/8	16 3/8	16 4/8	12	3 4/8	3 6/8	8	8	Santa Cruz Co., AZ	Lee E. Sullivan	Lee E. Sullivan	1996	39
124 7/8	15 3/8	17 1/8	11 3/8	4 6/8	4 7/8	8	5	Las Guijas Mts., AZ	Aubrey F. Powell	Aubrey F. Powell	1966	40
124 5/8	20	18 4/8	17 2/8	3 7/8	4	6	6	Pinal Co., AZ	C.J. Adair	C.J. Adair	1966	41
124 4/8	17 4/8	19	15	4 3/8	4 4/8	6	6	Yavapai Co., AZ	James W.P. Roe	James W.P. Roe	1971	42
124	17 6/8	16 4/8	12 7/8	4	4 2/8	7	6	Arizona	Unknown	George L. Cooper	1977	43
123 5/8	19 5/8	17 6/8	15 4/8	4 4/8	4 4/8	4	7	Cochise Co., AZ	William H. Nollsch	William H. Nollsch	1994	44
122 7/8	16 2/8	15 1/8	11 5/8	4	4	6	5	Sonora, MX	Edwin L. Robinson	Edwin L. Robinson	1992	45
122 6/8	16 7/8	16 6/8	12 4/8	4 2/8	4 2/8	6	7	Hidalgo Co., NM	Jack Samson	Jack Samson	1984	46
122 4/8	15 7/8	16 7/8	12	4	4	6	7	Cochise Co., AZ	Randy D. Goll	Randy D. Goll	1984	47
122 4/8	19 2/8	20	15 5/8	4 1/8	4 1/8	8	4	Sonora, MX	Robert P. Ellingson III	Robert P. Ellingson III	1997	47
122 2/8	17 2/8	16 5/8	13 4/8	4 4/8	4 4/8	4	7	Santa Cruz Co., AZ	Clifton E. Cox	Clifton E. Cox	1980	49
121 7/8	18 5/8	18 5/8	13 6/8	4 5/8	4 6/8	5	6	Gila Co., AZ	Ken Ashley	Ken Ashley	1988	50
121	16 6/8	16 5/8	14	3 6/8	3 5/8	8	6	Gila Co., AZ	James E. Stinson	James E. Stinson	1983	51
120 7/8	16 7/8	17	13 3/8	4 6/8	4 4/8	6	6	Pima Co., AZ	Carl E. Fasel	Carl E. Fasel	1981	52
120 7/8	17 2/8	17 6/8	15 2/8	5 1/8	4 7/8	6	6	Gila Co., AZ	David M. Conrad	David M. Conrad	1982	52
120 5/8	20 5/8	20	13 4/8	3 7/8	4	6	4	Santa Cruz Co., AZ	Jerry M. Myers	Jerry M. Myers	1970	54
120 2/8	14 4/8	17 5/8	11 5/8	4 3/8	4 3/8	8	8	Pima Co., AZ	Unknown	Mike Yeager	PR 1966	55
120 1/8	18 5/8	19	13 6/8	4 1/8	4	8	6	Santa Cruz Co., AZ	Gerald M. Kluzik	Gerald M. Kluzik	1981	56
120 1/8	16 5/8	17 6/8	15	3 4/8	3 6/8	7	8	Pima Co., AZ	Eugene S. Robinson	Eugene S. Robinson	1985	56
120 1/8	18 5/8	18 3/8	12 1/8	3 7/8	3 7/8	6	6	Sonora, MX	David A. Miller	David A. Miller	1991	56
133*	18 6/8	18 6/8	18 2/8	4 4/8	4 1/8	9	7	Greenlee Co., AZ	Linda A. Reese	Dee Charles	1993	
129 2/8*	18 7/8	18 7/8	16 4/8	4 7/8	4 5/8	4	8	Pima Co., AZ	Daniel D. King	Daniel D. King	1993	

* Final score is subject to revision by additional verifying measurements.

CATEGORY
COUES' WHITETAIL DEER
NON-TYPICAL ANTLERS

SCORE
150-3/8

HUNTER
JEFFREY K. VOLK (LEFT)
MICHAEL DUPERRET
(HUNTING PARTNER)

LOCATION
PIMA CO., AZ

DATE OF KILL
DECEMBER 1992

CATEGORY
COUES' WHITETAIL DEER
NON-TYPICAL ANTLERS

SCORE
122-4/8

HUNTER
ROBERT P. ELLINGSON III

LOCATION
SONORA, MX

DATE OF KILL
JANUARY 1997

CATEGORY
COUES' WHITETAIL DEER
NON-TYPICAL ANTLERS

SCORE
129-5/8

HUNTER
JAMES C. CORNELIUS

LOCATION
COCHISE CO., AZ

DATE OF KILL
NOVEMBER 1994

422

B&C HISTORY

ALDO LEOPOLD
1887-1948

He is considered the father of wildlife ecology. A renowned scientist and scholar, exceptional teacher and philosopher, he was considered conservation's most influential advocate. As a gifted writer, he is best known for his book, *A Sand County Almanac*, often acclaimed as this century's literary landmark in conservation. Born in Iowa, he took a degree in forestry at Yale and then joined the U.S. Forest Service, serving in the Arizona Territories. His cornerstone book, *Game Management* defined the fundamental skills and techniques for managing and restoring wildlife populations. He was a professional member of the Boone and Crockett Club. ∎

In the fall of 1980, Michael E. Laub left the gentle hills of Pennsylvania for the rough terrain of British Columbia in pursuit of a "childhood dream," a big-game wilderness hunt. Laub's consequential encounter with an enormous Canada moose (*Alces alces americana*) became a story for the records book.

Accompanying friends Sal Casino and Angelo Brocatello, the hunting party landed in a small plane in the outback of Vizer Creek, British Columbia. Gil Weins and three of his guides met the hunters and the next morning they mounted up and began a long search for moose and grizzly bear.

"On October 19th, after a couple of days of fly-camping, we were pretty demoralized. We hadn't even seen a rabbit. I was able to call my wife Carol via shortwave radio to tell her of our misfortune.

"After I spoke to my wife, Sal and I went out again with our guides. We had lunch around a lake, and then we split up. My guide, George, was on the trail of a moose. We got to the top of a mountain and looked down. To my surprise I saw a bull just grazing with his antlers glittering in the sun. The moose was at least 400 yards away, so we began the descent on our horses.

"I was so excited; but, I didn't realize how big the bull was because I had never seen a moose before. We kept moving down the mountain and I stopped to shoot, but missed.

The moose took off into the brush, and we continued down the mountain. I then saw the moose standing, his back toward me in the thick, high grass at about 250 yards, when I shot. He went down, got up again, and moved off. We got on our horses and galloped through the brush. We were behind and above the moose, the sun to our back. I was now 25 feet from my moose. I grabbed my rifle out of its scabbard and downed him with my last bullet.

"George was so excited that he jumped up and down like a little boy. He knew what I didn't, that this was a World's Record-sized moose."

Shot near Grayling River, British Columbia, Laub's trophy was officially scored at 242, and thus became the new World's Record for a Canada moose. ∎

BOUNDARIES FOR MOOSE

Three categories of moose are recognized for records keeping, with boundaries based on geographic lines. Canada moose includes trophies from Newfoundland and Canada (except for the Yukon and Northwest Territories), Minnesota, Maine, New Hampshire, North Dakota, and Vermont.

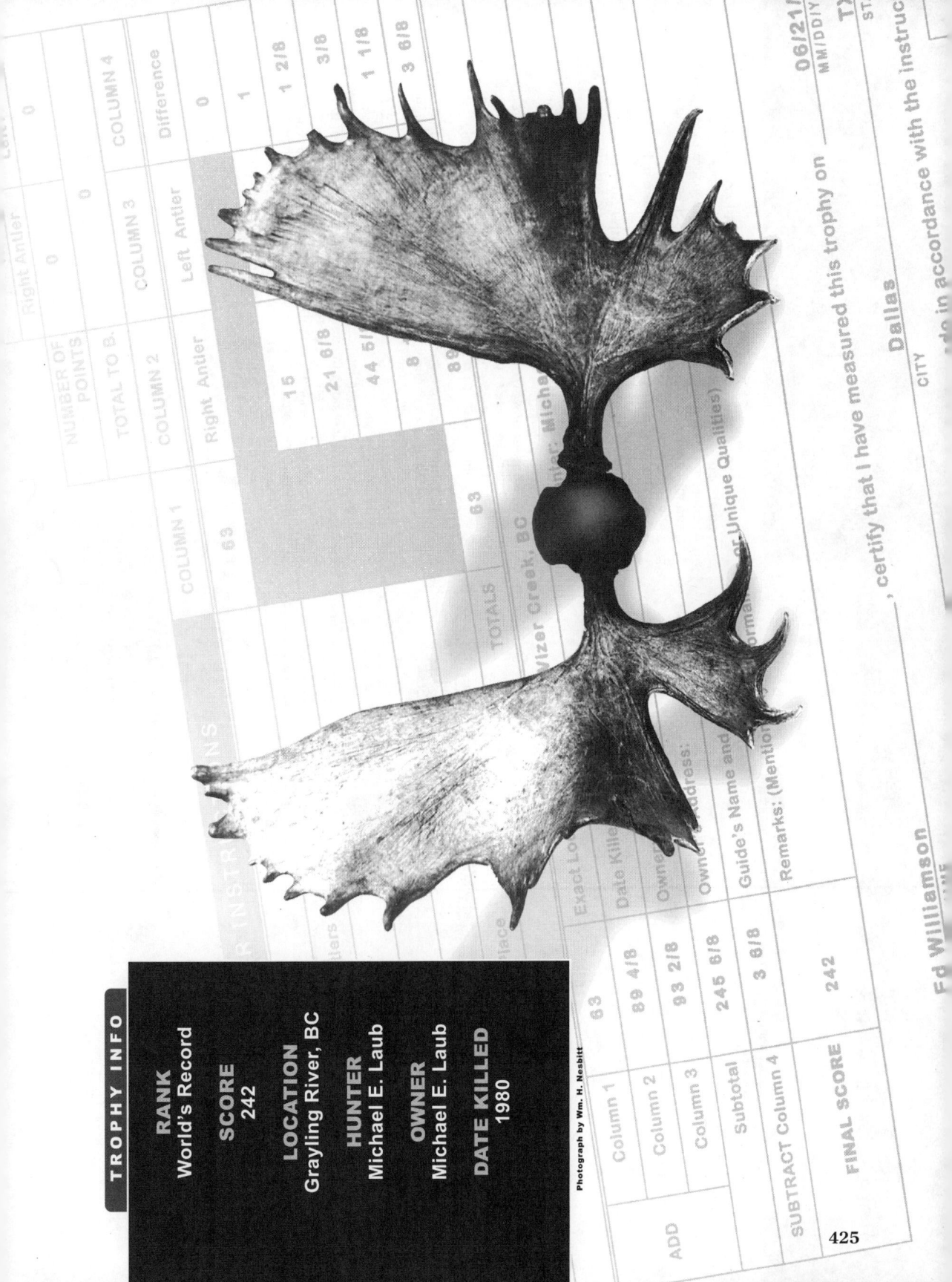

RANK
World's Record

SCORE
242

LOCATION
Grayling River, BC

HUNTER
Michael E. Laub

OWNER
Michael E. Laub

DATE KILLED
1980

Photograph by Wm. H. Nesbitt

ADD	Column 1	63	
	Column 2	89 4/8	
	Column 3	93 2/8	
	Subtotal	245 6/8	
SUBTRACT Column 4		3 6/8	
FINAL SCORE		242	

425

CANADA MOOSE
WORLD'S RECORD SCORECHART

Measurements must be made with a 1/4-inch wide flexible steel tape to the nearest one-eighth of an inch. Enter fractional figures in eighths, without reduction. Official measurements cannot be taken until antlers have air dried for at least 60 days after animal was killed.

A. Greatest Spread is measured between perpendiculars in a straight line at a right angle to the center line of the skull.

B. Number of Abnormal Points on Both Antlers: Abnormal points are those projections originating from normal points or from the upper or lower palm surface, or from the inner edge of palm (see illustration). Abnormal points must be at least one inch long, with length exceeding width at one inch or more of length.

C. Number of Normal Points: Normal points originate from the outer edge of palm. To be counted a point, a projection must be at least one inch long, with the length exceeding width at one inch or more of length. Be sure to verify whether or not each projection qualifies as a point.

D. Width of Palm is taken in contact with the under surface of palm, at a right angle to the inner edge of palm. The line of measurement should begin and end at the midpoint of the palm edge, which gives credit for the desirable character of palm thickness.

E. Length of Palm including Brow Palm is taken in contact with the surface along the underside of the palm, **parallel** to the inner edge, from dips between points at the top to dips between points (if present) at the bottom. If a bay is present, measure across the open bay if the proper line of measurement, parallel to **inner edge,** follows this path. The line of measurement should begin and end at the midpoint of the palm edge, which gives credit for the desirable character of palm thickness.

F. Circumference of Beam at Smallest Place is taken as illustrated.

Records of North American Big Game

BOONE AND CROCKETT CLUB®

250 Station Drive
Missoula, MT 59801
(406) 542-1888

OFFICIAL SCORING SYSTEM FOR NORTH AMERICAN BIG GAME TROPHIES

MOOSE

MINIMUM SCORES

	AWARDS	ALL-TIME
Canada	185	195
Alaska-Yukon	210	224
Wyoming	140	155

KIND OF MOOSE (check one)
- ☑ Canada
- ☐ Alaska-Yukon
- ☐ Wyoming

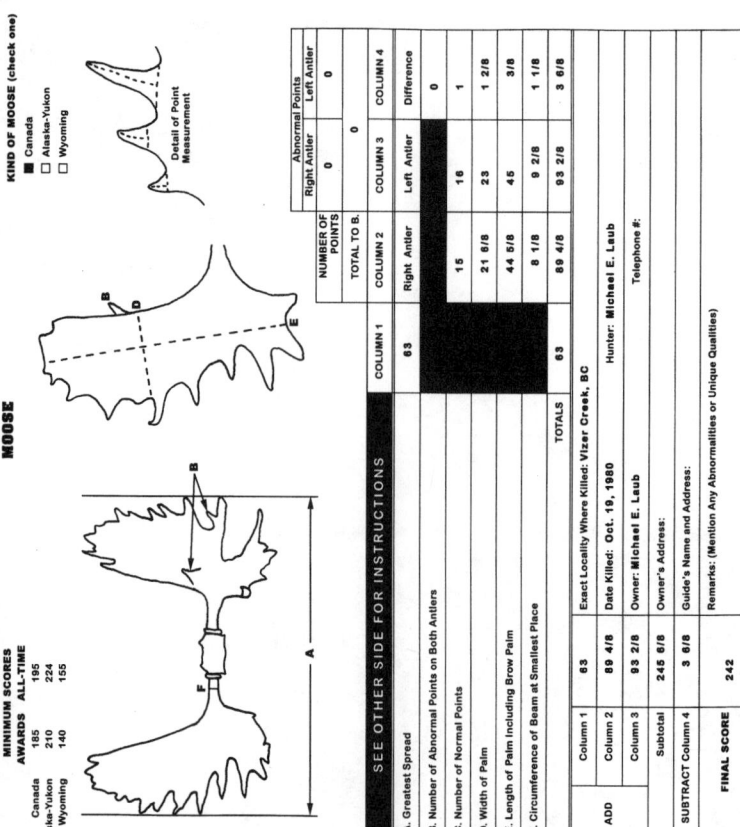

Detail of Point Measurement

SEE OTHER SIDE FOR INSTRUCTIONS	COLUMN 1	COLUMN 2	COLUMN 3	COLUMN 4
		Right Antler	Left Antler	Difference
		NUMBER OF POINTS		
		TOTAL TO B.		

Abnormal Points

	Right Antler	Left Antler
	0	0

	NUMBER OF POINTS	TOTAL TO B.
	0	0

	COLUMN 1	COLUMN 2 Right Antler	COLUMN 3 Left Antler	COLUMN 4 Difference
A. Greatest Spread	63			
B. Number of Abnormal Points on Both Antlers		15	16	1
C. Number of Normal Points		21 6/8	23	1 2/8
D. Width of Palm		44 5/8	45	3/8
E. Length of Palm Including Brow Palm		8 1/8	9 2/8	1 1/8
F. Circumference of Beam at Smallest Place		89 4/8	93 2/8	3 6/8
TOTALS	63			

ADD	Column 1	63
	Column 2	89 4/8
	Column 3	93 2/8
	Subtotal	245 6/8
SUBTRACT	Column 4	3 6/8
	FINAL SCORE	242

Exact Locality Where Killed: **Vizer Creek, BC**

Date Killed: **Oct. 19, 1980**   Hunter: **Michael E. Laub**

Owner: **Michael E. Laub**   Telephone #:

Owner's Address:

Guide's Name and Address:

Remarks: (Mention Any Abnormalities or Unique Qualities)

I, **Ed Williamson** , certify that I have measured this trophy on **06/21/83**
    PRINT NAME   MM/DD/YYYY

at **Dallas Museum of Natural History**   **Dallas**   **TX**
   STREET ADDRESS   CITY   STATE/PROVINCE

and that these measurements and data are, to the best of my knowledge and belief, made in accordance with the instructions given.

Witness: **Frank Cook**   Signature: **Ed Williamson**   I.D. Number:
                                            B&C OFFICIAL MEASURER

CANADA MOOSE

Alces alces americana and Alces alces andersoni

MINIMUM SCORE 195

Score	Greatest Spread	Length of Palm R	L	Width of Palm R	L	Circumference of Beam at Smallest Place R	L	Number of Normal Points R	L	Locality	Hunter	Owner	Date Killed	Rank
242	63	44 5/8	45	21 6/8	23	8 1/8	9 2/8	15	16	Grayling River, BC	Michael E. Laub	Michael E. Laub	1980	1
240 2/8	66 6/8	46 3/8	45 4/8	19	18 6/8	7 4/8	7 7/8	15	15	Teslin River, QC	Albertoni Ferruccio	Albertoni Ferruccio	1982	2
238 5/8	65 5/8	44 6/8	43 1/8	21	18 6/8	7 5/8	7 7/8	18	19	Bear Lake, QC	Silas H. Witherbee	B&C National Collection	1914	3
227 4/8	58 4/8	44	43 4/8	17 3/8	17 5/8	7 6/8	7 5/8	19	16	Cook Co., MN	Donald F. Blake	Donald F. Blake	1985	4
226 7/8	63 1/8	48 5/8	47	16 4/8	16 4/8	8 4/8	8 3/8	11	10	Whitecourt, AB	Tim Harbridge	Tim Harbridge	1978	5
226 6/8	63	44 3/8	42 2/8	18 1/8	18 7/8	7	7	15	15	Halfway River, BC	Richard Petersen	Richard Petersen	1977	6
225	60	45 7/8	46 1/8	14 6/8	14 3/8	7 4/8	7 2/8	17	15	Driftwood River, AB	Carl J. Buchanan	Carl J. Buchanan	1960	7
224 1/8	58 3/8	43 4/8	43	18 4/8	17 3/8	8 4/8	8 4/8	14	14	Nipawin, SK	Roy M. Hornseth	Roy M. Hornseth	1959	8
223 7/8	60 5/8	47 5/8	46	16 7/8	14 5/8	7 3/8	7	17	14	Buffalo Lake, MB	Pierre A. Lachance	Pierre A. Lachance	1985	9
223 5/8	64 7/8	46 1/8	47 1/8	17 4/8	14	7 4/8	7 2/8	12	12	Island Lake, MB	Native American	Jack E. Dunn	1980	10
223	56 2/8	48 4/8	48 2/8	13 6/8	14 5/8	7 6/8	7 3/8	15	14	Stikine River, BC	Donald G. Allen	Donald G. Allen	1995	11
222	59	46	47 1/8	14 3/8	14	7 6/8	7 4/8	15	14	Clearwater River, AB	Manuel Dominguez	Manuel Dominguez	1947	12
221 7/8	63 5/8	47 7/8	45 6/8	13 2/8	13 7/8	8 1/8	8 2/8	13	12	Goat Creek, BC	Roland Wilz	Roland Wilz	1971	13
221 4/8	64 4/8	48 6/8	47 7/8	15 2/8	11	8 6/8	8 7/8	14	11	Arborfield, SK	Ed Lutz	Ed Lutz	1959	14
221 4/8	66	40 1/8	41	15 7/8	15	7 5/8	8 1/8	16	15	Logan Mt., QC	Charles R. Roy	C.R. Roy & R. Roy	1988	15
220 3/8	67 5/8	41 6/8	46 6/8	17 2/8	15 6/8	8 2/8	7 7/8	11	13	Cassiar, BC	Unknown	Luxton Museum	PR 1954	16
219 7/8	65 5/8	40 1/8	44 2/8	16 4/8	16 4/8	7 4/8	7 6/8	16	13	East West Lake, ON	Kurt Skalitzky	Kurt Skalitzky	1989	17
219 2/8	62 2/8	40 5/8	39 6/8	18 7/8	15 2/8	7 5/8	7 4/8	17	19	Canada	Gift of W.B.O. Field to NCHH	Unknown	1924	18
219 1/8	64 1/8	45	43 1/8	15 5/8	13 7/8	7 6/8	7 4/8	14	13	Cold Fish Lake, BC	G. & P. Halvorson	G. & P. Halvorson	1974	19
218 6/8	58 2/8	42 6/8	40 4/8	15	15 4/8	8 7/8	8 6/8	16	16	Kennicott Lake, BC	Mike Popoff	Mike Popoff	1984	20
218 1/8	61 7/8	44 3/8	42 5/8	15	15	7 4/8	7 5/8	13	13	Chuchinra River, BC	Friedbert Prill	Friedbert Prill	1973	21
218	58 4/8	43 2/8	43 3/8	17	16 4/8	7	7 1/8	13	15	Wellman Lake, MB	Clifford S. Henderson	Bernie P. Nemetchek	1964	22
217 6/8	64 4/8	44 1/8	47 2/8	15	15	7 6/8	7 4/8	10	12	Cassiar Mts., BC	J. Barry Dyar	J. Barry Dyar	1977	23
217 4/8	63 2/8	42 1/8	44	19 4/8	15 2/8	7 6/8	7 6/8	17	12	Hart Mt., BC	Donna Loewenstein	Donna Loewenstein	1966	24
217 2/8	63 6/8	42 2/8	39 5/8	17 5/8	15 3/8	7	6 6/8	15	15	Firebag River, AB	Frank Baldwin	Carlysle Baldwin	1977	25
217 1/8	63 1/8	40 4/8	43 6/8	14 3/8	15	8 2/8	8 1/8	15	14	Liard River, BC	Wayne E. Dalgleish	Wayne E. Dalgleish	1984	26
216 7/8	59 3/8	41 6/8	44 2/8	17 2/8	15 4/8	7 4/8	7 4/8	17	14	Prophet River, BC	John G. Oltmanns	John G. Oltmanns	1971	27
216 3/8	58 5/8	43 6/8	46 2/8	14 6/8	15 3/8	8 3/8	8 4/8	16	12	Cassiar Mts., BC	Ross Ferguson	Ross Ferguson	1978	28
216 2/8	62 4/8	46 7/8	43 6/8	14 4/8	13 4/8	7 7/8	7 5/8	15	12	Cassiar Mts., BC	Don L. Corley	Don L. Corley	1984	29
216 1/8	71 5/8	38 1/8	37	14 1/8	14 4/8	8	8	14	14	Maine	H.M. Boice	Everhart Museum	1900	30
216	58 1/8	41 4/8	42 4/8	18 4/8	19 4/8	7 2/8	7 2/8	17	12	Dease Lake, BC	George A. Sinclair	George A. Sinclair	1981	30
215 4/8	64	41 4/8	42	13 4/8	13 4/8	6 6/8	6 7/8	14	15	Maine	Unknown	Albert Bierstadt	1880	32
215 3/8	53 1/8	43 7/8	43 4/8	18	14	7 6/8	7 5/8	16	20	Meekwap Lake, AB	Russell S. Watts, Sr.	Russell G. Watts, Jr.	1960	33
215 3/8	54 7/8	39 4/8	38 6/8	17 3/8	17 3/8	7 1/8	7 1/8	17	20	Latornell River, AB	Artie G. Brown	Artie G. Brown	1971	33
215 2/8	60 4/8	44 2/8	45 2/8	12 7/8	13 1/8	7 6/8	7 6/8	13	13	Cassiar Mts., BC	Milton J. Duffin	Milton J. Duffin	1976	35
215 1/8	62 3/8	42 6/8	44 1/8	14 4/8	13 3/8	7 2/8	7 2/8	13	14	Dease Lake, BC	Bert Klineburger	Bert Klineburger	1960	36
215	57 4/8	43	45 1/8	15 5/8	14	7 6/8	7 6/8	15	14	Ice Mt., BC	David H. Hilsberg	David H. Hilsberg	1985	37

Score	Greatest Spread	Length of Palm R	Length of Palm L	Width of Palm R	Width of Palm L	Circ. of Beam R	Circ. of Beam L	Points R	Points L	Locality	Hunter	Owner	Date	Rank
215	70	42 2/8	38 6/8	15 4/8	15 2/8	7 4/8	7 4/8	11	12	Teslin Lake, BC	Steven D. Kellesvig	Steven D. Kellesvig	1997	37
214 6/8	53 6/8	44 2/8	44 2/8	13 4/8	16	7 6/8	7 6/8	16	15	Narraway River, AB	Karl Weber	Karl Weber	1956	39
214 6/8	68	39 5/8	39 3/8	15	16 4/8	8 4/8	8 4/8	13	13	Dease River, BC	Herb Klein	Herb Klein	1960	39
214 6/8	56 2/8	45 5/8	42 3/8	19 6/8	17 4/8	7 4/8	7 3/8	14	12	Kennicott Lake, BC	Robert G. Burkhouse	Robert G. Burkhouse	1988	39
214 6/8	57	46 2/8	41 7/8	15 3/8	15 1/8	7 7/8	7 7/8	14	14	Red Lake, ON	Dan K. Brumm	D.K. Brumm & J. Krizsan	1991	39
214 4/8	62	42 2/8	38 6/8	17	15 7/8	7 5/8	7 5/8	14	16	Piscataquis Co., ME	Desmond Harvey	Desmond Harvey	1984	43
214 1/8	60 7/8	44 5/8	42 5/8	14 5/8	17 3/8	7 3/8	7 3/8	12	12	Teslin Lake, BC	John P. Costello II	John P. Costello II	1976	44
214	62 6/8	43	43 5/8	13 1/8	13 2/8	7	7 1/8	13	14	Alaska Hwy, Mile 100, BC	Karl Fritzsche	Karl Fritzsche	1968	45
214	62	41 2/8	38 5/8	17 2/8	17 3/8	7 2/8	7 1/8	15	13	North Brook, NF	Unknown	Sidney J. LeLuan, Sr.	PR 1988	45
213 6/8	58 6/8	39 7/8	41 6/8	19 1/8	18 4/8	8	7 5/8	13	17	Lesser Slave Lake, AB	Herbert R. Dobson	Herbert R. Dobson	1993	47
213 5/8	60 7/8	44 3/8	45 3/8	13 5/8	15 3/8	7 2/8	7 4/8	13	13	Prophet River, BC	Daniel T. Applebaker	Daniel T. Applebaker	1972	48
213 2/8	51 4/8	44	44	19	17 2/8	7 5/8	7 5/8	13	11	Atlin, BC	Ewald Krentz	Ewald Krentz	1971	49
213	63 2/8	41 4/8	39 6/8	15 4/8	15 2/8	7 7/8	7 7/8	12	12	Hines Creek, AB	Elwood Baird	Elwood Baird	1975	50
213	62 2/8	45 1/8	42 4/8	14 3/8	11 5/8	8 3/8	8 2/8	14	13	Stikine River, BC	Sam Sanders, Jr.	Sam Sanders, Jr.	1975	50
213	52	45	46 5/8	15	15 7/8	7 4/8	7 4/8	14	13	Liard River, BC	Hayden O. Woods, Sr.	Hayden O. Woods, Sr.	1976	50
213	59	42	41 7/8	15	14 3/8	7 3/8	7 2/8	14	14	Candle Lake, SK	Roger Mann	Roger Mann	1989	50
213	61 2/8	42 6/8	44	16 1/8	14	7 6/8	7 5/8	12	14	Gladys Lake, BC	Ronald A. Landree	Ronald A. Landree	1997	50
212 6/8	61	42 5/8	42 6/8	13 1/8	14 4/8	7 6/8	7 5/8	14	13	Love, SK	Robert J. Rogers	Robert J. Rogers	1966	55
212 6/8	60 6/8	38 1/8	38	18	20	8 1/8	8	13	14	Sikanni Chief River, BC	David B. Willis	David B. Willis	1977	55
212 5/8	60 5/8	40 4/8	43 4/8	13 4/8	13 6/8	8	8	14	16	Slave Lake, AB	R.W.H. Eben-Ebenau	R.W.H. Eben-Ebenau	1937	57
212 5/8	55 7/8	39 4/8	41 4/8	16 7/8	18 3/8	7 2/8	7	15	16	Marion Lake, BC	J. Clifton Jensen	J. Clifton Jensen	1974	57
212 3/8	56 3/8	47 6/8	40 2/8	18 6/8	15 2/8	8	8 2/8	17	15	Cassiar Mts., BC	Dean A. Bloomfield	Dean A. Bloomfield	1979	59
212 1/8	59 1/8	42	45	12 4/8	13 7/8	8 2/8	8 5/8	14	18	Fort Nelson River, BC	Glen S. Huntley	Glen S. Huntley	1995	60
212	54	39 4/8	39	16 4/8	17 4/8	7 4/8	7 4/8	16	16	Grayling River, BC	Arnold E. Dado	Arnold E. Dado	1984	61
212	58 4/8	41 7/8	43 5/8	13 6/8	13 5/8	7 1/8	7 2/8	14	14	Taku River, BC	William A. Van Alstine	William A. Van Alstine	1990	61
211 7/8	65 3/8	38 2/8	44 2/8	13 3/8	13 3/8	7 2/8	7 1/8	15	15	Pasquia Hills, SK	William H. Schweitzer	William H. Schweitzer	1978	63
211 6/8	56 6/8	40	39 2/8	18	17 6/8	7 1/8	7	15	17	Ft. St. John, BC	Jack Fries	Jack Fries	1977	64
211 6/8	58 6/8	43 2/8	43 4/8	14 4/8	14 4/8	7 6/8	7 6/8	11	11	Teslin River, BC	Ron Harris	Ron Harris	1994	64
211 6/8	61 7/8	46	42	14 4/8	18 7/8	8 3/8	8 6/8	12	10	Powell Lake, ON	Jerry R. Brocksmith	Jerry R. Brocksmith	1969	66
211 4/8	65	42	42	12 4/8	12 4/8	8 6/8	7 6/8	14	17	Pine Lake, QC	Walter Geismar	Walter Geismar	1949	67
211 4/8	64 6/8	41 7/8	40 6/8	12 4/8	12 4/8	8 4/8	7 5/8	12	12	Atlin, QC	William L. Frederick	William L. Frederick	1969	67
211 4/8	54	45 1/8	44 7/8	11 7/8	13 1/8	8 2/8	8 3/8	15	13	Sheslay River, BC	Daniel E. Gorecki	Daniel E. Gorecki	1989	67
211 4/8	63 6/8	36 2/8	37 4/8	13 4/8	16 4/8	7 6/8	7 6/8	15	14	Lake Madeleine, QC	Clement Chouinard	Michel Miouse	1992	67
211 3/8	54 1/8	40 1/8	40	15 7/8	18 1/8	7 1/8	7 2/8	17	16	Tochieka Range, BC	C. Thomas Manier	C. Thomas Manier	1978	71
211 1/8	57 7/8	41 7/8	41	18 1/8	14 1/8	7 3/8	7 1/8	15	15	Rabbit River, BC	Richard A. Jacobs	Richard A. Jacobs	1995	72
211	49	43 6/8	43 4/8	16 2/8	18 4/8	8	8 1/8	15	15	Grande Prairie, AB	Lester C. Hearn	Lester C. Hearn	1972	73
211	59 6/8	40 6/8	38 7/8	15 5/8	12 6/8	8 2/8	8 6/8	15	13	Mojikit Lake, ON	Charles R. Salfer	Charles R. Salfer	1987	73
210 7/8	70 1/8	40	40 2/8	14 4/8	12 6/8	8 1/8	8	11	12	Round Lake, ON	M.A. Kennedy	Royal Ontario Museum	1912	75
210 6/8	63 2/8	45 4/8	44 2/8	13 7/8	13 4/8	7 1/8	7	13	11	Sikanni Chief River, BC	Gerald Stecklein	Gerald Stecklein	1965	76
210 1/8	62 1/8	42 7/8	42 7/8	12 5/8	12 5/8	7 4/8	7 4/8	13	13	Sheep Creek, AB	R.V.D. Goltz	R.V.D. Goltz	1964	77
210	59 2/8	41 4/8	41 4/8	15 4/8	15 4/8	6 7/8	6 7/8	14	16	Sheep River, AB	Elton Boggs	Elton Boggs	1956	78
210	54 6/8	44 5/8	47 4/8	14 3/8	13 4/8	7 4/8	7 4/8	14	12	Cassiar Mts., BC	Richard J. Wristen	Richard J. Wristen	1978	78
210	53 4/8	42 3/8	39 2/8	19	18 4/8	7 5/8	7 5/8	15	13	Cold Fish Lake, BC	Glenroy G. Livingston	Glenroy G. Livingston	1990	78
209 7/8	53 3/8	43 1/8	43 5/8	12 7/8	12 6/8	7 3/8	7	15	15	Kakwa River, AB	Rolf Koelblinger	Rolf Koelblinger	1969	81
209 7/8	53 3/8	44 5/8	45 7/8	12 5/8	12 5/8	7	7 3/8	15	14	Cutbank River, AB	Alan D. Taylor	Alan D. Taylor	1970	81
209 7/8	54 3/8	45 3/8	42 2/8	15 3/8	15 2/8	7 2/8	7 2/8	13	13	Turnagain River, BC	Gordon R. Cole	Gordon R. Cole	1974	81
209 7/8	58 5/8	42	40 4/8	14	14 6/8	7 1/8	7 1/8	14	14	Cassiar Mts., BC	William M. Silva	William M. Silva	1976	81

Alces alces americana and Alces alces andersoni

Score	Greatest Spread	Length of Palm R	L	Width of Palm R	L	Circumference of Beam at Smallest Place R	L	Number of Normal Points R	L	Locality	Hunter	Owner	Date Killed	Rank
209 7/8	57 5/8	44 3/8	41	16 6/8	14 7/8	7 4/8	7 2/8	13	15	Dease River, BC	Michael D. Rochette	Michael D. Rochette	1988	81
209 6/8	64 6/8	39 4/8	44	12	13 5/8	7	7 2/8	14	14	Oba Lake, ON	Bruce McPherson	Bruce McPherson	1963	86
209 6/8	60 6/8	43 4/8	43 7/8	14	15 3/8	7	7 1/8	10	15	Jennings Lake, BC	Collins F. Kellogg	Collins F. Kellogg	1969	86
209 5/8	59 1/8	41 5/8	41 3/8	13 5/8	17 2/8	8 2/8	8 6/8	12	15	Malone Lake, QC	Harvey A. Kipp	Harvey A. Kipp	1953	88
209 5/8	68 3/8	41	41	13 3/8	13 4/8	7 6/8	7 7/8	10	9	Liard River, BC	Ronald B. Barker	Ronald B. Barker	1990	88
209 4/8	57 4/8	40 3/8	44 2/8	16 1/8	15	7 5/8	7 5/8	13	13	Hasler Creek, BC	Mike Nussbaumer	Mike Nussbaumer	1984	90
209 3/8	59 3/8	42 5/8	42 1/8	15 3/8	16 3/8	7 6/8	7 4/8	10	10	Cassiar Mts., BC	Hurnie H. Whitehead	Hurnie H. Whitehead	1978	91
209 2/8	59	44	50 4/8	12 5/8	12 5/8	7 4/8	7 5/8	12	11	Smoky River, AB	William R. Farmer	William R. Farmer	1970	92
209 1/8	55 5/8	40 6/8	41 4/8	13	13	7	7 2/8	16	11	Kenora, ON	David O. Moreton	David O. Moreton	1970	93
209	63	39 4/8	39	15	17 6/8	8	8	11	11	Manawaki, QC	George A. Krikory	George A. Krikory	1953	94
208 7/8	56 5/8	39 2/8	43 4/8	15 7/8	15	6 7/8	7 2/8	15	15	Hudson Bay, SK	Don Hendricks	Don Hendricks	1961	95
208 7/8	60 7/8	39 7/8	41 7/8	15	13 4/8	7 5/8	7 5/8	13	14	Telegraph Creek, BC	T.T. Stroup	T.T. Stroup	1968	95
208 6/8	63 2/8	39 4/8	44 6/8	15 3/8	16 4/8	6 7/8	7 2/8	11	15	The Pas, MB	Denver M. Wright	Denver M. Wright	1950	97
208 6/8	61 6/8	41	41 5/8	17 3/8	15 6/8	7 6/8	8	9	13	Hudson Bay, SK	Frank B. Miller	Frank B. Miller	1967	97
208 6/8	61	41 7/8	40 1/8	16 3/8	14	6 6/8	6 6/8	14	13	Ft. St. John, BC	Richard O. Vycital	Richard O. Vycital	1967	97
208 6/8	57 2/8	42 6/8	41 1/8	13 6/8	13 4/8	7 1/8	7 2/8	14	14	Catagua River, BC	Dominic Arone	Dominic Arone	1969	97
208 6/8	56	43 6/8	47 6/8	12 5/8	14 2/8	7 6/8	7 4/8	13	16	Pepaw Lake, SK	Maurice R. LaRose	Maurice R. LaRose	1976	97
208 6/8	61	41 2/8	41 1/8	14 7/8	14 5/8	7 1/8	7 2/8	11	13	Ketchum Lake, BC	Gailand K. Hann	Gailand K. Hann	1985	97
208 5/8	58 5/8	43 4/8	44 6/8	15 1/8	13 1/8	7 4/8	7 3/8	12	11	Muskwa River, BC	Gary D. Linsinbigler	Gary D. Linsinbigler	1969	103
208 4/8	52 2/8	46 4/8	45 5/8	16 4/8	12 4/8	8	8	14	12	Prophet River, BC	Vollrad J. von Berg	Vollrad J. von Berg	1967	104
208 4/8	61 4/8	42 6/8	41 5/8	16 4/8	19 5/8	7 3/8	7 4/8	10	8	Trutch Mt., BC	Charles H. Veasey	Charles H. Veasey	1976	104
208 4/8	58 7/8	43 4/8	44 4/8	14	15 3/8	7 2/8	7 2/8	10	19	Taku River, BC	Robert J. Matyas	Robert J. Matyas	1989	106
208 3/8	60 1/8	40 2/8	40 5/8	15	15 1/8	7	6 7/8	12	13	Hall Lake, BC	Theodore G. Yerasimides	Theodore G. Yerasimides	1991	106
208 3/8	53 5/8	45 4/8	44 5/8	14 5/8	12 2/8	8 4/8	8 5/8	13	12	Snowdon Range, BC	Ronald E. Gartner	Ronald E. Gartner	1997	106
208 2/8	61 2/8	40 1/8	40 7/8	11 6/8	12	7 5/8	7 6/8	14	14	Chetwynd, BC	Louis Carriere	Louis Carriere	1976	109
208 2/8	61 4/8	40 4/8	40 1/8	15 2/8	13 5/8	8 3/8	8 1/8	12	12	Coos Co., NH	Charles A. Covey, Sr.	Charles A. Covey, Sr.	1990	109
208 2/8	64 4/8	41 2/8	38 6/8	14	13 6/8	8 3/8	8 4/8	11	11	Beatty Creek, BC	Duane A. Enders	Duane A. Enders	1997	109
208 1/8	59 5/8	39 2/8	40 2/8	15 4/8	17 4/8	6 4/8	6 7/8	13	13	Halfway River, BC	Eugene F. Konopaski	Eugene F. Konopaski	1967	112
208 1/8	61 3/8	42 2/8	40	16 3/8	17 1/8	7	7 3/8	12	10	Cadomin, AB	Picked Up	E.F. Madole	1977	112
208 1/8	51 3/8	44 1/8	42	13 7/8	15 3/8	7 5/8	7 4/8	16	17	Elk Lake, ON	Florien Buch	Florien Buch	1991	112
208	58 2/8	41 7/8	40 7/8	14 1/8	12 3/8	7 7/8	7 5/8	14	16	Muskwa River, BC	William D. Phifer	William D. Phifer	1969	115
208	61 4/8	41 2/8	42 7/8	16	13 3/8	7 7/8	7 5/8	12	11	Legend Lake, AB	Reg Berry	Reg Berry	1977	115
208	62	40 7/8	40 5/8	13 4/8	11 6/8	7 6/8	7 5/8	15	13	Hotchkiss River, AB	Andy G. Petkus	Andy G. Petkus	1985	115
207 7/8	56 1/8	43 2/8	43	13 2/8	13 4/8	7 5/8	7 5/8	14	12	Hudson Bay, SK	Harold Read	Philip Schlegel	1956	118
207 7/8	52 3/8	47 3/8	46 3/8	14 2/8	16	7 1/8	7 3/8	11	10	Neaves Creek, BC	Mrs. George A. Strom, Jr.	Mrs. George A. Strom, Jr.	1960	118
207 7/8	62 5/8	40 1/8	40 2/8	14 1/8	15	8 2/8	7 3/8	11	15	Aroostook Co., ME	Michael C. Hall	Michael C. Hall	1991	118
207 6/8	71 4/8	41 6/8	38 1/8	13 6/8	12 5/8	7 3/8	7 3/8	11	10	Moccasin Lake, ON	Charles W. Reiley	Charles W. Reiley	1961	121
207 5/8	52 7/8	44 2/8	44	15 7/8	13 6/8	7 5/8	7 5/8	16	12	Ash Mt., BC	Robert E. Rabon	Robert E. Rabon	1984	122

Score	Greatest Spread	Length of Palm R	Length of Palm L	Width of Palm R	Width of Palm L	Circ. of Beam R	Circ. of Beam L	Points R	Points L	Locality	Hunter	Owner	Date	Rank
207 4/8	56 4/8	42 4/8	48	12 4/8	14	7 3/8	7 5/8	14	13	Long Lake, AB	Garry A. Debienne	Garry A. Debienne	1975	123
207 4/8	60 4/8	38 4/8	40 3/8	16 4/8	15 4/8	7 4/8	7 6/8	12	16	Sulphur Creek, AB	Willard L. Gamin	Willard L. Gamin	1980	123
207 4/8	51 2/8	43 3/8	43	14 1/8	14 4/8	7	7	14	15	Prophet River, BC	Arvin Harrell	Arvin Harrell	1981	123
207 3/8	70 1/8	31	31	15	16	7 7/8	7 5/8	16	15	Alberta	Unknown	Acad. Nat. Sci., Phil.	1905	126
207 3/8	59 3/8	39 3/8	40 3/8	14 6/8	14	7 6/8	7 5/8	13	13	Smoky River, AB	Robert L. Carmichael, Jr.	Robert L. Carmichael, Jr.	1974	126
207 3/8	53 5/8	40 5/8	41 5/8	15 3/8	15 6/8	6 7/8	6 7/8	14	14	Birch Mts., AB	Leo F. Neuls	Leo F. Neuls	1992	126
207 2/8	59 4/8	43	40 3/8	13 6/8	13 6/8	7 6/8	7 6/8	12	12	Hudson Bay, SK	A.L. Moore	A.L. Moore	1961	129
207 2/8	61 4/8	39 5/8	39 1/8	13 4/8	15 6/8	7 2/8	7 5/8	14	14	Indian Brook, NS	Claude Langley	Claude Langley	1994	129
207 1/8	60 3/8	40 4/8	39 7/8	13 2/8	15	7 2/8	7 5/8	13	13	Manning, AB	Gary Cumming	Gary Cumming	1971	131
207	61 6/8	43 4/8	45 7/8	12 4/8	15	7 7/8	7 5/8	9	12	Goose River, AB	O.D. Evans	O.D. Evans	1960	132
207	58 6/8	42 2/8	44 4/8	13 2/8	14 3/8	8	7 5/8	14	12	Nipisi Lake, AB	J.M. Kirkpatrick	J.M. Kirkpatrick	1966	132
207	60	47	43	12	12	7 4/8	7 5/8	12	11	Atlin, BC	Gerald Larsen	Gerald Larsen	1996	132
206 7/8	62 5/8	41	40 3/8	13 3/8	13 2/8	7 4/8	7 4/8	13	11	Somerset Co., ME	Stephen D. Cole	Stephen D. Cole	1984	135
206 7/8	61 7/8	44 5/8	40 7/8	14 7/8	16	7 6/8	7 6/8	17	9	Notikewin River, AB	Denis Drainville	Denis Drainville	1987	135
206 6/8	60 2/8	39 1/8	39 1/8	14	14 4/8	7 5/8	7 6/8	13	13	Smithers, BC	W.G. Reed	Louis Calder	1951	137
206 6/8	60 2/8	37 4/8	38 5/8	16 1/8	13 4/8	7 2/8	7 6/8	9	15	Black Sturgeon Lake, ON	Joseph J. Casey	Joseph J. Casey	1967	137
206 5/8	57 3/8	43 7/8	43 4/8	13	12 4/8	7 2/8	7 4/8	13	11	Assiniboine River, SK	Francis Peecock	Francis Peecock	1976	139
206 5/8	59 5/8	41 1/8	43 4/8	14 3/8	15 2/8	8	8	10	12	Peerless Lake, AB	Janet E. Spinks	Jonathan Spinks	1989	139
206 4/8	60	40 2/8	35 3/8	16	17 2/8	8 3/8	9 2/8	14	14	White River, ON	Ronald L. Porter	Ronald L. Porter	1975	141
206 4/8	56 2/8	41 3/8	41 6/8	13 3/8	14 4/8	7 3/8	7 4/8	15	13	Horseranch Mts., BC	Bill McCoy	Bill McCoy	1976	141
206 3/8	56 3/8	46 1/8	49	15	12 2/8	7 5/8	7 6/8	9	9	Windfall Creek, AB	Brian Richardson	Brian Richardson	1978	143
206 3/8	59 3/8	44 1/8	42 3/8	15 6/8	15	7 1/8	7 2/8	9	13	Hyland Lake, BC	John B. Barnhardt	John B. Barnhardt	1996	143
206 2/8	55 4/8	41 2/8	42 2/8	13 4/8	13	8 1/8	8 2/8	13	13	Trutch, BC	Richard M. Wilkey	Richard M. Wilkey	1976	145
206 2/8	61 2/8	44 2/8	40 4/8	14 1/8	14 1/8	8 4/8	8 7/8	10	13	Piscataquis Co., ME	Vernon Knott	Vernon Knott	1987	145
206 2/8	66 4/8	38 7/8	41 6/8	13 6/8	13 6/8	8 5/8	8 2/8	12	13	Manning, AB	Nick Denecky	Nick Denecky	1988	145
206 1/8	59 1/8	40 2/8	39 6/8	15 4/8	18 2/8	6 4/8	6 4/8	11	9	Brule, AB	Steven Rose	Steven Rose	1969	148
206 1/8	59 1/8	42 4/8	42 4/8	16 2/8	14 3/8	7 1/8	7 1/8	12	11	Klappan River, BC	Bert Varkonyi	Joe & Nini Varkonyi	1979	148
206 1/8	61 7/8	37 3/8	37 4/8	14 1/8	16 6/8	7 1/8	7 1/8	14	12	Aroostook Co., ME	Shawn LeClair	Shawn LeClair	1993	148
206	59 7/8	42 4/8	42	13 2/8	12 6/8	7 3/8	7 3/8	11	14	Gladys River, BC	Rory Kuchenbecker	Rory Kuchenbecker	1994	148
206	52 4/8	41 6/8	41 6/8	16 2/8	13 4/8	7 2/8	7 4/8	12	13	Trimble Lake, BC	Clifford E. Palmer	Clifford E. Palmer	1962	152
206	59 4/8	38 7/8	38 7/8	15 4/8	15 4/8	7 7/8	7 7/8	13	14	Moose Call Lake, BC	W.W. Harvie	W.W. Harvie	1965	152
206	54 4/8	40 3/8	40 3/8	16 2/8	16 2/8	7 3/8	7 1/8	13	13	Muskwa River, BC	C. Dale Hippensteel	C. Dale Hippensteel	1968	152
206	59 4/8	40 1/8	39 4/8	14 1/8	14 1/8	6 5/8	6 6/8	13	13	Halfway River, BC	Robert Lordahl	Robert Lordahl	1993	152
206	54 2/8	42 4/8	41 1/8	13 2/8	13 2/8	7 4/8	7 5/8	14	15	Gem Lake, BC	John H. Hoppe III	John H. Hoppe III	1997	152
205 7/8	64 3/8	41 2/8	38 6/8	12 4/8	12 4/8	6 4/8	6 5/8	13	16	Cook Co., MN	H. Chapman, C. Chapman, M. Chapman & J. Anderson	H. Chapman, C. Chapman, M. Chapman & J. Anderson	1987	157
205 6/8	56	41 5/8	40 4/8	12 4/8	14 4/8	6 7/8	7 1/8	15	17	Sheep Creek, AB	Rudiger Schwarz	Rudiger Schwarz	1959	158
205 6/8	55	42	41 7/8	14 3/8	16 5/8	8 2/8	8 1/8	12	11	Kechika River, BC	Len Eklund	Len Eklund	1968	158
205 6/8	54 2/8	42	41 4/8	14 1/8	16 6/8	7 6/8	7 5/8	14	13	Turnagain River, BC	Audrey E. Crabtree	Audrey E. Crabtree	1984	158
205 6/8	56 4/8	39	42 6/8	15 4/8	15 6/8	7 2/8	7 2/8	15	13	Badman Point, BC	K. James Malady III	K. James Malady III	1995	158
205 5/8	65 3/8	45	40	14 7/8	14 6/8	7 5/8	7 3/8	13	8	Vice Lake, ON	A.W. Winchester	A.W. Winchester	1959	162
205 5/8	55 3/8	43 3/8	43 4/8	13 7/8	17 6/8	7 4/8	7 4/8	12	13	Simonette River, AB	John G. Stelfox	John G. Stelfox	1965	162
205 5/8	54 1/8	41 1/8	41	12	13 4/8	8 1/8	8 1/8	15	17	Cassiar Mts., BC	Richard Trapp	Richard Trapp	1972	162
205 5/8	65 1/8	38 2/8	39 7/8	13 4/8	13 4/8	7 4/8	7 4/8	11	13	Bottineau Co., ND	Lloyd E. Burgard	Lloyd E. Burgard	1985	162
205 4/8	66 2/8	40 2/8	43 4/8	13 4/8	11 1/8	7 2/8	7 2/8	12	11	Bay Tree, AB	A. Iverson	Wally's Sporting Goods	1926	166

CANADA MOOSE

Alces alces americana and Alces alces andersoni

Score	Greatest Spread	Length of Palm R	Length of Palm L	Width of Palm R	Width of Palm L	Circumference of Beam at Smallest Place R	Circumference of Beam at Smallest Place L	Number of Normal Points R	Number of Normal Points L	Locality	Hunter	Owner	Date Killed	Rank
205 4/8	61 6/8	39 6/8	40 6/8	16 7/8	17	7 6/8	7 6/8	9	8	Kedahda Lake, BC	Jack Perisits, Jr.	Jack Perisits, Jr.	1970	166
205 3/8	62 5/8	44 2/8	37 6/8	14 7/8	13 3/8	8 2/8	8 4/8	13	12	Kleena Kleene, BC	Roger Dane	Roger Dane	1965	168
205 3/8	59 7/8	38 5/8	44 2/8	15 5/8	16 3/8	7 4/8	7 5/8	11	15	Liard Plateau, BC	Charles W. Melton	Charles W. Melton	1971	168
205 3/8	60 7/8	43 4/8	42 6/8	13 4/8	15 4/8	7	7 4/8	9	11	Cassiar Mts., BC	George R. Weeks	George R. Weeks	1985	168
205 2/8	57 2/8	39 4/8	39 7/8	13 2/8	14 3/8	7 3/8	7 2/8	17	14	Stikine Plateau, BC	Mike Papac	Mike Papac	1977	171
205 2/8	61 4/8	41	40 5/8	16	16 3/8	7 4/8	7 2/8	9	8	Serpentine River, NF	Picked Up	Gerard Beaulieu	1989	171
205 1/8	53 5/8	43 3/8	42	13 3/8	14 7/8	8 3/8	8 3/8	13	12	Cold Fish Lake, BC	A. Baltensweiler	A. Baltensweiler	1965	173
205 1/8	56 1/8	40 1/8	38 3/8	14	13 6/8	7 4/8	7 3/8	18	15	Atlin, BC	Joey H. Longpre	Joey H. Longpre	1994	173
205	57 4/8	36 2/8	35 4/8	17 2/8	19 4/8	7 4/8	7 4/8	16	14	Prophet River, MB	John E. Hammett, Jr.	John E. Hammett, Jr.	1944	175
205	56	42 7/8	41 6/8	11 6/8	14	7 1/8	7	14	16	Moose Lake, MB	Leif R. Langsjoen	Leif R. Langsjoen	1960	175
205	57 4/8	43 2/8	42 6/8	11 4/8	12	7 4/8	7 4/8	12	13	Cassiar, BC	James H. Bryant	James H. Bryant	1965	175
205	60 4/8	41	43	12	12	8 2/8	8 3/8	11	13	Cassiar Mts., BC	Earl I. Jones	Earl I. Jones	1978	175
205	58 2/8	42 6/8	42	15 1/8	15 1/8	7 3/8	7 2/8	9	9	Letain Lake, BC	Jesse Mengler	Jesse Mengler	1995	175
204 7/8	62 3/8	38 7/8	40 2/8	14 4/8	14 3/8	7 2/8	7	15	11	Prophet River, BC	Lewis Morgan	Lewis Morgan	1970	180
204 6/8	56 2/8	46 6/8	43 6/8	15 1/8	15 7/8	7 3/8	7 4/8	8	8	Hudson Bay, SK	Fred Smorodin	Fred Smorodin	1957	181
204 6/8	57	45 4/8	43 6/8	13 4/8	13 2/8	8 3/8	8 3/8	9	10	Heart Mts., BC	Timothy E. Walters	Timothy E. Walters	1995	181
204 4/8	54 4/8	40 3/8	40 2/8	13 5/8	12 2/8	6 5/8	6 4/8	16	16	Cassiar, BC	Unknown	B.C. Game Dept.	PR 1918	183
204 4/8	51 6/8	45 3/8	44 2/8	15	14 3/8	7 2/8	7 4/8	13	11	Germansen Mts., BC	Edward A. McLarney	Edward A. McLarney	1978	183
204 3/8	57 7/8	40 6/8	39 7/8	14	13 7/8	7 7/8	7 2/8	12	13	Prophet River, BC	W.T. Yoshimoto	W.T. Yoshimoto	1966	185
204 3/8	55 7/8	42 3/8	41	16 6/8	14 4/8	8	8	12	10	Summit Lake, BC	R. A. Schweitzer	R.A. Schweitzer	1970	185
204 3/8	56 5/8	43	41	15 2/8	14 4/8	7 3/8	7 4/8	11	11	Prophet River, BC	Daniel L. Rafferty	Daniel L. Rafferty	1986	185
204 2/8	52 4/8	36 3/8	38 3/8	16 1/8	16 7/8	7 4/8	7 3/8	16	16	Buckinghorse, BC	John C. Belcher	John C. Belcher	1955	188
204 2/8	60	37 6/8	38 4/8	16 2/8	14 2/8	7 1/8	7 2/8	14	13	The Pas, MB	Eddy Burkhartsmeir	Eddy Burkhartsmeir	1960	188
204 2/8	62	37 4/8	38 2/8	15 3/8	16 6/8	8 2/8	8 2/8	10	10	Duti Lake, BC	John M. Haugen	John M. Haugen	1966	188
204 2/8	62 2/8	41 4/8	41 1/8	16 6/8	14 5/8	7 2/8	7 2/8	8	9	Ice Mt., BC	J.E. Mason	J.E. Mason	1966	188
204 2/8	55 4/8	44 7/8	39 4/8	15 7/8	14 3/8	7 4/8	7 4/8	13	14	Muskwa River, BC	James C. Kolbe	James C. Kolbe	1969	188
204 2/8	58 6/8	36 2/8	41 7/8	19 1/8	18 4/8	7	7	11	16	Wawa, ON	Edward A. Hall	Edward A. Hall	1970	188
204 2/8	56 6/8	45	44 2/8	11 4/8	12 4/8	7	7 2/8	12	11	Tetsa River, BC	Alex Nesterenko	Alex Nesterenko	1973	188
204 2/8	65	41 6/8	39 5/8	15 1/8	13	7 1/8	7	11	10	Peace River, AB	Wilbur C. Savage	Wilbur C. Savage	1984	188
204 1/8	55 1/8	41 3/8	46 2/8	15	13 5/8	7	7 2/8	13	16	Ft. St. James, BC	Ed Cornish	Ed Cornish	1964	196
204 1/8	63 1/8	40 3/8	40 7/8	13	13	7 2/8	7 1/8	11	10	Eight Mile Creek, BC	Leroy C. Mooney	Leroy C. Mooney	1995	196
204	68 4/8	35	33 6/8	15 2/8	13	8	8	13	13	Elderslay, SK	R.E. McKenzie	R.E. McKenzie	1930	198
204	55	40 7/8	41 5/8	13 4/8	13 5/8	7 1/8	7 4/8	15	13	Lake Nipigon, ON	Gary C. Jacobson	Gary C. Jacobson	1965	198
204	57 6/8	42 6/8	43 6/8	16 3/8	13 4/8	7 4/8	7 3/8	11	10	Tachilta Lakes, BC	Karen White	Karen White	1997	198
203 7/8	63 3/8	41 3/8	39 6/8	10 7/8	11 6/8	7 7/8	7 5/8	12	12	Lodge, SK	F. Foarie	F. Foarie	1962	201
203 7/8	52 3/8	41 6/8	41 5/8	13 5/8	14 7/8	7 4/8	7 6/8	13	14	Kakwa River, AB	Dean A. Estes	Dean A. Estes	1987	201
203 7/8	53 1/8	40 3/8	42 2/8	18 2/8	15 4/8	7 4/8	7 4/8	15	12	Somerset Co., ME	Gary T. Brown	Gary T. Brown	1994	201
203 6/8	55	38 1/8	39	15 2/8	15 3/8	7	7	14	15	Jackfish Lake, AB	A. Stopson	A. Stopson	1955	204

Score	Greatest Spread	Length of Palm R	Length of Palm L	Width of Palm R	Width of Palm L	Circumference R	Circumference L	Points R	Points L	Locality	Hunter	Owner	Date	Rank
203 6/8	59 4/8	42 5/8	41 2/8	10 5/8	12 4/8	8 2/8	8 2/8	13	12	Hudson Bay, SK	Abraham Hassen	Abraham Hassen	1959	204
203 6/8	60	38 1/8	41 1/8	13	14	8	7 6/8	13	15	Rabbit River, BC	Bob V. Kelley	Bob V. Kelley	1969	204
203 6/8	58 4/8	39 1/8	39	12 2/8	12 5/8	8 3/8	8 3/8	13	14	Pink Mt., BC	Garth C. Hardy	Garth C. Hardy	1973	204
203 6/8	52 2/8	43	43 4/8	13 4/8	12 1/8	7 5/8	7 5/8	13	13	Turnagain River, BC	Larry R. Zilinski	Larry R. Zilinski	1986	204
203 6/8	58 4/8	41 5/8	42	11 6/8	12 2/8	7 3/8	7 3/8	12	13	Rhuda Lake, QC	Richard Cordes	Richard Cordes	1994	204
203 5/8	53 3/8	43 4/8	43 3/8	11 4/8	12 2/8	7 3/8	7 4/8	14	13	Overflowing River, MB	Lester Ochsner	Lester Ochsner	1957	210
203 5/8	56 3/8	43 1/8	41 7/8	13 1/8	13 2/8	7 6/8	7 5/8	16	10	Surmont Lake, AB	Daryl Goodine	Daryl Goodine	1984	210
203 5/8	59 5/8	39 2/8	45	13 5/8	13 1/8	8 4/8	8 1/8	12	12	Gladys Lake, BC	Harry Hoeft	Harry Hoeft	1984	210
203 4/8	55 6/8	38 4/8	40	13 2/8	13 2/8	8 1/8	8 1/8	14	15	Pink Mt., BC	John L. London	John L. London	1966	213
203 4/8	61	39 7/8	39 6/8	13 2/8	14 5/8	7 2/8	7 2/8	13	11	Graham River, BC	R. M. Frye	R.M. Frye	1970	213
203 4/8	55 2/8	43 4/8	43 4/8	14 1/8	14 1/8	7	7	11	11	Dease Lake, BC	John W. Goodwin	John W. Goodwin	1986	213
203 3/8	64 7/8	41	36 3/8	15 4/8	14	8 2/8	7 7/8	11	12	Leaf Lake, SK	Tom Skoretz	Tom Skoretz	1959	216
203 3/8	55 3/8	42	48 6/8	12 6/8	14 2/8	7 3/8	7 2/8	12	13	Hudson Bay Junct., SK	Murray Griffin	Murray Griffin	1965	216
203 3/8	53 3/8	40 6/8	42	17 6/8	16 2/8	7 4/8	7 5/8	11	10	Big Smoky River, AB	Ross D. Carrick	Ross D. Carrick	1971	216
203 3/8	58 3/8	39 1/8	40	17 6/8	16 2/8	7 4/8	7 1/8	10	13	Muskwa River, BC	John A. Kolman	John A. Kolman	1975	216
203 3/8	64 5/8	36 5/8	33 3/8	17 7/8	17 6/8	6 6/8	7 1/8	12	17	Ruggles Lake, ON	Alvin D. Chapman	Alvin D. Chapman	1983	216
203 3/8	59 3/8	38 6/8	38 3/8	12 4/8	12 4/8	7 1/8	7 1/8	14	11	Teslin Lake, BC	Russ LaFreniere	Russ LaFreniere	1988	216
203 2/8	69 2/8	32 7/8	32 6/8	17	16 1/8	7 1/8	8	11	12	Kvass Creek, AB	Frank C. Hibben	Frank C. Hibben	1958	222
203 2/8	59 6/8	39 3/8	38 3/8	13 4/8	15 7/8	8	8 1/8	12	14	Wapiti River, AB	David L. Savage	David L. Savage	1984	222
203 2/8	60 4/8	39 4/8	40 4/8	11 6/8	13 1/8	8 1/8	8 3/8	12	14	Bigstone River, MB	Corbett P. Smith	Corbett P. Smith	1994	222
203 2/8	56 1/8	37 4/8	37 6/8	14 2/8	15	7 6/8	7 6/8	15	13	Scoop Lake, BC	Dwight E. Farr, Jr.	Dwight E. Farr, Jr.	1980	222
203 1/8	52 3/8	43	42 2/8	14 4/8	14 2/8	7 3/8	7 3/8	14	13	Birch Mts., AB	Charles N. Johns	Charles N. Johns	1997	225
203 1/8	55	39	40	15 2/8	14	9 2/8	9 2/8	15	15	Fawcett, AB	A. Juckli	Mrs. A. Juckli	PR 1933	225
203	58 2/8	42	41 4/8	11	12 5/8	6 7/8	6 7/8	13	13	Cassiar, BC	Tom Lindahl	Tom Lindahl	1961	227
203	57 2/8	38 6/8	39 1/8	15 6/8	14	7 1/8	7 2/8	14	14	Cassiar, BC	Arvid F. Benson	Arvid F. Benson	1965	227
203	58 2/8	41 1/8	38 5/8	12 5/8	13 1/8	7 2/8	7 1/8	16	14	Pink Mt., BC	T. C. Britt, Jr.	T.C. Britt, Jr.	1966	227
203	61 2/8	39 1/8	42	14 2/8	15 3/8	7 4/8	7 6/8	13	10	Manning, AB	James Harbick	James Harbick	1967	227
203	55	43 1/8	44 2/8	15 3/8	12 1/8	7 6/8	7 6/8	12	11	Robb Lake, BC	Jerome Metcalfe	Jerome Metcalfe	1967	227
203	62	39 2/8	44 7/8	11 7/8	11 7/8	7 3/8	7 3/8	14	12	Graham River, BC	Harold L. Sperfslage	Harold L. Sperfslage	1975	227
203	67	42 2/8	42 2/8	13 4/8	14 6/8	7 4/8	7 4/8	9	10	Coast Range, BC	Picked Up	Neal Coleman	PR 1980	227
203	59	42 2/8	44	12 6/8	12 2/8	7	7	11	11	Bloodvein River, MB	R. Stearns, R. Sigurdson, R. Blowers & L. Walters	R. Stearns, R. Sigurdson, R. Blowers & L. Walters	1988	227
202 7/8	60 3/8	42	47 7/8	13 1/8	14 3/8	7 5/8	7 1/8	9	9	Prophet River, BC	Elbert Stiles	Elbert Stiles	1960	236
202 7/8	55 3/8	39 4/8	39 4/8	17 1/8	16	7 2/8	7 2/8	11	11	Atlin, BC	Robert H. Morgan	Robert H. Morgan	1973	236
202 7/8	57 1/8	43 4/8	46 3/8	15	11 5/8	7 6/8	7 1/8	10	11	Lower Manitou Lake, ON	Donald R. Anderson	Donald R. Anderson	1979	236
202 7/8	56 1/8	41 6/8	46 1/8	18 6/8	13 6/8	7 7/8	8 1/8	13	10	Frog River, BC	Malcom D. Dinges, Jr.	Malcom D. Dinges, Jr.	1980	236
202 6/8	58	43 1/8	40 3/8	11 4/8	11 7/8	7 4/8	7 4/8	14	13	Bee Peak, BC	Dennis J. Eakin	Dennis J. Eakin	1984	240
202 6/8	60 4/8	42	43 1/8	12	12 3/8	7 1/8	7 1/8	12	11	Chinchaga River, AB	Oliver Travers	Oliver Travers	1985	240
202 5/8	59 7/8	43 7/8	43 7/8	12	14	7 2/8	7 2/8	9	13	Alder Flats, AB	Fred J. Simpson	Carnegie Museum	1966	242
202 5/8	56 1/8	39 7/8	40 5/8	13 7/8	13 5/8	7 4/8	7 4/8	13	14	Harmon Lake, ON	Dale C. Curtis	Dale C. Curtis	1969	242
202 5/8	55 1/8	40	40 6/8	14 5/8	13 5/8	7 1/8	7 1/8	13	13	High Prairie, AB	Dean L. Walker	Dean L. Walker	1973	242
202 4/8	57	39 5/8	38 7/8	14 7/8	15 7/8	8 1/8	8	11	11	Chelan, SK	Picked Up	Harold Bergman	1955	245
202 4/8	58 2/8	41 2/8	41 4/8	13 6/8	13 4/8	8	8	10	10	Watson Lake, BC	Lloyd Nosler	Lloyd Nosler	1964	245
202 4/8	61 6/8	41	40 2/8	14 3/8	13 6/8	7 7/8	7 6/8	8	10	Prophet River, BC	Lyle Nosler	Lyle Nosler	1964	245
202 4/8	62 4/8	43 6/8	40 2/8	13 4/8	13 4/8	7 2/8	7 2/8	9	10	Stewart Lake, BC	Keith Wilson	Keith Wilson	1980	245
202 4/8	58	38 1/8	35 5/8	15 4/8	15 7/8	7 3/8	7 1/8	14	15	Margaree Valley, NS	Leo C. Horne	Leo C. Horne	1986	245
202 4/8	60 2/8	43	46 4/8	11 6/8	13 3/8	7 6/8	7 3/8	9	14	Glundebery Creek, BC	Neil Lawson	Neil Lawson	1988	245

CANADA MOOSE

Alces alces americana and Alces alces andersoni

Score	Greatest Spread	Length of Palm R	L	Width of Palm R	L	Circumference of Beam at Smallest Place R	L	Number of Normal Points R	L	Locality	Hunter	Owner	Date Killed	Rank
202 3/8	59 1/8	39 2/8	40 4/8	13	15 1/8	7 3/8	7 3/8	12	14	Cassiar, BC	Unknown	B.C. Game Dept.	PR 1918	251
202 3/8	53 5/8	43	39 4/8	19	16 2/8	7 6/8	7 5/8	13	12	Swan Hills, AB	Harold R. Wiese	Harold R. Wiese	1967	251
202 3/8	62 3/8	41	40 4/8	12 3/8	11 2/8	8 2/8	7 6/8	11	12	Grovedale, AB	Douglas R. Morris	Douglas R. Morris	1974	254
202 2/8	55 2/8	42	43 4/8	15	14	7 4/8	7 4/8	10	11	Cormorant, MB	Howard J. Lang	Howard J. Lang	1950	254
202 2/8	60 6/8	42 3/8	41 3/8	12 7/8	16 2/8	7 6/8	7 4/8	12	9	Goose Mt., AB	Fred Bartel	Fred Bartel	1956	254
202 2/8	56 4/8	40 4/8	44 5/8	12 7/8	13 5/8	7 4/8	7 4/8	13	13	Hines Creek, AB	Ralph Jumago	Ralph Jumago	1960	254
202 2/8	61 4/8	41	41	10 3/8	12 4/8	7 4/8	7 5/8	13	13	Turcotte Lake, QC	S.B. Fredenburgh, Jr.	S.B. Fredenburgh, Jr.	1962	254
202 2/8	59 2/8	36 6/8	38 3/8	16	17 6/8	6 6/8	7 4/8	12	13	Telegraph Creek, BC	George D. Young	George D. Young	1962	254
202 2/8	59	40 1/8	44 2/8	13 1/8	14 4/8	7 3/8	7 4/8	11	11	Atlin, BC	J.D. Kethley	J.D. Kethley	1966	254
202 2/8	59 4/8	38 1/8	37 4/8	12 4/8	15 4/8	7 4/8	7 3/8	14	14	King Brook, NB	Glen Gilks	Glen Gilks	1972	254
202 2/8	63 2/8	38	37	13	13 6/8	7 5/8	7 4/8	12	12	Wreck Cove Lakes, NS	Donald J. Sauveur	Donald J. Sauveur	1988	254
202 2/8	57 2/8	38 5/8	41 1/8	15	17 2/8	7 7/8	7 7/8	11	11	Swift River, BC	Jean Sirois	Jean Sirois	1991	254
202 1/8	66 7/8	43 3/8	39 3/8	13 1/8	13 4/8	7 1/8	7	9	8	Kawdy Mt., BC	Herman Kirn	Herman Kirn	1981	263
202 1/8	51 5/8	44 2/8	42 6/8	13 5/8	13 4/8	7	6 7/8	14	12	Graham River, BC	Thomas H. Morrison	Thomas H. Morrison	1981	263
202 1/8	54 3/8	40 7/8	40 3/8	14 6/8	15 3/8	7 2/8	7 2/8	11	11	Halfway River, BC	M. Toby Hobek	M. Toby Hobek	1990	263
202 1/8	57 1/8	39 6/8	40 3/8	13	13 3/8	6 6/8	7 1/8	13	14	Franklin Co., ME	Byron Beauregard	Byron Beauregard	1994	263
202	58	37	37 2/8	14	16 4/8	7	7 2/8	14	15	St. Jovite, QC	Ed Schmeller	Ed Schmeller	1942	267
202	61	39 2/8	42	14	15	7 3/8	7 2/8	10	10	Muskwa River, BC	Gordon C. Arndt	Gordon C. Arndt	1976	267
201 7/8	62 6/8	41 6/8	38 7/8	17 1/8	14 6/8	8	7 4/8	9	9	Tumbler Ridge, BC	Dale R. Duperreault	Dale R. Duperreault	1993	267
201 7/8	51 1/8	39 1/8	40 2/8	13 5/8	14 5/8	7 5/8	7 5/8	15	17	Saskatchewan	Gordon Lund	Gordon Lund	PR 1954	270
201 7/8	56 3/8	40 4/8	43 7/8	15	12 6/8	7 4/8	7 7/8	15	12	Cassiar Mts., BC	Clark A. Goetzmann	Clark A. Goetzmann	1968	270
201 7/8	56 5/8	38 3/8	41 1/8	15 2/8	12	7 2/8	7 2/8	15	16	Ft. St. John, BC	William J. Heiman	William J. Heiman	1969	270
201 7/8	57 5/8	40 2/8	40 3/8	14 6/8	13 3/8	7 5/8	7 4/8	14	11	Lake Co., MN	Dustin J. Benes	Dustin J. Benes	1994	270
201 6/8	60 2/8	37 5/8	40 3/8	15 4/8	16	7 5/8	7 5/8	10	14	Kechika Range, BC	Norman Lougheed	Norman Lougheed	1964	274
201 6/8	57 2/8	39	39 6/8	14 5/8	14	7 2/8	7 4/8	17	12	Colt Lake, BC	James C. Wood	James C. Wood	1965	274
201 6/8	59 4/8	38 7/8	39 6/8	15	16 3/8	7 2/8	7 2/8	10	15	Pink Mt., BC	John P. Blanchard	John P. Blanchard	1970	274
201 6/8	55 2/8	41 2/8	42	13 4/8	13 2/8	8	7 6/8	11	12	Cabin Lake, BC	Donald F. Gould	Donald F. Gould	1974	274
201 6/8	54 6/8	41 1/8	40 2/8	13 2/8	12	7 2/8	7 4/8	14	15	Toad River, BC	Dennis R. Gustafson	Dennis R. Gustafson	1982	274
201 6/8	59 6/8	39 5/8	36 7/8	13 6/8	16	7 3/8	7 3/8	13	18	Wapiti River, BC	Picked Up	Peter Christie	1989	274
201 6/8	54	39 5/8	39 4/8	17 1/8	18	7 6/8	7 6/8	12	13	Lake Co., MN	Dick, Bill, Ron & Joe Klesk	Joe Klesk	1993	274
201 5/8	56	43 3/8	42 1/8	12	13 1/8	6 6/8	6 7/8	12	14	Chukachida River, BC	Nelson T. Offutt	Nelson T. Offutt	1993	274
201 5/8	53 5/8	37	39	18	20	7	7	12	12	Omineca Mt., BC	C.L. Burnette	C.L. Burnette	1973	282
201 5/8	57 5/8	43 4/8	40 7/8	12 3/8	12 4/8	7 2/8	7 2/8	12	12	Calata Lake, BC	Klaus Schmidt	Klaus Schmidt	1994	282
201 4/8	49 2/8	42 7/8	42 3/8	15 2/8	13 3/8	7 3/8	7 3/8	15	13	Cold Fish Lake, BC	Charles E. Wilson, Jr.	Charles E. Wilson, Jr.	1957	284
201 4/8	56	36 6/8	34 5/8	18	19 2/8	7 1/8	7 2/8	17	13	Island Lake, QC	Silvene Bracalente	Silvene Bracalente	1962	284
201 4/8	54 4/8	43 5/8	42 1/8	16 1/8	15 5/8	7 2/8	7 3/8	10	10	Ospika River, BC	Bill Goosman	Bill Goosman	1964	284
201 4/8	55 2/8	46 6/8	42 6/8	12 4/8	11 4/8	7 3/8	7 3/8	12	12	Mt. Lady Laurier, BC	Peter L. Halbig	Peter L. Halbig	1968	284
201 4/8	56 6/8	41 4/8	44	12 4/8	14 1/8	6 7/8	6 7/8	12	15	Bougie Mt., BC	Dennis R. Mitchell	Dennis R. Mitchell	1987	284

Score										Locality	Hunter	Owner	Date Killed	Rank
201 4/8	56 6/8	42 1/8	43 3/8	12 4/8	14 1/8	7 6/8	8	10	14	Denetiah Lake, BC	Lee Frudden	Lee Frudden	1995	284
201 3/8	57 1/8	40	40 4/8	13 1/8	13 3/8	7	7	14	12	Swan Hills, AB	Earl C. Wood	Vale E. Wood	1967	290
201 2/8	56 4/8	41	40 6/8	13 2/8	14 4/8	7 3/8	7 2/8	12	13	Rocky Mt. House, AB	John B. Gibson	John B. Gibson	1955	291
201 2/8	62	40	43	11 2/8	13 2/8	7 6/8	7	11	12	Racing River, BC	Anthony Battaglia	Anthony Battaglia	1966	291
201 2/8	58	36 5/8	37 6/8	15	14 4/8	6 4/8	6 4/8	14	13	Upsala, ON	Daniel F. Volkmann	Daniel F. Volkmann	1969	291
201 2/8	63 6/8	34 6/8	34 1/8	15 3/8	15 1/8	7 7/8	7 4/8	13	12	Quebec	Diana Baglino	Diana Baglino	1971	291
201 2/8	53	40 7/8	38 4/8	13 1/8	13 7/8	7 4/8	7 5/8	15	15	Lesser Slave Lake, AB	B. Strain & B. Baergen	Bert Strain	1976	291
201 2/8	56 2/8	40 6/8	44	11	13 4/8	7 6/8	8 3/8	13	14	Crow River, QC	Richard P. Legare	Richard P. Legare	1994	291
201 2/8	55	41 3/8	42 5/8	13 4/8	16	7 2/8	7 2/8	11	11	Minaker River, BC	Marvin F. Mason	Marvin F. Mason	1996	291
201 1/8	53 5/8	39 6/8	42 4/8	15 7/8	15 7/8	7 5/8	8	11	11	Reserve, SK	O.A. Kjelshus	O.A. Kjelshus	1953	298
201 1/8	55 3/8	41 7/8	40	15 5/8	15	7 5/8	7 3/8	13	13	Big Sandy Lake, SK	John Longley	John Longley	1961	298
201 1/8	56 7/8	40 5/8	43	15 4/8	12 4/8	7 3/8	7	15	13	Slave Lake, AB	A.F. Harry	A.F. Harry	1967	298
201 1/8	61 3/8	41	45	16 6/8	13 1/8	7 5/8	7 2/8	11	11	Skeena Mts., BC	Wayne A. Tri	Wayne A. Tri	1978	298
201 1/8	57 5/8	38 3/8	40 3/8	11 6/8	14 5/8	8 5/8	8 6/8	13	14	Piscataquis Co., ME	Walter V. Scott	Walter V. Scott	1980	298
201 1/8	61 3/8	40 1/8	39	11 4/8	12	8 3/8	9 2/8	11	12	Lost Lake, BC	Kenneth C. Adair, Jr.	Kenneth C. Adair, Jr.	1992	298
201	55 4/8	38 2/8	42	14 4/8	15 1/8	8	8 2/8	13	11	Muskwa River, BC	J.H. Blu	J.H. Blu	1972	304
201	55 2/8	39 7/8	41	14 7/8	13 2/8	7 4/8	7 2/8	13	12	Sipanok Channel, SK	Clarence Saretsky	Clarence Saretsky	1974	304
201	54 4/8	43 4/8	42	14	13 1/8	8 5/8	8 1/8	13	13	Toad River, BC	Steven Ronshausen	Steven Ronshausen	1981	304
201	53 4/8	44 4/8	42 4/8	15 4/8	14 4/8	7 6/8	8	10	9	Wallace River, BC	Victor R. Tessier	Victor R. Tessier	1985	304
200 7/8	61 3/8	39 7/8	41 5/8	13 1/8	13 1/8	7 4/8	7 5/8	12	14	Grande Prairie, AB	John W. Benson	John W. Benson	1969	308
200 7/8	60 7/8	38 2/8	34 4/8	10 7/8	14 6/8	7 5/8	7	14	13	Spatsizi River, BC	G.C. Taylor	G.C. Taylor	1974	308
200 7/8	61 5/8	36 7/8	40 3/8	14 6/8	14 5/8	7 5/8	8 6/8	14	13	Muskwa River, BC	Stan Longyear	Stan Longyear	1984	308
200 7/8	56 5/8	41	38	12 3/8	16	7 6/8	7 7/8	11	14	Aroostook Co., ME	Ernest L. Leighton	Ernest L. Leighton	1988	308
200 7/8	63 3/8	42 7/8	39	13 3/8	14 7/8	7 7/8	8	9	9	Swan Lake, BC	Gary A. Markofer	Gary A. Markofer	1990	308
200 7/8	52 3/8	39 1/8	42 2/8	14 3/8	19 6/8	8	7 6/8	13	13	Muskwa River, BC	Teresa M. Mull	Teresa M. Mull	1995	308
200 6/8	50 2/8	41 5/8	39	13 5/8	13 5/8	7	6 7/8	14	14	Goodwin Lake, BC	Bill R. Moomey	Bill R. Moomey	1974	314
200 6/8	56 6/8	39	38 5/8	15	14 4/8	6 7/8	7	12	15	Turnagain River, BC	Kenneth M. Brown	Kenneth M. Brown	1986	314
200 5/8	61 1/8	39 1/8	39	11 2/8	11 5/8	6 4/8	6 4/8	13	13	Prophet River, BC	Chauncey Everard	Chauncey Everard	1967	316
200 5/8	63 1/8	38 3/8	39	11 4/8	12	7 7/8	7 7/8	11	11	Alberta	Ray Pierson	Ray Pierson	1967	316
200 5/8	58 1/8	37 6/8	39 2/8	13	13	7 6/8	7 4/8	14	14	Fort Nelson, BC	Everett L. Ashley	Everett L. Ashley	1975	316
200 5/8	59 1/8	39 1/8	41 1/8	16 3/8	13	7 5/8	7 7/8	15	15	Cassiar Mts., BC	G.L. Garrett	G.L. Garrett	1977	316
200 5/8	59 5/8	40 2/8	41 6/8	14	13 2/8	8	8 2/8	14	9	Robb Lake, BC	Richard L. Bostrom	Richard L. Bostrom	1985	316
200 5/8	66 5/8	36	37 2/8	14 6/8	15 3/8	7 3/8	8 2/8	11	9	Low Fog Creek, BC	Delmar L. Achenbach	Delmar L. Achenbach	1989	316
200 4/8	61	39 3/8	39 2/8	15 2/8	13 5/8	7	6 6/8	10	10	Deadmans Lake, BC	John Caputo	John Caputo	1950	322
200 4/8	61 4/8	38 2/8	39 2/8	14 2/8	16 2/8	6 6/8	7	10	10	Watson Lake, BC	Dan E. O'Neal, Jr.	Dan E. O'Neal, Jr.	1968	322
200 4/8	52	40	41 7/8	15	15 4/8	7 2/8	7 2/8	14	14	Muskwa River, BC	William W. Veigel	William W. Veigel	1971	322
200 4/8	59 2/8	42 3/8	40 1/8	15 3/8	15 1/8	6 7/8	7 1/8	9	10	Cassiar Mts., BC	Calvin D. Boatwright	Calvin D. Boatwright	1976	322
200 4/8	60	39 4/8	40	14 2/8	12 5/8	7 4/8	7 1/8	11	11	Adsit Lake, BC	Morris R. Nadeau	Morris R. Nadeau	1986	322
200 4/8	57 6/8	38 6/8	39	14 4/8	15	7 1/8	8 4/8	10	10	Kedahda Lake, BC	Brian Bergen	Brian Bergen	1990	322
200 4/8	52	39	40	13 6/8	15	8 4/8	7 6/8	14	14	Halfway River, BC	Harold Schmidt	Harold Schmidt	1993	322
200 4/8	52 4/8	41 2/8	39 7/8	15 1/8	15 3/8	8	7	13	12	Aulneau Pen., ON	Donald F. Holland	Donald F. Holland	1994	322
200 3/8	58 1/8	36 3/8	39	15	15	6 6/8	7 2/8	13	13	English River, ON	Jack Radke	Jack Radke	1966	330
200 3/8	59 3/8	43 6/8	41 1/8	11 3/8	11 5/8	8 1/8	6 7/8	10	11	Peace River, BC	Walter W. Kassner	Walter W. Kassner	1968	330
200 3/8	51 7/8	41 7/8	43	13 5/8	14	6 6/8	7 1/8	12	12	Cassiar Mts., BC	Don Stallings	Don Stallings	1971	330
200 3/8	53 1/8	40 6/8	38 6/8	13 7/8	14 3/8	7	6 7/8	16	16	Cypress Creek, BC	Raymond A. Racette	Raymond A. Racette	1984	330
200 3/8	56 7/8	40 1/8	41 5/8	13	14 1/8	6 5/8	6 7/8	14	12	Hixon, BC	Scott Paterson	Scott Paterson	1996	330
200 2/8	62	42	40 2/8	13 4/8	11 5/8	7 5/8	7 2/8	10	10	Atlin, BC	John Vigna	John Vigna	1965	335

CANADA MOOSE

Alces alces americana and Alces alces andersoni

Score	Greatest Spread	Length of Palm		Width of Palm		Circumference of Beam at Smallest Place		Number of Normal Points		Locality	Hunter	Owner	Date Killed	Rank
		R	L	R	L	R	L	R	L					
200 2/8	56 6/8	36 6/8	37 4/8	14 5/8	15 4/8	7 3/8	7 5/8	14	13	Pink Mt., BC	Danny Taylor	Danny Taylor	1970	335
200 1/8	56 7/8	39 7/8	41 2/8	12 7/8	12 2/8	8	8	12	13	Turcotte Lake, QC	George Clark, Jr.	George Clark, Jr.	1960	337
200 1/8	55 1/8	41 4/8	39 6/8	14 7/8	13 2/8	7 5/8	7 4/8	14	13	Whitebeech, SK	John J. Kuzma	John J. Kuzma	1966	337
200 1/8	52 7/8	46 2/8	46 6/8	11 6/8	10 2/8	7 1/8	7 2/8	12	10	Red Fern Lake, BC	M. Steven Weaver	M. Steven Weaver	1966	337
200	59	43	42 2/8	14 5/8	12 6/8	7	7	9	11	Cold Fish Lake, BC	G. Kenneth Whitehead	G. Kenneth Whitehead	1964	340
200	56 4/8	37 7/8	41 6/8	15 3/8	13 1/8	6 6/8	6 7/8	14	16	Lac Seul, ON	Robert B. Peregrine	Robert B. Peregrine	1966	340
200	59 2/8	40 3/8	41 1/8	14 1/8	12	7 4/8	7 5/8	11	12	Nass Lake, BC	Dan A. Pick	Dan A. Pick	1969	340
200	53	36 1/8	35 6/8	16	16 2/8	7 7/8	7 6/8	15	11	Muskwa River, BC	Roy V. Haskell	Roy V. Haskell	1978	340
200	59 2/8	44 3/8	41 2/8	11 2/8	11 4/8	7 7/8	7 7/8	10	11	Pelican Lake, AB	Terrance Krawec	Terrance Krawec	1993	340
197 7/8	62 3/8	32 6/8	33 2/8	16 6/8	13 4/8	7 6/8	7 4/8	15	15	Patapedia Lakes, QC	Frederick K. Barbour	Frederick K. Barbour	1911	345
197 7/8	46 5/8	41 6/8	40 3/8	17 5/8	15 7/8	7 3/8	7 3/8	13	13	Vanderhoof, BC	William Ilnisky	William Ilnisky	1978	345
197 7/8	54 3/8	40 2/8	44 3/8	14 6/8	17	7 6/8	7 7/8	13	10	Chukachida River, BC	Gregory M. Pacacha	Gregory M. Pacacha	1991	345
196 6/8	61 4/8	36 6/8	36 1/8	12 7/8	13 7/8	8 3/8	8 1/8	12	12	Cutbank River, AB	Steve Kalischuk	Steve Kalischuk	1960	348
196 6/8	51 4/8	40 2/8	40 6/8	14 4/8	14 6/8	7 3/8	7 4/8	12	13	Halfway River, BC	Jack Taylor	Jack Taylor	1973	348
196 6/8	57	39 7/8	39 7/8	14	13 4/8	7 4/8	7 5/8	11	13	Kledo Creek, BC	Rick L. McGowan	Rick L. McGowan	1975	348
196 6/8	60 6/8	37 3/8	41	13	12 7/8	8 2/8	8 6/8	11	11	Lake Co., MN	L.D. Holtegaard	L.D. Holtegaard, R. Smith, B. Nessler, & P. Nietz	1981	348
196 6/8	59	37	36 1/8	14 3/8	13 2/8	7 2/8	7	14	14	Cassiar Mts., BC	James D. Hoekstra	James D. Hoekstra	1986	348
196 6/8	58 6/8	40 6/8	40 2/8	13 6/8	14 6/8	7 4/8	7 4/8	9	11	St. Louis Co., MN	Arlo Manzke	Arlo Manzke	1993	348
196 5/8	55	38 5/8	39 5/8	13 2/8	12 6/8	8	7 7/8	13	14	Fort McMurray, AB	Thomas J. Skovron	Thomas J. Skovron	1997	348
196 5/8	53 3/8	38 5/8	39 7/8	13 1/8	15 3/8	7 3/8	7 4/8	14	15	Greenbush, SK	Tom Flanagan	Tom Flanagan	1955	355
196 5/8	61 7/8	38 7/8	39 2/8	15 2/8	14	8	8	10	8	Prairie River, SK	Clarence Slater	Clarence Slater	1955	355
196 5/8	58 7/8	41 2/8	38 2/8	13 3/8	15 7/8	7	6 6/8	12	12	Tootsee Lake, BC	Robert E. Alexander	James L. Clark	1992	355
196 5/8	64 3/8	38 1/8	39 3/8	13 6/8	13 6/8	7 6/8	7 6/8	9	8	Big Sand Lake, MB	Ronald J. Zockle	Ronald J. Zockle	1992	355
196 4/8	59	41	42	9 4/8	11 7/8	6 6/8	7 6/8	12	8	Drayton Valley, AB	Ollie Fedorus	Ollie Fedorus	1962	359
196 4/8	60	37 7/8	39 6/8	12 1/8	13	6 6/8	6 7/8	13	13	Dease Lake, BC	Peter Hohorst	Peter Hohorst	1968	359
196 4/8	58 6/8	40 1/8	40 4/8	12 2/8	14 1/8	7	7	11	11	Aroostook Co., ME	Richard Neal	Richard Neal	1983	359
196 4/8	56 4/8	36 6/8	38 5/8	14 4/8	14	7 6/8	7 3/8	13	13	Biencourt Lake, QC	Rodier Dumont	Rodier Dumont	1987	359
196 4/8	64	37 2/8	37	12 5/8	16 2/8	7 1/8	7 3/8	12	17	Kechika River, BC	John R. Shotzberger	John R. Shotzberger	1990	359
196 4/8	59 4/8	38 2/8	38 3/8	14	14 1/8	8 2/8	8 3/8	10	12	Seine River, ON	Robert K. Reuther	Robert K. Reuther	1994	359
196 3/8	49 7/8	43	45 1/8	13	12	7	7 6/8	11	14	Buckinghorse River, BC	Fain J. Little	Fain J. Little	1967	365
196 3/8	57 7/8	40 1/8	40 2/8	12 3/8	12 3/8	7 2/8	7 3/8	11	11	Sand River, AB	Douglas R. Lowe	Douglas R. Lowe	1977	365
196 3/8	69 3/8	33 7/8	34 6/8	12 3/8	14 3/8	7 6/8	7 6/8	11	13	Blanchard River, BC	James T. Walter	James T. Walter	1987	365
196 2/8	52 4/8	37 1/8	37 6/8	15 3/8	15 5/8	7 2/8	6 7/8	14	18	Glaslyn, SK	Allan Johnson	Allan Johnson	1956	368
196 2/8	57 4/8	41 5/8	43 7/8	11 3/8	12 2/8	6 7/8	7 1/8	11	11	Pasco Hills, SK	Mac B. Ford	Mac B. Ford	1969	368
196 2/8	63	38 7/8	37 1/8	14 1/8	15 1/8	7 3/8	7 3/8	10	14	English River, ON	Melvin Vetse	Melvin Vetse	1969	368
196 2/8	53 4/8	38 4/8	40	13 4/8	13	7 3/8	7 3/8	14	14	Kluayaz Lake, BC	William F. Jury	William F. Jury	1970	368

Score	Greatest Spread	Length of Palm R	Length of Palm L	Width of Palm R	Width of Palm L	Circ. R	Circ. L	Pts R	Pts L	Locality	Hunter	Owner	Date	Rank
199 2/8	52 6/8	41 6/8	43 1/8	11 6/8	11 6/8	7 6/8	8 2/8	12	12	Cut Beaver Lake, SK	Don Thorimbert	Don Thorimbert	1979	368
199 2/8	54 2/8	40 7/8	43 5/8	13 5/8	13 6/8	7	7 2/8	11	14	Teslin Lake, BC	Douglas Schnabel	Douglas Schnabel	1994	368
199 1/8	55 3/8	39 5/8	37	12 6/8	12 2/8	7 5/8	7 6/8	15	15	Mayerthorpe, AB	Unknown	Bennie Ziemmer	PR 1965	374
199 1/8	57 3/8	37 6/8	36 4/8	12 7/8	13	7 4/8	7 6/8	14	14	Dixonville, AB	Edward W. Filpula	Edward W. Filpula	1977	374
199 1/8	52 3/8	43 5/8	43 4/8	12 4/8	11 6/8	8	7 7/8	11	12	Iskut, BC	Larry Zilinski	Larry Zilinski	1979	374
199 1/8	51 5/8	43 4/8	43 4/8	11 6/8	13 3/8	7 4/8	7 5/8	11	12	Coutts River, AB	George J. Thimer	George J. Thimer	1983	374
199 1/8	56 3/8	43 1/8	41 5/8	13	14	6 6/8	6 6/8	10	13	Victoria Creek, BC	Bradley Bowden	Bradley Bowden	1986	374
199 1/8	58 1/8	38 2/8	41 2/8	13 4/8	13 1/8	7 5/8	7 6/8	12	13	Fox Back Ridge, NS	Joseph MacIsaac	Joseph MacIsaac	1994	374
199 1/8	58 3/8	42 1/8	46 4/8	12 2/8	14 1/8	7	7 2/8	9	12	Cassiar Mts., BC	Edward D. Yates	Edward D. Yates	1997	374
199	58 6/8	38	35 4/8	16	17	7 5/8	7 6/8	12	9	Hornepayne, ON	Harry T. Young	Harry T. Young	1967	381
199	57 4/8	38 4/8	37 4/8	14 3/8	14	7 2/8	7 4/8	12	11	Stikine River, BC	Francis O.N. Morris	Francis O.N. Morris	1968	381
199	61 4/8	36 6/8	35 5/8	12	13 2/8	8	8	14	16	Timmins, ON	Domenic V. Ripepi	Domenic V. Ripepi	1968	381
199	51 4/8	41 6/8	44 1/8	17 6/8	15 3/8	7 5/8	7 4/8	13	14	Fox Creek, AB	Ken McDonald	Merv Zaddery	1969	381
199	53 4/8	41 3/8	41 1/8	14 1/8	13 3/8	7 2/8	7 7/8	9	14	Trout Lake, BC	William R. Lee	William R. Lee	1982	381
199	58 6/8	36 7/8	36 6/8	14 1/8	13 5/8	7 6/8	7 2/8	11	15	Otter Lake, MB	Horace R. Cockerill	Horace R. Cockerill	1985	381
199	62 4/8	39 2/8	40 4/8	13 2/8	14 2/8	8	8	13	12	Piscataquis Co., ME	Darlene M. Ross	Darlene M. Ross	1993	381
198 7/8	53 6/8	40	42	14 4/8	14 5/8	7 1/8	7 1/8	9	11	Aconitum Lake, BC	Blair G. Fisher	Blair G. Fisher	1994	389
198 7/8	56 5/8	41 7/8	43	13 7/8	13 7/8	7 3/8	7 3/8	12	10	Hotchkiss, AB	R.A. Anderson	R.A. Anderson	1960	389
198 7/8	54 5/8	42 2/8	39 3/8	14 4/8	11 7/8	8 2/8	8 2/8	11	11	Monkman Pass, BC	A.E. Haddrell	A.E. Haddrell	1971	389
198 7/8	54 5/8	37 2/8	37 3/8	13 2/8	13	6 7/8	6 7/8	15	15	Manning, AB	Eugene G. McGee	Eugene G. McGee	1975	389
198 7/8	53 3/8	41 5/8	40	15	12	8 2/8	7 6/8	13	13	Coconino Creek, BC	Allan C. Endersby	Allan C. Endersby	1980	389
198 7/8	60 7/8	45 6/8	43 5/8	11 6/8	11 6/8	7 7/8	7 7/8	7	7	Copper River, BC	J. William Hofsink	J. William Hofsink	1985	389
198 6/8	52	40 6/8	39 4/8	14	13 1/8	6 6/8	7	15	14	Prophet River, BC	T.D. Braden	T.D. Braden	1973	394
198 6/8	53 4/8	40 6/8	40 7/8	13 6/8	13 6/8	7 3/8	7 1/8	11	11	Mt. Laurier, BC	Don Miller	Don Miller	1985	394
198 5/8	61 3/8	39 6/8	36	12 6/8	16 3/8	7 7/8	8	12	12	Stony Lake, BC	George Kalischuk	George Kalischuk	1962	396
198 5/8	57 1/8	40 3/8	40 3/8	16 4/8	13 5/8	8 5/8	8	6	9	Lake Nipigon, ON	Ohne L. Raasch	Ohne L. Raasch	1991	396
198 4/8	62 2/8	36 4/8	36 7/8	13 5/8	16	6 6/8	6 5/8	15	12	Serpentine Lake, BC	Randolph P. Wilson	Randolph P. Wilson	1976	398
198 4/8	58	39 2/8	40 2/8	13 7/8	16	7 1/8	7 3/8	10	10	Spatsizi Plateau, BC	Gordon J. Birgbauer, Jr.	Gordon J. Birgbauer, Jr.	1986	398
198 4/8	58 4/8	41 6/8	42 3/8	14 4/8	18 5/8	7 3/8	7 2/8	8	8	Nazcha Creek, BC	William H. Heafner	William H. Heafner	1994	398
198 3/8	53 5/8	43 3/8	39 6/8	17 4/8	12 7/8	7 1/8	7 2/8	11	11	Robb, BC	Bernholdt R. Nystrom	Bernholdt R. Nystrom	1973	398
198 3/8	60 3/8	40 3/8	43	10 5/8	14 1/8	7	7	12	16	Besa River, BC	Tommy D. Prance	Tommy D. Prance	1977	401
198 3/8	54 5/8	43	39 6/8	14 1/8	14 2/8	7 2/8	7 4/8	11	13	Tatshenshini River, BC	Wayne Patterson	Wayne Patterson	1993	401
198 3/8	58 3/8	37 4/8	37 4/8	12	14	7 5/8	7 3/8	16	14	Denetiah Lake, BC	Douglas J. Dee	Douglas J. Dee	1996	401
198 2/8	57 4/8	38	38 6/8	12 2/8	12 4/8	7 3/8	7	13	11	Whitecourt, AB	Glen Cox	Richard Jensen	1960	405
198 2/8	54 2/8	39 6/8	41 5/8	13 2/8	12	7	7	14	12	Beale Lake, BC	John O. Forster	John O. Forster	1963	405
198 2/8	53 4/8	43 6/8	42 5/8	12 6/8	12 2/8	6 7/8	7 1/8	11	11	Prairie River, BC	C.J. McElroy	C.J. McElroy	1967	405
198 2/8	59 4/8	36 5/8	41 5/8	15 6/8	17	7 1/8	7 1/8	14	14	Lake Co., MN	D.P. & H. Bradley	D.P. & H. Bradley	1973	405
198 2/8	57	40 7/8	38 6/8	11 4/8	12 7/8	7 5/8	7 3/8	13	13	Heart Mts., BC	Richard E. Radavich	Richard E. Radavich	1989	405
198 2/8	51 2/8	38 7/8	44 6/8	15 4/8	14 5/8	9 4/8	8	12	13	Carp Lake, BC	Harvey G. Underwood	Harvey G. Underwood	1994	405
198 1/8	58 1/8	43 6/8	38 6/8	14 2/8	15	7 4/8	8	10	10	Crow Wing Co., MN	Mr. Gustetson	Bob Coborn	PR 1920	411
198 1/8	56 5/8	42	42	12 1/8	12 1/8	7 7/8	7 5/8	9	13	Saskatchewan	Neil Oliver	Neil Oliver	1954	411
198 1/8	56 3/8	40	43 2/8	12 7/8	12 7/8	7 1/8	7 2/8	13	13	Dore Lake, SK	O. Dore	O. Dore	1966	411
198 1/8	63 5/8	40 3/8	34	12 4/8	11 6/8	7 6/8	8 6/8	12	15	Chapleau, ON	Chester Anderegg	Chester Anderegg	1968	411
198 1/8	50 7/8	39 5/8	41	16	17	7 3/8	8 1/8	15	13	Fraser River, BC	J. Henry Scown	J. Henry Scown	1973	411
198 1/8	55 7/8	42 4/8	42 7/8	13 6/8	13 6/8	7 3/8	7 5/8	13	14	Hluey Lakes, BC	Dale Campbell	Dale Campbell	1982	411
198	62 2/8	37 3/8	38 4/8	11 4/8	12	7	7	9	9	Cold Fish Lake, BC	Dan Edwards	Dan Edwards	1961	417
198	57	37	37 2/8	14 3/8	13	6 4/8	6 4/8	15	14	Hardwood Lake, ON	Weston Cook	Weston Cook	1963	417

CANADA MOOSE

Alces alces americana and Alces alces andersoni

Score	Greatest Spread	Length of Palm R	L	Width of Palm R	L	Circumference of Beam at Smallest Place R	L	Number of Normal Points R	L	Locality	Hunter	Owner	Date Killed	Rank
198	56 4/8	38 3/8	36 3/8	15 7/8	14 6/8	7 5/8	7 6/8	12	14	Crooked Lake, BC	J.W. Cornwall	J.W. Cornwall	1977	417
198	63 3/8	37	36 2/8	14 2/8	15	7	6 7/8	10	11	Upper Besa River, BC	Lloyd Schoenauer	Lloyd Schoenauer	1977	417
198	54 2/8	39 4/8	42 6/8	16 2/8	17	7 1/8	7 2/8	11	9	Pink Mt., BC	Wallace E. Anderson	Wallace E. Anderson	1982	417
197 7/8	55 7/8	44 1/8	40 6/8	11 5/8	13 3/8	7 6/8	7 5/8	11	11	Prophet River, BC	Paul W. Sharp	Paul W. Sharp	1963	422
197 7/8	59 7/8	39 6/8	40 1/8	11 4/8	12	7 6/8	7 6/8	10	11	Pink Mt., BC	Robert H. Ruth	Robert H. Ruth	1964	422
197 7/8	62 5/8	39	39	11 6/8	10 5/8	8	8 1/8	12	10	Swan Plain, SK	Gene Petryshyn	Gene Petryshyn	1971	422
197 7/8	56 3/8	40 2/8	40 7/8	14	15	7 5/8	7 4/8	9	9	Sikanni Chief River, BC	Nicholas M. Esposito	Nicholas M. Esposito	1974	422
197 7/8	49 7/8	42 7/8	43	13 6/8	13 6/8	7 3/8	7 5/8	10	10	Fish Lake, BC	Richard E. Glenz	Richard E. Glenz	1993	422
197 6/8	63 6/8	38 7/8	41 7/8	10 4/8	10 3/8	6 7/8	6 6/8	9	11	Willow Creek, AB	Helmut Vollmer	Helmut Vollmer	1960	427
197 6/8	52	37 3/8	39 3/8	14 2/8	13 4/8	7 1/8	7 1/8	15	15	Marion Lake, BC	Virgil W. Binkley	Virgil W. Binkley	1964	427
197 6/8	59 6/8	34 5/8	36 6/8	14 4/8	12 4/8	7	6 7/8	15	16	Pipestone River, ON	Howard E. Bennett	Howard E. Bennett	1973	427
197 5/8	56 7/8	42 1/8	38 2/8	13 1/8	13 2/8	7 2/8	7	12	12	Glaslyn, SK	Ernest Noble	Ernest Noble	1960	430
197 5/8	57 5/8	44	43 2/8	14 1/8	11 6/8	7 4/8	7 4/8	12	9	Simeon Lake, ON	Craig L. Chandonnet	Craig L. Chandonnet	1986	430
197 5/8	56 6/8	41 1/8	39 1/8	14 2/8	14 6/8	7 1/8	7 2/8	11	13	Stikine River, BC	Chad Clayburg	Chad Clayburg	1989	430
197 5/8	52 5/8	39 3/8	39 5/8	13 2/8	13 5/8	7 7/8	7 7/8	13	12	Peace River, AB	Angela Wolansky	Angela Wolansky	1993	430
197 5/8	56 1/8	44 4/8	42 6/8	12 2/8	14	6 6/8	6 7/8	9	11	Cassiar Mts., BC	Dennis D. Brust	Dennis D. Brust	1995	430
197 4/8	57 4/8	42 5/8	41 5/8	10 4/8	14 1/8	7	7	11	15	Telegraph Creek, BC	Gordon Best	Gordon Best	1968	435
197 4/8	51 4/8	36 4/8	37 1/8	16 4/8	17 2/8	8	8	12	15	Cassiar Mts., BC	Russell H. Underdahl	Russell H. Underdahl	1968	435
197 4/8	56 2/8	39 3/8	39 4/8	13 6/8	13	7 2/8	7 3/8	14	11	Atlin, BC	John Konrad	John Konrad	1973	435
197 4/8	54 4/8	41	42 4/8	12 2/8	12	7 4/8	7 6/8	11	13	Dease River, BC	Terry Jackson	Terry Jackson	1975	435
197 4/8	50 6/8	43 4/8	41 4/8	13 4/8	13 3/8	7 4/8	7 4/8	11	11	Kelly Creek, BC	Leonard O. Farlow	Leonard O. Farlow	1980	435
197 4/8	63 2/8	39 5/8	38 5/8	15	15 2/8	7	7	10	8	Cassiar Mts., BC	Michael J. Jacobson	Michael J. Jacobson	1986	435
197 4/8	49 4/8	40 3/8	41 3/8	13 2/8	13 5/8	7 3/8	7 3/8	14	13	Albany River, ON	Lee H. Monge	Lee H. Monge	1986	435
197 4/8	47 6/8	40 2/8	47 6/8	13 1/8	14 6/8	7 4/8	8 1/8	14	16	Inverness River, AB	Steve C. Klask	Steve C. Klask	1988	435
197 3/8	58 1/8	40 1/8	41 7/8	13 7/8	13 4/8	8	8	11	8	Sikanni Chief River, BC	Leslie Bowling	Leslie Bowling	1962	443
197 3/8	48 3/8	43 4/8	47 4/8	13	11 2/8	7 6/8	7 6/8	12	12	Cabin Lake, BC	W. Harrison	W. Harrison	1964	443
197 3/8	57 5/8	41 3/8	38 3/8	13 2/8	16 1/8	7 2/8	7 2/8	11	15	Firth Lake, BC	Gordon J. Pengelly	Gordon J. Pengelly	1973	443
197 3/8	50 1/8	39 7/8	39 5/8	13	13 2/8	7 1/8	7	14	14	Fleming Lake, MN	Peter Holland	Peter Holland	1976	443
197 2/8	58 4/8	39 1/8	37 4/8	17 4/8	17 2/8	6 5/8	6 6/8	8	8	St. Louis Co., MN	Paul W. Anthony	MN Dept. of Natl. Resc.	1906	447
197 2/8	56 4/8	37 6/8	38 4/8	10 6/8	12 2/8	7 7/8	8 2/8	14	15	Jackfish Lake, AB	Unknown	Ovar Uggen	1955	447
197 2/8	50 4/8	40 5/8	43 4/8	13	16 2/8	7 6/8	7 6/8	12	15	Terminus Mt., BC	Basil C. Bradbury	Basil C. Bradbury	1962	447
197 2/8	50	44	43 5/8	14 4/8	17 4/8	7 4/8	7 4/8	8	8	Liard Plateau, BC	George Roberts	George Roberts	1970	447
197 2/8	59 4/8	36 3/8	34 5/8	15 5/8	14	7 3/8	7 2/8	13	13	Hayes River, MB	John R. Schleicher	John R. Schleicher	1990	447
197 2/8	59 6/8	38 4/8	36 1/8	13 6/8	13 6/8	6 7/8	6 7/8	14	12	Penobscot Co., ME	Tabitha S. Dudley	Tabitha S. Dudley	1996	447
197 1/8	56 5/8	40 4/8	38 1/8	13 4/8	13 3/8	7 7/8	7 7/8	11	13	Tisdale, SK	Bill Hrechka	Bill Hrechka	1960	453
197 1/8	54 7/8	38 4/8	43 2/8	12 7/8	15 4/8	6 6/8	6 6/8	13	14	Pink Mt., BC	Allison R. Smith	Allison R. Smith	1963	453
197 1/8	53 3/8	38 5/8	39 7/8	14 4/8	14 6/8	7 6/8	8	11	12	Fir River, SK	Harold Kriger	Harold Kriger	1994	453
197	57 6/8	38	38 4/8	11 2/8	11 2/8	7 3/8	7 4/8	13	13	Cold Fish Lake, BC	George W. Hale	George W. Hale	1967	456

Score	Greatest Spread	Width of Palm R	Width of Palm L	Length of Palm R	Length of Palm L	Circumference R	Circumference L	Points R	Locality	Points L	Hunter	Owner	Date Killed	Rank
197	54 2/8	39 1/8	40	17 4/8	15 3/8	7 2/8	6 7/8	11	Brothers Lake, BC	10	William D. Phifer	William D. Phifer	1971	456
197	60 6/8	37 4/8	39 3/8	12 6/8	12 1/8	7 4/8	7 5/8	11	Swan Lake, BC	13	Carl E. Larson	Wild Kingdom Tax.	1975	456
197	48 4/8	41 2/8	40 4/8	14 2/8	13 6/8	7 2/8	7	16	Turnagain River, BC	13	Jack W. Lester, Jr.	Jack W. Lester, Jr.	1982	456
197	58	40 5/8	42 6/8	12	13 1/8	7 7/8	8	9	Chinchaga River, AB	13	Glen Mulzet	Glen Mulzet	1986	456
196 7/8	58 7/8	38 5/8	36 3/8	13 5/8	12 5/8	7	7	13	Weeks, SK	14	Ken Holloway	Ken Holloway	1961	461
196 7/8	54 1/8	39 4/8	39 5/8	14 7/8	13 3/8	7 5/8	7 4/8	11	Slave Lake, AB	13	Kathleen Wickersham	Ernest Wickersham	1967	461
196 7/8	50 7/8	41 2/8	39 5/8	20 4/8	13 7/8	7 4/8	7	13	Cassiar Mts., BC	13	Larry Herwick	Larry Herwick	1979	461
196 7/8	62 3/8	43	38 3/8	13 6/8	12	7 3/8	7 4/8	14	Pink Mt., BC	10	Tony J. Farace	Tony J. Farace	1984	461
196 7/8	55 7/8	40 1/8	40 2/8	12 2/8	13 7/8	7 2/8	7 1/8	11	Polk Co., MN	11	William H. Vollbrecht, Jr.	William H. Vollbrecht, Jr.	1985	461
196 7/8	50 1/8	40 2/8	42 2/8	14 4/8	14 2/8	6 7/8	7 1/8	12	Christina Falls, BC	14	David V. Collis	David V. Collis	1987	461
196 7/8	59 7/8	35 7/8	36 2/8	14 6/8	12 4/8	7 1/8	6 7/8	13	Lake Dumoine, QC	13	Claude Lapointe	Claude Lapointe	1993	461
196 7/8	49 6/8	43	43	14 6/8	12 6/8	6 6/8	6 6/8	15	Hines Creek, AB	11	Harry Kashuba	Harry Kashuba	1959	461
196 6/8	57	40 7/8	39 4/8	13 7/8	14 1/8	7 4/8	7 1/8	9	Atlin, BC	11	Dennis Downton	Dennis Downton	1969	468
196 6/8	57 6/8	36	38 2/8	16 4/8	16 3/8	7 1/8	7 3/8	10	Wapiti River, AB	12	John J. Seeliger	John J. Seeliger	1985	468
196 6/8	56	41 2/8	38	15 6/8	14 5/8	6 6/8	6 6/8	12	Scoop Lake, BC	11	Mark S. Coles	Mark S. Coles	1996	468
196 6/8	58 5/8	41 4/8	40 1/8	11 7/8	15 7/8	7	7 2/8	13	Stony Lake, BC	10	George Kalischuk	George Kalischuk	1963	468
196 5/8	53 3/8	42 3/8	43 7/8	12	14 4/8	7 4/8	7 2/8	13	Atlin, BC	11	Ernest Wilfong	Ernest Wilfong	1965	472
196 5/8	50 3/8	42 1/8	42 7/8	15 1/8	11 6/8	8 2/8	7 3/8	13	Cassiar, BC	11	Richard Pain	Richard Pain	1967	472
196 5/8	53 3/8	42 3/8	40 3/8	14	13 5/8	6 6/8	8 3/8	11	Medicine Lake, AB	13	Stan Reiser	Stan Reiser	1967	472
196 5/8	57 7/8	40 2/8	39 4/8	11 3/8	11 4/8	7 4/8	6 5/8	12	Telegraph Creek, BC	11	Paul Inzanti, Jr.	Paul Inzanti, Jr.	1969	472
196 5/8	62 5/8	41 4/8	39 3/8	11 5/8	11 7/8	7	7	11	Adsit Creek, BC	9	Loren D. Bliss	Loren D. Bliss	1980	472
196 5/8	53 7/8	38 2/8	36 7/8	16 4/8	16 4/8	7	7	14	Lake Co., MN	12	Brian S. Agnoli	Brian S. Agnoli	1981	472
196 4/8	46 6/8	37	37 4/8	18 1/8	14	7 6/8	7 2/8	13	Belcourt Lake, BC	12	Robert Agnello	Robert Agnello	1965	472
196 4/8	50 4/8	39 6/8	43 2/8	14	12 5/8	8	7 5/8	13	Perrault Falls, ON	13	A.H. Nettleship	A.H. Nettleship	1967	479
196 4/8	56 6/8	38 2/8	41 3/8	12	12 1/8	7 2/8	7 3/8	12	Sikanni Chief River, BC	13	W.C. Spencer	W.C. Spencer	1970	479
196 4/8	56 6/8	39 2/8	39 4/8	11 3/8	14 6/8	7 5/8	7 2/8	14	Kula Tan Tan River, BC	12	Arnold J. Kaslon	Arnold J. Kaslon	1972	479
196 4/8	53 2/8	43 2/8	38 6/8	14 6/8	16 5/8	7 3/8	7 1/8	11	Turnagain River, BC	13	George H. Biddle	George H. Biddle	1973	479
196 4/8	45 6/8	42 1/8	44 5/8	13 1/8	13 1/8	7 2/8	7 5/8	13	Pink Mt., BC	13	Gary Bloxham	Gary Bloxham	1973	479
196 4/8	60	36 2/8	36 6/8	13 6/8	16 3/8	7 1/8	7 6/8	9	Lake Co., MN	8	Roy H. Anderson	Roy H. Anderson	1977	479
196 4/8	57 4/8	41 6/8	41	10 4/8	13 6/8	7 5/8	7 4/8	13	Swan Lake, BC	13	Patricia Markofer	Patricia Markofer	1989	479
196 3/8	59 3/8	43 3/8	38 4/8	12 3/8	12 2/8	7 6/8	7 5/8	12	Abitibi Canyon, ON	12	Pelham Glasier	Pelham Glasier	1951	479
196 3/8	52 1/8	38 2/8	41 4/8	15 4/8	14 1/8	7 4/8	7 7/8	11	Green Lake, SK	11	Mike Spies	Mike Spies	1959	487
196 3/8	58 1/8	39 4/8	37 4/8	14 1/8	12 2/8	8 3/8	6 7/8	10	Cassiar Mts., BC	10	E. David Slye	E. David Slye	1967	487
196 2/8	59	43	39 4/8	12 4/8	12 4/8	7 4/8	7 1/8	10	Jack Pine, ON	10	William Picht	William Picht	1963	487
196 2/8	55 2/8	39 7/8	43	13 6/8	15 4/8	6 7/8	7 3/8	10	Anguille Mts., NF	12	Robert D. Smith	Robert D. Smith	1963	490
196 2/8	55 4/8	35 4/8	39 7/8	16 2/8	13 7/8	7 1/8	7 6/8	12	Cassiar Mts., BC	13	Bryan Upchurch	Bryan Upchurch	1975	490
196 2/8	56 6/8	41 4/8	37	14	14 3/8	7	7 4/8	14	Aroostook Co., ME	9	R.E. Gatchell & C. Dole	Robert E. Gatchell	1982	490
196 2/8	54	43	41 2/8	12 5/8	12 6/8	7 4/8	8 3/8	11	Pleasant Bay, NS	9	Richard M. Bouchard	Richard M. Bouchard	1992	490
196 2/8	52 2/8	42 6/8	42 6/8	14	12 5/8	8 2/8	7 5/8	10	Gardner Lake, AB	13	Edward Capes, Jr.	Edward Capes, Jr.	1992	490
196 2/8	54 2/8	41 2/8	41 2/8	12 5/8	10 7/8	7 4/8	7 1/8	13	Cassiar Mts., BC	11	Alan C. Cole	Alan C. Cole	1993	490
196 2/8	56 2/8	41 7/8	41 7/8	13	12 6/8	7 3/8	7 2/8	12	Meikle River, AB	9	Robert Kramer	R. Kramer & B. Friedel	1993	490
196 2/8	62 6/8	35 1/8	37	12 6/8	12 6/8	7 2/8	6 7/8	12	Essex Co., VT	11	Dale E. Potter	Dale E. Potter	1996	490
196 2/8	55 5/8	36 6/8	37	16 6/8	16 6/8	6 7/8	7 6/8	11	Endeavor, SK	13	G.N. Galbraith	G.N. Galbraith	1955	490
196 1/8	55 7/8	42 2/8	39 2/8	13 7/8	13 4/8	7 6/8	7 4/8	10	Jack Pine River, ON	16	M.H. Brown	M.H. Brown	1962	499
196 1/8	56 1/8	38	38 2/8	13 2/8	13 2/8	7 1/8	6 6/8	13	Atlin, BC	14	Cliff Schmidt	Cliff Schmidt	1966	499
196 1/8	49 1/8	42 2/8	42 2/8	11 3/8	11 2/8	7	7	13	Atlin, BC	13	H.J. Schwegler	H.J. Schwegler	1967	499
196 1/8	52 3/8	41 5/8	40 1/8	15 4/8	14 2/8	7 4/8	7 4/8	10	Frog River, BC	12	Robert McMurray	Robert McMurray	1968	499

CANADA MOOSE

Alces alces americana and Alces alces andersoni

Score	Greatest Spread	Length of Palm R	L	Width of Palm R	L	Circumference of Beam at Smallest Place R	L	Number of Normal Points R	L	Locality	Hunter	Owner	Date Killed	Rank
196 1/8	51 5/8	38 2/8	37 4/8	14 1/8	12 3/8	7 3/8	7 3/8	15	16	Ft. St. John, BC	Kanton R. Flemming	Kanton R. Flemming	1975	499
196 1/8	51 1/8	41 2/8	42 4/8	12 4/8	12 3/8	8 1/8	7 7/8	13	11	Penobscot Co., ME	Richard A. Record	Richard A. Record	1982	499
196 1/8	59 5/8	38 3/8	40 4/8	12 5/8	13 4/8	7 2/8	7 2/8	13	10	Fort Nelson, BC	Don C. Hurlbut	Don C. Hurlbut	1996	499
196	56 2/8	38 7/8	39 6/8	13 3/8	14 6/8	8	7 5/8	11	13	Pelican River, AB	Douglas A. Stoller	Douglas A. Stoller	1971	507
196	54 6/8	43 7/8	40 4/8	10 5/8	12 2/8	7	7	13	14	Tatuk Lake, BC	Erling E. Gull	Erling E. Gull	1980	507
196	53 6/8	39 2/8	40 3/8	13 1/8	15 5/8	6 6/8	6 7/8	12	12	Wollaston Lake, SK	Daryl V. Johannesen	Daryl V. Johannesen	1982	507
196	49 6/8	41	40 4/8	13 3/8	14 3/8	7 2/8	7 4/8	12	15	Birchwood Creek, AB	Gert B. Nielsen	Gert B. Nielsen	1990	507
196	57	38	38 4/8	15 5/8	12	7 6/8	7 4/8	13	12	Somerset Co., ME	Carol A. Hepfner	Carol A. Hepfner	1994	507
196	53 4/8	40 7/8	37 6/8	14 6/8	14	7 6/8	7 4/8	12	12	Franklin Co., ME	Richmond E. Yorke, Jr.	Richmond E. Yorke, Jr.	1994	507
195 7/8	56 3/8	37 4/8	40 3/8	12 6/8	13 5/8	7 6/8	7 4/8	13	12	Cassiar, BC	Donald F. Conway	Donald F. Conway	1965	513
195 7/8	54 1/8	37	41 7/8	14	13 6/8	7 1/8	7 2/8	13	13	Sheep Creek, AB	S.J. Blaupot Ten Cate	S.J. Blaupot Ten Cate	1966	513
195 7/8	56	38 6/8	38	11 3/8	11 3/8	8 4/8	8 4/8	15	12	Prophet River, BC	Earl Mumaw	Earl Mumaw	1957	515
195 6/8	53 4/8	38 2/8	39 1/8	12 7/8	13 6/8	7 2/8	7	13	14	Hudson Bay, SK	Charles Hamilton	Charles Hamilton	1964	515
195 6/8	59	44	43 2/8	13 1/8	13 2/8	7	7 1/8	10	14	Smoky River, AB	Ken G. Johnson	Ken G. Johnson	1966	515
195 6/8	56 2/8	42 6/8	43 4/8	12 2/8	12	7 2/8	7 2/8	11	12	Ft. St. John, BC	Louis M. Soetebeer	Louis M. Soetebeer	1969	515
195 6/8	48 6/8	42 4/8	42 3/8	12	13 7/8	8 1/8	8 2/8	11	16	Pasquia Hills, SK	Ray Eros	Ray Eros	1985	515
195 6/8	52 6/8	40 1/8	42 3/8	13 7/8	13 1/8	7 2/8	7 3/8	11	15	Denetiah Lake, BC	Scott S. Snyder	Scott S. Snyder	1995	515
195 5/8	57 7/8	36 6/8	40 6/8	12 5/8	16 4/8	7 4/8	7 7/8	12	13	Pink Mt., BC	Michael H. LaViolette	Michael H. LaViolette	1989	521
195 5/8	57 3/8	38 4/8	39 5/8	12 7/8	12 6/8	6 7/8	7	11	13	Uslika Lake, BC	Brad K. Smith	Brad K. Smith	1993	521
195 4/8	58	37 2/8	37 2/8	15 1/8	15	7 4/8	7 2/8	9	13	Pasquia Hills, SK	Henry Dyck	Henry Dyck	1955	523
195 4/8	65 2/8	39	40 2/8	11 4/8	10	7 1/8	7 1/8	9	9	Sheep Creek, AB	H.C. Early	H.C. Early	1957	523
195 4/8	57 6/8	38 4/8	39 2/8	12 4/8	13 3/8	8	7 7/8	11	10	Blanchard River, BC	William E. Lauffer	William E. Lauffer	1969	523
195 4/8	61	37 5/8	36 2/8	13 2/8	13 3/8	7 6/8	7 6/8	10	13	Whitecourt, AB	John E. Esslinger	John E. Esslinger	1971	523
195 4/8	54 6/8	38 7/8	39 4/8	13 4/8	13 6/8	8 1/8	8	13	10	Stikine River, BC	Manfred Beier	Manfred Beier	1976	523
195 4/8	57 4/8	37 7/8	40 6/8	11 3/8	16	7 3/8	7 2/8	13	13	Somerset Co., ME	Frank White	Frank White	1983	523
195 4/8	55 4/8	41 4/8	41 7/8	14 2/8	13 1/8	6 6/8	6 6/8	9	9	Turnagain Lake, BC	Fenton C. Carter	Fenton C. Carter	1985	523
195 4/8	52 2/8	39	39 4/8	13	13 1/8	6 5/8	6 5/8	13	16	Spatsizi Wilderness, BC	J.D. O'Rear	J.D. O'Rear	1985	523
195 4/8	52 4/8	43 4/8	39 5/8	12 3/8	12 1/8	7	6 6/8	13	16	Smoky River, AB	Thomas F. Wood	Thomas F. Wood	1996	523
195 3/8	63 3/8	36 2/8	37 1/8	14 3/8	13 5/8	7 2/8	7 1/8	9	9	Trembleur Lake, BC	Harry McCarter	Harry McCarter	1965	532
195 3/8	57 3/8	38 7/8	39 5/8	12 4/8	12 7/8	7 7/8	7 5/8	10	10	Atlin, BC	Jerome A. Ree	Jerome A. Ree	1965	532
195 3/8	52 5/8	39 5/8	38 7/8	13	12 5/8	6 7/8	7	13	14	Prophet River, BC	Ronald B. Sorensen	Ronald B. Sorensen	1967	532
195 3/8	54 1/8	38 2/8	40 1/8	12 5/8	13 7/8	7 6/8	7 6/8	12	12	Kechika Range, BC	Frank S. Kohar	Frank S. Kohar	1968	532
195 3/8	55 7/8	39 1/8	43 6/8	15	13 7/8	6 6/8	7	10	13	Chip Lake, AB	Elon Johnson	Elon Johnson	1984	532
195 3/8	55 7/8	39	37 1/8	16	15 6/8	6 7/8	6 7/8	10	10	Metsantan Lake, BC	Dwight L. Boettcher	Dwight L. Boettcher	1986	532
195 3/8	61 5/8	36 2/8	37	12 3/8	13 2/8	7 2/8	7 4/8	12	11	Duck Mt., MB	Nick Malchuk	Nick Malchuk	1994	532
195 2/8	60	39 4/8	39 2/8	12 7/8	11 1/8	7 3/8	7 2/8	10	13	Atlin, BC	Wilbert Hoffman	Wildl. Tax. Studios	1966	539
195 2/8	57 4/8	39 7/8	42 7/8	12 4/8	13 5/8	7 4/8	7 5/8	9	11	British Columbia	Len Anderson	Len Anderson	1967	539
195 2/8	56 2/8	41 6/8	40	10 3/8	13	7 1/8	7 4/8	12	14	Blanchard River, BC	Pat Archibald	Pat Archibald	1969	539

Score	Greatest Spread	Length of Palm R	Length of Palm L	Width of Palm R	Width of Palm L	Circ. R	Circ. L	Pts R	Pts L	Locality	Owner	Hunter	Date	Rank
195 2/8	60	33 5/8	39 2/8	14 5/8	19 5/8	7 3/8	7 4/8	12	15	Ignace, ON	Ervey W. Smith	Ervey W. Smith	1969	539
195 2/8	59 2/8	38 1/8	40	14 5/8	14 3/8	8 4/8	8 4/8	7	13	Lake Nipigon, ON	Danny E. Breivogel	Danny E. Breivogel	1974	539
195 2/8	54	37 4/8	39	13	14 4/8	7 1/8	7 3/8	13	13	Turnagain River, BC	Donald E. Franklin	Donald E. Franklin	1977	539
195 2/8	52	39 6/8	41 5/8	13 4/8	13 5/8	7 3/8	7 3/8	11	15	Ospika River, BC	John L. Fullmer	John L. Fullmer	1977	539
195 2/8	54 4/8	35	42	15 2/8	15 6/8	7 1/8	7 2/8	13	17	Piscataquis Co., ME	W.H. Gagnon, Jr.	W.H. Gagnon, Jr. & R.R. Gagnon	1980	539
195 2/8	57 2/8	41 6/8	42	12	12 3/8	7 3/8	7 2/8	8	8	Nuthinaw Mt., BC	Robert S. Curtis	Robert S. Curtis	1984	539
195 1/8	55 1/8	40	42 6/8	13	12 2/8	7 7/8	7 6/8	10	14	Berland River, AB	W.C. Kadatz	W.C. Kadatz	1962	548
195 1/8	55 3/8	39 5/8	39 5/8	11 5/8	11 6/8	8 1/8	7 5/8	12	11	Hudson Bay, SK	Walter Sukkau	Walter Sukkau	1964	548
195 1/8	56 3/8	38 5/8	39 1/8	13 7/8	14 7/8	7	6 7/8	10	11	British Columbia	Charles Waugaman	Charles Waugaman	1969	548
195 1/8	56 1/8	36	36 5/8	15 3/8	16	6 4/8	7 1/8	11	14	Muskwa River, BC	Buck Heide	Buck Heide	1979	548
195 1/8	61 5/8	39	34 2/8	14 1/8	15 1/8	7 2/8	5 7/8	13	13	Terminus Mt., BC	Modesta S. Williams	Modesta S. Williams	1982	548
195 1/8	58 7/8	38 3/8	38 3/8	11 5/8	12 2/8	7 3/8	7 3/8	11	11	Ash Mt., BC	H. Frank Grainger	H. Frank Grainger	1984	548
195 1/8	55 3/8	36 7/8	36 1/8	12 4/8	13 3/8	7 4/8	7 4/8	14	14	Goodwin Lake, BC	Delmar W. Welch	Delmar W. Welch	1986	548
195 1/8	54 1/8	38 7/8	40 3/8	12 6/8	12 3/8	7 2/8	7 2/8	12	13	Piscataquis Co., ME	Frank M. Harris	Frank M. Harris	1991	548
195	57 6/8	34 3/8	38 2/8	14 5/8	14	7 6/8	7 6/8	15	13	Little Codroy Pond, NF	J. Russell Allison	J. Russell Allison	1957	556
195	57 4/8	37 6/8	38 2/8	11 5/8	12 5/8	6 3/8	6 5/8	14	11	Turner Valley, AB	Bart Rockwell	Bart Rockwell	1958	556
195	58	37 3/8	42 1/8	13 1/8	12 7/8	7 2/8	7 3/8	13	10	Pontiac Co., QC	Roger Cashdollar	Roger Cashdollar	1966	556
195	52	41 5/8	40	14	15 2/8	7 4/8	8	13	11	Houston, BC	R. Starnes	R. Starnes	1966	556
195	54 6/8	38	37 2/8	15	14 6/8	7 3/8	7 1/8	11	11	Piscataquis Co., ME	Keith B. Gould	Keith B. Gould	1980	556
195	54 2/8	39	38 2/8	14	14 3/8	7 1/8	7 3/8	11	8	Lake Co., MN	Lewis N. Hostrawser	Lewis N. Hostrawser	1981	556
195	53 4/8	40 1/8	40	12 4/8	13 7/8	7 2/8	7 2/8	10	15	Piscatiquis Co., ME	Lester Whitten	Cecile D. Therrien	1982	556
195	61 4/8	37 4/8	36 6/8	14 3/8	14 3/8	8	8	10	9	Aroostook Co., ME	Sterling W. Waterman	Sterling W. Waterman	1982	556
228 6/8*	70	39 6/8	42 2/8	16 7/8	17 5/8	8 1/8	8 3/8	17	10	MacEachern Lake, NS	Brenton Holland	Glenwood Holland	1997	
226 1/8*	67 1/8	43	47 3/8	20	22 3/8	8 4/8	7 7/8	11	11	Cape North, NS	James A. Harris	James A. Harris	1995	
217 7/8*	58 1/8	44 6/8	42 4/8	19 2/8	19 6/8	8 1/8	8 1/8	15	15	Meat Cove, NS	David M. De Mille	David M. De Mille	1994	
213 4/8*	56 6/8	44 2/8	44 5/8	16	17 2/8	7 1/8	7 1/8	12	12	Muskwa River, BC	Gino Perri	Gino Perri	1993	

* Final score is subject to revision by additional verifying measurements.

CATEGORY
CANADA MOOSE

SCORE
215

HUNTER
STEVEN D. KELLESVIG

LOCATION
TESLIN LAKE, BC

DATE OF KILL
SEPTEMBER 1997

CATEGORY
CANADA MOOSE

SCORE
199-1/8

HUNTER
EDWARD D. YATES

LOCATION
CASSIAR MTS., BC

DATE OF KILL
SEPTEMBER 1997

CATEGORY
CANADA MOOSE

SCORE
196-6/8

HUNTER
MARK S. COLES

LOCATION
SCOOP LAKE, BC

DATE OF KILL
SEPTEMBER 1996

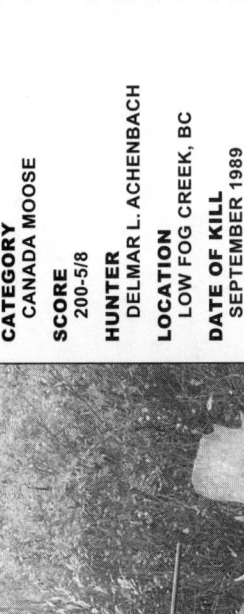

CATEGORY
CANADA MOOSE

SCORE
200-5/8

HUNTER
DELMAR L. ACHENBACH

LOCATION
LOW FOG CREEK, BC

DATE OF KILL
SEPTEMBER 1989

CATEGORY
CANADA MOOSE

SCORE
199-3/8

HUNTER
JAMES T. WALTER

LOCATION
BLANCHARD RIVER, BC

DATE OF KILL
SEPTEMBER 1987

CATEGORY
CANADA MOOSE

SCORE
208-3/8

HUNTER
ROBERT J. MATYAS

LOCATION
TAKU RIVER, BC

DATE OF KILL
OCTOBER 1989

443

It was during the late summer of 1994 that John A. Crouse caught the reflection of antlers belonging to an Alaska-Yukon moose near Fortymile River, Alaska.

"Suddenly, the bull stood up broadside to me and turned its head in our direction. My heart pounded. A slight breeze in our faces confirmed the bull didn't smell our scent. Could it have heard me whispering? I got back down over my scope. The bull stared at me. Ragged threads of velvet dangled from its front brow tines and gunny sack-size pieces draped from each palm.

"I tried to put the cross hairs behind its front shoulder but a branch blocked a clean shot. The bull stood as I inched to my right. My sights found the spot, and I squeezed the trigger. I heard the 'whump' of a solid hit and watched the bull leap into the air, whirl and run 180 feet before dropping to the ground. I chambered another round into my .270 Winchester and again found the bull in my scope.

"The bull stood its ground as I watched it for several seconds. I decided I didn't want the moose getting any farther from our camp. The second shot rocked the bull. In a final effort it tried to leap forward but its hind legs collapsed. The bull toppled over backwards, plowing its antlers into the soft earth."

Crouse and hunting partners, Dennis and Doug Chester, spent the remainder of that memorable September day, plus another full day and a half, butchering and packing the meat and the antlers back to their camp. Crouse knew the moose's rack was big – more than 60 inches wide. What he didn't figure was just how those antlers might fit into a Cessna.

When Charlie and Ron arrived with their Cubs, they were impressed with the rack. Charlie commented that it was the biggest set of antlers he had ever seen. Ron worried that we might not be able to get the antlers out with the small planes. He feared the wide palms might cause too much drag.

"I suggested we split the skull and put the antlers inside the airplane rather than tying them to the wing strut, but Charlie said, 'No way.' He said he wanted them scored by a Boone and Crockett Club official measurer. Charlie knew that trophies with split skulls are not eligible for entry in Boone and Crockett.

"The tips of the antlers were just a few short inches from the ground as they hung from the wing strut of Charlie's Cub. He decided to try and hop them over a few miles to an abandoned mine where they could land a larger plane to ferry them the rest of the way back to Tok. The plane, with its cumbersome load, quickly lifted off the ground and disappeared after a few minutes.

"I returned to Cordova just as the antlers arrived. The antlers did not fit into a Cessna 185, so a Cessna 206 with double cargo doors was flown out to retrieve them. A truck driver, on his route to Anchorage, brought them to Doug for storage. At the end of the 60-day drying period, Doug made the arrangements to have the antlers officially measured."

Upon receiving the news in late November, Crouse couldn't believe what he was told. Scored at 261-5/8, his trophy had set a new World's Record for Alaska-Yukon moose. ∎

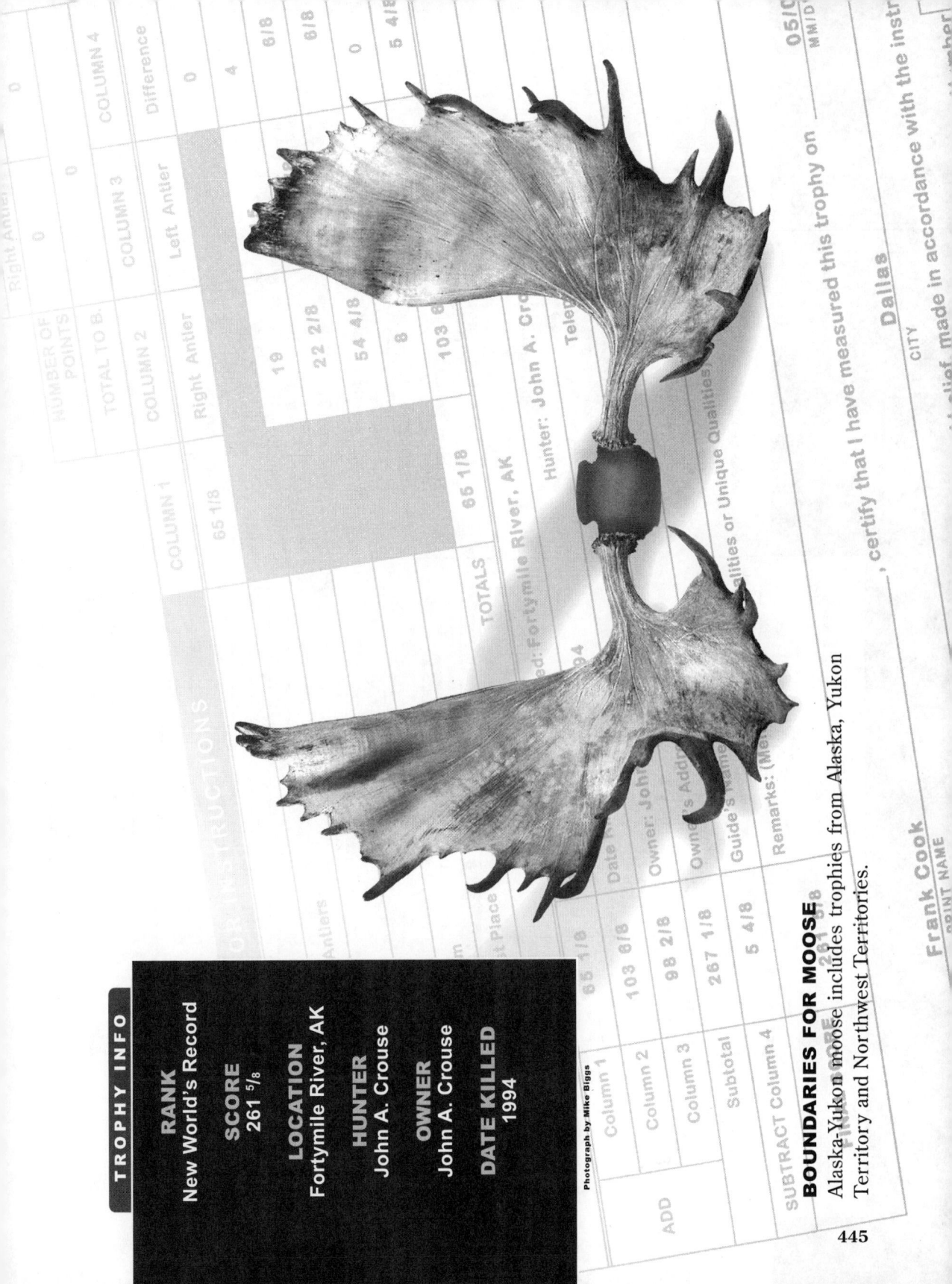

TROPHY INFO

RANK
New World's Record

SCORE
261 5/8

LOCATION
Fortymile River, AK

HUNTER
John A. Crouse

OWNER
John A. Crouse

DATE KILLED
1994

Photograph by Mike Biggs

BOUNDARIES FOR MOOSE

Alaska-Yukon moose includes trophies from Alaska, Yukon Territory and Northwest Territories.

445

Measurements must be made with a 1/4-inch wide flexible steel tape to the nearest one-eighth of an inch. Enter fractional figures in eighths, without reduction. Official measurements cannot be taken until antlers have air dried for at least 60 days after animal was killed.

A. Greatest Spread is measured between perpendiculars in a straight line at a right angle to the center line of the skull.

B. Number of Abnormal Points on Both Antlers: Abnormal points are those projections originating from normal points or from the upper or lower palm surface, or from the inner edge of palm (see illustration). Abnormal points must be at least one inch long, with length exceeding width at one inch or more of length.

C. Number of Normal Points: Normal points originate from the outer edge of palm. To be counted a point, a projection must be at least one inch long, with the length exceeding width at one inch or more of length. Be sure to verify whether or not each projection qualifies as a point.

D. Width of Palm is taken in contact with the under surface of palm, at a right angle to the inner edge of palm. The line of measurement should begin and end at the midpoint of the palm edge, which gives credit for the desirable character of palm thickness.

E. Length of Palm including Brow Palm is taken in contact with the surface along the underside of the palm, **parallel** to the inner edge, from dips between points at the top to dips between points (if present) at the bottom. If a bay is present, measure across the open bay if the proper line of measurement, parallel to **inner edge**, follows this path. The line of measurement should begin and end at the midpoint of the palm edge, which gives credit for the desirable character of palm thickness.

F. Circumference of Beam at Smallest Place is taken as illustrated.

Records of
North American
Big Game

250 Station Drive
Missoula, MT 59801
(406) 542-1888

BOONE AND CROCKETT CLUB®

OFFICIAL SCORING SYSTEM FOR NORTH AMERICAN BIG GAME TROPHIES

MOOSE

	MINIMUM SCORES	
	AWARDS	ALL-TIME
Canada	185	195
Alaska-Yukon	210	224
Wyoming	140	155

KIND OF MOOSE (check one)
☐ Canada
■ Alaska-Yukon
☐ Wyoming

Detail of Point Measurement

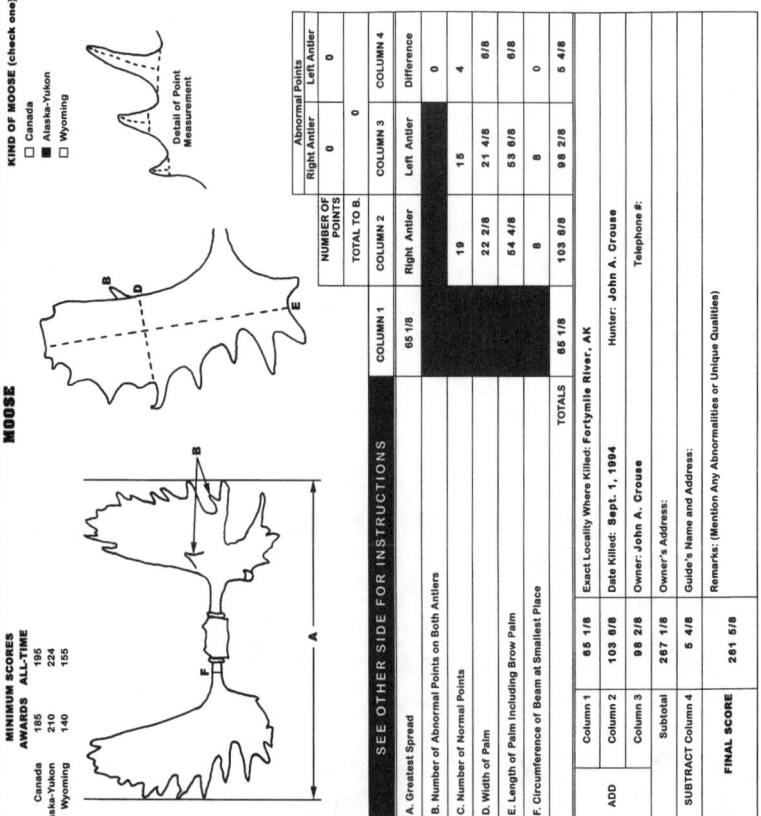

	Abnormal Points	
	Right Antler	Left Antler
	0	0

		NUMBER OF POINTS	COLUMN 2	COLUMN 3	COLUMN 4
			Right Antler	Left Antler	Difference
		TOTAL TO B.		0	
		19		15	4
			22 2/8	21 4/8	6/8
			54 4/8	53 6/8	6/8
		8		8	0
			103 6/8	98 2/8	5 4/8

SEE OTHER SIDE FOR INSTRUCTIONS	COLUMN 1
A. Greatest Spread	65 1/8
B. Number of Abnormal Points on Both Antlers	
C. Number of Normal Points	
D. Width of Palm	
E. Length of Palm Including Brow Palm	
F. Circumference of Beam at Smallest Place	
TOTALS	65 1/8

	Column 1	65 1/8
ADD	Column 2	103 6/8
	Column 3	98 2/8
	Subtotal	267 1/8
SUBTRACT Column 4	5 4/8
	FINAL SCORE	261 6/8

Exact Locality Where Killed: Fortymile River, AK

Date Killed: Sept. 1, 1994   Hunter: John A. Crouse

Owner: John A. Crouse   Telephone #:

Owner's Address:

Guide's Name and Address:

Remarks: (Mention Any Abnormalities or Unique Qualities)

I, _____ Frank Cook _____, certify that I have measured this trophy on _____ 05/01/95 _____
PRINT NAME   MM/DD/YYYY

at _____ Dallas Museum of Natural History _____   Dallas   TX
STREET ADDRESS   CITY   STATE/PROVINCE

and that these measurements and data are, to the best of my knowledge and belief, made in accordance with the instructions given.

Witness:: _____ Homer Saye _____ Signature:: _____ Frank Cook _____ I.D. Number ____
B&C OFFICIAL MEASURER

447

ALASKA-YUKON MOOSE

Alces alces gigas

MINIMUM SCORE 224

Score	Greatest Spread	Length of Palm		Width of Palm		Circumference of Beam at Smallest Place		Number of Normal Points		Locality	Hunter	Owner	Date Killed	Rank
		R	L	R	L	R	L	R	L					
261 5/8	65 1/8	54 4/8	53 6/8	22 2/8	21 4/8	8	8	19	15	Fortymile River, AK	John A. Crouse	John A. Crouse	1994	1
255	77	49 5/8	49 6/8	20 6/8	15 6/8	7 7/8	7 5/8	18	16	McGrath, AK	Kenneth Best	Kenneth Best	1978	2
251	77 4/8	46 3/8	51	17	29 6/8	7 7/8	8 1/8	18	17	Mt. Susitna, AK	Bert Klineburger	Bert Klineburger	1961	3
250 3/8	65 1/8	55 2/8	49 2/8	21 1/8	20	8 3/8	8 3/8	18	16	Kenai Pen., AK	Dyton A. Gilliland	Unknown	1947	4
249 6/8	67	47 7/8	48 2/8	22 1/8	21 1/8	7 3/8	7 5/8	15	15	Mother Goose Lake, AK	Josef Welle	Josef Welle	1967	5
249 3/8	75 3/8	51 6/8	53 1/8	17	18 6/8	7 2/8	7 2/8	11	12	Tikchik Lake, AK	John R. Johnson	John R. Johnson	1995	6
249 2/8	72	48 4/8	49 6/8	19 2/8	17	8 1/8	8 6/8	15	16	Alaska Range, AK	Henry S. Budney	Henry S. Budney	1967	7
249 1/8	69 5/8	46 6/8	43 2/8	21 2/8	22	8 2/8	8 4/8	17	17	Granite Mt., AK	David B. Parent	Earl D. Hahn	1982	8
248 7/8	73 1/8	47 1/8	47 1/8	20	22	7 4/8	7 4/8	14	19	Farewell Lake, AK	Loren G. Hammer	Loren G. Hammer	1967	9
248 5/8	68 7/8	54 3/8	46 5/8	19 6/8	19 5/8	7 5/8	8	17	16	Kenai Pen., AK	Bill Foster	Foster's Bighorn Rest.	1912	10
248 3/8	68 5/8	49 7/8	50 4/8	17 2/8	17 4/8	7 6/8	7 6/8	15	17	Natla River, NT	Myron A. Peterson	Myron A. Peterson	1988	11
248 1/8	77 5/8	47 5/8	48 5/8	18 3/8	18 6/8	8 2/8	8 3/8	13	16	Mulchatna River, AK	Bruce B. Hodson	Bruce B. Hodson	1970	12
247 5/8	73 1/8	46	46 1/8	19 6/8	21 4/8	9 4/8	9	15	15	Bering River, AK	Vol S. Davis, Jr.	Vol S. Davis, Jr.	1984	13
247 4/8	79 6/8	45 7/8	46 1/8	22 1/8	22 6/8	9	8 7/8	10	7	Iliamna Lake, AK	Gale L. Galloway	Gale L. Galloway	1970	14
247 2/8	66 4/8	48	48	18 4/8	19	7 7/8	7 7/8	17	16	Mackenzie Mts., NT	Harry Rogers	Harry Rogers	1978	15
247 2/8	70 4/8	50 6/8	52 4/8	18	16 5/8	9	9	12	12	Alagnak River, AK	Robert L. Marvin	Loaned to B&C Natl. Coll.	1981	15
246 5/8	77 5/8	48 7/8	48 4/8	16	17 6/8	7 5/8	7 4/8	13	15	Melozitna River, AK	Elmer Raphael	Elmer Raphael	1978	17
246 3/8	67 5/8	44 5/8	49 5/8	22 2/8	20 3/8	9	9 3/8	19	16	Kenai Pen., AK	Henry Hope	Henry Hope	1957	18
246 3/8	67 7/8	51 2/8	52 2/8	18 5/8	16 7/8	8 1/8	9 1/8	13	13	Redoubt Bay, AK	T.J. Hinkle	T.J. Hinkle	1993	18
246 1/8	75 3/8	48	46 3/8	18 6/8	18	8 3/8	8 5/8	12	16	Alaska Range, AK	Ralph Davies	Ralph Davies	1970	20
245 6/8	72 2/8	46 3/8	46 3/8	17	17 4/8	7 3/8	7 4/8	16	17	Wrangell Mts., AK	Philip S. Davidson	Philip S. Davidson	1970	21
245 3/8	73 3/8	49 3/8	51 3/8	16	15 4/8	8 5/8	9 5/8	14	13	Wien Lake, AK	Travis D. Thornley	Travis D. Thornley	1994	22
245 1/8	63 3/8	49 4/8	49 4/8	17 5/8	18 5/8	7 6/8	7 7/8	16	17	Kuskokwim River, AK	Ronald H. Barenz	Ronald H. Barenz	1995	23
244 6/8	64	52 1/8	52 4/8	18 4/8	15 4/8	8	7 6/8	16	15	Ogilvie Mts., YT	John F. Bruce	John F. Bruce	1995	24
244 4/8	67 4/8	51 2/8	49 1/8	20	18 7/8	8 6/8	8 5/8	13	14	Talkeetna Mts., AK	William H. Moore	Michael C. Horasanian	1953	25
244 3/8	72 3/8	48 6/8	47 2/8	19 4/8	19 7/8	7 2/8	7 3/8	12	12	Long Lake, AK	William F. Rae, Jr.	William F. Rae, Jr.	1973	26
244 2/8	71	48 4/8	48 4/8	15 4/8	16 6/8	7 5/8	7 5/8	15	15	Holy Cross, AK	Frank W. Dutton	Frank W. Dutton	1995	27
243 6/8	71 6/8	49 4/8	48 4/8	14 4/8	17 2/8	7 6/8	7 4/8	16	17	Mayo, YT	Carl Straub	Carl Straub	1971	28
243 6/8	69 4/8	49 6/8	50 6/8	15 6/8	21 1/8	8 1/8	7 5/8	17	14	Wrangell Mts., AK	John Ringstad	Loren St. Amand	1977	28
243	70	47 2/8	50 5/8	19 5/8	20 2/8	7 6/8	7 5/8	15	12	Kenai Pen., AK	D. Thompson & F. Walunga	Denny Thompson	1958	30
242 7/8	61 7/8	50 6/8	50 7/8	17 4/8	19 4/8	8 6/8	8 6/8	15	18	McGrath, AK	Leonard H. Wurman	Leonard H. Wurman	1995	31
242 6/8	63 6/8	51 4/8	50 4/8	16 7/8	16 7/8	8	7 5/8	16	15	Alaska	Unknown	Jonas Bros. Of Seattle	1954	32
242 6/8	65 6/8	45 6/8	46 1/8	16 6/8	18 4/8	8	8	18	18	Keele Range, AK	Spike Jorgensen	B. & T. Jorgensen	1994	32
242 4/8	69 2/8	46 1/8	49 2/8	15 6/8	15 6/8	8 6/8	8 6/8	16	17	Upper Susitna, AK	Helen S. Rusten	Carnegie Museum	1948	34
242 4/8	76	45 7/8	44 7/8	17 1/8	17 5/8	7 4/8	7 2/8	14	18	Nuyakuk River, AK	Ron D. DeRoest	Ron D. DeRoest	1995	34
242 3/8	67 3/8	46 6/8	46 2/8	19 3/8	21	7 3/8	7 5/8	15	15	Iliamna Lake, AK	Charles C. Parsons	Charles C. Parsons	1997	36
242 1/8	78 7/8	44 4/8	44	19 4/8	21 7/8	8 4/8	8 1/8	11	11	Alaska Pen., AK	H.S. Kamil	H.S. Kamil	1963	37
242	73 6/8	48 5/8	45 5/8	19 6/8	19 6/8	8	7 6/8	15	11	Homer, AK	Dan Jones	Dan Jones	1957	38

Score	Greatest Spread	Width of Palm R	Width of Palm L	Length of Palm R	Length of Palm L	Circ. of Beam R	Circ. of Beam L	Pts. R	Pts. L	Locality	By Whom Killed	Owner	Date	Rank
242	68	48 5/8	49 2/8	19 4/8	19 4/8	7 6/8	7 3/8	14	16	Grass Lakes, YT	Melvin R. Spohn	Melvin R. Spohn	1981	38
241 5/8	72 5/8	49 6/8	48 3/8	16 7/8	16	8 5/8	9	12	16	Neresna, AK	Lorene Ellis	Lorene Ellis	1962	40
241 5/8	67 5/8	46 5/8	46 7/8	19 1/8	16 3/8	8 2/8	8	16	16	Dawson City, YT	Ray C. Dillman	Ray C. Dillman	1971	40
241 4/8	72 1/8	48 1/8	47 7/8	19 6/8	20 6/8	7 3/8	7 1/8	16	10	Lower Ugashik Lake, AK	Bert A. McLay	John H. McLay	1986	40
241 5/8	76 6/8	47	47	16 4/8	15 3/8	8	8 2/8	14	13	King Salmon, AK	O.O. Parker & B. Bradley	O.O. Parker & B. Bradley	1960	43
241 4/8	72 5/8	48 1/8	46 7/8	17 7/8	21 7/8	8 5/8	8 4/8	13	12	Kenai Pen., AK	A.S. Reed	B&C National Collection	1900	44
240 7/8	80 5/8	43 4/8	43 2/8	18 6/8	16 2/8	8 7/8	8 7/8	11	15	Redoubt Bay, AK	Glenn B. Walker	Glenn B. Walker	1958	45
240 5/8	71 4/8	43 6/8	51 3/8	21 6/8	20 7/8	7 7/8	7 7/8	18	16	Ugashik Lakes, AK	Gene Buckles	Gene Buckles	1973	46
240 4/8	73 6/8	43 6/8	45	17	15 6/8	7 4/8	7 5/8	15	13	Alaska Pen., AK	Gregory C. McCann	Gregory C. McCann	1990	46
240 4/8	73 1/8	46 5/8	50 2/8	16 4/8	16 6/8	7 6/8	7 7/8	17	17	Huslia River, AK	Brady J. Drake	Brady J. Drake	1993	48
240 3/8	70 4/8	43 5/8	43 5/8	17 4/8	19 6/8	8 5/8	9	21	21	Yukon River, YT	Unknown	G. Kenneth Whitehead (PR)	1899	49
240 2/8	64 6/8	48 4/8	42 5/8	17 4/8	20 5/8	7 6/8	7 6/8	16	17	Noatak River, AK	Jake & Mae Jacobson	Jake & Mae Jacobson	1974	49
240 2/8	66 3/8	49 6/8	47 5/8	15 4/8	18 4/8	7 7/8	7 5/8	16	16	Wrangell Mts., AK	Forest Bigelow	Forest Bigelow	1973	51
240 1/8	70 3/8	44 4/8	41 2/8	20 4/8	20	8 1/8	8 2/8	16	15	Martin River, AK	Eugene B. Desjarlais	Eugene B. Desjarlais	1992	51
240 1/8	75 3/8	53 2/8	42 6/8	16 5/8	16 5/8	8 2/8	8 1/8	16	18	Koyukuk River, AK	Mark V. Cuppetilli	Mark V. Cuppetilli	1997	51
240 1/8	62 4/8	48 4/8	49 3/8	16 5/8	21	7 5/8	8 2/8	16	16	Beluga Mt., AK	Walter Renz	Walter Renz	1976	54
240	66 6/8	47 3/8	43 4/8	17 7/8	21 1/8	8 2/8	7 6/8	14	14	Rainy Pass, AK	Mrs. J. Watson Webb	Mrs. J. Watson Webb	1935	55
239 6/8	75 4/8	44 5/8	43 4/8	21 6/8	19 4/8	7 5/8	8 2/8	12	18	Mayo, YT	Dave Moses	Yukon Hist. Society	1950	55
239 6/8	70	52 7/8	47 6/8	14 7/8	21 5/8	8 2/8	9 2/8	15	14	Alaska Range, AK	James E. Egger	James E. Egger	1965	55
239 6/8	74 2/8	45 2/8	42 1/8	22 6/8	24 4/8	8 3/8	7 7/8	11	21	Tustumena Lake, AK	Richard R. Sawyer	Richard R. Sawyer	1988	55
239 4/8	75 5/8	42	45 3/8	20 2/8	19	7 7/8	8 6/8	13	16	Gold King, AK	Billy J. Morris	Billy J. Morris	1971	59
239 3/8	62 4/8	53 4/8	56	16 1/8	17 3/8	8	7 6/8	11	10	Alaska Pen., AK	Lars Degefors	Lars Degefors	1967	60
239 2/8	74	44 7/8	45 2/8	17 3/8	15 1/8	8 7/8	12 5/8	14	14	Bonnet Plume Range, YT	Tafford E. Oltz	Tafford E. Oltz	1978	60
239 2/8	65 7/8	47 4/8	47 2/8	20 6/8	14 6/8	9 2/8	8 2/8	18	17	Alaska Pen., AK	J. Paul Dittrich	J. Paul Dittrich	1962	62
239 2/8	67	45 1/8	48 1/8	15	15	7 6/8	8 7/8	14	14	Beluga Lake, AK	Peter W. Bading	Peter W. Bading	1961	63
239	74	51 2/8	50 4/8	13 7/8	13 7/8	12 1/8	8 2/8	10	13	Alaska Pen., AK	George J. Markham	George J. Markham	1967	63
238 4/8	73 4/8	49 6/8	52 4/8	14 6/8	14 6/8	8 2/8	8 4/8	12	12	Ugashik, AK	Alois A. Mauracher	Alois A. Mauracher	1973	63
238 3/8	67	46 1/8	48 6/8	16 7/8	16 7/8	8 7/8	8 3/8	15	15	Mackenzie Mts., NT	Burl A. Jones	Burl A. Jones	1973	66
238 2/8	69 2/8	47 4/8	48 4/8	15 6/8	14 4/8	8 4/8	9 6/8	15	15	Nushagak River, AK	Ira L. Kruger	Ira L. Kruger	1994	67
238 2/8	71 1/8	44	48	19 3/8	17 6/8	8 1/8	8 4/8	14	14	Lake Clark, AK	Frits Kielman	Frits Kielman	1973	68
238 1/8	72 4/8	46 3/8	45 6/8	18	22 1/8	7 7/8	8 5/8	11	13	Alaska Range, AK	Jeff Sievers	Jeff Sievers	1963	69
238	63 6/8	44	45 2/8	19 7/8	20 5/8	8 1/8	7 7/8	16	17	Anvil Range, YT	James F. Byers	James F. Byers	1977	69
238	74 5/8	43 5/8	43 5/8	21 4/8	25	8 3/8	9	9	16	Iliamna, AK	Joseph C. Anzalone	Joseph C. Anzalone	1972	71
237 7/8	69	48 4/8	47	17 6/8	16 1/8	8 5/8	8 6/8	11	15	Copper River, AK	Howard E. Thilenius II	Howard E. Thilenius II	1973	72
237 3/8	70 6/8	46 4/8	44 6/8	16	18 3/8	9	7 7/8	15	15	Mulchatna River, AK	Gary A. Smith	Gary A. Smith	1974	72
237	77 1/8	45 3/8	42 3/8	19 6/8	18 1/8	8 7/8	8 4/8	11	11	Dog Salmon River, AK	Peter Von Kap-Herr	Peter Von Kap-Herr	1971	74
237	67 1/8	46	48 2/8	18 3/8	15 6/8	8	7 5/8	11	17	Kenai Pen., AK	Leslie Maff	Temple Bros.	PR 1958	75
237	69 2/8	49 1/8	47 7/8	15 4/8	16 5/8	8 4/8	8 3/8	17	13	Talkeetna Mts., AK	Picked Up	Merle C. LaFortune	1970	76
236 7/8	71 6/8	48 7/8	51 1/8	14 5/8	14 1/8	8 4/8	9	13	12	Koyukuk River, AK	Jay Wattenbarger	Jay Wattenbarger	1994	76
236 7/8	64 4/8	45 2/8	47 6/8	16 5/8	18 7/8	7 7/8	8 1/8	12	16	Mid. Fork Twitya River, NT	James L. Chase	James L. Chase	1996	76
236 7/8	68 1/8	48 1/8	47 6/8	14 2/8	21 1/8	8 2/8	8 4/8	17	14	Beluga Mt., AK	Albert W. Erickson	Albert W. Erickson	1961	79
236 7/8	67 5/8	46 3/8	47 6/8	15 6/8	22 3/8	8 2/8	7 2/8	14	14	Talkeetna Mts., AK	Mario Pasquel	Mario Pasquel	1961	79
236 6/8	67 5/8	42 4/8	43	22	21 1/8	8 4/8	8 3/8	15	15	Koyukuk River, AK	Harry B. Markoskie	Harry B. Markoskie	1969	79
236 5/8	62 7/8	45 4/8	46 4/8	22 3/8	19 4/8	8	8 4/8	14	13	Kiana Lake, AK	Lane H. Drury	Lane H. Drury	1977	83
236 4/8	65 1/8	49 1/8	51 2/8	19 4/8	16 4/8	7 2/8	8 3/8	13	13	Farewell Lake, AK	Steven S. Bruggeman	Steven S. Bruggeman	1994	84
236 4/8	72 2/8	47 2/8	48 3/8	15 5/8	17 5/8	8 3/8	8 2/8	12	11	Blueberry Creek, AK	Heinrich Klimaszewski-Bletner	Heinrich Klimaszewski-Blettner	1991	84

ALASKA-YUKON MOOSE
Alces alces gigas

Score	Greatest Spread	Length of Palm R	L	Width of Palm R	L	Circumference of Beam at Smallest Place R	L	Number of Normal Points R	L	Locality	Hunter	Owner	Date Killed	Rank
236 3/8	68 1/8	46 4/8	49 3/8	16 4/8	17 7/8	8 2/8	8 1/8	14	13	Wood River, AK	Ronald Long	Ronald Long	1963	85
236 3/8	70 5/8	44 6/8	45 2/8	16 4/8	17 1/8	7 5/8	7 6/8	14	18	Lake Clark, AK	Gordon F. Wentzel	Gordon F. Wentzel	1973	85
236 2/8	68 4/8	46 4/8	52 2/8	18 3/8	16 6/8	8 1/8	8 6/8	14	16	Brusha Kama River, AK	Robert Harnish	Robert Harnish	1953	87
236 2/8	72	47	41 4/8	16 4/8	18 1/8	8 1/8	8 1/8	16	17	Upper Kiana Lake, AK	Marvin Henriksen	Marvin Henriksen	1964	87
236 2/8	73 6/8	41 6/8	42 1/8	23 1/8	22 6/8	8 3/8	8 2/8	9	14	Muddy River, AK	Richard J. Tomany	Richard J. Tomany	1993	87
236 1/8	66 7/8	44 3/8	43 5/8	16 3/8	18 4/8	7 5/8	8 1/8	17	20	Birch Creek, AK	D.T. Sharp	D.T. Sharp	1962	90
236 1/8	70 7/8	47 4/8	48	14 4/8	15 3/8	7 6/8	7 5/8	14	13	Black Lake, AK	Robert B. Ryan	Robert B. Ryan	1969	90
236 1/8	68 3/8	50	49 5/8	16 7/8	17 1/8	8 3/8	8 7/8	13	9	Alaska Range, AK	Dennis R. Johnson	Dennis R. Johnson	1980	90
236 1/8	67 5/8	45 2/8	48	18	21 2/8	8	8 2/8	13	14	Chikuminuk Lake, AK	Walter A. Brown	Walter A. Brown	1994	90
235 7/8	73 5/8	50 5/8	46 4/8	16 4/8	17 4/8	8 1/8	8 1/8	10	10	Dog Salmon River, AK	Gary R. Swanson	Gary R. Swanson	1966	94
235 7/8	69 3/8	50	50 2/8	17 4/8	15 6/8	7 5/8	7 4/8	11	10	Farewell Lake, AK	Wilhelm H. Koehler	Wilhelm H. Koehler	1974	94
235 6/8	74	44 3/8	46 2/8	15 7/8	16 2/8	8 1/8	8 1/8	13	13	Alaska	Frank Alexander	Univ. of Alaska	1952	96
235 6/8	65 2/8	46 4/8	51 6/8	20 4/8	21 6/8	9 2/8	8 2/8	13	10	Kenai Pen., AK	J.D. Rasmusson	J.D. Rasmusson	1959	96
235 5/8	69 1/8	46 3/8	47 4/8	14 6/8	15 6/8	7 1/8	7 3/8	15	15	Nowitna River, AK	Brian C. Ziegenfuss	Brian C. Ziegenfuss	1988	98
235 4/8	63 2/8	47 3/8	47 4/8	16 5/8	17 2/8	8 2/8	8 1/8	14	14	Tanana River, AK	Kenneth J. Dooley	Kenneth J. Dooley	1992	99
235 2/8	71 4/8	50 6/8	50 2/8	14 1/8	14 4/8	8 4/8	8 4/8	9	10	Rainy Pass, AK	Ralph Vogel	Ralph Vogel	1956	100
235 2/8	66 6/8	51 6/8	49	17 7/8	16 2/8	7 5/8	7 4/8	12	12	Post Lake, AK	Charles Bradley	Charles Bradley	1978	100
235 2/8	68	48 4/8	46 4/8	16 3/8	17	8	7 6/8	13	13	Iditarod River, AK	Glen D. Keil	Glen D. Keil	1992	100
235	71	47	45	14	15 5/8	8	8 3/8	15	16	Alaska Pen., AK	Otis Chandler	Otis Chandler	1964	103
235	74	45 2/8	45 1/8	15 4/8	14 3/8	8	8	15	13	Yellow River, AK	Peter Apokedak	Peter Apokedak	1966	103
235	71	47	46	16	17	8	8	12	14	Kateel River, AK	Ronald S. Peterson	Ronald S. Peterson	1976	103
234 4/8	74 4/8	50 7/8	49 1/8	16 7/8	16 3/8	8 1/8	7 5/8	12	8	Hewitt Lake, AK	W.L. Braun	W.L. Braun	1951	106
234 6/8	66 2/8	46 6/8	45 5/8	18 5/8	19 7/8	7 4/8	7 7/8	13	13	Alaska Range, AK	Bill Brown, Jr.	Bill Brown, Jr.	1987	106
234 6/8	74 6/8	46 6/8	46 1/8	15 7/8	20 5/8	8	8 3/8	10	13	Alaska Pen., AK	Lon O. Willer	Lon O. Willer	1991	106
234 4/8	62 4/8	48 3/8	45 2/8	16 4/8	17 1/8	8 2/8	8 3/8	18	16	Mayo Landing, YT	Edwin Edger	J.H. McEvoy	1962	109
234 4/8	70 6/8	43	42 6/8	18 3/8	17 4/8	7 5/8	8 1/8	14	16	Alaska Pen., AK	Herb Klein	Herb Klein	1967	109
234 4/8	69	47 1/8	48	18 2/8	17 5/8	8	8 1/8	11	12	Alaska Pen., AK	Robert P. Bliss	Robert P. Bliss	1969	109
234 4/8	66 6/8	47 4/8	44 4/8	17 4/8	16 6/8	7 5/8	7 7/8	16	15	Alaska	L.M. Hanson	L.M. Hanson	1969	109
234 4/8	71 4/8	47 6/8	49 2/8	14 2/8	15 6/8	8 6/8	8 4/8	11	11	Council, AK	Arden L. Peterson	Arden L. Peterson	1979	109
234 4/8	65 2/8	47 6/8	47 6/8	18 3/8	17 4/8	7 3/8	7 6/8	12	13	Teslin, YT	Bernard M. Stehelin	Bernard M. Stehelin	1995	109
234 2/8	58	52 6/8	51 6/8	16 7/8	16 6/8	8 5/8	8 5/8	15	11	Alaska Range, AK	Wakon I. Redbird	Wakon I. Redbird	1969	115
234 2/8	71 2/8	45 4/8	44 7/8	16 7/8	15 3/8	7 3/8	7 2/8	14	15	Fortymile River, AK	Orval R. Evans	Orval R. Evans	1973	115
234 2/8	70 4/8	45 2/8	46 1/8	17 5/8	17 5/8	8 1/8	8	14	11	Koyukuk River, AK	Oren Johnson	Oren Johnson	1975	115
234 2/8	71 4/8	49 2/8	47 6/8	13 7/8	14 7/8	7 7/8	7 6/8	12	14	Beluga Lake, AK	Eugene J. Smart	Eugene J. Smart	1989	115
234 2/8	66 6/8	47 7/8	45 4/8	16 1/8	15	8 2/8	8 3/8	15	17	Salcha River, AK	Robert C. Lang	Robert C. Lang	1991	115
234 1/8	71 3/8	41 4/8	43 2/8	19 2/8	18 1/8	7 6/8	7 6/8	16	14	Galena, AK	Michael J. Stowell	Michael J. Stowell	1977	120
234 1/8	68 5/8	44 2/8	46 4/8	17 2/8	17 2/8	7 2/8	7 2/8	14	16	Ditna River, AK	Richard C. Thompson	Richard C. Thompson	1992	120
234	68 4/8	46 4/8	43 3/8	18 6/8	17 3/8	8	8 1/8	14	14	Ugashik Lakes, AK	Richard C. Rubin	Richard C. Rubin	1968	122

Score	Greatest Spread	Width of Palm R	Width of Palm L	Length of Palm R	Length of Palm L	Circumference R	Circumference L	Points R	Points L	Locality	By Whom Killed	Owner	Date Killed	Rank
234	75 4/8	49 2/8	48 5/8	12 6/8	14 4/8	8	7 7/8	10	11	King Salmon, AK	Larry R. Price	Larry R. Price	1971	122
233 6/8	71 4/8	43 3/8	41	17 1/8	16 3/8	7 7/8	7 6/8	17	16	Kenai Pen., AK	A.S. Reed	Unknown	1900	124
233 6/8	76	42 2/8	50 2/8	20 5/8	19 3/8	8	7 2/8	10	12	Kenai Pen., AK	Otto Rohm	Otto Rohm	1964	124
233 6/8	63	50 5/8	49 2/8	20 3/8	15 6/8	6 7/8	8	13	14	Wrangell Mts., AK	Dan L. Quen	Dan L. Quen	1965	124
233 6/8	67 6/8	50 2/8	49 1/8	15	17 1/8	7 7/8	7	12	16	Galena, AK	Picked Up	Richard M. Reynolds	1995	124
233 5/8	77 5/8	41	44 1/8	14 5/8	18 3/8	7 6/8	8	15	18	Kenai Pen., AK	Picked Up	Am. Mus. Nat. Hist.	1938	128
233 5/8	65 7/8	46 3/8	45 1/8	18	20 6/8	8 5/8	7 6/8	15	13	Alaska Pen., AK	Jack S. Parker	Jack S. Parker	1968	128
233 5/8	71 3/8	45 4/8	50	15 4/8	18 2/8	8	8 5/8	14	17	Iliamna Lake, AK	Wayne Rattray	Wayne Rattray	1972	128
233 5/8	71 7/8	46 1/8	48 4/8	18 1/8	16 2/8	7 6/8	8 1/8	11	13	McGrath, AK	Art Beattie	Linda Beattie	1978	128
233 5/8	70 3/8	43 4/8	46 6/8	17 4/8	17 4/8	7 5/8	7 6/8	13	14	Telaquanna Lake, AK	Alvin A. Pierce	Alvin A. Pierce	1996	128
233 4/8	74 6/8	43 4/8	42 4/8	16 2/8	16 6/8	7 5/8	7 5/8	13	17	Kenai Pen., AK	Gift of C.H. Mackay to NCHH	Unknown	PR 1939	133
233 4/8	72 6/8	40 6/8	47 4/8	25 5/8	25 2/8	7 7/8	8	11	9	Kenai Pen., AK	Picked Up	Shawn T. Brown	PR 1972	133
233 4/8	70 4/8	50	45 5/8	16 4/8	15 7/8	8	8 3/8	14	12	Koyukuk River, AK	Arnold K. Wolf	Arnold K. Wolf	1993	133
233 3/8	66 1/8	46 7/8	48	15 6/8	16 3/8	8 7/8	8 7/8	12	11	Worm Lake, YT	James E. Nelson	James E. Nelson	1985	136
233 2/8	69 4/8	48 1/8	48 7/8	15 4/8	16 6/8	7 3/8	7 3/8	11	16	Chulitna River, AK	Joe L. Aprill	Elizabeth D. Aprill	1970	137
233	69	49 5/8	47 7/8	15 1/8	13 1/8	8	8	14	14	Merrill Pass, AK	Andrew F. Bjorge	Andrew F. Bjorge	1963	138
233	73 4/8	50 1/8	46 6/8	15 7/8	14 3/8	7 6/8	7 5/8	11	12	Dillinger River, AK	James N. McHolme	James N. McHolme	1976	138
232 7/8	67 1/8	46 1/8	48	15 6/8	15	8 3/8	8 4/8	12	12	Post Lake, AK	Andrew P. Schultze	Andrew P. Schultze	1996	140
232 6/8	65 6/8	45 3/8	42 7/8	19 6/8	18 7/8	7 7/8	7 7/8	17	9	Port Heiden, AK	Don C. Killom	Don C. Killom	1965	141
232 6/8	75	48 2/8	44 3/8	13 4/8	17 1/8	8 3/8	8 5/8	10	14	Port Heiden, AK	Gerald L. Lavenstein	Gerald L. Lavenstein	1967	141
232 6/8	74 2/8	43 3/8	48 1/8	18 1/8	15 4/8	7 1/8	7 2/8	9	15	Koyukuk River, AK	Chris M. Kendrick	Chris M. Kendrick	1994	141
232 5/8	65 1/8	43 3/8	45 4/8	18 1/8	18 6/8	8 3/8	8 3/8	11	13	Swede Lake, AK	Paul Bierdeman	Paul Bierdeman	1956	144
232 5/8	70 5/8	46 2/8	47 7/8	18 1/8	18 1/8	7 4/8	7 3/8	15	9	Ugashik Lakes, AK	Jack A. Shane, Sr.	Jack A. Shane, Sr.	1967	144
232 5/8	69 7/8	47 3/8	48 7/8	17	18 1/8	8	8	12	10	Lake Clark, AK	Wyatt B. Peek	Wyatt B. Peek	1987	144
232 5/8	67 1/8	49 6/8	49 6/8	16 6/8	17	7 2/8	7 3/8	9	13	Pilot Point, AK	Dennis M. Wick	Dennis M. Wick	1993	144
232 4/8	69 6/8	45	45	17 5/8	16 6/8	6 6/8	6 6/8	10	12	Talkeetna, AK	Ole Dahl	Boston Mus. Of Science	1950	148
232 4/8	67 4/8	47 7/8	48 3/8	15 4/8	17 5/8	7 4/8	7 4/8	13	13	Stewart River, YT	Patrick Seaman	Patrick Seaman	1968	148
232 4/8	68	45 2/8	46 7/8	17 4/8	17 1/8	8 1/8	8 2/8	12	12	Teklanika River, AK	Richard O. Cook	Richard O. Cook	1976	148
232 4/8	70 6/8	48	49 6/8	14 6/8	14 6/8	8 1/8	8 1/8	12	12	Matanuska Valley, AK	Jim Sakaguchi	Wendy Kleker	1979	148
232 4/8	63 4/8	46 1/8	48 2/8	19 5/8	17	7 3/8	7 3/8	10	14	Tok River, AK	Kenneth L. Klawunder	Kenneth L. Klawunder	1992	148
232 2/8	71	43	43 1/8	20 1/8	17	8 6/8	8 5/8	14	12	Alaska Pen., AK	Stewart G. Richards	Stewart G. Richards	1968	153
232 2/8	66 2/8	50 4/8	49 4/8	16 4/8	14 6/8	7 6/8	7 6/8	12	11	Wien Lake, AK	James E. Guist	James E. Guist	1988	153
232 1/8	67 3/8	47 3/8	45 2/8	16 7/8	16 7/8	8 7/8	8 7/8	12	12	Amos Lakes, AK	Buddy R. Donaldson	Buddy R. Donaldson	1990	155
232 1/8	69 5/8	45 7/8	47 4/8	14 7/8	14 2/8	7 5/8	7 5/8	12	12	Mackenzie Mts., NT	J.L. Madden	J.L. Madden	1994	155
232	66 6/8	47 3/8	50 7/8	17 4/8	18 3/8	7 6/8	7 4/8	10	11	Alaska Pen., AK	A.R. Buckles	A.R. Buckles	1967	157
232	63	55	55 3/8	14	14 5/8	7 4/8	7 4/8	8	9	Alaska Pen., AK	L.W. Bailey, Jr.	L.W. Bailey, Jr.	1969	157
232	65	47 5/8	46	17	15	9 6/8	9 4/8	15	14	King Salmon, AK	P.J. Grady	J. Michael Conoyer	1979	157
231 7/8	63 1/8	50 6/8	49 7/8	12 2/8	12 2/8	8 4/8	8 4/8	14	13	Talkeetna Mts., AK	T.A. Miller	T.A. Miller	1959	160
231 7/8	69 1/8	43 6/8	44	18	18	8 1/8	8 2/8	13	11	Red Paint Creek, AK	Larry D. Kropf	Larry D. Kropf	1983	160
231 7/8	69 5/8	49 5/8	49 7/8	16 5/8	17 3/8	8 2/8	8 1/8	11	13	Wood River, AK	Robert Kennedy	Robert Kennedy	1989	160
231 6/8	76	44 6/8	44 5/8	12 6/8	15 4/8	8 4/8	8 4/8	12	14	Kenai Pen., AK	Gift of C.H. Mackay to NCHH	Unknown	PR 1939	163
231 6/8	64 2/8	45 2/8	51 4/8	16 2/8	18	9	8 2/8	15	14	Lake Louise, AK	Paul Kunning	Paul Kunning	1966	163
231 6/8	65	45 5/8	46 6/8	18 5/8	18 1/8	7 6/8	7 6/8	13	13	Koyukuk River, AK	Don N. Bunker	Don N. Bunker	1990	163
231 6/8	59 6/8	48 5/8	48 6/8	17	17	8	8	13	13	Koyukuk River, AK	John W. Griffin	John W. Griffin	1996	163
231 5/8	73 1/8	48 4/8	44 4/8	17	15 4/8	7 7/8	7 6/8	12	16	Alaska Range, AK	Cecil M. Hopper	Cecil M. Hopper	1969	167

ALASKA-YUKON MOOSE

Alces alces gigas

Score	Greatest Spread	Length of Palm R	L	Width of Palm R	L	Circumference of Beam at Smallest Place R	L	Number of Normal Points R	L	Locality	Hunter	Owner	Date Killed	Rank
231 4/8	67 4/8	42 4/8	45 5/8	20 6/8	26 4/8	9 4/8	8 6/8	10	12	Alaska Pen., AK	George H. Landreth	George H. Landreth	1967	168
231 4/8	69 2/8	43 1/8	46 2/8	17	16 5/8	6 7/8	7 1/8	18	15	Steese Hwy., AK	Denver Perry	Denver Perry	1968	168
231 4/8	62 6/8	44	44 7/8	17 2/8	16 7/8	7 5/8	7 4/8	16	17	Alaska Range, AK	Peter J. Cassinelli	Peter J. Cassinelli	1977	168
231 4/8	67 4/8	46	44 4/8	17	17	7 5/8	7 4/8	13	15	Wood River, AK	H. Peter Blount	H. Peter Blount	1989	168
231 3/8	66 3/8	47 7/8	49 5/8	21 2/8	19 2/8	8 4/8	8 3/8	9	13	Kenai Pen., AK	Paula Rak	Paula Rak	1987	172
231 2/8	67	47 1/8	47 3/8	16 2/8	16	8	8	13	11	Brooks Range, AK	Lezlie D. Fickes	Lezlie D. Fickes	1972	173
231 1/8	66 5/8	49 3/8	49 6/8	15 4/8	14 1/8	7 6/8	7 6/8	12	11	Alaska Pen., AK	Frank N. Rome	Frank N. Rome	1976	174
231	67 6/8	42 7/8	45 5/8	18 1/8	17 4/8	7 2/8	7 3/8	14	17	Tazlina Glacier, AK	Stanley B. Hoagland	Stanley B. Hoagland	1963	175
231	67 2/8	45 6/8	46 3/8	17 3/8	19	7 6/8	8 1/8	11	12	Amber Bay, AK	Charles E. Guess	Charles E. Guess	1974	175
231	68	45 6/8	47 5/8	13 4/8	14 4/8	8 2/8	8 3/8	14	14	Kuskokwim River, AK	Larry S. Lewis	Larry S. Lewis	1994	175
231	61	47 2/8	48 1/8	14 1/8	17 1/8	7 5/8	8 1/8	16	16	Chisana River, AK	Steven J. DeRicco	Steven J. DeRicco	1995	175
230 6/8	67 6/8	48 6/8	46 6/8	16 2/8	17 6/8	7 4/8	7 4/8	11	13	Petersville, AK	Johnny Lamb	Johnny Lamb	1969	179
230 6/8	67 4/8	53 5/8	52 6/8	13 1/8	14 2/8	7 7/8	7 6/8	9	8	Innoko River, AK	Leslie R. Hunter	Leslie R. Hunter	1983	179
230 6/8	67 6/8	43 7/8	45	19 1/8	15 7/8	7 7/8	7 6/8	14	14	Deadlock Mt., AK	Vernon W. Van Wyk	Vernon W. Van Wyk	1995	179
230 5/8	68 7/8	54 4/8	53 2/8	15	14 5/8	9	8 4/8	6	6	Cordova, AK	John B. Pecel	John B. Pecel	1969	182
230 5/8	65 5/8	47 4/8	47	16 2/8	16 2/8	7 2/8	7 2/8	12	12	Port Heiden, AK	Brent Greenburg	Brent Greenburg	1972	182
230 5/8	71 5/8	43 4/8	44 2/8	17	14 6/8	7 3/8	7 2/8	22	14	Bonnet Plume Lake, YT	Walter P. Griffin	Walter P. Griffin	1978	182
230 5/8	64 1/8	46 7/8	48 2/8	15 3/8	16 4/8	8	8 2/8	13	14	Alaska Pen., AK	Lucky Christoph	Carl V. Christoph	1981	182
230 5/8	60 1/8	50	47 4/8	14 7/8	14 4/8	7 5/8	7 2/8	16	16	Hart River, YT	Charles H. Menzer	Charles H. Menzer	1988	182
230 5/8	70 3/8	49 7/8	50	13 7/8	12 4/8	7 7/8	7 6/8	13	10	Talkeetna River, AK	Wayne DiSarro	Wayne DiSarro	1989	182
230 4/8	61	50	50	15 2/8	19 5/8	7 4/8	7 5/8	12	12	Alaska Pen., AK	Louis Stojanovich	Louis Stojanovich	1993	188
230 3/8	69 1/8	49	47 1/8	15 1/8	18 3/8	8 3/8	8 5/8	10	15	Alaska Pen., AK	James H. Lieffers	James H. Lieffers	1963	189
230 2/8	66 4/8	45 1/8	47	15 6/8	16	8	8 2/8	14	15	Chelatna Lake, AK	G.O. Wiegner	G.O. Wiegner	1969	190
230 2/8	81 4/8	40 1/8	39 5/8	18 7/8	17	7 6/8	8	13	11	Iliamna Lake, AK	Peter Zipperle	Peter Zipperle	1972	190
230 2/8	70 2/8	46 5/8	46 2/8	17 1/8	17 2/8	8 1/8	8 3/8	9	11	Alaska Range, AK	Earl R. Hossman	C. Coldren	1975	190
230 1/8	65 3/8	45 7/8	47 4/8	18 5/8	25	8	7 7/8	10	12	Alaska Pen., AK	Walter Pfisterer	Walter Pfisterer	1960	193
230	70 4/8	43 5/8	45	18 5/8	19 7/8	7 3/8	7 6/8	14	10	Port Heiden, AK	Norman Garwood	Norman Garwood	1964	194
230	73	44 2/8	44 3/8	14 4/8	14 6/8	7 6/8	7 6/8	12	12	Miner River, YT	Gary L. Knepp	Gary L. Knepp	1979	194
230	72	44 7/8	45 2/8	16 4/8	16 2/8	8	7 7/8	12	10	Maclaren River, AK	Ronald D. Hocking	Ronald D. Hocking	1988	194
230	66	46 4/8	47 2/8	15 7/8	16 3/8	7 5/8	7 7/8	12	15	Ugashik River, AK	Angelo Poliseno	Angelo Poliseno	1991	194
230	70	43 1/8	45 6/8	16 5/8	19 5/8	8 4/8	8 2/8	13	12	Yellow River, AK	Patrick L. Kirsch	Patrick L. Kirsch	1993	194
230	70	46 4/8	47 2/8	15 4/8	19 5/8	7 4/8	7 4/8	11	11	Sleetmute, AK	Todd A. Horner	Todd A. Horner	1996	194
229 7/8	66 1/8	42 4/8	41 5/8	19 6/8	17 1/8	7 7/8	7 6/8	17	15	Wood River, AK	Bert Klineburger	Bert Klineburger	1964	200
229 7/8	66 1/8	46	46 2/8	19 2/8	20 7/8	8 6/8	8 5/8	8	13	King Salmon River, AK	Wilfred von Brand	Wilfred von Brand	1966	200
229 7/8	70 5/8	45 7/8	46 5/8	16 3/8	14	7 6/8	7 6/8	12	12	Kokwok River, AK	Patrick L. McDonald	Patrick L. McDonald	1990	200
229 6/8	60 4/8	48 4/8	51	17	18	8 1/8	8 3/8	11	11	Alaska Pen., AK	Robert H. Stewart	Robert H. Stewart	1963	203
229 6/8	67 2/8	47	45	17	19 6/8	8 2/8	8 2/8	12	11	Kenai Pen., AK	Barjona Meek	Barjona Meek	1973	203
229 6/8	64 6/8	45 6/8	45 4/8	17 2/8	17 2/8	7 4/8	7 4/8	12	12	Anvil Range, YT	Fritz Kemper	Fritz Kemper	1978	203

Score	Greatest Spread	Length of Palm R	Length of Palm L	Width of Palm R	Width of Palm L	Circumference R	Circumference L	Points R	Points L	By Whom Killed	Owner	Locality	Date Killed	Rank
229 6/8	61 2/8	43 1/8	45 4/8	16 6/8	25 4/8	7 3/8	7 7/8	17	20	Marvin H. Breitkreutz	Marvin H. Breitkreutz	Yanert Fort, AK	1988	203
229 5/8	64 7/8	45	45 4/8	16 2/8	16 6/8	7 1/8	7 2/8	14	15	Fred M. Poorman	Fred M. Poorman	McGrath, AK	1958	207
229 5/8	68 7/8	47 4/8	48 1/8	15	18	7 7/8	8	12	10	C.J. McElroy	C.J. McElroy	Kuichack River, AK	1966	207
229 4/8	63 4/8	42	43	21	21	8 4/8	8	12	13	W.M. Ellis	W.M. Ellis	Alaska Pen., AK	1963	209
229 4/8	72 7/8	45 6/8	46 2/8	15 1/8	18 6/8	7 6/8	8 4/8	10	13	Arnold H. Craine	Arnold H. Craine	Alaska Pen., AK	1968	209
229 4/8	66 6/8	44 4/8	46 6/8	16 7/8	17 1/8	8	8	12	13	Johnny Bunsen	Johnny Bunsen	Ogilvie Mts., YT	1996	212
229 2/8	73	43 5/8	43	17 4/8	15 7/8	8 2/8	8 2/8	12	12	Brian Yamamoto	Brian Yamamoto	Fortymile River, AK	1988	213
229 1/8	67 5/8	52	45	16 3/8	16 2/8	8 2/8	8	12	13	Duane E. Stroupe	Duane E. Stroupe	Talkeetna Mts., AK	1982	214
229	72 2/8	44 7/8	43 4/8	13 1/8	13 6/8	8	8	15	14	A. Knutson	A. Knutson	Wood River, AK	1957	214
229	62 4/8	47	45	19 3/8	20 1/8	6 7/8	6 7/8	12	13	William Bugh	William Bugh	Shaw Creek Flats, AK	1962	214
229	69	44 2/8	44	22 5/8	24	8	8	13	16	Paul R. Sharick	Paul R. Sharick	Mother Goose Lake, AK	1966	214
229	65 2/8	47 2/8	43 7/8	14	13 6/8	7 7/8	7 5/8	16	8	William G. Latimer	William G. Latimer	Wind River, YT	1973	214
229	67 2/8	47 3/8	44 4/8	16 5/8	17 2/8	7 5/8	7 3/8	14	13	Gary D. Myers	Gary D. Myers	Nushagak River, AK	1995	219
228 7/8	65 7/8	48 6/8	48 4/8	17 4/8	16 5/8	8 3/8	8 6/8	15	12	Berry B. Brooks	Berry B. Brooks	Wood River, AK	1958	219
228 7/8	63 7/8	42 1/8	45 2/8	13 5/8	13 6/8	8 4/8	8 3/8	12	13	David F. Bremner, Jr.	David F. Bremner, Jr.	Talkeetna Mts., AK	1959	219
228 7/8	70 7/8	46 3/8	42 2/8	22 1/8	13 5/8	8 2/8	8 2/8	13	12	Ray L. Aldridge	Ray L. Aldridge	Cantwell, AK	1964	219
228 7/8	70 1/8	47 5/8	44	20 2/8	15 5/8	9 2/8	8 5/8	12	13	Russell Matthes	Russell Matthes	Ugashik Lakes, AK	1969	219
228 6/8	65 6/8	43 6/8	44	18 1/8	18 4/8	8	8 1/8	13	12	R.D. Eichenour	R.D. Eichenour	Mulchatna River, AK	1968	223
228 6/8	72 6/8	47 3/8	48 6/8	16	18 1/8	8 4/8	8 2/8	12	13	E.L. Dosdall	E.L. Dosdall	Mulchatna River, AK	1975	223
228 6/8	63 4/8	49 4/8	44 7/8	15 3/8	14	6 7/8	7	13	16	Scott R. Sexson	Scott R. Sexson	Holitna River, AK	1978	223
228 6/8	69	44 4/8	47 6/8	14 2/8	15 5/8	7 7/8	7 7/8	11	13	David W. Doner	David W. Doner	Koyukuk River, AK	1988	223
228 6/8	70	42 4/8	43 7/8	19 5/8	14 2/8	8 3/8	7 7/8	12	11	John T. Jondal	John T. Jondal	Alganak River, AK	1992	223
228 5/8	78 3/8	48 4/8	48 4/8	20 1/8	15 3/8	8 2/8	8 2/8	11	15	Dale R. Wood	Dale R. Wood	Kenai Pen., AK	1960	228
228 5/8	54 3/8	47 6/8	47 4/8	18 4/8	16 4/8	9	8 1/8	15	14	Max Fugler	Max Fugler	Ugashik Bay, AK	1966	228
228 5/8	69 1/8	42	45 4/8	16	14	7 3/8	7 2/8	11	14	Edward A. Kneeland	Edward A. Kneeland	Kijik River, AK	1970	228
228 5/8	72 1/8	45	46 1/8	15 4/8	15 6/8	7 6/8	8	14	13	Larry B. Jamison	Larry B. Jamison	Wood River, AK	1979	228
228 5/8	68 3/8	47	47 5/8	16	15 3/8	8 2/8	7 6/8	12	12	Robert L. Nelson	Robert L. Nelson	Brooks Range, AK	1981	228
228 4/8	61 3/8	43 5/8	44 7/8	13 5/8	15 4/8	8	7	15	15	William E. Pipes III	William E. Pipes III	Bear Lake, AK	1994	228
228 4/8	58	45 6/8	44	16 2/8	16 3/8	8 5/8	8 4/8	19	14	G.W. Berry	G.W. Berry	Wrangell Mts., AK	1960	234
228 4/8	65 6/8	45 1/8	45 2/8	15 5/8	14 5/8	8 1/8	8 4/8	14	10	Ted T. Dabrowski	Ted T. Dabrowski	Bonnet Plume Lake, YT	1965	234
228 4/8	70	47 3/8	44 7/8	17 2/8	18 1/8	8 1/8	8	10	17	Tom W. Degefors	Tom W. Degefors	Alaska Pen., AK	1967	234
228 4/8	65 4/8	47 5/8	45 6/8	14 1/8	19 3/8	8 2/8	8 2/8	17	12	Hugh Beasley	Hugh Beasley	Wernecke Mts., YT	1968	234
228 4/8	71	44 1/8	47 3/8	13 5/8	15 2/8	7 6/8	7 5/8	12	10	Jesse C. Sprague	Jesse C. Sprague	Tagagawik River, AK	1983	234
228 3/8	68 4/8	49 2/8	47 5/8	15 1/8	15	7 3/8	7 5/8	10	13	John F. Walchli	John F. Walchli	Flattop Mt., AK	1991	240
228 2/8	70 7/8	40 5/8	48	15 3/8	15 4/8	7 5/8	7	13	15	Vern Mahoney	Vern Mahoney	Paxson Lake, AK	1953	241
228 2/8	66 6/8	46	41 4/8	15 4/8	16 3/8	8 3/8	7	15	15	Jerry D. Redick	Jerry D. Redick	Blair Lakes, AK	1979	241
228 1/8	66	45	45 6/8	14 5/8	14 1/8	8 5/8	8 2/8	14	11	James D. Chambers	James D. Chambers	Shotgun Creek, AK	1993	243
228 1/8	71 7/8	42 2/8	44	19 3/8	18 1/8	8 1/8	8 4/8	11	12	Bert Klineburger	Bert Klineburger	Mother Goose Lake, AK	1967	243
228	65 5/8	46 5/8	42 2/8	15	15 2/8	8 4/8	8 3/8	12	13	W.J. Brule	W.J. Brule	Rainy Pass, AK	1968	245
228	69 6/8	41 2/8	45 7/8	18	17	8	8 1/8	13	17	J.W. Dixon	J.W. Dixon	Rainy Pass, AK	1949	245
228	69 4/8	47	43 1/8	15 2/8	14 2/8	7 1/8	7 2/8	17	16	Wayne C. Eubank	Wayne C. Eubank	Talkeetna Mts., AK	1957	245
228	62 2/8	47 3/8	45 4/8	15 7/8	14 6/8	8 2/8	8 2/8	14	14	M.E. Davis, Jr.	M.E. Davis, Jr.	Alaska Pen., AK	1958	245
228	69	53 4/8	46 3/8	16 1/8	15 2/8	8 3/8	7 6/8	17	14	Peter W. Bading	Peter W. Bading	Mt. Susitna, AK	1963	245
228	67	47	45 4/8	15 6/8	20	7 2/8	7 4/8	12	16	Glen Miller	Glen Miller	Tonzona River, AK	1971	245
228	63 2/8	47 3/8	46 3/8	14 4/8	15 2/8	7 2/8	8 5/8	16	10	Michael J. Harlin	Michael J. Harlin	Koyukuk River, AK	1988	245
228	64 4/8	53 4/8	45 4/8	15 3/8	15 6/8	8 4/8	8 3/8	10	11	John S. Pangbron	John S. Pangbron	Cinder River, AK	1990	245
227 7/8	65 3/8	42 6/8	42 5/8	14 2/8	15	7 3/8	7 4/8	17	17	Thomas V. Scrivner	Jack V. Morkal	Savage River, AK	1966	252

ALASKA-YUKON MOOSE

Alces alces gigas

Score	Greatest Spread	Length of Palm R	L	Width of Palm R	L	Circumference of Beam at Smallest Place R	L	Number of Normal Points R	L	Locality	Hunter	Owner	Date Killed	Rank
227 7/8	65 3/8	46 2/8	49 1/8	17 1/8	18 2/8	7 7/8	8 2/8	10	10	Dog Salmon River, AK	John C. Davis	John C. Davis	1984	252
227 7/8	69 1/8	46	44 6/8	14 1/8	15	9	9 1/8	13	12	Koyuk River, AK	James R. Ryffel	James R. Ryffel	1986	252
227 7/8	71 1/8	44 5/8	46 4/8	13 5/8	13 1/8	8 3/8	8 1/8	14	13	Tonzona Creek, AK	Jim Fuchs	Jim Fuchs	1995	252
227 6/8	62 2/8	44 2/8	44 3/8	14	13 4/8	7	7 2/8	18	21	Soslota Creek, AK	Alex Cox	Alex Cox	1957	256
227 6/8	72 4/8	42	43	17	16 4/8	8 5/8	8 1/8	11	12	Nikabuna Lake, AK	James E. Curley	James E. Curley	1968	256
227 6/8	73 2/8	50 2/8	42 5/8	16 1/8	17 1/8	7 4/8	8 4/8	12	16	Martin River, AK	Jim Goodfellow, Jr.	Jim Goodfellow, Jr.	1977	256
227 6/8	61 5/8	49 3/8	45 2/8	17 6/8	22	9 5/8	9 2/8	11	11	Seward Pen., AK	Andrew Pellessier	Homer Westmark	1990	256
227 6/8	70 4/8	41 6/8	41 2/8	15 7/8	19 4/8	7 2/8	7	15	16	Kotzbue, AK	Hugh S. Wilson	Hugh S. Wilson	1992	256
227 5/8	72 1/8	41 4/8	43 6/8	18 4/8	18 2/8	8 4/8	8	11	10	Livengood, AK	James W. Keasling	James W. Keasling	1973	261
227 5/8	67 3/8	47 3/8	47 5/8	15 1/8	19 2/8	7 5/8	7 5/8	10	12	Alaska Pen., AK	Floyd F. Marrs	Floyd F. Marrs	1977	261
227 5/8	67 7/8	45	46 3/8	14 5/8	17 5/8	7 2/8	8	13	13	Susitna River, AK	Darryl G. Sanford	Darryl G. Sanford	1981	261
227 5/8	63 1/8	47 1/8	43 4/8	15 4/8	17 1/8	7 2/8	7 2/8	16	22	Divide Lake, NT	Joseph L. Bell	Joseph L. Bell	1986	261
227 5/8	74 5/8	43 2/8	43 4/8	18 7/8	17	8 3/8	8 2/8	9	8	Big River, AK	Adolf Hnup	Adolf Hnup	1994	261
227 4/8	75 4/8	39 6/8	45 4/8	17 4/8	20 4/8	7 6/8	7 6/8	12	11	Cinder River, AK	John Humphreys	John Humphreys	1963	266
227 4/8	56 2/8	48 4/8	46 6/8	21 4/8	19 2/8	8 6/8	8 5/8	13	11	Alaska Pen., AK	R.H. Platt	R.H. Platt	1965	266
227 4/8	71 2/8	51 4/8	46 4/8	14 5/8	14 1/8	8 6/8	8 4/8	10	9	Iliamna Lake, AK	Robert L. Hammond	Robert L. Hammond	1968	266
227 4/8	63	46	46 5/8	17	16 4/8	9 2/8	8 6/8	11	12	Kluane Lake, YT	Richard C. Wolff	Richard C. Wolff	1971	266
227 4/8	66	44 2/8	42 5/8	16 3/8	16 1/8	7 4/8	7 5/8	15	15	Elliott Lake, YT	Paul E. Wollenman	Paul E. Wollenman	1984	266
227 4/8	68 6/8	45 6/8	42 2/8	16 6/8	17 1/8	7 4/8	7 3/8	16	13	Harvey Lake, AK	David A. Coray	David A. Coray	1993	266
227 3/8	69 1/8	44 2/8	44 6/8	15	15 5/8	8	7 7/8	12	14	Tok River, AK	Walter W. Kellogg	Walter W. Kellogg	1967	272
227 3/8	72 1/8	41 2/8	41 4/8	13 7/8	15 1/8	8 4/8	8 4/8	14	14	Big River, AK	Ronald W. LeBeaumont	Ronald W. LeBeaumont	1996	272
227 2/8	69 6/8	44 6/8	44 1/8	16	15 1/8	8 4/8	8 5/8	11	12	Salana River, AK	Jules R. Ashlock	Jules R. Ashlock	1961	274
227 2/8	68 2/8	44 4/8	44 4/8	20	17 6/8	8 1/8	7 2/8	10	12	Port Heiden, AK	Pressley R. Rankin, Jr.	Pressley R. Rankin, Jr.	1966	274
227 2/8	70 4/8	41 7/8	41 6/8	14 7/8	15 1/8	7 6/8	7 6/8	14	15	Aniak River, AK	Donn W. Ulrich	Donn W. Ulrich	1980	274
227 2/8	67 6/8	48	49 5/8	17	13 2/8	8 4/8	8 4/8	13	10	Bonnet Plume Lake, YT	A.H. Clise	A.H. Clise	1982	274
227 2/8	62 6/8	46 2/8	46 7/8	14 5/8	15 2/8	7 7/8	8 1/8	14	17	Kuskokwim River, AK	Dennis Harms	Dennis Harms	1994	274
227 1/8	74 3/8	46 1/8	44 4/8	14	15 2/8	7 7/8	8 1/8	10	11	Aniak Lake, AK	Michael L. Caverly	Michael L. Caverly	1982	279
227 1/8	61 1/8	51 5/8	49 5/8	14	15 1/8	7 4/8	7 3/8	13	12	Mulchatna River, AK	Brett L. Foster	Brett L. Foster	1997	279
227	69	47 2/8	45 3/8	15 2/8	14 1/8	8 5/8	8 4/8	11	12	Rainy Pass, AK	John A. Mueller	John A. Mueller	1966	281
227	67 4/8	45 1/8	44 3/8	16 3/8	16 1/8	8 3/8	8 2/8	11	11	Ugashik Lakes, AK	Robert Loch	Robert Loch	1967	281
227	68 2/8	48 4/8	46 6/8	15 6/8	18	8 1/8	7 7/8	9	12	Ugashik Lakes, AK	Emil Underberg	Emil Underberg	1967	281
227	64 4/8	52	46	15 4/8	14 7/8	7 3/8	7 4/8	13	13	Ketchumstuk, AK	C.O. Tweedy, J. Albright & W. Burnette, Sr	C.O. Tweedy	1968	281
227	66 2/8	44 4/8	44 7/8	20 7/8	17	7 7/8	8	14	11	Farewell Lake, AK	Duke of Penaranda	Duke of Penaranda	1969	281
227	62 4/8	47 6/8	47 4/8	14 4/8	14 5/8	7 2/8	7 3/8	13	13	South Macmillan River, YT	Louis T. Hill	Louis T. Hill	1973	281
227	69 2/8	48 4/8	43 1/8	14 5/8	14 6/8	8 1/8	8 1/8	13	15	Susitna River, AK	L.E. Wold & W.A. Vollendorf	L.E. Wold	1978	281
227	66 2/8	43	41 1/8	16 1/8	17	8 1/8	8 1/8	15	19	Wood River, AK	Wayne G. Elwood	Wayne G. Elwood	1986	281

Score	Greatest Spread	Length of Palm R	Length of Palm L	Width of Palm R	Width of Palm L	Circ. of Beam R	Circ. of Beam L	Points R	Points L	Locality	Hunter	Owner	Date Killed	Rank
227	67 4/8	45 2/8	45 4/8	14 5/8	17 6/8	7 7/8	8 7/8	12	14	Iliamna River, AK	David S. Haeg	David S. Haeg	1987	281
227	74 2/8	44 6/8	48 4/8	15 1/8	17 3/8	8 4/8	8 4/8	8	14	Alaska Pen., AK	John A. Schumacher	John A. Schumacher	1987	281
226 7/8	63 5/8	47 3/8	46 2/8	13 2/8	12	7 4/8	7 3/8	16	16	Wood River, AK	M.D. Gilchrist	M.D. Gilchrist	1958	291
226 7/8	63 7/8	41	44 7/8	17 7/8	17 2/8	8 2/8	8 7/8	16	15	Yakutat, AK	Ray E. Buckwalter	Ray E. Buckwalter	1963	291
226 7/8	61 7/8	47 3/8	47	16 4/8	16 4/8	7 3/8	7 3/8	16	14	Nessling Range, YT	Eric Pilkington	Eric Pilkington	1965	291
226 7/8	63 3/8	43 3/8	47	16 5/8	16 7/8	7 6/8	8	14	14	Eagle, AK	David G. Martini	David G. Martini	1969	291
226 7/8	67 7/8	48 4/8	43 2/8	12 2/8	16 6/8	7 5/8	7 4/8	18	17	Ray River, AK	William A. Galster	William A. Galster	1972	291
226 7/8	58 3/8	52 5/8	50 7/8	13 6/8	15 1/8	7 5/8	7 5/8	14	12	Camp Creek, AK	Michael E. Carter	Michael E. Carter	1982	291
226 6/8	66 5/8	47	48	15 3/8	19	7 6/8	8	10	11	Alaska Pen., AK	Michael Z. Abrams	Michael Z. Abrams	1989	298
226 6/8	67	41 2/8	49	20 6/8	19 1/8	7 4/8	9	12	12	Alaska Pen., AK	George A. Waldriff	George A. Waldriff	1962	298
226 6/8	68	45 6/8	46 6/8	14	15 3/8	9 6/8	9 5/8	12	10	Nabesna River, AK	Ross L. Phillippi, Jr.	Ross L. Phillippi, Jr.	1968	298
226 5/8	70 4/8	45 4/8	41 1/8	18	17 4/8	7 4/8	7 6/8	12	12	Alaska Pen., AK	Gerald F. McNamara	Mac's Taxidermy	1979	301
226 5/8	61 3/8	44	44 4/8	16 4/8	17	8 1/8	8 1/8	15	14	Talkeetna Mts., AK	Lino Fred Vannelli	Lino Fred Vannelli	1979	301
226 5/8	68 5/8	44 5/8	46 1/8	13 4/8	13 4/8	7 7/8	7 7/8	14	13	Talkeetna Mts., AK	Wolfgang Porsche	Wolfgang Porsche	1981	301
226 5/8	72 5/8	46 4/8	43 5/8	16	15 5/8	7 2/8	8	13	10	King Salmon River, AK	Daniel E. Farr	Daniel E. Farr	1986	301
226 4/8	72 5/8	41	41 1/8	19	19 6/8	7	7	13	15	Fifteenmile River, YT	Tammy L. Wagner	Tammy L. Wagner	1996	305
226 4/8	70 6/8	44 2/8	44 6/8	15 4/8	14 4/8	7 1/8	7 3/8	12	12	Wood River, AK	Dan Auld, Jr.	Dan Auld, Jr.	1949	305
226 4/8	68	43 7/8	54 3/8	11 4/8	12 2/8	7 7/8	8	16	17	Charley River, AK	G.P. Nehrbas	AK Natl. Bank	1951	305
226 4/8	63	45 4/8	47	15	14 2/8	8	8	14	15	Rainy Pass, AK	W.B. Macomber	W.B. Macomber	1953	305
226 4/8	62 6/8	46	43 7/8	18 3/8	20	7 5/8	8	12	13	Paxson Lake, AK	L.M. Cole	L.M. Cole	1958	305
226 4/8	65 4/8	46	44 2/8	15 7/8	15 2/8	7 6/8	8	13	10	Chugach Mts., AK	R.E. Kelley	R.E. Kelley	1961	305
226 4/8	64 2/8	48 3/8	49	15 5/8	15	7 1/8	8	13	14	Talkeetna Mts., AK	Harold Froehle	Harold Froehle	1965	305
226 4/8	60 6/8	48	50 1/8	16 6/8	16	8	7 2/8	12	12	Dog Salmon River, AK	H.H. Ahlemann	H.H. Ahlemann	1968	305
226 4/8	73 2/8	45 3/8	42 7/8	15 6/8	17 7/8	8 4/8	8 4/8	9	10	Koyukuk River, AK	Paul H. Ruesch	Paul H. Ruesch	1990	314
226 3/8	68 2/8	42 7/8	46	15 6/8	17 5/8	7 4/8	7 4/8	13	14	Kuskokwim River, AK	Andrew R. Domas III	Andrew R. Domas III	1996	314
226 3/8	69 5/8	46	41 2/8	21	19 4/8	7 6/8	7 5/8	10	14	Lake Louise, AK	H.C. Ragsdale II	H.C. Ragsdale II	1958	314
226 3/8	65 5/8	45 4/8	45 4/8	20 6/8	17 1/8	8 2/8	8 2/8	11	10	Alaska Pen., AK	Lit Ng	Lit Ng	1967	314
226 2/8	65 1/8	42 6/8	42 2/8	16 4/8	18	8 3/8	8 3/8	13	14	Naknek, AK	Noel Thompson	Noel Thompson	1971	318
226 2/8	71 1/8	43 6/8	44 6/8	18 4/8	17 6/8	6 5/8	7 1/8	14	13	Big River, AK	Karl L. Strecker	Karl L. Strecker	1996	318
226 2/8	69	48 3/8	44 3/8	13 6/8	12 7/8	7 4/8	7 7/8	11	11	Talkeetna Mts., AK	T.L. Wynne, Jr.	T.L. Wynne, Jr.	1958	318
226 2/8	68	47 1/8	44 5/8	16 3/8	13	7 5/8	7 4/8	16	14	Kenai Pen., AK	Ottokar J. Skal	Ottokar J. Skal	1963	318
226 2/8	65 6/8	44	43	14 4/8	14 4/8	8	8	14	15	Bonnet Plume Lake, YT	Ted Dabrowski	Ted Dabrowski	1965	318
226 2/8	67 6/8	45	43 7/8	12 7/8	13 5/8	8 4/8	8 4/8	15	15	Elliot Lake, YT	Collins F. Kellogg, Sr.	Collins F. Kellogg, Sr.	1992	318
226 2/8	68 2/8	40 7/8	41 2/8	16 3/8	18 5/8	6 6/8	6 7/8	15	18	Koyukuk River, AK	Mel J. Tenneson	Mel J. Tenneson	1993	318
226 1/8	70 7/8	44 4/8	46 4/8	14 2/8	14 6/8	7 7/8	8	11	15	King Salmon Creek, AK	Tiney Mitchell	Tiney Mitchell	1971	323
226	66	46	48 5/8	17 4/8	16	8	8	10	12	Alaska Pen., AK	Robert L. Wesner	Robert L. Wesner	1963	324
226	67 2/8	46 6/8	44 1/8	17 4/8	20 7/8	7 2/8	8	11	11	Ft. Greely, AK	Jerry L. Bailey	Jerry L. Bailey	1970	324
226	58 2/8	46 5/8	46 3/8	18 6/8	18 4/8	8	8	11	14	Black Lake, AK	John Mike Behan	John Mike Behan	1972	324
226	64 4/8	47	45 4/8	13 4/8	17 6/8	7 6/8	8	13	11	Dillinger River, AK	Jerry E. Romanowski	Jerry E. Romanowski	1976	324
226	65	44 4/8	47 3/8	13 4/8	14 1/8	8 2/8	8 1/8	13	13	Alagnak River, AK	John H. Webster	John H. Webster	1985	324
226	60 2/8	48 6/8	46 4/8	15 3/8	17 1/8	8 2/8	8 5/8	13	17	Ketchumstuk Mt., AK	Donald P. Chase	Donald P. Chase	1993	324
226	63 2/8	47 6/8	45 4/8	16 3/8	18 2/8	8 5/8	8 4/8	11	13	Tsiu River, AK	Frank L. Fackovec	Frank L. Fackovec	1994	324
226	68 2/8	44	44	13 2/8	14 4/8	7 6/8	7 6/8	15	13	Willow Handle Lake, NT	M.R. James	M.R. James	1995	324
225 7/8	68 5/8	48 2/8	48 2/8	14 1/8	13 2/8	7 6/8	8 2/8	14	14	Wrangell Mts., AK	Lee Chambers	Lee Chambers	1969	332
225 7/8	68 7/8	50 7/8	45 2/8	19 1/8	13 2/8	8 2/8	8 4/8	11	13	Melozitna River, AK	John E. Stenehjem	John E. Stenehjem	1985	332
225 6/8	76 6/8	46 2/8	45 2/8	13 3/8	14 2/8	7 6/8	8 1/8	10	14	Alaska Pen., AK	Herman Kulhanek	Herman Kulhanek	1961	334
225 6/8	66 4/8	46 4/8	43 5/8	15	13 4/8	9 4/8	8 4/8	9	15	Alaska Pen., AK	Don Johnson	Don Johnson	1963	334

ALASKA-YUKON MOOSE

Alces alces gigas

Score	Greatest Spread	Length of Palm R	L	Width of Palm R	L	Circumference of Beam at Smallest Place R	L	Number of Normal Points R	L	Locality	Hunter	Owner	Date Killed	Rank
225 6/8	63 4/8	46 6/8	45 6/8	18 7/8	18 5/8	7 3/8	7 2/8	12	10	Alaska Range, AK	J.B. Copeland, Jr.	J.B. Copeland, Jr.	1968	334
225 6/8	57 6/8	47 4/8	47 6/8	14 2/8	16 4/8	8 2/8	8 3/8	14	18	St. George Creek, AK	Joseph G. Gaillard	Joseph G. Gaillard	1968	334
225 6/8	70 2/8	46 4/8	45	15 5/8	15 7/8	8 1/8	8 2/8	12	10	Farewell Station, AK	Daniel M. DiBenedetto, Sr.	Daniel M. DiBenedetto, Sr.	1973	334
225 6/8	75 2/8	43 2/8	38 5/8	14 3/8	15 2/8	8 2/8	8 4/8	14	14	Kenai Pen., AK	Willi Hilpert	Willi Hilpert	1973	334
225 6/8	66	46 7/8	46	13 4/8	16	8 3/8	8 3/8	12	12	Upper Mulchatna River, AK	O.B. Beard III	O.B. Beard III	1974	334
225 6/8	65 4/8	40 1/8	41	21 4/8	18 2/8	7 2/8	7 3/8	15	17	Spring Creek, AK	William D. Phifer	William D. Phifer	1975	334
225 6/8	67 2/8	43 4/8	42	15 4/8	16	8 6/8	8 6/8	13	13	Glennallen, AK	Eugene E. Wheeler	Eugene E. Wheeler	1981	334
225 6/8	67 2/8	43 4/8	44 4/8	17 2/8	18 2/8	8 5/8	8 4/8	10	12	Kugururok River, AK	H.I.H. Prince Abdorreza Pahlavi	H.I.H. Prince Abdorreza Pahlavi	1988	334
225 6/8	65	44 4/8	43 5/8	16 1/8	16 4/8	7 6/8	7 5/8	13	17	Ogilvie Mts., YT	George F. Dennis, Jr.	George F. Dennis, Jr.	1997	334
225 5/8	66 7/8	45	42 5/8	15 1/8	18 6/8	8 2/8	8 1/8	14	14	Unknown	Gift of C.H. Mackay to NCHH	Unknown	PR 1951	345
225 5/8	72 3/8	44	43 4/8	16	21 2/8	7 1/8	7 1/8	11	10	Port Heiden, AK	Harold Sill	Harold Sill	1964	345
225 5/8	65 5/8	45 4/8	46 4/8	16 2/8	14 7/8	7 5/8	7 5/8	13	13	High Lake, AK	Glen E. Park	Glen E. Park	1965	345
225 5/8	70 1/8	41 1/8	43	19 1/8	17 1/8	8 1/8	8	13	13	Alaska Range, AK	R. Pinamont & J. Albright	Robert Pinamont	1972	345
225 5/8	69 3/8	44 7/8	41 6/8	17 7/8	20 3/8	8	8 5/8	11	11	Farewell, AK	G. Jack Tankersley	G. Jack Tankersley	1975	345
225 5/8	66 3/8	44	49 1/8	15 2/8	13 6/8	8 3/8	8 3/8	14	14	Chandalar River, AK	William O. Dudley	William O. Dudley	1980	345
225 4/8	68 4/8	41 4/8	41	15 4/8	18 4/8	8	8	14	15	Alaska Pen., AK	Dolores F. Jones	Dolores F. Jones	1958	351
225 4/8	71	44 2/8	46 6/8	15 4/8	18 3/8	7 4/8	7 7/8	10	10	Stony River, AK	Leland R. McFarland	Leland R. McFarland	1969	351
225 4/8	66 6/8	47 2/8	48 3/8	14 1/8	16 1/8	8 2/8	8	10	14	Blackstone River, YT	Marc Korting	Marc Korting	1970	351
225 4/8	66 4/8	42 6/8	43 1/8	14 6/8	13 4/8	7 5/8	7 2/8	18	16	Cub Lake, AK	William McNamara	William McNamara	1979	351
225 3/8	70 3/8	43 4/8	45	16 3/8	16 4/8	7 5/8	8	10	10	Lake Clark, AK	George W. Robinson	George W. Robinson	1965	355
225 3/8	65 3/8	43 3/8	41 4/8	15	15 7/8	7 6/8	7 4/8	18	16	Tustumena Lake, AK	Harley E. Johnson	Harley E. Johnson	1983	355
225 3/8	69 7/8	43 1/8	43 1/8	15	15 4/8	6 5/8	6 6/8	13	14	Stony River, AK	David S. Haeg	David S. Haeg	1997	355
225 2/8	66 2/8	43 5/8	43	17	16 2/8	8 4/8	8 2/8	12	12	Wernecke Mts., YT	David V. Collis	David V. Collis	1984	358
225 2/8	65	39 6/8	43 4/8	22 1/8	19 2/8	9 1/8	10 7/8	16	16	Dog Salmon River, AK	Marvin D. Fuller	Marvin D. Fuller	1988	358
225 2/8	63	48	46 3/8	19 4/8	18 3/8	8 3/8	8 3/8	9	12	King Salmon, AK	Bob L. Chain, Jr.	Bob L. Chain, Jr.	1995	358
225 1/8	64 7/8	48 3/8	44	16 1/8	17 4/8	7 5/8	7 5/8	10	10	Alaska Pen., AK	James Ford	James Ford	1970	361
225 1/8	69 3/8	40 7/8	44	14 6/8	13 6/8	8 2/8	8 3/8	15	16	Alaska Range, AK	Richard C. Beall	Richard C. Beall	1978	361
225 1/8	73 1/8	43 4/8	44 5/8	17 4/8	15 6/8	8 2/8	8 2/8	12	11	Alagnak River, AK	J. & J. Hertel	J. & J. Hertel	1987	361
225 1/8	61 5/8	47 6/8	47 2/8	15 4/8	15 7/8	7	7	12	13	June Lake, NT	Bertha E. Thompson	Bertha E. Thompson	1987	361
225 1/8	62 5/8	46 2/8	53 5/8	17 7/8	18 4/8	8 1/8	8 2/8	9	9	King Salmon River, AK	Michaelangelo P. Ripepi	Michaelangelo P. Ripepi	1989	361
225	66 4/8	45 6/8	45	15 2/8	13	8 6/8	8 5/8	14	15	Kenai Pen., AK	Walter R. Peterson	Walter R. Peterson	1935	366
225	74	41	41 2/8	17	18 2/8	7 7/8	7 4/8	17	11	Livengood, AK	Bill Thomas	Univ. of Alaska	1952	366
225	65 2/8	40 7/8	41 2/8	15 4/8	17 4/8	8	8 1/8	16	20	Nelchina, AK	Jack D. Putnam	Denver Mus. Nat. Hist.	1961	366
225	65 4/8	50	49	15	14 7/8	7 7/8	7 7/8	8	*9	Alaska Range, AK	Basil C. Bradbury	Basil C. Bradbury	1963	366
225	72	45	47 5/8	14	16 1/8	7 4/8	7 6/8	10	15	Farewell Lake, AK	Lyman Strong	Lyman Strong	1965	366
225	58	47 4/8	45 7/8	15 2/8	17 5/8	8 3/8	8 5/8	14	17	Tok, AK	Bruce Dodson	Bruce Dodson	1974	366

Score	Greatest Spread	Length of Palm R	Length of Palm L	Width of Palm R	Width of Palm L	Circumference R	Circumference L	Points R	Points L	Locality	Hunter	Owner	Date Killed	Rank
225	70	44	44 1/8	13 1/8	15 2/8	8 7/8	10 2/8	12	14	Talkeetna Mts., AK	Eberhart Herzog	Eberhart Herzog	1981	366
225	61 2/8	46 2/8	46 1/8	15 3/8	15 7/8	7 4/8	7 3/8	13	17	Pelly River, YT	Glen H. Taylor	Glen H. Taylor	1985	366
224 7/8	71 5/8	48 1/8	42 2/8	16	17 3/8	7 3/8	7 3/8	12	11	Mt. Katmai, AK	Morris Roberts	Morris Roberts	1951	374
224 7/8	61 7/8	48 1/8	47 7/8	14 6/8	14 1/8	7 5/8	7 5/8	12	12	Ugashik Narrows, AK	Wayne Ewing	Wayne Ewing	1966	374
224 7/8	67 3/8	45 6/8	45 3/8	17 1/8	16 6/8	7 5/8	8 4/8	9	13	King Salmon, AK	Albert B. Fay	Albert B. Fay	1969	374
224 7/8	67 1/8	46 7/8	46 7/8	14 3/8	14 6/8	8 4/8	7 4/8	11	11	Koyukuk River, AK	Dennis E. Reiner	Dennis E. Reiner	1973	374
224 6/8	70 2/8	45 2/8	40 2/8	19 2/8	18 4/8	7 4/8	7 5/8	14	13	Farewell Lake, AK	Gust Pabst	Gust Pabst	1963	378
224 6/8	74 2/8	41 6/8	42 6/8	14 1/8	17 3/8	7 3/8	8 4/8	12	14	Alaska Pen., AK	Charles Bonnici	Charles Bonnici	1969	378
224 6/8	58 6/8	46	47	15	15	8 5/8	9 1/8	14	11	Cantwell, AK	Gene Sivell	Gene Sivell	1970	378
224 6/8	61 6/8	44 4/8	44 2/8	20 1/8	21 2/8	9 5/8	8 4/8	9	9	Lower Ugashik Lake, AK	Hugo Klinger	Hugo Klinger	1972	378
224 6/8	69 4/8	44 1/8	44 1/8	16 6/8	14	8 4/8	7 4/8	12	12	Little Tok River, AK	Edward J. Janus	Edward J. Janus	1974	378
224 6/8	62 6/8	47 3/8	46	19	15 4/8	7 4/8	8 2/8	13	14	Earn Lake, YT	Julian D. Weiant	Julian D. Weiant	1978	378
224 6/8	64 6/8	45 6/8	48 6/8	15	15 6/8	8 2/8	7 4/8	11	11	Stony River, AK	Bradford W. Reddick	Bradford W. Reddick	1993	378
224 6/8	64 4/8	47 4/8	45 5/8	15 1/8	15 2/8	7 4/8	7 5/8	12	14	Blackstone River, YT	Jerry Stefanitsis	Jerry Stefanitsis	1993	378
224 6/8	68 4/8	46 5/8	43 6/8	17 5/8	15 6/8	7 5/8	8	12	16	Koyukuk River, AK	Beattie J. Smith	Beattie J. Smith	1994	378
224 6/8	62 4/8	45 4/8	45 5/8	15 6/8	17 2/8	8	8 3/8	11	13	Post Lake, AK	Leonard H. Wurman	Leonard H. Wurman	1994	378
224 6/8	71	43 2/8	43 6/8	15 6/8	16 2/8	8 1/8	8 5/8	12	13	Koktuli River, AK	Alfred J. Ogella	Alfred J. Ogella	1994	378
224 5/8	68 1/8	45 1/8	47 2/8	16 4/8	18 7/8	8 5/8	8 5/8	11	13	Port Heiden, AK	Jon G. Koshell	Jon G. Koshell	1996	389
224 5/8	67 7/8	45 5/8	41 6/8	19 3/8	19 3/8	8 5/8	9 3/8	8	17	Fifteenmile River, YT	Joel B. Benner	Joel B. Benner	1964	389
224 5/8	72 1/8	40	38 1/8	17 6/8	17 4/8	6 5/8	8 2/8	10	12	Yuki River, AK	Steven B. Spaulding	Steven B. Spaulding	1986	389
224 5/8	65 1/8	44 6/8	40 3/8	20 6/8	20 4/8	7 7/8	8 3/8	14	9	Kandik River, YT	Charles W. Brammer	Charles W. Brammer	1986	389
224 5/8	66 5/8	40 4/8	50 4/8	23 2/8	25 5/8	8 3/8	8 2/8	12	10	Bering Glacier, AK	Steven L. Folkman	Steven L. Folkman	1988	389
224 5/8	68 3/8	48 3/8	46 5/8	15 3/8	15 2/8	8 2/8	7 2/8	7	13	Iliamna Lake, AK	William F. Rode	William F. Rode	1991	389
224 5/8	65 5/8	45 3/8	45	14 2/8	14 2/8	7 3/8	8	11	11	Bonnet Plume Lake, YT	Chris Brewer	Chris Brewer	1993	389
224 5/8	62 5/8	47 3/8	47	15	15 5/8	8 4/8	8 4/8	13	14	Bonnet Plume Lake, YT	Jerry E. Mason	Jerry E. Mason	1994	389
224 4/8	67	46 3/8	44 5/8	17 6/8	14 6/8	8 3/8	8 3/8	11	15	Cook's Inlet, AK	Dall Dew	Colorado Outdoor Journal	PR 1898	397
224 4/8	67	43 6/8	44 2/8	14 2/8	15	7 6/8	7 6/8	15	13	Unknown	Unknown	Buckhorn Mus. & Saloon, Ltd.	PR 1957	397
224 4/8	62	44 3/8	44 3/8	15 6/8	15	7 7/8	7 7/8	16	14	Fog Lakes, AK	C.A. Schwope	C.A. Schwope	1960	397
224 4/8	68 2/8	45 1/8	43 7/8	14 2/8	18	8 1/8	8	12	14	Alaska Pen., AK	James E. McFarland	James E. McFarland	1967	397
224 4/8	71 4/8	41 6/8	46 4/8	18 4/8	19 5/8	7 3/8	7 2/8	9	9	Alaska Range, AK	William M. Harrington	William M. Harrington	1970	397
224 4/8	66 6/8	46 5/8	48 5/8	18 4/8	16 2/8	7 4/8	7 4/8	14	9	Koyukuk River, AK	Philip C. Wahlbom	Philip C. Wahlbom	1976	397
224 4/8	63 6/8	45 2/8	45	16 2/8	16 4/8	7 7/8	7 7/8	13	12	Hess River, YT	Richard B. Limbach	Richard B. Limbach	1985	397
224 4/8	65 6/8	44 4/8	47	16 7/8	17 3/8	8	8 2/8	10	13	Iliamna Lake, AK	Norbert A. Prokosch	Norbert A. Prokosch	1986	397
224 3/8	58 1/8	44 3/8	48 7/8	16 5/8	19 6/8	8 2/8	8 1/8	14	12	Kenai Pen., AK	Carole Colclasure	Carole Colclasure	1962	405
224 3/8	71 7/8	47 4/8	43 2/8	18 4/8	18 4/8	8 2/8	8 4/8	11	12	Alaska Pen., AK	Alice J. Landreth	Alice J. Landreth	1967	405
224 3/8	61 5/8	47 3/8	46 4/8	13 5/8	13 5/8	7 3/8	8 2/8	15	14	Kenai Pen., AK	Gloria Reiter	Gloria Reiter	1969	405
224 3/8	67 7/8	44 4/8	44 7/8	14 7/8	14 7/8	7 1/8	7 3/8	11	12	Farewell Lake, AK	Arthur W. Dages	Arthur W. Dages	1993	405
224 2/8	70 4/8	45	46 6/8	15 3/8	17 4/8	8	7 1/8	10	12	Alligator Lake, YT	Arthur C. Popham, Jr.	Arthur C. Popham, Jr.	1950	409
224 2/8	63 2/8	43 7/8	43 5/8	14 3/8	13 3/8	8 7/8	8 1/8	14	11	Yukon	J.R. Gray	J.R. Gray	1951	409
224 2/8	61 2/8	48 1/8	48 6/8	13 6/8	16 4/8	8	7 7/8	12	14	Susitna River, AK	Donald E. Wicks	Donald E. Wicks	1963	409
224 2/8	60 2/8	42 6/8	46 2/8	16 4/8	13 6/8	7 6/8	7 6/8	15	12	Post Lake, AK	Wulf Nosofsky	Wulf Nosofsky	1965	409
224 2/8	58	49 4/8	49 4/8	13 6/8	16 1/8	7 7/8	7 7/8	12	11	Wood River Mts., AK	F. Jay Riley	F. Jay Riley	1987	409
224 2/8	62 2/8	48 4/8	47	16 1/8	15 5/8	7 3/8	7 3/8	11	14	Tatonduk River, YT	Thomas Covert	Thomas Covert	1992	409
224 2/8	69 4/8	45 4/8	42 3/8	15 1/8	15 6/8	8 1/8	8 1/8	12	13	Koyukuk River, AK	Mary S. Hubbard McIsaac	Mary S. Hubbard McIsaac	1995	409
224 2/8	68 4/8	43 6/8	48 3/8	18 2/8	18 2/8	7 4/8	7 6/8	10	12	Ogilvie Mts., YT	Edwin A. Lewis	Edwin A. Lewis	1996	409
224 1/8	67 3/8	44 6/8	46 6/8	15 6/8	18 7/8	7 7/8	8 4/8	10	10	Telaquana Lake, AK	Paul G. Curren	Paul G. Curren	1960	417

ALASKA-YUKON MOOSE

Alces alces gigas

Score	Greatest Spread	Length of Palm		Width of Palm		Circumference of Beam at Smallest Place		Number of Normal Points		Locality	Hunter	Owner	Date Killed	Rank
		R	L	R	L	R	L	R	L					
224 1/8	68 7/8	47 2/8	44	14 7/8	15 2/8	7 7/8	7 6/8	11	12	Port Salmon, AK	Graf Scheel-Plessen	Graf Scheel-Plessen	1965	417
224 1/8	68 7/8	45 4/8	44 6/8	15 2/8	13 1/8	7 6/8	7 6/8	14	12	Bear Lake, AK	Earl K. Wahl, Jr.	Earl K. Wahl, Jr.	1987	417
224 1/8	61 7/8	49 3/8	48 7/8	12 6/8	13	7 4/8	7 5/8	12	12	Fifteen Mile River, YT	Larry Lee	Larry Lee	1990	417
224 1/8	55 7/8	45 6/8	47 4/8	15 5/8	15 4/8	7 7/8	7 7/8	16	15	Mulchatna River, AK	Timothy D. Smithen	Timothy D. Smithen	1995	417
224	65 6/8	43 2/8	47 1/8	18 5/8	17 1/8	7 6/8	7 6/8	11	13	Alaska Range, AK	L.J. Pfeifer	L.J. Pfeifer	1977	422
224	66 6/8	42 6/8	44 4/8	15 6/8	14 5/8	7 2/8	7 3/8	15	14	Franklin Creek, AK	Vernon K. Lucas	Vernon K. Lucas	1994	422
224	65 4/8	45 3/8	53	14 7/8	14 2/8	7 5/8	7 7/8	12	12	Iliamna Lake, AK	Zane Streater	Zane Streater	1995	422
224	70 2/8	42 3/8	47	15 5/8	17	9 1/8	8 7/8	14	10	Aniak, AK	Larry W. Goehring	Larry W. Goehring	1997	422
249 6/8*	71 6/8	49 3/8	49 1/8	26 4/8	22 2/8	9 1/8	9 5/8	11	9	Pedro Bay, AK	David W. Boone	David W. Boone	1996	
242 6/8*	73	47 2/8	46 6/8	19 5/8	17 5/8	7 5/8	8 3/8	15	13	Aniak River, AK	Amour J. Lawson	Amour J. Lawson	1991	
240 4/8*	67	51 6/8	48 4/8	16	18 5/8	8 5/8	8 2/8	14	14	Meadow Creek, YT	Alistair Campbell	Alistair Campbell	1991	

* Final score is subject to revision by additional verifying measurements.

B&C HISTORY

GIFFORD PINCHOT
1865-1946

He was the first American professional forester; and served as the first Chief of the U.S. Forest Service. He was an early leader in crusading for the conservation of this nation's natural resources. He worked closely with President Theodore Roosevelt to engage the Governors of the States and the leaders of both Canada and Mexico in long-range planning to conserve the continent's resources. He served as Governor of Pennsylvania for two terms: 1923-27 and 1931-35. ■

459

CATEGORY
ALASKA-YUKON MOOSE

SCORE
242-7/8

HUNTER
LEONARD H. WURMAN

LOCATION
MCGRATH, AK

DATE OF KILL
SEPTEMBER 1995

CATEGORY
ALASKA-YUKON MOOSE

SCORE
227-3/8

HUNTER
RONALD W. LEBEAUMONT

LOCATION
BIG RIVER, AK

DATE OF KILL
SEPTEMBER 1996

CATEGORY
ALASKA-YUKON MOOSE

SCORE
230

HUNTER
ANGELO POLISENO

LOCATION
UGASHIK RIVER, AK

DATE OF KILL
SEPTEMBER 1991

460

CATEGORY
ALASKA-YUKON MOOSE

SCORE
224-3/8

HUNTER
ARTHUR W. DAGES

LOCATION
FAREWELL, AK

DATE OF KILL
SEPTEMBER 1993

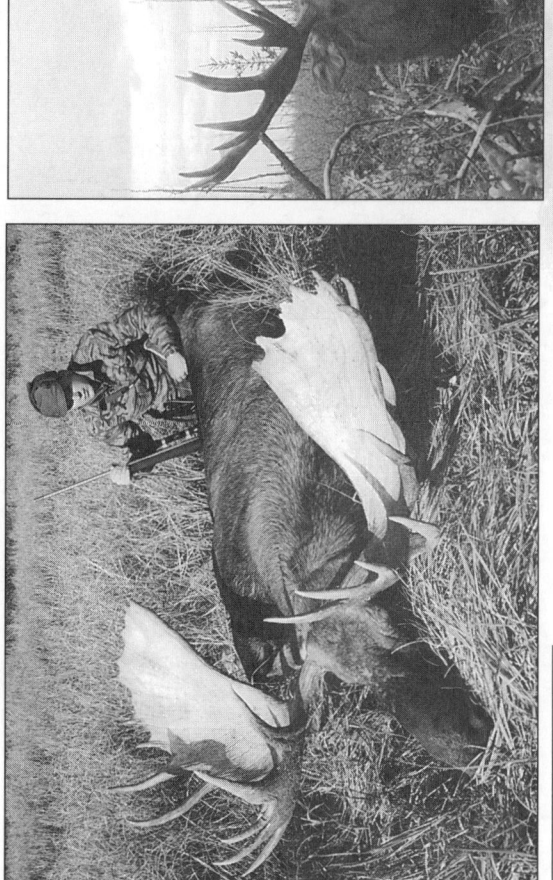

CATEGORY
ALASKA-YUKON MOOSE

SCORE
230

HUNTER
TODD A. HORNER

LOCATION
SLEETMUTE, AK

DATE OF KILL
SEPTEMBER 1996

CATEGORY
ALASKA-YUKON MOOSE

SCORE
237

HUNTER
JAMES L. CHASE

LOCATION
MID FORK TWITYA
RIVER, NT

DATE OF KILL
SEPTEMBER 1996

461

The World's Record Wyoming moose (*Alces alces shirasi*) was taken by John M. Oakley of Cheyenne. Shot during the 1952 season near Green River Lake, Wyoming, this specimen scored 205-4/8 at the national competition.

This Wyoming or Shiras moose was most likely stripping the delicate leaves from willow tips when Oakley spotted the reflection of the antlers as he made his way into the Gypsum Creek area of the Wind River Range. Because it can be difficult to judge the size of antlers against the immensity of a bull, Oakley did not know right off that the rack was of record size.

Having lived in Wyoming, Oakley had a healthy respect for the unpredictably of this animal, which is capable of moving extremely quickly. Bull's have been known to utilize their antlers as weapons, as well as symbols of intimidation.

Moose do not have strong vision but do possess extraordinary senses of smell and hearing. Making his stalk, Oakley had to be weary of the unpredictable gusts of wind that rush through the surrounding mountains.

Although they are the largest big game animal in North America, moose are usually taken down without too much difficulty. However, the bone in a moose's shoulder blade is heavy enough to deflect a bullet. Oakley had to shoot the powerful moose four times with 180-grain Speer bullets in .270 caliber hand loads.

The outcome was a new World's Record that edged ahead of the former record-holder, A.E. Chandler of Casper,

by the narrow margin of 3/8 of a point. Mounted and initially owned by J.L. Nevins and H.A. Yocum of Frontier Taxidermists, the prized Wyoming moose was later sold to the Jackson Hole Museum, Jackson, Wyoming. ■

BOUNDARIES FOR MOOSE

Wyoming (Shiras) moose includes trophies taken in Colorado, Idaho, Montana, Utah, Washington, and Wyoming.

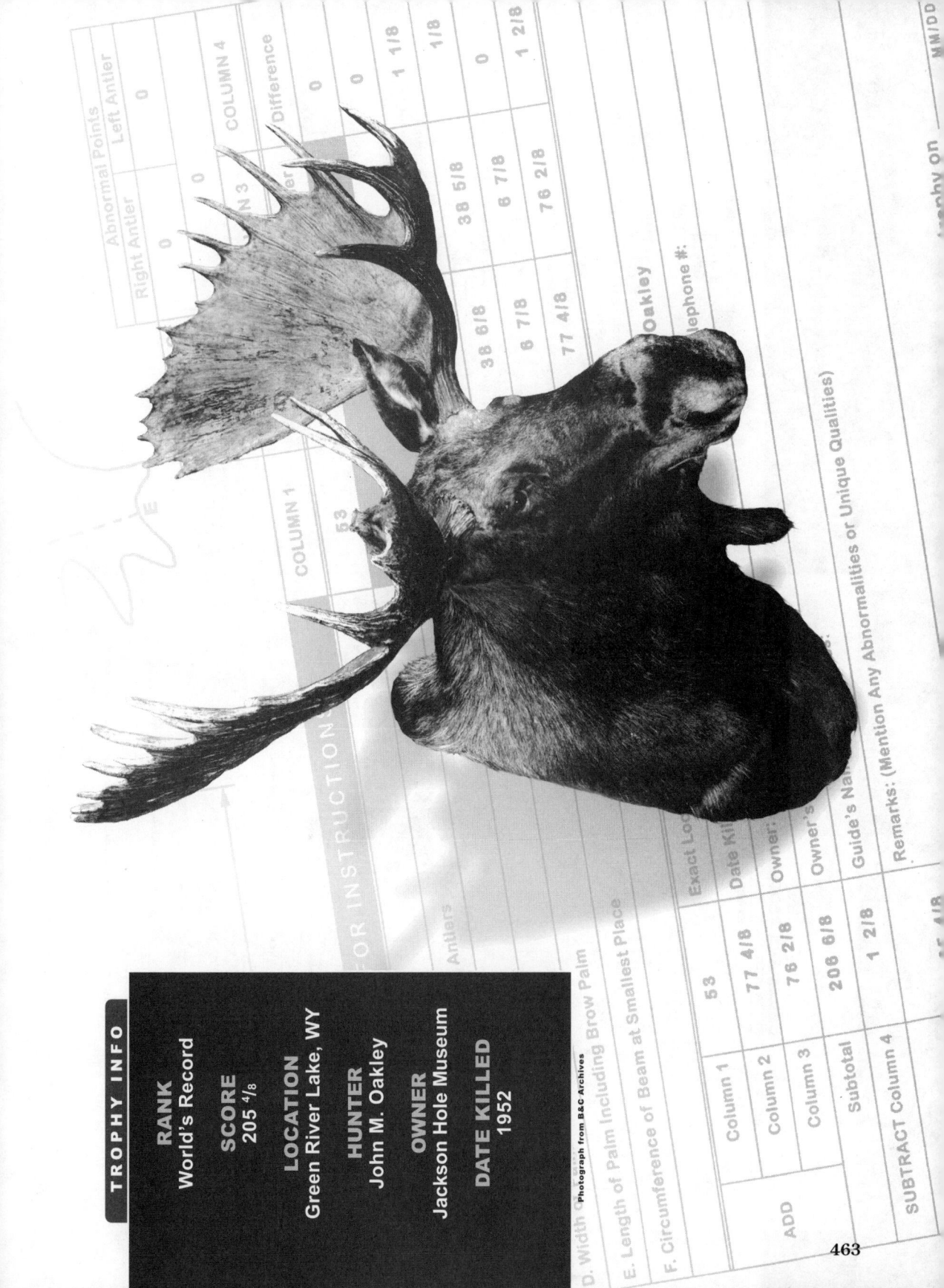

TROPHY INFO

RANK
World's Record

SCORE
205 4/8

LOCATION
Green River Lake, WY

HUNTER
John M. Oakley

OWNER
Jackson Hole Museum

DATE KILLED
1952

Photograph from B&C Archives

Measurements must be made with a 1/4-inch wide flexible steel tape to the nearest one-eighth of an inch. Enter fractional figures in eighths, without reduction. Official measurements cannot be taken until antlers have air dried for at least 60 days after animal was killed.

A. Greatest Spread is measured between perpendiculars in a straight line at a right angle to the center line of the skull.

B. Number of Abnormal Points on Both Antlers: Abnormal points are those projections originating from normal points or from the upper or lower palm surface, or from the inner edge of palm (see illustration). Abnormal points must be at least one inch long, with length exceeding width at one inch or more of length.

C. Number of Normal Points: Normal points originate from the outer edge of palm. To be counted a point, a projection must be at least one inch long, with the length exceeding width at one inch or more of length. Be sure to verify whether or not each projection qualifies as a point.

D. Width of Palm is taken in contact with the under surface of palm, at a right angle to the inner edge of palm. The line of measurement should begin and end at the midpoint of the palm edge, which gives credit for the desirable character of palm thickness.

E. Length of Palm including Brow Palm is taken in contact with the surface along the underside of the palm, **parallel** to the inner edge, from dips between points at the top to dips between points (if present) at the bottom. If a bay is present, measure across the open bay if the proper line of measurement, parallel to **inner edge**, follows this path. The line of measurement should begin and end at the midpoint of the palm edge, which gives credit for the desirable character of palm thickness.

F. Circumference of Beam at Smallest Place is taken as illustrated.

Records of
North American
Big Game

250 Station Drive
Missoula, MT 59801
(406) 542-1888

BOONE AND CROCKETT CLUB®

OFFICIAL SCORING SYSTEM FOR NORTH AMERICAN BIG GAME TROPHIES

MOOSE

MINIMUM SCORES	AWARDS	ALL-TIME
Canada	185	195
Alaska-Yukon	210	224
Wyoming	140	155

KIND OF MOOSE (check one)
☐ Canada
☐ Alaska-Yukon
■ Wyoming

Detail of Point Measurement

			NUMBER OF POINTS	Right Antler	Left Antler	Difference
				COLUMN 2	COLUMN 3	COLUMN 4
		Abnormal Points		Right Antler	Left Antler	
				0	0	

	COLUMN 1	NUMBER OF POINTS	Right Antler	Left Antler	Difference
			COLUMN 2	COLUMN 3	COLUMN 4
	53	TOTAL TO B.			
		15	15	15 6/8	0
		16 7/8	38 6/8	38 5/8	1 1/8
		6 7/8	6 7/8	1/8	
TOTALS	53	77 4/8	76 2/8	1 2/8	

SEE OTHER SIDE FOR INSTRUCTIONS		COLUMN 1	COLUMN 2	COLUMN 3	COLUMN 4
A. Greatest Spread		53			
B. Number of Abnormal Points on Both Antlers					
C. Number of Normal Points					
D. Width of Palm					
E. Length of Palm Including Brow Palm					
F. Circumference of Beam at Smallest Place					

ADD	Column 1	53	
	Column 2	77 4/8	
	Column 3	76 2/8	
	Subtotal	206 6/8	
SUBTRACT Column 4		1 2/8	
FINAL SCORE		**205 4/8**	

Exact Locality Where Killed: Green River Lake, WY

Date Killed: 1952   Hunter: John M. Oakley

Owner: Jackson Hole Museum   Telephone #:

Owner's Address:

Guide's Name and Address:

Remarks: (Mention Any Abnormalities or Unique Qualities)

I, _____, certify that I have measured this trophy on _____ MM/DD/YYYY

at _____
   STREET ADDRESS   PRINT NAME   CITY   STATE/PROVINCE

and that these measurements and data are, to the best of my knowledge and belief, made in accordance with the instructions given.

Witness: _____   Signature: _____   I.D. Number ☐

     B&C OFFICIAL MEASURER

465

WYOMING OR SHIRAS MOOSE

Alces alces shirasi

Score	Greatest Spread	Length of Palm		Width of Palm		Circumference of Beam at Smallest Place		Number of Normal Points		Locality	Hunter	Owner	Date Killed	Rank
		R	L	R	L	R	L	R	L					
205 4/8	53	38 6/8	38 5/8	16 7/8	15 6/8	6 7/8	6 7/8	15	15	Green River Lake, WY	John M. Oakley	Jackson Hole Museum	1952	1
205 1/8	56 5/8	40	40	13 3/8	14 2/8	7 7/8	7 7/8	13	13	Fremont Co., WY	Arthur E. Chandler	Arthur E. Chandler	1944	2
200 3/8	55 7/8	38 4/8	36 6/8	13 4/8	13 4/8	7	6 3/8	16	17	Lincoln Co., WY	Aldon L. Hale	Aldon L. Hale	1981	3
199 3/8	62 3/8	38 1/8	36 2/8	12 5/8	16 4/8	7 5/8	8 5/8	12	15	Elk City, ID	Reed T. Fisher	Reed T. Fisher	1957	4
199	48 4/8	40 4/8	42 1/8	12 1/8	11	7 7/8	7 6/8	17	16	Park Co., WY	Amos E. Hand	B. & M. Smith	1946	5
195 5/8	52 1/8	41 4/8	40	13	11	7	6 6/8	14	15	Atlantic Creek, WY	Alfred C. Berol	Alfred C. Berol	1933	6
195 1/8	55 7/8	43 1/8	35 6/8	15 1/8	14 5/8	7 3/8	7 2/8	14	14	Beaverhead Co., MT	C.M. Schmauch	C.M. Schmauch	1952	7
194 4/8	58 4/8	39	40	13 5/8	13	7 1/8	7	11	9	Jackson Co., CO	Jack A. Anderson	Jack A. Anderson	1995	8
188 4/8	50 2/8	34 3/8	36 4/8	15	15 3/8	6 6/8	6 7/8	13	13	Madison Co., ID	Vicki Grover	Vicki Grover	1976	9
186 3/8	56 7/8	37 1/8	38 3/8	11 3/8	11 6/8	6 4/8	6 2/8	18	10	Sublette Co., WY	Curt Mann	Curt Mann	1972	10
186 1/8	58 1/8	41 4/8	37 5/8	12 3/8	12 5/8	7 3/8	7	8	7	Ravalli Co., MT	Picked Up	G. Beechwood	1957	11
185 6/8	54	42 2/8	42	9 3/8	8 4/8	7 5/8	7 3/8	8	11	Sheridan Co., WY	Richard E. Jones, Jr.	Richard E. Jones, Jr.	1987	12
185 4/8	56 2/8	41 4/8	40	10 6/8	12 2/8	6 7/8	7	7	9	Sublette Co., WY	Robert C. Neely	Robert C. Neely	1959	13
185 1/8	47 1/8	38	36 2/8	14 2/8	14	7	6 6/8	12	14	Cache Co., UT	Lloyd E. Lish, Jr.	Lloyd E. Lish, Jr.	1993	14
185	52 2/8	37 1/8	36 1/8	12 2/8	11	6 7/8	6 6/8	13	15	Teton Co., WY	Isabelle Perry	Isabelle Perry	1961	15
184 7/8	56 3/8	33 7/8	33 6/8	13 1/8	14 1/8	7 7/8	7 3/8	11	10	Green River Lake, WY	Vern A. Bapst	Vern A. Bapst	1961	16
184 6/8	48 2/8	35 7/8	34 7/8	13 6/8	14	6 5/8	6 6/8	13	14	Bonneville Co., ID	Jacque J. Steele	Jacque J. Steele	1989	17
184 4/8	49	42 1/8	40 4/8	10 2/8	11	7	7	10	10	Fremont Co., WY	Jack C. Dow	Jack C. Dow	1948	18
183 4/8	57 2/8	36 7/8	35 4/8	11 5/8	14 4/8	7	7	9	13	Sublette Co., WY	Norb Voerding	Loaned to B&C Natl. Coll.	1940	19
183 3/8	56 7/8	35 4/8	37 7/8	13 4/8	12 2/8	7	7	12	9	Teton Co., WY	George E. Long	George E. Long	1993	20
183 2/8	45 6/8	37 5/8	38	13	13 6/8	6 1/8	6 2/8	12	15	Bear Lake Co., ID	Claudia R. Howell	Claudia R. Howell	1977	21
182 6/8	50	35 7/8	38	11 7/8	13	6 5/8	6 5/8	12	13	Spencer, ID	Charles A. Oswald	Charles A. Oswald	1957	22
182 6/8	48 2/8	34 6/8	38 3/8	12 4/8	13	6	6	14	15	Caribou Co., ID	Patricia A. Wood	Patricia A. Wood	1983	22
182 2/8	55 6/8	35 6/8	36 4/8	11 6/8	12 1/8	6 6/8	6 7/8	10	9	Teton Co., WY	Dick Gaudern	Dick Gaudern	1946	24
182	45 2/8	37 3/8	38 1/8	11 4/8	11 1/8	6 7/8	6 7/8	15	13	Sublette Co., WY	James R. Brougham	James R. Brougham	1969	25
182	51 7/8	36	34	14 2/8	11 6/8	6 6/8	6 4/8	16	13	Sheridan Co., WY	Picked Up	William E. Trapp	PR 1993	25
181 5/8	51 7/8	38 6/8	38 4/8	8 7/8	9 7/8	6 4/8	6 4/8	11	12	Bear River, UT	John W. Way	UT Div. of Wildl. Resc.	1958	27
181 3/8	53 6/8	39 1/8	40 3/8	12 6/8	10 6/8	8	7 3/8	12	7	Clearwater Co., ID	Thad L. Gilkey	Thad L. Gilkey	1997	28
180 7/8	48 3/8	37 2/8	37 1/8	12 4/8	10 2/8	6 7/8	6 7/8	15	12	Sublette Co., WY	Glen W. Beane	Glen W. Beane	1957	29
180 7/8	53 1/8	39 3/8	41	10 6/8	10 6/8	6 6/8	6 7/8	8	7	Sublette Co., WY	Donald Irwin	Donald Irwin	1976	29
180 3/8	49 3/8	32 6/8	32	13 5/8	14 6/8	6	5 7/8	14	16	Caribou Co., ID	Thomas R. McKenna	Thomas R. McKenna	1994	31
180 2/8	51 3/8	35 1/8	34 3/8	13 5/8	14 4/8	6 4/8	6 5/8	11	10	Weber Co., UT	Robert S. Mastronardi	Robert S. Mastronardi	1981	32
180	45 4/8	40 1/8	38 5/8	10 7/8	9 4/8	7 2/8	7 1/8	13	12	Green River, WY	L.W. Isaacs	L.W. Isaacs	1948	33
180	47	33 5/8	34 6/8	11 2/8	12 4/8	6 6/8	6 5/8	15	16	Pinedale, WY	Stuart W. Shepherd	Stuart W. Shepherd	1966	33
179 7/8	51 1/8	32 1/8	35 6/8	12 6/8	12 4/8	6 6/8	6 7/8	13	14	Gallatin Co., MT	John Williams	Powderhorn Sportsman Supply	1930	35
179 6/8	49 7/8	36 2/8	34 5/8	12 1/8	12 7/8	6 4/8	6 6/8	12	14	Greys River, WY	Serena Malech	Serena Malech	1972	36
179 6/8	52	35 2/8	38	12 7/8	14 3/8	6 6/8	6 7/8	9	10	Flathead Co., MT	Michael Clanton	Michael Clanton	1988	36

Score	Greatest Spread	Length of Palm R	Length of Palm L	Width of Palm R	Width of Palm L	Circ. of Beam R	Circ. of Beam L	Points R	Points L	Locality	Hunter	Owner	Date Killed	Rank
179 4/8	47 2/8	38 1/8	38 1/8	12 7/8	11 4/8	6 4/8	6 7/8	10	11	Teton Co., WY	John D. Seifert	John D. Seifert	1976	38
179 1/8	45 1/8	34 6/8	34 6/8	11 4/8	14 6/8	6 6/8	6 6/8	14	14	Nalley, WY	Stephen S. Fisher	Stephen S. Fisher	1964	39
179 1/8	49 7/8	36	38 4/8	11	11 6/8	6 5/8	6 6/8	12	11	Teton Co., WY	Marion J. Fonville	Marion J. Fonville	1987	39
178 7/8	52 5/8	37 1/8	37 1/8	10 1/8	9 7/8	6 1/8	6 2/8	11	9	Eagle Creek, WY	Loren L. Lutz	Loren L. Lutz	1956	41
178 7/8	48 3/8	42	36 3/8	12 6/8	10 4/8	7 2/8	7 1/8	15	16	Granite Co., MT	Jack A. Wilkinson	Jack A. Wilkinson	1994	41
178 6/8	55 2/8	33 4/8	31 3/8	13 3/8	10 4/8	6	5 7/8	14	14	Upper Hoback River, WY	Daniel T. Burch	Daniel T. Burch	1967	43
178 6/8	48 4/8	36 3/8	37 1/8	11 2/8	10 3/8	6 3/8	6 3/8	12	14	Sublette Co., WY	Charles Thornton	Charles Thornton	1973	43
178 5/8	46 3/8	33 5/8	31 2/8	14 6/8	16 6/8	6 4/8	6 1/8	20	11	Cache Co., UT	Barton R. Critchlow	Barton R. Critchlow	1985	45
178 5/8	47 7/8	34 3/8	38 3/8	13	12 7/8	7 1/8	7 4/8	12	9	Sheridan Co., WY	Jack A. Wilkinson	Jack A. Wilkinson	1991	45
178 3/8	58 5/8	38 3/8	36 6/8	8 4/8	9 3/8	6 7/8	6 7/8	11	11	Sublette Co., WY	Robert Dennis	Robert Dennis	1969	47
178 2/8	49 4/8	32 2/8	32 1/8	15 4/8	15 1/8	6 5/8	6 4/8	15	9	Sublette Co., WY	Ross J. Berlin	Ross J. Berlin	1972	48
178 1/8	50 3/8	37	36 5/8	11 4/8	10 6/8	6 6/8	6 6/8	12	12	Buffalo Park, WY	Walter Russell	Walter Russell	1956	49
178 1/8	49 7/8	36 7/8	38 4/8	12 6/8	10 2/8	6 4/8	6 4/8	11	11	Teton Co., WY	Harold L. Roby	Garvice E. Roby	1961	49
178 1/8	51 2/8	37 2/8	37 4/8	9 5/8	13 3/8	7	7 1/8	11	13	Madison Co., ID	Kevin W. Nichols	Kevin W. Nichols	1987	49
178	50 2/8	37	33 1/8	12 5/8	14 7/8	7	7	9	14	Thorofare River, WY	Earl Brahler	H.E. Wolfe	1959	51
177 6/8	49	35	34 3/8	14 7/8	13 7/8	6 7/8	6 2/8	12	12	Big Piney, WY	George F. Stewart, Jr.	George F. Stewart, Jr.	1965	52
177 6/8	52 3/8	30 1/8	31 2/8	14	11 5/8	6 5/8	6 5/8	14	11	Green River, WY	Walter C. Motta, Sr.	Walter C. Motta, Sr.	1956	52
177 5/8	51 7/8	38 1/8	35 3/8	11 2/8	11 4/8	6 6/8	6 7/8	12	12	Teton Co., WY	John R. Blanton	John R. Blanton	1985	54
177 5/8	51 4/8	33 3/8	33 2/8	11 4/8	10 7/8	6 4/8	6 1/8	14	14	Park Co., MT	Lawrence A. Allestad	Lawrence A. Allestad	1961	54
177 2/8	42 2/8	41 1/8	37	9 5/8	11 2/8	6 7/8	6 7/8	13	12	Jackson Co., CO	Steven P. Kugler	Steven P. Kugler	1995	56
177 2/8	50 3/8	35	34 2/8	11 4/8	12 5/8	6 1/8	5 7/8	14	12	Big Piney, WY	Mrs. Robert R. Jamieson	Mrs. Robert R. Jamieson	1966	56
177 1/8	53	32 4/8	32	11 6/8	11	7 3/8	7 2/8	14	10	Teton Co., WY	Elgin T. Gates	Elgin T. Gates	1947	58
177	50 5/8	36 4/8	37 6/8	11	11 4/8	6 5/8	6 1/8	10	12	Teton Co., WY	Jack G. Binkley	Jack G. Binkley	1977	59
176 7/8	48 4/8	35	35 4/8	10 4/8	11 2/8	6 5/8	6 7/8	12	11	Beaverhead Co., MT	Charles L. Walters	Charles L. Walters	1966	60
176 6/8	49 5/8	35 1/8	36 4/8	15 4/8	11 2/8	6 1/8	6 4/8	11	12	Caribou Co., ID	Justin P. Jones	Justin P. Jones	1995	61
176 5/8	50 6/8	35 4/8	33 5/8	10 7/8	12 6/8	7 3/8	7 3/8	11	12	Bonneville Co., ID	Diggs Lewis	Diggs Lewis	1972	62
176 4/8	47	35 1/8	34 4/8	12	11 4/8	6 2/8	6 3/8	13	14	Bingham Co., ID	Robert L. Johnston	Robert L. Johnston	1994	63
176 4/8	53 1/8	33	33 5/8	13 6/8	12 1/8	6 1/8	6 1/8	11	13	Bonneville Co., ID	Michael B. Messick	Michael B. Messick	1988	63
176 3/8	50 4/8	33 3/8	35	12 4/8	13	6 3/8	6 3/8	12	12	Cache Co., UT	Steven A. Barnard	Steven A. Barnard	1985	65
176 2/8	50 5/8	31 4/8	31 1/8	12 3/8	10 6/8	6 2/8	6 2/8	13	13	Teton Co., WY	Richard E. Green	Richard E. Green	1988	66
176 1/8	39 6/8	36 4/8	36 4/8	12 4/8	14 3/8	7	6 7/8	14	14	Weber Co., UT	Romaine L. Marshall	Romaine L. Marshall	1992	67
176	41 6/8	34 4/8	35 7/8	13 2/8	10 5/8	6 2/8	6 3/8	14	13	Spokane Co., WA	Robert A. Cox	Robert A. Cox	1973	68
175 6/8	62 5/8	29 2/8	29 5/8	10	12 5/8	7 2/8	7 1/8	10	13	Lincoln Co., WY	Picked Up	B&C National Collection	1992	69
175 3/8	50	31 6/8	34 6/8	11 6/8	11 4/8	7 1/8	7 2/8	12	13	Park Co., CO	Leon Gordon	Leon Gordon	1967	70
175 2/8	47 4/8	35 4/8	34 6/8	11 4/8	12 2/8	7 1/8	7 1/8	11	14	Hoback River, WY	Virgil A. Lair	Virgil A. Lair	1996	71
175 2/8	48 3/8	36 3/8	35 6/8	11 4/8	12 1/8	6 2/8	6 1/8	10	15	Squaw Creek, WY	George Tolan	George Tolan	1964	71
175 1/8	46 7/8	33 7/8	37 4/8	11 7/8	11 2/8	6 3/8	6 4/8	12	11	Park Co., MT	Denton C. Barker	Triangle C Ranch	1969	73
175 1/8	54 4/8	34	34	10	11 1/8	6 2/8	6 2/8	10	13	Teton Co., WY	Thomas J. Radoumis	Thomas J. Radoumis	1974	73
175	45 3/8	35 4/8	36 3/8	12 6/8	13 7/8	7 2/8	7 1/8	11	7	Idaho Co., ID	John W. Whalen, Jr.	John W. Whalen, Jr.	1988	75
174 7/8	49 5/8	37 1/8	35 7/8	13 7/8	11 5/8	7 4/8	7 4/8	12	11	Livingston, MT	Unknown	Brad Davis	PR 1995	76
174 7/8	50 2/8	33 1/8	34 3/8	13	9 5/8	6 4/8	6 4/8	8	11	Park Co., MT	Bill Cutler	Bill Cutler	1964	76
174 6/8	50 6/8	36	36 5/8	10 4/8	11	6 3/8	6 7/8	10	12	Park Co., MT	Picked Up	Duane A. Ferrell	1973	78
174 6/8	48	33 5/8	36 1/8	14 3/8	11	6 6/8	6 6/8	12	13	Gallatin Co., MT	L.C. Hulslander	L.C. Hulslander & K. Bennet	1981	78
174 4/8	45 4/8	37 2/8	36 3/8	11 5/8	10 1/8	7	7 1/8	11	13	Teton Co., WY	John F. Cross	John F. Cross	1965	81
174 4/8	46	35 1/8	33 2/8	11 4/8	11	7	7	13	13	Park Co., WY	Walter L. Gale	Walter L. Gale	1983	81
174 4/8	50 6/8	36 3/8	34 1/8	9 7/8	9 2/8	7 4/8	7 5/8	11	12	Lincoln Co., MT	Unknown	Mike Kropp	PR 1987	81

WYOMING OR SHIRAS MOOSE

Alces alces shirasi

Score	Greatest Spread	Length of Palm R	L	Width of Palm R	L	Circumference of Beam at Smallest Place R	L	Number of Normal Points R	L	Locality	Hunter	Owner	Date Killed	Rank
174 3/8	58 1/8	32 4/8	29 3/8	12 5/8	12 5/8	6 2/8	6 1/8	13	10	Idaho Co., ID	Paul L. White	Paul L. White	1981	84
174 2/8	46	32 2/8	32 1/8	14 3/8	13 3/8	6 5/8	6 5/8	12	14	Teton Co., WY	John R. Harju	John R. Harju	1980	85
173 7/8	46 5/8	37 3/8	36 7/8	9 6/8	10 3/8	7	7	10	11	Gallatin Co., MT	Rolf S. Dull	Rolf S. Dull	1988	86
173 6/8	50 4/8	30 6/8	34 4/8	13 7/8	13 3/8	7 4/8	7 4/8	10	12	Atlantic Creek, WY	Clyde Ormond	Clyde Ormond	1955	87
173 6/8	58	35 2/8	32 5/8	10 4/8	12 2/8	6 6/8	7	11	8	Teton Co., WY	David A. Yearsley	David A. Yearsley	1994	87
173 5/8	47 7/8	40 1/8	35 6/8	11 7/8	10 6/8	7 3/8	7 5/8	12	9	Weber Co., UT	C. Brent Morgan	C. Brent Morgan	1985	89
173 4/8	45 2/8	37 2/8	39 4/8	11 1/8	11 2/8	6 6/8	6 7/8	9	9	Sheridan Co., WY	Picked Up	D.V. Collis & R.R. Smith	1987	90
173 3/8	54 5/8	32 5/8	31 2/8	10 6/8	10 3/8	7 6/8	7 6/8	10	10	Flathead Co., MT	Tom Scheer	Tom Scheer	1976	91
173 2/8	58 4/8	34 4/8	34 1/8	8 4/8	10 4/8	6 6/8	6 6/8	8	10	Fremont Co., ID	Lula O. Jackson	Lula O. Jackson	1994	92
173 1/8	48 3/8	34 6/8	38	8 4/8	10	7 1/8	7 1/8	12	12	Madison Co., MT	Thomas L. Carter	Thomas L. Carter	1955	93
173 1/8	52 1/8	32 6/8	34 4/8	11 6/8	11 6/8	6	6	12	12	Sublette Co., WY	John C. Eklund	John C. Eklund	1970	93
173 1/8	48 3/8	35 5/8	35 2/8	11 6/8	10	6 1/8	6 1/8	11	11	Teton Co., WY	Raymond E. Pittman	Raymond E. Pittman	1995	93
173	49 4/8	33 1/8	35 3/8	11 2/8	12	6 4/8	6 3/8	11	13	Buffalo River, WY	Robert L. Hitch	Robert L. Hitch	1951	96
173	46	33 4/8	34	12 3/8	13	6 5/8	6 6/8	11	11	Cache Co., UT	Michael C. Leonhardt	Michael C. Leonhardt	1987	96
173	47 6/8	35 4/8	36 2/8	11	11 4/8	6 1/8	6 2/8	11	11	Flathead Co., MT	David A. Rose	David A. Rose	1991	96
173	53 6/8	33 4/8	31 1/8	13	11 4/8	6	6	11	12	Lincoln Co., MT	Ronald R. Higgins	Ronald R. Higgins	1994	96
172 6/8	41	35 1/8	35	11 3/8	11 3/8	6 4/8	6 4/8	13	13	Bridger Natl. For., WY	J.D. Bradley	J.D. Bradley	1970	100
172 4/8	42	35 4/8	33 1/8	12 4/8	14 4/8	6 5/8	6 6/8	13	17	Lincoln Co., MT	Tom DeShazer	Tom DeShazer	1956	101
172 4/8	50	32 3/8	36 4/8	10 1/8	10 5/8	6 6/8	6 6/8	12	12	Kilgore Creek, WY	Bill Jhun	Bill Jhun	1967	101
172 3/8	44 1/8	37 1/8	38 6/8	12	10 7/8	6 1/8	6 2/8	10	10	Pinedale, WY	Basil C. Bradbury	Basil C. Bradbury	1969	103
172 3/8	43 3/8	36	37	11	11 1/8	7 4/8	7 4/8	10	10	Silver Bow Co., MT	Derrold O. Paige	Derrold O. Paige	1995	103
172	51	36 6/8	38 4/8	8 7/8	9 6/8	6 7/8	6 7/8	10	12	Teton Co., WY	William D. Stewart	William D. Stewart	1954	105
172	46 2/8	35 7/8	38 5/8	9 3/8	10	6 5/8	6 5/8	11	11	Teton Co., WY	Holland C. McHenry	Holland C. McHenry	1980	105
171 7/8	58 3/8	30	33 5/8	9 5/8	9 5/8	6 1/8	6 1/8	11	13	Weber Co., UT	Kent G. Yearsley	Kent G. Yearsley	1981	107
171 7/8	52 3/8	33 2/8	33 6/8	11 1/8	11 1/8	6 7/8	6 5/8	10	11	Jackson Co., CO	Nancy A. Sommer	Nancy A. Sommer	1994	107
171 5/8	49 1/8	32 1/8	31 6/8	12 5/8	12 2/8	7 2/8	8	10	11	Fremont Co., ID	Rodney Chandler	Rodney Chandler	1967	109
171 3/8	51 5/8	37 7/8	37 2/8	9 5/8	10	7	7	8	6	Cache Co., UT	Picked Up	Ben J. Rossetto	PR 1975	110
171	50	34 4/8	37 5/8	10 3/8	10	6 6/8	6 6/8	9	9	Silver Bow Co., MT	Martin E. Carlson	Martin E. Carlson	1980	111
171 2/8	49 2/8	34 5/8	32	10 6/8	11 1/8	7 1/8	7 1/8	9	9	Teton Co., WY	Keith H. Hanson	Keith H. Hanson	1972	112
170 7/8	45 7/8	37 2/8	38 3/8	10 2/8	10 3/8	7 1/8	7	8	10	Lincoln Co., MT	Bruce C. Todd	Bruce C. Todd	1982	113
170 7/8	47 7/8	35 4/8	34 4/8	10 4/8	8 4/8	7 4/8	7 4/8	13	11	Sublette Co., WY	Don L. Corley	Don L. Corley	1983	113
170 6/8	50 2/8	35 6/8	34 2/8	8 7/8	11 7/8	6 1/8	6 1/8	12	11	Bridger Natl. For., WY	Unknown	Neil Blair	1965	115
170 6/8	47 6/8	38 1/8	35 1/8	9 7/8	11 6/8	7 4/8	7 5/8	9	12	Sublette Co., WY	Kenneth E. Myers	Kenneth E. Myers	1968	115
170 6/8	54 2/8	39	29 6/8	11 6/8	11 2/8	6 5/8	6 2/8	12	11	Cache Co., UT	Jim Vanderbeek	Jim Vanderbeek	1990	115
170 4/8	46 6/8	34 3/8	34 3/8	9 7/8	9 7/8	7 6/8	7 5/8	12	10	Warm Spring Creek, WY	Herbert L. Palmer	Herbert L. Palmer	1951	118
170 4/8	45 4/8	32 4/8	31	13 5/8	12 6/8	7 6/8	7 5/8	13	13	Flathead Co., MT	Arthur M. Nelson	Arthur M. Nelson	1987	118
170 4/8	49 2/8	35 5/8	34 6/8	11 3/8	10 3/8	6 4/8	6 4/8	11	9	Teton Co., WY	W.R. Titterington	W.R. Titterington	1989	118
170 4/8	51 2/8	33 7/8	34	9 3/8	12 7/8	6 3/8	6 5/8	10	11	Madison Co., MT	Michael W. Gallagher	Michael W. Gallagher	1996	118

Score										Locality	Owner	Hunter	Date	Rank
170 3/8	39 7/8	35 5/8	34 7/8	10 7/8	12 2/8	6 4/8	6 5/8	13	13	Lincoln Co., MT	Picked Up	Wayne Lundberg	1974	122
170	48 2/8	35	35 4/8	10 3/8	11 6/8	6 4/8	6 4/8	9	10	Bonneville Co., ID	Dean L. Brown	Dean L. Brown	1987	123
170	44 2/8	34 5/8	35	11 6/8	11 5/8	6 5/8	6 5/8	11	10	Teton Co., WY	Hazer K. Bulkley	Hazer K. Bulkley	1994	123
169 7/8	47 1/8	33 2/8	34 6/8	10 6/8	10 3/8	7	6 6/8	11	10	Lincoln Co., MT	William A. Stevens	William A. Stevens	1967	125
169 7/8	50 1/8	32 2/8	33 1/8	10 7/8	11 2/8	7 2/8	6 6/8	10	12	Weber Co., UT	Riley A. Bushman	Riley A. Bushman	1969	125
169 6/8	54 4/8	27 6/8	32 7/8	10 6/8	10 5/8	6 4/8	6 2/8	15	13	Wilson, WY	Howard Bennage	Howard Bennage	1958	127
169 5/8	52 5/8	32 1/8	30 4/8	12 3/8	11 1/8	7	6 7/8	10	11	Merna, WY	C. Von De Graaff	C. Von De Graaff	1959	128
169 4/8	40 6/8	35	35 2/8	12 1/8	11 3/8	7	7	11	11	Dubois, WY	Albert Wagner, Jr.	Albert Wagner, Jr.	1962	129
169 3/8	42 3/8	30 7/8	34	12	11 4/8	6 2/8	6 1/8	15	15	Lincoln Co., WY	Vannetta Marshinsky	Vannetta Marshinsky	1968	130
169 2/8	53 6/8	33 2/8	34 7/8	10 5/8	10 5/8	5 7/8	6 1/8	8	10	Lincoln Co., MT	Frank J. O'Connor	Frank J. O'Connor	1982	131
169 2/8	53	31 6/8	33 5/8	10 7/8	11 7/8	6 4/8	6 5/8	9	12	Park Co., MT	Sam A. Terakedis	Sam A. Terakedis	1995	131
169 1/8	54 5/8	31 4/8	31 1/8	9 4/8	9 4/8	6 2/8	6 2/8	9	12	Clark Co., ID	Carolyn Karvinen	Carolyn Karvinen	1966	133
169 1/8	48 1/8	33 4/8	33	12	13 1/8	6 4/8	6 4/8	9	11	Bonneville Co., ID	Picked Up	Michael J. Zwicker	1986	133
169 1/8	47 3/8	34 1/8	35 2/8	11 1/8	12 5/8	6 6/8	6 5/8	9	12	Flathead Co., MT	Frank J. Telling	Frank J. Telling	1994	133
169	52	33 3/8	33 4/8	8 6/8	8 7/8	7 3/8	7 3/8	9	9	Jackson Hole, WY	Shirley Straley	Shirley Straley	1963	136
169	46 4/8	36	33 5/8	11 4/8	12 7/8	6 2/8	6 1/8	7	9	Caribou Co., ID	Richard M. Hydzik	Richard M. Hydzik	1988	136
168 6/8	58	30 4/8	36	11 6/8	11 7/8	6 6/8	6 5/8	11	7	Park Co., WY	John A. Mahoney, Jr.	John A. Mahoney, Jr.	1957	138
168 6/8	48 2/8	36 3/8	36 3/8	10 2/8	10 3/8	6 6/8	6 6/8	12	10	Sublette Co., WY	Larry Petersen	Larry Petersen	1964	138
168 6/8	51 6/8	31 5/8	37 2/8	9 7/8	10	7 2/8	7 2/8	10	13	Sheridan Co., WY	James W. Owens	James W. Owens	1987	138
168 6/8	50	33 5/8	33 7/8	10 6/8	10 3/8	6 3/8	6 3/8	9	10	Park Co., MT	Jerry R. Blaquiere	Jerry R. Blaquiere	1992	138
168 3/8	43 3/8	36 2/8	39 6/8	13 2/8	12 4/8	6 6/8	6 6/8	13	7	Park Co., MT	Victoria L. Miller	Victoria L. Miller	1977	142
168 3/8	47 3/8	34 4/8	35 7/8	9 4/8	9 7/8	6 4/8	6 4/8	9	10	Teton Co., WY	Clyde E. Harnden	Clyde E. Harnden	1991	142
168 2/8	46 4/8	36 5/8	34 2/8	14	14 3/8	6 1/8	6 1/8	14	14	Bonneville Co., ID	Norman E. Stanley	Norman E. Stanley	1991	144
167 7/8	43 5/8	39 4/8	33 2/8	10 5/8	11	6 4/8	6 4/8	13	12	Gros Ventre, WY	Bonita Young	Bonita Young	1960	145
167 6/8	51	34 2/8	33 6/8	8 3/8	9 4/8	6 2/8	6 2/8	10	11	Teton Co., WY	Roger Wilmot	Roger Wilmot	1972	146
167 6/8	44	33 7/8	37	12 7/8	11 6/8	6 2/8	6 2/8	10	10	Beaverhead Co., MT	Peter A. Parini	Peter A. Parini	1981	146
167 4/8	47 4/8	34 6/8	32 4/8	11	11	6 4/8	6 4/8	10	10	Park Co., WY	Leo C. Chapel	Leo C. Chapel	1967	148
167 4/8	52	31 1/8	31 6/8	10 6/8	11	6 5/8	6 5/8	11	10	Summit Co., UT	L. Irvin Barnhart	L. Irvin Barnhart	1985	148
167 4/8	44 6/8	32	30 4/8	14 4/8	13 4/8	6 3/8	6 3/8	11	10	Morgan Co., UT	Roger L. Gregg	Roger L. Gregg	1991	148
167 3/8	43 7/8	37 5/8	33 7/8	12	10 1/8	6 6/8	6 6/8	12	11	Lincoln Co., MT	Timothy G. Coulson	Timothy G. Coulson	1974	151
167 3/8	49 1/8	36 5/8	30 5/8	12	12	6 4/8	6 4/8	12	10	Bonneville Co., ID	John K. Ryan	John K. Ryan	1984	151
167 1/8	45 1/8	32 6/8	34	11 7/8	10 6/8	6 4/8	6 4/8	11	11	Teton Co., WY	L. Stanley	L. Stanley	1964	153
167 1/8	48 1/8	32 7/8	30 7/8	10 7/8	11	6 7/8	6 7/8	11	11	Sublette Co., WY	Bob Housholder	Bob Housholder	1968	153
167 1/8	48 3/8	32 7/8	36 1/8	10	9 6/8	6 6/8	6 6/8	10	10	Caribou Co., ID	Ernest Saxton	Ernest Saxton	1969	153
167 1/8	46 7/8	30 5/8	31 3/8	12 1/8	12 4/8	7 2/8	7 2/8	12	12	Clearwater Co., ID	Richard E. Hardy	Richard E. Hardy	1987	153
167	46 6/8	35 4/8	35 4/8	8 7/8	12 1/8	6 6/8	6 6/8	12	9	Sublette Co., WY	Picked Up	Robert Dory	1976	157
167	46 2/8	38 6/8	34 2/8	9 5/8	10 5/8	6 4/8	6 4/8	10	13	Fremont Co., WY	LeRoy Castagno	LeRoy Castagno	1977	157
167	44 6/8	33 5/8	32 5/8	11 1/8	11 6/8	6 3/8	6 3/8	12	11	Lincoln Co., MT	Jeff Wisehart	Jeff Wisehart	1983	157
167	44 2/8	35 1/8	35 2/8	12 3/8	10 5/8	6 5/8	6 5/8	9	12	Sheridan Co., WY	David V. Collis	David V. Collis	1987	157
167	45 4/8	35 4/8	34 4/8	10 4/8	10 7/8	6 1/8	6 1/8	10	9	Broadwater Co., MT	Mac Vosbeck	Mac Vosbeck	1996	157
166 7/8	51 1/8	33 7/8	33 7/8	9 7/8	10	6 3/8	6 3/8	8	10	Gallatin Co., MT	Rodney R. Richardson	Rodney R. Richardson	1979	162
166 7/8	48 3/8	32 7/8	32 6/8	10 1/8	9	6 5/8	6 4/8	11	11	Gallatin Co., MT	Albert D. Williams	Albert D. Williams	1986	162
166 7/8	53 5/8	31 5/8	32 2/8	9 1/8	10 1/8	6 7/8	7	12	9	Bonneville Co., ID	Craig A. McBride	Craig A. McBride	1993	162
166 6/8	47 2/8	33	32 7/8	13 5/8	12 2/8	5 5/8	6 5/8	8	8	Lincoln Co., WY	Nancy J. Combs	Nancy J. Combs	1986	165
166 6/8	46 2/8	36 2/8	37 6/8	9 1/8	9 1/8	5 7/8	5 7/8	9	9	Weber Co., UT	George V. Aalberg	George V. Aalberg	1991	165
166 6/8	49 2/8	29 5/8	30 1/8	12	13 2/8	6 1/8	6 1/8	11	12	Bonneville Co., ID	LeRoy C. Meyer	LeRoy C. Meyer	1995	165
166 5/8	48 7/8	34 4/8	36	7 5/8	10 3/8	7 4/8	7 4/8	10	11	Teton Co., WY	R.G. De Graff	R.G. De Graff	1963	168

WYOMING OR SHIRAS MOOSE

Alces alces shirasi

Score	Greatest Spread	Length of Palm R	L	Width of Palm R	L	Circumference of Beam at Smallest Place R	L	Number of Normal Points R	L	Locality	Hunter	Owner	Date Killed	Rank
166 5/8	46 7/8	34 3/8	33 6/8	10 2/8	11 4/8	6 7/8	7 1/8	10	9	Lincoln Co., WY	James A. Grivet, Jr.	James A. Grivet, Jr.	1993	168
166 4/8	50	28 5/8	28 4/8	13 4/8	15 4/8	6 2/8	6 4/8	10	11	Bonneville Co., ID	Daniel J. Duggan	Daniel J. Duggan	1982	170
166 4/8	51 2/8	30 3/8	33 2/8	13 1/8	13 2/8	6 1/8	6 3/8	11	8	Caribou Co., ID	Diane G. Hall	Diane G. Hall	1985	170
166 3/8	50 1/8	34 2/8	32 4/8	8 7/8	9 7/8	6 6/8	6 6/8	10	10	Teton Co., WY	Terry Nilsen	Terry Nilsen	1970	172
166 3/8	48 5/8	37	35 2/8	11 6/8	9 6/8	6	5 7/8	8	11	Bonner Co., ID	Brian T. Farley	Brian T. Farley	1977	172
166 3/8	50 3/8	35 2/8	33 5/8	10 6/8	9 2/8	6 2/8	6 1/8	9	9	Lincoln Co., WY	T. Jefferson Cook	T. Jefferson Cook	1988	172
166 2/8	43 4/8	31 2/8	32 4/8	14 1/8	15 1/8	6	6 3/8	10	9	Morgan Co., UT	Michael F. Gleason	Michael F. Gleason	1990	175
166 1/8	46 3/8	34 4/8	29 7/8	13 6/8	13	6 2/8	6	11	11	Caribou Co., ID	Robert L. Christophersen	Robert L. Christophersen	1995	176
166	48 4/8	35 4/8	32 4/8	9 3/8	13	6 7/8	7	10	10	Tosi Creek, WY	Roscoe O. McKeehan	Roscoe O. McKeehan	1960	177
166	47	30	31	12	11 4/8	7	7	11	13	Glade Creek, WY	E.E. Hosafros	E. E. Hosafros	1961	177
166	48 4/8	34 1/8	33 5/8	14 7/8	9 7/8	6 2/8	6 3/8	10	9	Bonneville Co., ID	E. Ray Robinson	E. Ray Robinson	1977	177
166	42 4/8	39 6/8	38 2/8	8 7/8	9 1/8	6 5/8	6 7/8	9	8	Flathead Co., MT	Kathy A. Nagel	Kathy A. Nagel	1988	177
165 7/8	52 5/8	29 4/8	29 4/8	11	11	7 2/8	7 1/8	11	9	Clark Co., ID	Elden L. Perry	Elden L. Perry	1975	181
165 6/8	48 4/8	32	30 2/8	13 2/8	13 3/8	7 2/8	7 1/8	8	9	Bridger Lake, WY	Hugh W. Mildren	Larry Arndt	1959	182
165 6/8	48 4/8	33	33 5/8	11	11	6 5/8	6 6/8	8	9	Sublette Co., WY	Ray Snow	Don Boyer	1959	182
165 6/8	45	34 3/8	33 1/8	12 3/8	13 5/8	6	5 7/8	12	9	Weber Co., UT	Wayne J. Yamashita	Wayne J. Yamashita	1985	182
165 4/8	46 2/8	32 4/8	36 2/8	9 3/8	11 2/8	6 6/8	7	11	13	Sublette Co., WY	Paul A. Graham	Paul A. Graham	1970	185
165 4/8	51 2/8	32 3/8	33 5/8	9 5/8	9 2/8	6 4/8	6 5/8	12	9	Sheridan Co., WY	Jerry K. Hutchinson	Jerry K. Hutchinson	1993	185
165 4/8	50 6/8	31 4/8	31 4/8	11 3/8	11	5 7/8	5 7/8	11	9	Gallatin Co., MT	Jerry D. Johnson	Jerry D. Johnson	1994	185
165 3/8	53 7/8	39 3/8	33 6/8	8 6/8	7 4/8	6 4/8	6 6/8	11	8	Lincoln Co., WY	Brad H. Jacobs	Brad H. Jacobs	1990	188
165 2/8	43 6/8	32 2/8	32 2/8	10 4/8	12 6/8	6	6	12	13	Buffalo River, WY	Jock H. White	Jock H. White	1953	189
165 2/8	47 6/8	32 4/8	32 1/8	12	12 4/8	6 4/8	6 5/8	8	10	Fremont Co., ID	Harvey W. Lewis	Harvey W. Lewis	1964	189
165 2/8	45 4/8	27 7/8	28 4/8	14 2/8	14 4/8	5 6/8	5 7/8	12	12	Lincoln Co., WY	Ryley Z. Dawson	Ryley Z. Dawson	1969	189
165 2/8	43 6/8	33 3/8	32 1/8	11 6/8	10	6 5/8	6 5/8	14	12	Dubois, WY	Vernon Limbach	Vernon Limbach	1969	189
165 1/8	47 1/8	34	35 4/8	9	9 2/8	7	7 2/8	9	12	Lincoln Co., WY	Bern Whittaker	Bern Whittaker	1964	193
165 1/8	45 1/8	29 7/8	31	10 4/8	11	5 7/8	5 5/8	14	14	Teton Co., WY	Joseph M. Griset	Joseph M. Griset	1969	193
165 1/8	48 7/8	32	36	9 5/8	11 2/8	6 4/8	6 4/8	11	10	Lincoln Co., WY	Kenneth Madsen	Kenneth Madsen	1974	193
165	46 4/8	36 6/8	38 6/8	10 1/8	9 2/8	6 2/8	6 3/8	7	11	Gallatin Co., MT	Picked Up	Ray E. Brooks	1961	196
165	51 2/8	35	32	9 7/8	9 3/8	7 5/8	7 4/8	9	8	Fremont Co., WY	Charles A. Boyle	Charles A. Boyle	1965	196
164 7/8	52 1/8	30 2/8	34 1/8	9 7/8	9 5/8	6 4/8	6 4/8	10	10	Sublette Co., WY	Edmund J. Giebel	Edmund J. Giebel	1971	198
164 7/8	45 1/8	33 4/8	37 3/8	10	11 2/8	7 4/8	7 3/8	10	9	Fremont Co., ID	David F. Burk	Eugene H. Putnam	1973	198
164 7/8	47 3/8	38 1/8	31 4/8	11 3/8	11	7 3/8	7 2/8	9	10	Sheridan Co., WY	John D. Frost	John D. Frost	1988	198
164 7/8	54 3/8	33	28 2/8	12 6/8	11 3/8	6 5/8	6 6/8	11	9	Salt Lake Co., UT	Elizabeth Burrows	Elizabeth Burrows	1995	198
164 6/8	41	33 3/8	34 6/8	12 4/8	10 6/8	6 6/8	7	11	13	Bonneville Co., ID	Stanley M. Grover	Stanley M. Grover	1996	202
164 5/8	50 3/8	34 1/8	32 7/8	8 6/8	9 1/8	6 7/8	6 4/8	9	9	Pinedale, WY	Clifford G. McConnell	Clifford G. McConnell	1959	203
164 5/8	47 5/8	29 7/8	32 1/8	10 4/8	10 5/8	6 1/8	6 2/8	16	12	Teton Co., WY	Ernest L. Cummings	Ernest L. Cummings	1960	203
164 5/8	50 7/8	33	33 4/8	9 6/8	8 4/8	6 3/8	6 4/8	10	9	Lincoln Co., WY	Vernal J. Larsen	Vernal J. Larsen	1973	203
164 4/8	51 6/8	30 6/8	30 1/8	9 6/8	11 7/8	5 4/8	5 4/8	11	11	Flathead Co., MT	Picked Up	John Castles	PR 1954	206

Score	Greatest Spread	Length of Palm R	Length of Palm L	Width of Palm R	Width of Palm L	Circ. of Beam R	Circ. of Beam L	Points R	Points L	Locality	Hunter	Owner	Date	Rank
164 4/8	51 4/8	32	30 4/8	10 1/8	10 4/8	6 4/8	6 3/8	11	10	Cache Co., UT	Bruce N. Moss	Bruce N. Moss	1977	206
164 4/8	49	32 7/8	32	13	11 2/8	6 4/8	6 7/8	8	9	Morgan Co., UT	Craig S. Engelke	Craig S. Engelke	1987	206
164 4/8	40 4/8	32 6/8	34	11	10 7/8	6 2/8	6 5/8	12	10	Sheridan Co., WY	Warren D. Mischke	Warren D. Mischke	1991	206
164 4/8	49 4/8	34	34	10 3/8	9 5/8	6 3/8	6 2/8	8	12	Summit Co., UT	Roger P. Deschaine	Roger P. Deschaine	1994	211
164 3/8	48 5/8	31	36 1/8	10	10 3/8	7	7	11	11	Uinta Co., WY	Richard J. Gilmore	Richard J. Gilmore	1986	211
164 3/8	48 5/8	30 4/8	31 5/8	13	8 3/8	6 4/8	6 7/8	10	10	Cache Co., UT	Robert L. Jacobsen	Robert L. Jacobsen	1994	213
164 2/8	48 4/8	34	34 2/8	11	7 7/8	6 4/8	6 6/8	9	9	Spread Creek, WY	George Malouf	George Malouf	1966	213
164 2/8	51 4/8	34	34 6/8	7 7/8	10 2/8	6 4/8	6 4/8	8	8	Park Co., WY	Burton H. Ward	Burton H. Ward	1984	213
164 2/8	40	35 7/8	37 6/8	11 6/8	11 5/8	6 5/8	6 7/8	10	10	Teton Co., WY	Don L. Corley	Don L. Corley	1985	213
164 2/8	41 6/8	34 4/8	38 2/8	10 7/8	10 3/8	6 7/8	7	10	10	Morgan Co., UT	S. Kim Bonnett	S. Kim Bonnett	1986	213
164 2/8	51 6/8	32 3/8	30	11 3/8	9	7	6 5/8	9	9	Cache Co., UT	Karl E. Engelke	Karl E. Engelke	1987	213
164 2/8	43 6/8	34 2/8	33 5/8	10 3/8	7 1/8	6 5/8	7	11	12	Sublette Co., WY	Kenneth D. Rupp	Kenneth D. Rupp	1988	213
164 2/8	54 6/8	32 1/8	34 1/8	8 7/8	10 1/8	7	6 3/8	9	9	Teton Co., WY	Rick L. Parish	Rick L. Parish	1996	220
164 1/8	52 5/8	31 1/8	28 5/8	8 6/8	10 6/8	6 3/8	6 7/8	12	12	Skull Crack, UT	Blaine E. Worthen	Blaine E. Worthen	1975	221
164	55	26 3/8	29 3/8	11	11 4/8	6 7/8	7	12	12	Wilson, WY	V. Tullis & A. Van Noye	Victor Tullis	1955	221
164	43 4/8	30 4/8	31 3/8	13 2/8	10 3/8	6 2/8	6 3/8	12	12	Teton Co., WY	Clifford H. Rockhold	Clifford H. Rockhold	1984	223
163 7/8	49 7/8	31 4/8	34 5/8	11 3/8	11 6/8	6 3/8	6	11	9	Park Co., MT	William D. West	William D. West	1990	224
163 6/8	45 2/8	32 4/8	30 4/8	12	11	6	6	11	11	Teton Co., WY	Robert D. Rice	Robert D. Rice	1982	224
163 6/8	45 6/8	31 6/8	33	11 2/8	10	6 4/8	6 2/8	10	11	Grand Co., CO	Steve R. Countway	Steve R. Countway	1992	224
163 6/8	49 2/8	37 6/8	35 1/8	9	8 5/8	6 4/8	6 1/8	7	9	Lincoln Co., MT	Trent W. Warness	Trent W. Warness	1993	224
163 6/8	48 4/8	30 4/8	34 1/8	9 4/8	8 1/8	6 6/8	6 4/8	12	12	Madison Co., MT	Steven L. Blank	Steven L. Blank	1994	228
163 5/8	49 5/8	34	34 3/8	9 4/8	9 4/8	6 7/8	7	8	9	Bear Canyon, MT	John Olsen	John Olsen	1962	228
163 5/8	51 5/8	33 2/8	33 6/8	10 1/8	9 4/8	6 2/8	6 3/8	7	8	Teton Co., WY	Gordon Hay	Gordon Hay	1970	228
163 5/8	47 3/8	33 2/8	36 1/8	12 2/8	11 7/8	6 1/8	6	7	7	Teton Co., WY	Michael S. Greenwald	Michael S. Greenwald	1978	228
163 5/8	51 5/8	30 2/8	35 6/8	10 4/8	11 6/8	6 4/8	6 2/8	7	7	Lincoln Co., MT	Alfred E. Journey	Alfred E. Journey	1983	228
163 5/8	46 7/8	29 4/8	32	9 5/8	9 2/8	7 3/8	7 4/8	10	10	Madison Co., MT	Danny L. Johnerson	Danny L. Johnerson	1992	233
163 4/8	50	34	34	11	9 3/8	6 2/8	6 2/8	12	12	West Yellowstone, MT	Pete Hansen	Forest B. Fenn	1948	233
163 4/8	43 6/8	35 4/8	33 4/8	10	9 1/8	6 4/8	6 4/8	10	10	Teton Co., WY	Bruce C. Liddle	Bruce C. Liddle	1974	233
163 4/8	44 6/8	37 1/8	35 6/8	11 3/8	11 2/8	6 6/8	6 6/8	9	9	Bonneville Co., ID	Gerald E. Hill	Gerald E. Hill	1981	236
163 3/8	48 4/8	31 2/8	32 6/8	14 2/8	10 6/8	6 2/8	6 2/8	6	6	Lincoln Co., WY	Russell J. Smuin	Russell J. Smuin	1976	236
163 3/8	41 6/8	40 2/8	38 1/8	7 1/8	10	6 4/8	6 1/8	8	8	Fremont Co., ID	Lavonne A. Crews	Lavonne A. Crews	1985	236
163 3/8	46 6/8	33 7/8	32 1/8	10	9 6/8	6 7/8	6 4/8	9	9	Bonneville Co., ID	Judith A. Gordon	Judith A. Gordon	1988	239
163 1/8	44 3/8	31 3/8	32 4/8	10 2/8	9 3/8	6 2/8	6 6/8	10	10	Jackson, WY	Richard Butts	Richard Butts	1968	239
163 1/8	49 7/8	31 5/8	31 5/8	11 4/8	12 4/8	6 4/8	6 1/8	9	9	Sublette Co., WY	Gerald A. Hoefner	Gerald A. Hoefner	1974	239
163 1/8	48 1/8	31 5/8	31 2/8	10 3/8	9 1/8	6 1/8	5 7/8	11	11	Weber Co., UT	Randy K. Allen	Randy K. Allen	1992	239
163 1/8	52 7/8	29	28 4/8	11 7/8	7	5 7/8	5 7/8	10	10	Summit Co., UT	Brent V. Buhler	Brent V. Buhler	1994	243
163	44 4/8	32	36 3/8	11 3/8	12 6/8	6	6 6/8	12	12	Morgan Co., UT	Archie J. Nesbitt	Archie J. Nesbitt	1987	243
163	46 6/8	37 4/8	33 4/8	10 2/8	10 4/8	6 4/8	6 4/8	9	10	Lincoln Co., MT	Bob L. Summerfield	Bob L. Summerfield	1992	243
163	43	33 4/8	33 2/8	12 4/8	9 1/8	6	6 2/8	9	9	Morgan Co., UT	Lynn L. Wilcox	Lynn L. Wilcox	1992	246
162 6/8	49 4/8	35 3/8	34 1/8	9 1/8	8 6/8	6 7/8	6 3/8	9	8	Mineral Co., UT	Shawn R. Andres	Shawn R. Andres	1995	246
162 6/8	51 6/8	32 1/8	31 5/8	7	6 3/8	6 4/8	6 3/8	8	9	Uintah Co., UT	Mitchell S. Bastian	Mitchell S. Bastian	1987	248
162 4/8	42	32 1/8	31 5/8	12 6/8	11 4/8	6 1/8	6 1/8	13	13	Lincoln Co., WY	Gayle E. Hubert	Gayle E. Hubert	1991	248
162 4/8	51 7/8	29	28 4/8	11 4/8	10 3/8	5 7/8	5 7/8	12	12	Lincoln Co., MT	Lance K. Parks	Lance K. Parks	1991	248
162 4/8	49	33 3/8	36 3/8	10 3/8	10	6 3/8	6 3/8	7	7	Lincoln Co., MT	Kurt Spencer	Kurt Spencer	1991	248
162 2/8	46 7/8	30 6/8	31 3/8	10	13 2/8	6 5/8	6 5/8	14	14	Sublette Co., WY	Donald K. Irvine	Donald K. Irvine	1969	251
162 1/8	44 5/8	31 4/8	31 4/8	13 2/8	10 4/8	6 7/8	6 4/8	11	11	Teton Co., WY	Patrick L. Shanahan	Patrick L. Shanahan	1966	252
162	44 4/8	33 6/8	32 3/8	12 5/8	11 2/8	6 1/8	6 1/8	9	9	Upper Hoback, WY	Walter L. Flint	Walter L. Flint	1951	253

WYOMING OR SHIRAS MOOSE

Alces alces shirasi

Score	Greatest Spread	Length of Palm R	Length of Palm L	Width of Palm R	Width of Palm L	Circ. of Beam at Smallest Place R	Circ. of Beam at Smallest Place L	Normal Points R	Normal Points L	Locality	Hunter	Owner	Date Killed	Rank
162	48 6/8	29 6/8	34	10 3/8	10 7/8	6 4/8	6 7/8	10	10	Lincoln Co., WY	Joan Burnett	Dee J. Burnett	1963	253
162	42	33	34 4/8	9 6/8	11 5/8	6 2/8	6 2/8	13	11	Madison Co., MT	Joseph A. Aanes	Joseph A. Aanes	1984	253
162	53 4/8	29 5/8	29 3/8	12 6/8	12 1/8	7 3/8	6 6/8	6	6	Jackson Co., CO	Dennis W. Macy	Dennis W. Macy	1991	253
162	45 2/8	33 3/8	36	10 5/8	10	7 3/8	7	10	8	Flathead Co., MT	Wendell L. Ellsworth, Jr.	Wendell L. Ellsworth, Jr.	1992	253
162	51	32	32 7/8	9 6/8	9 3/8	7 1/8	7 3/8	7	8	Weber Co., UT	Joseph E. Ricca	Joseph E. Ricca	1994	253
161 7/8	48 7/8	31 7/8	31 2/8	10 7/8	10	6 4/8	6 2/8	10	8	Teton Co., ID	James Suitts	James Suitts	1992	259
161 6/8	51	30 6/8	32	9 6/8	10 4/8	5 7/8	6 1/8	10	9	Fremont Co., WY	Robert E. Novotny	Ernest Novotny	1944	260
161 6/8	46 6/8	33 2/8	32	10 2/8	10 4/8	6 2/8	6 2/8	9	9	Teton Co., WY	Bob G. Penny	Bob G. Penny	1989	260
161 5/8	46 3/8	28 6/8	29 7/8	11 6/8	12 2/8	6 1/8	6 2/8	11	11	Flathead Co., MT	Sharon L. Chase	Sharon L. Chase	1979	262
161 5/8	51 3/8	30 5/8	32 2/8	10 3/8	9 4/8	6	6 1/8	9	10	Cache Co., UT	Kenneth Hamilton	Kenneth Hamilton	1980	262
161 5/8	49 3/8	29 2/8	27 6/8	10 3/8	10 1/8	6 2/8	6 2/8	12	12	Cache Co., UT	Lloyd M. Owens	Lloyd M. Owens	1987	262
161 5/8	52 3/8	31 4/8	31	8 4/8	9 2/8	7 1/8	8 2/8	9	8	Sublette Co., WY	David S. Luzmoor	David S. Luzmoor	1993	262
161 4/8	51	32 4/8	35 3/8	10 1/8	10 6/8	6 6/8	6 6/8	10	11	Teton Co., WY	Don M. Sheaffer	Don M. Sheaffer	1958	266
161 4/8	52 6/8	29	35 3/8	11 7/8	9 4/8	6 3/8	6 4/8	10	11	Jackson, WY	Robert D. Lynn	Robert D. Lynn	1969	266
161 4/8	40 2/8	34 3/8	34 6/8	12 7/8	12 6/8	6 4/8	6 4/8	9	8	Teton Co., WY	Lynn C. Hill	Oliver Hill	1979	266
161 4/8	40 4/8	36 1/8	30 4/8	12 7/8	11 7/8	6 3/8	6 1/8	12	12	Bonneville Co., ID	Joe M. Coelho III	Joe M. Coelho III	1982	266
161 4/8	46	32 6/8	36 2/8	8 5/8	8 7/8	6 3/8	6 3/8	11	10	Bonneville Co., ID	Richard H. Meservey	Richard H. Meservey	1989	266
161 4/8	51 2/8	30 1/8	32 6/8	10 6/8	10 4/8	6 5/8	6 4/8	10	8	Teton Co., WY	Archie J. Nesbitt	Archie J. Nesbitt	1992	266
161 4/8	53	30 3/8	28 5/8	9 5/8	9 4/8	7 1/8	7 2/8	9	10	Park Co., MT	Spence J. Jahner	Spence J. Jahner	1994	266
161 2/8	50	34 4/8	27 4/8	11 3/8	11 4/8	6 6/8	6 6/8	11	8	Lincoln Co., MT	Stanley J. Evans	Stanley J. Evans	1982	273
161	51 4/8	31 6/8	33 1/8	8 4/8	10 3/8	6 4/8	6 5/8	11	8	Rich Co., UT	Picked Up	Robert G. Petersen	1984	273
161	37 2/8	34 3/8	33 1/8	10 4/8	12 1/8	6 2/8	6 4/8	12	13	Lincoln Co., MT	Charles M. Miller	Charles M. Miller	1990	274
161	50 6/8	29 7/8	29 7/8	9 6/8	13 6/8	6	6 2/8	10	14	Weber Co., UT	Paul J. Rivas	Paul J. Rivas	1992	274
161	43 5/8	32 4/8	32 7/8	10 2/8	10 6/8	6 7/8	7 2/8	9	10	Park Co., MT	Wes Synness	Wes Synness	1970	274
160 7/8	46 1/8	30	30 2/8	10 3/8	10 6/8	6	6	12	9	Lincoln Co., WY	Hugh E. Taylor	Hugh E. Taylor	1976	277
160 7/8	40 5/8	34	32 6/8	11 7/8	11 1/8	7 3/8	7 2/8	9	9	Lincoln Co., WY	Julian E. Sjostrom	Julian E. Sjostrom	1990	277
160 7/8	50 3/8	31 4/8	29 4/8	10 6/8	9 7/8	7 7/8	7 7/8	8	8	Cache Co., UT	Obert L. Haines	Obert L. Haines	1992	277
160 7/8	46 7/8	30 2/8	30 2/8	12 1/8	10 5/8	6 1/8	6 2/8	10	11	Bonneville Co., ID	Terry M. Jensen	Terry M. Jensen	1993	277
160 7/8	48 1/8	32 5/8	30	13	12 1/8	6 5/8	6 2/8	11	8	Wasatch Co., UT	Susan S. Willis	Susan S. Willis	1997	277
160 6/8	49	32 1/8	34 4/8	8 6/8	9 4/8	6	6 2/8	9	12	Pend Oreille Co., WA	Archie D. Wyles	Archie D. Wyles	1977	283
160 6/8	43 4/8	32	33 7/8	11	11	6 5/8	7 3/8	11	9	Sanders Co., MT	Ray E. Wolff	Ray E. Wolff	1987	283
160 6/8	40 4/8	33 3/8	33	10 5/8	10 7/8	6 4/8	6 4/8	11	9	Jackson Co., CO	Robert T. Goettl	Robert T. Goettl	1994	283
160 6/8	57	32	32	9 2/8	10 3/8	6 6/8	6 6/8	4	6	Mineral Co., MT	Dennis E. Althoff	Dennis E. Althoff	1995	283
160 5/8	53 7/8	30 2/8	35 6/8	9	12 7/8	6 1/8	6 1/8	8	10	Caribou Co., ID	Dale E. Lindstrom	Dale E. Lindstrom	1988	287
160 5/8	49 5/8	31 2/8	31 1/8	7 6/8	10 6/8	6 5/8	6 5/8	10	11	Bonneville Co., ID	Gary L. Sant	Gary L. Sant	1991	287
160 4/8	48	29 2/8	30 4/8	11 4/8	11 1/8	6 7/8	7	10	9	Lincoln Co., WY	Vic Dana	Fred's Taxidermy	1971	289
160 4/8	43 2/8	31 7/8	32 2/8	11 2/8	11	7 4/8	7 3/8	10	9	Beaverhead Co., MT	Morton L. Arkava	Morton L. Arkava	1980	289
160 4/8	47 6/8	31 6/8	32 6/8	7 4/8	10 4/8	7 1/8	7 2/8	10	10	Sheridan Co., WY	Don D. Morrison	Don D. Morrison	1993	289

Score	Greatest Spread	Width of Palm R	Width of Palm L	Length of Palm R	Length of Palm L	Circumference R	Circumference L	Points R	Points L	Locality	Hunter	Owner	Date	Rank
160 4/8	50 4/8	30 3/8	29 2/8	11	9 5/8	6 1/8	6 2/8	10	10	Jackson Co., CO	Ronald W. Madsen	Ronald W. Madsen	1996	289
160 3/8	45 3/8	30 2/8	31 2/8	11 7/8	12 7/8	7 3/8	7 6/8	11	8	Madison Co., MT	Tom Bugni	Tom Bugni	1959	293
160 3/8	45 1/8	31 3/8	34 2/8	9 6/8	12 4/8	6 4/8	6 6/8	10	14	Jackson Hole, WY	Jack Griset	Jack Griset	1967	293
160 3/8	49 3/8	29 6/8	31 4/8	9 4/8	11 6/8	5 4/8	6 2/8	10	12	Lincoln Co., WY	Eugene Heap	Eugene Heap	1970	293
160 3/8	50 1/8	29 4/8	29 4/8	10 2/8	10 1/8	6 1/8	6 1/8	10	10	Teton Co., WY	Joy L. Gage	Joy L. Gage	1981	293
160 3/8	50 1/8	33 2/8	32 4/8	9 4/8	11 1/8	6 3/8	6 3/8	7	9	Bonner Co., ID	Frederick Veltri	Frederick Veltri	1992	293
160 2/8	59 6/8	29	38	8 7/8	8 7/8	5 6/8	5 6/8	6	7	Lower Hoback, WY	Obby Agins	Obby Agins	1966	298
160 1/8	46 5/8	32 4/8	32 2/8	9 6/8	11 2/8	6 5/8	6 7/8	9	11	Sublette Co., WY	Nancy Burstad	Nancy Burstad	1996	299
159 6/8	49	32 4/8	31 3/8	7 3/8	8 7/8	6 6/8	6 6/8	10	11	Madison Co., ID	Max Bosworth	Max Bosworth	1985	300
159 6/8	45 2/8	33 2/8	32 6/8	9 6/8	10 3/8	7 2/8	7 1/8	8	11	Summit Co., UT	Dal Eyre	Dal Eyre	1991	300
159 6/8	36 2/8	33 3/8	35 1/8	9 2/8	9 4/8	5 6/8	6	9	12	Sheridan Co., WY	Jerry D. Blakeman	Jerry D. Blakeman	1992	300
159 5/8	49 5/8	32 5/8	31 6/8	10 1/8	10 1/8	7	6 7/8	8	8	Caribou Co., ID	Douglas C. Hall	Douglas C. Hall	1994	303
159 4/8	49 2/8	31 4/8	31 6/8	9 4/8	9 4/8	6 1/8	6	8	10	Teton Co., WY	Willis McAmis	Willis McAmis	1972	304
159 4/8	46	32	32 4/8	10 3/8	9 6/8	6 7/8	7 1/8	9	10	Fremont Co., ID	Lennard C. Bradley	Lennard C. Bradley	1983	304
159 4/8	45 6/8	33 1/8	32 6/8	10 2/8	10 4/8	6 3/8	6 5/8	7	12	Jackson Co., CO	Donald I. Poeschl	Donald I. Poeschl	1987	304
159 4/8	42 6/8	30 2/8	30 4/8	11 6/8	14	6 6/8	6 6/8	12	8	Weber Co., UT	Neal W. Darby	Neal W. Darby	1989	304
159 3/8	45 3/8	30 2/8	29 5/8	10 5/8	10 7/8	6 4/8	6 5/8	10	10	Pinedale, WY	C.J. McElroy	C.J. McElroy	1969	308
159 3/8	55 3/8	26 4/8	28	10	10 5/8	6 5/8	6 2/8	9	11	Idaho Co., ID	Rick E. Kramer	Rick E. Kramer	1980	308
159 3/8	41 5/8	30 7/8	30 6/8	10 7/8	10	6 2/8	6 1/8	11	13	Weber Co., UT	Carl O. Berube	Carl O. Berube	1983	308
159 3/8	46 7/8	31 7/8	31 7/8	11 4/8	11 6/8	6 1/8	6 5/8	10	9	Teton Co., WY	Tony D. Poulos	Tony D. Poulos	1983	308
159 2/8	53 4/8	34 1/8	30 2/8	11 4/8	10 6/8	7	7	6	10	Pine Creek, WY	Bud Toliver	Bud Toliver	1971	312
159 2/8	52 4/8	31 3/8	31	7 6/8	9 5/8	6 5/8	6 6/8	9	6	Lincoln Co., WY	Orlando J. Bernardi	Orlando J. Bernardi	1979	312
159 1/8	51 1/8	33 3/8	29	8 7/8	8 5/8	7 2/8	7 2/8	9	8	Sublette Co., WY	Robert W. Sievers	Mrs. R.B. McCullough	1967	314
159 1/8	47 3/8	31	30 2/8	12 6/8	9 2/8	5 7/8	5 7/8	9	9	Teton Co., WY	Eugene E. Hafen	Eugene E. Hafen	1989	314
159 1/8	54 1/8	30 2/8	33 1/8	10 1/8	12 4/8	5 4/8	5 5/8	8	7	Boundary Co., ID	Todd W. Egland	Todd W. Egland	1994	314
159	48 4/8	33 4/8	27 4/8	13 2/8	9 4/8	6	6	10	8	Jackson, WY	Earl F. Hayes	Earl F. Hayes	1953	317
159	41 2/8	35 6/8	28 4/8	9 4/8	9 6/8	6 7/8	6 7/8	8	12	Green River, WY	W.M. Hightower	W.M. Hightower	1962	317
159	48	30 7/8	30 5/8	10 6/8	9 5/8	7	7 7/8	10	8	Sheridan Co., WY	Bradley C. Wichman	Bradley C. Wichman	1990	317
158 7/8	47 2/8	35 1/8	34 1/8	9 4/8	10 2/8	6 2/8	6 2/8	12	11	Teton Co., WY	James A. Fanning	James A. Fanning	1992	317
158 6/8	47 1/8	32 4/8	28 6/8	11 2/8	9 4/8	6 2/8	6 3/8	9	11	Weber Co., UT	Donald E. Franklin	Donald E. Franklin	1985	321
158 6/8	40 6/8	31 3/8	33 3/8	9 2/8	12 1/8	6 2/8	6 1/8	13	13	Gallatin Co., MT	Fred Moger	Lance F. Hossack	1951	322
158 6/8	45 2/8	27 3/8	34	13 6/8	10 5/8	6	6	11	11	N. Hoback, WY	Geo. W. Hundley	Geo. W. Hundley	1970	322
158 5/8	42 6/8	36 1/8	29	9 6/8	12 2/8	6 3/8	6 4/8	8	8	Johnson Co., WY	Brian G. Griffin	Brian G. Griffin	1996	322
158 5/8	44 5/8	35	26 7/8	9 5/8	11 1/8	6 4/8	6 4/8	7	7	Trail Creek, WY	John J. Huseas	John J. Huseas	1953	325
158 5/8	47 3/8	33	26 3/8	11 7/8	11 2/8	7 5/8	7 2/8	8	8	Teton Co., WY	Albert Pantelis	Albert Pantelis	1967	325
158 5/8	40 1/8	30 5/8	31 6/8	10 5/8	12 2/8	6 1/8	6	13	13	Lincoln Co., WY	Caroline Nare	Caroline Nare	1979	325
158 4/8	42 1/8	35 2/8	33 3/8	11 1/8	14 6/8	6	6	8	8	Park Co., MT	Anthony W. Pollari	Anthony W. Pollari	1994	325
158 4/8	43 2/8	28 7/8	35 4/8	11 6/8	9 6/8	6 1/8	6 1/8	11	11	New Fork River, WY	Oscar Boyd	Oscar Boyd	1966	325
158 3/8	47	32	28	11 2/8	9 6/8	6 1/8	6 1/8	9	9	Teton Co., WY	Roy G. Hoover	Roy G. Hoover	1966	329
158 3/8	51 1/8	33 1/8	33 3/8	11 2/8	8 4/8	8 3/8	7 5/8	11	11	Teton Co., WY	Clyde E. Harnden	Clyde E. Harnden	1986	329
158 2/8	50 6/8	26	35 5/8	10 2/8	10 6/8	6 4/8	6 5/8	8	8	Pinedale, WY	Donald C. Rehwaldt	Donald C. Rehwaldt	1966	331
158 2/8	51	30 5/8	31 7/8	11 1/8	11 1/8	6 5/8	6 5/8	9	9	Clark Co., ID	Harold Vietz	Harold Vietz	1968	332
158 2/8	46 2/8	33 1/8	26 4/8	10 7/8	10 1/8	7 2/8	7 1/8	12	12	Cache Co., UT	Scott W. Crosbie	Scott W. Crosbie	1987	332
158 2/8	56	26 4/8	28	10 6/8	9	6 2/8	6 1/8	9	9	Summit Co., UT	Picked Up	Ralph E. Swiss	1991	332
158 2/8	46 4/8	31 7/8	33 3/8	11 6/8	10 6/8	7	6	8	8	Summit Co., UT	Thomas A. VonHatten	Thomas A. VonHatten	1995	332
158 1/8	42 5/8	35 4/8	35 5/8	8 7/8	10 3/8	6 5/8	6 5/8	9	9	Gravel Mt., UT	W.A. Kalkofen	W.A. Kalkofen	1966	337
158 1/8	46 3/8	30 4/8	31 7/8	10 3/8	10 3/8	6 4/8	6 4/8	10	10	Teton Co., WY	Fred L. Eales	Fred L. Eales	1984	337

WYOMING OR SHIRAS MOOSE

Alces alces shirasi

Score	Greatest Spread	Length of Palm R	L	Width of Palm R	L	Circumference of Beam at Smallest Place R	L	Number of Normal Points R	L	Locality	Hunter	Owner	Date Killed	Rank
158 1/8	47 7/8	32 2/8	31 3/8	11	11 2/8	6 6/8	6 7/8	6	7	Grand Co., CO	Ronald R. Pomeroy	Ronald R. Pomeroy	1993	337
158 1/8	44 3/8	29 2/8	28 5/8	11 6/8	11 3/8	6 7/8	6 7/8	11	10	Jackson Co., CO	Bill L. Olson	Bill L. Olson	1994	337
158 1/8	47 3/8	30 3/8	35 3/8	11 5/8	11 6/8	6 3/8	6 5/8	12	7	Summit Co., UT	Stephen W. Davis	Stephen W. Davis	1995	337
158	46 2/8	30 3/8	30 4/8	10 1/8	9 7/8	5 6/8	5 5/8	10	14	Bonneville Co., ID	Michael P. Dome	Michael P. Dome	1992	342
157 7/8	43 7/8	31 6/8	31 6/8	9 4/8	8 4/8	6 6/8	6 7/8	10	10	Teton Co., WY	Willard H. Leedy	Willard H. Leedy	1982	343
157 7/8	43 5/8	34 4/8	33 4/8	9 5/8	13 2/8	6	6	8	13	Flathead Co., MT	Jim M. Milligan	Jim M. Milligan	1982	343
157 7/8	52 3/8	32	30 3/8	8 4/8	10 6/8	5 7/8	6 1/8	8	10	Lincoln Co., WY	Patrick H. Roberts	Patrick H. Roberts	1988	343
157 7/8	47 1/8	33 3/8	29 1/8	11 4/8	10 7/8	6 3/8	6 4/8	9	10	Lincoln Co., MT	John K. Curry	John K. Curry	1997	343
157 6/8	47 2/8	27	29	13 2/8	12 2/8	6 1/8	6	10	12	Cache Co., UT	David W. Jensen	David W. Jensen	1977	347
157 6/8	47 2/8	35 4/8	33	8 4/8	9 7/8	6 6/8	6 6/8	7	8	Sublette Co., WY	Mrs. Kenneth Fortuna	Mrs. Kenneth Fortuna	1984	347
157 6/8	46 4/8	29 2/8	31 2/8	10	10 7/8	6 4/8	6 3/8	10	14	Morgan Co., UT	John L. Estes	John L. Estes	1987	347
157 5/8	41 5/8	33 2/8	34 1/8	10 2/8	9 5/8	6 1/8	6 1/8	9	12	Madison Co., ID	Lawrence Buckland	Lawrence Buckland	1987	350
157 4/8	50 2/8	28 1/8	26 2/8	10 6/8	11 1/8	6 5/8	6 5/8	11	10	Grey's River, WY	Mary B. Mikalis	Mary B. Mikalis	1969	351
157 4/8	42 6/8	30 5/8	30 5/8	10 1/8	9 1/8	5 5/8	5 5/8	12	12	Flathead Co., MT	Scott L. Davis	Scott L. Davis	1991	351
157 3/8	51 1/8	31 2/8	28	10	9 5/8	6 5/8	6 4/8	9	9	Sublette Co., WY	Teressa Ennis	Teressa Ennis	1983	353
157 3/8	41 3/8	28 6/8	28 6/8	12 2/8	12	6 2/8	6 2/8	12	11	Idaho Co., ID	Norman R. Fuchs	Norman R. Fuchs	1984	353
157 3/8	49 7/8	37 5/8	25 5/8	13 6/8	14	6 7/8	7	11	8	Bonneville Co., ID	George L. Vivian	George L. Vivian	1987	353
157 3/8	50 1/8	28 6/8	31	9 4/8	10	6 3/8	6 4/8	9	11	Teton Co., ID	Wenda W. Jones	Wenda W. Jones	1995	353
157 1/8	45 4/8	33	29 7/8	10 3/8	9 7/8	6	6	7	8	Lincoln Co., MT	Bob Stafford	Bob Stafford	1963	357
157 1/8	53 3/8	30 6/8	29 2/8	9	9 4/8	5 5/8	5 5/8	8	8	Pend Oreille Co., WA	William C. Phifer	William C. Phifer	1994	358
157	47 4/8	29 6/8	31 3/8	9 6/8	12 2/8	6 2/8	6 4/8	10	9	Fremont Co., WY	Fred S. Finley	Fred S. Finley	1962	359
157	47 2/8	29 1/8	26 7/8	11 6/8	11 6/8	6 3/8	6 2/8	10	10	Beaverhead Co., MT	Jason W. Roylance	Jason W. Roylance	1986	359
157	43 6/8	35 1/8	29 1/8	10 3/8	9 6/8	6 6/8	6 6/8	11	11	Teton Co., WY	Steven C. Rudd	Steven C. Rudd	1994	359
157	57	30 4/8	32 1/8	5 2/8	7	6 2/8	6 3/8	8	8	Madison Co., MT	Thomas E. Tillman	Thomas E. Tillman	1994	359
156 7/8	46 1/8	29 6/8	28	14 7/8	14 6/8	6 5/8	7 1/8	6	9	Ruby Mts., MT	Milton Burdick	Milton Burdick	1960	363
156 7/8	38 7/8	30 3/8	31	11 3/8	12 3/8	6 3/8	6 2/8	11	13	Deer Lodge Co., MT	Mike Munson	Mike Munson	1971	363
156 6/8	45 2/8	33 1/8	31 6/8	10 4/8	9	7 3/8	7	9	8	Teton Co., WY	Palmer Hegge	Palmer Hegge	1952	365
156 6/8	37	34	36	11 2/8	13 2/8	6 5/8	6 5/8	8	9	Devil's Basin, WY	Charlotte Bruce	Charlotte Bruce	1967	365
156 6/8	46 2/8	33 7/8	31 3/8	11	11 1/8	6 1/8	5 7/8	9	7	Sublette Co., WY	Richard A. Bonander	Richard A. Bonander	1979	365
156 6/8	43 2/8	31	29 4/8	10 4/8	11	6 7/8	6 6/8	10	10	Fremont Co., WY	Jan Liggett	J. Liggett & L. Liggett	1985	365
156 6/8	45 6/8	34 2/8	30 3/8	10 4/8	9 2/8	6 3/8	6	6	6	Lincoln Co., WY	Bryan Dexter	Bryan Dexter	1989	365
156 6/8	46 4/8	28	30 3/8	10 4/8	10 4/8	6 6/8	6 5/8	10	13	Cache Co., UT	Darin Seamons	Darin Seamons	1994	365
156 5/8	42 3/8	29 5/8	29 2/8	11 3/8	11 6/8	7 4/8	7 4/8	9	10	Teton Co., WY	George A. Nevills	George A. Nevills	1977	371
156 4/8	42 6/8	32 3/8	34 5/8	12 2/8	12 4/8	6 2/8	6 2/8	6	6	Gallatin River, MT	Paul Mako	Paul Mako	1960	372
156 4/8	51 2/8	29	32	8 6/8	9	6 7/8	6 7/8	8	9	Buffalo Horn Lake, MT	Vincent De Stefano	Vincent De Stefano	1966	372
156 4/8	49 6/8	28	30	9	9	5 7/8	5 7/8	11	12	Thorofare River, WY	Dean Johnson	Dean Johnson	1973	372
156 4/8	42 2/8	30 6/8	33 6/8	10 2/8	11	6 3/8	6 1/8	11	10	Caribou Co., ID	Reuben R. Barzee	Raelene Barzee	1991	372
156 3/8	48 1/8	33 1/8	30 5/8	11	10 6/8	6 6/8	7	6	8	Idaho Co., ID	Max D. Hunsaker	Max D. Hunsaker	1986	376

Score	Greatest Spread	Length of Palm R	Length of Palm L	Width of Palm R	Width of Palm L	Circ. of Beam R	Circ. of Beam L	Points R	Points L	Locality	By	Owner	Date Killed	Rank
156 3/8	39 3/8	33 1/8	32 3/8	10 3/8	11 3/8	6 6/8	6 6/8	10	9	Lincoln Co., MT	Arthur H. Baker	Arthur H. Baker	1993	376
156 3/8	43 7/8	34 4/8	34 4/8	8 7/8	8 6/8	6 2/8	6	9	7	Lincoln Co., MT	Thomas A. Steenberg	Thomas A. Steenberg	1997	376
156 2/8	43	40 7/8	31 4/8	10 2/8	10 1/8	7	7	8	9	Teton Co., WY	Gerda Prince	Gerda Prince	1970	379
156 2/8	46 6/8	31 4/8	30 5/8	8	9 5/8	6 1/8	6 1/8	10	10	Summit Co., UT	John G. Allred	John G. Allred	1980	379
156 2/8	41 6/8	30	32	10 4/8	9 7/8	6 4/8	6 3/8	8	10	Teton Co., WY	James A. Kent	James A. Kent	1988	379
156 2/8	42 4/8	31 4/8	31 3/8	10 1/8	10 4/8	7 5/8	7 3/8	9	10	Beaverhead Co., MT	Todd M. Gilstrap	Todd M. Gilstrap	1990	379
156 1/8	47 3/8	31 5/8	34 4/8	9 6/8	7 6/8	6 1/8	6	8	9	Lewis Creek, WY	Donald J. Krist	Donald J. Krist	1967	383
156 1/8	45 7/8	30 3/8	31 1/8	11	10 2/8	6 4/8	6 5/8	8	7	Glade Creek, WY	Joseph A. Merrill, Jr.	Joseph A. Merrill, Jr.	1973	383
156 1/8	40 1/8	33 2/8	32 5/8	12 3/8	13 6/8	6 2/8	6	8	11	Idaho Co., ID	John R. Lewinski	John R. Lewinski	1986	383
156	45 4/8	32 4/8	31 4/8	8 4/8	8	6 6/8	7	9	13	Missoula Co., MT	W.L. Rohrer	W.L. Rohrer	1957	386
156	43 4/8	31 2/8	29 1/8	11 6/8	10 3/8	6 1/8	6 1/8	11	8	Bonneville Co., ID	Bruce J. Thomson	Bruce J. Thomson	1990	386
156	50 2/8	29	30 2/8	9 6/8	9 1/8	6 2/8	6 2/8	10	8	Sublette Co., WY	Allen C. Capes	Allen C. Capes	1997	386
155 7/8	52 3/8	29 4/8	30 4/8	7 2/8	9 3/8	6	6	9	9	Ashton, ID	Robert H. Thomas	Robert H. Thomas	1972	389
155 7/8	44 5/8	34 7/8	34 4/8	11 1/8	9 3/8	6 6/8	6 6/8	9	9	Jackson Co., CO	Thomas A. Yukman	Thomas A. Yukman	1992	389
155 6/8	46	31 4/8	31 2/8	8 4/8	7 4/8	7 2/8	7 1/8	10	5	Jackson Hole, WY	Don Phillips	Don Phillips	1956	391
155 6/8	48 6/8	27 6/8	27 6/8	10 4/8	11 6/8	6 6/8	6 4/8	9	10	Jackson Hole, WY	Ralph Brumbaugh	Ralph Brumbaugh	1960	391
155 6/8	39 4/8	28	28 1/8	13	16 7/8	6 1/8	6 2/8	10	9	Upper Hoback, WY	Stephen N. Bean	Stephen N. Bean	1969	391
155 6/8	52 2/8	36 4/8	33 6/8	7 3/8	6 2/8	5 7/8	5 7/8	12	11	Summit Co., UT	Monika M. Anderson	Monika M. Anderson	1982	391
155 6/8	44 6/8	30	37 7/8	10 1/8	9 3/8	6 2/8	6 1/8	6	8	Lake Co., MT	Kenneth E. Trickey	Kenneth E. Trickey	1993	391
155 5/8	46	29 7/8	27 6/8	11	11 1/8	6 2/8	6 1/8	10	10	Fremont Co., ID	Debra L. Borresen	Debra L. Borresen	1994	397
155 5/8	41 5/8	30	31 4/8	11 3/8	11 3/8	6	5 5/8	10	12	Lincoln Co., MT	Robert D. Nolin	Robert D. Nolin	1979	397
155 5/8	52 7/8	29 4/8	31 2/8	8	8	5 7/8	5 7/8	11	10	Summit Co., UT	Michelle R. Liechty	Michelle R. Liechty	1989	397
155 5/8	48 1/8	30 7/8	30 3/8	9 4/8	10 5/8	6	6 6/8	8	10	Lincoln Co., WY	Robert B. Williams	Robert B. Williams	1994	397
155 4/8	51 2/8	31 2/8	31 2/8	9 2/8	8 7/8	6 3/8	6 2/8	7	8	Green River, WY	H.S. Jackman	H.S. Jackman	1964	400
155 4/8	46	29	31	12 6/8	11 4/8	6 1/8	6	10	9	Jackson, WY	Bud Weaver	Bud Weaver	1968	400
155 4/8	42 2/8	31	29	10 6/8	10 5/8	6	5 5/8	10	11	Lincoln Co., WY	Ralph Wood	Ralph Wood	1977	400
155 4/8	48 4/8	31 7/8	31 7/8	12 6/8	9 1/8	5 3/8	6 2/8	11	11	Lincoln Co., MT	H.E. Thompson, Jr.	H.E. Thompson, Jr.	1984	400
155 4/8	47 6/8	31 4/8	31 4/8	9 3/8	10 1/8	6 4/8	6 1/8	8	9	Morgan Co., UT	Michael C. Allen	Michael C. Allen	1987	400
155 3/8	43 6/8	30 2/8	30 2/8	9 2/8	9 3/8	6	6 6/8	10	8	Lincoln Co., WY	Rhonda S. Crank	Rhonda S. Crank	1989	408
155 3/8	48 2/8	28 7/8	28 7/8	9 5/8	10 6/8	5 7/8	6	10	10	Teton Co., WY	Mark A. Davidson	Mark A. Davidson	1992	408
155 3/8	38	30 6/8	30 6/8	12 7/8	13 3/8	6 2/8	6 4/8	12	11	Gallatin Co., MT	Jeffrey L. Griffith	Jeffrey L. Griffith	1994	408
155 3/8	52 3/8	27 4/8	27 4/8	9 7/8	9 2/8	6 6/8	6 3/8	9	8	Upper Yellowstone, WY	Am. Mus. Nat. Hist.	Harold E. Anthony	1934	408
155 3/8	49 5/8	30 2/8	30 2/8	8 5/8	9 5/8	6 1/8	6 2/8	8	8	Spread Creek, WY	Marty Fiorello	Marty Fiorello	1963	408
155 2/8	43 3/8	31 3/8	31 3/8	10 2/8	10 6/8	6	6 5/8	9	9	Sublette Co., WY	Tom J. Schwindt	Tom J. Schwindt	1973	413
155 2/8	49 5/8	23 4/8	23 4/8	13 3/8	14 7/8	6 4/8	6 5/8	10	9	Pend Oreille Co., WA	Thomas F. Kneeshaw	Thomas F. Kneeshaw	1983	413
155 2/8	48 3/8	30 2/8	30 2/8	10 3/8	9 4/8	6 3/8	6 2/8	11	9	Clark Co., ID	Louis E. Beardall	Louis E. Beardall	1994	413
155 2/8	47	28 3/8	28 3/8	10	9 4/8	6 2/8	6 4/8	9	11	Teton Co., WY	David M. Clark	Clarence Harris	1947	413
155 2/8	51 2/8	28 2/8	28 2/8	10 1/8	10 3/8	6 5/8	6 4/8	10	11	Dubois, WY	Clyde Thompson	Clyde Thompson	1954	413
155 1/8	46	29 2/8	29 2/8	9 4/8	8 6/8	6 5/8	6 6/8	10	10	Lolo Creek, MT	Virgil Fite	Edward Churchwell	1955	419
155 1/8	41 4/8	32 7/8	32 7/8	11 1/8	11 2/8	6 4/8	5 4/8	11	9	Teton Co., WY	Thomas F. Smith	Thomas F. Smith	1973	419
155 1/8	42 4/8	31 6/8	31 6/8	9 1/8	9 5/8	6 4/8	6 2/8	10	9	Weber Co., UT	David I. Dashnaw	David I. Dashnaw	1992	419
155 1/8	46 6/8	27 4/8	27 4/8	10 2/8	10 2/8	6 6/8	6 7/8	9	10	Sheridan Co., WY	Vicki M. Stites	Vicki M. Stites	1994	419
155 1/8	40 3/8	33 4/8	33 4/8	11	11	5 4/8	6 3/8	11	10	Yellowstone River, WY	T. Robert Johnson	T. Robert Johnson	1974	419
155 1/8	45 3/8	30 7/8	30 7/8	9 6/8	10 1/8	6 4/8	9 4/8	14	10	Madison Co., MT	Shawn G. Stewart	Shawn G. Stewart	1987	419
155 1/8	48 5/8	33 2/8	33 2/8	8 6/8	9 4/8	6 7/8	8 6/8	8	6	Teton Co., WY	John J. King	John J. King	1988	419
155 1/8	43 3/8	28 3/8	28 3/8	11 2/8	12 3/8	6 2/8	6 2/8	9	11	Cache Co., UT	Brian R. Nosker	Brian R. Nosker	1988	419
155 1/8	45 3/8	32 6/8	32 6/8	8 5/8	8	6 2/8	6 3/8	9	8	Beaverhead Co., MT	Katharine F. Heffner	Katharine F. Heffner	1990	419

WYOMING OR SHIRAS MOOSE

Alces alces shirasi

Score	Greatest Spread	Length of Palm R	Length of Palm L	Width of Palm R	Width of Palm L	Circumference of Beam at Smallest Place R	Circumference of Beam at Smallest Place L	Number of Normal Points R	Number of Normal Points L	Locality	Hunter	Owner	Date Killed	Rank
155	46 6/8	29 6/8	30	9	9 4/8	6 4/8	6 3/8	9	9	Jackson Hole, WY	Vernon Williams, Jr.	Vernon Williams, Jr.	1969	424
189 4/8*	53 2/8	38 4/8	40 5/8	14 2/8	13 6/8	6 7/8	7	13	9	Larimer Co., CO	Brad B. Schwindt	Brad B. Schwindt	1997	
184 3/8*	48 3/8	43 3/8	41 6/8	11 1/8	12	7 3/8	7 1/8	8	9	Fremont Co., ID	Craig J. Laughlin	Craig J. Laughlin	1993	

* Final score is subject to revision by additional verifying measurements.

CATEGORY
WYOMING MOOSE

SCORE
155-5/8

HUNTER
MICHELLE R. LIECHTY

LOCATION
SUMMIT CO., UT

DATE OF KILL
SEPTEMBER 1989

CATEGORY
WYOMING MOOSE

SCORE
157-1/8

HUNTER
WILLIAM C. PHIFER

LOCATION
PEND OREILLE CO., WA

DATE OF KILL
NOVEMBER 1994

CATEGORY
WYOMING MOOSE

SCORE
161-4/8

HUNTER
SPENCE J. JAHNER

LOCATION
PARK CO., MT

DATE OF KILL
OCTOBER 1994

CARIBOU BOUNDARIES

The various varieties of caribou, which vary widely in size and antler configuration, have required subdivision of the species into five different trophy categories: mountain, woodland, barren ground, Central Canada barren ground, and Quebec-Labrador. Prior to 1960, the classification of the different species and subspecies of the world was in disarray. At that time, Frank Banfield (a Canadian wildlife biologist) reviewed all of the available museum specimens of the world's caribou and reduced the number of valid subspecies. Among his conclusions were that the new world caribou and the old world reindeer should all be classified as one species, but that northern barren ground caribou differ from the more southerly distributed woodland caribou, both in Eurasia and in North America.

The largest antlered caribou from North America are the Grant's variety from Alaska and northern Yukon Territory. These caribou, called barren ground caribou for records-keeping purposes, have long, rounded main beams with very long top points. They also have the highest all-time records book

minimum entry score of 400 points. *(See below also for description of boundary between barren ground caribou and mountain caribou in Yukon Territory.)*

The so-called mountain caribou, now regarded as a variety of woodland caribou, is found in British Columbia, Alberta, southern Yukon Territory, and the Mackenzie Mountains of Northwest Territories. In Yukon Territory, the boundary (see map below) begins at the intersection of the Yukon River with the boundary between Yukon Territory and the state of Alaska. The boundary runs southeasterly following the Yukon River upstream to Dawson; then easterly and southerly along the Klondike Highway to Stewart Crossing; then easterly following the road to Mayo; then northeasterly following the south shore of McQuesten Lake; then easterly following the main drainage to the divide leading to Scougale Creek to its confluence with the Beaver River; then south following the Beaver River downstream to its confluence with the Rackla River; then southeasterly following the Rackla River downstream to its confluence with the Stewart River; then northeasterly following the Stewart River upstream to its confluence with the North Stewart River to the boundary between Yukon Territory and Northwest Territories. North of this line caribou are classified as **barren ground caribou** for records-keeping purposes, while those specimens taken south of this line are considered **mountain caribou.**

Central Canada barren ground caribou occur on Baffin Island and the mainland of Northwest Territories, as well as in northern Manitoba. The geographic boundaries in the mainland of Northwest Territories are: the Mackenzie River to the west; the north edge of the continent to the north (excluding

**CENTRAL CANADA
BARREN GROUND
CARIBOU BOUNDARY IN
MANITOBA (SHADED)**

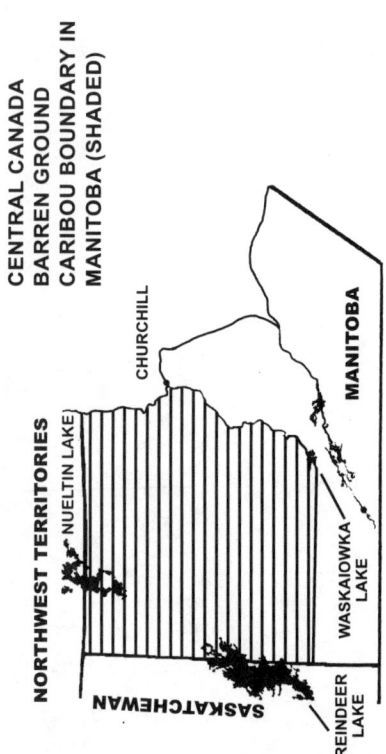

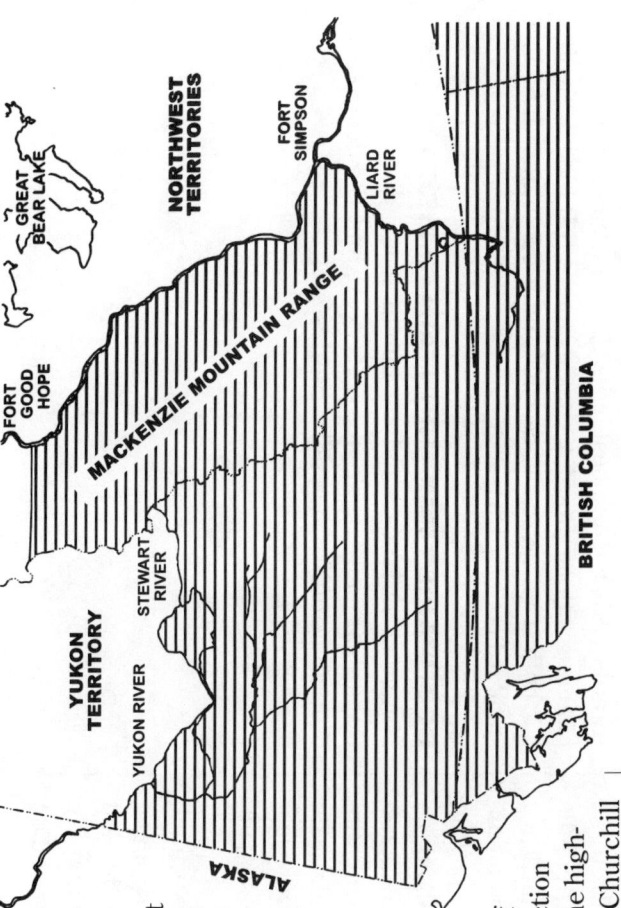

GREAT BEAR LAKE

NORTHWEST TERRITORIES

FORT GOOD HOPE

FORT SIMPSON

LIARD RIVER

MACKENZIE MOUNTAIN RANGE

YUKON TERRITORY

STEWART RIVER

YUKON RIVER

BRITISH COLUMBIA

ALASKA

NORTHERN BOUNDARY FOR MOUNTAIN CARIBOU (SHADED)

any islands except Baffin Island); Hudson's Bay to the east; and the southern boundary of Northwest Territories to the south.

The boundary (see map above) for Central Canada barren ground caribou in Manitoba begins at the point of intersection of the south limit of township 87 with the provincial boundary between the provinces of Manitoba and Saskatchewan. The boundary then follows this township line east to the point of confluence with Waskaiowka Lake. From there it proceeds in a northeasterly direction along the high-water mark of the north shore of the aforementioned lake following the sinuosities of the shoreline to the point of intersection with the water connection to Hale Lake. From this point, the high-water mark of the north shoreline is followed to the point of intersection with the Little Churchill River. Henceforth, it follows the high-water mark of the north or westerly shore of the Little Churchill River including expansions of the river into lakes to the point of confluence with the Churchill River. From there the boundary crosses the mouth of the Little Churchill River and follows the high-water mark on the south or easterly shore of the Churchill River to the community of Churchill located on Hudson Bay.

Caribou taken in Manitoba north of the above described boundary are now classified as Central Canada barren ground caribou.

The Quebec-Labrador caribou category was established in 1968. This large woodland caribou has very wide, long-beamed antlers with almost universally palmated bez formations. To have left these animals in competition with the woodland caribou of Newfoundland would have resulted in a complete swamping of the smaller-antlered woodland caribou from Newfoundland. Boundaries for Quebec-Labrador caribou are just as the name implies, Quebec and the Labrador region of Newfoundland.

Woodland caribou are eligible for entry from Nova Scotia, Newfoundland and New Brunswick. Woodland caribou occur sparingly all the way across Canada to southern British Columbia. Although there may be some open seasons in these provinces, they are not taken in large numbers anywhere. It would seem inappropriate to place such animals in competition with those from Newfoundland where they have been regularly hunted for more than 100 years. ∎

On September 15, 1976, Garry Beaubien's father took down a big bull from a herd of mountain caribou (*Rangifer montanus*) that the two hunters were stalking near the Turnagain River in British Columbia. Suddenly, something totally unexpected occurred.

From over a little knoll 200 yards to their left, ten bulls appeared on the horizon, with a massive bull in the lead. After a quick look at Beaubien and his father, the huge bull led the other nine back over the ridge and out of sight.

Hardly believing what he had just seen, Beaubien ran to the knoll as fast as he could and looked over. The bulls were several hundred yards away, running up a side hill. They had only 200 yards to go before they would go over the mountain top forever. Quickly lying down on the knoll and putting the cross hairs of his scope on the top of the bull's shoulder, Beaubien waited for him to stop. When he did, Beaubien carefully squeezed the trigger. His father, watching through binoculars, cried, "You shot way low". The bulls took off again for the top. The next time the bulls stopped they were just 100 yards from the summit. Beaubien aimed and fired again. His father told him that he had still shot too low.

Beaubien's heart was pounding mightily as he waited, hoping for one last chance. The big bull stopped just as he reached the skyline, the nine other bulls strung out behind him. Beaubien squeezed off his final effort, hoping that the 180 grain bullet from his .300 Winchester magnum would do

the job. As the rifle report died, his father yelled, "You got him!" Beaubien and his father watched through their binoculars for several minutes to make sure that he was indeed down for good.

Scoring 452 points, this mountain caribou replaced the long-standing World's Record trophy taken by G.L. Pop in 1923. The Pop caribou was later dropped from the records when it was discovered to have a split skull. Beaubien's trophy was recognized at the 16th North American Big Game Awards (1977) as the best in its category, and it was further honored with an award of the Sagamore Hill Medal, signifying both trophy excellence and a hunt exhibiting the finest standards of Fair Chase. ∎

BOUNDARIES FOR MOUNTAIN CARIBOU

Mountain caribou includes trophies from Alberta, British Columbia, southern Yukon Territory, and the Mackenzie Mountains of Northwest Territories.

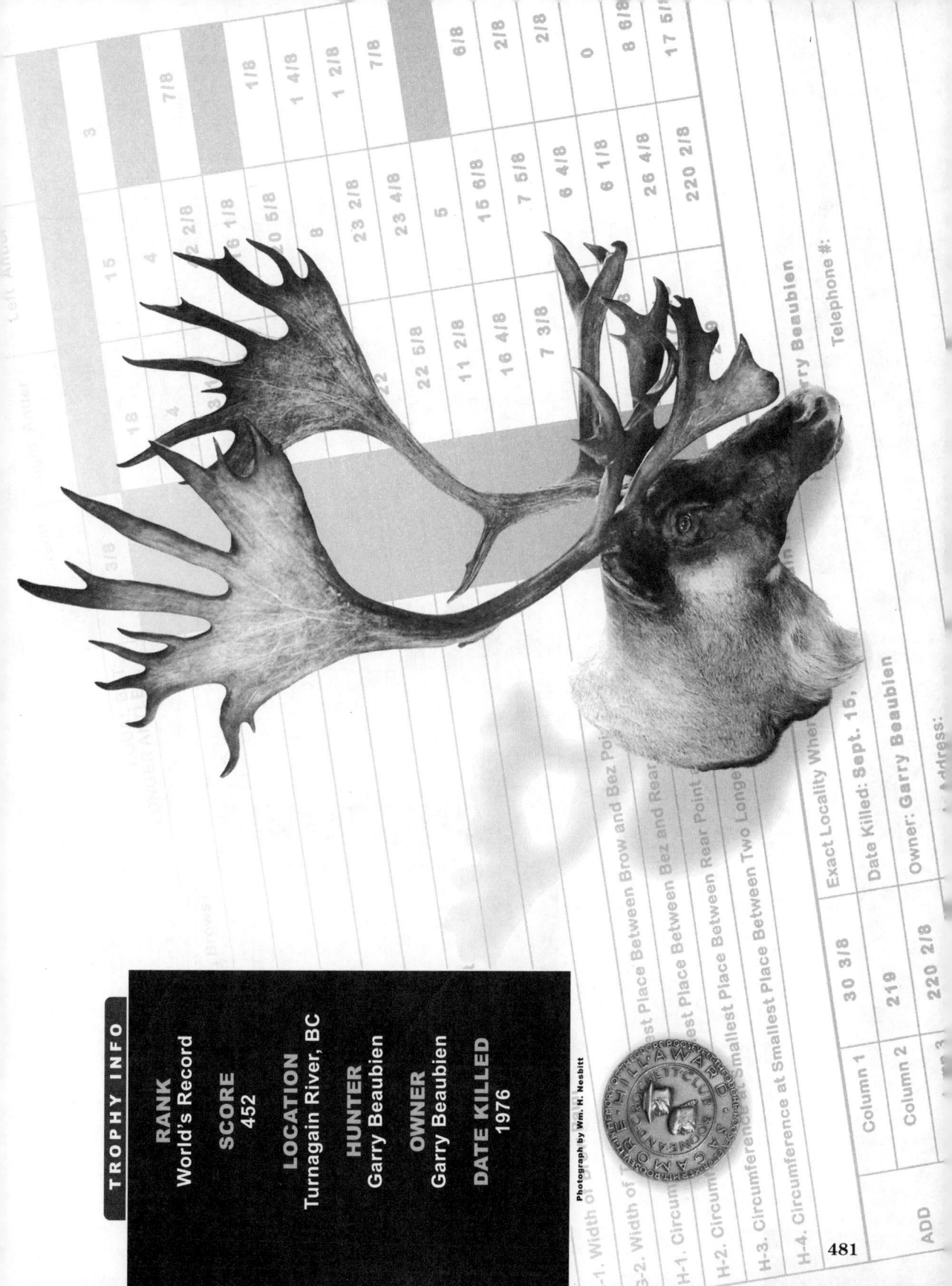

Photograph by Wm. H. Nesbitt

Column 1	30 3/8
Column 2	219
	220 2/8

ADD

Exact Locality Where ...
Date Killed: Sept. 15,
Owner: Garry Beaubien
Address:
Telephone #:

G-1. Width of ... est Place Between Brow and Bez Poi...
G-2. Width of ... est Place Between Bez and Rear Point
H-1. Circumference ...est Place Between Rear Point
H-2. Circumference ... Place Between ...
H-3. Circumference at Smallest Place Between Two Longe...
H-4. Circumference at Smallest Place

Records of
North American
Big Game

250 Station Drive
Missoula, MT 59801
(406) 542-1888

BOONE AND CROCKETT CLUB®

OFFICIAL SCORING SYSTEM FOR NORTH AMERICAN BIG GAME TROPHIES

CARIBOU

	MINIMUM SCORES	
	AWARDS	ALL-TIME
mountain	360	390
woodland	265	295
barren ground	375	400
Central Canada barren ground	345	360
Quebec-Labrador	365	375

Detail of Point Measurement

KIND OF CARIBOU (check one)
- ☑ mountain
- ☐ woodland
- ☐ barren ground
- ☐ Central Canada barren ground
- ☐ Quebec-Labrador

SEE OTHER SIDE FOR INSTRUCTIONS	COLUMN 1	COLUMN 2	COLUMN 3	COLUMN 4
	Spread Credit	Right Antler	Left Antler	Difference
A. Tip to Tip Spread	27 1/8			
B. Greatest Spread	33 3/8			
C. Inside Spread of Main Beams	30 3/8	SPREAD CREDIT MAY EQUAL BUT NOT EXCEED LONGER ANTLER	30 3/8	
D. Number of Points on Each Antler Excluding Brows		18	15	3
Number of Points on Each Brow		4	4	
E. Length of Main Beam		43 1/8	42 2/8	7/8
F-1. Length of Brow Palm or First Point		16 4/8	16 1/8	1/8
F-2. Length of Bez or Second Point		20 4/8	20 5/8	1/8
F-3. Length of Rear Point, If Present		6 4/8	8	1 4/8
F-4. Length of Second Longest Top Point		22	23 2/8	1 2/8
F-5. Length of Longest Top Point		22 5/8	23 4/8	7/8
G-1. Width of Brow Palm		11 2/8	5	6 2/8
G-2. Width of Top Palm		7 3/8	7 5/8	2/8
H-1. Circumference at Smallest Place Between Brow and Bez Point		6 6/8	6 4/8	2/8
H-2. Circumference at Smallest Place Between Bez and Rear Point		6 1/8	6 1/8	0
H-3. Circumference at Smallest Place Between Rear Point and First Top Point				
H-4. Circumference at Smallest Place Between Two Longest Top Palm Points		17 6/8	26 4/8	8 6/8
TOTALS	30 3/8	219	220 2/8	17 5/8

	Column 1	30 3/8	Exact Locality Where Killed: Turnagain River, BC	
ADD	Column 2	219	Date Killed: Sept. 15, 1976	Hunter: Garry Beaubien
	Column 3	220 2/8	Owner: Garry Beaubien	Telephone #:
	Subtotal	469 5/8	Owner's Address:	
SUBTRACT Column 4		17 5/8	Guide's Name and Address:	
FINAL SCORE		452	Remarks: (Mention Any Abnormalities or Unique Qualities)	

All measurements must be made with a 1/4-inch wide flexible steel tape to the nearest one-eighth of an inch. (Note: A flexible steel cable can be used to measure points and main beams only.) Enter fractional figures in eighths, without reduction. Official measurements cannot be taken until the antlers have air dried for at least 60 days after the animal was killed.

A. Tip to Tip Spread is measured between tips of main beams.

B. Greatest Spread is measured between perpendiculars at a right angle to the center line of the skull at widest part, whether across main beams or points.

C. Inside Spread of Main Beams is measured at a right angle to the center line of the skull at widest point between main beams. Enter this measurement again as the Spread Credit **if** it is less than or equal to the length of the longer antler; if greater, enter longer antler length for Spread Credit.

D. Number of Points on Each Antler: To be counted a point, a projection must be at least one-half inch long, with length exceeding width at one-half inch or more of length. Beam tip is counted as a point but not measured as a point. There are no "abnormal" points in caribou.

E. Length of Main Beam is measured from the center of the lowest outside edge of burr over the outer side to the most distant point of the main beam. The point of beginning is that point on the burr where the center line along the outer side of the beam intersects the burr, then following generally the line of the illustration.

F-1-2-3. Length of Points are measured from nearest edge of beam over outer curve to tip. Lay the tape along the outer curve of the beam so that the top edge of the tape coincides with the top edge of the beam on both sides of point to determine the baseline for point measurement. Record point lengths in appropriate blanks.

F-4-5. Length of Points are measured from the tip of the point to the top of the beam, then at a right angle to the bottom edge of beam. The Second Longest Top Point **cannot** be a point branch of the Longest Top Point.

G-1. Width of Brow is measured in a straight line from top edge to lower edge, as illustrated, with measurement line at a right angle to main axis of brow.

G-2. Width of Top Palm is measured from midpoint of lower edge of main beam to midpoint of a dip between points, at widest part of palm. The line of measurement begins and ends at midpoints of palm edges, which gives credit for palm thickness.

H-1-2-3-4. Circumferences are taken as illustrated for measurements. If brow point is missing, take H-1 at smallest point between burr and bez point. If rear point is missing, take H-2 and H-3 measurements at smallest place between bez and first top point. Do not depress the tape into any dips of the palm or main beam.

182

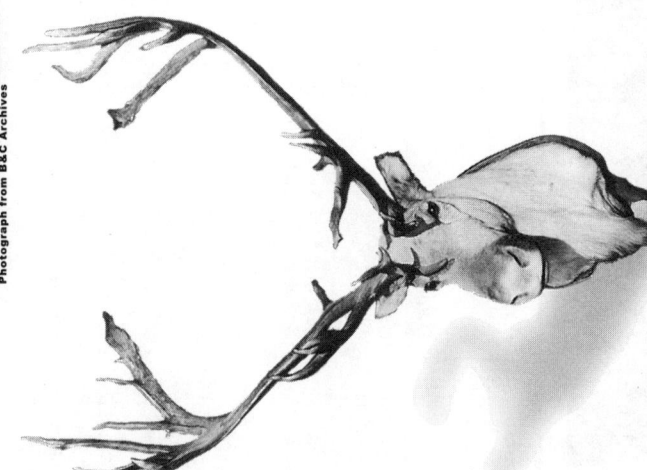

483

MINIMUM SCORE 390

Score	Length of Main Beam R	L	Inside Spread	Circumference at Smallest Place Between Brow and Bez Points R	L	Length of Brow Points R	L	Width of Brow Points R	L	Number of Points R	L	Locality	Hunter	Owner	Date Killed	Rank
452	43 1/8	42 2/8	30 3/8	7 3/8	7 5/8	16 4/8	16 1/8	11 2/8	5	22	19	Turnagain River, BC	Garry Beaubien	Garry Beaubien	1976	1
449 4/8	37 2/8	37 4/8	30 2/8	5 7/8	5 7/8	17 5/8	13 6/8	10 6/8	9 3/8	40	33	Fire Lake, YT	James R. Hollister	James R. Hollister	1989	2
448 6/8	51 3/8	51 5/8	40 2/8	6 6/8	6 6/8	18	18	10 6/8	1	24	20	Great Salmon Lake, YT	John Tomko	John Tomko	1965	3
446 2/8	55	53 5/8	40 2/8	7 5/8	7 2/8	14 7/8	13 2/8	9 3/8	5	20	14	Atlin, BC	Irvin Hardcastle	Loaned to B&C Natl. Coll.	1955	4
445 3/8	48 7/8	46 2/8	27 4/8	6 2/8	5 7/8	17 6/8	20 2/8	4 5/8	17 6/8	19	20	Cold Fish Lake, BC	John I. Moore	Buckhorn Mus. & Saloon, Ltd.	1958	5
444	52	52 1/8	38 2/8	6	6 1/8	8 6/8	20 2/8	1/8	15 7/8	16	25	Mountain River, NT	John A. Kolar	John A. Kolar	1984	6
444	42	43 1/8	35	6 4/8	6 5/8	15 6/8	17	8 1/8	7 3/8	20	23	Kechika Range, BC	James C. Johnson	James C. Johnson	1988	6
442 7/8	44 2/8	46 2/8	37 2/8	7	6 7/8	15 6/8	17 1/8	11 6/8	4 6/8	24	23	Spatsizi Plateau, BC	Jay L. Brasher	Jay L. Brasher	1984	8
441 5/8	49 4/8	46 2/8	33 1/8	7	6 7/8	19 2/8	21	15 3/8	4 7/8	24	19	Cold Fish Lake, BC	Drew W. Getgen	Carnegie Museum	1961	9
440	55 7/8	55 3/8	46 2/8	6	5 5/8	21	21	5 4/8	3 4/8	17	17	Carcajou River, NT	David P. McBrayer	David P. McBrayer	1990	10
438 4/8	43	42 2/8	33 2/8	7 1/8	6 5/8	19 4/8	18 1/8	14 3/8	5 2/8	25	24	Divide Lake, NT	Monte Sorgard	Monte Sorgard	1988	11
437 6/8	50 2/8	46	39 4/8	7 3/8	7 1/8	19	18 1/8	14 4/8	11 5/8	21	17	Willow Handle Lake, NT	M.R. James	M.R. James	1995	12
436 3/8	57	54 4/8	46 4/8	6 5/8	6 5/8	20 2/8	16 7/8	10 2/8	8	17	14	St. Cyr Range, YT	Randall W. Lawton	Randall W. Lawton	1985	13
436 1/8	43	43 3/8	34 4/8	6 2/8	6 1/8	19 4/8	18 1/8	13 6/8	5	24	23	June Lake, NT	Ronald K. Pettit	Ronald K. Pettit	1993	14
430 7/8	44 2/8	42	40 2/8	7 3/8	7 2/8	20 2/8	9 5/8	16 1/8	3 5/8	25	20	Ludwig Lake, BC	Gary D. Lloyd	Gary D. Lloyd	1987	15
428 5/8	42 5/8	47 2/8	35 2/8	7 4/8	7 1/8	17 1/8	16 1/8	12 3/8	10 4/8	21	22	Atlin, BC	Rafael Garcia Cano	Cascade Lodge	1968	16
428 4/8	56 6/8	55	37	7 4/8	7 4/8	15 4/8	15	17	15 7/8	19	19	Dease Lake, BC	Fred G. Kelly	Fred G. Kelly	1964	17
428 1/8	40 2/8	43 3/8	34 4/8	6 7/8	6 6/8	19 6/8	15	15 4/8	1/8	17	14	Ross River, YT	Picked Up	Jack R. Cook	1991	18
427 3/8	56 7/8	59	44 4/8	7 4/8	7 3/8	6	19 4/8	1/8	14 6/8	10	15	Pelly Mts., YT	Anna Chabara	Anna Chabara	1960	19
426 5/8	48 4/8	51 6/8	38 2/8	6 7/8	7	15 2/8	14 5/8	8	10	17	18	Pelly Mts., YT	Knut Wittfoth	Knut Wittfoth	1989	20
425 6/8	52 6/8	54 5/8	47	6 4/8	6 4/8	18 4/8	21 1/8	2 5/8	16	13	15	Kechika Range, BC	Victor E. Moss	Victor E. Moss	1988	21
425 1/8	55 3/8	52 2/8	34	7 3/8	7 7/8	10	20 2/8	1/8	17 6/8	12	25	Dease Lake, BC	Unknown	B&C National Collection	1917	22
424 3/8	47 7/8	49 5/8	43 5/8	6 7/8	7	16 6/8	16 2/8	10 7/8	8 5/8	22	22	Cold Fish Lake, BC	A.H. Clise	A.H. Clise	1968	23
424 2/8	47	46 4/8	37 3/8	6 1/8	6 2/8	15 2/8	15 2/8	9 7/8	7 2/8	20	19	Cold Fish Lake, BC	Howard Keeler	Howard Keeler	1954	24
423 7/8	46 2/8	45 3/8	34 4/8	7	6 5/8	14 5/8	14	10 3/8	4 3/8	16	16	Cold Fish Lake, BC	Edward E. Wilson	Edward E. Wilson	1963	25
423 6/8	42	40 5/8	33 1/8	6 3/8	6 4/8	16 3/8	17 6/8	13 4/8	6	21	23	Stikine Plateau, BC	Dwight Lewis	Dwight Lewis	1970	26
423 4/8	47 1/8	47 1/8	48 5/8	6 2/8	6 2/8	14 2/8	16	1 6/8	12 1/8	19	25	Cassiar, BC	Arvid F. Benson	Arvid F. Benson	1967	27
423 4/8	55 5/8	53 6/8	41 5/8	7 1/8	7 4/8	19 2/8	17 2/8	10 1/8	1 6/8	16	16	Divide Lake, NT	Les Jacobson	Les Jacobson	1988	27
423 1/8	51 6/8	50 6/8	32 3/8	6 7/8	7 2/8	20 7/8	18	6 3/8	11 2/8	18	18	Twitya River, NT	Carol S. Kraft	Carol S. Kraft	1987	29
422 7/8	45 4/8	44 7/8	36 5/8	7 1/8	7	15 4/8	19 3/8	1/8	13 2/8	17	20	Watson Lake, YT	Gary Lundstrom	Gary Lundstrom	1980	30
422 3/8	53 7/8	54 3/8	46	5 7/8	6 1/8	18 3/8	19 7/8	1/8	16 4/8	14	22	Keele Park, YT	Donald P. Smith, Jr.	Donald P. Smith, Jr.	1954	31
422 3/8	50 5/8	52	50	5 7/8	6	18 3/8	20 1/8	6 1/8	13 4/8	16	15	Little Dal Lake, NT	Dale L. Martin	Dale L. Martin	1976	31
422 2/8	65 1/8	62 2/8	50 5/8	7	7	15 4/8	15 4/8	8 3/8		22	14	Cassiar, BC	D.W. Bell	Acad. Nat. Sci., Phil.	1923	33
422 2/8	50 6/8	52 2/8	28 3/8	6 1/8	6 1/8	22 4/8	9 6/8	18 6/8	1/8	23	14	Mountain River, NT	Leroy A. Schommer	Leroy A. Schommer	1985	33
421 6/8	50 1/8	54 6/8	39 1/8	6 7/8	6 7/8	14 1/8	17 4/8	7 6/8	11 6/8	15	18	Arctic Red River, NT	Jerrell Coburn	Jerrell Coburn	1995	35
421 5/8	54	52 5/8	35 5/8	6 5/8	6 3/8	18 2/8	18	12 3/8	15 7/8	20	19	Aishihik Lake, YT	A.W. Fees, Jr.	A.W. Fees, Jr.	1971	36

Score										Pts	Pts	Locality	Hunter	Owner	Date Killed	Rank
421 4/8	42 5/8	40 2/8	25 6/8	6 2/8	6 2/8	15 4/8	13 5/8	7 6/8	7 7/8	25	22	Netson Lake, BC	Charlie D. Todd	Charlie D. Todd	1985	37
421 1/8	49 3/8	43 4/8	41 4/8	7 5/8	7 2/8	18 2/8	3 3/8	16 1/8	1/8	27	20	Taku Lake, YT	Lloyd Walker	Lloyd Walker	1961	38
420 5/8	45 1/8	44 7/8	40 4/8	6 2/8	6 2/8	19 2/8	13 3/8	13 3/8	6	27	17	Cold Fish Lake, BC	Maurice C. Perkins	Maurice C. Perkins	1961	39
420	59 6/8	62 3/8	44 3/8	5 7/8	6	22 7/8	14 2/8	20 2/8	8 4/8	21	15	Mackenzie Mts., NT	Martin C. Ernest	Martin C. Ernest	1978	40
420	51 3/8	52	42	6 7/8	5 7/8	15 2/8	18 5/8	9 7/8	12 6/8	17	16	Mountain River, NT	John D. Todd	John D. Todd	1985	40
419 6/8	52 2/8	50 2/8	42 2/8	8 2/8	8 2/8	19 5/8	16 1/8	13 4/8	11	21	18	Atlin Lake, BC	John Haefeli, Jr.	John Haefeli, Jr.	1964	42
419 5/8	50	50 3/8	37 1/8	6 7/8	6 7/8	18 4/8	17 6/8	15 1/8	1/8	20	16	Livingstone, YT	Charlie L. Bertani	Charlie L. Bertani	1977	43
419 3/8	51 2/8	49 5/8	40 7/8	7 2/8	7 1/8	18 1/8	20 5/8	2 4/8	13	15	13	Mt. Mye, YT	Clark A. Johnson	Clark A. Johnson	1981	44
417 7/8	47 4/8	50	36 4/8	6 4/8	6 3/8	6 5/8	17 5/8	1/8	12 2/8	13	21	Gladstone River, YT	Herman Peterson	Herman Peterson	1960	45
417 5/8	51	51 2/8	29 4/8	6 5/8	6 4/8	15 7/8	20 1/8	12 1/8	4 1/8	16	16	Fire Lake, YT	Marvin E. Egger	Marvin E. Egger	1986	46
417 4/8	43 7/8	43 2/8	30 3/8	6 1/8	6	18 7/8	18 6/8	12 6/8	6	21	16	Cassiar, BC	Elgin T. Gates	Elgin T. Gates	1953	47
417 1/8	49 4/8	49 5/8	42 4/8	6 4/8	6 4/8	21 1/8	10 6/8	6	14	15	16	Cold Fish Lake, BC	John E. Rhea	John E. Rhea	1959	47
417 1/8	49 5/8	51 5/8	40 6/8	7 2/8	7 5/8	11 6/8	17 3/8	1 5/8	14	19	16	Connally Lake, YT	Marlin P. Alt	Marlin P. Alt	1973	49
416 6/8	53 1/8	52 1/8	38 7/8	7 3/8	7 3/8	15 2/8	19 7/8	1/8	14 5/8	15	20	Little Dal Lake, NT	Patricia M. Dreeszen	Patricia M. Dreeszen	1984	50
416 4/8	50 1/8	47 2/8	46	6 3/8	6 4/8	14 7/8	12 3/8	10 3/8	1/8	14	18	Redstone River, NT	David D. Hill	David D. Hill	1980	51
416 3/8	42 2/8	40 2/8	31 5/8	8 2/8	8 3/8	11 1/8	15	3 7/8	11	24	26	Cold Fish Lake, BC	Charles E. Wilson, Jr.	Charles E. Wilson, Jr.	1970	52
416 1/8	52 6/8	51 2/8	47 6/8	7 4/8	7 4/8	18 3/8	18 5/8	2 3/8	11 3/8	12	13	Mountain Lake, NT	Stewart N. Shaft	Stewart N. Shaft	1985	52
416	50 2/8	50	42	6 1/8	6 1/8	18 2/8	20 1/8	8 2/8	9 5/8	13	13	Cold Fish Lake, BC	Clyde Williams	Clyde Williams	1966	54
415 3/8	57 1/8	53 5/8	45 2/8	7 1/8	7 3/8	16 5/8	16	6	14 3/8	13	16	Atlin, BC	R.W. Johnson	R.W. Johnson	1956	55
415 3/8	58 1/8	54 1/8	40 5/8	6 6/8	6 7/8	11 3/8	17	1/8	7 4/8	15	17	Pelly River, YT	Lee F. Olsen	Lee F. Olsen	1950	56
415 3/8	46 4/8	49	40 2/8	7 2/8	7 1/8	14 6/8	14 5/8	1/8	9 2/8	20	21	Cassiar, BC	James Keegan	James Keegan	1971	56
415 2/8	48 2/8	48 7/8	33 4/8	6 5/8	6 7/8	15	17 1/8	1 4/8	13	18	23	Mackenzie Mts., NT	Gerald Schroeder	Gerald Schroeder	1974	56
414 4/8	42 2/8	43 5/8	31	7 4/8	7 3/8	16 3/8	15 5/8	11 7/8	10	23	17	Lawson Lake, BC	Daniel E. Kelly	Daniel E. Kelly	1997	60
414 4/8	48 4/8	47 3/8	34	7 2/8	7 4/8	16 1/8	18 4/8	13 3/8	14	19	12	Arrowhead Lake, YT	Robert L. Pagel	Robert L. Pagel	1973	61
414 3/8	50 7/8	51 1/8	41 4/8	5 5/8	5 5/8	19 3/8	17 5/8	11	10 6/8	17	21	Watson Lake, BC	John H. Myaard	John H. Myaard	1971	61
414 3/8	48 3/8	48 2/8	40 2/8	7 1/8	7 2/8	3 1/8	16 1/8	1 2/8	10 4/8	16	19	Hoole River, YT	Kris M. Gustafson	Kris M. Gustafson	1984	63
414 1/8	54	53 4/8	28 2/8	7 7/8	7 3/8	15	15	11 2/8	5 3/8	15	17	Tweedsmuir Park, BC	Gary J. Deleenheer	Gary J. Deleenheer	1966	63
414 1/8	44 1/8	47	37 3/8	7 1/8	6 7/8	20 6/8	20 5/8	11 2/8	10 7/8	15	16	Kawdy Plateau, BC	Dan S. Muchow	Dan S. Muchow	1997	65
413 6/8	49 5/8	51 2/8	26	6 5/8	6 4/8	15 5/8	17 7/8	10	14 3/8	15	18	Cold Fish Lake, BC	D.W. Thiem	D.W. Thiem	1956	65
413 6/8	55	54 6/8	42 6/8	6 2/8	6 2/8	12 7/8	18 2/8	8 1/8	15 1/8	13	14	Johiah Lake, BC	Harold G. Vriend	Harold G. Vriend	1990	67
413 5/8	47 7/8	49	35 7/8	6 6/8	6 6/8	17 4/8	6 3/8	11 6/8	1 1/8	20	15	Dease Lake, BC	Bert Klineburger	Bert Klineburger	1960	67
413 4/8	49	49	36 4/8	6 6/8	6 6/8	20 2/8	19 2/8	11 6/8	2	17	27	Cassiar Mts., BC	Ira Jones	Ira Jones	1963	69
413 3/8	53 4/8	51 3/8	45 6/8	6 3/8	6 2/8	1	14 6/8	1/8	14 2/8	15	27	Atlin, BC	Mrs. R.S. Marvin, Jr.	Mrs. R.S. Marvin, Jr.	1956	70
413 2/8	42 3/8	39 6/8	35 1/8	6 2/8	7	8 3/8	18 4/8	1 6/8	15 4/8	17	10	Livingstone Creek, YT	Lawrence W. Dossman	Lawrence W. Dossman	1984	71
413 2/8	51 1/8	55	39 2/8	6 7/8	7	16	10 6/8	11 4/8	1/8	15	20	Atlin, BC	Mrs. Ramon Somavia	Mrs. Ramon Somavia	1955	72
413 2/8	41	44 1/8	40 3/8	8 7/8	7 6/8	15 6/8	13 6/8	6 7/8	9 6/8	19	14	Nisutlin Lake, YT	James V. Bosco, Sr.	James V. Bosco, Sr.	1935	72
413 2/8	44 4/8	49	31 6/8	7 1/8	7 1/8	18 4/8	7 2/8	13 6/8	1	16	26	Livingstone, YT	Lawrence W. Dossman	Lawrence W. Dossman	1975	72
413	43	46 7/8	25 7/8	7 5/8	6 4/8	17 1/8	19 6/8	4 4/8	14 4/8	22	18	Livingstone, YT	Mike J. Chirpich	Mike J. Chirpich	1977	75
413	51 4/8	53 7/8	43	6 5/8	6 5/8	15 4/8	16 7/8	8 3/8	7 4/8	14	14	Drury Lake, YT	James H. Russell	James H. Russell	1971	75
412 6/8	51 3/8	50 7/8	49 2/8	7 1/8	7 2/8	18 1/8	2 4/8	11 7/8	1/8	18	18	Kechika Range, BC	John J. Ottman	John J. Ottman	1988	77
412 6/8	50 3/8	53 6/8	47 3/8	6 3/8	6 2/8	18 1/8	2 6/8	12 3/8	1/8	15	15	Cassiar, BC	John R. Rinkevich	John R. Rinkevich	1968	77
412 6/8	48	47	47	7 3/8	7 2/8	16 5/8	17 4/8	10 6/8	10 3/8	18	18	Kechika Range, BC	Carol A. Domes	Carol A. Domes	1987	77
412 5/8	42 1/8	45 1/8	30 7/8	6 4/8	6	16 3/8	16 3/8	14 2/8	12 1/8	20	14	Grass Lakes, YT	Norman L. Meints	Norman L. Meints	1987	77
412 5/8	51 2/8	50 7/8	40 6/8	6 4/8	6 4/8	21 6/8	5 6/8	19 1/8	1/8	25	20	Black Fox Creek, BC	Tom Andres	Tom Andres	1991	81
412 4/8	49 7/8	50 2/8	38 5/8	6 6/8	6 5/8	15 6/8	17 6/8	10 2/8	9 6/8	21	25	Kechika Range, BC	Nolan Martins	Nolan Martins	1967	82
412 4/8	55 6/8	57 4/8	26	6 2/8	6 2/8	12 4/8	12 2/8	6	11	23	21	Cassiar Mts., BC	James F. Clarke	James F. Clarke	1929	82
412 4/8	48 1/8	51 3/8	33 3/8	6 7/8	7 3/8	19 4/8	14 1/8	14 2/8	8 2/8	18	15	Telegraph Creek, BC	Leon Mazzeo	Leon Mazzeo	1971	82

MOUNTAIN CARIBOU

Rangifer tarandus caribou

Score	Length of Main Beam R	L	Inside Spread	Circumference at Smallest Place Between Brow and Bez Points R	L	Length of Brow Points R	L	Width of Brow Points R	L	Number of Points R	L	Locality	Hunter	Owner	Date Killed	Rank
412 4/8	51 6/8	50	37 2/8	7 4/8	7 2/8	14 7/8	21 7/8	4 2/8	15 6/8	16	17	Ross River, YT	Barry E. Enders	Barry E. Enders	1984	82
412 3/8	49 2/8	48	36 3/8	6 2/8	6 3/8	18 2/8	12 2/8	14 5/8	3 7/8	16	16	Fort Nelson, BC	Elmer T. Newman	Gary F. Silc	1970	85
412 3/8	50 6/8	49 6/8	38 3/8	6 3/8	6 4/8	17 3/8	18	1 2/8	12 2/8	16	18	Mackenzie Mts., NT	James F. Willoughby	James F. Willoughby	1988	85
412	47 2/8	47 4/8	33 2/8	6 1/8	6 1/8	14	18	11 2/8	7 2/8	26	25	Dease River, BC	Herb Klein	Herb Klein	1960	87
412	43	47	37 2/8	7 3/8	7 3/8	11 6/8	16 4/8	1/8	11 3/8	21	19	Livingstone, YT	Arvo Walter Kannisto	Arvo Walter Kannisto	1974	87
412	47 7/8	52 4/8	40	6 5/8	6 5/8	17 6/8	16 1/8	12 4/8	5 1/8	14	14	Cassiar Mts., BC	Peter E. Paulos	Peter E. Paulos	1988	87
411 7/8	40 1/8	43 3/8	39 1/8	7 4/8	8 1/8	18	13 6/8	13 1/8	8 5/8	21	18	Fire Lake, YT	James C. Wondzell	James C. Wondzell	1991	90
411 2/8	49 2/8	49 1/8	30 7/8	6	8 1/8	17 2/8	18 3/8	11 6/8	11 2/8	20	21	Watson Lake, YT	John Csepp	John Csepp	1988	91
411 1/8	48 6/8	49 4/8	43	6 4/8	6 2/8	18 1/8	10	13 3/8	1/8	22	13	Norman Wells, NT	Elmer R. Kochans	Elmer R. Kochans	1981	92
411	39 5/8	40 5/8	31 6/8	7 6/8	7 5/8	20	17 2/8	14	10	17	17	Nisling Range, YT	Jack Odor	Jack Odor	1977	93
410 6/8	57 2/8	57 7/8	42 5/8	7	6 4/8	18 3/8	1 7/8	12 4/8	1/8	17	15	Keele Lake, YT	Robert L. Gilkey	Robert L. Gilkey	1986	94
410 3/8	48 5/8	47 7/8	34	6 6/8	6 2/8	17 3/8	5 4/8	16 1/8	1/8	27	19	Level Mts., BC	Stephen Sipes, Jr.	Stephen Sipes, Jr.	1985	95
410 1/8	53	53 2/8	41 2/8	7 3/8	7 1/8	16 7/8	18 7/8	9	5 7/8	9	18	Atlin, BC	Dale L. McCord	Dale L. McCord	1966	96
410 1/8	55 4/8	54 2/8	30 7/8	7	7 1/8	17 6/8	17 5/8	9 2/8	5 4/8	15	12	Cassiar Mts., BC	Charles J. Woodruff	Charles J. Woodruff	1970	96
410 1/8	52 4/8	53 7/8	39	6 6/8	7 6/8	19 5/8	18 1/8	16	10 1/8	22	21	Ram River, NT	Michael N. Anderson	Michael N. Anderson	1979	96
410	44 2/8	45 4/8	22 3/8	7 4/8	7 3/8	20 2/8	14 7/8	15 6/8	2 2/8	26	23	Level Mts., BC	James W. Reilly	James W. Reilly	1968	99
410	47	49 6/8	37 6/8	6 2/8	6 4/8	18 2/8	18 1/8	11 5/8	1 6/8	14	10	Deadwood Lake, BC	Joseph Mannino	Joseph Mannino	1986	99
409 7/8	46	45	44	7	7 5/8	20	18 6/8	9 3/8	15 6/8	17	20	Atlin, BC	Cliff Schmidt	Cliff Schmidt	1966	101
409 3/8	51 7/8	51 7/8	40 1/8	6 1/8	6 2/8	16 3/8	17 1/8	4	9 2/8	19	16	Divide Lake, NT	Eldon L. Thompson	Eldon L. Thompson	1986	101
409 3/8	41 4/8	42	36 4/8	7 7/8	7 7/8	20 4/8	7 2/8	15	3 1/8	13	13	Dease Lake, BC	Wilf Klingsat	Wilf Klingsat	1974	103
409 1/8	51 2/8	52 5/8	42 3/8	6 3/8	6 4/8	20	16 2/8	13 6/8	1/8	22	12	Ice Mt., BC	David M. George	David M. George	1966	104
409 1/8	45 3/8	46	30 6/8	7 2/8	7 4/8	14 4/8	14 3/8	10 6/8	12 4/8	22	24	Johanson Lake, BC	George L. Seifert	George L. Seifert	1968	104
409	48 2/8	44	48 2/8	7 7/8	8 1/8	18 6/8	11 4/8	14 1/8	1/8	18	14	Level Mts., BC	Larry A. Zullo	Larry A. Zullo	1978	106
408 7/8	43	43 7/8	34 1/8	6 1/8	6 1/8	14	15 2/8	6	8 4/8	18	16	Skeena River, BC	Gordon Baird	Gordon Baird	1966	107
408 4/8	48 6/8	47 6/8	35 6/8	6 7/8	6 7/8	14 7/8	16 4/8	1/8	6 2/8	16	16	Atlin, BC	Bradford O'Connor	Bradford O'Connor	1951	108
408 4/8	50 3/8	49 6/8	36 2/8	6 5/8	6 5/8	18	4 4/8	1/8	12 3/8	25	18	Mackenzie Mts., NT	Janet R. Johnson	Janet R. Johnson	1987	108
408 2/8	46 6/8	47	29	5 7/8	5 4/8	14 1/8	13 5/8	7 4/8	13 6/8	16	18	Spatsizi Plateau, BC	Michael M. Golightly	Michael M. Golightly	1985	110
408 2/8	46 6/8	46 3/8	32 5/8	7 6/8	7 2/8	8 3/8	18 2/8	1/8	14 7/8	19	24	Mt. Pike, YT	John T. Woloszyn	John T. Woloszyn	1994	110
408 2/8	51 2/8	51 2/8	30 5/8	9	6 5/8	16 4/8	18 6/8	3 7/8	13	20	21	Tsichu River, NT	Kristan Lashmore	Kristan Lashmore	1997	110
407 6/8	49	48 2/8	33 5/8	6 7/8	6 5/8	17 1/8	19 4/8	15	16	18	20	Cassiar Mts., YT	H.R. Safford III	H.R. Safford III	1968	113
407 6/8	50 1/8	45 2/8	36 5/8	7 3/8	6 7/8	17 1/8	13 4/8	10	9 2/8	20	14	Mackenzie Mts., NT	John K. Miller	John K. Miller	1989	113
407 5/8	42 7/8	45 5/8	40 6/8	6 7/8	6 5/8	17 4/8	16	9 6/8	1/8	16	14	Finlayson Lake, YT	Ken N. Booker	Ken N. Booker	1985	115
407 5/8	43 6/8	41 7/8	38 6/8	7	7	13 4/8	10 5/8	10 7/8	1/8	20	24	Tummel River, YT	William F. Calcagno, Jr.	William F. Calcagno, Jr.	1996	115
407 4/8	48 6/8	49 2/8	37 3/8	6 4/8	6 4/8	15 4/8	16 2/8	10 2/8	18 6/8	20	20	Buttle Creek, YT	Roy McLeod	Kerry Wagantall	1991	117
407 3/8	54 7/8	56 2/8	37 4/8	6 2/8	6 2/8	17 4/8	2 7/8	1/8	13 3/8	14	15	Keele River, NT	Roland Schwengler	Roland Schwengler	1984	118
407 3/8	46 3/8	48 2/8	35 3/8	6 7/8	6 6/8	16 3/8	15 2/8	11 6/8	1/8	17	17	Mackenzie Mts., NT	Tod L. Reichert	Tod L. Reichert	1996	118

Score												Locality	By whom killed	Owner	Date Killed	Rank
407 1/8	47 7/8	46 4/8	30	5 5/8	5 5/8	20 1/8	21	12 1/8	6 5/8	18	18	Lower Post, BC	Jack Jordon	Jack Jordon	1960	120
407	51 5/8	54 3/8	43 2/8	6 6/8	6 2/8	20 5/8	21 7/8	1 1/8	16 3/8	13	16	Watson Lake, BC	Len Anderson	Len Anderson	1967	121
407	51 4/8	54	42 1/8	7 1/8	6 5/8	6	19 6/8	7/8	10 6/8	18	14	Norman Wells, NT	Thomas P. Warner	Thomas P. Warner	1980	121
406 7/8	45 6/8	48 1/8	39 3/8	6 6/8	6 6/8	18 4/8	18 1/8	10 6/8	10 3/8	14	17	Tatlatui Lake, BC	Winston P. Woodman	Winston P. Woodman	1966	123
406 5/8	50 3/8	51 1/8	39 4/8	8 4/8	8 4/8	18 1/8	17 3/8	12 6/8	1 5/8	19	18	Mountain River, YT	Grover F. Glasner	Grover F. Glasner	1985	124
406 5/8	47 5/8	45 3/8	36 5/8	8 3/8	8 2/8	6 7/8	17 3/8	1/8	14 4/8	14	17	Tay Lake, YT	Ray J. Dennehy	Ray J. Dennehy	1988	124
406 4/8	43	44	30 3/8	6 6/8	6 6/8	17 5/8	17	11 5/8	10 1/8	18	14	Dawson Range, BC	Harold Ramberg	Harold Ramberg	1995	126
406 3/8	54	52 6/8	37 5/8	6 6/8	6 3/8	17 4/8	17	11 4/8	10 1/8	20	27	Kechika Range, BC	Basil C. Bradbury	B&C National Collection	1962	127
406 3/8	49 4/8	49 4/8	43 7/8	6	5 7/8	17 4/8	11 7/8	13 2/8	1/8	13	18	Drury Lake, YT	Robert T. Sanders	Robert T. Sanders	1997	127
406 2/8	54 2/8	54 2/8	48 2/8	6 4/8	6 5/8	19	16 3/8	1/8	10 3/8	12	9	Ross River, YT	Terrance D. Ferguson	Brian Hoffert	1994	129
406 1/8	43 4/8	41 5/8	35 6/8	6 6/8	6 4/8	3 7/8	19 3/8	12 4/8	4 6/8	21	9	Cassiar Mts., BC	Arvid F. Benson	Arvid F. Benson	1965	130
406	48 6/8	43 5/8	37 4/8	6 2/8	6 7/8	16	16	10 4/8	12 4/8	18	21	Tweedsmuir Park, BC	Bob Stewart	Bob Stewart	1964	131
406	54	53	42 1/8	7	6 7/8	16 4/8	17 6/8	5 7/8	11	18	17	Dawson Range, YT	John M. Domingos	John M. Domingos	1980	131
406	55 6/8	56 1/8	47	7 2/8	6 7/8	18 4/8	14 2/8	15	11	16	26	Jennings River, BC	R.D. Thomas, Jr.	R.D. Thomas, Jr.	1986	131
405 6/8	57 2/8	55 5/8	30	6 2/8	6 2/8	15	19	7 5/8	4 1/8	17	17	Watson Lake, BC	M.L. Walker	Marvin Walker	1968	134
405 4/8	52 5/8	51	38 3/8	6 3/8	6 7/8	17 2/8	13 3/8	13 3/8	7 4/8	14	14	Mackenzie Mts., NT	Robert J. Begeny	Robert J. Begeny	1976	135
404 6/8	44	40 5/8	36 4/8	8 2/8	7 2/8	16 4/8	19	5 6/8	9	14	14	Cold Fish Lake, BC	O.A. Campbell	O.A. Campbell	1959	136
404 4/8	43 7/8	45 2/8	45 2/8	6 2/8	6 2/8	16 4/8	17 4/8	8 4/8	15 6/8	23	26	Hess River, YT	Stanley W. Scruggs	Stanley W. Scruggs	1994	137
404 3/8	44	44	36	6 5/8	6 5/8	16 4/8	15	12	6 1/8	14	22	June Lake, NT	Myron A. Peterson	Myron A. Peterson	1980	138
404 2/8	48 2/8	48	40 2/8	5 4/8	5 4/8	16 2/8	18	8 6/8	7 4/8	23	15	Cassiar Mts., BC	Francis B. Wadelton	Francis B. Wadelton	1969	139
404 2/8	51 2/8	51 3/8	36 4/8	6	6	21 5/8	10 3/8	17 5/8	1/8	17	22	Mackenzie River, NT	Michael B. Murphy	Michael B. Murphy	1991	139
404 1/8	47 6/8	47 6/8	48	7	7	2 4/8	14 5/8	1	11 2/8	14	24	White River, YT	Perry Shankle	Perry Shankle	1955	141
404 1/8	52 5/8	53 6/8	36 5/8	7 3/8	7 4/8	5 2/8	22 2/8	16 5/8	16 5/8	29	12	Keele Peak, YT	Robert L. Gilkey	Robert L. Gilkey	1987	141
404	41	40	39 1/8	6 2/8	6 2/8	17	18	12 1/8	15 6/8	12	22	Teslin Lake, BC	Peter Hohn	Peter Hohn	1988	143
403 4/8	46 5/8	49	41 1/8	6	6	19 5/8	23 1/8	5 6/8	15 5/8	22	16	Keele River, NT	T.C. Britt, Jr.	T.C. Britt, Jr.	1968	144
403 4/8	49 7/8	50 7/8	36	6	6	23	7 7/8	1/8	19 6/8	21	16	Gem Lake, BC	Johann Gerdenits	Johann Gerdenits	1976	144
403 4/8	55	54 7/8	44 5/8	5 2/8	5 2/8	18 5/8	18 5/8	12 1/8	3 5/8	23	18	Carcajou River, NT	Julian B. White, Jr.	Julian B. White, Jr.	1988	144
403 3/8	44	46 1/8	32	6 3/8	6 1/8	17 1/8	10 3/8	12 1/8	1/8	12	26	Cassiar Mts., BC	Mrs. G.L. Gibbons	Mrs. G.L. Gibbons	1964	147
403 3/8	48 2/8	49 7/8	38 6/8	7 2/8	7	14	17	5 2/8	5 3/8	14	13	Gataga River, BC	Laurel E. Brown	Laurel E. Brown	1970	147
403 2/8	46	45 7/8	45 7/8	7 1/8	7	17 4/8	16	12 3/8	9 4/8	15	17	Ross River, BC	Gail W. Holderman	Gail W. Holderman	1989	147
403 2/8	47 4/8	51 3/8	51 3/8	7	7	17 6/8	17 4/8	14	10 6/8	16	16	Pelly Mts., YT	B.F. Briggs	B.F. Briggs	1963	150
403 2/8	45 3/8	43 4/8	43 4/8	7 6/8	8 2/8	8 2/8	21 1/8	10 4/8	14	13	13	Drury Lake, YT	Henry Macagni	Henry Macagni	1963	150
403 2/8	52 3/8	50 6/8	50 6/8	9	8 5/8	13 5/8	16 6/8	7 7/8	8 4/8	18	18	Ketchum Lake, BC	Andy Proksch	Andy Proksch	1978	150
403 2/8	50	52 2/8	31	7 2/8	7 2/8	10 7/8	17 7/8	7 7/8	11 1/8	24	16	Mountain River, NT	Reginald Zebedee	Reginald Zebedee	1986	150
402 7/8	52 2/8	48 3/8	41 5/8	7 3/8	5 2/8	20 5/8	18 5/8	12 6/8	15	24	18	Twitya River, NT	Percy Pyra	Percy Pyra	1984	154
402 6/8	47 1/8	47 7/8	36 6/8	5 2/8	6 4/8	6	6	14 7/8	1/8	17	14	Caesar Lakes, YT	Gladys M. Jamieson	Gladys M. Jamieson	1994	155
402 4/8	49 5/8	51 4/8	37 5/8	6 7/8	6 5/8	19 2/8	19 2/8	1	14 2/8	27	13	Level Mts., BC	Phillip Neuweiler	Phillip Neuweiler	1956	156
402 4/8	48 3/8	50 2/8	41 2/8	6 3/8	6 3/8	17 1/8	17 1/8	13 4/8	1/8	21	15	Mountain River, NT	Charles J. Gagliano	Charles J. Gagliano	1988	156
402 3/8	50 2/8	49 6/8	36 5/8	6 4/8	6 4/8	20 5/8	20 5/8	12	12 7/8	13	19	Dease Lake, BC	G.C.F. Dalziel	G.C.F. Dalziel	1958	158
402 1/8	49 6/8	47	40 5/8	7 1/8	6 7/8	7 5/8	7 5/8	1/8	14	15	19	Cottonwood Lake, BC	Collins F. Kellogg	Collins F. Kellogg	1969	159
402 1/8	47	47	39 4/8	7 1/8	7 1/8	16 2/8	16 2/8	11 4/8	9	19	20	Glenlyon Range, YT	Louis A. Rupp	Louis A. Rupp	1985	159
402	41 6/8	43 1/8	40 1/8	6 5/8	7 1/8	12 7/8	12 7/8	17 1/8	1/8	14	19	Tuya Lake, BC	Robert G. Frew	Robert G. Frew	1988	161
401 7/8	45	42 4/8	35 6/8	7 1/8	5 4/8	16 7/8	16 7/8	10	1 3/8	13	19	Mackenzie Mts., NT	Thomas E. South	Thomas E. South	1976	162
401 6/8	50 4/8	51 4/8	39 6/8	5 4/8	5 6/8	13 1/8	13 1/8	6 4/8	6 4/8	20	20	Mackenzie Mts., NT	Larry C. Fisher	Larry C. Fisher	1992	163
401 4/8	50 6/8	48 6/8	41 7/8	5 6/8	5 7/8	10 4/8	10 4/8	8 7/8	10 3/8	19	19	Dease Lake, BC	Hugh Bennett	Hugh Bennett	1961	164
401 2/8	43 7/8	46 6/8	32 1/8	6 2/8	7	15 7/8	15 7/8	11 1/8	1/8	14	14	Cassiar Mts., BC	Bernard W. McNamara	Bernard W. McNamara	1958	165
401 1/8	41 4/8	40	36 4/8	6 6/8	6 6/8	4 6/8	13 5/8	1 2/8	13 5/8	23	23	Cold Fish Lake, BC	P. Walsh	P. Walsh	1970	166

MOUNTAIN CARIBOU
Rangifer tarandus caribou

Score	Length of Main Beam R	L	Inside Spread	Circumference at Smallest Place Between Brow and Bez Points R	L	Length of Brow Points R	L	Width of Brow Points R	L	Number of Points R	L	Locality	Hunter	Owner	Date Killed	Rank
401 1/8	48	47 2/8	37 5/8	6 4/8	6 4/8	10 4/8	17 7/8	14	1/8	12	18	Arctic Red River, NT	Picked Up	L.M. Schmaus & S. Bowick	1986	166
401	42	41 6/8	36 4/8	8 4/8	8 5/8	16 1/8	11 6/8	11 2/8	3 5/8	15	15	Kechika Range, BC	H.I.H. Prince	H.I.H. Prince	1960	168
401													Abdorreza Pahlavi	Abdorreza Pahlavi		168
400 6/8	47 5/8	48 4/8	28 6/8	6 4/8	6 4/8	20 4/8	18 4/8	19 5/8	1/8	22	18	Mackenzie Mts., NT	James O. White	James O. White	1988	170
400 5/8	42 2/8	43 7/8	33 2/8	6 6/8	6 6/8	19	7 3/8	15 4/8	13 1/8	25	22	Aishihik Lake, YT	Armando J. Garcia	Armando J. Garcia	1987	171
400 5/8	44 6/8	44 6/8	34 4/8	6	6 3/8	17 3/8	19 3/8	11 6/8	4/8	14	18	Cassiar Mts., BC	Jack Fleishman, Jr.	Jack Fleishman, Jr.	1965	171
400 3/8	54 7/8	54 6/8	36 1/8	7 2/8	7 4/8	16 4/8	2 3/8	10	9 2/8	19	22	Nascha Creek, BC	W.A.K. Seale	W.A.K. Seale	1968	173
400 2/8	47 2/8	47	39 4/8	7	8 6/8	19	18 3/8	14 4/8	6/8	21	17	Cold Fish Lake, BC	Juan Brittingham	Juan Brittingham	1961	173
400 2/8	41 7/8	42 5/8	28 5/8	7 6/8	6 7/8	18 5/8	2 3/8	6 2/8	7	16	11	Caribou Mt., YT	Charles B. Heuring	Charles B. Heuring	1984	175
400	58 5/8	57 6/8	39 5/8	8	8 1/8	20 5/8	13 2/8	13 3/8	5 4/8	14	22	Dease Lake, BC	Stanley A. Chase	Stanley A. Chase	1973	176
400	37 1/8	39	31 1/8	6 5/8	6 4/8	13 7/8	14 4/8	9 6/8	6 1/8	19	14	Cold Fish Lake, BC	Charles P. Yarn, Jr.	Charles P. Yarn, Jr.	1965	176
400	54	53 6/8	37 4/8	6 4/8	6 4/8	17	14 2/8	6 4/8	8 7/8	18	24	Nahannie River, NT	Kevin Davidson	Kevin Davidson	1977	176
400	42 1/8	41	29	7	7	16 1/8	1 6/8	10 4/8	16 2/8	22	22	Little Rancheria River, BC	Allan Edwards	Allan Edwards	1988	176
400	50 2/8	45 4/8	36 3/8	7	7 1/8	19 5/8	17 4/8	14 1/8	6 5/8	24	18	Boya Lake, BC	Dale Selby	Dale Selby	1995	180
399 7/8	49 5/8	50 2/8	32 4/8	6 1/8	6 1/8	3 3/8	18 6/8	5/8	14 3/8	16	27	Eaglenest Range, BC	Robert J. Stevens	Robert J. Stevens	1967	180
399 7/8	43 2/8	41	37 5/8	6 5/8	6 5/8	18 3/8	17 6/8	12 3/8	12 2/8	15	16	Mackenzie Mts., NT	James J. McBride	James J. McBride	1989	180
399 7/8	46	44	37 1/8	5 6/8	5 6/8	18 5/8	17 3/8	13 6/8	4 1/8	26	18	Mackenzie Mts., NT	John E. Monek	John E. Monek	1994	183
399 6/8	47 2/8	49 2/8	33 2/8	8 4/8	8 6/8	14 4/8	17 6/8	3	7 5/8	20	17	Divide Lake, NT	Brooks Carmichael	Brooks Carmichael	1984	184
399 4/8	46 5/8	48	34 1/8	6 7/8	6 6/8	17 1/8	3 1/8	12 2/8	8 2/8	21	16	Cassiar Mts., BC	William R. Franklin	William R. Franklin	1969	184
399 4/8	45 1/8	45 1/8	38 1/8	5 6/8	5 7/8	15 1/8	16 6/8	8 2/8	12 4/8	19	18	Turnagain River, BC	Gerald L. Simpson	Gerald L. Simpson	1984	184
399 4/8	49 5/8	53 2/8	33	6 6/8	6 6/8	15 3/8	19 5/8	14 2/8	12 6/8	23	14	Mackenzie Mts., NT	Lawrence T. Keenan	Lawrence T. Keenan	1994	184
399 3/8	51 4/8	50 1/8	39 7/8	6 3/8	6 4/8	17 1/8	16	11 4/8	1/8	14	18	Mackenzie Mts., NT	Ilynn R. Schwartzberg	Ilynn R. Schwartzberg	1996	188
398 7/8	48 5/8	48 7/8	39	6 7/8	8	16 5/8	15 6/8	11 4/8	1	19	18	Ice Lakes, YT	F. David Thornberry	F. David Thornberry	1956	189
398 7/8	51 6/8	49	34 6/8	5 7/8	5 7/8	20	17 4/8	1 3/8	12 6/8	16	19	Cold Fish Lake, BC	George W. Hooker	George W. Hooker	1987	189
398 7/8	48 5/8	52 1/8	40 4/8	6 4/8	6 5/8	15 6/8	18	1/8	9 5/8	14	22	Mackenzie Mts., NT	Craig R. Johnson	Craig R. Johnson	1992	189
398 6/8	44 1/8	44 5/8	37 4/8	6 1/8	6 1/8	8	10 3/8	1/8	14 2/8	17	26	Cassiar Mts., BC	James Markle	James Markle	1992	192
398 3/8	44 7/8	42	34	6 6/8	6 4/8	19 4/8	11 1/8	11	7 6/8	21	13	Divide Lake, NT	John W. Zomer	John W. Zomer	1995	193
398 2/8	45 3/8	46 5/8	36 6/8	6 1/8	6 1/8	18 7/8	18 6/8	15	16 3/8	28	14	Spatsizi Plateau, BC	Udo Kerber	Udo Kerber	1995	193
398	54 4/8	56	38 6/8	7 1/8	7 1/8	19	16 7/8	14 3/8	11 6/8	18	18	Pelly Mts., YT	Warren Page	Warren Page	1970	194
398	47 1/8	44 2/8	36 5/8	6 3/8	6 2/8	18 6/8	14 5/8	10 2/8	12	14	12	Arctic Red River, NT	Michael F. Short	Michael F. Short	1982	195
398	47 1/8	49 4/8	39 1/8	6 2/8	6	15 5/8	15 3/8	11 1/8		22	23	Mackenzie Mts., NT	William J. Ostrom	William J. Ostrom	1994	195
397 6/8	46 4/8	47	35	5 7/8	5 7/8	4 7/8	17 3/8	6/8		13	20	Muncho Lake, BC	Tom Mould	Tom Mould	1960	197
397 4/8	46 1/8	43	34 1/8	6 6/8	6 6/8	14 6/8	18 1/8	11 6/8		17	20	Mountain River, NT	Kenn M. Haugen	Kenn M. Haugen	1993	198
397 4/8	42 4/8	40 7/8	30 1/8	5 6/8	5 5/8	16 6/8		14 1/8		20	17	June Lake, NT	Katherine A. Pyra	Katherine A. Pyra	1995	198
397 3/8	50	49	35	6 7/8	6 5/8	17		8 6/8		21	15	Mackenzie Mts., NT	Bob Donnelly	Bob Donnelly	1988	200
397 2/8	47	49	39 6/8	6 3/8	7 7/8	17 4/8		10 1/8		15	13	Glacier Lake, BC	Helmuth Katz	Helmuth Katz	1967	201

Score	Locality	Hunter	Owner	Date	Rank
397 2/8	Mackenzie Mts., NT	William J. Chronister	William J. Chronister	1978	201
396 7/8	Divide Lake, NT	Delbert E. Rieckers	Delbert E. Rieckers	1990	203
396 6/8	Mackenzie Mts., NT	Mark Cook	Mark Cook	1988	204
396 4/8	Cold Fish Lake, BC	L.W. Zimmerman	L.W. Zimmerman	1960	205
396 2/8	Cassiar Mts., BC	Peter C. Jurs	Peter C. Jurs	1964	206
396 2/8	Dease Lake, BC	David A. Smith	David A. Smith	1987	206
396 1/8	Drury Lake, YT	Ostell G. Penner	Ostell G. Penner	1985	208
396	Arctic Red River, NT	Hal Wheeler	Hal Wheeler	1993	209
395 7/8	Ice Lakes, YT	Tadeus S. Konieczka	Tadeus S. Konieczka	1982	210
395 7/8	O'Grady Lake, NT	Ralph Fleegle	R. Fleegle & D. Fleegle	1988	210
395 7/8	Mackenzie Mts., NT	Connie Blaszczak	Connie Blaszczak	1990	210
395 4/8	Atlin, BC	Ray Foerster	Ray Foerster	1960	213
395 4/8	Mackenzie Mts., NT	Carl V. Hancock, Jr.	Carl V. Hancock, Jr.	1997	213
395 3/8	Willow Creek, NT	Dwayne Moore	Dwayne Moore	1996	215
395 2/8	Cold Fish Lake, BC	D.A. Boyd	D.A. Boyd	1963	216
395 2/8	Dease Lake, BC	George H. Glass	George H. Glass	1963	216
395 2/8	Keele River, NT	George H. Fisher	George H. Fisher	1993	216
395 1/8	Prophet River, BC	V.B. Seigel	V.B. Seigel	1961	219
395	Mountain River, NT	Robert L. Williamson	Robert L. Williamson	1983	220
394 7/8	Wolf Creek, BC	Riley N. Ferguson	Riley N. Ferguson	1991	221
394 6/8	Cassiar, BC	Arcadio Guerra	Arcadio Guerra	1957	222
394 6/8	Divide Lake, NT	Richard A. Belotti	Richard A. Belotti	1987	222
394 6/8	Keele River, NT	Anthony T. Brazil	Anthony T. Brazil	1991	222
394 4/8	Ruby Range, YT	John R. Bloise	John R. Bloise	1985	225
394 3/8	Muncho Lake, BC	H.W. Julien	H.W. Julien	1965	226
394 3/8	Cassiar Mts., BC	Raymond A. Schneider	Raymond A. Schneider	1968	226
394 1/8	Cry Lake, BC	Ritchey Elliott	Catherine Mulvahill	1987	228
394	Turnagain River, BC	Robert E. Miller	Robert E. Miller	1968	229
394	Mackenzie Mts., NT	William E. Pipes III	William E. Pipes III	1974	230
393 6/8	Mackenzie Mts., NT	Steven S. Bruggeman	Steven S. Bruggeman	1988	230
393 6/8	Arctic Red River, NT	James K. McCasland	James K. McCasland	1988	230
393 6/8	Ross River, BC	Greg Kushnak	Greg Kushnak	1997	230
393 3/8	Mackenzie Mts., NT	Lonnie L. Ritchey	Lonnie L. Ritchey	1990	234
393 2/8	Tweedsmuir Park, BC	Harold Daye	Harold Daye	1960	235
393 1/8	Cassiar Dist., BC	Robert E. Miller	Robert E. Miller	1966	235
393	Grass Lakes, YT	Melvin R. Spohn	Melvin R. Spohn	1981	237
393	Mt. Thule, BC	William L. Searle	William L. Searle	1963	238
392 7/8	Ross River, BC	Robert C. Stephens	Robert C. Stephens	1993	238
392 7/8	Cassiar Mts., BC	Charles Haas	Charles Haas	1959	240
392 6/8	Atlin, BC	Earl H. Carlson	Wildl. Tax. Studios	1966	240
392 6/8	W. Toad River, BC	Daniel R. Bond	Daniel R. Bond	1966	240
392 5/8	Little Dal Lake, NT	Douglas M. Dreeszen	Douglas M. Dreeszen	1984	242
392 5/8	Cold Fish Lake, BC	Richard G. Van Vorst	Richard G. Van Vorst	1974	242
392 3/8	Arctic Red River, NT	Leo M. Schmaus	Leo M. Schmaus	1986	244
392 3/8	Kechika Range, BC	H.I.H. Prince Abdorreza Pahlavi	Game Council of Iran	1960	244
392 3/8	Ice Mt., BC	J.E. Mason	J.E. Mason	1966	246

489

MOUNTAIN CARIBOU

Rangifer tarandus caribou

Score	Length of Main Beam R	L	Inside Spread	Circumference at Smallest Place Between Brow and Bez Points R	L	Length of Brow Points R	L	Width of Brow Points R	L	Number of Points R	L	Locality	Hunter	Owner	Date Killed	Rank
392 3/8	47 7/8	45 4/8	32 4/8	6 6/8	6 3/8	16 6/8	17 2/8	9 3/8	6	15	12	Logan Mts., YT	Gordon Graham	Gordon Graham	1978	246
392 3/8	44 1/8	44	34 7/8	6 3/8	6 3/8	16 4/8	17 2/8	10 3/8	6 5/8	18	16	Dease Lake, BC	Ross H. Mann	Ross H. Mann	1984	246
392 2/8	45 6/8	43 1/8	30 7/8	5 2/8	5 2/8	16 3/8	17	8 4/8	11 6/8	18	22	Keele River, NT	Dale R. Hill	Dale R. Hill	1980	250
392 2/8	41 1/8	46	29 6/8	6 7/8	6 7/8	3 6/8	16 3/8	1/8	13	14	20	Fire Lake, YT	Michael L. Haydock	Michael L. Haydock	1989	250
392 1/8	39 4/8	46 2/8	38	7 4/8	7 5/8	17 4/8	17	7 4/8	7 1/8	17	13	Rabbit River, BC	Bob C. Jones	Bob C. Jones	1969	252
392	42 4/8	47 4/8	32 4/8	5 6/8	6 4/8	19 2/8	5 2/8	13 2/8	1	19	15	Twopete Mt., YT	David H. Crum	David H. Crum	1984	253
391 7/8	43 4/8	45 5/8	42 3/8	6 5/8	6 7/8	15 5/8	16 1/8	12	11	24	19	Cassiar, BC	Dorothy N. Benson	Dorothy N. Benson	1967	254
391 7/8	53 3/8	53	40 3/8	6 2/8	6 1/8	17 5/8	15 7/8	5 2/8	5 4/8	11	11	Glacier Lake, BC	Lowell C. Hansen II	Lowell C. Hansen II	1970	254
391 7/8	44 6/8	44 4/8	30 2/8	6 3/8	6 4/8	15 1/8	15 6/8	9	7 4/8	19	18	Mt. Rognaas, BC	Michael D. Miklosi	Michael D. Miklosi	1983	254
391 7/8	48 3/8	44 7/8	36 4/8	6 4/8	6	18 6/8	12 7/8	15 5/8	1/8	20	13	Keele River, NT	Dean Miller	Dean Miller	1994	254
391 5/8	46 3/8	43 7/8	34	5 7/8	6	18 3/8	21 2/8	19 4/8	17 6/8	18	21	Cassiar, BC	E.F. Ardourel	E.F. Ardourel	1960	258
391 4/8	48	46 2/8	37 6/8	6 6/8	6 3/8	19	15	6	10 4/8	15	16	Cassiar Mts., BC	Stan McKay	Stan McKay	1990	259
391 3/8	47 1/8	49	34 7/8	6 1/8	7 5/8	13 7/8	15	6 1/8	8	12	14	Mackenzie Mts., NT	William G. James	William G. James	1995	260
391 2/8	50 2/8	50	37 4/8	6 2/8	5 7/8	17 3/8	16 1/8	4 7/8	10 7/8	12	18	Drury Lake, YT	Nick Spiropolos	Nick Spiropolos	1970	261
391 2/8	49	52 5/8	40 4/8	5 6/8	5 5/8	22	21 2/8	5 3/8	11 3/8	14	13	Ruby Range, YT	William K. Hilton	William K. Hilton	1985	261
391 2/8	49 4/8	49 4/8	44 1/8	6 7/8	6 7/8	18 5/8	13 6/8	13	6 6/8	15	13	Twitya River, NT	Melvin E. Kraft	Melvin E. Kraft	1987	261
391 1/8	46 5/8	43 2/8	38 4/8	6 7/8	6 6/8	3	18 4/8	1/8	15 4/8	13	16	Atlin, BC	Bob Reinhold	Bob Reinhold	1963	264
391 1/8	49 1/8	47	36 4/8	6 7/8	6 6/8	14 6/8	13 3/8	8 7/8	2 5/8	16	17	Lonesome Creek, NT	Frank J. Kukurin	Frank J. Kukurin	1989	264
391	49 6/8	50 7/8	42 7/8	6 3/8	6 3/8	16 2/8	15 2/8	4 3/8	10 4/8	15	15	Blue River, BC	Aldo Guglielmini	Aldo Guglielmini	1976	266
391	38 5/8	39 4/8	37 7/8	7	7	7 4/8	17 1/8	1/8	11 7/8	19	20	Tuya Range, BC	Robert L. Gilkey	Robert L. Gilkey	1978	266
390 7/8	40 3/8	39	34 1/8	6 2/8	6	15 6/8	2 7/8	10	1/8	23	17	Tuya Lake, BC	John H. Epstein	John H. Epstein	1953	268
390 7/8	46	46 6/8	34	5 7/8	5 4/8	2 4/8	16 3/8	1/8	11 5/8	18	23	Snake River, BC	J.W.L. Monaghan	J.W.L. Monaghan	1963	268
390 6/8	42 3/8	45 6/8	24 4/8	6 2/8	6 2/8	15	14 2/8	13 1/8	15 3/8	24	25	N. Redstone River, NT	H. Hudson DeCray	H. Hudson DeCray	1995	270
390 5/8	51 7/8	48 7/8	45 1/8	7 3/8	7 1/8	6 6/8	18 3/8	3 6/8	6 6/8	12	12	Atlin, BC	Vern Cox	Vern Cox	1962	271
390 5/8	50 4/8	51 7/8	43	6 7/8	6 6/8	5	15	3/8	9 6/8	17	20	Semenot Hills, YT	Thomas F. Jeffcote	Thomas F. Jeffcote	1975	271
390 5/8	43 2/8	39 4/8	27 5/8	6 2/8	6 6/8	16 3/8	15 6/8	8 1/8	9 4/8	20	17	Drury Lake, YT	Robert D. Day	Robert D. Day	1986	271
390 5/8	44 4/8	45 7/8	35 3/8	5 6/8	5 7/8	15 3/8	17 6/8	9 7/8	9 2/8	23	17	Arctic Red River, NT	Arthur J. Bayer	Arthur J. Bayer	1994	271
390 4/8	39 2/8	39 3/8	36	5 6/8	6 2/8	16	18 2/8	11 5/8	7 5/8	20	18	Muncho Lake, BC	Dennis Dean	Dennis Dean	1963	275
390 4/8	37 4/8	38 5/8	37 5/8	7 4/8	7 5/8	18 2/8	17 4/8	11 7/8	13 4/8	17	19	Cassiar Mts., BC	Milo L. Blickenstaff	Milo L. Blickenstaff	1965	275
390 4/8	36 1/8	37 2/8	29 4/8	7 2/8	7 4/8	17 4/8	15 1/8	12 6/8	12 4/8	20	17	Halfway River, BC	Steven L. Rose	R. Lynn Ross	1965	275
390 4/8	57 3/8	57 6/8	42 1/8	5 4/8	5 4/8	2 4/8	19	1 1/8	12 4/8	15	17	Mountain River, NT	Jack R. Cook	Jack R. Cook	1981	275
390 3/8	54 2/8	54 6/8	37 2/8	7	6 6/8	17	1	11 5/8	2/8	15	14	Level Mts., NT	Donald S. Hopkins	Unknown	1928	279
390 3/8	55	56 6/8	47 2/8	7 4/8	8 1/8	18 2/8	16 5/8	8 7/8	1/8	12	12	Cassiar, BC	Orlando Bodeau	Orlando Bodeau	1953	279
390 2/8	41 7/8	41 3/8	34 7/8	5 6/8	5 6/8	16 7/8	16 6/8	14 3/8	4 5/8	19	18	Ice Lakes, YT	J. Michael Thornberry II	J. Michael Thornberry II	1996	281
390 2/8	44 4/8	43 7/8	31 2/8	5 7/8	6 1/8	11 1/8	11 1/8	1 1/8	16	12	18	Mackenzie Mts., NT	Charles M. Mendenhall	Charles M. Mendenhall	1997	281
390 1/8	47 1/8	50	40 4/8	6 3/8	6 7/8	17 1/8	6	14 3/8	1/8	21	16	Dease Lake, BC	W.A. Tharp	W.A. Tharp	1962	283

Score												Locality	Hunter	Owner	Date	Rank
390 ¹/₈	55 ²/₈	51 ⁶/₈	34 ¹/₈	6 ³/₈	6 ²/₈	17 ⁶/₈	18 ⁴/₈	12 ⁵/₈	2 ³/₈	15	11	Firesteel Lake, BC	Melvin K. Wolf	Melvin K. Wolf	1970	283
390	56 ⁷/₈	58 ³/₈	42 ³/₈	7	6 ³/₈	18 ⁶/₈	5 ³/₈	11 ¹/₈	¹/₈	15	18	Mackenzie Mts., NT	John R. Young	John R. Young	1985	285
434 ²/₈*	51 ¹/₈	51	35 ⁵/₈	7 ⁴/₈	7 ³/₈	16 ¹/₈	18 ²/₈	10 ²/₈	13 ⁴/₈	21	23	Fire Lake, YT	David Creamer	David Creamer	1995	
431 ⁴/₈*	50 ⁷/₈	48 ⁷/₈	38 ⁶/₈	5 ⁶/₈	5 ⁴/₈	17 ⁴/₈	18	6	12 ⁴/₈	15	20	Mackenzie Mts., NT	Henry S. Jennings III	Henry S. Jennings III	1991	
427 ¹/₈*	53 ⁴/₈	55 ¹/₈	35 ⁴/₈	7 ⁶/₈	6 ⁷/₈	19 ⁴/₈	10 ³/₈	9 ⁷/₈	¹/₈	23	16	Ice Lakes, YT	David Creamer	David Creamer	1996	
426 ⁶/₈*	56 ¹/₈	55	43 ²/₈	6	6	18 ¹/₈	21 ⁷/₈	5 ⁴/₈	16 ²/₈	17	16	Mackenzie Mts., NT	Kermit R. Hollingsworth	Kermit R. Hollingsworth	1997	
425 ⁵/₈*	52 ³/₈	55 ³/₈	42 ³/₈	6 ⁴/₈	9 ¹/₈	20 ²/₈	16 ⁷/₈	14 ⁵/₈	14 ⁴/₈	19	17	Mackenzie Mts., NT	Len H. Guldman	Len H. Guldman	1994	
418 ⁴/₈*	43	43 ⁶/₈	30 ³/₈	5 ⁶/₈	6	14 ⁵/₈	13	9 ⁷/₈	¹/₈	22	16	N. Redstone River, NT	L. Michael Ireland	L. Michael Ireland	1993	
414 ³/₈*	53 ⁶/₈	56	37 ⁴/₈	6 ²/₈	6 ²/₈	20 ³/₈	2 ⁷/₈	14	¹/₈	16	14	Jennings Lake, BC	Daniel Siepmann	Daniel Siepmann	1991	

* Final score is subject to revision by additional verifying measurements.

491

CATEGORY
MOUNTAIN CARIBOU

SCORE
421-6/8

HUNTER
JERRELL COBURN

LOCATION
ARCTIC RED RIVER., NT

DATE OF KILL
AUGUST 1995

CATEGORY
MOUNTAIN CARIBOU

SCORE
407-5/8

HUNTER
WILLIAM F. CALCAGNO, JR.

LOCATION
TUMMEL RIVER, YT

DATE OF KILL
SEPTEMBER 1996

492

CATEGORY
MOUNTAIN CARIBOU

SCORE
406-3/8

HUNTER
ROBERT T. SANDERS

LOCATION
DRURY LAKE, YT

DATE OF KILL
SEPTEMBER 1997

CATEGORY
MOUNTAIN CARIBOU

SCORE
390-6/8

HUNTER
H. HUDSON DECRAY

LOCATION
N. REDSTONE RIVER, NT

DATE OF KILL
SEPTEMBER 1995

CATEGORY
MOUNTAIN CARIBOU

SCORE
436-1/8

HUNTER
RONALD K. PETTIT

LOCATION
JUNE LAKE,, NT

DATE OF KILL
AUGUST 1993

WOODLAND CARIBOU
WORLD'S RECORD

Continuing to stand as the oldest World's Record, the top woodland caribou (*Rangifer tarandus caribou*) was shot in Newfoundland before 1910 and donated to the National Collection by the late Casimir de Rham.

The hunter who obtained the impressive mahogany colored antlers probably took his shot just before the rut in late summer, early fall when the animal's antlers had become fully developed and hardened. Newfoundland is considered the best hunting grounds for woodland trophies. Weighing upwards of 500 pounds, a particularly impressive woodland caribou will have a rack with as many as 40 tines. However, these are extremely difficult to count in the field, and other criteria must be considered such as rarer double shovels, as well as the size of the rack in proportion to the body.

Woodland caribou sometimes merely shift locally, and would have not moved much further than the southern part of the island during the autumn rut. Therefore, this trophy would have been hunted without too much concern for timing. If the animal was with the herd it would not have been overly difficult to track as the herd will leave a dark, obvious path on the delicate surface of the barrens. It is this soft terrain that allows them to be heard grazing from afar or clicking their heels as they move, and on a chilly, dank morning the hunter may even have spotted the rising vapor from the herd. Cover on the tundra is minimum, the ubiquitous bogs often make a stalk a cumbersome and wet task, and the wind is always a consideration. As the woodland caribou lowered

his head to graze upon the barrens for birch leaves or their mainstay, lichens, it would have proved difficult for the hunter to pick out the largest trophy without spooking the herd, which can suddenly move at 30 miles an hour.

Balancing all of these factors, this enormous woodland caribou was taken in a fair chase manner and exemplifies decades of Boone and Crockett's achievement in recording big game records. ■

BOUNDARIES FOR WOODLAND CARIBOU

Woodland caribou includes trophies from Nova Scotia, New Brunswick, and Newfoundland.

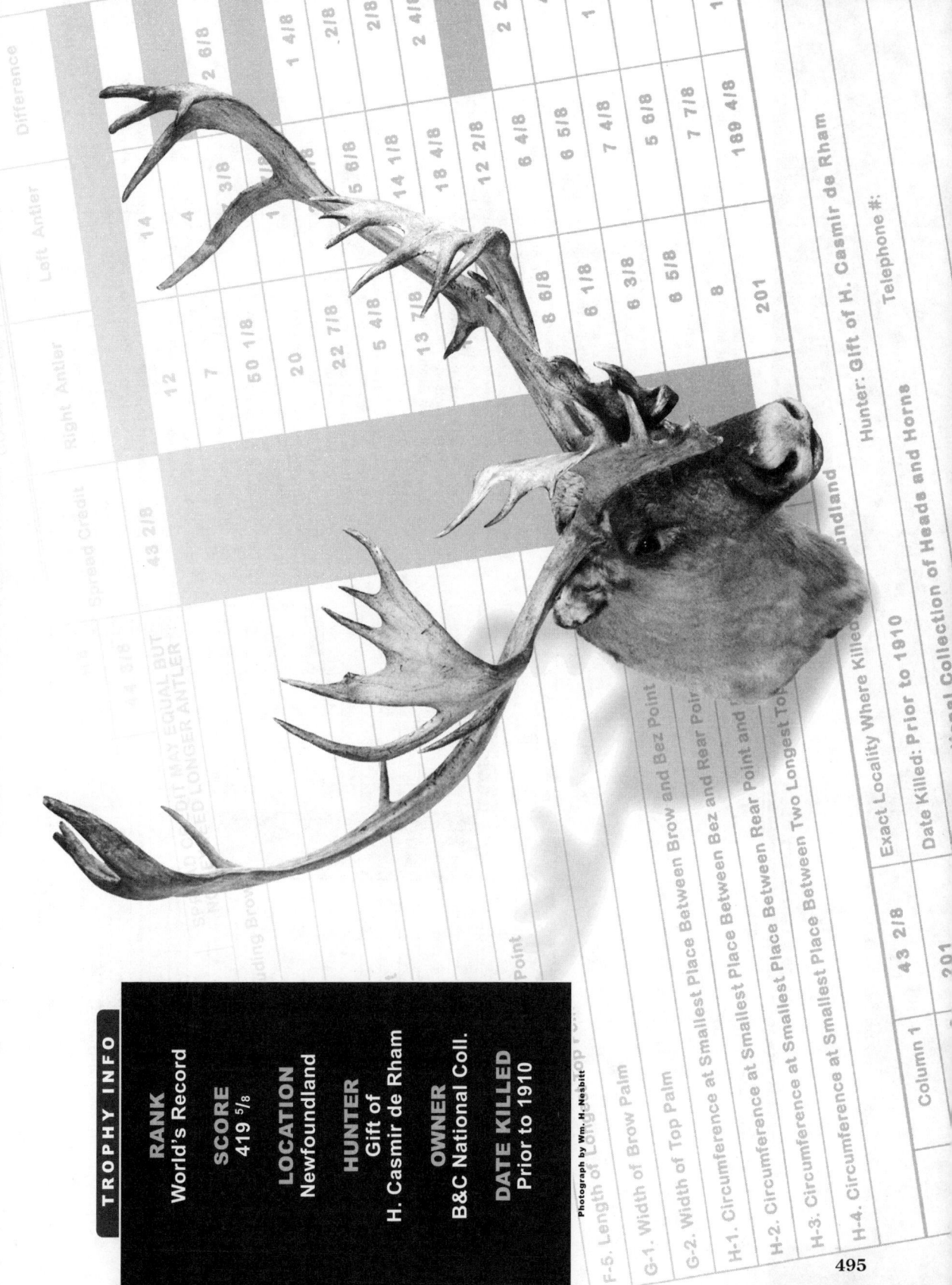

TROPHY INFO

RANK
World's Record

SCORE
419 5/8

LOCATION
Newfoundland

HUNTER
Gift of
H. Casmir de Rham

OWNER
B&C National Coll.

DATE KILLED
Prior to 1910

Photograph by Wm. H. Nesbitt

	Right Antler	Left Antler	Difference
	14		2 6/8
	7	3/8	1 4/8
50 1/8			2/8
20	5 6/8		2/8
22 7/8	14 1/8		2 4/8
5 4/8	18 4/8		
13 7/8	12 2/8		2 2/
8 6/8	6 4/8		4
6 1/8	6 5/8		1
6 3/8	7 4/8		
6 5/8	5 6/8		
8	7 7/8		1
201	189 4/8		

Spread Credit 43 2/8

SPREAD CREDIT MAY EQUAL BUT NOT EXCEED LONGER ANTLER 44 3/8

Hunter: Gift of H. Casmir de Rham
Telephone #:

Exact Locality Where Killed: Newfoundland
Date Killed: Prior to 1910

Gift of H. Casmir de Rham
National Collection of Heads and Horns

F-5. Length of Long
G-1. Width of Brow Palm
G-2. Width of Top Palm
H-1. Circumference at Smallest Place Between Brow and Bez Point
H-2. Circumference at Smallest Place Between Bez and Rear Point
H-3. Circumference at Smallest Place Between Rear Point and
H-4. Circumference at Smallest Place Between Two Longest To

	Column 1
	43 2/8
	201

WOODLAND CARIBOU
WORLD'S RECORD SCORECHART

All measurements must be made with a 1/4-inch wide flexible steel tape to the nearest one-eighth of an inch. (Note: A flexible steel cable can be used to measure points and main beams only.) Enter fractional figures in eighths, without reduction. Official measurements cannot be taken until the antlers have air dried for at least 60 days after the animal was killed.

A. Tip to Tip Spread is measured between tips of main beams.

B. Greatest Spread is measured between perpendiculars at a right angle to the center line of the skull at widest part, whether across main beams or points.

C. Inside Spread of Main Beams is measured at a right angle to the center line of the skull at widest point between main beams. Enter this measurement again as the Spread Credit **if** it is less than or equal to the length of the longer antler; if greater, enter longer antler length for Spread Credit.

D. Number of Points on Each Antler: To be counted a point, a projection must be at least one-half inch long, with length exceeding width at one-half inch or more of length. Beam tip is counted as a point but not measured as a point. There are no "abnormal" points in caribou.

E. Length of Main Beam is measured from the center of the lowest outside edge of burr over the outer side to the most distant point of the main beam. The point of beginning is that point on the burr where the center line along the outer side of the beam intersects the burr, then following generally the line of the illustration.

F-1-2-3. Length of Points are measured from nearest edge of beam over outer curve to tip. Lay the tape along the outer curve of the beam so that the top edge of the tape coincides with the top edge of the beam on both sides of point to determine the baseline for point measurement. Record point lengths in appropriate blanks.

F-4-5. Length of Points are measured from the tip of the point to the top of the beam, then at a right angle to the bottom edge of beam. The Second Longest Top Point **cannot** be a point branch of the Longest Top Point.

G-1. Width of Brow is measured in a straight line from top edge to lower edge, as illustrated, with measurement line at a right angle to main axis of brow.

G-2. Width of Top Palm is measured from midpoint of lower edge of main beam to midpoint of a dip between points, at widest part of palm. The line of measurement begins and ends at midpoints of palm edges, which gives credit for palm thickness.

H-1-2-3-4. Circumferences are taken as illustrated for measurements. If brow point is missing, take H-1 at smallest point between burr and bez point. If rear point is missing, take H-2 and H-3 measurements at smallest place between bez and first top point. Do not depress the tape into any dips of the palm or main beam.

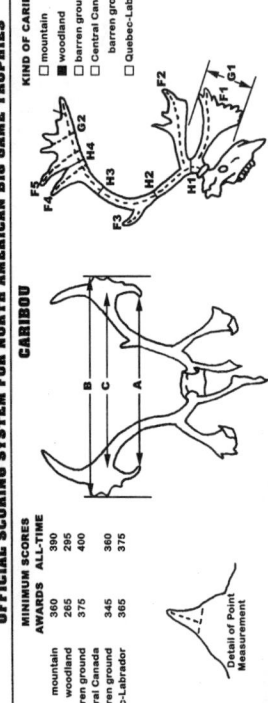

Records of
North American
Big Game

250 Station Drive
Missoula, MT 59801
(406) 542-1888

BOONE AND CROCKETT CLUB®
OFFICIAL SCORING SYSTEM FOR NORTH AMERICAN BIG GAME TROPHIES

CARIBOU

MINIMUM SCORES	AWARDS	ALL-TIME
mountain	360	390
woodland	265	295
barren ground	375	400
Central Canada barren ground	345	360
Quebec-Labrador barren ground	365	375

KIND OF CARIBOU (check one)
- ☐ mountain
- ☑ woodland
- ☐ barren ground
- ☐ Central Canada barren ground
- ☐ Quebec-Labrador barren ground

Detail of Point Measurement

SEE OTHER SIDE FOR INSTRUCTIONS

		COLUMN 1	COLUMN 2	COLUMN 3	COLUMN 4
		Spread Credit	Right Antler	Left Antler	Difference
A. Tip to Tip Spread	36 4/8				
B. Greatest Spread	44 3/8				
C. Inside Spread of Main Beams	43 2/8	SPREAD CREDIT MAY EQUAL BUT NOT EXCEED LONGER ANTLER	43 2/8			
D. Number of Points on Each Antler Excluding Brows			12	14	2
Number of Points on Each Brow			7	4	
E. Length of Main Beam			50 1/8	47 3/8	2 6/8
F-1. Length of Brow Palm or First Point			20	17 7/8	2
F-2. Length of Bez or Second Point			22 7/8	21 3/8	1 4/8
F-3. Length of Rear Point, if Present			5 4/8	5 6/8	2/8
F-4. Length of Second Longest Top Point			13 7/8	14 1/8	2/8
F-5. Length of Longest Top Point			16	18 4/8	2 4/8
G-1. Width of Brow Palm			17 6/8	12 2/8	
G-2. Width of Top Palm			8 6/8	6 4/8	2 2/8
H-1. Circumference at Smallest Place Between Brow and Bez Point			6 1/8	6 5/8	4/8
H-2. Circumference at Smallest Place Between Bez and Rear Point			6 3/8	7 4/8	1 1/8
H-3. Circumference at Smallest Place Between Rear Point and First Top Point			6 6/8	5 6/8	7/8
H-4. Circumference at Smallest Place Between Two Longest Top Palm Points			8	7 7/8	1/8
	TOTALS	43 2/8	201	189 4/8	14 1/8

ADD	Column 1	43 2/8	Exact Locality Where Killed: Newfoundland
	Column 2	201	Date Killed: Prior to 1910
	Column 3	189 4/8	Owner: National Collection of Heads and Horns
	Subtotal	433 6/8	Owner's Address:
SUBTRACT Column 4		14 1/8	Guide's Name and Address:
FINAL SCORE		419 5/8	Remarks: (Mention Any Abnormalities or Unique Qualities)

Hunter: Gift of H. Casmir de Rham   Telephone #:

COPYRIGHT © 1999 BY BOONE AND CROCKETT CLUB®

TROPHY INFO

RANK
2

SCORE
405 4/8

LOCATION
Gander River, NF

HUNTER
George H. Lesser

OWNER
Harold Pelly

DATE KILLED
1951

Photograph courtesy of the American Museum of Natural History

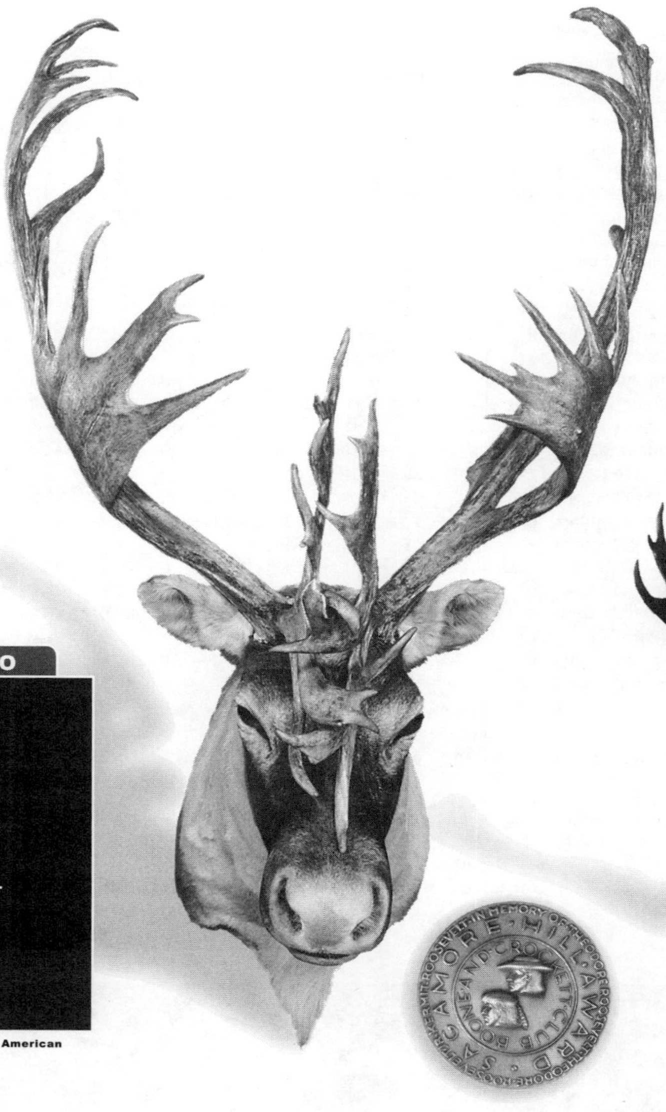

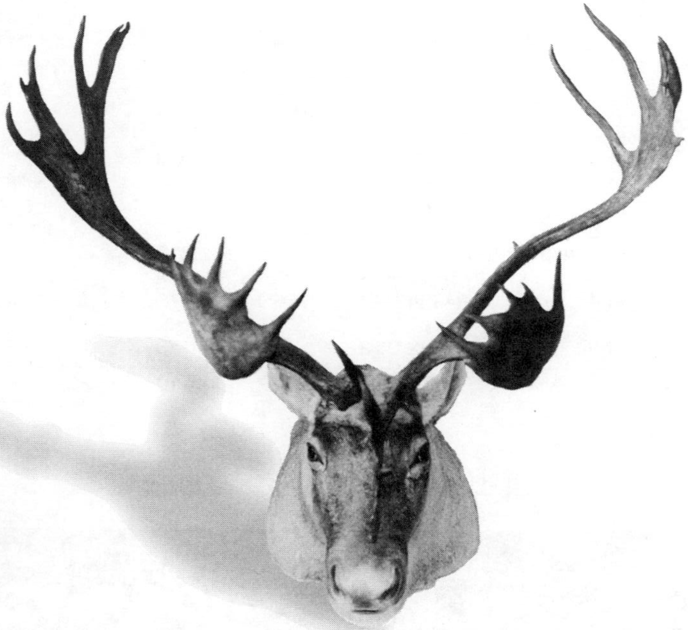

TROPHY INFO

RANK
6

SCORE
357 6/8

LOCATION
Gull River, NF

HUNTER
Picked Up

OWNER
Gerard R. Beaulieu

DATE KILLED
1988

Photograph courtesy of Gerard R. Beaulieu

WOODLAND CARIBOU

Rangifer tarandus caribou

Score	Length of Main Beam R	L	Inside Spread	Circumference at Smallest Place Between Brow and Bez Points R	L	Length of Brow Points R	L	Width of Brow Points R	L	Number of Points R	L	Locality	Hunter	Owner	Date Killed	Rank
419 5/8	50 1/8	47 3/8	43 2/8	6 1/8	6 5/8	20	17 7/8	17 6/8	12 2/8	19	18	Newfoundland	Gift of H. Casmir de Rham	B&C National Collection	PR 1910	1
405 4/8	**45**	**44**	**30 3/8**	**5 6/8**	**5 6/8**	**20 1/8**	**20 1/8**	**19 5/8**	**19 5/8**	**22**	**21**	**Gander River, NF**	**George H. Lesser**	**Harold Pelly**	**1951**	**2**
405 1/8	38	39 6/8	34	6 1/8	5 4/8	21 7/8	20 3/8	18 4/8	18 4/8	22	25	Millertown, NF	Robert V. Knutson	Robert V. Knutson	1966	3
380 2/8	47 3/8	45 7/8	36 7/8	5 6/8	5 6/8	21 7/8	22	16 6/8	16 6/8	22	18	Bonavista Bay, NF	Unknown	Crow's Nest Officers Club	1935	4
373 6/8	39 7/8	43 3/8	22 1/8	5 2/8	5 4/8	24 4/8	22 3/8	21	21	21	22	Newfoundland	Gift of J.B. Marvin, Jr.	Unknown	PR 1924	5
357 6/8	39 4/8	41 7/8	46 3/8	5 2/8	5 4/8	16	17 2/8	12 7/8	12 7/8	13	15	Gull River, NF	Picked Up	Gerard R. Beaulieu	1988	6
357 4/8	43 4/8	43 6/8	45 2/8	5 4/8	5	19 7/8	12 2/8	3 2/8	3 2/8	23	15	Mt. Peyton, NF	Picked Up	Harold Pelley	1968	7
356 7/8	42 5/8	43 7/8	31 6/8	5 2/8	5 2/8	19 3/8	19 2/8	16 4/8	16 4/8	15	18	Serpentine Lake, NB	F.W. Ayer	Carnegie Museum	1899	8
352 2/8	40	43 5/8	23 1/8	5 2/8	5 2/8	20 1/8	19 3/8	15 5/8	15 5/8	15	13	Deer Pond, NF	John McTurk, Jr.	John McTurk, Jr.	1996	9
350 3/8	44 4/8	41 7/8	45 2/8	5 4/8	5 5/8	17 2/8	17 1/8	7 4/8	7 4/8	14	16	Louse Lake, NF	William J. Chasko	William J. Chasko	1963	10
350 1/8	39 3/8	44	30 5/8	5 6/8	5 6/8	21 5/8	19 5/8	17 2/8	22	21	18	Gander, NF	Robert M. Lee	Robert M. Lee	1951	11
347 7/8	41 3/8	39 7/8	39 4/8	5 7/8	6 2/8	15 2/8	14 6/8	5 5/8	14	20	20	Gander River, NF	E.B. Warner	E.B. Warner	1951	12
347	45 3/8	43 1/8	33 3/8	5 5/8	5 5/8	14	19	3	13 1/8	17	15	Rocky Pond, NF	Gordon J. Birgbauer, Jr.	Gordon J. Birgbauer, Jr.	1984	13
346 6/8	39 2/8	39 2/8	32	6 3/8	6	15 1/8	15 6/8	12 5/8	10	17	17	Deer Pond, NF	Buck Taylor	Buck Taylor	1991	14
345 6/8	42 3/8	43	35 2/8	7 1/8	6 3/8	14	14 7/8	1 2/8	16 3/8	23	14	Lake Kaegudeck, NF	J.J. Veteto	J.J. Veteto	1968	15
345 2/8	39 7/8	39 7/8	28 2/8	6 6/8	6 7/8	17 3/8	16 5/8	16 3/8	17	18	19	Newfoundland	Wilson Potter	Unknown	1909	16
341 2/8	37 6/8	38 1/8	31	5 3/8	5 3/8	17	18 4/8	17	11	15	20	Grey River, NF	Karl Dore	Karl Dore	1984	17
341 2/8	38 7/8	38 6/8	38 1/8	5 6/8	6 1/8	15 2/8	16 3/8	13 2/8	13 2/8	13	15	Barachois Brook, NF	Harry L. Gunter	Harry L. Gunter	1986	17
340 7/8	38 6/8	40 3/8	31	5 4/8	5 4/8	15 2/8	16 4/8	10 2/8	15 1/8	15	17	Shanadithit Brook, NF	Gene Manion	Gene Manion	1964	19
340 2/8	46	44 6/8	27 2/8	6 1/8	6 1/8	17 5/8	17	15 1/8	13 4/8	15	16	Victoria River, NF	Dempsey Cape	Dempsey Cape	1966	20
340 2/8	40 2/8	41 1/8	35 3/8	5 1/8	4 7/8	16 1/8	16 3/8	10 2/8	13 4/8	17	17	Wall's Pond, NF	Jeff Lawton	Jeff Lawton	1971	20
339 2/8	50 6/8	50	30 5/8	8 6/8	8 6/8	1 3/8	1 3/8	13 2/8	13 1/8	10	12	New Gander, NF	Elgin T. Gates	Elgin T. Gates	1962	22
338 3/8	37 2/8	41 3/8	41 3/8	4 7/8	4 7/8	15 2/8	14 7/8	12 3/8	13 1/8	17	12	Avalon Pen., NF	Picked Up	Gerard Beaulieu	PR 1970	23
337	40 4/8	41	42 7/8	6 3/8	6 3/8	17	18	12 3/8	12 3/8	15	10	Gander, NF	Michael Savino	Michael Savino	1969	24
336 1/8	40 6/8	40 6/8	26 7/8	5 3/8	5 3/8	22 2/8	16 3/8	1/8	19 4/8	15	9	Barachois Brook, NF	Thomas W. Triplett	Thomas W. Triplett	1986	25
334 1/8	39 6/8	39 6/8	31	5 1/8	5 1/8	17 2/8	16 7/8	16	16	15	18	King George Lake, NF	John R. Blanton	John R. Blanton	1984	26
334	34 4/8	37 5/8	29 4/8	5 6/8	5 6/8	14 1/8	14 1/8	12 4/8	12 4/8	25	16	Red Indian Lake, NF	Grancel Fitz	Mrs. Grancel Fitz	1960	27
332 7/8	46 6/8	43 5/8	28 6/8	5	5	15 2/8	15 3/8	11 5/8	14 3/8	20	19	La Poile, NF	Donald A. Piombo	Donald A. Piombo	1979	28
332 6/8	30 4/8	28 3/8	26 3/8	4 7/8	6 6/8	15 5/8	16 6/8	15 3/8	12 5/8	14	19	Robinson Brook, NF	Picked Up	Harold Pelley	1990	29
332 3/8	38 3/8	35 2/8	31 4/8	6 6/8	5 7/8	15 1/8	13 3/8	10 1/8	13 6/8	19	20	Daniel's Harbour, NF	Shawn D. Perry	Shawn D. Perry	1996	30
332 2/8	35 6/8	36	27 6/8	6 2/8	6 2/8	17 2/8	16 3/8	13 4/8	16 2/8	23	18	Newfoundland	Gift of J.B. Marvin to NCHH	Unknown	PR 1924	31
332 2/8	35 5/8	36 7/8	28	6	6 2/8	16 1/8	15	13 6/8	13 5/8	25	21	Newfoundland	Gift of Grover Asmus to NCHH	Unknown	1932	31
331 2/8	46 2/8	48	40 6/8	5 6/8	5 6/8	17 2/8	18 4/8	14	11	11	11	Newfoundland	Frederick Brooks	Harvard Univ. Mus.	1881	33

Score	L.M.B. R	L.M.B. L	Inside Spread							Pts R	Pts L	Locality	Hunter	Owner	Date	Rank
330 5/8	31 2/8	34 2/8	26 6/8	5 4/8	5 5/8	15 4/8	15 3/8	13 4/8	11	22	23	New Brunswick	R.W. Gelbach	M.C. McQueen	1900	34
330 5/8	41 2/8	42 3/8	33 3/8	5 5/8	5 5/8	14 1/8	16 2/8	13 4/8	14 3/8	18	19	Meelpaeg, NF	Alex Kariotakis	Alex Kariotakis	1969	34
329 4/8	37 6/8	38 6/8	26 2/8	5 1/8	5	15 2/8	16	11 5/8	7 7/8	17	16	Robinsons River, NF	Timothy E. Fiedler	Timothy E. Fiedler	1980	36
329 2/8	40 1/8	44 2/8	32 1/8	5 4/8	5 4/8	16 6/8	14 5/8	12 2/8	10 2/8	15	14	Long Range Mts., NF	Thomas Robarts	Thomas Robarts	1991	37
328 2/8	35 4/8	38	31 1/8	5 4/8	5 4/8	15 4/8	17	12 5/8	13 6/8	18	17	Gulp Pond, NF	Michael E. Lombardo	Michael E. Lombardo	1968	38
327 7/8	44 2/8	44 3/8	32 1/8	5 6/8	5 6/8	15 4/8	12 7/8	13 5/8	11 2/8	18	17	Princes Pond, NF	Dermod O. Sullivan	Dermod O. Sullivan	1967	39
327 5/8	43 1/8	40 6/8	38 7/8	6 1/8	6 1/8	10 3/8	14 4/8	1/8	11 2/8	12	15	South Branch, NF	Mark L. Johansen	Mark L. Johansen	1986	40
327 3/8	39 3/8	39 3/8	27	4 6/8	4 6/8	16 1/8	17 3/8	6 4/8	14 3/8	18	18	Caribou Lake, NF	Conrad R. Bragg	Conrad R. Bragg	1962	41
326 3/8	41 2/8	40 4/8	31 1/8	6	6	14 1/8	15 7/8	11 3/8	9 7/8	23	21	Avalon Pen., NF	Harrold Clarke	Harrold Clarke	1971	42
326 2/8	39 5/8	41 1/8	31 7/8	5 7/8	5 7/8	15 5/8	12 4/8	9	8 2/8	17	13	Rocky Pond, NF	Thomas E. Phillippe, Jr.	Thomas E. Phillippe, Jr.	1975	43
325 4/8	42 4/8	41	36 1/8	5 6/8	5 6/8	14 1/8	12 4/8	10 7/8	10 7/8	11	17	Caribou Lake, NF	Lyle M. Paro	Lyle M. Paro	1981	44
325 3/8	43 5/8	45 2/8	34 3/8	6 1/8	6 1/8	13 3/8	12 1/8	7 4/8	10 7/8	18	15	Dashwoods Pond, NF	Daniel P. Amatuzzo	Daniel P. Amatuzzo	1983	45
325	45 7/8	44 5/8	42 6/8	6 2/8	6 2/8	12 6/8	16 5/8	1/8	2	17	14	Bear Pond, NF	Stanley T. Beers	Stanley T. Beers	1970	46
324 3/8	36 5/8	39 4/8	36 4/8	5 7/8	5 7/8	13 3/8	18 6/8	9	14 6/8	13	15	Conne River, NF	John B. Bazile	John B. Bazile	1996	47
323 6/8	43 5/8	42 5/8	50 2/8	5 4/8	5 4/8	16 4/8	16 2/8	11 7/8	10 2/8	13	10	Hynes Lake, NF	Martin W. Nasadowski	Martin W. Nasadowski	1969	48
322 6/8	40 7/8	41 6/8	33 3/8	5 2/8	5 2/8	2 5/8	16 1/8	1/8	12 7/8	10	14	Rocky Pond, NF	Wayne Karlin	Wayne Karlin	1988	49
322 5/8	37 5/8	36 7/8	37 1/8	5 7/8	5 7/8	14 7/8	15 1/8	14 3/8	10 7/8	14	14	Avalon Pen., NF	Richard F. Lewis	Richard F. Lewis	1977	50
322 3/8	40 2/8	38 1/8	35 1/8	4 5/8	5 3/8	13 2/8	15 3/8	8 3/8	9 6/8	12	12	Avalon Pen., NF	Angus J. Chafe	Angus J. Chafe	1969	51
322 2/8	40	40 4/8	25	5 6/8	5 6/8	15	14 7/8	13 5/8	14	15	20	Lloyds River, NF	Richard P. Navas	Richard P. Navas	1980	52
322 1/8	42 4/8	41 6/8	34 2/8	5 7/8	5 7/8	14 4/8	14 1/8	4 4/8	11	13	15	Cappahayden, NF	T.E. Best, Jr. & H.A. Chafe	Thomas E. Best, Jr.	1982	53
322 1/8	40 2/8	42 5/8	30 4/8	6	6	18	14 7/8	14 6/8	10 2/8	15	12	Avalon Pen., NF	Unknown	Gerard Beaulieu	PR 1991	53
322 1/8	47 4/8	40 5/8	38 5/8	6 1/8	5 5/8	16 2/8	17 5/8	12 7/8	17 2/8	13	16	Bay du Nord River, NF	Joby Quann	Myrtle Quann	1992	53
321 6/8	42 2/8	43 6/8	35 6/8	6 1/8	6 1/8	13 2/8	17 2/8	6 5/8	15 1/8	11	16	Princes Pond, NF	Henry Bondesen	Henry Bondesen	1966	56
320 7/8	37 4/8	40 6/8	34 4/8	5 5/8	5 5/8	15 3/8	16 4/8	8 5/8	11 7/8	15	17	La Poile, NF	David J. Coleman	David J. Coleman	1974	57
320 6/8	38 1/8	38 1/8	30 6/8	5	5	16 5/8	15 3/8	14 7/8	10 7/8	20	19	Long Range Mts., NF	Gary L. Benner	Gary L. Benner	1983	58
320 6/8	32	35	25 7/8	4 5/8	4 6/8	20 5/8	18 1/8	16 7/8	14	17	14	Crabbes River, NF	Joseph R. Levy	Joseph R. Levy	1983	58
320 2/8	39 4/8	39	34	5 1/8	5 2/8	15 5/8	17 3/8	12	6 4/8	12	17	Top Pond, NF	Donald F. Senter	Donald F. Senter	1984	60
319 5/8	40 6/8	37 1/8	38 3/8	5 4/8	5 2/8	15	15 4/8	11 4/8	3 1/8	17	15	Conne River, NF	Lloyd W. McClelland	Lloyd W. McClelland	1970	61
319 4/8	40 6/8	37 1/8	30 6/8	6	6	11 4/8	11 7/8	8 4/8	1 1/8	21	21	Long Range Mts., NF	William H. Taylor	William H. Taylor	1983	62
319	32 2/8	32 2/8	27 4/8	4 6/8	4 6/8	11 5/8	12 7/8	8 6/8	10 4/8	24	18	Fishels Brook, NF	Fred Waite	Fred Waite	1986	63
318 7/8	37 6/8	39 4/8	29 5/8	4 7/8	4 7/8	15 2/8	15 7/8	12 7/8	9 6/8	20	20	Deer Lake, NF	Alexander Thane	Alexander Thane	1951	64
318 7/8	38 7/8	38 1/8	27	5	5	13 4/8	14 2/8	11 2/8	13 3/8	17	16	Lake Margaret, NF	Edward J. Bugden	Edward J. Bugden	1973	64
318 6/8	37 7/8	41	34 4/8	5 2/8	5 2/8	12 6/8	14 3/8	8	11 4/8	16	15	Medonnegonix Lake, NF	Buck Taylor	Buck Taylor	1993	64
318 5/8	41	34 3/8	25 1/8	5 4/8	5 4/8	12 5/8	14 3/8	13 6/8	19	15	16	Mouse Pond, NF	C.T. Barnett	C.T. Barnett	1987	67
318 4/8	34 4/8	34 3/8	27 6/8	5 4/8	5 4/8	16 6/8	16 4/8	12 4/8	10 3/8	16	15	Island Pond, NF	Collins F. Kellogg, Sr.	Collins F. Kellogg, Sr.	1997	68
318 3/8	38 7/8	38 5/8	34 1/8	5 3/8	5 4/8	18 5/8	17	15 5/8	4 5/8	9	12	Great Rattling Brook, NF	Henry D. Frey	Henry D. Frey	1970	69
318 2/8	40	40	26 2/8	5 4/8	5 3/8	13 6/8	12 2/8	11 6/8	6 3/8	16	22	La Poile, NF	Van R. Johnson	Van R. Johnson	1977	70
317 7/8	40 2/8	37	38 4/8	5 2/8	5 4/8	16	16	10 4/8	12 3/8	18	20	Gander River, NF	W.H. Wilson	W.H. Wilson	1955	71
317 6/8	32	34 1/8	31 3/8	5 4/8	5 4/8	13 4/8	13 4/8	11 4/8	12 3/8	18	20	Walls Pond, NF	Laurence Brown	Laurence Brown	1967	72
316 3/8	45 2/8	45 2/8	30 7/8	5 4/8	5 4/8	17	18 2/8	18 2/8	15 2/8	15	9	Doyles, NF	Franklin H. Burns	Franklin H. Burns	1956	73
315 7/8	40 7/8	42	33 1/8	5 5/8	5 6/8	16 4/8	18	11 3/8	1 5/8	21	16	Sandy Pond Barrens, NF	George L. Harrison	Acad. Nat. Sci., Phil.	1897	74
315 6/8	43 3/8	46 1/8	33 5/8	5 5/8	5 5/8	14 2/8	16 4/8	11 3/8	11 1/8	16	9	Newton Lake, NF	W.H. Wilson	W.H. Wilson	1957	75
315 6/8	43 1/8	42 1/8	33 4/8	5 2/8	6 1/8	12 4/8	12	7 3/8	6 1/8	14	10	Sitdown Pond, NF	H.R. Wambold	H.R. Wambold	1966	76
315 1/8	40 4/8	39 5/8	34 4/8	5 7/8	5 1/8	12 4/8	14 7/8	5 1/8	11 1/8	13	13	Jubilee Lake, NF	James W. Beitler	James W. Beitler	1994	76
315 1/8	39 1/8	36	33 6/8	5 1/8	5 2/8	15 1/8	15 2/8	12 7/8	10 1/8	13	15	Hinds Plains, NF	Picked Up	Gerard Beaulieu	1977	78
314 7/8	42 4/8	42 4/8	34 2/8	5 2/8	5 2/8	14 6/8	14 7/8	9 6/8	3 4/8	12	16	Long Range Mts., NF	James J. McBride	James J. McBride	1982	79

WOODLAND CARIBOU
Rangifer tarandus caribou

Score	Main Beam R	Main Beam L	Inside Spread	Circ. Between Brow and Bez R	Circ. L	Length of Brow Points R	Length of Brow Points L	Width of Brow Points R	Width of Brow Points L	No. of Points R	No. of Points L	Locality	Hunter	Owner	Date Killed	Rank
314 2/8	47 2/8	47 3/8	24 7/8	5 7/8	5 7/8	13 1/8	12 1/8	9 7/8	3	13	12	Mt. Howley, NF	Picked Up	Tom Rose	1988	80
314	36 3/8	35	34 1/8	6 1/8	6	14 6/8	14	11 6/8	12 5/8	14	16	Rainy Lake, NF	Arnold H. Craine	Arnold H. Craine	1967	81
314	34 1/8	34 6/8	29 4/8	5 1/8	4 7/8	14 2/8	14 5/8	13 1/8	12 2/8	10	21	Long Range Mts., NF	Gordon J. Birgbauer, Jr.	Gordon J. Birgbauer, Jr.	1986	81
313 4/8	36 1/8	35	24 7/8	4 3/8	4 5/8	16 6/8	16	14 7/8	14 6/8	16	17	Cormacks Lake, NF	John Wirth, Jr.	John Wirth, Jr.	1993	83
313 3/8	40	42 1/8	25	5 3/8	5 3/8	15 5/8	14 2/8	9 4/8	11 4/8	18	17	Rainy Lake, NF	Jon Santangelo	Jon Santangelo	1971	84
313 3/8	33 3/8	32 2/8	29 5/8	5 7/8	5 5/8	12 3/8	10 5/8	11 2/8	9	20	17	Buchans Plateau, NF	Robert R. Kampstra	Robert R. Kampstra	1980	84
312 7/8	39 3/8	40 6/8	40 6/8	5 3/8	5 2/8	16 1/8	16 6/8	11 7/8	15 6/8	13	14	Crooked Lake, NF	Vernon L. Hanlin	Vernon L. Hanlin	1967	86
312 6/8	31 7/8	33 1/8	35 5/8	5 6/8	5 7/8	15 2/8	15 1/8	11 7/8	2 4/8	14	15	Victoria Lake, NF	Gordon T. Casey	Gordon T. Casey	1992	87
312 3/8	36 1/8	36 4/8	29 6/8	6 6/8	6 4/8	12 7/8	14 5/8	9 7/8	6 6/8	20	15	Stag Pond, NF	Max Meister	Max Meister	1976	88
311 6/8	40 5/8	43 6/8	40 4/8	5 1/8	5 2/8	13 3/8	13 3/8	4 6/8	14	17	14	Buchans Plateau, NF	Basil C. Bradbury	Basil C. Bradbury	1971	89
311 6/8	35 5/8	40 4/8	28	5 7/8	5 5/8	18 3/8	19 5/8	6 4/8	8	19	14	Grey River, NF	Edward R. Janas	Edward R. Janas	1986	89
310 3/8	42	42	29 6/8	5 4/8	5 5/8	12	12 3/8	9 3/8	8 7/8	13	14	Port aux Basques, NF	George C. Thompson, Jr.	George C. Thompson, Jr.	1987	91
309 4/8	38	36	34 2/8	5 5/8	5 5/8	15 2/8	16 2/8	5 6/8	13 6/8	15	12	Rainy Lake, NF	Ted Dreimans	Ted Dreimans	1962	92
309 3/8	43	43 3/8	33	5 3/8	5 2/8	15	16	13 3/8	13 6/8	15	15	Neola Paul Brook, NF	A.L. Levenseler	A.L. Levenseler	1967	93
309 2/8	40 2/8	36 5/8	30	6 5/8	5 6/8	18 3/8	14 7/8	9 4/8	11 4/8	16	19	Island Pond, NF	David J. DuFlo	David J. DuFlo	1996	94
309	42 3/8	44	33	5 1/8	5 3/8	2 1/8	15 3/8	17 5/8	1/8	16	15	Corner Brook, NF	Gilbert J. Heuer	Gilbert J. Heuer	1970	95
309	46 3/8	43 7/8	38 7/8	5 5/8	5 6/8	13	3 1/8	1/8	9 1/8	13	13	Alex Lake, NF	James E. Conklin	James E. Conklin	1981	95
308 7/8	38 5/8	40	29	4 7/8	5 1/8	14	16 2/8	10 5/8	10	12	12	Caribou Creek, NF	Remo Pizzagalli	Remo Pizzagalli	1994	97
308 1/8	29 3/8	30	31 3/8	5 5/8	5 5/8	11	13 2/8	10 2/8	8 3/8	16	19	Gaff Topsail, NF	Warren L. Miller	Warren L. Miller	1993	98
308	39 6/8	41 2/8	35 2/8	5 2/8	5 2/8	11 7/8	13 6/8	10 2/8	5 7/8	13	15	Shanadithit Brook, NF	L. Ben Hull	L. Ben Hull	1969	99
308	41 2/8	40 6/8	34 5/8	5 5/8	5 5/8	13 7/8	15 2/8	2 2/8	11 6/8	12	16	Meelpaeg, NF	Richard M. Moorehead	Richard M. Moorehead	1969	99
307 7/8	38 3/8	41	31 4/8	5 1/8	5 1/8	15 3/8	14 1/8	10 2/8	11 1/8	12	13	Grey River, NF	Roy S. Bowers	Roy S. Bowers	1993	101
307 5/8	38	39 5/8	34 5/8	5 6/8	5 4/8	16	16 4/8	15	2 2/8	19	13	White Bear Bay, NF	John K. Howard	John K. Howard	1938	102
307 1/8	35 4/8	37 2/8	30 5/8	5 3/8	5 2/8	16 4/8	17 1/8	11 6/8	14 1/8	16	17	Buchans Plateau, NF	Gary A. Laatsch	Gary A. Laatsch	1986	103
307 1/8	39 6/8	37 1/8	29 1/8	4 7/8	5 4/8	10 5/8	12 4/8	11 6/8	6 2/8	13	11	Conne River, NF	Michael J. Park	Michael J. Park	1987	103
307 1/8	39 6/8	40 5/8	40 5/8	5 1/8	5 4/8	16 7/8	14	10 3/8	12 2/8	11	16	Long Range Mts., NF	Kenneth W. Shafer, Jr.	Kenneth W. Shafer, Jr.	1997	103
306 7/8	31 5/8	42 4/8	23	5 4/8	5 4/8	7 7/8	17 1/8	15 2/8	1/8	15	10	Parsons Pond, NF	Gerard R. Beaulieu	Gerard R. Beaulieu	1992	106
306 6/8	37 1/8	31 6/8	28 7/8	5 5/8	8 6/8	15 5/8	15 4/8	12 7/8	12 1/8	13	17	Greenwood Brook, NF	Unknown	Harold Pelley	1988	107
306 4/8	34 3/8	42 2/8	29	5 1/8	5 1/8	14 1/8	14 7/8	10 4/8	10 4/8	11	11	Grand Lake, NF	Theodore R. Greenwood	Theodore R. Greenwood	1983	108
306 4/8	32 3/8	32 3/8	28 2/8	6 1/8	6	16 1/8	14 5/8	13	14 6/8	18	20	Harbour Deep, NF	Jack S. Zuidema	Jack S. Zuidema	1997	108
306 3/8	39	39 3/8	29 1/8	4 7/8	4 7/8	13 1/8	16 3/8	12 5/8	13	13	13	Millertown, NF	Gerhart H. Huber	Gerhart H. Huber	1966	110
306 2/8	41 3/8	39 7/8	37 3/8	5	4 7/8	12 5/8	13 1/8	10 2/8	9 5/8	17	20	Portage Lake, NF	Arnold Tonn	Arnold Tonn	1967	111
305 7/8	38 1/8	33	32 3/8	5	5	16 1/8	2	1/8	13 6/8	15	18	Grey River, NF	Jeffrey J. Eichhorst	Jeffrey J. Eichhorst	1980	112
305 5/8	36 4/8	25 5/8	25 5/8	4 5/8	4 6/8	13	13 1/8	11 7/8	10 6/8	17	17	Long Range Mts., NF	Collins F. Kellogg, Sr.	Collins F. Kellogg, Sr.	1989	113
305 1/8	37 4/8	36 6/8	28 2/8	5 2/8	5	13 5/8	11 5/8	10 2/8	11 7/8	17	19	Buchans Plateau, NF	Raymond M. Cappelli	Raymond M. Cappelli	1981	114
304 6/8	44 6/8	48 2/8	26 5/8	5 3/8	5 4/8	20 7/8	18 7/8	1 2/8	18 1/8	9	15	Middle Ridge, NF	Nat Levenson	Nat Levenson	1950	115

Score												Locality	By whom killed	Owner	Date Killed	Rank
304	38	40	33 5/8	5 1/8	5 2/8	12 1/8	12 2/8	4 4/8	10 6/8	13	14	Avalon Pen., NF	Unknown	Gerard Beaulieu	PR 1991	116
303 7/8	44	45	33 4/8	4 6/8	5 1/8	16 6/8	16 3/8	9	10 4/8	12	12	Blue Hills, NF	Charlie D. Todd	Charlie D. Todd	1986	117
302 7/8	51 4/8	50 5/8	29 1/8	5 7/8	6	18 4/8	11 3/8	16 4/8	1/8	14	10	Newfoundland	Gift of H.C. de Rham to NCHH	Unknown	PR 1910	118
302 5/8	40 6/8	41 3/8	29 5/8	5 4/8	5 4/8	15 5/8	15	9 4/8	11 3/8	11	11	La Poile, NF	L. Dale Gaugler	L. Dale Gaugler	1986	119
301 3/8	29 3/8	31 5/8	32 4/8	5	5	11 3/8	11 2/8	7 6/8	6 1/8	14	13	Buchans Plateau, NF	Robert C. Kaufman	Robert C. Kaufman	1988	120
301 1/8	38	39 3/8	27 4/8	5 2/8	5	15 2/8	13 6/8	12 2/8	9 3/8	15	13	Eastern Pond, NF	H.W. Doyle	H.W. Doyle	1953	121
301 1/8	39 5/8	40 6/8	29 1/8	5 3/8	5	13 3/8	13 3/8	8 3/8	12 5/8	11	14	Parsons Pond, NF	Gerard Beaulieu	Gerard Beaulieu	1991	121
300 5/8	41 3/8	40	37 7/8	6 1/8	5 3/8	11 4/8	18	2 4/8	14 6/8	15	13	Long Range Mts., NF	John L. Van Horn	John L. Van Horn	1983	123
300 3/8	33 1/8	31 4/8	31 6/8	5 2/8	5 1/8	13 1/8	12 7/8	11	9 3/8	22	20	St. Johns Co., NF	Craig A. LaBelle	Craig A. LaBelle	1991	124
300 1/8	38 7/8	36 7/8	34 6/8	5	5 2/8	16	16 3/8	2 4/8	13 6/8	12	12	Buchans Plateau, NF	Ernest J. Morgan	Ernest J. Morgan	1979	125
300 1/8	37 2/8	38 2/8	25 4/8	5	4 7/8	16 4/8	15 6/8	2 7/8	14	14	15	Terra Nova, NF	George Satterfield	George Satterfield	1996	125
299 7/8	43 7/8	42 3/8	36 2/8	5 2/8	5 3/8	12 1/8	12 3/8	9 3/8	8 2/8	12	14	Long Range Mts., NF	Edwin J. Tichy, Jr.	Edwin J. Tichy, Jr.	1985	127
299 7/8	42	41 7/8	29 2/8	5 6/8	5 4/8	8 7/8	17 7/8	1/8	15 6/8	11	18	Loon Lake, NF	Collins F. Kellogg, Sr.	Collins F. Kellogg, Sr.	1994	127
299 4/8	37 5/8	35 5/8	28 5/8	5 3/8	5 3/8	13 6/8	13 4/8	6 3/8	9 6/8	14	17	La Poile, NF	W.T. Yoshimoto	W.T. Yoshimoto	1973	129
299	36 3/8	37 4/8	35 1/8	4 4/8	4 5/8	12 6/8	10 6/8	9	9 7/8	15	15	La Poile, NF	Newton F. Moyer	Newton F. Moyer	1986	130
298 5/8	40 2/8	41 5/8	31 6/8	5 4/8	6	15	16 3/8	16 3/8	12 3/8	14	13	Pasadena, NF	C.J. McElroy	C.J. McElroy	1968	131
298 4/8	40 6/8	37 3/8	33 5/8	4 6/8	5	17 2/8	14 6/8	9 2/8	7 3/8	11	15	Lloyds River, NF	William A. Shaw	William A. Shaw	1987	132
298 4/8	33 2/8	35 1/8	25	5 3/8	5 6/8	14 3/8	15	2 2/8	12 3/8	14	15	Andrew Pond, NF	Roy K. McCollum	Roy K. McCollum	1994	132
298 2/8	37 4/8	35 7/8	30 2/8	6 1/8	5 6/8	15 1/8	15 5/8	9 4/8	7 6/8	15	11	Upper Humber River, NF	Picked Up	Gerard R. Beaulieu	1992	134
298	42 4/8	39 6/8	35	5 3/8	5 2/8	17	15 7/8	7 2/8	11 3/8	9	10	Buchans Plateau, NF	Stewart N. Shaft	Stewart N. Shaft	1982	135
298	37 4/8	36 4/8	31 4/8	5 4/8	5 1/8	15 1/8	14 5/8	11 5/8	11 5/8	13	12	Conne River, NF	Donald H. Reuter	Donald H. Reuter	1993	135
297 7/8	38 2/8	38 6/8	37 3/8	5 5/8	5 4/8	14 6/8	9	9 5/8	1/8	15	14	Princes Pond, NF	Richard C. Desjardins	Richard C. Desjardins	1996	137
297 5/8	32 4/8	33 3/8	29 7/8	5 5/8	5 5/8	13 4/8	12 5/8	9 1/8	6 4/8	17	13	Buchans Plateau, NF	Morton J. Greene	Morton J. Greene	1983	138
296 1/8	33 6/8	33	31 7/8	5 2/8	5 2/8	15 2/8	16 6/8	13 2/8	6	13	17	Goose Lake, NF	L. Reed Williams	L. Reed Williams	1993	139
295 4/8	40 4/8	38 1/8	26 7/8	5	5	14 4/8	15 6/8	9 5/8	14	16	14	Top Pond, NF	Robert L. Rex	Robert L. Rex	1966	140
295 4/8	41 5/8	41 1/8	28	5 2/8	5 2/8	16 5/8	14 5/8	12 2/8	9 6/8	18	16	South Branch, NF	Victor Pelletier	Victor Pelletier	1967	140
295	40 6/8	38 6/8	29 6/8	5 5/8	5 5/8	12 1/8	11 1/8	8 1/8	6 7/8	13	15	Parsons Pond, NF	Picked Up	Gerard R. Beaulieu	PR 1994	142
363 3/8*	34	35 2/8	27 5/8	5 4/8	5 4/8	17	15 2/8	14 4/8	11	21	12	Caribou Creek, NF	Michael T. DiFrancesco	Michael T. DiFrancesco	1994	
347 4/8*	38 2/8	40 1/8	30 3/8	5 2/8	5 2/8	15	17 4/8	14	11 3/8	17	16	Long Range Mts., NF	Allen G. Wilfong	Allen G. Wilfong	1993	
336 2/8*	48 7/8	47 1/8	36 3/8	6	6 1/8	17 1/8	16 6/8	13 7/8	2 7/8	15	16	Springdale, NF	E. Bruce White	E. Bruce White	1986	

* Final score is subject to revision by additional verifying measurements.

CATEGORY
WOODLAND CARIBOU

SCORE
306-7/8

HUNTER
GERARD R. BEAULIEU

LOCATION
PARSONS POND, NF

DATE OF KILL
SEPTEMBER 1992

CATEGORY
WOODLAND CARIBOU

SCORE
352-2/8

HUNTER
JOHN MCTURK, JR.

LOCATION
DEER POND, NF

DATE OF KILL
OCTOBER 1996

CATEGORY
WOODLAND CARIBOU

SCORE
324-3/8

HUNTER
JOHN B. BAZILE

LOCATION
CONNE RIVER, NF

DATE OF KILL
SEPTEMBER 1996

CATEGORY
WOODLAND CARIBOU

SCORE
296-1/8

HUNTER
L. REED WILLIAMS

LOCATION
GOOSE LAKE, NF

DATE OF KILL
SEPTEMBER 1993

Roger Hedgecock said that a trophy that would qualify for the Boone and Crockett records book had never been the objective of any of his hunting trips, but added that he can never remember sitting on a cold deer stand, rifle in hand, that thoughts of a record whitetail didn't cross his mind. Little did this hunter from North Carolina know that his destiny for a record book trophy did not lay in the foothills of the Blue Ridge Mountains, but along the tundra of Alaska, home of the barren ground caribou (*Rangifer tarandus*).

"I had never seen a caribou until September 25, 1987, the day we flew into a base camp that was located about 80 miles north of Nondalton, Alaska.

"The next day, about two miles from camp, I squeezed the trigger on my .300 Weatherby. It was nearly one o'clock, an hour-and-a-half after the guide, Bob Tracy, had spotted the animal and said we were going after it. I could detect some excitement in his voice as he pointed it out in a herd of about 20 caribou. As we slowly worked our way from Mosquito Creek across barren tundra, using ridges as shields, trying to reach the highest point nearest the herd, I kept remembering what Bob had said, 'If you have to look twice at the size of the rack, it ain't worth going after.'

"We were going and going hard. We crawled the last 200 yards. The cows, apparently sensing something was wrong, got up and started moving from left to right. Flat on my stomach, I was watching through my 3x9 Nikon scope. My eyes were watering, my vision was blurred, and I raised my head to wipe my eyes. At this point, I got my first really good look at the rack. Rack was all I could see. Quickly I put my binoculars before my eyes to take another look. I saw the rack, the head, and then the body. He was walking slowly behind the cows.

"As I eased the rifle into a shooting position, Bob was whispering, 'Wait. Wait. Give him just a little more time, and you, take your time. Make the first shot a good one.'

"Finally, after what seemed longer than the trip from North Carolina to Alaska, the big bull was clearly straight away, showing me his right shoulder. I fired! The animal spun completely around and just stood there. I fired again, and he spun completely around once again. Each time I could hear the impact of the 220 grain bullet. The novice of my caribou hunting came out. I asked Bob, 'Did I hit him?' He nodded his head and added, 'He'll die standing. Just wait, you have placed two bullets right on target.'

"The cows ran and the bull didn't, and I began feeling comfortable. Finally, the huge body crumbled to the tundra. At such a time I guess most hunters find something to worry about. I knew the hip boots were lighter as we walked the 200 yards, but I was worried about a broken tine, or just simply broken antlers. You allow a lot of things to pass through your mind. Bob's first words were comforting. 'It's a really big one,' he said, 'And it may make the book.'"

Shortly after the 20th Awards, Hedgecock agreed to a continuing loan of his new World's Record to the Club's collection at the Buffalo Bill Historical Center in Cody, Wyoming. ∎

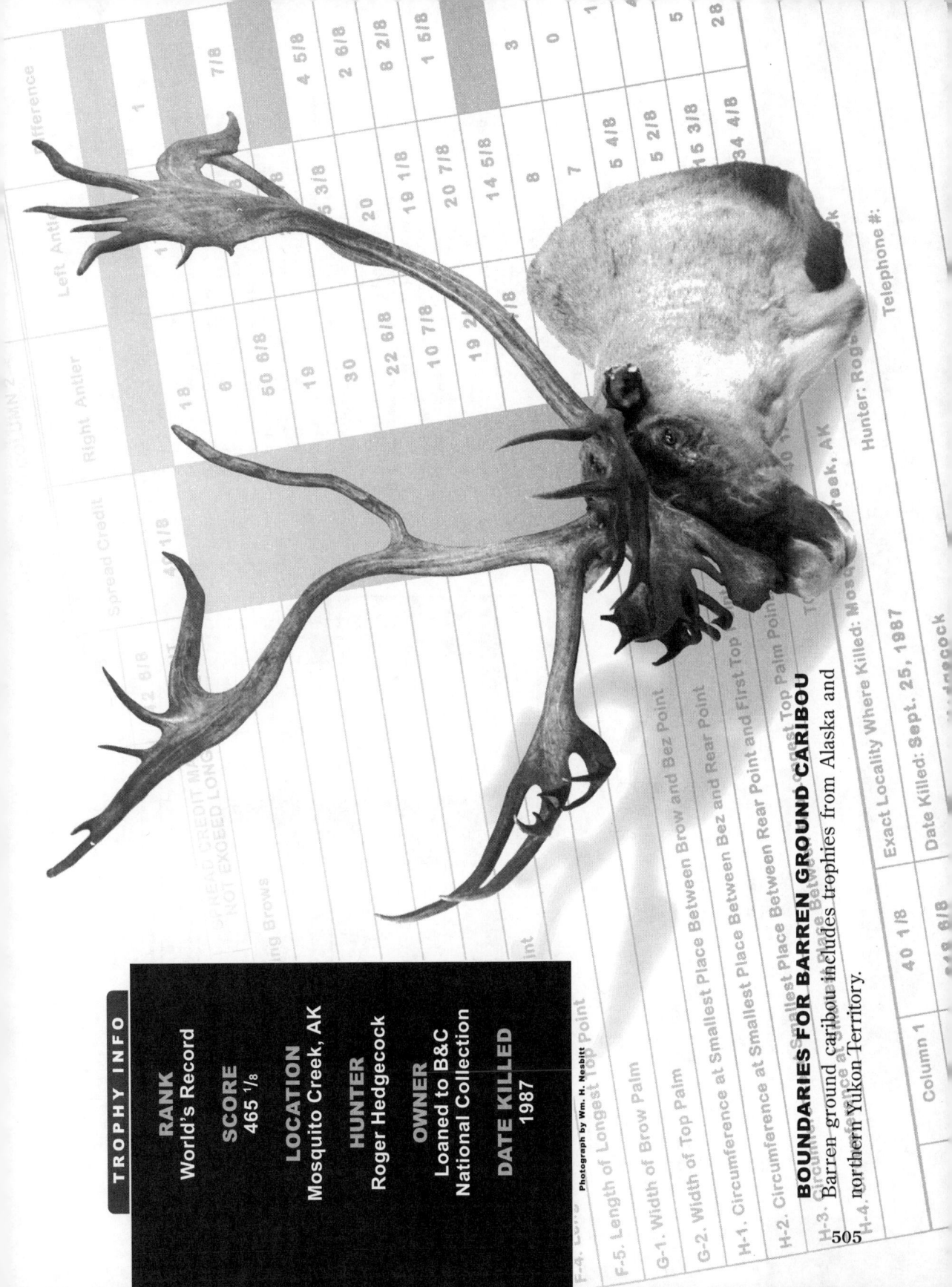

Photograph by Wm. H. Nesbitt

F-5. Length of Longest Top Point

G-1. Width of Brow Palm

G-2. Width of Top Palm

H-1. Circumference at Smallest Place Between Brow and Bez Point

H-2. Circumference at Smallest Place Between Bez and Rear Point

BOUNDARIES FOR BARREN GROUND CARIBOU

H-3. Barren-ground caribou includes trophies from Alaska and
H-4. northern Yukon Territory.

505

All measurements must be made with a 1/4-inch wide flexible steel tape to the nearest one-eighth of an inch. (Note: A flexible steel cable can be used to measure points and main beams only.) Enter fractional figures in eighths, without reduction. Official measurements cannot be taken until the antlers have air dried for at least 60 days after the animal was killed.

A. Tip to Tip Spread is measured between tips of main beams.

B. Greatest Spread is measured between perpendiculars at a right angle to the center line of the skull at widest part, whether across main beams or points.

C. Inside Spread of Main Beams is measured at a right angle to the center line of the skull at widest point between main beams. Enter this measurement again as the Spread Credit **if** it is less than or equal to the length of the longer antler; if greater, enter longer antler length for Spread Credit.

D. Number of Points on Each Antler: To be counted a point, a projection must be at least one-half inch long, with length exceeding width at one-half inch or more of length. Beam tip is counted as a point but not measured as a point. There are no "abnormal" points in caribou.

E. Length of Main Beam is measured from the center of the lowest outside edge of burr over the outer side to the most distant point of the main beam. The point of beginning is that point on the burr where the center line along the outer side of the beam intersects the burr, then following generally the line of the illustration.

F-1-2-3. Length of Points are measured from nearest edge of beam over outer curve to tip. Lay the tape along the outer curve of the beam so that the top edge of the tape coincides with the top edge of the beam on both sides of point to determine the baseline for point measurement. Record point lengths in appropriate blanks.

F-4-5. Length of Points are measured from the tip of the point to the top of the beam, then at a right angle to the bottom edge of beam. The Second Longest Top Point **cannot** be a point branch of the Longest Top Point.

G-1. Width of Brow is measured in a straight line from top edge to lower edge, as illustrated, with measurement line at a right angle to main axis of brow.

G-2. Width of Top Palm is measured from midpoint of lower edge of main beam to midpoint of a dip between points, at widest part of palm. The line of measurement begins and ends at midpoints of palm edges, which gives credit for palm thickness.

H-1-2-3-4. Circumferences are taken as illustrated for measurements. If brow point is missing, take H-1 at smallest point between burr and bez point. If rear point is missing, take H-2 and H-3 measurements at smallest place between bez and first top point. Do not depress the tape into any dips of the palm or main beam

---

Records of
North American
Big Game

BOONE AND CROCKETT CLUB®
250 Station Drive
Missoula, MT 59801
(406) 542-1888

OFFICIAL SCORING SYSTEM FOR NORTH AMERICAN BIG GAME TROPHIES

CARIBOU

	MINIMUM SCORES	
	AWARDS	ALL-TIME
mountain	360	390
woodland	265	295
Central Canada	375	400
barren ground	345	360
Quebec-Labrador	365	375

KIND OF CARIBOU (check one)
- ☐ mountain
- ☐ woodland
- ☑ barren ground
- ☐ Central Canada
- ☐ barren ground
- ☐ Quebec-Labrador

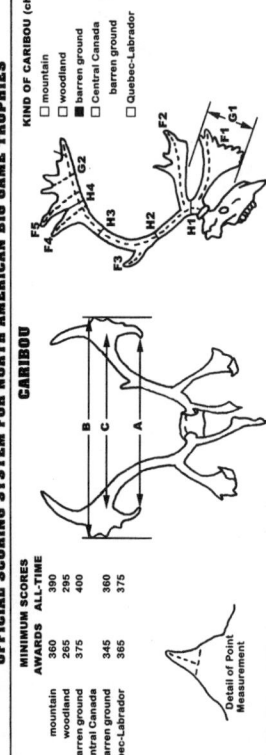

Detail of Point Measurement

SPREAD CREDIT MAY EQUAL BUT NOT EXCEED LONGER ANTLER

SEE OTHER SIDE FOR INSTRUCTIONS		COLUMN 1	COLUMN 2	COLUMN 3	COLUMN 4
		Spread Credit	Right Antler	Left Antler	Difference
A. Tip to Tip Spread	42 2/8				
B. Greatest Spread	42 6/8				
C. Inside Spread of Main Beams	40 1/8	40 1/8			
D. Number of Points on Each Antler Excluding Brows			18	17	1
Number of Points on Each Brow			8	8	
E. Length of Main Beam			50 6/8	49 7/8	7/8
F-1. Length of Brow Palm or First Point			19	20 4/8	1 4/8
F-2. Length of Bez or Second Point			30	25 3/8	4 5/8
F-3. Length of Rear Point, If Present			22 6/8	20	2 6/8
F-4. Length of Second Longest Top Point			10 7/8	19 1/8	8 2/8
F-5. Length of Longest Top Point			19 2/8	20 7/8	1 5/8
G-1. Width of Brow Palm			5	8	3
G-2. Width of Top Palm			7	7	0
H-1. Circumference at Smallest Place Between Brow and Bez Point			5 6/8	5 4/8	1/8
H-2. Circumference at Smallest Place Between Bez and Rear Point			4 6/8	5 2/8	4/8
H-3. Circumference at Smallest Place Between Rear Point and First Top Point			9 7/8	15 3/8	5 4/8
H-4. Circumference at Smallest Place Between Two Longest Top Palm Points					
	TOTALS	40 1/8	218 6/8	234 4/8	28 2/8

ADD	Column 1	40 1/8	Exact Locality Where Killed: Mosquito Creek, AK
	Column 2	218 6/8	Date Killed: Sept. 25, 1987
	Column 3	234 4/8	Owner: Roger Hedgecock
	Subtotal	493 3/8	Owner's Address:
SUBTRACT Column 4		28 2/8	Guide's Name and Address:
FINAL SCORE		465 1/8	Remarks: (Mention Any Abnormalities or Unique Qualities)

Hunter: Roger Hedgecock

Telephone #:

COPYRIGHT © 1999 BY BOONE AND CROCKETT CLUB®

506

507

BARREN GROUND CARIBOU

Rangifer tarandus granti

MINIMUM SCORE 400

Score	Length of Main Beam R	L	Inside Spread	Circumference at Smallest Place Between Brow and Bez Points R	L	Length of Brow Points R	L	Width of Brow Points R	L	Number of Points R	L	Locality	Hunter	Owner	Date Killed	Rank
465 1/8	50 6/8	49 7/8	40 1/8	7	7	19	20 4/8	9 7/8	14 5/8	24	23	Mosquito Creek, AK	Roger Hedgecock	Loaned to B&C Natl. Coll.	1987	1
464 6/8	54 1/8	56 1/8	34 5/8	7 6/8	6 6/8	19 6/8	19 4/8	11 1/8	13 6/8	19	17	Sharp Mt., AK	Frank Lobitz	Bass Pro Shops F. & W. Mus.	1988	2
463 6/8	51 2/8	51 5/8	46 7/8	5 7/8	6 1/8	18 2/8	24 6/8	12 7/8	21 4/8	22	23	Ugashik Lakes, AK	Ray Loesche	Ray Loesche	1967	3
461 6/8	53 2/8	55 3/8	35	8 6/8	8 4/8	20	18 2/8	16 4/8	12 4/8	29	21	Post River, AK	John V. Potter, Jr.	John V. Potter, Jr.	1976	4
461 4/8	59 1/8	61 4/8	44 4/8	7 2/8	7 2/8	22 5/8	21 1/8	15	6	19	15	Kenai Pen., AK	Buck D. Mantsch	Buck D. Mantsch	1994	5
459 6/8	58	59 3/8	40 6/8	7 1/8	7 1/8	19 4/8	18 3/8	16 5/8	4	30	17	Slana, AK	Floyd A. Blick	Floyd A. Blick	1954	6
458 6/8	68 2/8	66 6/8	41 6/8	6 1/8	5 6/8	18 6/8	15 7/8	9	2 3/8	21	17	Alaska Pen., AK	Joseph Shoaf	Joseph Shoaf	1968	7
458 2/8	55 2/8	54 4/8	45 3/8	5 4/8	5 6/8	20 6/8	21 3/8	10 6/8	15 2/8	15	21	Cinder River, AK	Josef Meran	Josef Meran	1967	8
458 1/8	54 1/8	56	38 6/8	6 6/8	7 2/8	15 1/8	20 5/8	1/8	20 6/8	21	29	Gulkana River, AK	W.J. Krause	W.J. Krause	1953	9
458 1/8	49 7/8	50	31 2/8	7 3/8	7 3/8	17 6/8	15 2/8	13 2/8	8 7/8	18	17	Alaska Range, AK	Bobbie E. Robinson	Bobbie E. Robinson	1963	9
457 6/8	50 4/8	50 2/8	38 3/8	5 7/8	7 2/8	18 2/8	19 1/8	8 5/8	15 3/8	27	17	Aniak River, AK	Timothy K. Kanady	Timothy K. Kanady	1994	11
456 6/8	53 1/8	55	43 5/8	7	7	9 4/8	19 3/8	1/8	16 6/8	27	28	Mulchatna River, AK	Dan Bottrell	Dan Bottrell	1965	12
456 1/8	63 3/8	59 7/8	48	6 7/8	6 7/8	23 1/8	25 6/8	8 3/8	13 1/8	22	31	Alaska Pen., AK	Kenneth R. Best	Bavarian Builders, Inc.	1978	13
455 6/8	49 6/8	48 6/8	41 1/8	7 3/8	7 3/8	21 1/8	19	10 5/8	15 3/8	22	26	Alaska Pen., AK	Fred H. Blatt, Jr.	Fred H. Blatt, Jr.	1979	14
454 3/8	57 3/8	58 1/8	44 6/8	9 4/8	7 4/8	22 6/8	21 4/8	19 2/8	2 3/8	19	17	Wrangell Mts., AK	Mary Brisbin	Mary Brisbin	1959	15
453 1/8	46 5/8	46 6/8	38 2/8	6 7/8	6 6/8	17	18 4/8	10 4/8	5 7/8	23	21	Tangle Lakes, AK	Mrs. Robert Dosdall	Mrs. Robert Dosdall	1955	16
453	50 6/8	51 3/8	35 5/8	11 2/8	6 5/8	20 6/8	15 7/8	20 6/8	5 2/8	36	18	Alaska Pen., AK	Ken Higginbotham	Ken Higginbotham	1984	17
452 6/8	60 1/8	57 2/8	56 6/8	6 3/8	6 2/8	5 1/8	20 6/8	1/8	14 4/8	17	22	Becharof Lake, AK	Gordon G. Chittick	Gordon G. Chittick	1983	18
451 6/8	54 7/8	54 1/8	31 2/8	7 3/8	6 3/8	19 4/8	18 6/8	13 4/8	9 4/8	23	19	Alaska Range, AK	Mrs. Leah Clemmons	Mrs. Leah Clemmons	1956	19
451 4/8	51 3/8	52 6/8	47 7/8	6 3/8	7 5/8	20	8 1/8	14 5/8	9 4/8	22	13	Wood River, AK	Q. Odell Robinson	Q. Odell Robinson	1980	20
450 6/8	58 1/8	59 4/8	55 5/8	6 1/8	6 2/8	19 4/8	21 6/8	11 5/8	11 4/8	15	16	Bonanza Hills, AK	David A. Fulbright	David A. Fulbright	1987	21
450 4/8	64 7/8	61	44 3/8	6 5/8	6 1/8	22 2/8	20 7/8	7 4/8	10 4/8	16	18	Alaska Pen., AK	Phillip D. Wagner	Phillip D. Wagner	1977	22
449 6/8	49 7/8	48 7/8	40 3/8	9 5/8	8 3/8	19 2/8	20	17	8 5/8	25	23	Lake Clark, AK	Dennis Burdick	Dennis Burdick	1984	23
449 4/8	50	47 5/8	46	6 3/8	6 3/8	17 1/8	19 1/8	11 5/8	12 7/8	18	23	Ugashik Lakes, AK	Frank Knies	Frank Knies	1965	24
449 1/8	45 3/8	43 5/8	42 5/8	5 6/8	5 7/8	20 6/8	23 2/8	11 5/8	16 5/8	16	24	Alaska Pen., AK	Eddie L. House	Eddie L. House	1979	25
449	47 7/8	48 5/8	36 6/8	7 3/8	6 5/8	17	16 2/8	13 5/8	4	20	24	Talkeetna Mts., AK	George L. Clark	George L. Clark	1960	26
448 6/8	50 5/8	51 1/8	40 5/8	8 4/8	7 3/8	20	13 3/8	15 1/8	7 5/8	22	24	Little Mulchatna Lake, AK	Morton P. Donohue	Morton P. Donohue	1968	27
448 3/8	56 5/8	59	45 3/8	6 2/8	6 2/8	20 3/8	20 5/8	8 1/8	14 1/8	15	19	Stony River, AK	Picked Up	William O. West	1987	28
448 2/8	60 2/8	56 5/8	41	5 7/8	6 1/8	21 7/8	15	17 6/8	1/8	23	15	Ogilvie River, YT	Glen E. Christman	Glen E. Christman	1997	29
448 1/8	54 7/8	56 4/8	42	6 5/8	6 3/8	16 7/8	24 2/8	4 2/8	21 4/8	18	20	Dog Salmon River, AK	Picked Up	Butch Hautanen	1982	30
447 7/8	59 4/8	58 5/8	49	7 5/8	6 5/8	17 2/8	23 4/8	4 6/8	14 3/8	18	19	Alaska Pen., AK	A.D. Heetderks	A.D. Heetderks	1966	31
447 5/8	54 1/8	57 1/8	48 5/8	6 1/8	6	17 2/8	20	13	14 4/8	24	22	Denali Hwy., AK	K.K. Anton	K.K. Anton	1957	32
447 5/8	52 3/8	50 3/8	42 5/8	6 6/8	7	19	18 5/8	15 6/8	16 7/8	26	21	Ugashik Lakes, AK	Neil C. McLaughlin	Neil C. McLaughlin	1971	32
447 5/8	52 4/8	52 4/8	48 5/8	7 4/8	6 7/8	17 1/8	17 1/8	14 4/8	13 6/8	26	22	Alaska Range, AK	Richard K. Tollison	Sandra L. Tollison	1978	32
447 4/8	58 3/8	59 5/8	52 7/8	5	5	17 1/8	19 5/8	11 6/8	12 1/8	20	24	Nelchina, AK	Bert Klineburger	Bert Klineburger	1964	35
446 6/8	58 2/8	55 5/8	48 5/8	5 7/8	6	20 5/8	23 6/8	1/8	17 5/8	15	19	Cinder River, AK	Cliff Thom	Cliff Thom	1966	36

Score									Pts.	Pts.	Locality	Hunter	Owner	Date Killed	Rank
446 3/8	56	58 1/8	45 2/8	12 2/8	6 4/8	7	17 4/8	11	15	18	Stuyahok River, AK	Marc C. Phillips	Marc C. Phillips	1993	37
444 5/8	44 6/8	46 4/8	51 2/8	18 2/8	7	6 6/8	3 3/8	5/8	25	17	Port Heiden, AK	Marshall Carr	Marshall Carr	1963	38
444 4/8	60 6/8	57 6/8	59	24 2/8	6 3/8	6	21 5/8	1/8	18	13	Mother Goose Lake, AK	S.W. Terry	S.W. Terry	1967	39
444 1/8	47 4/8	51	41 4/8	21 3/8	6	5 7/8	20 1/8	16 7/8	21	22	King Salmon River, AK	John C. Belcher	John C. Belcher	1967	40
443 7/8	51 6/8	50 3/8	45 1/8	22	6	5 7/8	19 4/8	15 7/8	19	21	Wrangell Mts., AK	A.E. Bruggeman	A.E. Bruggeman	1962	41
443 1/8	46 6/8	49 6/8	39 7/8	15 6/8	5 7/8	5 6/8	19 1/8	9 3/8	16	22	Denali Hwy., AK	Stephen Vacula	Stephen Vacula	1967	42
443 1/8	53 4/8	50 3/8	50 4/8	17 5/8	5 4/8	5 6/8	22	11 4/8	15	24	Kobuk River, AK	Ralph G. Colas	Ralph G. Colas	1988	42
443 1/8	60 6/8	60 6/8	51 7/8	20 2/8	6 1/8	6 3/8	16 6/8	8 7/8	12	15	Copper Creek, AK	Walter C. Dallis	Park A. Dallis	1994	42
443	57 1/8	57 6/8	37	10	6 2/8	6 3/8	21	1	22	18	Denali Hwy., AK	C.W. Hilbish	C.W. Hilbish	1958	45
443	50 7/8	50 5/8	41 4/8	17 4/8	6 7/8	6 3/8	19 6/8	14 4/8	21	23	Lime Village, AK	William R. Ellis III	William R. Ellis III	1978	45
442 2/8	62 6/8	62 7/8	48 7/8	24 2/8	7 1/8	8	7 2/8	5/8	22	14	Wood River, AK	Charles M. Bentley	Michael N. Bentley	1960	47
442 2/8	52 7/8	51 6/8	50	26 5/8	6	7	23 3/8	14 4/8	22	18	Kvichak River, AK	Todd C. Jacobson	Todd C. Jacobson	1996	47
442 1/8	45	50	38 2/8	14 4/8	7 1/8	7 4/8	21 6/8	17 5/8	17	26	Talkeetna Mts., AK	Jack C. Robb	Jack C. Robb	1958	49
441 6/8	51 5/8	53 7/8	47	22 3/8	6	6 3/8	5 3/8	1 1/8	20	13	Alaska Pen., AK	George Waldriff	George Waldriff	1962	50
441 4/8	55 6/8	53 3/8	37 2/8	20	6 2/8	5 7/8	15 1/8	14 4/8	17	15	Healy, AK	G.H. Gunn	G.H. Gunn	1968	51
441 3/8	51 3/8	52 3/8	52 7/8	16	5 1/8	5 2/8	18 6/8	1/8	15	20	Pilot Point, AK	Clifford H. Driskell	Clifford H. Driskell	1970	52
441 2/8	43 3/8	46 6/8	41 1/8	19 2/8	7 1/8	6 7/8	21 7/8	1	17	23	Tonzona River, AK	Dean W. Coffman	Dean W. Coffman	1964	53
440 3/8	59 6/8	56 4/8	44 2/8	13 6/8	6 2/8	6 4/8	17 2/8	1/8	11	15	Snowshoe Lake, AK	Ray Al Winchester	Demarest Mem. Museum	1953	54
440 2/8	54 2/8	56 5/8	38 5/8	15 3/8	7 7/8	7 3/8	14 4/8	11 3/8	19	19	Lake Clark, AK	James W. Vorhease	James W. Vorhease	1988	55
440 2/8	55 3/8	58 1/8	44 2/8	9 1/8	6 2/8	7	20 7/8	16 5/8	18	28	Blue Berry Creek, AK	Ed Shapiro	Ed Shapiro	1964	56
440 1/8	54	57	40 4/8	20 4/8	6 1/8	7 3/8	17 7/8	11	18	17	Kenai, AK	Picked Up	Marcia L. King	1972	56
440	50	50 1/8	48 1/8	18 3/8	6 5/8	6 1/8	16 1/8	12 6/8	18	17	Wood River, AK	David A. Schuller	David A. Schuller	1982	58
439 5/8	60 5/8	61 3/8	41 3/8	17 5/8	6 6/8	6 5/8	16 1/8	10 6/8	23	30	Mulchatna River, AK	Ted J. Forsi	Ted J. Forsi	1988	59
439 2/8	45 7/8	36 1/8	40 6/8	20 6/8	6 5/8	7 2/8	11 5/8	13 1/8	16	12	Talkeetna Mts., AK	Chris Klineburger	Chris Klineburger	1961	60
439 1/8	53 4/8	53 4/8	44 2/8	23 4/8	6 5/8	5 5/8	16	16	25	33	Egegik River, AK	Norman Tibbetts	Norman Tibbetts	1959	61
439 1/8	59 4/8	59	45 6/8	22 5/8	5 5/8	5 6/8	16 5/8	3 3/8	23	15	Iliamna Lake, AK	Edward L. Fuchs	Edward L. Fuchs	1955	62
439	62 5/8	60 2/8	46	2 4/8	5 6/8	7	18 4/8	10 4/8	12	15	Twin Lakes, AK	Thomas H. Lutsey	Thomas H. Lutsey	1955	62
438 6/8	50 4/8	47	53 4/8	21 1/8	5 5/8	5 7/8	15 3/8	1 1/8	19	22	Port Moller, AK	Joseph H. Johnson	Joseph H. Johnson	1976	64
438 4/8	52 4/8	51 6/8	45 2/8	19 3/8	6 3/8	5 3/8	18	16 6/8	27	23	Nushagak River, AK	Vincent P. Sullivan	Vincent P. Sullivan	1992	65
438 1/8	58 2/8	58 6/8	41 5/8	17 4/8	6 2/8	6 4/8	23	8 7/8	21	19	Maclaren River, AK	Donald W. Bunselmeier	Donald W. Bunselmeier	1981	66
438 1/8	60 6/8	55 4/8	53 6/8	23 5/8	7 5/8	6 2/8	17	2 2/8	18	12	Iliamna Lake, AK	Jerry L. Peterson	Jerry L. Peterson	1986	67
438	53 7/8	49	40 7/8	21 4/8	8 6/8	7 5/8	23	17	16	12	Ugashik Lakes, AK	Norman W. Gilmore	Norman W. Gilmore	1967	68
438	46 2/8	51	47	19 4/8	5 2/8	5 2/8	6 2/8	15	20	18	Lower Ugashik Lake, AK	Bert A. McLay	Bert A. McLay	1981	68
437 7/8	61 6/8	61 6/8	38 2/8	21 4/8	6 3/8	6 2/8	14	14 4/8	20	14	Alaska Pen., AK	Herb Klein	Herb Klein	1967	70
437 6/8	48 1/8	48 1/8	37 2/8	21 4/8	6 1/8	6 2/8	16 7/8	15 2/8	15	25	Nelchina River, AK	Don Flynn	Don Flynn	1959	71
437 4/8	48 5/8	50 7/8	38 6/8	5 1/8	6	7 2/8	23 3/8	14 4/8	21	22	Tangle Lakes, AK	Dennis Weston	Dennis Weston	1964	72
437 4/8	60	61 2/8	37 1/8	21 4/8	5 1/8	6	22 3/8	18 5/8	15	16	Port Heiden, AK	Joyce A. Houston	Joyce A. Houston	1987	72
437 3/8	59 3/8	57 2/8	50 5/8	13 6/8	7 2/8	6 7/8	19 5/8	16 5/8	19	19	Naknek, AK	C.J. McElroy	C.J. McElroy	1966	74
437 2/8	60 6/8	58 2/8	43 5/8	20 1/8	5 5/8	6 3/8	19 4/8	1 4/8	23	23	Mulchatna River, AK	Lyle W. Bentzen	Lyle W. Bentzen	1974	75
437 2/8	52 2/8	53	39 6/8	20 3/8	7	7 1/8	17 3/8	5	23	21	Crescent Lake, AK	Joseph C. Tennison	Joseph C. Tennison	1991	75
436 5/8	54 6/8	53 1/8	48	16 6/8	6	6 2/8	19 5/8	16	15	16	Chisana River, AK	Terry Overly	Terry Overly	1976	77
436 2/8	55 4/8	58 7/8	42 1/8	19 1/8	5 4/8	7 3/8	19 6/8	10 2/8	22	18	Nabesna, AK	Bill Ellis	Bill Ellis	1964	78
436 2/8	54 4/8	55	47 5/8	20 6/8	6	5 7/8	24 3/8	10 6/8	15	23	Alaska Pen., AK	A.R. Buckles	A.R. Buckles	1967	78
436 1/8	55 3/8	55	47 2/8	9 6/8	5 6/8	7 7/8	24 2/8	15 7/8	19	27	Port Moller, AK	Marvin L. Fergastad	Marvin L. Fergastad	1962	80
436 1/8	56 2/8	54	44 3/8	21 4/8	6 3/8	7 7/8	6 3/8	19 3/8	15	14	Iliamna Lake, AK	Robert S. Marvin	Robert S. Marvin	1987	80
435 7/8	55 7/8	51 5/8	39 4/8	18 1/8	7	6 3/8	18 1/8	21 5/8	19	16	McClaren Ridge, AK	Peter W. Bading	Peter W. Bading	1959	82
435 7/8	55 7/8	51 5/8	39 4/8	17 4/8	10 3/8	6 7/8	10 3/8	5 2/8	23	23	Wrangell Mts., AK	Fred Williams	Fred Williams	1964	82

BARREN GROUND CARIBOU
Rangifer tarandus granti

Score	Length of Main Beam R	L	Inside Spread	Circumference at Smallest Place Between Brow and Bez Points R	L	Length of Brow Points R	L	Width of Brow Points R	L	Number of Points R	L	Locality	Hunter	Owner	Date Killed	Rank
435 6/8	48 2/8	52 2/8	43	8 1/8	8 6/8	14 1/8	13 6/8	11 3/8	10	22	19	Farewell, AK	Henry Budny	Henry Budny	1960	84
435 6/8	53 1/8	53	41	6 2/8	5 7/8	4 3/8	17 4/8	1/8	11 4/8	17	24	Talkeetna Mts., AK	John M. Killian	John M. Killian	1960	84
435 5/8	53 6/8	54 3/8	37	6 7/8	6 7/8	18 4/8	20 6/8	11 1/8	14 4/8	22	19	Talkeetna Mts., AK	Mrs. Arnt Antonsen	Mrs. Arnt Antonsen	1960	86
435 3/8	51 2/8	50 3/8	41 7/8	7 7/8	7	23 7/8	12 1/8	18 1/8	2 7/8	19	13	Ugashik Lakes, AK	Robert E. Sass	Robert E. Sass	1963	87
435 3/8	54 1/8	52 4/8	48 6/8	6 3/8	6 2/8	3 1/8	20 6/8	1/8	11 7/8	14	13	Funny River, AK	David M. Bowen	David M. Bowen	1994	87
435 2/8	52 2/8	49 6/8	32 2/8	9 2/8	9 5/8	19 7/8	22 3/8	9 5/8	6 5/8	19	19	Naknek River, AK	Chris M. Kendrick	Chris M. Kendrick	1977	89
435 1/8	53 1/8	53 1/8	30 2/8	5 6/8	5 3/8	22 2/8	18 7/8	11 5/8	12 3/8	25	19	Alaska Range, AK	Kermit G. Johnson	Kermit G. Johnson	1970	90
435	51 1/8	51 6/8	55 1/8	6 1/8	6 2/8	22 5/8	20 7/8	3 4/8	12 6/8	15	23	King Salmon, AK	Warren F. Phillips	Warren F. Phillips	1983	91
434 6/8	53 2/8	51 5/8	35 2/8	6	6 2/8	24 6/8	11 4/8	14 7/8	1/8	30	16	Alinchak Bay, AK	Rodney R. Havens	Rodney R. Havens	1991	92
434 3/8	58 4/8	57 5/8	42 4/8	6 2/8	6	17 7/8	17 2/8	11 4/8	9	22	22	Tangle Lakes, AK	Bryant Flynn	Bryant Flynn	1953	93
434 3/8	53 2/8	53 6/8	45 6/8	5 2/8	5 3/8	18 2/8	18 4/8	11	5 7/8	23	18	Nushagak River, AK	John N. Pritchard	John N. Pritchard	1993	93
434 1/8	42 3/8	45 4/8	35 2/8	6 4/8	6 5/8	16	17 4/8	7 5/8	12 4/8	21	22	Tazlina, AK	Chuck Sutter	Chuck Sutter	1958	95
434	61 3/8	60	40 4/8	6 4/8	6 2/8	19 3/8	19 7/8	11 4/8	6 4/8	14	18	Little Nelchina River, AK	Joseph Brisco, Jr.	Joseph Brisco, Jr.	1955	96
434	51 6/8	48 6/8	44 3/8	6 1/8	6 1/8	20 1/8	19 4/8	15 4/8	14 2/8	21	16	King Salmon, AK	Roger W. Seiler	Roger W. Seiler	1959	96
433 7/8	51	52 4/8	28 6/8	5 7/8	6	19	19 4/8	7	15 3/8	34	34	Taylor Mt., AK	James C. Davis	James C. Davis	1993	98
433 6/8	59 2/8	56 7/8	41 2/8	6 4/8	6 2/8	15 5/8	20 4/8	10 1/8	15	25	21	Port Moller, AK	Paul M. Sweezey	Paul M. Sweezey	1968	99
433 4/8	59 4/8	59 7/8	57 2/8	6 3/8	6 2/8	23	8 4/8	18 2/8	1	22	13	Alaska Pen., AK	Herb Klein	Herb Klein	1964	100
433 3/8	50 2/8	50 2/8	33 6/8	6 1/8	6 6/8	19 1/8	22 7/8	10	14 5/8	16	21	Seventy Mile River, AK	Bronk Jorgensen	Bronk Jorgensen	1989	100
433 3/8	59 3/8	56	55 5/8	6	5 6/8	3 6/8	19 7/8	5/8	14 6/8	16	22	Port Heiden, AK	D.R. Klein	D.R. Klein	1966	102
433 1/8	54	56 4/8	32 1/8	6 5/8	6 2/8	26	10 6/8	19 1/8	1/8	17	12	Killey River, AK	Timothy D. Evans	Timothy D. Evans	1994	103
432 7/8	52 1/8	52 6/8	48 4/8	6 5/8	6 1/8	5 5/8	23 7/8	4	16 6/8	15	19	Black Lake, AK	John T. Swiss	John T. Swiss	1967	104
432 7/8	50 2/8	48 4/8	39 1/8	9	12 4/8	14 2/8	15 1/8	1/8	8 4/8	16	21	Healy River, AK	Anita Talerico	Frank Talerico	1982	104
432 5/8	55 6/8	55 4/8	48 1/8	5 5/8	5 4/8	7	21 1/8	17 2/8	1/8	23	15	Hick Creek, AK	Justin D. Hall	Justin D. Hall	1984	106
432 4/8	58 3/8	50 3/8	50	7 1/8	6 1/8	5 4/8	22	1	16 2/8	15	19	King Salmon, AK	Dan E. McCarty	Dan E. McCarty	1967	107
432 2/8	52 4/8	56	48 1/8	6	5 7/8	19	17 3/8	9 6/8	10 6/8	19	18	Iliamna Lake, AK	Thomas R. Reed, Jr.	Thomas R. Reed, Jr.	1988	108
432 1/8	54	53 3/8	49 7/8	6	5 7/8	10 1/8	22 3/8	1/8	15 5/8	15	25	Wide Bay, AK	Roy C. Jablonski	Roy C. Jablonski	1990	109
432	49 4/8	49 4/8	37 6/8	6	5 5/8	18 3/8	15 5/8	11 7/8	1/8	18	19	Upper Susitna River, AK	Theodore A. Warren	Theodore A. Warren	1955	110
432	52 1/8	51 5/8	42 4/8	7	5 5/8	10 1/8	15	4 6/8	12 1/8	21	22	Lake Louise, AK	Mike Walganski	Mike Walganski	1961	110
431 7/8	48	53 5/8	37 6/8	5 6/8	6	17 4/8	15	4	11 3/8	18	21	Nondalton, AK	Gordon S. Swift	Gordon S. Swift	1981	112
431 7/8	58 3/8	60 7/8	34 7/8	6 3/8	7 1/8	18	22 2/8	8 3/8	14 1/8	15	20	Egegik River, AK	David L. Dargis	David L. Dargis	1992	112
431 6/8	49 2/8	45 6/8	33 3/8	7 1/8	7		19 2/8		16 5/8	20	29	Clarence Lake, AK	Jack Hill	Jack Hill	1964	114
431 3/8	54 3/8	54 7/8	41 6/8	6 3/8	6 6/8	17	18 7/8	1 3/8	10 7/8	15	17	Talkeetna Mts., AK	Joseph R. Good	Joseph R. Good	1956	115
431 3/8	49	52 4/8	36 4/8	6 7/8	6 5/8	15 6/8	13 3/8	14	5 6/8	28	24	Cold Bay, AK	Gary D'Aigle	Gary D'Aigle	1973	115
431 3/8	54 1/8	51 7/8	35 4/8	6 7/8	7 3/8	18 4/8	18 7/8	14 1/8	10 7/8	20	20	Lake Clark, AK	William R. Lykken	William R. Lykken	1976	115
431 3/8	53 5/8	54 2/8	43	6 5/8	7 1/8	17 5/8	16 7/8	6 3/8	11 4/8	20	19	Mulchatna River, AK	Valerie E. King	Valerie E. King	1984	115
431	50 6/8	54 2/8	39	6 6/8	6 5/8	21	21	13 3/8	14 5/8	20	21	Port Heiden, AK	Ray B. Nienhaus	Ray B. Nienhaus	1966	119

Score	L. Main Beam R	L. Main Beam L	Inside Spread	Circ. R	Circ. L	Top Palm L. R	Top Palm L. L	Top Palm W. R	Top Palm W. L	Points R	Points L	Locality	Hunter	Owner	Date Killed	Rank
430 7/8	49	48 3/8	40 2/8	7 4/8	7 2/8	15 5/8	14	8	7 6/8	18	19	Susitna River, AK	James I. Roland	James I. Roland	1983	120
430 7/8	51 2/8	49 4/8	36 6/8	7 2/8	7 1/8	16 4/8	18 2/8	6 3/8	11	12	15	Mulchatna River, AK	Ted M. Labedz	Ted M. Labedz	1987	120
430 6/8	50 2/8	49 6/8	32 3/8	5 6/8	6	17 4/8	16 6/8	10 6/8	10 5/8	20	26	Talkeetna Mts., AK	Nelson Spencer	Nelson Spencer	1962	122
430 3/8	47	49 6/8	35 6/8	6 6/8	6 6/8	22	13 4/8	8 4/8	14 1/8	24	24	Gulkana River, AK	Troy Bogard	Troy Bogard	1954	123
430 3/8	57	54 1/8	46 4/8	8	8 5/8	17 3/8	6 1/8	9 5/8	6 6/8	22	17	Alaska Pen., AK	Michaux Nash, Jr.	Michaux Nash, Jr.	1968	123
430 2/8	57 7/8	53 6/8	44 5/8	6 2/8	6 4/8	18 3/8	20 4/8	5 6/8	15 2/8	23	16	Mother Goose Lake, AK	R.C. Parker	R.C. Parker	1959	125
430 2/8	53 1/8	54 3/8	44 1/8	6 1/8	6	22 4/8	17 3/8	5 6/8	10 6/8	15	20	Alaska Pen., AK	Ernest Milani	Ernest Milani	1961	125
430	52 4/8	56	36 4/8	6 6/8	6 1/8	21 6/8	19	6 7/8	17 3/8	15	17	Alaska Pen., AK	Richard A. Vozzi	Richard A. Vozzi	1991	127
429 6/8	51 1/8	49 7/8	40 3/8	8 7/8	8 7/8	14 3/8	19 1/8	8 7/8	9 2/8	20	16	Mulchatna River, AK	William Leffingwell	William Leffingwell	1990	128
429 5/8	56 5/8	48 4/8	39 5/8	6 3/8	6 3/8	18 3/8	9 1/8	6 6/8	5 4/8	17	14	Mulchatna River, AK	Jerry D. Downing	Jerry D. Downing	1986	129
429 4/8	50 6/8	51 5/8	30 7/8	5 7/8	5 3/8	18 6/8	10 6/8	5 7/8	5 4/8	21	24	Bonnet Plume, YT	R.G. Studemann	R.G. Studemann	1963	130
429 4/8	54 2/8	54 4/8	42 6/8	5 4/8	5 7/8	17 6/8	15 7/8	10 2/8	7	17	17	Mulchatna River, AK	Bruce C. Wassom	Bruce C. Wassom	1991	130
429 4/8	48 1/8	56 6/8	41 6/8	8 3/8	8 3/8	23	21 3/8	9 5/8	19 3/8	19	22	Alaska Pen., AK	Charles C. Parsons	Charles C. Parsons	1993	130
429 3/8	53 6/8	59	42 6/8	7 6/8	7	15 6/8	11 3/8	7	11 3/8	24	17	Mulchatna River, AK	Lem Crofton	Lem Crofton	1978	133
429 3/8	56	54 7/8	31 5/8	6	6	18 6/8	16 7/8	6	1 7/8	19	26	Juneau Lake, AK	Don Nickel	Don Nickel	1993	133
429 1/8	58	58	35	6	6 6/8	26	24	6 6/8	19	22	15	Alaska Range, AK	J.C. Phillips	Harvard Univ. Mus.	1928	135
429 1/8	49	46	43 6/8	6 6/8	5 4/8	16 6/8	17 2/8	8 7/8	8 7/8	21	20	Tyone Lake, AK	Ralph Marshall	Ralph Marshall	1960	135
429	50 3/8	51 6/8	48 6/8	5 4/8	5 4/8	18 6/8	16 1/8	8 6/8	10 3/8	18	19	Pinochle Creek, AK	William B. Ripley	William B. Ripley	1989	137
428 5/8	57	54 1/8	41	6 3/8	6	21 6/8	21 4/8	6 5/8	1 7/8	20	12	Iliamna Lake, AK	Linda J. Corley	Linda J. Corley	1983	138
428 1/8	62 6/8	62	49 1/8	6 4/8	6 4/8	23 1/8	3 2/8	14 6/8	1/8	12	9	Mulchatna River, AK	Ricky A. Beauchamp	Ricky A. Beauchamp	1987	139
428 1/8	53	55 3/8	38 1/8	6 1/8	6 2/8	19 4/8	24	3 7/8	12 4/8	19	20	Ivishak River, AK	Joseph A. Renfrow, Jr.	Joseph A. Renfrow, Jr.	1987	139
428 1/8	54 5/8	54 3/8	44 2/8	5 7/8	5 7/8	20 1/8	20 1/8	13 3/8	14 4/8	16	11	Tutna Lake, AK	Robert W. Roessel	Robert W. Roessel	1987	139
427 5/8	56 3/8	59 2/8	44 1/8	6 3/8	5 4/8	21 2/8	18 2/8	13 7/8	10 4/8	19	17	Talkeetna Mts., AK	Donald Parker	Donald Parker	1969	142
427 4/8	57 2/8	53 7/8	42 2/8	5 4/8	7 4/8	16	21 7/8	13 7/8	10 4/8	17	17	Aniak River, AK	Lad R. Neilson	Lad R. Neilson	1991	143
426 6/8	49	46	40 5/8	6 1/8	6 1/8	15 2/8	6 1/8	5 7/8	11 1/8	22	25	Cinder River, AK	John G. Merry, Jr.	John G. Merry, Jr.	1968	144
426 6/8	52 4/8	53 1/8	45 1/8	5 6/8	5 6/8	11 4/8	20	7 2/8	1/8	25	17	Anchorage, AK	Peter W. Bading	Peter W. Bading	1963	145
426 6/8	52 6/8	52 6/8	49 1/8	7 2/8	7 2/8	17 2/8	15 2/8	5 6/8	15 2/8	17	20	Alaska Range, AK	Dan Parker	Dan Parker	1971	145
426 6/8	51 6/8	53 4/8	39 4/8	5 4/8	4 6/8	16 2/8	5 7/8	7 6/8	10 3/8	18	12	King Salmon, AK	Donald E. Twa	Donald E. Twa	1993	145
426 4/8	54	58 1/8	47 5/8	5 5/8	5 5/8	21 4/8	13	5 5/8	2 4/8	14	14	Smelt Creek, AK	Chris Pickering	Chris Pickering	1996	145
426 4/8	59	56 6/8	44 5/8	6 1/8	6 1/8	18 1/8	13 5/8	6 1/8	1 7/8	16	16	Alaska Pen., AK	John S. Rohrer	John S. Rohrer	1987	149
426 3/8	52 6/8	54 4/8	37 6/8	6 3/8	6 5/8	18 1/8	3 2/8	6 3/8	15 5/8	15	22	Eureka, AK	C.C. Grey	C.C. Grey	1953	150
426 3/8	52 3/8	48 7/8	40 5/8	8 2/8	8	17	13 6/8	8 2/8	11 3/8	17	22	Wrangell Mts., AK	Richard Conroy	Richard Conroy	1961	150
426 3/8	53 2/8	54 4/8	44 3/8	8 3/8	8 3/8	19	24	8 3/8	1/8	19	18	Black Lake, AK	Lester W. Miller, Jr.	Lester W. Miller, Jr.	1963	150
426 2/8	50 3/8	56 4/8	37 4/8	6 1/8	6 7/8	37 4/8	1 6/8	6 1/8	22	22	22	Lake Clark, AK	Mark E. Carda	Mark E. Carda	1986	150
426 2/8	56 2/8	60 3/8	41 6/8	6 1/8	6 3/8	19 6/8	15 3/8	6 1/8	1/8	23	22	White River, YT	F.C. Havemeyer	Unknown	1912	154
426 2/8	48 5/8	47 5/8	43 4/8	6 1/8	5 7/8	20 4/8	4 7/8	5 7/8	8 2/8	20	23	Pumice Creek, AK	Raymond F. Fogarty	Raymond F. Fogarty	1991	154
426 2/8	55 2/8	55 5/8	47 6/8	6 3/8	6 3/8	17 3/8	7 3/8	9 5/8	1/8	18	20	Nushagak River, AK	John R. Herr, Jr.	John R. Herr, Jr.	1991	154
426 1/8	48 3/8	50 6/8	37	7	6 7/8	19	19 1/8	9 4/8	14 6/8	20	17	Coal Creek, AK	Dustin L. Sikes	Dustin L. Sikes	1993	157
426	53 5/8	52 5/8	42 1/8	6 5/8	6 7/8	19 1/8	8 4/8	8 4/8	11 1/8	22	20	Fog Lakes, AK	Larry F. Grout	Larry F. Grout	1981	158
426	54 2/8	58 2/8	40 6/8	5 4/8	5 6/8	18	2 7/8	1/8	13 6/8	18	27	Bear Creek, AK	Douglas E. Christiansen	Douglas E. Christiansen	1988	158
426	52 3/8	52 3/8	36 2/8	7 1/8	7 1/8	16 1/8	11 5/8	6 6/8	1/8	25	18	Hart River, YT	Peter C. Elarde, Jr.	Peter C. Elarde, Jr.	1990	158
425 6/8	45 4/8	49 2/8	32 2/8	6	7 4/8	19 3/8	11 4/8	6	18 6/8	18	18	Denali Hwy., AK	Sam Pancotto	Sam Pancotto	1960	161
425 5/8	53 2/8	55 5/8	39 4/8	7 4/8	7 2/8	14	1/8	7 4/8	10 1/8	15	19	Nabesna, AK	Frank Martin, Jr.	Frank Martin, Jr.	1965	161
425 5/8	52 6/8	48	31	7 2/8	7 2/8	19	4 3/8	7 2/8	13 4/8	15	19	Iliamna Lake, AK	Donald R. Barnes	Donald R. Barnes	1973	163
425 5/8	48 1/8	47 5/8	46 7/8	5 5/8	5 4/8	20 5/8	14 5/8	5 5/8	14 6/8	14	21	Becharof Lake, AK	Lavon L. Chittick	Lavon L. Chittick	1981	163
425 3/8	50 3/8	50	35	7 1/8	7 1/8	22 1/8	17 3/8	6 7/8	17 3/8	17	15	Igiugig, AK	William F. Peot	William F. Peot	1995	163
425 3/8	56 4/8	59	43 2/8	7	7	20 6/8	8	7 1/8	10 3/8	20	14	Iliamna Lake, AK	A.A. Bishop	A.A. Bishop	1982	166

BARREN GROUND CARIBOU

Rangifer tarandus granti

Score	Length of Main Beam R	L	Inside Spread	Circumference at Smallest Place Between Brow and Bez Points R	L	Length of Brow Points R	L	Width of Brow Points R	L	Number of Points R	L	Locality	Hunter	Owner	Date Killed	Rank
425 3/8	55 6/8	56 2/8	41	6 6/8	7 2/8	17 7/8	18 2/8	5 4/8	9 6/8	17	17	Moody Creek, AK	Ervin Hostetler	Ervin Hostetler	1983	166
425 3/8	49 4/8	50 3/8	39 2/8	5 6/8	5 3/8	19 4/8	16 1/8	6 5/8	9 5/8	16	15	Taylor Mts., AK	Val B. Jones	Val B. Jones	1990	166
425 3/8	57 2/8	55 7/8	52 6/8	5	5	19 1/8	14	11 6/8	1 4/8	18	13	Alaska Pen., AK	James T. Hartley	James T. Hartley	1996	166
425 2/8	46 7/8	48 2/8	35 2/8	6 4/8	6 5/8	16	17 2/8	7 5/8	12 3/8	20	21	McClaren Ridge, AK	Peter W. Bading	Peter W. Bading	1959	170
425	52 2/8	52 6/8	40 5/8	6 1/8	6 3/8	17 5/8	9 3/8	12 2/8	1/8	23	17	Susitna, AK	Elmer M. Rusten	Elmer M. Rusten	1952	171
425	45 1/8	45 2/8	36 7/8	5 6/8	5 3/8	20 3/8	21 6/8	15 1/8	7 7/8	22	22	Talkeetna Mts., AK	Thorne Donnelley	Thorne Donnelley	1959	171
425	47 1/8	52 4/8	36	7	6 3/8	8	23	1 3/8	18 5/8	18	32	Lake Louise, AK	H.E. O'Neal	H.E. O'Neal	1964	171
424 7/8	52 5/8	58 5/8	43 3/8	7 6/8	8 1/8	15 6/8	14 4/8	5 4/8	9	19	16	Denali Hwy., AK	Moyer Johnstone	Moyer Johnstone	1958	174
424 7/8	53 3/8	53 5/8	36 7/8	6 7/8	6 4/8	21 1/8	2 3/8	16 1/8	1/8	18	20	Alaska Range, AK	Dennis R. Johnson	Dennis R. Johnson	1980	174
424 7/8	58 3/8	54 5/8	45 4/8	6 4/8	6 4/8	3 7/8	25 2/8	1/8	18 5/8	14	17	Ugashik Lakes, AK	Robert C. Jones	Robert C. Jones	1981	174
424 7/8	53 7/8	54 6/8	41 6/8	7	6 7/8	21 7/8	18 7/8	11	13 7/8	13	14	Post River, AK	Roger E. Austin	Roger E. Austin	1988	174
424 6/8	50 5/8	53 6/8	39 2/8	7 3/8	7 3/8	16 6/8	20 7/8	1 3/8	13 4/8	19	17	Swan River, AK	Kenneth G. Rogowski	Kenneth G. Rogowski	1992	178
424 6/8	44 5/8	45 2/8	38 4/8	6 6/8	7 3/8	19 3/8	19 1/8	15 2/8	13 4/8	29	33	Nushagak River, AK	A. Mark Horvat	A. Mark Horvat	1995	178
424 4/8	51 4/8	47 4/8	43 6/8	6 5/8	6 4/8	17	17	11 3/8	8 1/8	18	20	Talkeetna Mts., AK	Wayne C. Eubank	Wayne C. Eubank	1959	180
424 4/8	55	52 5/8	47 5/8	7 1/8	7 6/8	19 6/8	19 5/8	14 2/8	1 6/8	18	13	Talkeetna Mts., AK	Karl Weber	Karl Weber	1959	180
424 4/8	57 7/8	55 4/8	42 4/8	6 3/8	6 6/8	17 1/8	16 7/8	3 4/8	7	14	16	Funny River, AK	Picked Up	Ted H. Spraker	1994	180
424 3/8	61	59	46	7 2/8	6 3/8	16 4/8	1 2/8	8 3/8	4/8	17	13	Lake Louise, AK	Dick Luckow	Dick Luckow	1959	183
424 3/8	51 7/8	52 1/8	48	5 5/8	5 5/8	14 6/8	14 6/8	13	4 5/8	23	14	Post River, AK	Guntram Rhomberg	Guntram Rhomberg	1966	183
424 2/8	51 1/8	49	43 3/8	6 2/8	6 1/8	12 2/8	22 4/8	1	17 7/8	16	13	Talkeetna Mts., AK	Morris Spencer	Morris Spencer	1962	185
424 2/8	50	46 1/8	38 4/8	6 5/8	7 4/8	20 1/8	19 7/8	7 4/8	16	18	26	Summit, AK	Myron Bethel	Myron Bethel	1976	185
424 2/8	57 2/8	58 2/8	40 2/8	5 3/8	5 4/8	15 5/8	19 1/8	10 4/8	15 6/8	17	19	King Salmon, AK	Samuel C. Johnson	Samuel C. Johnson	1978	185
424 1/8	52 5/8	52 4/8	46 6/8	6 2/8	6 2/8	17 6/8	19 4/8	9 1/8	4 6/8	16	17	Talkeetna Mts., AK	Lyle E. Reynolds	Lyle E. Reynolds	1960	188
424 1/8	43 5/8	43 4/8	32 7/8	6 7/8	6 2/8	16	1 7/8	13 4/8	5/8	37	24	Wrangell Mts., AK	Dan G. Best	Dan G. Best	1961	188
423 7/8	57 1/8	57	41 5/8	6 1/8	6 6/8	11 4/8	19 3/8	1/8	17 2/8	17	23	Mulchatna River, AK	Monte R. Ford	Monte R. Ford	1988	190
423 6/8	56 5/8	55 1/8	40 7/8	6 4/8	6 6/8	18 4/8	14 2/8	12 5/8	1/8	16	16	Alaska Pen., AK	Rex Hancock	Rex Hancock	1961	191
423 6/8	52 7/8	50 6/8	40 3/8	5 2/8	5 3/8	1 7/8	15 1/8	1/8	10 4/8	19	22	King Salmon River, AK	Henry N. Warren	Henry N. Warren	1978	191
423 6/8	55	54 7/8	47	5 6/8	5 6/8	17 2/8	10 7/8	11 3/8	3 2/8	25	17	Cinder River, AK	Gary F. Romaniw	Gary F. Romaniw	1981	191
423 6/8	53 4/8	52 1/8	39 3/8	6 2/8	6 4/8	18 4/8	18 4/8	8 1/8	14 4/8	18	22	Port Heiden, AK	James A. Prince, Jr.	James A. Prince, Jr.	1988	191
423 6/8	52 6/8	52 4/8	37 6/8	5 5/8	5 5/8	20 4/8	21 2/8	7 7/8	13 1/8	16	18	Hook Creek, AK	D. Alan Shreves	D. Alan Shreves	1996	191
423 3/8	59 3/8	59 4/8	41 1/8	5 6/8	6 2/8	19	19 2/8	8	16 2/8	17	21	Ferry, AK	Roy Maxwell	Roy Maxwell	1965	196
423 3/8	53 2/8	53 1/8	43 2/8	8 3/8	6 6/8	17	17	11 4/8	10 5/8	24	23	Maka Creek, AK	Julian E. White, Jr.	Julian E. White, Jr.	1993	196
423 2/8	51 1/8	50	45 7/8	7 2/8	7 3/8	18 3/8	15 6/8	13 5/8	11 3/8	19	16	Killey River, AK	Dennis H. Johns	Dennis H. Johns	1997	198
423 1/8	44 6/8	44	32 4/8	6 7/8	7 1/8	19 3/8	20 3/8	9 1/8	17	18	24	Tyone River, AK	Alva H. Rich	Alva H. Rich	1961	199
423	53 1/8	55 2/8	44 1/8	6 7/8	6 7/8	16	15 3/8	6 2/8	9 4/8	13	15	Gulkana River, AK	Lewis E. Yearout	Lewis E. Yearout	1956	200
423	43 5/8	43 7/8	40	5 6/8	7 2/8	6 7/8	16 7/8	3	11	14	15	Port Heiden, AK	Robert D. Jones	Robert D. Jones	1981	200
423	47 6/8	50	48	6 4/8	6 4/8	18 2/8	16 3/8	9 2/8	8 7/8	15	16	Panorama Mt., AK	Ronald R. Minard	Ronald R. Minard	1985	200

Score	L. Main Beam R	L. Main Beam L	Inside Spread	Circ. R	Circ. L	Width R	Width L	Length R	Length L	Pts R	Pts L	Locality	Hunter	Owner	Date Killed	Rank
422 7/8	50 6/8	51 5/8	37	6 2/8	6 2/8	21 1/8	20 2/8	9 1/8	15 1/8	20	21	Rainy Pass, AK	L. Arthur Cushman, Jr.	L. Arthur Cushman, Jr.	1961	203
422 6/8	49 4/8	48 6/8	47 3/8	6 3/8	6 3/8	16 4/8	14 5/8	11 2/8	6 6/8	19	13	Slana River, AK	Kirby Kiltz	Kirby Kiltz	1959	204
422 6/8	46 6/8	51 7/8	40	6 1/8	5 7/8	19 6/8	17	12 4/8	3 6/8	18	17	Matanuska River, AK	Stephen E. Skaggs	Stephen E. Skaggs	1978	204
422 6/8	55 4/8	55 6/8	45 4/8	6 3/8	7 1/8	20 6/8	18 6/8	4 4/8	15 6/8	16	18	Mother Goose Lake, AK	James B. Bloomer	James B. Bloomer	1987	204
422 6/8	51 3/8	51 4/8	41 7/8	6 2/8	6 2/8	22 4/8	19 3/8	17 4/8	3 4/8	23	16	Becharof Lake, AK	Richard-Salim F. Farah	Richard-Salim F. Farah	1993	204
422 5/8	50 4/8	45 4/8	34 4/8	9 4/8	6 6/8	20 2/8	17	15	5 5/8	16	19	Mt. Sanford, AK	John J. Heidel	John J. Heidel	1982	208
422 5/8	44 2/8	45 4/8	35 4/8	5 6/8	5 7/8	22	4 3/8	13 6/8	1 2/8	23	16	Snipe Lake, AK	Steven S. Lambe	Steven S. Lambe	1983	208
422 5/8	53 3/8	54 7/8	42 4/8	5 4/8	5 7/8	16 1/8	20 7/8	1/8	17 2/8	17	22	Alaska Pen., AK	Kirk D. Atter	Kirk D. Atter	1992	208
422 4/8	52 1/8	47 4/8	45 4/8	5 4/8	5 4/8	16 1/8	20 7/8	4 2/8	11 7/8	22	20	Iliamna Lake, AK	Bill Sims	Bill Sims	1973	211
422 3/8	49 2/8	49 3/8	37 4/8	6 3/8	6 2/8	20 7/8	19 3/8	13 4/8	11 4/8	22	20	Tangle Lakes, AK	Leroy G. Bohuslor	Leroy G. Bohuslor	1952	212
422 3/8	47	52 3/8	49	7 3/8	6	21 4/8	17 3/8	14 6/8	11 4/8	27	16	Hoholitna River, AK	Bradley A. Finch	Bradley A. Finch	1990	212
422 3/8	51	51 6/8	30 6/8	5 6/8	7 3/8	17 3/8	16 3/8	14 6/8	11 4/8	24	25	Hart River, YT	Steven B. Curtis	Steven B. Curtis	1996	212
422 1/8	42 3/8	45 7/8	37	7 6/8	5 6/8	16 3/8	15 4/8	14 6/8	11	27	27	Susitna River, AK	Warren Jones	Warren Jones	1961	215
422 1/8	57 3/8	59 3/8	54 4/8	6 1/8	5 7/8	22 4/8	17 4/8	14	1/8	21	21	King Salmon, AK	Jerry R. Jones	Jerry R. Jones	1981	215
422 1/8	49	49 2/8	36 1/8	6 6/8	8 1/8	19 7/8	17 5/8	16 7/8	14	21	21	Mulchatna River, AK	Thomas N. Govin	Thomas N. Govin	1987	215
422	53 5/8	51 5/8	40 6/8	6 7/8	6 7/8	20 1/8	17 5/8	15	15	22	22	Alaska Pen., AK	Debbie D. Burfiend	Debbie D. Burfiend	1993	218
421 7/8	55 6/8	48	33 6/8	7 2/8	7 3/8	17 5/8	16 5/8	10 7/8	15	20	15	Farewell Lake, AK	Richard K. Siller	Richard K. Siller	1958	219
421 7/8	50 1/8	50 5/8	36 6/8	6 6/8	7 5/8	16 5/8	11 3/8	1	1 4/8	22	20	Mosquito Creek, AK	Tom Teague	Tom Teague	1989	219
421 6/8	64 5/8	59 3/8	57	7 1/8	5 7/8	22 1/8	2 6/8	16 5/8	1	18	12	King Salmon, AK	Edwin W. Seiler	Edwin W. Seiler	1958	221
421 6/8	50 2/8	38 2/8	38 3/8	5 7/8	5 7/8	3 5/8	16 4/8	14 3/8	12	12	21	Cinder River, AK	Jerry A. Wilkinson	Jerry A. Wilkinson	1972	221
421 5/8	51 4/8	50	36 3/8	7 4/8	7 4/8	18 4/8	17 4/8	9	14	17	23	Port Moller, AK	John S. Clark	John S. Clark	1966	223
421 5/8	56 7/8	55 5/8	56	5 5/8	5 5/8	18 6/8	12 5/8	12 5/8	14	9		Upper Ugashik Lake, AK	Barry Barbour	Barry Barbour	1969	223
421 4/8	55 3/8	54 6/8	42 6/8	7 2/8	6 7/8	20 3/8	12 2/8	15 5/8	17	16		Denali Hwy., AK	D.G. Skagerberg	D.G. Skagerberg	1956	225
421 4/8	55	53 4/8	43	5 4/8	5 4/8	16 3/8	10	9 2/8	18	18		Denali Hwy., AK	John Schmidel	John Schmidel	1961	225
421 4/8	55 1/8	54 2/8	45 5/8	5 4/8	4 4/8	15 5/8	19 1/8	17	18	26		Twin Lakes, AK	Paul O'Hollaren	Paul O'Hollaren	1964	225
421 4/8	58 1/8	58 1/8	44 6/8	7 1/8	8 4/8	19	2 4/8	12 3/8	1/8	17	12	Kuskokwim River, AK	Dennis Harms	Dennis Harms	1967	225
421 4/8	44 6/8	47 3/8	32	6 3/8	6	18 7/8	19 2/8	22 2/8	1 6/8	15	22	Becharof Lake, AK	Ronnie L. Smith	Ronnie L. Smith	1993	225
421 2/8	48 7/8	49 7/8	37 1/8	6 2/8	6 2/8	21 2/8	19 2/8	12 7/8	18 1/8	22	19	Alaska	Unknown	Jonas Bros. of Seattle	1953	230
421 2/8	57 2/8	57	43 4/8	6	7	11 6/8	12 7/8	8 3/8	11 6/8	19	22	Cantwell, AK	Richard L. Miller	Richard L. Miller	1979	230
421 2/8	52 6/8	50 5/8	43 2/8	6 4/8	7	4 3/8	21 3/8	1/8	16 7/8	14	20	Boulder Creek, AK	Neal E. Osgood	Neal E. Osgood	1986	230
421 2/8	61 4/8	58	43 4/8	6 2/8	6 4/8	20 6/8	10 1/8	16 6/8	16 7/8	19	13	Lake Clark, AK	Ben C. Shafsky	Ben C. Shafsky	1993	230
421 2/8	53 2/8	54 3/8	38 1/8	5 6/8	6 3/8	19 1/8	19 3/8	3 6/8	11 5/8	23	19	Funny Lakes, AK	Robert W. Nelson	Robert W. Nelson	1995	230
421 1/8	47	51 4/8	37 3/8	7 4/8	7 4/8	18 2/8	19	10 5/8	10 5/8	24	21	Lake Louise, AK	Orel O. Parker	Orel O. Parker	1959	235
421 1/8	58 7/8	57 3/8	45 6/8	5 6/8	5 7/8	19 2/8	15 4/8	10 5/8	10 5/8	19	12	Ugashik Lakes, AK	Jack A. Shane, Sr.	Jack A. Shane, Sr.	1967	235
421 1/8	47 2/8	48 6/8	43 6/8	6	6	19 6/8	14 1/8	14 2/8	1/8	17	21	Alaska Pen., AK	Alice J. Landreth	Alice J. Landreth	1968	235
421 1/8	57 1/8	54 6/8	35 1/8	6 7/8	6 7/8	19	20 3/8	14 2/8	14 1/8	16	23	Maka Creek, AK	Larry G. Berry	Larry G. Berry	1994	235
421	56 4/8	54 6/8	49 1/8	7 3/8	6 1/8	20 3/8	9 7/8	14 1/8	20 3/8	23	19	Alaska Pen., AK	Lloyd W. Birdwell	Lloyd W. Birdwell	1970	239
421	55 5/8	57	44 7/8	6 4/8	6 4/8	18	10 7/8	7	18	14	20	Ugashik Lakes, AK	John M. Hangar	John M. Hangar	1988	239
420 7/8	56 2/8	55 2/8	45 3/8	5 5/8	5 5/8	23 6/8	21 4/8	2 4/8	1/8	16	14	Port Heiden, AK	Otis Chandler	Otis Chandler	1964	241
420 7/8	54 1/8	54 7/8	38 4/8	7 7/8	7 7/8	20 1/8	14 6/8	9 1/8	4/8	22	15	Farewell, AK	Vern G. Smith	Vern G. Smith	1967	241
420 6/8	45 6/8	47 6/8	36 4/8	6 3/8	6	16	10 2/8	10 2/8	1/8	27	21	Becharof Lake, AK	Glenn E. Anderson	Glenn E. Anderson	1982	243
420 6/8	56 4/8	57 4/8	46 1/8	5 4/8	5 7/8	20 1/8	5 2/8	5	5 2/8	12	14	Becharof Lake, AK	Steven H. Schaust	Steven H. Schaust	1983	243
420 5/8	53 7/8	49 1/8	40 2/8	6 1/8	5 7/8	18 1/8	19 3/8	11 2/8	11 3/8	18	13	Mulchatna River, AK	Ronald K. Hodges	Ronald K. Hodges	1986	245
420 4/8	59 4/8	57 4/8	42 4/8	8 6/8	8 5/8	12	18 2/8	17 2/8	17 2/8	11	16	Tangle Lakes, AK	J.W. Latham	J.W. Latham	1961	246
420 4/8	46 4/8	48	39 5/8	6 1/8	6 2/8	18 3/8	18 3/8	3 3/8	13 2/8	19	24	Dog Salmon River, AK	Gary R. Swanson	Gary R. Swanson	1966	246
420 4/8	55 5/8	58 4/8	46 4/8	6 3/8	6 3/8	18 2/8	18 2/8	12 5/8	7 3/8	21	14	Kaskanak Creek, AK	Robert J. Priewe	Robert J. Priewe	1991	246
420 4/8	55 5/8	53 5/8	46 2/8	6	7	21 3/8	18	14 4/8	1/8	17	19	Wolf Lake, AK	Thompson L. Hartlip	Thompson L. Hartlip	1994	246

BARREN GROUND CARIBOU
Rangifer tarandus granti

Score	Length of Main Beam R	L	Inside Spread	Circumference at Smallest Place Between Brow and Bez Points R	L	Length of Brow Points R	L	Width of Brow Points R	L	Number of Points R	L	Locality	Hunter	Owner	Date Killed	Rank
420 3/8	55	52 4/8	40 4/8	5 4/8	5 4/8	23	15 3/8	17 4/8	3	19	12	Alaska Pen., AK	W.M. Ellis	W.M. Ellis	1963	250
420 3/8	45 2/8	46 1/8	37 3/8	6 2/8	6	10 3/8	17	1/8	14 2/8	16	23	Cranberry Creek, AK	Robert A. Black	Robert A. Black	1994	250
420 2/8	48 1/8	48 1/8	35	6 7/8	7 5/8	19 4/8	18 2/8	12 6/8	12 2/8	26	25	Mulchatna River, AK	Bradley E. Groves	Bradley E. Groves	1994	252
420 1/8	59 2/8	57 2/8	40 4/8	6 3/8	6 3/8	22 7/8	21	5 4/8	17 4/8	15	19	Iliamna Lake, AK	A.E. Wilson	A.E. Wilson	1955	253
420 1/8	50 5/8	55 3/8	41 2/8	6 4/8	6 6/8	20	17 6/8	16 1/8	1/8	14	20	King Salmon River, AK	Frank N. Rome	Frank N. Rome	1983	253
420 1/8	56 1/8	54 2/8	37 6/8	7 2/8	7 3/8	17 2/8	13	1/8	1/8	18	15	Yanert Fork, AK	Michael H. Werner	Michael H. Werner	1984	253
420	50 2/8	50 5/8	42	7 1/8	7 3/8	17 6/8	13 1/8	13 4/8	13 1/8	20	17	Chisana, AK	John S. Newkam, Jr.	John S. Newkam, Jr.	1960	256
419 7/8	44	46 1/8	46 2/8	6 7/8	6 7/8	14 4/8	15 5/8	1 4/8	12 2/8	15	22	Aleutian Range, AK	Fred Dykema	Fred Dykema	1973	257
419 7/8	49 7/8	49 2/8	37 3/8	6 5/8	6 4/8	14 7/8	18 5/8	14 2/8	14 2/8	16	23	Alaska Pen., AK	Kenneth E. Hess	Kenneth E. Hess	1987	257
419 6/8	54 6/8	50 5/8	47 3/8	6 5/8	6 5/8	17 1/8	16 4/8	9 2/8	10 2/8	15	16	Dog Salmon River, AK	Ralph H. Eisaman	Ralph H. Eisaman	1971	259
419 6/8	53 7/8	51 3/8	41	6 2/8	6 1/8	16 3/8	19 3/8	9 4/8	12 4/8	18	21	Mulchatna River, AK	Robert P. Colson	Robert P. Colson	1993	259
419 5/8	43 6/8	45 3/8	29 7/8	7 5/8	7 5/8	14	15 4/8	8 7/8	10 7/8	22	22	Chisana, AK	Thomas F. Esper	Thomas F. Esper	1965	261
419 5/8	51 1/8	50 1/8	35 6/8	6 1/8	6 2/8	16 5/8	15 7/8	9 5/8	12 4/8	22	23	Mt. Drum, AK	Jerald T. Waite	Jerald T. Waite	1966	261
419 5/8	53 3/8	53 5/8	39 4/8	6 6/8	6 6/8	16 4/8	20 4/8	14 7/8	10 2/8	16	21	Nabesna, AK	Bernard Kendall	Bernard Kendall	1969	261
419 4/8	50	51 7/8	45 3/8	7 2/8	7 2/8	19 3/8	6 4/8	1/8	12 3/8	13	21	Rainy Pass, AK	Warren Page	Warren Page	1956	264
419 4/8	46 2/8	47 2/8	32	7 2/8	7	16 5/8	15 2/8	8 1/8	8 4/8	20	20	Talkeetna, AK	Dale Westenbarger	Dale Westenbarger	1965	264
419 4/8	57 3/8	57	46 6/8	6 1/8	6 4/8	17 4/8	19 3/8	9 6/8	7 5/8	17	16	King Salmon, AK	David C. Smith	David C. Smith	1987	264
419 3/8	45	45 4/8	35 5/8	8 1/8	7 4/8	18	15 3/8	13 1/8	1 2/8	26	21	Fairbanks, AK	Unknown	Ladd Air Force Base	PR 1953	267
419 3/8	54 2/8	52 3/8	37	7	7	20 2/8	19 3/8	7 7/8	11 7/8	14	17	Alaska Pen., AK	C. Driskell	C. Driskell	1965	267
419 3/8	53 1/8	53 1/8	40 5/8	7 4/8	7 4/8	18 7/8	3 6/8	17	1/8	17	15	Kenai River, AK	Allison L. Darsey	David A. Darsey	1992	267
419 3/8	52 2/8	52	42 5/8	6 1/8	6 1/8	21 5/8	19 6/8	15 1/8	12 2/8	12	17	Iliamna Lake, AK	Scott King	Scott King	1993	267
419 2/8	49 7/8	49 4/8	35 6/8	7	6 6/8	22 4/8	19 2/8	15 1/8	4 6/8	15	11	Iliamna Lake, AK	Roy F. Smith	Roy F. Smith	1987	271
419 2/8	53 5/8	55 3/8	37 2/8	6 6/8	6 2/8	19 2/8	19 1/8	12 6/8	5 7/8	19	16	Polly Creek, AK	Mark W. Linebarger	Mark W. Linebarger	1993	271
419 1/8	44 3/8	44 4/8	31 6/8	6 2/8	7 4/8	20 3/8	20	5	13	19	25	Ugashik River, AK	Ronald W. Madsen	Ronald W. Madsen	1987	273
419	45 2/8	44 2/8	35 5/8	7 4/8	7 4/8	14 1/8	15 7/8	8 2/8	9 1/8	24	19	Becharof Lake, AK	Ron L. Lerch	Ron L. Lerch	1966	274
419	42 3/8	46 5/8	35 3/8	6 4/8	6 4/8	17 4/8	11 6/8	1/8	11 4/8	12	24	Iliamna Lake, AK	Michael Clanton	Michael Clanton	1994	274
418 7/8	49 5/8	50	43	6	5 6/8	22 6/8	1 4/8	12	1/8	28	20	Nabesna River Valley, AK	Wayne Platt	Wayne Platt	1958	276
418 7/8	52 6/8	53 1/8	40 1/8	5 5/8	5 6/8	19 2/8	22 6/8	9	8 4/8	10	15	Mother Goose Lake, AK	Robert A. Epperson	Robert A. Epperson	1963	276
418 7/8	54 1/8	50 5/8	40 6/8	7	6 2/8	15 3/8	17	10 6/8	11 4/8	18	17	Hoholitna River, AK	O.B. Beard III	O.B. Beard III	1974	276
418 7/8	49 4/8	49 3/8	44	5 6/8	5 6/8	17 2/8	18 2/8	12 4/8	11 1/8	20	19	Cold Bay, AK	James E. Carson	James E. Carson	1974	276
418 7/8	48 7/8	54 1/8	38 2/8	6 4/8	7	17 3/8	18 2/8	5 7/8	13 2/8	15	15	Iliamna Lake, AK	Richard L. Deane	Richard L. Deane	1993	276
418 7/8	50 4/8	51 5/8	38	9 4/8	7 1/8	18 7/8	18 2/8	9 4/8	15 6/8	16	16	Nishlik Lake, AK	Kirby S. Kulbeck	Kirby S. Kulbeck	1994	276
418 6/8	59 6/8	60	53 1/8	6 6/8	6 7/8	17 2/8	22 3/8	12 5/8	3 3/8	12	15	Eureka, AK	William Curtis	F.A. Harrington	1949	282
418 6/8	59	55 5/8	34 4/8	6 4/8	6 1/8	22 3/8	6 1/8	1 2/8	6 1/8	17	21	Alaska Pen., AK	Otis Chandler	Otis Chandler	1964	282
418 6/8	58 5/8	53 4/8	40 7/8	5 6/8	5 6/8	20 6/8	6 1/8	1/8	15 1/8	11	18	Groundhog Mt., AK	Lloyd H. Richardson	Lloyd H. Richardson	1993	282
418 6/8	57 6/8	55 2/8	42 5/8	6 1/8	6 5/8	19 4/8	18	6 5/8	6 4/8	15	14	Alaska Pen., AK	V. Leland Richins	V. Leland Richins	1996	282

Score	L.R	L.L	(3)	(4)	(5)	(6)	(7)	(8)	(9)	R	L	Locality	Hunter	Owner	Date Killed	Rank
418 5/8	50 4/8	49 1/8	32 7/8	5 6/8	5 3/8	19 5/8	19 7/8	12 7/8	14 2/8	27	17	Hicks Creek, AK	Charles Brumbelow	Charles Brumbelow	1956	286
418 5/8	49 5/8	49 3/8	37 6/8	5 7/8	5 3/8	20 7/8	18	5 3/8	13 4/8	15	17	Kenai Mts., AK	Randall Yost	Randall Yost	1996	286
418 4/8	54 5/8	55	38 6/8	7 3/8	7 2/8	2 3/8	19	1/8	8 2/8	17	19	Ivishak River, AK	William O. Dudley	William O. Dudley	1979	288
418 3/8	52 6/8	51 5/8	50 4/8	6 2/8	5 6/8	18 7/8	19	5 2/8	8 2/8	12	13	Chistochina, AK	James H. Lahey	James H. Lahey	1961	289
418 3/8	52 7/8	52 5/8	45 5/8	5 6/8	6	12 1/8	19 1/8	1 3/8	5 1/8	15	17	Rainy Pass, AK	Aaron Saenz, Jr.	Aaron Saenz, Jr.	1964	289
418 3/8	47 1/8	46 5/8	39 6/8	7	7	18 7/8	19 3/8	11 4/8	1	21	12	High Lake, AK	Glen E. Park	Glen E. Park	1965	289
418 3/8	53	56	38 7/8	6 6/8	6 5/8	8	18 1/8	1	14 1/8	19	23	Aleutian Range, AK	Wayne Patton	Wayne Patton	1968	289
418 2/8	52 2/8	54 5/8	43 1/8	6 4/8	6	20 5/8	21 2/8	4	15 4/8	14	20	Big Susitna, AK	Forrest Boyce	Jack Dustin	1957	293
418 1/8	50 5/8	48 4/8	34 7/8	6	6	18 2/8	16 5/8	16 1/8	8	24	19	Denali Hwy., AK	Jerry Shepard	Jerry Shepard	1961	294
418 1/8	53 3/8	50 7/8	39 7/8	7	6 4/8	20	10 5/8	6 4/8	1/8	23	13	Caribou Creek, AK	Gary Joll	Gary Joll	1963	294
418 1/8	50 2/8	53 2/8	45 3/8	6 2/8	6 3/8	13 6/8	17	2 6/8	14 6/8	22	23	Chistochina, AK	Delbert H. Bullock	Delbert H. Bullock	1964	294
418 1/8	57 5/8	55 3/8	45 5/8	5 3/8	5 6/8	22	19	9 7/8	5 1/8	17	11	Becharof Lake, AK	William M. Beyl	William M. Beyl	1981	294
418	54 2/8	54	42 7/8	6 3/8	6 1/8	19 7/8	14 1/8	15 2/8	1/8	18	15	Alaska Range, AK	Richard L. McClellan	Richard L. McClellan	1978	298
418	54 6/8	53 6/8	47 3/8	7 5/8	7 6/8	17	20 4/8	1/8	14 4/8	12	17	Kenai, AK	Gary L. Zerbe	Gary L. Zerbe	1981	298
418	48	47 2/8	39 4/8	5 5/8	5 2/8	15 2/8	22 4/8	4 5/8	14 1/8	17	21	Becharof Lake, AK	Robert D. Lewallen	Robert D. Lewallen	1989	298
417 7/8	50 1/8	54 2/8	38 6/8	6 2/8	7 3/8	19 1/8	1 5/8	17	1/8	20	14	Tonzona River, AK	Fred T. Hecox	Fred T. Hecox	1983	301
417 7/8	54 2/8	58 5/8	46 5/8	6 7/8	6 3/8	15 6/8	10 7/8	9 7/8	7	14	10	Tyone River, AK	Edward D. Hull	Quint Hull	1987	301
417 7/8	50	49 2/8	27 3/8	6	6	21 7/8	18 3/8	18 3/8	13 7/8	25	17	Shotgun Creek, AK	Norman C. Wislef	Norman C. Wislef	1989	301
417 6/8	56 4/8	56 4/8	38 1/8	5 7/8	5 7/8	17 6/8	20 6/8	12 4/8	1 1/8	11	19	Talkeetna Mts., AK	Mrs. R.S. Mosiman	Mrs. R.S. Mosiman	1958	304
417 6/8	52 3/8	55 7/8	43 1/8	4 3/8	7 1/8	18 3/8	16 5/8	13 7/8	1/8	19	15	Alaska Pen., AK	William J. Miller	William J. Miller	1967	304
417 6/8	51 4/8	50	47 7/8	5 4/8	5 4/8	17 4/8	21 7/8	12 7/8	13 1/8	17	13	Nushagak River, AK	John M. Glover	John M. Glover	1988	304
417 5/8	55 2/8	60 4/8	46 2/8	6 1/8	6 1/8	17 4/8	16 4/8	6 1/8	12	12	17	Wrangell Mts., AK	Fred Packer	Fred Packer	1955	307
417 5/8	57 4/8	57	50 1/8	6 4/8	6 6/8	24 5/8	18 1/8	7 7/8	15	17	14	Alaska Range, AK	Richard K. Mellon	Richard K. Mellon	1959	307
417 5/8	51 3/8	53	35 2/8	6	5 5/8	18 4/8	19	12 1/8	12 4/8	12	16	Tangle Lakes, AK	Kurt C. Dunn	Kurt C. Dunn	1981	307
417 4/8	48 4/8	49 4/8	45 4/8	5 6/8	6	19 4/8	18 6/8	12 1/8	3 1/8	17	17	Mulchatna River, AK	R.D. Eichenour	R.D. Eichenour	1968	310
417 4/8	48 2/8	48 2/8	48 2/8	6	6 5/8	17	16 4/8	16 1/8	5 5/8	14	12	Mulchatna River, AK	Bradley P. Anderson	Bradley P. Anderson	1993	310
417 4/8	47 2/8	50 6/8	38 7/8	5 5/8	5	16 4/8	6	6	12 5/8	26	17	Lake Clark, AK	Gerald H. Nolen	Peter S. Nolen	1993	310
417 3/8	50 6/8	36 1/8	36 1/8	6 4/8	6 4/8	20 1/8	3 6/8	15 2/8	1/8	23	14	Twin Lakes, AK	Samuel B. Webb, Jr.	Samuel B. Webb, Jr.	1960	313
417 3/8	54 2/8	52 3/8	40 4/8	6 3/8	6 3/8	16 3/8	17 4/8	12	12 5/8	19	26	Alaska Pen., AK	Herb Klein	Herb Klein	1964	313
417 3/8	47 4/8	48 6/8	40 4/8	7 6/8	7 6/8	19 5/8	17 1/8	5	11	18	23	Alaska Pen., AK	Tyson Nichols	Tyson Nichols	1979	313
417 3/8	48 6/8	48 4/8	25 3/8	6	6	15 1/8	15 4/8	10 2/8	9 5/8	22	19	Fracture Creek, AK	L. Irvin Barnhart	L. Irvin Barnhart	1983	313
417 3/8	50 5/8	52	33 6/8	8 3/8	8 1/8	20	13 1/8	13 1/8	9	16	18	Mt. Sanford, AK	Dennis Brieske	Dennis Brieske	1984	313
417 2/8	52	52 3/8	38 3/8	8 3/8	8 3/8	17 5/8	11 1/8	11 1/8	13 1/8	13	22	White River, AK	Gary L. Todd	Gary L. Todd	1984	318
417 2/8	59 6/8	60 7/8	42 5/8	6 2/8	6 3/8	21 4/8	16 3/8	16 3/8	9	17	16	Chanuk Cr., AK	Roger O. Wyant	Roger O. Wyant	1989	318
417 1/8	55 1/8	61 5/8	42 5/8	5 6/8	6	20 6/8	14 6/8	14 6/8	9 5/8	15	13	Rainy Pass, AK	Sigurd Jensen	Sigurd Jensen	1956	320
417	51 5/8	57	37 2/8	6 5/8	6 2/8	11 1/8	20 2/8	1/8	14 7/8	14	17	Little Delta River, AK	Fred Bear	Fred Bear	1959	321
417	51 2/8	51 2/8	37 2/8	6 2/8	6 5/8	2	17 4/8	1/8	12 2/8	16	21	Mulchatna River, AK	Mark H. Young	Mark H. Young	1987	321
417	48	48	37	6 3/8	6 3/8	9 5/8	17 1/8	5	15 1/8	22	13	Bonanza Hills, AK	Richard A. Bergman	Richard A. Bergman	1991	321
417	61 3/8	61 1/8	40 1/8	1	1/8	21 1/8	15 4/8	9 3/8	15 2/8	13	21	Iliamna Lake, AK	Thomas D. Hess	Thomas D. Hess	1992	321
417	61 3/8	60 2/8	42 6/8	6 2/8	1/8	7 5/8	19 3/8	12 2/8	1/8	20	20	Dillingham, AK	Lowell N. Wacker	Lowell N. Wacker	1996	321
416 7/8	60 2/8	55	40 1/8	5 6/8	6 2/8	11 1/8	20 2/8	1	11 1/8	18	13	Clarence Lake, AK	James K. Harrower	James K. Harrower	1961	326
416 7/8	52 3/8	45 6/8	42 6/8	6 3/8	6 1/8	17 4/8	17 4/8	12 2/8	6	13	14	Mulchatna River, AK	Q.D. Edwards	Q.D. Edwards	1987	326
416 7/8	47 3/8	51 7/8	39 3/8	6 2/8	6	19 3/8	19	15 1/8	9 5/8	12	12	Windy Fork River, AK	William G. Hagerty	William G. Hagerty	1993	326
416 7/8	54 3/8	59 6/8	32 3/8	6 1/8	6 2/8	23 1/8	21 1/8	7 1/8	15 1/8	19	19	Nushagak River, AK	Robert D. Henderson	Robert D. Henderson	1994	326
416 6/8	54 3/8	51 7/8	43	6 1/8	6 1/8	18 5/8	18 5/8	7 5/8	15 1/8	20	17	Wood River, AK	A. Knutson	A. Knutson	1957	330
416 6/8	59 6/8	57 5/8	45 6/8	5 4/8	4 2/8	4 2/8	21 3/8	17	1/8	11	11	King Salmon, AK	F. Robert Bell	F. Robert Bell	1983	330
416 5/8	56 4/8	58 4/8	41	7	6 6/8	12 2/8	19 3/8	1	14 6/8	15	15	Mulchatna River, AK	R.D. Eichenour	R.D. Eichenour	1968	332

BARREN GROUND CARIBOU

Rangifer tarandus granti

Score	Length of Main Beam R	L	Inside Spread	Circumference at Smallest Place Between Brow and Bez Points R	L	Length of Brow Points R	L	Width of Brow Points R	L	Number of Points R	L	Locality	Hunter	Owner	Date Killed	Rank
416 5/8	51 2/8	51 4/8	36 4/8	6 4/8	6 5/8	17 7/8	4 5/8	12 3/8	1 4/8	31	21	Alaska Pen., AK	Jim Ford	Jim Ford	1970	332
416 5/8	53 1/8	51 1/8	52	6 5/8	6 5/8	21	14	17		23	14	Black Lake, AK	Merle L. Schreiner	Merle L. Schreiner	1993	332
416 4/8	56	54	37 5/8	7 4/8	7 4/8	13 6/8	16 2/8	7 3/8	13 2/8	15	21	Rainy Pass, AK	J. Watson Webb, Jr.	J. Watson Webb, Jr.	1934	335
416 4/8	45 1/8	45 7/8	41 4/8	8 4/8	7 6/8	20 7/8	18 6/8	5 1/8	14 4/8	17	20	Upper Ugashik Lake, AK	Russell Matthes	Russell Matthes	1969	335
416 4/8	56 7/8	54 2/8	48 6/8	5 6/8	6	15	19 6/8	3 6/8	10 4/8	13	18	Mulchatna River, AK	Willard L. Hubbard	Willard L. Hubbard	1983	335
416 4/8	49 3/8	52	44 3/8	6 4/8	6 3/8	16 7/8	17 6/8	12	10	18	20	American Pass, AK	Brett G. Alexander	Brett G. Alexander	1984	335
416 4/8	50 6/8	51 6/8	45 1/8	6	6 2/8	1 6/8	17 6/8	1/8	11 2/8	15	20	Lake Clark, AK	James E. Schoudel	James E. Schoudel	1993	335
416 4/8	50 6/8	51	34	7 2/8	6	17 1/8	18	10 3/8	13 6/8	22	21	Iliamna, AK	Tony L. Spriggs	Tony L. Spriggs	1995	335
416 3/8	52 1/8	51 3/8	44 2/8	7 5/8	7 4/8	15 4/8	17 4/8	9	8 3/8	13	17	Talkeetna Mts., AK	Karris Keirn	Karris Keirn	1958	341
416 3/8	53 4/8	52 7/8	38 3/8	6 2/8	5 6/8	18 6/8	19	16 1/8	14 5/8	24	18	Post Lake, AK	Gerald Scheuerman	Gerald Scheuerman	1961	341
416 3/8	58 1/8	59 7/8	46	7 5/8	8 2/8	20 7/8	10 1/8	13 2/8	1/8	13	11	Iliamna Lake, AK	Michael J. Ryan, Sr.	Michael J. Ryan, Sr.	1973	341
416 3/8	49 2/8	49 1/8	43 3/8	6 4/8	6 6/8	13 3/8	16 7/8	1 1/8	9 1/8	17	19	Port Heiden, AK	Charlie Martin	Charlie Martin	1981	341
416 3/8	56 6/8	56 7/8	35 1/8	5 3/8	5 4/8	20 1/8	20 1/8	6 3/8	14 6/8	13	18	Blackstone River, YT	Ken Vickerman	Ken Vickerman	1983	341
416 2/8	45 7/8	42 6/8	41 3/8	6 6/8	6 5/8	19 3/8	16 7/8	13 6/8	3 5/8	19	17	Kenakuchuk Creek, AK	Ed I. Zavadlov	Ed I. Zavadlov	1996	346
416 2/8	54 4/8	54 3/8	46 1/8	7 6/8	7	19 3/8	21	13 3/8	4 3/8	17	17	Nushagak River, AK	Shawn L. Wagner	Shawn L. Wagner	1997	346
416 1/8	52 6/8	52 7/8	37 5/8	6 2/8	6 2/8	15 3/8	19 1/8	1 2/8	15 2/8	11	20	Wrangell Mts., AK	William H. Warrick	William H. Warrick	1961	348
416 1/8	54 2/8	56 6/8	46 1/8	7	7		20 2/8	16		11	20	Farewell Lake, AK	K.T. Miller	K.T. Miller	1962	348
416 1/8	49 2/8	49 2/8	38 2/8	6 3/8	6 3/8	24	17 7/8	17 4/8	4 4/8	16	14	Crooked Creek, AK	Bill E. Slone	Bill E. Slone	1964	348
416 1/8	51 2/8	50 4/8	35	5 7/8	5 6/8	19	18 5/8	15	12 2/8	20	14	Little Mulchatna River, AK	M.E. Kulik	M.E. Kulik	1967	348
416 1/8	54 1/8	54 7/8	37 3/8	7 3/8	6 3/8	5	19 2/8	1/8	14 1/8	21	24	Becharof Lake, AK	Todd Rice	Todd Rice	1987	348
416 1/8	50	46	39 2/8	5 5/8	6 2/8	18 3/8	17	14	13 4/8	21	16	Lake Clark, AK	Rainer H. Unger	Rainer H. Unger	1987	348
416 1/8	57 4/8	57	34 5/8	6 1/8	6	21 5/8	19	17 4/8	9 7/8	17	16	Blackstone River, YT	Jack Franklin	Jack Franklin	1994	348
416	57 3/8	56 7/8	39 6/8	6 1/8	6	21 2/8	3 1/8	17 3/8	6/8	17	14	Ugashik, AK	Richard S. Farr	Richard S. Farr	1966	355
416	50 3/8	51 5/8	48	5 5/8	5 4/8	18 1/8	17 6/8	13 5/8	10	19	22	Alaska Pen., AK	Bill E. Hodson	Bill E. Hodson	1978	355
416	50 7/8	50 7/8	40 4/8	9 7/8	7 4/8	18 6/8	6 3/8	15 4/8	1/8	19	16	Stony River, AK	Charles F. Nadler	Charles F. Nadler	1985	355
415 7/8	55 2/8	53 5/8	45 3/8	6 3/8	6	16	16 7/8	15 5/8	10 2/8	19	25	Steese Hwy., AK	Howard Hill	Howard Hill	1958	358
415 7/8	51 2/8	52 2/8	40 3/8	6 3/8	6 3/8	18 2/8	12 6/8	12 7/8	7/8	14	14	Alaska Pen., AK	Richard A. Bengraff	Richard A. Bengraff	1981	358
415 7/8	64	63 1/8	45 4/8	6 1/8	6 3/8	17 4/8	21 4/8	8	10 7/8	19	12	Becharof Lake, AK	Alfred T. Bachman	Alfred T. Bachman	1989	358
415 7/8	51 5/8	53 2/8	38 2/8	6 7/8	7 3/8	17 2/8	17 6/8	13	11 3/8	21	17	Stuyahok River, AK	Barry N. Zimdars	Barry N. Zimdars	1992	358
415 6/8	50 6/8	47 5/8	40 7/8	5 1/8	6	19 4/8	16 6/8	13 5/8	12 5/8	19	19	Monsoon Lake, AK	Paul A. Szopa	Paul A. Szopa	1983	362
415 6/8	52 7/8	54 3/8	46 5/8	6	6	5 6/8	17 3/8	1/8	13 5/8	15	19	King Salmon River, AK	Paul G. Forslund	Paul G. Forslund	1995	362
415 5/8	49 2/8	52 6/8	39 2/8	6 1/8	5 7/8	17 6/8	17 4/8	6 6/8	11 7/8	19	20	King Salmon River, AK	Robert G. Barta	Robert G. Barta	1978	364
415 5/8	50 2/8	50 3/8	43 3/8	6 4/8	6 5/8	6 2/8	17 4/8	4 5/8	13 3/8	15	20	Whitefish Lake, AK	Jeffrey S. Sorg	Jeffrey S. Sorg	1982	364
415 4/8	56 3/8	56 7/8	35 7/8	6 5/8	6 5/8	19 1/8	7 7/8	12 3/8	5 4/8	20	16	Tyone River, AK	E.H. Miller	E.H. Miller	1956	366
415 4/8	54 7/8	53	39 2/8	5 5/8	5 4/8	20 3/8	22 3/8	15 7/8	9 7/8	22	18	Egegik River, AK	George J. Markham	George J. Markham	1967	366
415 4/8	58 5/8	60 6/8	60 7/8	5 6/8	5 6/8	3 6/8	17 5/8	10 4/8	1/8	15	23	Becharof Lake, AK	Max E. Chittick	Max E. Chittick	1980	366

Score									Pts.	Locality	No.	Owner	By Whom Killed	Date Killed	Rank
415 4/8	49 2/8	48	33	6	6 1/8	17 1/8	8 2/8	21 5/8	16	Watana Lake, AK	20	Kurt K. Knutson	Kurt K. Knutson	1981	366
415 4/8	50 3/8	49	44 7/8	6	7 1/8	16 1/8	12 2/8	16 5/8	16	Hoholitna River, AK	19	Franklin E. Phillips	Franklin E. Phillips	1997	366
415 3/8	49 6/8	50 1/8	41 2/8	5 6/8	5 5/8	13 6/8	14 3/8	17 5/8	17	Nenana River, AK	15	James H. Hunt	James H. Hunt	1983	371
415 3/8	51 4/8	46 4/8	30 1/8	5 4/8	5 1/8	17 6/8	12 4/8	17 2/8	21	Colville River, AK	24	Edward A. Rabalais	Edward A. Rabalais	1993	371
415 1/8	59	57 2/8	51 6/8	6 2/8	6 2/8	17 7/8	11 6/8	15	18	Becharof Lake, AK	22	L. Keith Mortensen	L. Keith Mortensen	1980	373
415	56 4/8	57	44 5/8	6 1/8	6 6/8	19 5/8	8 2/8	16 4/8	14	Alaska Pen., AK	22	Picked Up	William P. Bredesen, Jr.	1974	374
414 7/8	54 2/8	53 1/8	46 1/8	5 4/8	5 3/8	23 2/8	9 6/8	20 3/8	16	Alaska Pen., AK	17	Herb Klein	Herb Klein	1967	375
414 6/8	56	55 1/8	42 1/8	6	6 1/8	16 7/8	8 1/8	21 3/8	15	Denali Hwy., AK	10	Paul Patz	Paul Patz	1965	376
414 6/8	54	57 2/8	39 2/8	7 3/8	7 4/8	21 5/8	1 2/8	11 6/8	13	Yanert Fork, AK	22	Russell W. McInnis	Russell W. McInnis	1988	376
414 6/8	57 3/8	54 3/8	42 4/8	7	6 2/8	15 7/8	1/8	19 2/8	20	Rainy Pass, AK	16	Mahlon T. White	Mahlon T. White	1969	378
414 5/8	50 4/8	53	53	6	6 4/8	16 7/8	15 7/8	14 3/8	12	Miner River, AK	20	Gary L. Selig	Gary L. Selig	1979	378
414 5/8	53 5/8	53 4/8	39	7 4/8	5 5/8	3 6/8	1	10 4/8	12	Dog Salmon River, AK	27	Robert G. Good	Robert G. Good	1994	378
414 5/8	51 7/8	51 7/8	35 1/8	8 2/8	6 3/8	20 1/8	1 3/8	10 4/8	14	Shotgun Hills, AK	20	Douglas J. Aikin	Douglas J. Aikin	1995	378
414 4/8	42 3/8	44 1/8	32 2/8	5 6/8	7 2/8	17 3/8	15 5/8	20 7/8	21	Iliamna Lake, AK	23	Timothy F. McGinn	Timothy F. McGinn	1995	378
414 3/8	53 6/8	52 4/8	50 3/8	5 5/8	5 5/8	19 5/8	4/8	2 4/8	15	Naknek, AK	16	C.J. McElroy	C.J. McElroy	1966	383
414 3/8	54	55 6/8	39 4/8	7 1/8	7 1/8	16	10 5/8	9 1/8	14	Denali Hwy., AK	21	C.W. Hilbish	C.W. Hilbish	1958	384
414 3/8	54 2/8	54 4/8	49	7	6 2/8	21 1/8	6/8	16 3/8	14	Talkeetna Mts., AK	22	G.W. Berry	G.W. Berry	1960	384
414 3/8	46 3/8	54 5/8	40 1/8	6 2/8	6 3/8	17 2/8	12 1/8	16	16	Alaska Pen., AK	17	George H. Landreth	George H. Landreth	1967	384
414 3/8	57	49 3/8	47 2/8	6 4/8	6 3/8	16 4/8	11 6/8	5 2/8	17	Alaska Pen., AK	24	Robert Wessner	Robert Wessner	1969	384
414 3/8	50 1/8	50 6/8	40	5 5/8	5 5/8	18 2/8	11 6/8	14 4/8	16	Lake Clark, AK	17	Stanley J. Leger	Stanley J. Leger	1986	384
414 3/8	52 2/8	50 3/8	42 6/8	6 3/8	6 2/8	21 4/8	1 4/8	14 4/8	16	Tutna Lake, AK	18	Jim S. Campbell	Jim S. Campbell	1987	384
414 3/8	47 4/8	47 3/8	28 5/8	5 5/8	5 6/8	14 4/8	15 2/8	20 3/8	13	Nushagak Hills, AK	17	Robert D. Jones	Robert D. Jones	1991	384
414 2/8	53 4/8	53 6/8	36 1/8	6 5/8	9	20 3/8	1 2/8	17 7/8	13	Taylor Mts., AK	14	Robert J. Allen	Robert J. Allen	1989	391
414 2/8	58 7/8	53 5/8	32 5/8	7 4/8	7 4/8	17 7/8	3 4/8	14 2/8	15	Little Mulchatna River, AK	13	David B. Nielsen	David B. Nielsen	1992	391
414 1/8	45 1/8	46 4/8	35 7/8	11 2/8	11 2/8	10 2/8	13	16	27	Clarence Lake, AK	22	Jack Hill	Jack Hill	1964	393
414 1/8	43 2/8	43 4/8	43 4/8	6 4/8	6 4/8	15 3/8	13	19	21	Snake River, YT	20	Leslie Kish	Leslie Kish	1985	393
414 1/8	52 5/8	50 6/8	37 7/8	5 7/8	5 7/8	14 3/8	6 4/8	14 2/8	20	Iliamna Lake, AK	23	Richard J. Sands	Richard J. Sands	1989	393
414 1/8	44 7/8	44 6/8	33 3/8	6 6/8	6 6/8	17 4/8	12	15 1/8	18	Koktuli River, AK	18	Mark B. Nielsen	Mark B. Nielsen	1993	393
414 1/8	48 2/8	47 4/8	33 7/8	6 7/8	7	20 4/8	14	4 7/8	17	Beluga Lake, AK	17	Ted A. Clark	Ted A. Clark	1997	393
414	53 4/8	54 3/8	38 6/8	6 7/8	6 7/8	15 1/8	1/8	17 4/8	19	Upper Susitna, AK	21	Harold Gould	Harold Gould	1953	398
414	38 7/8	40 3/8	36 3/8	5 7/8	5 7/8	21	7 7/8	17 1/8	23	Little Nelchina River, AK	22	Temple Bros. Tax.	Picked Up	1954	398
414	48 6/8	48 1/8	39 7/8	6 3/8	6 3/8	17 2/8	14 2/8	17 2/8	14	Johnson River, AK	24	Donald W. Bunselmeier	Donald W. Bunselmeier	1988	398
413 7/8	49 4/8	51 6/8	40	6 4/8	6 4/8	14 1/8	10 4/8	17 2/8	19	Hart Lake, YT	20	Curt Curtis	Curt Curtis	1996	398
413 6/8	50	50 5/8	37	5 2/8	5 1/8	18 1/8	13 5/8	14 1/8	18	Nishlik Lake, AK	14	Nick J. Helterline	Nick J. Helterline	1994	402
413 6/8	57 4/8	59 2/8	44 5/8	6 1/8	6 6/8	19 3/8	12 6/8	18 1/8	18	Alaska Pen., AK	17	Ira Swartz	Ira Swartz	1967	403
413 6/8	51 2/8	51 1/8	39 3/8	6 1/8	6 2/8	2 7/8	8	19 3/8	20	Wrangell Mts., AK	14	Robert Reed	Robert Reed	1968	403
413 5/8	56 3/8	57	39 2/8	6	6	18	6/8	19 6/8	18	Alaska Pen., AK	20	Robert A. Patzer	Robert A. Patzer	1992	403
413 5/8	47 6/8	47 5/8	44 6/8	7 4/8	7 4/8	1 6/8	13 1/8	2 7/8	17	King Salmon River, AK	15	B&C National Collection	Basil C. Bradbury	1967	406
413 4/8	48 4/8	48 4/8	33 4/8	6	6	19 6/8	1	17 2/8	22	Kuskokwim River, AK	20	Walther Schmitz	Walther Schmitz	1969	406
413 4/8	50 4/8	50 4/8	38	5 5/8	5 5/8	19 6/8	16 4/8	1 6/8	13	Talkeetna Mts., AK	18	Louis Mussatto	Louis Mussatto	1964	408
413 3/8	52 1/8	52 1/8	37 4/8	5 2/8	5 2/8	5 7/8	13	20 4/8	15	Iliamna Lake, AK	29	Wright W. Allen	Wright W. Allen	1993	408
413 3/8	52 3/8	53	44	6 7/8	6 7/8	19 3/8	13 6/8	18	19	Denali Hwy., AK	12	Albert E. Greer	Albert E. Greer	1963	410
413 3/8	55 6/8	57 2/8	44 5/8	6 2/8	6 2/8	16 6/8	8 7/8	4 4/8	17	Whitefish Lake, AK	14	Larry D. Domson	Larry D. Domson	1984	411
413 2/8	53 3/8	54 1/8	39 5/8	6 1/8	5 7/8	15	12 6/8	20 5/8	14	Dry Tok Creek, AK	19	Todd A. Brewer	Todd A. Brewer	1994	411
413 1/8	59 3/8	57 3/8	40 5/8	5 7/8	5 7/8	16 6/8	8 7/8	19 7/8	14	Tyone River, AK	14	Walter Elam	Walter Elam	1959	413
413 1/8	52 6/8	54 1/8	36 2/8	6 1/8	6 2/8	15	9 2/8	16 1/8	22	Lake Clark, AK	18	Edward W. Threlkeld	Edward W. Threlkeld	1996	413
413	38 6/8	41 7/8	40 2/8	7	6 4/8	17 3/8	12 5/8	8 5/8	17	Tangle Lakes, AK	18	David J. Morlock	David J. Morlock	1956	415

517

BARREN GROUND CARIBOU

Rangifer tarandus granti

Score	Length of Main Beam R	L	Inside Spread	Circumference at Smallest Place Between Brow and Bez Points R	L	Length of Brow Points R	L	Width of Brow Points R	L	Number of Points R	L	Locality	Hunter	Owner	Date Killed	Rank
413	61 4/8	60 4/8	45 4/8	6 2/8	6	17 7/8	17 7/8	7 4/8	11 6/8	17	25	Aniakchak Crater, AK	M.G. Johnson	M.G. Johnson	1964	415
413	49 7/8	49 5/8	40 2/8	8 2/8	6 2/8	17 7/8	19	15 6/8	14 7/8	16	20	Mad River, AK	Larry G. Hurst	Larry G. Hurst	1992	415
412 7/8	51 2/8	48 7/8	31 6/8	8 6/8	7 5/8	11 6/8	14 4/8	2 5/8	9 6/8	20	28	Rainy Pass, AK	Ernst Von Hake	Ernst Von Hake	1963	418
412 7/8	56 2/8	56 2/8	41	5 6/8	6 3/8	16 2/8	14 6/8	10	7 5/8	18	16	Lake Clark, AK	William F. Rae, Jr.	William F. Rae, Jr.	1968	418
412 7/8	58 5/8	58 3/8	47 2/8	5 5/8	5 7/8	16 4/8	14 6/8	12 1/8	1/8	28	20	Tutna Lake, AK	Ernest C. Noble	Ernest C. Noble	1987	418
412 7/8	46 6/8	46 5/8	37	6 3/8	7 1/8	7 7/8	18 4/8	5 1/8	14 1/8	24	26	Hoholitna River, AK	Dale H. Maass	Dale H. Maass	1992	418
412 6/8	56 4/8	58	47	6	6 2/8	17	21 3/8	4 2/8	14 5/8	12	15	Alaska Pen., AK	John P. Nelson, Jr.	John P. Nelson, Jr.	1961	422
412 6/8	50 3/8	46 3/8	38 6/8	5 1/8	5 2/8	17 6/8	20 4/8	12 3/8	17 1/8	19	23	Port Moller, AK	Billy W. Green	Billy W. Green	1983	422
412 4/8	50 3/8	53 7/8	42 2/8	5	5	21 2/8	18 2/8	9 2/8	13 2/8	15	16	Eli River, AK	David R. Lautner	David R. Lautner	1992	424
412 4/8	49 7/8	49	42 3/8	6	6	14 5/8	20 3/8	1/8	10	13	20	Becharof Lake, AK	Terry M. Dittrich	Terry M. Dittrich	1997	424
412 3/8	50 6/8	55 5/8	41 3/8	6 1/8	6	20 6/8	14 6/8	15 4/8	8 6/8	18	13	Twin Lakes, AK	Inge Hill, Jr.	Inge Hill, Jr.	1965	426
412 3/8	61 5/8	62 5/8	50 1/8	5 6/8	5 5/8	22 6/8	8 7/8	14	1/8	18	11	King Salmon, AK	Larry Spiva	Larry Spiva	1983	426
412 3/8	59	60 2/8	40 5/8	5 6/8	5 6/8	21 4/8	23 2/8	15	7 6/8	15	13	Dog Salmon River, AK	John S. Alley	John S. Alley	1987	426
412 3/8	44 2/8	44 5/8	30 3/8	4 7/8	5 7/8	17 2/8	19	4 6/8	17 4/8	20	21	Squirrel River, AK	Jack D. Adams	Jack D. Adams	1991	426
412 3/8	54 5/8	54 6/8	43	5 7/8	6 1/8	21	2 2/8	15 2/8	1/8	18	14	Iliamna Lake, AK	Richard R. Lefler	Richard R. Lefler	1993	426
412 2/8	59 5/8	58 6/8	24 7/8	8 6/8	8 7/8	19	18 3/8	13 4/8	7	15	13	Slana, AK	William Kiltz	William Kiltz	1959	431
412 2/8	51 5/8	51 6/8	38 1/8	7 4/8	7 7/8	15 4/8	14 6/8	11 1/8	8 2/8	18	18	Gulkana River, AK	Danny K. Shepherd	Danny K. Shepherd	1993	431
412 2/8	47 2/8	46 2/8	44 1/8	7 2/8	7 4/8	15 2/8	16 2/8	11 6/8	14 3/8	21	22	Lake Clark, AK	William E. Pipes III	William E. Pipes III	1995	431
412 1/8	46	46 7/8	25 3/8	7 1/8	6 5/8	17 4/8	17 2/8	5 7/8	13 3/8	18	17	Tay Lake, YT	Dan Newlon	Dan Newlon	1963	434
412 1/8	44	46	44	6 4/8	6 1/8	8	19 2/8	18	16 6/8	17	26	Hoholitna River, AK	Daniel E. Lunde	Daniel E. Lunde	1986	434
412 1/8	54 5/8	51 5/8	47	6 1/8	6 1/8	19 6/8	18 5/8	14 1/8	3 3/8	19	18	Mulchatna River, AK	Sid A. Richards	Sid A. Richards	1993	434
412	43 6/8	47 2/8	40	8 3/8	8	19 6/8	20	13	13 4/8	27	29	Alaska Pen., AK	Paul T. Hartman	Paul T. Hartman	1966	437
411 7/8	57	53 2/8	46 4/8	7 3/8	7	3 3/8	23 3/8	20	1/8	12	21	Talkeetna Mts., AK	Walter J. Wojciuk	Walter J. Wojciuk	1960	438
411 7/8	59 7/8	60 2/8	49 1/8	5 6/8	5 7/8	20 5/8	4 4/8	18 2/8	1 1/8	16	10	Jimmy Lake, AK	Jack M. Matthews	Jack M. Matthews	1966	438
411 7/8	45 6/8	44 5/8	40	5 3/8	5 3/8	17	17 2/8	11 7/8	14 2/8	23	20	Dog Salmon River, AK	Benny B. Kerns	Benny B. Kerns	1983	438
411 7/8	53 2/8	55	41 2/8	6 4/8	6 4/8	12 1/8	20 6/8	1 2/8	16 2/8	14	19	Becharof Lake, AK	Douglas G. Bonetti	Douglas G. Bonetti	1987	438
411 7/8	53 6/8	51 1/8	39 1/8	7 4/8	6 5/8	3	17 3/8	1/8	14	16	20	Billy Creek, AK	David L. Richards	David L. Richards	1987	438
411 6/8	49 6/8	50 1/8	41	6 7/8	6 5/8	20 6/8	15 6/8	15 2/8	1 4/8	18	14	Becharof Lake, AK	Gary F. Sile	Gary F. Sile	1995	443
411 5/8	61 3/8	59 3/8	47	6	6	20 4/8	21 7/8	1/8	15 3/8	12	16	Alaska Pen., AK	H. Sagesser	Berne Mus. Nat. Hist.	1962	444
411 5/8	53 6/8	57 5/8	48	5 6/8	5 6/8	18 4/8	20 2/8	8 2/8	17 4/8	14	22	Big River, AK	Phillip D. Wagner	Phillip D. Wagner	1994	444
411 4/8	45 3/8	45 7/8	45 7/8	6 6/8	6 4/8	20 2/8	18 4/8	7 1/8	7 3/8	14	13	Lake Louise, AK	John Trautner	John Trautner	1960	446
411 4/8	49	45 7/8	34 1/8	6 5/8	6 6/8	17 6/8	18 1/8	13 7/8	7 3/8	16	17	Twin Lakes, AK	Richard R. Oberle	Richard R. Oberle	1973	446
411 4/8	56 4/8	57	42 2/8	6 3/8	6 1/8	16 1/8	10 4/8	1/8	10 4/8	12	12	Wood River, AK	Carol L. Schwabland	Carol L. Schwabland	1981	446
411 1/8	51 4/8	49 5/8	34 3/8	5 7/8	6	15 4/8	19 7/8	2 1/8	15 6/8	15	21	Hartman River, AK	Robert B. Hancock	Robert B. Hancock	1988	446
411 1/8	53 3/8	55 6/8	46 4/8	9 6/8	9 6/8	16 4/8	16 7/8	7 3/8	15 6/8	13	13	Wood River, AK	Luther W. Palmer	Luther W. Palmer	1984	450
411	43	43 3/8	32 2/8	8	8 1/8	17	18 2/8	15	9 4/8	22	19	Healy, AK	Michael A. Couch	Michael A. Couch	1969	451

Score	L. Main Beam R	L. Main Beam L	Inside Spread	Circ. R	Circ. L	Brow Palm R	Brow Palm L	Top Palm R	Top Palm L	Pts R	Pts L	Locality	By Whom Killed	Owner	Date	Rank
411	55 4/8	56 4/8	35 4/8	5 6/8	5 4/8	21 1/8	16	16	9 1/8	17	16	Wood River, AK	James C. Midcap	James C. Midcap	1970	451
411	59 6/8	55 7/8	54	6 4/8	8	13 1/8	16 7/8	3 4/8	9	13	16	Tutna Lake, AK	Joseph M. Negri	Joseph M. Negri	1986	451
411	53 1/8	49 6/8	36 4/8	6 7/8	7 2/8	22	7 1/8	14 2/8	1/8	20	14	Mt. Harper, AK	Gary L. Truitt	Gary L. Truitt	1987	451
410 7/8	53 5/8	52 4/8	32 7/8	6 3/8	6 1/8	21	16 6/8	15 4/8	6 2/8	24	16	Wrangell Mts., AK	John Belcher	John Belcher	1956	455
410 7/8	49 5/8	50 2/8	47 1/8	6 6/8	7	19	20 3/8	10 7/8	12 4/8	16	20	Talkeetna Mts., AK	Clifford F. Hood	Clifford F. Hood	1958	455
410 7/8	64 3/8	65 1/8	53 4/8	6	6 3/8	16 3/8	8 2/8	8 2/8		16	12	Becharof Lake, AK	Gordon G. Chittick	Gordon G. Chittick	1981	455
410 6/8	60 6/8	58 4/8	47 3/8	5 1/8	5 1/8	17 5/8	11 5/8	12 3/8	7/8	14	14	Chandalar Lake, AK	L.A. Miller	L.A. Miller	1953	458
410 6/8	60 3/8	64 2/8	53	5 3/8	5 2/8	1 5/8	16 7/8	14 7/8	1 1/8	31	25	Talkeetna Mts., AK	Elgin T. Gates	Elgin T. Gates	1960	458
410 6/8	53 2/8	54 7/8	40 7/8	6 7/8	6 4/8	19 3/8	12 4/8	14 7/8	7/8	16	11	Denali Hwy., AK	Ray W. Holler	Ray W. Holler	1965	458
410 6/8	57 5/8	56 2/8	41 5/8	6 2/8	6 6/8	18 7/8	17 3/8	1	14 1/8	20	28	Alaska Pen., AK	Jim Keeler	Jim Keeler	1966	458
410 6/8	55 2/8	56 5/8	41 1/8	6 1/8	7 3/8	3 5/8	17 3/8	13 2/8	1	12	13	Talkeetna Mts., AK	Melissa A. Everett	Melissa A. Everett	1988	458
410 5/8	51 7/8	52 4/8	52 4/8	7 3/8	6 2/8	16 7/8	17 2/8	16 7/8	9 7/8	15	13	Denali Hwy., AK	J.W. Jett	J.W. Jett	1960	463
410 5/8	51 4/8	51 4/8	33 6/8	6 2/8	6 1/8	15	18 7/8	15	15 6/8	22	21	Tanana Valley, AK	Bob Hagel	Bob Hagel	1961	463
410 5/8	58 3/8	56 7/8	31 3/8	7 5/8	7 5/8	15	21 3/8	16 5/8	4 7/8	19	20	McKinley Nat. Park, AK	Joseph M. Messana	Joseph M. Messana	1968	463
410 5/8	49 2/8	47 7/8	33 7/8	6 6/8	6 5/8	16 5/8	21 4/8	1	15 6/8	12	16	Wrangell Mts., AK	Lee Chambers	Lee Chambers	1969	463
410 5/8	57 2/8	57 5/8	35	6 4/8	6 4/8	15 5/8	15 2/8	14 2/8	9 2/8	18	18	Hunt River, AK	James W. Styler	James W. Styler	1981	463
410 3/8	48 6/8	52	48 3/8	5 7/8	7 2/8	4	20 3/8	1/8	11 6/8	11	19	Becharof Lake, AK	Marcus C. Deede	Marcus C. Deede	1987	470
410 3/8	58 2/8	53 7/8	43 1/8	6 1/8	7 5/8	17 3/8	21 5/8	1/8	21 7/8	13	13	Haines Lake, AK	Len F. Onorato	Len F. Onorato	1987	470
410 3/8	53 7/8	51 2/8	36 5/8	5 6/8	5 4/8	17 1/8	17 5/8	15 3/8	10 6/8	19	22	Lake Clark, AK	Donald J. Hotter III	Donald J. Hotter III	1979	470
410 2/8	57 6/8	56	46 3/8	6 1/8	5 7/8	13	21	1/8	12 7/8	13	20	Becharof Lake, AK	Lavon L. Chittick	Lavon L. Chittick	1981	473
410 2/8	55 2/8	57 4/8	41 7/8	5 7/8	5 6/8	17 7/8	17 7/8	10 2/8	12	15	16	Shotgun Hills, AK	David W. Nelson	David W. Nelson	1995	473
410	50 7/8	51	51	6 6/8	6 6/8	18 3/8	17 7/8	7 7/8	12 3/8	14	18	Rainy Pass, AK	Mrs. J. Watson Webb	Mrs. J. Watson Webb	1934	475
410	53 6/8	54 7/8	43 3/8	6 6/8	5 7/8	20 4/8	14 1/8	13 6/8	13 4/8	26	20	King Salmon, AK	Richard J. Gutherie	Richard J. Gutherie	1979	475
410	47 5/8	51 7/8	40	9 7/8	6 6/8	15 3/8	19 1/8	1/8	10 5/8	16	15	Fog Lakes, AK	Squee Shore	Squee Shore	1958	475
410	54 2/8	59	43 6/8	5 6/8	6 6/8	16 7/8	21	17 2/8	17 2/8	12	13	Nenana River, AK	Tom Grady	Tom Grady	1961	475
410	51 7/8	50 7/8	44 3/8	5 5/8	9 7/8	28 6/8	13 4/8		13 4/8	20	18	Alaska Pen., AK	C.G. Suits	C.G. Suits	1965	475
410	59 5/8	59 7/8	40 2/8	7 6/8	5 6/8	16 1/8	18 6/8	7 1/8	14 3/8	14	17	White River, AK	Dirk E. Brinkman	Dirk E. Brinkman	1974	475
409 7/8	56 7/8	55	42 4/8	6 6/8	5 5/8	19 4/8	19 6/8	7 5/8	11 1/8	17	18	Cinder River, AK	Joe B. Owen	Joe B. Owen	1990	480
409 7/8	50	50	42 4/8	8 2/8	7 6/8	20 6/8	4 5/8	13	13	15	16	Post Lake, AK	Werner Frey	Werner Frey	1963	480
409 7/8	51	47 6/8	42 1/8	8 4/8	7 7/8	11 7/8	17 5/8	1/8	13 5/8	15	18	Mulchatna River, AK	Christine H. Bukowski	Christine H. Bukowski	1992	480
409 7/8	54 5/8	52 7/8	27 5/8	6 3/8	7 1/8	19	10 4/8	14 6/8	1/8	20	16	Mulchatna River, AK	Lana K. Glowcheski	Lana K. Glowcheski	1994	480
409 7/8	45 2/8	46	34	6 4/8	7 7/8	15	22	16 6/8	16 6/8	25	25	Nuyakuk Lake, AK	Roy S. Bowers	Roy S. Bowers	1995	480
409 6/8	45	45 4/8	31 1/8	6 3/8	6 6/8	15 3/8	15 3/8	5 7/8	10 7/8	19	21	Wood River, AK	Stuart L.G. Rees	Stuart L.G. Rees	1983	484
409 6/8	54 7/8	55 5/8	33 2/8	6 7/8	8 2/8	15 3/8	17	10 4/8	10 1/8	19	22	King Salmon, AK	Romaine L. Marshall	Romaine L. Marshall	1993	484
409 6/8	46 2/8	48 7/8	47 1/8	6 1/8	5 7/8	20	19 6/8	16 4/8	13 1/8	23	23	Becharof Lake, AK	David N. Reppen	David N. Reppen	1993	484
409 5/8	46 2/8	47 1/8	47 1/8	6 3/8	6 1/8	22 5/8	16 7/8	13 1/8	4/8	17	14	Tyone Lake, AK	Ralph Marshall	Ralph Marshall	1960	487
409 5/8	48	47 1/8	35 6/8	6 3/8	6 3/8	21	11	15 6/8	9 3/8	19	13	Point Moller, AK	John S. Clark	John S. Clark	1966	487
409 5/8	44 5/8	48 1/8	28 1/8	6	6	13 7/8	17 1/8	4 6/8	13 1/8	25	15	Whitefish Lake, AK	Thomas M. Krueger	Thomas M. Krueger	1987	487
409 4/8	49 1/8	51 5/8	36 5/8	6 6/8	6 1/8	13 7/8	18 4/8	11 1/8	13 1/8	23	25	Alaska Range, AK	James C. Forrest	James C. Forrest	1988	487
409 4/8	54 4/8	51 4/8	36 5/8	6 3/8	6 6/8	17 6/8	17 6/8	14 7/8	9 2/8	23	23	Hicks Lake, AK	Raymond S. George	Raymond S. George	1990	487
409 4/8	54 7/8	53 6/8	33 6/8	6 3/8	6 3/8	14 4/8	14 4/8	10 4/8	10 4/8	14	14	Taylor Mts., AK	Lonnie R. Henriksen	Lonnie R. Henriksen	1995	487
409 4/8	57 3/8	58 2/8	41 1/8	6	6 6/8	18 2/8	14 4/8	10 3/8	2/8	17	14	Paxton Lake, AK	James Lundgren	James Lundgren	1950	493
409 4/8	47 4/8	58 2/8	33 6/8	5 7/8	5 7/8	16 2/8	15 7/8	10 3/8	7 7/8	17	17	Port Heiden, AK	Frank W. Ussery, Jr.	Frank W. Ussery, Jr.	1963	493
409 4/8	57	49 6/8	35 4/8	6 7/8	6 3/8	16 6/8	15 4/8	13 2/8	12 4/8	25	30	Mulchatna River, AK	L. John Sheppard	L. John Sheppard	1991	493
409 4/8	54 7/8	53 2/8	40 3/8	6	6 3/8	20 5/8	18 4/8	19 1/8	12 6/8	21	17	Becharof Lake, AK	Thomas L. Davidson	Thomas L. Davidson	1992	493
409 3/8	44 6/8	43 5/8	38 3/8	7	6 6/8	12 1/8	16 6/8	12	14 2/8	22	26	Whitefish Lake, AK	Charles E. Trojan	Charles E. Trojan	1992	493
409 3/8	54 5/8	54 7/8		6 3/8	6 2/8	24 7/8	12 5/8	18 6/8	1	20	13	King Salmon River, AK	Lit Ng	Lit Ng	1967	498

BARREN GROUND CARIBOU

Rangifer tarandus granti

Score	Length of Main Beam R	L	Inside Spread	Circumference at Smallest Place Between Bez and Brow Points R	L	Length of Brow Points R	L	Width of Brow Points R	L	Number of Points R	L	Locality	Hunter	Owner	Date Killed	Rank
409 3/8	55 5/8	53 5/8	35 2/8	6 4/8	6 2/8	20 3/8	21 4/8	15 3/8	1/8	19	13	Alaska Range, AK	James W. Rehm	James W. Rehm	1978	498
409 2/8	45 6/8	47 2/8	28 7/8	9	8	22	13 2/8	15 5/8	5 2/8	28	20	Chisana, AK	James B. Higgins	James B. Higgins	1967	500
409 2/8	53 2/8	53	40 6/8	5 5/8	6	21 3/8	19 7/8	7	12	15	20	Alaska Pen., AK	Herb Klein	Herb Klein	1967	500
409 2/8	47 2/8	46 6/8	46	6 2/8	6 2/8	16	17 4/8	12 4/8	12 6/8	20	24	Alaska Pen., AK	L.W. Bailey	L.W. Bailey	1969	500
409 2/8	51 3/8	56 7/8	39	6 1/8	6	29 1/8	6 6/8	15 7/8	1	22	13	King Salmon, AK	Jerry Ida	Jerry Ida	1990	500
409 2/8	52	50 5/8	35 5/8	6 5/8	6 5/8	1	18 4/8	1/8	14 2/8	15	21	Chulitna River, AK	Cynthia M. Buzby	Cynthia M. Buzby	1996	505
409 1/8	46 2/8	51 5/8	36 1/8	8	7 1/8	16 1/8	18 1/8	9 5/8	13 3/8	21	21	Alaska Pen., AK	Herb Klein	Herb Klein	1968	505
409 1/8	51	51	47 2/8	6 5/8	7 1/8	18 2/8	19 7/8	15	12 2/8	20	21	King Salmon, AK	Robert E. Deis	Robert E. Deis	1986	505
409 1/8	56 6/8	60	44 4/8	6 4/8	6 2/8	19 4/8	2	15 6/8	1/8	18	15	Nikabuna Lakes, AK	Stephen E. Warner	Stephen E. Warner	1986	505
409 1/8	48 2/8	51 5/8	43 6/8	6	6 1/8	18 5/8	19 1/8	14 7/8	5 4/8	20	17	Iliamna Lake, AK	Picked Up	Richard A. Link	1990	505
409	48 6/8	46 3/8	35 2/8	11	6 6/8	17 7/8	16 7/8	8 4/8	12 4/8	19	21	Chisana Valley, AK	William Burns	William Burns	1963	509
409	55 2/8	54 3/8	41 1/8	6	6	23	9 7/8	18 1/8	1/8	23	11	Port Heiden, AK	D.J. Lehman	D.J. Lehman	1967	509
409	55 1/8	51 1/8	40 2/8	7 5/8	7 7/8	19	13 2/8	9 7/8	9 5/8	15	11	Kuskokwim River, AK	Thomas B. May	Thomas B. May	1987	509
409	52	51 5/8	40 3/8	6	6	11	19 5/8	1/8	15 1/8	12	18	Nushagak Hills, AK	David J. Allen	David J. Allen	1993	509
409	52 4/8	53 6/8	36 5/8	6 1/8	6 1/8	18 3/8	2 5/8	15 6/8	1/8	23	13	Muklung Hills, AK	James J. McBride	James J. McBride	1996	509
408 7/8	55	53 7/8	45	6 6/8	6	15 6/8	16 1/8	6 5/8	9 7/8	19	19	Deadman Lake, AK	R.J. Brocker	R.J. Brocker	1950	514
408 7/8	41 6/8	42 7/8	37 5/8	8 6/8	8 5/8	16 5/8	12 2/8	11	1 1/8	18	16	Talkeetna Mts., AK	H.I.H. Prince Abdorreza Pahlavi	H.I.H. Prince Abdorreza Pahlavi	1960	514
408 6/8	54 4/8	54 7/8	39 6/8	6 4/8	7 1/8	18 1/8	10 7/8	9 7/8	3 3/8	14	13	Ingersol Lake, AK	John A. Du Puis	John A. Du Puis	1973	516
408 6/8	52 1/8	53 7/8	34	8 4/8	7 3/8	17 6/8	17 4/8	12 4/8	4 2/8	18	17	David River, AK	W.K. Leech	W.K. Leech	1979	516
408 6/8	52 2/8	51	39 3/8	10 5/8	9 1/8	4	18 7/8	1	12 6/8	14	17	Red Paint Creek, AK	Larry D. Kropf	Larry D. Kropf	1983	516
408 5/8	46 4/8	46 6/8	40 1/8	7	7 4/8	5 6/8	19 4/8	7/8	19 7/8	20	23	Talkeetna Mts., AK	Bill Lachenmaier	Bill Lachenmaier	1961	519
408 5/8	55 5/8	56 2/8	37 3/8	6 2/8	6 4/8	18 4/8	12 6/8	13 5/8	1 3/8	18	14	Lake Clark, AK	J.G. Blow	J.G. Blow	1968	519
408 5/8	48 1/8	49 1/8	35 5/8	7 3/8	7 4/8	17 3/8	21 4/8	9	11 1/8	17	15	Iliamna Lake, AK	David L. Mastolier	David L. Mastolier	1994	519
408 4/8	52 5/8	51	40 3/8	6 5/8	6 1/8	12 6/8	18 6/8	1	15 1/8	16	25	Susitna River, AK	Richard G. Drew	Richard G. Drew	1961	522
408 4/8	54 3/8	56 3/8	38 5/8	7	6 1/8	17 4/8	19 4/8	8 3/8	10 6/8	18	22	Sandy River, AK	Mrs. Ken McConnell	Mrs. Ken McConnell	1966	522
408 4/8	56	49 2/8	40 3/8	6 1/8	5 6/8	17 5/8	17 7/8	6 7/8	9	13	15	Alaska Pen., AK	Robert E.L. Wright	Robert E.L. Wright	1978	522
408 3/8	52 3/8	53 6/8	44 3/8	5 5/8	5 4/8	3	22 5/8	1/8	16 2/8	15	22	Becharof Lake, AK	Pete M. Baughman, Jr.	Pete M. Baughman, Jr.	1984	525
408 3/8	48 5/8	50 6/8	38 4/8	5 7/8	5 6/8	15 6/8	18 6/8	6 2/8	14 3/8	18	23	Port Heiden, AK	Harold L. Moore, Jr.	Harold L. Moore, Jr.	1985	525
408 2/8	50 6/8	51 6/8	35 4/8	6 3/8	6 1/8	20 7/8	20 1/8	7 5/8	13 7/8	13	13	Rainy Pass, AK	John S. Howell	John S. Howell	1966	527
408 2/8	52 6/8	52 6/8	50	5 6/8	6	13	14 5/8	11 3/8	4	13	13	Alaska Pen., AK	Robert J. Nellett	Robert J. Nellett	1966	527
408 2/8	58 4/8	59 5/8	48 5/8	6 7/8	6 3/8	18	20 3/8	8 6/8	8 2/8	19	18	Dog Salmon River, AK	Arlington F. Svoboda	Arlington F. Svoboda	1983	527
408 2/8	52 1/8	51 1/8	37 7/8	7 1/8	6 2/8	15 2/8	18 6/8	7 4/8	9 1/8	14	18	Bruskasna Creek, AK	Rod Boertje	Rod Boertje	1984	527
408 1/8	52 6/8	54	36 4/8	7	7 1/8	21 4/8	16	15	1/8	17	13	Wood River, AK	Max Lukin	Max Lukin	1964	531
408 1/8	53 6/8	52 4/8	39 6/8	5 4/8	5 6/8	7	19 2/8	1/8	13 4/8	12	19	Smelt Creek, AK	Eddie Clark	Eddie Clark	1986	531
408	46 1/8	48 2/8	32 4/8	6 2/8	6 2/8	15 5/8	16 6/8	10	13 7/8	25	30	Aniak River, AK	Renn G. Neilson	Renn G. Neilson	1991	533

Score	Length of Main Beam R	Length of Main Beam L	Inside Spread	No. Points R	No. Points L	Locality	Hunter	Owner	Date Killed	Rank
408	50 2/8	48 4/8	38	17	18	Becharof Lake, AK	James D. Knight	James D. Knight	1992	533
407 7/8	46 1/8	48	41 3/8	16	19	Caribou Creek, AK	Donald Kettlekamp	Donald Kettlekamp	1957	535
407 7/8	54 3/8	51	36 1/8	15	15	Alaska Pen., AK	Frank R. Fowler	Frank R. Fowler	1976	535
407 7/8	58 5/8	56	37 1/8	16	18	Kuskokwim River, AK	Robert Jacobsen	Robert Jacobsen	1982	535
407 7/8	49 6/8	54	42 2/8	15	22	Whitefish Lake, AK	Robert R. King	Robert R. King	1986	535
407 7/8	50 6/8	47 1/8	38 3/8	17	17	Post Lake, AK	Lyle D. Fett	Lyle D. Fett	1988	535
407 7/8	48 1/8	50 4/8	42 7/8	18	18	Mulchatna River, AK	Harold L. Biggs	Harold L. Biggs	1990	535
407 7/8	48 1/8	44 3/8	38 5/8	16	22	Shotgun Creek, AK	Roger O. Wyant	Roger O. Wyant	1994	535
407 6/8	55 7/8	54 5/8	30 5/8	18	25	Old Man Creek, AK	Gary A. French	Gary A. French	1991	542
407 6/8	57 3/8	55 7/8	39 3/8	18	18	Big Creek, AK	Edwin Epps	Edwin Epps	1993	542
407 5/8	45	49 5/8	46 1/8	13	18	Butte Creek, AK	J.H. Doolittle	J.H. Doolittle	1956	544
407 5/8	50 2/8	49 7/8	44 1/8	15	18	Becharof Lake, AK	Max E. Chittick	Max E. Chittick	1981	544
407 4/8	55	52 4/8	40 3/8	15	15	Reindeer Lake, AK	E.C. & D. Christiansen	E.C. & D. Christiansen	1993	547
407 3/8	58 1/8	56 6/8	45 1/8	13	11	Alaska Pen., AK	Pete Serafin	Pete Serafin	1966	548
407 3/8	57	55 5/8	44 4/8	20	14	Tetlin River, AK	O.F. Goeke	O.F. Goeke	1954	548
407 3/8	50	47 3/8	37 2/8	20	13	Chisana, AK	Lewis S. Kunkel, Jr.	Lewis S. Kunkel, Jr.	1964	548
407 3/8	56 3/8	56 6/8	43 2/8	30	13	Ugashik Lakes, AK	Gary J. Gray	Gary J. Gray	1981	548
407 2/8	56 6/8	49 3/8	40 2/8	19	14	Wolf Lake, AK	R. Douglas Isbell	R. Douglas Isbell	1993	553
407 2/8	49 3/8	51	51	14	15	Mulchatna River, AK	Richard D. Larson	Richard D. Larson	1994	553
407 2/8	49 5/8	49	41 1/8	22	15	Snowshoe Lake, AK	John P. Hale	John P. Hale	1962	553
407 2/8	47	50	35 4/8	22	24	Chandler Lake, AK	Steve Scheidness	Steve Scheidness	1974	553
407 1/8	47 6/8	44 6/8	31 4/8	22	18	Lake Clark, AK	Arthur L. Patterson	Arthur L. Patterson	1978	559
407 1/8	49 1/8	58 7/8	34 1/8	12	12	Kanuti River, AK	Leslie A. Olson	Leslie A. Olson	1981	559
407	62 4/8	52 2/8	45 6/8	25	14	Brooks Range, AK	Carol Kilian	Carol Kilian	1987	561
407	53 2/8	57 3/8	44 1/8	18	14	Mulchatna River, AK	James E. Stenga	James E. Stenga	1997	561
407	55	51 4/8	38 6/8	22	18	Mt. Watana, AK	James A. Jana	James A. Jana	1966	561
406 7/8	53 4/8	55 4/8	38 1/8	23	14	Charley River, AK	John J. Holcomb	John J. Holcomb	1997	564
406 7/8	51 2/8	54 2/8	33	18	16	Farewell Lake, AK	Ken Golden	Ken Golden	1962	564
406 4/8	52	49 2/8	35 4/8	13	16	Dog Salmon River, AK	Jack A. Wilkinson	Jack A. Wilkinson	1989	566
406 4/8	51 5/8	51 5/8	42	13	15	Becharof Lake, AK	Max E. Chittick	Max E. Chittick	1994	566
406 4/8	52 6/8	52 6/8	45	15	14	Cantwell, AK	W.F. Shoemaker	W.F. Shoemaker	1958	566
406 3/8	51 1/8	54	44 3/8	14	19	Hoholitna River, AK	Shawn T. Brown	Shawn T. Brown	1988	569
406 3/8	46 2/8	47 1/8	50 3/8	21	20	Denali Hwy., AK	D.L. Lucas	D.L. Lucas	1957	569
406 3/8	48 7/8	52 6/8	41 3/8	15	18	King Salmon, AK	Joe B. Reynolds	Joe B. Reynolds	1981	569
406 3/8	53 7/8	54	32 7/8	18	17	Stony River, AK	William T. Mailer	William T. Mailer	1993	569
406 2/8	53 6/8	52 7/8	34 1/8	17	17	Matanuska Valley, AK	Thomas J. Wright	Thomas J. Wright	1956	574
406 1/8				16	18	Kuskokwim River, AK	C. & D. Harms	Cheryl Harms	1967	576
406 1/8	65 4/8	59 2/8	41 6/8	17	22	Becharof Lake, AK	Gordon G. Chittick	Gordon G. Chittick	1980	576
406 1/8	49 5/8	50 6/8	57 4/8	23	17	Alaska Pen., AK	Harace R. Morgan	Harace R. Morgan	1980	576
406 1/8	49 7/8	50 2/8	50 6/8	14	13	Stuyahok River, AK	John C. Vickers	John C. Vickers	1991	576
406 1/8	51 7/8	53	50 3/8	13	13	Talkeetna Mts., AK	Herb Klein	Herb Klein	1960	576
406 1/8	48	50	35 6/8	13	16	Lake Louise, AK	Eugene Fetzer	Eugene Fetzer	1961	576
406 1/8	52 2/8	50	44 3/8	20	18	Moller Bay, AK	Harry H. Webb	Harry H. Webb	1953	576
406 1/8	50 2/8	52	45 7/8	16	16	Ugashik Lakes, AK	John A. Moody	John A. Moody	1983	576
406 1/8	56 5/8	56 5/8	51 2/8	15	16	Kvichak River, AK	John J. Jondal	John J. Jondal	1991	576
406 1/8	44 7/8	44	38	22	30	Big River, AK	Steven F. Lesikar	Steven F. Lesikar	1992	576
406 1/8	52 7/8	51 4/8	39 3/8	13	20	Killey River, AK	Roger H. Rosin	Roger H. Rosin	1997	576

BARREN GROUND CARIBOU

Rangifer tarandus granti

Score	Length of Main Beam		Inside Spread	Circumference at Smallest Place Between Brow and Bez Points		Length of Brow Points		Width of Brow Points		Number of Points		Locality	Hunter	Owner	Date Killed	Rank
	R	L		R	L	R	L	R	L	R	L					
406	50	49 7/8	30 5/8	7 7/8	7 5/8	6 4/8	19 5/8	1	15 2/8	14	19	Squaw Creek, AK	Elmo Strickland	Elmo Strickland	1960	581
406	50 4/8	47 3/8	36 1/8	7 4/8	7 2/8	23	11	18 3/8	1	17	12	Lake Louise, AK	C.J. Sullivan	C.J. Sullivan	1960	581
406	51 2/8	51 6/8	47 1/8	6 5/8	6 4/8	14	15 5/8	10 6/8	8	16	16	Fairbanks, AK	H.A. Cox, Jr.	H.A. Cox, Jr.	1968	581
406	58	53 1/8	46 6/8	6 6/8	6 6/8	16 7/8	15 4/8	12	1/8	13	10	Kenai, AK	Ernest A. Stirman	Ernest A. Stirman	1981	581
406	47 3/8	59 2/8	45	7 1/8	6 7/8	5 6/8	20 2/8	1 6/8	15	15	19	Black Lake, AK	William S. Lenz	William S. Lenz	1994	581
406	51 6/8	52	36	5 3/8	5 6/8	18 7/8	17 5/8	2 6/8	10 6/8	14	17	Hook Creek, AK	D. Alan Shreves	D. Alan Shreves	1996	581
405 7/8	57 2/8	58 4/8	57	6	6	19	11 6/8	11 6/8	15	15	16	Becharof Lake, AK	Max E. Chittick	Max E. Chittick	1983	587
405 7/8	47 4/8	43 2/8	39 1/8	7	6 2/8	18 2/8	18	12	3 2/8	15	17	Lake Clark, AK	Anthony Appel	Ronald Appel	1991	587
405 6/8	53 7/8	52	43	6 2/8	7 4/8	18 7/8	19	17 1/8	12	18	16	Taylor Mts., AK	John Burcham	John Burcham	1988	589
405 5/8	47 4/8	51 2/8	45 2/8	6 3/8	6 2/8	6 1/8	17 1/8	11 1/8	2/8	20	16	Paxton, AK	Maurice A. Stafford	Maurice A. Stafford	1956	590
405 5/8	47 7/8	48 7/8	36 4/8	5 6/8	5 6/8	17 3/8	19 6/8	2	16 6/8	17	24	Port Heiden, AK	James V. Pepa	James V. Pepa	1968	590
405 5/8	60 4/8	62 2/8	42 2/8	5 7/8	5 7/8	19 4/8	16 2/8	14 1/8	1 4/8	20	14	Joseph Creek, AK	Madeline M. Kelleyhouse	Madeline M. Kelleyhouse	1984	590
405 4/8	54 7/8	52 5/8	44 2/8	5 6/8	5 7/8	20 4/8	3	13	1	17	14	Denali Hwy., AK	Edna Conegys	Edna Conegys	1958	593
405 4/8	45 2/8	44 6/8	32 3/8	6 7/8	6 5/8	15 6/8	16 7/8	11 2/8	9 5/8	16	16	Little Nelchina, AK	Simon Jensen	Simon Jensen	1960	593
405 4/8	57 6/8	56 7/8	40 2/8	5 4/8	5 5/8	21 7/8	19 5/8	18 1/8	1/8	18	11	Mesa Mt., AK	Robert E. Lieberum	Robert E. Lieberum	1988	593
405 3/8	43	47 6/8	42	5 4/8	5 3/8	20 3/8	1 7/8	15 2/8	1/8	22	16	Becharof Lake, AK	Roy Ruiz	Roy Ruiz	1987	596
405 3/8	56 4/8	56 3/8	45 2/8	5 2/8	5 2/8	21 3/8	18 4/8	6 3/8	10 7/8	13	13	Dog Salmon River, AK	Earl T. Sweig	Earl T. Sweig	1992	596
405 3/8	49 6/8	51	37 2/8	7 4/8	7 3/8	6 2/8	17 7/8	1 1/8	11 4/8	18	20	Stuyahok River, AK	A. Mark Horvat	A. Mark Horvat	1993	596
405 2/8	46 6/8	46 4/8	43 4/8	6 5/8	6 6/8	18	17 4/8	1 1/8	13 5/8	17	22	Ochetna River, AK	Elbert E. Husted	Elbert E. Husted	1962	599
405 2/8	58 2/8	57 6/8	52 1/8	6 2/8	5 7/8	18	17 7/8	9 7/8	1/8	12	9	Alaska Pen., AK	Jose Garcia	Jose Garcia	1971	599
405 2/8	47 2/8	48 6/8	36 6/8	7 4/8	6 7/8	15 5/8	14 2/8	8 3/8	5 2/8	22	15	Mulchatna River, AK	Thomas J. Gallo	Thomas J. Gallo	1983	599
405 2/8	52 2/8	55 1/8	37 2/8	5 6/8	6 1/8	22 5/8	3	17	1/8	23	13	Lake Clark, AK	Jeff LaBour	Jeff LaBour	1991	599
405 1/8	45 6/8	46 7/8	35	9	7 4/8	12 4/8	17	1/8	9 6/8	20	23	Wood River, AK	Herb Klein	Herb Klein	1955	603
405 1/8	49 4/8	50 6/8	35 4/8	6 2/8	6	16 2/8	15	8 6/8	6 1/8	22	17	Denali Hwy., AK	W. Auckland	W. Auckland	1958	603
405 1/8	54 3/8	53 4/8	42	6 4/8	6 4/8	14	15 5/8	7 4/8	10 4/8	14	13	Rainy Pass, AK	W.D. Vogel	W.D. Vogel	1958	603
405 1/8	50 6/8	52 2/8	42 2/8	6 4/8	6 6/8	18	9 1/8	11 7/8	7/8	18	13	Talkeetna Mts., AK	Digvijay Sinh	Digvijay Sinh	1963	603
405 1/8	51 4/8	56 2/8	39 4/8	6 1/8	6 1/8	13 1/8	18 4/8	1/8	10 5/8	10	18	Bear Lake, AK	Ruth S. Kennedy	Ruth S. Kennedy	1983	603
405 1/8	56	53 7/8	37 4/8	5 3/8	5 3/8	16 2/8	19	4 2/8	8 1/8	10	10	Iliamna, AK	Fred W. Amyotte	Fred W. Amyotte	1987	603
405	55	54 3/8	42 2/8	5 3/8	5 1/8	19	19 4/8	11 6/8	6 5/8	17	14	Nushagak Hills, AK	Curtis C. Johnson	Curtis C. Johnson	1992	603
405	55 4/8	60 4/8	33 1/8	6 4/8	6 7/8	9 4/8	19 4/8	1/8	17 4/8	15	27	Susitna Valley, AK	E. Michael Rusten	E. Michael Rusten	1948	610
405	56 4/8	60 2/8	55 2/8	5 3/8	5 3/8	7/8	15 6/8	6/8	9 5/8	16	20	Port Heiden, AK	Lee W. Richie	Lee W. Richie	1963	610
405	45 4/8	43 6/8	31 6/8	7 5/8	8	8	16	1/8	9 1/8	15	20	Wrangell Mts., AK	Roger H. Belke	Roger H. Belke	1974	610
405	52 3/8	53	36 1/8	6 5/8	6 4/8	18	20 3/8	12 6/8	16 2/8	18	16	Stevens Creek, AK	John T. Lunenschloss	John T. Lunenschloss	1987	610
405	51 4/8	52 1/8	42 4/8	5	5 4/8	21 6/8	18 4/8	12 2/8	10 4/8	21	15	Hoholitna River, AK	Eugene R. Lewis	Eugene R. Lewis	1993	610
405	50 5/8	51 4/8	34	5 7/8	5 5/8	18 3/8	19 2/8	14 3/8	11 4/8	20	17	Nishlik Lake, AK	Jim P. Manley	Jim P. Manley	1995	610
405	48	49 4/8	39	5 6/8	5 2/8	19 1/8	18 4/8	12 7/8	9 2/8	20	17	Nushagak River, AK	Kurt D. Voge	Kurt D. Voge	1996	610

Score											Locality	No. of Points	Hunter	Owner	Date Killed	Rank
404 7/8	49 2/8	49 4/8	6 4/8	6 4/8	35	7 5/8	17	1	11 6/8	16	Wrangell Mts., AK	15	J.D. Waring	J.D. Waring	1959	617
404 7/8	52 4/8	49 3/8	8 1/8	7 6/8	41 2/8	17 4/8	17 7/8	14	7 4/8	15	Iliamna Lake, AK	14	M.E. Wackler	M.E. Wackler	1990	617
404 7/8	56 6/8	57 1/8	6 4/8	7 2/8	36 4/8	15 1/8	21 2/8	1/8	19 3/8	10	Harris Creek, AK	19	Brian M. Winter	Brian M. Winter	1994	617
404 6/8	53 1/8	52 6/8	7	6 2/8	49 6/8	19 7/8	19 3/8	13 4/8	9 2/8	12	Alaska Pen., AK	12	W.T. Yoshimoto	W.T. Yoshimoto	1961	620
404 6/8	48 7/8	47 2/8	6 2/8	6 1/8	42 5/8	7 2/8	7 2/8	14 1/8	1	19	King Salmon, AK	14	M.C. Worster	M.C. Worster	1963	620
404 6/8	56 6/8	54 6/8	6 4/8	6 5/8	36 5/8	7 1/8	23 4/8	7 4/8	1 1/8	14	King Salmon, AK	21	Henry A. Elias	Henry A. Elias	1965	620
404 6/8	49 5/8	50	6	6 4/8	43 5/8	19	7 4/8	7 4/8	19	20	Lake Clark, AK	17	Paul Hopkins	Paul Hopkins	1973	620
404 6/8	42 3/8	46 6/8	7 1/8	6 6/8	33 5/8	16 3/8	16 1/8	10 3/8	10 6/8	21	Cathedral Valley, AK	20	Doug Butler	Doug Butler	1980	620
404 6/8	54 1/8	54 2/8	5 3/8	5 3/8	38 4/8	16 1/8	15 7/8	9 5/8	11	22	Becharof Lake, AK	15	Victor Koenig	Victor Koenig	1981	620
404 6/8	46 1/8	47 1/8	8 6/8	6 1/8	39 4/8	23	2 1/8	11 6/8	1	17	Mulchatna River, AK	16	Dan M. Rudanovich	Dan M. Rudanovich	1983	620
404 6/8	53 6/8	51 7/8	6 3/8	6 1/8	46	17 6/8	11 5/8	11 5/8	1/8	17	Taylor Mts., AK	16	Daryl Stanley	Daryl Stanley	1988	620
404 6/8	48	46 3/8	6 2/8	6 5/8	37 5/8	16 2/8	19 4/8	11 5/8	14 3/8	13	Eureka, AK	12	Wayne W. Woods	Wayne W. Woods	1993	620
404 5/8	50 4/8	48 7/8	7 1/8	7 1/8	44 4/8	16 6/8	16 2/8	9 6/8	10 3/8	15	Taylor Hwy., AK	22	Charles C. Parsons	Charles C. Parsons	1950	629
404 5/8	45 4/8	47	6 4/8	6 4/8	32 4/8	16 4/8	17 2/8	15 1/8	20	18	Talkeetna Mts., AK	15	John C. Howard	John C. Howard	1960	629
404 5/8	54 5/8	55	6 2/8	6	33 7/8	16 2/8	17 4/8	11	11 2/8	18	Wood River, AK	24	J.W. Lawson	J.W. Lawson	1965	629
404 5/8	53 3/8	51 4/8	6 3/8	5 7/8	39 5/8	2 2/8	18 3/8	15 2/8	15 2/8	13	Wrangell Mts., AK	17	Robert D. Hancock, Jr.	Robert D. Hancock, Jr.	1983	629
404 4/8	53 4/8	53 4/8	5 5/8	7 3/8	35 1/8	17 6/8	7 7/8	1/8	1/8	19	Alaska Pen., AK	18	William B. Henley, Jr.	William B. Henley, Jr.	1962	633
404 4/8	53	40	5 7/8	6 1/8	40	16 6/8	18 7/8	10 2/8	7 5/8	16	Black River, AK	13	Peter Roemer	Camp Fire Club	1970	633
404 4/8	49 2/8	51 1/8	5 3/8	5 7/8	37 6/8	14 6/8	18 2/8	12 4/8	12 7/8	19	Becharof Lake, AK	14	Alfred E. Wochner	Alfred E. Wochner	1981	633
404 4/8	50 3/8	47	5 2/8	5 6/8	41 7/8	14 6/8	17 4/8	9 2/8	12 1/8	22	Moose Creek, AK	22	Bill Cade	Bill Cade	1984	633
404 4/8	48 2/8	50 7/8	6 4/8	5 2/8	44 1/8	14	16 7/8	7 2/8	11	17	Chilchitna River, AK	22	Dee Sanderson	Chuck J. Sanderson	1988	633
404 4/8	48 7/8	45 6/8	7 3/8	5 7/8	31 7/8	14 2/8	15 4/8	11 6/8	1/8	17	Titnuk Creek, AK	17	Mark S. Woltanski	Mark S. Woltanski	1988	633
404 4/8	54 2/8	51	7 1/8	6 1/8	41 6/8	15 2/8	15 4/8	12 6/8	13 6/8	16	Mulchatna River, AK	16	David O. Tinlin	David O. Tinlin	1992	633
404 4/8	51	48 5/8	6 7/8	6 7/8	32 7/8	12 4/8	18 2/8	1/8	13 6/8	17	Wood River, AK	27	Robert W. Stoeckmann	Robert W. Stoeckmann	1997	633
404 3/8	48 5/8	52 3/8	6 3/8	6 3/8	46 4/8	19	6	13 6/8	5/8	20	Brooks Range, AK	15	C.A. Stenger	C.A. Stenger	1968	641
404 3/8	52 1/8	46 4/8	4 7/8	4 7/8	47 1/8	14 1/8	13 4/8	9 2/8	6 6/8	25	Grant River, AK	18	Dwight C. Davis	Dwight C. Davis	1984	641
404 3/8	49 3/8	51 2/8	5 7/8	5 7/8	34 7/8	16 6/8	18 3/8	5	10 5/8	12	Upper Susitna, AK	14	Clifford R. Caldwell	Clifford R. Caldwell	1995	641
404 2/8	48	48	6	6	34 2/8	15 2/8	19 5/8	3 5/8	12 2/8	17	Talkeetna Mts., AK	24	Elmer M. Rusten	Elmer M. Rusten	1950	644
404 2/8	38 4/8	37	5 3/8	6 3/8	36 4/8	14 2/8	16 2/8	14 3/8	14 2/8	21	Port Heiden, AK	22	Ken Oldhem	Ken Oldhem	1959	644
404 2/8	58 6/8	59 4/8	5 4/8	6 3/8	41	18 7/8	4 6/8	16 2/8	1/8	20	Oshetna River, AK	16	Jon B. Chaney	Jon B. Chaney	1962	644
404 2/8	52 1/8	38 6/8	5 4/8	7 3/8	52 4/8	22 5/8	16 4/8	10	1/8	15	Nabesna, AK	22	Marven A. Henriksen	Marven A. Henriksen	1962	644
404 1/8	55	41	6 3/8	6 1/8	41	18	17 1/8	13 2/8	11 6/8	19	Wood River, AK	22	B.C. Varner	B.C. Varner	1955	648
404 1/8	45 2/8	48	6 4/8	7	41	18 4/8	14 7/8	14 7/8	14 3/8	18	Kvichak River, AK	16	Berry B. Brooks	Berry B. Brooks	1958	648
404 1/8	53 5/8	51 6/8	6 7/8	7 3/8	39 6/8	15 4/8	18 1/8	1/8	15 5/8	19	Nushagak Hills, AK	24	John Jondal	John Jondal	1988	648
404 1/8	54 2/8	52 6/8	6 2/8	7 1/8	37 6/8	15 2/8	18 7/8	2 4/8	15 3/8	19	Salmon Mts., YT	21	David W. Hanna	David W. Hanna	1993	648
404	52	55 2/8	8	8 1/8	36 2/8	19 5/8	17	9 4/8	1	17	Butte Creek, AK	14	Earl Faas	Earl Faas	1960	652
403 7/8	52 1/8	52 4/8	5 5/8	6 7/8	32	16 6/8	16 6/8	1 6/8	11 7/8	17	Port Moller, AK	22	John R. Copenhaver	John R. Copenhaver	1956	653
403 7/8	50 6/8	50 6/8	5 7/8	5 4/8	43 5/8	22 5/8	21 3/8	18	1 6/8	21	Cantwell, AK	15	Melvin Hetland	Melvin Hetland	1962	653
403 7/8	57 6/8	52 6/8	6 7/8	6 7/8	30	21 3/8	21	12	8	13	Halfway Mt., AK	14	Ben Bearse	Ben Bearse	1968	653
403 7/8	44 2/8	44	5 6/8	5 6/8	44	2 4/8	14 4/8	1/8	11 4/8	16	Holitna River, AK	18	Richard S. Hembroff	Richard S. Hembroff	1974	653
403 7/8	47 5/8	41 1/8	7 3/8	6 5/8	37 1/8	13 7/8	13 7/8	7	5 7/8	22	Talkeetna Mts., AK	25	Tony Weiss	Tony Weiss	1979	653
403 6/8	38 6/8	43 6/8	7 1/8	6 5/8	27 1/8	16 6/8	17 2/8	9 7/8	14 2/8	21	Denali Hwy., AK	14	Joe Nevins	Joe Nevins	1958	658
403 6/8	41 2/8	43 6/8	8	6 4/8	29 3/8	19 5/8	15 1/8	14 3/8	1	20	Denali Hwy., AK	19	Robert R. Opland	Robert R. Opland	1959	658
403 6/8	52 6/8	51 5/8	5 5/8	6 6/8	51 5/8	2 4/8	18	1	13 5/8	15	Port Heiden, AK	16	Jim Carpenter	Jim Carpenter	1960	658
403 6/8	48 5/8	47 2/8	5 7/8	6 6/8	47 2/8	18 2/8	2 2/8	13 2/8	6/8	23	Tyone River, AK	19	Gene Gall	Gene Gall	1967	658
403 6/8	47 2/8	47 4/8	6	5 7/8	34	17 5/8	17 5/8	10 2/8	9 2/8	16	Alaska Pen., AK	16	Frederick W. Fernelius	Frederick W. Fernelius	1981	658
403 6/8	51	49 6/8	6 2/8	6 2/8	46 3/8	16 5/8	18 4/8	7 2/8	8 4/8	15	Alaska Pen., AK	19	J. Leslie Rainey	J. Leslie Rainey	1989	658

BARREN GROUND CARIBOU

Rangifer tarandus granti

Score	Length of Main Beam R	L	Inside Spread	Circumference at Smallest Place Between Brow and Bez Points R	L	Length of Brow Points R	L	Width of Brow Points R	L	Number of Points R	L	Locality	Hunter	Owner	Date Killed	Rank
403 5/8	49 7/8	46 6/8	33 4/8	7 6/8	7 7/8	16 7/8	15 2/8	8 2/8	6	19	18	Tyone Lake, AK	Ralph E. Marshall	Ralph E. Marshall	1957	664
403 5/8	49 6/8	48 2/8	52 2/8	6 6/8	6 6/8	19	2 1/8	13	4/8	22	20	Talkeetna Mts., AK	Joe Van Daalwyk	Joe Van Daalwyk	1957	664
403 5/8	51 5/8	50 6/8	34 6/8	6 1/8	6 4/8	15	14	8 6/8	6 7/8	21	21	Lake Louise, AK	Marvin Kocurek	Marvin Kocurek	1961	664
403 5/8	57 6/8	57 2/8	46 3/8	5 6/8	6	20 4/8	19 7/8	11 2/8	14 5/8	15	15	King Salmon, AK	Gary A. Markofer	Gary A. Markofer	1986	664
403 5/8	44 5/8	45 1/8	27 4/8	6 7/8	6 7/8	19 6/8	3 3/8	14 2/8	2 2/8	15	12	Mulchatna River, AK	William H. Basil	William H. Basil	1987	664
403 5/8	47 4/8	50 7/8	37	7 6/8	6 7/8	13 6/8	16 6/8	10 1/8	13 2/8	18	20	New Stuyahok, AK	Lawrence E. Hodel	Lawrence E. Hodel	1996	664
403 4/8	43 5/8	42 7/8	29 6/8	7 4/8	7 4/8	21	20 4/8	15 4/8	5 2/8	18	14	Tazlina, AK	Harry L. Swank, Jr.	Harry L. Swank, Jr.	1959	670
403 4/8	50 1/8	50 5/8	39 7/8	6 2/8	6 3/8	13	21	1/8	17 2/8	14	19	Port Heiden, AK	Mrs. Jon B. Chaney	Mrs. Jon B. Chaney	1962	670
403 4/8	53 5/8	55 3/8	49 6/8	5 7/8	6	15 5/8	17 1/8	11 6/8	11 4/8	14	17	Alaska Pen., AK	Gerald Roland Gold	Gerald Roland Gold	1977	670
403 4/8	60 4/8	60 5/8	59 5/8	5 4/8	5 6/8	27 6/8	21 5/8	15 1/8	1/8	14	9	Becharof Lake, AK	Max E. Chittick	Max E. Chittick	1979	670
403 4/8	49 1/8	45 7/8	32 1/8	6 7/8	7	19 1/8	18 2/8	4 7/8	12 1/8	15	21	Kotsetna River, AK	Kevin J. Bores	Kevin J. Bores	1987	670
403 3/8	51	53 1/8	41	5 2/8	5 7/8	16 7/8	17 6/8	10 6/8	10 2/8	15	19	Nishlik Lake, AK	Adam J. Cummings	Adam J. Cummings	1994	675
403 3/8	49 4/8	49	35 4/8	6 7/8	6 1/8	18 3/8	18	13 6/8	8 2/8	19	20	Iliamna Lake, AK	Denton S. Haynes	Denton S. Haynes	1994	675
403 2/8	56 6/8	50	42 2/8	6 2/8	6	16 1/8	18 5/8	8	12 4/8	19	21	Deadman Lake, AK	Charles R. Green	Charles R. Green	1959	677
403 2/8	49 1/8	48 4/8	38 5/8	6 3/8	6 2/8	16 4/8	19 7/8	5 3/8	14 7/8	17	19	Eureka, AK	James S. Evans	James S. Evans	1960	677
403 2/8	59	59 3/8	42 4/8	5 1/8	5 1/8	20 7/8	22 2/8	13 6/8	8 3/8	16	14	Nushagak River, AK	Karen L. Morris	Karen L. Morris	1991	677
403 2/8	48 2/8	47	48 5/8	7 4/8	8	16 7/8	17 6/8	9 6/8	4 5/8	19	18	Stuyahok River, AK	John M. Arkley	John M. Arkley	1994	677
403 1/8	51	45 7/8	42 2/8	6 7/8	6 4/8	18 1/8	17 1/8	11 6/8	6	15	12	King Salmon, AK	James L. Corriea	James L. Corriea	1996	677
403 1/8	49 1/8	49 2/8	37 7/8	5 4/8	5 3/8	20 4/8	8 7/8	16	1/8	27	14	Pear Lake, AK	William M. Sowers	William M. Sowers	1981	682
403 1/8	54 5/8	51 5/8	45 6/8	6	6	22 4/8	16 3/8	14 6/8	1 7/8	14	14	Becharof Lake, AK	Linda J. McBride	Linda J. McBride	1988	682
403	53 2/8	50 2/8	43 6/8	6 1/8	6 1/8	16 3/8	14 5/8	1 7/8	8 1/8	13	16	Deadman Lake, AK	E.C. Lentz	E.C. Lentz	1955	684
403	56 2/8	54 7/8	39 1/8	7	7	18 6/8	4 2/8	14	1/8	20	10	Wood River, AK	Norman L. Akau, Jr.	Norman L. Akau, Jr.	1980	684
403	48 4/8	47 4/8	47 5/8	6 2/8	5 5/8	15 3/8	15 2/8	10 3/8	13 5/8	21	23	Brooks Range, AK	Jerry Imperial	Jerry Imperial	1985	684
403	62 5/8	63 3/8	37 6/8	6 7/8	6 1/8	19 5/8	16 2/8	3 6/8	10 1/8	12	16	Hoholitna River, AK	Patrick Meitin	Patrick Meitin	1993	684
402 7/8	48	46 4/8	28 6/8	6 7/8	8	19 6/8	11 7/8	1/8	8	17	25	Ogilvie Range, YT	E.J. Miller	E.J. Miller	1956	688
402 7/8	54 5/8	56 6/8	41 3/8	5 2/8	5 6/8	19 4/8	19 1/8	14 2/8	11 7/8	18	17	Nelchina, AK	Chris Klineburger	Chris Klineburger	1957	688
402 7/8	53 1/8	51 4/8	37	6 3/8	6 6/8	19 6/8	13 4/8	16 4/8	1/8	19	13	Sheep Creek, AK	David J. Palonis	David J. Palonis	1987	688
402 7/8	49 7/8	51 2/8	41 7/8	5 1/8	5 4/8	16 6/8	17 5/8	6 2/8	15 7/8	21	26	Becharof Lake, AK	Daniel P. Schilkey	Daniel P. Schilkey	1991	688
402 7/8	44	45 1/8	43 4/8	5 6/8	5 4/8	6 3/8	19 4/8	1/8	14 1/8	22	20	Grant Lake, AK	Daniel P. Harrington	Daniel P. Harrington	1996	688
402 6/8	49	54	33	7 1/8	7	14 6/8	15 6/8	8 4/8	9	15	18	Rainy Pass, AK	William Sleith	William Sleith	1961	693
402 6/8	52	50 4/8	43 4/8	5	4 7/8	15 2/8	16	8 4/8	7 2/8	22	18	Ugashik Lakes, AK	Vincent T. Ciaburri	Vincent T. Ciaburri	1977	693
402 6/8	53 6/8	51 6/8	51	5 7/8	5 5/8	2 3/8	19 1/8	1/8	15 3/8	14	19	King Salmon, AK	Daniel R. Nilles	Daniel R. Nilles	1985	693
402 6/8	59 4/8	58 3/8	54 6/8	5 7/8	5 6/8	21 2/8	14 6/8	15 2/8	1 4/8	17	13	Egegik, AK	Michael D. Odegard	Michael D. Odegard	1985	693
402 5/8	46 2/8	47 1/8	34 4/8	5 4/8	5 4/8	16 3/8	15 4/8	1 5/8	13 5/8	19	26	Old Crow, YT	J.M. Mouchet	Otto W. Geist	1958	697
402 5/8	48 4/8	52	42 1/8	5	5 1/8	17 4/8	16 3/8	1/8	14 2/8	12	15	Alaska Pen., AK	Robert C. Kaufman	Robert C. Kaufman	1978	697
402 5/8	53	54 2/8	41 3/8	6 2/8	6 4/8	17 3/8	5 6/8	1/8	4 6/8	19	21	Pilot Point, AK	Joseph P. Sebo, Jr.	Joseph P. Sebo, Jr.	1987	697

Score												Locality	By whom killed	Owner	Date Killed	Rank
402 5/8	51 5/8	50 1/8	34 6/8	5 2/8	6 2/8	18 5/8	19 2/8	12 1/8	14 5/8	14	18	Lake Clark, AK	Gene Thoney	Gene Thoney	1987	697
402 4/8	46 3/8	47 2/8	39 4/8	7 4/8	7 4/8	15 3/8	16 2/8	6 3/8	7 4/8	14	15	Clarence Lake, AK	John C. Heck	John C. Heck	1951	701
402 4/8	58	54 4/8	34 6/8	6 5/8	6 2/8	16 1/8	19 3/8	6 1/8	10 5/8	13	16	Rainy Pass, AK	Mahlon T. White	Mahlon T. White	1954	701
402 4/8	49 2/8	49 3/8	30 2/8	6	7 3/8	16 2/8	15 5/8	13 4/8	1/8	23	17	Talkeetna Mts., AK	Arvid F. Benson	Arvid F. Benson	1956	701
402 4/8	56 4/8	56	43 4/8	6 5/8	6 2/8	19 3/8	19 7/8	10 6/8	7	11	10	Talkeetna Mts., AK	W.L. Miers	W.L. Miers	1959	701
402 4/8	53 4/8	53 3/8	36 2/8	7	6 2/8	22 2/8	21 6/8	18 1/8	2 1/8	14	11	Glen Hwy., AK	Walter Pfisterer	Walter Pfisterer	1959	701
402 4/8	45	48	34 7/8	11 6/8	8 3/8	18 3/8	17	18 1/8	12 4/8	20	21	Talkeetna Mts., AK	A. Sweat	A. Sweat	1959	701
402 4/8	52 4/8	51 2/8	41 2/8	7	7 2/8	8 4/8	16 6/8	1 3/8	13 1/8	13	24	Nelchina, AK	Joseph Caputo	Joseph Caputo	1964	701
402 4/8	59 4/8	59 6/8	37 5/8	6 1/8	5 6/8	19 2/8	23 1/8	1 7/8	17 1/8	13	12	Port Heiden, AK	Walter Schubert	Walter Schubert	1965	701
402 4/8	47 6/8	49 6/8	44 4/8	6 4/8	6 1/8	17 5/8	17 5/8	10 4/8	13	15	14	Moose Lake, AK	Walter R. Willey	Walter R. Willey	1991	711
402 4/8	53 5/8	52 5/8	47	7 1/8	7 7/8	15 3/8	18 1/8	4 4/8	4 4/8	14	14	Mulchatna River, AK	James S. FonFerek	James S. FonFerek	1996	711
402 3/8	43 6/8	44 7/8	33 7/8	8 2/8	7 6/8	15 7/8	14 7/8	7	13 2/8	18	20	Tyone Lake, AK	Leon J. Brochu	Leon J. Brochu	1959	711
402 3/8	51 2/8	55 7/8	44	6 3/8	6 2/8	15 7/8	17 2/8	3 6/8	14 4/8	15	20	Denali Hwy., AK	Jerry Shepard	Jerry Shepard	1961	711
402 3/8	53 4/8	53 4/8	44 4/8	6 4/8	5 7/8	17 2/8	18	9 5/8	2 4/8	16	14	White Fish Lake, AK	Carol A. Rollings	Carol A. Rollings	1981	711
402 2/8	52 6/8	52 7/8	35 2/8	6 6/8	5 7/8	17 2/8	20 7/8	16 6/8	2 4/8	12	25	Swan Lake, AK	Frank Gregersen	Frank Gregersen	1994	715
402 2/8	54 4/8	53 1/8	49 1/8	6 1/8	6 3/8	19 6/8	18	16 6/8	1/8	20	18	Ugashik Lakes, AK	John Elmore	John Elmore	1964	715
402 2/8	46	46	39	5 6/8	5 6/8	17	16	2 7/8	12 2/8	17	16	Alaska Pen., AK	William K. Leech	William K. Leech	1977	715
402 2/8	57 4/8	54 6/8	38 2/8	7 1/8	2 3/8	2 3/8	19 4/8	1 2/8	16 6/8	16	23	Cathedral Bluff, AK	John T. Holzschuh	John T. Holzschuh	1983	715
402 1/8	50 5/8	47 3/8	38 2/8	6 2/8	6 2/8	18 2/8	20	1 2/8	13	15	20	Twin Lakes, AK	John H. Harvey, Jr.	John H. Harvey, Jr.	1987	719
402 1/8	55 5/8	56 2/8	54	6 3/8	7	21 1/8	4 1/8	17 5/8	1/8	19	11	Rainy Pass, AK	Cecil Glessner	Cecil Glessner	1966	719
402 1/8	52 1/8	54	32 4/8	7	7	1 1/8	17 7/8	4/8	14 3/8	16	24	Susitna River, AK	George V. Lenher	George V. Lenher	1967	719
402	48	49 2/8	43 6/8	6 2/8	6 2/8	23 4/8	16 5/8	13 1/8	6 2/8	19	16	Dago Creek, AK	Fredrick W. Thornton	Fredrick W. Thornton	1969	723
402	53 4/8	54 6/8	49 7/8	5 7/8	5 5/8	15 5/8	23 3/8	11 6/8	13 2/8	16	21	Mulchatna River, AK	John M. Gillette	John M. Gillette	1987	723
402	48 4/8	55 4/8	43 1/8	6 6/8	7 3/8	19 6/8	23 2/8	12 5/8	11 6/8	14	17	Talkeetna Mts., AK	Phillip Miller	Phillip Miller	1972	723
402	51 6/8	52 2/8	43 4/8	5 1/8	4 7/8	9 3/8	5	1/8	9 3/8	14	25	Ivishak River, AK	Clyde A. McLeod	Clyde A. McLeod	1983	723
402	51 4/8	57 3/8	45 6/8	5 2/8	5 2/8	15 4/8	18 3/8	15 4/8	5	17	22	Tundra Lake, AK	Vernon D. Holleman	Vernon D. Holleman	1986	723
402	49	49 6/8	32 5/8	6	6 2/8	10 7/8	19	12 3/8	17 7/8	20	17	Groundhog Mt., AK	Clyde A. James	Clyde A. James	1986	723
401 7/8	53 6/8	52 5/8	51 2/8	6 2/8	5 4/8	12 7/8	21	9 4/8	21 5/8	11	11	Alaska Pen., AK	James B. Haynes III	J.B. Haynes & Q.T. Hardtner	1988	729
401 7/8	48 4/8	49 4/8	44 2/8	5 4/8	5 7/8	7 1/8	19 3/8	16	7 1/8	19	16	Tyone Lake, AK	Roger O. Wyant	Roger O. Wyant	1990	729
401 7/8	55 6/8	55 5/8	35 5/8	7 3/8	9 3/8	15 4/8	18 3/8	5 2/8	21 2/8	16	15	Nabesna, AK	Eileen Marshall	Eileen Marshall	1961	729
401 7/8	59 3/8	56 2/8	35 1/8	6 6/8	7 3/8	19	18 1/8	16 5/8	17 6/8	18	24	Alaska Range, AK	Bill Copeland	Bill Copeland	1969	729
401 7/8	54 4/8	54 2/8	44 6/8	5 1/8	4 7/8	17 2/8	20 1/8	14	4 4/8	15	13	Stony River, AK	Glenn E. Allen	Glenn E. Allen	1979	729
401 7/8	53 7/8	50 4/8	36 4/8	5 5/8	5 1/8	18 1/8	4 2/8	11 7/8	1/8	22	18	Whitefish Lake, AK	Richard Berry	Richard Berry	1986	729
401 6/8	51 4/8	51 2/8	37 4/8	5 5/8	5 5/8	18 4/8	18	13 4/8	3 5/8	14	13	Tazlina, AK	Wesley W. Siegrist	Michael S. Siegrist	1986	734
401 6/8	41 4/8	40 4/8	40 5/8	6 6/8	6 2/8	13 7/8	13 7/8	7 5/8	9 4/8	29	27	Talkeetna Mts., AK	Lloyd Ronning	Lloyd Ronning	1958	734
401 6/8	45 2/8	49 7/8	39 4/8	6 6/8	6 6/8	15 6/8	15 6/8	5 6/8	7 6/8	18	14	Totatlanika River, AK	David Maroney	David Maroney	1961	734
401 6/8	50 4/8	50 2/8	37 6/8	6 5/8	6 3/8	17 7/8	17	10 2/8	11 1/8	15	10	Mt. Sanford, AK	Heinrich K. Springer	Heinrich K. Springer	1969	734
401 6/8	47 7/8	48 7/8	44 1/8	6 1/8	6 5/8	19	17 7/8	12 6/8	1/8	14	18	Deadman Lake, AK	Harold R. Clark	Harold R. Clark	1981	734
401 6/8	50 1/8	50 7/8	32 3/8	6 1/8	6 5/8	15 6/8	6 2/8	5 6/8	11 6/8	14	21	West Lake, AK	Richard W. Dean	Richard W. Dean	1986	734
401 5/8	53 7/8	52 2/8	41 5/8	6 6/8	6 5/8	14 5/8	18 7/8	7 1/8	11 4/8	14	14	Lake Louise, AK	Stephen J. McGrath	Stephen J. McGrath	1990	740
401 5/8	45 2/8	54 2/8	44 6/8	6 2/8	6 6/8	19 1/8	18 5/8	9 1/8	15 2/8	14	21	Rainy Pass, AK	Dale A. Hillmer	Dale A. Hillmer	1961	740
401 5/8	50 2/8	51 4/8	36 5/8	7	7 3/8	16 4/8	20 4/8	15 2/8	8 1/8	19	24	Mulchatna River, AK	Reed Sandvig	Reed Sandvig	1964	740
401 4/8	45 4/8	46 7/8	30 2/8	6 7/8	7	13 6/8	17	1/8	11 2/8	17	20	Talkeetna River, AK	Don N. Brown	Don N. Brown	1994	740
401 4/8	50	54 2/8	35 2/8	7 1/8	7 4/8	17 6/8	18 6/8	7	8	13	18	Wrangell Mts., AK	J. Donald Neill	J. Donald Neill	1961	743
401 4/8	52	53	32 5/8	7 1/8	5 3/8	14 3/8	14 1/8	9 1/8	1/8	20	18	Stuyahok River, AK	Gerald F. McNamara	Gerald F. McNamara	1968	743
401 4/8	61 4/8	63 5/8	48 4/8	7 2/8	7 1/8	17 4/8	17 4/8	10 7/8	7 4/8	17	14	Little Delta River, AK	Fred A. Wright	Fred A. Wright	1982	743
401 4/8	61 2/8	59 6/8	39 2/8	7 4/8	7	17 7/8	18 1/8	2 4/8	9 6/8	13	13	Little Delta River, AK	Danny R. Hart	Danny R. Hart	1983	743

BARREN GROUND CARIBOU
Rangifer tarandus granti

Score	Length of Main Beam R	L	Inside Spread	Circumference at Smallest Place Between Brow and Bez Points R	L	Length of Brow Points R	L	Width of Brow Points R	L	Number of Points R	L	Locality	Hunter	Owner	Date Killed	Rank
401 4/8	49 3/8	49	38 4/8	5 6/8	5 4/8	19 5/8	20 7/8	16 4/8	6 6/8	23	17	Becharof Lake, AK	Bill D. Reed	Bill D. Reed	1983	743
401 4/8	51 2/8	52 5/8	26 3/8	7 2/8	8	19 6/8	19	11 3/8	15 7/8	18	13	Little Nelchina River, AK	Francis M. Thistle	Francis M. Thistle	1957	748
401 3/8	51 2/8	51 2/8	35 6/8	6 2/8	6 1/8	16 4/8	15 6/8	9 5/8	9 6/8	18	21	Denali Hwy., AK	Norman Smith	Norman Smith	1959	748
401 3/8	57 5/8	56 4/8	42 7/8	6 3/8	6	9 4/8	16 5/8	1/8	13	14	18	Wrangell Mts., AK	Ronald Bergstrom	Ronald Bergstrom	1965	748
401 3/8	51 3/8	51 4/8	51 1/8	6 2/8	6 1/8	5 7/8	18 4/8	1/8	10 2/8	13	18	Black Creek, AK	Lonnie L. Ritchey	Lonnie L. Ritchey	1995	748
401 2/8	48 6/8	43 5/8	34 6/8	6 2/8	8	16 5/8	13 6/8	13 1/8	9 2/8	18	17	Alaska Range, AK	Robert B. Boone	Robert B. Boone	1959	752
401 2/8	50 5/8	54 2/8	42 4/8	6 5/8	6 4/8	17 2/8	13 6/8	11 6/8		16	14	Wood River, AK	William P. Ghiorso	William P. Ghiorso	1983	752
401 2/8	57 5/8	59 6/8	49 6/8	6 3/8	6 7/8	20 4/8	23 6/8	3 6/8	17	10	13	Mulchatna River, AK	Heidi J. Albrecht	Heidi J. Albrecht	1988	752
401 2/8	46	45 2/8	40 7/8	6 3/8	6 5/8	10 7/8	17 1/8	1	12 7/8	14	19	Iliamna Lake, AK	Jerome B. McElhannon	Jerome B. McElhannon	1992	752
401 2/8	49 1/8	51 4/8	31 4/8	7 2/8	6 5/8	20 6/8	13 4/8	13	4 2/8	18	19	Carin Mt., AK	Douglas D. Mosier	Douglas D. Mosier	1995	752
401 1/8	52	52 6/8	45 4/8	7 1/8	7 2/8	15 6/8	18	8 4/8	13 5/8	15	16	Nicholson Lake, AK	John P. Scribner	John P. Scribner	1956	757
401 1/8	53 4/8	54 4/8	40 5/8	6 1/8	6 6/8	6 2/8	19 5/8	1/8	17 6/8	11	21	Rainy Pass, AK	John Weirdsma	John Weirdsma	1961	757
401 1/8	61 5/8	57 2/8	47 3/8	5 6/8	6 2/8	22 4/8	18 7/8	9 2/8	1/8	13	10	Little Nelchina River, AK	Elton Aarestad	Elton Aarestad	1964	757
401 1/8	54 4/8	51	44	6 4/8	7 4/8	17	19 6/8	7 4/8	14 5/8	17	17	Nondalton, AK	Anton L. Cerro	Anton L. Cerro	1973	757
401 1/8	51 1/8	51 1/8	43 7/8	7 1/8	7	15 1/8		11 1/8		22	12	Big River, AK	Roger L. Gregg	Roger L. Gregg	1977	757
401 1/8	60 6/8	53 6/8	43 5/8	6 2/8	7	19 3/8	19 4/8	16 5/8	6 5/8	20	14	King Salmon, AK	Edward W. Ratcliff	Edward W. Ratcliff	1984	757
401 1/8	47 2/8	45 5/8	30 2/8	7 1/8	5 4/8	17 2/8	17 1/8	6 7/8	8 2/8	15	16	Mt. Harper, AK	John J. Auman	John J. Auman	1992	757
401	61 4/8	58	46	7	7 1/8	20	14 4/8	8	8	16	19	Talkeetna Mts., AK	Louis Mussatto	Louis Mussatto	1964	764
401	55 2/8	56 2/8	37	8 6/8	7 3/8	18 3/8	19 4/8	11 7/8	4	18	14	Red Devil, AK	Joseph L. LaNou	Joseph L. LaNou	1984	764
401	53 5/8	56 5/8	46 7/8	5	5 2/8	20	17 5/8	10 2/8	1/8	17	16	Iliamna Lake, AK	Joe C. Simmons	Joe C. Simmons	1986	764
401	49 2/8	49 2/8	41 6/8	7 4/8	8 2/8	12 3/8	9 6/8	4 4/8	1/8	18	16	Iliamna Lake, AK	Thomas R. Reed III	Thomas R. Reed III	1988	764
400 6/8	51 1/8	50 7/8	38	6 5/8	7 4/8	11 7/8	13 7/8	6 2/8	9 6/8	14	19	Chisana, AK	Harry L. Thompson	Harry L. Thompson	1966	768
400 5/8	57 6/8	57 7/8	38 1/8	7 5/8	7 2/8	8 2/8	21 4/8	1	18	12	22	Alaska Pen., AK	E.J. Hansen	E.J. Hansen	1964	769
400 5/8	54 5/8	51	47 4/8	5 4/8	5 5/8	25 4/8	20 7/8	18 2/8	8 2/8	13	12	Port Heiden, AK	Picked Up	H. Bruce Freeman	1984	769
400 5/8	57 2/8	55 4/8	44 3/8	6 4/8	7	4	16 4/8	14 7/8	14 7/8	15	21	Iliamna Lake, AK	K. James Malady III	K. James Malady III	1987	769
400 5/8	58	59	43 3/8	5 3/8	5	19 3/8	16 5/8	11 1/8	11 7/8	11	20	Cinder River, AK	Brian Peterson	Brian Peterson	1988	769
400 5/8	51 7/8	51 1/8	42 3/8	6	6 1/8	16 6/8	17 4/8	9	5 6/8	13	16	Whitefish Lake, AK	John E. Alexander	John E. Alexander	1990	769
400 4/8	48 1/8	49 4/8	29 1/8	7	6 6/8	22 3/8	21 2/8	16 4/8	4 6/8	16	14	Fortymile River, AK	Arnold O. Burton	Arnold O. Burton	1985	774
400 4/8	54 1/8	54	42	6 2/8	6 2/8	16 3/8	7 7/8	13 1/8	1/8	20	15	Mulchatna River, AK	Darryl G. Sanford	Darryl G. Sanford	1996	774
400 3/8	57 3/8	58 3/8	40	7 6/8	7 4/8	17 3/8	4	12	4/8	20	13	Wood River, AK	Berry B. Brooks	Berry B. Brooks	1958	776
400 3/8	42 1/8	41 2/8	33 5/8	5 6/8	5 7/8	18 1/8	18 1/8	1/8	13 6/8	15	19	Talkeetna, AK	S.H. Sampson	S.H. Sampson	1959	776
400 3/8	52	35	45 4/8	7 5/8	7 4/8	8 4/8	23 5/8	16	1	13	15	Ingersoll Lake, AK	Peter H. Merlin	Peter H. Merlin	1970	776
400 3/8	49 2/8	49	42	5 7/8	5 6/8	17 2/8	19 6/8	9 7/8	9 2/8	19	14	Cinder River, AK	Mervin Bergstrom	Mervin Bergstrom	1975	776
400 3/8	49 5/8	47 6/8	39 4/8	6 2/8	6	19	2 1/8	15 3/8	1/8	19	26	Alaska Pen., AK	James Swartout	James Swartout	1978	776
400 3/8	59 6/8	58 3/8	43	6 1/8	6	19 4/8	2 1/8	14 1/8	1/8	16	10	Hook Lake, AK	James L. Horneck	James L. Horneck	1983	776
400 3/8	52 6/8	56 7/8	46	6 1/8	5 7/8	18 2/8	10 5/8	4 2/8	15 4/8	15	21	Painter Creek, AK	Stephen R. Hurt	Stephen R. Hurt	1987	776

Score												Locality	Owner	Hunter	Date	Rank
400 3/8	57 7/8	54 7/8	50 3/8	5 7/8	6 2/8	7 3/8	19 4/8	1/8	13 4/8	10	13	Iliamna Lake, AK	Steven R. Crawford	Steven R. Crawford	1991	776
400 3/8	52 1/8	51	42 3/8	6 5/8	6 4/8	17 6/8	9 3/8	13	1/8	21	18	Nushagak River, AK	Stephen G. Jolley	Stephen G. Jolley	1991	776
400 3/8	58 1/8	57 2/8	46 6/8	5 1/8	5 6/8	3 3/8	18 7/8	1 4/8	13 5/8	13	21	Otter Lake, AK	George W. Swierkos	George W. Swierkos	1991	776
400 3/8	61 1/8	55 6/8	43 1/8	5 5/8	5 5/8	19	16 7/8	11 4/8	2 5/8	19	16	Kvichak River, AK	Larry Crnkovich	Larry Crnkovich	1993	776
400 2/8	60	60 4/8	50	7 2/8	9 4/8		24 4/8	17	17	14	22	King Salmon, AK	Richard O. Burns III	Richard O. Burns III	1982	787
400 1/8	51 3/8	50 3/8	42	6 7/8	6 3/8	5 3/8	14 1/8	6/8	10 1/8	15	19	Denali Hwy., AK	Wilbur T. Gamble	Wilbur T. Gamble	1963	788
400 1/8	59 3/8	59 5/8	43	5 6/8	5 5/8	18	15 5/8	10 2/8	1	17	16	Monahan Flats, AK	C.H. Dana, Jr.	C.H. Dana, Jr.	1965	788
400 1/8	48 6/8	48 4/8	31 1/8	5 7/8	5 7/8	16	16 6/8	6 4/8	7	13	18	Alaska Pen., AK	Lillie E. Kriss	Lillie E. Kriss	1972	788
400 1/8	56 4/8	55	41 5/8	6 5/8	7	20 4/8	2	12 1/8	1/8	17	14	Iliamna Lake, AK	David L. Pfiester	David L. Pfiester	1992	788
400 1/8	49 3/8	47 6/8	38 1/8	6 3/8	5 4/8	18 4/8	15 5/8	9 3/8	13 2/8	17	17	Naknek River, AK	Ronald L. Petersen, Jr.	Ronald L. Petersen, Jr.	1996	788
400	47 6/8	50 4/8	30 5/8	8 1/8	5 6/8	3	17	1/8	10 6/8	13	19	Anchorage, AK	C.C. Irving	C.C. Irving	1959	793
400	57 4/8	56 7/8	37 4/8	7 4/8	6	18 7/8	19	12 3/8	11 6/8	14	16	Alaska Pen., AK	Bert Klineburger	Bert Klineburger	1961	793
400	45	46 5/8	44 1/8	5	5	16 4/8		12 1/8	7/8	24	16	Nelchina, AK	Webb Hilgar	Webb Hilgar	1962	793
400	53 1/8	53 1/8	37	5 5/8	5 5/8	20 2/8	21 2/8	1	14 4/8	9	19	Lake Louise, AK	George Moerlein	George Moerlein	1962	793
400	54 3/8	56 1/8	35 1/8	7 1/8	7 1/8	19 6/8	16 6/8	17 2/8	1/8	17	8	King Salmon, AK	G.O. Wiegner	G.O. Wiegner	1970	793
400	48	50	39 6/8	6 4/8	6	15 3/8	17 1/8	12	1 4/8	19	15	Caribou Lake, AK	Donald J. Giottonini, Jr.	Donald J. Giottonini, Jr.	1983	793
400	54 3/8	53 1/8	31 1/8	6 3/8	6	6	17		9	18	20	White Fish Lake, AK	Thomas K. Willard	Thomas K. Willard	1984	793
400	49 5/8	48 1/8	39 6/8	6 1/8	6 1/8	21 1/8	19 1/8	14 1/8	2 1/8	19	19	Lake Aleknagik, AK	Monty D. McCormick	Monty D. McCormick	1987	793
400	45 4/8	48 7/8	36 5/8	7	7 5/8	9 1/8	18 4/8	1/8	15 5/8	18	25	Mulchatna River, AK	Francis W. Rosendale	Francis W. Rosendale	1991	793
444*	51 2/8	51 1/8	49 6/8	8 3/8	9 5/8	19 7/8	17 1/8	16 4/8	6 6/8	18	17	Sparrevon, AK	Thomas R. Kean	Thomas R. Kean	1997	793
435 5/8*	50 1/8	50 2/8	41	6 7/8	6 7/8	17 1/8	17 7/8	12 3/8	13	21	19	Alaska Pen., AK	Kip R. Carroll	Kip R. Carroll	1997	793

* Final score is subject to revision by additional verifying measurements.

CATEGORY
BARREN GROUND
CARIBOU

SCORE
446-3/8

HUNTER
MARC C. PHILLIPS

LOCATION
STUYAHOK RIVER, AK

DATE OF KILL
SEPTEMBER 1993

CATEGORY
BARREN GROUND
CARIBOU

SCORE
405-2/8

HUNTER
JEFF LABOUR

LOCATION
LAKE CLARK, AK

DATE OF KILL
SEPTEMBER 1991

CATEGORY
BARREN GROUND
CARIBOU

SCORE
414-5/8

HUNTER
ROBERT G. GOOD

LOCATION
DOG SALMON RIVER, AK

DATE OF KILL
SEPTEMBER 1994

Hunting Central Canada barren ground caribou in the Northwest Territories during the late summer of 1994, Donald J. Hotter III was faced with the ultimate decision. "Is this the bull I want?" Taking heed from an experienced friend, Wes Vining, president of The Trophy Connection in Cody, Wyoming, Hotter's decision was narrowed to two potential trophies the hunters spotted near Humpy Lake on September 11.

"We saw lots of antlers through our binoculars. Two bulls were worth a closer look. We examined them for 20 to 30 minutes. 'The third bull from the left has fantastic bottoms, good tops and outstanding main beam length,' Wes said. I agreed.

"We asked Leon Wellin, our guide, how to get to the bulls. He suggested we go back to the boat, circle a ridge and climb above the caribou to relocate and intercept them. Everything worked perfectly and our guide knew the ground like the back of his hand. After about 30 minutes, we were in place and found the caribou feeding at a fast walk up a valley, so we hurried ahead to intercept. Everything went as planned, and the bulls were feeding straight up the anticipated route.

"'Not that bull. I know the bull I was looking at had better palms,' I heard Wes whisper. 'Not that one. He's too narrow.'

"On it went with Wes' whisperings until the fifth bull stepped out and Wes said, 'That's the bull. Look at those palms and bez!'

"I concentrated on this one bull as it slowly walked behind a ridge and out of sight. I rushed farther up the ridge and hoped to see the bull again. The other bulls saw my movement and became alert. I heard Wes say the bull was only 100 yards in front of me, but I still couldn't see it.

"I sneaked forward and saw the bull. I looked over my shoulder to ask Wes if this was the bull and could see by the excitement in his eyes that it was. I asked if I should shoot and he responded that if I didn't, he would shoot for me. My shot was an easy 100 yards downhill, standing, one-shot kill.

"I had killed the new World's Record Central Canada barren ground caribou by 10 a.m. on the first morning of the hunt. We all knew we had an exceptional bull but we were hesitant to dream of the final score. We taped the antlers and thought we made a mistake. Back at camp, we measured and remeasured the antlers, each time getting a slightly different score. 'This is some kind of trophy,' Wes kept saying."

After packing out the prized caribou from Humpy Lake, the trophy was taken back to Cody where resident and official Boone and Crockett Club measurer, Bob Hanson, measured the caribou rack with a score of 428-1/8 points. The score smashed the old World's Record by more than 16 points! Later in May of 1995, when the Judges' Panel officially measured the rack in Dallas, the final score would ascend even further to 433-4/8 points. ∎

BOUNDARIES FOR CENTRAL CANADA BARREN GROUND CARIBOU

Central Canada barren ground caribou occur on Baffin Island and the mainland of N.W.T., with geographic boundaries of the Mackenzie River to the west; the north edge of the continent to the north (excluding any island except Baffin Island); Hudson's Bay to the east; and the southern boundary of N.W.T. to the south. In 1994, the boundary was expanded to include the northwest corner of Manitoba north of the south limit of township 87 and west of the Little Churchill River, Churchill River, and Hudson Bay.

TROPHY INFO

RANK
New World's Record

SCORE
433 4/8

LOCATION
Humpy Lake, NT

HUNTER
Donald J. Hotter III

OWNER
Bass Pro Shops
F & W Museum

DATE KILLED
1994

CENTRAL CANADA BARREN GROUND CARIBOU
WORLD'S RECORD SCORECHART

Records of
North American
Big Game

250 Station Drive
Missoula, MT 59801
(406) 542-1888

BOONE AND CROCKETT CLUB®
OFFICIAL SCORING SYSTEM FOR NORTH AMERICAN BIG GAME TROPHIES

	MINIMUM SCORES	
	AWARDS	ALL-TIME
mountain	360	390
woodland	265	295
barren ground	375	400
Central Canada barren ground	345	360
Quebec-Labrador	365	375

KIND OF CARIBOU (check one)
- ☐ mountain
- ☐ woodland
- ☐ barren ground
- ☒ Central Canada barren ground
- ☐ Quebec-Labrador

CARIBOU

Detail of Point Measurement

SEE OTHER SIDE FOR INSTRUCTIONS	COLUMN 1	COLUMN 2	COLUMN 3	COLUMN 4
	Spread Credit	Right Antler	Left Antler	Difference
A. Tip to Tip Spread	32 6/8			
B. Greatest Spread	41 5/8			
C. Inside Spread of Main Beams	40 3/8	SPREAD CREDIT MAY EQUAL BUT NOT EXCEED LONGER ANTLER	40 3/8	
D. Number of Points on Each Antler Excluding Brows		24	18	6
Number of Points on Each Brow		5	8	
E. Length of Main Beam		48 7/8	49 4/8	5/8
F-1. Length of Brow Palm or First Point		18 3/8	18 2/8	
F-2. Length of Bez or Second Point		20 7/8	23	2 1/8
F-3. Length of Rear Point, If Present		2 2/8	2 2/8	0
F-4. Length of Second Longest Top Point		17 5/8	19 3/8	1 6/8
F-5. Length of Longest Top Point		25 2/8	23 4/8	1 6/8
G-1. Width of Brow Palm		10 1/8	14 1/8	
G-2. Width of Top Palm		5 1/8	6 7/8	1 6/8
H-1. Circumference at Smallest Place Between Brow and Bez Point		4 6/8	4 4/8	2/8
H-2. Circumference at Smallest Place Between Bez and Rear Point		4 4/8	4 4/8	0
H-3. Circumference at Smallest Place Between Rear Point and First Top Point		4 4/8	4 4/8	0
H-4. Circumference at Smallest Place Between Two Longest Top Palm Points		9 7/8	13 3/8	3 4/8
TOTALS	40 3/8	201 1/8	209 6/8	17 6/8

ADD	Column 1	40 3/8	Exact Locality Where Killed: Humpy Lake, NT
	Column 2	201 1/8	Date Killed: Sept. 11, 1994 — Hunter: Donald J. Hotter
	Column 3	209 6/8	Owner: Bass Pro Shops F. & W. Museum — Telephone #:
	Subtotal	451 2/8	Owner's Address:
SUBTRACT Column 4		17 6/8	Guide's Name and Address:
FINAL SCORE		484 4/8	Remarks: (Mention Any Abnormalities or Unique Qualities)

All measurements must be made with a 1/4-inch wide flexible steel tape to the nearest one-eighth of an inch. (Note: A flexible steel cable can be used to measure points and main beams only.) Enter fractional figures in eighths, without reduction. Official measurements cannot be taken until the antlers have air dried for at least 60 days after the animal was killed.

A. Tip to Tip Spread is measured between tips of main beams.

B. Greatest Spread is measured between perpendiculars at a right angle to the center line of the skull at widest part, whether across main beams or points.

C. Inside Spread of Main Beams is measured at a right angle to the center line of the skull at widest point between main beams. Enter this measurement again as the Spread Credit **if** it is less than or equal to the length of the longer antler; if greater, enter longer antler length for Spread Credit.

D. Number of Points on Each Antler: To be counted a point, a projection must be at least one-half inch long, with length exceeding width at one-half inch or more of length. Beam tip is counted as a point but not measured as a point. There are no "abnormal" points in caribou.

E. Length of Main Beam is measured from the center of the lowest outside edge of burr over the outer side to the most distant point of the main beam. The point of beginning is that point on the burr where the center line along the outer side of the beam intersects the burr, then following generally the line of the illustration.

F-1-2-3. Length of Points are measured from nearest edge of beam over outer curve to tip. Lay the tape along the outer curve of the beam so that the top edge of the tape coincides with the top edge of the beam on both sides of point to determine the baseline for point measurement. Record point lengths in appropriate blanks.

F-4-5. Length of Points are measured from the tip of the point to the top of the beam, then at a right angle to the bottom edge of beam. The Second Longest Top Point **cannot** be a point branch of the Longest Top Point.

G-1. Width of Brow is measured in a straight line from top edge to lower edge, as illustrated, with measurement line at a right angle to main axis of brow.

G-2. Width of Top Palm is measured from midpoint of lower edge of main beam to midpoint of a dip between points, at widest part of palm. The line of measurement begins and ends at midpoints of palm edges, which gives credit for palm thickness.

H-1-2-3-4. Circumferences are taken as illustrated for measurements. If brow point is missing, take H-1 at smallest point between burr and bez point. If rear point is missing, take H-2 and H-3 measurements at smallest place between bez and first top point. Do not depress the tape into any dips of the palm or main beam.

CENTRAL CANADA BARREN GROUND CARIBOU

MINIMUM SCORE 345

Rangifer tarandus groenlandicus

Score	Length of Main Beam R	L	Inside Spread	Circumference at Smallest Place Between Brow and Bez Points R	L	Length of Brow Points R	L	Width of Brow Points R	L	Number of Points R	L	Locality	Hunter	Owner	Date Killed	Rank
433 4/8	48 7/8	49 4/8	40 3/8	4 6/8	4 4/8	18 3/8	18 2/8	10 1/8	14 1/8	29	26	Humpy Lake, NT	Donald J. Hotter III	Bass Pro Shops F. & W. Mus.	1994	1
426 1/8	55 5/8	58 2/8	38 1/8	6	7 1/8	18 3/8	15 3/8	14 1/8	5 7/8	19	15	Humpy Lake, NT	Al Kuntz	Al Kuntz	1994	2
424 7/8	57 1/8	54	49 5/8	6 2/8	6 5/8	20 5/8	14 4/8	14 7/8	1 4/8	18	16	Manitoba	Unknown	Luxton Museum	PR 1954	3
412 6/8	50 2/8	49 3/8	36 2/8	4 5/8	4 6/8	18 6/8	20	6 3/8	15 7/8	17	19	MacKay Lake, NT	James H. Wooten	James H. Wooten	1989	4
408 4/8	52 2/8	51 1/8	38 7/8	4 6/8	4 6/8	21 2/8	18 2/8	8 6/8	15 5/8	17	23	Rendez-vous Lake, NT	Tom W. Barry	Tom W. Barry	1982	5
408 3/8	47 1/8	46 2/8	31 5/8	4 7/8	5 1/8	18 1/8	14 6/8	12 3/8	9	15	14	Rendez-vous Lake, NT	Jon Vanderhoef	Jon Vanderhoef	1987	6
408 3/8	49 4/8	49 2/8	44 2/8	5 1/8	5 1/8	13 6/8	14 6/8	8 1/8	12 4/8	17	17	MacKay Lake, NT	Ronald VanGilder	Ronald VanGilder	1996	6
408 2/8	46 4/8	47	39 1/8	4 2/8	4 4/8	16 3/8	16	10 7/8	18 3/8	20	25	Courageous Lake, NT	Raymond H. Bonar	Raymond H. Bonar	1985	8
407 6/8	52 7/8	53 1/8	35 1/8	5 2/8	5 2/8	16 1/8	16 1/8	6 1/8	13 4/8	12	17	Repulse Bay, NT	Kendall J. Bauer	Kendall J. Bauer	1996	9
407 2/8	54 1/8	54 4/8	36 4/8	5 5/8	5 4/8	19 7/8	17 7/8	15	15 4/8	21	16	Kugaryuak River, NT	James G. Empey	James G. Empey	1990	10
401 1/8	53	52 5/8	40	5 6/8	5 6/8	17	17 1/8	12	11	14	15	Courageous Lake, NT	Richard B. Limbach	Richard B. Limbach	1989	11
401	54 3/8	57 1/8	35 5/8	4 7/8	4 6/8	19 6/8	20	13	6 5/8	14	14	Courageous Lake, NT	John H. Smith	John H. Smith	1992	12
400 6/8	51 2/8	50	27 2/8	4 6/8	5 5/8	12 6/8	20 5/8	14 2/8	14 2/8	19	26	Rendez-vous Lake, NT	Dale L. Zeigler	Loaned to B&C Natl. Coll.	1986	13
400 6/8	56 5/8	56 7/8	37 3/8	5	5 3/8	16 6/8	16 5/8	14 3/8	14 1/8	28	19	Humpy Lake, NT	William G. Farley	William G. Farley	1996	13
398 4/8	46 3/8	44 1/8	31 3/8	5	5 4/8	17 6/8	18 3/8	13 7/8	7 7/8	23	23	Rendez-vous Lake, NT	Robert M. Hazlewood	Robert M. Hazlewood	1986	15
398 3/8	47 7/8	45 3/8	31 7/8	5 4/8	5 4/8	17 1/8	18 4/8	3 2/8	13 6/8	26	25	Rendez-vous Lake, NT	Jim Moellman	Jim Moellman	1991	16
398 1/8	52 3/8	52 1/8	34 3/8	5	5	16 5/8	16 5/8	12 4/8	12 6/8	20	19	Lac de Gras, NT	Glen P. Rupe	Glen P. Rupe	1987	17
395 3/8	49 3/8	49 5/8	31 4/8	4 5/8	4 7/8	15 7/8	16 2/8	11 1/8	7 5/8	20	18	Courageous Lake, NT	George O. Poston	George O. Poston	1985	18
394 7/8	50 1/8	53 1/8	42 6/8	5	5	17	17 2/8	2 5/8	14	18	26	MacKay Lake, NT	Alfred E. Journey	Alfred E. Journey	1988	19
394 3/8	49 3/8	49 6/8	28 1/8	5 2/8	5 6/8	14 4/8	18 5/8	13 3/8	19 4/8	23	22	Rendez-vous Lake, NT	John P. Poston	John P. Poston	1986	20
394 3/8	54 3/8	52 2/8	35	5 3/8	4 6/8	19 5/8	16 6/8	8 4/8	18 4/8	20	21	Courageous Lake, NT	James R. Adams, Jr.	James R. Adams, Jr.	1997	20
393 4/8	47 3/8	48 3/8	24 6/8	5 3/8	5 4/8	19	21 3/8	4 2/8	18 7/8	19	25	Courageous Lake, NT	Robert G. Koffman	Robert G. Koffman	1987	22
391 7/8	54 2/8	52 6/8	41 4/8	6 1/8	5 5/8	16 6/8	17 7/8	2	15	14	17	Lake Providence, NT	Bert Varkonyi	Joey Varkonyi	1986	23
391 1/8	54 4/8	52 4/8	38 6/8	5 7/8	6 6/8	16 5/8	18 1/8	14 1/8	13 6/8	18	18	MacKay Lake, NT	Jack L. Odor	Jack L. Odor	1995	23
391 1/8	47 1/8	50 5/8	25	5 4/8	5 5/8	20 6/8	15 1/8	11 2/8	13 6/8	23	18	MacKay Lake, NT	Grady E. Maggard, Jr.	Grady E. Maggard, Jr.	1988	25
390 4/8	43 5/8	44 2/8	28	4 7/8	4 7/8	16	16 7/8	5 1/8	11 2/8	27	24	Courageous Lake, NT	Joseph Pinkas	Joseph Pinkas	1987	26
390 3/8	55 4/8	54 1/8	43 5/8	5	4 7/8	18 3/8	17	5 5/8	15 5/8	20	8	Courageous Lake, NT	Patrick H. Ackerman	Patrick H. Ackerman	1988	27
390 2/8	63	61 3/8	37	6	6 1/8	17 1/8	16 4/8	13 5/8	9 3/8	19	18	Little Marten Lake, NT	Daniel Butzler	Daniel Butzler	1989	28
389 6/8	51 3/8	52 7/8	40 2/8	6 2/8	5 6/8	16 4/8	16 3/8	5	12 6/8	19	18	Point Lake, NT	George E. Kimmel	George E. Kimmel	1997	29
389 4/8	48 4/8	50 2/8	27 3/8	5 3/8	5	19 4/8	19	12 3/8	14 7/8	24	18	Point Lake, NT	William D. Backman, Jr.	William D. Backman, Jr.	1989	30
389 2/8	43 7/8	53 3/8	39 4/8	4 7/8	5	14	12 4/8	8 5/8	5 1/8	15	16	Desteffany Lake, NT	Gordon W. Russell	Mike Howden	1989	31
389 1/8	51 4/8	53	35 2/8	5 2/8	5 3/8	18 5/8	16	8 1/8	10 6/8	21	20	Little Marten Lake, NT	Stewart N. Shaft	Stewart N. Shaft	1995	32
388 6/8	51 7/8	49 7/8	30	6 1/8	5 6/8	16 6/8	16	14 1/8	10 7/8	25	21	Lynn Lake, MB	Carl E. Houghton	Carl E. Houghton	1996	33
388 4/8	52 1/8	54	40 4/8	5 3/8	5 5/8	13	15 1/8	6 5/8	11 6/8	14	19	Point Lake, NT	Robert S. Everson	Robert S. Everson	1996	34
387 6/8	50 5/8	50 5/8	31 6/8	6 1/8	6 5/8	16 2/8	21 4/8	1/8	19	11	17	Rendez-vous Lake, NT	Michael Andres	Michael Andres	1994	35
387 5/8	47 3/8	49 5/8	38 6/8	6 2/8	6 5/8	18 3/8	17	8 6/8	15 4/8	18	21	Courageous Lake, NT	Brian L. Dam	Brian L. Dam	1995	36

Score	Main Beam R	Main Beam L	Inside Spread	Circ. R	Circ. L	Width of Brow R	Width of Brow L	Points R	Points L	Locality	Hunter	Owner	Date Killed	Rank
387 1/8	47 4/8	49	38 5/8	5 7/8	5 2/8	15 2/8	13 4/8	13	20	Courageous Lake, NT	James J. McBride	James J. McBride	1987	37
387 1/8	49 1/8	47	30 7/8	7 1/8	5 2/8	15 6/8	13 4/8	23	23	Point Lake, NT	Blair C. Rumble	Blair C. Rumble	1996	37
386 7/8	47 6/8	47 2/8	40 1/8	5 3/8	5 4/8	16 1/8	11 6/8	17	20	Little Marten Lake, NT	Michael C. Jesch	Michael C. Jesch	1995	39
386 4/8	54 6/8	51 1/8	26 6/8	5	5 5/8	12	7 4/8	18	14	Rendez-vous Lake, NT	Victor E. Moss	Victor E. Moss	1993	40
386 3/8	52 4/8	52 1/8	28 2/8	5 7/8	6 1/8	16 5/8	12 2/8	24	25	Rendez-vous Lake, NT	Picked Up	Jerome T. Loendorf	1988	41
386 3/8	43 1/8	42 6/8	38	6 1/8	5 4/8	14 7/8	9 4/8	18	20	Tsoko Lake, NT	Roger A. Hansen	Roger A. Hansen	1989	41
386	48	38	33 5/8	5 4/8	5 4/8	15 6/8	4 1/8	16	18	Parry Pen., NT	Bernard Sippin	Bernard Sippin	1988	43
385 5/8	54 7/8	48 1/8	40 2/8	5 4/8	4 5/8	17 3/8	13	17	14	Little Marten Lake, NT	C. Page Senn	C. Page Senn	1991	44
385 4/8	49 4/8	51 4/8	31 4/8	4 5/8	4 3/8	20 5/8	11 2/8	17	17	Humpy Lake, NT	James S. Nelson IV	James S. Nelson IV	1997	45
385 1/8	57 5/8	57 4/8	41	4 4/8	5 2/8	3 3/8	1/8	18	11	Lake Providence, NT	Paul Wisness	Paul Wisness	1987	46
384 3/8	49	50 1/8	39	4 3/8	6 2/8	14 6/8	13 4/8	21	21	Lake Providence, NT	John Branneky	John Branneky	1991	47
384 3/8	46	47 5/8	29 6/8	5 1/8	5 2/8	18 3/8	9 1/8	16	16	Rendez-vous Lake, NT	John S. Walkenhauer	J.S. & J. Walkenhauer	1994	47
383 7/8	50 4/8	50 2/8	31 4/8	7 2/8	4 6/8	17 4/8	15	16	28	Rendez-vous Lake, NT	Michael L. Chaffin	Michael L. Chaffin	1988	49
383 6/8	50 2/8	50 3/8	40 7/8	5 3/8	6	2 4/8	12 6/8	14	17	Little Marten Lake, NT	Shawn R. Andres	Shawn R. Andres	1991	50
383 1/8	55	54	36 2/8	4 6/8	5 5/8	13 5/8	1/8	17	12	Desteffany Lake, NT	Roger J. Larson	Roger J. Larson	1989	51
382 7/8	53 4/8	55 4/8	30 2/8	5	5 1/8	19 4/8	10 4/8	15	15	Rendez-vous Lake, NT	Steve MacKenzie	Steve MacKenzie	1989	52
382 6/8	47 4/8	47 3/8	32 4/8	5 1/8	5 6/8	13 2/8	14 1/8	17	18	Courageous Lake, NT	James C. Johnson	James C. Johnson	1990	53
382 3/8	49 7/8	44 6/8	31 3/8	5 6/8	6 4/8	16 3/8	12 4/8	20	26	Courageous Lake, NT	Patrick T. Stanosheck	Patrick T. Stanosheck	1989	54
382 2/8	56	56 1/8	37 1/8	6	8 2/8	14 1/8	9 2/8	17	15	Courageous Lake, NT	Earle H. Harder	Earle H. Harder	1985	55
382 2/8	47 4/8	50 1/8	30 7/8	6 2/8	5 1/8	17 4/8	11 2/8	19	20	Paulatuk, NT	William H. Taylor	William H. Taylor	1986	55
382 1/8	51 5/8	50 5/8	32 2/8	8 2/8	5	19	14 7/8	19	16	Courageous Lake, NT	Kevin J. McCormick	Kevin J. McCormick	1983	57
381 3/8	51 4/8	52 7/8	33 3/8	5	5 2/8	17 5/8	16 1/8	17	22	Lake Providence, NT	Vicki L. St. Germaine	Vicki L. St. Germaine	1989	58
381 2/8	54 3/8	54 4/8	34 3/8	6	6	19	11 3/8	14	16	Point Lake, NT	Jim Anderson	Jim Anderson	1989	59
381	52	54 1/8	35 4/8	6 2/8	6 2/8	16 4/8	15 7/8	15	17	Little Marten Lake, NT	Scott D. Fink	Scott D. Fink	1988	60
381	43 6/8	47 6/8	33 5/8	4 4/8	5 4/8	16	14 7/8	19	25	Little Marten Lake, NT	Anne Marie Freed	Anne Marie Freed	1995	60
380 6/8	48 2/8	49 1/8	34 5/8	4 7/8	4 3/8	15 4/8	16 2/8	17	20	Courageous Lake, NT	Brian G. Edgerton	Brian G. Edgerton	1990	62
380 4/8	52 1/8	52 5/8	36 1/8	4 4/8	4 5/8	16	12	17	18	Lac de Gras, NT	James R. Crawford	James R. Crawford	1987	63
380 2/8	49 1/8	50 3/8	40	6	6	13 7/8	3 1/8	19	15	MacKay Lake, NT	Richard B. Martin	Richard B. Martin	1990	64
379 2/8	54 2/8	54 6/8	37 6/8	5 7/8	5 1/8	18 6/8	7 3/8	18	15	Courageous Lake, NT	Wesley V. Hazen	Wesley V. Hazen	1992	65
379 1/8	51 3/8	50	36 3/8	5 1/8	5 1/8	16 7/8	13 2/8	16	16	Courageous Lake, NT	Gordon B. Knipe	Gordon B. Knipe	1989	66
379 1/8	53 1/8	49 6/8	35	6 1/8	6	17 2/8	7 3/8	16	13	Courageous Lake, NT	Lester I. Pearmine	Lester I. Pearmine	1989	66
378 7/8	54 6/8	53 6/8	33 6/8	5 2/8	6 1/8	14	13 1/8	23	17	Courageous Lake, NT	Ronald R. Ragan	Ronald R. Ragan	1996	68
378 2/8	50 4/8	52 4/8	38 2/8	4 6/8	5 2/8	18 5/8	9 1/8	12	17	Courageous Lake, NT	James A. Erickson	James A. Erickson	1989	69
377 7/8	56 2/8	56 3/8	35 6/8	5 1/8	5 1/8	18 5/8	13 5/8	18	19	Courageous Lake, NT	John C. Clumpner	John C. Clumpner	1994	70
377 5/8	47 2/8	48 6/8	31 2/8	6 1/8	5 5/8	16 6/8	16 7/8	17	24	Winter Lake, NT	Warren D. St. Germaine	Warren D. St. Germaine	1985	71
377 5/8	49	49	41	4 7/8	6 1/8	1 1/8	11 7/8	16	12	Humpy Lake, NT	Terry L. Miller	Terry L. Miller	1995	71
377 2/8	54 7/8	54 5/8	38 7/8	5 3/8	5 3/8	15 7/8	1/8	16	15	Reid Lake, NT	Daryl Ouillette	Daryl Ouillette	1992	73
376 5/8	55 4/8	54	38 2/8	5 3/8	5 5/8	13 4/8	8 2/8	14	19	Snare Lake, NT	Gary L. Temple	Gary L. Temple	1987	74
376 4/8	48 5/8	46 6/8	37 7/8	6	6	17	10 5/8	15	21	MacKay Lake, NT	David Emken	David Emken	1990	75
376 3/8	49 7/8	49 1/8	29 4/8	6 2/8	6 2/8	14	11	16	9	Courageous Lake, NT	Dennis C. Ault	Dennis C. Ault	1991	76
376 1/8	54 3/8	52 4/8	32 4/8	4 3/8	4 5/8	17 1/8	1/8	11	22	Warburton Bay, NT	John L. Campbell	John L. Campbell	1995	77
375 6/8	55 2/8	53 6/8	35	4 6/8	4 3/8	14	7 7/8	20	16	Jolly Lake, NT	William L. Pederson	William L. Pederson	1996	78
375 4/8	52	53 1/8	43 4/8	5 2/8	4 7/8	17 1/8	13	14	13	Little Marten Lake, NT	Richard J. Wristen	Richard J. Wristen	1995	79
375	56 3/8	53 7/8	34 3/8	4 4/8	4 4/8	14	1/8	17	21	Courageous Lake, NT	Hal L. Shockey	Hal L. Shockey	1994	80
374 7/8	57 7/8	55 3/8	41 2/8	5 7/8	5 7/8	2 7/8	19 1/8	17	19	Little Marten Lake, NT	Scott D. Fink	Scott D. Fink	1988	81
374 6/8	45 2/8	47 2/8	31 5/8	4 6/8	4 6/8	16 2/8	12 6/8	19	14	Courageous Lake, NT	Anna Marie Pavlik	Anna Marie Pavlik	1995	82
374 5/8	54	53 1/8	37 7/8	5 4/8	5 4/8	21 7/8	15 5/8	14	19	Jolly Lake, NT	Bill LaSalle	Bill LaSalle	1996	83

Rangifer tarandus groenlandicus

Score	Length of Main Beam R	Length of Main Beam L	Inside Spread	Circ. at Smallest Place Between Brow and Bez Points R	Circ. L	Length of Brow Points R	Length of Brow Points L	Width of Brow Points R	Width of Brow Points L	Number of Points R	Number of Points L	Locality	Hunter	Owner	Date Killed	Rank
374	54	52 5/8	36 7/8	5	5 2/8	21 1/8	19 4/8	8	13 6/8	17	15	Jolly Lake, NT	Kim Aliprandini	Kim Aliprandini	1995	84
373 7/8	49 5/8	49 4/8	39 1/8	5 7/8	5 2/8	15 1/8	13 4/8	11	4 6/8	15	16	Little Marten Lake, NT	William Vaznis	William Vaznis	1989	85
373 5/8	52 5/8	53 4/8	43 2/8	6	6 3/8	18 4/8	17 6/8	11	11 5/8	15	13	Courageous Lake, NT	Wayne H. Kingsley	Wayne H. Kingsley	1989	86
373 1/8	52 1/8	53 6/8	38 7/8	5 2/8	5	15 5/8	15 4/8	9 4/8	11 7/8	14	14	Point Lake, NT	Gary A. Bingham	Gary A. Bingham	1989	87
373	53 2/8	55 2/8	23 3/8	4 4/8	4 5/8	20 2/8	16 6/8	15 5/8	11 4/8	14	16	Lake Providence, NT	Dean G. Fletcher	Dean G. Fletcher	1987	88
372 7/8	56 3/8	56 4/8	47 5/8	5 3/8	5 6/8	17 5/8	2 2/8	13 6/8	1/8	21	13	Little Marten Lake, NT	Ronald V. Hurlburt	Ronald V. Hurlburt	1989	89
372 5/8	48 2/8	48 2/8	32 2/8	5 3/8	5	16 5/8	16 5/8	12	8	14	13	Courageous Lake, NT	Charles L. Cleis	Charles L. Cleis	1990	90
372 4/8	49 3/8	48 3/8	33 6/8	5 3/8	6	6 5/8	15 2/8	1/8	10	18	24	Lac de Gras, NT	Raymond C. Hunt	Raymond C. Hunt	1987	91
372 2/8	48 2/8	47 3/8	36 1/8	5 1/8	5 3/8	14 4/8	15 7/8	9 4/8	11 6/8	16	19	MacKay Lake, NT	Ronald L. Chapman	Ronald L. Chapman	1990	92
371 7/8	45 1/8	44 5/8	28 1/8	5 4/8	6	15 2/8	12 4/8	12 2/8	2 6/8	15	15	Courageous Lake, NT	Robert C. Kaufman	Robert C. Kaufman	1984	93
371 7/8	49	48 3/8	32 6/8	4 7/8	5 1/8	5 2/8	17 6/8	1/8	14 2/8	22	16	Little Marten Lake, NT	David J. Richey, Sr.	David J. Richey, Sr.	1990	93
371 3/8	53 7/8	52 5/8	28 5/8	6 3/8	10 4/8	16 5/8	14 3/8	14	4 6/8	20	19	Lake Providence, NT	John C. Pitts	John C. Pitts	1993	95
371 2/8	53 3/8	53 4/8	42 2/8	4 4/8	4 5/8	14 5/8	1 7/8	10 4/8	1/8	15	14	Courageous Lake, NT	James M. Arnold	James M. Arnold	1992	96
371 1/8	56 3/8	58	37 1/8	5 5/8	5 7/8	19 7/8	17	12 6/8	5	17	13	Courageous Lake, NT	Jon R. Stephens	Jon R. Stephens	1984	97
371 1/8	50 3/8	48 4/8	44	5 6/8	5 1/8	14 7/8	17	9 4/8	10	16	17	MacKay Lake, NT	Dan Brockman	Dan Brockman	1990	97
371	47 4/8	43 5/8	36 5/8	4 6/8	6 4/8	14 3/8	16 2/8	13 2/8	10 7/8	19	15	MacKay Lake, NT	Phillip Henry	Phillip Henry	1988	99
371	54 4/8	54 1/8	37 4/8	5 3/8	5 5/8	19 1/8	17 1/8	16 2/8	15 2/8	17	13	Jolly Lake, NT	Ronald E. Kohler	Ronald E. Kohler	1995	99
370 5/8	55 5/8	57 3/8	32 7/8	5 7/8	6 6/8	17	17 1/8	5	1/8	16	17	Muskox Lake, NT	Neill A. Murphy	Neil A. Murphy	1978	101
370 3/8	46	45 4/8	31 6/8	5 1/8	5 4/8	14 6/8	14 5/8	9 3/8	11 3/8	21	19	MacKay Lake, NT	A. Oscar Carlson	A. Oscar Carlson	1996	102
370 2/8	41 1/8	41 6/8	22 6/8	7	6 4/8	14 2/8	14 2/8	10 7/8	7 6/8	26	19	Rendez-vous Lake, NT	Victor E. Moss	Victor E. Moss	1989	103
369 7/8	52 1/8	50	28 4/8	5 2/8	4 6/8	19 1/8	5/8	15 2/8	1/8	16	19	Rendez-vous Lake, NT	Philip L. Wright	Hedwig Vogel-Wright	1986	104
369 7/8	49 1/8	49 6/8	24 4/8	6 2/8	5	14 6/8	5/8	9 3/8	1/8	20	19	Caribou Lake, MB	Warren Johnson	Warren Johnson	1992	104
369 3/8	48 6/8	45 1/8	38 6/8	4 5/8	5 4/8	14 2/8	4 6/8	6 6/8	11 3/8	16	22	Lynn Lake, MB	Lloyd J. Fink	Lloyd J. Fink	1996	106
369 1/8	50 3/8	51 4/8	43	5	5 6/8	14 2/8	14 2/8	4 5/8	7 6/8	15	14	Seahorse Lake, NT	Barry D. Taylor	Barry D. Taylor	1985	107
369	52 6/8	53	33 2/8	5 4/8	6 6/8	17	16 5/8	6 5/8	13 5/8	12	16	Destteffany Lake, NT	William J. Burwash	William J. Burwash	1991	108
368 7/8	56	56 4/8	43 7/8	5 6/8	6 6/8	15 2/8	1 2/8	13 6/8	4 6/8	16	17	Courageous Lake, NT	Kent T. Michaelson	Kent T. Michaelson	1988	109
368 7/8	58 4/8	56 1/8	36 4/8	5 2/8	5 2/8	17 3/8	14	14	14	17	21	Courageous Lake, NT	Richard Fitch	Richard Fitch	1989	109
368 5/8	55 7/8	56	41 6/8	5 4/8	5 4/8	14 7/8	18	12 3/8	11 1/8	15	17	Point Lake, NT	Douglas G. Kirchhoff	Douglas G. Kirchhoff	1987	111
368 5/8	46	48 2/8	36 5/8	5 3/8	5 3/8	15 2/8	11	3 2/8	9 4/8	17	19	Point Lake, NT	Robert S. Everson	Robert S. Everson	1996	111
368 4/8	47 5/8	48 6/8	25	5 1/8	5 1/8	15 3/8	10 1/8	15 3/8	2 2/8	21	16	Rocher Lake, NT	Henry C. Gilbertson	Henry C. Gilbertson	1997	113
368 3/8	48	49 4/8	29 4/8	5	5 6/8	16 1/8	17 6/8	1/8	11 4/8	12	11	Courageous Lake, NT	Kent T. Michaelson	Kent T. Michaelson	1988	114
368 2/8	54	55 4/8	39 4/8	4 5/8	5 2/8	14 3/8	15 3/8	11	10 6/8	15	12	Rendez-vous Lake, NT	David P. Jacobson	David P. Jacobson	1988	115
368 2/8	51 7/8	51 7/8	31 7/8	6 7/8	4 6/8	15	15	13	8	19	15	MacKay Lake, NT	Patrick M. Condie	Patrick M. Condie	1995	115
367 5/8	48 3/8	52	33 2/8	5	6 7/8	18 6/8	15 7/8	13 5/8	11 5/8	21	25	Little Marten Lake, NT	Allen R. Prince	Allen R. Prince	1996	117
367 2/8	51	49 4/8	35 7/8	5 2/8	5 6/8	16 2/8	15 2/8	12 2/8	4 3/8	19	17	MacKay Lake, NT	James L. White	James L. White	1989	118
366 4/8	52 1/8	53 6/8	34 1/8	5 2/8	5 2/8	18	15 2/8	15 4/8	8 7/8	17	12	Courageous Lake, NT	William H. Moyer	William H. Moyer	1995	119
366 2/8	54	54 1/8	38 7/8	4 7/8	4 6/8	20 1/8	5 4/8	14 5/8	1/8	18	11	Point Lake, NT	John O. Plahn	John O. Plahn	1993	120

Score	Measurements	Locality	Owner	Hunter	Date Killed	Rank
366	47 1/8 45 4/8 32 5/8 4 5/8 4 4/8 13 2/8 10 4/8 8 7/8 7 6/8 18 23	Courageous Lake, NT	Arthur C. Peckham, Jr.	Arthur C. Peckham, Jr.	1987	121
365 7/8	52 2/8 54 2/8 32 4/8 5 5 1/8 16 3/8 14 2/8 13 2/8 8 2/8 15 14	Little Marten Lake, NT	Ralph Madden	Ralph Madden	1989	122
365 6/8	42 5/8 44 3/8 34 5/8 5 2/8 5 6/8 15 5/8 16 6/8 11 4/8 9 16 18	Lake Providence, NT	Jeffrey M. Farnsworth	Jeffrey M. Farnsworth	1994	123
365 5/8	53 5/8 54 4/8 36 1/8 5 2/8 5 1/8 16 6/8 16 8 6/8 11 3/8 15 12	Humpy Lake, NT	Garrett T. Bayrd	Garrett T. Bayrd	1996	123
365 5/8	47 2/8 54 4/8 31 1/8 9 3/8 8 2/8 15 6/8 5 5 4/8 14 14	Coppermine River, NT	David P. Jacobson	David P. Jacobson	1975	125
365 3/8	51 2/8 52 3/8 39 5 2 1/8 2 1/8 1/8 10 6/8 16 16	Courageous Lake, NT	Rob W. Shatzko	Rob W. Shatzko	1997	125
365 2/8	44 3/8 44 3/8 27 5/8 5 2/8 5 2/8 13 4/8 10 5/8 1/8 10 4/8 14 23	Courageous Lake, NT	Lilly Pinkas	Lilly Pinkas	1987	127
365 1/8	46 3/8 48 28 4/8 5 6/8 5 5/8 17 1/8 17 3/8 10 5/8 17 3/8 26 23	Snare River, NT	William M. Leitner	William M. Leitner	1987	128
365	49 4/8 47 32 1/8 5 2/8 5 1/8 18 2/8 18 2/8 15 4/8 16 20	Courageous Lake, NT	Frederick E. Haskell	Frederick E. Haskell	1987	129
364 7/8	48 4/8 50 7/8 36 5 14 7/8 11 4/8 15 4/8 10 4/8 16 15	Little Marten Lake, NT	Robin Bonner	Robin Bonner	1989	130
364 6/8	44 6/8 44 6/8 34 6/8 5 4 6/8 13 6 6/8 11 1/8 15 12	Lake Providence, NT	Bert Varkonyi	Nini Varkonyi	1986	131
364 4/8	51 3/8 51 6/8 36 3/8 5 5/8 5 2/8 15 7/8 15 4/8 10 16 13	Point Lake, NT	Rodger E. Warwick	Rodger E. Warwick	1991	132
364 3/8	48 48 40 2/8 4 4/8 4 6/8 11 3/8 13 2/8 7 5/8 10 6/8 16 19	Little Marten Lake, NT	Robin Bonner	Robin Bonner	1989	133
364	42 4/8 46 1/8 33 1/8 5 4/8 6 1/8 15 7/8 14 3/8 13 1/8 9 7/8 23 18	Pellatt Lake, NT	James D. Mierzwiak	James D. Mierzwiak	1996	134
364	45 1/8 46 2/8 32 3/8 5 4 6/8 15 6/8 14 7/8 11 5/8 8 5/8 21 17	Commonwealth Lake, MB	James F. Mervenne	James F. Mervenne	1996	135
363 7/8	47 5/8 48 34 6/8 5 5 15 2/8 14 8 2/8 14 4/8 14 17	Glover Lake, MB	Dean Toth	Dean Toth	1997	135
363 6/8	47 6/8 47 39 5/8 5 5/8 5 5/8 15 4/8 12 6/8 7 6/8 7 6/8 19 17	Humpy Lake, NT	Jeffrey M. Grab	Jeffrey M. Grab	1996	137
363 5/8	47 6/8 47 5/8 29 3/8 4 7/8 4 5/8 14 5/8 12 5/8 6 1/8 13 2/8 16 14	MacKay Lake, NT	Gary A. Jackson	Gary A. Jackson	1988	138
362 2/8	48 1/8 48 4/8 35 5 1/8 4 6/8 15 6/8 15 4/8 4 5/8 12 3/8 16 16	MacKay Lake, NT	Robert J. Gribble	Robert J. Gribble	1995	139
362 1/8	53 2/8 51 2/8 25 6/8 7 6 4/8 9 7/8 18 2/8 6 2/8 14 4/8 12 21	Courageous Lake, NT	John D. Frost	John D. Frost	1994	140
362 1/8	50 3/8 53 4/8 28 4/8 4 7/8 4 7/8 13 6/8 6 5/8 5 4/8 4 4/8 12 16	Rendez-vous Lake, NT	Victor E. Moss	Victor E. Moss	1989	141
362 1/8	49 49 37 4 6/8 4 6/8 8 2/8 22 1/8 18 3/8 13 16	Courageous Lake, NT	Larry H. Beller	Larry H. Beller	1991	141
362	53 4/8 54 36 4/8 6 5 5/8 19 16 4/8 14 13 6/8 13 18	Humpy Lake, NT	Robert W. Ehle	Robert W. Ehle	1997	141
361 7/8	51 1/8 50 6/8 35 2/8 5 5/8 5 2/8 11 3/8 19 1/8 1/8 13 6/8 15 15	Little Marten Lake, NT	William H. Oliver	William H. Oliver	1990	144
361 5/8	47 2/8 47 3/8 32 4/8 4 4/8 4 6/8 12 15 1/8 1/8 14 6/8 15 23	Point Lake, NT	Rick L. Clark	Rick L. Clark	1997	145
361 4/8	43 44 5/8 31 2/8 4 2/8 4 2/8 15 4/8 13 2/8 1 2/8 10 4/8 17 17	Courageous Lake, NT	Jack Lamb	Jack Lamb	1986	146
361 3/8	53 6/8 53 6/8 41 2/8 5 1/8 4 7/8 17 2/8 12 7/8 12 7/8 7 7/8 22 10	Lake Providence, NT	Grant M. St. Germaine	Grant M. St. Germaine	1988	147
361 1/8	47 4/8 50 1/8 31 2/8 5 4/8 4 7/8 18 7/8 9 2/8 14 5/8 3 14 23	Point Lake, NT	Neil Harles	Neil Harles	1991	148
361 1/8	49 5/8 49 6/8 29 4/8 5 4/8 5 4/8 6 5/8 18 6/8 2 3/8 14 1/8 10 11	Rendez-vous Lake, NT	Barry Jacobson	Barry Jacobson	1994	148
361	51 2/8 51 5/8 31 7/8 5 7/8 6 2/8 17 6/8 16 2/8 13 10 4/8 18 15	Winter Lake, NT	Warren D. St. Germaine	Warren D. St. Germaine	1984	150
360 6/8	46 3/8 47 2/8 31 2/8 6 3/8 6 3/8 13 1/8 2 5/8 1/8 18 13	Courageous Lake, NT	Paul E. Opfermann	Paul E. Opfermann	1988	150
360 6/8	49 5/8 48 7/8 26 7/8 5 4/8 5 4/8 6 4/8 14 6/8 10 4/8 1/8 24 18	Cape Dorset, NT	Ronald E. Gray	Ronald E. Gray	1985	152
360 5/8	50 3/8 51 5/8 39 7/8 4 7/8 5 1/8 18 2/8 18 1/8 12 2/8 15 3/8 17 14	Little Marten Lake, NT	Allen R. Prince	Allen R. Prince	1996	152
360 3/8	54 4/8 53 4/8 37 4/8 5 1/8 5 7/8 14 6/8 18 1/8 10 4/8 18 3/8 15 14	Humpy Lake, NT	William Vaznis	William Vaznis	1994	154
360 3/8	49 4/8 50 4/8 38 4 5/8 5 18 2/8 19 6/8 14 4/8 16 16	MacKay Lake, NT	Michael J. Spence	Michael J. Spence	1995	154
360 2/8	49 1/8 45 1/8 38 7/8 4 7/8 4 6/8 15 5/8 15 2/8 1/8 11 7/8 13 15	Point Lake, NT	Sharon Ziegenhagen	Sharon Ziegenhagen	1988	156
360	54 4/8 54 4/8 36 6/8 5 1/8 4 6/8 17 2/8 17 2/8 14 4/8 13 13	Humpy Lake, NT	William Vaznis	William Vaznis	1993	156
359 7/8	52 4/8 52 4/8 33 5/8 5 2/8 5 1/8 17 2/8 19 1/8 7 7/8 13 7/8 13 15	Point Lake, NT	Gary L. Vogel	Gary L. Vogel	1996	156
359 6/8	52 50 1/8 43 4/8 5 4/8 5 1/8 13 2/8 19 5/8 7 6/8 11 5/8 13 15	Obstruction Rapids, NT	George Bishop	George Bishop	1989	159
359 3/8	47 46 2/8 46 2/8 5 6/8 5 1/8 2 5/8 15 4/8 1/8 11 2/8 11 17	Courageous Lake, NT	Brian L. Dam	Brian L. Dam	1995	160
359 2/8	48 6/8 48 2/8 39 6/8 5 2/8 5 2/8 12 6/8 16 2/8 2 6/8 12 1/8 18 15	Ellice River, NT	Gerald L. Warnock	Gerald L. Warnock	1988	161
359	50 1/8 49 7/8 34 3/8 4 3/8 4 7/8 17 16 4/8 12 4/8 6 1/8 15 15	Humpy Lake, NT	Michael P. Kennedy	Michael P. Kennedy	1997	161
358 6/8	46 6/8 47 1/8 32 4 4/8 4 6/8 16 6/8 16 4/8 13 6/8 13 13	Nejanilini Lake, MB	John C. Hinchey	John C. Hinchey	1992	163
358 6/8	43 4/8 46 4/8 38 4 5/8 4 5/8 14 7/8 14 3/8 11 3/8 11 3/8 21 13	Point Lake, NT	Sean J. Lancaster	Sean J. Lancaster	1996	164
358 6/8	48 48 6/8 30 6/8 5 5/8 5 3/8 14 7/8 13 2/8 11 1/8 6 6/8 13 13	Courageous Lake, NT	Gregory S. Oliver	Gregory S. Oliver	1997	165
357 6/8	45 1/8 46 2/8 28 4 7/8 5 4/8 17 20 3 5/8 15 3/8 16 16	Courageous Lake, NT	Jose L. Perez	Jose L. Perez	1997	165
357 6/8	45 1/8 46 2/8 28 4 7/8 5 4/8 17 20 3 5/8 15 3/8 16 16	Rendez-vous Lake, NT	Nathan Andres	Nathan Andres	1994	167

CENTRAL CANADA BARREN GROUND CARIBOU

Rangifer tarandus groenlandicus

Score	Length of Main Beam R	L	Inside Spread	Circumference at Smallest Place Between Brow and Bez Points R	L	Length of Brow Points R	L	Width of Brow Points R	L	Number of Points R	L	Locality	Hunter	Owner	Date Killed	Rank
357 5/8	48	47	27 5/8	5 2/8	5	19	13 5/8	7 2/8	11 3/8	18	17	Undine Lake, NT	Barry D. Taylor	Barry D. Taylor	1985	168
357 5/8	50 5/8	49 4/8	27 6/8	6 2/8	6 1/8	16 2/8	14	13 7/8	12 6/8	11	17	MacKay Lake, NT	Glenn E. Thompson	Glenn E. Thompson	1992	168
357 4/8	51 5/8	50 5/8	30 2/8	5	5	16 4/8	15 7/8	9 2/8	11 1/8	14	17	MacKay Lake, NT	Glenn E. Hisey	Glenn E. Hisey	1997	170
357 3/8	50	48	31 5/8	4 6/8	5	4 2/8	18 7/8	1/8	14 2/8	20	15	Jolly Lake, NT	William L. Pederson	William L. Pederson	1996	171
357 1/8	45 6/8	45	30 3/8	5	5 2/8	18 3/8	18 4/8	16 2/8	12 4/8	12	21	Courageous Lake, NT	Richard N. Gubler	Richard N. Gubler	1988	172
357 1/8	49 3/8	48 7/8	33	4 4/8	4 5/8	18 3/8	16 5/8	13 2/8	7 4/8	18	16	Courageous Lake, NT	Kaye Poston	Kaye Poston	1983	173
357 1/8	48	45 2/8	40 3/8	4 4/8	4 5/8	14 5/8	16 3/8	10 3/8	12 7/8	20	12	Courageous Lake, NT	Charles D. Day	Charles D. Day	1991	173
357	49 5/8	48 2/8	28 6/8	5	5 5/8	13 1/8	18 2/8	5 2/8	16 1/8	21	16	MacKay Lake, NT	Robert C. Harrison	Robert C. Harrison	1987	175
356 5/8	49 2/8	49 1/8	28	5 1/8	5 1/8	14 1/8	16	9 2/8	14	22	19	Lake Providence, NT	David Spina	David Spina	1992	176
356 4/8	47 2/8	45 4/8	33 6/8	5	5	19 7/8	18	6 4/8	12 1/8	16	15	Bathurst Inlet, NT	George R. Skaggs	George R. Skaggs	1988	177
356 4/8	47	44 7/8	29 6/8	4 6/8	4 7/8	16 5/8	16 5/8	7 7/8	1 5/8	23	20	MacKay Lake, NT	Patrick M. Condie	Patrick M. Condie	1995	177
356 4/8	47 1/8	47 2/8	29 7/8	5 6/8	5 6/8	18 5/8	11 6/8	15 5/8	1 5/8	13	16	MacKay Lake, NT	Ken Kamstra	Ken Kamstra	1997	177
356 2/8	49	48	31 5/8	7	7 5/8	13		10 5/8		23	17	Arctic Bay, NT	James E. Mockerman	James E. Mockerman	1987	180
356 2/8	52 4/8	52 5/8	38 1/8	4 7/8	4 5/8	13 3/8	16	1 3/8	12 5/8	13	13	Coppermine River, NT	Duane Schroh	Duane Schroh	1987	180
356 1/8	51 2/8	49 4/8	36 7/8	5 7/8	5 3/8	8 1/8	18 2/8	1/8	16 1/8	13	16	Little Marten Lake, NT	Lloyd R. Broadwater	Lloyd R. Broadwater	1989	180
356 1/8	51	54 3/8	31 7/8	5 4/8	5 3/8	17	16 4/8	7 1/8	10 3/8	9	17	Little Marten Lake, NT	Barry J. Mitchell	Barry J. Mitchell	1988	183
355 6/8	47	48 6/8	40 3/8	5 4/8	5 7/8	4	16 4/8	7 1/8	13 2/8	16	16	Warburton Bay, NT	Stanley Godfrey	Stanley Godfrey	1988	184
355 6/8	48 6/8	51	30 2/8	4 5/8	4 5/8	17 3/8	20 7/8	1 2/8	14 4/8	15	14	Lake Providence, NT	Robert L. Kammerer	Robert L. Kammerer	1991	184
355 5/8	44 5/8	43 5/8	42 7/8	5	5 4/8	13 3/8	14 3/8	6 4/8	6 4/8	18	16	Rendez-vous Lake, NT	Shawn R. Andres	Shawn R. Andres	1991	186
355 4/8	48	48 7/8	36 7/8	4 7/8	5	15 4/8	15 3/8	3 4/8	12 2/8	16	11	Humpy Lake, NT	Jeffrey M. Grab	Jeffrey M. Grab	1996	187
355 3/8	42 4/8	41 6/8	36 2/8	5 1/8	5 1/8	15 1/8	15 1/8	11 5/8	10 4/8	24	25	Commonwealth Lake, MB	Charles M. Bloom	Charles M. Bloom	1996	188
355 2/8	48 5/8	48 5/8	32 6/8	5 4/8	5	14 7/8	14 4/8	11 4/8	9 6/8	16	18	Point Lake, NT	Edward F. Harles	Edward F. Harles	1991	189
355 2/8	44 1/8	44 5/8	36 4/8	4 6/8	5	17 5/8	16 7/8	11	11	15	18	Little Marten Lake, NT	Tom Balis	Tom Balis	1995	189
355	49 3/8	49 3/8	36 4/8	4 5/8	4 4/8	13 7/8	18 1/8	3 5/8	11 1/8	10	14	Little Marten Lake, NT	Marlowe D. Kottke	Marlowe D. Kottke	1992	191
355	39 3/8	35	18 5/8	5 3/8	5 5/8	17 6/8	16 1/8	17 3/8	14 7/8	21	27	Obstruction Rapids, NT	William G. Farley	William G. Farley	1996	191
354 7/8	52	51 2/8	38	5 1/8	4 6/8	14 7/8	6/8	11 5/8	1/8	12	17	Lynn Lake, MB	James A. Plett	James A. Plett	1994	193
354 3/8	47 4/8	49	40 1/8	4 6/8	5 2/8	15 6/8	5 6/8	11 5/8	1/8	14	15	Lac de Gras, NT	Brooks Carmichael	Brooks Carmichael	1987	194
354 2/8	51 2/8	51 2/8	29 4/8	5 7/8	5 7/8	18 3/8	5 6/8	1/8	14 4/8	16	13	Little Marten Lake, NT	Greg C. Bond	Greg C. Bond	1996	195
354 2/8	48 1/8	49 1/8	33 1/8	4 5/8	4 7/8	20 1/8	15 4/8	18	1 2/8	14	21	Point Lake, NT	Steven F. Burke	Steven F. Burke	1997	195
354 1/8	53 6/8	51 5/8	36 6/8	4 7/8	4 7/8	14	15 4/8	6 6/8	11 3/8	15	19	Humpy Lake, NT	Eugene M. McDaniel, Jr.	Eugene M. McDaniel, Jr.	1994	197
354	47 7/8	47 3/8	38	6 7/8	6 3/8	9 1/8	15 4/8	10 4/8	1/8	15	22	Winter River, NT	Robert W. Logan	Robert W. Logan	1996	198
353 7/8	46 3/8	48 5/8	31 4/8	5 1/8	5 1/8	2 2/8	15 3/8	13 7/8	1/8	15	25	Little Marten Lake, NT	William G. Freed	William G. Freed	1995	199
353 6/8	49 6/8	50 4/8	33 1/8	4 4/8	4 6/8	17 5/8	7 5/8	1/8	13 1/8	19	14	MacKay Lake, NT	Peter D. Scholl	Peter D. Scholl	1993	200
353 4/8	46 5/8	45 3/8	41	4 7/8	5	15 7/8	15 7/8	10 5/8		20	20	Lac de Gras, NT	Joseph P. Prinzi	Joseph P. Prinzi	1988	201
353 3/8	45 7/8	45 6/8	27 7/8	5	5 1/8	19 5/8	1 5/8	16 3/8	1/8	18	12	Courageous Lake, NT	Collins F. Kellogg	Collins F. Kellogg	1987	202
353 3/8	45 1/8	46 6/8	33 6/8	5 1/8	5	14	15 2/8	7	6 5/8	14	15	Jolly Lake, NT	Richard W. Anderson	Richard W. Anderson	1996	202
353 2/8	51 2/8	51 5/8	32 7/8	6 3/8	6 4/8	16 1/8	16 2/8	11 6/8	11 6/8	16	21	Rendez-vous Lake, NT	Roy C. Ewen	Roy C. Ewen	1988	204

Score	Locality	Hunter	Owner	Date	Rank
353 2/8	Humpy Lake, NT	Mike Kistler	Mike Kistler	1995	204
352 2/8	Rendez-vous Lake, NT	Steven R. Dunwell	Steven R. Dunwell	1996	206
351 7/8	Point Lake, NT	Jeffrey M. Turner	Jeffrey M. Turner	1987	207
351 1/8	MacKay Lake, NT	Reagan Dunn	Reagan Dunn	1997	207
351 1/8	Robin Lake, NT	Gary D. Cooney	Gary D. Cooney	1981	209
350 7/8	Courageous Lake, NT	Daryl W. Schreiner	Daryl W. Schreiner	1986	210
350 4/8	Parry Pen, NT	Donald F. Senter	Donald F. Senter	1985	211
350 4/8	Rendez-vous Lake, NT	Victor E. Moss	Victor E. Moss	1993	211
350 4/8	Point Lake, NT	Pete Doney	Pete Doney	1996	211
350 2/8	Lac de Gras, NT	Rex Baker	Rex Baker	1993	214
350 1/8	Ellice River, NT	Thomas D. Suedmeier	Thomas D. Suedmeier	1989	215
348 6/8	Rocher Lake, NT	Gary F. Silc	Gary F. Silc	1997	216
348 4/8	Rendez-vous Lake, NT	Morgan D. Silvers	Morgan D. Silvers	1996	217
348 3/8	Courageous Lake, NT	Thomas A. McIntyre	Thomas A. McIntyre	1987	218
348 3/8	Rendez-vous Lake, NT	William Mitchell	William Mitchell	1991	218
348 1/8	Warburton Bay, NT	David R. Coupland	David R. Coupland	1992	220
348 1/8	Warburton Bay, NT	Tom Foss	Tom Foss	1993	220
348 1/8	MacKay Lake, NT	Fred S. Youngblood	Fred S. Youngblood	1989	222
348	Rocher Lake, NT	Harry Kaczmarek	Harry Kaczmarek	1997	222
347 6/8	Paulatuk, NT	Don L. Corley	Don L. Corley	1985	224
347 3/8	Warburton Bay, NT	John L. Campbell	John L. Campbell	1995	224
347 3/8	Little Marten Lake, NT	Greg C. Bond	Greg C. Bond	1996	224
347 3/8	MacKay Lake, NT	Anne McGarvey	Anne McGarvey	1996	227
347 2/8	Courageous Lake, NT	Harold B. Van Hoy	Harold B. Van Hoy	1986	228
347 1/8	Point Lake, NT	Sharon Ziegenhagen	Sharon Ziegenhagen	1988	228
347 1/8	Point Lake, NT	Jim Anderson	Jim Anderson	1989	230
347	Rendez-vous Lake, NT	Michael A. Dunwell	Michael A. Dunwell	1996	230
347	Courageous Lake, NT	Rick Berreth	Picked Up	1992	232
346 4/8	Point Lake, NT	John J. McSherry	John J. McSherry	1993	232
346 4/8	Courageous Lake, NT	James D. Verbrugge	James D. Verbrugge	1996	232
346 4/8	Obstruction Rapids, NT	Fred H. Palmer	Fred H. Palmer	1988	232
346 2/8	Little Marten Lake, NT	Jack R. Cook	Jack R. Cook	1989	235
346 2/8	Rendez-vous Lake, NT	J.A. & J. Walkenhauer	James A. Walkenhauer	1994	235
346 2/8	Big Lake, NT	Dan Murphy	Dan Murphy	1979	235
346 1/8	Courageous Lake, NT	Glenn St. Charles	Glenn St. Charles	1987	238
346 1/8	Little Marten Lake, NT	Hugo P. Fleckner	Hugo P. Fleckner	1991	238
346 1/8	Farmie Lake, MB	Wes Plett	Wes Plett	1995	238
346 1/8	Rendez-vous Lake, NT	David P. Jacobson	David P. Jacobson	1988	238
345 7/8	Lake Providence, NT	Wayne Stewart	Wayne Stewart	1991	242
345 7/8	Courageous Lake, NT	Anna Marie Pavlik	Anna Marie Pavlik	1995	242
345 3/8	MacKay Lake, NT	Thomas J. Reardon	Thomas J. Reardon	1987	244
345 3/8	MacKay Lake, NT	R.E. Smith	R.E. Smith	1992	245
345 2/8	Contwoyto Lake, NT	John P. Burdette	John P. Burdette	1993	245
345 2/8	Nejanilini Lake, MB	Robert J. Fox	Robert J. Fox	1996	247
345 1/8	MacKay Lake, NT	W.J. Burns	W.J. Burns	1991	247
345 1/8	Little Marten Lake, NT	Marc N. Shaft	Marc N. Shaft	1997	249
398 3/8*	Nejanilini Lake, MB	Peter Wiebe	Peter Wiebe	1994	249

* Final score is subject to revision by additional verifying measurements.

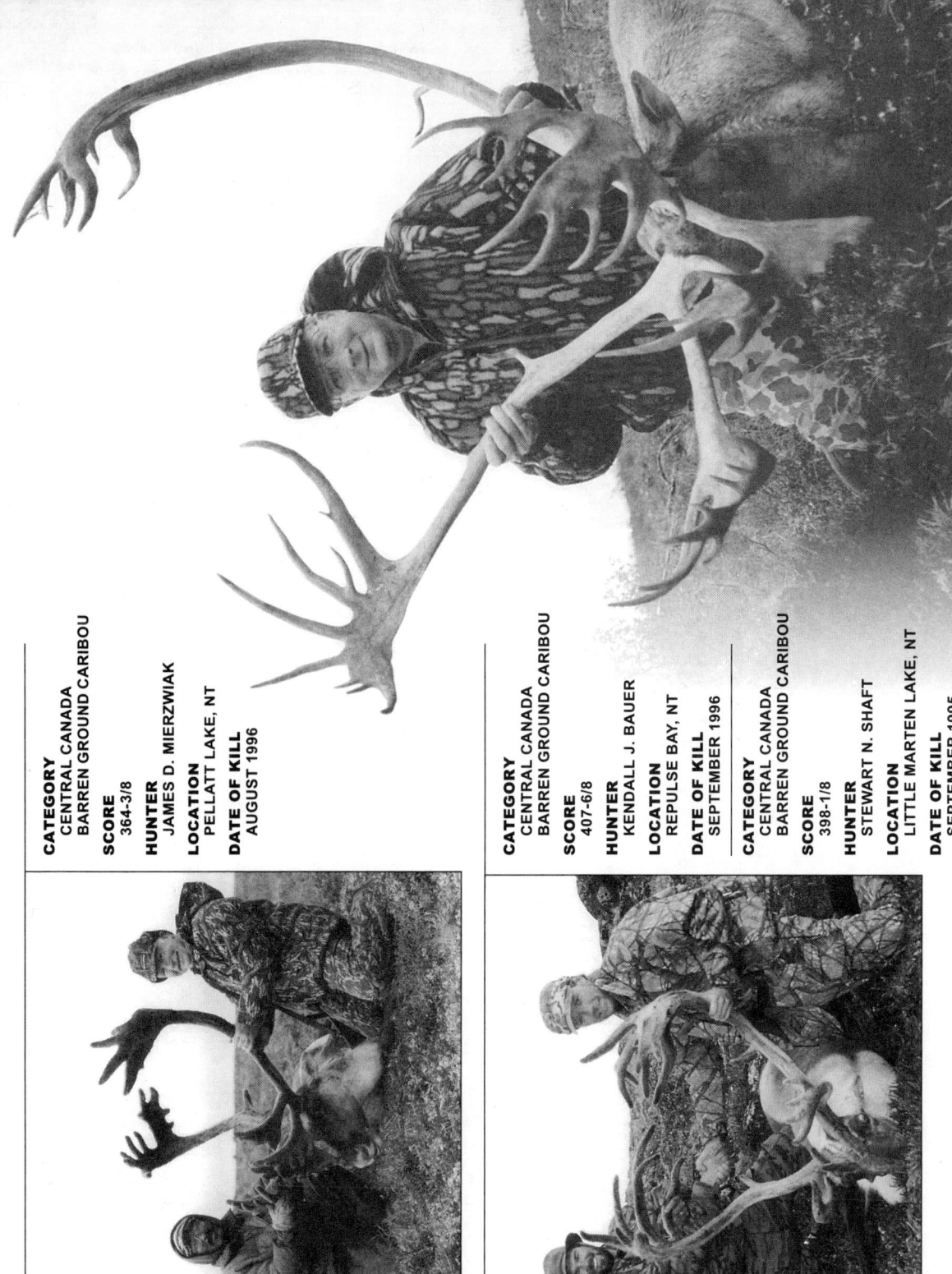

CATEGORY
CENTRAL CANADA
BARREN GROUND CARIBOU

SCORE
364-3/8

HUNTER
JAMES D. MIERZWIAK

LOCATION
PELLATT LAKE, NT

DATE OF KILL
AUGUST 1996

CATEGORY
CENTRAL CANADA
BARREN GROUND CARIBOU

SCORE
407-6/8

HUNTER
KENDALL J. BAUER

LOCATION
REPULSE BAY, NT

DATE OF KILL
SEPTEMBER 1996

CATEGORY
CENTRAL CANADA
BARREN GROUND CARIBOU

SCORE
398-1/8

HUNTER
STEWART N. SHAFT

LOCATION
LITTLE MARTEN LAKE, NT

DATE OF KILL
SEPTEMBER 1995

QUEBEC-LABRADOR CARIBOU
WORLD'S RECORD

This fine caribou trophy makes one wonder how many potential big game World's Records were already taken by the Inuit during their long tradition of hunting in North America. The trophy is one of the few specimens of the rare caribou race from Labrador. It was shot by Zack Elbow near Nain, Canada, during the winter of 1931 and later picked up by Charles Ray Peck who recorded an account of his find.

"During the summer of 1932, I was cruising home from Norway on a chartered Norwegian sealing vessel. When we reached Nain, a small village on the Labrador coast, we had our first sight of trees and of continental North America, so we decided to explore a fjord that ran inland for perhaps 50 miles to the northwest. As a sort of guide, we took along from the village an Eskimo named Zack Elbow for we had gathered that we might see some caribou and find some good trout fishing. We stayed at the head of the fjord for several days. While some of the party were enjoying the fishing, my friend Hoff Benjamin and I went caribou hunting with the Eskimo, who understood no English.

"Mosquitos were extremely bothersome, but the first day we saw two or three small caribou, which I did not shoot. This seemed to irritate the Eskimo. However, by the next day I had succeeded in conveying to him that I was hunting for 'big Tuktu.' So we proceeded overland, I would say about 12 miles, to a spot where Zack had shot a couple of bulls, for meat, during the previous winter. When he led us to this place

I could see two huge heads lying on the ground, 50 yards away. Foxes, of course, had eaten everything thar Zack had left except the bones. We tossed a coin to see whether Hoff Benjamin or I would be the possessor of the larger head. I won."

This head, presented to the Boone and Crockett Club's National Collection of Heads and Horns by Peck in 1951, is the highest scoring caribou ever recorded. As the picture below shows, these Quebec-Labrador heads often differ markedly from those of the caribou races in the western part of the continent. ■

TROPHY INFO

RANK
World's Record

SCORE
474 6/8

LOCATION
Nain, LB

HUNTER
Zack Elbow

OWNER
B&C Natl. Collection

DATE KILLED
1931

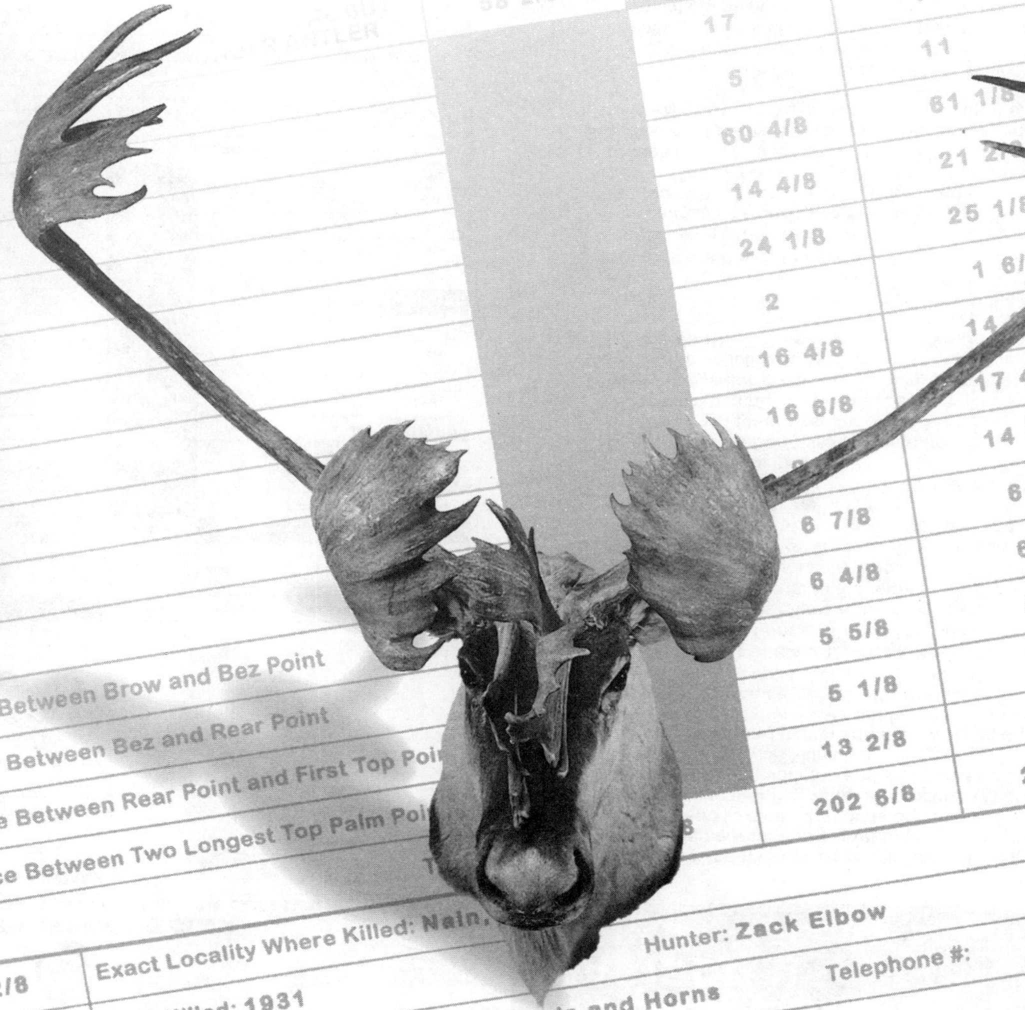

G-1. Width of Brow
G-2. Width of Top Palm
H-1. Circumference at Smallest Place Between Brow and Bez Point
H-2. Circumference at Smallest Place Between Bez and Rear Point
H-3. Circumference at Smallest Place Between Rear Point and First Top Poi
H-4. Circumference at Smallest Place Between Two Longest Top Palm Poi
58 2/8
17
5
60 4/8
14 4/8
24 1/8
2
16 4/8
16 6/8
6 7/8
6 4/8
5 5/8
5 1/8
13 2/8
202 6/8
19
11
61 1/8
25 1/8
1 6/8
17 4/8
14 6/8
6 5/8
6 1/8
5 7/8
5 3/8
12 5/8
222 3/8
2
5/8
2/8
2 2/8
6/8
2/8
3/8
2/8
2/8
ADD
Column 1
58 2/8
Column 2
202 6/8
Column 3
222 3/8
Exact Locality Where Killed: Nain,
Hunter: Zack Elbow
Date Killed: 1931
Telephone #:
Owner: National Collection of Heads and Horns
Owner's Address:

Photograph by Wm. H. Nesbitt

QUEBEC-LABRADOR CARIBOU

WORLD'S RECORD SCORECHART

Records of
North American
Big Game

250 Station Drive
Missoula, MT 59801
(406) 542-1888

BOONE AND CROCKETT CLUB®

OFFICIAL SCORING SYSTEM FOR NORTH AMERICAN BIG GAME TROPHIES

CARIBOU

KIND OF CARIBOU (check one)
- ☐ mountain
- ☐ woodland
- ☐ barren ground
- ☐ Central Canada barren ground
- ■ Quebec-Labrador

	MINIMUM SCORES AWARDS	ALL-TIME
mountain	360	390
woodland	265	295
barren ground	375	400
Central Canada barren ground	345	360
Quebec-Labrador	365	375

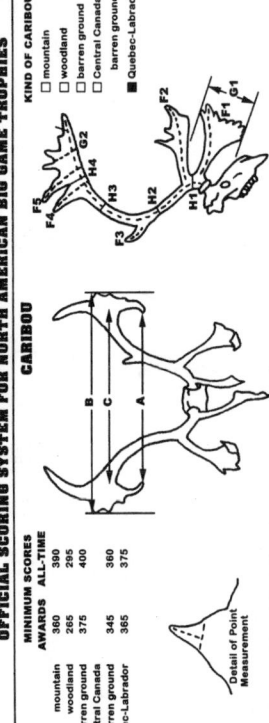

Detail of Point Measurement

SEE OTHER SIDE FOR INSTRUCTIONS		COLUMN 1	COLUMN 2	COLUMN 3	COLUMN 4
		Spread Credit	Right Antler	Left Antler	Difference
A. Tip to Tip Spread	41 3/8				
B. Greatest Spread	60 3/8				
C. Inside Spread of Main Beams	58 2/8	SPREAD CREDIT MAY EQUAL BUT NOT EXCEED LONGER ANTLER	58 2/8			
D. Number of Points on Each Antler Excluding Brows					2
Number of Points on Each Brow			17	19	
E. Length of Main Beam			5	11	
F-1. Length of Brow Palm or First Point			60 4/8	61 1/8	5/8
F-2. Length of Bez or Second Point			14 4/8	21 2/8	
F-3. Length of Rear Point, If Present			24 1/8	25 1/8	1
F-4. Length of Second Longest Top Point			2	2	2/8
F-5. Length of Longest Top Point			16 4/8	14 2/8	2 2/8
G-1. Width of Brow Palm			16 6/8	17 4/8	6/8
G-2. Width of Top Palm			9	14 6/8	
H-1. Circumference at Smallest Place Between Brow and Bez Point			6 7/8	6 5/8	2/8
H-2. Circumference at Smallest Place Between Bez and Rear Point			6 4/8	6 1/8	3/8
H-3. Circumference at Smallest Place Between Rear Point and First Top Point			5 5/8	5 7/8	2/8
H-4. Circumference at Smallest Place Between Two Longest Top Palm Points			5 1/8	5 3/8	2/8
			13 2/8	12 5/8	5/8
TOTALS	58 2/8	202 6/8	222 3/8	8 5/8

	Column 1	58 2/8	Exact Locality Where Killed: Nain, Labrador	
ADD	Column 2	202 6/8	Date Killed: 1931	Hunter: Zack Elbow
	Column 3	222 3/8	Owner: National Collection of Heads and Horns	Telephone #:
	Subtotal	483 3/8	Owner's Address:	
SUBTRACT Column 4		8 5/8	Guide's Name and Address:	
FINAL SCORE		474 6/8	Remarks: (Mention Any Abnormalities or Unique Qualities)	

COPYRIGHT © 1999 BY BOONE AND CROCKETT CLUB®

All measurements must be made with a 1/4-inch wide flexible steel tape to the nearest one-eighth of an inch. (Note: A flexible steel cable can be used to measure points and main beams only.) Enter fractional figures in eighths, without reduction. Official measurements cannot be taken until the antlers have air dried for at least 60 days after the animal was killed.

A. Tip to Tip Spread is measured between tips of main beams.

B. Greatest Spread is measured between perpendiculars at a right angle to the center line of the skull at widest part, whether across main beams or points.

C. Inside Spread of Main Beams is measured at a right angle to the center line of the skull at widest point between main beams. Enter this measurement again as the Spread Credit **if** it is less than or equal to the length of the longer antler; if greater, enter longer antler length for Spread Credit.

D. Number of Points on Each Antler: To be counted a point, a projection must be at least one-half inch long, with length exceeding width at one-half inch or more of length. Beam tip is counted as a point but not measured as a point. There are no "abnormal" points in caribou.

E. Length of Main Beam is measured from the center of the lowest outside edge of burr over the outer side to the most distant point of the main beam. The point of beginning is that point on the burr where the center line along the outer side of the beam intersects the burr, then following generally the line of the illustration.

F-1-2-3. Length of Points are measured from nearest edge of beam over outer curve to tip. Lay the tape along the outer curve of the beam so that the top edge of the tape coincides with the top edge of the beam on both sides of point to determine the baseline for point measurement. Record point lengths in appropriate blanks.

F-4-5. Length of Points are measured from the tip of the point to the top of the beam, then at a right angle to the bottom edge of beam. The Second Longest Top Point **cannot** be a point branch of the Longest Top Point.

G-1. Width of Brow is measured in a straight line from top edge to lower edge, as illustrated, with measurement line at a right angle to main axis of brow.

G-2. Width of Top Palm is measured from midpoint of lower edge of main beam to midpoint of a dip between points, at widest part of palm. The line of measurement begins and ends at midpoints of palm edges, which gives credit for palm thickness.

H-1-2-3-4. Circumferences are taken as illustrated for measurements. If brow point is missing, take H-1 at smallest point between burr and bez point. If rear point is missing, take H-2 and H-3 measurements at smallest place between bez and first top point. Do not depress the tape into any dips of the palm or main beam.

QUEBEC-LABRADOR CARIBOU

Rangifer tarandus from Quebec and Labrador

MINIMUM SCORE 375

Score	Length of Main Beam R	Length of Main Beam L	Inside Spread	Circ. at Smallest Place Between Brow and Bez Points R	Circ. L	Length of Brow Points R	Length of Brow Points L	Width of Brow Points R	Width of Brow Points L	Number of Points R	Number of Points L	Locality	Hunter	Owner	Date Killed	Rank
474 6/8	60 4/8	61 1/8	58 2/8	6 4/8	6 1/8	14 4/8	21 2/8	9	14 6/8	22	30	Nain, LB	Zack Elbow	B&C National Collection	1931	1
464 4/8	55 7/8	54 2/8	54 5/8	5 6/8	5 5/8	19 2/8	19 5/8	2 1/8	14 1/8	18	23	Tunulic River, QC	James A. DeLuca	James A. DeLuca	1983	2
460 6/8	59 4/8	56 5/8	49 2/8	5 1/8	5 2/8	16 6/8	21 4/8	13 6/8	18 4/8	22	24	Ungava Bay, QC	Lynn D. McLaud	Lynn D. McLaud	1978	3
439 1/8	56 6/8	59 1/8	42	6 7/8	5 7/8	17 7/8	20 2/8	12 3/8	13 7/8	11	22	Ungava Bay, QC	Don Tomberlin	Don Tomberlin	1985	4
438 2/8	59 3/8	55 4/8	52 7/8	5 3/8	5 3/8	8	21 1/8	1/8	19 1/8	17	25	Beach Camp, QC	Ronald R. Ragan	Ronald R. Ragan	1975	5
434 7/8	51 2/8	52	44 5/8	4 7/8	5 1/8	16 3/8	20 6/8	14 7/8	8 6/8	25	22	Mistinibi Lake, QC	Don L. Corley	Don L. Corley	1983	6
434 3/8	50 6/8	53 7/8	54	5 6/8	5 4/8	16 2/8	20 1/8	9 7/8	16 1/8	28	28	George River, QC	Dewey Mark	Dewey Mark	1973	7
433 2/8	44 2/8	41 1/8	41 1/8	5 6/8	5 6/8	20 1/8	20 3/8	7/8	16 7/8	22	22	Lake Otelnuk, QC	Robert E. McNeill	Robert E. McNeill	1986	8
431 6/8	53 4/8	56	46 1/8	5 4/8	5 6/8	16 5/8	20 5/8	3 6/8	15 1/8	19	18	Tunulik River, QC	Carol A. Mauch	Carol A. Mauch	1984	9
430 7/8	52 2/8	56 4/8	47	6 2/8	6 5/8	11	20 6/8	1 7/8	17 4/8	22	33	George River, QC	Larry Barnett	Larry Barnett	1978	10
429 6/8	55 1/8	59 1/8	50 1/8	5 6/8	5 5/8	21 6/8	2 1/8	19 1/8	1/8	15	12	Ford Lake, QC	George Shultz	George Shultz	1972	11
428 2/8	51 6/8	50 1/8	48 3/8	5 4/8	5 4/8	18 1/8	18 5/8	13 1/8	14 6/8	21	21	Mistinibi Lake, QC	Charles E. Wilson, Jr.	Charles E. Wilson, Jr.	1980	12
428 5/8	51 5/8	52 1/8	38 5/8	6	6	14 7/8	15 3/8	9 2/8	12	26	30	George River, QC	Cayetano G. Arriola, Jr.	Cayetano G. Arriola, Jr.	1975	13
427	56 1/8	57 6/8	48 2/8	6 4/8	6 6/8	16 6/8	14 7/8	14 4/8	2 7/8	21	15	Ungava Bay, QC	David Walker	David Walker	1984	14
425 7/8	52 5/8	51 4/8	41 3/8	6 4/8	6	16 6/8	21 5/8	18	12 2/8	19	15	Lake Natuak, QC	Patricio M. Sada	Patricio M. Sada	1993	15
424 1/8	55 3/8	55 3/8	47 6/8	6 2/8	5 5/8	16 2/8	18 3/8	9 4/8	14 6/8	18	22	Serigny River, QC	Brad Case	Brad Case	1989	16
421 4/8	52 7/8	54 4/8	53 5/8	6 2/8	5 7/8	17 2/8	5 6/8	12 2/8	1/8	20	16	George River, QC	Maurice J. Southmayd	Maurice J. Southmayd	1979	17
417	53 2/8	57 4/8	52 1/8	5 7/8	5 4/8	16 2/8	21 3/8	10 1/8	12 3/8	24	16	Caniapiscau River, QC	John A. Picard	John A. Picard	1994	18
416 5/8	45 3/8	47 7/8	47 4/8	4 7/8	4 7/8	13 1/8	16	6 4/8	11	28	27	George River, QC	Collins F. Kellogg	Collins F. Kellogg	1978	19
416 1/8	48	45 2/8	38 4/8	5 1/8	5 1/8	21 2/8	16 4/8	15 7/8	11 4/8	25	20	Lake Amichinatwayach, QC	Thomas R. Conrardy	Thomas R. Conrardy	1995	20
416	52	50 3/8	50	5 3/8	5 2/8	21 2/8	20 7/8	14	15 5/8	17	20	Lake Consigny, QC	Ricardo L. Garza	Ricardo L. Garza	1989	21
415 5/8	54 6/8	52 4/8	46	5	5 2/8	17 3/8	18 2/8	8 2/8	16 6/8	15	21	George River, QC	George E. Poleshock	George E. Poleshock	1980	22
414 7/8	62 4/8	66	43 6/8	5 1/8	5 1/8	2 3/8	21 5/8	1/8	16 6/8	16	22	Schefferville, QC	Peggy A. Vallery	Peggy A. Vallery	1980	23
414	42 7/8	43 5/8	41	6	6	15 1/8	13 7/8	8 3/8	8 1/8	22	23	George River Lodge, QC	James E. McCarthy	James E. McCarthy	1974	24
412 2/8	53 6/8	52 1/8	45 5/8	6 4/8	6	13 3/8	16	13 1/8	11 1/8	16	22	Whale River, QC	Daniel E. Merrell	Daniel E. Merrell	1972	25
411 7/8	51	51 7/8	52 5/8	7	8 2/8	13 7/8	14	5 6/8	4 1/8	9	14	Mistinibi Lake, QC	Rudolf Sand	Rudolf Sand	1973	26
411 1/8	53 2/8	49 2/8	56 6/8	5 2/8	5 3/8	17 6/8	22 4/8	8 5/8	13	14	19	Tunulik River, QC	Leon Orzechowski	Leon Orzechowski	1978	26
410 7/8	61 4/8	63 4/8	48	5 7/8	6	16 7/8	3 2/8	17 7/8	1/8	18	18	Mistinibi Lake, QC	David H. Crum	David H. Crum	1980	28
410 6/8	50 7/8	51 2/8	54	5 1/8	5 1/8	19 5/8	17 5/8	13 5/8	13 4/8	19	23	Caniapiscau Lake, QC	Stephen C. Lockhart	Stephen C. Lockhart	1989	29
410 6/8	59 4/8	60 4/8	40 6/8	5 7/8	5 6/8	17 5/8	17 2/8	14	8 7/8	26	22	George River, QC	Kenneth E. Goslant	Kenneth E. Goslant	1974	30
410 4/8	44 5/8	42 4/8	46 4/8	6 1/8	5 7/8	13 4/8	17 2/8	14 6/8	10 7/8	25	24	George River, QC	Gail W. Holderman	Gail W. Holderman	1979	30
410	52 4/8	51 6/8	48 6/8	6 2/8	6 2/8	16 5/8	16	12	10 7/8	18	18	Pons River, QC	Don Young	Don Young	1988	32
409 6/8	56	55 6/8	52 1/8	6 2/8	5	21 1/8	22 4/8	12 2/8	8	15	16	Lake Nachicapau, QC	Charles L. Buechel, Jr.	Charles L. Buechel, Jr.	1987	33
409 5/8	51 2/8	50 6/8	51 1/8	5 1/8	5 2/8	14	16 2/8	8 7/8	11	18	20	Mistinibi Lake, QC	George H. Fearons	George H. Fearons	1982	34
408 5/8	48 7/8	49 1/8	43	5 2/8	5 4/8	16	16 1/8	12 4/8	12 6/8	28	22	Tunulik Lake, QC	Robert F. Cook	Robert F. Cook	1979	35
408 4/8	57 2/8	47 6/8	45	5 3/8	5 3/8	21 6/8	20 7/8	15 4/8	1 7/8	19	14	Mistinibi Lake, QC	Lee Frudden	Lee Frudden	1980	36

Score	Length of Main Beam R	Length of Main Beam L	Inside Spread	By whom killed	Owner	Locality	Date Killed	Rank
408 4/8	53 2/8	53 1/8	46 1/8	Richard H. Propp	Richard H. Propp	Ungava Bay, QC	1985	36
408	55 2/8	55 1/8	44 6/8	Bernard W. Masino	Bernard W. Masino	Caniapiscau River, QC	1987	38
407 7/8	54 6/8	56 3/8	42 1/8	Robert L. Sprinkle, Jr.	Robert L. Sprinkle, Jr.	Tunulik Lake, QC	1979	39
407 5/8	50 3/8	50	45 3/8	Jeffrey S. Baker	Jeffrey S. Baker	Lake Moyer, QC	1988	40
406 3/8	58 5/8	59	46 3/8	Trevor H.S. Povah	Trevor H.S. Povah	Delay River, QC	1989	41
406 2/8	49	48 7/8	48 7/8	Michael R. Miggins	Michael R. Miggins	Caniapiscau River, QC	1987	42
406	45 6/8	44 3/8	43 2/8	Thomas A. Rue	Thomas A. Rue	Narcy Lake, QC	1988	43
405 4/8	55	56 1/8	51 3/8	Jerry Ippolito	Jerry Ippolito	Tunulik River, QC	1980	44
405 2/8	52	53	44 6/8	Herbert J. Englemann	Herbert J. Englemann	De Pas River, QC	1979	45
405	53 1/8	54 4/8	51 4/8	Chester Gluck	Chester Gluck	Knob Lake, QC	1964	46
404 6/8	46 4/8	46 4/8	40 4/8	Daniel W. Inserra	Daniel W. Inserra	Ungava Bay, QC	1979	47
404 5/8	53 4/8	57 6/8	42 6/8	Robert E. Prittinen	Robert E. Prittinen	Camp Tuktu, QC	1980	48
404 2/8	53 3/8	50 4/8	46	Paul Bambara	Paul Bambara	George River, QC	1985	49
404	49 5/8	50 4/8	51 7/8	Ernest W. Foster, Jr.	Ernest W. Foster, Jr.	Sagler Fiord, LB	1985	50
403 5/8	46 1/8	48 2/8	48 2/8	L.C. Harold	L.C. Harold	Schefferville, QC	1982	51
403 4/8	58 6/8	61	42 4/8	John A. Gulius	John A. Gulius	Ungava Bay, QC	1975	52
403 3/8	54 3/8	54 2/8	41 5/8	Bernard W. Masino	Bernard W. Masino	Caniapiscau River, QC	1987	53
403 2/8	47 3/8	50 2/8	43	James R. Blankenheim	James R. Blankenheim	Samuel Lake, QC	1989	55
403	51 2/8	51 1/8	48 1/8	Ralph Cervo	Ralph Cervo	Thibault Lake, QC	1983	56
402 6/8	47 7/8	45 1/8	35 2/8	Barbara A. Shuler	Barbara A. Shuler	Caniapiscau River, QC	1985	57
402 2/8	56 4/8	54	47	John T. Richards, Jr.	John T. Richards, Jr.	Kuujjuaq, QC	1986	58
402	60 2/8	53 4/8	48 3/8	Paul B. Brunner	Paul B. Brunner	George River, QC	1980	59
401 3/8	54 2/8	53 6/8	48 5/8	Theodore L. Greenwood	Theodore L. Greenwood	Mistinibi Lake, QC	1981	60
401 3/8	57 1/8	57 6/8	49 4/8	Arthur J. Pelon	Arthur J. Pelon	Koksoak River, QC	1986	60
401 2/8	49 4/8	49	48 1/8	C. Gordon Demeritt	C. Gordon Demeritt	Ungava Bay, QC	1988	62
401 1/8	57	58 3/8	58 3/8	Bruce Hartel	Bruce Hartel	Indian River, QC	1981	63
401	49 7/8	51	49 2/8	Claude E. Genet	Claude E. Genet	George River, QC	1966	64
400 5/8	51	52 7/8	44 4/8	Robert A. Krizek	Robert A. Krizek	George River, QC	1979	65
400 5/8	51 2/8	52 6/8	37 7/8	M. Farrel Gosman	M. Farrel Gosman	Tunulic River, QC	1978	65
400 4/8	52 4/8	46 1/8	46 1/8	Dennis E. Moos	Dennis E. Moos	Mistinibi Lake, QC	1980	67
400 3/8	46	46	52 5/8	Dale D. Wieand	Dale D. Wieand	George River, QC	1977	68
400 1/8	54 5/8	56 2/8	47 3/8	Charles E. Putt	Charles E. Putt	Pons River, QC	1988	69
400	56 6/8	53 1/8	53 1/8	Ronald L. Boucher	Ronald L. Boucher	Pons River, QC	1986	70
400	51 1/8	51 6/8	51 1/8	John C. Sullivan, Jr.	John C. Sullivan, Jr.	George River, QC	1978	70
399 7/8	56 4/8	58 2/8	58 2/8	Elwood Larsen	Elwood Larsen	Fort Chimo, QC	1986	72
399 5/8	53	50 4/8	50 4/8	David L. George	David L. George	George River, QC	1968	73
399 3/8	55	56	58	William E. Johnson	William E. Johnson	Desbergeres Lake, QC	1996	74
399 3/8	54 2/8	52 2/8	45	George E. Rommler	George E. Rommler	Dihourse Lake, QC	1980	74
398 4/8	57 7/8	59 3/8	45 3/8	Gary R. Smock	Gary R. Smock	Pons River, QC	1980	76
398 4/8	55 1/8	53 5/8	48 6/8	Bob Bates	Bob Bates	Tunulik River, QC	1980	77
398 3/8	52 7/8	51 1/8	48 3/8	Jack Schwabland	Jack Schwabland	Tunulik River, QC	1987	78
398 1/8	54 4/8	53	45	Anthony L. Pinnavaia, Sr.	Anthony L. Pinnavaia, Sr.	Ford Lake, QC	1977	79
397 6/8	54 3/8	55 7/8	49	George H. Fearons	George H. Fearons	Lac Vallerenne, QC	1988	80
397 5/8	48 5/8	49 4/8	52 4/8	Charles J. Spies	Charles J. Spies	George River, QC	1983	81
397 5/8	54 2/8	53	47	Stanley M. Boots	Stanley M. Boots	George River, QC	1988	81
397 4/8	53 1/8	54 4/8	57 4/8	John R. Connelly	John R. Connelly	Caniapiscau River, QC	1988	83
397 4/8	48 1/8	51 2/8	49 4/8	Gary A. Perin	Gary A. Perin	Serigny River, QC	1987	83

QUEBEC-LABRADOR CARIBOU

Rangifer tarandus from Quebec and Labrador

Score	Length of Main Beam R	Length of Main Beam L	Inside Spread	Circumference at Smallest Place Between Brow and Bez Points R	Circumference at Smallest Place Between Brow and Bez Points L	Length of Brow Points R	Length of Brow Points L	Width of Brow Points R	Width of Brow Points L	Number of Points R	Number of Points L	Locality	Hunter	Owner	Date Killed	Rank
397 3/8	43 2/8	45 6/8	42 3/8	5 7/8	5 6/8	18	15 4/8	15 7/8	10 7/8	23	19	Black Duck Bay, LB	Hal W. Johnson	Hal W. Johnson	1994	84
397 2/8	43 5/8	47 7/8	46 2/8	6	5 6/8	2 1/8	17 1/8	1/8	12 7/8	21	21	Twin River Lodge, QC	Fred W. Sheaman, Jr.	Fred W. Sheaman, Jr.	1969	85
397 1/8	56 6/8	56 6/8	61 1/8	5 2/8	5 2/8	18 1/8	2	8 5/8	1/8	19	17	George River, QC	Morris Weinstein	Morris Weinstein	1972	86
397	54 2/8	54 2/8	40	5 1/8	5 1/8	14	15 1/8	14 1/8	15 4/8	19	22	Ungava Bay, QC	Charles T. Sheley	Charles T. Sheley	1979	87
396 5/8	46 7/8	47 7/8	39 3/8	5 7/8	5 5/8	15 4/8	19 4/8	1/8	15 3/8	21	23	Tunulik River, QC	Charles W. Dixon	Charles W. Dixon	1979	88
396 4/8	59 7/8	59 2/8	46 4/8	6	5 6/8	20 3/8	20 2/8	17 1/8	8 6/8	16	17	George River Lodge, QC	Robert S. Carroll	Robert S. Carroll	1974	89
396 4/8	45 4/8	46 7/8	40	5 5/8	5 7/8	19 4/8	16 7/8	11 4/8	13 6/8	16	21	Lake Gerido, QC	Jerry McDonald	Jerry McDonald	1992	89
396 3/8	53 1/8	52	38 7/8	5 1/8	5 1/8	19 3/8	16 3/8	14 2/8	1	21	18	Pons River, QC	Glenn M. Smith	Glenn M. Smith	1986	91
396 2/8	54 1/8	55 2/8	48 5/8	6 4/8	7 3/8	17 5/8	11 4/8	13 4/8	6 2/8	19	14	George River, QC	John E. Clark	John E. Clark	1980	92
396	55 2/8	57 2/8	42 5/8	5 3/8	5 1/8	21 5/8	21 3/8	8 3/8	16 2/8	17	20	Ungava Bay, QC	Edwin L. DeYoung	Edwin L. DeYoung	1989	93
396	53 4/8	50 5/8	40 2/8	5 3/8	5 3/8	18 6/8	17 1/8	16 4/8	12 5/8	19	16	Black Duck Bay, LB	Hal W. Johnson	Hal W. Johnson	1994	93
396	55 4/8	58 3/8	51	5 5/8	5 4/8	1	18 7/8	1/8	14 3/8	15	22	Ungava Bay, QC	Bruce S. Markham	Bruce S. Markham	1979	95
395 5/8	55 5/8	51 2/8	44 6/8	5 6/8	5 6/8	16	18	1/8	14 4/8	19	24	George River, QC	Kurt Roenspies	Kurt Roenspies	1990	96
395	41	40 5/8	37 3/8	5 2/8	5 2/8	16	5 7/8	12 4/8	1/8	27	24	Kamawapakich Lake, QC	Michael R. Carlson	Michael R. Carlson	1994	97
394 7/8	54 6/8	52 2/8	48 5/8	5 4/8	5 5/8	17	17 3/8	13	12 1/8	15	17	Ungava Bay, QC	Norbert D. Bremer	Norbert D. Bremer	1989	98
394 5/8	51 1/8	48 4/8	42 7/8	5 1/8	5 4/8	19 4/8	17 7/8	2 6/8	11 4/8	17	15	De Pas River, QC	William A. O'Connor	William A. O'Connor	1980	99
394 4/8	44 1/8	44 2/8	38 2/8	5 7/8	5 1/8	13 5/8	7 6/8	10	13 5/8	22	21	Rogers Lake, QC	Gregg D. Dunkel	Gregg D. Dunkel	1988	99
394 4/8	58 4/8	55 4/8	54 2/8	5 4/8	6 2/8	20 4/8	7 2/8	1/8	13 7/8	14	13	Fiddle Lake, QC	Robert Hammond	Robert Hammond	1967	101
394 4/8	49 1/8	50 6/8	41	5 6/8	5 4/8	18 5/8	1 1/8	12	1	13	16	Mistinibi Lake, QC	Paul E. Robey	Paul E. Robey	1981	101
394 2/8	52 6/8	52 6/8	46 5/8	4 2/8	4 2/8	19 3/8	19 1/8	4 4/8	13	16	19	Ungava Region, QC	James F. Tappan	James F. Tappan	1967	103
394 1/8	50 2/8	52 1/8	42 4/8	5 6/8	5 4/8	19 6/8	18 5/8	10 7/8	12 1/8	22	17	Lake Ballantyne, QC	Donald A. Cowe	Donald A. Cowe	1993	103
394 1/8	54 2/8	51 6/8	48	6	5 6/8	5	18	4/8	15 2/8	13	21	Ungava Bay, QC	Nancy J. Alward	Nancy J. Alward	1988	105
394	50 7/8	54 2/8	40 1/8	4 7/8	5	16 7/8	9 4/8	12 5/8	1/8	22	16	George River, QC	Rick Ullery	Rick Ullery	1975	106
393 6/8	55 6/8	50 3/8	52 4/8	5 1/8	5 3/8	17 4/8	15 5/8	4 3/8	9 7/8	12	14	Ungava Bay, QC	Arthur Bashore	Arthur Bashore	1971	107
393 5/8	45 1/8	57 4/8	53 5/8	6 1/8	6 2/8	18 2/8	17 5/8	14 4/8	11 3/8	17	13	George River, QC	Michael J. Merritt	Michael J. Merritt	1978	107
393 5/8	47 7/8	42 1/8	41 7/8	5 3/8	5 3/8	18 4/8	16 7/8	15 4/8	11 1/8	24	26	Caniapiscau River, QC	Donald J. Coughlin	Donald J. Coughlin	1995	107
393 3/8	55 3/8	49 5/8	30	5 1/8	5 1/8	18 7/8	16 2/8	14	11 7/8	27	22	Petite Baleine River, QC	Gary A. Borton	Gary A. Borton	1995	110
393 2/8	52 2/8	56 6/8	48 4/8	5 6/8	4 4/8	19 1/8	18 2/8	9 7/8	14	15	19	Lake Natuak, QC	Dale Stangil	Dale Stangil	1989	111
392 6/8	55	52 4/8	52 5/8	5 2/8	5 2/8	18 5/8	17 5/8	6 4/8	8 7/8	20	17	Lake Consigny, QC	Thomas L. Vaux	Thomas L. Vaux	1988	112
392 6/8	48	53 4/8	45 6/8	5 2/8	5 2/8	17 3/8	7 2/8	5 3/8	14	20	20	Schefferville, QC	Robert Henn	Robert Henn	1979	113
392 4/8	52 4/8	47	35 2/8	4 4/8	4 4/8	17 4/8	17 4/8	14	13 3/8	24	25	George River, QC	Kerry W. Blanton	Kerry W. Blanton	1983	114
392 4/8	50 7/8	53 4/8	44 7/8	5 2/8	5 2/8	18 5/8	17 3/8	12 2/8	1/8	16	14	Caniapiscau River, QC	Michael E. Ingold	Michael E. Ingold	1988	114
392 4/8	57 3/8	52 4/8	52 7/8	6	5 4/8	12	11 6/8	10 6/8	12 6/8	15	17	Nulluluak Lake, QC	Charles L. McConn	Charles L. McConn	1993	114
392 3/8	51 4/8	57 1/8	43 4/8	5 4/8	5 6/8	16 7/8	18 2/8	2 4/8	13	19	20	Ungava Region, QC	Frank J. Blaha, Jr.	Frank J. Blaha, Jr.	1978	117
392 3/8	51 2/8	51 2/8	44 6/8	4 6/8	4 6/8	1 4/8	14 6/8	1/8	12 6/8	19	19	Baleine River, QC	John D. Sheaffer	John D. Sheaffer	1988	117
392 3/8	51	50 5/8	46 1/8	4 7/8	5 7/8	23	21 5/8	14 2/8	5 7/8	16	19	Pons River, QC	Louis J. Lorenzo	Louis J. Lorenzo	1991	117

Score										Points R	Points L	Locality	Hunter	Owner	Date Killed	Rank
392 1/8	56 6/8	55 2/8	40 5/8	4 6/8	4 6/8	3 5/8	20 4/8	1/8	15 6/8	15	23	Tunulik River, QC	Salvatore A. Gusmano	Salvatore A. Gusmano	1981	120
392 1/8	55	53 4/8	41	5 6/8	5 6/8	12 4/8	16 4/8	3 7/8	14	15	18	George River, QC	Donald F. Senter	Donald F. Senter	1983	120
391 7/8	56 3/8	56	51 3/8	6 1/8	6 2/8	16 3/8	19 6/8	1/8	13 4/8	15	18	George River, QC	Alex Kariotakis	Alex Kariotakis	1974	122
391 4/8	60 4/8	57	54 7/8	5 3/8	5 3/8	15	19 3/8	2 4/8	13 6/8	13	15	Tunulik River, QC	Kenneth J. Gerstung	Kenneth J. Gerstung	1979	123
391 2/8	49 2/8	48 3/8	46 4/8	5 6/8	5 6/8	15 1/8	16 1/8	9 4/8	12 6/8	24	24	Kakiattukallak Lake, QC	Dale E. Toweill	Dale E. Toweill	1994	124
391	48 3/8	47 2/8	39 2/8	5 2/8	5 2/8	15 1/8	18 2/8	13 2/8	13 4/8	24	19	Wolf Lake, QC	Robert G. Burkhouse	Robert G. Burkhouse	1993	125
390 5/8	54	54 4/8	47 4/8	6 4/8	6 7/8	8	20	1/8	13 4/8	15	17	Mistinibi Lake, QC	Thomas J. Merkley	Thomas J. Merkley	1979	126
390 5/8	51 3/8	51 2/8	53 7/8	5 4/8	5 4/8	14 1/8	17	8	13 5/8	16	21	Agnew River, QC	Walter Brennen	Walter Brennen	1996	126
390 4/8	54	55 2/8	42 1/8	5 5/8	5 4/8	18 4/8	14 6/8	12	6 5/8	14	14	George River, QC	James E. Prevost	James E. Prevost	1979	128
390 4/8	49 6/8	52 2/8	48 5/8	4 7/8	4 5/8	17 2/8	10 7/8	10 5/8	1/8	18	18	Caniapiscau River, QC	John W. Flies	John W. Flies	1990	128
390 3/8	54	52 4/8	47 2/8	6 1/8	6 3/8		14 6/8		12 5/8	14	17	George River, QC	John Daniels	John Daniels	1972	130
390	53	55	46 4/8	5 4/8	5 2/8	15 4/8	18 4/8	1 2/8	14	12	16	Schefferville, QC	Samuel March, Jr.	Samuel March, Jr.	1982	131
389 7/8	54 2/8	56 3/8	48 4/8	5 7/8	5 7/8	15 6/8	12 4/8	9 5/8	1 5/8	18	16	Ford Lake, QC	Carl F. Gernold	Carl F. Gernold	1989	132
389 6/8	56 5/8	55 4/8	46 4/8	5 2/8	5 2/8	13 3/8	18 4/8	1	15 1/8	13	21	Echo Lake, QC	James T. Luxem	James T. Luxem	1993	133
389 5/8	50 4/8	49 6/8	42 1/8	5 4/8	5 2/8	14 3/8	18 4/8	9 4/8	16 1/8	19	21	Lake Ronald, QC	Christopher H. Kantianis	Christopher H. Kantianis	1995	134
389 5/8	48 7/8	49 5/8	46 1/8	4 7/8	4 7/8	2 5/8	21	1/8	16 6/8	14	20	Pons River, QC	Henry R. Binette	Henry R. Binette	1973	134
389 4/8	48 3/8	51 5/8	39 6/8	6	5 3/8	6	19 5/8	2	17 6/8	21	25	Ungava Region, QC	Eugene M. Decker	Eugene M. Decker	1983	136
389 4/8	48 4/8	49 4/8	40 5/8	5 6/8	5 5/8	20 1/8	18 1/8	6 6/8	14	16	21	Mistinibi Lake, QC	Don L. Corley	Don L. Corley	1995	136
389 4/8	53 1/8	58 4/8	41 7/8	5 7/8	5 5/8	13 4/8	17 7/8	6 6/8	14	12	14	Potier River, QC	Donald L. Sagner	Donald L. Sagner	1987	136
389 1/8	51 2/8	50 6/8	40 4/8	7 4/8	7 1/8	6 7/8	14 2/8	13 2/8	10 5/8	16	16	Tunulic River, QC	George Dempsey	George Dempsey	1990	139
388 6/8	53 3/8	57	42	7 1/8	7 1/8	18 5/8	17 4/8	13 2/8	1 7/8	23	13	George River, QC	Rodney A. Scott	Rodney A. Scott	1987	140
388 4/8	52 7/8	52 5/8	58 1/8	5 7/8	5 5/8	17 4/8	14 4/8	12 1/8	10	18	17	Koksoak River, QC	Charlie D. Todd	Charlie D. Todd	1987	141
388	55	54 5/8	53	5 5/8	5 2/8	21 5/8	18 3/8	6 5/8	1/8	15	12	Caniapiscau River, QC	Henry O. Fromm	Henry O. Fromm	1985	142
387 7/8	52 1/8	42 7/8	42 7/8	6 1/8	6 2/8	2 2/8	17 4/8	1	13 1/8	21	22	George River, QC	Michael Yeck	Michael Yeck	1987	143
387 7/8	53 2/8	52 1/8	55 1/8	5 3/8	5 3/8	18	15	17	17	17	23	George River, QC	John Downing	John Downing	1987	143
387 6/8	52 1/8	53 3/8	37 4/8	5 5/8	5 5/8	18 5/8	18 2/8	13	6 2/8	14	19	Ungava Bay, QC	Fred N. Huston, Sr.	Fred N. Huston, Sr.	1988	145
387 5/8	53 2/8	56	53	5 2/8	5 2/8	12 6/8	14 5/8	12 6/8	1	17	14	Ungava Bay, QC	Phil N. Alward	Phil N. Alward	1989	146
387 5/8	56 5/8	57 2/8	46 7/8	7 1/8	5 7/8	10 5/8	16 1/8	5 7/8	13 2/8	17	14	Abloviak Fjord, QC	Frederick S. Fish	Frederick S. Fish	1987	146
387 4/8	42 2/8	39 5/8	47 7/8	5 4/8	5 4/8	13 2/8	17 2/8	11 7/8	9 5/8	18	18	Delay River, QC	Larry E. Smith	Larry E. Smith	1988	148
387 3/8	44 5/8	47 2/8	45 2/8	5 3/8	5 3/8	16 5/8	18 6/8	14 6/8	9 5/8	18	20	Whale River, QC	Michael Karboski	Michael Karboski	1986	148
387 1/8	53 4/8	53 4/8	61 1/8	5 7/8	5 7/8	17 5/8	17	14 6/8	11 4/8	14	18	Tunulik Lake, QC	Jay G. St. Charles	Jay G. St. Charles	1984	150
386 7/8	53 4/8	54 7/8	47	5 7/8	5 7/8	1	17	1/8	14	14	18	Tunulik River, QC	Larry Hoff	Larry Hoff	1979	151
386 3/8	54 3/8	54 7/8	47 3/8	6 6/8	6 4/8	18 6/8	7	14 5/8	1/8	17	14	George River, QC	Arthur C. Sadowski	Arthur C. Sadowski	1980	152
386 1/8	49 6/8	49 4/8	44 1/8	5	5	12 7/8	18 3/8	2 7/8	14 5/8	17	17	Mistinibi Lake, QC	W.T. Yoshimoto	W.T. Yoshimoto	1991	153
385 5/8	52 1/8	53	53	5 4/8	5 4/8	12 1/8	17 2/8	1/8	12 1/8	14	15	Pons River, QC	George D. Berger	George D. Berger	1990	154
385 5/8	57	58 1/8	48 6/8	5	5 2/8	4 5/8	20 4/8	1/8	13 6/8	16	14	Koksoak River, QC	Donald E. Eberman	Donald E. Eberman	1986	155
385 2/8	46 4/8	46 4/8	48 1/8	5 1/8	5 4/8	19 3/8	18 2/8	10 3/8	13 6/8	20	14	George River, QC	David G. Noble	David G. Noble	1982	156
385 1/8	51	49 7/8	47 1/8	6	6	10 3/8	15 3/8	10	20	George River, QC	James J. McBride	James J. McBride	1983	157
385	57 4/8	56	50 4/8	5 1/8	5	20 6/8	20 7/8	6	5	15	20	George River, QC	Daniel B. Kahle	Daniel B. Kahle	1990	158
385	55	55 1/8	54 4/8	5 1/8	5 1/8	19 3/8	16 3/8	12 3/8	11 5/8	19	15	Delay River, QC	Dan E. Stimmell	Dan E. Stimmell	1994	159
384 7/8	46 1/8	45 7/8	57 6/8	5 2/8	5 2/8	19 7/8	19 4/8	11 7/8	11 4/8	17	16	Pons Lake, QC	George P. Mann	George P. Mann	1991	160
384 5/8	50	50 1/8	50 1/8	4 7/8	4 7/8	21 5/8	14 5/8	16 5/8	1/8	20	13	Lake Demitte, QC	Arthur J. Petroff	Arthur J. Petroff	1979	161
384 4/8	53 4/8	52 1/8	46 6/8	6	5 7/8	17 3/8	12 7/8	12 7/8	18	15	Mistinibi Lake, QC	Stewart N. Shaft	Stewart N. Shaft	1986	162
384 4/8	50 4/8	52 1/8	48	5 2/8	5 2/8	7 3/8	12 7/8	7 3/8	19	19	Abloviak Fiord, QC	Brian L. Dam	Brian L. Dam	1987	162
384 4/8	46 4/8	46 5/8	42 4/8	4 7/8	4 7/8	16	17 5/8	7	10 5/8	18	19	Baleine River, QC	Elmer R. Luce, Jr.	Elmer R. Luce, Jr.	1996	162
384 3/8	48 3/8	45 6/8	36 3/8	4 4/8	4 8/8	20 3/8	17 2/8	4 5/8	11	14	15	Pons River, QC	Louie Kitcoff	Louie Kitcoff	1991	165
384 2/8	45 2/8	46 6/8	49	5 2/8	5 4/8	17 3/8	15 1/8	8 5/8	19	23	Baleine River, QC	Elmer R. Luce, Jr.	Elmer R. Luce, Jr.	1987	166

QUEBEC-LABRADOR CARIBOU

Rangifer tarandus from Quebec and Labrador

Score	Length of Main Beam R	Length of Main Beam L	Inside Spread	Circ. at Smallest Place Between Brow and Bez Points R	Circ. L	Length of Brow Points R	Length of Brow Points L	Width of Brow Points R	Width of Brow Points L	Number of Points R	Number of Points L	Locality	Hunter	Owner	Date Killed	Rank
384 2/8	47 6/8	51 4/8	40 6/8	6	5 3/8	16 7/8	18 1/8	13 5/8	14	20	16	Pons Lake, QC	Jonathan S. Warke	Jonathan S. Warke	1991	166
383 7/8	52 4/8	51 2/8	45 3/8	5 2/8	5	18 4/8	19 3/8	4 3/8	14	15	14	George River Lodge, QC	Clayton C. Dovey, Jr.	Clayton C. Dovey, Jr.	1969	168
383 7/8	47 3/8	49 5/8	46 7/8	4 6/8	5 1/8	15	15 7/8	10 6/8	15 5/8	18	23	Lake Loudin, QC	Roger M. Schmitt	Roger M. Schmitt	1988	168
383 5/8	51 4/8	52 2/8	53 5/8	5 1/8	5 3/8	19 1/8	15 7/8	13 4/8	1 1/8	16	13	Ungava Bay, QC	Fred S. DeHaan	Fred S. DeHaan	1986	170
383 4/8	51 4/8	50 7/8	55	5 5/8	5 6/8	19 1/8	17 7/8	10 6/8	2	12	12	Tunulic River, QC	Peter Smith	Peter Smith	1982	171
383 4/8	50 3/8	50	36 1/8	5 3/8	5 1/8	17 2/8	18 6/8	12 7/8	11 6/8	15	17	Caniapiscau River, QC	Roy Jebb, Jr.	Roy Jebb, Jr.	1984	171
383 4/8	46 2/8	43 6/8	40 2/8	5	5	18 2/8	18 6/8	13	15	16	23	Ungava Pen., QC	Jon D. Johnson	Jon D. Johnson	1995	171
383 2/8	50 2/8	50 7/8	50 1/8	5 7/8	6 1/8	4 5/8	16 1/8	12 4/8	1/8	16	19	Abloviak Fjord, QC	Steven N. Mitchell	Steven N. Mitchell	1991	174
382 7/8	51 6/8	53 3/8	42 6/8	6 6/8	6 2/8	17 3/8	6 7/8	1 4/8	14 7/8	15	14	George River, QC	Ralph Zampella	Ralph Zampella	1972	175
382 7/8	49 7/8	49 6/8	43	4 7/8	5 1/8	20 1/8	17 7/8	16 7/8	15 4/8	21	23	Glinel Lake, QC	Howard F. Lemon	Howard F. Lemon	1995	175
382 7/8	48 1/8	48 6/8	46 5/8	4 4/8	4 4/8	12 6/8	14 7/8	2 6/8	7 5/8	15	17	Nulluluak Lake, QC	Steve A. Rivet	Steve A. Rivet	1996	175
382 5/8	50 4/8	50 5/8	33	5 5/8	5 6/8	17 1/8	15 1/8	10 5/8	7 2/8	13	17	Lake Diane, QC	Wayne R. Martka	Wayne R. Martka	1990	178
382 5/8	53	56	39 6/8	4 6/8	4 4/8	23 1/8	19 4/8	16 2/8	7	18	22	Caniapiscau River, QC	Greg L. Farnworth	Greg L. Farnworth	1993	178
382 5/8	52 1/8	51 4/8	42 5/8	4 4/8	4 5/8	20 4/8	22	14 3/8	16 7/8	16	17	Bienville Lake, QC	L. Reed Breight	L. Reed Breight	1997	178
382 3/8	53 5/8	53 5/8	53 6/8	5 5/8	5 6/8	4 2/8	15 1/8	1/8	12	17	23	Mistinibi Lake, QC	W.T. Yoshimoto	W.T. Yoshimoto	1979	181
382 3/8	48 1/8	50 2/8	45 5/8	6 6/8	5 7/8	15 5/8	17 7/8	12 3/8	13 5/8	16	24	Wayne Lake, QC	Timothy D. Gildersleeve	Timothy D. Gildersleeve	1987	181
381 7/8	59 3/8	59 1/8	54 4/8	5 4/8	6 2/8	16	1 2/8	10 2/8	5 7/8	19	14	Ungava Region, QC	John R. Oakes	John R. Oakes	1971	183
381 7/8	59	55 7/8	53 2/8	5 1/8	5 1/8	19 5/8	1 2/8	1/8	16 1/8	13	16	Nulluluak Lake, QC	Walter J. Manning	Walter J. Manning	1988	183
381 6/8	47 5/8	48 2/8	45 2/8	5 2/8	5 2/8	16 5/8	16 3/8	6 4/8	8	22	23	Indian Lake, QC	Donald A. Lawrence	Donald A. Lawrence	1987	185
381 6/8	51 2/8	51 1/8	41 5/8	5 1/8	5 2/8	18 5/8	14 2/8	11 4/8	10	19	18	Ungava Bay, QC	James B. Wessinger	James B. Wessinger	1987	185
381 6/8	53 7/8	51 2/8	42 2/8	4 6/8	4 6/8	18 2/8	15 4/8	15 1/8	6 5/8	15	13	Pons River, QC	Chris S. Marshall	Chris S. Marshall	1990	185
381 4/8	48 6/8	47 5/8	38 5/8	5	5	2 4/8	16 2/8	4/8	14 5/8	16	18	Kamaywapakich Lake, QC	Steve T. Bartolomucci	Steve T. Bartolomucci	1994	188
381 3/8	52	52 3/8	60	5 1/8	5	14 3/8	4 3/8	4/8	14 5/8	11	15	Ungava Bay, QC	Edward J. Pallay	Edward J. Pallay	1982	189
381 3/8	53 6/8	53 6/8	46	7	7	1 4/8	20 6/8	1/8	14 7/8	15	16	Kogaluk, LB	Basil C. Bradbury	Basil C. Bradbury	1949	190
381 2/8	51 6/8	54 4/8	45 4/8	5 4/8	5 4/8	9	17 6/8	1	12 6/8	19	25	Caniapiscau River, QC	Donald P. Travis	Donald P. Travis	1986	190
381 2/8	49 3/8	50 5/8	45 5/8	5 1/8	5 2/8	16 2/8	14 5/8	9 1/8	8 5/8	17	18	Wayne Lake, QC	Vincent P. Cina, Sr.	Vincent P. Cina, Sr.	1990	190
381 1/8	48 3/8	49 1/8	53 2/8	4 5/8	4 5/8	19 4/8	18 2/8	13 2/8	15	17	21	Tudor Lake, QC	Collins F. Kellogg, Jr.	Collins F. Kellogg, Jr.	1970	193
381 1/8	56	53 3/8	47 2/8	6	5 6/8	16 4/8	2	8 4/8	1/8	17	15	Koksoak River, QC	Arthur J. Pelon	Arthur J. Pelon	1984	193
381	53 5/8	55 2/8	48 6/8	6	4 7/8	5 1/8	19	13 4/8	4 7/8	17	13	Ungava Bay, QC	Jeff S. Koster	Jeff S. Koster	1990	195
381	49 4/8	50 3/8	45 6/8	5	5 1/8	18 4/8	18 4/8	9 4/8	13 4/8	18	13	Riviere Aux Feuilles, QC	Wayne F. Kilgore	Wayne F. Kilgore	1992	195
380 7/8	54 4/8	55 6/8	49 4/8	5 7/8	5 6/8	18 4/8	19 4/8	1/8	15 3/8	16	18	Tunulik River, QC	Joseph P. Toth	Joseph P. Toth	1986	197
380 6/8	47 5/8	48 6/8	44 3/8	6	6	17	12	8 2/8	1 6/8	14	18	Mistinibi Lake, QC	Paul F. Barnhart	Paul F. Barnhart	1980	198
380 6/8	53 5/8	54	46 7/8	6 2/8	5 6/8	16 4/8	6 1/8	13 5/8	1/8	15	14	Lake May, QC	Steven L. Fair	Steven L. Fair	1993	198
380 5/8	52 7/8	55 5/8	53 3/8	6 2/8	5 5/8	17 2/8	16 4/8	10 3/8	5 1/8	16	19	Fiddle Lake, QC	Herb Dittmar	Herb Dittmar	1966	200
380 5/8	51 7/8	51 3/8	47 6/8	5 4/8	5 3/8	18 6/8	18 6/8	4 6/8	12 7/8	18	16	Lake Gerido, QC	Dan D. Boy	Dan D. Boy	1987	200
380 5/8	45 3/8	45 3/8	44 4/8	5 2/8	4 7/8	13	17 7/8	6 5/8	13 5/8	14	16	Ungava Bay, QC	William G. Freed	William G. Freed	1992	200

Score	L.M.B. R	L.M.B. L	Inside Spread	Locality	Hunter	Owner	Date	Rank
380 4/8	58	60 2/8	44 4/8	Whale River, QC	John A. Yeager	John A. Yeager	1979	203
380 4/8	55	55 5/8	50 3/8	Pons River, QC	Ronald S. Newman	Ronald S. Newman	1990	203
380 2/8	53 4/8	51	48 6/8	Fort Chimo, QC	B.N. McCrum	B.N. McCrum	1967	205
380 2/8	53 4/8	55	39 6/8	George River, QC	Roger R. Card	Roger R. Card	1980	205
380 2/8	62 4/8	65	55 5/8	George River, QC	Randal L. Diehl	Randal L. Diehl	1980	205
379 7/8	49 7/8	46 5/8	44 2/8	Serigny River, QC	Gary A. Perin	Gary A. Perin	1987	208
379 7/8	49	50 2/8	50 2/8	Baleine River, QC	Michael C. Dysh	Michael C. Dysh	1990	208
379 6/8	42 7/8	47 2/8	41 6/8	Wade Lake, LB	Unknown	Gerard Beaulieu	1985	210
379 6/8	49 4/8	49 2/8	42 5/8	Long Lake, QC	Ted K. Jaycox	Ted K. Jaycox	1986	210
379 6/8	45 6/8	47	44 4/8	Caniapiscau River, QC	John W. Czerwinski	John W. Czerwinski	1987	210
379 6/8	45 7/8	50 1/8	48 2/8	Pons River, QC	Christopher J. Cass	Christopher J. Cass	1993	210
379 5/8	52 1/8	54 6/8	52 7/8	George River, QC	Frank R. Heller	Frank R. Heller	1978	214
379 3/8	60 2/8	59 7/8	50 6/8	Tunulik River, QC	Thomas L. Cash	Thomas L. Cash	1988	215
379 3/8	62 2/8	64 2/8	41	Ungava Bay, QC	Bruce E. Cepicky	Bruce E. Cepicky	1988	215
378 6/8	56	56 6/8	56 6/8	Ford River, QC	Vivian Sleight	Vivian Sleight	1973	217
378 6/8	54	52 4/8	40 4/8	Tunulliq Lake, QC	Scott M. Showalter	Scott M. Showalter	1982	217
378 3/8	45 6/8	50 1/8	41	Wendell Lake, QC	Terry E. Lefever	Terry E. Lefever	1988	219
378 2/8	54 3/8	53 5/8	40	Ungava Bay, QC	James B. Wessinger	James B. Wessinger	1987	220
378 2/8	46 5/8	47 4/8	53 7/8	Martine Lake, QC	Robert A. Ritter	Robert A. Ritter	1991	220
378 1/8	53	44	44	Ungava Pen., QC	Theodore M. Schall	Theodore M. Schall	1985	222
378	45 5/8	51 2/8	49 6/8	George River, QC	Dick Ullery	Dick Ullery	1975	223
377 7/8	51	45 4/8	40 6/8	Lake Brisson, QC	David Read	David Read	1983	224
377 7/8	49 3/8	49 7/8	40 4/8	Ungava Bay, QC	Joseph Mannino	Joseph Mannino	1985	224
377 7/8	45 3/8	48	42 7/8	Maricourt Lake, QC	James O. Kingsley	James O. Kingsley	1992	224
377 7/8	47 2/8	45 7/8	47 1/8	Caniapiscau River, QC	Daniel C. Craft	Daniel C. Craft	1993	224
377 7/8	45 7/8	47 2/8	41 6/8	Kamaywapakich Lake, QC	Christopher Vozzo	Christopher Vozzo	1997	224
377 6/8	51 1/8	45 1/8	41 5/8	George River, QC	Normand Poulin	Normand Poulin	1976	229
377 3/8	45 1/8	49 5/8	43 1/8	Ungava Bay, QC	Arlo J. Spiess	Arlo J. Spiess	1985	230
377 2/8	56 2/8	48 4/8	42 5/8	Lac du Rougemont, QC	Albert O. Toaldo	Albert O. Toaldo	1992	231
377 1/8	53 6/8	58 6/8	49 7/8	Mistinibi Lake, QC	James H. Meckes, Jr.	James H. Meckes, Jr.	1980	232
377 1/8	55 6/8	54 5/8	48	Rainbow Lake, QC	David J. Richey, Sr.	David J. Richey, Sr.	1990	232
377	48 1/8	55 5/8	49 4/8	George River, QC	Stanley R. Smith	Stanley R. Smith	1975	234
376 7/8	51 5/8	49 6/8	51	Lake Lachine, QC	Edward A. Mertins	Edward A. Mertins	1990	235
376 6/8	50 1/8	53 5/8	52 5/8	George River, QC	C.J. McElroy	C.J. McElroy	1969	236
376 5/8	45 6/8	50 6/8	45 4/8	Ungava Bay, QC	John D. Powers	John D. Powers	1981	237
376 4/8	40 1/8	48 7/8	48	Schefferville, QC	Carl J. Los	Carl J. Los	1970	238
376 3/8	53	42 4/8	28	George River, QC	Norman Clausen	Norman Clausen	1973	239
376 2/8	49 5/8	53 6/8	46 2/8	Ungava Region, QC	Don Peters	Don Peters	1969	240
376	50 3/8	50 4/8	47 6/8	Schefferville, QC	Charles Lanzarone	Charles Lanzarone	1980	241
375 5/8	61 1/8	50 4/8	44	Lake Patu, QC	Burnell R. Kauffman	Burnell R. Kauffman	1985	242
375 4/8	55 7/8	58 6/8	41	Du Gue River, QC	Arden Bancroft	Arden Bancroft	1989	243
375 3/8	51 2/8	54 1/8	55 3/8	North Tudor Lake, QC	Collins F. Kellogg	Collins F. Kellogg	1970	244
375 2/8	50 2/8	52 3/8	46 4/8	Caniapiscau River, QC	Gerald A. Gredell	Gerald A. Gredell	1987	245
375 1/8	56 2/8	52 2/8	37 3/8	George River, QC	Norma J. Laros	Norma J. Laros	1975	246
375	52 2/8	56 1/8	55 3/8	Ungava Bay, QC	Ronald R. Pomery	Ronald R. Pomery	1986	247
375	52 2/8	53 7/8	46 1/8	Fritz Lake, QC	Donald A. Boyer	Donald A. Boyer	1978	248
375	48 6/8	52 3/8	40	Ungava Bay, QC	Glenn M. Smith	Glenn M. Smith	1986	248

QUEBEC-LABRADOR CARIBOU

Rangifer tarandus from Quebec and Labrador

Score	Length of Main Beam R	L	Inside Spread	Circumference at Smallest Place Between Brow and Bez Points R	L	Length of Brow Points R	L	Width of Brow Points R	L	Number of Points R	L	Locality	Hunter	Owner	Date Killed	Rank
375	50 4/8	50 2/8	52 2/8	5 1/8	5 2/8	16 2/8	18 2/8	6 6/8	13 2/8	11	11	Caniapiscau River, QC	Ronald Hurlburt	Ronald Hurlburt	1987	248
375	53 4/8	52 3/8	36	5 1/8	5 2/8	12 4/8	19 1/8	1/8	16	15	18	Tunulik River, QC	Kenneth G. Straub	Kenneth G. Straub	1989	248
441 7/8*	52 3/8	51 7/8	44	5 6/8	5 7/8	21 6/8	20 5/8	6 7/8	14 5/8	25	23	Lake Arbique, QC	Larry R. Waldron	Larry R. Waldron	1993	
409 2/8*	50 1/8	51 6/8	40 6/8	5 7/8	5 5/8	2 1/8	18 6/8	1 2/8	11 1/8	28	23	Lake Demitte, QC	Eric P. Obernberger	Eric P. Obernberger	1993	
405 1/8*	51 2/8	52	52	4 6/8	4 6/8	15 7/8	17	2 4/8	12 6/8	16	16	Nullualuk Lake, QC	Henry C. Gilbertson	Henry C. Gilbertson	1988	
400 5/8*	47 2/8	47 7/8	45 1/8	5 3/8	5 1/8	17 4/8	18 6/8	8 6/8	16 2/8	24	26	Marin Lake, QC	Wilhelm Hollstein	Wilhelm Hollstein	1995	

* Final score is subject to revision by additional verifying measurements.

CATEGORY
QUEBEC-LABRADOR
CARIBOU

SCORE
416-1/8

HUNTER
THOMAS R. CONRARDY

LOCATION
LAKE AMICHINATWAYACH,
QC

DATE OF KILL
SEPTEMBER 1995

CATEGORY
QUEBEC-LABRADOR
CARIBOU

SCORE
379-7/8

HUNTER
MICHAEL C. DYSH

LOCATION
BALEINE RIVER, QC

DATE OF KILL
SEPTEMBER 1990

CATEGORY
QUEBEC-LABRADOR
CARIBOU

SCORE
386-3/8

HUNTER
W.T. YOSHIMOTO

LOCATION
MISTINIBI LAKE, QC

DATE OF KILL
SEPTEMBER 1980

PRONGHORN
WORLD'S RECORD

Good news finally arrived for Arizona rancher, Michael J. O'Haco, Jr., in August 1985 when he received a pronghorn permit after having been rejected 19 previous times. O'Haco and hunting partner, Phil Donnelly, immediately set out to scout the unit he had drawn for in Coconino County.

O'Haco also did a little research on pronghorn (*Antilocapra americana*), which ended up giving him the edge he needed in relocating the one big buck that he knew to be exceptional. After spotting the buck a week before the hunt, the hunters kept a close eye on the potential trophy all the way up to the September afternoon and evening before the hunt.

"We drove to within a mile of where the buck and his does had bedded down for the night. It was still an hour before daylight. We discussed how we would make our stalk, and tried to visualize all aspects of the stalk so there would be no mistakes.

"Finally, it was light enough to make a move. We had to crawl over a fence and then use the scattered cedar trees for cover. We moved slowly. When we were about 300 yards from where we had seen them the night before, I spotted the does but couldn't see the buck. Now we were crawling slowly and easily. When we were about 200 yards from the pronghorn, something caught my eye to the left. It was a buck. Phil was about 20 yards to my left. The buck was looking straight at me, with a slight right turn, and I could see just part of a shoulder. Not being able to tell if it was the big one, I whispered to

Phil, 'Is that him?' I knew the buck was big, but I couldn't see the prong from my angle. Phil said, 'That's him.' I shot. The buck broke and ran. I thought I had missed.

"I jammed another shell into my rifle. The buck slowed down, then stopped and looked back. I shot again, nothing. The adrenaline was really pumping through my body, and I couldn't hold the cross hairs steady. Phil said to use his shoulder for a rest, but he was shaking worse than I was. I took a deep breath, got my composure, and squeezed."

Two days later, O'Haco had Jerry Walters, an official Arizona state measurer, sized up the buck. Walters came up with a 95-2/8 green score. After the 60-day drying period, the buck was officially scored by Mike Cupell, a Boone and Crockett measurer for entry into the records program. It was beginning to look like O'Haco just might have a new World's Record on his hands.

At the 19th Awards Program, O'Haco's World's Record trophy, scoring 93-4/8 points, and the fine, fair chase hunt for it, received special recognition with the Sagamore Hill Award, the highest award given by the Club. This was the first time ever that the Sagamore Hill Award was bestowed upon a pronghorn trophy. ■

COLUMN 2

	Left Horn	Difference
	17 4/8	2/8
	7	1/8
		3/8
		1/8
		1/8
	2/8	2/8
	47 6/8	1 2/8

TOTALS   47

Exact Locality Where Killed: Coconino Co., AZ

Date Killed: Sept. 20, 1985

Owner: Michael J. O'Haco, Jr.

Owner's Address:

Guide's Name and Address:

Remarks: (Mention Any Abnormalities)

	Column 2
ADD	94 6/8
SUBTRACT	1 2/8
FINAL SCORE	93 4/8

Photograph courtesy of Michael J. O'Haco, Jr.

TROPHY INFO

RANK
World's Record

SCORE
93 4/8

LOCATION
Coconino Co., Az

HUNTER
Michael J. O'Haco, Jr.

OWNER
Michael J. O'Haco, Jr.

DATE KILLED
1985

certified this trophy on 05/13/8
MM/DD/YY

Vegas
CITY

NV
STATE

Walter H. White
PRINT NAME

Walter H. White
MEASURER

I.D. Number

to the best of my knowledge and belief, made in accordance with the instruct

Nevada State Museum

PRONGHORN
WORLD'S RECORD SCORECHART

All measurements must be made with a 1/4-inch wide flexible steel tape to the nearest one-eighth of an inch, without reduction. Official measurements cannot be taken until horns have air dried for at least 60 days after the animal was killed.

A. Tip to Tip Spread is measured between tips of horns.

B. Inside Spread of Main Beams is measured at a right angle to the center line of the skull, at widest point between main beams.

C. Length of Horn is measured on the outside curve on the general line illustrated. The line taken will vary with different heads, depending on the direction of their curvature. Measure along the center of the outer curve from tip of horn to a point in line with the lowest edge of the base, using a straight edge to establish the line end.

D-1. Circumference of Base is measured at a right angle to axis of horn. **Do not** follow irregular edge of horn; the line of measurement must be entirely on horn material.

D-2-3-4. Divide measurement C of longer horn by four. Starting at base, mark **both** horns at these quarters (even though the other horn is shorter) and measure circumferences at these marks. If the prong interferes with D-2, move the measurement down to just below the swelling of the prong. If D-3 falls in the swelling of the prong, move the measurement up to just above the prong.

E. Length of Prong: Measure from the tip of the prong **along the upper edge** of the outer side to the horn; then continue around the horn to a point at the rear of the horn where a straight edge across the back of both horns touches the horn, with the latter part being at a right angle to the long axis of horn.

Records of
North American
Big Game

250 Station Drive
Missoula, MT 59801
(406) 542-1888

MINIMUM SCORES
AWARDS ALL-TIME
80   82

BOONE AND CROCKETT CLUB®

OFFICIAL SCORING SYSTEM FOR NORTH AMERICAN BIG GAME TROPHIES

PRONGHORN

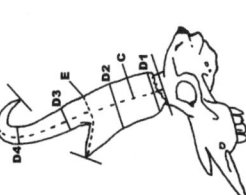

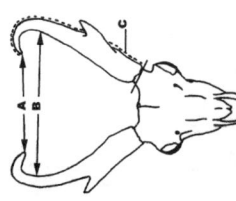

SEE OTHER SIDE FOR INSTRUCTIONS		COLUMN 1	COLUMN 2	COLUMN 3
		Right Horn	Left Horn	Difference
A. Tip to Tip Spread	8 1/8			
B. Inside Spread of Main Beams	12 5/8			
C. Length of Horn		17 6/8	17 4/8	2/8
D-1. Circumference of Base		6 7/8	7	1/8
D-2. Circumference at First Quarter		6 7/8	7 2/8	3/8
D-3. Circumference at Second Quarter		4 3/8	4 4/8	1/8
D-4. Circumference at Third Quarter		3 1/8	3 2/8	1/8
E. Length of Prong		8	8 2/8	2/8
TOTALS		47	47 6/8	1 2/8

ADD	Column 1	47	Exact Locality Where Killed: Coconino Co., AZ
	Column 2	47 6/8	Date Killed: Sept. 20, 1985 · Hunter: Michael J. O'Haco, Jr.
	Subtotal	94 6/8	Owner: Michael J. O'Haco, Jr. · Telephone #:
SUBTRACT Column 3		1 2/8	Owner's Address:
FINAL SCORE		93 4/8	Guide's Name and Address:
			Remarks: (Mention Any Abnormalities or Unique Qualities)

I, __Walter H. White__ , certify that I have measured this trophy on __05/13/86__
PRINT NAME   MM/DD/YYYY

at __Nevada State Museum__   __Las Vegas__   __NV__
STREET ADDRESS   CITY   STATE/PROVINCE

and that these measurements and data are, to the best of my knowledge and belief, made in accordance with the instructions given.

Witness: __George Tsukamoto__   Signature: __Walter H. White__   I.D. Number _____
                                            B&C OFFICIAL MEASURER

557

PRONGHORN

Antilocapra americana and related subspecies

MINIMUM SCORE 82

Score	Length of Horn R	Length of Horn L	Circumference of Base R	Circumference of Base L	Circumference at Third Quarter R	Circumference at Third Quarter L	Inside Spread	Tip to Tip Spread	Length of Prong R	Length of Prong L	Locality	Hunter	Owner	Date Killed	Rank
93 4/8	17 6/8	17 4/8	6 7/8	7	3 1/8	3 2/8	12 5/8	8 1/8	8	8 2/8	Coconino Co., AZ	Michael J. O'Haco, Jr.	Michael J. O'Haco, Jr.	1985	1
93	18 1/8	18 2/8	7 2/8	7	2 5/8	2 6/8	10 1/8	6 5/8	7 6/8	7 2/8	Yavapai Co., AZ	Edwin L. Wetzler	Loaned to B&C Natl. Coll.	1975	2
92 6/8	16 4/8	16 4/8	7 2/8	7 1/8	3 1/8	3 1/8	12 4/8	9 5/8	7 3/8	7 4/8	Coconino Co., AZ	Sam Jaksick, Jr.	Sam Jaksick, Jr.	1991	3
91 6/8	17 2/8	17 1/8	7 6/8	7 6/8	3 3/8	2 7/8	13 4/8	9	7	7 3/8	Coconino Co., AZ	Steven E. Hopkins	Steven E. Hopkins	1992	4
91 4/8	20 1/8	20	7 4/8	7	2 6/8	2 6/8	12	11 3/8	4 5/8	5 3/8	Arizona	Wilson Potter	Unknown	1899	5
91 4/8	15 1/8	15 2/8	7 7/8	7 7/8	3 2/8	3 4/8	10 4/8	9 4/8	7	7	Weld Co., CO	Bob Schneidmiller	Bob Schneidmiller	1965	5
91 4/8	17 1/8	17	7 3/8	7 1/8	3 3/8	3 2/8	13 5/8	10 1/8	4 4/8	4 7/8	Garfield Co., MT	Donald W. Yates	Donald W. Yates	1977	5
91 1/8	18 4/8	18 5/8	6 7/8	6 6/8	3	3	9	3 3/8	6 2/8	6 1/8	Lincoln Co., NM	Robert S. Guevara	Robert S. Guevara	1996	8
91	16 6/8	16 4/8	7 1/8	7 1/8	2 6/8	3	10 3/8	3	7 2/8	7 2/8	Carbon Co., WY	J. Ivan Kitch	J. Ivan Kitch	1964	9
91	16 2/8	15 6/8	7 1/8	7 1/8	3	3 1/8	14 1/8	11 7/8	5 6/8	5 5/8	Rawlins, WY	Fred Starling	Fred Starling	1967	9
91	17 7/8	17 5/8	6 7/8	6 7/8	2 5/8	2 5/8	14	8 2/8	7 1/8	7 3/8	Humboldt Co., NV	Steve W. Dustin	Steve W. Dustin	1990	9
90 6/8	16 2/8	16 4/8	6 4/8	7 4/8	2 5/8	2 5/8	17 2/8	15 2/8	7 5/8	7 5/8	Weston Co., WY	Allen Douglas	Richard J. Macy	1943	12
90 6/8	17 5/8	17 5/8	7 1/8	6 7/8	3 4/8	3 4/8	9 5/8	3 4/8	5 4/8	5 2/8	Catron Co., NM	John P. Grimmett	John P. Grimmett	1986	12
90 6/8	16 3/8	16 4/8	7	7 3/8	3 4/8	3 4/8	13 2/8	8 6/8	5 7/8	6 1/8	Natrona Co., WY	Richard J. Guthrie	Richard J. Guthrie	1989	12
90 4/8	18 1/8	18 3/8	6 5/8	6 5/8	2 6/8	2 6/8	10 3/8	2 7/8	7	6 4/8	Yavapai Co., AZ	Joe P. Fornara	Joe P. Fornara	1984	15
90 4/8	18 2/8	18 6/8	6 5/8	6 6/8	3	3	10 1/8	4	6	6	Hudspeth Co., TX	Walter O. Ford III	Walter O. Ford III	1994	15
90	19 4/8	19 5/8	7	7	2 7/8	3	10 1/8	8	4 7/8	4 6/8	Guano Creek, OR	E.C. Starr	E.C. Starr	1942	17
90	17	17 2/8	7	7	3 2/8	3 2/8	6	3 4/8	5 7/8	5 6/8	Yavapai Co., AZ	Marvin N. Zieser	Marvin N. Zieser	1995	17
89 6/8	18 3/8	18	6 5/8	6 4/8	2 6/8	2 7/8	9 4/8	4	7 1/8	7 3/8	Seligman, AZ	J.W. Johnson	J.W. Johnson	1959	19
89 6/8	17 5/8	17 6/8	7 3/8	7 1/8	2 6/8	2 6/8	11 1/8	6 5/8	6 1/8	6 2/8	Rawlins, WY	Mary C. Kircher	Mary C. Kircher	1961	19
89 6/8	17 2/8	17 4/8	7	7	2 6/8	2 6/8	12 5/8	11 1/8	7 4/8	7 2/8	Rosebud Co., MT	Jim Ollom	Jim Ollom	1973	19
89 6/8	18 2/8	18	7	6 7/8	3	2 7/8	9 7/8	3 3/8	6 3/8	6 3/8	Coconino Co., AZ	James W. Barrett	James W. Barrett	1987	19
89 6/8	18 7/8	19	6 1/8	6	3	3	12 4/8	8	6	5 6/8	Colfax Co., NM	Hudson DeCray	B&C National Collection	1989	19
89 6/8	16 6/8	17	7 4/8	7 5/8	3 1/8	3 3/8	10 2/8	5 1/8	6 4/8	6 2/8	Coconino Co., AZ	Sam Jaksick, Jr.	Sam Jaksick, Jr.	1993	19
89 6/8	16 5/8	16 2/8	7 3/8	7 3/8	3 3/8	3 2/8	11 1/8	5 2/8	6 1/8	6 1/8	Yavapai Co., AZ	Sam Jaksick, Jr.	Sam Jaksick, Jr.	1996	19
89 4/8	17 6/8	17 4/8	7 2/8	7 2/8	2 5/8	2	13 5/8	9 7/8	6 3/8	6	Ferris, WY	John T. Peddy	John T. Peddy	1957	26
89 4/8	17 2/8	17	7 1/8	7 1/8	3 2/8	3 2/8	12	8 5/8	6 5/8	5 6/8	Laramie Co., WY	Roy Vail	Roy Vail	1958	26
89 4/8	16	15 4/8	7 4/8	7 4/8	3 2/8	2 6/8	9 4/8	3 2/8	6 6/8	6 3/8	Sierra Co., NM	P.K. Colquitt, Jr.	Thomas V. Schrivner	1961	26
89 4/8	17 2/8	17 5/8	6 7/8	6 7/8	3	3	10 4/8	5	5 3/8	5 4/8	Humboldt Co., NV	Richard Steinmetz	Richard Steinmetz	1977	26
89 4/8	17 7/8	17 3/8	7 2/8	7 2/8	3 3/8	3 5/8	11 3/8	4 1/8	5 5/8	5 2/8	Uintah Co., UT	Charles A. Grimmett	Charles A. Grimmett	1988	26
89 4/8	17 6/8	17 4/8	7 4/8	7 1/8	3 6/8	3 6/8	11 1/8	1 5/8	5 1/8	6	Catron Co., NM	Brady J. Smith	Brady J. Smith	1996	26
89 2/8	18 6/8	18 4/8	6 5/8	6 5/8	2 6/8	3	7 6/8	4 4/8	6	5 2/8	Grant Co., NM	Jerry Saint	NM Dept. of Game & Fish	1975	32
89 2/8	17 1/8	17 1/8	7	7	3 1/8	3 1/8	9 6/8	6 6/8	5 7/8	6	Moffat Co., CO	Gerald Scott	Gerald Scott	1982	32
89 2/8	17 2/8	17 2/8	6 7/8	6 7/8	2 7/8	3	12 1/8	8 6/8	5 6/8	5 6/8	Cochise Co., AZ	Rene J. Dube, Jr.	Rene J. Dube, Jr.	1985	32
89 2/8	16 3/8	16 3/8	7 2/8	7 2/8	3	3	9 6/8	4 4/8	7 2/8	6 7/8	Hudspeth Co., TX	Jack E. Beal	Jack E. Beal	1987	32
89 2/8	17 4/8	17 1/8	6 6/8	6 6/8	2 5/8	2 4/8	12 5/8	8 6/8	7	7 1/8	Washoe Co., NV	Jaime L. Fuentes	Jaime L. Fuentes	1990	32
89 2/8	15 4/8	15 4/8	6 6/8	6 6/8	2 6/8	2 6/8	10	4 4/8	8	8	Washoe Co., NV	Marjorie A. Puryear	Marjorie A. Puryear	1990	32
89 2/8	17 2/8	17 1/8	7 4/8	7 4/8	2 6/8	2 7/8	11 7/8	4 7/8	6 2/8	5 7/8	Mora Co., NM	Michael R. Memmer	Michael R. Memmer	1991	32

Score	Length of Horn R	Length of Horn L	Circ. of Base R	Circ. of Base L	Circ. Third Qtr. R	Circ. Third Qtr. L	Inside Spread	Tip to Tip	Length of Prong R	Length of Prong L	Locality	By Whom Killed	Owner	Date Killed	Rank
89 2/8	17 4/8	17 1/8	6 6/8	6 6/8	2 5/8	2 5/8	8 1/8	2 4/8	6 6/8	6 6/8	Lincoln Co., WY	Harold P. Wales	Harold P. Wales	1991	32
89	17	16 3/8	7 1/8	7 2/8	3	3 1/8	11	5 2/8	6 5/8	6 5/8	Lassen Co., CA	George W. Conant	Picked Up	1985	40
89	16 1/8	16	7 4/8	7 3/8	3	2 6/8	11 2/8	8	6 5/8	7 1/8	Sweetwater Co., WY	Willis E. Haines	Willis E. Haines	1985	40
89	18	18 1/8	7	6 7/8	2 6/8	2 5/8	10 2/8	3 5/8	6 2/8	6	Lincoln Co., NM	Arthur E. Long	Arthur E. Long	1985	40
89	16 2/8	16 2/8	6 6/8	6 7/8	3 1/8	3 1/8	10 2/8	4 5/8	6 4/8	6 5/8	Catron Co., NM	Charles A. Grimmett	Picked Up	1989	40
89	16 3/8	16 3/8	7 5/8	7 5/8	2 5/8	2 4/8	10	5	6 2/8	5 6/8	Sweetwater Co., WY	Douglas G. DeVivo	Douglas G. DeVivo	1993	40
89	17 4/8	17 5/8	7	7	2 7/8	3	11 7/8	4 1/8	5 2/8	5 1/8	Hudspeth Co., TX	Wallace P. Riddell	Wallace P. Riddell	1996	40
88 6/8	18 7/8	18 6/8	7 2/8	6 6/8	2 4/8	2 4/8	11 7/8	10 1/8	6 2/8	6 3/8	Socorro Co., NM	J. Lyn Perry	J. Lyn Perry	1976	46
88 6/8	18	17 7/8	6 6/8	6 6/8	2 6/8	2 6/8	15 4/8	11 5/8	6 7/8	5 5/8	Washoe Co., NV	Bruce L. Zeller	Bruce L. Zeller	1986	46
88 6/8	16 4/8	16 6/8	7 5/8	6 4/8	2 6/8	2 6/8	8 4/8	4 7/8	5 6/8	4 6/8	White Pine Co., NV	William W. Diekmann	William W. Diekmann	1987	46
88 6/8	18 4/8	18 4/8	7 6/8	7 6/8	3 1/8	3 1/8	12	12	5 5/8	5 7/8	Brewster Co., TX	John W. Houchins	John W. Houchins	1988	46
88 6/8	16 5/8	16 5/8	6 3/8	6 3/8	3 1/8	3	15 6/8	12 7/8	5 7/8	5 7/8	Catron Co., NM	Gerald Roland Gold	Gerald Roland Gold	1990	46
88 6/8	16 3/8	16 3/8	7 2/8	7 3/8	3 1/8	3 1/8	13 6/8	12 2/8	5 7/8	6 2/8	Socorro Co., NM	Grant L. Perry	Grant L. Perry	1991	46
88 6/8	18 1/8	18	7 2/8	6 6/8	2 3/8	2 7/8	15 3/8	11 2/8	6	6 3/8	Washoe Co., NV	Kerry E. Kilgore	Kerry E. Kilgore	1992	46
88 6/8	19	18 4/8	6 2/8	6 5/8	3 1/8	3 1/8	18 2/8	15 6/8	5 6/8	5 4/8	Yavapai Co., AZ	Jerry P. Carver	Jerry P. Carver	1993	46
88 6/8	17 4/8	17 3/8	6 6/8	6 6/8	3 1/8	3 1/8	16	16	5 1/8	5 1/8	Mora Co., NM	John D. Fetcho	John D. Fetcho	1993	46
88 6/8	17 3/8	16 5/8	7 3/8	6 5/8	2 7/8	2 7/8	6 7/8	6 7/8	5 6/8	5 6/8	Humboldt Co., NV	Werner Estes	Werner Estes	1994	46
88 6/8	17 2/8	17 7/8	6 5/8	7 1/8	3 1/8	3 4/8	14 3/8	11 2/8	5 6/8	5 4/8	Colfax Co., NM	John C. Henkel	John C. Henkel	1995	46
88 6/8	15 1/8	15	7 7/8	7 7/8	3 4/8	3 2/8	9	5 7/8	4	5 6/8	Washoe Co., NV	Todd B. Jaksick	Todd B. Jaksick	1996	46
88 6/8	16 6/8	17 1/8	7 3/8	7 4/8	3 2/8	2 6/8	10	5 4/8	7 2/8	7 2/8	Fremont Co., WY	Terry N. TenBoer	Terry N. TenBoer	1974	58
88 4/8	17 7/8	17 6/8	7	7	2 6/8	3	15 6/8	11 6/8	5 7/8	5 1/8	Humboldt Co., NV	Clifford J. Heaverne	Clifford J. Heaverne	1983	58
88 4/8	19 2/8	18 6/8	6 5/8	6 4/8	2 5/8	2 5/8	13 4/8	10 4/8	5	5 3/8	Coconino Co., AZ	Harold R. Edgemon	Harold R. Edgemon	1984	58
88 4/8	18	17 5/8	6 4/8	7	3 7/8	3 4/8	13 2/8	13 4/8	5 3/8	4 6/8	Coconino Co., AZ	Randall W. Smith	Randall W. Smith	1985	58
88 4/8	16 5/8	16 2/8	7	6 6/8	2 1/8	3	8	8	6 4/8	5 7/8	Catron Co., NM	Doug W. Kasey	Doug W. Kasey	1987	58
88 4/8	17 7/8	17 7/8	6 7/8	7 1/8	3 2/8	2 7/8	13 7/8	13 7/8	5 6/8	5 6/8	Yavapai Co., AZ	Arthur C. Savoini	Arthur C. Savoini	1988	58
88 4/8	18 1/8	18 2/8	6 6/8	7	3	3 2/8	10	10	5 6/8	5 3/8	Coconino Co., AZ	Arthur R. Dubs	Arthur R. Dubs	1990	58
88 4/8	18	18	6 6/8	6 6/8	3 1/8	3	11 4/8	11 4/8	5 4/8	5 3/8	Cochise Co., AZ	Tom R. Braun	Tom R. Braun	1991	58
88 4/8	16 3/8	16 3/8	6 6/8	6 4/8	3 4/8	3	10 1/8	6 1/8	5 4/8	6 2/8	Catron Co., NM	R. Steve Bass	R. Steve Bass	1997	58
88 4/8	15 7/8	16 4/8	6 4/8	6 6/8	3 2/8	3 4/8	10 1/8	6 6/8	6 3/8	6 2/8	Coconino Co., AZ	Sam Jaksick, Jr.	Sam Jaksick, Jr.	1997	58
88 2/8	17 2/8	17 2/8	7	7	3 2/8	3 2/8	17 3/8	5 3/8	6 2/8	6 2/8	Carter Co., MT	Carl T. Clapp	Carl T. Clapp	1955	68
88 2/8	18 2/8	18 2/8	6 2/8	6 2/8	2 6/8	2 6/8	14	14	6 2/8	6 2/8	Navajo Co., AZ	John M. Griffith, Jr.	John M. Griffith, Jr.	1983	68
88 2/8	17 4/8	16 5/8	6 6/8	6 5/8	3 1/8	3 1/8	11 4/8	8 4/8	7 2/8	5 3/8	Sweetwater Co., WY	Annette D. Lynch	Annette D. Lynch	1983	68
88 2/8	16 7/8	16 7/8	6 6/8	6 6/8	3	2 6/8	20 5/8	20	5 3/8	5 7/8	Yavapai Co., AZ	Larry D. Saylor	Larry D. Saylor	1984	68
88 2/8	18	17 5/8	6 6/8	6 6/8	3 4/8	3	10 6/8	5 5/8	6 4/8	6 4/8	Apache Co., AZ	D.J. Hollinger & B. Howard	Bob Howard	1987	68
88 2/8	18 2/8	18 1/8	6 3/8	6 4/8	2 7/8	2 7/8	13 4/8	10 6/8	5 6/8	5 2/8	Carbon Co., UT	James M. Machac	James M. Machac	1989	68
88 2/8	17 6/8	18 1/8	6 7/8	6 7/8	2 5/8	2 4/8	16 4/8	12 1/8	5 4/8	7	Mohave Co., AZ	Peter E. Mangelsdorf	Peter E. Mangelsdorf	1989	68
88 2/8	16 1/8	15 7/8	7 2/8	7 2/8	3	3 2/8	11 3/8	6 4/8	7	7	Goshen Co., WY	William P. Price	William P. Price	1991	68
88 2/8	17 2/8	17 4/8	7	7 4/8	2 6/8	2 5/8	13 7/8	13 1/8	6 7/8	6 4/8	Natrona Co., WY	John J. Heidel	John J. Heidel	1992	68
88 2/8	15 7/8	15 7/8	7 4/8	7	2 7/8	2 7/8	13 1/8	10 5/8	6 4/8	6	Washoe Co., NV	Todd B. Jaksick	Todd B. Jaksick	1997	68
88	17 3/8	17	7	7 4/8	2 5/8	2 7/8	10 5/8	7 7/8	6	5 6/8	Sweet Grass Co., MT	William S. Amos	William S. Amos	1971	78
88	16 6/8	17 1/8	7 4/8	7	2 7/8	3	12 7/8	7 5/8	5 5/8	5 1/8	Coconino Co., AZ	Richard J. Hallock	Richard J. Hallock	1973	78
88	17 1/8	16 1/8	7 1/8	7 4/8	3	2 6/8	9 4/8	5 1/8	7 4/8	7 3/8	Hudspeth Co., TX	Gibson D. Lewis	Gibson D. Lewis	1986	78
88	17 1/8	17 4/8	7	7 1/8	2 6/8	2 7/8	8 7/8	6 6/8	5 7/8	6 1/8	Chaves Co., NM	Grant L. Perry	Grant L. Perry	1988	78
88	16 1/8	16 1/8	6 6/8	6 6/8	2 7/8	3	14 1/8	9	6 1/8	6	Uinta Co., WY	John V. Lockard	John V. Lockard	1990	78
88	16 7/8	17 1/8	6 6/8	6 6/8	2 7/8	3 1/8	13	9 4/8	6 2/8	6 2/8	Natrona Co., WY	F. Miles Hartung	F. Miles Hartung	1992	78
88	16 6/8	16 5/8	6 5/8	6 5/8	3 1/8	3 1/8	11 6/8	8	6 2/8	6 3/8	Apache Co., AZ	Richard L. Hazelwood	Richard L. Hazelwood	1992	78
88	18 6/8	18 1/8	6 5/8	6 5/8	2 6/8	2 6/8	9	3 1/8	5 5/8	5 5/8	Lincoln Co., NM	Vincent C. Gunn	Vincent C. Gunn	1994	78

PRONGHORN

Antilocapra americana and related subspecies

Score	Length of Horn R	L	Circumference of Base R	L	Circumference at Third Quarter R	L	Inside Spread	Tip to Tip Spread	Length of Prong R	L	Locality	Hunter	Owner	Date Killed	Rank
87 6/8	17	16 7/8	7	7 4/8	2 6/8	2 6/8	15 2/8	12 1/8	5 3/8	5 2/8	Fremont Co., WY	William I. Crump	William I. Crump	1963	86
87 6/8	15	15 2/8	7 2/8	7 2/8	3 1/8	3 1/8	10 4/8	6 3/8	7 2/8	7 1/8	Fremont Co., WY	Frank Schuele	Frank Schuele	1975	86
87 6/8	17 2/8	17 5/8	6 6/8	6 6/8	2 7/8	2 7/8	14 4/8	9 5/8	5 6/8	6	Coconino Co., AZ	Thomas R. Roberts	Thomas R. Roberts	1986	86
87 6/8	15 3/8	15 3/8	7 6/8	7 6/8	2 6/8	2 6/8	13 6/8	11 2/8	7 1/8	7	Fremont Co., WY	Karey H. Stebner	Karey H. Stebner	1991	86
87 6/8	16 2/8	16	7 1/8	7 1/8	3 1/8	3 1/8	11 5/8	9 2/8	6 2/8	6 1/8	Socorro Co., NM	Paul A. Stewart	Paul A. Stewart	1993	86
87 6/8	14 7/8	15	7	7 1/8	3 4/8	3 5/8	13 2/8	10 3/8	6 7/8	6 5/8	Socorro Co., NM	Len H. Guldman	Len H. Guldman	1996	86
87 4/8	17 5/8	17 3/8	6 4/8	6 3/8	2 5/8	2 6/8	11 5/8	6 3/8	6 4/8	6 3/8	Gillette, WY	Stanley Scott	Stanley Scott	1961	92
87 4/8	16	17 4/8	7 1/8	7 1/8	4 7/8	3 4/8	11 2/8	12	6	6 4/8	Modoc Co., CA	Lynn M. Greene	Lynn M. Greene	1971	92
87 4/8	17 2/8	17 2/8	6 3/8	6 7/8	2 6/8	3 4/8	9 4/8	2 4/8	6 5/8	6 5/8	Modoc Co., CA	Ron L. Reasor	Ron L. Reasor	1979	92
87 4/8	16 2/8	16 3/8	7	6 7/8	3 2/8	3 7/8	8 3/8	4 1/8	5 4/8	5 4/8	Socorro Co., NM	Enoch D. Brandenburg	Enoch D. Brandenburg	1987	92
87 4/8	16 7/8	16 5/8	6 6/8	6 6/8	2 6/8	2 7/8	11 7/8	7 2/8	6 1/8	6 1/8	Mora Co., NM	Anthony J. Garrett	Anthony J. Garrett	1987	92
87 4/8	16 2/8	16 1/8	7 1/8	7 2/8	3	3	11 6/8	7 2/8	5 6/8	5 5/8	Socorro Co., NM	Kevin B. Oliver	Kevin B. Oliver	1993	92
87 4/8	17	17 2/8	6 6/8	6 5/8	3	3	8 2/8	2 7/8	5 5/8	5 2/8	Colfax Co., NM	Clay T. Robertson	Clay T. Robertson	1994	92
87 4/8	16	16 3/8	7	7 3/8	3 5/8	3 5/8	8 6/8	3 3/8	6	5 5/8	Coconino Co., AZ	Ken D. Langford	Ken D. Langford	1995	92
87 4/8	16 1/8	15 7/8	6 6/8	6 6/8	3 5/8	3 5/8	9 7/8	4 4/8	5 5/8	5 4/8	Socorro Co., NM	Lesa A. Hall	Lesa A. Hall	1997	92
87 4/8	15 4/8	16	6 4/8	6 4/8	3	2 7/8	9 1/8	6 1/8	6 7/8	7	Eureka Co., NV	Nick Owen	Nick Owen	1997	92
87 2/8	16 4/8	17	6 7/8	6 7/8	2 4/8	2 4/8	13 3/8	11 4/8	7 4/8	7 2/8	Lake Co., OR	Ronald E. Hills	Ronald E. Hills	1966	102
87 2/8	16 3/8	16 1/8	6 5/8	6 4/8	2 5/8	2 4/8	13 5/8	11	7 4/8	7 5/8	Fremont Co., WY	Scott A. Trabing	Scott A. Trabing	1973	102
87 2/8	17 5/8	17 4/8	6 7/8	6 6/8	2 5/8	2 4/8	10 7/8	4 2/8	6 7/8	6 4/8	Sweetwater Co., WY	Jay R. Anderson	Jay R. Anderson	1975	102
87 2/8	16 2/8	16 2/8	6 7/8	6 7/8	2 5/8	2 4/8	12 2/8	10 4/8	7	6 7/8	Humboldt Co., NV	Steve Young	Steve Young	1975	102
87 2/8	16	16 1/8	7 2/8	7 1/8	2 7/8	2 7/8	12 1/8	9	6 3/8	6 4/8	Niobrara Co., WY	Stephen M. Cameron	Stephen M. Cameron	1976	102
87 2/8	16 5/8	16 5/8	7 4/8	7 4/8	4 1/8	4 2/8	14 2/8	10 2/8	6	5 7/8	Carbon Co., WY	Lee Miller	Lee Miller	1976	102
87 2/8	16 5/8	17	7	7	2 7/8	3	13 6/8	10	5 6/8	5 5/8	Chaves Co., NM	Charles A. Grimmett	Charles A. Grimmett	1988	102
87 2/8	19 1/8	18 4/8	7	7 2/8	3 2/8	2 6/8	14 3/8	8 2/8	5 1/8	5 2/8	Humboldt Co., NV	Jared R. Nuffer	Jared R. Nuffer	1988	102
87 2/8	16 4/8	16 5/8	7	7	2 3/8	2 4/8	11 7/8	8	7 2/8	6 4/8	Washoe Co., NV	Pierre M. Leautier	Pierre M. Leautier	1989	102
87 2/8	17 6/8	18 1/8	7 1/8	7 1/8	2 6/8	2 7/8	10 2/8	3 4/8	5 6/8	6	Catron Co., NM	Roy Holdridge	Roy Holdridge	1991	102
87 2/8	16 6/8	16 7/8	7 6/8	7 4/8	3 1/8	2 7/8	15 6/8	12 4/8	5 1/8	4 6/8	Colfax Co., NM	Calvin H. Rabb, Jr.	Calvin H. Rabb, Jr.	1991	102
87 2/8	17	17 2/8	7	7	2 6/8	2 7/8	14 4/8	8 7/8	5 7/8	5 7/8	Yavapai Co., AZ	Ervin G. Rothfuss II	Ervin G. Rothfuss II	1991	102
87 2/8	15 6/8	15 6/8	6 4/8	6 4/8	2 6/8	2 6/8	10 5/8	6 5/8	6 6/8	6 7/8	Mora Co., NM	Stephen C. LeBlanc	Stephen C. LeBlanc	1992	102
87 2/8	17 4/8	17 2/8	7 4/8	7 4/8	2 3/8	2 2/8	9 4/8	5 6/8	6 1/8	6	Humboldt Co., NV	James M. Machac	James M. Machac	1992	102
87 2/8	16 6/8	16 7/8	6 5/8	6 7/8	3	2 7/8	14 7/8	11 1/8	6 3/8	6 1/8	Humboldt Co., NV	Gary D. Bader	Gary D. Bader	1994	102
87 2/8	17 2/8	17	7 2/8	7 2/8	2 6/8	2 5/8	12	6 4/8	5 4/8	5 2/8	Washoe Co., NV	Jay T. Gunter	Jay T. Gunter	1994	102
87 2/8	17 6/8	18 3/8	6 5/8	6 5/8	2 6/8	3	10 4/8	3 6/8	5 4/8	5 3/8	Yavapai Co., AZ	Brian F. Dolan	Brian F. Dolan	1996	102
87	16 2/8	15 6/8	7 3/8	7 3/8	2 7/8	2 3/8	16	12 2/8	6 3/8	7	Hudspeth Co., TX	E.R. Rinehart	E.R. Rinehart	1959	119
87	17 6/8	17 4/8	6 3/8	6 3/8	3 2/8	3 1/8	15 4/8	10 4/8	5 2/8	5 3/8	Magdalena, NM	Picked Up	John L. Stein	1970	119
87	16 2/8	16 1/8	6 3/8	6 3/8	2 7/8	2 7/8	10 6/8	4 7/8	6 4/8	6 5/8	Washoe Co., NV	William E. Walker	William E. Walker	1970	119
87	15 7/8	15 7/8	7 1/8	7	2 4/8	2 4/8	10 5/8	5	6 1/8	6 4/8	Sweetwater Co., WY	Dell J. Barnes	Dell J. Barnes	1976	119
87	17 2/8	17 2/8	6 4/8	6 6/8	2 5/8	2 7/8	10 7/8	6 4/8	6 2/8	5 7/8	Lake Co., OR	JoAnn Hathaway	JoAnn Hathaway	1976	119

Score	Length of Horn	Circ. of Base R	Circ. of Base L	Circ. Third Quarter R	Circ. Third Quarter L	Inside Spread	Tip to Tip Spread	Length of Prong R	Length of Prong L	Owner	Hunter	Locality	Date	Rank
87	16 3/8	6 5/8	6 4/8	2 6/8	2 6/8	11 4/8	7 4/8	7 2/8	6 5/8	William S. Salisbury	William S. Salisbury	Sweetwater Co., WY	1983	119
87	16	6 4/8	6 4/8	3 2/8	3 2/8	11 5/8	5 6/8	6 1/8	6 2/8	David J. Braun	David J. Braun	Cochise Co., AZ	1984	119
87	17	6 6/8	6 6/8	2 5/8	2 7/8	10 4/8	8 2/8	6 1/8	6 6/8	Duane Stanworth	Duane Stanworth	Millard Co., UT	1984	119
87	16 2/8	6 7/8	7 1/8	2 6/8	2 4/8	12 3/8	6 7/8	6	6 4/8	Laurie Scott	Laurie Scott	Catron Co., NM	1987	119
87	15 1/8	7 4/8	7 4/8	2 7/8	2 7/8	18 2/8	17 1/8	5 4/8	5 4/8	Wayne Blue	Wayne Blue	Ochiltree Co., TX	1988	119
87	16 4/8	6 7/8	6 6/8	3	3	10 5/8	5 7/8	6 3/8	6 2/8	Robbie A. Jochim	Robbie A. Jochim	Yavapai Co., AZ	1989	119
87	16 5/8	6 7/8	6 5/8	3 1/8	3	9 1/8	2 6/8	5 2/8	5 3/8	Darrell J. Woodahl	Darrell J. Woodahl	Chouteau Co., MT	1990	119
87	16 2/8	6 6/8	6 6/8	2 6/8	2 6/8	9 6/8	5 2/8	8	7 4/8	Shane A. Siewert	Shane A. Siewert	Rosebud Co., MT	1991	119
87	16 3/8	8 1/8	8	2 5/8	2 5/8	11 5/8	11	6	6 4/8	Jim S. Vilos	Jim S. Vilos	Lincoln Co., WY	1991	119
87	16 1/8	7	7	3 3/8	3 2/8	9 5/8	7 3/8	6 1/8	5 6/8	John P. Grimmett	John P. Grimmett	Coconino Co., AZ	1994	119
87	16 1/8	7 2/8	7 1/8	3 2/8	3 2/8	13	8 3/8	5 7/8	6 1/8	Sam Jaksick, Jr.	Sam Jaksick, Jr.	Yavapai Co., AZ	1995	119
87	16 5/8	6 3/8	6 4/8	3 1/8	3	12 4/8	7 5/8	6 1/8	5 5/8	Garnet L. Kingsland	Garnet L. Kingsland	Yavapai Co., AZ	1995	119
87	16	6 6/8	6 6/8	3	3	13 6/8	13 5/8	6 4/8	6	Heidi A. Gunnell	Jeff K. Gunnell	Yavapai Co., AZ	1996	119
87	17 4/8	6 7/8	6 7/8	2 3/8	2 3/8	10 4/8	5 2/8	6	6	Donald R. Hilts	Donald R. Hilts	Washoe Co., NV	1997	119
86 6/8	17 3/8	6 7/8	6 7/8	2 4/8	2 4/8	15 3/8	9 6/8	5	5	Unknown	Unknown	South Dakota	PR 1940	138
86 6/8	18 7/8	6 3/8	6 3/8	2 6/8	2 7/8	12 4/8	7 1/8	6	6	Gene Tolle	Gene Tolle	Anderson Mesa, AZ	1941	138
86 6/8	17 4/8	6 4/8	6 3/8	2 6/8	2 7/8	15 5/8	13 4/8	6	6	Stanley Sinclair	Stanley Sinclair	Rock Springs, WY	1952	138
86 6/8	16 5/8	6 5/8	6 6/8	2 4/8	2 4/8	9 7/8	6 5/8	6 1/8	6	C.M. Chandler	C.M. Chandler	Rawlins, WY	1953	138
86 6/8	16 2/8	6 6/8	6 6/8	2 6/8	2 6/8	8 1/8	3 4/8	5 2/8	5 5/8	Dale Nealis	Dale Nealis	Jefferson Co., ID	1961	138
86 6/8	17 5/8	6 3/8	6 3/8	2 6/8	2 6/8	9 6/8	6 1/8	6 1/8	6	Louis R. Dees	Louis R. Dees	Yavapai Co., AZ	1963	138
86 6/8	16 3/8	7	7	3	3	11 6/8	9 4/8	6	6	Chuck Sanger	Chuck Sanger	Carbon Co., WY	1968	138
86 6/8	16 5/8	6 3/8	6 3/8	2 6/8	2 6/8	8 4/8	2 5/8	6 4/8	6 4/8	Richard A. Fruchey	Richard A. Fruchey	Fremont Co., WY	1973	138
86 6/8	15 3/8	7	7	2 6/8	2 6/8	9 3/8	6	7	7	Mrs. Arvid J. Siegel	Mrs. Arvid J. Siegel	Sublette Co., WY	1974	138
86 6/8	17 3/8	7 1/8	7	2 6/8	2 6/8	10 2/8	6	6 6/8	6 7/8	Ralph C. Stayner	Ralph C. Stayner	Coconino Co., AZ	1980	138
86 6/8	17	7	7	3 1/8	3 1/8	14	9 1/8	5 4/8	5 6/8	Rebecca J. Hall	Rebecca J. Hall	Humboldt Co., NV	1981	138
86 6/8	18 3/8	6 5/8	6 5/8	3	3	8 7/8	5 6/8	5 3/8	5 3/8	Glenn A. Eiden	Glenn A. Eiden	Sublette Co., WY	1983	138
86 6/8	15 5/8	7 3/8	7 3/8	2 6/8	2 6/8	11 2/8	10 5/8	7	7	Lloyd D. Kindsfater	Lloyd D. Kindsfater	Albany Co., WY	1983	138
86 6/8	17 1/8	7	7	2 6/8	2 6/8	12 4/8	11 2/8	5 1/8	5 1/8	John H. Bevel	John H. Bevel	Catron Co., NM	1986	138
86 6/8	15 5/8	6 7/8	6 6/8	2 7/8	2 7/8	11	7 6/8	5 1/8	5 1/8	Troy T. Hall	Troy T. Hall	Carbon Co., WY	1987	138
86 6/8	16 7/8	6 6/8	7	2 7/8	2 7/8	8 5/8	4 3/8	6 2/8	6 2/8	Peter L. Bright	Peter L. Bright	Hudspeth Co., TX	1988	138
86 6/8	14 2/8	7 5/8	7 5/8	3 1/8	3 2/8	6	2 2/8	6 1/8	6	Scott R. Dell	Scott R. Dell	Perkins Co., SD	1990	138
86 6/8	17	7 1/8	7 1/8	2 7/8	2 7/8	11 3/8	5 2/8	6 5/8	6 5/8	Ben E. Stayner	Ben E. Stayner	Coconino Co., AZ	1991	138
86 6/8	16 3/8	6 7/8	6 7/8	2 4/8	2 5/8	13 3/8	11 1/8	6 6/8	6 6/8	Glen H. Taylor	Glen H. Taylor	Fremont Co., WY	1991	138
86 6/8	18	6 6/8	6 6/8	2 6/8	2 6/8	8 4/8	4 2/8	6	6	Norman E. Gammons	Norman E. Gammons	Coconino Co., AZ	1992	138
86 6/8	16 2/8	6 4/8	6 4/8	2 4/8	2 4/8	11	7 2/8	6 2/8	6 1/8	Rodney D. Glaser	Rodney D. Glaser	Bent Co., CO	1992	138
86 6/8	16 6/8	6 6/8	6 6/8	2 5/8	2 5/8	7 7/8	4 4/8	6 2/8	6 2/8	Johnny Unser	Johnny Unser	Blaine Co., ID	1992	138
86 6/8	17 2/8	7 2/8	7 2/8	2 6/8	2 6/8	9 4/8	9 4/8	6	6	Harry L. Hussey	Harry L. Hussey	Coconino Co., AZ	1993	138
86 6/8	16	7	7	3	3	8 1/8	8 1/8	6 5/8	6 5/8	James M. Machac	James M. Machac	Yavapai Co., AZ	1993	138
86 6/8	16 1/8	7	6 7/8	2 7/8	2 7/8	13 5/8	10 1/8	6 5/8	6 5/8	Gary L. White	Gary L. White	Carbon Co., WY	1993	138
86 6/8	16 7/8	7 1/8	7	2 6/8	2 6/8	18 4/8	18 2/8	5 7/8	6 1/8	George V. Escobedo	George V. Escobedo	Coconino Co., AZ	1994	138
86 6/8	16 6/8	6 6/8	7 2/8	2 7/8	2 7/8	10 6/8	6	5 4/8	5 4/8	Scott E. Raubach	Scott E. Raubach	Jackson Co., CO	1995	138
86 6/8	16 7/8	6 7/8	6 6/8	2 7/8	2 5/8	10 5/8	10 5/8	6	6	Joseph R. Maynard	Joseph R. Maynard	Moffat Co., CO	1972	138
86 4/8	15 7/8	6 4/8	6 4/8	2 7/8	2 7/8	10 4/8	6 4/8	6 4/8	6 4/8	James W. Greer	James W. Greer	Lake Co., OR	1976	165
86 4/8	18	7 4/8	7 4/8	2 7/8	2 7/8	11	6	6 7/8	6 4/8	John D. Higginbotham	John D. Higginbotham	Navajo Co., AZ	1979	165
86 4/8	17	7 2/8	7 6/8	3	2 6/8	9	6 7/8	5 3/8	6 6/8	Rex A. Behrends	Rex A. Behrends	Sweetwater Co., WY	1980	165
86 4/8	17 2/8	7 2/8	7 2/8	3	3	9	6 6/8	4 1/8	5 3/8	Richard E. Hueckstaedt	Richard E. Hueckstaedt	Sweetwater Co., WY	1982	165
86 4/8	17 2/8	6 6/8	6 6/8	2 5/8	2 5/8	9 1/8	2	6 1/8	5 5/8	Bruce D. Gallio	Bruce D. Gallio	Washoe Co., NV	1983	165

PRONGHORN

Antilocapra americana americana and related subspecies

Score	Length of Horn R	L	Circumference of Base R	L	Circumference at Third Quarter R	L	Inside Spread	Tip to Tip Spread	Length of Prong R	L	Locality	Hunter	Owner	Date Killed	Rank
86 4/8	15 7/8	15 7/8	7 2/8	7 2/8	2 6/8	2 5/8	12 6/8	9	5 4/8	5 3/8	Catron Co., NM	H. James Tonkin, Jr.	H. James Tonkin, Jr.	1987	165
86 4/8	16 4/8	16 4/8	7	6 7/8	2 4/8	2 4/8	11 2/8	7 5/8	6 6/8	6 5/8	Fremont Co., WY	Gerald G. Korell	Gerald G. Korell	1989	165
86 4/8	16 1/8	16	6 7/8	6 6/8	3 1/8	3 1/8	8 7/8	5 7/8	6	6 1/8	Hay Lake, SK	Gerald W. Bien	Gerald W. Bien	1990	165
86 4/8	16 7/8	16 7/8	6 4/8	6 5/8	3 1/8	3 1/8	9	2 4/8	5 5/8	5 6/8	Billings Co., ND	Greg A. Ganje	Greg A. Ganje	1990	165
86 4/8	16 6/8	16 5/8	7 2/8	7	3 2/8	3 1/8	15	14	5 7/8	5 7/8	Coconino Co., AZ	Arthur R. Dubs	Arthur R. Dubs	1991	165
86 4/8	16 6/8	17 5/8	6 4/8	6 4/8	2 3/8	2 1/8	14 6/8	13	6 5/8	7	Malheur Co., OR	Nicholas J. Vidan	Nicholas J. Vidan	1991	165
86 4/8	17 3/8	17 4/8	6 6/8	6 6/8	2 6/8	2 5/8	10 7/8	4 2/8	5 4/8	5 4/8	Harney Co., OR	Sam L. Wilkins, Jr.	Sam L. Wilkins, Jr.	1991	165
86 4/8	17 5/8	16 5/8	6 6/8	6 7/8	3	3	14	9 5/8	6	6 1/8	Coconino Co., AZ	Sam Jaksick, Jr.	Sam Jaksick, Jr.	1992	165
86 4/8	16 6/8	15 7/8	7 2/8	7 2/8	2 7/8	2 6/8	9 3/8	5 3/8	5 5/8	6 1/8	Uinta Co., AZ	Randy L. Mair	Randy L. Mair	1992	165
86 4/8	15 7/8	16	6 4/8	6 4/8	3 1/8	3 1/8	10 3/8	7 6/8	6 2/8	6 1/8	Rosebud Co., MT	Dennis J. Giese	Dennis J. Giese	1995	165
86 4/8	16 2/8	16 2/8	6 7/8	6 7/8	3 2/8	3 1/8	9 3/8	3 6/8	5 6/8	5 4/8	Las Animas Co., CO	Nicholas R. Russo	Nicholas R. Russo	1996	165
86 4/8	18 2/8	18 5/8	6 7/8	6 7/8	2 5/8	2 6/8	7 7/8	8 1/8	5 6/8	5 2/8	Catron Co., NM	Robert J. Seeds	Robert J. Seeds	1996	165
86 4/8	16 2/8	16 1/8	6 3/8	6 3/8	3 1/8	3	11	10	6 2/8	6	Elko Co., NV	Travis Branzell	Travis Branzell	1997	165
86 2/8	16 7/8	16 6/8	6 5/8	6 5/8	3 1/8	3	13 5/8	8 1/8	6 2/8	6 1/8	Brooks, AB	S. Prescott Fay	Boston Mus. Science	1913	184
86 2/8	16 6/8	16 6/8	6 4/8	6 3/8	3 1/8	3	11 4/8	10	7	6 1/8	Manville, WY	J.J. Hartnett	Roy Vail	1952	184
86 2/8	15 6/8	15 6/8	6 3/8	6 4/8	3 1/8	3	11	5 7/8	8 3/8	8 4/8	Otero Co., NM	Robert B. West	Dorothy West	1957	184
86 2/8	16	16 2/8	7 1/8	6 6/8	2 6/8	2 4/8	9 7/8	5 4/8	6 5/8	6 5/8	Coconino Co., AZ	Eugene Anderson	Eugene Anderson	1961	184
86 2/8	16 7/8	16 6/8	6 6/8	6 6/8	2 3/8	2 7/8	11 7/8	4 7/8	5 4/8	5	Du Gas, AZ	Rex Earl	Rex Earl	1962	184
86 2/8	15	15 2/8	7 6/8	7 6/8	2 7/8	3	9	5 6/8	6	5 6/8	Casper, WY	William W. Brummet	William W. Brummet	1963	184
86 2/8	17 6/8	17 6/8	6 3/8	6 3/8	2 7/8	3	10 6/8	7 4/8	5 3/8	5 3/8	Coconino Co., AZ	Jon H. Bryan	Jon H. Bryan	1970	184
86 2/8	16 7/8	16 1/8	6 5/8	6 6/8	2 6/8	2 6/8	12 1/8	7 2/8	6 6/8	6 4/8	Carbon Co., WY	Mike Davich	Mike Davich	1974	184
86 2/8	17 7/8	17 6/8	6 4/8	6 4/8	3	3	14 2/8	9 1/8	4 5/8	4 4/8	Ft. Apache Res., AZ	Jack Pierce	Jack Pierce	1974	184
86 2/8	16 6/8	16 2/8	6 4/8	6 4/8	3 2/8	3 1/8	12 3/8	9 4/8	6	6	Big Horn Co., WY	Robert Temme	Robert Temme	1974	184
86 2/8	17 2/8	17	7	7	3 2/8	3 1/8	12 6/8	10 7/8	5 6/8	5 7/8	Carbon Co., WY	Harold J. Rollison	Harold J. Rollison	1975	184
86 2/8	16 4/8	16 5/8	7 7/8	7 7/8	2 7/8	2 6/8	14 3/8	9 6/8	5	5 1/8	Fremont Co., WY	Douglas B. Stromberg	Douglas B. Stromberg	1976	184
86 2/8	17 3/8	17 3/8	6 7/8	7	2 6/8	2 5/8	13 7/8	13 7/8	5	5	Carbon Co., WY	James Poydack	James Poydack	1977	184
86 2/8	17 4/8	17 1/8	7 5/8	7 5/8	2 4/8	2 6/8	7 5/8	5	6 1/8	6 3/8	Sweetwater Co., WY	J. Robert Tigner	J. Robert Tigner	1980	184
86 2/8	16 5/8	17	7 5/8	7 5/8	3 2/8	2 4/8	14 3/8	8 1/8	5 2/8	5 1/8	El Paso Co., CO	Maurice Cutting	Maurice Cutting	1981	184
86 2/8	15 2/8	15	6 6/8	6 4/8	3 6/8	3 2/8	9 6/8	5 6/8	5	4 6/8	Hartley Co., TX	Ernie Davis	Ernie Davis	1983	184
86 2/8	17 2/8	17 1/8	6 4/8	6 7/8	2 6/8	3	11 4/8	7 3/8	5 2/8	5 3/8	Washoe Co., NV	Daniel E. Warren	Daniel E. Warren	1983	184
86 2/8	16 5/8	16 3/8	6 7/8	6 7/8	3	3	17	15 3/8	6 2/8	6 6/8	Yavapai Co., AZ	Vincent J. Conti	Vincent J. Conti	1986	184
86 2/8	15 1/8	15 1/8	7 4/8	7 4/8	2 5/8	2 7/8	10 6/8	10 1/8	4 7/8	5	Sweetwater Co., WY	Kurt A. Mari	Kurt A. Mari	1988	184
86 2/8	17 5/8	17 6/8	6 5/8	6 5/8	2 7/8	2 7/8	15 6/8	13 4/8	7 1/8	6 6/8	Coconino Co., AZ	Scott J. Reger	Scott J. Reger	1988	184
86 2/8	15 3/8	15 4/8	7 1/8	7 1/8	2 4/8	2 4/8	12 1/8	10	6 6/8	6 2/8	Sweetwater Co., WY	Brian T. Gabbitas	Brian T. Gabbitas	1990	184
86 2/8	17	16 3/8	7 3/8	7 3/8	2 7/8	2 5/8	9 2/8	2 6/8	6 1/8	6 2/8	Sweetwater Co., WY	Geraldine Hazzard	Leonard L. Arnold	1991	184
86 2/8	16 4/8	16 4/8	7 3/8	7 3/8	2 5/8	2 6/8	9 2/8	4	6 2/8	5 3/8	Sweetwater Co., WY	Daniel Daugherty	Daniel Daugherty	1991	184
86 2/8	18	17 4/8	6 5/8	6 5/8	3 2/8	3 3/8	9 3/8	7	3 4/8	3 6/8	Mora Co., NM	Hub R. Grounds	Hub R. Grounds	1992	184
86 2/8	17 1/8	17 2/8	7 1/8	7 2/8	2 6/8	2 6/8	11 4/8	6 3/8	5 5/8	5 1/8	Mora Co., NM	Len H. Guldman	Len H. Guldman	1993	184

Score										Locality	Hunter	Owner	Date	Rank
86 2/8	16 7/8	16 7/8	7	7 1/8	3 1/8	3 2/8	11	4 6/8	5	Colfax Co., NM	James D. Knight	James D. Knight	1994	184
86 2/8	17 2/8	17 2/8	7	7 2/8	2 7/8	2 7/8	9 1/8	4 4/8	4 6/8	Pershing Co., NV	Matthew K. Morris	Matthew K. Morris	1994	184
86 2/8	15 2/8	15	7 1/8	7 1/8	3 3/8	3	11	8 1/8	5 4/8	Humboldt Co., NV	David C. Rahn	David C. Rahn	1994	184
86 2/8	17 1/8	17	6 5/8	6 4/8	3	2 7/8	14 3/8	2 7/8	5 3/8	Coconino Co., AZ	Gregg L. Warne	Gregg L. Warne	1995	184
86 2/8	17 2/8	17 4/8	5 7/8	5 7/8	2 4/8	3 2/8	7 1/8	3 2/8	5	Yavapai Co., AZ	James E. Stark	James E. Stark	1996	184
86 2/8	15 5/8	16 2/8	6 6/8	6 6/8	4 3/8	4 4/8	9 6/8	3	5 2/8	Coconino Co., AZ	Jeffery A. Alt	Jeffery A. Alt	1997	184
86	17 3/8	18	7	7 2/8	3 4/8	3 4/8	6 6/8	3 4/8	6	Medicine Bow, WY	Jack R. Campbell	Jack R. Campbell	1959	215
86	16 2/8	16 1/8	6 7/8	6 7/8	2 5/8	2 3/8	12 6/8	3 4/8	6 4/8	Coconino Co., AZ	Richard R. Barney	Richard R. Barney	1969	215
86	15	16 3/8	7	7 3/8	3 2/8	3 3/8	9 7/8	4 1/8	4 4/8	Carter Co., MT	Jamie Byrne	Jamie Byrne	1972	215
86	17 1/8	15	7 1/8	7 2/8	2 7/8	2 7/8	13 6/8	11 6/8	6 6/8	Fremont Co., WY	Robert Hall	Robert Hall	1973	215
86	16 4/8	16 4/8	6 7/8	6 6/8	2 7/8	3	11 3/8	7 6/8	6 7/8	Yavapai Co., AZ	Ruth McCasland	Ruth McCasland	1975	215
86	17 3/8	17 3/8	6 6/8	6 7/8	2 7/8	3 1/8	14 3/8	12 4/8	5 5/8	Valley Co., MT	Ernie Freebury	Ernie Freebury	1981	215
86	16	16	6 5/8	7 1/8	2 4/8	2 3/8	10 1/8	4 2/8	6 5/8	Sweetwater Co., WY	F.A. Oliver	F.A. Oliver	1981	215
86	16 5/8	16 1/8	6 5/8	7 1/8	3	3	9 4/8	4 2/8	5 6/8	Natrona Co., WY	David H. Crum	David H. Crum	1983	215
86	16	16 5/8	6 7/8	6 5/8	2 4/8	2 4/8	10 4/8	7 2/8	6 6/8	McCone Co., MT	Danny L. Curtiss	Danny L. Curtiss	1983	215
86	16 4/8	16 6/8	6 6/8	6 6/8	2 5/8	2 5/8	9 2/8	4 3/8	6	Wibaux Co., MT	Raymond G. Marciniak	Raymond G. Marciniak	1984	215
86	16 3/8	16 4/8	7 1/8	7 1/8	4 1/8	4 3/8	6 6/8	2 2/8	3 5/8	Apache Co., AZ	Charles R. Sprung	Charles R. Sprung	1984	215
86	14 2/8	14 5/8	7 4/8	7 5/8	2 6/8	2 6/8	10 2/8	6 7/8	7	Lake Co., OR	Frank Biggs	Frank Biggs	1985	215
86	17	17 1/8	6 3/8	6 2/8	2 4/8	2 3/8	0	7 4/8	6 2/8	De Baca Co., NM	Bennie F. Hromadka	Bennie F. Hromadka	1985	215
86	15 2/8	15	7 4/8	7 3/8	2 7/8	2 6/8	12 6/8	8 1/8	6 3/8	Coconino Co., AZ	John S. Harrison	John S. Harrison	1986	215
86	16 2/8	16 2/8	7	7	2 6/8	2 5/8	11 7/8	7 6/8	6 7/8	Sierra Co., NM	Vicki L. Leonard	Vicki L. Leonard	1987	215
86	16	15 6/8	7	7	2 6/8	3 1/8	13 4/8	10 6/8	6 2/8	Lassen Co., CA	David A. Tye	David A. Tye	1987	215
86	14 6/8	14 2/8	8 1/8	7 7/8	2 7/8	3	12	10	5 2/8	Rosebud Co., MT	William E. Butler	William E. Butler	1989	215
86	15 4/8	15 4/8	6 5/8	6 5/8	3 1/8	3 3/8	10 2/8	7 4/8	6	Apache Co., MT	Jennifer C. Flaherty	Jennifer C. Flaherty	1990	215
86	16 1/8	16	6 7/8	6 7/8	3 1/8	3 3/8	11	7 5/8	6 3/8	Catron Co., NM	Picked Up	NM Dept. Game & Fish	1990	215
86	15 5/8	15 5/8	7 1/8	7	2 5/8	2 6/8	11 4/8	6 3/8	5 4/8	Natrona Co., WY	Bruce L. Bummer	Bruce L. Bummer	1991	215
86	16 6/8	16 7/8	6 7/8	6 7/8	2 7/8	2 6/8	10 2/8	6	6 2/8	Sweetwater Co., WY	Jason K. Faigl	Jason K. Faigl	1991	215
86	17 1/8	16 5/8	6 6/8	6 5/8	2 6/8	2 6/8	11 2/8	5	6 4/8	Catron Co., NM	Armando J. Garcia	Armando J. Garcia	1991	215
86	17	16 4/8	6 5/8	6 4/8	2 6/8	2 6/8	10 6/8	5 6/8	6 6/8	Garfield Co., UT	Lynn M. Greene	Lynn M. Greene	1991	215
86	16 2/8	16 4/8	7	7	2 6/8	2 7/8	8 7/8	2 8/8	6 4/8	Sweetwater Co., WY	William H. Miller	William H. Miller	1991	215
86	16 5/8	16 4/8	6 4/8	6 3/8	2 5/8	2 7/8	9 5/8	3 4/8	5 4/8	Socorro Co., NM	Joseph C. Sawyers	Joseph C. Sawyers	1991	215
86	15	15 6/8	6 2/8	6 2/8	2 7/8	2 7/8	14 4/8	12 3/8	5 4/8	Carter Co., MT	Keith L. Folk	Keith L. Folk	1992	215
86	17 3/8	16 1/8	6 7/8	6 5/8	2 7/8	3 1/8	13 1/8	11 2/8	5 5/8	Coconino Co., AZ	Walter E. George	Walter E. George	1992	215
86	16	16	6 7/8	6 7/8	3	3	10 6/8	4 6/8	5	Coconino Co., AZ	Sam Jaksick, Jr.	Sam Jaksick, Jr.	1994	215
86	16	16 3/8	6 4/8	6 4/8	3 2/8	3 2/8	11 2/8	3 2/8	4 5/8	Colfax Co., NM	Robert D. Jones	Robert D. Jones	1994	215
86	16 5/8	16 4/8	6 5/8	6 6/8	3 3/8	3 3/8	10	3 6/8	6 4/8	Coconino Co., AZ	Robin W. Bechtel	Robin W. Bechtel	1995	215
86	15	15	7 4/8	7 2/8	3	3	8 6/8	6 1/8	6 2/8	Gunnison Co., CO	James R. Dawson	James R. Dawson	1995	215
86	17 3/8	17 2/8	6 7/8	6 6/8	2 7/8	2 7/8	7 5/8	2 3/8	5 4/8	Washoe Co., NV	Len H. Guldman	Len H. Guldman	1995	215
86	15 5/8	15 6/8	7 1/8	7 1/8	2 6/8	2 6/8	9 4/8	4 4/8	6 2/8	Converse Co., WY	Charles J. White	Charles J. White	1995	215
86	14 1/8	15	6 7/8	6 7/8	3 4/8	3 4/8	9 1/8	7 2/8	6 6/8	Hudspeth Co., TX	Len H. Guldman	Len H. Guldman	1996	215
85 6/8	17 2/8	17 2/8	6 4/8	6 4/8	3 5/8	3 1/8	12 1/8	10 4/8	4 6/8	Fergus Co., MT	H.H. Applegate	H.H. Applegate	1951	249
85 6/8	16 4/8	16 4/8	6 4/8	6 4/8	3 5/8	3 1/8	12 1/8	10 6/8	6	Carbon Co., WY	B.L. Holman	B.L. Holman	1953	249
85 6/8	17 5/8	18	6 4/8	6 4/8	2 6/8	2 6/8	7 7/8	3 4/8	5 6/8	Chugwater, WY	Louis C. Morrison	Louis C. Morrison	1955	249
85 6/8	16 3/8	15 1/8	6 3/8	6 4/8	3 4/8	3 2/8	12 5/8	7 3/8	5 3/8	Chihuahua, MX	Juan A. Saenz	Juan A. Saenz	1955	249
85 6/8	15	15 4/8	7 1/8	7 4/8	2 7/8	3 1/8	6	2 2/8	6	Sioux Co., NE	Gerald R. Larson	Gerald R. Larson	1962	249
85 6/8	16 2/8	16 1/8	6 6/8	6 5/8	2 6/8	2 6/8	12 5/8	9 6/8	6 4/8	Brooks, AB	Oliver Ost	Oliver Ost	1964	249
85 6/8	18 4/8	18 1/8	6	6	2 6/8	2 4/8	6 5/8	0	6 1/8	Socorro Co., NM	V.F. Tannich	V.F. Tannich	1965	249

PRONGHORN

Antilocapra americana americana and related subspecies

Score	Length of Horn R	L	Circumference of Base R	L	Circumference at Third Quarter R	L	Inside Spread	Tip to Tip Spread	Length of Prong R	L	Locality	Hunter	Owner	Date Killed	Rank
85 6/8	16	15 6/8	7	6 5/8	3	2 7/8	10 6/8	6 1/8	6 3/8	6 1/8	Boise City, OK	R.L. Williams	R.L. Williams	1966	249
85 6/8	16 4/8	16 1/8	6 6/8	6 5/8	3	3	9 1/8	5 1/8	6 1/8	6	Beaverhead Co., MT	Vern Hensley	Vern Hensley	1968	249
85 6/8	15 2/8	15 2/8	7 2/8	7 2/8	2 7/8	2 7/8	13 4/8	10 6/8	7	6 7/8	Rock Springs, WY	C.J. McElroy	C.J. McElroy	1969	249
85 6/8	16 3/8	15 7/8	6 2/8	6 2/8	3	3	10	9	4 4/8	4 4/8	Sweetwater Co., WY	E. Tom Thorne	E. Tom Thorne	1969	249
85 6/8	16 5/8	16 5/8	6 2/8	6 2/8	3	3	9 7/8	5 6/8	5 2/8	5 3/8	Sweetwater Co., WY	Roger A. Perkins	Roger A. Perkins	1971	249
85 6/8	16	16	6 5/8	6 5/8	2 5/8	2 5/8	13 1/8	8	6 2/8	6 2/8	Humboldt Co., NV	Thomas R. Pitts	Thomas R. Pitts	1973	249
85 6/8	16 4/8	16 5/8	6 4/8	6 5/8	2 5/8	2 6/8	9 6/8	4 4/8	6 4/8	6 4/8	Yavapai Co., AZ	Randy Modisett	Randy Modisett	1974	249
85 6/8	18 3/8	18 2/8	6 6/8	6 4/8	2 6/8	2 6/8	7 7/8	4 7/8	5 2/8	4 3/8	Carbon Co., WY	Robert F. Johnston	Robert F. Johnston	1977	249
85 6/8	16 1/8	16	7	7 1/8	2 6/8	2 5/8	11 2/8	8 7/8	6 2/8	6 1/8	Natrona Co., WY	Terrie L. Morrison	Terrie L. Morrison	1980	249
85 6/8	15 4/8	15 5/8	7 3/8	7 4/8	2 6/8	2 6/8	7 4/8	3	5 5/8	5 6/8	Carbon Co., WY	James M. Jagusch	James M. Jagusch	1981	249
85 6/8	15 7/8	16	6 7/8	6 7/8	2 7/8	2 7/8	9 4/8	4 3/8	5 4/8	5 5/8	Sweetwater Co., WY	Mark E. Nedrow	Mark E. Nedrow	1981	249
85 6/8	15 7/8	16 1/8	7 4/8	7 4/8	3	2 6/8	12 6/8	9 3/8	6 2/8	6 2/8	Navajo Co., AZ	C. Boyd Austin	C. Boyd Austin	1987	249
85 6/8	16 2/8	16 4/8	6 4/8	6 4/8	2 4/8	2 6/8	9	3	6 7/8	6 7/8	Sweetwater Co., WY	Steven J. Vanlerberghe	Steven J. Vanlerberghe	1988	249
85 6/8	15 7/8	15 7/8	7 6/8	7 6/8	2 6/8	2 6/8	8 6/8	2 3/8	5 5/8	5 5/8	Sweetwater Co., WY	Duane M. Smith	Duane M. Smith	1989	249
85 6/8	16 6/8	16 6/8	6 5/8	6 5/8	3	2 7/8	10 6/8	9 4/8	6	6	Carbon Co., WY	Herman A. Hatfield	Herman A. Hatfield	1990	249
85 6/8	17	16 7/8	7	7	2 5/8	2 5/8	11	4 7/8	5 6/8	5 4/8	Mora Co., NM	Michael J. Loomis	Michael J. Loomis	1990	249
85 6/8	16 3/8	16 5/8	6 2/8	6 2/8	2 5/8	2 5/8	8	1 7/8	6 5/8	6 6/8	Emery Co., UT	Jerry L. Oveson	Jerry L. Oveson	1991	249
85 6/8	15 4/8	15 4/8	7 2/8	7 2/8	2 6/8	2 6/8	8 3/8	3	6 4/8	6 2/8	Sweetwater Co., WY	Robert C. Sexton	Robert C. Sexton	1992	249
85 6/8	18 1/8	18	6 3/8	6 3/8	2 6/8	2 6/8	17 1/8	13	6 1/8	5 7/8	Coconino Co., AZ	Gene Coon	Gene Coon	1993	249
85 6/8	17 1/8	17 1/8	6 5/8	6 5/8	2 7/8	2 6/8	11 6/8	6 6/8	6 7/8	5 3/8	Mora Co., NM	Edward C. Joseph	Edward C. Joseph	1994	249
85 6/8	16 3/8	16 5/8	6 6/8	6 6/8	2 6/8	2 6/8	12 6/8	8 1/8	6 1/8	6	Yavapai Co., AZ	James W.P. Roe	James W.P. Roe	1994	249
85 6/8	15 4/8	15 4/8	7	7	3 1/8	2 7/8	11 1/8	7 3/8	5 6/8	5 4/8	Colfax Co., NM	Robert D. Jones	Robert D. Jones	1995	249
85 6/8	16 2/8	16 1/8	6 6/8	6 6/8	3 6/8	3 4/8	13 2/8	12 4/8	5 5/8	5 4/8	Coconino Co., AZ	Kevin E. Rector	Kevin E. Rector	1996	249
85 4/8	16 6/8	16 5/8	7 4/8	7 5/8	2 3/8	2 2/8	11 6/8	8 4/8	7 3/8	6 5/8	Rawlins, WY	Paul C. Himelright	Paul C. Himelright	1960	279
85 4/8	17 2/8	16 5/8	6 1/8	6 1/8	2 6/8	2 5/8	10 7/8	6 2/8	6 2/8	6 2/8	Campbell Co., WY	Eugene D. Springen	Eugene D. Springen	1962	279
85 4/8	15 3/8	15 3/8	7 2/8	7 2/8	2 7/8	2 7/8	7 6/8	4 1/8	6 2/8	6 3/8	Saratoga, WY	Carlyn J. Ourada	Carlyn J. Ourada	1969	279
85 4/8	16	16 6/8	7 6/8	6 7/8	3	2 7/8	11 1/8	10 2/8	6 4/8	6 2/8	Rosebud Co., MT	Calvin F. Mayes	Calvin F. Mayes	1973	279
85 4/8	16 6/8	16 6/8	7 4/8	7 4/8	2 5/8	2 5/8	10 2/8	2 2/8	6 2/8	5 5/8	Washoe Co., NV	Mario E. Gildone	Mario E. Gildone	1977	279
85 4/8	17 2/8	17 1/8	6 4/8	6 3/8	2 5/8	2 6/8	15 1/8	11 1/8	6 1/8	6	Washoe Co., NV	Maryanne Robinson	M. & M. Robinson	1981	279
85 4/8	16	16	6 7/8	7	2 6/8	2 6/8	7 3/8	3 3/8	6 5/8	6 4/8	Sweetwater Co., WY	Lee Frudden	Lee Frudden	1982	279
85 4/8	17 2/8	17 3/8	6 3/8	6 6/8	2 7/8	2 7/8	11 4/8	9 4/8	6 7/8	6 2/8	Mora Co., NM	Roger B. Heemeier	Roger B. Heemeier	1982	279
85 4/8	16 4/8	17 1/8	7	7	3	3	13	9 3/8	5 5/8	5 7/8	Fremont Co., WY	Jerry A. Martin	Jerry A. Martin	1982	279
85 4/8	15 5/8	15 6/8	6 7/8	6 7/8	2 5/8	2 5/8	8 4/8	2 3/8	6 3/8	6 3/8	Fremont Co., WY	Roger E. Udovich	Roger E. Udovich	1982	279
85 4/8	17 7/8	17 3/8	6 3/8	6 1/8	2 5/8	2 7/8	9 1/8	4 2/8	6 3/8	5 7/8	Lemhi Co., ID	Michael Wolf	Michael Wolf	1982	279
85 4/8	17	16 6/8	6 7/8	6 7/8	2 7/8	2 7/8	9 3/8	6	5 3/8	5 7/8	Sweetwater Co., WY	E. Jay Dawson	E. Jay Dawson	1983	279
85 4/8	16 1/8	15 7/8	7	7 1/8	2 4/8	2 4/8	10 4/8	5 6/8	7 1/8	6 7/8	Sioux Co., NE	John W. Hlavacek	John W. Hlavacek	1983	279
85 4/8	18 1/8	18 4/8	6 4/8	6 4/8	2 4/8	2 5/8	17 4/8	13 5/8	5 4/8	5 5/8	Apache Co., AZ	Don L. Corley	Don L. Corley	1985	279
85 4/8	17 6/8	17 3/8	7	7	2 6/8	2 4/8	14 1/8	12 2/8	5 3/8	6	Lake Co., OR	Edna J. Kettenburg	Edna J. Kettenburg	1985	279

Score	L.R	L.L	Circ.R	Circ.L	3Q.R	3Q.L	Prong R	Prong L	Spread	Tip	Locality	Hunter	By Whom Killed	Date	Rank
85 4/8	16 5/8	16 5/8	6 7/8	6 7/8	2 7/8	2 6/8	9 3/8	4 1/8	5 4/8	6 1/8	Yavapai Co., AZ	Steven C. Dunn	Steven C. Dunn	1987	279
85 4/8	17 2/8	17 2/8	6 7/8	6 6/8	2 7/8	2 7/8	17 2/8	13 4/8	5 1/8	5 3/8	Washoe Co., NV	Peter K. Beers	Peter K. Beers	1988	279
85 4/8	16 5/8	16 6/8	6 6/8	6 6/8	2 6/8	2 5/8	15 1/8	11 1/8	5 6/8	6	Butte Co., ID	Picked Up	S. Eric Krasa	1988	279
85 4/8	16 4/8	16 4/8	6 6/8	6 6/8	3	2 7/8	9 2/8	5 1/8	5 4/8	5 1/8	Millard Co., UT	David J. Carter	David J. Carter	1989	279
85 4/8	16 6/8	16 6/8	6 7/8	6 6/8	2 6/8	3	9 2/8	1 1/8	6	5 5/8	Rosebud Co., MT	John A. Hill	John A. Hill	1989	279
85 4/8	16 4/8	16 4/8	6 6/8	6 5/8	3	3	7	1	6	5 7/8	Coconino Co., AZ	Lester E. Bradley	Lester E. Bradley	1990	279
85 4/8	16	16 2/8	6 6/8	6 5/8	2 6/8	3	11 2/8	8 3/8	5 7/8	5 4/8	Harney Co., OR	Van G. Decker	Van G. Decker	1990	279
85 4/8	16 5/8	16 5/8	6 4/8	6 4/8	2 7/8	3	12 5/8	7 7/8	5 4/8	5 4/8	Coconino Co., AZ	Don W. Drew	Don R. Drew	1990	279
85 4/8	16	16 6/8	6 6/8	6 6/8	3 1/8	3 3/8	12 6/8	3 7/8	6 1/8	6	Lassen Co., CA	Jeff R. Rogers	Jeff R. Rogers	1990	279
85 4/8	16 6/8	16 7/8	6 6/8	7	2 6/8	2 6/8	8 4/8	8 5/8	4 4/8	4 2/8	Washoe Co., NV	Gregg A. Menter	Gregg A. Menter	1991	279
85 4/8	15 5/8	15 7/8	6 4/8	6 4/8	2 6/8	2 6/8	12 5/8	5 6/8	7 3/8	6 4/8	Torrance Co., NM	James D. Moreland	James D. Moreland	1991	279
85 4/8	17 4/8	17 2/8	6	6	2 5/8	2 4/8	9 7/8	8	4 5/8	4 4/8	De Baca Co., NM	Samuel S. Pattillo	Samuel S. Pattillo	1991	279
85 4/8	15 6/8	15 6/8	7	7	2 6/8	3	11 4/8	10 2/8	4	4 2/8	Catron Co., NM	Tanya M. Horwath	Tanya M. Horwath	1992	279
85 4/8	15 5/8	15 6/8	6 7/8	6 7/8	2 6/8	2 6/8	12 3/8	9 1/8	6	6 1/8	Nye Co., NV	E. William Almberg	E. William Almberg	1993	279
85 4/8	17	16 6/8	6 5/8	6 7/8	2 6/8	2 6/8	12 5/8	8 2/8	6	5 6/8	Campbell Co., WY	Ronald R. Mobley	Ronald R. Mobley	1993	279
85 4/8	16 4/8	16 4/8	6 7/8	6 7/8	2 6/8	2 6/8	12 4/8	4 4/8	6 3/8	6	Coconino Co., AZ	Edward Boutonnet	Edward Boutennet	1994	279
85 4/8	16 5/8	16 6/8	6 3/8	6 4/8	2 5/8	2 7/8	8 4/8	7 6/8	6	5 7/8	Catron Co., NM	Thomas J. Chavez	Thomas J. Chavez	1995	279
85 4/8	16 3/8	16 5/8	6 2/8	6 2/8	2 7/8	2 7/8	13 3/8	7 6/8	6 1/8	6 1/8	Cibola Co., NM	David M. Asal	David M. Asal	1996	279
85 4/8	18 1/8	18 1/8	6 1/8	6 2/8	3 2/8	3 2/8	15 1/8	13 4/8	5 2/8	5 2/8	Mohave Co., AZ	Ralph C. Stayner	Ralph C. Stayner	1996	279
85 4/8	17 4/8	17 6/8	6 4/8	6 4/8	2 6/8	2 3/8	11 1/8	3 5/8	4 7/8	6 3/8	Crook Co., OR	David T. Boyle	David T. Boyle	1997	279
85 2/8	16 3/8	16 4/8	7 1/8	6 4/8	2 6/8	2 6/8	9 6/8	5 2/8	6 7/8	6 3/8	Saratoga, WY	Russell Cutter	Russell Cutter	1957	314
85 2/8	17 4/8	17 6/8	7 2/8	7 1/8	2 6/8	2 6/8	12 4/8	2	5 6/8	5 4/8	Yavapai Co., AZ	Robert C. Bogart	Robert C. Bogart	1963	314
85 2/8	15 4/8	15 4/8	7 1/8	7 1/8	2 6/8	2 6/8	7 2/8	2	5 4/8	5 4/8	Lower Sweetwater, WY	John Kereszturi	John Kereszturi	1963	314
85 2/8	16 3/8	16 2/8	6 3/8	6 3/8	2 6/8	2 6/8	12 2/8	11 1/8	6 1/8	6	Maple Creek, SK	Glen A. Lewis	George Hooey	1964	314
85 2/8	17	17	6 2/8	7	2 7/8	2 7/8	12 1/8	8	5 1/8	5 3/8	Bow City, AB	Howard M. Stephens	Eric Wilson	1964	314
85 2/8	14 3/8	14 4/8	6 6/8	6 6/8	2 4/8	3	10 6/8	8	6 4/8	6 3/8	Sublette Co., WY	Mike Wilson	Mike Wilson	1966	314
85 2/8	16	16	6 6/8	6 3/8	2 5/8	3	14	11 5/8	6 4/8	7 4/8	Johnson Co., WY	Robert P. Murphy	Robert P. Murphy	1968	314
85 2/8	16 6/8	16 6/8	6 3/8	6 2/8	2 6/8	2 6/8	10 3/8	7 4/8	6 3/8	6 1/8	Sweetwater Co., WY	Mario Shassetz	Mario Shassetz	1968	314
85 2/8	17 1/8	14 4/8	6 2/8	7 6/8	2 6/8	2 6/8	11 1/8	5 6/8	6 3/8	6 1/8	S. Wamsutter, WY	William G. Hepworth	William G. Hepworth	1970	314
85 2/8	14 4/8	14 4/8	7 6/8	7 2/8	2 6/8	2 6/8	11 7/8	9 7/8	4 6/8	4 6/8	Carbon Co., WY	Daryl L. Frank	Daryl L. Frank	1973	314
85 2/8	15 7/8	15 6/8	7 1/8	7 1/8	2 6/8	2 6/8	8 3/8	8 2/8	6 4/8	6 4/8	Lincoln Co., WY	James R. Gunter	James R. Gunter	1976	314
85 2/8	15 6/8	15 6/8	6 6/8	7	2 5/8	2 5/8	12 5/8	12 5/8	4 6/8	5 2/8	Colfax Co., NM	Rick H. Jackson	Rick H. Jackson	1976	314
85 2/8	17 4/8	17 5/8	7	7	2 7/8	2 7/8	9 4/8	6 1/8	4 6/8	5 2/8	Carbon Co., WY	Paul M. Ostrander	Paul M. Ostrander	1977	314
85 2/8	16 4/8	16 3/8	6 7/8	7	3	3	8 5/8	4 3/8	5 6/8	4 3/8	Colfax Co., NM	John D. Pearson	John D. Pearson	1977	314
85 2/8	17 7/8	17 1/8	6 7/8	7 1/8	3	3	11 1/8	4 7/8	5	4 3/8	Colfax Co., NM	Robert Spears	Robert Spears	1977	314
85 2/8	15 2/8	15 1/8	7 3/8	7 5/8	2 4/8	2 5/8	10 5/8	6 3/8	4	4 1/8	Baker Co., OR	Roland W. Anthony	Roland W. Anthony	1978	314
85 2/8	14 4/8	14 4/8	5 7/8	6 7/8	2 5/8	2 7/8	9 7/8	6 7/8	6 7/8	5 7/8	Carbon Co., WY	James H. Hastings	James H. Hastings	1979	314
85 2/8	16 1/8	16 1/8	6 7/8	7	2 5/8	2 7/8	13 4/8	11 7/8	7	7	Lake Co., OR	Eldon L. Buckner	Eldon L. Buckner	1981	314
85 2/8	15 4/8	15 4/8	7 3/8	7 6/8	3 2/8	3 2/8	8	4 1/8	7 3/8	7	Fremont Co., WY	Richard A. Fruchey	Richard A. Fruchey	1981	314
85 2/8	16	15 5/8	6 5/8	6 4/8	2 6/8	2 6/8	12	8 4/8	6 2/8	6 5/8	Natrona Co., WY	Margery H.T. Torrey	Margery H.T. Torrey	1981	314
85 2/8	17 4/8	17 3/8	6 1/8	6 1/8	2 7/8	2 6/8	9 3/8	8 4/8	5 4/8	5 7/8	Carbon Co., WY	Patrick R. Adams	Patrick R. Adams	1982	314
85 2/8	16 3/8	16 3/8	6 7/8	6 6/8	2 7/8	2 5/8	14 3/8	10 5/8	6 2/8	6 2/8	Coconino Co., AZ	Philip S. Leiendecker	Philip S. Leiendecker	1982	314
85 2/8	16 7/8	16 7/8	7	7	3	3	11 6/8	6 1/8	5 3/8	6 1/8	Sweetwater Co., WY	L. Bill Miller	L. Bill Miller	1982	314
85 2/8	16 1/8	16 1/8	7	7	2 7/8	2 7/8	10 5/8	7 1/8	5 5/8	5 1/8	Rosebud Co., MT	Dale R. Brauer	Dale R. Brauer	1983	314
85 2/8	17 3/8	17 1/8	7 2/8	7	2 6/8	2 6/8	12	7 2/8	5 2/8	5 1/8	Colfax Co., NM	S.X. Callahan III	S.X. Callahan III	1983	314
85 2/8	17 1/8	17 2/8	6 4/8	6 4/8	2 4/8	2 4/8	14 1/8	13 2/8	5 1/8	6 6/8	Emery Co., UT	Marvin L. Thayn	Marvin L. Thayn	1986	314
85 2/8	16	18	6 6/8	6 6/8	2 7/8	2 7/8	13	9 2/8	6	5 7/8	Socorro Co., NM	L. Steve Waide	L. Steve Waide	1986	314

PRONGHORN

Antilocapra americana americana and related subspecies

Score	Length of Horn R	L	Circumference of Base R	L	Circumference at Third Quarter R	L	Inside Spread	Tip to Tip Spread	Length of Prong R	L	Locality	Hunter	Owner	Date Killed	Rank
85 2/8	16 4/8	16 3/8	6 6/8	6 6/8	2 7/8	2 6/8	7 1/8	2 2/8	6 3/8	5 7/8	Navajo Co., AZ	Robert A. Dodson	Robert A. Dodson	1989	314
85 2/8	16 4/8	16 4/8	6 6/8	6 4/8	2 7/8	3	7 5/8	2 6/8	7	5 4/8	Natrona Co., WY	J. Brendan Bummer	J. Brendan Bummer	1990	314
85 2/8	15	14 7/8	7 1/8	7 1/8	3	2 7/8	10 3/8	7 3/8	6 3/8	5 7/8	McKenzie Co., ND	Michael A. Palmer	Michael A. Palmer	1990	314
85 2/8	17	16 7/8	6 5/8	6 3/8	2 7/8	2 7/8	12 3/8	7 4/8	5 4/8	6	Baker Co., OR	Gordon C. Van Patten	Gordon C. Van Patten	1990	314
85 2/8	16 5/8	17	7 1/8	7 2/8	2 3/8	2 3/8	12 6/8	10 7/8	5 4/8	6 2/8	Harney Co., OR	Sharon L. Ganos	Sharon L. Ganos	1992	314
85 2/8	15 7/8	15 6/8	7	6 6/8	2 7/8	2 7/8	11 1/8	7 1/8	5 7/8	5 6/8	Unita Co., WY	Michael D. Wayman	Michael D. Wayman	1994	314
85 2/8	17	16 2/8	7 1/8	7	2 7/8	2 6/8	10 3/8	6 1/8	5 5/8	6 5/8	Coconino Co., AZ	Donald E. Wyckoff	Donald E. Wyckoff	1994	314
85 2/8	16 3/8	16 3/8	7	6 6/8	2 3/8	2 4/8	10 4/8	5 7/8	6 3/8	6 4/8	Carbon Co., WY	Michael S. Carrico	Michael S. Carrico	1996	314
85 2/8	16 4/8	16 2/8	6 7/8	7	2 3/8	3	6 4/8	0 4/8	5 3/8	5 2/8	Natrona Co., WY	Dwight O. Wicker	Dwight O. Wicker	1996	314
85	15 3/8	14 7/8	7 4/8	7 4/8	2 7/8	2 7/8	11 1/8	6 1/8	6	5 6/8	Douglas, WY	Floyd Bishop	Floyd Bishop	1937	350
85	16 5/8	16 4/8	6 5/8	6 5/8	2 6/8	2 6/8	13 2/8	9 6/8	5 2/8	5 3/8	Campbell Co., WY	O.P. Nicholson	Johnson Co. Museum	1937	350
85	15 3/8	15 2/8	7 4/8	7 4/8	2 5/8	2 5/8	11	10 1/8	6 4/8	6	Henderson, NM	Ron Vance	Ron Vance	1943	350
85	17 5/8	17 4/8	5 5/8	5 5/8	2 5/8	2 5/8	9 7/8	7 2/8	6 2/8	6 3/8	Washoe Co., NV	Walter C. Bell	Walter C. Bell	1949	350
85	18	18 1/8	6 5/8	6 4/8	2 6/8	2 5/8	18 2/8	14 4/8	5 1/8	5 1/8	Plush, OR	Ernest E. Puddy	Ernest E. Puddy	1949	350
85	14 7/8	15 1/8	6 4/8	6 4/8	3	3	14 4/8	12 2/8	5 3/8	5 6/8	Brothers, OR	Orlo Flock	Orlo Flock	1955	350
85	15	15	6 6/8	6 5/8	3 1/8	3 1/8	14 1/8	10 7/8	5 7/8	6	Raleigh, ND	Archie Malm	Archie Malm	1958	350
85	15 5/8	15 6/8	6	6	3	3	9 6/8	8 1/8	4 5/8	5 3/8	Sage Creek Basin, WY	Robert A. Hill	Robert A. Hill	1959	350
85	19 3/8	18 7/8	6 4/8	6 2/8	3 2/8	2 4/8	14 1/8	8 5/8	5 3/8	4 7/8	Williams, AZ	Donovan E. Smith	Donovan E. Smith	1959	350
85	17 3/8	17 5/8	6 6/8	6 6/8	2 7/8	2 7/8	17 3/8	14 4/8	5	5 1/8	Forsyth, MT	John M. Broadwell	John M. Broadwell	1961	350
85	15 4/8	15 4/8	6 6/8	6 4/8	3 2/8	3 2/8	10	5 4/8	4 6/8	5	Brusett, MT	Unknown	Frank McKeever	PR 1962	350
85	16	15 7/8	7	7	2 5/8	2 5/8	8 6/8	4 6/8	5 6/8	5 7/8	Rawlins, WY	Clarence J. Becker	Clarence J. Becker	1965	350
85	16 1/8	15 6/8	6 7/8	7	2 7/8	2 7/8	10 4/8	7 4/8	6 7/8	6 2/8	Garfield Co., MT	W.A. Delaney	W.A. Delaney	1965	350
85	14 5/8	14 4/8	8 1/8	7 6/8	2 7/8	2 7/8	11 5/8	10 2/8	5 7/8	5 6/8	Saratoga, WY	Benny E. Bechtol	Benny E. Bechtol	1968	350
85	16 2/8	16 2/8	6 6/8	6 6/8	3	3	14 1/8	9 1/8	5 7/8	6	Rawlins, WY	H.H. Eighmy	H.H. Eighmy	1969	350
85	15 4/8	15 6/8	7 2/8	7	2 4/8	3	13 2/8	8 7/8	6 5/8	6 1/8	Uinta Co., WY	Joan Beachler	Joan Beachler	1974	350
85	16 3/8	16 1/8	6 3/8	6 4/8	3	3	9 2/8	3 5/8	5 5/8	5 5/8	Torrance Co., NM	Stephen A. Nisbet	Stephen A. Nisbet	1975	350
85	17 3/8	17 7/8	6 2/8	6 4/8	3 2/8	3 2/8	13 5/8	8 5/8	4 7/8	5 1/8	Yavapai Co., AZ	David M. Sanders	David M. Sanders	1976	350
85	18 2/8	18 5/8	6 4/8	6 5/8	2 6/8	2 6/8	13 1/8	9	5	5 3/8	Sierra Co., NM	Charles R. Bowen	Charles R. Bowen	1977	350
85	16 5/8	16 5/8	6 6/8	6 5/8	2 5/8	2 5/8	10 6/8	7 2/8	6	5 7/8	Lake Co., OR	Frank R. Biggs	Frank R. Biggs	1978	350
85	16 5/8	16 6/8	6 4/8	6 4/8	2 7/8	2 6/8	10 2/8	5 2/8	5 6/8	5 6/8	Lincoln Co., WY	Ross M. Wilde	Ross M. Wilde	1980	350
85	16 2/8	16	6 6/8	6 6/8	2 5/8	2 5/8	12 7/8	9 4/8	6 1/8	6 1/8	Carbon Co., WY	Kelly W. Hepworth	Kelly W. Hepworth	1982	350
85	16 6/8	16 6/8	6 3/8	6 3/8	2 7/8	2 7/8	10 2/8	3 5/8	6 2/8	5 5/8	Hudspeth Co., TX	Vernon Dodd	Vernon Dodd	1984	350
85	17	17 2/3	6 2/8	6 2/8	2 6/8	2 5/8	11 7/8	8 4/8	6 1/8	6 3/8	Millard Co., UT	Scott C. Rowley	Scott C. Rowley	1984	350
85	16 1/8	16	6 5/8	6 6/8	2 7/8	2 7/8	13 1/8	8 2/8	4 4/8	4 4/8	Garfield Co., MT	Jeff M. Busse	Jeff M. Busse	1988	350
85	17 4/8	18	6	6	2 6/8	2 6/8	17	13 6/8	5 5/8	5 6/8	Hudspeth Co., TX	Ronnie L. Hinze	Ronnie L. Hinze	1988	350
85	16 6/8	16 7/8	6 5/8	6 6/8	3	3	11 4/8	8 3/8	5	5	Rosebud Co., MT	Daniel D. Ova	Daniel D. Ova	1988	350
85	15 5/8	15 3/8	6 6/8	6 6/8	2 6/8	2 6/8	9 4/8	4 3/8	6 6/8	6 6/8	Sweetwater Co., WY	Ronald L. Barber	Ronald L. Barber	1989	350
85	17 5/8	18 1/8	6 6/8	6 3/8	2 7/8	2 7/8	10 7/8	3 1/8	5 3/8	5 2/8	Coconino Co., AZ	John L. Neely	John L. Neely	1989	350

Score	Length of Horn	Circ. of Base R	Circ. of Base L	Circ. Third Qtr. R	Circ. Third Qtr. L	Inside Spread	Tip to Tip	Prong R	Prong L	Hunter	Owner	Locality	Date	Rank
85	15 7/8	7 3/8	7 2/8	2 5/8	2 4/8	7 3/8	4 5/8	6 4/8	6 3/8	Mary A. Barbour	Mary A. Barbour	Sweetwater Co., WY	1990	350
85	17	7	7	2 5/8	2 4/8	15 2/8	10 6/8	5 3/8	5 2/8	Ernie Davis	Ernie Davis	De Baca Co., NM	1991	350
85	15 1/8	7 2/8	7 3/8	3 3/8	3 4/8	12	9 7/8	5	5	Jess Jones	Jess Jones	Socorro Co., NM	1992	350
85	16 2/8	6 2/8	6 2/8	3	3	13	10 5/8	6 1/8	5 7/8	Charles R. Senter	Charles R. Senter	Dallam Co., TX	1992	350
85	16 6/8	6 5/8	6 5/8	3	3	12 3/8	8 2/8	5 4/8	5 3/8	Craig R. Johnson	Craig R. Johnson	Yavapai Co., AZ	1993	350
85	15 5/8	6 6/8	6 7/8	2 7/8	2 6/8	16	13 4/8	6 3/8	5 6/8	Ruth L. Tasa	Ruth L. Tasa	Coconino Co., AZ	1994	350
85	15 7/8	6 4/8	6 4/8	3 1/8	2 7/8	16	6 5/8	6 4/8	6 4/8	Rebecca R. Thomas	Rebecca R. Thomas	Yavapai Co., AZ	1994	350
85	15 1/8	5 3/8	7 2/8	2 6/8	2 6/8	12 1/8	5 6/8	6 3/8	5 7/8	Theodore Heimburger	Theodore Heimburger	Carbon Co., WY	1995	350
85	16 1/8	7 1/8	7 1/8	3	3	13	11 1/8	4 6/8	4 6/8	Mark B. Steffen	Mark B. Steffen	Natrona Co., WY	1997	350
84 6/8	15 7/8	7 3/8	7 3/8	2 3/8	2 4/8	7	1	6 2/8	5 6/8	William A. Shaw	William A. Shaw	Modoc Co., CA	1942	388
84 6/8	16 5/8	6 7/8	6 6/8	2 6/8	2 6/8	14 6/8	11 2/8	6 7/8	5 5/8	Elgin T. Gates	Elgin T. Gates	Anderson Mesa, AZ	1955	388
84 6/8	17 1/8	6 1/8	6 1/8	2 6/8	2 6/8	12 2/8	10 5/8	6 2/8	6 7/8	Jim Calkins	Jim Calkins	Slate Creek, WY	1956	388
84 6/8	16 4/8	6 5/8	6 5/8	2 4/8	2 4/8	10 5/8	3 4/8	6 1/8	5 5/8	Roger D. Ramsay	Roger D. Ramsay	Laramie, WY	1958	388
84 6/8	16 3/8	6	6 3/8	2 7/8	2 7/8	8 3/8	7 4/8	4 5/8	4 7/8	Elmer Rupert	Elmer Rupert	Laramie Peak, WY	1961	388
84 6/8	16	7 2/8	7 2/8	3	3	11 3/8	6 6/8	5	4 6/8	Joseph Nelson	Joseph Nelson	Alliance, NE	1962	388
84 6/8	17 3/8	7 1/8	7 1/8	3	3	12 1/8	12 4/8	5 4/8	4 4/8	Dick Cone	Dick Cone	Fremont Co., WY	1963	388
84 6/8	16 3/8	6 4/8	6 4/8	2 7/8	2 7/8	14 6/8	7	5	5	John Kastner	John Kastner	Sinclair, WY	1963	388
84 6/8	15 4/8	6 4/8	6 4/8	3	3	11 1/8	7	5 4/8	5 5/8	D.R. Knoll	D.R. Knoll	Harney Co., OR	1963	388
84 6/8	17	7 4/8	7	3 6/8	3 5/8	7 4/8	11 1/8	6 1/8	5 3/8	J.E. Edwards	J.E. Edwards	Jenner, AB	1964	388
84 6/8	16 6/8	6 7/8	6 7/8	2 4/8	2 4/8	14 6/8	11	5 2/8	4 7/8	John G. Carroll	John G. Carroll	Johnson Co., WY	1965	388
84 6/8	15 7/8	7	7	3	3 5/8	12	6 2/8	7	7	W. Daniel English	W. Daniel English	Rock Springs, WY	1966	388
84 6/8	17	6 2/8	6 2/8	2 5/8	2 5/8	10 6/8	16	5 3/8	5 1/8	Claus Karlson	Claus Karlson	Custer Co., ID	1966	388
84 6/8	16	6 6/8	6 6/8	2 6/8	2 6/8	17	5 4/8	6 4/8	6 4/8	John E. Mohritz	John E. Mohritz	Casper, WY	1966	388
84 6/8	16 2/8	6 4/8	6 3/8	2 4/8	2 3/8	11 2/8	3 5/8	7	6 7/8	George M. Owen	George M. Owen	Navajo Co., AZ	1966	388
84 6/8	15 5/8	6 1/8	6 5/8	2 5/8	2 5/8	8 5/8	5 1/8	5 6/8	5 5/8	Robert Ziker	Robert Ziker	Poison Spider Creek, WY	1966	388
84 6/8	16 2/8	7 6/8	7 6/8	2 3/8	2 3/8	10 2/8	13 6/8	6 5/8	5 1/8	Leland C. Lehman	Leland C. Lehman	Modoc Co., CA	1969	388
84 6/8	16 5/8	6 2/8	6 2/8	2 3/8	2 3/8	10 4/8	8 6/8	5 2/8	5 2/8	Bob Dixon	Bob Dixon	Boquillas Ranch, AZ	1970	388
84 6/8	19 4/8	6 1/8	6 1/8	2 5/8	2 5/8	18	5 1/8	5 7/8	4 5/8	Donald Smith	Donald Smith	Ft. Apache Res., AZ	1972	388
84 6/8	15 7/8	6 5/8	6 5/8	3 5/8	3 6/8	13 5/8	7 1/8	5 4/8	5 2/8	James C. MacLachlan	James C. MacLachlan	Moffat Co., CO	1975	388
84 6/8	16 3/8	7	7	2 6/8	2 6/8	11	5	5 6/8	5 7/8	Richard Mosley	Richard Mosley	Garden Co., NE	1978	388
84 6/8	15 6/8	6 1/8	6 1/8	2 7/8	2 7/8	10 2/8	11 4/8	6 3/8	6 1/8	Earnest Anacleto	Earnest Anacleto	Modoc Co., CA	1980	388
84 6/8	16 4/8	6 2/8	6 2/8	2 6/8	2 6/8	9 7/8	5	4 4/8	4 4/8	Pat McCarty	Pat McCarty	Lincoln Co., NV	1980	388
84 6/8	17 1/8	7 3/8	7 3/8	2 6/8	2 6/8	13 6/8	3 2/8	5 1/8	5 2/8	Lloyd B. Miller	Lloyd B. Miller	Washoe Co., NV	1980	388
84 6/8	15 4/8	7 2/8	7 3/8	2 6/8	2 6/8	10	8 3/8	6 6/8	6 4/8	W. Bruce Mouw	W. Bruce Mouw	Natrona Co., WY	1980	388
84 6/8	16 2/8	6 5/8	6 5/8	2 5/8	2 5/8	8 5/8	7 4/8	6 5/8	6 4/8	Martin Vavra	Martin Vavra	Baker Co., OR	1981	388
84 6/8	14 1/8	7 3/8	7 1/8	3 3/8	3 2/8	11 1/8	8 4/8	6 5/8	6 2/8	James E. Egger	James E. Egger	Fremont Co., WY	1981	388
84 6/8	16 7/8	6 5/8	6 2/8	2 4/8	2 4/8	9 2/8	7 6/8	7 1/8	7 1/8	Robb D. Hitchcock	Robb D. Hitchcock	Carbon Co., WY	1982	388
84 6/8	15 4/8	7 2/8	7 2/8	2 4/8	2 4/8	11 4/8	1 5/8	6 5/8	6 5/8	David L. Thompson	David L. Thompson	Sweetwater Co., WY	1983	388
84 6/8	17	6 3/8	6 3/8	2 7/8	2 7/8	11 5/8	4 2/8	6	5 4/8	Sherl L. Chapman	Sherl L. Chapman	Lemhi Co., ID	1983	388
84 6/8	16 3/8	6 3/8	6 3/8	3 2/8	3 2/8	8	9 3/8	5 2/8	5 3/8	Paul Herring	Paul Herring	Carbon Co., WY	1986	388
84 6/8	16 7/8	6 4/8	6 4/8	3 1/8	3 1/8	16 5/8	11 1/8	7 1/8	5	Ernie Davis	Ernie Davis	Hudspeth Co., TX	1986	388
84 6/8	16	6	6 1/8	2 4/8	2 4/8	8 6/8	5	4 7/8	5	Charles D. Tuttle	Charles D. Tuttle	Hudspeth Co., TX	1987	388
84 6/8	15 4/8	7 7/8	7 2/8	3	3	11 7/8	6	6	6 3/8	William P. Boone	William P. Boone	Mora Co., NM	1989	388
84 6/8	16 1/8	6	6	2 4/8	2 7/8	8 5/8	2 2/8	5 6/8	5 5/8	John P. Grimmett	John P. Grimmett	Catron Co., NM	1989	388
84 6/8	16 3/8	6 3/8	6 3/8	3 1/8	3 1/8	13 2/8	11 2/8	6 7/8	6 7/8	Melvin E. Killman	Melvin E. Killman	Sweetwater Co., WY	1990	388
84 6/8	16 4/8	6 4/8	6 4/8	2 5/8	2 5/8	6 3/8	6 4/8	6 3/8	6 3/8	Gary Caraccioli	Gary Caraccioli	Lassen Co., CA	1990	388
84 6/8	16	6 7/8	6 7/8	2 6/8	2 5/8	7 6/8	3 7/8	6 6/8	6 5/8	Warren N. Pearce	Warren N. Pearce	Natrona Co., WY	1990	388

PRONGHORN

Antilocapra americana americana and related subspecies

Score	Length of Horn R	L	Circumference of Base R	L	Circumference at Third Quarter R	L	Inside Spread	Tip to Tip Spread	Length of Prong R	L	Locality	Hunter	Owner	Date Killed	Rank
84 6/8	15 7/8	15 4/8	7	7 2/8	2 7/8	2 7/8	9 3/8	6 4/8	5 3/8	5 6/8	Hutchinson Co., TX	Rex A. Umbarger	Rex A. Umbarger	1990	388
84 6/8	15 2/8	15 3/8	7 3/8	7 4/8	2 6/8	2 5/8	11 3/8	9 6/8	6	5 7/8	Carbon Co., WY	Myron J. Wakkuri	Myron J. Wakkuri	1990	388
84 6/8	16 4/8	16 1/8	6 5/8	6 3/8	3	2 4/8	8 4/8	3 6/8	6 4/8	6 5/8	Cochise Co., AZ	David J. Braun	David J. Braun	1991	388
84 6/8	17 1/8	17 1/8	6 4/8	6 1/8	2 6/8	2 4/8	12 4/8	8 2/8	5 6/8	5 6/8	Coconino Co., AZ	Jerrell F. Coburn	Jerrell F. Coburn	1991	388
84 6/8	16 5/8	16 6/8	6 4/8	6 4/8	2 5/8	2 5/8	12 4/8	6 7/8	6 2/8	6 2/8	Socorro Co., NM	Charles A. Grimmett	Charles A. Grimmett	1991	388
84 6/8	16 3/8	16 4/8	6 4/8	6 4/8	2 4/8	2 5/8	7 2/8	1 2/8	4 6/8	5 3/8	Fremont Co., WY	Karen L. Jenson	Karen L. Jenson	1991	388
84 6/8	15 5/8	15 6/8	7 1/8	7	3 1/8	3 1/8	12	8 2/8	5 3/8	5 3/8	Carbon Co., WY	Brian T. King	Brian T. King	1991	388
84 6/8	14 6/8	15	6 6/8	6 6/8	2 7/8	2 6/8	14 5/8	11 7/8	5 6/8	5 2/8	Converse Co., WY	Michael R. Land	Michael R. Land	1991	388
84 6/8	16 1/8	15 7/8	6 6/8	6 6/8	3 1/8	3	11 1/8	7 4/8	5 5/8	5 6/8	Mora Co., NM	Linda J. McBride	Linda J. McBride	1991	388
84 6/8	16 2/8	16 2/8	6 5/8	6 5/8	2 3/8	2 3/8	10 2/8	5 2/8	7	6 5/8	Lake Co., OR	Patrick R. McConnell	Patrick R. McConnell	1991	388
84 6/8	17 4/8	17 5/8	7 1/8	6 7/8	2 4/8	2 5/8	13 4/8	11 6/8	4 6/8	4 6/8	Mora Co., NM	Robert Model	Robert Model	1991	388
84 6/8	17	16 4/8	6 4/8	6 5/8	3	3 2/8	11 4/8	6 4/8	6	5 4/8	Lincoln Co., NM	Jay B. Robert	Jay B. Robert	1991	388
84 6/8	16 3/8	16 2/8	6 2/8	6 2/8	2 4/8	2 4/8	15 2/8	11 4/8	5 7/8	6	Mora Co., NM	Donald W. Martin	Donald W. Martin	1992	388
84 6/8	16 2/8	16 1/8	7 2/8	7	2 7/8	3	9 3/8	3 1/8	5 5/8	5 4/8	Carter Co., MT	Daniel Goodman	Daniel Goodman	1993	388
84 6/8	15 3/8	15 3/8	7	7	2 4/8	2 4/8	14 6/8	11 4/8	7 2/8	7	Petroleum Co., MT	Daniel S. Wentz	Daniel S. Wentz	1993	388
84 6/8	15 2/8	15 2/8	7 4/8	7 4/8	3 1/8	3 2/8	10 6/8	4 7/8	5 2/8	5 2/8	Natrona Co., WY	Brian J. Bummer	Brian J. Bummer	1994	388
84 6/8	16	15 2/8	7	6 7/8	2 6/8	2 6/8	13 7/8	12	6	6	Mora Co., NM	Walter O. Ford, Jr.	Walter O. Ford, Jr.	1994	388
84 6/8	16 4/8	16 1/8	6 6/8	6 6/8	2 4/8	2 5/8	8 1/8	2	6 6/8	7	Emery Co., UT	Tomme L. Gold	Tomme L. Gold	1995	388
84 6/8	16 5/8	16 1/8	7	7 2/8	2 6/8	2 6/8	7 6/8	2	5 6/8	5 2/8	Mora Co., NM	Ilynn Guldman	Ilynn Guldman	1995	388
84 6/8	16 7/8	16 7/8	6 6/8	6 6/8	2 7/8	3	10 7/8	5 5/8	5 4/8	5 5/8	Rosebud Co., MT	John W. Lane	John W. Lane	1995	388
84 6/8	16	16	6 3/8	6 5/8	3 1/8	3	10 4/8	6 4/8	6 3/8	6 2/8	Socorro Co., NM	Kevin A. Teston	Kevin A. Teston	1996	388
84 6/8	15 2/8	15 4/8	8	7 5/8	3	2 6/8	13 3/8	9	5 4/8	5 4/8	Colfax Co., NM	Robert D. Jones	Robert D. Jones	1997	388
84 6/8	17 4/8	17	6 3/8	6 3/8	2 6/8	2 6/8	8 2/8	3 1/8	5 5/8	5 2/8	Socorro Co., NM	David A. Miller	David A. Miller	1997	388
84 6/8	17 5/8	16 7/8	6 6/8	6 5/8	3	3	10 3/8	4 7/8	5 7/8	5 3/8	Yellowstone Co., MT	Michael E. Schieno	Michael E. Schieno	1997	388
84 4/8	16 3/8	16 3/8	7 1/8	7	2 5/8	2 5/8	9 6/8	6	5 3/8	5 3/8	Carbon Co., WY	A.A. Carrey	A.A. Carrey	1944	450
84 4/8	16 4/8	16 2/8	6 2/8	6 2/8	2 6/8	2 6/8	12 7/8	9 2/8	7 6/8	7 5/8	Chihuahua, MX	Julio Estrada	Julio Estrada	1945	450
84 4/8	15 7/8	15 6/8	7 2/8	7 4/8	2 6/8	2 6/8	10 6/8	5 5/8	5 2/8	6 3/8	North Dakota	Dale Linderman	Dale Linderman	PR 1952	450
84 4/8	16	16	5 5/8	5 5/8	2 7/8	2 7/8	14 4/8	13 7/8	5 1/8	5	Fremont Co., WY	Ernest R. Novotny	Ernest R. Novotny	1954	450
84 4/8	16 6/8	16 5/8	6 1/8	6 1/8	2 6/8	2 6/8	10 3/8	4 2/8	6 3/8	6 2/8	Tripp Co., SD	Roy Hazuka	Roy Hazuka	1962	450
84 4/8	15 6/8	15 7/8	7 5/8	7 5/8	2 4/8	2 4/8	14 7/8	10 3/8	5 6/8	5 7/8	Rawlins, WY	Eloise Kees	Eloise Kees	1962	450
84 4/8	18 4/8	18	7	7	3	3	13	8 4/8	5 7/8	3 4/8	Seligman, AZ	Garth A. Brown	Garth A. Brown	1964	450
84 4/8	14 7/8	14 6/8	7 4/8	7 4/8	2 6/8	2 6/8	9 1/8	5 7/8	5 7/8	6 2/8	Baggs, WY	Tom Elberson	Tom Elberson	1966	450
84 4/8	17	17 1/8	6 4/8	6 4/8	2 4/8	2 4/8	11 1/8	5 1/8	5 6/8	5 6/8	Sweetwater Co., WY	Harvey B. Bartley	Harvey B. Bartley	1970	450
84 4/8	16 2/8	16 2/8	6	6	2 3/8	2 3/8	13	8	7 1/8	7	Carbon Co., WY	William G. Mackey	William G. Mackey	1972	450
84 4/8	14 5/8	14 7/8	6 7/8	7 1/8	2 6/8	2 6/8	12 6/8	8 6/8	6 1/8	6 5/8	Lake Co., OR	Gene Cormie	Gene Cormie	1973	450
84 4/8	16	16	6 4/8	6 5/8	2 4/8	2 4/8	12 3/8	7 3/8	6 6/8	6 6/8	Lincoln Co., WY	George Kirkman	George Kirkman	1973	450
84 4/8	16 3/8	16 4/8	7 2/8	7 2/8	2 4/8	2 3/8	13 3/8	7 7/8	5 6/8	5 6/8	Washoe Co., NV	Frances M. Hansell	Frances M. Hansell	1974	450
84 4/8	17	16 5/8	7 2/8	7 2/8	2 3/8	2 3/8	9 6/8	7 4/8	6	6 1/8	Fields, OR	John H. Johnson	John H. Johnson	1974	450

Score	L. Horn R	L. Horn L	Circ. Base R	Circ. Base L	Circ. 3rd Qtr R	Circ. 3rd Qtr L	Inside Spread	Tip to Tip	Prong R	Prong L	Locality	Hunter	Owner	Date	Rank
84 4/8	15	15 3/8	7 5/8	7 2/8	2 6/8	2 6/8	6 5/8	4 6/8	6 6/8	5 6/8	Carbon Co., WY	Stephen C. LeBlanc	Stephen C. LeBlanc	1976	450
84 4/8	15 6/8	16	7 4/8	7 4/8	3	3 1/8	10 4/8	6 6/8	5 1/8	5 3/8	Carbon Co., WY	John C. Sjogren	John C. Sjogren	1976	450
84 4/8	17 1/8	16 6/8	6 2/8	6 3/8	2 2/8	2 3/8	15 6/8	13 7/8	6	5 3/8	Modoc Co., CA	J. Bob Johnson	J. Bob Johnson	1978	450
84 4/8	16 3/8	16 3/8	7	6 7/8	3	2 3/8	14 6/8	12 5/8	6 7/8	5 4/8	Sweetwater Co., WY	Frankie Miller	Frankie Miller	1979	450
84 4/8	17 7/8	17 6/8	6 5/8	6 5/8	2 3/8	2 7/8	13 6/8	8 1/8	7 4/8	4 6/8	Lake Co., OR	Rodger D. Bates	Rodger D. Bates	1980	450
84 4/8	17 2/8	17	6 5/8	6 5/8	3	3	8 3/8	4 1/8	6 5/8	6	Sweetwater Co., WY	Lee Frudden	Lee Frudden	1981	450
84 4/8	16 1/8	16 4/8	6 4/8	6 5/8	2 6/8	2 7/8	15	12 2/8	6 5/8	5 5/8	Carbon Co., WY	Jack A. Berger	Jack A. Berger	1982	450
84 4/8	15	15	7 4/8	7 4/8	3	3	9 6/8	7 3/8	6 5/8	5 5/8	Carbon Co., WY	William J. Stokes	William J. Stokes	1982	450
84 4/8	15 4/8	15 2/8	6 2/8	6 3/8	2 6/8	2 5/8	13 6/8	10	7	6 6/8	Fremont Co., WY	Michael P. Hauffe	Michael P. Hauffe	1983	450
84 4/8	17 5/8	17 3/8	7 3/8	7 2/8	3	3	7 5/8	4 6/8	7 4/8	5 5/8	Yavapai Co., AZ	John E. Jerome, Jr.	John E. Jerome, Jr.	1983	450
84 4/8	16 6/8	16 7/8	6	6	2 5/8	2 5/8	14 4/8	8 6/8	6 3/8	4 5/8	Fremont Co., WY	William R. Suranyi	William R. Suranyi	1983	450
84 4/8	16 4/8	16 2/8	6 3/8	7 4/8	3	2 5/8	9	5 1/8	7 2/8	4 3/8	Phillips Co., MT	Donald W. Hellhake	Donald W. Hellhake	1984	450
84 4/8	16	16 4/8	7 2/8	6 7/8	2 4/8	2 5/8	8 4/8	4 4/8	6	7	Natrona Co., WY	Joe L. Ficken	Joe L. Ficken	1985	450
84 4/8	17	17 4/8	6 7/8	7	2 5/8	2 3/8	15	11	7 4/8	5 5/8	Deschutes Co., OR	Rick Ward	Rick Ward	1985	450
84 4/8	17 3/8	17 3/8	6 2/8	7	2 4/8	2 5/8	7 5/8	1 7/8	6 7/8	5 2/8	Emery Co., UT	Bruce Gordon	Bruce Gordon	1986	450
84 4/8	16 4/8	16 5/8	6 5/8	7	2 7/8	2 6/8	8 3/8	4	6 2/8	5 7/8	Sweetwater Co., WY	Mike D. McKell	Mike D. McKell	1986	450
84 4/8	16 1/8	16 4/8	7	7 2/8	2 6/8	2 6/8	7 3/8	2 5/8	6 7/8	5 7/8	Prairie Co., MT	Duane R. Pisk	Duane R. Pisk	1988	450
84 4/8	17 1/8	17 1/8	7	6 2/8	2 7/8	2 7/8	11 6/8	8 2/8	7	5 1/8	Washoe Co., NV	Tracy A. Tripp	Tracy A. Tripp	1989	450
84 4/8	14 7/8	15 1/8	7 2/8	6 2/8	2 7/8	2 7/8	8 6/8	4 6/8	7 2/8	5 6/8	Fremont Co., WY	Lyle D. Fruchey	Lyle D. Fruchey	1990	450
84 4/8	17 1/8	17	6 1/8	7	3	2 4/8	12 2/8	6 4/8	6 2/8	6 2/8	Humboldt Co., NV	Shawn R. Hall	Shawn R. Hall	1990	450
84 4/8	16 1/8	15 7/8	7	6 7/8	2 4/8	2 6/8	11 7/8	10 4/8	7	5 2/8	Cutbank Creek, AB	Cameron C. Owen	Cameron C. Owen	1990	450
84 4/8	14 2/8	14 1/8	6 7/8	6 2/8	2 6/8	3 7/8	8 6/8	4 4/8	7	6 1/8	Logan Co., KS	Corey Urban	Corey Urban	1991	450
84 4/8	15 7/8	15 7/8	6 4/8	6 3/8	2 5/8	2 5/8	13 4/8	9 7/8	6 2/8	6 2/8	Mora Co., NM	Kenneth L. Ebbens	Kenneth L. Ebbens	1991	450
84 4/8	16 7/8	16 5/8	6 3/8	6 6/8	2 6/8	2 7/8	12 2/8	6 4/8	6 2/8	5 7/8	Hudspeth Co., TX	Larry R. Price	Larry R. Price	1991	450
84 4/8	16 6/8	17	6 6/8	6	2 7/8	2 7/8	15	11 6/8	6 6/8	5	Union Co., NM	Walter R. Schreiner, Jr.	Walter R. Schreiner, Jr.	1991	450
84 4/8	16	15 6/8	7	7 1/8	3	3 2/8	13 7/8	14	7	4 5/8	Natrona Co., WY	Barry N. Strang	Barry N. Strang	1992	450
84 4/8	16 6/8	16 4/8	6 4/8	6 7/8	2 5/8	2 5/8	8 7/8	2 5/8	7 1/8	6	Sweetwater Co., WY	Clint N. Gibson	Clint N. Gibson	1992	450
84 4/8	15 6/8	15 5/8	6 7/8	7 1/8	2 4/8	2 4/8	10 3/8	9	6 7/8	6 5/8	Carbon Co., WY	Kirby C. Hornbeck	Kirby C. Hornbeck	1992	450
84 4/8	16 5/8	16 5/8	7 1/8	7 2/8	2 6/8	2 6/8	10 7/8	6 1/8	7 1/8	4 4/8	Fremont Co., WY	Jeff A. Schweighart	Jeff A. Schweighart	1992	450
84 4/8	15 4/8	16	6 7/8	6 6/8	2 7/8	2 6/8	7 4/8	4	7 2/8	5 6/8	Humboldt Co., NV	Stuart W. Shepherd	Stuart W. Shepherd	1992	450
84 4/8	14 4/8	14 3/8	6 6/8	6 3/8	3	2 7/8	10 2/8	7 3/8	7	6 4/8	Humboldt Co., NV	Rebecca L. Webley	Rebecca L. Webley	1993	450
84 4/8	15 3/8	15 4/8	6 6/8	6 6/8	3	3	10 6/8	7 2/8	7	5 4/8	Yavapai Co., AZ	Eric D. Olson	Eric D. Olson	1994	450
84 4/8	17 5/8	17 4/8	6 5/8	6 5/8	3	2 6/8	13 5/8	9 2/8	6 5/8	4 7/8	Mora Co., NM	Ross F. Adams	Ross F. Adams	1995	450
84 4/8	17	17	6 3/8	6 3/8	2 6/8	3	15	12 2/8	6 5/8	5 7/8	Socorro Co., NM	Dennis J. Sites	Dennis J. Sites	1996	450
84 4/8	16 6/8	16 6/8	6 6/8	6 3/8	3 1/8	3 1/8	9 5/8	3 6/8	6 3/8	5 4/8	Sweetwater River, WY	Reuben R. Tipton III	Reuben R. Tipton III	1996	450
84 2/8	16 6/8	16 6/8	6 7/8	6 3/8	2 6/8	2 6/8	10 2/8	5 7/8	6 6/8	5 2/8	Pumpkin Buttes, WY	Kermit Platt	Kermit Platt	1952	499
84 2/8	15 4/8	15	7 1/8	7 1/8	3 1/8	3	11 4/8	11	6 3/8	4 4/8	Sage Creek Basin, WY	John B. Miller	John B. Miller	1957	499
84 2/8	16 4/8	16 4/8	7	7	3 2/8	2 5/8	10 2/8	6 1/8	6 3/8	4 6/8	Natrona Co., WY	Aydeen Auld	Aydeen Auld	1959	499
84 2/8	16 2/8	16 5/8	7	7	2 5/8	2 3/8	7 5/8	1 7/8	6 4/8	6	Uinta Co., WY	William Fisher	William Fisher	1960	499
84 2/8	16	16 3/8	7 1/8	7	2 6/8	2 5/8	11 5/8	7 6/8	7	6 2/8	Rawlins, WY	Ross Lukenbill	Ross Lukenbill	1965	499
84 2/8	15 7/8	16	7 1/8	7	3	2 5/8	10 2/8	5 1/8	6 1/8	6 1/8	Fremont Co., WY	Armin O. Baltensweiler	Armin O. Baltensweiler	1966	499
84 2/8	16 2/8	16 1/8	7 3/8	7 1/8	2 6/8	2 6/8	12 3/8	8 6/8	5 6/8	5 5/8	Big Piney, WY	Edward S. Friend	Edward S. Friend	1967	499
84 2/8	14 6/8	14 7/8	6 5/8	6 5/8	3	3	7 2/8	7 1/8	6 6/8	7 1/8	Ft. Apache Res., AZ	Lawrence M. Kick	Lawrence M. Kick	1967	499
84 2/8	17 7/8	17 7/8	6 1/8	6 1/8	2 7/8	2 7/8	12 1/8	7 6/8	6	6 5/8	Fremont Co., WY	Frank E. White	Frank E. White	1968	499
84 2/8	15	15	7 6/8	7 6/8	2 4/8	2 4/8	13 4/8	11 7/8	7 5/8	4 6/8	Humboldt Co., NV	Lee Arce	Lee Arce	1970	499
84 2/8	17 4/8	17 4/8	7 2/8	7 2/8	2 4/8	2 4/8	8 4/8	5 4/8	7 2/8	4 1/8	Fremont Co., WY	Gerald A. Lent	Gerald A. Lent	1970	499
84 2/8	15 2/8	15	6	6	2 7/8	2 6/8	11 6/8	8 2/8	6	4 7/8	Natrona Co., WY	Donald F. Mahnke	Donald F. Mahnke	1971	499

PRONGHORN

Antilocapra americana americana and related subspecies

Score	Length of Horn R	L	Circumference of Base R	L	Circumference at Third Quarter R	L	Inside Spread	Tip to Tip Spread	Length of Prong R	L	Locality	Hunter	Owner	Date Killed	Rank
84 2/8	16 4/8	16 4/8	7	7	2 6/8	2 6/8	15 1/8	11 2/8	5 2/8	5 2/8	Albany Co., WY	George Panagos, Jr.	George Panagos, Jr.	1972	499
84 2/8	16 6/8	16 7/8	6 6/8	6 5/8	2 6/8	2 6/8	8 4/8	3 7/8	5 4/8	5 3/8	Apache Co., AZ	Alaine D. Neal	Alaine D. Neal	1973	499
84 2/8	17 1/8	17 1/8	5 7/8	5 7/8	2 4/8	2 4/8	8 7/8	1 1/8	7	6 7/8	Abbott, NM	George H. Ray III	George H. Ray III	1974	499
84 2/8	16 4/8	17 2/8	6 6/8	6 6/8	2 5/8	2 6/8	16	11 4/8	5 6/8	6	Meade Co., SD	John Hostetter	John Hostetter	1975	499
84 2/8	16	16 1/8	6 7/8	6 7/8	2 7/8	3	9 7/8	7	4 5/8	4 2/8	Carbon Co., WY	William O. Queen	William O. Queen	1975	499
84 2/8	17 4/8	17 4/8	6 5/8	6 5/8	2 6/8	2 4/8	11 2/8	8 1/8	4 5/8	4 3/8	Sweetwater Co., WY	Bill Jordan	Bill Jordan	1976	499
84 2/8	15 2/8	15 2/8	7 3/8	7 1/8	2 6/8	2 5/8	13	12 1/8	5 6/8	5 6/8	Carbon Co., WY	Kenneth Mellin	Kenneth Mellin	1976	499
84 2/8	16 4/8	16 3/8	6 4/8	6 3/8	3	3	8 2/8	5 1/8	5 5/8	6 1/8	Humboldt Co., NV	David Perondi	David Perondi	1976	499
84 2/8	15 5/8	15 7/8	7 3/8	7 2/8	2 4/8	2 5/8	14 2/8	13	5 6/8	5 7/8	Carbon Co., WY	Glenn F. Galbraith	Glenn F. Galbraith	1977	499
84 2/8	15 4/8	15 5/8	7	7 1/8	2 7/8	2 7/8	9	9 6/8	4 6/8	4 5/8	Modoc Co., CA	Unknown	Jess Jones	PR 1978	499
84 2/8	15 4/8	15 2/8	7 4/8	7 4/8	2 5/8	2 5/8	12 3/8	8	6 2/8	6 2/8	Fremont Co., WY	William D. Baldwin	William D. Baldwin	1980	499
84 2/8	15 5/8	15 6/8	7	7	2 4/8	2 4/8	6 4/8	2	6 6/8	6 6/8	Humboldt Co., NV	James R. Puryear	James R. Puryear	1980	499
84 2/8	15 3/8	15 3/8	7 2/8	7 2/8	2 4/8	2 4/8	16 2/8	13 4/8	6	5 7/8	Sweetwater Co., WY	Richard D. Ullery	Richard D. Ullery	1980	499
84 2/8	17	17 3/8	6 6/8	6 5/8	2 6/8	2 7/8	12 2/8	10 2/8	5 4/8	5 6/8	Sweetwater Co., WY	John V. Wilgus	John V. Wilgus	1980	499
84 2/8	15 5/8	16 1/8	6 2/8	6 2/8	2 7/8	3 1/8	9 1/8	5 2/8	6 2/8	6 7/8	Modoc Co., CA	Larry A. Owens, Sr.	Larry A. Owens, Sr.	1981	499
84 2/8	17 2/8	17 4/8	6 2/8	6 3/8	2 6/8	2 6/8	14 6/8	10 4/8	6 1/8	6	Powder River Co., MT	Sam C. Borla	Sam C. Borla	1982	499
84 2/8	16 4/8	16 2/8	6 7/8	6 6/8	2 4/8	2 6/8	13 7/8	10 3/8	6	6	Malheur Co., OR	Matt J. Brundridge	Matt J. Brundridge	1982	499
84 2/8	17	16 6/8	6 4/8	6 3/8	2 5/8	2 4/8	12 2/8	8 4/8	6 1/8	6 1/8	Coconino Co., AZ	Michael A. Cromer	Michael A. Cromer	1982	499
84 2/8	16	16	6 6/8	6 6/8	2 4/8	2 4/8	10	5 2/8	5 5/8	5 6/8	Carbon Co., WY	Ernest L. Tollini	Ernest L. Tollini	1982	499
84 2/8	15 5/8	15 6/8	6 5/8	6 5/8	2 5/8	2 5/8	9 3/8	4 5/8	6 5/8	6 1/8	Carbon Co., WY	Mike Clegg	Mike Clegg	1983	499
84 2/8	16 5/8	16 4/8	7 4/8	7 4/8	3	3	9 2/8	5 1/8	5 1/8	4 6/8	Natrona Co., WY	Allen J. Hogan	Allen J. Hogan	1983	499
84 2/8	17 2/8	17 3/8	6 4/8	6 4/8	2 4/8	2 5/8	8 5/8	2 2/8	5 6/8	5 4/8	Washoe Co., NV	Judy Taylor	Judy Taylor	1983	499
84 2/8	16 6/8	16 7/8	6 2/8	6 2/8	2 7/8	2 7/8	9 1/8	6 6/8	5 3/8	5 2/8	Coconino Co., AZ	William R. Vaughn	William R. Vaughn	1983	499
84 2/8	16	16 2/8	6 5/8	6 5/8	3	3	13 2/8	11	5 6/8	5 6/8	Fremont Co., WY	John Monje	John Monje	1985	499
84 2/8	15	15	6 7/8	6 6/8	3	2 6/8	12 5/8	10 2/8	6 2/8	6	White Pine Co., NV	Paul E. Podborny	Paul E. Podborny	1985	499
84 2/8	16	16	7 4/8	7 3/8	2 5/8	2 5/8	13 2/8	12	4 6/8	4 2/8	Washoe Co., NV	Eugene E. Belli	Eugene E. Belli	1986	499
84 2/8	16	16 2/8	7	7	2 3/8	2 3/8	12	7 2/8	6 2/8	6 4/8	Yellowstone Co., MT	Jim B. Cherpeski	Jim B. Cherpeski	1986	499
84 2/8	14 5/8	14 2/8	6 7/8	6 7/8	2 6/8	2 6/8	7 2/8	6 7/8	6 2/8	6 4/8	Carter Co., MT	Robert Cunningham	Robert Cunningham	1986	499
84 2/8	16 4/8	18 2/8	6 2/8	6 2/8	2 5/8	2 6/8	11 1/8	6 5/8	6 1/8	6 1/8	Coconino Co., AZ	Kevin B. Call	Kevin B. Call	1987	499
84 2/8	15 2/8	15 1/8	6 1/8	6	2 7/8	2 7/8	11 3/8	7 2/8	5 5/8	5 2/8	Baker Co., OR	Paul W. Schon	Paul W. Schon	1987	499
84 2/8	17	16 7/8	6 2/8	6 1/8	2 7/8	2 7/8	13 1/8	7 7/8	6 2/8	6 1/8	Hudspeth Co., TX	Sam H. Gann IV	Sam H. Gann IV	1988	499
84 2/8	16	16	6 6/8	6 5/8	2 3/8	2 3/8	10	4	7	6 6/8	Yavapai Co., AZ	Brian Murray	Brian Murray	1988	499
84 2/8	16 1/8	16 3/8	6 2/8	6 2/8	2 4/8	2 4/8	16 5/8	13	6	7	Hudspeth Co., TX	W. Wayne Spahn	W. Wayne Spahn	1988	499
84 2/8	15 7/8	15 7/8	6 7/8	6 7/8	2 7/8	2 7/8	9 2/8	4 6/8	6 5/8	7 1/8	Weld Co., CO	M. Wayne Hoeben	M. Wayne Hoeben	1989	499
84 2/8	15 7/8	15 1/8	7 1/8	7 1/8	2 5/8	2 5/8	10 1/8	6 3/8	6 2/8	6 2/8	Fremont Co., WY	Boyd E. Sharp, Jr.	Boyd E. Sharp, Jr.	1989	499
84 2/8	16 4/8	16 2/8	6 5/8	6 5/8	2 5/8	2 5/8	11 6/8	7 3/8	5 4/8	6 2/8	Mora Co., NM	Scott Steinkruger	Scott Steinkruger	1989	499
84 2/8	15 3/8	15 5/8	7 3/8	7 3/8	2 6/8	2 6/8	9 3/8	5 1/8	6 1/8	5 5/8	Washakie Co., WY	Douglas D. Stinnette	Douglas D. Stinnette	1989	499
84 2/8	17 1/8	16 2/8	7 1/8	7 1/8	2 5/8	2 4/8	12	7 7/8	6 7/8	6 2/8	San Miguel Co., NM	Larry R. Griffin	Larry R. Griffin	1990	499

Score	C1	C2	C3	C4	C5	C6	C7	C8	C9	C10	Locality	Hunter	Owner	Date	Rank
84 2/8	5 7/8	6	5	9 6/8	2 5/8	2 4/8	7 2/8	7 2/8	15 6/8	15 4/8	Carbon Co., MT	Patrick I. Kalloch	Patrick I. Kalloch	1990	499
84 2/8	6	5 6/8	1 3/8	8 5/8	2 6/8	2 6/8	6 3/8	6 5/8	16 6/8	16 7/8	Harney Co., OR	Douglas J. Modey	Douglas J. Modey	1990	499
84 2/8	6 3/8	6 4/8	8 4/8	9 3/8	2 5/8	2 4/8	7	7 1/8	15 7/8	15 7/8	Sweetwater Co., WY	Kurt D. Olson	Kurt D. Olson	1990	499
84 2/8	7 1/8	6 3/8	2 2/8	11 1/8	2 6/8	2 6/8	7	7	15	15 2/8	Carbon Co., WY	Robert G. Wimpenny	Robert G. Wimpenny	1991	499
84 2/8	7	7	12 6/8	7 2/8	2 7/8	2 6/8	6 7/8	6 7/8	16	15 6/8	Jackson Co., CO	Jerrald L. Copple	Jerrald L. Copple	1991	499
84 2/8	5 5/8	7 5/8	8 2/8	12 6/8	2 6/8	2 3/8	7 5/8	7 5/8	15 5/8	16	Fremont Co., WY	Carl A. Engler	Carl A. Engler	1991	499
84 2/8	5	6 4/8	8 2/8	12 4/8	2 7/8	2 6/8	6 5/8	6 6/8	17 2/8	17 2/8	Quay Co., NM	Marvin S. Keating	Marvin S. Keating	1991	499
84 2/8	6 6/8	6 7/8	4 1/8	9 1/8	2 6/8	2 6/8	6 4/8	6 5/8	15 5/8	15 4/8	Box Elder Co., UT	O. Brent Maw	O. Brent Maw	1991	499
84 2/8	5 3/8	6 6/8	6 6/8	11 7/8	2 6/8	2 5/8	6 6/8	6 6/8	17 3/8	17 3/8	Mora Co., NM	Ralph C. Stayner	Ralph C. Stayner	1991	499
84 2/8	6 1/8	7	6 6/8	9 6/8	2 6/8	2 6/8	6 6/8	6 6/8	16 4/8	16 4/8	Carbon Co., WY	Lynn Woodard	Lynn Woodard	1992	499
84 2/8	6 2/8	6 4/8	3 1/8	9 6/8	2 7/8	2 6/8	6 4/8	6 6/8	16	16 1/8	Carbon Co., WY	Timothy A. Barnhart	Timothy A. Barnhart	1992	499
84 2/8	3 1/8	6 1/8	10 1/8	9 1/8	3	2 7/8	7 3/8	7 1/8	13 7/8	13 5/8	Harney Co., OR	Delbert W. Case	Delbert W. Case	1992	499
84 2/8	7 3/8	7 2/8	5 3/8	12 2/8	2 4/8	2 5/8	6 6/8	6 6/8	15 3/8	15 4/8	Lassen Co., CA	Bernard P. Fuhrmann	Bernard P. Fuhrmann	1993	499
84 2/8	6 1/8	5 3/8	4 1/8	9 6/8	2 6/8	2 6/8	6 4/8	6 6/8	16 4/8	16 3/8	Dewey Co., SD	Steven G. Sparks	Steven G. Sparks	1993	499
84 2/8	5 1/8	4 1/8	2	8 2/8	3	3	6 6/8	6 6/8	16 4/8	17 3/8	Carbon Co., WY	Ernie Davis	Ernie Davis	1994	499
84 2/8	6	6	4 4/8	8 3/8	2 4/8	2 4/8	5 6/8	5 7/8	17 4/8	17 3/8	Hartley Co., TX	Gary J. Farotte	Gary J. Farotte	1994	499
84 2/8	5 3/8	5 6/8	4 4/8	10 4/8	2 5/8	2 5/8	6 3/8	6 3/8	17 1/8	17 1/8	Humboldt Co., NV	Don Perrien	Don Perrien	1994	499
84 2/8	6 6/8	6 4/8	3 2/8	9 6/8	2 4/8	2 4/8	6 2/8	6 2/8	17 3/8	17	Modoc Co., CA	Glen R. Barthold	Glen R. Barthold	1995	499
84 2/8	5 2/8	4 7/8	2 5/8	9 1/8	2 2/8	2 2/8	7	7	17 5/8	17 5/8	Washoe Co., NV	Jared Mason	Jared Mason	1995	499
84 2/8	5 4/8	5 5/8	9 5/8	11 6/8	2 3/8	2 3/8	7 4/8	7 5/8	15 3/8	15 2/8	Sweetwater Co., WY	Timothy M. Storey	Timothy M. Storey	1995	499
84 2/8	5 5/8	5 6/8	13 4/8	14 7/8	2 7/8	2 6/8	8	8	13 6/8	13 6/8	Sweetwater Co., WY	Ben P. Carlson	Ben P. Carlson	1996	499
84 2/8	6	6	3 2/8	9 3/8	2 5/8	2 5/8	7 2/8	7	16 1/8	16	Natrona Co., WY	Sandi K. Fruchey	Sandi K. Fruchey	1996	499
84 2/8	6 2/8	6 3/8	3 4/8	7 3/8	2 5/8	2 5/8	7	7	15 4/8	15 4/8	Fremont Co., WY	Caleb Miller	Caleb Miller	1996	499
84 2/8	6 1/8	5 5/8	4 7/8	8 5/8	3 1/8	3 1/8	6 2/8	6 2/8	16 5/8	16 4/8	Yavapai Co., AZ	William R. Kincade	William R. Kincade	1997	499
84	5 6/8	4 7/8	4 7/8	10 3/8	2 6/8	2 6/8	6 6/8	6 6/8	16 1/8	15 7/8	Baca Co., CO	Jack Henrey	Jack Henrey	1955	573
84	3 3/8	3 5/8	10 6/8	14 1/8	3 7/8	3 7/8	7 2/8	7 2/8	16	16	Lost Cabin, WY	Mrs. Lodisa Pipher	Mrs. Lodisa Pipher	1956	573
84	5 2/8	5	11 1/8	14 2/8	2 6/8	2 6/8	6 4/8	6 4/8	17 1/8	17 1/8	Meadowdale, WY	Walter Tibbs	Walter Tibbs	1959	573
84	5 3/8	6	5 6/8	10 6/8	2 7/8	2 7/8	6 2/8	6 3/8	17 2/8	16 4/8	Yavapai Co., AZ	Fred J. Brogle	Fred J. Brogle	1960	573
84	6 4/8	6 4/8	8	11 2/8	3	3	6	6	16	15 6/8	Campbell Co., WY	Edward Sturla	Edward Sturla	1960	573
84	5 7/8	6	13 6/8	14 4/8	3 1/8	3 1/8	6 6/8	6 6/8	16 1/8	16	Pinedale, WY	Pat Swarts	Pat Swarts	1960	573
84	5 2/8	5 5/8	9	11 4/8	2 4/8	2 4/8	6 4/8	6 6/8	16 6/8	16 4/8	Sage Creek, WY	Ross F. Adams	Ross F. Adams	1961	573
84	6	6	8 2/8	12 1/8	2 7/8	2 7/8	6 7/8	7 1/8	16 7/8	17 1/8	Coconino Co., AZ	Mrs. T.H. Green	Mrs. T.H. Green	1964	573
84	5 1/8	5 3/8	12 5/8	13 4/8	3 1/8	3	6 4/8	6 4/8	17 1/8	16 5/8	Carbon Co., WY	Robert E. Novotny	Robert E. Novotny	1964	573
84	6 1/8	6 2/8	3	11 2/8	3	3	6 3/8	6 3/8	16 5/8	16 5/8	Fremont Co., WY	John M. Sell	John M. Sell	1964	573
84	6 2/8	6 5/8	5 2/8	8 6/8	2 5/8	2 5/8	6 6/8	7	16	16	Rawlins, WY	George Vandervalk	George Vandervalk	1966	573
84	4 7/8	5 7/8	6 7/8	12 2/8	2 6/8	2 6/8	7 1/8	7 1/8	17	17	Milk River, AB	Christian Heyden	Christian Heyden	1967	573
84	5 3/8	6 4/8	3	8	3	3	6 6/8	6 4/8	16 4/8	16 3/8	Washington Co., CO	Leonard Lahr	Leonard Lahr	1967	573
84	6 4/8	6 7/8	12 2/8	14 7/8	2 4/8	2 5/8	6 7/8	6 7/8	15 5/8	15 4/8	Leola, SD	W.E. Cherry	W.E. Cherry	1968	573
84	7 1/8	6 4/8	8 7/8	11 6/8	2 6/8	2 6/8	6 5/8	6 5/8	15 4/8	15 4/8	Chouteau Co., MT	Robert L. Mallory	Robert L. Mallory	1969	573
84	6 4/8	6 2/8	9	14 2/8	2 4/8	2 3/8	6 2/8	6 7/8	15 6/8	16 2/8	Washoe Co., NV	Fred Morgan	Fred Morgan	1969	573
84	4 6/8	4 6/8	11 5/8	11 5/8	2 7/8	2 7/8	7	7	14 4/8	14 4/8	Red Desert, WY	Russ Allen	Russ Allen	1970	573
84	6 7/8	6 6/8	3 5/8	7 3/8	2 6/8	2 6/8	6 7/8	6 7/8	16 6/8	16 6/8	Carbon Co., NV	Gary D. Bader	Gary D. Bader	1970	573
84	6 3/8	6 6/8	2 3/8	8 6/8	2 4/8	2 4/8	6 7/8	6 7/8	16 5/8	16 3/8	Albany Co., WY	Andy Pfaff	Andy Pfaff	1972	573
84	6	7	11 4/8	14 1/8	2 5/8	2 5/8	7	7	15	15 2/8	Sublette Co., WY	Dick Reilly	Dick Reilly	1974	573
84	4 5/8	5	15 7/8	17 6/8	2 4/8	2 3/8	6 4/8	6 4/8	18 6/8	18 2/8	Presidio Co., TX	W. Wayne Roye	W. Wayne Roye	1977	573
84	5 5/8	5 4/8	8 3/8	11 6/8	2 5/8	2 5/8	6 6/8	6 6/8	16 3/8	16 3/8	Sioux Co., NE	Harvey Y. Suetsugu	Harvey Y. Suetsugu	1977	573
84	5 2/8	5 2/8	4 7/8	10 6/8	3	2 6/8	6 4/8	6 5/8	16 7/8	16 7/8	Coconino Co., AZ	Robert F. Veazey	Robert F. Veazey	1979	573

PRONGHORN

Antilocapra americana americana and related subspecies

Score	Length of Horn R	L	Circumference of Base R	L	Circumference at Third Quarter R	L	Inside Spread	Tip to Tip Spread	Length of Prong R	L	Locality	Hunter	Owner	Date Killed	Rank
84	14 7/8	14 5/8	7 6/8	7 3/8	3	3	11 1/8	10	6 3/8	6	Natrona Co., WY	Bill E. Boatman	Bill E. Boatman	1980	573
84	17 6/8	17 4/8	6 2/8	6 1/8	2 6/8	2 5/8	6	5 3/8	6	5 3/8	Washoe Co., NV	Jamie L. Kent	Jamie L. Kent	1980	573
84	17 6/8	17 5/8	6 1/8	6 2/8	2 7/8	2 7/8	13 6/8	8 2/8	5	4 7/8	Yavapai Co., AZ	James O. Pierce	James O. Pierce	1980	573
84	16 1/8	16 4/8	6 7/8	6 6/8	2 5/8	2 7/8	11 2/8	5 7/8	6 4/8	5 6/8	Fremont Co., WY	Joel E. Hensley	Joel E. Hensley	1981	573
84	16	15 6/8	6 3/8	6 3/8	2 4/8	2 3/8	14 2/8	12 6/8	5	4 6/8	Blaine Co., ID	Charles R. Hisaw	Charles R. Hisaw	1981	573
84	15 2/8	15 7/8	7 1/8	7 2/8	2 4/8	2 4/8	15 3/8	13 6/8	6 2/8	6 2/8	Fremont Co., WY	Victor M. McCullough	Victor M. McCullough	1981	573
84	16	15 4/8	7	7	2 7/8	2 5/8	12 6/8	9 1/8	6 2/8	6 3/8	Carbon Co., WY	Dudley R. Elmgren	Dudley R. Elmgren	1982	573
84	16 7/8	16 3/8	7	6 6/8	2 5/8	2 5/8	10 4/8	6 4/8	5 2/8	5 4/8	Sweetwater Co., WY	Richard H. Maddock	Richard H. Maddock	1982	573
84	15 5/8	15 5/8	6 6/8	6 4/8	3 4/8	3 1/8	15 1/8	11 2/8	5 1/8	5 2/8	Coconino Co., AZ	Fred J. Nobbe, Jr.	Fred J. Nobbe, Jr.	1982	573
84	16 7/8	16 4/8	6 6/8	6 6/8	2 5/8	2 4/8	10 6/8	6	6 1/8	6	Sweetwater Co., WY	Lorio Verzasconi	Lorio Verzasconi	1982	573
84	16 2/8	16 2/8	6 4/8	6 5/8	3	3 2/8	12	9 5/8	5 3/8	5 1/8	Mora Co., NM	Roger B. Coit	Roger B. Coit	1983	573
84	16 4/8	16 4/8	6 3/8	6 3/8	2 6/8	2 6/8	11 6/8	7 4/8	5 6/8	5 7/8	Sweetwater Co., WY	Dennis W. Gallegos	Dennis W. Gallegos	1983	573
84	14 6/8	14 5/8	7 2/8	7 2/8	3	3	11 1/8	7 5/8	6 1/8	5 5/8	Sheridan Co., NE	Wayne M. Kelly	Wayne M. Kelly	1983	573
84	17 2/8	17 2/8	6 5/8	6 4/8	3	2 7/8	9 3/8	5 4/8	4 5/8	5 2/8	Bennett Co., SD	Paul R. Nelson	Paul R. Nelson	1983	573
84	16 7/8	16 6/8	6 5/8	6 5/8	2 4/8	2 3/8	10 4/8	6 4/8	6 3/8	6 3/8	Natrona Co., WY	Dale A. Ableidinger	Dale A. Ableidinger	1984	573
84	16	16	6 4/8	6 5/8	2 7/8	2 7/8	10	7 6/8	5 7/8	6 1/8	Washoe Co., NV	Bert F. Carder	Bert F. Carder	1984	573
84	17 4/8	17 2/8	6 7/8	6 7/8	3	2 6/8	18	14	4 5/8	4 5/8	Colfax Co., NM	David S. Dickenson	David S. Dickenson	1984	573
84	17 4/8	16 2/8	6 7/8	6 6/8	3 1/8	3	10 3/8	4 6/8	5 7/8	5 2/8	Yavapai Co., AZ	Fredrick T. Lau	Fredrick T. Lau	1985	573
84	16 4/8	16 3/8	6 7/8	6 6/8	2 7/8	2 7/8	9 7/8	5 7/8	5 6/8	5 5/8	Dawson Co., MT	Jeff S. Trangmoe	Jeff S. Trangmoe	1985	573
84	16 3/8	16 1/8	6 7/8	6 6/8	2 5/8	2 4/8	11	5 4/8	6	6	Lassen Co., CA	Al J. Accurso, Jr.	Al J. Accurso, Jr.	1986	PR 573
84	15 2/8	15 3/8	6 2/8	6 3/8	2 5/8	2 4/8	12 3/8	8	7 1/8	7 2/8	Campbell Co., WY	Unknown	J. Michael Conoyer	1986	573
84	16 4/8	16 2/8	7 2/8	7 2/8	2 6/8	2 6/8	10	6 3/8	5 7/8	5 3/8	Lake Co., OR	Del J. DeSart	Del J. DeSart	1986	573
84	16 7/8	17 2/8	6 6/8	6 7/8	2 6/8	2 4/8	12 6/8	7 3/8	5 4/8	5 2/8	Sierra Co., NM	Mike W. Leonard	Mike W. Leonard	1987	573
84	16 2/8	16 7/8	6 5/8	6 6/8	2 7/8	3 1/8	14 7/8	16 6/8	5 5/8	6 1/8	Yavapai Co., AZ	James K. McCasland	James K. McCasland	1987	573
84	15 6/8	16 7/8	6 2/8	6 2/8	3	3	12 3/8	11 1/8	5 6/8	5 6/8	Harney Co., OR	James E. Baley	James E. Baley	1988	573
84	17	16 7/8	6 6/8	6 5/8	2 4/8	2 4/8	11 7/8	8 6/8	5 7/8	5 7/8	Custer Co., MT	Don A. Bryendl	Don A. Bryendl	1988	573
84	14 2/8	14 5/8	7	7 1/8	3 1/8	3 2/8	11 1/8	7 3/8	5 4/8	5 3/8	Colfax Co., NM	Ruel T. Holt	Ruel T. Holt	1988	573
84	17 5/8	17 6/8	6 2/8	6 3/8	2 3/8	2 4/8	18 5/8	14 3/8	5 5/8	5 6/8	Hudspeth Co., TX	Gibson D. Lewis	Gibson D. Lewis	1988	573
84	16 3/8	16 3/8	6 6/8	6 6/8	2 7/8	2 7/8	11 3/8	8	5 3/8	5 3/8	Elko Co., NV	Larri R. Naveran	Larri R. Naveran	1989	573
84	15 6/8	15 7/8	6 6/8	6 5/8	2 6/8	2 6/8	11 3/8	6 1/8	5 6/8	5 5/8	Navajo Co., AZ	Alan K. Nulliner	Alan K. Nulliner	1989	573
84	17 2/8	17 4/8	6 6/8	6 6/8	2 4/8	2 4/8	14 6/8	8 5/8	5	4 6/8	Washoe Co., NV	Roger D. Puccinelli	Roger D. Puccinelli	1989	573
84	14 7/8	15 6/8	7	6 7/8	2 3/8	2 4/8	13 1/8	10 2/8	7 4/8	7	Lassen Co., CA	Larry R. Brower	Larry R. Brower	1990	573
84	16 2/8	16 2/8	6 5/8	6 5/8	2 5/8	2 5/8	9 7/8	6 2/8	5 5/8	5 3/8	Sweetwater Co., WY	Robert E. Bergquist	Robert E. Bergquist	1991	573
84	16 2/8	16 2/8	6 4/8	6 3/8	2 6/8	3	10 6/8	7 2/8	5 2/8	5 5/8	Coconino Co., AZ	William B. Bullock	William B. Bullock	1991	573
84	15 5/8	15 4/8	6 4/8	6 6/8	3 2/8	3 1/8	8 4/8	7 1/8	5 3/8	5 3/8	Mora Co., NM	Charles F. Marsh	Charles F. Marsh	1991	573
84	17 2/8	17 4/8	6 4/8	6 6/8	2 2/8	2 2/8	7	2 3/8	6 4/8	6 6/8	Humboldt Co., NV	Andrew M. Specht	Andrew M. Specht	1991	573
84	17	17 4/8	6 4/8	6 4/8	2 6/8	2 7/8	9 1/8	3 7/8	5 2/8	5 1/8	Apache Co., AZ	Charlinda Webster	Charlinda Webster	1991	573
84	15	15 2/8	7 2/8	7 2/8	2 7/8	3	10 4/8	5 2/8	5 3/8	5 4/8	Fremont Co., WY	John J. Weust	John J. Weust	1991	573

Score	Length of Horn R	Length of Horn L	Prong R	Prong L	Tip to Tip Spread	Inside Spread	Circ. 3rd Qtr. R	Circ. 3rd Qtr. L	Circ. Base R	Circ. Base L	Locality	Owner	Hunter	Date	Page
84	16 2/8	16 6/8	5 4/8	5 1/8	6 4/8	10 2/8	3 1/8	3	6 5/8	6 6/8	Mora Co., NM	Joseph J. Bongiovi, Jr.	Joseph J. Bongiovi, Jr.	1992	573
84	16 3/8	16 4/8	5 3/8	5 6/8	6 6/8	12 5/8	3	2 6/8	6 4/8	6 4/8	Mora Co., NM	Mel L. Helm	Mel L. Helm	1992	573
84	15 6/8	15 6/8	6	5 7/8	4 4/8	8 7/8	2 7/8	2 7/8	6 6/8	6 6/8	Washoe Co., NV	Timothy H. Humes	Timothy H. Humes	1993	573
84	16 6/8	17	5 3/8	5 3/8	8 7/8	14 5/8	2 6/8	2 6/8	6 2/8	6 2/8	Coconino Co., AZ	Paul F. Musser	Paul F. Musser	1993	573
84	15 1/8	15	5 2/8	5 6/8	14 4/8	16 4/8	2 7/8	2 7/8	7 6/8	8 2/8	Sioux Co., NE	Royce S. Schaeffer	Royce S. Schaeffer	1993	573
84	16 3/8	16 1/8	5 5/8	5 5/8	3 6/8	9 4/8	2 6/8	2 6/8	7 2/8	7 2/8	Jackson Co., CO	Barry A. Weaver	Barry A. Weaver	1993	573
84	17 1/8	16 5/8	5	5	8 1/8	9 4/8	3 2/8	3 3/8	6 6/8	6 5/8	Mora Co., NM	Orlando J. Suris	Orlando J. Suris	1995	573
84	15 5/8	15 7/8	5 6/8	5 5/8	0 4/8	5 5/8	3 4/8	3 3/8	7 1/8	7	Grand Co., UT	Ken E. Ashley	Ken E. Ashley	1996	573
84	16 5/8	15 7/8	6 1/8	5 7/8	5 3/8	10 4/8	2 7/8	2 7/8	6 7/8	7 3/8	Otero Co., NM	Doug C. Brooks	Doug C. Brooks	1996	573
84	15 3/8	15 2/8	5 5/8	6	10 5/8	13 6/8	2 5/8	2 5/8	6 5/8	6 6/8	Hudspeth Co., TX	Robert O. Crow	Robert O. Crow	1997	573
84	17 5/8	17 2/8	5 4/8	5 7/8	5 7/8	11 6/8	2 5/8	2 5/8	6 7/8	6 5/8	Sweetwater Co., WY	Craig L. Kling	Craig L. Kling	1997	573
83 6/8	16 4/8	17	5 4/8	6	6	12 4/8	2 5/8	2 5/8	6 6/8	6 6/8	Coconino Co., AZ	Marvin Redburn	Marvin Redburn	1950	645
83 6/8	16	16	5 6/8	5 4/8	9 6/8	13	3 3/8	3 2/8	6 4/8	6 4/8	Sheridan Co., WY	John T. Yarrington	John T. Yarrington	1951	645
83 6/8	16 3/8	16	5 2/8	4 6/8	11	12 7/8	3	2 7/8	7 1/8	7	Saratoga, WY	Bob Herbison	Bob Herbison	1955	645
83 6/8	16 4/8	16 3/8	5 3/8	5 1/8	8 6/8	12 6/8	2 7/8	2 7/8	6 6/8	6 6/8	Chino Valley, AZ	Max Durfee	Max Durfee	1960	645
83 6/8	16 1/8	16 1/8	5 7/8	6 3/8	8 3/8	10 2/8	2 7/8	2 7/8	7	6 7/8	Plainview, SD	Bernie Wanhanen	Bernie Wanhanen	1960	645
83 6/8	15 4/8	15 3/8	5 7/8	6 3/8	6 3/8	10 4/8	2 5/8	2 5/8	6 7/8	7	Poison Spider, WY	Robert Ziker	Robert Ziker	1960	645
83 6/8	16 5/8	16 6/8	4 4/8	4 5/8	10 6/8	15 6/8	3 1/8	3 2/8	6 4/8	7 1/8	Yavapai Co., AZ	C.J. Adair	C.J. Adair	1961	645
83 6/8	17 4/8	17 3/8	5 6/8	5 6/8	6 7/8	10 6/8	3	3	6	6 4/8	Williams, AZ	Dave Blair	Dave Blair	1961	645
83 6/8	17 5/8	15 7/8	5 2/8	5	10 7/8	8 6/8	2 5/8	2 5/8	6 3/8	6 3/8	Hudspeth Co., TX	Jim Perry	Jim Perry	1963	645
83 6/8	15 7/8	15 5/8	5 7/8	5 7/8	5 6/8	8 3/8	2 5/8	2 4/8	7 2/8	7	Alcova, WY	Donald G. Gebers	Donald G. Gebers	1964	645
83 6/8	15 6/8	15 2/8	6 2/8	6 2/8	6 1/8	10 3/8	2 6/8	2 7/8	7	7 2/8	Hudspeth Co., TX	Basil C. Bradbury	Basil C. Bradbury	1966	645
83 6/8	15 2/8	19 1/8	6 7/8	6 6/8	6 7/8	11 7/8	2 6/8	2 6/8	6 5/8	6 6/8	Meridian, OR	Dale E. Beattie	Dale E. Beattie	1967	645
83 6/8	18 4/8	16 4/8	4 4/8	4 5/8	8 3/8	7 7/8	2 6/8	2 6/8	6 2/8	6 1/8	Motley Co., TX	Ron Vandiver	Ron Vandiver	1967	645
83 6/8	16 6/8	15	4 7/8	5	5 6/8	10	3	3	6 3/8	6 3/8	Black Tank, AZ	George M. Lewis	George M. Lewis	1968	645
83 6/8	15	15 7/8	5 4/8	6 3/8	10 4/8	13 4/8	3	3	6 5/8	6 5/8	Sweetwater Co., WY	R.L. Brown, Jr.	R.L. Brown, Jr.	1970	645
83 6/8	15 6/8	15 1/8	5 1/8	5 2/8	4 1/8	9 3/8	2 5/8	2 5/8	7 2/8	7 4/8	Lake Co., OR	Dennis E. Carter	Dennis E. Carter	1972	645
83 6/8	15	14 3/8	5 6/8	5 7/8	11 2/8	14 2/8	2 7/8	2 7/8	7 2/8	7 2/8	Sweetwater Co., WY	Betty J. Oliver	Betty J. Oliver	1974	645
83 6/8	14 4/8	16 2/8	6 2/8	6 2/8	7 4/8	7 4/8	2 6/8	2 6/8	6 4/8	6 4/8	Divide, SK	Leslie Banford	Leslie Banford	1975	645
83 6/8	15 6/8	16	6 6/8	6 6/8	10	10 4/8	2 1/8	2 2/8	7 1/8	7 1/8	Park Co., WY	D.F. & T. Holt	Don F. Holt	1975	645
83 6/8	15 4/8	16 6/8	5 5/8	5 4/8	7	11 4/8	2 6/8	2 6/8	6 1/8	6 1/8	Sweetwater Co., WY	Dennis D. Seipp	Dennis D. Seipp	1975	645
83 6/8	16	16 6/8	6 4/8	6 4/8	2	7 1/8	2 6/8	2 6/8	6 4/8	6 4/8	Modoc Co., CA	William B. Steig	William B. Steig	1977	645
83 6/8	16 6/8	17 4/8	6 3/8	6 1/8	7 7/8	11 6/8	2 5/8	2 5/8	6 3/8	6 4/8	Wamsutter, WY	James A. White	James A. White	1980	645
83 6/8	15 4/8	14 7/8	5 4/8	6 1/8	6	9 2/8	2 7/8	2 7/8	7 4/8	7 5/8	Carbon Co., WY	Jack F. Schakel	Jack F. Schakel	1981	645
83 6/8	16 1/8	16 4/8	4 5/8	5	5	9 1/8	2 4/8	2 3/8	6 2/8	6 2/8	Humboldt Co., NV	Harold J. Ward	Harold J. Ward	1981	645
83 6/8	14 7/8	15 2/8	4 4/8	4 5/8	11 6/8	6 5/8	2 6/8	2 8/8	7 5/8	7 4/8	Washoe Co., NV	Robert A. Colon	Robert A. Colon	1982	645
83 6/8	16 3/8	16 1/8	6 5/8	5	2	8 5/8	3	3	6 1/8	6 2/8	Lincoln Co., NM	James R. Doverspike	James R. Doverspike	1982	645
83 6/8	15	16 7/8	6 6/8	6 6/8	6 6/8	10 2/8	2 6/8	2 7/8	6 1/8	6 7/8	Big Horn Co., MT	Michael Ferri	Michael Ferri	1982	645
83 6/8	17 2/8	15 1/8	6 4/8	6 4/8	2 5/8	7 1/8	2 5/8	2 3/8	6 3/8	6 5/8	Natrona Co., WY	Ronald K. Morrison	Ronald K. Morrison	1982	645
83 6/8	15 7/8	16 3/8	6 4/8	5 7/8	11	12 5/8	2 5/8	2 3/8	6 6/8	6 6/8	Sweetwater Co., WY	Robert Gilbert	Robert Gilbert	1983	645
83 6/8	16 2/8	15 7/8	5 4/8	5 8/8	8 4/8	12 6/8	2 5/8	2 5/8	6 5/8	7	Carbon Co., WY	Douglas L. Hancock	Douglas L. Hancock	1983	645
83 6/8	15 6/8	15 7/8	6	6 1/8	7 6/8	11	2 3/8	2 3/8	6 2/8	6 2/8	Jackson Co., CO	Cylestine A. Manguso	Cylestine A. Manguso	1983	645
83 6/8	15 6/8	16	5 6/8	6 3/8	11 6/8	15 5/8	2 4/8	2 3/8	7 4/8	7 5/8	Lake Co., OR	Barbara J. Smallwood	Barbara J. Smallwood	1983	645
83 6/8	16 1/8	16 1/8	6 2/8	6	9 6/8	12 7/8	2 6/8	2 6/8	6 4/8	6 3/8	Washoe Co., NV	Arthur L. Biggs	Arthur L. Biggs	1984	645
83 6/8	15 6/8	16 1/8	6 2/8	6 3/8	9 6/8	12	2 6/8	2 6/8	6 6/8	6 4/8	Millard Co., UT	Mitchell S. Bastian	Mitchell S. Bastian	1985	645
83 6/8	16 7/8	17	5 2/8	5 1/8	5 6/8	10 6/8	2 7/8	3	6 3/8	6 3/8	Colfax Co., NM	Stephen C. LeBlanc	Stephen C. LeBlanc	1985	645
83 6/8	16 1/8	15 7/8	5 1/8	6	11 5/8	15 2/8	2 5/8	2 4/8	6 4/8	6 5/8	Catron Co., NM	Charles A. Grimmett	Charles A. Grimmett	1986	645

PRONGHORN

Antilocapra americana americana and related subspecies

Score	Length of Horn R	L	Circumference of Base R	L	Circumference at Third Quarter R	L	Inside Spread	Tip to Tip Spread	Length of Prong R	L	Locality	Hunter	Owner	Date Killed	Rank
83 6/8	15 4/8	15 4/8	7 3/8	7 4/8	2 4/8	2 2/8	13 1/8	9 6/8	6 2/8	5 6/8	Colfax Co., NM	LeGrand C. Kirby III	LeGrand C. Kirby III	1986	645
83 6/8	16 6/8	16 5/8	6 5/8	6 4/8	2 6/8	2 6/8	13 3/8	10	5 4/8	5 2/8	De Baca Co., NM	Ben L. Mueller	Ben L. Mueller	1986	645
83 6/8	14 7/8	15	6 5/8	6 5/8	2 7/8	2 6/8	9 4/8	7 7/8	6 2/8	6 6/8	Fremont Co., WY	Carl N. Anderson	Carl N. Anderson	1987	645
83 6/8	14 3/8	14 3/8	7 5/8	7 5/8	2 7/8	2 6/8	7	3 3/8	5 7/8	5 7/8	Carbon Co., WY	Thomas D. Widiker	Thomas D. Widiker	1987	645
83 6/8	15 7/8	15 7/8	6 4/8	6 3/8	3 1/8	3	9 6/8	3 5/8	5 7/8	6	Hudspeth Co., TX	A. Alan Griffin	A. Alan Griffin	1988	645
83 6/8	16 3/8	16 3/8	6 4/8	6 4/8	2 4/8	2 4/8	9 1/8	4 3/8	5 6/8	6 4/8	Harney Co., OR	Lyle W. Crawford	Lyle W. Crawford	1990	645
83 6/8	16 2/8	16 3/8	7 1/8	7	2 6/8	2 5/8	10 2/8	5 3/8	5 3/8	5 4/8	Harney Co., OR	John S. Hansen	John S. Hansen	1990	645
83 6/8	17	17 2/8	6 6/8	6 6/8	3 1/8	3	16	11 4/8	4 5/8	4 1/8	Washoe Co., NV	P.D. Kiser	P.D. Kiser	1990	645
83 6/8	15 4/8	15 2/8	7 2/8	7 2/8	2 3/8	2 3/8	13 4/8	10	5 5/8	5 6/8	Yavapai Co., AZ	Michael J. Rusing	Michael J. Rusing	1990	645
83 6/8	15 1/8	15	6 5/8	6 5/8	2 5/8	2 5/8	6	1 5/8	6 5/8	6 4/8	Fremont Co., WY	Stuart W. Shepherd	Stuart W. Shepherd	1990	645
83 6/8	16 4/8	16 6/8	6 5/8	6 5/8	2 4/8	2 4/8	9 6/8	6	5 6/8	5 7/8	Carbon Co., WY	Rod F. Waeckerlin	Rod F. Waeckerlin	1990	645
83 6/8	15 7/8	16	6 3/8	6 1/8	2 6/8	2 6/8	11 4/8	6 7/8	5 6/8	6 2/8	Yavapai Co., AZ	Roland J. Chooljian	Roland J. Chooljian	1991	645
83 6/8	17 1/8	17 3/8	6	6 1/8	3 2/8	2 7/8	9 5/8	4 3/8	5 2/8	5 4/8	Socorro Co., NM	William W. Klein	William W. Klein	1991	645
83 6/8	16 5/8	16 5/8	6 4/8	6 4/8	2 7/8	3	11 7/8	7	5 2/8	5	Humboldt Co., NV	Sam Lair	Sam Lair	1991	645
83 6/8	16 4/8	16 6/8	6 3/8	6 4/8	3	3	13 6/8	10	5	5 1/8	Mora Co., NM	Brody J. Bonnett	Brody J. Bonnett	1992	645
83 6/8	15 2/8	15 2/8	6 5/8	6 5/8	3 1/8	3	9	5 4/8	6	6 5/8	Rosebud Co., MT	William E. Butler	William E. Butler	1992	645
83 6/8	16 1/8	16 1/8	6 4/8	6 4/8	3 1/8	3	13 5/8	13 6/8	5 4/8	5 6/8	Yavapai Co., AZ	Jerry T. Harper	Jerry T. Harper	1992	645
83 6/8	15 6/8	15 5/8	6 7/8	6 6/8	2 4/8	2 4/8	10 4/8	5 7/8	6 2/8	6 2/8	Lake Co., OR	Brian R. Hayes	Brian R. Hayes	1992	645
83 6/8	16 6/8	16 5/8	6 6/8	7	2 6/8	2 6/8	9 5/8	4 1/8	5	4 7/8	Carbon Co., WY	John T. Johnson	John T. Johnson	1992	645
83 6/8	16 6/8	16 7/8	6 1/8	6 3/8	2 5/8	2 5/8	10 6/8	6	5 6/8	5 5/8	Mora Co., NM	Edward C. Joseph	Edward C. Joseph	1992	645
83 6/8	17	17	6 4/8	6 3/8	2 7/8	2 6/8	10 3/8	5 3/8	5 4/8	5 4/8	Campbell Co., WY	Loy D. Peters	Loy D. Peters	1992	645
83 6/8	16 3/8	16 3/8	6 6/8	6 6/8	2 4/8	2 4/8	14	10 7/8	5 7/8	5 6/8	Hot Springs Co., WY	Robert J. Ruiz	Robert J. Ruiz	1992	645
83 6/8	16 4/8	16 2/8	7	7	2 4/8	2 4/8	9 4/8	3 3/8	6 2/8	6	Sublette Co., WY	Delores Ball	Delores Ball	1993	645
83 6/8	15 4/8	15 4/8	6 6/8	6 6/8	2 7/8	2 7/8	14 2/8	11 4/8	6 2/8	6 1/8	Mora Co., NM	Richard E. Joseph	Richard E. Joseph	1993	645
83 6/8	16 4/8	16 4/8	6	6	2 6/8	2 6/8	10 1/8	6 4/8	6 4/8	6 7/8	Malheur Co., OR	Kenneth L. Barstad	Kenneth L. Barstad	1994	645
83 6/8	15 6/8	15 4/8	8	8	2 6/8	2 6/8	10 6/8	8 1/8	4 2/8	4 7/8	Jackson Co., CO	Stephen H. Porter	Stephen H. Porter	1994	645
83 6/8	16 5/8	16 3/8	7 3/8	7 3/8	3 1/8	3 2/8	14 4/8	10 4/8	4 4/8	5	Socorro Co., NM	John W. Bishop	John W. Bishop	1995	645
83 6/8	16 4/8	16 7/8	6 6/8	6 5/8	2 3/8	2 5/8	10 3/8	4 3/8	6 3/8	6	Natrona Co., WY	Miles B. Bundy	Miles B. Bundy	1996	645
83 6/8	17	16 6/8	6 7/8	6 7/8	2 5/8	2 4/8	11 3/8	4 3/8	5 4/8	5 7/8	Rosebud Co., MT	Douglas B. Colombik	Douglas B. Colombik	1996	645
83 5/8	16 7/8	16 1/8	6 3/8	6 3/8	2 5/8	3	11 5/8	7 7/8	5 2/8	5 4/8	Hudspeth Co., TX	James N. Gallagher, Jr.	James N. Gallagher, Jr.	1996	645
83 6/8	16 1/8	16	6 7/8	6 7/8	3 1/8	3	13 6/8	11 7/8	5 5/8	5 1/8	Socorro Co., NM	Ilynn Guldman	Ilynn Guldman	1996	645
83 6/8	16 3/8	16 5/8	6 5/8	6 5/8	2 4/8	2 4/8	11 3/8	7 7/8	5 6/8	5 3/8	Fremont Co., WY	Roger L. McCosker	Roger L. McCosker	1997	645
83 6/8	16 1/8	16 4/8	6 6/8	7	2 7/8	2 7/8	8	1 4/8	5 7/8	6	Humboldt Co., NV	Terry D. Scott	Terry D. Scott	1997	645
83 4/8	17	16 2/8	6 4/8	6 2/8	2 6/8	2 6/8	14 1/8	11 1/8	6 4/8	6 1/8	Farson, WY	Geo. E. MacGillivray	Geo. E. MacGillivray	1951	714
83 4/8	16 7/8	17	6 6/8	7	2 7/8	2 5/8	10 4/8	6 7/8	5 2/8	5 2/8	Miles City, MT	J. Louis Mann	J. Louis Mann	1954	714
83 4/8	18 1/8	17 6/8	6 4/8	6 3/8	2 4/8	2 2/8	16	14 2/8	5 6/8	5 2/8	Arizona	O. Patton	William N. Henry	1956	714
83 4/8	17	17	6 4/8	6 4/8	2 6/8	2 4/8	10 2/8	5 7/8	5	4 6/8	Navajo Co., AZ	Mrs. Don Lambert	Mrs. Don Lambert	1961	714
83 4/8	14	14 4/8	6 7/8	6 7/8	3 5/8	3 4/8	12 5/8	10 1/8	6 4/8	6 2/8	Watford City, ND	Dean Etl	Dean Etl	1964	714

Score											Locality	Owner	Hunter	Date	Rank
83 4/8	15 6/8	15 6/8	6 1/8	6 1/8	3 2/8	3 1/8	11 3/8	6 3/8	4 6/8	4 6/8	Shoshoni, WY	Collins F. Kellogg	Collins F. Kellogg	1965	714
83 4/8	16	15 7/8	6 4/8	6 4/8	2 4/8	2 4/8	10 5/8	5 7/8	7	6 6/8	Boone, CO	Mahlon T. White	Mahlon T. White	1966	714
83 4/8	15 6/8	15 5/8	7	7	2 4/8	2 6/8	9 6/8	6 7/8	5 4/8	5 3/8	Wamsutter, WY	Kenneth L. Swanson	Kenneth L. Swanson	1967	714
83 4/8	15 5/8	15 7/8	7 2/8	7 1/8	2 4/8	2 5/8	11 1/8	7 1/8	5 2/8	5 4/8	Craig, CO	Albert Johnson	Albert Johnson	1969	714
83 4/8	16 2/8	16 1/8	6 3/8	6 4/8	2 6/8	2 5/8	15 4/8	12 2/8	5 5/8	5 7/8	Red Desert, WY	David W. Knowles	David W. Knowles	1970	714
83 4/8	16 2/8	16 2/8	6 6/8	6 6/8	2 4/8	2 5/8	12	10 1/8	5	5 1/8	Carbon Co., WY	Billy C. Randall	Billy C. Randall	1970	714
83 4/8	17 1/8	17	6 6/8	6 6/8	2 6/8	2 6/8	15 5/8	10 6/8	5	5	Hoback Rim, WY	F. Larry Storey	F. Larry Storey	1973	714
83 4/8	17	17 1/8	6 5/8	6 5/8	2 7/8	2 7/8	6 2/8	1 3/8	4 5/8	4 6/8	Coconino Co., AZ	Cheryl Alderman	Cheryl Alderman	1974	714
83 4/8	15 3/8	15 6/8	7 2/8	7 2/8	2 4/8	2 4/8	8 1/8	2 2/8	5 3/8	5 1/8	Fremont Co., WY	James G. Allard	James G. Allard	1974	714
83 4/8	17 2/8	17 1/8	7	7	2 6/8	2 6/8	14 6/8	9 5/8	5 5/8	5 6/8	Coconino Co., AZ	Thomas A. Dunlap	Thomas A. Dunlap	1974	714
83 4/8	16	16	6 2/8	6 3/8	2 5/8	2 5/8	9	3 2/8	5 3/8	4 6/8	Fremont Co., WY	Ruth Muller	Ruth Muller	1974	714
83 4/8	17 3/8	17 2/8	6 3/8	6 4/8	2 6/8	2 7/8	9 5/8	5 3/8	5 5/8	5 1/8	Fremont Co., WY	Robert B. Cragoe, Sr.	Robert B. Cragoe, Sr.	1975	714
83 4/8	16	17	6 5/8	6 5/8	2 7/8	2 7/8	10 6/8	6 6/8	5 1/8	5 1/8	De Baca Co., NM	Glenn C. Conner	Glenn C. Conner	1977	714
83 4/8	16 3/8	16 2/8	7 2/8	7 2/8	2 5/8	2 5/8	9 4/8	3 6/8	6 6/8	6 6/8	Harney Co., OR	Craig Foster	Craig Foster	1977	714
83 4/8	16 4/8	16 4/8	6 6/8	6 6/8	3	3	10 4/8	5 3/8	9 4/8	9 4/8	Box Butte Co., NE	Derald E. Morgan	Derald E. Morgan	1977	714
83 4/8	15 3/8	15 3/8	6 3/8	6 3/8	2 6/8	2 6/8	10 3/8	6 4/8	5 3/8	5 5/8	Washoe Co., NV	James R. Cobb	James R. Cobb	1978	714
83 4/8	15 2/8	16 1/8	6 6/8	6 6/8	2 5/8	3	10 2/8	6	6 4/8	6 4/8	Uinta Co., WY	Velma O'Neil	Velma O'Neil	1978	714
83 4/8	16 3/8	16 7/8	6 5/8	6 5/8	2 5/8	2 5/8	8 6/8	2 4/8	5 2/8	6 2/8	Sweetwater Co., WY	Otis T. Page	Otis T. Page	1978	714
83 4/8	14 6/8	14 7/8	6 3/8	6 3/8	2 3/8	2 2/8	9	3 5/8	7 4/8	7	Lake Co., OR	Thomas A. Jones	Thomas A. Jones	1980	714
83 4/8	15 4/8	15 5/8	6 6/8	6 7/8	3 1/8	3 1/8	13	10 1/8	5 3/8	5 1/8	Rosebud Co., MT	James D. Cameron	James D. Cameron	1981	714
83 4/8	16 6/8	16 6/8	6 4/8	6 4/8	2 5/8	2 5/8	11 4/8	5 6/8	5 4/8	5 4/8	Custer Co., ID	Wayne L. Coleman	Wayne L. Coleman	1981	714
83 4/8	16 7/8	17	6 1/8	6 1/8	2 7/8	2 7/8	10 3/8	4 6/8	5	5 1/8	Harding Co., SD	John R. Simpson	John R. Simpson	1981	714
83 4/8	17 5/8	17 3/8	6 5/8	6 5/8	2 4/8	2 3/8	6 7/8	0	6 3/8	5 7/8	Natrona Co., WY	Gerald J. Ahles	Gerald J. Ahles	1982	714
83 4/8	17 4/8	17	7 4/8	7 4/8	2 6/8	2 6/8	9 4/8	4 6/8	5	5 2/8	Colfax Co., NM	James H. Hoffman	James H. Hoffman	1982	714
83 4/8	16 4/8	16 6/8	6 4/8	6 4/8	2 3/8	2 3/8	10 1/8	2 7/8	6 4/8	6 2/8	Prairie Co., MT	L.H. Lindquist	L.H. Lindquist	1982	714
83 4/8	14 1/8	14 2/8	6 5/8	6 5/8	3 2/8	3 2/8	8 5/8	4	6 3/8	6 2/8	Jackson Co., CO	Cynthia L. Welle	Cynthia L. Welle	1982	714
83 4/8	18	18	7	6 7/8	3	3	9 3/8	6 2/8	4 6/8	3 1/8	Carbon Co., WY	Ronald K. Pettit	Ronald K. Pettit	1983	714
83 4/8	17 3/8	17 4/8	6 4/8	6 4/8	3 2/8	3 2/8	13 3/8	6 2/8	4 4/8	4 4/8	Coconino Co., AZ	Duane D. Backhaus	Duane D. Backhaus	1984	714
83 4/8	16 7/8	17	6 4/8	6 4/8	3 2/8	3	14 1/8	10 2/8	5 4/8	5 1/8	Lake Co., OR	Donald R. Davidson	Donald R. Davidson	1984	714
83 4/8	16 2/8	16 3/8	6 4/8	7	2 7/8	2 5/8	13 2/8	8 5/8	5 4/8	5 1/8	Yavapai Co., AZ	Glenn E. Leslie, Jr.	Glenn E. Leslie, Jr.	1984	714
83 4/8	17 5/8	17 5/8	6	6	2 7/8	2 7/8	10 7/8	8	5 3/8	5	Coconino Co., AZ	Arthur A. Smith	Arthur A. Smith	1984	714
83 4/8	16 4/8	16 5/8	6 1/8	6 1/8	3 2/8	3 2/8	12 4/8	9 1/8	5 2/8	5 2/8	Mora Co., NM	Brent Arrant	Brent Arrant	1986	714
83 4/8	17 2/8	17 4/8	6 3/8	6 3/8	2 7/8	2 7/8	8 4/8	1 6/8	4 6/8	4 6/8	Foremost, AB	Brian J. Gathercole	Brian J. Gathercole	1988	714
83 4/8	16 3/8	16 2/8	6 6/8	6 1/8	2 6/8	2 6/8	16 1/8	13 7/8	6	6	Wildhorse, AB	Ralph L. Cervo	Ralph L. Cervo	1989	714
83 4/8	16 6/8	16 7/8	6 4/8	6 4/8	2 6/8	2 6/8	9	3 6/8	6	6	Colfax Co., NM	David M. Lackie	David M. Lackie	1989	714
83 4/8	15 5/8	15 5/8	6 4/8	6 4/8	2 4/8	2 4/8	11 6/8	7 2/8	6 3/8	5 3/8	Sweetwater Co., WY	Charles R. Monroe	Charles R. Monroe	1989	714
83 4/8	17 2/8	15 3/8	7	7	2 6/8	2 4/8	10	4 3/8	6	5 2/8	Maple Creek, SK	Lynn P. Needham	Lynn P. Needham	1989	714
83 4/8	15 7/8	15 6/8	6 2/8	6 3/8	2 6/8	2 6/8	10 2/8	6 4/8	6	6 3/8	Carbon Co., UT	John R. Stevens	John R. Stevens	1989	714
83 4/8	15 5/8	16	6 4/8	6 4/8	2 5/8	2 5/8	15 5/8	12 4/8	7	5 2/8	Colfax Co., NM	Louie Alcon	Louie Alcon	1990	714
83 4/8	15 4/8	15 4/8	6 2/8	6 7/8	2 6/8	2 7/8	10 7/8	7 7/8	6 2/8	6 2/8	Sublette Co., WY	Heath Harrower	Heath Harrower	1990	714
83 4/8	15 5/8	15 5/8	6 6/8	6 6/8	2 4/8	2 4/8	15 5/8	12 4/8	6 3/8	6 3/8	Socorro Co., NM	Michael T. Miller	Michael T. Miller	1990	714
83 4/8	15 6/8	15 6/8	7	7	2 7/8	2 7/8	8 5/8	3 2/8	5 5/8	5 5/8	Moffat Co., CO	Brad A. Winder	Brad A. Winder	1990	714
83 4/8	16 7/8	16 7/8	6 2/8	6 2/8	2 7/8	2 5/8	9 3/8	4 5/8	6 2/8	6 4/8	Custer Co., ID	Michael J. Felton	Michael J. Felton	1991	714
83 4/8	15 6/8	15 6/8	5 4/8	5 4/8	3	2 6/8	10 2/8	5 1/8	4 7/8	5 2/8	Butte Co., ID	Sandie L. Goodson	Sandie L. Goodson	1991	714
83 4/8	16 1/8	16 1/8	6	6 1/8	2 6/8	2 6/8	10 2/8	5 1/8	6	6	Hudspeth Co., TX	Carl H. Green	Carl H. Green	1991	714
83 4/8	16 4/8	16 4/8	6 2/8	6 5/8	2 4/8	2 4/8	8 7/8	4 5/8	6 1/8	6 1/8	Moffat Co., CO	Rodney R. Hall, Jr.	Rodney R. Hall, Jr.	1991	714
83 4/8	18 3/8	18	6	5 7/8	2 3/8	2 4/8	10 3/8	8 4/8	6	5 6/8	Hudspeth Co., TX	Eduardo Padilla	Eduardo Padilla	1991	714

Score	Length of Horn R	L	Circumference of Base R	L	Circumference at Third Quarter R	L	Inside Spread	Tip to Tip Spread	Length of Prong R	L	Locality	Hunter	Owner	Date Killed	Rank
83 4/8	16 4/8	16 4/8	6 4/8	6 4/8	2 5/8	2 6/8	11 7/8	6 5/8	5 5/8	5 4/8	Elko Co., NV	Eugene E. Schain	Eugene E. Schain	1991	714
83 4/8	17 3/8	17 2/8	6 5/8	6 4/8	2 5/8	2 3/8	10	5	5 5/8	5 4/8	Humboldt Co., NV	William J. Swartz, Jr.	William J. Swartz, Jr.	1991	714
83 4/8	17 2/8	17 3/8	6	6	2 4/8	2 4/8	8 6/8	3 3/8	5 3/8	5 2/8	Socorro Co., NM	Randy W. Tonkin	Randy W. Tonkin	1991	714
83 4/8	15 7/8	16	6 6/8	7	3	3	14 7/8	11 5/8	6	5 2/8	Mora Co., NM	Jeffrey D. Warren	Jeffrey D. Warren	1991	714
83 4/8	17 3/8	16 7/8	6 3/8	6 3/8	2 3/8	2 2/8	8	4 7/8	6 3/8	6 4/8	Washoe Co., NV	Robert J. Cornelius	Robert J. Cornelius	1992	714
83 4/8	14 5/8	14 7/8	7 2/8	7 2/8	2 7/8	3	6 3/8	2 3/8	5 4/8	5 4/8	Carter Co., MT	Angelo J. Feroleto	Angelo J. Feroleto	1992	714
83 4/8	16 6/8	16 1/8	6 3/8	6 2/8	3	3	9 6/8	6	6 3/8	5 4/8	Hudspeth Co., TX	Ray O. Herzog	Ray O. Herzog	1992	714
83 4/8	17 5/8	17 5/8	6 3/8	6 3/8	2 5/8	2 6/8	12	6 7/8	5	4 6/8	Otero Co., NM	Harold W. Lisby	Harold W. Lisby	1992	714
83 4/8	14 3/8	14 4/8	7 4/8	7 4/8	2 5/8	2 5/8	13 4/8	12 1/8	6 3/8	6 2/8	Natrona Co., WY	Jerry A. Stoll	Jerry A. Stoll	1992	714
83 4/8	15 2/8	14 4/8	6 7/8	6 7/8	3 5/8	3 6/8	10 4/8	9 5/8	5	5	Weld Co., CO	Delmar C. Brewer	Delmar C. Brewer	1993	714
83 4/8	14 5/8	15	7	7	2 5/8	2 6/8	9 4/8	7	6 1/8	6 2/8	Sweetwater Co., WY	Keith A. Dana	Keith A. Dana	1994	714
83 4/8	15 7/8	16 2/8	6 5/8	6 5/8	3 2/8	3 1/8	8 3/8	1 6/8	5 1/8	5	Yavapai Co., AZ	Michael K. Giboney	Michael K. Giboney	1994	714
83 4/8	17 5/8	17 2/8	6 2/8	6 2/8	2 2/8	2 3/8	17	15	5 6/8	6 1/8	Washoe Co., NV	Thomas V. Guio	Thomas V. Guio	1994	714
83 4/8	15 6/8	16	6	5 7/8	3	3	10 1/8	5 3/8	6 1/8	6 1/8	Colfax Co., NM	Mark B. Henkel	Mark B. Henkel	1994	714
83 4/8	15 6/8	15 6/8	7 1/8	7	2 5/8	2 4/8	11 5/8	7 6/8	6 3/8	6 1/8	Lassen Co., CA	Jason W. Langslet	Jason W. Langslet	1994	714
83 4/8	16 2/8	16 2/8	6 6/8	6 6/8	2 5/8	2 6/8	11 5/8	11 4/8	5 3/8	5 4/8	Uintah Co., UT	Ben Dattage	Alan L. Dattage	1995	714
83 4/8	17 1/8	16 4/8	6 1/8	6 3/8	2 5/8	2 5/8	17 1/8	14 1/8	5 6/8	5 6/8	Washakie Co., WY	Chad D. Heiser	Chad D. Heiser	1995	714
83 4/8	16 3/8	16 3/8	6 4/8	6 4/8	2 3/8	2 3/8	7 6/8	3 2/8	5 6/8	5 4/8	Malheur Co., OR	Tom D. Johansen	Holly Johansen	1995	714
83 4/8	16	16	7	7	2 7/8	2 7/8	10	5 6/8	5 1/8	5 1/8	Socorro Co., NM	David A. Miller	David A. Miller	1995	714
83 4/8	16 5/8	16 4/8	6 6/8	6 6/8	3	3	16 3/8	14 6/8	5 3/8	4 6/8	Navajo Co., AZ	Christopher H. Sipe	Christopher H. Sipe	1995	714
83 4/8	17 1/8	17 2/8	6 4/8	6 3/8	2 5/8	2 4/8	11 5/8	5 1/8	5 3/8	5 3/8	Socorro Co., NM	Holley W. Lacey	Holley W. Lacey	1996	714
83 4/8	18 2/8	18 2/8	6	5 7/8	3	2 6/8	10 1/8	3 2/8	4 5/8	4 3/8	Hudspeth Co., TX	Thomas C. Merritt	Thomas C. Merritt	1997	714
83 2/8	16 6/8	17 1/8	6 2/8	6 1/8	2 4/8	2 5/8	16 5/8	15 3/8	6	6	Arminto, WY	Edward H. Bohlin	Edward H. Bohlin	1951	788
83 2/8	16 1/8	16	7	6 7/8	2 5/8	2 6/8	12 3/8	10 4/8	5 2/8	4 7/8	Newcastle, WY	Rupert Chisholm	Rupert Chisholm	1953	788
83 2/8	15 3/8	14 7/8	8 2/8	8 2/8	2 4/8	2 1/8	8 5/8	6 3/8	6 3/8	6 7/8	Campbell Co., WY	Phillip M. Hodge	Phillip M. Hodge	1955	788
83 2/8	15 5/8	16 1/8	6 3/8	6 3/8	2 3/8	2 5/8	9 5/8	5	6 4/8	6 5/8	Atlantic City, WY	James S. Kleinhammer	James S. Kleinhammer	1958	788
83 2/8	15 2/8	15 5/8	6 2/8	6 2/8	2 4/8	2 6/8	9 6/8	6 5/8	6 6/8	7 1/8	Jeffrey City, WY	Harry G.M. Jopson	Harry G.M. Jopson	1961	788
83 2/8	16 5/8	16 3/8	6 5/8	6 5/8	2 7/8	2 7/8	8 1/8	7 6/8	5 2/8	5	Kaycee, WY	R.B. Nienhaus	R.B. Nienhaus	1961	788
83 2/8	14 7/8	14 7/8	6 2/8	6 2/8	2 5/8	2 5/8	9 7/8	6	4 6/8	4 5/8	Fergus Co., MT	Steven G. Ard	Steven G. Ard	1962	788
83 2/8	16 3/8	16	6 4/8	6 4/8	3	2 7/8	9 3/8	4 3/8	6	6	Ferris Mt., WY	Ron Vance	Ron Vance	1962	788
83 2/8	16 7/8	16 7/8	6 1/8	6 1/8	2 4/8	2 4/8	11 2/8	7 6/8	5 4/8	5 4/8	Capitan, NM	Lee H. Ingalls	Lee H. Ingalls	1969	788
83 2/8	16 7/8	16 7/8	7 1/8	7	2 4/8	2 4/8	14 3/8	12 4/8	5 2/8	5	Sweetwater Co., WY	Allen Tanner	Allen Tanner	1970	788
83 2/8	16 7/8	15 2/8	6 4/8	6 4/8	2 7/8	2 6/8	12	7 4/8	6 2/8	6 4/8	Coconino Co., AZ	Vernon E. North	Vernon E. North	1972	788
83 2/8	17 1/8	17 1/8	6 5/8	6 6/8	2 4/8	2 3/8	8	2 4/8	5 1/8	5	Washoe Co., NV	David Pohl	David Pohl	1972	788
83 2/8	17	17	6 2/8	6 3/8	2 5/8	2 5/8	13 1/8	9 2/8	5 3/8	5 3/8	Culberson Co., TX	Jim Smith	Jim Smith	1972	788
83 2/8	17 7/8	17 7/8	6 7/8	6 7/8	2 4/8	2 5/8	9 4/8	6 2/8	5	5 4/8	Coconino Co., AZ	Russell Fischer	Russell Fischer	1973	788
83 2/8	16 2/8	16 2/8	6 1/8	6 2/8	2 4/8	2 6/8	11	8 4/8	7 1/8	7 2/8	Carbon Co., WY	Ray Freitas	Ray Freitas	1973	788
83 2/8	16	15 6/8	6 1/8	6 1/8	3	3	8 3/8	5 5/8	5 2/8	5 2/8	Park Co., WY	Dwight Brunsvold	Dwight Brunsvold	1974	788

Score	L. Horn R	L. Horn L	Circ. Base R	Circ. Base L	Circ. 3rd Qtr R	Circ. 3rd Qtr L	Prong R	Prong L	Inside Spread	Tip to Tip	Locality	Hunter	Owner	Date	Rank
83 2/8	16 2/8	16 4/8	6	6 1/8	2 7/8	2 6/8	10 6/8	4 1/8	6 1/8	6 5/8	Rolling Hills, AB	Dennis A. Andrews	Dennis A. Andrews	1975	788
83 2/8	17 4/8	17 5/8	6 2/8	6 3/8	3 2/8	3 1/8	12 6/8	6 3/8	6 3/8	4 4/8	Yavapai Co., AZ	J. Mike Foley	J. Mike Foley	1975	788
83 2/8	14 5/8	14 5/8	6 5/8	6 6/8	2 6/8	2 6/8	12 4/8	10	6 6/8	7 6/8	Carter Co., MT	Joseph Henderson	Joseph Henderson	1975	788
83 2/8	17	16 3/8	6 7/8	7	2 4/8	2 5/8	15 4/8	12 6/8	7	5 1/8	Yavapai Co., AZ	Ralph Koepke	Ralph Koepke	1975	788
83 2/8	17	17	6 2/8	6 2/8	2 6/8	2 5/8	15	11 3/8	6 2/8	5 4/8	Coconino Co., AZ	Edmond C. Morton	Edmond C. Morton	1975	788
83 2/8	14 5/8	14 5/8	7	6 6/8	3 2/8	3 2/8	9 5/8	7 7/8	6 6/8	5 1/8	Jackson Co., CO	James R. Mosman	James R. Mosman	1975	788
83 2/8	16	16	7	6 7/8	2 6/8	2 5/8	11 6/8	7 5/8	6 7/8	5 1/8	Harding Co., SD	Kathleen Prestjohn	Kathleen Prestjohn	1975	788
83 2/8	15 2/8	15 6/8	6	6 1/8	2 5/8	2 6/8	11	4 1/8	6 1/8	7 5/8	Medicine Hat, AB	Roger H. Stone	Roger H. Stone	1975	788
83 2/8	15 2/8	15 6/8	6 4/8	6 4/8	2 5/8	2 7/8	9	2 6/8	6 4/8	5	Cochise Co., AZ	Keith L. Miller	Keith L. Miller	1976	788
83 2/8	15 6/8	14 6/8	7 1/8	7 1/8	2 7/8	3	13	10 6/8	7 1/8	5 1/8	Goshen Co., WY	William E. Patterson	William E. Patterson	1976	788
83 2/8	14 6/8	15 2/8	7 1/8	6 6/8	3	3 2/8	14	10 5/8	6 6/8	6 1/8	Natrona Co., WY	Dean L. Johnson	Dean L. Johnson	1977	788
83 2/8	15 2/8	16	7 1/8	6 5/8	2 7/8	2 7/8	10 5/8	4 4/8	6 5/8	6	Sweet Grass Co., MT	Dennis E. Moos	Dennis E. Moos	1977	788
83 2/8	16	16 1/8	6 5/8	6 7/8	2 4/8	2 5/8	10 7/8	4 6/8	6 7/8	9 6/8	Socorro Co., NM	Charles M. McLaughlin	Charles M. McLaughlin	1979	788
83 2/8	16 1/8	17 7/8	6 5/8	6 4/8	2 6/8	2 6/8	15	9 1/8	6 4/8	4 6/8	Humboldt Co., NV	Robert E. Stopper	Robert E. Stopper	1979	788
83 2/8	17 2/8	17 2/8	6 2/8	6 2/8	2 6/8	2 5/8	16 1/8	13	6 2/8	4 7/8	Roosevelt Co., NM	Danny L. Tivis	Danny L. Tivis	1979	788
83 2/8	16 2/8	16 2/8	6 6/8	6 6/8	2 5/8	2 7/8	8 5/8	5 2/8	6 6/8	4 7/8	Musselshell Co., MT	Caroll M. Lumpkin, Jr.	Caroll M. Lumpkin, Jr.	1980	788
83 2/8	16 2/8	16 3/8	6 4/8	6 4/8	3	2 5/8	12 1/8	7 2/8	6 4/8	5 2/8	Beaverhead Co., MT	Scott Withers	Scott Withers	1980	788
83 2/8	16	16	7	7	2 7/8	2 7/8	10 1/8	8	7	6 1/8	Natrona Co., WY	Bill E. Boatman	Bill E. Boatman	1981	788
83 2/8	15 1/8	15 2/8	6 7/8	6 4/8	2 6/8	3	9 5/8	5 6/8	6 4/8	6 2/8	Natrona Co., WY	Andy Van Patten	Andy Van Patten	1981	788
83 2/8	17 2/8	16 4/8	6 4/8	6 4/8	3 1/8	2 6/8	7 2/8	6 7/8	6 4/8	5 7/8	Fremont Co., WY	Benjamin T. Tonn	Benjamin T. Tonn	1981	788
83 2/8	16 3/8	16 6/8	7 5/8	7 4/8	2 4/8	2 4/8	7 1/8	2 2/8	7 4/8	6	Harney Co., OR	Gary L. Wilfert	Gary L. Wilfert	1981	788
83 2/8	16 6/8	17 3/8	6 2/8	6 2/8	2 5/8	2 5/8	12 2/8	7 3/8	6 2/8	5 3/8	Campbell Co., WY	Dwayne A. Anderson	Dwayne A. Anderson	1982	788
83 2/8	17 4/8	16 1/8	6 4/8	6 4/8	2 7/8	2 7/8	8	2 4/8	6 4/8	4 6/8	Brewster Co., TX	Richard T. Delgado	Richard T. Delgado	1982	788
83 2/8	16 1/8	16 5/8	6	6	3 2/8	3 2/8	8 7/8	3 5/8	6	4 7/8	Coconino Co., AZ	Gilbert S. Garside	Gilbert S. Garside	1982	788
83 2/8	16 4/8	15 2/8	7 4/8	7 4/8	2 7/8	3 1/8	11 5/8	11 2/8	7 4/8	5 3/8	Natrona Co., WY	Gary A. Campbell	Gary A. Campbell	1983	788
83 2/8	16 2/8	16 5/8	6	6	2 7/8	2 6/8	12	3 5/8	6	6 5/8	Carter Co., MT	Martin Crane	Martin Crane	1983	788
83 2/8	16 1/8	16 3/8	6 6/8	6 6/8	3 1/8	3 1/8	9 1/8	10 1/8	6 6/8	5 2/8	Mora Co., NM	James E. Davenport, Jr.	James E. Davenport, Jr.	1983	788
83 2/8	14 6/8	14 6/8	7 3/8	7 3/8	3	2 6/8	14 3/8	11 1/8	7 3/8	5 4/8	Lake Co., OR	Clyde L. Dehlinger	Clyde L. Dehlinger	1983	788
83 2/8	16 4/8	16 2/8	6 5/8	6 5/8	2 6/8	2 2/8	13 5/8	3 4/8	6 5/8	6 2/8	Uinta Co., WY	Earl H. Heninger	Earl H. Heninger	1983	788
83 2/8	16 2/8	16 6/8	6 5/8	6 4/8	2 2/8	2 5/8	8 6/8	3 7/8	6 4/8	5 3/8	Sweetwater Co., WY	Donald W. Kramer	Donald W. Kramer	1983	788
83 2/8	16 3/8	17	7	6 7/8	2 4/8	2 6/8	9 5/8	6 5/8	6 7/8	5 5/8	Lake Co., OR	Richard L. Smith	Richard L. Smith	1983	788
83 2/8	15 2/8	15 7/8	7	6 6/8	2 6/8	2 6/8	12 3/8	7	6 6/8	3 6/8	Apache Co., AZ	Robert A. Stacy	Robert A. Stacy	1983	788
83 2/8	17 3/8	17 4/8	6 2/8	6 3/8	3	3	12 4/8	6 6/8	6 3/8	4 6/8	Coconino Co., AZ	Delroy Western	Delroy Western	1983	788
83 2/8	16 2/8	15	7	6 4/8	3 3/8	3 1/8	11 4/8	7 3/8	6 4/8	6	Cochise Co., AZ	Jim Tomlin	B&C National Collection	1984	788
83 2/8	15 7/8	15 6/8	6 2/8	6 2/8	3 2/8	3 2/8	8 5/8	4 5/8	6 2/8	4 7/8	Coconino Co., AZ	Matthew Dominy	Matthew Dominy	1984	788
83 2/8	17	17 1/8	6 6/8	6 6/8	2 6/8	2 6/8	9 7/8	4 5/8	6 6/8	4 7/8	Colfax Co., NM	Stephen C. LeBlanc	Stephen C. LeBlanc	1984	788
83 2/8	17 2/8	17 2/8	6 1/8	6 1/8	3 1/8	3 1/8	9 5/8	3 3/8	6 1/8	4 3/8	Lincoln Co., NV	Linda P. Allen	Linda P. Allen	1985	788
83 2/8	16 6/8	16 7/8	7 1/8	7	3 2/8	3 2/8	15 3/8	14	7	4 6/8	Thomas Co., KS	Charles M. Barnett	Charles M. Barnett	1985	788
83 2/8	16	16	6 4/8	6 3/8	3 1/8	3 2/8	10 2/8	3 4/8	6 3/8	6	Cochise Co., AZ	Neil G. Sutherland II	Neil G. Sutherland II	1986	788
83 2/8	16	15 6/8	6 3/8	6 3/8	2 7/8	2 7/8	9 3/8	3 7/8	6 3/8	4 7/8	Sweetwater Co., WY	Rob M. Knight	Rob M. Knight	1987	788
83 2/8	17 1/8	17 1/8	6	6	2 6/8	2 6/8	10 1/8	4 5/8	6	5 2/8	Coconino Co., AZ	H. Keith Neitch	H. Keith Neitch	1988	788
83 2/8	17 2/8	17 2/8	6 2/8	6 2/8	2 4/8	2 4/8	9 6/8	9 6/8	6 2/8	5 5/8	Mora Co., NM	Patrick F. Taylor	Patrick F. Taylor	1988	788
83 2/8	16 3/8	16 7/8	6 2/8	6 2/8	3 1/8	2 7/8	13 6/8	9 3/8	6 2/8	3 6/8	Hartley Co., TX	Ernie Davis	Ernie Davis	1989	788
83 2/8	16	16	7	7	3	3	11 2/8	9	7	4 1/8	Socorro Co., NM	Arthur R. Dubs	Arthur R. Dubs	1989	788
83 2/8	15	16	7 1/8	7	2 7/8	3 3/8	8 4/8	2 3/8	7	5 5/8	Rosebud Co., MT	Anthony J. Emmerich	Anthony J. Emmerich	1989	788
83 2/8	17 2/8	17 2/8	6 2/8	6 3/8	2 4/8	2 4/8	12 6/8	9 2/8	6 3/8	5 5/8	Sweet Grass Co., MT	Daniel Phariss	Daniel Phariss	1989	788
83 2/8	15 6/8	16 3/8	6 2/8	6 1/8	3 1/8	2 7/8	16 5/8	15 2/8	6 1/8	6 2/8	Navajo Co., AZ	Ray V. Pogue	Ray V. Pogue	1989	788

PRONGHORN

Antilocapra americana and related subspecies

Score	Length of Horn R	L	Circumference of Base R	L	Circumference at Third Quarter R	L	Inside Spread	Tip to Tip Spread	Length of Prong R	L	Locality	Hunter	Owner	Date Killed	Rank
83 2/8	16 3/8	16 1/8	6 3/8	6 3/8	2 4/8	2 4/8	10 3/8	7	6 3/8	6 2/8	Rosebud Co., MT	Gary M. Van Dyke	Gary M. Van Dyke	1989	788
83 2/8	15 1/8	15 1/8	6 7/8	6 6/8	2 7/8	2 7/8	6 7/8	1 4/8	5	4 6/8	Natrona Co., WY	Dean Albanis	Dean Albanis	1990	788
83 2/8	14 2/8	14 6/8	6 6/8	6 6/8	2 6/8	2 7/8	10 5/8	5 5/8	7 2/8	7	Modoc Co., CA	David T. Eveland	David T. Eveland	1990	788
83 2/8	16 2/8	16 2/8	6 4/8	6 4/8	2 5/8	2 5/8	9 4/8	4	5	5 1/8	Washoe Co., NV	Steve F. Holmes	Steve F. Holmes	1990	788
83 2/8	14 5/8	15	7	7	3 4/8	3 2/8	11 4/8	10 5/8	5 4/8	5	Uinta Co., WY	John W. McGehee	John W. McGehee	1990	788
83 2/8	16	16	6 6/8	6 6/8	2 7/8	3	10	6 7/8	4 7/8	4 7/8	Carter Co., MT	Donald W. Mindemann, Jr.	Donald W. Mindemann, Jr.	1990	788
83 2/8	16 1/8	16 4/8	6 7/8	7 1/8	2 5/8	2 6/8	13 1/8	9 7/8	5 5/8	5 6/8	Carbon Co., WY	Thomas W. Popham	Thomas W. Popham	1990	788
83 2/8	16 1/8	16 1/8	6 6/8	6 5/8	2 6/8	2 7/8	9 6/8	6 5/8	5 3/8	5 2/8	Natrona Co., WY	Robert B. Poskie	Robert B. Poskie	1990	788
83 2/8	16 1/8	15 6/8	6 7/8	6 6/8	3	2 7/8	13 2/8	9 5/8	5 7/8	5 7/8	Carbon Co., WY	Robert H. Ruegge	Robert H. Ruegge	1990	788
83 2/8	17 1/8	16 2/8	6 6/8	6 6/8	2 2/8	2 2/8	12 3/8	7 2/8	5 7/8	6 1/8	Custer Co., MT	Eric S. Doeden	Eric S. Doeden	1991	788
83 2/8	15 1/8	14 7/8	6 6/8	6 6/8	2 6/8	2 5/8	10 7/8	10 6/8	6	6 4/8	Albany Co., WY	Shawn E. Dovey	Shawn E. Dovey	1991	788
83 2/8	17	16 6/8	7	6 7/8	2 4/8	2 4/8	11 6/8	6 3/8	5 2/8	5 2/8	Fremont Co., WY	John M. Dunsworth	John M. Dunsworth	1991	788
83 2/8	17 3/8	17	6 3/8	6 4/8	2 4/8	2 4/8	14 1/8	10 3/8	5 6/8	5 5/8	Harney Co., OR	Patricia A. Kaiser	Patricia A. Kaiser	1991	788
83 2/8	16 6/8	16 6/8	6 2/8	6 3/8	2 4/8	2 4/8	11 4/8	6 4/8	5 7/8	5 6/8	Colfax Co., NM	Robert J. Seeds	Robert J. Seeds	1991	788
83 2/8	15 7/8	15 6/8	6 2/8	6 2/8	3 2/8	3 2/8	9 6/8	6 6/8	5 5/8	5 6/8	Mineral Co., NV	Victor Trujillo	Victor Trujillo	1991	788
83 2/8	15 5/8	15 3/8	6 3/8	6 3/8	2 4/8	2 3/8	12 1/8	11 5/8	6 6/8	6 4/8	Lassen Co., CA	Timothy L. Hartin	Timothy L. Hartin	1992	788
83 2/8	15 2/8	15 3/8	7	7	2 4/8	2 4/8	10 2/8	5 2/8	5 5/8	5 6/8	Natrona Co., WY	Sharnell I. Kamish	Sharnell I. Kamish	1992	788
83 2/8	17 1/8	17	6 2/8	6 2/8	2 3/8	2 4/8	8 4/8	4 3/8	4 6/8	4 7/8	Carbon Co., WY	Kelly L. Sandry	Kelly L. Sandry	1992	788
83 2/8	17 7/8	18	6	6	2 6/8	2 7/8	11 7/8	6 2/8	4 5/8	4 5/8	Apache Co., AZ	R. Steve Bass	R. Steve Bass	1993	788
83 2/8	14 3/8	14 7/8	6 5/8	6 6/8	2 4/8	2 4/8	14 7/8	12 7/8	6 7/8	6 7/8	Coconino Co., AZ	Benjamin Piper	Benjamin Piper	1993	788
83 2/8	16 3/8	16 2/8	6 1/8	6 1/8	3 1/8	3 1/8	11 5/8	9 7/8	5 1/8	5	Apache Co., AZ	Susanne W. Queenan	Susanne W. Queenan	1993	788
83 2/8	14 2/8	14 2/8	6 7/8	7	3 7/8	3 6/8	7 6/8	3 6/8	6 6/8	6 2/8	Mora Co., NM	Robert J. Seeds	Robert J. Seeds	1993	788
83 2/8	17	16 6/8	6 4/8	6 4/8	2 4/8	2 5/8	11 5/8	6 5/8	5 7/8	5 5/8	Sage Creek, AB	Leslie C. Wall	Leslie C. Wall	1993	788
83 2/8	17 6/8	18	6 2/8	6 1/8	2 5/8	2 5/8	12 4/8	9 4/8	4 2/8	5 2/8	Coconino Co., AZ	Fred F. Brown	Fred F. Brown	1994	788
83 2/8	15 5/8	15 2/8	6 7/8	6 6/8	2 6/8	2 6/8	13 6/8	11 3/8	5 5/8	5 7/8	Box Elder Co., UT	Larry D. Elliott	Larry D. Elliott	1994	788
83 2/8	18 1/8	18 4/8	6	6	2 7/8	2 7/8	7 3/8	1 1/8	5 2/8	4 5/8	Apache Co., AZ	John W. Whitcomb	John W. Whitcomb	1994	788
83 2/8	17 4/8	16 7/8	5 6/8	5 6/8	2 7/8	2 4/8	10 2/8	5 1/8	6 1/8	5 7/8	Colfax Co., NM	Herbert W. Eplee	Herbert W. Eplee	1995	788
83 2/8	16 5/8	16 6/8	6 4/8	6 4/8	2 4/8	2 3/8	14 4/8	10 5/8	6 4/8	6 6/8	Catron Co., NM	Robert M. Kahute	Robert M. Kahute	1995	788
83 2/8	16 4/8	16 1/8	6 5/8	6 3/8	2 7/8	2 5/8	8 2/8	3 4/8	6 1/8	5 6/8	Lea Co., NM	W. Don Byers	W. Don Byers	1996	788
83 2/8	16 6/8	16 6/8	6 2/8	6 4/8	3 2/8	3 2/8	12 5/8	10 4/8	4 7/8	4 6/8	Catron Co., NM	Stephen K. May	Stephen K. May	1996	788
83 2/8	15 2/8	15 5/8	6 7/8	6 7/8	2 7/8	2 7/8	8 2/8	4	5 3/8	5 5/8	Albany Co., WY	Felix A. Nieves	Felix A. Nieves	1996	788
83 2/8	16 4/8	16 4/8	6 6/8	6 6/8	3	3	8 6/8	4	5 3/8	5 2/8	Navajo Co., AZ	David W. Pearson	David W. Pearson	1996	788
83 2/8	16	15 6/8	6 6/8	6 6/8	2 5/8	2 5/8	8 4/8	4 1/8	5 6/8	5 6/8	Emery Co., UT	Kirk D. Taylor	Kirk D. Taylor	1996	788
83 2/8	15 7/8	16 2/8	7	7 1/8	2 5/8	2 7/8	11	7	4 6/8	5 2/8	Natrona Co., WY	Gerald M. Schroder	Gerald M. Schroder	1997	788
83	16 2/8	16 5/8	6 4/8	6 3/8	3	3	16 2/8	16 4/8	4 1/8	5 1/8	Shirley Basin, WY	Duncan G. Weibel	Duncan G. Weibel	1946	885
83	15 7/8	15 4/8	7 1/8	7	2 5/8	2 5/8	9 1/8	3 1/8	5 5/8	5 4/8	Rawlins, WY	Richard Eisner	Richard Eisner	1951	885
83	15 3/8	15 3/8	6 4/8	6 2/8	3 2/8	3 4/8	11 5/8	7 2/8	5 5/8	5	Hartley Co., TX	William G. Kendrick	William G. Kendrick	1953	885
83	15 2/8	14 7/8	6 5/8	6 4/8	3	3 1/8	12 2/8	9 1/8	5 4/8	6	Heber, AZ	Grady L. Beard	Grady L. Beard	1954	885

Rank	Length R	Length L	Circ. Base R	Circ. Base L	D R	D L	Tip to Tip	Inside Spread	Prong R	Prong L	Locality	Trophy Owner	Hunter	Date	Score
83	14 4/8	15 2/8	7 6/8	7 2/8	2 2/8	2 4/8	8 7/8	10 4/8	6 2/8	6 4/8	Casper, WY	Tom R. Frye	Tom R. Frye	1954	885
83	15 2/8	15 1/8	6 5/8	6 4/8	2 5/8	2 5/8	13 4/8	14 6/8	6 5/8	6 2/8	Saratoga, WY	Dave Erickson	Dave Erickson	1957	885
83	16 4/8	16 1/8	6 7/8	6 4/8	3	2 6/8	11 4/8	13 7/8	5 2/8	5 2/8	Rawlins, WY	Melvin Birks	Melvin Birks	1960	885
83	16	16 1/8	6 4/8	6 4/8	2 7/8	2 7/8	5 1/8	11	5 7/8	5 7/8	Lame Deer, MT	G.E. Badgley	G.E. Badgley	1961	885
83	16 3/8	16 7/8	6 2/8	6 2/8	2 3/8	2 3/8	5 7/8	11	5 6/8	6 1/8	Lake Co., OR	Ken Smith	Ken Smith	1962	885
83	15 4/8	15 2/8	7 1/8	7 2/8	2 6/8	3	9 3/8	13 4/8	5 3/8	6 1/8	Plevna, MT	Joseph P. Burger	Joseph P. Burger	1963	885
83	16 6/8	17 1/8	6 5/8	6 6/8	3	2 5/8	3 7/8	8 7/8	5 4/8	4 3/8	Thatcher, CO	M.A. May	M.A. May	1965	885
83	16 2/8	16 5/8	6 7/8	6 3/8	2 5/8	2 5/8	8 3/8	12 5/8	5 5/8	5 5/8	Boyero, CO	Henry H. Zietz	Henry H. Zietz	1965	885
83	18 2/8	18 2/8	6 2/8	6 6/8	2 5/8	3	8 5/8	11	4 4/8	4 2/8	Navajo Co., AZ	Joseph R. Rencher	Joseph R. Rencher	1970	885
83	16 3/8	16 2/8	7	6 2/8	3 1/8	2 5/8	8	11	4 6/8	4 4/8	Wamsutter, WY	Marlene Simons	Marlene Simons	1970	885
83	16 1/8	16 2/8	6 2/8	6 2/8	2 5/8	2 6/8	10 4/8	13 6/8	6 4/8	6 5/8	Moffat Co., CO	Michael Coleman	Michael Coleman	1971	885
83	16	15 5/8	6 6/8	6 6/8	2 6/8	2 4/8	5	9	5	5	Springer, NM	Ronald E. McKinney	Ronald E. McKinney	1973	885
83	16	16 3/8	7	7	2 5/8	2 6/8	4 1/8	10 2/8	5 6/8	4 6/8	Fremont Co., WY	Robert Cragoe, Jr.	Robert Cragoe, Jr.	1974	885
83	16 2/8	16 5/8	6 4/8	6 3/8	3	3	6 4/8	11	5 7/8	6	Colfax Co., NM	Jim Hoots	Jim Hoots	1975	885
83	16 5/8	17	6 4/8	6 1/8	2 5/8	2 5/8	9 6/8	13 5/8	5 6/8	5 2/8	Yavapai Co., AZ	Artie L. Thrower	Artie L. Thrower	1975	885
83	17	16 6/8	6 4/8	6 2/8	2 7/8	2 7/8	12 5/8	15	5 7/8	5 2/8	Wagon Mound, NM	Dale R. Leonard	Dale R. Leonard	1976	885
83	16 2/8	16 2/8	6 1/8	6 5/8	3 2/8	3 3/8	10 7/8	11 6/8	5 7/8	5 4/8	Valley Co., MT	Timothy R. Logan	Timothy R. Logan	1976	885
83	16 2/8	16 4/8	6 3/8	6 2/8	2 5/8	2 5/8	4 2/8	11 2/8	6 4/8	6 3/8	Harding Co., NM	Stephen C. LeBlanc	Stephen C. LeBlanc	1977	885
83	16 5/8	16 5/8	6 6/8	6 4/8	2 6/8	2 6/8	5	9 5/8	6 1/8	6 4/8	Lake Co., OR	Francis G. Dalrymple	Francis G. Dalrymple	1978	885
83	16	16 1/8	6 4/8	7 1/8	2 4/8	2 6/8	2 2/8	9 5/8	6 1/8	6 2/8	Sweetwater Co., WY	Douglas Grantham	Douglas Grantham	1978	885
83	16 2/8	16 2/8	7	6 2/8	2 6/8	2 4/8	14 2/8	8 3/8	5 3/8	5 3/8	Sublette Co., WY	Kenneth D. Knight	Kenneth D. Knight	1978	885
83	17 1/8	17 1/8	6 2/8	6 4/8	2 7/8	2 6/8	10 5/8	15	5 2/8	5 3/8	Sublette Co., WY	Thomas A. Scott	Thomas A. Scott	1978	885
83	16 1/8	16 4/8	6 4/8	6 4/8	2 6/8	2 7/8	7 5/8	14 2/8	5 3/8	5 4/8	Washington Co., CO	Gina R. Cass	Gina R. Cass	1979	885
83	16	16	7 5/8	7 5/8	2 6/8	2 6/8	1 2/8	11 1/8	5 3/8	5 1/8	Sweetwater Co., WY	Glen W. Coates	Glen W. Coates	1979	885
83	16 2/8	16 4/8	6 4/8	6 4/8	3 1/8	3 2/8	8 5/8	8 1/8	4	4 2/8	Custer Co., SD	Edward J. Schauer	Edward J. Schauer	1979	885
83	16	16 3/8	5 5/8	5 5/8	2 6/8	2 5/8	1 7/8	10 1/8	5 7/8	5 7/8	Hudspeth Co., TX	Ernie Davis	Ernie Davis	1980	885
83	15 7/8	15 5/8	6 4/8	6 4/8	2 4/8	2 4/8	4 7/8	8 1/8	5 6/8	5 6/8	Lake Co., OR	Jerry J. Peacore	Jerry J. Peacore	1980	885
83	15 6/8	15 6/8	5 5/8	5 5/8	3 1/8	3 1/8	5 6/8	11 1/8	6 2/8	5 4/8	Sweetwater Co., WY	Keith Penner	Keith Penner	1980	885
83	15 4/8	15 4/8	7 3/8	7	2 4/8	2 4/8	6 1/8	7 7/8	5 2/8	6 6/8	Campbell Co., WY	Richard S. Alford	Richard S. Alford	1982	885
83	16 4/8	16 5/8	6 3/8	6 3/8	2 6/8	2 6/8	4 4/8	8 6/8	5 7/8	5 2/8	Meade Co., SD	Randy A. Cammack	Randy A. Cammack	1982	885
83	15 7/8	15 7/8	6 4/8	6 3/8	2 5/8	2 5/8	4 6/8	9	6 6/8	5 4/8	Washoe Co., NV	Richard J. Depaoli	Richard J. Depaoli	1982	885
83	15 6/8	15 6/8	6 2/8	6 4/8	2 5/8	2 5/8	9 3/8	10 6/8	5 5/8	5 5/8	Albany Co., NV	Mark T. Gleason	Mark T. Gleason	1982	885
83	15 4/8	15 6/8	7	6 6/8	2 5/8	2 5/8	8 4/8	13 6/8	5 5/8	5 4/8	Humboldt Co., NV	Thomas S. Kelley	Thomas S. Kelley	1983	885
83	15 7/8	15 7/8	7 2/8	7	2 6/8	2 6/8	7	10 1/8	5 6/8	5 4/8	Colfax Co., NM	John W. Ladd	John W. Ladd	1983	885
83	16	16	7 1/8	7	2 4/8	2 4/8	9 3/8	9 6/8	5 6/8	5 4/8	Carbon Co., WY	Frederick L. Proffit	Frederick L. Proffit	1983	885
83	15 3/8	15 5/8	7	7	3	3	7 7/8	13 3/8	5 2/8	5 6/8	Box Butte Co., NE	Lynda G. Sydow	Lynda G. Sydow	1984	885
83	12 6/8	13	7	7	3 5/8	3 7/8	1 2/8	13 4/8	5 4/8	5 2/8	Jackson Co., CO	Charles J. Cesar	Charles J. Cesar	1985	885
83	15 6/8	15 1/8	6 6/8	6 6/8	2 6/8	2 7/8	6 4/8	11 7/8	5 6/8	5 6/8	Fremont Co., WY	Thomas A. Dremel	Thomas A. Dremel	1985	885
83	15 5/8	15 5/8	7 1/8	7 1/8	2 7/8	2 6/8	13 6/8	12 6/8	5 4/8	5 4/8	Sweetwater Co., WY	Clifford Rockhold	Clifford Rockhold	1985	885
83	16 5/8	17 1/8	7 1/8	7 1/8	2 6/8	2 6/8	7 7/8	10 1/8	4 5/8	4 5/8	Humboldt Co., NV	Lenda Z. Azcarate	Lenda Z. Azcarate	1986	885
83	16 6/8	16 6/8	6 4/8	6 4/8	2 6/8	2 6/8	10 1/8	8 5/8	5	5	Modoc Co., CA	Richard Bishop	Richard Bishop	1986	885
83	15 2/8	15 2/8	6 6/8	6 6/8	2 6/8	2 6/8	10 7/8	13 6/8	5	5	Manyberries, AB	Rae E. Cervo	Rae E. Cervo	1986	885
83	15 5/8	15 3/8	7 1/8	7 2/8	2 4/8	2 4/8	9 4/8	10 7/8	4 7/8	4 7/8	Baker Co., OR	Richard R. Mason	Richard R. Mason	1986	885
83	15 4/8	15 4/8	7 2/8	7 2/8	2 6/8	2 6/8	9	9 4/8	5 7/8	5 7/8	Natrona Co., WY	Gerald Utrup	Gerald Utrup	1986	885
83	17 2/8	17 5/8	6	6	2 4/8	2 4/8	6	9	5 7/8	5 7/8	Catron Co., NM	Dan L. Harper	Dan L. Harper	1987	885
83	16 4/8	16 6/8	7	7	2 3/8	2 4/8	4 2/8	6	6 1/8	6 1/8	Emery Co., UT	Dennis G. McElvain	Dennis G. McElvain	1987	885
83	15 7/8	15 6/8	7 1/8	7	2 6/8	2 6/8		8 5/8	5 7/8	5 1/8	Albany Co., WY	Robert J. Miller	Robert J. Miller	1987	885

PRONGHORN

Antilocapra americana americana and related subspecies

Score	Length of Horn R	L	Circumference of Base R	L	Circumference at Third Quarter R	L	Inside Spread	Tip to Tip Spread	Length of Prong R	L	Locality	Hunter	Owner	Date Killed	Rank
83	15 1/8	15	7	7 1/8	2 6/8	2 5/8	9 3/8	7	5 6/8	5 4/8	Washoe Co., NV	Christopher T. Rores	Christopher T. Rores	1987	885
83	17 1/8	17	6 4/8	6 4/8	3 2/8	3 2/8	12 1/8	8 6/8	3 7/8	4 4/8	Graham Co., AZ	Marvin R. Selke	Marvin R. Selke	1987	885
83	17 2/8	16 2/8	6 6/8	6 4/8	3 2/8	2 5/8	11 3/8	9 6/8	5 2/8	5 7/8	Moffat Co., CO	Marvin L. Shepard	Marvin L. Shepard	1987	885
83	15 4/8	15 2/8	6 4/8	6 4/8	3 1/8	3	8	3	5 5/8	5	Washoe Co., NV	Edward J. Smith	Edward J. Smith	1987	885
83	17	17 2/8	6 2/8	6 2/8	2 7/8	3	15 3/8	12 2/8	5 5/8	5 5/8	Coconino Co., AZ	Billie F. Bechtel	Billie F. Bechtel	1988	885
83	17 4/8	17 4/8	6 1/8	6	3	3	14 4/8	10	5	4	Sierra Co., NM	Steven A. Berry	Steven A. Berry	1988	885
83	16 4/8	16 2/8	6 4/8	6 4/8	3 2/8	3 1/8	16 2/8	16 4/8	4 3/8	4 5/8	Washakie Co., WY	Gordon E. Deromedi	Gordon E. Deromedi	1988	885
83	16	16	6 4/8	6 4/8	2 6/8	2 6/8	14 6/8	11	5 4/8	5 4/8	Fremont Co., WY	Douglas R. Dow	Douglas R. Dow	1988	885
83	15 6/8	15 6/8	6 6/8	6 7/8	2 6/8	2 6/8	5 4/8	8 4/8	5 6/8	5 2/8	Jackson Co., CO	Douglas A. Weimer	Douglas A. Weimer	1988	885
83	16 5/8	16	7	6 7/8	2 3/8	2 1/8	13 1/8	9 7/8	6 2/8	6 3/8	Carbon Co., WY	Gary Duggins	Gary Duggins	1989	885
83	16 5/8	16 3/8	6 3/8	6 7/8	3 1/8	3 5/8	16 2/8	13 7/8	4 7/8	4 5/8	Sheridan Co., WY	Tom W. Housh	Tom W. Housh	1989	885
83	16 4/8	16 4/8	6 5/8	6 4/8	2 5/8	2 5/8	15 7/8	15 3/8	5 4/8	5 2/8	Moffat Co., CO	Mike Wallers	Mike Wallers	1989	885
83	15 7/8	15 7/8	7 1/8	7	2 5/8	2 4/8	11 1/8	7 6/8	6	5 7/8	Carbon Co., WY	Robert G. Wimpenny	Robert G. Wimpenny	1989	885
83	17 1/8	17	6 4/8	6 3/8	2 7/8	2 6/8	13 1/8	8 5/8	5 1/8	4 6/8	Socorro Co., NM	David A. Berry	David A. Berry	1990	885
83	15 4/8	15 2/8	6 4/8	6 4/8	2 4/8	2 4/8	9 4/8	6	6 7/8	6 4/8	Fremont Co., WY	Tom Covert	Tom Covert	1990	885
83	16 1/8	15 6/8	7 2/8	7 2/8	3	3 1/8	11 2/8	7	4 3/8	5 2/8	Perkins Co., SD	Dick D. Knock	Dick D. Knock	1990	885
83	17 4/8	17 4/8	6 3/8	6 1/8	3	2 6/8	9 3/8	8 1/8	5 3/8	4 6/8	Greenlee Co., AZ	Paul E. Palmer	Paul E. Palmer	1990	885
83	15 4/8	15 6/8	7	7	2 5/8	2 4/8	9 2/8	6 1/8	5	5 6/8	Mora Co., NM	Gerald W. Pullin	Gerald W. Pullin	1990	885
83	16 1/8	15 6/8	6 2/8	6 1/8	2 7/8	2 6/8	10 1/8	4	5 7/8	5 6/8	Lincoln Co., NM	Robert M. Rogulic	Robert M. Rogulic	1990	885
83	16 2/8	16 2/8	6 7/8	6 7/8	3	2 6/8	8 1/8	6	4 5/8	4 4/8	Coconino Co., AZ	Michael L. Allen	Michael L. Allen	1991	885
83	16 5/8	16 5/8	6 2/8	6 3/8	2 5/8	2 5/8	16 3/8	12 4/8	5 2/8	5 4/8	Otero Co., NM	Steven A. Baldock	Steven A. Baldock	1991	885
83	14	14 5/8	7	7	2 4/8	2 4/8	10 4/8	7 7/8	6 6/8	6 6/8	Lincoln Co., NM	Johnny Bliznak	Johnny Bliznak	1991	885
83	16	16	7 3/8	7 3/8	2 3/8	2 3/8	9 3/8	3 4/8	5 7/8	6	Sweetwater Co., WY	Arnold DeCastro	Arnold DeCastro	1991	885
83	16 3/8	16 2/8	6 4/8	6 4/8	2 5/8	2 5/8	10	5 5/8	5 6/8	5 3/8	Carbon Co., WY	Roger M. Green	Roger M. Green	1991	885
83	16 2/8	16 4/8	6 6/8	6 6/8	2 6/8	2 7/8	10 7/8	7 3/8	5 3/8	4 7/8	Uinta Co., WY	Florence Kitchel	Florence Kitchel	1991	885
83	17 2/8	17 1/8	6 1/8	6 2/8	3 1/8	3 1/8	15 2/8	6 2/8	4 4/8	4 4/8	Hudspeth Co., TX	Larry P. Panebaker	Larry P. Panebaker	1991	885
83	17 4/8	17 2/8	6 4/8	6 6/8	2 6/8	3	12	7 6/8	5	4 7/8	Coconino Co., AZ	Gene Sewell	Gene Sewell	1991	885
83	17	17 2/8	6 7/8	6 5/8	2 6/8	2 5/8	10 3/8	5 2/8	4 6/8	5 4/8	Carbon Co., WY	Gerald A. Steele	Gerald A. Steele	1991	885
83	16 1/8	16	6 3/8	6 3/8	2 6/8	2 6/8	12 6/8	9	4 2/8	4 7/8	Lake Co., OR	Wil L. Wilson	Wil L. Wilson	1991	885
83	15 1/8	15 3/8	7 1/8	7	2 6/8	2 5/8	14	13 4/8	5 5/8	5 3/8	Washoe Co., NV	Joseph A. Burkhamer	Joseph A. Burkhamer	1992	885
83	15 6/8	16	6 6/8	6 7/8	2 4/8	2 7/8	10 2/8	6 4/8	5 5/8	5 6/8	Carbon Co., WY	Mark D. Gaines	Mark D. Gaines	1992	885
83	15 5/8	15 3/8	6 2/8	6 3/8	2 7/8	3	10 2/8	5 3/8	6 1/8	5 7/8	Juab Co., UT	Alan L. Pfiefer	Alan L. Pfiefer	1992	885
83	15 3/8	15 2/8	7 2/8	7	2 7/8	2 7/8	8	5 4/8	5 7/8	4 7/8	Kimball Co., NE	Mayda M. Zimmerman	Mayda M. Zimmerman	1992	885
83	16 6/8	16 6/8	6	6	3 1/8	3 1/8	13 5/8	10 6/8	5 2/8	5 2/8	Milk River, AB	Lyle G. Andersen	Lyle G. Andersen	1993	885
83	16 5/8	16 5/8	6 1/8	6	2 6/8	2 5/8	9 5/8	5 6/8	5 5/8	5 4/8	Colfax Co., NM	W. Douglas Appling	W. Douglas Appling	1993	885
83	16	16	6 6/8	6 6/8	2 7/8	2 6/8	8 7/8	7 2/8	5 1/8	5	Las Animas Co., CO	Mike R. Caldarella	Mike R. Caldarella	1993	885
83	15 7/8	15 5/8	6 4/8	6 3/8	2 7/8	2 7/8	10 6/8	6 2/8	5 4/8	5 2/8	Colfax Co., NM	Robert D. Jones	Robert D. Jones	1993	885
83	16 3/8	17	7 5/8	7 5/8	2 7/8	2 6/8	7 4/8	1 6/8	5 1/8	4 4/8	Weld Co., CO	Gregory A. Peters	Gregory A. Peters	1993	885

Score	Length of Horn R	Length of Horn L	Circ. of Base R	Circ. of Base L	Circ. 2nd Q R	Circ. 2nd Q L	Circ. 3rd Q R	Circ. 3rd Q L	Tip to Tip Spread	Inside Spread	Prong R	Prong L	Locality	Hunter	Owner	Date	Rank
83	15 7/8	16 2/8	7	7	2 5/8	2 5/8	2 5/8	2 5/8	6 3/8	2 4/8	5 3/8	5 3/8	Carbon Co., WY	John L. Anderson	John L. Anderson	1994	885
83	15 6/8	16	6 1/8	6 1/8	2 6/8	2 6/8	2 7/8	2 6/8	8 1/8	3 3/8	6 6/8	6 6/8	Chouteau Co., MT	Brad Burney	Brad Burney	1994	885
83	15 6/8	16	6 7/8	6 7/8	2 6/8	2 6/8	2 6/8	2 6/8	10 7/8	7 4/8	5 3/8	5 1/8	Humboldt Co., NV	Harvey J. Estes	Harvey J. Estes	1994	885
83	15 7/8	16	7	7 1/8	2 4/8	2 4/8	2 4/8	2 4/8	12 5/8	9 7/8	5 7/8	5 3/8	Mora Co., NM	Ralph L. Galyan	Ralph L. Galyan	1994	885
83	16	16	7 1/8	7 1/8	2 6/8	2 6/8	2 6/8	2 6/8	13 4/8	8 6/8	5 2/8	5 6/8	Mora Co., NM	Len H. Guldman	Len H. Guldman	1994	885
83	15 2/8	14 6/8	7 2/8	7 2/8	2 5/8	2 5/8	2 6/8	2 5/8	8 1/8	5 5/8	6 2/8	6 4/8	Sweetwater Co., WY	William M. Henry III	William M. Henry III	1994	885
83	16 4/8	16 5/8	6 1/8	6 2/8	2 3/8	2 3/8	2 7/8	2 7/8	9 1/8	4 5/8	4 5/8	5 2/8	Carbon Co., WY	Jeffery K. Harrow	Jeffery K. Harrow	1995	885
83	15 2/8	15 1/8	7 3/8	7 3/8	3	3	2 6/8	2 6/8	11 2/8	10 2/8	5 3/8	5 2/8	Sweetwater Co., WY	David P. Nicholson	David P. Nicholson	1995	885
83	16 7/8	17 2/8	6 1/8	6 1/8	2 6/8	2 6/8	2 4/8	2 4/8	9 4/8	7	5 2/8	5 3/8	Custer Co., ID	Stanley T. Riddle	Stanley T. Riddle	1995	885
83	15 2/8	15 6/8	6 7/8	6 7/8	2 4/8	2 4/8	2 5/8	2 5/8	9 1/8	5	5 6/8	5 7/8	Carbon Co., WY	Todd D. Pope	Todd D. Pope	1996	885
83	15 4/8	15 1/8	6 7/8	6 7/8	2 5/8	2 5/8	2 5/8	2 5/8	9 6/8	5	6 5/8	6 5/8	Carbon Co., WY	John P. Hornbeck	John P. Hornbeck	1997	885
83	17 2/8	17	7	7	2 3/8	2 3/8	2 5/8	2 5/8	12 1/8	7 3/8	5 1/8	5 1/8	Natrona Co., WY	Unknown	G.S. Peterson	1948	885
82 6/8	15 4/8	15 6/8	6 5/8	6 5/8	3 3/8	3 2/8	2 5/8	2 5/8	16 3/8	5 6/8	5 6/8	5 6/8	Navajo Co., AZ	Joe D. Sutton	Joe D. Sutton	1951	985
82 6/8	16	16 2/8	6 4/8	6 4/8	2 6/8	2 6/8	2 6/8	2 6/8	12 1/8	14 2/8	5 1/8	6 2/8	Angora, NE	Harold C. Rusk	NE Game & Parks Comm.	1954	985
82 6/8	16 6/8	17	6 7/8	6 7/8	2 6/8	2 6/8	3 2/8	3 2/8	14 3/8	11 5/8	5	5	Prairie Co., MT	Gordon Spears	Gordon Spears	1954	985
82 6/8	15 4/8	15 4/8	6 4/8	6 4/8	2 4/8	2 4/8	2 6/8	2 6/8	14	14	5 1/8	5	Jelm Mt., WY	Guy Murdock	Guy Murdock	1955	985
82 6/8	15 2/8	15 2/8	6 7/8	6 7/8	2 6/8	2 6/8	2 6/8	2 6/8	14 2/8	11	6	6	Glad Valley, SD	D.M. Davis	D.M. Davis	1958	985
82 6/8	17 3/8	17 3/8	7 1/8	7 2/8	2 6/8	2 6/8	3 1/8	3 1/8	11 7/8	9 1/8	5	5	Butte Co., SD	P.T. Theodore	P.T. Theodore	1958	985
82 6/8	17 6/8	17 4/8	5 7/8	6	3	3	2 7/8	2 7/8	10 4/8	3 5/8	5 6/8	5 5/8	Yavapai Co., AZ	Vaughan Rock	Vaughan Rock	1959	985
82 6/8	14 6/8	14 6/8	6 4/8	6 4/8	2 7/8	2 7/8	2 7/8	2 7/8	13 5/8	9 4/8	4 7/8	5 3/8	Gillette, WY	R.R. Kirchner	R.R. Kirchner	1961	985
82 6/8	15 6/8	15 6/8	6 7/8	6 7/8	2 7/8	2 7/8	2 3/8	2 3/8	8 3/8	2 6/8	6 2/8	5 2/8	Sweetwater Co., WY	A.L. Bruner	A.L. Bruner	1962	985
82 6/8	16 6/8	16 4/8	6 2/8	6 2/8	2 3/8	2 3/8	2 3/8	2 3/8	11	5 3/8	5 4/8	5 7/8	Lake Co., OR	Kenneth Smith	Kenneth Smith	1963	985
82 6/8	15 4/8	15 7/8	6 7/8	6 7/8	2 7/8	2 7/8	2 7/8	2 7/8	11 3/8	5 7/8	6 3/8	6 3/8	Natrona Co., WY	William S. Martin	William S. Martin	1964	985
82 6/8	15 2/8	15 4/8	6 4/8	6 4/8	2 4/8	2 4/8	2 4/8	2 4/8	14 2/8	8 1/8	6 5/8	6 2/8	Sweetwater Co., WY	James C. Klum	James C. Klum	1965	985
82 6/8	17 6/8	17 4/8	6	6	2 5/8	2 7/8	2 7/8	2 7/8	9 1/8	11 7/8	4 6/8	4 7/8	Ft. Apache Res., AZ	Robert L. Martin	Robert L. Martin	1965	985
82 6/8	14 2/8	14 1/8	7 6/8	7 7/8	2 6/8	2 6/8	2 6/8	2 6/8	10 4/8	9 1/8	5 5/8	5 7/8	Alcova, WY	J. & V. Johnson	New Park Hotel	1965	985
82 6/8	15 6/8	15 6/8	7 5/8	7 5/8	3	3	2 6/8	2 6/8	12 5/8	10 4/8	5	6	Converse Co., WY	Paul W. Tomlin	Paul W. Tomlin	1965	985
82 6/8	17 3/8	17 3/8	6 2/8	6 2/8	2 6/8	2 6/8	2 7/8	2 7/8	8 6/8	8 3/8	4 4/8	4 2/8	Mora Co., NM	R.L. Wakefield	R.L. Wakefield	1967	985
82 6/8	17 2/8	17 3/8	6 5/8	6 5/8	2 7/8	2 7/8	3	3	14 6/8	10 2/8	4 2/8	4	Round Mt., AZ	Dennis L. Fife	Dennis L. Fife	1967	985
82 6/8	15 1/8	15 2/8	7	7	2 6/8	2 6/8	2 6/8	2 6/8	10 5/8	1 6/8	6 1/8	6 5/8	Rocky Ford, CO	Henry A. Helmke	Henry A. Helmke	1967	985
82 6/8	15 2/8	15 2/8	6 7/8	6 7/8	2 6/8	2 6/8	2 6/8	2 6/8	10 5/8	8 6/8	6 1/8	6 5/8	Fremont Co., WY	Terry N. TenBoer	Terry N. TenBoer	1967	985
82 6/8	16 3/8	16 4/8	6 4/8	6 4/8	2 4/8	2 4/8	2 4/8	2 4/8	10	4 7/8	5 5/8	5 5/8	Farson, WY	Ronald O. West	Ronald O. West	1969	985
82 6/8	16	15 7/8	6 7/8	6 7/8	3	3	3	3	10 2/8	5 1/8	5 4/8	5 4/8	Uinta Co., WY	Barry Hyken	Barry Hyken	1969	985
82 6/8	15 3/8	15 4/8	6 6/8	6 6/8	2 4/8	2 4/8	2 5/8	2 5/8	8 6/8	5 2/8	6 3/8	5 4/8	Carbon Co., WY	John M. Sell	John M. Sell	1970	985
82 6/8	14 4/8	14	7 5/8	7 5/8	3 1/8	3 1/8	2 4/8	2 4/8	9	7 6/8	6 1/8	6	Sweetwater Co., WY	Keith F. Dunbar	Keith F. Dunbar	1970	985
82 6/8	15 3/8	15 3/8	6 4/8	6 4/8	3 1/8	3 1/8	2 3/8	2 3/8	5 1/8	5 1/8	5 4/8	6	Custer Co., MT	George E. Sanquist	George E. Sanquist	1970	985
82 6/8	16 5/8	16 4/8	6 3/8	6 3/8	2 3/8	2 3/8	2 5/8	2 5/8	15 4/8	5 4/8	6 1/8	6 1/8	Socorro Co., NM	Lawrence D. Vigil	Lawrence D. Vigil	1971	985
82 6/8	16 3/8	16 3/8	6 3/8	6 3/8	2 5/8	2 5/8	2 7/8	2 7/8	8 4/8	2 7/8	6 2/8	5	Natrona Co., WY	Kenneth Niedan	Kenneth Niedan	1973	985
82 6/8	16 1/8	15 5/8	6 2/8	6 3/8	2 7/8	2 7/8	2 7/8	2 7/8	10 7/8	8 4/8	6 6/8	6 7/8	Medicine Bow, WY	Raymond Freitas	Raymond Freitas	1975	985
82 6/8	15 4/8	15 4/8	6 1/8	6 1/8	2 7/8	2 7/8	3 5/8	3 5/8	9 2/8	4 6/8	5	4 6/8	Carbon Co., WY	Roger D. George	Roger D. George	1977	985
82 6/8	16 3/8	16	6 3/8	6 2/8	2 7/8	2 7/8	2 7/8	2 7/8	13	7 4/8	4 6/8	5 2/8	Modoc Co., CA	Dennis McClelland	Dennis McClelland	1978	985
82 6/8	16 6/8	17 2/8	6 6/8	6 6/8	2 2/8	2 2/8	2 2/8	2 2/8	10 5/8	6	5 1/8	5 2/8	Catron Co., NM	David Chavez	David Chavez	1978	985
82 6/8	15 5/8	15 6/8	6 3/8	6 3/8	2 5/8	2 5/8	2 6/8	2 6/8	10 6/8	6 4/8	6 4/8	6 4/8	Weld Co., CO	Chester N. Erwin	Ronald G. Erwin	1978	985
82 6/8	14 5/8	14 5/8	6 6/8	6 6/8	2 1/8	2 1/8	2 7/8	2 7/8	11 2/8	7 5/8	7 2/8	7 2/8	Grant Co., OR	A. Paul Malstrom	A. Paul Malstrom	1980	985
82 6/8	15 6/8	15 7/8	6 5/8	6 5/8	2 7/8	2 7/8	2 7/8	2 7/8	8	5 3/8	5 5/8	5 3/8	Hudspeth Co., TX	L.A. Grelling	L.A. Grelling	1980	985
82 6/8	15 3/8	15 3/8	6 4/8	6 5/8	2 6/8	2 6/8	2 6/8	2 6/8	10 5/8	8 2/8	6 5/8	6 1/8	Carbon Co., WY	Robert J. Smith	Robert J. Smith	1980	985
82 6/8	16 1/8	16 1/8	7 4/8	7 4/8	2 4/8	2 4/8	2 6/8	2 6/8	8 7/8	2 1/8	5 2/8	5 2/8	Natrona Co., WY	Bill E. Boatman	Bill E. Boatman	1982	985

PRONGHORN

Antilocapra americana americana and related subspecies

Score	Length of Horn R	L	Circumference of Base R	L	Circumference at Third Quarter R	L	Inside Spread	Tip to Tip Spread	Length of Prong R	L	Locality	Hunter	Owner	Date Killed	Rank
82 6/8	15	15	7 2/8	6 7/8	2 5/8	2 5/8	10	6	5 3/8	5 5/8	Carbon Co., WY	Dailen R. Jones	Dailen R. Jones	1982	985
82 6/8	15 3/8	15 4/8	6 6/8	6 6/8	2 6/8	2 6/8	12	9	5 6/8	6 1/8	Carter Co., MT	Lloyd R. Norvell	Lloyd R. Norvell	1982	985
82 6/8	15 5/8	16	6 5/8	6 4/8	2 5/8	2 6/8	9 2/8	6 3/8	6 3/8	5 6/8	Natrona Co., WY	Eugene Turner, Jr.	Eugene Turner, Jr.	1982	985
82 6/8	16 7/8	16 6/8	6 2/8	6 2/8	2 6/8	2 6/8	11 3/8	8 3/8	4 7/8	5	Mora Co., NM	Donald R. Warren	Donald R. Warren	1982	985
82 6/8	14 6/8	15	7 5/8	7 2/8	2 5/8	2 6/8	14 6/8	12 3/8	6 3/8	5 6/8	Carbon Co., WY	Kenneth E. Grail	Kenneth E. Grail	1983	985
82 6/8	17 1/8	17 4/8	6 6/8	6 5/8	2 2/8	2 2/8	11 1/8	4 5/8	5 2/8	5 3/8	Washoe Co., NV	Michael J. Lange	Michael J. Lange	1983	985
82 6/8	15 6/8	15 4/8	6 3/8	6 2/8	2 5/8	2 4/8	15 7/8	13	6 3/8	6 2/8	Yavapai Co., AZ	Joseph C. Cancilliere	Joseph C. Cancilliere	1984	985
82 6/8	16 3/8	16 4/8	6 1/8	6	2 5/8	2 4/8	13 7/8	10 1/8	6 4/8	5 2/8	Yellowstone Co., MT	Robert M. Labert	Robert M. Labert	1984	985
82 6/8	16 3/8	16 2/8	6 2/8	6 2/8	2 4/8	2 4/8	8 4/8	2 5/8	6 4/8	5 2/8	Sweetwater Co., WY	Craig B. Argyle	Craig B. Argyle	1985	985
82 6/8	17 3/8	17	6	6	2 5/8	2 6/8	9 5/8	5 1/8	5 4/8	5 3/8	Custer Co., ID	William P. Benscoter	William P. Benscoter	1985	985
82 6/8	15 7/8	15 5/8	7 2/8	7 3/8	2 2/8	2 3/8	14 5/8	10 6/8	6 2/8	6	Natrona Co., WY	Michael L. Brownell	Michael L. Brownell	1985	985
82 6/8	15 4/8	15 3/8	6 6/8	6 5/8	2 4/8	2 3/8	10 5/8	4 3/8	6 4/8	7 1/8	Yavapai Co., AZ	Roy T. Hume	Roy T. Hume	1985	985
82 6/8	16 2/8	16 4/8	6 5/8	6 3/8	2 6/8	2 6/8	12 4/8	9 3/8	6 1/8	5 6/8	Larimer Co., CO	James D. Brink	James D. Brink	1986	985
82 6/8	17	17 1/8	6 3/8	6 3/8	2 5/8	2 5/8	10	4 4/8	5 6/8	5 2/8	Lake Co., OR	Steve W. Thompson	Steve W. Thompson	1986	985
82 6/8	16 6/8	16 7/8	7	7	2 5/8	2 5/8	13 3/8	8 4/8	5 3/8	5 5/8	Lake Co., OR	Wayne W. Wingert	Wayne W. Wingert	1986	985
82 6/8	15 2/8	15 3/8	7	7	2 5/8	2 6/8	8 5/8	3 2/8	5 7/8	6 1/8	Natrona Co., WY	Tom Covert	Tom Covert	1987	985
82 6/8	15 7/8	15 5/8	6 2/8	6 2/8	3 1/8	3 1/8	15 3/8	11 7/8	6 1/8	5 7/8	Lemhi Co., ID	Richard W. Feagan	Richard W. Feagan	1988	985
82 6/8	17	16 6/8	6 6/8	6 4/8	2 5/8	2 4/8	9 3/8	2	5 6/8	5 5/8	Washoe Co., NV	David E. Messmann	David E. Messmann	1988	985
82 6/8	16 1/8	15 4/8	6 2/8	6 2/8	2 5/8	2 4/8	12 4/8	8 2/8	6 2/8	6 6/8	Sweetwater Co., WY	Roy D. Sessions	Roy D. Sessions	1988	985
82 6/8	16 2/8	16 6/8	6 3/8	6 4/8	2 5/8	2 4/8	10 7/8	8 1/8	6	6 2/8	Malheur Co., OR	Terrence L. Vaughan	Terrence L. Vaughan	1988	985
82 6/8	15 4/8	15 5/8	7 2/8	7 1/8	2 3/8	2 4/8	12 1/8	7 2/8	6 3/8	5 7/8	Humboldt Co., NV	Darren K. Bader	Darren K. Bader	1989	985
82 6/8	17 3/8	17 5/8	6 3/8	6 3/8	2 6/8	2 5/8	12 4/8	9 7/8	4 7/8	4 6/8	Humboldt Co., NV	Christopher C. Hornbarger	Christopher C. Hornbarger	1989	985
82 6/8	16	15 4/8	6 7/8	6 6/8	3	3	8 6/8	4 1/8	5 7/8	5 7/8	Campbell Co., WY	Richard H. Stasiak	Richard H. Stasiak	1989	985
82 6/8	17 4/8	17 6/8	6 3/8	6 3/8	2 4/8	2 4/8	11	5 5/8	6	4 7/8	Fremont Co., WY	Ronald E. Cebuhar	Ronald E. Cebuhar	1990	985
82 6/8	16 2/8	16 3/8	6 3/8	6 3/8	2 6/8	2 6/8	12 1/8	8 7/8	6 1/8	6 1/8	Catron Co., NM	H. James Tonkin, Jr.	H. James Tonkin, Jr.	1990	985
82 6/8	16 2/8	16 2/8	7	6 7/8	2 4/8	2 6/8	13 3/8	9 6/8	5 7/8	5	Harney Co., OR	Garry L. Whitmore	Garry L. Whitmore	1990	985
82 6/8	16 3/8	16 2/8	6 1/8	6 2/8	3	3	8	1 6/8	5 2/8	5 7/8	Cypress Lake, SK	Jack Clary	Jack Clary	1991	985
82 6/8	17 6/8	18	6	6	2 3/8	2 5/8	13	8 6/8	5 1/8	5	Hudspeth Co., TX	Louise G. Davis	Louise G. Davis	1991	985
82 6/8	15 4/8	15 1/8	6 7/8	6 6/8	2 5/8	2 5/8	9 1/8	4 6/8	5 6/8	5 6/8	Carbon Co., WY	Rebecca J. Miller	Rebecca J. Miller	1991	985
82 6/8	15 7/8	15 6/8	6 6/8	6 5/8	2 6/8	2 4/8	12 5/8	9 1/8	6	5 7/8	Sweetwater Co., WY	Timothy L. Schuckman	Timothy L. Schuckman	1991	985
82 6/8	16 4/8	16 3/8	6 1/8	6 1/8	2 5/8	2 5/8	9 4/8	7 3/8	6 2/8	6 2/8	Mora Co., NM	Gilbert T. Adams	Gilbert T. Adams	1992	985
82 6/8	16 4/8	16 3/8	7	7 1/8	2 2/8	2 2/8	13 2/8	10 1/8	6 4/8	6	Rich Co., UT	Robby Aston	Robby Aston	1992	985
82 6/8	16	15 7/8	6 4/8	6 4/8	2 5/8	2 5/8	10 5/8	7 6/8	7	6 5/8	Modoc Co., CA	Mary L. Crabtree	Mary L. Crabtree	1992	985
82 6/8	16 6/8	16 6/8	6 5/8	6 5/8	2 3/8	2 4/8	14 1/8	10 6/8	5 6/8	5 6/8	Modoc Co., CA	Kevin D. Fabig	Kevin D. Fabig	1992	985
82 6/8	15	15	6 6/8	7	2 5/8	2 5/8	9 5/8	5 3/8	6 2/8	6 3/8	Natrona Co., WY	William S. Franzen	William S. Franzen	1992	985
82 6/8	15 2/8	16	7 4/8	7 3/8	2 7/8	2 4/8	8 7/8	2 5/8	6	5 5/8	Fremont Co., WY	Lyle D. Fruchey	Lyle D. Fruchey	1992	985
82 6/8	16 2/8	16 1/8	6 6/8	6 6/8	2 6/8	2 6/8	13 5/8	8 4/8	5 7/8	5 3/8	Goshen Co., WY	Edward A. Greaves	Edward A. Greaves	1992	985
82 6/8	15 7/8	16	7 5/8	7 3/8	2 5/8	2 5/8	9 7/8	4 2/8	5 1/8	5 2/8	Sweetwater Co., WY	Joe Ingrao	Joe Ingrao	1992	985

Score	Length of Horn R	Length of Horn L	Circumference of Base R	Circumference of Base L	Inside Spread	Tip to Tip Spread	Circ. at Third Quarter R	Circ. at Third Quarter L	Length of Prong R	Length of Prong L	Locality	Hunter	Owner	Date Killed	Rank
82 6/8	15 6/8	16	7	6 7/8	14	13 2/8	2 6/8	3	4 6/8	4 7/8	Sweetwater Co., WY	Brian T. King	Brian T. King	1992	985
82 6/8	16 2/8	16 1/8	6 5/8	6 4/8	9	4 1/8	2 6/8	2 6/8	5 5/8	5 2/8	Juab Co., UT	David B. Nielsen	David B. Nielsen	1992	985
82 6/8	16 1/8	15 5/8	6 1/8	6	7 1/8	0 5/8	2 6/8	2 7/8	6 6/8	6 2/8	Lincoln Co., NM	Michael R. Tiffany	Michael R. Tiffany	1992	985
82 6/8	16	16 2/8	6 4/8	6 4/8	10 2/8	5 2/8	2 6/8	2 6/8	5	5 3/8	Milk River, AB	Darryl D. Bartos	Darryl D. Bartos	1993	985
82 6/8	17 7/8	17 6/8	6 5/8	6 5/8	15 2/8	8	2 4/8	2 3/8	5 2/8	5 1/8	Mora Co., NM	Ernie Davis	Ernie Davis	1993	985
82 6/8	15 5/8	15 4/8	7	6 7/8	8	5 4/8	2 4/8	2 5/8	4 7/8	6 2/8	Sweetwater Co., WY	Tim A. Erich	Tim A. Erich	1993	985
82 6/8	16 4/8	16 4/8	7	7	10 7/8	7 3/8	2 6/8	2 4/8	5 3/8	4 7/8	Mora Co., NM	Linda J. McBride	Linda J. McBride	1993	985
82 6/8	15 2/8	15 4/8	7 4/8	7 4/8	11 5/8	12 7/8	2 7/8	2 6/8	5 2/8	6 3/8	Carbon Co., WY	Lawrence L. Searles	Lawrence L. Searles	1994	985
82 6/8	16	16 2/8	6 6/8	6 6/8	13 5/8	6	2 7/8	2 6/8	6 1/8	5	Hudspeth Co., TX	Linda J. McBride	Linda J. McBride	1995	985
82 6/8	14 3/8	14 4/8	6 2/8	6 6/8	12 7/8	11 7/8	2 4/8	2 7/8	5 2/8	6 1/8	Rio Grande Co., CO	Hammond R. Collins	Hammond R. Collins	1995	985
82 6/8	17 3/8	17 2/8	6 1/8	6 2/8	6	6 5/8	2 5/8	2 4/8	5 4/8	5 2/8	Navajo Co., AZ	Alan Hamberlin	Alan Hamberlin	1995	985
82 6/8	16 4/8	16 5/8	6 1/8	6 1/8	9 4/8	4 6/8	2 7/8	2 4/8	5 1/8	5 3/8	Washoe Co., NV	John M. Porter	John M. Porter	1996	985
82 6/8	17 4/8	17 4/8	6 5/8	6 5/8	11 7/8	6 7/8	2 6/8	2 5/8	5 4/8	5 3/8	Navajo Co., AZ	Noel J. Poux	Noel J. Poux	1996	985
82 6/8	16	16 1/8	6 3/8	6 2/8	6 5/8	3 1/8	2 2/8	2 6/8	4 4/8	4 4/8	Washoe Co., NV	Richard Tripp	Richard Tripp	1996	985
82 6/8	17 1/8	17	6 2/8	6 2/8	8 5/8	4 4/8	2 5/8	2 6/8	5 2/8	5 2/8	Yavapai Co., AZ	Paul S. Keltner	Paul S. Keltner	1997	985
82 4/8	16 4/8	16 4/8	6 1/8	6	3 1/8	6 5/8	2 5/8	2 2/8	6	6	California	Bill Foster	Foster's Bighorn Rest.	1930	1074
82 4/8	16 1/8	16 1/8	6 5/8	6 5/8	4 4/8	5 6/8	2 4/8	2 5/8	4 4/8	6 1/8	Saratoga, WY	Helen R. Peterson	Helen R. Peterson	1945	1074
82 4/8	16 6/8	16 6/8	6 2/8	6 2/8	6 5/8	11 2/8	2 5/8	2 7/8	6 5/8	5 4/8	Park Co., MT	William E. Randall	William E. Randall	1947	1074
82 4/8	14 2/8	14 2/8	6 6/8	6 6/8	11 2/8	6 7/8	2 7/8	2 4/8	6 1/8	5 3/8	Catron Co., NM	C.J. Boyd	C.J. Boyd	1952	1074
82 4/8	16 7/8	17	7 6/8	7 6/8	12 3/8	7 4/8	2 5/8	2 6/8	5 4/8	5 6/8	Ferris Mt., WY	Donald Anderson	Donald Anderson	1959	1074
82 4/8	16 1/8	15 2/8	6 1/8	6 1/8	10	8 7/8	2 7/8	3	5 4/8	5 4/8	Seligman, AZ	Cleo E. Wallace	Cleo E. Wallace	1959	1074
82 4/8	16 2/8	16 6/8	6 5/8	6 6/8	11 1/8	10	3	2 4/8	5 3/8	5 3/8	Campbell Co., WY	Fred J. Brogle	Fred J. Brogle	1960	1074
82 4/8	16 4/8	16 2/8	6 6/8	6 6/8	13 1/8	6 3/8	3	3	5 3/8	4 7/8	Shirley Basin, WY	Walter B. Hester	Walter B. Hester	1960	1074
82 4/8	16 7/8	16 4/8	6 1/8	6 4/8	14 2/8	4 1/8	2 2/8	2 2/8	5 6/8	5 6/8	Poison Spider, WY	Clarence Meddock	Clarence Meddock	1961	1074
82 4/8	16 1/8	16 7/8	6	6	16 5/8	7 3/8	2 4/8	2 4/8	5 3/8	5 3/8	Green Mt., WY	Forrest H. Burnett	Forrest H. Burnett	1962	1074
82 4/8	17	16 1/8	6 6/8	6 6/8	10 4/8	11 4/8	2 4/8	2 4/8	5 4/8	5 6/8	Shirley Basin, WY	G.C. Cunningham	G.C. Cunningham	1962	1074
82 4/8	15 2/8	16 1/8	6 2/8	6 2/8	11 1/8	6 1/8	2 4/8	2 4/8	5 4/8	5 4/8	Springerville, AZ	Malcolm Silvia	Malcolm Silvia	1962	1074
82 4/8	16 3/8	15 2/8	6 7/8	6 7/8	10 5/8	5 7/8	2 4/8	2 6/8	6 1/8	4 6/8	Medicine Hat, AB	Nick Mandryk	Nick Mandryk	1963	1074
82 4/8	16 6/8	16 3/8	7 5/8	7 5/8	16 1/8	5 4/8	2 5/8	2 4/8	4 6/8	5 7/8	Park Co., CO	Mrs. Cotton Gordon	Mrs. Cotton Gordon	1964	1074
82 4/8	16 6/8	16 5/8	6 2/8	6 2/8	9	7 1/8	2 3/8	2 5/8	5 4/8	5 4/8	Seligman, AZ	Glenn Olson	Glenn Olson	1965	1074
82 4/8	15 5/8	16 6/8	6 1/8	6 2/8	11	4 3/8	2 7/8	2 3/8	5	5	Ingomar, MT	L.P. Treaster	L.P. Treaster	1965	1074
82 4/8	15 1/8	15 5/8	6 2/8	6 1/8	9	7 1/8	2 4/8	2 6/8	5 5/8	5 6/8	Natrona Co., WY	Charles P. Weber	Charles P. Weber	1966	1074
82 4/8	13 6/8	13 6/8	6 4/8	6 4/8	11	4 5/8	2 5/8	2 4/8	5 1/8	5 6/8	Laramie, WY	Noel Weidner	Noel Weidner	1966	1074
82 4/8	15 6/8	15 6/8	6 7/8	6 3/8	6 4/8	6 4/8	2 6/8	2 4/8	5 6/8	6	Butte, ND	E.J. Weigel	E.J. Weigel	1966	1074
82 4/8	16 1/8	15 3/8	6 5/8	6 1/8	10 7/8	10 7/8	2 5/8	2 5/8	6 1/8	6 4/8	Pecos Co., TX	Ben H. Moore, Jr.	Ben H. Moore, Jr.	1967	1074
82 4/8	15 6/8	15 6/8	6 2/8	6 1/8	14	6 3/8	3	2 5/8	5 1/8	5 1/8	Washoe Co., NV	James R. Stoner, Jr.	James R. Stoner, Jr.	1969	1074
82 4/8	15 1/8	15 3/8	6 6/8	6 6/8	12 1/8	6 4/8	2 5/8	2 6/8	5 6/8	5 4/8	Lake Co., OR	Charles R. Waite	Charles R. Waite	1969	1074
82 4/8	16 1/8	16 1/8	6 5/8	6 6/8	8 7/8	8 5/8	2 4/8	2 6/8	5 4/8	5 4/8	Humboldt Co., NV	Robert C. Lawson	Robert C. Lawson	1970	1074
82 4/8	17 2/8	17 2/8	6 6/8	6 5/8	8 5/8	4	2 6/8	2 6/8	3 6/8	3 6/8	Brewster Co., TX	Joseph W. Burkett III	Joseph W. Burkett III	1971	1074
82 4/8	16 4/8	16	6 5/8	6 7/8	9 7/8	6 3/8	3	3	5 2/8	5 6/8	Platte Co., WY	Dwight E. Farr	William R. Brewer	1972	1074
82 4/8	14 5/8	17 2/8	6 4/8	6 4/8	10 7/8	5	2 7/8	2 7/8	5	5 2/8	Coconino Co., AZ	Robert J. Hallock	Robert J. Hallock	1973	1074
82 4/8	14 4/8	16 4/8	6 2/8	6 2/8	11 7/8	10 6/8	2 5/8	2 5/8	5 5/8	5 5/8	Converse Co., WY	J.A. Merrill, Jr. & C. Davis	J.A. Merrill, Jr.	1973	1074
82 4/8	16 3/8	14 3/8	7	7	9 5/8	5 5/8	3	3 1/8	5 4/8	5 5/8	Rosebud Co., MT	Norman G. Kern	Norman G. Kern	1974	1074
82 4/8	16	14 6/8	6 2/8	6 3/8	11	9 3/8	3 1/8	3	6	6	Cimarron, NM	Ronald E. McKinney	Ronald E. McKinney	1974	1074
82 4/8	16 7/8	16 3/8	6 3/8	6 2/8	11 2/8	6 1/8	2 4/8	2 4/8	5 6/8	5 7/8	Custer Co., MT	Harry Zirwas	Harry Zirwas	1974	1074
82 4/8	17	16 7/8	6 2/8	6 1/8	10 2/8	6 1/8	2 6/8	2 6/8	5 2/8	5 2/8	Slope Co., ND	Marlin J. Kapp	Marlin J. Kapp	1975	1074
82 4/8	17 2/8	17 2/8	6 2/8	6 2/8	11 6/8	7 6/8	2 4/8	2 4/8	5 3/8	5	Coconino Co., AZ	David S. Hibbert	David S. Hibbert	1976	1074

PRONGHORN

Antilocapra americana americana and related subspecies

Score	Length of Horn R	L	Circumference of Base R	L	Circumference at Third Quarter R	L	Inside Spread	Tip to Tip Spread	Length of Prong R	L	Locality	Hunter	Owner	Date Killed	Rank
82 4/8	15 3/8	15 3/8	6 4/8	6 3/8	2 5/8	2 4/8	13 5/8	10 4/8	6 3/8	7	Lassen Co., CA	Brad L. Ayotte	Brad L. Ayotte	1977	1074
82 4/8	15	15	6 4/8	6 4/8	2 6/8	2 6/8	9 4/8	4	6 4/8	6 4/8	Sublette Co., WY	Larry W. Cross	Larry W. Cross	1977	1074
82 4/8	14 7/8	14 7/8	7	7	3	2 7/8	11 7/8	8 7/8	5 2/8	5 4/8	Richland Co., MT	Lloyd Holland	Lloyd Holland	1977	1074
82 4/8	16 3/8	16 4/8	6 6/8	6 4/8	2 5/8	2 5/8	11 1/8	5 4/8	5 6/8	5 4/8	Fremont Co., WY	Wayne D. Kleinman	Wayne D. Kleinman	1977	1074
82 4/8	16	15 5/8	6 4/8	6 6/8	2 5/8	2 2/8	14 1/8	14 2/8	5 7/8	5 7/8	Washakie Co., WY	Greg Warner	Greg Warner	1977	1074
82 4/8	16	16 1/8	6 6/8	6 6/8	2 5/8	2 5/8	12 3/8	8 1/8	5 2/8	5	Carter Co., MT	James A. White	James A. White	1977	1074
82 4/8	15 4/8	15 2/8	6 6/8	6 6/8	2 4/8	2 4/8	12 2/8	7 1/8	5 5/8	5 6/8	Modoc Co., CA	Mark Hansen	Mark Hansen	1978	1074
82 4/8	16 5/8	16 5/8	6 4/8	6 3/8	2 7/8	2 7/8	9 1/8	5 3/8	5 2/8	5 1/8	Sweetwater Co., WY	Fred B. Keyes	Fred B. Keyes	1978	1074
82 4/8	14 6/8	14 7/8	6 6/8	6 5/8	2 7/8	2 7/8	13 7/8	11 7/8	6 4/8	6 4/8	Carbon Co., WY	Michael Boender	Michael Boender	1979	1074
82 4/8	15 4/8	15 5/8	6 6/8	6 4/8	2 5/8	2 5/8	9 4/8	4 5/8	5 3/8	5 3/8	Millard Co., UT	William R. Houston	William R. Houston	1979	1074
82 4/8	16 2/8	16 3/8	7	6 7/8	2 3/8	2 4/8	8 1/8	6 2/8	5 5/8	5 3/8	Siskiyou Co., CA	Rodney F. Royer	Rodney F. Royer	1979	1074
82 4/8	17 6/8	17 3/8	6	6	2 5/8	2 5/8	11 2/8	6	5 2/8	5 4/8	Hudspeth Co., TX	Ray A. Acker, Sr.	Ray A. Acker, Sr.	1980	1074
82 4/8	15 1/8	15 2/8	6 6/8	6 6/8	2 4/8	2 4/8	12 1/8	10 3/8	6 1/8	6 3/8	Carbon Co., WY	Barry L. Alger	Barry L. Alger	1980	1074
82 4/8	15 7/8	16 2/8	6 1/8	6 3/8	2 4/8	2 5/8	14 6/8	9 7/8	6 1/8	6 2/8	White Pine Co., NV	Tom I. Papagna, Jr.	Tom I. Papagna, Jr.	1980	1074
82 4/8	15 1/8	15 1/8	6 2/8	6 2/8	3	3	10 2/8	8 2/8	6	6 1/8	Socorro Co., NM	Clyde C. Brumley	Clyde C. Brumley	1981	1074
82 4/8	14 7/8	14 6/8	6 7/8	7 2/8	2 5/8	2 6/8	9 7/8	6 6/8	6 3/8	6 4/8	Campbell Co., WY	Larry L. Helgerson	Larry L. Helgerson	1981	1074
82 4/8	15 3/8	15 2/8	6 5/8	6 3/8	3	3	8 7/8	4 6/8	6 4/8	6 2/8	Moffat Co., CO	Charles W. Klaassens	Charles W. Klaassens	1981	1074
82 4/8	17	16 6/8	6 3/8	6 4/8	2 4/8	2 4/8	9 2/8	3 3/8	5 4/8	5 4/8	Sweetwater Co., WY	Donald R. Williamson	Donald R. Williamson	1981	1074
82 4/8	16 2/8	16 1/8	6 4/8	6 4/8	2 6/8	2 6/8	9 2/8	4 5/8	5 5/8	5 3/8	Natrona Co., WY	Edgar M. Artecona	Edgar M. Artecona	1982	1074
82 4/8	15 1/8	15 1/8	6 6/8	6 6/8	2 5/8	2 5/8	10 6/8	9 1/8	5 7/8	5 7/8	Carbon Co., WY	John T. Butters	John T. Butters	1982	1074
82 4/8	16 6/8	16 6/8	6 3/8	6 3/8	3	3	10 6/8	5 4/8	5	5 4/8	Union Co., NM	John W. Saunders	John W. Saunders	1982	1074
82 4/8	16 6/8	16 1/8	6 6/8	6 5/8	2 3/8	2 4/8	8 1/8	2 6/8	5 7/8	5 4/8	Washoe Co., NV	Vernon E. Benney	Vernon E. Benney	1983	1074
82 4/8	16 1/8	16 1/8	7	7	2 4/8	2 4/8	5 2/8	2	5 2/8	5 2/8	Natrona Co., WY	Bill E. Boatman	Bill E. Boatman	1983	1074
82 4/8	15 5/8	16	6 4/8	6 3/8	3	3	12	10 5/8	5 6/8	5 4/8	Carbon Co., WY	Merlyn J. Kiel	Merlyn J. Kiel	1983	1074
82 4/8	15 6/8	15 6/8	6 6/8	6 6/8	2 4/8	2 6/8	9 4/8	5 3/8	5 6/8	5 6/8	Sweetwater Co., WY	Richard E. Knox, Jr.	Richard E. Knox, Jr.	1983	1074
82 4/8	15 5/8	15 3/8	6 4/8	6 4/8	2 7/8	2 5/8	8	3 6/8	6	5 6/8	Navajo Co., AZ	Perry H. Finger	Perry H. Finger	1984	1074
82 4/8	16 4/8	16 4/8	6 3/8	6 4/8	2 6/8	2 6/8	11 2/8	5 6/8	5	5 4/8	Humboldt Co., NV	Frank K. Azcarate, Jr.	Frank K. Azcarate, Jr.	1985	1074
82 4/8	15 5/8	16 1/8	6 4/8	6 5/8	2 7/8	2 7/8	8 6/8	5 2/8	5 3/8	5 4/8	Sweetwater Co., WY	W.A. Chambers	W.A. Chambers	1985	1074
82 4/8	16	15 5/8	6 6/8	6 6/8	2 6/8	2 7/8	9	4	5 3/8	5 3/8	Rosebud Co., MT	Robert B. DeLattre	Robert B. DeLattre	1985	1074
82 4/8	16 3/8	15 6/8	6 4/8	6 5/8	3	3 1/8	14 1/8	9 6/8	5 3/8	6 2/8	Hudspeth Co., TX	Ernest Elbert, Jr.	Ernest Elbert, Jr.	1985	1074
82 4/8	16 4/8	16 6/8	6 5/8	6 3/8	3 1/8	3 2/8	12 1/8	7	4 7/8	4 7/8	Lassen Co., CA	Bob Freed	Bob Freed	1985	1074
82 4/8	15	15	6 6/8	7	2 5/8	2 5/8	13 3/8	10 5/8	6 6/8	6 3/8	Saguache Co., CO	Michael J. Atwood, Sr.	Michael J. Atwood, Sr.	1986	1074
82 4/8	15 5/8	15 5/8	7	7	2 5/8	2 4/8	9 3/8	5	5 6/8	5 7/8	Campbell Co., WY	Robert J. Anderson	Robert J. Anderson	1987	1074
82 4/8	15 3/8	15 3/8	7 1/8	7 2/8	2 4/8	2 6/8	11 5/8	7 4/8	5 2/8	4 7/8	Colfax Co., NM	John A. Jones	John A. Jones	1987	1074
82 4/8	16 1/8	16 2/8	6 6/8	6 7/8	2 4/8	2 5/8	9 4/8	3 5/8	5 7/8	6 2/8	Sweetwater Co., WY	Eric M. Berg	Eric M. Berg	1988	1074
82 4/8	17 1/8	16 6/8	6 4/8	6 2/8	2 4/8	2 4/8	11 6/8	6 6/8	5 6/8	6 2/8	Humboldt Co., NV	Michael K. McBeath	Michael K. McBeath	1988	1074
82 4/8	17 1/8	17 2/8	6	6	2 5/8	2 4/8	9 5/8	7 4/8	6 1/8	5 4/8	Custer Co., ID	Ronald E. Pruyn	Ronald E. Pruyn	1988	1074
82 4/8	17 1/8	15 4/8	6 4/8	6 4/8	3 1/8	2 7/8	8 5/8	6 2/8	6	5 7/8	Yavapai Co., AZ	Chris Skoczylas	Chris Skoczylas	1988	1074

Score	Length R	Length L	Circ. Base R	Circ. Base L	Circ. 3rd Qtr R	Circ. 3rd Qtr L	Tip to Tip Spread	Inside Spread	Prong R	Prong L	Locality	Hunter	Owner	Date Killed	Rank
82 4/8	15 3/8	15 3/8	6 2/8	6 3/8	3	3	6 2/8	11	5 3/8	5 5/8	Yellowstone Co., MT	Jon J. Wilson	Jon J. Wilson	1988	1074
82 4/8	16 5/8	16 2/8	6 5/8	6 5/8	2 3/8	2 3/8	7 2/8	11 4/8	6 2/8	6 1/8	Fremont Co., WY	Ben L. Adamson	Ben L. Adamson	1989	1074
82 4/8	15 2/8	15 1/8	6 2/8	6 4/8	3 1/8	3 1/8	12 6/8	14 1/8	5 4/8	5 4/8	Box Elder Co., UT	Curtis K. Blasingame	Curtis K. Blasingame	1989	1074
82 4/8	16 6/8	16	6 2/8	6 2/8	3 4/8	2 6/8	17 4/8	19 1/8	6	6	Hudspeth Co., TX	Peter L. Bright	Peter L. Bright	1989	1074
82 4/8	15 6/8	15 6/8	6 2/8	6 2/8	2 7/8	2 6/8	3	9 2/8	5 4/8	5 6/8	Graham Co., AZ	Daniel C. Hicks	Daniel C. Hicks	1989	1074
82 4/8	15 6/8	15 6/8	6 3/8	6 2/8	2 7/8	2 7/8	3 4/8	8 4/8	5 6/8	5 7/8	Colfax Co., NM	Roy G. Jones	Roy G. Jones	1989	1074
82 4/8	14 4/8	14 4/8	7	7 1/8	2 4/8	2 4/8	11 5/8	8 4/8	6 5/8	5 7/8	Fremont Co., WY	James M. Machac	James M. Machac	1989	1074
82 4/8	14 5/8	14 5/8	7 2/8	7 2/8	2 5/8	2 5/8	11	12 6/8	6 1/8	6 6/8	Carbon Co., WY	Lance E. Novak	Lance E. Novak	1989	1074
82 4/8	14 2/8	14 2/8	6 6/8	6 6/8	3	3	12 6/8	13 2/8	5 4/8	6 3/8	Jackson Co., CO	Loren D. Reid	Loren D. Reid	1989	1074
82 4/8	16 4/8	16 5/8	6 6/8	6 6/8	2 6/8	3	13 5/8	11 4/8	5 5/8	5 1/8	Humboldt Co., NV	Richard Vanderkous	Richard Vanderkous	1989	1074
82 4/8	15	15	6 6/8	6 8/8	2 5/8	2 6/8	9 1/8	12 1/8	6 3/8	6 2/8	Converse Co., WY	Larry E. Zumbrum	Larry E. Zumbrum	1989	1074
82 4/8	15 2/8	15 2/8	6 7/8	6 6/8	2 4/8	2 4/8	8 3/8	8 3/8	7 4/8	7 3/8	Natrona Co., WY	Robert W. Genner	Robert W. Genner	1990	1074
82 4/8	15 2/8	15 2/8	6 5/8	6 3/8	2 6/8	2 4/8	9 5/8	8 3/8	6 5/8	6 5/8	McKenzie Co., ND	Nathan S. Gilbertson	Nathan S. Gilbertson	1990	1074
82 4/8	17 1/8	17	5 7/8	6	2 4/8	2 4/8	13 6/8	9 5/8	6	6 3/8	San Juan Co., UT	Wayne A. Hines	Wayne A. Hines	1990	1074
82 4/8	15 5/8	15 5/8	6 4/8	6 5/8	3 6/8	3	11 7/8	13 6/8	6 4/8	5 2/8	Converse Co., WY	Farrell M. McQuiddy	Farrell M. McQuiddy	1990	1074
82 4/8	15 6/8	15 4/8	6 4/8	6 1/8	2 5/8	2 5/8	8 2/8	12 5/8	6 1/8	5 6/8	Fremont Co., WY	James J. Person	James J. Person	1990	1074
82 4/8	17 6/8	17 6/8	5 4/8	5 4/8	2 5/8	2 5/8	3 3/8	12 2/8	5 2/8	5 2/8	Mora Co., NM	Gilbert T. Adams	Gilbert T. Adams	1991	1074
82 4/8	14	15	7	7	3	3	11 2/8	9 7/8	6 4/8	6 1/8	Apache Co., AZ	Robin W. Bechtel	Robin W. Bechtel	1991	1074
82 4/8	15	14	6 7/8	7	3	3	7 5/8	12 5/8	5 7/8	5 7/8	Judith Basin Co., MT	Sarah M. Brown	Sarah M. Brown	1991	1074
82 4/8	15 5/8	15 7/8	6	6	2 5/8	2 6/8	5 6/8	12 3/8	5	5	Box Elder Co., UT	Roudy Christensen	Roudy Christensen	1991	1074
82 4/8	16 3/8	16 4/8	6 7/8	7	2 6/8	2 4/8	9 6/8	10 1/8	5 2/8	5 5/8	Hot Springs Co., WY	Brett W. Jones	Brett W. Jones	1991	1074
82 4/8	16 4/8	16 5/8	6 4/8	6 4/8	2 4/8	2 4/8	15 2/8	12 4/8	6 3/8	6 3/8	Sweetwater Co., WY	Robert S. Lund	Robert S. Lund	1991	1074
82 4/8	15 5/8	15 5/8	6	6 1/8	2 5/8	2 5/8	4 7/8	10 1/8	6 2/8	6 5/8	Mora Co., NM	Dan E. McBride	Dan E. McBride	1991	1074
82 4/8	17 2/8	16	6 1/8	5 7/8	2 3/8	2 3/8	6 3/8	6 3/8	5 5/8	5 5/8	Cascade Co., MT	John P. Michalies	John P. Michalies	1991	1074
82 4/8	16	15 6/8	6 5/8	6 5/8	2 7/8	2 7/8	8 2/8	8 2/8	6 1/8	6 1/8	Moffat Co., CO	S. Wayne Olson	S. Wayne Olson	1991	1074
82 4/8	15 5/8	15 5/8	7 2/8	7	2 3/8	2 3/8	9 4/8	4 5/8	5 7/8	5 7/8	Uinta Co., WY	Velma O'Neil	Velma O'Neil	1991	1074
82 4/8	17	16 6/8	6 3/8	6 6/8	2 4/8	2 3/8	2 6/8	9	5 2/8	5 1/8	Mora Co., NM	Kenneth G. Planet	Kenneth G. Planet	1991	1074
82 4/8	15 4/8	15 4/8	7 1/8	7 1/8	2 5/8	2 6/8	8 4/8	12 2/8	6 3/8	5 5/8	Sweetwater Co., WY	Justin C. Shadrick	Justin C. Shadrick	1991	1074
82 4/8	16 5/8	16 6/8	6 6/8	6 7/8	2 4/8	2 4/8	2 6/8	8 6/8	5 4/8	5 4/8	Treasure Co., MT	David W. Shannon	David W. Shannon	1991	1074
82 4/8	16 3/8	16 2/8	6	6	2 3/8	2 3/8	5	9 7/8	4 7/8	4 7/8	Washoe Co., NV	Dean C. Tischler	Dean C. Tischler	1991	1074
82 4/8	15 5/8	17	6 6/8	7	2 7/8	2 7/8	9 7/8	11 2/8	5	5	Natrona Co., WY	Hubert C. Wightman	Hubert C. Wightman	1991	1074
82 4/8	16 7/8	16 4/8	6 2/8	6 2/8	2 6/8	2 6/8	8 6/8	10	5 1/8	5 5/8	Harney Co., OR	Terry L. Greene	Terry L. Greene	1992	1074
82 4/8	15 7/8	15 7/8	6 4/8	6 5/8	2 4/8	2 4/8	3 5/8	8 5/8	5 5/8	6 1/8	Milk River, AB	Carey Karl	Carey Karl	1992	1074
82 4/8	15 5/8	15 5/8	6 6/8	6 3/8	2 3/8	2 3/8	9 7/8	13 4/8	7	7	Jefferson Co., MT	Tom R. Osborne	Tom R. Osborne	1992	1074
82 4/8	15 5/8	15 4/8	6 6/8	6 6/8	2 4/8	2 4/8	10 7/8	10 7/8	5 6/8	5 4/8	Colfax Co., NM	Robert J. Seeds	Robert J. Seeds	1992	1074
82 4/8	16 1/8	15 4/8	6 1/8	6 2/8	2 3/8	2 3/8	4 1/8	7 2/8	6 3/8	6 3/8	Carbon Co., WY	David Shadrick	David Shadrick	1992	1074
82 4/8	16 2/8	15 5/8	6 6/8	6	2 7/8	2 3/8	7 6/8	9 3/8	6	6	Washoe Co., NV	Sydney M. Smith	Sydney M. Smith	1992	1074
82 4/8	16	16	6 2/8	6 3/8	2 4/8	2 4/8	1 6/8	6 5/8	6	6	Moffat Co., CO	Brad A. Winder	Brad A. Winder	1992	1074
82 4/8	14 6/8	14 4/8	7 2/8	7 1/8	3 2/8	3	10 3/8	11 7/8	5 6/8	5 6/8	Park Co., WY	Dan Barngrover	Dan Barngrover	1993	1074
82 4/8	16 5/8	16 5/8	6 4/8	6	2 6/8	2 6/8	4	9	5 1/8	5 2/8	Fergus Co., MT	Scott D. Boelman	Scott D. Boelman	1993	1074
82 4/8	14 2/8	16 5/8	6 7/8	6 7/8	2 6/8	2 5/8	5 3/8	8 7/8	4 6/8	5	Hudspeth Co., TX	Bruce Kettler	Bruce Kettler	1993	1074
82 4/8	14 4/8	14 2/8	7	6 7/8	2 5/8	2 5/8	7 6/8	10 1/8	6 2/8	6	Elko Co., NV	Paul M. Adams	Paul M. Adams	1994	1074
82 4/8	15 6/8	15 4/8	6 4/8	6 4/8	2 7/8	2 7/8	6 5/8	10 2/8	5 4/8	5 4/8	Mora Co., NM	Luke C. Kellogg	Luke C. Kellogg	1994	1074
82 4/8	16	16 4/8	6 3/8	6 3/8	3 1/8	3	2 6/8	8 1/8	5 3/8	5 3/8	Moffat Co., CO	Brad A. Winder	Brad A. Winder	1994	1074
82 4/8	16 4/8	16 1/8	6 4/8	6 1/8	3 2/8	3	8 4/8	13 2/8	4 5/8	4 4/8	Deaf Smith Co., TX	Russell W. Casteel	Russell W. Casteel	1995	1074
82 4/8	15 7/8	16 1/8	7 1/8	7	2 4/8	2 4/8	4	8 5/8	5 4/8	5 4/8	Mora Co., NM	Len H. Guldman	Len H. Guldman	1995	1074
82 4/8	16 7/8	15 4/8	6 3/8	6 4/8	3	3	8 3/8	11 2/8	6	6	Socorro Co., NM	Jess T. Jones	Jess T. Jones	1995	1074

PRONGHORN

Antilocapra americana americana and related subspecies

Score	Length of Horn R	L	Circumference of Base R	L	Circumference at Third Quarter R	L	Inside Spread	Tip to Tip Spread	Length of Prong R	L	Locality	Hunter	Owner	Date Killed	Rank
82 4/8	15 4/8	15 4/8	6 6/8	6 7/8	2 7/8	2 6/8	8 4/8	5 5/8	5 5/8	6 2/8	Niobrara Co., WY	William F. King	William F. King	1995	1074
82 4/8	16 6/8	16 6/8	6 4/8	6 4/8	2 7/8	2 7/8	12 2/8	8 7/8	5	5	Liberty Co., MT	Stuart Stone	Stuart Stone	1995	1074
82 4/8	17 5/8	17 2/8	6 1/8	6 1/8	2 5/8	2 4/8	11 6/8	6 2/8	5 4/8	5 6/8	Coconino Co., AZ	Tom Bowman	Tom Bowman	1996	1074
82 4/8	15 6/8	15 5/8	6 5/8	6 5/8	2 4/8	2 3/8	9 6/8	7 2/8	5 6/8	6	Carbon Co., WY	Kristopher P. Cobbley	Kristopher P. Cobbley	1996	1074
82 4/8	17 4/8	17 1/8	6 1/8	6 2/8	2 4/8	2 3/8	12 1/8	7 1/8	5 4/8	5 2/8	Hudspeth Co., TX	Gerald P. McBride	Gerald P. McBride	1996	1074
82 4/8	16	16	6 6/8	6 6/8	2 7/8	2 7/8	12 1/8	9	5 6/8	5 1/8	Socorro Co., NM	Gerald L. Warnock	Gerald L. Warnock	1996	1074
82 4/8	16 1/8	16	6 5/8	6 4/8	2 6/8	2 6/8	9 4/8	4 1/8	5 4/8	5 1/8	Mora Co., NM	Dennis J. Sites	Dennis J. Sites	1997	1074
82 4/8	14 7/8	14 7/8	6 4/8	6 4/8	2 6/8	2 6/8	10 3/8	7 3/8	5	5	Colfax Co., NM	Kevin W. Underwood	Kevin W. Underwood	1997	1074
82 2/8	16 7/8	16 7/8	5 7/8	6	2 4/8	2 4/8	14 5/8	13 4/8	6 2/8	6 3/8	Chaves Co., NM	Harvey Pirtle	Glenn Marshall	1939	1199
82 2/8	14 5/8	14 4/8	7 1/8	7 1/8	3 1/8	2 7/8	8 2/8	4 4/8	5 4/8	5 5/8	Henderson, NM	Ron Vance	Ron Vance	1947	1199
82 2/8	16 6/8	16 5/8	6 4/8	6 4/8	2 4/8	2 4/8	15 7/8	11 1/8	5 5/8	5 7/8	Split Rock, WY	Herb Klein	Herb Klein	1952	1199
82 2/8	17 4/8	17 3/8	6 4/8	6 3/8	2 6/8	2 5/8	14 1/8	10	4 2/8	4 4/8	Anderson Mesa, AZ	Roy Stevens	Roy Stevens	1953	1199
82 2/8	17 2/8	17 2/8	6 2/8	6 2/8	2 5/8	2 5/8	11 3/8	5 5/8	5 4/8	5 4/8	Weld Co., CO	James Gertson, Jr.	Howard E. Bates	1955	1199
82 2/8	16	16	6 4/8	6 2/8	2 6/8	2 4/8	8 6/8	5 5/8	6 3/8	5 7/8	Rawlins, WY	Thomas B. McNeill	Thomas B. McNeill	1955	1199
82 2/8	15 4/8	15 4/8	6 4/8	6 4/8	3 1/8	3	8 6/8	4 4/8	5	5	Saratoga, WY	J.E. Prothroe	J.E. Prothroe	1955	1199
82 2/8	16 5/8	16 6/8	6 4/8	6 3/8	3	3	10 5/8	4 5/8	4 4/8	4 4/8	Hettinger, ND	Art Score	Art Score	1957	1199
82 2/8	15 7/8	15 7/8	7	7 1/8	2 4/8	2 7/8	13 2/8	8 6/8	6	6 1/8	Sage Creek, WY	Glenn P. Anderson	Glenn P. Anderson	1959	1199
82 2/8	16 5/8	16 2/8	6 2/8	6 1/8	2 4/8	2 4/8	13 2/8	10 3/8	5 5/8	5 5/8	Williams, AZ	Fred Udine	Fred Udine	1959	1199
82 2/8	17 1/8	16 4/8	6 4/8	6 4/8	2 6/8	2 6/8	13	6 7/8	5 4/8	5 1/8	Anderson Mesa, AZ	Bill Gray	Bill Gray	1960	1199
82 2/8	16 2/8	16 2/8	6 4/8	6 5/8	2 4/8	2 7/8	6 4/8	4 4/8	5 6/8	5 2/8	Park Co., WY	Don A. Johnson	Don A. Johnson	1960	1199
82 2/8	16 2/8	16 2/8	6 6/8	6 6/8	2 7/8	2 7/8	13 2/8	10 5/8	4 6/8	4 6/8	Sierra Blanca, TX	Charles Nichols	Charles Nichols	1960	1199
82 2/8	16 7/8	16 5/8	6	6	2 6/8	2 6/8	11 1/8	5	6	5 4/8	Arpan, SD	Dell Shanks	Dell Shanks	1960	1199
82 2/8	16 1/8	16 2/8	6 3/8	6 3/8	2 3/8	2 4/8	10 2/8	6	6 2/8	6 6/8	Crook Co., WY	John P. Wood	John P. Wood	1961	1199
82 2/8	16 1/8	16	6 6/8	6 6/8	3 1/8	3	14	9	5	5	Shirley Basin, WY	T.C. Gonya	T.C. Gonya	1961	1199
82 2/8	17 2/8	16 6/8	6	6	2 4/8	2 4/8	7 2/8	12 6/8	6 2/8	6 3/8	New Mexico	Joan V. Gordon	Joan V. Gordon	1961	1199
82 2/8	16 2/8	16 2/8	6 3/8	6 4/8	2 7/8	2 7/8	11 2/8	7 1/8	5 2/8	5 5/8	Poison Spider, WY	Unknown	Robert F. Ziker	1961	1199
82 2/8	15 4/8	15 4/8	6 6/8	6 6/8	2 4/8	2 3/8	10 1/8	5	5 6/8	6	Lewis & Clark Co., MT	Leo M. Bergthold	Leo M. Bergthold	1963	1199
82 2/8	15 7/8	15 6/8	7 1/8	6 5/8	2 7/8	2 6/8	11 4/8	6 4/8	5 2/8	5 3/8	Casper, WY	Frank Gardner	Frank Gardner	1963	1199
82 2/8	16	16	6 4/8	6 4/8	2 5/8	2 6/8	13 1/8	9	6 3/8	5 7/8	Lavina, MT	W.J. Morrelle	W.J. Morrelle	1963	1199
82 2/8	15 7/8	16	7	7	3	3	11 7/8	7 6/8	5 2/8	5 1/8	Hanna, AB	Rita Shumka	C.W. Edwards	1964	1199
82 2/8	16 2/8	16 1/8	6 6/8	6 6/8	2 6/8	2 6/8	12	9 4/8	5	5	Laramie, WY	Susan W. Tupper	Susan W. Tupper	1964	1199
82 2/8	16 3/8	16 2/8	6 2/8	6 2/8	2 6/8	2 6/8	13 2/8	9 1/8	5 4/8	5 2/8	Knappen, AB	Ken Bosch	Ken Bosch	1965	1199
82 2/8	16 4/8	16 2/8	6 3/8	6 3/8	2 6/8	2 6/8	10 2/8	4 1/8	5 3/8	5 2/8	Foremost, AB	Les Gordon	Les Gordon	1966	1199
82 2/8	16 6/8	16 3/8	6 5/8	6 4/8	2 5/8	2 6/8	11	11 4/8	5	5	Bowen, ND	Lee Atkinson	Sioux Sport Goods	1966	1199
82 2/8	14 7/8	15	6 4/8	6 5/8	2 4/8	2 4/8	9 1/8	5 6/8	6 2/8	6 2/8	Weld Co., CO	Mrs. Paul Goodwin	Mrs. Paul Goodwin	1967	1199
82 2/8	15 7/8	15 7/8	6 6/8	6 4/8	2 5/8	2 4/8	9 6/8	4 5/8	6	6 1/8	Powderville, MT	Morrel W. Ivie	Morrel W. Ivie	1969	1199
82 2/8	15	15 4/8	6 5/8	6 6/8	2 5/8	2 6/8	11 2/8	7 3/8	6 4/8	6 6/8	Vivian, SD	Larry K. Lantz	Larry K. Lantz	1969	1199
82 2/8	16 4/8	16 3/8	6 7/8	6 7/8	2 7/8	2 6/8	10 3/8	8 1/8	5 3/8	6 2/8	Natrona Co., WY	R.O. Marshall, Jr.	R.O. Marshall, Jr.	1970	1199

Score	L. R	L. L	Circ. R	Circ. L	D. R	D. L	Spread 1	Spread 2	Tip	Locality	Hunter	Owner	Date	Rank
82 2/8	17 3/8	17 2/8	6 7/8	7 2/8	1 7/8	1 5/8	7 1/8	3 1/8	4 7/8	Wild Horse, AB	Adam Schmick	Adam Schmick	1970	1199
82 2/8	15 5/8	15 7/8	6 6/8	6 6/8	2 6/8	2 6/8	10 7/8	4 4/8	5 7/8	Fergus Co., MT	Carl Aus	Carl Aus	1971	1199
82 2/8	16 2/8	16 5/8	6 4/8	6 5/8	2 4/8	2 6/8	13	8 3/8	5 4/8	Coconino Co., AZ	William L. Butler	William L. Butler	1973	1199
82 2/8	15 5/8	15 5/8	6 4/8	6 4/8	2 7/8	2 7/8	9 6/8	5 7/8	5 5/8	Treasure Co., MT	Joseph A. Balmelli	Joseph A. Balmelli	1974	1199
82 2/8	15	15 2/8	6	6	2 4/8	2 4/8	10 2/8	9 4/8	5 2/8	Fremont Co., WY	Collins F. Kellogg	Collins F. Kellogg	1974	1199
82 2/8	15 2/8	15 3/8	6 3/8	6 2/8	2 7/8	2 4/8	7 7/8	3 3/8	5 7/8	Gillette, WY	Gary Simonson	Gary Simonson	1975	1199
82 2/8	15 2/8	15 3/8	7 1/8	6 6/8	2 6/8	2 7/8	8 7/8	5 7/8	6 1/8	Duchesne Co., UT	David L. Peterson	David L. Peterson	1976	1199
82 2/8	15 3/8	14 7/8	6 6/8	6 6/8	2 5/8	2 6/8	13 2/8	9 6/8	6 3/8	Harney Co., OR	Dean Dunson	Dean Dunson	1977	1199
82 2/8	16	15 6/8	6 2/8	6 1/8	3	2 5/8	13 2/8	10	5 4/8	Morgan Co., CO	Kenneth L. Kelly	Kenneth L. Kelly	1977	1199
82 2/8	15 6/8	16	6 1/8	6 1/8	2 4/8	3	12 4/8	9	7	Lassen Co., CA	Del S. Oliver	Del S. Oliver	1978	1199
82 2/8	16 6/8	16 4/8	6 3/8	6 4/8	2 4/8	2 4/8	15	11	6 1/8	Otero Co., NM	Heber Simmons, Jr.	Heber Simmons, Jr.	1978	1199
82 2/8	16 2/8	16 2/8	6 5/8	6 5/8	2 3/8	2 4/8	12 2/8	8	5 6/8	Apache Co., AZ	Richard L. Simmons, Sr.	Richard L. Simmons, Sr.	1978	1199
82 2/8	15 3/8	15 2/8	6 7/8	6 7/8	2 5/8	2 6/8	15 5/8	14 5/8	5 7/8	Carbon Co., WY	Jerry G. Hagen	Jerry G. Hagen	1980	1199
82 2/8	15 1/8	15	6 6/8	6 6/8	2 6/8	2 5/8	9 5/8	7	6 4/8	Lake Co., OR	Richard R. Delfs	Richard R. Delfs	1981	1199
82 2/8	15 7/8	15 3/8	7 2/8	7 1/8	2 7/8	2 6/8	16 1/8	14 1/8	6 2/8	Natrona Co., WY	Wade Dumont	Wade Dumont	1981	1199
82 2/8	17 3/8	17 4/8	6 6/8	6 3/8	2 3/8	2 7/8	11 7/8	11 7/8	5 3/8	Niobrara Co., WY	W.L. McMillan	W.L. McMillan	1981	1199
82 2/8	15 5/8	15 4/8	6 2/8	6 2/8	2 6/8	2 6/8	10 2/8	4 3/8	5 4/8	Butte Co., ID	Jon L. Wadkins	Jon L. Wadkins	1982	1199
82 2/8	16 7/8	16 7/8	6 1/8	6 1/8	2 7/8	2 6/8	11 1/8	5 6/8	5 6/8	Brewster Co., TX	McLean Bowman	McLean Bowman	1982	1199
82 2/8	14 5/8	14 7/8	6 5/8	6 5/8	2 4/8	2 4/8	9 5/8	6 2/8	6 2/8	Sweetwater Co., WY	Gregg R. Landrum	Gregg R. Landrum	1982	1199
82 2/8	16 6/8	16 4/8	6 4/8	6 4/8	2 6/8	2 6/8	11 5/8	8 6/8	4 7/8	Washoe Co., NV	Thomas O. Malone	Thomas O. Malone	1982	1199
82 2/8	16 2/8	16 2/8	6 2/8	6 4/8	2 7/8	2 7/8	13 2/8	11	4 7/8	Fremont Co., WY	Michael C. Meeker	Michael C. Meeker	1982	1199
82 2/8	17	16 6/8	6 6/8	6 5/8	2 4/8	2 6/8	8 4/8	5 6/8	4 7/8	Valley Co., MT	David D. Rittenhouse	David D. Rittenhouse	1982	1199
82 2/8	15 6/8	15 6/8	6 3/8	6 3/8	2 5/8	2 5/8	14 1/8	13 6/8	5 6/8	Carbon Co., WY	Larry J. Thoney	Larry J. Thoney	1983	1199
82 2/8	16 4/8	16 4/8	6 4/8	6 4/8	2 4/8	2 4/8	13 1/8	9 2/8	5 5/8	Fremont Co., WY	Richard L. Bostrom	Richard L. Bostrom	1983	1199
82 2/8	16 2/8	16 2/8	6 4/8	6 2/8	2 6/8	2 7/8	9 5/8	3 5/8	5 4/8	Garfield Co., MT	William E. Butler	William E. Butler	1983	1199
82 2/8	16	16 1/8	6 1/8	6 1/8	2 7/8	2 7/8	10 2/8	6	6	Navajo Co., AZ	Collins L. Cochran	Collins L. Cochran	1983	1199
82 2/8	15 7/8	16 6/8	6 6/8	6 6/8	2 6/8	2 6/8	10 3/8	10	5 4/8	Washakie Co., WY	Carol Greet	Carol Greet	1983	1199
82 2/8	16 3/8	16 3/8	6 2/8	6 2/8	2 4/8	2 5/8	13 3/8	8 3/8	5 6/8	Fremont Co., WY	Evelyn A. Maxon	Evelyn A. Maxon	1983	1199
82 2/8	14	14 3/8	7 6/8	7	2 4/8	2 4/8	10 4/8	8 4/8	6 2/8	Sweetwater Co., WY	Peter B. Shaw	Peter B. Shaw	1983	1199
82 2/8	16 5/8	15 7/8	6 4/8	6	2 7/8	2 7/8	15	11	5	Navajo Co., AZ	A.T. Boulinghouse	A.T. Boulinghouse	1983	1199
82 2/8	16 5/8	16	6 3/8	6 3/8	2 3/8	2 4/8	10 5/8	6 3/8	6 1/8	Butte Co., ID	John L. Stein	John L. Stein	1983	1199
82 2/8	18 2/8	18 7/8	6 1/8	6 1/8	2 4/8	2 4/8	9 5/8	5 5/8	5 2/8	Humboldt Co., NV	Chris Tiller	Chris Tiller	1983	1199
82 2/8	15 7/8	15 6/8	6 3/8	6 2/8	2 5/8	2 5/8	12 6/8	8 7/8	6 3/8	Hartley Co., TX	David E. Boyles, Sr.	David E. Boyles, Sr.	1984	1199
82 2/8	15 1/8	15 4/8	6 1/8	6 3/8	2 7/8	2 7/8	10	4 7/8	6 1/8	Fremont Co., WY	Ernie Davis	Ernie Davis	1984	1199
82 2/8	15 4/8	16	6 3/8	6 6/8	3	3	12	12	6 4/8	Sweetwater Co., WY	Charles D. Day	Charles D. Day	1984	1199
82 2/8	16	16 7/8	6 6/8	6	2 4/8	2 4/8	13 4/8	9 4/8	6 4/8	Siskiyou Co., CA	William Holland	William Holland	1984	1199
82 2/8	17 3/8	17 3/8	6 2/8	6 2/8	2 2/8	2 5/8	11 7/8	8 6/8	6 2/8	Natrona Co., WY	Laird E. Marshall	Laird E. Marshall	1984	1199
82 2/8	16	15 6/8	7 1/8	7 1/8	2 5/8	2 5/8	12 1/8	6 1/8	4 7/8	Humboldt Co., NV	Michael D. Samuelson	Michael D. Samuelson	1984	1199
82 2/8	15 2/8	15	6 5/8	6	3	3	9 4/8	5	5 2/8	Fergus Co., MT	Andrew S. Burnett	Andrew S. Burnett	1986	1199
82 2/8	16	17 2/8	6 3/8	6	3 1/8	3	11 1/8	9 3/8	4 7/8	Natrona Co., WY	Patricia M. Dreeszen	Patricia M. Dreeszen	1986	1199
82 2/8	15 2/8	16 4/8	6 7/8	6 2/8	2 7/8	2 7/8	10 2/8	7 6/8	5 4/8	Torrance Co., NM	Steven N. Levin	Steven N. Levin	1986	1199
82 2/8	17	17 3/8	6 2/8	6 2/8	2 7/8	3 2/8	8 6/8	3 4/8	4 4/8	Converse Co., WY	Michael F. Killoy	Michael F. Killoy	1987	1199
82 2/8	14 1/8	14 1/8	7 3/8	7	2 6/8	2 6/8	15 6/8	14 2/8	6	Catron Co., NM	Barbara Moore	Barbara Moore	1987	1199
82 2/8	16 5/8	16 5/8	6	6	2 6/8	2 6/8	11	6 7/8	5 5/8	Mohave Co., AZ	Harry J. Turiello	Harry J. Turiello	1987	1199
82 2/8	15 6/8	14 7/8	6 3/8	6 3/8	2 7/8	2 7/8	10 3/8	4 6/8	6 2/8	Rosebud Co., MT	Ronald D. Wood	Ronald D. Wood	1987	1199
82 2/8	14 6/8	15 7/8	6 1/8	6 7/8	2 6/8	2 6/8	8 1/8	5 6/8	6 1/8	Navajo Co., AZ	Cory Nissen	Cory Nissen	1988	1199
82 2/8	16	16	6 3/8	6	2 5/8	2 6/8	14 1/8	13 4/8	5 7/8	Navajo Co., AZ	Brian Reece	Brian Reece	1988	1199
82 2/8	16 2/8	15 7/8	6 4/8	6	2 5/8	2 5/8	7 7/8	2 6/8	6 3/8	Carbon Co., WY	Robert Depellegrini	Robert Depellegrini	1989	1199

PRONGHORN

Antilocapra americana americana and related subspecies

Score	Length of Horn R	L	Circumference of Base R	L	Circumference at Third Quarter R	L	Inside Spread	Tip to Tip Spread	Length of Prong R	L	Locality	Hunter	Owner	Date Killed	Rank
82 2/8	16 2/8	16 6/8	6	6	2 5/8	2 6/8	9 5/8	3 4/8	6 3/8	6 4/8	Fremont Co., WY	John A. Monje	John A. Monje	1989	1199
82 2/8	16 1/8	15 6/8	6 4/8	6 5/8	2 5/8	2 5/8	12 1/8	5 5/8	6 1/8	6 2/8	Natrona Co., WY	Valentine Novicki II	Valentine Novicki II	1989	1199
82 2/8	17	16 7/8	6 1/8	6 2/8	2 4/8	2 4/8	16 3/8	12 1/8	5	5 6/8	Middle Creek Res., AB	Donald P. Penner	Donald P. Penner	1989	1199
82 2/8	16 4/8	17	6 2/8	6 3/8	2 6/8	3 1/8	10 4/8	6 1/8	6 3/8	4 6/8	Catron Co., NM	Todd Garrison	Todd Garrison	1990	1199
82 2/8	16	15 5/8	6 6/8	6 5/8	2 6/8	2 5/8	14 2/8	10 1/8	5 4/8	5 3/8	Washoe Co., NV	Robert E. Hill	Robert E. Hill	1990	1199
82 2/8	14 4/8	14 4/8	6 6/8	6 5/8	3 1/8	3	10 5/8	6 6/8	6	5 2/8	Colfax Co., NM	Virgil A. Lair	Virgil A. Lair	1990	1199
82 2/8	15 5/8	15 6/8	6 4/8	6 4/8	2 5/8	2 5/8	10 3/8	7 6/8	5 2/8	5 4/8	Mora Co., NM	Allen E. Thomas	Allen E. Thomas	1990	1199
82 2/8	16 2/8	16 5/8	6 6/8	6 4/8	3 1/8	3 1/8	9 3/8	7 1/8	4 5/8	4 6/8	Weston Co., WY	Scott H. Eia	Scott H. Eia	1991	1199
82 2/8	18 7/8	19 4/8	5 6/8	5 6/8	2 3/8	2 3/8	17 7/8	15 4/8	4 5/8	4 5/8	Modoc Co., CA	Rod Eisenbeis	Rod Eisenbeis	1991	1199
82 2/8	15 6/8	15 5/8	7 4/8	7 2/8	2 4/8	2 5/8	9 7/8	7 7/8	6 2/8	5 4/8	Natrona Co., WY	Brian G. Elliott	Brian G. Elliott	1991	1199
82 2/8	15 1/8	15 7/8	7 1/8	7	2 7/8	2 7/8	10 6/8	8 2/8	5 1/8	5 3/8	Coconino Co., AZ	Dale H. Haggard	Dale H. Haggard	1991	1199
82 2/8	17 2/8	16 7/8	6 3/8	6 4/8	2 5/8	2 5/8	11 1/8	5	5 1/8	5	Sierra Co., NM	Gerald S. Janos	Gerald S. Janos	1991	1199
82 2/8	14 5/8	14 6/8	7	7 1/8	2 5/8	2 5/8	10 3/8	6 7/8	6 1/8	6 1/8	Carbon Co., WY	Roger T. Ralph	Roger T. Ralph	1991	1199
82 2/8	17	16 7/8	6 2/8	6 2/8	2 4/8	2 4/8	9	3 4/8	6 1/8	6 1/8	Dewey Co., SD	Alan Ruhlman	Alan Ruhlman	1991	1199
82 2/8	16 6/8	16 5/8	6 2/8	6 2/8	2 5/8	2 6/8	11	7	5	5 2/8	Slope Co., ND	Marty Beard	Marty Beard	1992	1199
82 2/8	16 4/8	16 3/8	6 2/8	6 2/8	2 5/8	2 6/8	10	5 2/8	5 5/8	5 5/8	Butte Co., SD	Bernerd E. Emery	Bernerd E. Emery	1992	1199
82 2/8	15	15	7	6 7/8	3 3/8	3 3/8	8 2/8	2 7/8	4 6/8	4 6/8	Catron Co., NM	Sam Jaksick, Jr.	Sam Jaksick, Jr.	1992	1199
82 2/8	16 5/8	16 6/8	6 5/8	6 5/8	2 4/8	2 3/8	17 3/8	14 4/8	5 1/8	5	Sweetwater Co., WY	Dan E. McBride	Dan E. McBride	1992	1199
82 2/8	16 2/8	16 2/8	6 2/8	6 2/8	2 6/8	3	10 4/8	5 7/8	4 7/8	5	Colfax Co., NM	Cooper Moore	Cooper Moore	1992	1199
82 2/8	17 1/8	17	6	5 7/8	2 4/8	2 4/8	9 1/8	4 5/8	5 6/8	6	Quay Co., NM	Lonnie L. Ritchey	Lonnie L. Ritchey	1992	1199
82 2/8	16 1/8	16 1/8	6 3/8	6 2/8	2 6/8	2 7/8	7 7/8	2 6/8	5 3/8	5 2/8	Mora Co., NM	Anses Joseph, Jr.	Anses Joseph, Jr.	1993	1199
82 2/8	17 5/8	17 2/8	6 3/8	6 3/8	2 5/8	2 5/8	9	6 7/8	5	5 4/8	Big Horn Co., MT	Valley C. Sian	Valley C. Sian	1993	1199
82 2/8	16 5/8	16 4/8	6	5 7/8	2 5/8	2 5/8	10 2/8	4 3/8	6 2/8	6	Coconino Co., AZ	Charles M. Wiedmaier	Charles M. Wiedmaier	1993	1199
82 2/8	16 6/8	16 3/8	5 6/8	5 6/8	2 3/8	2 2/8	11 5/8	8 5/8	6 7/8	6 6/8	Socorro Co., NM	Mark A. Cadwallader	Mark A. Cadwallader	1994	1199
82 2/8	15 5/8	15 5/8	6 2/8	6 3/8	3 1/8	3	10 5/8	5 3/8	5	5	Catron Co., NM	David Fulson	David Fulson	1994	1199
82 2/8	15 7/8	16	6 7/8	6 7/8	2 7/8	3	9	5 2/8	5	4 5/8	Sweetwater Co., WY	Casey Hunter	Casey Hunter	1994	1199
82 2/8	16	16	7	7	2 6/8	3 4/8	9 4/8	5 7/8	5 1/8	4 2/8	Carbon Co., WY	Richard D. Lumpkins	Richard D. Lumpkins	1994	1199
82 2/8	14 6/8	14 5/8	6 5/8	6 4/8	3 1/8	3 2/8	8	4 3/8	5 3/8	5 3/8	Washoe Co., NV	Mark A. Mannens	Mark A. Mannens	1994	1199
82 2/8	16	16 2/8	6 1/8	6 1/8	3	3	9 4/8	5 2/8	5 3/8	5 4/8	Yavapai Co., AZ	Jason L. Sims	Jason L. Sims	1994	1199
82 2/8	16 1/8	16 1/8	7 3/8	7 1/8	3 1/8	3 1/8	12 5/8	8	4 7/8	4 6/8	Mora Co., NM	Edward C. Joseph	Edward C. Joseph	1995	1199
82 2/8	17 2/8	17	6 4/8	6 4/8	1 7/8	1 7/8	16 4/8	15 6/8	5	4 4/8	Socorro Co., NM	David L. Swenson	David L. Swenson	1995	1199
82 2/8	16 1/8	16	6 4/8	6 6/8	2 3/8	2 3/8	11 6/8	7	6 4/8	6 6/8	Washoe Co., NV	Kent Burroughs	Kent Burroughs	1996	1199
82 2/8	15 5/8	16 6/8	6 7/8	6 4/8	2 6/8	2 6/8	12 1/8	7	5 5/8	5 4/8	Colfax Co., NM	Robert D. Jones	Robert D. Jones	1996	1199
82 2/8	16 6/8	16 2/8	6 4/8	6 4/8	2 6/8	2 5/8	8 7/8	2 6/8	5 1/8	4 7/8	Hudspeth Co., TX	Dan E. McBride	Dan E. McBride	1996	1199
82 2/8	16 4/8	16 2/8	6 4/8	6 3/8	2 6/8	2 6/8	10 5/8	5 2/8	5 3/8	5 4/8	Socorro Co., NM	David A. Miller	David A. Miller	1996	1199
82 2/8	16 4/8	16 5/8	6 3/8	6 2/8	3 1/8	3 2/8	10 6/8	7 4/8	4 6/8	4 4/8	Socorro Co., NM	William S. Pickett III	William S. Pickett III	1996	1199
82 2/8	16 4/8	17	6 6/8	6 2/8	2 4/8	2 2/8	8 4/8	7 4/8	5 6/8	6 2/8	Pershing Co., NV	Randy C. Rasley	Randy C. Rasley	1996	1199
82 2/8	15 2/8	14 5/8	6 6/8	6 6/8	2 7/8	3	9 3/8	5	5 4/8	5 4/8	Colfax Co., NM	Bill K. Ritchey	Bill K. Ritchey	1996	1199

Score	Length of Horn R	Length of Horn L	Circ. of Base R	Circ. of Base L	Circ. 3rd Qtr R	Circ. 3rd Qtr L	Inside Spread	Tip to Tip	Prong R	Prong L	Locality	By Whom Killed	Owner	Date	Rank
82 2/8	16 2/8	16 2/8	7 2/8	7 2/8	2 4/8	2 3/8	8 6/8	7 2/8	5 3/8	5 3/8	Converse Co., WY	David Tinson	David Tinson	1996	1199
82	17 4/8	17 4/8	6 2/8	6 4/8	3 2/8	3 2/8	14 6/8	11 6/8	3 4/8	4	Pahsimeroi Valley, ID	Elmer Keith	Elmer Keith	1936	1315
82	15 4/8	15 5/8	6 7/8	6 7/8	2 5/8	2 5/8	12 4/8	6 3/8	5 4/8	5 4/8	Catron Co., NM	Floyd Todd	Floyd Todd	1947	1315
82	16 2/8	15 6/8	6 4/8	6 4/8	3	3	11	7 2/8	5	5 2/8	Mormon Lake, AZ	Bob Housholder	Bob Housholder	1949	1315
82	16 2/8	16 2/8	6 4/8	6 2/8	2 6/8	2 4/8	13 1/8	10 4/8	5 6/8	6	Shirley Basin, WY	Earl Fisher	Earl Fisher	1951	1315
82	17 7/8	17 4/8	6 5/8	6 5/8	3	2 5/8	16	11 7/8	3 5/8	3 4/8	Williams, AZ	Paul D. Hosman	Paul D. Hosman	1951	1315
82	16 1/8	15 6/8	6 7/8	6 7/8	2 6/8	2 5/8	11 4/8	5	5 2/8	4 7/8	Anderson Mesa, AZ	Mrs. C.C. Cooper	Mrs. C.C. Cooper	1953	1315
82	17 4/8	17 5/8	6	6 1/8	2 7/8	2 7/8	12 3/8	5 6/8	4 5/8	4 6/8	Santa Rosa, NM	Frank C. Hibben	Frank C. Hibben	1955	1315
82	15	14 6/8	6 7/8	6 7/8	2 7/8	3	10 3/8	7 6/8	5 6/8	5 5/8	Bow Island, AB	R.F. Dunmire	R.F. Dunmire	1957	1315
82	15 2/8	15 2/8	7	7	3	2 5/8	12 3/8	7 6/8	5 6/8	5 3/8	Limon, CO	Walt Paulk	Walt Paulk	1958	1315
82	14 7/8	14 6/8	6 7/8	6 6/8	2 5/8	2 7/8	9 4/8	8 1/8	6 3/8	5 7/8	Sage Creek, WY	Mrs. Ramon Somavia	Mrs. Ramon Somavia	1960	1315
82	16	16 4/8	6 2/8	6 5/8	2 6/8	2 7/8	12 2/8	8 2/8	6	5 7/8	Encampment, WY	G.A. Surface	G.A. Surface	1960	1315
82	15 5/8	15 6/8	6 7/8	6 7/8	2 7/8	2 4/8	10 3/8	6 1/8	5 2/8	5	Natrona Co., WY	Fred Deiss	Fred Deiss	1961	1315
82	15 4/8	15 4/8	6 1/8	6 1/8	2 3/8	2 6/8	11 1/8	6 4/8	6 4/8	6 3/8	Shirley Basin, WY	Norman Miller	Norman Miller	1961	1315
82	16 1/8	16	6 3/8	6 4/8	2 6/8	2 6/8	9 5/8	7 6/8	5 2/8	5	Shirley Basin, WY	Henry Macagni	Henry Macagni	1962	1315
82	14 6/8	14 6/8	6 6/8	6	2 6/8	2 4/8	11	6 3/8	6 2/8	6 2/8	Hartley Co., TX	Walter O. Ford, Jr.	Walter O. Ford, Jr.	1964	1315
82	15 3/8	15 3/8	5 6/8	5 6/8	2 4/8	2 6/8	9	9	5	5 7/8	Arco, ID	Ernest L. Ellis, Jr.	Ernest L. Ellis, Jr.	1965	1315
82	17	16	6	6 1/8	2 7/8	2 6/8	12 1/8	6 4/8	6	6	McKinley Co., NM	W.R. Phillips	W.R. Phillips	1965	1315
82	16 1/8	16	6 6/8	6 6/8	2 6/8	2 6/8	12 7/8	11 4/8	4 3/8	3 2/8	Navajo Co., AZ	John Welch III	John Welch III	1965	1315
82	15 2/8	15	6	6	2 5/8	2 7/8	8 4/8	7	5 2/8	5 3/8	Eston, SK	Dennis Crowe	Dennis Crowe	1966	1315
82	16 5/8	16 3/8	6 1/8	6 4/8	2 5/8	2 3/8	9 3/8	8 4/8	6 7/8	6 7/8	Lake Co., OR	Eldon Hayes	Eldon Hayes	1966	1315
82	14 6/8	14 6/8	6 4/8	6	2 4/8	3 4/8	8 7/8	9 3/8	5 7/8	5 7/8	Garfield Co., MT	Dean V. Ashton	Dean V. Ashton	1968	1315
82	15 5/8	15	6 5/8	6 5/8	3	3 4/8	10 1/8	8 7/8	7	6	Carbon Co., WY	C.W. Hermanson	C.W. Hermanson	1968	1315
82	15 4/8	15 4/8	7 1/8	7 1/8	3	2 4/8	8	7	5 4/8	5 4/8	Farson, WY	Larry N. Garner	Larry N. Garner	1969	1315
82	17 2/8	17	6 2/8	6 2/8	2 6/8	2 3/8	11 2/8	13 1/8	6	6	Albany Co., WY	Edwin J. Keppner	Edwin J. Keppner	1969	1315
82	14	14 3/8	7 4/8	7 2/8	2 4/8	3 2/8	13	13	6	5 5/8	Wamsutter, WY	Frank Simons	Frank Simons	1969	1315
82	16 1/8	16 4/8	6 7/8	6 5/8	2 6/8	2 6/8	12 3/8	8 6/8	5 2/8	5 5/8	Carbon Co., WY	Martin J. Stuart	Martin J. Stuart	1969	1315
82	16 2/8	16 1/8	6 4/8	6 4/8	2 5/8	2 5/8	10 1/8	5	5 3/8	5 3/8	Washoe Co., NV	Oliver V. Iveson	Oliver V. Iveson	1970	1315
82	14 5/8	14 6/8	6 4/8	6 4/8	3 4/8	2 4/8	11 2/8	7 1/8	4 3/8	5 2/8	Brewster Co., TX	Joseph W. Burkett III	Joseph W. Burkett III	1972	1315
82	16 2/8	16 2/8	6 1/8	6 1/8	3 4/8	2 4/8	9 3/8	7 3/8	5 2/8	5 2/8	Sweet Rock, WY	Alphonse Cuomo, Jr.	Alphonse Cuomo, Jr.	1973	1315
82	14 1/8	13 6/8	7	6 6/8	2 4/8	2 3/8	10 1/8	8	6	6	Sublette Co., WY	Gary D. Jorgensen	Gary D. Jorgensen	1973	1315
82	15 2/8	15 3/8	6 6/8	6 6/8	2 5/8	2 3/8	11 2/8	5 4/8	5 7/8	6 1/8	Coconino Co., AZ	Jerry R. Killman	Jerry R. Killman	1973	1315
82	16 4/8	16 4/8	6 6/8	6 6/8	3 2/8	3 2/8	13	7 3/8	6 6/8	7 3/8	Garfield Co., MT	Don E. Traughber	Don E. Traughber	1973	1315
82	15	15	7 3/8	7 1/8	3 2/8	2 5/8	11	7 2/8	3 4/8	2 6/8	Wolf Point, MT	Raymond A. Gould	Raymond A. Gould	1974	1315
82	16	16	6	6	2 5/8	2 6/8	10 3/8	7 3/8	5 6/8	5 7/8	Carbon Co., WY	Reg. R. Smith	Reg. R. Smith	1974	1315
82	17 7/8	17 6/8	5 4/8	5 5/8	2 2/8	2 6/8	8 2/8	5 6/8	5 7/8	5 7/8	Campbell Co., WY	Gilbert Steinen, Jr.	Gilbert Steinen, Jr.	1975	1315
82	16 4/8	16 3/8	7	7 5/8	2 7/8	2 7/8	10 3/8	5	6	6	Lake Co., OR	Calvin M. Auvil	Calvin M. Auvil	1976	1315
82	14 1/8	13 6/8	7	6 6/8	3 2/8	3	9 6/8	9	4 4/8	4 4/8	Sweetwater Co., WY	Starla L. Cairns	Starla L. Cairns	1976	1315
82	15 2/8	15 3/8	6 6/8	6 6/8	2 3/8	2 5/8	2 7/8	9	5 6/8	5 6/8	Wallace Co., KS	Curtis R. Penner	Curtis R. Penner	1976	1315
82	16 4/8	16 4/8	6 2/8	6 2/8	2 3/8	2 3/8	8 2/8	11 4/8	5 4/8	5 4/8	Fremont Co., WY	Daniel R. Hahn	Daniel R. Hahn	1977	1315
82	15	15	6	6	3 2/8	3	10 3/8	7 1/8	5 4/8	5 4/8	Carbon Co., WY	Peck Rollison	Peck Rollison	1977	1315
82	16	16	5 4/8	5 5/8	2 4/8	2 2/8	9	6	5 4/8	5 4/8	Hartley Co., TX	John A. Wright	John A. Wright	1977	1315
82	17 7/8	17 6/8	5 5/8	5 5/8	2 4/8	2 4/8	12 7/8	7	5 4/8	5	Otero Co., NM	Robert E. Anton	Robert E. Anton	1978	1315
82	16 4/8	16 3/8	6 2/8	6 2/8	2 7/8	2 5/8	12 6/8	6 2/8	5 4/8	5 4/8	Fremont Co., WY	John J. Eichhorn	John J. Eichhorn	1978	1315
82	16 4/8	16 4/8	6 2/8	6 2/8	2 5/8	2 5/8	10 3/8	8 7/8	5 1/8	4 2/8	Hudspeth Co., TX	Luther V. Oliver	Luther V. Oliver	1978	1315
82	17 1/8	17 4/8	6 4/8	6 4/8	3 1/8	3 1/8	0	0	4 2/8	4 4/8	Culberson Co., TX	Charles Seidensticker	Charles Seidensticker	1978	1315
82	14 5/8	15 1/8	6 7/8	6 7/8	2 4/8	2 4/8	10 7/8	6 7/8	6 3/8	6 5/8	Sweetwater Co., WY	Dan B. Artery	Dan B. Artery	1979	1315

Antilocapra americana americana and related subspecies

Score	Length of Horn R	L	Circumference of Base R	L	Circumference at Third Quarter R	L	Inside Spread	Tip to Tip Spread	Length of Prong R	L	Locality	Hunter	Owner	Date Killed	Rank
82	17	17	6 4/8	6 3/8	2 5/8	2 4/8	8 6/8	6 4/8	4 6/8	5 1/8	Brewster Co., TX	Peggy F. Brady	Peggy F. Brady	1979	1315
82	16 1/8	16 1/8	6 5/8	6 4/8	2 6/8	2 6/8	12 6/8	7 3/8	5 5/8	5 5/8	Lassen Co., CA	Robert D. Luna, Jr.	Robert D. Luna, Jr.	1979	1315
82	16 1/8	16	7	6 7/8	2 6/8	2 5/8	9	2 1/8	5 2/8	4 6/8	Fremont Co., WY	Steven E. Clingman	Steven E. Clingman	1980	1315
82	16 6/8	16	6 3/8	6 2/8	2 2/8	2 2/8	15	11 5/8	5 5/8	5 2/8	Natrona Co., WY	Theresa Fulfaro	Theresa Fulfaro	1980	1315
82	16 3/8	16 5/8	6 3/8	6 4/8	2 6/8	2 5/8	9 6/8	3 5/8	5 5/8	5 5/8	Coconino Co., AZ	Fred W. Fernow, Jr.	Fred W. Fernow, Jr.	1981	1315
82	16 1/8	16	6 1/8	6 1/8	2 2/8	2 2/8	14	10 1/8	6 4/8	6 4/8	Washoe Co., NV	Jerry L. Nelms	Jerry L. Nelms	1981	1315
82	17	17	6 2/8	6 1/8	2 4/8	2 4/8	6 6/8	1 6/8	5 5/8	5 4/8	Lincoln Co., WY	Tom Crank	Tom Crank	1982	1315
82	15 6/8	15 6/8	7	7	2 6/8	2 6/8	8 4/8	2 6/8	5 2/8	5 2/8	Crook Co., WY	Jay D. Hacklin	Jay D. Hacklin	1982	1315
82	15 5/8	15 3/8	6 2/8	6 2/8	2 6/8	2 5/8	10 4/8	6 3/8	6 2/8	6 4/8	Fremont Co., WY	Thomas O. Martens	Thomas O. Martens	1982	1315
82	16 2/8	16 1/8	6 5/8	6 6/8	2 5/8	2 5/8	12	8 3/8	5 2/8	5 1/8	Natrona Co., WY	Joseph P. Prinzi	Joseph P. Prinzi	1982	1315
82	15 2/8	15 2/8	6 5/8	6 4/8	3 1/8	3	10	6 4/8	5 2/8	5 4/8	Carbon Co., WY	Eric J. Swanson	Eric J. Swanson	1982	1315
82	14 1/8	14	7 2/8	7 1/8	2 5/8	2 5/8	10 6/8	7 5/8	6 2/8	6 1/8	Sweetwater Co., WY	Brett A. Ward	Brett A. Ward	1982	1315
82	15	14 5/8	7	7 1/8	2 6/8	2 6/8	12	10 6/8	5 5/8	5 5/8	Carbon Co., WY	Albert Gregg	Albert Gregg	1983	1315
82	16 2/8	15 6/8	6 5/8	6 5/8	2 4/8	2 4/8	7 2/8	1	5 7/8	5 7/8	Washoe Co., NV	Jack D. Bothwell	Jack D. Bothwell	1984	1315
82	16 5/8	16 3/8	6 1/8	6 4/8	2 3/8	2 4/8	14 1/8	10 1/8	5 6/8	5 6/8	Quay Co., NM	Donald E. Fritz	Donald E. Fritz	1984	1315
82	16	15 7/8	6 2/8	6 3/8	2 6/8	2 7/8	9 6/8	5	5	5 3/8	Coconino Co., AZ	Charles L. Holland	Charles L. Holland	1984	1315
82	15 5/8	16 1/8	6 7/8	6 6/8	2 5/8	2 7/8	8 4/8	3	5 6/8	5 6/8	Carbon Co., WY	James A. Rademacher	James A. Rademacher	1986	1315
82	16 4/8	17	6 3/8	6 4/8	2 5/8	2 5/8	10 2/8	7 4/8	5 3/8	5	Johnson Co., WY	Thomas F. Williams	Thomas F. Williams	1986	1315
82	16 1/8	16	6 6/8	6 5/8	2 4/8	2 4/8	11 6/8	7 5/8	6	5 3/8	Apache Co., AZ	Leonard J. Imperial	Leonard J. Imperial	1987	1315
82	17 4/8	18	5 6/8	5 6/8	2 7/8	2 7/8	18	16 2/8	4 6/8	4 5/8	Graham Co., AZ	James P. Kniffin	James P. Kniffin	1987	1315
82	15 4/8	15 4/8	6 6/8	6 6/8	2 6/8	2 6/8	8 4/8	5 7/8	5 6/8	4 6/8	Alberta	Peter M. Parkyn	Peter M. Parkyn	1987	1315
82	16 4/8	16 2/8	6 4/8	6 4/8	2 4/8	2 3/8	7 5/8	3 2/8	5 7/8	5 7/8	Sweetwater Co., WY	Jeffrey A. Schalow	Jeffrey A. Schalow	1987	1315
82	15 3/8	15 3/8	6 6/8	6 5/8	2 3/8	2 2/8	7 2/8	3 4/8	6 2/8	6 2/8	Elko Co., NV	Roger L. Curry	Roger L. Curry	1988	1315
82	15 7/8	15 7/8	6 3/8	6 3/8	3	3	14 4/8	11	5 3/8	5 4/8	Billings Co., ND	Curtis D. Decker	Curtis D. Decker	1988	1315
82	17 1/8	16 6/8	6 4/8	6 3/8	2 4/8	2 3/8	11 5/8	6 5/8	5 5/8	5 4/8	Fremont Co., WY	Timothy A. Kiefer	Timothy A. Kiefer	1988	1315
82	16	15 3/8	6 4/8	6 4/8	2 6/8	2 6/8	11	8 1/8	4 6/8	4 6/8	Harding Co., NM	Andrew J. Ortega	Andrew J. Ortega	1988	1315
82	14 2/8	14 3/8	7 2/8	7 2/8	2 5/8	2 3/8	9 3/8	5 4/8	5 7/8	5 3/8	Carbon Co., WY	Donald L. Soderberg	Donald L. Soderberg	1988	1315
82	14 3/8	14 3/8	7 2/8	7 2/8	2 3/8	2 3/8	11 5/8	10 2/8	6 3/8	6 2/8	Carbon Co., WY	Becky Strand	Becky Strand	1988	1315
82	16 7/8	17	6 3/8	6 4/8	2 5/8	2 6/8	11 2/8	6	4 6/8	4 4/8	Mora Co., NM	H.P. Wood	H.P. Wood	1988	1315
82	14 4/8	14 3/8	7 6/8	7 6/8	2 5/8	2 6/8	10 6/8	8 6/8	5 5/8	5 6/8	Sweetwater Co., WY	Mark E. Gillespie	Mark E. Gillespie	1989	1315
82	15 4/8	15 6/8	6	6 1/8	2 5/8	2 5/8	10 2/8	4 1/8	5 4/8	5 5/8	Mohave Co., AZ	Jeff K. Gunnell	Jeff K. Gunnell	1989	1315
82	16 2/8	15 7/8	6 7/8	6 5/8	2 2/8	2 2/8	10 6/8	5 4/8	5 5/8	5 5/8	Washoe Co., NV	James E. Puryear	James E. Puryear	1989	1315
82	16 2/8	16 2/8	6 4/8	6 4/8	2 4/8	2 4/8	9 5/8	5 5/8	6 3/8	6 4/8	Lincoln Co., WY	Michael H. Romney	Michael H. Romney	1989	1315
82	15 5/8	15 5/8	6 2/8	6 1/8	2 7/8	2 7/8	8 6/8	5	5 6/8	5 4/8	Natrona Co., WY	Victor Colonna	Victor Colonna	1990	1315
82	15 3/8	15 2/8	6 4/8	6 3/8	2 6/8	2 7/8	8 2/8	4	5	5 5/8	Albany Co., WY	Phil Darnell	Phil Darnell	1990	1315
82	15	15 1/8	7	7 1/8	2 3/8	2 4/8	8 4/8	6	6 5/8	5 6/8	Carbon Co., WY	Allen A. Ehrke	Allen A. Ehrke	1990	1315
82	16 6/8	16 2/8	6 3/8	6 4/8	3	3	8 6/8	4 5/8	4 5/8	4 6/8	Moffat Co., CO	Len H. Guldman	Len H. Guldman	1990	1315
82	16 2/8	16	7	6 7/8	2 6/8	2 6/8	9 6/8	5 5/8	5	5 3/8	Washakie Co., WY	Jake Hanson	Jake Hanson	1990	1315

Score	Length of Horn R	Length of Horn L	Circ. of Base R	Circ. of Base L	Circ. 3rd Qtr R	Circ. 3rd Qtr L	Inside Spread	Tip to Tip	Prong R	Prong L	Locality	Hunter	Owner	Date	Rank
82	15 7/8	16 2/8	6 3/8	6 4/8	2 4/8	2 5/8	10 3/8	4 6/8	6 1/8	5 7/8	Mora Co., NM	Todd S. Hyden	Todd S. Hyden	1990	1315
82	17 4/8	17 3/8	6 2/8	6 2/8	2 4/8	2 5/8	8 2/8	2 7/8	4 7/8	4 7/8	Washoe Co., NV	Paul J. Jesch	Paul J. Jesch	1990	1315
82	17	17 2/8	6 6/8	6 6/8	3	3	9 2/8	3	3 5/8	5 1/8	Lincoln Co., NM	Steve A. Marasovich, Jr.	Steve A. Marasovich, Jr.	1990	1315
82	16 5/8	16 7/8	6 2/8	6 1/8	2 4/8	2 4/8	16 3/8	12 3/8	5 2/8	5	Slope Co., ND	Todd M. Quinn	Todd M. Quinn	1990	1315
82	17 6/8	17 4/8	6 3/8	6 4/8	2 5/8	2 5/8	8 7/8	4 4/8	5 4/8	4 5/8	Hudspeth Co., TX	E. Scott Smith	E. Scott Smith	1990	1315
82	16	16	6 3/8	6 3/8	2 4/8	2 4/8	10 4/8	8 1/8	6 1/8	7	Albany Co., WY	James T. Sprinkle	James T. Sprinkle	1990	1315
82	15 3/8	15 4/8	6 5/8	6 5/8	3	3	12	8 7/8	4 5/8	4 3/8	Lassen Co., CA	Tommy B. Esperance	Tommy B. Esperance	1991	1315
82	15 7/8	15 3/8	7 1/8	7 1/8	2 5/8	2 7/8	11 4/8	7 2/8	4 3/8	4 4/8	Mora Co., NM	Charlie Hooser	Raymond R. Gonzales	1991	1315
82	15 7/8	15 7/8	6 4/8	6 4/8	2 7/8	2 7/8	9 7/8	5 3/8	4 6/8	5	Washoe Co., NV	James D. Jones	James D. Jones	1991	1315
82	15 4/8	15	7 3/8	7 3/8	2 5/8	2 5/8	10 6/8	7 3/8	5 3/8	4 3/8	Lassen Co., CA	Joseph D. Nolan	Joseph D. Nolan	1991	1315
82	16 3/8	16 4/8	6 5/8	6 5/8	2 6/8	2 6/8	9 7/8	4 2/8	4 6/8	5 4/8	Converse Co., WY	Rick P. Sakovitz	Rick P. Sakovitz	1991	1315
82	16 2/8	16 2/8	6 1/8	6 1/8	2 7/8	2 7/8	9 5/8	3 7/8	5 3/8	5 4/8	Frenchman River, SK	Larry Schmidt	Larry Schmidt	1991	1315
82	13 4/8	13 2/8	7 1/8	7	3	3	11 7/8	10 6/8	6 4/8	3 7/8	Carbon Co., WY	Andrew W. Serres	Andrew W. Serres	1991	1315
82	16 4/8	16 4/8	6 5/8	6 5/8	3	3	7	0 1/8	4 1/8	6 3/8	Cochise Co., AZ	Brad Wedding	Brad Wedding	1991	1315
82	16 2/8	16 3/8	6 3/8	6 4/8	2 4/8	2 4/8	6 3/8	8 6/8	5 1/8	4 1/8	Washoe Co., NV	Richard T. Adams	Richard T. Adams	1992	1315
82	16 2/8	16 1/8	6	6	2 5/8	2 5/8	13 3/8	6 3/8	5	5 3/8	Catron Co., NM	Spence Dupree	Spence Dupree	1992	1315
82	15 4/8	15 7/8	6 4/8	6 4/8	2 6/8	2 6/8	8 3/8	6 6/8	5 3/8	6 2/8	Carbon Co., WY	Jeffrey L. Engel	Jeffrey L. Engel	1992	1315
82	16 5/8	16 5/8	6 3/8	6 3/8	2 5/8	2 5/8	10 7/8	6 6/8	5 5/8	5 7/8	Sweetwater Co., WY	Dennis L. Haan	Dennis L. Haan	1992	1315
82	16 3/8	16 3/8	6 4/8	6 4/8	2 5/8	2 5/8	10 1/8	4 4/8	5 5/8	5 4/8	Rosebud Co., MT	Denver W. Holt	Denver W. Holt	1992	1315
82	16 1/8	16 1/8	6 4/8	6 4/8	2 6/8	2 6/8	13 6/8	10 2/8	5 5/8	5 5/8	Colfax Co., NM	Kyle G. Hyden	Kyle G. Hyden	1992	1315
82	15	15	7 1/8	7 2/8	2 6/8	2 6/8	10	7 6/8	6	5 6/8	Garfield Co., MT	Kip K. Karges	Kip K. Karges	1992	1315
82	16 3/8	16 3/8	6 5/8	6 5/8	2 5/8	2 5/8	7	2 5/8	4 7/8	4 7/8	Mora Co., NM	Luke C. Kellogg	Luke C. Kellogg	1992	1315
82	16 2/8	16 1/8	6 1/8	6 1/8	2 5/8	2 7/8	10 7/8	5 4/8	6 1/8	5 6/8	Catron Co., NM	Donald K. Lash	Donald K. Lash	1992	1315
82	16 1/8	16	6 4/8	6 4/8	2 6/8	3	9 2/8	3	4 4/8	4 6/8	Colfax Co., NM	Maurice R. Strawn	Maurice R. Strawn	1992	1315
82	16 5/8	16 5/8	6 7/8	7	2 5/8	2 5/8	12	7 4/8	6 7/8	6 3/8	Colfax Co., NM	James D. Verbrugge	James D. Verbrugge	1992	1315
82	15 7/8	15 4/8	7	7	2 6/8	2 7/8	10 3/8	6 4/8	7	5 3/8	Rich Co., UT	William B. Bullen	William B. Bullen	1993	1315
82	17 1/8	17 1/8	6 4/8	6 4/8	2 7/8	3	13 5/8	9	7	7	Milk River, AB	Lance Hartley	Lance Hartley	1993	1315
82	17 4/8	17 3/8	6 2/8	6 2/8	2 6/8	2 6/8	6 3/8	1 3/8	4 6/8	4 3/8	Apache Co., AZ	Shane D. Koury	Shane D. Koury	1993	1315
82	15 4/8	15 4/8	6 3/8	6 3/8	2 5/8	2 5/8	11 1/8	6 3/8	5 2/8	6 3/8	Slope Co., ND	Sherry L. Niesar	Sherry L. Niesar	1993	1315
82	15	15	6	6	2 4/8	2 4/8	15 6/8	14	6 3/8	5 6/8	Colfax Co., NM	David R. Raemisch	David R. Raemisch	1993	1315
82	17 6/8	17 4/8	6 2/8	6 2/8	2 6/8	2 6/8	13	7 7/8	5 6/8	5 5/8	Lincoln Co., NM	Nicholas A. Baldock	Nicholas A. Baldock	1994	1315
82	16 2/8	16 2/8	6 2/8	6 2/8	2 5/8	2 5/8	9 7/8	4 3/8	4 1/8	4 1/8	Harney Co., OR	Errol W. Claire	Errol W. Claire	1994	1315
82	16 4/8	16 4/8	6 1/8	6 1/8	3	3	15 2/8	9 2/8	5 2/8	5 1/8	Navajo Co., AZ	Earl A. Petznick, Jr.	Earl A. Petznick, Jr.	1994	1315
82	15 3/8	15 4/8	6	6	2 4/8	2 4/8	9 5/8	4 6/8	5 7/8	5 2/8	Colfax Co., NM	R. Terrell McCombs	R. Terrell McCombs	1995	1315
82	15 4/8	15	6 6/8	6 6/8	2 6/8	2 6/8	11 4/8	8 4/8	5 2/8	5 2/8	Banner Co., NE	Timothy H. Ruzicka	Timothy H. Ruzicka	1995	1315
82	16 3/8	16 2/8	6 4/8	6 4/8	2 5/8	2 5/8	11 7/8	6 5/8	4 3/8	4 3/8	Humboldt Co., NV	Joseph D. Anelli	Joseph D. Anelli	1996	1315
82	16 2/8	16 2/8	6 6/8	6 6/8	2 4/8	2 4/8	11	5 5/8	5 4/8	5	Catron Co., NM	Mark J. Etcheberry	Mark J. Etcheberry	1996	1315
82	16 4/8	16 4/8	6 2/8	6 2/8	2 3/8	2 4/8	8 7/8	5 5/8	5 4/8	6	Washoe Co., NV	Robert A. Johnson	Robert A. Johnson	1996	1315
82	15 3/8	15 2/8	7 1/8	7 1/8	2 4/8	2 4/8	13 2/8	9 1/8	5 4/8	5 3/8	Rosebud Co., MT	Gary L. Reed	Gary L. Reed	1996	1315
82	15 4/8	15 6/8	6 3/8	6 3/8	3	3	8 2/8	4	5 4/8	5 2/8	Malheur Co., OR	Ursula E. Sporrer-Cain	Ursula E. Sporrer-Cain	1996	1315
82	16 3/8	15 4/8	6 6/8	6 6/8	2 4/8	2 4/8	9 5/8	4 2/8	6 5/8	6	Humboldt Co., NV	Donald D. Van Dyken	Donald D. Van Dyken	1996	1315
82	16 4/8	16 2/8	6 2/8	6 2/8	2 4/8	2 4/8	9 6/8	2 5/8	6 2/8	6 3/8	Lincoln Co., NM	Russell J. Jackson	Russell J. Jackson	1997	1315
82	15 1/8	15 1/8	6 6/8	6 7/8	3 1/8	3	9 6/8	5 6/8	5	5	Logan Co., CO	Andrew R. Paxton	Andrew R. Paxton	1997	1315
90 4/8*	19 4/8	19 4/8	6 2/8	6 2/8	3 5/8	3 3/8	12 4/8	9 2/8	6 2/8	5 2/8	Coconino Co., AZ	Paul R. Langford	Paul R. Langford	1995	
89 2/8*	15 7/8	15 5/8	8	7 6/8	3 3/8	3 3/8	9 7/8	7 3/8	5 5/8	5 5/8	Carbon Co., WY	Sharon M. Carson	Sharon M. Carson	1991	

* Final score is subject to revision by additional verifying measurements.

591

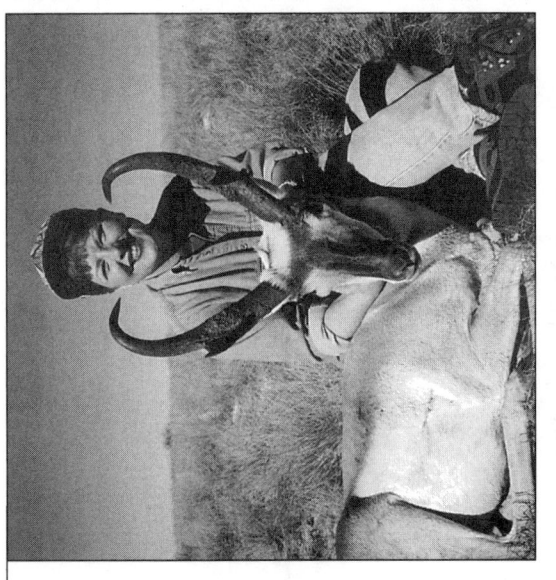

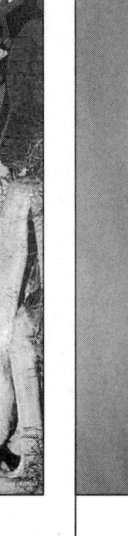

CATEGORY
PRONGHORN

SCORE
83-4/8

HUNTER
HOLLEY W. LACEY

LOCATION
SOCORRO CO., NM

DATE OF KILL
SEPTEMBER 1996

CATEGORY
PRONGHORN

SCORE
87-2/8

HUNTER
STEPHEN C. LeBLANC

LOCATION
MORA CO., NM

DATE OF KILL
AUGUST 1992

CATEGORY
PRONGHORN

SCORE
83-6/8

HUNTER
JOHN W. BISHOP

LOCATION
SOCORRO CO., NM

DATE OF KILL
SEPTEMBER 1995

CATEGORY
PRONGHORN

SCORE
84-4/8

HUNTER
DENNIS J. SITES

LOCATION
MORA CO., NM

DATE OF KILL
AUGUST 1996

CATEGORY
PRONGHORN

SCORE
89-4/8

HUNTER
BRADY J. SMITH

LOCATION
CATRON CO., NM

DATE OF KILL
AUGUST 1996

CATEGORY
PRONGHORN

SCORE
85

HUNTER
MARK B. STEFFEN

LOCATION
NATRONA CO., WY

DATE OF KILL
AUGUST 1997

593

For years, tourists visiting Yellowstone National Park have been awed by a bison skull that hangs in the Chief Ranger's office in Mammoth Hot Springs. This replica is based off the original skull that is currently stored in the Albright Visitor Center. Shot by Chief Ranger Sam Woodring in 1926, "Old Tex" was not taken for sport but in the course of reducing the Yellowstone Park herd in order to balance it with the land's grazing capacity.

The record was almost toppled by a very outstanding trophy shot by Samuel Israel in Northwest Territories in 1961, with a score of 136-2/8. Though the Canadian subspecies of the wood bison is considered to have a larger head than the plains bison, its horns are not necessarily as large as confirmed by Woodring's long-standing record of 136-4/8. The dense cushioning of matted hair between their wide, black crescent horns, said to be thick enough to stop a bullet, is used as a sort of shock absorber when colliding with a competitor during the rut. It is an awesome sight, but at times devastating as a horn can deliver a mortal wound.

Bison are capable of galloping up to 32 miles per hour and have been known to charge careless tourists who have approached too closely. However, this supreme power along with an immense appearance is really their only means of defense. Consequently, the plains bison became an easy target for market shooters who greatly contributed to their ruthless butchering in the late nineteenth century. This act was a tragic blow to the Plains Indians who were dependent on these animals for meat, clothes, shelter, fuel and as the basis of their culture. By the turn of the century fewer than a thousand bison were in existence. Luckily, there was a call to rescue their plight by organizations and individuals such as Theodore Roosevelt, founder of the Boone and Crockett Club, and William T. Hornaday, an early Club member and founder of the Bison Society and the National Bison Range in western Montana. ∎

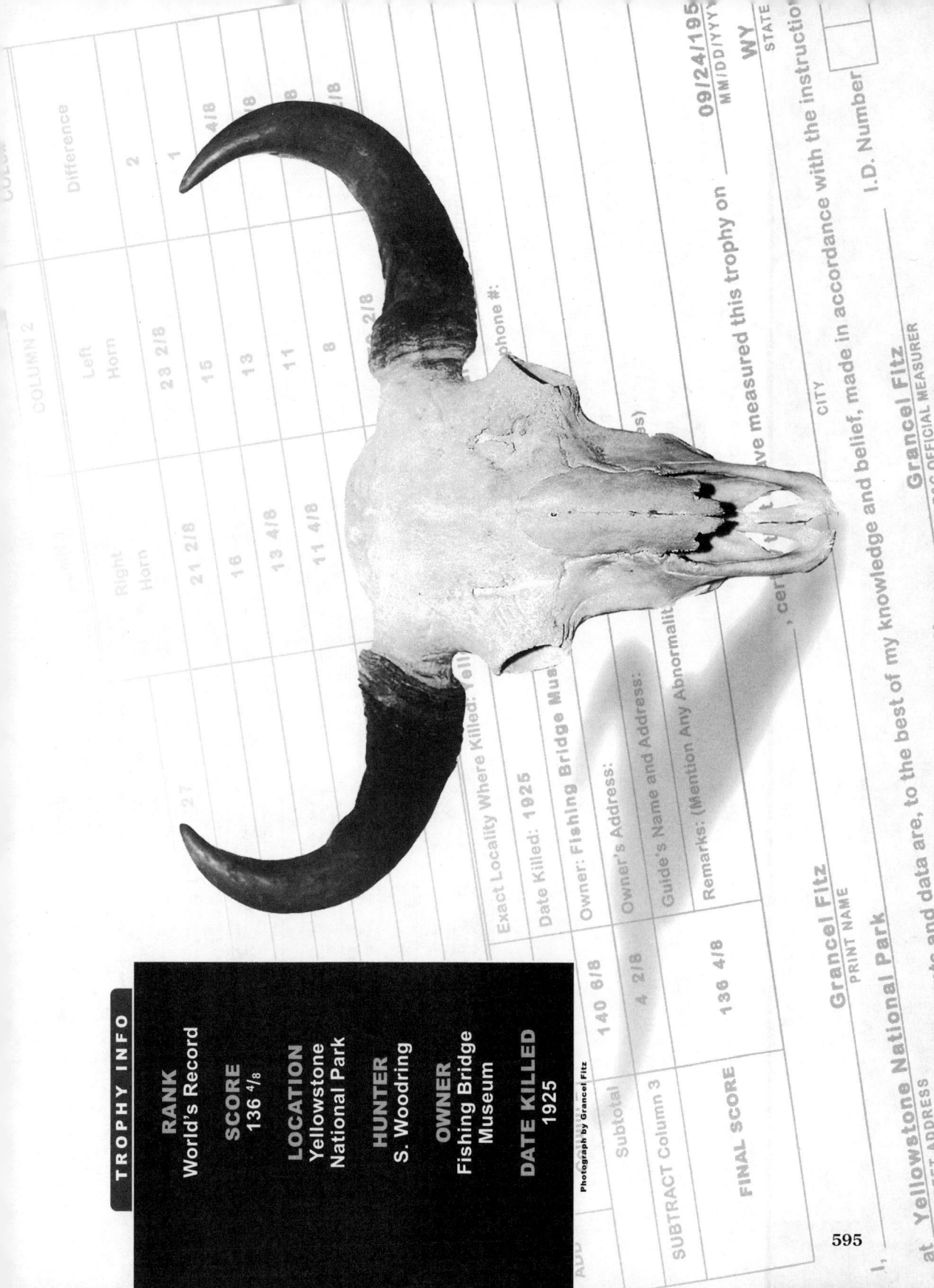

Photograph by Grancel Fitz

TROPHY INFO

RANK
World's Record

SCORE
136 4/8

LOCATION
Yellowstone National Park

HUNTER
S. Woodring

OWNER
Fishing Bridge Museum

DATE KILLED
1925

	COLUMN 2		Difference
	Right Horn	Left Horn	2
		28 2/8	4/8 · 1
	21 2/8	15	
	16	13	
	13 4/8	11	
	11 4/8	8	
	2 7		

Exact Locality Where Killed: Yell...

Date Killed: 1925

Owner: Fishing Bridge Mus...

Owner's Address:

Guide's Name and Address:

Remarks: (Mention Any Abnormalit...

Subtotal   140 6/8

SUBTRACT Column 3   4 2/8

FINAL SCORE   136 4/8

...ve measured this trophy on _____ 09/24/195_
MM/DD/YYY

..., cer... ...re...

...urements and data are, to the best of my knowledge and belief, made in accordance with the instructio...

signature: _____

Grancel Fitz
PRINT NAME

Grancel Fitz
B&C OFFICIAL MEASURER

WY
STATE

CITY

I.D. Number

I, _____

at **Yellowstone National Park**
STREET ADDRESS

595

All measurements must be made with a 1/4-inch wide flexible steel tape to the nearest one-eighth of an inch. Wherever it is necessary to change direction of measurement, mark a control point and swing tape at this point. Enter fractional figures in eighths, without reduction. Official measurements cannot be taken until horns have air dried for at least 60 days after the animal was killed.

A. Greatest Spread is measured between perpendiculars at a right angle to the center line of the skull.

B. Tip to Tip Spread is measured between tips of horns.

C. Length of Horn is measured from the lowest point on underside over outer curve to a point in line with the tip. Use a straight edge, perpendicular to horn axis, to end the measurement, if necessary.

D-1. Circumference of Base is measured at right angle to axis of horn. **Do not** follow the irregular edge of horn; the line of measurement must be entirely on horn material.

D-2-3-4. Divide measurement C of **longer** horn by four. Starting at base, mark **both** horns at these quarters (even though the other horn is shorter) and measure the circumferences at these marks, with measurements taken at right angles to horn axis.

Records of
North American
Big Game

BOONE AND CROCKETT CLUB®

250 Station Drive
Missoula, MT 59801
(406) 542-1888

OFFICIAL SCORING SYSTEM FOR NORTH AMERICAN BIG GAME TROPHIES

MINIMUM SCORES
AWARDS ALL-TIME
115   115

BISON

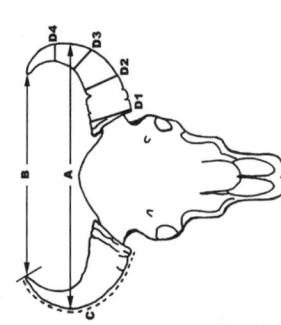

SEE OTHER SIDE FOR INSTRUCTIONS		COLUMN 1	COLUMN 2	COLUMN 3
		Right Horn	Left Horn	Difference
A. Greatest Spread	35 3/8			
B. Tip to Tip Spread	27			
C. Length of Horn		21 2/8	23 2/8	2
D-1. Circumference of Base		16	15	1
D-2. Circumference at First Quarter		13 4/8	13	4/8
D-3. Circumference at Second Quarter		11 4/8	11	4/8
D-4. Circumference at Third Quarter		8 2/8	8	2/8
	TOTALS	70 4/8	70 2/8	4 2/8

ADD	Column 1	70 4/8
	Column 2	70 2/8
	Subtotal	140 6/8
SUBTRACT Column 3		4 2/8
FINAL SCORE		136 4/8

Exact Locality Where Killed: **Yellowstone National Park, WY**

Date Killed: **1925**   Hunter: **B. Woodring**

Owner: **Fishing Bridge Museum**   Telephone #:

Owner's Address:

Guide's Name and Address:

Remarks: (Mention Any Abnormalities or Unique Qualities)

I, **Grancel Fitz** , certify that I have measured this trophy on **09/24/1951**
PRINT NAME   MM/DD/YYYY

at **Yellowstone National Park**   **WY**
STREET ADDRESS   CITY   STATE/PROVINCE

and that these measurements and data are, to the best of my knowledge and belief, made in accordance with the instructions given.

Witness: _____   Signature: **Grancel Fitz** _____ I.D. Number _____
                                              B&C OFFICIAL MEASURER

TROPHY INFO

RANK
2

SCORE
136 $^{2}/_{8}$

LOCATION
Northwest Territories

HUNTER
Samuel Israel

OWNER
Samuel Israel

DATE KILLED
1961

Photograph by Alex Rota

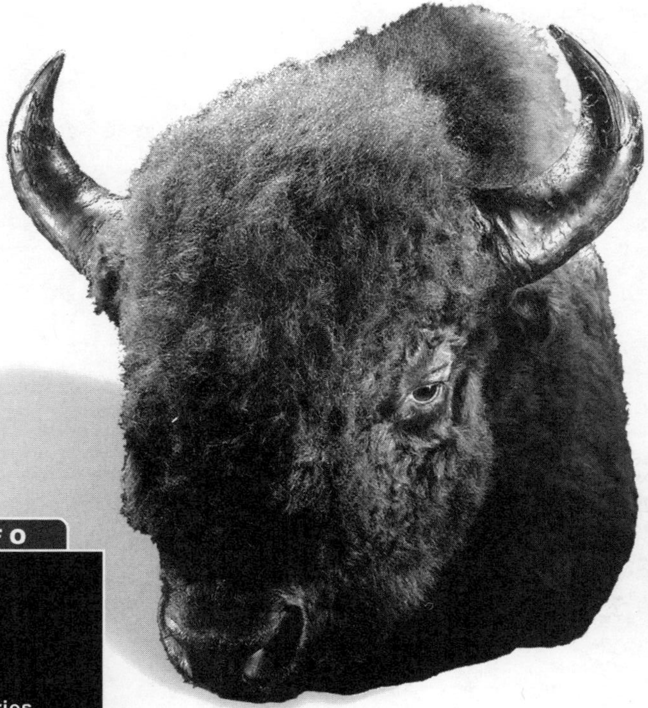

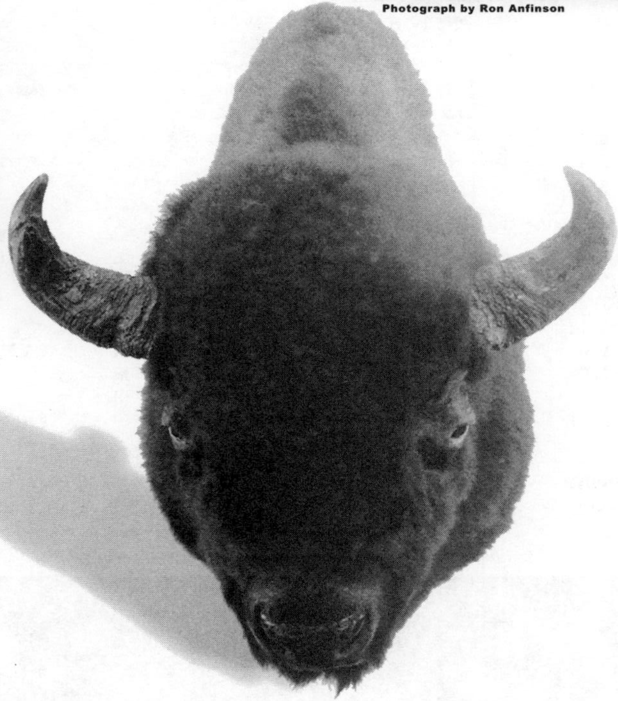

TROPHY INFO

RANK
3

SCORE
135

LOCATION
Custer Co., SD

HUNTER
Remo Pizzagalli

OWNER
Remo Pizzagalli

DATE KILLED
1995

Photograph by Ron Anfinson

Bison bison bison and Bison bison athabascae

Score	Length of Horn R	L	Circumference of Base R	L	Circumference at Third Quarter R	L	Greatest Spread	Tip to Tip Spread	Locality	Hunter	Owner	Date Killed	Rank
136 4/8	21 2/8	23 2/8	16	15	8 2/8	8	35 3/8	27	Yellowstone Natl. Park, WY	S. Woodring	Fishing Bridge Museum	1925	1
136 2/8	19	18 6/8	18 4/8	18 4/8	6 5/8	6 7/8	30 1/8	22 3/8	Northwest Territories	Samuel Israel	Samuel Israel	1961	2
135	18 2/8	18	16	15 4/8	8 6/8	8 7/8	32 2/8	28 4/8	Custer Co., SD	Remo Pizzagalli	Remo Pizzagalli	1995	3
134 2/8	21 2/8	20 6/8	14 4/8	14 7/8	8 6/8	7 6/8	33 7/8	26 2/8	Park Co., WY	Picked Up	H.A. Moore	1977	4
133 4/8	19 2/8	18 6/8	17	17	7	7	29 2/8	21 2/8	Great Slave Lake, AB	Mike Dempsey	Natl. Mus. of Canada	1935	5
132 2/8	21 2/8	22 2/8	16 4/8	16 7/8	6	7 5/8	35 2/8	26 6/8	Unknown	James H. Lockhart	Carnegie Museum	PR 1939	6
132 2/8	21 7/8	21 7/8	14 1/8	14 1/8	6 6/8	6 5/8	32 6/8	24 3/8	Sweet Grass, AB	Ken Cooper	Univ. of Sask.	1961	6
131 6/8	20 5/8	20 6/8	15	15	7	7	30	20 7/8	Hell Roaring Creek, MT	Picked Up	Univ. of Mont. Zool. Mus.	1945	8
130 6/8	24 2/8	23 5/8	14 3/8	14 1/8	6	6	34 1/8	20 1/8	Falaise Lake, NT	Rene Picard	Rene Picard	1992	9
129	21 1/8	20 2/8	14 1/8	14 4/8	6 6/8	7 5/8	29 4/8	18 6/8	Big Horn Mts., WY	Picked Up	George S. Burnap, Jr.	1953	10
128 6/8	19 1/8	18 7/8	17 1/8	16 7/8	7 5/8	7 5/8	33 2/8	25	Northwest Territories	Bert Klineburger	Bert Klineburger	1960	11
128 6/8	19 5/8	20	15 2/8	15 4/8	6 3/8	6 4/8	35 1/8	33 6/8	Custer Co., SD	Rick E. Matzick	Rick E. Matzick	1996	11
128 4/8	18 4/8	18 5/8	14 6/8	14 6/8	8 2/8	8 4/8	28 1/8	20 4/8	Yellowstone Natl. Park, WY	Unknown	U.S. Natl. Museum	1913	13
128 4/8	18 7/8	18 6/8	15 1/8	14 7/8	7 6/8	7 4/8	31	23 5/8	Custer Co., SD	Stephanie Altimus	Wildl. Mus. of the West	1989	13
128	21 5/8	20 4/8	14 5/8	14 6/8	6 6/8	5 7/8	23 7/8	27	Custer Co., SD	Larry L. Altimus	Larry L. Altimus	1990	15
127 6/8	19 2/8	20 1/8	15 6/8	15 3/8	5 5/8	6	31 2/8	22 2/8	Northwest Territories	Leslie Bowling	Leslie Bowling	1961	16
127 6/8	19 5/8	19 6/8	15 5/8	15 3/8	6 3/8	6 4/8	32 2/8	25 3/8	Northwest Territories	Wilbur Hilgar	Wilbur Hilgar	1961	16
127	21 7/8	22 3/8	13 2/8	13 6/8	6 6/8	7 7/8	29	18 4/8	Canada	Unknown	Raymond Brown	1899	18
127	18 7/8	19	15 6/8	14 5/8	6 7/8	7 1/8	26 3/8	23 5/8	Custer Co., SD	Henry E. McLemore	Henry E. McLemore	1980	18
127	19 6/8	19 5/8	14 4/8	14 5/8	8 6/8	8 6/8	30 6/8	25 4/8	Coconino Co., AZ	William G. Cummard II	William G. Cummard II	1997	18
126 6/8	19 6/8	19 6/8	15 2/8	15 1/8	7 2/8	7 3/8	27 6/8	18 2/8	Gillette, WY	D.C. Basolo, Jr.	D.C. Basolo, Jr.	1963	21
126 6/8	20 7/8	21 1/8	14 2/8	14 4/8	6 2/8	6 2/8	30 3/8	19 6/8	Garfield Co., UT	Holland D. Butler	Holland D. Butler	1990	21
126 4/8	18 7/8	18 7/8	15	14 6/8	6 5/8	6 2/8	29	22	Park Co., MT	Picked Up	Matthew J. Young	1990	23
126 2/8	17 4/8	18 3/8	15 6/8	15 6/8	7 2/8	7	30 4/8	24 3/8	Yellowstone River, MT	Picked Up	Edward J. Melby	1935	24
126 2/8	18 3/8	18 1/8	16 2/8	16	6 2/8	6 4/8	29 6/8	21 7/8	Fort Smith, NT	V.N. Holderman	V.N. Holderman	1961	24
126 2/8	20 1/8	20 5/8	16 2/8	16	5 4/8	5 7/8	32 2/8	23 6/8	Custer Co., SD	Norman F. Taylor	Norman F. Taylor	1994	24
126	20 2/8	20 3/8	15	15 4/8	5 7/8	5 4/8	27 2/8	13 2/8	Slave River, NT	Edward A. Feser	Edward A. Feser	1975	27
126	18 1/8	21	15	15 2/8	6 4/8	7 2/8	31 7/8	24 6/8	Wrangell Mts., AK	Walter H. Hammer	Walter H. Hammer	1977	27
126	18 2/8	19 1/8	15 6/8	15 4/8	5 6/8	5 6/8	32 1/8	29 1/8	Custer Co., SD	Brian K. Yeoman	Brian K. Yeoman	1994	27
125 6/8	19 4/8	19 4/8	15	15 4/8	6 2/8	6	30 2/8	24	Yellowstone Natl. Park, WY	Lee L. Coleman	Jackson Hole Museum	1958	30
125 6/8	17 2/8	17 7/8	14	14	8	8	26 7/8	21 6/8	Park Co., WY	Unknown	James Patterson	PR 1970	30
125 6/8	19 2/8	20	15	15 3/8	5 7/8	6 2/8	31 2/8	24 6/8	Custer Co., SD	Edward Orestad	Edward Orestad	1991	30
125 4/8	19 6/8	19 5/8	14 7/8	14 6/8	6 3/8	5 7/8	31 5/8	25	Custer Co., SD	C. Brent Morgan	C. Brent Morgan	1986	33
125 2/8	19 7/8	20	14 3/8	13 4/8	6 7/8	7 1/8	28 4/8	19 5/8	Montana	Unknown	O.P. Chisholm	PR 1891	34
125 2/8	18 6/8	19	14 2/8	14 1/8	8	7 6/8	31 6/8	26 2/8	Park Co., MT	Richard Olson	Richard Olson	1989	34
125 2/8	18 4/8	17 7/8	14 7/8	14 3/8	8	8 2/8	33 2/8	29 1/8	Custer Co., SD	Robert J. Fair	Robert J. Fair	1992	34
125 2/8	17 4/8	17	15 1/8	15 2/8	8 1/8	8 2/8	29 2/8	24 4/8	Custer Co., SD	Romaine L. Marshall	Romaine L. Marshall	1993	34
125	19 7/8	20	14 4/8	14 4/8	6 1/8	6	28	20 3/8	Manitoba	Unknown	James Fredrick	1928	38

Score	Length of Horn R	Length of Horn L	Circ. of Base R	Circ. of Base L	Circ. Third Quarter R	Circ. Third Quarter L	Greatest Spread	Tip to Tip Spread	Locality	Hunter	Owner	Date Killed	Rank
125	18 7/8	18 7/8	14 5/8	15	6 6/8	6 2/8	28 3/8	18 5/8	Fort Smith, NT	Leonard J. Ostrom	Leonard J. Ostrom	1959	38
125	18 4/8	18 7/8	15 7/8	15 3/8	6	6	28 1/8	21 6/8	Halfway River, BC	Mary-Anne Faiers	Mary-Anne Faiers	1996	38
124 6/8	20 2/8	20 3/8	15 2/8	15 1/8	6 1/8	6 5/8	30 1/8	21 7/8	Wyoming	Lord Rendlesham	B&C National Collection	1892	41
124 6/8	18 2/8	18 2/8	14 1/8	14 3/8	7 2/8	8 1/8	30 7/8	25 6/8	Custer Co., SD	Picked Up	Dick Rossum	1991	41
124 4/8	20 4/8	20 4/8	14 7/8	15 4/8	6 1/8	6 4/8	31 6/8	24	Copper River, AK	Earl E. Knutson	Earl E. Knutson	1965	43
124 4/8	19 4/8	20	15 1/8	15 1/8	5 7/8	5 6/8	29 3/8	20 4/8	Delta Junction, AK	Mike Stagno	Mike Stagno	1975	43
124 4/8	19 6/8	19 6/8	15	14 6/8	6 3/8	6 2/8	30	23 3/8	Delta Junction, AK	Ted J. Forsi, Jr.	Ted J. Forsi, Jr.	1992	43
124 4/8	18 5/8	18	14 7/8	15	7	7 6/8	31 1/8	27 2/8	Custer Co., SD	Anthony J. Visentin	Anthony J. Visentin	1994	47
124 2/8	17 6/8	17 5/8	16 3/8	16 2/8	6 2/8	6 6/8	32 4/8	28 4/8	Fort Smith, NT	Margaret Buckner	Margaret Buckner	1960	47
124 2/8	17 2/8	17 2/8	14 6/8	14 6/8	7 4/8	7 6/8	31 3/8	27 3/8	Custer Co., SD	Stuart Godin	Stuart Godin	1975	47
124 2/8	17 6/8	17 2/8	15 6/8	15 6/8	6 6/8	6 4/8	31	25 2/8	Chitina River, AK	Robert E. Day	Robert E. Day	1976	47
124 2/8	19 1/8	18 4/8	14 4/8	14 4/8	6 6/8	6 4/8	30 6/8	24 4/8	Custer Co., SD	Robert D. Taylor	Robert D. Taylor	1986	47
124 2/8	19	18 3/8	14 5/8	15 6/8	6 7/8	6 5/8	29 4/8	23 7/8	Delta Junction, AK	Gary D. Wolfe	Gary D. Wolfe	1990	52
124	18 4/8	18 3/8	15 4/8	15 4/8	7 2/8	7	29 7/8	20 4/8	Jardine, MT	Unknown	Kerry Constan	1962	52
124	18 3/8	19	13 3/8	14	5 7/8	5 1/8	25 5/8	18 6/8	Slave River, NT	Rudolf Sand	Rudolf Sand	1972	52
124	21 2/8	20 4/8	15 6/8	16	7 6/8	7 7/8	30 6/8	16 6/8	Hook Lake, NT	Manfred Kurtz	Manfred Kurtz	1973	52
124	16 6/8	16 3/8	15 4/8	14 2/8	6 1/8	5 4/8	33 2/8	22 4/8	Coconino Co., AZ	Philip A. Sturgill	Philip A. Sturgill	1984	52
124	19 4/8	19 2/8	14 2/8	14	6 4/8	7 6/8	33	27 6/8	Custer Co., SD	William H. Smith	William H. Smith	1991	52
124	19	18 4/8	14	14 6/8	6 4/8	6 1/8	33 1/8	28	Custer Co., SD	Jack S. Snider	Jack S. Snider	1993	58
124	18	18	14 5/8	14 5/8	6 5/8	5 4/8	31	26 4/8	Northwest Territories	J.S. Sanders	J.S. Sanders	1961	58
123 6/8	20	19	14 3/8	14 3/8	5 4/8	5 1/8	25	20 7/8	Gillette, WY	D.C. Basolo, Jr.	D.C. Basolo, Jr.	1963	58
123 6/8	20 4/8	18	14 1/8	14 2/8	5 2/8	7 2/8	29	15 2/8	Calais Lake, NT	Warren D. St. Germaine	Warren D. St. Germaine	1988	61
123 6/8	18	17 6/8	16 1/8	16	5 4/8	5 4/8	28 6/8	22 3/8	Yellowstone Natl. Park, WY	Harry Trishman	James B. Minter	1924	61
123 4/8	19 6/8	19 5/8	14 2/8	14 2/8	5 7/8	6 3/8	29 4/8	21 4/8	Yellowstone Natl. Park, WY	Picked Up	C. Watters & D. Moore	1956	61
123 4/8	18	18	16	15 6/8	6 2/8	6 4/8	32 5/8	21 5/8	Delta Junction, AK	Donald A. Prescott	Donald A. Prescott	1963	61
123 4/8	20	20 7/8	15 1/8	15 4/8	6	6	29 2/8	22 5/8	Gillette, WY	H.I.H. Prince Abdorreza Pahlavi	H.I.H. Prince Abdorreza Pahlavi	1967	61
123 4/8	20 2/8	20 2/8	15 5/8	15 5/8	5 4/8	5 2/8	26	19	Fort Smith, NT	Earl H. Harris	Earl H. Harris	1969	66
123 4/8	18 6/8	18 1/8	14 5/8	14 5/8	7 5/8	7 3/8	29 1/8	21 4/8	Custer Co., SD	Tim P. Matzinger	Tim P. Matzinger	1983	66
123 2/8	17 4/8	16 2/8	15 4/8	15 4/8	6	6	28	22 1/8	Garfield Co., UT	Carl R. Albrecht	Carl R. Albrecht	1986	66
123 2/8	18 3/8	18 1/8	13 6/8	14 2/8	7 4/8	7 6/8	32	26 4/8	Chitina River, AK	Gerald H. Phillips	Gerald H. Phillips	1987	69
123 2/8	19	18 5/8	15 2/8	14 7/8	6 1/8	5 7/8	27 6/8	24	Custer Co., SD	Jerry Ippolito	Jerry Ippolito	1990	70
123	16 4/8	17	14 5/8	14 3/8	8	7	31 4/8	24 7/8	Big Delta, AK	Unknown	Chuck Sutter	1950	70
122 6/8	20 3/8	19 3/8	15 2/8	14 5/8	5 3/8	5 4/8	29 4/8	16 5/8	Park Co., MT	Picked Up	James J. Darr	1991	72
122 6/8	18 3/8	18 3/8	14 5/8	14 5/8	7 1/8	6 5/8	26 4/8	23 7/8	Garfield Co., UT	Greg Harper	Greg Harper	1978	72
122 4/8	20 4/8	20 4/8	14 4/8	14 4/8	5	5	25	19 6/8	Custer Co., UT	Donald F. Senter	Donald F. Senter	1989	72
122 4/8	18 4/8	18 5/8	14 6/8	14 2/8	5 6/8	6 6/8	29 4/8	27 2/8	Garfield Co., UT	Shawn M. Ward	Shawn M. Ward	1991	72
122 4/8	19 1/8	19 2/8	14	14	6 3/8	5 7/8	33 2/8	26 2/8	Custer Co., SD	Robert D. Jones	Robert D. Jones	1995	76
122 4/8	20 5/8	20 4/8	13 4/8	14 1/8	6 4/8	6 4/8	32 7/8	23 2/8	Absarokee Wilder., MT	Picked Up	H.E. Lillis	1953	76
122 2/8	18 4/8	18	14 1/8	14 1/8	7 3/8	6 2/8	29 6/8	19 1/8	Fort Greely, AK	McClaren Johnson, Jr.	McClaren Johnson, Jr.	PR 1961	76
122 2/8	19 2/8	19 2/8	14 4/8	14 2/8	6 2/8	6 2/8	28 4/8	20 3/8	Northwest Territories	A. Sanford	A. Sanford	1961	76
122 2/8	18 2/8	18 2/8	14 4/8	14 3/8	7 4/8	7 4/8	28 6/8	27 5/8	Gillette, WY	Tom R. Bowles	Tom R. Bowles	1963	81
122 2/8	18 1/8	20 1/8	15 4/8	15 4/8	6 1/8	6 1/8	31 5/8	22 6/8	Lawrence Co., SD	Kenneth H. Jones	Kenneth H. Jones	1986	81
122	18 5/8	18 3/8	16 1/8	16	5	5	29 4/8	29 1/8	Hook Lake, NT	Picked Up	Robert C. Jones	1974	81
122	19 3/8	19 6/8	15 1/8	15 2/8	5 3/8	5 3/8	30 4/8	29 4/8	Goodpastor River, AK	Charles W. Jackson	Charles W. Jackson	1989	84
122	19 1/8	19 4/8	15 2/8	15 2/8	5 2/8	5 2/8	29 3/8	25 3/8	Gerstle River, AK	Richard Voss	Richard Voss	1990	84
121 6/8	19 4/8	20 3/8	14 6/8	14 6/8	5 7/8	5 5/8	29 3/8	21 3/8	Wayne Co., UT	Ardell K. Woolsey	Ardell K. Woolsey	1974	84

BISON

Bison bison bison and Bison bison athabascae

Score	Length of Horn R	L	Circumference of Base R	L	Circumference at Third Quarter R	L	Greatest Spread	Tip to Tip Spread	Locality	Hunter	Owner	Date Killed	Rank
121 6/8	18 2/8	18 2/8	14 3/8	14 3/8	7	7 2/8	29 3/8	23 7/8	Custer Co., SD	Jon R. Stephens	Jon R. Stephens	1982	84
121 6/8	18 6/8	18 6/8	13 4/8	13 3/8	7 4/8	7 3/8	32 4/8	30 3/8	Custer Co., SD	Thomas H. Coe	Thomas H. Coe	1991	84
121 4/8	21 1/8	22 1/8	13 5/8	14	5 3/8	5 3/8	29 7/8	18 7/8	Custer, MT	Picked Up	Martin Sorensen, Jr.	1962	87
121 4/8	19 2/8	18 3/8	15 3/8	14 5/8	6 2/8	6 7/8	31 4/8	26 4/8	Custer Co., SD	Glen Taylor	Glen Taylor	1993	87
121 2/8	16	14 7/8	16	16 3/8	8 2/8	8	29 4/8	25 6/8	Ogalala Sioux G. R., SD	Robert B. Peregrine	Robert B. Peregrine	1972	89
121 2/8	18	18 6/8	14	14 3/8	6 3/8	7	28 3/8	17 2/8	Fort Smith, NT	W.C. Whitt	W.C. Whitt	1972	89
121 2/8	18 1/8	18 4/8	15	15 1/8	5 5/8	6	28 4/8	21 4/8	Custer Co., SD	Robert L. Trupe	Robert L. Trupe	1979	89
121 2/8	16 7/8	17 2/8	13 4/8	14 1/8	7 4/8	5 1/8	30 4/8	25 3/8	Custer Co., SD	Bradley D. Hanson	Bradley D. Hanson	1988	89
121 2/8	20 1/8	20 4/8	14	14 1/8	4 6/8	5 1/8	29	21 6/8	Garfield Co., UT	Travis S. Myers	Travis S. Myers	1995	89
121	16 7/8	17 2/8	14 3/8	14 2/8	7 1/8	7 1/8	29 2/8	21 5/8	Slave River, NT	Franz M. Wilhelmsen	Franz M. Wilhelmsen	1959	94
121	20 4/8	18 3/8	14 4/8	14 4/8	6 4/8	6 4/8	28 5/8	20	Shoshone Natl. For., WY	Picked Up	G.A. Cadwalader	PR 1965	94
121	17 4/8	18 2/8	14 4/8	15 2/8	6 6/8	7 1/8	28	21 7/8	House Rock, AZ	Larry R. French	Larry R. French	1965	94
121	18 2/8	18	14 4/8	14 4/8	6 6/8	6 7/8	27 6/8	19 6/8	Big Horn Co., MT	Picked Up	Larry Edgar	1972	94
121	19 2/8	18 2/8	14 5/8	14 6/8	5 7/8	5 4/8	30 2/8	24 6/8	Custer Co., SD	Dave Ramey	Dave Ramey	1978	94
121	17 6/8	17 4/8	15 2/8	15 4/8	7 5/8	6 1/8	25 5/8	19 5/8	Custer Co., SD	Wilson W. Crook III	Wilson W. Crook III	1982	94
121	17 2/8	17 5/8	14 4/8	15 1/8	7	7 2/8	29 6/8	23 3/8	Park Co., MT	Dale K. Jackson	Dale K. Jackson	1986	94
121	17 4/8	18 2/8	14 3/8	14 2/8	7	6 5/8	29 2/8	22 4/8	Custer Co., SD	James J. Ceccolini	James J. Ceccolini	1992	94
121	15 7/8	16 4/8	14 7/8	15	7 6/8	7 5/8	28	22 2/8	Custer Co., SD	Jerry Landa	Jerry Landa	1993	94
120 6/8	17	17 4/8	15 3/8	15 2/8	5 6/8	5 3/8	31 2/8	29 6/8	Delta Junction, AK	George R. Horner	George R. Horner	1950	103
120 6/8	18 2/8	18 2/8	15 3/8	15 3/8	5 3/8	5 3/8	29 6/8	24 7/8	Hook Lake, NT	George W. Parker	George W. Parker	1961	103
120 6/8	17 7/8	17 5/8	15 6/8	15 7/8	5 2/8	5 3/8	29	25 6/8	Afton, WY	Bernard Domries	Bernard Domries	1968	103
120 6/8	17	16 6/8	14 4/8	14 4/8	7 3/8	7	29 1/8	24 1/8	Custer Co., SD	Louis Vaughn	Louis Vaughn	1968	103
120 6/8	20 7/8	19 6/8	15 2/8	16 1/8	5 1/8	5	31 3/8	24	Gillette, WY	C.J. McElroy	C.J. McElroy	1970	103
120 6/8	16 5/8	16 3/8	13 7/8	14 7/8	7 6/8	7	28 2/8	24	Park Co., WY	Picked Up	James Patterson	PR 1970	103
120 6/8	17 4/8	18	15 3/8	15 1/8	6 2/8	6 2/8	29 1/8	24	Coconino Co., AZ	Greg V. Parker	Greg V. Parker	1975	103
120 6/8	18	18 3/8	15 6/8	15 3/8	5 1/8	5 3/8	29 1/8	26 4/8	Custer Co., SD	Lucky Simpson	Lucky Simpson	1985	103
120 6/8	15 1/8	14 4/8	14 3/8	14 2/8	8 2/8	9	28	25	Custer Co., SD	Douglas M. Dreeszen	Douglas M. Dreeszen	1988	103
120 6/8	17 3/8	16 6/8	14 6/8	14 3/8	6 6/8	6 3/8	27	20	Park Co., MT	Matthew P. Wheeler	Matthew P. Wheeler	1989	103
120 6/8	19 5/8	18 7/8	14 6/8	14 5/8	6 4/8	5 7/8	31 6/8	24 7/8	Custer Co., SD	William D. Bradley	William D. Bradley	1996	103
120 6/8	19 4/8	19 4/8	14 4/8	14 3/8	6 2/8	6 3/8	29 7/8	21	Pink Mt., BC	Chester L. Greene	Chester L. Greene	1996	103
120 4/8	20 4/8	20 6/8	14	14	5 1/8	5 2/8	29 2/8	17 3/8	Northwest Territories	Charles H. Stoll	Charles H. Stoll	1961	115
120 4/8	17 1/8	17	14 5/8	14 5/8	7 1/8	7 1/8	28 7/8	23 2/8	Custer Co., SD	Philip L. Nare	Philip L. Nare	1974	115
120 4/8	17 5/8	17 2/8	14 6/8	15	7 4/8	7 3/8	30 4/8	26 3/8	Custer Co., SD	Dale L. Martin	Dale L. Martin	1983	115
120 2/8	17 6/8	17 2/8	14 1/8	14 6/8	6 1/8	6 6/8	27 7/8	21 1/8	Slave River, NT	Unknown	Mrs. Malcom McKenzie	1960	118
120 2/8	19 7/8	20	15 1/8	15 2/8	5 1/8	5	31 3/8	27 6/8	Delta Junction, AK	James M. Hill	James M. Hill	1978	118
120 2/8	18 2/8	17 4/8	14 3/8	14 2/8	7	6 4/8	31 5/8	26 6/8	Custer Co., SD	Richard A. Bonander	Richard A. Bonander	1996	118
120 2/8	21	20 2/8	16	15 7/8	4 5/8	4 5/8	28 7/8	18 1/8	Lamar River, WY	Frank Oberhansley	Natl. Park Service	1939	121
120	15 1/8	17	14 6/8	14 7/8	7 1/8	7 1/8	28 1/8	24 4/8	Big Delta, AK	Unknown	Robert C. Reeve	1950	121

Score	L.H. R	L.H. L	C.B. R	C.B. L	C.Q. R	C.Q. L	Gr. Spr.	Tip to Tip	Locality	Hunter	Owner	Date	Rank
120	18 1/8	20 2/8	16	16 2/8	4 5/8	5 1/8	29 5/8	23	Big Delta, AK	Thomas B. Hite	Thomas B. Hite	1983	121
120	18 4/8	19 3/8	15 3/8	15 5/8	5	5 3/8	31 2/8	27 6/8	Park Co., MT	Luke G. Eighorn	Luke G. Eighorn	1986	121
120	19 5/8	19 4/8	14 4/8	14 2/8	5	5	28 4/8	22 3/8	Wayne Co., UT	Bryant S. Furness	Bryant S. Furness	1986	121
120	18 2/8	16 6/8	15 4/8	15	5 6/8	6 6/8	31 5/8	27 7/8	Custer Co., SD	Donald G. Allen	Donald G. Allen	1994	121
119 6/8	17 5/8	18 5/8	15	14 7/8	6 4/8	6 3/8	25 7/8	16	Northwest Territories	Patrick Britell	Patrick Britell	1961	127
119 6/8	19 6/8	20	15 1/8	14 6/8	6 2/8	5	30 6/8	23 1/8	Big Delta, AK	Ann Denardo	Ann Denardo	1961	127
119 6/8	18 1/8	18	15 1/8	15 2/8	6 2/8	6 2/8	28 4/8	20 3/8	Northwest Territories	Pitt Sanders	Pitt Sanders	1961	127
119 6/8	17 5/8	18 4/8	14 5/8	14 6/8	5 3/8	5 5/8	28 6/8	21 3/8	Fort Smith, NT	Sheldon H. Weinstein	Sheldon H. Weinstein	1975	127
119 6/8	18 4/8	19 4/8	14 2/8	13 7/8	6 2/8	6 1/8	23 1/8	30 4/8	Custer Co., SD	Charles E. Ferguson	Charles E. Ferguson	1985	127
119 4/8	20	19	14 2/8	14 2/8	5 6/8	5 3/8	32	25 4/8	Gillette, WY	Glenn Ellingson	Glenn Ellingson	1961	132
119 4/8	17	17 4/8	15 4/8	15 4/8	6 6/8	6	29	24 6/8	Gillette, WY	Walt Paulk	Walt Paulk	1962	132
119 4/8	19 2/8	19 4/8	13 4/8	13 3/8	6 6/8	7	25 6/8	15 4/8	Yellowstone Natl. Park, WY	Picked Up	Jim Ford	1970	132
119 4/8	18	17 3/8	16 1/8	15 6/8	5 4/8	5 5/8	30 6/8	24 5/8	Coconino Co., AZ	Dorothy B. Gilliam	Dorothy B. Gilliam	1980	132
119 4/8	17 7/8	17 7/8	14 2/8	14	6 2/8	6 5/8	30 4/8	24 4/8	Custer Co., SD	Paul L.C. Snider	Paul L.C. Snider	1992	132
119 2/8	18 1/8	18 5/8	15 5/8	15 1/8	6 2/8	5 4/8	27 5/8	18 1/8	Ravalli Co., MT	Unknown	Harold G. Arnold	1975	137
119 2/8	19 6/8	19 3/8	14 4/8	14 4/8	5	5 1/8	26 6/8	15 4/8	San Juan Co., UT	Janice N. Wahlstrom	Janice N. Wahlstrom	1979	137
119 2/8	16 7/8	17 4/8	14 6/8	14 5/8	6 2/8	6 2/8	29 5/8	24 4/8	Custer Co., SD	Merlynn K. Jones	Merlynn K. Jones	1986	137
119 2/8	18 6/8	19 6/8	14 6/8	14 2/8	6 4/8	6 5/8	28 7/8	21 3/8	Custer Co., SD	John L. Van Horn	John L. Van Horn	1986	137
119 2/8	17 4/8	17 2/8	14	14 4/8	6 4/8	7	28 3/8	21 5/8	Coconino Co., AZ	James R. Brown	James R. Brown	1988	137
119 2/8	19	17 7/8	15 1/8	15	5 7/8	5 5/8	31 7/8	27 6/8	Park Co., MT	Michael D. Cadwell	Michael D. Cadwell	1988	137
119 2/8	19 2/8	19 2/8	13 5/8	13 4/8	6 1/8	5 5/8	30	21 6/8	Black Rapids Glacier, AK	Picked Up	Ashley L. Thompson	1991	137
119	17 6/8	17 4/8	13 6/8	13 5/8	6 2/8	6 7/8	25 4/8	16 4/8	Fort Smith, NT	John H. Epp	John H. Epp	1960	144
119	18 6/8	18 6/8	15 1/8	15 1/8	4 7/8	5	25 4/8	18	Hook Lake, NT	John G. Zelenka	John G. Zelenka	1971	144
119	16 7/8	16 7/8	14 5/8	14 6/8	6 4/8	6 4/8	27 2/8	18 7/8	Coconino Co., AZ	Melvin C. Kincaid	Melvin C. Kincaid	1983	144
118 6/8	18	18 1/8	14	14	7 1/8	7 1/8	28 7/8	19 1/8	Northwest Territories	Herb Klein	Herb Klein	1960	147
118 6/8	17 2/8	16 6/8	15 3/8	15 2/8	6	5 6/8	29	22 4/8	Fort Smith, NT	W.J. Nixon	W.J. Nixon	1960	147
118 6/8	15 4/8	17 1/8	15 6/8	15 6/8	6 2/8	5 7/8	27 3/8	20 6/8	Fort Smith, NT	D.N. Rowe	D.N. Rowe	1960	147
118 6/8	19 1/8	18	15 1/8	14 7/8	5 3/8	4 7/8	28 7/8	22 6/8	Fort Smith, NT	Charles Sides	Charles Sides	1960	147
118 6/8	16 2/8	16 5/8	15 4/8	14 2/8	7	7	29 7/8	26 3/8	Big Horn Co., MT	Richard P. Platz	Richard P. Platz	1961	147
118 6/8	15 3/8	14	15 4/8	14 3/8	7 1/8	7 6/8	28 2/8	25	Lake Co., MT	Basil C. Bradbury	Basil C. Bradbury	1968	147
118 6/8	19 6/8	19 6/8	15 2/8	15 2/8	4 6/8	4 6/8	31 1/8	23 6/8	Hook Lake, NT	Jack A. Shane, Sr.	Jack A. Shane, Sr.	1968	147
118 6/8	17 6/8	16 6/8	16 4/8	16 4/8	6 3/8	6 2/8	31 1/8	26	Garfield Co., UT	G.A. Treschow	G.A. Treschow	1972	147
118 6/8	20 1/8	20 2/8	14 2/8	14 1/8	5	5	29	23 1/8	Custer Co., SD	David G. Hansen	David G. Hansen	1975	147
118 6/8	17 7/8	17 5/8	15 6/8	16	5 4/8	5 5/8	30 4/8	24 7/8	Copper River, AK	Joel J. Torgerson	Joel J. Torgerson	1981	147
118 6/8	17 7/8	17 7/8	13 2/8	13 2/8	7 1/8	7	29 1/8	22 3/8	Custer Co., SD	G. Michael Miller	G. Michael Miller	1988	147
118 6/8	18 7/8	18	14	14 3/8	6 6/8	5 6/8	33 5/8	29	Copper River, AK	William J. Ahern	William J. Ahern	1992	147
118 6/8	17 3/8	18 3/8	14 5/8	14 5/8	6 6/8	5 4/8	31	25 5/8	Custer Co., SD	Robert B. Williams	Robert B. Williams	1995	147
118 4/8	18 1/8	18 1/8	14 4/8	14 4/8	5 7/8	6	28 4/8	23 6/8	Copper River, AK	Jim Harrower	Jim Harrower	1964	160
118 4/8	20 1/8	20 3/8	15 2/8	15 2/8	4 5/8	4 5/8	28 4/8	21 3/8	Pine Ridge Indian Res., SD	Mary L. Pipp	Mary L. Pipp	1972	160
118 4/8	20	19 4/8	14 3/8	14 3/8	5 1/8	4 6/8	27 5/8	20 2/8	Garfield Co., UT	Robert B. Williams	Robert B. Williams	1986	160
118 4/8	20 2/8	20 2/8	14 2/8	14 2/8	4 6/8	5	26 6/8	14 4/8	Davis Co., UT	Ronald J. Dallin	Ronald J. Dallin	1987	160
118 4/8	17 5/8	19 1/8	13 7/8	13 6/8	6 6/8	6 4/8	32	27	Custer Co., SD	Patrick C. Allen	Patrick C. Allen	1992	160
118 2/8	19 4/8	18 7/8	14 7/8	15 4/8	4 6/8	4 6/8	31	28	Wyoming	Snow Museum	Sidney Snow	PR 1900	165
118 2/8	18 6/8	19 1/8	14 1/8	14 2/8	5 3/8	5 3/8	28 2/8	22 4/8	Pierre, SD	Earl Mumaw	Earl Mumaw	1962	165
118 2/8	19 1/8	19 6/8	14 4/8	14 4/8	5 2/8	5 4/8	29	18 4/8	Houserock Valley, AZ	Fred Shook	Fred Shook	1967	165
118 2/8	18 1/8	18 7/8	14 3/8	14 7/8	4 6/8	5 4/8	30 5/8	23 5/8	Teton Co., WY	Steven C. Kobold	Steven C. Kobold	1990	165
118 2/8	17 7/8	16 5/8	15	15 5/8	5 4/8	5 4/8	29 4/8	25	Custer Co., SD	Robert M. McCarten	Robert M. McCarten	1993	165

BISON

Bison bison bison and Bison bison athabascae

Score	Length of Horn R	L	Circumference of Base R	L	Circumference at Third Quarter R	L	Greatest Spread	Tip to Tip Spread	Locality	Hunter	Owner	Date Killed	Rank
118 2/8	14 6/8	15	14 3/8	14 1/8	8 7/8	8 6/8	28 1/8	22 3/8	Custer Co., SD	Robert D. Jones	Robert D. Jones	1995	165
118	17 4/8	18 6/8	15	15 4/8	6 2/8	6 2/8	29 4/8	21	Yellowstone Natl. Park, WY	Unknown	Alfred C. Berol	1927	171
118	17 2/8	17 3/8	13 7/8	14 2/8	6 7/8	7	30	26 2/8	Crow Indian Res., MT	Pete Laird	Curt Laird	1956	171
118	16	16	16	16	5 7/8	5 7/8	27 6/8	20 2/8	Gillette, WY	D.C. Basolo, Jr.	D.C. Basolo, Jr.	1962	171
118	17 4/8	16 7/8	14 1/8	16	6	6	25 5/8	19	Garfield Co., UT	John Goldenstein	John Goldenstein	1962	171
118	18 4/8	19 4/8	15 1/8	15 1/8	5	5 1/8	31 7/8	29 1/8	Custer Co., SD	Harry T. Scharfenberg	Harry T. Scharfenberg	1984	171
118	18 7/8	18 1/8	14 2/8	14	5 4/8	4 7/8	29 3/8	25 1/8	Garfield Co., UT	Sharon G. Polley	Sharon G. Polley	1994	171
117 6/8	18 2/8	17 6/8	14 2/8	14 1/8	5 6/8	6 2/8	30 6/8	25 6/8	Farewell, AK	Thomas R. Keele	Thomas R. Keele	1975	177
117 6/8	17 5/8	17 4/8	13 5/8	13 5/8	5 6/8	5 5/8	26	20 4/8	Garfield Co., UT	Sheldon D. Worthen	Sheldon D. Worthen	1977	177
117 6/8	17 4/8	16 4/8	14 5/8	14 5/8	6	6 6/8	27 4/8	23	Park Co., MT	Thomas D. Roe	Thomas D. Roe	1988	177
117 4/8	16 3/8	16 5/8	15 4/8	15 6/8	6	6 7/8	29	23	Custer Co., SD	Thomas J. Radoumis	Thomas J. Radoumis	1973	180
117 2/8	17 6/8	17 3/8	14	14 2/8	6 5/8	6 3/8	30	25	Garfield Co., UT	Don Genessy	Don Genessy	1960	181
117 2/8	18 7/8	18 7/8	14 6/8	14 6/8	4 7/8	4 5/8	27	16	Gillette, WY	D.C. Basolo, Jr.	D.C. Basolo, Jr.	1963	181
117 2/8	19	19 4/8	14 2/8	14 4/8	5	5	31	27	Campbell Co., WY	Leroy Van Buggenum	Leroy Van Buggenum	1968	181
117 2/8	17 7/8	17 7/8	14 1/8	14 1/8	5 6/8	6	28 5/8	24 4/8	Park Co., MT	Donald E. Franklin	Donald E. Franklin	1986	181
117 2/8	19 1/8	18 6/8	14 6/8	14 2/8	5	4 7/8	27 5/8	18 4/8	Wayne Co., UT	Tony K. Cross	Tony K. Cross	1987	181
117 2/8	16 6/8	16 3/8	15	14 6/8	6 1/8	5 4/8	27 3/8	23 1/8	Garfield Co., UT	L. Scot Jenkins	L. Scot Jenkins	1987	181
117	18 2/8	18	14 4/8	14 1/8	6 3/8	5 4/8	30 6/8	25	Fort Smith, NT	Fred Burke	Fred Burke	1960	187
117	17 4/8	17 6/8	15 1/8	15 2/8	5 4/8	5	28 4/8	22 7/8	Gillette, WY	D.C. Basolo, Jr.	D.C. Basolo, Jr.	1963	187
117	18 4/8	18 5/8	15	15 3/8	4 6/8	5 4/8	29 5/8	26	Dadina River, AK	Joe Van Conia	Joe Van Conia	1965	187
117	19	19 3/8	14 6/8	14 6/8	4 6/8	5	29 6/8	29 6/8	Delta Junction, AK	William T. Warren	William T. Warren	1978	187
117	19 6/8	20 2/8	14 6/8	14 5/8	4 4/8	4 5/8	30 4/8	24 3/8	Donnelly Dome, AK	Debra S. Darland	Debra S. Darland	1981	187
117	17 7/8	17 6/8	14 2/8	14 2/8	6 1/8	6 6/8	29	23 7/8	Delta Junction, AK	Elizabeth B. McConkey	Elizabeth B. McConkey	1981	187
117	19 5/8	19 7/8	14	14 2/8	5	5	29 4/8	26 4/8	Farewell, AK	Kevin G. Meyer	Kevin G. Meyer	1982	187
117	19	18 4/8	13 6/8	14	6	6	28 4/8	19 6/8	Custer Co., SD	William E. Butler	William E. Butler	1986	187
117	19 3/8	19 3/8	14 3/8	14 2/8	4 6/8	4 6/8	27 6/8	21	Delta Junction, AK	Rodney D. Bradford	Rodney D. Bradford	1994	187
116 6/8	16 2/8	15 4/8	14 7/8	14 6/8	6 5/8	6 3/8	32 7/8	38 1/8	Raymond Ranch, AZ	Unknown	Jack Brooks	1954	196
116 6/8	16 3/8	15 7/8	13 6/8	13 7/8	7	7 6/8	28	24	Custer Co., SD	Merle G. Smith	Merle G. Smith	1974	196
116 6/8	19 4/8	19 4/8	14 3/8	14 2/8	4 5/8	4 4/8	29 5/8	24 6/8	Coconino Co., AZ	Stanley W. Gaines	Stanley W. Gaines	1977	196
116 6/8	19 1/8	18 5/8	14 3/8	14 1/8	5	5 6/8	30 5/8	25	Post River, AK	Elizabeth A. Bassney	Elizabeth A. Bassney	1990	196
116 6/8	17 5/8	17 7/8	13 2/8	13 2/8	6 2/8	5 5/8	29 4/8	20 5/8	Garfield Co., UT	Chris S. Eggli	Chris S. Eggli	1990	196
116 4/8	21	20 5/8	12 2/8	13 1/8	5 5/8	5 7/8	29 2/8	17 5/8	Donnelly Dome, AK	F. Glaser & R. Tremblay	Univ. of Alaska	1954	201
116 4/8	16 7/8	16 3/8	15	14 6/8	7	5 7/8	28	22	Gillette, WY	D.C. Basolo, Jr.	D.C. Basolo, Jr.	1963	201
116 4/8	18 4/8	18 1/8	14	13 6/8	6 3/8	5 6/8	27 4/8	19 3/8	Pink Mt., BC	Jerry E. Mason	Jerry E. Mason	1992	201
116 2/8	18	18 2/8	15	14 5/8	4 6/8	4 7/8	30 4/8	26 6/8	Alberta	Casper Whitney	B&C National Collection	1907	204
116 2/8	20 3/8	20 5/8	13 4/8	14 1/8	4 5/8	4 6/8	30 3/8	23 4/8	Osage Co., OK	Harold A. Yocum	Harold A. Yocum	1943	204
116 2/8	17 1/8	17 3/8	17	16 6/8	4 7/8	5	25 6/8	18 1/8	Slave River, NT	Jim Wellman	Jim Wellman	1960	204
116 2/8	18 4/8	20	14 2/8	14 3/8	5	5 2/8	23 2/8	23 2/8	Delta Junction, AK	Alma Eades	Alma Eades	1963	204

Score	Length of Horn R	L	Circ. of Base R	L	Circ. at Third Quarter R	L	Greatest Spread	Tip to Tip Spread	Locality	Hunter	Owner	Date Killed	Rank
116 2/8	17 4/8	17 3/8	14 4/8	14 4/8	5 3/8	6 4/8	33	28 5/8	Hook Lake, NT	Jerry Bick	Jerry Bick	1970	204
116 2/8	16 5/8	16 4/8	14 3/8	14 4/8	6 2/8	6 2/8	25 3/8	17	Hook Lake, NT	Jens K. Touborg	Jens K. Touborg	1972	204
116 2/8	19 6/8	18 4/8	14 3/8	14 4/8	5 2/8	4 4/8	28 7/8	20 2/8	Custer Co., SD	James B. Wade	James B. Wade	1976	204
116 2/8	19 4/8	19 3/8	13 3/8	13 6/8	5 1/8	4 7/8	27 3/8	18 5/8	Garfield Co., UT	Jed D. Topham	Jed D. Topham	1989	204
116 2/8	18 2/8	19 4/8	13 2/8	13	6 4/8	6	29 4/8	20 4/8	Custer Co., SD	Gene C. Lasch	Gene C. Lasch	1995	204
116	15	15 4/8	15 5/8	15 4/8	6 5/8	6 4/8	27 4/8	20 6/8	Gillette, WY	D.C. Basolo, Jr.	D.C. Basolo, Jr.	1962	213
116	17 2/8	18	14 6/8	14 7/8	5 5/8	5 6/8	30 4/8	24 6/8	Copper River, AK	Tony Oney	Tony Oney	1964	213
116	17 5/8	18 1/8	14 2/8	14 6/8	5 4/8	5 3/8	30 1/8	23 7/8	Coconino Co., AZ	John Renkema, Jr.	John Renkema, Jr.	1977	213
116	19 2/8	19 2/8	14 3/8	14 3/8	5 1/8	4 6/8	27 1/8	19 1/8	Garfield Co., UT	Gary B. Brosig	Gary B. Brosig	1995	213
115 6/8	18 5/8	18 2/8	14	14	5 4/8	6	33	25	Big Delta, AK	Barbara A. Nagengast	Barbara A. Nagengast	1963	217
115 6/8	15 3/8	17	14 3/8	14 6/8	6 4/8	6	25 5/8	21	Park Co., MT	Hilary J. Benbenek	Hilary J. Benbenek	1989	217
115 6/8	16 7/8	16 6/8	13 6/8	13 4/8	7 7/8	7 2/8	31 2/8	25	Custer Co., SD	C.J. Fuller	C.J. Fuller	1991	217
115 4/8	22 5/8	20 5/8	14	14 3/8	4 3/8	3 7/8	31	23 6/8	Nickolai Village, AK	Picked Up	Robert D. Jones	1994	221
115 4/8	17 4/8	18	14 6/8	14	4 7/8	5 1/8	28 3/8	20 4/8	Sanders Co., MT	Glenn W. Slade, Jr.	Glenn W. Slade, Jr.	1961	221
115 4/8	19 4/8	19 7/8	14	13 7/8	4 6/8	5 1/8	0	0	Delta Junction, AK	W.S. Jarusiewicz	W.S. Jarusiewicz	1963	221
115 4/8	19 1/8	19	14	13 4/8	5	5	27 1/8	15 4/8	Hook Lake, NT	Robert C. Jones	Robert C. Jones	1974	221
115 4/8	19 4/8	20	13 2/8	13 4/8	5 2/8	5 5/8	29 6/8	22 6/8	Chitina River, AK	Ronald A. Sturgeon	Ronald A. Sturgeon	1979	221
115 4/8	17 7/8	17 4/8	14 1/8	13 4/8	5 7/8	5 7/8	29 3/8	24 1/8	Garfield Co., UT	Roger Stewart	Roger Stewart	1984	221
115 4/8	19 6/8	19 4/8	13 4/8	13 7/8	5	5 1/8	32 1/8	25 7/8	Gerstle River, AK	Robert F. Wiese	Robert F. Wiese	1987	221
115 4/8	19 1/8	20 2/8	13 7/8	13 7/8	4 7/8	5 3/8	29 4/8	20	Gerstle River, AK	Frank H. Talerico	Frank H. Talerico	1990	221
115 4/8	16	16 4/8	15 3/8	15 3/8	5 3/8	5 2/8	27 4/8	24	Garfield Co., UT	Kirk S. Jessop	Kirk S. Jessop	1992	221
115 4/8	18 2/8	18 6/8	14 2/8	14 2/8	4 2/8	5 4/8	28 5/8	24	Delta Junction, AK	Barbara G. Rekowski	Barbara G. Rekowski	1992	221
115 4/8	19 4/8	19 5/8	13 7/8	14	5	5 1/8	31	22 4/8	Pink Mt., BC	Jim Popil	Jim Popil	1996	221
115 2/8	16 2/8	17 2/8	13 6/8	14	6 7/8	7 2/8	28 2/8	23 2/8	Black Hills, SD	Unknown	John H. Brandt	1969	231
115 2/8	18 2/8	19 1/8	15 2/8	14 7/8	4 3/8	5 6/8	28 6/8	21	Custer Co., SD	J.P. Moon, Jr.	J.P. Moon, Jr.	1983	231
115 2/8	17	17 4/8	14	14	5 4/8	5 4/8	28 4/8	24 1/8	Garfield Co., UT	Marsha Nickle	Marsha Nickle	1986	231
115	17 4/8	18 3/8	13 6/8	14 3/8	5 3/8	4 7/8	28 2/8	18 1/8	Fort Smith, NT	Jules R. Ashlock	Jules R. Ashlock	1973	234
115	19 2/8	16 6/8	15	15	5 4/8	6 2/8	29 3/8	27 6/8	Custer Co., SD	Rodger E. Warwick	Rodger E. Warwick	1982	234
115	16	18 6/8	14 2/8	14	5 6/8	5 3/8	30 3/8	25 6/8	Custer Co., SD	August Benz, Jr.	August Benz, Jr.	1983	234
115	18 1/8	17 4/8	12 4/8	14 4/8	5 1/8	5	26	18	Custer Co., UT	LaMar K. Cox	LaMar K. Cox	1985	234
115	18 2/8	19 2/8	13 4/8	13 4/8	7 2/8	6	30	23 2/8	Custer Co., SD	Picked Up	Oscar P. Barkhurst	1987	234
115	18 2/8	18 5/8	13 2/8	13 3/8	5	5 6/8	27 3/8	18 6/8	Davis Co., UT	Willie T. Southern	Willie T. Southern	1990	234
115	17 3/8	17	13 2/8	13 1/8	7 2/8	7 3/8	26 4/8	26 1/8	Park Co., MT	Picked Up	Joanne L. Flesch	1992	234
115	17	17 6/8	13 5/8	13 6/8	5 2/8	5	27 6/8	24 4/8	Garfield Co., UT	Michael D. Vincent	Michael D. Vincent	1993	234
135*	23	24 4/8	14 1/8	14 4/8	6	7	31 3/8	20	Park Co., MT	Picked Up	William H. Hoppe	1997	
129 6/8*	18 6/8	19	15	15	8	7 7/8	29 6/8	22 4/8	Custer Co., SD	Terry E. Wink	Terry E. Wink	1992	
127 6/8*	19	19	16 2/8	16 4/8	5 6/8	5 6/8	30	22 5/8	Falaise Lake, NT	Brian R. Edmondson	Brian R. Edmondson	1992	

* Final score is subject to revision by additional verifying measurements.

CATEGORY
BISON

SCORE
119-4/8

HUNTER
PAUL L.C. SNIDER

LOCATION
CUSTER CO., SD

DATE OF KILL
AUGUST 1992

CATEGORY
BISON

SCORE
118-2/8

HUNTER
ROBERT D. JONES

LOCATION
CUSTER CO., SD

DATE OF KILL
JANUARY 1995

CATEGORY
BISON

SCORE
128-6/8

HUNTER
RICK E. MATZICK

LOCATION
CUSTER CO., SD

DATE OF KILL
DECEMBER 1996

B&C HISTORY

A. PHIMISTER PROCTOR
1860-1950

Generally considered to be one of the nation's greatest sculptor's, he worked in bronze and specialized in horses, cowboys, Indians, and wildlife. He first came to prominence at the Columbian Exposition in Chicago in 1893. His work appears throughout the U.S.; in Chicago, New York City, Washington, D.C., Kansas City and Denver. His art was on display at the Paris Exposition in 1900, for which he earned his first "Gold Medal" and membership in the National Academy. He contributed to the design of the Boone and Crockett Club "medallion" that is awarded for high achievement in hunting, conservation and service to the Club, and serves as the Club's logo. ∎

Fate smiled on E.C. Haase on the morning of September 15, 1949. A World's Record mountain goat (*Oreamnos americanus*) was the first mountain goat this hunter encountered upon his initial climb up the sheer slopes of the Babine Mountains.

Having packed out from Smithers, British Columbia, Haase and his guide, Allen Fletcher, were hunting out of their newly established camp. As they made their way over the precipitous hunting grounds, they spotted a huge solitary billy at about 300 yards.

It is very difficult to identify the age or even sex of a goat unless a close stalk is made. A good, experienced guide can usually tell the sex of a goat, but not from the length of the horn. A male's horns tend to be thicker at the base with a more even curve than those of a nanny. More significantly, billies have a gland, posterior to the base of each horn, that is visible from some angles.

Unlike other big game that have to keep their senses keen, a mountain goat does not usually dart instantly when it senses danger. However, this one disappeared into its lofty realm before a shot could be fired. The Rocky Mountain goat is a climbing machine built with short stout legs that maintain their balance upon the crags. When they saw the mountain goat again, a few minutes later, the range had stretched to nearly 400 yards, with no way to get closer.

The hunters knew that their lives depended on not making a misstep as they studied the position of the white animal. Haase, shooting prone with a .30-06, killed the goat with his third shot, and although it fell off the ledge and rolled down the mountain for several hundred feet, it lodged in a snowbank with its horns undamaged.

With a long-standing World's Record score of 56-6/8, this trophy will most likely continue to be admired well into the next century by visitors viewing the National Collection of Heads and Horns in the Buffalo Bill Historical Center, Cody, Wyoming. Haase willed the trophy to the Boone and Crockett Club's National Collection of Heads and Horns on his deathbed. ∎

TROPHY INFO

RANK
World's Record

SCORE
56 6/8

LOCATION
Babine Mts., BC

HUNTER
E.C. Haase

OWNER
B&C Natl. Collection

DATE KILLED
1949

Photograph from B&C Archives

ROCKY MOUNTAIN GOAT
WORLD'S RECORD SCORECHART

Records of
North American
Big Game

250 Station Drive
Missoula, MT 59801
(406) 542-1888

BOONE AND CROCKETT CLUB®
OFFICIAL SCORING SYSTEM FOR NORTH AMERICAN BIG GAME TROPHIES
ROCKY MOUNTAIN GOAT

MINIMUM SCORES
AWARDS ALL-TIME
47   50

All measurements must be made with a 1/4-inch wide flexible steel tape to the nearest one-eighth of an inch. Wherever it is necessary to change direction of measurement, mark a control point and swing tape at this point. Enter fractional figures in eighths, without reduction. Official measurements cannot be taken until horns have air dried for at least 60 days after the animal was killed.

A. Greatest Spread is measured between perpendiculars at a right angle to the center line of the skull.

B. Tip to Tip spread is measured between tips of the horns.

C. Length of Horn is measured from the lowest point in front over outer curve to a point in line with tip.

D-1. Circumference of Base is measured at a right angle to axis of horn. Do not follow irregular edge of horn; the line of measurement must be entirely on horn material.

D-2-3-4. Divide measurement C of longer horn by four. Starting at base, mark **both** horns at these quarters (even though the other horn is shorter) and measure circumferences at these marks, with measurements taken at right angles to horn axis.

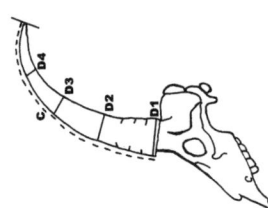

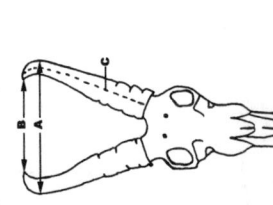

SEE OTHER SIDE FOR INSTRUCTIONS		COLUMN 1	COLUMN 2	COLUMN 3
		Right Horn	Left Horn	Difference
A. Greatest Spread	9 2/8			
B. Tip to Tip Spread	9			
C. Length of Horn		12	12	0
D-1. Circumference of Base		6 4/8	6 4/8	0
D-2. Circumference at First Quarter		4 7/8	4 6/8	1/8
D-3. Circumference at Second Quarter		3 2/8	3 1/8	1/8
D-4. Circumference at Third Quarter		2	2	0
	TOTALS	28 5/8	28 3/8	2/8

ADD	Column 1	28 5/8
	Column 2	28 3/8
	Subtotal	57
SUBTRACT Column 3		2/8
FINAL SCORE		56 6/8

Exact Locality Where Killed: **Babine Mountains, BC**

Date Killed: **1949**   Hunter: **E.C. Haase**

Owner: **B&C National Collection**

Owner's Address:

Guide's Name and Address:

Remarks: (Mention Any Abnormalities or Unique Qualities)

I, __**Grancel Fitz**__
     PRINT NAME
, certify that I have measured this trophy on __**01/28/1950**__
                                                         MM/DD/YYYY

at **American Museum of Natural History** _____ **New York** _____ **NY**
        STREET ADDRESS   CITY   STATE/PROVINCE

and that these measurements and data are, to the best of my knowledge and belief, made in accordance with the instructions given.

Witness: __**Samuel B. Webb**__   Signature: __**Grancel Fitz**__   I.D. Number _____
                                                      B&C OFFICIAL MEASURER

609

ROCKY MOUNTAIN GOAT

Oreamnos americanus americanus and related subspecies

MINIMUM SCORE 50

Score	Length of Horn R	L	Circumference of Base R	L	Circumference at Third Quarter R	L	Greatest Spread	Tip tp Tip Spread	Locality	Hunter	Owner	Date Killed	Rank
56 6/8	12	12	6 4/8	6 4/8	2	2	9 2/8	9	Babine Mts., BC	E.C. Haase	B&C National Collection	1949	1
56 2/8	11 5/8	11 5/8	5 5/8	5 5/8	2 1/8	2 1/8	7 2/8	6 4/8	Helm Bay, AK	W.H. Jackson	B&C National Collection	1933	2
56 2/8	11 3/8	11 3/8	6 3/8	6 4/8	2 1/8	2	8 6/8	8 3/8	Hedley, BC	Picked Up	Robert Kitto	1969	2
56	10 4/8	10 6/8	6 1/8	6	2 5/8	2 6/8	6 7/8	6 4/8	Kenai Pen., AK	Peter W. Bading	Peter W. Bading	1963	4
55 6/8	10 5/8	10 4/8	6 1/8	6 1/8	2 2/8	2 1/8	7 6/8	6 3/8	Blunt Mt., BC	Picked Up	Jack Adams	1970	5
55 2/8	10 6/8	11	6 2/8	6 3/8	2	2 1/8	7 6/8	7 2/8	Oliver Creek, BC	Patrick P. Moleski	Patrick P. Moleski	1994	6
55	11 7/8	11 7/8	5 4/8	5 3/8	2	2	8 3/8	6 4/8	Cleveland Pen., AK	Elmer W. Copstead	Jonas Bros. of Seattle	1939	7
55	12 1/8	12 1/8	5 2/8	5 1/8	2 2/8	2	7 7/8	5 5/8	Alex. Archipelago, AK	James Wilson	James Wilson	1969	7
55	11 4/8	11 2/8	6 2/8	6 2/8	2	2	7	5 5/8	Cleveland Pen., AK	David K. Mueller	David K. Mueller	1997	7
54 6/8	10 5/8	11 3/8	6 2/8	6 2/8	1 7/8	1 7/8	8 3/8	7 5/8	Coquihalla Mts., BC	Fred D. Fouty	Fred D. Fouty	1959	10
54 6/8	10 7/8	11 2/8	6	6	2 3/8	2 3/8	7 5/8	6 5/8	Telkwa Range, BC	Mrs. V. Goudie	Mrs. V. Goudie	1964	10
54 6/8	11 3/8	11 3/8	5 6/8	5 5/8	2	2	7 6/8	5 5/8	Reflection Lake, AK	Lue Wilson, Jr.	Lue Wilson, Jr.	1979	10
54 6/8	11 3/8	11 2/8	5 7/8	5 7/8	2	2	8 1/8	7 7/8	Chupaka Mts., BC	Dennis F. Gaines	Dennis F. Gaines	1991	10
54 6/8	11 3/8	11 2/8	6 2/8	6 1/8	1 7/8	1 7/8	7 6/8	6 3/8	Bowser Lake, BC	Perley E. Holmes	Perley E. Holmes	1993	10
54 2/8	11	11	6 3/8	6 3/8	1 6/8	1 7/8	10 1/8	10	Fairmont Range, BC	Ira McLemore	Ira McLemore	1947	15
54 2/8	11 2/8	11 4/8	6	5 7/8	1 7/8	1 7/8	10	9 3/8	Hastings Arm, BC	Rupert Maier	Rupert Maier	1963	15
54 2/8	10 3/8	10 4/8	6	5 7/8	2 2/8	2 2/8	8 2/8	7 4/8	Cassiar Mts., BC	Richard J. Wristen	Richard J. Wristen	1978	15
54 2/8	11	10 6/8	6 2/8	6 2/8	2	2	9 6/8	9 4/8	Cassiar Mts., BC	Raymond M. Stenger	Raymond M. Stenger	1979	15
54 2/8	10 5/8	10 5/8	6 2/8	6 2/8	2 1/8	2 1/8	7 5/8	6 7/8	Mt. Meehaus, BC	Denis J. Chagnon	Denis J. Chagnon	1989	15
54 2/8	11 6/8	12	5 4/8	5 4/8	1 7/8	1 7/8	7 2/8	5 2/8	Yes Bay, AK	Wally L. Grover	Wally L. Grover	1991	15
54	11 2/8	11 1/8	6 2/8	6 2/8	2	2	9 2/8	9 2/8	Bow Summit, AB	Native American	N.K. Luxton	1907	21
54	11	11	6 1/8	6 1/8	2	2	8 1/8	8 1/8	Terminus Mt., BC	Herb Klein	Herb Klein	1965	21
54	10 7/8	10 6/8	6	6 1/8	2 1/8	2 1/8	9 1/8	8 5/8	Sicintine Range, BC	Thomas R. VanEvery	Thomas R. VanEvery	1994	21
53 6/8	11 1/8	11 2/8	5 7/8	5 7/8	1 7/8	1 7/8	9 4/8	8 4/8	Telegraph Creek, BC	V.D.E. Smith	V.D.E. Smith	1954	24
53 6/8	10 7/8	10 7/8	6	6	1 7/8	1 7/8	7 6/8	6 6/8	Tumeka Lake, BC	Robert H. Edwards	Robert H. Edwards	1972	24
53 6/8	10 3/8	10 3/8	5 7/8	5 7/8	2 1/8	2 1/8	7 7/8	7 5/8	Elko Co., NV	Robert D. Kennedy	Robert D. Kennedy	1978	24
53 6/8	10 6/8	10 6/8	6	6	2	2	8 6/8	8	Sheslay River, BC	Dan Stobbe	Dan Stobbe	1987	24
53 6/8	10 4/8	10 6/8	6	6	2	2	8 3/8	8 2/8	Telegraph Creek, BC	Steven M. Gross	Steven M. Gross	1991	24
53 6/8	10 6/8	10 5/8	6	6	2	2	7 4/8	6 7/8	Stikine River, BC	John Creyke	John Creyke	1926	24
53 4/8	11 4/8	11 2/8	5 7/8	5 7/8	1 7/8	1 7/8	9 2/8	8 7/8	Coldstream Creek, BC	R.J. Pop	Herb Klein	1952	29
53 4/8	10 6/8	11	6	6	1 7/8	1 7/8	8 1/8	7 4/8	Kitimat, BC	Fred Hahn	Fred Hahn	1966	29
53 4/8	11 4/8	9 5/8	5 6/8	6 6/8	2	2 3/8	7	6	Bella Coola, BC	Darryl Hodson	Darryl Hodson	1966	29
53 4/8	11 4/8	11 3/8	5 5/8	5 5/8	2	2	9 2/8	8 7/8	Cassiar Mts., BC	William Rohlfs	William Rohlfs	1971	29
53 4/8	10 6/8	10 3/8	6 2/8	6 2/8	2	2	7	5 2/8	Mt. Horetzky, BC	Jackie O. Arnold	Jackie O. Arnold	1980	29
53 4/8	10 4/8	10 6/8	6 1/8	6 1/8	2	2	8 5/8	8 1/8	Beggerlay Creek, BC	Joe Hamelink	Joe Hamelink	1986	29
53 4/8	10 5/8	10 5/8	6 1/8	6 1/8	2	2	9 4/8	8 6/8	Sheslay River, BC	Gregory A. Hurst	Gregory A. Hurst	1996	29
53 2/8	11 1/8	11 1/8	5 6/8	5 6/8	2	2	8 7/8	7 7/8	Cassiar Mts., BC	W. Reuen Fisher	W. Reuen Fisher	1945	37
53 2/8	10 6/8	11	5 7/8	5 7/8	2	2	6 6/8	5 6/8	Ketchikan, AK	Charles E. Slajer	Charles E. Slajer	1966	37

Score	Length R	Length L	Circ. Base R	Circ. Base L	Circ. 3rd Qtr. R	Circ. 3rd Qtr. L	Greatest Spread	Tip to Tip	Locality	Hunter	Owner	Date Killed	Rank
53 2/8	10 7/8	11 1/8	6 3/8	6 3/8	1 6/8	1 7/8	7 7/8	7 2/8	Mt. Findlay, BC	Glenn Welsh	Glenn Welsh	1971	37
53 2/8	11 2/8	11 5/8	5 4/8	5 4/8	1 7/8	2	7	6 1/8	Halfmoon Lake, AK	Robert A. Hewitt	Robert A. Hewitt	1980	37
53 2/8	10 3/8	10 3/8	5 7/8	6	2 1/8	2 1/8	7 6/8	7 2/8	Skeena River, BC	Robin B. Freeman	Robin B. Freeman	1985	37
53 2/8	10 1/8	10	5 6/8	5 6/8	2 1/8	2 1/8	8 4/8	8	Skagway, AK	Charles R. Heath	Charles R. Heath	1965	37
53 2/8	10 7/8	10 6/8	5 7/8	5 7/8	1 7/8	1 7/8	6 5/8	6 2/8	Skeena-Copper Rivers, BC	John A. Paetkau	John W. Kroeker	1967	37
53	9 7/8	10	6 2/8	6 2/8	2	2	6	7 4/8	James Creek, BC	Manfred Beier	Manfred Beier	1968	42
53	11 2/8	10 5/8	6	6	2 1/8	2 1/8	8 1/8	8 7/8	Cassiar Mts., BC	Jack Thorndike	Jack Thorndike	1970	42
53	10 4/8	10 4/8	6 1/8	6 1/8	2	2	8 7/8	4 7/8	Aaron Mt., AK	John Sturgeon	John Sturgeon	1973	42
53	11	11	6	6	2	2	6 5/8	8 1/8	Homer, AK	Robert W. Hertz, Jr.	Robert W. Hertz, Jr.	1974	42
53	10 4/8	10 7/8	6	6	2	2	8 2/8	9 3/8	Sheslay Mt., BC	Wallace E. Sills	Wallace E. Sills	1985	42
53	10 7/8	10 7/8	5 7/8	5 7/8	1 7/8	2	9 3/8	9 3/8	Tagish Lake, BC	Larry W. White	Larry W. White	1987	42
53	11	10 7/8	5 4/8	5 4/8	2	2	8 6/8	8 5/8	Toms Creek, BC	Tommy B. Lee, Jr.	Tommy B. Lee, Jr.	1988	42
53	10 7/8	11 2/8	5 7/8	5 7/8	2	2	8 1/8	7 5/8	Morice River, BC	Elizabeth D. Saunders	Rob Saunders	1989	42
53	11	10 6/8	6	6	1 7/8	2	7 1/8	6 2/8	Skeena River, BC	Russil Tanner	Russil Tanner	1990	42
53	10 4/8	10 7/8	5 5/8	5 5/8	1 7/8	2	8	7 4/8	Nahlin River, BC	James T. Kruger	James T. Kruger	1992	42
53	11 4/8	11	6	6	2	2	8 5/8	7 3/8	Tahltan River, BC	Terry Schulist	Terry Schulist	1997	42
53	11	11 4/8	6	6	2	2	7 4/8	8 2/8	Idaho Co., ID	Farrell M. Trenary	Farrell M. Trenary	1933	42
53	11 4/8	11	5 7/8	5 7/8	2	2	8 3/8	7 4/8	Kootenay, BC	A.C. Gilbert	Jules V. Lane	1935	42
52 6/8	11 4/8	11 4/8	5 1/8	5 1/8	1 6/8	1 7/8	7 5/8	5 6/8	Whatcom Co., WA	Arie Vanderhoek, Jr.	Arie Vanderhoek, Jr.	1966	55
52 6/8	10 1/8	10 1/8	5 7/8	5 7/8	2 3/8	2 1/8	6 5/8	8 1/8	Cold Fish Lake, BC	Stanley W. Glasscock	Stanley W. Glasscock	1967	55
52 6/8	10 2/8	10 5/8	6	6	2 1/8	2 1/8	8 3/8	5 5/8	Ashnola Valley, BC	Brian Chipperfield	Brian Chipperfield	1968	55
52 6/8	11 1/8	11 1/8	5 7/8	5 7/8	2	2	6 3/8	7	Vernon, BC	Robert B. Procter	Robert B. Procter	1968	55
52 6/8	10 3/8	10 3/8	6 3/8	6 3/8	2	2	7 5/8	7 4/8	Terrace, BC	R.P. Kolterman	R.P. Kolterman	1971	55
52 6/8	10 4/8	10 2/8	5 6/8	5 6/8	2	2	8 2/8	7 6/8	Cassiar Mts., BC	H. Scott Whyel	H. Scott Whyel	1981	55
52 6/8	10 5/8	10 5/8	6	6	1 7/8	2	7 6/8	6	Foch Lake, BC	A.S. Griffin, Jr.	A.S. Griffin, Jr.	1985	55
52 6/8	10 4/8	10 4/8	5 5/8	5 5/8	2 1/8	2 1/8	7 1/8	6 4/8	Reflection Lake, AK	Timothy F. McGinn	Timothy F. McGinn	1985	55
52 6/8	11 3/8	11 2/8	5 7/8	5 7/8	1 6/8	1 7/8	8 2/8	7 3/8	Park Co., CO	Lyle K. Willmarth	Lyle K. Willmarth	1988	55
52 6/8	10 5/8	10 5/8	5 7/8	5 7/8	2 1/8	2 1/8	6 7/8	6 7/8	Inklin River, BC	Anthony C. Ruggeri	Anthony C. Ruggeri	1993	55
52 6/8	10	10 5/8	5 6/8	5 6/8	2	2	8 2/8	7 3/8	Skeena River, BC	Michael Moleski	Michael Moleski	1996	55
52 4/8	10 6/8	10 6/8	5 7/8	5 7/8	2 1/8	2 1/8	7 6/8	7 2/8	Okanogan Co., WA	Richard Shatto	Richard Shatto	1962	68
52 4/8	11	11	5 7/8	5 7/8	2	2	7 1/8	6	Whatcom Co., WA	John W. Bullene	John W. Bullene	1965	68
52 4/8	10 1/8	10 1/8	6	6	2	2	6 7/8	6 6/8	Colt Lake, BC	George P. Jackson, Jr.	George P. Jackson, Jr.	1965	68
52 4/8	10 6/8	10 6/8	5 7/8	5 7/8	2	2	9 1/8	8 6/8	Terminus Mt., BC	Herb Klein	Herb Klein	1965	68
52 4/8	11	11	6	6	2	2	7 6/8	2	Sheep Creek, WA	R.C. Dukart	R.C. Dukart	1967	68
52 4/8	10	10 2/8	5 7/8	5 7/8	2	2	6	10	Cassiar, BC	Otto Machek	Otto Machek	1968	68
52 4/8	10 7/8	10 6/8	6	6	2 1/8	2 1/8	5 7/8	7 7/8	Spectrum Range, BC	Kelly Good	Kelly Good	1973	68
52 4/8	10 1/8	10 1/8	5 6/8	5 6/8	2 1/8	2 1/8	8 2/8	7 3/8	Rock Island Lake, BC	Joe E. Coleman	Joe E. Coleman	1976	68
52 4/8	10 1/8	10 2/8	5 3/8	5 3/8	2 1/8	2 1/8	8 2/8	7 5/8	Skeena Mts., BC	Hardy Murr	Hardy Murr	1977	68
52 4/8	10 6/8	10 6/8	6	6	1 6/8	1 7/8	8 1/8	7 5/8	Taku River, BC	Fritz Stork	Fritz Stork	1985	68
52 4/8	10	10	5 7/8	5 7/8	1 7/8	1 6/8	7 3/8	6 6/8	Granite Basin Lake, AK	Scott D. Hansen	Scott D. Hansen	1988	68
52 4/8	9 6/8	9 7/8	6	6	2	2	10 1/8	10	Sicintine Lake, BC	Albert C. Nassan	Albert C. Nassan	1992	68
52 4/8	10 6/8	10 7/8	5 6/8	5 6/8	2	2	7 2/8	7 1/8	Keremeos, BC	Jerrell Coburn	Jerrell Coburn	1994	68
52 2/8	11	11 3/8	6	6	2	2	8 3/8	8	Swan Lake, BC	A.C. Gilbert	The Old State House	1938	81
52 2/8	10 3/8	10 3/8	6	6	2	2	7 1/8	6	Cassiar, BC	Frank H. Schramm	Frank H. Schramm	1947	81
52 2/8	10 1/8	10 1/8	5 6/8	5 6/8	2	2	10 3/8	7 6/8	Hastings Arm, BC	Ernest Dietschi	Ernest Dietschi	1963	81
52 2/8	10 4/8	10 2/8	5 7/8	5 7/8	2	2	8 2/8	8 2/8	Copper River, AK	Fritz Maier	Fritz Maier	1964	81
52 2/8	10 3/8	10 3/8	5 7/8	5 7/8	1 7/8	1 7/8	6 5/8	5 3/8	Bella Bella, BC	William B. Chivers	William B. Chivers	1965	81

ROCKY MOUNTAIN GOAT

Oreamnos americanus americanus and related subspecies

Score	Length of Horn R	Length of Horn L	Circumference of Base R	Circumference of Base L	Circumference at Third Quarter R	Circumference at Third Quarter L	Greatest Spread	Tip to Tip Spread	Locality	Hunter	Owner	Date Killed	Rank
52 2/8	10 7/8	10 7/8	5 2/8	5 2/8	1 7/8	1 7/8	8	7 5/8	Boca De Quadra, AK	Dan Hook	Dan Hook	1968	81
52 2/8	11	11	5 4/8	5 5/8	2	1 7/8	6 7/8	7 1/8	Boca De Quadra, AK	Doug Vann	Doug Vann	1968	81
52 2/8	10 6/8	10 6/8	5 6/8	5 6/8	2	1 7/8	8 5/8	8	Whatcom Co., WA	Al Hershey	Al Hershey	1969	81
52 2/8	10 5/8	10 5/8	5 7/8	5 7/8	2	2	8 2/8	7 7/8	Seward, AK	Donald R. Platt, Sr.	Donald R. Platt, Sr.	1969	81
52 2/8	11	11 1/8	6 1/8	6	1 6/8	1 6/8	9 3/8	8 3/8	Cassiar Mts., BC	Peter Fenchak	Peter Fenchak	1970	81
52 2/8	10 6/8	10 4/8	6 1/8	6	1 7/8	1 6/8	6 7/8	5 2/8	Mt. Cronin, BC	Vinko Strgar	Vinko Strgar	1972	81
52 2/8	10 6/8	10 5/8	5 6/8	5 6/8	1 7/8	1 7/8	8 2/8	7 5/8	Chelan Co., WA	John W. Lane	John W. Lane	1973	81
52 2/8	10	10	5 7/8	6	1 7/8	1 7/8	9 4/8	8 6/8	Cold Fish Lake, BC	Larry Bonetti	Larry Bonetti	1975	81
52 2/8	10 1/8	10 2/8	5 4/8	5 4/8	1 5/8	1 6/8	8 4/8	8 3/8	Kutcho Creek, BC	J.C. Page	J.C. Page	1975	81
52 2/8	10 1/8	10 1/8	5 6/8	6 1/8	2	1 7/8	6 7/8	6 4/8	Chelan Co., WA	Thomas A. Lovas	Thomas A. Lovas	1976	81
52 2/8	10 2/8	10 4/8	6	6 1/8	1 6/8	1 7/8	7	6 2/8	Chelan Co., WA	Nat Steele	Nat Steele	1980	81
52 2/8	10 4/8	10 4/8	5 6/8	5 6/8	2	2	7 3/8	7	Lewis & Clark Co., MT	Charles N. Johns	Charles N. Johns	1981	81
52 2/8	10 2/8	10	6 2/8	6 1/8	2	2	7 5/8	7 1/8	Sheslay River, BC	Frank L. Stukel	Frank L. Stukel	1984	81
52 2/8	11 1/8	11 1/8	5 5/8	5 5/8	1 7/8	1 7/8	6 7/8	6	Mt. Meehaus, BC	George A. Angello, Jr.	George A. Angello, Jr.	1988	81
52 2/8	11	10 5/8	5 4/8	5 4/8	1 7/8	1 7/8	9 5/8	9 3/8	Little Oliver Creek, BC	James K. Hansen	James K. Hansen	1988	81
52 2/8	10 5/8	10 6/8	5 6/8	5 6/8	2	2	10	9 7/8	Sheslay River, BC	Steve Parks	Steve Parks	1988	81
52 2/8	10 6/8	10 2/8	5 7/8	5 7/8	2	2	7 5/8	7 1/8	Bradfield Canal, AK	C. Wayne Treadway	C. Wayne Treadway	1988	81
52 2/8	10 2/8	10 2/8	5 4/8	5 4/8	2 1/8	2 1/8	6 7/8	6 2/8	Cassiar Mts., BC	Debbie S. Sanowski	Debbie S. Sanowski	1989	81
52 2/8	10 2/8	10 3/8	5 7/8	5 7/8	1 7/8	1 7/8	7 7/8	6 6/8	Lynn Canal, AK	Charles F. Roy	Charles F. Roy	1990	81
52 2/8	10 4/8	10 2/8	6 1/8	6 1/8	1 6/8	1 6/8	6 5/8	5 7/8	Fife Creek, BC	George M. Klein	George M. Klein	1991	81
52 2/8	10 2/8	10 2/8	5 7/8	5 7/8	1 7/8	1 7/8	6 4/8	6 2/8	Elko Co., NV	Daniel E. Warren	Daniel E. Warren	1994	81
52 2/8	10 1/8	10 1/8	6	6	2	2	7 1/8	6 3/8	Seton Lake, BC	Jerry M. Smith	Jerry M. Smith	1995	81
52 2/8	10 2/8	10 2/8	5 6/8	5 6/8	1 7/8	1 7/8	8 2/8	7 4/8	Resurrection Bay, AK	James L. Kedrowski	James L. Kedrowski	1997	81
52	10 1/8	10 4/8	6 1/8	6 1/8	2	2	8 6/8	8 4/8	Cassiar, BC	Walter R. Peterson	Walter R. Peterson	1937	109
52	10 4/8	10	5 6/8	5 6/8	2	2	9	9	Tweedsmuir Park, BC	Chester G. Moore	Chester G. Moore	1946	109
52	10 3/8	10 3/8	5 4/8	5 4/8	2 1/8	2 1/8	6 7/8	4 5/8	Jumbo Mt., WA	Clyde Lewis	Clyde Lewis	1948	109
52	10 7/8	11	5 4/8	5 4/8	1 7/8	1 7/8	7 4/8	6 7/8	Watson Peak, AK	Harold M. Wright	Harold M. Wright	1957	109
52	10 6/8	10 3/8	5 6/8	5 6/8	2	2	6 7/8	6 2/8	Idaho Co., ID	Charlie T. Knox	Charlie T. Knox	1959	109
52	10 2/8	10 3/8	5 7/8	5 7/8	2	1 7/8	7 6/8	7 5/8	Mission Ridge, BC	B. Naimark	B. Naimark	1960	109
52	10 4/8	11	6	6	2 1/8	2 1/8	8 7/8	8 2/8	Bulkley Range, BC	Ingvar Wickstrom	Ingvar Wickstrom	1960	109
52	10 1/8	10 2/8	5 7/8	5 7/8	1 7/8	1 7/8	7 2/8	6 1/8	Kootenay River, BC	Howard Paish	Howard Paish	1961	109
52	10 3/8	10 2/8	5 7/8	5 7/8	2 1/8	2	7 4/8	7 1/8	Coquihalla, BC	Fred D. Fouty	Fred D. Fouty	1962	109
52	10	10	6	6	2	2	7 3/8	7	Sundial Lake, AK	Arnold W. Johnson	Arnold W. Johnson	1962	109
52	11 4/8	11 3/8	5 3/8	5 3/8	2	2	7	4 5/8	Boca De Quadra, AK	James Todahl	James Todahl	1962	109
52	10 1/8	10 2/8	5 7/8	5 7/8	2	2	9 1/8	7 6/8	Skeena River, BC	R.H. Simonds	R.H. Simonds	1963	109
52	10 5/8	10 6/8	6	6 1/8	1 7/8	1 7/8	7 2/8	6	Kitsumgallum Lake, BC	Manfred Beier	Manfred Beier	1965	109
52	9 7/8	10	5 6/8	5 6/8	2 1/8	2 1/8	8	7 5/8	Hart Mt., BC	Donna Loewenstein	Donna Loewenstein	1965	109
52	10 1/8	10 2/8	5 5/8	5 4/8	2	2	6 3/8	5 4/8	Southgate River, BC	R.T. Ostby	R.T. Ostby	1966	109

Score	Length of Horn	Circumf. of Base R	Circumf. of Base L	Circumf. Third Quarter	Greatest Spread	Tip to Tip Spread	Locality	Owner	By Whom Killed	Date Killed	Rank
52	10 2/8	6 1/8	6 1/8	2	6 1/8	5 3/8	Okanogan Co., WA	E.W. Butler	E.W. Butler	1967	109
52	10 7/8	5 4/8	5 4/8	1 7/8	9 6/8	9 2/8	Auke Bay, AK	Kenneth L. Klawunder	Kenneth L. Klawunder	1968	109
52	9 7/8	5 6/8	5 6/8	2	7 5/8	7	Skagit Co., WA	John C. Casebeer	John C. Casebeer	1970	109
52	10 1/8	6	6 1/8	1 7/8	8 5/8	8	Chelan Co., WA	Robert A. Beckton	Robert A. Beckton	1971	109
52	10 3/8	5 6/8	5 7/8	2 2/8	7	5 7/8	Camp Island Lake, BC	C.N. Hoffman	C.N. Hoffman	1971	109
52	9 4/8	5 7/8	6	2 1/8	8 4/8	7 7/8	Skeena Mts., BC	William F. Jury	William F. Jury	1971	109
52	11	6	6 1/8	1 6/8	7	6 3/8	Kispiox Range, BC	John W. Allen	John W. Allen	1974	109
52	10 1/8	5 6/8	5 6/8	2	7	5 3/8	Elko Co., NV	Les Boni	Les Boni	1978	109
52	10 2/8	6	6 2/8	2 1/8	6 3/8	5 7/8	Whatcom Co., WA	George W. Bowen	George W. Bowen	1978	109
52	10 4/8	6	5 3/8	1 7/8	7 4/8	7 5/8	Mt. Saint Elias, AK	Terry L. Friske	Terry L. Friske	1980	109
52	10 6/8	6 2/8	5 6/8	1 6/8	8 1/8	8 1/8	Horn Cliffs, AK	Jack W. McKernan	Jack W. McKernan	1981	109
52	12 1/8	5 3/8	5 7/8	2	8 1/8	7 4/8	Burnie Lake, BC	Paul R. Levan	Paul R. Levan	1983	109
52	10 2/8	5 6/8	5 6/8	2	7 4/8	7 4/8	Old Tom Creek, BC	Dusty R. Cooper	Dusty R. Cooper	1986	109
52	10 5/8	5 7/8	5 6/8	2 2/8	7	6 3/8	Telegraph Creek, BC	Britt W. Wilson	Britt W. Wilson	1986	109
52	9 7/8	5 6/8	5 6/8	2 1/8	5 3/8	5 2/8	Yes Bay, AK	Roddy Shelton	Roddy Shelton	1987	109
52	10	5 7/8	5 7/8	2	8	7	Shemes River, BC	Russil Tanner	Russil Tanner	1990	109
52	10 2/8	5 4/8	5 4/8	2	7 4/8	6 4/8	Whatcom Co., WA	Gary W. Cunningham	Gary W. Cunningham	1991	109
51 6/8	10 3/8	6 1/8	6 1/8	1 7/8	8 7/8	8 3/8	Telegraph Creek, BC	John S. McCormick, Jr.	John S. McCormick, Jr.	1936	141
51 6/8	10 6/8	5 6/8	5 6/8	2	7 5/8	7 4/8	Mile 402, AK	E.J. Blumenshine	E.J. Blumenshine	1948	141
51 6/8	10 3/8	5 6/8	5 6/8	2	6 3/8	6 2/8	Lake Co., MT	Glenn Conklin	Glenn Conklin	1958	141
51 6/8	10 4/8	5 6/8	5 6/8	2	8 4/8	8 2/8	Wolf Creek, MT	Jim B. Beard	Jim B. Beard	1963	141
51 6/8	11 2/8	5 6/8	5 7/8	1 7/8	7 4/8	6 7/8	Flathead Co., MT	John J. Allmaras	John J. Allmaras	1965	141
51 6/8	10 2/8	5 6/8	5 6/8	2	7 7/8	7	Telegraph Creek, BC	John Caputo, Sr.	John Caputo, Sr.	1965	141
51 6/8	10	5 1/8	5 1/8	1 6/8	9 3/8	9 1/8	Atlin, BC	Bill Slikker	Bill Slikker	1965	141
51 6/8	10 4/8	5 6/8	5 6/8	1 7/8	7 5/8	7 1/8	Kildala River, BC	Lorne Hallman	Lorne Hallman	1966	141
51 6/8	11 5/8	5 7/8	5 6/8	1 7/8	13	13	Cassiar Mts., BC	Bruce N. Spencer	Bruce N. Spencer	1966	141
51 6/8	10 4/8	5 7/8	5 7/8	1 7/8	7 4/8	5 7/8	Copper-Skeena Rivers, BC	Henry Dyck	Henry Dyck	1967	141
51 6/8	10 1/8	6	5 7/8	2	6 6/8	6 6/8	Ecstall River, BC	W.A. Kristmanson	W.A. Kristmanson	1967	141
51 6/8	10	5 6/8	5 6/8	2	6 2/8	6 2/8	The Pinnacles Mt., BC	Michael Bigford	Michael Bigford	1968	141
51 6/8	10 7/8	5 7/8	5 7/8	1 7/8	8 4/8	8 4/8	Telegraph Creek, BC	Basil C. Bradbury	Basil C. Bradbury	1968	141
51 6/8	10 2/8	5 6/8	5 6/8	1 6/8	7	7	Wrangell Mts., AK	John R. Braun	John R. Braun	1968	141
51 6/8	10 1/8	5 6/8	5 6/8	1 6/8	10	9 7/8	Turnagain River, BC	Stephen W. Cook	Stephen W. Cook	1968	141
51 6/8	11 3/8	5 4/8	5 4/8	1 5/8	7 7/8	7 5/8	Clearwater Creek, BC	Frans Fait	Frans Fait	1968	141
51 6/8	10 5/8	6 1/8	6 1/8	1 7/8	9 2/8	8 7/8	Skeena-Exstew Rivers, BC	Roy K. Pysher	Roy K. Pysher	1968	141
51 6/8	10 3/8	6	6	2	6 3/8	7 1/8	Hobo Creek, BC	Ellis D. Skidmore	Ellis D. Skidmore	1969	141
51 6/8	10 3/8	5 5/8	5 5/8	1 7/8	6 6/8	5	Burns Lake, BC	Roderick Martin	Roderick Martin	1970	141
51 6/8	10	5 7/8	5 7/8	2	6 6/8	5 1/8	Tongass Natl. For., AK	James M. Remza	James M. Remza	1970	141
51 6/8	10 7/8	5 5/8	5 5/8	1 7/8	7 2/8	6 3/8	Bradfield River, AK	H.D. Costello	H.D. Costello	1973	141
51 6/8	10 5/8	5 7/8	5 7/8	1 7/8	6	5 2/8	Cleveland Pen., AK	Des F. Hinds	Des F. Hinds	1974	141
51 6/8	10 3/8	5 4/8	5 4/8	1 7/8	6	4 5/8	Snohomish Co., WA	David Brousseau	David Brousseau	1975	141
51 6/8	11	6	6	1 7/8	6 5/8	7	Mt. Allard, BC	Donald G. Oldenburg	Donald G. Oldenburg	1977	141
51 6/8	10 5/8	5 6/8	5 6/8	1 6/8	7 3/8	7 6/8	Ketchikan, AK	William E. Bond	William E. Bond	1978	141
51 6/8	10 3/8	5 4/8	5 4/8	1 7/8	8 6/8	5 4/8	Zymoetz River, BC	Harry McCowan	Harry McCowan	1980	141
51 6/8	10 3/8	5 6/8	5 6/8	2	6 6/8	5 4/8	Mt. Carthew, BC	J.C. Priebe & W.A. Bolles	J.C. Priebe & W.A. Bolles	1980	141
51 6/8	10 1/8	5 7/8	5 7/8	1 6/8	6 5/8	7 2/8	Kaza Lake, BC	Michael L. Ward	Michael L. Ward	1980	141
51 6/8	10 2/8	5 7/8	5 7/8	2	7 7/8	5 5/8	Behm Canal, AK	Michael J. Simon	John M. Mitchell	1981	141
51 6/8	9 7/8	5 4/8	5 4/8	2 2/8	6 4/8	6 4/8	Snohomish Co., WA	John M. Mitchell	Michael J. Simon	1981	141
51 6/8	10 2/8	5 5/8	5 5/8	2 1/8	6 5/8	6	Tyee Lake, AK	Daniel G. Bowden	Daniel G. Bowden	1982	141

ROCKY MOUNTAIN GOAT

Oreamnos americanus americanus and related subspecies

Score	Length of Horn R	L	Circumference of Base R	L	Circumference at Third Quarter R	L	Greatest Spread	Tip tp Tip Spread	Locality	Hunter	Owner	Date Killed	Rank
51 6/8	10 6/8	10 5/8	5 3/8	5 3/8	2	2	7 1/8	6	Leduc Lake, AK	Steve Lepschat	Steve Lepschat	1982	141
51 6/8	10 2/8	10 4/8	5 6/8	5 5/8	2	2 1/8	6 3/8	5 1/8	Lake Rowena, AK	George T. Law	George T. Law	1983	141
51 6/8	9 6/8	9 6/8	5 6/8	5 5/8	2	2	6	4 4/8	Cleveland Pen., AK	Michael L. Ward	Michael L. Ward	1983	141
51 6/8	10 1/8	10 3/8	6	6	1 5/8	1 6/8	7 7/8	7 4/8	Bonneville Co., ID	K. Rands Wiley	K. Rands Wiley	1983	141
51 6/8	10 5/8	10 4/8	5 5/8	5 5/8	1 7/8	1 7/8	7 1/8	6 1/8	Snohomish Co., WA	Edward M. Beitner	Edward M. Beitner	1984	141
51 6/8	10 3/8	10 5/8	6	6 1/8	1 7/8	1 7/8	6 5/8	5 6/8	Whatcom Co., WA	Desmond J Iverson	Desmond J. Iverson	1985	141
51 6/8	10 3/8	10 2/8	5 7/8	5 7/8	1 7/8	1 7/8	7 3/8	7 1/8	Spatsizi Plateau, BC	Gary R. Schneider	Gary R. Schneider	1986	141
51 6/8	10 2/8	10 4/8	5 7/8	6	1 7/8	2	8	6 6/8	McGavin Creek, BC	Charles H. Menzer	Charles H. Menzer	1987	141
51 6/8	10 1/8	10 1/8	5 6/8	5 6/8	2	2	7	6 3/8	Chita Creek, BC	Anthony D. Tindall	Anthony D. Tindall	1989	141
51 6/8	10	9 6/8	5 4/8	5 4/8	2	2	6 6/8	6 2/8	Snohomish Co., WA	Terry L. Wagner	Terry L. Wagner	1990	141
51 6/8	11	10 7/8	5 4/8	5 5/8	1 7/8	1 7/8	7 2/8	6 3/8	Gallatin Co., MT	Todd E. Barry	Todd E. Barry	1994	141
51 6/8	9 6/8	9 5/8	6	6	2	2 1/8	6 7/8	6 2/8	Lillooet, BC	Greg C. Bond	Greg C. Bond	1997	141
51 4/8	11	11 2/8	5 6/8	5 6/8	1 6/8	1 6/8	8 4/8	7 6/8	Kootenay, BC	Herb Klein	Herb Klein	1946	183
51 4/8	11 3/8	11 5/8	5 4/8	5 5/8	1 6/8	1 6/8	7 4/8	7 3/8	Ella River, BC	Lee G. Smith	Walter Ozorowski	1950	183
51 4/8	10 2/8	10 1/8	5 6/8	5 6/8	2	2	6 6/8	5 7/8	Cold Fish Lake, BC	George W. Hooker	George W. Hooker	1956	183
51 4/8	10	10	5 6/8	5 6/8	1 7/8	1 7/8	0	6 7/8	Jarvis Lake, BC	G.F. Juhl	G.F. Juhl	1960	183
51 4/8	10	10	5 7/8	5 7/8	2	2	7	6 2/8	Cassiar, BC	Adolf Doerre	Adolf Doerre	1961	183
51 4/8	10 4/8	10 3/8	5 6/8	5 6/8	1 6/8	1 6/8	9 3/8	9 3/8	Cold Fish Lake, BC	Dan Edwards	Dan Edwards	1961	183
51 4/8	10 3/8	10 3/8	5 6/8	5 6/8	1 7/8	1 7/8	6 3/8	5 7/8	Cleveland Pen., AK	Allen E. Linn	Allen E. Linn	1961	183
51 4/8	10 2/8	10 2/8	5 5/8	5 4/8	1 7/8	1 7/8	6 6/8	6	Boca De Quadra, AK	Charles E. Simmons	Charles E. Simmons	1961	183
51 4/8	10 5/8	10 7/8	5 6/8	5 6/8	1 6/8	1 6/8	7 1/8	6 6/8	Kenai Pen., AK	Alan Olson	Alan Olson	1962	183
51 4/8	9 5/8	9 5/8	5 6/8	5 6/8	1 6/8	1 6/8	7 4/8	6 7/8	Chugach Mts., AK	Donald A. Turcke	Donald A. Turcke	1964	183
51 4/8	10 6/8	10 7/8	5 4/8	5 4/8	1 7/8	1 7/8	8 1/8	7 6/8	Kechika Range, BC	W.C. Dabney, Jr.	W.C. Dabney, Jr.	1965	183
51 4/8	11 1/8	11 3/8	5 3/8	5 3/8	1 7/8	1 7/8	6 3/8	4 1/8	Boca De Quadra, AK	Arthur N. Wilson, Jr.	Arthur N. Wilson, Jr.	1965	183
51 4/8	10 1/8	9 7/8	5 7/8	6 1/8	1 7/8	1 7/8	7 4/8	7 2/8	Sheep Creek, AB	Russell A. Fischer	Russell A. Fischer	1967	183
51 4/8	10 1/8	10 2/8	6	6	2	2	7 4/8	6 5/8	Coast Range, BC	S. Lantenhammer	S. Lantenhammer	1967	183
51 4/8	10 6/8	10 5/8	5 7/8	5 7/8	1 6/8	1 6/8	6 6/8	5 4/8	Clearwater Creek, BC	Richard H. Leedy	Richard H. Leedy	1967	183
51 4/8	9 5/8	9 6/8	6	6	2	2	7 1/8	6 2/8	Toad River, BC	Bill Goosman	Bill Goosman	1970	183
51 4/8	10 3/8	10 3/8	5 6/8	5 6/8	2	2	8	7 4/8	Bowen Lake, AK	Ted A. Dedmon	Ted A. Dedmon	1971	183
51 4/8	10 2/8	10 4/8	5 7/8	5 6/8	2	2	8 4/8	8	Terrace, BC	George A. Shaw	George A. Shaw	1972	183
51 4/8	10 2/8	10 1/8	5 4/8	5 4/8	1 7/8	1 7/8	6 7/8	5 5/8	Chelan Co., WA	Virgil N. Carpenter	Virgil N. Carpenter	1973	183
51 4/8	10 4/8	10 2/8	5 7/8	5 7/8	1 7/8	1 7/8	7 2/8	6 4/8	Ketchikan, AK	Kevin Downey	Kevin Downey	1973	183
51 4/8	11	11	5 6/8	5 6/8	1 7/8	1 7/8	6 2/8	5 5/8	Stikine River, AK	Donald E. Fossen	Donald E. Fossen	1973	183
51 4/8	10 2/8	10 3/8	5 7/8	6	2	2 1/8	7 4/8	7 1/8	Stikine Range, BC	L.A. Candelaria	L.A. Candelaria	1974	183
51 4/8	10 4/8	10 5/8	5 6/8	5 6/8	2	2	8 5/8	8 1/8	Mt. Edziza, BC	A. Coe Frankhauser	A. Coe Frankhauser	1974	183
51 4/8	9 4/8	9 7/8	5 7/8	5 7/8	1 7/8	1 7/8	9 3/8	8 6/8	Pine Lake, BC	Charles H. Duke, Jr.	Charles H. Duke, Jr.	1975	183
51 4/8	10 2/8	10 5/8	5 6/8	5 5/8	2 1/8	2 1/8	8 1/8	7 4/8	Bulkley Mts., BC	Gordon Hannas	Gordon Hannas	1976	183
51 4/8	10 4/8	10 4/8	5 4/8	5 6/8	1 6/8	1 6/8	8 6/8	8 6/8	Kodiak Island, AK	Ron Eller	Ron Eller	1978	183

Score	Length of Horn R	Length of Horn L	Circ. of Base R	Circ. of Base L	Circ. 3rd Quarter R	Circ. 3rd Quarter L	Tip to Tip Spread	Locality			Date	Rank
51 4/8	9 7/8	9 7/8	6	6	2	2	8 1/8	Telegraph Creek, BC	Casey G. Terry	Casey G. Terry	1979	183
51 4/8	9 7/8	9 7/8	5 6/8	5 7/8	2	2	5 1/8	Big Wideen River, BC	Steven D. Skipper	Steven D. Skipper	1980	183
51 4/8	10 2/8	10 4/8	6 1/8	6 1/8	1 7/8	1 7/8	7 5/8	Montana	Unknown	James Fredrick	PR 1981	183
51 4/8	10 1/8	10 1/8	5 6/8	5 6/8	1 7/8	1 7/8	6 5/8	Halfmoon Lake, AK	Kurt W. Kuehl	Kurt W. Kuehl	1982	183
51 4/8	10 3/8	10 1/8	5 6/8	5 7/8	1 7/8	1 7/8	6 2/8	Chouteau Co., MT	Larry W. Lander	Larry W. Lander	1983	183
51 4/8	10 1/8	10 4/8	5 4/8	5 4/8	2 1/8	2 1/8	7 5/8	Little Oliver Creek, BC	JoAnn F. Flemming	JoAnn F. Flemming	1985	183
51 4/8	10 7/8	10 4/8	5 4/8	5 4/8	1 7/8	1 7/8	7 1/8	Snohomish Co., WA	Theodore H. Kiser	Theodore H. Kiser	1985	183
51 4/8	10 4/8	10 1/8	5 7/8	5 7/8	1 7/8	1 7/8	7 2/8	Gallatin Co., MT	Jack D. Yadon	Jack D. Yadon	1986	183
51 4/8	10 1/8	10 1/8	5 6/8	5 7/8	1 7/8	1 7/8	7 5/8	Taku River, BC	Bernard Sippin	Bernard Sippin	1987	183
51 4/8	10 3/8	10 3/8	5 4/8	5 6/8	1 7/8	1 6/8	8 1/8	Maiyuk Creek, BC	John P. Katrichak	John P. Katrichak	1988	183
51 4/8	11	11	5 4/8	5 4/8	1 7/8	1 7/8	7 4/8	Tahltan River, BC	Wayne H. Kingsley	Wayne H. Kingsley	1988	183
51 4/8	11 1/8	10	5 7/8	5 7/8	1 7/8	1 7/8	8 7/8	Nass River, BC	Scott McDonald	Scott McDonald	1988	183
51 4/8	10	10 6/8	5 6/8	5 6/8	2	2	6 3/8	Sheslay River, BC	Daniel E. Gorecki	Daniel E. Gorecki	1989	183
51 4/8	9 5/8	10 1/8	6	6	2 1/8	1 7/8	7 4/8	Bradley Lake, AK	Paul H. Ross	Paul H. Ross	1989	183
51 4/8	10 1/8	10	6	6	1 7/8	2	7 7/8	Beaverhead Co., MT	Shawn M. Probst	Shawn M. Probst	1990	183
51 4/8	9 7/8	9 7/8	5 7/8	5 7/8	1 7/8	1 7/8	6 3/8	Salt Lake Co., UT	Joyce A. Christensen	Joyce A. Christensen	1993	183
51 4/8	10 2/8	10 2/8	5 7/8	5 6/8	2	2	6 4/8	Nanika Lake, BC	Reg Meisner	Reg Meisner	1995	183
51 4/8	10 1/8	10 1/8	5 7/8	5 7/8	2	2	7 2/8	Scoop Lake, BC	Robert McCarter	Robert McCarter	1997	183
51 4/8	10 7/8	10 6/8	6	6	1 6/8	1 6/8	6 5/8	Kootenay, BC	Teddy MacLachlan	W.K. Porter	1925	183
51 2/8	10 2/8	10 4/8	6 1/8	6 1/8	1 6/8	1 6/8	7 7/8	Hard Scrabble Pass, AB	Justus von Lengerke	Justus von Lengerke	1937	227
51 2/8	10 1/8	10 1/8	5 4/8	5 4/8	2	2	7 5/8	Katalla, AK	John Goeres	John Goeres	1943	227
51 2/8	10	10	6 1/8	6 1/8	2	2	8 1/8	Mt. Robson, BC	E.T. Reilly	E.T. Reilly	1948	227
51 2/8	10 6/8	10 6/8	5 7/8	5 7/8	1 6/8	1 6/8	6 6/8	Cassiar, BC	Elmer E. Rasmuson	Elmer E. Rasmuson	1952	227
51 2/8	10 4/8	10 6/8	5 6/8	5 5/8	1 6/8	1 5/8	7 2/8	Bulkley Range, BC	Mrs. Billie Gardiner	Mrs. Billie Gardiner	1959	227
51 2/8	10	10 4/8	6	5 5/8	1 7/8	1 6/8	7 7/8	Kechika Range, BC	Paul A. Bagalio	Paul A. Bagalio	1965	227
51 2/8	9 6/8	9 6/8	5 7/8	5 7/8	2	2	7	Gataga River, BC	Robert C. McAtee	Robert C. McAtee	1965	227
51 2/8	9 3/8	9 2/8	6 1/8	6 1/8	2 1/8	2	7 5/8	Anchorage, AK	Wade Charles	Wade Charles	1966	227
51 2/8	10 3/8	10 3/8	5 6/8	5 6/8	2 2/8	2	7 7/8	Atlin, BC	Nolan Martins	Nolan Martins	1967	227
51 2/8	9 6/8	10 3/8	5 6/8	5 5/8	2	2	8 4/8	Atlin Lake, BC	Walter O. Johnston	Walter O. Johnston	1968	227
51 2/8	10 3/8	10	5 7/8	5 7/8	2	2	7 4/8	Vetter Peak, BC	Tracy Skead	Tracy Skead	1969	227
51 2/8	10 1/8	10 3/8	5 6/8	5 6/8	1 7/8	1 7/8	7 4/8	Kechika Range, BC	W.A. McKay	W.A. McKay	1970	227
51 2/8	10 4/8	10 1/8	5 5/8	5 6/8	2	2	6 4/8	Wrangell Mts., AK	John E. Meyers	John E. Meyers	1971	227
51 2/8	10 5/8	10 7/8	5 2/8	5 3/8	2 2/8	2	8 2/8	Skeena Mts., BC	Michael A. Wright	Michael A. Wright	1972	227
51 2/8	10 3/8	10 3/8	5 6/8	5 6/8	1 7/8	1 7/8	8 4/8	Tsetia Creek, BC	Douglas V. Turner	Douglas V. Turner	1973	227
51 2/8	10 4/8	10 2/8	5 5/8	5 5/8	2	2	7 3/8	Pend Oreille Co., WA	William R. Stevens	William R. Stevens	1975	227
51 2/8	10 2/8	10	6	6	1 7/8	2	6 4/8	Morice Lake, BC	G. Fitchett & L. Austin	George Fitchett	1978	227
51 2/8	10 4/8	10	5 4/8	5 4/8	1 7/8	1 7/8	10 4/8	Marker Lake, YT	James K. Montgomery	James K. Montgomery	1978	227
51 2/8	10 6/8	10 5/8	5 5/8	5 5/8	1 7/8	1 7/8	6 4/8	Idaho Co., ID	Lorraine Ravary	Lorraine Ravary	1980	227
51 2/8	10 3/8	10 4/8	5 4/8	5 5/8	2	2	7 7/8	Kittitas Co., WA	Michael W. Duby	Michael W. Duby	1980	227
51 2/8	10 6/8	10 6/8	5 3/8	5 4/8	2	2	8 3/8	Chilkat Mt., AK	Terry L. Friske	Terry L. Friske	1981	227
51 2/8	10 7/8	10 6/8	6 1/8	6 1/8	1 6/8	1 6/8	6 5/8	Swan Lake, BC	John Dobish	John Dobish	1981	227
51 2/8	9 6/8	9 6/8	5 5/8	5 6/8	2	2	8 1/8	Duti Lake, BC	T.J. Tucker	T.J. Tucker	1981	227
51 2/8	10 4/8	10 2/8	5 5/8	5 5/8	2	2	7	Tyee Lake, AK	David L. Bowden	David L. Bowden	1982	227
51 2/8	10	10 2/8	5 5/8	5 6/8	2 1/8	2 1/8	5 7/8	Okanogan Co., WA	Richard D. Grant	Richard D. Grant	1982	227
51 2/8	10 1/8	10 1/8	5 6/8	5 6/8	1 7/8	1 7/8	6 6/8	Kaustua Creek, BC	Duane Pankratz	Duane Pankratz	1982	227
51 2/8	10 5/8	10 5/8	6	5 7/8	1 7/8	1 7/8	7 4/8	Glennallen, AK	Kirk Z. Smith	Kirk Z. Smith	1982	227
51 2/8	10 4/8	10	5 5/8	5 5/8	2	2	8 3/8	Nass River, BC	Larry Zilinski	Larry Zilinski	1982	227

ROCKY MOUNTAIN GOAT

Oreamnos americanus americanus and related subspecies

Score	Length of Horn R	L	Circumference of Base R	L	Circumference at Third Quarter R	L	Greatest Spread	Tip tp Tip Spread	Locality	Hunter	Owner	Date Killed	Rank
51 2/8	9 1/8	9 1/8	5 5/8	5 5/8	2 4/8	2 4/8	7 4/8	6 6/8	Taku River, BC	Charles W. Schmidt	Charles W. Schmidt	1985	227
51 2/8	10 1/8	10 1/8	5 6/8	5 6/8	1 7/8	1 7/8	6 7/8	6 6/8	Crown Mt., AK	Robert L. Hales	Robert L. Hales	1986	227
51 2/8	10 2/8	10 2/8	5 4/8	5 4/8	2	2	7	6 2/8	Mt. Guanton, BC	Charles R. McKinley	Charles R. McKinley	1986	227
51 2/8	9 7/8	9 7/8	5 5/8	5 6/8	2	2	6 2/8	5 3/8	Snehumption Creek, BC	Raymond C. Croissant	Raymond C. Croissant	1989	227
51 2/8	10 6/8	10 7/8	5 5/8	5 6/8	1 7/8	1 7/8	7 2/8	6 2/8	Cassiar Mts., BC	Robert A. Lenzini	Robert A. Lenzini	1991	227
51 2/8	10 6/8	11	5 6/8	5 5/8	1 7/8	1 7/8	8	7 2/8	Taku River, BC	John H. Garnett, Sr.	John H. Garnett, Sr.	1992	227
51 2/8	10 2/8	10 4/8	6	6	1 6/8	1 7/8	8 1/8	7 2/8	Moose Creek, AK	Michael R. Morava	Michael R. Morava	1993	227
51 2/8	10 6/8	10 5/8	5 5/8	5 6/8	1 7/8	1 7/8	7 7/8	7 2/8	Hugh Creek, BC	Gerhard Volz	Gerhard Volz	1993	227
51 2/8	11	10 6/8	5 7/8	5 7/8	1 5/8	1 6/8	8 1/8	6 4/8	Washout Creek, BC	Brian L. Davis	Brian L. Davis	1994	227
51 2/8	10 6/8	10 1/8	5 6/8	5 6/8	2	2	6 5/8	6 2/8	Bond Sound, BC	Richard R. Ford	Richard R. Ford	1994	227
51 2/8	9 7/8	10	6 1/8	6 1/8	1 6/8	1 7/8	7 5/8	7 2/8	Nahlin Mt., BC	Daniel W. Brockman	Daniel W. Brockman	1995	227
51	9 6/8	10	5 7/8	5 7/8	2	2	8 2/8	7 7/8	Morice River, BC	Warren Bodeker	Warren Bodeker	1958	267
51	9 6/8	9 5/8	5 6/8	5 6/8	2 2/8	2 1/8	6 6/8	6 1/8	Resurrection Bay, AK	Peter W. Bading	Peter W. Bading	1961	267
51	9 4/8	9 4/8	5 5/8	5 6/8	2 1/8	2 1/8	5 6/8	4 4/8	Terrace, BC	Gerald Prosser	Gerald Prosser	1962	267
51	11	10 6/8	5 7/8	5 7/8	1 7/8	1 6/8	7 2/8	6 4/8	Smithers, BC	John Strban	John Strban	1962	267
51	10 2/8	10 6/8	5 4/8	5 4/8	2	2	7 5/8	6 1/8	Butte Inlet, BC	Reuben C. Carlson	Reuben C. Carlson	1963	267
51	10 7/8	11	5 7/8	5 7/8	1 6/8	1 7/8	7 1/8	6 6/8	Kootenay Range, BC	Norbert M. Welch	Norbert M. Welch	1963	267
51	10	10	5 6/8	5 6/8	2	2	7 6/8	7	Dease Lake, BC	W.M. Rudd	W.M. Rudd	1964	267
51	10 2/8	10 2/8	5 5/8	5 5/8	1 7/8	1 7/8	7 4/8	7 3/8	Telegraph Creek, BC	John Caputo, Jr.	John Caputo, Jr.	1965	267
51	10 3/8	10 3/8	5 2/8	5 2/8	1 6/8	1 6/8	7 2/8	6 2/8	Flathead Co., MT	Johnny Powell	Johnny Powell	1965	267
51	10 6/8	10 4/8	5 6/8	5 3/8	1 7/8	1 7/8	7 1/8	5 5/8	Alaska Panhandle, AK	Donald W. Moody	Donald W. Moody	1966	267
51	10 2/8	10 2/8	5 5/8	5 6/8	2	2	8 3/8	7 7/8	Okanagan, BC	Earl Dawson	Earl Dawson	1967	267
51	10 1/8	10 6/8	6	6	1 7/8	1 7/8	7 3/8	6 6/8	Tete Jaune, BC	George Hanschen	George Hanschen	1967	267
51	9 6/8	9 6/8	5 7/8	5 7/8	2	1 7/8	7 3/8	7 2/8	Hart Mt., BC	Marvin F. Lawrence	Marvin F. Lawrence	1967	267
51	10 2/8	10 2/8	5 5/8	5 5/8	2	2	8	7 3/8	Telegraph Creek, BC	George McCullough	George McCullough	1967	267
51	10 6/8	10 1/8	5 5/8	5 5/8	2	2	9 2/8	9	Terrace, BC	Gary Townsend	Gary Townsend	1967	267
51	10 4/8	10 4/8	5 5/8	5 7/8	1 6/8	1 7/8	7 3/8	7 3/8	Nuka Bay, AK	Curt Henning	Curt Henning	1968	267
51	9 4/8	9 5/8	5 7/8	5 6/8	1 7/8	1 7/8	5 6/8	5 5/8	McBride, BC	Ervin Voelk	Ervin Voelk	1968	267
51	10 5/8	10 5/8	5 6/8	5 6/8	1 6/8	1 7/8	8 3/8	7 6/8	Lillooet, BC	Helmut Krieger	Helmut Krieger	1969	267
51	10	9 6/8	5 6/8	5 5/8	2	2 1/8	6 6/8	6	Yakutat, AK	Robert Sinko	Robert Sinko	1971	267
51	10 2/8	10 2/8	5 2/8	5 2/8	2	2	6 6/8	5 7/8	Snohomish Co., WA	David T. Lewis	David T. Lewis	1972	267
51	10 3/8	10 3/8	5 7/8	5 7/8	1 7/8	1 7/8	8	7 5/8	Findlay Creek, BC	Sharon Robey	Sharon Robey	1978	267
51	10 3/8	10 6/8	5 7/8	6	1 6/8	1 6/8	0	0	Ravalli Co., MT	John K. Frederikson	John K. Frederikson	1979	267
51	10 4/8	10 4/8	5 6/8	5 6/8	1 7/8	1 7/8	7 2/8	5 7/8	Tahtsa Lake, BC	Vernon J. Boose	Vernon J. Boose	1981	267
51	10 4/8	10 5/8	5 5/8	5 5/8	1 7/8	1 7/8	7 3/8	6 6/8	Snohomish Co., WA	John W. Lane	John W. Lane	1982	267
51	9 7/8	9 5/8	5 7/8	5 7/8	1 7/8	1 7/8	6	4 6/8	Granite Basin, AK	Gerry D. Downey	Gerry D. Downey	1983	267
51	10 7/8	10 7/8	5 3/8	5 4/8	1 6/8	1 6/8	6 4/8	5 6/8	Gallatin Co., MT	Ronald K. Lewis	Ronald K. Lewis	1984	267
51	10 4/8	10 3/8	5 6/8	5 6/8	1 7/8	1 7/8	7 3/8	6 7/8	Sheslay River, BC	Steven M. Sullivan	Steven M. Sullivan	1985	267

Score									Locality	Hunter	Owner	Date Killed	Rank
51	8 4/8	2 3/8	2 2/8	5 7/8	6	8 6/8	7 5/8	7 2/8	Salt Lake Co., UT	Andrea L. Shaffer	Andrea L. Shaffer	1987	267
51	10 4/8	1 6/8	1 6/8	5 6/8	5 5/8	10 4/8	8 3/8	8 2/8	Skilak Glacier, AK	Mark A. Gaede	Mark A. Gaede	1988	267
51	10 3/8	1 7/8	2	5 5/8	5 5/8	10 3/8	7	6 4/8	Clear Creek Co., CO	Janice L. Hemingson	Janice L. Hemingson	1988	267
51	10 1/8	1 7/8	1 7/8	6	6	10	6 2/8	7 1/8	Serrated Peak, BC	Philip E. Blacher, Jr.	Philip E. Blacher, Jr.	1989	267
51	10 4/8	2	1 7/8	5 4/8	5 4/8	10 7/8	6 1/8	5 5/8	Cleveland Pen., AK	Lynn K. Herbert	Lynn K. Herbert	1989	267
51	10 2/8	1 7/8	1 7/8	5 6/8	5 5/8	10 3/8	6 1/8	5	Wrangell, AK	Kerry Kammer	Kerry Kammer	1992	267
51	9 3/8	1 7/8	1 7/8	5 6/8	5 6/8	9 6/8	6 4/8	5 7/8	Yakima Co., WA	Stephanie L. Peyser	Stephanie L. Peyser	1992	267
51	10 2/8	1 6/8	1 7/8	6 2/8	6 1/8	10 1/8	7	6 3/8	Nanika Lake, BC	Gary Eby	Gary Eby	1993	267
51	10 2/8	1 6/8	2	5 5/8	5 5/8	10 2/8	7 1/8	6 7/8	Similkameen River, BC	Charles H. Veasey	Charles H. Veasey	1993	267
51	9 6/8	2	2	5 7/8	5 7/8	9 6/8	6 6/8	6 2/8	Morice Lake, BC	Keith Thompson	Keith Thompson	1994	267
51	10 3/8	1 6/8	1 6/8	5 6/8	5 6/8	10 2/8	6 4/8	5 3/8	Granite Creek, BC	Erich Unterberger	Erich Unterberger	1996	267
50 6/8	10 1/8	2	1 7/8	5 7/8	5 7/8	10 3/8	7 1/8	6 4/8	Cassiar, BC	W.N. Beach	W.N. Beach	1918	305
50 6/8	10 4/8	2	1 5/8	5 4/8	5 4/8	10 1/8	9	7 1/8	Cassiar, BC	Clement B. Newbold	Clement B. Newbold	1926	305
50 6/8	11	1 6/8	1 6/8	5 4/8	5 4/8	11 1/8	5 4/8	4 3/8	Flathead Co., MT	Charlie Shaw	Picked Up	1936	305
50 6/8	9 4/8	2 1/8	2 1/8	5 7/8	5 7/8	9 4/8	7 7/8	7 6/8	Similkameen, BC	John D. Rempel	Peter Braun	1939	305
50 6/8	10 2/8	1 7/8	1 7/8	5 6/8	5 5/8	10 2/8	6 7/8	6 7/8	Cordova, AK	Ralph E. Renner	Ralph E. Renner	1950	305
50 6/8	10 7/8	2	2	5 4/8	5 7/8	10 1/8	8 3/8	8 3/8	Cassiar, BC	Peter Schramm	Peter Schramm	1950	305
50 6/8	9 6/8	1 6/8	1 6/8	5 5/8	5 5/8	11 2/8	9 1/8	8	Telegraph Creek, BC	Wayne C. Eubank	Wayne C. Eubank	1953	305
50 6/8	9 5/8	1 7/8	1 7/8	5 7/8	5 7/8	9 6/8	7 4/8	7 2/8	Telegraph Creek, BC	A.J. Duany	A.J. Duany	1954	305
50 6/8	10 1/8	2	2 1/8	5 7/8	5 7/8	10 1/8	8	7 3/8	Knik River, AK	C.M. Van Meter	C.M. Van Meter	1956	305
50 6/8	10 3/8	2	2	5 6/8	5 6/8	10 2/8	7 1/8	5 7/8	Boca De Quadra Inlet, AK	Lyman Reynoldson	Lyman Reynoldson	1957	305
50 6/8	9 6/8	2	2	5 7/8	5 6/8	10 3/8	8 2/8	7 5/8	Kenai Pen., AK	Elgin T. Gates	Elgin T. Gates	1961	305
50 6/8	10 2/8	2	2	5 6/8	5 7/8	9 6/8	7 1/8	5 6/8	Maxan Lake, BC	K.J. Nysven	K.J. Nysven	1961	305
50 6/8	10 4/8	1 7/8	1 6/8	6	6	10	7 4/8	6 6/8	Cold Fish Lake, BC	Howard Boazman	Howard Boazman	1962	305
50 6/8	9 6/8	1 7/8	1 7/8	6	6	10 5/8	9 4/8	8 3/8	Gataga River, BC	Herb Klein	Herb Klein	1963	305
50 6/8	10	2	1 6/8	5 5/8	5 7/8	10 4/8	6 1/8	5 5/8	Keremeos, BC	Bill Postill	Bill Postill	1963	305
50 6/8	10 3/8	2 1/8	2 1/8	6	6	9 4/8	9 2/8	8 6/8	Atlin, BC	G. Vernon Boggs	G. Vernon Boggs	1964	305
50 6/8	10 1/8	2 1/8	2 1/8	5 2/8	5 3/8	10 3/8	7	7 5/8	Cold Fish Lake, BC	Armin Baltensweiler	Armin Baltensweiler	1965	305
50 6/8	9 7/8	2	1 7/8	5 7/8	5 6/8	10 1/8	8 7/8	7 4/8	Cassiar Mts., BC	Ernest Granum	Ernest Granum	1965	305
50 6/8	10 1/8	1 7/8	1 7/8	5 7/8	5 7/8	9 6/8	8 7/8	8 1/8	Klappan Range, BC	Larry P. Miller	Larry P. Miller	1965	305
50 6/8	9 3/8	1 7/8	1 7/8	6 2/8	6 1/8	9 3/8	6 2/8	6	Kechika Range, BC	Unknown	Basil C. Bradbury	1965	305
50 6/8	9 2/8	2	2	6 1/8	6 1/8	9 5/8	6 7/8	6 3/8	Hedley, BC	Donald J. Robb	Donald J. Robb	1965	305
50 6/8	10 2/8	1 5/8	1 5/8	6 1/8	6 1/8	10 3/8	6	5 7/8	Mt. Antero, CO	Leroy C. Wood	Leroy C. Wood	1965	305
50 6/8	10 1/8	1 7/8	1 7/8	5 3/8	5 3/8	10 1/8	7 5/8	7 3/8	Ashnola River, BC	Robert C. Bateson	Robert C. Bateson	1966	305
50 6/8	9 5/8	2 1/8	2 1/8	5 5/8	5 6/8	9 6/8	6 6/8	5 6/8	Skeena River, BC	G. Best	G. Best	1966	305
50 6/8	10 1/8	1 7/8	1 7/8	5 6/8	5 7/8	10 7/8	8 3/8	8 2/8	Toad River, BC	Walt Paulk	Walt Paulk	1966	305
50 6/8	10 2/8	1 7/8	1 7/8	5 6/8	5 6/8	10 4/8	6 6/8	6 5/8	Horsethief Creek, BC	Bill Pitt	Bill Pitt	1966	305
50 6/8	9 7/8	2	1 7/8	5 7/8	5 7/8	9 7/8	5 7/8	5 7/8	Black Hills, SD	Lloyd Weaver	Lloyd Weaver	1967	305
50 6/8	9 4/8	2 2/8	2 2/8	5 4/8	5 5/8	9 4/8	7 3/8	7 1/8	Kenai Mts., AK	Stephen D. LaBelle	Stephen D. LaBelle	1971	305
50 6/8	10 4/8	1 6/8	1 6/8	5 5/8	5 5/8	10 4/8	8 4/8	8 1/8	Dease Lake, BC	John H. Epp	John H. Epp	1972	305
50 6/8	10 1/8	2	2	5 5/8	5 5/8	9 7/8	8 5/8	8 3/8	Chelan Co., WA	Raymond J. Hammer	Raymond J. Hammer	1973	305
50 6/8	10 1/8	1 7/8	1 7/8	5 7/8	5 7/8	10	7 7/8	7 2/8	Kechika Range, BC	Dennis Laabs	Dennis Laabs	1973	305
50 6/8	10	2 1/8	2 1/8	6	6 1/8	8 7/8	7 2/8	6 5/8	Kenai Pen., AK	Jack Allen	Jack Allen	1974	305
50 6/8	10 3/8	1 7/8	1 7/8	5 5/8	5 5/8	10 2/8	7 6/8	7 2/8	Cassiar Mts., BC	Kenneth E. Bishop	Kenneth E. Bishop	1979	305
50 6/8	9 5/8	2	2	5 6/8	5 5/8	9 5/8	5 5/8	5 7/8	Johnston Lake, BC	Brian A. Halina	Brian A. Halina	1979	305
50 6/8	10 3/8	1 7/8	1 7/8	5 7/8	5 7/8	10 5/8	7 1/8	6 1/8	Klastline River, BC	Glenn E. Hisey	Glenn E. Hisey	1979	305
50 6/8	10 3/8	1 6/8	1 6/8	5 7/8	5 7/8	10 3/8	7 1/8	6 1/8	Dutch Creek, BC	Tom Housh	Tom Housh	1982	305

ROCKY MOUNTAIN GOAT

Oreamnos americanus americanus and related subspecies

Score	Length of Horn R	L	Circumference of Base R	L	Circumference at Third Quarter R	L	Greatest Spread	Tip tp Tip Spread	Locality	Hunter	Owner	Date Killed	Rank
50 6/8	10 4/8	10 4/8	5 5/8	5 4/8	2	2	7 4/8	7	Stewart, BC	Harry J. McCowan	Harry J. McCowan	1983	305
50 6/8	10	10	5 7/8	5 7/8	1 7/8	1 7/8	7 5/8	7 2/8	Okanogan Co., WA	Jerrel R. Harmon	Jerrel R. Harmon	1984	305
50 6/8	10 3/8	10 3/8	5 5/8	5 5/8	1 7/8	1 6/8	9 5/8	9 5/8	Day Harbor, AK	Steen Henriksen	Steen Henriksen	1984	305
50 6/8	11 2/8	11 7/8	5 5/8	5 5/8	1 5/8	1 5/8	7 7/8	7 7/8	Beaverfoot Range, BC	Kelley Knight	Kelley Knight	1984	305
50 6/8	11	10 5/8	6	5 7/8	2	1 6/8	7 3/8	6 2/8	Little Oliver Creek, BC	David J. Flemming	David J. Flemming	1985	305
50 6/8	10	10	5 6/8	5 7/8	1 7/8	1 7/8	6 5/8	6 3/8	Okanogan Co, WA	Susan M. Fletcher	Susan M. Fletcher	1985	305
50 6/8	9 6/8	9 7/8	5 7/8	6	1 6/8	1 7/8	5 7/8	5 4/8	Salt Lake Co., UT	Picked Up	UT Div. of Wildl. Resc.	1985	305
50 6/8	10 5/8	10 5/8	5 6/8	5 6/8	1 6/8	1 7/8	6 7/8	6 5/8	Chelan Co., WA	David L. Metzler	David L. Metzler	1986	305
50 6/8	10 1/8	9 7/8	5 4/8	5 4/8	1 7/8	1 7/8	8 2/8	7 7/8	Okanogan Co., WA	Monica M. Knight	Monica M. Knight	1987	305
50 6/8	10 1/8	10 1/8	5 6/8	5 6/8	1 7/8	1 7/8	6 2/8	5 6/8	Williams Lake, BC	Norwood N. Kern	Norwood N. Kern	1988	305
50 6/8	9 5/8	9 5/8	5 6/8	5 6/8	1 7/8	1 7/8	6 6/8	6 2/8	Salt Lake Co., UT	Macie J. Manire	Macie J. Manire	1988	305
50 6/8	9 7/8	9 7/8	5 7/8	5 7/8	1 6/8	1 7/8	7 6/8	7 6/8	Belcourt Creek, BC	Cameron Todd	Cameron Todd	1988	305
50 6/8	10 5/8	10 5/8	5 6/8	5 6/8	1 6/8	1 7/8	7 2/8	7 1/8	Kootenay Mt., BC	Ted A. Trout	Ted A. Trout	1988	305
50 6/8	10 3/8	10 3/8	5 6/8	5 5/8	1 7/8	1 7/8	6 5/8	6 1/8	Chouteau Co., MT	Craig L. Nowak	Craig L. Nowak	1990	305
50 6/8	10 2/8	10 2/8	5 4/8	5 5/8	2	1 7/8	8 1/8	7 7/8	Chopaka Mts., BC	John D. Chalk III	John D. Chalk III	1991	305
50 6/8	10	10	5 6/8	5 7/8	1 7/8	1 7/8	5 3/8	3 5/8	Coldstream Creek, BC	Richard P. Price	Richard P. Price	1991	305
50 6/8	10 2/8	10 5/8	5 5/8	5 5/8	1 6/8	1 7/8	9	8 6/8	Atlin Lake, BC	John R. Busby	John R. Busby	1992	305
50 6/8	10 2/8	10 3/8	6	6	1 6/8	1 6/8	6	5 2/8	Lardeau River, BC	Rod Smaldon	Rod Smaldon	1993	305
50 6/8	11 2/8	10 1/8	5 5/8	5 5/8	2	2	8	7 1/8	Whatcom Co., WA	James C. Zevely	James C. Zevely	1993	305
50 6/8	10 1/8	10	6	6	2	2	7 6/8	7 1/8	Castle Creek, BC	Curtis Neudorf	Curtis Neudorf	1996	305
50 6/8	10 5/8	10 4/8	5 4/8	5 4/8	1 7/8	1 7/8	6 1/8	5	Cleveland Pen., AK	Stephen Elenberger	Stephen Elenberger	1997	305
50 6/8	9 5/8	9 5/8	6	6	1 7/8	1 7/8	8 1/8	7 6/8	Chugach Mts., AK	Bill Gregory	Bill Gregory	1997	305
50 4/8	12 1/8	12 4/8	4 6/8	4 6/8	1 6/8	1 7/8	7 1/8	6 4/8	Cassiar, BC	A. Bryan Williams	Mrs. N.S. Gooch	PR 1916	363
50 4/8	10 2/8	10 3/8	5 4/8	5 4/8	2	2	7 4/8	7	Cassiar, BC	George E. Burghard	George E. Burghard	1925	363
50 4/8	10 1/8	10 2/8	5 5/8	5 5/8	1 7/8	1 7/8	7 2/8	6 5/8	Telegraph Creek, BC	John S. McCormick, Jr.	John S. McCormick, Jr.	1936	363
50 4/8	10 2/8	10 4/8	5 2/8	5 3/8	2	2	7	5 5/8	Brazeau River, AB	Walter B. McClurkan	Walter B. McClurkan	1942	363
50 4/8	11 1/8	11 1/8	5	5	2	2	7	5 2/8	Stikine River, AK	W.F. Littleton	W.F. Littleton	1953	363
50 4/8	10 4/8	10 5/8	5 6/8	5 6/8	1 7/8	2 1/8	7 1/8	6	Bull River, BC	Albert Markstein	Albert Markstein	1954	363
50 4/8	10 1/8	9 7/8	5 4/8	5 4/8	2 1/8	1 7/8	8 2/8	7 1/8	Cold Fish Lake, BC	Joseph Smith	Joseph Smith	1955	363
50 4/8	10	10	5 6/8	5 6/8	1 6/8	1 7/8	6 5/8	6 4/8	Okanogan Mts., WA	Neil Castner	Neil Castner	1956	363
50 4/8	10 1/8	10	5 6/8	5 6/8	1 6/8	1 6/8	8	7 1/8	Cold Fish Lake, BC	Patrick Britell	Patrick Britell	1957	363
50 4/8	10 2/8	10 1/8	5 1/8	5 1/8	1 7/8	1 7/8	0	0	Seward, AK	Picked Up	A.D. Stenger	PR 1957	363
50 4/8	10 2/8	10 1/8	5 5/8	5 5/8	2	2	7 2/8	6 3/8	Bennett Lake, YT	H. Kennedy	H. Kennedy	1958	363
50 4/8	9 6/8	9 6/8	5 6/8	5 6/8	1 7/8	1 7/8	8 1/8	7 5/8	Chugach Mts., AK	Elmer A. Patson	Elmer A. Patson	1958	363
50 4/8	10 4/8	10 4/8	5 4/8	5 4/8	2	2	7 4/8	6 7/8	Cold Fish Lake, BC	L.A. Wunsch	L.A. Wunsch	1958	363
50 4/8	10 3/8	10 2/8	5 6/8	5 6/8	2	2	6 6/8	5 1/8	Okanogan, WA	Bob Hazelbrook	Bob Hazelbrook	1960	363
50 4/8	10 1/8	10 2/8	5 6/8	5 6/8	1 6/8	1 6/8	7 7/8	6 7/8	Smithers, BC	A.S. Langan	A.S. Langan	1960	363
50 4/8	10 2/8	10 3/8	5 1/8	5 1/8	2 1/8	2 1/8	7	7	Chilco Lake, BC	C. Marc Miller	C. Marc Miller	1960	363

Score									Locality	Hunter	Owner	Date	Rank
50 4/8	10 2/8	10	5 6/8	5 6/8	1 7/8	1 7/8	8 1/8	7 6/8	Kenai Pen., AK	Gordon Best	G. Best & R. Reed	1962	363
50 4/8	10 1/8	10	5 4/8	5 4/8	2	2	7 5/8	7	Atlin Lake, BC	Wendell Bever	Wendell Bever	1962	363
50 4/8	9 3/8	9 3/8	5 5/8	5 5/8	2 1/8	2 1/8	6 3/8	5 4/8	Mt. Stoyoma, BC	Frank S.T. Bradley	Frank S.T. Bradley	1962	363
50 4/8	10 1/8	9 7/8	5 6/8	5 7/8	2	1 7/8	7	6 2/8	White Sales Mt., BC	Robert McDonald	Robert McDonald	1962	363
50 4/8	9 7/8	10	5 7/8	5 4/8	1 7/8	1 7/8	7 2/8	7 2/8	Kechika Range, BC	G.W. Hawkins	G.W. Hawkins	1963	363
50 4/8	10 5/8	10 6/8	5 4/8	5 5/8	1 6/8	1 6/8	7 2/8	6 7/8	Cape Yakataga, AK	Lynn M. Castle	Lynn M. Castle	1964	363
50 4/8	10 3/8	10 4/8	5 5/8	5 5/8	1 7/8	1 7/8	7 6/8	6 6/8	Lake Kinniskan, BC	Michel Boel	Michel Boel	1965	363
50 4/8	10	10	5 7/8	5 6/8	1 6/8	1 6/8	7 1/8	5 4/8	Wrangell Mts., AK	Charles S. Moses	Charles S. Moses	1965	363
50 4/8	9 4/8	9 4/8	5 6/8	5 5/8	1 5/8	2 1/8	8 1/8	8	Smoky River, AB	Terry Thrift, Jr.	Terry Thrift, Jr.	1965	363
50 4/8	9 6/8	9 6/8	5 5/8	5 5/8	2 1/8	2 1/8	7 3/8	7 6/8	Atlin, BC	Raymond Bartram	Raymond Bartram	1966	363
50 4/8	10 2/8	10 2/8	5 5/8	5 4/8	2	2	8	6 2/8	McDonald Lake, BC	Henry P. Foradora	Henry P. Foradora	1966	363
50 4/8	9 6/8	9 6/8	5 4/8	5 4/8	1 7/8	1 7/8	8	7 5/8	Sloko Lake, BC	John Haefeli	John Haefeli	1966	363
50 4/8	10 2/8	10 3/8	5 5/8	5 5/8	1 7/8	1 7/8	6	5 1/8	Revelstoke, BC	George Lines	Picked Up	1966	363
50 4/8	10 4/8	10 3/8	5 5/8	5 4/8	1 7/8	1 7/8	7 3/8	7 7/8	Seward, AK	Frank W. Pinkerton	Frank W. Pinkerton	1966	363
50 4/8	10 5/8	10 3/8	5 4/8	5 3/8	1 7/8	1 7/8	7 3/8	5 4/8	Winstanley Lakes, AK	James R. Simms	James R. Simms	1966	363
50 4/8	10 5/8	10 5/8	5 3/8	5 3/8	1 6/8	1 6/8	7 2/8	6 3/8	Black Hills, SD	Robert M. Aalseth	Robert M. Aalseth	1967	363
50 4/8	10 1/8	10 1/8	5 5/8	5 5/8	1 7/8	1 7/8	9 2/8	9 2/8	Cassiar Mts., BC	Donovan N. Branch	Donovan N. Branch	1967	363
50 4/8	10 2/8	10 2/8	5 4/8	5 4/8	1 7/8	1 7/8	8 4/8	7 6/8	Telegraph Creek, BC	T.T. Stroup	T.T. Stroup	1968	363
50 4/8	10 1/8	10 1/8	6	6	1 7/8	2	6 5/8	5 4/8	Turnagain River, BC	Howard S. Duffield	Howard S. Duffield	1969	363
50 4/8	11	11	5 5/8	5 4/8	1 7/8	1 7/8	7 1/8	5 1/8	Stikine River, AK	Donald E. Fossen	Donald E. Fossen	1973	363
50 4/8	10 3/8	10 4/8	6	6	1 6/8	1 6/8	7 7/8	7 7/8	Lewis & Clark Co., MT	Donald C. Thelen	Robert F. Thelen	1974	363
50 4/8	10	10 2/8	5 6/8	5 7/8	1 7/8	1 7/8	7 1/8	7 5/8	Dease Lake, BC	James T. Knutson	James T. Knutson	1975	363
50 4/8	9 7/8	9 6/8	5 7/8	5 5/8	2	1 7/8	6 6/8	6 6/8	Pennington Co., SD	Floyd J. Campbell	Floyd J. Campbell	1978	363
50 4/8	10 4/8	10 4/8	5 5/8	5 5/8	1 7/8	1 6/8	7	6 4/8	Wrangell Mts., AK	Leonard O. Farlow	Leonard O. Farlow	1978	363
50 4/8	10	10	5 5/8	5 7/8	1 6/8	1 7/8	6 7/8	5 7/8	Bingay Creek, BC	C.P. Podrasky	C.P. Podrasky	1981	363
50 4/8	10 4/8	10 4/8	5 7/8	5 7/8	2	2	9 1/8	9	Stikine Canyon, BC	Reuben F. Gerecke	Reuben F. Gerecke	1982	363
50 4/8	10 3/8	10 3/8	5 7/8	5 3/8	1 6/8	1 7/8	7 7/8	7 3/8	Mt. Cummins, BC	Rod Aune	Rod Aune	1984	363
50 4/8	10 6/8	10 6/8	5 3/8	5 6/8	1 7/8	1 7/8	8	7 5/8	Icy Bay, AK	David W. Dillard	David W. Dillard	1985	363
50 4/8	10 6/8	10 7/8	5 6/8	5 6/8	1 7/8	1 4/8	7 4/8	6 4/8	Leduc Lake, AK	James M. Judd	James M. Judd	1985	363
50 4/8	10 1/8	10 1/8	5 6/8	5 6/8	1 7/8	1 7/8	6 4/8	5 6/8	Missoula Co., MT	Bill R. Tillerson	Bill R. Tillerson	1985	363
50 4/8	10	10	5 4/8	5 4/8	1 7/8	1 7/8	5 6/8	5	Madison Co., MT	Corey M. Halvorson	Corey M. Halvorson	1986	363
50 4/8	11	11	5 5/8	5 5/8	1 6/8	1 7/8	5 6/8	4 4/8	Beaver Lake, BC	Richard G. Henke	Richard G. Henke	1986	363
50 4/8	9 7/8	10	5 6/8	5 5/8	1 7/8	1 6/8	6 2/8	5 5/8	Lewis & Clark Co., MT	Don St. Clair	Don St. Clair	1986	363
50 4/8	10	10 1/8	5 5/8	5 5/8	1 6/8	1 7/8	6 7/8	6 7/8	Bonneville Co., ID	William D. Stoddard	William D. Stoddard	1986	363
50 4/8	9 7/8	10 2/8	5 5/8	5 5/8	1 7/8	2 1/8	8 2/8	7 5/8	Cassiar Mts., BC	Charles Reichenau	Charles Reichenau	1991	363
50 4/8	9 7/8	10	5 5/8	5 5/8	1 7/8	1 7/8	7	6 1/8	Jug Lake, BC	Larry W. Steeley	Larry W. Steeley	1991	363
50 4/8	10 4/8	10 4/8	5 4/8	5 4/8	1 7/8	1 7/8	8 1/8	8	Tahtsa Lake, BC	Melvin Bromels	Melvin Bromels	1992	363
50 4/8	10 4/8	10 3/8	5 6/8	5 6/8	1 7/8	1 7/8	7 6/8	7 3/8	Puget Bay, AK	Ross Darst	Ross Darst	1992	363
50 4/8	9 4/8	9 5/8	5 6/8	5 6/8	2 1/8	2 1/8	8 3/8	7 4/8	Palliser River, BC	Ernie F. Knight	Ernie F. Knight	1992	363
50 4/8	10	10	5 4/8	5 4/8	2	2	7	7 7/8	Eaglenest Range, BC	Paul Green	Paul Green	1993	363
50 4/8	10 1/8	10 1/8	5 6/8	5 5/8	1 6/8	1 6/8	6 3/8	6 2/8	Stikine River, AK	Thomas R. LeMasters	Thomas R. LeMasters	1994	363
50 4/8	10 2/8	10 2/8	5 6/8	5 5/8	1 7/8	1 7/8	7 7/8	5 7/8	Lewis & Clark Co., MT	Glenn P. Anderson	Glenn P. Anderson	1995	363
50 4/8	10 3/8	10 3/8	5 5/8	5 5/8	1 7/8	1 7/8	7 4/8	7 4/8	Tuktsayda Mt., BC	Mike Young	Mike Young	1995	363
50 4/8	10 1/8	10 1/8	6 1/8	6 1/8	1 7/8	1 7/8	8 6/8	7 6/8	Kakesta Mt., BC	Mark S. Calkins	Mark S. Calkins	1996	363
50 4/8	10 2/8	10 2/8	5 6/8	5 6/8	1 7/8	1 7/8	7	6 1/8	Telegraph Creek, BC	Emile Matte	Emile Matte	1996	363
50 4/8	10	10	5 5/8	5 5/8	1 7/8	1 7/8	7	7 7/8	Fox River, AK	Alvin Schmoyer	Alvin Schmoyer	1996	363
50 4/8	10 1/8	10 4/8	5 5/8	5 5/8	1 7/8	1 7/8	6 7/8	6 3/8	Gallatin Co., MT	William J. Swartz, Jr.	William J. Swartz, Jr.	1996	363

ROCKY MOUNTAIN GOAT

Oreamnos americanus and related subspecies

Score	Length of Horn R	L	Circumference of Base R	L	Circumference at Third Quarter R	L	Greatest Spread	Tip to Tip Spread	Locality	Hunter	Owner	Date Killed	Rank
50 4/8	10 5/8	10 6/8	5 4/8	5 4/8	1 7/8	1 7/8	8	7	Inklin River, BC	Ricardo L. Garza	Ricardo L. Garza	1997	363
50 2/8	10 4/8	10 4/8	5 6/8	5 6/8	1 6/8	1 6/8	8 5/8	8 4/8	Swan Lake, BC	A.C. Gilbert	A.C. Gilbert	1938	427
50 2/8	9 5/8	9 7/8	5 6/8	5 6/8	2	2	7 4/8	6 7/8	Taseko Lakes, BC	L.W. Howell	L.W. Howell	1952	427
50 2/8	10	10	5 5/8	5 5/8	2	2	7 4/8	7 4/8	Cold Fish Lake, BC	T.A. Walker	Univ. of B.C.	1952	427
50 2/8	10	10	5 6/8	5 6/8	1 7/8	1 7/8	7	6 4/8	Blue Goat Mt., WA	Picked Up	Charles F. Martinsen	1956	427
50 2/8	10 4/8	10 3/8	5 4/8	5 5/8	1 6/8	1 6/8	6 6/8	6 6/8	Pentagon Mt., MT	Guy Brash	Guy Brash	1957	427
50 2/8	9 7/8	10	5 4/8	5 4/8	1 5/8	1 6/8	6 2/8	6	Unknown	Unknown	Buckhorn Mus. & Saloon, Ltd.	PR 1957	427
50 2/8	10 4/8	10 3/8	5 4/8	5 4/8	1 6/8	1 6/8	7 2/8	7 2/8	Turnagain River, BC	John La Rocca	John La Rocca	1957	427
50 2/8	10	10 1/8	5 6/8	5 5/8	2	1 7/8	8	7 6/8	Okanogan Co, WA	Victor E. Moss	Victor E. Moss	1957	427
50 2/8	10 1/8	10 3/8	5 5/8	5 6/8	1 7/8	1 7/8	8	7 4/8	Shuswap Creek, BC	Nolan Rad	Nolan Rad	1958	427
50 2/8	10 2/8	10 2/8	5 5/8	5 6/8	1 6/8	1 6/8	7 2/8	6	Sheridan Glacier, AK	Leslie B. Maxwell	Leslie B. Maxwell	1959	427
50 2/8	10 2/8	10 2/8	5 5/8	5 5/8	1 7/8	1 6/8	6 3/8	5 2/8	Smithers, BC	William Stallone	William Stallone	1960	427
50 2/8	9 4/8	9 1/8	5 6/8	5 6/8	2 1/8	2	7 4/8	7 2/8	Ft. St. John, BC	Billy Ross	Billy Ross	1962	427
50 2/8	10 1/8	10 1/8	5 6/8	5 6/8	1 6/8	1 6/8	8 4/8	8 2/8	Sukunka River, BC	Robert C. Sutton	Robert C. Sutton	1962	427
50 2/8	10 5/8	9 5/8	6	6	2	1 7/8	7 3/8	7 3/8	Cassiar, BC	James E. Kelley	James E. Kelley	1963	427
50 2/8	11 2/8	10 6/8	5 5/8	5 6/8	1 6/8	1 6/8	8 4/8	7 7/8	Elk Valley, BC	Emile Gele	Emile Gele	1964	427
50 2/8	10 2/8	10 2/8	5 6/8	5 6/8	1 6/8	1 7/8	7 5/8	7 3/8	Koch Creek, BC	Pat Archibald	Pat Archibald	1965	427
50 2/8	10 2/8	10 1/8	5 4/8	5 4/8	1 7/8	1 7/8	6 4/8	5 5/8	Chehalis Lake, BC	Fred E. Harper	Fred E. Harper	1965	427
50 2/8	10 4/8	10 3/8	5 5/8	5 5/8	1 6/8	1 6/8	8	7 2/8	Ravalli Co., MT	Mark J. Jakobson	Mark J. Jakobson	1965	427
50 2/8	10 5/8	10 3/8	5 4/8	5 4/8	1 6/8	1 7/8	6 6/8	5 2/8	Invermere, BC	Laszlo Molnar	Laszlo Molnar	1965	427
50 2/8	10 7/8	11	5 4/8	5 3/8	1 7/8	1 7/8	8 4/8	8 1/8	Atlin, BC	Walter F. Ramage	Walter F. Ramage	1965	427
50 2/8	10 6/8	10 7/8	5 5/8	5 5/8	1 6/8	1 6/8	6 5/8	5 6/8	Skeena River, BC	Jack E. Monet	Jack E. Monet	1966	427
50 2/8	10	10	5 5/8	5 5/8	1 6/8	1 6/8	7 4/8	6 5/8	Chelan Co., WA	Ned Shiflett	Ned Shiflett	1966	427
50 2/8	10 2/8	10 3/8	5 6/8	5 6/8	1 4/8	1 5/8	6 3/8	5 1/8	Telkwa, BC	A.W. Phillips	A.W. Phillips	1967	427
50 2/8	9 4/8	9 4/8	5 3/8	5 4/8	2	2	7 4/8	7	Cassiar, BC	John A. Mueller	John A. Mueller	1968	427
50 2/8	10 1/8	10 1/8	6	5 7/8	2	2	7 5/8	7 5/8	Lynn Canal, AK	Jacques M. Norvell, Sr.	Jacques M. Norvell, Sr.	1968	427
50 2/8	10	9 6/8	6	5 7/8	1 7/8	1 7/8	6 4/8	6	Lake Chelan, WA	Gary L. Aichlmayr	Gary L. Aichlmayr	1969	427
50 2/8	10 5/8	10 2/8	5 3/8	5 4/8	1 7/8	2	6 5/8	5	Ecstall River, BC	Thomas J. Perry	Thomas J. Perry	1970	427
50 2/8	9 7/8	9 5/8	5 5/8	5 5/8	1 7/8	2	6 7/8	6 2/8	Juneau, AK	Jerry Kressin	Jerry Kressin	1971	427
50 2/8	10 1/8	10 2/8	5 6/8	5 6/8	1 7/8	1 7/8	7 1/8	6 2/8	Tumeka Lake, BC	Dan M. Edwards, Jr.	Dan M. Edwards, Jr.	1972	427
50 2/8	10 1/8	10 1/8	5 3/8	5 3/8	1 7/8	1 7/8	7 2/8	7 5/8	Dease Lake, BC	Carl K. Beaudry	Carl K. Beaudry	1975	427
50 2/8	10 6/8	10 6/8	5 4/8	5 4/8	1 6/8	1 6/8	8 7/8	8 2/8	Stikine River, BC	R.H. Weaver	R.H. Weaver	1976	427
50 2/8	9 7/8	9 7/8	5 6/8	5 6/8	1 7/8	1 7/8	7 3/8	6 4/8	Cassiar Mts., BC	Ron Ragan	Ron Ragan	1978	427
50 2/8	9 7/8	9 6/8	5 7/8	5 7/8	2	1 7/8	7 5/8	7 5/8	Ice Mt., BC	J.S. Van Alsburg	J.S. Van Alsburg	1978	427
50 2/8	10 2/8	10 2/8	5 4/8	5 6/8	1 7/8	1 7/8	6 5/8	5 4/8	Eagle Lake, AK	Dale E. Gibbons	Dale E. Gibbons	1982	427
50 2/8	10 1/8	10	5 6/8	5 6/8	1 7/8	1 7/8	6 6/8	5 5/8	Pemberton, BC	Weldon Talbot	Weldon Talbot	1982	427
50 2/8	9 3/8	9 1/8	5 7/8	5 7/8	1 7/8	1 7/8	6 7/8	6 3/8	Okanogan Co., WA	Richard J. Wristen	Richard J. Wristen	1982	427

Score	Length of Horn R	Length of Horn L	Circ. of Base R	Circ. of Base L	Circ. 3rd Quarter R	Circ. 3rd Quarter L	Tip to Tip Spread	Greatest Spread	Locality	By Whom Killed	Owner	Date Killed	Rank
50 4/8	10 7/8	10 5/8	5 5/8	5 4/8	1 6/8	1 6/8	1 6/8	7 2/8	Skeena, BC	Clarence J. Fields	Clarence J. Fields	1983	427
50 2/8	10 3/8	10 3/8	5 5/8	5 5/8	1 6/8	1 6/8	1 6/8	7 4/8	Mt. Stockdale, BC	James C. King	James C. King	1983	427
50 2/8	10 1/8	10 1/8	5 5/8	5 4/8	2	2	2	7 3/8	Kildala River, BC	Philip Perrone	Philip Perrone	1983	427
50 2/8	10 3/8	10 2/8	5 6/8	5 6/8	1 6/8	1 6/8	1 6/8	6 7/8	Chouteau Co., MT	Robert E. Young	Robert E. Young	1983	427
50 2/8	10 5/8	10 5/8	5 4/8	5 4/8	1 6/8	1 6/8	1 6/8	6 3/8	Bleasdell Creek, BC	Daniel Fediuk	Daniel Fediuk	1984	427
50 2/8	9 4/8	9 5/8	5 6/8	5 6/8	1 7/8	1 7/8	1 7/8	6 5/8	Snohomish Co., WA	Wayne E. Ritter	Wayne E. Ritter	1985	427
50 2/8	9 7/8	9 5/8	5 6/8	5 6/8	1 7/8	1 7/8	1 7/8	6 4/8	Kudwat Creek, BC	William R. Orth	William R. Orth	1986	427
50 2/8	9 2/8	9 2/8	5 7/8	5 7/8	1 7/8	1 7/8	1 7/8	6 6/8	Sicintine Range, BC	Roger L. Pock	Roger L. Pock	1988	427
50 2/8	9 6/8	10	5 6/8	5 6/8	1 7/8	1 7/8	1 7/8	7 5/8	Kitimat, BC	Steven M. Cooper	Steven M. Cooper	1990	427
50 2/8	10	9 7/8	5 6/8	5 6/8	1 6/8	1 7/8	1 7/8	7 3/8	Kenai Pen., AK	David W. Doner	David W. Doner	1992	427
50 2/8	9 7/8	10 6/8	5 4/8	5 5/8	1 6/8	1 6/8	1 6/8	6 4/8	Whatcom Co., WA	Darrel Van Kekerix	Darrel Van Kekerix	1992	427
50 2/8	10 4/8	10 1/8	5 5/8	5 5/8	1 6/8	1 7/8	1 6/8	7	Bonneville Co., ID	Arnae R. Hillam	Arnae R. Hillam	1993	427
50 2/8	10 1/8	10 1/8	5 5/8	5 5/8	1 6/8	1 7/8	1 6/8	9	Gataga River, BC	Wilson S. Stout	Wilson S. Stout	1993	427
50 2/8	10 1/8	10 2/8	5 6/8	5 6/8	2	2	2	4 3/8	Niblack Hollow, AK	Stan Colton	Stan Colton	1994	427
50 2/8	10 4/8	10 7/8	5 5/8	5 5/8	1 7/8	1 7/8	1 7/8	8 2/8	Kluachon Lake, BC	Eugene E. Hafen	Eugene E. Hafen	1994	427
50 2/8	10 7/8	10 1/8	5 5/8	5 5/8	1 7/8	1 7/8	1 7/8	5 5/8	Hidden Basin, AK	Chester J. McConnell, Jr.	Chester J. McConnell, Jr.	1994	427
50 2/8	10 1/8	10 2/8	5 5/8	5 5/8	1 6/8	1 6/8	1 6/8	7 2/8	Flameau Creek, BC	Robert Reisert	Robert Reisert	1994	427
50 2/8	9 6/8	9 6/8	5 6/8	5 6/8	1 7/8	1 7/8	1 7/8	7 3/8	Meziadin Lake, BC	John A. Monk	John A. Monk	1995	427
50 2/8	10	10	5 6/8	6	1 7/8	2	2	7 1/8	Chukachida River, BC	Lynn C. Street	Lynn C. Street	1995	427
50 2/8	10 1/8	10 1/8	5 7/8	5 7/8	1 7/8	1 7/8	1 7/8	5 1/8	Goldstream River, BC	Jo-Anne Meissner	Jo-Anne Meissner	1996	427
50 2/8	10 2/8	9 4/8	5 5/8	5 5/8	1 7/8	1 6/8	1 6/8	8 2/8	Kenai Pen., AK	William G. Boyce	William G. Boyce	1997	427
50 2/8	10 1/8	10 1/8	5 6/8	5 6/8	1 7/8	1 7/8	1 7/8	6 5/8	Idaho Co., ID	Joseph M. Coelho III	Joseph M. Coelho III	1997	427
50	9 7/8	9 4/8	5 6/8	5 6/8	1 6/8	1 6/8	1 6/8	7	Klinaklini River, BC	Powhatan Robinson	Camp Fire Club	1916	485
50	10 6/8	10 6/8	5 5/8	5 7/8	1 6/8	1 6/8	1 6/8	6 4/8	Rudyerd Bay, AK	Joseph H. Keeney	Joseph H. Keeney	1946	485
50	10	10	5 6/8	5 6/8	1 7/8	1 7/8	1 7/8	7 1/8	Cassiar Mts., BC	James King	James King	1947	485
50	10 1/8	9 4/8	5 4/8	5 4/8	2	2	2	7 6/8	Okanogan Co., WA	John Hutchinson	Ralph Hutchinson	1950	485
50	10 1/8	9 6/8	6	6	1 7/8	1 7/8	1 7/8	6 4/8	Kenai Pen., AK	Coke Elms	Coke Elms	1956	485
50	9 3/8	10 2/8	5 6/8	5 6/8	1 7/8	1 7/8	1 7/8	6 7/8	Prophet River, BC	Frank C. Hibben	Frank C. Hibben	1956	485
50	9 6/8	9 7/8	5 6/8	5 7/8	2 1/8	2	2 1/8	5 5/8	Keremeos Mt., BC	Robert Quaedvlieg	Robert Quaedvlieg	1956	485
50	9 4/8	9 4/8	5 4/8	5 6/8	1 7/8	1 7/8	1 7/8	6 6/8	Flathead River, MT	Gene Biddle	Gene Biddle	1957	485
50	10 2/8	10 2/8	5 5/8	5 5/8	1 5/8	1 6/8	1 5/8	5 6/8	Squaw Creek, ID	William A. Callaway	William H. Lockhart	1959	485
50	10 6/8	10 6/8	5 7/8	5 7/8	2	2	2	6 4/8	Cape Yakataga, AK	Edward I. Worst	Edward I. Worst	1960	485
50	10	10	5 6/8	5 6/8	1 7/8	1 7/8	1 7/8	6	K-Mountain, BC	Fred D. Fouty	Fred D. Fouty	1961	485
50	10	9 4/8	5 7/8	5 7/8	1 6/8	1 6/8	1 6/8	5 4/8	Bear Point, ID	Aaron U. Jones	Aaron U. Jones	1961	485
50	9 4/8	10 1/8	5 6/8	5 6/8	1 7/8	1 6/8	1 6/8	7 3/8	Girdwood, AK	Franklin Maus	Franklin Maus	1961	485
50	9 6/8	10 2/8	5 6/8	5 6/8	1 6/8	1 6/8	1 6/8	6 6/8	Grand Forks, BC	Norman Dawson, Jr.	Norman Dawson, Jr.	1962	485
50	9 3/8	10	6	6	2	2	2	6 6/8	Lake Chelan, WA	Ed Pariseu	Ed Pariseu	1962	485
50	9 6/8	10 2/8	5 5/8	5 5/8	2 2/8	2 1/8	2 2/8	6 7/8	Telegraph Creek, BC	Anthony Bechik	Anthony Bechik	1963	485
50	10 1/8	9 4/8	5 4/8	5 4/8	2	2	2	6 1/8	Lincoln, MT	James A. Gunn III	James A. Gunn III	1963	485
50	10 3/8	10 1/8	5 3/8	5 3/8	1 6/8	1 6/8	1 6/8	8 2/8	Gataga River, BC	Herb Klein	Herb Klein	1963	485
50	10	10 3/8	5 7/8	5 7/8	1 7/8	1 7/8	1 7/8	6 4/8	Oroville, WA	G. Pickering	G. Pickering	1963	485
50	10 3/8	10 2/8	5 4/8	5 4/8	1 7/8	1 7/8	1 7/8	6 4/8	Spatsizi, BC	William L. Searle	William L. Searle	1963	485
50	9 4/8	9 4/8	5 4/8	5 4/8	2 1/8	2 2/8	2 1/8	7 5/8	Halfway River, BC	Victor Tullis	Victor Tullis	1963	485
50	9 5/8	9 5/8	5 7/8	5 7/8	1 7/8	1 7/8	1 7/8	5 1/8	Blue Sheep Lake, BC	O.A. McClintock	O.A. McClintock	1964	485
50	10 3/8	10 3/8	5 5/8	5 5/8	1 6/8	1 6/8	1 6/8	6 6/8	Smithers, BC	John Rienhart	John Rienhart	1964	485
50	10 7/8	10 7/8	5 4/8	5 4/8	1 5/8	1 5/8	1 5/8	6	Keremeos, BC	Charles Barry	Charles Barry	1965	485
50	9 6/8	9 6/8	5 4/8	5 4/8	2	2	2	6 7/8	Keremeos, BC	Picked Up	Robert Kitto	1965	485

ROCKY MOUNTAIN GOAT
Oreamnos americanus and related subspecies

Score	Length of Horn R	L	Circumference of Base R	L	Circumference at Third Quarter R	L	Greatest Spread	Tip to Tip Spread	Locality	Hunter	Owner	Date Killed	Rank
50	10 4/8	10 6/8	5 3/8	5 3/8	1 6/8	1 7/8	6 5/8	5 6/8	Hope, BC	Peter Konrad	Peter Konrad	1965	485
50	9 7/8	10 1/8	5 4/8	5 5/8	2	2 1/8	7 7/8	6 2/8	Heart Peaks, BC	Bob Loewenstein	Bob Loewenstein	1965	485
50	10 1/8	10	5 6/8	5 6/8	1 6/8	1 6/8	8 2/8	8	Chilkat Range, AK	Jacques M. Norvell	Jacques M. Norvell	1965	485
50	10	10 1/8	5 5/8	5 6/8	2	2	7 2/8	7 2/8	Morice River, BC	Dennis A. Sperling	Dennis A. Sperling	1965	485
50	11 2/8	11 2/8	5	5	1 6/8	1 7/8	8 1/8	7 6/8	Petersburg, AK	James Briggs	James Briggs	1966	485
50	9 3/8	9 6/8	6	5 7/8	1 6/8	1 7/8	6 2/8	5 2/8	Lake Chelan, WA	Don Francis	Don Francis	1966	485
50	10 1/8	10 1/8	5 6/8	5 7/8	1 6/8	1 7/8	8 3/8	8 3/8	Seward, AK	John Lee	John Lee	1966	485
50	9 7/8	9 6/8	5 6/8	5 7/8	1 7/8	1 7/8	6 3/8	5 6/8	Nass River, BC	Vernon Rydde	Vernon Rydde	1966	485
50	9 6/8	9 7/8	5 6/8	5 6/8	1 7/8	1 7/8	6 6/8	5 4/8	Tatla Lake, BC	Jack Close	Jack Close	1967	485
50	10 3/8	10 3/8	5 4/8	5 4/8	1 6/8	1 7/8	7 5/8	7 4/8	Kenai Pen., AK	A.P. Funk	A.P. Funk	1967	485
50	9 7/8	9 6/8	5 4/8	5 4/8	2	2	7 5/8	7 3/8	Nass River, BC	D.E. O'Shea	D.E. O'Shea	1967	485
50	10 2/8	10 2/8	5 4/8	5 4/8	1 6/8	1 6/8	7 3/8	6 7/8	Cassiar Mts., BC	Arthur M. Scully, Jr.	Arthur M. Scully, Jr.	1967	485
50	10	10	5 4/8	5 4/8	2	2	8 6/8	8 6/8	Cassiar Mts., BC	E. David Slye	E. David Slye	1967	485
50	9 6/8	9 6/8	5 5/8	5 5/8	1 7/8	1 7/8	7 6/8	7 6/8	Whittier, AK	Myron D. Cowell	Myron D. Cowell	1968	485
50	9 7/8	9 7/8	5 2/8	5 2/8	2	2	7 4/8	6 5/8	Hastings Arm, BC	Walter J. Eisele	Walter J. Eisele	1968	485
50	10 2/8	10 2/8	5 4/8	5 4/8	1 7/8	1 7/8	6	4 6/8	Chelan Co., WA	Carl Lewis	Carl Lewis	1968	485
50	10 2/8	10 2/8	5 4/8	5 4/8	1 6/8	1 6/8	7 1/8	6 2/8	Skagway, AK	Don Sather	Don Sather	1968	485
50	10 5/8	10 6/8	5 5/8	5 5/8	1 5/8	1 5/8	6 6/8	6	St. Mary River, BC	Frederick Brahniuk	Frederick Brahniuk	1969	485
50	9 7/8	9 7/8	5 6/8	5 7/8	1 6/8	1 7/8	5	4 3/8	Chelan Co., WA	John F. Hooper	William R. Hooper	1970	485
50	9 6/8	9 6/8	5 2/8	5 2/8	2	2	8 6/8	5 7/8	Lake Kitchener, BC	Aubrey W. Minshall	Aubrey W. Minshall	1971	485
50	10 2/8	10 3/8	5 2/8	5 3/8	2	2	8 6/8	8 6/8	Port Dick, AK	Neil Smith	Neil Smith	1972	485
50	9 6/8	9 6/8	5 5/8	5 5/8	1 7/8	1 7/8	6 5/8	6	Hendon River, BC	R.A. Wiseman	R.A. Wiseman	1973	485
50	10	10 3/8	5 6/8	5 6/8	1 7/8	1 7/8	8 3/8	8	Goodwin Lake, BC	Bill Moomey	Bill Moomey	1974	485
50	9 6/8	9 7/8	5 6/8	5 5/8	1 7/8	1 7/8	6 4/8	6	Rudyerd Bay, AK	Gerry D. Downey	Gerry D. Downey	1975	485
50	10 1/8	10 1/8	5 4/8	5 3/8	2	1 7/8	7 3/8	6 5/8	Gataga River, BC	Jerald T. Waite	Jerald T. Waite	1975	485
50	9 7/8	9 7/8	5 4/8	5 4/8	1 7/8	1 7/8	8 2/8	7 7/8	Cassiar Mts., BC	Gordon A. Read	Gordon A. Read	1976	485
50	10 2/8	10 2/8	5 6/8	5 6/8	1 7/8	1 7/8	7 5/8	7 5/8	Terrace, BC	Joe Zucchiatti	Joe Zucchiatti	1976	485
50	10 3/8	10 5/8	5 5/8	5 5/8	1 6/8	1 6/8	8 2/8	7 5/8	Cassiar Mts., BC	Murray B. Wilson	Murray B. Wilson	1977	485
50	10 2/8	10 1/8	5 3/8	5 2/8	1 7/8	1 7/8	8 2/8	7 4/8	Prince William Sound, AK	Ernest H. Youngs	Ernest H. Youngs	1978	485
50	10 1/8	10 2/8	5 6/8	5 6/8	1 6/8	1 7/8	7 4/8	6 6/8	Skeena Mts., BC	Dee J. Burnett	Dee J. Burnett	1982	485
50	10 3/8	10 2/8	5 5/8	5 6/8	2	2	8 2/8	7	Yeth Creek, BC	Michael Follett	Michael Follett	1983	485
50	9 2/8	9 2/8	5 2/8	5 2/8	1 7/8	1 7/8	7 1/8	7 1/8	Bonneville Co., ID	Charles E. Wood	Charles E. Wood	1983	485
50	10 1/8	10 1/8	5 4/8	5 4/8	1 7/8	1 7/8	7 4/8	8	Inklin River, BC	John V. Macaluso	John V. Macaluso	1984	485
50	9 7/8	10	5 6/8	5 7/8	1 6/8	1 6/8	7 1/8	7	Kodiak Island, AK	Terry R. Stockman	Terry R. Stockman	1986	485
50	9 5/8	9 7/8	5 7/8	5 7/8	1 6/8	1 6/8	6 7/8	6 1/8	Yohetta Creek, BC	Terry R. Wagner	Terry R. Wagner	1986	485
50	10 3/8	10 6/8	5 5/8	5 5/8	1 6/8	1 6/8	6 7/8	6 1/8	Lincoln Co., MT	Wayne Hill	Wayne Hill	1988	485
50	9 7/8	9 7/8	5 5/8	5 5/8	1 7/8	1 7/8	7 7/8	7 7/8	Nass River, BC	Murray McDonald	Murray McDonald	1988	485
50	10 2/8	10 2/8	5 6/8	5 6/8	2	2	8 1/8	7 4/8	Rapid River, BC	Michael D. Rowe	Michael D. Rowe	1988	485

Score								Locality	Hunter	Owner	Date Killed	Rank
50	10 2/8	10 5/8	5 6/8	5 6/8	1 6/8	1 7/8	6 3/8	5	Bradfield Canal, AK	James L. Beskin	James L. Beskin	1989	485
50	10 1/8	9 7/8	5 2/8	5 2/8	2	2	7 4/8	6 3/8	Snohomish Co., WA	Jeffrey J. Nelson	Jeffrey J. Nelson	1989	485
50	10 3/8	10 2/8	5 5/8	5 5/8	1 7/8	1 7/8	7 7/8	7 3/8	Palliser River, BC	Louis B. Wood, Jr.	Louis B. Wood, Jr.	1989	485
50	10 4/8	10 2/8	5 4/8	5 5/8	1 7/8	1 6/8	6 2/8	5 7/8	King Co., WA	Spencer C. Davis	Spencer C. Davis	1990	485
50	9 1/8	9 3/8	5 6/8	5 6/8	2	2	7 3/8	7 1/8	Thunder Mt., BC	Jimmy E. Dixon	Jimmy E. Dixon	1990	485
50	9 3/8	9 3/8	5 7/8	5 7/8	2	2	6 4/8	5 3/8	Checats Lake, AK	Mark W. Agnew	Mark W. Agnew	1992	485
50	10 2/8	10	5 7/8	5 7/8	1 7/8	1 7/8	7 1/8	6 5/8	Bradley Lake, AK	John L. Hendrix	John L. Hendrix	1992	485
50	9 6/8	9 6/8	5 7/8	5 7/8	1 6/8	1 7/8	7 3/8	7	Elko Co., NV	Tammy H. Bawcom	Tammy H. Bawcom	1993	485
50	10 1/8	10	5 6/8	5 6/8	1 6/8	1 6/8	7	6 3/8	Kodiak Island, AK	Michael K. Odin	Michael K. Odin	1993	485
50	9 6/8	9 6/8	5 4/8	5 6/8	1 6/8	1 6/8	6 7/8	6	Kenai Pen., AK	Les Rainey	Les Rainey	1993	485
50	9 6/8	10 2/8	5 6/8	5 6/8	1 6/8	1 7/8	7 1/8	6 2/8	Elk River, BC	Santo Rocca	Santo Rocca	1993	485
50	9 4/8	9 4/8	5 6/8	5 6/8	1 7/8	1 7/8	6 6/8	6 2/8	Utah Co., UT	Ned W. Walker	Ned W. Walker	1994	485
50	10 7/8	10 7/8	5 4/8	5 4/8	1 7/8	1 5/8	7 3/8	6 5/8	Brewer Creek, BC	Donald L. Butler	Donald L. Butler	1995	485
50	10	10	5 6/8	5 6/8	1 7/8	1 7/8	8	8	Dease Lake, BC	Beau Beck	Beau Beck	1996	485
50	10	9 5/8	5 5/8	5 5/8	2	2	7 7/8	7 1/8	Flint Creek, BC	Doug H. Cundy	Doug H. Cundy	1996	485
50	10 2/8	10 4/8	5 4/8	5 4/8	1 6/8	1 6/8	7 6/8	7 4/8	Clark Co., ID	Brian G. Edgerton	Brian G. Edgerton	1996	485
50	9 7/8	9 6/8	5 4/8	5 4/8	1 7/8	1 7/8	6 3/8	5 2/8	Salt Lake Co., UT	Brad B. Kimball	Brad B. Kimball	1996	485
53 6/8*	10 2/8	10 2/8	6	6	2 1/8	2	7 2/8	7	Shoemaker Creek, BC	Brian D. Shepherd	Brian D. Shepherd	1991	485
53 6/8*	10 3/8	10 3/8	6 2/8	6 2/8	2	2	6 5/8	5 7/8	Stikine River, BC	Charles W. Bateman	Charles W. Bateman	1995	485

* Final score is subject to revision by additional verifying measurements.

CATEGORY
ROCKY MOUNTAIN GOAT

SCORE
50

HUNTER
MICHAEL K. ODIN

LOCATION
KODIAK ISLAND, AK

DATE OF KILL
OCTOBER 1993

CATEGORY
ROCKY MOUNTAIN GOAT

SCORE
51-4/8

HUNTER
REG MEISNER

LOCATION
NANIKA LAKE, BC

DATE OF KILL
OCTOBER 1995

CATEGORY
ROCKY MOUNTAIN GOAT

SCORE
52-6/8

HUNTER
ANTHONY C. RUGGERI

LOCATION
INKLIN RIVER, BC

DATE OF KILL
OCTOBER 1993

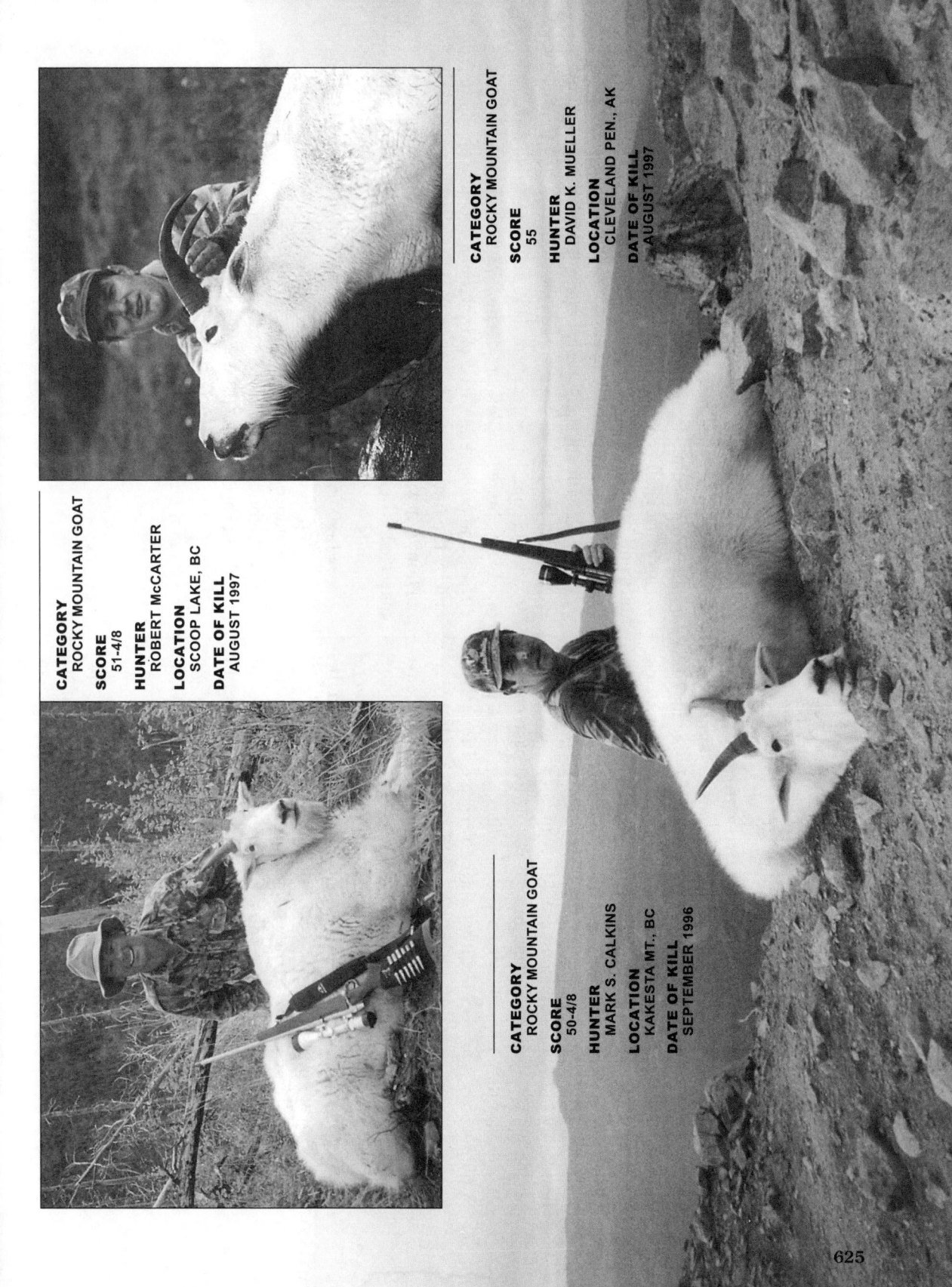

CATEGORY
ROCKY MOUNTAIN GOAT

SCORE
51-4/8

HUNTER
ROBERT McCARTER

LOCATION
SCOOP LAKE, BC

DATE OF KILL
AUGUST 1997

CATEGORY
ROCKY MOUNTAIN GOAT

SCORE
50-4/8

HUNTER
MARK S. CALKINS

LOCATION
KAKESTA MT., BC

DATE OF KILL
SEPTEMBER 1996

CATEGORY
ROCKY MOUNTAIN GOAT

SCORE
55

HUNTER
DAVID K. MUELLER

LOCATION
CLEVELAND PEN., AK

DATE OF KILL
AUGUST 1997

MUSKOX

NEW WORLD'S RECORD

Only a year after a successful bow hunt for Cape Buffalo in South Africa, Robert A. Black began thinking about his next hunt — one without bugs. He decided to hunt muskox (*Ovibos moschatus*). After choosing a reputable outfitter, Black began to plan his adventure to the frozen world of Northwest Territories.

"I arrived at Coppermine on March 25, 1996, and met Frank, my Inuit guide for the hunt. My equipment and I were placed on a snowmobile sled, and we set off for base camp. On the first day, 100 miles from Coppermine, we saw a herd of 65 muskox, but decided it would be very hard to stalk a herd that large with little or no cover. On the second day we left early to go scouting, and after several hours we spotted a group of 15, including two nice bulls. Prior to beginning the stalk, we watched the herd to see what direction they were grazing. Fortunately, a small snowbank separated us from the herd, providing the only cover for miles.

"As the herd moved slowly toward me, I prepared for the shot. The bull was broadside at 40 yards when I removed my hands from the mittens, and drew my bow. My point of aim was just to the right of the bull's left shoulder. I made my shot, just like I had practiced except for one small detail. With the adrenaline pumping, my natural instincts took over and I failed to bend my wrist to compensate for the additional clothing. Consequently, the bow string hit my coat, causing the arrow to strike seven inches to the left, resulting in impact directly at his left shoulder joint. The Muzzy broadhead shat- tered the shoulder joint of this huge animal; however, the arrow only penetrated through the joint. I immediately nocked another arrow and started to draw my bow. If you have ever been really, really cold and tried to draw a bow, you will understand my embarrassment when I could not get the bow drawn! This is one of those times when you have a very brief, intense talk with yourself and try again. I drew and again I hit exactly seven inches left of where I was aiming. This time the broadhead completely penetrated the animal. The whole herd, minus one huge bull, left the scene. The bull did not go over 20 feet, and collapsed. We quickly skinned and quartered him, and by the time we had the meat loaded on the sled, a good portion of it was already frozen. I was surprised to see how massive his head was. The skull cap and horns alone weighed 60 pounds."

At -50°F, Black had taken the first good bull he had a chance for, but he had no idea what the Boone and Crockett score would be until his return to the U.S. Scored at 127 points, the bull was declared a new Boone and Crockett Club World's Record at the 23rd Awards Program in Reno, Nevada, in 1998. It was also declared Pope and Young Club's World's Record at their 20th Recording Period in Edmonton Alberta, in 1997. ■

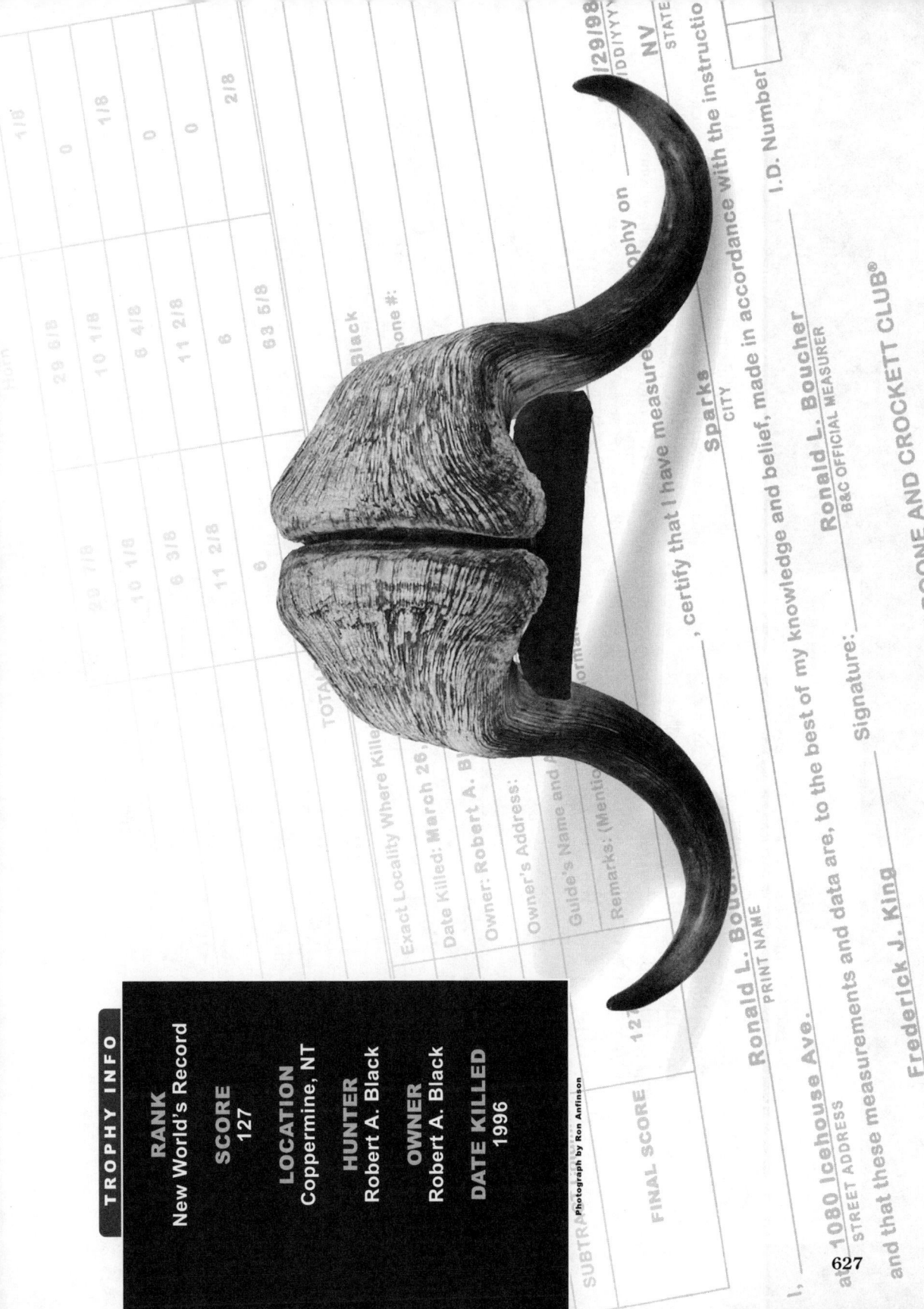

TROPHY INFO

RANK
New World's Record

SCORE
127

LOCATION
Coppermine, NT

HUNTER
Robert A. Black

OWNER
Robert A. Black

DATE KILLED
1996

Photograph by Ron Anfinson

	Horn		
	1/8		1/8
	29 6/8	0	0
	10 1/8		1/8
	6 4/8	0	
	11 2/8	0	
	6	0	
	63 5/8		2/8

	29 7/8
	10 1/8
	6 3/8
	11 2/8
	6

Black

TOTAL

Exact Locality Where Kille

Date Killed: March 26,

Owner: Robert A. Bl

Owner's Address:

Guide's Name and

Remarks: (Mentic

SUBTRA

FINAL SCORE

12

Ronald L. Bouch
PRINT NAME

I, , certify that I have measure
ophy on

Sparks
CITY

29/98
D/YYY

NV
STATE

I.D. Number

and that these measurements and data are, to the best of my knowledge and belief, made in accordance with the instructio

Signature:

Ronald L. Boucher
B&C OFFICIAL MEASURER

I,

at 1080 Icehouse Ave.
STREET ADDRESS

Witness:

Frederick J. King

© 1999 BY BOONE AND CROCKETT CLUB®

627

MUSKOX
WORLD'S RECORD SCORECHART

All measurements must be made with a 1/4-inch wide flexible steel tape and adjustable calipers to the nearest one-eighth of an inch. Enter fractional figures in eighths, without reduction. Official measurements cannot be taken until horns have air dried for at least 60 days after the animal was killed.

A. Greatest Spread is measured between perpendiculars at a right angle to the center line of the skull.

B. Tip to Tip Spread is measured between tips of horns.

C. Length of Horn is measured along center of upper horn surface, staying within curve of horn as illustrated, to a point in line with tip. Attempt to free the connective tissue between the horns at the center of the boss to determine the lowest point of horn material on each side. Hook the tape under the lowest point of the horn and measure the length of horn, with the measurement line maintained in the center of the upper surface of horn following the converging lines to the horn tip.

D-1. Width of Boss is measured with calipers at greatest width of the boss, with measurement line forming a right angle with horn axis. It is often helpful to measure D-1 before C, marking the midpoint of the boss as the correct path of C.

D-2-3-4. Divide measurement C of longer horn by four. Starting at base, mark **both** horns at these quarters (even though the other horn is shorter). Then, using calipers, measure width of boss at D-2, making sure the measurement is at a right angle to horn axis and in line with the D-2 mark. Circumferences are then measured at D-3 and D-4, with measurements being taken at right angles to horn axis.

Records of
North American
Big Game

250 Station Drive
Missoula, MT 59801
(406) 542-1888

BOONE AND CROCKETT CLUB®
OFFICIAL SCORING SYSTEM FOR NORTH AMERICAN BIG GAME TROPHIES

MINIMUM SCORES
AWARDS 105   ALL-TIME 105

MUSKOX

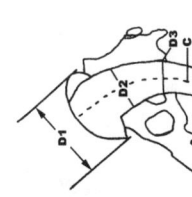

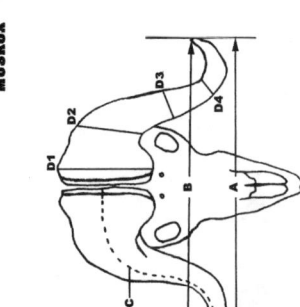

SEE OTHER SIDE FOR INSTRUCTIONS			COLUMN 1 Right Horn	COLUMN 2 Left Horn	COLUMN 3 Difference
A. Greatest Spread			30 4/8		
B. Tip to Tip Spread			29 5/8		
C. Length of Horn			29 7/8	29 6/8	1/8
D-1. Width of Boss			10 1/8	10 1/8	0
D-2. Width at First Quarter			6 3/8	6 4/8	1/8
D-3. Circumference at Second Quarter			11 2/8	11 2/8	0
D-4. Circumference at Third Quarter			6	6	0
		TOTALS	63 5/8	63 5/8	2/8
ADD	Column 1	63 5/8	Exact Locality Where Killed: Coppermine, NT		
	Column 2	63 5/8	Date Killed: March 26, 1996	Hunter: Robert A. Black	
	Subtotal	127 2/8	Owner: Robert A. Black	Telephone #:	
SUBTRACT Column 3		2/8	Owner's Address:		
			Guide's Name and Address:		
FINAL SCORE		127	Remarks: (Mention Any Abnormalities or Unique Qualities)		

I, __Ronald L. Boucher__ , certify that I have measured this trophy on __04/29/98__
    PRINT NAME   MM/DD/YYYY

at __1080 Icehouse Ave.__ __Sparks__ __NV__
    STREET ADDRESS   CITY   STATE/PROVINCE

and that these measurements and data are, to the best of my knowledge and belief, made in accordance with the instructions given.

Witness: __Frederick J. King__   Signature: __Ronald L. Boucher__   I.D. Number _____
                                                         B&C OFFICIAL MEASURER

Photograph by Ron Anfinson

TROPHY INFO

RANK
3

SCORE
125 4/8

LOCATION
Perry River, NT

HUNTER
Steven Persson

OWNER
Steven Persson

DATE KILLED
1995

TROPHY INFO

RANK
2

SCORE
126

LOCATION
Coppermine, NT

HUNTER
Eric Llanes

OWNER
Eric Llanes

DATE KILLED
1997

Photograph by Ron Anfinson

Ovibos moschatus moschatus and certain related subspecies

Score	Length of Horn R	L	Width of Boss R	L	Circumference at Third Quarter R	L	Greatest Spread	Tip to Tip Spread	Locality	Hunter	Owner	Date Killed	Rank
127	29 7/8	29 1/8	10 1/8	10 1/8	6	6	30 4/8	29 5/8	Coppermine, NT	Robert A. Black	Robert A. Black	1996	1
126	30	29 1/8	10 1/8	10 1/8	6 2/8	6	29 7/8	29	Coppermine, NT	Eric Llanes	Eric Llanes	1997	2
125 4/8	28 1/8	27 6/8	10 1/8	10 4/8	5 7/8	5 7/8	29	28 4/8	Perry River, NT	Steven Persson	Steven Persson	1995	3
125 2/8	27 2/8	27 1/8	10 5/8	10 2/8	6 5/8	6 4/8	30 4/8	30 1/8	Bay Chimo, NT	Donald Nicholson	Donald Nicholson	1988	4
125	30 2/8	31 6/8	10 4/8	10 1/8	5	6 3/8	31 4/8	30 5/8	Bay Chimo, NT	Stephen A. Kroflich	Stephen A. Kroflich	1990	5
124 6/8	30 1/8	29 6/8	9 2/8	9	6	5 7/8	31 4/8	31	Perry River, NT	Robert D. Jones	Robert D. Jones	1988	6
124 6/8	27 2/8	27 6/8	11 1/8	11	6	6 2/8	28 2/8	27 3/8	Tree River, NT	John V. Lattimore, Jr.	John V. Lattimore, Jr.	1995	6
123 6/8	28 1/8	28 3/8	10 4/8	10 5/8	6 2/8	6 5/8	31 2/8	31	Northwest Territories	Unknown	Sam Pancotto	PR 1976	8
122 6/8	28 3/8	29 3/8	9 7/8	9 6/8	5 7/8	7 1/8	27 2/8	26 6/8	Kent Pen., NT	Jeffery L. Meyerl	Jeffery L. Meyerl	1993	9
122 4/8	27 6/8	27 6/8	10 7/8	11	5 6/8	5 5/8	30 2/8	29 4/8	Rendez-vous Lake, NT	William R. Powers	William R. Powers	1991	10
122 4/8	27 5/8	28 7/8	11 3/8	11 1/8	6 1/8	5 2/8	29 2/8	27 2/8	Asiak River, NT	Bruce T. Berger	Bruce T. Berger	1993	10
122	29	28 1/8	10	9 7/8	6 5/8	5 7/8	30 5/8	30 3/8	Perry River, NT	Picked Up	Robert J. Decker	1979	12
122	30 2/8	30 6/8	10 3/8	10 6/8	5 2/8	5 4/8	31 1/8	30 6/8	Kikerk Lake, NT	Bill McDowell	Bill McDowell	1994	12
121 6/8	28 2/8	29	9 7/8	9 6/8	5 6/8	6 2/8	32 4/8	32 2/8	Cambridge Bay, NT	Tom Gross	Tom Gross	1986	14
121	28 2/8	29 6/8	9 7/8	9 7/8	5 5/8	6 4/8	31 4/8	31	Ellice River, NT	Picked Up by J.G. Stelfox	B&C National Collection	1983	15
121	29	27	10 5/8	10 6/8	6 4/8	5 5/8	28 5/8	28	Inulik Lake, NT	Richard N. Gubler	Richard N. Gubler	1994	15
120 6/8	28 6/8	30	11 3/8	11 1/8	4 7/8	5 3/8	25 7/8	22 4/8	Coppermine River, NT	Ralph E. Post	Ralph E. Post	1993	17
120 2/8	27 6/8	28 7/8	10 1/8	10 3/8	5 7/8	6	28 6/8	26 7/8	Inulik Lake, NT	Mike Stockton	Mike Stockton	1994	18
120	28 5/8	28 3/8	10 6/8	10 2/8	5 4/8	5 2/8	28 4/8	27	Rendez-vous Lake, NT	Jim Moellman	Jim Moellman	1989	19
119 6/8	29 4/8	29 2/8	10 2/8	10 2/8	5 2/8	5 1/8	27	24 1/8	Coppermine River, NT	Glenn M. Smith	Glenn M. Smith	1994	20
119 4/8	28 7/8	29 1/8	9 5/8	10	5 4/8	5 4/8	29 1/8	28 7/8	McNaughton River, NT	Picked Up	Robert D. Jones	1991	21
119 4/8	29 1/8	28 4/8	9 6/8	9 6/8	6 1/8	5 5/8	28 4/8	26 7/8	Back River, NT	Michael N. Van Handel	Michael N. Van Handel	1997	21
119	27 2/8	27 2/8	9 2/8	8 7/8	6 4/8	6 2/8	28 6/8	28 6/8	Ellice River, NT	Greg C. Bond	Greg C. Bond	1995	23
118 6/8	27 5/8	28 2/8	10 4/8	9 7/8	5 2/8	5 2/8	29 3/8	28 3/8	Bay Chimo, NT	Doyle V. Toliver	Doyle V. Toliver	1989	24
118 6/8	29 4/8	28 5/8	10 4/8	10 1/8	5 7/8	6	28 5/8	27 1/8	Bay Chimo, NT	Lance K. Parks	Lance K. Parks	1993	24
118 4/8	28 3/8	29 1/8	9 3/8	9 4/8	5 4/8	5 7/8	32	31 6/8	Perry Island, NT	Lawrence T. Epping	Lawrence T. Epping	1990	26
118 2/8	27 2/8	27 2/8	10 6/8	10 4/8	5 2/8	5 4/8	26 7/8	24 6/8	Rendez-vous Lake, NT	Victor E. Moss	Victor E. Moss	1989	27
118	28 4/8	28 7/8	9 4/8	9 3/8	5 2/8	5 1/8	27 3/8	24 6/8	Rendez-vous Lake, NT	Roy L. Jacobs	Roy L. Jacobs	1996	28
117 6/8	27 7/8	27 2/8	9	9 4/8	5 6/8	5 6/8	29 2/8	27 3/8	Victoria Island, NT	James D. Verbrugge	James D. Verbrugge	1996	29
117	29 5/8	29 6/8	9 2/8	9 3/8	5 2/8	5 2/8	30 3/8	29 4/8	Perry Island, NT	Robert D. Jones	Robert D. Jones	1989	30
117	26	25 7/8	10 1/8	10 4/8	6 5/8	6 5/8	28 5/8	28 3/8	Cambridge Bay, NT	Jay Archibald	Jay Archibald	1996	30
116 6/8	26 3/8	26 6/8	10 2/8	10 4/8	5 7/8	5 4/8	27 2/8	25 4/8	Ellice River, NT	George M. Dirgo	George M. Dirgo	1996	32
116 6/8	26	26 6/8	9 7/8	9 7/8	4 7/8	5 3/8	24 4/8	22 4/8	Rendez-vous Lake, NT	Picked Up	Hubert R. Kennedy	PR 1991	32
116 4/8	27 3/8	28 5/8	11	10 7/8	5 1/8	5 3/8	28 2/8	27 3/8	Coppermine, NT	Rob W. Shatzko	Rob W. Shatzko	1996	32
116 2/8	29 7/8	28 2/8	10 4/8	10 4/8	6 1/8	4 4/8	26 4/8	24 2/8	Inulik Lake, NT	Russell G. Brice	Russell G. Brice	1994	35
115 6/8	28 2/8	27 5/8	10 1/8	10	5 7/8	5 5/8	27 1/8	26 6/8	Perry Island, NT	Delbert E. Rieckers	Delbert E. Rieckers	1988	36
115 6/8	28 3/8	29 5/8	9 4/8	9 6/8	4 3/8	5 1/8	28 5/8	26 3/8	Rendez-vous Lake, NT	Hubert R. Kennedy	Hubert R. Kennedy	1990	36
115 4/8	28	28 5/8	8 7/8	9 4/8	5 4/8	5 4/8	26 1/8	25 1/8	Adelaide Pen., NT	Jack A. Wilkinson	Jack A. Wilkinson	1992	38

Score									Locality	Hunter	Owner	Date Killed	Rank
115 4/8	27 7/8	30	9 4/8	9 2/8	5 2/8	6	28 3/8	27 5/8	Bay Chimo, NT	Richard Persson	Richard Persson	1995	38
115 4/8	27	29 1/8	11 3/8	11 2/8	4	5 3/8	30 7/8	29 7/8	Coppermine, NT	James D. Verbrugge	James D. Verbrugge	1995	38
115 2/8	27 3/8	27 2/8	9 1/8	9 3/8	5 3/8	5 2/8	31 5/8	30 7/8	Perry Island, NT	Richard A. Jones	Richard A. Jones	1988	41
115	26	26	10 6/8	10 2/8	5 4/8	5 4/8	27	27	Ellesmere Island, NT	I.S. Wombath	Harvard Univ. Mus.	1900	42
114 6/8	25 7/8	25 7/8	9 7/8	9 6/8	5 2/8	5 4/8	28 3/8	27 7/8	Kent Pen., NT	Archie J. Nesbitt	Archie J. Nesbitt	1989	43
114 4/8	28 1/8	27 7/8	9 2/8	9 1/8	5	4 7/8	25 5/8	22 4/8	Banks Island, NT	Don L. Corley	Don L. Corley	1985	44
114 4/8	25 5/8	26 5/8	11	10 4/8	5 1/8	5 7/8	31 5/8	31 2/8	Melville Sound, NT	Robert D. Taylor	Robert D. Taylor	1996	44
114 2/8	29 6/8	29 4/8	9 5/8	9 7/8	5 2/8	5 2/8	26	25 5/8	Hudson Bay, NT	Monjo	Carnegie Mus.	1910	46
114 2/8	27 6/8	25 5/8	9 7/8	10 2/8	6 2/8	5 6/8	26 6/8	26 1/8	Ellice River, NT	Gary Loghry	Gary Loghry	1990	46
114 2/8	26 6/8	27 4/8	10 4/8	10 2/8	5	5 6/8	26	24 6/8	Rendez-vous Lake, NT	James C. Johnson	James C. Johnson	1991	46
114	26	25 7/8	9 5/8	9 6/8	5 4/8	5 2/8	27 6/8	27	Rendez-vous Lake, NT	Richard E. Aniballi	Richard E. Aniballi	1992	49
113 6/8	27 5/8	28	9 1/8	9 1/8	5 1/8	4 7/8	26 4/8	24 6/8	Rendez-vous Lake, NT	Shawn Andres	Shawn Andres	1990	50
113 6/8	27 3/8	28 3/8	9 7/8	9 6/8	5 2/8	5	29 1/8	28	Kikerk Lake, NT	Ronald J. Pavlik	Ronald J. Pavlik	1994	50
113 4/8	29	28	8 7/8	9 3/8	5 5/8	5 1/8	28 6/8	28 4/8	Ellice River, NT	Steve Munier	Steve Munier	1988	52
113 4/8	28 2/8	27 2/8	9 5/8	9 6/8	5 7/8	5 4/8	28 2/8	27 4/8	Bathurst Inlet, NT	George R. Skaggs	George R. Skaggs	1988	52
113 4/8	27 1/8	27 2/8	9 7/8	9 6/8	5 2/8	5 4/8	28 6/8	27 2/8	Paulatuk, NT	Duane Fujiye	Duane Fujiye	1996	52
113 2/8	28	29	8 5/8	8 6/8	4 7/8	4 7/8	29 5/8	28 5/8	Barren Grounds, NT	Gift of H. Casmir de Rham	B&C National Collection	PR 1910	55
113 2/8	26 6/8	26 7/8	9 7/8	10 1/8	4 7/8	5 1/8	28	26 1/8	Swan Lake, NT	Basil C. Bradbury	Basil C. Bradbury	1982	55
113 2/8	26 6/8	28	9 4/8	9	5 2/8	5 1/8	23 6/8	22 4/8	Kuuk River, NT	Roger L. Gregg	Roger L. Gregg	1992	55
113 2/8	27 4/8	28 2/8	10	10 1/8	4 5/8	5	28 7/8	28 3/8	Inulik Lake, NT	William H. Crawford	William H. Crawford	1994	55
113	27 6/8	27 1/8	9 4/8	9	5 4/8	5 6/8	30	29 6/8	Bay Chimo, NT	David B. Dentoni, Sr.	David B. Dentoni, Sr.	1990	59
113	27 2/8	27 5/8	10 1/8	10 4/8	5	5 1/8	27 1/8	25 2/8	Rendez-vous Lake, NT	Picked Up	Victor E. Moss	PR 1990	59
112 6/8	28 4/8	26 7/8	10 6/8	11 4/8	5 6/8	4 5/8	25 1/8	23 3/8	Paulatuk, NT	Picked Up	Roger A. Hansen	1988	61
112 6/8	25 7/8	27 3/8	10 7/8	11	4 2/8	5 5/8	30 2/8	30	Coppermine, NT	Al Houston	Al Houston	1995	61
112 4/8	27 5/8	27 5/8	8 2/8	8 2/8	5	5	31 1/8	30 2/8	Thirty Mile Lake, NT	Joe Scotti	Neale Wortley	1983	63
112 4/8	31 2/8	30 4/8	9 2/8	9	5	4 2/8	27 7/8	25 5/8	Victoria Island, NT	Patrick H. Ackerman	Patrick H. Ackerman	1992	63
112 4/8	25 2/8	25 6/8	10 3/8	10	5 2/8	5	27 7/8	28 3/8	Rendez-vous Lake, NT	Victor E. Moss	Victor E. Moss	1992	63
112 2/8	27 7/8	27 3/8	9 1/8	9 1/8	4 7/8	4 6/8	27 4/8	24	Rendez-vous Lake, NT	Michael E. Kuglitsch	Michael E. Kuglitsch	1994	66
111 6/8	24 7/8	26 1/8	9	9 1/8	4 6/8	7 4/8	27 7/8	26 1/8	Perry River, NT	Robert H. Hanson	Robert H. Hanson	1987	67
111 6/8	25 4/8	26 3/8	9 5/8	9 3/8	5 4/8	5 7/8	29 1/8	29	Ellice River, NT	William G. Farley	William G. Farley	1990	67
111 6/8	26 4/8	26 3/8	9 2/8	9 7/8	4 2/8	4 7/8	27 7/8	27 4/8	Nunivak Island, AK	Danny Pankoski	Danny Pankoski	1991	67
111 6/8	27 4/8	26 2/8	9 4/8	9 7/8	5	4 5/8	26 5/8	24 6/8	Rendez-vous Lake, NT	Richard J. Larson	Richard J. Larson	1992	67
111 4/8	24 3/8	24 4/8	10 1/8	10 2/8	5 2/8	5 3/8	26 4/8	25 3/8	Prince of Wales Island, NT	J. William Kerr	J. William Kerr	1970	71
111 4/8	27 6/8	27 4/8	9 1/8	8 6/8	5 3/8	5 2/8	28 4/8	28	Nightmute, AK	B. & T. Jorgensen	Picked Up	1988	71
111 4/8	27 7/8	27 4/8	9 3/8	9 5/8	5 2/8	5 1/8	23 6/8	22 5/8	Kaleet River, NT	Collins F. Kellogg, Sr.	Collins F. Kellogg, Sr.	1993	71
111 2/8	28 1/8	26 5/8	10 1/8	10 1/8	5 5/8	4 4/8	28 1/8	26 4/8	Perry River, NT	Douglas G. Williams	Douglas G. Williams	1987	74
111 2/8	26 4/8	26 6/8	8 4/8	8 6/8	5 4/8	5 7/8	26 3/8	25 6/8	Nunivak Island, AK	Willard G. Waite	Willard G. Waite	1989	74
111 2/8	27	27 1/8	8 3/8	8 1/8	6	5 4/8	27 7/8	27 5/8	Nunivak Island, AK	David L. Richards	David L. Richards	1990	74
111 2/8	26 2/8	26 6/8	9 5/8	10	5 1/8	5 1/8	23	21 1/8	Rendez-vous Lake, NT	Mark A. Adams	Mark A. Adams	1991	74
111 2/8	26 7/8	28 1/8	9	9 6/8	4 5/8	5 3/8	28 1/8	27 5/8	Coppermine, NT	Robert W. Kubick	Robert W. Kubick	1991	74
111 2/8	25 2/8	25 2/8	10	10	5 6/8	5 4/8	26 7/8	25 5/8	Coppermine, NT	Douglas G. Lynn	Douglas G. Lynn	1995	74
111	27 4/8	26 6/8	9 7/8	9 3/8	4 6/8	5	26 7/8	24 5/8	Rendez-vous Lake, NT	Michael Andres	Michael Andres	1994	80
111	26 1/8	26 2/8	8 1/8	9 1/8	5 2/8	5 2/8	26	25	Paulatuk, NT	Dale L. Hedgpeth	Dale L. Hedgpeth	1994	80
110 6/8	27	27	8 2/8	8	5 2/8	5 6/8	26 6/8	26 1/8	McNaughton River, NT	Hugo K. Kilian	Hugo K. Kilian	1992	82
110 4/8	27 6/8	26 6/8	9 3/8	9 4/8	5	4 5/8	28 1/8	27	Holman Island, NT	Adam Ovilek	Roger Britton	1981	83
110 4/8	26 3/8	25 3/8	9	9 2/8	5 4/8	5 4/8	26 1/8	25 7/8	Thelon River, NT	Picked Up	H.P.L. Kiliaan	1982	83

MUSKOX

Ovibos moschatus moschatus and certain related subspecies

Score	Length of Horn R	L	Width of Boss R	L	Circumference at Third Quarter R	L	Greatest Spread	Tip to Tip Spread	Locality	Hunter	Owner	Date Killed	Rank
110 4/8	25	25 1/8	10	10	5	5 4/8	28 3/8	27 2/8	Holman Island, NT	William M. Phillippe, Jr.	William M. Phillippe, Jr.	1982	83
110 4/8	26	26	9 6/8	9 6/8	4 5/8	5	25 6/8	21 5/8	Banks Island, NT	David V. Collis	David V. Collis	1985	83
110 4/8	27	27 2/8	8 6/8	8 4/8	5 3/8	5 4/8	28	27 4/8	Nelson Island, AK	William McNamara	William McNamara	1993	83
110 2/8	25 6/8	26 4/8	9 2/8	9 5/8	5	5	27 1/8	25 6/8	Delesse Lake, NT	Michael T. Warn	Michael T. Warn	1995	88
110	26 2/8	26 6/8	8 6/8	9 1/8	4 6/8	5 4/8	28	26 4/8	Banks Island, NT	William R. Ellis III	William R. Ellis III	1982	89
110	26 6/8	26 4/8	8 5/8	8 6/8	5 4/8	5 1/8	27	26 1/8	Sadlerochit River, AK	Ronald L. Deis	Ronald L. Deis	1985	89
110	26 2/8	25 2/8	9 7/8	9 6/8	5	5 7/8	28 7/8	28 4/8	Pelly Island, AK	Jurgen Blattgerste	Jurgen Blattgerste	1990	89
109 6/8	27 2/8	27 2/8	8 4/8	8 1/8	5 1/8	5 1/8	26 6/8	26 2/8	Nelson Island, AK	Brent R. Akers	Brent R. Akers	1986	92
109 6/8	26 1/8	25 4/8	9 7/8	10 1/8	5 3/8	5	26 6/8	25 1/8	Victoria Island, NT	Virgil R. Graber	Virgil R. Graber	1987	92
109 6/8	27 5/8	27 4/8	9	9	5 1/8	4 6/8	27 3/8	26 6/8	Nunivak Island, AK	Scott Hebertson	Scott Hebertson	1988	92
109 6/8	26 2/8	26 3/8	8 6/8	8 5/8	5 2/8	4 5/8	23 4/8	21 5/8	Rendez-vous Lake, NT	F. Dee Rea	F. Dee Rea	1994	92
109 6/8	27 3/8	26 5/8	9 2/8	10	4 6/8	4 5/8	27 4/8	26 6/8	Victoria Island, NT	Harold B. Biggs	Harold B. Biggs	1996	92
109 4/8	25	26	9 4/8	9 4/8	4 6/8	5 7/8	27	25 6/8	Banks Island, NT	James M. Domokos	James M. Domokos	1981	97
109 4/8	25 4/8	26	9 7/8	9 4/8	5 2/8	5 3/8	28 1/8	27 5/8	Nunivak Island, AK	Carolyn Elledge	Carolyn Elledge	1983	97
109 4/8	26 2/8	26 4/8	8 6/8	8 4/8	5 3/8	5 4/8	27	26 1/8	Nelson Island, AK	Jeff C. Rogers	Jeff C. Rogers	1986	97
109 4/8	26 1/8	26 3/8	8 1/8	8	5 3/8	5 5/8	26 3/8	25 4/8	Canning River, AK	Gregory L. Venable	Gregory L. Venable	1990	97
109 4/8	25 3/8	26 5/8	9 2/8	9	5 4/8	5 7/8	28 1/8	27 6/8	Nunivak Island, AK	David R. Lautner	David R. Lautner	1991	97
109 2/8	27	26 6/8	9 1/8	8 7/8	4 6/8	4 2/8	26 4/8	23 5/8	Parry Pen., NT	Douglas J. Dollhopf	Douglas J. Dollhopf	1983	102
109 2/8	28	26 6/8	9 7/8	9 1/8	5 4/8	4 2/8	25 6/8	23	Banks Island, NT	Audrey E. Crabtree	Audrey E. Crabtree	1985	102
109	27 1/8	27	8 1/8	8 1/8	5	5	30 5/8	27 7/8	Nunivak Island, AK	Ron D. King	Ron D. King	1986	104
109	26	26 4/8	9	8 7/8	5 2/8	5 4/8	27 2/8	26 5/8	Ellice River, NT	Gerald L. Warnock	Gerald L. Warnock	1988	104
109	27 3/8	26 6/8	8 2/8	8 4/8	5 2/8	4 5/8	26 2/8	25 6/8	Nunivak Island, AK	Butch Hautanen	Butch Hautanen	1989	104
109	26 2/8	24 3/8	9 2/8	9 2/8	5 4/8	5 7/8	26 1/8	28	Ellice River, NT	Thomas D. Suedmeier	Thomas D. Suedmeier	1989	104
109	26 5/8	26 5/8	8 2/8	8 1/8	5 4/8	5 7/8	24 7/8	24 5/8	Nunivak Island, AK	James A. Reid	James A. Reid	1991	104
109	27 7/8	30	9 1/8	9 2/8	4 2/8	4	23 3/8	20	Rendez-vous Lake, NT	George B. Hubbard, Jr.	George B. Hubbard, Jr.	1993	104
108 6/8	25 1/8	25 1/8	10 1/8	10	5	5	28 5/8	27 3/8	Banks Island, NT	William M. Wheless III	William M. Wheless III	1980	110
108 6/8	25 3/8	25 7/8	8 7/8	8 3/8	5 7/8	5 7/8	27 7/8	27 6/8	Nunivak Island, AK	James P. Moon, Jr.	James P. Moon, Jr.	1985	110
108 6/8	24 7/8	26 1/8	10 5/8	10 4/8	5	5 2/8	27	24 5/8	Sachs Harbour, NT	Charles D. Lein	Charles D. Lein	1986	110
108 6/8	26 2/8	26 1/8	8 1/8	7 7/8	5 3/8	5 6/8	26 6/8	26 4/8	Nunivak Island, AK	William C. Cloyd	William C. Cloyd	1991	110
108 6/8	27 2/8	27	7 6/8	7 7/8	5 6/8	5 1/8	26 6/8	26 4/8	Nunivak Island, AK	Joseph E. Hardy	Joseph E. Hardy	1991	110
108 6/8	26 7/8	28	9	8 6/8	4 1/8	5 1/8	26 3/8	26	Nunivak Island, AK	Loren B. Hollers	Loren B. Hollers	1991	110
108 6/8	25 7/8	25 6/8	8 7/8	8 7/8	5 1/8	5 1/8	28	27 2/8	Nunivak Island, AK	Travis D. House	Travis D. House	1994	110
108 4/8	25	23	9 1/8	9 3/8	6 6/8	6 7/8	25 3/8	23 1/8	Hornaday River, NT	Picked Up	Dan Murphy	PR 1976	117
108 4/8	27	26 3/8	9 2/8	9 4/8	4 5/8	4 6/8	25 5/8	23 6/8	Banks Island, NT	James W. Owens	James W. Owens	1981	117
108 4/8	25 4/8	26 3/8	9 7/8	10 2/8	4 4/8	5 6/8	26 2/8	26 6/8	Banks Island, NT	Herman A. Bennett	Herman A. Bennett	1982	117
108 4/8	27	26 7/8	8 3/8	8 4/8	5 1/8	5	27 1/8	26 3/8	Nunivak Island, AK	Jaci A. Crace	Jaci A. Crace	1986	117
108 4/8	26 5/8	26 6/8	8 2/8	8 2/8	4 7/8	5	24 5/8	24 2/8	Nunivak Island, AK	Lloyd E. Laborde	Lloyd E. Laborde	1986	117
108 4/8	27 2/8	27 4/8	7 7/8	8	5	5	28 5/8	28 3/8	Nunivak Island, AK	Jerry M. Wylie	Jerry M. Wylie	1989	117

Score	Length of Horn R	Length of Horn L	Width of Boss R	Width of Boss L	Circ. R	Circ. L	Greatest Spread	Tip to Tip	Locality	Hunter	Owner	Date	Rank
108 4/8	26	26 1/8	9 6/8	10 4/8	4 7/8	5 4/8	28	26 6/8	Kikerk Lake, NT	Daryl W. Schreiner	Daryl W. Schreiner	1994	117
108 4/8	24 7/8	28	11 4/8	10 7/8	4 4/8	6 1/8	29 6/8	28 6/8	Coppermine, NT	Deborah K. DeBruyn	Deborah K. DeBruyn	1997	117
108 2/8	25 3/8	27	8 5/8	8 5/8	4 7/8	5 3/8	29	28 2/8	Ellice River, NT	Jerald E. Mason	Jerald E. Mason	1989	125
108 2/8	25 3/8	25 7/8	9 3/8	9 3/8	4 7/8	6	25 3/8	24 2/8	Lady Franklin Point, NT	Perry Harwell	Perry Harwell	1990	125
108	24 5/8	25 2/8	9 4/8	10 1/8	4 6/8	5 4/8	26 5/8	24	Hudson Bay, NT	Native American	N.K. Luxton	1890	127
108	24 5/8	25 5/8	9	9 5/8	5 2/8	6 2/8	27	26	Barren Grounds, NT	Gift of J.B. Marvin	Unknown	PR 1951	127
108	24 6/8	26 5/8	7 4/8	8 7/8	5 6/8	5 6/8	25 3/8	26 6/8	Nunivak Island, AK	Helga Schroeder	Helga Schroeder	1978	127
108	30 1/8	30 4/8	9 4/8	7 4/8	4 2/8	5	25 6/8	23 4/8	Cape Mendenhall, AK	Donald E. Franklin	Donald E. Franklin	1983	127
108	26 6/8	25 7/8	9 4/8	9 4/8	5 1/8	5	25 6/8	25 3/8	Paulatuk, NT	Don McVittie	Don McVittie	1985	127
108	26 7/8	25 7/8	9 4/8	9 4/8	4 4/8	4 5/8	28 2/8	25 6/8	Sachs Harbour, NT	John G. Munsinger	John G. Munsinger	1988	127
108	26 5/8	25 3/8	9	9 1/8	5	5	26 7/8	26 2/8	Perry River, NT	Robert D. Jones	Robert D. Jones	1990	127
108	26 1/8	26 1/8	8 4/8	8 4/8	5 1/8	5 1/8	28 5/8	27 1/8	Nunivak Island, AK	Terrance E. Burlew	Terrance E. Burlew	1990	127
108	27	25 6/8	8 7/8	8 7/8	6 1/8	5 1/8	28 1/8	26 3/8	Queen Maud Gulf, NT	Archie J. Nesbitt	Archie J. Nesbitt	1993	127
108	25 2/8	24 1/8	10 6/8	10 1/8	5 2/8	4 7/8	23 7/8	28 2/8	Victoria Island, NT	David L. Currier	David L. Currier	1993	127
108	26 7/8	27 4/8	9 2/8	9 2/8	4 3/8	4 3/8	27 4/8	28 5/8	Victoria Island, NT	George F. Dennis, Jr.	George F. Dennis, Jr.	1993	127
108	26 2/8	26 3/8	9 5/8	9 2/8	4 5/8	5 1/8	24 7/8	27 6/8	Rendez-vous Lake, NT	Thomas J. Merkley	Thomas J. Merkley	1994	127
108	24 7/8	24 7/8	9 4/8	9 4/8	5 1/8	5 4/8	28 7/8	28 1/8	Victoria Island, NT	Robert C. Balkman	Robert C. Balkman	1994	127
108	26 5/8	27 7/8	9 6/8	9 6/8	4 7/8	5	25 5/8	21 1/8	Brock River, NT	Craig W. Barnes	Craig W. Barnes	1974	127
108	26 2/8	26 1/8	9 3/8	9 5/8	5 5/8	5	27 3/8	23 7/8	Melville Island, NT	Picked Up	D.C. Thomas	1976	127
108	25 3/8	25 6/8	8 3/8	8 3/8	5	5	26 5/8	27 4/8	Nunivak Island, AK	John H. Taucher II	John H. Taucher II	1982	127
107 6/8	25 2/8	26	9 7/8	9 7/8	4 7/8	4 1/8	26	22 7/8	Victoria Island, NT	Picked Up	John Behrns	1988	141
107 6/8	27 4/8	26 6/8	9 6/8	9 4/8	4 7/8	5 1/8	25 4/8	23 6/8	Pellatt Lake, NT	Robert A. Skrzypek	Robert A. Skrzypek	1989	141
107 6/8	26 7/8	26 4/8	9 5/8	9 2/8	5 6/8	5 4/8	24 4/8	27 7/8	Perry River, NT	Robert L. Killett	Robert L. Killett	1996	141
107 6/8	25 2/8	25 5/8	9 2/8	8 2/8	5 3/8	5 4/8	25 6/8	24 6/8	Banks Island, NT	John M. Schaffter	John M. Schaffter	1993	141
107 4/8	26 1/8	25 7/8	8	8	4 5/8	5 4/8	26 4/8	25 2/8	Canada	George Vaux	Acad. Nat. Sci., Phil.	PR 1951	147
107 4/8	26 2/8	27 2/8	9 2/8	9 3/8	4 6/8	4 5/8	27 2/8	24	Victoria Island, NT	Craig T. Boddington	Craig T. Boddington	1981	147
107 4/8	25 3/8	24 7/8	9 4/8	9 4/8	4 5/8	5	28	25 7/8	Banks Island, NT	Jack Fiske	Jack Fiske	1981	147
107 4/8	25 2/8	26 6/8	9	9	5	5	26 3/8	27 2/8	Cape Mohican, AK	Tommy L. Ramsey	Tommy L. Ramsey	1990	147
107 4/8	26 6/8	26 4/8	8 4/8	8 1/8	4 6/8	4 6/8	29 4/8	24 5/8	Victoria Island, NT	Vernon J. Boose	Vernon J. Boose	1992	147
107 4/8	26 3/8	26 3/8	8 1/8	9 1/8	5 4/8	5 4/8	29 2/8	26 1/8	Nunivak Island, AK	Timothy A. Gleason	Timothy A. Gleason	1992	147
107 4/8	25	25 2/8	9 3/8	9 1/8	5 3/8	5 1/8	29 4/8	29 1/8	Contwoyto Lake, NT	John P. Burdette	John P. Burdette	1993	147
107 4/8	26 1/8	27 2/8	9 7/8	9 7/8	5 6/8	6	27 6/8	27 7/8	Kent Pen., NT	Raymond Venissat	Raymond Venissat	1993	147
107 2/8	26 7/8	24 7/8	8 6/8	9 1/8	5 3/8	5	28	29 2/8	Greenland	Bill Foster	Foster's Bighorn Rest.	PR 1945	155
107 2/8	26 1/8	26 6/8	9	8 1/8	4 5/8	5	27 6/8	26 2/8	Nunivak Island, AK	William A. Keller	William A. Keller	1977	155
107 2/8	26 1/8	25	8 1/8	8 4/8	5 6/8	4 6/8	27 3/8	27 3/8	Nunivak Island, AK	Normand Poulin	Normand Poulin	1977	155
107 2/8	26 3/8	24 7/8	8 4/8	9	5 2/8	5 4/8	27 4/8	27 4/8	Nunivak Island, AK	Jacob Metzger	Jacob Metzger	1978	155
107 2/8	25	25 2/8	9 1/8	9	5 2/8	5 4/8	23	24 4/8	Cambridge Bay, NT	Picked Up	Manfred Huellbusch	1979	155
107 2/8	26 2/8	26 4/8	9	9 1/8	4 5/8	5 2/8	24 6/8	21 4/8	Banks Island, NT	Karen K. Jacobsen	Karen K. Jacobsen	1987	155
107	26 6/8	27 1/8	9 1/8	8 5/8	4 3/8	4 5/8	27 3/8	26 2/8	Rendez-vous Lake, NT	Terence L. Andres	Terence L. Andres	1994	162
107	26 3/8	26 6/8	8 5/8	8 4/8	4 6/8	5	27 3/8	26 1/8	Nunivak Island, AK	Russell Reed	Russell Reed	1978	162
107	24 3/8	25	9 1/8	9 4/8	5 4/8	5 2/8	24 6/8	23 5/8	Delesse Lake, NT	Franco Mazzucchelli	Franco Mazzucchelli	1981	162
107	26 1/8	24 7/8	9 7/8	10 1/8	5 5/8	4 2/8	24 6/8	22 7/8	Holman Island, NT	I.D. Shapiro	I.D. Shapiro	1982	162
107	26 1/8	25 5/8	9 3/8	9	4 7/8	5	24	26 2/8	Rendez-vous Lake, NT	Jack W. Claypoole	Jack W. Claypoole	1993	162
107	26 1/8	25 7/8	8 7/8	8 5/8	4 6/8	5	25 4/8	24	Falaise Lake, NT	Robert D. Hansen	Robert D. Hansen	1994	167
106 6/8	27 3/8	28 1/8	8 6/8	8 3/8	4 5/8	5 3/8	25 4/8	25 4/8	Greenland	Unknown	Rudolf Sand	1930	167
106 6/8	25	27 3/8	8 5/8	8 2/8	5 3/8	6	26 7/8	26 4/8	Greenland	Alvin Pedersen	Zool. Mus., Copenhagen	1935	167
106 6/8	25 1/8	25 1/8	8 3/8	8 4/8	5	5	28	27 6/8	Nunivak Island, AK	Bert Klineburger	Bert Klineburger	1959	167

Ovibos moschatus moschatus and certain related subspecies

Score	Length of Horn R	L	Width of Boss R	L	Circumference at Third Quarter R	L	Greatest Spread	Tip to Tip Spread	Locality	Hunter	Owner	Date Killed	Rank
106 6/8	26 1/8	27 1/8	8 6/8	8 6/8	4 7/8	4 7/8	27 5/8	27 2/8	Nunivak Island, AK	Ethel D. Leedy	Ethel D. Leedy	1975	167
106 6/8	26 1/8	26 3/8	9 3/8	9	4 7/8	5	27	25	Sachs Harbour, NT	John R. Blanton	John R. Blanton	1984	167
106 6/8	26 2/8	26 3/8	7 7/8	8 1/8	5	5	26 1/8	25 4/8	Nunivak Island, AK	Jerald M. Finney	Jerald M. Finney	1987	167
106 6/8	26 2/8	25	8 2/8	8 3/8	5 6/8	5 4/8	27 6/8	27 4/8	Roberts Mt., AK	Jack D. Adams	Jack D. Adams	1993	167
106 6/8	26	27 3/8	9 5/8	9 5/8	4 2/8	4 7/8	27 3/8	26 1/8	Sachs Harbour, NT	James R. Gall	James R. Gall	1995	167
106 6/8	27 2/8	25 4/8	9 3/8	10	5 6/8	4 4/8	29	28 6/8	Bay Chimo, NT	David G. Miller	David G. Miller	1996	167
106 6/8	25 6/8	25 1/8	9 3/8	8 1/8	5 2/8	4 6/8	26 7/8	26 1/8	Holman, NT	David A. Justmann	David A. Justmann	1997	167
106 4/8	25 7/8	25 7/8	8 1/8	8 4/8	5 1/8	4 7/8	28 1/8	28	Karon Lake, AK	R. Kim Francisco	R. Kim Francisco	1985	177
106 4/8	25 5/8	25 4/8	9 2/8	9 3/8	5	5	25 1/8	22 6/8	Banks Island, NT	Keith C. Halstead	Keith C. Halstead	1986	177
106 4/8	25 6/8	26 2/8	8 4/8	8 2/8	4 7/8	4 7/8	26 2/8	25 3/8	Nunivak Island, AK	Richard McIntyre	Richard McIntyre	1988	177
106 4/8	26 4/8	26 4/8	8 1/8	8	4 7/8	5	26	25 3/8	Sadlerochit River, AK	Donald L. Willis	Donald L. Willis	1990	177
106 4/8	25	25 2/8	8 5/8	8 3/8	5 3/8	5 3/8	27 6/8	27 4/8	Nunivak Island, AK	Paulette R. Knutson	Paulette R. Knutson	1992	177
106 4/8	26 5/8	28 1/8	9 5/8	9 5/8	4	5 2/8	25 1/8	24 3/8	Sachs Harbour, NT	James E. Kapuscinski	James E. Kapuscinski	1994	177
106 2/8	26 2/8	27 2/8	8 4/8	8 1/8	4 5/8	5 2/8	25 4/8	24 5/8	Kuparuk River, AK	David F. Neel	David F. Neel	1995	177
106 2/8	26	25 6/8	8 4/8	8 2/8	4 7/8	4 4/8	29 6/8	29 4/8	Nunivak Island, AK	L.G. Sullivan	L.G. Sullivan	1977	184
106 2/8	24 6/8	25 2/8	9	9	6	5 2/8	27	26 4/8	Nunivak Island, AK	Frank N. Rome	Frank N. Rome	1985	184
106 2/8	25 2/8	25 3/8	9 3/8	9 4/8	5 7/8	4 7/8	25	21 2/8	Victoria Island, NT	Lawrence T. Epping	Lawrence T. Epping	1986	184
106 2/8	26 4/8	25 7/8	7 6/8	8 1/8	4 7/8	5 3/8	27 6/8	26 7/8	Perry River, NT	Jack Downing	Jack Downing	1988	184
106 2/8	25 4/8	26 5/8	9 1/8	9	5	5 2/8	26 6/8	26 6/8	Nunivak Island, AK	Elwin J. Lawler	Elwin J. Lawler	1990	184
106 2/8	25 7/8	25 2/8	8 5/8	8 6/8	5 7/8	5 1/8	26 2/8	25 6/8	Canning River, AK	Carl L. Yowell	Carl L. Yowell	1990	184
106 2/8	25 2/8	25 1/8	8 7/8	9	5 4/8	5 4/8	25 5/8	24 4/8	Cambridge Bay, NT	Donald E. Twa	Donald E. Twa	1991	184
106	26 3/8	25 1/8	10 4/8	10 5/8	4 4/8	4 5/8	27	27	Nunivak Island, AK	Gail W. Holderman	Gail W. Holderman	1976	191
106	26 5/8	26 5/8	8 6/8	9	5 1/8	4 2/8	26 4/8	25 1/8	Banks Island, NT	Norman F. Taylor	Norman F. Taylor	1981	191
106	26 1/8	25 2/8	8	8 2/8	5 3/8	5	27 4/8	27 2/8	Canning River, AK	Darrel W. Sauder	Darrel W. Sauder	1983	191
106	25 1/8	25 2/8	8 6/8	8 6/8	5	4 6/8	26 6/8	26 4/8	Rendez-vous Lake, NT	Lanny L. Walker	Lanny L. Walker	1988	191
105 6/8	27 2/8	27	9 4/8	9 6/8	4 4/8	5 2/8	27	24 6/8	Barren Grounds, NT	Unknown	Snow Museum	1890	195
105 6/8	25 2/8	25 1/8	8 5/8	8 7/8	5 5/8	5	25 2/8	24 4/8	Nunivak Island, AK	Lynn M. Castle	Lynn M. Castle	1977	195
105 6/8	25 6/8	25 2/8	8 4/8	8 4/8	5	4 6/8	27 2/8	26 4/8	Nunivak Island, AK	William K. Leech	William K. Leech	1977	195
105 6/8	26	25 2/8	9 2/8	9 1/8	4 5/8	4 5/8	25 7/8	23 6/8	Nunivak Island, AK	Gary E. Brown	Gary E. Brown	1978	195
105 6/8	26	24 7/8	9 4/8	9 6/8	4 6/8	4 6/8	27 5/8	25 6/8	Sachs Harbour, NT	Donald J. Craite	Donald J. Craite	1987	195
105 6/8	25 2/8	25 6/8	9	8 7/8	4 6/8	5 1/8	23 6/8	21 5/8	Coronation Gulf, NT	James A. Hale	James A. Hale	1987	195
105 6/8	26 2/8	26 6/8	7 7/8	7 7/8	5 2/8	5	29 5/8	29 2/8	Nunivak Island, AK	Henry M. Hills III	Henry M. Hills III	1987	195
105 6/8	25	26	9 7/8	9 5/8	4 3/8	5 2/8	27 1/8	26 5/8	Banks Island, NT	Bernard Sippin	Bernard Sippin	1988	195
105 6/8	25	28	9 3/8	9 3/8	4 2/8	5 4/8	26	25 4/8	Ellice River, NT	Christopher J. Harvey	Christopher J. Harvey	1992	195
105 6/8	26 5/8	26 5/8	9 4/8	9 5/8	4 1/8	4	23 6/8	22 7/8	Montresor River, NT	David J. DuFlo	David J. DuFlo	1993	195
105 6/8	25 5/8	26 3/8	8	8 1/8	5 6/8	5	27 5/8	27 3/8	Nunivak Island, AK	Gregory A. Stoick	Gregory A. Stoick	1993	195
105 6/8	26 6/8	26	8 3/8	8 2/8	4 4/8	4 6/8	26 2/8	25	Rendez-vous Lake, NT	Jody C. Hostetler	Jody C. Hostetler	1996	195
105 6/8	25 5/8	25 5/8	8 5/8	8 4/8	5 1/8	4 6/8	26 1/8	23 3/8	Rendez-vous Lake, NT	Paul E. Hostetler	Paul E. Hostetler	1996	195

Score	Length of Horn R	Length of Horn L	Width of Boss R	Width of Boss L	Width of Horn R	Width of Horn L	Greatest Spread	Tip to Tip Spread	Locality	By Whom Killed	Owner	Date Killed	Rank
105 4/8*	26	26	8 2/8	8 2/8	4 7/8	4 6/8	27	26 2/8	Nunivak Island, AK	Sam C. Arnett III	Sam C. Arnett III	1976	208
105 4/8	25 7/8	25 7/8	8 2/8	8 3/8	5	4 6/8	27	26 6/8	Nunivak Island, AK	Robert E. Speegle	Robert E. Speegle	1976	208
105 4/8	26	25 7/8	8 1/8	8 1/8	5 2/8	5	26 3/8	25 1/8	Nunivak Island, AK	Jean Louis L'Ecuyer	Jean Louis L'Ecuyer	1978	208
105 4/8	25 4/8	25 4/8	8 1/8	8 2/8	5 2/8	5 1/8	25 6/8	24 4/8	Nunivak Island, AK	Curtis S. Williams	Curtis S. Williams	1978	208
105 4/8	25 4/8	25 3/8	8 7/8	9 1/8	4 6/8	4 6/8	28	27	Nunivak Island, AK	Roland Stickney	Roland Stickney	1979	208
105 4/8	26 3/8	26 3/8	8 3/8	8 6/8	5 1/8	4 3/8	29 4/8	29	Nunivak Island, AK	Joseph A. Carr	Joseph A. Carr	1984	208
105 4/8	26 4/8	26 7/8	7 7/8	8	4 5/8	4 7/8	27 3/8	26 3/8	Nunivak Island, AK	John D. Frost	John D. Frost	1986	208
105 4/8	25 4/8	25 6/8	9 5/8	9 4/8	4 6/8	5 1/8	26 4/8	25 4/8	Sachs Harbour, NT	William H. Bynum	William H. Bynum	1989	208
105 4/8	27	27	8 6/8	8 2/8	4 5/8	4 5/8	24 3/8	23 2/8	Bluenose Lake, NT	George P. Mann	George P. Mann	1990	208
105 4/8	26 1/8	26 1/8	8 3/8	8 3/8	5 4/8	5 7/8	27 7/8	27 6/8	Nunivak Island, AK	Frederick D. Overly	Frederick D. Overly	1994	208
105 4/8	25 7/8	25 5/8	9 5/8	9 3/8	4 7/8	4 7/8	25 4/8	24 4/8	Banks Island, NT	Jerry Boettcher	Jerry Boettcher	1996	208
105 4/8	26	26	7 5/8	7 4/8	5 3/8	5 3/8	27 5/8	26 7/8	Nunivak Island, AK	G.A. Treschow	G.A. Treschow	1978	208
105 2/8	26 1/8	25 3/8	8 2/8	8 1/8	6	5 4/8	25 6/8	24	Nunivak Island, AK	F. Phillips Williamson	F. Phillips Williamson	1978	219
105 2/8	25 6/8	25 5/8	8 3/8	8 3/8	4 6/8	5	27 2/8	26 4/8	Nunivak Island, AK	David A. Schuller	David A. Schuller	1982	219
105 2/8	24 4/8	24 5/8	9 6/8	9 6/8	4 5/8	5 2/8	25 1/8	23 7/8	Richardson River, NT	Ronald L. Fuller	Ronald L. Fuller	1988	219
105 2/8	27	27	9 2/8	9 1/8	4 4/8	5 1/8	26 5/8	26	Gjaa Haven, NT	James J. McBride	James J. McBride	1991	219
105 2/8	25 4/8	25 4/8	8 6/8	8 6/8	4 7/8	4 4/8	27 7/8	27 7/8	Nunivak Island, AK	Michael L. Frost, Jr.	Michael L. Frost, Jr.	1993	219
105 2/8	24 2/8	24 2/8	8 3/8	8 3/8	5 4/8	5 2/8	25 6/8	24 6/8	Banks Island, NT	Thomas A. Shimak, Sr.	Thomas A. Shimak, Sr.	1993	219
105 2/8	25 5/8	25 5/8	8	7 7/8	5 2/8	4 7/8	27 3/8	27	Nelson Island, AK	Samuel H. Schurig	Samuel H. Schurig	1994	219
105 2/8	26 5/8	26 5/8	8 3/8	8 3/8	4 7/8	4 7/8	24 4/8	23 4/8	Hudson Bay, NT	Indian	N.K. Luxton	1905	219
105	26	26	8 7/8	8 2/8	4 7/8	4 7/8	26 7/8	26 1/8	Nunivak Island, AK	Carlo Bonomi	Carlo Bonomi	1976	227
105	25 7/8	25 7/8	8 4/8	9	4 6/8	4 6/8	27 7/8	27	Nunivak Island, AK	Dan H. Brainard	Dan H. Brainard	1977	227
105	26 2/8	26 2/8	8 5/8	8 3/8	4 5/8	4 5/8	27 5/8	26	Bering Sea, AK	Jack M. Holland, Jr.	Jack M. Holland, Jr.	1977	227
105	24 7/8	24 7/8	9 1/8	8 4/8	5 1/8	5 4/8	24 6/8	24	Cambridge Bay, NT	Picked Up	Manfred Huellbusch	1979	227
105	26 2/8	26 2/8	9 2/8	9 2/8	4 5/8	4 3/8	24 3/8	19	Cambridge Bay, NT	Norman L. Epley	Norman L. Epley	1989	227
105	27 1/8	27 1/8	8 1/8	7 7/8	4 4/8	4 6/8	27 4/8	27 1/8	Nelson Island, AK	Unknown	Thomas W. Oates	PR 1992	227
105	27 2/8	27 2/8	8 3/8	8 4/8	6	4 5/8	26 2/8	26	Nunivak Island, AK	William O. West	William O. West	1992	227
105	25 7/8	25 7/8	9 4/8	9 4/8	4 1/8	4 7/8	26 6/8	24 7/8	Banks Island, NT	Robert B. Nancarrow	Robert B. Nancarrow	1995	227
105	23 5/8	23 5/8	9 2/8	9 2/8	4 7/8	5 4/8	27 1/8	25 6/8	Victoria Island, NT	Kenneth L. Jenson	Kenneth L. Jenson	1996	227
126 2/8*	29 4/8	29 4/8	11	11	5 7/8	5 5/8	28 3/8	27 1/8	Coppermine, NT	Fred Gonzales	Fred Gonzales	1996	
122 4/8*	27 4/8	27 4/8	10 5/8	10 7/8	6	5 6/8	29 5/8	29 2/8	Kikirk Lake, NT	Bill Pastorek	Bill Pastorek	1996	
122 4/8*	29 2/8	29 2/8	11	11 7/8	6	5 4/8	29 2/8	28 3/8	Coppermine River, NT	Larry C. Fisher	Larry C. Fisher	1997	
122 2/8*	27 6/8	27 6/8	10 4/8	10 1/8	6 1/8	6 2/8	31 1/8	30 2/8	Coppermine, NT	Michael K. McKenzie	Michael K. McKenzie	1995	
118 6/8*	28 3/8	28 3/8	10	10	5 5/8	5 1/8	29 4/8	26 5/8	Rendez-vous Lake, NT	John J. Grabenstein	John J. Grabenstein	1994	

* Final score is subject to revision by additional verifying measurements.

CATEGORY
MUSKOX

SCORE
127
WORLD'S RECORD

HUNTER
ROBERT A. BLACK

LOCATION
COPPERMINE, NT

DATE OF KILL
MARCH 1996

CATEGORY
MUSKOX

SCORE
113-6/8

HUNTER
RONALD J. PAVLIK

LOCATION
KIKERK LAKE, NT

DATE OF KILL
MARCH 1994

CATEGORY
MUSKOX

SCORE
117-6/8

HUNTER
JAMES D. VERBRUGGE

LOCATION
VICTORIA ISLAND, NT

DATE OF KILL
OCTOBER 1996

636

CATEGORY
MUSKOX

SCORE
105-6/8

HUNTER
DAVID J. DUFLO

LOCATION
MONTRESOR RIVER, NT

DATE OF KILL
APRIL 1993

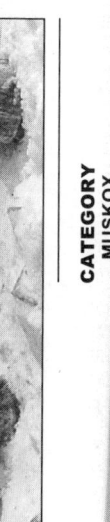

CATEGORY
MUSKOX

SCORE
122-6/8

HUNTER
JEFFERY L. MEYERL

LOCATION
KENT PEN., NT

DATE OF KILL
MARCH 1993

CATEGORY
MUSKOX

SCORE
105-2/8

HUNTER
THOMAS A. SHIMAK, SR.

LOCATION
BANKS ISLAND, NT

DATE OF KILL
SEPTEMBER 1993

BIGHORN SHEEP
WORLD'S RECORD

Taken in Blind Canyon, Alberta, in 1911 by Twin Butte rancher Fred Weiller, this trophy would undergo a North American odyssey lasting nearly a half century. Weiller killed the bighorn ram (*Ovis canadensis canadensis*) with one shot using a Model 1894 Winchester .30-30. After having the 70 pound trophy mounted, Weiller hung the ram's head on the wall of his ranch house without ever having it officially measured.

Nearly 30 years later, Clarence Baird, a former ranch hand who took over after Weiller passed on, finally agreed to enter the bighorn in the Willow Valley Trophy Club Awards. Unofficially scored at 208-2/8, the bighorn was recognized after all those years as a potential World's Record. In order to make the measurement official, it was requested that the ram's head be sent to the Boone and Crockett Club's 12th Competition in 1965 at the Carnegie Museum in Pittsburgh, Pennsylvania.

Initially wary of having the trophy leave his safeguard, Baird agreed to have it shipped by train. Little did he know that his worse fears would come true when the head was lost for a month due to a railway strike. To everyone's relief the trophy was eventually located and continued its voyage to the Carnegie Museum where it was officially scored at 208 -1/8. The new World's Record was put on exhibit at the 12th Competition (now called Awards) before making the long trip from Pittsburgh back to Alberta. Despite enticing offers, the head

remained hanging at the Baird house where it was admired by visitors for years.

However, the story behind the World's Record bighorn sheep does not have a happy ending. Nearly as sad as the fact that Weiller never received credit in his own lifetime was the event that occurred in December 1971. Two weeks before Christmas, the Baird house was engulfed in flames and the 60 year old trophy went up in a puff of smoke. ■

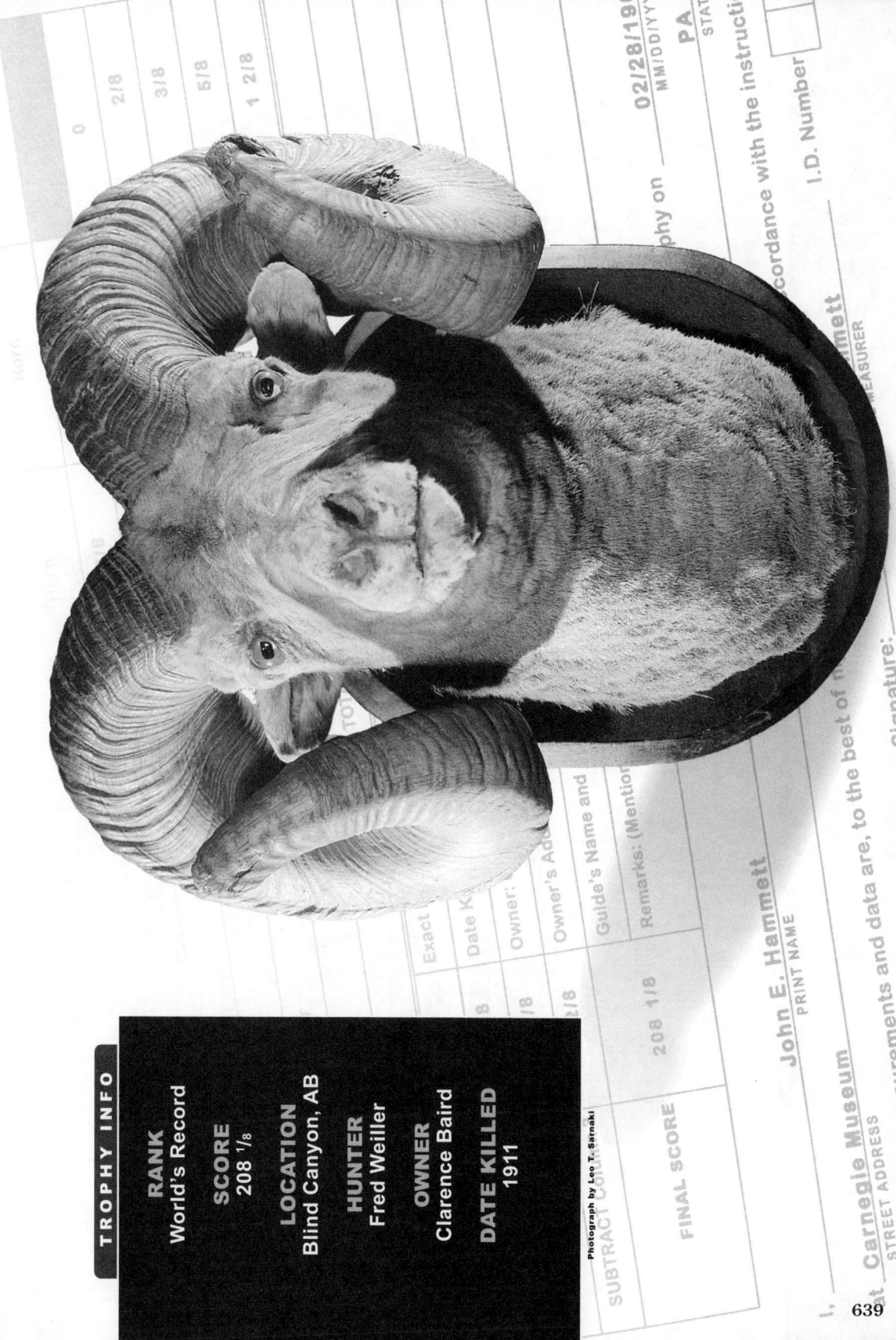

TROPHY INFO

RANK
World's Record

SCORE
208 1/8

LOCATION
Blind Canyon, AB

HUNTER
Fred Weiller

OWNER
Clarence Baird

DATE KILLED
1911

All measurements must be made with a 1/4-inch wide flexible steel tape to the nearest one-eighth of an inch. Enter fractional figures in eighths, without reduction. Official measurements cannot be taken until horns have air dried for at least 60 days after the animal was killed.

A. Greatest Spread is measured between perpendiculars at a right angle to the center line of the skull.

B. Tip to Tip Spread is measured between tips of horns.

C. Length of Horn is measured from the lowest point in front on outer curve to a point in line with tip. **Do not** press tape into depressions. The low point of the outer curve of the horn is considered to be the low point of the frontal portion of the horn, situated above and slightly medial to the eye socket (not the outside edge). Use a straight edge, perpendicular to horn axis, to end measurement on "broomed" horns.

D-1. Circumference of Base is measured at a right angle to axis of horn. **Do not** follow irregular edge of horn; the line of measurement must be entirely on horn material.

D-2-3-4. Divide measurement C of longer horn by four. Starting at base, mark **both** horns at these quarters (even though the other horn is shorter) and measure circumferences at these marks, with measurements taken at right angles to horn axis.

Records of
North American
Big Game

250 Station Drive
Missoula, MT 59801
(406) 542-1888

BOONE AND CROCKETT CLUB®
OFFICIAL SCORING SYSTEM FOR NORTH AMERICAN BIG GAME TROPHIES

SHEEP

MINIMUM SCORES

	AWARDS	ALL-TIME
bighorn	175	180
desert	165	168
Dall's	160	170
Stone's	165	170

KIND OF SHEEP (check one)
- ■ bighorn
- ☐ desert
- ☐ Dall's
- ☐ Stone's

PLUG NUMBER

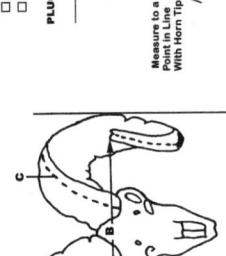

Measure to a
Point in Line
With Horn Tip

SEE OTHER SIDE FOR INSTRUCTIONS	COLUMN 1	COLUMN 2	COLUMN 3
	Right Horn	Left Horn	Difference
A. Greatest Spread (Is Often Tip to Tip Spread)	22 6/8		
B. Tip to Tip Spread	19 3/8		
C. Length of Horn	44 7/8	45	0
D-1. Circumference of Base	16 5/8	16 5/8	2/8
D-2. Circumference at First Quarter	16 1/8	16 3/8	3/8
D-3. Circumference at Second Quarter	15 1/8	15 4/8	5/8
D-4. Circumference at Third Quarter	11 2/8	11 7/8	1 2/8
TOTALS	104	105 3/8	

ADD	Column 1	104	
	Column 2	105 3/8	
	Subtotal	209 3/8	
SUBTRACT Column 3		1 2/8	
FINAL SCORE		**208 1/8**	

Exact Locality Where Killed: **Blind Canyon, AB**

Date Killed: **1911**   Hunter: **Fred Weiller**

Owner: **Clarence Baird**   Telephone #:

Owner's Address:

Guide's Name and Address:

Remarks: (Mention Any Abnormalities or Unique Qualities)

I, **John E. Hammett** , certify that I have measured this trophy on **02/28/1966**
PRINT NAME   MM/DD/YYYY

at **Carnegie Museum**   **Pittsburgh**   **PA**
STREET ADDRESS   CITY   STATE/PROVINCE

and that these measurements and data are, to the best of my knowledge and belief, made in accordance with the instructions given.

Witness: **George T. Church, Jr.**   Signature: **John E. Hammett**   I.D. Number
B&C OFFICIAL MEASURER

641

BIGHORN SHEEP

Ovis canadensis canadensis and certain related subspecies

MINIMUM SCORE 180

Score	Length of Horn		Circumference of Base		Circumference at Third Quarter		Greatest Spread	Tip tp Tip Spread	Locality	Hunter	Owner	Date Killed	Rank
	R	L	R	L	R	L							
208 1/8	44 7/8	45	16 5/8	16 5/8	11 2/8	11 7/8	22 6/8	19 3/8	Blind Canyon, AB	Fred Weiler	Clarence Baird	1911	1
207 2/8	45	45 2/8	15 6/8	16	11 6/8	11 7/8	23 1/8	19 3/8	Oyster Creek, AB	Martin Bovey	Martin Bovey	1924	2
206 3/8	44 4/8	44 3/8	15 7/8	15 7/8	12 1/8	12 1/8	21 4/8	21 4/8	Burnt Timber Creek, AB	Picked Up	Gordon L. Magnussen	1955	3
204 7/8	43 1/8	41 6/8	17 1/8	16 7/8	11 4/8	11 7/8	23 4/8	18 6/8	Granite Co., MT	James R. Weatherly	James R. Weatherly	1993	4
204	49 4/8	48 2/8	15 2/8	15 3/8	10 5/8	10 2/8	23 7/8	23 7/8	Sheep Creek, BC	James Simpson	Am. Mus. Nat. Hist.	1920	5
203 5/8	43 2/8	41 5/8	17 2/8	17 4/8	11 3/8	10 2/8	20 7/8	23 4/8	Beaverhead Co., MT	Picked Up	MT Dept. Fish, Wildl. & Parks	1992	6
203 4/8	43 1/8	42 5/8	16 4/8	16 4/8	11 3/8	11 1/8	25 4/8	19 4/8	Sheep River, AB	Katherine A. Pyra	Katherine A. Pyra	1992	7
202 3/8	41	40 7/8	17 2/8	17 2/8	11	11	25 3/8	26 2/8	Granite Co., MT	Richard B. Wiant	Richard B. Wiant	1992	8
202 2/8	46 7/8	44 5/8	15 5/8	15 2/8	11	10 6/8	23 2/8	23 2/8	Panther River, AB	Tom Kerquits	Unknown	1918	9
202	46 5/8	45 1/8	15 2/8	15 3/8	10 4/8	10 4/8	22 6/8	22 5/8	Canmore, AB	Picked Up	AB Fish & Wildl. Div.	1987	10
201 2/8	43 2/8	42 4/8	16 3/8	16 3/8	10 7/8	10 7/8	22 3/8	17 6/8	Nikanassin Range, AB	Larry Strawson	Larry Strawson	1997	11
201 1/8	44	43 7/8	15 5/8	15 5/8	11 3/8	11 4/8	25	25	Jasper, AB	Picked Up	A.H. Hilbert	1932	12
201 1/8	49 2/8	44 5/8	15 2/8	15 1/8	9 4/8	9 2/8	26 2/8	25 6/8	Cross River, BC	David L. Onerheim	David L. Onerheim	1987	12
200 7/8	42 4/8	43 3/8	16 5/8	16 7/8	9	9	22 5/8	20 3/8	Fernie, BC	H.J. Johnson	Royal Ontario Museum	1902	14
200 6/8	45 7/8	49 2/8	15 2/8	15 2/8	9 2/8	9 1/8	28 5/8	28 3/8	Deer Lodge Co., MT	Lester A. Kish	Lester A. Kish	1990	14
200 2/8	42 4/8	43 6/8	16 7/8	16 7/8	9 2/8	9 6/8	23 7/8	23 7/8	Blaine Co., MT	Eugene R. Knight	Eugene R. Knight	1991	16
200 1/8	44 3/8	44	15 1/8	15 1/8	11 6/8	11 3/8	23	23	Brazeau River, AB	Unknown	Norman Lougheed	1937	17
200 1/8	40 4/8	41 3/8	16 3/8	16 3/8	11 3/8	11 3/8	22 2/8	18 5/8	Alberta	Picked Up	Otis Chandler	1955	17
200	44	44 1/8	16 1/8	16 2/8	10 4/8	10 1/8	23 3/8	22 6/8	Granite Co., MT	Mavis M. Lorenz	Mavis M. Lorenz	1993	17
200	40 6/8	41 6/8	16 4/8	16 3/8	10 7/8	10 1/8	22	19 6/8	Wind River Range, WY	Mr. Crawford	Duncan Weibel	1883	20
199 6/8	42 6/8	43 6/8	16 2/8	16 4/8	9 6/8	9 7/8	22 7/8	21 6/8	Granite Co., MT	Kevin E. Williams	Kevin E. Williams	1993	21
199 3/8	42 4/8	45 3/8	16	16	10	11	22 2/8	20 6/8	Sanders Co., MT	Michael D. Turner	Michael D. Turner	1992	22
199 2/8	42 6/8	42 4/8	17 3/8	17 2/8	9 4/8	9 2/8	25 5/8	25 2/8	Granite Co., MT	Marvin C. Skinner	Marvin C. Skinner	1995	23
199 1/8	43 5/8	42 4/8	16	16	10 1/8	10	22 2/8	22 2/8	Salmo, BC	Picked Up	Fort Steele Heritage Town	1993	24
199	45	45 4/8	15 1/8	15	10 3/8	10 6/8	22 5/8	22 5/8	Spences Bridge, BC	Picked Up	Parliament Bldg., B.C.	1969	25
198 6/8	43 4/8	43 6/8	15 4/8	15	10 7/8	11 3/8	24 6/8	24 6/8	Alberta	Bill Foster	Foster's Bighorn Rest.	PR 1947	26
198 1/8	42 4/8	41 3/8	15 6/8	15 6/8	12	11 3/8	23 3/8	23 3/8	Saskatchewan Lake, AB	Herb Klein	Herb Klein	1965	27
198	42 4/8	43 4/8	16 5/8	16 5/8	10	9 4/8	25	18 4/8	Wallowa Co., OR	Todd B. Jaksick	Todd B. Jaksick	1988	28
197 7/8	43 2/8	42 7/8	14 7/8	15	11 4/8	11 5/8	21 6/8	21 2/8	Wallowa Co., OR	Picked Up	OR Fish & Wildl. Div.	1986	29
197 7/8	42 5/8	42 6/8	16 5/8	16 4/8	9 4/8	9 5/8	23 4/8	23 1/8	Sanders Co., MT	Daniel R. Schwenk	Daniel R. Schwenk	1992	29
197 7/8	45 4/8	44 5/8	15 4/8	16 1/8	9 2/8	9 3/8	24 1/8	21 2/8	Nez Perce Co., ID	Picked Up	Bob Landrus	1996	29
197 5/8	41 1/8	42 4/8	15 7/8	16 1/8	11 1/8	11	22 3/8	22 3/8	Deer Lodge Co., MT	Arthur R. Dubs	Arthur R. Dubs	1987	32
197 3/8	44 7/8	43 4/8	14 6/8	14 6/8	10 6/8	11 1/8	23 4/8	18 3/8	Alberta	Bill Foster	Foster's Bighorn Rest.	PR 1947	33
197 2/8	39 1/8	42 3/8	17	17	9 5/8	9 6/8	23 4/8	20	East Kootenay, BC	Picked Up	Victoria Fish & Game Assn.	PR 1930	34
197 1/8	44 3/8	45 4/8	15 7/8	16 5/8	8 5/8	9 4/8	28 7/8	28 7/8	Sanders Co., MT	Armand H. Johnson	Armand H. Johnson	1979	35
197 1/8	42	41 5/8	16 5/8	16 4/8	10 5/8	10 6/8	23 5/8	23 2/8	Granite Co., MT	Lee Hart	Lee Hart	1990	35
197 1/8	41 2/8	40 7/8	16 5/8	16 6/8	10 4/8	10 2/8	20 7/8	18 4/8	Granite Co., MT	Mary E. Schroeder	Mary E. Schroeder	1992	35
196 7/8	41 1/8	40 4/8	17 4/8	17 4/8	10	9 7/8	23 2/8	18 1/8	Yarrow Creek, AB	George W. Biron	George W. Biron	1968	38

Score	Length R	Length L	Circumference of Base R	Circumference of Base L	Circumference Third Quarter R	Circumference Third Quarter L	Greatest Spread	Tip to Tip	Locality	Hunter	Owner	Date	Rank
196 7/8	43	40 7/8	16 3/8	16 2/8	10 1/8	9 7/8	20 2/8	20	Granite Co., MT	Keith J. Koprivica	Keith J. Koprivica	1990	38
196 6/8	41 2/8	40 4/8	16 4/8	16 4/8	10 1/8	9 7/8	22 6/8	19 4/8	Badlands, ND	Howard Eaton	Richard K. Mellon	1880	40
196 6/8	45 2/8	44 2/8	16 1/8	15 7/8	8 7/8	9 3/8	23	23	Wardner, BC	Jim Buss	Jim Buss	1961	40
196 5/8	41 5/8	42	16 2/8	16 1/8	10 7/8	10 6/8	22 2/8	19 1/8	Brazeau River, AB	Donald S. Hopkins	Donald S. Hopkins	1924	42
196 5/8	39 5/8	41 6/8	16	16	11 4/8	11 4/8	24 4/8	21 2/8	Alberta	Bill Foster	Foster's Bighorn Rest.	1938	42
196 5/8	45 2/8	44 3/8	14 5/8	14 6/8	10 4/8	10 4/8	24 5/8	19 2/8	Sun River, MT	Don Anderson	Don Anderson	1961	42
196 4/8	40 6/8	40 2/8	15 4/8	15 4/8	12	12	24	21 4/8	Badlands Natl. Park, SD	Picked Up	SD Game, Fish & Parks Dept.	1984	45
196 4/8	40 4/8	45	16	16	10 5/8	10 1/8	24 2/8	22 7/8	Silver Bow Co., MT	Verne O. Barnett	Verne O. Barnett	1991	45
196 4/8	45	44 5/8	16	16 1/8	11 4/8	11 5/8	22 7/8	16 5/8	Cadomin, AB	Rick Stelter	Rick Stelter	1996	45
196 4/8	43 7/8	42 4/8	16 2/8	16	11 5/8	11 5/8	21 6/8	22 1/8	Highwood, AB	Joseph F. Kubasek	Joseph F. Kubasek	1953	48
196 2/8	42 4/8	42 4/8	16 2/8	16 2/8	9 5/8	10	22 2/8	24 5/8	Sanders Co., MT	Earl V. Cole	Earl V. Cole	1993	48
196 2/8	44 6/8	43 6/8	14 7/8	14 6/8	11 2/8	11 3/8	24 5/8	22 6/8	Cadomin, AB	Al Leary	Al Leary	1962	48
196	44 7/8	44 3/8	15	15	10 3/8	10 2/8	22 6/8	24	Nez Perce Co., ID	Richard N. Aznaran	Richard N. Aznaran	1994	50
196	45 3/8	43 3/8	16 5/8	16 5/8	7 7/8	9 1/8	24	19 4/8	Montana	Unknown	Dole & Bailey, Inc.	1890	50
195 7/8	45 4/8	44 3/8	15 5/8	16 5/8	8 6/8	9 2/8	23	18 6/8	Line Creek, BC	Danny Whiting	Danny Whiting	1994	52
195 6/8	41	41 4/8	16 3/8	16 5/8	9 7/8	10	22 2/8	19 4/8	Castle River, AB	R.E. Woodward	R.E. Woodward	1965	53
195 5/8	41 5/8	40 2/8	16 3/8	16 3/8	10 4/8	10 4/8	23		Bow River, AB	Native American	N.K. Luxton	1890	54
195 5/8	43	43 6/8	14 5/8	14 7/8	11 3/8	11 1/8	29 6/8	29 6/8	Deer Lodge Co., MT	Thomas J. Matosich	Thomas J. Matosich	1986	55
195 4/8	46 2/8	41	16 1/8	16 3/8	11 1/8	11 1/8	22 2/8	20 7/8	West Sundre, AB	Jim Neeser	Jim Neeser	1961	55
195 3/8	42 3/8	42 4/8	15 7/8	15 6/8	9	10 1/8	24 7/8	23 2/8	Missoula Co., MT	Leonard G. Thompson	Leonard G. Thompson	1990	57
195 3/8	44 5/8	43 4/8	15 4/8	15 4/8	10 1/8	9	22 3/8	21 3/8	Granite Co., MT	Craig R. Johnson	Craig R. Johnson	1994	57
195 3/8	40 4/8	41 7/8	15 3/8	15 5/8	9	11 1/8	26 7/8	26 7/8	Sun River, MT	Gold White	Lee M. Ford	1911	57
195	44 2/8	38 4/8	15	15	11 6/8	11	23 6/8	19 6/8	Ram River, AB	G.M. De Witt	G.M. De Witt	1944	60
194 7/8	42 4/8	42 5/8	16 2/8	16 2/8	11 2/8	10 3/8	23 7/8	22 4/8	Granite Co., MT	Rick L. Barkell	Rick L. Barkell	1992	61
194 7/8	40 4/8	39 5/8	15 1/8	15 3/8	10 3/8	10 5/8	20 3/8	17 4/8	Storm Mt., AB	Bryan M. Watts	Bryan M. Watts	1957	61
194 6/8	42	41 6/8	16 4/8	16 4/8	10 7/8	10 5/8	22 2/8	20 6/8	Sheep River, AB	Picked Up	Harry McElroy	1966	63
194 3/8	40 4/8	41 3/8	16 4/8	16 4/8	10 4/8	10 6/8	22 4/8	21 4/8	Beaverhead Co., MT	Glenn M. Smith	Glenn M. Smith	1992	64
194 3/8	44 2/8	41 3/8	15 3/8	15 6/8	10 3/8	10 3/8	21 4/8	18 7/8	Panther River, AB	Picked Up	N.K. Luxton	1930	64
194 2/8	45 2/8	45 2/8	16 4/8	16 4/8	9 4/8	9 7/8	20 7/8	18 1/8	Cadomin, AB	Al D. Kuffner	Al D. Kuffner	1994	66
194 2/8	42 7/8	42 7/8	15 7/8	15 7/8	10 2/8	10 2/8	23 5/8	21 2/8	Nez Perce Co., ID	George R. Harms	George R. Harms	1995	66
194 1/8	42 2/8	42 2/8	16	16	10 1/8	10 6/8	22 3/8	16 7/8	Alberta	Bill Foster	Foster's Bighorn Rest.	PR 1947	68
194	44	42 6/8	16 2/8	16 2/8	10 6/8	10	24	18 1/8	Yarrow Creek, AB	F.H. Riggall	F.H. Riggall	1906	69
194	39 4/8	42 4/8	16	16 4/8	9 4/8	9 3/8	22 1/8	17 4/8	Cameron Pass, CO	F. Cotter	Herbert J. Havemann	1954	70
193 6/8	41	42 6/8	15 4/8	15 4/8	10 2/8	10 6/8	23 7/8	22 7/8	Tornado Pass, BC	John Stuber	John Stuber	1956	70
193 6/8	40 5/8	40 5/8	16 5/8	16 4/8	9 7/8	9 7/8	22 6/8	20 1/8	Granite Co., MT	Michael L. Girard	Michael L. Girard	1986	70
193 6/8	40 4/8	39 6/8	15 6/8	15 7/8	10 6/8	11 1/8	23 3/8	22 6/8	Granite Co., MT	Kenneth L. Getz	Kenneth L. Getz	1992	70
193 6/8	40 2/8	42	16 4/8	16 4/8	9 7/8	9 6/8	22 4/8	23 3/8	Granite Co., MT	Rex V. Blackwell	Rex V. Blackwell	1997	76
193 5/8	40 6/8	41 4/8	16 2/8	16 3/8	11 1/8	9 5/8	23	19 4/8	Sheep River, AB	Gary H. Cain	Gary H. Cain	1990	76
193 5/8	43 1/8	41 2/8	16 4/8	16 4/8	9 6/8	8 4/8	26 7/8	23	Lincoln Co., MT	Al Bratkovich	Al Bratkovich	1993	78
193 4/8	42 2/8	42 2/8	16 3/8	16 3/8	9 5/8	10 6/8	22 3/8	26 7/8	Silver Bow Co., MT	Thomas R. Webster	Thomas R. Webster	1990	79
193 3/8	39	40 4/8	15 7/8	15 7/8	10 4/8	10 2/8	22 4/8	17 1/8	Coleman, AB	George Hagglund	George Hagglund	1952	80
193 3/8	42 1/8	39 7/8	16 5/8	16 5/8	10	10	23 2/8	19 1/8	Sanders Co., MT	Jerry Landa	Jerry Landa	1989	80
193 2/8	39 7/8	42 6/8	16	16	10	9	21 7/8	20	Luscar Mt., AB	Marion McLean	Marion McLean	1994	80
193 2/8	42 2/8	44 5/8	15 1/8	15 2/8	10 1/8	9 7/8	23 6/8	21 7/8	Spences Bridge, BC	M. Da Rosa	M. Da Rosa	1961	82
193 1/8	44 5/8	41 7/8	15 5/8	15 5/8	9 7/8	9 7/8	19 7/8	21 4/8	Missoula Co., MT	Bonnie A. Ford	Bonnie A. Ford	1982	82
193 1/8	41 7/8	39 2/8	16 3/8	16 4/8	10 3/8	10 3/8	22 1/8	15	Ewin Creek, BC	Gary N. Goode	Gary N. Goode	1989	82
193	40 1/8	43 5/8	14 6/8	14 6/8	9 7/8	10 1/8		22 1/8	Spences Bridge, BC	Norman Holland	Norman Holland	1971	85

BIGHORN SHEEP

Ovis canadensis canadensis and certain related subspecies

Score	Length of Horn R	L	Circumference of Base R	L	Circumference at Third Quarter R	L	Greatest Spread	Tip to Tip Spread	Locality	Hunter	Owner	Date Killed	Rank
193	39 2/8	41 2/8	16 3/8	16 4/8	9 6/8	9 7/8	23	21 7/8	Granite Co., MT	Phillip S. Benson	Phillip S. Benson	1992	85
192 7/8	40 6/8	41 3/8	16 2/8	16 3/8	10	9 5/8	21 3/8	21 3/8	Granite Co., MT	Raymond J. Dvorak	Raymond J. Dvorak	1989	87
192 6/8	44 6/8	43 2/8	14 2/8	14 2/8	10 7/8	11 1/8	22 1/8	22 1/8	Clearwater, AB	Edward L. Fuchs	Edward L. Fuchs	1943	88
192 5/8	42 7/8	44 2/8	14 3/8	14 2/8	10 6/8	10 3/8	24	24	Sun River, MT	Unknown	Leyton Z. Yearout	1963	89
192 5/8	39 5/8	40 2/8	15 4/8	15 6/8	11 4/8	11 4/8	21 2/8	17 4/8	Clearwater River, AB	James Allan	James Allan	1977	89
192 4/8	38 4/8	41 2/8	16 1/8	16 1/8	10 6/8	10 4/8	22	18 6/8	Mt. Gregg, AB	Eric Satre	Eric Satre	1992	91
192 3/8	40 7/8	40 7/8	15 6/8	15 4/8	10 5/8	11 3/8	22 7/8	18 4/8	Alberta	Henry Graves, Jr.	Unknown	PR 1931	92
192 3/8	40 6/8	40 7/8	15 4/8	15 5/8	10 5/8	10 5/8	20 5/8	17 6/8	Granite Co., MT	Robert L. Sandman	Robert L. Sandman	1991	92
192 3/8	42 4/8	42 3/8	16 2/8	16 1/8	8 5/8	8 4/8	22 2/8	21 6/8	Teton Co., MT	Darwin T. Scott	Darwin T. Scott	1995	92
192 2/8	45 2/8	43	16	15 6/8	8 3/8	8 3/8	21	21	Sanders Co., MT	Richard W. Browne	Richard W. Browne	1968	95
192 2/8	40 5/8	40 5/8	16 7/8	16 7/8	8 6/8	9 2/8	22	17 6/8	Sanders Co., MT	Michael A. Jorgenson	Michael A. Jorgenson	1978	95
192 2/8	43 3/8	41 7/8	16 2/8	16 1/8	8 4/8	9 1/8	22 2/8	21 3/8	Granite Co., MT	John P. Steele	John P. Steele	1991	95
192 2/8	40 7/8	40 1/8	17 1/8	17 1/8	8 1/8	8 6/8	22	21 3/8	Sanders Co., MT	Charles M. LaRance	Dale Manning	1995	95
192 1/8	42 7/8	42 4/8	16	16 2/8	9 1/8	8 6/8	22 4/8	19 1/8	Deer Lodge Co., MT	Mitchell A. Thorson	Mitchell A. Thorson	1987	99
192	41 6/8	42 4/8	15 1/8	15	10	10 3/8	21 5/8	20 1/8	Narrow Creek, AB	Henry Mitchell	Henry Mitchell	1910	100
192	43 3/8	42 7/8	15 5/8	15 6/8	9	9 6/8	24 2/8	24 2/8	Wallowa Co., OR	H. James Tonkin	H. James Tonkin	1991	100
191 7/8	40 4/8	41 1/8	15	15	11 1/8	11 6/8	23 3/8	21 4/8	Lake Co., CO	Emory Whilton	Kern Co. (Calif.) Mus.	1901	102
191 7/8	44	41 7/8	15 3/8	15 3/8	9 6/8	8 7/8	24 4/8	22 2/8	Lake Co., MT	Picked Up	Univ. of Mont. Zool. Mus.	1961	102
191 7/8	41 6/8	42 3/8	16	15 3/8	10 2/8	10 2/8	24	22	Alberta	Clarence Hardy	Russel Vanslett	PR 1961	102
191 7/8	41 3/8	40 4/8	16	15 7/8	10 1/8	9 5/8	24 3/8	24	Granite Co., MT	Steven L. Gingras	Steven L. Gingras	1984	102
191 7/8	41 3/8	40 6/8	15 6/8	15 7/8	8 6/8	9 4/8	21 2/8	21 7/8	Missoula Co., MT	Carl W. Schmidt	Carl W. Schmidt	1989	102
191 7/8	39 5/8	40 6/8	16	16	9 7/8	10 2/8	21 4/8	18 2/8	Granite Co., MT	Dale E. Garrison	Dale E. Garrison	1996	102
191 7/8	41 4/8	41 3/8	16 5/8	16 6/8	8 3/8	8 4/8	23 3/8	20 6/8	Sanders Co., MT	Michael L. Knaff	Michael L. Knaff	1996	102
191 6/8	40	42 2/8	15 6/8	15 5/8	9 7/8	10 3/8	23 3/8	22 6/8	Smoky River, AB	Picked Up	Carl M. Borgh	1944	109
191 6/8	41 7/8	41 5/8	16	16 1/8	9 7/8	9	25	23 6/8	Silver Bow Co., MT	James G. Dennehy	James G. Dennehy	1992	109
191 6/8	41 6/8	41 4/8	16 2/8	16 3/8	8 4/8	8 5/8	24 5/8	23 6/8	Missoula Co., MT	Shelley Goodman	Shelley Goodman	1993	109
191 6/8	43 4/8	46 4/8	14 6/8	14 6/8	9 4/8	9 2/8	23 2/8	20 4/8	Granite Co., MT	Blair G. McGavin	Blair G. McGavin	1995	109
191 5/8	40 2/8	40 3/8	15 6/8	15 6/8	10 2/8	10 1/8	22 1/8	15	Dinwoody Creek, WY	Oris Miller	Oris Miller	1954	113
191 4/8	42 4/8	41 4/8	14 6/8	15	10 2/8	9 7/8	22 6/8	22 3/8	Lincoln Co., MT	Picked Up	Ed Boyes	PR 1961	114
191 4/8	44 3/8	39 3/8	15 7/8	16	9 6/8	9 3/8	23 6/8	20 3/8	Wallowa Co., OR	Sam Jaksick, Jr.	Sam Jaksick, Jr.	1987	114
191 4/8	41 5/8	42 5/8	16	16	9 1/8	10 1/8	26	25 6/8	Missoula Co., MT	Roy R. Wickman	Roy R. Wickman	1994	114
191 4/8	40 7/8	41 7/8	15 5/8	15 4/8	10	10 4/8	20 5/8	17	Line Creek, BC	Stephen Babijowski	Stephen Babijowski	1996	114
191 3/8	40 7/8	42 4/8	15	14 7/8	10 5/8	10 5/8	22 1/8	20 7/8	Canada	Unknown	A.H. Hilbert	PR 1930	118
191 3/8	42 3/8	40	14 6/8	14 7/8	10 4/8	10 7/8	21 4/8	15 2/8	Natal, BC	John A. Morais	John A. Morais	1960	118
191 3/8	39 6/8	38 1/8	16 1/8	16 1/8	11 1/8	10 6/8	20	18 3/8	Cadomin, AB	Tony Oney	Tony Oney	1966	118
191 3/8	40	39 3/8	15 7/8	15 7/8	10 3/8	10 4/8	21	19	Sanders Co., MT	Robert A. Larsson	Robert A. Larsson	1994	118
191 2/8	41 5/8	42 1/8	15 3/8	15 3/8	10 5/8	10 5/8	22	20 5/8	Brazeau River, AB	Donald S. Hopkins	Donald S. Hopkins	1937	122
191 2/8	45 6/8	44 2/8	15 2/8	15 2/8	7 7/8	8 4/8	24 5/8	24 5/8	Grassmere, BC	Donald F. Letcher	Donald F. Letcher	1965	122

Score	Length of Horn R	Length of Horn L	Circ. of Base R	Circ. of Base L	Circ. Third Quarter R	Circ. Third Quarter L	Greatest Spread	Tip to Tip Spread	Locality	Hunter	Owner	Date Killed	Rank
191 2/8	42	41	14 5/8	14 5/8	10 6/8	10 4/8	22 1/8	19 4/8	Leyland Mt., AB	Rick J. Tymchuk	Rick J. Tymchuk	1982	122
191 2/8	39 5/8	38 7/8	16 1/8	16 1/8	10 5/8	10 2/8	22 1/8	21 4/8	Sanders Co., MT	Charles V. Gordon	Charles V. Gordon	1993	122
191 2/8	39 6/8	41 4/8	15 6/8	15 6/8	9 7/8	10	23	17 4/8	Fording River, BC	Ryan D. Jones	Ryan D. Jones	1993	122
191 1/8	39 6/8	39 4/8	15 2/8	15 3/8	10 7/8	9 6/8	19 6/8	16 4/8	Huerfano Co., CO	Timothy K. Rushing	Timothy K. Rushing	1997	128
191 1/8	40 1/8	42	15 3/8	15	10	10 7/8	22	19 6/8	Cadomin, AB	Frank Nuspel	Frank Nuspel	1962	128
191 1/8	39 3/8	39 2/8	15 4/8	15 1/8	11 1/8	8 2/8	25 1/8	18 3/8	Castle River, AB	Picked Up	E.B. Cunningham	PR 1967	128
191 1/8	43 2/8	43 3/8	16	16	9	9	25 1/8	25 1/8	Wolverine Creek, AB	James R. Gaines	James R. Gaines	1990	128
191	44	40 1/8	15 6/8	15 4/8	11	11	21 6/8	21 6/8	Sheep River, AB	Harvey Pyra	Harvey Pyra	1991	132
191	40 4/8	39	15 3/8	15 4/8	9 1/8	9	22 5/8	18	Kvass Creek, AB	Joseph W. Dent	Joseph W. Dent	1962	132
191	39	39 2/8	15 4/8	16 5/8	9 1/8	9	24	22 2/8	Granite Co., MT	Harry W. Miller	Harry W. Miller	1985	132
191	39 2/8	40 4/8	16 1/8	16	9 6/8	9 6/8	21 1/8	21	Sanders Co., MT	Lenora L. Liberty	Lenora L. Liberty	1995	132
190 7/8	40 4/8	39 4/8	15 7/8	16	10	10	23 4/8	18 7/8	Sanders Co., MT	Terri Stoneman	Terri Stoneman	1988	135
190 7/8	39 4/8	39 6/8	15 4/8	15 4/8	9 7/8	9 7/8	25 2/8	24 7/8	Lewis & Clark Co., MT	Rodney H. Eaton	Rodney H. Eaton	1992	135
190 7/8	39 6/8	38 4/8	16 5/8	16 5/8	9 6/8	9 3/8	23 4/8	19 1/8	Apache Co., AZ	Jeffery P. Augustine	Jeffery P. Augustine	1995	135
190 6/8	42 5/8	40 5/8	15 2/8	15	9 2/8	9 2/8	23 3/8	23 3/8	Fernie, BC	J.J. Osman	J.J. Osman	1950	138
190 6/8	39 1/8	44 4/8	14 7/8	14 7/8	11	11	22	15 4/8	Elko, BC	Charles Weikert	Charles Weikert	1970	138
190 6/8	42 4/8	37 1/8	16 7/8	15 5/8	11 1/8	11	25 5/8	25 7/8	Missoula Co., MT	Arthur R. Dubs	Arthur R. Dubs	1986	138
190 6/8	46 3/8	41 5/8	15 5/8	15 7/8	8 7/8	9	23	17 3/8	Granite Co., MT	Scott A. Campbell	Scott A. Campbell	1990	138
190 6/8	37 5/8	40 6/8	15 7/8	15 7/8	9 7/8	8 4/8	24 7/8	22 2/8	Gregg River, AB	H. Gene Warren	H. Gene Warren	1991	138
190 6/8	42 3/8	40 1/8	15 2/8	15 2/8	9 2/8	9 2/8	22	20 3/8	Sanders Co., MT	Mike Wasylyshen	Mike Wasylyshen	1994	138
190 6/8	40 6/8	39 5/8	16	16	10 1/8	9 4/8	24	23 2/8	Sanders Co., MT	Timothy B. Johnston	Timothy B. Johnston	1995	138
190 5/8	41 1/8	41 2/8	17	16 7/8	9	9	24	16 7/8	Brazeau River, AB	Julio Estrada	Julio Estrada	1936	145
190 5/8	40 2/8	41 6/8	15 5/8	15 5/8	8 6/8	8 4/8	24 5/8	24 5/8	Missoula Co., MT	John J. Ottman	John J. Ottman	1985	145
190 5/8	40 3/8	39 3/8	15 6/8	16 1/8	9 2/8	9 2/8	24 2/8	23 4/8	Missoula Co., MT	Chris L. Mostad	Chris L. Mostad	1986	145
190 5/8	41 5/8	40 1/8	16 1/8	16 1/8	9 4/8	9 4/8	25 2/8	19 2/8	Asotin Co., WA	Picked Up	WA Dept. of Fish & Wildl.	1995	145
190 5/8	43 5/8	43 2/8	16	16	10 4/8	10 5/8	23	20 5/8	Blaine Co., MT	Wilbur J. Helzer	Wilbur J. Helzer	1996	145
190 5/8	40 4/8	40 4/8	15 4/8	15 1/8	11 7/8	11 7/8	21	17	Taos Co., NM	Donald E. Wenner	Donald E. Wenner	1996	145
190 4/8	40 2/8	40 1/8	16 2/8	16	11 1/8	12	19 4/8	19	Berry's Creek, AB	Bernard A. Fiedeldey, Jr.	Bernard A. Fiedeldey, Jr.	1996	151
190 3/8	38 6/8	39 5/8	16 5/8	15 1/8	8 3/8	8 3/8	22 6/8	21 7/8	Highwood, AB	Nick Sekella	Nick Sekella	1953	152
190 3/8	41 1/8	41 6/8	16 4/8	16	10 3/8	10 4/8	21 7/8	21 7/8	Sun River, MT	F.P. Murray	F.P. Murray	1957	152
190 2/8	39 2/8	37 6/8	16 4/8	16 4/8	9 7/8	10 2/8	22 4/8	18 1/8	Sanders Co., MT	Duane Dauenhauer	Duane Dauenhauer	1992	154
190 2/8	44 6/8	41 2/8	14 7/8	14 5/8	9 4/8	9 2/8	23 3/8	22 5/8	Sanders Co., MT	Scott W. Johnson	Scott W. Johnson	1994	154
190 1/8	41 6/8	40 3/8	15 7/8	15 1/8	9 2/8	9 2/8	23 4/8	21	Missoula Co., MT	Joseph C. Turner	Joseph C. Turner	1987	156
190 1/8	39 3/8	41	15 6/8	15 6/8	10	10	24	17 4/8	Nez Perce Co., ID	Gary E. Hansen	Gary E. Hansen	1996	156
190	39 6/8	40	15 4/8	15 4/8	10 5/8	10 5/8	22 1/8	14	Alberta	Native American	Acad. Nat. Sci., Phil.	1901	158
190	40 7/8	39 7/8	15 1/8	15 2/8	10 3/8	10 2/8	19 4/8	19 4/8	Brazeau River, AB	Donald S. Hopkins	Acad. Nat. Sci., Phil.	1927	158
190	40 5/8	40 1/8	16	15 4/8	10 2/8	10 5/8	22 6/8	22	Granite Co., MT	Rick L. Williams	Rick L. Williams	1991	158
189 7/8	40 4/8	39 1/8	16 2/8	15 4/8	10 3/8	9 7/8	21 5/8	21 5/8	Clearwater Forest, AB	George Bugbee	Sally Bugbee	1928	161
189 7/8	40 5/8	41 4/8	15 6/8	15 6/8	9 1/8	9	21 3/8	17 1/8	Ribbon Lake, AB	Ovar Uggen	Ovar Uggen	1957	161
189 6/8	41	40 6/8	15 4/8	15 4/8	9 4/8	9 3/8	23 4/8	20 1/8	Highwood Range, AB	Unknown	Earl Johnson	1928	163
189 6/8	40 6/8	40 6/8	15 5/8	15	9 4/8	9 4/8	21 6/8	14 1/8	Swan Lake, BC	Billy Stork	A.C. Gilbert	1936	163
189 6/8	42 7/8	42 4/8	15 6/8	15 7/8	8 3/8	8 2/8	23 6/8	23 3/8	Sanders Co., MT	Eric C. Hastings	Eric C. Hastings	1995	163
189 5/8	42 4/8	41 5/8	15 2/8	15 2/8	9	8 7/8	22	21 3/8	Valley Co., MT	Picked Up	Andy Strommen	PR 1918	166
189 5/8	38 6/8	40 1/8	16	16	9 4/8	9 3/8	23	20 4/8	Yarrow Creek, AB	Allan Foster	Allan Foster	1963	166
189 5/8	39 4/8	42 3/8	15 4/8	15 3/8	9 3/8	10 1/8	22 3/8	21	Deer Lodge Co., MT	Lawrence A. Jany	Lawrence A. Jany	1990	166
189 4/8	41	40 4/8	14 5/8	14 7/8	11 2/8	11 4/8	23 3/8	21	Park Co., WY	Picked Up	Dale McWilliams	1975	169
189 4/8	39 2/8	41 2/8	15 7/8	16	9 6/8	9 7/8	19 6/8	19 3/8	Nikanassin Range, AB	Colleen Bodenchuk	Colleen Bodenchuk	1976	169

BIGHORN SHEEP

Ovis canadensis canadensis and certain related subspecies

Score	Length of Horn R	L	Circumference of Base R	L	Circumference at Third Quarter R	L	Greatest Spread	Tip tp Tip Spread	Locality	Hunter	Owner	Date Killed	Rank
189 3/8	40 3/8	41 2/8	14 4/8	14 4/8	11 3/8	11 4/8	18 6/8	17 2/8	Panther River, AB	Picked Up	George Browne	1928	171
189 3/8	43 7/8	43	14 2/8	14 4/8	10 1/8	9 4/8	22 3/8	22 3/8	Spences Bridge, BC	Bert Walkem	Bert Walkem	1964	171
189 3/8	40 7/8	40 4/8	16 6/8	16 4/8	8 4/8	8 5/8	23	19 1/8	Teton Co., MT	R.L. Kennedy	R.L. Kennedy	1983	171
189 3/8	40 1/8	41 4/8	16 6/8	16 6/8	8 5/8	8	23 2/8	21 6/8	Asotin Co., WA	Edwin L. Harris	Edwin L. Harris	1987	171
189 2/8	41	39	15 6/8	15 5/8	9 7/8	9 7/8	24	20 2/8	Canal Flat, BC	Robert Lemaster	Robert Lemaster	1962	175
189 2/8	40 7/8	40 3/8	16 6/8	16 6/8	8 1/8	8 2/8	26	25 6/8	Sanders Co., MT	Linda Phillips	Linda Phillips	1989	175
189 1/8	40 5/8	42	14 7/8	14 5/8	10 5/8	10 5/8	21 3/8	17 4/8	Alberta	Bill Foster	Foster's Bighorn Rest.	PR 1947	177
189 1/8	37 3/8	38	15 7/8	15 6/8	11 1/8	10 5/8	19	20 7/8	Sheep River, AB	Patrick J. Downey	Patrick J. Downey	1986	177
189 1/8	39 3/8	39 6/8	16 4/8	16 4/8	9	9 1/8	21 6/8	18	Lost Creek, BC	Les J. Husband	Les J. Husband	1992	177
189	39	41	15 4/8	15 4/8	9 7/8	9 4/8	19 5/8	17	Highwood River, AB	Hanson Bearspaw	W.S. Armstrong	1917	180
189	40 1/8	41 5/8	15 3/8	15 4/8	9 5/8	9 3/8	21 3/8	20 5/8	Granite Co., MT	Mark M. Morgan	Mark M. Morgan	1991	180
189	40 4/8	37 4/8	15 6/8	15 7/8	10 3/8	10	22 4/8	17 2/8	Panther River, AB	Picked Up	D. James Turner	1994	180
189	43 1/8	39 3/8	15 6/8	15 6/8	8 7/8	8 6/8	26	24 3/8	Blaine Co., MT	Greg D. Beach	Greg D. Beach	1997	180
188 7/8	41	40 1/8	14 6/8	14 5/8	10 4/8	11 1/8	21 3/8	18	Ram Creek, AB	William N. Beach	William N. Beach	1928	184
188 7/8	43 1/8	41 4/8	14 6/8	15 1/8	9 6/8	9 7/8	25 6/8	25 6/8	Bow Valley, AB	Picked Up	Joseph Kovach	PR 1952	184
188 7/8	40 1/8	41	14 6/8	14 6/8	10 6/8	10 6/8	24	17	Gannet Peak, WY	James Huffman	James Huffman	1962	184
188 7/8	41 2/8	44 5/8	15 1/8	15	9	8 7/8	24 4/8	23 6/8	Gallatin Range, MT	Alden B. Walrath	Alden B. Walrath	1965	184
188 7/8	40 5/8	40 4/8	14 6/8	14 7/8	10 6/8	10 5/8	22	22	Wallowa Co., OR	Nick J. Gianopoulos	Nick J. Gianopoulos	1986	184
188 7/8	44 7/8	39 6/8	15 7/8	15 7/8	8 4/8	8 2/8	26 6/8	26 4/8	Silver Bow Co., MT	Jerry J. Joseph	Jerry J. Joseph	1990	184
188 7/8	39 5/8	39 4/8	15 2/8	15	10 2/8	10 2/8	22 5/8	18 4/8	Whitehorse Creek, AB	Wally Nicklin	Wally Nicklin	1995	184
188 6/8	40 1/8	38 1/8	17 1/8	17 1/8	8 3/8	8 4/8	24 7/8	20 5/8	Highwood, AB	Steve Kubasek	Steve Kubasek	1953	191
188 6/8	40	40	15 1/8	15 1/8	10 7/8	10 7/8	20 4/8	16 4/8	Onion Lake, AB	Martin M. Reddy	Martin M. Reddy	1985	191
188 6/8	40	40	15 4/8	15 4/8	10 3/8	10 5/8	21 7/8	20 6/8	Deer Lodge Co., MT	Mike J. Bartoletti	Mike J. Bartoletti	1991	191
188 5/8	40 4/8	41 1/8	15 5/8	15 5/8	9 4/8	9 5/8	23 1/8	21 3/8	Alberta	Bill Foster	Foster's Bighorn Rest.	PR 1947	194
188 5/8	38 7/8	39 4/8	15 5/8	15 6/8	10 1/8	10 1/8	21 4/8	19 2/8	Sun River, MT	Bruce McCracken	Bruce McCracken	1955	194
188 5/8	41	38 7/8	15 3/8	15 3/8	10 6/8	10 5/8	20 3/8	19	Simpson River, BC	Patrick Deuling	Patrick Deuling	1985	194
188 5/8	40 5/8	39 2/8	15 2/8	15 3/8	10 3/8	10 2/8	20 6/8	18 2/8	Sanders Co., MT	Richard L. Grimes	Richard L. Grimes	1990	194
188 5/8	43 1/8	41	15 1/8	15 1/8	9 1/8	9 3/8	19 2/8	17 3/8	Burnt Timber Creek, AB	Robert P. Erickson	Robert P. Erickson	1993	194
188 5/8	39 2/8	39 5/8	15 2/8	15 4/8	10 4/8	10 5/8	21 2/8	19	Luscar Mt., AB	Dwayne Oneski	Dwayne Oneski	1997	194
188 4/8	41	45 4/8	14 6/8	14 5/8	11	9 1/8	27	27	Clearwater, AB	Unknown	Norman Lougheed	1936	200
188 4/8	40 2/8	40	16 2/8	16 1/8	8 5/8	8 6/8	21 1/8	19 4/8	Opal Range, AB	Robert Zebedee	Robert Zebedee	1977	200
188 4/8	39	40 4/8	15 7/8	15 7/8	9 5/8	10	22 4/8	22 4/8	Ravalli Creek, MT	Sandy Rose	Sandy Rose	1978	200
188 4/8	40 4/8	37 4/8	15 7/8	15 7/8	9 5/8	9 5/8	23 6/8	17 4/8	Blaine Co., MT	Lanny L. Walker	Lanny L. Walker	1991	200
188 4/8	42 5/8	41 1/8	15 7/8	15 7/8	8 1/8	9	23 2/8	22 6/8	Sanders Co., MT	Dean M. Vaughan	Dean M. Vaughan	1993	200
188 4/8	37 4/8	39 2/8	16	16	10	10 6/8	21 1/8	20	Blaine Co., MT	Brian W. Evans	Brian W. Evans	1997	200
188 3/8	40 6/8	39 7/8	16 1/8	16 1/8	9	9	25 2/8	21	White Swan Lake, BC	A.C. Gilbert	The Old State House	1940	206
188 3/8	40 6/8	40 5/8	15 4/8	15 4/8	9	9	21 6/8	17 2/8	Surprise Lake, BC	Herb Klein	Herb Klein	1950	206
188 3/8	42 1/8	38	16	16	9 4/8	9 2/8	20 6/8	20 6/8	Alberta	Arthur Smith	Arthur Smith	1959	206

Score	Length R	Length L	Circ. Base R	Circ. Base L	Circ. 3rd Q R	Circ. 3rd Q L	Tip to Tip	Greatest Spread	Locality	Hunter	Owner	Date	Rank
188 3/8	39 1/8	39 6/8	15 6/8	15 6/8	9 5/8	9 7/8	15 4/8	21 6/8	Burnt Timber Creek, AB	Walter O. Ford, Jr.	Walter O. Ford, Jr.	1966	206
188 3/8	39 3/8	39 6/8	15 3/8	15 3/8	10 4/8	10 4/8	14	22 1/8	Gibraltar Mt., AB	Leslie Kish	Leslie Kish	1981	206
188 3/8	40	40 7/8	15 4/8	15 5/8	9 6/8	9 7/8	23 1/8	24	Deer Lodge Co., MT	Paul J. Druyvestein	Paul J. Druyvestein	1986	206
188 3/8	40 4/8	39 3/8	15 4/8	15 2/8	10 7/8	11	20 6/8	23 6/8	Granite Co., MT	Larry J. Antonich	Larry J. Antonich	1990	206
188 3/8	40	39 7/8	16	16	9	8 7/8	20 1/8	25 1/8	Sheep River, AB	Katherine A. Pyra	Katherine A. Pyra	1991	206
188 2/8	40	40 6/8	15 4/8	15 5/8	9 3/8	10 4/8	19	21 4/8	Sun River, MT	Bruce Neal	Bruce Neal	1912	214
188 2/8	45 4/8	44 2/8	13 6/8	13 6/8	9 7/8	9 7/8	22 7/8	23 4/8	Panther River, AB	Unknown	Harvey A. Trimble	1932	214
188 2/8	40 4/8	40 6/8	15 1/8	15 1/8	10 5/8	10 5/8	21 1/8	22 4/8	Sun River, MT	J.R. Pfeifer	J.R. Pfeifer	1958	214
188 2/8	38 5/8	37 7/8	15 6/8	15 7/8	10 4/8	10 4/8	15	21 7/8	Kananaskis, AB	Terry Webber	Terry Webber	1961	214
188 2/8	42 5/8	42 5/8	15 6/8	15 6/8	8 4/8	8 4/8	25 7/8	25 7/8	Spences Bridge, BC	Romeo Leduc	Romeo Leduc	1982	214
188 2/8	43	42 2/8	15 6/8	15 6/8	7 7/8	8 1/8	24 1/8	24 3/8	Deer Lodge Co., MT	Walter F. Smith	Walter F. Smith	1986	214
188 2/8	39 4/8	42	15 5/8	15 5/8	9 1/8	9 5/8	25 2/8	25 6/8	Beaverhead Co., MT	Corey J. Buhl	Corey J. Buhl	1992	214
188 2/8	40 6/8	40 4/8	17	17	8	8	25 3/8	25 4/8	Granite Co., MT	Donald O. Cure	Donald O. Cure	1994	214
188 1/8	44 3/8	42 2/8	14 3/8	14 7/8	9 6/8	9 2/8	25 3/8	25 3/8	Lincoln Co., MT	Alfred E. Journey	Alfred E. Journey	1980	222
188 1/8	38 5/8	39 4/8	16 6/8	16 5/8	9 2/8	9 2/8	21	26 4/8	Sanders Co., MT	Patti L. Lewis	Patti L. Lewis	1984	222
188 1/8	40 1/8	40 4/8	15 1/8	15 1/8	10	10	23 4/8	23 4/8	Blaine Co., MT	Curtis L. Kostelecky	Curtis L. Kostelecky	1991	222
188	41 6/8	41 6/8	15 4/8	15	10 2/8	10 2/8	16 6/8	21 2/8	Kananaskis River, AB	C. Allenhof	C. Allenhof	1958	225
188	39 1/8	39 5/8	15 2/8	15	10 6/8	10 6/8	13 4/8	23 7/8	Kananaskis Summit, AB	Ted Howell	Ted Howell	1963	225
188	41 1/8	41	16 2/8	16 2/8	10 4/8	10	16 4/8	20 5/8	Cardinal River, AB	Lawrence N. Baraniuk	Lawrence N. Baraniuk	1986	225
188	39 2/8	41 3/8	15 7/8	15 7/8	8 4/8	10 5/8	21 2/8	22 2/8	Asotin Co., WA	Glen A. Landrus	Glen A. Landrus	1995	225
187 7/8	41 6/8	40 1/8	15 5/8	15 5/8	8 3/8	8 4/8	18	24 2/8	Sanders Co., MT	Richard L. Carlson	Richard L. Carlson	1994	229
187 7/8	41 6/8	39 2/8	15 3/8	15 3/8	9	8 3/8	19 1/8	22 6/8	Missoula Co., MT	Ronald C. Gibson	Ronald C. Gibson	1995	229
187 7/8	40 5/8	44 2/8	15 4/8	15 4/8	9 1/8	9 1/8	20	22 6/8	Little Elbow River, AB	David W. Sowers	David W. Sowers	1995	229
187 7/8	41 7/8	42 3/8	14 7/8	14 7/8	10 2/8	9 1/8	20	21 7/8	Granite Co., MT	Richard M. Mierva	Richard M. Mierva	1996	229
187 6/8	43 4/8	43 2/8	14 5/8	14 7/8	8 4/8	8 2/8	24 2/8	24 2/8	Salmon River, ID	Picked Up	Dwight Smith	1951	233
187 6/8	42 1/8	38 7/8	15 1/8	15	9 2/8	9 2/8	21 4/8	21 4/8	Chase, BC	L. McNary & J. Langer	Lloyd McNary	1956	233
187 6/8	44	42	14 5/8	14 7/8	8 4/8	8 2/8	24 3/8	24 3/8	Ram River, AB	George W. Parker	George W. Parker	1961	233
187 6/8	39 3/8	39 7/8	14 5/8	15 2/8	7 6/8	8 4/8	15	22 3/8	Wildhay River, AB	Jim Papst	Jim Papst	1967	233
187 6/8	39 4/8	38	16	14 7/8	11 3/8	8 4/8	23 1/8	23 2/8	Deer Lodge Co., MT	William H. Shurte	William H. Shurte	1984	233
187 6/8	40 1/8	40 4/8	15 6/8	15 6/8	8 7/8	8 7/8	12	21	Ghost River, AB	Gerald Molnar	Gerald Molnar	1988	233
187 6/8	38	43 6/8	15 2/8	16	8 4/8	8 4/8	20 1/8	20 7/8	Fergus Co., MT	Gordon L. Lencioni	Gordon L. Lencioni	1995	233
187 5/8	39 3/8	39 5/8	14 4/8	15 7/8	10 7/8	10 7/8	21 2/8	21 2/8	Glacier Natl. Park, MT	Olmstead, Dow, & Hawley	MT Dept. Fish, Wildl. & Parks	1956	240
187 5/8	40 5/8	42	16 1/8	15 2/8	9 6/8	9 6/8	22	22 1/8	Butcher Creek, AB	Vince Bruder	Vince Bruder	1958	240
187 5/8	42 4/8	39 7/8	14 7/8	14 4/8	10 2/8	10 3/8	25 4/8	26 1/8	Teton Co., WY	William R. Flagg	William R. Flagg	1967	240
187 5/8	45 7/8	38 4/8	15 6/8	15 5/8	8	8 7/8	22 2/8	23	Spences Bridge, BC	J. David Smith	J. David Smith	1969	240
187 5/8	39 6/8	43 1/8	16 5/8	16 7/8	8 7/8	8 7/8	20 5/8	22 6/8	El Paso Co., CO	Picked Up	Michael D. Swanson	1988	240
187 5/8	40 5/8	39 7/8	15 5/8	15 4/8	8 3/8	9 3/8	21 1/8	24 1/8	Granite Co., MT	Polly A. Tate	Polly A. Tate	1997	240
187 4/8	39 5/8	37 4/8	15 3/8	15 5/8	8 4/8	8 2/8	19	26 4/8	Crystal Creek, WY	Picked Up	Melvin R. Fowlkes	1970	246
187 4/8	40 5/8	39 3/8	16 2/8	16 2/8	9 3/8	8 3/8	19 2/8	20 4/8	Ram Range, AB	John F. Snyder	John F. Snyder	1978	246
187 4/8	35	39 3/8	15 4/8	15 4/8	10 7/8	9 4/8	23 5/8	24 4/8	Deer Lodge Co., MT	Dorothy A. Pennington	Dorothy A. Pennington	1991	246
187 3/8	39 2/8	40 3/8	16 2/8	16 1/8	9 6/8	9 6/8	20	21 4/8	Sundre, AB	Stan Burrell	Stan Burrell	1953	249
187 3/8	40 4/8	41 7/8	15 3/8	15 4/8	8 3/8	8 3/8	22 7/8	22 7/8	Elbow River, AB	Sam R. Sloan	Sam R. Sloan	1962	249
187 3/8	42	43 1/8	14 7/8	15 1/8	8 4/8	8 4/8	21 4/8	21 4/8	Lytton, BC	R.G. Jones & P.B. Wilmot	R. George Jones	1973	249
187 2/8	40 3/8	39 4/8	15 6/8	14 7/8	9 3/8	9 3/8	19 7/8	22 4/8	McDonald Creek, AB	Ernest F. Greenwood	Ernest F. Greenwood	1965	252
187 2/8	38 4/8	38 3/8	15 1/8	15 6/8	10 3/8	10 3/8	17 3/8	22 2/8	Plateau Mt., AB	Randy Jackson	Randy Jackson	1984	252
187 2/8	41 1/8	40 4/8	17	17	7 7/8	7 7/8	20 1/8	24 2/8	Asotin Co., WA	Roger S. Brazier	Roger S. Brazier	1986	252
187 2/8	39 2/8	39 2/8	15 7/8	15 7/8	8 6/8	8 6/8	22 6/8	23 1/8	Granite Co., MT	Donald A. Chamberlain	Donald A. Chamberlain	1987	252

BIGHORN SHEEP

Ovis canadensis canadensis and certain related subspecies

Score	Length of Horn R	Length of Horn L	Circumference of Base R	Circumference of Base L	Circumference at Third Quarter R	Circumference at Third Quarter L	Greatest Spread	Tip to Tip Spread	Locality	Hunter	Owner	Date Killed	Rank
187 2/8	36 3/8	37 1/8	16 5/8	16 5/8	9 7/8	9 7/8	22 4/8	20	Thornton Creek, AB	John Gehan	John Gehan	1988	252
187 2/8	42 4/8	39 4/8	15 7/8	15 5/8	8 3/8	8 7/8	22 2/8	21 5/8	Granite Co., MT	Chuck Houtz	Chuck Houtz	1988	252
187 2/8	40 3/8	41 1/8	16	16 1/8	8 4/8	8 7/8	21 1/8	20 2/8	Beaverhead Co., MT	Charles R. Moe	Charles R. Moe	1994	252
187 1/8	41 3/8	41 4/8	15 5/8	15 4/8	9 1/8	9 1/8	21	21	White Swan Lake, BC	Lucius A. Chase	Lucius A. Chase	1961	259
187 1/8	41 5/8	43 4/8	15	15	9 1/8	8 5/8	23 4/8	23	Fallen Timber Creek, AB	Picked Up	Joe Blakemore	1968	259
187 1/8	41	38 5/8	15 6/8	15 7/8	9	9 3/8	22 6/8	15 2/8	Red Deer River, AB	Richard B. Smith	Richard B. Smith	1984	259
187 1/8	40 7/8	40 4/8	14 5/8	14 4/8	10 5/8	10 3/8	23 4/8	23 4/8	Deer Lodge Co., MT	David J. Etzwiler	David J. Etzwiler	1985	259
187 1/8	40	40 3/8	15 6/8	15	8 7/8	8 5/8	25	25	Deer Lodge Co., MT	Jeffrey A. Mikunda	Jeffrey A. Mikunda	1995	259
187	39	39 4/8	15	15	10 5/8	10 4/8	22 6/8	17 4/8	Wind River Mts., WY	Ralph E. Platt	Ralph E. Platt	1963	264
187	36 6/8	38	15 6/8	15 7/8	10 3/8	10 6/8	23 4/8	22 7/8	Colorado	Picked Up	E.H. Brown	PR 1964	264
187	37 7/8	38 1/8	16	16 1/8	10	10 2/8	17 6/8	22 5/8	Unknown	Unknown	Dale Selby	PR 1968	264
187	40 6/8	40 6/8	15 5/8	15 5/8	8 4/8	8 6/8	22 2/8	20 7/8	Sanders Co., MT	Bruce L. Hartford	Bruce L. Hartford	1978	264
187	37 4/8	38 4/8	16 3/8	16 5/8	9 4/8	9 7/8	25	22 4/8	Sanders Co., MT	Richard F. Lukes	Richard F. Lukes	1980	264
187	40 4/8	38 6/8	16	15 7/8	9 4/8	8 6/8	15	22 7/8	Elbow River, AB	Ralph Cervo	Ralph Cervo	1981	264
187	39 6/8	38	16 7/8	17	8 1/8	8 1/8	20	21 7/8	Highwood Range, AB	Sten B. Lundberg	Sten B. Lundberg	1984	264
187	40 6/8	40 4/8	16 4/8	16 4/8	7 6/8	8	21 6/8	21 6/8	Deer Lodge Co., MT	Wayne E. Bousfield	Wayne E. Bousfield	1985	264
187	41 3/8	41 3/8	16	16	8 2/8	8 2/8	24 4/8	24 4/8	Sanders Co., MT	Mark S. Eaton	Mark S. Eaton	1985	264
187	39 3/8	39 7/8	16	15 7/8	8 7/8	8 5/8	22	22 4/8	Granite Co., MT	Norman C. Dunkle	Norman C. Dunkle	1989	264
187	39	38 4/8	15 2/8	15 2/8	10 3/8	11	22 1/8	22 1/8	Sanders Co., MT	William V. Kuchera	William V. Kuchera	1990	264
187	40 4/8	39 4/8	15 5/8	15 5/8	10	9 6/8	20 4/8	17 4/8	Granite Co., MT	Pearl Foust	Pearl Foust	1991	264
187	38 7/8	39 4/8	16 3/8	16 3/8	9 6/8	8 7/8	22 4/8	19 7/8	Sanders Co., MT	Jim Zumbo	Jim Zumbo	1995	264
186 7/8	34 3/8	40 2/8	15 6/8	15 5/8	10 5/8	10 5/8	22 4/8	18 6/8	Burnt Timber, AB	C.J. McElroy	C.J. McElroy	1965	277
186 7/8	40 1/8	38 4/8	16 1/8	16	9	9	24 3/8	19	Ghost River, AB	D. James Turner	D. James Turner	1990	277
186 7/8	40 1/8	39 4/8	15 1/8	15	10 2/8	10 2/8	22 1/8	21 4/8	Asotin Co., WA	Ron Willenborg	Ron Willenborg	1991	277
186 6/8	39 4/8	38 4/8	16 2/8	16 3/8	10	10	23 6/8	18 7/8	East Kootenay, BC	Jerry Mortimer	Jerry Mortimer	1959	280
186 6/8	39 1/8	39 7/8	15 1/8	15 2/8	10 2/8	10 4/8	22	17 4/8	Whitehorse Creek, AB	Philip H. R. Stepney	Prov. Mus. Alta.	1978	280
186 6/8	41 7/8	42 7/8	15 7/8	15 7/8	7 3/8	7 4/8	22 3/8	21 6/8	Whitman Co., WA	Picked Up	Inland Empire Big Game Council	1983	280
186 6/8	38 6/8	38 2/8	16 3/8	16 3/8	8 7/8	8 7/8	23 3/8	18 5/8	Highwood River, AB	Ross Nikonchuk	Ross Nikonchuk	1984	280
186 6/8	41 2/8	40 2/8	15	15	9 6/8	9 6/8	22 5/8	18 7/8	Tornado Creek, BC	Clive J. Endicott	Clive J. Endicott	1988	280
186 6/8	39 1/8	37 5/8	15 2/8	15 3/8	11 1/8	10 5/8	22 3/8	20 4/8	Sanders Co., MT	Bill Mitchell	Bill Mitchell	1988	280
186 6/8	41 1/8	41 1/8	15 4/8	15 4/8	8 5/8	8 6/8	22 3/8	21 6/8	Granite Co., MT	Carol K. Chudy	Carol K. Chudy	1991	280
186 6/8	39 4/8	40	15 3/8	15 4/8	10 1/8	9 1/8	20 4/8	15	Sheep River, AB	Percy Pyra	Percy Pyra	1991	280
186 6/8	40 2/8	38 2/8	16 2/8	16 1/8	9 2/8	9 2/8	25 2/8	24 4/8	Granite Co., MT	Anthony D. Orizotti	Anthony D. Orizotti	1995	280
186 6/8	41	40 6/8	14 1/8	14 4/8	9	10 6/8	19 6/8	17 4/8	Whitehorse Creek, AB	Brian T. Panylyk	Brian T. Panylyk	1995	280
186 5/8	42 4/8	41 3/8	14 5/8	14 6/8	10 6/8	9 4/8	24 4/8	21 6/8	Panther River, AB	Picked Up	Belmore Browne	1936	290
186 5/8	42 6/8	42 1/8	15	15	9 4/8	8 3/8	25 6/8	25 6/8	Shell Rock, ID	Lea J. Bacos	Lea J. Bacos	1953	290
186 5/8	38 6/8	38 3/8	15 3/8	15 7/8	10 1/8	8 2/8	22	17 7/8	Blind Canyon, AB	Picked Up	AB Fish & Wildl. Div.	1983	290

Score	Length R	Length L	Base R	Base L			Spread		Locality	Hunter	Owner	Date	Rank
186⁵/₈	40⁷/₈	41	16¹/₈	16¹/₈	8	8⁶/₈	23⁶/₈	23⁶/₈	Beaverhead Co., MT	Gary L. Peltomaa	Gary L. Peltomaa	1989	290
186⁵/₈	38⁴/₈	37⁵/₈	15⁷/₈	15⁶/₈	9⁶/₈	9⁷/₈	22³/₈	23⁶/₈	Sanders Co., MT	Robert G. Blenker	Robert G. Blenker	1991	290
186⁵/₈	38	37⁵/₈	17³/₈	17²/₈	8²/₈	8⁵/₈	25	25	Blaine Co., MT	Gary A. Morton	Gary A. Morton	1995	290
186⁵/₈	39⁵/₈	40	15⁴/₈	15⁴/₈	9²/₈	9²/₈	25²/₈	25²/₈	Missoula Co., MT	Paul Bjerke	Paul Bjerke	1996	290
186⁵/₈	38⁷/₈	40	16⁶/₈	16⁸/₈	8⁴/₈	8⁴/₈	22	22	Sanders Co., MT	Cathryn Powell	Cathryn Powell	1997	290
186⁴/₈	39¹/₈	38	15⁷/₈	15⁶/₈	9³/₈	9	19	19	Fording River, BC	M.C. Baher	M.C. Baher	1942	298
186⁴/₈	38⁴/₈	40⁵/₈	17³/₈	17²/₈	8¹/₈	8⁴/₈	20²/₈	20²/₈	Rocky Mt. House, AB	Robert B. Johnson	Robert B. Johnson	1960	298
186⁴/₈	39⁷/₈	39⁷/₈	16²/₈	16³/₈	8¹/₈	8⁴/₈	21⁷/₈	21⁷/₈	Mt. Assiniboine, BC	Shirley A. Malbery	Shirley A. Malbery	1990	298
186⁴/₈	40⁴/₈	40⁴/₈	14⁴/₈	14⁴/₈	9⁶/₈	9⁶/₈	23⁶/₈	23⁶/₈	Sanders Co., MT	C.F. Dupuis & I. Dupuis	Picked Up	1995	298
186³/₈	40⁴/₈	41⁸/₈	14¹/₈	14¹/₈	10⁴/₈	10⁴/₈	20	20	Tyrrell Creek, AB	John H. Batten	Picked Up	1949	302
186³/₈	41⁷/₈	41	14¹/₈	14¹/₈	11¹/₈	10⁶/₈	22¹/₈	22⁴/₈	Ventre-Flat, WY	John Evasco	John Evasco	1953	302
186³/₈	38¹/₈	36	16¹/₈	16	10	10	22⁴/₈	22⁴/₈	Castle River, AB	Ed Burton	Ed Burton	1954	302
186³/₈	42	41¹/₈	15³/₈	15³/₈	8³/₈	8⁶/₈	21⁶/₈	21⁶/₈	Fernie, BC	Thomas Krall	Thomas Krall	1963	302
186³/₈	41	42³/₈	15¹/₈	15¹/₈	8⁷/₈	8²/₈	20¹/₈	20¹/₈	Simpson River, BC	James A. Walls	James A. Walls	1981	302
186³/₈	43⁴/₈	40⁵/₈	14¹/₈	14¹/₈	9⁷/₈	10²/₈	23	23³/₈	Grant Co., NM	Clyde Reed	Clyde Reed	1992	302
186³/₈	39	40¹/₈	14⁶/₈	14⁶/₈	10⁶/₈	10⁴/₈	23⁵/₈	23³/₈	Emery Co., UT	Stephen C. Walker	Stephen C. Walker	1992	302
186²/₈	41⁷/₈	42¹/₈	14	14	9⁷/₈	9⁴/₈	21¹/₈	21⁴/₈	Cadomin, AB	R.A. Craig	R.A. Craig	1936	309
186²/₈	42³/₈	41³/₈	14⁵/₈	14⁶/₈	9⁴/₈	9⁴/₈	24²/₈	24²/₈	Clearwater River, AB	Picked Up	Picked Up	1954	309
186²/₈	40³/₈	40¹/₈	15¹/₈	15³/₈	9⁵/₈	9⁷/₈	21⁴/₈	20⁶/₈	Sheep Creek, AB	G.A. Reiche	G.A. Reiche	1960	309
186²/₈	37	38⁴/₈	15⁷/₈	15⁷/₈	9⁴/₈	10	20¹/₈	20¹/₈	Junction Mt., AB	Robert R. Willis	Robert R. Willis	1978	309
186²/₈	40	41⁴/₈	16	16	8³/₈	8	22²/₈	22²/₈	Rabbit Creek, BC	Lanny E. Kniert	Lanny E. Kniert	1982	309
186²/₈	39⁶/₈	39⁴/₈	16¹/₈	16¹/₈	8⁴/₈	8⁵/₈	23³/₈	22	Little Elbow River, AB	John Liefso	John Liefso	1982	309
186²/₈	40	41	16¹/₈	16¹/₈	8¹/₈	8⁵/₈	20⁷/₈	17⁴/₈	Riverside Mt., BC	Paul A. Templin	Paul A. Templin	1983	309
186¹/₈	43²/₈	44⁵/₈	16⁴/₈	16⁴/₈	6⁷/₈	6⁵/₈	24⁵/₈	24⁵/₈	Yellowstone Park, MT	James K. Weatherford	William H. Dirrett	1913	316
186¹/₈	39⁴/₈	39⁴/₈	15²/₈	15³/₈	10	10⁴/₈	15⁶/₈	15⁶/₈	Highwood, AB	Terry J. Webber	Terry J. Webber	1959	316
186¹/₈	41⁵/₈	41²/₈	15³/₈	15⁴/₈	8²/₈	8²/₈	20⁷/₈	19¹/₈	Sun River Canyon, MT	Glen Roberts	Glen Roberts	1961	316
186¹/₈	39⁵/₈	40²/₈	15⁴/₈	15⁶/₈	8²/₈	8³/₈	22	17⁴/₈	Waterton Natl. Park, AB	Robert Thompson	Picked Up	PR 1966	316
186¹/₈	39⁵/₈	38	15³/₈	15⁴/₈	10²/₈	9⁶/₈	20⁴/₈	20⁴/₈	Cougar Mt., AB	Alan E. Schroeder	Alan E. Schroeder	1989	316
186¹/₈	41⁴/₈	41	16¹/₈	16⁸/₈	9²/₈	9¹/₈	20⁴/₈	18	Fergus Co., MT	Henry M. Kengerski	Henry M. Kengerski	1993	316
186¹/₈	36⁷/₈	41²/₈	14⁶/₈	14⁶/₈	10⁴/₈	10⁴/₈	20⁶/₈	20⁴/₈	Fremont Co., WY	Warren V. Spriggs, Sr.	Picked Up	1994	316
186	38⁵/₈	40²/₈	15	15	9³/₈	9³/₈	22	18⁶/₈	Sparwood, BC	H. Bruce Freeman	Unknown	PR 1910	323
186	40⁴/₈	39	16	16	8⁷/₈	8⁴/₈	19⁵/₈	19⁵/₈	Clearwater, AB	Herb Hamilton	Herb Hamilton	1964	323
186	39⁴/₈	39	14⁶/₈	14⁶/₈	10⁶/₈	10⁶/₈	21	21	Granite Co., MT	Dale W. Hoth	Dale W. Hoth	1981	323
186	40⁶/₈	40²/₈	15⁴/₈	15³/₈	9⁷/₈	9⁶/₈	22	20⁴/₈	Line Creek, BC	Sam W. Stephenson	Sam W. Stephenson	1991	323
185⁷/₈	40³/₈	40⁴/₈	15	15	9⁶/₈	9⁶/₈	21	17³/₈	Panther River, AB	J.F. Blakemore	J.F. Blakemore	1961	327
185⁷/₈	41²/₈	41³/₈	14	14	10⁶/₈	10³/₈	22⁵/₈	17³/₈	Mystery Lake, AB	Jim Baballa	Jim Baballa	1962	327
185⁷/₈	35	37³/₈	14⁴/₈	14⁴/₈	13	13	20³/₈	17⁵/₈	Ural, MT	Curtis Gatson	Curtis Gatson	1962	327
185⁷/₈	38⁷/₈	38²/₈	15⁵/₈	15⁶/₈	10	10	21⁵/₈	17¹/₈	Burnt Timber Creek, AB	John T. Blackwell	John T. Blackwell	1967	327
185⁷/₈	40³/₈	41	15⁶/₈	15⁶/₈	8⁴/₈	8⁴/₈	21⁵/₈	21	Botanie Creek, BC	William J. Pincock	William J. Pincock	1988	327
185⁶/₈	40²/₈	40²/₈	14⁷/₈	14⁷/₈	9⁶/₈	9⁶/₈	20⁴/₈	21	Ghost River, AB	William D. Cox	William D. Cox	1959	332
185⁶/₈	39⁶/₈	38⁴/₈	15²/₈	15²/₈	9⁷/₈	9⁷/₈	20⁴/₈	20	Granite Co., MT	James M. Milligan	James M. Milligan	1990	332
185⁶/₈	38⁴/₈	36⁶/₈	15⁶/₈	15⁶/₈	10²/₈	10²/₈	21	18³/₈	Granite Co., MT	Donald A. Dwyer	Donald A. Dwyer	1992	332
185⁵/₈	39¹/₈	39⁴/₈	14⁷/₈	14⁸/₈	10¹/₈	10⁵/₈	22⁴/₈	18	Black Diamond, AB	Gordon Lait	Picked Up	1962	335
185⁵/₈	40⁵/₈	40	15²/₈	15²/₈	8⁷/₈	9	23⁴/₈	23⁴/₈	Lemhi Co., ID	W.R. Franklin	W.R. Franklin	1963	335
185⁵/₈	39³/₈	40⁵/₈	15⁵/₈	15⁵/₈	8²/₈	8²/₈	24³/₈	18⁴/₈	Simpson River, BC	Thomas R. VanEvery	Thomas R. VanEvery	1995	335
185⁴/₈	42⁶/₈	41	13⁶/₈	13⁶/₈	9⁷/₈	10	24³/₈	21²/₈	Wind River Mts., WY	Elgin T. Gates	Elgin T. Gates	1954	338
185⁴/₈	40⁶/₈	40⁸/₈	14⁵/₈	14⁵/₈	10¹/₈	10¹/₈	22⁴/₈	20	Saskatchewan River, AB	Herb Klein	Herb Klein	1963	338

649

BIGHORN SHEEP

Ovis canadensis canadensis and certain related subspecies

Score	Length of Horn R	L	Circumference of Base R	L	Circumference at Third Quarter R	L	Greatest Spread	Tip tp Tip Spread	Locality	Hunter	Owner	Date Killed	Rank
185 4/8	38 5/8	40 5/8	15 4/8	15 4/8	8 5/8	10	24	19 4/8	Highwood River, AB	W. Erdman	M.R. Wagner	1964	338
185 4/8	40 2/8	40 2/8	14 4/8	14 4/8	10 1/8	10 1/8	22	20 4/8	Canyon Creek, AB	Edith J. Nagy	Edith J. Nagy	1981	338
185 4/8	39 5/8	38 5/8	16 6/8	16 3/8	8 2/8	8 2/8	27 3/8	27 3/8	Granite Co., MT	Lawrence R. Simkins	Lawrence R. Simkins	1986	338
185 4/8	40 5/8	39 3/8	16 4/8	16 3/8	8 7/8	8 3/8	21 7/8	21 7/8	Deer Lodge Co., MT	Douglas C. Landers	Douglas C. Landers	1987	338
185 4/8	38 4/8	40 4/8	15	14 7/8	10 4/8	10 4/8	21	18 4/8	Barrier Mt., AB	Ronald K. Smith	Ronald K. Smith	1988	338
185 4/8	40 7/8	40 3/8	14 5/8	14 6/8	9 7/8	10 2/8	20 5/8	20 3/8	Lewis & Clark Co., MT	Darlene K. Kechely	Darlene K. Kechely	1992	338
185 4/8	41 1/8	39 3/8	15 6/8	15 7/8	8 7/8	8 3/8	25	22 2/8	Missoula Co., MT	Thomas J. Dux	Thomas J. Dux	1993	338
185 4/8	38 4/8	37 4/8	16	16	9 2/8	9 5/8	23 1/8	17	Blaine Co., MT	Eugene W. Bell	Eugene W. Bell	1995	338
185 3/8	39 6/8	39 5/8	16 3/8	16 3/8	8	8 1/8	21 5/8	13 4/8	Natal, BC	H. Beard	Myles Travis	1921	348
185 3/8	39 4/8	38 3/8	14 7/8	15 1/8	10 2/8	10 2/8	22	17 4/8	Lewis & Clark Co., MT	Richard Tyler	Richard Tyler	1954	348
185 3/8	39 5/8	39	16	16	9 6/8	9 1/8	21	20 5/8	Fremont Co., CO	Leonard L. Kiser	Leonard L. Kiser	1955	348
185 3/8	40 3/8	39 6/8	14 6/8	14 7/8	10 1/8	9 5/8	23 4/8	19 4/8	Lillooet, BC	Glen E. Park	Glen E. Park	1964	348
185 3/8	39 3/8	40 2/8	15 4/8	15 6/8	10 1/8	10 6/8	21 4/8	15 6/8	Banff, AB	Unknown	E. Kent. Univ.	PR 1974	348
185 3/8	38 1/8	40 6/8	15 7/8	15 7/8	9 4/8	9 3/8	22 6/8	17 6/8	Sanders Co., MT	Chad R. Jones	Chad R. Jones	1990	348
185 3/8	40 1/8	39 6/8	14 6/8	14 6/8	10 1/8	10 2/8	22 5/8	18 6/8	Grand Co., UT	Picked Up	Ute Indian Tribe	1990	348
185 3/8	36 7/8	38 2/8	17 2/8	17 2/8	8	8 2/8	22	16 4/8	Kananaskis, AB	Bruce Stewart	Bruce Stewart	1996	348
185 3/8	38 1/8	38 4/8	15 7/8	15 6/8	9 3/8	10 2/8	22 3/8	19 1/8	Granite Co., MT	John C. Lundt	John C. Lundt	1997	348
185 2/8	42 2/8	38	15 6/8	16	8 5/8	8 6/8	21	17 3/8	Unknown	Unknown	Art Esslinger	1930	357
185 2/8	38 1/8	37 1/8	16	16	10 4/8	9 7/8	20 1/8	20 1/8	Big Creek, ID	Edson Piers	Edson Piers	1962	357
185 2/8	40 6/8	41	15 3/8	15 3/8	8 7/8	8 6/8	23 2/8	20 1/8	Spences Bridge, BC	J.C. Atkinson	J.C. Atkinson	1965	357
185 2/8	38 1/8	37 5/8	16 5/8	16 5/8	9 1/8	8 5/8	22 4/8	21	Fremont Co., CO	Robert W. Wallace	Robert W. Wallace	1978	357
185 2/8	38 5/8	41 3/8	15 5/8	15 1/8	8 6/8	9 2/8	21 4/8	20 4/8	Teton Co., MT	Picked Up	Tim French	1980	357
185 2/8	39 2/8	38	15	15 2/8	11 3/8	10 3/8	22 7/8	17	Phillips Co., MT	Patrick R. Trujillo	Patrick R. Trujillo	1992	357
185 2/8	40 5/8	40 3/8	16	16	8 5/8	8 3/8	23 1/8	22 4/8	Missoula Co., MT	Mayline K. Robertson	Mayline K. Robertson	1996	357
185 1/8	41 3/8	40 6/8	14 5/8	14 4/8	9 3/8	9 6/8	22 7/8	19 2/8	Dubois, WY	B.N. Lively	B.N. Lively	1953	364
185 1/8	40 1/8	38 6/8	15 3/8	15 3/8	9 2/8	8 7/8	23	15 2/8	Tornado Mt., BC	Vincent Kehm	Vincent Kehm	1958	364
185 1/8	40 2/8	37 5/8	15 7/8	15 7/8	9 4/8	9	23 2/8	18 2/8	Big Horn River, AB	Chris Klineburger	Chris Klineburger	1962	364
185 1/8	40 5/8	37 6/8	16	16	8 3/8	8 7/8	21 7/8	18	Sheep River, AB	Garner D. Jacobs	Garner D. Jacobs	1989	364
185 1/8	38	38 5/8	16 4/8	16 2/8	8 5/8	9	25 1/8	22 4/8	Blaine Co., MT	Mark K. Weiser	Mark K. Weiser	1989	364
185 1/8	41	40 1/8	14 2/8	14 1/8	11	10 7/8	21	17 6/8	Lewis & Clark Co., MT	Eugene R. Lewis	Eugene R. Lewis	1990	364
185 1/8	36 2/8	37 7/8	16 4/8	16 4/8	9 2/8	10 5/8	24 6/8	18	Greenlee Co., AZ	Gary L. Asmus	Gary L. Asmus	1994	364
185 1/8	38	39 1/8	16 2/8	16 3/8	9	9	22 2/8	18 2/8	Sanders Co., MT	Marcus M. Nichols	Marcus M. Nichols	1994	364
185	40 1/8	39 5/8	14 7/8	16 2/8	8 4/8	8 2/8	22	19 4/8	Alberta	Gift of Lynford Biddle	Acad. Nat. Sci., Phil.	1901	372
185	39 1/8	39 1/8	14 7/8	14 7/8	10 4/8	10 4/8	23	17 6/8	Green River, WY	Floyd J. Stalnaker	Elsie Stalnaker	1913	372
185	38 6/8	41 2/8	15 1/8	15 2/8	9 2/8	9 4/8	18 4/8	17 7/8	Mitchell River, BC	Mr. & Mrs. N.A. Meckstroth	Mr. & Mrs. N.A. Meckstroth	1963	372
185	40 4/8	39 4/8	15 1/8	15 1/8	9 3/8	8 6/8	20 2/8	17 2/8	Cadomin, AB	Rita Oney	Rita Oney	1966	372
185	40	40 ††	14 7/8	15	10	10	23 3/8	18 1/8	Sanders Co., MT	Patrick M. Woolard	Patrick M. Woolard	1992	372
185	41 2/8	38 2/8	15 5/8	15 5/8	8 6/8	8 6/8	22 3/8	21 1/8	Missoula Co., MT	William G. Crandall	William G. Crandall	1994	372

Score	Length of Horn R	Length of Horn L	Circumference of Base R	Circumference of Base L	Circumference 3rd Quarter R	Circumference 3rd Quarter L	Greatest Spread	Tip to Tip Spread	Locality	By Whom Killed	Owner	Date Killed	Rank
184 7/8	40 4/8	39 5/8	14 6/8	14 7/8	9 5/8	9 4/8	23 5/8	23 5/8	Westhorse Mts., ID	Cecil Dodge	Cecil Dodge	1953	378
184 7/8	37 6/8	37 7/8	15	15 3/8	10 4/8	10 2/8	22 3/8	20	Glenwood Springs, CO	Picked Up	Mark E. Cook	1960	378
184 7/8	39 1/8	40 4/8	15 4/8	15 4/8	9	8 5/8	25 2/8	25 2/8	Harney Co., OR	Thomas P. Weil	Thomas P. Weil	1997	378
184 6/8	38 7/8	39 1/8	15 1/8	15 4/8	10 4/8	10 2/8	21 3/8	21 3/8	Unknown	Unknown	George Ostashek	PR 1920	381
184 6/8	40 1/8	40 1/8	15 2/8	15 1/8	9 7/8	9 6/8	21 5/8	21 5/8	Brazeau River, AB	Grancel Fitz	Mrs. Grancel Fitz	1954	381
184 6/8	41 2/8	41 2/8	14 4/8	14 4/8	9 6/8	9 4/8	21	21	Castle Mt., MT	E.L. Anderson	E.L. Anderson	1962	381
184 6/8	40	40 4/8	14 2/8	14 2/8	10 2/8	10 5/8	23 7/8	20 6/8	Jackson Hole, WY	Johnny Kretschman	Johnny Kretschman	1976	381
184 6/8	39 4/8	39 2/8	16 3/8	16 3/8	8 1/8	7 6/8	21 1/8	21 1/8	Little Elbow River, AB	Alex Cornett	Alex Cornett	1991	381
184 6/8	37 7/8	37 3/8	15 4/8	15 4/8	10 2/8	10 1/8	19 7/8	17 3/8	Sanders Co., MT	William J. Alexander	William J. Alexander	1994	381
184 6/8	40 2/8	40 6/8	15 7/8	15 7/8	8 1/8	8 2/8	24 7/8	24 4/8	Granite Co., MT	Klinton K. Curtis	Klinton K. Curtis	1995	381
184 6/8	37 6/8	40 4/8	16 5/8	16 5/8	8 6/8	8 5/8	23 4/8	20 2/8	Ravalli Co., MT	Bruce A. Hover	Bruce A. Hover	1996	381
184 6/8	39 1/8	37 5/8	16 5/8	16 5/8	8 4/8	8 4/8	20 2/8	19 7/8	Wallowa Co., OR	Bill A. Richichi	Bill A. Richichi	1997	381
184 5/8	41	41	16 6/8	16 5/8	6 6/8	6 7/8	22 4/8	21 1/8	Salmon River, ID	Mark D. Armstrong	Mark D. Armstrong	1939	391
184 5/8	38 5/8	37 4/8	15 7/8	15 7/8	9 4/8	9 4/8	22 3/8	20 7/8	Clearwater, AB	Ted Biladeau	Ted Biladeau	1942	391
184 5/8	39 2/8	41 1/8	15 1/8	15 1/8	9 6/8	9 6/8	20 2/8	17 6/8	Burnt Timber Creek, AB	G.C. Matthews	G.C. Matthews	1960	391
184 5/8	41 6/8	42 3/8	14 7/8	14 1/8	9 7/8	9 6/8	22 1/8	22 1/8	Rock Lake, AB	Berry B. Brooks	Berry B. Brooks	1960	391
184 5/8	39 2/8	39 1/8	14 7/8	14 7/8	10 6/8	10 4/8	22 1/8	18 3/8	Ruby Lake, AB	Bill Bodenchuk	Clifford Wolfe	1965	391
184 5/8	40 1/8	40 1/8	15 3/8	15 4/8	9 3/8	9 3/8	22 5/8	21 4/8	Luscar Creek, AB	Picked Up	John G. Stelfox	1976	391
184 5/8	39	40 5/8	15	15 1/8	10	10	22	18 2/8	Asotin Co., WA	Doug W. Whiteside	Doug W. Whiteside	1994	391
184 4/8	41 6/8	37 7/8	16 3/8	16	7 7/8	9 1/8	21 3/8	22 1/8	Smoky River, AB	Thomas J. Pawlacyk	Thomas J. Pawlacyk	1946	398
184 4/8	39 2/8	39 2/8	16	16	8 1/8	8 4/8	22 3/8	17 4/8	Sun River, MT	W.C. Barthman	W.C. Barthman	1948	398
184 4/8	38 5/8	38 5/8	14 4/8	14 7/8	10 1/8	10 1/8	21 5/8	17 7/8	Custer Co., ID	Picked Up	Stanley V. Potts	1981	398
184 4/8	39 5/8	39 5/8	16	16 1/8	8 4/8	8 5/8	22 4/8	18 5/8	Granite Co., MT	Kevin R. Bouley	Kevin R. Bouley	1988	398
184 4/8	36 7/8	37 5/8	15 7/8	15 4/8	10 5/8	10 1/8	24 6/8	23 7/8	Exshaw Creek, AB	Kenneth F. Bills	Kenneth F. Bills	1993	398
184 4/8	39 3/8	39 3/8	16 3/8	16 3/8	8 7/8	8 6/8	21 2/8	18 1/8	Kindersley Creek, BC	James C. Johnson	James C. Johnson	1993	398
184 4/8	38 6/8	38 4/8	15 5/8	15 5/8	9 5/8	9 6/8	22 7/8	17 4/8	Park Co., MT	Cliff Harden	Cliff Harden	1994	398
184 4/8	40 6/8	40 6/8	14 6/8	15	10 2/8	11	19 6/8	19 6/8	Ravalli Co., MT	Brenda M. Lewis	Brenda M. Lewis	1994	398
184 3/8	38 3/8	38 2/8	15 6/8	15 6/8	9 2/8	9 2/8	22	19 4/8	Gunnison Co., CO	Billy Prior	Daniel C. Harrington	1915	406
184 3/8	37 4/8	37 7/8	15 2/8	15 4/8	10 2/8	10 2/8	21 6/8	22	Cadomin, AB	John H. Marcum	John H. Marcum	1969	406
184 3/8	39 7/8	39 7/8	14 1/8	14	11 6/8	11	22	21	Carbon Co., MT	Picked Up	Monte Berzel	1977	406
184 3/8	41	41 7/8	14 2/8	14 2/8	10	10	21 4/8	18 2/8	Burnt Timber Creek, AB	Terrance S. Marcum	Terrance S. Marcum	1988	406
184 3/8	42 4/8	41 7/8	15 3/8	15 4/8	7 4/8	7 4/8	24 2/8	23 7/8	Sanders Co., MT	Charles Hall	Charles Hall	1992	406
184 3/8	39 5/8	39 4/8	16 3/8	16 3/8	8 4/8	8 2/8	18 6/8	18 6/8	Hinton, AB	James S. Robinson	James S. Robinson	1994	406
184 3/8	41 6/8	38 1/8	15 7/8	15 7/8	8 2/8	8 5/8	19	19	Missoula Co., MT	James A. Schott	James A. Schott	1995	406
184 2/8	37 6/8	37 6/8	15 4/8	15 4/8	10 7/8	10 1/8	24	24	Middle Mts., WY	William Underwood	William Underwood	1959	413
184 2/8	38 7/8	40 3/8	15	15	9 4/8	9 4/8	20 1/8	18 4/8	Drinnan Creek, AB	John H. Epstein	John H. Epstein	1963	413
184 2/8	41	40 6/8	15 1/8	15 1/8	8 6/8	8 5/8	20 7/8	20 1/8	Elk Valley, BC	Bernard A. Fiedeldey, Jr.	Bernard A. Fiedeldey, Jr.	1992	413
184 2/8	39 3/8	40 1/8	15 1/8	15 1/8	9 2/8	9 2/8	21 7/8	17	Granite Co., MT	Keith Bomstad	Keith Bomstad	1996	413
184 1/8	40 2/8	38 1/8	15 3/8	15 2/8	9 6/8	9 6/8	23	22 5/8	Vaseux Lake, BC	Bob McDowell	Bob McDowell	1960	417
184 1/8	38 7/8	38 1/8	15 2/8	15 2/8	8 5/8	8 7/8	22 5/8	23 1/8	Alberta	Bob Wood	N. Am. Wildl. Mus.	1964	417
184 1/8	38 7/8	39	17	17	8 1/8	7 6/8	23 1/8	21 7/8	Castle River, AB	E.B. Cunningham	E.B. Cunningham	1965	417
184 1/8	39 4/8	39 4/8	15 4/8	15 2/8	9 3/8	9 3/8	24	23 5/8	Panther River, AB	Picked Up	Paul Ujfalusi	1966	417
184 1/8	39	39	15 7/8	15 7/8	9 5/8	9 5/8	25	13 5/8	Silver Bow Co., MT	John D. Truzzoline	John D. Truzzoline	1990	417
184 1/8	38 1/8	38 4/8	16 6/8	16 5/8	8 3/8	8 2/8	22 1/8	16 1/8	Fording River, BC	Cam McGregor	Cam McGregor	1995	417
184 1/8	38 6/8	38 3/8	15 1/8	15	9 7/8	9 7/8	22 3/8	22 3/8	Cadomin Creek, AB	David F. Thomson	David F. Thomson	1997	417
184	40 5/8	37 7/8	14 7/8	14 6/8	9 4/8	9 2/8	22 4/8	22 3/8	Valley Co., ID	Picked Up	LaVarr Jacklin	1949	424

BIGHORN SHEEP

Ovis canadensis canadensis and certain related subspecies

Score	Length of Horn		Circumference of Base		Circumference at Third Quarter		Greatest Spread	Tip tp Tip Spread	Locality	Hunter	Owner	Date Killed	Rank
	R	L	R	L	R	L							
184	41 1/8	41 1/8	14 2/8	14 1/8	10	10	20 5/8	19	Ghost River, AB	W.D. Norwood	W.D. Norwood	1955	424
184	39 1/8	39 1/8	14 7/8	14 7/8	10 1/8	10 3/8	21 6/8	21 6/8	Sun River, MT	Carl Mehmke	Carl Mehmke	1957	424
184	35	36 4/8	16 2/8	16 1/8	10 6/8	11	21	20	Cardston, AB	August Glander	August Glander	1969	424
184	37 5/8	39 5/8	16 4/8	16 3/8	8 2/8	8 7/8	21	20	Sanders Co., MT	Don Robinson	Don Robinson	1980	424
184	40 4/8	43 4/8	15	15	8 2/8	8 3/8	25 5/8	25 5/8	Deer Lodge Co., MT	Dave Bisch	Dave Bisch	1988	424
184	39	40 2/8	14 4/8	14 4/8	10 2/8	10 4/8	22	19 7/8	Mineral Co., MT	Ronald A. Snyder	Ronald A. Snyder	1991	424
184	39 4/8	32	16 2/8	16 4/8	9 5/8	9 4/8	25	22	Missoula Co., MT	Billy J. Olsen	Billy J. Olsen	1997	424
183 7/8	41 1/8	40	14 4/8	14 4/8	9 6/8	9 4/8	23	20 5/8	Saskatchewan River, AB	Basil C. Bradbury	Basil C. Bradbury	1968	432
183 7/8	43 5/8	35 2/8	17	17	7 5/8	6 6/8	24 4/8	23	Beaverhead Co., MT	James C. Garrett	James C. Garrett	1983	432
183 7/8	41	41 1/8	15 1/8	15 1/8	8 4/8	8 2/8	24 3/8	24 3/8	Sanders Co., MT	Lyndell C. Stahn	Lyndell C. Stahn	1988	432
183 7/8	39 2/8	39 3/8	16	16 1/8	8 2/8	8 2/8	21 5/8	18 3/8	Garfield Co., WA	Klaus H. Meyn	Klaus H. Meyn	1990	432
183 7/8	39 1/8	39 2/8	15 5/8	15 5/8	8 7/8	8 6/8	23 7/8	21 6/8	Granite Co., MT	Gordon H. Brandenburger	Gordon H. Brandenburger	1992	432
183 7/8	38 1/8	39	16	16 2/8	8 4/8	8 4/8	20 5/8	20 2/8	Nez Perce Co., ID	Michael L. Lohman	Michael L. Lohman	1993	432
183 7/8	37 4/8	37 1/8	16 4/8	16 4/8	9	9	23 2/8	23	Beaverhead Co., MT	Arthur E. Nuthak	Arthur E. Nuthak	1993	432
183 7/8	38 3/8	39 6/8	16	16	8 5/8	8 7/8	23 6/8	16 2/8	Huerfano Co., CO	Mark D. Thomson	Mark D. Thomson	1997	432
183 6/8	37 2/8	37 2/8	15 5/8	15 5/8	9 2/8	9 6/8	20 4/8	17 4/8	Fernie, BC	Unknown	Fred Braatz	1930	440
183 6/8	39 7/8	39 3/8	14 6/8	14 6/8	9 7/8	10	21 4/8	15 7/8	Natal, BC	Mrs. A.L. Musser	A.L. Musser	1947	440
183 6/8	40 1/8	39 5/8	14 3/8	14 4/8	10 2/8	10 2/8	19 5/8	18 1/8	Castle River, AB	George Hagglund	George Hagglund	1959	440
183 6/8	37 2/8	38	15 4/8	15 4/8	10	10	21 4/8	23 4/8	Highwood Range, AB	K. Fred Coleman	K. Fred Coleman	1977	440
183 6/8	37 6/8	36 4/8	16 5/8	16 6/8	9	9	23 4/8	23 4/8	Ravalli Co., MT	Sandra L. Gann	Les Towner	1985	440
183 6/8	37 4/8	37 4/8	16	16	9 3/8	9 4/8	24	22 4/8	Silver Bow Co., MT	Emmett O. Riordan	Emmett O. Riordan	1986	440
183 6/8	38 4/8	39	15 6/8	15 6/8	8 7/8	8 6/8	23 2/8	14 4/8	Wallowa Co., OR	Tom R. Croswell	Tom R. Croswell	1992	440
183 6/8	36	36	16 2/8	16 2/8	9 5/8	10 1/8	21 7/8	15 3/8	Teton Co., MT	Greg D. Gilbert	Greg D. Gilbert	1992	440
183 6/8	37 1/8	36 1/8	17 2/8	17 2/8	8 1/8	8	21 4/8	21	Blaine Co., MT	John H. Miller	John H. Miller	1992	440
183 6/8	38 5/8	40 3/8	14 7/8	14 7/8	9 6/8	9 7/8	23 6/8	17 6/8	Granite Co., MT	Janice J. Kauffman	Janice J. Kauffman	1993	440
183 6/8	39	37 6/8	15 2/8	15 2/8	9 7/8	9 6/8	23 5/8	17 7/8	Lewis Co., ID	Earl G. Lunceford, Jr.	Earl G. Lunceford, Jr.	1993	440
183 6/8	38 3/8	40 7/8	16 7/8	16 7/8	7 5/8	7 2/8	22 3/8	20 4/8	Blaine Co., MT	Kathy M. Peterson	Kathy M. Peterson	1995	440
183 5/8	37 4/8	37 3/8	16 2/8	16 3/8	9 2/8	9 3/8	21 6/8	17 2/8	Mystery Lake, AB	Paul J. Inzanti	Paul J. Inzanti	1960	452
183 5/8	38 2/8	39 3/8	15 6/8	15 6/8	9 2/8	9 2/8	19 4/8	18 7/8	Marble Creek, ID	Joseph T. Pelton	Joseph T. Pelton	1961	452
183 5/8	37 7/8	39	15 3/8	15 3/8	9 5/8	10 1/8	22	16 1/8	Burnt Timber, AB	Jay H. Giese	Jay H. Giese	1966	452
183 5/8	36 7/8	37	16 1/8	16 1/8	9 6/8	9 5/8	24 7/8	24 7/8	Granite Co., MT	Sandy C. Antonich	Sandy C. Antonich	1982	452
183 5/8	39 4/8	41 5/8	15	15	9 1/8	9 2/8	22	22	Lemhi Co., ID	Ronald D. Carlson	Ronald D. Carlson	1989	452
183 5/8	39 3/8	37 6/8	16 5/8	16 5/8	8 4/8	8 5/8	21 6/8	21 2/8	Phillips Co., MT	Dee Strickler	Jack F. Strickler	1993	452
183 4/8	33 4/8	39	16	16	10 4/8	10 4/8	22 3/8	18 2/8	Sweet Grass Co., MT	Basil C. Bradbury	Basil C. Bradbury	1965	458
183 4/8	42	36 6/8	14 5/8	14 5/8	9 7/8	9 4/8	21 2/8	21 1/8	Mystery Lake, AB	Armando Tomasso	Armando Tomasso	1967	458
183 4/8	38 4/8	37 6/8	15 4/8	15 6/8	9 5/8	9 4/8	20 4/8	20 4/8	C.M. Russell Game Range, MT	Mrs. Gordon Pagenkopf	Mrs. Gordon Pagenkopf	1970	458
183 4/8	38 2/8	39 2/8	16 1/8	16 2/8	8 6/8	8 1/8	18	13 7/8	Granite Co., MT	Karen Throckmorton	Karen Throckmorton	1987	458

Score	Length R	Length L	Circ. Base R	Circ. Base L	Circ. 3rd Qtr R	Circ. 3rd Qtr L	Tip to Tip	Greatest Spread	Locality	Hunter	Owner	Date	Rank
183 4/8	39 1/8	37 5/8	16 6/8	16 4/8	8 1/8	7 6/8	14 2/8	22 6/8	Chauncey Creek, BC	Stewart Cockshutt	Stewart Cockshutt	1990	458
183 4/8	39 2/8	38 6/8	16 1/8	16 1/8	8	8	21 2/8	21 2/8	Galatea Creek, AB	Karlo Miklic	Karlo Miklic	1990	458
183 4/8	39	39 6/8	16	16	8 2/8	8	20 3/8	21 2/8	Lewis & Clark Co., MT	Lynn E. Valtinson	Lynn E. Valtinson	1991	458
183 4/8	38 4/8	38 4/8	16	15 6/8	9 3/8	9 3/8	19	22 7/8	Sanders Co., MT	Clinton R. Fitchett	Clinton R. Fitchett	1996	458
183 4/8	41	40	15	15 1/8	9 2/8	7 7/8	19 3/8	21 4/8	Granite Co., MT	Robert D. Mattie	Robert D. Mattie	1996	458
183 4/8	42 3/8	41 7/8	15 1/8	15 1/8	7 7/8	8 3/8	24 3/8	24 5/8	Lewis & Clark Co., MT	Jack R. Sater	Jack R. Sater	1997	458
183 3/8	41	38 1/8	16	15 6/8	8	10 7/8	23 5/8	24 5/8	Clearwater River, AB	John Coston	John Coston	1961	468
183 3/8	37 3/8	38 4/8	15 3/8	15 3/8	10 1/8	8 2/8	16 2/8	22	Sanders Co., MT	C.J. McElroy	C.J. McElroy	1969	468
183 3/8	38 7/8	39 4/8	16 4/8	16 6/8	7 7/8	6 7/8	15 6/8	21	Sanders Co., MT	John P. Dilley	John P. Dilley	1981	468
183 3/8	42 7/8	42 4/8	15 2/8	15 2/8	7 4/8	7 4/8	27 4/8	27 4/8	Sanders Co., MT	Edward W. Blackwood	Rocky Mt. Elk Foundation	1985	468
183 3/8	40 4/8	41 1/8	15 4/8	15 4/8	7 5/8	7 6/8	21 5/8	21 5/8	Mt. Sparrowhawk, AB	Ilse R. Knight	Ilse R. Knight	1986	468
183 3/8	38 3/8	37 4/8	16 4/8	16 4/8	9 5/8	9 6/8	18 4/8	20 5/8	Silver Bow Co., MT	Gregory Kondro	Gregory Kondro	1989	468
183 3/8	37 5/8	37 4/8	16 1/8	16 1/8	9 2/8	8 5/8	19 4/8	22 6/8	Beaverhead Co., MT	Travis R. Schuessler	Travis R. Schuessler	1990	468
183 3/8	39 3/8	39 4/8	15 5/8	15 5/8	9 5/8	9 3/8	21 7/8	21 7/8	Granite Co., MT	Austin S. Rosenbaum	Austin S. Rosenbaum	1993	468
183 3/8	36 6/8	40 3/8	15 3/8	15 3/8	11 1/8	11 5/8	21 2/8	23	Snake-Indian River, AB	Terry R. Screnar	Terry R. Screnar	1996	468
183 2/8	39 4/8	39 2/8	14 3/8	14 3/8	9 4/8	9 6/8	17 6/8	20	Smoky River, AB	O. Fowler & J. Brewster	Fred Brewster	1919	477
183 2/8	39 4/8	38	15 7/8	15 7/8	9 7/8	9 7/8	19 6/8	19 6/8	Sun River, MT	Frank C. Hibben	Frank C. Hibben	1957	477
183 2/8	39 4/8	39 4/8	14 7/8	14 7/8	9	8 6/8	23 2/8	23 2/8	Clearwater River, MT	Earl Hofland	Earl Hofland	1957	477
183 2/8	39 6/8	39	15 1/8	15 1/8	8	8 4/8	23 1/8	23 1/8	Granite Co., MT	Joseph C. Sellitti	Joseph C. Sellitti	1981	477
183 2/8	38 4/8	39	15 2/8	15 2/8	7 4/8	7 7/8	22 3/8	22 3/8	Deer Lodge Co., MT	John L. Wozniak	John L. Wozniak	1984	477
183 2/8	41	37 1/8	16	16	8 5/8	8 6/8	23 7/8	23 7/8	Bow River, AB	Phillip Demers	Phillip Demers	1985	477
183 2/8	38 2/8	40 4/8	16 2/8	16 2/8	7 3/8	7 6/8	20 5/8	20 5/8	Sanders Co., MT	Guy R. Woods	Guy R. Woods	1985	477
183 2/8	41 4/8	41	15 4/8	15 7/8	8 1/8	8 1/8	21 1/8	21 1/8	Sanders Co., MT	Alma E. Arnold	Alma E. Arnold	1986	477
183 2/8	40 2/8	40 2/8	16 3/8	16 2/8	8 7/8	8 5/8	23 6/8	23 6/8	Granite Co., MT	Thorne R. Johnson	Thorne R. Johnson	1987	477
183 2/8	39 5/8	36 3/8	15 4/8	15 4/8	9	9 1/8	28 2/8	28 2/8	Simpson River, BC	Scott R. Rossow	Scott R. Rossow	1988	477
183 2/8	39 4/8	39 6/8	15 3/8	15 4/8	8 6/8	9 4/8	20 2/8	20 2/8	Prospect Creek, AB	Robert T. White	Robert T. White	1988	477
183 2/8	39	39	15 2/8	15 2/8	9 3/8	9 2/8	21 4/8	21 4/8	Grizzly Creek, AB	Bruce E. Williams	Bruce E. Williams	1989	477
183 2/8	37 5/8	37 1/8	16 1/8	16 1/8	9 1/8	8 5/8	20 4/8	20 4/8	Park Co., WY	William J. Herchuk	William J. Herchuk	1993	477
183 2/8	41 6/8	40 4/8	14 6/8	14 6/8	9 3/8	9 4/8	17 7/8	26	Silver Bow Co., MT	T.K. Atkinson	T.K. Atkinson	1994	477
183 1/8	41	37 1/8	15 2/8	15 2/8	8 3/8	8 3/8	26	26	Silver Bow Co., MT	Jeffrey T. Fisher	Jeffrey T. Fisher	1994	477
183 1/8	34 7/8	36	16	16	9	9	24 6/8	24 6/8	Unknown	Unknown	Jonas Bros. of Seattle	PR 1939	492
183 1/8	38 4/8	38 4/8	16 2/8	16 2/8	9 7/8	8 5/8	22 4/8	22 4/8	S. Platte Canyon, CO	Harold C. Eastwood	Harold C. Eastwood	1957	492
183 1/8	36 7/8	37 2/8	15 5/8	15 5/8	9	9 3/8	20	20	Kootenay River, BC	W. Vernon Walsh	W. Vernon Walsh	1962	492
183 1/8	36 1/8	36 1/8	16 1/8	16 1/8	10 3/8	10 5/8	16 7/8	24 5/8	Fraser River, BC	Karl P. Willms	Karl P. Willms	1977	492
183 1/8	36 2/8	36 2/8	16	16	8 7/8	8 6/8	18 4/8	22 2/8	Mt. Sparrowhawk, AB	Randy Ward	Randy Ward	1984	492
183 1/8	36 1/8	39 5/8	15 4/8	15 4/8	9	9 5/8	16 3/8	22	Deer Lodge Co., MT	Jeffrey R. Shellenberg	Jeffrey R. Shellenberg	1990	492
183 1/8	39 6/8	39 6/8	14 6/8	14 5/8	8 5/8	8 7/8	20 2/8	20 3/8	Granite Co., MT	Stephen E. Brown	Stephen E. Brown	1993	492
183 1/8	41 1/8	39 3/8	15 4/8	15 5/8	9 4/8	9	20 4/8	22 7/8	Sanders Co., MT	Robert A. Parker	Robert A. Parker	1993	492
183 1/8	39 3/8	38 1/8	16 2/8	16 2/8	8 4/8	9 5/8	18 4/8	22	Wallowa Co., OR	Kenneth W. Kirsch	Kenneth W. Kirsch	1994	492
183	39 4/8	39	15 1/8	15 5/8	8 2/8	9 4/8	18 2/8	21 2/8	Sanders Co., MT	Diana L. Ross	Diana L. Ross	1994	492
183	37 5/8	38	15 5/8	15 5/8	10 3/8	8 4/8	21 7/8	22	Teton Basin, WY	William A. Baillie-Grohman	John H. Batten	1876	502
183	39 2/8	39 1/8	15 4/8	15 4/8	8 3/8	8 4/8	17 6/8	21 4/8	Clearwater River, AB	John H. Batten	John H. Batten	1931	502
183	38	40	15 1/8	15 1/8	9	9	15 6/8	19 4/8	Cadomin, AB	Otis Chandler	Otis Chandler	1969	502
183	38	38 6/8	14 1/8	14 1/8	10 5/8	10 4/8	21 5/8	21 5/8	Solomon Creek, AB	Picked Up	William Gosney	1977	502
183	40 5/8	40 7/8	13 7/8	13 7/8	9 2/8	9 2/8	21 1/8	21 1/8	Ram River, AB	Robert G. Morgan	Robert G. Morgan	1980	502
183	38	38 4/8	15 5/8	15 5/8	9 4/8	9 2/8	19 4/8	20 2/8	Galatea Mt., AB	Mario G. Giustini	Mario G. Giustini	1996	502
182 7/8	40 5/8	40 5/8	15	15 1/8	9 2/8	9 4/8	15 6/8	22	Alberta	G.L. Gibbons	G.L. Gibbons	1963	508

BIGHORN SHEEP

Ovis canadensis canadensis and certain related subspecies

Score	Length of Horn R	L	Circumference of Base R	L	Circumference at Third Quarter R	L	Greatest Spread	Tip to Tip Spread	Locality	Hunter	Owner	Date Killed	Rank
182 7/8	37 6/8	38 5/8	16 4/8	16 6/8	7 6/8	8 1/8	22 1/8	17	Line Creek, BC	Kevin J. Galla	Kevin J. Galla	1989	508
182 7/8	39	37 5/8	14 7/8	15	10 6/8	9 7/8	21	19	Harlequin Creek, AB	Bob Wasylyshen	Bob Wasylyshen	1997	508
182 6/8	37 5/8	37 5/8	15 2/8	15 2/8	10	9 7/8	23 7/8	20 4/8	Lake Louise, AB	Picked Up	Howard Bronsdon	1952	511
182 6/8	39 6/8	38	14 3/8	14 4/8	10 2/8	10	22 4/8	18	Salmon River, ID	Picked Up	Wayne Demaray	1963	511
182 6/8	38 4/8	37 4/8	14 6/8	15	10 5/8	10 3/8	21 7/8	15 5/8	Burnt Timber, AB	Mrs. W.E. Anderson	Mrs. W.E. Anderson	1964	511
182 6/8	39 2/8	39	15	15	9 7/8	9 4/8	22	18 6/8	Wildhay River, AB	Jim Papst	Jim Papst	1968	511
182 6/8	40 4/8	40 4/8	14 6/8	14 5/8	9	9 1/8	22 6/8	22 6/8	Lower Salmon River, ID	Glenn H. Schubert	Deloras A. Schubert	1970	511
182 6/8	40 6/8	39 2/8	16 1/8	16	7 6/8	7 7/8	22 6/8	19 6/8	Sanders Co., MT	Terrence Pond	Terrence Pond	1978	511
182 6/8	42	40 4/8	16	16	7	7 1/8	25 7/8	25 3/8	Deer Lodge Co., MT	Kirk G. Stovall	Kirk G. Stovall	1990	511
182 6/8	40 1/8	40 3/8	15	15 2/8	9	8 4/8	23	22 1/8	Ravalli Co., MT	Robert S. Wood	Robert S. Wood	1993	511
182 6/8	42 1/8	40 5/8	14 2/8	14 4/8	9 1/8	9 1/8	22	22	Blaine Co., MT	Mike Crites	Mike Crites	1996	511
182 6/8	42	40	15	14 7/8	8 1/8	8 2/8	22	21 2/8	Missoula Co., MT	Shawn M. Conrad	Shawn M. Conrad	1997	511
182 6/8	39 4/8	36 4/8	15 5/8	15 5/8	8 7/8	9	24 4/8	23 1/8	Redcap Mt., AB	Glenn Funfer	Glenn Funfer	1997	511
182 5/8	44 1/8	42 4/8	13 7/8	14	9 3/8	8 4/8	23 1/8	23 1/8	Alberta	John D. Hazen	Unknown	1918	522
182 5/8	37 7/8	38 6/8	16 6/8	16 6/8	8 2/8	7 3/8	19 4/8	16	Brazeau Forest, AB	H.A. Yocum	H.A. Yocum	1941	522
182 5/8	40 3/8	39 4/8	15	15 2/8	8 6/8	8 4/8	22 7/8	13 4/8	Bull River, BC	Ralph W. Stearns	Ralph W. Stearns	1950	522
182 5/8	42 1/8	40 4/8	15 2/8	15 2/8	7 5/8	7 3/8	20 2/8	20	Sun River, MT	Martin Alzheimer	Martin Alzheimer	1955	522
182 5/8	39 1/8	36 4/8	15 5/8	15 4/8	9 4/8	9 4/8	21 4/8	20 6/8	Narraway River, AB	John C. Seidensticker	John C. Seidensticker	1959	522
182 5/8	38 1/8	38 4/8	15	14 7/8	9 6/8	9 6/8	21 2/8	15 6/8	Storm Mt., AB	W. Glaser	W. Glaser	1961	522
182 5/8	38 4/8	37 3/8	16	16	9 2/8	8 7/8	21 2/8	13 1/8	Junction Creek, AB	Robert F. Brooks	Robert F. Brooks	1978	522
182 5/8	38	38 7/8	14 7/8	14 7/8	9 6/8	9 6/8	21 2/8	20 7/8	Missoula Co., MT	Brad A. Sweeney	Brad A. Sweeney	1996	522
182 5/8	38 3/8	37 4/8	15 7/8	16 2/8	9	9 1/8	20 7/8	18 6/8	Lewis & Clark Co., MT	Gary M. Zadick	Gary M. Zadick	1996	522
182 5/8	38 5/8	39	15 1/8	15 1/8	9 2/8	9 2/8	20 2/8	15	Rocky Mt. House, AB	Chris Blower	Chris Blower	1997	522
182 4/8	35 4/8	35 2/8	16 4/8	16 4/8	10	9 4/8	24	22 5/8	Waterton, CO	William D. Jenkins	William D. Jenkins	1956	532
182 4/8	37	35 4/8	15 4/8	15 3/8	11 2/8	10 4/8	23	21	Wind River, WY	Hubert Weibel	Hubert Weibel	1956	532
182 4/8	36 7/8	37 7/8	16 1/8	16 3/8	8 5/8	8 7/8	23 5/8	17 6/8	S. Castle River, AB	Leon Atwood	Leon Atwood	1962	532
182 4/8	38 4/8	39 2/8	15 5/8	15 5/8	8 4/8	8 2/8	22 1/8	19 1/8	Kananaskis Summit, AB	Ted Howell	Ted Howell	1964	532
182 4/8	38 3/8	37 5/8	15	14 6/8	10 6/8	10 5/8	22 1/8	18 2/8	Turtle Creek, WY	Russell C. Cutter	Russell C. Cutter	1968	532
182 4/8	41 1/8	40 5/8	15	15	8 1/8	8 4/8	22	18 4/8	Edgewater, BC	William N. Ward	William N. Ward	1969	532
182 4/8	40 2/8	40	15 3/8	15 4/8	8 2/8	8 1/8	23 1/8	20	Spences Bridge, BC	Don Ticehurst	Don Ticehurst	1973	532
182 4/8	38 4/8	41 2/8	15 4/8	15 2/8	8 2/8	9	22 5/8	17 2/8	Mary Ann Creek, BC	Jack Bridgewater	Jack Bridgewater	1981	532
182 4/8	38 6/8	35 6/8	15 3/8	15 5/8	11 1/8	10 1/8	23 2/8	23 2/8	Wallowa Co., OR	Randy Craddock	Randy Craddock	1981	532
182 4/8	35 7/8	36 3/8	16 2/8	16 2/8	9 7/8	9 7/8	22 4/8	19	Blind Canyon, AB	Alan W. Foster	Alan W. Foster	1981	532
182 4/8	39 3/8	39 3/8	15 5/8	15 5/8	9 7/8	8 4/8	21 5/8	19	Sanders Co., MT	Thorne R. Johnson	Thorne R. Johnson	1989	532
182 3/8	38 7/8	38 2/8	15 4/8	15 4/8	9 1/8	9 5/8	20	18 1/8	Montana	Unknown	Joseph P. Scurti	PR 1949	543
182 3/8	38 3/8	37 4/8	14 6/8	14 6/8	10 2/8	10 4/8	22	16 2/8	Banff, AB	Gift of Madison Grant to NCHH	Unknown	PR 1951	543
182 3/8	37 2/8	37 3/8	15 3/8	15 2/8	10 4/8	10 4/8	21 7/8	17	Teton River, MT	Geoffrey A. Morrison	Geoffrey A. Morrison	1969	543

Score	L. Horn R	L. Horn L	Circ. Base R	Circ. Base L	Circ. 3rd Qtr R	Circ. 3rd Qtr L	Greatest Spread	Tip to Tip	Locality	Owner	Hunter	Date	Rank
182 3/8	38 6/8	37 1/8	16	16	8 3/8	8 7/8	23 7/8	18 6/8	West Sulphur River, AB	Robert Highberg	Robert Highberg	1980	543
182 3/8	38 7/8	39 2/8	15 6/8	15 6/8	9 4/8	8 7/8	20 6/8	20 1/8	Pigeon Mt., AB	Len H. Guldman	Len H. Guldman	1990	543
182 2/8	40 3/8	40 1/8	14 5/8	14 5/8	9 7/8	9 6/8	21 4/8	21	Shoshone N. Fork, WY	Herb Klein	Herb Klein	1934	548
182 2/8	40 7/8	40 1/8	15	15	8 7/8	8 6/8	23 4/8	20 4/8	Dubois, WY	Larry Pate	George Pate	1960	548
182 2/8	39 5/8	39 7/8	15 2/8	15 2/8	9 1/8	9 4/8	21 4/8	17 4/8	Ram River, AB	Louise McConnell	Louise McConnell	1961	548
182 2/8	36	36	15 4/8	15 4/8	10	10	21 3/8	16	Sulphur River, AB	Roy Everest	Unknown	1963	548
182 2/8	39 7/8	39 7/8	14 5/8	15	10 2/8	9 4/8	23 3/8	21 2/8	Wildhay River, AB	James H. Duke, Jr.	James H. Duke, Jr.	1967	548
182 2/8	36 4/8	35 4/8	16 1/8	16 1/8	9 1/8	9 1/8	23 3/8	18 7/8	Rocky Creek, AB	Randy A. Desabrais	Randy A. Desabrais	1982	548
182 2/8	37 5/8	39 1/8	14 5/8	14 7/8	10 1/8	10 1/8	22 5/8	21 3/8	Park Co., MT	Rodney W. Cole	Rodney W. Cole	1985	548
182 2/8	39 3/8	39 7/8	16 1/8	16 1/8	7 7/8	8	23 1/8	23 5/8	Beaverhead Co., MT	Raymond L. Cote	Raymond L. Cote	1989	548
182 2/8	38 5/8	38 7/8	15 1/8	15 7/8	9 6/8	9 3/8	19 7/8	19 1/8	Silver Bow Co., MT	John T. LaPierre	John T. LaPierre	1990	548
182 2/8	39	40 2/8	14 7/8	14 4/8	9 1/8	8	22 2/8	22 2/8	Lewis & Clark Co., MT	Ben E. Arps	Picked Up	1996	548
182 1/8	41 5/8	39	13 1/8	14 7/8	9 2/8	9 3/8	22 2/8	23 5/8	Salmon River, ID	Anson Eddy	Anson Eddy	PR 1959	558
182 1/8	35 4/8	39 3/8	15 2/8	15 2/8	11 2/8	11 6/8	24 6/8	24	Lemhi Co., ID	Leonard C. Miller, Sr.	Leonard C. Miller, Sr.	1963	558
182 1/8	38 3/8	37 4/8	15 2/8	15 1/8	9 4/8	9 4/8	22 1/8	17 3/8	Panther River, AB	W.H. Slikker	W.H. Slikker	1966	558
182 1/8	37 7/8	37 4/8	16	16 2/8	8 5/8	8 5/8	20 1/8	18 2/8	Crowsnest Lake, AB	John Truant	John Truant	1970	558
182 1/8	39	39 3/8	16 1/8	16 1/8	7 6/8	7	22 4/8	22 4/8	Silver Bow Co., MT	Eric L. Jacobson	Eric L. Jacobson	1990	558
182 1/8	37 7/8	38 3/8	15	15	7 6/8	8 2/8	23 5/8	22 6/8	Ravalli Co., MT	Bret A. Sourbrine	Bret A. Sourbrine	1994	558
182 1/8	39 2/8	38 3/8	14 6/8	14 6/8	9 7/8	8 7/8	22 2/8	21 7/8	Granite Co., MT	Roy H. Rogers	Picked Up	1995	558
182	40	41	14 5/8	14 7/8	8 5/8	8 7/8	24	24	Salmon River, ID	Elmer Keith	Elmer Keith	1957	565
182	41	37 6/8	15	14 7/8	9 2/8	9 1/8	21 5/8	17 4/8	Canal Flat, BC	Allen Cudworth	Allen Cudworth	1958	565
182	37 5/8	36 7/8	15 6/8	15 7/8	9 7/8	9 7/8	21	16 4/8	Pincher Creek, AB	Delton Smith	Delton Smith	1958	565
182	39 1/8	41 7/8	15 2/8	15	8 3/8	7 6/8	23 5/8	23 3/8	Lewis & Clark Co., MT	Allan L. Davies	Allan L. Davies	1981	565
182	38 4/8	38 4/8	14 4/8	14 3/8	10 4/8	10 4/8	19	17 4/8	Mt. Kidd, AB	Dirk Kieft	Picked Up	1982	565
182	37 4/8	39 2/8	15 3/8	15 3/8	8 6/8	8 1/8	20 3/8	20 4/8	Mt. Kidd, AB	Dwayne W. Oneski	Dwayne W. Oneski	1982	565
182	39 7/8	40 1/8	15 2/8	15 2/8	8	7 1/8	20 4/8	20 4/8	Murray Creek, BC	Nancy J. Koopman	Nancy J. Koopman	1986	565
182	40 7/8	39 5/8	16 2/8	16 3/8	7 3/8	7 3/8	22 5/8	22 2/8	Wallowa Co., OR	Dale R. Dotson	Dale R. Dotson	1988	565
182	39 4/8	39 6/8	15	15 1/8	8 7/8	9 4/8	20 1/8	19 1/8	Sanders Co., MT	Kevin K. Harris	Kevin K. Harris	1988	565
182	37	38 6/8	15 3/8	15 1/8	10 4/8	9 6/8	22 1/8	20 2/8	Deer Lodge Co., MT	George A. Kovacich	George A. Kovacich	1988	565
182	39 4/8	37 5/8	16 2/8	16 2/8	8 2/8	8 2/8	24 4/8	24 4/8	Wigwam River, BC	Grant W. Markoski	Grant W. Markoski	1990	565
182	38 3/8	38 1/8	15	15	8 7/8	9	24	24	Saguache Co., CO	Ralph G. Hejny	Ralph G. Hejny	1992	565
182	39 6/8	39 6/8	15 2/8	15 2/8	9 4/8	9 4/8	21 1/8	17 2/8	Missoula Co., MT	Jeff S. Putnam	Jeff S. Putnam	1993	565
182	38 3/8	38 1/8	16 2/8	16 2/8	8 1/8	8 1/8	22 4/8	20 3/8	Mineral Co., MT	Billy D. Queen	Billy D. Queen	1994	565
182	37 4/8	38	14 4/8	14 4/8	10 6/8	10 5/8	25 6/8	20 7/8	Las Animas Co., CO	U.S. Army	Picked Up	1994	565
181 7/8	40	40 4/8	15 6/8	15 6/8	8 1/8	8 1/8	22 6/8	22 6/8	Missoula Co., MT	Kenneth B. Henegar	Kenneth B. Henegar	1996	581
181 7/8	39 2/8	39 1/8	14 3/8	14 2/8	10 5/8	10 5/8	20 7/8	20 4/8	Coal Branch, AB	John Caputo	John Caputo	1962	581
181 7/8	36 5/8	36 2/8	16 5/8	16 4/8	8 4/8	8 4/8	20 6/8	20	Elko, BC	Percy McGregor	Percy McGregor	1974	581
181 7/8	38 3/8	39	15 1/8	15 1/8	9 4/8	9 4/8	21 1/8	19	Hinton, AB	Ben Morris	Darla J. Smith	1980	581
181 7/8	39 5/8	40 6/8	14 7/8	14 7/8	8 6/8	8 6/8	21 1/8	21 1/8	Sundre, AB	Dennis G. Overguard	Dennis G. Overguard	1980	581
181 7/8	39 1/8	38 4/8	15 1/8	15 1/8	9 1/8	9	20	19	Kakwa River, AB	Donald C. Fobert	Donald C. Fobert	1983	581
181 7/8	38	38 7/8	15 5/8	15 5/8	8 6/8	8 3/8	23 2/8	22 7/8	Cataract Creek, AB	Michael J. Hogan	Michael J. Hogan	1984	581
181 7/8	39 4/8	39 4/8	15 3/8	15 3/8	8 4/8	9	22	22	Teton Co., MT	Deborah Conway	Deborah Conway	1991	581
181 7/8	36 1/8	38 2/8	16	16	8 5/8	8 4/8	23 2/8	21 7/8	Granite Co., MT	Don Syrud	Don Syrud	1991	581
181 7/8	35 5/8	36 2/8	15	15	12	12	21 2/8	16 4/8	Taos Co., NM	Reuben R. Tipton III	Reuben R. Tipton III	1994	581
181 6/8	37	37 2/8	15 4/8	15 2/8	9 5/8	9 5/8	18	14 4/8	Ghost River, AB	L.C. Nowlin	L.C. Nowlin	PR 1940	590
181 6/8	38 1/8	38 5/8	15	15 1/8	10	9 6/8	20 6/8	16 1/8	Prospect Creek, AB	Wayne Tarnasky	Wayne Tarnasky	1983	590
181 6/8	36 4/8	38 2/8	17	16 7/8	8 4/8	8 4/8	23 4/8	20 6/8	Gunnison Co., CO	Paula D. Darner	Paula D. Darner	1986	590

BIGHORN SHEEP

Ovis canadensis canadensis and certain related subspecies

Score	Length of Horn R	L	Circumference of Base R	L	Circumference at Third Quarter R	L	Greatest Spread	Tip to Tip Spread	Locality	Hunter	Owner	Date Killed	Rank
181 6/8	40 5/8	39 5/8	15 2/8	15 2/8	8 4/8	8	26	24 4/8	Teton Co., WY	Richard L. Grabowski	Richard L. Grabowski	1989	590
181 6/8	38 3/8	39 7/8	14 7/8	14 7/8	9 1/8	8 4/8	22 2/8	22 2/8	Blaine Co., MT	Betty L. Ramsey	Betty L. Ramsey	1989	590
181 6/8	39 3/8	37 3/8	14 7/8	15	9 4/8	9 3/8	23 1/8	20	Graham Co., AZ	Terrance S. Marcum	Terrance S. Marcum	1995	590
181 5/8	42	40 1/8	15 2/8	15 1/8	8	7 6/8	21	20 2/8	Ghost River, AB	J.S. Parker	J.S. Parker	1954	596
181 5/8	39 1/8	37	15 6/8	15 6/8	8 4/8	9 3/8	23 2/8	21 2/8	Custer Co., MT	Picked Up	W.S. Maloit	1959	596
181 5/8	36 7/8	39 2/8	15 4/8	15 3/8	9	8 7/8	23 4/8	23 4/8	Elbow River, AB	Ernest F. Dill	Ernest F. Dill	1961	596
181 5/8	39 6/8	40 1/8	15 5/8	15 3/8	8 4/8	7 6/8	22 7/8	22 7/8	Sun River, MT	Walter L. Bodie	Walter L. Bodie	1965	596
181 5/8	41 5/8	37 6/8	14 2/8	14 4/8	10	10 2/8	21 4/8	20 4/8	Burnt Timber Creek, AB	George H. Glass	George H. Glass	1967	596
181 5/8	38 4/8	39 3/8	14 4/8	14 6/8	9 2/8	9 6/8	23 5/8	19	Park Co., WY	Keith Frick	Keith Frick	1972	596
181 5/8	39 3/8	37	16 4/8	16 3/8	7 3/8	7 5/8	20	15 4/8	Fisher Range, AB	Reginald Zebedee	Reginald Zebedee	1982	596
181 5/8	38 1/8	34 4/8	16 2/8	16 2/8	9 4/8	9 2/8	23	18	Pigeon Mt., AB	Paul S. Inzanti, Jr.	Paul S. Inzanti, Jr.	1984	596
181 5/8	39 6/8	39 5/8	15 4/8	15 4/8	8 1/8	8 1/8	21 4/8	17 4/8	Goat Range, AB	Christian D. Pagenkopf	Christian D. Pagenkopf	1984	596
181 5/8	39	38 1/8	15 3/8	15 2/8	9 7/8	9 2/8	22 6/8	20	Lemhi Co., ID	David Freel	David Freel	1986	596
181 5/8	39	37 7/8	15 7/8	16	9	8 3/8	19 5/8	13 4/8	Kootenay River, BC	Arthur V. Parsons	Arthur V. Parsons	1986	596
181 5/8	36 2/8	35 5/8	16	16	9 5/8	10 4/8	23 3/8	22 5/8	Lewis & Clark Co., MT	Pamela J. Bennett	Pamela J. Bennett	1989	596
181 5/8	39 1/8	38 2/8	15 3/8	15 4/8	8 7/8	8 4/8	21 2/8	20 1/8	Teton Co., MT	Neil L. Hamm	Neil L. Hamm	1990	596
181 5/8	39	39 1/8	15 3/8	15 2/8	9	9 3/8	24 4/8	23 4/8	Deer Lodge Co., MT	Roy A. Wiant	David P. Moore	1990	596
181 5/8	37 4/8	36 7/8	14 6/8	14 6/8	10 4/8	10 4/8	21 7/8	14 3/8	Sanders Co., MT	Peter J. Bachmeier	Peter J. Bachmeier	1995	596
181 4/8	40	40 5/8	15 1/8	15 2/8	8 2/8	8 4/8	22	21 1/8	Sulphur River, AB	John E. Hammett	John E. Hammett	1938	611
181 4/8	38 6/8	41 2/8	14 6/8	14 4/8	8 5/8	8 5/8	22 2/8	22 2/8	Castle River, AB	Cliff Johnson	Cliff Johnson	1957	611
181 4/8	36	36 2/8	15 1/8	15 1/8	11 1/8	11 1/8	23	21	Dubois, WY	Jack Adams	Jack Adams	1959	611
181 4/8	38 5/8	39 1/8	15 1/8	15 3/8	8 6/8	9	23 1/8	19 6/8	Cadomin, AB	John Caputo	John Caputo	1961	611
181 4/8	43	43 4/8	16	16	6 2/8	6 7/8	29 4/8	29 4/8	Gallatin Co., MT	Richard D. Gilman	Richard D. Gilman	1967	611
181 4/8	41 3/8	39 7/8	15 2/8	15 2/8	8	7 7/8	22 5/8	22 5/8	Lewis & Clark Co., MT	Picked Up	William L. Wesland	1973	611
181 4/8	39	37 6/8	15 1/8	15 1/8	9	9 1/8	22	18 6/8	Spray Lake, AB	George R. Willows	George R. Willows	1974	611
181 4/8	41	41 2/8	16 1/8	16	6 5/8	6 6/8	21 4/8	21 4/8	Deer Lodge Co., MT	Gerald P. Wendt	Gerald P. Wendt	1978	611
181 4/8	37	39	16 2/8	16 3/8	8 4/8	8 3/8	24 3/8	24 3/8	Lewis & Clark Co., MT	Donel G. Hayes	Donel G. Hayes	1980	611
181 4/8	38 3/8	41 3/8	16 2/8	16 4/8	6 7/8	6 7/8	24	24	Granite Co., MT	Michael B. Murphy	Michael B. Murphy	1987	611
181 4/8	38 6/8	36 4/8	16 4/8	16 5/8	7 5/8	7 3/8	19 4/8	11 7/8	Mt. Evans-Thomas, AB	William E. MacDougall	William E. MacDougall	1988	611
181 4/8	35 7/8	36 7/8	16 3/8	16 3/8	8 5/8	9 2/8	22 3/8	21	Granite Co., MT	Bronwyn M. Price	Bronwyn M. Price	1989	611
181 4/8	38 3/8	31 1/8	17	17	9	9	23 5/8	19 3/8	Greenlee Co., AZ	Timothy R. Lacy, Sr.	Timothy R. Lacy, Sr.	1991	611
181 4/8	38 7/8	38 7/8	15 6/8	15 5/8	7 7/8	8 2/8	21 4/8	13 6/8	Burnt Timber Creek, AB	Lambert VanDongen	Lambert VanDongen	1991	611
181 4/8	40 4/8	40 2/8	16 2/8	15 2/8	8 2/8	8 1/8	22 1/8	21 5/8	Sanders Co., MT	Thomas L. Judge	Thomas L. Judge	1992	611
181 4/8	38 1/8	38 5/8	16 2/8	16 4/8	8 1/8	8 1/8	20 4/8	18 4/8	Granite Co., MT	Jacob A. Streitz	Jacob A. Streitz	1992	611
181 4/8	36 3/8	35 7/8	15 1/8	15 1/8	10 7/8	10 6/8	22 5/8	18	Saguache Co., CO	Darrel L. Moberly	Darrel L. Moberly	1994	611
181 4/8	40 1/8	39 5/8	15 6/8	15 6/8	7 6/8	7 4/8	21 3/8	17 6/8	Wildhorse Creek, BC	Dan VanZanten	Dan VanZanten	1994	611
181 3/8	39 3/8	39 6/8	15 1/8	14 6/8	9 4/8	9 1/8	25	21	Clearwater River, AB	Phil Temple	Phil Temple	1951	629
181 3/8	38 2/8	39 3/8	15 1/8	15 2/8	9 2/8	9 4/8	20 4/8	14 4/8	Big Horn Creek, AB	Earl Foss	Earl Foss	1960	629

Score	L. Horn R	L. Horn L	Circ. Base R	Circ. Base L	Circ. 3rd Qtr R	Circ. 3rd Qtr L	Greatest Spread	Tip to Tip	Locality	Hunter	Owner	Date	Rank
181 3/8	37 2/8	36 7/8	15	17	8	8 1/8	20 4/8	15 4/8	Park Co., CO	Richard L. Rudeen	Richard L. Rudeen	1963	629
181 3/8	38 6/8	37 7/8	14 7/8	14 7/8	9 3/8	9 3/8	20 4/8	19 6/8	Clearwater River, AB	Joseph T. Pelton	Joseph T. Pelton	1966	629
181 3/8	38 3/8	38 4/8	14 7/8	15	9 5/8	9 5/8	21 4/8	15	Beartooth Plateau, MT	Olav E. Nelson	Olav E. Nelson	1970	629
181 3/8	39	39	15 4/8	14 6/8	8 3/8	8 2/8	22 3/8	19 4/8	Lincoln Co., MT	Lowell Olin	Lowell Olin	1977	629
181 3/8	38 4/8	39 5/8	14 7/8	15	9 3/8	9	20 6/8	20 3/8	Lake Co., MT	Picked Up	J. Michael Conoyer	1978	629
181 3/8	37 5/8	37 4/8	15	15	10 5/8	10 5/8	19	15 3/8	Cardinal River, AB	Randy Babala	Randy Babala	1980	629
181 3/8	39 1/8	41 2/8	15 6/8	15 5/8	8 1/8	7 7/8	21 2/8	20 5/8	Granite Co., MT	David D. Rittenhouse	David D. Rittenhouse	1980	629
181 3/8	39	39	15 5/8	15 6/8	8 2/8	8 5/8	21 2/8	20 5/8	Lewis & Clark Co., MT	Elmer T. Crawford	Elmer T. Crawford	1986	629
181 3/8	38 5/8	38 3/8	14 7/8	14 5/8	9 2/8	9 1/8	22 6/8	22 1/8	Wallowa Co., OR	Michael L. Taylor	Michael L. Taylor	1987	629
181 3/8	37 3/8	40 2/8	15 1/8	14 7/8	9 2/8	9 6/8	20 2/8	16 4/8	Fairholme Range, AB	Eldon Hoff	Eldon Hoff	1989	629
181 3/8	39	39 2/8	15 1/8	15	10 2/8	10 2/8	23 3/8	21 4/8	Grant Co., NM	Dan Pocapalia	Dan Pocapalia	1990	629
181 3/8	36 7/8	39	15	15	8 4/8	8 4/8	23 5/8	23 5/8	Deer Lodge Co., MT	Kenneth B. Fitte	Kenneth B. Fitte	1997	629
181 2/8	42	39 2/8	16 1/8	16 2/8	8 5/8	8 2/8	24 6/8	24 6/8	Teton Basin, WY	Michael Huppuch	Philip Schlegel	1901	643
181 2/8	41 1/8	41 4/8	14	14	10 1/8	9 5/8	21 2/8	19 6/8	Highwood River, AB	Ralph Rink	George Beach	1946	643
181 2/8	40 5/8	40 7/8	13 7/8	14	7 2/8	7 5/8	22 4/8	22 4/8	McBride, BC	Alfred Saulnier	Alfred Saulnier	1966	643
181 2/8	39 2/8	40 2/8	15 4/8	15 4/8	10	10 2/8	20 5/8	16 4/8	Timber Creek, AB	Jason G. Hindes	Jason G. Hindes	1985	643
181 2/8	40 3/8	40 3/8	14 1/8	14 1/8	8 7/8	8 7/8	23 7/8	23 7/8	Lewis & Clark Co., MT	Brandon C. Johns	Brandon C. Johns	1987	643
181 2/8	41 3/8	41 3/8	14 3/8	14 3/8	7 5/8	7 5/8	21	21	Granite Co., NM	Tom J. Lewis	Tom J. Lewis	1989	643
181 2/8	37 1/8	37 3/8	15 3/8	15 4/8	9 4/8	7 6/8	20 7/8	20 4/8	Fergus Co., MT	Leda R. McReynolds	Leda R. McReynolds	1991	643
181 2/8	40	40 6/8	15 5/8	15 5/8	7 6/8	9 5/8	21 4/8	21	Ghost River, AB	Mike Michalezki	Mike Michalezki	1991	643
181 2/8	38 4/8	38 4/8	15	15 1/8	8 6/8	7 6/8	19 5/8	19 5/8	Whiteswan Lake, BC	Larry Tooze	Larry Tooze	1995	643
181 2/8	36	36 4/8	15 4/8	15 4/8	9 5/8	8 5/8	21 6/8	16 2/8	Gregg River, AB	Mike Michalezki	Mike Michalezki	1997	643
181 1/8	38 2/8	38 5/8	15 3/8	15 3/8	11	9 5/8	20 4/8	15 1/8	Cooke City, MT	Larry L. Altimus	Larry L. Altimus	1969	653
181 1/8	38 7/8	35	14	14 2/8	9 1/8	10	17 3/8	15	Spray Lakes Reservoir, AB	G. Robert Willows	G. Robert Willows	1977	653
181 1/8	38 2/8	40 3/8	15 5/8	15 4/8	8 5/8	9 1/8	22 5/8	21	Scalp Creek, AB	James Mills	James Mills	1984	653
181 1/8	39 4/8	39 3/8	15	15 5/8	9 5/8	8 5/8	20 6/8	22 5/8	Deer Lodge Co., MT	Thomas R. Puccinelli	Thomas R. Puccinelli	1984	653
181 1/8	39	38 5/8	14 4/8	14 5/8	8 5/8	9 4/8	22	17 4/8	Mt. Inflexible, AB	Carl Gallant	Carl Gallant	1987	653
181 1/8	39 3/8	38 5/8	15 3/8	15 4/8	7 7/8	8 3/8	20 6/8	21	Sanders Co., MT	David O. Conrad	David O. Conrad	1993	653
181 1/8	40 4/8	39 2/8	16 3/8	16 3/8	7 5/8	8 3/8	20 3/8	20 3/8	Sanders Co., MT	Darren J. Page	Darren J. Page	1995	653
181	39 4/8	38 3/8	14 7/8	14 7/8	7 4/8	7 5/8	22 5/8	17 4/8	Kootenay, BC	A.E. Matthew	A.E. Matthew	1950	660
181	40 5/8	45 7/8	14 1/8	13 7/8	7 7/8	7 7/8	26 1/8	17 6/8	Lincoln Co., MT	Hal Kanzler	Hal Kanzler	1960	660
181	39 2/8	39 6/8	15 2/8	15 2/8	8 3/8	8 3/8	21	15	Brule, AB	Picked Up	G.W. Warner	1963	660
181	37 6/8	39 2/8	15 5/8	15 5/8	9	8 6/8	23	19 1/8	Mystery Lake, AB	Peter Lazio	Peter Lazio	1967	660
181	38 7/8	37	15 3/8	15 2/8	11 1/8	11	19 1/8	18 1/8	Simpson Creek, BC	Walt Failor	Walt Failor	1968	660
181	39 1/8	37 5/8	15	15	7 7/8	7 7/8	22 4/8	22 4/8	Kindersley Creek, BC	Karl Dorr	Karl Dorr	1989	660
181	38	41 1/8	16 7/8	16 7/8	6 4/8	5 7/8	25	18 1/8	Granite Co., MT	Misty D. Fischer	Misty D. Fischer	1995	660
181	38 2/8	43	15 4/8	15 4/8	8 6/8	8 2/8	21 6/8	18	Missoula Co., MT	Daniel M. Rockwood	Daniel M. Rockwood	1995	660
180 7/8	38 3/8	40 6/8	14	14	10 3/8	10 1/8	19 6/8	19 6/8	Park Co., WY	Picked Up	Jay Thomas	1979	668
180 7/8	39 2/8	39 2/8	14 6/8	14 6/8	9 3/8	9 3/8	22 6/8	22 2/8	Clearwater River, AB	Kevin Peters	Kevin Peters	1989	668
180 7/8	40 5/8	38 1/8	16	16	7 7/8	7 6/8	25 3/8	25 3/8	Sanders Co., MT	Raymond J. Smith	Raymond J. Smith	1990	668
180 7/8	38 7/8	37 4/8	14 6/8	15	9 2/8	9 2/8	19 4/8	15 4/8	Line Creek, BC	Kevin J. Galla	Kevin J. Galla	1991	668
180 7/8	41	39 4/8	15	14 6/8	8 4/8	8 4/8	24 4/8	24 4/8	Deer Lodge Co., MT	Jack D. Shanstrom	Jack D. Shanstrom	1991	668
180 6/8	38 2/8	42	15 7/8	15 7/8	11 2/8	8 1/8	22 7/8	22 1/8	Seebe, AB	Ted Trueblood	Ted Trueblood	1956	673
180 6/8	37	37	15 2/8	15 2/8	8 6/8	8 4/8	22 5/8	15	Bull River, BC	Walter J. Ruehle	Walter J. Ruehle	1962	673
180 6/8	35	34 2/8	15 6/8	15 6/8	10 6/8	10 6/8	22 5/8	17	Texas Creek, CO	Picked Up	Jack Putnam	PR 1963	673
180 6/8	37 4/8	35 6/8	16	16	8 4/8	8 4/8	21	21	Flat Creek, AB	G.I. Franklin	G.I. Franklin	1964	673
180 6/8	37 5/8	38 3/8	15	15 1/8	9 6/8	9 7/8	21 3/8	16 4/8	Panther Creek, AB	C.D. Sharp	C.D. Sharp	1966	673

Ovis canadensis canadensis and certain related subspecies

Score	Length of Horn R	L	Circumference of Base R	L	Circumference at Third Quarter R	L	Greatest Spread	Tip tp Tip Spread	Locality	Hunter	Owner	Date Killed	Rank
180 6/8	37 2/8	36 4/8	16	16	9 2/8	8 7/8	21	17 2/8	Junction Creek, AB	Spencer T. Nichols	Spencer T. Nichols	1981	673
180 6/8	39 6/8	39 4/8	15	15	8 7/8	8 4/8	22	19 1/8	Mineral Co., MT	Roberta A. Hartford	Roberta A. Hartford	1982	673
180 6/8	37	37 6/8	14 7/8	15	10 1/8	10	22 7/8	18 6/8	Park Co., WY	Dwight Lyman	Dwight Lyman	1982	673
180 6/8	37 1/8	37 7/8	15 7/8	15 7/8	8 4/8	8 7/8	21 4/8	17 5/8	Forbidden Creek, AB	Dennis H. Russell	Dennis H. Russell	1984	673
180 6/8	38 7/8	37 7/8	16 2/8	16 2/8	7 5/8	7 6/8	24 4/8	24	Sanders Co., MT	Bob L. Jacks	Bob L. Jacks	1990	673
180 6/8	36 2/8	39	16 2/8	16 2/8	7 6/8	8	21 1/8	18 7/8	Ewin Pass, BC	Sam W. Stephenson	Sam W. Stephenson	1992	673
180 6/8	38 6/8	38 6/8	15 2/8	15 3/8	8 5/8	8 4/8	21 6/8	19 4/8	Columbia Co., WA	Karie K. Kominski	Karie K. Kominski	1994	673
180 5/8	39 4/8	39 5/8	13 6/8	13 5/8	10 7/8	11	22	17 6/8	Wind River Mts., WY	Alfred Hume	Alfred Hume	1960	685
180 5/8	38 1/8	38 2/8	14 6/8	14 6/8	10	10	21 1/8	19 4/8	Sun River, MT	Robert W. Boucher	Robert W. Boucher	1966	685
180 5/8	38	39 3/8	14 3/8	14 3/8	9 6/8	10 3/8	19 4/8	19 4/8	Salmon River, ID	Emerson Hall	Emerson Hall	1968	685
180 5/8	37 1/8	35	15 5/8	15 4/8	9 4/8	9 4/8	22 4/8	15 4/8	Waterton Lake, BC	Victor T. Zarnock, Jr.	Victor T. Zarnock, Jr.	1972	685
180 5/8	40 5/8	39 4/8	15 4/8	15 4/8	8 1/8	7 6/8	20	18 6/8	Lewis & Clark Co., MT	William J. McRae	William J. McRae	1980	685
180 5/8	37 3/8	36	15 3/8	15 3/8	9 5/8	9 6/8	22 1/8	16 2/8	Ghost River, AB	Robert W. Hodge	Robert W. Hodge	1985	685
180 5/8	41 4/8	41 7/8	14 7/8	14 7/8	7 5/8	7 6/8	27 2/8	27 1/8	Sanders Co., MT	Raymond J. Baenen	Raymond J. Baenen	1986	685
180 5/8	40 2/8	40 2/8	14 4/8	14 2/8	9 5/8	10	21 6/8	21	Lemhi Co., ID	Eugene L. Chesler	Eugene L. Chesler	1990	685
180 5/8	38 7/8	38 7/8	15 5/8	15 3/8	8 2/8	8 1/8	21 2/8	19 6/8	Blaine Co., MT	Mark D. Farnam	Mark D. Farnam	1990	685
180 5/8	39 4/8	38 3/8	16	16	8 3/8	8 2/8	22 3/8	16 4/8	Chouteau Co., MT	Edward J. Lehman	Edward J. Lehman	1994	685
180 4/8	39	41 4/8	14 5/8	14 5/8	8	8 2/8	22 5/8	22	Smoky River, AB	H.P. Brandenburg	H.P. Brandenburg	1924	695
180 4/8	40 2/8	38 2/8	15 5/8	15 4/8	8 3/8	8	21 2/8	20	White Swan Lake, BC	John Barton	John Barton	1936	695
180 4/8	35 6/8	38 2/8	15	15	10 7/8	9 3/8	22	17	Lake Louise, AB	Unknown	Martin Bonack	PR 1951	695
180 4/8	38	39	14 2/8	14 2/8	10 6/8	10 6/8	22 3/8	18 2/8	Coal Branch, AB	R.G.F. Brown	R.G.F. Brown	1962	695
180 4/8	38	38 4/8	15	15	8 7/8	9	19 7/8	18 6/8	Moosehorn Lake, AB	Maynard Mathews	Maynard Mathews	1964	695
180 4/8	41	39	14	14	10 1/8	9 6/8	21 4/8	18 3/8	Simpson River, BC	Picked Up	Sharon Buck	1967	695
180 4/8	38 6/8	39 2/8	13 6/8	13 6/8	10 3/8	10 5/8	20 6/8	20 6/8	Park Co., WY	Picked Up	Sam L. Beasom	1974	695
180 4/8	34 7/8	35 5/8	15 4/8	15 5/8	10 1/8	10 2/8	21 2/8	13 1/8	Thistle Creek, AB	Paul H. Chance	Paul H. Chance	1975	695
180 4/8	40 1/8	40 1/8	15 4/8	15 4/8	7 6/8	7 5/8	22 6/8	20 2/8	Luscar Mt., AB	Jerry L. Christian	Jerry L. Christian	1979	695
180 4/8	40 6/8	38 2/8	14 5/8	14 5/8	9 2/8	9 3/8	23 2/8	22	Deer Lodge Co., MT	Jan J. Henry	Jan J. Henry	1983	695
180 4/8	39 1/8	37 5/8	14 6/8	14 7/8	9 4/8	9	25 2/8	24 6/8	Sanders Co., AB	Terry F. Brown	Terry F. Brown	1991	695
180 4/8	39 4/8	39 2/8	14	14	10	10 2/8	20	17 2/8	Skeleton Creek, AB	James W. Campbell	James W. Campbell	1991	695
180 4/8	40 2/8	40	14 3/8	14 4/8	8 4/8	8 4/8	23 1/8	23	Lemhi Co., ID	Maxallen D. Jackson	Maxallen D. Jackson	1993	695
180 3/8	38 6/8	40 1/8	15 1/8	15 1/8	8 6/8	9 3/8	20 1/8	19	Bow Lake, AB	Robert D. Layton	Robert D. Layton	1942	708
180 3/8	39 6/8	39 7/8	16 2/8	16	7 1/8	7 1/8	22 1/8	22 1/8	Sulphur River, AB	W.D. Parker	W.D. Parker	1955	708
180 3/8	41	36 7/8	15 4/8	15 5/8	8	8 1/8	19 7/8	19 7/8	Ghost River, AB	Art Brewster	Art Brewster	1960	708
180 3/8	37 5/8	38 6/8	14 6/8	14 4/8	9 4/8	10 1/8	22 6/8	19	Sheep Creek, WY	Picked Up	Loren L. Lutz	1962	708
180 3/8	36 1/8	37 2/8	15 4/8	15 2/8	9 6/8	10	22	19 4/8	Jakey's Fork, WY	Eugene Schilling	Eugene Schilling	1962	708
180 3/8	38 1/8	39 4/8	15	14 7/8	9 4/8	9	21 4/8	17	Ghost River, AB	J.E. Edwards	J.E. Edwards	1964	708
180 3/8	39 5/8	39 4/8	14 6/8	15	8 7/8	9	23 2/8	23 2/8	Wallowa Co., OR	Kirk W. Jones	Kirk W. Jones	1979	708
180 3/8	40 7/8	40 2/8	14 4/8	14 4/8	8 5/8	8 3/8	22 7/8	22 7/8	Lemhi Co., MT	Picked Up	R. Munn & F. Porter	1982	708

Score	Length of Horn R	Length of Horn L	Circ. of Base R	Circ. of Base L	Circ. 3rd Qtr R	Circ. 3rd Qtr L	Greatest Spread	Tip to Tip Spread	Locality	By whom killed	Owner	Date Killed	Rank
180 3/8	35 5/8	38 2/8	16 3/8	16 4/8	8 2/8	8 3/8	24 4/8	21 5/8	Silver Bow Co., MT	Robert C. Carlson	Robert C. Carlson	1983	708
180 3/8	37	37 7/8	15 1/8	15 2/8	9 5/8	9 5/8	23	19	Park Co., WY	Robert G. Curtis	Robert G. Curtis	1984	708
180 3/8	39 4/8	39 1/8	15 3/8	15 3/8	8 5/8	8 1/8	22 5/8	19 6/8	Mineral Co., MT	J. Ray Lake	J. Ray Lake	1984	708
180 3/8	37 5/8	41 4/8	15 2/8	15 3/8	7 7/8	8 3/8	23 4/8	23 4/8	Silver Bow Co., MT	Scott A. Shuey	Scott A. Shuey	1985	708
180 3/8	37 1/8	38	15 5/8	15 5/8	9	8 6/8	21	19	Sanders Co., MT	Calvin L. Pomrenke	Calvin L. Pomrenke	1986	708
180 3/8	38	38 1/8	15 5/8	15 5/8	8 3/8	9 3/8	19 3/8	19 3/8	Ravalli Co., MT	Terry Frey	Terry Frey	1988	708
180 3/8	35 1/8	37 2/8	14 6/8	15 4/8	9 4/8	9 7/8	24	15 6/8	Greenlee Co., AZ	James A. Gerrettie II	James A. Gerrettie II	1988	708
180 3/8	40 4/8	40 3/8	15	15	8 1/8	8	25 6/8	25 6/8	Chouteau Co., MT	Scott D. Rubin	Scott D. Rubin	1989	708
180 3/8	38 4/8	38 5/8	15 1/8	15 3/8	8 7/8	8 7/8	23 1/8	22 4/8	Deer Lodge Co., MT	Max E. Leishman	Max E. Leishman	1990	708
180 3/8	41 6/8	32 5/8	16 4/8	16 4/8	9 1/8	7 3/8	25	22 4/8	Beaverhead Co., MT	James M. Linscott	James M. Linscott	1990	708
180 3/8	38 3/8	37 4/8	15 4/8	15 4/8	8 6/8	8 3/8	22 1/8	15 4/8	Sheep Creek, AB	Barry Gramlich	Barry Gramlich	1992	708
180 3/8	37 6/8	36 5/8	15 2/8	15 2/8	10	10	19 5/8	17 6/8	Mora Co., NM	Ronald D. Rod	Ronald D. Rod	1992	708
180 3/8	40 4/8	38 1/8	16 1/8	15 5/8	7 6/8	8 3/8	23 1/8	21 2/8	Asotin Co., WA	Brian J. Greenhaw	Brian J. Greenhaw	1993	708
180 3/8	41 5/8	36	16	16	9	7 6/8	23 4/8	16 6/8	Greenlee Co., AZ	Hoover L. Lee	Hoover L. Lee	1993	708
180 3/8	36 6/8	36 1/8	16 2/8	16 2/8	9 2/8	9	22 4/8	16 7/8	Nez Perce Co., ID	Don R. Scoles	Don R. Scoles	1994	708
180 3/8	38 7/8	39 4/8	14 6/8	14 7/8	8 6/8	8 5/8	26 4/8	26 2/8	Fergus Co., MT	Dan T. Brelsford	Dan T. Brelsford	1995	708
180 3/8	37 5/8	38 4/8	16 5/8	16 5/8	7 5/8	8	23 7/8	23 3/8	Sanders Co., MT	Daniel C. Wahle	Daniel C. Wahle	1995	708
180 2/8	38	39 2/8	15	14 4/8	10 2/8	10 4/8	21	14	British Columbia	James T. Wilson	Kevin D. O'Connell	1928	733
180 2/8	36 4/8	38 6/8	15	15 1/8	9	9	20 4/8	20 4/8	Cecelia Lake, BC	Dan Auld	Dan Auld	1950	733
180 2/8	39 3/8	38 1/8	14 1/8	14 1/8	10 6/8	10	20 7/8	20 3/8	Salmon River, ID	Ralph Puckett	Ralph Puckett	1958	733
180 2/8	38 6/8	37 2/8	14 6/8	14 6/8	10 3/8	10	21 1/8	15	Burnt Timber Creek, AB	Ruth Mahoney	Ruth Mahoney	1963	733
180 2/8	39 5/8	39 5/8	15 3/8	15 4/8	7 7/8	7 6/8	21 1/8	19 1/8	Invermere, BC	Lyle O. Fett	Lyle O. Fett	1982	733
180 2/8	37 6/8	37 4/8	15 2/8	15	10 1/8	9 5/8	20 1/8	12 7/8	Ewin Creek, BC	Bob Hildebrandt	Bob Hildebrandt	1988	733
180 2/8	38 2/8	40 2/8	15 2/8	15 2/8	8 5/8	8 6/8	19 5/8	16 3/8	Cross River, BC	Daryl Stech	Daryl Stech	1989	733
180 2/8	39 1/8	39 1/8	14 5/8	14 4/8	9 1/8	9 1/8	22	20 2/8	Lincoln Co., MT	Bradley S. Osler	Bradley S. Osler	1990	733
180 2/8	35 3/8	35 7/8	15 6/8	15 6/8	9 7/8	10	21 1/8	14 2/8	Warden Rock, AB	Brian N. Holthe	Brian N. Holthe	1991	733
180 2/8	39 2/8	39 4/8	15 3/8	15 3/8	7 7/8	8	19	18 5/8	Rocky Creek, AB	Donald R. Smith	Donald R. Smith	1993	733
180 2/8	39	39 2/8	15	15 1/8	8 3/8	8 2/8	25 4/8	25 4/8	Lemhi Co., ID	Picked Up	Thomas C. Pike	1994	733
180 2/8	36 5/8	40 3/8	16 3/8	15 4/8	8 2/8	7 1/8	26 2/8	26 2/8	Missoula Co., MT	Joel D. Cusker	Joel D. Cusker	1994	733
180 1/8	40 5/8	34 5/8	15 2/8	16 5/8	7 1/8	10 7/8	21 5/8	18 1/8	Kootenay River, BC	Gerry Favreau	Gerry Favreau		746
180 1/8	36 4/8	37 2/8	15 4/8	15 1/8	10 3/8	9 1/8	22 1/8	18 4/8	Sugarloaf Mt., CO	Picked Up	Henry Zietz	1947	746
180 1/8	36 5/8	40 6/8	15 4/8	15 3/8	9 1/8	8 3/8	23 3/8	20 5/8	Green River, WY	John N. Leonard	John N. Leonard	1953	746
180 1/8	36 1/8	40 2/8	14 7/8	15 2/8	8 5/8	8 5/8	20 4/8	18	Sun River, MT	Dennis Reichelt	Dennis Reichelt	1958	746
180 1/8	39 5/8	39 7/8	15	15	8 3/8	9 4/8	23	23	Salmon River, ID	Picked Up	C.A. Schwope	1959	746
180 1/8	39 6/8	34 5/8	14	15 3/8	9 4/8	9 6/8	22 7/8	17 4/8	Kootenay Mts., BC	Gary E. Brown	Gary E. Brown	1963	746
180 1/8	37 3/8	37 6/8	15 4/8	14 6/8	10 4/8	10	16 5/8	16 5/8	Gannet Peak, WY	Wilbur Rickett	Wilbur Rickett	1964	746
180 1/8	37 6/8	34 3/8	14 4/8	14 4/8	10	9 5/8	22 4/8	19 1/8	Ghost River, AB	Lloyd E. Zeman	Jenifer D. Schmidt	1968	746
180 1/8	36 4/8	38 1/8	15 6/8	15 7/8	9 7/8	8 1/8	22 5/8	18 2/8	Castle River, AB	Don W. Caldwell	Don W. Caldwell	1969	746
180 1/8	37 6/8	37 4/8	15 7/8	15 7/8	8 1/8	8 1/8	18 6/8	18 6/8	Nye, MT	Ira H. Kent	Ira H. Kent	1974	746
180 1/8	37 4/8	37 4/8	16 4/8	16 4/8	8 1/8	7 2/8	20	20	Sanders Co., MT	Gene N. Meyer	Gene N. Meyer	1976	746
180 1/8	41 3/8	35 3/8	15	15	7	9 7/8	28 6/8	28 6/8	Deer Lodge Co., MT	Arden Holden	Arden Holden	1979	746
180 1/8	37 4/8	35 4/8	15 4/8	15 4/8	7 7/8	8	19 4/8	16	Coral Creek, AB	Leonard W. King	Leonard W. King	1983	746
180 1/8	37 6/8	37 7/8	16	16	7 7/8	6 3/8	21 4/8	14 6/8	Cougar Mt., AB	Norman Howg	Norman Howg	1984	746
180 1/8	38 5/8	42 6/8	15 7/8	15 7/8	6 3/8	7 5/8	24 3/8	24 3/8	Granite Co., MT	Leonard W. Bowen	Leonard W. Bowen	1985	746
180 1/8	38	37 1/8	16 4/8	16 4/8	7 6/8	8 2/8	19 3/8	19 3/8	Sanders Co., MT	Bruce P. Allen	Bruce P. Allen	1986	746
180 1/8	39 4/8	38 5/8	15	15	8 2/8	8 5/8	23 1/8	20 7/8	Custer Co., ID	Leland S. Speakes, Jr.	Leland S. Speakes, Jr.	1987	746
180 1/8	36 2/8	38 1/8	15 4/8	15 4/8	9 5/8	9 6/8	19 2/8	17 4/8	Granite Co., MT	Scott M. Willumsen	Scott M. Willumsen	1989	746

BIGHORN SHEEP

Ovis canadensis canadensis and certain related subspecies

Score	Length of Horn R	L	Circumference of Base R	L	Circumference at Third Quarter R	L	Greatest Spread	Tip tp Tip Spread	Locality	Hunter	Owner	Date Killed	Rank
180 1/8*	40	39 5/8	14 1/8	14 2/8	9 3/8	9 1/8	22 6/8	22 4/8	Lemhi Co., ID	JoAnn Basso	JoAnn Basso	1990	746
180 1/8	37 4/8	37 3/8	15 2/8	15 2/8	9 2/8	9	22 7/8	18 2/8	Clear Creek Co., CO	Charles W. Hanawalt	Charles W. Hanawalt	1990	746
180 1/8	37 7/8	35 3/8	16	16 1/8	8 4/8	9	21	19 3/8	Drinnan Mt., AB	Everitt N. Davis	Everitt N. Davis	1992	746
180 1/8	39 1/8	34 4/8	16 1/8	16 2/8	8	9 5/8	25 1/8	22 2/8	Greenlee Co., AZ	Mark E. McCullough	Mark E. McCullough	1994	746
180 1/8	37 2/8	37 1/8	16 1/8	16 1/8	8 3/8	8 5/8	23 2/8	23 1/8	Granite Co., MT	Dan Beck	Dan Beck	1995	746
180	37 1/8	38 7/8	15	15	9 4/8	10	22	18 2/8	Seebe, AB	Anson Brooks	Anson Brooks	1956	768
180	39 1/8	37 1/8	15	15 2/8	9 4/8	9 6/8	21	19 4/8	Forbidden Creek, AB	James Haugland	James Haugland	1958	768
180	38 1/8	38 3/8	15 2/8	15 2/8	9	9	21 5/8	18 2/8	Kootenay, BC	Walter L. Bjorkman	Walter L. Bjorkman	1963	768
180	37 6/8	37 1/8	14 4/8	14 4/8	10 4/8	10 4/8	22 3/8	22 3/8	Panther Creek, AB	Walter R. Schubert	Walter R. Schubert	1966	768
180	38 5/8	41 1/8	14 5/8	14 5/8	8 3/8	8 4/8	24	23 4/8	Lewis & Clark Co., MT	James G. Braddee, Jr.	James G. Braddee, Jr.	1978	768
180	39 6/8	39 2/8	15 3/8	15 3/8	8	8	22 4/8	20 6/8	Wallowa Co., OR	F. Carter Kerns	F. Carter Kerns	1978	768
180	38 5/8	37 3/8	15 4/8	15 4/8	9	8 4/8	20 4/8	16 3/8	Whitehorse Creek, AB	Philip H. R. Stepney	Prov. Mus. Alta.	1978	768
180	40 2/8	37 2/8	15 3/8	15 4/8	8 2/8	8 7/8	22 6/8	22 6/8	Granite Co., MT	Jerry E. Gallagher	Jerry E. Gallagher	1980	768
180	40 2/8	40 2/8	14 5/8	14 5/8	8 4/8	8 4/8	25	25	Wallowa Co., OR	Jerome V. Epping	Jerome V. Epping	1984	768
180	39 7/8	40 1/8	15 5/8	15 5/8	7 5/8	7 4/8	22 2/8	22 2/8	Granite Co., MT	Jim A. Crepeau	Jim A. Crepeau	1986	768
180	37 1/8	39 5/8	15 6/8	15 6/8	7 7/8	8 1/8	21 6/8	21 6/8	Beaverhead Co., MT	Kory McGavin	Kory McGavin	1988	768
180	38 2/8	40	14 4/8	14 6/8	9 2/8	9 1/8	21 2/8	20 6/8	Lewis & Clark Co., MT	Brian J. Boehm	Brian J. Boehm	1989	768
180	38 1/8	37 5/8	15 3/8	15 2/8	9 1/8	9	23 1/8	22 4/8	Deer Lodge Co., MT	Michael P. Lorello	Michael P. Lorello	1990	768
180	37 4/8	37	15 3/8	15 5/8	9 2/8	9 1/8	21	17 4/8	Granite Co., MT	Thomas I. Jenni	Thomas I. Jenni	1991	768
180	40 5/8	40 1/8	14 4/8	14 7/8	8 4/8	8 6/8	20 7/8	19 5/8	Lemhi Co., ID	A. Oscar Carlson	A. Oscar Carlson	1993	768
180	38 5/8	40 1/8	14 6/8	14 7/8	8 2/8	8 5/8	22 3/8	17 2/8	Fortress Mt., AB	Mike Michalezki	Mike Michalezki	1993	768
180	37 1/8	36 1/8	15 3/8	15 3/8	9 7/8	9 3/8	21 6/8	16 2/8	Mist Creek, AB	Morgan Williams	Morgan Williams	1995	768
180	37 1/8	37 3/8	15 5/8	15 5/8	9 3/8	8 7/8	21 6/8	20 5/8	Sanders Co., MT	Gino R. Fasano	Gino R. Fasano	1996	768
180	40	37 4/8	14 6/8	15 1/8	9 3/8	9	20 7/8	18 6/8	Granite Co., MT	William J. Leehan	William J. Leehan	1996	768
201 5/8*	44 6/8	44 5/8	15 2/8	15 3/8	11 2/8	10 7/8	23 6/8	22 4/8	Pincher Creek, AB	Percy Pyra	Percy Pyra	1973	
196 6/8*	39 4/8	40	16 5/8	16 5/8	10 7/8	11 2/8	23 2/8	18 1/8	Granite Co., MT	Luke B. Ostby	Luke B. Ostby	1995	

* Final score is subject to revision by additional verifying measurements.

B&C HISTORY

FREDERICK COURTENEY SELOUS 1851-1917

Perhaps the greatest of all African hunters, he was born in London, England, and educated at Rugby School. His dreams and ambitions took him to Southern Africa in 1871 where, at the age of 19, he undertook his legendary career as an elephant hunter and explorer. As a naturalist, his interests were diverse; he was ranked as one of the leading ornithologists of his day. He is credited with securing Mashonaland (later Rhodesia) for Britain in 1890. A gifted writer, he authored *A Hunter's Wanderings in Africa*, capturing the imagination of his native England. President Roosevelt considered him a hero and great friend, leading to his membership in the Boone and Crockett Club in 1907. He hunted throughout the American West and Canada. He returned to Africa to fight with the British in World War I and was killed in battle at Beho-Beho Ridge in Tanganyika on January 4, 1917. He was 65. ∎

CATEGORY
BIGHORN SHEEP

SCORE
191-7/8

HUNTER
DALE E. GARRISON

LOCATION
GRANITE CO., MT

DATE OF KILL
SEPTEMBER 1996

CATEGORY
BIGHORN SHEEP

SCORE
181-1/8

HUNTER
DAVID O. CONRAD

LOCATION
SANDERS CO., MT

DATE OF KILL
OCTOBER 1993

CATEGORY
BIGHORN SHEEP

SCORE
180-3/8

HUNTER
DONALD D. ROD

LOCATION
MORA CO., NM

DATE OF KILL
SEPTEMBER 1992

CATEGORY
BIGHORN SHEEP

SCORE
182-6/8

HUNTER
ROBERT S. WOOD

LOCATION
RAVALLI CO., MT

DATE OF KILL
NOVEMBER 1993

CATEGORY
BIGHORN SHEEP

SCORE
188

HUNTER
GLEN A. LANDRUS

LOCATION
ASOTIN CO., WA

DATE OF KILL
SEPTEMBER 1995

CATEGORY
BIGHORN SHEEP

SCORE
201-2/8

HUNTER
LARRY STRAWSON

LOCATION
NIKANASSIN RANGE, AB

DATE OF KILL
AUGUST 1997

Carl M. Scrivens of Jackson, Wyoming, has taken impressive desert sheep (*Ovis canadensis nelsoni*) in the past, but this accomplished hunter has not yet shot a ram that had topped the extraordinary trophy he found in 1941.

In a 1992 article for *Wild Sheep*, Scrivens gave an account of his discovery that occurred during a hunting trip on the Baja Peninsula of Mexico and his subsequent determination to obtain the trophy.

"We finally arrived at our destination, a remote rancho on the southern end of the Sierra San Pedro Martir. While the vaqueros were rounding up the mules, we took a stroll around the rancho. We looked inside an old dilapidated wagon, and there was a skull and horns of a desert ram. What a head it was!!! My brothers and family were fairly knowledgeable about the size of desert rams, but this beat anything we had ever seen — and I was determined to have it before we left."

Scrivens added that he wished he had more background on the actual circumstances of the hunt for this ram.

"The history of the taking of this head is meager. According to the vaqueros at the rancho, the ram had been killed the previous year by a native American meat hunter, who left the head lying. A vaquero brought the head to the rancho.

"When I acquired the head there was still a scrap of hide adhered to the skull, and it was black. Frequently rams with black, or nearly black pelts are found in that area. We hunted this same area at later times and took other rams, but none as large as the one I bartered for."

Scrivens' find was measured by Samuel Webb of the Boone and Crockett Club in 1946 and scored at 205-1/8 points. By 1992, the trophy still held the World's Record and was bequeathed to the Arizona Desert Bighorn Sheep Society of which Scrivens has been a lifelong member. After locating a suitable cape for the ram from the Arizona Department of Fish and Game, the restored mount was hung in the Buffalo Bill Historical Center in Cody, Wyoming, on June 27, 1992. ∎

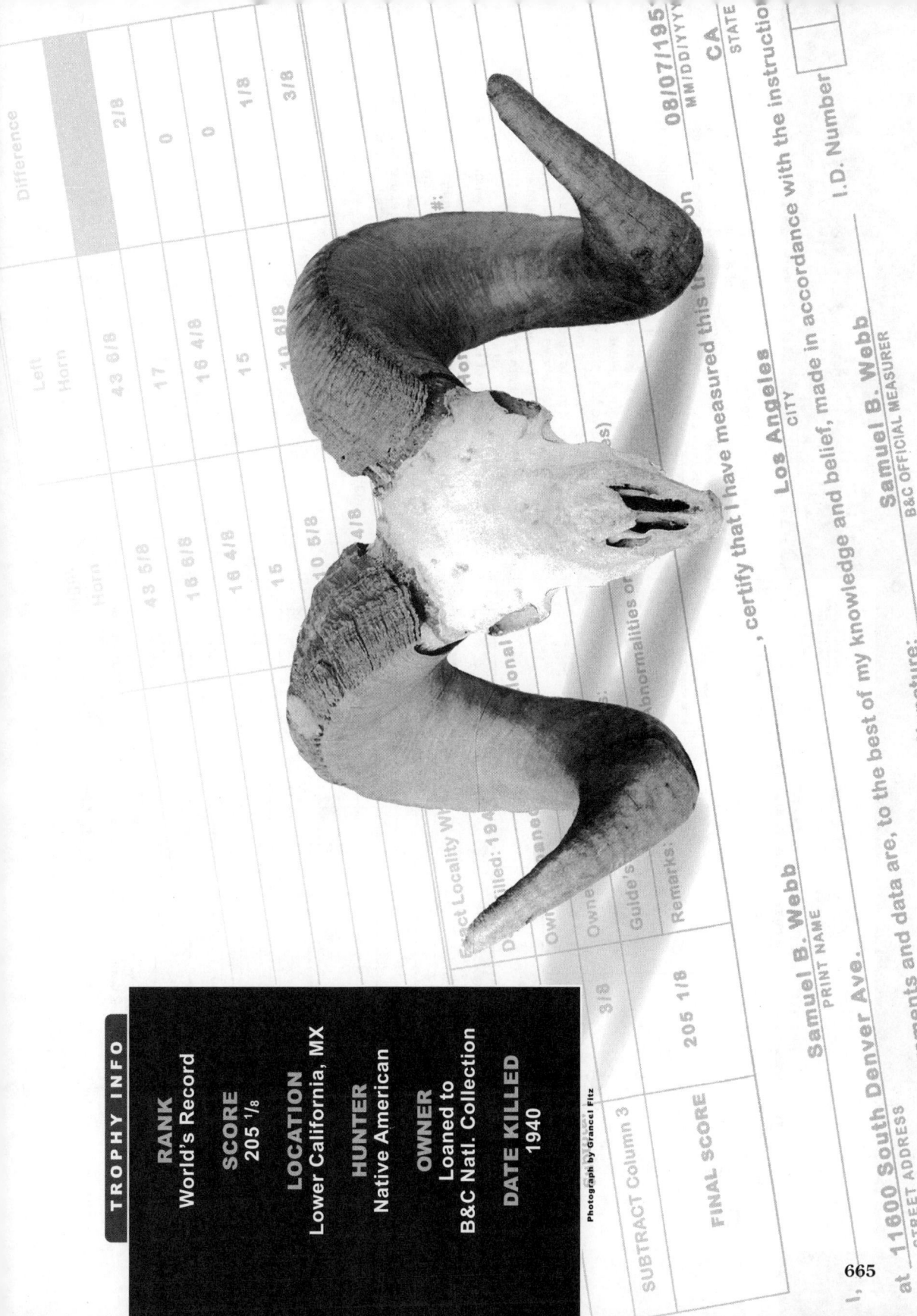

TROPHY INFO

RANK
World's Record

SCORE
205 1/8

LOCATION
Lower California, MX

HUNTER
Native American

OWNER
Loaned to
B&C Natl. Collection

DATE KILLED
1940

Photograph by Grancel Fitz

	Right Horn	Left Horn	Difference
	43 5/8	43 6/8	2/8
	16 6/8	17	0
	16 4/8	16 4/8	0
	15	15	1/8
	10 5/8	10 6/8	3/8
	4/8		

SUBTRACT Column 3   3/8

FINAL SCORE   205 1/8

I, _____, certify that I have measured this trophy

on **08/07/195_** at **Los Angeles**
MM/DD/YYYY   CITY

CA
STATE

and that these measurements and data are, to the best of my knowledge and belief, made in accordance with the instructions

Samuel B. Webb
PRINT NAME

Signature: _____

at **11600 South Denver Ave.**
STREET ADDRESS

I.D. Number _____

Samuel B. Webb
B&C OFFICIAL MEASURER

ROCKETT CLUB®

665

All measurements must be made with a 1/4-inch wide flexible steel tape to the nearest one-eighth of an inch. Enter fractional figures in eighths, without reduction. Official measurements cannot be taken until horns have air dried for at least 60 days after the animal was killed.

A. Greatest Spread is measured between perpendiculars at a right angle to the center line of the skull.

B. Tip to Tip Spread is measured between tips of horns.

C. Length of Horn is measured from the lowest point in front on outer curve to a point in line with tip. **Do not** press tape into depressions. The low point of the outer curve of the horn is considered to be the low point of the frontal portion of the horn, situated above and slightly medial to the eye socket (not the outside edge). Use a straight edge, perpendicular to horn axis, to end measurement on "broomed" horns.

D-1. Circumference of Base is measured at a right angle to axis of horn. **Do not** follow irregular edge of horn; the line of measurement must be entirely on horn material.

D-2-3-4. Divide measurement C of longer horn by four. Starting at base, mark **both** horns at these quarters (even though the other horn is shorter) and measure circumferences at these marks, with measurements taken at right angles to horn axis.

Records of
North American
Big Game

250 Station Drive
Missoula, MT 59801
(406) 542-1888

BOONE AND CROCKETT CLUB®
OFFICIAL SCORING SYSTEM FOR NORTH AMERICAN BIG GAME TROPHIES

SHEEP

MINIMUM SCORES		
	AWARDS	ALL-TIME
bighorn	175	180
desert	165	168
Dall's	160	170
Stone's	165	170

KIND OF SHEEP (check one)
- ☐ bighorn
- ■ desert
- ☐ Dall's
- ☐ Stone's

PLUG NUMBER

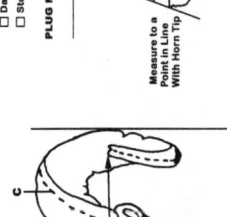

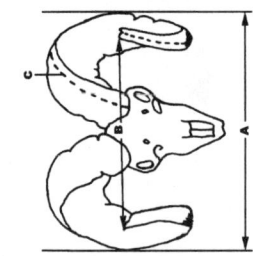

Measure to a
Point in Line
With Horn Tip

SEE OTHER SIDE FOR INSTRUCTIONS		COLUMN 1	COLUMN 2	COLUMN 3
		Right Horn	Left Horn	Difference
A. Greatest Spread (Is Often Tip to Tip Spread)	25 5/8			
B. Tip to Tip Spread	25 5/8			
C. Length of Horn		43 5/8	43 6/8	2/8
D-1. Circumference of Base		16 6/8	17	
D-2. Circumference at First Quarter		16 4/8	16 4/8	0
D-3. Circumference at Second Quarter		15	15	0
D-4. Circumference at Third Quarter		10 5/8	10 6/8	1/8
TOTALS		102 4/8	103	3/8

ADD	Column 1	102 4/8	Exact Locality Where Killed: **Lower California, MX**
	Column 2	103	Date Killed: **1940** Hunter: **Native American**
	Subtotal	205 4/8	Owner: **Loaned to B&C National Collection of Heads and Horns** Telephone #:
SUBTRACT Column 3		3/8	Owner's Address:
FINAL SCORE		205 1/8	Guide's Name and Address:
			Remarks: (Mention Any Abnormalities or Unique Qualities)

I, **Samuel B. Webb**
      PRINT NAME
, certify that I have measured this trophy on **08/07/1951**
                   MM/DD/YYYY

at **11600 South Denver Ave.**   **Los Angeles**   **CA**
  STREET/ADDRESS   CITY   STATE/PROVINCE

and that these measurements and data are, to the best of my knowledge and belief, made in accordance with the instructions given.

Witness: **Carl M. Scrivens**   Signature: **Samuel B. Webb**   I.D. Number:
                                     B&C OFFICIAL MEASURER

DESERT SHEEP

Ovis canadensis nelsoni and certain related subspecies

MINIMUM SCORE 168

Score	Length of Horn R	L	Circumference of Base R	L	Circumference at Third Quarter R	L	Greatest Spread	Tip tp Tip Spread	Locality	Hunter	Owner	Date Killed	Rank
205 1/8	43 5/8	43 6/8	16 6/8	17	10 5/8	10 6/8	25 5/8	25 5/8	Lower Calif., MX	Native American	Loaned to B&C Natl. Coll.	1940	1
201 3/8	45 5/8	46 2/8	15 5/8	15 5/8	11 2/8	11 5/8	20 4/8	20	Pima Co., AZ	Picked Up	Greg Koons	1982	2
197 4/8	44	43 4/8	15 7/8	15 7/8	10 5/8	10	23 7/8	23 7/8	Lower Calif., MX	Gift of H.M. Beck	Acad. Nat. Sci., Phil.	1892	3
197 1/8	42 3/8	41 6/8	16 1/8	16 1/8	10 5/8	11	26	26	Graham Co., AZ	Arthur R. Dubs	Arthur R. Dubs	1988	4
192 5/8	41 6/8	42 3/8	15	15 1/8	10 6/8	10 4/8	25 4/8	25	Baja Calif., MX	Javier Lopez del Bosque	Javier Lopez del Bosque	1979	5
191 6/8	42	43 4/8	15 4/8	15 3/8	9 6/8	9 3/8	23 4/8	23 4/8	Baja Calif., MX	Lit Ng	Lit Ng	1968	6
191 3/8	40	41 3/8	16 5/8	16 5/8	9 5/8	9 5/8	24 1/8	24 1/8	Mexico	Picked Up	Snow Museum	PR 1952	7
191 2/8	38 4/8	40 4/8	16 2/8	16 2/8	9 1/8	10 7/8	21 6/8	17 2/8	Baja Calif., MX	Claude Bourguignon	Claude Bourguignon	1982	8
191 1/8	39 3/8	39 2/8	16 4/8	16 4/8	10	10	19 3/8	19 2/8	Baja Calif., MX	Bruno Scherrer	Bruno Scherrer	1981	9
190 3/8	41	43 7/8	15 3/8	15 5/8	9 1/8	9 1/8	23 7/8	23 7/8	Arizona	Unknown	Bruce R. Kemp, Sr.	1903	10
189 3/8	39 5/8	39 4/8	15 4/8	15 4/8	10 3/8	11	21 3/8	21 3/8	Lower Calif., MX	M.B. Silva	M.B. Silva	1939	11
189	41	40 2/8	16 6/8	16 7/8	8 7/8	8 7/8	23 2/8	23 2/8	Gila Co., AZ	Sam Jaksick, Jr.	Sam Jaksick, Jr.	1988	12
188 4/8	40 2/8	40 2/8	15 4/8	15 6/8	10 2/8	10 1/8	21 5/8	19	Grant Co., NM	Picked Up	NM Dept. of Game & Fish	1992	13
188 2/8	43	43	14 4/8	14 5/8	9 5/8	9 4/8	27 3/8	27 3/8	Baja Calif., MX	A. Cal Rossi, Jr.	A. Cal Rossi, Jr.	1974	14
187 7/8	39 6/8	39 5/8	15 7/8	15 7/8	9 4/8	9 4/8	21 4/8	16 6/8	Pima Co., AZ	Carl A. Mattias, Sr.	Carl A. Mattias, Sr.	1982	15
187 6/8	42	40	15 2/8	15 2/8	10 1/8	10 1/8	23 5/8	23 5/8	Baja Calif., MX	Ed Stedman, Jr.	Ed Stedman, Jr.	1976	16
187 5/8	38 4/8	40 5/8	16 2/8	16 2/8	9	9 4/8	21 4/8	20 6/8	Baja Calif., MX	Romulo Sanchez Mireles	Romulo Sanchez Mireles	1969	17
187 3/8	39 2/8	39 7/8	15 1/8	15 2/8	10 2/8	10 5/8	21	21	Sonora, MX	Herb Klein	Herb Klein	1952	18
187 3/8	39 1/8	39 2/8	16	16	10 2/8	10 3/8	17 6/8	17 6/8	Sonora, MX	Oscar J. Brooks	Oscar J. Brooks	1955	18
187 1/8	39 3/8	39 3/8	15 4/8	15 4/8	10	10	24 3/8	22	Yuma Co., AZ	Rick Wood	Rick Wood	1996	20
187	39 1/8	39 5/8	16	16	9 3/8	9 5/8	24 5/8	24 5/8	Lower Calif., MX	Unknown	Snow Museum	PR 1952	21
187	40 4/8	40 2/8	15 2/8	15 2/8	9 6/8	10	26	26	Kofa Mts., AZ	Louis R. Dees	Louis R. Dees	1965	21
187	41 4/8	42 4/8	15 4/8	15 4/8	9 6/8	9 2/8	28	28	California	Picked Up	CA Dept. of Fish & Game	PR 1970	21
186 5/8	38 3/8	38 4/8	14 7/8	14 7/8	11 3/8	11 3/8	22	20 1/8	Sonora, MX	F.B. Heider	O.M. Corbett	1927	24
186 3/8	41 1/8	39	15 7/8	16	9 3/8	9 4/8	24	22 3/8	Gila Co., AZ	Steven E. Wright	Steven E. Wright	1990	25
186 2/8	40 5/8	38 3/8	16	16	9	9 1/8	21 1/8	20 7/8	Maricopa Co., AZ	Ralph Grossman	Ralph Grossman	1961	26
186 2/8	40 6/8	40 2/8	14 6/8	14 7/8	10	10	20 2/8	23	Baja Calif., MX	Robert P. Miller	Robert P. Miller	1981	26
186	37	36	15 7/8	16	11 7/8	11 7/8	21 4/8	19	Arizona	Unknown	J. Michael Conoyer	1960	28
186	38 2/8	38 4/8	15 4/8	15 5/8	10 6/8	10 6/8	22 3/8	19 5/8	Yuma Co., AZ	Gerry W. Nikolaus	Gerry W. Nikolaus	1979	28
185 3/8	39 5/8	40	16	16	10 2/8	9 2/8	22 3/8	19 7/8	Baja Calif., MX	Graciano Guichard	Graciano Guichard	1970	30
185 3/8	38 3/8	39 4/8	16 1/8	16 1/8	8 7/8	9	23 2/8	19 6/8	Baja Calif., MX	Robert L. Williamson	Robert L. Williamson	1987	30
185 2/8	39 7/8	38 7/8	15 5/8	15 6/8	9	9 3/8	19 4/8	16 3/8	Baja Calif., MX	Wilmer C. Hansen	Wilmer C. Hansen	1972	32
185 2/8	39 2/8	39 2/8	15 4/8	15 4/8	10 4/8	10 4/8	25 2/8	25 2/8	Baja Calif., MX	Albert Pellizzari	Albert Pellizzari	1978	32
185 2/8	41	40 2/8	15 7/8	15 7/8	8 2/8	9	21 1/8	20 3/8	Graham Co., AZ	John W. Harris	John W. Harris	1982	32
185	39 4/8	39 2/8	15 7/8	15 7/8	8 7/8	9	20 3/8	18 6/8	San Borjas Mts., MX	Alice J. Landreth	Alice J. Landreth	1969	35
185	38 6/8	37 2/8	16 4/8	16 4/8	8 7/8	8 7/8	24 5/8	21	Baja Calif., MX	Miguel Zaldivar De Valasco	Miguel Zaldivar De Valasco	1979	35
184 6/8	42	40 6/8	14 6/8	15	9 4/8	9 2/8	29 4/8	29 4/8	Kofa Mts., AZ	W.A. Rudd	W.A. Rudd	1965	37
184 6/8	39 4/8	38 4/8	16 2/8	16 3/8	8 5/8	8 7/8	22 5/8	21 1/8	Baja Calif., MX	Burton L. Smith, Sr.	Burton L. Smith, Sr.	1973	37

Score	L. Horn R	L. Horn L	Circ. Base R	Circ. Base L	Circ. 3rd Qtr R	Circ. 3rd Qtr L	Greatest Spread	Tip to Tip	Locality	Hunter	Owner	Date Killed	Rank
184 6/8	42 6/8	41	15	15 1/8	8 4/8	8 3/8	27 1/8	26 6/8	Nye Co., NV	Alfred L. Raiche, Sr.	Alfred L. Raiche, Sr.	1988	37
184 5/8	40 1/8	37 4/8	15 1/8	15 1/8	10	10 3/8	22 4/8	21 2/8	Baja Calif., MX	Steven L. Rose	Steven L. Rose	1967	40
184 4/8	38 6/8	39	15 5/8	16	9 2/8	9 4/8	20 6/8	21	Baja Calif., MX	H. Clayton Poole	H. Clayton Poole	1966	41
184 4/8	43 1/8	45 3/8	13 7/8	13 5/8	8 6/8	8 6/8	26 4/8	26 4/8	Santa Teresa Mts., AZ	Picked Up	AZ Game & Fish Dept.	1967	41
184 4/8	40 4/8	40	15 2/8	15 2/8	9	9	22	22	Baja Calif., MX	Clint Heiber	Clint Heiber	1978	41
184 2/8	40 4/8	37 2/8	15 4/8	15 4/8	9 2/8	9 2/8	22 1/8	22 1/8	Pinal Co., AZ	Everett A. Hodge	Everett A. Hodge	1988	44
184 1/8	38 5/8	40	15 2/8	15 2/8	9 3/8	9 4/8	22	20 1/8	Papago Indian Res., AZ	Ralph J. Murrietta	Ollie O. Barney, Jr.	1965	45
184	40 1/8	38 7/8	14 6/8	14 6/8	10 1/8	9 7/8	25 4/8	25 4/8	Santa Rosa Mts., CA	Picked Up	Fred L. Jones	1955	46
184	41 6/8	40 4/8	15 4/8	15 4/8	8 3/8	8 7/8	25 6/8	25 6/8	Baja Calif., MX	Thomas J. Brimhall	Thomas J. Brimhall	1981	46
183 7/8	39 3/8	40 3/8	15 4/8	16	9 5/8	9 3/8	23 5/8	23 5/8	Gonzaga, MX	Glenn Napierskie	Glenn Napierskie	1970	48
183 3/8	40	40 3/8	16	13 7/8	10 4/8	9 6/8	24 7/8	24 1/8	Pinkley, AZ	Picked Up	Organ Pipe Cactus Natl. Mon.	1957	49
183 2/8	39 4/8	41 6/8	15 2/8	15 2/8	9	9	25 3/8	25 3/8	Lower Calif., MX	George H. Gould	Unknown	1894	50
183 2/8	39 7/8	38 1/8	15 2/8	15 2/8	9 7/8	9 6/8	23	23	Clark Co., NV	Gerald A. Lent	Gerald A. Lent	1976	50
183 2/8	37 6/8	37	14 7/8	14 7/8	10 7/8	11 1/8	14 2/8	14 2/8	Pima Co., AZ	Picked Up	LeRoy Van Buggenum	1987	50
183 2/8	40 5/8	41 5/8	15 2/8	15 2/8	8 3/8	8 6/8	27 2/8	27 2/8	Clark Co., NV	Alan G. Means	Alan G. Means	1988	50
182 6/8	39 2/8	37 6/8	14 6/8	14 6/8	11	10 7/8	22	20 6/8	Colorado River, AZ	Picked Up	John E. Luster	1956	54
182 6/8	41 6/8	38 6/8	15 4/8	15 4/8	8 2/8	8 4/8	23 4/8	23 4/8	Baja Calif., MX	Rita Oney	Rita Oney	1976	54
182 5/8	36	35 5/8	16 3/8	16 4/8	9 4/8	9 6/8	22 2/8	22 2/8	Pima Co., AZ	Charles W. Fisher	Charles W. Fisher	1972	56
182 5/8	39	39 1/8	15 5/8	15 5/8	8 6/8	9 2/8	22 6/8	22 6/8	Baja Calif., MX	Duane H. Loomis	Duane H. Loomis	1972	56
182 4/8	39 7/8	39 3/8	14 6/8	14 5/8	9 6/8	9 7/8	21 1/8	21 1/8	Lower Calif., MX	Picked Up	C.G. Clare	1958	58
182 4/8	37	37 4/8	14 7/8	14 5/8	10	10 2/8	22 3/8	22 3/8	Riverside Co., CA	Picked Up	Orson Morgan	1963	58
182 3/8	38 5/8	37 6/8	15	15	10 5/8	10 1/8	22 1/8	22 1/8	Lower Calif., MX	Elgin T. Gates	Elgin T. Gates	1940	60
182 3/8	39 3/8	40	14 6/8	14 7/8	9 3/8	9 5/8	22	22	Baja Calif., MX	Robert Zachrich	Robert Zachrich	1978	60
182 2/8	39 5/8	39 5/8	15 3/8	15 3/8	9 3/8	9	22 3/8	22 3/8	Graham Co., AZ	Beverly M. Nuessle	Beverly M. Nuessle	1986	62
182 1/8	39 6/8	39 6/8	15 4/8	15 4/8	8 4/8	7 3/8	22 2/8	22 2/8	Graham Co., AZ	James W. Ferguson	James W. Ferguson	1984	63
182 1/8	37	37	14 7/8	14 7/8	10 2/8	10 1/8	23 6/8	23 6/8	Baja Calif., MX	Jesus H. Garza-Villarreal	Jesus H. Garza-Villarreal	1984	63
182	36 6/8	37	15 6/8	15 6/8	9 2/8	9 2/8	22 1/8	22 1/8	Baja Calif., MX	John M. Griffith, Jr.	John M. Griffith, Jr.	1974	65
181 6/8	42 2/8	39	16 1/8	16 1/8	8 5/8	9	24	24	Sonora, MX	George W. Parker	George W. Parker	1939	66
181 5/8	39 2/8	41 3/8	15 2/8	15 1/8	8 7/8	8 7/8	24 1/8	24 1/8	Sheep Mt. Range, NV	David Ingram	David Ingram	1962	67
181 5/8	36 7/8	36 3/8	16 1/8	16 1/8	10 3/8	10 3/8	22	20 1/8	Baja Calif., MX	Elvin Hawkins	Elvin Hawkins	1978	67
181 4/8	39	38 4/8	15 3/8	15 3/8	9 4/8	9 5/8	22 2/8	19 2/8	Graham Co., AZ	Mark A. Clark	Mark A. Clark	1995	69
181 4/8	38 3/8	39 2/8	15 2/8	15 2/8	8 6/8	9 4/8	21 6/8	21 7/8	Hidalgo Co., NM	Thomas J. Pawlacyk	Thomas J. Pawlacyk	1995	69
181 2/8	37	37	15	15	10 6/8	10 6/8	21 7/8	21 1/8	Sonora, MX	Ira C. Green	Ira C. Green	1939	71
180 7/8	40	38 1/8	15 4/8	15 4/8	9 1/8	9 6/8	22 5/8	21 5/8	Baja Calif., MX	Geo. H. Landreth	Geo. H. Landreth	1969	72
180 7/8	37 7/8	34 4/8	15 6/8	15 6/8	9 6/8	9 6/8	20 6/8	20 6/8	Baja Calif., MX	Jack Atcheson, Jr.	Jack Atcheson, Jr.	1978	72
180 7/8	38	38 1/8	15 2/8	15 1/8	9 3/8	9 4/8	22 6/8	16 3/8	Yuma Co., AZ	Michael J. Pace	Michael J. Pace	1991	72
180 6/8	38 6/8	39	14 7/8	14 7/8	10 2/8	10	26	26	Mohave Co., AZ	Larry F. Snead	Larry F. Snead	1993	75
180 4/8	35 7/8	37 3/8	16 1/8	16 3/8	9	8 6/8	19 1/8	18 4/8	Dragon Teeth Mt., AZ	Raymond White	Raymond White	1966	76
180 4/8	36 7/8	37 5/8	16 2/8	16 2/8	9 4/8	9 5/8	21 5/8	17 3/8	Yuma Co., AZ	Weldon A. Rogers	Weldon A. Rogers	1990	76
180 3/8	38 1/8	40 2/8	15 1/8	15 1/8	9	9 1/8	20 3/8	20 3/8	Baja Calif., MX	Arthur R. Dubs	Arthur R. Dubs	1966	78
180 3/8	39 2/8	39 5/8	14 6/8	14 5/8	9 4/8	9	22 4/8	22 4/8	Baja Calif., MX	Fritz A. Nachant	Fritz A. Nachant	1970	78
180 3/8	38	37 5/8	15	14 7/8	10 2/8	9 4/8	21 7/8	17	Yuma Co., AZ	James K. McCasland	James K. McCasland	1978	78
180 2/8	37 2/8	38 5/8	15 1/8	15 1/8	9 3/8	9 3/8	21 6/8	19 1/8	Baja Calif., MX	Emory C. Thompson	Emory C. Thompson	1985	82
180 2/8	36 2/8	36 4/8	15 4/8	15 4/8	9 7/8	10 1/8	22 4/8	21 4/8	Baja Calif., MX	Hector Aguilar Parada	Hector Aguilar Parada	1988	82
180 2/8	41 2/8	39 6/8	14 4/8	14 4/8	8 7/8	9 7/8	22 6/8	21 1/8	Baja Calif., MX	Bernard Sippin	Bernard Sippin	1988	82
180 2/8	39 6/8	39 6/8	14 4/8	14 4/8	10	10	21 5/8	17 1/8	La Paz Co., AZ	Bruce Liddy	Bruce Liddy	1992	85
180 1/8	37 4/8	39 1/8	14 3/8	14 3/8	9 6/8	9 3/8	22 5/8	22 2/8	Tank Mts., AZ	Picked Up	Calvin C. Wallerich	1960	85

DESERT SHEEP

Ovis canadensis nelsoni and certain related subspecies

Score	Length of Horn R	L	Circumference of Base R	L	Circumference at Third Quarter R	L	Greatest Spread	Tip to Tip Spread	Locality	Hunter	Owner	Date Killed	Rank
180 1/8	36 5/8	35 4/8	16 5/8	16 5/8	9 1/8	8 5/8	22 4/8	21 5/8	Pima Co., AZ	Robert A. Christy	Robert A. Christy	1986	85
180 1/8	38 1/8	38 2/8	15 1/8	15 4/8	9	8 7/8	26 7/8	26 5/8	Mohave Co., AZ	Gary D. Barcom	Gary D. Barcom	1996	85
180	36 1/8	36 1/8	15 6/8	15 6/8	9 4/8	10 1/8	21 3/8	17 3/8	Pima Co., AZ	Clifford W. Saylor	Clifford W. Saylor	1976	88
180	38 2/8	38 5/8	15 2/8	15 2/8	9	9 2/8	22	20 6/8	Clark Co., NV	John V. Zenz	John V. Zenz	1980	88
179 7/8	38 7/8	36 4/8	15 3/8	15 3/8	10 2/8	9 4/8	25 4/8	23 5/8	Clark Co., NV	Sal Quilici	NV State Museum	1978	90
179 7/8	37 5/8	37 2/8	15 2/8	15 2/8	8 7/8	9 2/8	19 5/8	0	Baja Calif., MX	George W. Vogt	George W. Vogt	1978	90
179 7/8	37 6/8	37 5/8	16	16 1/8	8 4/8	9	24 3/8	24 3/8	Baja Calif., MX	Paul E. Robey	Paul E. Robey	1979	90
179 6/8	39 1/8	39 1/8	16	16	7 5/8	7 4/8	24	24	Baja Calif., MX	Don L. Corley	Don L. Corley	1978	93
179 5/8	37	36 7/8	16 5/8	16 5/8	8 2/8	8 4/8	21 2/8	19 4/8	Pima Co., AZ	Brian F. Dolan	Brian F. Dolan	1995	94
179 4/8	38 1/8	37 3/8	15 3/8	15 4/8	9 4/8	9 7/8	21	19 6/8	Baja Calif., MX	Mrs. Carroll Pistell	Mrs. Carroll Pistell	1969	95
179 4/8	38 1/8	37 7/8	15 5/8	15 6/8	8 7/8	8 5/8	26 6/8	26 6/8	Baja Calif., MX	Ronald J. Wade	Ronald J. Wade	1987	95
179 2/8	36 5/8	35 7/8	16 2/8	16 2/8	9 1/8	9 1/8	20 5/8	19 3/8	Baja Calif., MX	Jim Buss	Jim Buss	1966	97
179 2/8	38 2/8	37	15 2/8	15 2/8	9 6/8	9 4/8	21 2/8	21 2/8	Baja Calif., MX	Francisco Salido	Francisco Salido	1968	97
179 2/8	36 7/8	36 7/8	14 7/8	14 7/8	9 7/8	9 6/8	20 4/8	20 4/8	Clark Co., NV	Andy S. Burnett	Andy S. Burnett	1979	97
179 2/8	38 3/8	40 1/8	15 1/8	15 2/8	9 3/8	9 3/8	23 4/8	23	Clark Co., NV	Tammy H. Bawcom	Tammy H. Bawcom	1988	97
179 2/8	38	35 2/8	15 2/8	15 2/8	9 4/8	9 4/8	28 6/8	27 5/8	Nye Co., NV	John V. Zenz II	John V. Zenz II	1994	97
179 2/8	38 2/8	37 2/8	14 1/8	15 4/8	11 2/8	10 6/8	23 7/8	18 3/8	Cochise Co., AZ	Steven E. Krook	Steven E. Krook	1996	97
179 1/8	36 1/8	38 2/8	15 4/8	15 5/8	8 4/8	8 6/8	21 4/8	18 4/8	Baja Calif., MX	W.J. Boynton, Jr.	W.J. Boynton, Jr.	1974	103
179 1/8	39 5/8	40	14 4/8	14 4/8	9	9	25 1/8	24 5/8	Clark Co., NV	Gary D. Selmi	Gary D. Selmi	1989	103
179	37 3/8	36 1/8	16 2/8	16 1/8	8 5/8	8 6/8	19 4/8	18 7/8	Baja Calif., MX	Graciano G. Michel	Graciano G. Michel	1970	105
178 7/8	39 1/8	36	16 2/8	16 2/8	8	7 5/8	20 5/8	20	Hidalgo Co., NM	L.P. McKinney	Frank McKinney	1921	106
178 7/8	36 7/8	37	15 4/8	15 4/8	9 7/8	10 1/8	23	22 6/8	Sauceda Mts., AZ	Picked Up	Edward Hunt	1962	106
178 7/8	35 2/8	36 3/8	15 2/8	15 2/8	9 7/8	10 2/8	29 5/8	29 5/8	Mohave Co., AZ	Earle H. Smith	Earle H. Smith	1981	106
178 7/8	39 6/8	39 5/8	14 6/8	14 7/8	8 7/8	9	28 1/8	27	Mohave Co., AZ	Ronald A. Norman	Ronald A. Norman	1994	106
178 6/8	39 6/8	39 4/8	14 3/8	14 4/8	9 1/8	9	27	27	Colorado River, NV	E.A. Goldman	U.S. Natl. Museum	1913	110
178 6/8	37 2/8	37	14 6/8	14 6/8	10 2/8	10 2/8	22 3/8	18 5/8	Sonora, MX	Oscar J. Brooks	Oscar J. Brooks	1950	110
178 6/8	37 2/8	36 6/8	15 7/8	15 7/8	8 4/8	8 3/8	21 4/8	21 4/8	Baja Calif., MX	Hobson L. Sanderson, Jr.	Hobson L. Sanderson, Jr.	1981	110
178 5/8	35 2/8	36 5/8	15 5/8	15 5/8	9 5/8	9 2/8	23 4/8	22	Lincoln Co., NV	William A. Bertelson	William A. Bertelson	1984	113
178 5/8	37 7/8	37 2/8	15 3/8	15 3/8	8 7/8	8 7/8	21 2/8	20 2/8	La Paz Co., AZ	Wayne B. Smith	Wayne B. Smith	1993	113
178 4/8	38 3/8	35 3/8	15 5/8	15 5/8	9 5/8	9 1/8	22 3/8	20	Pima Co., AZ	Ken Broyles	Ken Broyles	1971	115
178 4/8	36 4/8	36 2/8	15 6/8	15 6/8	9	9 2/8	20 4/8	19 2/8	Baja Calif., MX	Henry Culp	Henry Culp	1978	115
178 4/8	40 4/8	39 2/8	14 1/8	13 7/8	9 6/8	10	25 7/8	25 7/8	Clark Co., NV	Stephen E. Aiazzi	Stephen E. Aiazzi	1985	115
178 2/8	38 6/8	36 2/8	14 2/8	14 2/8	10 1/8	10 4/8	23 5/8	22 4/8	Clark Co., NV	Kenneth A. Brunk	Kenneth A. Brunk	1989	118
178 1/8	34	40 1/8	15	14 6/8	9 5/8	10 2/8	19 7/8	18	Maricopa Co., AZ	Michael Holt	Michael Holt	1970	119
178 1/8	36 1/8	39 4/8	14 5/8	14 4/8	9 6/8	9 5/8	25 4/8	25 1/8	Lincoln Co., NV	David R. Montrose	David R. Montrose	1993	119
178 1/8	36 2/8	36 1/8	15 2/8	15 4/8	9 1/8	9 5/8	18 1/8	18 1/8	Sonora, MX	Dennis H. Dunn	Dennis H. Dunn	1997	119
178	38 3/8	37 3/8	15	14 6/8	9 3/8	9 6/8	21 4/8	19 4/8	Baja Calif., MX	Basil C. Bradbury	Basil C. Bradbury	1969	122
178	36	37	16	16	8 6/8	9	22	22	Sonora, MX	Aaron Saenz, Jr.	Aaron Saenz, Jr.	1969	122

Score	Length of Horn R	L	Circumference of Base R	L	Circ. at Third Quarter R	L	Tip to Tip Spread	Greatest Spread	Locality	Hunter	Owner	Date Killed	Rank
178	35 4/8	38 2/8	16	16	8 2/8	8 2/8	24	24	Baja Calif., MX	James G. Lagiss	James G. Lagiss	1980	122
177 7/8	39 7/8	38 6/8	15 3/8	15 1/8	8	8 3/8	26 5/8	26 5/8	San Boros Mts., MX	Jerald T. Waite	Jerald T. Waite	1972	125
177 7/8	38 1/8	37 4/8	15 1/8	15	9 2/8	9 2/8	19 2/8	20 5/8	Baja Calif., MX	Richard C. Hansen	Richard C. Hansen	1973	125
177 7/8	37	37 7/8	15	14 7/8	9 5/8	9 5/8	19 5/8	21	Mohave Co., AZ	William C. Duffy, Jr.	William C. Duffy, Jr.	1981	125
177 7/8	36 5/8	36	15 4/8	15 4/8	9 5/8	9 3/8	20 5/8	24	Yuma Co., AZ	J. Dorsey Smith	J. Dorsey Smith	1983	125
177 7/8	34 2/8	38 1/8	16 1/8	16 2/8	8 4/8	8 3/8	23 3/8	27 6/8	Graham Co., AZ	William N. Willis	William N. Willis	1989	125
177 4/8	38	42	14 4/8	14 4/8	8 3/8	8 1/8	27 6/8	25 5/8	Lower Calif., MX	Earl A. Garrettson	William Foster	1912	130
177 4/8	38	37	14 6/8	14 5/8	9 3/8	9 4/8	24	15 7/8	Baja Calif., MX	Herb Klein	Herb Klein	1966	130
177 4/8	36 7/8	35 7/8	15 1/8	14 7/8	9 5/8	9 4/8	18 7/8	20 3/8	Baja Calif., MX	Joe Osterbauer	Joe Osterbauer	1978	130
177 4/8	36 5/8	35 5/8	15 2/8	15 2/8	9 5/8	9 3/8	20 3/8	21	Pima Co., AZ	Mark D. Morris	Mark D. Morris	1990	130
177 3/8	38 4/8	38 3/8	14 2/8	14 3/8	9 6/8	10 4/8	21	22 6/8	Lower Calif., MX	F. Stephens	U.S. Natl. Museum	1902	134
177 3/8	37 5/8	37 3/8	14 5/8	14 3/8	8 7/8	8 7/8	22 6/8	21 7/8	Yuma Co., AZ	George I. Parker	George I. Parker	1968	134
177 3/8	38	38	15 2/8	15 4/8	8 4/8	8 4/8	21 7/8	19 4/8	Baja Calif., MX	Arthur W. Carlsberg	Arthur W. Carlsberg	1970	134
177 3/8	37 5/8	37	16 2/8	16	8	10 4/8	19 4/8	19	Baja Calif., MX	Don McBride	Don McBride	1980	134
177 3/8	37	36	15	15 1/8	11	8 7/8	19	28 5/8	Clark Co., NV	Ralph W. McClintock	Ralph W. McClintock	1980	134
177 2/8	34 6/8	36 3/8	15 3/8	15 2/8	8 4/8	9	28 5/8	20 2/8	Clark Co., NV	Robert M. Bransford	Robert M. Bransford	1966	139
177 2/8	39 2/8	34 4/8	15 3/8	15 3/8	9 3/8	9 1/8	20 2/8	23	San Borjas Mts., MX	Lloyd E. Zeman	Jenifer D. Schmidt	1970	139
177 1/8	37 1/8	37 1/8	15 2/8	15 2/8	9 1/8	9	23	21 7/8	Yuma Co., AZ	Robert Fritzinger	Robert Fritzinger	1976	139
177 1/8	37	36	15 5/8	15 4/8	8 6/8	8 6/8	21 7/8	21 4/8	Yuma Co., AZ	Julian W. Chancellor	Julian W. Chancellor	1992	139
177	36 4/8	36 4/8	15 6/8	15 6/8	8 6/8	8 6/8	21 4/8	22 5/8	Pima Co., AZ	Michael A. Jensen	Michael A. Jensen	1978	143
177	36 1/8	36 2/8	15 2/8	15 2/8	8 2/8	8 2/8	22 5/8	21	Baja Calif., MX	G. Dale Monson	G. Dale Monson	1982	143
177	37 6/8	38 5/8	15 4/8	15 1/8	8 3/8	8 1/8	21	19	Yuma Co., AZ	Michael A. Longoria	Michael A. Longoria	1994	143
177	37 6/8	39 1/8	15 4/8	15 4/8	9	9	18 1/8	21 3/8	Baja Calif., MX	Alain Ferraris	Alain Ferraris	1966	146
177	36 4/8	36 2/8	14 6/8	15 1/8	9 2/8	9 1/8	18	19 6/8	Sonora Desert, MX	Herb Klein	Herb Klein	1969	146
177	35 4/8	37	15 7/8	15 7/8	9 1/8	9 2/8	20	23 2/8	Baja Calif., MX	Roy A. Woodward	Roy A. Woodward	1969	146
176 7/8	38	36 6/8	15	14 7/8	8 7/8	9 2/8	17 3/8	27 6/8	Clark Co., NV	Scott J. Weyrick	Scott J. Weyrick	1996	150
176 6/8	38 1/8	37 4/8	14 2/8	14 2/8	8 3/8	8 2/8	22 7/8	21 3/8	Mexico	Bill Foster	Foster's Bighorn Rest.	PR 1967	151
176 6/8	38	39 2/8	14 6/8	14 6/8	7 6/8	8 6/8	27 6/8	23 2/8	Kofa Range, AZ	Picked Up	D.B. Sanford	1957	151
176 6/8	37 4/8	36 1/8	13 6/8	14 1/8	10 7/8	10 5/8	20 2/8	22 1/8	Santa Rosa Mts., CA	Picked Up	John C. Belcher	PR 1958	151
176 6/8	39 6/8	38 2/8	14 6/8	15 5/8	8 2/8	8 2/8	23 3/8	21 7/8	Pinal Co., AZ	Travis R. Holder	Travis R. Holder	1984	151
176 5/8	36 3/8	37	15 6/8	14 6/8	9	9 4/8	22 1/8	20	Clark Co., NV	Douglas E. Wendt	Douglas E. Wendt	1989	155
176 5/8	39	38	14 4/8	15 6/8	8 7/8	8 4/8	20	28 3/8	Baja Calif., MX	Fernando Garcia	Fernando Garcia	1968	155
176 5/8	35 7/8	38 5/8	15 6/8	15 6/8	8 4/8	8 6/8	28 3/8	19 5/8	Clark Co., NV	Allan R. Sundell	Kent A. Sundell	1979	155
176 5/8	39 7/8	36 4/8	15 6/8	16 4/8	9 1/8	9 1/8	14 5/8	22 6/8	Baja Calif., MX	Douglas J. Dollhopf	Douglas J. Dollhopf	1983	155
176 5/8	36 6/8	38	14 1/8	14 1/8	8 6/8	9 4/8	21	22 6/8	Cochise Co., AZ	William R. Whitworth	William R. Whitworth	1995	155
176 4/8	38 6/8	38 1/8	15 4/8	15	9 4/8	9 4/8	23 6/8	23 2/8	Pima Co., AZ	Benjamin J. Hooper	Benjamin J. Hooper	1996	160
176 4/8	38	38 6/8	15 1/8	15 2/8	8 4/8	8 3/8	23 2/8	21 6/8	Lower Calif., MX	E.W. Funcke	U.S. Natl. Museum	1905	160
176 4/8	36 7/8	37 2/8	14	13 6/8	9 7/8	10 1/8	21 6/8	20 6/8	Baja Calif., MX	Picked Up	Leland Brand	1973	160
176 4/8	35 2/8	38 2/8	16	16	7 7/8	7 7/8	20 6/8	19 2/8	Pinal Co., AZ	Robbie A. Brown	Robert L. Brown	1985	160
176 3/8	34 5/8	38 3/8	15	15 1/8	10 2/8	9 6/8	19 2/8	21 1/8	Yuma Co., AZ	Gail Ferguson	Gail Ferguson	1988	164
176 3/8	35 2/8	36 2/8	16 5/8	16 4/8	9	8 5/8	19 7/8	29 1/8	Baja Calif., MX	William L. Baker, Jr.	William L. Baker, Jr.	1974	164
176 3/8	37 5/8	34 5/8	16	15 3/8	9 2/8	9	21 1/8	19 7/8	Baja Calif., MX	Joe E. Coleman	Joe E. Coleman	1976	164
176 3/8	36	37 1/8	15 3/8	15 3/8	8 5/8	8 2/8	29 1/8	23 1/8	Baja Calif., MX	C.J. McElroy	C.J. McElroy	1978	164
176 2/8	36 6/8	36	15 7/8	15 7/8	8 4/8	8 4/8	19 7/8	21 5/8	Baja Calif., MX	Richard Wehling	Richard Wehling	1978	168
176 2/8	35 6/8	36 6/8	14 3/8	14 3/8	8 4/8	9 6/8	23 1/8	19 4/8	Clark Co., NV	F. Lorin Ronnow	F. Lorin Ronnow	1957	168
176 2/8	38 1/8	36 6/8	15 1/8	15	10	8 4/8	22 4/8	22 4/8	Yuma Co., AZ	Vicki L. Clark	Vicki L. Clark	1980	168
176 2/8	38 2/8	36	15 3/8	15 3/8	8 4/8	8 4/8	21 5/8	21 6/8	Clark Co., NV	Christine J. Burrows	Christine J. Burrows	1981	168

DESERT SHEEP

Ovis canadensis nelsoni and certain related subspecies

Score	Length of Horn R	Length of Horn L	Circumference of Base R	Circumference of Base L	Circumference at Third Quarter R	Circumference at Third Quarter L	Greatest Spread	Tip to Tip Spread	Locality	Hunter	Owner	Date Killed	Rank
176 2/8	38 6/8	37 4/8	14 4/8	14 4/8	8 7/8	9	21	21	Pinal Co., AZ	D. Mark Exline	D. Mark Exline	1982	168
176 2/8	34	37	15 2/8	15 2/8	9 1/8	9 5/8	23	21 2/8	Clark Co., NV	Jack Oberly	Jack Oberly	1983	168
176 1/8	37 2/8	36 6/8	15	15 1/8	9 2/8	9 2/8	25 3/8	25 3/8	Baja Calif., MX	N.J. Segal, Jr.	N.J. Segal, Jr.	1972	173
176 1/8	36 6/8	36 4/8	14 6/8	15 1/8	9 3/8	9 4/8	21 6/8	20	Pinal Co., AZ	Warren A. Adams	Warren A. Adams	1985	173
176 1/8	37 7/8	38 2/8	15 1/8	15 4/8	8 3/8	8	21 5/8	21 1/8	Clark Co., NV	Tim L. Iverson	Tim L. Iverson	1985	173
176 1/8	37	34 7/8	15 6/8	16	8 4/8	8 4/8	22 4/8	22 4/8	Pima Co., AZ	Don Petersen	Don Petersen	1988	173
176	38 3/8	39 7/8	15 1/8	15 1/8	7 4/8	8 1/8	22 1/8	20 5/8	Sonora, MX	Fritz Katz	Fritz Katz	1941	177
176	37 2/8	38 2/8	14 4/8	15 1/8	9	9 4/8	25	25	Black Mts., AZ	Picked Up	R.A. Wagner	1954	177
176	37 4/8	34 2/8	15 5/8	15 5/8	9 2/8	9 2/8	21 4/8	18 4/8	Kofa Mts., AZ	Robin Underdown	Robin Underdown	1966	177
176	34 6/8	34 2/8	17 1/8	17 1/8	8 3/8	8 3/8	19 6/8	17	Sonora, MX	Ollie O. Barney	Ollie O. Barney	1968	177
176	36	36	15 4/8	15 4/8	9	9 1/8	18 2/8	18 2/8	Baja Calif., MX	Paul J. Inzanti	Paul J. Inzanti	1982	177
176	36 2/8	35 6/8	14 6/8	14 6/8	10 2/8	10	19 1/8	16 4/8	Baja Calif., MX	Pedro S. Montano	Pedro S. Montano	1986	177
175 7/8	35 7/8	35 4/8	15	15 1/8	9 7/8	9 3/8	22 4/8	22	Yuma Co., AZ	J. Don McGaffee	J. Don McGaffee	1978	183
175 7/8	39 5/8	38 6/8	14	14	8 6/8	9 2/8	22 5/8	22 5/8	Yuma Co., AZ	Fred W. Jerome	Fred W. Jerome	1979	183
175 7/8	36 7/8	37	15 2/8	15 1/8	9 4/8	9 6/8	22 4/8	19	Pinal Co., AZ	Tracy L. Contreras	Tracy L. Contreras	1980	183
175 6/8	35 5/8	36 1/8	14 1/8	14	10 2/8	10 4/8	21 2/8	17 5/8	San Diego Co., CA	Picked Up	Anza-Borrego Desert State Park	1951	186
175 6/8	35 3/8	35 3/8	16 1/8	16 3/8	8 5/8	8 3/8	18 6/8	18 6/8	Baja Calif., MX	Jack Leeds	Jack Leeds	1976	186
175 6/8	36 6/8	36 4/8	14 3/8	14 3/8	9 6/8	9 6/8	21	21	Lincoln Co., NV	Denny L. Frook	Denny L. Frook	1977	186
175 6/8	33 3/8	35 5/8	16	16	9 4/8	9 1/8	22	20 6/8	Pima Co., AZ	Robert F. Lebo	Robert F. Lebo	1977	186
175 6/8	35 2/8	35 2/8	16	16	8 7/8	9 1/8	20	17 4/8	Baja Calif., MX	William C. Cloyd	William C. Cloyd	1984	186
175 6/8	34 5/8	35 1/8	15 5/8	15 6/8	9	9 3/8	22 4/8	18 4/8	Yuma Co., AZ	Robert A. Brannan	Robert A. Brannan	1994	186
175 6/8	37 1/8	37 7/8	15 4/8	15 2/8	8 7/8	8 6/8	25 3/8	24 7/8	Clark Co., NV	David L. Mode	David L. Mode	1994	186
175 4/8	36	36 4/8	15	15 4/8	8 4/8	8 4/8	20 6/8	19 3/8	Yuma, AZ	Picked Up	Tom D. Moore	1956	193
175 4/8	37 2/8	36	15	14 4/8	9 4/8	10	21 4/8	21 4/8	Maricopa Co., AZ	Picked Up	Robert B. Thompson	1963	193
175 4/8	37 3/8	36 5/8	14 4/8	14 6/8	9 3/8	9 3/8	21 6/8	19	Baja Calif., MX	Tony Oney	Tony Oney	1968	193
175 4/8	36 4/8	37 4/8	14 7/8	14 7/8	8 7/8	8 7/8	22 3/8	21 6/8	Plomosa Mts., AZ	J. James Froelich	J. James Froelich	1969	193
175 4/8	36 3/8	36 1/8	14 3/8	14 2/8	10 1/8	10 1/8	21 6/8	18 4/8	Yuma Co., AZ	Anton E. Rimsza	Anton E. Rimsza	1982	193
175 4/8	36 6/8	36 6/8	15	15 4/8	8 5/8	8 7/8	20 7/8	17 5/8	Pima Co., AZ	David R. Howell	David R. Howell	1991	193
175 3/8	37	37 3/8	14 5/8	14 5/8	8 6/8	9 2/8	21 2/8	21 2/8	Lincoln Co., NV	Robert Fagan	Robert Fagan	1968	199
175 3/8	35 6/8	35 3/8	15 4/8	15 3/8	9 4/8	9 2/8	21 6/8	18 4/8	Plomosa Mts., AZ	M.S. MacCollum	M.S. MacCollum	1968	199
175 3/8	38 2/8	38 3/8	14 5/8	14 5/8	8 5/8	8 5/8	22	19 4/8	Yuma Co., AZ	Patrick E. Hurley	Patrick E. Hurley	1981	199
175 3/8	37 5/8	39 4/8	14	14	9 2/8	9 4/8	19 1/8	17 7/8	Baja Calif., MX	Isidro Lopez-Del Bosque	Isidro Lopez-Del Bosque	1984	199
175 2/8	37 4/8	37 4/8	14 3/8	14 3/8	9 1/8	9 4/8	21 5/8	17 3/8	Baja Calif., MX	K.C. Brown	K.C. Brown	1966	203
175 2/8	36 4/8	36 4/8	14 2/8	15 2/8	9 2/8	8 5/8	17 4/8	17 1/8	Yuma Co., AZ	Ted Phoenix	Ted Phoenix	1995	203
175 2/8	36 1/8	37 3/8	15 6/8	15 6/8	7 7/8	8 4/8	23 4/8	21 2/8	Riverside Co., CA	David E. Combs	David E. Combs	1996	203
175 1/8	36 4/8	37 3/8	15 2/8	15 1/8	8 2/8	8 5/8	19 3/8	19 3/8	Mexico	Bill Foster	Foster's Bighorn Rest.	1950	206
175 1/8	36 5/8	37 2/8	14 7/8	15	9 4/8	8 7/8	19 4/8	17 4/8	Sonora, MX	Unknown	Paul W. Hughes	1952	206
175 1/8	37 2/8	38 3/8	14 2/8	14 2/8	9 2/8	8 5/8	20 1/8	20 1/8	Lamb Springs, NV	D.B. Walkington	D.B. Walkington	1965	206

Score	Length of Horn R	Length of Horn L	Circ. of Base R	Circ. of Base L	Circ. Third Qtr R	Circ. Third Qtr L	Greatest Spread	Tip to Tip Spread	Locality	Hunter	Owner	Date Killed	Rank
175 1/8	37 1/8	37	14 6/8	14 6/8	9 5/8	9 2/8	25 7/8	25 7/8	Clark Co., NV	Wayne C. Matley	Wayne C. Matley	1966	206
175 1/8	37 1/8	37 1/8	13 7/8	13 7/8	8 6/8	9 3/8	20 5/8	22 6/8	Riverside Co., CA	Picked Up	George F. Stewart, Jr.	PR 1967	206
175 1/8	36 6/8	35 5/8	15 2/8	15 2/8	8 7/8	8 7/8	31 1/8	18 6/8	Baja Calif., MX	C.J. Wimer	C.J. Wimer	1977	206
175 1/8	36 4/8	37 3/8	15 2/8	15 2/8	8 4/8	8 4/8	23 1/8	23 1/8	Clark Co., NV	Lenda Z. Azcarate	Lenda Z. Azcarate	1979	206
175 1/8	36 2/8	36 1/8	15	15 1/8	9	9 6/8	23 7/8	23 7/8	Clark Co., NV	Lloyd G. Bare	Lloyd G. Bare	1980	206
175 1/8	34 4/8	36 5/8	15 2/8	15 2/8	10 5/8	10 1/8	23 2/8	22	San Bernardino Co., CA	William J. Conner	William J. Conner	1989	206
175	34 2/8	34 7/8	15	15	10	9 2/8	21 6/8	20	Sonora, MX	Arthur D. Bailey	Arthur D. Bailey	1993	216
175	35	36	15 3/8	15 3/8	8 4/8	8 7/8	22 4/8	22 4/8	Yuma Co., AZ	Juan A. Saenz, Jr.	Juan A. Saenz, Jr.	1969	216
175	37 4/8	33 6/8	15	15	9 2/8	9 6/8	20 4/8	18 4/8	Clark Co., NV	Harry B. Cook	Harry B. Cook	1982	216
175	37 4/8	37 6/8	14 6/8	14 6/8	9 5/8	8 6/8	26 6/8	26 6/8	Baja Calif., MX	Timothy P. Ryan	Timothy P. Ryan	1983	216
175	35 6/8	36 4/8	15	15	9 3/8	9 4/8	20 6/8	20 2/8	Pima, AZ	Craig Leerberg	Craig Leerberg	1990	216
174 7/8	37	35 1/8	13 5/8	13 5/8	9 3/8	9 4/8	20 3/8	19 6/8	Arizona	Picked Up	Robert J. Kirkpatrick	PR 1968	220
174 7/8	37 1/8	37	15 6/8	15 7/8	8 7/8	9 4/8	23 3/8	21	Clark Co., NV	Picked Up	Nathan Frisby	1974	220
174 7/8	35 1/8	38 4/8	15 6/8	15 6/8	8 6/8	8 5/8	23 5/8	23 1/8	Clark Co., NV	Herman H. Storey, Jr.	Herman S. Storey, Jr.	1980	220
174 7/8	35 7/8	35	15 6/8	15 6/8	9 1/8	9 3/8	19 6/8	19 6/8	Clark Co., NV	Cleldon E. Nelson	Cleldon E. Nelson	1987	220
174 6/8	41 4/8	35 4/8	13 6/8	13 6/8	8 7/8	9 4/8	29	29	Clark Co., NV	Michael J. Ellena	Michael J. Ellena	1993	225
174 6/8	39	41 7/8	15	15	8 1/8	8 7/8	22 1/8	0	Barstow, CA	Picked Up	Thomas Hodges	1941	225
174 6/8	34 6/8	38 4/8	14 7/8	14 7/8	10 1/8	8 6/8	25 4/8	25 4/8	Clark Co., NV	Ron W. Biggs	Ron W. Biggs	1980	225
174 5/8	37 4/8	34 6/8	15 6/8	15 6/8	8 6/8	9 1/8	21 4/8	17	Pima Co., AZ	Collins L. Cochran	Collins L. Cochran	1992	228
174 5/8	34 7/8	35 4/8	15 7/8	15 7/8	9 2/8	9 3/8	18 7/8	21 4/8	Baja Calif., MX	Stanley S. Gray	Stanley S. Gray	1972	228
174 4/8	34 6/8	34 6/8	14 6/8	14	9 3/8	9 3/8	25 1/8	18 7/8	Clark Co., NV	Roseanne K. Wilkinson	Roseanne K. Wilkinson	1980	230
174 4/8	36 4/8	37 5/8	14 2/8	14 2/8	9 4/8	9 4/8	19 4/8	25 1/8	Maricopa Co., AZ	Picked Up	Robert B. Thompson	1963	230
174 4/8	36	36	15 2/8	15 5/8	8 3/8	7 5/8	20 6/8	19 4/8	Baja Calif., MX	Jack Walters	Jack Walters	1966	230
174 3/8	37 2/8	36 6/8	15 5/8	15 5/8	7 6/8	7 6/8	25 7/8	20 6/8	Clark Co., NV	Stanley R. Galvin, Jr.	Stanley R. Galvin, Jr.	1983	234
174 2/8	36 6/8	37 2/8	14 4/8	14 4/8	9 1/8	9	21 4/8	26 2/8	Clark Co., NV	Larry G. Marshall	Larry G. Marshall	1983	235
174 2/8	38 1/8	38 4/8	14 4/8	14 4/8	7 6/8	7 6/8	24 4/8	18 5/8	Baja Calif., MX	Kathy E. Seaberg	K.E. & G. Seaberg	1981	235
174 2/8	37	36	15 7/8	15 7/8	7 5/8	7 6/8	20 4/8	23 5/8	Las Vegas, NV	Basil C. Bradbury	Basil C. Bradbury	1968	235
174 2/8	37	38 2/8	14 1/8	14	10 1/8	10 1/8	21 7/8	18 3/8	Mohave Co., AZ	Thomas R. McElhenney	Thomas R. McElhenney	1969	235
174 2/8	35 3/8	36 1/8	14 7/8	14 7/8	9 7/8	9 7/8	25 5/8	21 7/8	Lincoln Co., NV	Susan C. Nelson	Susan C. Nelson	1979	235
174	36 1/8	35 6/8	15 3/8	15 6/8	8 3/8	8 1/8	26	25 5/8	Mohave Co., AZ	Larry M. Evans	Larry M. Evans	1982	241
174	35 6/8	40 4/8	14 4/8	15	9 3/8	9 3/8	30 3/8	26	Maricopa Co., AZ	Howard Grounds	Howard Grounds	1984	241
174	40 4/8	33 4/8	15 4/8	15 3/8	9 4/8	9 4/8	24 4/8	30 1/8	Lower Calif., MX	Debi L. Adair	Debi L. Adair	1987	241
174	33 4/8	38 4/8	15 4/8	14 4/8	7 6/8	7 4/8	25 2/8	21 6/8	Yuma, AZ	E.W. Funcke	Harvard Univ. Mus.	1911	241
174	38 4/8	40	15 2/8	15 4/8	8	8	21 5/8	25 2/8	Sonora, MX	Wynn Robestal	U.S. Fish & Wild. Serv.	1913	241
174	36 4/8	37 4/8	15 6/8	15 5/8	9 5/8	9 6/8	19 4/8	21	McCullough Mts., NV	Frank C. Hibben	Frank C. Hibben	1940	241
174	37 2/8	36 2/8	15 2/8	15 2/8	9 1/8	9 1/8	24 4/8	18	Pima Co., AZ	Picked Up	William H. Pogue	PR 1958	241
173 7/8	36 6/8	37 4/8	14 3/8	14 2/8	8 7/8	8 7/8	22	24 4/8	Baja Calif., MX	George Martin	George Martin	1978	249
173 7/8	37 4/8	37 1/8	14 3/8	14 3/8	10 1/8	10 2/8	23	20	Clark Co., NV	James W. Owens	James W. Owens	1983	249
173 7/8	31 6/8	34 4/8	14 5/8	14 3/8	8 4/8	8 4/8	22	23	La Paz Co., AZ	H. James Tonkin, Jr.	H. James Tonkin, Jr.	1990	249
173 7/8	36 3/8	35 1/8	13 1/8	13 4/8	10 2/8	10 4/8	22 1/8	17 5/8	Kofa Mts., AZ	Craig R. Johnson	Craig R. Johnson	1993	249
173 6/8	37 2/8	38 2/8	15 6/8	15 6/8	9 1/8	9 1/8	24 5/8	18	La Paz Co., AZ	William L. Snider	William L. Snider	1965	254
173 6/8	35 5/8	35 5/8	14 6/8	14 6/8	8 6/8	8 6/8	22 2/8	19 3/8	Anza-Borrego Desert, CA	Picked Up	Anza-Borrego Desert State Park	1971	254
173 6/8	37 2/8	37	15	15	9 3/8	9 3/8	22 5/8	22 2/8	Baja Calif., MX	Erwin Dykstra	Erwin Dykstra	1978	254
173 6/8	36 5/8	36 5/8	15 3/8	15 3/8	9 2/8	9 3/8	20	22 5/8	Yuma Co., AZ	John C. Marsalla	John C. Marsalla	1982	254
173 6/8	34 7/8	34 6/8	14 2/8	14 2/8	10 2/8	10 2/8	18 3/8	21 4/8	Sonora, MX	A. Oscar Carlson	A. Oscar Carlson	1996	254
173 6/8	37	37	14 4/8	14 6/8	8	8	22 4/8	17 5/8	Yuma Co., AZ	Picked Up	Bob Housholder	1953	254
173 6/8	37 5/8	37 5/8	16 2/8	16 2/8	8 4/8	8 4/8	20 5/8	20 5/8	Baja Calif., MX	Fritz A. Nachant	Fritz A. Nachant	1969	254

Score	Length of Horn R	L	Circumference of Base R	L	Circumference at Third Quarter R	L	Greatest Spread	Tip to Tip Spread	Locality	Hunter	Owner	Date Killed	Rank
173 6/8	36 2/8	35 6/8	15 6/8	15 7/8	8	7 5/8	22 4/8	23	Mohave Co., AZ	Steve Clonts	Steve Clonts	1991	254
173 5/8	37	37 1/8	15 1/8	15 3/8	8 4/8	8 6/8	20 7/8	20 4/8	Baja Calif., MX	James H. Duke, Jr.	James H. Duke, Jr.	1969	257
173 5/8	35 4/8	34 5/8	15 1/8	15 1/8	9	8 7/8	22 2/8	22 2/8	Baja Calif., MX	John H. Batten	John H. Batten	1975	257
173 5/8	37 1/8	36 6/8	15 1/8	15	8 6/8	8 6/8	23 4/8	23 4/8	Clark Co., NV	Buddy H. Fujii	Buddy H. Fujii	1980	257
173 5/8	36 6/8	34 5/8	15 2/8	15 1/8	9 3/8	8 7/8	24 4/8	19 7/8	Yuma Co., AZ	David C. Root	David C. Root	1983	257
173 5/8	37 1/8	34 2/8	15 2/8	15	9	9	19 2/8	15 1/8	Sonora, MX	Douglas G. Williams	Douglas G. Williams	1983	257
173 5/8	37 3/8	36 2/8	14 4/8	14 4/8	8 3/8	8 3/8	22	21 3/8	Baja Calif., MX	Patrick C. Allen	Patrick C. Allen	1987	257
173 5/8	37 5/8	36 6/8	-14 6/8	14 5/8	8 2/8	8 3/8	21 6/8	20 4/8	Clark Co., NV	Dale O. Millerin	Dale O. Millerin	1987	257
173 5/8	35 4/8	36 3/8	14 6/8	15 4/8	8 2/8	8 7/8	21	20 4/8	Baja Calif., MX	John P. Reilly	John P. Reilly	1989	257
173 4/8	35 4/8	36 6/8	15 5/8	15 6/8	8 1/8	8	21 3/8	21 3/8	Muleje Baja, MX	Victor M. Ruiza	Victor M. Ruiza	1966	265
173 4/8	35	33 4/8	16	16	8 4/8	8 2/8	23 1/8	23 1/8	Clark Co., NV	Ira H. Kent	Ira H. Kent	1978	265
173 4/8	34 6/8	33 6/8	16 2/8	16 2/8	8 2/8	9	19 7/8	15	Sonora, MX	Walter Snoke	Walter Snoke	1978	265
173 4/8	34	33 4/8	15 4/8	15 4/8	9 4/8	9 4/8	25 7/8	25 4/8	Mohave Co., AZ	Gordon M. Osborn	Gordon M. Osborn	1989	265
173 4/8	33 7/8	35 7/8	14 4/8	14 3/8	10	10 5/8	20 5/8	17 7/8	San Bernardino Co., CA	Jerry K. Chandler	Jerry K. Chandler	1993	265
173 4/8	33 5/8	33 7/8	16 2/8	16 3/8	8 7/8	8 7/8	20 3/8	20	Sonora, MX	Robert E. Manger	Robert E. Manger	1993	265
173 4/8	34 4/8	34 2/8	15 6/8	15 6/8	8 6/8	8 7/8	24 1/8	24 1/8	Nye Co., NV	Seth Puryear	Seth Puryear	1995	265
173 3/8	36 6/8	36 1/8	14 5/8	14 5/8	8 6/8	8 5/8	21 1/8	17 7/8	Baja Calif., MX	M. Alessio Robles	M. Alessio Robles	1956	272
173 3/8	36 2/8	36 3/8	15 5/8	15 5/8	8 1/8	8 2/8	21 3/8	20 3/8	Sonora, MX	Gaston Cano	Gaston Cano	1968	272
173 3/8	36 6/8	37 3/8	14 6/8	14 7/8	8 6/8	8 4/8	22 3/8	22 3/8	Baja Calif., MX	Roy A. Schultz	Roy A. Schultz	1971	272
173 3/8	37	37 7/8	15	15 1/8	8 4/8	8 6/8	22	22	Baja Calif., MX	Dale R. Leonard	Dale R. Leonard	1972	272
173 3/8	40 5/8	38	13 7/8	14 6/8	8 2/8	8 1/8	0	0	Baja Calif., MX	Tim C. Boyd	Tim C. Boyd	1981	272
173 3/8	36	36 3/8	15 3/8	15 3/8	8 2/8	8 3/8	21 6/8	19 1/8	Mohave Co., AZ	Donald E. Franklin	Donald E. Franklin	1982	272
173 3/8	36 4/8	35 1/8	14 6/8	14 7/8	8 7/8	9	23 4/8	22 5/8	Maricopa Co., AZ	James D. Thorne	James D. Thorne	1989	272
173 2/8	34 7/8	35 3/8	15 4/8	15 4/8	8 6/8	8 5/8	25 3/8	25 3/8	Little Horn Mts., AZ	Joseph J. Sobotka	Joseph J. Sobotka	1969	279
173 2/8	36 3/8	36 1/8	15 5/8	15 2/8	8 4/8	8 2/8	21 4/8	19 6/8	Baja Calif., MX	Ernest Righetti	Ernest Righetti	1974	279
173 2/8	35 2/8	34 6/8	15 4/8	14 5/8	8 6/8	8 6/8	21 5/8	21 5/8	Baja Calif., MX	Marion H. Scott	Marion H. Scott	1978	279
173 2/8	35 4/8	35 6/8	15 1/8	15 1/8	8 6/8	9 1/8	26 1/8	25 4/8	Lincoln Co., NV	Ken G. Gerg	Ken G. Gerg	1990	279
173 2/8	36 4/8	35 4/8	15 5/8	15 6/8	8 5/8	9 2/8	23 4/8	20 6/8	Pima Co., AZ	Ben H. Mattausch	Ben H. Mattausch	1994	279
173 1/8	37 1/8	35 2/8	14 1/8	14 5/8	9 4/8	9	21	21	Little Horn Mts., AZ	Picked Up	Duane J. Hall	1960	284
173 1/8	37 5/8	32 6/8	14 6/8	14 6/8	9	11	25 4/8	25 4/8	Lincoln Co., NV	Picked Up	Billy D. Stoddard	1965	284
173 1/8	32 6/8	30 7/8	15 4/8	15 3/8	11	11 6/8	24 4/8	23	Tulelake, CA	Picked Up	Natl. Park Service	1968	284
173 1/8	37 4/8	40 1/8	14	13 1/8	7 7/8	9 7/8	21 3/8	18	Sonora Desert, MX	Picked Up	Herb Klein	1969	284
173 1/8	37 1/8	37	14 3/8	14 4/8	9 1/8	8 3/8	27 5/8	27 5/8	Clark Co., NV	Chris Hurtado	Chris Hurtado	1975	284
173 1/8	36 5/8	36	14 7/8	14 7/8	9 5/8	9 5/8	24	24	Lincoln Co., NV	Michael D. Rowe	Michael D. Rowe	1988	284
173 1/8	35 6/8	36 5/8	14 5/8	14 5/8	8 7/8	8 7/8	20 3/8	16 4/8	Yuma Co., AZ	Robert S. Holyoak	Robert S. Holyoak	1994	284
173	36	38	15	15	8 2/8	8 4/8	24 4/8	21 4/8	Lower Calif., MX	Henry H. Blagden	Henry H. Blagden	1914	291
173	36 1/8	38 3/8	14 6/8	14 6/8	8 4/8	9 1/8	19 1/8	19 1/8	Sheep Mt. Range, NV	Gilbert A. Helsel	Gilbert A. Helsel	1960	291
173	36	35 2/8	14 3/8	14 3/8	9 4/8	9	21 6/8	16 6/8	Aguila Mts., AZ	Picked Up	C.G. Clare	1961	291

Score								Locality	By Whom Killed	Owner	Date	Rank
173	35 6/8	15 1/8	15 4/8	8 7/8	8 3/8	20 7/8	20 1/8	Baja Calif., MX	James H. Russell	James H. Russell	1970	291
173	37 1/8	13 6/8	14	10 3/8	10 5/8	20	17 5/8	Maricopa Co., AZ	Stephen K. Weisser	Stephen K. Weisser	1973	291
173	39	15	15	8 3/8	8 3/8	24	24	Baja Calif., MX	Charles Oyer	Charles Oyer	1975	291
173	35	15 5/8	15 6/8	8 2/8	8 3/8	20 4/8	17 2/8	Baja Calif., MX	P. Franklin Bays, Jr.	P. Franklin Bays, Jr.	1976	291
173	35 1/8	16	16 1/8	8 1/8	8 1/8	20 2/8	19 4/8	Baja Calif., MX	Tom W. Housh	Tom W. Housh	1988	291
173	35 4/8	15 3/8	15 3/8	9 4/8	9 4/8	21 3/8	21 3/8	Maricopa Co., AZ	Jim L. Boyer	Jim L. Boyer	1993	291
173	34	15 2/8	15 3/8	8 6/8	8 5/8	21 4/8	20 4/8	Cochise Co., AZ	Jon A. Ancell	Jon A. Ancell	1997	291
172 7/8	34 1/8	15	15 2/8	9 3/8	9 3/8	20 5/8	19 4/8	Baja Calif., MX	Mahlon T. White	Mahlon T. White	1969	301
172 7/8	34 1/8	15	15	9 7/8	9 5/8	22 1/8	22 1/8	Gila Co., AZ	Picked Up	Michael T. Miller	1990	301
172 7/8	35 1/8	14 4/8	14 4/8	10	10	22	22	Clark Co., NV	William R. Slattery	William R. Slattery	1992	301
172 6/8	38 5/8	13 4/8	13 5/8	9	9	23 7/8	23 7/8	Baja Calif., MX	Otis Chandler	Otis Chandler	1966	304
172 6/8	37 1/8	15 5/8	15 7/8	8 7/8	8 7/8	21 2/8	21 2/8	Baja Calif., MX	Graciano Guichard	Graciano Guichard	1969	304
172 6/8	36 3/8	14 3/8	14 3/8	8 4/8	8 4/8	20 3/8	20 3/8	Yuma Co., AZ	Norman F. Mathews	Norman F. Mathews	1977	304
172 6/8	36	15 3/8	15 5/8	8 5/8	8 2/8	19 1/8	19	Pima Co., AZ	Paul H. Harrison	Paul H. Harrison	1981	304
172 6/8	36 4/8	13 7/8	14	9 6/8	10 1/8	19 6/8	19 6/8	Yuma Co., AZ	Larry J. Landes	Larry J. Landes	1981	304
172 6/8	36 5/8	14 3/8	14 2/8	8 2/8	8 4/8	24 5/8	24 5/8	Gila Co., AZ	Byron Wiley	Byron Wiley	1986	304
172 6/8	37 2/8	14 2/8	14 3/8	8 7/8	8 1/8	19 1/8	19 1/8	Gila Co., AZ	Richard P. Carlsberg	Richard P. Carlsberg	1989	304
172 6/8	35	15 2/8	15 3/8	9 2/8	9 2/8	20 6/8	20 6/8	Sonora, MX	Lloyd O. Barrow	Lloyd O. Barrow	1969	304
172 5/8	36 4/8	14 4/8	14 4/8	10	9 6/8	19 6/8	19 6/8	Baja Calif., MX	G. David Edwards	G. David Edwards	1973	311
172 5/8	36	15 5/8	15 4/8	8	8	21 3/8	21 3/8	Baja Calif., MX	Daniel Smith	Daniel Smith	1975	311
172 5/8	35 2/8	15 2/8	15 2/8	9	8 3/8	19 2/8	19 2/8	Clark Co., NV	Charles W. Knittle	Charles W. Knittle	1976	311
172 5/8	40 3/8	13 3/8	12 6/8	8 2/8	8 6/8	26 5/8	26 5/8	White Mts., CA	Picked Up	Danny Lowe	1978	311
172 4/8	36 2/8	14 6/8	15 5/8	8 3/8	8 3/8	22 1/8	22 1/8	Yuma Co., AZ	Margaret Wood	Margaret Wood	1958	316
172 4/8	36	14 4/8	15	8 4/8	8 4/8	23	23	Yuma Co., AZ	Picked Up	Donald Ogan	1964	316
172 4/8	40	14 5/8	14 4/8	7 6/8	8	25	25	Clark Co., NV	Scott D. Oxborrow	Scott D. Oxborrow	1983	316
172 4/8	33 4/8	15 1/8	15 3/8	9 3/8	9 2/8	21 4/8	21 4/8	Baja Calif., MX	Hector Aguilar Parada	Hector Aguilar Parada	1985	316
172 4/8	37 2/8	15 4/8	15 4/8	8	8	25 5/8	25 5/8	Yuma Co., AZ	William J. Paul	William J. Paul	1987	316
172 4/8	36 4/8	14 1/8	14 1/8	9 3/8	8 6/8	29 5/8	29 5/8	Mohave Co., AZ	Densel M. Strang	Densel M. Strang	1989	316
172 3/8	35 6/8	14 7/8	14 7/8	9 5/8	9 5/8	20 3/8	20 3/8	Lincoln Co., NV	Craig S. Boyack	Craig S. Boyack	1990	324
172 3/8	36 2/8	14 4/8	14 3/8	9	8 7/8	23 6/8	23 6/8	Coconino Co., AZ	Frank J. Tucek	Frank J. Tucek	1993	324
172 3/8	34 6/8	15 1/8	15	9 6/8	9 6/8	21 5/8	21 5/8	Sauceda Mts., AZ	Wayne Grippin	Wayne Grippin	1962	324
172 3/8	32 5/8	15 2/8	15	9 2/8	9	23 1/8	23 1/8	Clark Co., NV	Ronald L. Giovanetti	Ronald L. Giovanetti	1980	324
172 3/8	34 6/8	14 5/8	15 2/8	9 4/8	9	20 1/8	20 1/8	Baja Calif., MX	H. Varley Grantham	H. Varley Grantham	1980	324
172 2/8	35 1/8	14 3/8	14 5/8	9 5/8	9 4/8	21 2/8	21 2/8	Clark Co., NV	John F. Lohse	John F. Lohse	1982	329
172 2/8	36 3/8	14 7/8	14 7/8	9 5/8	8 4/8	16 2/8	20 2/8	Pima Co., AZ	Loren G. Pederson, Jr.	Loren G. Pederson, Jr.	1985	329
172 2/8	38	16 1/8	15	7 3/8	7 4/8	27 1/8	27 1/8	Baja Calif., MX	W.E. Humphrey	WA State Mus.	1909	329
172 2/8	36 5/8	15 4/8	15 1/8	8 5/8	8 6/8	20 2/8	20 2/8	Baja Calif., MX	Herb Klein	Herb Klein	1966	329
172 2/8	35 2/8	15 3/8	15 4/8	8 6/8	9	19 1/8	19 1/8	Baja Calif., MX	Armando de la Parra	Armando de la Parra	1966	329
172 2/8	35	14 2/8	14 8/8	8 6/8	8 5/8	22 6/8	22 6/8	Clark Co., NV	Ralph A. Shoberg	Ralph A. Shoberg	1986	329
172 2/8	37 1/8	14 4/8	14 2/8	8 7/8	8 4/8	22 2/8	22 2/8	Baja Calif., MX	Verner J. Fisher, Jr.	Verner J. Fisher, Jr.	1988	329
172 2/8	35 3/8	15 1/8	15 3/8	9	8 7/8	19 6/8	22 2/8	Clark Co., NV	Fred Fortier	Fred Fortier	1989	329
172 2/8	36 4/8	14	13 7/8	10	10 1/8	21 8/8	21 1/8	Baja Calif., MX	Nicholas J. Coussoulis	Nicholas J. Coussoulis	1990	329
172 1/8	36	15	15 2/8	8 4/8	8 4/8	14	23	Kofa Range, AZ	Picked Up	AZ Game & Fish Dept.	1953	336
172 1/8	35 3/8	14 5/8	14 3/8	9 3/8	9 2/8	21 4/8	22 6/8	Clark Co., NV	Robert F. Sievert	Robert F. Sievert	1985	336
172 1/8	35 5/8	14 7/8	14 6/8	8 6/8	9 2/8	20 4/8	20 7/8	Baja Calif., MX	Greg A. Strait	Greg A. Strait	1989	336
172	33	15	15	8 4/8	8 6/8	30 2/8	30 2/8	Tulelake, CA	Picked Up	Natl. Park Service	1963	339
172	34 6/8	15	15	8 7/8	8 7/8	20 6/8	20 6/8	Baja Calif., MX	Robert O. Cromwell	Robert O. Cromwell	1974	339

DESERT SHEEP

Ovis canadensis nelsoni and certain related subspecies

Score	Length of Horn R	L	Circumference of Base R	L	Circumference at Third Quarter R	L	Greatest Spread	Tip tp Tip Spread	Locality	Hunter	Owner	Date Killed	Rank
172	34 5/8	34 5/8	16 4/8	16 1/8	8 3/8	8 5/8	21 3/8	20 3/8	Baja Calif., MX	Bill Silveira	Bill Silveira	1974	339
172	36 4/8	36	14 2/8	14 3/8	9 3/8	9 2/8	22 4/8	22 4/8	Clark Co., NV	Mike W. Steele	Mike W. Steele	1986	339
172	34	36 4/8	14 6/8	14 4/8	9 4/8	9 3/8	23 3/8	22 5/8	Clark Co., NV	Jerry J. Long	Jerry J. Long	1987	339
172	36 7/8	37 3/8	15 1/8	14 7/8	8 5/8	8 6/8	25 7/8	25 7/8	Clark Co., NV	Dan Pocapalia	Dan Pocapalia	1988	339
172	35	35	15 4/8	15 3/8	8 2/8	8 2/8	22 1/8	24 6/8	Lincoln Co., NV	Gary R. Quarisa	Gary R. Quarisa	1993	339
171 7/8	33 1/8	32 6/8	16 1/8	15 7/8	8 6/8	8 6/8	19 7/8	17 7/8	Baja Calif., MX	Joan Leeds	Joan Leeds	1976	346
171 7/8	33 7/8	35 2/8	15 2/8	15 4/8	9 7/8	9 7/8	22 1/8	21 4/8	Baja Calif., MX	Don L. Corley	Don L. Corley	1978	346
171 7/8	35 3/8	36 2/8	15	15	9	9 1/8	20 2/8	18 2/8	Graham Co., AZ	Roger J. Stolp	Roger J. Stolp	1985	346
171 7/8	34 7/8	33 2/8	15 6/8	15 4/8	8 7/8	9 4/8	21 5/8	18 4/8	La Paz Co., AZ	Robert M.H. Gray	Robert M.H. Gray	1987	346
171 7/8	36 6/8	36 3/8	14	14 3/8	9 2/8	9 3/8	22 7/8	21 5/8	Clark Co., NV	John R. Chase	John R. Chase	1990	346
171 7/8	36 4/8	35 3/8	15 1/8	15 2/8	8 1/8	8 2/8	21 5/8	21 5/8	Yuma Co., AZ	John F. Heskett	John F. Heskett	1990	346
171 6/8	37 2/8	36 4/8	14	13 4/8	9 5/8	9 4/8	20 1/8	20 1/8	Kofa Range, AZ	Harvey Davison	Harvey Davison	1953	352
171 6/8	36 4/8	36	15 6/8	15 6/8	7 6/8	8 3/8	21	18 2/8	Baja Calif., MX	Earl H. Harris	Earl H. Harris	1968	352
171 6/8	35 6/8	35 2/8	14	14	10	10 1/8	23	20 7/8	Lincoln Co., NV	William A. Molini	William A. Molini	1977	352
171 5/8	38 6/8	38 1/8	15 5/8	15 4/8	7	7	23	23	Sonora, MX	Julio Estrada	Julio Estrada	1931	355
171 5/8	33 3/8	35	15 4/8	15 5/8	8 6/8	8 7/8	20	18 4/8	Baja Calif., MX	Dan L. Quen	Dan L. Quen	1968	355
171 5/8	35 3/8	35 4/8	15 2/8	15 4/8	8 7/8	8 7/8	21 4/8	20	Baja Calif., MX	Roberto M. del Campo	Roberto M. del Campo	1969	355
171 5/8	35 6/8	35 3/8	14 7/8	15	9 1/8	8 7/8	19 3/8	19 3/8	Baja Calif., MX	C.J. McElroy	C.J. McElroy	1969	355
171 5/8	36 4/8	36 3/8	14 3/8	14 5/8	8 7/8	8 5/8	21 4/8	21 4/8	Sonora, MX	Picked Up	Robert C. Jones	1970	355
171 5/8	34 3/8	32 4/8	15 3/8	15 4/8	9 3/8	9 6/8	21 7/8	20 4/8	Clark Co., NV	Edward M. Evans	Edward M. Evans	1977	355
171 5/8	35 3/8	35 4/8	14 5/8	14 6/8	9 3/8	9	20 5/8	20 5/8	Clark Co., NV	George Hueftle	George Hueftle	1977	355
171 5/8	34 6/8	34 7/8	14 7/8	15	9	8 4/8	22 3/8	18	Yuma Co., AZ	Miles R. Brown	Miles R. Brown	1989	355
171 5/8	33 2/8	33 3/8	15 1/8	15 2/8	9 6/8	10 2/8	22	23 6/8	Lincoln Co., NV	James D. Buonamici	James D. Buonamici	1989	355
171 5/8	36 7/8	34 2/8	16 2/8	16 2/8	7 6/8	7 5/8	20 5/8	19 7/8	Baja Calif., MX	Marshall J. Collins, Jr.	Marshall J. Collins, Jr.	1994	355
171 4/8	35 1/8	34 7/8	14	14	10 2/8	10	19 4/8	19 4/8	Bullion Mts., CA	Picked Up	Fred L. Jones	1950	365
171 4/8	37 4/8	37 6/8	13 6/8	13 6/8	8 3/8	8 3/8	23	22 6/8	Clark Co., NV	Jerry P. Devin	Jerry P. Devin	1976	365
171 4/8	33 6/8	35	15 1/8	15 1/8	8 6/8	9 2/8	21 4/8	20 2/8	Maricopa Co., AZ	Unknown	Clarence House	PR 1979	365
171 4/8	35 4/8	35	14 4/8	14 4/8	10	10	21 4/8	20 4/8	San Bernardino Co., CA	Leon A. Pimentel	Leon A. Pimentel	1989	365
171 3/8	36 7/8	36 4/8	14 3/8	14 3/8	8 5/8	8 4/8	22 2/8	22 2/8	Anvil Mt., AZ	George Stewart, Jr.	George Stewart, Jr.	1961	369
171 3/8	34 2/8	34 3/8	15 5/8	15 6/8	8 2/8	8 5/8	19 7/8	16 1/8	Crater Mts., AZ	Raymond I. Skipper, Jr.	Raymond I. Skipper, Jr.	1971	369
171 3/8	38 1/8	37	14	14 2/8	9	8 6/8	24	23 5/8	Clark Co., NV	Daniel T. Magee	Daniel T. Magee	1980	369
171 3/8	37 6/8	38 1/8	14 1/8	14 2/8	9	9 2/8	26	25	Lincoln Co., NV	Roy F. Lerg	Roy D. Lerg	1984	369
171 3/8	35 3/8	35 2/8	13 7/8	14 1/8	9 1/8	9 5/8	23 5/8	24 2/8	Mojave Co., NV	Picked Up	Dan Priest	1985	369
171 3/8	35 5/8	37	16 5/8	16 4/8	7 5/8	7 2/8	19 5/8	19 4/8	Baja Calif., MX	Milton Schultz, Jr.	Milton Schultz, Jr.	1995	369
171 2/8	35 2/8	35 6/8	14 2/8	14 3/8	8 6/8	9 2/8	21 2/8	18 3/8	Growler Mts., AZ	David E. Brown	David E. Brown	1967	369
171 2/8	35 1/8	36 7/8	14 4/8	14 4/8	8 6/8	8 5/8	20 2/8	20 2/8	Clark Co., NV	Bill R. Balsi, Jr.	Bill R. Balsi, Jr.	1979	375
171 2/8	34 4/8	35	15 4/8	14 3/8	8 2/8	8 4/8	24	24	Baja Calif., MX	David L. Harshbarger	David L. Harshbarger	1983	375
171 2/8	38	38 2/8	14 6/8	14 3/8	9 3/8	9 4/8	21 6/8	21 4/8	Yuma Co., AZ	Lauren W. Hogan	Lauren W. Hogan	1984	375

Score									Locality	Owner	By Whom Taken	Date	Rank
171 2/8	35 2/8	35 6/8	15	14 7/8	9 3/8	9 1/8	17 3/8	21	Baja Calif., MX	L. Irvin Barnhart	L. Irvin Barnhart	1992	375
171 2/8	34 6/8	34 6/8	15 4/8	15 4/8	8 3/8	8 1/8	20 4/8	21 1/8	Coconino Co., AZ	Merlynn K. Jones	Merlynn K. Jones	1994	375
171 1/8	35 4/8	35 1/8	16 4/8	16 4/8	7 6/8	7 2/8	19 1/8	19 1/8	Yuma Co., AZ	Elizabeth Barganski	Elizabeth Barganski	1959	381
171 1/8	36 4/8	36 7/8	14 3/8	14 4/8	8 2/8	8 3/8	19 7/8	22 2/8	Palomas Mts., AZ	James F. Pierce	James F. Pierce	1967	381
171 1/8	35 2/8	35 3/8	15	14 7/8	9 2/8	8 6/8	25 2/8	25 2/8	Clark Co., NV	Ray W. Diehl	Ray W. Diehl	1979	381
171 1/8	36 6/8	36 6/8	15	15	8 1/8	8 3/8	22	22	Yuma Co., AZ	Robert J. Cordes III	Robert J. Cordes III	1988	381
171 1/8	37 4/8	33 4/8	14 5/8	14 6/8	8 7/8	8 1/8	22 6/8	23 1/8	Mohave Co., AZ	Gary C. Bateman	Gary C. Bateman	1991	381
171 1/8	36 2/8	35 1/8	15	15	8 1/8	8 6/8	18	21	Yuma Co., AZ	Robert J. Zent	Robert J. Zent	1991	381
171 1/8	36 1/8	35 6/8	13 7/8	13 6/8	8 5/8	8 1/8	23 2/8	23 4/8	Churchill Co., NV	Vincent L. Euse	Vincent L. Euse	1993	381
171 1/8	37 5/8	37 4/8	15	15 1/8	8 5/8	8 3/8	24 4/8	25	Mohave Co., AZ	Donald G. McMurry	Donald G. McMurry	1993	381
171 1/8	34 6/8	34 5/8	15 1/8	15 1/8	8 4/8	8 4/8	25	24	Mohave Co., AZ	William H. Smith	William H. Smith	1995	381
171	36	36 2/8	14 3/8	14 4/8	8 7/8	8 6/8	19 4/8	20 3/8	Sauceda Mts., AZ	Kelly S. Neal, Jr.	Kelly S. Neal, Jr.	1969	390
171	36 2/8	35 4/8	14 4/8	14 6/8	8 6/8	9 3/8	22 1/8	22 1/8	Baja Calif., MX	George S. Gayle III	George S. Gayle III	1975	390
171	36 4/8	36 1/8	14 5/8	14 7/8	9 3/8	8 5/8	21 4/8	23 1/8	Clark Co., NV	Richard A. Bell	Richard A. Bell	1986	390
171	36 1/8	37 1/8	14 7/8	14 7/8	8 5/8	8 5/8	17	18 3/8	Pima Co., AZ	Don J. Parks, Jr.	Don J. Parks, Jr.	1986	390
171	35 5/8	35 4/8	14 2/8	14 5/8	7 7/8	8 1/8	24 4/8	24 4/8	Clark Co., NV	Toni M. Venturacci	Toni M. Venturacci	1986	390
171	37 5/8	37 1/8	14 7/8	15	7 7/8	8 2/8	26	26 5/8	Mohave Co., AZ	Michael L. Gwaltney	Michael L. Gwaltney	1990	390
171	36 1/8	35 4/8	15 1/8	15 3/8	8 2/8	8 6/8	27 2/8	27 2/8	Mohave Co., AZ	Tanner D. Henry	Tanner D. Henry	1994	390
170 7/8	35 4/8	35 4/8	16	16	8	8 1/8	22 5/8	22 5/8	Sonora Desert, MX	Herb Klein	Herb Klein	1962	397
170 7/8	35 5/8	35 4/8	14	14 2/8	9 3/8	8 2/8	21 5/8	21 5/8	Baja Calif., MX	Michaux Nash, Jr.	Michaux Nash, Jr.	1964	397
170 7/8	38 1/8	36 4/8	14 4/8	14 4/8	9 7/8	9 5/8	17 6/8	19 2/8	Baja Calif., MX	John T. Blackwell	John T. Blackwell	1966	397
170 7/8	32 7/8	37	15	15	8 2/8	8	21 4/8	21 4/8	Baja Calif., MX	Daniel B. Moore	Daniel B. Moore	1979	397
170 7/8	36 5/8	36 1/8	15 3/8	15 3/8	8 7/8	8	18 7/8	24 1/8	Pima Co., AZ	Barbara J. Ridgeway	Barbara J. Ridgeway	1984	397
170 7/8	33	35 7/8	14 6/8	14 6/8	8 1/8	8 2/8	23 1/8	24 1/8	Mohave Co., AZ	Dale A. Kelling	Dale A. Kelling	1987	397
170 7/8	37	36 1/8	15 2/8	15 4/8	8 4/8	8 7/8	19 3/8	22 6/8	Yuma Co., AZ	Gary L. Major	Gary L. Major	1989	397
170 7/8	34 1/8	35 4/8	15 4/8	14 2/8	9 4/8	9 5/8	24 2/8	24 2/8	Clark Co., NV	John V. Zenz	Picked Up	1991	397
170 7/8	34 3/8	34 3/8	14 2/8	13 7/8	9 5/8	10 1/8	23 7/8	24 3/8	Clark Co., NV	Richard D. Kendall	Richard D. Kendall	1995	397
170 6/8	34 7/8	34 7/8	13 7/8	15 3/8	8	10 2/8	23 1/8	23 1/8	San Bernardino Co., CA	John M. Parrish	Picked Up	1960	406
170 6/8	33 3/8	33 3/8	14	14	8 4/8	7 5/8	20 7/8	21 6/8	Little Horn Mts., AZ	Dale Wagner	Dale Wagner	1963	406
170 6/8	36 7/8	36 3/8	15 3/8	15 6/8	7 7/8	7 7/8	20 5/8	20 5/8	Baja Calif., MX	Enrique Cervera Cicero	Enrique Cervera Cicero	1968	406
170 6/8	35 2/8	34 6/8	15 6/8	16 3/8	7 7/8	7 3/8	21 4/8	21 4/8	Baja Calif., MX	Gino Perfetto	Gino Perfetto	1968	406
170 6/8	36 1/8	36 3/8	16 3/8	13 7/8	7 3/8	8 4/8	22 6/8	22 6/8	Clark Co., NV	Roy Gamblin	Roy Gamblin	1977	406
170 6/8	39 4/8	36 1/8	13 7/8	14 2/8	8 4/8	9 4/8	24	25	Nye Co., NV	Donald A. Leveille	Donald A. Leveille	1986	406
170 6/8	36 4/8	35 4/8	14 2/8	15 1/8	9 4/8	8 2/8	17 4/8	19 4/8	Yuma Co., AZ	Bryan L. Rogers	Bryan L. Rogers	1986	406
170 6/8	34 1/8	36 7/8	15	15 1/8	8 2/8	8 4/8	24	24	Clark Co., NV	Lacel Bland	Picked Up	1991	406
170 6/8	36 3/8	36 3/8	15 1/8	14 4/8	8 4/8	8	20 4/8	22	Pima Co., AZ	Andrew D. Langmade	Andrew D. Langmade	1991	406
170 6/8	35 6/8	35 6/8	15 1/8	13 6/8	8 4/8	8 1/8	21 4/8	20 3/8	Graham Co., AZ	William A. Keebler	William A. Keebler	1993	406
170 5/8	36 3/8	34	14 4/8	15	8 1/8	9 1/8	17 6/8	24 4/8	Death Valley, CA	Fred L. Jones	Picked Up	1955	416
170 5/8	34	38 5/8	13 6/8	15 2/8	9 1/8	8 2/8	23 1/8	19 3/8	Baja Calif., MX	Bill Lewis	Bill Lewis	1969	416
170 5/8	34 2/8	35 7/8	15 2/8	16 1/8	8 2/8	8 6/8	22 6/8	23 1/8	Pima Co., AZ	David Chavez	David Chavez	1972	416
170 5/8	32 2/8	32 2/8	16 1/8	15	8 6/8	9 4/8	23 1/8	22 6/8	Clark Co., NV	George W. Wilkinson, Jr.	George W. Wilkinson, Jr.	1976	416
170 5/8	35 2/8	34 7/8	15	14 4/8	9 5/8	9	21 2/8	21 2/8	Yuma Co., AZ	James R. Ammons	James R. Ammons	1995	416
170 4/8	34 7/8	34 7/8	15 2/8	15 1/8	9	8 7/8	17 3/8	19 3/8	Mohave Co., AZ	John H. Houzenga, Jr.	John H. Houzenga, Jr.	1961	421
170 4/8	36	35	14 1/8	14 3/8	9	9	19 3/8	20 2/8	Clark Co., NV	Robert E. Coons	Robert E. Coons	1971	421
170 4/8	36	34 6/8	15 7/8	16	10 1/8	9 1/8	20 2/8	18 7/8	Baja Calif., MX	Don Turner	Don Turner	1980	421
170 4/8	32 6/8	34 2/8	16 2/8	16 2/8	7 6/8	8 3/8	18 7/8	24	Baja Calif., MX	Stephen P. Connell	Stephen P. Connell	1986	421
170 4/8	34 7/8	35 7/8	15 1/8	15	8 3/8	8 3/8	24	18 7/8	Baja Calif., MX	Edward J. Huxen	Edward J. Huxen	1988	421

Ovis canadensis nelsoni and certain related subspecies

Score	Length of Horn R	L	Circumference of Base R	L	Circumference at Third Quarter R	L	Greatest Spread	Tip to Tip Spread	Locality	Hunter	Owner	Date Killed	Rank
170 4/8	34 5/8	32 1/8	15 2/8	15 3/8	8 6/8	8 5/8	23 6/8	23	Lincoln Co., NV	Robert Del Porto	Robert Del Porto	1989	421
170 4/8	33 4/8	35	14 6/8	14 6/8	9 2/8	10	19 4/8	17 4/8	La Paz Co., AZ	Oscar B. Oland	Oscar B. Oland	1992	421
170 3/8	32	34 3/8	16 2/8	16 2/8	7 6/8	8 7/8	19 2/8	19 2/8	Sonora, MX	Frank C. Hibben	Frank C. Hibben	1935	428
170 3/8	35 3/8	36 2/8	15	15	7 5/8	7 7/8	19 7/8	18	Chemehuevi Mts., AZ	James B. Lingo	James B. Lingo	1970	428
170 3/8	32 5/8	32 4/8	16	16	9 1/8	9 3/8	20 2/8	15 5/8	Hermosillo, MX	Michael Follett	Michael Follett	1979	428
170 3/8	35 5/8	35 6/8	14 1/8	14 4/8	8 4/8	9	23 6/8	23	Yuma Co., AZ	Gary V. Harmon	Gary V. Harmon	1979	428
170 3/8	35	35 7/8	14 2/8	14 2/8	9 6/8	9 6/8	23 3/8	23 3/8	Lincoln Co., NV	Robert S. Mastronardi	Robert S. Mastronardi	1982	428
170 3/8	36 2/8	35 6/8	13 6/8	14 4/8	9 5/8	9 5/8	23 4/8	19 3/8	La Paz Co., AZ	Tracy L. Wilkinson	Tracy L. Wilkinson	1982	428
170 3/8	35 1/8	36 1/8	14	14	9 2/8	9 2/8	20 6/8	18	La Paz Co., AZ	Rick P. Palmer	Rick P. Palmer	1989	428
170 2/8	35 2/8	36 4/8	15	15 2/8	8	8 4/8	20 1/8	20 1/8	Baja Calif., MX	Richard Buffington	Richard Buffington	1966	435
170 2/8	37 7/8	34 7/8	14 7/8	14 4/8	8 2/8	8 4/8	24 1/8	24 1/8	Clark Co., NV	Landon D. Mack	Landon D. Mack	1977	435
170 2/8	37 2/8	35	15 4/8	15 4/8	8	7 5/8	21 3/8	20 4/8	Baja Calif., MX	James W. Owens	James W. Owens	1978	435
170 2/8	34 4/8	34 2/8	15	15	9 5/8	9 4/8	18 1/8	18	Baja Calif., MX	A. Verne Crowell	A. Verne Crowell	1979	435
170 2/8	34 5/8	33 7/8	14 6/8	14 6/8	9 2/8	9 1/8	21 2/8	16	Sonora, MX	Leonard E. Brewster	Leonard E. Brewster	1982	435
170 2/8	36	35 2/8	15 1/8	15 1/8	8 1/8	8 2/8	21 7/8	21 7/8	Baja Calif., MX	David C. Southard, Jr.	David C. Southard, Jr.	1982	435
170 2/8	37 6/8	37 2/8	15 3/8	15 2/8	7	7 4/8	24 7/8	24 7/8	Clark Co., NV	Raymond B. Graber II	Raymond B. Graber II	1987	435
170 2/8	34 2/8	35	14 4/8	14 5/8	9 4/8	10	21 6/8	19 5/8	Yuma Co., AZ	Lance K. Parks	Lance K. Parks	1987	435
170 2/8	33	33	14 7/8	14 7/8	10 1/8	10 1/8	21	18 7/8	Yuma Co., AZ	Valentino J. Pugnea	Valentino J. Pugnea	1987	435
170 2/8	34 1/8	34 5/8	14 4/8	14 5/8	9 5/8	9 5/8	24	22 6/8	Mohave Co., AZ	Wily S. Addis	Wily S. Addis	1992	435
170 2/8	36 3/8	36 1/8	15 6/8	15 6/8	7 3/8	7	24	24	Maricopa Co., AZ	Gregory C. Hintze	Gregory C. Hintze	1996	435
170 1/8	34 6/8	34 7/8	14 6/8	15	8 6/8	9	19 1/8	18 2/8	Baja Calif., MX	Fred T. LaBean	Fred T. LaBean	1969	446
170 1/8	40 3/8	34 2/8	13 6/8	13 6/8	8 5/8	8 3/8	25 4/8	25 4/8	Mineral Co., NV	Picked Up	NV Dept. of Wildl.	1969	446
170 1/8	37 1/8	37	15 3/8	15 5/8	7 1/8	7 1/8	22 4/8	22 4/8	Baja Calif., MX	Arthur E. Davis	Arthur E. Davis	1972	446
170 1/8	36	36 3/8	15 3/8	15 3/8	7 7/8	7 7/8	19 2/8	16 5/8	Baja Calif., MX	Edward V. Wilson	Edward V. Wilson	1974	446
170 1/8	34 4/8	35 3/8	15 4/8	14 2/8	8 4/8	8 4/8	20 4/8	18 4/8	Clark Co., NV	William F. Zenz, Jr.	William F. Zenz, Jr.	1980	446
170 1/8	35 5/8	35 4/8	14 3/8	14 2/8	8 7/8	9 1/8	20 1/8	19 5/8	Baja Calif., MX	Alfred Barone	Alfred Barone	1984	446
170 1/8	36 1/8	35 2/8	14 3/8	14 5/8	8 4/8	8 5/8	24 5/8	24 2/8	Mineral Co., NV	Jeff Lund	Jeff Lund	1994	446
170	33	33	15 5/8	15 5/8	9 1/8	9 1/8	21 4/8	19 5/8	Little Horn Mts., AZ	Ivan L. Shiflet	Ivan L. Shiflet	1966	453
170	37 4/8	33 4/8	15 2/8	15 1/8	7 7/8	7 6/8	22 2/8	21 7/8	Baja Calif., MX	Warren K. Parker	Warren K. Parker	1970	453
170	33	34 6/8	14 2/8	14 2/8	9 6/8	10 2/8	20 7/8	18 5/8	Clark Co., NV	Lee R. Williamson	Lee R. Williamson	1972	453
170	35 2/8	35 2/8	14 6/8	14 5/8	8 6/8	8 6/8	19 5/8	19 5/8	Baja Calif., MX	Rudolf Sand	Rudolf Sand	1973	453
170	34 7/8	34 1/8	14 5/8	14 4/8	10 1/8	9 5/8	21 2/8	21 2/8	Clark Co., NV	Jim Lathrop, Jr.	Jim Lathrop, Jr.	1976	453
170	35 6/8	35 2/8	14 2/8	14	9	9	20 1/8	19 4/8	Clark Co., NV	Roy A. Walker	Roy A. Walker	1985	453
170	36 2/8	36	15	14 7/8	9 6/8	9 6/8	22 3/8	21 4/8	Yuma Co., AZ	Cheryl Machac	Cheryl Machac	1988	453
170	36	33 4/8	15	14 5/8	9 1/8	9 2/8	24 2/8	23 4/8	Mohave Co., AZ	Ross F. Adams	Ross F. Adams	1993	453
169 7/8	35 3/8	35 2/8	14 6/8	14 6/8	8 3/8	8 4/8	20 4/8	19 5/8	Baja Calif., MX	Harold Hallick	Harold Hallick	1971	461
169 7/8	35 5/8	34 6/8	15 2/8	15 2/8	8	7 6/8	26 1/8	26	Nye Co., NV	William R. Rohel	William R. Rohel	1993	461
169 6/8	35 2/8	35 6/8	14 1/8	14	9 3/8	9 5/8	21 2/8	21 2/8	Baja Calif., MX	William M. Wheless III	William M. Wheless III	1974	463

Score	Length R	Length L	Base R	Base L	Qtr R	Qtr L	Greatest Spread	Tip to Tip	Locality	Owner	Hunter	Date	Rank
169 6/8	36 4/8	36 6/8	15 3/8	15	7 4/8	7 3/8	21	20 1/8	Baja Calif., MX	Richard L. Larson	Richard L. Larson	1985	463
169 6/8	33 5/8	34 1/8	14	14 2/8	10	10 2/8	22	20 5/8	Yuma Co., AZ	Gary S. Sitton	Gary S. Sitton	1986	463
169 6/8	37 2/8	37	13 6/8	14	9 1/8	9	20 7/8	18 4/8	San Bernardino Co., CA	Charles E. Cook	Charles E. Cook	1989	463
169 6/8	38 2/8	36	13 3/8	13 5/8	9 3/8	9 3/8	23	21 7/8	Clark Co., NV	Harold D. Humes	Harold D. Humes	1990	463
169 6/8	33 4/8	36 4/8	15 3/8	15 2/8	7 7/8	8 1/8	25 4/8	25 4/8	Nye Co., NV	Kevin B. Oliver	Kevin B. Oliver	1994	463
169 5/8	34 5/8	34 3/8	14 3/8	14 4/8	9 1/8	9 1/8	23	19	Muddy Mts., NV	Peter Dietrick	Peter Dietrick	1962	469
169 5/8	35 1/8	35	15	15	8	8 1/8	20	18 7/8	Baja Calif., MX	Leonard W. Gilman	Leonard W. Gilman	1969	469
169 5/8	35 3/8	35 4/8	15 4/8	15 4/8	8 2/8	8 2/8	20 4/8	20 4/8	San Borjas Mts., MX	John T. Blackwell	John T. Blackwell	1970	469
169 5/8	35 5/8	35	15	15	9	8 7/8	18 2/8	16 3/8	Baja Calif., MX	Gunter M. Paefgen	Gunter M. Paefgen	1975	469
169 5/8	33 6/8	33 7/8	15 7/8	16	7 6/8	8 3/8	21 6/8	21 6/8	Baja Calif., MX	Emerson Hall	Emerson Hall	1978	469
169 5/8	34	33 7/8	15 1/8	15 1/8	8 7/8	8 6/8	20 7/8	18 4/8	Yuma Co., AZ	Brad J. Ullery	Brad J. Ullery	1981	469
169 5/8	33	34 5/8	15 2/8	15 1/8	8 4/8	8 5/8	18 6/8	18 4/8	Coconino Co., AZ	Terrance S. Marcum	Terrance S. Marcum	1990	469
169 5/8	31 3/8	33	15 2/8	15 2/8	9 6/8	9 5/8	19 6/8	19 6/8	Mesa Co., CO	Steven K. Allen	Steven K. Allen	1996	469
169 5/8	36 6/8	37 7/8	14	14 1/8	8 3/8	8 6/8	22 4/8	22 1/8	Clark Co., NV	Gwendolyn C. Jaksick-Dixon	Gwendolyn C. Jaksick-Dixon	1996	469
169 4/8	36	36	15 4/8	15 4/8	8 4/8	8 4/8	25 4/8	25 4/8	Lower Calif., MX	Henry H. Blagden	Henry H. Blagden	1914	478
169 4/8	34 4/8	34 6/8	14 3/8	14 1/8	9 6/8	10 5/8	21	18 5/8	Hart Tank, AZ	Greg Diley	Picked Up	PR 1970	478
169 4/8	35 6/8	35 6/8	14 5/8	14 4/8	8 4/8	8 5/8	18	18	Baja Calif., MX	Lowell C. Hansen II	Lowell C. Hansen II	1974	478
169 4/8	33 6/8	36	14 6/8	14 7/8	9 2/8	8 5/8	22 7/8	22 5/8	Quartzite, AZ	Maurice D. Mathews	Maurice D. Mathews	1975	478
169 4/8	39	37 2/8	15	15	6 6/8	6 7/8	19 4/8	19 4/8	Baja Calif., MX	James A. Bush, Jr.	James A. Bush, Jr.	1981	478
169 4/8	34 4/8	34 2/8	14 6/8	14 6/8	9 4/8	9 1/8	23 3/8	20 4/8	San Bernardino Co., CA	Jefre R. Bugni	Jefre R. Bugni	1989	478
169 4/8	35	35 2/8	15 1/8	15 1/8	8 1/8	8 1/8	22 5/8	21 5/8	Baja Calif., MX	Steven D. Bacon	Steven D. Bacon	1990	478
169 4/8	32 2/8	34 4/8	15 3/8	15 3/8	9 2/8	9 4/8	21 2/8	20	Coconino Co., AZ	Warren K. Winkler	Warren K. Winkler	1990	478
169 4/8	36 6/8	33 6/8	14 3/8	14 3/8	8 5/8	8 4/8	21 3/8	18 4/8	Maricopa Co., AZ	David T. Demaree	David T. Demaree	1993	478
169 3/8	35 3/8	35	15 7/8	16	7 2/8	7 2/8	20 4/8	20 4/8	Sonora, MX	Unknown	Unknown	PR 1939	487
169 3/8	33 3/8	38 2/8	15	15	8	8	23	22	Pima Co., AZ	Don L. Mattausch	Don L. Mattausch	1979	487
169 2/8	34 5/8	34 7/8	14	13 7/8	9 6/8	9 7/8	21 2/8	21 2/8	White Mts., CA	Fred L. Jones	Picked Up	1951	489
169 2/8	33 7/8	34 7/8	15 2/8	15 2/8	8 4/8	8 3/8	20 4/8	18 3/8	Baja Calif., MX	Joe Osterbauer	Joe Osterbauer	1977	489
169 2/8	35 5/8	34 7/8	15 5/8	15 4/8	7 5/8	7 5/8	20 4/8	18 4/8	Baja Calif., MX	Steve F. Reiter	Steve F. Reiter	1984	489
169 2/8	36 2/8	36 1/8	14 6/8	14 6/8	8 1/8	8 1/8	23 4/8	23 4/8	Clark Co., NV	Richard M. McDrew	Richard M. McDrew	1986	489
169 2/8	33 4/8	34 4/8	15 1/8	15 2/8	8 5/8	8 6/8	21 3/8	21	La Paz Co., AZ	Jim F. Phelps	Jim F. Phelps	1988	489
169 2/8	35 3/8	34 3/8	14 2/8	14 2/8	10	9 1/8	23 7/8	23 4/8	Mohave Co., AZ	William A. Doty	Picked Up	1991	489
169 1/8	33 4/8	33 7/8	14 4/8	14 4/8	10	10	20 6/8	15 5/8	Lower Calif., MX	William W. Renfrew	Picked Up	1953	495
169 1/8	35	34 1/8	14 2/8	14 2/8	9 1/8	9 1/8	22 4/8	22 4/8	Chocolate Mts., AZ	Dan Oliver	Dan Oliver	1966	495
169 1/8	35 6/8	38 7/8	15	15	7 3/8	7 1/8	25 4/8	25 4/8	Baja Calif., MX	James W. Owens	James W. Owens	1977	495
169 1/8	34 4/8	35 5/8	14	14	10 1/8	7 1/8	21 6/8	21 6/8	Clark Co., NV	Lee M. Smith, Jr.	Lee M. Smith, Jr.	1979	495
169 1/8	36	36 7/8	14 7/8	15	7 1/8	7	23 6/8	23 5/8	Clark Co., NV	Vernon C. Tays	Vernon C. Tays	1987	495
169	36 1/8	36 3/8	15 6/8	14 7/8	6 4/8	6 5/8	22 3/8	22 2/8	Baja Calif., MX	WA State Mus.	W.E. Humphrey	1909	500
169	37	36	13 4/8	14	8	8 4/8	27	27	Yuma Co., AZ	Dean Bowdoin	Dean Bowdoin	1964	500
169	34 3/8	35 3/8	15 3/8	15 1/8	7 7/8	8	21	21	Baja Calif., MX	Gordon L. Shuster	Gordon L. Shuster	1980	500
169	35 2/8	35 2/8	13 6/8	13 6/8	10	10	20 5/8	20 5/8	Baja Calif., MX	Arthur L. Wehner	Arthur L. Wehner	1980	500
169	36 4/8	36 4/8	15 2/8	15 2/8	7 6/8	7 6/8	25 6/8	16 1/8	Clark Co., NV	Charles E. Sibley	Charles E. Sibley	1986	500
169	35 4/8	35	15	15	8 5/8	8 2/8	22 1/8	16 3/8	Maricopa Co., AZ	C. Ames Thompson	C. Ames Thompson	1988	500
168 7/8	34 1/8	35	14 6/8	14 4/8	8 6/8	8 6/8	22 2/8	21 4/8	Aquila Mts., AZ	John Carr	John Carr	1969	506
168 7/8	35	33 7/8	16	16	8 1/8	7 7/8	21 4/8	18 4/8	Baja Calif., MX	Larry R. Price	Larry R. Price	1973	506
168 7/8	36 2/8	36 7/8	14 6/8	14 7/8	7 5/8	7 6/8	20 1/8	22	Baja Calif., MX	Gary Davis	Gary Davis	1975	506
168 7/8	36 5/8	33 2/8	14 6/8	14 7/8	8 2/8	8 7/8	22	22	Clark Co., NV	Robert Darakjy	Robert Darakjy	1978	506

DESERT SHEEP

Ovis canadensis nelsoni and certain related subspecies

Score	Length of Horn R	L	Circumference of Base R	L	Circumference at Third Quarter R	L	Greatest Spread	Tip tp Tip Spread	Locality	Hunter	Owner	Date Killed	Rank
168 7/8	33 4/8	33 7/8	14 7/8	14 7/8	9 3/8	9 2/8	20 6/8	20 6/8	Lincoln Co., NV	Melvin J. Lowe	Melvin J. Lowe	1981	506
168 7/8	36 1/8	36	14 3/8	14 6/8	8 7/8	8 5/8	19 7/8	17 5/8	Sonora, MX	Kevin A. Dettler	Kevin A. Dettler	1997	506
168 6/8	35 2/8	33 4/8	14	14 2/8	10 1/8	9 6/8	19 7/8	16 4/8	Sonora, MX	Jack O'Connor	Jack O'Connor	1946	512
168 6/8	36 4/8	36 2/8	14 2/8	14 3/8	7 7/8	7 6/8	22 5/8	21 7/8	Little Horn Mts., AZ	Dean Bowdoin	Dean Bowdoin	1966	512
168 6/8	35 2/8	36 6/8	13 5/8	13 3/8	9	9 2/8	22 4/8	22 4/8	Lincoln Co., NV	Von A. Mitton	Von A. Mitton	1966	512
168 6/8	34 6/8	35 2/8	15 2/8	15 2/8	7 6/8	8 2/8	19	16 3/8	Sierra De Jaraguay, MX	Jack A. Shane, Sr.	Jack A. Shane, Sr.	1972	512
168 6/8	36 4/8	37 4/8	13 5/8	13 7/8	8 6/8	9 2/8	21 2/8	22 2/8	Yuma Co., AZ	Frances B. Boggess	Frances B. Boggess	1980	512
168 5/8	36 5/8	34 4/8	13 6/8	13 7/8	9 1/8	9 4/8	23 6/8	23 6/8	Arizona	Picked Up	Don McBride	PR 1961	517
168 5/8	36 1/8	33 6/8	14	14	9 3/8	10	20 7/8	18	Castle Dome Peak, AZ	Tommy G. Moore	Tommy G. Moore	1966	517
168 5/8	34 7/8	34 4/8	14 5/8	14 5/8	8 7/8	8 4/8	21 1/8	17 3/8	Aquila Mts., AZ	David C. Thornburg	David C. Thornburg	1969	517
168 5/8	34 6/8	34 6/8	14 3/8	14 3/8	8 7/8	9	18 3/8	18 2/8	Sonora, MX	Lionel Heinrich	Lionel Heinrich	1982	517
168 5/8	35 5/8	34 4/8	15	15	8	8	24 1/8	22 1/8	Clark Co., NV	Joseph Machac	Joseph Machac	1989	517
168 4/8	34 4/8	33 6/8	15 4/8	15 4/8	8 4/8	8 7/8	18 5/8	17 4/8	Baja Calif., MX	Russell C. Cutter	Russell C. Cutter	1964	522
168 4/8	32 3/8	35 3/8	15	15	9 1/8	8 4/8	25 4/8	25	Kofa Game Range, AZ	Judy Franks	Judy Franks	1965	522
168 4/8	35	35 4/8	16 3/8	16 3/8	7 2/8	7	21 2/8	20 3/8	Pima Co., AZ	Jerald S. Wagner	Jerald S. Wagner	1977	522
168 4/8	35 5/8	36 3/8	13 6/8	13 5/8	9	9 4/8	18 5/8	18 5/8	Baja Calif., MX	W.T. Yoshimoto	W.T. Yoshimoto	1978	522
168 4/8	37 2/8	37	15 2/8	15 1/8	7 2/8	7 1/8	23 4/8	23 4/8	Baja Calif., MX	Dan L. Duncan	Dan L. Duncan	1979	522
168 4/8	36	35 4/8	14 2/8	14 5/8	8 2/8	7 7/8	18 7/8	18 7/8	Baja Calif., MX	John Whitcombe	John Whitcombe	1983	522
168 4/8	34 7/8	35 5/8	14 6/8	14 7/8	8 3/8	8 5/8	25 2/8	24 4/8	Mohave Co., AZ	Louise B. Ellison	Louise B. Ellison	1984	522
168 4/8	35 5/8	35 5/8	15 3/8	15 3/8	7 3/8	7 5/8	23 5/8	23 5/8	Clark Co., NV	James M. Machac	James M. Machac	1987	522
168 4/8	33 6/8	35	14 6/8	14 5/8	9	8 7/8	22 6/8	22 6/8	Nye Co., NV	David E. Underwood	David E. Underwood	1992	522
168 4/8	36 4/8	36 4/8	16	15 7/8	6 6/8	6 6/8	20 6/8	20 6/8	Pima Co., AZ	Carl L. Plasterer	Carl L. Plasterer	1995	522
168 4/8	34 2/8	33 4/8	13 6/8	14	10 2/8	10 4/8	23 1/8	19 5/8	Yuma Co., AZ	Dan L. Mattausch	Dan L. Mattausch	1996	522
168 3/8	34 5/8	34 2/8	15 5/8	15 5/8	8	7 6/8	17 6/8	17 4/8	Sand Tank Mts., AZ	Homer Coppinger	Homer Coppinger	1960	533
168 3/8	35	34 3/8	14	14 5/8	9 6/8	9 2/8	19 1/8	17 6/8	Yuma Co., AZ	Leanna G. Mendenhall	Leanna G. Mendenhall	1975	533
168 3/8	34 6/8	35	15 1/8	15	9	8 4/8	21 6/8	20 1/8	Maricopa Co., AZ	Peter C. Knagge	Peter C. Knagge	1985	533
168 3/8	35 4/8	37 1/8	13 6/8	13 5/8	9 3/8	9 4/8	24 2/8	24	Clark Co., NV	Leonard L. Lerg	Leonard L. Lerg	1985	533
168 3/8	34	32 3/8	14 3/8	14 4/8	10 1/8	9 3/8	23	20 2/8	Garfield Co., UT	Douglas L. Marx	Douglas L. Marx	1996	533
168 2/8	34 4/8	35 2/8	14 7/8	14 6/8	8	8 4/8	21 6/8	21 6/8	Baja Calif., MX	George H. Glass	George H. Glass	1964	538
168 2/8	34 7/8	34 1/8	15 5/8	15 6/8	7 4/8	7 5/8	20 7/8	14	Sonora, MX	Sergio Rios Aguilera	Sergio Rios Aguilera	1968	538
168 2/8	34 1/8	34 7/8	14 4/8	14 4/8	9	8 5/8	21 4/8	19 7/8	Clark Co., NV	Marie F. Reuter	Marie F. Reuter	1969	538
168 2/8	33 6/8	34 7/8	15 3/8	15 3/8	8 1/8	8 5/8	22 2/8	19 3/8	Clark Co., NV	Charles J. Lindberg	Charles J. Lindberg	1971	538
168 2/8	34 1/8	35 5/8	14 7/8	15 1/8	8 3/8	8 1/8	22	22	Yuma Co., AZ	Ervin Black	Ervin Black	1972	538
168 2/8	33 5/8	34 5/8	14	14	9 2/8	9 5/8	23 3/8	23 3/8	Lincoln Co., NV	Dale Deming	Dale Deming	1977	538
168 2/8	37	36	13 6/8	13 6/8	10 2/8	9 3/8	20	19 4/8	Lincoln Co., NV	Lee A. Raine	Lee A. Raine	1982	538
168 2/8	35 7/8	37 1/8	14 3/8	14 4/8	7 7/8	8 2/8	25 3/8	25 3/8	Clark Co., NV	Ronald E. Brown	Ronald E. Brown	1983	538
168 2/8	35 1/8	33 1/8	15 1/8	15 1/8	8 4/8	8 3/8	19 6/8	19	Baja Calif., MX	Roger R. Card	Roger R. Card	1985	538
168 2/8	34 6/8	36	13 5/8	14	8 7/8	9 1/8	24	23	Yuma Co., AZ	Ralph C. Stayner	Ralph C. Stayner	1985	538

Score								Locality	Owner	Hunter	Date	Rank
168 2/8*	34 4/8	35 4/8	14 3/8	14 3/8	8 4/8	9	20 7/8	19 1/8	Culberson Co., TX	Ben Hollingsworth, Jr.	Ben Hollingsworth, Jr.	1993	538
168 1/8	34 3/8	37 6/8	15	15	8	7 7/8	24 4/8	24 4/8	Lower Calif., MX	G.L. Harrison	Acad. Nat. Sci., Phil.	1903	549
168 1/8	34 4/8	34 5/8	14 1/8	14 1/8	8 6/8	9 2/8	20 7/8	18 3/8	Baja Calif., MX	James C. Nystrom	James C. Nystrom	1969	549
168 1/8	32 3/8	31 6/8	16 1/8	16 1/8	8 6/8	8 4/8	19 4/8	18 5/8	Pima Co., AZ	Jeff R. Snodgrass	Jeff R. Snodgrass	1970	549
168 1/8	34 6/8	34 6/8	14 4/8	14 6/8	8 5/8	8 7/8	22 2/8	22 2/8	Baja Calif., MX	C.R. Palmer	C.R. Palmer	1979	549
168 1/8	32 2/8	34 3/8	15 2/8	15 2/8	8 5/8	9	20	15 4/8	Sonora, MX	David V. Collis	David V. Collis	1985	549
168 1/8	35 6/8	36 5/8	14 6/8	14 6/8	7 1/8	7 3/8	23	21 1/8	Clark Co., NV	Richard L. Deane	Richard L. Deane	1988	549
168 1/8	31 4/8	31 1/8	15 2/8	15 2/8	9 6/8	9 5/8	21 2/8	20 4/8	Yuma Co., AZ	Charles H. Criss	Charles H. Criss	1996	549
168	35	35	14	14	10	9	25	25	Lamb Springs, NV	Leslie H. Farr	Leslie H. Farr	1966	556
168	34 4/8	34 4/8	14 6/8	15	8 3/8	8 6/8	21 4/8	21 1/8	Clark Co., NV	Edward Friel	Edward Friel	1969	556
168	34 6/8	35 6/8	15 1/8	15 1/8	8	8 3/8	21 1/8	21 1/8	Baja Calif., MX	Lee Frudden	Lee Frudden	1972	556
168	35 4/8	35 4/8	14 3/8	14 2/8	9 1/8	9	23	23	Clark Co., NV	Leonard M. Faike	Leonard M. Faike	1973	556
168	34 3/8	33 1/8	14 6/8	14 4/8	8 4/8	9 3/8	18 4/8	17 4/8	Mohave Co., AZ	Robert L. Fletcher	Robert L. Fletcher	1974	556
168	35 2/8	37 2/8	14 6/8	14 6/8	6 6/8	6 5/8	26 3/8	26 3/8	Mohave Co., AZ	Tom H. Martin	Tom H. Martin	1980	556
168	35 6/8	36 4/8	14 2/8	14 2/8	8 4/8	8 1/8	23 5/8	22 2/8	Clark Co., NV	Dennis K. Evans	Dennis K. Evans	1981	556
168	35 3/8	35 1/8	14 6/8	14 6/8	8 3/8	8 2/8	25	20	Mojave Co., AZ	Picked Up	Dean Priest	1984	556
168	34	34	14 3/8	14 3/8	9 2/8	8 7/8	21	20	Mohave Co., AZ	Perry H. Finger	Perry H. Finger	1985	556
168	35	35 4/8	15 4/8	15 4/8	7 7/8	7 7/8	20	19 4/8	Baja Calif., MX	Carl E. Jacobson	Carl E. Jacobson	1985	556
168	35 4/8	34 2/8	15 4/8	15 4/8	8 1/8	8 2/8	21 6/8	18 2/8	Pinal Co., AZ	Peter A. Inorio	Peter A. Inorio	1986	556
168	34 2/8	32 4/8	15 5/8	14 7/8	9 2/8	9 1/8	25 3/8	24 5/8	Mohave Co., AZ	Joseph D. Lynch	Joseph D. Lynch	1987	556
168	33 4/8	33 4/8	14 6/8	14 7/8	8 1/8	8 1/8	20 5/8	20 1/8	Yuma Co., AZ	Alan D. Maynard	Alan D. Maynard	1987	556
168	36 7/8	36 3/8	14 1/8	14 2/8	8 7/8	8 7/8	19 6/8	17 3/8	Baja Calif., MX	Mclean Bowman	Mclean Bowman	1989	556
168	35 2/8	35 2/8	14 1/8	14 6/8	9	9	20 5/8	19	Yuma Co., AZ	Richard M. Cordova	Richard M. Cordova	1991	556
168	34 3/8	34 1/8	14 6/8	14 3/8	9 2/8	9 1/8	22	20 6/8	San Bernardino Co., CA	Charles L. Rensing	Charles L. Rensing	1992	556
168	35 6/8	37 2/8	14 3/8	13 3/8	9 5/8	9 5/8	22 1/8	17 3/8	San Bernardino Co., CA	Ron Smith	Ron Smith	1992	556
168	32 6/8	32 6/8	14 3/8	14 3/8	9 6/8	9 4/8	19 5/8	16 5/8	Yuma Co., AZ	Kenneth L. Blank	Kennth L. Blank	1993	556
188 2/8*	38 2/8	37 4/8	16 3/8	16 2/8	10 3/8	10 6/8	24 3/8	21 5/8	Maricopa Co., AZ	Jerry Fletcher	Jerry Fletcher	1993	556
180 4/8*	36 4/8	36 4/8	15 7/8	15 7/8	9 4/8	9 6/8	19 1/8	18 3/8	Baja Calif., MX	John B. Brelsford	John B. Brelsford	1993	556

* Final score is subject to revision by additional verifying measurements.

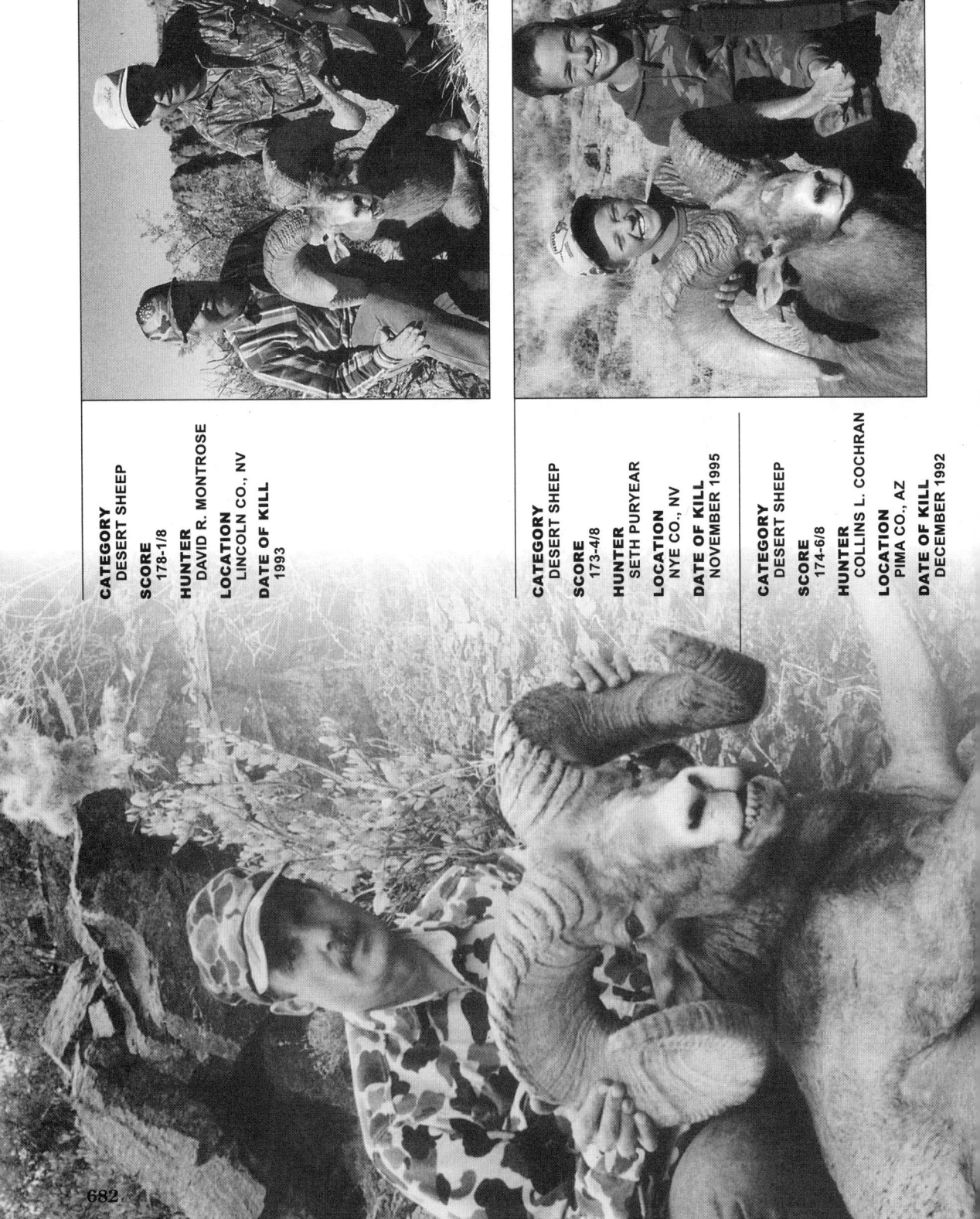

CATEGORY
DESERT SHEEP

SCORE
178-1/8

HUNTER
DAVID R. MONTROSE

LOCATION
LINCOLN CO., NV

DATE OF KILL
1993

CATEGORY
DESERT SHEEP

SCORE
173-4/8

HUNTER
SETH PURYEAR

LOCATION
NYE CO., NV

DATE OF KILL
NOVEMBER 1995

CATEGORY
DESERT SHEEP

SCORE
174-6/8

HUNTER
COLLINS L. COCHRAN

LOCATION
PIMA CO., AZ

DATE OF KILL
DECEMBER 1992

682

CATEGORY
DESERT SHEEP

SCORE
181-4/8

HUNTER
THOMAS J. PAWLACYK

LOCATION
HIDALGO CO., NM

DATE OF KILL
DECEMBER 1995

CATEGORY
DESERT SHEEP

SCORE
175-2/8

HUNTER
TED PHOENIX

LOCATION
YUMA CO., AZ

DATE OF KILL
DECEMBER 1995

CATEGORY
DESERT SHEEP

SCORE
170-6/8

HUNTER
WILLIAM A. KEEBLER

LOCATION
GRAHAM CO., AZ

DATE OF KILL
DECEMBER 1993

683

DALL'S SHEEP
WORLD'S RECORD

Having gained the experience he needed on some earlier hunts for Dall's sheep (*Ovis dalli dalli*) in Alaska, Harry Swank, Jr., a resident of Anchorage, decided to try for a really outstanding ram in the Wrangell Mountains. He knew that there were some wonderful heads to be found there, even though the World's Record up to that time had come from the Chugach Mountains. Swank's story occurred in September, 1961, and it offers another good example of trophy hunting at its very best.

"A man must want a trophy pretty badly to put in all that time, and that man was me. So last season I went into the wild Wrangell Mountains of Alaska with my hunting partner, Perley Jones, and guide, Jack Wilson. From Jack's base camp at Gulkana we made a number of reconnaissance flights deep into the mountains and finally, picked an area that was so shockingly rough and remote that it is seldom, if ever, visited by hunters. Then in September, I was put down on a big, tilted glacier, an operation that called for infinite skill. The country was as hostile as any a man is likely to meet; forbidding glaciers bounded by treacherous crevasses; cliffs whose sheer faces seemed insurmountable and the weather was miserable.

"After a good night's sleep, Perley and I made a blood-curdling descent down the side of the main glacier into the valley of a lesser one. Moving slowly up the canyon we carefully glassed the surrounding ridges. There were sheep, but nothing that looked like a World's Record. By now it was well into the afternoon, but I decided to have a look at what lay beyond the next hill. The hill proved to be farther away than I'd estimated and the sun was getting dangerously low when I finally glassed the valley beyond it. Seeing nothing, I was about to return to camp when two rams suddenly appeared on a ridge a quarter mile away. One was only a youngster but the other was huge — bigger than any sheep I'd ever seen.

"Caught out in the open, there was nothing I could do but try to get closer to the ram, and strangely enough I managed to get within a few hundred yards of it before the young sheep noticed me and started to act nervous. Groaning inwardly, I dropped to the ground and brought my .264 against my shoulder, the great white sheep moved closer to the edge of the ridge and peered down curiously. Instantly I brought the cross hairs to bear, but as my finger tightened on the trigger, doubts began to assail me. Should I shoot or wait? I was not sure he was of world-record stature, and if I shot him my hunt would be over for the year. Maybe-Wham! The rifle went off almost by itself, before I'd made up my mind. The big ram leaped convulsively, then slumped to the ground. By now it was almost dark. Not until the next morning did I know my seven-year quest was over. Carefully I measured the curl. The head was a new World's Record! Later on, the Boone and Crockett Club officially scored it at 189-6/8 points."

This trophy won the coveted Sagamore Hill Award in the 1961 Competition, signifying both trophy excellence and a hunt exhibiting the finest standards of Fair Chase. ∎

	Right Horn	Left Horn	Difference
		47 7/8	1/8
	48 5/8	14 6/8	1/8
	14 6/8		1/8
	/8	/8	2/8
	/8	/8	5/8

TOTALS

Exact Locality... lled: Wrangell

Date Killed: 19

Owner: Mrs. H... Swank,

Owner's Address.

Guide's Name and Address

Remarks: (Mention Any Ab

5/8

189 6/8

I certify that I have measured this trophy on **12/08/19**
MM/DD/YY

at **5 Tudor City Place**
STREET ADDRESS

New York **NY**
CITY STATE

I.D. Number

that these measurements and data are, to the best of my knowledge and belief, made in accordance with the instructi

Signature: _____

Grancel Fitz
PRINT NAME

Grancel Fitz
B&C OFFICIAL MEASURER

685

DALL'S SHEEP
WORLD'S RECORD SCORECHART

All measurements must be made with a 1/4-inch wide flexible steel tape to the nearest one-eighth of an inch. Enter fractional figures in eighths, without reduction. Official measurements cannot be taken until horns have air dried for at least 60 days after the animal was killed.

A. Greatest Spread is measured between perpendiculars at a right angle to the center line of the skull.

B. Tip to Tip Spread is measured between tips of horns.

C. Length of Horn is measured from the lowest point in front on outer curve to a point in line with tip. **Do not** press tape into depressions. The low point of the outer curve of the horn is considered to be the low point of the frontal portion of the horn, situated above and slightly medial to the eye socket (not the outside edge). Use a straight edge, perpendicular to horn axis, to end measurement on "broomed" horns.

D-1. Circumference of Base is measured at a right angle to axis of horn. **Do not** follow irregular edge of horn; the line of measurement must be entirely on horn material.

D-2-3-4. Divide measurement C of longer horn by four. Starting at base, mark **both** horns at these quarters (even though the other horn is shorter) and measure circumferences at these marks, with measurements taken at right angles to horn axis.

Records of
North American
Big Game

250 Station Drive
Missoula, MT 59801
(406) 542-1888

BOONE AND CROCKETT CLUB®
OFFICIAL SCORING SYSTEM FOR NORTH AMERICAN BIG GAME TROPHIES

SHEEP

MINIMUM SCORES		
	AWARDS	ALL-TIME
bighorn	175	180
desert	165	168
Dall's	160	170
Stone's	165	170

KIND OF SHEEP (check one)
☐ bighorn
☐ desert
☑ Dall's
☐ Stone's

PLUG NUMBER

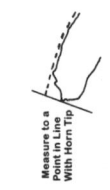

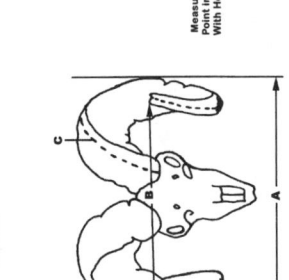

Measure to a
Point in Line
With Horn Tip

SEE OTHER SIDE FOR INSTRUCTIONS	COLUMN 1	COLUMN 2	COLUMN 3
	Right Horn	Left Horn	Difference
A. Greatest Spread (Is Often Tip to Tip Spread)	34 3/8		
B. Tip to Tip Spread	34 3/8		
C. Length of Horn	48 5/8	47 7/8	
D-1. Circumference of Base	14 5/8	14 6/8	1/8
D-2. Circumference at First Quarter	13 5/8	13 6/8	1/8
D-3. Circumference at Second Quarter	11 6/8	11 7/8	1/8
D-4. Circumference at Third Quarter	6 5/8	6 7/8	2/8
TOTALS	95 2/8	95 1/8	5/8

ADD	Column 1	95 2/8	Exact Locality Where Killed: Wrangell Mts., AK
	Column 2	95 1/8	Date Killed: 1961	Hunter: Harry L. Swank, Jr.
	Subtotal	190 3/8	Owner: Mrs. Harry L. Swank, Jr.	Telephone #:
SUBTRACT Column 3		5/8	Owner's Address:
FINAL SCORE		**189 6/8**	Guide's Name and Address:
			Remarks: (Mention Any Abnormalities or Unique Qualities)

I, _____ Grancel Fitz _____, certify that I have measured this trophy on ___12/08/1961___
       PRINT NAME   MM/DD/YYYY

at ___5 Tudor City Place___   ___New York___   ___NY___
   STREET ADDRESS   CITY   STATE/PROVINCE

and that these measurements and data are, to the best of my knowledge and belief, made in accordance with the instructions given.

Witness: ___Elmer Rusten___   Signature: ___Grancel Fitz___   I.D. Number _____
                                             B&C OFFICIAL MEASURER

TROPHY INFO

RANK
2

SCORE
185 $^{6}/_{8}$

LOCATION
Chugach Mts., AK

HUNTER
Frank Cook

OWNER
Frank Cook

DATE KILLED
1956

Photograph from B&C Archives

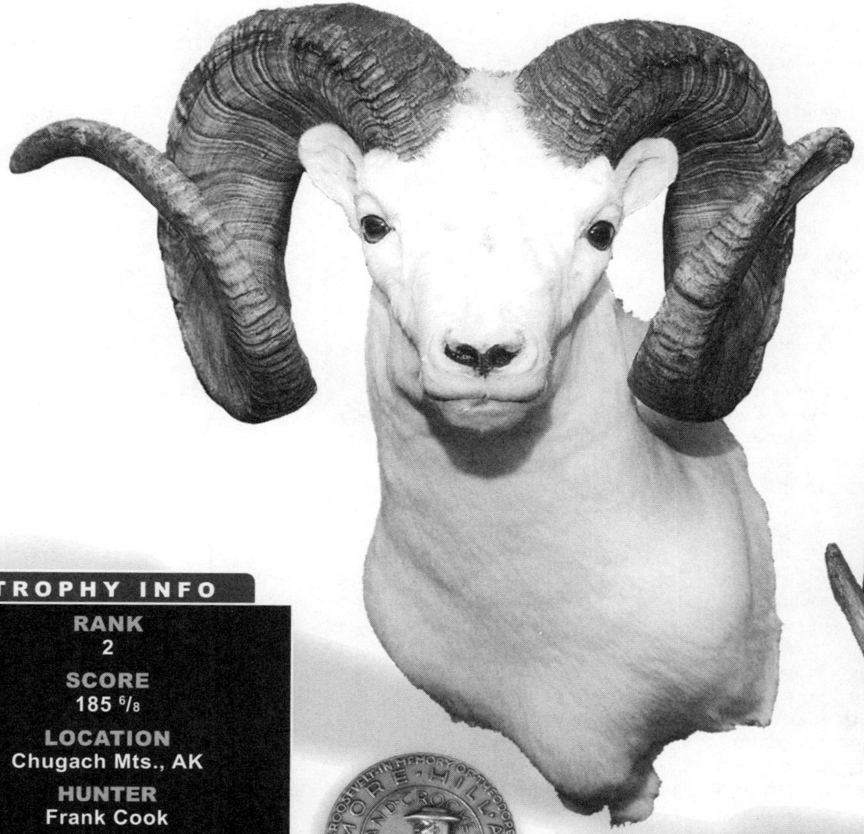

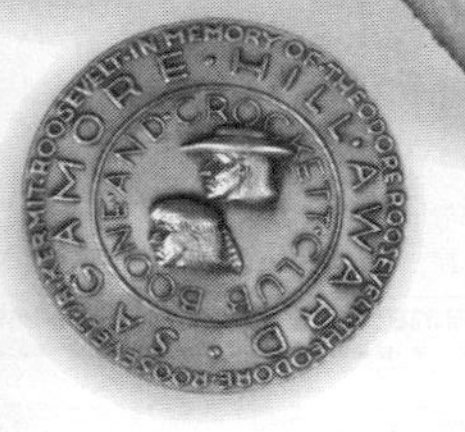

TROPHY INFO

RANK
10

SCORE
182 $^{2}/_{8}$

LOCATION
Champagne, YT

HUNTER
Earl J. Thee

OWNER
Earl J. Thee

DATE KILLED
1948

Photograph from B&C Archives

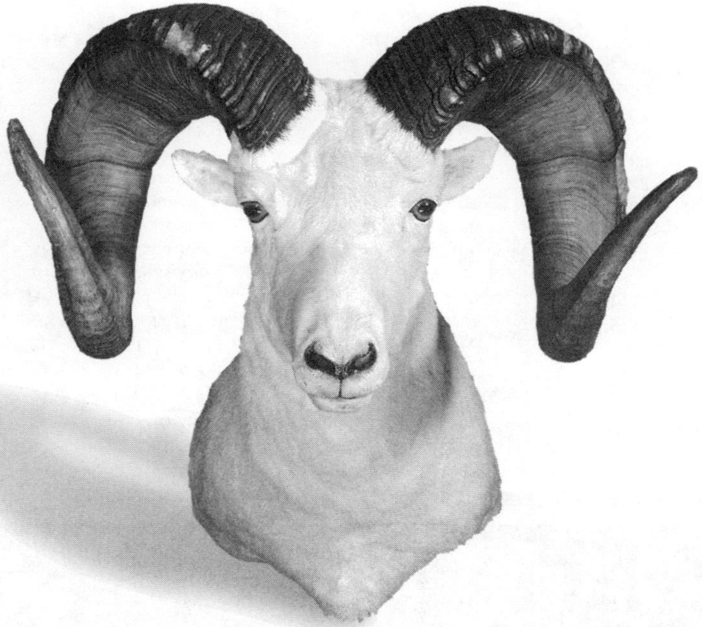

DALL'S SHEEP

Ovis dalli dalli and Ovis dalli kenaiensis

MINIMUM SCORE 170

Score	Length of Horn R	L	Circumference of Base R	L	Circumference at Third Quarter R	L	Greatest Spread	Tip tp Tip Spread	Locality	Hunter	Owner	Date Killed	Rank
189 6/8	48 5/8	47 7/8	14 5/8	14 6/8	6 5/8	6 7/8	34 3/8	34 3/8	Wrangell Mts., AK	Harry L. Swank, Jr.	Harry L. Swank, Jr.	1961	1
185 6/8	49 4/8	44 2/8	14	13 7/8	6 6/8	7 3/8	24 3/8	24 3/8	Chugach Mts., AK	Frank Cook	Frank Cook	1956	2
185 4/8	43 6/8	40 4/8	14 7/8	14 7/8	9 4/8	9 3/8	20 7/8	20 7/8	Chugach Mts., AK	Jack W. Lentfer	Jack W. Lentfer	1964	3
184 1/8	43 6/8	46	14 1/8	14 3/8	9	7 6/8	21 6/8	21 6/8	Wrangell Mts., AK	B.L. Burkholder	B.L. Burkholder	1958	4
184	44 6/8	44 4/8	14 2/8	14 2/8	7 1/8	7 2/8	24 5/8	24 5/8	Chugach Mts., AK	Thomas C. Sheets	Thomas C. Sheets	1962	5
183 6/8	46 5/8	47 4/8	13 6/8	13 6/8	6 4/8	6 4/8	31	31	Wrangell Mts., AK	Tony Oney	Tony Oney	1963	6
183 6/8	48	47 4/8	14	13 6/8	6 2/8	6 5/8	33 4/8	33 4/8	Alaska Range, AK	Jonathan T. Summar, Jr.	Jonathan T. Summar, Jr.	1965	7
183 4/8	45 7/8	45 1/8	13 7/8	14	7 1/8	7 6/8	27 7/8	27 7/8	Whitehorse, YT	W. Newhall	Robert E. Barnes	1924	8
183	42 3/8	39 3/8	14 6/8	14 6/8	9 5/8	9 5/8	22 5/8	19 4/8	Wrangell Mts., AK	Gene M. Effler	Gene M. Effler	1959	9
182 6/8	44 4/8	43 6/8	14 1/8	14 5/8	7 2/8	7 1/8	23 4/8	23 4/8	Champagne, YT	Earl J. Thee	Earl J. Thee	1948	10
182	38 6/8	39	15 2/8	15 2/8	10 1/8	10 1/8	0	0	Kenai Pen., AK	Picked Up	C.E. Lyons	PR 1969	11
181 6/8	44 4/8	44 4/8	14 5/8	14 5/8	6 4/8	6 6/8	27 2/8	27 2/8	Knik River, AK	Matthew Lahti	Unknown	1930	12
181 6/8	47 3/8	47 5/8	14 6/8	14 4/8	5 7/8	6 2/8	28 7/8	28 7/8	Atlin, BC	Robert Landis	Robert Landis	1969	12
181 5/8	46 2/8	46 5/8	14	14 1/8	6	6 2/8	32 6/8	32 6/8	McCarthy, AK	Bud Nelson	Bud Nelson	1953	14
181 3/8	42 6/8	42 5/8	15 2/8	15 1/8	7 4/8	7 6/8	24 2/8	24 2/8	Wrangell Mts., AK	James K. Harrower	James K. Harrower	1961	15
181 3/8	46 6/8	46 5/8	13	13	6 5/8	6 5/8	28 3/8	28 3/8	Hartman River, AK	Carl E. Jacobson	Carl E. Jacobson	1989	15
181	46 3/8	46 7/8	13 4/8	13 6/8	6 2/8	6 4/8	28 7/8	28 7/8	Mt. Selous, AK	George C. Morris, Sr.	George C. Morris, Sr.	1962	17
180 7/8	44 2/8	44 1/8	14 7/8	14 5/8	6 4/8	6 4/8	30 1/8	30 1/8	Wrangell Mts., AK	Robert W. Engstrom	Robert W. Engstrom	1973	18
180 6/8	43 1/8	43 7/8	14 1/8	14 1/8	7 2/8	7 2/8	27	25 3/8	Kluane Lake, YT	Moose Johnson	Ollie Wirth	1953	19
180 6/8	42 4/8	44 2/8	14 2/8	15	6 2/8	7	26 5/8	26 5/8	Yukon	Billy Jack	Yukon Govt.	1966	19
180 3/8	45 7/8	46 2/8	13 4/8	13 5/8	6 6/8	6 5/8	29 1/8	29 1/8	Johnson River, AK	P.A. Johnson & J.N. Brennan	P.A. Johnson & J.N. Brennan	1950	21
180 1/8	39 2/8	46 1/8	14 6/8	15 2/8	7 2/8	7	27	27	Wrangell Mts., AK	Harry H. Wilson	Harry H. Wilson	1961	22
180	39 2/8	40 6/8	14 6/8	14 4/8	8 2/8	8 1/8	23	21	Grand View, AK	Nellie Neal	Nellie Neal	1917	23
179 7/8	45 6/8	45 5/8	13	13	6 4/8	7 4/8	27 2/8	27 2/8	Kenai Pen., AK	A.B. Learned	A.B. Learned	1936	24
179 6/8	41 5/8	41 5/8	14 6/8	14 6/8	7	7	28 3/8	28 3/8	Chugach Mts., AK	J.H. Esslinger	J.H. Esslinger	1959	25
179 5/8	40 7/8	41 4/8	14 5/8	14 4/8	8	8	26 2/8	26 2/8	Kluane Lake, YT	George E. Thompson	George E. Thompson	1956	26
179 1/8	44 5/8	44 2/8	14 2/8	14 2/8	6 4/8	7	27	27	Chugach Mts., AK	Boyd Howard	Boyd Howard	1957	27
178 7/8	40 7/8	40 4/8	14 6/8	14 7/8	7 5/8	7 3/8	24	23 7/8	Chugach Mts., AK	Daniel A. Story	Daniel A. Story	1954	28
178 6/8	42 4/8	42 2/8	13 6/8	13 2/8	8 2/8	8 5/8	25 5/8	25 5/8	Knik River, AK	V.A. Morgan	V.A. Morgan	1934	29
178 6/8	40 2/8	40 4/8	15 6/8	15 6/8	7	7	30 2/8	30 2/8	Champagne, YT	B.V. Seigel	B.V. Seigel	1964	29
178 3/8	45 3/8	43 6/8	13 5/8	13 4/8	7	6 4/8	23 6/8	23 6/8	Alaska Hwy., YT	William H. Miller	William H. Miller	1947	31
178 3/8	43 2/8	42 5/8	13 7/8	14	6 6/8	6 7/8	27 1/8	27 1/8	Chugach Mts., AK	Sam Jaksick, Jr.	Sam Jaksick, Jr.	1966	31
178 2/8	45 6/8	46 4/8	13	13	6 3/8	6 5/8	26 3/8	26 3/8	Pelly Mts., YT	Eric W. French	Eric W. French	1958	33
178 2/8	45 4/8	42 2/8	14 6/8	14 2/8	6	6 3/8	31 5/8	31 5/8	Wrangell Mts., AK	Wilbur Ternyik	Wilbur Ternyik	1958	33
178 1/8	45 7/8	43 6/8	13 4/8	13 5/8	7 1/8	6 2/8	23 6/8	23 6/8	Wrangell Mts., AK	Unknown	Jeff Sievers	PR 1950	35
178 1/8	45 7/8	44	14	13 7/8	7 4/8	7 3/8	28	28	Chugach Mts., AK	J.S. Lichtenfels	J.S. Lichtenfels	1956	35
178	43 4/8	43	15	15	6 4/8	6 4/8	30 2/8	30 2/8	Chitina River, AK	Frank C. Hibben	Frank C. Hibben	1963	37

Score							Locality	Hunter	Owner	Date	Rank
177 7/8	44 5/8	45	14	14 3/8	6 3/8	6 2/8	Chugach Mts., AK	William R. Champlain	William R. Champlain	1965	38
177 6/8	43 3/8	44 3/8	14 2/8	14 4/8	6 2/8	6 1/8	Chugach Mts., AK	Chris Klineburger	Chris Klineburger	1957	39
177 5/8	41 7/8	43 2/8	13 2/8	13 2/8	8 7/8	9 1/8	Rainy Pass, AK	F. Edmond Blanc	F. Edmond Blanc	1937	40
177 5/8	44	43 5/8	14 4/8	14 4/8	6	6	Kenai Pen., AK	John Swiss	John Swiss	1959	40
177 5/8	44 1/8	44	14	14 1/8	6 4/8	6 6/8	Wrangell Mts., AK	Elgin T. Gates	Elgin T. Gates	1961	40
177 4/8	43 2/8	44	14 1/8	14 1/8	6 3/8	6 4/8	Aishihik Lake, YT	Eleanor O'Connor	Loaned to B&C Natl. Coll.	1963	43
177 4/8	44	43 6/8	14 2/8	14 3/8	6 2/8	6 2/8	Wrangell Mts., AK	Rita Oney	Rita Oney	1963	43
177 4/8	45 4/8	44 4/8	14	14	6 1/8	6	Chugach Mts., AK	Robert Kraai	Robert Kraai	1977	43
177 2/8	42 4/8	43 4/8	13 6/8	13 6/8	7	7	Kenai Pen., AK	Luke Elwell	Luke Elwell	1936	46
177 2/8	38	40 6/8	15 2/8	15 2/8	7 3/8	7 2/8	Chugach Mts., AK	Harry H. Wilson	Harry H. Wilson	1960	46
177 1/8	43 4/8	43 3/8	13 6/8	13 6/8	6 6/8	6 6/8	Kenai Pen., AK	C.R. Cross, Jr.	C.R. Cross, Jr.	1907	48
177 1/8	43 7/8	44	13	13 1/8	7	7 1/8	Ship Creek, AK	Oliver Towsen	Oliver Towsen	1940	48
177 1/8	45 3/8	44 6/8	14	14	6	5 7/8	Chugach Mts., AK	Jim Milito	Jim Milito	1971	48
177 1/8	44 3/8	45 4/8	13 5/8	13 5/8	6 2/8	6 1/8	Mackenzie River, NT	Joseph Scott	Joseph Scott	1973	48
177	44 6/8	44 6/8	13 6/8	13 7/8	6	6	Chugach Mts., AK	Paul E. Huling	Paul E. Huling	1959	52
176 7/8	43 5/8	42 2/8	14 7/8	14 6/8	6 3/8	6 1/8	Sifton Range, YT	Jack O'Connor	Jack O'Connor	1950	53
176 7/8	41 2/8	42	14 7/8	14 7/8	6 6/8	6 6/8	Wrangell Mts., AK	Vic S. Sears	Vic S. Sears	1960	53
176 6/8	43	43	15	15	5 7/8	5 7/8	Wrangell Mts., AK	Ed Bilderback	Ed Bilderback	1959	55
176 6/8	43 1/8	43 1/8	14 3/8	14 3/8	6 2/8	6 4/8	Chugach Mts., AK	Charles H. Rohrer	Charles H. Rohrer	1982	55
176 5/8	44 4/8	44 7/8	13 1/8	13 1/8	6 4/8	6 6/8	Mayo, YT	C.L. Bestoule	C.L. Bestoule	1960	57
176 4/8	45	45	13 3/8	13	6 5/8	6 6/8	Donjek, YT	Mrs. Jacquot	Olof Erickson	1933	58
176 4/8	46 2/8	40 6/8	13 6/8	13 6/8	7 2/8	7	Knik River, AK	Philip English	Philip English	1954	58
176 4/8	43 5/8	43 5/8	13 7/8	13 7/8	6 4/8	6 4/8	Mt. River, NT	Daniel E. Yaeger	Daniel E. Yaeger	1973	58
176 3/8	41 2/8	41 7/8	14	14	6 7/8	7 6/8	Champagne, YT	Lloyd Ronning	Lloyd Ronning	1953	61
176 2/8	40 4/8	42 2/8	14 4/8	14 4/8	6 4/8	7	Ruby Range, YT	H.W. Meisch	H.W. Meisch	1957	62
176 2/8	40 7/8	41 3/8	13 4/8	13 4/8	8 4/8	8 2/8	Chugach Mts., AK	J. Martin Benchoff	J. Martin Benchoff	1963	62
176 2/8	41 6/8	42	14 3/8	14 4/8	7	7 1/8	Knik River, AK	Donald P. Chase	Donald P. Chase	1978	62
176	40 4/8	42	14 2/8	14 2/8	7	7	Chugach Mts., AK	John S. Lahti	John S. Lahti	1930	65
176	42	41 6/8	14 7/8	15	6 5/8	6 4/8	Chugach Mts., AK	William D. Backman, Jr.	William D. Backman, Jr.	1960	65
176	39	38 4/8	14 3/8	15	9 6/8	7 6/8	Tonsina Lake, AK	Horace E. Groff	Horace E. Groff	1960	65
176	42	43	14 3/8	14 3/8	6 4/8	6 4/8	Alaska	Picked Up	T.H. Rowe	PR 1960	65
176	46 4/8	45 4/8	13 2/8	14 2/8	6	6	Wrangell Mts., AK	Harold Meeker	Harold Meeker	1965	65
176	41 2/8	41 4/8	15	15	6	6	Wrangell Mts., AK	Paul D. Weingart	Paul D. Weingart	1974	65
175 6/8	40 4/8	46 6/8	13 4/8	13 4/8	6 6/8	6 7/8	Ruby Range, YT	John K. Hansen	John K. Hansen	1960	71
175 6/8	42 3/8	42 7/8	14 7/8	14 6/8	6 2/8	6 2/8	Yukon	William E. Portman	William E. Portman	1966	71
175 5/8	43 7/8	43 7/8	13 5/8	13 5/8	6 4/8	6 4/8	Chugach Mts., AK	Ben C. Boynton	Ben C. Boynton	1971	71
175 5/8	41 4/8	42 3/8	13 4/8	13 4/8	7 4/8	7 5/8	Chugach Mts., AK	Harry Anderson	Harry Anderson	1955	74
175 4/8	42	42	14	14	7	6 7/8	Wrangell Mts., AK	Swen Honkola	Swen Honkola	1958	75
175 3/8	37 6/8	40 3/8	14 4/8	14 4/8	8 2/8	8 3/8	Wrangell Mts., AK	Burt Ahlstrom	Burt Ahlstrom	1959	76
175 2/8	40 4/8	46 6/8	14 4/8	14 4/8	6 2/8	6 3/8	Chitina River, AK	Henry Boyden	Henry Boyden	1936	77
175 2/8	41 4/8	42	14 3/8	14 3/8	6 6/8	6 6/8	Wrangell Mts., AK	Grant Smith	Grant Smith	1963	77
175 2/8	41 7/8	43 3/8	14 2/8	14 2/8	6 6/8	6 6/8	Chugach Mts., AK	Miles Hajny	Miles Hajny	1969	77
175 2/8	43 3/8	44 2/8	15	15	7 3/8	7 3/8	Wrangell Mts., AK	Russell A. Reed	Russell A. Reed	1983	77
175 1/8	42 3/8	44 2/8	14	14	6 4/8	6 4/8	Talkeetna Mts., AK	Dale Caldwell	Dale Caldwell	1957	81
175 1/8	42 1/8	37	14 2/8	14 3/8	8	8 2/8	Wrangell Mts., AK	Herman F. Wyman	Herman F. Wyman	1964	81
175 1/8	41	40 7/8	14 3/8	14 3/8	6 7/8	6 7/8	Chugach Mts., AK	Edward A. Champlain	Edward A. Champlain	1965	81
175 1/8	41 3/8	39	15	15	7 4/8	6 4/8	Wrangell Mts., AK	John M. Griffith, Jr.	John M. Griffith, Jr.	1976	81

DALL'S SHEEP

Ovis dalli dalli and Ovis dalli kenaiensis

Score	Length of Horn R	L	Circumference of Base R	L	Circumference at Third Quarter R	L	Greatest Spread	Tip to Tip Spread	Locality	Hunter	Owner	Date Killed	Rank
175	42 4/8	42 7/8	14 2/8	14 2/8	6 4/8	6 3/8	23 2/8	23 2/8	Kenai Pen., AK	Russel Gainer	Russel Gainer	1959	85
175	42 7/8	42 7/8	13 7/8	14	6 6/8	6 4/8	23 4/8	23 4/8	Chugach Mts., AK	Arthur R. Dubs	Arthur R. Dubs	1961	85
174 7/8	44 5/8	44	13 3/8	13 3/8	6 6/8	6 5/8	26 5/8	26 5/8	Lake Arkell, YT	J.J. Elliott	J.J. Elliott	1924	87
174 7/8	41 3/8	40 4/8	13 7/8	13 7/8	8 2/8	8	19 7/8	19 7/8	Chugach Mts., AK	Leroy Holen	Leroy Holen	1957	87
174 7/8	42 2/8	40 3/8	13 7/8	14	7 4/8	7 7/8	28 2/8	28 2/8	Aishihik Lake, YT	Abe Goldberg	Abe Goldberg	1962	87
174 7/8	43 1/8	43	13 5/8	13 7/8	6 6/8	6 6/8	29	29	Wrangell Mts., AK	R.W. Ulman	R.W. Ulman	1962	87
174 7/8	44 6/8	42 1/8	13 6/8	13 4/8	7	6 5/8	29	29	Chitina River, AK	Ray B. Nienhaus	Ray B. Nienhaus	1966	87
174 6/8	47 4/8	43	12 6/8	13	5 6/8	5 6/8	26	29	Carcross, YT	Billy Smith	Acad. Nat. Sci., Phil.	1927	92
174 6/8	46 6/8	43	13	13	7 1/8	6 1/8	25 4/8	25 4/8	Sifton Range, YT	Herb Klein	Herb Klein	1950	92
174 6/8	45 2/8	45	13 1/8	13 1/8	9 4/8	6 2/8	28 5/8	28 5/8	Wrangell Mts., AK	Warren W. Wilbur	Warren W. Wilbur	1952	92
174 6/8	40 5/8	40 3/8	14 4/8	14 3/8	6 6/8	6 7/8	26 3/8	26 3/8	Wrangell Mts., AK	Peter W. Bading	Peter W. Bading	1963	92
174 6/8	41 3/8	43 5/8	14 4/8	14 5/8	6 4/8	6 1/8	28 2/8	28 2/8	Wheaton, YT	Herbert Carlson	Herbert Carlson	1963	92
174 6/8	42	42 4/8	14	13 6/8	6 7/8	7	23 7/8	24 1/8	Chugach Mts., AK	Bill Silveira	Bill Silveira	1969	92
174 6/8	40 1/8	40 7/8	15 3/8	15 4/8	6 4/8	6 4/8	20 4/8	20 4/8	Wrangell Mts., AK	Tod Reichert	Tod Reichert	1976	92
174 6/8	41 2/8	41 2/8	14	14	6 7/8	7 3/8	27 3/8	27 2/8	Wrangell Mts., AK	Don L. Corley	Don L. Corley	1978	92
174 5/8	40 4/8	43 5/8	14 2/8	14 2/8	6 4/8	6 4/8	22 3/8	22 3/8	Kenai Mts., AK	C.A. Brauch	C.A. Brauch	1959	100
174 5/8	40 5/8	42 2/8	14 5/8	14 5/8	7 2/8	6 4/8	27 1/8	27 1/8	Raft Creek, YT	Marvin Wood	Marvin Wood	1961	100
174 5/8	43 4/8	42 3/8	13 7/8	14 1/8	6 5/8	6 6/8	26 1/8	26 1/8	Kusawa Lake, YT	Lawrence J. Kolar	Lawrence J. Kolar	1973	100
174 5/8	43	42 3/8	14 2/8	14 1/8	6 1/8	6	26 4/8	26 4/8	Barnard Glacier, AK	Rodney Lane	Rodney Lane	1995	100
174 5/8	42 2/8	40 7/8	14 1/8	14 1/8	6 2/8	6 1/8	22	22	Chugach Mts., AK	Carl W. Schmidt	Carl W. Schmidt	1996	100
174 4/8	41	41 4/8	13 5/8	13 6/8	8 1/8	8 5/8	22	21 3/8	Wrangell Mts., AK	Lloyd Walker	Lloyd Walker	1959	105
174 4/8	42 2/8	41 6/8	13 7/8	13 7/8	8	7 4/8	20 1/8	20 1/8	Wrangell Mts., AK	Robert L. Jenkins	Robert L. Jenkins	1963	105
174 4/8	40 3/8	40 5/8	15 1/8	14 7/8	6 4/8	6 7/8	23 7/8	23 5/8	Chugach Mts., AK	Lawrence T. Keenan	Lawrence T. Keenan	1976	105
174 4/8	42 1/8	41 3/8	15 1/8	15	6 3/8	6 4/8	27 5/8	27 3/8	Snowcap Mt., AK	Brenton J. Whaley	Brenton J. Whaley	1992	105
174 3/8	43 2/8	43 1/8	14 3/8	14 2/8	6 2/8	6 2/8	24	24	Wrangell Mts., AK	John J. Liska	John J. Liska	1963	109
174 3/8	42 1/8	42 4/8	14 1/8	14 2/8	6 4/8	6 5/8	25 6/8	25 4/8	Nahannie Range, NT	Nick Trenke	Nick Trenke	1979	109
174 2/8	41 5/8	41 5/8	14 2/8	14 2/8	6 4/8	6 3/8	26 4/8	26 4/8	Talkeetna Mts., AK	William J. Konesky	William J. Konesky	1958	111
174 2/8	40 7/8	41 5/8	14 4/8	14 4/8	7 4/8	7	22	22	Wrangell Mts., AK	Jerry L. Beason	Jerry L. Beason	1961	111
174 2/8	41 4/8	43 4/8	13 7/8	14	6 3/8	6 4/8	31 1/8	31 1/8	Coast Mts., YT	Clarence Hinkle	Clarence Hinkle	1963	111
174 1/8	40	42 7/8	14 5/8	14 4/8	6 4/8	6 4/8	25	25	Ruby Range, YT	Lawrence S. Kellogg	T.A. Alujevic	1958	114
174 1/8	43 6/8	43 3/8	14 1/8	14 1/8	6	6	30 7/8	30 7/8	Wrangell Mts., AK	Sven Johanson	Sven Johanson	1960	114
174	40 7/8	42 3/8	13 5/8	13 7/8	7 6/8	7 4/8	21 7/8	21 7/8	Kenai Pen., AK	Basil C. Bradbury	James B. Sisco III	1960	116
174	42 4/8	45	14	14	6 1/8	6 1/8	27	27	Wrangell Mts., AK	Howard Gilmore, Jr.	Howard Gilmore, Jr.	1969	116
174	43 3/8	44 7/8	14 4/8	14 3/8	5 5/8	5 7/8	32 1/8	31 6/8	Wrangell Mts., AK	Dan Parker	Dan Parker	1972	116
174	43 5/8	42 1/8	14 3/8	14 4/8	5 7/8	5 4/8	29	29 2/8	Alaska Range, AK	Harry R. Hannon	Harry R. Hannon	1976	116
174	42 6/8	41 2/8	14 2/8	14 3/8	6 1/8	6 1/8	23 4/8	23 4/8	Keele River, NT	Kelly R. Elmer	Kelly R. Elmer	1997	116
173 7/8	44 1/8	42 4/8	13 7/8	13 7/8	6 2/8	6 5/8	26	26	Twitya River, NT	Lewis W. Lindemer	Lewis W. Lindemer	1970	121
173 6/8	42 6/8	43 2/8	14 2/8	14 5/8	6 1/8	6 4/8	29 3/8	29 3/8	Talkeetna Mts., AK	Frank Cook	Frank Cook	1961	122

Score	Length R	Length L	Base R	Base L	Qtr R	Qtr L	Tip Spread	Greatest Spread	Locality	Hunter	Owner	Date	Rank
173 6/8	36 2/8	41 6/8	15	15 1/8	7 2/8	7 2/8	24 6/8	24 6/8	Wrangell Mts., AK	Gene Effler	Gene Effler	1964	122
173 6/8	40 2/8	40 2/8	14 6/8	14 7/8	5 4/8	5 4/8	30 4/8	30 4/8	Keele River, NT	John M. Azevedo	John M. Azevedo	1975	122
173 6/8	43 6/8	43 6/8	13 7/8	13 7/8	5 6/8	5 6/8	28 1/8	28 1/8	Robertson River, AK	Thomas A. Berg	Thomas A. Berg	1992	122
173 5/8	41 6/8	45 3/8	13	12 7/8	6 7/8	7	24 6/8	24 6/8	Ruby Range, YT	John E. Hammett	John E. Hammett	1949	126
173 5/8	45 2/8	45 1/8	13 2/8	13 1/8	5 6/8	5 7/8	30 6/8	30 7/8	Chitina, AK	Dene Leonard, Jr.	Dene Leonard, Jr.	1959	126
173 5/8	38 5/8	38 2/8	13 7/8	13 7/8	9 3/8	9 3/8	19 6/8	21 1/8	Wrangell Mts., AK	B.L. Burkholder	B.L. Burkholder	1960	126
173 5/8	42 1/8	42 1/8	13 2/8	13 2/8	5 4/8	5 4/8	28	28	Chugach Mts., AK	Richard T. Kopsack	Richard T. Kopsack	1961	126
173 5/8	43 4/8	43 4/8	13 4/8	13 4/8	7 2/8	7 2/8	22 2/8	23 3/8	Champagne, YT	Edmund D. Patterson, Jr.	Edmund D. Patterson, Jr.	1963	126
173 5/8	41 4/8	41 3/8	13 2/8	13 2/8	6 7/8	6 7/8	24 2/8	24 2/8	Lake Clark, AK	Melvin C. Paxton	Melvin C. Paxton	1968	126
173 5/8	40 2/8	40 5/8	14 2/8	14 5/8	6 3/8	6 3/8	25 6/8	25 6/8	Chugach Mts., AK	Keith A. Douglas	Keith A. Douglas	1993	126
173 4/8	43 5/8	43 5/8	13 6/8	13 6/8	5 7/8	5 7/8	29 7/8	29 7/8	Primrose River, YT	W.R. Collier	W.R. Collier	1962	133
173 4/8	42	42	14	14	6 4/8	6 4/8	29 7/8	29 7/8	Wrangell Mts., AK	James Harrower	James Harrower	1963	133
173 4/8	41 1/8	41 1/8	13 7/8	14 6/8	6 4/8	6 6/8	30 6/8	31 1/8	Chitina Glacier, AK	Robert W. Kubick	Robert W. Kubick	1967	133
173 4/8	41 7/8	41 5/8	14 7/8	13 6/8	6 6/8	6 6/8	26 4/8	26 4/8	Troublesome Creek, AK	David G. Urban	David G. Urban	1991	133
173 3/8	43 5/8	43	13 6/8	13 5/8	6 4/8	6 5/8	28 4/8	28 4/8	Tonsina Lake, AK	James St. Amour	James St. Amour	1957	137
173 3/8	40 1/8	40 4/8	13 5/8	15	6 2/8	6 1/8	27 5/8	27 5/8	Whitehorse, YT	Francis Bouchard	Francis Bouchard	1961	137
173 3/8	44 6/8	44 7/8	15	13 3/8	5 6/8	5 6/8	28 6/8	28 6/8	Chugach Mts., AK	Howard Haney	Howard Haney	1961	137
173 3/8	42 2/8	42 2/8	13 3/8	13 1/8	6 2/8	6 2/8	19 4/8	19 4/8	Kenai Pen., AK	Spud Dillon	Spud Dillon	1961	137
173 3/8	39 7/8	44 4/8	13 7/8	13 7/8	6 4/8	6 4/8	25 3/8	25 3/8	Wrangell Mts., AK	Basil C. Bradbury	Basil C. Bradbury	1968	137
173 3/8	42	42	13 4/8	13 5/8	7 4/8	6 4/8	22 3/8	22 3/8	Alaska Range, AK	Arthur L. Spicer	Arthur L. Spicer	1970	137
173 3/8	44	43 7/8	13 3/8	13 4/8	5 3/8	5 4/8	30 2/8	30 2/8	Cache Lake, NT	Lester Behrns	Lester Behrns	1980	137
173 2/8	35 2/8	45	14 4/8	14 4/8	6 2/8	5 5/8	23 3/8	25 2/8	Wrangell Mts., AK	J.H. Shelton	J.H. Shelton	1958	144
173 1/8	46 4/8	41 5/8	14 3/8	14 3/8	6	6	26 7/8	20 1/8	Kenai Pen., AK	W.R. Shellhorn	D. Shellhorn	1936	145
173 1/8	41 2/8	39 7/8	13 2/8	13 2/8	7 3/8	7 4/8	21 7/8	18 4/8	Dawson Range, YT	Bill Goosman	Bill Goosman	1972	145
173	40 3/8	40 3/8	15	15	6 3/8	6 3/8	28 6/8	28 6/8	Whitehorse, YT	Earl DuBois	Earl DuBois	1961	147
173	42	42	13 5/8	13 5/8	6 4/8	6 4/8	28 1/8	28 1/8	Wrangell Mts., AK	Ken Knudson	Ken Knudson	1961	147
173	45 2/8	45 2/8	13 4/8	13 4/8	5 4/8	5 5/8	33	33	Wrangell Mts., AK	Bob Merz	Bob Merz	1966	147
173	40 5/8	41 5/8	13 3/8	13 5/8	7 2/8	7 2/8	20 5/8	20 5/8	Chugach Mts., AK	J.C. Hemming	J.C. Hemming	1970	147
173	40 6/8	43	14 7/8	14 7/8	5 7/8	5 7/8	27 7/8	28 3/8	Wrangell Mts., AK	Charles A. Pohland	Charles A. Pohland	1971	147
173	43 6/8	44	13 5/8	13 5/8	6	6	28	28	Chugach Mts., AK	Thomas Clark	Thomas Clark	1975	147
172 7/8	40 4/8	41 6/8	14	13 7/8	6 6/8	6 7/8	24 1/8	24 3/8	Chugach Mts., AK	Daniel G. Montgomery	Daniel G. Montgomery	1991	155
172 7/8	41 6/8	40 1/8	14 2/8	14 1/8	6 6/8	6 6/8	28	28	Mackenzie Mts., NT	F. Michael Parkowski	F. Michael Parkowski	1991	155
172 7/8	40 1/8	43	14 2/8	14 2/8	6 3/8	6 2/8	25 1/8	25 1/8	Chugach Mts., AK	Peter W. Bading	Peter W. Bading	1961	155
172 7/8	39 1/8	39	14 4/8	14 2/8	7 7/8	7 7/8	25 1/8	25 1/8	Wrangell Mts., AK	Ralph Cox	Ralph Cox	1971	155
172 6/8	43 7/8	42 6/8	14 4/8	14 4/8	6 1/8	6 1/8	24	24 2/8	Alaska Range, AK	George Faerber	Buckhorn Mus. & Saloon, Ltd.	1976	158
172 6/8	40 3/8	40 3/8	13 4/8	13 4/8	7 7/8	7 7/8	20 6/8	22	Kusawa Lake, YT	John I. Moore	John I. Moore	1955	158
172 6/8	38 7/8	41 7/8	14 2/8	14 2/8	8	8	27 7/8	27 7/8	Nabesna River, AK	J.C. Phillips	J.C. Phillips	1956	158
172 6/8	41 2/8	41 2/8	13 5/8	13 6/8	6 6/8	6 6/8	25 6/8	25 6/8	Chugach Mts., AK	Ruby Wyatt	Ruby Wyatt	1960	158
172 6/8	43 5/8	43 3/8	13 5/8	13 5/8	6 4/8	6 4/8	33	33	Chugach Mts., AK	Richard Kopsack	Richard Kopsack	1963	158
172 6/8	41 2/8	41 2/8	14 2/8	14 1/8	6 4/8	6 4/8	28 5/8	28 5/8	Wrangell Mts., AK	Alvin W. Huba, Jr.	Alvin W. Huba, Jr.	1968	158
172 6/8	40	40 4/8	15	15	7	7	30 3/8	30 3/8	Gerstle River, AK	John A. Shilling	John A. Shilling	1968	158
172 6/8	41 7/8	41 7/8	14 1/8	14 1/8	6 3/8	6 3/8	29	29	Radelet Creek, BC	Norman W. Dougan	Norman W. Dougan	1972	158
172 6/8	43 2/8	43 2/8	13 6/8	13 6/8	5 7/8	5 7/8	28 5/8	28 5/8	Chandalar River, AK	Robert M. Welch	Robert M. Welch	1974	158
172 6/8	43 1/8	43 1/8	14	14	5 5/8	5 5/8	30 1/8	30 3/8	Wrangell Mts., AK	Robert J. Wykel	Robert J. Wykel	1976	158
172 5/8	40 2/8	41 2/8	15	15	5 7/8	5 7/8	28 5/8	29	Mountain River, NT	Edmond D. Henley	Edmond D. Henley	1983	168
172 5/8	43 4/8	43 4/8	13 2/8	12 7/8	7	7	29 4/8	29 4/8	Knik Glacier, AK	Picked Up	Howard G. Romig	1932	168
172 5/8	42 1/8	42	13 4/8	13 4/8	6 6/8	6 4/8	26 3/8	26 3/8	Mt. Arkell, YT	Stuart Hall	Stuart Hall	1957	168

DALL'S SHEEP

Ovis dalli dalli and Ovis dalli kenaiensis

Score	Length of Horn R	L	Circumference of Base R	L	Circumference at Third Quarter R	L	Greatest Spread	Tip to Tip Spread	Locality	Hunter	Owner	Date Killed	Rank
172 5/8	42	41 3/8	14 5/8	14 6/8	5 7/8	5 6/8	32	32	Wrangell Mts., AK	William T. Ellis	William T. Ellis	1960	168
172 5/8	38 7/8	39 2/8	14 7/8	15 3/8	6 5/8	6 7/8	33 7/8	33 1/8	Caribou Creek, YT	Harold J. Lund	Harold J. Lund	1963	168
172 5/8	41 5/8	42	14 4/8	14 2/8	8 6/8	6 2/8	27 1/8	27 1/8	Yukon	S.P. Viezner	S.P. Viezner	1964	168
172 5/8	41 1/8	41 6/8	14 1/8	14 1/8	6 3/8	6 2/8	29 7/8	29 7/8	Knik River, AK	Miles G. France	Miles G. France	1969	168
172 5/8	42	41 3/8	13	13	7 6/8	7 3/8	21 6/8	21 6/8	Talbot Creek, YT	Lloyd E. Zeman	Jenifer D. Schmidt	1959	168
172 4/8	42 4/8	41 4/8	14 2/8	14 2/8	6 4/8	6 6/8	26 1/8	26 1/8	Wrangell Mts., AK	W.A. Bailey, Jr.	W.A. Bailey, Jr.	1960	175
172 4/8	43 4/8	42 6/8	13 1/8	13 1/8	7 2/8	6 7/8	24 3/8	24 3/8	Wrangell Mts., AK	H.E. Eldred	H.E. Eldred	1960	175
172 4/8	39 5/8	45 1/8	14 1/8	14	5 6/8	5 6/8	27 5/8	27 5/8	Chugach Mts., AK	Raymond Capossela	Raymond Capossela	1963	175
172 4/8	41 1/8	42 1/8	14 2/8	14 2/8	6 1/8	6	31 3/8	31 3/8	Primrose Lake, YT	Walter Sutton	Walter Sutton	1968	175
172 4/8	40 6/8	42	14 6/8	15	6 4/8	6 3/8	26 6/8	26 6/8	Mackenzie Mts., NT	Leslie C. Finger	Leslie C. Finger	1985	175
172 3/8	41 5/8	41 2/8	13 5/8	13 6/8	6 6/8	6 6/8	25 1/8	25	Chugach Mts., AK	Chuck Moe	Chuck Moe	1979	180
172 3/8	42 7/8	41 6/8	14 2/8	14 2/8	6 5/8	6 1/8	21 1/8	21 1/8	Granite Lake, YT	William E. Medley II	William E. Medley II	1980	180
172 3/8	41 4/8	41 7/8	14 1/8	14 2/8	6 4/8	6 6/8	23	22 7/8	Mackenzie Mts., NT	Dan L. Johnerson	Dan L. Johnerson	1989	180
172 3/8	45	41 3/8	14	13 7/8	5 5/8	5 6/8	27 2/8	27 2/8	Alaska Range, AK	Joseph C. LoMonaco	Joseph C. LoMonaco	1992	180
172 2/8	45 7/8	44 7/8	13 2/8	13 2/8	5 5/8	6	32	32	Copper River, AK	C.J. McElroy	C.J. McElroy	1977	184
172 2/8	43 1/8	43 3/8	13 5/8	13 4/8	6 2/8	6 3/8	26 6/8	26 4/8	Chugach Mts., AK	Michael L. Kasterin	Michael L. Kasterin	1986	184
172 2/8	42 3/8	41 3/8	13 4/8	13 5/8	6 5/8	6 5/8	23	22 7/8	Chugach Mts., AK	Ethan Williams	Ethan Williams	1988	184
172 2/8	41 1/8	42 5/8	13 2/8	13 2/8	7 3/8	7	23 6/8	23 6/8	McCarthy, AK	Picked Up	John W. Adams	1996	184
172 1/8	40	39 7/8	14 2/8	14 2/8	6 4/8	6 6/8	24 3/8	24 3/8	Wrangell Mts., AK	Kirk Gay	Kirk Gay	1958	188
172 1/8	39 7/8	39	15 4/8	15 3/8	7	6 5/8	26	26	Wrangell Mts., AK	Horace Groff	Horace Groff	1961	188
172 1/8	38 5/8	38	14 1/8	14 1/8	7	7	21 7/8	21 3/8	Chugach Mts., AK	E.F. Craig	E.F. Craig	1963	188
172 1/8	42	41 7/8	14 5/8	14 6/8	6	6 2/8	25 6/8	25 6/8	Wrangell Mts., AK	Walter E. Cox	Walter E. Cox	1966	188
172 1/8	43	38 7/8	14 4/8	14 4/8	5 7/8	5 7/8	29 2/8	29 2/8	Kuskokwim River, AK	Ken M. Wilson	Ken M. Wilson	1973	188
172	41 3/8	41 7/8	14 5/8	14 6/8	6 2/8	5 7/8	26 2/8	26 2/8	Wrangell Mts., AK	Carroll W. Gibbs	Carroll W. Gibbs	1957	193
172	43 6/8	44 6/8	13 6/8	13 6/8	5 6/8	6	26 1/8	26 1/8	Chugach Mts., AK	M.L. Magnusson	M.L. Magnusson	1957	193
172	41 6/8	42	13 5/8	13 5/8	6 4/8	7	25 3/8	25 3/8	Sheep Mt., YT	Ray Hoffman III	Ray Hoffman III	1961	193
172	36	39	15	15 1/8	8	8	22 6/8	20	Chugach Mts., AK	Ward Gay, Jr.	Ward Gay, Jr.	1962	193
172	41 4/8	41 4/8	14 4/8	14 2/8	6 2/8	6 2/8	22 3/8	22 3/8	Sekwi Mt., NT	J.D. Martin, Jr.	J.D. Martin, Jr.	1978	193
171 7/8	45 2/8	42 7/8	13 1/8	13 1/8	6	6 7/8	27 6/8	27 6/8	McCarthy, AK	Eugene E. Saxton	Eugene E. Saxton	1953	198
171 7/8	43 2/8	41 3/8	13 5/8	13 4/8	6 2/8	6 1/8	25 4/8	25 4/8	Talkeetna Mts., AK	Paul S. Lawrence	Paul S. Lawrence	1960	198
171 7/8	39 5/8	38	15 6/8	15 7/8	6	6 2/8	25 6/8	25 6/8	Wrangell Mts., AK	Kenneth Knudson	Kenneth Knudson	1963	198
171 7/8	41 4/8	40 1/8	13 3/8	13 3/8	7 6/8	7 3/8	24 4/8	24 4/8	Chugach Mts., AK	Herb Klein	Herb Klein	1964	198
171 7/8	41 5/8	40 2/8	14 6/8	14 4/8	6 1/8	6 3/8	22 6/8	22 2/8	Chugach Mts., AK	Frank Cook	Frank Cook	1965	198
171 7/8	40 4/8	40 5/8	14 1/8	14 2/8	6 3/8	6 3/8	28 2/8	28 2/8	Wrangell Mts., AK	Brent R. Hanks	Brent R. Hanks	1983	198
171 7/8	42 7/8	43	13 1/8	13 1/8	6 7/8	6 6/8	25 1/8	25 1/8	Robertson River, AK	David C. Sharp	David C. Sharp	1987	198
171 6/8	38 7/8	42 5/8	14	13 7/8	6 5/8	6 4/8	28 4/8	28 4/8	Wrangell Mts., AK	Charles C. Parsons	Charles C. Parsons	1955	205
171 6/8	42 7/8	42 3/8	13 7/8	14	6 3/8	6 2/8	30 7/8	30 7/8	Wrangell Mts., AK	Ross Jardine	Ross Jardine	1960	205
171 6/8	35 3/8	42	14 7/8	14 7/8	6 5/8	6 7/8	24 3/8	24 3/8	Chugach Mts., AK	C.J. McElroy	C.J. McElroy	1969	205

Score	Length of Horn R	Length of Horn L	Circumference of Base R	Circumference of Base L	Circumference Third Quarter R	Circumference Third Quarter L	Greatest Spread	Tip to Tip Spread	Locality	Hunter	Owner	Date Killed	Rank
171 6/8	40 2/8	44 2/8	13 7/8	13 7/8	6 2/8	6 3/8	30 3/8	30 3/8	Ivishak River, AK	Charles W. Troutman	Charles W. Troutman	1987	205
171 6/8	42 1/8	41 5/8	14 7/8	14 6/8	5 6/8	5 6/8	23 5/8	23 5/8	Chugach Mts., AK	Mark D. Truax	Mark D. Truax	1992	205
171 6/8	41	42	14 5/8	14 5/8	5 5/8	5 4/8	24 3/8	24 2/8	Canyon Creek, YT	George F. Dennis, Jr.	George F. Dennis, Jr.	1993	205
171 5/8	41 6/8	41 7/8	14 1/8	14 3/8	5 7/8	6 1/8	26 5/8	26 5/8	Chugach Mts., AK	Justin L. Smith	Justin L. Smith	1963	211
171 5/8	41	40 3/8	14 4/8	14 4/8	6 7/8	6 7/8	22 1/8	22 1/8	Nabesna Glacier, AK	John F. Saltz	John F. Saltz	1983	211
171 4/8	40 5/8	40 6/8	13 6/8	13 6/8	6 2/8	5 7/8	23 4/8	23 4/8	Kenai Pen., AK	C.R. Wright	C.R. Wright	1936	213
171 4/8	39 4/8	40 6/8	15	15	5 7/8	6 6/8	28	28	Whitehorse, YT	Howard Creason	Howard Creason	1969	213
171 4/8	41 5/8	41 5/8	14 6/8	14 6/8	6 7/8	5 6/8	26	26	Wrangell Mts., AK	Robert V. Walker	Robert V. Walker	1971	213
171 3/8	44 3/8	45 2/8	13 5/8	13 5/8	5 6/8	7 7/8	34 2/8	34 2/8	Wood River, AK	R.R.M. Carpenter	Acad. Nat. Sci., Phil.	1940	216
171 3/8	40 1/8	40 1/8	13 5/8	13	6 7/8	7 5/8	27 2/8	27 2/8	Coal Creek, AK	W.W. Fultz	W.W. Fultz	1955	216
171 3/8	41 2/8	41 2/8	14	13 6/8	6 3/8	6 2/8	30 3/8	30 3/8	Chugach Mts., AK	Perley Colbeth	Perley Colbeth	1958	216
171 3/8	42 3/8	42	13 3/8	13 3/8	7 3/8	7 3/8	29 2/8	29 2/8	Wrangell Mts., AK	Arthur R. Dubs	Arthur R. Dubs	1962	216
171 3/8	44	36 3/8	14 6/8	14 6/8	6 3/8	6 7/8	26 4/8	25 6/8	Wrangell Mts., AK	Doug McRae, Sr.	Doug McRae, Sr.	1972	216
171 3/8	41 1/8	41 1/8	14	14	6	6 7/8	26 6/8	26 4/8	Chugach Mts., AK	Michael J. Ebner	Michael J. Ebner	1977	216
171 3/8	42 2/8	42 2/8	14	14	5 6/8	5 7/8	32 2/8	32 2/8	Carcajou River, NT	Colin J. Kure	Colin J. Kure	1980	216
171 3/8	42 3/8	42 1/8	14	13 6/8	5 4/8	5 6/8	22 2/8	22 2/8	Chugach Mts., AK	Anthony R. Russ	Anthony R. Russ	1988	216
171 2/8	42 4/8	42 4/8	13 6/8	14 7/8	7 6/8	7 6/8	24 3/8	24 1/8	Wrangell Mts., AK	Gordon Madole	Gordon Madole	1956	224
171 2/8	38 1/8	36 3/8	14 7/8	12 3/8	9 4/8	9 3/8	21 6/8	21 6/8	Ruby Range, YT	Picked Up	William J. Joslin	1960	224
171 2/8	40	39 4/8	12 4/8	14 3/8	7 1/8	7 1/8	19 6/8	19 6/8	Kluane Range, YT	Phil Temple	Phil Temple	1972	224
171 2/8	39 6/8	39 6/8	14 3/8	14 3/8	7	6	24 1/8	23 7/8	Wrangell Mts., AK	Rudolpho Valladolid	Rudolpho Valladolid	1974	224
171 1/8	41 2/8	41 2/8	14 7/8	14 6/8	6 5/8	6	26 4/8	26 4/8	Wrangell Mts., AK	Picked Up	Dick Gunlogson	1968	228
171 1/8	45	44 1/8	12 1/8	12 1/8	6 2/8	6 6/8	24	24	Kusawa Lake, YT	Maurice G. Katz	Maurice G. Katz	1970	228
171 1/8	42	42 5/8	13 7/8	13 7/8	6 1/8	6	22 3/8	22 2/8	Robertson River, AK	Beuron A. McKenzie	Beuron A. McKenzie	1971	228
171 1/8	40 7/8	40 6/8	13 2/8	13 1/8	6 5/8	6	26 2/8	26 2/8	Chugach Mts., AK	Emil V. Nelson	Emil V. Nelson	1988	228
171	43 2/8	42 7/8	13 5/8	13 5/8	6	5 7/8	30 4/8	30 4/8	Carcross, YT	Henry Brockhouse	Henry Brockhouse	1955	232
171	42 7/8	43 1/8	14	14	5 6/8	8	20 6/8	19 3/8	Chugach Mts., AK	Raymond Capossela	Raymond Capossela	1961	232
171	36 7/8	39 3/8	13 7/8	13 7/8	8 3/8	6 2/8	26 7/8	26 7/8	Alligator Lake, YT	D. Graham	D. Graham	1968	232
171	42 1/8	41 1/8	14	14	6 2/8	6 3/8	26 3/8	26 3/8	Ruby Range, YT	Harry T. Scharfenberg	Harry T. Scharfenberg	1977	232
171	40 6/8	41 2/8	13 6/8	13 6/8	6 3/8	6 1/8	29	29	Greyling Creek, AK	Michael M. Stitzel	Michael M. Stitzel	1986	232
171	41 2/8	40 6/8	14 2/8	14 2/8	6 1/8	6 4/8	28 6/8	28 6/8	Little Tok River, AK	Kenneth L. House	Kenneth L. House	1992	232
171	43	42 5/8	13 4/8	13 3/8	6 4/8	6 4/8	26 3/8	26 3/8	Kenai Pen., AK	David Jones	David Jones	1963	232
170 7/8	41 4/8	41 4/8	14 6/8	14 6/8	5 4/8	5 4/8	25 7/8	25 7/8	Wrangell Mts., AK	Richard Stingley	Richard Stingley	1965	238
170 7/8	35 3/8	36 6/8	15 2/8	15 2/8	7 1/8	7 2/8	29 5/8	29 5/8	Wrangell Mts., AK	Thomas Sperstad	Thomas Sperstad	1969	238
170 7/8	42	42	14 4/8	14 4/8	6 3/8	6 3/8	25 4/8	24 5/8	Chugach Mts., AK	Gerald L. Warnock	Gerald L. Warnock	1970	238
170 7/8	36	36 5/8	14	14 2/8	9 1/8	9 1/8	25 7/8	25 7/8	Trench Lake, NT	Wayne G. Myers	Wayne G. Myers	1974	238
170 7/8	40 6/8	40 7/8	14 2/8	14 2/8	6	6	29	29	Wrangell Mts., AK	Unknown	J. Michael Conoyer	1980	238
170 7/8	41 5/8	41 5/8	14	14	6 4/8	6 4/8	25 3/8	24 6/8	Chugach Mts., AK	Kenneth P. Meinzer	Kenneth P. Meinzer	1992	238
170 6/8	41 7/8	41 5/8	13 5/8	13 5/8	6 4/8	5 6/8	26 4/8	26 4/8	Wrangell Mts., AK	Joseph A. Tedesco	Joseph A. Tedesco	1959	245
170 6/8	41 5/8	41 7/8	14 1/8	14 1/8	5 6/8	6 6/8	28 2/8	28 2/8	Wrangell Mts., AK	George Stelious	George Stelious	1962	245
170 6/8	39 2/8	39 2/8	14 7/8	14	6 6/8	6 1/8	26 4/8	26 4/8	Wrangell Mts., AK	Robert V. Broadbent	Robert V. Broadbent	1965	245
170 6/8	42 2/8	42 4/8	13 6/8	12 7/8	6 1/8	6	30	30 1/8	Teepee Mt., BC	Steve Snider	Jon K. Mahoney	1983	245
170 5/8	44	44	13 4/8	13 7/8	5 5/8	5 4/8	21 3/8	21 3/8	Nabesna River, AK	J.S. Rutherford	J.S. Rutherford	1956	249
170 5/8	41 4/8	41 7/8	12 7/8	14 6/8	7 6/8	7 4/8	25 1/8	25 1/8	Wrangell Mts., AK	W.A. Fisher	W.A. Fisher	1959	249
170 5/8	42 1/8	42 1/8	13 7/8	14 1/8	6 3/8	6 4/8	25 6/8	25 6/8	Wrangell Mts., AK	Gene Sperstad	Gene Sperstad	1961	249
170 5/8	42 2/8	40 7/8	14 1/8	14 6/8	6 3/8	5 5/8	25 2/8	25 2/8	Nutzotin Mts., AK	Dorothy Andersen	Larry Folger	1965	249
170 5/8	41 2/8	42 1/8	14	14	5 3/8	5 2/8	28	28	Chugach Mts., AK	Harry C. Heckendorn	Harry C. Heckendorn	1972	249
170 5/8	39 4/8	41 3/8	14	15	7	6 4/8	18 6/8	19 2/8	S. Nahanni River, NT	Lionel G. Heinrich	Lionel G. Heinrich	1987	249

DALL'S SHEEP

Ovis dalli dalli and Ovis dalli kenaiensis

Score	Length of Horn R	L	Circumference of Base R	L	Circumference at Third Quarter R	L	Greatest Spread	Tip tp Tip Spread	Locality	Hunter	Owner	Date Killed	Rank
170 5/8	41 4/8	41 1/8	14 4/8	14 4/8	6 2/8	6	25 3/8	25 1/8	Hawkins Glacier, AK	Terrance S. Marcum	Terrance S. Marcum	1997	249
170 4/8	44 2/8	38	13 5/8	13 6/8	6 4/8	6 4/8	29 3/8	29 3/8	Wrangell Mts., AK	Harry L. Swank, Jr.	Harry L. Swank, Jr.	1962	256
170 4/8	40 2/8	40 6/8	14 4/8	14 4/8	6 2/8	6 4/8	21 3/8	21 3/8	Ruby Range, YT	Harold C. Casey	Harold C. Casey	1964	256
170 4/8	41 2/8	41 2/8	14 2/8	14 2/8	6 3/8	6 4/8	23 6/8	23 6/8	Brooks Range, AK	Donald E. Harrell	Donald E. Harrell	1979	256
170 4/8	41 3/8	41 3/8	13 5/8	13 5/8	6 7/8	6 7/8	26 3/8	26 3/8	Ogilvie River, YT	Charles L. Baldridge	Charles L. Baldridge	1987	256
170 4/8	43 1/8	43 7/8	13 2/8	13 2/8	6	6 3/8	25 7/8	25 6/8	Eklutna River, AK	Robert L. Lynch	Robert L. Lynch	1994	256
170 3/8	42 1/8	42 1/8	14	14	6	6 1/8	25 6/8	25 6/8	Talkeetna Mts., AK	William C. Cloyd	William C. Cloyd	1995	256
170 3/8	40	40 3/8	14 2/8	14 2/8	6 2/8	6 2/8	22	22	Kenai Pen., AK	Vance Corrigan	Vance Corrigan	1957	262
170 3/8	39 7/8	43	14 2/8	14 2/8	6 2/8	6 2/8	28	28	Wrangell Mts., AK	J.A. Tadesco	J.A. Tadesco	1960	262
170 3/8	41 5/8	42 4/8	14 2/8	14 2/8	5 6/8	5 7/8	27 7/8	27 7/8	Wrangell Mts., AK	Willie Bogner, Sr.	Willie Bogner, Sr.	1961	262
170 3/8	42 4/8	43 5/8	13 2/8	13 2/8	5 7/8	6 4/8	31 2/8	31 2/8	Chugach Mts., AK	William H. Smith	William H. Smith	1961	262
170 3/8	40 6/8	40 3/8	13 7/8	13 7/8	6 7/8	6 6/8	23 7/8	23 7/8	Alaska Range, AK	James W. Thompson	James W. Thompson	1986	262
170 3/8	42	38 7/8	14 2/8	14 2/8	6 1/8	6 2/8	25 4/8	25 4/8	Chugach Mts., AK	Gene N. Meyer	Gene N. Meyer	1996	262
170 2/8	40 5/8	41 3/8	14 1/8	14 1/8	5 6/8	6 1/8	22 2/8	22 2/8	Kenai Pen., AK	C.R. Wright	C.R. Wright	1935	268
170 2/8	39 7/8	39 7/8	14 5/8	14 5/8	6 2/8	6 4/8	25 3/8	25 3/8	Champagne, YT	Walter Butcher	Walter Butcher	1956	268
170 2/8	39 5/8	41 7/8	15 3/8	15 3/8	5 6/8	5 6/8	23 3/8	23 3/8	Tonsina Creek, AK	R.J. Uhl	R.J. Uhl	1959	268
170 2/8	38 7/8	39 7/8	13 6/8	13 6/8	7 6/8	7 6/8	19 6/8	19 6/8	Chugach Mts., AK	Donald Stroble	Donald Stroble	1961	268
170 2/8	37 2/8	38	14 7/8	14 7/8	7	6 7/8	20 6/8	19 4/8	Kenai Pen., AK	Lee Miller	Lee Miller	1963	268
170 2/8	40 3/8	40	14 6/8	14 6/8	6 2/8	6 2/8	27 2/8	27 2/8	Wrangell Mts., AK	C. Driskell	C. Driskell	1965	268
170 2/8	41	40	14 5/8	14 5/8	5 7/8	5 7/8	28 3/8	28 3/8	Wrangell Mts., AK	Jim Baballa	Jim Baballa	1967	268
170 2/8	38 2/8	37 6/8	13 6/8	13 6/8	8 2/8	9 2/8	21	20 5/8	Robertson River, AK	John W. Redmond	John W. Redmond	1970	268
170 2/8	41 2/8	41 4/8	13 6/8	13 6/8	6 4/8	6 4/8	25 7/8	25 7/8	Talkeetna Mts., AK	H. Albertas Hall	H. Albertas Hall	1971	268
170 2/8	40	40	14 4/8	14 4/8	6 4/8	7	26 6/8	23 6/8	Wrangell Mts., AK	Bernard J. Meinerz	Bernard J. Meinerz	1972	268
170 2/8	42 7/8	42 7/8	13 4/8	13 4/8	5 7/8	6	29 2/8	29 2/8	Snake River, YT	Norman M. Thachuk	Norman M. Thachuk	1982	268
170 2/8	41 1/8	41 1/8	14	14	6 6/8	6 6/8	21 4/8	21 2/8	Mackenzie Mts., NT	Alan Means	Alan Means	1991	268
170 2/8	39 6/8	39	14 3/8	14 3/8	6 4/8	6 2/8	29 2/8	29	Hunter Creek, AK	James C. Becker	James C. Becker	1993	268
170 2/8	41	41	13 6/8	13 6/8	6 4/8	6 4/8	27	27	Talkeetna Mts., AK	Robert L. Hodson	Robert L. Hodson	1995	268
170 1/8	42	42 7/8	13 5/8	13 5/8	6 5/8	6 7/8	28	28	Donjek, YT	Unknown	Acad. Nat. Sci., Phil.	1921	282
170 1/8	40 1/8	41	14 5/8	14 5/8	6 3/8	6 2/8	25 4/8	25 4/8	Mt. Arkell, YT	Ed Steiner	Ed Steiner	1955	282
170 1/8	40 2/8	40 3/8	13 2/8	13 2/8	7 6/8	7 5/8	22	22	Wrangell Mts., AK	Chester Beer	Chester Beer	1959	282
170 1/8	41 4/8	41 1/8	14	14	5 5/8	5 5/8	24 5/8	24 5/8	Chugach Mts., AK	James A. Kirsch	James A. Kirsch	1961	282
170 1/8	38	37 3/8	14 2/8	14 2/8	8 2/8	8 2/8	20 3/8	20 5/8	Wrangell Mts., AK	W.T. Yoshimoto	W.T. Yoshimoto	1967	282
170	42	42 2/8	13 1/8	13 1/8	6 1/8	6 1/8	30 1/8	30 1/8	Wrangell Mts., AK	Ralph Morava, Jr.	Ralph Morava, Jr.	1954	287
170	40 6/8	42 2/8	14 3/8	14 3/8	6 1/8	6 1/8	27 3/8	27 3/8	Nabesna River, AK	Raymond A. Talbott	Raymond A. Talbott	1958	287
170	40 2/8	39 4/8	13 4/8	13 4/8	7 5/8	8 2/8	23 3/8	23 3/8	Kluane Lake, YT	Herb Graham	Herb Graham	1959	287
170	41 5/8	42 5/8	13 6/8	13 6/8	6 1/8	6	23 4/8	23 4/8	Wrangell Mts., AK	Mrs. Melvin Soder	Mrs. Melvin Soder	1961	287
170	41 6/8	42	13 3/8	13 3/8	6 4/8	6 5/8	23 5/8	23 5/8	Farewell Lake, AK	Frank G. Merz	Frank G. Merz	1983	287
170	41 7/8	42 7/8	14	14	5 7/8	5 6/8	24 4/8	24 4/8	Haley Creek, AK	Larry C. Munn	Larry C. Munn	1985	287

Score									Hunter	Owner	Locality	Date	Rank
170	38 7/8	40 7/8	14	14 1/8	6 6/8	6 5/8	24	24	Clark Johnson	Clark Johnson	Snake River, YT	1988	287
170	40 5/8	37 7/8	14	13 6/8	7 2/8	7 2/8	22 1/8	22 1/8	Russell Scribner	Russell Scribner	Chugach Mts., AK	1988	287
170	41 1/8	40 1/8	13 7/8	13 7/8	6 7/8	6 6/8	28 2/8	28 2/8	Philipp Heuchert	Philipp Heuchert	Arctic Red River, NT	1991	287
170	39 5/8	37 1/8	14	14	7 4/8	7 4/8	21 6/8	19 2/8	Mark W. Bills	Mark W. Bills	Ptarmigan Creek, AK	1993	287
170	42 4/8	42	13 2/8	13 2/8	6 3/8	6	26	26	Picked Up	John Greenwood	Chugach Mts., AK	1996	287
176*	46	44 4/8	14 4/8	14 5/8	5 5/8	5 3/8	31 4/8	31 4/8	Roscoe D. Uscola	Roscoe D. Uscola	Tok, AK	1995	
172 6/8*	41	41	14 1/8	14 1/8	7 2/8	7 6/8	27	27	John P. Bast	John P. Bast	White Mts., AK	1995	

* Final score is subject to revision by additional verifying measurements.

CATEGORY
DALL'S SHEEP

SCORE
170-5/8

HUNTER
TERRANCE S. MARCUM

LOCATION
HAWKINS GLACIER, AK

DATE OF KILL
AUGUST 1997

CATEGORY
DALL'S SHEEP

SCORE
174

HUNTER
KELLY R. ELMER

LOCATION
KEELE RIVER, NT

DATE OF KILL
SEPTEMBER 1997

CATEGORY
DALL'S SHEEP

SCORE
170-7/8

HUNTER
KENNETH P. MEINZER

LOCATION
CHUGACH MTS., AK

DATE OF KILL
1993

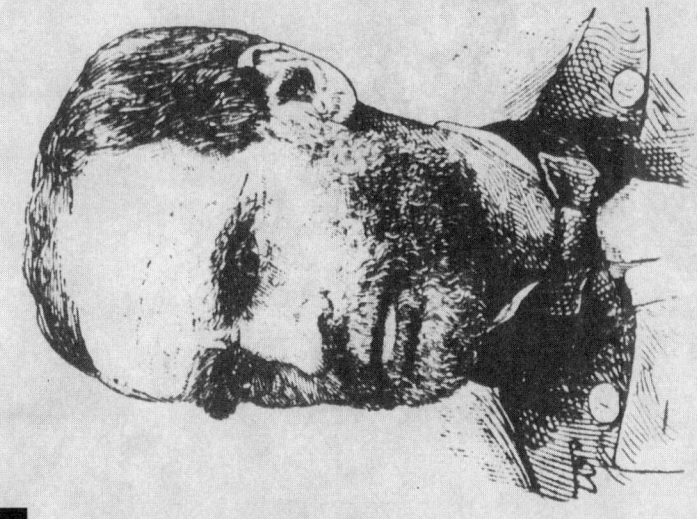

GENERAL WILLIAM TECUMSEH SHERMAN
1820-1891

Ranked second only to General Ulysses S. Grant as the greatest northern commander in the Civil War, Gen. Sherman was considered a master of modern warfare. He was born in Ohio in 1820 and later went to West Point. He saw service in California during the Mexican War and later became the head of Louisiana University. He resigned that position in 1861 to rejoin the Army of the North. As a commander, he led his troops at Bull Run, Shiloh and, in 1864, in the defining campaign of his career, took Atlanta, defeating Confederate commander General Joseph E. Johnson. With Grant as President, Sherman became commander of the U.S. Army until retiring in 1884. He moved to New York City in 1886 and died there in 1891. ■

697

STONE'S SHEEP
WORLD'S RECORD

L.S. Chadwick was enterprising enough to hunt Stone's sheep (*Ovis dalli stonei*) in the upper Muskwa River country of British Columbia in 1936, long before the Alcan Highway made a formerly virgin game range more accessible. He was accompanied by Roy Hargreaves, with whom he had hunted several times in that region as well as local guides Walter (Curly) Cochrane and Frank Golata.

On the evening the campsite was reached, Hargreaves looked the country over with a 20x spotting scope and saw a few sheep on a distant mountain. The next morning the whole party rode over in that direction, and in the early afternoon they saw three rams on the skyline of a ridge, about a mile and a half away. The horses were left with the guides while Chadwick started off with Hargreaves for the final approach.

"We went up pretty fast for a man close to 62 years of age, but when my hatband, which was tight, banked up a large pool of perspiration, I would remove the hat and scoop off several handfuls of water, take a short rest, then plod on toward the top, with dry mouth and my shoes slowly filling with perspiration.

"When we arrived at the top, the sheep were gone, as was to be expected, but we sighted them down in the Muskwa Valley, two thousand feet or more below. Then down over the rock slide with sore feet and trembling knees we went, until we got to within about 200 yards of them. We stopped

and took movies of the three and I undertook to shoot the big one.

"My first shot was low, through his brisket. I used the scope for the first time. He started off at a terrible speed and I started to pour lead into him. I shot four times, one of these hitting him lightly in the hip. Roy followed him on the run and, when he started up the mountain, he could not keep up with the other rams and this gave Roy a chance to get in the finishing shot.

"He fell down a sharp ravine into a little brook. I was about all in and, of course, could not keep up with Roy. It was a very bad place to get to, but we both got down to the sheep without a fall, and when we got to him, we saw that he was well worth the hard work.

"He had the most magnificent head I had ever seen, but not an overly large body. He had two almost perfect horns. The right horn was slightly broken on the end and only measured 50-4/8 inches. The left horn was pointed clear to the end and measured 52-1/8 inches. They were both a little over 15-3/8 inches at the base and the spread was 31-2/8 inches. All told, he was the finest head I had ever seen. If he is not a record head, he is close to it."

Scored at a World's Record 196-6/8, this is the only recorded ram ever taken in North America with horns over 50 inches long, and it is widely regarded as the best big game trophy this continent has produced. ■

TROPHY INFO

RANK
World's Record

SCORE
196 6/8

LOCATION
Muskwa River, BC

HUNTER
L.S. Chadwick

OWNER
B&C National
Collection

DATE KILLED
1936

Photograph by Wm. H. Nesbitt

STONE'S SHEEP
WORLD'S RECORD SCORECHART

All measurements must be made with a 1/4-inch wide flexible steel tape to the nearest one-eighth of an inch. Enter fractional figures in eighths, without reduction. Official measurements cannot be taken until horns have air dried for at least 60 days after the animal was killed.

A. Greatest Spread is measured between perpendiculars at a right angle to the center line of the skull.

B. Tip to Tip Spread is measured between tips of horns.

C. Length of Horn is measured from the lowest point in front on outer curve to a point in line with tip. **Do not** press tape into depressions. The low point of the outer curve of the horn is considered to be the low point of the frontal portion of the horn, situated above and slightly medial to the eye socket (not the outside edge). Use a straight edge, perpendicular to horn axis, to end measurement on "broomed" horns.

D-1. Circumference of Base is measured at a right angle to axis of horn. **Do not** follow irregular edge of horn; the line of measurement must be entirely on horn material.

D-2-3-4. Divide measurement C of longer horn by four. Starting at base, mark **both** horns at these quarters (even though the other horn is shorter) and measure circumferences at these marks, with measurements taken at right angles to horn axis.

Records of
North American
Big Game

250 Station Drive
Missoula, MT 59801
(406) 542-1888

BOONE AND CROCKETT CLUB®

OFFICIAL SCORING SYSTEM FOR NORTH AMERICAN BIG GAME TROPHIES

SHEEP

MINIMUM SCORES	AWARDS	ALL-TIME
bighorn	175	180
desert	165	168
Dall's	160	170
Stone's	165	170

KIND OF SHEEP (check one)
- ☐ bighorn
- ☐ desert
- ☐ Dall's
- ☑ Stone's

PLUG NUMBER

Measure to a Point in Line With Horn Tip

SEE OTHER SIDE FOR INSTRUCTIONS		COLUMN 1 Right Horn	COLUMN 2 Left Horn	COLUMN 3 Difference
A. Greatest Spread (Is Often Tip to Tip Spread)	31			
B. Tip to Tip Spread	31			
C. Length of Horn		50 1/8	51 5/8	1 4/8
D-1. Circumference of Base		14 6/8	14 6/8	0
D-2. Circumference at First Quarter		14 1/8	14 2/8	1/8
D-3. Circumference at Second Quarter		11 7/8	12 1/8	2/8
D-4. Circumference at Third Quarter		6 6/8	7	2/8
	TOTALS	97 5/8	99 6/8	5/8

ADD	Column 1	97 5/8	Exact Locality Where Killed: Muskwa River, BC
	Column 2	99 6/8	Date Killed: 1936 — Hunter: L.S. Chadwick
	Subtotal	197 3/8	Owner: B&C National Collection of Heads and Horns — Telephone #:
SUBTRACT Column 3		5/8	Owner's Address:
FINAL SCORE		196 6/8	Guide's Name and Address:
			Remarks: (Mention Any Abnormalities or Unique Qualities)

I, **Grancel Fitz**   , certify that I have measured this trophy on **04/10/1951**
  PRINT NAME   MM/DD/YYYY

at **American Museum of Natural History**   **New York**   **NY**
   STREET ADDRESS   CITY   STATE/PROVINCE

and that these measurements and data are, to the best of my knowledge and belief, made in accordance with the instructions given.

Witness: _____ **Samuel B. Webb**   Signature: **Grancel Fitz**   I.D. Number: _____
                                                              B&C OFFICIAL MEASURER

STONE'S SHEEP

Ovis dalli stonei

MINIMUM SCORE 170

Score	Length of Horn R	L	Circumference of Base R	L	Circumference at Third Quarter R	L	Greatest Spread	Tip to Tip Spread	Locality	Hunter	Owner	Date Killed	Rank
196 6/8	50 1/8	51 5/8	14 6/8	14 6/8	6 6/8	7	31	31	Muskwa River, BC	L.S. Chadwick	B&C National Collection	1936	1
190	46 6/8	46 6/8	15 2/8	15 1/8	6 5/8	6 6/8	30 6/8	30 6/8	Sikanni River, BC	Norman Blank	Norman Blank	1962	2
189 6/8	48 2/8	46 2/8	14 7/8	14 7/8	7 2/8	7 4/8	28	28	Blue Sheep Lake, BC	G.C.F. Dalziel	G.C.F. Dalziel	1965	3
187 4/8	43	44	14 6/8	14 6/8	8 4/8	8 4/8	22	22	Ospika River, BC	Paul D. Weingart	Paul D. Weingart	1970	4
185 3/8	45 6/8	44 3/8	15 7/8	15 7/8	6 1/8	5 7/8	29 3/8	29 3/8	Prophet River, BC	Felipe Palau	Felipe Palau	1970	5
184 6/8	43	43 4/8	15 6/8	15 6/8	7 1/8	7 1/8	28 4/8	28 4/8	Prophet River, BC	Joseph H. Shirk	Mrs. C. Barnaby	1948	6
184 4/8	44 4/8	45	15 4/8	15 3/8	6 3/8	6 4/8	26 3/8	26 3/8	Hudson Hope, BC	John W. Pitney	Am. Mus. Nat. Hist.	1936	7
184 3/8	44 3/8	46	14 1/8	14 2/8	8	7	28 6/8	28 6/8	Colt Lake, BC	Lloyd E. Hall	Lloyd E. Hall	1963	8
184 2/8	42 1/8	42 3/8	16 2/8	16 2/8	7 1/8	7 1/8	24 4/8	24 4/8	Blue Sheep Lake, BC	G.C.F. Dalziel	G.C.F. Dalziel	1964	9
184 2/8	47 5/8	45 3/8	14 2/8	14 4/8	6 6/8	6 3/8	31 3/8	31 3/8	Colt Lake, BC	Herb Klein	Herb Klein	1965	9
183 7/8	44 4/8	42 7/8	14 7/8	15	7 3/8	7 5/8	22 5/8	22 3/8	Kechika Range, BC	Arthur R. Dubs	Arthur R. Dubs	1966	12
183 7/8	44 3/8	45 5/8	13 7/8	13 7/8	7	7 5/8	23 7/8	23 7/8	Hudson Hope, BC	Picked Up	Bill Beattie	1961	12
183 5/8	43 3/8	43 2/8	14 7/8	14 7/8	7 1/8	7	20 5/8	19	Dease Lake, BC	Otis Chandler	Otis Chandler	1966	14
183 5/8	43 3/8	44	14 7/8	14 4/8	8 1/8	8	25 7/8	25 7/8	Sikanni Chief River, BC	Picked Up	B. & D. Beattie	1962	14
183 3/8	44 6/8	44 1/8	15	15	6 6/8	6 4/8	20 1/8	22 6/8	Muncho Lake, BC	Jeff Browne	Jeff Browne	1990	16
183 3/8	43	42 2/8	14 7/8	14 4/8	6 6/8	6 6/8	26 3/8	26 1/8	Kechika Range, BC	John Caputo, Jr.	John Caputo, Jr.	1961	16
183 2/8	49 2/8	44 7/8	13 4/8	13 4/8	6 7/8	5 7/8	25	25	Terminus Mt., BC	Picked Up	Herb Klein	1969	18
183 1/8	44 1/8	43 5/8	15 6/8	15 6/8	7 6/8	7	27	27	Buckinghorse River, BC	Keith Brown	Keith Brown	1971	19
183	44 7/8	46 4/8	14 1/8	14 4/8	6 7/8	7 1/8	29 6/8	29 5/8	Cassiar Mts., BC	Robert S. Jackson	Robert S. Jackson	1968	20
183	45 4/8	44 4/8	14	14	7 6/8	7 6/8	25 3/8	25 3/8	Muskwa River, BC	T.E. Shillingburg	T.E. Shillingburg	1937	20
183	44	44 6/8	14 5/8	14 6/8	7 3/8	7	25 7/8	25 7/8	Kechika Range, BC	John Caputo, Sr.	John Caputo, Sr.	1966	20
182 6/8	45 6/8	44 6/8	14 6/8	14 6/8	6 5/8	6 5/8	27 6/8	27 6/8	Cassiar Mts., BC	Gordon Studer	Gordon Studer	1967	23
182 6/8	46 1/8	45 7/8	14 4/8	14 4/8	6 6/8	6 6/8	26 3/8	26 2/8	Cassiar Mts., BC	Alex Cox	Alex Cox	1959	23
182 4/8	43	42 2/8	15 1/8	15 1/8	7 1/8	7 1/8	24 7/8	24 7/8	Redfern Lake, BC	James P. Winters	James P. Winters	1970	25
182 3/8	42 5/8	41 7/8	14 6/8	14 6/8	7 7/8	7 7/8	24	24	Chlotapecta Creek, BC	Gary F. Bogner	Gary F. Bogner	1987	26
182 3/8	45 1/8	45 6/8	14 5/8	14 6/8	6 3/8	6 4/8	31 4/8	31 2/8	Telegraph Creek, BC	Mrs. John Crowe	Mrs. John Crowe	1967	26
182	43	44 7/8	14 5/8	14 5/8	7	7	26 6/8	26 6/8	Kechika Range, BC	Hallett Ward, Jr.	Hallett Ward, Jr.	1967	28
182	41	42	15 4/8	15 4/8	8	8 2/8	27	27	Prophet River, BC	John E. Hammett, Jr.	John E. Hammett, Jr.	1944	28
182	45 6/8	45 4/8	14 2/8	14 2/8	6 7/8	7 1/8	26 4/8	26 4/8	Sand Pile Lake, BC	Al Robbins	Al Robbins	1963	28
181 7/8	45 1/8	44 5/8	14 4/8	14 4/8	6 5/8	6 5/8	26	26	Gataga Mts., BC	Gary Moore	Gary Moore	1965	31
181 4/8	43 3/8	43 4/8	15 1/8	15 1/8	6 4/8	6 5/8	26 5/8	26 5/8	Cassiar Mts., BC	Norman Lougheed	Norman Lougheed	1965	32
181 3/8	39	45 2/8	14 3/8	14 3/8	7 6/8	7 6/8	23 6/8	23 6/8	Burnt Rose Lake, BC	Lloyd E. Zeman	Jenifer D. Schmidt	1970	33
181	44 3/8	44 6/8	15	14 7/8	6 4/8	6 4/8	27 2/8	27 2/8	Toad River, BC	Jerry E. Dahl	Jerry E. Dahl	1971	34
180 7/8	44 3/8	44 7/8	14 3/8	14 3/8	6 2/8	6 3/8	30 5/8	30 5/8	Watson Lake, BC	C.W. Houle	C.W. Houle	1967	35
180 7/8	41 4/8	42 3/8	15	14 7/8	7 2/8	7 3/8	26 6/8	26 6/8	Hudson Hope, BC	Don Beattie	Don Beattie	1945	35
180 5/8	44	43 1/8	14 7/8	14 6/8	6 6/8	6 7/8	26 2/8	26 2/8	Sand Pile Lake, BC	David S. Loos	David S. Loos	1967	37
180 5/8	40 5/8	43	14 1/8	14 2/8	7 7/8	7 7/8	22 4/8	22 2/8	Hudson Hope, BC	David Slutker	David Slutker	1966	37
180 5/8	38 5/8	38 5/8	15 1/8	15 2/8	9 1/8	9 1/8	23 2/8	19	Prophet River, BC	Joseph Madonia	Joseph Madonia	1970	37

Score	Length R	Length L	Circ. Base R	Circ. Base L	Circ. 3rd Qtr. R	Circ. 3rd Qtr. L	Greatest Spread	Tip to Tip	Locality	Hunter	Owner	Date	Rank
180 4/8	44 4/8	44 4/8	14 2/8	14 3/8	6 6/8	6 6/8	23 6/8	23 6/8	Kechika Range, BC	Tucker Davis	Tucker Davis	1965	39
180 3/8	44 5/8	45 6/8	14 2/8	14 3/8	6 3/8	6	29	29	Telegraph Creek, BC	John B. Winsor	John B. Winsor	1966	40
180 2/8	44 4/8	44	14 2/8	14 2/8	6 5/8	7	26 3/8	26 3/8	Burnt Rose Lake, BC	E.L. Cook	E.L. Cook	1970	41
179 7/8	42 7/8	42 2/8	14 5/8	14 4/8	7 7/8	8	24 7/8	24 7/8	Prophet River, BC	Bill Thomas	Bill Thomas	1963	42
179 7/8	44	43 3/8	14 2/8	14 2/8	7 5/8	7 1/8	28	0	Ice Mt., BC	J.E. Mason	J.E. Mason	1966	42
179 5/8	39 4/8	44 5/8	13 6/8	13 7/8	8 6/8	9	21 3/8	21 3/8	Cassiar Mts., BC	Ralph W. Hull	Ralph W. Hull	1963	44
179 3/8	43 2/8	39 3/8	14 5/8	14 6/8	7 5/8	7 3/8	21 3/8	21 3/8	Pink Mt., BC	Gerald E. Howe	Gerald E. Howe	1970	45
179 3/8	45 4/8	44 7/8	14 2/8	14 3/8	6 3/8	6 5/8	24	24	Gathto Creek, BC	Gary J. Powell	Gary J. Powell	1970	45
179 2/8	43 3/8	43 3/8	13 6/8	13 7/8	6 6/8	7 2/8	26 3/8	26 3/8	Toad River, BC	Dennis Callison	Dennis Callison	1957	47
179 1/8	40 2/8	40 5/8	13 7/8	14 5/8	8 4/8	8 2/8	26 6/8	22 6/8	Eydee Creek, BC	Jack McNeill	Jack McNeill	1967	48
179 1/8	41 7/8	44 4/8	15	15 1/8	6 5/8	6 7/8	26 6/8	19 2/8	Muskwa River, BC	Cliff C. Cory	Cliff C. Cory	1987	48
178 7/8	44 4/8	45 5/8	13 6/8	13 6/8	7 3/8	7	28 3/8	26	Kechika River, BC	W.C. Waldron	W.C. Waldron	1967	50
178 3/8	39 3/8	48	13 6/8	13 6/8	7	6 3/8	26	28 3/8	Moody Lake, BC	J. Martin Benchoff	J. Martin Benchoff	1966	51
178 2/8	43 4/8	43 4/8	14 4/8	14 4/8	6 4/8	6 5/8	24 2/8	26	Muskwa River, BC	Don S. Hopkins	Don S. Hopkins	1948	52
178 2/8	43 6/8	43 6/8	14 2/8	14 2/8	6 4/8	7 4/8	27 6/8	27 6/8	Tuchodi Lakes, BC	Ross Peck	Ross Peck	1963	52
178 2/8	40 7/8	41 1/8	14 7/8	14 6/8	7 4/8	7 1/8	24 2/8	24 2/8	Moody Lake, BC	Raymond G. Speer	Raymond G. Speer	1966	52
178 1/8	43 3/8	45	14	14	6 7/8	6	24	26 4/8	Gataga Mts., BC	Dan Auld	Dan Auld	1960	55
178 1/8	44 3/8	43 7/8	14 2/8	14 2/8	7 1/8	8 5/8	26 6/8	27 4/8	Watson Lake, BC	James C. Maly	James C. Maly	1963	55
177 7/8	43 2/8	43 2/8	13 4/8	13 5/8	6	6 6/8	27 4/8	31	Skookum Mt., YT	Ira H. Kent	Ira H. Kent	1968	57
177 7/8	40 2/8	41 5/8	14 2/8	14 4/8	8 7/8	6 3/8	31	24 3/8	Frog River, BC	Don Palmer	Don Palmer	1968	57
177 6/8	44 7/8	43 1/8	14 3/8	13 7/8	6 6/8	9	24 3/8	27 5/8	Kechika Range, BC	John Caputo, Sr.	John Caputo, Sr.	1961	59
177 6/8	44 4/8	44 4/8	14	14	6 3/8	7	27 5/8	28 4/8	Sikanni Chief River, BC	Steven L. Rose	Steven L. Rose	1961	59
177 6/8	39 1/8	39 3/8	13 7/8	14 5/8	9	6 5/8	28 4/8	22 7/8	Turnagain River, BC	Byron Dalziel	Byron Dalziel	1970	59
177 5/8	44	44	14 5/8	14 2/8	6 7/8	8	22 7/8	26 2/8	Telegraph Creek, BC	Paul O'Hollaren	Paul O'Hollaren	1967	62
177 5/8	45 2/8	45 2/8	14 2/8	13 2/8	6 6/8	7 2/8	27 6/8	27 6/8	Toad River, BC	Dewey Rawlings	Dewey Rawlings	1969	62
177 4/8	44 2/8	44 2/8	14 5/8	14 4/8	6 3/8	6 4/8	24 2/8	24 2/8	Watson Lake, YT	Edgar A. Robertson	Edgar A. Robertson	1968	64
177 3/8	42 1/8	42	13 7/8	13 5/8	8 1/8	6 5/8	23 4/8	23 4/8	Toad River, BC	John Huml	John Huml	1969	65
177 2/8	42 2/8	42	13 5/8	13 4/8	7 5/8	6 1/8	22 4/8	22 4/8	Racing River, BC	Robert H. Kunzli	Robert H. Kunzli	1959	66
177 2/8	44 5/8	44 3/8	13 7/8	13 4/8	6 2/8	6 1/8	24 6/8	24 6/8	Atlin, BC	Delmar Aldrich	Delmar Aldrich	1964	66
177 2/8	40 4/8	40 4/8	15 1/8	15 1/8	6 4/8	7 1/8	29 2/8	29 2/8	Ft. St. John, BC	Ted T. Dabrowski	Ted T. Dabrowski	1967	66
177 2/8	42 4/8	42 4/8	13 6/8	14	9	6 4/8	20 7/8	20 7/8	Watson Lake, YT	Keith Thompson	Keith Thompson	1969	66
177 2/8	38 1/8	38 1/8	14 5/8	14 5/8	8 7/8	8 1/8	29 4/8	29 4/8	Cassiar Mts., BC	H.H. Kissinger	H.H. Kissinger	1970	66
177 1/8	43 1/8	43 1/8	14 6/8	14 6/8	6 1/8	6 6/8	27 7/8	27 7/8	Redfern Lake, BC	Unknown	W.H. Kirk	1923	71
177 1/8	44	44	15	15	6	7 1/8	23 5/8	23 5/8	Mt. Lady Laurier, BC	Chet Gifford	Chet Gifford	1963	71
177 1/8	40 7/8	40 6/8	14 2/8	14 2/8	6 6/8	6	27	27 2/8	Muskwa River, BC	Gerald A. Paille	Gerald A. Paille	1986	71
177	42 1/8	42 1/8	15 3/8	15 3/8	8 1/8	6	25 6/8	25 4/8	Prophet River, BC	Wade Martin	Wade Martin	1960	74
177	36	36	15	15	6 6/8	6 7/8	21 6/8	18 6/8	Sikanni Chief River, BC	Don R. Hughes	Don R. Hughes	1988	74
176 7/8	44 5/8	44 5/8	13 3/8	13 3/8	7	8 3/8	29	29	Dease Lake, BC	Thomas M. Dye	Thomas M. Dye	1966	76
176 7/8	41 6/8	41 6/8	15	15 2/8	6	5 5/8	25 3/8	25 3/8	Rabbit River, BC	George H. Rhoads	George H. Rhoads	1971	76
176 6/8	44 2/8	44 2/8	14	14	6	7	24 3/8	24 3/8	Cassiar Mts., BC	Donald J. Robb	Donald J. Robb	1969	78
176 5/8	40	40	14 4/8	14 6/8	7 4/8	6 6/8	23	23	Muskwa River, BC	T.E. Shillingburg	T.E. Shillingburg	1947	79
176 4/8	42 7/8	39 7/8	13 6/8	13 6/8	8 3/8	6 4/8	28 1/8	28 1/8	Prophet River, BC	Jim Caves	Jim Caves	1959	80
176 4/8	45 3/8	44 5/8	14 3/8	14 3/8	5 5/8	6 3/8	24	23 6/8	Gataga River, BC	David C. Coleman	David C. Coleman	1980	80
176 4/8	41	41 2/8	14 6/8	14 6/8	7	6 3/8	23 6/8	23 6/8	Tuchodi River, BC	James M. Peek	James M. Peek	1993	80
176 3/8	40 7/8	40 2/8	15 4/8	15 4/8	6 4/8	6 4/8	23 6/8	24	Prophet River, BC	O.B. Kahn	O.B. Kahn	1965	83
176 3/8	44	44	14 2/8	14 2/8	6 3/8	6 3/8	28 3/8	28 3/8	Cassiar Mts., BC	Gene Klineburger	Gene Klineburger	1965	83
176 3/8	42 7/8	43 4/8	15	15	5 5/8	5 5/8	29 4/8	29 2/8	Nabesche River, BC	Kenneth W. Kleiman	Kenneth W. Kleiman	1973	83

STONE'S SHEEP

Ovis dalli stonei

Score	Length of Horn R	L	Circumference of Base R	L	Circumference at Third Quarter R	L	Greatest Spread	Tip tp Tip Spread	Locality	Hunter	Owner	Date Killed	Rank
176 3/8	45	38 7/8	14 4/8	14 4/8	7 2/8	6 5/8	23	23	Wokkpash Creek, BC	Hub R. Grounds	Hub R. Grounds	1987	83
176 2/8	41 6/8	44	14 4/8	14 4/8	6 1/8	6 1/8	26 7/8	26 7/8	Prophet River, BC	W.A. Newmiller	W.A. Newmiller	1958	87
176 1/8	36 3/8	39 2/8	15	15	8 7/8	7 7/8	22 6/8	18 6/8	Richard Creek, BC	James Milito	James Milito	1967	88
176 1/8	40 7/8	36	15	15	7 4/8	7 6/8	21 7/8	19 7/8	Pink Mt., BC	Roland Schroeder	Roland Schroeder	1968	88
176 1/8	43 3/8	43 2/8	14 1/8	14 1/8	6 5/8	6 5/8	25 4/8	25 4/8	Watson Lake, BC	Elgin T. Gates	Elgin T. Gates	1969	88
176	45 7/8	41 1/8	13 7/8	13 6/8	6 6/8	7	25 4/8	25 4/8	Cassiar Mts., BC	Walter O. Ford, Jr.	Walter O. Ford, Jr.	1967	91
176	39	41 2/8	15 2/8	15 2/8	6 5/8	6 4/8	23 6/8	23 6/8	Tetsa River, BC	Ron Sedor	Ron Sedor	1988	91
176	41 2/8	40 2/8	14 2/8	14 4/8	8 1/8	8 1/8	21 6/8	21 6/8	Tuchodi Lakes, BC	Terry Filas	Terry Filas	1989	91
175 6/8	41 4/8	39 6/8	14 7/8	14 7/8	7 2/8	7 2/8	24 2/8	24 4/8	Prophet River, BC	Jack O'Connor	Jack O'Connor	1946	94
175 6/8	40 4/8	40 6/8	13 3/8	13 7/8	8 7/8	9	23 1/8	23 1/8	Terminus Mt., BC	Irvin Hart	Irvin Hart	1964	94
175 6/8	42 1/8	37 1/8	15 5/8	15 5/8	7	7 1/8	21 1/8	20 7/8	Turnagain River, BC	Lester C. Brewick	Lester C. Brewick	1967	94
175 6/8	43 2/8	43 4/8	14 1/8	13 7/8	6 6/8	6 7/8	29 2/8	29 2/8	Blue Sheep Lake, BC	John M. Griffith, Jr.	John M. Griffith, Jr.	1971	94
175 6/8	39 2/8	39 2/8	14 1/8	14 1/8	8 4/8	8 4/8	20 4/8	20	Tuchodi River, BC	Roy D. Brown	Roy D. Brown	1992	94
175 5/8	42 5/8	42 6/8	14 4/8	14 2/8	6 2/8	6 3/8	22	22	Pelly Mts., YT	John Caputo	John Caputo	1953	99
175 5/8	42 4/8	41 5/8	14	14	6 6/8	6 7/8	21 6/8	21 6/8	Top Lake, BC	Richard Buffington	Richard Buffington	1964	99
175 5/8	46 3/8	43 4/8	13 5/8	13 5/8	5 5/8	5 4/8	28	27 7/8	Hudson Hope, BC	Jim Papst	Jim Papst	1966	99
175 4/8	46 6/8	48	12 6/8	12 5/8	5 5/8	5 5/8	30 6/8	30 6/8	Lake Kinniskan, BC	Richard Stough	Richard Stough	1961	102
175 4/8	41 2/8	41 2/8	14	14 2/8	7 3/8	7 5/8	23 6/8	23 6/8	Frog River, BC	Robert McMurray	Robert McMurray	1968	102
175 4/8	42 2/8	42	14 7/8	14 6/8	6 3/8	6 2/8	28 1/8	28 1/8	Colt Lake, BC	Marsh Dear	Marsh Dear	1970	102
175 4/8	40 1/8	36 3/8	14 4/8	14 4/8	8	7 7/8	22 2/8	19 4/8	Prophet River, BC	Sam C. Arnett III	Sam C. Arnett III	1972	102
175 4/8	38 2/8	38	15	15	8	8	23 7/8	21 1/8	Muskwa River, BC	Robert M. Case	Robert M. Case	1980	102
175 3/8	43	42 5/8	14 2/8	14 2/8	6 4/8	6 4/8	26	26	Pelly Mts., YT	Pat S. McInturff	Pat S. McInturff	1962	107
175 2/8	41 3/8	42 3/8	12 7/8	12 7/8	8 7/8	9 2/8	22	21 6/8	Tetsa River, BC	Stanley Walchuk, Jr.	Stanley Walchuk, Jr.	1992	108
175	42 2/8	41 6/8	14 2/8	14 2/8	6 5/8	6 5/8	26 5/8	26 5/8	Hudson Hope, BC	Harry M. Haywood	Harry M. Haywood	1949	109
175	40 5/8	41 3/8	14 1/8	14 2/8	7	7 1/8	22	21 5/8	Cassiar, BC	John Sochor	John Sochor	1962	109
175	42 6/8	42 6/8	13 7/8	13 7/8	6 3/8	6 5/8	28 5/8	28 5/8	Cold Fish Lake, BC	Chris Reynolds	Chris Reynolds	1963	109
175	42 4/8	43 2/8	14 2/8	14 1/8	6 1/8	6 2/8	24	24	Colt Lake, BC	Warren Page	Warren Page	1965	109
175	40 4/8	42	14	14 1/8	8 2/8	7 6/8	22 5/8	20 1/8	Toad River, BC	William E. Butler	William E. Butler	1975	109
174 7/8	41 6/8	42 3/8	14 6/8	14 5/8	6 7/8	6 4/8	21 7/8	21 7/8	Cassiar, BC	John W. Hull	John W. Hull	1962	114
174 7/8	38 2/8	38 3/8	13 7/8	14	9 3/8	9 1/8	19 6/8	17	Summit Lake, BC	John D. Chalk III	John D. Chalk III	1989	114
174 6/8	38 6/8	38 2/8	14 5/8	14 5/8	7 7/8	8	21 4/8	19 7/8	Watson Lake, BC	Philip English	Philip English	1965	116
174 5/8	42 1/8	41 4/8	14 1/8	14 1/8	6 1/8	6	30 2/8	30 2/8	Stikine River, BC	Hugh J. O'Dower	Hugh J. O'Dower	1952	117
174 5/8	41 4/8	41 5/8	14 1/8	14 1/8	7 3/8	7 3/8	24 7/8	24 7/8	Sikanni Chief River, BC	Joseph W. Quarto	Joseph W. Quarto	1965	117
174 5/8	36 7/8	39	14 6/8	14 6/8	8 3/8	8 4/8	20 7/8	20 2/8	Prophet River, BC	Craig R. Johnson	Craig R. Johnson	1989	117
174 4/8	40 6/8	41 2/8	14 6/8	14 6/8	8	8 2/8	27 4/8	27 4/8	Dease Lake, BC	Alice J. Landreth	Alice J. Landreth	1964	120
174 4/8	42 6/8	42	14 5/8	14 6/8	6	5 6/8	24 6/8	24 6/8	Ram Lake, BC	Walter Smetaniuk	Walter Smetaniuk	1966	120
174 4/8	40	40 2/8	15	15	6 7/8	6 7/8	22 6/8	21	Dall Lake, BC	Darrell Orth	Darrell Orth	1990	120
174 4/8	42 3/8	41 1/8	14 3/8	14 3/8	6 3/8	6 2/8	22 6/8	22 5/8	Drury Lake, YT	Samuel E. Sanders	Samuel E. Sanders	1997	120

Score	Length of Horn R	L	Circ. of Base R	L	Circ. Third Quarter R	L	Greatest Spread	Tip to Tip	Locality	Hunter	Owner	Date Killed	Rank
174 3/8	41 2/8	40 1/8	13 4/8	13 5/8	7 5/8	8	20 5/8	20 5/8	Racing River, BC	Lash Callison	Lash Callison	1959	124
174 3/8	39 4/8	41 5/8	14 6/8	14 6/8	7 3/8	6 4/8	21 6/8	21 6/8	Top Lake, BC	W.E. Fisher	W.E. Fisher	1964	124
174 3/8	37	38 5/8	14 4/8	14 6/8	8 7/8	8 6/8	21	21 6/8	Cassiar Mts., BC	Gordon Studer	Gordon Studer	1966	124
174 3/8	40 3/8	40 6/8	15	15 1/8	6 1/8	6 4/8	24	24	Tuchodi Lakes, BC	Lydell Johnson	Lydell Johnson	1993	124
174 2/8	46 4/8	46 2/8	13 3/8	13 3/8	5 4/8	5 3/8	33	33	Watson Lake, BC	G.C.F. Dalziel	G.C.F. Dalziel	1962	128
174 2/8	42 2/8	46 2/8	12 5/8	12 4/8	6 5/8	6 5/8	26 3/8	26 3/8	W. Toad River, BC	Unknown	N.B. Sorenson	PR 1969	128
174 2/8	39 7/8	39 1/8	15 1/8	15 1/8	6 7/8	6 6/8	22 5/8	22 5/8	Toad River, BC	Bill Hicks, Jr.	Bill Hicks, Jr.	1990	128
174 2/8	38 2/8	39 2/8	15 4/8	15 6/8	5 4/8	6 6/8	26 6/8	26 4/8	Redfern Lake, BC	Wilf Klingsat	Wilf Klingsat	1990	128
174 2/8	42 2/8	40 7/8	14	14	7	7 6/8	23	23	Cold Fish Lake, BC	Roberto De La Garza	Roberto De La Garza	1961	128
174 1/8	39 2/8	42 3/8	14 7/8	15 2/8	5 2/8	5 2/8	25	25	Gold Bar, BC	Henry O. Carlson	Henry O. Carlson	1962	132
174 1/8	41 1/8	43 3/8	14 4/8	14 4/8	6 4/8	6 2/8	25 3/8	25 3/8	Mt. Winston, BC	Norman A. Hill	Norman A. Hill	1967	132
174 1/8	44 6/8	41 4/8	14 1/8	14 2/8	6 5/8	6 7/8	23 5/8	23 5/8	Muskwa River, BC	Gary Powell	Gary Powell	1974	132
174 1/8	41 6/8	41	14	13 6/8	6 2/8	6 7/8	22 7/8	22 7/8	Muskwa River, BC	Wade Martin	Wade Martin	1961	132
174	40	40	14 1/8	14 1/8	6 4/8	6 4/8	27	27	Cassiar Mts., BC	Russell Castner	Russell Castner	1966	136
174	40 1/8	38 4/8	14 1/8	14 1/8	6 6/8	6 7/8	26 3/8	26 3/8	Cassiar Mts., BC	George H. Glass	George H. Glass	1966	136
174	44 2/8	41	14 5/8	14 6/8	6 5/8	6 6/8	20 3/8	19 4/8	Muskwa Area, BC	W.R. Collie	W.R. Collie	1972	136
174	44 3/8	40 1/8	15 2/8	15 3/8	6 3/8	6 4/8	25 1/8	24 7/8	Muskwa River, BC	R.L. Gearhart	R.L. Gearhart	1983	136
173 7/8	39 6/8	43 5/8	13 4/8	13 4/8	7	6 2/8	27 2/8	27 2/8	Stikine River, BC	Vernon D.E. Smith	Vernon D.E. Smith	1960	141
173 7/8	38 4/8	44 2/8	13 2/8	13 3/8	5 7/8	6	29 7/8	29 7/8	Cassiar, BC	Fred F. Wells	Fred F. Wells	1961	141
173 7/8	41 5/8	41 4/8	13 4/8	14 3/8	8 7/8	8 3/8	25	25	Gataga River, BC	H.L. Hale	H.L. Hale	1968	141
173 7/8	47 3/8	41 5/8	15	15	8 3/8	8 6/8	16	16	Tetsa River, BC	Eugene P. LaSota	Eugene P. LaSota	1973	141
173 7/8	43 4/8	43 1/8	13 4/8	14	6 6/8	5 3/8	21 5/8	21 5/8	Rabbit River, BC	Terry J. Ridley	Terry J. Ridley	1994	141
173 6/8	41 4/8	43 4/8	13 5/8	14 5/8	6 4/8	6 4/8	25 2/8	25 2/8	Halfway River, BC	Lynn Ross	Lynn Ross	1957	146
173 6/8	41 5/8	41 4/8	14	14 4/8	6 2/8	6 3/8	28 2/8	28 2/8	Terminus Mt., BC	Chester A. Crago	Chester A. Crago	1962	146
173 6/8	41 4/8	43	14 4/8	14 2/8	6 3/8	6 5/8	30 4/8	30 4/8	Kechika Range, BC	Russell C. Cutter	Russell C. Cutter	1965	146
173 6/8	45 4/8	40 7/8	14 1/8	14 1/8	7 2/8	7	25 6/8	25 6/8	Muskwa River, BC	W. Michalsky	W. Michalsky	1965	146
173 6/8	42 5/8	41 5/8	13 4/8	13 4/8	6 5/8	6 5/8	22 6/8	22 6/8	Toad River, BC	Peter C. Swenson	Peter C. Swenson	1993	146
173 5/8	42 3/8	42	14 3/8	14 2/8	6 5/8	6 5/8	26 2/8	26 2/8	Peace River, BC	Unknown	Melvin Shearer	1933	151
173 5/8	40	42	14 3/8	14 3/8	6 3/8	5 7/8	23 2/8	23 2/8	Hudson Hope, BC	G.F. Moore	G.F. Moore	1963	151
173 5/8	40 2/8	41 5/8	15 2/8	15 4/8	6 2/8	6 2/8	22 4/8	22 4/8	Rose Mt., YT	Karl Fritzsche	Karl Fritzsche	1972	151
173 5/8	41 6/8	41 2/8	13 4/8	13 3/8	6	6	22 3/8	22 3/8	Muskwa River, BC	Valerie Carter-Green	Valerie Carter-Green	1994	151
173 4/8	39	42	14 1/8	14 1/8	7 7/8	7 7/8	20 4/8	20 4/8	Cassiar, BC	Charles F. Haas	Charles F. Haas	1960	155
173 4/8	41	41	15	15	6 2/8	6 2/8	28 5/8	28 5/8	Telegraph Creek, BC	L. Iverson	L. Iverson	1961	155
173 4/8	39 4/8	41 5/8	14	14	7 4/8	6 4/8	22 4/8	22 4/8	Dease Lake, BC	George I. Parker	George I. Parker	1963	155
173 4/8	41 3/8	41 3/8	14	14 2/8	9 4/8	9	27	27	Dease Lake, BC	John T. Blackwell	John T. Blackwell	1964	155
173 4/8	39 6/8	40 2/8	14 4/8	14 2/8	8 1/8	8 1/8	23	23	Watson Lake, YT	Harry S. Rinker	Harry S. Rinker	1964	155
173 4/8	41 2/8	41 2/8	14 4/8	15 4/8	6 2/8	6 1/8	26 4/8	26 4/8	Cold Fish Lake, BC	Roger Britton	Roger Britton	1986	155
173 4/8	42 4/8	42 4/8	15 4/8	14 2/8	6 2/8	7	24 7/8	24 7/8	Schooler Creek, BC	Wade Nielsen	Wade Nielsen	1992	155
173 4/8	43 3/8	43	14 3/8	14 7/8	6 6/8	5 5/8	22 4/8	22 4/8	Muncho Lake, BC	Harold L. Brander	Harold L. Brander	1996	155
173 4/8	44	44	14 7/8	15	5 4/8	6 6/8	26 4/8	26 4/8	Through Creek, BC	Peter W. Spear	Peter W. Spear	1997	155
173 3/8	38 3/8	38 3/8	13 4/8	13 4/8	6	8	28	28	Toad River, BC	H.L. Vidricksen	H.L. Vidricksen	1960	164
173 3/8	41 5/8	42 6/8	14 6/8	14 6/8	8 3/8	5 5/8	20 6/8	19 3/8	Tuchodi Lakes, BC	George S. Gayle III	George S. Gayle III	1972	164
173 3/8	39 3/8	38 6/8	14 4/8	14 4/8	5 5/8	6 6/8	26 4/8	26 4/8	Racing River, BC	Dick Sullivan	Dick Sullivan	1982	164
173 3/8	41 6/8	41 2/8	15 3/8	15 3/8	6 3/8	6 2/8	21 6/8	20 6/8	Sikanni Chief River, BC	Ray M. Fabri	Ray M. Fabri	1992	164
173 2/8	41 2/8	41 2/8	14 4/8	14 3/8	6 2/8	5 7/8	24 6/8	24 6/8	Cassiar Mts., BC	John Caputo	John Caputo	1962	168
173 2/8	44 4/8	45	13 2/8	13 2/8	5 7/8	6 6/8	26 5/8	26 5/8	Cassiar Mts., BC	William Warrick	William Warrick	1963	168
173 1/8	40 1/8	41 2/8	14	14	7	6 7/8	24 5/8	24 5/8	Halfway River, BC	Frank H. Rogers	Frank H. Rogers	1962	170

STONE'S SHEEP

Ovis dalli stonei

Score	Length of Horn R	L	Circumference of Base R	L	Circumference at Third Quarter R	L	Greatest Spread	Tip tp Tip Spread	Locality	Hunter	Owner	Date Killed	Rank
173 1/8	40 4/8	41 3/8	14 7/8	14 7/8	6	6 3/8	27 4/8	27 4/8	Cassiar Mts., BC	Charles F. Nadler	Charles F. Nadler	1967	170
173 1/8	41 3/8	40	14 1/8	14 2/8	7 2/8	7 2/8	21 6/8	21 6/8	Summit Lake, BC	Henry L. Baddley	Henry L. Baddley	1979	170
173	39 4/8	38	14 4/8	14 4/8	8	8	26	26	Muskwa River, BC	Elmer Keith	Elmer Keith	1937	173
173	34	45	15	15	7 4/8	7 1/8	24 2/8	24 2/8	Gataga River, BC	Wilson Southwell	Wilson Southwell	1958	173
173	40 3/8	41 3/8	13 6/8	13 7/8	7 2/8	7 5/8	23 4/8	21 4/8	Prophet River, BC	Merrimen M. Watkins	Merrimen M. Watkins	1965	173
173	42	42 2/8	14 2/8	14 3/8	5 6/8	5 6/8	22 5/8	22 5/8	Watson Lake, YT	E.P. Gray	E.P. Gray	1968	173
173	42	42 2/8	13 6/8	14	6 6/8	6 5/8	23 2/8	23 2/8	Prophet River, BC	Robert E. Hammond	Robert E. Hammond	1969	173
173	42 5/8	42 3/8	14	14	5 6/8	5 6/8	27 1/8	27 1/8	Cold Fish Lake, BC	A.H. Clise	A.H. Clise	1970	173
173	41 5/8	42 5/8	14 1/8	13 7/8	5 5/8	5 7/8	24 3/8	24 3/8	Alaska Hwy, Mile 422, BC	Garland N. Teich	Garland N. Teich	1971	173
173	41 4/8	42 4/8	13 6/8	13 5/8	6 6/8	7	24	23 5/8	Rapid River, BC	Bill Silveira	Bill Silveira	1983	173
173	41 7/8	42 7/8	13 3/8	13 3/8	6 4/8	6 5/8	25 5/8	25 5/8	Racing River, BC	Len J. Smith	Len J. Smith	1995	173
173	41 7/8	41 7/8	14 2/8	14 2/8	6 2/8	6 2/8	27 7/8	27 6/8	Cassiar Mts., BC	Michael J. Borel	Michael J. Borel	1997	173
172 7/8	40 4/8	39 5/8	14 3/8	14 4/8	6 6/8	6 6/8	24 1/8	24 1/8	Prophet River, BC	Harry M. Haywood	Harry M. Haywood	1956	183
172 7/8	40 7/8	42 4/8	14 7/8	14 7/8	5 4/8	6	25 3/8	25 3/8	Summit Lake, BC	A. Tony Mathisen	A. Tony Mathisen	1958	183
172 7/8	42 7/8	42 2/8	13 7/8	13 7/8	6 3/8	6	25 1/8	25 1/8	Cassiar Mts., BC	Wayne C. Eubank	Wayne C. Eubank	1963	183
172 7/8	46 3/8	35	14	14	6 4/8	6 4/8	21 2/8	21 2/8	Cassiar Mts., BC	Orval H. Ause	Orval H. Ause	1968	183
172 7/8	37 7/8	37	15	14 6/8	7 5/8	7 7/8	23	20	Cassiar Mts., BC	Greg Williams	Greg Williams	1976	183
172 6/8	36 4/8	37	14 6/8	15	8 3/8	8 4/8	19 1/8	19 1/8	Sikanni Chief River, BC	Mrs. Maitland Armstrong	Mrs. Maitland Armstrong	1962	188
172 6/8	40 2/8	41 6/8	14 2/8	14 3/8	6 5/8	7	22	22	Gataga River, BC	Basil C. Bradbury	Basil C. Bradbury	1968	188
172 6/8	36 4/8	36 2/8	14 6/8	15	8 6/8	8 4/8	21 3/8	15 3/8	Muskwa River, BC	Andrew A. Samuels, Jr.	Andrew A. Samuels, Jr.	1969	188
172 6/8	42	41 6/8	14 5/8	14 4/8	6 2/8	6 1/8	27 5/8	27 5/8	Dall Lake, BC	Robert J. Rood	Robert J. Rood	1971	188
172 6/8	41 2/8	41	14 5/8	14 5/8	6 2/8	6 3/8	22 7/8	22 5/8	Toad River, BC	Robert E. Zaiglin	Robert E. Zaiglin	1995	188
172 5/8	40 3/8	40 4/8	14 2/8	14 2/8	7 2/8	7 1/8	24 5/8	24 5/8	Liard River, BC	Jack N. Allen	Jack N. Allen	1959	193
172 5/8	38 7/8	40	14 7/8	14 7/8	6 6/8	6 6/8	24 6/8	23	Blue Sheep Lake, BC	John Deromedi	John Deromedi	1989	193
172 5/8	43 2/8	42 5/8	14 1/8	14 1/8	5 7/8	5 4/8	26 1/8	26 1/8	Kechika River, BC	William B. McClelland	William B. McClelland	1991	193
172 4/8	42 2/8	42	13 7/8	13 5/8	6 1/8	5 7/8	29 4/8	29 4/8	Halfway River, BC	Cecil V. Mumbert	Cecil V. Mumbert	1958	196
172 4/8	40 4/8	41 6/8	14 4/8	14 2/8	6 4/8	6 4/8	25	25	Dease Lake, BC	John T. Blackwell	John T. Blackwell	1963	196
172 4/8	37 2/8	38	15 2/8	15 5/8	6 6/8	6 2/8	27 5/8	27 5/8	Prophet River, BC	William A. Miller	William A. Miller	1969	196
172 4/8	39 6/8	42	14 1/8	14 2/8	7	7	25 3/8	25 3/8	Watson Lake, BC	Julian Gutierrez	Julian Gutierrez	1970	196
172 4/8	37 3/8	41 7/8	14 4/8	14 3/8	6 4/8	7	23 3/8	23 1/8	Muskwa River, BC	L.A. Denson	L.A. Denson	1971	196
172 4/8	41 1/8	41 1/8	15 1/8	15 1/8	6	6 1/8	28 2/8	28 2/8	Mile Creek, BC	H.D. Miller	H.D. Miller	1980	196
172 4/8	40 5/8	40 5/8	14 4/8	14 4/8	5 7/8	5 7/8	24 4/8	24	Sikanni Chief River, BC	Ben F. Carter III	Ben F. Carter III	1997	196
172 3/8	37 1/8	38 4/8	14 2/8	14 2/8	8 4/8	8 3/8	23 1/8	17 2/8	Sandbar Creek, BC	John La Rocca	John La Rocca	1957	203
172 3/8	41 6/8	42 3/8	14 3/8	14 4/8	5 7/8	5 7/8	27 6/8	27 6/8	Pelly Mts., YT	Walter R. Michael	Walter R. Michael	1960	203
172 3/8	45 1/8	45 2/8	13	13	5 5/8	5 7/8	28	28	Cold Fish Lake, BC	Juan Brittingham	Juan Brittingham	1961	203
172 3/8	39 3/8	39 6/8	15 5/8	15 5/8	6 6/8	6	20 2/8	20 2/8	Ospika Drainage, BC	Mark Swenson	Mark Swenson	1964	203
172 3/8	41 5/8	41 4/8	14 5/8	14 5/8	6 2/8	6 1/8	23 4/8	23 4/8	Dall Lake, BC	Paul M. Rothermel, Jr.	Paul M. Rothermel, Jr.	1965	203
172 3/8	38 6/8	38 7/8	15 1/8	15 2/8	6 2/8	6 5/8	25 1/8	25 1/8	Muskwa River, BC	Ken W. Scheer	Ken W. Scheer	1985	203

Score											Location	Hunter	Owner	Date	Rank
172 2/8	41 1/8	41 1/8	14 1/8	14 2/8	14 1/8	14 1/8	6	6 5/8	21 1/8	21 4/8	Prophet River, BC	George F. Crain	George F. Crain	1961	209
172 2/8	40 4/8	38 2/8	14 3/8	14 4/8	14 4/8	14 3/8	7	6 7/8	21 1/8	21 4/8	Muskwa River, BC	Arvid F. Benson	Arvid F. Benson	1963	209
172 2/8	42 4/8	42 2/8	14 4/8	14 4/8	14 4/8	14 4/8	5 4/8	5 6/8	29	29	Prophet River, BC	S.E. Burrell	S.E. Burrell	1967	209
172 2/8	41 6/8	41 6/8	14 2/8	14 2/8	14 2/8	14 2/8	8	7 4/8	23 1/8	23 1/8	Sikanni Chief River, BC	John B. Collier IV	John B. Collier IV	1967	209
172 2/8	39 6/8	42 2/8	14	14	14 2/8	14	6 6/8	7 7/8	26 4/8	26 4/8	Cassiar Mts., BC	Michaux Nash, Jr.	Michaux Nash, Jr.	1967	209
172 2/8	41 6/8	41 2/8	14 4/8	14 5/8	14 4/8	14 4/8	6 1/8	6	28 4/8	28 4/8	Akie River, BC	O.J. Baggenstoss	O.J. Baggenstoss	1968	209
172 2/8	39	38 4/8	14 4/8	14 4/8	14 4/8	14 4/8	7 3/8	7 4/8	18 2/8	20 2/8	Prophet River, BC	Larry Ciejka	Larry Ciejka	1977	209
172 2/8	40 6/8	41 6/8	14 4/8	14 4/8	14 4/8	14 4/8	6 3/8	6 2/8	22 1/8	22 1/8	Chlotapecta Creek, BC	Merle Freyborg	Merle Freyborg	1992	209
172 1/8	41 5/8	41	13	13	13	13	9 2/8	9 2/8	30	30	Dease Lake, BC	W.M. Rudd	W.M. Rudd	1964	217
172 1/8	37 6/8	34 5/8	14 2/8	14 2/8	14 2/8	14	9 1/8	9 1/8	19	19	Cassiar Mts., BC	Keith M. Kissinger	Keith M. Kissinger	1968	217
172 1/8	39	40 5/8	14 4/8	14 4/8	14 4/8	14 4/8	6 7/8	7 1/8	23 2/8	23 2/8	Alaska Hwy., BC	Robert Murdock	Robert Murdock	1968	217
172 1/8	40 2/8	38 1/8	14 2/8	14 2/8	14 2/8	14 2/8	7 3/8	7	23 2/8	23 2/8	Burnt Rose Lake, BC	John K. De Broux	John K. De Broux	1970	217
172 1/8	40 3/8	41	14 3/8	14 2/8	14 3/8	14 2/8	6 4/8	7 2/8	20 2/8	20 5/8	Muskwa River, BC	Greg L. Stires	Greg L. Stires	1984	217
172	39 2/8	40 2/8	15	15	15	15	6 5/8	6 4/8	23 2/8	23 2/8	Hudson Hope, BC	Don Stewart	Don Stewart	1961	222
172	45 5/8	43 3/8	13	12 7/8	13	13	6 2/8	6 2/8	25 7/8	25 7/8	Atlin, BC	Thomas E. Francis	Thomas E. Francis	1964	222
172	40 2/8	41 6/8	14 2/8	14 2/8	14 5/8	14 2/8	6 1/8	6 2/8	25 2/8	25 2/8	Pelly Creek, BC	Robert A. Lubeck	Robert A. Lubeck	1968	222
172	40 2/8	40	14 5/8	14 5/8	14 2/8	14 4/8	6	6 1/8	29	29	Prairie River, BC	C.J. McElroy	C.J. McElroy	1969	222
172	41 2/8	40 2/8	14 3/8	14 2/8	14 2/8	14 2/8	6 1/8	6 2/8	26 6/8	26 6/8	Denetiah Lake, BC	Michael G. Meeker	Michael G. Meeker	1969	222
172	41 2/8	41 4/8	14	14	14 3/8	14 2/8	6 2/8	6 2/8	25 1/8	25 1/8	Toad River, BC	David G. Kidder	David G. Kidder	1975	222
172	40 6/8	40 2/8	13 4/8	13 4/8	13 4/8	13 4/8	6 7/8	6 5/8	23	23	Toad River, BC	Steve Best	Steve Best	1988	222
171 7/8	38 6/8	38 6/8	14 2/8	14 1/8	14 1/8	14 2/8	7 5/8	7 3/8	23 6/8	23 6/8	Akie River, BC	Henry K. Leworthy	Henry K. Leworthy	1966	229
171 7/8	38 3/8	39	13 7/8	14 1/8	13 7/8	14 1/8	8 7/8	8 5/8	20 4/8	20 4/8	Island Lake, BC	Martin F. Wood	Martin F. Wood	1970	229
171 7/8	43 2/8	41 3/8	14 1/8	14 1/8	14 1/8	14 1/8	5 6/8	5 6/8	30 2/8	30 2/8	Cache Creek, BC	Kenneth A. Jeronimus	Kenneth A. Jeronimus	1974	229
171 7/8	42 3/8	39 6/8	14 1/8	14 2/8	14 2/8	14 1/8	6 3/8	6 2/8	23 5/8	23 5/8	Toad River, BC	Larry Jenkins	Larry Jenkins	1988	229
171 6/8	41	41	13 4/8	13 4/8	13 4/8	13 4/8	8	8	27 4/8	27 4/8	Gataga River, BC	Dan Auld	Dan Auld	1958	233
171 6/8	39 2/8	39 2/8	14 4/8	14 2/8	14 4/8	14 2/8	5 3/8	5 4/8	27 1/8	27 1/8	Cassiar Mts., BC	John Caputo, Sr.	John Caputo, Sr.	1960	233
171 6/8	43	42 6/8	14	14 1/8	14 5/8	14 2/8	6 4/8	7 2/8	24 6/8	24 6/8	Trimble Lake, BC	Roy E. Stare	Roy E. Stare	1962	233
171 6/8	42 6/8	37	14 4/8	14 5/8	14 5/8	14 7/8	10 2/8	8 3/8	21 6/8	21 6/8	Muskwa River, BC	William I. Spencer	William I. Spencer	1963	233
171 6/8	37	41 2/8	14 7/8	14 7/8	14 7/8	14 7/8	6	6 4/8	23 5/8	23 5/8	Dease Lake, BC	Michaux Nash, Jr.	Michaux Nash, Jr.	1965	233
171 6/8	39 2/8	39 6/8	16	16	16	16	6 3/8	6 7/8	21 3/8	21 3/8	Gataga River, BC	D.R. Seabaugh	D.R. Seabaugh	1971	233
171 6/8	37 6/8	38 4/8	15 5/8	15 5/8	15 5/8	15 5/8	6 7/8	6 3/8	23 5/8	24 7/8	Prophet River, BC	Don Haemmerlein	Don Haemmerlein	1977	233
171 6/8	38 4/8	42 4/8	14 2/8	14	14 2/8	14	6	6 3/8	24 7/8	24 7/8	Rock Island Lake, BC	William K. Mortlock	William K. Mortlock	1988	233
171 5/8	42 4/8	37 1/8	14	14	14 4/8	14 2/8	8 6/8	8 6/8	20 3/8	20 3/8	Tuchodi Lakes, BC	Win Condict	Win Condict	1951	241
171 5/8	37 2/8	42 3/8	13 4/8	14	13 4/8	14 4/8	6 1/8	6 2/8	26	26 1/8	Dease Lake, BC	C.E. Krieger	C.E. Krieger	1962	241
171 5/8	42 4/8	42 6/8	13 4/8	13 5/8	13 5/8	13 4/8	6 2/8	6 3/8	25 6/8	25 6/8	Muncho Lake, BC	H.W. Julien	H.W. Julien	1966	241
171 5/8	44 1/8	40	13 4/8	13 5/8	13 5/8	13 4/8	5 5/8	6 2/8	20 1/8	20 1/8	Toad River, BC	H.W. Julien	H.W. Julien	1969	241
171 5/8	38 6/8	36 3/8	14 1/8	14 1/8	14 2/8	14 1/8	8 5/8	8 5/8	20 1/8	20 1/8	Prophet River, BC	John Whitcombe	John Whitcombe	1981	241
171 4/8	37 2/8	45 3/8	14 2/8	14 7/8	14 7/8	14 2/8	6 1/8	6	24	24	Prophet River, BC	L.A. Denson	L.A. Denson	1963	246
171 4/8	37	38 4/8	14 2/8	14 2/8	14 2/8	14 2/8	6 2/8	6 3/8	23 3/8	23 3/8	Trutch, BC	Charles F. Waterman	Charles F. Waterman	1964	246
171 4/8	39	38 4/8	14 4/8	14 6/8	14 6/8	14 4/8	7 4/8	7 6/8	22 2/8	22 2/8	Cassiar Mts., BC	Robert R. Bridges	Robert R. Bridges	1966	246
171 4/8	45 4/8	45	13 5/8	13 6/8	13 6/8	13 5/8	5 4/8	5 4/8	29 7/8	29 7/8	Turnagain River, BC	George H. Landreth	George H. Landreth	1966	246
171 4/8	42 5/8	43 5/8	13 6/8	13 6/8	13 6/8	13 6/8	5 7/8	6 1/8	29 7/8	29 7/8	Turnagain River, BC	Lewis M. Mull	Lewis M. Mull	1966	246
171 4/8	45	43 5/8	13 1/8	13 2/8	13 2/8	13 1/8	5 4/8	5 4/8	28 4/8	28 4/8	Cassiar Mts., BC	William A. Kelly	William A. Kelly	1969	246
171 4/8	39	34 4/8	15 5/8	15 6/8	15 6/8	15 5/8	7 2/8	7	25 6/8	25 6/8	Lower Besa River, BC	Peter Hochleitner	Peter Hochleitner	1977	246
171 3/8	43	42 7/8	14	13 6/8	13 6/8	14	6	6	30 4/8	30 4/8	Kechika Range, BC	H.I.H. Prince Abdorreza Pahlavi	H.I.H. Prince Abdorreza Pahlavi	1960	253
171 3/8	37 7/8	37	14	14	14 1/8	14	8 4/8	8 7/8	21 7/8	21 3/8	Horseshoe Lake, YT	Jack G. Giannola	Jack G. Giannola	1973	253

STONE'S SHEEP

Ovis dalli stonei

Score	Length of Horn R	L	Circumference of Base R	L	Circumference at Third Quarter R	L	Greatest Spread	Tip to Tip Spread	Locality	Hunter	Owner	Date Killed	Rank
171 3/8	39 2/8	38 5/8	14 1/8	14	7 4/8	7 3/8	22 4/8	22 4/8	Besa River, BC	Dale Webber	Dale Webber	1984	253
171 2/8	42 5/8	42 5/8	13 5/8	13 6/8	6 4/8	6 6/8	24 3/8	24 3/8	Muskwa River, BC	Bernard J. Brown	Bernard J. Brown	1953	256
171 2/8	41 2/8	41	13 7/8	13 7/8	6 3/8	6	26 2/8	26 2/8	Pelly Mts., YT	Jack Tillotson	Jack Tillotson	1955	256
171 2/8	41 6/8	43	13 6/8	13 6/8	5 7/8	6 2/8	27 2/8	27 2/8	Cold Fish Lake, BC	Robert Brittingham	Robert Brittingham	1961	256
171 2/8	44 1/8	43 1/8	12 7/8	12 7/8	5 7/8	5 6/8	27 3/8	27 3/8	Pelly Lake, BC	Robert M. Mallett	Robert M. Mallett	1966	256
171 2/8	41	39 6/8	14 3/8	14 4/8	6 7/8	6 6/8	21 6/8	20 6/8	Cassiar Mts., BC	G.A. Treschow	G.A. Treschow	1966	256
171 2/8	38	45 4/8	13	13 3/8	6 2/8	7 2/8	20 4/8	20 4/8	Telegraph Creek, BC	Picked Up	John Crowe	PR 1967	256
171 2/8	39 1/8	40 3/8	15 2/8	15 3/8	5 7/8	6	25 1/8	25 1/8	Colt Lake, BC	Roscoe Hurd	Roscoe Hurd	1967	256
171 2/8	42	42 2/8	13 5/8	13 5/8	6 3/8	6	26 3/8	26 3/8	Cassiar, BC	Herb Parsons	Herb Parsons	1969	256
171	41	42	14	14 2/8	6	6	30	30	Cassiar, BC	Wilson Potter	Harvard Univ. Mus.	1906	264
171	40 3/8	39 7/8	15	15	5 5/8	5 5/8	28 7/8	28 7/8	Sandbar Creek, BC	John La Rocca	John La Rocca	1958	264
171	40	40	14 2/8	14 2/8	6 4/8	6 4/8	25 5/8	25 5/8	Halfway River, BC	S.J. Seidensticker	S.J. Seidensticker	1962	264
171	41 7/8	41 3/8	14	14 2/8	5 7/8	5 7/8	24 7/8	24 7/8	Cassiar Mts., BC	Sam Jaksick, Jr.	Sam Jaksick, Jr.	1967	264
171	35 6/8	40 6/8	14 4/8	14 4/8	6 7/8	6 7/8	22 3/8	22 3/8	Wrede Creek, BC	Jack Feightner	Jack Feightner	1972	264
171	38 5/8	38 7/8	14 7/8	15	6 1/8	6 1/8	24 5/8	24 5/8	Ice Mt., BC	David P. Jacobson	David P. Jacobson	1974	264
171	41	44 4/8	13 4/8	13 5/8	5 7/8	6	27 1/8	27 1/8	Cassiar Mts., BC	Ed Stedman, Jr.	Ed Stedman, Jr.	1974	264
171	39 5/8	40 1/8	14 7/8	14 7/8	6 2/8	6 4/8	21 3/8	18 6/8	Burnt Rose Lake, BC	John Drift	John Drift	1977	264
171	40 2/8	39 6/8	14 6/8	14 5/8	6	5 7/8	20 6/8	20 5/8	Ice Lakes, YT	Terrance S. Marcum	Terrance S. Marcum	1992	264
170 7/8	41 2/8	41 5/8	13 3/8	13 3/8	7	7 1/8	26 5/8	26 5/8	Watson Lake, BC	Ed Ball	Ed Ball	1960	273
170 7/8	44 5/8	41 4/8	13 2/8	13 3/8	6 1/8	6 1/8	28	28	Watson Lake, YT	Richard G. Peters	Richard G. Peters	1962	273
170 7/8	39 6/8	39 5/8	14 4/8	15	6 3/8	6 1/8	19 6/8	19 6/8	Prophet River, BC	John J. LoMonaco	John J. LoMonaco	1963	273
170 7/8	38	38 1/8	14 2/8	14	7 7/8	8	19 7/8	19	Prophet River, BC	Ted Howell	Ted Howell	1964	273
170 7/8	37 5/8	38 4/8	14 5/8	14 5/8	7 3/8	7 4/8	24 6/8	18 1/8	Tuchodi Lakes, BC	Robert C. Ries	Robert C. Ries	1965	273
170 7/8	39 2/8	41 1/8	14 4/8	14 4/8	6 3/8	6 2/8	28 1/8	28 1/8	Telegraph Creek, BC	R.B. England	R.B. England	1966	273
170 7/8	37 3/8	38 6/8	14 6/8	14 6/8	7 2/8	7 2/8	23	22 3/8	Cassiar Mts., BC	W.G. Rathmann	W.G. Rathmann	1971	273
170 6/8	42 2/8	42 4/8	13 7/8	13 6/8	6 4/8	6 2/8	32	32	Pink Mt., BC	Unknown	J. Michael Conoyer	1960	280
170 6/8	42	41	13 7/8	14	6 5/8	6 3/8	24 4/8	24 4/8	Peace River, BC	C.A. Freese	C.A. Freese	1960	280
170 6/8	41	41	14	14	6	6	27 4/8	27 4/8	Gataga River, BC	Herb Klein	Herb Klein	1963	280
170 6/8	43	42 2/8	13 4/8	13 5/8	5 6/8	5 7/8	22 2/8	22 2/8	Pelly Creek, BC	Jon A. Jourdonnais	Jon A. Jourdonnais	1968	280
170 6/8	40 6/8	41	14 1/8	14 2/8	6 3/8	6 3/8	25 3/8	25 3/8	Kechika Range, BC	Ferdinand Stemann	Ferdinand Stemann	1970	280
170 6/8	41 6/8	37 6/8	14	14 1/8	6 6/8	7	25 5/8	25 5/8	Tuchodi Lakes, BC	Larry Tooze	Larry Tooze	1986	280
170 6/8	43 5/8	45 1/8	12 6/8	12 6/8	6 3/8	6 2/8	26 3/8	26 3/8	Anvil Range, YT	John A. Capdeville	John A. Capdeville	1991	280
170 6/8	40 2/8	40 4/8	14 2/8	14 2/8	6 5/8	6 4/8	22 6/8	22 6/8	Anvil Range, YT	Alan A. Terril	Alan A. Terril	1997	280
170 5/8	43 2/8	43 3/8	13 5/8	13 4/8	5 5/8	6 1/8	29 6/8	29 6/8	Cassiar, BC	John W. Beban	John W. Beban	1956	288
170 5/8	40 4/8	40 1/8	14 4/8	14 4/8	6	6	29 5/8	29 5/8	Prophet River, BC	E.R. Wells	E.R. Wells	1967	288
170 5/8	41 3/8	39	14	14 2/8	6 4/8	6 7/8	21 2/8	21 2/8	Toad River, BC	Jay Stewart	Jay Stewart	1969	288
170 5/8	40 7/8	40 6/8	14	14	6 2/8	6 4/8	24 3/8	24 3/8	Prophet River, BC	Robert E. Speegle	Robert E. Speegle	1983	288
170 5/8	41 1/8	42 2/8	14 1/8	14 1/8	6 1/8	6 4/8	25 4/8	25 4/8	Sharktooth Mt., BC	Steven J. DeRicco	Steven J. DeRicco	1990	288

Score	Length of Horn R	Length of Horn L	Circ. of Base R	Circ. of Base L	Circ. 3rd Qtr R	Circ. 3rd Qtr L	Greatest Spread	Tip to Tip	Locality	Hunter	Owner	Date	Rank
170 5/8	41 7/8	41 4/8	14	14	6 3/8	6 3/8	25 2/8	24 7/8	Fox Mt., YT	Mark R. Redman	Mark R. Redman	1990	288
170 5/8	42 4/8	41 5/8	14 6/8	14 6/8	5 3/8	5 3/8	25 7/8	25 7/8	Turnagain River, BC	George L. Wilson	George L. Wilson	1995	288
170 5/8	40 4/8	42 1/8	13 4/8	13 4/8	7	7	23 1/8	22 4/8	Williston Lake, BC	Chuck Pridgeon	Chuck Pridgeon	1996	288
170 5/8	40 6/8	38 1/8	14 4/8	14 2/8	7	7	20 3/8	20 3/8	Muskwa River, BC	Kenneth R. Hamer	Kenneth R. Hamer	1997	288
170 5/8	39	39 7/8	15 3/8	15 5/8	5 6/8	5 1/8	27 5/8	27 4/8	Prophet River, BC	Don W. Hansen	Don W. Hansen	1997	288
170 4/8	42 7/8	42 5/8	13 4/8	13 4/8	6	6	33 1/8	33 1/8	Pelly Mts., YT	William Fisher	William Fisher	1957	298
170 4/8	42	42	13 4/8	13 4/8	5 7/8	6 1/8	26 4/8	26 4/8	Telegraph Creek, BC	Joseph T. Pelton	Joseph T. Pelton	1963	298
170 4/8	39 4/8	40	14	14	6 1/8	6 4/8	22	20 4/8	Toad River, BC	Fred Sothmann	Fred Sothmann	1963	298
170 4/8	40 7/8	39 3/8	14 2/8	14 2/8	6 4/8	6 3/8	21 6/8	21 6/8	Dease Lake, BC	Melvin A. Hetland	Melvin A. Hetland	1965	298
170 4/8	40	40 4/8	14 3/8	14 3/8	6 3/8	6 4/8	21 3/8	22 4/8	Watson Lake, BC	W. Brandon Macomber	W. Brandon Macomber	1966	298
170 4/8	41 2/8	40	14 4/8	14 4/8	6 4/8	6 2/8	26 1/8	26 1/8	Pink Mt., BC	Rita Oney	Rita Oney	1966	298
170 4/8	32	41 4/8	14 6/8	14 6/8	8	8 4/8	22	24	Muskwa River, BC	Donald P. Eickhoff	E.C. Eickhoff	1968	298
170 4/8	42 2/8	40 2/8	13 5/8	13 5/8	6 4/8	6 4/8	25 4/8	25 2/8	Mt. Edziza, BC	William J. Pollard	William J. Pollard	1974	307
170 4/8	38 5/8	40 5/8	14 2/8	14 1/8	6 4/8	6 4/8	19 7/8	18 2/8	Muncho Lake, BC	James G. Petersen	James G. Petersen	1997	307
170 3/8	41 3/8	40 2/8	13 7/8	13 7/8	6 2/8	6 2/8	22 3/8	22 3/8	Sikanni, BC	W.A.K. Seale	W.A.K. Seale	1961	307
170 3/8	39 6/8	40 7/8	14	14	6 3/8	6 3/8	28	28	Kechika Range, BC	Basil C. Bradbury	Basil C. Bradbury	1965	307
170 3/8	37 5/8	38 2/8	14 6/8	14 6/8	6 5/8	6 5/8	22 4/8	22 4/8	Ospika Area, BC	Ray E. Bigler	Ray E. Bigler	1972	311
170 3/8	41	41 1/8	14	14	6 3/8	6 1/8	25 7/8	25 7/8	Muncho Lake, BC	Michael H. Baldwin	Michael H. Baldwin	1997	311
170 2/8	43 2/8	43 2/8	13 4/8	13 3/8	6 4/8	6 4/8	25 4/8	25 4/8	Beale Lake, BC	John Forester	John Forester	1963	311
170 2/8	35	35 2/8	14 5/8	14 6/8	8 2/8	8 2/8	21 6/8	21 6/8	Richards Creek, BC	Herbert A. Leupold	Herbert A. Leupold	1965	311
170 2/8	39	39	14 7/8	15	6 5/8	6 5/8	22 6/8	22 6/8	Halfway River, BC	Steven L. Rose	Steven L. Rose	1967	311
170 2/8	41	41	14 7/8	14 7/8	6 2/8	6 2/8	26	26	Keohka River, BC	Fritz A. Nachant	Fritz A. Nachant	1970	311
170 2/8	39 4/8	39 4/8	14 2/8	14 2/8	6	6	21 7/8	21 2/8	Muskwa River, BC	James S. Griffin	James S. Griffin	1972	311
170 2/8	43 2/8	43 2/8	14 1/8	14 1/8	6 3/8	6 3/8	23 6/8	23 6/8	Turnagain River, BC	Jerald T. Waite	Jerald T. Waite	1976	311
170 2/8	36 2/8	37	14 2/8	14 2/8	8 2/8	8	20 7/8	19 4/8	Townsley Creek, BC	Robert L. Williamson	Robert L. Williamson	1981	311
170 2/8	41	41	14 5/8	14 3/8	6 1/8	6 1/8	24 2/8	24 2/8	Racing River, BC	Bill Stevenson	Bill Stevenson	1983	311
170 2/8	40 4/8	40 4/8	14 5/8	14 5/8	6 1/8	6 1/8	25 3/8	25 3/8	Prophet River, BC	Steve J. Polich	Steve J. Polich	1984	311
170 2/8	39 5/8	39 5/8	14 2/8	14 2/8	6 6/8	6 6/8	27 1/8	27 1/8	Cutbank Creek, BC	Brett M. Moore	Brett M. Moore	1987	311
170 2/8	41 6/8	41 6/8	14 1/8	14 1/8	5 6/8	5 6/8	27 2/8	27 2/8	Blue Lake, BC	Ralph L. Albright	Ralph L. Albright	1995	311
170 1/8	43 1/8	42	13 3/8	13 1/8	6	6	30 7/8	30 7/8	Ram Creek, BC	George W. Young	George W. Young	1965	322
170 1/8	39 4/8	38 1/8	14 6/8	14 7/8	6 2/8	6 2/8	24 6/8	24 6/8	Needham Creek, BC	Kim Cox	Kim Cox	1966	322
170 1/8	39 2/8	43 7/8	13 4/8	13 4/8	6 1/8	6 1/8	21 5/8	21 5/8	Cassiar Mts., BC	Roy Fukunaga	Roy Fukunaga	1974	322
170 1/8	43 2/8	42 3/8	12 5/8	12 5/8	6 2/8	6 2/8	27 5/8	27 5/8	Rabbit River, BC	James H. Duke, Jr.	James H. Duke, Jr.	1976	322
170 1/8	40	40 1/8	14 1/8	14 1/8	6 4/8	6 4/8	24 7/8	24 7/8	Prophet River, BC	Frank F. Azcarate	Frank F. Azcarate	1985	322
170 1/8	39 7/8	39 2/8	14 4/8	14 4/8	5 7/8	5 7/8	23	23	Pelly Lake, BC	Kenneth Baker, Jr.	Kenneth Baker, Jr.	1995	322
170 1/8	39 5/8	39 5/8	14 4/8	14 4/8	6 2/8	6 2/8	23	23	The Pillar, BC	Lawrence W. Dossman	Lawrence W. Dossman	1995	322
170 1/8	39	39	15 2/8	15 2/8	5 6/8	5 6/8	26 4/8	23 1/8	Prophet River, BC	Dwight Clower	Dwight Clower	1997	322
170	42 4/8	38 6/8	14 1/8	14 2/8	5 4/8	5 2/8	24 3/8	24 3/8	Prophet River, BC	Walter B. McClurkan	Walter B. McClurkan	1945	330
170	39 2/8	43 4/8	13 7/8	13 5/8	6	6	25	25	Cold Fish Lake, BC	Howard Boazman	Howard Boazman	1962	330
170	42	37	14 1/8	14 1/8	6 3/8	6 3/8	22 4/8	22 4/8	Alaska Hwy., BC	Arthur Gordon	Arthur Gordon	1965	330
170	39 2/8	39 2/8	14 5/8	14 5/8	6 4/8	6 4/8	22 3/8	22 3/8	Cassiar Mts., BC	Neil Castner	Neil Castner	1966	330
170	40 1/8	40 1/8	14 2/8	14 2/8	6 4/8	6 4/8	16 5/8	21 5/8	Cassiar Mts., BC	Glen E. Park	Glen E. Park	1967	330
170	39 4/8	39 4/8	13 6/8	13 7/8	7 2/8	7 3/8	17 5/8	21	Tetsa River, BC	Owen R. Walker	Owen R. Walker	1967	330
170	41	41	14	14	6 4/8	6 4/8	20 6/8	20 6/8	Prophet River, BC	Jim Nystrom	Jim Nystrom	1968	330
170	40	39 2/8	15 4/8	15 4/8	5 2/8	5 2/8	22 6/8	22 6/8	Muskwa River, BC	W.J. Boynton III	W.J. Boynton III	1970	330
170	42 3/8	43 7/8	13 2/8	13 2/8	6 1/8	6 1/8	29 2/8	29 2/8	Gataga River, BC	Paul L.C. Snider	Paul L.C. Snider	1970	330
170	37	37 6/8	14 6/8	14 6/8	7 4/8	7 4/8	18 1/8	22 2/8	Prophet River, BC	Doug Heinrich	Doug Heinrich	1992	330

STONE'S SHEEP

Ovis dalli stonei

Score	Length of Horn R	L	Circumference of Base R	L	Circumference at Third Quarter R	L	Greatest Spread	Tip to Tip Spread	Locality	Hunter	Owner	Date Killed	Rank
170	35 4/8	37	14 1/8	14 1/8	8 4/8	8 5/8	19 6/8	17 1/8	Toad River, BC	Rick Davis	Rick Davis	1993	330
170	42 2/8	42	13 4/8	13 6/8	6 1/8	6 1/8	23 3/8	23 1/8	Toad River, BC	Robert M. Hall	Robert M. Hall	1995	330
170	41 3/8	39 1/8	14 2/8	14 2/8	5 7/8	5 7/8	23 2/8	23	Muncho Lake, BC	Ken Jagersma	Ken Jagersma	1996	330
178 4/8*	45 2/8	46 2/8	14 6/8	14 4/8	5 6/8	5 6/8	25 7/8	26 2/8	Johiah Lake, BC	Robert Joseph	Robert Joseph	1997	
178 2/8*	43	42 4/8	14 6/8	14 6/8	7	6 7/8	25 2/8	25 1/8	Ram Creek, BC	Roger M. Britton	Roger M. Britton	1993	
177 4/8*	41 5/8	42 1/8	14 4/8	14 3/8	7 2/8	7 3/8	25	24 6/8	Racing River, BC	Floyd W. Ternier	F.W. & C. Ternier	1994	
177 1/8*	44 7/8	45 2/8	14	14	5 6/8	6	31	31	Muskwa River, BC	Kevin H. Olmstead	Kevin H. Olmstead	1993	
176 4/8*	45	43	14	14 3/8	6 2/8	6 3/8	31	31	Burnt Rose Lake, BC	Michael G. Adams	Michael G. Adams	1994	
176*	42	40	15 2/8	15 2/8	6 4/8	6 5/8	25 1/8	25 1/8	Gathto Creek, BC	Dyrk T. Eddie	Dyrk T. Eddie	1997	

* Final score is subject to revision by additional verifying measurements.

CATEGORY
STONE'S SHEEP

SCORE
170-2/8

HUNTER
RALPH L. ALBRIGHT

LOCATION
BLUE LAKE, BC

DATE OF KILL
AUGUST 1995

CATEGORY
STONE'S SHEEP

SCORE
170

HUNTER
ROBERT M. HALL

LOCATION
TOAD RIVER, BC

DATE OF KILL
AUGUST 1995

CATEGORY
STONE'S SHEEP

SCORE
178-4/8

HUNTER
ROBERT JOSEPH

LOCATION
JOHIAH LAKE, BC

DATE OF KILL
AUGUST 1997

ACKNOWLEDGEMENTS

RECORDS OF NORTH AMERICAN BIG GAME

DATA COMPILED WITH THE ABLE ASSISTANCE OF:

C. Randall Byers - Chair, Boone and Crockett Club's Records Committee

Jack Reneau - Director of Big Game Records, Boone and Crockett Club

Chris Tonkinson - Assistant to Director of Big Game Records, Boone and Crockett Club

Sandy Poston - Administrative Assistant, Boone and Crockett Club

Mary Armour - Support Specialist, Boone and Crockett Club

Bill Sawyer - Business Manager, Boone and Crockett Club

WORLD'S RECORD ACCOUNTS GATHERED AND EDITED BY:

Jeffrey Buchanan Miller - Jackson, Wyoming

BOOK, DUST JACKET AND COVER DESIGNED BY:

Julie L. Tripp - Director of Publications, Boone and Crockett Club

ALASKA BROWN BEAR PAINTING BY:

Bob Kuhn - Emeritus Member, Boone and Crockett Club

COPY EDITING BY:

George A. Bettas - Vice President of Communications, Boone and Crockett Club

C. Randall Byers - Chair, Boone and Crockett Club's Records Committee

Jack Reneau - Director of Big Game Records, Boone and Crockett Club

PRINTED AND BOUND HARDCOVER TRADE EDITIONS BY:

R.R. Donnelley & Sons Company

Crawfordsville, Indiana

LIMITED EDITIONS BINDING BY:

Campbell-Logan Bindery

Minneapolis, Minnesota